Sam Bayliss

International Financial Reporting Standards (IFRSs™) 2005

including International Accounting Standards (IASs™) and Interpretations as at 1 January 2005

International Financial Reporting Standards (IFRSs™) 2005

including International Accounting Standards (IASs™) and Interpretations as at 1 January 2005

The full text of all International Financial Reporting Standards extant at 1 January 2005

International Accounting Standards Board®
30 Cannon Street
London EC4M 6XH
United Kingdom

Telephone: +44 (0)20 7246 6410
Fax: +44 (0)20 7246 6411
Email: iasb@iasb.org

Publications Telephone: +44 (0)20 7332 2730
Publications Fax: +44 (0)20 7332 2749
Publications Email: publications@iasb.org
Web: www.iasb.org

IFRSs together with their accompanying documents are issued by the International Accounting Standards Board (IASB)

30 Cannon Street, London EC4M 6XH, United Kingdom.
Tel: +44 (0)20 7246 6410 Fax: +44 (0)20 7246 6411
Email: iasb@iasb.org Web: www.iasb.org

ISBN: 1-904230-79-2

IASCF Publications Department
30 Cannon Street, London EC4M 6XH, United Kingdom.
Telephone: +44 (0)20 7332 2730 Fax: +44 (0)20 7332 2749
Email: publications@iasb.org Web: www.iasb.org

Acknowledgements:

Cover designed and produced in the United Kingdom by Buckmans. Telephone: +44 (0)20 7770 6040

Contents

Interpretations

Changes in this edition

This section is a brief guide to the changes since the 2004 edition that are incorporated in this edition of the Bound Volume of International Financial Reporting Standards.

Introduction

The main changes in this edition of the Bound Volume are the inclusion of:

- a new Standard–IFRS 6
- five Interpretations–IFRICs 1–5
- amendments to IASs 19 and 39 and to SIC-12
- amendments to other IFRSs resulting from these pronouncements.

New Standards

Details of the new Standard and Interpretations included in this edition are as follows.

IFRS 6

IFRS 6 *Exploration for and Evaluation of Mineral Resources* specifies the financial reporting for those activities. The IFRS is required to be applied from 1 January 2006, but earlier application is encouraged.

Other Standards

The Board issued amendments to two Standards–IAS 19 and IAS 39. Those amendments have been incorporated into the text of those Standards in this edition of the Bound Volume.

The amendments to IAS 19 *Employee Benefits* (on actuarial gains and losses, group plans and disclosures) have various effective dates. The mandatory requirements are required to be applied for annual periods beginning on or after 1 January 2006, but earlier application is encouraged. The amendments include an option that may be used for annual periods ending on or after 16 December 2004. There are consequential effects if an entity changes its accounting policies to reflect the amendments.

The amendments to IAS 39 *Financial Instruments: Recognition and Measurement* (on transition and initial recognition of financial assets and financial liabilities) are required to be applied to annual periods beginning on or after 1 January 2005 (or earlier if IAS 39 and IAS 32 *Financial Instruments: Disclosure and Presentation* are applied to an earlier period).

IFRIC 1–IFRIC 5

The five Interpretations developed by the International Financial Reporting Interpretations Committee (IFRIC) are:

- IFRIC 1 *Changes in Existing Decommissioning, Restoration and Similar Liabilities*
- IFRIC 2 *Members' Shares in Co-operative Entities and Similar Instruments*
- IFRIC 3 *Emission Rights*
- IFRIC 4 *Determining whether an Arrangement contains a Lease*

- IFRIC 5 *Rights to Interests arising from Decommissioning, Restoration and Environmental Rehabilitation Funds*

In addition, the IFRIC issued an amendment to the Interpretation SIC-12 *Consolidation—Special Purpose Entities.* The amendment was effective from 1 January 2005, and it is incorporated in the text of SIC-12 in this edition of the Bound Volume.

IFRIC 1 is required to be applied for annual periods beginning on or after 1 September 2004, and IFRIC 2 for annual periods from 1 January 2005. IFRIC 3 is to be applied for annual periods from 1 March 2005 and IFRICs 4 and 5 for annual periods from 1 January 2006.

Earlier application of IFRICs 3–5 is encouraged.

Several of the documents mentioned above included amendments to other pronouncements; those amendments have been incorporated into the text of the pronouncements affected.

Other material that has changed

The Glossary of Terms and the Index have been revised.

Up–to–date text of documents

The text of this edition of the Bound Volume includes the latest versions of all IFRSs (including IASs) issued up to 31 December 2004 and required to be applied on 1 January 2005 or from a future date.

New presentation

Until now, documents that were originated by IASC have been reprinted in their original typeface, and those developed by the Board have been printed in a different typeface. There were other presentational differences, of which perhaps the most obvious was the use by IASC of bold italic type to denote mandatory requirements, whereas the Board uses **bold roman** type to denote the main principles (as explained in paragraph 14 of the *Preface to International Financial Reporting Standards*). The documents published in this Bound Volume have been set in new typefaces and styles of headings, common to all documents, that are intended to enhance the readability of the text. In particular, text that was formerly set in bold italics is now generally set in bold roman.

In addition, numerous other formatting changes have been introduced to ensure that all Standards and Interpretations are similar in appearance. These changes include:

- reformatted tables
- consistent use of footnotes
- normalised heading levels, ie headings of the same level will be the same size.

Introduction

The International Accounting Standards Board (IASB), based in London, began operations in 2001. The IASB is committed to developing, in the public interest, a single set of high quality, global accounting standards that require transparent and comparable information in general purpose financial statements. In pursuit of this objective, the IASB co-operates with other accounting standard-setters to achieve convergence in accounting standards around the world. The 14 IASB members (12 of whom are full-time) have a broad range of professional backgrounds and have liaison responsibilities throughout the world. The nineteen Trustees of the IASC Foundation select, oversee and fund the IASB. The major accounting firms, private financial institutions and industrial companies throughout the world, central and development banks, and other international and professional organisations provide financial support to the organisation.

Trustees

The Trustees are responsible for directing the IASC Foundation's activities. The Trustees appoint IASB members, the Standards Advisory Council and the International Financial Reporting Interpretations Committee. The Trustees also have responsibility for constitutional changes.

The Trustees are individuals who bring together a diversity of perspective and experience. Under the existing Constitution of the IASC Foundation most recently revised in 2002, the Trustees are appointed so that there are six from North America, six from Europe, four from the Asia/Pacific region, and three others from any area, as long as geographical balance is maintained. Five of the nineteen Trustees are selected after consultation with the International Federation of Accountants. The Constitution requires the Trustees to have at least one member designated a preparer, a user and an academic–each selected after consultation with relevant international organisations. The remaining eleven Trustees were 'at-large' appointments. The existing Trustees follow similar procedures in selecting subsequent Trustees to fill vacancies.

The Trustees are currently reviewing the constitutional arrangements, as is required every five years, and expect to announce their decisions in the course of 2005.

The IASB

The IASB has sole responsibility for setting accounting standards. The foremost qualification for IASB membership is technical expertise and the Trustees exercise their best judgement to ensure that the IASB is not dominated by any particular constituency or regional interest. The Constitution requires that at least five IASB members have a background as practising auditors, at least three have a background in the preparation of financial statements, at least three have a background as users of financial statements, and at least one has an academic background. Seven of the fourteen IASB members have defined responsibility for liaison with one or more national standard-setters. The publication of a standard, exposure draft, or final IFRIC Interpretation requires approval by eight of the IASB's fourteen members. At 1 January 2005, the IASB members were:

Sir David Tweedie, *Chairman*

Thomas E Jones, *Vice-Chairman*

Professor Mary E Barth *(part-time)*

Hans-Georg Bruns *(Liaison with the German standard-setter)*

Anthony T Cope

Jan Engström

Robert P Garnett

Gilbert Gélard *(Liaison with the French standard-setter)*

James J Leisenring *(Liaison with the US standard-setter)*

Warren J McGregor *(Liaison with the Australian and New Zealand standard-setters)*

Patricia L O'Malley *(Liaison with the Canadian standard-setter)*

John T Smith *(part-time)*

Geoffrey Whittington *(Liaison with the UK standard-setter)*

Tatsumi Yamada *(Liaison with the Japanese standard-setter)*

The IASB issues a Board decision summary promptly after each IASB meeting. This report is published in electronic format on the IASB Website.

Standards Advisory Council

The Standards Advisory Council (SAC) provides a formal vehicle for further groups and individuals having diverse geographical and functional backgrounds to give advice to the IASB and, at times, to advise the Trustees. The Trustees attach particular importance to the perspective that the SAC can bring to the IASB's role and mandate. At present the SAC comprises about fifty members. It has the objective of (a) giving advice to the IASB on priorities in the IASB's work, (b) informing the IASB of the implications of proposed standards for users and preparers of financial statements and (c) giving other advice to the IASB or the Trustees. The SAC normally meets at least three times a year. It is to be consulted by the IASB on all major projects and its meetings are open to the public.

The Trustees are in the process of reorganising the SAC and expect to announce a new SAC in the second half of 2005.

International Financial Reporting Interpretations Committee

The International Financial Reporting Interpretations Committee (IFRIC) is appointed by the IASC Foundation Trustees to assist the IASB in establishing and improving standards of financial accounting and reporting for the benefit of users, preparers and auditors of financial statements. The Trustees established the IFRIC in March 2002, when it replaced the previous interpretations committee, the Standing Interpretations Committee (SIC). The role of the IFRIC is to provide timely guidance on newly identified financial reporting issues not specifically addressed in the IASB's standards (IFRSs) or issues where unsatisfactory or conflicting interpretations have developed, or seem likely to develop. It thus promotes the rigorous and uniform application of IFRSs.

The IFRIC assists the IASB in achieving international convergence of accounting standards by working with similar groups sponsored by national standard-setters to reach similar conclusions on issues where underlying standards are substantially similar.

The IFRIC has twelve voting members in addition to a non-voting Chair. The Chair has the right to speak to the technical issues being considered but not to vote. The Trustees, as they deem necessary, may appoint as non-voting observers regulatory organisations, whose representatives have the right to attend and speak at meetings. Currently, the International Organization of Securities Commissions (IOSCO) and the European Commission are non-voting observers.

The IASB issues an IFRIC decision summary promptly after each IFRIC meeting. This report is published in electronic format on the IASB Website.

IASB staff

A staff based in London, and headed by the Chairman of the IASB, supports the IASB. At the time of printing, the technical staff includes people from Australia, Bangladesh, China, Germany, India, Ireland, Korea, New Zealand, Russia, South Africa, the United Kingdom and the United States.

Due process

IASB due process

IFRSs are developed through a formal system of due process and broad international consultation that involves accountants, financial analysts and other users of financial statements, the business community, stock exchanges, regulatory and legal authorities, academics and other interested individuals and organisations from around the world. The IASB consults, in public meetings, the SAC on major projects, agenda decisions and work priorities, and discusses technical matters in meetings that are open to public observation. Formal due process for projects normally, but not necessarily, involves the following steps (the steps that are required under the terms of the IASC Foundation Constitution are indicated by an asterisk*):

(a) the staff are asked to identify and review all the issues associated with the topic and to consider the application of the IASB *Framework* to the issues;

(b) study of national accounting requirements and practice and an exchange of views about the issues with national standard-setters;

(c) consulting the SAC about the advisability of adding the topic to the IASB's agenda;*

(d) formation of an advisory group to give advice to the IASB on the project;

(e) publishing for public comment a discussion document;

(f) publishing for public comment an exposure draft approved by at least eight members of the IASB, including any dissenting opinions held by IASB members;*

(g) publishing within an exposure draft a basis for conclusions;

(h) consideration of all comments received within the comment period on discussion documents and exposure drafts;*

(i) consideration of the desirability of holding a public hearing and of the desirability of conducting field tests and, if considered desirable, holding such hearings and conducting such tests;

(j) approval of a standard by at least eight members of the IASB and inclusion in the published standard of any dissenting opinions;* and

(k) publishing within a standard a basis for conclusions, explaining, among other things, the steps in the IASB's due process and how the IASB dealt with public comments on the exposure draft.

The Trustees are currently undertaking a review of the IASB's consultative procedures and are seeking public comment on a handbook of those procedures, developed by the IASB.

IFRIC due process

Interpretations of IFRSs are developed through a formal due process that involves accountants, financial analysts and other users of financial statements, the business community, stock exchanges, regulatory and legal authorities, academics and other interested individuals and organisations from around the world. The IFRIC discusses technical matters in meetings that are open to public observation. The due process for each project normally, but not necessarily, involves the following steps (the steps that are required under the terms of the IASC Foundation Constitution are indicated by an asterisk*):

(a) the staff are asked to identify and review all the issues associated with the topic and to consider the application of the IASB *Framework* to the issues;

(b) study of national accounting requirements and practice and an exchange of views about the issues with national standard-setters, including national committees that have responsibility for interpretations of national standards;

(c) publication of a draft Interpretation for public comment if no more than three IFRIC members have voted against the proposal;*

(d) consideration of all comments received within the comment period on a draft Interpretation;*

(e) approval by the IFRIC of an Interpretation if no more than three IFRIC members have voted against the Interpretation after considering public comments on the draft Interpretation;* and

(f) approval of the Interpretation by at least eight members of the IASB.*

Voting

The publication of an exposure draft, a standard or a final Interpretation requires approval by eight of the fourteen members of the IASB. The Trustees have agreed to raise the requirement to nine of the fourteen members upon completion of the Constitution Review. Other decisions of the IASB, including the publication of a discussion paper, require a simple majority of the members of the IASB present at a meeting that is attended by at least 60 per cent of the members of the IASB, in person or by telecommunications. The IASB has full discretion over the development and pursuit of its technical agenda.

Each member of the IFRIC has one vote on an Interpretation. Nine voting IFRIC members constitute a quorum. Members vote in accordance with their own independent views, not as representatives voting according to the views of any firm, organisation or constituency with which they may be associated. Approval of draft or final Interpretations requires that not more than three voting members vote against the draft or final Interpretation.

Openness of meetings

(a) Meetings of the Trustees, the IASB and the IFRIC are all open to public observation. However, certain IASB discussions (normally about selection, appointment and other personnel issues) are held in private.

(b) The IASB continues to explore how technology can be used to overcome geographical barriers and other logistical problems and thus facilitate public observation of open meetings. The introduction of audio and video and webcasting on the IASB Website are examples of recent innovations.

(c) The agenda for each meeting of the Trustees, the IASB, the SAC and the IFRIC is published in advance on the IASB's Website, which also publishes promptly a summary of the technical decisions made at IASB and IFRIC meetings and, where appropriate, decisions of the Trustees.

(d) When the IASB issues a standard or an Interpretation, it publishes a basis for conclusions to explain the rationale behind the conclusions and to provide background information that may help users of IFRSs to apply them in practice. The IASB also publishes its members' dissenting opinions on standards.

Comment periods

The IASB publishes each exposure draft of a standard and discussion documents for public comment, with a normal comment period of 90 days. In certain circumstances, the IASB may expose proposals for a longer or shorter period. Draft IFRIC Interpretations are normally exposed for a 60-day comment period, although a shorter period of not less than 30 days may be used in certain circumstances.

Co-ordination with due process of other accounting standard-setters

The IASB meets the chairmen of its partner and other accounting standard-setters regularly. In addition, staff members of the IASB and partner standard-setters co-operate on a daily basis on projects, sharing resources whenever necessary and appropriate. Close co-ordination between the IASB's due process and the due process of national standard-setters is important to the success of the IASB. As far as possible, the IASB aims to integrate its due process with national due process. In addition, those IASB members having liaison responsibilities with accounting standard-setters provide a mechanism for more regular contact.

Opportunities for input

The development of an International Financial Reporting Standard (IFRS) involves an open, public process of debating technical issues and evaluating input sought through several mechanisms. Opportunities for interested parties to participate in the development of IFRSs include, depending on the nature of the project:

(a) participation in the development of views as a member of the SAC;

(b) participation in advisory groups;

(c) submission of an issue to the IFRIC (see the IASB Website for details);

(d) submission of a comment letter in response to a discussion document;

(e) submission of a comment letter in response to an exposure draft;

(f) participation in public round-table discussions; and

(g) participation in field visits and field tests.

The IASB publishes an annual report on its activities during the past year and priorities for the next year. This report provides a basis and opportunity for comment by interested parties.

Preface to International Financial Reporting Standards

The *Preface to International Financial Reporting Standards* sets out the objectives and due process of the IASB and explains the scope, authority and timing of application of IFRSs.

IASB *Framework*

The IASB has a *Framework for the Preparation and Presentation of Financial Statements*. The *Framework* assists the IASB:

(a) in the development of future IFRSs and in its review of existing IFRSs; and

(b) in promoting the harmonisation of regulations, accounting standards and procedures relating to the presentation of financial statements by providing a basis for reducing the number of alternative accounting treatments permitted by IFRSs.

In addition, the Framework may assist:

(a) preparers of financial statements in applying IFRSs and in dealing with topics that have yet to form the subject of a Standard or an Interpretation;

(b) auditors in forming an opinion on whether financial statements conform with IFRSs;

(c) users of financial statements in interpreting the information contained in financial statements prepared in conformity with IFRSs; and

(d) those who are interested in the work of IASB, providing them with information about its approach to the formulation of accounting standards.

The *Framework* is not a part of IFRSs. However, when developing an accounting policy in the absence of a standard or an Interpretation that specifically applies to an item, an entity's management is required to refer to, and consider the applicability of, the concepts in the *Framework* (see IAS 8 *Accounting Policies, Changes in Accounting Estimates and Errors*).

In a limited number of cases there may be a conflict between the *Framework* and a requirement within a standard or an Interpretation. In those cases where there is a conflict, the requirements of the standard or Interpretation prevail over those of the *Framework*.

Accounting standards

The IASB publishes its standards in a series of pronouncements called International Financial Reporting Standards (IFRSs). Upon its inception the IASB adopted the body of International Accounting Standards (IASs) issued by its predecessor, the Board of the International Accounting Standards Committee. The term 'International Financial Reporting Standards' includes IFRSs, IFRIC Interpretations, IASs and SIC Interpretations.

Benchmark and allowed alternative treatments

In some cases, IASs permit different treatments for given transactions and events. In limited cases, one treatment is identified as the 'benchmark treatment' and the other as the 'allowed alternative treatment'. The financial statements of an entity may appropriately be described as being prepared in accordance with IFRSs whether they use the benchmark treatment or the allowed alternative treatment.

The IASB's objective is to require like transactions and events to be accounted for and reported in a like way and unlike transactions and events to be accounted for and reported differently, both within an entity over time and among entities. Consequently, the IASB intends not to permit choices in accounting treatment. Also, the IASB has reconsidered, and will continue to reconsider, those transactions and events for which IASs permit a choice of accounting treatment, with the objective of reducing the number of those choices.

Staff advice

The IASB's Operating Procedures do not generally allow IASB staff to give advice on the meaning of IFRSs.

Current technical activities

Details of the IASB's and the IFRIC's current technical activities, including the progress of the IASB's and the IFRIC's deliberations, are available on the IASB Website. As projects are completed, the IASB expects to add new projects including, potentially, those listed as 'other topics' on the IASB Website. The IFRIC adds topics to its agenda on the basis of an assessment of issues submitted to it by constituents.

The IASB reports on its technical projects in its quarterly newsletter, *IASB Insight*, and on its Website. The IASB publishes a report on its decisions promptly after each IASB meeting in *IASB Update*. The IFRIC publishes a report on its decisions promptly after each IFRIC meeting in *IFRIC Update*.

IASB/IASC Foundation publications and translations

The IASC Foundation (IASCF) holds the copyright of all publications issued or approved by the IASB including International Financial Reporting Standards, International Accounting Standards, Interpretations, exposure drafts, and other IASB publications except where the IASCF has expressly waived copyright on portions of that material. For more information regarding the IASCF copyright, please refer to the copyright notice at the front of this volume or the IASCF Website.

Approved translations of International Financial Reporting Standards are available in over 30 languages, including all major European and Asian languages. The IASCF will consider making approved translations available in other languages. For more information, contact the IASCF's Commercial Director.

Although the IASCF makes every reasonable effort to translate IFRSs into other languages on a timely basis, a rigorous process must be followed to ensure that the translations are as accurate as possible. For that reason, there may well be a lag between when a standard or an Interpretation is issued by the IASB (in English) and when it is issued in other languages. Further details are available on the IASB Website (www.iasb.org/resources/translations.asp) and from the IASCF Publications department.

More information

The IASB Website, at www.iasb.org, provides news, updates and other resources related to the IASB and the IASCF. The latest publications and subscription services can be ordered from the IASCF Shop at www.iasb.org/shop.

For more information about the IASB, or to obtain copies of its publications and details of the IASCF's subscription services, visit the IASB Website at www.iasb.org, or write to:

IASC Foundation Publications Department
30 Cannon Street,
London EC4M 6XH,
United Kingdom

Telephone: +44 (0)20 7332 2730
Fax: +44 (0)20 7332 2749
Email: publications@iasb.org

Website: www.iasb.org

IASC Foundation Constitution (revised)

Foreword

This Constitution was approved in its original form by the Board of the former International Accounting Standards Committee (IASC) in March 2000 and by the members of IASC at a meeting in Edinburgh on 24 May 2000.

At its meeting in December 1999, the IASC Board had appointed a Nominating Committee to select the first Trustees. These Trustees were nominated on 22 May 2000 and took office on 24 May 2000 as a result of the approval of the Constitution.

In execution of their duties under the Constitution, the Trustees formed the International Accounting Standards Committee Foundation on 6 February 2001. As a consequence of a resolution by the Trustees, Part C of the Constitution approved on 24 May 2000 ceased to have effect.

Reflecting the Trustees' decision to create the International Financial Reporting Interpretations Committee, and following public consultation, the Constitution was revised on 5 March 2002. Subsequently the Trustees amended the Constitution, with effect from 8 July 2002, to reflect other changes that had taken place since the formation of the IASC Foundation.

IASC Foundation Constitution

(approved by the Members of IASC at a meeting in Edinburgh, Scotland on 24 May 2000 and revised by the IASC Foundation Trustees on 5 March 2002 and 8 July 2002)

This Constitution consists of Part A and Part B. Part A deals with the organisation's name and objectives, and the membership and appointment of Trustees. Part B sets out the provisions that came into effect when the Trustees formed the International Accounting Standards Committee Foundation on 6 February 2001, following a Trustees' Resolution. In accordance with the Trustees' decision, Part C of the Constitution approved on 24 May 2000 no longer pertains.

Part A

Name and objectives

1 The name of the organisation shall be the International Accounting Standards Committee Foundation (abbreviated as "IASC Foundation"). The International Accounting Standards Board (abbreviated as "IASB"), whose structure and functions are laid out in Sections 19–33, shall be the standard-setting body of the IASC Foundation.

2 The objectives of the IASC Foundation are:

(a) to develop, in the public interest, a single set of high quality, understandable and enforceable global accounting standards that require high quality, transparent and comparable information in financial statements and other financial reporting to help participants in the world's capital markets and other users make economic decisions;

(b) to promote the use and rigorous application of those standards; and

(c) to bring about convergence of national accounting standards and International Accounting Standards and International Financial Reporting Standards to high quality solutions.

Governance of the IASC Foundation

3 The governance of the IASC Foundation shall rest with the Trustees and such other governing organs as may be appointed by the Trustees in accordance with the provisions of this Constitution. The Trustees shall use their best endeavours to ensure that the requirements of this Constitution are observed; however, they are empowered to make minor variations in the interest of feasibility of operation if such variations are agreed by 75% of all the Trustees.

Trustees

4 The Trustees shall comprise nineteen individuals. The nineteen individuals selected by the Nominating Committee as Trustees prior to the coming into effect of this Constitution shall comprise the initial Trustees of the IASC Foundation.

5 The Trustees shall be responsible for the selection of all subsequent Trustees to fill vacancies caused by routine retirement or other reason. In making such selection,

the Trustees shall be bound by the criteria set forth in Sections 6, 7 and 8 and in particular shall undertake mutual consultation with international organisations as set out in Section 7, for the purpose of selecting an individual with a similar background to that of the retiring Trustee, where the retiring Trustee was selected through a process of mutual consultation with one or more international organisations.

6 All Trustees shall be required to show a firm commitment to the IASC Foundation and the IASB as a high quality global standard-setter, to be financially knowledgeable, and to have an ability to meet the time commitment. Each Trustee shall have an understanding of, and be sensitive to, international issues relevant to the success of an international organisation responsible for the development of high quality global accounting standards for use in the world's capital markets and by other users. The mix of Trustees shall be representative of the world's capital markets and a diversity of geographical and professional backgrounds. The Trustees shall be required to commit formally to acting in the public interest in all matters. In order to ensure a broad international basis, there shall be:

- six Trustees appointed from North America;
- six Trustees appointed from Europe;
- four Trustees appointed from the Asia/Pacific region; and
- three Trustees appointed from any area, subject to establishing overall geographical balance.

7 Five of the nineteen Trustees shall be nominated by the International Federation of Accountants (IFAC), subject to a process of mutual consultation between IFAC and the Nominating Committee or the Trustees, as the case may be, to ensure that prospective IFAC nominees are consistent with the maintenance of a balance of geographical and professional backgrounds. Two of the five Trustees nominated by IFAC shall normally be senior partners/executives from prominent international accounting firms. Three of the other Trustees shall be selected after consultation with international organisations of preparers, users and academics for the purpose of obtaining one Trustee from each of those backgrounds. Organisations consulted shall include the International Association of Financial Executives Institutes, the International Council of Investment Associations and the International Association for Accounting Education and Research and/or other organisations of similar standing.

8 Eleven *at-large* Trustees shall also be selected. The *at-large* designation indicates that such Trustees are not appointed through the consultation process with constituency organisations (IFAC, preparers, users or academics). *At-large* Trustees are expected to bring to the IASC Foundation strong public interest backgrounds that are complementary to those of Trustees nominated through the constituency process. The Trustees shall establish procedures for inviting suggestions for appointments of *at-large* Trustees from relevant organisations and for allowing individuals to put forward their own names.

9 Trustees shall normally be appointed for a term of three years, renewable once: in order to provide continuity, some of the initial Trustees will serve staggered terms so as to retire after four or five years.

10 Subject to the voting requirements in Section 15, the Trustees may terminate the appointment of an individual as a Trustee on grounds of poor performance, misbehaviour or incapacity.

11 The Chairman of the Trustees shall be appointed by the Trustees from among their own number.

12 The Trustees shall meet at least twice each year and shall be remunerated by the IASC Foundation with an annual fee and a per-meeting fee, commensurate with the responsibilities assumed, such fees to be determined by the Trustees. Expenses of travel on IASC Foundation business shall be met by the IASC Foundation.

13 In addition to the powers and duties set out in Section 14, the Trustees may make such operational commitments and other arrangements as they deem necessary to achieve the organisation's objectives, including, but without limitation, leasing premises and agreeing contracts of employment with IASB members.

14 The Trustees shall:

(a) assume responsibility for fundraising;

(b) establish or amend operating procedures for the Trustees;

(c) determine the legal entity under which the IASC Foundation shall operate, provided always that such legal entity shall be a Foundation or other body corporate conferring limited liability on its members and that the legal documents establishing such legal entity shall incorporate provisions to achieve the same requirements as the provisions contained in this Constitution;

(d) review in due course the location of the IASC Foundation, both as regards its legal base and its operating location;

(e) investigate the possibility of seeking charitable or similar status for the IASC Foundation in those countries where such status would assist fundraising;

(f) open their meetings to the public but may, at their discretion, hold certain discussions (normally only about selection, appointment and other personnel issues, and funding) in private; and

(g) publish an annual report on the IASC Foundation's activities, including audited financial statements and priorities for the coming year.

15 There shall be a quorum for meetings of the Trustees if 60% of the Trustees are present in person or by telecommunications: Trustees shall not be represented by alternates. Each Trustee shall have one vote and a simple majority of those voting shall be required to take decisions on matters other than termination of the appointment of a Trustee, amendments to the Constitution, or minor variations made in the interest of feasibility of operations, in which cases a 75% majority of all Trustees shall be required; voting by proxy shall not be permitted on any issue. In the event of a tied vote, the Chairman shall have an additional casting vote.

Part B

Trustees

16 In addition to the duties set out in Part A, the Trustees shall:

(a) appoint the members of the IASB, including those who will serve in liaison capacities with national standard-setters, and establish their contracts of service and performance criteria;

(b) appoint the members of the International Financial Reporting Interpretations Committee and the Standards Advisory Council;

(c) review annually the strategy of the IASC Foundation and the IASB and its effectiveness;

(d) approve annually the budget of the IASC Foundation and determine the basis for funding;

(e) review broad strategic issues affecting accounting standards, promote the IASC Foundation and its work and promote the objective of rigorous application of International Accounting Standards and International Financial Reporting Standards, provided that the Trustees shall be excluded from involvement in technical matters relating to accounting standards;

(f) establish and amend operating procedures for the IASB, the International Financial Reporting Interpretations Committee and the Standards Advisory Council;

(g) approve amendments to this Constitution after following a due process, including consultation with the Standards Advisory Council and publication of an Exposure Draft for public comment and subject to the voting requirements given in Section 15; and

(h) exercise all powers of the IASC Foundation except for those expressly reserved to the IASB, the International Financial Reporting Interpretations Committee and the Standards Advisory Council.

17 The Trustees may terminate the appointment of a member of the IASB, the International Financial Reporting Interpretations Committee or the Standards Advisory Council, on grounds of poor performance, misbehaviour, incapacity or other failure to comply with contractual requirements and the Trustees shall develop procedures for such termination.

18 The accountability of the Trustees shall be ensured *inter alia* through:

(a) a commitment made by each Trustee to act in the public interest;

(b) their undertaking a review of the entire structure of the IASC Foundation and its effectiveness, such review to include consideration of changing the geographical distribution of Trustees in response to changing global economic conditions, and publishing the proposals of that review for public comment, the review commencing three years after the coming into force of this Constitution, with the objective of implementing any agreed changes five years after the coming into force of this Constitution (6 February 2006, five years after the date of the incorporation of the IASC Foundation); and

(c) their undertaking a similar review subsequently every five years.

IASB

19 The IASB shall comprise fourteen members, appointed by the Trustees under Section 16(a), of whom twelve shall be full-time members (the expression "full-time" meaning that the members concerned commit all of their time in paid employment to the IASC Foundation) and two part-time members (the expression "part-time" meaning that the members concerned commit less than all of their time in paid employment to the IASC Foundation). The work of the IASB shall not be invalidated by its failure at any time to have a full complement of fourteen members, although the Trustees shall use their best endeavours to achieve a full complement.

20 The foremost qualification for membership of the IASB shall be technical expertise. The Trustees shall select members of the IASB so that it will comprise a group of people representing, within that group, the best available combination of technical skills and background experience of relevant international business and market conditions in order to contribute to the development of high quality, global accounting standards. No individual shall be both a Trustee and an IASB member at the same time.

21 The selection of members of the IASB shall not be based on geographical representation. The Trustees shall ensure that the IASB is not dominated by any particular constituency or geographical interest. In particular, when making appointments to the IASB, the Trustees shall observe the general parameters set out in the *Criteria for IASB Members* which are attached to this Constitution.

22 To achieve a balance of perspectives and experience, a minimum of five members of the IASB shall have a background as practising auditors, a minimum of three a background in the preparation of financial statements, a minimum of three a background as users of financial statements, and at least one an academic background. The Trustees shall select IASB members so that, at the beginning of their initial terms, there is a balance of recent and earlier experience in each category of members.

23 Seven of the full-time members of the IASB will be expected to have formal liaison responsibilities with national standard-setters in order to promote the convergence of national accounting standards and International Accounting Standards and International Financial Reporting Standards but shall not be voting members of the national standard-setters: the selection process will therefore necessarily involve consultation between the Trustees and the national standard-setters concerned.

24 Each full-time and part-time member of the IASB shall agree contractually to act in the public interest and to have regard to the IASB Framework (as amended from time to time) in deciding on and revising standards.

25 The Trustees shall appoint one of the full-time members as Chairman of the IASB, who shall also be the Chief Executive of the IASC Foundation. One of the full-time members of the IASB shall also be designated by the Trustees as Vice-Chairman,

whose role shall be to chair meetings of the IASB in the absence of the Chairman in unusual circumstances (such as illness). The appointment of the Chairman and the designation as Vice-Chairman shall be for such term as the Trustees decide. The title of Vice-Chairman would not imply that the individual concerned is the Chairman-elect.

26 Members of the IASB shall be appointed for a term of up to five years, renewable once. The Trustees shall develop rules and procedures to ensure that the IASB is, and is seen to be, independent, and, in particular, on appointment, full-time members of the IASB shall sever all employment relationships with current employers and shall not hold any position giving rise to economic incentives which might call into question their independence of judgement in setting accounting standards. Secondments and any rights to return to an employer would therefore not be permitted. Part-time members of the IASB would not be expected to sever all other employment arrangements.

27 The terms of appointment of members of the IASB shall be staggered so that not all members retire at once. To accomplish this, the Trustees shall consider initial terms of three years for some members, four years for others and a full five years for the remaining initial members.

28 Full-time and part-time members of the IASB shall be remunerated at rates commensurate with the respective responsibilities assumed: such rates shall be determined by the Trustees. Expenses of travel on IASB business shall be met by the IASC Foundation.

29 The IASB shall meet at such times and locations as it determines: meetings of the IASB shall be open to the public, but certain discussions (normally only about selection, appointment and other personnel issues) may be held in private at the discretion of the IASB.

30 Each member of the IASB shall have one vote. On both technical and other matters, proxy voting shall not be permitted nor shall members of the IASB be entitled to appoint alternates to attend meetings. In the event of a tied vote, on a decision that is to be made by a simple majority of the members of the IASB present at a meeting in person or by telecommunications, the Chairman shall have an additional casting vote.

31 The publication of an Exposure Draft, International Accounting Standard, International Financial Reporting Standard, or final Interpretation of the International Financial Reporting Interpretations Committee shall require approval by eight of the fourteen members of the IASB. Other decisions of the IASB, including the publication of a Draft Statement of Principles or discussion paper, shall require a simple majority of the members of the IASB present at a meeting that is attended by at least 60% of the members of the IASB, in person or by telecommunications.

32 The IASB shall:

(a) have complete responsibility for all IASB technical matters including the preparation and issuing of International Accounting Standards, International Financial Reporting Standards, and Exposure Drafts, each of which shall include any dissenting opinions, and final approval of Interpretations by the International Financial Reporting Interpretations Committee;

(b) publish an Exposure Draft on all projects and normally publish a Draft Statement of Principles or other discussion document for public comment on major projects;

(c) have full discretion over the technical agenda of the IASB and over project assignments on technical matters: in organising the conduct of its work, the IASB may outsource detailed research or other work to national standard-setters or other organisations;

(d) (i) establish procedures for reviewing comments made within a reasonable period on documents published for comment,

(ii) normally form Steering Committees or other types of specialist advisory groups to give advice on major projects,

(iii) consult the Standards Advisory Council on major projects, agenda decisions and work priorities and

(iv) normally issue bases for conclusions with International Accounting Standards, International Financial Reporting Standards, and Exposure Drafts;

(e) consider holding public hearings to discuss proposed standards, although there is no requirement to hold public hearings for every project; and

(f) consider undertaking field tests (both in developed countries and in emerging markets) to ensure that proposed standards are practical and workable in all environments, although there is no requirement to undertake field tests for every project.

33 The authoritative text of any Exposure Draft or International Accounting Standard or International Financial Reporting Standard or Draft or final Interpretation shall be that published by the IASB in the English language. The IASB may publish authorised translations or give authority to others to publish translations of the authoritative text of Exposure Drafts and International Accounting Standards and International Financial Reporting Standards and Draft and final Interpretations.

International Financial Reporting Interpretations Committee

34 The International Financial Reporting Interpretations Committee shall comprise twelve voting members, appointed by the Trustees under Section 16(b) for renewable terms of three years. The Trustees shall appoint a member of the IASB, the Director of Technical Activities or another senior member of the IASB staff, or another appropriately qualified individual, to chair the Committee. The Chair has the right to speak to the technical issues being considered but not to vote. The Trustees, as they deem necessary, shall appoint as non-voting observers representatives of regulatory organisations, who shall have the right to attend and speak at meetings. Expenses of travel on Committee business shall be met by the IASC Foundation.

35 The Committee shall meet as and when required and nine voting members present in person or by telecommunications shall constitute a quorum: one or two IASB members shall be designated by the IASB and shall attend meetings as non-voting observers; other members of the IASB may attend and speak at the meetings. On exceptional occasions, members of the Committee may be allowed to send non-voting alternates, at the discretion of the Chair of the Committee. Members wishing to nominate an alternate should seek the consent of the Chair in advance of the meeting concerned. Meetings of the Committee shall be open to the public, but certain discussions (normally only about selection, appointment and other personnel issues) may be held in private at the Committee's discretion.

36 Each member of the Committee shall have one vote. Members vote in accordance with their own independent views, not as representatives voting according to the views of any firm, organisation or constituency with which they may be associated. Proxy voting shall not be permitted. Approval of Draft or final Interpretations shall require that not more than three voting members vote against the Draft or final Interpretation.

37 The Committee shall:

(a) interpret the application of International Accounting Standards (IASs) and International Financial Reporting Standards (IFRSs) and provide timely guidance on financial reporting issues not specifically addressed in IASs and IFRSs, in the context of the IASB Framework, and undertake other tasks at the request of the IASB;

(b) in carrying out its work under (a) above, have regard to the IASB's objective of working actively with national standard-setters to bring about convergence of national accounting standards and IASs and IFRSs to high quality solutions;

(c) publish after clearance by the IASB Draft Interpretations for public comment and consider comments made within a reasonable period before finalising an Interpretation; and

(d) report to the IASB and obtain its approval for final Interpretations.

Standards Advisory Council

38 The Standards Advisory Council, whose members shall be appointed by the Trustees under Section 16(b), provides a forum for participation by organisations and individuals, with an interest in international financial reporting, having diverse geographical and functional backgrounds, with the objective of (a) giving advice to the IASB on agenda decisions and priorities in the IASB's work, (b) informing the IASB of the views of the organisations and individuals on the Council on major standard-setting projects and (c) giving other advice to the IASB or the Trustees.

39 The Council shall comprise thirty or more members, having a diversity of geographical and professional backgrounds, appointed for renewable terms of three years. The Chairman of the IASB shall chair the Council.

40 The Council shall normally meet at least three times a year. Meetings shall be open to the public. The Council shall be consulted by the IASB in advance of IASB decisions on major projects and by the Trustees in advance of any proposed changes to this Constitution.

Chief Executive and Staff

41 As provided under Section 25, the Chairman of the IASB shall also be the Chief Executive of the IASC Foundation, and shall be subject to supervision by the Trustees.

42 The Chief Executive shall be responsible for the staffing of the IASB, which shall include a Director of Technical Activities appointed by the Chief Executive in consultation with the Trustees: the Director of Technical Activities, while not a member of the IASB, shall be entitled to participate in the debate but not to vote at meetings of the IASB and the International Financial Reporting Interpretations Committee.

43 A Director of Operations and a Commercial Director shall also be appointed by the Chief Executive in consultation with the Trustees. They shall have responsibility for publications and copyright, communications, administration, and finance under the supervision of the Chief Executive and for fundraising under the supervision of the Trustees.

Administration

44 The administrative office of the IASC Foundation shall be located in such location as may be determined by the Trustees in accordance with Section 14(d).

45 The IASC Foundation shall be a legal entity as determined by the Trustees and shall be governed by this Constitution and by any laws which apply to such legal entity, including, if appropriate, laws applicable because of the location of its registered office.

46 The IASC Foundation shall be bound by the signature(s) of such person or persons as may be duly authorised by the Trustees.

Annex
International Accounting Standards Committee Foundation Criteria for IASB Members

The following would represent criteria for IASB membership:

1 **Demonstrated Technical Competency and Knowledge of Financial Accounting and Reporting.** All members of the IASB, regardless of whether they are from the accounting profession, preparers, users, or academics, should have demonstrated a high level of knowledge and technical competency in financial accounting and reporting. The credibility of the IASB and its individual members and the effectiveness and efficiency of the organisation will be enhanced with members who have such knowledge and skills.

2 **Ability to Analyse.** IASB members should have demonstrated the ability to analyse issues and consider the implications of that analysis for the decision-making process.

3 **Communication Skills.** Effective oral and written communication skills are necessary. These skills include the ability to communicate effectively in private meetings with IASB members, in public meetings, and in written materials such as accounting standards, speeches, articles, memos and correspondence with constituents. Communication skills also include the ability to listen to and consider the views of others. While a working knowledge of English is necessary, there should not be discrimination in selection against those for whom English is not their first language.

4 **Judicious Decision-making.** IASB members should be capable of considering varied viewpoints, weighing the evidence presented in an impartial fashion, and reaching well-reasoned and supportable decisions in a timely fashion.

5 **Awareness of the Financial Reporting Environment.** High quality financial reporting will be affected by the financial, business and economic environment. IASB members should have an understanding of the global economic environment in which the IASB operates. This global awareness should include awareness of business and financial reporting issues that are relevant to, and affect the quality of, transparent financial reporting and disclosure in the various capital markets worldwide.

6 **Ability to Work in a Collegial Atmosphere.** Members should be able to show respect, tact and consideration for one another's and constituents' views. Members must be able to work with one another in reaching consensus views based on the IASB's objective of developing high quality and transparent financial reporting. Members must be able to put the objective of the IASB above individual philosophies and interests.

7 **Integrity, Objectivity and Discipline.** The credibility of members should be demonstrated through their integrity and objectivity. This includes intellectual integrity as well as integrity in dealing with fellow IASB members and constituents. Members should demonstrate an ability to be objective in reaching decisions. Members also should demonstrate an ability to show rigorous discipline and carry a demanding workload.

8 **Commitment to the IASC Foundation's Mission and Public Interest.** Members should be committed to achieving the objective of the IASC Foundation of establishing international accounting and financial reporting standards that are of high quality, comparable, and transparent. A candidate for the IASB also should be committed to serving the public interest through a private standard-setting process.

Preface to International Financial Reporting Standards

This Preface is issued to set out the objectives and due process of the International Accounting Standards Board and to explain the scope, authority and timing of application of International Financial Reporting Standards. The Preface was approved in April 2002 and supersedes the Preface published in January 1975 (amended November 1982).

1 The International Accounting Standards Board (IASB) was established in 2001 as part of the International Accounting Standards Committee (IASC) Foundation. The governance of the IASC Foundation rests with nineteen Trustees. The Trustees' responsibilities include appointing the members of the IASB and associated councils and committees, as well as securing financing for the organisation. The IASB comprises twelve full-time and two part-time members. Approval of International Financial Reporting Standards (IFRSs) and related documents, such as the *Framework for the Preparation and Presentation of Financial Statements*, exposure drafts, and other discussion documents, is the responsibility of the IASB.

2 The International Financial Reporting Interpretations Committee (IFRIC) comprises twelve voting members and a non-voting Chairman, all appointed by the Trustees. The role of the IFRIC is to prepare interpretations of IFRSs for approval by the IASB and, in the context of the *Framework*, to provide timely guidance on financial reporting issues not specifically addressed in IFRSs. The IFRIC replaced the former Standing Interpretations Committee (SIC) in 2002.

3 The Standards Advisory Council (SAC) is appointed by the Trustees. It provides a formal vehicle for participation by organisations and individuals with an interest in international financial reporting. The participants have diverse geographical and functional backgrounds. The SAC's objective is to give advice to the IASB on priorities and on major standard-setting projects.

4 The IASB was preceded by the Board of IASC, which came into existence on 29 June 1973 as a result of an agreement by professional accountancy bodies in Australia, Canada, France, Germany, Japan, Mexico, the Netherlands, the United Kingdom and Ireland, and the United States of America. A revised Agreement and Constitution were signed in November 1982. The Constitution was further revised in October 1992 and May 2000 by the IASC Board. Under the May 2000 Constitution, the professional accountancy bodies adopted a mechanism enabling the appointed Trustees to put the May 2000 Constitution into force. The Trustees activated the new Constitution in January 2001, and revised it in March 2002.

5 At its meeting on 20 April 2001, the IASB passed the following resolution:

> "All Standards and Interpretations issued under previous Constitutions continue to be applicable unless and until they are amended or withdrawn. The International Accounting Standards Board may amend or withdraw International Accounting Standards and SIC Interpretations issued under previous Constitutions of IASC as well as issue new Standards and Interpretations."

When the term IFRSs is used in this Preface, it includes standards and interpretations approved by the IASB, and International Accounting Standards (IASs) and SIC interpretations issued under previous Constitutions.

Objectives of the IASB

6 The objectives of the IASB are:

(a) to develop, in the public interest, a single set of high quality, understandable and enforceable global accounting standards that require high quality, transparent and comparable information in financial statements and other financial reporting to help participants in the various capital markets of the world and other users of the information to make economic decisions;

(b) to promote the use and rigorous application of those standards; and

(c) to work actively with national standard-setters to bring about convergence of national accounting standards and IFRSs to high quality solutions.

Scope and authority of International Financial Reporting Standards

7 The IASB achieves its objectives primarily by developing and publishing IFRSs and promoting the use of those standards in general purpose financial statements and other financial reporting. Other financial reporting comprises information provided outside financial statements that assists in the interpretation of a complete set of financial statements or improves users' ability to make efficient economic decisions. In developing IFRSs, the IASB works with national standard-setters to maximise the convergence of IFRSs and national standards.

8 IFRSs set out recognition, measurement, presentation and disclosure requirements dealing with transactions and events that are important in general purpose financial statements. They may also set out such requirements for transactions and events that arise mainly in specific industries. IFRSs are based on the *Framework*, which addresses the concepts underlying the information presented in general purpose financial statements. The objective of the *Framework* is to facilitate the consistent and logical formulation of IFRSs. The *Framework* also provides a basis for the use of judgement in resolving accounting issues.

9 IFRSs are designed to apply to the general purpose financial statements and other financial reporting of all profit-oriented entities. Profit-oriented entities include those engaged in commercial, industrial, financial and similar activities, whether organised in corporate or in other forms. They include organisations such as mutual insurance companies and other mutual cooperative entities that provide dividends or other economic benefits directly and proportionately to their owners, members or participants. Although IFRSs are not designed to apply to not-for-profit activities in the private sector, public sector or government, entities with such activities may find them appropriate. The Public Sector Committee of the International Federation of Accountants (PSC) has issued a Guideline stating that IFRSs are applicable to government business entities. The PSC prepares accounting standards for governments and other public sector entities, other than government business entities, based on IFRSs.

10 IFRSs apply to all general purpose financial statements. Such financial statements are directed towards the common information needs of a wide range of users, for example, shareholders, creditors, employees and the public at large. The objective of financial statements is to provide information about the financial position, performance and cash flows of an entity that is useful to those users in making economic decisions.

11 A complete set of financial statements includes a balance sheet, an income statement, a statement showing either all changes in equity or changes in equity other than those arising from capital transactions with owners and distributions to owners, a cash flow statement, and accounting policies and explanatory notes. In the interest of timeliness and cost considerations and to avoid repeating information previously reported, an entity may provide less information in its interim financial statements than in its annual financial statements. IAS 34 *Interim Financial Reporting* prescribes the minimum content of complete or condensed financial statements for an interim period. The term 'financial statements' includes a complete set of financial statements prepared for an interim or annual period, and condensed financial statements for an interim period.

12 In some cases, IASC permitted different treatments for given transactions and events. Usually, one treatment is identified as the 'benchmark treatment' and the other as the 'allowed alternative treatment'. The financial statements of an entity may appropriately be described as being prepared in accordance with IFRSs whether they use the benchmark treatment or the allowed alternative treatment.

13 The IASB's objective is to require like transactions and events to be accounted for and reported in a like way and unlike transactions and events to be accounted for and reported differently, both within an entity over time and among entities. Consequently, the IASB intends not to permit choices in accounting treatment. Also, the IASB has reconsidered, and will continue to reconsider, those transactions and events for which IASs permit a choice of accounting treatment, with the objective of reducing the number of those choices.

14 Standards approved by the IASB include paragraphs in bold type and plain type, which have equal authority. Paragraphs in bold type indicate the main principles. An individual standard should be read in the context of the objective stated in that standard and this Preface.

15 Interpretations of IFRSs are prepared by the IFRIC to give authoritative guidance on issues that are likely to receive divergent or unacceptable treatment, in the absence of such guidance.

16 IAS 1 *Presentation of Financial Statements* includes the following requirement:

> "An entity whose financial statements comply with IFRSs shall make an explicit and unreserved statement of such compliance in the notes. Financial statements shall not be described as complying with IFRSs unless they comply with all the requirements of IFRSs."

17 Any limitation of the scope of an IFRS is made clear in the standard.

Due process

18 IFRSs are developed through an international due process that involves accountants, financial analysts and other users of financial statements, the business community, stock exchanges, regulatory and legal authorities, academics and other interested individuals and organisations from around the world. The IASB consults, in public meetings, the SAC on major projects, agenda decisions and work priorities, and discusses technical matters in meetings that are open to public observation. Due process for projects normally, but not necessarily, involves the following steps (the steps that are required under the terms of the IASC Foundation Constitution are indicated by an asterisk*):

(a) the staff are asked to identify and review all the issues associated with the topic and to consider the application of the *Framework* to the issues;

(b) study of national accounting requirements and practice and an exchange of views about the issues with national standard-setters;

(c) consulting the SAC about the advisability of adding the topic to the IASB's agenda;*

(d) formation of an advisory group to give advice to the IASB on the project;

(e) publishing for public comment a discussion document;

(f) publishing for public comment an exposure draft approved by at least eight votes of the IASB, including any dissenting opinions held by IASB members;*

(g) publishing within an exposure draft a basis for conclusions;

(h) consideration of all comments received within the comment period on discussion documents and exposure drafts;*

(i) consideration of the desirability of holding a public hearing and of the desirability of conducting field tests and, if considered desirable, holding such hearings and conducting such tests;

(j) approval of a standard by at least eight votes of the IASB and inclusion in the published standard of any dissenting opinions;* and

(k) publishing within a standard a basis for conclusions, explaining, among other things, the steps in the IASB's due process and how the IASB dealt with public comments on the exposure draft.

19 Interpretations of IFRSs are developed through an international due process that involves accountants, financial analysts and other users of financial statements, the business community, stock exchanges, regulatory and legal authorities, academics and other interested individuals and organisations from around the world. The IFRIC discusses technical matters in meetings that are open to public observation. The due process for each project normally, but not necessarily, involves the following steps (the steps that are required under the terms of the IASC Foundation Constitution are indicated by an asterisk*):

(a) the staff are asked to identify and review all the issues associated with the topic and to consider the application of the *Framework* to the issues;

(b) study of national accounting requirements and practice and an exchange of views about the issues with national standard-setters, including national committees that have responsibility for interpretations of national standards;

(c) publication of a draft interpretation for public comment if no more than three IFRIC members have voted against the proposal;*

(d) consideration of all comments received within the comment period on a draft interpretation;*

(e) approval by the IFRIC of an interpretation if no more than three IFRIC members have voted against the interpretation after considering public comments on the draft interpretation;* and

(f) approval of the interpretation by at least eight votes of the IASB.*

Timing of application of International Financial Reporting Standards

20 IFRSs apply from a date specified in the document. New or revised IFRSs set out transitional provisions to be applied on their initial application.

21 The IASB has no general policy of exempting transactions occurring before a specific date from the requirements of new IFRSs. When financial statements are used to monitor compliance with contracts and agreements, a new IFRS may have consequences that were not foreseen when the contract or agreement was finalised. For example, covenants contained in banking and loan agreements may impose limits on measures shown in a borrower's financial statements. The IASB believes the fact that financial reporting requirements evolve and change over time is well understood and would be known to the parties when they entered into the agreement. It is up to the parties to determine whether the agreement should be insulated from the effects of a future IFRS, or, if not, the manner in which it might be renegotiated to reflect changes in reporting rather than changes in the underlying financial condition.

22 Exposure drafts are issued for comment and their proposals are subject to revision. Until the effective date of an IFRS, the requirements of any IFRS that would be affected by proposals in an exposure draft remain in force.

Language

23 The approved text of any discussion document, exposure draft, or IFRS is that approved by the IASB in the English language. The IASB may approve translations in other languages, provided that the translation is prepared in accordance with a process that provides assurance of the quality of the translation, and the IASB may license other translations.

Framework for the Preparation and Presentation of Financial Statements

The IASB Framework was approved by the IASC Board in April 1989 for publication in July 1989, and adopted by the IASB in April 2001.

CONTENTS

Preface

Financial statements are prepared and presented for external users by many entities around the world. Although such financial statements may appear similar from country to country, there are differences which have probably been caused by a variety of social, economic and legal circumstances and by different countries having in mind the needs of different users of financial statements when setting national requirements.

These different circumstances have led to the use of a variety of definitions of the elements of financial statements; that is, for example, assets, liabilities, equity, income and expenses. They have also resulted in the use of different criteria for the recognition of items in the financial statements and in a preference for different bases of measurement. The scope of the financial statements and the disclosures made in them have also been affected.

The International Accounting Standards Committee (IASC) is committed to narrowing these differences by seeking to harmonise regulations, accounting standards and procedures relating to the preparation and presentation of financial statements. It believes that further harmonisation can best be pursued by focusing on financial statements that are prepared for the purpose of providing information that is useful in making economic decisions.

The Board of IASC believes that financial statements prepared for this purpose meet the common needs of most users. This is because nearly all users are making economic decisions, for example, to:

(a) decide when to buy, hold or sell an equity investment;

(b) assess the stewardship or accountability of management;

(c) assess the ability of the entity to pay and provide other benefits to its employees;

(d) assess the security for amounts lent to the entity;

(e) determine taxation policies;

(f) determine distributable profits and dividends;

(g) prepare and use national income statistics; or

(h) regulate the activities of entities.

The Board recognises, however, that governments, in particular, may specify different or additional requirements for their own purposes. These requirements should not, however, affect financial statements published for the benefit of other users unless they also meet the needs of those other users.

Financial statements are most commonly prepared in accordance with an accounting model based on recoverable historical cost and the nominal financial capital maintenance concept. Other models and concepts may be more appropriate in order to meet the objective of providing information that is useful for making economic decisions although there is presently no consensus for change. This *Framework* has been developed so that it is applicable to a range of accounting models and concepts of capital and capital maintenance.

Introduction

Purpose and status

1 This *Framework* sets out the concepts that underlie the preparation and presentation of financial statements for external users. The purpose of the *Framework* is to:

(a) assist the Board of IASC in the development of future International Accounting Standards and in its review of existing International Accounting Standards;

(b) assist the Board of IASC in promoting harmonisation of regulations, accounting standards and procedures relating to the presentation of financial statements by providing a basis for reducing the number of alternative accounting treatments permitted by International Accounting Standards;

(c) assist national standard-setting bodies in developing national standards;

(d) assist preparers of financial statements in applying International Accounting Standards and in dealing with topics that have yet to form the subject of an International Accounting Standard;

(e) assist auditors in forming an opinion as to whether financial statements conform with International Accounting Standards;

(f) assist users of financial statements in interpreting the information contained in financial statements prepared in conformity with International Accounting Standards; and

(g) provide those who are interested in the work of IASC with information about its approach to the formulation of International Accounting Standards.

2 This *Framework* is not an International Accounting Standard and hence does not define standards for any particular measurement or disclosure issue. Nothing in this *Framework* overrides any specific International Accounting Standard.

3 The Board of IASC recognises that in a limited number of cases there may be a conflict between the *Framework* and an International Accounting Standard. In those cases where there is a conflict, the requirements of the International Accounting Standard prevail over those of the *Framework*. As, however, the Board of IASC will be guided by the *Framework* in the development of future Standards and in its review of existing Standards, the number of cases of conflict between the *Framework* and International Accounting Standards will diminish through time.

4 The *Framework* will be revised from time to time on the basis of the Board's experience of working with it.

Scope

5 The *Framework* deals with:

(a) the objective of financial statements;

(b) the qualitative characteristics that determine the usefulness of information in financial statements;

(c) the definition, recognition and measurement of the elements from which financial statements are constructed; and

(d) concepts of capital and capital maintenance.

6 The *Framework* is concerned with general purpose financial statements (hereafter referred to as "financial statements") including consolidated financial statements. Such financial statements are prepared and presented at least annually and are directed toward the common information needs of a wide range of users. Some of these users may require, and have the power to obtain, information in addition to that contained in the financial statements. Many users, however, have to rely on the financial statements as their major source of financial information and such financial statements should, therefore, be prepared and presented with their needs in view. Special purpose financial reports, for example, prospectuses and computations prepared for taxation purposes, are outside the scope of this *Framework*. Nevertheless, the *Framework* may be applied in the preparation of such special purpose reports where their requirements permit.

7 Financial statements form part of the process of financial reporting. A complete set of financial statements normally includes a balance sheet, an income statement, a statement of changes in financial position (which may be presented in a variety of ways, for example, as a statement of cash flows or a statement of funds flow), and those notes and other statements and explanatory material that are an integral part of the financial statements. They may also include supplementary schedules and information based on or derived from, and expected to be read with, such statements. Such schedules and supplementary information may deal, for example, with financial information about industrial and geographical segments and disclosures about the effects of changing prices. Financial statements do not, however, include such items as reports by directors, statements by the chairman, discussion and analysis by management and similar items that may be included in a financial or annual report.

8 The *Framework* applies to the financial statements of all commercial, industrial and business reporting entities, whether in the public or the private sectors. A reporting entity is an entity for which there are users who rely on the financial statements as their major source of financial information about the entity.

Users and their information needs

9 The users of financial statements include present and potential investors, employees, lenders, suppliers and other trade creditors, customers, governments and their agencies and the public. They use financial statements in order to satisfy some of their different needs for information. These needs include the following:

(a) *Investors.* The providers of risk capital and their advisers are concerned with the risk inherent in, and return provided by, their investments. They need information to help them determine whether they should buy, hold or sell. Shareholders are also interested in information which enables them to assess the ability of the entity to pay dividends.

(b) *Employees.* Employees and their representative groups are interested in information about the stability and profitability of their employers. They are also interested in information which enables them to assess the ability of the entity to provide remuneration, retirement benefits and employment opportunities.

(c) *Lenders.* Lenders are interested in information that enables them to determine whether their loans, and the interest attaching to them, will be paid when due.

(d) *Suppliers and other trade creditors.* Suppliers and other creditors are interested in information that enables them to determine whether amounts owing to them will be paid when due. Trade creditors are likely to be interested in an entity over a shorter period than lenders unless they are dependent upon the continuation of the entity as a major customer.

(e) *Customers.* Customers have an interest in information about the continuance of an entity, especially when they have a long-term involvement with, or are dependent on, the entity.

(f) *Governments and their agencies.* Governments and their agencies are interested in the allocation of resources and, therefore, the activities of entities. They also require information in order to regulate the activities of entities, determine taxation policies and as the basis for national income and similar statistics.

(g) *Public.* Entities affect members of the public in a variety of ways. For example, entities may make a substantial contribution to the local economy in many ways including the number of people they employ and their patronage of local suppliers. Financial statements may assist the public by providing information about the trends and recent developments in the prosperity of the entity and the range of its activities.

10 While all of the information needs of these users cannot be met by financial statements, there are needs which are common to all users. As investors are providers of risk capital to the entity, the provision of financial statements that meet their needs will also meet most of the needs of other users that financial statements can satisfy.

11 The management of an entity has the primary responsibility for the preparation and presentation of the financial statements of the entity. Management is also interested in the information contained in the financial statements even though it has access to additional management and financial information that helps it carry out its planning, decision-making and control responsibilities. Management has the ability to determine the form and content of such additional information in order to meet its own needs. The reporting of such information, however, is beyond the scope of this *Framework*. Nevertheless, published financial statements are based on the information used by management about the financial position, performance and changes in financial position of the entity.

The objective of financial statements

12 The objective of financial statements is to provide information about the financial position, performance and changes in financial position of an entity that is useful to a wide range of users in making economic decisions.

13 Financial statements prepared for this purpose meet the common needs of most users. However, financial statements do not provide all the information that users may need to make economic decisions since they largely portray the financial effects of past events and do not necessarily provide non-financial information.

14 Financial statements also show the results of the stewardship of management, or the accountability of management for the resources entrusted to it. Those users who wish to assess the stewardship or accountability of management do so in order that they may make economic decisions; these decisions may include, for example, whether to hold or sell their investment in the entity or whether to reappoint or replace the management.

Financial position, performance and changes in financial position

15 The economic decisions that are taken by users of financial statements require an evaluation of the ability of an entity to generate cash and cash equivalents and of the timing and certainty of their generation. This ability ultimately determines, for example, the capacity of an entity to pay its employees and suppliers, meet interest payments, repay loans and make distributions to its owners. Users are better able to evaluate this ability to generate cash and cash equivalents if they are provided with information that focuses on the financial position, performance and changes in financial position of an entity.

16 The financial position of an entity is affected by the economic resources it controls, its financial structure, its liquidity and solvency, and its capacity to adapt to changes in the environment in which it operates. Information about the economic resources controlled by the entity and its capacity in the past to modify these resources is useful in predicting the ability of the entity to generate cash and cash equivalents in the future. Information about financial structure is useful in predicting future borrowing needs and how future profits and cash flows will be distributed among those with an interest in the entity; it is also useful in predicting how successful the entity is likely to be in raising further finance. Information about liquidity and solvency is useful in predicting the ability of the entity to meet its financial commitments as they fall due. Liquidity refers to the availability of cash in the near future after taking account of financial commitments over this period. Solvency refers to the availability of cash over the longer term to meet financial commitments as they fall due.

17 Information about the performance of an entity, in particular its profitability, is required in order to assess potential changes in the economic resources that it is likely to control in the future. Information about variability of performance is important in this respect. Information about performance is useful in predicting the capacity of the entity to generate cash flows from its existing resource base. It is also useful in forming judgements about the effectiveness with which the entity might employ additional resources.

18 Information concerning changes in the financial position of an entity is useful in order to assess its investing, financing and operating activities during the reporting period. This information is useful in providing the user with a basis to assess the ability of the entity to generate cash and cash equivalents and the needs of the entity to utilise those cash flows. In constructing a statement of changes in financial position, funds can be defined in various ways, such as all financial resources, working capital, liquid assets or cash. No attempt is made in this *Framework* to specify a definition of funds.

19 Information about financial position is primarily provided in a balance sheet. Information about performance is primarily provided in an income statement. Information about changes in financial position is provided in the financial statements by means of a separate statement.

20 The component parts of the financial statements interrelate because they reflect different aspects of the same transactions or other events. Although each statement provides information that is different from the others, none is likely to serve only a single purpose or provide all the information necessary for particular needs of users. For example, an income statement provides an incomplete picture of performance unless it is used in conjunction with the balance sheet and the statement of changes in financial position.

Notes and supplementary schedules

21 The financial statements also contain notes and supplementary schedules and other information. For example, they may contain additional information that is relevant to the needs of users about the items in the balance sheet and income statement. They may include disclosures about the risks and uncertainties affecting the entity and any resources and obligations not recognised in the balance sheet (such as mineral reserves). Information about geographical and industry segments and the effect on the entity of changing prices may also be provided in the form of supplementary information.

Underlying assumptions

Accrual basis

22 In order to meet their objectives, financial statements are prepared on the accrual basis of accounting. Under this basis, the effects of transactions and other events are recognised when they occur (and not as cash or its equivalent is received or paid) and they are recorded in the accounting records and reported in the financial statements of the periods to which they relate. Financial statements prepared on the accrual basis inform users not only of past transactions involving the payment and receipt of cash but also of obligations to pay cash in the future and of resources that represent cash to be received in the future. Hence, they provide the type of information about past transactions and other events that is most useful to users in making economic decisions.

Going concern

23 The financial statements are normally prepared on the assumption that an entity is a going concern and will continue in operation for the foreseeable future.

Hence, it is assumed that the entity has neither the intention nor the need to liquidate or curtail materially the scale of its operations; if such an intention or need exists, the financial statements may have to be prepared on a different basis and, if so, the basis used is disclosed.

Qualitative characteristics of financial statements

24 Qualitative characteristics are the attributes that make the information provided in financial statements useful to users. The four principal qualitative characteristics are understandability, relevance, reliability and comparability.

Understandability

25 An essential quality of the information provided in financial statements is that it is readily understandable by users. For this purpose, users are assumed to have a reasonable knowledge of business and economic activities and accounting and a willingness to study the information with reasonable diligence. However, information about complex matters that should be included in the financial statements because of its relevance to the economic decision-making needs of users should not be excluded merely on the grounds that it may be too difficult for certain users to understand.

Relevance

26 To be useful, information must be relevant to the decision-making needs of users. Information has the quality of relevance when it influences the economic decisions of users by helping them evaluate past, present or future events or confirming, or correcting, their past evaluations.

27 The predictive and confirmatory roles of information are interrelated. For example, information about the current level and structure of asset holdings has value to users when they endeavour to predict the ability of the entity to take advantage of opportunities and its ability to react to adverse situations. The same information plays a confirmatory role in respect of past predictions about, for example, the way in which the entity would be structured or the outcome of planned operations.

28 Information about financial position and past performance is frequently used as the basis for predicting future financial position and performance and other matters in which users are directly interested, such as dividend and wage payments, security price movements and the ability of the entity to meet its commitments as they fall due. To have predictive value, information need not be in the form of an explicit forecast. The ability to make predictions from financial statements is enhanced, however, by the manner in which information on past transactions and events is displayed. For example, the predictive value of the income statement is enhanced if unusual, abnormal and infrequent items of income or expense are separately disclosed.

Materiality

29 The relevance of information is affected by its nature and materiality. In some cases, the nature of information alone is sufficient to determine its relevance. For example, the reporting of a new segment may affect the assessment of the

risks and opportunities facing the entity irrespective of the materiality of the results achieved by the new segment in the reporting period. In other cases, both the nature and materiality are important, for example, the amounts of inventories held in each of the main categories that are appropriate to the business.

30 Information is material if its omission or misstatement could influence the economic decisions of users taken on the basis of the financial statements. Materiality depends on the size of the item or error judged in the particular circumstances of its omission or misstatement. Thus, materiality provides a threshold or cut-off point rather than being a primary qualitative characteristic which information must have if it is to be useful.

Reliability

31 To be useful, information must also be reliable. Information has the quality of reliability when it is free from material error and bias and can be depended upon by users to represent faithfully that which it either purports to represent or could reasonably be expected to represent.

32 Information may be relevant but so unreliable in nature or representation that its recognition may be potentially misleading. For example, if the validity and amount of a claim for damages under a legal action are disputed, it may be inappropriate for the entity to recognise the full amount of the claim in the balance sheet, although it may be appropriate to disclose the amount and circumstances of the claim.

Faithful representation

33 To be reliable, information must represent faithfully the transactions and other events it either purports to represent or could reasonably be expected to represent. Thus, for example, a balance sheet should represent faithfully the transactions and other events that result in assets, liabilities and equity of the entity at the reporting date which meet the recognition criteria.

34 Most financial information is subject to some risk of being less than a faithful representation of that which it purports to portray. This is not due to bias, but rather to inherent difficulties either in identifying the transactions and other events to be measured or in devising and applying measurement and presentation techniques that can convey messages that correspond with those transactions and events. In certain cases, the measurement of the financial effects of items could be so uncertain that entities generally would not recognise them in the financial statements; for example, although most entities generate goodwill internally over time, it is usually difficult to identify or measure that goodwill reliably. In other cases, however, it may be relevant to recognise items and to disclose the risk of error surrounding their recognition and measurement.

Substance over form

35 If information is to represent faithfully the transactions and other events that it purports to represent, it is necessary that they are accounted for and presented in accordance with their substance and economic reality and not merely their legal form. The substance of transactions or other events is not always consistent with that which is apparent from their legal or contrived form. For example, an entity

may dispose of an asset to another party in such a way that the documentation purports to pass legal ownership to that party; nevertheless, agreements may exist that ensure that the entity continues to enjoy the future economic benefits embodied in the asset. In such circumstances, the reporting of a sale would not represent faithfully the transaction entered into (if indeed there was a transaction).

Neutrality

36 To be reliable, the information contained in financial statements must be neutral, that is, free from bias. Financial statements are not neutral if, by the selection or presentation of information, they influence the making of a decision or judgement in order to achieve a predetermined result or outcome.

Prudence

37 The preparers of financial statements do, however, have to contend with the uncertainties that inevitably surround many events and circumstances, such as the collectability of doubtful receivables, the probable useful life of plant and equipment and the number of warranty claims that may occur. Such uncertainties are recognised by the disclosure of their nature and extent and by the exercise of prudence in the preparation of the financial statements. Prudence is the inclusion of a degree of caution in the exercise of the judgements needed in making the estimates required under conditions of uncertainty, such that assets or income are not overstated and liabilities or expenses are not understated. However, the exercise of prudence does not allow, for example, the creation of hidden reserves or excessive provisions, the deliberate understatement of assets or income, or the deliberate overstatement of liabilities or expenses, because the financial statements would not be neutral and, therefore, not have the quality of reliability.

Completeness

38 To be reliable, the information in financial statements must be complete within the bounds of materiality and cost. An omission can cause information to be false or misleading and thus unreliable and deficient in terms of its relevance.

Comparability

39 Users must be able to compare the financial statements of an entity through time in order to identify trends in its financial position and performance. Users must also be able to compare the financial statements of different entities in order to evaluate their relative financial position, performance and changes in financial position. Hence, the measurement and display of the financial effect of like transactions and other events must be carried out in a consistent way throughout an entity and over time for that entity and in a consistent way for different entities.

40 An important implication of the qualitative characteristic of comparability is that users be informed of the accounting policies employed in the preparation of the financial statements, any changes in those policies and the effects of such changes. Users need to be able to identify differences between the accounting policies for like transactions and other events used by the same entity from period

to period and by different entities. Compliance with International Accounting Standards, including the disclosure of the accounting policies used by the entity, helps to achieve comparability.

41 The need for comparability should not be confused with mere uniformity and should not be allowed to become an impediment to the introduction of improved accounting standards. It is not appropriate for an entity to continue accounting in the same manner for a transaction or other event if the policy adopted is not in keeping with the qualitative characteristics of relevance and reliability. It is also inappropriate for an entity to leave its accounting policies unchanged when more relevant and reliable alternatives exist.

42 Because users wish to compare the financial position, performance and changes in financial position of an entity over time, it is important that the financial statements show corresponding information for the preceding periods.

Constraints on relevant and reliable information

Timeliness

43 If there is undue delay in the reporting of information it may lose its relevance. Management may need to balance the relative merits of timely reporting and the provision of reliable information. To provide information on a timely basis it may often be necessary to report before all aspects of a transaction or other event are known, thus impairing reliability. Conversely, if reporting is delayed until all aspects are known, the information may be highly reliable but of little use to users who have had to make decisions in the interim. In achieving a balance between relevance and reliability, the overriding consideration is how best to satisfy the economic decision-making needs of users.

Balance between benefit and cost

44 The balance between benefit and cost is a pervasive constraint rather than a qualitative characteristic. The benefits derived from information should exceed the cost of providing it. The evaluation of benefits and costs is, however, substantially a judgemental process. Furthermore, the costs do not necessarily fall on those users who enjoy the benefits. Benefits may also be enjoyed by users other than those for whom the information is prepared; for example, the provision of further information to lenders may reduce the borrowing costs of an entity. For these reasons, it is difficult to apply a cost-benefit test in any particular case. Nevertheless, standard-setters in particular, as well as the preparers and users of financial statements, should be aware of this constraint.

Balance between qualitative characteristics

45 In practice a balancing, or trade-off, between qualitative characteristics is often necessary. Generally the aim is to achieve an appropriate balance among the characteristics in order to meet the objective of financial statements. The relative importance of the characteristics in different cases is a matter of professional judgement.

True and fair view/fair presentation

46 Financial statements are frequently described as showing a true and fair view of, or as presenting fairly, the financial position, performance and changes in financial position of an entity. Although this *Framework* does not deal directly with such concepts, the application of the principal qualitative characteristics and of appropriate accounting standards normally results in financial statements that convey what is generally understood as a true and fair view of, or as presenting fairly such information.

The elements of financial statements

47 Financial statements portray the financial effects of transactions and other events by grouping them into broad classes according to their economic characteristics. These broad classes are termed the elements of financial statements. The elements directly related to the measurement of financial position in the balance sheet are assets, liabilities and equity. The elements directly related to the measurement of performance in the income statement are income and expenses. The statement of changes in financial position usually reflects income statement elements and changes in balance sheet elements; accordingly, this *Framework* identifies no elements that are unique to this statement.

48 The presentation of these elements in the balance sheet and the income statement involves a process of sub-classification. For example, assets and liabilities may be classified by their nature or function in the business of the entity in order to display information in the manner most useful to users for purposes of making economic decisions.

Financial position

49 The elements directly related to the measurement of financial position are assets, liabilities and equity. These are defined as follows:

(a) An asset is a resource controlled by the entity as a result of past events and from which future economic benefits are expected to flow to the entity.

(b) A liability is a present obligation of the entity arising from past events, the settlement of which is expected to result in an outflow from the entity of resources embodying economic benefits.

(c) Equity is the residual interest in the assets of the entity after deducting all its liabilities.

50 The definitions of an asset and a liability identify their essential features but do not attempt to specify the criteria that need to be met before they are recognised in the balance sheet. Thus, the definitions embrace items that are not recognised as assets or liabilities in the balance sheet because they do not satisfy the criteria for recognition discussed in paragraphs 82 to 98. In particular, the expectation that future economic benefits will flow to or from an entity must be sufficiently certain to meet the probability criterion in paragraph 83 before an asset or liability is recognised.

51 In assessing whether an item meets the definition of an asset, liability or equity, attention needs to be given to its underlying substance and economic reality and

not merely its legal form. Thus, for example, in the case of finance leases, the substance and economic reality are that the lessee acquires the economic benefits of the use of the leased asset for the major part of its useful life in return for entering into an obligation to pay for that right an amount approximating to the fair value of the asset and the related finance charge. Hence, the finance lease gives rise to items that satisfy the definition of an asset and a liability and are recognised as such in the lessee's balance sheet.

52 Balance sheets drawn up in accordance with current International Accounting Standards may include items that do not satisfy the definitions of an asset or liability and are not shown as part of equity. The definitions set out in paragraph 49 will, however, underlie future reviews of existing International Accounting Standards and the formulation of further Standards.

Assets

53 The future economic benefit embodied in an asset is the potential to contribute, directly or indirectly, to the flow of cash and cash equivalents to the entity. The potential may be a productive one that is part of the operating activities of the entity. It may also take the form of convertibility into cash or cash equivalents or a capability to reduce cash outflows, such as when an alternative manufacturing process lowers the costs of production.

54 An entity usually employs its assets to produce goods or services capable of satisfying the wants or needs of customers; because these goods or services can satisfy these wants or needs, customers are prepared to pay for them and hence contribute to the cash flow of the entity. Cash itself renders a service to the entity because of its command over other resources.

55 The future economic benefits embodied in an asset may flow to the entity in a number of ways. For example, an asset may be:

(a) used singly or in combination with other assets in the production of goods or services to be sold by the entity;

(b) exchanged for other assets;

(c) used to settle a liability; or

(d) distributed to the owners of the entity.

56 Many assets, for example, property, plant and equipment, have a physical form. However, physical form is not essential to the existence of an asset; hence patents and copyrights, for example, are assets if future economic benefits are expected to flow from them to the entity and if they are controlled by the entity.

57 Many assets, for example, receivables and property, are associated with legal rights, including the right of ownership. In determining the existence of an asset, the right of ownership is not essential; thus, for example, property held on a lease is an asset if the entity controls the benefits which are expected to flow from the property. Although the capacity of an entity to control benefits is usually the result of legal rights, an item may nonetheless satisfy the definition of an asset even when there is no legal control. For example, know-how obtained from a development activity may meet the definition of an asset when, by keeping that know-how secret, an entity controls the benefits that are expected to flow from it.

58 The assets of an entity result from past transactions or other past events. Entities normally obtain assets by purchasing or producing them, but other transactions or events may generate assets; examples include property received by an entity from government as part of a programme to encourage economic growth in an area and the discovery of mineral deposits. Transactions or events expected to occur in the future do not in themselves give rise to assets; hence, for example, an intention to purchase inventory does not, of itself, meet the definition of an asset.

59 There is a close association between incurring expenditure and generating assets but the two do not necessarily coincide. Hence, when an entity incurs expenditure, this may provide evidence that future economic benefits were sought but is not conclusive proof that an item satisfying the definition of an asset has been obtained. Similarly the absence of a related expenditure does not preclude an item from satisfying the definition of an asset and thus becoming a candidate for recognition in the balance sheet; for example, items that have been donated to the entity may satisfy the definition of an asset.

Liabilities

60 An essential characteristic of a liability is that the entity has a present obligation. An obligation is a duty or responsibility to act or perform in a certain way. Obligations may be legally enforceable as a consequence of a binding contract or statutory requirement. This is normally the case, for example, with amounts payable for goods and services received. Obligations also arise, however, from normal business practice, custom and a desire to maintain good business relations or act in an equitable manner. If, for example, an entity decides as a matter of policy to rectify faults in its products even when these become apparent after the warranty period has expired, the amounts that are expected to be expended in respect of goods already sold are liabilities.

61 A distinction needs to be drawn between a present obligation and a future commitment. A decision by the management of an entity to acquire assets in the future does not, of itself, give rise to a present obligation. An obligation normally arises only when the asset is delivered or the entity enters into an irrevocable agreement to acquire the asset. In the latter case, the irrevocable nature of the agreement means that the economic consequences of failing to honour the obligation, for example, because of the existence of a substantial penalty, leave the entity with little, if any, discretion to avoid the outflow of resources to another party.

62 The settlement of a present obligation usually involves the entity giving up resources embodying economic benefits in order to satisfy the claim of the other party. Settlement of a present obligation may occur in a number of ways, for example, by:

(a) payment of cash;

(b) transfer of other assets;

(c) provision of services;

(d) replacement of that obligation with another obligation; or

(e) conversion of the obligation to equity.

An obligation may also be extinguished by other means, such as a creditor waiving or forfeiting its rights.

63 Liabilities result from past transactions or other past events. Thus, for example, the acquisition of goods and the use of services give rise to trade payables (unless paid for in advance or on delivery) and the receipt of a bank loan results in an obligation to repay the loan. An entity may also recognise future rebates based on annual purchases by customers as liabilities; in this case, the sale of the goods in the past is the transaction that gives rise to the liability.

64 Some liabilities can be measured only by using a substantial degree of estimation. Some entities describe these liabilities as provisions. In some countries, such provisions are not regarded as liabilities because the concept of a liability is defined narrowly so as to include only amounts that can be established without the need to make estimates. The definition of a liability in paragraph 49 follows a broader approach. Thus, when a provision involves a present obligation and satisfies the rest of the definition, it is a liability even if the amount has to be estimated. Examples include provisions for payments to be made under existing warranties and provisions to cover pension obligations.

Equity

65 Although equity is defined in paragraph 49 as a residual, it may be sub-classified in the balance sheet. For example, in a corporate entity, funds contributed by shareholders, retained earnings, reserves representing appropriations of retained earnings and reserves representing capital maintenance adjustments may be shown separately. Such classifications can be relevant to the decision-making needs of the users of financial statements when they indicate legal or other restrictions on the ability of the entity to distribute or otherwise apply its equity. They may also reflect the fact that parties with ownership interests in an entity have differing rights in relation to the receipt of dividends or the repayment of contributed equity.

66 The creation of reserves is sometimes required by statute or other law in order to give the entity and its creditors an added measure of protection from the effects of losses. Other reserves may be established if national tax law grants exemptions from, or reductions in, taxation liabilities when transfers to such reserves are made. The existence and size of these legal, statutory and tax reserves is information that can be relevant to the decision-making needs of users. Transfers to such reserves are appropriations of retained earnings rather than expenses.

67 The amount at which equity is shown in the balance sheet is dependent on the measurement of assets and liabilities. Normally, the aggregate amount of equity only by coincidence corresponds with the aggregate market value of the shares of the entity or the sum that could be raised by disposing of either the net assets on a piecemeal basis or the entity as a whole on a going concern basis.

68 Commercial, industrial and business activities are often undertaken by means of entities such as sole proprietorships, partnerships and trusts and various types of government business undertakings. The legal and regulatory framework for such entities is often different from that applying to corporate entities. For example, there may be few, if any, restrictions on the distribution to owners or other

beneficiaries of amounts included in equity. Nevertheless, the definition of equity and the other aspects of this *Framework* that deal with equity are appropriate for such entities.

Performance

69 Profit is frequently used as a measure of performance or as the basis for other measures, such as return on investment or earnings per share. The elements directly related to the measurement of profit are income and expenses. The recognition and measurement of income and expenses, and hence profit, depends in part on the concepts of capital and capital maintenance used by the entity in preparing its financial statements. These concepts are discussed in paragraphs 102 to 110.

70 The elements of income and expenses are defined as follows:

(a) Income is increases in economic benefits during the accounting period in the form of inflows or enhancements of assets or decreases of liabilities that result in increases in equity, other than those relating to contributions from equity participants.

(b) Expenses are decreases in economic benefits during the accounting period in the form of outflows or depletions of assets or incurrences of liabilities that result in decreases in equity, other than those relating to distributions to equity participants.

71 The definitions of income and expenses identify their essential features but do not attempt to specify the criteria that would need to be met before they are recognised in the income statement. Criteria for the recognition of income and expenses are discussed in paragraphs 82 to 98.

72 Income and expenses may be presented in the income statement in different ways so as to provide information that is relevant for economic decision-making. For example, it is common practice to distinguish between those items of income and expenses that arise in the course of the ordinary activities of the entity and those that do not. This distinction is made on the basis that the source of an item is relevant in evaluating the ability of the entity to generate cash and cash equivalents in the future; for example, incidental activities such as the disposal of a long-term investment are unlikely to recur on a regular basis. When distinguishing between items in this way consideration needs to be given to the nature of the entity and its operations. Items that arise from the ordinary activities of one entity may be unusual in respect of another.

73 Distinguishing between items of income and expense and combining them in different ways also permits several measures of entity performance to be displayed. These have differing degrees of inclusiveness. For example, the income statement could display gross margin, profit or loss from ordinary activities before taxation, profit or loss from ordinary activities after taxation, and profit or loss.

Income

74 The definition of income encompasses both revenue and gains. Revenue arises in the course of the ordinary activities of an entity and is referred to by a variety of different names including sales, fees, interest, dividends, royalties and rent.

75 Gains represent other items that meet the definition of income and may, or may not, arise in the course of the ordinary activities of an entity. Gains represent increases in economic benefits and as such are no different in nature from revenue. Hence, they are not regarded as constituting a separate element in this *Framework*.

76 Gains include, for example, those arising on the disposal of non-current assets. The definition of income also includes unrealised gains; for example, those arising on the revaluation of marketable securities and those resulting from increases in the carrying amount of long-term assets. When gains are recognised in the income statement, they are usually displayed separately because knowledge of them is useful for the purpose of making economic decisions. Gains are often reported net of related expenses.

77 Various kinds of assets may be received or enhanced by income; examples include cash, receivables and goods and services received in exchange for goods and services supplied. Income may also result from the settlement of liabilities. For example, an entity may provide goods and services to a lender in settlement of an obligation to repay an outstanding loan.

Expenses

78 The definition of expenses encompasses losses as well as those expenses that arise in the course of the ordinary activities of the entity. Expenses that arise in the course of the ordinary activities of the entity include, for example, cost of sales, wages and depreciation. They usually take the form of an outflow or depletion of assets such as cash and cash equivalents, inventory, property, plant and equipment.

79 Losses represent other items that meet the definition of expenses and may, or may not, arise in the course of the ordinary activities of the entity. Losses represent decreases in economic benefits and as such they are no different in nature from other expenses. Hence, they are not regarded as a separate element in this *Framework*.

80 Losses include, for example, those resulting from disasters such as fire and flood, as well as those arising on the disposal of non-current assets. The definition of expenses also includes unrealised losses, for example, those arising from the effects of increases in the rate of exchange for a foreign currency in respect of the borrowings of an entity in that currency. When losses are recognised in the income statement, they are usually displayed separately because knowledge of them is useful for the purpose of making economic decisions. Losses are often reported net of related income.

Capital maintenance adjustments

81 The revaluation or restatement of assets and liabilities gives rise to increases or decreases in equity. While these increases or decreases meet the definition of income and expenses, they are not included in the income statement under certain concepts of capital maintenance. Instead these items are included in equity as capital maintenance adjustments or revaluation reserves. These concepts of capital maintenance are discussed in paragraphs 102 to 110 of this *Framework*.

Recognition of the elements of financial statements

82 Recognition is the process of incorporating in the balance sheet or income statement an item that meets the definition of an element and satisfies the criteria for recognition set out in paragraph 83. It involves the depiction of the item in words and by a monetary amount and the inclusion of that amount in the balance sheet or income statement totals. Items that satisfy the recognition criteria should be recognised in the balance sheet or income statement. The failure to recognise such items is not rectified by disclosure of the accounting policies used nor by notes or explanatory material.

83 An item that meets the definition of an element should be recognised if:

(a) it is probable that any future economic benefit associated with the item will flow to or from the entity; and

(b) the item has a cost or value that can be measured with reliability.

84 In assessing whether an item meets these criteria and therefore qualifies for recognition in the financial statements, regard needs to be given to the materiality considerations discussed in paragraphs 29 and 30. The interrelationship between the elements means that an item that meets the definition and recognition criteria for a particular element, for example, an asset, automatically requires the recognition of another element, for example, income or a liability.

The probability of future economic benefit

85 The concept of probability is used in the recognition criteria to refer to the degree of uncertainty that the future economic benefits associated with the item will flow to or from the entity. The concept is in keeping with the uncertainty that characterises the environment in which an entity operates. Assessments of the degree of uncertainty attaching to the flow of future economic benefits are made on the basis of the evidence available when the financial statements are prepared. For example, when it is probable that a receivable owed to an entity will be paid, it is then justifiable, in the absence of any evidence to the contrary, to recognise the receivable as an asset. For a large population of receivables, however, some degree of non-payment is normally considered probable; hence an expense representing the expected reduction in economic benefits is recognised.

Reliability of measurement

86 The second criterion for the recognition of an item is that it possesses a cost or value that can be measured with reliability as discussed in paragraphs 31 to 38 of this *Framework*. In many cases, cost or value must be estimated; the use of reasonable estimates is an essential part of the preparation of financial statements and does not undermine their reliability. When, however, a reasonable estimate cannot be made the item is not recognised in the balance sheet or income statement. For example, the expected proceeds from a lawsuit may meet the definitions of both an asset and income as well as the probability criterion for recognition; however, if it is not possible for the claim to be measured reliably, it

should not be recognised as an asset or as income; the existence of the claim, however, would be disclosed in the notes, explanatory material or supplementary schedules.

87 An item that, at a particular point in time, fails to meet the recognition criteria in paragraph 83 may qualify for recognition at a later date as a result of subsequent circumstances or events.

88 An item that possesses the essential characteristics of an element but fails to meet the criteria for recognition may nonetheless warrant disclosure in the notes, explanatory material or in supplementary schedules. This is appropriate when knowledge of the item is considered to be relevant to the evaluation of the financial position, performance and changes in financial position of an entity by the users of financial statements.

Recognition of assets

89 An asset is recognised in the balance sheet when it is probable that the future economic benefits will flow to the entity and the asset has a cost or value that can be measured reliably.

90 An asset is not recognised in the balance sheet when expenditure has been incurred for which it is considered improbable that economic benefits will flow to the entity beyond the current accounting period. Instead such a transaction results in the recognition of an expense in the income statement. This treatment does not imply either that the intention of management in incurring expenditure was other than to generate future economic benefits for the entity or that management was misguided. The only implication is that the degree of certainty that economic benefits will flow to the entity beyond the current accounting period is insufficient to warrant the recognition of an asset.

Recognition of liabilities

91 A liability is recognised in the balance sheet when it is probable that an outflow of resources embodying economic benefits will result from the settlement of a present obligation and the amount at which the settlement will take place can be measured reliably. In practice, obligations under contracts that are equally proportionately unperformed (for example, liabilities for inventory ordered but not yet received) are generally not recognised as liabilities in the financial statements. However, such obligations may meet the definition of liabilities and, provided the recognition criteria are met in the particular circumstances, may qualify for recognition. In such circumstances, recognition of liabilities entails recognition of related assets or expenses.

Recognition of income

92 Income is recognised in the income statement when an increase in future economic benefits related to an increase in an asset or a decrease of a liability has arisen that can be measured reliably. This means, in effect, that recognition of income occurs simultaneously with the recognition of increases in assets or decreases in liabilities (for example, the net increase in assets arising on a sale of goods or services or the decrease in liabilities arising from the waiver of a debt payable).

93 The procedures normally adopted in practice for recognising income, for example, the requirement that revenue should be earned, are applications of the recognition criteria in this *Framework*. Such procedures are generally directed at restricting the recognition as income to those items that can be measured reliably and have a sufficient degree of certainty.

Recognition of expenses

94 Expenses are recognised in the income statement when a decrease in future economic benefits related to a decrease in an asset or an increase of a liability has arisen that can be measured reliably. This means, in effect, that recognition of expenses occurs simultaneously with the recognition of an increase in liabilities or a decrease in assets (for example, the accrual of employee entitlements or the depreciation of equipment).

95 Expenses are recognised in the income statement on the basis of a direct association between the costs incurred and the earning of specific items of income. This process, commonly referred to as the matching of costs with revenues, involves the simultaneous or combined recognition of revenues and expenses that result directly and jointly from the same transactions or other events; for example, the various components of expense making up the cost of goods sold are recognised at the same time as the income derived from the sale of the goods. However, the application of the matching concept under this *Framework* does not allow the recognition of items in the balance sheet which do not meet the definition of assets or liabilities.

96 When economic benefits are expected to arise over several accounting periods and the association with income can only be broadly or indirectly determined, expenses are recognised in the income statement on the basis of systematic and rational allocation procedures. This is often necessary in recognising the expenses associated with the using up of assets such as property, plant, equipment, goodwill, patents and trademarks; in such cases the expense is referred to as depreciation or amortisation. These allocation procedures are intended to recognise expenses in the accounting periods in which the economic benefits associated with these items are consumed or expire.

97 An expense is recognised immediately in the income statement when an expenditure produces no future economic benefits or when, and to the extent that, future economic benefits do not qualify, or cease to qualify, for recognition in the balance sheet as an asset.

98 An expense is also recognised in the income statement in those cases when a liability is incurred without the recognition of an asset, as when a liability under a product warranty arises.

Measurement of the elements of financial statements

99 Measurement is the process of determining the monetary amounts at which the elements of the financial statements are to be recognised and carried in the balance sheet and income statement. This involves the selection of the particular basis of measurement.

100 A number of different measurement bases are employed to different degrees and in varying combinations in financial statements. They include the following:

(a) *Historical cost.* Assets are recorded at the amount of cash or cash equivalents paid or the fair value of the consideration given to acquire them at the time of their acquisition. Liabilities are recorded at the amount of proceeds received in exchange for the obligation, or in some circumstances (for example, income taxes), at the amounts of cash or cash equivalents expected to be paid to satisfy the liability in the normal course of business.

(b) *Current cost.* Assets are carried at the amount of cash or cash equivalents that would have to be paid if the same or an equivalent asset was acquired currently. Liabilities are carried at the undiscounted amount of cash or cash equivalents that would be required to settle the obligation currently.

(c) *Realisable (settlement) value.* Assets are carried at the amount of cash or cash equivalents that could currently be obtained by selling the asset in an orderly disposal. Liabilities are carried at their settlement values; that is, the undiscounted amounts of cash or cash equivalents expected to be paid to satisfy the liabilities in the normal course of business.

(d) *Present value.* Assets are carried at the present discounted value of the future net cash inflows that the item is expected to generate in the normal course of business. Liabilities are carried at the present discounted value of the future net cash outflows that are expected to be required to settle the liabilities in the normal course of business.

101 The measurement basis most commonly adopted by entities in preparing their financial statements is historical cost. This is usually combined with other measurement bases. For example, inventories are usually carried at the lower of cost and net realisable value, marketable securities may be carried at market value and pension liabilities are carried at their present value. Furthermore, some entities use the current cost basis as a response to the inability of the historical cost accounting model to deal with the effects of changing prices of non-monetary assets.

Concepts of capital and capital maintenance

Concepts of capital

102 A financial concept of capital is adopted by most entities in preparing their financial statements. Under a financial concept of capital, such as invested money or invested purchasing power, capital is synonymous with the net assets or equity of the entity. Under a physical concept of capital, such as operating capability, capital is regarded as the productive capacity of the entity based on, for example, units of output per day.

103 The selection of the appropriate concept of capital by an entity should be based on the needs of the users of its financial statements. Thus, a financial concept of capital should be adopted if the users of financial statements are primarily concerned with the maintenance of nominal invested capital or the purchasing power of invested capital. If, however, the main concern of users is with the operating capability of the entity, a physical concept of capital should be used.

The concept chosen indicates the goal to be attained in determining profit, even though there may be some measurement difficulties in making the concept operational.

Concepts of capital maintenance and the determination of profit

104 The concepts of capital in paragraph 102 give rise to the following concepts of capital maintenance:

(a) *Financial capital maintenance.* Under this concept a profit is earned only if the financial (or money) amount of the net assets at the end of the period exceeds the financial (or money) amount of net assets at the beginning of the period, after excluding any distributions to, and contributions from, owners during the period. Financial capital maintenance can be measured in either nominal monetary units or units of constant purchasing power.

(b) *Physical capital maintenance.* Under this concept a profit is earned only if the physical productive capacity (or operating capability) of the entity (or the resources or funds needed to achieve that capacity) at the end of the period exceeds the physical productive capacity at the beginning of the period, after excluding any distributions to, and contributions from, owners during the period.

105 The concept of capital maintenance is concerned with how an entity defines the capital that it seeks to maintain. It provides the linkage between the concepts of capital and the concepts of profit because it provides the point of reference by which profit is measured; it is a prerequisite for distinguishing between an entity's return on capital and its return of capital; only inflows of assets in excess of amounts needed to maintain capital may be regarded as profit and therefore as a return on capital. Hence, profit is the residual amount that remains after expenses (including capital maintenance adjustments, where appropriate) have been deducted from income. If expenses exceed income the residual amount is a loss.

106 The physical capital maintenance concept requires the adoption of the current cost basis of measurement. The financial capital maintenance concept, however, does not require the use of a particular basis of measurement. Selection of the basis under this concept is dependent on the type of financial capital that the entity is seeking to maintain.

107 The principal difference between the two concepts of capital maintenance is the treatment of the effects of changes in the prices of assets and liabilities of the entity. In general terms, an entity has maintained its capital if it has as much capital at the end of the period as it had at the beginning of the period. Any amount over and above that required to maintain the capital at the beginning of the period is profit.

108 Under the concept of financial capital maintenance where capital is defined in terms of nominal monetary units, profit represents the increase in nominal money capital over the period. Thus, increases in the prices of assets held over the period, conventionally referred to as holding gains, are, conceptually, profits. They may not be recognised as such, however, until the assets are disposed of in an

exchange transaction. When the concept of financial capital maintenance is defined in terms of constant purchasing power units, profit represents the increase in invested purchasing power over the period. Thus, only that part of the increase in the prices of assets that exceeds the increase in the general level of prices is regarded as profit. The rest of the increase is treated as a capital maintenance adjustment and, hence, as part of equity.

109 Under the concept of physical capital maintenance when capital is defined in terms of the physical productive capacity, profit represents the increase in that capital over the period. All price changes affecting the assets and liabilities of the entity are viewed as changes in the measurement of the physical productive capacity of the entity; hence, they are treated as capital maintenance adjustments that are part of equity and not as profit.

110 The selection of the measurement bases and concept of capital maintenance will determine the accounting model used in the preparation of the financial statements. Different accounting models exhibit different degrees of relevance and reliability and, as in other areas, management must seek a balance between relevance and reliability. This *Framework* is applicable to a range of accounting models and provides guidance on preparing and presenting the financial statements constructed under the chosen model. At the present time, it is not the intention of the Board of IASC to prescribe a particular model other than in exceptional circumstances, such as for those entities reporting in the currency of a hyperinflationary economy. This intention will, however, be reviewed in the light of world developments.

International Financial Reporting Standard 1

First-time Adoption of International Financial Reporting Standards

This version includes amendments resulting from the following amendments issued in 2004: IFRICs 1 and 4; IFRS 6; Amendment to IAS 19 Employee Benefits—Actuarial Gains and Losses, Group Plans and Disclosures; *Amendment to IAS 39* Financial Instruments: Recognition and Measurement—Transition and Initial Recognition of Financial Assets and Financial Liabilities.

CONTENTS

International Financial Reporting Standard 1 *First-time Adoption of International Financial Reporting Standards* (IFRS 1) is set out in paragraphs 1–47E and Appendices A–C. All the paragraphs have equal authority. Paragraphs in **bold type** state the main principles. Terms defined in Appendix A are in *italics* the first time they appear in the Standard. Definitions of other terms are given in the Glossary for International Financial Reporting Standards. IFRS 1 should be read in the context of its objective and the Basis for Conclusions, the *Preface to International Financial Reporting Standards* and the *Framework for the Preparation and Presentation of Financial Statements*. IAS 8 *Accounting Policies, Changes in Accounting Estimates and Errors* provides a basis for selecting and applying accounting policies in the absence of explicit guidance.

Introduction

Reasons for issuing the IFRS

IN1 The IFRS replaces SIC-8 *First-time Application of IASs as the Primary Basis of Accounting*. The Board developed this IFRS to address concerns that:

(a) some aspects of SIC-8's requirement for full retrospective application caused costs that exceeded the likely benefits for users of financial statements. Moreover, although SIC-8 did not require retrospective application when this would be impracticable, it did not explain whether a first-time adopter should interpret impracticability as a high hurdle or a low hurdle and it did not specify any particular treatment in cases of impracticability.

(b) SIC-8 could require a first-time adopter to apply two different versions of a Standard if a new version were introduced during the periods covered by its first financial statements prepared under IASs and the new version prohibited retrospective application.

(c) SIC-8 did not state clearly whether a first-time adopter should use hindsight in applying recognition and measurement decisions retrospectively.

(d) there was some doubt about how SIC-8 interacted with specific transitional provisions in individual Standards.

Main features of the IFRS

IN2 The IFRS applies when an entity adopts IFRSs for the first time by an explicit and unreserved statement of compliance with IFRSs.

IN3 In general, the IFRS requires an entity to comply with each IFRS effective at the reporting date for its first IFRS financial statements. In particular, the IFRS requires an entity to do the following in the opening IFRS balance sheet that it prepares as a starting point for its accounting under IFRSs:

(a) recognise all assets and liabilities whose recognition is required by IFRSs;

(b) not recognise items as assets or liabilities if IFRSs do not permit such recognition;

(c) reclassify items that it recognised under previous GAAP as one type of asset, liability or component of equity, but are a different type of asset, liability or component of equity under IFRSs; and

(d) apply IFRSs in measuring all recognised assets and liabilities.

IN4 The IFRS grants limited exemptions from these requirements in specified areas where the cost of complying with them would be likely to exceed the benefits to users of financial statements. The IFRS also prohibits retrospective application of IFRSs in some areas, particularly where retrospective application would require judgements by management about past conditions after the outcome of a particular transaction is already known.

IN5 The IFRS requires disclosures that explain how the transition from previous GAAP to IFRSs affected the entity's reported financial position, financial performance and cash flows.

IN6 An entity is required to apply the IFRS if its first IFRS financial statements are for a period beginning on or after 1 January 2004. Earlier application is encouraged.

Changes from previous requirements

IN7 Like SIC-8, the IFRS requires retrospective application in most areas. Unlike SIC-8, the IFRS:

(a) includes targeted exemptions to avoid costs that would be likely to exceed the benefits to users of financial statements, and a small number of other exceptions for practical reasons.

(b) clarifies that an entity applies the latest version of IFRSs.

(c) clarifies how a first-time adopter's estimates under IFRSs relate to the estimates it made for the same date under previous GAAP.

(d) specifies that the transitional provisions in other IFRSs do not apply to a first-time adopter.

(e) requires enhanced disclosure about the transition to IFRSs.

International Financial Reporting Standard 1 First-time Adoption of International Financial Reporting Standards

Objective

1 The objective of this IFRS is to ensure that an entity's *first IFRS financial statements*, and its interim financial reports for part of the period covered by those financial statements, contain high quality information that:

(a) is transparent for users and comparable over all periods presented;

(b) provides a suitable starting point for accounting under *International Financial Reporting Standards (IFRSs)*; and

(c) can be generated at a cost that does not exceed the benefits to users.

Scope

2 An entity shall apply this IFRS in:

(a) its first IFRS financial statements; and

(b) each interim financial report, if any, that it presents under IAS 34 *Interim Financial Reporting* for part of the period covered by its first IFRS financial statements.

3 An entity's first IFRS financial statements are the first annual financial statements in which the entity adopts IFRSs, by an explicit and unreserved statement in those financial statements of compliance with IFRSs. Financial statements under IFRSs are an entity's first IFRS financial statements if, for example, the entity:

(a) presented its most recent previous financial statements:

  (i) under national requirements that are not consistent with IFRSs in all respects;

  (ii) in conformity with IFRSs in all respects, except that the financial statements did not contain an explicit and unreserved statement that they complied with IFRSs;

  (iii) containing an explicit statement of compliance with some, but not all, IFRSs;

  (iv) under national requirements inconsistent with IFRSs, using some individual IFRSs to account for items for which national requirements did not exist; or

  (v) under national requirements, with a reconciliation of some amounts to the amounts determined under IFRSs;

(b) prepared financial statements under IFRSs for internal use only, without making them available to the entity's owners or any other external users;

(c) prepared a reporting package under IFRSs for consolidation purposes without preparing a complete set of financial statements as defined in IAS 1 *Presentation of Financial Statements*; or

(d) did not present financial statements for previous periods.

4 This IFRS applies when an entity first adopts IFRSs. It does not apply when, for example, an entity:

(a) stops presenting financial statements under national requirements, having previously presented them as well as another set of financial statements that contained an explicit and unreserved statement of compliance with IFRSs;

(b) presented financial statements in the previous year under national requirements and those financial statements contained an explicit and unreserved statement of compliance with IFRSs; or

(c) presented financial statements in the previous year that contained an explicit and unreserved statement of compliance with IFRSs, even if the auditors qualified their audit report on those financial statements.

5 This IFRS does not apply to changes in accounting policies made by an entity that already applies IFRSs. Such changes are the subject of:

(a) requirements on changes in accounting policies in IAS 8 *Accounting Policies, Changes in Accounting Estimates and Errors*; and

(b) specific transitional requirements in other IFRSs.

Recognition and measurement

Opening IFRS balance sheet

6 An entity shall prepare an *opening IFRS balance sheet* at the *date of transition to IFRSs*. This is the starting point for its accounting under IFRSs. An entity need not present its opening IFRS balance sheet in its first IFRS financial statements.

Accounting policies

7 An entity shall use the same accounting policies in its opening IFRS balance sheet and throughout all periods presented in its first IFRS financial statements. Those accounting policies shall comply with each IFRS effective at the reporting date for its first IFRS financial statements, except as specified in paragraphs 13–34.

8 An entity shall not apply different versions of IFRSs that were effective at earlier dates. An entity may apply a new IFRS that is not yet mandatory if it permits early application.

Example: Consistent application of latest version of IFRSs

Background

The reporting date for entity A's first IFRS financial statements is 31 December 2005. Entity A decides to present comparative information in those financial statements for one year only (see paragraph 36). Therefore, its date of transition to IFRSs is the beginning of business on 1 January 2004 (or, equivalently, close of business on 31 December 2003). Entity A presented financial statements under its *previous GAAP* annually to 31 December each year up to, and including, 31 December 2004.

Application of requirements

Entity A is required to apply the IFRSs effective for periods ending on 31 December 2005 in:

(a) preparing its opening IFRS balance sheet at 1 January 2004; and

(b) preparing and presenting its balance sheet for 31 December 2005 (including comparative amounts for 2004), income statement, statement of changes in equity and cash flow statement for the year to 31 December 2005 (including comparative amounts for 2004) and disclosures (including comparative information for 2004).

If a new IFRS is not yet mandatory but permits early application, entity A is permitted, but not required, to apply that IFRS in its first IFRS financial statements.

9 The transitional provisions in other IFRSs apply to changes in accounting policies made by an entity that already uses IFRSs; they do not apply to a *first-time adopter's* transition to IFRSs, except as specified in paragraphs 25D, 34A and 34B.

10 Except as described in paragraphs 13–34, an entity shall, in its opening IFRS balance sheet:

(a) recognise all assets and liabilities whose recognition is required by IFRSs;

(b) not recognise items as assets or liabilities if IFRSs do not permit such recognition;

(c) reclassify items that it recognised under previous GAAP as one type of asset, liability or component of equity, but are a different type of asset, liability or component of equity under IFRSs; and

(d) apply IFRSs in measuring all recognised assets and liabilities.

11 The accounting policies that an entity uses in its opening IFRS balance sheet may differ from those that it used for the same date using its previous GAAP. The resulting adjustments arise from events and transactions before the date of transition to IFRSs. Therefore, an entity shall recognise those adjustments directly in retained earnings (or, if appropriate, another category of equity) at the date of transition to IFRSs.

12 This IFRS establishes two categories of exceptions to the principle that an entity's opening IFRS balance sheet shall comply with each IFRS:

(a) paragraphs 13–25F grant exemptions from some requirements of other IFRSs.

(b) paragraphs 26–34B prohibit retrospective application of some aspects of other IFRSs.

Exemptions from other IFRSs

13 An entity may elect to use one or more of the following exemptions:

(a) business combinations (paragraph 15);

(b) *fair value* or revaluation as *deemed cost* (paragraphs 16–19);

(c) employee benefits (paragraph 20);

(d) cumulative translation differences (paragraphs 21 and 22);

(e) compound financial instruments (paragraph 23);

(f) assets and liabilities of subsidiaries, associates and joint ventures (paragraphs 24 and 25);

(g) designation of previously recognised financial instruments (paragraph 25A);

(h) share-based payment transactions (paragraphs 25B and 25C);

(i) insurance contracts (paragraph 25D);

(j) decommissioning liabilities included in the cost of property, plant and equipment (paragraph 25E);

(k) leases (paragraph 25F); and

(l) fair value measurement of financial assets or financial liabilities at initial recognition (paragraph 25G).

An entity shall not apply these exemptions by analogy to other items.

14 Some exemptions below refer to fair value. IFRS 3 *Business Combinations* explains how to determine the fair values of identifiable assets and liabilities acquired in a business combination. An entity shall apply those explanations in determining fair values under this IFRS, unless another IFRS contains more specific guidance on the determination of fair values for the asset or liability in question. Those fair values shall reflect conditions that existed at the date for which they were determined.

Business combinations

15 An entity shall apply the requirements in Appendix B to business combinations that the entity recognised before the date of transition to IFRSs.

Fair value or revaluation as deemed cost

16 An entity may elect to measure an item of property, plant and equipment at the date of transition to IFRSs at its fair value and use that fair value as its deemed cost at that date.

17 A first-time adopter may elect to use a previous GAAP revaluation of an item of property, plant and equipment at, or before, the date of transition to IFRSs as deemed cost at the date of the revaluation, if the revaluation was, at the date of the revaluation, broadly comparable to:

(a) fair value; or

(b) cost or depreciated cost under IFRSs, adjusted to reflect, for example, changes in a general or specific price index.

18 The elections in paragraphs 16 and 17 are also available for:

(a) investment property, if an entity elects to use the cost model in IAS 40 *Investment Property*; and

(b) intangible assets that meet:

(i) the recognition criteria in IAS 38 *Intangible Assets* (including reliable measurement of original cost); and

(ii) the criteria in IAS 38 for revaluation (including the existence of an active market).

An entity shall not use these elections for other assets or for liabilities.

19 A first-time adopter may have established a deemed cost under previous GAAP for some or all of its assets and liabilities by measuring them at their fair value at one particular date because of an event such as a privatisation or initial public offering. It may use such event-driven fair value measurements as deemed cost for IFRSs at the date of that measurement.

Employee benefits

20 Under IAS 19 *Employee Benefits*, an entity may elect to use a 'corridor' approach that leaves some actuarial gains and losses unrecognised. Retrospective application of this approach requires an entity to split the cumulative actuarial gains and losses from the inception of the plan until the date of transition to IFRSs into a recognised portion and an unrecognised portion. However, a first-time adopter may elect to recognise all cumulative actuarial gains and losses at the date of transition to IFRSs, even if it uses the corridor approach for later actuarial gains and losses. If a first-time adopter uses this election, it shall apply it to all plans.

20A An entity may disclose the amounts required by paragraph 120A(p) as the amounts are determined for each accounting period prospectively from the transition date.

Cumulative translation differences

21 IAS 21 *The Effects of Changes in Foreign Exchange Rates* requires an entity:

(a) to classify some translation differences as a separate component of equity; and

(b) on disposal of a foreign operation, to transfer the cumulative translation difference for that foreign operation (including, if applicable, gains and losses on related hedges) to the income statement as part of the gain or loss on disposal.

22 However, a first-time adopter need not comply with these requirements for cumulative translation differences that existed at the date of transition to IFRSs. If a first-time adopter uses this exemption:

(a) the cumulative translation differences for all foreign operations are deemed to be zero at the date of transition to IFRSs; and

(b) the gain or loss on a subsequent disposal of any foreign operation shall exclude translation differences that arose before the date of transition to IFRSs and shall include later translation differences.

Compound financial instruments

23 IAS 32 *Financial Instruments: Disclosure and Presentation* requires an entity to split a compound financial instrument at inception into separate liability and equity components. If the liability component is no longer outstanding, retrospective application of IAS 32 involves separating two portions of equity. The first portion is in retained earnings and represents the cumulative interest accreted on the liability component. The other portion represents the original equity component. However, under this IFRS, a first-time adopter need not separate these two portions if the liability component is no longer outstanding at the date of transition to IFRSs.

Assets and liabilities of subsidiaries, associates and joint ventures

24 If a subsidiary becomes a first-time adopter later than its parent, the subsidiary shall, in its financial statements, measure its assets and liabilities at either:

(a) the carrying amounts that would be included in the parent's consolidated financial statements, based on the parent's date of transition to IFRSs, if no adjustments were made for consolidation procedures and for the effects of the business combination in which the parent acquired the subsidiary; or

(b) the carrying amounts required by the rest of this IFRS, based on the subsidiary's date of transition to IFRSs. These carrying amounts could differ from those described in (a):

(i) when the exemptions in this IFRS result in measurements that depend on the date of transition to IFRSs.

(ii) when the accounting policies used in the subsidiary's financial statements differ from those in the consolidated financial statements. For example, the subsidiary may use as its accounting policy the cost model in IAS 16 *Property, Plant and Equipment*, whereas the group may use the revaluation model.

A similar election is available to an associate or joint venture that becomes a first-time adopter later than an entity that has significant influence or joint control over it.

25 However, if an entity becomes a first-time adopter later than its subsidiary (or associate or joint venture) the entity shall, in its consolidated financial statements, measure the assets and liabilities of the subsidiary (or associate or joint venture) at the same carrying amounts as in the financial statements of the subsidiary (or associate or joint venture), after adjusting for consolidation and

equity accounting adjustments and for the effects of the business combination in which the entity acquired the subsidiary. Similarly, if a parent becomes a first-time adopter for its separate financial statements earlier or later than for its consolidated financial statements, it shall measure its assets and liabilities at the same amounts in both financial statements, except for consolidation adjustments.

Designation of previously recognised financial instruments

25A IAS 39 *Financial Instruments: Recognition and Measurement* (as revised in 2003) permits a financial instrument to be designated on initial recognition as a financial asset or financial liability at fair value through profit or loss or as available for sale. Despite this requirement, an entity is permitted to make such a designation at the date of transition to IFRSs.

Share-based payment transactions

25B A first-time adopter is encouraged, but not required, to apply IFRS 2 *Share-based Payment* to equity instruments that were granted on or before 7 November 2002. A first-time adopter is also encouraged, but not required, to apply IFRS 2 to equity instruments that were granted after 7 November 2002 that vested before the later of (a) the date of transition to IFRSs and (b) 1 January 2005. However, if a first-time adopter elects to apply IFRS 2 to such equity instruments, it may do so only if the entity has disclosed publicly the fair value of those equity instruments, determined at the measurement date, as defined in IFRS 2. For all grants of equity instruments to which IFRS 2 has not been applied (eg equity instruments granted on or before 7 November 2002), a first-time adopter shall nevertheless disclose the information required by paragraphs 44 and 45 of IFRS 2. If a first-time adopter modifies the terms or conditions of a grant of equity instruments to which IFRS 2 has not been applied, the entity is not required to apply paragraphs 26–29 of IFRS 2 if the modification occurred before the later of (a) the date of transition to IFRSs and (b) 1 January 2005.

25C A first-time adopter is encouraged, but not required, to apply IFRS 2 to liabilities arising from share-based payment transactions that were settled before the date of transition to IFRSs. A first-time adopter is also encouraged, but not required, to apply IFRS 2 to liabilities that were settled before 1 January 2005. For liabilities to which IFRS 2 is applied, a first-time adopter is not required to restate comparative information to the extent that the information relates to a period or date that is earlier than 7 November 2002.

Insurance contracts

25D A first-time adopter may apply the transitional provisions in IFRS 4 *Insurance Contracts*. IFRS 4 restricts changes in accounting policies for insurance contracts, including changes made by a first-time adopter.

Changes in existing decommissioning, restoration and similar liabilities included in the cost of property, plant and equipment

25E IFRIC 1 *Changes in Existing Decommissioning, Restoration and Similar Liabilities* requires specified changes in a decommissioning, restoration or similar liability to be added to or deducted from the cost of the asset to which it relates; the adjusted depreciable amount of the asset is then depreciated prospectively over its remaining useful life. A first-time adopter need not comply with these requirements for changes in such liabilities that occurred before the date of transition to IFRSs. If a first-time adopter uses this exemption, it shall:

(a) measure the liability as at the date of transition to IFRSs in accordance with IAS 37;

(b) to the extent that the liability is within the scope of IFRIC 1, estimate the amount that would have been included in the cost of the related asset when the liability first arose, by discounting the liability to that date using its best estimate of the historical risk-adjusted discount rate(s) that would have applied for that liability over the intervening period; and

(c) calculate the accumulated depreciation on that amount, as at the date of transition to IFRSs, on the basis of the current estimate of the useful life of the asset, using the depreciation policy adopted by the entity under IFRSs.

Leases

IFRIC 4 Determining whether an Arrangement contains a Lease

25F A first-time adopter may apply the transitional provisions in IFRIC 4 *Determining whether an Arrangement contains a Lease*. Therefore, a first-time adopter may determine whether an arrangement existing at the date of transition to IFRSs contains a lease on the basis of facts and circumstances existing at that date.

Fair value measurement of financial assets or financial liabilities

25G Notwithstanding the requirements of paragraphs 7 and 9, an entity may apply the requirements in the last sentence of IAS 39 paragraph AG76, and paragraph AG76A, in either of the following ways:

(a) prospectively to transactions entered into after 25 October 2002; or

(b) prospectively to transactions entered into after 1 January 2004.

Exceptions to retrospective application of other IFRSs

26 This IFRS prohibits retrospective application of some aspects of other IFRSs relating to:

(a) derecognition of financial assets and financial liabilities (paragraph 27);

(b) hedge accounting (paragraphs 28–30);

(c) estimates (paragraphs 31–34); and

(d) assets classified as held for sale and discontinued operations.

Derecognition of financial assets and financial liabilities

27 Except as permitted by paragraph 27A, a first-time adopter shall apply the derecognition requirements in IAS 39 prospectively for transactions occurring on or after 1 January 2004. In other words, if a first-time adopter derecognised non-derivative financial assets or non-derivative financial liabilities under its previous GAAP as a result of a transaction that occurred before 1 January 2004, it shall not recognise those assets and liabilities under IFRSs (unless they qualify for recognition as a result of a later transaction or event).

27A Notwithstanding paragraph 27, an entity may apply the derecognition requirements in IAS 39 retrospectively from a date of the entity's choosing, provided that the information needed to apply IAS 39 to financial assets and financial liabilities derecognised as a result of past transactions was obtained at the time of initially accounting for those transactions.

Hedge accounting

28 As required by IAS 39 *Financial Instruments: Recognition and Measurement*, at the date of transition to IFRSs, an entity shall:

(a) measure all derivatives at fair value; and

(b) eliminate all deferred losses and gains arising on derivatives that were reported under previous GAAP as if they were assets or liabilities.

29 An entity shall not reflect in its opening IFRS balance sheet a hedging relationship of a type that does not qualify for hedge accounting under IAS 39 (for example, many hedging relationships where the hedging instrument is a cash instrument or written option; where the hedged item is a net position; or where the hedge covers interest risk in a held-to-maturity investment). However, if an entity designated a net position as a hedged item under previous GAAP, it may designate an individual item within that net position as a hedged item under IFRSs, provided that it does so no later than the date of transition to IFRSs.

30 If, before the date of transition to IFRSs, an entity had designated a transaction as a hedge but the hedge does not meet the conditions for hedge accounting in IAS 39 the entity shall apply paragraphs 91 and 101 of IAS 39 (as revised in 2003) to discontinue hedge accounting. Transactions entered into before the date of transition to IFRSs shall not be retrospectively designated as hedges.

Estimates

31 An entity's estimates under IFRSs at the date of transition to IFRSs shall be consistent with estimates made for the same date under previous GAAP (after adjustments to reflect any difference in accounting policies), unless there is objective evidence that those estimates were in error.

32 An entity may receive information after the date of transition to IFRSs about estimates that it had made under previous GAAP. Under paragraph 31, an entity shall treat the receipt of that information in the same way as non-adjusting events after the balance sheet date under IAS 10 *Events after the Balance Sheet Date*. For example, assume that an entity's date of transition to IFRSs is 1 January 2004 and new information on 15 July 2004 requires the revision of an estimate made under previous GAAP at 31 December 2003. The entity shall not reflect that new information in its opening IFRS balance sheet (unless the estimates need adjustment for any differences in accounting policies or there is objective evidence that the estimates were in error). Instead, the entity shall reflect that new information in its income statement (or, if appropriate, other changes in equity) for the year ended 31 December 2004.

33 An entity may need to make estimates under IFRSs at the date of transition to IFRSs that were not required at that date under previous GAAP. To achieve consistency with IAS 10, those estimates under IFRSs shall reflect conditions that

existed at the date of transition to IFRSs. In particular, estimates at the date of transition to IFRSs of market prices, interest rates or foreign exchange rates shall reflect market conditions at that date.

34 Paragraphs 31–33 apply to the opening IFRS balance sheet. They also apply to a comparative period presented in an entity's first IFRS financial statements, in which case the references to the date of transition to IFRSs are replaced by references to the end of that comparative period.

Assets classified as held for sale and discontinued operations

34A IFRS 5 requires that it shall be applied prospectively to non-current assets (or disposal groups) that meet the criteria to be classified as held for sale and operations that meet the criteria to be classified as discontinued after the effective date of the IFRS. IFRS 5 permits an entity to apply the requirements of the IFRS to all non-current assets (or disposal groups) that meet the criteria to be classified as held for sale and operations that meet the criteria to be classified as discontinued after any date before the effective date of the IFRS, provided the valuations and other information needed to apply the IFRS were obtained at the time those criteria were originally met.

34B An entity with a date of transition to IFRSs before 1 January 2005 shall apply the transitional provisions of IFRS 5. An entity with a date of transition to IFRSs on or after 1 January 2005 shall apply IFRS 5 retrospectively.

Presentation and disclosure

35 This IFRS does not provide exemptions from the presentation and disclosure requirements in other IFRSs.

Comparative information

36 To comply with IAS 1 *Presentation of Financial Statements*, an entity's first IFRS financial statements shall include at least one year of comparative information under IFRSs.

Exemption from the requirement to restate comparative information for IAS 39 and IFRS 4

36A In its first IFRS financial statements, an entity that adopts IFRSs before 1 January 2006 shall present at least one year of comparative information, but this comparative information need not comply with IAS 32, IAS 39 and IFRS 4. An entity that chooses to present comparative information that does not comply with IAS 32, IAS 39 and IFRS 4 in its first year of transition shall:

(a) apply its previous GAAP in the comparative information to financial instruments within the scope of IAS 32 and IAS 39 and to insurance contracts within the scope of IFRS 4;

(b) disclose this fact together with the basis used to prepare this information; and

(c) disclose the nature of the main adjustments that would make the information comply with IAS 32, IAS 39 and IFRS 4. The entity need not quantify those adjustments. However, the entity shall treat any adjustment between the balance sheet at the comparative period's reporting date (ie the balance sheet that includes comparative information under previous GAAP) and the balance sheet at the start of the *first IFRS reporting period* (ie the first period that includes information that complies with IAS 32, IAS 39 and IFRS 4) as arising from a change in accounting policy and give the disclosures required by paragraph 28(a)–(e) and (f)(i) of IAS 8 *Accounting Policies, Changes in Accounting Estimates and Errors*. Paragraph 28(f)(i) applies only to amounts presented in the balance sheet at the comparative period's reporting date.

In the case of an entity that chooses to present comparative information that does not comply with IAS 32, IAS 39 and IFRS 4, references to the 'date of transition to IFRSs' shall mean, in the case of those Standards only, the beginning of the first IFRS reporting period.

Exemption from the requirement to provide comparative disclosures for IFRS 6

36B An entity that adopts IFRSs before 1 January 2006 and chooses to adopt IFRS 6 *Exploration for and Evaluation of Mineral Resources* before 1 January 2006 need not present the disclosures required by IFRS 6 for comparative periods in its first IFRS financial statements.

Historical summaries

37 Some entities present historical summaries of selected data for periods before the first period for which they present full comparative information under IFRSs. This IFRS does not require such summaries to comply with the recognition and measurement requirements of IFRSs. Furthermore, some entities present comparative information under previous GAAP as well as the comparative information required by IAS 1. In any financial statements containing historical summaries or comparative information under previous GAAP, an entity shall:

(a) label the previous GAAP information prominently as not being prepared under IFRSs; and

(b) disclose the nature of the main adjustments that would make it comply with IFRSs. An entity need not quantify those adjustments.

Explanation of transition to IFRSs

38 An entity shall explain how the transition from previous GAAP to IFRSs affected its reported financial position, financial performance and cash flows.

Reconciliations

39 To comply with paragraph 38, an entity's first IFRS financial statements shall include:

(a) reconciliations of its equity reported under previous GAAP to its equity under IFRSs for both of the following dates:

(i) the date of transition to IFRSs; and

(ii) the end of the latest period presented in the entity's most recent annual financial statements under previous GAAP;

(b) a reconciliation of the profit or loss reported under previous GAAP for the latest period in the entity's most recent annual financial statements to its profit or loss under IFRSs for the same period; and

(c) if the entity recognised or reversed any impairment losses for the first time in preparing its opening IFRS balance sheet, the disclosures that IAS 36 *Impairment of Assets* would have required if the entity had recognised those impairment losses or reversals in the period beginning with the date of transition to IFRSs.

40 The reconciliations required by paragraph 39(a) and (b) shall give sufficient detail to enable users to understand the material adjustments to the balance sheet and income statement. If an entity presented a cash flow statement under its previous GAAP, it shall also explain the material adjustments to the cash flow statement.

41 If an entity becomes aware of errors made under previous GAAP, the reconciliations required by paragraph 39(a) and (b) shall distinguish the correction of those errors from changes in accounting policies.

42 IAS 8 does not deal with changes in accounting policies that occur when an entity first adopts IFRSs. Therefore, IAS 8's requirements for disclosures about changes in accounting policies do not apply in an entity's first IFRS financial statements.

43 If an entity did not present financial statements for previous periods, its first IFRS financial statements shall disclose that fact.

Designation of financial assets or financial liabilities

43A An entity is permitted to designate a previously recognised financial asset or financial liability as a financial asset or financial liability at fair value through profit or loss or as available for sale in accordance with paragraph 25A. The entity shall disclose the fair value of any financial assets or financial liabilities designated into each category and the classification and carrying amount in the previous financial statements.

Use of fair value as deemed cost

44 If an entity uses fair value in its opening IFRS balance sheet as deemed cost for an item of property, plant and equipment, an investment property or an intangible asset (see paragraphs 16 and 18), the entity's first IFRS financial statements shall disclose, for each line item in the opening IFRS balance sheet:

(a) the aggregate of those fair values; and

(b) the aggregate adjustment to the carrying amounts reported under previous GAAP.

Interim financial reports

45 To comply with paragraph 38, if an entity presents an interim financial report under IAS 34 *Interim Financial Reporting* for part of the period covered by its first IFRS financial statements, the entity shall satisfy the following requirements in addition to the requirements of IAS 34:

(a) Each such interim financial report shall, if the entity presented an interim financial report for the comparable interim period of the immediately preceding financial year, include reconciliations of:

(i) its equity under previous GAAP at the end of that comparable interim period to its equity under IFRSs at that date; and

(ii) its profit or loss under previous GAAP for that comparable interim period (current and year-to-date) to its profit or loss under IFRSs for that period.

(b) In addition to the reconciliations required by (a), an entity's first interim financial report under IAS 34 for part of the period covered by its first IFRS financial statements shall include the reconciliations described in paragraph 39(a) and (b) (supplemented by the details required by paragraphs 40 and 41) or a cross-reference to another published document that includes these reconciliations.

46 IAS 34 requires minimum disclosures, which are based on the assumption that users of the interim financial report also have access to the most recent annual financial statements. However, IAS 34 also requires an entity to disclose 'any events or transactions that are material to an understanding of the current interim period'. Therefore, if a first-time adopter did not, in its most recent annual financial statements under previous GAAP, disclose information material to an understanding of the current interim period, its interim financial report shall disclose that information or include a cross-reference to another published document that includes it.

Effective date

47 An entity shall apply this IFRS if its first IFRS financial statements are for a period beginning on or after 1 January 2004. Earlier application is encouraged. If an entity's first IFRS financial statements are for a period beginning before 1 January 2004 and the entity applies this IFRS instead of SIC-8 *First-time Application of IASs as the Primary Basis of Accounting*, it shall disclose that fact.

47A An entity shall apply the amendments in paragraphs 13(j) and 25E for annual periods beginning on or after 1 September 2004. If an entity applies IFRIC 1 *Changes in Existing Decommissioning, Restoration and Similar Liabilities* for an earlier period, these amendments shall be applied for that earlier period.

47B An entity shall apply the amendments in paragraphs 13(k) and 25F for annual periods beginning on or after 1 January 2006. If an entity applies IFRIC 4 *Determining whether an Arrangement contains a Lease* for an earlier period, these amendments shall be applied for that earlier period.

47C An entity shall apply the amendments in paragraph 36B for annual periods beginning on or after 1 January 2006. If an entity applies IFRS 6 *Exploration for and Evaluation of Mineral Resources* for an earlier period, these amendments shall be applied for that earlier period.

47D An entity shall apply the amendments in paragraph 20A for annual periods beginning on or after 1 January 2006. If an entity applies the amendments to

IAS 19 *Employee Benefits—Actuarial Gains and Losses, Group Plans and Disclosures* for an earlier period, these amendments shall be applied for that earlier period.

47E An entity shall apply the amendments in paragraphs 13(l) and 25G for annual periods beginning on or after 1 January 2005. If an entity applies the amendments to IAS 39 *Financial Instruments: Recognition and Measurement—Transition and Initial Recognition of Financial Assets and Financial Liabilities* for an earlier period, these amendments shall be applied for that earlier period.

Appendix A
Defined terms

This appendix is an integral part of the IFRS.

date of transition to IFRSs	The beginning of the earliest period for which an entity presents full comparative information under IFRSs in its **first IFRS financial statements**.
deemed cost	An amount used as a surrogate for cost or depreciated cost at a given date. Subsequent depreciation or amortisation assumes that the entity had initially recognised the asset or liability at the given date and that its cost was equal to the deemed cost.
fair value	The amount for which an asset could be exchanged, or a liability settled, between knowledgeable, willing parties in an arm's length transaction.
first IFRS financial statements	The first annual financial statements in which an entity adopts **International Financial Reporting Standards (IFRSs)**, by an explicit and unreserved statement of compliance with IFRSs.
first IFRS reporting period	The reporting period ending on the **reporting date** of an entity's **first IFRS financial statements**.
first-time adopter	An entity that presents its **first IFRS financial statements**.
International Financial Reporting Standards (IFRSs)	Standards and Interpretations adopted by the International Accounting Standards Board (IASB). They comprise: (a) International Financial Reporting Standards; (b) International Accounting Standards; and (c) Interpretations originated by the International Financial Reporting Interpretations Committee (IFRIC) or the former Standing Interpretations Committee (SIC).
opening IFRS balance sheet	An entity's balance sheet (published or unpublished) at the **date of transition to IFRSs**.
previous GAAP	The basis of accounting that a **first-time adopter** used immediately before adopting IFRSs.
reporting date	The end of the latest period covered by financial statements or by an interim financial report.

Appendix B
Business combinations

This appendix is an integral part of the IFRS.

B1 A first-time adopter may elect not to apply IFRS 3 *Business Combinations* retrospectively to past business combinations (business combinations that occurred before the date of transition to IFRSs). However, if a first-time adopter restates any business combination to comply with IFRS 3, it shall restate all later business combinations and shall also apply IAS 36 *Impairment of Assets* (as revised in 2004) and IAS 38 *Intangible Assets* (as revised in 2004) from that same date. For example, if a first-time adopter elects to restate a business combination that occurred on 30 June 2002, it shall restate all business combinations that occurred between 30 June 2002 and the date of transition to IFRSs, and it shall also apply IAS 36 (as revised in 2004) and IAS 38 (as revised in 2004) from 30 June 2002.

B1A An entity need not apply IAS 21 *The Effects of Changes in Foreign Exchange Rates* (as revised in 2003) retrospectively to fair value adjustments and goodwill arising in business combinations that occurred before the date of transition to IFRSs. If the entity does not apply IAS 21 retrospectively to those fair value adjustments and goodwill, it shall treat them as assets and liabilities of the entity rather than as assets and liabilities of the acquiree. Therefore, those goodwill and fair value adjustments either are already expressed in the entity's functional currency or are non-monetary foreign currency items, which are reported using the exchange rate applied under previous GAAP.

B1B An entity may apply IAS 21 retrospectively to fair value adjustments and goodwill arising in either:

(a) all business combinations that occurred before the date of transition to IFRSs; or

(b) all business combinations that the entity elects to restate to comply with IFRS 3, as permitted by paragraph B1 above.

B2 If a first-time adopter does not apply IFRS 3 retrospectively to a past business combination, this has the following consequences for that business combination:

(a) The first-time adopter shall keep the same classification (as an acquisition by the legal acquirer, a reverse acquisition by the legal acquiree, or a uniting of interests) as in its previous GAAP financial statements.

(b) The first-time adopter shall recognise all its assets and liabilities at the date of transition to IFRSs that were acquired or assumed in a past business combination, other than:

(i) some financial assets and financial liabilities derecognised under previous GAAP (see paragraph 27); and

(ii) assets, including goodwill, and liabilities that were not recognised in the acquirer's consolidated balance sheet under previous GAAP and also would not qualify for recognition under IFRSs in the separate balance sheet of the acquiree (see paragraph B2(f)–B2(i)).

The first-time adopter shall recognise any resulting change by adjusting retained earnings (or, if appropriate, another category of equity), unless the change results from the recognition of an intangible asset that was previously subsumed within goodwill (see paragraph B2(g)(i)).

(c) The first-time adopter shall exclude from its opening IFRS balance sheet any item recognised under previous GAAP that does not qualify for recognition as an asset or liability under IFRSs. The first-time adopter shall account for the resulting change as follows:

   (i) the first-time adopter may have classified a past business combination as an acquisition and recognised as an intangible asset an item that does not qualify for recognition as an asset under IAS 38 *Intangible Assets*. It shall reclassify that item (and, if any, the related deferred tax and minority interests) as part of goodwill (unless it deducted goodwill directly from equity under previous GAAP, see paragraph B2(g)(i) and B2(i)).

   (ii) the first-time adopter shall recognise all other resulting changes in retained earnings.*

(d) IFRSs require subsequent measurement of some assets and liabilities on a basis that is not based on original cost, such as fair value. The first-time adopter shall measure these assets and liabilities on that basis in its opening IFRS balance sheet, even if they were acquired or assumed in a past business combination. It shall recognise any resulting change in the carrying amount by adjusting retained earnings (or, if appropriate, another category of equity), rather than goodwill.

(e) Immediately after the business combination, the carrying amount under previous GAAP of assets acquired and liabilities assumed in that business combination shall be their deemed cost under IFRSs at that date. If IFRSs require a cost-based measurement of those assets and liabilities at a later date, that deemed cost shall be the basis for cost-based depreciation or amortisation from the date of the business combination.

(f) If an asset acquired, or liability assumed, in a past business combination was not recognised under previous GAAP, it does not have a deemed cost of zero in the opening IFRS balance sheet. Instead, the acquirer shall recognise and measure it in its consolidated balance sheet on the basis that IFRSs would require in the balance sheet of the acquiree. To illustrate: if the acquirer had not, under its previous GAAP, capitalised finance leases acquired in a past business combination, it shall capitalise those leases in its consolidated financial statements, as IAS 17 *Leases* would require the acquiree to do in its IFRS balance sheet. Conversely, if an asset or liability was subsumed in goodwill under previous GAAP but would have been recognised separately under IFRS 3, that asset or liability remains in goodwill unless IFRSs would require its recognition in the financial statements of the acquiree.

---

* Such changes include reclassifications from or to intangible assets if goodwill was not recognised under previous GAAP as an asset. This arises if, under previous GAAP, the entity (a) deducted goodwill directly from equity or (b) did not treat the business combination as an acquisition.

(g) The carrying amount of goodwill in the opening IFRS balance sheet shall be its carrying amount under previous GAAP at the date of transition to IFRSs, after the following three adjustments:

   (i) If required by paragraph B2(c)(i) above, the first-time adopter shall increase the carrying amount of goodwill when it reclassifies an item that it recognised as an intangible asset under previous GAAP. Similarly, if paragraph B2(f) requires the first-time adopter to recognise an intangible asset that was subsumed in recognised goodwill under previous GAAP, the first-time adopter shall decrease the carrying amount of goodwill accordingly (and, if applicable, adjust deferred tax and minority interests).

   (ii) A contingency affecting the amount of the purchase consideration for a past business combination may have been resolved before the date of transition to IFRSs. If a reliable estimate of the contingent adjustment can be made and its payment is probable, the first-time adopter shall adjust the goodwill by that amount. Similarly, the first-time adopter shall adjust the carrying amount of goodwill if a previously recognised contingent adjustment can no longer be measured reliably or its payment is no longer probable.

   (iii) Regardless of whether there is any indication that the goodwill may be impaired, the first-time adopter shall apply IAS 36 *Impairment of Assets* in testing the goodwill for impairment at the date of transition to IFRSs and in recognising any resulting impairment loss in retained earnings (or, if so required by IAS 36, in revaluation surplus). The impairment test shall be based on conditions at the date of transition to IFRSs.

(h) No other adjustments shall be made to the carrying amount of goodwill at the date of transition to IFRSs. For example, the first-time adopter shall not restate the carrying amount of goodwill:

   (i) to exclude in-process research and development acquired in that business combination (unless the related intangible asset would qualify for recognition under IAS 38 in the balance sheet of the acquiree);

   (ii) to adjust previous amortisation of goodwill;

   (iii) to reverse adjustments to goodwill that IFRS 3 would not permit, but were made under previous GAAP because of adjustments to assets and liabilities between the date of the business combination and the date of transition to IFRSs.

(i) If the first-time adopter recognised goodwill under previous GAAP as a deduction from equity:

   (i) it shall not recognise that goodwill in its opening IFRS balance sheet. Furthermore, it shall not transfer that goodwill to the income statement if it disposes of the subsidiary or if the investment in the subsidiary becomes impaired.

   (ii) adjustments resulting from the subsequent resolution of a contingency affecting the purchase consideration shall be recognised in retained earnings.

(j) Under its previous GAAP, the first-time adopter may not have consolidated a subsidiary acquired in a past business combination (for example, because the parent did not regard it as a subsidiary under previous GAAP or did not prepare consolidated financial statements). The first-time adopter shall adjust the carrying amounts of the subsidiary's assets and liabilities to the amounts that IFRSs would require in the subsidiary's balance sheet. The deemed cost of goodwill equals the difference at the date of transition to IFRSs between:

(i) the parent's interest in those adjusted carrying amounts; and

(ii) the cost in the parent's separate financial statements of its investment in the subsidiary.

(k) The measurement of minority interests and deferred tax follows from the measurement of other assets and liabilities. Therefore, the above adjustments to recognised assets and liabilities affect minority interests and deferred tax.

B3 The exemption for past business combinations also applies to past acquisitions of investments in associates and of interests in joint ventures. Furthermore, the date selected for paragraph B1 applies equally for all such acquisitions.

Appendix C
Amendments to other IFRSs

The amendments in this appendix become effective for annual financial statements covering periods beginning on or after 1 January 2004. If an entity applies this IFRS for an earlier period, these amendments become effective for that earlier period.

* * * * *

The amendments contained in this appendix when this Standard was issued in 2003 have been incorporated into the relevant pronouncements published in this volume.

Approval of IFRS 1 by the Board

International Financial Reporting Standard 1 *First-time Adoption of International Financial Reporting Standards* was approved for issue by the fourteen members of the International Accounting Standards Board.

Sir David Tweedie	Chairman
Thomas E Jones	Vice-Chairman
Mary E Barth	
Hans-Georg Bruns	
Anthony T Cope	
Robert P Garnett	
Gilbert Gélard	
James J Leisenring	
Warren J McGregor	
Patricia L O'Malley	
Harry K Schmid	
John T Smith	
Geoffrey Whittington	
Tatsumi Yamada	

CONTENTS

paragraphs

BASIS FOR CONCLUSIONS ON IFRS 1 FIRST-TIME ADOPTION OF INTERNATIONAL FINANCIAL REPORTING STANDARDS

Basis for Conclusions on IFRS 1 First-time Adoption of International Financial Reporting Standards

This Basis for Conclusions accompanies, but is not part of, IFRS 1.

Introduction

BC1 This Basis for Conclusions summarises the International Accounting Standards Board's considerations in reaching the conclusions in IFRS 1 *First-time Adoption of International Financial Reporting Standards.* Individual Board members gave greater weight to some factors than to others.

BC2 SIC-8 *First-time Application of IASs as the Primary Basis of Accounting*, issued in 1998, dealt with matters that arose when an entity first adopted IASs. In 2001, the Board began a project to review SIC-8. In July 2002, the Board published ED 1 *First-time Application of International Financial Reporting Standards*, with a comment deadline of 31 October 2002. The Board received 83 comment letters on ED 1.

BC3 This project took on added significance because of the requirement that listed European Union companies should adopt International Financial Reporting Standards (IFRSs) in their consolidated financial statements from 2005. Several other countries have announced that they will permit or require entities to adopt IFRSs in the next few years. Nevertheless, the Board's aim in developing the IFRS was to find solutions that will be appropriate for any entity, in any part of the world, regardless of whether adoption occurs in 2005 or at a different time.

Scope

BC4 The IFRS applies to an entity that presents its first IFRS financial statements (a first-time adopter). Some suggested that an entity should not be regarded as a first-time adopter if its previous financial statements contained an explicit statement of compliance with IFRSs, except for specified (and explicit) departures. They argued that an explicit statement of compliance establishes that an entity regards IFRSs as its basis of accounting, even if the entity does not comply with every requirement of every IFRS. Some regarded this argument as especially strong if an entity previously complied with all recognition and measurement requirements of IFRSs, but did not give some required disclosures—for example, segmental disclosures that IAS 14 *Segment Reporting* requires or the explicit statement of compliance with IFRSs that IAS 1 *Presentation of Financial Statements* requires.

BC5 To implement that approach, it would be necessary to establish how many departures are needed—and how serious they must be—before an entity would conclude that it has not adopted IFRSs. In the Board's view, this would lead to complexity and uncertainty. Also, an entity should not be regarded as having adopted IFRSs if it does not give all disclosures required by IFRSs, because that approach would diminish the importance of disclosures and undermine efforts to promote full compliance with IFRSs. Therefore, the IFRS contains a simple test that gives an unambiguous answer: an entity has adopted IFRSs if, and only if, its financial statements contain an explicit and unreserved statement of compliance with IFRSs (paragraph 3 of the IFRS).

BC6 If an entity's financial statements in previous years contained that statement, any material disclosed or undisclosed departures from IFRSs are errors. The entity applies IAS 8 *Accounting Policies, Changes in Accounting Estimates and Errors* in correcting them.

Basic concepts

Useful information for users

BC7 In developing recognition and measurement requirements for an entity's opening IFRS balance sheet, the Board referred to the objective of financial statements, as set out in the *Framework for the Preparation and Presentation of Financial Statements*. The *Framework* states that the objective of financial statements is to provide information about the financial position, performance and changes in financial position of an entity that is useful to a wide range of users in making economic decisions.

BC8 The *Framework* identifies four qualitative characteristics that make information in financial statements useful to users. In summary, the information should be:

(a) readily understandable by users.

(b) relevant to the decision-making needs of users.

(c) reliable, in other words financial statements should:

   (i) represent faithfully the transactions and other events they either purport to represent or could reasonably be expected to represent;

   (ii) represent transactions and other events in accordance with their substance and economic reality and not merely their legal form;

   (iii) be neutral, that is to say, free from bias;

   (iv) contend with the uncertainties that inevitably surround many events and circumstances by the exercise of prudence; and

   (v) be complete within the bounds of materiality and cost.

(d) comparable with information provided by the entity in its financial statements through time and with information provided in the financial statements of other entities.

Comparability

BC9 The previous paragraph notes the need for comparability. Ideally, a regime for first-time adoption of IFRSs would achieve comparability:

(a) within an entity over time;

(b) between different first-time adopters; and

(c) between first-time adopters and entities that already apply IFRSs.

BC10 SIC-8 gave priority to ensuring comparability between a first-time adopter and entities that already applied IASs. It was based on the principle that a first-time adopter should comply with the same Standards as an entity that already applied IASs. However, the Board decided that it is more important to achieve comparability over time within a first-time adopter's first IFRS financial statements and between different entities adopting IFRSs for the first time at a given date; achieving comparability between first-time adopters and entities that already apply IFRSs is a secondary objective.

Current version of IFRSs

BC11 Paragraphs 7–9 of the IFRS require a first-time adopter to apply the current version of IFRSs, without considering superseded or amended versions. This:

(a) enhances comparability, because the information in a first-time adopter's first IFRS financial statements is prepared on a consistent basis over time;

(b) gives users comparative information prepared using later versions of IFRSs that the Board regards as superior to superseded versions; and

(c) avoids unnecessary costs.

BC12 In general, the transitional provisions in other IFRSs do not apply to a first-time adopter (paragraph 9 of the IFRS). Some of these transitional provisions require or permit an entity already reporting under IFRSs to apply a new requirement prospectively. These provisions generally reflect a conclusion that one or both of the following factors are present in a particular case:

(a) Retrospective application may be difficult or involve costs exceeding the likely benefits. The IFRS permits prospective application in specific cases where this could occur (paragraphs BC30–BC73).

(b) There is a danger of abuse if retrospective application would require judgements by management about past conditions after the outcome of a particular transaction is already known. The IFRS prohibits retrospective application in some areas where this could occur (paragraphs BC74–BC84).

BC13 Some have suggested three further reasons for permitting or requiring prospective application in some cases:

(a) to alleviate unforeseen consequences of a new IFRS if another party uses financial statements to monitor compliance with a contract or agreement. However, in the Board's view, it is up to the parties to an agreement to determine whether to insulate the agreement from the effects of a future IFRS and, if not, how they might renegotiate it so that it reflects changes in the underlying financial condition rather than changes in reporting (paragraph 21 of the *Preface to International Financial Reporting Standards*).

(b) to give a first-time adopter the same accounting options as an entity that already applies IFRSs. However, permitting prospective application by a first-time adopter would conflict with the Board's primary objective of comparability within an entity's first IFRS financial statements (paragraph BC10). Therefore, the Board did not adopt a general policy of giving first-time adopters the same accounting options of prospective application that existing IFRSs give to entities that already apply IFRSs. Paragraphs BC20–BC23 discuss one specific case, namely derecognition of financial assets and financial liabilities.

(c) to avoid difficult distinctions between changes in estimates and changes in the basis for making estimates. However, a first-time adopter need not make this distinction in preparing its opening IFRS balance sheet, so the IFRS does not include exemptions on these grounds. If an entity becomes aware of errors made under previous GAAP, the IFRS requires it to disclose the correction of the errors (paragraph 41 of the IFRS).

BC14 The Board will consider case by case when it issues a new IFRS whether a first-time adopter should apply that IFRS retrospectively or prospectively. The Board expects that retrospective application will be appropriate in most cases, given its primary objective of comparability over time within a first-time adopter's first IFRS financial statements. However, if the Board concludes in a particular case that prospective application by a first-time adopter is justified, it will amend the IFRS on first-time adoption of IFRSs. As a result, IFRS 1 will contain all material on first-time adoption of IFRSs and other IFRSs will not refer to first-time adopters (except, when needed, in the Basis for Conclusions and consequential amendments).

BC15 Under the proposals in ED 1, a first-time adopter could have elected to apply IFRSs as if it had always applied IFRSs. This alternative approach was intended mainly to help an entity that did not wish to use any of the exemptions proposed in ED 1 because it had already been accumulating information under IFRSs without presenting IFRS financial statements. To enable an entity using this approach to use the information it had already accumulated, ED 1 would have required it to consider superseded versions of IFRSs if more recent versions required prospective application. However, as explained in paragraphs BC28 and BC29, the Board abandoned ED 1's all-or-nothing approach to exemptions. Because this eliminated the reason for the alternative approach, the Board deleted it in finalising the IFRS.

Opening IFRS balance sheet

BC16 An entity's opening IFRS balance sheet is the starting point for its accounting under IFRSs. The following paragraphs explain how the Board used the *Framework* in developing recognition and measurement requirements for the opening IFRS balance sheet.

Recognition

BC17 The Board considered a suggestion that the IFRS should not require a first-time adopter to investigate transactions that occurred before the beginning of a 'look back' period of, say, three to five years before the date of transition to IFRSs. Some argued that this would be a practical way for a first-time adopter to give a high level of transparency and comparability, without incurring the cost of investigating very old transactions. They noted two particular precedents for transitional provisions that have permitted an entity to omit some assets and liabilities from its balance sheet:

(a) A previous version of IAS 39 *Financial Instruments: Recognition and Measurement* prohibited restatement of securitisation, transfer or other derecognition transactions entered into before the beginning of the financial year in which it was initially applied.

(b) Some national accounting standards and IAS 17 *Accounting for Leases* (superseded in 1997 by IAS 17 *Leases*) permitted prospective application of a requirement for lessees to capitalise finance leases. Under this approach, a lessee would not be required to recognise finance lease obligations and the related leased assets for leases that began before a specified date.

BC18 However, limiting the look back period could lead to the omission of material assets or liabilities from an entity's opening IFRS balance sheet. Material omissions would undermine the understandability, relevance, reliability and comparability of an entity's first IFRS financial statements. Therefore, the Board concluded that an entity's opening IFRS balance sheet should:

(a) include all assets and liabilities whose recognition is required by IFRSs, except:

 (i) some financial assets or financial liabilities derecognised under previous GAAP before the date of transition to IFRSs (paragraphs BC20–BC23); and

 (ii) goodwill and other assets acquired, and liabilities assumed, in a past business combination that were not recognised in the acquirer's consolidated balance sheet under previous GAAP and also would not qualify for recognition under IFRSs in the balance sheet of the acquiree (paragraphs BC31–BC40).

(b) not report items as assets or liabilities if they do not qualify for recognition under IFRSs.

BC19 Some financial instruments may be classified as equity under previous GAAP but as financial liabilities under IAS 32 *Financial Instruments: Disclosure and Presentation*. Some respondents to ED 1 requested an extended transitional period to enable the issuer of such instruments to renegotiate contracts that refer to debt-equity ratios. However, although a new IFRS may have unforeseen consequences if another party uses financial statements to monitor compliance with a contract or agreement, that possibility does not, in the Board's view, justify prospective application (paragraph BC13(a)).

Derecognition under previous GAAP

BC20 An entity may have derecognised financial assets or financial liabilities under its previous GAAP that do not qualify for derecognition under IAS 39. ED 1 proposed that a first-time adopter should recognise those assets and liabilities in its opening IFRS balance sheet. Some respondents to ED 1 requested the Board to permit or require a first-time adopter not to restate past derecognition transactions, on the following grounds:

(a) Restating past derecognition transactions would be costly, especially if restatement involves determining the fair value of retained servicing assets and liabilities and other components retained in a complex securitisation.

Furthermore, it may be difficult to obtain information on financial assets held by transferees that are not under the transferor's control.

(b) Restatement undermines the legal certainty expected by parties who entered into transactions on the basis of the accounting rules in effect at the time.

(c) IAS 39 did not, before the improvements proposed in June 2002, require (or even permit) entities to restate past derecognition transactions. Without a similar exemption, first-time adopters would be unfairly disadvantaged.

(d) Retrospective application would not result in consistent measurement, as entities would need to recreate information about past transactions with the benefit of hindsight.

BC21 The Board had considered these arguments in developing ED 1. The Board's reasons for the proposal in ED 1 were as follows:

(a) The omission of material assets or liabilities would undermine the understandability, relevance, reliability and comparability of an entity's financial statements. Many of the transactions under discussion are large and will have effects for many years.

(b) Such an exemption would be inconsistent with the June 2002 Exposure Draft of improvements to IAS 39.

(c) The Board's primary objective is to achieve comparability over time within an entity's first IFRS financial statements. Prospective application by a first-time adopter would conflict with that primary objective, even if prospective application were available to entities already applying IFRSs.

(d) Although a new IFRS may have unforeseen consequences if another party uses financial statements to monitor compliance with a contract or agreement, that possibility does not justify prospective application (paragraph BC13(a)).

BC22 Nevertheless, in finalising the IFRS, the Board concluded that it would be premature to require a treatment different from the current version of IAS 39 before completing the proposed improvements to IAS 39. Accordingly, the IFRS originally required the same treatment as the then current version of IAS 39 for derecognition transactions before the effective date of the then current version of IAS 39, namely that any financial assets or financial liabilities derecognised under previous GAAP before financial years beginning on 1 January 2001 remain derecognised. The Board agreed that when it completed the improvements to IAS 39, it might amend or delete this exemption.

BC22A The Board reconsidered this issue in completing the revision of IAS 39 in 2003. The Board decided to retain the transition requirements as set out in IFRS 1, for the reasons given in paragraph BC20. However, the Board amended the date from which prospective application was required to transactions that occur on or after 1 January 2004 in order to overcome the practical difficulties of restating transactions that had been derecognised before that date.

BC22B The Board also noted that financial statements that include financial assets and financial liabilities that would otherwise be omitted under the provisions of the IFRS would be more complete and therefore more useful to users of financial statements. The Board therefore decided to permit retrospective application of the derecognition requirements. It also decided that retrospective application should be limited to cases when the information needed to apply the IFRS to past transactions was obtained at the time of initially accounting for those transactions. This limitation prevents the unacceptable use of hindsight.

BC23 The Board removed from IAS 39 the following consequential amendments to IAS 39 made when IFRS 1 was issued, because, for first-time adopters, these clarifications are clear in paragraphs IG26–IG31 and IG53 of the guidance on implementing IFRS 1. These were:

(a) the clarification that an entity is required to apply IAS 39 to all derivatives or other interests retained after a derecognition transaction, even if the transaction occurred before the effective date of IAS 39; and

(b) the confirmation that there are no exemptions for special purpose entities that existed before the date of transition to IFRSs.

Measurement

BC24 The Board considered whether it should require a first-time adopter to measure all assets and liabilities at fair value in the opening IFRS balance sheet. Some argued that this would result in more relevant information than an aggregation of costs incurred at different dates, or of costs and fair values. However, the Board concluded that a requirement to measure all assets and liabilities at fair value at the date of transition to IFRSs would be unreasonable, given that an entity may use an IFRS-compliant cost-based measurement before and after that date for some items.

BC25 The Board decided as a general principle that a first-time adopter should measure all assets and liabilities recognised in its opening IFRS balance sheet on the basis required by the relevant IFRSs. This is needed for an entity's first IFRS financial statements to present understandable, relevant, reliable and comparable information.

Benefits and costs

BC26 The *Framework* acknowledges that the need for a balance between the benefits of information and the cost of providing it may constrain the provision of relevant and reliable information. The Board considered these cost-benefit constraints and developed targeted exemptions from the general principle described in paragraph BC25. SIC-8 did not include specific exemptions of this kind, although it provided general exemptions from:

(a) retrospective adjustments to the opening balance of retained earnings 'when the amount of the adjustment relating to prior periods cannot be reasonably determined'.

(b) provision of comparative information when it is 'impracticable' to provide such information.

BC27 The Board expects that most first-time adopters will begin planning on a timely basis for the transition to IFRSs. Accordingly, in balancing benefits and costs, the Board took as its benchmark an entity that plans the transition well in advance and can collect most information needed for its opening IFRS balance sheet at, or very soon after, the date of transition to IFRSs.

BC28 ED 1 proposed that a first-time adopter should use either all the exemptions in ED 1 or none. However, some respondents disagreed with this all-or-nothing approach for the following reasons:

(a) Many of the exemptions are not interdependent, so there is no conceptual reason to condition use of one exemption on use of other exemptions.

(b) Although it is necessary to permit some exemptions on pragmatic grounds, entities should be encouraged to use as few exemptions as possible.

(c) Some of the exemptions proposed in ED 1 were implicit options because they relied on the entity's own judgement of undue cost or effort and some others were explicit options. Only a few exemptions were really mandatory.

(d) Unlike the other exceptions to retrospective application, the requirement to apply hedge accounting prospectively was not intended as a pragmatic concession on cost-benefit grounds. Retrospective application in an area that relies on designation by management would not be acceptable, even if an entity applied all other aspects of IFRSs retrospectively.

BC29 The Board found these comments persuasive. In finalising the IFRS, the Board grouped the exceptions to retrospective application into two categories:

(a) Some exceptions consist of optional exemptions (paragraphs BC30–BC63).

(b) The other exceptions prohibit full retrospective application of IFRSs to some aspects of derecognition (paragraphs BC20–BC23), hedge accounting (paragraphs BC75–BC80), and estimates (paragraph BC84).

Exemptions from other IFRSs

BC30 An entity may elect to use one or more of the following exemptions:

(a) business combinations (paragraphs BC31–BC40);

(b) fair value or revaluations as deemed cost (paragraphs BC41–BC47);

(c) employee benefits (paragraphs BC48–BC52);

(d) cumulative translation differences (paragraphs BC53–BC55);

(e) compound financial instruments (paragraphs BC56–BC58);

(f) assets and liabilities of subsidiaries, associates and joint ventures (paragraphs BC59–BC63);

(g) designation of previously recognised financial instruments (paragraph BC63A); and

(h) share-based payment transactions (paragraph 63B).

Business combinations

BC31 The following paragraphs discuss various aspects of accounting for business combinations that an entity recognised under previous GAAP before the date of transition to IFRSs:

(a) whether retrospective restatement of past business combinations should be prohibited, permitted or required (paragraphs BC32–BC34).

(b) whether an entity should recognise assets acquired and liabilities assumed in a past business combination if it did not recognise them under previous GAAP (paragraph BC35).

(c) whether an entity should restate amounts assigned to the assets and liabilities of the combining entities if previous GAAP brought forward unchanged their pre-combination carrying amounts (paragraph BC36).

(d) whether an entity should restate goodwill for adjustments made in its opening IFRS balance sheet to the carrying amounts of assets acquired and liabilities assumed in past business combinations (paragraphs BC37–BC40).

BC32 Retrospective application of IFRS 3 *Business Combinations* could require an entity to recreate data that it did not capture at the date of a past business combination and make subjective estimates about conditions that existed at that date. These factors could reduce the relevance and reliability of the entity's first IFRS financial statements. Therefore, ED 1 would have prohibited restatement of past business combinations (unless an entity used the proposed alternative approach, discussed in paragraph BC15, of applying IFRSs as if it had always applied IFRSs). Some respondents agreed, arguing that restatement of past business combinations would involve subjective, and potentially selective, use of hindsight that would diminish the relevance and reliability of financial statements.

BC33 Other respondents disagreed. They argued that:

(a) effects of business combination accounting can last for many years. Previous GAAP may differ significantly from IFRSs, and in some countries there are no accounting requirements at all for business combinations. Previous GAAP balances might not result in decision-useful information in these countries.

(b) restatement is preferable and may not involve as much cost or effort for more recent business combinations.

BC34 In the light of these comments, the Board concluded that restatement of past business combinations is conceptually preferable, although for cost-benefit reasons this should be permitted but not required. The Board decided to place some limits on this election and noted that information is more likely to be available for more recent business combinations. Therefore, if a first-time adopter restates any business combination, the IFRS requires it to restate all later business combinations (paragraph B1 of Appendix B of the IFRS).

BC35 If an entity did not recognise a particular asset or liability under previous GAAP at the date of the business combination, ED 1 proposed that its deemed cost under IFRSs would be zero. As a result, the entity's opening IFRS balance sheet would not have included that asset or liability if IFRSs permit or require a cost-based measurement. Some respondents to ED 1 argued that this would be an unjustifiable departure from the principle that the opening IFRS balance sheet should include all assets and liabilities. The Board agreed with that conclusion. Therefore, paragraph B2(f) of Appendix B of the IFRS requires that the acquirer should recognise those assets and liabilities and measure them on the basis that IFRSs would require in the separate balance sheet of the acquiree.

BC36 Under previous GAAP, an entity might have brought forward unchanged the pre-combination carrying amounts of the combining entities' assets and liabilities. Some argued that it would be inconsistent to use these carrying amounts as deemed cost under IFRSs, given that the IFRS does not permit the use of similar carrying amounts as deemed cost for assets and liabilities that were not acquired in a business combination. However, the Board identified no specific form of past business combination, and no specific form of accounting for past business combinations, for which it would not be acceptable to bring forward cost-based measurements made under previous GAAP.

BC37 Although the IFRS treats amounts assigned under previous GAAP to goodwill and other assets acquired and liabilities assumed in a past business combination as their deemed cost under IFRSs at the date of the business combination, an entity needs to adjust their carrying amounts in its opening IFRS balance sheet, as follows.

(a) Assets and liabilities measured under IFRSs at fair value or other forms of current value: remeasure to fair value or that other current value.

(b) Assets (other than goodwill) and liabilities for which IFRSs apply a cost-based measurement: adjust the accumulated depreciation or amortisation since the date of the business combination if it does not comply with IFRSs. Depreciation is based on deemed cost, which is the carrying amount under previous GAAP immediately following the business combination.

(c) Assets (other than goodwill) and liabilities not recognised under previous GAAP: measure on the basis that IFRSs would require in the separate balance sheet of the acquiree.

(d) Items that do not qualify for recognition as assets and liabilities under IFRSs: eliminate from the opening IFRS balance sheet.

BC38 The Board considered whether a first-time adopter should recognise the resulting adjustments by restating goodwill. Because intangible assets and goodwill are closely related, the Board decided that a first-time adopter should restate goodwill when it:

(a) eliminates an item that was recognised under previous GAAP as an intangible asset but does not qualify for separate recognition under IFRSs; or

(b) recognises an intangible asset that was subsumed within goodwill under previous GAAP.

However, to avoid costs that would exceed the likely benefits to users, the IFRS prohibits restatement of goodwill for most other adjustments reflected in the opening IFRS balance sheet, unless a first-time adopter elects to apply IFRS 3 retrospectively (paragraph B2(g) of the IFRS).

BC39 To minimise the possibility of double-counting an item that was included in goodwill under previous GAAP, and is included under IFRSs either within the measurement of another asset or as a deduction from a liability, the IFRS requires an entity to test goodwill recognised in its opening IFRS balance sheet for impairment (paragraph B2(g)(iii) of the IFRS). This does not prevent the implicit recognition of internally generated goodwill that arose after the date of the business combination. However, the Board concluded that an attempt to exclude such internally generated goodwill would be costly and lead to arbitrary results.

BC40 Some respondents to ED 1 suggested that a formal impairment test should be required only if there is a possibility of double-counting–ie when additional, previously unrecognised, assets relating to a past business combination are recognised in the opening IFRS balance sheet (or an indicator of impairment is present). However, the Board decided that a first-time adopter should carry out a formal impairment test of all goodwill recognised in its opening IFRS balance sheet, as previous GAAP might not have required a test of comparable rigour.

Fair value or revaluation as deemed cost

BC41 Some measurements under IFRSs are based on an accumulation of past costs or other transaction data. If an entity has not previously collected the necessary information, collecting or estimating it retrospectively may be costly. To avoid excessive cost, ED 1 proposed that an entity could use the fair value of an item of property, plant and equipment at the date of transition to IFRSs as its deemed cost at that date if determining a cost-based measurement under IFRSs would involve undue cost or effort.

BC42 In finalising the IFRS, the Board noted that reconstructed cost data might be less relevant to users, and less reliable, than current fair value data. Furthermore, the Board concluded that balancing costs and benefits was a task for the Board when it sets accounting requirements rather than for entities when they apply those requirements. Therefore, the IFRS permits an entity to use fair value as deemed cost in some cases without any need to demonstrate undue cost or effort.

BC43 Some expressed concerns that the use of fair value would lead to lack of comparability. However, cost is generally equivalent to fair value at the date of acquisition. Therefore, the use of fair value as the deemed cost of an asset means that an entity will report the same cost data as if it had acquired an asset with the same remaining service potential at the date of transition to IFRSs. If there is any lack of comparability, it arises from the aggregation of costs incurred at different dates, rather than from the targeted use of fair value as deemed cost for some assets. The Board regarded this approach as justified to solve the unique problem of introducing IFRSs in a cost-effective way without damaging transparency.

BC44 The IFRS restricts the use of fair value as deemed cost to those assets for which reconstructing costs is likely to be of limited benefit to users and particularly onerous: property, plant and equipment, investment property (if an entity elects to use the cost method in IAS 40 *Investment Property*) and intangible assets that meet restrictive criteria (paragraphs 16 and 18 of the IFRS).

BC45 Under the revaluation model in IAS 16 *Property, Plant and Equipment*, if an entity revalues an asset, it must revalue all assets in that class. This restriction prevents selective revaluation of only those assets whose revaluation would lead to a particular result. Some suggested a similar restriction on the use of fair value as deemed cost. However, IAS 36 *Impairment of Assets* requires an impairment test if there is any indication that an asset is impaired. Thus, if an entity uses fair value as deemed cost for assets whose fair value is above cost, it cannot ignore indications that the recoverable amount of other assets may have fallen below their carrying amount. Therefore, the IFRS does not restrict the use of fair value as deemed cost to entire classes of asset.

BC46 Some revaluations under previous GAAP might be more relevant to users than original cost. If so, it would not be reasonable to require time-consuming and expensive reconstruction of a cost that complies with IFRSs. In consequence, the IFRS permits an entity to use amounts determined using previous GAAP as deemed cost for IFRSs in the following cases:

(a) if an entity revalued one of the assets described in paragraph BC44 using its previous GAAP and the revaluation met specified criteria (paragraphs 17 and 18 of the IFRS).

(b) if an entity established a deemed cost under previous GAAP for some or all assets and liabilities by measuring them at their fair value at one particular date because of an event such as a privatisation or initial public offering (paragraph 19 of the IFRS).

BC47 Paragraph 17 of the IFRS refers to revaluations that are broadly comparable to fair value or reflect an index applied to a cost that is broadly comparable to cost determined under IFRSs. It may not always be clear whether a previous revaluation was intended as a measure of fair value or differs materially from fair value. The flexibility in this area permits a cost-effective solution for the unique problem of transition to IFRSs. It allows a first-time adopter to establish a deemed cost using a measurement that is already available and is a reasonable starting point for a cost-based measurement.

Employee benefits

BC48 If an entity elects to use the 'corridor' approach in IAS 19 *Employee Benefits*, full retrospective application of IAS 19 would require the entity to determine actuarial gains or losses for each year since the inception of the plan in order to determine the net cumulative unrecognised gains or losses at the date of transition to IFRSs. The Board concluded that this would not benefit users and would be costly. Therefore, the IFRS permits a first-time adopter to recognise all actuarial gains or losses up to the date of transition to IFRSs, even if its accounting policy under IAS 19 involves leaving some later actuarial gains and losses unrecognised (paragraph 20 of the IFRS).

BC49 The revision of IAS 19 in 1998 increased the reported employee benefit liabilities of some entities. IAS 19 permitted entities to amortise that increase over up to five years. Some suggested a similar transitional treatment for first-time adopters. However, the Board has no general policy of exempting transactions occurring before a specific date from the requirements of new IFRSs (paragraph 21 of the *Preface to International Financial Reporting Standards*). Therefore, the Board did not include a similar transitional provision for first-time adopters.

BC50 An entity's first IFRS financial statements may reflect measurements of pension liabilities at three dates: the reporting date, the end of the comparative year and the date of transition to IFRSs. Some suggested that obtaining three separate actuarial valuations for a single set of financial statements would be costly. Therefore, they proposed that the Board should permit an entity to use a single actuarial valuation, based, for example, on assumptions valid at the reporting date, with service costs and interest costs based on those assumptions for each of the periods presented.

BC51 However, the Board concluded that a general exemption from the principle of measurement at each date would conflict with the objective of providing understandable, relevant, reliable and comparable information for users. If an entity obtains a full actuarial valuation at one or two of these dates and rolls that (those) valuation(s) forward or back to the other date(s), any such roll forward or roll back needs to reflect material transactions and other material events (including changes in market prices and interest rates) between those dates (IAS 19, paragraph 57).

BC52 Some suggested that the Board should exempt a first-time adopter from the requirement to identify and amortise the unvested portion of past service cost at the date of transition to IFRSs. However, this requirement is less onerous than the retrospective application of the corridor for actuarial gains and losses because it does not require the recreation of data since the inception of the plan. The Board concluded that no exemption was justified for past service cost.

Cumulative translation differences

BC53 IAS 21 *The Effects of Changes in Foreign Exchange Rates* requires an entity to classify some cumulative translation differences (CTDs) relating to a net investment in a foreign operation as a separate component of equity. The entity transfers the CTDs to the income statement on subsequent disposal of the foreign operation. The proposals in ED 1 would have permitted a first-time adopter to use the CTDs under previous GAAP as the deemed CTDs under IFRSs if reconstructing CTDs would have involved undue cost or effort.

BC54 Some respondents to ED 1 argued that it would be more transparent and comparable to exempt an entity from the requirement to identify CTDs at the date of transition to IFRSs, for the following reasons:

(a) An entity might know the aggregate CTDs, but might not know the amount for each subsidiary. If so, it could not transfer that amount to the income statement on disposal of that subsidiary. This would defeat the objective of identifying CTDs as a separate component of equity.

(b) The amount of CTDs under previous GAAP might be inappropriate as it might be affected by adjustments made on transition to IFRSs to assets and liabilities of foreign entities.

BC55 The Board found these arguments persuasive. Therefore, a first-time adopter need not identify the CTDs at the date of transition to IFRSs (paragraphs 21 and 22 of the IFRS). The first-time adopter need not show that identifying the CTDs would involve undue cost or effort.

Compound financial instruments

BC56 IAS 32 *Financial Instruments: Disclosure and Presentation* requires an entity to split a compound financial instrument at inception into separate liability and equity components. Even if the liability component is no longer outstanding, retrospective application of IAS 32 would involve separating two portions of equity. The first portion is in retained earnings and represents the cumulative interest accreted on the liability component. The other portion represents the original equity component of the instrument.

BC57 Some respondents to ED 1 argued that separating these two portions would be costly if the liability component of the compound instrument is no longer outstanding at the date of transition to IFRSs. The Board agreed with those comments. Therefore, if the liability component is no longer outstanding at the date of transition to IFRSs, a first-time adopter need not separate the cumulative interest on the liability component from the equity component (paragraph 23 of the IFRS).

BC58 Some respondents requested an exemption for compound instruments even if still outstanding at the date of transition to IFRSs. One possible approach would be to use the fair value of the components at the date of transition to IFRSs as deemed cost. However, as the IFRS does not include any exemptions for financial liabilities, the Board concluded that it would be inconsistent to create such an exemption for the liability component of a compound instrument.

Assets and liabilities of subsidiaries, associates and joint ventures

BC59 A subsidiary may have reported to its parent in the previous period using IFRSs without presenting a full set of financial statements under IFRSs. If the subsidiary subsequently begins to present financial statements that contain an explicit and unreserved statement of compliance with IFRSs, it becomes a first-time adopter at that time. This might compel the subsidiary to keep two parallel sets of accounting records based on different dates of transition to IFRSs, because some measurements under the IFRS depend on the date of transition to IFRSs.

BC60 In developing ED 1, the Board concluded that a requirement to keep two parallel sets of records would be burdensome and not be beneficial to users. Therefore, ED 1 proposed that a subsidiary would not be treated as a first-time adopter for recognition and measurement purposes if the subsidiary was consolidated in IFRS financial statements for the previous period and all owners of the minority interests consented.

BC61 Some respondents to ED 1 opposed the exemption, on the following grounds:

(a) The exemption would not eliminate all differences between the group reporting package and the subsidiary's own financial statements. The reporting package does not constitute a full set of financial statements, the parent may have made adjustments to the reported numbers (for example, if pension cost adjustments were made centrally), and the group materiality threshold may be higher than for the subsidiary.

(b) The Board's objective of comparability between different entities adopting IFRSs for the first time at the same date (paragraph BC10) should apply equally to any entity, including subsidiaries, particularly if the subsidiary's debt or equity securities are publicly traded.

BC62 However, the Board retained the exemption because it will ease some practical problems. Although the exemption does not eliminate all differences between the subsidiary's financial statements and a group reporting package, it does reduce them. Furthermore, the exemption does not diminish the relevance and reliability of the subsidiary's financial statements because it permits a measurement that is already acceptable under IFRSs in the consolidated financial statements of the parent. Therefore, the Board also eliminated the proposal in ED 1 that the exemption should be conditional on the consent of minorities.

BC63 In finalising the IFRS, the Board simplified the description of the exemption for a subsidiary that adopts IFRSs after its parent. Under the IFRS, the subsidiary may measure its assets and liabilities at the carrying amounts that would be included in the parent's consolidated financial statements, based on the parent's date of transition to IFRSs, if no adjustments were made for consolidation procedures and for the effects of the business combination in which the parent acquired the subsidiary. Alternatively, it may elect to measure them at the carrying amounts required by the rest of the IFRS, based on the subsidiary's date of transition to IFRSs. The Board also extended the exemption to an associate or joint venture that becomes a first-time adopter later than an entity that has significant influence or joint control over it (paragraph 24 of the IFRS). However, if a parent adopts IFRSs later than a subsidiary, the parent cannot, in its consolidated financial statements, elect to change IFRS measurements that the subsidiary has already used in its financial statements, except to adjust for consolidation procedures and for the effects of the business combination in which the parent acquired the subsidiary (paragraph 25 of the IFRS).

Designation of previously recognised financial instruments

BC63A IAS 39 (as revised in 2003) permits an entity to designate, on initial recognition only, a financial instrument as (a) a financial asset or financial liability at fair value through profit or loss or (b) available for sale. Despite this requirement, an entity that had already applied IFRSs before the effective date of IAS 39 (as revised in 2003) may, on initial application of IAS 39 (as revised in 2003), so designate a previously recognised financial instrument. The Board decided to treat first-time adopters in the same way as entities that already apply IFRSs. Accordingly, a first-time adopter of IFRSs may similarly designate a previously recognised financial instrument at the date of transition to IFRSs. Such an entity is required to disclose the amount of previously recognised financial instruments that it so designates.

Share-based payment transactions

BC63B IFRS 2 *Share-based Payment* contains various transitional provisions. For example, for equity-settled share-based payment arrangements, IFRS 2 requires an entity to apply IFRS 2 to shares, share options or other equity instruments that were granted after 7 November 2002 and had not vested at the effective date of IFRS 2. IFRS 2 is effective for annual periods beginning on or after 1 January 2005. There are also transitional arrangements for liabilities arising from cash-settled share-based payment transactions, and for modifications of the terms or conditions of a grant of equity instruments to which IFRS 2 has not been applied, if the modification occurs after the effective date of IFRS 2. The Board decided that, in general, first-time adopters should be treated in the same way as entities that already apply IFRSs. For example, a first-time adopter should not be required to apply IFRS 2 to equity instruments that were granted on or before 7 November 2002. Similarly, a first-time adopter should not be required to apply IFRS 2 to equity instruments that were granted after 7 November 2002 if those equity instruments vested before 1 January 2005. In addition, the Board decided that a first-time adopter should not be required to apply IFRS 2 to equity instruments that were granted after 7 November 2002 if those equity instruments vested before the date of transition to IFRSs. Similarly, the Board decided that a first-time adopter should not be required to apply IFRS 2 to liabilities arising from cash-settled share-based payment transactions if those liabilities were settled before 1 January 2005, or before the date of transition to IFRSs.

Changes in existing decommissioning, restoration and similar liabilities included in the cost of property, plant and equipment

BC63C IFRIC 1 *Changes in Existing Decommissioning, Restoration and Similar Liabilities* requires specified changes in decommissioning, restoration and similar liabilities to be added to, or deducted from, the cost of the assets to which they relate, and the adjusted depreciable amount to be depreciated prospectively over the remaining useful life of those assets. Retrospective application of this requirement at the date of transition would require an entity to construct a historical record of all such adjustments that would have been made in the past. In many cases this will not be practicable. The Board agreed that, as an alternative to complying with this requirement, an entity should be permitted to include in the depreciated cost of the asset, at the date of transition to IFRSs, an amount calculated by discounting the liability at that date back to, and depreciating it from, when the liability was first incurred.

Leases

BC63D IFRIC 4 *Determining whether an Arrangement contains a Lease* contains transitional provisions because the IFRIC acknowledged the practical difficulties raised by full retrospective application of the Interpretation, in particular the difficulty of going back potentially many years and making a meaningful assessment of whether the arrangement satisfied the criteria at that time. The Board decided to treat first-time adopters in the same way as entities that already apply IFRSs.

Other possible exemptions rejected

BC64 The Board considered and rejected suggestions for other exemptions. Each such exemption would have moved the IFRS away from a principles-based approach, diminished transparency for users, decreased comparability over time within an entity's first IFRS financial statements and created additional complexity. In the Board's view, any cost savings generated would not have outweighed these disadvantages. Paragraphs BC65–BC73 discuss some of the specific suggestions the Board considered, for embedded derivatives, hyperinflation, intangible assets and transaction costs on financial instruments.

Embedded derivatives

BC65 IAS 39 *Financial Instruments: Recognition and Measurement* requires an entity to account separately for some embedded derivatives at fair value. Some respondents to ED 1 argued that retrospective application of this requirement would be costly. Some suggested either an exemption from retrospective application of this requirement, or a requirement or option to use the fair value of the host instrument at the date of transition to IFRSs as its deemed cost at that date.

BC66 The Board noted that US GAAP provides an option in this area. Under the transitional provisions of SFAS 133 *Accounting for Derivative Instruments and Hedging Activities*, an entity need not account separately for some pre-existing embedded derivatives. Nevertheless, the Board concluded that the failure to measure embedded derivatives at fair value would diminish the relevance and reliability of an entity's first IFRS financial statements. The Board also observed that IAS 39 addresses an inability to measure an embedded derivative and the host contract separately. In such cases, IAS 39 requires an entity to measure the entire combined contract at fair value.

Hyperinflation

BC67 Some argued that the cost of restating financial statements for the effects of hyperinflation in periods before the date of transition to IFRSs would exceed the benefits, particularly if the currency is no longer hyperinflationary. However, the Board concluded that such restatement should be required, because hyperinflation can make unadjusted financial statements meaningless or misleading.

Intangible assets

BC68 For the following reasons, some proposed that a first-time adopter's opening IFRS balance sheet should exclude intangible assets that it did not recognise under previous GAAP:

(a) Using hindsight to assess retrospectively when the recognition criteria for intangible assets were met could be subjective, open up possibilities for manipulation and involve costs that might exceed the benefits to users.

(b) The benefits expected from intangible assets are often not related directly to the costs incurred. Therefore, capitalising the costs incurred is of limited benefit to users, particularly if the costs were incurred in the distant past.

(c) Such an exclusion would be consistent with the transitional provisions in IAS 38 *Intangible Assets*. These encourage (but do not require) the recognition of intangible assets acquired in a previous business combination that was an acquisition and prohibit the recognition of all other previously unrecognised intangible assets.

BC69 In many cases, internally generated intangible assets do not qualify for recognition under IAS 38 at the date of transition to IFRSs because an entity did not, under previous GAAP, accumulate cost information or did not carry out contemporaneous assessments of future economic benefits. In these cases, there is no need for a specific requirement to exclude those assets. Furthermore, when these assets do not qualify for recognition, first-time adopters will not generally, in the Board's view, need to perform extensive work to reach this conclusion.

BC70 In other cases, an entity may have accumulated and retained sufficient information about costs and future economic benefits to determine which intangible assets (whether internally generated or acquired in a business combination or separately) qualify under IAS 38 for recognition in its opening IFRS balance sheet. If that information is available, no exclusion is justified.

BC71 Some argued that fair value should be used as deemed cost for intangible assets in the opening IFRS balance sheet (by analogy with a business combination). ED 1 would not have permitted this. However, in finalising the IFRS, the Board concluded that this approach should be available for those intangible assets for which IFRSs already permit fair value measurements. Therefore, under the IFRS, a first-time adopter may elect to use fair value or some previous GAAP revaluations of intangible assets as deemed cost for IFRSs, but only if the intangible assets meet:

(a) the recognition criteria in IAS 38 (including reliable measurement of original cost); and

(b) the criteria in IAS 38 for revaluation (including the existence of an active market) (paragraph 18 of the IFRS).

Transaction costs: financial instruments

BC72 To determine the amortised cost of a financial asset or financial liability using the effective interest method, it is necessary to determine the transaction costs incurred when the asset or liability was originated. Some respondents to ED 1 argued that determining these transaction costs could involve undue cost or effort for financial assets or financial liabilities originated long before the date of transition to IFRSs. They suggested that the Board should permit a first-time adopter:

(a) to use the fair value of the financial asset or financial liability at the date of transition to IFRSs as its deemed cost at that date; or

(b) to determine amortised cost without considering transaction costs.

BC73 In the Board's view, the unamortised portion of transaction costs at the date of transition to IFRSs is unlikely to be material for most financial assets and financial liabilities. Even when the unamortised portion is material, reasonable estimates should be possible. Therefore, the Board created no exemption in this area.

Retrospective designation

BC74 The Board considered practical implementation difficulties that could arise from the retrospective application of aspects of IAS 39 *Financial Instruments: Recognition and Measurement*:

(a) hedge accounting (paragraphs BC75–BC80);

(b) the treatment of cumulative fair value changes on available-for-sale financial assets at the date of transition to IFRSs (paragraphs BC81–BC83); and

(c) 'day 1' gain or loss recognition (paragraph BC83A).

Hedge accounting

BC75 Before beginning their preparations for adopting IAS 39 (or a local standard based on IAS 39), it is unlikely that most entities would have adopted IAS 39's criteria for (a) documenting hedges at their inception and (b) testing the hedges for effectiveness, even if they intended to continue the same hedging strategies after adopting IAS 39. Furthermore, retrospective designation of hedges (or retrospective reversal of their designation) could lead to selective designation of some hedges to report a particular result.

BC76 To overcome these problems, the transitional requirements in IAS 39 require an entity already applying IFRSs to apply the hedging requirements prospectively when it adopts IAS 39. As the same problems arise for a first-time adopter, the IFRS requires prospective application by a first-time adopter.

BC77 ED 1 included a redrafted version of the transitional provisions in IAS 39 and related *Questions and Answers* (Q&As) developed by the IAS 39 Implementation Guidance Committee. The Board confirmed in the Basis for Conclusions published with ED 1 that it did not intend the redrafting to create substantive changes. However, in the light of responses to ED 1, the Board decided in finalising IFRS 1 that the redrafting would not make it easier for first-time adopters and others to understand and apply the transitional provisions and Q&As. However, the project to improve IAS 32 and IAS 39 resulted in certain amendments to the transition requirements. In addition, this project incorporated selected other Q&As (ie not on transition) into IAS 39. The Board therefore took this opportunity to consolidate all the guidance for first-time adopters in one place, by incorporating the Q&As on transition into IFRS 1.

BC78 Some respondents to ED 1 asked the Board to clarify what would happen if hedge accounting under previous GAAP involved hedging relationships of a type that does not qualify for hedge accounting under IAS 39. The problem can be seen most clearly for a hedge of a net position (macro hedge). If a first-time adopter were to use hedge accounting in its opening IFRS balance sheet for a hedge of a net position, this would involve either:

(a) recognising deferred debits and credits that are not assets and liabilities (for a fair value hedge); or

(b) deferring gains or losses in equity when there is, at best, a weak link to an underlying item that defines when they should be transferred to the income statement (for a cash flow hedge).

BC79 As either of these treatments would diminish the relevance and reliability of an entity's first IFRS financial statements, the Board decided that an entity should not apply hedge accounting in its opening IFRS balance sheet to a hedge of a net position that does not qualify as a hedged item under IAS 39. However, the Board concluded that it would be reasonable (and consistent with IAS 39, paragraph 133) to permit a first-time adopter to designate an individual item as a hedged item within the net position, provided that it does so no later than the date of transition to IFRSs, to prevent selective designation. For similar reasons, the Board prohibited hedge accounting in the opening IFRS balance sheet for any hedging relationship of a type that does not qualify for hedge accounting under IAS 39 (see paragraph 29 of the IFRS).

BC80 Some respondents to ED 1 suggested that an entity adopting IFRSs for the first time in 2005 could not meet IAS 39's documentation and effectiveness criteria by the date of transition to IFRSs (1 January 2004 for many entities). Some requested an exemption from these criteria until the beginning of the latest period covered by the first IFRS financial statements (1 January 2005 for many entities). However, for the following reasons, the Board did not create an exemption in this area:

(a) The Board's primary objective is comparability within a first-time adopter's first IFRS financial statements and between different first-time adopters switching to IFRSs at the same time (paragraph BC10).

(b) The continuation of previous GAAP hedge accounting practices could permit the non-recognition of derivatives or the recognition of deferred debits and credits that are not assets and liabilities.

(c) The Board's benchmark for cost-benefit assessments was an entity that has planned the transition to IFRSs and is able to collect the necessary information at, or very soon after, the date of transition to IFRSs (paragraph BC27). Entities should not be 'rewarded' by concessions if they failed to plan for transition, nor should that failure be allowed to undermine the integrity of their opening IFRS balance sheet. Entities switching to IFRSs in 2005 need to have their hedge accounting systems in place by the beginning of 2004. In the Board's view, that is a challenging but achievable timetable. Entities preparing to switch to IFRSs in 2004 should have been aware of the implications of IAS 39 already and the Exposure Draft of improvements to IAS 39, published in June 2002, proposed very few changes in this area, so delayed transition is not justified for these entities either.

Available-for-sale financial assets

BC81 Retrospective application of IAS 39 to available-for-sale financial assets requires a first-time adopter to recognise the cumulative fair value changes in a separate component of equity in the opening IFRS balance sheet, and transfer those fair value changes to the income statement on subsequent disposal or impairment of the asset. This could allow, for example, selective classification of assets with cumulative gains as available for sale (with subsequent transfers to the income statement on disposal) and assets with cumulative losses as held for trading (with no transfers on disposal).

BC82 IAS 39 confirmed the proposal in the Exposure Draft of June 2002 to give an entity that already applies IFRSs an option to designate any financial asset as at fair value through profit or loss when it first applies the proposed improvements. Although this requirement could increase the risk of selective classification by first-time adopters of the kind discussed in the previous paragraph, the Board noted that an entity could achieve a similar result by selective disposal of some assets before the date of transition to IFRSs. Therefore, the Board concluded that it should treat first-time adopters in the same way as entities that already apply IFRSs by requiring retrospective application.

BC83 Some respondents to ED 1 commented that the cost of determining the amount to be included in a separate component of equity would exceed the benefits. However, the Board noted that these costs would be minimal if a first-time adopter carried the available-for-sale financial assets under previous GAAP at cost or the lower of cost and market value. These costs might be more significant if it carried them at fair value, but in that case it might well classify the assets as held for trading. Therefore, the Board made no changes to ED 1's proposal that a first-time adopter should apply IAS 39 retrospectively to available-for-sale financial assets.

BC83A IFRS 1 originally required retrospective application of the 'day 1' gain or loss recognition requirements in IAS 39, paragraph AG76. After the revised IAS 39 was issued, constituents raised concerns that retrospective application would diverge from the requirements of US GAAP, would be difficult and expensive to implement, and might require subjective assumptions about what was observable and what was not. In response to these concerns, the Board decided to permit entities to apply the requirements in the last sentence of IAS 39 paragraph AG76, and paragraph AG76A, in any one of the following ways:

(a) retrospectively;

(b) prospectively to transactions entered into after 25 October 2002; or

(c) prospectively to transactions entered into after 1 January 2004.

Estimates

BC84 An entity will have made estimates under previous GAAP at the date of transition to IFRSs. Events between that date and the reporting date for the entity's first IFRS financial statements might suggest a need to change those estimates. Some of those events might qualify as adjusting events under IAS 10 *Events after the Balance Sheet Date*. However, if the entity made those estimates on a basis consistent with IFRSs, the Board concluded that it would be more helpful to users—and more consistent with IAS 8 *Accounting Policies, Changes in Accounting Estimates and Errors*—to recognise the revision of those estimates as income or expense in the period when the entity made the revision, rather than in preparing the opening IFRS balance sheet (paragraphs 31–34 of the IFRS).

Presentation and disclosure

Comparative information

BC85 IAS 1 *Presentation of Financial Statements* requires an entity to disclose comparative information (under IFRSs) for the previous period. Some suggested that a first-time adopter should disclose comparative information for more than one previous period. For entities that already apply IFRSs, users normally have access to financial statements prepared on a comparable basis for several years. However, this is not the case for a first-time adopter.

BC86 Nevertheless, the Board did not require a first-time adopter to present more comparative information than IAS 1 requires, because such a requirement would impose costs out of proportion to the benefits to users, and increase the risk that preparers might need to make arbitrary assumptions in applying hindsight.

BC87 ED 1 proposed that if the first IFRS financial statements include more than one year of comparative information, the additional comparative information should comply with IFRSs. Some respondents to ED 1 noted that some regulators require entities to prepare more than two years of comparatives. They argued the following:

(a) A requirement to restate two years of comparatives would impose excessive costs and lead to arbitrary restatements that might be biased by hindsight.

(b) Consider an entity adopting IFRSs in 2005 and required by its regulator to give two years of comparatives. Its date of transition to IFRSs would be 1 January 2003—several months before the publication of the IFRS and of the standards resulting from the Improvements project. This could contradict the Board's assertion in paragraph BC27 above that most preparers could gather most information they need for their opening IFRS balance sheet at, or soon after, the date of transition to IFRSs.

BC88 In response to these comments, the Board deleted this proposal. Instead, if a first-time adopter elects to give more than one year of comparative information, the additional comparative information need not comply with IFRSs, but the IFRS requires the entity:

(a) to label previous GAAP information prominently as not being prepared under IFRSs.

(b) to disclose the nature of the main adjustments that would make it comply with IFRSs (paragraph 37 of the IFRS).

BC89 Some respondents to ED 1 suggested that it would be onerous to prepare comparative information under IAS 32 and IAS 39 about financial instruments. They suggested that an entity should be able to apply IAS 39 prospectively from the beginning of the year of its first IFRS financial statements (eg 1 January 2005 for many first-time adopters). They noted that US companies were not required to restate comparatives on the introduction of SFAS 133 *Accounting for Derivative Instruments and Hedging Activities*. However, given the Board's emphasis on comparability within the first IFRS financial statements (paragraph BC10) and the assumption of timely planning (paragraph BC27), the Board introduced no general exemption in this area.

BC89A Nevertheless, the Board noted that the revised IAS 32 and IAS 39 were not issued until December 2003. Additionally, the Board's decision to re-expose its proposals for portfolio hedges of interest rate risk had the effect that some of the requirements will not be finalised until early 2004. The Board was sympathetic to concerns that entities that will be required to comply with IFRSs for the first time in 2005 could not make a timely transition to IFRSs because IAS 39 will not be issued in final form until after the start of 2004. Therefore, the Board decided to exempt entities adopting IFRSs for the first time before 1 January 2006 from producing comparative information that complies with IAS 32 and IAS 39, as revised in 2003, in their first IFRS financial statements. The disclosures in paragraph 36A inform users of the lack of comparability.

Historical summaries

BC90 Some entities choose, or are required, to present in their financial statements historical summaries of selected data covering periods before the first period for which they present full comparative information. Some argued that an entity should present this information under IFRSs, to ensure comparability over time. However, the Board concluded that such a requirement would cause costs out of proportion to the benefit to users. The IFRS requires disclosure of the nature of the main adjustments needed to make historical summaries included in financial statements or interim financial reports comply with IFRSs (paragraph 37 of the IFRS). Historical summaries published outside financial statements or interim financial reports are beyond the scope of the IFRS.

Explanation of transition to IFRSs

BC91 The IFRS requires disclosures about the effect of the transition from previous GAAP to IFRSs. The Board concluded that such disclosures are essential, in the first (annual) IFRS financial statements as well as in interim financial reports (if any), because they help users understand the effect and implications of the transition to IFRSs and how they need to change their analytical models to make the best use of information presented using IFRSs. The required disclosures relate to both:

(a) the most recent information published under previous GAAP, so that users have the most up-to-date information; and

(b) the date of transition to IFRSs. This is an important focus of attention for users, preparers and auditors because the opening IFRS balance sheet is the starting point for accounting under IFRSs.

BC92 Paragraph 39(a) and (b) of the IFRS requires reconciliations of equity and profit or loss. The Board concluded that users would also find it helpful to have information about the other adjustments that affect the opening IFRS balance sheet but do not appear in these reconciliations. Because a reconciliation could be voluminous, the IFRS requires disclosure of narrative information about these adjustments, as well as about adjustments to the cash flow statement (paragraph 40 of the IFRS).

BC93 Paragraph 41 of the IFRS states that the reconciliations should distinguish changes in accounting policies from the correction of errors. Some respondents to ED 1 argued that complying with this requirement could be difficult or costly. However, the Board concluded that both components are important and their disclosure should be required because:

(a) information about changes in accounting policies helps explain the transition to IFRSs.

(b) information about errors helps users assess the reliability of financial information. Furthermore, a failure to disclose the effect of material errors would obscure the 'results of the stewardship of management, or the accountability of management for the resources entrusted to it' (*Framework*, paragraph 14).

BC94 For impairment losses (and reversals) recognised in preparing the opening IFRS balance sheet, paragraph 39(c) of the IFRS requires the disclosures that IAS 36 *Impairment of Assets* would require if those impairment losses (and reversals) were recognised during the period beginning with the date of transition to IFRSs. The rationale for this requirement is that there is inevitably subjectivity about impairment losses. This disclosure provides transparency about impairment losses recognised on transition to IFRSs. These losses might otherwise receive less attention than impairment losses recognised in earlier or later periods.

BC95 Paragraph 44 of the IFRS requires disclosures about the use of fair value as deemed cost. Although the adjustment arising from the use of this exemption appears in the reconciliations discussed above, this more specific disclosure highlights it. Furthermore, this exemption differs from the other exemptions that might apply for property, plant and equipment (previous GAAP revaluation or event-driven fair value measurement). The latter two exemptions do not lead to a restatement on transition to IFRSs because they apply only if the measurement was already used in previous GAAP financial statements.

Interim financial reports

BC96 IAS 34 *Interim Financial Reporting* states that the interim financial report is 'intended to provide an update on the latest complete set of annual financial statements' (paragraph 6). Thus, IAS 34 requires less disclosure in interim financial statements than IFRSs require in annual financial statements. However, an entity's interim financial report under IAS 34 is less helpful to users if the entity's latest annual financial statements were prepared using previous GAAP than if they were prepared under IFRSs. Therefore, the Board concluded that a first-time adopter's first interim financial report under IAS 34 should include sufficient information to enable users to understand how the transition to IFRSs affected previously reported annual, as well as interim, figures (paragraphs 45 and 46 of the IFRS).

BC97 [Deleted]

CONTENTS

LIST OF EXAMPLES

Guidance on implementing IFRS 1 First-time Adoption of International Financial Reporting Standards

This guidance accompanies, but is not part of, IFRS 1.

Introduction

IG1 This implementation guidance:

(a) explains how the requirements of the IFRS interact with the requirements of some other IFRSs (paragraphs IG2–IG62, IG64 and IG65). This explanation addresses those IFRSs that are most likely to involve questions that are specific to first-time adopters.

(b) includes an illustrative example to show how a first-time adopter might disclose how the transition to IFRSs affected its reported financial position, financial performance and cash flows, as required by paragraphs 39(a) and (b), 40 and 41 of the IFRS (paragraph IG63).

IAS 10 *Events after the Balance Sheet Date*

IG2 Except as described in paragraph IG3, an entity applies IAS 10 in determining whether:

(a) its opening IFRS balance sheet reflects an event that occurred after the date of transition to IFRSs; and

(b) comparative balance sheet amounts in its first IFRS financial statements reflect an event that occurred after the end of that comparative period.

IG3 Paragraphs 31–34 of the IFRS require some modifications to the principles in IAS 10 when a first-time adopter determines whether changes in estimates are adjusting or non-adjusting events at the date of transition to IFRSs (or, when applicable, the end of the comparative period). Cases 1 and 2 below illustrate those modifications. In case 3 below, paragraphs 31-34 of the IFRS do not require modifications to the principles in IAS 10.

(a) Case 1—Previous GAAP required estimates of similar items for the date of transition to IFRSs, using an accounting policy that is consistent with IFRSs. In this case, the estimates under IFRSs need to be consistent with estimates made for that date under previous GAAP, unless there is objective evidence that those estimates were in error (see IAS 8 *Accounting Policies, Changes in Accounting Estimates and Errors*). The entity reports later revisions to those estimates as events of the period in which it makes the revisions, rather than as adjusting events resulting from the receipt of further evidence about conditions that existed at the date of transition to IFRSs.

(b) Case 2—Previous GAAP required estimates of similar items for the date of transition to IFRSs, but the entity made those estimates using accounting policies that are not consistent with its accounting policies under IFRSs. In this case, the estimates under IFRSs need to be consistent with the estimates required under previous GAAP for that date (unless there is objective evidence that those estimates were in error), after adjusting for the difference in accounting policies. The opening IFRS balance sheet reflects those adjustments for the difference in accounting policies. As in case 1, the entity reports later revisions to those estimates as events of the period in which it makes the revisions.

For example, previous GAAP may have required an entity to recognise and measure provisions on a basis consistent with IAS 37 *Provisions, Contingent Liabilities and Contingent Assets*, except that the previous GAAP measurement was on an undiscounted basis. In this example, the entity uses the estimates under previous GAAP as inputs in making the discounted measurement required by IAS 37.

(c) Case 3—Previous GAAP did not require estimates of similar items for the date of transition to IFRSs. Estimates under IFRSs for that date reflect conditions existing at that date. In particular, estimates of market prices, interest rates or foreign exchange rates at the date of transition to IFRSs reflect market conditions at that date. This is consistent with the distinction in IAS 10 between adjusting events after the balance sheet date and non-adjusting events after the balance sheet date.

IG Example 1 Estimates

Background

Entity A's first IFRS financial statements have a reporting date of 31 December 2005 and include comparative information for one year. In its previous GAAP financial statements for 31 December 2003 and 2004, entity A:

(a) made estimates of accrued expenses and provisions at those dates;

(b) accounted on a cash basis for a defined benefit pension plan; and

(c) did not recognise a provision for a court case arising from events that occurred in September 2004. When the court case was concluded on 30 June 2005, entity A was required to pay 1,000 and paid this on 10 July 2005.

In preparing its first IFRS financial statements, entity A concludes that its estimates under previous GAAP of accrued expenses and provisions at 31 December 2003 and 2004 were made on a basis consistent with its accounting policies under IFRSs. Although some of the accruals and provisions turned out to be overestimates and others to be underestimates, entity A concludes that its estimates were reasonable and that, therefore, no error had occurred. As a result, accounting for those over- and underestimates involves the routine adjustment of estimates under IAS 8.

Continued from previous page

IG Example 1 Estimates

Application of requirements

In preparing its opening IFRS balance sheet at 1 January 2004 and in its comparative balance sheet at 31 December 2004, entity A:

(a) does not adjust the previous estimates for accrued expenses and provisions; and

(b) makes estimates (in the form of actuarial assumptions) necessary to account for the pension plan under IAS 19 *Employee Benefits.* Entity A's actuarial assumptions at 1 January 2004 and 31 December 2004 do not reflect conditions that arose after those dates. For example, entity A's:

  (i) discount rates at 1 January 2004 and 31 December 2004 for the pension plan and for provisions reflect market conditions at those dates; and

  (ii) actuarial assumptions at 1 January 2004 and 31 December 2004 about future employee turnover rates do not reflect conditions that arose after those dates—such as a significant increase in estimated employee turnover rates as a result of a curtailment of the pension plan in 2005.

The treatment of the court case at 31 December 2004 depends on the reason why entity A did not recognise a provision under previous GAAP at that date.

Assumption 1 – Previous GAAP was consistent with IAS 37 *Provisions, Contingent Liabilities and Contingent Assets.* Entity A concluded that the recognition criteria were not met. In this case, entity A's assumptions under IFRSs are consistent with its assumptions under previous GAAP. Therefore, entity A does not recognise a provision at 31 December 2004.

Assumption 2 – Previous GAAP was not consistent with IAS 37. Therefore, entity A develops estimates under IAS 37. Under IAS 37, an entity determines whether an obligation exists at the balance sheet date by taking account of all available evidence, including any additional evidence provided by events after the balance sheet date. Similarly, under IAS 10 *Events after the Balance Sheet Date*, the resolution of a court case after the balance sheet date is an adjusting event after the balance sheet date if it confirms that the entity had a present obligation at that date. In this instance, the resolution of the court case confirms that entity A had a liability in September 2004 (when the events occurred that gave rise to the court case). Therefore, entity A recognises a provision at 31 December 2004. Entity A measures that provision by discounting the 1,000 paid on 10 July 2005 to its present value, using a discount rate that complies with IAS 37 and reflects market conditions at 31 December 2004.

IG4 Paragraphs 31–34 of the IFRS do not override requirements in other IFRSs that base classifications or measurements on circumstances existing at a particular date. Examples include:

(a) the distinction between finance leases and operating leases (see IAS 17 *Leases*);

(b) the restrictions in IAS 38 *Intangible Assets* that prohibit capitalisation of expenditure on an internally generated intangible asset if the asset did not qualify for recognition when the expenditure was incurred; and

(c) the distinction between financial liabilities and equity instruments (see IAS 32 *Financial Instruments: Disclosure and Presentation*).

IAS 12 *Income Taxes*

IG5 An entity applies IAS 12 to temporary differences between the carrying amount of the assets and liabilities in its opening IFRS balance sheet and their tax bases.

IG6 Under IAS 12, the measurement of current and deferred tax reflects tax rates and tax laws that have been enacted or substantively enacted by the balance sheet date. An entity accounts for the effect of changes in tax rates and tax laws when those changes are enacted or substantively enacted.

IAS 16 *Property, Plant and Equipment**

IG7 If an entity's depreciation methods and rates under previous GAAP are acceptable under IFRSs, it accounts for any change in estimated useful life or depreciation pattern prospectively from when it makes that change in estimate (paragraphs 31 and 32 of the IFRS and paragraph 61 of IAS 16). However, in some cases, an entity's depreciation methods and rates under previous GAAP may differ from those that would be acceptable under IFRSs (for example, if they were adopted solely for tax purposes and do not reflect a reasonable estimate of the asset's useful life). If those differences have a material effect on the financial statements, the entity adjusts accumulated depreciation in its opening IFRS balance sheet retrospectively so that it complies with IFRSs.

IG8 An entity may elect to use one of the following amounts as the deemed cost of an item of property, plant and equipment:

(a) fair value at the date of transition to IFRSs (paragraph 16 of the IFRS), in which case the entity gives the disclosures required by paragraph 44 of the IFRS;

(b) a revaluation under previous GAAP that meets the criteria in paragraph 17 of the IFRS; or

(c) fair value at the date of an event such as a privatisation or initial public offering (paragraph 19 of the IFRS).

IG9 Subsequent depreciation is based on that deemed cost and starts from the date for which the entity established the fair value measurement or revaluation.

IG10 If an entity chooses as its accounting policy the revaluation model in IAS 16 for some or all classes of property, plant and equipment, it presents the cumulative revaluation surplus as a separate component of equity. The revaluation surplus at the date of transition to IFRSs is based on a comparison of the carrying amount of

* as revised in 2003

the asset at that date with its cost or deemed cost. If the deemed cost is the fair value at the date of transition to IFRSs, the entity gives the disclosures required by paragraph 44 of the IFRS.

IG11 If revaluations under previous GAAP did not satisfy the criteria in paragraph 17 or 19 of the IFRS, an entity measures the revalued assets in its opening balance sheet on one of the following bases:

(a) cost (or deemed cost) less any accumulated depreciation and any accumulated impairment losses under the cost model in IAS 16;

(b) deemed cost, being the fair value at the date of transition to IFRSs (paragraph 16 of the IFRS); or

(c) revalued amount, if the entity adopts the revaluation model in IAS 16 as its accounting policy under IFRSs for all items of property, plant and equipment in the same class.

IG12 IAS 16 requires each part of an item of property, plant and equipment with a cost that is significant in relation to the total cost of the item to be depreciated separately. However, IAS 16 does not prescribe the unit of measure for recognition of an asset, ie what constitutes an item of property, plant and equipment. Thus, judgement is required in applying the recognition criteria to an entity's specific circumstances (see IAS 16, paragraphs 9 and 43).

IG13 In some cases, the construction or commissioning of an asset results in an obligation for an entity to dismantle or remove the asset and restore the site on which the asset stands. An entity applies IAS 37 *Provisions, Contingent Liabilities and Contingent Assets* in recognising and measuring any resulting provision. The entity applies IAS 16 in determining the resulting amount included in the cost of the asset, before depreciation and impairment losses. Items such as depreciation and, when applicable, impairment losses cause differences between the carrying amount of the liability and the amount included in the carrying amount of the asset. An entity accounts for changes in such liabilities in accordance with IFRIC 1 *Changes in Existing Decommissioning, Restoration and Similar Liabilities.* However, paragraph 25E of IFRS 1 provides an exemption for changes that occurred before the date of transition to IFRSs, and prescribes an alternative treatment where the exemption is used. An example of the first-time adoption of IFRIC 1, which illustrates the use of this exemption, is given at paragraphs IG201–IG203.

IAS 17 *Leases*[*]

IG14 At the date of transition to IFRSs, a lessee or lessor classifies leases as operating leases or finance leases on the basis of circumstances existing at the inception of the lease (IAS 17, paragraph 13). In some cases, the lessee and the lessor may agree to change the provisions of the lease, other than by renewing the lease, in a manner that would have resulted in a different classification in accordance with IAS 17 had the changed terms been in effect at the inception of the lease. If so, the revised agreement is considered as a new agreement over its term. However, changes in estimates (for example, changes in estimates of the economic life or of

[*] as revised in 2003

the residual value of the leased property) or changes in circumstances (for example, default by the lessee) do not give rise to a new classification of a lease.

IG15 When IAS 17 was revised in 1997, the net cash investment method for recognising finance income of lessors was eliminated. IAS 17 permits finance lessors to eliminate this method prospectively. However, the transitional provisions in IAS 17 do not apply to an entity's opening IFRS balance sheet (paragraph 9 of the IFRS). Therefore, a finance lessor measures finance lease receivables in its opening IFRS balance sheet as if the net cash investment method had never been permitted.

IG16 SIC-15 *Operating Leases—Incentives* applies to lease terms beginning on or after 1 January 1999. However, a first-time adopter applies SIC-15 to all leases, whether they started before or after that date.

IAS 18 *Revenue*

IG17 If an entity has received amounts that do not yet qualify for recognition as revenue under IAS 18 (for example, the proceeds of a sale that does not qualify for revenue recognition), the entity recognises the amounts received as a liability in its opening IFRS balance sheet and measures that liability at the amount received.

IAS 19 *Employee Benefits*

IG18 At the date of transition to IFRSs, an entity applies IAS 19 in measuring net employee benefit assets or liabilities under defined benefit plans, but it may elect to recognise all cumulative actuarial gains or losses from the inception of the plan until the date of transition to IFRSs even if its accounting policy under IAS 19 will involve leaving some later actuarial gains and losses unrecognised (paragraph 20 of the IFRS). The transitional provisions in IAS 19 do not apply to an entity's opening IFRS balance sheet (paragraph 9 of the IFRS).

IG19 An entity's actuarial assumptions at the date of transition to IFRSs are consistent with actuarial assumptions made for the same date under previous GAAP (after adjustments to reflect any difference in accounting policies), unless there is objective evidence that those assumptions were in error (paragraph 31 of the IFRS). The impact of any later revisions to those assumptions is an actuarial gain or loss of the period in which the entity makes the revisions.

IG20 An entity may need to make actuarial assumptions at the date of transition to IFRSs that were not necessary under its previous GAAP. Such actuarial assumptions do not reflect conditions that arose after the date of transition to IFRSs. In particular, discount rates and the fair value of plan assets at the date of transition to IFRSs reflect market conditions at that date. Similarly, the entity's actuarial assumptions at the date of transition to IFRSs about future employee turnover rates do not reflect a significant increase in estimated employee turnover rates as a result of a curtailment of the pension plan that occurred after the date of transition to IFRSs (paragraph 32 of the IFRS).

IG21 In many cases, an entity's first IFRS financial statements will reflect measurements of employee benefit obligations at three dates: the reporting date, the date of the comparative balance sheet and the date of transition to IFRSs. IAS 19 encourages an entity to involve a qualified actuary in the measurement of all material post-employment benefit obligations. To minimise costs, an entity may request a qualified actuary to carry out a detailed actuarial valuation at one or two of these dates and roll the valuation(s) forward or back to the other date(s). Any such roll forward or roll back reflects any material transactions and other material events (including changes in market prices and interest rates) between those dates (IAS 19, paragraph 57).

IAS 21 *The Effects of Changes in Foreign Exchange Rates**

IG21A An entity may, under previous GAAP, have treated goodwill arising on the acquisition of a foreign operation and any fair value adjustments to the carrying amounts of assets and liabilities arising on the acquisition of that foreign operation as assets and liabilities of the entity rather than as assets and liabilities of the foreign operation. If so, the entity is permitted to apply prospectively the requirements of paragraph 47 of IAS 21 to all acquisitions occurring after the date of transition to IFRSs.

IFRS 3 *Business Combinations*

IG22 The following examples illustrate the effect of Appendix B of the IFRS, assuming that a first-time adopter uses the exemption.

IG Example 2 Business combination

Background

Entity B's first IFRS financial statements have a reporting date of 31 December 2005 and include comparative information for 2004 only. On 1 July 2001, entity B acquired 100 per cent of subsidiary C. Under its previous GAAP, entity B:

(a) classified the business combination as an acquisition by entity B.

(b) measured the assets acquired and liabilities assumed at the following amounts under previous GAAP at 31 December 2003 (date of transition to IFRSs):

(i) identifiable assets less liabilities for which IFRSs require cost-based measurement at a date after the business combination: 200 (with a tax base of 150 and an applicable tax rate of 30 per cent).

(ii) pension liability (for which the present value of the defined benefit obligation measured under IAS 19 *Employee Benefits* is 130 and the fair value of plan assets is 100): nil (because entity B used a pay-as-you-go cash method of accounting for pensions under its previous GAAP). The tax base of the pension liability is also nil.

(iii) goodwill: 180.

(c) did not, at the date of acquisition, recognise deferred tax arising from temporary differences associated with the identifiable assets acquired and liabilities assumed.

* as revised in 2003

Continued from previous page

IG Example 2 Business combination

Application of requirements

In its opening (consolidated) IFRS balance sheet, entity B:

(a) classifies the business combination as an acquisition by entity B even if the business combination would have qualified under IFRS 3 as a reverse acquisition by subsidiary C (paragraph B2(a) of the IFRS).

(b) does not adjust the accumulated amortisation of goodwill. Entity B tests the goodwill for impairment under IAS 36 *Impairment of Assets* and recognises any resulting impairment loss, based on conditions that existed at the date of transition to IFRSs. If no impairment exists, the carrying amount of the goodwill remains at 180 (paragraph B2(g)).

(c) for those net identifiable assets acquired for which IFRSs require cost-based measurement at a date after the business combination, treats their carrying amount under previous GAAP immediately after the business combination as their deemed cost at that date (paragraph B2(e)).

(d) does not restate the accumulated depreciation and amortisation of the net identifiable assets in (c), unless the depreciation methods and rates under previous GAAP result in amounts that differ materially from those required under IFRSs (for example, if they were adopted solely for tax purposes and do not reflect a reasonable estimate of the asset's useful life under IFRSs). If no such restatement is made, the carrying amount of those assets in the opening IFRS balance sheet equals their carrying amount under previous GAAP at the date of transition to IFRSs (200) (paragraph IG7).

(e) if there is any indication that identifiable assets are impaired, tests those assets for impairment, based on conditions that existed at the date of transition to IFRSs (see IAS 36).

(f) recognises the pension liability, and measures it, at the present value of the defined benefit obligation 130 less the fair value of the plan assets (100), giving a carrying amount of 30, with a corresponding debit of 30 to retained earnings (paragraph B2(d)). However, if subsidiary C had already adopted IFRSs in an earlier period, entity B would measure the pension liability at the same amount as in subsidiary C's financial statements (paragraph 25 of the IFRS and IG Example 9).

Continued from previous page

IG Example 2 Business combination

(g) recognises a net deferred tax liability of 6 (20 at 30 per cent) arising from:

(i) the taxable temporary difference of 50 (200 less 150) associated with the identifiable assets acquired and non-pension liabilities assumed, less

(ii) the deductible temporary difference of 30 (30 less nil) associated with the pension liability.

The entity recognises the resulting increase in the deferred tax liability as a deduction from retained earnings (paragraph B2(k) of the IFRS). If a taxable temporary difference arises from the initial recognition of the goodwill, entity B does not recognise the resulting deferred tax liability (paragraph 15(a) of IAS 12 *Income Taxes*).

IG Example 3 Business combination—restructuring provision

Background

Entity D's first IFRS financial statements have a reporting date of 31 December 2005 and include comparative information for 2004 only. On 1 July 2003, entity D acquired 100 per cent of subsidiary E. Under its previous GAAP, entity D recognised an (undiscounted) restructuring provision of 100 that would not have qualified as an identifiable liability under IFRS 3. The recognition of this restructuring provision increased goodwill by 100. At 31 December 2003 (date of transition to IFRSs), entity D:

(a) had paid restructuring costs of 60; and

(b) estimated that it would pay further costs of 40 in 2004, and that the effects of discounting were immaterial. At 31 December 2003, those further costs did not qualify for recognition as a provision under IAS 37 *Provisions, Contingent Liabilities and Contingent Assets*.

Application of requirements

In its opening IFRS balance sheet, entity D:

(a) does not recognise a restructuring provision (paragraph B2(c) of the IFRS).

(b) does not adjust the amount assigned to goodwill. However, entity D tests the goodwill for impairment under IAS 36 *Impairment of Assets*, and recognises any resulting impairment loss (paragraph B2(g)).

(c) as a result of (a) and (b), reports retained earnings in its opening IFRS balance sheet that are higher by 40 (before income taxes, and before recognising any impairment loss) than in the balance sheet at the same date under previous GAAP.

IG Example 4 Business combination—intangible assets

Background

Entity F's first IFRS financial statements have a reporting date of 31 December 2005 and include comparative information for 2004 only. On 1 July 2001, entity F acquired 75 per cent of subsidiary G. Under its previous GAAP, entity F assigned an initial carrying amount of 200 to intangible assets that would not have qualified for recognition under IAS 38 *Intangible Assets*. The tax base of the intangible assets was nil, giving rise to a deferred tax liability (at 30 per cent) of 60.

On 31 December 2003 (the date of transition to IFRSs), the carrying amount of the intangible assets under previous GAAP was 160, and the carrying amount of the related deferred tax liability was 48 (30 per cent of 160).

Application of requirements

Because the intangible assets do not qualify for recognition as separate assets under IAS 38, entity F transfers them to goodwill, together with the related deferred tax liability (48) and minority interests (paragraph B2(g)(i) of the IFRS). The related minority interests amount to 28 (25 per cent of [160 − 48 = 112]). Thus, the increase in goodwill is 84—intangible assets (160) less deferred tax liability (48) less minority interests (28.)

Entity F tests the goodwill for impairment under IAS 36 *Impairment of Assets* and recognises any resulting impairment loss, based on conditions that existed at the date of transition to IFRSs (paragraph B2(g)(iii) of the IFRS).

IG Example 5 Business combination—goodwill deducted from equity and treatment of related intangible assets

Background

Entity H acquired a subsidiary before the date of transition to IFRSs. Under its previous GAAP, entity H:

(a) recognised goodwill as an immediate deduction from equity;

(b) recognised an intangible asset of the subsidiary that does not qualify for recognition as an asset under IAS 38; and

(c) did not recognise an intangible asset of the subsidiary that would qualify under IAS 38 *Intangible Assets* for recognition as an asset in the financial statements of the subsidiary. The subsidiary held the asset at the date of its acquisition by entity H.

Continued from previous page

IG Example 5 Business combination—goodwill deducted from equity and treatment of related intangible assets

Application of requirements

In its opening IFRS balance sheet, entity H:

(a) does not recognise the goodwill, as it did not recognise the goodwill as an asset under previous GAAP (paragraph B2(g)–B2(i)).

(b) does not recognise the intangible asset that does not qualify for recognition as an asset under IAS 38. Because entity H deducted goodwill from equity under its previous GAAP, the elimination of this intangible asset reduces retained earnings (paragraph B2(c)(ii)).

(c) recognises the intangible asset that qualifies under IAS 38 for recognition as an asset in the financial statements of the subsidiary, even though the amount assigned to it under previous GAAP in entity H's consolidated financial statements was nil (paragraph B2(f)). The recognition criteria in IAS 38 include the availability of a reliable measurement of cost (paragraphs IG45–IG48) and entity H measures the asset at cost less accumulated depreciation and less any impairment losses identified under IAS 36. Because entity H deducted goodwill from equity under its previous GAAP, the recognition of this intangible asset increases retained earnings (paragraph B2(c)(ii)). However, if this intangible asset had been subsumed in goodwill recognised as an asset under previous GAAP, entity H would have decreased the carrying amount of that goodwill accordingly (and, if applicable, adjusted deferred tax and minority interests) (paragraph B2(g)(i)).

IG Example 6 Business combination—subsidiary not consolidated under previous GAAP

Background

Parent J's date of transition to IFRSs is 1 January 2004. Under its previous GAAP, parent J did not consolidate its 75 per cent subsidiary K, acquired in a business combination on 15 July 2001. On 1 January 2004:

(a) the cost of parent J's investment in subsidiary K is 180.

(b) under IFRSs, subsidiary K would measure its assets at 500 and its liabilities (including deferred tax under IAS 12) at 300. On this basis, subsidiary K's net assets are 200 under IFRSs.

Continued from previous page

IG Example 6 Business combination—subsidiary not consolidated under previous GAAP

Application of requirements

Parent J consolidates subsidiary K. The consolidated balance sheet at 1 January 2004 includes:

(a) subsidiary K's assets at 500 and liabilities at 300;

(b) minority interests of 50 (25 per cent of [500 – 300]); and

(c) goodwill of 30 (cost of 180 less 75 per cent of [500 – 300]) (paragraph B2(j)). Parent J tests the goodwill for impairment under IAS 36 *Impairment of Assets* and recognises any resulting impairment loss, based on conditions that existed at the date of transition to IFRSs (paragraph B2(g)(iii)).

IG Example 7 Business combination—finance lease not capitalised under previous GAAP

Background

Parent L's date of transition to IFRSs is 1 January 2004. Parent L acquired subsidiary M on 15 January 2001 and did not capitalise subsidiary M's finance leases. If subsidiary M prepared financial statements under IFRSs, it would recognise finance lease obligations of 300 and leased assets of 250 at 1 January 2004.

Application of requirements

In its consolidated opening IFRS balance sheet, parent L recognises finance lease obligations of 300 and leased assets of 250, and charges 50 to retained earnings (paragraph B2(f)).

IAS 23 *Borrowing Costs*

IG23 On first adopting IFRSs, an entity adopts a policy of capitalising borrowing costs (IAS 23 allowed alternative treatment) or not capitalising them (IAS 23 benchmark treatment). The entity applies that policy consistently in its opening IFRS balance sheet and in all periods presented in its first IFRS financial statements. However, if the entity established a deemed cost for an asset, the entity does not capitalise borrowing costs incurred before the date of the measurement that established the deemed cost.

IG24 Under the allowed alternative treatment, IAS 23 requires disclosure of interest capitalised during the period. Neither IAS 23 nor the IFRS requires disclosure of the cumulative amount capitalised.

IG25 IAS 23 contains transitional provisions that encourage retrospective application, but permit an entity that adopts the allowed alternative treatment to capitalise (prospectively) only those borrowing costs incurred after the effective date of IAS 23 that meet the criteria for capitalisation. However, if a first-time adopter adopts the IAS 23 allowed alternative treatment, the IFRS requires retrospective application of that treatment, even for periods before the effective date of IAS 23 (paragraph 9 of the IFRS).

IAS 27 *Consolidated and Separate Financial Statements*

IG26 A first-time adopter consolidates all subsidiaries that it controls, unless IAS 27 requires otherwise.

IG27 If a first-time adopter did not consolidate a subsidiary under previous GAAP, then:

(a) in its consolidated financial statements, the first-time adopter measures the subsidiary's assets and liabilities at the same carrying amounts as in the IFRS financial statements of the subsidiary, after adjusting for consolidation procedures and for the effects of the business combination in which it acquired the subsidiary (paragraph 25 of the IFRS). If the subsidiary has not adopted IFRSs in its financial statements, the carrying amounts described in the previous sentence are those that IFRSs would require in those financial statements (paragraph B2(j) of the IFRS).

(b) if the parent acquired the subsidiary in a business combination before the date of transition to IFRS, the parent recognises goodwill, as explained in IG Example 6.

(c) if the parent did not acquire the subsidiary in a business combination because it created the subsidiary, the parent does not recognise goodwill.

IG28 When a first-time adopter adjusts the carrying amounts of assets and liabilities of its subsidiaries in preparing its opening IFRS balance sheet, this may affect minority interests and deferred tax.

IG29 IG Examples 8 and 9 illustrate paragraphs 24 and 25 of the IFRS, which address cases where a parent and its subsidiary become first-time adopters at different dates.

IG Example 8 Parent adopts IFRSs before subsidiary

Background

Parent N presents its (consolidated) first IFRS financial statements in 2005. Its foreign subsidiary O, wholly owned by parent N since formation, prepares information under IFRSs for internal consolidation purposes from that date, but subsidiary O does not present its first IFRS financial statements until 2007.

Continued from previous page

IG Example 8 Parent adopts IFRSs before subsidiary

Application of requirements

If subsidiary O applies paragraph 24(a) of the IFRS, the carrying amounts of its assets and liabilities are the same in both its opening IFRS balance sheet at 1 January 2006 and parent N's consolidated balance sheet (except for adjustments for consolidation procedures) and are based on parent N's date of transition to IFRSs.

Alternatively, subsidiary O may, under paragraph 24(b) of the IFRS, measure all its assets or liabilities based on its own date of transition to IFRSs (1 January 2006). However, the fact that subsidiary O becomes a first-time adopter in 2007 does not change the carrying amounts of its assets and liabilities in parent N's consolidated financial statements.

IG Example 9 Subsidiary adopts IFRSs before parent

Background

Parent P presents its (consolidated) first IFRS financial statements in 2007. Its foreign subsidiary Q, wholly owned by parent P since formation, presented its first IFRS financial statements in 2005. Until 2007, subsidiary Q prepared information for internal consolidation purposes under parent P's previous GAAP.

Application of requirements

The carrying amounts of subsidiary Q's assets and liabilities at 1 January 2006 are the same in both parent P's (consolidated) opening IFRS balance sheet and subsidiary Q's financial statements (except for adjustments for consolidation procedures) and are based on subsidiary Q's date of transition to IFRSs. The fact that parent P becomes a first-time adopter in 2007 does not change those carrying amounts (paragraph 25 of the IFRS).

IG30 Paragraphs 24 and 25 of the IFRS do not override the following requirements:

(a) to apply Appendix B of the IFRS to assets acquired, and liabilities assumed, in a business combination that occurred before the acquirer's date of transition to IFRSs. However, the acquirer applies paragraph 25 to new assets acquired, and liabilities assumed, by the acquiree after that business combination and still held at the acquirer's date of transition to IFRSs.

(b) to apply the rest of the IFRS in measuring all assets and liabilities for which paragraphs 24 and 25 are not relevant.

(c) to give all disclosures required by the IFRS as of the first-time adopter's own date of transition to IFRSs.

IG31 Paragraph 24 of the IFRS applies if a subsidiary becomes a first-time adopter later than its parent, for example if the subsidiary previously prepared a reporting package under IFRSs for consolidation purposes but did not present a full set of financial statements under IFRSs. This may be relevant not only when a subsidiary's reporting package complies fully with the recognition and measurement requirements of IFRSs, but also when it is adjusted centrally for matters such as post-balance sheet events review and central allocation of pension costs. For the disclosure required by paragraph 41 of the IFRS, adjustments made centrally to an unpublished reporting package are not corrections of errors. However, paragraph 24 does not permit a subsidiary to ignore misstatements that are immaterial to the consolidated financial statements of its parent but material to its own financial statements.

IAS 29 *Financial Reporting in Hyperinflationary Economies*

IG32 An entity complies with IAS 21 *The Effects of Changes in Foreign Exchange Rates* in determining its functional currency and presentation currency. When the entity prepares its opening IFRS balance sheet, it applies IAS 29 to any periods during which the economy of the functional currency or presentation currency was hyperinflationary.

IG33 An entity may elect to use the fair value of an item of property, plant and equipment at the date of transition to IFRSs as its deemed cost at that date (paragraph 16 of the IFRS), in which case it gives the disclosures required by paragraph 44 of the IFRS.

IG34 If an entity elects to use the exemptions in paragraphs 16–19 of the IFRS, it applies IAS 29 to periods after the date for which the revalued amount or fair value was determined.

IAS 32 *Financial Instruments: Disclosure and Presentation**

IG35 In its opening IFRS balance sheet, an entity applies the criteria in IAS 32 to classify financial instruments issued (or components of compound instruments issued) as either financial liabilities or equity instruments in accordance with the substance of the contractual arrangement when the instrument first satisfied the recognition criteria in IAS 32 (paragraphs 15 and 30), without considering events after that date (other than changes to the terms of the instruments).

IG36 For compound instruments outstanding at the date of transition to IFRSs, an entity determines the initial carrying amounts of the components on the basis of circumstances existing when the instrument was issued (IAS 32, paragraph 30). An entity determines those carrying amounts using the version of IAS 32 effective at the reporting date for its first IFRS financial statements. If the liability component is no longer outstanding at the date of transition to IFRSs, a first-time adopter need not separate the initial equity component of the instrument from the cumulative interest accreted on the liability component (paragraph 23 of the IFRS).

IAS 34 *Interim Financial Reporting*

IG37 IAS 34 applies if an entity is required, or elects, to present an interim financial report in accordance with IFRSs. Accordingly, neither IAS 34 nor the IFRS requires an entity:

(a) to present interim financial reports that comply with IAS 34; or

* as revised in 2003

(b) to prepare new versions of interim financial reports presented under previous GAAP. However, if an entity does prepare an interim financial report under IAS 34 for part of the period covered by its first IFRS financial statements, the entity restates the comparative information presented in that report so that it complies with IFRSs.

IG38 An entity applies the IFRS in each interim financial report that it presents under IAS 34 for part of the period covered by its first IFRS financial statements. In particular, paragraph 45 of the IFRS requires an entity to disclose various reconciliations (see IG Example 10).

IG Example 10 Interim financial reporting

Background

Entity R's first IFRS financial statements have a reporting date of 31 December 2005, and its first interim financial report under IAS 34 is for the quarter ended 31 March 2005. Entity R prepared previous GAAP annual financial statements for the year ended 31 December 2004, and prepared quarterly reports throughout 2004.

Application of requirements

In each quarterly interim financial report for 2005, entity R includes reconciliations of:

(a) its equity under previous GAAP at the end of the comparable quarter of 2004 to its equity under IFRSs at that date; and

(b) its profit or loss under previous GAAP for the comparable quarter of 2004 (current and year-to-date) to its profit or loss under IFRSs.

In addition to the reconciliations required by (a) and (b) and the disclosures required by IAS 34, entity R's interim financial report for the first quarter of 2005 includes reconciliations of (or a cross-reference to another published document that includes these reconciliations):

(a) its equity under previous GAAP at 1 January 2004 and 31 December 2004 to its equity under IFRSs at those dates; and

(b) its profit or loss for 2004 under previous GAAP to its profit or loss for 2004 under IFRSs.

Continued from previous page

IG Example 10 Interim financial reporting

Each of the above reconciliations gives sufficient detail to enable users to understand the material adjustments to the balance sheet and income statement. Entity R also explains the material adjustments to the cash flow statement.

If entity R becomes aware of errors made under previous GAAP, the reconciliations distinguish the correction of those errors from changes in accounting policies.

If entity R did not, in its most recent annual financial statements under previous GAAP, disclose information material to an understanding of the current interim period, its interim financial reports for 2005 disclose that information or include a cross-reference to another published document that includes it (paragraph 46 of the IFRS).

IAS 36 *Impairment of Assets* and IAS 37 *Provisions, Contingent Liabilities and Contingent Assets*

IG39 An entity applies IAS 36 in:

(a) determining whether any impairment loss exists at the date of transition to IFRSs; and

(b) measuring any impairment loss that exists at that date, and reversing any impairment loss that no longer exists at that date. An entity's first IFRS financial statements include the disclosures that IAS 36 would have required if the entity had recognised those impairment losses or reversals in the period beginning with the date of transition to IFRSs (paragraph 39(c) of the IFRS).

IG40 The estimates used to determine whether an entity recognises an impairment loss or provision (and to measure any such impairment loss or provision) at the date of transition to IFRSs are consistent with estimates made for the same date under previous GAAP (after adjustments to reflect any difference in accounting policies), unless there is objective evidence that those estimates were in error (paragraphs 31 and 32 of the IFRS). The entity reports the impact of any later revisions to those estimates as an event of the period in which it makes the revisions.

IG41 In assessing whether it needs to recognise an impairment loss or provision (and in measuring any such impairment loss or provision) at the date of transition to IFRSs, an entity may need to make estimates for that date that were not necessary under its previous GAAP. Such estimates and assumptions do not reflect conditions that arose after the date of transition to IFRSs (paragraph 33 of the IFRS).

IG42 The transitional provisions in IAS 36 and IAS 37 do not apply to an entity's opening IFRS balance sheet (paragraph 9 of the IFRS).

IG43 IAS 36 requires the reversal of impairment losses in some cases. If an entity's opening IFRS balance sheet reflects impairment losses, the entity recognises any later reversal of those impairment losses in the income statement (except when IAS 36 requires the entity to treat that reversal as a revaluation). This applies to both impairment losses recognised under previous GAAP and additional impairment losses recognised on transition to IFRSs.

IAS 38 *Intangible Assets*[*]

IG44 An entity's opening IFRS balance sheet:

(a) excludes all intangible assets and other intangible items that do not meet the criteria for recognition under IAS 38 at the date of transition to IFRSs; and

(b) includes all intangible assets that meet the recognition criteria in IAS 38 at that date, except for intangible assets acquired in a business combination that were not recognised in the acquirer's consolidated balance sheet under previous GAAP and also would not qualify for recognition under IAS 38 in the separate balance sheet of the acquiree (see paragraph B2(f) of Appendix B of the IFRS).

IG45 The criteria in IAS 38 require an entity to recognise an intangible asset if, and only if:

(a) it is probable that the future economic benefits that are attributable to the asset will flow to the entity; and

(b) the cost of the asset can be measured reliably.

IAS 38 supplements these two criteria with further, more specific, criteria for internally generated intangible assets.

IG46 Under paragraphs 65 and 71 of IAS 38, an entity capitalises the costs of creating internally generated intangible assets prospectively from the date when the recognition criteria are met. IAS 38 does not permit an entity to use hindsight to conclude retrospectively that these recognition criteria are met. Therefore, even if an entity concludes retrospectively that a future inflow of economic benefits from an internally generated intangible asset is probable and the entity is able to reconstruct the costs reliably, IAS 38 prohibits it from capitalising the costs incurred before the date when the entity both:

(a) concludes, based on an assessment made and documented at the date of that conclusion, that it is probable that future economic benefits from the asset will flow to the entity; and

(b) has a reliable system for accumulating the costs of internally generated intangible assets when, or shortly after, they are incurred.

IG47 If an internally generated intangible asset qualifies for recognition at the date of transition to IFRSs, an entity recognises the asset in its opening IFRS balance sheet even if it had recognised the related expenditure as an expense under previous GAAP. If the asset does not qualify for recognition under IAS 38 until a later date, its cost is the sum of the expenditure incurred from that later date.

IG48 The criteria discussed in paragraph IG45 also apply to an intangible asset acquired separately. In many cases, contemporaneous documentation prepared to support

* as revised in 2004

the decision to acquire the asset will contain an assessment of the future economic benefits. Furthermore, as explained in paragraph 26 of IAS 38, the cost of a separately acquired intangible asset can usually be measured reliably.

IG49 For an intangible asset acquired in a business combination before the date of transition to IFRSs, its carrying amount under previous GAAP immediately after the business combination is its deemed cost under IFRSs at that date (paragraph B2(e) of the IFRS). If that carrying amount was zero, the acquirer does not recognise the intangible asset in its consolidated opening IFRS balance sheet, unless it would qualify under IAS 38, applying the criteria discussed in paragraphs IG45–IG48, for recognition at the date of transition to IFRSs in the balance sheet of the acquiree (paragraph B2(f) of the IFRS). If those recognition criteria are met, the acquirer measures the asset on the basis that IAS 38 would require in the balance sheet of the acquiree. The resulting adjustment affects goodwill (paragraph B2(g)(i) of the IFRS).

IG50 A first-time adopter may elect to use the fair value of an intangible asset at the date of an event such as a privatisation or initial public offering as its deemed cost at the date of that event (paragraph 19 of the IFRS), provided that the intangible asset qualifies for recognition under IAS 38 (paragraph 10 of the IFRS). In addition, if, and only if, an intangible asset meets both the recognition criteria in IAS 38 (including reliable measurement of original cost) and the criteria in IAS 38 for revaluation (including the existence of an active market), a first-time adopter may elect to use one of the following amounts as its deemed cost (paragraph 18 of the IFRS):

(a) fair value at the date of transition to IFRSs (paragraph 16 of the IFRS), in which case the entity gives the disclosures required by paragraph 44 of the IFRS; or

(b) a revaluation under previous GAAP that meets the criteria in paragraph 17 of the IFRS.

IG51 If an entity's amortisation methods and rates under previous GAAP would be acceptable under IFRSs, the entity does not restate the accumulated amortisation in its opening IFRS balance sheet. Instead, the entity accounts for any change in estimated useful life or amortisation pattern prospectively from the period when it makes that change in estimate (paragraph 31 of the IFRS and paragraph 104 of IAS 38). However, in some cases, an entity's amortisation methods and rates under previous GAAP may differ from those that would be acceptable under IFRSs (for example, if they were adopted solely for tax purposes and do not reflect a reasonable estimate of the asset's useful life). If those differences have a material effect on the financial statements, the entity adjusts the accumulated amortisation in its opening IFRS balance sheet retrospectively so that it complies with IFRSs (paragraph 31 of the IFRS).

IAS 39 *Financial Instruments: Recognition and Measurement*[*]

IG52 An entity recognises and measures all financial assets and financial liabilities in its opening IFRS balance sheet in accordance with IAS 39, except as specified in paragraphs 27–30 of the IFRS, which address derecognition and hedge accounting, and paragraph 36A, which permits an exemption from restating comparative information.

Recognition

IG53 An entity recognises all financial assets and financial liabilities (including all derivatives) that qualify for recognition under IAS 39 and have not yet qualified for derecognition under IAS 39, except non-derivative financial assets and non-derivative financial liabilities derecognised under previous GAAP before 1 January 2004, to which the entity does not choose to apply paragraph 27A (see paragraphs 27 and 27A of the IFRS). For example, an entity that does not apply paragraph 27A does not recognise assets transferred in a securitisation, transfer or other derecognition transaction that occurred before 1 January 2004 if those transactions qualified for derecognition under previous GAAP. However, if the entity uses the same securitisation arrangement or other derecognition arrangement for further transfers after 1 January 2004, those further transfers qualify for derecognition only if they meet the derecognition criteria of IAS 39.

IG54 An entity does not recognise financial assets and financial liabilities that do not qualify for recognition under IAS 39, or have already qualified for derecognition under IAS 39.

Embedded derivatives

IG55 When IAS 39 requires an entity to separate an embedded derivative from a host contract, the initial carrying amounts of the components at the date when the instrument first satisfies the recognition criteria in IAS 39 reflect circumstances at that date (IAS 39, paragraph 11). If the entity cannot determine the initial carrying amounts of the embedded derivative and host contract reliably, it treats the entire combined contract as a financial instrument held for trading (IAS 39, paragraph 12). This results in fair value measurement (except when the entity cannot determine a reliable fair value, see IAS 39, paragraph 46(c)), with changes in fair value recognised in profit or loss.

Measurement

IG56 In preparing its opening IFRS balance sheet, an entity applies the criteria in IAS 39 to identify those financial assets and financial liabilities that are measured at fair value and those that are measured at amortised cost. In particular:

(a) to comply with IAS 39, paragraph 51, classification of financial assets as held-to-maturity investments relies on a designation made by the entity in applying IAS 39 reflecting the entity's intention and ability at the date of transition to IFRSs. It follows that sales or transfers of held-to-maturity investments before the date of transition to IFRSs do not trigger the 'tainting' rules in IAS 39, paragraph 9.

* as revised in 2003

(b) to comply with IAS 39, paragraph 9, the category of 'loans and receivables' refers to the circumstances when the financial asset first satisfied the recognition criteria in IAS 39.

(c) under IAS 39, paragraph 9, derivative financial assets and derivative financial liabilities are always deemed held for trading (except for a derivative that is a designated and effective hedging instrument). The result is that an entity measures all derivative financial assets and derivative financial liabilities at fair value.

(d) to comply with IAS 39, paragraph 50, an entity classifies a non-derivative financial asset or non-derivative financial liability in its opening IFRS balance sheet as at fair value through profit or loss if, and only if, the asset or liability was:

(i) acquired or incurred principally for the purpose of selling or repurchasing it in the near term;

(ii) at the date of transition to IFRSs, part of a portfolio of identified financial instruments that were managed together and for which there was evidence of a recent actual pattern of short-term profit-taking; or

(iii) designated as at fair value through profit or loss at the date of transition to IFRSs.

(e) to comply with IAS 39, paragraph 9, available-for-sale financial assets are those non-derivative financial assets that are designated as available for sale and those non-derivative financial assets that are not in any of the previous categories.

IG57 For those financial assets and financial liabilities measured at amortised cost in the opening IFRS balance sheet, an entity determines their cost on the basis of circumstances existing when the assets and liabilities first satisfied the recognition criteria in IAS 39. However, if the entity acquired those financial assets and financial liabilities in a past business combination, their carrying amount under previous GAAP immediately following the business combination is their deemed cost under IFRSs at that date (paragraph B2(e) of the IFRS).

IG58 An entity's estimates of loan impairments at the date of transition to IFRSs are consistent with estimates made for the same date under previous GAAP (after adjustments to reflect any difference in accounting policies), unless there is objective evidence that those assumptions were in error (paragraph 31 of the IFRS). The entity treats the impact of any later revisions to those estimates as impairment losses (or, if the criteria in IAS 39 are met, reversals of impairment losses) of the period in which it makes the revisions.

Transition adjustments

IG58A An entity shall treat an adjustment to the carrying amount of a financial asset or financial liability as a transition adjustment to be recognised in the opening balance of retained earnings at the date of transition to IFRSs only to the extent that it results from adopting IAS 39. Because all derivatives, other than those that are designated and effective hedging instruments, are classified as held for trading, the differences between the previous carrying amount (which may have been zero) and the fair value of the derivatives are recognised as an adjustment of the balance of retained earnings at the beginning of the financial year in which IAS 39 is initially applied (other than for a derivative that is a designated and effective hedging instrument).

IG58B IAS 8 (as revised in 2003) applies to adjustments resulting from changes in estimates. If an entity is unable to determine whether a particular portion of the adjustment is a transition adjustment or a change in estimate, it treats that portion as a change in accounting estimate under IAS 8, with appropriate disclosures (IAS 8, paragraphs 32–40).

IG59 An entity may, under its previous GAAP, have measured investments at fair value and recognised the revaluation gain directly in equity. If an investment is classified as at fair value through profit or loss, the pre-IAS 39 revaluation gain that had been recognised in equity is reclassified into retained earnings on initial application of IAS 39. If, on initial application of IAS 39, an investment is classified as available for sale, then the pre-IAS 39 revaluation gain is recognised in a separate component of equity. Subsequently, the entity recognises gains and losses on the available-for-sale financial asset in that separate component of equity until the investment is impaired, sold, collected or otherwise disposed of. On subsequent derecognition or impairment of the available-for-sale financial asset, the entity transfers to profit or loss the cumulative gain or loss remaining in equity (IAS 39, paragraph 55(b)).

Hedge accounting

IG60 Paragraphs 28–30 of the IFRS deal with hedge accounting. The designation and documentation of a hedge relationship must be completed on or before the date of transition to IFRSs if the hedge relationship is to qualify for hedge accounting from that date. Hedge accounting can be applied prospectively only from the date that the hedge relationship is fully designated and documented.

IG60A An entity may, under its previous GAAP, have deferred or not recognised gains and losses on a fair value hedge of a hedged item that is not measured at fair value. For such a fair value hedge, an entity adjusts the carrying amount of the hedged item at the date of transition to IFRSs. The adjustment is the lower of:

(a) that portion of the cumulative change in the fair value of the hedged item that reflects the designated hedged risk and was not recognised under previous GAAP; and

(b) that portion of the cumulative change in the fair value of the hedging instrument that reflects the designated hedged risk and, under previous GAAP, was either (i) not recognised or (ii) deferred in the balance sheet as an asset or liability.

IG60B An entity may, under its previous GAAP, have deferred gains and losses on a cash flow hedge of a forecast transaction. If, at the date of transition to IFRSs, the hedged forecast transaction is not highly probable, but is expected to occur, the entire deferred gain or loss is recognised in equity. Any net cumulative gain or loss that has been reclassified to equity on initial application of IAS 39 remains in equity until (a) the forecast transaction subsequently results in the recognition of a non-financial asset or non-financial liability, (b) the forecast transaction affects profit or loss or (c) subsequently circumstances change and the forecast transaction is no longer expected to occur, in which case any related net cumulative gain or loss that had been recognised directly in equity is recognised in profit or loss. If the hedging instrument is still held, but the hedge does not qualify as a cash flow hedge under IAS 39, hedge accounting is no longer appropriate starting from the date of transition to IFRSs.

IAS 40 *Investment Property*

IG61 An entity that adopts the fair value model in IAS 40 measures its investment property at fair value at the date of transition to IFRSs. The transitional requirements of IAS 40 do not apply (paragraph 9 of the IFRS).

IG62 An entity that adopts the cost model in IAS 40 applies paragraphs IG7–IG13 on property, plant and equipment.

Explanation of transition to IFRSs

IG63 Paragraphs 39(a) and (b), 40 and 41 of the IFRS require a first-time adopter to disclose reconciliations that give sufficient detail to enable users to understand the material adjustments to the balance sheet, income statement and, if applicable, cash flow statement. Paragraph 39(a) and (b) requires specific reconciliations of equity and profit or loss. IG Example 11 shows one way of satisfying these requirements.

IG Example 11 Reconciliation of equity and profit or loss

Background

An entity first adopted IFRSs in 2005, with a date of transition to IFRSs of 1 January 2004. Its last financial statements under previous GAAP were for the year ended 31 December 2004.

Application of requirements

The entity's first IFRS financial statements include the reconciliations and related notes shown below.

Among other things, this example includes a reconciliation of equity at the date of transition to IFRSs (1 January 2004). The IFRS also requires a reconciliation at the end of the last period presented under previous GAAP (not included in this example).

In practice, it may be helpful to include cross-references to accounting policies and supporting analyses that give further explanation of the adjustments shown in the reconciliations below.

If a first-time adopter becomes aware of errors made under previous GAAP, the reconciliations distinguish the correction of those errors from changes in accounting policies (paragraph 41 of the IFRS). This example does not illustrate disclosure of a correction of an error.

Continued from previous page

IG Example 11 Reconciliation of equity and profit or loss

Reconciliation of equity at 1 January 2004 (date of transition to IFRSs)

Note		*Previous GAAP*	*Effect of transition to IFRSs*	*IFRSs*
1	Property, plant and equipment	8,299	100	8,399
2	Goodwill	1,220	150	1,370
2	Intangible assets	208	(150)	58
3	Financial assets	3,471	420	3,891
	Total non-current assets	13,198	520	13,718
	Trade and other receivables	3,710	0	3,710
4	Inventories	2,962	400	3,362
5	Other receivables	333	431	764
	Cash and cash equivalents	748	0	748
	Total current assets	7,753	831	8,584
	Total assets	20,951	1,351	22,302
	Interest-bearing loans	9,396	0	9,396
	Trade and other payables	4,124	0	4,124
6	Employee benefits	0	66	66
7	Restructuring provision	250	(250)	0
	Current tax liability	42	0	42
8	Deferred tax liability	579	460	1,039
	Total liabilities	14,391	276	14,667
	Total assets less total liabilities	6,560	1,075	7,635
	Issued capital	1,500	0	1,500
3	Revaluation reserve	0	294	294
5	Hedging reserve	0	302	302
9	Retained earnings	5,060	479	5,539
	Total equity	6,560	1,075	7,635

Continued from previous page

IG Example 11 Reconciliation of equity and profit or loss

Notes to the reconciliation of equity at 1 January 2004:

1 Depreciation was influenced by tax requirements under previous GAAP, but under IFRSs reflects the useful life of the assets. The cumulative adjustment increased the carrying amount of property, plant and equipment by 100.

2 Intangible assets under previous GAAP included 150 for items that are transferred to goodwill because they do not qualify for recognition as intangible assets under IFRSs.

3 Financial assets are all classified as available-for-sale under IFRSs and are carried at their fair value of 3,891. They were carried at cost of 3,471 under previous GAAP. The resulting gains of 294 (420, less related deferred tax of 126) are included in the revaluation reserve.

4 Inventories include fixed and variable production overhead of 400 under IFRSs, but this overhead was excluded under previous GAAP.

5 Unrealised gains of 431 on unmatured forward foreign exchange contracts are recognised under IFRSs, but were not recognised under previous GAAP. The resulting gains of 302 (431, less related deferred tax of 129) are included in the hedging reserve because the contracts hedge forecast sales.

6 A pension liability of 66 is recognised under IFRSs, but was not recognised under previous GAAP, which used a cash basis.

7 A restructuring provision of 250 relating to head office activities was recognised under previous GAAP, but does not qualify for recognition as a liability under IFRSs.

8 The above changes increased the deferred tax liability as follows:

Revaluation reserve (note 3)	126
Hedging reserve (note 5)	129
Retained earnings	205
Increase in deferred tax liability	460

Because the tax base at 1 January 2004 of the items reclassified from intangible assets to goodwill (note 2) equalled their carrying amount at that date, the reclassification did not affect deferred tax liabilities.

Continued from previous page

IG Example 11 Reconciliation of equity and profit or loss

9 The adjustments to retained earnings are as follows:

Depreciation (note 1)	100
Production overhead (note 4)	400
Pension liability (note 6)	(66)
Restructuring provision (note 7)	250
Tax effect of the above	(205)
Total adjustment to retained earnings	479

Reconciliation of profit or loss for 2004

Note		*Previous GAAP*	*Effect of transition to IFRSs*	*IFRSs*
	Revenue	20,910	0	20,910
1,2,3	Cost of sales	(15,283)	(97)	(15,380)
	Gross profit	5,627	(97)	5,530
1	Distribution costs	(1,907)	(30)	(1,937)
1,4	Administrative expenses	(2,842)	(300)	(3,142)
	Finance income	1,446	0	1,446
	Finance costs	(1,902)	0	(1,902)
	Profit before tax	422	(427)	(5)
5	Tax expense	(158)	128	(30)
	Net profit (loss)	264	(299)	(35)

Notes to the reconciliation of profit or loss for 2004:

1 A pension liability is recognised under IFRSs, but was not recognised under previous GAAP. The pension liability increased by 130 during 2004, which caused increases in cost of sales (50), distribution costs (30) and administrative expenses (50).

2 Cost of sales is higher by 47 under IFRSs because inventories include fixed and variable production overhead under IFRSs but not under previous GAAP.

3 Depreciation was influenced by tax requirements under previous GAAP, but reflects the useful life of the assets under IFRSs. The effect on the profit for 2004 was not material.

Continued from previous page

IG Example 11 Reconciliation of equity and profit or loss

4	A restructuring provision of 250 was recognised under previous GAAP at 1 January 2004, but did not qualify for recognition under IFRS until the year ended 31 December 2004. This increases administrative expenses for 2004 under IFRSs.
5	Adjustments 1–4 above lead to a reduction of 128 in deferred tax expense.

Explanation of material adjustments to the cash flow statement for 2004:

Income taxes of 133 paid during 2004 are classified as operating cash flows under IFRSs, but were included in a separate category of tax cash flows under previous GAAP. There are no other material differences between the cash flow statement presented under IFRSs and the cash flow statement presented under previous GAAP.

IFRS 2 *Share-based Payment*

IG64 A first-time adopter is encouraged, but not required, to apply IFRS 2 *Share-based Payment* to equity instruments that were granted after 7 November 2002 that vested before the later of (a) the date of transition to IFRSs and (b) 1 January 2005.

IG65 For example, if an entity's date of transition to IFRSs is 1 January 2004, the entity applies IFRS 2 to shares, share options or other equity instruments that were granted after 7 November 2002 and had not yet vested at 1 January 2005. Conversely, if an entity's date of transition to IFRSs is 1 January 2010, the entity applies IFRS 2 to shares, share options or other equity instruments that were granted after 7 November 2002 and had not yet vested at 1 January 2010.

[Paragraphs IG66–IG200 reserved for possible guidance on future standards]

IFRIC Interpretations

IFRIC 1 *Changes in Existing Decommissioning, Restoration and Similar Liabilities*

IG201 IAS 16 requires the cost of an item of property, plant and equipment to include the initial estimate of the costs of dismantling and removing the asset and restoring the site on which it is located. IAS 37 requires the liability, both initially and subsequently, to be measured at the amount required to settle the present obligation at the balance sheet date, reflecting a current market-based discount rate.

IG202 IFRIC 1 requires that, subject to specified conditions, changes in an existing decommissioning, restoration or similar liability are added to or deducted from the cost of the related asset. The resulting depreciable amount of the asset is depreciated over its useful life, and the periodic unwinding of the discount on the liability is recognised in profit or loss as it occurs.

IG203 Paragraph 25E of IFRS 1 provides a transitional exemption. Instead of retrospectively accounting for changes in this way, entities can include in the depreciated cost of the asset an amount calculated by discounting the liability at the date of transition to IFRSs back to, and depreciating it from, when the liability was first incurred. IG Example 201 illustrates the effect of applying this exemption, assuming that the entity accounts for its property, plant and equipment using the cost model.

IG Example 201 Changes in existing decommissioning, restoration and similar liabilities

Background

An entity's first IFRS financial statements have a reporting date of 31 December 2005 and include comparative information for 2004 only. Its date of transition to IFRSs is therefore 1 January 2004.

The entity acquired an energy plant on 1 January 2001, with a life of 40 years.

As at the date of transition to IFRSs, the entity estimates the decommissioning cost in 37 years' time to be 470, and estimates that the appropriate risk-adjusted discount rate for the liability is 5 per cent. It judges that the appropriate discount rate has not changed since 1 January 2001.

Application of requirements

The decommissioning liability recognised at the transition date is 77 (470 discounted for 37 years at 5 per cent).

Discounting this liability back for a further three years to 1 January 2001 gives an estimated liability at acquisition, to be included in the cost of the asset, of 67. Accumulated depreciation on the asset is 67 × 3/40 = 5.

The amounts recognised in the opening IFRS balance sheet on the date of transition to IFRSs (1 January 2004) are, in summary:

Decommissioning cost included in cost of plant	67
Accumulated depreciation	(5)
Decommissioning liability	(77)
Net assets/retained earnings	(15)

IFRIC 4 *Determining whether an Arrangement contains a Lease*

IG204 IFRIC 4 specifies criteria for determining, at the inception of an arrangement, whether the arrangement contains a lease. It also specifies when an arrangement should be reassessed subsequently.

IG205 Paragraph 25F of IFRS 1 provides a transitional exemption. Instead of determining retrospectively whether an arrangement contains a lease at the inception of the arrangement and subsequently reassessing that arrangement as required in the periods before transition to IFRSs, entities may determine whether arrangements in existence on the date of transition to IFRSs contain leases by applying paragraphs 6–9 of IFRIC 4 to those arrangements on the basis of facts and circumstances existing on that date.

IG Example 202 Determining whether an arrangement contains a Lease

Background

An entity's first IFRS financial statements have a reporting date of 31 December 2007 and include comparative information for 2006 only. Its date of transition to IFRSs is therefore 1 January 2006.

On 1 January 1995, the entity entered into a take-or-pay arrangement to supply gas. On 1 January 2000, there was a change in the contractual terms of the arrangement.

Application of requirements

On 1 January 2006, the entity may determine whether the arrangement contains a lease by applying the criteria in paragraphs 6–9 of IFRIC 4 on the basis of facts and circumstances existing on that date. Alternatively, the entity applies those criteria on the basis of facts and circumstances existing on 1 January 1995 and reassesses the arrangement on 1 January 2000. If the arrangement is determined to contain a lease, the entity follows the guidance in paragraphs IG14–IG16.

International Financial Reporting Standard 2

Share-based Payment

This version includes amendments resulting from IFRSs issued up to 31 December 2004.

CONTENTS

International Financial Reporting Standard 2 *Share-based Payment* (IFRS 2) is set out in paragraphs 1–60 and Appendices A–C. All the paragraphs have equal authority. Paragraphs in **bold type** state the main principles. Terms defined in Appendix A are in *italics* the first time they appear in the Standard. Definitions of other terms are given in the Glossary for International Financial Reporting Standards. IFRS 2 should be read in the context of its objective and the Basis for Conclusions, the *Preface to International Financial Reporting Standards* and the *Framework for the Preparation and Presentation of Financial Statements*. IAS 8 *Accounting Policies, Changes in Accounting Estimates and Errors* provides a basis for selecting and applying accounting policies in the absence of explicit guidance.

Introduction

Reasons for issuing the IFRS

IN1 Entities often grant shares or share options to employees or other parties. Share plans and share option plans are a common feature of employee remuneration, for directors, senior executives and many other employees. Some entities issue shares or share options to pay suppliers, such as suppliers of professional services.

IN2 Until this IFRS was issued, there was no IFRS covering the recognition and measurement of these transactions. Concerns were raised about this gap in IFRSs, given the increasing prevalence of share-based payment transactions in many countries.

Main features of the IFRS

IN3 The IFRS requires an entity to recognise share-based payment transactions in its financial statements, including transactions with employees or other parties to be settled in cash, other assets, or equity instruments of the entity. There are no exceptions to the IFRS, other than for transactions to which other Standards apply.

IN4 The IFRS sets out measurement principles and specific requirements for three types of share-based payment transactions:

(a) equity-settled share-based payment transactions, in which the entity receives goods or services as consideration for equity instruments of the entity (including shares or share options);

(b) cash-settled share-based payment transactions, in which the entity acquires goods or services by incurring liabilities to the supplier of those goods or services for amounts that are based on the price (or value) of the entity's shares or other equity instruments of the entity; and

(c) transactions in which the entity receives or acquires goods or services and the terms of the arrangement provide either the entity or the supplier of those goods or services with a choice of whether the entity settles the transaction in cash or by issuing equity instruments.

IN5 For equity-settled share-based payment transactions, the IFRS requires an entity to measure the goods or services received, and the corresponding increase in equity, directly, at the fair value of the goods or services received, unless that fair value cannot be estimated reliably. If the entity cannot estimate reliably the fair value of the goods or services received, the entity is required to measure their value, and the corresponding increase in equity, indirectly, by reference to the fair value of the equity instruments granted. Furthermore:

(a) for transactions with employees and others providing similar services, the entity is required to measure the fair value of the equity instruments granted, because it is typically not possible to estimate reliably the fair value of employee services received. The fair value of the equity instruments granted is measured at grant date.

(b) for transactions with parties other than employees (and those providing similar services), there is a rebuttable presumption that the fair value of the goods or services received can be estimated reliably. That fair value is measured at the date the entity obtains the goods or the counterparty renders service. In rare cases, if the presumption is rebutted, the transaction is measured by reference to the fair value of the equity instruments granted, measured at the date the entity obtains the goods or the counterparty renders service.

(c) for goods or services measured by reference to the fair value of the equity instruments granted, the IFRS specifies that vesting conditions, other than market conditions, are not taken into account when estimating the fair value of the shares or options at the relevant measurement date (as specified above). Instead, vesting conditions are taken into account by adjusting the number of equity instruments included in the measurement of the transaction amount so that, ultimately, the amount recognised for goods or services received as consideration for the equity instruments granted is based on the number of equity instruments that eventually vest. Hence, on a cumulative basis, no amount is recognised for goods or services received if the equity instruments granted do not vest because of failure to satisfy a vesting condition (other than a market condition).

(d) the IFRS requires the fair value of equity instruments granted to be based on market prices, if available, and to take into account the terms and conditions upon which those equity instruments were granted. In the absence of market prices, fair value is estimated, using a valuation technique to estimate what the price of those equity instruments would have been on the measurement date in an arm's length transaction between knowledgeable, willing parties.

(e) the IFRS also sets out requirements if the terms and conditions of an option or share grant are modified (eg an option is repriced) or if a grant is cancelled, repurchased or replaced with another grant of equity instruments. For example, irrespective of any modification, cancellation or settlement of a grant of equity instruments to employees, the IFRS generally requires the entity to recognise, as a minimum, the services received measured at the grant date fair value of the equity instruments granted.

IN6 For cash-settled share-based payment transactions, the IFRS requires an entity to measure the goods or services acquired and the liability incurred at the fair value of the liability. Until the liability is settled, the entity is required to remeasure the fair value of the liability at each reporting date and at the date of settlement, with any changes in value recognised in profit or loss for the period.

IN7 For share-based payment transactions in which the terms of the arrangement provide either the entity or the supplier of goods or services with a choice of whether the entity settles the transaction in cash or by issuing equity instruments, the entity is required to account for that transaction, or the components of that transaction, as a cash-settled share-based payment transaction if, and to the extent that, the entity has incurred a liability to settle in cash (or other assets), or as an equity-settled share-based payment transaction if, and to the extent that, no such liability has been incurred.

IN8 The IFRS prescribes various disclosure requirements to enable users of financial statements to understand:

(a) the nature and extent of share-based payment arrangements that existed during the period;

(b) how the fair value of the goods or services received, or the fair value of the equity instruments granted, during the period was determined; and

(c) the effect of share-based payment transactions on the entity's profit or loss for the period and on its financial position.

International Financial Reporting Standard 2
Share-based Payment

Objective

1 The objective of this IFRS is to specify the financial reporting by an entity when it undertakes a *share-based payment transaction*. In particular, it requires an entity to reflect in its profit or loss and financial position the effects of share-based payment transactions, including expenses associated with transactions in which *share options* are granted to employees.

Scope

2 An entity shall apply this IFRS in accounting for all share-based payment transactions including:

(a) *equity-settled share-based payment transactions*, in which the entity receives goods or services as consideration for *equity instruments* of the entity (including shares or share options),

(b) *cash-settled share-based payment transactions*, in which the entity acquires goods or services by incurring liabilities to the supplier of those goods or services for amounts that are based on the price (or value) of the entity's shares or other equity instruments of the entity, and

(c) transactions in which the entity receives or acquires goods or services and the terms of the arrangement provide either the entity or the supplier of those goods or services with a choice of whether the entity settles the transaction in cash (or other assets) or by issuing equity instruments,

except as noted in paragraphs 5 and 6.

3 For the purposes of this IFRS, transfers of an entity's equity instruments by its shareholders to parties that have supplied goods or services to the entity (including employees) are share-based payment transactions, unless the transfer is clearly for a purpose other than payment for goods or services supplied to the entity. This also applies to transfers of equity instruments of the entity's parent, or equity instruments of another entity in the same group as the entity, to parties that have supplied goods or services to the entity.

4 For the purposes of this IFRS, a transaction with an employee (or other party) in his/her capacity as a holder of equity instruments of the entity is not a share-based payment transaction. For example, if an entity grants all holders of a particular class of its equity instruments the right to acquire additional equity instruments of the entity at a price that is less than the fair value of those equity instruments, and an employee receives such a right because he/she is a holder of equity instruments of that particular class, the granting or exercise of that right is not subject to the requirements of this IFRS.

5 As noted in paragraph 2, this IFRS applies to share-based payment transactions in which an entity acquires or receives goods or services. Goods includes inventories, consumables, property, plant and equipment, intangible assets and other

non-financial assets. However, an entity shall not apply this IFRS to transactions in which the entity acquires goods as part of the net assets acquired in a business combination to which IFRS 3 *Business Combinations* applies. Hence, equity instruments issued in a business combination in exchange for control of the acquiree are not within the scope of this IFRS. However, equity instruments granted to employees of the acquiree in their capacity as employees (eg in return for continued service) are within the scope of this IFRS. Similarly, the cancellation, replacement or other modification of *share-based payment arrangements* because of a business combination or other equity restructuring shall be accounted for in accordance with this IFRS.

6 This IFRS does not apply to share-based payment transactions in which the entity receives or acquires goods or services under a contract within the scope of paragraphs 8–10 of IAS 32 *Financial Instruments: Disclosure and Presentation* (as revised in 2003) or paragraphs 5–7 of IAS 39 *Financial Instruments: Recognition and Measurement* (as revised in 2003).

Recognition

7 **An entity shall recognise the goods or services received or acquired in a share-based payment transaction when it obtains the goods or as the services are received. The entity shall recognise a corresponding increase in equity if the goods or services were received in an equity-settled share-based payment transaction, or a liability if the goods or services were acquired in a cash-settled share-based payment transaction.**

8 **When the goods or services received or acquired in a share-based payment transaction do not qualify for recognition as assets, they shall be recognised as expenses.**

9 Typically, an expense arises from the consumption of goods or services. For example, services are typically consumed immediately, in which case an expense is recognised as the counterparty renders service. Goods might be consumed over a period of time or, in the case of inventories, sold at a later date, in which case an expense is recognised when the goods are consumed or sold. However, sometimes it is necessary to recognise an expense before the goods or services are consumed or sold, because they do not qualify for recognition as assets. For example, an entity might acquire goods as part of the research phase of a project to develop a new product. Although those goods have not been consumed, they might not qualify for recognition as assets under the applicable IFRS.

Equity-settled share-based payment transactions

Overview

10 **For equity-settled share-based payment transactions, the entity shall measure the goods or services received, and the corresponding increase in equity, directly, at the fair value of the goods or services received, unless that fair value cannot be estimated reliably. If the entity cannot estimate reliably the fair value of the goods or services received, the entity shall**

measure their value, and the corresponding increase in equity, indirectly, by reference to* the fair value of the equity instruments granted.

11 To apply the requirements of paragraph 10 to transactions with *employees and others providing similar services*,† the entity shall measure the fair value of the services received by reference to the fair value of the equity instruments granted, because typically it is not possible to estimate reliably the fair value of the services received, as explained in paragraph 12. The fair value of those equity instruments shall be measured at *grant date*.

12 Typically, shares, share options or other equity instruments are granted to employees as part of their remuneration package, in addition to a cash salary and other employment benefits. Usually, it is not possible to measure directly the services received for particular components of the employee's remuneration package. It might also not be possible to measure the fair value of the total remuneration package independently, without measuring directly the fair value of the equity instruments granted. Furthermore, shares or share options are sometimes granted as part of a bonus arrangement, rather than as a part of basic remuneration, eg as an incentive to the employees to remain in the entity's employ or to reward them for their efforts in improving the entity's performance. By granting shares or share options, in addition to other remuneration, the entity is paying additional remuneration to obtain additional benefits. Estimating the fair value of those additional benefits is likely to be difficult. Because of the difficulty of measuring directly the fair value of the services received, the entity shall measure the fair value of the employee services received by reference to the fair value of the equity instruments granted.

13 To apply the requirements of paragraph 10 to transactions with parties other than employees, there shall be a rebuttable presumption that the fair value of the goods or services received can be estimated reliably. That fair value shall be measured at the date the entity obtains the goods or the counterparty renders service. In rare cases, if the entity rebuts this presumption because it cannot estimate reliably the fair value of the goods or services received, the entity shall measure the goods or services received, and the corresponding increase in equity, indirectly, by reference to the fair value of the equity instruments granted, measured at the date the entity obtains the goods or the counterparty renders service.

Transactions in which services are received

14 If the equity instruments granted *vest* immediately, the counterparty is not required to complete a specified period of service before becoming unconditionally entitled to those equity instruments. In the absence of evidence to the contrary, the entity shall presume that services rendered by the counterparty as consideration for the equity instruments have been received.

* This IFRS uses the phrase 'by reference to' rather than 'at', because the transaction is ultimately measured by multiplying the fair value of the equity instruments granted, measured at the date specified in paragraph 11 or 13 (whichever is applicable), by the number of equity instruments that vest, as explained in paragraph 19.

† In the remainder of this IFRS, all references to employees also includes others providing similar services.

In this case, on grant date the entity shall recognise the services received in full, with a corresponding increase in equity.

15 If the equity instruments granted do not vest until the counterparty completes a specified period of service, the entity shall presume that the services to be rendered by the counterparty as consideration for those equity instruments will be received in the future, during the *vesting period*. The entity shall account for those services as they are rendered by the counterparty during the vesting period, with a corresponding increase in equity. For example:

(a) if an employee is granted share options conditional upon completing three years' service, then the entity shall presume that the services to be rendered by the employee as consideration for the share options will be received in the future, over that three-year vesting period.

(b) if an employee is granted share options conditional upon the achievement of a performance condition and remaining in the entity's employ until that performance condition is satisfied, and the length of the vesting period varies depending on when that performance condition is satisfied, the entity shall presume that the services to be rendered by the employee as consideration for the share options will be received in the future, over the expected vesting period. The entity shall estimate the length of the expected vesting period at grant date, based on the most likely outcome of the performance condition. If the performance condition is a *market condition*, the estimate of the length of the expected vesting period shall be consistent with the assumptions used in estimating the fair value of the options granted, and shall not be subsequently revised. If the performance condition is not a market condition, the entity shall revise its estimate of the length of the vesting period, if necessary, if subsequent information indicates that the length of the vesting period differs from previous estimates.

Transactions measured by reference to the fair value of the equity instruments granted

Determining the fair value of equity instruments granted

16 For transactions measured by reference to the fair value of the equity instruments granted, an entity shall measure the fair value of equity instruments granted at the *measurement date*, based on market prices if available, taking into account the terms and conditions upon which those equity instruments were granted (subject to the requirements of paragraphs 19–22).

17 If market prices are not available, the entity shall estimate the fair value of the equity instruments granted using a valuation technique to estimate what the price of those equity instruments would have been on the measurement date in an arm's length transaction between knowledgeable, willing parties. The valuation technique shall be consistent with generally accepted valuation methodologies for pricing financial instruments, and shall incorporate all factors and assumptions that knowledgeable, willing market participants would consider in setting the price (subject to the requirements of paragraphs 19–22).

18 Appendix B contains further guidance on the measurement of the fair value of shares and share options, focusing on the specific terms and conditions that are common features of a grant of shares or share options to employees.

Treatment of vesting conditions

19 A grant of equity instruments might be conditional upon satisfying specified *vesting conditions.* For example, a grant of shares or share options to an employee is typically conditional on the employee remaining in the entity's employ for a specified period of time. There might be performance conditions that must be satisfied, such as the entity achieving a specified growth in profit or a specified increase in the entity's share price. Vesting conditions, other than market conditions, shall not be taken into account when estimating the fair value of the shares or share options at the measurement date. Instead, vesting conditions shall be taken into account by adjusting the number of equity instruments included in the measurement of the transaction amount so that, ultimately, the amount recognised for goods or services received as consideration for the equity instruments granted shall be based on the number of equity instruments that eventually vest. Hence, on a cumulative basis, no amount is recognised for goods or services received if the equity instruments granted do not vest because of failure to satisfy a vesting condition, eg the counterparty fails to complete a specified service period, or a performance condition is not satisfied, subject to the requirements of paragraph 21.

20 To apply the requirements of paragraph 19, the entity shall recognise an amount for the goods or services received during the vesting period based on the best available estimate of the number of equity instruments expected to vest and shall revise that estimate, if necessary, if subsequent information indicates that the number of equity instruments expected to vest differs from previous estimates. On vesting date, the entity shall revise the estimate to equal the number of equity instruments that ultimately vested, subject to the requirements of paragraph 21.

21 Market conditions, such as a target share price upon which vesting (or exercisability) is conditioned, shall be taken into account when estimating the fair value of the equity instruments granted. Therefore, for grants of equity instruments with market conditions, the entity shall recognise the goods or services received from a counterparty who satisfies all other vesting conditions (eg services received from an employee who remains in service for the specified period of service), irrespective of whether that market condition is satisfied.

Treatment of a reload feature

22 For options with a *reload feature*, the reload feature shall not be taken into account when estimating the fair value of options granted at the measurement date. Instead, a *reload option* shall be accounted for as a new option grant, if and when a reload option is subsequently granted.

After vesting date

23 Having recognised the goods or services received in accordance with paragraphs 10–22, and a corresponding increase in equity, the entity shall make no subsequent adjustment to total equity after vesting date. For example, the

entity shall not subsequently reverse the amount recognised for services received from an employee if the vested equity instruments are later forfeited or, in the case of share options, the options are not exercised. However, this requirement does not preclude the entity from recognising a transfer within equity, ie a transfer from one component of equity to another.

If the fair value of the equity instruments cannot be estimated reliably

24 The requirements in paragraphs 16–23 apply when the entity is required to measure a share-based payment transaction by reference to the fair value of the equity instruments granted. In rare cases, the entity may be unable to estimate reliably the fair value of the equity instruments granted at the measurement date, in accordance with the requirements in paragraphs 16–22. In these rare cases only, the entity shall instead:

(a) measure the equity instruments at their *intrinsic value*, initially at the date the entity obtains the goods or the counterparty renders service and subsequently at each reporting date and at the date of final settlement, with any change in intrinsic value recognised in profit or loss. For a grant of share options, the share-based payment arrangement is finally settled when the options are exercised, are forfeited (eg upon cessation of employment) or lapse (eg at the end of the option's life).

(b) recognise the goods or services received based on the number of equity instruments that ultimately vest or (where applicable) are ultimately exercised. To apply this requirement to share options, for example, the entity shall recognise the goods or services received during the vesting period, if any, in accordance with paragraphs 14 and 15, except that the requirements in paragraph 15(b) concerning a market condition do not apply. The amount recognised for goods or services received during the vesting period shall be based on the number of share options expected to vest. The entity shall revise that estimate, if necessary, if subsequent information indicates that the number of share options expected to vest differs from previous estimates. On vesting date, the entity shall revise the estimate to equal the number of equity instruments that ultimately vested. After vesting date, the entity shall reverse the amount recognised for goods or services received if the share options are later forfeited, or lapse at the end of the share option's life.

25 If an entity applies paragraph 24, it is not necessary to apply paragraphs 26–29, because any modifications to the terms and conditions on which the equity instruments were granted will be taken into account when applying the intrinsic value method set out in paragraph 24. However, if an entity settles a grant of equity instruments to which paragraph 24 has been applied:

(a) if the settlement occurs during the vesting period, the entity shall account for the settlement as an acceleration of vesting, and shall therefore recognise immediately the amount that would otherwise have been recognised for services received over the remainder of the vesting period.

(b) any payment made on settlement shall be accounted for as the repurchase of equity instruments, ie as a deduction from equity, except to the extent that the payment exceeds the intrinsic value of the equity instruments, measured at the repurchase date. Any such excess shall be recognised as an expense.

Modifications to the terms and conditions on which equity instruments were granted, including cancellations and settlements

26 An entity might modify the terms and conditions on which the equity instruments were granted. For example, it might reduce the exercise price of options granted to employees (ie reprice the options), which increases the fair value of those options. The requirements in paragraphs 27–29 to account for the effects of modifications are expressed in the context of share-based payment transactions with employees. However, the requirements shall also be applied to share-based payment transactions with parties other than employees that are measured by reference to the fair value of the equity instruments granted. In the latter case, any references in paragraphs 27–29 to grant date shall instead refer to the date the entity obtains the goods or the counterparty renders service.

27 The entity shall recognise, as a minimum, the services received measured at the grant date fair value of the equity instruments granted, unless those equity instruments do not vest because of failure to satisfy a vesting condition (other than a market condition) that was specified at grant date. This applies irrespective of any modifications to the terms and conditions on which the equity instruments were granted, or a cancellation or settlement of that grant of equity instruments. In addition, the entity shall recognise the effects of modifications that increase the total fair value of the share-based payment arrangement or are otherwise beneficial to the employee. Guidance on applying this requirement is given in Appendix B.

28 If the entity cancels or settles a grant of equity instruments during the vesting period (other than a grant cancelled by forfeiture when the vesting conditions are not satisfied):

(a) the entity shall account for the cancellation or settlement as an acceleration of vesting, and shall therefore recognise immediately the amount that otherwise would have been recognised for services received over the remainder of the vesting period.

(b) any payment made to the employee on the cancellation or settlement of the grant shall be accounted for as the repurchase of an equity interest, ie as a deduction from equity, except to the extent that the payment exceeds the fair value of the equity instruments granted, measured at the repurchase date. Any such excess shall be recognised as an expense.

(c) if new equity instruments are granted to the employee and, on the date when those new equity instruments are granted, the entity identifies the new equity instruments granted as replacement equity instruments for the cancelled equity instruments, the entity shall account for the granting of replacement equity instruments in the same way as a modification of the original grant of equity instruments, in accordance with paragraph 27 and the guidance in Appendix B. The incremental fair value granted is the difference between the fair value of the replacement equity instruments and the net fair value of the cancelled equity instruments, at the date the replacement equity instruments are granted. The net fair value of the cancelled equity instruments is their fair value, immediately before the cancellation, less the amount of any payment made to the employee on cancellation of the equity instruments that is accounted for as a deduction from equity in accordance with (b) above. If the entity does not identify new equity instruments granted as replacement equity instruments for the cancelled equity instruments, the entity shall account for those new equity instruments as a new grant of equity instruments.

29 If an entity repurchases vested equity instruments, the payment made to the employee shall be accounted for as a deduction from equity, except to the extent that the payment exceeds the fair value of the equity instruments repurchased, measured at the repurchase date. Any such excess shall be recognised as an expense.

Cash-settled share-based payment transactions

30 **For cash-settled share-based payment transactions, the entity shall measure the goods or services acquired and the liability incurred at the fair value of the liability. Until the liability is settled, the entity shall remeasure the fair value of the liability at each reporting date and at the date of settlement, with any changes in fair value recognised in profit or loss for the period.**

31 For example, an entity might grant share appreciation rights to employees as part of their remuneration package, whereby the employees will become entitled to a future cash payment (rather than an equity instrument), based on the increase in the entity's share price from a specified level over a specified period of time. Or an entity might grant to its employees a right to receive a future cash payment by granting to them a right to shares (including shares to be issued upon the exercise of share options) that are redeemable, either mandatorily (eg upon cessation of employment) or at the employee's option.

32 The entity shall recognise the services received, and a liability to pay for those services, as the employees render service. For example, some share appreciation rights vest immediately, and the employees are therefore not required to complete a specified period of service to become entitled to the cash payment. In the absence of evidence to the contrary, the entity shall presume that the services rendered by the employees in exchange for the share appreciation rights have been received. Thus, the entity shall recognise immediately the services received and a liability to pay for them. If the share appreciation rights do not vest until the employees have completed a specified period of service, the entity shall recognise the services received, and a liability to pay for them, as the employees render service during that period.

33 The liability shall be measured, initially and at each reporting date until settled, at the fair value of the share appreciation rights, by applying an option pricing model, taking into account the terms and conditions on which the share appreciation rights were granted, and the extent to which the employees have rendered service to date.

Share-based payment transactions with cash alternatives

34 **For share-based payment transactions in which the terms of the arrangement provide either the entity or the counterparty with the choice of whether the entity settles the transaction in cash (or other assets) or by issuing equity instruments, the entity shall account for that transaction, or the components of that transaction, as a cash-settled share-based payment transaction if, and to the extent that, the entity has incurred a liability to settle in cash or other assets, or as an equity-settled share-based payment transaction if, and to the extent that, no such liability has been incurred.**

Share-based payment transactions in which the terms of the arrangement provide the counterparty with a choice of settlement

35 If an entity has granted the counterparty the right to choose whether a share-based payment transaction is settled in cash* or by issuing equity instruments, the entity has granted a compound financial instrument, which includes a debt component (ie the counterparty's right to demand payment in cash) and an equity component (ie the counterparty's right to demand settlement in equity instruments rather than in cash). For transactions with parties other than employees, in which the fair value of the goods or services received is measured directly, the entity shall measure the equity component of the compound financial instrument as the difference between the fair value of the goods or services received and the fair value of the debt component, at the date when the goods or services are received.

36 For other transactions, including transactions with employees, the entity shall measure the fair value of the compound financial instrument at the measurement date, taking into account the terms and conditions on which the rights to cash or equity instruments were granted.

37 To apply paragraph 36, the entity shall first measure the fair value of the debt component, and then measure the fair value of the equity component—taking into account that the counterparty must forfeit the right to receive cash in order to receive the equity instrument. The fair value of the compound financial instrument is the sum of the fair values of the two components. However, share-based payment transactions in which the counterparty has the choice of settlement are often structured so that the fair value of one settlement alternative is the same as the other. For example, the counterparty might have the choice of receiving share options or cash-settled share appreciation rights. In such cases, the fair value of the equity component is zero, and hence the fair value of the compound financial instrument is the same as the fair value of the debt component. Conversely, if the fair values of the settlement alternatives differ, the fair value of the equity component usually will be greater than zero, in which case the fair value of the compound financial instrument will be greater than the fair value of the debt component.

* In paragraphs 35–43, all references to cash also include other assets of the entity.

38 The entity shall account separately for the goods or services received or acquired in respect of each component of the compound financial instrument. For the debt component, the entity shall recognise the goods or services acquired, and a liability to pay for those goods or services, as the counterparty supplies goods or renders service, in accordance with the requirements applying to cash-settled share-based payment transactions (paragraphs 30–33). For the equity component (if any), the entity shall recognise the goods or services received, and an increase in equity, as the counterparty supplies goods or renders service, in accordance with the requirements applying to equity-settled share-based payment transactions (paragraphs 10–29).

39 At the date of settlement, the entity shall remeasure the liability to its fair value. If the entity issues equity instruments on settlement rather than paying cash, the liability shall be transferred direct to equity, as the consideration for the equity instruments issued.

40 If the entity pays in cash on settlement rather than issuing equity instruments, that payment shall be applied to settle the liability in full. Any equity component previously recognised shall remain within equity. By electing to receive cash on settlement, the counterparty forfeited the right to receive equity instruments. However, this requirement does not preclude the entity from recognising a transfer within equity, ie a transfer from one component of equity to another.

Share-based payment transactions in which the terms of the arrangement provide the entity with a choice of settlement

41 For a share-based payment transaction in which the terms of the arrangement provide an entity with the choice of whether to settle in cash or by issuing equity instruments, the entity shall determine whether it has a present obligation to settle in cash and account for the share-based payment transaction accordingly. The entity has a present obligation to settle in cash if the choice of settlement in equity instruments has no commercial substance (eg because the entity is legally prohibited from issuing shares), or the entity has a past practice or a stated policy of settling in cash, or generally settles in cash whenever the counterparty asks for cash settlement.

42 If the entity has a present obligation to settle in cash, it shall account for the transaction in accordance with the requirements applying to cash-settled share-based payment transactions, in paragraphs 30–33.

43 If no such obligation exists, the entity shall account for the transaction in accordance with the requirements applying to equity-settled share-based payment transactions, in paragraphs 10–29. Upon settlement:

(a) if the entity elects to settle in cash, the cash payment shall be accounted for as the repurchase of an equity interest, ie as a deduction from equity, except as noted in (c) below.

(b) if the entity elects to settle by issuing equity instruments, no further accounting is required (other than a transfer from one component of equity to another, if necessary), except as noted in (c) below.

(c) if the entity elects the settlement alternative with the higher fair value, as at the date of settlement, the entity shall recognise an additional expense for the excess value given, ie the difference between the cash paid and the fair value of the equity instruments that would otherwise have been issued, or the difference between the fair value of the equity instruments issued and the amount of cash that would otherwise have been paid, whichever is applicable.

Disclosures

44 An entity shall disclose information that enables users of the financial statements to understand the nature and extent of share-based payment arrangements that existed during the period.

45 To give effect to the principle in paragraph 44, the entity shall disclose at least the following:

(a) a description of each type of share-based payment arrangement that existed at any time during the period, including the general terms and conditions of each arrangement, such as vesting requirements, the maximum term of options granted, and the method of settlement (eg whether in cash or equity). An entity with substantially similar types of share-based payment arrangements may aggregate this information, unless separate disclosure of each arrangement is necessary to satisfy the principle in paragraph 44.

(b) the number and weighted average exercise prices of share options for each of the following groups of options:

(i) outstanding at the beginning of the period;

(ii) granted during the period;

(iii) forfeited during the period;

(iv) exercised during the period;

(v) expired during the period;

(vi) outstanding at the end of the period; and

(vii) exercisable at the end of the period.

(c) for share options exercised during the period, the weighted average share price at the date of exercise. If options were exercised on a regular basis throughout the period, the entity may instead disclose the weighted average share price during the period.

(d) for share options outstanding at the end of the period, the range of exercise prices and weighted average remaining contractual life. If the range of exercise prices is wide, the outstanding options shall be divided into ranges that are meaningful for assessing the number and timing of additional shares that may be issued and the cash that may be received upon exercise of those options.

46 **An entity shall disclose information that enables users of the financial statements to understand how the fair value of the goods or services received, or the fair value of the equity instruments granted, during the period was determined.**

47 If the entity has measured the fair value of goods or services received as consideration for equity instruments of the entity indirectly, by reference to the fair value of the equity instruments granted, to give effect to the principle in paragraph 46, the entity shall disclose at least the following:

(a) for share options granted during the period, the weighted average fair value of those options at the measurement date and information on how that fair value was measured, including:

(i) the option pricing model used and the inputs to that model, including the weighted average share price, exercise price, expected volatility, option life, expected dividends, the risk-free interest rate and any other inputs to the model, including the method used and the assumptions made to incorporate the effects of expected early exercise;

(ii) how expected volatility was determined, including an explanation of the extent to which expected volatility was based on historical volatility; and

(iii) whether and how any other features of the option grant were incorporated into the measurement of fair value, such as a market condition.

(b) for other equity instruments granted during the period (ie other than share options), the number and weighted average fair value of those equity instruments at the measurement date, and information on how that fair value was measured, including:

(i) if fair value was not measured on the basis of an observable market price, how it was determined;

(ii) whether and how expected dividends were incorporated into the measurement of fair value; and

(iii) whether and how any other features of the equity instruments granted were incorporated into the measurement of fair value.

(c) for share-based payment arrangements that were modified during the period:

(i) an explanation of those modifications;

(ii) the incremental fair value granted (as a result of those modifications); and

(iii) information on how the incremental fair value granted was measured, consistently with the requirements set out in (a) and (b) above, where applicable.

48 If the entity has measured directly the fair value of goods or services received during the period, the entity shall disclose how that fair value was determined, eg whether fair value was measured at a market price for those goods or services.

49 If the entity has rebutted the presumption in paragraph 13, it shall disclose that fact, and give an explanation of why the presumption was rebutted.

50 An entity shall disclose information that enables users of the financial statements to understand the effect of share-based payment transactions on the entity's profit or loss for the period and on its financial position.

51 To give effect to the principle in paragraph 50, the entity shall disclose at least the following:

(a) the total expense recognised for the period arising from share-based payment transactions in which the goods or services received did not qualify for recognition as assets and hence were recognised immediately as an expense, including separate disclosure of that portion of the total expense that arises from transactions accounted for as equity-settled share-based payment transactions;

(b) for liabilities arising from share-based payment transactions:

(i) the total carrying amount at the end of the period; and

(ii) the total intrinsic value at the end of the period of liabilities for which the counterparty's right to cash or other assets had vested by the end of the period (eg vested share appreciation rights).

52 If the information required to be disclosed by this IFRS does not satisfy the principles in paragraphs 44, 46 and 50, the entity shall disclose such additional information as is necessary to satisfy them.

Transitional provisions

53 For equity-settled share-based payment transactions, the entity shall apply this IFRS to grants of shares, share options or other equity instruments that were granted after 7 November 2002 and had not yet vested at the effective date of this IFRS.

54 The entity is encouraged, but not required, to apply this IFRS to other grants of equity instruments if the entity has disclosed publicly the fair value of those equity instruments, determined at the measurement date.

55 For all grants of equity instruments to which this IFRS is applied, the entity shall restate comparative information and, where applicable, adjust the opening balance of retained earnings for the earliest period presented.

56 For all grants of equity instruments to which this IFRS has not been applied (eg equity instruments granted on or before 7 November 2002), the entity shall nevertheless disclose the information required by paragraphs 44 and 45.

57 If, after the IFRS becomes effective, an entity modifies the terms or conditions of a grant of equity instruments to which this IFRS has not been applied, the entity shall nevertheless apply paragraphs 26–29 to account for any such modifications.

58 For liabilities arising from share-based payment transactions existing at the effective date of this IFRS, the entity shall apply the IFRS retrospectively. For these liabilities, the entity shall restate comparative information, including adjusting the opening balance of retained earnings in the earliest period presented for

which comparative information has been restated, except that the entity is not required to restate comparative information to the extent that the information relates to a period or date that is earlier than 7 November 2002.

59 The entity is encouraged, but not required, to apply retrospectively the IFRS to other liabilities arising from share-based payment transactions, for example, to liabilities that were settled during a period for which comparative information is presented.

Effective date

60 An entity shall apply this IFRS for annual periods beginning on or after 1 January 2005. Earlier application is encouraged. If an entity applies the IFRS for a period beginning before 1 January 2005, it shall disclose that fact.

Appendix A
Defined terms

This appendix is an integral part of the IFRS.

cash-settled share-based payment transaction — A **share-based payment transaction** in which the entity acquires goods or services by incurring a liability to transfer cash or other assets to the supplier of those goods or services for amounts that are based on the price (or value) of the entity's shares or other equity instruments of the entity.

employees and others providing similar services — Individuals who render personal services to the entity and either (a) the individuals are regarded as employees for legal or tax purposes, (b) the individuals work for the entity under its direction in the same way as individuals who are regarded as employees for legal or tax purposes, or (c) the services rendered are similar to those rendered by employees. For example, the term encompasses all management personnel, ie those persons having authority and responsibility for planning, directing and controlling the activities of the entity, including non-executive directors.

equity instrument — A contract that evidences a residual interest in the assets of an entity after deducting all of its liabilities.[*]

equity instrument granted — The right (conditional or unconditional) to an **equity instrument** of the entity conferred by the entity on another party, under a **share-based payment arrangement**.

equity-settled share-based payment transaction — A **share-based payment transaction** in which the entity receives goods or services as consideration for **equity instruments** of the entity (including shares or **share options**).

fair value — The amount for which an asset could be exchanged, a liability settled, or an **equity instrument granted** could be exchanged, between knowledgeable, willing parties in an arm's length transaction.

grant date — The date at which the entity and another party (including an employee) agree to a **share-based payment arrangement**, being when the entity and the counterparty have a shared understanding of the terms and conditions of the arrangement. At grant date the entity confers on the counterparty the right to cash, other assets, or **equity instruments** of the entity, provided the specified **vesting conditions**, if any, are met. If that agreement is subject to an approval process (for example, by shareholders), grant date is the date when that approval is obtained.

intrinsic value — The difference between the **fair value** of the shares to which the counterparty has the (conditional or unconditional) right to subscribe or which it has the right to receive, and the price (if any) the counterparty is (or will be) required to pay for those shares. For example, a **share option** with an exercise price of CU15,[†] on a share with a **fair value** of CU20, has an intrinsic value of CU5.

---

* The *Framework* defines a liability as a present obligation of the entity arising from past events, the settlement of which is expected to result in an outflow from the entity of resources embodying economic benefits (ie an outflow of cash or other assets of the entity).

† In this appendix, monetary amounts are denominated in 'currency units' (CU).

market condition	A condition upon which the exercise price, vesting or exercisability of an **equity instrument** depends that is related to the market price of the entity's **equity instruments**, such as attaining a specified share price or a specified amount of **intrinsic value** of a **share option**, or achieving a specified target that is based on the market price of the entity's **equity instruments** relative to an index of market prices of **equity instruments** of other entities.
measurement date	The date at which the **fair value** of the **equity instruments granted** is measured for the purposes of this IFRS. For transactions with **employees and others providing similar services**, the measurement date is **grant date**. For transactions with parties other than employees (and those providing similar services), the measurement date is the date the entity obtains the goods or the counterparty renders service.
reload feature	A feature that provides for an automatic grant of additional **share options** whenever the option holder exercises previously granted options using the entity's shares, rather than cash, to satisfy the exercise price.
reload option	A new **share option** granted when a share is used to satisfy the exercise price of a previous share option.
share-based payment arrangement	An agreement between the entity and another party (including an employee) to enter into a **share-based payment transaction**, which thereby entitles the other party to receive cash or other assets of the entity for amounts that are based on the price of the entity's shares or other **equity instruments** of the entity, or to receive **equity instruments** of the entity, provided the specified **vesting conditions**, if any, are met.
share-based payment transaction	A transaction in which the entity receives goods or services as consideration for **equity instruments** of the entity (including shares or **share options**), or acquires goods or services for amounts that are based on the price of the entity's shares or other **equity instruments** of the entity.
share option	A contract that gives the holder the right, but not the obligation, to subscribe to the entity's shares at a fixed or determinable price for a specified period of time.
vest	To become an entitlement. Under a **share-based payment arrangement**, a counterparty's right to receive cash, other assets, or **equity instruments** of the entity vests upon satisfaction of any specified **vesting conditions**.
vesting conditions	The conditions that must be satisfied for the counterparty to become entitled to receive cash, other assets or **equity instruments** of the entity, under a **share-based payment arrangement**. Vesting conditions include service conditions, which require the other party to complete a specified period of service, and performance conditions, which require specified performance targets to be met (such as a specified increase in the entity's profit over a specified period of time).
vesting period	The period during which all the specified **vesting conditions** of a **share-based payment arrangement** are to be satisfied.

Appendix B
Application Guidance

This appendix is an integral part of the IFRS.

Estimating the fair value of equity instruments granted

B1 Paragraphs B2–B41 of this appendix discuss measurement of the fair value of shares and share options granted, focusing on the specific terms and conditions that are common features of a grant of shares or share options to employees. Therefore, it is not exhaustive. Furthermore, because the valuation issues discussed below focus on shares and share options granted to employees, it is assumed that the fair value of the shares or share options is measured at grant date. However, many of the valuation issues discussed below (eg determining expected volatility) also apply in the context of estimating the fair value of shares or share options granted to parties other than employees at the date the entity obtains the goods or the counterparty renders service.

Shares

B2 For shares granted to employees, the fair value of the shares shall be measured at the market price of the entity's shares (or an estimated market price, if the entity's shares are not publicly traded), adjusted to take into account the terms and conditions upon which the shares were granted (except for vesting conditions that are excluded from the measurement of fair value in accordance with paragraphs 19–21).

B3 For example, if the employee is not entitled to receive dividends during the vesting period, this factor shall be taken into account when estimating the fair value of the shares granted. Similarly, if the shares are subject to restrictions on transfer after vesting date, that factor shall be taken into account, but only to the extent that the post-vesting restrictions affect the price that a knowledgeable, willing market participant would pay for that share. For example, if the shares are actively traded in a deep and liquid market, post-vesting transfer restrictions may have little, if any, effect on the price that a knowledgeable, willing market participant would pay for those shares. Restrictions on transfer or other restrictions that exist during the vesting period shall not be taken into account when estimating the grant date fair value of the shares granted, because those restrictions stem from the existence of vesting conditions, which are accounted for in accordance with paragraphs 19–21.

Share options

B4 For share options granted to employees, in many cases market prices are not available, because the options granted are subject to terms and conditions that do not apply to traded options. If traded options with similar terms and conditions do not exist, the fair value of the options granted shall be estimated by applying an option pricing model.

B5 The entity shall consider factors that knowledgeable, willing market participants would consider in selecting the option pricing model to apply. For example, many employee options have long lives, are usually exercisable during the period between vesting date and the end of the options' life, and are often exercised early. These factors should be considered when estimating the grant date fair value of the options. For many entities, this might preclude the use of the Black-Scholes-Merton formula, which does not allow for the possibility of exercise before the end of the option's life and may not adequately reflect the effects of expected early exercise. It also does not allow for the possibility that expected volatility and other model inputs might vary over the option's life. However, for share options with relatively short contractual lives, or that must be exercised within a short period of time after vesting date, the factors identified above may not apply. In these instances, the Black-Scholes-Merton formula may produce a value that is substantially the same as a more flexible option pricing model.

B6 All option pricing models take into account, as a minimum, the following factors:

(a) the exercise price of the option;

(b) the life of the option;

(c) the current price of the underlying shares;

(d) the expected volatility of the share price;

(e) the dividends expected on the shares (if appropriate); and

(f) the risk-free interest rate for the life of the option.

B7 Other factors that knowledgeable, willing market participants would consider in setting the price shall also be taken into account (except for vesting conditions and reload features that are excluded from the measurement of fair value in accordance with paragraphs 19–22).

B8 For example, a share option granted to an employee typically cannot be exercised during specified periods (eg during the vesting period or during periods specified by securities regulators). This factor shall be taken into account if the option pricing model applied would otherwise assume that the option could be exercised at any time during its life. However, if an entity uses an option pricing model that values options that can be exercised only at the end of the options' life, no adjustment is required for the inability to exercise them during the vesting period (or other periods during the options' life), because the model assumes that the options cannot be exercised during those periods.

B9 Similarly, another factor common to employee share options is the possibility of early exercise of the option, for example, because the option is not freely transferable, or because the employee must exercise all vested options upon cessation of employment. The effects of expected early exercise shall be taken into account, as discussed in paragraphs B16–B21.

B10 Factors that a knowledgeable, willing market participant would not consider in setting the price of a share option (or other equity instrument) shall not be taken into account when estimating the fair value of share options (or other equity instruments) granted. For example, for share options granted to employees, factors that affect the value of the option from the individual employee's perspective only are not relevant to estimating the price that would be set by a knowledgeable, willing market participant.

Inputs to option pricing models

B11 In estimating the expected volatility of and dividends on the underlying shares, the objective is to approximate the expectations that would be reflected in a current market or negotiated exchange price for the option. Similarly, when estimating the effects of early exercise of employee share options, the objective is to approximate the expectations that an outside party with access to detailed information about employees' exercise behaviour would develop based on information available at the grant date.

B12 Often, there is likely to be a range of reasonable expectations about future volatility, dividends and exercise behaviour. If so, an expected value should be calculated, by weighting each amount within the range by its associated probability of occurrence.

B13 Expectations about the future are generally based on experience, modified if the future is reasonably expected to differ from the past. In some circumstances, identifiable factors may indicate that unadjusted historical experience is a relatively poor predictor of future experience. For example, if an entity with two distinctly different lines of business disposes of the one that was significantly less risky than the other, historical volatility may not be the best information on which to base reasonable expectations for the future.

B14 In other circumstances, historical information may not be available. For example, a newly listed entity will have little, if any, historical data on the volatility of its share price. Unlisted and newly listed entities are discussed further below.

B15 In summary, an entity should not simply base estimates of volatility, exercise behaviour and dividends on historical information without considering the extent to which the past experience is expected to be reasonably predictive of future experience.

Expected early exercise

B16 Employees often exercise share options early, for a variety of reasons. For example, employee share options are typically non-transferable. This often causes employees to exercise their share options early, because that is the only way for the employees to liquidate their position. Also, employees who cease employment are usually required to exercise any vested options within a short period of time, otherwise the share options are forfeited. This factor also causes the early exercise of employee share options. Other factors causing early exercise are risk aversion and lack of wealth diversification.

B17 The means by which the effects of expected early exercise are taken into account depends upon the type of option pricing model applied. For example, expected early exercise could be taken into account by using an estimate of the option's expected life (which, for an employee share option, is the period of time from grant date to the date on which the option is expected to be exercised) as an input into an option pricing model (eg the Black-Scholes-Merton formula). Alternatively, expected early exercise could be modelled in a binomial or similar option pricing model that uses contractual life as an input.

B18 Factors to consider in estimating early exercise include:

(a) the length of the vesting period, because the share option typically cannot be exercised until the end of the vesting period. Hence, determining the valuation implications of expected early exercise is based on the assumption that the options will vest. The implications of vesting conditions are discussed in paragraphs 19–21.

(b) the average length of time similar options have remained outstanding in the past.

(c) the price of the underlying shares. Experience may indicate that the employees tend to exercise options when the share price reaches a specified level above the exercise price.

(d) the employee's level within the organisation. For example, experience might indicate that higher-level employees tend to exercise options later than lower-level employees (discussed further in paragraph B21).

(e) expected volatility of the underlying shares. On average, employees might tend to exercise options on highly volatile shares earlier than on shares with low volatility.

B19 As noted in paragraph B17, the effects of early exercise could be taken into account by using an estimate of the option's expected life as an input into an option pricing model. When estimating the expected life of share options granted to a group of employees, the entity could base that estimate on an appropriately weighted average expected life for the entire employee group or on appropriately weighted average lives for subgroups of employees within the group, based on more detailed data about employees' exercise behaviour (discussed further below).

B20 Separating an option grant into groups for employees with relatively homogeneous exercise behaviour is likely to be important. Option value is not a linear function of option term; value increases at a decreasing rate as the term lengthens. For example, if all other assumptions are equal, although a two-year option is worth more than a one-year option, it is not worth twice as much. That means that calculating estimated option value on the basis of a single weighted average life that includes widely differing individual lives would overstate the total fair value of the share options granted. Separating options granted into several groups, each of which has a relatively narrow range of lives included in its weighted average life, reduces that overstatement.

B21 Similar considerations apply when using a binomial or similar model. For example, the experience of an entity that grants options broadly to all levels of employees might indicate that top-level executives tend to hold their options longer than middle-management employees hold theirs and that lower-level employees tend to exercise their options earlier than any other group. In addition, employees who are encouraged or required to hold a minimum amount of their employer's equity instruments, including options, might on average exercise options later than employees not subject to that provision. In those situations, separating options by groups of recipients with relatively homogeneous exercise behaviour will result in a more accurate estimate of the total fair value of the share options granted.

Expected volatility

B22 Expected volatility is a measure of the amount by which a price is expected to fluctuate during a period. The measure of volatility used in option pricing models is the annualised standard deviation of the continuously compounded rates of return on the share over a period of time. Volatility is typically expressed in annualised terms that are comparable regardless of the time period used in the calculation, for example, daily, weekly or monthly price observations.

B23 The rate of return (which may be positive or negative) on a share for a period measures how much a shareholder has benefited from dividends and appreciation (or depreciation) of the share price.

B24 The expected annualised volatility of a share is the range within which the continuously compounded annual rate of return is expected to fall approximately two-thirds of the time. For example, to say that a share with an expected continuously compounded rate of return of 12 per cent has a volatility of 30 per cent means that the probability that the rate of return on the share for one year will be between −18 per cent (12% − 30%) and 42 per cent (12% + 30%) is approximately two-thirds. If the share price is CU100 at the beginning of the year and no dividends are paid, the year-end share price would be expected to be between CU83.53 (CU100 × $e^{-0.18}$) and CU152.20 (CU100 × $e^{0.42}$) approximately two-thirds of the time.

B25 Factors to consider in estimating expected volatility include:

(a) implied volatility from traded share options on the entity's shares, or other traded instruments of the entity that include option features (such as convertible debt), if any.

(b) the historical volatility of the share price over the most recent period that is generally commensurate with the expected term of the option (taking into account the remaining contractual life of the option and the effects of expected early exercise).

(c) the length of time an entity's shares have been publicly traded. A newly listed entity might have a high historical volatility, compared with similar entities that have been listed longer. Further guidance for newly listed entities is given below.

(d) the tendency of volatility to revert to its mean, ie its long-term average level, and other factors indicating that expected future volatility might differ from past volatility. For example, if an entity's share price was extraordinarily volatile for some identifiable period of time because of a failed takeover bid or a major restructuring, that period could be disregarded in computing historical average annual volatility.

(e) appropriate and regular intervals for price observations. The price observations should be consistent from period to period. For example, an entity might use the closing price for each week or the highest price for the week, but it should not use the closing price for some weeks and the highest price for other weeks. Also, the price observations should be expressed in the same currency as the exercise price.

Newly listed entities

B26 As noted in paragraph B25, an entity should consider historical volatility of the share price over the most recent period that is generally commensurate with the expected option term. If a newly listed entity does not have sufficient information on historical volatility, it should nevertheless compute historical volatility for the longest period for which trading activity is available. It could also consider the historical volatility of similar entities following a comparable period in their lives. For example, an entity that has been listed for only one year and grants options with an average expected life of five years might consider the pattern and level of historical volatility of entities in the same industry for the first six years in which the shares of those entities were publicly traded.

Unlisted entities

B27 An unlisted entity will not have historical information to consider when estimating expected volatility. Some factors to consider instead are set out below.

B28 In some cases, an unlisted entity that regularly issues options or shares to employees (or other parties) might have set up an internal market for its shares. The volatility of those share prices could be considered when estimating expected volatility.

B29 Alternatively, the entity could consider the historical or implied volatility of similar listed entities, for which share price or option price information is available, to use when estimating expected volatility. This would be appropriate if the entity has based the value of its shares on the share prices of similar listed entities.

B30 If the entity has not based its estimate of the value of its shares on the share prices of similar listed entities, and has instead used another valuation methodology to value its shares, the entity could derive an estimate of expected volatility consistent with that valuation methodology. For example, the entity might value its shares on a net asset or earnings basis. It could consider the expected volatility of those net asset values or earnings.

Expected dividends

B31 Whether expected dividends should be taken into account when measuring the fair value of shares or options granted depends on whether the counterparty is entitled to dividends or dividend equivalents.

B32 For example, if employees were granted options and are entitled to dividends on the underlying shares or dividend equivalents (which might be paid in cash or applied to reduce the exercise price) between grant date and exercise date, the options granted should be valued as if no dividends will be paid on the underlying shares, ie the input for expected dividends should be zero.

B33 Similarly, when the grant date fair value of shares granted to employees is estimated, no adjustment is required for expected dividends if the employee is entitled to receive dividends paid during the vesting period.

B34 Conversely, if the employees are not entitled to dividends or dividend equivalents during the vesting period (or before exercise, in the case of an option), the grant date valuation of the rights to shares or options should take expected dividends into account. That is to say, when the fair value of an option grant is estimated, expected dividends should be included in the application of an option pricing model. When the fair value of a share grant is estimated, that valuation should be reduced by the present value of dividends expected to be paid during the vesting period.

B35 Option pricing models generally call for expected dividend yield. However, the models may be modified to use an expected dividend amount rather than a yield. An entity may use either its expected yield or its expected payments. If the entity uses the latter, it should consider its historical pattern of increases in dividends. For example, if an entity's policy has generally been to increase dividends by approximately 3 per cent per year, its estimated option value should not assume a fixed dividend amount throughout the option's life unless there is evidence that supports that assumption.

B36 Generally, the assumption about expected dividends should be based on publicly available information. An entity that does not pay dividends and has no plans to do so should assume an expected dividend yield of zero. However, an emerging entity with no history of paying dividends might expect to begin paying dividends during the expected lives of its employee share options. Those entities could use an average of their past dividend yield (zero) and the mean dividend yield of an appropriately comparable peer group.

Risk-free interest rate

B37 Typically, the risk-free interest rate is the implied yield currently available on zero-coupon government issues of the country in whose currency the exercise price is expressed, with a remaining term equal to the expected term of the option being valued (based on the option's remaining contractual life and taking into account the effects of expected early exercise). It may be necessary to use an appropriate substitute, if no such government issues exist or circumstances indicate that the implied yield on zero-coupon government issues is not representative of the risk-free interest rate (for example, in high inflation economies). Also, an appropriate substitute should be used if market participants would typically determine the risk-free interest rate by using that substitute, rather than the implied yield of zero-coupon government issues, when estimating the fair value of an option with a life equal to the expected term of the option being valued.

Capital structure effects

B38 Typically, third parties, not the entity, write traded share options. When these share options are exercised, the writer delivers shares to the option holder. Those shares are acquired from existing shareholders. Hence the exercise of traded share options has no dilutive effect.

B39 In contrast, if share options are written by the entity, new shares are issued when those share options are exercised (either actually issued or issued in substance, if shares previously repurchased and held in treasury are used). Given that the shares will be issued at the exercise price rather than the current market price at the date of exercise, this actual or potential dilution might reduce the share price, so that the option holder does not make as large a gain on exercising as on exercising an otherwise similar traded option that does not dilute the share price.

B40 Whether this has a significant effect on the value of the share options granted depends on various factors, such as the number of new shares that will be issued on exercise of the options compared with the number of shares already issued. Also, if the market already expects that the option grant will take place, the market may have already factored the potential dilution into the share price at the date of grant.

B41 However, the entity should consider whether the possible dilutive effect of the future exercise of the share options granted might have an impact on their estimated fair value at grant date. Option pricing models can be adapted to take into account this potential dilutive effect.

Modifications to equity-settled share-based payment arrangements

B42 Paragraph 27 requires that, irrespective of any modifications to the terms and conditions on which the equity instruments were granted, or a cancellation or settlement of that grant of equity instruments, the entity should recognise, as a minimum, the services received measured at the grant date fair value of the equity instruments granted, unless those equity instruments do not vest because of failure to satisfy a vesting condition (other than a market condition) that was specified at grant date. In addition, the entity should recognise the effects of modifications that increase the total fair value of the share-based payment arrangement or are otherwise beneficial to the employee.

B43 To apply the requirements of paragraph 27:

(a) if the modification increases the fair value of the equity instruments granted (eg by reducing the exercise price), measured immediately before and after the modification, the entity shall include the incremental fair value granted in the measurement of the amount recognised for services received as consideration for the equity instruments granted. The incremental fair value granted is the difference between the fair value of the modified equity instrument and that of the original equity instrument, both estimated as at the date of the modification. If the modification occurs during the vesting period, the incremental fair value granted is included in the measurement of the amount recognised for services received over the period from the modification date until the date when the modified equity instruments vest, in addition to the amount based on the grant date fair value of the original equity instruments, which is recognised over the remainder of the original vesting period. If the modification occurs after vesting date, the incremental fair value granted is recognised immediately, or over the vesting period if the employee is required to complete an additional period of service before becoming unconditionally entitled to those modified equity instruments.

(b) similarly, if the modification increases the number of equity instruments granted, the entity shall include the fair value of the additional equity instruments granted, measured at the date of the modification, in the measurement of the amount recognised for services received as consideration for the equity instruments granted, consistently with the requirements in (a) above. For example, if the modification occurs during the vesting period, the fair value of the additional equity instruments granted is included in the measurement of the amount recognised for services received over the period from the modification date until the date when the additional equity instruments vest, in addition to the amount based on the grant date fair value of the equity instruments originally granted, which is recognised over the remainder of the original vesting period.

(c) if the entity modifies the vesting conditions in a manner that is beneficial to the employee, for example, by reducing the vesting period or by modifying or eliminating a performance condition (other than a market condition, changes to which are accounted for in accordance with (a) above), the entity shall take the modified vesting conditions into account when applying the requirements of paragraphs 19–21.

B44 Furthermore, if the entity modifies the terms or conditions of the equity instruments granted in a manner that reduces the total fair value of the share-based payment arrangement, or is not otherwise beneficial to the employee, the entity shall nevertheless continue to account for the services received as consideration for the equity instruments granted as if that modification had not occurred (other than a cancellation of some or all the equity instruments granted, which shall be accounted for in accordance with paragraph 28). For example:

(a) if the modification reduces the fair value of the equity instruments granted, measured immediately before and after the modification, the entity shall not take into account that decrease in fair value and shall continue to measure the amount recognised for services received as consideration for the equity instruments based on the grant date fair value of the equity instruments granted.

(b) if the modification reduces the number of equity instruments granted to an employee, that reduction shall be accounted for as a cancellation of that portion of the grant, in accordance with the requirements of paragraph 28.

(c) if the entity modifies the vesting conditions in a manner that is not beneficial to the employee, for example, by increasing the vesting period or by modifying or adding a performance condition (other than a market condition, changes to which are accounted for in accordance with (a) above), the entity shall not take the modified vesting conditions into account when applying the requirements of paragraphs 19–21.

Appendix C
Amendments to other IFRSs

The amendments in this appendix become effective for annual financial statements covering periods beginning on or after 1 January 2005. If an entity applies this IFRS for an earlier period, these amendments become effective for that earlier period.

* * * * *

The amendments contained in this appendix when this Standard was issued in 2004 have been incorporated into the relevant pronouncements published in this volume.

Approval of IFRS 2 by the Board

International Financial Reporting Standard 2 *Share-based Payment* was approved for issue by the fourteen members of the International Accounting Standards Board.

Sir David Tweedie	Chairman
Thomas E Jones	Vice-Chairman
Mary E Barth	
Hans-Georg Bruns	
Anthony T Cope	
Robert P Garnett	
Gilbert Gélard	
James J Leisenring	
Warren J McGregor	
Patricia L O'Malley	
Harry K Schmid	
John T Smith	
Geoffrey Whittington	
Tatsumi Yamada	

CONTENTS

Basis for Conclusions on IFRS 2 Share-based Payment

This Basis for Conclusions accompanies, but is not part of, IFRS 2.

Introduction

BC1 This Basis for Conclusions summarises the International Accounting Standards Board's considerations in reaching the conclusions in IFRS 2 *Share-based Payment*. Individual Board members gave greater weight to some factors than to others.

BC2 Entities often issue[*] shares or share options to pay employees or other parties. Share plans and share option plans are a common feature of employee remuneration, not only for directors and senior executives, but also for many other employees. Some entities issue shares or share options to pay suppliers, such as suppliers of professional services.

BC3 Until the issue of IFRS 2, there has been no International Financial Reporting Standard (IFRS) covering the recognition and measurement of these transactions. Concerns have been raised about this gap in international standards. For example, the International Organization of Securities Commissions (IOSCO), in its 2000 report on international standards, stated that IASC (the IASB's predecessor body) should consider the accounting treatment of share-based payment.

BC4 Few countries have standards on the topic. This is a concern in many countries, because the use of share-based payment has increased in recent years and continues to spread. Various standard-setting bodies have been working on this issue. At the time the IASB added a project on share-based payment to its agenda in July 2001, some standard-setters had recently published proposals. For example, the German Accounting Standards Committee published a draft accounting standard *Accounting for Share Option Plans and Similar Compensation Arrangements* in June 2001. The UK Accounting Standards Board led the development of the Discussion Paper *Accounting for Share-based Payment*, published in July 2000 by IASC, the ASB and other bodies represented in the G4+1.[†] The Danish Institute of State Authorised Public Accountants issued a Discussion Paper *The Accounting Treatment of Share-based Payment* in April 2000. More recently, in December 2002, the Accounting Standards Board of Japan published a Summary Issues Paper on share-based payment. In March 2003, the US Financial Accounting Standards Board (FASB) added to its agenda a project to review US accounting requirements on share-based payment. Also, the Canadian Accounting Standards Board (AcSB) recently completed its project on share-based payment. The AcSB standard requires recognition of all share-based payment transactions,

* The word 'issue' is used in a broad sense. For example, a transfer of shares held in treasury (own shares held) to another party is regarded as an 'issue' of equity instruments. Some argue that if options or shares are granted with vesting conditions, they are not 'issued' until those vesting conditions have been satisfied. However, even if this argument is accepted, it does not change the Board's conclusions on the requirements of the IFRS, and therefore the word 'issue' is used broadly, to include situations in which equity instruments are conditionally transferred to the counterparty, subject to the satisfaction of specified vesting conditions.

† The G4+1 comprised members of the national accounting standard-setting bodies of Australia, Canada, New Zealand, the UK and the US, and IASC.

including transactions in which share options are granted to employees (discussed further in paragraphs BC281 and BC282).

BC5 Users of financial statements and other commentators are calling for improvements in the accounting treatment of share-based payment. For example, the proposal in the IASC/G4+1 Discussion Paper and ED 2 *Share-based Payment*, that share-based payment transactions should be recognised in the financial statements, resulting in an expense when the goods or services are consumed, received strong support from investors and other users of financial statements. Recent economic events have emphasised the importance of high quality financial statements that provide neutral, transparent and comparable information to help users make economic decisions. In particular, the omission of expenses arising from share-based payment transactions with employees has been highlighted by investors, other users of financial statements and other commentators as causing economic distortions and corporate governance concerns.

BC6 As noted above, the Board began a project to develop an IFRS on share-based payment in July 2001. In September 2001, the Board invited additional comment on the IASC/G4+1 Discussion Paper, with a comment deadline of 15 December 2001. The Board received over 270 letters. During the development of ED 2, the Board was also assisted by an Advisory Group, consisting of individuals from various countries and with a range of backgrounds, including persons from the investment, corporate, audit, academic, compensation consultancy, valuation and regulatory communities. The Board received further assistance from other experts at a panel discussion held in New York in July 2002. In November 2002, the Board published an Exposure Draft, ED 2 *Share-based Payment*, with a comment deadline of 7 March 2003. The Board received over 240 letters. The Board also worked with the FASB after that body added to its agenda a project to review US accounting requirements on share-based payment. This included participating in meetings of the FASB's Option Valuation Group and meeting the FASB to discuss convergence issues.

Scope

BC7 Much of the controversy and complexity surrounding the accounting for share-based payment relates to employee share options. However, the scope of IFRS 2 is broader than that. It applies to transactions in which shares or other equity instruments are granted to employees. It also applies to transactions with parties other than employees, in which goods or services are received as consideration for the issue of shares, share options or other equity instruments. The term 'goods' includes inventories, consumables, property, plant and equipment, intangible assets and other non-financial assets. Lastly, the IFRS applies to payments in cash (or other assets) that are 'share-based' because the amount of the payment is based on the price of the entity's shares or other equity instruments, eg cash share appreciation rights.

Broad-based employee share plans, including employee share purchase plans

BC8 Some employee share plans are described as 'broad-based' or 'all-employee' plans, in which all (or virtually all) employees have the opportunity to participate, whereas other plans are more selective, covering individual or specific groups of employees (eg senior executives). Employee share purchase plans are often broad-based plans. Typically, employee share purchase plans provide employees with an opportunity to buy a specific number of shares at a discounted price, ie at an amount that is less than the fair value of the shares. The employee's entitlement to discounted shares is usually conditional upon specific conditions being satisfied, such as remaining in the service of the entity for a specified period.

BC9 The issues that arise with respect to employee share purchase plans are:

(a) are these plans somehow so different from other employee share plans that a different accounting treatment is appropriate?

(b) even if the answer to the above question is 'no', are there circumstances, such as when the discount is very small, when it is appropriate to exempt employee share purchase plans from an accounting standard on share-based payment?

BC10 Some respondents to ED 2 argued that broad-based employee share plans should be exempt from an accounting standard on share-based payment. The reason usually given was that these plans are different from other types of employee share plans and, in particular, are not a part of remuneration for employee services. Some argued that requiring the recognition of an expense in respect of these types of plans was perceived to be contrary to government policy to encourage employee share ownership. In contrast, other respondents saw no difference between employee share purchase plans and other employee share plans, and argued that the same accounting requirements should therefore apply. However, some suggested that there should be an exemption if the discount is small.

BC11 The Board concluded that, in principle, there is no reason to treat broad-based employee share plans, including broad-based employee share purchase plans, differently from other employee share plans (the issue of 'small' discounts is considered later). The Board noted that the fact that these schemes are available only to employees is in itself sufficient to conclude that the benefits provided represent employee remuneration. Moreover, the term 'remuneration' is not limited to remuneration provided as part of an individual employee's contract: it encompasses all benefits provided to employees. Similarly, the term services encompasses all benefits provided by the employees in return, including increased productivity, commitment or other enhancements in employee work performance as a result of the incentives provided by the share plan.

BC12 Moreover, distinguishing regular employee services from the additional benefits received from broad-based employee share plans would not change the conclusion that it is necessary to account for such plans. No matter what label is placed on the benefits provided by employees–or the benefits provided by the entity–the transaction should be recognised in the financial statements.

BC13 Furthermore, that governments in some countries have a policy of encouraging employee share ownership is not a valid reason for according these types of plans a different accounting treatment, because it is not the role of financial reporting to give favourable accounting treatment to particular transactions to encourage entities to enter into them. For example, governments might wish to encourage entities to provide pensions to their employees, to lessen the future burden on the state, but that does not mean that pension costs should be excluded from the financial statements. To do so would impair the quality of financial reporting. The purpose of financial reporting is to provide information to users of financial statements, to assist them in making economic decisions. The omission of expenses from the financial statements does not change the fact that those expenses have been incurred. The omission of expenses causes reported profits to be overstated and hence the financial statements are not neutral, are less transparent and comparable, and are potentially misleading to users.

BC14 There remains the question whether there should be an exemption for some plans, when the discount is small. For example, FASB Statement of Financial Accounting Standards No. 123 *Accounting for Stock-Based Compensation* contains an exemption for employee share purchase plans that meet specified criteria, of which one is that the discount is small.

BC15 On the one hand, it seems reasonable to exempt an employee share purchase plan if it has substantially no option features and the discount is small. In such situations, the rights given to the employees under the plan probably do not have a significant value, from the entity's perspective.

BC16 On the other hand, even if one accepts that an exemption is appropriate, specifying its scope is problematic, eg deciding what constitutes a small discount. Some argue that a 5 per cent discount from the market price (as specified in SFAS 123) is too high, noting that a block of shares can be sold on the market at a price close to the current share price. Furthermore, it could be argued that it is unnecessary to exempt these plans from the standard. If the rights given to the employees do not have a significant value, this suggests that the amounts involved are immaterial. Because it is not necessary to include immaterial information in the financial statements, there is no need for a specific exclusion in an accounting standard.

BC17 For the reasons given in the preceding paragraph, the Board concluded that broad-based employee share plans, including broad-based employee share purchase plans, should not be exempted from the IFRS.

BC18 However, the Board noted that there might be instances when an entity engages in a transaction with an employee in his/her capacity as a holder of equity instruments, rather than in his/her capacity as an employee. For example, an entity might grant all holders of a particular class of its equity instruments the right to acquire additional equity instruments of the entity at a price that is less than the fair value of those equity instruments. If an employee receives such a right because he/she is a holder of that particular class of equity instruments, the Board concluded that the granting or exercise of that right should not be subject to the requirements of the IFRS, because the employee has received that right in his/her capacity as a shareholder, rather than as an employee.

Transfers of equity instruments to employees

BC19 In some situations, an entity might not issue shares or share options to employees (or other parties) direct. Instead, a shareholder (or shareholders) might transfer equity instruments to the employees (or other parties).

BC20 Under this arrangement, the entity has received services (or goods) that were paid for by its shareholders. The arrangement could be viewed as being, in substance, two transactions—one transaction in which the entity has reacquired equity instruments for nil consideration, and a second transaction in which the entity has received services (or goods) as consideration for equity instruments issued to the employees (or other parties).

BC21 The second transaction is a share-based payment transaction. Therefore, the Board concluded that the entity should account for transfers of equity instruments by shareholders to employees or other parties in the same way as other share-based payment transactions. The Board reached the same conclusion with respect to transfers of equity instruments of the entity's parent, or of another entity within the same group as the entity, to the entity's employees or other suppliers.

BC22 However, such a transfer is not a share-based payment transaction if the transfer of equity instruments to an employee or other party is clearly for a purpose other than payment for goods or services supplied to the entity. This would be the case, for example, if the transfer is to settle a shareholder's personal obligation to an employee that is unrelated to employment by the entity, or if the shareholder and employee are related and the transfer is a personal gift because of that relationship.

Transactions within the scope of IFRS 3 *Business Combinations*

BC23 An entity might acquire goods (or other non-financial assets) as part of the net assets acquired in a business combination for which the consideration paid included shares or other equity instruments issued by the entity. Because IFRS 3 applies to the acquisition of assets and issue of shares in connection with a business combination, that is the more specific standard that should be applied to that transaction.

BC24 Therefore, equity instruments issued in a business combination in exchange for control of the acquiree are not within the scope of IFRS 2. However, equity instruments granted to employees of the acquiree in their capacity as employees, eg in return for continued service, are within the scope of IFRS 2. Also, the cancellation, replacement, or other modifications to share-based payment arrangements because of a business combination or other equity restructuring should be accounted for in accordance with IFRS 2.

Transactions within the scope of IAS 32 *Financial Instruments: Disclosure and Presentation* and IAS 39 *Financial Instruments: Recognition and Measurement*

BC25 The IFRS includes consequential amendments to IAS 32 and IAS 39 (both as revised in 2003) to exclude from their scope transactions within the scope of IFRS 2.

BC26 For example, suppose the entity enters into a contract to purchase cloth for use in its clothing manufacturing business, whereby it is required to pay cash to the counterparty in an amount equal to the value of 1,000 of the entity's shares at the date of delivery of the cloth. The entity will acquire goods and pay cash at an amount based on its share price. This meets the definition of a share-based payment transaction. Moreover, because the contract is to purchase cloth, which is a non-financial item, and the contract was entered into for the purpose of taking delivery of the cloth for use in the entity's manufacturing business, the contract is not within the scope of IAS 32 and IAS 39.

BC27 The scope of IAS 32 and IAS 39 includes contracts to buy non-financial items that can be settled net in cash or another financial instrument, or by exchanging financial instruments, with the exception of contracts that were entered into and continue to be held for the purpose of the receipt or delivery of a non-financial item in accordance with the entity's expected purchase, sale or usage requirements. A contract that can be settled net in cash or another financial instrument or by exchanging financial instruments includes (a) when the terms of the contract permit either party to settle it net in cash or another financial instrument or by exchanging financial instruments; (b) when the ability to settle net in cash or another financial instrument, or by exchanging financial instruments, is not explicit in the terms of the contract, but the entity has a practice of settling similar contracts net in cash or another financial instrument, or by exchanging financial instruments (whether with the counterparty, by entering into offsetting contracts, or by selling the contract before its exercise or lapse); (c) when, for similar contracts, the entity has a practice of taking delivery of the underlying and selling it within a short period after delivery for the purpose of generating a profit from short-term fluctuations in price or dealer's margin; and (d) when the non-financial item that is the subject of the contract is readily convertible to cash (IAS 32, paragraphs 8–10 and IAS 39, paragraphs 5–7).

BC28 The Board concluded that the contracts discussed in paragraph BC27 should remain within the scope of IAS 32 and IAS 39 and they are therefore excluded from the scope of IFRS 2.

Recognition of equity-settled share-based payment transactions

BC29 When it developed ED 2, the Board first considered conceptual arguments relating to the recognition of an expense arising from equity-settled share-based payment transactions, including arguments advanced by respondents to the Discussion Paper and other commentators. Some respondents who disagreed with the recognition of an expense arising from particular share-based payment transactions (ie those involving employee share options) did so for practical, rather than conceptual, reasons. The Board considered those practical issues later (see paragraphs BC294–BC310).

BC30 The Board focused its discussions on employee share options, because that is where most of the complexity and controversy lies, but the question of whether expense recognition is appropriate is broader than that–it covers all transactions involving the issue of shares, share options or other equity instruments to employees or suppliers of goods and services. For example, the Board noted that arguments made by respondents and other commentators against expense recognition are directed solely at employee share options. However, if conceptual arguments made against recognition of an expense in relation to employee share options are valid (eg that there is no cost to the entity), those arguments ought to apply equally to transactions involving other equity instruments (eg shares) and to equity instruments issued to other parties (eg suppliers of professional services).

BC31 The rationale for recognising all types of share-based payment transactions–irrespective of whether the equity instrument is a share or a share option, and irrespective of whether the equity instrument is granted to an employee or to some other party–is that the entity has engaged in a transaction that is in essence the same as any other issue of equity instruments. In other words, the entity has received resources (goods or services) as consideration for the issue of shares, share options or other equity instruments. It should therefore account for the inflow of resources (goods or services) and the increase in equity. Subsequently, either at the time of receipt of the goods or services or at some later date, the entity should also account for the expense arising from the consumption of those resources.

BC32 Many respondents to ED 2 agreed with this conclusion. Of those who disagreed, some disagreed in principle, some disagreed for practical reasons, and some disagreed for both reasons. The arguments against expense recognition in principle were considered by the Board when it developed ED 2, as were the arguments against expense recognition for practical reasons, as explained below and in paragraphs BC294–BC310.

BC33 Arguments commonly made against expense recognition include:

(a) the transaction is between the shareholders and the employees, not the entity and the employees.

(b) the employees do not provide services for the options.

(c) there is no cost to the entity, because no cash or other assets are given up; the shareholders bear the cost, in the form of dilution of their ownership interests, not the entity.

(d) the recognition of an expense is inconsistent with the definition of an expense in the conceptual frameworks used by accounting standard-setters, including the IASB's *Framework for the Preparation and Presentation of Financial Statements*.

(e) the cost borne by the shareholders is recognised in the dilution of earnings per share (EPS); if the transaction is recognised in the entity's accounts, the resulting charge to the income statement would mean that EPS is 'hit twice'.

(f) requiring the recognition of a charge would have adverse economic consequences, because it would discourage entities from introducing or continuing employee share plans.

'The entity is not a party to the transaction'

BC34 Some argue that the effect of employee share plans is that the existing shareholders transfer some of their ownership interests to the employees and that the entity is not a party to this transaction.

BC35 The Board did not accept this argument. Entities, not shareholders, set up employee share plans and entities, not shareholders, issue share options to their employees. Even if that were not the case, eg if shareholders transferred shares or share options direct to the employees, this would not mean that the entity is not a party to the transaction. The equity instruments are issued in return for services rendered by the employees and the entity, not the shareholders, receives those services. Therefore, the Board concluded that the entity should account for the services received in return for the equity instruments issued. The Board noted that this is no different from other situations in which equity instruments are issued. For example, if an entity issues warrants for cash, the entity recognises the cash received in return for the warrants issued. Although the effect of an issue, and subsequent exercise, of warrants might be described as a transfer of ownership interests from the existing shareholders to the warrant holders, the entity nevertheless is a party to the transaction because it receives resources (cash) for the issue of warrants and further resources (cash) for the issue of shares upon exercise of the warrants. Similarly, with employee share options, the entity receives resources (employee services) for the issue of the options and further resources (cash) for the issue of shares on the exercise of options.

'The employees do not provide services'

BC36 Some who argue that the entity is not a party to the transaction counter the points made above with the argument that employees do not provide services for the options, because the employees are paid in cash (or other assets) for their services.

BC37 Again, the Board was not convinced by this argument. If it were true that employees do not provide services for their share options, this would mean that entities are issuing valuable share options and getting nothing in return. Employees do not pay cash for the share options they receive. Hence, if they do not provide services for the options, the employees are providing nothing in return. If this were true, by issuing such options the entity's directors would be in breach of their fiduciary duties to their shareholders.

BC38 Typically, shares or share options granted to employees form one part of their remuneration package. For example, an employee might have a remuneration package consisting of a basic cash salary, company car, pension, healthcare benefits, and other benefits including shares and share options. It is usually not possible to identify the services received in respect of individual components of that remuneration package, eg the services received in respect of healthcare benefits. But that does not mean that the employee does not provide services for those healthcare benefits. Rather, the employee provides services for the entire remuneration package.

BC39 In summary, shares, share options or other equity instruments are granted to employees because they are employees. The equity instruments granted form a part of their total remuneration package, regardless of whether that represents a large part or a small part.

'There is no cost to the entity, therefore there is no expense'

BC40 Some argue that because share-based payments do not require the entity to sacrifice any cash or other assets, there is no cost to the entity, and therefore no expense should be recognised.

BC41 The Board regards this argument as unsound, because it overlooks that:

(a) every time an entity receives resources as consideration for the issue of equity instruments, there is no outflow of cash or other assets, and on every other occasion the resources received as consideration for the issue of equity instruments are recognised in the financial statements; and

(b) the expense arises from the consumption of those resources, not from an outflow of assets.

BC42 In other words, irrespective of whether one accepts that there is a cost to the entity, an accounting entry is required to recognise the resources received as consideration for the issue of equity instruments, just as it is on other occasions when equity instruments are issued. For example, when shares are issued for cash, an entry is required to recognise the cash received. If a non-monetary asset, such as plant and machinery, is received for those shares instead of cash, an entry is required to recognise the asset received. If the entity acquires another business or entity by issuing shares in a business combination, the entity recognises the net assets acquired.

BC43 The recognition of an expense arising out of such a transaction represents the consumption of resources received, ie the 'using up' of the resources received for the shares or share options. In the case of the plant and machinery mentioned above, the asset would be depreciated over its expected life, resulting in the recognition of an expense each year. Eventually, the entire amount recognised for the resources received when the shares were issued would be recognised as an expense (including any residual value, which would form part of the measurement of the gain or loss on disposal of the asset). Similarly, if another business or entity is acquired by an issue of shares, an expense is recognised when the assets acquired are consumed. For example, inventories acquired will be recognised as an expense when sold, even though no cash or other assets were disbursed to acquire those inventories.

BC44 The only difference in the case of employee services (or other services) received as consideration for the issue of shares or share options is that usually the resources received are consumed immediately upon receipt. This means that an expense for the consumption of resources is recognised immediately, rather than over a period of time. The Board concluded that the timing of consumption does not change the principle; the financial statements should recognise the receipt and consumption of resources, even when consumption occurs at the same time as, or soon after, receipt. This point is discussed further in paragraphs BC45-BC53.

'Expense recognition is inconsistent with the definition of an expense'

BC45 Some have questioned whether recognition of an expense arising from particular share-based payment transactions is consistent with accounting standard-setters' conceptual frameworks, in particular, the *Framework*, which states:

> Expenses are decreases in economic benefits during the accounting period in the form of outflows or *depletions of assets* or incurrences of liabilities that result in decreases in equity, other than those relating to distributions to equity participants. (paragraph 70, emphasis added)

BC46 Some argue that if services are received in a share-based payment transaction, there is no transaction or event that meets the definition of an expense. They contend that there is no outflow of assets and that no liability is incurred. Furthermore, because services usually do not meet the criteria for recognition as an asset, it is argued that the consumption of those services does not represent a depletion of assets.

BC47 The *Framework* defines an asset and explains that the term 'asset' is not limited to resources that can be recognised as assets in the balance sheet (*Framework*, paragraphs 49 and 50). Although services to be received in the future might not meet the definition of an asset,* services are assets when received. These assets are usually consumed immediately. This is explained in FASB Statement of Financial Accounting Concepts No. 6 *Elements of Financial Statements*:

> Services provided by other entities, including personal services, cannot be stored and are received and used simultaneously. They can be assets of an entity only momentarily—as the entity receives and uses them—although their use may create or add value to other assets of the entity... (paragraph 31)

BC48 This applies to all types of services, eg employee services, legal services and telephone services. It also applies irrespective of the form of payment. For example, if an entity purchases services for cash, the accounting entry is:

Dr Services Received

Cr Cash paid

BC49 Sometimes, those services are consumed in the creation of a recognisable asset, such as inventories, in which case the debit for services received is capitalised as part of a recognised asset. But often the services do not create or form part of a recognisable asset, in which case the debit for services received is charged immediately to the income statement as an expense. The debit entry above (and the resulting expense) does not represent the cash outflow—that is what the credit entry was for. Nor does it represent some sort of balancing item, to make the accounts balance. The debit entry above represents the resources received, and the resulting expense represents the consumption of those resources.

* For example, the entity might not have control over future services.

BC50 The same analysis applies if the services are acquired with payment made in shares or share options. The resulting expense represents the consumption of services, ie a depletion of assets.

BC51 To illustrate this point, suppose that an entity has two buildings, both with gas heating, and the entity issues shares to the gas supplier instead of paying cash. Suppose that, for one building, the gas is supplied through a pipeline, and so is consumed immediately upon receipt. Suppose that, for the other building, the gas is supplied in bottles, and is consumed over a period of time. In both cases, the entity has received assets as consideration for the issue of equity instruments, and should therefore recognise the assets received, and a corresponding contribution to equity. If the assets are consumed immediately (the gas received through the pipeline), an expense is recognised immediately; if the assets are consumed later (the gas received in bottles), an expense is recognised later when the assets are consumed.

BC52 Therefore, the Board concluded that the recognition of an expense arising from share-based payment transactions is consistent with the definition of an expense in the *Framework*.

BC53 The FASB considered the same issue and reached the same conclusion in SFAS 123:

> Some respondents pointed out that the definition of expenses in FASB Concepts Statement No. 6, *Elements of Financial Statements*, says that expenses result from outflows or using up of assets or incurring of liabilities (or both). They asserted that because the issuance of stock options does not result in the incurrence of a liability, no expense should be recognised. The Board agrees that employee stock options are not a liability–like stock purchase warrants, employee stock options are equity instruments of the issuer. However, equity instruments, including employee stock options, are valuable financial instruments and thus are issued for valuable consideration, which...for employee stock options is employee services. Using in the entity's operations the benefits embodied in the asset received results in an expense... (Concepts Statement 6, paragraph 81, footnote 43, notes that, in concept most expenses decrease assets. However, if receipt of an asset, such as services, and its use occur virtually simultaneously, the asset often is not recorded.) [paragraph 88]

'Earnings per share is "hit twice"'

BC54 Some argue that any cost arising from share-based payment transactions is already recognised in the dilution of earnings per share (EPS). If an expense were recognised in the income statement, EPS would be 'hit twice'.

BC55 However, the Board noted that this result is appropriate. For example, if the entity paid the employees in cash for their services and the cash was then returned to the entity, as consideration for the issue of share options, the effect on EPS would be the same as issuing those options direct to the employees.

BC56 The dual effect on EPS simply reflects the two economic events that have occurred: the entity has issued shares or share options, thereby increasing the number of shares included in the EPS calculation–although, in the case of options, only to the extent that the options are regarded as dilutive–and it has also consumed the resources it received for those options, thereby decreasing earnings. This is illustrated by the plant and machinery example mentioned in paragraphs BC42 and BC43. Issuing shares affects the number of shares in the EPS calculation, and the consumption (depreciation) of the asset affects earnings.

BC57 In summary, the Board concluded that the dual effect on diluted EPS is not double-counting the effects of a share or share option grant—the same effect is not counted twice. Rather, two different effects are each counted once.

'Adverse economic consequences'

BC58 Some argue that to require recognition (or greater recognition) of employee share-based payment would have adverse economic consequences, in that it might discourage entities from introducing or continuing employee share plans.

BC59 Others argue that if the introduction of accounting changes did lead to a reduction in the use of employee share plans, it might be because the requirement for entities to account properly for employee share plans had revealed the economic consequences of such plans. They argue that this would correct the present economic distortion, whereby entities obtain and consume resources by issuing valuable shares or share options without accounting for those transactions.

BC60 In any event, the Board noted that the role of accounting is to report transactions and events in a neutral manner, not to give 'favourable' treatment to particular transactions to encourage entities to engage in those transactions. To do so would impair the quality of financial reporting. The omission of expenses from the financial statements does not change the fact that those expenses have been incurred. Hence, if expenses are omitted from the income statement, reported profits are overstated. The financial statements are not neutral, are less transparent and are potentially misleading to users. Comparability is impaired, given that expenses arising from employee share-based payment transactions vary from entity to entity, from sector to sector, and from year to year. More fundamentally, accountability is impaired, because the entities are not accounting for transactions they have entered into and the consequences of those transactions.

Measurement of equity-settled share-based payment transactions

BC61 To recognise equity-settled share-based payment transactions, it is necessary to decide how the transactions should be measured. The Board began by considering how to measure share-based payment transactions in principle. Later, it considered practical issues arising from the application of its preferred measurement approach. In terms of accounting principles, there are two basic questions:

(a) which measurement basis should be applied?

(b) when should that measurement basis be applied?

BC62 To answer these questions, the Board considered the accounting principles applying to equity transactions. The *Framework* states:

> Equity is the residual interest in the assets of the enterprise after deducting all of its liabilities...The amount at which equity is shown in the balance sheet is dependent upon the measurement of assets and liabilities. Normally, the aggregate amount of equity only by coincidence corresponds with the aggregate market value of the shares of the enterprise... (paragraphs 49 and 67)

BC63 The accounting equation that corresponds to this definition of equity is:

> assets minus liabilities equals equity

BC64 Equity is a residual interest, dependent on the measurement of assets and liabilities. Therefore, accounting focuses on recording changes in the left side of the equation (assets minus liabilities, or net assets), rather than the right side. Changes in equity arise from changes in net assets. For example, if an entity issues shares for cash, it recognises the cash received and a corresponding increase in equity. Subsequent changes in the market price of the shares do not affect the entity's net assets and therefore those changes in value are not recognised.

BC65 Hence, the Board concluded that, when accounting for an equity-settled share-based payment transaction, the primary accounting objective is to account for the goods or services received as consideration for the issue of equity instruments. Therefore, equity-settled share-based payment transactions should be accounted for in the same way as other issues of equity instruments, by recognising the consideration received (the change in net assets), and a corresponding increase in equity.

BC66 Given this objective, the Board concluded that, in principle, the goods or services received should be measured at their fair value at the date when the entity obtains those goods or as the services are received. In other words, because a change in net assets occurs when the entity obtains the goods or as the services are received, the fair value of those goods or services at that date provides an appropriate measure of the change in net assets.

BC67 However, for share-based payment transactions with employees, it is usually difficult to measure directly the fair value of the services received. As noted earlier, typically shares or share options are granted to employees as one component of their remuneration package. It is usually not possible to identify the services rendered in respect of individual components of that package. It might also not be possible to measure independently the fair value of the total package, without measuring directly the fair value of the equity instruments granted. Furthermore, options or shares are sometimes granted as part of a bonus arrangement, rather than as a part of basic remuneration, eg as an incentive to the employees to remain in the entity's employ, or to reward them for their efforts in improving the entity's performance. By granting share options, in addition to other remuneration, the entity is paying additional remuneration to obtain additional benefits. Estimating the fair value of those additional benefits is likely to be difficult.

BC68 Given these practical difficulties in measuring directly the fair value of the employee services received, the Board concluded that it is necessary to measure the other side of the transaction, ie the fair value of the equity instruments granted, as a surrogate measure of the fair value of the services received. In this context, the Board considered the same basic questions, as mentioned above:

(a) which measurement basis should be applied?

(b) when should that measurement basis be applied?

Measurement basis

BC69 The Board discussed the following measurement bases, to decide which should be applied in principle:

(a) historical cost

(b) intrinsic value

(c) minimum value

(d) fair value.

Historical cost

BC70 In jurisdictions where legislation permits, entities commonly repurchase their own shares, either directly or through a vehicle such as a trust, which are used to fulfil promised grants of shares to employees or the exercise of employee share options. A possible basis for measuring a grant of options or shares would be the historical cost (purchase price) of its own shares that an entity holds (own shares held), even if they were acquired before the award was made.

BC71 For share options, this would entail comparing the historical cost of own shares held with the exercise price of options granted to employees. Any shortfall would be recognised as an expense. Also, presumably, if the exercise price exceeded the historical cost of own shares held, the excess would be recognised as a gain.

BC72 At first sight, if one simply focuses on the cash flows involved, the historical cost basis appears reasonable: there is a cash outflow to acquire the shares, followed by a cash inflow when those shares are transferred to the employees (the exercise price), with any shortfall representing a cost to the entity. If the cash flows related to anything other than the entity's own shares, this approach would be appropriate. For example, suppose ABC Ltd bought shares in another entity, XYZ Ltd, for a total cost of CU500,000,* and later sold the shares to employees for a total of CU400,000. The entity would recognise an expense for the CU100,000 shortfall.

* All monetary amounts in this Basis for Conclusions are denominated in 'currency units' (CU).

BC73 But when this analysis is applied to the entity's own shares, the logic breaks down. The entity's own shares are not an asset of the entity.* Rather, the shares are an interest in the entity's assets. Hence, the distribution of cash to buy back shares is a return of capital to shareholders, and should therefore be recognised as a decrease in equity. Similarly, when the shares are subsequently reissued or transferred, the inflow of cash is an increase in shareholders' capital, and should therefore be recognised as an increase in equity. It follows that no revenue or expense should be recognised. Just as the issue of shares does not represent revenue to the entity, the repurchase of those shares does not represent an expense.

BC74 Therefore, the Board concluded that historical cost is not an appropriate basis upon which to measure equity-settled share-based payment transactions.

Intrinsic value

BC75 An equity instrument could be measured at its intrinsic value. The intrinsic value of a share option at any point in time is the difference between the market price of the underlying shares and the exercise price of the option.

BC76 Often, employee share options have zero intrinsic value at the date of grant—commonly the exercise price is at the market value of the shares at grant date. Therefore, in many cases, valuing share options at their intrinsic value at grant date is equivalent to attributing no value to the options.

BC77 However, the intrinsic value of an option does not fully reflect its value. Options sell in the market for more than their intrinsic value. This is because the holder of an option need not exercise it immediately and benefits from any increase in the value of the underlying shares. In other words, although the ultimate benefit realised by the option holder is the option's intrinsic value at the date of exercise, the option holder is able to realise that future intrinsic value because of having held the option. Thus, the option holder benefits from the right to participate in future gains from increases in the share price. In addition, the option holder benefits from the right to defer payment of the exercise price until the end of the option term. These benefits are commonly referred to as the option's 'time value'.

BC78 For many options, time value represents a substantial part of their value. As noted earlier, many employee share options have zero intrinsic value at grant date, and hence the option's value consists entirely of time value. In such cases, ignoring time value by applying the intrinsic value method at grant date understates the value of the option by 100 per cent.

---

* The Discussion Paper discusses this point: Accounting practice in some jurisdictions may present own shares acquired as an asset, but they lack the essential feature of an asset—the ability to provide future economic benefits. The future economic benefits usually provided by an interest in shares are the right to receive dividends and the right to gain from an increase in value of the shares. When a company has an interest in its own shares, it will receive dividends on those shares only if it elects to pay them, and such dividends do not represent a gain to the company, as there is no change in net assets: the flow of funds is simply circular. Whilst it is true that a company that holds its own shares in treasury may sell them and receive a higher amount if their value has increased, a company is generally able to issue shares to third parties at (or near) the current market price. Although there may be legal, regulatory or administrative reasons why it is easier to sell shares that are held as treasury shares than it would be to issue new shares, such considerations do not seem to amount to a fundamental contrast between the two cases. (Footnote to paragraph 4.7)

BC79 The Board concluded that, in general, the intrinsic value measurement basis is not appropriate for measuring share-based payment transactions, because omitting the option's time value ignores a potentially substantial part of an option's total value. Measuring share-based payment transactions at such an understated value would fail to represent those transactions faithfully in the financial statements.

Minimum value

BC80 A share option could be measured at its minimum value. Minimum value is based on the premise that someone who wants to buy a call option on a share would be willing to pay at least (and the option writer would demand at least) the value of the right to defer payment of the exercise price until the end of the option's term. Therefore, minimum value can be calculated using a present value technique. For a dividend-paying share, the calculation is:

(a) the current price of the share, minus

(b) the present value of expected dividends on that share during the option term (if the option holder does not receive dividends), minus

(c) the present value of the exercise price.

BC81 Minimum value can also be calculated using an option pricing model with an expected volatility of effectively zero (not exactly zero, because some option pricing models use volatility as a divisor, and zero cannot be a divisor).

BC82 The minimum value measurement basis captures part of the time value of options, being the value of the right to defer payment of the exercise price until the end of the option's term. It does not capture the effects of volatility. Option holders benefit from volatility because they have the right to participate in gains from increases in the share price during the option term without having to bear the full risk of loss from decreases in the share price. By ignoring volatility, the minimum value method produces a value that is lower, and often much lower, than values produced by methods designed to estimate the fair value of an option.

BC83 The Board concluded that minimum value is not an appropriate measurement basis, because ignoring the effects of volatility ignores a potentially large part of an option's value. As with intrinsic value, measuring share-based payment transactions at the option's minimum value would fail to represent those transactions faithfully in the financial statements.

Fair value

BC84 Fair value is already used in other areas of accounting, including other transactions in which non-cash resources are acquired through the issue of equity instruments. For example, a business acquisition is measured at the fair value of the consideration given, including the fair value of any equity instruments issued by the entity.

BC85 Fair value, which is the amount at which an equity instrument granted could be exchanged between knowledgeable, willing parties in an arm's length transaction, captures both intrinsic value and time value and therefore provides a measure of the share option's total value (unlike intrinsic value or minimum value). It is the value that reflects the bargain between the entity and its employees, whereby the entity has agreed to grant share options to employees for their services to the entity. Hence, measuring share-based payment transactions at fair value ensures that those transactions are represented faithfully in the financial statements, and consistently with other transactions in which the entity receives resources as consideration for the issue of equity instruments.

BC86 Therefore, the Board concluded that shares, share options or other equity instruments granted should be measured at their fair value.

BC87 Of the respondents to ED 2 who addressed this issue, many agreed with the proposal to measure the equity instruments granted at their fair value. Some respondents who disagreed with the proposal, or who agreed with reservations, expressed concerns about measurement reliability, particularly in the case of smaller or unlisted entities. The issues of measurement reliability and unlisted entities are discussed in paragraphs BC294–BC310 and BC137–BC144, respectively.

Measurement date

BC88 The Board first considered at which date the fair value of equity instruments should be determined for the purpose of measuring share-based payment transactions with employees (and others providing similar services).[*] The possible measurement dates discussed were grant date, service date, vesting date and exercise date. Much of this discussion was in the context of share options rather than shares or other equity instruments, because only options have an exercise date.

BC89 In the context of an employee share option, grant date is when the entity and the employee enter into an agreement, whereby the employee is granted rights to the share option, provided that specified conditions are met, such as the employee's remaining in the entity's employ for a specified period. Service date is the date when the employee renders the services necessary to become entitled to the share option.[†] Vesting date is the date when the employee has satisfied all the conditions necessary to become entitled to the share option. For example, if the employee is required to remain in the entity's employ for three years, vesting date is at the end of that three-year period. Exercise date is when the share option is exercised.

* When the Board developed the proposals in ED 2, it focused on the measurement of equity-settled transactions with employees and with parties other than employees. ED 2 did not propose a definition of the term 'employees'. When the Board reconsidered the proposals in ED 2 in the light of comments received, it discussed whether the term might be interpreted too narrowly. This could result in a different accounting treatment of services received from individuals who are regarded as employees (eg for legal or tax purposes) and substantially similar services received from other individuals. The Board therefore concluded that the requirements of the IFRS for transactions with employees should also apply to transactions with other parties providing similar services. This includes services received from (1) individuals who work for the entity under its direction in the same way as individuals who are regarded as employees for legal or tax purposes and (2) individuals who are not employees but who render personal services to the entity similar to those rendered by employees. All references to employees therefore includes other parties providing similar services.

† Service date measurement theoretically requires the entity to measure the fair value of the share option at each date when services are received. For pragmatic reasons, an approximation would probably be used, such as the fair value of the share option at the end of each accounting period, or the value of the share option measured at regular intervals during each accounting period.

BC90 To help determine the appropriate measurement date, the Board applied the accounting concepts in the *Framework* to each side of the transaction. For transactions with employees, the Board concluded that grant date is the appropriate measurement date, as explained in paragraphs BC91–BC105. The Board also considered some other issues, as explained in paragraphs BC106–BC118. For transactions with parties other than employees, the Board concluded that delivery date is the appropriate measurement date (ie the date the goods or services are received, referred to as service date in the context of transactions with employees), as explained in paragraphs BC119–BC128.

The debit side of the transaction

BC91 Focusing on the debit side of the transaction means focusing on measuring the fair value of the resources received. This measurement objective is consistent with the primary objective of accounting for the goods or services received as consideration for the issue of equity instruments (see paragraphs BC64–BC66). The Board therefore concluded that, in principle, the goods or services received should be measured at their fair value at the date when the entity obtains those goods or as the services are received.

BC92 However, if the fair value of the services received is not readily determinable, then a surrogate measure must be used, such as the fair value of the share options or shares granted. This is the case for employee services.

BC93 If the fair value of the equity instruments granted is used as a surrogate measure of the fair value of the services received, both vesting date and exercise date measurement are inappropriate because the fair value of the services received during a particular accounting period is not affected by subsequent changes in the fair value of the equity instrument. For example, suppose that services are received during years 1-3 as the consideration for share options that are exercised at the end of year 5. For services received in year 1, subsequent changes in the value of the share option in years 2-5 are unrelated to, and have no effect on, the fair value of those services when received.

BC94 Service date measurement measures the fair value of the equity instrument at the same time as the services are received. This means that changes in the fair value of the equity instrument during the vesting period affect the amount attributed to the services received. Some argue that this is appropriate, because, in their view, there is a correlation between changes in the fair value of the equity instrument and the fair value of the services received. For example, they argue that if the fair value of a share option falls, so does its incentive effects, which causes employees to reduce the level of services provided for that option, or demand extra remuneration. Some argue that when the fair value of a share option falls because of a general decline in share prices, remuneration levels also fall, and therefore service date measurement reflects this decline in remuneration levels.

BC95 The Board concluded, however, that there is unlikely to be a high correlation between changes in the fair value of an equity instrument and the fair value of the services received. For example, if the fair value of a share option doubles, it is unlikely that the employees work twice as hard, or accept a reduction in the rest of their remuneration package. Similarly, even if a general rise in share prices is accompanied by a rise in remuneration levels, it is unlikely that there is a high correlation between the two. Furthermore, it is likely that any link between share prices and remuneration levels is not universally applicable to all industry sectors.

BC96 The Board concluded that, at grant date, it is reasonable to presume that the fair value of both sides of the contract are substantially the same, ie the fair value of the services expected to be received is substantially the same as the fair value of the equity instruments granted. This conclusion, together with the Board's conclusion that there is unlikely to be a high correlation between the fair value of the services received and the fair value of the equity instruments granted at later measurement dates, led the Board to conclude that grant date is the most appropriate measurement date for the purposes of providing a surrogate measure of the fair value of the services received.

The credit side of the transaction

BC97 Although focusing on the debit side of the transaction is consistent with the primary accounting objective, some approach the measurement date question from the perspective of the credit side of the transaction, ie the issue of an equity instrument. The Board therefore considered the matter from this perspective too.

Exercise date

BC98 Under exercise date measurement, the entity recognises the resources received (eg employee services) for the issue of share options, and also recognises changes in the fair value of the option until it is exercised or lapses. Thus, if the option is exercised, the transaction amount is ultimately 'trued up' to equal the gain made by the option holder on exercise of the option. However, if the option lapses at the end of the exercise period, any amounts previously recognised are effectively reversed, hence the transaction amount is ultimately trued up to equal zero. The Board rejected exercise date measurement because it requires share options to be treated as liabilities, which is inconsistent with the definition of liabilities in the *Framework*. Exercise date measurement requires share options to be treated as liabilities because it requires the remeasurement of share options after initial recognition, which is inappropriate if the share options are equity instruments. A share option does not meet the definition of a liability, because it does not contain an obligation to transfer cash or other assets.

Vesting date, service date and grant date

BC99 The Board noted that the IASC/G4+1 Discussion Paper supported vesting date measurement, and rejected grant date and service date measurement, because it concluded that the share option is not issued until vesting date. It noted that the employees must perform their side of the arrangement by providing the necessary services and meeting any other performance criteria before the entity is obliged to perform its side of the arrangement. The provision of services by the employees is not merely a condition of the arrangement, it is the consideration they use to 'pay' for the share option. Therefore, the Discussion Paper concluded, in economic terms the share option is not issued until vesting date. Because the entity performs its side of the arrangement on vesting date, that is the appropriate measurement date.

BC100 The Discussion Paper also proposed recognising an accrual in equity during the vesting period to ensure that the services are recognised when they are received.

It proposed that this accrual should be revised on vesting date to equal the fair value of the share option at that date. This means that amounts credited to equity during the vesting period will be subsequently remeasured to reflect changes in the value of that equity interest before vesting date. That is inconsistent with the *Framework* because equity interests are not subsequently remeasured, ie any changes in their value are not recognised. The Discussion Paper justified this remeasurement by arguing that because the share option is not issued until vesting date, the option is not being remeasured. The credit to equity during the vesting period is merely an interim measure that is used to recognise the partially completed transaction.

BC101 However, the Board noted that even if one accepts that the share option is not issued until vesting date, this does not mean that there is no equity interest until then. If an equity interest exists before vesting date, that interest should not be remeasured. Moreover, the conversion of one type of equity interest into another should not, in itself, cause a change in total equity, because no change in net assets has occurred.

BC102 Some supporters of vesting date suggest that the accrual during the performance period meets the definition of a liability. However, the basis for this conclusion is unclear. The entity is not required to transfer cash or other assets to the employees. Its only commitment is to issue equity instruments.

BC103 The Board concluded that vesting date measurement is inconsistent with the *Framework*, because it requires the remeasurement of equity.

BC104 Service date measurement does not require remeasurement of equity interests after initial recognition. However, as explained earlier, the Board concluded that incorporating changes in the fair value of the share option into the transaction amount is unlikely to produce an amount that fairly reflects the fair value of the services received, which is the primary objective.

BC105 The Board therefore concluded that, no matter which side of the transaction one focuses upon (ie the receipt of resources or the issue of an equity instrument), grant date is the appropriate measurement date under the *Framework*, because it does not require remeasurement of equity interests and it provides a reasonable surrogate measure of the fair value of the services received from employees.

Other issues

IAS 32 Financial Instruments: Disclosure and Presentation

BC106 As discussed above, under the definitions of liabilities and equity in the *Framework*, both shares and share options are equity instruments, because neither instrument requires the entity to transfer cash or other assets. Similarly, all contracts or arrangements that will be settled by the entity issuing shares or share options are classified as equity. However, this differs from the distinction between liabilities and equity applied in IAS 32. Although IAS 32 also considers, in its debt/equity distinction, whether an instrument contains an obligation to transfer cash or other assets, this is supplemented by a second criterion, which considers whether the number of shares to be issued (and cash to be received) on settlement is fixed or variable. IAS 32 classifies a contract that will or may be settled in the entity's own equity instruments as a liability if the contract is a non-derivative for which the entity is or may be obliged to deliver a variable number of the entity's own equity instruments; or a derivative that will or may be settled other than by the exchange of a fixed amount of cash or another financial asset for a fixed number of the entity's own equity instruments.

BC107 In some cases, the number of share options to which employees are entitled varies. For example, the number of share options to which the employees will be entitled on vesting date might vary depending on whether, and to the extent that, a particular performance target is exceeded. Another example is share appreciation rights settled in shares. In this situation, a variable number of shares will be issued, equal in value to the appreciation of the entity's share price over a period of time.

BC108 Therefore, if the requirements of IAS 32 were applied to equity-settled share-based payment transactions, in some situations an obligation to issue equity instruments would be classified as a liability. In such cases, final measurement of the transaction would be at a measurement date later than grant date.

BC109 The Board concluded that different considerations applied in developing IFRS 2. For example, drawing a distinction between fixed and variable option plans and requiring a later measurement date for variable option plans has undesirable consequences, as discussed in paragraphs BC272–BC275.

BC110 The Board concluded that the requirements in IAS 32, whereby some obligations to issue equity instruments are classified as liabilities, should not be applied in the IFRS on share-based payment. The Board recognises that this creates a difference between IFRS 2 and IAS 32. Before deciding whether and how that difference should be eliminated, the Board concluded that it is necessary to address this issue in a broader context, as part of a fundamental review of the definitions of liabilities and equity in the *Framework*, particularly because this is not the only debt/equity classification issue that has arisen in the share-based payment project, as explained below.

Suggestions to change the definitions of liabilities and equity

BC111 In concluding that, for transactions with employees, grant date is the appropriate measurement date under the *Framework*, the Board noted that some respondents to ED 2 and the Discussion Paper support other measurement dates because they believe that the definitions of liabilities and equity in the *Framework* should be revised.

BC112 For example, some supporters of vesting date argue that receipt of employee services between grant date and vesting date creates an obligation for the entity to pay for those services, and that the method of settlement should not matter. In other words, it should not matter whether that obligation is settled in cash or in equity instruments—both ought to be treated as liabilities. Therefore, the definition of a liability should be modified so that all types of obligations, however settled, are included in liabilities. But it is not clear that this approach would necessarily result in vesting date measurement. A share option contains an obligation to issue shares. Hence, if all types of obligations are classified as liabilities, then a share option would be a liability, which would result in exercise date measurement.

BC113 Some support exercise date measurement on the grounds that it produces the same accounting result as 'economically similar' cash-settled share-based payments. For example, it is argued that share appreciation rights (SARs) settled in cash are substantially similar to SARs settled in shares, because in both cases the employee receives consideration to the same value. Also, if the SARs are settled in shares and the shares are immediately sold, the employee ends up in exactly the same position as under a cash-settled SAR, ie with cash equal to the appreciation in the entity's share price over the specified period. Similarly, some argue that share options and cash-settled SARs are economically similar. This is particularly true when the employee realises the gain on the exercise of share options by selling the shares immediately after exercise, as commonly occurs. Either way, the employee ends up with an amount of cash that is based on the appreciation of the share price over a period of time. If cash-settled transactions and equity-settled transactions are economically similar, the accounting treatment should be the same.

BC114 However, it is not clear that changing the distinction between liabilities and equity to be consistent with exercise date measurement is the only way to achieve the same accounting treatment. For example, the distinction could be changed so that cash-settled employee share plans are measured at grant date, with the subsequent cash payment debited directly to equity, as a distribution to equity participants.

BC115 Others who support exercise date measurement do not regard share option holders as part of the ownership group, and therefore believe that options should not be classified as equity. Option holders, some argue, are only potential owners of the entity. But it is not clear whether this view is held generally, ie applied to all types of options. For example, some who support exercise date measurement for employee share options do not necessarily advocate the same approach for share options or warrants issued for cash in the market. However, any revision to the definitions of liabilities and equity in the *Framework* would affect the classification of all options and warrants issued by the entity.

BC116 Given that there is more than one suggestion to change the definitions of liabilities and equity, and these suggestions have not been fully explored, it is not clear exactly what changes to the definitions are being proposed.

BC117 Moreover, the Board concluded that these suggestions should not be considered in isolation, because changing the distinction between liabilities and equity affects all sorts of financial interests, not just those relating to employee share plans. All of the implications of any suggested changes should be explored in a broader project to review the definitions of liabilities and equity in the *Framework*. If such a review resulted in changes to the definitions, the Board would then consider whether the IFRS on share-based payment should be revised.

BC118 Therefore, after considering the issues discussed above, the Board confirmed its conclusion that grant date is the appropriate date at which to measure the fair value of the equity instruments granted for the purposes of providing a surrogate measure of the fair value of services received from employees.

Share-based payment transactions with parties other than employees

BC119 In many share-based payment transactions with parties other than employees, it should be possible to measure reliably the fair value of the goods or services received. The Board therefore concluded that the IFRS should require an entity to presume that the fair value of the goods or services received can be measured reliably. However, in rare cases in which the presumption is rebutted, it is necessary to measure the transaction at the fair value of the equity instruments granted.

BC120 Some measurement issues that arise in respect of share-based payment transactions with employees also arise in transactions with other parties. For example, there might be performance (ie vesting) conditions that must be met before the other party is entitled to the shares or share options. Therefore, any conclusions reached on how to treat vesting conditions in the context of share-based payment transactions with employees also apply to transactions with other parties.

BC121 Similarly, performance by the other party might take place over a period of time, rather than on one specific date, which again raises the question of the appropriate measurement date.

BC122 SFAS 123 does not specify a measurement date for share-based payment transactions with parties other than employees, on the grounds that this is usually a minor issue in such transactions. However, the date at which to estimate the fair value of equity instruments issued to parties other than employees is specified in the US interpretation EITF 96-18 *Accounting for Equity Instruments That Are Issued to Other Than Employees for Acquiring, or in Conjunction with Selling, Goods or Services*:

> [The measurement date is] the earlier of the following:
>
> (a) The date at which a commitment for performance by the counterparty to earn the equity instruments is reached (a "performance commitment"), or
>
> (b) The date at which the counterparty's performance is complete. (extract from Issue 1, footnotes excluded)

BC123 The second of these two dates corresponds to vesting date, because vesting date is when the other party has satisfied all the conditions necessary to become unconditionally entitled to the share options or shares. The first of the two dates does not necessarily correspond to grant date. For example, under an employee

---

* ED 2 proposed that equity-settled share-based payment transactions should be measured at the fair value of the goods or services received, or by reference to the fair value of the equity instruments granted, whichever fair value is more readily determinable. For transactions with parties other than employees, ED 2 proposed that there should be a rebuttable presumption that the fair value of the goods or services received is the more readily determinable fair value. The Board reconsidered these proposed requirements when finalising the IFRS. It concluded that it would be more consistent with the primary accounting objective (explained in paragraphs BC64–BC66) to require equity-settled share-based payment transactions to be measured at the fair value of the goods or services received, unless that fair value cannot be estimated reliably (eg in transactions with employees). For transactions with parties other than employees, the Board concluded that, in many cases, it should be possible to measure reliably the fair value of the goods or services received, as noted above. Hence, the Board concluded that the IFRS should require an entity to presume that the fair value of the goods or services received can be measured reliably.

share plan, the employees are (usually) not committed to providing the necessary services, because they are usually able to leave at any time. Indeed, EITF 96-18 makes it clear that the fact that the equity instrument will be forfeited if the counterparty fails to perform is not sufficient evidence of a performance commitment (Issue 1, footnote 3). Therefore, in the context of share-based payment transactions with parties other than employees, if the other party is not committed to perform, there would be no performance commitment date, in which case the measurement date would be vesting date.

BC124 Accordingly, under SFAS 123 and EITF 96-18, the measurement date for share-based payment transactions with employees is grant date, but for transactions with other parties the measurement date could be vesting date, or some other date between grant date and vesting date.

BC125 In developing the proposals in ED 2, the Board concluded that for transactions with parties other than employees that are measured by reference to the fair value of the equity instruments granted, the equity instruments should be measured at grant date, the same as for transactions with employees.

BC126 However, the Board reconsidered this conclusion during its redeliberations of the proposals in ED 2. The Board considered whether the delivery (service) date fair value of the equity instruments granted provided a better surrogate measure of the fair value of the goods or services received from parties other than employees than the grant date fair value of those instruments. For example, some argue that if the counterparty is not firmly committed to delivering the goods or services, the counterparty would consider whether the fair value of the equity instruments at the delivery date is sufficient payment for the goods or services when deciding whether to deliver the goods or services. This suggests that there is a high correlation between the fair value of the equity instruments at the date the goods or services are received and the fair value of those goods or services. The Board noted that it had considered and rejected a similar argument in the context of transactions with employees (see paragraphs BC94 and BC95). However, the Board found the argument more compelling in the case of transactions with parties other than employees, particularly for transactions in which the counterparty delivers the goods or services on a single date (or over a short period of time) that is substantially later than grant date, compared with transactions with employees in which the services are received over a continuous period that typically begins on grant date.

BC127 The Board was also concerned that permitting entities to measure transactions with parties other than employees on the basis of the fair value of the equity instruments at grant date would provide opportunities for entities to structure transactions to achieve a particular accounting result, causing the carrying amount of the goods or services received, and the resulting expense for the consumption of those goods or services, to be understated.

BC128 The Board therefore concluded that for transactions with parties other than employees in which the entity cannot measure reliably the fair value of the goods or services received at the date of receipt, the fair value of those goods or services should be measured indirectly, based on the fair value of the equity instruments granted, measured at the date the goods or services are received.

Fair value of employee share options

BC129 The Board spent much time discussing how to measure the fair value of employee share options, including how to take into account common features of employee share options, such as vesting conditions and non-transferability. These discussions focused on measuring fair value at grant date, not only because the Board regarded grant date as the appropriate measurement date for transactions with employees, but also because more measurement issues arise at grant date than at later measurement dates. In reaching its conclusions in ED 2, the Board received assistance from the project's Advisory Group and from a panel of experts. During its redeliberations of the proposals in ED 2, the Board considered comments by respondents and advice received from valuation experts on the FASB's Option Valuation Group.

BC130 Market prices provide the best evidence of the fair value of share options. However, share options with terms and conditions similar to employee share options are seldom traded in the markets. The Board therefore concluded that, if market prices are not available, it will be necessary to apply an option pricing model to estimate the fair value of share options.

BC131 The Board decided that it is not necessary or appropriate to prescribe the precise formula or model to be used for option valuation. There is no particular option pricing model that is regarded as theoretically superior to the others, and there is the risk that any model specified might be superseded by improved methodologies in the future. Entities should select whichever model is most appropriate in the circumstances. For example, many employee share options have long lives, are usually exercisable during the period between vesting date and the end of the option's life, and are often exercised early. These factors should be considered when estimating the grant date fair value of share options. For many entities, this might preclude the use of the Black-Scholes-Merton formula, which does not take into account the possibility of exercise before the end of the share option's life and may not adequately reflect the effects of expected early exercise. This is discussed further below (paragraphs BC160–BC162).

BC132 All option pricing models take into account the following option features:

- the exercise price of the option
- the current market price of the share
- the expected volatility of the share price
- the dividends expected to be paid on the shares
- the rate of interest available in the market
- the term of the option.

BC133 The first two items define the intrinsic value of a share option; the remaining four are relevant to the share option's time value. Expected volatility, dividends and interest rate are all based on expectations over the option term. Therefore, the option term is an important part of calculating time value, because it affects the other inputs.

BC134 One aspect of time value is the value of the right to participate in future gains, if any. The valuation does not attempt to predict what the future gain will be, only the amount that a buyer would pay at the valuation date to obtain the right to participate in any future gains. In other words, option pricing models estimate the value of the share option at the measurement date, not the value of the underlying share at some future date.

BC135 The Board noted that some argue that any estimate of the fair value of a share option is inherently uncertain, because it is not known what the ultimate outcome will be, eg whether the share option will expire worthless or whether the employee (or other party) will make a large gain on exercise. However, the valuation objective is to measure the fair value of the rights granted, not to predict the outcome of having granted those rights. Hence, irrespective of whether the option expires worthless or the employee makes a large gain on exercise, that outcome does not mean that the grant date estimate of the fair value of the option was unreliable or wrong.

BC136 A similar analysis applies to the argument that share options do not have any value until they are in the money, ie the share price is greater than the exercise price. This argument refers to the share option's intrinsic value only. Share options also have a time value, which is why they are traded in the markets at prices greater than their intrinsic value. The option holder has a valuable right to participate in any future increases in the share price. So even share options that are at the money have a value when granted. The subsequent outcome of that option grant, even if it expires worthless, does not change the fact that the share option had a value at grant date.

Application of option pricing models to unlisted and newly listed entities

BC137 As explained above, two of the inputs to an option pricing model are the entity's share price and the expected volatility of its share price. For an unlisted entity, there is no published share price information. The entity would therefore need to estimate the fair value of its shares (eg based on the share price of similar entities that are listed, or on a net assets or earnings basis). It would also need to estimate the expected volatility of that value.

BC138 The Board considered whether unlisted entities should be permitted to use the minimum value method instead of a fair value measurement method. The minimum value method is explained earlier, in paragraphs BC80–BC83. Because it excludes the effects of expected volatility, the minimum value method produces a value that is lower, often much lower, than that produced by methods designed to estimate the fair value of an option. Therefore, the Board discussed how an unlisted entity could estimate expected volatility.

BC139 An unlisted entity that regularly issues share options or shares to employees (or other parties) might have an internal market for its shares. The volatility of the internal market share prices provides a basis for estimating expected volatility. Alternatively, an entity could use the historical or implied volatility of similar entities that are listed, and for which share price or option price information is available, as the basis for an estimate of expected volatility. This would be appropriate if the entity has estimated the value of its shares by reference to the share prices of these similar listed entities. If the entity has instead used another methodology to value its shares, the entity could derive an estimate of expected volatility consistent with that methodology. For example, the entity might value its shares on the basis of net asset values or earnings, in which case it could use the expected volatility of those net asset values or earnings as a basis for estimating expected share price volatility.

BC140 The Board acknowledged that these approaches for estimating the expected volatility of an unlisted entity's shares are somewhat subjective. However, the Board thought it likely that, in practice, the application of these approaches would result in underestimates of expected volatility, rather than overestimates, because entities were likely to exercise caution in making such estimates, to ensure that the resulting option values are not overstated. Therefore, estimating expected volatility is likely to produce a more reliable measure of the fair value of share options granted by unlisted entities than an alternative valuation method, such as the minimum value method.

BC141 Newly listed entities would not need to estimate their share price. However, like unlisted entities, newly listed entities could have difficulties in estimating expected volatility when valuing share options, because they might not have sufficient historical share price information upon which to base an estimate of expected volatility.

BC142 SFAS 123 requires such entities to consider the historical volatility of similar entities during a comparable period in their lives:

> For example, an entity that has been publicly traded for only one year that grants options with an average expected life of five years might consider the pattern and level of historical volatility of more mature entities in the same industry for the first six years the stock of those entities were publicly traded. (paragraph 285b)

BC143 The Board concluded that, in general, unlisted and newly listed entities should not be exempt from a requirement to apply fair value measurement and that the IFRS should include implementation guidance on estimating expected volatility for the purposes of applying an option pricing model to share options granted by unlisted and newly listed entities.

BC144 However, the Board acknowledged that there might be some instances in which an entity—such as (but not limited to) an unlisted or newly listed entity—cannot estimate reliably the grant date fair value of share options granted. In this situation, the Board concluded that the entity should measure the share option at its intrinsic value, initially at the date the entity obtains the goods or the counterparty renders service and subsequently at each reporting date until the final settlement of the share-based payment arrangement, with the effects of the remeasurement recognised in profit or loss. For a grant of share options, the share-based payment arrangement is finally settled when the options are exercised, forfeited (eg upon cessation of employment) or lapse (eg at the end of the option's life). For a grant of shares, the share-based payment arrangement is finally settled when the shares vest or are forfeited.

Application of option pricing models to employee share options

BC145 Option pricing models are widely used in, and accepted by, the financial markets. However, there are differences between employee share options and traded share options. The Board considered the valuation implications of these differences, with assistance from its Advisory Group and other experts, including experts in the FASB's Option Valuation Group, and comments made by respondents to ED 2. Employee share options usually differ from traded options in the following ways, which are discussed further below:

(a) there is a vesting period, during which time the share options are not exercisable;

(b) the options are non-transferable;

(c) there are conditions attached to vesting which, if not satisfied, cause the options to be forfeited; and

(d) the option term is significantly longer.

Inability to exercise during the vesting period

BC146 Typically, employee share options have a vesting period, during which the options cannot be exercised. For example, a share option might be granted with a ten-year life and a vesting period of three years, so the option is not exercisable for the first three years and can then be exercised at any time during the remaining seven years. Employee share options cannot be exercised during the vesting period because the employees must first 'pay' for the options, by providing the necessary services. Furthermore, there might be other specified periods during which an employee share option cannot be exercised (eg during a closed period).

BC147 In the finance literature, employee share options are sometimes called Bermudian options, being partly European and partly American. An American share option can be exercised at any time during the option's life, whereas a European share option can be exercised only at the end of the option's life. An American share option is more valuable than a European share option, although the difference in value is not usually significant.

BC148 Therefore, other things being equal, an employee share option would have a higher value than a European share option and a lower value than an American share option, but the difference between the three values is unlikely to be significant.

BC149 If the entity uses the Black-Scholes-Merton formula, or another option pricing model that values European share options, there is no need to adjust the model for the inability to exercise an option in the vesting period (or any other period), because the model already assumes that the option cannot be exercised during that period.

BC150 If the entity uses an option pricing model that values American share options, such as the binomial model, the inability to exercise an option during the vesting period can be taken into account in applying such a model.

BC151 Although the inability to exercise the share option during the vesting period does not, in itself, have a significant effect on the value of the option, there is still the question whether this restriction has an effect when combined with non-transferability. This is discussed in the following section.

BC152 The Board therefore concluded that:

(a) if the entity uses an option pricing model that values European share options, such as the Black-Scholes-Merton formula, no adjustment is required for the inability to exercise the options during the vesting period, because the model already assumes that they cannot be exercised during that period.

(b) if the entity uses an option pricing model that values American share options, such as a binomial model, the application of the model should take account of the inability to exercise the options during the vesting period.

Non-transferability

BC153 From the option holder's perspective, the inability to transfer a share option limits the opportunities available when the option has some time yet to run and the holder wishes either to terminate the exposure to future price changes or to liquidate the position. For example, the holder might believe that over the remaining term of the share option the share price is more likely to decrease than to increase. Also, employee share option plans typically require employees to exercise vested options within a fixed period of time after the employee leaves the entity, or to forfeit the options.

BC154 In the case of a conventional share option, the holder would sell the option rather than exercise it and then sell the shares. Selling the share option enables the holder to receive the option's fair value, including both its intrinsic value and remaining time value, whereas exercising the option enables the holder to receive intrinsic value only.

BC155 However, the option holder is not able to sell a non-transferable share option. Usually, the only possibility open to the option holder is to exercise it, which entails forgoing the remaining time value. (This is not always true. The use of other derivatives, in effect, to sell or gain protection from future changes in the value of the option is discussed later.)

BC156 At first sight, the inability to transfer a share option could seem irrelevant from the entity's perspective, because the entity must issue shares at the exercise price upon exercise of the option, no matter who holds it. In other words, from the entity's perspective, its commitments under the contract are unaffected by whether the shares are issued to the original option holder or to someone else. Therefore, in valuing the entity's side of the contract, from the entity's perspective, non-transferability seems irrelevant.

BC157 However, the lack of transferability often results in early exercise of the share option, because that is the only way for the employees to liquidate their position. Therefore, by imposing the restriction on transferability, the entity has caused the option holder to exercise the option early, thereby resulting in the loss of time value. For example, one aspect of time value is the value of the right to defer payment of the exercise price until the end of the option term. If the option is exercised early because of non-transferability, the entity receives the exercise price much earlier than it would otherwise have done.

BC158 Non-transferability is not the only reason why employees might exercise share options early. Other reasons include risk aversion, lack of wealth diversification, and termination of employment (typically, employees must exercise vested options soon after termination of employment; otherwise the options are forfeited).

BC159 Recent accounting standards and proposed standards (including ED 2) address the issue of early exercise by requiring the expected life of a non-transferable share option to be used in valuing it, rather than the contractual option term. Expected life can be estimated either for the entire share option plan or for subgroups of employees participating in the plan. The estimate takes into account factors such as the length of the vesting period, the average length of time similar options have remained outstanding in the past and the expected volatility of the underlying shares.

BC160 However, comments from respondents to ED 2 and advice received from valuation experts during the Board's redeliberations led the Board to conclude that using a single expected life as an input into an option pricing model (eg the Black-Scholes-Merton formula) was not the best solution for reflecting in the share option valuation the effects of early exercise. For example, such an approach does not take into account the correlation between the share price and early exercise. It would also mean that the share option valuation does not take into account the possibility that the option might be exercised at a date that is later than the end of its expected life. Therefore, in many instances, a more flexible model, such as a binomial model, that uses the share option's contractual life as an input and takes into account the possibility of early exercise on a range of different dates in the option's life, allowing for factors such as the correlation between the share price and early exercise and expected employee turnover, is likely to produce a more accurate estimate of the option's fair value.

BC161 Binomial lattice and similar option pricing models also have the advantage of permitting the inputs to the model to vary over the share option's life. For example, instead of using a single expected volatility, a binomial lattice or similar option pricing model can allow for the possibility that volatility might change over the share option's life. This would be particularly appropriate when valuing share options granted by entities experiencing higher than usual volatility, because volatility tends to revert to its mean over time.

BC162 For these reasons, the Board considered whether it should require the use of a more flexible model, rather than the more commonly used Black-Scholes-Merton formula. However, the Board concluded that it was not necessary to prohibit the use of the Black-Scholes-Merton formula, because there might be instances in which the formula produces a sufficiently reliable estimate of the fair value of the share options granted. For example, if the entity has not granted many share options, the effects of applying a more flexible model might not have a material impact on the entity's financial statements. Also, for share options with relatively short contractual lives, or share options that must be exercised within a short period of time after vesting date, the issues discussed in paragraph BC160 may not be relevant, and hence the Black-Scholes-Merton formula may produce a value that is substantially the same as that produced by a more flexible option pricing model. Therefore, rather than prohibit the use of the Black-Scholes-Merton formula, the Board concluded that the IFRS should include guidance on selecting the most appropriate model to apply. This includes the requirement that the entity should consider factors that knowledgeable, willing market participants would consider in selecting the option pricing model to apply.

BC163 Although non-transferability often results in the early exercise of employee share options, some employees can mitigate the effects of non-transferability, because they are able, in effect, to sell the options or protect themselves from future changes in the value of the options by selling or buying other derivatives. For example, the employee might be able, in effect, to sell an employee share option by entering into an arrangement with an investment bank whereby the employee sells a similar call option to the bank, ie an option with the same exercise price and term. A zero-cost collar is one means of obtaining protection from changes in the value of an employee share option, by selling a call option and buying a put option.

BC164 However, it appears that such arrangements are not always available. For example, the amounts involved have to be sufficiently large to make it worthwhile for the investment bank, which would probably exclude many employees (unless a collective arrangement was made). Also, it appears that investment banks are unlikely to enter into such an arrangement unless the entity is a top listed company, with shares traded in a deep and active market, to enable the investment bank to hedge its own position.

BC165 It would not be feasible to stipulate in an accounting standard that an adjustment to take account of non-transferability is necessary only if the employees cannot mitigate the effects of non-transferability through the use of other derivatives. However, using expected life as an input into an option pricing model, or modelling early exercise in a binomial or similar model, copes with both situations. If employees were able to mitigate the effects of non-transferability by using derivatives, this would often result in the employee share options being exercised later than they would otherwise have been. By taking this factor into account, the estimated fair value of the share option would be higher, which makes sense, given that non-transferability is not a constraint in this case. If the employees cannot mitigate the effects of non-transferability through the use of derivatives, they are likely to exercise the share options much earlier than is optimal. In this case, allowing for the effects of early exercise would significantly reduce the estimated value of the share option.

BC166 This still leaves the question whether there is a need for further adjustment for the combined effect of being unable to exercise or transfer the share option during the vesting period. In other words, the inability to exercise a share option does not, in itself, appear to have a significant effect on its value. But if the share option cannot be transferred and cannot be exercised, and assuming that other derivatives are not available, the holder is unable to extract value from the share option or protect its value during the vesting period.

BC167 However, it should be noted why these restrictions are in place: the employee has not yet 'paid' for the share option by providing the required services (and fulfilling any other performance conditions). The employee cannot exercise or transfer a share option to which he/she is not yet entitled. The share option will either vest or fail to vest, depending on whether the vesting conditions are satisfied. The possibility of forfeiture resulting from failure to fulfil the vesting conditions is taken into account through the application of the modified grant date method (discussed in paragraphs BC170–BC184).

BC168 Moreover, for accounting purposes, the objective is to estimate the fair value of the share option, not the value from the employee's perspective. The fair value of any item depends on the expected amounts, timing, and uncertainty of the future cash flows relating to the item. The share option grant gives the employee the right to subscribe to the entity's shares at the exercise price, provided that the vesting conditions are satisfied and the exercise price is paid during the specified period. The effect of the vesting conditions is considered below. The effect of the share option being non-exercisable during the vesting period has already been considered above, as has the effect of non-transferability. There does not seem to be any additional effect on the expected amounts, timing or uncertainty of the future cash flows arising from the combination of non-exercisability and non-transferability during the vesting period.

BC169 After considering all of the above points, the Board concluded that the effects of early exercise, because of non-transferability and other factors, should be taken into account when estimating the fair value of the share option, either by modelling early exercise in a binomial or similar model, or using expected life rather than contracted life as an input into an option pricing model, such as the Black-Scholes-Merton formula.

Vesting conditions

BC170 Employee share options usually have vesting conditions. The most common condition is that the employee must remain in the entity's employ for a specified period, say three years. If the employee leaves during that period, the options are forfeited. There might also be other performance conditions, eg that the entity achieves a specified growth in share price or earnings.

BC171 Vesting conditions ensure that the employees provide the services required to 'pay' for their share options. For example, the usual reason for imposing service conditions is to retain staff; the usual reason for imposing other performance conditions is to provide an incentive for the employees to work towards specified performance targets.

BC172 Some argue that the existence of vesting conditions does not necessarily imply that the value of employee share options is significantly less than the value of traded share options. The employees have to satisfy the vesting conditions to fulfil their side of the arrangement. In other words, the employees' performance of their side of the arrangement is what they do to pay for their share options. Employees do not pay for the options with cash, as do the holders of traded share options; they pay with their services. Having to pay for the share options does not make them less valuable. On the contrary, it proves that the share options are valuable.

BC173 Others argue that the possibility of forfeiture without compensation for part-performance suggests that the share options are less valuable. The employees might partly perform their side of the arrangement, eg by working for part of the period, then have to leave for some reason, and forfeit the share options without compensation for that part performance. If there are other performance conditions, such as achieving a specified growth in the share price or earnings, the employees might work for the entire vesting period, but fail to meet the vesting conditions and therefore forfeit the share options.

BC174 Similarly, some argue that the entity would take into account the possibility of forfeiture when entering into the agreement at grant date. In other words, in deciding how many share options to grant in total, the entity would allow for expected forfeitures. Hence, if the objective is to estimate at grant date the fair value of the entity's commitments under the share option agreement, that valuation should take into account that the entity's commitment to fulfil its side of the option agreement is conditional upon the vesting conditions being satisfied.

BC175 In developing the proposals in ED 2, the Board concluded that the valuation of rights to share options or shares granted to employees (or other parties) should take into account all types of vesting conditions, including both service conditions and performance conditions. In other words, the grant date valuation should be reduced to allow for the possibility of forfeiture due to failure to satisfy the vesting conditions.

BC176 Such a reduction might be achieved by adapting an option pricing model to incorporate vesting conditions. Alternatively, a more simplistic approach might be applied. One such approach is to estimate the possibility of forfeiture at grant date, and reduce the value produced by an option pricing model accordingly. For example, if the valuation calculated using an option pricing model was CU15, and the entity estimated that 20 per cent of the share options would be forfeited because of failure to satisfy the vesting conditions, allowing for the possibility of forfeiture would reduce the grant date value of each option granted from CU15 to CU12.

BC177 The Board decided against proposing detailed guidance on how the grant date value should be adjusted to allow for the possibility of forfeiture. This is consistent with the Board's objective of setting principles-based standards. The measurement objective is to estimate fair value. That objective might not be achieved if detailed, prescriptive rules were specified, which would probably become outdated by future developments in valuation methodologies.

BC178 However, respondents to ED 2 raised a variety of concerns about the inclusion of vesting conditions in the grant date valuation. Some respondents were concerned about the practicality and subjectivity of including non-market performance conditions in the share option valuation. Some were also concerned about the practicality of including service conditions in the grant date valuation, particularly in conjunction with the units of service method proposed in ED 2 (discussed further in paragraphs BC203–BC217).

BC179 Some respondents suggested the alternative approach applied in SFAS 123, referred to as the modified grant date method. Under this method, service conditions and non-market performance conditions are excluded from the grant date valuation (ie the possibility of forfeiture is not taken into account when estimating the grant date fair value of the share options or other equity instruments, thereby producing a higher grant date fair value), but are instead taken into account by requiring the transaction amount to be based on the number of equity instruments that eventually vest. Under this method, on a cumulative basis, no amount is recognised for goods or services received if the equity instruments granted do not vest because of failure to satisfy a vesting condition (other than a market condition), eg the counterparty fails to complete a specified service period, or a performance condition (other than a market condition) is not satisfied.

BC180 After considering respondents' comments and obtaining further advice from valuation experts, the Board decided to adopt the modified grant date method applied in SFAS 123. However, the Board decided that it should not permit the choice available in SFAS 123 to account for the effects of expected or actual forfeitures of share options or other equity instruments because of failure to satisfy a service condition. For a grant of equity instruments with a service condition, SFAS 123 permits an entity to choose at grant date to recognise the services received based on an estimate of the number of share options or other equity instruments expected to vest, and to revise that estimate, if necessary, if subsequent information indicates that actual forfeitures are likely to differ from previous estimates. Alternatively, an entity may begin recognising the services received as if all the equity instruments granted that are subject to a service requirement are expected to vest. The effects of forfeitures are then recognised when those forfeitures occur, by reversing any amounts previously recognised for services received as consideration for equity instruments that are forfeited.

BC181 The Board decided that the latter method should not be permitted. Given that the transaction amount is ultimately based on the number of equity instruments that vest, it is appropriate to estimate the number of expected forfeitures when recognising the services received during the vesting period. Furthermore, by ignoring expected forfeitures until those forfeitures occur, the effects of reversing any amounts previously recognised might result in a distortion of remuneration expense recognised during the vesting period. For example, an entity that experiences a high level of forfeitures might recognise a large amount of remuneration expense in one period, which is then reversed in a later period.

BC182 Therefore, the Board decided that the IFRS should require an entity to estimate the number of equity instruments expected to vest and to revise that estimate, if necessary, if subsequent information indicates that actual forfeitures are likely to differ from previous estimates.

BC183 Under SFAS 123, market conditions (eg a condition involving a target share price, or specified amount of intrinsic value on which vesting or exercisability is conditioned) are included in the grant date valuation, without subsequent reversal. That is to say, when estimating the fair value of the equity instruments at grant date, the entity takes into account the possibility that the market condition may not be satisfied. Having allowed for that possibility in the grant date valuation of the equity instruments, no adjustment is made to the number of equity instruments included in the calculation of the transaction amount, irrespective of the outcome of the market condition. In other words, the entity recognises the goods or services received from a counterparty that satisfies all other vesting conditions (eg services received from an employee who remains in service for the specified service period), irrespective of whether that market condition is satisfied. The treatment of market conditions therefore contrasts with the treatment of other types of vesting conditions. As explained in paragraph BC179, under the modified grant date method, vesting conditions are not taken into account when estimating the fair value of the equity instruments at grant date, but are instead taken into account by requiring the transaction amount to be based on the number of equity instruments that eventually vest.

BC184 The Board considered whether it should apply the same approach to market conditions as is applied in SFAS 123. It might be argued that it is not appropriate to distinguish between market conditions and other types of performance conditions, because to do so could create opportunities for arbitrage, or cause an economic distortion by encouraging entities to favour one type of performance condition over another. However, the Board noted that it is not clear what the result would be. On the one hand, some entities might prefer the 'truing up' aspect of the modified grant date method, because it permits a reversal of remuneration expense if the condition is not met. On the other hand, if the performance condition is met, and it has not been incorporated into the grant date valuation (as is the case when the modified grant date method is used), the expense will be higher than it would otherwise have been (ie if the performance condition had been incorporated into the grant date valuation). Furthermore, some entities might prefer to avoid the potential volatility caused by the truing up mechanism. Therefore, it is not clear whether having a different treatment for market and non-market performance conditions will necessarily cause entities to favour market conditions over non-market performance conditions, or vice versa. Furthermore, the practical difficulties that led the Board to conclude that non-market performance conditions should be dealt with via the modified grant date method rather than being included in the grant date valuation do not apply to market conditions, because market conditions can be incorporated into option pricing models. Moreover, it is difficult to distinguish between market conditions, such as a target share price, and the market condition that is inherent in the option itself, ie that the option will be exercised only if the share price on the date of exercise exceeds the exercise price. For these reasons, the Board concluded that the IFRS should apply the same approach as is applied in SFAS 123.

Option term

BC185 Employee share options often have a long contractual life, eg ten years. Traded options typically have short lives, often only a few months. Estimating the inputs required by an option pricing model, such as expected volatility, over long periods can be difficult, giving rise to the possibility of significant estimation error. This is not usually a problem with traded share options, given their much shorter lives.

BC186 However, some share options traded over the counter have long lives, such as ten or fifteen years. Option pricing models are used to value them. Therefore, contrary to the argument sometimes advanced, option pricing models can be (and are being) applied to long-lived share options.

BC187 Moreover, the potential for estimation error is mitigated by using a binomial or similar model that allows for changes in model inputs over the share option's life, such as expected volatility, and interest and dividend rates, that could occur and the probability of those changes occurring during the term of the share option. The potential for estimation error is further mitigated by taking into account the possibility of early exercise, either by using expected life rather than contracted life as an input into an option pricing model or by modelling exercise behaviour in a binomial or similar model, because this reduces the expected term of the share option. Because employees often exercise their share options relatively early in the share option's life, the expected term is usually much shorter than contracted life.

Other features of employee share options

BC188 Whilst the features discussed above are common to most employee share options, some might include other features. For example, some share options have a reload feature. This entitles the employee to automatic grants of additional share options whenever he/she exercises previously granted share options and pays the exercise price in the entity's shares rather than in cash. Typically, the employee is granted a new share option, called a reload option, for each share surrendered when exercising the previous share option. The exercise price of the reload option is usually set at the market price of the shares on the date the reload option is granted.

BC189 When SFAS 123 was developed, the FASB concluded that, ideally, the value of the reload feature should be included in the valuation of the original share option at grant date. However, at that time the FASB believed that it was not possible to do so. Accordingly, SFAS 123 does not require the reload feature to be included in the grant date valuation of the original share option. Instead, reload options granted upon exercise of the original share options are accounted for as a new share option grant.

BC190 However, recent academic research indicates that it is possible to value the reload feature at grant date, eg Saly, Jagannathan and Huddart (1999).* However, if significant uncertainties exist, such as the number and timing of expected grants of reload options, it might not be practicable to include the reload feature in the grant date valuation.

BC191 When it developed ED 2, the Board concluded that the reload feature should be taken into account, where practicable, when measuring the fair value of the share options granted. However, if the reload feature was not taken into account, then when the reload option is granted, it should be accounted for as a new share option grant.

BC192 Many respondents to ED 2 agreed with the proposals in ED 2. However, some disagreed. For example, some disagreed with there being a choice of treatments. Some respondents supported always treating reload options granted as new grants whereas others supported always including the reload feature in the grant date valuation. Some expressed concerns about the practicality of including the reload feature in the grant date valuation. After reconsidering this issue, the Board

* P J Saly, R Jagannathan and S J Huddart. 1999. Valuing the Reload Features of Executive Stock Options. *Accounting Horizons* 13 (3): 219-240.

concluded that the reload feature should not be included in the grant date valuation and therefore all reload options granted should be accounted for as new share option grants.

BC193 There may be other features of employee (and other) share options that the Board has not yet considered. But even if the Board were to consider every conceivable feature of employee (and other) share options that exist at present, new features might be developed in the future.

BC194 The Board therefore concluded that the IFRS should focus on setting out clear principles to be applied to share-based payment transactions, and provide guidance on the more common features of employee share options, but should not prescribe extensive application guidance, which would be likely to become outdated.

BC195 Nevertheless, the Board considered whether there are share options with such unusual or complex features that it is too difficult to make a reliable estimate of their fair value and, if so, what the accounting treatment should be.

BC196 SFAS 123 states that 'it should be possible to reasonably estimate the fair value of most stock options and other equity instruments at the date they are granted' (paragraph 21). However, it states that, 'in unusual circumstances, the terms of the stock option or other equity instrument may make it virtually impossible to reasonably estimate the instrument's fair value at the date it is granted'. The standard requires that, in such situations, measurement should be delayed until it is possible to estimate reasonably the instrument's fair value. It notes that this is likely to be the date at which the number of shares to which the employee is entitled and the exercise price are determinable. This could be vesting date. The standard requires that estimates of compensation expense for earlier periods (ie until it is possible to estimate fair value) should be based on current intrinsic value.

BC197 The Board thought it unlikely that entities could not reasonably determine the fair value of share options at grant date, particularly after excluding vesting conditions* and reload features from the grant date valuation. The share options form part of the employee's remuneration package, and it seems reasonable to presume that an entity's management would consider the value of the share options to satisfy itself that the employee's remuneration package is fair and reasonable.

BC198 When it developed ED 2, the Board concluded that there should be no exceptions to the requirement to apply a fair value measurement basis, and therefore it was not necessary to include in the proposed IFRS specific accounting requirements for share options that are difficult to value.

BC199 However, after considering respondents' comments, particularly with regard to unlisted entities, the Board reconsidered this issue. The Board concluded that, in rare cases only, in which the entity could not estimate reliably the grant date fair value of the equity instruments granted, the entity should measure the equity instruments at intrinsic value, initially at grant date and subsequently at each reporting date until the final settlement of the share-based payment arrangement,

* ie vesting conditions other than market conditions.

with the effects of the remeasurement recognised in profit or loss. For a grant of share options, the share-based payment arrangement is finally settled when the share options are exercised, are forfeited (eg upon cessation of employment) or lapse (eg at the end of the option's life). For a grant of shares, the share-based payment arrangement is finally settled when the shares vest or are forfeited. This requirement would apply to all entities, including listed and unlisted entities.

Recognition and measurement of services received in an equity-settled share-based payment transaction

During the vesting period

BC200 In an equity-settled share-based payment transaction, the accounting objective is to recognise the goods or services received as consideration for the entity's equity instruments, measured at the fair value of those goods or services when received. For transactions in which the entity receives employee services, it is often difficult to measure directly the fair value of the services received. In this case, the Board concluded that the fair value of the equity instruments granted should be used as a surrogate measure of the fair value of the services received. This raises the question how to use that surrogate measure to derive an amount to attribute to the services received. Another related question is how the entity should determine when the services are received.

BC201 Starting with the latter question, some argue that shares or share options are often granted to employees for past services rather than future services, or mostly for past services, irrespective of whether the employees are required to continue working for the entity for a specified future period before their rights to those shares or share options vest. Conversely, some argue that shares or share options granted provide a future incentive to the employees and those incentive effects continue after vesting date, which implies that the entity receives services from employees during a period that extends beyond vesting date. For share options in particular, some argue that employees render services beyond vesting date, because employees are able to benefit from an option's time value between vesting date and exercise date only if they continue to work for the entity (since usually a departing employee must exercise the share options within a short period, otherwise they are forfeited).

BC202 However, the Board concluded that if the employees are required to complete a specified service period to become entitled to the shares or share options, this requirement provides the best evidence of when the employees render services in return for the shares or share options. Consequently, the Board concluded that the entity should presume that the services are received during the vesting period. If the shares or share options vest immediately, it should be presumed that the entity has already received the services, in the absence of evidence to the contrary. An example of when immediately vested shares or share options are not for past services is when the employee concerned has only recently begun working for the entity, and the shares or share options are granted as a signing bonus. But in this situation, it might nevertheless be necessary to recognise an expense immediately, if the future employee services do not meet the definition of an asset.

BC203 Returning to the first question in paragraph BC200, when the Board developed ED 2 it developed an approach whereby the fair value of the shares or share options granted, measured at grant date and allowing for all vesting conditions, is divided by the number of units of service expected to be received to determine the deemed fair value of each unit of service subsequently received.

BC204 For example, suppose that the fair value of share options granted, before taking into account the possibility of forfeiture, is CU750,000. Suppose that the entity estimates the possibility of forfeiture because of failure of the employees to complete the required three-year period of service is 20 per cent (based on a weighted average probability), and hence it estimates the fair value of the options granted at CU600,000 (CU750,000 × 80%). The entity expects to receive 1,350 units of service over the three-year vesting period.

BC205 Under the units of service method proposed in ED 2, the deemed fair value per unit of service subsequently received is CU444.44 (CU600,000/1,350). If everything turns out as expected, the amount recognised for services received is CU600,000 (CU444.44 × 1,350).

BC206 This approach is based on the presumption that there is a fairly bargained contract at grant date. Thus the entity has granted share options valued at CU600,000 and expects to receive services valued at CU600,000 in return. It does not expect all share options granted to vest because it does not expect all employees to complete three years' service. Expectations of forfeiture because of employee departures are taken into account when estimating the fair value of the share options granted, and when determining the fair value of the services to be received in return.

BC207 Under the units of service method, the amount recognised for services received during the vesting period might exceed CU600,000, if the entity receives more services than expected. This is because the objective is to account for the services subsequently received, not the fair value of the share options granted. In other words, the objective is not to estimate the fair value of the share options granted and then spread that amount over the vesting period. Rather, the objective is to account for the services subsequently received, because it is the receipt of those services that causes a change in net assets and hence a change in equity. Because of the practical difficulty of valuing those services directly, the fair value of the share options granted is used as a surrogate measure to determine the fair value of each unit of service subsequently received, and therefore the transaction amount is dependent upon the number of units of service actually received. If more are received than expected, the transaction amount will be greater than CU600,000. If fewer services are received, the transaction amount will be less than CU600,000.

BC208 Hence, a grant date measurement method is used as a practical expedient to achieve the accounting objective, which is to account for the services actually received in the vesting period. The Board noted that many who support grant date measurement do so for reasons that focus on the entity's commitments under the contract, not the services received. They take the view that the entity has conveyed to its employees valuable equity instruments at grant date and that the accounting objective should be to account for the equity instruments conveyed. Similarly, supporters of vesting date measurement argue that the entity does not convey valuable equity instruments to the employees until vesting date, and that the accounting objective should be to account for the equity instruments conveyed at vesting date. Supporters of exercise date measurement argue that, ultimately, the valuable equity instruments conveyed by the entity to the employees are the shares issued on exercise date and the objective should be to account for the value given up by the entity by issuing equity instruments at less than their fair value.

BC209 Hence all of these arguments for various measurement dates are focused entirely on what the entity (or its shareholders) has given up under the share-based payment arrangement, and accounting for that sacrifice. Therefore, if 'grant date measurement' were applied as a matter of principle, the primary objective would be to account for the value of the rights granted. Depending on whether the services have already been received and whether a prepayment for services to be received in the future meets the definition of an asset, the other side of the transaction would either be recognised as an expense at grant date, or capitalised as a prepayment and amortised over some period of time, such as over the vesting period or over the expected life of the share option. Under this view of grant date measurement, there would be no subsequent adjustment for actual outcomes. No matter how many share options vest or how many share options are exercised, that does not change the value of the rights given to the employees at grant date.

BC210 Therefore, the reason why some support grant date measurement differs from the reason why the Board concluded that the fair value of the equity instruments granted should be measured at grant date. This means that some will have different views about the consequences of applying grant date measurement. Because the units of service method is based on using the fair value of the equity instruments granted, measured at grant date, as a surrogate measure of the fair value of the services received, the total transaction amount is dependent upon the number of units of service received.

BC211 Some respondents to ED 2 disagreed with the units of service method in principle, because they did not accept that the fair value of the services received should be the accounting focus. Rather, the respondents focused on accounting for the 'cost' of the equity instruments issued (ie the credit side of the transaction rather than the debit side), and took the view that if the share options or shares are forfeited, no cost was incurred, and thus any amounts recognised previously should be reversed, as would happen with a cash-settled transaction.

BC212 Some respondents also disagreed with the treatment of performance conditions under the units of service method, because if the employee completes the required service period but the equity instruments do not vest because of the performance condition not being satisfied, there is no reversal of amounts recognised during the vesting period. Some argue that this result is unreasonable because, if the performance condition is not satisfied, then the employee did not perform as required, hence it is inappropriate to recognise an expense for services received or consumed, because the entity did not receive the specified services.

BC213 The Board considered and rejected the above arguments made against the units of service method in principle. For example, the Board noted that the objective of accounting for the services received, rather than the cost of the equity instruments issued, is consistent with the accounting treatment of other issues of equity instruments, and with the IASB *Framework*. With regard to performance conditions, the Board noted that the strength of the argument in paragraph BC212 depends on the extent to which the employee has control or influence over the achievement of the performance target. One cannot necessarily conclude that the non-attainment of the performance target is a good indication that the employee has failed to perform his/her side of the arrangement (ie failed to provide services).

BC214 Therefore, the Board was not persuaded by those respondents who disagreed with the units of service method in principle. However, the Board also noted that some respondents raised practical concerns about the method. Some respondents regarded the units of service method as too complex and burdensome to apply in practice. For example, if an entity granted share options to a group of employees but did not grant the same number of share options to each employee (eg the number might vary according to their salary or position in the entity), it would be necessary to calculate a different deemed fair value per unit of service for each individual employee (or for each subgroup of employees, if there are groups of employees who each received the same number of options). Then the entity would have to track each employee, to calculate the amount to recognise for each employee. Furthermore, in some circumstances, an employee share or share option scheme might not require the employee to forfeit the shares or share options if the employee leaves during the vesting period in specified circumstances. Under the terms of some schemes, employees can retain their share options or shares if they are classified as a 'good leaver', eg a departure resulting from circumstances not within the employee's control, such as compulsory retirement, ill health or redundancy. Therefore, in estimating the possibility of forfeiture, it is not simply a matter of estimating the possibility of employee departure during the vesting period. It is also necessary to estimate whether those departures will be 'good leavers' or 'bad leavers'. And because the share options or shares will vest upon departure of 'good leavers', the expected number of units to be received and the expected length of the vesting period will be shorter for this group of employees. These factors would need to be incorporated into the application of the units of service method.

BC215 Some respondents also raised practical concerns about applying the units of service method to grants with performance conditions. These concerns include the difficulty of incorporating non-market and complex performance conditions into the grant date valuation, the additional subjectivity that this introduces, and that it was unclear how to apply the method when the length of the vesting period is not fixed, because it depends on when a performance condition is satisfied.

BC216 The Board considered the practical concerns raised by respondents, and obtained further advice from valuation experts concerning the difficulties highlighted by respondents of including non-market performance conditions in the grant date valuation. Because of these practical considerations, the Board concluded that the units of service method should not be retained in the IFRS. Instead, the Board decided to adopt the modified grant date method applied in SFAS 123. Under this method, service conditions and non-market performance conditions are excluded from the grant date valuation (ie the possibility of forfeiture is not taken into account when estimating the grant date fair value of the share options or other equity instruments, thereby producing a higher grant date fair value), but are instead taken into account by requiring that the transaction amount be based on the number of equity instruments that eventually vest.* Under this method, on a cumulative basis, no amount is recognised for goods or services received if the equity instruments granted do not vest because of failure to satisfy a vesting condition (other than a market condition), eg the counterparty fails to complete a specified service period, or a performance condition (other than a market condition) is not satisfied.

BC217 However, as discussed earlier (paragraphs BC180–BC182), the Board decided that it should not permit the choice available in SFAS 123 to account for the effects of expected or actual forfeitures of share options or other equity instruments because of failure to satisfy a service condition. The Board decided that the IFRS should require an entity to estimate the number of equity instruments expected to vest and to revise that estimate, if necessary, if subsequent information indicates that actual forfeitures are likely to differ from previous estimates.

Share options that are forfeited or lapse after the end of the vesting period

BC218 Some share options might not be exercised. For example, a share option holder is unlikely to exercise a share option if the share price is below the exercise price throughout the exercise period. Once the last date for exercise is passed, the share option will lapse.

BC219 The lapse of a share option at the end of the exercise period does not change the fact that the original transaction occurred, ie goods or services were received as consideration for the issue of an equity instrument (the share option). The lapsing of the share option does not represent a gain to the entity, because there is no change to the entity's net assets. In other words, although some might see such an event as being a benefit to the remaining shareholders, it has no effect on the entity's financial position. In effect, one type of equity interest (the share option holders' interest) becomes part of another type of equity interest (the shareholders' interest). The Board therefore concluded that the only accounting entry that might be required is a movement within equity, to reflect that the share options are no longer outstanding (ie as a transfer from one type of equity interest to another).

BC220 This is consistent with the treatment of other equity instruments, such as warrants issued for cash. When warrants subsequently lapse unexercised, this is not treated as a gain; instead the amount previously recognised when the warrants were issued remains within equity.†

BC221 The same analysis applies to equity instruments that are forfeited after the end of the vesting period. For example, an employee with vested share options typically

* The treatment of market conditions is discussed in paragraphs BC183 and BC184. As noted in paragraph BC184, the practical difficulties that led the Board to conclude that non-market conditions should be dealt with via the modified grant date method rather than being included in the grant date valuation do not apply to market conditions, because market conditions can be incorporated into option pricing models.

† However, an alternative approach is followed in some jurisdictions (eg Japan and the UK), where the entity recognises a gain when warrants lapse. But under the *Framework*, recognising a gain on the lapse of warrants would be appropriate only if warrants were liabilities, which they are not.

must exercise those options within a short period after cessation of employment, otherwise the options are forfeited. If the share options are not in the money, the employee is unlikely to exercise the options and hence they will be forfeited. For the same reasons as are given in paragraph BC219, no adjustment is made to the amounts previously recognised for services received as consideration for the share options. The only accounting entry that might be required is a movement within equity, to reflect that the share options are no longer outstanding.

Modifications to the terms and conditions of share-based payment arrangements

BC222 An entity might modify the terms of or conditions under which the equity instruments were granted. For example, the entity might reduce the exercise price of share options granted to employees (ie reprice the options), which increases the fair value of those options. During the development of ED 2, the Board focused mainly on the repricing of share options.

BC223 The Board noted that the IASC/G4+1 Discussion Paper argued that if the entity reprices its share options it has, in effect, replaced the original share option with a more valuable share option. The entity presumably believes that it will receive an equivalent amount of benefit from doing so, because otherwise the directors would not be acting in the best interests of the entity or its shareholders. This suggests that the entity expects to receive additional or enhanced employee services equivalent in value to the incremental value of the repriced share options. The Discussion Paper therefore proposed that the incremental value given (ie the difference between the value of the original share option and the value of the repriced share option, as at the date of repricing) should be recognised as additional remuneration expense. Although the Discussion Paper discussed repricing in the context of vesting date measurement, SFAS 123, which applies a grant date measurement basis for employee share-based payment, contains reasoning similar to that in the Discussion Paper.

BC224 This reasoning seems appropriate if grant date measurement is applied on the grounds that the entity made a payment to the employees on grant date by granting them valuable rights to equity instruments of the entity. If the entity is prepared to replace that payment with a more valuable payment, it must believe it will receive an equivalent amount of benefit from doing so.

BC225 The same conclusion is drawn if grant date measurement is applied on the grounds that some type of equity interest is created at grant date, and thereafter changes in the value of that equity interest accrue to the option holders as equity participants, not as employees. Repricing is inconsistent with the view that share option holders bear changes in value as equity participants. Hence it follows that the incremental value has been granted to the share option holders in their capacity as employees (rather than equity participants), as part of their remuneration for services to the entity. Therefore additional remuneration expense arises in respect of the incremental value given.

BC226 It could be argued that if (a) grant date measurement is used as a surrogate measure of the fair value of the services received and (b) the repricing occurs between grant date and vesting date and (c) the repricing merely restores the share option's original value at grant date, then the entity may not receive additional services. Rather, the repricing might simply be a means of ensuring that the entity receives the services it originally expected to receive when the share options were granted. Under this view, it is not appropriate to recognise additional remuneration expense to the extent that the repricing restores the share option's original value at grant date.

BC227 Some argue that the effect of a repricing is to create a new deal between the entity and its employees, and therefore the entity should estimate the fair value of the repriced share options at the date of repricing to calculate a new measure of the fair value of the services received subsequent to repricing. Under this view, the entity would cease using the grant date fair value of the share options when measuring services received after the repricing date, but without reversal of amounts recognised previously. The entity would then measure the services received between the date of repricing and the end of the vesting period by reference to the fair value of the modified share options, measured at the date of repricing. If the repricing occurs after the end of the vesting period, the same process applies. That is to say, there is no adjustment to previously recognised amounts, and the entity recognises—either immediately or over the vesting period, depending on whether the employees are required to complete an additional period of service to become entitled to the repriced share options—an amount equal to the fair value of the modified share options, measured at the date of repricing.

BC228 In the context of measuring the fair value of the equity instruments as a surrogate measure of the fair value of the services received, after considering the above points, the Board concluded when it developed ED 2 that the incremental value granted on repricing should be taken into account when measuring the services received, because:

(a) there is an underlying presumption that the fair value of the equity instruments, at grant date, provides a surrogate measure of the fair value of the services received. That fair value is based on the share option's original terms and conditions. Therefore, if those terms or conditions are modified, the modification should be taken into account when measuring the services received.

(b) a share option that will be repriced if the share price falls is more valuable than one that will not be repriced. Therefore, by presuming at grant date that the share option will not be repriced, the entity underestimated the fair value of that option. The Board concluded that, because it is impractical to include the possibility of repricing in the estimate of fair value at grant date, the incremental value granted on repricing should be taken into account as and when the repricing occurs.

BC229 Many of the respondents to ED 2 who addressed the issue of repricing agreed with the proposed requirements. After considering respondents' comments, the Board decided to retain the approach to repricing as proposed in ED 2, ie recognise the incremental value granted on repricing, in addition to continuing to recognise amounts based on the fair value of the original grant.

BC230 The Board also discussed situations in which repricing might be effected by cancelling share options and issuing replacement share options. For example, suppose an entity grants at-the-money share options with an estimated fair value of CU20 each. Suppose the share price falls, so that the share options become significantly out of the money, and are now worth CU2 each. Suppose the entity is considering repricing, so that the share options are again at the money, which would result in them being worth, say, CU10 each. (Note that the share options are still worth less than at grant date, because the share price is now lower. Other things being equal, an at-the-money option on a low priced share is worth less than an at-the-money option on a high priced share.)

BC231 Under ED 2's proposed treatment of repricing, the incremental value given on repricing (CU10 − CU2 = CU8 increment in fair value per share option) would be accounted for when measuring the services rendered, resulting in the recognition of additional expense, ie additional to any amounts recognised in the future in respect of the original share option grant (valued at CU20). If the entity instead cancelled the existing share options and then issued what were, in effect, replacement share options, but treated the replacement share options as a new share option grant, this could reduce the expense recognised. Although the new grant would be valued at CU10 rather than incremental value of CU8, the entity would not recognise any further expense in respect of the original share option grant, valued at CU20. Although some regard such a result as appropriate (and consistent with their views on repricing, as explained in paragraph BC227), it is inconsistent with the Board's treatment of repricing.

BC232 By this means, the entity could, in effect, reduce its remuneration expense if the share price falls, without having to increase the expense if the share price rises (because no repricing would be necessary in this case). In other words, the entity could structure a repricing so as to achieve a form of service date measurement if the share price falls and grant date measurement if the share price rises, ie an asymmetrical treatment of share price changes.

BC233 When it developed ED 2, the Board concluded that if an entity cancels a share or share option grant during the vesting period (other than cancellations because of employees' failing to satisfy the vesting conditions), it should nevertheless continue to account for services received, as if that share or share option grant had not been cancelled. In the Board's view, it is very unlikely that a share or share option grant would be cancelled without some compensation to the counterparty, either in the form of cash or replacement share options. Moreover, the Board saw no difference between a repricing of share options and a cancellation of share options followed by the granting of replacement share options at a lower exercise price, and therefore concluded that the accounting treatment should be the same. If cash is paid on the cancellation of the share or share option grant, the Board concluded that the payment should be accounted for as the repurchase of an equity interest, ie as a deduction from equity.

BC234 The Board noted that its proposed treatment means that an entity would continue to recognise services received during the remainder of the original vesting period, even though the entity might have paid cash compensation to the counterparty upon cancellation of the share or share option grant. The Board discussed an alternative approach applied in SFAS 123: if an entity settles unvested shares or share options in cash, those shares or share options are treated as having immediately vested. The entity is required to recognise immediately an expense for the amount of compensation expense that would otherwise have been recognised during the remainder of the original vesting period. Although the Board would have preferred to adopt this approach, it would have been difficult to apply in the context of the proposed accounting method in ED 2, given that there is not a specific amount of unrecognised compensation expense—the amount recognised in the future would have depended on the number of units of service received in the future.

BC235 Many respondents who commented on the treatment of cancellations disagreed with the proposals in ED 2. They commented that it was inappropriate to continue recognising an expense after a grant has been cancelled. Some suggested other approaches, including the approach applied in SFAS 123. After considering these comments, and given that the Board had decided to replace the units of service method with the modified grant date method in SFAS 123, the Board concluded that it should adopt the same approach as applied in SFAS 123 to cancellations and settlements. Under SFAS 123, a settlement (including a cancellation) is regarded as resulting in the immediate vesting of the equity instruments. The amount of remuneration expense measured at grant date but not yet recognised is recognised immediately at the date of settlement or cancellation.

BC236 In addition to the above issues, during its redeliberation of the proposals in ED 2 the Board also considered more detailed issues relating to modifications and cancellations. Specifically, the Board considered:

(a) a modification that results in a decrease in fair value (ie the fair value of the modified instrument is less than the fair value of the original instrument, measured at the date of the modification).

(b) a change in the number of equity instruments granted (increase and decrease).

(c) a change in services conditions, thereby changing the length of the vesting period (increase and decrease).

(d) a change in performance conditions, thereby changing the probability of vesting (increase and decrease).

(e) a change in the classification of the grant, from equity to liabilities.

BC237 The Board concluded that having adopted a grant date measurement method, the requirements for modifications and cancellations should ensure that the entity cannot, by modifying or cancelling the grant of shares or share options, avoid recognising remuneration expense based on the grant date fair values. Therefore, the Board concluded that, for arrangements that are classified as equity-settled arrangements (at least initially), the entity must recognise the grant date fair value of the equity instruments over the vesting period, unless the employee fails to vest in those equity instruments under the terms of the original vesting conditions.

Share appreciation rights settled in cash

BC238 Some transactions are 'share-based', even though they do not involve the issue of shares, share options or any other form of equity instrument. Share appreciation rights (SARs) settled in cash are transactions in which the amount of cash paid to the employee (or another party) is based upon the increase in the share price over a specified period, usually subject to vesting conditions, such as the employee's remaining with the entity during the specified period. (Note that the following discussion focuses on SARs granted to employees, but also applies to SARs granted to other parties.)

BC239 In terms of accounting concepts, share-based payment transactions involving an outflow of cash (or other assets) are different from transactions in which goods or services are received as consideration for the issue of equity instruments.

BC240 In an equity-settled transaction, only one side of the transaction causes a change in assets, ie an asset (services) is received but no assets are disbursed. The other side of the transaction increases equity; it does not cause a change in assets. Accordingly, not only is it not necessary to remeasure the transaction amount upon settlement, it is not appropriate, because equity interests are not remeasured.

BC241 In contrast, in a cash-settled transaction, both sides of the transaction cause a change in assets, ie an asset (services) is received and an asset (cash) is ultimately disbursed. Therefore, no matter what value is attributed to the first asset (services received), eventually it will be necessary to recognise the change in assets when the second asset (cash) is disbursed. Thus, no matter how the transaction is accounted for between the receipt of services and the settlement in cash, it will be 'trued up' to equal the amount of cash paid out, to account for both changes in assets.

BC242 Because cash-settled SARs involve an outflow of cash (rather than the issue of equity instruments) cash SARs should be accounted for in accordance with the usual accounting for similar liabilities. That sounds straightforward, but there are some questions to consider:

(a) should a liability be recognised before vesting date, ie before the employees have fulfilled the conditions to become unconditionally entitled to the cash payment?

(b) if so, how should that liability be measured?

(c) how should the expense be presented in the income statement?

Is there a liability before vesting date?

BC243 It could be argued that the entity does not have a liability until vesting date, because the entity does not have a present obligation to pay cash to the employees until the employees fulfil the conditions to become unconditionally entitled to the cash; between grant date and vesting date there is only a contingent liability.

BC244 The Board noted that this argument applies to all sorts of employee benefits settled in cash, not just SARs. For example, it could be argued that an entity has no liability for pension payments to employees until the employees have met the specified vesting conditions. This argument was considered by IASC in IAS 19 *Employee Benefits*. The Basis for Conclusions states:

> Paragraph 54 of the new IAS 19 summarises the recognition and measurement of liabilities arising from defined benefit plans...Paragraph 54 of the new IAS 19 is based on the definition of, and recognition criteria for, a liability in IASC's *Framework*...The Board believes that an enterprise has an obligation under a defined benefit plan when an employee has rendered service in return for the benefits promised under the plan...The Board believes that an obligation exists even if a benefit is not vested, in other words if the employee's right to receive the benefit is conditional upon future employment. For example, consider an enterprise that provides a benefit of 100 to employees who remain in service for two years. At the end of the first year, the employee and the enterprise are not in the same position as at the beginning of the first year, because the employee will only need to work for one year, instead of two, before becoming entitled to the benefit. Although there is a possibility that the benefit may not vest, that difference is an obligation and, in the Board's view, should result in the recognition of a liability at the end of the first year. The measurement of that obligation at its present value reflects the enterprise's best estimate of the probability that the benefit may not vest. (IAS 19, Basis for Conclusions, paragraphs 11–14)

BC245 Therefore, the Board concluded that, to be consistent with IAS 19, which covers other cash-settled employee benefits, a liability should be recognised in respect of cash-settled SARs during the vesting period, as services are rendered by the employees. Thus, no matter how the liability is measured, the Board concluded that it should be accrued over the vesting period, to the extent that the employees have performed their side of the arrangement. For example, if the terms of the arrangement require the employees to perform services over a three-year period, the liability would be accrued over that three-year period, consistently with the treatment of other cash-settled employee benefits.

How should the liability be measured?

BC246 A simple approach would be to base the accrual on the entity's share price at the end of each reporting period. If the entity's share price increased over the vesting period, expenses would be larger in later reporting periods compared with earlier reporting periods. This is because each reporting period will include the effects of (a) an increase in the liability in respect of the employee services received during that reporting period and (b) an increase in the liability attributable to the increase in the entity's share price during the reporting period, which increases the amount payable in respect of past employee services received.

BC247 This approach is consistent with SFAS 123 (paragraph 25) and FASB Interpretation No. 28 *Accounting for Stock Appreciation Rights and Other Variable Stock Option or Award Plans*.

BC248 However, this is not a fair value approach. Like share options, the fair value of SARs includes both their intrinsic value (the increase in the share price to date) and their time value (the value of the right to participate in future increases in the share price, if any, that may occur between the valuation date and the settlement date). An option pricing model can be used to estimate the fair value of SARs.

BC249 Ultimately, however, no matter how the liability is measured during the vesting period, the liability—and therefore the expense—will be remeasured, when the SARs are settled, to equal the amount of the cash paid out. The amount of cash paid will be based on the SARs' intrinsic value at the settlement date. Some support measuring the SAR liability at intrinsic value for this reason, and because intrinsic value is easier to measure.

BC250 The Board concluded that measuring SARs at intrinsic value would be inconsistent with the fair value measurement basis applied, in most cases, in the rest of the IFRS. Furthermore, although a fair value measurement basis is more complex to apply, it was likely that many entities would be measuring the fair value of similar instruments regularly, eg new SAR or share option grants, which would provide much of the information required to remeasure the fair value of the SAR at each reporting date. Moreover, because the intrinsic value measurement basis does not include time value, it is not an adequate measure of either the SAR liability or the cost of services consumed.

BC251 The question of how to measure the liability is linked with the question how to present the associated expense in the income statement, as explained below.

How should the associated expense be presented in the income statement?

BC252 SARs are economically similar to share options. Hence some argue that the accounting treatment of SARs should be the same as the treatment of share options, as discussed earlier (paragraph BC113). However, as noted in paragraphs BC240 and BC241, in an equity-settled transaction there is one change in net assets (the goods or services received) whereas in a cash-settled transaction there are two changes in net assets (the goods or services received and the cash or other assets paid out). To differentiate between the effects of each change in net assets in a cash-settled transaction, the expense could be separated into two components:

- an amount based on the fair value of the SARs at grant date, recognised over the vesting period, in a manner similar to accounting for equity-settled share-based payment transactions, and
- changes in estimate between grant date and settlement date, ie all changes required to remeasure the transaction amount to equal the amount paid out on settlement date.

BC253 In developing ED 2, the Board concluded that information about these two components would be helpful to users of financial statements. For example, users of financial statements regard the effects of remeasuring the liability as having little predictive value. Therefore, the Board concluded that there should be separate disclosure, either on the face of the income statement or in the notes, of that portion of the expense recognised during each accounting period that is attributable to changes in the estimated fair value of the liability between grant date and settlement date.

BC254 However, some respondents to ED 2 disagreed with the proposed disclosure, arguing that it was burdensome and inappropriate to require the entity to account for the transaction as a cash-settled transaction and also calculate, for the purposes of the disclosure, what the transaction amount would have been if the arrangement was an equity-settled transaction.

BC255 The Board considered these comments and also noted that its decision to adopt the SFAS 123 modified grant date method will make it more complex for entities to determine the amount to disclose, because it will be necessary to distinguish between the effects of forfeitures and the effects of fair value changes when calculating the amount to disclose. The Board therefore concluded that the disclosure should not be retained as a mandatory requirement, but instead should be given as an example of an additional disclosure that entities should consider providing. For example, entities with a significant amount of cash-settled arrangements that experience significant share price volatility will probably find that the disclosure is helpful to users of their financial statements.

Share-based payment transactions with cash alternatives

BC256 Under some employee share-based payment arrangements the employees can choose to receive cash instead of shares or share options, or instead of exercising share options. There are many possible variations of share-based payment arrangements under which a cash alternative may be paid. For example, the employees may have more than one opportunity to elect to receive the cash alternative, eg the employees may be able to elect to receive cash instead of shares or share options on vesting date, or elect to receive cash instead of exercising the share options. The terms of the arrangement may provide the entity with a choice of settlement, ie whether to pay the cash alternative instead of issuing shares or share options on vesting date or instead of issuing shares upon the exercise of the share options. The amount of the cash alternative may be fixed or variable and, if variable, may be determinable in a manner that is related, or unrelated, to the price of the entity's shares.

BC257 The IFRS contains different accounting methods for cash-settled and equity-settled share-based payment transactions. Hence, if the entity or the employee has the choice of settlement, it is necessary to determine which accounting method should be applied. The Board considered situations when the terms of the arrangement provide (a) the employee with a choice of settlement and (b) the entity with a choice of settlement.

The terms of the arrangement provide the employee with a choice of settlement

BC258 Share-based payment transactions without cash alternatives do not give rise to liabilities under the *Framework*, because the entity is not required to transfer cash or other assets to the other party. However, this is not so if the contract between the entity and the employee gives the employee the contractual right to demand the cash alternative. In this situation, the entity has an obligation to transfer cash to the employee and hence a liability exists. Furthermore, because the employee has the right to demand settlement in equity instead of cash, the employee also has a conditional right to equity instruments. Hence, on grant date the employee was granted rights to a compound financial instrument, ie a financial instrument that includes both debt and equity components.

BC259 It is common for the alternatives to be structured so that the fair value of the cash alternative is always the same as the fair value of the equity alternative, eg where the employee has a choice between share options and SARs. However, if this is not so, then the fair value of the compound financial instrument will usually exceed both the individual fair value of the cash alternative (because of the possibility that the shares or share options may be more valuable than the cash alternative) and that of the shares or options (because of the possibility that the cash alternative may be more valuable than the shares or options).

BC260 Under IAS 32, a financial instrument that is accounted for as a compound instrument is separated into its debt and equity components, by allocating the proceeds received for the issue of a compound instrument to its debt and equity components. This entails determining the fair value of the liability component and then assigning the remainder of the proceeds received to the equity component. This is possible if those proceeds are cash or non-cash consideration whose fair value can be reliably measured. If that is not the case, it will be necessary to estimate the fair value of the compound instrument itself.

BC261 The Board concluded that the compound instrument should be measured by first valuing the liability component (the cash alternative) and then valuing the equity component (the equity instrument)—with that valuation taking into account that the employee must forfeit the cash alternative to receive the equity instrument—and adding the two component values together. This is consistent with the approach adopted in IAS 32, whereby the liability component is measured first and the residual is allocated to equity. If the fair value of each settlement alternative is always the same, then the fair value of the equity component of the compound instrument will be zero and hence the fair value of the compound instrument will be the same as the fair value of the liability component.

BC262 The Board concluded that the entity should separately account for the services rendered in respect of each component of the compound financial instrument, to ensure consistency with the IFRS's requirements for equity-settled and cash-settled share-based payment transactions. Hence, for the debt component, the entity should recognise the services received, and a liability to pay for those services, as the employees render services, in the same manner as other cash-settled share-based payment transactions (eg SARs). For the equity component (if any), the entity should recognise the services received, and an increase in equity, as the employees render services, in the same way as other equity-settled share-based payment transactions.

BC263 The Board concluded that the liability should be remeasured to its fair value as at the date of settlement, before accounting for the settlement of the liability. This ensures that, if the entity settles the liability by issuing equity instruments, the resulting increase in equity is measured at the fair value of the consideration received for the equity instruments issued, being the fair value of the liability settled.

BC264 The Board also concluded that, if the entity pays cash rather than issuing equity instruments on settlement, any contributions to equity previously recognised in respect of the equity component should remain in equity. By electing to receive cash rather than equity instruments, the employee has surrendered his/her rights to receive equity instruments. That event does not cause a change in net assets and hence there is no change in total equity. This is consistent with the Board's conclusions on other lapses of equity instruments (see paragraphs BC218–BC221).

The terms of the arrangement provide the entity with a choice of settlement

BC265 For share-based payment transactions in which the terms of the arrangement provide the entity with a choice of whether to settle in cash or by issuing equity instruments, the entity would need first to determine whether it has an obligation to settle in cash and therefore does not, in effect, have a choice of settlement. Although the contract might specify that the entity can choose whether to settle in cash or by issuing equity instruments, the Board concluded that the entity will have an obligation to settle in cash if the choice of settlement in equity has no commercial substance (eg because the entity is legally prohibited from issuing shares), or if the entity has a past practice or a stated policy of settling in cash, or generally settles in cash whenever the counterparty asks for cash settlement. The entity will also have an obligation to settle in cash if the shares issued (including shares issued upon the exercise of share options) are redeemable, either mandatorily (eg upon cessation of employment) or at the counterparty's option.

BC266 During its redeliberations of the proposals in ED 2, the Board noted that the classification as liabilities or equity of arrangements in which the entity appears to have the choice of settlement differs from the classification under IAS 32, which requires such an arrangement to be classified either wholly as a liability (if the contract is a derivative contract) or as a compound instrument (if the contract is a non-derivative contract). However, consistently with its conclusions on the other differences between IFRS 2 and IAS 32 (see paragraphs BC106–BC110), the Board decided to retain this difference, pending the outcome of its longer-term Concepts project, which includes reviewing the definitions of liabilities and equity.

BC267 Even if the entity is not obliged to settle in cash until it chooses to do so, at the time it makes that election a liability will arise for the amount of the cash payment. This raises the question how to account for the debit side of the entry. It could be argued that any difference between (a) the amount of the cash payment and (b) the total expense recognised for services received and consumed up to the date of settlement (which would be based on the grant date value of the equity settlement alternative) should be recognised as an adjustment to the employee remuneration expense. However, given that the cash payment is to settle an equity interest, the Board concluded that it is consistent with the *Framework* to treat the cash payment as the repurchase of an equity interest, ie as a deduction from equity. In this case, no adjustment to remuneration expense is required on settlement.

BC268 However, the Board concluded that an additional expense should be recognised if the entity chooses the settlement alternative with the higher fair value because, given that the entity has voluntarily paid more than it needed to, presumably it expects to receive (or has already received) additional services from the employees in return for the additional value given.

Overall conclusions on accounting for employee share options

BC269 The Board first considered all major issues relating to the recognition and measurement of share-based payment transactions, and reached conclusions on those issues. It then drew some overall conclusions, particularly on the treatment of employee share options, which is one of the most controversial aspects of the project. In arriving at those conclusions, the Board considered the following issues:

- convergence with US GAAP
- recognition versus disclosure of expenses arising from employee share-based payment transactions
- reliability of measurement of the fair value of employee share options.

Convergence with US GAAP

BC270 Some respondents to the Discussion Paper and ED 2 urged the Board to develop an IFRS that was based on existing requirements under US generally accepted accounting principles (US GAAP).

BC271 More specifically, respondents urged the Board to develop a standard based on SFAS 123. However, given that convergence of accounting standards was commonly given as a reason for this suggestion, the Board considered US GAAP overall, not just one aspect of it. The main pronouncements of US GAAP on share-based payment are Accounting Principles Board Opinion No. 25 *Accounting for Stock Issued to Employees*, and SFAS 123.

APB 25

BC272 APB 25 was issued in 1972. It deals with employee share plans only, and draws a distinction between non-performance-related (fixed) plans and performance-related and other variable plans.

BC273 For fixed plans, an expense is measured at intrinsic value (ie the difference between the share price and the exercise price), if any, at grant date. Typically, this results in no expense being recognised for fixed plans, because most share options granted under fixed plans are granted at the money. For performance-related and other variable plans, an expense is measured at intrinsic value at the measurement date. The measurement date is when both the number of shares or share options that the employee is entitled to receive and the exercise price are fixed. Because this measurement date is likely to be much later than grant date, any expense is subject to uncertainty and, if the share price is increasing, the expense for performance-related plans would be larger than for fixed plans.

BC274 In SFAS 123, the FASB noted that APB 25 is criticised for producing anomalous results and for lacking any underlying conceptual rationale. For example, the requirements of APB 25 typically result in the recognition of an expense for performance-related share options but usually no expense is recognised for fixed share options. This result is anomalous because fixed share options are usually more valuable at grant date than performance-related share options. Moreover, the omission of an expense for fixed share options impairs the quality of financial statements:

> The resulting financial statements are less credible than they could be, and the financial statements of entities that use fixed employee share options extensively are not comparable to those of entities that do not make significant use of fixed options. (SFAS 123, paragraph 56)

BC275 The Discussion Paper, in its discussion of US GAAP, noted that the different accounting treatments for fixed and performance-related plans also had the perverse effect of discouraging entities from setting up performance-related employee share plans.

SFAS 123

BC276 SFAS 123 was issued in 1995. It requires recognition of share-based payment transactions with parties other than employees, based on the fair value of the shares or share options issued or the fair value of the goods or services received, whichever is more reliably measurable. Entities are also encouraged, but not required, to apply the fair value accounting method in SFAS 123 to share-based payment transactions with employees. Generally speaking, SFAS 123 draws no distinction between fixed and performance-related plans.

BC277 If an entity applies the accounting method in APB 25 rather than that in SFAS 123, SFAS 123 requires disclosures of pro forma net income and earnings per share in the annual financial statements, as if the standard had been applied. Recently, a significant number of major US companies have voluntarily adopted the fair value accounting method in SFAS 123 for transactions with employees.

BC278 The FASB regards SFAS 123 as superior to APB 25, and would have preferred recognition based on the fair value of employee options to be mandatory, not optional. SFAS 123 makes it clear that the FASB decided to permit the disclosure-based alternative for political reasons, not because it thought that it was the best accounting solution:

> ...the Board...continues to believe that disclosure is not an adequate substitute for recognition of assets, liabilities, equity, revenues and expenses in financial statements...The Board chose a disclosure-based solution for stock-based employee compensation to bring closure to the divisive debate on this issue–not because it believes that solution is the best way to improve financial accounting and reporting. (SFAS 123, paragraphs 61 and 62)

BC279 Under US GAAP, the accounting treatment of share-based payment transactions differs, depending on whether the other party to the transaction is an employee or non-employee, and whether the entity chooses to apply SFAS 123 or APB 25 to transactions with employees. Having a choice of accounting methods is generally regarded as undesirable. Indeed, the Board recently devoted much time and effort to developing improvements to existing international standards, one of the objectives of which is to eliminate choices of accounting methods.

BC280 Research in the US demonstrates that choosing one accounting method over the other has a significant impact on the reported earnings of US entities. For example, research by Bear Stearns and Credit Suisse First Boston on the S&P 500 shows that, had the fair value measurement method in SFAS 123 been applied for the purposes of recognising an expense for employee stock-based compensation, the earnings of the S&P 500 companies would have been significantly lower, and that the effect is growing. The effect on reported earnings is substantial in some sectors, where companies make heavy use of share options.

BC281 The Canadian Accounting Standards Board (AcSB) recently completed its project on share-based payment. In accordance with the AcSB's policy of harmonising

Canadian standards with those in the US, the AcSB initially proposed a standard that was based on US GAAP, including APB 25. After considering respondents' comments, the AcSB decided to delete the guidance drawn from APB 25. The AcSB reached this decision for various reasons, including that, in its view, the intrinsic value method is flawed. Also, incorporating the requirements of APB 25 into an accounting standard would result in preparers of financial statements incurring substantial costs for which users of financial statements would derive no benefit—entities would spend a great deal of time and effort on understanding the rules and then redesigning option plans, usually by deleting existing performance conditions, to avoid recognising an expense in respect of such plans, thereby producing no improvement in the accounting for share option plans.

BC282 The Canadian standard was initially consistent with SFAS 123. That included permitting a choice between fair value-based accounting for employee stock-based compensation expense in the income statement and disclosure of pro forma amounts in the notes to both interim and annual financial statements. However, the AcSB recently amended its standard to remove the choice between recognition and disclosure, and therefore expense recognition is mandatory for financial periods beginning on or after 1 January 2004.

BC283 Because APB 25 contains serious flaws, the Board concluded that basing an IFRS on it is unlikely to represent much, if any, improvement in financial reporting. Moreover, the perverse effects of APB 25, particularly in discouraging performance-related share option plans, may cause economic distortions. Accounting standards are intended to be neutral, not to give favourable or unfavourable accounting treatments to particular transactions to encourage or discourage entities from entering into those transactions. APB 25 fails to achieve that objective. Performance-related employee share plans are common in Europe (performance conditions are often required by law) and in other parts of the world outside the US, and investors are calling for greater use of performance conditions. Therefore, the Board concluded that introducing an accounting standard based on APB 25 would be inconsistent with its objective of developing high quality accounting standards.

BC284 That leaves SFAS 123. Comments from the FASB, in the SFAS 123 Basis for Conclusions, and from the Canadian AcSB when it developed a standard based on SFAS 123, indicate that both standard-setters regard it as inadequate, because it permits a choice between recognition and disclosure. (This issue is discussed further below.) The FASB added to its agenda in March 2003 a project to review US accounting requirements on share-based payment, including removing the disclosure alternative in SFAS 123, so that expense recognition is mandatory. The Chairman of the FASB commented:

> Recent events have served as a reminder to all of us that clear, credible and comparable financial information is essential to the health and vitality of our capital market system. In the wake of the market meltdown and corporate reporting scandals, the FASB has received numerous requests from individual and institutional investors, financial analysts and many others urging the Board to mandate the expensing of the compensation cost relating to employee stock options...While a number of major companies have voluntarily opted to reflect these costs as an expense in reporting their earnings, other companies continue to show these costs in the footnotes to their financial statements. In addition, a move to require an expense treatment would be

> consistent with the FASB's commitment to work toward convergence between U.S. and international accounting standards. In taking all of these factors into consideration, the Board concluded that it was critical that it now revisit this important subject. (FASB News Release, 12 March 2003)

BC285 During the Board's redeliberations of the proposals in ED 2, the Board worked with the FASB to achieve convergence of international and US standards, to the extent possible, bearing in mind that the FASB was at an earlier stage in its project—the FASB was developing an Exposure Draft to revise SFAS 123 whereas the IASB was finalising its IFRS. The Board concluded that, although convergence is an important objective, it would not be appropriate to delay the issue of the IFRS, because of the pressing need for a standard on share-based payment, as explained in paragraphs BC2BC5. In any event, at the time the IASB concluded its deliberations, a substantial amount of convergence had been achieved. For example, the FASB agreed with the IASB that all share-based payment transactions should be recognised in the financial statements, measured on a fair value measurement basis, including transactions in which share options are granted to employees. Hence, the FASB agreed that the disclosure alternative in SFAS 123 should be eliminated.

BC286 The IASB and FASB also agreed that, once both boards have issued final standards on share-based payment, the two boards will consider undertaking a convergence project, with the objective of eliminating any remaining areas of divergence between international and US standards on this topic.

Recognition versus disclosure

BC287 A basic accounting concept is that disclosure of financial information is not an adequate substitute for recognition in the financial statements. For example, the *Framework* states:

> Items that meet the recognition criteria should be recognised in the balance sheet or income statement. The failure to recognise such items is not rectified by disclosure of the accounting policies used nor by notes or explanatory material. (paragraph 82)

BC288 A key aspect of the recognition criteria is that the item can be measured with reliability. This issue is discussed further below. Therefore, this discussion focuses on the 'recognition versus disclosure' issue in principle, not on measurement reliability. Once it has been determined that an item meets the criteria for recognition in the financial statements, failing to recognise it is inconsistent with the basic concept that disclosure is not an adequate substitute for recognition.

BC289 Some disagree with this concept, arguing that it makes no difference whether information is recognised in the financial statements or disclosed in the notes. Either way, users of financial statements have the information they require to make economic decisions. Hence, they believe that note disclosure of expenses arising from particular employee share-based payment transactions (ie those involving awards of share options to employees), rather than recognition in the income statement, is acceptable.

BC290 The Board did not accept this argument. The Board noted that if note disclosure is acceptable, because it makes no difference whether the expense is recognised or disclosed, then recognition in the financial statements must also be acceptable for the same reason. If recognition is acceptable, and recognition rather than mere disclosure accords with the accounting principles applied to all other expense items, it is not acceptable to leave one particular expense item out of the income statement.

BC291 The Board also noted that there is significant evidence that there is a difference between recognition and disclosure. First, academic research indicates that whether information is recognised or merely disclosed affects market prices (eg Barth, Clinch and Shibano, 2003).* If information is disclosed only in the notes, users of financial statements have to expend time and effort to become sufficiently expert in accounting to know (a) that there are items that are not recognised in the financial statements, (b) that there is information about those items in the notes, and (c) how to assess the note disclosures. Because gaining that expertise comes at a cost, and not all users of financial statements will become accounting experts, information that is merely disclosed may not be fully reflected in share prices.

BC292 Second, both preparers and users of financial statements appear to agree that there is an important difference between recognition and disclosure. Users of financial statements have strongly expressed the view that all forms of share-based payment, including employee share options, should be recognised in the financial statements, resulting in the recognition of an expense when the goods or services received are consumed, and that note disclosure alone is inadequate. Their views have been expressed by various means, including:

(a) users' responses to the Discussion Paper and ED 2.

(b) the 2001 survey by the Association for Investment Management and Research of analysts and fund managers—83 per cent of survey respondents said the accounting method for all share-based payment transactions should require recognition of an expense in the income statement.

(c) public comments by users of financial statements, such as those reported in the press or made at recent US Senate hearings.

BC293 Preparers of financial statements also see a major difference between recognition and disclosure. For example, some preparers who responded to the Discussion Paper and ED 2 were concerned that unless expense recognition is required in all countries, entities that are required to recognise an expense would be at a competitive disadvantage compared with entities that are permitted a choice between recognition and disclosure. Comments such as these indicate that preparers of financial statements regard expense recognition as having consequences that are different from those of disclosure.

Reliability of measurement

BC294 One reason commonly given by those who oppose the recognition of an expense arising from transactions involving grants of share options to employees is that it is not possible to measure those transactions reliably.

* M E Barth, G Clinch and T Shibano. 2003. Market Effects of Recognition and Disclosure. *Journal of Accounting Research* 41(4): 581-609.

BC295 The Board discussed these concerns about reliability, after first putting the issue into context. For example, the Board noted that when estimating the fair value of share options, the objective is to measure that fair value at the measurement date, not the value of the underlying share at some future date. Some regard the fair value estimate as inherently uncertain because it is not known, at the measurement date, what the final outcome will be, ie how much the gain on exercise (if any) will be. However, the valuation does not attempt to estimate the future gain, only the amount that the other party would pay to obtain the right to participate in any future gains. Therefore, even if the share option expires worthless or the employee makes a large gain on exercise, this does not mean that the grant date estimate of the fair value of that option was unreliable or wrong.

BC296 The Board also noted that accounting often involves making estimates, and therefore reporting an estimated fair value is not objectionable merely because that amount represents an estimate rather than a precise measure. Examples of other estimates made in accounting, which may have a material effect on the income statement and the balance sheet, include estimates of the collectability of doubtful debts, estimates of the useful life of fixed assets and the pattern of their consumption, and estimates of employee pension liabilities.

BC297 However, some argue that including in the financial statements an estimate of the fair value of employee share options is different from including other estimates, because there is no subsequent correction of the estimate. Other estimates, such as employee pension costs, will ultimately be revised to equal the amount of the cash paid out. In contrast, because equity is not remeasured, if the estimated fair value of employee share options is recognised, there is no remeasurement of the fair value estimate—unless exercise date measurement is used—so any estimation error is permanently embedded in the financial statements.

BC298 The FASB considered and rejected this argument in developing SFAS 123. For example, for employee pension costs, the total cost is never completely trued up unless the scheme is terminated, the amount attributed to any particular year is never trued up, and it can take decades before the amounts relating to particular employees are trued up. In the meantime, users of financial statements have made economic decisions based on the estimated costs.

BC299 Moreover, the Board noted that if no expense (or an expense based on intrinsic value only, which is typically zero) is recognised in respect of employee share options, that also means that there is an error that is permanently embedded in the financial statements. Reporting zero (or an amount based on intrinsic value, if any) is never trued up.

BC300 The Board also considered the meaning of reliability. Arguments about whether estimates of the fair value of employee share options are sufficiently reliable focus on one aspect of reliability only—whether the estimate is free from material error. The *Framework*, in common with the conceptual frameworks of other accounting standard-setters, makes it clear that another important aspect of reliability is whether the information can be depended upon by users of financial statements to represent faithfully what it purports to represent. Therefore, in assessing whether a particular accounting method produces reliable financial information, it is necessary to consider whether that information is representationally faithful.

This is one way in which reliability is linked to another important qualitative characteristic of financial information, relevance.

BC301 For example, in the context of share-based payment, some commentators advocate measuring employee share options at intrinsic value rather than fair value, because intrinsic value is regarded as a much more reliable measure. Whether intrinsic value is a more reliable measure is doubtful—it is certainly less subject to estimation error, but is unlikely to be a representationally faithful measure of remuneration. Nor is intrinsic value a relevant measure, especially when measured at grant date. Many employee share options are issued at the money, so have no intrinsic value at grant date. A share option with no intrinsic value consists entirely of time value. If a share option is measured at intrinsic value at grant date, zero value is attributed to the share option. Therefore, by ignoring time value, the amount attributed to the share option is 100 per cent understated.

BC302 Another qualitative characteristic is comparability. Some argue that, given the uncertainties relating to estimating the fair value of employee share options, it is better for all entities to report zero, because this will make financial statements more comparable. They argue that if, for example, for two entities the 'true' amount of expense relating to employee share options is CU500,000, and estimation uncertainties cause one entity to report CU450,000 and the other to report CU550,000, the two entities' financial statements would be more comparable if both reported zero, rather than these divergent figures.

BC303 However, it is unlikely that any two entities will have the same amount of employee share-based remuneration expense. Research (eg by Bear Stearns and Credit Suisse First Boston) indicates that the expense varies widely from industry to industry, from entity to entity, and from year to year. Reporting zero rather than an estimated amount is likely to make the financial statements much less comparable, not more comparable. For example, if the estimated employee share-based remuneration expense of Company A, Company B and Company C is CU10,000, CU100,000 and CU1,000,000 respectively, reporting zero for all three companies will not make their financial statements comparable.

BC304 In the context of the foregoing discussion of reliability, the Board addressed the question whether transactions involving share options granted to employees can be measured with sufficient reliability for the purpose of recognition in the financial statements. The Board noted that many respondents to the Discussion Paper asserted that this is not possible. They argue that option pricing models cannot be applied to employee share options, because of the differences between employee options and traded options.

BC305 The Board considered these differences, with the assistance of the project's Advisory Group and other experts, and has reached conclusions on how to take account of these differences when estimating the fair value of employee share options, as explained in paragraphs BC145–BC199. In doing so, the Board noted that the objective is to measure the fair value of the share options, ie an estimate of what the price of those equity instruments would have been on grant date in an arm's length transaction between knowledgeable, willing parties. The valuation methodology applied should therefore be consistent with valuation methodologies that market participants would use for pricing similar financial instruments, and should incorporate all factors and assumptions that knowledgeable, willing market participants would consider in setting the price.

BC306 Hence, factors that a knowledgeable, willing market participant would not consider in setting the price of an option are not relevant when estimating the fair value of shares, share options or other equity instruments granted. For example, for share options granted to employees, factors that affect the value of the option from the individual employee's perspective only are not relevant to estimating the price that would be set by a knowledgeable, willing market participant. Many respondents' comments about measurement reliability, and the differences between employee share options and traded options, often focused on the value of the option from the employee's perspective. Therefore, the Board concluded that the IFRS should emphasise that the objective is to estimate the fair value of the share option, not an employee-specific value.

BC307 The Board noted that there is evidence to support a conclusion that it is possible to make a reliable estimate of the fair value of employee share options. First, there is academic research to support this conclusion (eg Carpenter 1998, Maller, Tan and Van De Vyver 2002).* Second, users of financial statements regard the estimated fair values as sufficiently reliable for recognition in the financial statements. Evidence of this can be found in a variety of sources, such as the comment letters received from users of financial statements who responded to the Discussion Paper and ED 2. Users' views are important, because the objective of financial statements is to provide high quality, transparent and comparable information to help users make economic decisions. In other words, financial statements are intended to meet the needs of users, rather than preparers or other interest groups. The purpose of setting accounting standards is to ensure that, wherever possible, the information provided in the financial statements meets users' needs. Therefore, if the people who use the financial statements in making economic decisions regard the fair value estimates as sufficiently reliable for recognition in the financial statements, this provides strong evidence of measurement reliability.

BC308 The Board also noted that, although the FASB decided to permit a choice between recognition and disclosure of expenses arising from employee share-based payment transactions, it did so for non-technical reasons, not because it agreed with the view that reliable measurement was not possible:

> The Board continues to believe that use of option-pricing models, as modified in this statement, will produce estimates of the fair value of stock options that are sufficiently reliable to justify recognition in financial statements. Imprecision in those estimates does not justify failure to recognize compensation cost stemming from employee stock options. That belief underlies the Board's encouragement to entities to adopt the fair value based method of recognizing stock-based employee compensation cost in their financial statements. (SFAS 123, Basis for Conclusions, paragraph 117)

* J N Carpenter. 1998. The exercise and valuation of executive stock options. *Journal of Financial Economics* 48: 127-158.
R A Maller, R Tan and M Van De Vyver. 2002. How Might Companies Value ESOs? *Australian Accounting Review* 12 (1): 11-24.

BC309 In summary, if expenses arising from grants of share options to employees are omitted from the financial statements, or recognised using the intrinsic value method (which typically results in zero expense) or the minimum value method, there will be a permanent error embedded in the financial statements. So the question is, which accounting method is more likely to produce the smallest amount of error and the most relevant, comparable information–a fair value estimate, which might result in some understatement or overstatement of the associated expense, or another measurement basis, such as intrinsic value (especially if measured at grant date), that will definitely result in substantial understatement of the associated expense?

BC310 Taking all of the above into consideration, the Board concluded that, in virtually all cases, the estimated fair value of employee share options at grant date can be measured with sufficient reliability for the purposes of recognising employee share-based payment transactions in the financial statements. The Board therefore concluded that, in general, the IFRS on share-based payment should require a fair value measurement method to be applied to all types of share-based payment transactions, including all types of employee share-based payment. Hence, the Board concluded that the IFRS should not allow a choice between a fair value measurement method and an intrinsic value measurement method, and should not permit a choice between recognition and disclosure of expenses arising from employee share-based payment transactions.

Consequential amendments to other Standards

Tax effects of share-based payment transactions

BC311 Whether expenses arising from share-based payment transactions are deductible, and if so, whether the amount of the tax deduction is the same as the reported expense and whether the tax deduction arises in the same accounting period, varies from country to country.

BC312 If the amount of the tax deduction is the same as the reported expense, but the tax deduction arises in a later accounting period, this will result in a deductible temporary difference under IAS 12 *Income Taxes*. Temporary differences usually arise from differences between the carrying amount of assets and liabilities and the amount attributed to those assets and liabilities for tax purposes. However, IAS 12 also deals with items that have a tax base but are not recognised as assets and liabilities in the balance sheet. It gives an example of research costs that are recognised as an expense in the financial statements in the period in which the costs are incurred, but are deductible for tax purposes in a later accounting period. The Standard states that the difference between the tax base of the research costs, being the amount that will be deductible in a future accounting period, and the carrying amount of nil is a deductible temporary difference that results in a deferred tax asset (IAS 12, paragraph 9).

BC313 Applying this guidance indicates that if an expense arising from a share-based payment transaction is recognised in the financial statements in one accounting period and is tax-deductible in a later accounting period, this should be accounted for as a deductible temporary difference under IAS 12. Under that Standard, a deferred tax asset is recognised for all deductible temporary differences to the extent that it is probable that taxable profit will be available against which the deductible temporary difference can be used (IAS 12, paragraph 24).

BC314 Whilst IAS 12 does not discuss reverse situations, the same logic applies. For example, suppose the entity is able to claim a tax deduction for the total transaction amount at the date of grant but the entity recognises an expense arising from that transaction over the vesting period. Applying the guidance in IAS 12 suggests that this should be accounted for as a taxable temporary difference, and hence a deferred tax liability should be recognised.

BC315 However, the amount of the tax deduction might differ from the amount of the expense recognised in the financial statements. For example, the measurement basis applied for accounting purposes might not be the same as that used for tax purposes, eg intrinsic value might be used for tax purposes and fair value for accounting purposes. Similarly, the measurement date might differ. For example, US entities receive a tax deduction based on intrinsic value at the date of exercise in respect of some share options, whereas for accounting purposes an entity applying SFAS 123 would recognise an expense based on the option's fair value, measured at the date of grant. There could also be other differences in the measurement method applied for accounting and tax purposes, eg differences in the treatment of forfeitures or different valuation methodologies applied.

BC316 SFAS 123 requires that, if the amount of the tax deduction exceeds the total expense recognised in the financial statements, the tax benefit for the excess deduction should be recognised as additional paid-in capital, ie as a direct credit to equity. Conversely, if the tax deduction is less than the total expense recognised for accounting purposes, the write-off of the related deferred tax asset in excess of the benefits of the tax deduction is recognised in the income statement, except to the extent that there is remaining additional paid-in capital from excess tax deductions from previous share-based payment transactions (SFAS 123, paragraph 44).

BC317 At first sight, it may seem questionable to credit or debit directly to equity amounts that relate to differences between the amount of the tax deduction and the total recognised expense. The tax effects of any such differences would ordinarily flow through the income statement. However, some argue that the approach in SFAS 123 is appropriate if the reason for the difference between the amount of the tax deduction and the recognised expense is that a different measurement date is applied.

BC318 For example, suppose grant date measurement is used for accounting purposes and exercise date measurement is used for tax purposes. Under grant date measurement, any changes in the value of the equity instrument after grant date accrue to the employee (or other party) in their capacity as equity participants. Therefore, some argue that any tax effects arising from those valuation changes should be credited to equity (or debited to equity, if the value of the equity instrument declines).

BC319 Similarly, some argue that the tax deduction arises from an equity transaction (the exercise of options), and hence the tax effects should be reported in equity. It can also be argued that this treatment is consistent with the requirement in IAS 12 to account for the tax effects of transactions or events in the same way as the entity accounts for those transactions or events themselves. If the tax deduction relates to both an income statement item and an equity item, the associated tax effects should be allocated between the income statement and equity.

BC320 Others disagree, arguing that the tax deduction relates to employee remuneration expense, ie an income statement item only, and therefore all of the tax effects of the deduction should be recognised in the income statement. The fact that the taxing authority applies a different method in measuring the amount of the tax deduction does not change this conclusion. A further argument is that this treatment is consistent with the *Framework*, because reporting amounts directly in equity would be inappropriate, given that the government is not an owner of the entity.

BC321 The Board noted that, if one accepts that it might be appropriate to debit/credit to equity the tax effect of the difference between the amount of the tax deduction and the total recognised expense where that difference relates to changes in the value of equity interests, there could be other reasons why the amount of the tax deduction differs from the total recognised expense. For example, grant date measurement may be used for both tax and accounting purposes, but the valuation methodology used for tax purposes might produce a higher value than the methodology used for accounting purposes (eg the effects of early exercise might be ignored when valuing an option for tax purposes). The Board saw no reason why, in this situation, the excess tax benefits should be credited to equity.

BC322 In developing ED 2, the Board concluded that the tax effects of share-based payment transactions should be recognised in the income statement by being taken into account in the determination of tax expense. It agreed that this should be explained in the form of a worked example in a consequential amendment to IAS 12.

BC323 During the Board's redeliberation of the proposals in ED 2, the Board reconsidered the points above, and concluded that the tax effects of an equity-settled share-based payment transaction should be allocated between the income statement and equity. The Board then considered how this allocation should be made and related issues, such as the measurement of the deferred tax asset.

BC324 Under IAS 12, the deferred tax asset for a deductible temporary difference is based on the amount the taxation authorities will permit as a deduction in future periods. Therefore, the Board concluded that the measurement of the deferred tax asset should be based on an estimate of the future tax deduction. If changes in the share price affect that future tax deduction, the estimate of the expected future tax deduction should be based on the current share price.

BC325 These conclusions are consistent with the proposals in ED 2 concerning the measurement of the deferred tax asset. However, this approach differs from SFAS 123, which measures the deferred tax asset on the basis of the cumulative recognised expense. The Board rejected the SFAS 123 method of measuring the deferred tax asset because it is inconsistent with IAS 12. As noted above, under IAS 12, the deferred tax asset for a deductible temporary difference is based on the amount the taxation authorities will permit as a deduction in future periods. If a later measurement date is applied for tax purposes, it is very unlikely that the tax deduction will ever equal the cumulative expense, except by coincidence. For example, if share options are granted to employees, and the entity receives a tax deduction measured as the difference between the share price and the exercise price at the date of exercise, it is extremely unlikely that the tax deduction will ever equal the cumulative expense. By basing the measurement of the deferred tax asset on the cumulative expense, the SFAS 123 method is likely to result in the understatement or overstatement of the deferred tax asset. In some situations, such as when share options are significantly out of the money, SFAS 123 requires the entity to continue to recognise a deferred tax asset even when the possibility of the entity recovering that asset is remote. Continuing to recognise a deferred tax asset in this situation is not only inconsistent with IAS 12, it is inconsistent with the definition of an asset in the *Framework*, and the requirements of other IFRSs for the recognition and measurement of assets, including requirements to assess impairment.

BC326 The Board also concluded that:

(a) if the tax deduction received (or expected to be received, measured as described in paragraph BC324) is less than or equal to the cumulative expense, the associated tax benefits received (or expected to be received) should be recognised as tax income and included in profit or loss for the period.

(b) if the tax deduction received (or expected to be received, measured as described in paragraph BC324) exceeds the cumulative expense, the excess associated tax benefits received (or expected to be received) should be recognised directly in equity.

BC327 The above allocation method is similar to that applied in SFAS 123, with some exceptions. First, the above allocation method ensures that the total tax benefits recognised in the income statement in respect of a particular share-based payment transaction do not exceed the tax benefits ultimately received. The Board disagreed with the approach in SFAS 123, which sometimes results in the total tax benefits recognised in the income statement exceeding the tax benefits ultimately received because, in some situations, SFAS 123 permits the unrecovered portion of the deferred tax asset to be written off to equity.

BC328 Second, the Board concluded that the above allocation method should be applied irrespective of why the tax deduction received (or expected to be received) differs from the cumulative expense. The SFAS 123 method is based on US tax legislation, under which the excess tax benefits credited to equity (if any) arise from the use of a later measurement date for tax purposes. The Board agreed with respondents who commented that the accounting treatment must be capable of being applied in various tax jurisdictions. The Board was concerned that requiring entities to examine the reasons why there is a difference between the tax deduction and the cumulative expense, and then account for the tax effects accordingly, would be too complex to be applied consistently across a wide range of different tax jurisdictions.

BC329 The Board noted that it might need to reconsider its conclusions on accounting for the tax effects of share-based payment transactions in the future, for example, if the Board reviews IAS 12 more broadly.

Accounting for own shares held

BC330 IAS 32 requires the acquisition of treasury shares to be deducted from equity, and no gain or loss is to be recognised on the sale, issue or cancellation of treasury shares. Consideration received on the subsequent sale or issue of treasury shares is credited to equity.

BC331 This is consistent with the *Framework*. The repurchase of shares and their subsequent reissue or transfer to other parties are transactions with equity participants that should be recognised as changes in equity. In accounting terms, there is no difference between shares that are repurchased and cancelled, and shares that are repurchased and held by the entity. In both cases, the repurchase involves an outflow of resources to shareholders (ie a distribution), thereby reducing shareholders' investment in the entity. Similarly, there is no difference between a new issue of shares and an issue of shares previously repurchased and held in treasury. In both cases, there is an inflow of resources from shareholders, thereby increasing shareholders' investment in the entity. Although accounting practice in some jurisdictions treats own shares held as assets, this is not consistent with the definition of assets in the *Framework* and the conceptual frameworks of other standard-setters, as explained in the Discussion Paper (footnote to paragraph 4.7 of the Discussion Paper, reproduced earlier in the footnote to paragraph BC73).

BC332 Given that treasury shares are treated as an asset in some jurisdictions, it will be necessary to change that accounting treatment when this IFRS is applied, because otherwise an entity would be faced with two expense items—an expense arising from the share-based payment transaction (for the consumption of goods and services received as consideration for the issue of an equity instrument) and another expense arising from the write-down of the 'asset' for treasury shares issued or transferred to employees at an exercise price that is less than their purchase price.

BC333 Hence, the Board concluded that the requirements in the relevant paragraphs of IAS 32 regarding treasury shares should also be applied to treasury shares purchased, sold, issued or cancelled in connection with employee share plans or other share-based payment arrangements.

CONTENTS

paragraphs

GUIDANCE ON IMPLEMENTING IFRS 2 SHARE-BASED PAYMENT

Guidance on Implementing IFRS 2 Share-based Payment

This guidance accompanies, but is not part of, IFRS 2.

Definition of grant date

IG1 IFRS 2 defines grant date as the date at which the entity and the employee (or other party providing similar services) agree to a share-based payment arrangement, being when the entity and the counterparty have a shared understanding of the terms and conditions of the arrangement. At grant date the entity confers on the counterparty the right to cash, other assets, or equity instruments of the entity, provided the specified vesting conditions, if any, are met. If that agreement is subject to an approval process (for example, by shareholders), grant date is the date when that approval is obtained.

IG2 As noted above, grant date is when both parties agree to a share-based payment arrangement. The word 'agree' is used in its usual sense, which means that there must be both an offer and acceptance of that offer. Hence, the date at which one party makes an offer to another party is not grant date. The date of grant is when that other party accepts the offer. In some instances, the counterparty explicitly agrees to the arrangement, eg by signing a contract. In other instances, agreement might be implicit, eg for many share-based payment arrangements with employees, the employees' agreement is evidenced by their commencing to render services.

IG3 Furthermore, for both parties to have agreed to the share-based payment arrangement, both parties must have a shared understanding of the terms and conditions of the arrangement. Therefore, if some of the terms and conditions of the arrangement are agreed on one date, with the remainder of the terms and conditions agreed on a later date, then grant date is on that later date, when all of the terms and conditions have been agreed. For example, if an entity agrees to issue share options to an employee, but the exercise price of the options will be set by a compensation committee that meets in three months' time, grant date is when the exercise price is set by the compensation committee.

IG4 In some cases, grant date might occur after the employees to whom the equity instruments were granted have begun rendering services. For example, if a grant of equity instruments is subject to shareholder approval, grant date might occur some months after the employees have begun rendering services in respect of that grant. The IFRS requires the entity to recognise the services when received. In this situation, the entity should estimate the grant date fair value of the equity instruments (eg by estimating the fair value of the equity instruments at the end of the reporting period), for the purposes of recognising the services received during the period between service commencement date and grant date. Once the date of grant has been established, the entity should revise the earlier estimate so that the amounts recognised for services received in respect of the grant are ultimately based on the grant date fair value of the equity instruments.

Measurement date for transactions with parties other than employees

IG5 For transactions with parties other than employees (and others providing similar services) that are measured by reference to the fair value of the equity instruments granted, paragraph 13 of IFRS 2 requires the entity to measure that fair value at the date the entity obtains the goods or the counterparty renders service.

IG6 If the goods or services are received on more than one date, the entity should measure the fair value of the equity instruments granted on each date when goods or services are received. The entity should apply that fair value when measuring the goods or services received on that date.

IG7 However, an approximation could be used in some cases. For example, if an entity received services continuously during a three-month period, and its share price did not change significantly during that period, the entity could use the average share price during the three-month period when estimating the fair value of the equity instruments granted.

Transitional arrangements

IG8 In paragraph 54 of IFRS 2, the entity is encouraged, but not required, to apply the requirements of the IFRS to other grants of equity instruments (ie grants other than those specified in paragraph 53 of the IFRS), if the entity has disclosed publicly the fair value of those equity instruments, measured at the measurement date. For example, such equity instruments include equity instruments for which the entity has disclosed in the notes to its financial statements the information required in the US by SFAS 123 *Accounting for Stock-based Compensation*.

Illustrative examples

Equity-settled share-based payment transactions

IG9 For equity-settled transactions measured by reference to the fair value of the equity instruments granted, paragraph 19 of IFRS 2 states that vesting conditions, other than market conditions,* are not taken into account when estimating the fair value of the shares or share options at the measurement date (ie grant date, for transactions with employees and others providing similar services). Instead, vesting conditions are taken into account by adjusting the number of equity instruments included in the measurement of the transaction amount so that, ultimately, the amount recognised for goods or services received as consideration for the equity instruments granted is based on the number of equity instruments that eventually vest. Hence, on a cumulative basis, no amount is recognised for goods or services received if the equity instruments granted do not vest because of failure to satisfy a vesting condition, eg the counterparty fails to complete a specified service period, or a performance condition is not satisfied. This accounting method is known as the modified grant date method, because the number of equity instruments included in the determination of the transaction amount is adjusted to reflect the outcome of the vesting conditions, but no

* In the remainder of this paragraph, the discussion of vesting conditions excludes market conditions, which are subject to the requirements of paragraph 21 of IFRS 2.

adjustment is made to the fair value of those equity instruments. That fair value is estimated at grant date (for transactions with employees and others providing similar services) and not subsequently revised. Hence, neither increases nor decreases in the fair value of the equity instruments after grant date are taken into account when determining the transaction amount (other than in the context of measuring the incremental fair value transferred if a grant of equity instruments is subsequently modified).

IG10 To apply these requirements, paragraph 20 of IFRS 2 requires the entity to recognise the goods or services received during the vesting period based on the best available estimate of the number of equity instruments expected to vest and to revise that estimate, if necessary, if subsequent information indicates that the number of equity instruments expected to vest differs from previous estimates. On vesting date, the entity revises the estimate to equal the number of equity instruments that ultimately vested (subject to the requirements of paragraph 21 concerning market conditions).

IG11 In the examples below, the share options granted all vest at the same time, at the end of a specified period. In some situations, share options or other equity instruments granted might vest in instalments over the vesting period. For example, suppose an employee is granted 100 share options, which will vest in instalments of 25 share options at the end of each year over the next four years. To apply the requirements of the IFRS, the entity should treat each instalment as a separate share option grant, because each instalment has a different vesting period, and hence the fair value of each instalment will differ (because the length of the vesting period affects, for example, the likely timing of cash flows arising from the exercise of the options).

IG Example 1

Background

An entity grants 100 share options to each of its 500 employees. Each grant is conditional upon the employee working for the entity over the next three years. The entity estimates that the fair value of each share option is CU15.[(a)]

On the basis of a weighted average probability, the entity estimates that 20 per cent of employees will leave during the three-year period and therefore forfeit their rights to the share options.

Application of requirements

Scenario 1

If everything turns out exactly as expected, the entity recognises the following amounts during the vesting period, for services received as consideration for the share options.

Year	Calculation	Remuneration expense for period	Cumulative remuneration expense
		CU	CU
1	50,000 options × 80% × CU15 × ⅓ years	200,000	200,000
2	(50,000 options × 80% × CU15 × ⅔ years) – CU200,000	200,000	400,000
3	(50,000 options × 80% × CU15 × 3/3 years) – CU400,000	200,0000	600,000

Continued from previous page

IG Example 1

Scenario 2

During year 1, 20 employees leave. The entity revises its estimate of total employee departures over the three-year period from 20 per cent (100 employees) to 15 per cent (75 employees). During year 2, a further 22 employees leave. The entity revises its estimate of total employee departures over the three-year period from 15 per cent to 12 per cent (60 employees). During year 3, a further 15 employees leave. Hence, a total of 57 employees forfeited their rights to the share options during the three-year period, and a total of 44,300 share options (443 employees × 100 options per employee) vested at the end of year 3.

Year	Calculation	Remuneration expense for period CU	Cumulative remuneration expense CU
1	50,000 options × 85% × CU15 × ⅓ years	212,500	212,500
2	(50,000 options × 88% × CU15 × ⅔ years) – CU212,500	227,500	440,000
3	(44,300 options × CU15) – CU440,000	224,500	664,500

(a) In this example, and in all other examples in this guidance, monetary amounts are denominated in 'currency units' (CU).

IG12 In Example 1, the share options were granted conditionally upon the employees' completing a specified service period. In some cases, a share option or share grant might also be conditional upon the achievement of a specified performance target. Examples 2, 3 and 4 illustrate the application of the IFRS to share option or share grants with performance conditions (other than market conditions, which are discussed in paragraph IG5 and illustrated in Examples 5 and 6). In Example 2, the length of the vesting period varies, depending on when the performance condition is satisfied. Paragraph 15 of the IFRS requires the entity to estimate the length of the expected vesting period, based on the most likely outcome of the performance condition, and to revise that estimate, if necessary, if subsequent information indicates that the length of the vesting period is likely to differ from previous estimates.

IG Example 2

Grant with a performance condition, in which the length of the vesting period varies

Background

At the beginning of year 1, the entity grants 100 shares each to 500 employees, conditional upon the employees' remaining in the entity's employ during the vesting period. The shares will vest at the end of year 1 if the entity's earnings increase by more than 18 per cent; at the end of year 2 if the entity's earnings increase by more than an average of 13 per cent per year over the two-year period; and at the end of year 3 if the entity's earnings increase by more than an average of 10 per cent per year over the three-year period. The shares have a fair value of CU30 per share at the start of year 1, which equals the share price at grant date. no dividends are expected to be paid over the three-year period.

By the end of year 1, the entity's earnings have increased by 14 per cent, and 30 employees have left. The entity expects that earnings will continue to increase at a similar rate in year 2, and therefore expects that the shares will vest at the end of year 2. The entity expects, on the basis of a weighted average probability, that a further 30 employees will leave during year 2, and therefore expects that 440 employees will vest in 100 shares each at the end of year 2.

By the end of year 2, the entity's earnings have increased by only 10 per cent and therefore the shares do not vest at the end of year 2. 28 employees have left during the year. The entity expects that a further 25 employees will leave during year 3, and that the entity's earnings will increase by at least 6 per cent, thereby achieving the average of 10 per cent per year.

By the end of year 3, 23 employees have left and the entity's earnings had increased by 8 per cent, resulting in an average increase of 10.67 per cent per year. Therefore, 419 employees received 100 shares at the end of year 3.

Application of requirements

Year	Calculation	Remuneration expense for period	Cumulative remuneration expense
		CU	CU
1	440 employees × 100 shares × CU30 × ½	660,000	660,000
2	(417 employees × 100 shares × CU30 × ⅔) – CU660,000	174,000	834,000
3	(419 employees × 100 shares × CU30 × 3⁄3) – CU834,000	423,000	1,257,000

IG Example 3

Grant with a performance condition, in which the number of equity instruments varies

Background

At the beginning of year 1, Entity A grants share options to each of its 100 employees working in the sales department. The share options will vest at the end of year 3, provided that the employees remain in the entity's employ, and provided that the volume of sales of a particular product increases by at least an average of 5 per cent per year. If the volume of sales of the product increases by an average of between 5 per cent and 10 per cent per year, each employee will receive 100 share options. If the volume of sales increases by an average of between 10 per cent and 15 per cent each year, each employee will receive 200 share options. If the volume of sales increases by an average of 15 per cent or more, each employee will receive 300 share options.

On grant date, Entity A estimates that the share options have a fair value of CU20 per option. Entity A also estimates that the volume of sales of the product will increase by an average of between 10 per cent and 15 per cent per year, and therefore expects that, for each employee who remains in service until the end of year 3, 200 share options will vest. The entity also estimates, on the basis of a weighted average probability, that 20 per cent of employees will leave before the end of year 3.

By the end of year 1, seven employees have left and the entity still expects that a total of 20 employees will leave by the end of year 3. Hence, the entity expects that 80 employees will remain in service for the three-year period. Product sales have increased by 12 per cent and the entity expects this rate of increase to continue over the next 2 years.

By the end of year 2, a further five employees have left, bringing the total to 12 to date. The entity now expects only three more employees will leave during year 3, and therefore expects a total of 15 employees will have left during the three-year period, and hence 85 employees are expected to remain. Product sales have increased by 18 per cent, resulting in an average of 15 per cent over the two years to date. The entity now expects that sales will average 15 per cent or more over the three-year period, and hence expects each sales employee to receive 300 share options at the end of year 3.

By the end of year 3, a further two employees have left. Hence, 14 employees have left during the three-year period, and 86 employees remain. The entity's sales have increased by an average of 16 per cent over the three years. Therefore, each of the 86 employees receive 300 share options.

Continued from previous page

IG Example 3

Application of requirements

Year	Calculation	Remuneration expense for period CU	Cumulative remuneration expense CU
1	80 employees × 200 options × CU20 × ⅓	106,667	106,667
2	(85 employees × 300 options × CU20 × ⅔) – CU106,667	233,333	340,000
3	(86 employees × 300 options × CU20 × 3/3) – CU340,000	176,000	516,000

IG Example 4

Grant with a performance condition, in which the exercise price varies

Background

At the beginning of year 1, an entity grants to a senior executive 10,000 share options, conditional upon the executive's remaining in the entity's employ until the end of year 3. The exercise price is CU40. However, the exercise price drops to CU30 if the entity's earnings increase by at least an average of 10 per cent per year over the three-year period.

On grant date, the entity estimates that the fair value of the share options, with an exercise price of CU30, is CU16 per option. If the exercise price is CU40, the entity estimates that the share options have a fair value of CU12 per option.

During year 1, the entity's earnings increased by 12 per cent, and the entity expects that earnings will continue to increase at this rate over the next two years. The entity therefore expects that the earnings target will be achieved, and hence the share options will have an exercise price of CU30.

During year 2, the entity's earnings increased by 13 per cent, and the entity continues to expect that the earnings target will be achieved.

During year 3, the entity's earnings increased by only 3 per cent, and therefore the earnings target was not achieved. The executive completes three years' service, and therefore satisfies the service condition. Because the earnings target was not achieved, the 10,000 vested share options have an exercise price of CU40.

Continued from previous page

IG Example 4

Application of requirements

Because the exercise price varies depending on the outcome of a performance condition that is not a market condition, the effect of that performance condition (ie the possibility that the exercise price might be CU40 and the possibility that the exercise price might be CU30) is not taken into account when estimating the fair value of the share options at grant date. Instead, the entity estimates the fair value of the share options at grant date under each scenario (ie exercise price of CU40 and exercise price of CU30) and ultimately revises the transaction amount to reflect the outcome of that performance condition, as illustrated below.

Year	Calculation	Remuneration expense for period	Cumulative remuneration expense
		CU	CU
1	10,000 options × CU16 × ⅓	53,333	53,333
2	(10,000 options × CU16 × ⅔) – CU53,333	53,334	106,667
3	(10,000 options × CU12 × 3/3) – CU106,667	13,333	120,000

IG13 Paragraph 21 of the IFRS requires market conditions, such as a target share price upon which vesting (or exercisability) is conditional, to be taken into account when estimating the fair value of the equity instruments granted. Therefore, for grants of equity instruments with market conditions, the entity recognises the goods or services received from a counterparty who satisfies all other vesting conditions (eg services received from an employee who remains in service for the specified period of service), irrespective of whether that market condition is satisfied. Example 5 illustrates these requirements.

IG Example 5

Grant with a market condition

Background

At the beginning of year 1, an entity grants to a senior executive 10,000 share options, conditional upon the executive remaining in the entity's employ until the end of year 3. However, the share options cannot be exercised unless the share price has increased from CU50 at the beginning of year 1 to above CU65 at the end of year 3. If the share price is above CU65 at the end of year 3, the share options can be exercised at any time during the next seven years, ie by the end of year 10.

The entity applies a binomial option pricing model, which takes into account the possibility that the share price will exceed CU65 at the end of year 3 (and hence the share options become exercisable) and the possibility that the share price will not exceed CU65 at the end of year 3 (and hence the options will be forfeited). It estimates the fair value of the share options with this market condition to be CU24 per option.

Continued from previous page

IG Example 5

Application of requirements

Because paragraph 21 of the IFRS requires the entity to recognise the services received from a counterparty who satisfies all other vesting conditions (eg services received from an employee who remains in service for the specified service period), irrespective of whether that market condition is satisfied, it makes no difference whether the share price target is achieved. The possibility that the share price target might not be achieved has already been taken into account when estimating the fair value of the share options at grant date. Therefore, if the entity expects the executive to complete the three-year service period, and the executive does so, the entity recognises the following amounts in years 1, 2 and 3:

Year	Calculation	Remuneration expense for period	Cumulative remuneration expense
		CU	CU
1	10,000 options × CU24 × ⅓	80,000	80,000
2	(10,000 options × CU24 × ⅔) – CU80,000	80,000	160,000
3	(10,000 options × CU24) – CU160,000	80,000	240,000

As noted above, these amounts are recognised irrespective of the outcome of the market condition. However, if the executive left during year 2 (or year 3), the amount recognised during year 1 (and year 2) would be reversed in year 2 (or year 3). This is because the service condition, in contrast to the market condition, was not taken into account when estimating the fair value of the share options at grant date. Instead, the service condition is taken into account by adjusting the transaction amount to be based on the number of equity instruments that ultimately vest, in accordance with paragraphs 19 and 20 of the IFRS.

IG14 In Example 5, the outcome of the market condition did not change the length of the vesting period. However, if the length of the vesting period varies depending on when a performance condition is satisfied, paragraph 15 of the IFRS requires the entity to presume that the services to be rendered by the employees as consideration for the equity instruments granted will be received in the future, over the expected vesting period. The entity is required to estimate the length of the expected vesting period at grant date, based on the most likely outcome of the performance condition. If the performance condition is a market condition, the estimate of the length of the expected vesting period must be consistent with the assumptions used in estimating the fair value of the share options granted, and is not subsequently revised. Example 6 illustrates these requirements.

IG Example 6

Grant with a market condition, in which the length of the vesting period varies

Background

At the beginning of year 1, an entity grants 10,000 share options with a ten-year life to each of ten senior executives. The share options will vest and become exercisable immediately if and when the entity's share price increases from CU50 to CU70, provided that the executive remains in service until the share price target is achieved.

The entity applies a binomial option pricing model, which takes into account the possibility that the share price target will be achieved during the ten-year life of the options, and the possibility that the target will not be achieved. The entity estimates that the fair value of the share options at grant date is CU25 per option. From the option pricing model, the entity determines that the mode of the distribution of possible vesting dates is five years. In other words, of all the possible outcomes, the most likely outcome of the market condition is that the share price target will be achieved at the end of year 5. Therefore, the entity estimates that the expected vesting period is five years. The entity also estimates that two executives will have left by the end of year 5, and therefore expects that 80,000 share options (10,000 share options × 8 executives) will vest at the end of year 5.

Throughout years 1–4, the entity continues to estimate that a total of two executives will leave by the end of year 5. However, in total three executives leave, one in each of years 3, 4 and 5. The share price target is achieved at the end of year 6. Another executive leaves during year 6, before the share price target is achieved.

Application of requirements

Paragraph 15 of the IFRS requires the entity to recognise the services received over the expected vesting period, as estimated at grant date, and also requires the entity not to revise that estimate. Therefore, the entity recognises the services received from the executives over years 1–5. Hence, the transaction amount is ultimately based on 7,000 share options (10,000 share options × 7 executives who remain in service at the end of year 5). Although another executive left during year 6, no adjustment is made, because the executive had already completed the expected vesting period of 5 years. Therefore, the entity recognises the following amounts in years 1–5:

Continued from previous page

IG Example 6

Year	Calculation	Remuneration expense for period	Cumulative remuneration expense
		CU	CU
1	80,000 options × CU25 × ⅕	400,000	400,000
2	(80,000 options × CU25 × ⅖) – CU400,000	400,000	800,000
3	(80,000 options × CU25 × ⅗) – CU800,000	400,000	1,200,000
4	(80,000 options × CU25 × ⅘) – CU1,600,000	400,000	1,600,000
5	(70,000 options × CU25) – CU1,600,000	150,000	1,750,000

IG15 Paragraphs 26–29 and B42–B44 of the IFRS set out requirements that apply if a share option is repriced (or the entity otherwise modifies the terms or conditions of a share-based payment arrangement). Examples 7–9 illustrate some of these requirements.

IG Example 7

Grant of share options that are subsequently repriced

Background

At the beginning of year 1, an entity grants 100 share options to each of its 500 employees. Each grant is conditional upon the employee remaining in service over the next three years. The entity estimates that the fair value of each option is CU15. On the basis of a weighted average probability, the entity estimates that 100 employees will leave during the three-year period and therefore forfeit their rights to the share options.

Suppose that 40 employees leave during year 1. Also suppose that by the end of year 1, the entity's share price has dropped, and the entity reprices its share options, and that the repriced share options vest at the end of year 3. The entity estimates that a further 70 employees will leave during years 2 and 3, and hence the total expected employee departures over the three-year vesting period is 110 employees. During year 2, a further 35 employees leave, and the entity estimates that a further 30 employees will leave during year 3, to bring the total expected employee departures over the three-year vesting period to 105 employees. During year 3, a total of 28 employees leave, and hence a total of 103 employees ceased employment during the vesting period. For the remaining 397 employees, the share options vested at the end of year 3.

The entity estimates that, at the date of repricing, the fair value of each of the original share options granted (ie before taking into account the repricing) is CU5 and that the fair value of each repriced share option is CU8.

Continued from previous page

IG Example 7

Application of requirements

Paragraph 27 of the IFRS requires the entity to recognise the effects of modifications that increase the total fair value of the share-based payment arrangement or are otherwise beneficial to the employee. If the modification increases the fair value of the equity instruments granted (eg by reducing the exercise price), measured immediately before and after the modification, paragraph B43(a) of Appendix B requires the entity to include the incremental fair value granted (ie the difference between the fair value of the modified equity instrument and that of the original equity instrument, both estimated as at the date of the modification) in the measurement of the amount recognised for services received as consideration for the equity instruments granted. If the modification occurs during the vesting period, the incremental fair value granted is included in the measurement of the amount recognised for services received over the period from the modification date until the date when the modified equity instruments vest, in addition to the amount based on the grant date fair value of the original equity instruments, which is recognised over the remainder of the original vesting period.

The incremental value is CU3 per share option (CU8 – CU5). This amount is recognised over the remaining two years of the vesting period, along with remuneration expense based on the original option value of CU15.

The amounts recognised in years 1–3 are as follows:

Year	Calculation	Remuneration expense for period	Cumulative remuneration expense
		CU	CU
1	(500 – 110) employees × 100 options × CU15 × ⅓	195,000	195,000
2	(500 – 105) employees × 100 options × (CU15 × ⅔ + CU3 × ½) – CU195,000	259,250	454,250
3	(500 – 103) employees × 100 options × (CU15 + CU3) – CU454,250	260,350	714,600

IG Example 8

Grant of shares, with a cash alternative subsequently added

Background

At the beginning of year 1, the entity grants ,000 share options to each member of its sales team, conditional upon the employee's remaining in the entity's employ for three years, and the team selling more than 50,000 units of a particular product over the three-year period. The fair value of the share options is CU15 per option at the date of grant.

During year 2, the entity increases the sales target to 100,000 units. By the end of year 3, the entity has sold 50,000 units, and the share options are forfeited. Twelve members of the sales team have remained in service for the three-year period.

Application of requirements

Paragraph 20 of the IFRS requires, for a performance condition that is not a market condition, the entity to recognise the services received during the vesting period based on the best available estimate of the number of equity instruments expected to vest and to revise that estimate, if necessary, if subsequent information indicates that the number of equity instruments expected to vest differs from previous estimates. On vesting date, the entity revises the estimate to equal the number of equity instruments that ultimately vested. However, paragraph 27 of the IFRS requires, irrespective of any modifications to the terms and conditions on which the equity instruments were granted, or a cancellation or settlement of that grant of equity instruments, the entity to recognise, as a minimum, the services received, measured at the grant date fair value of the equity instruments granted, unless those equity instruments do not vest because of failure to satisfy a vesting condition (other than a market condition) that was specified at grant date. Furthermore, paragraph B44(c) of Appendix B specifies that, if the entity modifies the vesting conditions in a manner that is not beneficial to the employee, the entity does not take the modified vesting conditions into account when applying the requirements of paragraphs 19–21 of the IFRS.

Continued from previous page

IG Example 8

Therefore, because the modification to the performance condition made it less likely that the share options will vest, which was not beneficial to the employee, the entity takes no account of the modified performance condition when recognising the services received. Instead, it continues to recognise the services received over the three-year period based on the original vesting conditions. Hence, the entity ultimately recognises cumulative remuneration expense of CU180,000 over the three-year period (12 employees × 1,000 options × CU15).

The same result would have occurred if, instead of modifying the performance target, the entity had increased the number of years of service required for the share options to vest from three years to ten years. Because such a modification would make it less likely that the options will vest, which would not be beneficial to the employees, the entity would take no account of the modified service condition when recognising the services received. Instead, it would recognise the services received from the twelve employees who remained in service over the original three-year vesting period.

IG Example 9

Grant with a market condition, in which the length of the vesting period varies

Background

At the beginning of year 1, the entity grants 10,000 shares with a fair value of CU33 per share to a senior executive, conditional upon the completion of three years' service. By the end of year 2, the share price has dropped to CU25 per share. At that date, the entity adds a cash alternative to the grant, whereby the executive can choose whether to receive 10,000 shares or cash equal to the value of 10,000 shares on vesting date. The share price is CU22 on vesting date.

Continued from previous page

IG Example 9

Application of requirements

Paragraph 27 of the IFRS requires, irrespective of any modifications to the terms and conditions on which the equity instruments were granted, or a cancellation or settlement of that grant of equity instruments, the entity to recognise, as a minimum, the services received measured at the grant date fair value of the equity instruments granted, unless those equity instruments do not vest because of failure to satisfy a vesting condition (other than a market condition) that was specified at grant date. Therefore, the entity recognises the services received over the three-year period, based on the grant date fair value of the shares.

Furthermore, the addition of the cash alternative at the end of year 2 creates an obligation to settle in cash. In accordance with the requirements for cash-settled share-based payment transactions (paragraphs 30–33 of the IFRS), the entity recognises the liability to settle in cash at the modification date, based on the fair value of the shares at the modification date and the extent to which the specified services have been received. Furthermore, the entity remeasures the fair value of the liability at each reporting date and at the date of settlement, with any changes in fair value recognised in profit or loss for the period. Therefore, the entity recognises the following amounts:

Continued from previous page

IG Example 9

Year	Calculation	Expense	Equity	Liability
		CU	CU	CU
1	Remuneration expense for year: 10,000 shares × CU33 × ⅓	110,000	110,000	
2	Remuneration expense for year: (10,000 shares × CU33 × ⅔) – CU110,000	110,000	110,000	
	Reclassify equity to liabilities: 10,000 shares × CU25 × ⅔		(166,667)	166,667
3	Remuneration expense for year: (10,000 shares × CU33 × 3⁄3) – CU220,000	110,000	26,667 (a)	83,333 (a)
	Adjust liability to closing fair value: (CU166,667 + CU83,333) – (CU22 × 10,000 shares)	(30,000)		(30,000)
	Total	300,000	80,000	220,000

(a) Allocated between liabilities and equity, to bring in the final third of the liability based on the fair value of the shares as at the date of the modification.

IG16 Paragraph 24 of the IFRS requires that, in rare cases only, in which the IFRS requires the entity to measure an equity-settled share-based payment transaction by reference to the fair value of the equity instruments granted, but the entity is unable to estimate reliably that fair value at the specified measurement date (eg grant date, for transactions with employees), the entity shall instead measure the transaction using an intrinsic value measurement method. Paragraph 24 also contains requirements on how to apply this method. The following example illustrates these requirements.

IG Example 10

Grant of share options that is accounted for by applying the intrinsic value method

Background

At the beginning of year 1, an entity grants 1,000 share options to 50 employees. The share options will vest at the end of year 3, provided the employees remain in service until then. The share options have a life of 10 years. The exercise price is CU60 and the entity's share price is also CU60 at the date of grant.

At the date of grant, the entity concludes that it cannot estimate reliably the fair value of the share options granted.

At the end of year 1, three employees have ceased employment and the entity estimates that a further seven employees will leave during years 2 and 3. Hence, the entity estimates that 80 per cent of the share options will vest.

Two employees leave during year 2, and the entity revises its estimate of the number of share options that it expects will vest to 86 per cent.

Two employees leave during year 3. Hence, 43,000 share options vested at the end of year 3.

The entity's share price during years 1–10, and the number of share options exercised during years 4–10, are set out below. Share options that were exercised during a particular year were all exercised at the end of that year.

Year	Share price at year-end	Number of share options exercised at year-end
1	63	0
2	65	0
3	75	0
4	88	6,000
5	100	8,000
6	90	5,000
7	96	9,000
8	105	8,000
9	108	5,000
10	115	2,000

Continued from previous page

IG Example 10

Application of requirements

In accordance with paragraph 24 of the IFRS, the entity recognises the following amounts in years 1–10.

Year	Calculation	Expense for period	Cumulative expense
		CU	CU
1	50,000 options × 80% × (CU63 –CU60) × ⅓ years	40,000	40,000
2	50,000 options × 86% × (CU65 –CU60) × ⅔ years – CU40,000	103,333	143,333
3	43,000 options × (CU75 – CU60) – CU143,333	501,667	645,000
4	37,000 outstanding options × (CU88 – CU75) + 6,000 exercised options × (CU88 – CU75)	559,000	1,204,000
5	29,000 outstanding options × (CU100 – CU88) + 8,000 exercised options × (CU100 – CU88)	444,000	1,648,000
6	24,000 outstanding options × (CU90 – CU100) + 5,000 exercised options × (CU90 – CU100)	(290,000)	1,358,000
7	15,000 outstanding options × (CU96 – CU90) + 9,000 exercised options × (CU96 – CU90)	144,000	1,502,000
8	7,000 outstanding options × (CU105 – CU96) + 8,000 exercised options × (CU105 – CU96)	135,000	1,637,000
9	2,000 outstanding options × (CU108 – CU105) + 5,000 exercised options × (CU108 – CU105)	21,000	1,658,000
10	2,000 exercised options × (CU115 – CU108)	14,000	1,672,000

IG17 There are many different types of employee share and share option plans. The following example illustrates the application of IFRS 2 to one particular type of plan–an employee share purchase plan. Typically, an employee share purchase plan provides employees with the opportunity to purchase the entity's shares at a discounted price. The terms and conditions under which employee share purchase plans operate differ from country to country. That is to say, not only are there many different types of employee share and share options plans, there are

also many different types of employee share purchase plans. Therefore, the following example illustrates the application of IFRS 2 to one specific employee share purchase plan.

IG Example 11

Employee share purchase plan

Background

An entity offers all its 1,000 employees the opportunity to participate in an employee share purchase plan. The employees have two weeks to decide whether to accept the offer. Under the terms of the plan, the employees are entitled to purchase a maximum of 100 shares each. The purchase price will be 20 per cent less than the market price of the entity's shares at the date the offer is accepted, and the purchase price must be paid immediately upon acceptance of the offer. All shares purchased must be held in trust for the employees, and cannot be sold for five years. The employee is not permitted to withdraw from the plan during that period. For example, if the employee ceases employment during the five-year period, the shares must nevertheless remain in the plan until the end of the five-year period. Any dividends paid during the five-year period will be held in trust for the employees until the end of the five-year period.

In total, 800 employees accept the offer and each employee purchases, on average, 80 shares, ie the employees purchase a total of 64,000 shares. The weighted-average market price of the shares at the purchase date is CU30 per share, and the weighted-average purchase price is CU24 per share.

Continued from previous page

IG Example 11

Application of requirements

For transactions with employees, IFRS 2 requires the transaction amount to be measured by reference to the fair value of the equity instruments granted (IFRS 2, paragraph 11). To apply this requirement, it is necessary first to determine the type of equity instrument granted to the employees. Although the plan is described as an employee share purchase plan (ESPP), some ESPPs include option features and are therefore, in effect, share option plans. For example, an ESPP might include a 'look-back feature', whereby the employee is able to purchase shares at a discount, and choose whether the discount is applied to the entity's share price at the date of grant or its share price at the date of purchase. Or an ESPP might specify the purchase price, and then allow the employees a significant period of time to decide whether to participate in the plan. Another example of an option feature is an ESPP that permits the participating employees to cancel their participation before or at the end of a specified period and obtain a refund of amounts previously paid into the plan.

However, in this example, the plan includes no option features. The discount is applied to the share price at the purchase date, and the employees are not permitted to withdraw from the plan.

Another factor to consider is the effect of post-vesting transfer restrictions, if any. Paragraph B3 of IFRS 2 states that, if shares are subject to restrictions on transfer after vesting date, that factor should be taken into account when estimating the fair value of those shares, but only to the extent that the post-vesting restrictions affect the price that a knowledgeable, willing market participant would pay for that share. For example, if the shares are actively traded in a deep and liquid market, post-vesting transfer restrictions may have little, if any, effect on the price that a knowledgeable, willing market participant would pay for those shares.

Continued from previous page

IG Example 11

In this example, the shares are vested when purchased, but cannot be sold for five years after the date of purchase. Therefore, the entity should consider the valuation effect of the five-year post-vesting transfer restriction. This entails using a valuation technique to estimate what the price of the restricted share would have been on the purchase date in an arm's length transaction between knowledgeable, willing parties. Suppose that, in this example, the entity estimates that the fair value of each restricted share is CU28. In this case, the fair value of the equity instruments granted is CU4 per share (being the fair value of the restricted share of CU28 less the purchase price of CU24). Because 64,000 shares were purchased, the total fair value of the equity instruments granted is CU256,000.

In this example, there is no vesting period. Therefore, in accordance with paragraph 14 of IFRS 2, the entity should recognise an expense of CU256,000 immediately.

However, in some cases, the expense relating to an ESPP might not be material. IAS 8 *Accounting Policies, Changes in Accounting Policies and Errors* states that the accounting policies in IFRSs need not be applied when the effect of applying them is immaterial (IAS 8, paragraph 8). IAS 8 also states that an omission or misstatement of an item is material if it could, individually or collectively, influence the economic decisions of users taken on the basis of the financial statements. Materiality depends on the size and nature of the omission or misstatement judged in the surrounding circumstances. The size or nature of the item, or a combination of both, could be the determining factor (IAS 8, paragraph 5). Therefore, in this example, the entity should consider whether the expense of CU256,000 is material.

Cash-settled share-based payment transactions

IG18 Paragraphs 30–33 of the IFRS set out requirements for transactions in which an entity acquires goods or services by incurring liabilities to the supplier of those goods or services in amounts based on the price of the entity's shares or other equity instruments. The entity is required to recognise initially the goods or services acquired, and a liability to pay for those goods or services, when the entity obtains the goods or as the services are rendered, measured at the fair value of the liability. Thereafter, until the liability is settled, the entity is required to recognise changes in the fair value of the liability.

IG19 For example, an entity might grant share appreciation rights to employees as part of their remuneration package, whereby the employees will become entitled to a future cash payment (rather than an equity instrument), based on the increase in the entity's share price from a specified level over a specified period of time. If the share appreciation rights do not vest until the employees have completed a specified period of service, the entity recognises the services received, and a liability to pay for them, as the employees render service during that period. The liability is measured, initially and at each reporting date until settled, at the fair value of the share appreciation rights, by applying an option pricing model, and the extent to which the employees have rendered service to date. Changes in fair value are recognised in profit or loss. Therefore, if the amount recognised for the services received was included in the carrying amount of an asset recognised in the entity's balance sheet (eg inventory), the carrying amount of that asset is not adjusted for the effects of the liability remeasurement. Example 12 illustrates these requirements.

IG Example 12

Background

An entity grants 100 cash share appreciation rights (SARs) to each of its 500 employees, on condition that the employees remain in its employ for the next three years.

During year 1, 35 employees leave. The entity estimates that a further 60 will leave during years 2 and 3. During year 2, 40 employees leave and the entity estimates that a further 25 will leave during year 3. During year 3, 22 employees leave. At the end of year 3, 150 employees exercise their SARs, another 140 employees exercise their SARs at the end of year 4 and the remaining 113 employees exercise their SARs at the end of year 5.

The entity estimates the fair value of the SARs at the end of each year in which a liability exists as shown below. At the end of year 3, all SARs held by the remaining employees vest. The intrinsic values of the SARs at the date of exercise (which equal the cash paid out) at the end of years 3, 4 and 5 are also shown below.

Continued from previous page

IG Example 12

Year	Fair value	Intrinsic value
1	CU14.40	
2	CU15.50	
3	CU18.20	CU15.00
4	CU21.40	CU20.00
5		CU25.00

Application of requirements

Year	Calculation		Equity CU	Liability CU
1	(500 – 95) employees × 100 SARs × CU14.40 × ⅓		194,400	194,400
2	(500 – 100) employees × 100 SARs × CU15.50 × ⅔ – CU194,400		218,933	413,333
3	(500 – 97 – 150) employees × 100 SARs × CU18.20 – CU413,333	47,127		460,460
	+ 150 employees × 100 SARs × CU15.00	225,000		
	Total		272,127	
4	(253 – 140) employees × 100 SARs × CU21.40 – CU460,460	(218,640)		241,820
	+ 140 employees × 100 SARs × CU20.00	280,000		
	Total		61,360	
5	CU0 – CU241,820	(241,820)		0
	+ 113 employees × 100 SARs × CU25.00	282,500		
	Total		40,680	
	Total		787,500	

Share-based payment arrangements with cash alternatives

IG20 Some employee share-based payment arrangements permit the employee to choose whether to receive cash or equity instruments. In this situation, a compound financial instrument has been granted, ie a financial instrument with debt and equity components. Paragraph 37 of the IFRS requires the entity to estimate the fair value of the compound financial instrument at grant date, by first measuring the fair value of the debt component, and then measuring the fair value of the equity component—taking into account that the employee must forfeit the right to receive cash to receive the equity instrument.

IG21 Typically, share-based payment arrangements with cash alternatives are structured so that the fair value of one settlement alternative is the same as the other. For example, the employee might have the choice of receiving share options or cash share appreciation rights. In such cases, the fair value of the equity component will be zero, and hence the fair value of the compound financial instrument will be the same as the fair value of the debt component. However, if the fair values of the settlement alternatives differ, usually the fair value of the equity component will be greater than zero, in which case the fair value of the compound financial instrument will be greater than the fair value of the debt component.

IG22 Paragraph 38 of the IFRS requires the entity to account separately for the services received in respect of each component of the compound financial instrument. For the debt component, the entity recognises the services received, and a liability to pay for those services, as the counterparty renders service, in accordance with the requirements applying to cash-settled share-based payment transactions. For the equity component (if any), the entity recognises the services received, and an increase in equity, as the counterparty renders service, in accordance with the requirements applying to equity-settled share-based payment transactions. Example 13 illustrates these requirements.

IG Example 13

Background

An entity grants to an employee the right to choose either 1,000 phantom shares, ie a right to a cash payment equal to the value of 1,000 shares, or 1,200 shares. The grant is conditional upon the completion of three years' service. If the employee chooses the share alternative, the shares must be held for three years after vesting date.

At grant date, the entity's share price is CU50 per share. At the end of years 1, 2 and 3, the share price is CU52, CU55 and CU60 respectively. The entity does not expect to pay dividends in the next three years. After taking into account the effects of the post-vesting transfer restrictions, the entity estimates that the grant date fair value of the share alternative is CU48 per share.

At the end of year 3, the employee chooses:

Scenario 1: The cash alternative

Scenario 2: The equity alternative

Continued from previous page

IG Example 13

Application of requirements

The fair value of the equity alternative is CU57,600 (1,200 shares × CU48). The fair value of the cash alternative is CU50,000 (1,000 phantom shares × CU50). Therefore, the fair value of the equity component of the compound instrument is CU7,600 (CU57,600 – CU50,000).

The entity recognises the following amounts:

Year		Expense	Equity	Liability
		CU	CU	CU
1	Liability component: (1,000 × CU52 × ⅓)	17,333		17,333
	Equity component: (CU7,600 × ⅓)	2,533	2,533	
2	Liability component: (1,000 × CU55 × ⅔) – CU110,000	19,333		19,333
	Equity component: (CU7,600 × ⅓)	2,533	2,533	
3	Liability component: (1,000 × CU60) – CU36,666	23,334		23,334
	Equity component: (CU7,600 × ⅓)	2,534	2,534	
End Year 3	Scenario 1: cash of CU60,000 paid			(60,000)
	Scenario 1 totals	67,600	7,600	0
	Scenario 2: 1,200 shares issued		60,000	(60,000)
	Scenario 2 totals	67,600	67,600	0

Illustrative disclosures

IG23 The following example illustrates the disclosure requirements in paragraphs 44–52 of the IFRS.*

Extract from the Notes to the Financial Statements of Company Z for the year ended 31 December 2005.

Share-based Payment

During the period ended 31 December 2005, the Company had four share-based payment arrangements, which are described below.

* Note that the illustrative example is not intended to be a template or model and is therefore not exhaustive. For example, it does not illustrate the disclosure requirements in paragraphs 47(c), 48 and 49 of the IFRS.

Type of arrangement	Senior management share option plan	General employee share option plan	Executive share plan	Senior management share appreciation cash plan
Date of grant	1 January 2004	1 January 2005	1 January 2005	1 July 2005
Number granted	50,000	75,000	50,000	25,000
Contractual life	10 years	10 years	N/A	10 years
Vesting conditions	1.5 years' service and achievement of a share price target, which was achieved.	Three years' service.	Three years' service and achievement of a target growth in earnings per share.	Three years' service and achievement of a target increase in market share.

The estimated fair value of each share option granted in the general employee share option plan is CU23.60. This was calculated by applying a binomial option pricing model. The model inputs were the share price at grant date of CU50, exercise price of CU50, expected volatility of 30 per cent, no expected dividends, contractual life of ten years, and a risk-free interest rate of 5 per cent. To allow for the effects of early exercise, it was assumed that the employees would exercise the options after vesting date when the share price was twice the exercise price. Historical volatility was 40 per cent, which includes the early years of the Company's life; the Company expects the volatility of its share price to reduce as it matures.

The estimated fair value of each share granted in the executive share plan is CU50.00, which is equal to the share price at the date of grant.

Further details of the two share option plans are as follows:

	2004		2005	
	Number of options	Weighted average exercise price	Number of options	Weighted average exercise price
Outstanding at start of year	0	–	45,000	CU40
Granted	50,000	CU40	75,000	CU50
Forfeited	(5,000)	CU40	(8,000)	CU46
Exercised	0	–	(4,000)	CU40
Outstanding at end of year	45,000	CU40	103,000	CU46
Exercisable at end of year	0	CU40	38,000	CU40

The weighted average share price at the date of exercise for share options exercised during the period was CU52. The options outstanding at 31 December 2005 had an exercise price of CU40 or CU50, and a weighted average remaining contractual life of 8.64 years.

	2004	2005
	CU	CU
Expense arising from share-based payment transactions	495,000	1,105,867
Expense arising from share and share option plans	495,000	1,007,000
Closing balance of liability for cash share appreciation plan	–	98,867
Expense arising from increase in fair value of liability for cash share appreciation plan	–	9,200

International Financial Reporting Standard 3

Business Combinations

This version includes amendments resulting from IFRSs issued up to 31 December 2004.

CONTENTS

International Financial Reporting Standard 3 *Business Combinations* (IFRS 3) is set out in paragraphs 1–87 and Appendices A–C. All the paragraphs have equal authority. Paragraphs in **bold type** state the main principles. Terms defined in Appendix A are in *italics* the first time they appear in the Standard. Definitions of other terms are given in the Glossary for International Financial Reporting Standards. IFRS 3 should be read in the context of its objective and the Basis for Conclusions, the *Preface to International Financial Reporting Standards* and the *Framework for the Preparation and Presentation of Financial Statements*. IAS 8 *Accounting Policies, Changes in Accounting Estimates and Errors* provides a basis for selecting and applying accounting policies in the absence of explicit guidance.

Introduction

IN1 International Financial Reporting Standard 3 *Business Combinations* (IFRS 3) replaces IAS 22 *Business Combinations*. The IFRS also replaces the following Interpretations:

- SIC-9 *Business Combinations—Classification either as Acquisitions or Unitings of Interests*
- SIC-22 *Business Combinations—Subsequent Adjustment of Fair Values and Goodwill Initially Reported*
- SIC-28 *Business Combinations—"Date of Exchange" and Fair Value of Equity Instruments*.

Reasons for issuing the IFRS

IN2 IAS 22 permitted business combinations to be accounted for using one of two methods: the pooling of interests method or the purchase method. Although IAS 22 restricted the use of the pooling of interests method to business combinations classified as unitings of interests, analysts and other users of financial statements indicated that permitting two methods of accounting for substantially similar transactions impaired the comparability of financial statements. Others argued that requiring more than one method of accounting for such transactions created incentives for structuring those transactions to achieve a desired accounting result, particularly given that the two methods produce quite different results.

IN3 These factors, combined with the prohibition of the pooling of interests method in Australia, Canada and the United States, prompted the International Accounting Standards Board to examine whether, given that few combinations were understood to be accounted for in accordance with IAS 22 using the pooling of interests method, it would be advantageous for international standards to converge with those in Australia and North America by also prohibiting the method.

IN4 Accounting for business combinations varied across jurisdictions in other respects as well. These included the accounting for goodwill and intangible assets acquired in a business combination, the treatment of any excess of the acquirer's interest in the fair values of identifiable net assets acquired over the cost of the business combination, and the recognition of liabilities for terminating or reducing the activities of an acquiree.

IN5 Furthermore, IAS 22 contained an option in respect of how the purchase method could be applied: the identifiable assets acquired and liabilities assumed could be measured initially using either a benchmark treatment or an allowed alternative treatment. The benchmark treatment resulted in the identifiable assets acquired and liabilities assumed being measured initially at a combination of fair values (to the extent of the acquirer's ownership interest) and pre-acquisition carrying amounts (to the extent of any minority interest). The allowed alternative treatment resulted in the identifiable assets acquired and liabilities assumed being measured initially at their fair values as at the date of acquisition. The Board believes that permitting similar transactions to be accounted for in dissimilar ways impairs the usefulness of the information provided to users of financial statements, because both comparability and reliability are diminished.

IN6 Therefore, this IFRS has been issued to improve the quality of, and seek international convergence on, the accounting for business combinations, including:

(a) the method of accounting for business combinations;

(b) the initial measurement of the identifiable assets acquired and liabilities and contingent liabilities assumed in a business combination;

(c) the recognition of liabilities for terminating or reducing the activities of an acquiree;

(d) the treatment of any excess of the acquirer's interest in the fair values of identifiable net assets acquired in a business combination over the cost of the combination; and

(e) the accounting for goodwill and intangible assets acquired in a business combination.

Main features of the IFRS

IN7 This IFRS:

(a) requires all business combinations within its scope to be accounted for by applying the purchase method.

(b) requires an acquirer to be identified for every business combination within its scope. The acquirer is the combining entity that obtains control of the other combining entities or businesses.

(c) requires an acquirer to measure the cost of a business combination as the aggregate of: the fair values, at the date of exchange, of assets given, liabilities incurred or assumed, and equity instruments issued by the acquirer, in exchange for control of the acquiree; plus any costs directly attributable to the combination.

(d) requires an acquirer to recognise separately, at the acquisition date, the acquiree's identifiable assets, liabilities and contingent liabilities that satisfy the following recognition criteria at that date, regardless of whether they had been previously recognised in the acquiree's financial statements:

(i) in the case of an asset other than an intangible asset, it is probable that any associated future economic benefits will flow to the acquirer, and its fair value can be measured reliably;

(ii) in the case of a liability other than a contingent liability, it is probable that an outflow of resources embodying economic benefits will be required to settle the obligation, and its fair value can be measured reliably; and

(iii) in the case of an intangible asset or a contingent liability, its fair value can be measured reliably.

(e) requires the identifiable assets, liabilities and contingent liabilities that satisfy the above recognition criteria to be measured initially by the acquirer at their fair values at the acquisition date, irrespective of the extent of any minority interest.

(f) requires goodwill acquired in a business combination to be recognised by the acquirer as an asset from the acquisition date, initially measured as the excess of the cost of the business combination over the acquirer's interest in the net fair value of the acquiree's identifiable assets, liabilities and contingent liabilities recognised in accordance with (d) above.

(g) prohibits the amortisation of goodwill acquired in a business combination and instead requires the goodwill to be tested for impairment annually, or more frequently if events or changes in circumstances indicate that the asset might be impaired, in accordance with IAS 36 *Impairment of Assets*.

(h) requires the acquirer to reassess the identification and measurement of the acquiree's identifiable assets, liabilities and contingent liabilities and the measurement of the cost of the business combination if the acquirer's interest in the net fair value of the items recognised in accordance with (d) above exceeds the cost of the combination. Any excess remaining after that reassessment must be recognised by the acquirer immediately in profit or loss.

(i) requires disclosure of information that enables users of an entity's financial statements to evaluate the nature and financial effect of:

  (i) business combinations that were effected during the period;

  (ii) business combinations that were effected after the balance sheet date but before the financial statements are authorised for issue; and

  (iii) some business combinations that were effected in previous periods.

(j) requires disclosure of information that enables users of an entity's financial statements to evaluate changes in the carrying amount of goodwill during the period.

Changes from previous requirements

IN8 The main changes from IAS 22 are described below.

Method of accounting

IN9 This IFRS requires all business combinations within its scope to be accounted for using the purchase method. IAS 22 permitted business combinations to be accounted for using one of two methods: the pooling of interests method for combinations classified as unitings of interests and the purchase method for combinations classified as acquisitions.

Recognising the identifiable assets acquired and liabilities and contingent liabilities assumed

IN10 This IFRS changes the requirements in IAS 22 for separately recognising as part of allocating the cost of a business combination:

(a) liabilities for terminating or reducing the activities of the acquiree; and

(b) contingent liabilities of the acquiree.

This IFRS also clarifies the criteria for separately recognising intangible assets of the acquiree as part of allocating the cost of a combination.

IN11 This IFRS requires an acquirer to recognise liabilities for terminating or reducing the activities of the acquiree as part of allocating the cost of the combination only when the acquiree has, at the acquisition date, an existing liability for restructuring recognised in accordance with IAS 37 *Provisions, Contingent Liabilities and Contingent Assets*. IAS 22 required an acquirer to recognise as part of allocating the cost of a business combination a provision for terminating or reducing the activities of the acquiree that was not a liability of the acquiree at the acquisition date, provided the acquirer satisfied specified criteria.

IN12 This IFRS requires an acquirer to recognise separately the acquiree's contingent liabilities (as defined in IAS 37) at the acquisition date as part of allocating the cost of a business combination, provided their fair values can be measured reliably. Such contingent liabilities were, in accordance with IAS 22, subsumed within the amount recognised as goodwill or negative goodwill.

IN13 IAS 22 required an intangible asset to be recognised if, and only if, it was probable that the future economic benefits attributable to the asset would flow to the entity, and its cost could be measured reliably. The probability recognition criterion is not included in this IFRS because it is always considered to be satisfied for intangible assets acquired in business combinations. Additionally, this IFRS includes guidance clarifying that the fair value of an intangible asset acquired in a business combination can normally be measured with sufficient reliability to qualify for recognition separately from goodwill. If an intangible asset acquired in a business combination has a finite useful life, there is a rebuttable presumption that its fair value can be measured reliably.

Measuring the identifiable assets acquired and liabilities and contingent liabilities assumed

IN14 IAS 22 included a benchmark and an allowed alternative treatment for the initial measurement of the identifiable net assets acquired in a business combination, and therefore for the initial measurement of any minority interests. This IFRS requires the acquiree's identifiable assets, liabilities and contingent liabilities recognised as part of allocating the cost of the combination to be measured initially by the acquirer at their fair values at the acquisition date. Therefore, any minority interest in the acquiree is stated at the minority's proportion of the net fair values of those items. This is consistent with IAS 22's allowed alternative treatment.

Subsequent accounting for goodwill

IN15 This IFRS requires goodwill acquired in a business combination to be measured after initial recognition at cost less any accumulated impairment losses. Therefore, the goodwill is not amortised and instead must be tested for impairment annually, or more frequently if events or changes in circumstances indicate that it might be impaired. IAS 22 required acquired goodwill to be systematically amortised over its useful life, and included a rebuttable presumption that its useful life could not exceed twenty years from initial recognition.

Excess of acquirer's interest in the net fair value of acquiree's identifiable assets, liabilities and contingent liabilities over cost

IN16 This IFRS requires the acquirer to reassess the identification and measurement of the acquiree's identifiable assets, liabilities and contingent liabilities and the measurement of the cost of the combination if, at the acquisition date, the acquirer's interest in the net fair value of those items exceeds the cost of the combination. Any excess remaining after that reassessment must be recognised by the acquirer immediately in profit or loss. In accordance with IAS 22, any excess of the acquirer's interest in the net fair value of the identifiable assets and liabilities acquired over the cost of the acquisition was accounted for as negative goodwill as follows:

(a) to the extent that it related to expectations of future losses and expenses identified in the acquirer's acquisition plan, it was required to be carried forward and recognised as income in the same period in which the future losses and expenses were recognised.

(b) to the extent that it did not relate to expectations of future losses and expenses identified in the acquirer's acquisition plan, it was required to be recognised as income as follows:

    (i) for the amount of negative goodwill not exceeding the aggregate fair value of acquired identifiable non-monetary assets, on a systematic basis over the remaining weighted average useful life of the identifiable depreciable assets.

    (ii) for any remaining excess, immediately.

Business Combinations

Objective

1 The objective of this IFRS is to specify the financial reporting by an entity when it undertakes a *business combination.* In particular, it specifies that all business combinations should be accounted for by applying the purchase method. Therefore, the acquirer recognises the acquiree's identifiable assets, liabilities and *contingent liabilities* at their *fair values* at the *acquisition date*, and also recognises *goodwill*, which is subsequently tested for impairment rather than amortised.

Scope

2 Except as described in paragraph 3, entities shall apply this IFRS when accounting for business combinations.

3 This IFRS does not apply to:

(a) business combinations in which separate entities or *businesses* are brought together to form a *joint venture.*

(b) *business combinations involving entities or businesses under common control.*

(c) business combinations involving two or more *mutual entities.*

(d) business combinations in which separate entities or businesses are brought together to form a *reporting entity* by contract alone without the obtaining of an ownership interest (for example, combinations in which separate entities are brought together by contract alone to form a dual listed corporation).

Identifying a business combination

4 A business combination is the bringing together of separate entities or businesses into one reporting entity. The result of nearly all business combinations is that one entity, the acquirer, obtains *control* of one or more other businesses, the acquiree. If an entity obtains control of one or more other entities that are not businesses, the bringing together of those entities is not a business combination. When an entity acquires a group of assets or net assets that does not constitute a business, it shall allocate the cost of the group between the individual identifiable assets and liabilities in the group based on their relative fair values at the date of acquisition.

5 A business combination may be structured in a variety of ways for legal, taxation or other reasons. It may involve the purchase by an entity of the equity of another entity, the purchase of all the net assets of another entity, the assumption of the liabilities of another entity, or the purchase of some of the net assets of another entity that together form one or more businesses. It may be effected by the issue of equity instruments, the transfer of cash, cash equivalents or other assets, or a combination thereof. The transaction may be between the shareholders of the combining entities or between one entity and the shareholders of another entity. It may involve the establishment of a new entity to control the combining entities or net assets transferred, or the restructuring of one or more of the combining entities.

6 A business combination may result in a parent-subsidiary relationship in which the acquirer is the *parent* and the acquiree a *subsidiary* of the acquirer. In such circumstances, the acquirer applies this IFRS in its consolidated financial statements. It includes its interest in the acquiree in any separate financial statements it issues as an investment in a subsidiary (see IAS 27 *Consolidated and Separate Financial Statements*).

7 A business combination may involve the purchase of the net assets, including any goodwill, of another entity rather than the purchase of the equity of the other entity. Such a combination does not result in a parent-subsidiary relationship.

8 Included within the definition of a business combination, and therefore the scope of this IFRS, are business combinations in which one entity obtains control of another entity but for which the date of obtaining control (ie the acquisition date) does not coincide with the date or dates of acquiring an ownership interest (ie the *date or dates of exchange*). This situation may arise, for example, when an investee enters into share buy-back arrangements with some of its investors and, as a result, control of the investee changes.

9 This IFRS does not specify the accounting by venturers for interests in joint ventures (see IAS 31 *Interests in Joint Ventures*).

Business combinations involving entities under common control

10 A business combination involving entities or businesses under common control is a business combination in which all of the combining entities or businesses are ultimately controlled by the same party or parties both before and after the business combination, and that control is not transitory.

11 A group of individuals shall be regarded as controlling an entity when, as a result of contractual arrangements, they collectively have the power to govern its financial and operating policies so as to obtain benefits from its activities. Therefore, a business combination is outside the scope of this IFRS when the same group of individuals has, as a result of contractual arrangements, ultimate collective power to govern the financial and operating policies of each of the combining entities so as to obtain benefits from their activities, and that ultimate collective power is not transitory.

12 An entity can be controlled by an individual, or by a group of individuals acting together under a contractual arrangement, and that individual or group of individuals may not be subject to the financial reporting requirements of IFRSs. Therefore, it is not necessary for combining entities to be included as part of the same consolidated financial statements for a business combination to be regarded as one involving entities under common control.

13 The extent of *minority interests* in each of the combining entities before and after the business combination is not relevant to determining whether the combination involves entities under common control. Similarly, the fact that one of the combining entities is a subsidiary that has been excluded from the consolidated financial statements of the group in accordance with IAS 27 is not relevant to determining whether a combination involves entities under common control.

Method of accounting

14 **All business combinations shall be accounted for by applying the purchase method.**

15 The purchase method views a business combination from the perspective of the combining entity that is identified as the acquirer. The acquirer purchases net assets and recognises the assets acquired and liabilities and contingent liabilities assumed, including those not previously recognised by the acquiree. The measurement of the acquirer's assets and liabilities is not affected by the transaction, nor are any additional assets or liabilities of the acquirer recognised as a result of the transaction, because they are not the subjects of the transaction.

Application of the purchase method

16 Applying the purchase method involves the following steps:

(a) identifying an acquirer;

(b) measuring the cost of the business combination; and

(c) allocating, at the acquisition date, the cost of the business combination to the assets acquired and liabilities and contingent liabilities assumed.

Identifying the acquirer

17 **An acquirer shall be identified for all business combinations. The acquirer is the combining entity that obtains control of the other combining entities or businesses.**

18 Because the purchase method views a business combination from the acquirer's perspective, it assumes that one of the parties to the transaction can be identified as the acquirer.

19 Control is the power to govern the financial and operating policies of an entity or business so as to obtain benefits from its activities. A combining entity shall be presumed to have obtained control of another combining entity when it acquires more than one-half of that other entity's voting rights, unless it can be demonstrated that such ownership does not constitute control. Even if one of the combining entities does not acquire more than one-half of the voting rights of another combining entity, it might have obtained control of that other entity if, as a result of the combination, it obtains:

(a) power over more than one-half of the voting rights of the other entity by virtue of an agreement with other investors; or

(b) power to govern the financial and operating policies of the other entity under a statute or an agreement; or

(c) power to appoint or remove the majority of the members of the board of directors or equivalent governing body of the other entity; or

(d) power to cast the majority of votes at meetings of the board of directors or equivalent governing body of the other entity.

20 Although sometimes it may be difficult to identify an acquirer, there are usually indications that one exists. For example:

(a) if the fair value of one of the combining entities is significantly greater than that of the other combining entity, the entity with the greater fair value is likely to be the acquirer;

(b) if the business combination is effected through an exchange of voting ordinary equity instruments for cash or other assets, the entity giving up cash or other assets is likely to be the acquirer; and

(c) if the business combination results in the management of one of the combining entities being able to dominate the selection of the management team of the resulting combined entity, the entity whose management is able so to dominate is likely to be the acquirer.

21 In a business combination effected through an exchange of equity interests, the entity that issues the equity interests is normally the acquirer. However, all pertinent facts and circumstances shall be considered to determine which of the combining entities has the power to govern the financial and operating policies of the other entity (or entities) so as to obtain benefits from its (or their) activities. In some business combinations, commonly referred to as reverse acquisitions, the acquirer is the entity whose equity interests have been acquired and the issuing entity is the acquiree. This might be the case when, for example, a private entity arranges to have itself 'acquired' by a smaller public entity as a means of obtaining a stock exchange listing. Although legally the issuing public entity is regarded as the parent and the private entity is regarded as the subsidiary, the legal subsidiary is the acquirer if it has the power to govern the financial and operating policies of the legal parent so as to obtain benefits from its activities. Commonly the acquirer is the larger entity; however, the facts and circumstances surrounding a combination sometimes indicate that a smaller entity acquires a larger entity. Guidance on the accounting for reverse acquisitions is provided in paragraphs B1–B15 of Appendix B.

22 When a new entity is formed to issue equity instruments to effect a business combination, one of the combining entities that existed before the combination shall be identified as the acquirer on the basis of the evidence available.

23 Similarly, when a business combination involves more than two combining entities, one of the combining entities that existed before the combination shall be identified as the acquirer on the basis of the evidence available. Determining the acquirer in such cases shall include a consideration of, amongst other things, which of the combining entities initiated the combination and whether the assets or revenues of one of the combining entities significantly exceed those of the others.

Cost of a business combination

24 **The acquirer shall measure the cost of a business combination as the aggregate of:**

(a) the fair values, at the date of exchange, of assets given, liabilities incurred or assumed, and equity instruments issued by the acquirer, in exchange for control of the acquiree; plus

(b) any costs directly attributable to the business combination.

25 The acquisition date is the date on which the acquirer effectively obtains control of the acquiree. When this is achieved through a single exchange transaction, the date of exchange coincides with the acquisition date. However, a business combination may involve more than one exchange transaction, for example when it is achieved in stages by successive share purchases. When this occurs:

(a) the cost of the combination is the aggregate cost of the individual transactions; and

(b) the date of exchange is the date of each exchange transaction (ie the date that each individual investment is recognised in the financial statements of the acquirer), whereas the acquisition date is the date on which the acquirer obtains control of the acquiree.

26 Assets given and liabilities incurred or assumed by the acquirer in exchange for control of the acquiree are required by paragraph 24 to be measured at their fair values at the date of exchange. Therefore, when settlement of all or any part of the cost of a business combination is deferred, the fair value of that deferred component shall be determined by discounting the amounts payable to their present value at the date of exchange, taking into account any premium or discount likely to be incurred in settlement.

27 The published price at the date of exchange of a quoted equity instrument provides the best evidence of the instrument's fair value and shall be used, except in rare circumstances. Other evidence and valuation methods shall be considered only in the rare circumstances when the acquirer can demonstrate that the published price at the date of exchange is an unreliable indicator of fair value, and that the other evidence and valuation methods provide a more reliable measure of the equity instrument's fair value. The published price at the date of exchange is an unreliable indicator only when it has been affected by the thinness of the market. If the published price at the date of exchange is an unreliable indicator or if a published price does not exist for equity instruments issued by the acquirer, the fair value of those instruments could, for example, be estimated by reference to their proportional interest in the fair value of the acquirer or by reference to the proportional interest in the fair value of the acquiree obtained, whichever is the more clearly evident. The fair value at the date of exchange of monetary assets given to equity holders of the acquiree as an alternative to equity instruments may also provide evidence of the total fair value given by the acquirer in exchange for control of the acquiree. In any event, all aspects of the combination, including significant factors influencing the negotiations, shall be considered. Further guidance on determining the fair value of equity instruments is set out in IAS 39 *Financial Instruments: Recognition and Measurement*.

28 The cost of a business combination includes liabilities incurred or assumed by the acquirer in exchange for control of the acquiree. Future losses or other costs expected to be incurred as a result of a combination are not liabilities incurred or assumed by the acquirer in exchange for control of the acquiree, and are not, therefore, included as part of the cost of the combination.

29 The cost of a business combination includes any costs directly attributable to the combination, such as professional fees paid to accountants, legal advisers, valuers and other consultants to effect the combination. General administrative costs, including the costs of maintaining an acquisitions department, and other costs that cannot be directly attributed to the particular combination being accounted for are not included in the cost of the combination: they are recognised as an expense when incurred.

30 The costs of arranging and issuing financial liabilities are an integral part of the liability issue transaction, even when the liabilities are issued to effect a business combination, rather than costs directly attributable to the combination. Therefore, entities shall not include such costs in the cost of a business combination. In accordance with IAS 39, such costs shall be included in the initial measurement of the liability.

31 Similarly, the costs of issuing equity instruments are an integral part of the equity issue transaction, even when the equity instruments are issued to effect a business combination, rather than costs directly attributable to the combination. Therefore, entities shall not include such costs in the cost of a business combination. In accordance with IAS 32 *Financial Instruments: Disclosure and Presentation*, such costs reduce the proceeds from the equity issue.

Adjustments to the cost of a business combination contingent on future events

32 When a business combination agreement provides for an adjustment to the cost of the combination contingent on future events, the acquirer shall include the amount of that adjustment in the cost of the combination at the acquisition date if the adjustment is *probable* and can be measured reliably.

33 A business combination agreement may allow for adjustments to the cost of the combination that are contingent on one or more future events. The adjustment might, for example, be contingent on a specified level of profit being maintained or achieved in future periods, or on the market price of the instruments issued being maintained. It is usually possible to estimate the amount of any such adjustment at the time of initially accounting for the combination without impairing the reliability of the information, even though some uncertainty exists. If the future events do not occur or the estimate needs to be revised, the cost of the business combination shall be adjusted accordingly.

34 However, when a business combination agreement provides for such an adjustment, that adjustment is not included in the cost of the combination at the time of initially accounting for the combination if it either is not probable or cannot be measured reliably. If that adjustment subsequently becomes probable

and can be measured reliably, the additional consideration shall be treated as an adjustment to the cost of the combination.

35 In some circumstances, the acquirer may be required to make a subsequent payment to the seller as compensation for a reduction in the value of the assets given, equity instruments issued or liabilities incurred or assumed by the acquirer in exchange for control of the acquiree. This is the case, for example, when the acquirer guarantees the market price of equity or debt instruments issued as part of the cost of the business combination and is required to issue additional equity or debt instruments to restore the originally determined cost. In such cases, no increase in the cost of the business combination is recognised. In the case of equity instruments, the fair value of the additional payment is offset by an equal reduction in the value attributed to the instruments initially issued. In the case of debt instruments, the additional payment is regarded as a reduction in the premium or an increase in the discount on the initial issue.

Allocating the cost of a business combination to the assets acquired and liabilities and contingent liabilities assumed

36 **The acquirer shall, at the acquisition date, allocate the cost of a business combination by recognising the acquiree's identifiable assets, liabilities and contingent liabilities that satisfy the recognition criteria in paragraph 37 at their fair values at that date, except for non-current assets (or disposal groups) that are classified as held for sale in accordance with IFRS 5** *Non-current Assets Held for Sale and Discontinued Operations*, **which shall be recognised at fair value less costs to sell. Any difference between the cost of the business combination and the acquirer's interest in the net fair value of the identifiable assets, liabilities and contingent liabilities so recognised shall be accounted for in accordance with paragraphs 51–57.**

37 **The acquirer shall recognise separately the acquiree's identifiable assets, liabilities and contingent liabilities at the acquisition date only if they satisfy the following criteria at that date:**

- **(a) in the case of an asset other than an** *intangible* **asset, it is probable that any associated future economic benefits will flow to the acquirer, and its fair value can be measured reliably;**
- **(b) in the case of a liability other than a contingent liability, it is probable that an outflow of resources embodying economic benefits will be required to settle the obligation, and its fair value can be measured reliably;**
- **(c) in the case of an intangible asset or a contingent liability, its fair value can be measured reliably.**

38 The acquirer's income statement shall incorporate the acquiree's profits and losses after the acquisition date by including the acquiree's income and expenses based on the cost of the business combination to the acquirer. For example, depreciation expense included after the acquisition date in the acquirer's income

statement that relates to the acquiree's depreciable assets shall be based on the fair values of those depreciable assets at the acquisition date, ie their cost to the acquirer.

39 Application of the purchase method starts from the acquisition date, which is the date on which the acquirer effectively obtains control of the acquiree. Because control is the power to govern the financial and operating policies of an entity or business so as to obtain benefits from its activities, it is not necessary for a transaction to be closed or finalised at law before the acquirer obtains control. All pertinent facts and circumstances surrounding a business combination shall be considered in assessing when the acquirer has obtained control.

40 Because the acquirer recognises the acquiree's identifiable assets, liabilities and contingent liabilities that satisfy the recognition criteria in paragraph 37 at their fair values at the acquisition date, any minority interest in the acquiree is stated at the minority's proportion of the net fair value of those items. Paragraphs B16 and B17 of Appendix B provide guidance on determining the fair values of the acquiree's identifiable assets, liabilities and contingent liabilities for the purpose of allocating the cost of a business combination.

Acquiree's identifiable assets and liabilities

41 In accordance with paragraph 36, the acquirer recognises separately as part of allocating the cost of the combination only the identifiable assets, liabilities and contingent liabilities of the acquiree that existed at the acquisition date and satisfy the recognition criteria in paragraph 37. Therefore:

(a) the acquirer shall recognise liabilities for terminating or reducing the activities of the acquiree as part of allocating the cost of the combination only when the acquiree has, at the acquisition date, an existing liability for restructuring recognised in accordance with IAS 37 *Provisions, Contingent Liabilities and Contingent Assets*; and

(b) the acquirer, when allocating the cost of the combination, shall not recognise liabilities for future losses or other costs expected to be incurred as a result of the business combination.

42 A payment that an entity is contractually required to make, for example, to its employees or suppliers in the event that it is acquired in a business combination is a present obligation of the entity that is regarded as a contingent liability until it becomes probable that a business combination will take place. The contractual obligation is recognised as a liability by that entity in accordance with IAS 37 when a business combination becomes probable and the liability can be measured reliably. Therefore, when the business combination is effected, that liability of the acquiree is recognised by the acquirer as part of allocating the cost of the combination.

43 However, an acquiree's restructuring plan whose execution is conditional upon its being acquired in a business combination is not, immediately before the business combination, a present obligation of the acquiree. Nor is it a contingent liability of the acquiree immediately before the combination because it is not a possible obligation arising from a past event whose existence will be confirmed only by the occurrence or non-occurrence of one or more uncertain future events not wholly

within the control of the acquiree. Therefore, an acquirer shall not recognise a liability for such restructuring plans as part of allocating the cost of the combination.

44 The identifiable assets and liabilities that are recognised in accordance with paragraph 36 include all of the acquiree's assets and liabilities that the acquirer purchases or assumes, including all of its financial assets and financial liabilities. They might also include assets and liabilities not previously recognised in the acquiree's financial statements, eg because they did not qualify for recognition before the acquisition. For example, a tax benefit arising from the acquiree's tax losses that was not recognised by the acquiree before the business combination qualifies for recognition as an identifiable asset in accordance with paragraph 36 if it is probable that the acquirer will have future taxable profits against which the unrecognised tax benefit can be applied.

Acquiree's intangible assets

45 In accordance with paragraph 37, the acquirer recognises separately an intangible asset of the acquiree at the acquisition date only if it meets the definition of an intangible asset in IAS 38 *Intangible Assets* and its fair value can be measured reliably. This means that the acquirer recognises as an asset separately from goodwill an in-process research and development project of the acquiree if the project meets the definition of an intangible asset and its fair value can be measured reliably. IAS 38 provides guidance on determining whether the fair value of an intangible asset acquired in a business combination can be measured reliably.

46 A non-monetary asset without physical substance must be identifiable to meet the definition of an intangible asset. In accordance with IAS 38, an asset meets the identifiability criterion in the definition of an intangible asset only if it:

(a) is separable, ie capable of being separated or divided from the entity and sold, transferred, licensed, rented or exchanged, either individually or together with a related contract, asset or liability; or

(b) arises from contractual or other legal rights, regardless of whether those rights are transferable or separable from the entity or from other rights and obligations.

Acquiree's contingent liabilities

47 Paragraph 37 specifies that the acquirer recognises separately a contingent liability of the acquiree as part of allocating the cost of a business combination only if its fair value can be measured reliably. If its fair value cannot be measured reliably:

(a) there is a resulting effect on the amount recognised as goodwill or accounted for in accordance with paragraph 56; and

(b) the acquirer shall disclose the information about that contingent liability required to be disclosed by IAS 37.

Paragraph B16(l) of Appendix B provides guidance on determining the fair value of a contingent liability.

48 **After their initial recognition, the acquirer shall measure contingent liabilities that are recognised separately in accordance with paragraph 36 at the higher of:**

(a) the amount that would be recognised in accordance with IAS 37, and

(b) the amount initially recognised less, when appropriate, cumulative amortisation recognised in accordance with IAS 18 ***Revenue*****.**

49 The requirement in paragraph 48 does not apply to contracts accounted for in accordance with IAS 39 *Financial Instruments: Recognition and Measurement*. However, loan commitments excluded from the scope of IAS 39 that are not commitments to provide loans at below-market interest rates are accounted for as contingent liabilities of the acquiree if, at the acquisition date, it is not probable that an outflow of resources embodying economic benefits will be required to settle the obligation or if the amount of the obligation cannot be measured with sufficient reliability. Such a loan commitment is, in accordance with paragraph 37, recognised separately as part of allocating the cost of a combination only if its fair value can be measured reliably.

50 Contingent liabilities recognised separately as part of allocating the cost of a business combination are excluded from the scope of IAS 37. However, the acquirer shall disclose for those contingent liabilities the information required to be disclosed by IAS 37 for each class of provision.

Goodwill

51 **The acquirer shall, at the acquisition date:**

(a) recognise goodwill acquired in a business combination as an asset; and

(b) initially measure that goodwill at its cost, being the excess of the cost of the business combination over the acquirer's interest in the net fair value of the identifiable assets, liabilities and contingent liabilities recognised in accordance with paragraph 36.

52 Goodwill acquired in a business combination represents a payment made by the acquirer in anticipation of future economic benefits from assets that are not capable of being individually identified and separately recognised.

53 To the extent that the acquiree's identifiable assets, liabilities or contingent liabilities do not satisfy the criteria in paragraph 37 for separate recognition at the acquisition date, there is a resulting effect on the amount recognised as goodwill (or accounted for in accordance with paragraph 56). This is because goodwill is measured as the residual cost of the business combination after recognising the acquiree's identifiable assets, liabilities and contingent liabilities.

54 **After initial recognition, the acquirer shall measure goodwill acquired in a business combination at cost less any accumulated impairment losses.**

55 Goodwill acquired in a business combination shall not be amortised. Instead, the acquirer shall test it for impairment annually, or more frequently if events or changes in circumstances indicate that it might be impaired, in accordance with IAS 36 *Impairment of Assets*.

Excess of acquirer's interest in the net fair value of acquiree's identifiable assets, liabilities and contingent liabilities over cost

56 **If the acquirer's interest in the net fair value of the identifiable assets, liabilities and contingent liabilities recognised in accordance with paragraph 36 exceeds the cost of the business combination, the acquirer shall:**

(a) reassess the identification and measurement of the acquiree's identifiable assets, liabilities and contingent liabilities and the measurement of the cost of the combination; and

(b) recognise immediately in profit or loss any excess remaining after that reassessment.

57 A gain recognised in accordance with paragraph 56 could comprise one or more of the following components:

(a) errors in measuring the fair value of either the cost of the combination or the acquiree's identifiable assets, liabilities or contingent liabilities. Possible future costs arising in respect of the acquiree that have not been reflected correctly in the fair value of the acquiree's identifiable assets, liabilities or contingent liabilities are a potential cause of such errors.

(b) a requirement in an accounting standard to measure identifiable net assets acquired at an amount that is not fair value, but is treated as though it is fair value for the purpose of allocating the cost of the combination. For example, the guidance in Appendix B on determining the fair values of the acquiree's identifiable assets and liabilities requires the amount assigned to tax assets and liabilities to be undiscounted.

(c) a bargain purchase.

Business combination achieved in stages

58 A business combination may involve more than one exchange transaction, for example when it occurs in stages by successive share purchases. If so, each exchange transaction shall be treated separately by the acquirer, using the cost of the transaction and fair value information at the date of each exchange transaction, to determine the amount of any goodwill associated with that transaction. This results in a step-by-step comparison of the cost of the individual investments with the acquirer's interest in the fair values of the acquiree's identifiable assets, liabilities and contingent liabilities at each step.

59 When a business combination involves more than one exchange transaction, the fair values of the acquiree's identifiable assets, liabilities and contingent liabilities may be different at the date of each exchange transaction. Because:

(a) the acquiree's identifiable assets, liabilities and contingent liabilities are notionally restated to their fair values at the date of each exchange transaction to determine the amount of any goodwill associated with each transaction; and

(b) the acquiree's identifiable assets, liabilities and contingent liabilities must then be recognised by the acquirer at their fair values at the acquisition date, any adjustment to those fair values relating to previously held interests of the acquirer is a revaluation and shall be accounted for as such. However, because this revaluation arises on the initial recognition by the acquirer of the acquiree's assets, liabilities and contingent liabilities, it does not signify that the acquirer has elected to apply an accounting policy of revaluing those items after initial recognition in accordance with, for example, IAS 16 *Property, Plant and Equipment*.

60 Before qualifying as a business combination, a transaction may qualify as an investment in an associate and be accounted for in accordance with IAS 28 *Investments in Associates* using the equity method. If so, the fair values of the investee's identifiable net assets at the date of each earlier exchange transaction will have been determined previously in applying the equity method to the investment.

Initial accounting determined provisionally

61 The initial accounting for a business combination involves identifying and determining the fair values to be assigned to the acquiree's identifiable assets, liabilities and contingent liabilities and the cost of the combination.

62 If the initial accounting for a business combination can be determined only provisionally by the end of the period in which the combination is effected because either the fair values to be assigned to the acquiree's identifiable assets, liabilities or contingent liabilities or the cost of the combination can be determined only provisionally, the acquirer shall account for the combination using those provisional values. The acquirer shall recognise any adjustments to those provisional values as a result of completing the initial accounting:

(a) within twelve months of the acquisition date; and

(b) from the acquisition date. Therefore:

   (i) the carrying amount of an identifiable asset, liability or contingent liability that is recognised or adjusted as a result of completing the initial accounting shall be calculated as if its fair value at the acquisition date had been recognised from that date.

   (ii) goodwill or any gain recognised in accordance with paragraph 56 shall be adjusted from the acquisition date by an amount equal to the adjustment to the fair value at the acquisition date of the identifiable asset, liability or contingent liability being recognised or adjusted.

   (iii) comparative information presented for the periods before the initial accounting for the combination is complete shall be presented as if the initial accounting had been completed from the acquisition date. This includes any additional depreciation, amortisation or other profit or loss effect recognised as a result of completing the initial accounting.

Adjustments after the initial accounting is complete

63 Except as outlined in paragraphs 33, 34 and 65, adjustments to the initial accounting for a business combination after that initial accounting is complete shall be recognised only to correct an error in accordance with IAS 8 *Accounting Policies, Changes in Accounting Estimates and Errors*. Adjustments to the initial accounting for a business combination after that accounting is complete shall not

be recognised for the effect of changes in estimates. In accordance with IAS 8, the effect of a change in estimates shall be recognised in the current and future periods.

64 IAS 8 requires an entity to account for an error correction retrospectively, and to present financial statements as if the error had never occurred by restating the comparative information for the prior period(s) in which the error occurred. Therefore, the carrying amount of an identifiable asset, liability or contingent liability of the acquiree that is recognised or adjusted as a result of an error correction shall be calculated as if its fair value or adjusted fair value at the acquisition date had been recognised from that date. Goodwill or any gain recognised in a prior period in accordance with paragraph 56 shall be adjusted retrospectively by an amount equal to the fair value at the acquisition date (or the adjustment to the fair value at the acquisition date) of the identifiable asset, liability or contingent liability being recognised (or adjusted).

Recognition of deferred tax assets after the initial accounting is complete

65 If the potential benefit of the acquiree's income tax loss carry-forwards or other deferred tax assets did not satisfy the criteria in paragraph 37 for separate recognition when a business combination is initially accounted for but is subsequently realised, the acquirer shall recognise that benefit as income in accordance with IAS 12 *Income Taxes*. In addition, the acquirer shall:

(a) reduce the carrying amount of goodwill to the amount that would have been recognised if the deferred tax asset had been recognised as an identifiable asset from the acquisition date; and

(b) recognise the reduction in the carrying amount of the goodwill as an expense.

However, this procedure shall not result in the creation of an excess as described in paragraph 56, nor shall it increase the amount of any gain previously recognised in accordance with paragraph 56.

Disclosure

66 An acquirer shall disclose information that enables users of its financial statements to evaluate the nature and financial effect of business combinations that were effected:

(a) during the period.

(b) after the balance sheet date but before the financial statements are authorised for issue.

67 To give effect to the principle in paragraph 66(a), the acquirer shall disclose the following information for each business combination that was effected during the period:

(a) the names and descriptions of the combining entities or businesses.

(b) the acquisition date.

(c) the percentage of voting equity instruments acquired.

(d) the cost of the combination and a description of the components of that cost, including any costs directly attributable to the combination. When equity instruments are issued or issuable as part of the cost, the following shall also be disclosed:

   (i) the number of equity instruments issued or issuable; and

   (ii) the fair value of those instruments and the basis for determining that fair value. If a published price does not exist for the instruments at the date of exchange, the significant assumptions used to determine fair value shall be disclosed. If a published price exists at the date of exchange but was not used as the basis for determining the cost of the combination, that fact shall be disclosed together with: the reasons the published price was not used; the method and significant assumptions used to attribute a value to the equity instruments; and the aggregate amount of the difference between the value attributed to, and the published price of, the equity instruments.

(e) details of any operations the entity has decided to dispose of as a result of the combination.

(f) the amounts recognised at the acquisition date for each class of the acquiree's assets, liabilities and contingent liabilities, and, unless disclosure would be impracticable, the carrying amounts of each of those classes, determined in accordance with IFRSs, immediately before the combination. If such disclosure would be impracticable, that fact shall be disclosed, together with an explanation of why this is the case.

(g) the amount of any excess recognised in profit or loss in accordance with paragraph 56, and the line item in the income statement in which the excess is recognised.

(h) a description of the factors that contributed to a cost that results in the recognition of goodwill—a description of each intangible asset that was not recognised separately from goodwill and an explanation of why the intangible asset's fair value could not be measured reliably—or a description of the nature of any excess recognised in profit or loss in accordance with paragraph 56.

(i) the amount of the acquiree's profit or loss since the acquisition date included in the acquirer's profit or loss for the period, unless disclosure would be impracticable. If such disclosure would be impracticable, that fact shall be disclosed, together with an explanation of why this is the case.

68 The information required to be disclosed by paragraph 67 shall be disclosed in aggregate for business combinations effected during the reporting period that are individually immaterial.

69 If the initial accounting for a business combination that was effected during the period was determined only provisionally as described in paragraph 62, that fact shall also be disclosed together with an explanation of why this is the case.

70 To give effect to the principle in paragraph 66(a), the acquirer shall disclose the following information, unless such disclosure would be impracticable:

(a) the revenue of the combined entity for the period as though the acquisition date for all business combinations effected during the period had been the beginning of that period.

(b) the profit or loss of the combined entity for the period as though the acquisition date for all business combinations effected during the period had been the beginning of the period.

If disclosure of this information would be impracticable, that fact shall be disclosed, together with an explanation of why this is the case.

71 To give effect to the principle in paragraph 66(b), the acquirer shall disclose the information required by paragraph 67 for each business combination effected after the balance sheet date but before the financial statements are authorised for issue, unless such disclosure would be impracticable. If disclosure of any of that information would be impracticable, that fact shall be disclosed, together with an explanation of why this is the case.

72 An acquirer shall disclose information that enables users of its financial statements to evaluate the financial effects of gains, losses, error corrections and other adjustments recognised in the current period that relate to business combinations that were effected in the current or in previous periods.

73 To give effect to the principle in paragraph 72, the acquirer shall disclose the following information:

(a) the amount and an explanation of any gain or loss recognised in the current period that:

(i) relates to the identifiable assets acquired or liabilities or contingent liabilities assumed in a business combination that was effected in the current or a previous period; and

(ii) is of such size, nature or incidence that disclosure is relevant to an understanding of the combined entity's financial performance.

(b) if the initial accounting for a business combination that was effected in the immediately preceding period was determined only provisionally at the end of that period, the amounts and explanations of the adjustments to the provisional values recognised during the current period.

(c) the information about error corrections required to be disclosed by IAS 8 for any of the acquiree's identifiable assets, liabilities or contingent liabilities, or changes in the values assigned to those items, that the acquirer recognises during the current period in accordance with paragraphs 63 and 64.

74 An entity shall disclose information that enables users of its financial statements to evaluate changes in the carrying amount of goodwill during the period.

75 To give effect to the principle in paragraph 74, the entity shall disclose a reconciliation of the carrying amount of goodwill at the beginning and end of the period, showing separately:

(a) the gross amount and accumulated impairment losses at the beginning of the period;

(b) additional goodwill recognised during the period except goodwill included in a disposal group that, on acquisition, meets the criteria to be classified as held for sale in accordance with IFRS 5;

(c) adjustments resulting from the subsequent recognition of deferred tax assets during the period in accordance with paragraph 65;

(d) goodwill included in a disposal group classified as held for sale in accordance with IFRS 5 and goodwill derecognised during the period without having previously been included in a disposal group classified as held for sale;

(e) impairment losses recognised during the period in accordance with IAS 36;

(f) net exchange differences arising during the period in accordance with IAS 21 *The Effects of Changes in Foreign Exchange Rates*;

(g) any other changes in the carrying amount during the period; and

(h) the gross amount and accumulated impairment losses at the end of the period.

76 The entity discloses information about the recoverable amount and impairment of goodwill in accordance with IAS 36 in addition to the information required to be disclosed by paragraph 75(e).

77 If in any situation the information required to be disclosed by this IFRS does not satisfy the objectives set out in paragraphs 66, 72 and 74, the entity shall disclose such additional information as is necessary to meet those objectives.

Transitional provisions and effective date

78 Except as provided in paragraph 85, this IFRS shall apply to the accounting for business combinations for which the agreement date is on or after 31 March 2004. This IFRS shall also apply to the accounting for:

(a) goodwill arising from a business combination for which the agreement date is on or after 31 March 2004; or

(b) any excess of the acquirer's interest in the net fair value of the acquiree's identifiable assets, liabilities and contingent liabilities over the cost of a business combination for which the agreement date is on or after 31 March 2004.

Previously recognised goodwill

79 An entity shall apply this IFRS prospectively, from the beginning of the first annual period beginning on or after 31 March 2004, to goodwill acquired in a business combination for which the agreement date was before 31 March 2004, and to goodwill arising from an interest in a jointly controlled entity obtained before 31 March 2004 and accounted for by applying proportionate consolidation. Therefore, an entity shall:

(a) from the beginning of the first annual period beginning on or after 31 March 2004, discontinue amortising such goodwill;

(b) at the beginning of the first annual period beginning on or after 31 March 2004, eliminate the carrying amount of the related accumulated amortisation with a corresponding decrease in goodwill; and

(c) from the beginning of the first annual period beginning on or after 31 March 2004, test the goodwill for impairment in accordance with IAS 36 (as revised in 2004).

80 If an entity previously recognised goodwill as a deduction from equity, it shall not recognise that goodwill in profit or loss when it disposes of all or part of the business to which that goodwill relates or when a cash-generating unit to which the goodwill relates becomes impaired.

Previously recognised negative goodwill

81 The carrying amount of negative goodwill at the beginning of the first annual period beginning on or after 31 March 2004 that arose from either

(a) a business combination for which the agreement date was before 31 March 2004 or

(b) an interest in a jointly controlled entity obtained before 31 March 2004 and accounted for by applying proportionate consolidation

shall be derecognised at the beginning of that period, with a corresponding adjustment to the opening balance of retained earnings.

Previously recognised intangible assets

82 The carrying amount of an item classified as an intangible asset that either

(a) was acquired in a business combination for which the agreement date was before 31 March 2004 or

(b) arises from an interest in a jointly controlled entity obtained before 31 March 2004 and accounted for by applying proportionate consolidation

shall be reclassified as goodwill at the beginning of the first annual period beginning on or after 31 March 2004, if that intangible asset does not at that date meet the identifiability criterion in IAS 38 (as revised in 2004).

Equity accounted investments

83 For investments accounted for by applying the equity method and acquired on or after 31 March 2004, an entity shall apply this IFRS in the accounting for:

(a) any acquired goodwill included in the carrying amount of that investment. Therefore, amortisation of that notional goodwill shall not be included in the determination of the entity's share of the investee's profits or losses.

(b) any excess included in the carrying amount of the investment of the entity's interest in the net fair value of the investee's identifiable assets, liabilities and contingent liabilities over the cost of the investment. Therefore, an entity shall include that excess as income in the determination of the entity's share of the investee's profits or losses in the period in which the investment is acquired.

84 For investments accounted for by applying the equity method and acquired before 31 March 2004:

(a) an entity shall apply this IFRS on a prospective basis, from the beginning of the first annual period beginning on or after 31 March 2004, to any acquired goodwill included in the carrying amount of that investment. Therefore, an entity shall, from that date, discontinue including the amortisation of that goodwill in the determination of the entity's share of the investee's profits or losses.

(b) an entity shall derecognise any negative goodwill included in the carrying amount of that investment at the beginning of the first annual period beginning on or after 31 March 2004, with a corresponding adjustment to the opening balance of retained earnings.

Limited retrospective application

85 An entity is permitted to apply the requirements of this IFRS to goodwill existing at or acquired after, and to business combinations occurring from, any date before the effective dates outlined in paragraphs 78–84, provided:

(a) the valuations and other information needed to apply the IFRS to past business combinations were obtained at the time those combinations were initially accounted for; and

(b) the entity also applies IAS 36 (as revised in 2004) and IAS 38 (as revised in 2004) prospectively from that same date, and the valuations and other information needed to apply those Standards from that date were previously obtained by the entity so that there is no need to determine estimates that would need to have been made at a prior date.

Withdrawal of other pronouncements

86 This IFRS supersedes IAS 22 *Business Combinations* (as issued in 1998).

87 This IFRS supersedes the following Interpretations:

(a) SIC-9 *Business Combinations—Classification either as Acquisitions or Unitings of Interests*;

(b) SIC-22 *Business Combinations—Subsequent Adjustment of Fair Values and Goodwill Initially Reported*; and

(c) SIC-28 *Business Combinations—"Date of Exchange" and Fair Value of Equity Instruments*.

Appendix A
Defined terms

This appendix is an integral part of the IFRS.

acquisition date The date on which the acquirer effectively obtains control of the acquiree.

agreement date The date that a substantive agreement between the combining parties is reached and, in the case of publicly listed entities, announced to the public. In the case of a hostile takeover, the earliest date that a substantive agreement between the combining parties is reached is the date that a sufficient number of the acquiree's owners have accepted the acquirer's offer for the acquirer to obtain control of the acquiree.

business An integrated set of activities and assets conducted and managed for the purpose of providing:

(a) a return to investors; or

(b) lower costs or other economic benefits directly and proportionately to policyholders or participants.

A business generally consists of inputs, processes applied to those inputs, and resulting outputs that are, or will be, used to generate revenues. If **goodwill** is present in a transferred set of activities and assets, the transferred set shall be presumed to be a business.

business combination The bringing together of separate entities or **businesses** into one **reporting entity**.

business combination involving entities or businesses under common control A **business combination** in which all of the combining entities or **businesses** ultimately are **controlled** by the same party or parties both before and after the combination, and that **control** is not transitory.

contingent liability Contingent liability has the meaning given to it in IAS 37 *Provisions, Contingent Liabilities and Contingent Assets*, ie:

(a) a possible obligation that arises from past events and whose existence will be confirmed only by the occurrence or non-occurrence of one or more uncertain future events not wholly within the control of the entity; or

(b) a present obligation that arises from past events but is not recognised because:

   (i) it is not **probable** that an outflow of resources embodying economic benefits will be required to settle the obligation; or

   (ii) the amount of the obligation cannot be measured with sufficient reliability.

control The power to govern the financial and operating policies of an entity or business so as to obtain benefits from its activities.

date of exchange	When a **business combination** is achieved in a single exchange transaction, the date of exchange is the **acquisition date**. When a **business combination** involves more than one exchange transaction, for example when it is achieved in stages by successive share purchases, the date of exchange is the date that each individual investment is recognised in the financial statements of the acquirer.
fair value	The amount for which an asset could be exchanged, or a liability settled, between knowledgeable, willing parties in an arm's length transaction.
goodwill	Future economic benefits arising from assets that are not capable of being individually identified and separately recognised.
intangible asset	Intangible asset has the meaning given to it in IAS 38 *Intangible Assets*, ie an identifiable non-monetary asset without physical substance.
joint venture	Joint venture has the meaning given to it in IAS 31 *Interests in Joint Ventures*, ie a contractual arrangement whereby two or more parties undertake an economic activity that is subject to joint control.
minority interest	That portion of the profit or loss and net assets of a **subsidiary** attributable to equity interests that are not owned, directly or indirectly through **subsidiaries**, by the **parent**.
mutual entity	An entity other than an investor-owned entity, such as a mutual insurance company or a mutual cooperative entity, that provides lower costs or other economic benefits directly and proportionately to its policyholders or participants.
parent	An entity that has one or more **subsidiaries**.
probable	More likely than not.
reporting entity	An entity for which there are users who rely on the entity's general purpose financial statements for information that will be useful to them for making decisions about the allocation of resources. A reporting entity can be a single entity or a group comprising a **parent** and all of its **subsidiaries**.
subsidiary	An entity, including an unincorporated entity such as a partnership, that is **controlled** by another entity (known as the **parent**).

Appendix B Application supplement

This appendix is an integral part of the IFRS.

Reverse acquisitions

B1 As noted in paragraph 21, in some business combinations, commonly referred to as reverse acquisitions, the acquirer is the entity whose equity interests have been acquired and the issuing entity is the acquiree. This might be the case when, for example, a private entity arranges to have itself 'acquired' by a smaller public entity as a means of obtaining a stock exchange listing. Although legally the issuing public entity is regarded as the parent and the private entity is regarded as the subsidiary, the legal subsidiary is the acquirer if it has the power to govern the financial and operating policies of the legal parent so as to obtain benefits from its activities.

B2 An entity shall apply the guidance in paragraphs B3–B15 when accounting for a reverse acquisition.

B3 Reverse acquisition accounting determines the allocation of the cost of the business combination as at the acquisition date and does not apply to transactions after the combination.

Cost of the business combination

B4 When equity instruments are issued as part of the cost of the business combination, paragraph 24 requires the cost of the combination to include the fair value of those equity instruments at the date of exchange. Paragraph 27 notes that, in the absence of a reliable published price, the fair value of the equity instruments can be estimated by reference to the fair value of the acquirer or the fair value of the acquiree, whichever is more clearly evident.

B5 In a reverse acquisition, the cost of the business combination is deemed to have been incurred by the legal subsidiary (ie the acquirer for accounting purposes) in the form of equity instruments issued to the owners of the legal parent (ie the acquiree for accounting purposes). If the published price of the equity instruments of the legal subsidiary is used to determine the cost of the combination, a calculation shall be made to determine the number of equity instruments the legal subsidiary would have had to issue to provide the same percentage ownership interest of the combined entity to the owners of the legal parent as they have in the combined entity as a result of the reverse acquisition. The fair value of the number of equity instruments so calculated shall be used as the cost of the combination.

B6 If the fair value of the equity instruments of the legal subsidiary is not otherwise clearly evident, the total fair value of all the issued equity instruments of the legal parent before the business combination shall be used as the basis for determining the cost of the combination.

Preparation and presentation of consolidated financial statements

B7 Consolidated financial statements prepared following a reverse acquisition shall be issued under the name of the legal parent, but described in the notes as a continuation of the financial statements of the legal subsidiary (ie the acquirer for accounting purposes). Because such consolidated financial statements represent a continuation of the financial statements of the legal subsidiary:

(a) the assets and liabilities of the legal subsidiary shall be recognised and measured in those consolidated financial statements at their pre-combination carrying amounts.

(b) the retained earnings and other equity balances recognised in those consolidated financial statements shall be the retained earnings and other equity balances of the legal subsidiary immediately before the business combination.

(c) the amount recognised as issued equity instruments in those consolidated financial statements shall be determined by adding to the issued equity of the legal subsidiary immediately before the business combination the cost of the combination determined as described in paragraphs B4–B6. However, the equity structure appearing in those consolidated financial statements (ie the number and type of equity instruments issued) shall reflect the equity structure of the legal parent, including the equity instruments issued by the legal parent to effect the combination.

(d) comparative information presented in those consolidated financial statements shall be that of the legal subsidiary.

B8 Reverse acquisition accounting applies only in the consolidated financial statements. Therefore, in the legal parent's separate financial statements, if any, the investment in the legal subsidiary is accounted for in accordance with the requirements in IAS 27 *Consolidated and Separate Financial Statements* on accounting for investments in an investor's separate financial statements.

B9 Consolidated financial statements prepared following a reverse acquisition shall reflect the fair values of the assets, liabilities and contingent liabilities of the legal parent (ie the acquiree for accounting purposes). Therefore, the cost of the business combination shall be allocated by measuring the identifiable assets, liabilities and contingent liabilities of the legal parent that satisfy the recognition criteria in paragraph 37 at their fair values at the acquisition date. Any excess of the cost of the combination over the acquirer's interest in the net fair value of those items shall be accounted for in accordance with paragraphs 51–55. Any excess of the acquirer's interest in the net fair value of those items over the cost of the combination shall be accounted for in accordance with paragraph 56.

Minority interest

B10 In some reverse acquisitions, some of the owners of the legal subsidiary do not exchange their equity instruments for equity instruments of the legal parent. Although the entity in which those owners hold equity instruments (the legal subsidiary) acquired another entity (the legal parent), those owners shall be treated as a minority interest in the consolidated financial statements prepared after the reverse acquisition. This is because the owners of the legal subsidiary that do not exchange their equity instruments for equity instruments of the legal parent have an interest only in the results and net assets of the legal subsidiary, and not in the results and net assets of the combined entity. Conversely, all of the owners of the legal parent, notwithstanding that the legal parent is regarded as the acquiree, have an interest in the results and net assets of the combined entity.

B11 Because the assets and liabilities of the legal subsidiary are recognised and measured in the consolidated financial statements at their pre-combination carrying amounts, the minority interest shall reflect the minority shareholders' proportionate interest in the pre-combination carrying amounts of the legal subsidiary's net assets.

Earnings per share

B12 As noted in paragraph B7(c), the equity structure appearing in the consolidated financial statements prepared following a reverse acquisition reflects the equity structure of the legal parent, including the equity instruments issued by the legal parent to effect the business combination.

B13 For the purpose of calculating the weighted average number of ordinary shares outstanding (the denominator) during the period in which the reverse acquisition occurs:

(a) the number of ordinary shares outstanding from the beginning of that period to the acquisition date shall be deemed to be the number of ordinary shares issued by the legal parent to the owners of the legal subsidiary; and

(b) the number of ordinary shares outstanding from the acquisition date to the end of that period shall be the actual number of ordinary shares of the legal parent outstanding during that period.

B14 The basic earnings per share disclosed for each comparative period before the acquisition date that is presented in the consolidated financial statements following a reverse acquisition shall be calculated by dividing the profit or loss of the legal subsidiary attributable to ordinary shareholders in each of those periods by the number of ordinary shares issued by the legal parent to the owners of the legal subsidiary in the reverse acquisition.

B15 The calculations outlined in paragraphs B13 and B14 assume that there were no changes in the number of the legal subsidiary's issued ordinary shares during the comparative periods and during the period from the beginning of the period in which the reverse acquisition occurred to the acquisition date. The calculation of earnings per share shall be appropriately adjusted to take into account the effect of a change in the number of the legal subsidiary's issued ordinary shares during those periods.

Allocating the cost of a business combination

B16 This IFRS requires an acquirer to recognise the acquiree's identifiable assets, liabilities and contingent liabilities that satisfy the relevant recognition criteria at their fair values at the acquisition date. For the purpose of allocating the cost of a business combination, the acquirer shall treat the following measures as fair values:

(a) for financial instruments traded in an active market the acquirer shall use current market values.

(b) for financial instruments not traded in an active market the acquirer shall use estimated values that take into consideration features such as price-earnings ratios, dividend yields and expected growth rates of comparable instruments of entities with similar characteristics.

(c) for receivables, beneficial contracts and other identifiable assets the acquirer shall use the present values of the amounts to be received, determined at appropriate current interest rates, less allowances for uncollectibility and collection costs, if necessary. However, discounting is not required for short-term receivables, beneficial contracts and other identifiable assets when the difference between the nominal and discounted amounts is not material.

(d) for inventories of:

   (i) finished goods and merchandise the acquirer shall use selling prices less the sum of (1) the costs of disposal and (2) a reasonable profit allowance for the selling effort of the acquirer based on profit for similar finished goods and merchandise;

   (ii) work in progress the acquirer shall use selling prices of finished goods less the sum of (1) costs to complete, (2) costs of disposal and (3) a reasonable profit allowance for the completing and selling effort based on profit for similar finished goods; and

   (iii) raw materials the acquirer shall use current replacement costs.

(e) for land and buildings the acquirer shall use market values.

(f) for plant and equipment the acquirer shall use market values, normally determined by appraisal. If there is no market-based evidence of fair value because of the specialised nature of the item of plant and equipment and the item is rarely sold, except as part of a continuing business, an acquirer may need to estimate fair value using an income or a depreciated replacement cost approach.

(g) for intangible assets the acquirer shall determine fair value:

   (i) by reference to an active market as defined in IAS 38 *Intangible Assets*; or

   (ii) if no active market exists, on a basis that reflects the amounts the acquirer would have paid for the assets in arm's length transactions between knowledgeable willing parties, based on the best information available (see IAS 38 for further guidance on determining the fair values of intangible assets acquired in business combinations).

(h) for net employee benefit assets or liabilities for defined benefit plans the acquirer shall use the present value of the defined benefit obligation less the fair value of any plan assets. However, an asset is recognised only to the extent that it is probable it will be available to the acquirer in the form of refunds from the plan or a reduction in future contributions.

(i) for tax assets and liabilities the acquirer shall use the amount of the tax benefit arising from tax losses or the taxes payable in respect of profit or loss in accordance with IAS 12 *Income Taxes*, assessed from the perspective of the combined entity. The tax asset or liability is determined after allowing for the tax effect of restating identifiable assets, liabilities and contingent liabilities to their fair values and is not discounted.

(j) for accounts and notes payable, long-term debt, liabilities, accruals and other claims payable the acquirer shall use the present values of amounts to be disbursed in settling the liabilities determined at appropriate current interest rates. However, discounting is not required for short-term liabilities when the difference between the nominal and discounted amounts is not material.

(k) for onerous contracts and other identifiable liabilities of the acquiree the acquirer shall use the present values of amounts to be disbursed in settling the obligations determined at appropriate current interest rates.

(l) for contingent liabilities of the acquiree the acquirer shall use the amounts that a third party would charge to assume those contingent liabilities. Such an amount shall reflect all expectations about possible cash flows and not the single most likely or the expected maximum or minimum cash flow.

B17 Some of the above guidance requires fair values to be estimated using present value techniques. If the guidance for a particular item does not refer to the use of present value techniques, such techniques may be used in estimating the fair value of that item.

Appendix C
Amendments to other IFRSs

The amendments in this appendix shall be applied to the accounting for business combinations for which the agreement date is on or after 31 March 2004, and to the accounting for any goodwill and intangible assets acquired in those business combinations. In all other respects, these amendments shall be applied for annual periods beginning on or after 31 March 2004.

However, if an entity elects in accordance with paragraph 85 to apply IFRS 3 from any date before the effective dates outlined in paragraphs 78–84, it shall also apply these amendments prospectively from that same date.

* * * * *

The amendments contained in this appendix when this IFRS was issued in 2004 have been incorporated into the relevant pronouncements published in this volume.

Approval of IFRS 3 by the Board

International Financial Reporting Standard 3 *Business Combinations* was approved for issue by twelve of the fourteen members of the International Accounting Standards Board. Professor Whittington and Mr Yamada dissented. Their dissenting opinions are set out after the Basis for Conclusions on IFRS 3.

Sir David Tweedie	Chairman
Thomas E Jones	Vice-Chairman
Mary E Barth	
Hans-Georg Bruns	
Anthony T Cope	
Robert P Garnett	
Gilbert Gélard	
James J Leisenring	
Warren J McGregor	
Patricia L O'Malley	
Harry K Schmid	
John T Smith	
Geoffrey Whittington	
Tatsumi Yamada	

CONTENTS

paragraphs

BASIS FOR CONCLUSIONS
IFRS 3 BUSINESS COMBINATIONS

Basis for Conclusions on IFRS 3 Business Combinations

This Basis for Conclusions accompanies, but is not part of, IFRS 3.

Introduction

BC1 This Basis for Conclusions summarises the Board's considerations in reaching the conclusions in IFRS 3 *Business Combinations*. Individual Board members gave greater weight to some factors than to others.

BC2 IAS 22 *Business Combinations* (revised in 1998) specified the accounting for business combinations. In 2001 the Board began a project to review IAS 22 as part of its initial agenda, with the objective of improving the quality of, and seeking international convergence on, the accounting for business combinations. The Board's project on business combinations has two phases. As part of the first phase, the Board published in December 2002 ED 3 *Business Combinations*, together with an Exposure Draft of proposed related amendments to IAS 38 *Intangible Assets* and IAS 36 *Impairment of Assets*, with a comment deadline of 4 April 2003. The Board received 136 comment letters.

BC3 The first phase resulted in the Board issuing simultaneously the IFRS and revised versions of IAS 36 and IAS 38. The Board's intention in developing the IFRS as part of the first phase of the project was not to reconsider all of the requirements in IAS 22. Instead, the Board's primary focus was on:

(a) the method of accounting for business combinations;

(b) the initial measurement of the identifiable assets acquired and liabilities and contingent liabilities assumed in a business combination;

(c) the recognition of liabilities for terminating or reducing the activities of an acquiree;

(d) the treatment of any excess of the acquirer's interest in the fair value of identifiable net assets acquired in a business combination over the cost of the combination; and

(e) the accounting for goodwill and intangible assets acquired in a business combination.

BC4 Therefore, a number of the requirements in the IFRS were carried forward from IAS 22 without reconsideration by the Board. This Basis for Conclusions identifies those requirements but does not discuss them in detail.

BC5 The second phase of the Business Combinations project includes consideration of:

(a) issues arising in respect of the application of the purchase method, including its application to:

(i) business combinations involving two or more mutual entities; and

(ii) business combinations in which separate entities are brought together to form a reporting entity by contract alone without the obtaining of an ownership interest. This includes combinations in which separate entities are brought together by contract to form a dual listed corporation.

(b) the accounting for business combinations in which separate entities or businesses are brought together to form a joint venture, including possible applications for 'fresh start' accounting.

(c) the accounting for business combinations involving entities under common control.

Definition of a business combination

BC6 A business combination is defined in the IFRS as 'the bringing together of separate entities or businesses into one reporting entity'.

BC7 The Board concluded that the definition of a business combination should be broad enough to encompass all transactions that meet the business combination definition in IAS 22, ie all transactions or other events in which separate entities or businesses are brought together into one economic entity, regardless of the form of the transaction. In developing ED 3 and the ensuing IFRS, the Board considered the following description contained in the US Financial Accounting Standards Board's Statement of Financial Accounting Standards No. 141 *Business Combinations* (SFAS 141):

> a business combination occurs when an entity acquires net assets that constitute a business or acquires equity interests of one or more other entities and obtains control over that entity or entities. (paragraph 9)

BC8 The Board was concerned whether the above description would, in fact, encompass all transactions or other events in which separate entities or businesses are brought together into one economic entity. That concern stemmed from the use of the term 'acquires' in the above description, and its implication that a business combination is always the result of one entity acquiring control of one or more other entities or businesses, ie that all business combinations are acquisitions. The Board concluded that it should not rule out the possibility of some transaction or other event occurring or being structured in which separate entities or businesses are brought together into one economic entity, but without one of the combining entities acquiring control of the other combining entities or businesses. Therefore, the Board decided to develop a more general definition.

BC9 Given the Board's desire for the definition to encompass all transactions or other events that are, in substance, business combinations, regardless of their form, the Board decided to retain the IAS 22 definition, but with two modifications. The first was to remove the reference in that definition to the form that IAS 22 asserts a business combination might take (ie a uniting of interests or an acquisition). The second was to replace the reference to 'economic entity' with 'reporting entity' for consistency with the IASB's *Framework for the Preparation and Presentation of Financial Statements*. Paragraph 8 of the *Framework* states that it is concerned with the financial statements of reporting enterprises, and that a reporting enterprise is 'an enterprise for which there are users who rely on the financial statements as their major source of financial information about the enterprise.' The definition of reporting entity in the IFRS also clarifies that a reporting entity can be a single entity or a group comprising a parent and all of its subsidiaries.

Definition of a business

BC10 ED 3 proposed to define a business combination as 'the bringing together of separate entities or operations of entities into one reporting entity'. Many respondents to ED 3 asked for additional guidance on identifying when an entity or a group of assets or net assets comprises an operation and when, therefore, the acquisition of an entity or a group of assets or net assets should be accounted for in accordance with the IFRS. As a result:

(a) references in ED 3 to 'operations' have been replaced in the IFRS with 'businesses'.

(b) 'business' has been defined in the IFRS (Appendix A) as follows:

> An integrated set of activities and assets conducted and managed for the purpose of providing:
>
> (a) a return to investors; or
>
> (b) lower costs or other economic benefits directly and proportionately to policyholders or participants.
>
> A business generally consists of inputs, processes applied to those inputs, and resulting outputs that are, or will be, used to generate revenues. If goodwill is present in a transferred set of activities and assets, the transferred set shall be presumed to be a business.

(c) additional guidance has been included in the IFRS to clarify that if an entity obtains control over one or more other entities that are not businesses, the bringing together of those entities is not a business combination. When a group of assets that does not constitute a business is acquired, the cost of the group of assets should be allocated between the individual identifiable assets in the group based on their relative fair values.

Replacing 'operations' with 'businesses'

BC11 As noted above, ED 3 proposed to define a business combination as 'the bringing together of separate entities or operations of entities into one reporting entity'. The Board observed that the definition of a discontinuing operation in IAS 35 *Discontinuing Operations* incorporates a definition of an operation for the purpose of applying the requirements in IAS 35. Similarly, the IFRS arising from ED 4 *Disposal of Non-current Assets and Presentation of Discontinued Operations* will include a definition of an operation to ensure its consistent application. The Board decided that it should eliminate any possible connection between the IFRS and the notion of an operation embedded in any current or future Standard on discontinuing operations. Therefore, the Board decided to replace references to operations in ED 3 with businesses, and to include in the IFRS guidance on identifying when an entity or a group of assets or net assets constitutes a business.

Defining a business

BC12 Given its objective of seeking international convergence on the accounting for business combinations, the Board considered as its starting point the definition of a business and the related guidance in the US Emerging Issues Task Force (EITF) Consensus 98-3 *Determining Whether a Nonmonetary Transaction Involves Receipt of Productive Assets or of a Business.* For the reasons discussed in paragraphs BC13–BC15, the Board decided to proceed with a definition of a business that differs from the EITF's definition in the following ways:

(a) the IFRS definition does not require a business to be self-sustaining;

(b) the IFRS definition does not include a presumption that a transferred set of activities and assets in the development stage that has not commenced planned principal operations cannot be a business;

(c) the IFRS definition includes a presumption that a transferred set of activities and assets is a business when that transferred set includes goodwill; and

(d) the IFRS definition can also be applied in assessing whether an integrated set of activities and assets of a mutual entity is a business.

BC13 A transferred set of activities and assets must be self-sustaining to meet the EITF's definition of a business. The Board concluded that such a requirement is too narrow because it excludes some transferred sets of activities and assets that include goodwill (ie future economic benefits arising from assets that are not capable of being individually identified and separately recognised) and are, in substance, businesses. For example, the EITF's definition excludes from business combination accounting transactions in which one entity (the acquirer) acquires a business (the acquiree) with the intention of completely integrating the acquiree with its existing operations, but without taking over the acquiree's systems and senior management. Indeed, not taking over the existing systems and senior management may be a major part of the synergistic cost savings the acquirer is striving to achieve through the business combination. The Board concluded that an acquirer's decision not to retain all of the employees and not to acquire systems does not mean the net assets it acquired are not a business.

BC14 EITF 98-3 includes the presumption that if a transferred set of activities and assets is in the development stage and has not commenced planned principal operations, the set cannot be a business. The Board observed that a development stage entity might often include significant resources in the nature of goodwill. Those resources might arise, for example, from employment contracts with development engineers, a new technology nearing the final stage of development, the work performed to develop markets and customers or protocols and systems. The Board concluded that it would be more representationally faithful to account for the acquisition of such a transferred set as a business combination, thereby recognising any goodwill as a separate asset rather than having the value attributable to that goodwill subsumed within the carrying amounts of the other assets in the transferred set. Therefore, the Board decided not to include a similar presumption in the IFRS. The Board further concluded that to be representationally faithful, *any* transferred set of assets that includes goodwill should be accounted for as a business combination. Therefore, the Board decided that the definition of a business should include a presumption that if a transferred set of activities and assets includes goodwill, the transferred set should be presumed to be a business.

BC15 The EITF's definition states that the set of assets must be managed for the purpose of 'providing a return to investors'. The Board agreed that this would preclude sets of activities and assets of mutual entities from being regarded as businesses when those sets are, in substance, businesses. This is because a mutual entity is defined in the IFRS as 'an entity other than an investor-owned entity, such as a mutual insurance company or a mutual cooperative entity, that provides lower costs or other economic benefits directly and proportionately to its policyholders or participants.' The Board decided that:

(a) the definition of a business should be able to be applied in assessing whether an integrated set of activities and assets of a mutual entity is a business; and

(b) therefore, a business should be defined in the IFRS as an integrated set of activities and assets conducted and managed for the purpose of providing a return to investors *or* lower costs or other economic benefits directly and proportionately to policyholders or participants.

Scope

Scope exclusions (paragraphs 2 and 3)

BC16 The IFRS does not apply to:

(a) business combinations in which separate entities or businesses are brought together to form a joint venture.

(b) business combinations involving entities or businesses under common control.

(c) business combinations involving two or more mutual entities.

(d) business combinations in which separate entities or businesses are brought together to form a reporting entity by contract alone without the obtaining of an ownership interest (for example, combinations in which separate entities are brought together by contract alone to form a dual listed corporation).

IAS 22 similarly did not deal with the formation of joint ventures or transactions among enterprises under common control. However, IAS 22 included within its scope combinations involving two or more mutual entities, and combinations in which separate entities or businesses are brought together to form a reporting entity by contract alone without the obtaining of an ownership interest.

Business combinations involving the formation of a joint venture

BC17 Although the treatment by venturers of interests in joint ventures is addressed in IAS 31 *Interests in Joint Ventures*, the Board has not yet considered the accounting by a joint venture upon its formation. The issues involved relate to broader 'new basis' issues that the Board intends to address as part of the second phase of its Business Combinations project.

BC18 However, in developing ED 3 and the IFRS, the Board considered whether it should amend the definition of joint control in IAS 31. The Board decided to consider this issue because it was concerned that its decision to eliminate the pooling of interests method (see paragraphs BC37–BC55) would create incentives for business combinations to be structured to meet the definition of a joint venture. A joint venture is defined in IAS 31 as 'a contractual arrangement whereby two or more parties undertake an economic activity that is subject to joint control.' Joint control was defined as 'the contractually agreed sharing of control over an economic activity.'

BC19 The Board considered as a starting point the following definition proposed in the 1999 G4+1 discussion paper *Reporting Interests in Joint Ventures and Similar Arrangements* :

> Joint control over an enterprise exists when no one party alone has the power to control its strategic operating, investing, and financing decisions, but two or more parties together can do so, and each of the parties sharing control (joint venturers) must consent.

BC20 In developing ED 3, the Board decided that the definition of joint control should be more closely aligned with the definition proposed by the G4+1. ED 3 proposed amending the definition of joint control as follows:

> **Joint control ~~is the contractually agreed sharing of control~~ over an economic activity exists only when the financial and operating decisions relating to the activity require the unanimous consent of the parties sharing control (the venturers).**

BC21 Many respondents to ED 3 suggested that, unlike the definition proposed by the G4+1, the above definition would result in a joint venture existing only when unanimous consent is required for all, rather than just strategic, financial and operating decisions. They recommended that the Board retain the former definition of joint control in IAS 31, pending a comprehensive review of that Standard.

BC22 The Board agreed with the respondents' concerns that requiring unanimous consent on all financial and operating decisions would narrow by too far the types of arrangements meeting the definition of a joint venture. However, the Board remained concerned that the former definition of joint control could result in the requirement to apply the purchase method being circumvented when a business combination involves the owners of multiple businesses (for example, multiple medical practices) agreeing to combine their businesses into a new entity (sometimes referred to as rollup transactions). In such circumstances, the owners of the combining businesses could avoid the requirement to apply the purchase method by contractually agreeing that all the essential strategic operating, investing, and financing decisions require the consent of a majority of the owners. The Board concluded that in the absence of a contractual agreement requiring unanimous consent to strategic operating, investing and financing decisions of the parties sharing control, such transactions should be accounted for by applying the purchase method.

BC23 As a result, the Board decided to amend the definition of joint control as follows:

> **Joint control is the contractually agreed sharing of control over an economic activity, and exists only when the strategic financial and operating decisions relating to the activity require the unanimous consent of the parties sharing control (the venturers).**

Business combinations involving entities under common control (paragraphs 10–13)

BC24 Because the first phase of the project primarily dealt with the issues identified in paragraph BC3, the Board also decided to defer until the second phase of the project consideration of the accounting for business combinations involving entities or businesses under common control.

BC25 The former Standing Interpretations Committee (SIC) received numerous requests to clarify the types of transactions that were within the IAS 22 scope exclusion for transactions among enterprises under common control. The SIC concluded that, in the absence of authoritative guidance, the identification of transactions within the scope exclusion was likely to receive divergent or unacceptable treatment. Therefore, the SIC agreed in December 2000 to add this issue to its agenda. The SIC had not, however, completed its deliberations by the time the Board began the first phase of its Business Combinations project. In developing ED 3 and the IFRS the Board reached the same view as the SIC and agreed that the IFRS replacing IAS 22 should include authoritative guidance on this issue.

BC26 Because the IFRS addresses the accounting for business combinations and not other transactions, the Board concluded that the nature of the scope exclusion would be better expressed as 'business combinations involving entities or businesses under common control' rather than 'transactions among enterprises under common control'.

BC27 The IFRS defines a business combination involving entities or businesses under common control as a business combination in which all of the combining entities or businesses ultimately are controlled by the same party or parties both before and after the combination, and that control is not transitory. In arriving at this definition, and the related guidance in paragraphs 10–13, the Board first considered the meaning of common control. The Board noted that control is defined in IFRSs as the power to govern the financial and operating policies of an entity or business so as to obtain benefits from its activities. This definition requires consideration of direct and indirect relationships and is not limited to control by another entity; control can, for example, rest with an individual or a group of individuals acting collectively under contractual arrangements. In addition, the definition of control means that control of an entity can exist irrespective of the extent of minority interest in that entity. The Board also noted that the ordinary meaning of 'common' is a similarity shared by two or more things. Therefore, the Board concluded that entities or businesses are under common control when the same party or parties have the power to govern the financial and operating policies of those entities or businesses so as to obtain benefits from their activities. The Board further concluded that for a business combination to involve entities or businesses under common control, the combining entities or businesses would need to be controlled by the same party or parties both before and after the combination.

BC28 The Board noted the concern expressed by some that business combinations between parties acting at arm's length could be structured through the use of 'grooming' transactions so that, for a brief period immediately before the combination, the combining entities or businesses are under common control. In this way, it might be possible for combinations that would otherwise be accounted for in accordance with the IFRS using the purchase method to be accounted for using some other method. Thus, the Board decided that for a business combination to be excluded from the scope of the IFRS as one involving entities or businesses under common control, the combining entities or businesses should be controlled by the same party or parties both before and after the combination, and that control should not be transitory.

Combinations involving mutual entities or the bringing together of separate entities to form a reporting entity by contract alone

BC29 The Board decided to exclude from the scope of the IFRS the following business combinations:

(a) combinations involving two or more mutual entities.

(b) combinations in which separate entities are brought together to form a reporting entity by contract alone without the obtaining of an ownership interest. This includes combinations in which separate entities are brought together by contract to form a dual listed corporation.

BC30 ED 3 did not propose to exclude such transactions from the scope of the IFRS, but instead proposed to delay the application of the IFRS to the accounting for such transactions until the Board issues guidance on the application of the purchase method to those transactions. In developing ED 3, the Board observed that differences between the ownership structures of mutual entities (such as mutual insurance companies or mutual cooperative entities) and those of investor-owned entities give rise to complications in applying the purchase method to business combinations involving two or more mutual entities. Similarly, the Board noted that complications arise in applying the purchase method to combinations involving the formation of a reporting entity by contract alone without the obtaining of an ownership interest. The Board decided to propose in ED 3 that until those issues are resolved as part of the second phase of the Business Combinations project, the accounting for such transactions should continue to be dealt with by IAS 22.

BC31 During its redeliberations, the Board observed that continuing to apply IAS 22 to such transactions would result in them being classified either as unitings of interests or as acquisitions. If such a transaction were classified as a uniting of interests, it would be required by IAS 22 to be accounted for by applying the pooling of interests method. The Board decided that this would not be consistent with its conclusion that there are no circumstances in which the pooling of interests method provides information superior to that provided by the purchase method (see paragraphs BC50–BC53). The Board also observed that if such a transaction were classified as an acquisition, it would be required by IAS 22 to be accounted for by applying the purchase method, but a different version of the purchase method from that contained in the IFRS. The Board considered it troublesome that two versions of the purchase method might coexist for a period of time, particularly given that the two versions might produce quite different results. For example, unlike the IFRS, IAS 22 would require goodwill amortisation and permit restructuring plans that do not meet the definition of a liability to be recognised as a provision as part of allocating the cost of the combination.

BC32 The Board then considered whether entities should be required to apply the IFRS to such transactions, focusing its discussion on two issues that might arise in applying the purchase method to those transactions. The first was the proposition that it might be difficult to identify the acquirer. The second was the concern that such transactions normally do not involve the payment of any readily measurable consideration. Thus, difficulties would arise in estimating the cost of the business combination and any goodwill acquired in the combination.

BC33 On the first issue, the Board reaffirmed its conclusion outlined in paragraphs BC54 and BC55.

BC34 On the second issue, the Board decided that until it develops as part of the second phase of its Business Combinations project guidance on applying the purchase method to such transactions, the IFRS should include such transactions within its scope. However, the IFRS should require the aggregate fair value of the acquiree's identifiable assets, liabilities and contingent liabilities to be treated as the deemed cost of the business combination. Therefore, until guidance is developed as part of the second phase of the Business Combinations project on estimating the fair value of an acquiree when the combination does not involve readily measurable consideration, no goodwill would arise in the accounting for such transactions. The Board decided, however, that it would not be appropriate to incorporate this interim solution into the IFRS without first exposing it for public comment. Therefore, given the Board's desire to issue the IFRS before the end of March 2004, the Board decided:

(a) to proceed with publishing the IFRS before the end of March 2004, but to exclude such transactions from its scope.

(b) to publish at about the same time as the IFRS an exposure draft proposing a limited amendment to the IFRS whereby such transactions would be included within the scope of the IFRS, but with the aggregate fair value of the acquiree's identifiable assets, liabilities and contingent liabilities being treated as the deemed cost of the combination.

Scope inclusions (paragraph 8)

BC35 The Board concluded that, because the first phase of the project dealt primarily with the issues identified in paragraph BC3, the IFRS should apply to the same transactions as IAS 22. The Board observed that the definition of a business combination in IAS 22, and therefore the scope of IAS 22, included combinations in which one entity obtains control of another, but for which the date of obtaining control (the acquisition date) does not coincide with the date of acquiring an ownership interest (the date of exchange). This might occur, for example, when an investee enters into share buy-back arrangements with some of its investors and, as a result of those arrangements, control of the investee changes.

BC36 However, the Board noted that some constituents might not have appreciated this implication of IAS 22's scope. Accordingly, the Board decided that the IFRS should explicitly state that such transactions are within its scope.

Method of accounting (paragraph 14)

BC37 ED 3 proposed, and the IFRS requires, all business combinations within its scope to be accounted for using the purchase method. IAS 22 permitted business combinations to be accounted for using one of two methods: the pooling of interests method for combinations classified as unitings of interests and the purchase method for combinations classified as acquisitions.

BC38 Although IAS 22 tightly restricted the scope of business combinations that could be accounted for using the pooling of interests method, analysts and other users of financial statements indicated that permitting two methods of accounting for business combinations impaired the comparability of financial statements. Others indicated that requiring more than one method of accounting for substantially similar transactions created incentives for structuring transactions to achieve a desired accounting result, particularly given that the two methods produce substantially different results. These factors, combined with the prohibition of the pooling of interests method in Australia, Canada and the United States, prompted the Board to examine whether, given that few combinations were understood to be accounted for in accordance with IAS 22 using the pooling of interests method, it would be advantageous for international standards to converge with those in Australia and North America by also prohibiting the method.

BC39 After considering all the information and arguments put before it, including case studies drawn from situations encountered in practice, the Board concluded that most business combinations result in one entity obtaining control of another entity (or entities) or business(es), and therefore that an acquirer could be identified for most combinations. However, the Board decided that it should not, in the first phase of its project, rule out the possibility of a business combination occurring (other than a combination involving the formation of a joint venture) in which one of the combining entities does not obtain control of the other combining entity or entities (often referred to as a 'true merger' or 'merger of equals').

BC40 Therefore, the Board focused first on the appropriate method of accounting for business combinations in which one entity obtains control of another entity or business. Next it considered the method of accounting that should be applied to those business combinations within the scope of the IFRS for which one of the combining entities does not obtain control of the other combining entity (or entities), assuming such transactions exist.

BC41 For the reasons discussed in paragraphs BC44–BC46, the Board concluded that the purchase method is the appropriate method of accounting for business combinations in which one entity obtains control of another entity (or entities) or business(es).

BC42 As discussed in paragraphs BC47–BC49, the Board concluded that the IFRS arising from the first phase of the project should also require the purchase method to be applied to those combinations within its scope for which one of the combining entities does not obtain control of the other combining entity. The Board acknowledged, however, that a case might be made for using the 'fresh start' method to account for such business combinations. The fresh start method derives from the view that a new entity emerges as a result of such a business combination. Therefore, a case can be made that the assets and liabilities of each of the combining entities, including assets and liabilities not previously recognised, should be recognised by the new entity at their fair values. However, the Board observed that to the best of its knowledge the fresh start method is not currently applied in any jurisdiction in accounting for business combinations, and that one of the primary aims of the first phase of the project is to seek international convergence on the method(s) of accounting for combinations. Therefore, the Board committed itself to exploring in a future phase of its Business Combinations project whether the fresh start method might be applied to some combinations. The Board noted, however, that business combinations to which the fresh start method might be applied would not necessarily be all of those that would be classified by IAS 22 as unitings of interests and accounted for by applying the pooling of interests method. Consequently, the pooling of interests method in IAS 22 could not simply be replaced with the fresh start method.

BC43 Most of the respondents to ED 3 supported the proposal to eliminate the pooling of interests method and require all business combinations to be accounted for by applying the purchase method, pending the Board's future consideration of whether the fresh start method might be applied to some combinations.

Business combinations in which one of the combining entities obtains control

BC44 The Board concluded that the purchase method is the only appropriate method of accounting for business combinations in which one entity obtains control of one or more other entities or businesses. The purchase method views a combination from the perspective of the combining entity that is the acquirer (ie the combining entity that obtains control of the other combining entities or businesses). The acquirer purchases net assets and recognises in its financial statements the assets acquired and liabilities and contingent liabilities assumed, including those not previously recognised by the acquiree. The nature of the consideration exchanged does not affect the recognition or measurement of the assets acquired and liabilities and contingent liabilities assumed. Because the exchange transaction is assumed to result from arm's length bargaining between independent parties, the values exchanged are presumed to be equal. The measurement of the acquirer's assets and liabilities is not affected by the transaction, nor are any additional assets or liabilities of the acquirer recognised as a result of the transaction, because they are not involved in the transaction. Therefore, the purchase method faithfully represents the underlying economics of business combinations in which one entity obtains control of another entity or business.

BC45 The *Framework* notes that one of the objectives of financial statements is to show the accountability of management for the resources entrusted to it. Because the purchase method recognises the values exchanged in a business combination, it provides users of an entity's financial statements with more useful information for assessing the investment made by management and the subsequent performance of that investment. In addition, by recognising at their fair values all of the assets acquired and liabilities and contingent liabilities assumed, the purchase method impounds information from the current transaction about the expected future cash flows associated with the assets acquired and liabilities and contingent liabilities assumed, thereby providing greater predictive value.

BC46 The Board considered the assertion that identifying the fair values of assets acquired and liabilities and contingent liabilities assumed in such business combinations is too costly or too difficult, particularly when the assets and liabilities are not traded regularly. The Board concluded that the benefits of obtaining more useful financial information by applying the purchase method outweigh the costs to obtain fair values, and that an understanding by the acquirer of the fair values of the assets acquired and the liabilities and contingent liabilities assumed would be necessary to arrive at an acceptable exchange value for the combination. Therefore, any additional costs or difficulties associated with recognising those assets, liabilities and contingent liabilities at their fair values are unlikely to be significant.

Business combinations in which none of the combining entities obtains control

BC47 As noted above, the Board decided that it should not, in the first phase of its Business Combinations project, rule out the possibility of a combination occurring (other than a combination involving the formation of a joint venture) in which one of the combining entities does not obtain control of the other combining entity or entities. Such combinations are sometimes referred to as 'true mergers' or 'mergers of equals'.

BC48 The Board concluded that even if 'true mergers' exist and were to be accounted for using a method other than the purchase method, suitable non-arbitrary and unambiguous criteria would be needed to distinguish those transactions from business combinations in which one entity obtains control of another entity (or entities). The Board observed that such criteria do not exist at present and, based on the history of the pooling of interests method, would be likely to take considerable time, and be extremely difficult, to develop. The Board also noted that:

(a) one of its primary aims in the first phase of the project is to seek international convergence on the method(s) of accounting for business combinations.

(b) permitting more than one method of accounting for combinations would create incentives for structuring transactions to achieve a desired accounting result, particularly given that the different methods (ie the purchase method and the pooling of interests method) produce significantly different accounting results.

(c) true mergers, assuming they exist, are likely to be rare.

(d) it does not follow that the pooling of interests method is the appropriate method of accounting for true mergers, assuming they exist. For the reasons outlined in paragraphs BC50–BC53, the Board concluded that in no circumstances does the pooling of interests method provide information superior to that provided by the purchase method, and that if true mergers were to be accounted for using a method other than the purchase method, the 'fresh start' method was likely to be more appropriate than the pooling of interests method.

BC49 Therefore, the Board concluded that the IFRS arising from the first phase of the project should require all business combinations to be accounted for by applying the purchase method. However, as discussed in paragraph BC42, the Board committed itself to exploring in a future phase of its Business Combinations project whether the 'fresh start' method might be applied to some combinations.

Reasons for rejecting the pooling of interests method

BC50 IAS 22 permitted business combinations to be accounted for using one of two methods: the pooling of interests method or the purchase method. These methods were not regarded as alternatives for the same form of business combination either in IAS 22 or the equivalent accounting standards in other jurisdictions that permitted the use of the two methods. Rather, each method applied to a specific form of business combination: the purchase method to those that were acquisitions (ie business combinations in which one entity obtains control of another entity or business), and the pooling of interests method to those that were 'true mergers' or 'unitings of interest'. Standard-setters disagree about the precise meaning of the term 'true merger'. However, the Board's deliberations on applying the pooling of interests method to true mergers focused on combinations in which one of the combining entities does not obtain control of the other combining entity or entities. The Board concluded that the pooling of interests method should not be applied to such transactions because in no circumstances does it provide information superior to that provided by the purchase method.

BC51 Use of the pooling of interests method was limited to business combinations in which equity was the predominant form of consideration. Assets and liabilities of the combining entities were carried forward at their pre-combination book values, and no additional assets or liabilities were recognised as a result of the combination. The Board considered the assertion that the pooling of interests method is appropriate for true mergers because, in such transactions, ownership interests are completely or substantially continued, no new equity is invested and no assets are distributed, post-combination ownership interests are proportional to those before the combination, and the intention is to have a uniting of commercial strategies. The Board rejected these arguments, noting that although a combination effected by an exchange of equity instruments results in the continuation of ownership interests, those interests *change* as a result of the combination. The owners of the combining entities have, as a result of the combination, a residual interest in the net assets of the combined entity. The information provided by applying the pooling of interests method would fail to reflect this and would therefore lack relevance. Because the assets and liabilities of all the combining entities would be recognised at their pre-combination book values rather than at their fair values at the date of the combination, users of the combined entity's financial statements would be unable to assess reasonably the nature, timing and extent of future cash flows expected to arise from the combined entity as a result of a combination. Furthermore, the Board does not accept that the nature of the consideration tendered (equity interests in the case of true mergers) should dictate how the assets and liabilities of the combining entities are recognised.

BC52 The Board also considered the assertion that the pooling of interests method properly portrays true mergers as a transaction between the owners of the combining entities rather than between the combining entities. The Board rejected this assertion, noting that business combinations are initiated by, and take place as a result of, a transaction between the entities themselves. It is the entities, and not their owners, that engage in the negotiations necessary to carry out the combination, although obviously the owners must eventually participate in and approve the transaction.

BC53 The *Framework* notes that one of the objectives of financial statements is to show the accountability of management for the resources entrusted to it. The Board observed that the pooling of interests method is an exception to the general principle that exchange transactions are accounted for at the fair values of the items exchanged. Because it ignores the values exchanged in the business combination, the information provided by applying the pooling of interests method does not hold management accountable for the investment made and its subsequent performance.

Business combinations in which it is difficult to identify an acquirer

BC54 The Board observed that in some business combinations, domestic legal, taxation or economic factors can make it extremely difficult to identify an acquirer. This can occur, for example, when entities of similar sizes or capitalisations come together through industry restructurings, with existing managements and staff retained and integrated. The Board considered arguments about whether such factors could make it impossible to identify an acquirer in a business combination and, if so, whether the pooling of interests method should be permitted in such circumstances. The Board also considered whether applying the purchase method to combinations for which identifying the acquirer is difficult could result in an arbitrary selection of an acquirer and therefore be detrimental to the comparability of accounting information. As part of its deliberations, the Board considered case studies that related to situations encountered in practice.

BC55 Whilst acknowledging that it could be difficult to identify an acquirer in some rare circumstances, the Board did not agree that exceptions to applying the purchase method should be permitted. The Board concluded that in no circumstances does the pooling of interests method provide superior information to that provided by the purchase method, even if identifying the acquirer is problematic.

Application of the purchase method

Identifying an acquirer (paragraphs 17–23)

BC56 As proposed in ED 3, the IFRS carries forward from IAS 22 the principle that, in a business combination accounted for using the purchase method, the acquirer is the combining entity that obtains control of the other combining entities or businesses. In developing ED 3 and the IFRS, the Board observed that the use of the control concept as the basis for identifying the acquirer is consistent with the use of the control concept in IAS 27 *Consolidated and Separate Financial Statements* to define the boundaries of the reporting entity and provide the basis for establishing the existence of a parent-subsidiary relationship. The IFRS also carries forward the guidance in paragraphs 10 and 11 of IAS 22 on control and identifying an acquirer.

Identifying an acquirer in a business combination effected through an exchange of equity interests (paragraph 21)

BC57 In developing ED 3 and the IFRS, the Board decided not to carry forward paragraph 12 of IAS 22, which provided guidance on identifying which of the combining entities is the acquirer when one entity (say entity A) obtains ownership of the equity instruments of another entity (entity B) but, as part of the exchange transaction, issues enough of its own voting equity instruments as purchase consideration for control of the combined entity to pass to the owners of entity B. IAS 22 described such a situation as a reverse acquisition and required the entity whose owners control the combined entity to be treated as the acquirer. The Board observed that such an approach to identifying the acquirer presumed that for any business combination effected through an exchange of equity interests, the entity whose owners control the combined entity is always the entity with the power to govern the financial and operating policies of the other entity so as to obtain benefits from its activities. The Board observed that this is not always the case and that carrying forward such a presumption to the IFRS would in effect override the control concept for identifying the acquirer.

BC58 The Board noted that the control concept focuses on the relationship between two entities, in particular, whether one entity has the power to govern the financial and operating policies of another so as to obtain benefits from its activities. Therefore, the Board concluded that fundamental to identifying the acquirer in a business combination is a consideration of the relationship between the combining entities to determine which of them has, as a consequence of the combination, the power to govern the financial and operating policies of the other so as to obtain benefits from its activities. The Board concluded that this should be the case irrespective of the form of the purchase consideration.

BC59 The Board also observed that there might be instances in which the acquirer is the entity whose equity interests have been acquired and the issuing entity is the acquiree. This might occur, for example, when a private entity arranges to have itself 'acquired' by a smaller public entity through an exchange of equity interests as a means of obtaining a stock exchange listing and, as part of the agreement, the directors of the public entity resign and are replaced with directors appointed by the private entity and its former owners. The Board observed that in such circumstances, the private entity (ie the legal subsidiary) has the power to govern the financial and operating policies of the combined entity so as to obtain benefits from its activities. Therefore, treating the legal subsidiary as the acquirer in such circumstances is consistent with applying the control concept for identifying the acquirer.

BC60 As a result, the Board concluded that the IFRS should require the acquirer in a business combination effected through an issue of equity interests to be identified on the basis of a consideration of all pertinent facts and circumstances, including but not limited to the relative ownership interests of the owners of the combining entities, to determine which of those entities has the power to govern the financial and operating policies of the other so as to obtain benefits from its activities. Respondents to ED 3 generally supported this conclusion.

BC61 The Board also considered the assertion that, although consistent with the control concept, treating the legal subsidiary as the acquirer in the circumstances described in paragraph BC59 produces an accounting result that:

(a) is difficult for users to understand; and

(b) provides less relevant information than would be the case if the legal parent (ie the entity providing the consideration) were treated as the acquirer.

The Board concluded that treating the legal parent as the acquirer in such circumstances places the form of the transaction over its substance, thereby providing less useful information than is provided using the control concept to identify the acquirer. Therefore, the Board concluded that the IFRS should not include any departures from the control concept to identify an acquirer.

Identifying an acquirer when a new entity is formed to effect a business combination (paragraphs 22 and 23)

BC62 ED 3 proposed, and the IFRS requires, that when a new entity is formed to issue equity instruments to effect a business combination, one of the combining entities that existed before the combination should be identified as the acquirer on the basis of the evidence available. In deciding to include this requirement in the IFRS, the Board identified two approaches to the purchase method that had been applied in various jurisdictions. The first approach viewed business combinations from the perspective of one of the combining entities that existed before the combination, ie the acquirer must be one of the combining entities that existed before the combination and therefore cannot be a new entity formed to issue equity instruments to effect a combination. The second approach viewed business combinations from the perspective of the entity, which could be a newly formed entity, providing the consideration, ie the acquirer must be the entity providing the consideration. The Board noted that whereas some jurisdictions had interpreted IAS 22 as requiring the acquirer to be identified as one of the combining entities that existed before the combination, other jurisdictions had interpreted IAS 22 as requiring the entity, which could be a newly formed entity, providing the purchase consideration to be treated as the acquirer.

BC63 The Board observed that if a new entity is formed to issue equity instruments to effect a business combination between, for example, two other entities, viewing the combination from the perspective of the entity providing the consideration would result in the newly formed entity applying the purchase method to each of the two other combining entities. This would, in effect, produce a business combination accounted for as a fresh start. The Board noted that this would potentially provide users of the financial statements with more relevant information than an approach in which one of the pre-existing combining entities must be treated as the acquirer.

BC64 The Board also noted that some of the issues that arise under an approach in which one of the pre-existing combining entities must be treated as the acquirer do not arise if the entity providing the purchase consideration is treated as the acquirer. For example, treating one of several combining entities as the acquirer when those separate entities are brought together to form a new consolidated group might require one of those pre-existing entities to be arbitrarily selected as the acquirer. The Board agreed that the usefulness of the information provided in such circumstances is questionable. If the entity providing the purchase consideration is treated as the acquirer, that entity would be regarded as having obtained control of each of the pre-existing combining entities and would therefore apply the purchase method to each of the combining entities.

BC65 The Board also considered the assertion that treating as the acquirer a new entity formed to issue equity instruments to effect a business combination places the form of the transaction over its substance, because the new entity may have no economic substance. The formation of such entities is often related to legal, tax or other business considerations that do not affect the identification of the acquirer. For example, a combination between two entities that is structured so that one entity directs the formation of a new entity to issue equity instruments to the owners of both of the combining entities is, in substance, no different from a transaction in which one of the combining entities directly acquires the other. Therefore, the transaction should be accounted for in the same way as a transaction in which one of the combining entities directly acquires the other. Those supporting this approach argue that to do otherwise would impair the usefulness of the information provided to users about the combination, because both comparability and reliability (which rests on the notions of accounting for the substance of transactions and representational faithfulness, ie that similar transactions are accounted for in the same way) are diminished.

BC66 In developing ED 3 and the IFRS, the Board concluded that the users of an entity's financial statements are provided with more useful information about a business combination when that information represents faithfully the transaction it purports to represent. Therefore, the Board concluded that the IFRS should adopt the approach in which a business combination is viewed from the perspective of one of the combining entities that existed before the combination. In other words, the acquirer must be one of the combining entities that existed before the combination and therefore cannot be a new entity formed to issue equity instruments to effect a combination.

Cost of a business combination (paragraphs 24–35)

BC67 As proposed in ED 3, the IFRS carries forward from IAS 22, without reconsideration, the principle that the cost of a business combination should be measured by the acquirer as the aggregate of: the fair values, at the date of exchange, of assets given, liabilities incurred or assumed, and equity instruments issued by the acquirer, in exchange for control over the acquiree; plus any costs directly attributable to the business combination. The IFRS also incorporates, without reconsideration:

(a) the requirements of SIC-28 *Business Combinations—"Date of Exchange" and Fair Value of Equity Instruments* on the distinction between the date of exchange and the acquisition date, and, with one amendment (see paragraph BC69), measuring the fair value of equity instruments issued as part of the cost of a business combination;

(b) the requirement previously in paragraph 23 of IAS 22 on the treatment of the cost of a business combination when settlement of all or any part of that cost is deferred; and

(c) the requirements previously in paragraphs 65–70 of IAS 22 on adjustments to the cost of a business combination.

The Board is reconsidering these requirements as part of the second phase of its project.

BC68 The Basis for Conclusions on SIC-28 provided information on how the former Standing Interpretations Committee reached its consensus on the issues in (a) above (ie the distinction between the date of exchange and the acquisition date, and measuring the fair value of equity instruments issued as part of the cost of a combination). That Basis for Conclusions stated the following:

> ...when an acquisition is achieved in stages, the distinction between the date of acquisition and the date of the exchange transaction is important. When an acquisition is achieved in one exchange transaction there is no distinction between the date of exchange and the date of acquisition. Sub-paragraph 100(a) of the *Framework* indicates that when assets are recorded at their historical cost, the assets are recorded at the fair value of the purchase consideration given to acquire them at the time of their acquisition. Therefore, when a business is acquired in one exchange transaction (i.e., not in stages), the fair value of the purchase consideration given is determined when control ... of the net assets and operations of the acquiree is effectively transferred to the acquirer. When a business is acquired in stages (e.g., successive share purchases), the fair value of the purchase consideration given at each stage is determined when each individual investment is recognised in the financial statements of the acquirer.
>
> ...marketable securities issued by the acquirer are measured at their fair value, which is their market price as at the date of the exchange transaction, provided that undue fluctuations or the narrowness of the market do not make the market price an unreliable indicator. Under IAS 39, an investment in an equity instrument is measured at its fair value, except in specified circumstances. Equity instruments have only one fair value in a market. IAS 39 ... indicates that the existence of published price quotations in an active market is normally the best evidence of fair value. Therefore, estimates of premiums for large, and discounts for small, blocks of equity instruments issued in comparison to that exchanged in observable transactions are not considered. When the published price of a quoted equity instrument on the date of an exchange is

determined to be an unreliable indicator of its fair value, the information necessary to reliably estimate the effect of the undue fluctuation or market narrowness at that date is unlikely to be available due to the many factors that affect prices. Consequently, other evidence and valuation methods for determining fair value are considered only in the rare circumstance when it can be demonstrated that the published price is an unreliable indicator and that the other evidence and valuation methods provide a more reliable estimate of the equity instrument's fair value at the date of exchange.

BC69 SIC-28 stated that the published price of an equity instrument issued as part of the cost of a business combination is an unreliable indicator of fair value only when it has been affected by an undue price fluctuation or a narrowness of the market. The Board is of the view that the only circumstance in which the published price of an equity instrument is an unreliable indicator of its fair value is when the published price has been affected by the thinness of the market. Therefore, the Board decided to amend accordingly the requirements of SIC-28 included in the IFRS.

BC70 As proposed in ED 3, the IFRS includes additional guidance clarifying that future losses or other costs expected to be incurred as a result of a business combination cannot be included as part of the cost of the combination. The Board observed that those future losses or other costs do not satisfy the definition of a liability and therefore are not liabilities incurred by the acquirer in exchange for control over the acquiree, nor liabilities of the acquiree assumed by the acquirer. In the Board's view, future losses or other costs expected to be incurred as a result of a business combination should not have been included as part of the 'cost of acquisition' in accordance with IAS 22, but the Board noted that this was not stated explicitly in IAS 22. The IFRS states explicitly that this is the case to ensure that future losses or other costs expected to be incurred as a result of a business combination are treated consistently by all entities.

Costs directly attributable to the business combination (paragraphs 29–31)

BC71 Paragraph 25 of IAS 22 indicated that direct costs relating to an acquisition include the costs of registering and issuing equity instruments, and professional fees paid to accountants, legal advisers, valuers and other consultants to effect the acquisition. The Board noted that treating the costs of registering and issuing equity instruments as costs directly attributable to a business combination is inconsistent with the treatment of such costs in the jurisdictions of its partner standard-setters. It is also inconsistent with the conclusion reached by the G4+1 group of standard-setters at its meeting in August 1998, namely that transaction costs arising on the issue of equity instruments are an integral part of the equity issue transaction and should be recognised directly in equity as a reduction of the proceeds of the equity instruments. The Board observed that treating the transaction costs as a reduction of the proceeds of the equity instruments issued is consistent with the treatment of such costs in accordance with IAS 32 *Financial Instruments: Disclosure and Presentation* in circumstances involving the issue of equity instruments other than to effect a business combination.

BC72 Therefore, the Board concluded that the IFRS should not carry forward the requirement in IAS 22 for the costs of registering and issuing equity instruments to be treated as costs directly attributable to a business combination.

BC73 As part of the first phase of the project, the Board considered issues raised by constituents as part of the Improvements project that related to IAS 22. One of the issues raised was whether the costs of arranging financial liabilities for the purpose of acquisition financing are costs directly attributable to the acquisition and therefore part of the cost of acquisition. Consistently with its conclusions about the costs of registering and issuing equity instruments, the Board concluded that the costs of arranging and issuing financial liabilities are an integral part of the liability and, in accordance with IAS 39 *Financial Instruments: Recognition and Measurement*, should be included in the initial measurement of the liability rather than as part of the costs directly attributable to a business combination.

Allocating the cost of a business combination (paragraphs 36–60)

Recognising the identifiable assets acquired and liabilities and contingent liabilities assumed (paragraphs 36–50)

BC74 With the exception of the separate recognition of an acquiree's intangible assets, the IFRS carries forward the general principle previously in paragraphs 19 and 26–28 of IAS 22. That principle required an acquirer to recognise separately, from the acquisition date, the acquiree's identifiable assets and liabilities at that date that can be measured reliably and for which it is probable that any associated future economic benefits will flow to, or resources embodying economic benefits will flow from, the acquirer. The IFRS also carries forward:

(a) the requirement previously in paragraph 19 of IAS 22 for the acquirer's income statement to incorporate the acquiree's profits and losses from the acquisition date;

(b) the guidance previously in paragraph 20 of IAS 22 on determining the acquisition date; and

(c) the prohibition previously in paragraph 29 of IAS 22 on recognising as part of allocating the cost of a business combination provisions for future losses or other costs expected to be incurred as a result of the combination.

BC75 However, the IFRS changes the requirements previously in IAS 22 on separately recognising the following items as part of allocating the cost of a combination:

(a) provisions for terminating or reducing the activities of the acquiree; and

(b) contingent liabilities of the acquiree.

The IFRS also clarifies the criteria for separately recognising intangible assets of the acquiree as part of allocating the cost of a combination, and includes guidance on the treatment of payments that an entity is contractually required to make if it is acquired in a business combination.

Provisions for terminating or reducing the activities of the acquiree

BC76 IAS 22 contained one exception to the general principle that an acquirer should recognise separately, from the acquisition date, only those liabilities of the acquiree that existed at the acquisition date and satisfy the recognition criteria. The exception related to provisions for terminating or reducing the activities of the acquiree that were not liabilities of the acquiree at the acquisition date.

Paragraph 31 of IAS 22 required the acquirer to recognise as part of allocating the cost of a combination a provision for terminating or reducing the activities of the acquiree (a 'restructuring provision') that was not a liability of the acquiree at the acquisition date, provided the acquirer had satisfied the following criteria:

(a) at or before the acquisition date it had developed the main features of a plan that involved terminating or reducing the activities of the acquiree and related to:

  (i) compensating employees of the acquiree for terminating their employment;

  (ii) closing the facilities of the acquiree;

  (iii) eliminating product lines of the acquiree; or

  (iv) terminating contracts of the acquiree that had become onerous because the acquirer had communicated to the other party, at or before the acquisition date, that the contract would be terminated;

(b) raised a valid expectation in those affected by the plan that the plan will be implemented by announcing, at or before the acquisition date, the plan's main features; and

(c) by the earlier of three months after the acquisition date and the date when the annual financial statements are authorised for issued, developed those main features into a detailed formal plan.

BC77 The general criteria for identifying and recognising restructuring provisions are in IAS 37 *Provisions, Contingent Liabilities and Contingent Assets*. IAS 37 states that a constructive obligation to restructure (and therefore a liability) arises only when the entity has developed a detailed formal plan for the restructuring and either raised a valid expectation in those affected that it will carry out the restructuring by publicly announcing details of the plan or begun implementing the plan. Such a liability is required to be recognised in accordance with IAS 37 when it is probable that an outflow of resources embodying economic benefits will be required to settle the obligation, and a reliable estimate can be made of the amount of the obligation.

BC78 The Board observed that the requirement in IAS 22 for the acquirer to recognise a restructuring provision that was not a liability of the acquiree at the acquisition date provided specified criteria were met leads to different accounting, depending on whether a plan to restructure arose in connection with, or in the absence of, a business combination. The Board agreed that it should not, as part of its Business Combinations project, reconsider the general requirements in IAS 37 on the identification and recognition of restructuring provisions, but that it should consider whether the differences in accounting should be carried forward in the IFRS arising from the first phase of that project.

BC79 In developing ED 3 and the IFRS, the Board considered the view that a restructuring provision that was not a liability of the acquiree at the date of acquisition should nonetheless be recognised by the acquirer as part of allocating the cost of the combination if the decision to terminate or reduce the activities of the acquiree is communicated at or before the acquisition date to those likely to be affected and, within a limited time after the acquisition date, a detailed formal plan for the restructuring is developed. Those supporting this view, including some respondents to ED 3, argued that:

(a) the estimated cost of terminating or reducing the activities of the acquiree would have influenced the price paid by the acquirer for the acquiree and therefore should be taken into account in measuring goodwill; and

(b) the acquirer is committed to the costs of terminating or reducing the activities of the acquiree as a result of the business combination: in other words, the combination is the past event that gives rise to a present obligation to terminate or reduce the activities of the acquiree.

BC80 The Board rejected these arguments, noting that the price paid by the acquirer would also be influenced by future losses and other 'unavoidable' costs that relate to the future conduct of the business, such as costs of investing in new systems. Such costs are not recognised as liabilities as part of allocating the cost of the business combination because they do not represent liabilities or contingent liabilities of the acquiree at the acquisition date, although the expected future outflows may affect the value of existing recognised assets. The Board also agreed that it is inconsistent to argue that when a business combination gives rise to 'unavoidable' restructuring costs, the combination is a past event giving rise to a present obligation, but to prohibit recognition of a liability for other 'unavoidable' costs to be incurred as a result of the combination as part of allocating the cost.

BC81 The Board also noted the assertion that the necessary condition for the existence of a constructive obligation for restructuring is the creation of a valid expectation in those affected that it will carry out the restructuring by beginning implementation or by a sufficiently specific announcement. As a result, some argue that satisfying the criteria previously in paragraph 31 of IAS 22 is sufficient to establish the existence, at the acquisition date, of a liability for terminating or reducing the activities of the acquiree. Based on the *Framework*, a liability for terminating or reducing the activities of the acquiree does not exist at the acquisition date unless at that date there is a present obligation (legal or constructive) for the costs of terminating or reducing the acquiree's activities arising from past events, the settlement of which is expected to result in an outflow from the entity of resources embodying economic benefits. Based on the conclusions reached in IAS 37, this will be the case only when, before the acquisition date, firm contracts for the restructuring have been entered into, or a detailed formal plan for the restructuring has been developed, and a valid expectation has been raised in those affected (either by a public announcement of the main features of the plan or by the start of its implementation) that the restructuring will be carried out. The Board decided that any reconsideration of the necessary conditions that must be satisfied for a constructive obligation for restructuring to exist should be part of a future project on IAS 37, and not part of the Business Combinations project, because it relates to broader issues associated with the existence of obligations for restructurings generally.

BC82 The Board concluded that if the criteria previously in paragraph 31 of IAS 22 for the recognition of a restructuring provision were carried forward, similar items would be accounted for in dissimilar ways because the timing of the recognition of restructuring provisions would differ, depending on whether a plan to restructure arises in connection with, or in the absence of, a business combination. The Board agreed that this would impair the usefulness of the information provided to users about an entity's plans to restructure, because both comparability and reliability would be diminished.

BC83 The Board considered the concern expressed by some that removing the exception in IAS 22 would simply open the way to accounting that achieves the same result by other means. For example, the acquiree, on the instructions of the acquirer, might enter into obligations to restructure the business before the formal transfer of control. The Board considered the suggestions that to overcome the potential for entities to structure business combinations so as to achieve a desired outcome, the IFRS should require either of the following:

(a) prohibiting restructuring provisions that *are* recognised liabilities of the acquiree at the acquisition date from being recognised as part of allocating the cost of the combination (and therefore from the determination of goodwill or any excess of the acquirer's interest in the net fair value of the acquiree's identifiable net assets over the cost of the combination). Under such an approach, the acquiree's existing liability would be excluded from the acquiree's pre-combination net assets and instead treated as arising after the combination.

(b) continuing to permit recognition of restructuring provisions that are not liabilities of the acquiree at the acquisition date as part of allocating the cost of the combination provided that, within a limited time after the combination, the decision to terminate or reduce the activities of the acquiree is communicated to those likely to be affected, and a detailed formal plan for the restructuring is developed.

BC84 The Board observed that for the acquirer to have, in effect, the 'free choice' to recognise a liability as part of allocating the cost of the business combination requires such a level of cooperation between the acquirer and acquiree that the acquiree, on the instructions of the acquirer, would enter into obligations to restructure the business before the formal transfer of control. The Board concluded that possible cooperation between parties to a combination does not provide sufficient justification for departing from the *Framework* and treating post-combination liabilities as arising before the combination or pre-combination liabilities as arising after the combination.

BC85 Moreover, if the acquirer can compel the acquiree to incur obligations, then it is likely that the acquirer already controls the acquiree, given that control is the power to govern the financial and operating policies of an entity so as to obtain benefits from its activities. If, alternatively, the acquirer suggests that negotiations cannot proceed until the acquiree arranges, for example, to restructure its workforce, and the acquiree takes the steps necessary to satisfy the recognition criteria for restructuring provisions in IAS 37, then those obligations are pre-combination obligations of the acquiree and, in the Board's view, should be recognised as part of allocating the cost of the combination.

BC86 The Board considered the assertion that another way in which an acquirer could achieve the same result as that previously achieved for restructuring provisions under IAS 22 would be for the acquirer to recognise the restructuring provision either as part of the cost of the business combination, ie as a liability incurred by the acquirer in exchange for control of the acquiree, or as a contingent liability of the acquiree.* The Board noted that a provision for restructuring the acquiree could be recognised by the acquirer, and therefore included as part of the cost of the combination, only if the criteria in IAS 37 for recognising a restructuring provision are satisfied. In other words, the acquirer, at or before the acquisition date, must have developed a detailed formal plan for the restructuring and raised a valid expectation in those affected that it will carry out the restructuring by publicly announcing the main features of the plan or beginning its implementation. These criteria are not the same as the criteria previously in IAS 22 for recognising restructuring provisions as part of allocating the cost of a combination. Therefore, the Board disagreed that an acquirer can recognise a provision for restructuring the acquiree as part of the cost of the combination to achieve virtually the same result as that previously available under IAS 22.

BC87 Consequently, the Board concluded that liabilities for terminating or reducing the activities of the acquiree should be recognised by the acquirer as part of allocating the cost of the business combination only when the acquiree has, at the acquisition date, an existing liability for restructuring recognised in accordance with IAS 37. A majority of respondents to ED 3 supported this conclusion.

Intangible assets

BC88 The IFRS requires an acquirer to recognise separately at the acquisition date an intangible asset of the acquiree, but only when it meets the definition of an intangible asset in IAS 38 *Intangible Assets* and its fair value can be measured reliably. A non-monetary asset without physical substance must be identifiable to meet the definition of an intangible asset. In accordance with IAS 38, an asset meets the identifiability criterion in the definition of an intangible asset only if it arises from contractual or other legal rights or is separable. Previously IAS 22 required an acquirer to recognise any identifiable asset of the acquiree separately from goodwill at the acquisition date if it was probable that any associated future economic benefits would flow to the acquirer and the asset could be measured reliably. The previous version of IAS 38 clarified that the definition of an intangible asset required an intangible asset to be identifiable to distinguish it from goodwill. However, it did not define 'identifiability', but stated that an intangible asset could be distinguished from goodwill if the asset was separable, though separability was not a necessary condition for identifiability. Therefore, previously under international standards, to be recognised separately from goodwill an intangible asset would have to be identifiable and reliably measurable, and it would have to be probable that any associated future economic benefits would flow to the acquirer.

BC89 Changes during 2001 to the requirements in Canadian and United States standards on the separate recognition of intangible assets acquired in a business combination prompted the Board to consider whether it also should explore this issue as part of the first phase of its Business Combinations project. The Board observed that intangible assets comprise an increasing proportion of the assets of

* See paragraphs BC107–BC110 for a discussion of this latter point.

many entities, and that intangible assets acquired in a business combination were often included in the amount recognised as goodwill, despite the previous requirements in IAS 22 and the previous version of IAS 38 that they should be recognised separately from goodwill. The Board also agreed with the conclusion reached in IAS 22 and by the Canadian and US standard-setters that the usefulness of financial statements would be enhanced if intangible assets acquired in a business combination were distinguished from goodwill. Therefore, the Board concluded that IAS 38 and the IFRS arising from the first phase of the project should provide a definitive basis for identifying and recognising intangible assets acquired in a business combination separately from goodwill.

BC90 The Board focused its deliberations first on intangible assets, other than in-process research and development projects, acquired in a business combination. Paragraphs BC91–BC103 outline those deliberations. The Board then considered whether the criteria for recognising those intangible assets separately from goodwill should also be applied to in-process research and development projects acquired in a business combination, and concluded that they should. The Board's reasons for reaching this conclusion are outlined in paragraphs BC104–BC106.

BC91 In revising IAS 38 and developing the IFRS, the Board affirmed the view contained in the previous version of IAS 38 that identifiability is the characteristic that conceptually distinguishes other intangible assets from goodwill. The Board concluded that to provide a definitive basis for identifying and recognising intangible assets separately from goodwill, the concept of identifiability needed to be articulated more clearly.

BC92 Consistently with the guidance in the previous version of IAS 38, the Board concluded that an intangible asset can be distinguished from goodwill if it is separable, ie capable of being separated or divided from the entity and sold, transferred, licensed, rented or exchanged. Therefore, in the context of intangible assets, separability signifies identifiability, and intangible assets with that characteristic that are acquired in a business combination should be recognised as assets separately from goodwill.

BC93 However, again consistently with the guidance in the previous version of IAS 38, the Board concluded that separability is not the only indication of identifiability. The Board observed that, in contrast to goodwill, the values of many intangible assets arise from rights conveyed legally by contract or statute. In the case of acquired goodwill, its value arises from the collection of assembled assets that make up an acquired entity or the value created by assembling a collection of assets through a business combination, such as the synergies that are expected to result from combining two or more entities or businesses. The Board also observed that, although many intangible assets are both separable and arise from contractual-legal rights, some contractual-legal rights establish property interests that are not readily separable from the entity as a whole. For example, under the laws of some jurisdictions some licences granted to an entity are not transferable except by sale of the entity as a whole. The Board concluded that the fact that an intangible asset arises from contractual or other legal rights is a characteristic that distinguishes it from goodwill. Therefore, intangible assets with that characteristic that are acquired in a business combination should be recognised as assets separately from goodwill.

BC94 As outlined in paragraph BC88, the previous Standards required an intangible asset acquired in a business combination and determined to be identifiable also to satisfy the following recognition criteria to be recognised as an asset separately from goodwill:

(a) it must be probable that any associated future economic benefits will flow to the acquirer; and

(b) it must be reliably measurable.

BC95 ED 3 and the Exposure Draft of Proposed Amendments to IAS 38 proposed that the above recognition criteria would, with the exception of an assembled workforce, always be satisfied for an intangible asset acquired in a business combination. Therefore, those criteria were not included in ED 3. ED 3 proposed requiring an acquirer to recognise separately at the acquisition date all of the acquiree's intangible assets as defined in IAS 38, other than an assembled workforce. After considering respondents' comments, the Board decided:

(a) to proceed with the proposal that the probability recognition criterion is always considered to be satisfied for intangible assets acquired in a business combination.

(b) not to proceed with the proposal that, with the exception of an assembled workforce, sufficient information should always exist to measure reliably the fair value of an intangible asset acquired in a business combination.

BC96 In developing ED 3 and the IFRS, the Board observed that the fair value of an intangible asset reflects market expectations about the probability that the future economic benefits associated with the intangible asset will flow to the acquirer. In other words, the effect of probability is reflected in the fair value measurement of an intangible asset. The Board concluded that, given its decision to require the acquirer to recognise the acquiree's intangible assets satisfying the relevant criteria at their fair values as part of allocating the cost of a business combination, the probability recognition criterion need not be included in the IFRS. The Board observed that this highlights a general inconsistency between the recognition criteria for assets and liabilities in the *Framework* (which states that an item meeting the definition of an element should be recognised only if it is probable that any future economic benefits associated with the item will flow to or from the entity, and the item can be measured reliably) and the fair value measurements required in, for example, a business combination. However, the Board concluded that the role of probability as a criterion for recognition in the *Framework* should be considered more generally as part of a forthcoming Concepts project.

BC97 In developing ED 3 and the IAS 38 Exposure Draft, the Board had concluded that, except for an assembled workforce, sufficient information could reasonably be expected to exist to measure reliably the fair value of an asset that has an underlying contractual or legal basis or is capable of being separated from the entity. Respondents generally disagreed with this conclusion, arguing that:

(a) it might not always be possible to measure reliably the fair value of an asset that has an underlying contractual or legal basis or is capable of being separated from the entity.

(b) a similar presumption does not exist in IFRSs for identifiable tangible assets acquired in a business combination. Indeed, the Board decided when developing the IFRS to carry forward from IAS 22 the general principle that an acquirer should recognise separately from goodwill the acquiree's identifiable tangible assets, but only provided they can be measured reliably.

BC98 Additionally, as part of its consultative process, the Board conducted field visits and round-table discussions during the comment period for the Exposure Draft.* Field visit and round-table participants were asked a series of questions aimed at improving the Board's understanding of whether there might exist non-monetary assets without physical substance that are separable or arise from legal or other contractual rights, but for which there may *not* be sufficient information to measure fair value reliably.

BC99 The field visit and round-table participants provided numerous examples of intangible assets they had acquired in recent business combinations whose fair values might not be reliably measurable. For example, one participant acquired water acquisition rights as part of a business combination. The rights are extremely valuable to many manufacturers operating in the same jurisdiction as the participant—the manufacturers cannot acquire water and, in many cases, cannot operate their plants without them. Local authorities grant the rights at little or no cost, but in limited numbers, for fixed periods (normally 10 years), and renewal is certain at little or no cost. The rights cannot be sold other than as part of the sale of a business as a whole, therefore there exists no secondary market in the rights. If a manufacturer hands the rights back to the local authority, it is prohibited from reapplying. The participant argued that it could not value these rights separately from its businesses (and therefore from the goodwill), because the businesses would cease to exist without the rights.

BC100 After considering respondents' comments and the experiences of field visit and round-table participants, the Board concluded that, in some instances, there might not be sufficient information to measure reliably the fair value of an intangible asset separately from goodwill, notwithstanding that the asset is 'identifiable'. The Board observed that the intangible assets whose fair values respondents and field visit and round-table participants could not measure reliably arose either:

(a) from legal or other contractual rights and are not separable (ie could be transferred only as part of the sale of a business as a whole); or

(b) from legal or other contractual rights and are separable (ie capable of being separated or divided from the entity and sold, transferred, licensed, rented or exchanged, either individually or together with a related contract, asset or liability), but there is no history or evidence of exchange transactions for the

* The field visits were conducted from early December 2002 to early April 2003, and involved IASB members and staff in meetings with 41 companies in Australia, France, Germany, Japan, South Africa, Switzerland and the United Kingdom. IASB members and staff also took part in a series of round-table discussions with auditors, preparers, accounting standard-setters and regulators in Canada and the United States on implementation issues encountered by North American companies during first-time application of US Statements of Financial Accounting Standards 141 *Business Combinations* and 142 *Goodwill and Other Intangible Assets*, and the equivalent Canadian Handbook Sections, which were issued in June 2001.

same or similar assets, and otherwise estimating fair value would be dependent on variables whose effect is not measurable.

BC101 Nevertheless, the Board remained of the view that the usefulness of financial statements would be enhanced if intangible assets acquired in a business combination were distinguished from goodwill, particularly given the Board's decision to regard goodwill as an indefinite-lived asset that is not amortised. The Board also remained concerned that failing the reliability of measurement recognition criterion might be inappropriately used by entities as a basis for not recognising intangible assets separately from goodwill. For example, IAS 22 and the previous version of IAS 38 required an acquirer to recognise an intangible asset of the acquiree separately from goodwill at the acquisition date if it was probable that any associated future economic benefits would flow to the acquirer and the asset's fair value could be measured reliably. The Board observed when developing ED 3 that although intangible assets constitute an increasing proportion of the assets of many entities, those acquired in business combinations were often included in the amount recognised as goodwill, despite the requirements in IAS 22 and the previous version of IAS 38 that they should be recognised separately from goodwill.

BC102 Therefore, although the Board decided not to proceed with the proposal that, with the exception of an assembled workforce, sufficient information should always exist to measure reliably the fair value of an intangible asset acquired in a business combination, the Board also decided:

(a) to clarify in IAS 38 that the fair value of an intangible asset acquired in a business combination can normally be measured with sufficient reliability for it to be recognised separately from goodwill. When, for the estimates used to measure an intangible asset's fair value, there is a range of possible outcomes with different probabilities, that uncertainty enters into the measurement of the asset's fair value, rather than demonstrates an inability to measure fair value reliably.

(b) to include in IAS 38 a rebuttable presumption that the fair value of a finite-lived intangible asset acquired in a business combination can be measured reliably.

(c) to clarify in IAS 38 that the only circumstances in which it might not be possible to measure reliably the fair value of an intangible asset acquired in a business combination are when the intangible asset arises from legal or other contractual rights and it either (i) is not separable or (ii) is separable but there is no history or evidence of exchange transactions for the same or similar assets and otherwise estimating fair value would be dependent on variables whose effect is not measurable.

(d) to include in the IFRS a requirement for entities to disclose a description of each asset that meets the definition of an intangible asset and was acquired in a business combination during the period but was not recognised separately from goodwill, and an explanation of why its fair value could not be measured reliably.

BC103 Some respondents and field visit participants suggested that it might also not be possible to measure reliably the fair value of an intangible asset when it is separable, but only together with a related contract, asset or liability (ie it is not individually separable), there is no history of exchange transactions for the same or similar assets on a stand-alone basis, and, because the related items produce jointly the same cash flows, the fair value of each could be estimated only by arbitrarily allocating those cash flows between the two items. The Board disagreed that such circumstances provide a basis for subsuming the value of the intangible asset within the carrying amount of goodwill. Although some intangible assets are so closely related to other identifiable assets or liabilities that they are usually sold as a 'package', it would still be possible to measure reliably the fair value of that 'package'. Therefore, the Board decided to include the following clarifications in IAS 38:

(a) when an intangible asset acquired in a business combination is separable but only together with a related tangible or intangible asset, the acquirer recognises the group of assets as a single asset separately from goodwill if the individual fair values of the assets in the group are not reliably measurable.

(b) similarly, an acquirer recognises as a single asset a group of complementary intangible assets constituting a brand if the individual fair values of the complementary assets are not reliably measurable. If the individual fair values of the complementary assets are reliably measurable, the acquirer may recognise them as a single asset separately from goodwill, provided the individual assets have similar useful lives.

BC104 As noted in paragraph BC90, the Board also considered whether the criteria for recognising intangible assets separately from goodwill should also be applied to in-process research and development projects acquired in a business combination, and concluded that they should. In reaching this conclusion, the Board observed that the criteria in IAS 22 and the previous version of IAS 38 for recognising an intangible asset acquired in a business combination separately from goodwill applied to all intangible assets, including in-process research and development projects. Therefore, the effect of those Standards was that any intangible item acquired in a business combination was recognised as an asset separately from goodwill when it was identifiable and could be measured reliably, and it was probable that any associated future economic benefits would flow to the acquirer. If those criteria were not satisfied, the expenditure on that item, which was included in the cost of the combination, was attributed to goodwill.

BC105 The Board could see no conceptual justification for changing the approach in IAS 22 and the previous version of IAS 38 of using the same criteria for all intangible assets acquired in a business combination when assessing whether those assets should be recognised separately from goodwill. The Board concluded that adopting different criteria would impair the usefulness of the information provided to users about the assets acquired in a combination, because both comparability and reliability would be diminished.

BC106 Some respondents to ED 3 and the IAS 38 Exposure Draft expressed concern that applying the same criteria to all intangible assets acquired in a business combination to assess whether they should be recognised separately from goodwill results in treating some in-process research and development projects acquired in business combinations differently from similar projects started internally. The Board acknowledged this point. However, it concluded that this does not provide a basis for subsuming those acquired intangible assets within goodwill. Rather, it highlights a need to reconsider the view taken in IAS 38 that an intangible asset can never exist in respect of an in-process research project and can exist in respect of an in-process development project only once all of the criteria for deferral in IAS 38 have been satisfied. The Board concluded that such a reconsideration is outside the scope of its Business Combinations project.

Contingent liabilities

BC107 ED 3 proposed, and the IFRS requires, an acquirer to recognise separately the acquiree's contingent liabilities (as defined in IAS 37 *Provisions, Contingent Liabilities and Contingent Assets*) at the acquisition date as part of allocating the cost of a business combination, provided their fair values can be measured reliably. In reaching its decision to include this requirement in the IFRS, the Board observed that provisions for terminating or reducing the activities of an acquiree that were previously recognised in accordance with paragraph 31 of IAS 22 as part of allocating the cost of a combination (but which the IFRS prohibits from being so recognised; see paragraphs BC76–BC87) are not contingent liabilities of the acquiree. A contingent liability is defined in IAS 37 as (a) a possible obligation that arises from past events and whose existence will be confirmed only by the occurrence or non-occurrence of one or more uncertain future events not wholly within the control of the entity, or (b) a present obligation that arises from past events but is not recognised either because it is not probable that an outflow of resources embodying economic benefits will be required to settle the obligation or because the amount of the obligation cannot be measured with sufficient reliability. In the case of provisions for terminating or reducing the activities of an acquiree that were previously recognised in accordance with paragraph 31 of IAS 22, there is no present obligation, nor is there a possible obligation arising from a past event whose existence will be confirmed only by the occurrence or non-occurrence of one or more uncertain future events not wholly within the control of the entity.

BC108 However, some respondents to ED 3 suggested that the acquiree and acquirer could agree for the acquiree to take the steps necessary to satisfy the recognition criteria for restructuring provisions in IAS 37, but to make the execution of the plan conditional on the acquiree being acquired in a business combination. This could circumvent the prohibition in the IFRS on recognising restructuring provisions as part of allocating the cost of a combination. Unlike the circumstances contemplated by the Board in paragraph BC85, if the business combination does not take place the acquiree is under no obligation to proceed with the plan. Respondents suggested that, in such circumstances, it might be possible to argue that the restructuring plan is, before the business combination, either one of the following:

(a) a possible obligation of the acquiree that arises from past events and whose existence will be confirmed only by the occurrence or non-occurrence of one or more uncertain future events. Therefore, the acquirer could recognise it as a contingent liability of the acquiree when allocating the cost of the combination.

(b) a present obligation of the acquiree that is regarded as a contingent liability until it becomes probable that a business combination will occur. This obligation could then be recognised as a liability by the acquiree, in accordance with IAS 37, when a business combination becomes probable and the liability can be measured reliably. Respondents suggested that this would be consistent with paragraph 41 of ED 3 (with slightly revised wording, that paragraph is now paragraph 42 of the IFRS), which stated that 'A payment that an entity is contractually required to make to, for example, its employees or suppliers in the event it is acquired in a business combination is a present obligation of that entity that is regarded as a contingent liability until it becomes probable that a business combination will take place. The contractual obligation is recognised as a liability by that entity under IAS 37 when a business combination becomes probable and the liability can be measured reliably. Therefore, when the business combination is effected, that liability of the acquiree is recognised by the acquirer as part of allocating the cost of the combination.'

BC109 The Board disagreed that a restructuring plan whose execution is conditional on a business combination is either (a) a possible obligation of the acquiree that, before the business combination, meets part (a) of the definition of a contingent liability, or (b) a present obligation of the acquiree that is regarded as a contingent liability until it becomes probable that a business combination will take place. This is because:

(a) a possible obligation meets the definition of a contingent liability only when it satisfies all of the following criteria:

(i) it arises from past events;

(ii) its existence will be confirmed only by the occurrence or non-occurrence of one or more uncertain future events; and

(iii) the uncertain future event(s) is (are) not wholly within the control of the entity.

The Board concluded that a restructuring plan whose execution is conditional on a business combination, although meeting the criteria in (i) and (ii) above, fails to meet the criterion in (iii). This is because the uncertain future event (ie being acquired in a business combination) is generally within the acquiree's control.

(b) the acquiree has not, before the business combination, established a present obligation. In accordance with paragraph 72 of IAS 37, a constructive obligation to restructure arises only when an entity has:

(i) a detailed formal plan for the restructuring; and

(ii) raised a valid expectation in those affected that it will carry out the restructuring by starting to implement that plan or announcing its main features to those affected by it.

The Board concluded that if execution of the plan is conditional on the acquiree being acquired in a business combination, then the criterion in (ii) has not been satisfied. Even if the main features of the plan were announced to those that would be affected by it, the 'valid expectation' would be conditional on the entity being acquired in a business combination—a possibility that is not provided for in the wording of paragraph 72 of IAS 37.

BC110 Therefore, to avoid any confusion or possibility of circumventing the Board's intention in relation to the treatment of restructuring provisions, the Board decided to clarify in paragraph 43 of the IFRS that an acquiree's restructuring plan whose execution is conditional upon it being acquired in a business combination is not, immediately before the business combination, a present obligation of the acquiree, nor is it a contingent liability of the acquiree. Therefore, an acquirer shall not recognise such restructuring plans as part of allocating the cost of the combination.

BC111 In developing ED 3 and the IFRS, the Board observed that although a contingent liability of the acquiree is not recognised by the acquiree before the business combination, that contingent liability has a fair value, the amount of which reflects market expectations about any uncertainty surrounding the possibility that an outflow of resources embodying economic benefits will be required to settle the possible or present obligation. As a result, the existence of contingent liabilities of the acquiree has the effect of depressing the price that an acquirer is prepared to pay for the acquiree, ie the acquirer has, in effect, been paid to assume an obligation in the form of a reduced purchase price for the acquiree.

BC112 The Board observed that this highlights an inconsistency between the recognition criteria applying to liabilities and contingent liabilities in IAS 37 and the *Framework* (both of which permit liability recognition only when it is probable that an outflow of resources embodying economic benefits will be required to settle a present obligation) and the fair value measurement of the cost of a business combination. Indeed, the probability recognition criterion applying to liabilities in IAS 37 and the *Framework* is fundamentally inconsistent with any fair value or expected value basis of measurement because expectations about the probability that an outflow of resources embodying economic benefits will be required to settle a possible or present obligation will be reflected in the measurement of that possible or present obligation. However, the Board agreed that the role of probability in the *Framework* should be considered more generally as part of a forthcoming Concepts project.

BC113 The Board also observed that the principles in IAS 37 had been developed largely for provisions that are generated internally, not obligations that the entity has been paid to assume. This is not dissimilar from situations in which assets are recognised as a result of the business combination, even though they would not be recognised had they been generated internally. For example, some internally generated intangible assets are not permitted to be recognised by an entity, but would be recognised by an acquirer as part of allocating the cost of acquiring that entity.

BC114 In developing ED 3 the Board proposed that a contingent liability recognised as part of allocating the cost of a business combination should be excluded from the scope of IAS 37 and measured after initial recognition at fair value with changes in fair value recognised in profit or loss until settled or the uncertain future event described in the definition of a contingent liability is resolved. While considering respondents' comments on this issue, the Board noted that measuring such contingent liabilities after initial recognition at fair value would be inconsistent with the conclusions it reached on the accounting for financial guarantees and commitments to provide loans at below-market interest rates when revising IAS 39 *Financial Instruments: Recognition and Measurement*.

BC115 The Board decided to amend the proposal in ED 3 for consistency with IAS 39. Therefore, the IFRS requires contingent liabilities recognised as part of allocating the cost of a combination to be measured after their initial recognition at the higher of:

(a) the amount that would be recognised in accordance with IAS 37, and

(b) the amount initially recognised less, when appropriate, cumulative amortisation recognised in accordance with IAS 18 *Revenue*.

The Board observed that not specifying the subsequent accounting might result in some or all of these contingent liabilities inappropriately being derecognised immediately after the combination.

BC116 To avoid any confusion over the interaction between IAS 39 and the above requirement, the Board also decided to clarify in the IFRS that:

(a) the above requirement does not apply to contracts accounted for in accordance with IAS 39.

(b) loan commitments excluded from the scope of IAS 39 that are not commitments to provide loans at below-market interest rates are accounted for as contingent liabilities of the acquiree if, at the acquisition date, it is not probable that an outflow of resources embodying economic benefits will be required to settle the obligation or if the amount of the obligation cannot be measured with sufficient reliability. Such a loan commitment is recognised separately as part of allocating the cost of a combination only if its fair value can be measured reliably.

BC117 The Board is considering as part of the second phase of its Business Combinations project whether items meeting the definition in IAS 37 of contingent assets should also be recognised separately as part of allocating the cost of a business combination. However, the Board decided that it was necessary to address contingent liabilities of the acquiree in the first phase of its project, given that it had agreed to reconsider the requirements in IAS 22 for the treatment of negative goodwill as part of that first phase. The Board observed that negative goodwill as determined in accordance with IAS 22 could have arisen as a result of, amongst other things, failure to recognise contingent liabilities of the acquiree that the acquirer had been paid to take on in the form of a reduced purchase price.

Contractual obligations of the acquiree for which payment is triggered by a business combination

BC118 The IFRS clarifies that a payment an acquiree is contractually required to make, for example, to its employees or suppliers in the event it is acquired in a business combination, would be recognised by the acquirer as part of allocating the cost of the combination. The Board agreed that before the business combination, such a contractual arrangement gives rise to a present obligation of the acquiree. That present obligation meets the IAS 37 definition of a contingent liability until it becomes probable that a business combination will take place. Once it becomes probable that a business combination will take place, the obligation should, in accordance with IAS 37, be recognised as a liability by the acquiree provided it can be measured reliably. Therefore, when the business combination is effected, the liability is recognised by the acquirer as part of allocating the cost of the combination.

BC119 The Board concluded that the treatment in IAS 22 of such obligations was ambiguous, and that the IFRS should therefore clarify their treatment.

BC120 However, as outlined in paragraphs BC108–BC110, the Board clarified that an acquiree's restructuring plan whose execution is conditional on the acquiree being acquired in a business combination is not, immediately before the business combination, a present obligation of the acquiree.

Measuring the identifiable assets acquired and liabilities and contingent liabilities incurred or assumed (paragraphs 36 and 40)

BC121 IAS 22 included a benchmark and an allowed alternative treatment for the initial measurement of the identifiable net assets acquired in a business combination, and therefore for the initial measurement of any minority interests. The Board agreed that permitting similar transactions to be accounted for in dissimilar ways impairs the usefulness of the information provided to users of financial reports, because both comparability and reliability are diminished. The Board concluded that the quality of Standards would be improved by omitting the option that existed in IAS 22 from the IFRS arising from the first phase of its Business Combinations project. ED 3 proposed, and the IFRS requires, the acquiree's identifiable assets, liabilities and contingent liabilities recognised as part of allocating the cost of the business combination to be measured initially by the acquirer at their fair values at the acquisition date. Therefore, any minority interest in the acquiree will be stated at the minority's proportion of the net fair value of those items. Almost all of the respondents to ED 3 supported the proposal, which was consistent with the allowed alternative treatment in IAS 22.

BC122 Applying IAS 22's benchmark treatment, the acquirer would have initially measured each of the acquiree's identifiable assets and liabilities at the aggregate of:

(a) its fair value at the date of the exchange transaction, but only to the extent of the ownership interest obtained by the acquirer in the exchange transaction; and

(b) the minority's proportion of its pre-combination carrying amount.

BC123 In assessing IAS 22's benchmark treatment, the Board noted that the requirement in IAS 27 *Consolidated and Separate Financial Statements* to prepare consolidated financial statements is driven by the existence of a group. The objective of consolidated financial statements is to provide users with relevant and reliable financial information about the resources under the control of the parent entity so as to reflect that the related entities operate as a single economic entity. Therefore, under IAS 27 the consolidated financial statements for the group are intended to reflect the performance of that group and the resources under the control of the parent entity, irrespective of the extent of the ownership interest held. As a result, IAS 27 requires consolidation of all of the identifiable assets and liabilities of the controlled entity; a proportionate approach to the preparation of consolidated financial statements is not permitted. Accordingly, with the exception of goodwill arising on the acquisition of a subsidiary, 100 per cent of a subsidiary's assets and liabilities are included in the consolidated financial statements from the date on which the parent obtains control of that subsidiary, irrespective of the ownership interest held in the subsidiary.

BC124 The Board concluded that the mixed measurement reported in accordance with IAS 22's benchmark treatment was inconsistent with the consolidation approach in IAS 27 and with the objective of providing users with relevant and reliable financial information about the resources under the control of the parent entity.

BC125 The Board noted that the allowed alternative treatment provided users with information about the fair values at the acquisition date of the acquiree's identifiable assets and liabilities, together with any minority interest in those fair values. The Board concluded that this treatment was consistent with the consolidation approach adopted in IAS 27 and the objective of consolidated financial statements because the information it provided enabled users to better assess the cash-generating abilities of the identifiable net assets acquired in the business combination. The Board also noted that the allowed alternative treatment provided users of the group's consolidated financial statements with more useful information for assessing the accountability of management for the resources entrusted to it.

BC126 The Board considered the view that, notwithstanding the use in IAS 27 of control to define the boundaries of a group, the focus of consolidated financial statements remains the owners of the parent. On that basis, and because the cost of a business combination relates only to the percentage of the identifiable net assets acquired by the parent, those identifiable net assets should be measured at their fair values only to the extent of the parent's interest obtained in the exchange transaction. In other words, the minority's proportionate interest in the identifiable net assets acquired by the parent is not part of the exchange transaction and therefore should be stated on the basis of pre-combination carrying amounts. Those supporting this approach argue that it is consistent with the requirement in IAS 22 to recognise only the amount of goodwill acquired by the parent based on the parent's ownership interest, rather than the amount of goodwill controlled by the parent as a result of the combination.

BC127 However, the Board concluded that the use in IAS 27 of control to define the boundaries of a group remains fundamental to identifying the objective of consolidated financial statements, even if the intended focus of those statements were the owners of the parent. In a consolidation model whose intended focus is the owners of the parent but which uses control to define the boundaries of the group, the objective of the consolidated financial statements for that group would be to provide information to the owners of the parent about the resources under their control, irrespective of the extent of the ownership interest held by the parent in those resources. The Board concluded that information about the fair values at the acquisition date of the acquiree's identifiable assets, liabilities and contingent liabilities provides the owners of the parent with more useful information about the resources under their control than the mixed measurement reported under the benchmark treatment.

BC128 The Board nonetheless observed that the requirement in IAS 22 to recognise only the amount of goodwill acquired by the parent based on the parent's ownership interest, rather than the amount of goodwill controlled by the parent as a result of the business combination, is problematic. The Board saw this as a flaw in the way that IAS 22 interacted with IAS 27 rather than an indication that consolidated financial statements prepared in accordance with IAS 27 are intended to reflect only the resources attributable to owners of the parent on the basis of the ownership interests held by the parent. The Board concluded that if this were indeed the objective of consolidated financial statements, then a proportionate approach to consolidation for all of the assets acquired and liabilities assumed in a business combination would be the only approach to satisfy that objective. The Board is reconsidering the requirement to recognise only the amount of goodwill acquired by the parent on the basis of the parent's ownership interest as part of the second phase of its Business Combinations project.

Goodwill (paragraphs 51–55)

Initial recognition of goodwill as an asset

BC129 ED 3 proposed, and the IFRS requires, goodwill acquired in a business combination to be recognised by the acquirer as an asset and initially measured as the excess of the cost of the combination over the acquirer's interest in the net fair value of the acquiree's identifiable assets, liabilities and contingent liabilities. Almost all of the respondents to ED 3 supported these proposals. Except for the effect on the measurement of acquired goodwill of recognising the acquiree's contingent liabilities (see paragraphs BC107–BC117), these requirements are consistent with the requirements previously in IAS 22. However, the Board decided that the IFRS should not confuse measurement techniques with concepts and therefore, unlike IAS 22, the IFRS defines goodwill in terms of its nature rather than its measurement. In particular, the IFRS defines goodwill as future economic benefits arising from assets that are not capable of being individually identified and separately recognised.

BC130 In developing ED 3 and the IFRS, the Board observed that when goodwill is measured as a residual, it could comprise the following components:

(a) the fair value of the 'going concern' element of the acquiree. The going concern element represents the ability of the acquiree to earn a higher rate of return on an assembled collection of net assets than would be expected from those net assets operating separately. That value stems from the synergies of the net assets of the acquiree, as well as from other benefits such as factors related to market imperfections, including the ability to earn monopoly profits and barriers to market entry.

(b) the fair value of the expected synergies and other benefits from combining the acquiree's net assets with those of the acquirer. Those synergies and other benefits are unique to each business combination, and different combinations produce different synergies and, hence, different values.

(c) overpayments by the acquirer.

(d) errors in measuring and recognising the fair value of either the cost of the business combination or the acquiree's identifiable assets, liabilities or contingent liabilities, or a requirement in an accounting standard to measure those identifiable items at an amount that is not fair value.

BC131 The Board observed that the third and fourth components conceptually are not part of goodwill and not assets, whereas the first and second components conceptually *are* part of goodwill. The Board described those first and second components as 'core goodwill', and focused its analysis first on whether core goodwill should be recognised as an asset.

BC132 An asset is defined in the *Framework* as a resource controlled by the entity as a result of past events and from which future economic benefits are expected to flow to the entity. Paragraph 53 of the *Framework* states that 'The future economic benefit embodied in an asset is the potential to contribute, directly or indirectly, to the flow of cash and cash equivalents to the enterprise.' The Board concluded that core goodwill represents resources from which future economic benefits are expected to flow to the entity. In considering whether core goodwill represents a resource *controlled* by the entity, the Board considered the assertion that core goodwill arises, at least in part, through factors such as a well-trained workforce, loyal customers etc, and that these factors cannot be regarded as controlled by the entity because the workforce could leave and the customers go elsewhere. However, the Board concluded that in the case of core goodwill, control is provided by means of the acquirer's power to direct the policies and management of the acquiree. Therefore, the Board concluded that core goodwill meets the *Framework's* definition of an asset.

BC133 The Board then considered whether including the third and fourth components identified in paragraph BC130 in the measurement of acquired goodwill should prevent goodwill from being recognised by the acquirer as an asset. To the extent that acquired goodwill includes those components, it includes items that are not assets. Thus, including them in the asset described as goodwill would not be representationally faithful.

BC134 The Board observed that it would not be feasible to determine the amount attributable to each of the components of acquired goodwill. Although there might be problems with representational faithfulness in recognising all of the components as an asset labelled goodwill, there are corresponding problems with the alternative of recognising all of the components immediately as an expense. In other words, to the extent that the measurement of acquired goodwill includes core goodwill, recognising that asset as an expense is also not representationally faithful.

BC135 The Board concluded that goodwill acquired in a business combination and measured as a residual is likely to consist primarily of core goodwill at the acquisition date, and that recognising it as an asset is more representationally faithful than recognising it as an expense.

Subsequent accounting for goodwill

BC136 ED 3 proposed, and the IFRS requires, goodwill acquired in a business combination to be carried after initial recognition at cost less any accumulated impairment losses. Therefore, the goodwill is not permitted to be amortised and instead must be tested for impairment annually, or more frequently if events or changes in circumstances indicate that it might be impaired, in accordance with

IAS 36 *Impairment of Assets*. IAS 22 required acquired goodwill to be amortised on a systematic basis over the best estimate of its useful life. There was a rebuttable presumption that its useful life did not exceed twenty years from initial recognition. If that presumption was rebutted, acquired goodwill was required to be tested for impairment in accordance with the previous version of IAS 36 at least at each financial year-end, even if there was no indication that it was impaired.

BC137 In considering the appropriate accounting for acquired goodwill after its initial recognition, the Board examined the following three approaches:

(a) straight-line amortisation but with an impairment test whenever there is an indication that the goodwill might be impaired;

(b) non-amortisation but with an impairment test annually or more frequently if events or changes in circumstances indicate that the goodwill might be impaired; and

(c) permitting entities a choice between approaches (a) and (b).

BC138 The Board concluded, and the respondents to ED 3 that expressed a clear view on this issue generally agreed, that entities should not be allowed a choice between approaches (a) and (b). Permitting such choices impairs the usefulness of the information provided to users of financial statements because both comparability and reliability are diminished.

BC139 The respondents to ED 3 that expressed a clear view on this issue generally supported approach (a). They put forward the following arguments in support of that approach:

(a) acquired goodwill is an asset that is consumed and replaced with internally generated goodwill. Amortisation therefore ensures that the acquired goodwill is recognised in profit or loss and no internally generated goodwill is recognised as an asset in its place, consistently with the general prohibition in IAS 38 on the recognition of internally generated goodwill.

(b) conceptually, amortisation is a method of allocating the cost of acquired goodwill over the periods it is consumed, and is consistent with the approach taken to other intangible and tangible fixed assets that do not have indefinite useful lives. Indeed, entities are required to determine the useful lives of items of property, plant and equipment, and allocate their depreciable amounts on a systematic basis over those useful lives. There is no conceptual reason for treating acquired goodwill differently.

(c) the useful life of acquired goodwill cannot be predicted with a satisfactory level of reliability, nor can the pattern in which that goodwill diminishes be known. However, systematic amortisation over an albeit arbitrary period provides an appropriate balance between conceptual soundness and operationality at an acceptable cost: it is the only practical solution to an intractable problem.

BC140 In considering these comments, the Board agreed that achieving an acceptable level of reliability in the form of representational faithfulness, while at the same time striking some balance between what is practicable, was the primary challenge it faced in deliberating the subsequent accounting for goodwill. The Board observed that the useful life of acquired goodwill and the pattern in which it diminishes generally are not possible to predict, yet its amortisation depends on such predictions. As a result, the amount amortised in any given period can at best be described as an arbitrary estimate of the consumption of acquired goodwill during that period. The Board acknowledged that if goodwill is an asset, in some sense it must be true that goodwill acquired in a business combination is being consumed and replaced by internally generated goodwill, provided that an entity is able to maintain the overall value of goodwill (by, for example, expending resources on advertising and customer service). However, consistently with the view it reached in developing ED 3, the Board remained doubtful about the usefulness of an amortisation charge that reflects the consumption of acquired goodwill, whilst the internally generated goodwill replacing it is not recognised. Therefore, the Board reaffirmed the conclusion it reached in developing ED 3 that straight-line amortisation of goodwill over an arbitrary period fails to provide useful information. The Board noted that both anecdotal and research evidence supports this view.

BC141 In considering respondents' comments summarised in paragraph BC139(b), the Board noted that although the useful lives of both goodwill and tangible fixed assets are directly related to the period over which they are expected to generate net cash inflows for the entity, the expected physical utility to the entity of a tangible fixed asset places an upper limit on the asset's useful life. In other words, unlike goodwill, the useful life of a tangible fixed asset could never extend beyond the asset's expected physical utility to the entity.

BC142 The Board reaffirmed the view it reached in developing ED 3 that if a rigorous and operational impairment test could be devised, more useful information would be provided to users of an entity's financial statements under an approach in which goodwill is not amortised, but instead tested for impairment annually or more frequently if events or changes in circumstances indicate that the goodwill might be impaired. After considering respondents' comments to the Exposure Draft of Proposed Amendments to IAS 36 on the form that such an impairment test should take, the Board concluded that a sufficiently rigorous and operational impairment test could be devised. Its deliberations on the form that the impairment test should take are included in the Basis for Conclusions on IAS 36.

Excess of acquirer's interest in the net fair value of acquiree's identifiable assets, liabilities and contingent liabilities over cost (paragraphs 56 and 57)

BC143 In some business combinations, the acquirer's interest in the net fair value of the acquiree's identifiable assets, liabilities and contingent liabilities exceeds the cost of the combination. That excess, commonly referred to as negative goodwill, is referred to below as the excess.

BC144 ED 3 proposed, and the IFRS requires, that if an excess exists, the acquirer should:

(a) first reassess the identification and measurement of the acquiree's identifiable assets, liabilities and contingent liabilities and the measurement of the cost of the combination; and

(b) recognise immediately in profit or loss any excess remaining after that reassessment.

BC145 Respondents to ED 3 generally did not support the proposal to recognise immediately in profit or loss any excess remaining after the reassessment. Their objections were based on the following views:

(a) any such excess is likely to arise because of expectations of future losses and expenses.

(b) recognising the excess immediately in profit or loss would not be representationally faithful to the extent it arises because of measurement errors or because of a requirement in an accounting standard to measure identifiable net assets acquired at an amount that is not fair value, but is treated as though it is fair value for the purpose of allocating the cost of the combination.

(c) the proposal is inconsistent with historical cost accounting.

BC146 In considering respondents' comments, the Board agreed that most business combinations are exchange transactions in which each party receives and sacrifices equal value. As a result, the existence of an excess might indicate that:

(a) the values attributed to the acquiree's identifiable assets have been overstated;

(b) identifiable liabilities and/or contingent liabilities of the acquiree have been omitted or the values attributed to those items have been understated; or

(c) the values assigned to the items comprising the cost of the business combination have been understated.

BC147 The Board reaffirmed its previous conclusions that an excess should rarely remain if the valuations inherent in the accounting for a business combination are properly performed and all of the acquiree's identifiable liabilities and contingent liabilities have been properly identified and recognised. Therefore, when such an excess exists, the acquirer should first reassess the identification and measurement of the acquiree's identifiable assets, liabilities and contingent liabilities and the measurement of the cost of the business combination.

BC148 The Board further observed that any excess remaining after the reassessment could comprise one or more of the following components:

(a) errors that remain, notwithstanding the reassessment, in recognising or measuring the fair value of either the cost of the combination or the acquiree's identifiable assets, liabilities or contingent liabilities.

(b) a requirement in an accounting standard to measure identifiable net assets acquired at an amount that is not fair value, but is treated as though it is fair value for the purpose of allocating the cost of the combination.

(c) a bargain purchase. This might occur, for instance, when the seller of a business wishes to exit from that business for other than economic reasons and is prepared to accept less than its fair value as consideration.

BC149 The Board disagreed with the view that expectations of future losses and expenses could give rise to an excess. Although expectations of future losses and expenses have the effect of depressing the price that an acquirer is prepared to pay for the acquiree, the net fair value of the acquiree's identifiable assets, liabilities and contingent liabilities will be similarly affected. For example, assume the present value of the expected future cash flows of a business is 100 provided 20 is spent on restructuring the business, but only 30 if no restructuring is done. Assume also there is no goodwill in the business. Any acquirer would therefore be prepared to pay 80 to acquire the business, provided it too could generate the additional cash flows as a result of the restructuring. The fair value of the business is therefore 80. This amount is compared with the net fair value of the acquiree's identifiable assets, liabilities and contingent liabilities. The net fair value of those items is also 80 and not 100, because the costs of 20 needed to generate the value of 100 have not yet been incurred. In other words, expectations of future losses and expenses are reflected in the fair value of the acquiree's identifiable assets, liabilities and contingent liabilities. The Board observed that a possible cause of the errors referred to in paragraph BC148(a) is a failure to reflect correctly the fair value of the acquiree's identifiable assets, liabilities or contingent liabilities in their current location and condition, reflecting their current level of performance.

BC150 In developing ED 3 and the IFRS, the Board considered the appropriate treatment for an excess comprising the components identified in paragraph BC148 by assessing whether it should be recognised:

(a) as a reduction in the values attributed to some of the acquiree's identifiable net assets (for example, by reducing proportionately the values attributed to the acquiree's identifiable assets without readily observable market prices);

(b) as a separate liability; or

(c) immediately in profit or loss.

Recognising the excess as a reduction in the values attributed to some net assets

BC151 The Board considered the view that recognising an excess by reducing the values attributed to the acquiree's identifiable net assets is appropriate because it is consistent with the historical cost accounting method, in that it does not recognise the total net assets acquired above the total cost of those assets. The Board rejected this view, noting that, to the extent the excess comprises the first and third components in paragraph BC148, the reduction in the values allocated to each of the acquiree's identifiable net assets would inevitably be arbitrary and, therefore, not representationally faithful. The resulting amount recognised for each item would not be cost, nor would it be fair value. Such an approach raises further issues in respect of the subsequent measurement of those items. For example, if the acquirer reduces proportionately the fair values attributed to the acquiree's identifiable assets without readily observable market prices, that reduction would be immediately reversed for any of those assets that are measured after initial recognition on a fair value basis.

BC152 To the extent the excess comprises the second component in paragraph BC148, reducing the values assigned to the acquiree's identifiable net assets that *are* required to be initially measured by the acquirer at their fair values also would not be representationally faithful.

BC153 The Board observed that although conceptually any guidance on determining the values to be assigned by the acquirer to the acquiree's identifiable net assets should be consistent with a fair value measurement objective, this is not currently the case under IFRSs. Allocating an excess comprising the second component in paragraph BC148 to those items that *are not* initially measured by the acquirer at their fair values would nonetheless result in those items being initially recognised by the acquirer at their fair values at the acquisition date. However, the Board decided that such an approach would not be appropriate at this time because:

(a) it is reconsidering as part of the second phase of its Business Combinations project those requirements in IFRSs that result in the acquirer initially recognising identifiable net assets acquired at amounts that are not fair values but are treated as though they are fair values for the purpose of allocating the cost of the combination.

(b) it would raise further issues in respect of the subsequent measurement of those items similar to those identified in paragraph BC151. For example, measuring the acquiree's deferred tax assets at their fair values at the acquisition date would involve discounting the nominal tax benefits to their present values. This is inconsistent with IAS 12 *Income Taxes*, which requires deferred tax assets to be measured at nominal amounts. Therefore, the effect of the discounting would be immediately reversed by IAS 12.

Recognising the excess as a separate liability

BC154 The Board observed that an excess comprising any of the components identified in paragraph BC148 does not meet the definition of a liability and that its recognition as such would not be representationally faithful. The Board also observed that recognition as a liability also raises the issue of when, if ever, the credit balance should be reduced.

Recognising the excess immediately in profit or loss

BC155 The Board concluded that the most representationally faithful treatment of that part of an excess arising from a bargain purchase is immediate recognition in profit or loss. The Board further concluded that separately identifying the amount of an excess that is attributable to each of the first and second components identified in paragraph BC148 is not feasible.

BC156 As a result, the Board concluded that:

(a) the most appropriate treatment for any excess remaining after the acquirer performs the necessary reassessments is immediate recognition in profit or loss; and

(b) for each business combination occurring during the reporting period, the acquirer should be required to disclose the amount and a description of the nature of any such excess.

Business combination achieved in stages (paragraphs 58–60)

BC157 The IFRS carries forward the requirements in paragraphs 36–38 of IAS 22 on the accounting for business combinations achieved in stages by, for example, successive share purchases. The Board will reconsider those requirements as part of the second phase of its Business Combinations project.

BC158 However, the Board received a large number of requests from its constituents for guidance on the practical application of paragraphs 36–38 of IAS 22. As a result, the Board:

(a) clarified in the IFRS that accounting for adjustments to the fair values of the acquiree's identifiable assets, liabilities and contingent liabilities as revaluations to the extent that they relate to the acquirer's previously held ownership interests does not signify that the acquirer has elected to apply an accounting policy of revaluing those items after initial recognition.

(b) developed an example illustrating the application of the requirements in paragraphs 58–60 of the IFRS. That example is included in the Illustrative Examples accompanying the IFRS.

Initial accounting determined provisionally (paragraphs 61–65)

BC159 The IFRS changes the requirements in paragraphs 71–74 of IAS 22 on the subsequent recognition of, or changes in the values assigned to, the acquiree's identifiable assets and liabilities. When the initial accounting for a business combination can be determined only provisionally by the end of the reporting period in which the combination occurs, ED 3 proposed, and IFRS 3 requires, the acquirer to account for the combination using those provisional values. This will be the case if either the fair values to be assigned to the acquiree's identifiable assets, liabilities or contingent liabilities or the cost of the combination can be determined only provisionally by the acquirer by the end of the reporting period in which the combination occurs. The IFRS also requires:

(a) any adjustments to those provisional values as a result of completing the initial accounting to be recognised from the acquisition date and within twelve months of the acquisition date.

(b) with a few specified exceptions, adjustments to the initial accounting for a combination after that initial accounting is complete to be recognised only to correct an error in accordance with IAS 8 *Accounting Policies, Changes in Accounting Estimates and Errors*. Therefore, the initial accounting for the combination cannot be amended for the effects of changes in accounting estimates after the combination.

BC160 In contrast, IAS 22 required:

(a) the acquiree's identifiable assets and liabilities that did not satisfy the criteria for separate recognition at the time of initially accounting for a business combination to be subsequently recognised by the acquirer when they satisfy those criteria; and

(b) the values assigned to the acquiree's identifiable assets and liabilities to be adjusted by the acquirer when additional evidence became available to assist with estimating the values of those items at the acquisition date.

In accordance with IAS 22, the acquirer recognised any such adjustment by adjusting the amount assigned to goodwill or negative goodwill, but only provided the adjustment was made by the end of the first annual reporting period that began after the business combination, and only to the extent the adjustment did not increase the carrying amount of goodwill above its recoverable amount. Otherwise, the adjustment was required to be recognised in profit or loss.

BC161 In developing ED 3 and the IFRS, the Board observed that one of the objectives of accounting for a business combination is for the acquirer to recognise all of the acquiree's identifiable assets, liabilities and contingent liabilities that existed and satisfied the criteria for separate recognition at the acquisition date at their fair values at that date. The Board concluded that the requirements in IAS 22 for subsequently recognising the acquiree's identifiable assets and liabilities could, in some instances, have resulted in a business combination being accounted for in a way that was inconsistent with this objective. This would have been the case if, for example, an asset of the acquiree that did not satisfy the criteria for recognition separately from goodwill at the time of initially accounting for the combination subsequently satisfied those criteria because of an event taking place after the acquisition date but before the end of the first annual reporting period beginning after the combination.

BC162 However, the Board also observed that normally it is not possible for an acquirer to obtain before the acquisition date all of the information necessary to achieve, immediately after the acquisition date, the objective described in paragraph BC161. Consequently, it is often not possible for an acquirer to finalise the accounting for the combination for some time thereafter. The Board therefore concluded that the IFRS should, without modifying the objective described in paragraph BC161, provide an acquirer with some period of time after the acquisition date to finalise the accounting for a business combination. The Board also concluded that a maximum time period in which to finalise that accounting, although arbitrary, is necessary to prevent the accounting from being adjusted indefinitely. The Board concluded that a 12-month maximum period is reasonable.

BC163 Respondents to ED 3 generally supported the above approach. The minority that disagreed questioned whether a 12-month period for completing the initial accounting would be sufficient. However, there was no clear consensus amongst respondents as to what an appropriate alternative period might be, nor did the respondents clarify why their proposed alternatives might be any less arbitrary than that proposed by the Board in ED 3.

Adjustments after the initial accounting is complete (paragraphs 63–65)

BC164 The Board began its deliberations on when adjustments to the initial accounting for a business combination after that accounting is complete should be required by first considering the other circumstances in which IFRSs require or permit the accounting for a transaction to be retrospectively adjusted. In accordance with

IAS 8, in the absence of a change in an accounting policy, an entity is required to adjust its financial statements retrospectively only to correct an error. The Board concluded that it would be inconsistent for the IFRS to require or permit retrospective adjustments to the accounting for a business combination other than to correct an error. Therefore, the Board decided that, with the three exceptions discussed in paragraphs BC165–BC169, the IFRS should require an acquirer to adjust the initial accounting for a combination after that accounting is complete only to correct an error in accordance with IAS 8. Almost all of the respondents to ED 3 supported such a requirement.

BC165 Two of the three exceptions to this requirement relate to adjustments to the cost of a business combination after the initial accounting for the combination is complete. Those exceptions are discussed in paragraphs BC166 and BC167. The third relates to the subsequent recognition by the acquirer of the acquiree's deferred tax assets that did not satisfy the criteria for separate recognition when initially accounting for the business combination. This exception is discussed in paragraphs BC168 and BC169.

Adjustments to the cost of a business combination after the initial accounting is complete

BC166 When a business combination agreement provides for an adjustment to the cost of the combination contingent on future events, paragraph 32 of the IFRS requires the amount of the adjustment to be included in the cost of the combination at the acquisition date if the adjustment is probable and can be measured reliably. In accordance with paragraph 33, if the amount of the adjustment is included in the cost of the combination at the time of initially accounting for the combination but the future events do not occur or the estimate needs to be revised, the cost of the combination must be adjusted accordingly. In accordance with paragraph 34, if the amount of the adjustment is *not* included in the cost of the combination at the time of initially accounting for the combination and the adjustment subsequently becomes probable and can be measured reliably, the cost of the combination must also be adjusted accordingly. The requirements in paragraphs 33 and 34 of the IFRS are two exceptions to the principle adopted by the Board that the initial accounting for a business combination should be adjusted after that accounting is complete only to correct an error.

BC167 As noted in paragraph BC67, the IFRS carries forward from IAS 22, without reconsideration, the requirements on adjustments to the cost of a business combination contingent on future events. The Board is reconsidering those requirements, and therefore the two related exceptions to the principle that the initial accounting for a business combination can be adjusted only to correct an error, as part of the second phase of its Business Combinations project.

Recognition of deferred tax assets after the initial accounting is complete (paragraph 65)

BC168 IAS 22 contained an exception to the requirements outlined in paragraph BC160 for the subsequent recognition of the acquiree's identifiable assets and liabilities. That exception arose because of the accounting required by IAS 22 when the potential benefit of the acquiree's income tax loss carry-forwards or other deferred tax assets not satisfying the criteria for separate recognition when the business combination was initially accounted for was subsequently realised.

BC169 Paragraph 65 of the IFRS carries forward from IAS 22, without reconsideration, the requirements for accounting for the subsequent realisation of such potential tax benefits. These requirements:

(a) are also an exception to the principle adopted by the Board that the initial accounting for a business combination should be adjusted after that accounting is complete only to correct an error; and

(b) are being reconsidered by the Board as part of the second phase of its Business Combinations project.

Disclosure (paragraphs 66–77)

BC170 In line with the Board's aim of articulating in IFRSs the broad principles underpinning a required accounting treatment, the Board decided that the IFRS should state explicitly the objectives that the various disclosure requirements are intended to meet. To that end, the Board identified the following three disclosure objectives:

(a) to provide the users of an acquirer's financial statements with information that enables them to evaluate the nature and financial effect of business combinations that were effected during the reporting period or after the balance sheet date but before the financial statements are authorised for issue.

(b) to provide the users of an acquirer's financial statements with information that enables them to evaluate the financial effects of gains, losses, error corrections and other adjustments recognised in the current period that relate to business combinations that were effected in the current period or in previous periods.

(c) to provide the users of an acquirer's financial statements with information that enables them to evaluate changes in the carrying amount of goodwill during the period.

BC171 The Board began its discussion of the disclosure requirements necessary to meet these objectives by assessing the disclosure requirements in SIC-28 *Business Combinations—"Date of Exchange" and Fair Value of Equity Instruments* and IAS 22. The Board concluded that information disclosed in accordance with SIC-28 about equity instruments issued as part of the cost of a business combination helps to meet the first of the three objectives outlined above. Therefore, the Board decided to carry forward to the IFRS the disclosure requirements in SIC-28.

BC172 The Board also concluded that information previously disclosed in accordance with IAS 22 about business combinations classified as acquisitions and goodwill helps to meet the objectives outlined above. Therefore, the Board decided to carry forward to the IFRS the related disclosure requirements in IAS 22, amended as necessary to reflect the Board's other decisions in this project. For example, IAS 22 required disclosure of the amount of any adjustment during the period to goodwill or negative goodwill resulting from subsequent identification or changes in value of the acquiree's identifiable assets and liabilities. In line with the

Board's decision that an acquirer should, with specified exceptions, adjust the initial accounting for a combination after that accounting is complete only to correct an error (see paragraphs BC164–BC169), the IAS 22 disclosure requirement has been amended in the IFRS to require disclosure of information about error corrections required to be disclosed by IAS 8 *Accounting Policies, Changes in Accounting Estimates and Errors*.

BC173 The Board then assessed whether any additional disclosure requirements should be included in the IFRS to ensure that the three disclosure objectives outlined in paragraph BC170 are met. Mindful of the aim to seek international convergence on the accounting for business combinations, the Board, in making its assessment, considered the disclosure requirements in the corresponding domestic standards of each of its partner standard-setters.

BC174 As a result, and after considering respondents' comments on ED 3, the Board identified, and decided to include in the IFRS, the following additional disclosure requirements that it concluded would help to meet the first of the three disclosure objectives outlined in paragraph BC170:

(a) for each business combination that was effected during the period:

  (i) the amounts recognised at the acquisition date for each class of the acquiree's assets, liabilities and contingent liabilities, and, unless disclosure would be impracticable, the carrying amounts of each of those classes, determined in accordance with IFRSs, immediately before the combination. If such disclosure would be impracticable, that fact must be disclosed, together with an explanation of why this is the case.

  (ii) a description of the factors that contributed to a cost that results in the recognition of goodwill—including a description of each intangible asset that was not recognised separately from goodwill and an explanation of why the intangible asset's fair value could not be measured reliably—or a description of the nature of an excess (ie an excess of the acquirer's interest in the net fair value of the acquiree's identifiable assets, liabilities and contingent liabilities over the cost).

  (iii) the amount of the acquiree's profit or loss since the acquisition date included in the acquirer's profit or loss for the period, unless disclosure would be impracticable. If such disclosure would be impracticable, that fact must be disclosed, together with an explanation of why this is the case.

(b) the information required to be disclosed for each business combination that was effected during the period in aggregate for business combinations that are individually immaterial.

(c) the revenue and profit or loss of the combined entity for the period as though the acquisition date for all business combinations that were effected during the period had been the beginning of that period, unless such disclosure would be impracticable.

BC175 The Board further decided that, to aid in meeting the second disclosure objective outlined in paragraph BC170, the IFRS should also require disclosure by the acquirer of the amount and an explanation of any gain or loss recognised in the current period that:

(a) relates to the identifiable assets acquired or liabilities or contingent liabilities assumed in a business combination that was effected in the current or a previous period; and

(b) is of such size, nature or incidence that disclosure is relevant to an understanding of the combined entity's financial performance.

BC176 In relation to the third disclosure objective outlined in paragraph BC170, the Board concluded that the requirement to disclose a reconciliation of the carrying amount of goodwill at the beginning and end of the period should be amended to require separate disclosure of net exchange differences arising during the period.

BC177 After deciding on these additional disclosure requirements, the Board observed that there might be situations in which the information disclosed under the specific requirements does not completely satisfy the three disclosure objectives outlined in paragraph BC170. The Board therefore agreed that the IFRS should require disclosure in these situations of such additional information as is necessary to meet those objectives.

BC178 Paragraph 67 of the IFRS also requires that when equity instruments are issued or issuable as part of the cost of a business combination, the acquirer should disclose the number of equity instruments issued or issuable, the fair value of those instruments, and the basis for determining that fair value. The Board concluded that, although IAS 22 did not explicitly require disclosure of this information, it should have nonetheless been provided by the acquirer as part of disclosing the cost of acquisition and a description of the purchase consideration paid or contingently payable in accordance with paragraph 87(b) of IAS 22. The Board decided that to avoid the IFRS being inconsistently applied, the IFRS should explicitly require disclosure of this information.

Transitional provisions and effective date (paragraphs 78–85)

BC179 Except as discussed in paragraphs BC181–BC184, the IFRS applies to the accounting for business combinations for which the agreement date is on or after 31 March 2004 (ie the date the IFRS was issued), and to the accounting for any goodwill or excess arising from such a business combination.

BC180 The Board observed that requiring the IFRS to be applied retrospectively to all business combinations for which the agreement date is before the date the IFRS was issued might improve the comparability of financial information. However, such an approach would be problematic for the following reasons:

(a) it is likely to be impossible for many business combinations because the information needed may not exist or may no longer be obtainable.

(b) it requires the determination of estimates that would have been made at a prior date, and therefore raises problems in relation to the role of hindsight—in particular, whether the benefit of hindsight should be included or excluded from those estimates and, if excluded, how the effect of hindsight can be separated from the other factors existing at the date for which the estimates are required.

The Board concluded that the problems associated with applying the IFRS retrospectively, on balance, outweigh the benefit of improved comparability of financial information.

Limited retrospective application (paragraph 85)

BC181 The Board then considered whether retrospective application of the IFRS to business combinations for which the agreement date is before the date the IFRS is issued should nonetheless be permitted. In developing ED 3 the Board concluded that this would have the effect of providing preparers of financial statements with an option in respect of transitional provisions, thereby undermining both the comparability of financial information and the Board's efforts to eliminate options from IFRSs. Therefore, ED 3 proposed prohibiting retrospective application of the IFRS to combinations for which the agreement date is before the date the IFRS is issued.

BC182 Some respondents to ED 3 were concerned that prohibiting retrospective application of the IFRS to combinations for which the agreement date is before the date the IFRS is issued would not be consistent with the option provided to first-time adopters in IFRS 1 *First-time Adoption of International Financial Reporting Standards*. IFRS 1 permits a first-time adopter to restate a past business combination to comply with IFRSs, provided it also restates all later business combinations. In considering this issue, the Board observed the following:

(a) requiring the IFRS to be applied retrospectively to *all* past business combinations would be problematic for the reasons described in paragraph BC180.

(b) IFRS preparers that are also US registrants would have the necessary information to apply US Statements of Financial Accounting Standards 141 *Business Combinations* and 142 *Goodwill and Other Intangible Assets*, from the effective date of those Standards. The availability of that information would make application of the IFRS and the revised versions of IAS 36 and IAS 38 practicable from at least that same date.

BC183 The Board noted that giving entities the option of applying the IFRS to past business combinations from any date before the IFRS's effective dates would impair the comparability of financial information. However, the Board also noted that the issue of any new or revised IFRS reflects its opinion that application of that IFRS will result in more useful information being provided to users about an entity's financial position, performance or cash flows. On that basis, a case exists for permitting, and indeed encouraging, entities to apply a new or revised IFRS before its effective date. The Board concluded that if it were practicable for an entity to apply the IFRS from any date before the IFRS's effective dates, users of the entity's financial statements would be provided with more useful information than was previously the case under IAS 22. The Board concluded that the benefit of providing users with more useful information about an entity's financial position and performance by allowing limited retrospective application of this IFRS outweighs the disadvantages of potentially diminished comparability.

BC184 Therefore, unlike the proposals in ED 3, the IFRS permits entities to apply the requirements of the IFRS from any date before the effective dates outlined in paragraphs 78–84 of the IFRS, provided:

(a) the valuations and other information needed to apply the IFRS to past business combinations were obtained at the time those combinations were initially accounted for; and

(b) the entity also applies the revised versions of IAS 36 and IAS 38 prospectively from that same date, and the valuations and other information needed to apply those Standards from that date were previously obtained by the entity so that there would be no need to determine estimates that would need to have been made at a prior date.

Previously recognised goodwill (paragraphs 79 and 80)

BC185 The requirement to apply the IFRS to the accounting for business combinations for which the agreement date is on or after the date the IFRS is issued (or from an earlier date if the entity elects to apply paragraph 85 of the IFRS) raises a number of additional issues. One is whether goodwill acquired in a business combination for which the agreement date was before the date the IFRS is first applied should continue to be accounted for after that date in accordance with the requirements in IAS 22 (ie amortised and impairment tested), or in accordance with the requirements in the IFRS (ie impairment tested only). A similar issue exists for negative goodwill arising from a business combination for which the agreement date was before the date the IFRS is first applied. This latter issue is discussed in paragraphs BC189–BC195.

BC186 Consistently with its earlier decision about the accounting for goodwill after initial recognition (see paragraphs BC136–BC142), the Board concluded that non-amortisation of goodwill in conjunction with testing for impairment is the most representationally faithful method of accounting for goodwill and therefore should be applied in all circumstances, including to goodwill acquired in a business combination for which the agreement date was before the date the IFRS is first applied. The Board also concluded that if amortisation of such goodwill were to continue after the date the IFRS is first applied, financial statements would suffer the same lack of comparability that persuaded the Board to reject a mixed approach to accounting for goodwill, ie allowing entities a choice between amortisation and impairment testing.

BC187 As a result, the Board concluded that the IFRS should be applied prospectively, from the beginning of the first annual period beginning on or after the date the IFRS is issued (or from an earlier date if the entity elects to apply paragraph 85 of the IFRS), to:

(a) goodwill acquired in a business combination for which the agreement date was before the date the IFRS is first applied; and

(b) goodwill arising from an interest in a jointly controlled entity obtained before the date the IFRS is first applied and accounted for by applying proportionate consolidation.

BC188 In response to comments received on ED 3, the IFRS also clarifies that if an entity previously recognised goodwill as a deduction from equity, it should not recognise that goodwill in profit or loss if it disposes of all or part of the business to which that goodwill relates or if a cash-generating unit to which the goodwill relates becomes impaired.

Previously recognised negative goodwill (paragraph 81)

BC189 The Board considered whether the carrying amount of negative goodwill arising from a business combination for which the agreement date was *before* the date the IFRS is issued (or from an earlier date if the entity elects to apply paragraph 85 of the IFRS) should:

(a) continue to be accounted for after the date the IFRS is first applied in accordance with the requirements in IAS 22, ie deferred and recognised in profit or loss in future periods by matching the excess against the related future losses and/or expenses; or

(b) be derecognised on the date the IFRS is first applied with a corresponding adjustment to the opening balance of retained earnings.

BC190 In considering this issue, the Board observed that IAS 22 did not permit an acquirer to recognise the acquiree's contingent liabilities at the acquisition date as part of allocating the cost of a business combination. The Board also observed that the application of IAS 22 in practice would probably have resulted in liabilities arising as a consequence of the combination that were not liabilities of the acquiree immediately before the combination being incorrectly recognised as part of allocating the cost of the combination. Therefore, the carrying amount of negative goodwill arising from a combination for which the agreement date was *before* the date the IFRS is first applied is likely to comprise one or more of the following components:

(a) unrecognised contingent liabilities of the acquiree at the acquisition date.

(b) errors in measuring the fair value of either the consideration paid or the identifiable net assets acquired. These measurement errors could, for example, relate to a failure properly to reflect expectations of future losses and expenses in the market value of the acquiree's identifiable net assets.

(c) a requirement in an accounting standard to measure identifiable net assets acquired at an amount that is not fair value.

(d) a bargain purchase.

BC191 The Board concluded that with the exception of the acquiree's contingent liabilities, the above components do not satisfy the definition of a liability. Therefore, they should not continue to be recognised as deferred credits in the balance sheet after the date the IFRS is first applied.

BC192 The Board noted that, to the extent the carrying amount of negative goodwill on the date the IFRS is first applied comprises contingent liabilities of the acquiree at the acquisition date, those contingent liabilities may or may not have been resolved. If the contingent liability *has* been resolved, the related expense (if any) will have been recognised by the combined entity in profit or loss. The Board therefore concluded that any component of the carrying amount of negative goodwill that relates to contingent liabilities of the acquiree that have been resolved should be derecognised on the date the IFRS is first applied.

BC193 The Board observed that if a contingent liability included within the carrying amount of negative goodwill at the date the IFRS is first applied has not been resolved, the portion of the carrying amount attributable to that contingent liability might, in theory, be able to be isolated and carried forward as a liability after the date the IFRS is first applied. However, the Board agreed that isolating the contingent liability is likely to be extremely difficult in practice: the information needed may not exist or may no longer be obtainable. In addition, it requires the determination of estimates that would have been made at a prior date, and therefore raises problems in relation to the role of hindsight.

BC194 Furthermore, IAS 22 required negative goodwill to be deferred and recognised as income in future periods by matching the excess against the related future losses and/or expenses that were identified in the acquirer's plan for the acquisition and could be measured reliably. To the extent the negative goodwill did not relate to expectations of future losses and expenses that were identified in the acquirer's plan and could be measured reliably, an amount not exceeding the aggregate fair values of the identifiable non-monetary assets acquired was recognised as income on a systematic basis over the remaining weighted average useful life of the identifiable depreciable assets acquired. Any remaining negative goodwill was recognised as income immediately. Therefore, if the acquiree's unresolved contingent liability was not identified in the acquirer's plan for the acquisition, some or all of that contingent liability would have been recognised as income before the date the IFRS is first applied, adding an additional layer of complexity to trying to isolate the portion of the carrying amount attributable to the unresolved contingent liability.

BC195 On the basis of these arguments, the Board concluded that the IFRS should require derecognition of the full carrying amount of negative goodwill at the beginning of the first annual period beginning on or after the date the IFRS is issued (or at an earlier date if the entity elects to apply paragraph 85 of the IFRS), with a corresponding adjustment to the opening balance of retained earnings.

Previously recognised intangible assets (paragraph 82)

BC196 The IFRS clarifies the criteria for recognising intangible assets separately from goodwill. The Board therefore considered whether entities should be required to apply those criteria to reassess:

(a) the carrying amount of intangible assets acquired in business combinations for which the agreement date was before the date the IFRS is issued (or at an earlier date if the entity elects to apply paragraph 85 of the IFRS) and reclassify as goodwill any that do not meet the criteria for separate recognition; and

(b) the carrying amount of goodwill acquired in business combinations for which the agreement date was before the date the IFRS is issued (or at an earlier date if the entity elects to apply paragraph 85 of the IFRS) and reclassify as an identifiable intangible asset any component of the goodwill that meets the criteria for separate recognition.

BC197 The Board noted that determining whether a recognised intangible asset meets the criteria for recognition separately from goodwill would be fairly straightforward, and that requiring reclassification as goodwill if the criteria are not met would improve the comparability of financial statements. However, identifying and reclassifying intangible assets that meet those criteria but were previously subsumed in goodwill would be problematic for the same reasons that it would be problematic to require retrospective application of the requirements in the IFRS to all past business combinations.

BC198 As a result, the Board concluded that the IFRS should require the criteria for recognising intangible assets separately from goodwill to be applied only to reassess the carrying amounts of recognised intangible assets acquired in business combinations for which the agreement date was before the date the IFRS is issued (or at an earlier date if the entity elects to apply paragraph 85 of the IFRS). The IFRS should not require the criteria to be applied to reassess the carrying amount of goodwill acquired before the date the IFRS is first applied.

BC199 The Board noted that the transitional provisions in the previous version of IAS 38 *Intangible Assets* permitted, but did not require, retrospective reclassification of an intangible asset acquired in a business combination that was an acquisition and subsumed within goodwill but which satisfied the criteria in IAS 22 and the previous version of IAS 38 for recognition separately from goodwill. However, the Board observed that adopting such an approach in the IFRS would have the effect of providing preparers of financial statements with an option in respect of transitional provisions, thereby undermining both the comparability of financial information and the Board's efforts to eliminate options from IFRSs. The Board further observed that such an option was likely to act as an incentive to restate financial statements only if that restatement serves to benefit the entity in some way. Therefore, the Board decided that the IFRS should also not permit the option of applying the criteria for recognising intangible assets separately from goodwill to goodwill acquired before the date the IFRS is first applied.

Equity accounted investments (paragraphs 83 and 84)

BC200 Consistently with its decision that the IFRS should apply to the accounting for business combinations for which the agreement date is on or after the date the IFRS is issued and any goodwill or excess arising from such combinations (or from an earlier date if the entity elects to apply paragraph 85 of the IFRS), the Board agreed that the IFRS should also apply to the accounting for any goodwill or excess included in the carrying amount of an equity accounted investment acquired on or after the date the IFRS is first applied. Therefore, if the carrying amount of the investment includes goodwill, amortisation of that notional goodwill should not be included in the determination of the investor's share of the investee's profit or loss. If the carrying amount of the investment includes an excess, the amount of that excess should be included as income in the determination of the investor's share of the investee's profit or loss in the period in which the investment is acquired.

BC201 However, as outlined in paragraph BC185, the requirement for the IFRS to be applied to the accounting for goodwill or any excess arising from business combinations for which the agreement date is on or after the date the IFRS is issued (or from an earlier date if the entity elects to apply paragraph 85 of the IFRS) raises a number of additional issues. One is whether goodwill acquired in a combination for which the agreement date was *before* the date the IFRS is first applied should be accounted for after that date in accordance with IAS 22 or the IFRS. Another is whether the carrying amount of negative goodwill arising from a combination for which the agreement date was *before* the date the IFRS is first applied should be accounted for after that date as a deferred credit in accordance with IAS 22 or derecognised.

BC202 Related to these issues are questions of whether, for equity accounted investments acquired *before* the date the IFRS is first applied, an investor should calculate its share of the investee's profit or loss *after* that date by:

(a) in the case of an investment that notionally includes goodwill within its carrying amount, continuing to include an adjustment for the amortisation of that goodwill; or

(b) in the case of an investment that notionally includes negative goodwill in its carrying amount, continuing to reflect the deferral and matching approach required by IAS 22 for that negative goodwill.

BC203 For the reasons the Board concluded that previously recognised goodwill should be accounted for after the date the IFRS is first applied by applying the requirements in the IFRS (see paragraphs BC186 and BC187), the Board also concluded that any goodwill included in the carrying amount of an equity accounted investment acquired *before* the date the IFRS is first applied should be accounted for after that date by applying the requirements in the IFRS. Therefore, amortisation of that notional goodwill should not be included in the determination of the investor's share of the investee's profit or loss.

BC204 Similarly, for the reasons the Board concluded that previously recognised negative goodwill should be derecognised (see paragraphs BC189–BC195), the Board also concluded that any negative goodwill included in the carrying amount of an equity accounted investment acquired *before* the date the IFRS is first applied should be derecognised at the date the IFRS is first applied, with a corresponding adjustment to the opening balance of retained earnings.

Dissenting opinions on IFRS 3

Dissent of Geoffrey Whittington and Tatsumi Yamada

DO1 Professor Whittington and Mr Yamada dissent from the issue of this Standard.

DO2 Professor Whittington dissents on three grounds: first, the Board's decision to defer consideration of 'fresh start' accounting rather than implementing it immediately in place of pooling of interests accounting; second, the recognition criteria for intangible assets acquired and contingent liabilities assumed in a business combination; and third, the abolition of the amortisation of goodwill.

DO3 Mr Yamada dissents because he objects to the abolition of the amortisation of goodwill.

Fresh start accounting

DO4 Professor Whittington notes that fresh start accounting treats the business combination as creating a new entity. It therefore requires revaluation of all the assets of the combining entities (including, when the method is applied in its purest form, goodwill) at current value at the date of the combination. In effect, it applies the purchase method to both parties to the combination. It therefore provides, in Professor Whittington's view, an appropriate representation of the economic reality of a 'true merger' or 'uniting of interests' in which all parties to the combination are radically affected by the transaction. The fresh start approach is long established in the accounting literature and a version of it (the new entity method) was suggested in E22 (1981) *Accounting for Business Combinations*, the exposure draft that preceded IAS 22 (1983) *Accounting for Business Combinations*. Professor Whittington believes that further consideration of this method should not have been deferred.

DO5 Professor Whittington also believes that while IFRS 3 correctly acknowledges that true mergers may exist (see paragraphs BC40–BC42 and BC47), it may underestimate the range of business combinations that might be included in this category. In Professor Whittington's view, a 'true acquisition' may be characterised as being similar to an investment by the acquiring business, which may extend the business but does not radically affect the existing activities of the acquirer. A 'true merger' on the other hand leads to a radical change in the conduct of all existing activities. Between these two extremes is a range of business combinations that fall less easily into one category or the other. When the pooling of interests method was the alternative accounting treatment available for mergers (as in IAS 22), the radical differences between the outcome of applying that method and the purchase method led to the possibility of accounting arbitrage across the merger/acquisition boundary (as is suggested in paragraph BC48(b)). Professor Whittington believes that because the fresh start method is, in effect, an extension of the purchase method, the incentives for such arbitrage would probably be less were the fresh start method substituted for the pooling of interests method as the appropriate treatment for mergers.

DO6 Professor Whittington believes that IFRS 3 is correct in its prohibition of the pooling of interests method, because that method does not take account of the values arising from the business combination transaction. However, IFRS 3 is wrong to substitute the purchase method for the pooling of interests method, enforcing the identification of an acquirer even when this is acknowledged to be extremely difficult and may fail to capture the economic substance of the transaction, as in the case of the 'roll-up transactions' described in paragraph BC22. In such circumstances, the fresh start method should be permitted.

Recognition criteria for intangible assets acquired and contingent liabilities assumed in a business combination

DO7 Professor Whittington dissents from the recognition criteria in paragraph 37 insofar as they exempt intangible assets acquired and contingent liabilities assumed in a business combination from the requirement that the inflows or outflows of benefits will probably flow to the acquirer. The Board acknowledges in paragraphs BC96 and BC112 that this is inconsistent with the *Framework* and, in the case of contingent liabilities, with IAS 37 *Provisions, Contingent Liabilities and Contingent Assets*. Professor Whittington believes that such a step should not be taken in advance of a full review of the recognition criteria in the *Framework*.

Abolition of goodwill amortisation

DO8 Professor Whittington and Mr Yamada observe that the amortisation of goodwill is a well-established and well-understood practice. The requirements of IAS 22, including the rebuttable presumption of a 20-year useful life and an impairment test, appear to have given rise to no obvious difficulties.

DO9 Professor Whittington and Mr Yamada believe that the benefits of amortisation are its simplicity, its transparency and its precise targeting of the acquired goodwill, as opposed to the internally generated goodwill of the acquiring entity or the subsequent internally generated goodwill. The result is that management is made accountable for its expenditure on goodwill.

DO10 Professor Whittington and Mr Yamada acknowledge that two valid criticisms are made of amortisation: it is arbitrary, although not necessarily more arbitrary than the amortisation of other assets, and there is little evidence it is of significant value to users, as indicated by empirical studies of its impact on share prices. However, Professor Whittington and Mr Yamada believe that the arbitrariness can be overcome to a large extent by the additional use of impairment tests (as was required by IAS 22), and that the lack of immediate impact of amortisation on share prices does not negate the benefits of accountability. Indeed, it can reasonably be argued that the measurement of goodwill is intrinsically unreliable, and that a transparent if somewhat arbitrary method, such as amortisation, is less likely to mislead the market than the impairment-only approach required in IFRS 3, which, in the view of Professor Whittington and Mr Yamada, purports to capture economic reality but fails to do so.

DO11 Professor Whittington and Mr Yamada also believe that the abolition of goodwill amortisation in favour of an impairment-only approach is inconsistent with the general principle that internally generated goodwill should not be recognised. They agree with the Board's analysis in paragraphs BC130 and BC131 regarding the components of 'core goodwill', and note that the Board correctly acknowledges in paragraph BC140 that core goodwill acquired in a business combination is consumed over time and replaced by internally generated goodwill, provided that an entity is able to maintain the overall value of goodwill. In other words, the acquired core goodwill has a limited useful life, notwithstanding that it might be difficult to determine that useful life otherwise than in an arbitrary manner. Professor Whittington and Mr Yamada therefore believe that the amortisation of acquired goodwill over its useful life to reflect its consumption over that useful life is more representationally faithful than the impairment-only approach required by IFRS 3, even if the useful life and pattern of consumption can be determined only arbitrarily. The potential for arbitrariness does not provide sufficient grounds for ignoring the fact that the value of the acquired goodwill diminishes over its useful life as it is consumed. Thus, Professor Whittington and Mr Yamada are of the view that amortisation with regular impairment testing should be the required method of accounting for goodwill after its initial recognition. Professor Whittington and Mr Yamada note that the respondents to ED 3 that expressed a clear view on this issue generally supported straight-line amortisation (provided there is no evidence that an alternative pattern of amortisation is more representationally faithful) coupled with an impairment test whenever there is an indication that the goodwill might be impaired (see paragraph BC139). Professor Whittington and Mr Yamada agree with these respondents, and disagree with the Board's analysis of their comments (as set out in paragraphs BC140 and BC141).

DO12 Professor Whittington is additionally concerned that in rejecting amortisation, IFRS 3 puts its faith in a potentially unreliable impairment test that inevitably cannot separate out subsequent internally generated goodwill and has other weaknesses that require attention. Until greater experience of such tests has been accumulated, it cannot be established that they pass the cost/benefit test for the majority of entities affected. The costs of the impairment tests are likely to be high and the benefits may be diminished by their potential unreliability. Thus, amortisation supplemented by an impairment test (as was required by IAS 22) should be retained as the required method of accounting for goodwill. Professor Whittington is of the view that annual impairment tests without amortisation could be permitted as an alternative treatment when it is possible to rebut the presumption that goodwill has a determinable life. In such cases, impairment testing can be regarded as an alternative technique for achieving a similar objective to amortisation (measuring the consumption of goodwill), rather than being in direct conflict with the method previously required by IAS 22. This treatment of goodwill would also be consistent with the treatment of intangible assets. Neither method will achieve the objective of measuring the consumption of goodwill perfectly: accounting for goodwill is one of the most difficult problems in financial reporting, and the difficulty arises from the nature of goodwill.

DO13 Mr Yamada shares Professor Whittington's concern that, in rejecting amortisation, IFRS 3 puts its faith in a potentially unreliable impairment-only approach that inevitably cannot separate out subsequent internally generated goodwill and has other weaknesses that require attention. Mr Yamada views the impairment-only approach for goodwill as particularly unsatisfactory because of the failure of the impairment test in IAS 36 *Impairment of Assets* to eliminate the internally generated goodwill of the acquiring entity at the acquisition date and internally generated goodwill accruing after a business combination. He believes that including these items in the measure of goodwill will inappropriately provide 'cushions' against recognising impairment losses that have in fact occurred in respect of the acquired goodwill. Such 'cushions', combined with the abolition of the amortisation of acquired goodwill, will improperly result in an entity recognising internally generated goodwill as an asset, up to the amount initially recognised for the acquired goodwill. Mr Yamada acknowledges that many of the 'cushioning' problems existed, to a certain extent, under the previous approach in IAS 22 and IAS 36 *Impairment of Assets* of amortising goodwill in conjunction with regular impairment testing using the 'one-step' impairment test in the previous version of IAS 36. However, he believes that the previous approach provided more appropriate information because it ensured that the carrying amount of acquired goodwill was reduced to zero at the end of its useful life, even though there was a degree of arbitrariness in determining that useful life and the pattern of the acquired goodwill's consumption. The previous approach also ensured that, ultimately, no internally generated goodwill could be recognised. Under IFRS 3, if a business combination is so successful that the recoverable amount of a cash-generating unit to which goodwill has been allocated continues to exceed its carrying amount, the goodwill allocated to that unit will continue indefinitely to be recognised at its fair value at the acquisition date. Mr Yamada does not agree that this is a representationally faithful method of accounting for an asset that is consumed over time and replaced by internally generated goodwill. He believes that the previous approach provided a more transparent and representationally faithful method of accounting for acquired goodwill than the impairment-only approach required by IFRS 3.

DO14 Mr Yamada notes the Board's conclusion, as set out in paragraph BC142, that if a rigorous and operational impairment test could be devised, more useful information would be provided under an approach in which goodwill is not amortised, but instead tested for impairment annually or more frequently if events or changes in circumstances indicate that the goodwill might be impaired. Mr Yamada is of the view that the Board's decision to withdraw the 'two-step' impairment test for goodwill proposed in the Exposure Draft of Proposed Amendments to IAS 36, in favour of retaining the 'one-step' approach to measuring impairments of goodwill in the previous version of IAS 36 does not meet the requirement of 'a rigorous and operational impairment test'. He is also of the view that the requirement in paragraph 104(a) of IAS 36 for impairment losses to be allocated first to reduce the carrying amount of any goodwill allocated to a cash-generating unit is inconsistent with the view set out in paragraph BC132 that 'core goodwill' represents resources from which future economic benefits are expected to flow to the entity. This inconsistency strengthens Mr Yamada's view that the impairment-only approach is not a transparent and representationally faithful method of accounting for acquired goodwill. Nevertheless he welcomes the Board's decision to retain the 'one-step' approach to measuring impairments of goodwill because he believes that the requirements proposed in the Exposure Draft of Proposed Amendments to IAS 36 for measuring the implied value of goodwill were extremely complex, unduly burdensome, and would have resulted in a hypothetical measure unrelated to the acquired goodwill being tested for impairment.

DO15 With regard to intangible assets other than goodwill, Mr Yamada agrees with the Board's conclusion, as set out in paragraphs BC74 and BC75 of the Basis for Conclusions on IAS 38 *Intangible Assets*, that there are some such assets that have indefinite useful lives and that should not, therefore, be amortised. Mr Yamada believes that intangible assets with indefinite useful lives are fundamentally different in nature from goodwill. Therefore, although he disagrees with the abolition of amortisation of goodwill, he agrees with the abolition of amortisation of intangible assets with indefinite useful lives.

DO16 Mr Yamada notes the concern expressed by some that amortising goodwill but not amortising intangible assets with indefinite useful lives increases the potential for intangible assets to be misclassified at the acquisition date. However, Mr Yamada agrees with the Board's conclusion, as set out in paragraph BC49 of the Basis for Conclusions on IAS 38, that adopting the separability and contractual or other legal rights criteria provides a reasonably definitive basis for separately identifying and recognising intangible assets acquired in a business combination. Therefore, differences between the subsequent treatment of goodwill and intangible assets with indefinite useful lives would not, in his view, increase the potential for intangible assets to be misclassified at the acquisition date.

Contents

IFRS 3 Business Combinations Illustrative Examples

These examples accompany, but are not part of, IFRS 3.

Examples of items acquired in a business combination that meet the definition of an intangible asset

The following guidance provides examples of items acquired in a business combination that meet the definition of an intangible asset and are therefore recognised under IFRS 3 *Business Combinations* separately from goodwill, provided that their fair values can be measured reliably. To meet the definition of an intangible asset a non-monetary asset without physical substance must be identifiable, ie it must arise from contractual or other legal rights or be separable.

The examples provided below are not intended to be an exhaustive list of items acquired in a business combination that meet the definition of an intangible asset. A non-monetary asset without physical substance acquired in a business combination might meet the identifiability criterion for identification as an intangible asset but not be included in this guidance.

Assets designated with the symbol # are those that meet the definition of an intangible asset because they arise from contractual or other legal rights. Assets designated with the symbol * do not arise from contractual or other legal rights, but meet the definition of an intangible asset because they are separable. Assets designated with the symbol # might also be separable; however, separability is not a necessary condition for an asset to meet the contractual-legal criterion.

A Marketing-related intangible assets

1 Trademarks, trade names, service marks, collective marks and certification marks #

Trademarks are words, names, symbols or other devices used in trade to indicate the source of a product and to distinguish it from the products of others. A service mark identifies and distinguishes the source of a service rather than a product. Collective marks are used to identify the goods or services of members of a group. Certification marks are used to certify the geographical origin or other characteristics of a good or service.

Trademarks, trade names, service marks, collective marks and certification marks may be protected legally through registration with governmental agencies, continuous use in commerce, or by other means. Provided it is protected legally through registration or other means, a trademark or other mark acquired in a business combination is an intangible asset that meets the contractual-legal criterion. Otherwise, a trademark or other mark acquired in a business combination can meet the definition of an intangible asset provided the separability criterion is met, which would normally be the case.

The terms 'brand' and 'brand name' are often used as synonyms for trademarks and other marks. However, the former are general marketing terms that are typically used to refer to a group of complementary assets such as a trademark (or service mark) and its related trade name, formulas, recipes and technological expertise.

2 Internet domain names #

An Internet domain name is a unique alphanumeric name that is used to identify a particular numeric Internet address. Registration of a domain name creates an association between that name and a designated computer on the Internet for the period of the registration. Those registrations are renewable. A registered domain name acquired in a business combination is an intangible asset that meets the contractual-legal criterion.

3 Trade dress (unique colour, shape or package design) #

4 Newspaper mastheads #

5 Non-competition agreements #

B Customer-related intangible assets

1 Customer lists *

A customer list consists of information about customers, such as their name and contact information. A customer list may also be in the form of a database that includes other information about the customers such as their order history and demographic information. A customer list does not generally arise from contractual or other legal rights. However, customer lists are valuable and are frequently leased or exchanged. Therefore, a customer list acquired in a business combination normally meets the separability criterion for identification as an intangible asset. However, a customer list acquired in a business combination would not meet that criterion if the terms of confidentiality or other agreements prohibit an entity from selling, leasing or otherwise exchanging information about its customers.

2 Order or production backlog #

An order or production backlog arises from contracts such as purchase or sales orders. An order or production backlog acquired in a business combination meets the contractual-legal criterion for identification as an intangible asset, even if the purchase or sales orders are cancellable.

3 Customer contracts and the related customer relationships #

If an entity establishes relationships with its customers through contracts, those customer relationships arise from contractual rights. Therefore, customer contracts and the related customer relationships acquired in a business combination meet the contractual-legal criterion for identification as intangible assets. This will be the case even if confidentiality or other contractual terms prohibit the sale or transfer of a contract separately from the acquired entity or business.

Customer relationships also meet the contractual-legal criterion for identification as intangible assets when an entity has a practice of establishing contracts with its customers, regardless of whether a contract exists at the date of acquisition.

As noted in B2, an order or a production backlog arises from contracts such as purchase or sales orders, and is therefore also considered a contractual right. Consequently, if an entity has customer relationships with its customers through these types of contracts, the customer relationships also arise from contractual rights, and therefore meet the contractual-legal criterion for identification as intangible assets.

4 Non-contractual customer relationships *

If a customer relationship acquired in a business combination does not arise from a contract, the relationship is an intangible asset if it meets the separability criterion. Exchange transactions for the same asset or a similar asset provide evidence of separability of a non-contractual customer relationship and might also provide information about exchange prices that should be considered when estimating fair value.

C Artistic-related intangible assets

Artistic-related assets acquired in a business combination meet the criteria for identification as intangible assets if they arise from contractual or legal rights such as those provided by copyright. Copyrights can be transferred either in whole through assignments or in part through licensing agreements. An entity is not precluded from recognising a copyright intangible asset and any related assignments or licence agreements as a single asset, provided they have similar useful lives.

1 Plays, operas and ballets #

2 Books, magazines, newspapers and other literary works #

3 Musical works such as compositions, song lyrics and advertising jingles #

4 Pictures and photographs #

5 Video and audiovisual material, including films, music videos and television programmes #

D Contract-based intangible assets

1 Licensing, royalty and standstill agreements #

2 Advertising, construction, management, service or supply contracts #

3 Lease agreements #

4 Construction permits #

5 Franchise agreements #

6 Operating and broadcasting rights #

7 Use rights such as drilling, water, air, mineral, timber-cutting and route authorities #

8 Servicing contracts such as mortgage servicing contracts #

Contracts to service financial assets are one particular type of contract-based intangible asset. While servicing is inherent in all financial assets, it becomes a distinct asset (or liability):

(a) when contractually separated from the underlying financial asset by sale or securitisation of the assets with servicing retained; or

(b) through the separate purchase and assumption of the servicing.

If mortgage loans, credit card receivables or other financial assets are acquired in a business combination with servicing retained, the inherent servicing rights are not a separate intangible asset because the fair value of those servicing rights is included in the measurement of the fair value of the acquired financial asset.

9 Employment contracts that are beneficial contracts from the perspective of the employer because the pricing of those contracts is below their current market value #

E Technology-based intangible assets

1 Patented technology #

2 Computer software and mask works #

If computer software and program formats acquired in a business combination are protected legally, such as by patent or copyright, they meet the contractual-legal criterion for identification as intangible assets.

Mask works are software permanently stored on a read-only memory chip as a series of stencils or integrated circuitry. Mask works may have legal protection. Mask works with legal protection that are acquired in a business combination also meet the contractual-legal criterion for identification as intangible assets.

3 Unpatented technology *

4 Databases *

Databases are collections of information, often stored in electronic form (such as on computer disks or files). A database that includes original works of authorship may be entitled to copyright protection. If a database acquired in a business combination is protected by copyright, it meets the contractual-legal criterion for identification as an intangible asset. However, a database typically includes information created as a consequence of an entity's normal operations, such as customer lists, or specialised information such as scientific data or credit information. Databases that are not protected by copyright can be, and often are, exchanged, licensed or leased to others in their entirety or in part. Therefore, even if the future economic benefits from a database do not arise from legal rights, a database acquired in a business combination meets the separability criterion for identification as an intangible asset.

5 Trade secrets such as secret formulas, processes or recipes #

If the future economic benefits from a trade secret acquired in a business combination are legally protected, that asset meets the contractual-legal criterion for identification as an intangible asset. Otherwise, trade secrets acquired in a business combination meet the definition of an intangible asset only if the separability criterion is met, which is often likely to be the case.

Customer relationship intangible assets acquired in a business combination

The following examples illustrate the recognition in accordance with IFRS 3 *Business Combinations* of customer relationship intangible assets acquired in a business combination.

Example 1

Background

Parent obtained control of Supplier in a business combination on 31 December 20X4. Supplier has a five-year agreement to supply goods to Buyer. Both Supplier and Parent believe that Buyer will renew the supply agreement at the end of the current contract. The supply agreement is not separable.

Analysis

The supply agreement (whether cancellable or not) meets the contractual-legal criterion for identification as an intangible asset, and therefore is recognised separately from goodwill, provided its fair value can be measured reliably. Additionally, because Supplier establishes its relationship with Buyer through a contract, the customer relationship with Buyer meets the contractual-legal criterion for identification as an intangible asset. Therefore, the customer relationship intangible asset is also recognised separately from goodwill provided its fair value can be measured reliably. In determining the fair value of the customer relationship, Parent considers assumptions such as the expected renewal of the supply agreement.

Example 2

Background

Parent obtained control of Subsidiary in a business combination on 31 December 20X4. Subsidiary manufactures goods in two distinct lines of business–sporting goods and electronics. Customer purchases from Subsidiary both sporting goods and electronics. Subsidiary has a contract with Customer to be its exclusive provider of sporting goods. However, there is no contract for the supply of electronics to Customer. Both Subsidiary and Parent believe that there is only one overall customer relationship between Subsidiary and Customer.

Analysis

The contract to be Customer's exclusive supplier of sporting goods (whether cancellable or not) meets the contractual-legal criterion for identification as an intangible asset, and is therefore recognised separately from goodwill, provided its fair value can be measured reliably. Additionally, because Subsidiary establishes its relationship with Customer through a contract, the customer relationship with Customer meets the contractual-legal criterion for identification as an intangible asset. Therefore, the customer relationship intangible asset is also recognised separately from goodwill, provided its fair value can be measured reliably. Because there is only one customer relationship with Customer, the fair value of that relationship incorporates assumptions regarding Subsidiary's relationship with Customer related to both sporting goods and electronics.

However, if both Parent and Subsidiary believed there were separate customer relationships with Customer—one for sporting goods and another for electronics—the customer relationship with respect to electronics would be assessed by Parent to determine whether it meets the separability criterion for identification as an intangible asset.

Example 3

Background

Entity A obtained control of Entity B in a business combination on 31 December 20X4. Entity B does business with its customers solely through purchase and sales orders. At 31 December 20X4, Entity B has a backlog of customer purchase orders from 60 per cent of its customers, all of whom are recurring customers. The other 40 per cent of Entity B's customers are also recurring customers. However, as of 31 December 20X4, Entity B does not have any open purchase orders or other contracts with those customers.

Analysis

The purchase orders from 60 per cent of Entity B's customers (whether cancellable or not) meet the contractual-legal criterion for identification as intangible assets, and are therefore recognised separately from goodwill, provided their fair values can be measured reliably. Additionally, because Entity B has established its relationship with 60 per cent of its customers through contracts, those customer relationships meet the contractual-legal criterion for identification as an intangible asset. Therefore, the customer relationship intangible asset is also recognised separately from goodwill provided its fair value can be measured reliably.

Because Entity B has a practice of establishing contracts with the remaining 40 per cent of its customers, its relationship with those customers also arises through contractual rights, and therefore meets the contractual-legal criterion for identification as an intangible asset. Entity A recognises this customer relationship separately from goodwill, provided its fair value can be measured reliably, even though Entity B does not have contracts with those customers at 31 December 20X4.

Example 4

Background

Parent obtained control of Insurer in a business combination on 31 December 20X4. Insurer has a portfolio of one-year motor insurance contracts that are cancellable by policyholders. A reasonably predictable number of policyholders renew their insurance contracts each year.

Analysis

Because Insurer establishes its relationships with policyholders through insurance contracts, the customer relationship with policyholders meets the contractual-legal criterion for identification as an intangible asset. Therefore, the customer relationship intangible asset is recognised separately from goodwill, provided its fair value can be measured reliably. In determining the fair value of the customer relationship intangible asset, Parent considers estimates of renewals and cross-selling. IAS 36 *Impairment of Assets* and IAS 38 *Intangible Assets* apply to the customer relationship intangible asset.

In determining the fair value of the liability relating to the portfolio of insurance contracts, Parent considers estimates of cancellations by policyholders. IFRS 4 *Insurance Contracts* permits, but does not require, an expanded presentation that splits the fair value of acquired insurance contracts into two components:

(a) a liability measured in accordance with the insurer's accounting policies for insurance contracts that it issues; and

(b) an intangible asset, representing the fair value of the contractual rights and obligations acquired, to the extent that the liability does not reflect that fair value. This intangible asset is excluded from the scope of IAS 36 and IAS 38. After the business combination, Parent is required to measure that intangible asset on a basis consistent with the measurement of the related insurance liability.

Reverse acquisitions

The following example illustrates the application of the guidance on reverse acquisition accounting provided as an application supplement in paragraphs B1–B15 of Appendix B of IFRS 3 *Business Combinations*.

Example 5

This example illustrates the accounting for a reverse acquisition in which Entity A, the entity issuing equity instruments and therefore the legal parent, is acquired in a reverse acquisition by Entity B, the legal subsidiary, on 30 September 20X1. The accounting for any income tax effects is ignored in this example:

Balance sheets of A and B immediately before the business combination

	A	B
	CU	CU
Current assets	500	700
Non-current assets	1,300	3,000
	1,800	3,700
Current liabilities	300	600
Non-current liabilities	400	1,100
	700	1,700
Owners' equity		
Retained earnings	800	1,400
Issued equity		
100 ordinary shares	300	
60 ordinary shares		600
	1,100	2,000
	1,800	3,700

Other information

(a) On 30 September 20X1, A issues 2½ shares in exchange for each ordinary share of B. All of B's shareholders exchange their shares in B. Therefore, A issues 150 ordinary shares in exchange for all 60 ordinary shares of B.

(b) The fair value of each ordinary share of B at 30 September 20X1 is CU40. The quoted market price of A's ordinary shares at that date is CU12.

(c) The fair values of A's identifiable assets and liabilities at 30 September 20X1 are the same as their carrying amounts, with the exception of non-current assets. The fair value of A's non-current assets at 30 September 20X1 is CU1,500.

Calculating the cost of the business combination

As a result of the issue of 150 ordinary shares by A, B's shareholders own 60 per cent of the issued shares of the combined entity (ie 150 shares out of 250 issued shares). The remaining 40 per cent are owned by A's shareholders. If the business combination had taken place in the form of B issuing additional ordinary shares to A's shareholders in exchange for their ordinary shares in A, B would have had to issue 40 shares for the ratio of ownership interest in the combined entity to be the same. B's shareholders would then own 60 out of the 100 issued shares of B and therefore 60 per cent of the combined entity.

As a result, the cost of the business combination is CU1,600 (ie 40 shares each with a fair value of CU40).

Measuring goodwill

Goodwill is measured as the excess of the cost of the business combination over the net fair value of A's identifiable assets and liabilities. Therefore, goodwill is measured as follows:

	CU	CU
Cost of the business combination		1,600
Net fair value of A's identifiable assets and liabilities:		
Current assets	500	
Non-current assets	1,500	
Current liabilities	(300)	
Non-current liabilities	(400)	1,300
Goodwill		300

Consolidated balance sheet at 30 September 20X1

	CU
Current assets [CU700 + CU500]	1,200
Non-current assets [CU3,000 + CU1,500]	4,500
Goodwill	300
	6,000
Current liabilities [CU600 + CU300]	900
Non-current liabilities [CU1,100 + CU400]	1,500
	2,400
Owners' equity	
Retained earnings	1,400
Issued equity	
250 ordinary shares [CU600 + CU1,600][(a)]	2,200
	3,600
	6,000

(a) In accordance with paragraph B7(c) of IFRS 3, the amount recognised as issued equity instruments in the consolidated financial statements is determined by adding to the issued equity of the legal subsidiary immediately before the business combination [CU600] the cost of the combination [CU1,600]. However, the equity structure appearing in the consolidated financial statements (ie the number and type of equity instruments issued) must reflect the equity structure of the legal parent, including the equity instruments issued by the legal parent to effect combination.

Earnings per share

Assume that B's profit for the annual period ending 31 December 20X0 was CU600, and that the consolidated profit for the annual period ending 31 December 20X1 is CU800. Assume also that there was no change in the number of ordinary shares issued by B during the annual period ending 31 December 20X0 and during the period from 1 January 20X1 to the date of the reverse acquisition (30 September 20X1).

Earnings per share for the annual period ending 31 December 20X1 is calculated as follows:

Number of shares deemed to be outstanding for the period from 1 January 20X1 to the acquisition date (ie the number of ordinary shares issued by A in the reverse acquisition)	150
Number of shares outstanding from the acquisition date to 31 December 20X1	250
Weighted average number of ordinary shares outstanding [(150 × 9/12) + (250 × 3/12)]	175
Earnings per share [800/175]	CU4.57

Restated earnings per share for the annual period ending 31 December 20X0 is 4.00 (ie the profit of B of 600 divided by the number of ordinary shares issued by A in the reverse acquisition).

Minority interest

In the above example, assume that only 56 of B's ordinary shares are tendered for exchange rather than all 60. Because A issues 2½ shares in exchange for each ordinary share of B, A issues only 140 (rather than 150) shares. As a result, B's shareholders own 58.3 per cent of the issued shares of the combined entity (ie 140 shares out of 240 issued shares).

The cost of the business combination is calculated by assuming that the combination had taken place in the form of B issuing additional ordinary shares to the shareholders of A in exchange for their ordinary shares in A. In calculating the number of shares that would have to be issued by B, the minority interest is ignored. The majority shareholders own 56 shares of B. For this to represent a 58.3 per cent ownership interest, B would have had to issue an additional 40 shares. The majority shareholders would then own 56 out of the 96 issued shares of B and therefore 58.3 per cent of the combined entity.

As a result, the cost of the business combination is CU1,600 (ie 40 shares each with a fair value of CU40). This is the same amount as when all 60 of B's ordinary shares are tendered for exchange. The cost of the combination does not change simply because some of B's shareholders do not participate in the exchange.

The minority interest is represented by the 4 shares of the total 60 shares of B that are not exchanged for shares of A. Therefore, the minority interest is 6.7 per cent. The minority interest reflects the minority shareholders' proportionate interest in the pre-combination carrying amounts of the net assets of the legal subsidiary. Therefore, the consolidated balance sheet is adjusted to show a minority interest of 6.7 per cent of the pre-combination carrying amounts of B's net assets (ie CU134 or 6.7 per cent of CU2,000).

The consolidated balance sheet at 30 September 20X1 reflecting the minority interest is as follows:

	CU
Current assets [CU700 + CU500]	1,200
Non-current assets [CU3,000 + CU1,500]	4,500
Goodwill	300
	6,000
Current liabilities [CU600 + CU300]	900
Non-current liabilities [CU1,100 + CU400]	1,500
	2,400
Owners' equity	
Retained earnings [CU1,400 × 93.3%]	1,306
Issued equity	2,160
240 ordinary shares [CU560 + CU1,600]	
Minority interest	134
	3,600
	6,000

Business combination achieved in stages

The following example illustrates the application of the guidance on business combinations achieved in stages in paragraphs 58–60 of IFRS 3 *Business Combinations*. In particular, it deals with successive share purchases that result in an investee previously accounted for at fair value being included as a subsidiary in the consolidated financial statements.

Immediately following the example is a discussion of the outcome of applying the guidance in paragraphs 58–60 of IFRS 3 to the example assuming the investee had previously been accounted for at cost or by applying the equity method, rather than at fair value.

Example 6

Investor acquires a 20 per cent ownership interest in Investee (a service company) on 1 January 20X1 for CU3,500,000 cash. At that date, the fair value of Investee's identifiable assets is CU10,000,000, and the carrying amount of those assets is CU8,000,000. Investee has no liabilities or contingent liabilities at that date. The following shows Investee's balance sheet at 1 January 20X1 together with the fair values of the identifiable assets:

	Carrying amounts	Fair values
	CU	CU
Cash and receivables	2,000,000	2,000,000
Land	6,000,000	8,000,000
	8,000,000	10,000,000
Issued equity: 1,000,000 ordinary shares	5,000,000	
Retained earnings	3,000,000	
	8,000,000	

During the year ended 31 December 20X1, Investee reports a profit of CU6,000,000 but does not pay any dividends. In addition, the fair value of Investee's land increases by CU3,000,000 to CU11,000,000. However, the amount recognised by Investee in respect of the land remains unchanged at CU6,000,000. The following shows Investee's balance sheet at 31 December 20X1 together with the fair values of the identifiable assets:

	Carrying amounts	Fair values
	CU	CU
Cash and receivables	8,000,000	8,000,000
Land	6,000,000	11,000,000
	14,000,000	19,000,000
Issued equity: 1,000,000 ordinary shares	5,000,000	
Retained earnings	9,000,000	
	14,000,000	

On 1 January 20X2, Investor acquires a further 60 per cent ownership interest in Investee for CU22,000,000 cash, thereby obtaining control. Before obtaining control, Investor does *not* have significant influence over Investee, and accounts for its initial 20 per cent investment at fair value with changes in value included in profit or loss. Investee's ordinary shares have a quoted market price at 31 December 20X1 of CU30 per share.*

Throughout the period 1 January 20X1 to 1 January 20X2, Investor's issued equity was CU30,000,000. Investor's only asset apart from its investment in Investee is cash.

Accounting for the initial investment before obtaining control

Investor's initial 20 per cent investment in Investee is measured at CU3,500,000. However, Investee's 1,000,000 ordinary shares have a quoted market price at 31 December 20X1 of CU30 per share. Therefore, the carrying amount of Investor's initial 20 per cent investment is remeasured in Investor's financial statements to CU6,000,000 at 31 December 20X1, with the CU2,500,000 increase recognised in profit or loss for the period. Therefore, Investor's balance sheet at 31 December 20X1, before the acquisition of the additional 60 per cent ownership interest, is as follows:

	CU
Cash	26,500,000
Investment in Investee	6,000,000
	32,500,000
Issued equity	30,000,000
Retained earnings	2,500,000
	32,500,000

* Therefore, Investee's market capitalisation at 31 December 20X1 is CU30,000,000. However, Investor paid CU22,000,000 for the additional 60 per cent of the issued shares and control of Investee on 1 January 20X2. This indicates that Investor paid a significant premium for control of Investee.

Accounting for the business combination

Paragraph 25 of IFRS 3 states that when a business combination involves more than one exchange transaction, the cost of the combination is the aggregate cost of the individual transactions, with the cost of each individual transaction determined at the date of each exchange transaction (ie the date that each individual investment is recognised in the acquirer's financial statements). This means that for this example, the cost to Investor of the business combination is the aggregate of the cost of the initial 20 per cent ownership interest (CU3,500,000) plus the cost of the subsequent 60 per cent ownership interest (CU22,000,000), irrespective of the fact that the carrying amount of the initial 20 per cent interest has changed.

In addition, and in accordance with paragraph 58 of IFRS 3, each transaction must be treated separately to determine the goodwill on that transaction, using cost and fair value information at the date of each exchange transaction. Therefore, Investor recognises the following amounts for goodwill in its consolidated financial statements:

For the 20% ownership interest costing CU3,500,000:

goodwill = 3,500,000 – [20% × 10,000,000] =	CU1,500,000

For the 60% ownership interest costing CU22,000,000:

goodwill = 22,000,000 – [60% × 19,000,000] =	CU10,600,000

The following shows Investor's consolidation worksheet (all amounts in CU) immediately after the acquisition of the additional 60 per cent ownership interest in Investee, together with consolidation adjustments and associated explanations:

	Investor	Investee	Consolidation Adjustments Dr	Consolidation Adjustments Cr	Consolidated	
Net Assets						
Cash and receivables	4,500	8,000			12,500	
Investment in Investee	28,000	–		2,500 (2) 3,500 (3) 22,000 (4)	–	
Land	–	6,000	5,000 (1)		11,000	See note (a)
Goodwill	–	–	1,500 (3) 10,600 (4)		12,100	See note (b)
	32,500	14,000			35,600	
Issued equity	30,000	5,000	1,000 (3) 3,000 (4) 1,000 (5)		30,000	See note (c)
Asset revaluation surplus	–	–	400 (3) 3,000 (4) 1,000 (5)	5,000 (1)	600	See note (d)
Retained earnings	2,500	9,000	2,500 (2) 600 (3) 5,400 (4) 1,800 (5)		1,200	See note (e)
Minority interest	–	–		3,800 (5)	3,800	See note (a)
	32,500	14,000			35,600	

Consolidation Adjustments

		Dr	Cr
(1)	Land	5,000	
	Asset revaluation surplus		5,000
	To recognise Investee's identifiable assets at fair values at the acquisition date		
(2)	Retained earnings	2,500	
	Investment in Investee		2,500
	To restate the initial 20 per cent investment in Investee to cost		
(3)	Issued equity [20% × 5,000]	1,000	
	Asset revaluation surplus [20% × 2,000[(a)]]	400	
	Retained earnings [20% × 3,000]	600	
	Goodwill	1,500	
	Investment in Investee		3,500
	To recognise goodwill on the initial 20 per cent investment in Investee and record the elimination of that investment against associated equity balances		
(4)	Issued equity [60% × 5,000]	3,000	
	Asset revaluation surplus [60% × 5,000]	3,000	
	Retained earnings [60% × 9,000]	5,400	
	Goodwill	10,600	
	Investment in Investee		22,000
	To recognise goodwill on the subsequent 60 per cent investment in Investee and record elimination of that investment against associated equity balances		
(5)	Issued equity [20% × 5,000]	1,000	
	Asset revaluation surplus [20% × 5,000]	1,000	
	Retained earnings [20% × 9,000]	1,800	
	Minority interest (in issued equity)		1,000
	Minority interest (in asset revaluation surplus)		1,000
	Minority interest (in retained earnings)		1,800
	To recognise the minority interest in the Investee		

(a) The CU2,000,000 asset revaluation surplus represents the amount by which the fair value of Investee's land at the date of the first exchange transaction exceeds its carrying amount; the carrying amount of the land at the date Investor acquired the initial 20 per cent interest was CU6,000,000, but its fair value was CU8,000,000. In accordance with paragraph 58 of IFRS 3, each transaction must be treated separately for the purpose of determining the amount of goodwill on that transaction, using cost and fair value information at the date of each exchange transaction.

Notes

The above consolidation adjustments result in:

(a) Investee's identifiable net assets being stated at their full fair values at the date Investor obtains control of Investee. This means that the 20 per cent minority interest in Investee also is stated at the minority's 20 per cent share of the fair values of Investee's identifiable net assets.

(b) goodwill being recognised from the acquisition date at an amount based on treating each exchange transaction separately and using cost and fair value information at the date of each exchange transaction.

(c) issued equity of CU30,000,000 comprising the issued equity of Investor of CU30,000,000.

(d) an asset revaluation surplus of CU600,000. This amount reflects that part of the increase in the fair value of Investee's identifiable net assets after the acquisition of the initial 20 per cent interest that is attributable to that initial 20 per cent interest [20% × CU3,000,000].

(e) a retained earnings balance of CU1,200,000. This amount reflects the changes in Investee's retained earnings after Investor acquired its initial 20 per cent interest that is attributable to that 20 per cent interest [20% × CU6,000,000].

Therefore, the effect of applying the requirements in IFRS 3 to business combinations involving successive share purchases for which the investment was previously accounted for at fair value with changes in value included in profit or loss is to cause:

- changes in the fair value of previously held ownership interests to be reversed (so that the carrying amounts of those ownership interests are restated to cost).
- changes in the investee's retained earnings and other equity balances after each exchange transaction to be included in the post-combination consolidated financial statements to the extent that they relate to the previously held ownership interests.

Applying IFRS 3 if the investee had previously been accounted for at cost or using the equity method

As discussed above, paragraph 25 of IFRS 3 requires the cost of a business combination involving more than one exchange transaction to be measured as the aggregate cost of the individual transactions, with the cost of each individual transaction determined at the date of each exchange transaction (ie the date that each individual investment is recognised in the acquirer's financial statements). Therefore, irrespective of whether the initial 20 per cent investment in Investee is accounted for at cost, by applying the equity method or at fair value, the cost to Investor of the combination is the aggregate of the cost of the initial 20 per cent ownership interest (CU3,500,000) plus the cost of the subsequent 60 per cent ownership interest (CU22,000,000).

In addition, and again irrespective of whether the initial 20 per cent investment in Investee is accounted for at cost, by applying the equity method or at fair value, each transaction must be treated separately for the purpose of determining the amount of goodwill on that transaction, using cost and fair value information at the date of each exchange transaction.

Therefore, the effect of applying IFRS 3 to any business combination involving successive share purchases is to cause:

- any changes in the carrying amount of previously held ownership interests to be reversed (so that the carrying amounts of those ownership interests are restated to cost).
- changes in the investee's retained earnings and other equity balances after each exchange transaction to be included in the post-combination consolidated financial statements to the extent that they relate to the previously held ownership interests.

Consequently, the consolidated financial statements immediately after Investor acquires the additional 60 per cent ownership interest and obtains control of Investee would be the same irrespective of the method used to account for the initial 20 per cent investment in Investee before obtaining control.

Changes in the values assigned to the acquiree's identifiable assets

Completing the initial accounting for a business combination

The following example illustrates the application of the guidance in paragraph 62 of IFRS 3 *Business Combinations* on completing the initial accounting for a business combination when the acquirer has, at the end of the first period after the combination, accounted for the combination using provisional values. This example does not address the accounting for any income tax effects arising from the adjustments.

IFRS 3 requires the acquirer to account for a business combination using provisional values if the initial accounting for a business combination can be determined only provisionally by the end of the reporting period in which the combination is effected. The acquirer is required to recognise any adjustments to those provisional values as a result of completing the initial accounting:

(a) within twelve months of the acquisition date; and

(b) from the acquisition date. Therefore:

  (i) the carrying amount of an identifiable asset, liability or contingent liability that is recognised or adjusted as a result of completing the initial accounting is calculated as if its fair value at the acquisition date had been recognised from that date.

  (ii) goodwill or any gain recognised in accordance with paragraph 56 is adjusted from the acquisition date by an amount equal to the adjustment to the fair value at the acquisition date of the identifiable asset, liability or contingent liability being recognised or adjusted.

  (iii) comparative information presented for the periods before the initial accounting for the combination is complete is presented as if the initial accounting had been completed from the acquisition date. This includes any additional depreciation, amortisation or other profit or loss effects recognised as a result of completing the initial accounting.

Example 7

An entity prepares financial statements for annual periods ending on 31 December and does not prepare interim financial statements. The entity was the acquirer in a business combination on 30 September 20X4. The entity sought an independent appraisal for an item of property, plant and equipment acquired in the combination. However, the appraisal was not finalised by the time the entity completed its 20X4 annual financial statements. The entity recognised in its 20X4 annual financial statements a provisional fair value for the asset of CU30,000, and a provisional value for acquired goodwill of CU100,000. The item of property, plant and equipment had a remaining useful life at the acquisition date of five years.

Four months after the acquisition date, the entity received the independent appraisal, which estimated the asset's fair value at the acquisition date at CU40,000.

As outlined in paragraph 62 of IFRS 3, the acquirer is required to recognise any adjustments to provisional values as a result of completing the initial accounting from the acquisition date.

Therefore, in the 20X5 financial statements, an adjustment is made to the opening carrying amount of the item of property, plant and equipment. That adjustment is measured as the fair value adjustment at the acquisition date of CU10,000, less the additional depreciation that would have been recognised had the asset's fair value at the acquisition date been recognised from that date (CU500 for three months' depreciation to 31 December 20X4). The carrying amount of goodwill is also adjusted for the reduction in value at the acquisition date of CU10,000, and the 20X4 comparative information is restated to reflect this adjustment and to include additional depreciation of CU500 relating to the year ended 31 December 20X4.

In accordance with paragraph 69 of IFRS 3, the entity discloses in its 20X4 financial statements that the initial accounting for the business combination has been determined only provisionally, and explains why this is the case. In accordance with paragraph 73(b) of IFRS 3, the entity discloses in its 20X5 financial statements the amounts and explanations of the adjustments to the provisional values recognised during the current reporting period. Therefore, the entity discloses that:

- the fair value of the item of property, plant and equipment at the acquisition date has been increased by CU10,000 with a corresponding decrease in goodwill; and
- the 20X4 comparative information is restated to reflect this adjustment and to include additional depreciation of CU500 relating to the year ended 31 December 20X4.

Error corrections

The following examples illustrate the application of the guidance in paragraphs 63 and 64 of IFRS 3 on the accounting for error corrections related to the initial accounting for a business combination. These examples do not address the accounting for any income tax effects arising from the adjustments.

With three exceptions,* IFRS 3 requires adjustments to be made to the initial accounting for a business combination after that initial accounting is complete only to correct an error in accordance with IAS 8 *Accounting Policies, Changes in Accounting Estimates and Errors*. After that accounting is completed, adjustments cannot be recognised for the effect of changes in accounting estimates. In accordance with IAS 8, the effect of a change in an accounting estimate is

* Two of the three exceptions relate to adjustments to the cost of a business combination after the initial accounting for the combination is complete. The third relates to the subsequent recognition by the acquirer of the acquiree's deferred tax assets that did not satisfy the criteria for separate recognition when initially accounting for the business combination.

recognised prospectively. IAS 8 provides guidance on distinguishing corrections of errors from changes in accounting estimates.

Example 8

An entity prepares financial statements for annual periods ending on 31 December and does not prepare interim financial statements. The entity was the acquirer in a business combination on 30 September 20X1. As part of the initial accounting for that combination, the entity recognised goodwill of CU100,000. The carrying amount of goodwill at 31 December 20X1 was CU100,000.

During 20X2, the entity becomes aware of an error relating to the amount initially allocated to property, plant and equipment assets acquired in the business combination. In particular, CU20,000 of the CU100,000 initially allocated to goodwill should be allocated to property, plant and equipment assets that had a remaining useful life at the acquisition date of five years.

As outlined in paragraph 64 of IFRS 3, IAS 8 requires the correction of an error to be accounted for retrospectively, and for the financial statements to be presented as if the error had never occurred by correcting the error in the comparative information for the prior period(s) in which it occurred.

Therefore, in the 20X2 financial statements, an adjustment is made to the opening carrying amount of property, plant and equipment assets. That adjustment is measured as the fair value adjustment at the acquisition date of CU20,000 less the amount that would have been recognised as depreciation of the fair value adjustment (CU1,000 for three months' depreciation to 31 December 20X1). The carrying amount of goodwill is also adjusted for the reduction in value at the acquisition date of CU20,000, and the 20X1 comparative information is restated to reflect this adjustment and to include additional depreciation of CU1,000 relating to the year ended 31 December 20X1.

In accordance with IAS 8, the entity discloses in its 20X2 financial statements the nature of the error and that, as a result of correcting that error, an adjustment was made to the carrying amount of property, plant and equipment. The entity also discloses that:

- the fair value of property, plant and equipment assets at the acquisition date has been increased by CU20,000 with a corresponding decrease in goodwill; and
- the 20X1 comparative information is restated to reflect this adjustment and to include additional depreciation of CU1,000 relating to the year ended 31 December 20X1.

Example 9

This example assumes the same facts as in Example 8, except that the amount initially allocated to property, plant and equipment assets is decreased by CU20,000 to correct the error, rather than increased by CU20,000. This example also assumes that the entity determines that the recoverable amount of the additional goodwill is only CU17,000 at 31 December 20X1.

In the 20X2 financial statements, the opening carrying amount of property, plant and equipment assets is reduced by CU19,000, being the fair value adjustment at the acquisition date of CU20,000 less CU1,000 in depreciation expense recognised for the three-month period to 31 December 20X1. The carrying amount of goodwill is increased by CU17,000, being the increase in value at the acquisition date of CU20,000 less a CU3,000 impairment loss to reflect that the carrying amount of the adjustment exceeds its recoverable amount. The 20X1 comparative information is restated to reflect this adjustment and to exclude the CU1,000 depreciation and include the CU3,000 impairment loss.

In accordance with IAS 8, the entity discloses in its 20X2 financial statements the nature of the error and that, as a result of correcting that error, an adjustment was made to the carrying amount of property, plant and equipment. The entity also discloses that:

- the fair value of property, plant and equipment assets at the acquisition date has been decreased by CU20,000 with a corresponding increase in goodwill; and
- the 20X1 comparative information is restated to reflect this adjustment and to exclude CU1,000 depreciation recognised during the year ended 31 December 20X1 and include a CU3,000 impairment loss for goodwill relating to the year ended 31 December 20X1.

International Financial Reporting Standard 4

Insurance Contracts

CONTENTS

International Financial Reporting Standard 4 *Insurance Contracts* (IFRS 4) is set out in paragraphs 1–45 and Appendices A–C. All the paragraphs have equal authority. Paragraphs in **bold type** state the main principles. Terms defined in Appendix A are in *italics* the first time they appear in the Standard. Definitions of other terms are given in the Glossary for International Financial Reporting Standards. IFRS 4 should be read in the context of its objective and the Basis for Conclusions, the *Preface to International Financial Reporting Standards* and the *Framework for the Preparation and Presentation of Financial Statements*. IAS 8 *Accounting Policies, Changes in Accounting Estimates and Errors* provides a basis for selecting and applying accounting policies in the absence of explicit guidance.

Introduction

Reasons for issuing the IFRS

IN1 This is the first IFRS to deal with insurance contracts. Accounting practices for insurance contracts have been diverse, and have often differed from practices in other sectors. Because many entities will adopt IFRSs in 2005, the International Accounting Standards Board has issued this IFRS:

(a) to make limited improvements to accounting for insurance contracts until the Board completes the second phase of its project on insurance contracts.

(b) to require any entity issuing insurance contracts (an insurer) to disclose information about those contracts.

IN2 This IFRS is a stepping stone to phase II of this project. The Board is committed to completing phase II without delay once it has investigated all relevant conceptual and practical questions and completed its full due process.

Main features of the IFRS

IN3 The IFRS applies to all insurance contracts (including reinsurance contracts) that an entity issues and to reinsurance contracts that it holds, except for specified contracts covered by other IFRSs. It does not apply to other assets and liabilities of an insurer, such as financial assets and financial liabilities within the scope of IAS 39 *Financial Instruments: Recognition and Measurement*. Furthermore, it does not address accounting by policyholders.

IN4 The IFRS exempts an insurer temporarily (ie during phase I of this project) from some requirements of other IFRSs, including the requirement to consider the Framework in selecting accounting policies for insurance contracts. However, the IFRS:

(a) prohibits provisions for possible claims under contracts that are not in existence at the reporting date (such as catastrophe and equalisation provisions).

(b) requires a test for the adequacy of recognised insurance liabilities and an impairment test for reinsurance assets.

(c) requires an insurer to keep insurance liabilities in its balance sheet until they are discharged or cancelled, or expire, and to present insurance liabilities without offsetting them against related reinsurance assets.

IN5 The IFRS permits an insurer to change its accounting policies for insurance contracts only if, as a result, its financial statements present information that is more relevant and no less reliable, or more reliable and no less relevant. In particular, an insurer cannot introduce any of the following practices, although it may continue using accounting policies that involve them:

(a) measuring insurance liabilities on an undiscounted basis.

(b) measuring contractual rights to future investment management fees at an amount that exceeds their fair value as implied by a comparison with current fees charged by other market participants for similar services.

(c) using non-uniform accounting policies for the insurance liabilities of subsidiaries.

IN6 The IFRS permits the introduction of an accounting policy that involves remeasuring designated insurance liabilities consistently in each period to reflect current market interest rates (and, if the insurer so elects, other current estimates and assumptions). Without this permission, an insurer would have been required to apply the change in accounting policies consistently to all similar liabilities.

IN7 An insurer need not change its accounting policies for insurance contracts to eliminate excessive prudence. However, if an insurer already measures its insurance contracts with sufficient prudence, it should not introduce additional prudence.

IN8 There is a rebuttable presumption that an insurer's financial statements will become less relevant and reliable if it introduces an accounting policy that reflects future investment margins in the measurement of insurance contracts.

IN9 When an insurer changes its accounting policies for insurance liabilities, it may reclassify some or all financial assets as 'at fair value through profit or loss'.

IN10 The IFRS:

(a) clarifies that an insurer need not account for an embedded derivative separately at fair value if the embedded derivative meets the definition of an insurance contract.

(b) requires an insurer to unbundle (ie account separately for) deposit components of some insurance contracts, to avoid the omission of assets and liabilities from its balance sheet.

(c) clarifies the applicability of the practice sometimes known as 'shadow accounting'

(d) permits an expanded presentation for insurance contracts acquired in a business combination or portfolio transfer.

(e) addresses limited aspects of discretionary participation features contained in insurance contracts or financial instruments.

IN11 The IFRS requires disclosure to help users understand:

(a) the amounts in the insurer's financial statements that arise from insurance contracts.

(b) the amount, timing and uncertainty of future cash flows from insurance contracts.

IN12 Entities should apply the IFRS for annual periods beginning on or after 1 January 2005, but earlier application is encouraged. An insurer need not apply some aspects of the IFRS to comparative information that relates to annual periods beginning before 1 January 2005.

Potential impact of future proposals

IN13 The Board expects to approve Exposure Drafts in the second quarter of 2004 that will propose amendments to:

(a) the treatment of financial guarantees and credit insurance contracts; and

(b) the option in IAS 39 that permits an entity to designate financial assets and financial liabilities as 'at fair value through profit or loss'.

International Financial Reporting Standard 4 Insurance Contracts

Objective

1 The objective of this IFRS is to specify the financial reporting for *insurance contracts* by any entity that issues such contracts (described in this IFRS as an *insurer*) until the Board completes the second phase of its project on insurance contracts. In particular, this IFRS requires:

(a) limited improvements to accounting by insurers for insurance contracts.

(b) disclosure that identifies and explains the amounts in an insurer's financial statements arising from insurance contracts and helps users of those financial statements understand the amount, timing and uncertainty of future cash flows from insurance contracts.

Scope

2 An entity shall apply this IFRS to:

(a) insurance contracts (including *reinsurance contracts*) that it issues and reinsurance contracts that it holds.

(b) financial instruments that it issues with a *discretionary participation feature* (see paragraph 35). IAS 32 *Financial Instruments: Disclosure and Presentation* requires disclosure about financial instruments, including financial instruments that contain such features.

3 This IFRS does not address other aspects of accounting by insurers, such as accounting for financial assets held by insurers and financial liabilities issued by insurers (see IAS 32 and IAS 39 *Financial Instruments: Recognition and Measurement*), except in the transitional provisions in paragraph 45.

4 An entity shall not apply this IFRS to:

(a) product warranties issued directly by a manufacturer, dealer or retailer (see IAS 18 *Revenue* and IAS 37 *Provisions, Contingent Liabilities and Contingent Assets*).

(b) employers' assets and liabilities under employee benefit plans (see IAS 19 *Employee Benefits* and IFRS 2 *Share-based Payment*) and retirement benefit obligations reported by defined benefit retirement plans (see IAS 26 *Accounting and Reporting by Retirement Benefit Plans*).

(c) contractual rights or contractual obligations that are contingent on the future use of, or right to use, a non-financial item (for example, some licence fees, royalties, contingent lease payments and similar items), as well as a lessee's residual value guarantee embedded in a finance lease (see IAS 17 *Leases*, IAS 18 *Revenue* and IAS 38 *Intangible Assets*).

(d) financial guarantees that an entity enters into or retains on transferring to another party financial assets or financial liabilities within the scope of IAS 39, regardless of whether the financial guarantees are described as financial guarantees, letters of credit or insurance contracts (see IAS 39).

(e) contingent consideration payable or receivable in a business combination (see IFRS 3 *Business Combinations*).

(f) *direct insurance contracts* that the entity holds (ie direct insurance contracts in which the entity is the *policyholder*). However, a *cedant* shall apply this IFRS to reinsurance contracts that it holds.

5 For ease of reference, this IFRS describes any entity that issues an insurance contract as an insurer, whether or not the issuer is regarded as an insurer for legal or supervisory purposes.

6 A reinsurance contract is a type of insurance contract. Accordingly, all references in this IFRS to insurance contracts also apply to reinsurance contracts.

Embedded derivatives

7 IAS 39 requires an entity to separate some embedded derivatives from their host contract, measure them at *fair value* and include changes in their fair value in profit or loss. IAS 39 applies to derivatives embedded in an insurance contract unless the embedded derivative is itself an insurance contract.

8 As an exception to the requirement in IAS 39, an insurer need not separate, and measure at fair value, a policyholder's option to surrender an insurance contract for a fixed amount (or for an amount based on a fixed amount and an interest rate), even if the exercise price differs from the carrying amount of the host *insurance liability*. However, the requirement in IAS 39 does apply to a put option or cash surrender option embedded in an insurance contract if the surrender value varies in response to the change in a financial variable (such as an equity or commodity price or index), or a non-financial variable that is not specific to a party to the contract. Furthermore, that requirement also applies if the holder's ability to exercise a put option or cash surrender option is triggered by a change in such a variable (for example, a put option that can be exercised if a stock market index reaches a specified level).

9 Paragraph 8 applies equally to options to surrender a financial instrument containing a discretionary participation feature.

Unbundling of deposit components

10 Some insurance contracts contain both an insurance component and a *deposit component*. In some cases, an insurer is required or permitted to *unbundle* those components:

(a) unbundling is required if both the following conditions are met:

(i) the insurer can measure the deposit component (including any embedded surrender options) separately (ie without considering the insurance component).

(ii) the insurer's accounting policies do not otherwise require it to recognise all obligations and rights arising from the deposit component.

(b) unbundling is permitted, but not required, if the insurer can measure the deposit component separately as in (a)(i) but its accounting policies require it to recognise all obligations and rights arising from the deposit component, regardless of the basis used to measure those rights and obligations.

(c) unbundling is prohibited if an insurer cannot measure the deposit component separately as in (a)(i).

11 The following is an example of a case when an insurer's accounting policies do not require it to recognise all obligations arising from a deposit component. A cedant receives compensation for losses from a *reinsurer*, but the contract obliges the cedant to repay the compensation in future years. That obligation arises from a deposit component. If the cedant's accounting policies would otherwise permit it to recognise the compensation as income without recognising the resulting obligation, unbundling is required.

12 To unbundle a contract, an insurer shall:

(a) apply this IFRS to the insurance component.

(b) apply IAS 39 to the deposit component.

Recognition and measurement

Temporary exemption from some other IFRSs

13 Paragraphs 10–12 of IAS 8 *Accounting Policies, Changes in Accounting Estimates and Errors* specify criteria for an entity to use in developing an accounting policy if no IFRS applies specifically to an item. However, this IFRS exempts an insurer from applying those criteria to its accounting policies for:

(a) insurance contracts that it issues (including related acquisition costs and related intangible assets, such as those described in paragraphs 31 and 32); and

(b) reinsurance contracts that it holds.

14 Nevertheless, this IFRS does not exempt an insurer from some implications of the criteria in paragraphs 10–12 of IAS 8. Specifically, an insurer:

(a) shall not recognise as a liability any provisions for possible future claims, if those claims arise under insurance contracts that are not in existence at the reporting date (such as catastrophe provisions and equalisation provisions).

(b) shall carry out the *liability adequacy test* described in paragraphs 15–19.

(c) shall remove an insurance liability (or a part of an insurance liability) from its balance sheet when, and only when, it is extinguished—ie when the obligation specified in the contract is discharged or cancelled or expires.

(d) shall not offset:

(i) *reinsurance assets* against the related insurance liabilities; or

(ii) income or expense from reinsurance contracts against the expense or income from the related insurance contracts.

(e) shall consider whether its reinsurance assets are impaired (see paragraph 20).

Liability adequacy test

15 **An insurer shall assess at each reporting date whether its recognised insurance liabilities are adequate, using current estimates of future cash flows under its insurance contracts. If that assessment shows that the**

carrying amount of its insurance liabilities (less related deferred acquisition costs and related intangible assets, such as those discussed in paragraphs 31 and 32) is inadequate in the light of the estimated future cash flows, the entire deficiency shall be recognised in profit or loss.

16 If an insurer applies a liability adequacy test that meets specified minimum requirements, this IFRS imposes no further requirements. The minimum requirements are the following:

(a) The test considers current estimates of all contractual cash flows, and of related cash flows such as claims handling costs, as well as cash flows resulting from embedded options and guarantees.

(b) If the test shows that the liability is inadequate, the entire deficiency is recognised in profit or loss.

17 If an insurer's accounting policies do not require a liability adequacy test that meets the minimum requirements of paragraph 16, the insurer shall:

(a) determine the carrying amount of the relevant insurance liabilities* less the carrying amount of:

(i) any related deferred acquisition costs; and

(ii) any related intangible assets, such as those acquired in a business combination or portfolio transfer (see paragraphs 31 and 32). However, related reinsurance assets are not considered because an insurer accounts for them separately (see paragraph 20).

(b) determine whether the amount described in (a) is less than the carrying amount that would be required if the relevant insurance liabilities were within the scope of IAS 37 *Provisions, Contingent Liabilities and Contingent Assets*. If it is less, the insurer shall recognise the entire difference in profit or loss and decrease the carrying amount of the related deferred acquisition costs or related intangible assets or increase the carrying amount of the relevant insurance liabilities.

18 If an insurer's liability adequacy test meets the minimum requirements of paragraph 16, the test is applied at the level of aggregation specified in that test. If its liability adequacy test does not meet those minimum requirements, the comparison described in paragraph 17 shall be made at the level of a portfolio of contracts that are subject to broadly similar risks and managed together as a single portfolio.

19 The amount described in paragraph 17(b) (ie the result of applying IAS 37) shall reflect future investment margins (see paragraphs 27–29) if, and only if, the amount described in paragraph 17(a) also reflects those margins.

* The relevant insurance liabilities are those insurance liabilities (and related deferred acquisition costs and related intangible assets) for which the insurer's accounting policies do not require a liability adequacy test that meets the minimum requirements of paragraph 16.

Impairment of reinsurance assets

20 If a cedant's reinsurance asset is impaired, the cedant shall reduce its carrying amount accordingly and recognise that impairment loss in profit or loss. A reinsurance asset is impaired if, and only if:

(a) there is objective evidence, as a result of an event that occurred after initial recognition of the reinsurance asset, that the cedant may not receive all amounts due to it under the terms of the contract; and

(b) that event has a reliably measurable impact on the amounts that the cedant will receive from the reinsurer.

Changes in accounting policies

21 Paragraphs 22–30 apply both to changes made by an insurer that already applies IFRSs and to changes made by an insurer adopting IFRSs for the first time.

22 An insurer may change its accounting policies for insurance contracts if, and only if, the change makes the financial statements more relevant to the economic decision-making needs of users and no less reliable, or more reliable and no less relevant to those needs. An insurer shall judge relevance and reliability by the criteria in IAS 8.

23 To justify changing its accounting policies for insurance contracts, an insurer shall show that the change brings its financial statements closer to meeting the criteria in IAS 8, but the change need not achieve full compliance with those criteria. The following specific issues are discussed below:

(a) current interest rates (paragraph 24);

(b) continuation of existing practices (paragraph 25);

(c) prudence (paragraph 26);

(d) future investment margins (paragraphs 27–29); and

(e) shadow accounting (paragraph 30).

Current market interest rates

24 An insurer is permitted, but not required, to change its accounting policies so that it remeasures designated insurance liabilities* to reflect current market interest rates and recognises changes in those liabilities in profit or loss. At that time, it may also introduce accounting policies that require other current estimates and assumptions for the designated liabilities. The election in this paragraph permits an insurer to change its accounting policies for designated liabilities, without applying those policies consistently to all similar liabilities as IAS 8 would otherwise require. If an insurer designates liabilities for this election, it shall continue to apply current market interest rates (and, if applicable, the other current estimates and assumptions) consistently in all periods to all these liabilities until they are extinguished.

* In this paragraph, insurance liabilities include related deferred acquisition costs and related intangible assets, such as those discussed in paragraphs 31 and 32.

Continuation of existing practices

25 An insurer may continue the following practices, but the introduction of any of them does not satisfy paragraph 22:

(a) measuring insurance liabilities on an undiscounted basis.

(b) measuring contractual rights to future investment management fees at an amount that exceeds their fair value as implied by a comparison with current fees charged by other market participants for similar services. It is likely that the fair value at inception of those contractual rights equals the origination costs paid, unless future investment management fees and related costs are out of line with market comparables.

(c) using non-uniform accounting policies for the insurance contracts (and related deferred acquisition costs and related intangible assets, if any) of subsidiaries, except as permitted by paragraph 24. If those accounting policies are not uniform, an insurer may change them if the change does not make the accounting policies more diverse and also satisfies the other requirements in this IFRS.

Prudence

26 An insurer need not change its accounting policies for insurance contracts to eliminate excessive prudence. However, if an insurer already measures its insurance contracts with sufficient prudence, it shall not introduce additional prudence.

Future investment margins

27 An insurer need not change its accounting policies for insurance contracts to eliminate future investment margins. However, there is a rebuttable presumption that an insurer's financial statements will become less relevant and reliable if it introduces an accounting policy that reflects future investment margins in the measurement of insurance contracts, unless those margins affect the contractual payments. Two examples of accounting policies that reflect those margins are:

(a) using a discount rate that reflects the estimated return on the insurer's assets; or

(b) projecting the returns on those assets at an estimated rate of return, discounting those projected returns at a different rate and including the result in the measurement of the liability.

28 An insurer may overcome the rebuttable presumption described in paragraph 27 if, and only if, the other components of a change in accounting policies increase the relevance and reliability of its financial statements sufficiently to outweigh the decrease in relevance and reliability caused by the inclusion of future investment margins. For example, suppose that an insurer's existing accounting policies for insurance contracts involve excessively prudent assumptions set at inception and a discount rate prescribed by a regulator without direct reference to market conditions, and ignore some embedded options and guarantees. The insurer might make its financial statements more relevant and no less reliable by switching to a comprehensive investor-oriented basis of accounting that is widely used and involves:

(a) current estimates and assumptions;

(b) a reasonable (but not excessively prudent) adjustment to reflect risk and uncertainty;

(c) measurements that reflect both the intrinsic value and time value of embedded options and guarantees; and

(d) a current market discount rate, even if that discount rate reflects the estimated return on the insurer's assets.

29 In some measurement approaches, the discount rate is used to determine the present value of a future profit margin. That profit margin is then attributed to different periods using a formula. In those approaches, the discount rate affects the measurement of the liability only indirectly. In particular, the use of a less appropriate discount rate has a limited or no effect on the measurement of the liability at inception. However, in other approaches, the discount rate determines the measurement of the liability directly. In the latter case, because the introduction of an asset-based discount rate has a more significant effect, it is highly unlikely that an insurer could overcome the rebuttable presumption described in paragraph 27.

Shadow accounting

30 In some accounting models, realised gains or losses on an insurer's assets have a direct effect on the measurement of some or all of (a) its insurance liabilities, (b) related deferred acquisition costs and (c) related intangible assets, such as those described in paragraphs 31 and 32. An insurer is permitted, but not required, to change its accounting policies so that a recognised but unrealised gain or loss on an asset affects those measurements in the same way that a realised gain or loss does. The related adjustment to the insurance liability (or deferred acquisition costs or intangible assets) shall be recognised in equity if, and only if, the unrealised gains or losses are recognised directly in equity. This practice is sometimes described as 'shadow accounting'.

Insurance contracts acquired in a business combination or portfolio transfer

31 To comply with IFRS 3 *Business Combinations*, an insurer shall, at the acquisition date, measure at fair value the insurance liabilities assumed and *insurance assets* acquired in a business combination. However, an insurer is permitted, but not required, to use an expanded presentation that splits the fair value of acquired insurance contracts into two components:

(a) a liability measured in accordance with the insurer's accounting policies for insurance contracts that it issues; and

(b) an intangible asset, representing the difference between (i) the fair value of the contractual insurance rights acquired and insurance obligations assumed and (ii) the amount described in (a). The subsequent measurement of this asset shall be consistent with the measurement of the related insurance liability.

32 An insurer acquiring a portfolio of insurance contracts may use the expanded presentation described in paragraph 31.

33 The intangible assets described in paragraphs 31 and 32 are excluded from the scope of IAS 36 *Impairment of Assets* and IAS 38 *Intangible Assets*. However, IAS 36 and IAS 38 apply to customer lists and customer relationships reflecting the expectation of future contracts that are not part of the contractual insurance rights and contractual insurance obligations that existed at the date of a business combination or portfolio transfer.

Discretionary participation features

Discretionary participation features in insurance contracts

34 Some insurance contracts contain a discretionary participation feature as well as a *guaranteed element*. The issuer of such a contract:

(a) may, but need not, recognise the guaranteed element separately from the discretionary participation feature. If the issuer does not recognise them separately, it shall classify the whole contract as a liability. If the issuer classifies them separately, it shall classify the guaranteed element as a liability.

(b) shall, if it recognises the discretionary participation feature separately from the guaranteed element, classify that feature as either a liability or a separate component of equity. This IFRS does not specify how the issuer determines whether that feature is a liability or equity. The issuer may split that feature into liability and equity components and shall use a consistent accounting policy for that split. The issuer shall not classify that feature as an intermediate category that is neither liability nor equity.

(c) may recognise all premiums received as revenue without separating any portion that relates to the equity component. The resulting changes in the guaranteed element and in the portion of the discretionary participation feature classified as a liability shall be recognised in profit or loss. If part or all of the discretionary participation feature is classified in equity, a portion of profit or loss may be attributable to that feature (in the same way that a portion may be attributable to minority interests). The issuer shall recognise the portion of profit or loss attributable to any equity component of a discretionary participation feature as an allocation of profit or loss, not as expense or income (see IAS 1 *Presentation of Financial Statements*).

(d) shall, if the contract contains an embedded derivative within the scope of IAS 39, apply IAS 39 to that embedded derivative.

(e) shall, in all respects not described in paragraphs 14–20 and 34(a)(d), continue its existing accounting policies for such contracts, unless it changes those accounting policies in a way that complies with paragraphs 21–30.

Discretionary participation features in financial instruments

35 The requirements in paragraph 34 also apply to a financial instrument that contains a discretionary participation feature. In addition:

(a) if the issuer classifies the entire discretionary participation feature as a liability, it shall apply the liability adequacy test in paragraphs 15–19 to the whole contract (ie both the guaranteed element and the discretionary participation feature). The issuer need not determine the amount that would result from applying IAS 39 to the guaranteed element.

(b) if the issuer classifies part or all of that feature as a separate component of equity, the liability recognised for the whole contract shall not be less than the amount that would result from applying IAS 39 to the guaranteed element. That amount shall include the intrinsic value of an option to surrender the contract, but need not include its time value if paragraph 9 exempts that option from measurement at fair value. The issuer need not disclose the amount that would result from applying IAS 39 to the guaranteed element, nor need it present that amount separately. Furthermore, the issuer need not determine that amount if the total liability recognised is clearly higher.

(c) although these contracts are financial instruments, the issuer may continue to recognise the premiums for those contracts as revenue and recognise as an expense the resulting increase in the carrying amount of the liability.

Disclosure

Explanation of recognised amounts

36 **An insurer shall disclose information that identifies and explains the amounts in its financial statements arising from insurance contracts.**

37 To comply with paragraph 36, an insurer shall disclose:

(a) its accounting policies for insurance contracts and related assets, liabilities, income and expense.

(b) the recognised assets, liabilities, income and expense (and, if it presents its cash flow statement using the direct method, cash flows) arising from insurance contracts. Furthermore, if the insurer is a cedant, it shall disclose:

(i) gains and losses recognised in profit or loss on buying reinsurance; and

(ii) if the cedant defers and amortises gains and losses arising on buying reinsurance, the amortisation for the period and the amounts remaining unamortised at the beginning and end of the period.

(c) the process used to determine the assumptions that have the greatest effect on the measurement of the recognised amounts described in (b). When practicable, an insurer shall also give quantified disclosure of those assumptions.

(d) the effect of changes in assumptions used to measure insurance assets and insurance liabilities, showing separately the effect of each change that has a material effect on the financial statements.

(e) reconciliations of changes in insurance liabilities, reinsurance assets and, if any, related deferred acquisition costs.

Amount, timing and uncertainty of cash flows

38 **An insurer shall disclose information that helps users to understand the amount, timing and uncertainty of future cash flows from insurance contracts.**

39 To comply with paragraph 38, an insurer shall disclose:

(a) its objectives in managing risks arising from insurance contracts and its policies for mitigating those risks.

(b) those terms and conditions of insurance contracts that have a material effect on the amount, timing and uncertainty of the insurer's future cash flows.

(c) information about *insurance risk* (both before and after risk mitigation by reinsurance), including information about:

(i) the sensitivity of profit or loss and equity to changes in variables that have a material effect on them.

(ii) concentrations of insurance risk.

(iii) actual claims compared with previous estimates (ie claims development). The disclosure about claims development shall go back to the period when the earliest material claim arose for which there is still uncertainty about the amount and timing of the claims payments, but need not go back more than ten years. An insurer need not disclose this information for claims for which uncertainty about the amount and timing of claims payments is typically resolved within one year.

(d) the information about interest rate risk and credit risk that IAS 32 would require if the insurance contracts were within the scope of IAS 32.

(e) information about exposures to interest rate risk or market risk under embedded derivatives contained in a host insurance contract if the insurer is not required to, and does not, measure the embedded derivatives at fair value.

Effective date and transition

40 The transitional provisions in paragraphs 41–45 apply both to an entity that is already applying IFRSs when it first applies this IFRS and to an entity that applies IFRSs for the first-time (a first-time adopter).

41 An entity shall apply this IFRS for annual periods beginning on or after 1 January 2005. Earlier application is encouraged. If an entity applies this IFRS for an earlier period, it shall disclose that fact.

Disclosure

42 An entity need not apply the disclosure requirements in this IFRS to comparative information that relates to annual periods beginning before 1 January 2005, except for the disclosures required by paragraph 37(a) and (b) about accounting policies, and recognised assets, liabilities, income and expense (and cash flows if the direct method is used).

43 If it is impracticable to apply a particular requirement of paragraphs 10–35 to comparative information that relates to annual periods beginning before 1 January 2005, an entity shall disclose that fact. Applying the liability adequacy test (paragraphs 15–19) to such comparative information might sometimes be impracticable, but it is highly unlikely to be impracticable to apply other requirements of paragraphs 10–35 to such comparative information. IAS 8 explains the term 'impracticable'.

44 In applying paragraph 39(c)(iii), an entity need not disclose information about claims development that occurred earlier than five years before the end of the first financial year in which it applies this IFRS. Furthermore, if it is impracticable, when an entity first applies this IFRS, to prepare information about claims development that occurred before the beginning of the earliest period for which an entity presents full comparative information that complies with this IFRS, the entity shall disclose that fact.

Redesignation of financial assets

45 When an insurer changes its accounting policies for insurance liabilities, it is permitted, but not required, to reclassify some or all of its financial assets as 'at fair value through profit or loss'. This reclassification is permitted if an insurer changes accounting policies when it first applies this IFRS and if it makes a subsequent policy change permitted by paragraph 22. The reclassification is a change in accounting policy and IAS 8 applies.

Appendix A Defined terms

This appendix is an integral part of the IFRS.

cedant — The **policyholder** under a **reinsurance contract**.

deposit component — A contractual component that is not accounted for as a derivative under IAS 39 and would be within the scope of IAS 39 if it were a separate instrument.

direct insurance contract — An **insurance contract** that is not a **reinsurance contract**.

discretionary participation feature — A contractual right to receive, as a supplement to **guaranteed benefits**, additional benefits:

(a) that are likely to be a significant portion of the total contractual benefits;

(b) whose amount or timing is contractually at the discretion of the issuer; and

(c) that are contractually based on:

(i) the performance of a specified pool of contracts or a specified type of contract;

(ii) realised and/or unrealised investment returns on a specified pool of assets held by the issuer; or

(iii) the profit or loss of the company, fund or other entity that issues the contract.

fair value — The amount for which an asset could be exchanged, or a liability settled, between knowledgeable, willing parties in an arm's length transaction.

financial risk — The risk of a possible future change in one or more of a specified interest rate, financial instrument price, commodity price, foreign exchange rate, index of prices or rates, credit rating or credit index or other variable, provided in the case of a non-financial variable that the variable is not specific to a party to the contract.

guaranteed benefits — Payments or other benefits to which a particular **policyholder** or investor has an unconditional right that is not subject to the contractual discretion of the issuer.

guaranteed element — An obligation to pay **guaranteed benefits**, included in a contract that contains a **discretionary participation feature**.

insurance asset — An **insurer's** net contractual rights under an insurance contract.

insurance contract — A contract under which one party (the **insurer**) accepts significant **insurance risk** from another party (the **policyholder**) by agreeing to compensate the policyholder if a specified uncertain future event (the **insured event**) adversely affects the policyholder. (See Appendix B for guidance on this definition.)

insurance liability — An **insurer's** net contractual obligations under an **insurance contract**.

insurance risk — Risk, other than **financial risk**, transferred from the holder of a contract to the issuer.

insured event	An uncertain future event that is covered by an **insurance contract** and creates **insurance risk**.
insurer	The party that has an obligation under an **insurance contract** to compensate a **policyholder** if an **insured event** occurs.
liability adequacy test	An assessment of whether the carrying amount of an **insurance liability** needs to be increased (or the carrying amount of related deferred acquisition costs or related intangible assets decreased), based on a review of future cash flows.
policyholder	A party that has a right to compensation under an **insurance contract** if an **insured event** occurs.
reinsurance assets	A **cedant's** net contractual rights under a **reinsurance contract**.
reinsurance contract	An **insurance contract** issued by one insurer (the **reinsurer**) to compensate another insurer (the **cedant**) for losses on one or more contracts issued by the cedant.
reinsurer	The party that has an obligation under a **reinsurance contract** to compensate a **cedant** if an **insured event** occurs.
unbundle	Account for the components of a contract as if they were separate contracts.

Appendix B
Definition of an insurance contract

This appendix is an integral part of the IFRS.

B1 This appendix gives guidance on the definition of an insurance contract in Appendix A. It addresses the following issues:

(a) the term 'uncertain future event' (paragraphs B2–B4);

(b) payments in kind (paragraphs B5–B7);

(c) insurance risk and other risks (paragraphs B8–B17);

(d) examples of insurance contracts (paragraphs B18–B21);

(e) significant insurance risk (paragraphs B22–B28); and

(f) changes in the level of insurance risk (paragraphs B29 and B30).

Uncertain future event

B2 Uncertainty (or risk) is the essence of an insurance contract. Accordingly, at least one of the following is uncertain at the inception of an insurance contract:

(a) whether an *insured event* will occur;

(b) when it will occur; or

(c) how much the insurer will need to pay if it occurs.

B3 In some insurance contracts, the insured event is the discovery of a loss during the term of the contract, even if the loss arises from an event that occurred before the inception of the contract. In other insurance contracts, the insured event is an event that occurs during the term of the contract, even if the resulting loss is discovered after the end of the contract term.

B4 Some insurance contracts cover events that have already occurred, but whose financial effect is still uncertain. An example is a reinsurance contract that covers the direct insurer against adverse development of claims already reported by policyholders. In such contracts, the insured event is the discovery of the ultimate cost of those claims.

Payments in kind

B5 Some insurance contracts require or permit payments to be made in kind. An example is when the insurer replaces a stolen article directly, instead of reimbursing the policyholder. Another example is when an insurer uses its own hospitals and medical staff to provide medical services covered by the contracts.

B6 Some fixed-fee service contracts in which the level of service depends on an uncertain event meet the definition of an insurance contract in this IFRS but are not regulated as insurance contracts in some countries. One example is a maintenance contract in which the service provider agrees to repair specified equipment after a malfunction. The fixed service fee is based on the expected number of malfunctions, but it is uncertain whether a particular machine will break down. The malfunction of the equipment adversely affects its owner and the contract compensates the owner (in kind, rather than cash). Another example is a contract for car breakdown services in which the provider agrees, for a fixed annual fee, to provide roadside assistance or tow the car to a nearby garage. The latter contract could meet the definition of an insurance contract even if the provider does not agree to carry out repairs or replace parts.

B7 Applying the IFRS to the contracts described in paragraph B6 is likely to be no more burdensome than applying the IFRSs that would be applicable if such contracts were outside the scope of this IFRS:

(a) There are unlikely to be material liabilities for malfunctions and breakdowns that have already occurred.

(b) If IAS 18 *Revenue* applied, the service provider would recognise revenue by reference to the stage of completion (and subject to other specified criteria). That approach is also acceptable under this IFRS, which permits the service provider (i) to continue its existing accounting policies for these contracts unless they involve practices prohibited by paragraph 14 and (ii) to improve its accounting policies if so permitted by paragraphs 22–30.

(c) The service provider considers whether the cost of meeting its contractual obligation to provide services exceeds the revenue received in advance. To do this, it applies the liability adequacy test described in paragraphs 15–19 of this IFRS. If this IFRS did not apply to these contracts, the service provider would apply IAS 37 *Provisions, Contingent Liabilities and Contingent Assets* to determine whether the contracts are onerous.

(d) For these contracts, the disclosure requirements in this IFRS are unlikely to add significantly to disclosures required by other IFRSs.

Distinction between insurance risk and other risks

B8 The definition of an insurance contract refers to insurance risk, which this IFRS defines as risk, other than *financial risk* , transferred from the holder of a contract to the issuer. A contract that exposes the issuer to financial risk without significant insurance risk is not an insurance contract.

B9 The definition of financial risk in Appendix A includes a list of financial and non-financial variables. That list includes non-financial variables that are not specific to a party to the contract, such as an index of earthquake losses in a particular region or an index of temperatures in a particular city. It excludes non-financial variables that are specific to a party to the contract, such as the occurrence or non-occurrence of a fire that damages or destroys an asset of that party. Furthermore, the risk of changes in the fair value of a non-financial asset is not a financial risk if the fair value reflects not only changes in market prices for such assets (a financial variable) but also the condition of a specific non-financial asset held by a party to a contract (a non-financial variable). For example, if a guarantee of the residual value of a specific car exposes the guarantor to the risk of changes in the car's physical condition, that risk is insurance risk, not financial risk.

B10 Some contracts expose the issuer to financial risk, in addition to significant insurance risk. For example, many life insurance contracts both guarantee a minimum rate of return to policyholders (creating financial risk) and promise death benefits that at some times significantly exceed the policyholder's account balance (creating insurance risk in the form of mortality risk). Such contracts are insurance contracts.

B11 Under some contracts, an insured event triggers the payment of an amount linked to a price index. Such contracts are insurance contracts, provided the payment that is contingent on the insured event can be significant. For example, a life-contingent annuity linked to a cost-of-living index transfers insurance risk because payment is triggered by an uncertain event—the survival of the annuitant. The link to the price index is an embedded derivative, but it also transfers insurance risk. If the resulting transfer of insurance risk is significant, the embedded derivative meets the definition of an insurance contract, in which case it need not be separated and measured at fair value (see paragraph 7 of this IFRS).

B12 The definition of insurance risk refers to risk that the insurer accepts from the policyholder. In other words, insurance risk is a pre-existing risk transferred from the policyholder to the insurer. Thus, a new risk created by the contract is not insurance risk.

B13 The definition of an insurance contract refers to an adverse effect on the policyholder. The definition does not limit the payment by the insurer to an amount equal to the financial impact of the adverse event. For example, the definition does not exclude 'new-for-old' coverage that pays the policyholder sufficient to permit replacement of a damaged old asset by a new asset. Similarly, the definition does not limit payment under a term life insurance contract to the financial loss suffered by the deceased's dependants, nor does it preclude the payment of predetermined amounts to quantify the loss caused by death or an accident.

B14 Some contracts require a payment if a specified uncertain event occurs, but do not require an adverse effect on the policyholder as a precondition for payment. Such a contract is not an insurance contract even if the holder uses the contract to mitigate an underlying risk exposure. For example, if the holder uses a derivative to hedge an underlying non-financial variable that is correlated with cash flows from an asset of the entity, the derivative is not an insurance contract because payment is not conditional on whether the holder is adversely affected by a reduction in the cash flows from the asset. Conversely, the definition of an insurance contract refers to an uncertain event for which an adverse effect on the policyholder is a contractual precondition for payment. This contractual precondition does not require the insurer to investigate whether the event actually caused an adverse effect, but permits the insurer to deny payment if it is not satisfied that the event caused an adverse effect.

B15 Lapse or persistency risk (ie the risk that the counterparty will cancel the contract earlier or later than the issuer had expected in pricing the contract) is not insurance risk because the payment to the counterparty is not contingent on an uncertain future event that adversely affects the counterparty. Similarly, expense risk (ie the risk of unexpected increases in the administrative costs associated with the servicing of a contract, rather than in costs associated with insured events) is not insurance risk because an unexpected increase in expenses does not adversely affect the counterparty.

B16 Therefore, a contract that exposes the issuer to lapse risk, persistency risk or expense risk is not an insurance contract unless it also exposes the issuer to insurance risk. However, if the issuer of that contract mitigates that risk by using a second contract to transfer part of that risk to another party, the second contract exposes that other party to insurance risk.

B17 An insurer can accept significant insurance risk from the policyholder only if the insurer is an entity separate from the policyholder. In the case of a mutual insurer, the mutual accepts risk from each policyholder and pools that risk. Although policyholders bear that pooled risk collectively in their capacity as owners, the mutual has still accepted the risk that is the essence of an insurance contract.

Examples of insurance contracts

B18 The following are examples of contracts that are insurance contracts, if the transfer of insurance risk is significant:

(a) insurance against theft or damage to property.

(b) insurance against product liability, professional liability, civil liability or legal expenses.

(c) life insurance and prepaid funeral plans (although death is certain, it is uncertain when death will occur or, for some types of life insurance, whether death will occur within the period covered by the insurance).

(d) life-contingent annuities and pensions (ie contracts that provide compensation for the uncertain future event—the survival of the annuitant or pensioner—to assist the annuitant or pensioner in maintaining a given standard of living, which would otherwise be adversely affected by his or her survival).

(e) disability and medical cover.

(f) surety bonds, fidelity bonds, performance bonds and bid bonds (ie contracts that provide compensation if another party fails to perform a contractual obligation, for example an obligation to construct a building).

(g) credit insurance that provides for specified payments to be made to reimburse the holder for a loss it incurs because a specified debtor fails to make payment when due under the original or modified terms of a debt instrument. These contracts could have various legal forms, such as that of a financial guarantee, letter of credit, credit derivative default product or insurance contract. However, these contracts are outside the scope of this IFRS if the entity entered into them, or retained them, on transferring to another party financial assets or financial liabilities within the scope of IAS 39 (see paragraph 4(d)).

(h) product warranties. Product warranties issued by another party for goods sold by a manufacturer, dealer or retailer are within the scope of this IFRS. However, product warranties issued directly by a manufacturer, dealer or retailer are outside its scope, because they are within the scope of IAS 18 *Revenue* and IAS 37 *Provisions, Contingent Liabilities and Contingent Assets*.

(i) title insurance (ie insurance against the discovery of defects in title to land that were not apparent when the insurance contract was written). In this case, the insured event is the discovery of a defect in the title, not the defect itself.

(j) travel assistance (ie compensation in cash or in kind to policyholders for losses suffered while they are travelling). Paragraphs B6 and B7 discuss some contracts of this kind.

(k) catastrophe bonds that provide for reduced payments of principal, interest or both if a specified event adversely affects the issuer of the bond (unless the specified event does not create significant insurance risk, for example if the event is a change in an interest rate or foreign exchange rate).

(l) insurance swaps and other contracts that require a payment based on changes in climatic, geological or other physical variables that are specific to a party to the contract.

(m) reinsurance contracts.

B19 The following are examples of items that are not insurance contracts:

(a) investment contracts that have the legal form of an insurance contract but do not expose the insurer to significant insurance risk, for example life insurance contracts in which the insurer bears no significant mortality risk (such contracts are non-insurance financial instruments or service contracts, see paragraphs B20 and B21).

(b) contracts that have the legal form of insurance, but pass all significant insurance risk back to the policyholder through non-cancellable and enforceable mechanisms that adjust future payments by the policyholder as a direct result of insured losses, for example some financial reinsurance contracts or some group contracts (such contracts are normally non-insurance financial instruments or service contracts, see paragraphs B20 and B21).

(c) self-insurance, in other words retaining a risk that could have been covered by insurance (there is no insurance contract because there is no agreement with another party).

(d) contracts (such as gambling contracts) that require a payment if a specified uncertain future event occurs, but do not require, as a contractual precondition for payment, that the event adversely affects the policyholder. However, this does not preclude the specification of a predetermined payout to quantify the loss caused by a specified event such as death or an accident (see also paragraph B13).

(e) derivatives that expose one party to financial risk but not insurance risk, because they require that party to make payment based solely on changes in one or more of a specified interest rate, financial instrument price, commodity price, foreign exchange rate, index of prices or rates, credit rating or credit index or other variable, provided in the case of a non-financial variable that the variable is not specific to a party to the contract (see IAS 39).

(f) a financial guarantee contract (or letter of credit, credit derivative default product or credit insurance contract) that requires payments even if the holder has not incurred a loss on the failure of the debtor to make payments when due (see IAS 39).

(g) contracts that require a payment based on a climatic, geological or other physical variable that is not specific to a party to the contract (commonly described as weather derivatives).

(h) catastrophe bonds that provide for reduced payments of principal, interest or both, based on a climatic, geological or other physical variable that is not specific to a party to the contract.

B20 If the contracts described in paragraph B19 create financial assets or financial liabilities, they are within the scope of IAS 39. Among other things, this means that the parties to the contract use what is sometimes called deposit accounting, which involves the following:

(a) one party recognises the consideration received as a financial liability, rather than as revenue.

(b) the other party recognises the consideration paid as a financial asset, rather than as an expense.

B21 If the contracts described in paragraph B19 do not create financial assets or financial liabilities, IAS 18 applies. Under IAS 18, revenue associated with a transaction involving the rendering of services is recognised by reference to the stage of completion of the transaction if the outcome of the transaction can be estimated reliably.

Significant insurance risk

B22 A contract is an insurance contract only if it transfers significant insurance risk. Paragraphs B8–B21 discuss insurance risk. The following paragraphs discuss the assessment of whether insurance risk is significant.

B23 Insurance risk is significant if, and only if, an insured event could cause an insurer to pay significant additional benefits in any scenario, excluding scenarios that lack commercial substance (ie have no discernible effect on the economics of the transaction). If significant additional benefits would be payable in scenarios that have commercial substance, the condition in the previous sentence may be met even if the insured event is extremely unlikely or even if the expected (ie probability-weighted) present value of contingent cash flows is a small proportion of the expected present value of all the remaining contractual cash flows.

B24 The additional benefits described in paragraph B23 refer to amounts that exceed those that would be payable if no insured event occurred (excluding scenarios that lack commercial substance). Those additional amounts include claims handling and claims assessment costs, but exclude:

(a) the loss of the ability to charge the policyholder for future services. For example, in an investment-linked life insurance contract, the death of the policyholder means that the insurer can no longer perform investment management services and collect a fee for doing so. However, this economic loss for the insurer does not reflect insurance risk, just as a mutual fund manager does not take on insurance risk in relation to the possible death of the client. Therefore, the potential loss of future investment management fees is not relevant in assessing how much insurance risk is transferred by a contract.

(b) waiver on death of charges that would be made on cancellation or surrender. Because the contract brought those charges into existence, the waiver of these charges does not compensate the policyholder for a pre-existing risk. Hence, they are not relevant in assessing how much insurance risk is transferred by a contract.

(c) a payment conditional on an event that does not cause a significant loss to the holder of the contract. For example, consider a contract that requires the issuer to pay one million currency units if an asset suffers physical damage causing an insignificant economic loss of one currency unit to the holder. In this contract, the holder transfers to the insurer the insignificant risk of losing one currency unit. At the same time, the contract creates non-insurance risk that the issuer will need to pay 999,999 currency units if the specified event occurs. Because the issuer does not accept significant insurance risk from the holder, this contract is not an insurance contract.

(d) possible reinsurance recoveries. The insurer accounts for these separately.

B25 An insurer shall assess the significance of insurance risk contract by contract, rather than by reference to materiality to the financial statements.* Thus, insurance risk may be significant even if there is a minimal probability of material losses for a whole book of contracts. This contract-by-contract assessment makes it easier to classify a contract as an insurance contract. However, if a relatively homogeneous book of small contracts is known to consist of contracts that all transfer insurance risk, an insurer need not examine each contract within that book to identify a few non-derivative contracts that transfer insignificant insurance risk.

B26 It follows from paragraphs B23–B25 that if a contract pays a death benefit exceeding the amount payable on survival, the contract is an insurance contract unless the additional death benefit is insignificant (judged by reference to the contract rather than to an entire book of contracts). As noted in paragraph B24(b), the waiver on death of cancellation or surrender charges is not included in this assessment if this waiver does not compensate the policyholder for a pre-existing risk. Similarly, an annuity contract that pays out regular sums for the rest of a policyholder's life is an insurance contract, unless the aggregate life-contingent payments are insignificant.

B27 Paragraph B23 refers to additional benefits. These additional benefits could include a requirement to pay benefits earlier if the insured event occurs earlier and the payment is not adjusted for the time value of money. An example is whole life insurance for a fixed amount (in other words, insurance that provides a fixed death benefit whenever the policyholder dies, with no expiry date for the cover). It is certain that the policyholder will die, but the date of death is

* For this purpose, contracts entered into simultaneously with a single counterparty (or contracts that are otherwise interdependent) form a single contract.

uncertain. The insurer will suffer a loss on those individual contracts for which policyholders die early, even if there is no overall loss on the whole book of contracts.

B28 If an insurance contract is unbundled into a deposit component and an insurance component, the significance of insurance risk transfer is assessed by reference to the insurance component. The significance of insurance risk transferred by an embedded derivative is assessed by reference to the embedded derivative.

Changes in the level of insurance risk

B29 Some contracts do not transfer any insurance risk to the issuer at inception, although they do transfer insurance risk at a later time. For example, consider a contract that provides a specified investment return and includes an option for the policyholder to use the proceeds of the investment on maturity to buy a life-contingent annuity at the current annuity rates charged by the insurer to other new annuitants when the policyholder exercises the option. The contract transfers no insurance risk to the issuer until the option is exercised, because the insurer remains free to price the annuity on a basis that reflects the insurance risk transferred to the insurer at that time. However, if the contract specifies the annuity rates (or a basis for setting the annuity rates), the contract transfers insurance risk to the issuer at inception.

B30 A contract that qualifies as an insurance contract remains an insurance contract until all rights and obligations are extinguished or expire.

Appendix C
Amendments to other IFRSs

The amendments in this appendix shall be applied for annual periods beginning on or after 1 January 2005. If an entity adopts this IFRS for an earlier period, these amendments shall be applied for that earlier period.

* * * * *

The amendments contained in this appendix when this IFRS was issued in 2004 have been incorporated into the relevant pronouncements published in this volume.

Approval of IFRS 4 by the Board

International Financial Reporting Standard 4 *Insurance Contracts* was approved for issue by eight of the fourteen members of the International Accounting Standards Board. Professor Barth and Messrs Garnett, Gélard, Leisenring, Smith and Yamada dissented. Their dissenting opinions are set out after the Basis for Conclusions on IFRS 4.

Sir David Tweedie	Chairman
Thomas E Jones	Vice-Chairman
Mary E Barth	
Hans-Georg Bruns	
Anthony T Cope	
Robert P Garnett	
Gilbert Gélard	
James J Leisenring	
Warren J McGregor	
Patricia L O'Malley	
Harry K Schmid	
John T Smith	
Geoffrey Whittington	
Tatsumi Yamada	

CONTENTS

paragraphs

BASIS FOR CONCLUSIONS ON IFRS 4 INSURANCE CONTRACTS

Basis for Conclusions on IFRS 4 Insurance Contracts

This Basis for Conclusions accompanies, but is not part of, IFRS 4.

Introduction

BC1 This Basis for Conclusions summarises the International Accounting Standards Board's considerations in reaching the conclusions in IFRS 4 *Insurance Contracts*. Individual Board members gave greater weight to some factors than to others.

Background

BC2 The Board decided to develop an International Financial Reporting Standard (IFRS) on insurance contracts because:

(a) there was no IFRS on insurance contracts, and insurance contracts were excluded from the scope of existing IFRSs that would otherwise have been relevant (eg IFRSs on provisions, financial instruments, intangible assets).

(b) accounting practices for insurance contracts were diverse, and also often differed from practices in other sectors.

BC3 The Board's predecessor organisation, the International Accounting Standards Committee (IASC), set up a Steering Committee in 1997 to carry out the initial work on this project. In December 1999, the Steering Committee published an *Issues Paper*, which attracted 138 comment letters. The Steering Committee reviewed the comment letters and concluded its work by developing a report to the Board in the form of a *Draft Statement of Principles* (DSOP). The Board started discussing the DSOP in November 2001. The Board did not approve the DSOP or invite formal comments on it, but made it available to the public on the IASB's Website.

BC4 Few insurers report using IFRSs at present, although many more are expected to do so from 2005. Because it was not feasible to complete this project for implementation in 2005, the Board split the project into two phases so that insurers could implement some aspects in 2005. The Board published its proposals for phase I in July 2003 as ED 5 *Insurance Contracts*. The deadline for comments was 31 October 2003 and the Board received 135 responses. After reviewing the responses, the Board issued IFRS 4 in March 2004.

BC5 The Board's objectives for phase I were:

(a) to make limited improvements to accounting practices for insurance contracts, without requiring major changes that may need to be reversed in phase II.

(b) to require disclosure that (i) identifies and explains the amounts in an insurer's financial statements arising from insurance contracts and (ii) helps users of those financial statements understand the amount, timing and uncertainty of future cash flows from insurance contracts.

Tentative conclusions for phase II

BC6 The Board sees phase I as a stepping stone to phase II and is committed to completing phase II without delay once it has investigated all relevant conceptual and practical questions and completed its due process. In January 2003, the Board reached the following tentative conclusions for phase II:

(a) The approach should be an asset-and-liability approach that would require an entity to identify and measure directly the contractual rights and obligations arising from insurance contracts, rather than create deferrals of inflows and outflows.

(b) Assets and liabilities arising from insurance contracts should be measured at their fair value, with the following two caveats:

(i) Recognising the lack of market transactions, an entity may use entity-specific assumptions and information when market-based information is not available without undue cost and effort.

(ii) In the absence of market evidence to the contrary, the estimated fair value of an insurance liability shall not be less, but may be more, than the entity would charge to accept new contracts with identical contractual terms and remaining maturity from new policyholders. It follows that an insurer would not recognise a net gain at inception of an insurance contract, unless such market evidence is available.

(c) As implied by the definition of fair value:

(i) an undiscounted measure is inconsistent with fair value.

(ii) expectations about the performance of assets should not be incorporated into the measurement of an insurance contract, directly or indirectly (unless the amounts payable to a policyholder depend on the performance of specific assets).

(iii) the measurement of fair value should include an adjustment for the premium that marketplace participants would demand for risks and mark-up in addition to the expected cash flows.

(iv) fair value measurement of an insurance contract should reflect the credit characteristics of that contract, including the effect of policyholder protections and insurance provided by governmental bodies or other guarantors.

(d) The measurement of contractual rights and obligations associated with the closed book of insurance contracts should include future premiums specified in the contracts (and claims, benefits, expenses, and other additional cash flows resulting from those premiums) if, and only if:

(i) policyholders hold non-cancellable continuation or renewal rights that significantly constrain the insurer's ability to reprice the contract to rates that would apply for new policyholders whose characteristics are similar to those of the existing policyholders; and

(ii) those rights will lapse if the policyholders stop paying premiums.

(e) Acquisition costs should be recognised as an expense when incurred.

(f) The Board will consider two more questions later in phase II:

  (i) Should the measurement model unbundle the individual elements of an insurance contract and measure them individually?

  (ii) How should an insurer measure its liability to holders of participating contracts?

BC7 In two areas, those tentative conclusions differ from the IASC Steering Committee's recommendations in the DSOP:

(a) the use of a fair value measurement objective rather than entity-specific value. However, that change is not as significant as it might seem because entity-specific value as described in the DSOP is indistinguishable in most respects from estimates of fair value determined using measurement guidance that the Board has tentatively adopted in phase II of its project on business combinations.

(b) the criteria used to determine whether measurement should reflect future premiums and related cash flows (paragraph BC6(d)).

BC8 Since January 2003, constraints on Board and staff resources have prevented the Board from continuing work to determine whether its tentative conclusions for phase II can be developed into a standard that is consistent with the IASB *Framework* and workable in practice. The Board intends to return to phase II of the project in the second quarter of 2004. It plans to focus at that time on both conceptual and practical issues, as in any project. Only after completing its deliberations will the Board proceed with an Exposure Draft of a proposed IFRS. The Board's deliberations in all projects include a consideration of alternatives and whether those alternatives represent conceptually superior approaches to financial reporting issues. Consequently, the Board will examine existing practices throughout the world to ascertain whether any could be deemed to be a superior answer suitable for international adoption.

BC9 As discussed in paragraph BC84, ED 5 proposed a 'sunset clause', which the Board deleted in finalising the IFRS. Although respondents generally opposed the sunset clause, many applauded the Board's signal of its commitment to complete phase II without delay.

Scope

BC10 Some argued that the IFRS should deal with all aspects of financial reporting by insurers, to ensure that the financial reporting for insurers is internally consistent. They noted that regulatory requirements, and some national accounting requirements, often cover all aspects of an insurer's business. However, for the following reasons, the IFRS deals with insurance contracts of all entities and does not address other aspects of accounting by insurers:

(a) It would be difficult, and perhaps impossible, to create a robust definition of an insurer that could be applied consistently from country to country. Among other things, an increasing number of entities have major activities in both insurance and other areas.

(b) It would be undesirable for an insurer to account for a transaction in one way and for a non-insurer to account in a different way for the same transaction.

(c) The project should not reopen issues addressed by other IFRSs, unless specific features of insurance contracts justify a different treatment. Paragraphs BC166–BC180 discuss the treatment of assets backing insurance contracts.

Definition of insurance contract

BC11 The definition of an insurance contract determines which contracts are within the scope of IFRS 4 rather than other IFRSs. Some argued that phase I should use existing national definitions of insurance contracts, on the following grounds:

(a) Before phase II gives guidance on applying IAS 39 *Financial Instruments: Recognition and Measurement* to difficult areas such as discretionary participation features and cancellation and renewal rights, it would be premature to require insurers to apply IAS 39 to contracts that contain these features and rights.

(b) The definition adopted for phase I may need to be amended again for phase II. This could compel insurers to make extensive changes twice in a short time.

BC12 However, in the Board's view, it is unsatisfactory to base the definition used in IFRSs on local definitions that may vary from country to country and may not be most relevant for deciding which IFRS ought to apply to a particular type of contract.

BC13 Some expressed concerns that the adoption of a particular definition by the IASB could lead ultimately to inappropriate changes in definitions used for other purposes, such as insurance law, insurance supervision or tax. The Board emphasises that any definition used in IFRSs is solely for financial reporting and is not intended to change or pre-empt definitions used for other purposes.

BC14 Various Standards issued by IASC used definitions or descriptions of insurance contracts to exclude insurance contracts from their scope. The scope of IAS 37 *Provisions, Contingent Liabilities and Contingent Assets* and of IAS 38 *Intangible Assets* excluded provisions, contingent liabilities, contingent assets and intangible assets that arise in insurance enterprises from contracts with policyholders. IASC used this wording when its insurance project had just started, to avoid prejudging whether the project would address insurance contracts or a broader class of contracts. Similarly, the scope of IAS 18 *Revenue* excluded revenue arising from insurance contracts of insurance enterprises.

BC15 The following definition of insurance contracts was used to exclude insurance contracts from the scope of an earlier version of IAS 32 *Financial Instruments: Disclosure and Presentation* and IAS 39.

> An insurance contract is a contract that exposes the insurer to identified risks of loss from events or circumstances occurring or discovered within a specified period, including death (in the case of an annuity, the survival of the annuitant), sickness, disability, property damage, injury to others and business interruption.

BC16 This definition was supplemented by a statement that IAS 32 and IAS 39 did, nevertheless, apply when a financial instrument 'takes the form of an insurance contract but principally involves the transfer of financial risks.'

BC17 For the following reasons, the Board discarded the previous definition in IAS 32 and IAS 39:

(a) The definition gave a list of examples, but did not define the characteristics of the risks that it was intended to include.

(b) A clearer definition reduces the uncertainty about the meaning of the phrase 'principally involves the transfer of financial risks'. This will help insurers adopting IFRSs for the first-time ('first-time adopters') in 2005 and minimises the likelihood of further changes in classification for phase II. Furthermore, the previous test could have led to many contracts being classified as financial instruments even though they transfer significant insurance risk.

BC18 In developing a new definition, the Board also considered US GAAP. The main FASB statements for insurers deal with financial reporting by insurance entities and do not define insurance contracts explicitly. However, paragraph 1 of SFAS 113 *Accounting and Reporting for Reinsurance of Short-Duration and Long-Duration Contracts* states:

> Insurance provides indemnification against loss or liability from specified events and circumstances that may occur or be discovered during a specified period. In exchange for a payment from the policyholder (a premium), an insurance enterprise agrees to pay the policyholder if specified events occur or are discovered.

BC19 Paragraph 6 of SFAS 113 applies to any transaction, regardless of its form, that indemnifies an insurer against loss or liability relating to insurance risk. The glossary appended to SFAS 113 defines insurance risk as:

> The risk arising from uncertainties about both (a) the ultimate amount of net cash flows from premiums, commissions, claims, and claim settlement expenses paid under a contract (often referred to as underwriting risk) and (b) the timing of the receipt and payment of those cash flows (often referred to as timing risk). Actual or imputed investment returns are not an element of insurance risk. Insurance risk is fortuitous—the possibility of adverse events occurring is outside the control of the insured.

BC20 Having reviewed these definitions from US GAAP, the Board developed a new definition of insurance contract for the IFRS and expects to use the same definition for phase II. The following aspects of the definition are discussed below:

(a) insurance risk (paragraphs BC21–BC24);

(b) insurable interest (paragraphs BC25–BC29);

(c) quantity of insurance risk (paragraphs BC30–BC37);

(d) expiry of insurance-contingent rights and obligations (paragraphs BC38 and BC39);

(e) unbundling (paragraphs BC40–BC54); and

(f) weather derivatives (paragraphs BC55–BC60).

Insurance risk

BC21 The definition of an insurance contract in the IFRS focuses on the feature that causes accounting problems unique to insurance contracts, namely insurance risk. The definition of insurance risk excludes financial risk, defined using a list of risks that also appears in IAS 39's definition of a derivative.

BC22 Some contracts have the legal form of insurance contracts but do not transfer significant insurance risk to the issuer. Some argue that all such contracts should be treated as insurance contracts, for the following reasons:

(a) These contracts are traditionally described as insurance contracts and are generally subject to regulation by insurance supervisors.

(b) Phase I will not achieve great comparability between insurers because it will permit a diverse range of treatments for insurance contracts. It would be preferable to ensure consistency at least within a single insurer.

(c) Accounting for some contracts under IAS 39 and others under local GAAP is unhelpful to users. Moreover, some argued that IAS 39 contains insufficient, and possibly inappropriate, guidance for investment contracts.*

(d) The guidance proposed in ED 5 on significant insurance risk was too vague, would be applied inconsistently and relied on actuarial resources in short supply in many countries.

BC23 However, as explained in the *Framework*, financial statements should reflect economic substance and not merely legal form. Furthermore, accounting arbitrage could occur if the addition of an insignificant amount of insurance risk made a significant difference to the accounting. Therefore, the Board decided that contracts described in the previous paragraph should not be treated as insurance contracts for financial reporting.

BC24 Some respondents suggested that an insurance contract is any contract under which the policyholder exchanges a fixed amount (ie the premium) for an amount payable if an insured event occurs. However, not all insurance contracts have explicit premiums (eg insurance cover bundled with some credit card contracts). Adding a reference to premiums would have introduced no more clarity and might have required more supporting guidance and explanations.

Insurable interest

BC25 In some countries, the legal definition of insurance requires that the policyholder or other beneficiary should have an insurable interest in the insured event. For the following reasons, the definition proposed in 1999 by the former IASC Steering Committee in the Issues Paper did not refer to insurable interest:

(a) Insurable interest is defined in different ways in different countries. Also, it is difficult to find a simple definition of insurable interest that is adequate for such different types of insurance as insurance against fire, term life insurance and annuities.

(b) Contracts that require payment if a specified uncertain future event occurs cause similar types of economic exposure, whether or not the other party has an insurable interest.

* 'Investment contract' is an informal term referring to a contract issued by an insurer that does not expose the insurer to significant insurance risk and is therefore within the scope of IAS 39.

BC26 Because the definition proposed in the Issues Paper did not include a notion of insurable interest, it would have encompassed gambling. Several commentators on the Issues Paper stressed the important social, moral, legal and regulatory differences between insurance and gambling. They noted that policyholders buy insurance to reduce risk, whereas gamblers take on risk (unless they use a gambling contract as a hedge). In the light of these comments, the definition of an insurance contract in the IFRS incorporates the notion of insurable interest. Specifically, it refers to the fact that the insurer accepts risk from the policyholder by agreeing to compensate the policyholder if an uncertain event adversely affects the policyholder. The notion of insurable interest also appears in the definition of financial risk, which refers to a non-financial variable not specific to a party to the contract.

BC27 This reference to an adverse effect is open to the objections set out in paragraph BC25. However, without this reference, the definition of an insurance contract might have captured any prepaid contract to provide services whose cost is uncertain (see paragraphs BC74–BC76 for further discussion). This would have extended the meaning of the term 'insurance contract' too far beyond its traditional meaning.

BC28 Some respondents to ED 5 were opposed to including the notion of insurable interest, on the following grounds:

(a) In life insurance, there is no direct link between the adverse event and the financial loss to the policyholder. Moreover, it is not clear that survival adversely affects an annuitant. Any contract that is contingent on human life should meet the definition of insurance contract.

(b) This notion excludes some contracts that are, in substance, used as insurance, such as weather derivatives (see paragraphs BC55–BC60 for further discussion). The test should be whether there is a reasonable expectation of some indemnification to policyholders. A tradable contract could be brought within the scope of IAS 39.

(c) It would be preferable to eliminate the notion of insurable interest and replace it with the notion that insurance is a business that involves assembling risks into a pool that is managed together.

BC29 The Board decided to retain the notion of insurable interest because it gives a principle-based distinction, particularly between insurance contracts and other contracts that happen to be used for hedging. Furthermore, it is preferable to base a distinction on the type of contract, rather than the way an entity manages a contract or group of contracts. Moreover, the Board decided that it was unnecessary to refine this notion for a life insurance contract or life-contingent annuity, because such contracts typically provide for a predetermined amount to quantify the adverse effect (see paragraph B13 of the IFRS).

Quantity of insurance risk

BC30 Paragraphs B22–B28 of Appendix B of the IFRS discuss how much insurance risk must be present before a contract qualifies as an insurance contract. In developing this material, the Board noted the conditions in US GAAP for a contract to be treated as an insurance contract. SFAS 113 requires two conditions for a contract to be eligible for reinsurance accounting, rather than deposit accounting:

(a) the contract transfers significant insurance risk from the cedant to the reinsurer (which does not occur if the probability of a significant variation in either the amount or timing of payments by the reinsurer is remote); and

(b) either:

  (i) there is a reasonable possibility that the reinsurer will suffer a significant loss (based on the present value of all cash flows between the ceding and assuming enterprises under reasonably possible outcomes); or

  (ii) the reinsurer has assumed substantially all of the insurance risk relating to the reinsured portions of the underlying insurance contracts (and the cedant has retained only insignificant insurance risk on the reinsured portions).

BC31 Under paragraph 8 of SFAS 97 *Accounting and Reporting by Insurance Enterprises for Certain Long-Duration Contracts and for Realized Gains and Losses from the Sale of Investments*, an annuity contract is considered an insurance contract unless (a) the probability that life contingent payments will be made is remote* or (b) the present value of the expected life-contingent payments relative to the present value of all expected payments under the contract is insignificant.

BC32 The Board noted that some practitioners use the following guideline in applying US GAAP: a reasonable possibility of a significant loss is a 10 per cent probability of a 10 per cent loss. In this light, the Board considered whether it should define the amount of insurance risk in quantitative terms in relation to, for example:

(a) the probability that payments under the contract will exceed the expected (ie probability-weighted average) level of payments; or

(b) a measure of the range of outcomes, such as the range between the highest and lowest level of payments or the standard deviation of payments.

BC33 Quantitative guidance creates an arbitrary dividing line that results in different accounting treatments for similar transactions that fall marginally on different sides of the line. It also creates opportunities for accounting arbitrage by encouraging transactions that fall marginally on one side or the other of the line. For these reasons, the IFRS does not include quantitative guidance.

BC34 The Board also considered whether it should define the significance of insurance risk by referring to materiality, which the *Framework* describes as follows. 'Information is material if its omission or misstatement could influence the economic decisions of users taken on the basis of the financial statements.' However, a single contract, or even a single book of similar contracts, could rarely generate a loss that is material in relation to the financial statements as a whole. Therefore, the IFRS defines the significance of insurance risk in relation to the individual contract (paragraph B25). The Board had two reasons for this:

* Paragraph 8 of SFAS 97 notes that the term remote is defined in paragraph 3 of SFAS 5 *Accounting for Contingencies* as 'the chance of the future event or events occurring is slight.'

(a) Although insurers manage contracts on a portfolio basis, and often measure them on that basis, the contractual rights and obligations arise from individual contracts.

(b) An assessment contract by contract is likely to increase the proportion of contracts that qualify as insurance contracts. If a relatively homogeneous book of contracts is known to consist of contracts that all transfer insurance risk, the Board did not intend to require insurers to examine each contract within that book to identify a few non-derivative contracts that transfer insignificant insurance risk (paragraph B25 of the IFRS). The Board intended to make it easier, not harder, for a contract to meet the definition.

BC35 The Board also rejected the notion of defining the significance of insurance risk by expressing the expected (ie probability-weighted) average of the present values of the adverse outcomes as a proportion of the expected present value of all outcomes, or as a proportion of the premium. This notion had some intuitive appeal because it would consider both amount and probability. However, it would have meant that a contract could start as an investment contract (ie a financial liability) and become an insurance contract as time passes or probabilities are reassessed. In the Board's view, requiring continuous monitoring over the life of the contract would be too onerous. Instead, the Board adopted an approach that requires this decision to be made once only, at the inception of a contract. The guidance in paragraphs B22–B28 of the IFRS focuses on whether insured events could cause an insurer to pay additional amounts, judged contract by contract.

BC36 Some respondents objected to ED 5's proposal that insurance risk would be significant if a single plausible event could cause a loss that is more than trivial. They suggested that such a broad notion of significant insurance risk might permit abuse. Instead, they suggested referring to a reasonable possibility of a significant loss. However, the Board rejected this suggestion because it would have required insurers to monitor the level of insurance risk continually, which could have given rise to frequent reclassifications. It might also have been too difficult to apply this notion to remote catastrophic scenarios; indeed, some respondents asked the Board to clarify whether the assessment should include such scenarios. In finalising the IFRS, the Board clarified the terminology by (a) replacing the notion of a plausible scenario with an explanation of the need to ignore scenarios that have no commercial substance and (b) replacing the term 'trivial' with the term 'insignificant'.

BC37 Some respondents asked the Board to clarify the basis of comparison for the significance test, because of uncertainty about the meaning of the phrase 'net cash flows arising from the contract' in ED 5. Some suggested that this would require a comparison with the profit that the issuer expects from the contract. However, the Board had not intended this reading, which would have led to the absurd conclusion that any contract with a profitability of close to zero might qualify as an insurance contract. In finalising the IFRS, the Board confirmed in paragraphs B22–B28 that:

(a) the comparison is between the amounts payable if an insured event occurs and the amounts payable if no insured event occurs. Implementation

Guidance in IG Example 1.3 addresses a contract in which the death benefit in a unit-linked contract is 101 per cent of the unit value.

(b) surrender charges that might be waived on death are not relevant in assessing how much insurance risk a contract transfers because their waiver does not compensate the policyholder for a pre-existing risk. Implementation Guidance in IG Examples 1.23 and 1.24 is relevant.

Expiry of insurance-contingent rights and obligations

BC38 Some respondents suggested that a contract should no longer be treated as an insurance contract after all insurance-contingent rights and obligations have expired. However, this suggestion could have required insurers to set up new systems to identify these contracts. Therefore, paragraph B30 states that an insurance contract remains an insurance contract until all rights and obligations expire. IG Example 2.19 in the Implementation Guidance addresses dual-trigger contracts.

BC39 Some respondents suggested that a contract should not be regarded as an insurance contract if the insurance-contingent rights and obligations expire after a very short time. The IFRS includes material that may be relevant: paragraph B23 explains the need to ignore scenarios that lack commercial substance and paragraph B24(b) notes that there is no significant transfer of pre-existing risk in some contracts that waive surrender penalties on death.

Unbundling

BC40 The definition of an insurance contact distinguishes insurance contracts within the scope of the IFRS from investments and deposits within the scope of IAS 39. However, many insurance contracts contain a significant deposit component (ie a component that would, if it were a separate instrument, be within the scope of IAS 39). Indeed, virtually all insurance contracts have an implicit or explicit deposit component, because the policyholder is generally required to pay premiums before the period of risk; therefore, the time value of money is likely to be one factor that insurers consider in pricing contracts.

BC41 To reduce the need for guidance on the definition of an insurance contract, some argue that an insurer should 'unbundle' the deposit component from the insurance component. Unbundling has the following consequences:

(a) The insurance component is measured as an insurance contract.

(b) The deposit component is measured under IAS 39 at either amortised cost or fair value. This might not be consistent with the basis used for insurance contracts.

(c) Premium receipts for the deposit component are recognised not as revenue, but rather as changes in the deposit liability. Premium receipts for the insurance element are typically recognised as revenue.

(d) A portion of the transaction costs incurred at inception is allocated to the deposit component if this allocation has a material effect.

BC42 Supporters of unbundling deposit components argue that:

(a) an entity should account in the same way for the deposit component of an insurance contract as for an otherwise identical financial instrument that does not transfer significant insurance risk.

(b) the tendency in some countries for banks to own insurers (and vice versa) and the similarity of products offered by the insurance and fund management sectors suggest that insurers, banks and fund managers should account for the deposit component in a similar manner.

(c) many groups sell products ranging from pure investments to pure insurance, with all variations in between. Unbundling would avoid sharp discontinuities in the accounting between a product that transfers just enough insurance risk to be an insurance contract, and another product that falls marginally on the other side of the line.

(d) financial statements should make a clear distinction between premium revenue derived from products that transfer significant insurance risk and premium receipts that are, in substance, investment or deposit receipts.

BC43 The Issues Paper published in 1999 proposed that the deposit component should be unbundled if it is either disclosed explicitly to the policyholder or clearly identifiable from the terms of the contract. However, commentators on the Issues Paper generally opposed unbundling, giving the following reasons:

(a) The components are closely interrelated and the value of the bundled product is not necessarily equal to the sum of the individual values of the components.

(b) Unbundling would require significant and costly systems changes.

(c) Contracts of this kind are a single product, regulated as insurance business by insurance supervisors and should be treated in a similar way for financial reporting.

(d) Some users of financial statements would prefer that either all products are unbundled or no products are unbundled, because they regard information about gross premium inflows as important. A consistent use of a single measurement basis might be more useful as an aid to economic decisions than mixing one measurement basis for the deposit component with another measurement basis for the insurance component.

BC44 In the light of these arguments, the DSOP proposed that an insurer or policyholder should not unbundle these components. However, that was against the background of an assumption that the treatments of the two components would be reasonably similar. This may not be the case in phase I, because phase I permits a wide range of accounting treatments for insurance components. Nevertheless, the Board did not wish to require costly changes in phase I that might be reversed in phase II. Therefore, the Board decided to require unbundling only when it is easiest to perform and the effect is likely to be greatest (paragraphs 10–12 of the IFRS and IG Example 3 in the Implementation Guidance).

BC45 The Board acknowledges that there is no clear conceptual line between the cases when unbundling is required and the cases when unbundling is not required.

At one extreme, the Board regards unbundling as appropriate for large customised contracts, such as some financial reinsurance contracts, if a failure to unbundle them could lead to the complete omission from the balance sheet of material contractual rights and obligations. This may be especially important if a contract was deliberately structured to achieve a specific accounting result. Furthermore, the practical problems cited in paragraph BC43 are much less significant for these contracts.

BC46 At the other extreme, unbundling the surrender values in a large portfolio of traditional life insurance contracts would require significant systems changes beyond the intended scope of phase I. Furthermore, failing to unbundle these contracts would affect the measurement of these liabilities, but not lead to their complete omission from the insurer's balance sheet. In addition, a desire to achieve a particular accounting result is much less likely to influence the precise structure of these transactions.

BC47 The option for the policyholder to surrender a traditional life insurance contract at an amount that differs significantly from its carrying amount is an embedded derivative and IAS 39 would require the insurer to separate it and measure it at fair value. That treatment would have the same disadvantages, described in the previous paragraph, as unbundling the surrender value. Therefore, paragraph 8 of the IFRS exempts an insurer from applying this requirement to some surrender options embedded in insurance contracts. However, the Board saw no conceptual or practical reason to create such an exemption for surrender options in non-insurance financial instruments issued by insurers or by others.

BC48 Some respondents opposed unbundling in phase I on the following grounds, in addition to the reasons given in paragraph BC43:

(a) Insurance contracts are, in general, designed, priced and managed as packages of benefits. Furthermore, the insurer cannot unilaterally terminate the agreement or sell parts of it. In consequence, any unbundling required solely for accounting would be artificial. Insurance contracts should not be unbundled unless the structure of the contract is clearly artificial.

(b) Unbundling may require extensive systems changes that would increase the administrative burden for 2005 and not be needed for phase II.

(c) There would be no need to require unbundling if the Board strengthened the liability adequacy test, defined significant insurance risk more narrowly and confirmed that contracts combined artificially are separate contracts.

(d) The unbundling conditions in ED 5 were vague and did not explain the underlying principle.

(e) Because ED 5 did not propose recognition criteria, insurers would use local GAAP to judge whether assets and liabilities were omitted. This would defeat the stated reason for unbundling.

(f) If a contract is unbundled, the premium for the deposit component is recognised not as premium revenue but as a balance sheet movement (ie as a deposit receipt). Requiring this would be premature before the Board completes its project on reporting comprehensive income.

BC49 Some suggested other criteria for unbundling:

(a) All contracts should be unbundled, or unbundling should always be permitted at least. Unbundling is required in Australia and New Zealand.

(b) All non-insurance components (for example, service components) should be unbundled, not only deposit components.

(c) Unbundling should be required only when the components are completely separable, or when there is an account in the name of the policyholder.

(d) Unbundling could affect the presentation of revenue more than it affects liability recognition. Therefore, unbundling should also be required if it would have a significant effect on reported revenue and is easy to perform.

BC50 Some respondents argued that the test for unbundling should be two-sided (ie the cash flows of the insurance component and the investment component do not interact) rather than the one-sided test proposed in ED 5 (ie the cash flows from the insurance component do not affect the cash flows from the deposit component). Here is an example where this might make a difference: in some life insurance contracts, the death benefit is the difference between (a) a fixed amount and (b) the value of a deposit component (for example, a unit-linked investment). The deposit component can be measured independently, but the death benefit depends on the unit value so the insurance component cannot be measured independently.

BC51 The Board decided that phase I should not require insurers to set up systems to unbundle the products described in the previous paragraph. However, the Board decided to rely on the condition that provides an exemption from unbundling if all the rights and obligations under the deposit component are recognised. If this condition is not met, unbundling is appropriate.

BC52 Some argued that it is irrelevant whether the insurance component affects the deposit component. They suggested that a deposit component exists if the policyholder will receive a minimum fixed amount of future cash flows in the form of either a return of premium (if no insured event occurs) or an insurance recovery (if an insured event occurs). However, the Board noted that this focus on a single cash flow would not result in unbundling if a financial instrument and an insurance contract are combined artificially into a single contract and the cash flows from one component offset cash flows from the other component. The Board regarded that result as inappropriate and open to abuse.

BC53 In summary, the Board retained the approach broadly as in ED 5. This requires unbundling if that is needed to ensure the recognition of rights and obligations arising from the deposit component and those rights and obligations can be measured separately. If only the second of these conditions is met, the IFRS permits unbundling, but does not require it.

BC54 Some respondents suggested that if a contract has been artificially separated through the use of side letters, the separate components of the contract should be considered together. The Board did not address this because it is a wider issue for the Board's possible future work on linkage (ie accounting for separate transactions that are connected in some way). The footnote to paragraph B25 refers to simultaneous contracts with the same counterparty.

Weather derivatives

BC55 The scope of IAS 39 previously excluded contracts that require a payment based on climatic, geological, or other physical variables (if based on climatic variables, sometimes described as weather derivatives). It is convenient to divide these contracts into two categories:

(a) contracts that require a payment only if a particular level of the underlying climatic, geological, or other physical variables adversely affects the contract holder. These are insurance contracts as defined in the IFRS.

(b) contracts that require a payment based on a specified level of the underlying variable regardless of whether there is an adverse effect on the contract holder. These are derivatives and the IFRS removes a previous scope exclusion to bring them within the scope of IAS 39.

BC56 The previous scope exclusion was created mainly because the holder might use such a derivative in a way that resembles the use of an insurance contract. However, the definition of an insurance contract in the IFRS now provides a principled basis for deciding which of these contracts are treated as insurance contracts and which are treated as derivatives. Therefore, the Board removed the scope exclusion from IAS 39 (see paragraph C3 of Appendix C of the IFRS). Such contracts are within the scope of the IFRS if payment is contingent on changes in a physical variable that is specific to a party to the contract, and within the scope of IAS 39 in all other cases.

BC57 Some respondents suggested that a weather derivative should be treated as:

(a) an insurance contract if it is expected to be highly effective in mitigating an existing risk exposure.

(b) a derivative financial instrument otherwise.

BC58 Some argued that some weather derivatives are, in substance, insurance contracts. For example, under some contracts, the policyholder can claim a fixed sum based on rainfall levels at the nearest weather station. The contract was purchased to provide insurance against low rainfall but was structured like this because of difficulties in measuring actual loss suffered and because of the moral hazard of having a rainfall gauge on the policyholder's property. It can reasonably be expected that the rainfall at the nearest weather station will affect the holder, but the physical variable specified in the contract (ie rainfall) is not specific to a party to the contract. Similarly, some insurers use weather derivatives as a hedge against insurance contracts they issue and view them as similar to reinsurance.

BC59 Some suggested that weather derivatives should be excluded from the scope of the IFRS because they are tradable instruments that behave like other derivatives and have an observable market value, rather than because there is no contractual link between the holder and the event that triggers payment.

BC60 The IFRS distinguishes an insurance contract (in which an adverse effect on the policyholder is a contractual precondition for payment) from other instruments, such as derivatives and weather derivatives (in which an adverse effect is not a contractual precondition for payment, although the counterparty may, in fact, use the instrument to hedge an existing exposure). In the Board's view, this is an important and useful distinction. It is much easier to base a classification on the terms of the contract than on an assessment of the counterparty's motive (ie hedging or trading). Consequently, the Board made no change to ED 5's proposals for the treatment of weather derivatives.

Scope exclusions

BC61 The scope of the IFRS excludes various items that may meet the definition of insurance contracts, but are, or will be, covered by existing or proposed future IFRSs (paragraph 4). The following paragraphs discuss:

(a) financial guarantees and insurance against credit risk (paragraphs BC62–BC68);

(b) product warranties (paragraphs BC69–BC72);

(c) accounting by policyholders (paragraph BC73); and

(d) prepaid service contracts (paragraphs BC74–BC76).

Financial guarantees and insurance against credit risk

BC62 Some contracts require specified payments to reimburse the holder for a loss it incurs if a specified debtor fails to make payment when due under the original or modified terms of a debt instrument. If the resulting risk transfer is significant, these contracts meet the definition of an insurance contract. Some of these contracts have the legal form of an insurance contract and others have the legal form of a financial guarantee or letter of credit. In the Board's view, although this difference in legal form may be associated in some cases with differences in substance, the same accounting requirements should, in principle, apply to all contracts with similar substance.

BC63 Some took the view that the scope of IAS 39 should include all contracts that provide cover against credit risk, on the following grounds:

(a) Although credit insurers manage credit risk by pooling individual risk within a portfolio, banks also do this in managing the credit risk in a portfolio of financial guarantees. Although banks may rely more on collateral, this is no reason to require a different accounting treatment.

(b) Banks manage credit risk embedded in their financial assets, and there is no reason to require them to apply a different standard to credit risk embedded in financial guarantees.

(c) Credit risk is commonly traded in capital markets, even if the specific forms of credit risk embedded in some forms of credit insurance are not traded.

(d) As noted above, some financial guarantees were already within the scope of IAS 39. To ensure consistent reporting, the scope of IAS 39 should include all contracts that provide protection against similar exposures.

BC64 Some argued that insurance against credit risk is different from a financial guarantee and should be within the scope of IFRS 4, on the following grounds:

(a) Insurance against credit risk is often arranged by the seller of goods and protects the seller against default by the buyer. The fact that default is generally outside the control of the seller, and so is fortuitous, allows the use of stochastic methods to estimate future cash flows arising from the contract, because they are random and not subject to moral hazard. By contrast, some financial guarantees, such as some letters of credit, are arranged at the request of the party whose obligation is being guaranteed. Default on such guarantees is partly under the control of that party.

(b) Insurance against credit risk is part of an insurer's overall insurance activity, and is managed as part of a diversified portfolio in the same way as other insurance activities.

(c) A credit insurer may refuse to pay a claim if the policyholder did not give full disclosure and may delay payment while a claim is investigated, whereas a guarantor is often required to pay on first notice of a default.

(d) A credit insurer faces risks similar to those arising in some other insurance contracts. For example, a contract may require payments (either to the debtor or to the creditor) if a debtor's income is reduced by specified adverse events such as unemployment or illness, regardless of whether the debtor continues to make loan payments when due. The issuer of this contract may face risks similar to those faced by a guarantor of the loan.

(e) Including these contracts within the scope of IAS 39 would compel credit insurers to change their accounting immediately, unlike issuers of other types of insurance contract. Furthermore, some credit insurance contracts contain features, such as cancellation and renewal rights and profit-sharing features, that the Board will not resolve until phase II.

BC65 When the Board developed ED 5, the following contracts were already within the scope of IAS 39 and the Board concluded that they should remain so:

(a) a financial guarantee given or retained by a transferor when it derecognises financial assets or financial liabilities. In general, IAS 39 prevents the derecognition of the transferred asset or liability when such a guarantee exists.

(b) a financial guarantee that does not meet the definition of an insurance contract.

BC66 Other financial guarantees were within the scope of IAS 37 *Provisions, Contingent Liabilities and Contingent Assets*. In June 2002, an Exposure Draft of amendments to IAS 39 proposed that IAS 39 should deal with all financial guarantees at initial recognition, but that the subsequent measurement of some financial guarantees should remain within the scope of IAS 37. In finalising the revision of IAS 39, issued in December 2003, the Board decided that the issuer of the financial guarantees described in paragraph BC62 (ie those that meet the definition of an insurance contract) should initially recognise them at fair value, and subsequently measure them at the higher of (a) the amount recognised under IAS 37 and (b) the amount initially recognised less, where appropriate, cumulative amortisation recognised in accordance with IAS 18 *Revenue*.

BC67 In finalising IFRS 4, the Board reached the following conclusions:

(a) Financial guarantees can have various legal forms, such as that of a financial guarantee, letter of credit, credit default contract or insurance contract. The accounting should not depend on their legal form.

(b) A financial guarantee contract should be within the scope of IAS 39 if it is not an insurance contract, as defined in IFRS 4. A financial guarantee qualifies as an insurance contract if it requires the issuer to make specified payments to reimburse the holder for a loss it incurs because a specified debtor fails to make payment when due under the original or modified terms of a debt instrument, provided that the resulting risk transfer is significant.

(c) If an insurance contract is a financial guarantee contract incurred or retained on transferring to another party financial assets or financial liabilities within the scope of IAS 39, the issuer should apply IAS 39 to that contract (even though the contract is an insurance contract, as defined).

(d) Unless (c) applies, the measurement described in the last sentence of paragraph BC66 is appropriate for a financial guarantee contract that meets the definition of an insurance contract. However, the Board acknowledged the need to expose this conclusion for comment. Mindful of the need to develop a 'stable platform' of Standards for 2005, the Board decided to finalise IFRS 4 without specifying the accounting for these contracts and to develop an Exposure Draft on this topic. In the meantime, the liability adequacy test in paragraphs 15–19 may be particularly relevant if the insurer's accounting policies would not otherwise require it to recognise a liability at the inception of the contract.

(e) ED 5 proposed that guarantees incurred or retained on derecognition of a non-financial asset or non-financial liability should be treated in the same way as guarantees incurred or retained on derecognition of a financial asset or financial liability. However, no respondents commented on the substance of this proposal and entities responding to ED 5 were not the entities most likely to be affected by this proposal. Therefore, the Board decided to delete the proposal in finalising IFRS 4. It follows that financial guarantees incurred or retained on the transfer of a non-financial asset:

   (i) are within the scope of IFRS 4 if they meet the definition of an insurance contract (pending amendments from the Exposure Draft discussed in (d)). Among other things, this means that the guarantee given is subject to the liability adequacy test described in paragraphs 15–19 of the IFRS.

   (ii) are not recognised separately if they prevent the derecognition of a non-financial asset, for example if they mean that the transfer does not meet the revenue recognition criteria in IAS 18. In such case, the proceeds received are typically recognised as a liability.

   (iii) otherwise, are within the scope of IAS 39.

BC68 Some respondents asked the Board to give specific guidance on accounting for financial guarantees received. However, the Board decided that this would not be appropriate. For contracts classified as insurance contracts, the beneficiary of the guarantee is a policyholder; policyholder accounting is beyond the scope of IFRS 4.

For contracts within the scope of IAS 39, the beneficiary applies IAS 39; the application of IAS 39 to other contracts is beyond the scope of this project.

Product warranties

BC69 A product warranty clearly meets the definition of an insurance contract if an entity issues it on behalf of another party (such as a manufacturer, dealer or retailer). The scope of the IFRS includes such warranties.

BC70 A product warranty issued directly by a manufacturer, dealer or retailer also meets the definition of an insurance contract. Although some might think of this as 'self-insurance', the risk retained arises from existing contractual obligations towards the customer. Some may reason that the definition of insurance contracts should exclude such direct warranties because they do not involve a transfer of risk from buyer to seller, but rather a crystallisation of an existing responsibility. However, in the Board's view, excluding these warranties from the definition of insurance contracts would complicate the definition for only marginal benefit.

BC71 Although such direct warranties create economic exposures similar to warranties issued on behalf of the manufacturer, dealer or retailer by another party (ie the insurer), the scope of the IFRS excludes them because they are closely related to the underlying sale of goods and because IAS 37 addresses product warranties. IAS 18 deals with the revenue received for such warranties.

BC72 In a separate project, the Board is exploring an asset and liability approach to revenue recognition. If this approach is implemented, the accounting model for these direct product warranties may change.

Accounting by policyholders

BC73 The IFRS does not address accounting and disclosure by policyholders for direct insurance contracts because the Board does not regard this as a high priority for phase I. The Board intends to address accounting by policyholders in phase II (see IASB *Update* February 2002 for the Board's discussion of accounting by policyholders). IFRSs address some aspects of accounting by policyholders for insurance contracts:

(a) IAS 37 addresses accounting for reimbursements from insurers for expenditure required to settle a provision.

(b) IAS 16 addresses some aspects of compensation from third parties for property, plant and equipment that was impaired, lost or given up.

(c) Because policyholder accounting is outside the scope of the IFRS, the hierarchy of criteria in paragraphs 10–12 of IAS 8 *Accounting Policies, Changes in Accounting Estimates and Errors* applies to policyholder accounting (see paragraphs BC77–BC86).

(d) A policyholder's rights and obligations under insurance contracts are outside the scope of IAS 32 and IAS 39.

Prepaid service contracts

BC74 Some respondents noted that the definition proposed in ED 5 captured some prepaid contracts to provide services whose cost is uncertain. Because these contracts are not normally regarded as insurance contracts, these respondents suggested that the Board should change the definition or exclude these contracts from the scope of the IFRS. Respondents cited two specific examples.

(a) Fixed fee service contracts if the level of service depends on an uncertain event, for example maintenance contracts if the service provider agrees to repair specified equipment after a malfunction. The fixed service fee is based on the expected number of malfunctions, although it is uncertain that the machines will actually break down. The malfunction of the equipment adversely affects its owner and the contract compensates the owner (in kind, rather than cash).

(b) Some car breakdown assistance if (i) each breakdown has little incremental cost because employed patrols provide most of the assistance, (ii) the motorist pays for all parts and repairs, (iii) the service provider's only responsibility is to take the car to a specified destination (eg the nearest garage, home or the original destination), (iv) the need to provide assistance (and the related cost) is known within hours and (v) the number of call-outs is limited.

BC75 The Board saw no conceptual reason to change either the definition of insurance contracts or the scope of the IFRS in the light of the two examples cited by respondents. Paragraphs B6 and B7 of the IFRS note that complying with the IFRS in phase I is unlikely to be particularly burdensome in these two examples, for materiality reasons. The Board may need to review this conclusion in phase II.

BC76 Some respondents argued that the proposals in ED 5 were directed primarily at entities that are generally regarded as insurers. They suggested that the Board should not impose these proposals on entities that have a relatively small amount of a given transaction type. The Board concluded that these comments were primarily about materiality. IAS 1 *Presentation of Financial Statements* and IAS 8 address materiality and the Board decided that no further guidance or specific exemption was needed in this case.

Temporary exemption from some other IFRSs

BC77 Paragraphs 10–12 of IAS 8 specify a hierarchy of criteria that an entity should use in developing an accounting policy if no IFRS applies specifically to an item. Without changes made in the IFRS, an insurer adopting IFRSs in 2005 would have needed to assess whether its accounting policies for insurance contracts comply with these requirements. In the absence of guidance, there might have been uncertainty about what would be acceptable. Establishing what would be acceptable could have been costly and some insurers might have made major changes in 2005 followed by further significant changes in phase II.

BC78 To avoid unnecessary disruption for both users and preparers in phase I that would not have eased the transition to phase II, the Board decided to limit the need for insurers to change their existing accounting policies for insurance contracts. The Board did this by the following measures:

(a) creating a temporary exemption from the hierarchy in IAS 8 that specifies the criteria an entity uses in developing an accounting policy if no IFRS applies specifically to an item. The exemption applies to insurers, but not to policyholders.

(b) limiting the impact of that exemption from the hierarchy by five specific requirements (relating to catastrophe provisions, liability adequacy, derecognition, offsetting and impairment of reinsurance assets, see paragraphs BC87–BC114).

(c) permitting some existing practices to continue but prohibiting their introduction (paragraphs BC123–BC146).

BC79 Some respondents opposed the exemption from the hierarchy on the grounds that it would permit too much diversity and allow fundamental departures from the *Framework* that could prevent an insurer's financial statements from presenting information that is understandable, relevant, reliable and comparable. The Board did not grant the exemption from the hierarchy in IAS 8 lightly, but took this unusual step to minimise disruption in 2005 for both users (eg lack of continuity of trend data) and preparers (eg systems changes).

BC80 ED 6 *Exploration for and Evaluation of Mineral Resources* proposes a temporary exemption from paragraphs 11 and 12 of IAS 8 (ie sources of guidance), but not from paragraph 10 (ie relevance and reliability). That proposed exemption is narrower than in IFRS 4 because ED 6 leaves a relatively narrow range of issues unaddressed. In contrast, because IFRS 4 leaves many significant aspects of accounting for insurance contracts until phase II, a requirement to apply paragraph 10 of IAS 8 to insurance contracts would have had much more pervasive effects and insurers would have needed to address matters such as completeness, substance over form and neutrality.

BC81 Some suggested that the Board should specifically require an insurer to follow its national accounting requirements (national GAAP) in accounting for insurance contracts during phase I, to prevent selection of accounting policies that do not form a comprehensive basis of accounting to achieve a predetermined result ('cherry-picking'). However, defining national GAAP would have posed problems. Further definitional problems could have arisen because some insurers do not apply the national GAAP of their own country. For example, some non-US insurers with a US listing apply US GAAP. Moreover, it is unusual and, arguably, beyond the Board's mandate to impose requirements set by another body.

BC82 In addition, an insurer might wish to improve its accounting policies to reflect other accounting developments with no counterpart in national GAAP. For example, an insurer adopting IFRSs for the first time might wish to amend its accounting policies for insurance contracts for greater consistency with accounting policies that it uses for contracts within the scope of IAS 39. Similarly, an insurer might wish to improve its accounting for embedded options and guarantees by addressing both their time value and their intrinsic value, even if no similar improvements are made to its national GAAP.

BC83 Therefore, the Board decided that an insurer could continue to follow the accounting policies that it was using when it first applied the phase I requirements, with some exceptions noted below. An insurer could also improve those accounting policies if specified criteria are met (see paragraphs 21–30 of the IFRS).

BC84 The criteria in paragraphs 10–12 of IAS 8 include relevance and reliability. Granting an exemption from those criteria, even temporarily, is a highly unusual step. The Board was prepared to contemplate that step only as part of an orderly and relatively fast transition to phase II. Because the exemption is so exceptional, ED 5 proposed that it would apply only for accounting periods beginning before 1 January 2007. Some described this time limit as a 'sunset clause'.

BC85 Many respondents opposed the sunset clause. They argued the following:

(a) If the exemption expired in 2007 before phase II is in force, there would be considerable confusion, disruption and cost for both users and preparers. It would not be appropriate to penalise users and preparers if the Board does not complete phase II on time.

(b) The sunset clause might be perceived as putting pressure on the Board to complete phase II without adequate consultation, investigation and testing.

The Board accepted the validity of these objections to the sunset clause and deleted it.

BC86 The Board decided to maintain some requirements that follow from the criteria in IAS 8. The Board acknowledges that it is difficult to make piecemeal changes to recognition and measurement practices in phase I because many aspects of accounting for insurance contracts are interrelated with aspects that will not be completed until phase II. However, abandoning these particular requirements would detract from the relevance and reliability of an insurer's financial statements to an unacceptable degree. Moreover, these requirements are not interrelated to a great extent with other aspects of recognition and measurement and the Board does not expect phase II to reverse these requirements. The following points are discussed below:

(a) catastrophe and equalisation provisions (paragraphs BC87–BC93)

(b) liability adequacy (paragraphs BC94–BC104)

(c) derecognition (paragraph BC105)

(d) offsetting (paragraph BC106)

(e) impairment of reinsurance assets (paragraphs BC107–BC114).

Catastrophe and equalisation provisions

BC87 Some insurance contracts expose the insurer to infrequent but severe catastrophic losses caused by events such as damage to nuclear installations or satellites or earthquake damage. Some jurisdictions permit or require catastrophe provisions for contracts of this type. The catastrophe provisions are generally built up gradually over the years out of the premiums received, usually following a prescribed formula, until a specified limit is reached. They are intended to be used on the occurrence of a future catastrophic loss that is covered by current or future contracts of this type. Some countries also permit or require equalisation provisions to cover random fluctuations of claim expenses around the expected value of claims for some types of insurance contract (eg hail, credit, guarantee and fidelity insurance) using a formula based on experience over a number of years.

BC88 Those who favour recognising catastrophe or equalisation provisions as liabilities base their view on one or more of the following arguments:

(a) Such provisions represent a deferral of unearned premiums that are designed to provide for events that are not expected, on average, to occur in any single contract period but are expected to occur over an entire cycle of several contract periods. Although contracts cover only one period in form, in substance contracts are commonly renewed, leading to pooling of risks over time rather than within a single period. Indeed, some jurisdictions make it difficult for an insurer to stop offering insurance against some forms of risk, such as hurricanes.

(b) In some jurisdictions, an insurer is required to segregate part of the premium (the catastrophe premium). The catastrophe premium is not available for distribution to shareholders (except on liquidation) and, if the insurer transfers the contract to another insurer, it must also transfer the catastrophe premium.

(c) In years when no catastrophe occurs (or when claims are abnormally low), such provisions portray an insurer's long-term profitability faithfully because they match the insurer's costs and revenue over the long term. Also, they show a pattern of profit similar to one obtained through reinsurance, but with less cost and administrative burden.

(d) Such provisions enhance solvency protection by restricting the amounts distributed to shareholders and by restricting a weak company's ability to expand or enter new markets.

(e) Such provisions encourage insurers to accept risks that they might otherwise decline. Some countries reinforce this encouragement with tax deductions.

BC89 For the following reasons, the IFRS prohibits the recognition as a liability of provisions for possible future claims under contracts that are not in existence at the reporting date (such as catastrophe and equalisation provisions):

(a) Such provisions are not liabilities as defined in the *Framework*, because the insurer has no present obligation for losses that will occur after the end of the current contract period. As the *Framework* states, the matching concept does not allow the recognition of items in the balance sheet that do not meet the definition of assets or liabilities. Recognising deferred credits as if they were liabilities would diminish the relevance and reliability of an insurer's financial statements.

(b) Even if the insurance law requires an insurer to segregate catastrophe premiums so that they are not available for distribution to shareholders in any circumstances, earnings on those segregated premiums will ultimately be available to shareholders. Therefore, those segregated amounts are appropriately classified as equity, not as a liability.

(c) Recognising such provisions obscures users' ability to examine the impact of past catastrophes and does not contribute to their analysis of an insurer's exposure to future catastrophes. Given adequate disclosure, knowledgeable users understand that some types of insurance expose an insurer to infrequent but severe losses. Moreover, the analogy with reinsurance contracts is irrelevant, because reinsurance actually changes the insurer's risk profile.

(d) The objective of general purpose financial statements is not to enhance solvency but to provide information that is useful to a wide range of users for economic decisions. Moreover, the recognition of provisions does not, by itself, enhance solvency. However, if the objective of financial statements were to enhance solvency and such provisions were an appropriate means of enhancing solvency, it would follow that the insurer should recognise the entire provision immediately, rather than accumulating it over time. Furthermore, if catastrophes (or unusual experience) in one period are independent of those in other periods, the insurer should not reduce the liability when a catastrophe (or unusually bad experience) occurs. Also, if diversification over time were a valid basis for accounting, above-average losses in early years should be recognised as assets, yet proponents of catastrophe and equalisation provisions do not advocate this.

(e) Recognising catastrophe or equalisation provisions is not the only way to limit distributions to shareholders. Other measures, such as solvency margin requirements and risk-based capital requirements, could play an important role. Another possibility is for an insurer to segregate a portion of its equity for retention to meet possible losses in future years.

(f) The objective of general purpose financial statements is not to encourage or discourage particular transactions or activities, but to report neutral information about transactions and activities. Therefore, accounting requirements should not try to encourage insurers to accept or decline particular types of risks.

(g) If an insurer expects to continue writing catastrophe cover, presumably it believes that the future business will be profitable. It would not be representationally faithful to recognise a liability for future contracts that are expected to be profitable.

(h) There is no objective way to measure catastrophe and equalisation provisions, unless an arbitrary formula is used.

BC90 Some suggested that it is not appropriate to eliminate catastrophe and equalisation provisions in phase I as a piecemeal amendment to existing approaches. However, the Board concluded that it could prohibit these provisions without undermining other components of existing approaches. There is no credible basis for arguing that catastrophe or equalisation 'provisions' are recognisable liabilities under IFRSs and there is no realistic prospect that the Board will permit them in phase II. Indeed, as noted above, paragraphs 10–12 of IAS 8 require an entity to consider various criteria in developing an accounting policy for an item if no IFRS applies specifically to that item. In the Board's view, if the IFRS had not suspended that requirement, it would clearly have prohibited the recognition of such items as a liability. Accordingly, the IFRS preserves this prohibition (see paragraph 14(a) of the IFRS).

BC91 Some respondents presented additional arguments for permitting the recognition of catastrophe and equalisation provisions as a liability:

(a) Some insurers measure insurance contracts without margins for risk, but instead recognise catastrophe or equalisation provisions. If catastrophe provisions are eliminated in phase I, this change might be partly reversed in phase II if insurers are then required to include margins for risk.

(b) Some insurers regard these provisions as relating partly to existing contracts and partly to future contracts. Splitting these components may be difficult and involve systems changes that might not be needed in phase II.

BC92 For the following reasons, these arguments did not persuade the Board:

(a) Present imperfections in the measurement of recognisable liabilities do not justify the recognition of other items that do not meet the definition of a liability.

(b) Additions to these provisions are often based on a percentage of premium revenue. If the risk period has already expired, that premium does not relate to an existing contractual obligation. If the risk period has not yet fully expired, the related portion of the premium relates to an existing contractual obligation, but most existing models defer all the related premium as unearned premium, so recognising an additional provision would be double-counting (unless the contract were known to be underpriced).

BC93 Accordingly, the Board retained the proposal in ED 5 to eliminate these provisions. However, although the IFRS prohibits their recognition as a liability, it does not prohibit the segregation of a component of equity. Changes in a component of equity are not recognised in profit or loss. IAS 1 requires a statement of changes in equity.

Liability adequacy

BC94 Many existing accounting models have tests to confirm that insurance liabilities are not understated, and that related amounts recognised as assets, such as deferred acquisition costs, are not overstated. The precise form of the test depends on the underlying measurement approach. However, there is no guarantee that these tests exist everywhere and the credibility of IFRSs could suffer if an insurer claims to comply with IFRSs but fails to recognise material and reasonably foreseeable losses arising from existing contractual obligations. To avoid this, the IFRS requires a liability adequacy test* (see paragraphs 15–19).

BC95 The Board's intention was not to introduce piecemeal elements of a parallel measurement model, but to create a mechanism that reduces the possibility that material losses remain unrecognised during phase I. With this in mind, paragraph 16 of the IFRS defines minimum requirements that an insurer's existing test must meet. If the insurer does not apply a test that meets those requirements, it must apply a test specified by the Board. To specify a test on a basis that already exists in IFRSs and minimise the need for exceptions to existing principles, the Board decided to draw on IAS 37.

* ED 5 described this as a 'loss recognition test'.

BC96 The liability adequacy test also applies to deferred acquisition costs and to intangible assets representing the contractual rights acquired in a business combination or portfolio transfer. As a result, when the Board revised IAS 36 *Impairment of Assets* in 2004, it excluded deferred acquisition costs and those intangible assets from the scope of IAS 36.

BC97 The Board considered whether it should retain the impairment model in IAS 36 for deferred acquisition costs, and perhaps also the related insurance liabilities. However, the IAS 36 model cannot be applied to deferred acquisition costs alone, without also considering the cash flows relating to the recognised liability. Indeed, some insurers capitalise acquisition costs implicitly through deductions in the measurement of the liability. Moreover, it would be confusing and difficult to apply this model to liabilities without some re-engineering. In the Board's view, it is simpler to use a model that is designed for liabilities, namely the IAS 37 model. In practice, a re–engineered IAS 36 model and IAS 37 might not lead to very different results.

BC98 Some respondents suggested that the Board should specify that the cash flows considered in a liability adequacy test should include the effect of embedded options and guarantees, such as guaranteed annuity rates. They expressed concerns that many national practices have not required insurers to recognise these exposures, which can be very large.

BC99 Although the Board's objective was not to develop a detailed liability adequacy test, it observed that the size of exposures to embedded guarantees and options and the failings of many national practices in this area warranted specific requirements, even in phase I. Accordingly, the Board decided that the minimum requirements for an existing liability adequacy test should include considering cash flows resulting from embedded options and guarantees. The Board did not specify how those cash flows should be considered but noted that an insurer would consider this matter in developing disclosures of its accounting policies. If an existing liability adequacy test does not meet the minimum requirements, a comparison is made with the measurement that IAS 37 would require. IAS 37 refers to the amount that an entity would rationally pay to settle the obligation or transfer it to a third party. Implicitly, this amount would consider the possible effect of embedded options and guarantees.

BC100 ED 5 did not specify the level of aggregation for the liability adequacy test and some respondents asked the Board to clarify this. Paragraph 18 of the IFRS confirms that the aggregation requirements of the existing liability adequacy test apply if the test meets the minimum requirements specified in paragraph 16 of the IFRS. If that test does not meet those minimum requirements, there is no conceptual justification for offsetting a loss on one contract against an otherwise unrecognisable gain on another contract. However, the Board concluded that a contract-by-contract assessment would impose costs that exceed the likely benefits to users. Therefore, paragraph 18 states that the comparison is made at the level of a portfolio of contracts that are subject to broadly similar risks and managed together as a portfolio. More precise definition would be difficult and is not needed, given the Board's restricted objective of ensuring at least a minimum level of testing for the limited life of phase I.

BC101 It is beyond the scope of phase I to create a detailed accounting regime for insurance contracts. Therefore, the IFRS does not specify:

(a) what criteria determine when existing contracts end and future contracts start.

(b) whether or how the cash flows are discounted to reflect the time value of money or adjusted for risk and uncertainty.

(c) whether the liability adequacy test considers both the time value and the intrinsic value of embedded options and guarantees.

(d) whether additional losses recognised because of the liability adequacy test are recognised by reducing the carrying amount of deferred acquisition costs or by increasing the carrying amount of the related insurance liabilities.

BC102 Some respondents asked the Board to clarify that no formal liability adequacy test is needed if an entity can demonstrate that its method of measuring insurance liabilities means that they are not understated. Paragraph 15 of the IFRS requires an insurer to 'assess whether its recognised insurance liabilities are adequate, using current estimates of future cash flows'. The fundamental point is that future cash flows must be considered in some way, and not merely be assumed to support the existing carrying amount. The IFRS does not specify the precise means of ensuring this, as long as the minimum requirements in paragraph 16 are met.

BC103 Some respondents read the liability adequacy test proposed in ED 5 as requiring fair value measurement as a minimum. That was not the Board's intention. An insurer needs to refer to IAS 37 only if the minimum requirements in paragraph 16 are not met.

BC104 Some respondents noted that many existing liability adequacy tests require measurements that do not include a risk margin. However, IAS 37 requires such a margin. To achieve consistency, these respondents suggested that a liability adequacy test under IAS 37 should also exclude these margins. The Board did not adopt this suggestion. The idea behind using IAS 37 for phase I was to take an existing measurement basis 'off the shelf' rather than create a new model.

Derecognition

BC105 The Board identified no reasons why derecognition requirements for insurance liabilities and insurance assets should differ from those for financial liabilities and financial assets. Therefore, the derecognition requirements for insurance liabilities are the same as for financial liabilities (see paragraph 14(c) of the IFRS). However, because derecognition of financial assets is a controversial topic, the IFRS does not address derecognition of insurance assets.

Offsetting

BC106 A cedant (ie the insurer that is the policyholder under a reinsurance contract) does not normally have a right to offset amounts due from a reinsurer against amounts due to the underlying policyholder. Normal offsetting criteria prohibit offsetting when no such right exists. When these criteria are not met, a gross presentation gives a clearer picture of the cedant's rights and obligations, and related income and expense (see paragraph 14(d) of the IFRS).

Reinsurance assets

Impairment of reinsurance assets

BC107 ED 5 proposed that a cedant should apply IAS 36 *Impairment of Assets* to its reinsurance assets. Respondents opposed this proposal for the following reasons:

(a) This would compel many cedants to change their accounting model for reinsurance contracts in a way that is inconsistent with the accounting for the underlying direct insurance liability.

(b) IAS 36 would require the cedant to address matters that are beyond the scope of phase I for the underlying direct insurance liability, such as the cash flows to be discounted, the discount rate and the approach to risk. Some saw IAS 36 as an indirect way of imposing something similar to a fair value model. There would also have been systems implications.

(c) Reinsurance assets are essentially a form of financial asset and should be subject, for impairment testing, to IAS 39 rather than IAS 36.

BC108 The Board concluded that an impairment test for phase I (a) should focus on credit risk (arising from the risk of default by the reinsurer and also from disputes over coverage) and (b) should not address matters arising from the measurement of the underlying direct insurance liability. The Board decided that the most appropriate way to achieve this was an incurred loss model based on that in IAS 39 (see paragraph 20 of the IFRS).

Gains and losses on buying reinsurance

BC109 The IFRS defines a reinsurance contract as an insurance contract issued by one insurer (the reinsurer) to compensate another insurer (the cedant) for losses on one or more contracts issued by the cedant. One consequence is that the level of insurance risk required to meet the definition of an insurance contract is the same for a reinsurance contract as for a direct insurance contract.

BC110 National accounting requirements often define reinsurance contracts more strictly than direct insurance contracts to avoid distortion through contracts that have the legal form of reinsurance but do not transfer significant insurance risk (sometimes known as financial reinsurance). One source of such distortions is the failure to discount many non-life insurance claims liabilities. If the insurer buys reinsurance, the premium paid to the reinsurer reflects the present value of the liability and is, therefore, less than the previous carrying amount of the liability. Reporting a gain on buying the reinsurance is not representationally faithful if no economic gain occurred at that time. The accounting gain arises largely because of the failure to use discounting for the underlying liability. Similar problems arise if the underlying insurance liability is measured with excessive prudence.

BC111 The Board decided that it would not use the definition of a reinsurance contract to address these problems because the Board found no conceptual reason to define a reinsurance contract more or less strictly than a direct insurance contract. Instead, ED 5 addressed these problems through the following proposals:

(a) prohibiting derecognition if the liability is not extinguished (paragraphs 14(c) of the IFRS and BC105) and prohibiting the offsetting of reinsurance assets against the related direct insurance liabilities (paragraphs 14(d) of the IFRS and BC106).

(b) requiring unbundling in some cases (paragraphs 10–12 of the IFRS, IG Example 3 in the Implementation Guidance and paragraphs BC40–BC54).

(c) limiting the recognition of gains when an insurer buys reinsurance.

BC112 Respondents to ED 5 generally opposed the proposal described in paragraph BC111(c), on the following grounds:

(a) These piecemeal amendments to existing accounting models were beyond the scope of phase I and would require new systems that might not be needed in phase II.

(b) The proposals would have been difficult to apply to more complex reinsurance contracts, including excess of loss contracts and contracts that reinsure different layers of a portfolio of underlying direct insurance contracts.

(c) The proposals would have created inconsistencies with the measurement of the underlying direct insurance contracts.

(d) The artificial gain recognised at inception of some reinsurance contracts mitigates an artificial loss that arose earlier from excessive prudence or lack of discounting. If the net exposure has been reduced by reinsurance, there is no reason to continue to overstate the original liability.

(e) Any deferral of profit on buying reinsurance should be recognised as a liability, not as a reduction in the carrying amount of the reinsurance asset. This would permit assets and liabilities relating to the same underlying insurance contracts to be measured on a consistent basis and would also be consistent with other accounting bases such as US GAAP.

(f) Any restrictions in phase I should be targeted more precisely at financial reinsurance transactions (ie transactions that do not meet the definition of an insurance contract or that have significant financial components) or contracts that provide retroactive cover (ie ones that cover events that have already occurred).

(g) The liability adequacy test and unbundling proposals would have provided sufficient safeguards against the recognition of excessive profits.

BC113 The Board considered limiting the proposed requirements to cases where significant distortions in reported profit were most likely to occur, for example retroactive contracts. However, developing such a distinction would have been time-consuming and difficult, and there would have been no guarantee of success. The Board also considered drawing on requirements in US GAAP but decided not to include detailed requirements of this kind as a temporary and only partly effective solution. The proposals in ED 5 were an attempt to develop a simpler temporary solution. The responses indicated that the proposed solution contained too many imperfections to achieve its purpose.

BC114 The Board decided to delete the proposal in ED 5 and replace it with a specific disclosure requirement for gains and losses that arose on buying reinsurance (see paragraph 37(b) of the IFRS).

Other existing practices

BC115 The IFRS does not address:

(a) acquisition costs (paragraphs BC116–BC119);

(b) salvage and subrogation (paragraphs BC120 and BC121); and

(c) policy loans (paragraph BC122).

Acquisition costs

BC116 Acquisition costs are the costs that an insurer incurs to sell, underwrite and initiate a new insurance contract. The IFRS neither prohibits nor requires the deferral of acquisition costs, nor does it prescribe what acquisition costs are deferrable, the period and method of their amortisation or whether an insurer should present deferred acquisition costs as an asset or as a reduction in insurance liabilities. The treatment of deferred acquisition costs is an integral part of existing models and cannot be amended easily without a more fundamental review of those models in phase II.

BC117 The treatment of acquisition costs for insurance contracts in phase I may differ from the treatment of transaction costs incurred for investment contracts (ie financial liabilities). IAS 39 requires specified transaction costs to be presented as a deduction in determining the initial carrying amount of a financial liability. The Board did not wish to create exceptions to the definition of the transaction costs to which this treatment applies. Those costs may be defined more broadly or more narrowly than the acquisition costs that an insurer is required or permitted to defer using its existing accounting policies.

BC118 Some entities incur significant costs in originating long-term savings contracts. Some respondents argued that most, if not all, of these costs relate to the right to charge future investment management fees rather than to the financial liability that is created when the first instalment is received. They asked the Board to clarify whether the cost of originating those rights could be recognised as a separate asset rather than as a deduction in determining the initial carrying amount of the financial liability. They noted that this treatment would:

(a) simplify the application of the effective interest method for a financial liability carried at amortised cost.

(b) prevent the recognition of a misleading loss at inception for a financial liability that contains a demand feature and is carried at fair value. IAS 39 states that the fair value of such a liability is not less than the amount payable on demand (discounted, if applicable, from the first date when that amount could be required to be paid).

BC119 In response to these comments, the Board decided that incremental costs directly attributable to securing an investment management contract should be recognised as an asset if they meet specified criteria, and that incremental costs should be defined in the same way as in IAS 39. The Board clarified these points by adding guidance to the appendix of IAS 18 *Revenue*.

Salvage and subrogation

BC120 Some insurance contracts permit the insurer to sell (usually damaged) property acquired in settling the claim (ie salvage). The insurer may also have the right to pursue third parties for payment of some or all costs (ie subrogation). The Board will consider salvage and subrogation in phase II.

BC121 In the following two related areas, the IFRS does not amend IAS 37:

(a) Gains on the expected disposal of assets are not taken into account in measuring a provision, even if the expected disposal is closely linked to the event giving rise to the provision. Instead, an entity recognises gains on expected disposals of assets at the time specified by the IFRS dealing with the assets concerned (paragraphs 51 and 52 of IAS 37).

(b) Paragraphs 53–58 of IAS 37 address reimbursements for some or all of the expenditure required to settle a provision.

The Board is working on a project to amend various aspects of IAS 37.

Policy loans

BC122 Some insurance contracts permit the policyholder to obtain a loan from the insurer. The DSOP proposed that an insurer should treat these loans as a prepayment of the insurance liability, rather than as the creation of a separate financial asset. Because the Board does not regard this issue as a priority, phase I does not address it.

Changes in accounting policies

Relevance and reliability

BC123 IAS 8 prohibits a change in accounting policies that is not required by an IFRS, unless the change will result in the provision of reliable and more relevant information. Although the Board wished to avoid imposing unnecessary changes in phase I, it saw no need to exempt insurers from the requirement to justify changes in accounting policies. Therefore, paragraph 22 of the IFRS permits an insurer to change its accounting policies for insurance contracts if, and only if, the change makes the financial statements more relevant and no less reliable or more reliable and no less relevant, judged by the criteria in IAS 8.* As the Board's conclusions for phase II develop (see paragraphs BC6–BC8), they will give insurers further context for judgements about whether a change in accounting policies will make their financial statements more relevant and reliable.

* Unlike IAS 8, paragraph 22 of the IFRS permits changes in accounting policies that make the financial statements more reliable and no less relevant. This permits improvements that make financial statements more reliable even if they do not achieve full reliability. In IAS 8 and the *Framework*, reliability is not synonymous with verifiability but includes characteristics such as neutrality and substance over form.

BC124 The IFRS contains further specific requirements supporting paragraph 22:

(a) paragraph 24 permits an insurer to change its accounting policies for some insurance liabilities that it designates, without satisfying the normal requirement in IAS 8 that an accounting policy should be applied to all similar items (paragraphs BC174–BC177).

(b) paragraph 25 permits the following practices to continue but prohibits their introduction:

   (i) measuring insurance liabilities on an undiscounted basis (paragraphs BC126 and BC127).

   (ii) measuring contractual rights to future investment management fees at an amount that exceeds their fair value as implied by a comparison with current fees charged by other market participants for similar services (paragraphs BC128–BC130).

   (iii) using non-uniform accounting policies for the insurance contracts of subsidiaries (paragraphs BC131 and BC132).

(c) paragraph 26 prohibits the introduction of additional prudence if an insurer already measures insurance liabilities with sufficient prudence (paragraph BC133).

(d) paragraphs 27–29 create a rebuttable presumption against the introduction of future investment margins in the measurement of insurance contracts (paragraphs BC134–BC144).

(e) paragraph 30 addresses 'shadow accounting' (paragraphs BC181–BC184).

(f) paragraph 45 permits an insurer to redesignate financial assets as 'at fair value through profit or loss' when it changes its accounting policies for insurance liabilities (paragraphs BC145 and BC146).

BC125 Some respondents suggested that phase I should not permit changes in accounting policies, to prevent lack of comparability (especially within a country) and management discretion to make arbitrary changes. However, the Board decided to permit changes in accounting policies for insurance contracts if they make the financial statements more relevant and no less reliable, or more reliable and no less relevant.

Discounting

BC126 In present practice, most general insurance claims liabilities are not discounted. In the Board's view, discounting of insurance liabilities results in financial statements that are more relevant and reliable. However, because the Board will not address discount rates and the basis for risk adjustments until phase II, the Board concluded that it could not require discounting in phase I. Nevertheless, the IFRS prohibits a change from an accounting policy that involves discounting to one that does not involve discounting (paragraph 25(a)).

BC127 Some respondents to ED 5 opposed discounting for contracts in which almost all the cash flows are expected to arise within one year, on materiality and cost-benefit grounds. The Board decided to create no specific exemption for these liabilities, because the normal materiality criteria in IAS 8 apply.

Investment management fees

BC128 Under some insurance contracts, the insurer is entitled to receive a periodic investment management fee. Some suggest that the insurer should, in determining the fair value of its contractual rights and obligations, discount the estimated future cash flows at a discount rate that reflects the risks associated with the cash flows. Some insurers use this approach in determining embedded values.

BC129 However, in the Board's view, this approach can lead to results that are not consistent with a fair value measurement. If the insurer's contractual asset management fee is in line with the fee charged by other insurers and asset managers for comparable asset management services, the fair value of the insurer's contractual right to that fee would be approximately equal to what it would cost insurers and asset managers to acquire similar contractual rights.* Therefore, paragraph 25(b) of the IFRS confirms that an insurer cannot introduce an accounting policy that measures those contractual rights at more than their fair value as implied by fees charged by others for comparable services; however, if an insurer's existing accounting policies involve such measurements, it may continue to use them in phase I.

BC130 The Board's agenda includes a project on revenue recognition.

Uniform accounting policies on consolidation

BC131 IAS 27 *Consolidated and Separate Financial Statements* requires entities to use uniform accounting policies. However, under current national requirements, some insurers consolidate subsidiaries without conforming the measurement of insurance liabilities using the subsidiaries' own local GAAP to the accounting policies used by the rest of the group.

BC132 The use of non-uniform accounting policies reduces the relevance and reliability of financial statements. However, prohibiting this would force some insurers to change their accounting policies for the insurance liabilities of some subsidiaries in phase I. This could have required systems changes that might no longer be needed in phase II. Therefore, the Board decided that an insurer already using non-uniform accounting policies for insurance contracts could continue to do so in phase I. However, if an insurer already uses uniform accounting policies for insurance contracts, it could not switch to a policy of using non-uniform accounting policies (paragraph 25(c) of the IFRS).

Excessive prudence

BC133 Insurers sometimes measure insurance liabilities on what is intended to be a highly prudent basis that lacks the neutrality required by the *Framework*. However, phase I does not define how much prudence is appropriate and cannot, therefore, eliminate excessive prudence. Consequently, the IFRS does not attempt to prohibit existing measurements of insurance liabilities that lack neutrality because of excessive prudence. Nevertheless, it prohibits the introduction of additional prudence if an insurer already measures insurance liabilities with

* This approach is consistent with the discussion of servicing rights and obligations in IAS 39.

sufficient prudence (see paragraph 26 of the IFRS). The liability adequacy test in paragraphs 15–19 addresses the converse problem of understated insurance liabilities.

Future investment margins

BC134 In the Board's view, the cash flows from an asset are irrelevant for the measurement of a liability (unless those cash flows affect (a) the cash flows arising from the liability or (b) the credit characteristics of the liability). Many existing measurement practices for insurance liabilities conflict with this principle because they use a discount rate based on the estimated return from the assets that are deemed to back the insurance liabilities. However, the Board concluded that it could not eliminate these practices until phase II gives guidance on discount rates and the basis for risk adjustments.

BC135 ED 5 stated that an accounting policy change makes financial statements less relevant and reliable if it introduces a practice of including future investment margins. On the following grounds, some respondents opposed this proposal, which would have prohibited the introduction of any measurements that reflect future investment margins:

(a) The proposal prejudges a phase II issue. Most actuaries and insurers believe that a fair value measure (ie one calibrated to transactions involving insurance contracts) must include some consideration of asset performance because product pricing, reinsurance and market transactions are observed to reflect this feature.

(b) A current market rate results in more relevant and reliable information than an out-of-date discount rate prescribed by a regulator, even if the current market rate reflects expected asset returns.

(c) Asset-based discount rates are a feature of most existing national systems, including some modern systems that use current estimates of future cash flows and current (albeit asset-based) discount rates. The prohibition proposed in ED 5 would have prevented an insurer from replacing its existing accounting policies for insurance contracts with another comprehensive basis of accounting for insurance contracts that is, in aggregate, more relevant and reliable despite the disadvantage of using an asset-based discount rate.

(d) Because US GAAP uses an asset-based discount rate for some insurance liabilities, the prohibition would have prevented insurers from adopting US GAAP for their insurance liabilities in phase I. This would have been unfair because some insurers that have already adopted IFRSs apply US GAAP to their insurance contracts and could continue to do so in phase I.

BC136 In the light of these comments, the Board replaced the prohibition proposed in ED 5 with a rebuttable presumption, which could be overcome if the other components of a change in accounting policies increase the relevance and reliability of an insurer's financial statements sufficiently to outweigh the disadvantage of introducing the practice in question (see paragraph 28 of the IFRS for an example).

BC137 The IFRS identifies two practices that include future investment margins in the measurement of insurance liabilities: (a) using a discount rate that reflects the estimated return on the insurer's assets,* (b) projecting the returns on those assets at an estimated rate of return, discounting those projected returns at a different rate and including the result in the measurement of the liability. Some suggested that (b) should be eliminated in phase I because they regarded it as less acceptable than (a). However, the Board noted that although (b) appears more obviously incorrect than (a), these two practices have the same effect and are logically equivalent.

Future investment margins and embedded value

BC138 In addition to considering asset-based discount rates in general, the Board also considered a specific measurement technique that, at least in present practice, typically reflects future investment margins, namely embedded value. Embedded value is an indirect method of measuring an insurance liability. Indirect methods measure the liability by discounting all cash flows arising from both the book of insurance contracts and the assets supporting the book, to arrive at a net measurement for the contracts and supporting assets. The measurement of the assets is then deducted to arrive at a measurement of the book of contracts.† In contrast, direct methods measure the liability by discounting future cash flows arising from the book of insurance contracts only. If the same assumptions are made in both methods, direct and indirect methods can produce the same results.§

BC139 Life insurers in an increasing number of countries disclose embedded value information. Most disclose this information outside the financial statements or as supplementary information (usually unaudited), but a few use it as a measurement in their balance sheets.

BC140 Some respondents felt that embedded value methodology is far more relevant and reliable than most local accounting methods, and insurers should be permitted to adopt it. They noted that embedded values are often an important consideration in determining prices for acquisitions of insurers and of blocks of insurance contracts. Furthermore, embedded value and similar indirect methods are often used in accounting for the insurance liabilities assumed in these acquisitions.

* Some approaches attempt to find a portfolio of assets ('replicating portfolio') with characteristics that replicate the characteristics of the liability very closely. If such a portfolio can be found, it may be appropriate to use the expected return on the replicating portfolio as the discount rate for the liability, with suitable adjustments for differences in their characteristics. However, replicating portfolio approaches should not be regarded as using an asset-based discount rate because they attempt to measure the characteristics of the liability. They are not based on the characteristics of the actual assets held, which may or may not match those of the liability.

† If embedded values are recognised in the balance sheet, they are typically presented as two components: an insurance liability and a separate intangible asset. This is similar to the expanded presentation that the IFRS permits in a business combination or portfolio transfer.

§ Luke N. Girard, *Market Value of Insurance Liabilities: Reconciling the Actuarial Appraisal and Option Pricing Methods*, North American Actuarial Journal, Volume 4, Number 1

BC141 For the following reasons, some suggested that phase I should prohibit embedded value measurements in the balance sheet.

(a) Embedded value approaches are largely unregulated at present and there is diversity in their application. For example, some view the methods used to reflect risk as fairly crude, diverse and not always fully consistent with capital market prices.

(b) Embedded value methods today typically involve two practices whose introduction ED 5 regarded as unacceptable:

(i) reflecting future investment margins in the measurement of the 'embedded value' asset associated with insurance liabilities (see paragraphs BC134–BC144).

(ii) measuring contractual rights to future investment management fees at an amount that exceeds their fair value as implied by a comparison with current fees charged by other market participants for similar services (see paragraphs BC128–BC130).

(c) In current practice, embedded values are generally determined on a single best estimate basis that does not reflect the full range of possible outcomes. This does not generally adequately address embedded guarantees and options, such as embedded interest rate guarantees. Until recently, embedded values would have ignored these items if they were out of the money. Indeed, in some cases, they might have been ignored even if they were in the money, because of assumptions about future investment performance. More attention is now being devoted to these options and guarantees and embedded value methods may begin to address them more rigorously, but that development is not yet complete.

BC142 However, for the following reasons, the IFRS permits continued use of embedded value measurements:

(a) One objective of phase I is to avoid disturbing existing practice for insurance contracts, unless a change creates a significant improvement and leads in a direction consistent with the likely direction of phase II. Prohibiting the continued use of embedded values would not meet that criterion.

(b) Embedded value methods are based on estimates of future cash flows, not an accumulation of past transactions. The advantages of this may, in some cases, outweigh the disadvantage of including future investment margins. Therefore, eliminating embedded value methods may not result in more relevant and reliable financial statements in every case.

(c) Given that the Board did not prohibit asset-based discount rates for other measurements of insurance liabilities in phase I, there is no compelling reason in phase I to prohibit embedded value measurements that contain future investment margins.

(d) Although embedded value measurements today typically include future investment margins, some practitioners have suggested improving embedded value methods by adjusting the asset cash flows fully for risk to make them consistent with market prices.

BC143 It follows from the Board's conclusions on relevance and reliability (paragraphs BC123–BC125), investment management fees (paragraphs BC128–BC130) and future investment margins (paragraphs BC134–BC137) that an insurer can introduce embedded value measurements in its balance sheet only if all the following conditions are met:

(a) the new accounting policy will result in more relevant and reliable financial statements (paragraph 22 of the IFRS). This is not an automatic decision and will depend on a comparison of the insurer's existing accounting with the way in which it intends to apply embedded value.

(b) this increase in relevance and reliability is sufficient to overcome the rebuttable presumption against including future investment margins (paragraph 29 of the IFRS).

(c) the embedded values include contractual rights to future investment management fees at an amount that does not exceed their fair value as implied by a comparison with current fees charged by other market participants for similar services (paragraph 25(b) of the IFRS and paragraphs BC128–BC130).

BC144 In some measurement approaches, the discount rate is used to determine the present value of a future profit margin, which is then attributed to different periods using a formula. However, in other approaches (such as most applications of embedded value), the discount rate determines the measurement of the liability directly. The Board concluded that it is highly unlikely that an insurer could overcome the rebuttable presumption in the latter case (see paragraph 29 of the IFRS).

Redesignation of financial assets

BC145 When an insurer changes its accounting policies for insurance liabilities, it is permitted, but not required, to reclassify some or all financial assets as 'at fair value through profit or loss'. This permits an insurer to avoid artificial mismatches when it improves its accounting policies for insurance liabilities. The Board also decided:

(a) not to restrict redesignation to assets backing the insurance contracts for which the accounting policies were changed. The Board did not wish to create unnecessary barriers for those insurers that wish to move to a more consistent measurement basis that reflects fair values.

(b) not to introduce an option to reclassify financial assets as 'available for sale'. Such reclassification would have caused changes in carrying amount to be recognised directly in equity for assets, but in profit or loss for insurance liabilities. An insurer can avoid this inconsistency by classifying the financial assets as 'at fair value through profit or loss'.

BC146 IAS 39 permits redesignation of assets in specified circumstances when an entity adopts the revised IAS 39. IFRS 1 *First-time Adoption of International Financial Reporting Standards* contains corresponding provisions for first-time adopters.

Acquisition of insurance contracts in business combinations and portfolio transfers

BC147 When an entity acquires another entity in a business combination, IFRS 3 *Business Combinations* requires the acquirer to measure at fair value the identifiable assets and liabilities acquired. Similar requirements exist under many national accounting frameworks. Nevertheless, in practice, insurers have often used an expanded presentation that splits the fair value of acquired insurance contracts into two components:

(a) a liability measured in accordance with the insurer's accounting policies for insurance contracts that it issues; and

(b) an intangible asset, representing the difference between (i) the fair value of the contractual insurance rights acquired and insurance obligations assumed and (ii) the amount described in (a). Life insurers often describe this intangible asset by names such as the present value of in force business (PVIF), present value of future profits (PVFP or PVP) or value of business acquired (VOBA). Similar principles apply in non-life insurance, for example if claims liabilities are not discounted.

BC148 For the following reasons, the Board decided to permit these existing practices during phase I (paragraph 31 of the IFRS):

(a) One objective of phase I is to avoid prejudging most phase II issues and to avoid requiring systems changes for phase I that might need to be reversed for phase II. In the meantime, disclosure about the nature of, and changes in, the related intangible asset provides transparency for users.

(b) The IFRS gives no guidance on how to determine the fair value of the insurance liabilities, because that would be premature in phase I. Thus, fair values identified during phase I might need to be changed in phase II.

(c) It may be difficult to integrate a fair value measurement at the date of a business combination into subsequent insurance contract accounting without requiring systems changes that could become obsolete in phase II.

BC149 The intangible asset described above is generally amortised over the estimated life of the contracts. Some insurers use an interest method of amortisation, which appears appropriate for an asset that essentially comprises the present value of a set of contractual cash flows. However, it is doubtful whether IAS 38 *Intangible Assets* would have permitted its use. Therefore, the Board decided that this asset should remain outside the scope of IAS 38 and its subsequent measurement should be consistent with the measurement of the related insurance liability (paragraph 31(b) of the IFRS). Because this asset would be covered by the liability adequacy test in paragraphs 15–19, the Board also excluded it from the scope of IAS 36 *Impairment of Assets*.

BC150 IAS 36 and IAS 38 still apply to customer lists and customer relationships reflecting the expectation of contracts that are not part of the contractual insurance rights and contractual insurance obligations that existed at the date of a business combination. An illustrative example published with IFRS 3 deals with customer relationships acquired together with a portfolio of one-year motor insurance contracts.

BC151 Measurements of the intangible asset described in paragraph BC147(b) sometimes include future investment margins. Those margins are subject to the same requirements as future investment margins included in the measurement of the related insurance liability (see paragraphs BC134–BC144).

BC152 In some cases, an insurer's accounting policies under previous GAAP (ie those used before it adopted IFRSs) involved measuring the intangible asset described in paragraph BC147(b) on a basis derived from the carrying amounts of other assets and liabilities. In such cases, if an entity changes the measurements of its assets and liabilities on adopting IFRSs for the first time, shadow accounting may become relevant (see paragraphs BC181–BC184 for a discussion of shadow accounting).

BC153 Some respondents requested an exemption from fair value measurement for insurance liabilities assumed in a business combination. They argued that there is still too much uncertainty about how fair value should be defined and determined. However, insurers have apparently been able to cope with the existing requirements in IFRSs and in national standards. The Board saw no compelling reason for a new exemption.

Discretionary participation features

BC154 Some insurance contracts contain a discretionary participation feature as well as a guaranteed element. The insurer has discretion over the amount and/or timing of distributions to policyholders, although that discretion may be subject to some contractual constraints (including related legal and regulatory constraints) and competitive constraints. Distributions are typically made to policyholders whose contracts are still in force when the distribution is made. Thus, in many cases, a change in the timing of a distribution means that a different generation of policyholders will benefit.

BC155 Although the issuer has contractual discretion over distributions, it is usually likely that current or future policyholders will ultimately receive some part of the accumulated surplus available, at the reporting date, for distribution to holders of contracts with discretionary participation features (ie distributable surplus). The main accounting question is whether that part of the distributable surplus is a liability or a component of equity. The Board will explore that question in phase II.

BC156 Features of this kind are found not only in insurance contracts but also in some investment contracts (ie financial liabilities). Requiring a particular accounting treatment in phase I for investment contracts with these features would create the risk that the Board might decide on a different treatment in phase II. Furthermore, in some cases, holders of insurance contracts and investment contracts have a contractual right to share in discretionary payments out of the same pool of assets. If the Board required a particular treatment for the discretionary participation features of the investment contracts in phase I, it might prejudge the treatment of these features in insurance contracts that are linked to the same pool of assets.

BC157 For these reasons, the Board decided not to address most aspects of the accounting treatment of such features in phase I, in either insurance contracts or investment contracts. However, paragraphs 34 and 35 of the IFRS confirm that it is unacceptable to classify a discretionary participation feature as an intermediate category that is neither liability nor equity, because this would be inconsistent with the *Framework*. If a balance sheet item does not meet the *Framework's* definition of, and recognition criteria for, assets or liabilities, that item is included in equity.

BC158 Furthermore, ED 5 proposed a requirement for the issuer of an investment contract containing such a feature to recognise a liability measured at no less than the amount that would result from applying IAS 39 to the guaranteed element of the contract. Because issuers need not determine the IAS 39 measurement of the guaranteed element if the total recognised liability is clearly higher, ED 5 noted the Board's expectation that issuers would not need extensive new systems to comply with this requirement.

BC159 Some respondents objected that determining the result of applying IAS 39 to the guaranteed element would either have virtually no effect (in which case the requirement would be unnecessary) or require extensive new systems (causing costs exceeding the likely benefit to users). In finalising the IFRS, the Board adopted a more flexible approach that limits the need for systems to apply IAS 39 to the guaranteed element alone, while still requiring some rigour to avoid the understatement of the financial liability. Specifically, paragraph 35 permits two approaches for a discretionary participation feature in a financial liability:

(a) The issuer may classify the entire discretionary participation feature as a liability, but need not separate it from the guaranteed element (and so need not determine the result of applying IAS 39 to the guaranteed element). An issuer choosing this approach is required to apply the liability adequacy test in paragraphs 15–19 of the IFRS to the contract.

(b) The issuer may classify part or all of the feature as a separate component of equity. If so, the liability recognised cannot be less than the result of applying IAS 39 to the guaranteed element. The issuer need not determine that measurement if the total liability recognised is clearly higher.

BC160 There may be timing differences between accumulated profits under IFRSs and distributable surplus (ie the accumulated amount that is contractually eligible for distribution to holders of discretionary participation features). For example, distributable surplus may exclude unrealised investment gains that are recognised under IFRSs. The resulting timing differences are analogous, in some respects, to temporary differences between the carrying amounts of assets and liabilities and their tax bases. The IFRS does not address the classification of these timing differences because the Board will not determine until phase II whether the distributable surplus is all equity, all liability or part equity and part liability.

BC161 The factor that makes it difficult to determine the appropriate accounting for these features is constrained discretion, in other words, the combination of discretion and constraints on that discretion. If participation features lack discretion, they are embedded derivatives and within the scope of IAS 39.

BC162 The definition of a discretionary participation feature does not capture an unconstrained contractual discretion to set a 'crediting rate' that is used to credit interest or other returns to policyholders (as found in the contracts described in some countries as 'universal life' contracts). Some view these features as similar to discretionary participation features because crediting rates are constrained by market forces and the insurer's resources. The Board will revisit the treatment of these features in phase II.

BC163 Some respondents asked the Board to clarify the treatment of premiums received for financial instruments containing discretionary participation features. Conceptually the premium for the guaranteed element is not revenue, but the treatment of the premium for the discretionary participation feature could depend on matters that will not be resolved until phase II. Furthermore, requiring the premium to be split could involve system changes that might become redundant in phase II. To avoid unnecessary disruption in phase I, the Board decided that entities could continue presenting premiums as revenue, with a corresponding expense representing the change in the liability.

BC164 Conceptually, if part or all of a discretionary participation feature is classified as a component of equity, the related portion of the premium should not be included in profit or loss. However, the Board concluded that requiring each incoming premium to be split would require systems changes beyond the scope of phase I. Therefore, the Board decided that an issuer could recognise the entire premium as revenue without separating the portion that relates to the equity component. However, the Board confirmed that the portion of profit or loss attributable to the equity component is presented as an allocation of profit or loss (in a manner similar to the presentation of minority interests), not as expense or income.

BC165 Some suggested that investment contracts containing a discretionary participation feature should be excluded from the fair value disclosure required by IAS 32. They noted both conceptual and practical problems in determining the fair value of an instrument of this kind. However, instead of creating a new exclusion from the required disclosure of fair value, the Board added new paragraph 91A to IAS 32. This extends existing requirements in IAS 32 governing those unquoted equity instruments whose fair value cannot be determined reliably.

Issues related to IAS 39

Assets held to back insurance contracts

BC166 The IFRS does not address financial or non-financial assets held by insurers to back insurance contracts. IAS 39 identifies four categories of financial asset, with three different accounting treatments. In developing IAS 39, the Board's predecessor (IASC) acknowledged that most countries had a mixed measurement model, measuring some financial assets at amortised cost and others at fair value. IASC decided to retain, but regulate and structure, the different approaches as follows:

(a) financial assets classified as 'at fair value through profit or loss' (including all financial assets held for trading) are measured at fair value, with all changes in their fair value recognised in profit or loss. Furthermore, all derivatives are deemed to be held for trading, and hence measured at fair value, because this is the only method that provides sufficient transparency in the financial statements.

(b) available-for-sale assets (ie those that do not fall into any of the other categories) are measured at fair value, with changes in their fair value recognised in equity until the asset is derecognised or becomes impaired. Measurement at fair value is appropriate given that available-for-sale assets may be sold in response to, for example, changes in market prices or a liquidity shortage.

(c) assets with a fixed maturity may be measured at amortised cost if the entity intends to hold them to maturity and shows that it has the ability to do so. This treatment is based on the view of some that changes in market prices are irrelevant if an asset is held to maturity because those changes will reverse before maturity (unless the asset becomes impaired).

(d) loans and receivables are measured at amortised cost. IASC was persuaded that there are difficulties in estimating the fair value of such loans, and that further progress was needed in valuation techniques before fair value should be required.

BC167 Some expressed concerns that accounting mismatches would arise in phase I if financial assets (particularly interest-bearing investments) held to back insurance contracts are measured at fair value under IAS 39 whilst insurance liabilities are measured on a different basis. If the insurer classifies the assets as 'available for sale', this difference in measurement basis would not affect profit or loss but it could lead to some volatility in equity. Some do not regard that volatility as a faithful representation of changes in the insurer's financial position. In developing ED 5, after discussing various suggestions for reducing that volatility,* the Board decided:

(a) not to relax the criteria in IAS 39 for classifying financial assets as 'held to maturity'. Relaxing those criteria would undermine the fundamental assertion that an entity has both the intent and ability to hold the assets until maturity. The Board noted that an insurer may be able to classify some of its fixed maturity financial assets as held to maturity if it intends not to sell them before maturity and, in addition to meeting the other conditions set out in IAS 39, concludes that an unexpected increase in lapses or claims would not compel it to sell those assets (except in the 'disaster scenario' discussed in IAS 39 paragraph AG21).

(b) not to create a new category of assets carried at amortised cost: assets held to back insurance liabilities. The creation of such a category would lead to a need for arbitrary distinctions and complex attribution procedures that would not make an insurer's financial statements more relevant and reliable, and could require insurers to develop costly systems. The Board reviewed a precedent that exists in Japan for such a category, but was not persuaded that the procedures adopted there can overcome these difficulties. Moreover, if an insurer may sell assets in response to, for example, changes in market prices or a liquidity shortage, the only appropriate measurement is fair value.

* The Board discussed this subject at its meeting in November 2002. It was also one of the major topics raised by insurance participants at two half-day sessions during the financial instruments round-tables in March 2003. Before finalising ED 5, the Board discussed the subject again in April 2003.

(c) not to create a new category of 'available-for-settlement' liabilities, analogous to available-for-sale assets, measured at fair value, with changes in fair value recognised in equity. The creation of such a category would make it necessary to find some basis for distinguishing between that category and the existing category of non-trading financial liabilities, or to permit a free choice of accounting treatments. The Board has identified no basis for such a distinction, nor for deciding which of these two categories would be the new residual category. Furthermore, creating such a category could require insurers to develop new systems with no certainty that those systems would be needed in phase II.

BC168 In developing ED 5, the Board concluded that the reasons given above outweigh the effects of any accounting mismatch on an insurer's reported equity. Therefore, the Board decided not to exempt insurers from these existing requirements, even temporarily.

BC169 Insurers may be particularly sensitive to equity reported in general purpose financial statements in some countries where this amount is used in assessing compliance with regulatory capital requirements. However, although insurance supervisors are important users of general purpose financial statements, those financial statements are not directed at specific needs of insurance supervisors that other users do not share. Furthermore, supervisors generally have the power to obtain additional information that meets their specific needs. In the Board's view, creating new exemptions from IAS 39 in this area would not have been the best way to meet the common needs of users (including insurance supervisors) of an insurer's general purpose financial statements.

BC170 Some argued that banks enjoy an 'advantage' that is not available to insurers. Under IAS 39, a bank may measure its core banking-book assets and liabilities (loans and receivables and non-trading financial liabilities) at amortised cost, whereas an insurer would have no such option for many of the assets held to back its core insurance activities. However, as noted in paragraph BC166(d), IASC permitted amortised cost measurement for loans and receivables because it had concerns about difficulties in establishing their fair value. This factor does not apply to many assets held by insurers to back insurance liabilities.

BC171 Many of the respondents to ED 5 urged the Board to explore ways of reducing the accounting mismatch described above. The Board discussed this subject at length at all three meetings at which it discussed the responses to ED 5 before finalising the IFRS. In addition, the Board discussed it with the Standards Advisory Council. It was also raised at a meeting of the Board's Insurance Advisory Committee in September 2003, which six Board members attended together with the project staff. Individual Board members and staff also had many discussions with interested parties, including users, insurers, actuaries, auditors and regulators.

BC172 It is important to distinguish two different types of mismatch:

(a) *accounting mismatch* arises if changes in economic conditions affect assets and liabilities to the same extent, but the carrying amounts of those assets and liabilities do not respond equally to those economic changes. Specifically, accounting mismatch occurs if an entity uses different measurement bases for assets and liabilities.

(b) *economic mismatch* arises if the values of, or cash flows from, assets and liabilities respond differently to changes in economic conditions. It is worth noting that economic mismatch is not necessarily eliminated by an asset-liability management programme that involves investing in assets to provide the optimal risk-return trade-off for the package of assets and liabilities.

BC173 Ideally, a measurement model would report all the economic mismatch that exists and would not report any accounting mismatch. The Board considered various alternatives, observing that all had advantages and disadvantages. Some alternatives would have amended IAS 39 to extend the use of cost or amortised cost measurements. However, the Board noted the following:

(a) Fair value is a more relevant measurement than amortised cost for financial assets that an entity might sell in response to changing market and other conditions.

(b) In its response to ED 5, the Association for Investment Management and Research (AIMR) strongly urged the Board not to extend the use of amortised cost in IAS 39. The AIMR is a non-profit professional association of more than 67,200 financial analysts, portfolio managers, and other investment professionals in 116 countries.

(c) An accounting model that measured both assets and liabilities at amounts based on current interest rates would provide information about the degree of economic mismatch. A model that measured both at historical values, or ignored the time value of money in measuring some insurance liabilities, would not. Financial analysts often observe that information about economic mismatch is very important to them.

(d) Some suggested that insurers wish to follow a strategy that involves holding fixed maturity investments to maturity, with some flexibility to sell investments if insurance claims or lapses are unusually high. They recommended relaxing restrictions in IAS 39 so that insurers using such a strategy could use the held-to-maturity category more easily. However, in discussions with individual Board members and staff, insurers generally indicated that they also wished to keep the flexibility to make sales in the light of changing demographic and economic conditions so that they can seek the best trade-off between risk and return. That is a valid and understandable business objective, but it is difficult to argue that cost could be more relevant than fair value in such cases. Although IAS 32 requires disclosure of the fair value of financial assets carried at amortised cost, disclosure does not rectify inappropriate measurement.

(e) Some noted that they wished to keep the flexibility to sell corporate bonds before a major downgrade occurs. They viewed the guidance in IAS 39 as restricting their ability to do this. Moreover, because a 'tainting' requirement in IAS 39 prohibits the use of the held-to-maturity category after most sales from this category, insurers are reluctant to use this classification for corporate bonds. The application guidance in IAS 39 gives examples of cases when sales of held-to-maturity investments do not 'taint' all other such investments. For example, paragraph AG22(a) of IAS 39 refers to a sale following a significant deterioration in the issuer's creditworthiness.

The Board noted that some appeared to read that guidance as limited to changes in a credit rating by an external credit rating agency, although the guidance also refers to internal ratings that meet particular criteria.

(f) The Japanese precedent mentioned in paragraph BC167(b) creates some discipline by placing restrictions on the use of amortised cost, but for systems or other reasons not all insurers in Japan adopt this approach. Furthermore, this approach permits a cost approach if the durations (ie average maturities) of insurance liabilities match those of the related assets within a specified band of 80–125 per cent. If any economic mismatch arises within that band, this approach does not recognise it. In addition, gains and losses on selling assets held at amortised cost are generally recognised immediately in profit or loss (except that some gains are deferred and amortised if sales are not compatible with the duration matching strategy).

(g) Some Board members and staff met representatives of major European insurers to explore the possibility of (i) extending the use of amortised cost if specified, relatively strict, criteria are met and (ii) combining that with a simplified attempt to identify 'ineffectiveness' resulting from the fact that the assets and liabilities would not respond identically to changes in interest rates. This approach would have avoided some of the practical and conceptual problems inherent in the Japanese approach discussed above. However, this untried approach had been developed at short notice and not all details had been worked through. Moreover, many insurers may not be able or willing to invest in systems that could need amendment in phase II.

(h) That a mixed measurement model can create an accounting mismatch is undeniable. Furthermore, it costs time and money for insurers to explain the effects even to sophisticated users. Insurers are very concerned that less sophisticated users may misinterpret the resulting information. If a simple, transparent and conceptually acceptable way could have been found to eliminate the accounting mismatch at an acceptable cost without also obscuring the economic mismatch, that change might have been beneficial. However, the Board could find no such way in the short term. The Board also noted that any change could have required major systems changes and that there appeared to be no consensus among insurers on a single method.

(i) Extending the use of amortised cost would have created an inconsistency with US GAAP. The accounting mismatch described in paragraphs BC167 and BC172 has existed for some years in US GAAP, which requires insurers to account for their financial assets in broadly the same way as under IAS 39. Furthermore, the US Financial Accounting Standards Board decided in January 2004 not to add to its agenda a project to reconsider US GAAP for investments held by life insurance companies.

BC174 In the light of these considerations, the Board concluded that changing the measurement requirements in IAS 39 for financial assets, even temporarily, would diminish the relevance and reliability of an insurer's financial statements. The Board observed that the accounting mismatch arose more from imperfections in existing measurement models for insurance liabilities than from deficiencies in the measurement of the assets. It would have been a retrograde step to try to mitigate the accounting mismatch by adopting a less relevant measurement of the assets—a measurement that would also have obscured some of the economic mismatch.

BC175 The Board considered whether it could mitigate the accounting mismatch by permitting improvements to the measurement of insurance liabilities. The Board noted that introducing a current market-based discount rate for insurance liabilities rather than a historical discount rate would improve the relevance and reliability of an insurer's financial statements. Therefore, such a change would have been permitted by the proposals in ED 5 and is also permitted by the IFRS. However, IAS 8 requires consistent accounting policies for similar transactions. For systems and other reasons, some insurers may not wish, or be able, in phase I to introduce a current market-based discount rate for all insurance liabilities.

BC176 The Board concluded that the increase in relevance and reliability from introducing a current discount rate could outweigh the disadvantages of permitting accounting policies that are not applied consistently to all similar liabilities. Accordingly, the Board decided to permit, but not require, an insurer to change its accounting policies so that it remeasures designated insurance liabilities for changes in interest rates. This election permits a change in accounting policies that is applied to some liabilities, but not to all similar liabilities as IAS 8 would otherwise require. The Board noted that insurers might sometimes be able to develop simplified models that give a reasonable estimate of the effect of interest rate changes.

BC177 The Board also noted the following:

(a) No single proposal would have eliminated the accounting mismatch for a broad cross-section of insurers without also obscuring the economic mismatch.

(b) No single proposal would have been acceptable to a broad cross-section of insurers.

(c) No single proposal could have been implemented by a broad cross-section of insurers without major systems changes. In other words, no solution was available that built on common industry approaches and systems. Furthermore, the systems needed to implement successfully the approach discussed with some European insurers (see paragraph BC173(g)) would also allow the approach permitted by paragraph 24 of the IFRS (adjusting designated liabilities for changes in interest rates). Indeed, paragraph 24 imposes fewer restrictions than the approach discussed with European insurers because it does not require the assets to match the liability cash flows closely, since any mismatch in cash flows is reflected in profit or loss.

(d) Adjusting the discount rate for designated liabilities will not eliminate all the accounting mismatch described above and some, perhaps many, insurers will choose not to make that adjustment. The reasons for this are as follows:

(i) As noted above, many insurers may not have systems to adjust liabilities for changes in interest rates and may not wish to develop such systems, even for designated liabilities as opposed to all liabilities.

(ii) Changes in discount rates would not affect the measurement of insurance liabilities that are carried at an accumulated account value.

(iii) Changes in discount rates would not affect the measurement of financial liabilities with a demand feature, because IAS 39 states that their fair value is not less than the amount payable on demand (discounted, if applicable, from the first date when that amount could be required to be paid). Although this last point is not strictly relevant for insurance contracts, many life insurers issue investment contracts for which it is relevant.

BC178 In summary, the Board decided not to amend existing measurement requirements in IAS 39 for financial assets because such amendments would have reduced the relevance and reliability of financial statements to an unacceptable extent. Although such amendments could have eliminated some of the accounting mismatch, they would also have obscured any economic mismatch that exists. The following points summarise amendments made to ED 5 that might mitigate the accounting mismatch in some cases, as well as relevant observations made by the Board:

(a) The Board decided to permit, but not require, an insurer to change its accounting policies so that it remeasures designated insurance liabilities for changes in interest rates (see paragraph BC176).

(b) The Board clarified the applicability of the practice sometimes known as 'shadow accounting' (paragraphs BC181–BC184).

(c) The Board amended IAS 40 *Investment Property* to permit two separate elections when an entity selects the fair value model or the cost model for investment property. One election is for investment property backing contracts (which could be either insurance contracts or financial instruments) that pay a return linked directly to the fair value of, or returns from, specified assets including that investment property. The other election is for all other investment property (see paragraph C12 of the IFRS).

(d) The Board observed that some entities appeared to have misread the application guidance in IAS 39 on sales of held-to-maturity investments following a significant deterioration in the issuer's creditworthiness. Specifically, as noted in paragraph 173(e), some appeared to have read it as limited to changes in a credit rating by an external credit rating agency, although the guidance also refers to internal ratings that meet particular criteria.

(e) The Board observed that IAS 1 and IAS 32 do not preclude a presentation identifying a separate component of equity to report a portion of the change (and cumulative change) in the carrying amount of fixed-maturity available-for-sale financial assets. An insurer could use such a presentation to highlight the effect on equity of changes in interest rates that (i) changed the carrying amount of assets but (ii) did not change the carrying amount of liabilities that respond economically to those changing interest rates.

BC179 IAS 40 permits an entity to use a fair value model for investment property, but IAS 16 does not permit this model for owner-occupied property. An entity may measure its owner-occupied property at fair value using the revaluation model in

IAS 16, but changes in its fair value must be recognised in revaluation surplus rather than in profit or loss. Some insurers regard their owner-occupied property as an investment and prefer to use a fair value model for it. However, the Board decided not to make piecemeal changes to IAS 16 and IAS 40 at this stage.

BC180 The Board noted that shadow accounting (paragraphs BC181–BC184) may be relevant if there is a contractual link between payments to policyholders and the carrying amount of, or returns from, owner-occupied property. If an insurer elects to use shadow accounting, changes in the measurement of the liability resulting from revaluations of the property are recognised directly in equity, through the statement of changes in equity.

Shadow accounting

BC181 In some accounting models, realised gains or losses on an insurer's assets have a direct effect on the measurement of some or all of its insurance liabilities.*

BC182 When many of those models were constructed, unrealised gains and most unrealised losses were not recognised in financial statements. Some of those models were extended later to require some financial assets to be measured at fair value, with changes in fair value recognised directly in equity (ie the same treatment as for available-for-sale financial assets under IAS 39). When this happened, a practice sometimes known as 'shadow accounting' was developed with the following two features:

(a) A recognised but unrealised gain or loss on an asset affects the measurement of the insurance liability in the same way that a realised gain or loss does.

(b) If unrealised gains or losses on an asset are recognised directly in equity, the resulting change in the carrying amount of the insurance liability is also recognised in equity.

BC183 Some respondents asked the Board to clarify whether the proposals in ED 5 permitted shadow accounting. The Board concluded the following:

(a) In principle, gains and losses on an asset should not influence the measurement of an insurance liability (unless the gains or losses on the asset alter the amounts payable to policyholders). Nevertheless, this is a feature of some existing measurement models for insurance liabilities and the Board decided that it was not feasible to eliminate this practice in phase I (see paragraph BC134 for further discussion in the context of future investment margins).

(b) Shadow accounting permits all recognised gains and losses on assets to affect the measurement of insurance liabilities in the same way, regardless of whether (i) the gains and losses are realised or unrealised and (ii) unrealised gains and losses are recognised in profit or loss or directly in equity. This is a logical application of a feature of some existing models.

* Throughout this section, references to insurance liabilities are also relevant for (a) related deferred acquisition costs and (b) intangible assets relating to insurance contracts acquired in a business combination or portfolio transfer.

(c) Because the Board does not expect that feature of existing models to survive in phase II, insurers should not be required to develop systems to apply shadow accounting.

(d) If an unrealised gain or loss on an asset triggers a shadow accounting adjustment to a liability, that adjustment should be recognised in the same way as the unrealised gain or loss.

(e) In some cases and to some extent, shadow accounting might mitigate volatility caused by differences between the measurement basis for assets and the measurement basis for insurance liabilities. However, that is a by-product of shadow accounting and not its primary purpose.

BC184 Paragraph 30 of the IFRS permits, but does not require, shadow accounting. The Implementation Guidance includes an illustrative example to show how shadow accounting might become relevant in an environment where the accounting for assets changes so that unrealised gains are recognised (IG Example 4). Because the Board does not expect the feature underlying the use of shadow accounting to survive in phase II, the Board decided not to give further guidance.

Investment contracts

BC185 Many insurers issue investment contracts (ie financial instruments that do not transfer enough insurance risk to qualify as insurance contracts). Under IAS 39, the issuer measures investment contracts at either amortised cost or, with appropriate designation at inception, at fair value. Some aspects of the measurements under IAS 39 differ from the measurements that are often used at present under national accounting requirements for these contracts:

(a) The definition and treatment of transaction costs under IAS 39 may differ from the definition and treatment of acquisition costs in some national requirements.

(b) The condition in IAS 39 for treating a modification of a financial liability (or the exchange of the new liability for an old liability) as an extinguishment of the original liability may differ from equivalent national requirements.

(c) Future cash flows from assets do not affect the amortised cost or fair value of investment contract liabilities (unless the cash flows from the liabilities are contractually linked to the cash flows from the assets).

(d) The amortised cost of a financial liability is not adjusted when market interest rates change, even if the return on available assets is below the effective interest rate on the liability (unless the change in rates causes the liability cash flows to change).

(e) The fair value of a financial liability with a demand feature is not less than the amount payable on demand.

(f) The fair value of a financial instrument reflects its credit characteristics.

(g) Premiums received for an investment contract are not recognised as revenue under IAS 39, but as balance sheet movements, in the same way as a deposit received.

BC186 Some argued that the Board should not require insurers to change their accounting for investment contracts in phase I because the scope of phase I is intended to be limited and because the current treatment of such contracts is often very similar to the treatment of insurance contracts. However, the Board saw no reason to delay the application of IAS 39 to contracts that do not transfer significant insurance risk. The Board noted that some of these contracts have features, such as long maturities, recurring premiums and high initial transaction costs, that are less common in other financial instruments. Nevertheless, applying a single set of accounting requirements to all financial instruments will make an insurer's financial statements more relevant and reliable.

BC187 Some contracts within the scope of IAS 39 grant cancellation or renewal rights to the holder. The cancellation or renewal rights are embedded derivatives and IAS 39 requires the issuer to measure them separately at fair value if they are not closely related to their host contract (unless the issuer elects to measure the entire contract at fair value).

Embedded derivatives

BC188 Some suggested that the Board should exempt insurers from the requirement to separate embedded derivatives contained in a host insurance contract and measure them at fair value under IAS 39. They argued that:

(a) separating these derivatives would require extensive and costly systems changes that might not be needed for phase II.

(b) some of these derivatives are intertwined with the host insurance contract in a way that would make separate measurement arbitrary and perhaps misleading, because the fair value of the whole contract might differ from the sum of the fair values of its components.

BC189 Some suggested that the inclusion of embedded options and guarantees in the cash flows used for a liability adequacy test could permit the Board to exempt some embedded derivatives from fair value measurement under IAS 39. Most proponents of this exemption implied that including only the intrinsic value of these items (ie without their time value) would suffice. However, because excluding the time value of these items could make an entity's financial statements much less relevant and reliable, the Board did not create such an exemption.

BC190 In the Board's view, fair value is the only relevant measurement basis for derivatives, because it is the only method that provides sufficient transparency in the financial statements. The cost of most derivatives is nil or immaterial. Hence if derivatives were measured at cost, they would not be included in the balance sheet and their success (or otherwise) in reducing risk, or their role in increasing risk, would not be visible. In addition, the value of derivatives often changes disproportionately in response to market movements (put another way, they are highly leveraged or carry a high level of risk). Fair value is the only measurement basis that can capture this leveraged nature of derivatives—information that is essential to communicate to users the nature of the rights and obligations inherent in derivatives.

BC191 IAS 39 requires entities to account separately for derivatives embedded in non-derivative contracts. This is necessary:

(a) to ensure that contractual rights and obligations that create similar risk exposures are treated in the same way whether or not they are embedded in a non-derivative contract.

(b) to counter the possibility that entities might seek to avoid the requirement to measure derivatives at fair value by embedding a derivative in a non-derivative contract.

BC192 The requirement to separate embedded derivatives already applied to a host contract of any kind before the IFRS was issued. Exempting insurance contracts from that existing requirement would have been a retrograde step. Furthermore, much of the effort needed to measure embedded derivatives at fair value arises from the need to identify the derivatives and from other steps that will still be needed if the Board requires fair value measurement for phase II. In the Board's view, the incremental effort needed to identify the embedded derivatives separately in phase I is relatively small and is justified by the increased transparency that fair value measurement brings. IG Example 2 in the Implementation Guidance gives guidance on the treatment of various forms of embedded derivative.

BC193 Some embedded derivatives meet the definition of an insurance contract. It would be contradictory to require a fair value measurement in phase I of an insurance contract that is embedded in a larger contract when such measurement is not required for a stand-alone insurance contract. Therefore, the IFRS confirms that this is not required (paragraph 8). For the same reason, the Board concluded that an embedded derivative is closely related to the host insurance contract if the embedded derivative and host insurance contract are so interdependent that an entity cannot measure the embedded derivative separately (see new paragraph AG33(h) of IAS 39). Without this conclusion, paragraph 12 of IAS 39 would have required the insurer to measure the entire contract at fair value. An alternative approach would have been to retain that requirement, but require measurement at cost if an insurance contract cannot be measured reliably at fair value in its entirety, building on a similar treatment in IAS 39 for unquoted equity instruments. However, the Board did not intend to require fair value measurement for insurance contracts in phase I. Therefore, the Board decided not to require this even when it is possible to measure reliably the fair value of an insurance contract containing an embedded derivative.

BC194 The Board acknowledges that insurers need not, during phase I, recognise some potentially large exposures to items such as guaranteed annuity options and guaranteed minimum death benefits. These items create risks that many regard as predominantly financial, but if the payout is contingent on an event that creates significant insurance risk, these embedded derivatives meet the definition of an insurance contract. The IFRS requires specific disclosures about these items (paragraph 39(e)). In addition, the liability adequacy test requires an entity to consider them (see paragraphs BC94–BC104).

Elimination of internal items

BC195 Some respondents suggested that financial instruments issued by one entity to a life insurer in the same group should not be eliminated from the group's consolidated financial statements if the life insurer's assets are earmarked as security for policyholders' savings.

BC196 The Board noted that these financial instruments are not assets and liabilities from the group's perspective. The Board saw no justification for departing from the general principle that all intragroup transactions are eliminated, even if they are between components of an entity that have different stakeholders, for example policyholder funds and shareholder funds. However, although the transactions are eliminated, they may affect future cash flows. Hence, they may be relevant in measuring liabilities.

BC197 Some respondents argued that non-elimination would be consistent with the fact that financial instruments issued can (unless they are non-transferable) be plan assets in defined benefit plans under IAS 19 *Employee Benefits*. However, the Board did not view IAS 19 as a precedent in this area. IAS 19 requires a presentation net of plan assets because investment in plan assets reduces the obligation (IAS 19 Basis for Conclusions paragraph 66). This presentation does not result in the recognition of new assets and liabilities.

Income taxes

BC198 Some respondents argued that discounting should be required, or at least permitted, for deferred tax relating to insurance contracts. The Board noted that discounting of a temporary difference is not relevant if an item's tax base and carrying amount are both determined on a present value basis.

Disclosure

BC199 The disclosure requirements are designed as a pair of high level principles, supplemented by some specified disclosures to meet those objectives. Implementation Guidance, published in a separate booklet, discusses how an insurer might satisfy the requirements.

BC200 Although they agreed that insurers should be allowed flexibility in determining the levels of aggregation and amount of disclosure, some respondents suggested that the Board should introduce more specific and standardised disclosure requirements. Others suggested that the draft Implementation Guidance published with ED 5 was at too high a level to ensure consistency and comparability and that its non-mandatory nature might diminish its usefulness. Some were concerned that different levels of aggregation by different insurers could reduce comparability.

BC201 Nevertheless, the Board retained ED 5's approach. The Board viewed this as superior to requiring a long list of detailed and descriptive disclosures, because concentrating on the underlying principles:

(a) makes it easier for insurers to understand the rationale for the requirements, which promotes compliance.

(b) avoids 'hard-wiring' into the IFRS disclosures that may become obsolete, and encourages experimentation that will lead to improvements as techniques develop.

(c) avoids requiring specific disclosures that may not be needed to meet the underlying objectives in the circumstances of every insurer and could lead to information overload that obscures important information in a mass of detail.

(d) gives insurers flexibility to decide on an appropriate level of aggregation that enables users to see the overall picture but without combining information that has different characteristics.

BC202 Some respondents expressed the following general concerns about the proposed disclosure requirements in ED 5:

(a) The proposed volume of disclosure was excessive and some of it would duplicate extensive material included in some countries in prudential returns.

(b) Some of the proposed disclosures would be difficult and costly to prepare and audit, make it difficult to prepare timely financial statements and provide users with little value.

(c) The proposals in ED 5 would require excessive disclosure of sensitive pricing information and other confidential proprietary information.

(d) Some of the disclosures exceeded those required in other industries, which singled out insurers unfairly. Some felt that the level of disclosure would be particularly burdensome for small insurers, whereas others referred to the difficulty of aggregating information in a meaningful way for large international groups.

BC203 The two principles and most of the supporting requirements are applications of existing requirements in IFRSs, or relatively straightforward analogies with existing IFRS requirements (particularly IAS 32). The Board's project on financial risk and other amendments to financial instruments disclosures may lead to amendments to IAS 32 that could require consequential amendments to the disclosures for insurance contracts. Furthermore, that project will consider possible disclosures in various areas that IFRS 4 does not address (eg capital and solvency requirements, market risk, liquidity risk and operational risk).

BC204 Many respondents asked the Board to clarify the status of the Implementation Guidance. In particular, some felt that the Implementation Guidance appeared to impose detailed and voluminous requirements that contradicted the Board's stated intention in paragraph BC201. In response to requests from respondents, the Board added paragraph IG12 to clarify the status of the implementation guidance on disclosure.

BC205 Some suggested that some of the disclosures, particularly those that are qualitative rather than quantitative or convey management's assertions about possible future developments, should be located outside the financial statements in a financial review by management. However, in the Board's view, the disclosure requirements are all essential and should be part of the financial statements.

BC206 Some argued that the disclosure requirements could be particularly onerous and less relevant for a subsidiary, especially if the parent guarantees the liabilities or the parent reinsures all the liabilities. However, the Board decided that no exemptions from the disclosure principles were justified. Nevertheless, the high level and flexible approach adopted by the Board enables a subsidiary to disclose the required information in a way that suits its circumstances.

BC207 Some respondents expressed concerns that the disclosure proposals in ED 5 might require extensive systems changes in phase I that might not be needed in phase II. The Board expects that both disclosure principles will remain largely unchanged for phase II, although the guidance to support them may need refinement because different information will be available and because insurers will have experience of developing systems to meet the disclosure principles in phase I.

Materiality

BC208 Some respondents expressed concerns that the IFRS (reinforced by the Implementation Guidance) might require disclosure of excessively detailed information that might not be beneficial to users. In response to these concerns, the Board included in the Implementation Guidance a discussion of materiality taken from IAS 1.

BC209 Some respondents suggested that some of the qualitative disclosures should not be subject to the normal materiality threshold, which might, in their view, lead to excessive disclosure. They proposed using different terminology, such as 'significant', to reinforce that message. However, the Board noted that not requiring disclosure of material information would be inconsistent with the definition of materiality. Thus, the Board concluded that the disclosure should, in general, rely solely on the normal definition of materiality.

BC210 In one place, the IFRS refers to a different notion. Paragraph 37(c) refers to 'the assumptions that have the greatest effect on the measurement of' assets, liabilities, income and expense arising from insurance contracts. Because many assumptions could be relevant, the Board decided to narrow the scope of the disclosure somewhat.

Explanation of recognised amounts

Assumptions

BC211 The first disclosure principle in the IFRS requires disclosure of amounts in an insurer's balance sheet and income statement that arise from insurance contracts (paragraph 36 of the IFRS). In support of this principle, paragraph 37(c) and (d) requires disclosure about assumptions and changes in assumptions. The disclosure of assumptions both assists users in testing reported information for sensitivity to changes in those assumptions and enhances their confidence in the transparency and comparability of the information.

BC212 Some expressed concerns that information about assumptions and changes in assumptions might be costly to prepare and of limited usefulness. There are many possible assumptions that could be disclosed: excessive aggregation would result in meaningless information, whereas excessive disaggregation could be costly, lead to information overload, and reveal commercially sensitive information. In response to these concerns, the disclosure about the assumptions focuses on the process used to derive them.

BC213 Some respondents argued that it is difficult to disclose meaningful information about changes in interdependent assumptions. As a result, an analysis by sources of change often depends on the order in which the analysis is performed. To acknowledge this difficulty, the IFRS does not specify a rigid format or contents for this analysis. This allows insurers to analyse the changes in a way that meets the objective of the disclosure and is appropriate for the risks they face and the systems that they have, or can enhance at a reasonable cost.

Changes in insurance liabilities

BC214 Paragraph 37(e) of the IFRS requires a reconciliation of changes in insurance liabilities, reinsurance assets and, if any, deferred acquisition costs. IAS 37 requires broadly comparable disclosure of changes in provisions, but the scope of IAS 37 excludes insurance contracts. Disclosure about changes in deferred acquisition costs is important because some existing methods use adjustments to deferred acquisition costs as a means of recognising some effects of remeasuring the future cash flows from an insurance contract (for example, to reflect the result of a liability adequacy test).

Amount, timing and uncertainty of cash flows

BC215 The second disclosure principle in the IFRS requires disclosure of information that helps users understand the amount, timing and uncertainty of future cash flows from insurance contracts (paragraph 38 of the IFRS). The Implementation Guidance supporting this principle builds largely on existing requirements in IFRSs, particularly the disclosures for financial instruments in IAS 32.

BC216 Some respondents read the draft Implementation Guidance accompanying ED 5 as implying that the IFRS would require disclosures of estimated cash flows. That was not the Board's intention because insurers cannot be expected to have systems to prepare detailed estimates of cash flows in phase I (beyond what is needed for the liability adequacy test). The Board revised the Implementation Guidance to emphasise that the second disclosure principle requires disclosure **about** cash flows (ie disclosure that helps users understand their amount, timing and uncertainty), not disclosure **of** cash flows.

Insurance risk

BC217 For insurance risk (paragraph 39(c)), the disclosures are intended to be consistent with the spirit of the disclosures required by IAS 32. The usefulness of particular disclosures about insurance risk depends on the circumstances of a particular insurer. Therefore, the requirements are written in general terms to allow practice in this area to evolve.

Sensitivity analysis

BC218 Paragraph 39(c)(i) requires disclosure of a sensitivity analysis. The Board decided not to include specific requirements that may not be appropriate in every case and could impede the development of more useful forms of disclosure or become obsolete.

BC219 IAS 32 requires disclosure of a sensitivity analysis only for assumptions that are not supported by observable market prices or rates. However, because the IFRS does not require a specific method of accounting for embedded options and guarantees, including some that are partly dependent on observable market prices or rates, paragraph 39(c)(i) requires a sensitivity analysis for all variables that have a material effect, including variables that are observable market prices or rates.

Claims development

BC220 Paragraph 39(c)(iii) requires disclosure about claims development. The US Securities and Exchange Commission requires property and casualty insurers to provide a table showing the development of provisions for unpaid claims and claim adjustment expenses for the previous ten years, if the provisions exceed 50 per cent of equity. The Board noted that the period of ten years is arbitrary and decided instead to set the period covered by this disclosure by reference to the length of the claims settlement cycle. Therefore, the IFRS requires that the disclosure should go back to the period when the earliest material claim arose for which there is still uncertainty about the amount and timing of the claims payments, but need not go back more than ten years (subject to transitional exemptions in paragraph 44 of the IFRS). Furthermore, the proposal applies to all insurers, not only to property and casualty insurers. However, because an insurer need not disclose this information for claims for which uncertainty about the amount and timing of claims payments is typically resolved within one year, it is unlikely that many life insurers would need to give this disclosure.

BC221 In the US, disclosure of claims development is generally presented in management's discussion and analysis, rather than in the financial statements. However, this disclosure is important because it gives users insights into the uncertainty surrounding estimates about future claims, and also indicates whether a particular insurer has tended to overestimate or underestimate ultimate payments. Therefore, the IFRS requires it in the financial statements.

Probable maximum loss

BC222 Some suggested that an insurer–particularly a general insurer–should disclose the probable maximum loss (PML) that it would expect if a reasonably extreme event occurred. For example, an insurer might disclose the loss that it would suffer from a severe earthquake of the kind that would be expected to recur every one hundred years, on average. However, given the lack of a widely agreed definition of PML, the Board concluded that it is not feasible to require disclosure of PML or similar measures.

Exposures to interest rate risk or market risk

BC223 As discussed in paragraphs BC193 and BC194, the Board confirmed that an insurer need not account at fair value for embedded derivatives that meet the definition of an insurance contract, but also create material exposures to interest rate risk or market risk. For many insurers, these exposures can be large. Therefore, paragraph 39(e) of the IFRS specifically requires disclosures about these exposures.

Fair value of insurance liabilities and insurance assets

BC224 ED 5 proposed that an insurer should disclose the fair value of its insurance liabilities and insurance assets. This proposal was intended (a) to give useful information to users of an insurer's financial statements and (b) to encourage insurers to begin work on systems that use updated information, to minimise the transition period for phase II.

BC225 Some respondents supported the proposed disclosure of fair value, arguing that it is important information for users. Some felt that this would be particularly important given the range of measurement practices in phase I. However, many respondents (including some who supported a fair value disclosure requirement in principle) suggested that the Board should delete this requirement or suspend it until phase II is completed. They offered the following arguments:

(a) Requiring such disclosure would be premature before the Board resolves significant issues about fair value measurement and gives adequate guidance on how to determine fair value. The lack of guidance would lead to lack of comparability for users, place unreasonable demands on preparers and pose problems of auditability. Furthermore, disclosure cannot rectify that lack of comparability because it is difficult to describe the features of different models clearly and concisely.

(b) Disclosure by 2006 (as proposed in ED 5) would be impracticable because insurers would not have time to create and test the necessary systems.

(c) Expecting insurers to begin work on an unknown objective would be costly and waste time. Furthermore, in the absence of agreed methods for developing fair value, the systems developed for phase I disclosures of fair value might need changes for phase II.

(d) The proposal asked for a mandate for the IASB to interpret its own requirement before explaining what it means.

BC226 The Board did not view the proposed requirement to disclose fair value as conditional on the measurement model for phase II. In the Board's view, disclosure of the fair value of insurance liabilities and insurance assets would provide relevant and reliable information for users even if phase II does not result in a fair value model. However, the Board agreed with respondents that requiring disclosure of fair value would not be appropriate at this stage.

Summary of changes from ED 5

BC227 The following is a summary of the main changes from ED 5 to the IFRS. The Board:

(a) clarified aspects of the definition of an insurance contract (paragraphs BC36 and BC37).

(b) clarified the requirement to unbundle deposit components in some (limited) circumstances (paragraphs BC40–BC54).

(c) deleted the 'sunset clause' proposed in ED 5 (paragraphs BC84 and BC85).

(d) clarified the need to consider embedded options and guarantees in a liability adequacy test (paragraph BC99) and clarified the level of aggregation for the liability adequacy test (paragraph BC100).

(e) replaced the impairment test for reinsurance assets. Instead of referring to IAS 36 (which contained no scope exclusion for reinsurance assets before the Board issued IFRS 4), the test will refer to IAS 39 (paragraphs BC107 and BC108).

(f) deleted the proposed ban on recognising a gain at inception of a reinsurance contract, and replaced this with a disclosure requirement (paragraphs BC109–BC114).

(g) clarified the treatment of acquisition costs for contracts that involve the provision of investment management services (paragraphs BC118 and BC119).

(h) changed the prohibition on introducing asset-based discount rates into a rebuttable presumption (paragraphs BC134–BC144).

(i) clarified aspects of the treatment of discretionary participation features (paragraphs BC154–BC165) and created an explicit new exemption from the requirement to separate, and measure at fair value, some options to surrender a contract with a discretionary participation feature (paragraph 9 of the IFRS).

(j) introduced an option for an insurer to change its accounting policies so that it remeasures designated insurance liabilities in each period for changes in interest rates. This election permits a change in accounting policies that is applied to some liabilities, but not to all similar liabilities as IAS 8 would otherwise require (paragraphs BC174–BC177).

(k) amended IAS 40 to permit two separate elections for investment property when an entity selects the fair value model or the cost model. One election is for investment property backing contracts that pay a return linked directly to the fair value of, or returns from, that investment property. The other election is for all other investment property (paragraph BC178).

(l) clarified the applicability of shadow accounting (paragraphs BC181–BC184).

(m) clarified that an embedded derivative is closely related to the host insurance contract if they are so interdependent that an entity cannot measure the embedded derivative separately (ie without considering the host contract) (paragraph BC193).

(n) clarified that the Implementation Guidance does not impose new disclosure requirements (paragraph BC204).

(o) deleted the proposed requirement to disclose the fair value of insurance contracts from 2006 (paragraphs BC224–BC226).

(p) provided an exemption from applying most disclosure requirements for insurance contracts to comparatives that relate to 2004 (paragraphs 42–44 of the IFRS).

(q) confirmed that unit-denominated payments can be measured at current unit values, for both insurance contracts and investment contracts, avoiding the apparent need to separate an 'embedded derivative' (paragraph AG33(g) of IAS 39, inserted by paragraph C8 of the IFRS).

Dissenting opinions on IFRS 4

DO1 Professor Barth and Messrs Garnett, Gélard, Leisenring, Smith and Yamada dissent from the issue of IFRS 4.

Dissent of Mary E Barth, Robert P Garnett, Gilbert Gélard, James J Leisenring and John T Smith

DO2 Messrs Garnett and Gélard dissent for the reasons given in paragraphs DO3 and DO4 and Mr Garnett also dissents for the reasons given in paragraphs DO5 and DO6. Professor Barth and Messrs Leisenring and Smith dissent for the reasons given in paragraphs DO3–DO8 and Mr Smith also dissents for the reasons given in paragraphs DO9–DO13.

Temporary exemption from paragraphs 10–12 of IAS 8

DO3 Professor Barth and Messrs Garnett, Gélard, Leisenring and Smith dissent because IFRS 4 exempts an entity from applying paragraphs 10–12 of IAS 8 *Accounting Policies, Changes in Accounting Estimates and Errors* when accounting for insurance and reinsurance contracts. They believe that all entities should be required to apply these paragraphs. These Board members believe that the requirements in IAS 8 have particular relevance and applicability when an IFRS lacks specificities, as does IFRS 4, which allows the continuation of a variety of measurement bases for insurance and reinsurance contracts. Because of the failure to consider the IASB *Framework*, continuation of such practices may result in the inappropriate recognition of, or inappropriate failure to recognise, assets, liabilities, equity, income and expense. In these Board members' view, if an entity cannot meet the basic requirements of paragraphs 10–12 of IAS 8, it should not be allowed to describe its financial statements as being in accordance with International Financial Reporting Standards.

DO4 These Board members' concerns are heightened by the delay in completing phase II of the Board's project on accounting for insurance contracts. Although phase II is on the Board's active agenda, it is unlikely that the Board will be able to develop an IFRS on insurance contracts in the near term. Accordingly, it is likely that the exemption from IAS 8 will be in place for some time.

Future investment margins and shadow accounting

DO5 Professor Barth and Messrs Garnett, Leisenring and Smith dissent for the further reason that they would not permit entities to change their accounting policies for insurance and reinsurance contracts to policies that include using future investment margins in the measurement of insurance liabilities. They agree with the view expressed in paragraph BC134 that cash flows from an asset are irrelevant for the measurement of a liability (unless those cash flows affect the cash flows arising from the liability or the credit characteristics of the liability). Therefore, they believe that changing to an accounting policy for insurance contracts that uses future investment margins to measure liabilities arising from insurance contracts reduces the relevance and reliability of an insurer's financial statements. They do not believe that other aspects of an accounting model for insurance contracts can outweigh this reduction.

DO6 These four Board members also would not permit entities to change their accounting policies for insurance and reinsurance contracts to policies that include using what is called shadow accounting. They do not believe that the changes in the carrying amount of insurance liabilities (including related deferred acquisition costs and intangible assets) under shadow accounting should be recognised directly in equity. That these changes in the measurement of the liability are calculated on the basis of changes in the measurement of assets is irrelevant. These Board members believe that these changes in insurance liabilities result in expenses that under the IASB *Framework* should be recognised in profit or loss.

Financial instruments with a discretionary participation feature

DO7 Professor Barth and Messrs Leisenring and Smith would not permit entities to account for a financial instrument with a discretionary participation feature on a basis that differs from that required by IAS 32 *Financial Instruments: Disclosure and Presentation* and IAS 39 *Financial Instruments: Recognition and Measurement*. Those Standards require entities to separate the components of a compound financial instrument, recognise the liability component initially at fair value, and attribute any residual to the equity component. These three Board members believe that the difficulty in determining whether a discretionary participation feature is a liability or equity does not preclude applying the measurement requirements in IAS 39 to the liability and equity components once the entity makes that determination. These three Board members believe that an entity would misstate interest expense if the financial liability component is not initially measured at its fair value.

DO8 These three Board members would require entities to ensure in all cases that the liability recognised for financial instruments with a discretionary participation feature is no less than the amount that would result from applying IAS 39 to the guaranteed element. Paragraph 35 of IFRS 4 requires this if an entity classifies none or some of the feature as a liability, but not if it classifies all of the feature as a liability.

Financial instruments

DO9 Mr Smith also dissents from IFRS 4 because he believes it defines insurance contracts too broadly and makes unnecessary exceptions to the scope of IAS 32 and IAS 39. In his view, this permits the structuring of contractual provisions to avoid the requirements of those Standards, diminishing their effectiveness and adding considerable complexity in interpreting and applying them and IFRS 4. He believes that many of the exceptions, based on the desire to avoid systems changes, are unnecessary because they generally are unrelated to the second phase of the project on insurance contracts, and they create a disincentive to enhance systems before the second phase of that project is completed. Mr Smith believes that IAS 32 and IAS 39 already contain the appropriate solutions when measurements cannot be made reliably and those solutions make systems limitations transparent.

DO10 Paragraph 10 of IFRS 4 requires an insurer to unbundle a deposit component of an insurance contract if the insurer can measure the deposit component separately and the insurer's accounting policies do not otherwise require it to recognise all rights and obligations arising from the deposit component. Mr Smith notes that the deposit component consists entirely of financial liabilities or financial assets. Therefore, he believes that the deposit component of all insurance contracts should be unbundled. Mr Smith notes that IAS 32 already requires the liability component of a compound financial instrument to be separated at its fair value with any residual accounted for as equity. He believes this approach could be applied by analogy when an insurance contract contains a financial liability and would represent a superior solution.

DO11 IFRS 4 amends IAS 39 by stating that an embedded derivative and the host insurance contract are closely related if they are so interdependent that the entity cannot measure the embedded derivative separately. This creates an exemption from the requirement in IAS 39 to account for such embedded derivatives at fair value. Mr Smith disagrees with that change. In particular, if a contract permits a policyholder to obtain a derivative-based cash settlement in lieu of maintaining insurance, Mr Smith believes that the derivative-based cash settlement alternative is a financial liability and should be measured at fair value.

DO12 For the contracts discussed in the previous paragraph, Mr Smith believes that IAS 39 already provides a superior solution that will not promote structuring to take advantage of an exception to IAS 39. It requires the entire contract to be measured at fair value when an embedded derivative cannot be reliably separated from the host contract. However, Mr Smith would amend IAS 39 to require measurement at cost if a contract cannot be measured reliably at fair value in its entirety and contains a significant insurance component as well as an embedded derivative. This amendment would be consistent with similar requirements in IAS 39 for unquoted equity instruments. To make systems limitations more transparent, Mr Smith would add the disclosure required by IAS 32, including the fact that fair value cannot be measured reliably, a description of the insurance contracts in question, their carrying amounts, an explanation of why fair value cannot be measured reliably and, if possible, the range of estimates within which fair value is likely to fall.

DO13 Mr Smith would exclude from the definition of an insurance contract those contracts that are regarded as transferring significant insurance risk at inception only because they include a pricing option permitting the holder to purchase insurance at a specified price at a later date. He would also exclude from the definition those contracts in which the insurance component has expired. He believes that any remaining obligation is a financial instrument that should be accounted for under IAS 39.

Dissent of Tatsumi Yamada

DO14 Mr Yamada dissents from the issue of IFRS 4 because he believes that it does not resolve appropriately the mismatch in measurement base between financial assets of insurers and their insurance liabilities. Specifically:

(a) he disagrees with the inclusion of an option to introduce a current discount rate for designated insurance liabilities.

(b) he believes that the Board should have provided a practicable means to reduce the effect of the accounting mismatch using methods based partly on some existing practices that involve broader, but constrained, use of amortised cost.

Option to introduce a current discount rate

DO15 Mr Yamada disagrees with paragraph 24 of the IFRS, which creates an option to introduce a current market-based discount rate for designated insurance liabilities. He has sympathy for the view expressed in paragraph BC175 that introducing a current market-based discount rate for insurance liabilities rather than a historical discount rate would improve the relevance and reliability of an insurer's financial statements. However, as explained in paragraph BC126, 'the Board will not address discount rates and the basis for risk adjustments until phase II.' Therefore, Mr Yamada believes that it is not appropriate to deal with measurement of insurance liabilities in phase I of this project.

DO16 In addition, Mr Yamada believes that there should be a stringent test to assess whether changes in the carrying amount of the designated insurance liabilities mitigate the changes in carrying amount of financial assets. Without such a test, management will have a free choice to decide the extent to which it introduces remeasurement of insurance liabilities. Therefore, he does not agree with the Board's conclusion in paragraph BC176 that 'the increase in relevance and reliability from introducing a current discount rate could outweigh the disadvantages of permitting accounting policies that are not applied consistently to all similar liabilities'.

DO17 Furthermore, the option introduced by paragraph 24 is not an effective way to reduce the accounting mismatch, in Mr Yamada's view. He agrees with the Board's analysis that 'many insurers may not have systems to adjust liabilities for changes in interest rates and may not wish to develop such systems, even for designated liabilities as opposed to all liabilities', as explained in paragraph BC177(d)(i).

Assets held to back insurance liabilities

DO18 As stated in paragraph BC171, many of the respondents to ED 5 urged the Board to explore ways of reducing the accounting mismatch. Mr Yamada notes that IFRS 4 provides some limited solutions for the accounting mismatch by clarifying that shadow accounting can be used and amending IAS 40 to permit two separate elections when an entity selects the fair value model or the cost model for investment property. IFRS 4 also provides an option to introduce a current market-based discount rate for designated insurance liabilities but, for reasons given in paragraphs DO15–DO17, Mr Yamada does not support that option.

DO19 Mr Yamada believes that it would have been appropriate to provide a more broadly applicable way of mitigating the effect of the accounting mismatch. Because phase I is only a stepping stone to phase II, Mr Yamada is of the view that the only practicable solution in the short term is one based on the existing practices of insurers. He believes that if remeasurement of insurance liabilities by a current market-based discount rate is allowed as means of resolving the mismatch, a new category of assets carried at amortised cost such as the Japanese 'debt securities earmarked for policy reserve' (DSR) should also have been allowed in phase I.

DO20 Although Mr Yamada acknowledges that the DSR approach would not lead to more relevant and reliable measurements, he notes that insurers have several years' experience of using this approach, which was created in 2000 when Japan introduced an accounting standard for financial instruments that is similar to IASs 32 and 39. He believes that no perfect solution is available in phase I and together with the disclosure of fair value information required by IAS 32, the DSR approach would provide a reasonable solution for phase I. Therefore he does not agree with the Board's conclusion in paragraph BC178 that amending the existing measurement requirements in IAS 39 for financial assets 'would have reduced the relevance and reliability of financial statements to an unacceptable extent'. Indeed, Mr Yamada believes the exemption in IFRS 4 from paragraphs 10–12 of IAS 8 could impair the relevance and reliability of financial statements more than introducing the DSR approach would have done.

CONTENTS

Guidance on Implementing IFRS 4 Insurance Contracts

This guidance accompanies, but is not part of, IFRS 4.

Introduction

IG1 This implementation guidance:

(a) illustrates which contracts and embedded derivatives are within the scope of the IFRS (see paragraphs IG2–IG4).

(b) includes an example of an insurance contract containing a deposit component that needs to be unbundled (paragraph IG5).

(c) illustrates shadow accounting (paragraphs IG6–IG10).

(d) discusses how an insurer might satisfy the disclosure requirements in the IFRS (paragraphs IG11–IG71).

Definition of insurance contract

IG2 IG Example 1 illustrates the application of the definition of an insurance contract. The example does not illustrate all possible circumstances.

IG Example 1: Application of the definition of an insurance contract		
Contract type		***Treatment in phase I***
1.1	Insurance contract (see definition in Appendix A of the IFRS and guidance in Appendix B).	Within the scope of the IFRS, unless covered by scope exclusions in paragraph 4 of the IFRS. Some embedded derivatives and deposit components must be separated (see IG Examples 2 and 3 and paragraphs 7–12 of the IFRS).
1.2	Death benefit that could exceed amounts payable on surrender or maturity.	Insurance contract (unless contingent amount is insignificant in all scenarios that have commercial substance). Insurer could suffer a significant loss on an individual contract if the policyholder dies early. See IG Examples 1.23–27 for further discussion of surrender penalties.
1.3	A unit-linked contract that pays benefits linked to the fair value of a pool of assets. The benefit is 100 per cent of the unit value on surrender or maturity and 101 per cent of the unit value on death.	This contract contains a deposit component (100 per cent of unit value) and an insurance component (additional death benefit of 1 per cent). Paragraph 10 of the IFRS permits unbundling (but requires it only if the insurance component is material and the issuer would not otherwise recognise all obligations and rights arising under the deposit component). If the insurance component is not unbundled, the whole contract is an investment contract because the insurance component is insignificant in relation to the whole contract.
1.4	Life-contingent annuity.	Insurance contract (unless contingent amount is insignificant in all scenarios that have commercial substance). Insurer could suffer a significant loss on an individual contract if the annuitant survives longer than expected.
1.5	Pure endowment. The insured person receives a payment on survival to a specified date, but beneficiaries receive nothing if the insured person dies before then.	Insurance contract (unless the transfer of insurance risk is insignificant). If a relatively homogeneous book of pure endowments is known to consist of contracts that all transfer insurance risk, the insurer may classify the entire book as insurance contracts without examining each contract to identify a few non-derivative pure endowments that transfer insignificant insurance risk (see paragraph B25).
1.6	Deferred annuity: policyholder will receive, or can elect to receive, a life-contingent annuity at rates guaranteed at inception.	Insurance contract (unless the transfer of insurance risk is insignificant). The contract transfers mortality risk to the insurer at inception, because the insurer might have to pay significant additional benefits for an individual contract if the annuitant elects to take the life-contingent annuity and survives longer than expected (unless the contingent amount is insignificant in all scenarios that have commercial substance).

Continued from previous page

IG Example 1: Application of the definition of an insurance contract

Contract type		*Treatment in phase I*
1.7	Deferred annuity: policyholder will receive, or can elect to receive, a life-contingent annuity at rates prevailing when the annuity begins.	Not an insurance contract at inception, if the insurer can reprice the mortality risk without constraints. Within the scope of IAS 39 *Financial Instruments: Recognition and Measurement* unless the contract contains a discretionary participation feature. Will become an insurance contract when the annuity rate is fixed (unless the contingent amount is insignificant in all scenarios that have commercial substance).
1.8	Investment contract[(a)] that does not contain a discretionary participation feature.	Within the scope of IAS 39.
1.9	Investment contract containing a discretionary participation feature.	Paragraph 35 of the IFRS sets out requirements for these contracts, which are excluded from the scope of IAS 39.
1.10	Investment contract in which payments are contractually linked (with no discretion) to returns on a specified pool of assets held by the issuer.	Within the scope of IAS 39. Payments denominated in unit values representing the fair value of the specified assets are measured at current unit value (see paragraph AG33(g) of Appendix A of IAS 39).
1.11	Contract that requires specified payments to reimburse the holder for a loss it incurs because a specified debtor fails to make payment when due under the original or modified terms of a debt instrument. The contract may have various legal forms (eg insurance contract, financial guarantee or letter of credit).	Insurance contract. Within the scope of the IFRS, unless the contract was entered into or retained on the transfer of financial assets or financial liabilities within the scope of IAS 39. If the issuer's accounting policies do not require it to recognise a liability at inception, the liability adequacy test in paragraphs 15–19 of the IFRS may be particularly relevant. The legal form of the contract does not affect its recognition and measurement.
1.12	A financial guarantee that does not, as a precondition for payment, require that the holder is exposed to, and has incurred a loss on, the failure of the debtor to make payments on the guaranteed asset when due. An example of such a contract is one that requires payments in response to changes in a specified credit rating or credit index.	Not an insurance contract. Within the scope of IAS 39.

Continued from previous page **IG Example 1: Application of the definition of an insurance contract**		
Contract type		***Treatment in phase I***
1.13	Guarantee fund established by contract. The contract requires all participants to pay contributions to the fund so that it can meet obligations incurred by participants (and, perhaps, others). Participants would typically be from a single industry, eg insurance, banking or travel.	The contract that establishes the guarantee fund is an insurance contract (see IG Example 1.11).
1.14	Guarantee fund established by law.	The commitment of participants to contribute to the fund is not established by a contract, so there is no insurance contract. Within the scope of IAS 37 *Provisions, Contingent Liabilities and Contingent Assets*.
1.15	Residual value insurance or residual value guarantee. Guarantee by one party of the fair value at a future date of a non-financial asset held by a beneficiary of the insurance or guarantee.	Insurance contract within the scope of the IFRS (unless changes in the condition of the asset have an insignificant effect). The risk of changes in the fair value of the non-financial asset is not a financial risk because the fair value reflects not only changes in market prices for such assets (a financial variable) but also the condition of the specific asset held (a non-financial variable). However, if the contract compensates the beneficiary only for changes in market prices and not for changes in the condition of the beneficiary's asset, the contract is a derivative and within the scope of IAS 39. Residual value guarantees given by a lessee under a finance lease are within the scope of IAS 17 *Leases*.
1.16	Product warranties issued directly by a manufacturer, dealer or retailer.	Insurance contracts, but excluded from the scope of the IFRS (see IAS 18 *Revenue* and IAS 37).
1.17	Product warranties issued by a third party.	Insurance contracts, no scope exclusion. Same treatment as other insurance contracts.
1.18	Group insurance contract that gives the insurer an enforceable and non-cancellable contractual right to recover all claims paid out of future premiums, with appropriate compensation for the time value of money.	Insurance risk is insignificant. Therefore, the contract is a financial instrument within the scope of IAS 39. Servicing fees are within the scope of IAS 18 (recognise as services are provided, subject to various conditions).

Continued from previous page

IG Example 1: Application of the definition of an insurance contract

Contract type		***Treatment in phase I***
1.19	Catastrophe bond: bond in which principal, interest payments or both are reduced if a specified triggering event occurs and the triggering event does not include a condition that the issuer of the bond suffered a loss.	Financial instrument with embedded derivative. Both the holder and the issuer measure the embedded derivative at fair value.
1.20	Catastrophe bond: bond in which principal, interest payments or both are reduced significantly if a specified triggering event occurs and the triggering event includes a condition that the issuer of the bond suffered a loss.	The contract is an insurance contract, and contains an insurance component (with the issuer as policyholder and the holder as the insurer) and a deposit component. (a) If specified conditions are met, paragraph 10 of the IFRS requires the holder to unbundle the deposit component and apply IAS 39 to it. (b) The issuer accounts for the insurance component as reinsurance if it uses the bond for that purpose. If the issuer does not use the insurance component as reinsurance, it is not within the scope of the IFRS, which does not address accounting by policyholders for direct insurance contracts. (c) Under paragraph 13 of the IFRS, the holder could continue its existing accounting for the insurance component, unless that involves the practices prohibited by paragraph 14.
1.21	An insurance contract issued by an insurer to a defined benefit pension plan covering the employees of the insurer, or of another entity consolidated within the same financial statements as the insurer.	The contract will generally be eliminated from the financial statements, which will include: (a) the full amount of the pension obligation under IAS 19 *Employee Benefits*, with no deduction for the plan's rights under the contract. (b) no liability to policyholders under the contract. (c) the assets backing the contract.
1.22	An insurance contract issued to employees as a result of a defined contribution pension plan. The contractual benefits for employee service in the current and prior periods are not contingent on future service. The insurer also issues similar contracts on the same terms to third parties.	Insurance contract within the scope of the IFRS. If the employer pays part or all of the employee's premiums, the payment by the employer is an employee benefit within the scope of IAS 19. See also IAS 19, paragraphs 39–42 and 104–104D. Furthermore, a 'qualifying insurance policy' as defined in IAS 19 need not meet the definition of an insurance contract in this IFRS.

Continued from previous page

IG Example 1: Application of the definition of an insurance contract

Contract type		***Treatment in phase I***
1.23	Loan contract containing a prepayment fee that is waived if prepayment results from the borrower's death.	Not an insurance contract. Before entering into the contract, the borrower faced no risk corresponding to the prepayment fee. Hence, although the loan contract exposes the lender to mortality risk, it does not transfer a pre-existing risk from the borrower. Thus, the risk associated with the possible waiver on death of the prepayment fee is not insurance risk (paragraphs B12 and B24(b) of Appendix B of the IFRS).
1.24	Loan contract that waives repayment of the entire loan balance if the borrower dies.	This contract contains a deposit component (the loan) and an insurance component (waiver of the loan balance on death, equivalent to a cash death benefit). If specified conditions are met, paragraph 10 of the IFRS requires or permits unbundling. If the insurance component is not unbundled, the contract is an insurance contract if the insurance component is significant in relation to the whole contract.
1.25	A contract permits the issuer to deduct a market value adjustment (MVA) from surrender values or death benefits to reflect current market prices for the underlying assets. The contract does not permit an MVA for maturity benefits.	The policyholder obtains an additional survival benefit because no MVA is applied at maturity. That benefit is a pure endowment (see IG Example 1.5). If the risk transferred by that benefit is significant, the contract is an insurance contract.
1.26	A contract permits the issuer to deduct an MVA from surrender values or maturity payments to reflect current market prices for the underlying assets. The contract does not permit an MVA for death benefits.	The policyholder obtains an additional death benefit because no MVA is applied on death. If the risk transferred by that benefit is significant, the contract is an insurance contract.

Continued from previous page

IG Example 1: Application of the definition of an insurance contract

	Contract type	*Treatment in phase I*
1.27	A contract permits the issuer to deduct an MVA from surrender payments to reflect current market prices for the underlying assets. The contract does not permit an MVA for death and maturity benefits. The amount payable on death or maturity is the amount originally invested plus interest.	The policyholder obtains an additional benefit because no MVA is applied on death or maturity. However, that benefit does not transfer insurance risk from the policyholder because it is certain that the policyholder will live or die and the amount payable on death or maturity is adjusted for the time value of money (see paragraph B27 of the IFRS). The contract is an investment contract. This contract combines the two features discussed in IG Examples 1.25 and 1.26. When considered separately, those two features transfer insurance risk. However, when combined, they do not transfer insurance risk. Therefore, it is not appropriate to separate this contract into two 'insurance' components. If the amount payable on death were not adjusted in full for the time value of money, or were adjusted in some other way, the contract might transfer insurance risk. If that insurance risk is significant, the contract is an insurance contract.
1.28	A contract meets the definition of an insurance contract. It was issued by one entity in a group (for example a captive insurer) to another entity in the same group.	If the entities present individual or separate financial statements, they treat the contract as an insurance contract in those individual or separate financial statements (see IAS 27 *Consolidated and Separate Financial Statements*). The transaction is eliminated from the group's consolidated financial statements. If the intragroup contract is reinsured with a third party that is not part of the group, the reinsurance contract is treated as a direct insurance contract in the consolidated financial statements because the intragroup contract is eliminated on consolidation.
1.29	An agreement that entity A will compensate entity B for losses on one or more contracts issued by entity B that do not transfer significant insurance risk.	The contract is an insurance contract if it transfers significant insurance risk from entity B to entity A, even if some or all of the individual contracts do not transfer significant insurance risk to entity B. The contract is a reinsurance contract if any of the contracts issued by entity B are insurance contracts. Otherwise, the contract is a direct insurance contract.

(a) The term 'investment contract' is an informal term used for ease of discussion. It refers to a financial instrument that does not meet the definition of an insurance contract.

Embedded derivatives

IG3 IAS 39 requires an entity to separate embedded derivatives that meet specified conditions from the host instrument that contains them, measure the embedded derivatives at fair value and recognise changes in their fair value in profit or loss. However, an insurer need not separate an embedded derivative that itself meets the definition of an insurance contract (paragraph 7 of the IFRS). Nevertheless, separation and fair value measurement of such an embedded derivative are not prohibited if the insurer's existing accounting policies require such separation, or if an insurer changes its accounting policies and that change meets the criteria in paragraph 22 of the IFRS.

IG4 IG Example 2 illustrates the treatment of embedded derivatives contained in insurance contracts and investment contracts. The term 'investment contract' is an informal term used for ease of discussion. It refers to a financial instrument that does not meet the definition of an insurance contract. The example does not illustrate all possible circumstances. Throughout the example, the phrase 'fair value measurement is required' indicates that the issuer of the contract is required:

(a) to measure the embedded derivative at fair value and include changes in its fair value in profit or loss.

(b) to separate the embedded derivative from the host contract, unless it measures the entire contract at fair value and includes changes in that fair value in profit or loss.

IG Example 2: Embedded derivatives

	Type of embedded derivative	***Treatment if embedded in a host insurance contract***	***Treatment if embedded in a host investment contract***
2.1	Death benefit linked to equity prices or equity index, payable only on death or annuitisation and not on surrender or maturity.	The equity-index feature is an insurance contract (unless the life-contingent payments are insignificant), because the policyholder benefits from it only when the insured event occurs. Fair value measurement is not required (but not prohibited).	Not applicable. The entire contract is an insurance contract (unless the life-contingent payments are insignificant).
2.2	Death benefit that is the greater of: (a) unit value of an investment fund (equal to the amount payable on surrender or maturity); and (b) guaranteed minimum.	Excess of guaranteed minimum over unit value is a death benefit (similar to the payout on a dual trigger contract, see IG Example 2.19). This meets the definition of an insurance contract (unless the life-contingent payments are insignificant) and fair value measurement is not required (but not prohibited).	Not applicable. The entire contract is an insurance contract (unless the life-contingent payments are insignificant).

Continued from previous page

IG Example 2: Embedded derivatives

	Type of embedded derivative	***Treatment if embedded in a host insurance contract***	***Treatment if embedded in a host investment contract***
2.3	Option to take a life-contingent annuity at guaranteed rate (combined guarantee of interest rates and mortality charges).	The embedded option is an insurance contract (unless the life-contingent payments are insignificant). Fair value measurement is not required (but not prohibited).	Not applicable. The entire contract is an insurance contract (unless the life-contingent payments are insignificant).
2.4	Embedded guarantee of minimum interest rates in determining surrender or maturity values that is at or out of the money on issue, and not leveraged.	The embedded guarantee is not an insurance contract (unless significant payments are life-contingent[a]. However, it is closely related to the host contract (paragraph AG33(b) of Appendix A of IAS 39). Fair value measurement is not required (but not prohibited). If significant payments are life-contingent, the contract is an insurance contract and contains a deposit component (the guaranteed minimum). However, an insurer is not required to unbundle the contract if it recognises all obligations arising from the deposit component (paragraph 10 of the IFRS). If cancelling the deposit component requires the policyholder to cancel the insurance component, the two cancellation options may be interdependent; if the option to cancel the deposit component cannot be measured separately (ie without considering the other option), both options are regarded as part of the insurance component (paragraph AG33(h) of IAS 39).	Fair value measurement is not permitted (paragraph AG33(b) of IAS 39).
2.5	Embedded guarantee of minimum interest rates in determining surrender or maturity values: in the money on issue, or leveraged.	The embedded guarantee is not an insurance contract (unless the embedded guarantee is life-contingent to a significant extent). Fair value measurement is required (paragraph AG33(b) of IAS 39).	Fair value measurement is required (paragraph AG33(b) of IAS 39).

Continued from previous page

IG Example 2: Embedded derivatives

Type of embedded derivative		Treatment if embedded in a host insurance contract	Treatment if embedded in a host investment contract
2.6	Embedded guarantee of minimum annuity payments if the annuity payments are contractually linked to investment returns or asset prices:		
	(a) guarantee relates only to payments that are life-contingent.	The embedded guarantee is an insurance contract (unless the life-contingent payments are insignificant). Fair value measurement is not required (but not prohibited).	Not applicable. The entire contract is an insurance contract (unless the life-contingent payments are insignificant).
	(b) guarantee relates only to payments that are not life-contingent.	The embedded derivative is not an insurance contract. Fair value measurement is required (unless the guarantee is regarded as closely related to the host contract because the guarantee is an unleveraged interest floor that is at or out of the money at inception, see paragraph AG33(b) of IAS 39).	Fair value measurement is required (unless the guarantee is regarded as closely related to the host contract because the guarantee is an unleveraged interest floor that is at or out of the money at inception, see paragraph AG33(b) of IAS 39).
	(c) policyholder can elect to receive life-contingent payments or payments that are not life-contingent, and the guarantee relates to both. When the policyholder makes its election, the issuer cannot adjust the pricing of the life-contingent payments to reflect the risk that the insurer assumes at that time (see paragraph B29 of the IFRS for discussion of contracts with separate accumulation and payout phases).	The embedded option to benefit from a guarantee of life-contingent payments is an insurance contract (unless the life-contingent payments are insignificant). Fair value measurement is not required (but not prohibited). The embedded option to receive payments that are not life-contingent ('the second option') is not an insurance contract. However, because the second option and the life-contingent option are alternatives, their fair values are interdependent. If they are so interdependent that the issuer cannot measure the second option separately (ie without considering the life-contingent option), the second option is closely related to the insurance contract. In that case, fair value measurement is not required (but not prohibited).	Not applicable. The entire contract is an insurance contract (unless the life-contingent payments are insignificant).

Continued from previous page

IG Example 2: Embedded derivatives

Type of embedded derivative		***Treatment if embedded in a host insurance contract***	***Treatment if embedded in a host investment contract***
2.7	Embedded guarantee of minimum equity returns on surrender or maturity.	The embedded guarantee is not an insurance contract (unless the embedded guarantee is life-contingent to a significant extent) and is not closely related to the host insurance contract. Fair value measurement is required.	Fair value measurement is required.
2.8	Equity-linked return available on surrender or maturity.	The embedded derivative is not an insurance contract (unless the equity-linked return is life-contingent to a significant extent) and is not closely related to the host insurance contract. Fair value measurement is required.	Fair value measurement is required.
2.9	Embedded guarantee of minimum equity returns that is available only if the policyholder elects to take a life-contingent annuity.	The embedded guarantee is an insurance contract (unless the life-contingent payments are insignificant), because the policyholder can benefit from the guarantee only by taking the annuity option (whether annuity rates are set at inception or at the date of annuitisation). Fair value measurement is not required (but not prohibited).	Not applicable. The entire contract is an insurance contract (unless the life-contingent payments are insignificant).
2.10	Embedded guarantee of minimum equity returns available to the policyholder as either (a) a cash payment, (b) a period-certain annuity or (c) a life-contingent annuity, at annuity rates prevailing at the **date of annuitisation.**	If the guaranteed payments are not contingent to a significant extent on survival, the option to take the life-contingent annuity does not transfer insurance risk until the policyholder opts to take the annuity. Therefore, the embedded guarantee is not an insurance contract and is not closely related to the host insurance contract. Fair value measurement is required. If the guaranteed payments are contingent to a significant extent on survival, the guarantee is an insurance contract (similar to a pure endowment). Fair value measurement is not required (but not prohibited).	Fair value measurement is required.

Continued from previous page

IG Example 2: Embedded derivatives

	Type of embedded derivative	***Treatment if embedded in a host insurance contract***	***Treatment if embedded in a host investment contract***
2.11	Embedded guarantee of minimum equity returns available to the policyholder as either (a) a cash payment (b) a period-certain annuity or (c) a life-contingent annuity, at annuity rates set at **inception**.	The whole contract is an insurance contract from inception (unless the life-contingent payments are insignificant). The option to take the life-contingent annuity is an embedded insurance contract, so fair value measurement is not required (but not prohibited). The option to take the cash payment or the period-certain annuity ('the second option') is not an insurance contract (unless the option is contingent to a significant extent on survival), so it must be separated. However, because the second option and the life-contingent option are alternatives, their fair values are interdependent. If they are so interdependent that the issuer cannot measure the second option separately (ie without considering the life-contingent option), the second option is closely related to the host insurance contract. In that case, fair value measurement is not required (but not prohibited).	Not applicable.
2.12	Policyholder option to surrender a contract for a cash surrender value specified in a schedule (ie not indexed and not accumulating interest).	Fair value measurement is not required (but not prohibited: paragraph 8 of the IFRS). The surrender value may be viewed as a deposit component, but the IFRS does not require an insurer to unbundle a contract if it recognises all its obligations arising under the deposit component (paragraph 10).	The surrender option is closely related to the host contract if the surrender value is approximately equal to the amortised cost at each exercise date (paragraph AG30(g) of IAS 39). Otherwise, the surrender option is measured at fair value.

Continued from previous page

IG Example 2: Embedded derivatives

Type of embedded derivative		*Treatment if embedded in a host insurance contract*	*Treatment if embedded in a host investment contract*
2.13	Policyholder option to surrender a contract for account value based on a principal amount and a fixed or variable interest rate (or based on the fair value of a pool of interest-bearing securities), possibly after deducting a surrender charge.	Same as for a cash surrender value (IG Example 2.12).	Same as for a cash surrender value (IG Example 2.12).
2.14	Policyholder option to surrender a contract for a surrender value based on an equity or commodity price or index.	The option is not closely related to the host contract (unless the option is life-contingent to a significant extent). Fair value measurement is required (paragraphs 8 of the IFRS and AG30(d) and (e) of IAS 39).	Fair value measurement is required (paragraph AG30(d) and (e) of IAS 39).
2.15	Policyholder option to surrender a contract for account value equal to the fair value of a pool of equity investments, possibly after deducting a surrender charge.	If the insurer measures that portion of its obligation at account value, no further adjustment is needed for the option (unless the surrender value differs significantly from account value) (see paragraph AG33(g) of IAS 39). Otherwise, fair value measurement is required.	If the insurer regards the account value as the amortised cost or fair value of that portion of its obligation, no further adjustment is needed for the option (unless the surrender value differs significantly from account value). Otherwise, fair value measurement is required.
2.16	Contractual feature that provides a return contractually linked (with no discretion) to the return on specified assets.	The embedded derivative is not an insurance contract and is not closely related to the contract (paragraph AG30(h) of IAS 39). Fair value measurement is required.	Fair value measurement is required.

Continued from previous page

IG Example 2: Embedded derivatives

Type of embedded derivative		Treatment if embedded in a host insurance contract	Treatment if embedded in a host investment contract
2.17	Persistency bonus paid at maturity in cash (or as a period-certain annuity).	The embedded derivative (option to receive the persistency bonus) is not an insurance contract (unless the persistency bonus is life-contingent to a significant extent). Insurance risk does not include lapse or persistency risk (paragraph B15 of the IFRS). Fair value measurement is required.	An option or automatic provision to extend the remaining term to maturity of a debt instrument is not closely related to the host debt instrument unless there is a concurrent adjustment to the approximate current market rate of interest at the time of the extension (paragraph AG30(c) of IAS 39). If the option or provision is not closely related to the host instrument, fair value measurement is required.
2.18	Persistency bonus paid at maturity as an enhanced life-contingent annuity.	The embedded derivative is an insurance contract (unless the life-contingent payments are insignificant). Fair value measurement is not required (but not prohibited).	Not applicable. The entire contract is an insurance contract (unless the life-contingent payments are insignificant).
2.19	Dual trigger contract, eg contract requiring a payment that is contingent on a breakdown in power supply that adversely affects the holder (first trigger) and a specified level of electricity prices (second trigger). The contingent payment is made only if both triggering events occur.	The embedded derivative is an insurance contract (unless the first trigger lacks commercial substance). A contract that qualifies as an insurance contract, whether at inception or later, remains an insurance contract until all rights and obligations are extinguished or expire (paragraph B30 of the IFRS). Therefore, although the remaining exposure is similar to a financial derivative after the insured event has occurred, the embedded derivative is still an insurance contract and fair value measurement is not required (but not prohibited).	Not applicable. The entire contract is an insurance contract (unless the first trigger lacks commercial substance).

Continued from previous page

IG Example 2: Embedded derivatives

	Type of embedded derivative	***Treatment if embedded in a host insurance contract***	***Treatment if embedded in a host investment contract***
2.20	non-guaranteed participating dividend contained in a life insurance contract. The amount is contractually at the discretion of the insurer but is contractually based on the insurer's actual experience on the related block of insurance contracts.	The contract contains a discretionary participation feature, rather than an embedded derivative (paragraph 34 of the IFRS).	Not applicable. The entire contract is an insurance contract (unless the life-contingent payments are insignificant).

(a) Payments are life-contingent if they are contingent on death or contingent on survival.

Unbundling a deposit component

IG5 Paragraph 10 of the IFRS requires an insurer to unbundle some insurance contracts that contain a deposit component. IG Example 3 illustrates this requirement. Although arrangements of this kind are more common in reinsurance, the same principle applies in direct insurance. However, unbundling is not required if the insurer recognises all obligations or rights arising from the deposit component.

IG Example 3: Unbundling a deposit component of a reinsurance contract

Background

A reinsurance contract has the following features:

(a) The cedant pays premiums of CU10[(a)] every year for five years.

(b) An experience account is established, equal to 90 per cent of cumulative premiums (including the additional premiums discussed in (c) below) less 90 per cent of cumulative claims.

(c) If the balance in the experience account is negative (ie cumulative claims exceed cumulative premiums), the cedant pays an additional premium equal to the experience account balance divided by the number of years left to run on the contract.

(d) At the end of the contract, if the experience account balance is positive (ie cumulative premiums exceed cumulative claims), it is refunded to the cedant; if the balance is negative, the cedant pays the balance to the reinsurer as an additional premium.

(e) Neither party can cancel the contract before maturity.

(f) The maximum loss that the reinsurer is required to pay in any period is CU200.

This contract is an insurance contract because it transfers significant insurance risk to the reinsurer. For example, in case 2 discussed below, the reinsurer is required to pay additional benefits with a present value, in year 1, of CU35, which is clearly significant in relation to the contract.

The following discussion addresses the accounting by the reinsurer. Similar principles apply to the accounting by the cedant.

(a) In this Implementation Guidance monetary amounts are denominated in 'currency units' (CU).

Continued from previous page

IG Example 3: Unbundling a deposit component of a reinsurance contract

Application of requirements: case 1—no claims

If there are no claims, the cedant will receive CU45 in year 5 (90 per cent of the cumulative premiums of CU50). In substance, the cedant has made a loan, which the reinsurer will repay in one instalment of CU45 in year 5.

If the reinsurer's accounting policies require it to recognise its contractual liability to repay the loan to the cedant, unbundling is permitted but not required. However, if the reinsurer's accounting policies would not require it to recognise the liability to repay the loan, the reinsurer is required to unbundle the contract (paragraph 10 of the IFRS).

If the reinsurer is required, or elects, to unbundle the contract, it does so as follows. Each payment by the cedant has two components: a loan advance (deposit component) and a payment for insurance cover (insurance component). Applying IAS 39 to the deposit component, the reinsurer is required to measure it initially at fair value. Fair value could be determined by discounting the future cash flows from the deposit component. Assume that an appropriate discount rate is 10 per cent and that the insurance cover is equal in each year, so that the payment for insurance cover is the same in every year. Each payment of CU10 by the cedant is then made up of a loan advance of CU6.7 and an insurance premium of CU3.3.

The reinsurer accounts for the insurance component in the same way that it accounts for a separate insurance contract with an annual premium of CU3.3.

The movements in the loan are shown below.

Year	Opening balance	Interest at 10 per cent	Advance (repayment)	Closing balance
	CU	CU	CU	CU
0	0.00	0.00	6.70	6.70
1	6.70	0.67	6.70	14.07
2	14.07	1.41	6.70	22.18
3	22.18	2.22	6.70	31.09
4	31.09	3.11	6.70	40.90
5	40.90	4.10	(45.00)	0.00
Total		11.50	(11.50)	

Continued from previous page

IG Example 3: Unbundling a deposit component of a reinsurance contract

Application of requirements: case 2—claim of CU150 in year 1

Consider now what happens if the reinsurer pays a claim of CU150 in year 1. The changes in the experience account, and resulting additional premiums, are as follows.

Year	Premium	Additional premium	Total premium	Cumulative premium	Claims	Cumulative claims	Cumulative premiums less claims	Experience account
	CU	CU	CU	CU	CU	CU	CU	CU
0	10	0	10	10	0	0	10	9
1	10	0	10	20	(150)	(150)	(130)	(117)
2	10	39	49	69	0	(150)	(81)	(73)
3	10	36	46	115	0	(150)	(35)	(31)
4	10	31	41	156	0	(150)	6	6
		106	156		(150)			

Continued from previous page

IG Example 3: Unbundling a deposit component of a reinsurance contract

Incremental cash flows because of the claim in year 1

The claim in year 1 leads to the following incremental cash flows, compared with case 1:

Year	Additional premium	Claims	Refund in case 2	Refund in case 1	Net incremental cash flow	Present value at 10 per cent
	CU	CU	CU	CU	CU	CU
0	0	0			0	0
1	0	(150)			(150)	(150)
2	39	0			39	35
3	36	0			36	30
4	31	0			31	23
5	0	0	(6)	(45)	39	27
Total	106	(150)	(6)	(45)	(5)	(35)

The incremental cash flows have a present value, in year 1, of CU35 (assuming a discount rate of 10 per cent is appropriate). Applying paragraphs 10–12 of the IFRS, the cedant unbundles the contract and applies IAS 39 to this deposit component (unless the cedant already recognises its contractual obligation to repay the deposit component to the reinsurer). If this were not done, the cedant might recognise the CU150 received in year 1 as income, and the incremental payments in years 2–5 as expenses. However, in substance, the reinsurer has paid a claim of CU35 and made a loan of CU115 (CU150 less CU35) that will be repaid in instalments.

The following table shows the changes in the loan balance. The table assumes that the original loan shown in case 1 and the new loan in case 2 met the criteria for offsetting in IAS 32. Amounts shown in the table are rounded.

Continued from previous page

IG Example 3: Unbundling a deposit component of a reinsurance contract

Loan to (from) the reinsurer

Year	Opening balance	Interest at 10 per cent	Payments per original schedule	Additional payments in case 2	Closing balance
	CU	CU	CU	CU	CU
0	–	–	6	–	6
1	6	1	7	(115)	(101)
2	(101)	(10)	7	39	(65)
3	(65)	(7)	7	36	(29)
4	(29)	(3)	6	31	5
5	5	1	(45)	39	0
Total		(18)	(12)	(30)	

Shadow accounting

IG6 Paragraph 30 of the IFRS permits, but does not require, a practice sometimes described as 'shadow accounting'. IG Example 4 illustrates shadow accounting.

IG7 Shadow accounting is not the same as fair value hedge accounting under IAS 39 and will not usually have the same effect. Under IAS 39, a non-derivative financial asset or non-derivative financial liability may be designated as a hedging instrument only for a hedge of foreign currency risk.

IG8 Shadow accounting is not applicable for liabilities arising from investment contracts (ie contracts within the scope of IAS 39) because the underlying measurement of those liabilities (including the treatment of related transaction costs) does not depend on asset values or asset returns. However, shadow accounting may be applicable for a discretionary participation feature within an investment contract if the measurement of that feature depends on asset values or asset returns.

IG9 Shadow accounting is not applicable if the measurement of an insurance liability is not driven directly by realised gains and losses on assets held. For example, assume that financial assets are measured at fair value and insurance liabilities are measured using a discount rate that reflects current market rates but does not depend directly on the actual assets held. The measurements of the assets and the liability both reflect changes in interest rates, but the measurement of the liability does not depend directly on the carrying amount of the assets held. Therefore, shadow accounting is not applicable and changes in the carrying amount of the liability are recognised in profit or loss because IAS 1 *Presentation of Financial Statements* requires all items of income or expense to be recognised in profit or loss unless a Standard or Interpretation requires otherwise.

IG10 Shadow accounting may be relevant if there is a contractual link between payments to policyholders and the carrying amount of, or returns from, owner-occupied property. If an entity uses the revaluation model in IAS 16 *Property, Plant and Equipment*, it recognises changes in the carrying amount of the owner-occupied property in revaluation surplus. If it also elects to use shadow accounting, the changes in the measurement of the insurance liability resulting from revaluations of the property are also recognised in revaluation surplus.

IG Example 4: Shadow accounting

Background

Under some national requirements for some insurance contracts, deferred acquisition costs (DAC) are amortised over the life of the contract as a constant proportion of estimated gross profits (EGP). EGP includes investment returns, including realised (but not unrealised) gains and losses. Interest is applied to both DAC and EGP, to preserve present value relationships. For simplicity, this example ignores interest and ignores re-estimation of EGP.

At the inception of a contract, insurer A has DAC of CU20 relating to that contract and the present value, at inception, of EGP is CU100. In other words, DAC is 20 per cent of EGP at inception. Thus, for each CU1 of realised gross profits, insurer A amortises DAC by CU0.20. For example, if insurer A sells assets and recognises a gain of CU10, insurer A amortises DAC by CU2 (20 per cent of CU10).

Before adopting IFRSs for the first time in 2005, insurer A measured financial assets on a cost basis. (Therefore, EGP under those national requirements considers only realised gains and losses.) However, under IFRSs, it classifies its financial assets as available for sale. Thus, insurer A measures the assets at fair value and recognises changes in their fair value directly in equity, through the statement of changes in equity. In 2005, insurer A recognises unrealised gains of CU10 on the assets backing the contract.

In 2006, insurer A sells the assets for an amount equal to their fair value at the end of 2005 and, to comply with IAS 39, transfers the now-realised gain of CU10 from equity to profit or loss.

Application of paragraph 30 of the IFRS

Paragraph 30 of the IFRS permits, but does not require, insurer A to adopt shadow accounting. If insurer A adopts shadow accounting, it amortises DAC in 2005 by an additional CU2 (20 per cent of CU10) as a result of the change in the fair value of the assets. Because insurer A recognised the change in their fair value in equity, it recognises the additional amortisation of CU2 directly in equity, through the statement of changes in equity.

When insurer A sells the assets in 2006, it makes no further adjustment to DAC, but transfers DAC amortisation of CU2 relating to the now-realised gain from equity to profit or loss.

In summary, shadow accounting treats an unrealised gain in the same way as a realised gain, except that the unrealised gain and resulting DAC amortisation are (a) recognised in equity rather than in profit or loss and (b) transferred to profit or loss when the gain on the asset becomes realised.

If insurer A does not adopt shadow accounting, unrealised gains on assets do not affect the amortisation of DAC.

Disclosure

Purpose of this guidance

IG11 The guidance in paragraphs IG12–IG71 suggests possible ways to apply the disclosure requirements in paragraphs 36–39 of the IFRS. As explained in paragraph 1(b) of the IFRS, the objective of the disclosures is to identify and explain the amounts in an insurer's financial statements arising from insurance contracts and help users of those financial statements understand the amount, timing and uncertainty of future cash flows from insurance contracts.

IG12 An insurer decides in the light of its circumstances how much detail it gives to satisfy those requirements, how much emphasis it places on different aspects of the requirements and how it aggregates information to display the overall picture without combining information that has materially different characteristics. To satisfy the requirements, an insurer would not typically need to disclose all the information suggested in the guidance. This guidance does not create additional requirements.

IG13 IAS 1 *Presentation of Financial Statements* (as revised in 2003) requires an entity to 'provide additional disclosures when compliance with the specific requirements in IFRSs is insufficient to enable users to understand the impact of particular transactions, other events and conditions on the entity's financial position and financial performance'.

IG14 For convenience, this Implementation Guidance discusses each disclosure requirement in the IFRS separately. In practice, disclosures would normally be presented as an integrated package and individual disclosures may satisfy more than one requirement. For example, information about the terms and conditions of insurance contracts may help to convey information about insurance risk and interest rate risk.

Materiality

IG15 IAS 1 notes that a specific disclosure requirement in a Standard or an Interpretation need not be satisfied if the information is not material. IAS 1 defines materiality as follows:

> Omissions or misstatements of items are material if they could, individually or collectively, influence the economic decisions of users taken on the basis of the financial statements. Materiality depends on the size and nature of the omission or misstatement judged in the surrounding circumstances. The size or nature of the item, or a combination of both, could be the determining factor.

IG16 IAS 1 also explains the following:

> Assessing whether an omission or misstatement could influence economic decisions of users, and so be material, requires consideration of the characteristics of those users. The *Framework for the Preparation and Presentation of Financial Statements* states in paragraph 25 that 'users are assumed to have a reasonable knowledge of business and economic activities and accounting and a willingness to study the information with reasonable diligence.' Therefore, the assessment needs to take into account how users with such attributes could reasonably be expected to be influenced in making economic decisions.

Explanation of recognised amounts (paragraphs 36 and 37 of the IFRS)

Accounting policies

IG17 IAS 1 requires disclosure of accounting policies and paragraph 37(a) of the IFRS highlights this requirement. In developing disclosures about accounting policies for insurance contracts, insurers might need to address the treatment of, for example, some or all of the following, if applicable:

(a) premiums (including the treatment of unearned premiums, renewals and lapses, premiums collected by agents and brokers but not yet passed on and premium taxes or other levies on premiums).

(b) fees or other charges made to policyholders.

(c) acquisition costs (including a description of their nature).

(d) claims incurred (both reported and not reported), claims handling costs (including a description of their nature) and liability adequacy tests (including a description of the cash flows included in the test, whether and how the cash flows are discounted and the treatment of embedded options and guarantees in those tests, see paragraphs 15–19 of the IFRS). An insurer might disclose whether insurance liabilities are discounted and, if they are discounted, explain the methodology used.

(e) the objective of methods used to adjust insurance liabilities for risk and uncertainty (for example, in terms of a level of assurance or level of sufficiency) the nature of those models, and the source of information used in the models.

(f) embedded options and guarantees (including a description of whether (i) the measurement of insurance liabilities reflects the intrinsic value and time value of these items and (ii) their measurement is consistent with observed current market prices).

(g) discretionary participation features (including a clear statement of how the insurer applies paragraphs 34 and 35 of the IFRS in classifying that feature as a liability or as a component of equity) and other features that permit policyholders to share in investment performance.

(h) salvage, subrogation or other recoveries from third parties.

(i) reinsurance held.

(j) underwriting pools, coinsurance and guarantee fund arrangements.

(k) insurance contracts acquired in business combinations and portfolio transfers, and the treatment of related intangible assets.

(l) as required by IAS 1, the judgements, apart from those involving estimations, management has made in the process of applying the accounting policies that have the most significant effect on the amounts recognised in the financial statements. The classification of discretionary participation features is an example of an accounting policy that might have a significant effect.

IG18 If the financial statements disclose supplementary information, for example embedded value information, that is not prepared on the basis used for other measurements in the financial statements, it might be appropriate to explain the basis. Disclosures about embedded value methodology might include information similar to that described in paragraph IG17, as well as disclosure of whether, and how, embedded values are affected by estimated returns from assets and by locked-in capital and how those effects are estimated.

Assets, liabilities, income and expense

IG19 Paragraph 37(b) of the IFRS requires an insurer to disclose the assets, liabilities, income and expenses that arise from insurance contracts. If an insurer presents its cash flow statement using the direct method, paragraph 37(b) requires it also to disclose the cash flows that arise from insurance contracts. The IFRS does not require disclosure of specific items. The following paragraphs discuss how an insurer might satisfy those general requirements.

IG20 IAS 1 requires minimum disclosures on the face of the balance sheet. To satisfy those requirements, an insurer might need to present separately on the face of its balance sheet the following amounts arising from insurance contracts:

(a) liabilities under insurance contracts and reinsurance contracts issued.

(b) assets under insurance contracts and reinsurance contracts issued.

(c) assets under reinsurance ceded. Under paragraph 14(d)(i) of the IFRS, these assets are not offset against the related insurance liabilities.

IG21 Neither IAS 1 nor the IFRS prescribes the descriptions and ordering of the line items presented on the face of the balance sheet. An insurer could amend the descriptions and ordering to suit the nature of its transactions.

IG22 IAS 1 requires disclosure, either on the face of the balance sheet or in the notes, of subclassifications of the line items presented, classified in a manner appropriate to the entity's operations. The subclassifications of insurance liabilities that require separate disclosure will depend on the circumstances, but might include items such as:

(a) unearned premiums.

(b) claims reported by policyholders.

(c) claims incurred but not reported (IBNR).

(d) provisions arising from liability adequacy tests.

(e) provisions for future non-participating benefits.

(f) liabilities or components of equity relating to discretionary participation features (see paragraphs 34 and 35 of the IFRS). If an insurer classifies these features as a component of equity, disclosure is needed to comply with IAS 1, which requires an entity to disclose 'a description of the nature and purpose of each reserve within equity'.

(g) receivables and payables related to insurance contracts (amounts currently due to and from agents, brokers and policyholders related to insurance contracts).

(h) non-insurance assets acquired by exercising rights to recoveries.

IG23 Similar subclassifications may also be appropriate for reinsurance assets, depending on their materiality and other relevant circumstances. For assets under insurance contracts and reinsurance contracts issued, an insurer might need to distinguish:

(a) deferred acquisition costs; and

(b) intangible assets relating to insurance contracts acquired in business combinations or portfolio transfers.

IG24 IAS 1 lists minimum line items that an entity should present on the face of its income statement. It also requires the presentation of additional line items when this is necessary to present fairly the entity's financial performance. To satisfy these requirements, an insurer might need to disclose the following amounts on the face of its income statement:

(a) revenue from insurance contracts issued (without any reduction for reinsurance held).

(b) income from contracts with reinsurers.

(c) expense for policyholder claims and benefits (without any reduction for reinsurance held).

(d) expenses arising from reinsurance held.

IG25 IAS 18 requires an entity to disclose the amount of each significant category of revenue recognised during the period, and specifically requires disclosure of revenue arising from the rendering of services. Although revenue from insurance contracts is outside the scope of IAS 18, similar disclosures may be appropriate for insurance contracts. The IFRS does not prescribe a particular method for recognising revenue and various models exist:

(a) Under some models, an insurer recognises premiums earned during the period as revenue and recognises claims arising during the period (including estimates of claims incurred but not reported) as an expense.

(b) Under some other models, an insurer recognises premiums received as revenue and at the same time recognises an expense representing the resulting increase in the insurance liability.

(c) Under yet other models, an insurer reports premiums received as deposit receipts. Its reported revenue comprises charges for items such as mortality, whilst its reported policyholder claims and benefits comprise the claims and benefits related to those charges.

IG26 IAS 1 requires additional disclosure of various items of income and expense. To satisfy these requirements, an insurer might need to disclose the following additional items, either on the face of its income statement or in the notes:

(a) acquisition costs (distinguishing those recognised as an expense immediately from the amortisation of deferred acquisition costs).

(b) the effect of changes in estimates and assumptions.

(c) losses recognised as a result of applying liability adequacy tests.

(d) for insurance liabilities measured on a discounted basis:

(i) accretion of interest to reflect the passage of time; and

(ii) the effect of changes in discount rates.

(e) distributions or allocations to holders of contracts that contain discretionary participation features. The portion of profit or loss that relates to any equity component of those contracts is an allocation of profit or loss, not expense or income (paragraph 34(c) of the IFRS).

IG27 Some insurers present a detailed analysis of the sources of their earnings from insurance activities either in the income statement, or as a complement to an income statement presented in a more traditional format. Such an analysis may provide useful information about both the income and expense of the current period and the risk exposures faced during the period.

IG28 The items described in paragraph IG26 are not offset against income or expense arising from reinsurance held (paragraph 14(d)(ii) of the IFRS).

IG29 Paragraph 37(b) also requires specific disclosure about gains or losses recognised on buying reinsurance. This disclosure informs users about gains or losses that may, using some measurement models, arise from imperfect measurements of the underlying direct insurance liability. Furthermore, some measurement models require a cedant to defer some of those gains and losses and amortise them over the period of the related risk exposures, or some other period. Paragraph 37(b) also requires a cedant to disclose information about such deferred gains and losses.

IG30 If an insurer does not adopt uniform accounting policies for the insurance liabilities of its subsidiaries, it might need to disaggregate the disclosures about amounts reported in its financial statements to give meaningful information about amounts determined using different accounting policies.

Significant assumptions and other sources of estimation uncertainty

IG31 Paragraph 37(c) of the IFRS requires an insurer to describe the process used to determine the assumptions that have the greatest effect on the measurement of assets, liabilities, income and expense arising from insurance contracts and, when practicable, give quantified disclosure of those assumptions. For some disclosures, such as discount rates or assumptions about future trends or general inflation, it may be relatively easy to disclose the assumptions used (aggregated at a reasonable but not excessive level, where necessary). For other assumptions, such as mortality tables, it may not be practicable to disclose quantified assumptions because there are too many, in which case it is more important to describe the process used to generate the assumptions.

IG32 The description of the process used to determine assumptions might include a summary of the most significant of the following:

(a) the objective of the assumptions. For example, an insurer might disclose whether the assumptions are intended to be neutral estimates of the most likely or expected outcome ('best estimates') or to provide a given level of assurance or level of sufficiency. If they are intended to provide a quantitative or qualitative level of assurance, an insurer might disclose that level.

(b) the source of data used as inputs for the assumptions that have the greatest effect. For example, an insurer might disclose whether the inputs are internal, external or a mixture of the two. For data derived from detailed studies that are not carried out annually, an insurer might disclose the criteria used to determine when the studies are updated and the date of the latest update.

(c) the extent to which the assumptions are consistent with observable market prices or other published information.

(d) a description of how past experience, current conditions and other relevant benchmarks are taken into account in developing estimates and assumptions. If a relationship would normally be expected between experience and future results, an insurer might explain the reasons for using assumptions that differ from past experience and indicate the extent of the difference.

(e) a description of how the insurer developed assumptions about future trends, such as changes in mortality, healthcare costs or litigation awards.

(f) an explanation of how the insurer identifies correlations between different assumptions.

(g) the insurer's policy in making allocations or distributions for contracts with discretionary participation features, the related assumptions that are reflected in the financial statements, the nature and extent of any significant uncertainty about the relative interests of policyholders and shareholders in the unallocated surplus associated with those contracts, and the effect on the financial statements of any changes during the period in that policy or those assumptions.

(h) the nature and extent of uncertainties affecting specific assumptions. In addition, to comply with paragraphs 116–122 of IAS 1, an insurer may need to disclose that it is reasonably possible, based on existing knowledge, that outcomes within the next financial year that are different from assumptions could require a material adjustment to the carrying amount of insurance liabilities and insurance assets. Paragraph 120 of IAS 1 gives further guidance on this disclosure.

IG33 The IFRS does not prescribe specific assumptions that would be disclosed, because different assumptions will be more significant for different types of contract.

Changes in assumptions

IG34 Paragraph 37(d) of the IFRS requires an insurer to disclose the effect of changes in assumptions used to measure insurance assets and insurance liabilities. This is consistent with IAS 8, which requires disclosure of the nature and amount of a change in an accounting estimate that has an effect in the current period or is expected to have an effect in future periods.

IG35 Assumptions are often interdependent. When this is the case, analysis of changes by assumption may depend on the order in which the analysis is performed and may be arbitrary to some extent. Therefore, the IFRS does not specify a rigid format or content for this analysis. This allows insurers to analyse the changes in a way that meets the objective of the disclosure and is appropriate for their particular circumstances. If practicable, an insurer might disclose separately the impact of changes in different assumptions, particularly if changes in some assumptions have an adverse effect and others have a beneficial effect. An insurer might also describe the impact of interdependencies between assumptions and the resulting limitations of any analysis of the effect of changes in assumption.

IG36 An insurer might disclose the effects of changes in assumptions both before and after the impact of reinsurance held, especially if the insurer expects a significant change in the nature or extent of its reinsurance programme or if an analysis before reinsurance is relevant for an analysis of the credit risk arising from reinsurance held.

Changes in insurance liabilities and related items

IG37 Paragraph 37(e) of the IFRS requires an insurer to disclose reconciliations of changes in insurance liabilities. It also requires disclosure of movements in reinsurance assets. An insurer need not disaggregate those movements into broad classes, but might do that if different forms of analysis are more relevant for different types of liability. The movements might include:

(a) the carrying amount at the beginning and end of the period.

(b) additional insurance liabilities arising during the period.

(c) cash paid.

(d) income and expense included in profit or loss.

(e) liabilities acquired from, or transferred to, other insurers.

(f) net exchange differences arising on the translation of the financial statements into a different presentation currency, and on the translation of a foreign operation into the presentation currency of the reporting entity.

IG38 An insurer discloses the movements in insurance liabilities and reinsurance assets in all prior periods for which it reports full comparative information.

IG39 Paragraph 37(e) of the IFRS also requires an insurer to disclose movements in deferred acquisition costs, if applicable. The reconciliation might disclose:

(a) the carrying amount at the beginning and end of the period.

(b) the amounts incurred during the period.

(c) the amortisation for the period.

(d) impairment losses recognised during the period.

(e) other movements categorised by cause and type.

IG40 An insurer may have recognised intangible assets related to insurance contracts acquired in a business combination or portfolio transfer. IAS 38 *Intangible Assets* contains disclosure requirements for intangible assets, including a requirement to give a reconciliation of movements in intangible assets. The IFRS does not require additional disclosures about these assets.

Amount, timing and uncertainty of future cash flows (paragraphs 38 and 39 of the IFRS)

IG41 The disclosures about the risk, timing and uncertainty of future cash flows are based on two foundations:

(a) There should be a balance between quantitative and qualitative disclosures, enabling users to understand the nature of risk exposures and their potential impact.

(b) Disclosures should be consistent with how management perceives its activities and risks, and the methods that management uses to manage those risks. This approach is likely:

(i) to generate information that has more predictive value than information based on assumptions and methods that management does not use, for instance, in considering the insurer's ability to react to adverse situations.

(ii) to be more effective in adapting to the continuing change in risk measurement and management techniques and developments in the external environment over time.

IG42 In developing disclosures to satisfy paragraphs 38 and 39 of the IFRS, an insurer would decide in the light of its circumstances how it would aggregate information to display the overall picture without combining information that has materially different characteristics, so that the information is useful. An insurer might group insurance contracts into broad classes in ways that are appropriate for the nature of the information to be disclosed, taking into account matters such as the risks covered, the characteristics of the contracts and the measurement basis applied. The broad classes may correspond to classes established for legal or regulatory purposes, but the IFRS does not require this.

IG43 Under IAS 14 *Segment Reporting*, the identification of reportable segments reflects differences in the risks and returns of an entity's products and services. IAS 14 takes the position that the segments identified in an organisational and management structure and internal financial reporting system normally provide an appropriate segmentation for financial reporting. An insurer might adopt a similar approach to identify broad classes of insurance contracts for disclosure purposes, although it might be appropriate to disaggregate disclosures down to the next level. For example, if an insurer identifies life insurance as a reportable segment for IAS 14, it might be appropriate to report separate information about, say, life insurance, annuities in the accumulation phase and annuities in the payout phase.

IG44 IAS 32 *Financial Instruments: Disclosure and Presentation* (as revised in 2003) gives the following guidance on the level of detail to be disclosed about financial instruments, which is also appropriate for insurance contracts.

Determining the level of detail to be disclosed about particular financial instruments requires the exercise of judgement taking into account the relative significance of those instruments. It is necessary to strike a balance between overburdening financial statements with excessive detail that may not assist users of financial statements and obscuring important information as a result of too much aggregation. For example, when an entity is party to a large number of financial instruments with similar characteristics and no single contract is individually material, a summary by classes of instruments is appropriate. On the other hand, information about an individual instrument may be important when it is, for example, a material component of an entity's capital structure.

IG45 In identifying broad classes for separate disclosure, an insurer might consider the need to indicate the level of uncertainty associated with the risks underwritten, to inform users whether outcomes are likely to be within a wider or a narrower range. For example, an insurer might disclose information about exposures where there are significant amounts of provisions for claims incurred but not reported (IBNR) or where outcomes and risks are unusually difficult to assess (eg asbestos).

IG46 It may be useful to disclose sufficient information about the broad classes identified to permit a reconciliation to relevant line items on the balance sheet.

IG47 Information about the extent and nature of insurance contracts is more useful if it highlights any relationship between insurance contracts (and between insurance contracts and other items, such as financial instruments) that can affect the amount, timing or uncertainty of an entity's future cash flows. The extent to which a risk exposure is altered by the relationship among the assets and liabilities might be apparent to users from information about the terms and conditions of insurance contracts (see paragraph IG49), but in some cases further disclosure might be useful.

Risk management objectives and policies for mitigating insurance risk

IG48 Paragraph 39(a) of the IFRS requires an insurer to disclose its objectives in managing risks arising from insurance contracts and its policies for mitigating those risks. Such discussion provides a valuable additional perspective that is independent of the specific contracts outstanding at a particular time. An insurer might disclose, for example:

(a) its policies for accepting insurance risks, including selection and approval of risks to be insured, use of limits and use of options and avoiding undue concentrations of risk; the underwriting strategy to ensure that there are appropriate risk classification and premium levels. These disclosures might include a combination of narrative descriptions and specific quantified data, as appropriate to the nature of the insurance contracts and their relative significance to the insurer.

(b) the methods it uses to assess and monitor insurance risk exposures both for individual types of risks insured and overall, such as internal risk measurement models, sensitivity analyses, scenario analyses, and stress testing, and how it integrates them into its operating activities. Useful disclosure might include a summary description of the approach used, associated assumptions and parameters (including confidence intervals, computation frequencies and historical observation periods) and strengths and limitations of the approach.

(c) methods it employs to limit or transfer insurance risk exposures, such as retention limits and the use of reinsurance.

(d) the extent to which insurance risks are assessed and managed on an entity-wide basis.

(e) asset and liability management (ALM) techniques.

(f) commitments received (or given) to issue (contribute) additional debt or equity capital when specified events occur.

Terms and conditions of insurance contracts

IG49 Paragraph 39(b) of the IFRS requires an insurer to disclose those terms and conditions of insurance contracts that have a material effect on the amount, timing and uncertainty of future cash flows arising from insurance contracts. To achieve this, an insurer might disclose the more significant of the following for each broad class of insurance liabilities, and reinsurance assets held:

(a) the nature of the risk covered, with a brief summary description of the class (such as annuities, pensions, other life insurance, motor, property and liability).

(b) concentrations of insurance risk, interest rate risk, credit risk or foreign exchange risk and the extent to which reinsurance or policyholder participation features mitigate those risks (see paragraphs IG55–IG58 for further discussion).

(c) a summary of significant guarantees, and of the levels at which guarantees of market prices or interest rates are likely to alter the insurer's cash flows materially.

(d) claims development information (see paragraphs IG59–IG61 for further discussion).

(e) the basis for determining investment returns credited to policyholders, such as whether the returns are fixed, based contractually on the return of specified assets or partly or wholly subject to the insurer's discretion.

(f) the general nature of participation features whereby policyholders share in the performance (and related risks) of individual contracts, pools of contracts or entities, including the general nature of any formula for the participation and the extent of any discretion held by the insurer.

IG50 An insurer might also disclose the following information, which need not be disaggregated by broad classes:

(a) information about the estimated timing of the net cash inflows and outflows resulting from recognised insurance liabilities, and reinsurance assets. To comply with IAS 1, the information would need to distinguish items falling due within one year from items falling due later. In addition, an insurer might disclose summary information about items falling due after one year (such as the estimated weighted average maturity of those items) or a more detailed analysis by time periods. The IFRS does not require an insurer to disclose the amounts of the estimated cash flows: an analysis, by estimated timing, of the amounts recognised in the balance sheet is sufficient.

(b) a summary narrative description of how the amounts in (a) could change if policyholders exercised lapse or surrender options in different ways.

(c) if applicable, the average discount rate or interest rate implicit in the measurement of insurance liabilities for each period described in (a).

(d) the sensitivity of profit or loss and equity to changes in key variables (see paragraphs IG52–IG54 for further discussion).

(e) the terms of any obligation or contingent obligation for the insurer to contribute to government or other guarantee funds (see also IAS 37 *Provisions, Contingent Liabilities and Contingent Assets*).

(f) segregation requirements that are intended to protect policyholders by restricting the use of some of the insurer's assets.

Insurance risk

IG51 Paragraph 39(c) of the IFRS requires disclosures about insurance risk. Disclosures to satisfy this requirement might build on the following foundations:

(a) Information about insurance risk is consistent with (though naturally less detailed than) the information provided internally to the board of directors and chief executive officer, so that users can assess the insurer's financial position, performance and cash flows 'through the eyes of management'.

(b) Information about risk exposures might report exposures both gross and net of reinsurance (or other risk mitigating elements, such as catastrophe bonds issued or policyholder participation features), especially if the insurer expects a significant change in the nature or extent of its reinsurance programme or if an analysis before reinsurance is relevant for an analysis of the credit risk arising from reinsurance held.

(c) In reporting quantitative information about insurance risk, an insurer might disclose the methods used, the strengths and limitations of those methods, the assumptions made, and the effect of reinsurance, policyholder participation and other mitigating elements.

(d) Insurers might classify risk along more than one dimension. For example, life insurers might classify contracts by both the level of mortality risk and the level of investment risk. It may sometimes be convenient to display this information in a matrix format.

(e) If an insurer's risk exposures at the reporting date are unrepresentative of its exposures during the period, it might be useful to disclose that fact.

(f) The following disclosures required by paragraph 39 of the IFRS might also be relevant:

  (i) the sensitivity of reported profit or loss and equity to changes in variables that have a material effect on them.

  (ii) concentrations of insurance risk.

(iii) the development of prior year insurance liabilities.

Sensitivity analysis

IG52 Paragraph 39(c)(i) of the IFRS requires disclosure about the sensitivity of profit or loss and equity to changes in variables that have a material effect on them. Sensitivity analysis might be qualitative, and preferably also quantitative. An insurer might, if feasible without undue cost or effort, explain the impact of correlations between key variables. Although sensitivity tests can provide useful information, such tests have limitations. An insurer might disclose the strengths and limitations of sensitivity analyses performed.

IG53 Informative disclosure might avoid giving a misleading sensitivity analysis if there are significant non-linearities in sensitivities to variables that have a material effect. For example, if a change of 1 per cent in a variable has a negligible effect, but a change of 1.1 per cent has a material effect, it might be misleading to disclose the effect of a 1 per cent change without further explanation.

IG54 Sensitivity analysis helps to meet the requirement to disclose information about the amount, timing and uncertainty of cash flows. However, to permit meaningful aggregation, the required sensitivity disclosure does not refer directly to the cash flows but instead focuses on summary indicators, namely profit or loss and equity.

Concentrations of insurance risk

IG55 Paragraph 39(c)(ii) of the IFRS refers to the need to disclose concentrations of insurance risk. Such concentration could arise from, for example:

(a) a single insurance contract, or a small number of related contracts, for instance, when an insurance contract covers low-frequency, high-severity risks such as earthquakes.

(b) single incidents that expose an insurer to risk under several different types of insurance contract. For example, a major terrorist incident could create exposure under life insurance contracts, property insurance contracts, business interruption and civil liability.

(c) exposure to unexpected changes in trends, for example, unexpected changes in human mortality or in policyholder behaviour.

(d) exposure to possible major changes in financial market conditions that could cause options held by policyholders to come into the money. For example, when interest rates decline significantly, interest rate and annuity guarantees may result in significant losses.

(e) significant litigation or legislative risks that could cause a large single loss, or have a pervasive effect on many contracts.

(f) correlations and interdependencies between different risks.

(g) significant non-linearities, such as stop-loss or excess of loss features, especially if a key variable is close to a level that triggers a material change in future cash flows.

(h) geographical and sectoral concentrations. The guidance in IAS 14 *Segment Reporting* may help an insurer to identify these.

IG56 Disclosure of concentrations of insurance risk might include a description of the shared characteristic that identifies each concentration and an indication of the possible exposure, both before and after reinsurance held, associated with all insurance liabilities sharing that characteristic.

IG57 Disclosure about an insurer's historical performance on low-frequency, high-severity risks might be one way to help users to assess cash flow uncertainty associated with those risks. Consider an insurance contract that covers an earthquake that is expected to happen every 50 years, on average. If the insured event occurs during the current contract period, the insurer will report a large loss. If the insured event does not occur during the current period, the insurer will report a profit. Without adequate disclosure of the source of historical profits, it could be misleading for the insurer to report 49 years of reasonable profits, followed by one large loss; users may misinterpret the insurer's long-term ability to generate cash flows over the complete cycle of 50 years. Therefore, it might be useful to describe the extent of the exposure to risks of this kind and the estimated frequency of losses. If circumstances have not changed significantly, disclosure of the insurer's experience with this exposure may be one way to convey information about estimated frequencies.

IG58 For regulatory or other reasons, some entities produce special purpose financial statements that report catastrophe or equalisation reserves as liabilities. Those reserves are a component of equity under IFRSs. IAS 1 requires an entity to disclose 'a description of the nature and purpose of each reserve within equity'.

Claims development

IG59 Paragraph 39(c)(iii) of the IFRS requires disclosure of claims development information (subject to transitional relief in paragraph 44). Informative disclosure reconciles this information to amounts reported in the balance sheet. An insurer might disclose unusual claims expenses or developments separately, allowing users to identify the underlying trends in performance.

IG60 As explained in paragraph 39(c)(iii) of the IFRS, disclosures about claims development are not required for claims for which uncertainty about the amount and timing of claims payments is typically resolved within one year. Therefore, these disclosures are not normally required for most life insurance contracts. Furthermore, claims development disclosure is not normally needed for annuity contracts because each periodic payment arises, in effect, from a separate claim about which there is no uncertainty.

IG61 IG Example 5 shows one possible format for presenting claims development information. Other possible formats might, for example, present information by accident year rather than underwriting year. Although the example illustrates a format that might be useful if insurance liabilities are discounted, the IFRS does not require discounting (paragraph 25(a) of the IFRS).

IG Example 5: Disclosure of claims development

This example illustrates a possible format for a claims development table for a general insurer. The top half of the table shows how the insurer's estimates of total claims for each underwriting year develop over time. For example, at the end of 20X1, the insurer estimated that it would pay claims of 680 for insured events relating to insurance contracts underwritten in 20X1. By the end of 20X2, the insurer had revised the estimate of cumulative claims (both those paid and those still to be paid) to 673.

The lower half of the table reconciles the cumulative claims to the amount appearing in the balance sheet. First, the cumulative payments are deducted to give the cumulative unpaid claims for each year on an undiscounted basis. Second, if the claims liabilities are discounted, the effect of discounting is deducted to give the carrying amount in the balance sheet.

Underwriting year	*20X1*	*20X2*	*20X3*	*20X4*	*20X5*	*Total*
	CU	CU	CU	CU	CU	CU
Estimate of cumulative claims:						
At end of underwriting year	680	790	823	920	968	
One year later	673	785	840	903		
Two years later	692	776	845			
Three years later	697	771				
Four years later	702					
Estimate of cumulative claims	702	771	845	903	968	
Cumulative payments	(702)	(689)	(570)	(350)	(217)	
	–	82	275	553	751	1,713
Effect of discounting	–	(14)	(68)	(175)	(285)	(547)
Present value recognised in the balance sheet	–	68	207	378	466	1,166

Interest rate risk and credit risk

IG62 Paragraph 39(d) of the IFRS requires an insurer to disclose information about interest rate risk and credit risk. The information required is the same as that required by IAS 32 (to the extent not already covered by the disclosures discussed above).

IG63 If an insurer considers that lapse behaviour is likely to be sensitive to interest rates, the insurer might disclose that fact and state whether the disclosures about interest rate risk reflect that interdependence.

IG64 Informative disclosure includes information about the extent to which policyholder participation features mitigate or compound interest rate risk.

IG65 For an insurer, disclosure about credit risk might be particularly important for reinsurance contracts held and for credit risk assumed under credit insurance contracts and financial guarantees. Balances due from agents or brokers may also be subject to credit risk.

Exposures to interest rate risk or market risk under embedded derivatives

IG66 Paragraph 39(e) of the IFRS requires an insurer to disclose information about exposures to interest rate risk or market risk under embedded derivatives contained in a host insurance contract if the insurer is not required to, and does not, measure the embedded derivative at fair value (for example, guaranteed annuity options and guaranteed minimum death benefits).

IG67 An example of a contract containing a guaranteed annuity option is one in which the policyholder pays a fixed monthly premium for thirty years. At maturity, the policyholder can elect to take either (a) a lump sum equal to the accumulated investment value or (b) a lifetime annuity at a rate guaranteed at inception (ie when the contract started). For policyholders electing to receive the annuity, the insurer could suffer a significant loss if interest rates decline substantially or if the policyholder lives much longer than the average. The insurer is exposed to both interest rate risk and significant insurance risk (mortality risk) and a transfer of insurance risk occurs at inception, because the insurer fixed the price for mortality risk at that date. Therefore, the contract is an insurance contract from inception. Moreover, the embedded guaranteed annuity option itself meets the definition of an insurance contract, and so separation is not required.

IG68 An example of a contract containing minimum guaranteed death benefits is one in which the policyholder pays a monthly premium for 30 years. Most of the premiums are invested in a mutual fund. The rest is used to buy life cover and to cover expenses. On maturity or surrender, the insurer pays the value of the mutual fund units at that date. On death before final maturity, the insurer pays the greater of (a) the current unit value and (b) a fixed amount. This contract could be viewed as a hybrid contract comprising (a) a mutual fund investment and (b) an embedded life insurance contract that pays a death benefit equal to the fixed amount less the current unit value (but zero if the current unit value is more than the fixed amount).

IG69 Both these embedded derivatives meet the definition of an insurance contract if the insurance risk is significant. However, in both cases interest rate risk or market risk may be much more significant than the mortality risk. If interest rates or equity markets fall substantially, these guarantees would be well in the money. Given the long-term nature of the guarantees and the size of the exposures, an insurer might face extremely large losses. Therefore, an insurer might place particular emphasis on disclosures about such exposures.

IG70 Useful disclosures about such exposures might include:

(a) the sensitivity analysis discussed above.

(b) information about the levels when these exposures start to have a material effect (paragraph IG49(c)).

(c) the fair value of the embedded derivative, although neither the IFRS nor IAS 32 requires disclosure of that fair value.

Key performance indicators

IG71 Some insurers present disclosures about what they regard as key performance indicators, such as lapse and renewal rates, total sum insured, average cost per claim, average number of claims per contract, new business volumes, claims ratio, expense ratio and combined ratio. The IFRS does not require such disclosures. However, such disclosures might be a useful way for an insurer to explain its financial performance during the period and to give an insight into the amount, timing and uncertainty of its future cash flows.

International Financial Reporting Standard 5

Non-current Assets Held for Sale and Discontinued Operations

CONTENTS

International Financial Reporting Standard 5 *Non-current Assets Held for Sale and Discontinued Operations* (IFRS 5) is set out in paragraphs 1–45 and Appendices A–C. All the paragraphs have equal authority. Paragraphs in **bold type** state the main principles. Terms defined in Appendix A are in *italics* the first time they appear in the Standard. Definitions of other terms are given in the Glossary for International Financial Reporting Standards. IFRS 5 should be read in the context of its objective and the Basis for Conclusions, the *Preface to International Financial Reporting Standards* and the *Framework for the Preparation and Presentation of Financial Statements*. IAS 8 *Accounting Policies, Changes in Accounting Estimates and Errors* provides a basis for selecting and applying accounting policies in the absence of explicit guidance.

Introduction

Reasons for issuing the IFRS

IN1 International Financial Reporting Standard 5 *Non-current Assets Held for Sale and Discontinued Operations* (IFRS 5) sets out requirements for the classification, measurement and presentation of non-current assets held for sale and replaces IAS 35 *Discontinuing Operations*.

IN2 Achieving convergence of accounting standards around the world is one of the prime objectives of the International Accounting Standards Board. In pursuit of that objective, one of the strategies adopted by the Board has been to enter into a memorandum of understanding with the Financial Accounting Standards Board (FASB) in the United States that sets out the two boards' commitment to convergence. As a result of that understanding the boards have undertaken a joint short-term project with the objective of reducing differences between IFRSs and US GAAP that are capable of resolution in a relatively short time and can be addressed outside major projects.

IN3 One aspect of that project involves the two boards considering each other's recent standards with a view to adopting high quality accounting solutions. The IFRS arises from the IASB's consideration of FASB Statement No. 144 *Accounting for the Impairment or Disposal of Long-Lived Assets* (SFAS 144), issued in 2001.

IN4 SFAS 144 addresses three areas: (i) the impairment of long-lived assets to be held and used, (ii) the classification, measurement and presentation of assets held for sale and (iii) the classification and presentation of discontinued operations. The impairment of long-lived assets to be held and used is an area in which there are extensive differences between IFRSs and US GAAP. However, those differences were not thought to be capable of resolution in a relatively short time. Convergence on the other two areas was thought to be worth pursuing within the context of the short-term project.

IN5 The IFRS achieves substantial convergence with the requirements of SFAS 144 relating to assets held for sale, the timing of the classification of operations as discontinued and the presentation of such operations.

Main features of the IFRS

IN6 The IFRS:

(a) adopts the classification 'held for sale'.

(b) introduces the concept of a disposal group, being a group of assets to be disposed of, by sale or otherwise, together as a group in a single transaction, and liabilities directly associated with those assets that will be transferred in the transaction.

(c) specifies that assets or disposal groups that are classified as held for sale are carried at the lower of carrying amount and fair value less costs to sell.

(d) specifies that an asset classified as held for sale, or included within a disposal group that is classified as held for sale, is not depreciated.

(e) specifies that an asset classified as held for sale, and the assets and liabilities included within a disposal group classified as held for sale, are presented separately on the face of the balance sheet.

(f) withdraws IAS 35 *Discontinuing Operations* and replaces it with requirements that:

   (i) change the timing of the classification of an operation as discontinued. IAS 35 classified an operation as discontinuing at the earlier of (a) the entity entering into a binding sale agreement and (b) the board of directors approving and announcing a formal disposal plan. The IFRS classifies an operation as discontinued at the date the operation meets the criteria to be classified as held for sale or when the entity has disposed of the operation.

   (ii) specify that the results of discontinued operations are to be shown separately on the face of the income statement.

   (iii) prohibit retroactive classification of an operation as discontinued, when the criteria for that classification are not met until after the balance sheet date.

International Financial Reporting Standard 5 Non-current Assets Held for Sale and Discontinued Operations

Objective

1 The objective of this IFRS is to specify the accounting for assets held for sale, and the presentation and disclosure of *discontinued operations*. In particular, the IFRS requires:

(a) assets that meet the criteria to be classified as held for sale to be measured at the lower of carrying amount and *fair value* less *costs to sell*, and depreciation on such assets to cease; and

(b) assets that meet the criteria to be classified as held for sale to be presented separately on the face of the balance sheet and the results of discontinued operations to be presented separately in the income statement.

Scope

2 The classification and presentation requirements of this IFRS apply to all recognised *non-current assets*[*] and to all *disposal groups* of an entity. The measurement requirements of this IFRS apply to all recognised non-current assets and disposal groups (as set out in paragraph 4), except for those assets listed in paragraph 5 which shall continue to be measured in accordance with the Standard noted.

3 Assets classified as non-current in accordance with IAS 1 *Presentation of Financial Statements* (as revised in 2003) shall not be reclassified as *current assets* until they meet the criteria to be classified as held for sale in accordance with this IFRS. Assets of a class that an entity would normally regard as non-current that are acquired exclusively with a view to resale shall not be classified as current unless they meet the criteria to be classified as held for sale in accordance with this IFRS.

4 Sometimes an entity disposes of a group of assets, possibly with some directly associated liabilities, together in a single transaction. Such a disposal group may be a group of *cash-generating units*, a single cash-generating unit, or part of a cash-generating unit.[†] The group may include any assets and any liabilities of the entity, including current assets, current liabilities and assets excluded by paragraph 5 from the measurement requirements of this IFRS. If a non-current asset within the scope of the measurement requirements of this IFRS is part of a disposal group, the measurement requirements of this IFRS apply to the group as a whole, so that the group is measured at the lower of its carrying amount and fair

* For assets classified according to a liquidity presentation, non-current assets are assets that include amounts expected to be recovered more than twelve months after the balance sheet date. Paragraph 3 applies to the classification of such assets.

† However, once the cash flows from an asset or group of assets are expected to arise principally from sale rather than continuing use, they become less dependent on cash flows arising from other assets, and a disposal group that was part of a cash-generating unit becomes a separate cash-generating unit.

value less costs to sell. The requirements for measuring the individual assets and liabilities within the disposal group are set out in paragraphs 18, 19 and 23.

5 The measurement provisions of this IFRS* do not apply to the following assets, which are covered by the Standards listed, either as individual assets or as part of a disposal group:

(a) deferred tax assets (IAS 12 *Income Taxes*).

(b) assets arising from employee benefits (IAS 19 *Employee Benefits*).

(c) financial assets within the scope of IAS 39 *Financial Instruments: Recognition and Measurement*.

(d) non-current assets that are accounted for in accordance with the fair value model in IAS 40 *Investment Property*.

(e) non-current assets that are measured at fair value less estimated point-of-sale costs in accordance with IAS 41 *Agriculture*.

(f) contractual rights under insurance contracts as defined in IFRS 4 *Insurance Contracts*.

Classification of non-current assets (or disposal groups) as held for sale

6 **An entity shall classify a non-current asset (or disposal group) as held for sale if its carrying amount will be recovered principally through a sale transaction rather than through continuing use.**

7 For this to be the case, the asset (or disposal group) must be available for immediate sale in its present condition subject only to terms that are usual and customary for sales of such assets (or disposal groups) and its sale must be *highly probable*.

8 For the sale to be highly probable, the appropriate level of management must be committed to a plan to sell the asset (or disposal group), and an active programme to locate a buyer and complete the plan must have been initiated. Further, the asset (or disposal group) must be actively marketed for sale at a price that is reasonable in relation to its current fair value. In addition, the sale should be expected to qualify for recognition as a completed sale within one year from the date of classification, except as permitted by paragraph 9, and actions required to complete the plan should indicate that it is unlikely that significant changes to the plan will be made or that the plan will be withdrawn.

9 Events or circumstances may extend the period to complete the sale beyond one year. An extension of the period required to complete a sale does not preclude an asset (or disposal group) from being classified as held for sale if the delay is caused by events or circumstances beyond the entity's control and there is sufficient evidence that the entity remains committed to its plan to sell the asset (or disposal group). This will be the case when the criteria in Appendix B are met.

* Other than paragraphs 18 and 19, which require the assets in question to be measured in accordance with other applicable IFRSs.

10 Sale transactions include exchanges of non-current assets for other non-current assets when the exchange has commercial substance in accordance with IAS 16 *Property, Plant and Equipment*.

11 When an entity acquires a non-current asset (or disposal group) exclusively with a view to its subsequent disposal, it shall classify the non-current asset (or disposal group) as held for sale at the acquisition date only if the one-year requirement in paragraph 8 is met (except as permitted by paragraph 9) and it is highly probable that any other criteria in paragraphs 7 and 8 that are not met at that date will be met within a short period following the acquisition (usually within three months).

12 If the criteria in paragraphs 7 and 8 are met after the balance sheet date, an entity shall not classify a non-current asset (or disposal group) as held for sale in those financial statements when issued. However, when those criteria are met after the balance sheet date but before the authorisation of the financial statements for issue, the entity shall disclose the information specified in paragraph 41(a), (b) and (d) in the notes.

Non-current assets that are to be abandoned

13 An entity shall not classify as held for sale a non-current asset (or disposal group) that is to be abandoned. This is because its carrying amount will be recovered principally through continuing use. However, if the disposal group to be abandoned meets the criteria in paragraph 32(a)–(c), the entity shall present the results and cash flows of the disposal group as discontinued operations in accordance with paragraphs 33 and 34 at the date on which it ceases to be used. non-current assets (or disposal groups) to be abandoned include non-current assets (or disposal groups) that are to be used to the end of their economic life and non-current assets (or disposal groups) that are to be closed rather than sold.

14 An entity shall not account for a non-current asset that has been temporarily taken out of use as if it had been abandoned.

Measurement of non-current assets (or disposal groups) classified as held for sale

Measurement of a non-current asset (or disposal group)

15 **An entity shall measure a non-current asset (or disposal group) classified as held for sale at the lower of its carrying amount and fair value less costs to sell.**

16 If a newly acquired asset (or disposal group) meets the criteria to be classified as held for sale (see paragraph 11), applying paragraph 15 will result in the asset (or disposal group) being measured on initial recognition at the lower of its carrying amount had it not been so classified (for example, cost) and fair value less costs to sell. Hence, if the asset (or disposal group) is acquired as part of a business combination, it shall be measured at fair value less costs to sell.

17 When the sale is expected to occur beyond one year, the entity shall measure the costs to sell at their present value. Any increase in the present value of the costs to sell that arises from the passage of time shall be presented in profit or loss as a financing cost.

18 Immediately before the initial classification of the asset (or disposal group) as held for sale, the carrying amounts of the asset (or all the assets and liabilities in the group) shall be measured in accordance with applicable IFRSs.

19 On subsequent remeasurement of a disposal group, the carrying amounts of any assets and liabilities that are not within the scope of the measurement requirements of this IFRS, but are included in a disposal group classified as held for sale, shall be remeasured in accordance with applicable IFRSs before the fair value less costs to sell of the disposal group is remeasured.

Recognition of impairment losses and reversals

20 An entity shall recognise an impairment loss for any initial or subsequent write-down of the asset (or disposal group) to fair value less costs to sell, to the extent that it has not been recognised in accordance with paragraph 19.

21 An entity shall recognise a gain for any subsequent increase in fair value less costs to sell of an asset, but not in excess of the cumulative impairment loss that has been recognised either in accordance with this IFRS or previously in accordance with IAS 36 *Impairment of Assets*.

22 An entity shall recognise a gain for any subsequent increase in fair value less costs to sell of a disposal group:

(a) to the extent that it has not been recognised in accordance with paragraph 19; but

(b) not in excess of the cumulative impairment loss that has been recognised, either in accordance with this IFRS or previously in accordance with IAS 36, on the non-current assets that are within the scope of the measurement requirements of this IFRS.

23 The impairment loss (or any subsequent gain) recognised for a disposal group shall re duce (or increase) the carrying amount of the non-current assets in the group that are within the scope of the measurement requirements of this IFRS, in the order of allocation set out in paragraphs 104(a) and (b) and 122 of IAS 36 (as revised in 2004).

24 A gain or loss not previously recognised by the date of the sale of a non-current asset (or disposal group) shall be recognised at the date of derecognition. Requirements relating to derecognition are set out in:

(a) paragraphs 67–72 of IAS 16 (as revised in 2003) for property, plant and equipment, and

(b) paragraphs 112–117 of IAS 38 *Intangible Assets* (as revised in 2004) for intangible assets.

25 An entity shall not depreciate (or amortise) a non-current asset while it is classified as held for sale or while it is part of a disposal group classified as held for sale. Interest and other expenses attributable to the liabilities of a disposal group classified as held for sale shall continue to be recognised.

Changes to a plan of sale

26 If an entity has classified an asset (or disposal group) as held for sale, but the criteria in paragraphs 7–9 are no longer met, the entity shall cease to classify the asset (or disposal group) as held for sale.

27 The entity shall measure a non-current asset that ceases to be classified as held for sale (or ceases to be included in a disposal group classified as held for sale) at the lower of:

(a) its carrying amount before the asset (or disposal group) was classified as held for sale, adjusted for any depreciation, amortisation or revaluations that would have been recognised had the asset (or disposal group) not been classified as held for sale, and

(b) its *recoverable amount* at the date of the subsequent decision not to sell.*

28 The entity shall include any required adjustment to the carrying amount of a non-current asset that ceases to be classified as held for sale in income† from continuing operations in the period in which the criteria in paragraphs 7–9 are no longer met. The entity shall present that adjustment in the same income statement caption used to present a gain or loss, if any, recognised in accordance with paragraph 37.

29 If an entity removes an individual asset or liability from a disposal group classified as held for sale, the remaining assets and liabilities of the disposal group to be sold shall continue to be measured as a group only if the group meets the criteria in paragraphs 79. Otherwise, the remaining non-current assets of the group that individually meet the criteria to be classified as held for sale shall be measured individually at the lower of their carrying amounts and fair values less costs to sell at that date. Any non-current assets that do not meet the criteria shall cease to be classified as held for sale in accordance with paragraph 26.

Presentation and disclosure

30 An entity shall present and disclose information that enables users of the financial statements to evaluate the financial effects of discontinued operations and disposals of non-current assets (or disposal groups).

Presenting discontinued operations

31 A *component* of an entity comprises operations and cash flows that can be clearly distinguished, operationally and for financial reporting purposes, from the rest of the entity. In other words, a component of an entity will have been a cash-generating unit or a group of cash-generating units while being held for use.

* If the non-current asset is part of a cash-generating unit, its recoverable amount is the carrying amount that would have been recognised after the allocation of any impairment loss arising on that cash-generating unit in accordance with IAS 36.

† Unless the asset is property, plant and equipment or an intangible asset that had been revalued in accordance with IAS 16 or IAS 38 before classification as held for sale, in which case the adjustment shall be treated as a revaluation increase or decrease.

32 A discontinued operation is a component of an entity that either has been disposed of, or is classified as held for sale, and

(a) represents a separate major line of business or geographical area of operations,

(b) is part of a single co-ordinated plan to dispose of a separate major line of business or geographical area of operations or

(c) is a subsidiary acquired exclusively with a view to resale.

33 An entity shall disclose:

(a) a single amount on the face of the income statement comprising the total of:

(i) the post-tax profit or loss of discontinued operations and

(ii) the post-tax gain or loss recognised on the measurement to fair value less costs to sell or on the disposal of the assets or disposal group(s) constituting the discontinued operation.

(b) an analysis of the single amount in (a) into:

(i) the revenue, expenses and pre-tax profit or loss of discontinued operations;

(ii) the related income tax expense as required by paragraph 81(h) of IAS 12;

(iii) the gain or loss recognised on the measurement to fair value less costs to sell or on the disposal of the assets or disposal group(s) constituting the discontinued operation; and

(iv) the related income tax expense as required by paragraph 81(h) of IAS 12.

The analysis may be presented in the notes or on the face of the income statement. If it is presented on the face of the income statement it shall be presented in a section identified as relating to discontinued operations, ie separately from continuing operations. The analysis is not required for disposal groups that are newly acquired subsidiaries that meet the criteria to be classified as held for sale on acquisition (see paragraph 11).

(c) the net cash flows attributable to the operating, investing and financing activities of discontinued operations. These disclosures may be presented either in the notes or on the face of the financial statements. These disclosures are not required for disposal groups that are newly acquired subsidiaries that meet the criteria to be classified as held for sale on acquisition (see paragraph 11).

34 An entity shall re-present the disclosures in paragraph 33 for prior periods presented in the financial statements so that the disclosures relate to all operations that have been discontinued by the balance sheet date for the latest period presented.

35 Adjustments in the current period to amounts previously presented in discontinued op erations that are directly related to the disposal of a discontinued operation in a prior period shall be classified separately in discontinued

operations. The nature and amount of such adjustments shall be disclosed. Examples of circumstances in which these adjustments may arise include the following:

(a) the resolution of uncertainties that arise from the terms of the disposal transaction, such as the resolution of purchase price adjustments and indemnification issues with the purchaser.

(b) the resolution of uncertainties that arise from and are directly related to the operations of the component before its disposal, such as environmental and product warranty obligations retained by the seller.

(c) the settlement of employee benefit plan obligations, provided that the settlement is directly related to the disposal transaction.

36 If an entity ceases to classify a component of an entity as held for sale, the results of operations of the component previously presented in discontinued operations in accordance with paragraphs 33–35 shall be reclassified and included in income from continuing operations for all periods presented. The amounts for prior periods shall be described as having been re-presented.

Gains or losses relating to continuing operations

37 Any gain or loss on the remeasurement of a non-current asset (or disposal group) classified as held for sale that does not meet the definition of a discontinued operation shall be included in profit or loss from continuing operations.

Presentation of a non-current asset or disposal group classified as held for sale

38 An entity shall present a non-current asset classified as held for sale and the assets of a disposal group classified as held for sale separately from other assets in the balance sheet. The liabilities of a disposal group classified as held for sale shall be presented separately from other liabilities in the balance sheet. Those assets and liabilities shall not be offset and presented as a single amount. The major classes of assets and liabilities classified as held for sale shall be separately disclosed either on the face of the balance sheet or in the notes, except as permitted by paragraph 39. An entity shall present separately any cumulative income or expense recognised directly in equity relating to a non-current asset (or disposal group) classified as held for sale.

39 If the disposal group is a newly acquired subsidiary that meets the criteria to be classified as held for sale on acquisition (see paragraph 11), disclosure of the major classes of assets and liabilities is not required.

40 An entity shall not reclassify or re-present amounts presented for non-current assets or for the assets and liabilities of disposal groups classified as held for sale in the balance sheets for prior periods to reflect the classification in the balance sheet for the latest period presented.

Additional disclosures

41 An entity shall disclose the following information in the notes in the period in which a non-current asset (or disposal group) has been either classified as held for sale or sold:

(a) a description of the non-current asset (or disposal group);

(b) a description of the facts and circumstances of the sale, or leading to the expected disposal, and the expected manner and timing of that disposal;

(c) the gain or loss recognised in accordance with paragraphs 20–22 and, if not separately presented on the face of the income statement, the caption in the income statement that includes that gain or loss;

(d) if applicable, the segment in which the non-current asset (or disposal group) is presented in accordance with IAS 14 *Segment Reporting*.

42 If either paragraph 26 or paragraph 29 applies, an entity shall disclose, in the period of the decision to change the plan to sell the non-current asset (or disposal group), a description of the facts and circumstances leading to the decision and the effect of the decision on the results of operations for the period and any prior periods presented.

Transitional provisions

43 The IFRS shall be applied prospectively to non-current assets (or disposal groups) that meet the criteria to be classified as held for sale and operations that meet the criteria to be classified as discontinued after the effective date of the IFRS. An entity may apply the requirements of the IFRS to all non-current assets (or disposal groups) that meet the criteria to be classified as held for sale and operations that meet the criteria to be classified as discontinued after any date before the effective date of the IFRS, provided the valuations and other information needed to apply the IFRS were obtained at the time those criteria were originally met.

Effective date

44 An entity shall apply this IFRS for annual periods beginning on or after 1 January 2005. Earlier application is encouraged. If an entity applies the IFRS for a period beginning before 1 January 2005, it shall disclose that fact.

Withdrawal of IAS 35

45 This IFRS supersedes IAS 35 *Discontinuing Operations*.

Appendix A
Defined terms

This appendix is an integral part of the IFRS.

cash-generating unit The smallest identifiable group of assets that generates cash inflows that are largely independent of the cash inflows from other assets or groups of assets.

component of an entity Operations and cash flows that can be clearly distinguished, operationally and for financial reporting purposes, from the rest of the entity.

costs to sell The incremental costs directly attributable to the disposal of an asset (or **disposal group**), excluding finance costs and income tax expense.

current asset An asset that satisfies any of the following criteria:

(a) it is expected to be realised in, or is intended for sale or consumption in, the entity's normal operating cycle;

(b) it is held primarily for the purpose of being traded;

(c) it is expected to be realised within twelve months after the balance sheet date; or

(d) it is cash or a cash equivalent asset unless it is restricted from being exchanged or used to settle a liability for at least twelve months after the balance sheet date.

discontinued operation A **component of an entity** that either has been disposed of or is classified as held for sale and:

(a) represents a separate major line of business or geographical area of operations,

(b) is part of a single co-ordinated plan to dispose of a separate major line of business or geographical area of operations or

(c) is a subsidiary acquired exclusively with a view to resale.

disposal group A group of assets to be disposed of, by sale or otherwise, together as a group in a single transaction, and liabilities directly associated with those assets that will be transferred in the transaction. The group includes goodwill acquired in a business combination if the group is a **cash-generating unit** to which goodwill has been allocated in accordance with the requirements of paragraphs 80–87 of IAS 36 *Impairment of Assets* (as revised in 2004) or if it is an operation within such a cash-generating unit.

fair value The amount for which an asset could be exchanged, or a liability settled, between knowledgeable, willing parties in an arm's length transaction.

firm purchase commitment An agreement with an unrelated party, binding on both parties and usually legally enforceable, that (a) specifies all significant terms, including the price and timing of the transactions, and (b) includes a disincentive for non-performance that is sufficiently large to make performance **highly probable.**

highly probable Significantly more likely than **probable**.

non-current asset An asset that does not meet the definition of a **current asset**.

probable More likely than not.

recoverable amount	The higher of an asset's **fair value** less **costs to sell** and its **value in use**.
value in use	The present value of estimated future cash flows expected to arise from the continuing use of an asset and from its disposal at the end of its useful life.

Appendix B
Application supplement

This appendix is an integral part of the IFRS.

Extension of the period required to complete a sale

B1 As noted in paragraph 9, an extension of the period required to complete a sale does not preclude an asset (or disposal group) from being classified as held for sale if the delay is caused by events or circumstances beyond the entity's control and there is sufficient evidence that the entity remains committed to its plan to sell the asset (or disposal group). An exception to the one-year requirement in paragraph 8 shall therefore apply in the following situations in which such events or circumstances arise:

(a) at the date an entity commits itself to a plan to sell a non-current asset (or disposal group) it reasonably expects that others (not a buyer) will impose conditions on the transfer of the asset (or disposal group) that will extend the period required to complete the sale, and:

    (i) actions necessary to respond to those conditions cannot be initiated until after a *firm purchase commitment* is obtained, and

    (ii) a firm purchase commitment is highly probable within one year.

(b) an entity obtains a firm purchase commitment and, as a result, a buyer or others unexpectedly impose conditions on the transfer of a non-current asset (or disposal group) previously classified as held for sale that will extend the period required to complete the sale, and:

    (i) timely actions necessary to respond to the conditions have been taken, and

    (ii) a favourable resolution of the delaying factors is expected.

(c) during the initial one-year period, circumstances arise that were previously considered unlikely and, as a result, a non-current asset (or disposal group) previously classified as held for sale is not sold by the end of that period, and:

    (i) during the initial one-year period the entity took action necessary to respond to the change in circumstances,

    (ii) the non-current asset (or disposal group) is being actively marketed at a price that is reasonable, given the change in circumstances, and

    (iii) the criteria in paragraphs 7 and 8 are met.

Appendix C
Amendments to other IFRSs

The amendments in this appendix shall be applied for annual periods beginning on or after 1 January 2005. If an entity adopts this IFRS for an earlier period, these amendments shall be applied for that earlier period.

* * * * *

The amendments contained in this appendix when this IFRS was issued in 2004 have been incorporated into the relevant pronouncements published in this volume.

Approval of IFRS 5 by the Board

International Financial Reporting Standard 5 *Non-current Assets Held for Sale and Discontinued Operations* was approved for issue by twelve of the fourteen members of the International Accounting Standards Board. Messrs Cope and Schmid dissented. Their dissenting opinions are set out after the Basis for Conclusions on IFRS 5.

Sir David Tweedie	Chairman
Thomas E Jones	Vice-Chairman
Mary E Barth	
Hans-Georg Bruns	
Anthony T Cope	
Robert P Garnett	
Gilbert Gélard	
James J Leisenring	
Warren J McGregor	
Patricia L O'Malley	
Harry K Schmid	
John T Smith	
Geoffrey Whittington	
Tatsumi Yamada	

CONTENTS

paragraphs

BASIS FOR CONCLUSIONS ON IFRS 5 NON-CURRENT ASSETS HELD FOR SALE AND DISCONTINUED OPERATIONS

Basis for Conclusions on IFRS 5 Non-current Assets Held for Sale and Discontinued Operations

This Basis for Conclusions accompanies, but is not part of, IFRS 5.

Introduction

BC1 This Basis for Conclusions summarises the International Accounting Standards Board's considerations in reaching the conclusions in IFRS 5 *Non-current Assets Held for Sale and Discontinued Operations*. Individual Board members gave greater weight to some factors than to others.

BC2 In September 2002 the Board agreed to add a short-term convergence project to its active agenda. The objective of the project is to reduce differences between IFRSs and US GAAP that are capable of resolution in a relatively short time and can be addressed outside major projects. The project is a joint project with the US Financial Accounting Standards Board (FASB).

BC3 As part of the project, the two boards agreed to review each other's deliberations on each of the selected possible convergence topics, and choose the highest quality solution as the basis for convergence. For topics recently considered by either board, there is an expectation that whichever board has more recently deliberated that topic will have the higher quality solution.

BC4 As part of the review of topics recently considered by the FASB, the Board discussed the requirements of SFAS 144 *Accounting for the Impairment or Disposal of Long-Lived Assets*, as they relate to assets held for sale and discontinued operations. The Board did not consider the requirements of SFAS 144 relating to the impairment of assets held for use. Impairment of such assets is an issue that is being addressed in the IASB research project on measurement being led by the Canadian Accounting Standards Board.

BC5 Until the issue of IFRS 5, the requirements of SFAS 144 on assets held for sale and discontinued operations differed from IFRSs in the following ways:

(a) if specified criteria are met, SFAS 144 requires non-current assets that are to be disposed of to be classified as held for sale. Such assets are remeasured at the lower of carrying amount and fair value less costs to sell and are not depreciated or amortised. IFRSs did not require non-current assets that are to be disposed of to be classified separately or measured differently from other non-current assets.

(b) the definition of discontinued operations in SFAS 144 was different from the definition of discontinuing operations in IAS 35 *Discontinuing Operations* and the presentation of such operations required by the two standards was also different.

BC6 As discussed in more detail below, the Board concluded that introducing a classification of assets that are held for sale would substantially improve the information available to users of financial statements about assets to be sold.

BC7 The Board published its proposals in an Exposure Draft, ED 4 *Disposal of Non-current Assets and Presentation of Discontinued Operations*, in July 2003 with a comment deadline of 24 October 2003. The Board received over 80 comment letters on the Exposure Draft.

Scope of the IFRS

BC8 In ED 4, the Board proposed that the IFRS should apply to all non-current assets except:

(a) goodwill,

(b) financial instruments within the scope of IAS 39 *Financial Instruments: Recognition and Measurement*,

(c) financial assets under leases, and

(d) deferred tax assets and assets arising from employee benefits.

BC9 In reconsidering the scope, the Board noted that the use of the term 'non-current' caused the following problems:

(a) assets that are acquired with the intention of resale were clearly intended to be within the scope of ED 4, but would also be within the definition of current assets and so might be thought to be excluded. The same was true for assets that had been classified as non-current but were now expected to be realised within twelve months.

(b) it was not clear how the scope would apply to assets presented in accordance with a liquidity presentation.

BC10 The Board noted that it had not intended that assets classified as non-current in accordance with IAS 1 *Presentation of Financial Statements* would be reclassified as current assets simply because of management's intention to sell or because they reached their final twelve months of expected use by the entity. The Board decided to clarify in IFRS 5 that assets classified as non-current are not reclassified as current assets until they meet the criteria to be classified as held for sale in accordance with the IFRS. Further, assets of a class that an entity would normally regard as non-current and are acquired exclusively with a view to resale are not classified as current unless they meet the criteria to be classified as held for sale in accordance with the IFRS.

BC11 In relation to assets presented in accordance with a liquidity presentation, the Board decided that non-current should be taken to mean assets that include amounts expected to be recovered more than twelve months after the balance sheet date.

BC12 These clarifications ensure that all assets of the type normally regarded by the entity as non-current will be within the scope of the IFRS.

BC13 The Board also reconsidered the exclusions from the scope proposed in ED 4. The Board noted that the classification and presentation requirements of the IFRS are applicable to all non-current assets and concluded that any exclusions should relate only to the measurement requirements. In relation to the measurement requirements, the Board decided that non-current assets should be excluded only if (i) they are already carried at fair value with changes in fair value recognised in profit or loss or (ii) there would be difficulties in determining their fair value less costs to sell. The Board therefore concluded that only the following non-current assets should be excluded from the measurement requirements of the IFRS:

Assets already carried at fair value with changes in fair value recognised in profit or loss:

(a) financial assets within the scope of IAS 39 *Financial Instruments: Recognition and Measurement.**

(b) non-current assets that have been accounted for using the fair value model in IAS 40 *Investment Property*.

(c) non-current assets that have been measured at fair value less estimated point-of-sale costs in accordance with IAS 41 *Agriculture*.

Assets for which there might be difficulties in determining their fair value

(a) deferred tax assets.

(b) assets arising from employee benefits.

(c) assets arising from insurance contracts.

BC14 The Board acknowledged that the scope of the IFRS would differ from that of SFAS 144 but noted that SFAS 144 covers the impairment of non-current assets held for use as well as those held for sale. Furthermore, other requirements in US GAAP affect the scope of SFAS 144. The Board therefore concluded that convergence with the scope of SFAS 144 would not be possible.

Classification of non-current assets to be disposed of as held for sale

BC15 Under SFAS 144, long-lived assets are classified as either (i) held and used or (ii) held for sale. Before the issue of this IFRS, no distinction was made in IFRSs between non-current assets held and used and non-current assets held for sale, except in relation to financial instruments.

BC16 The Board considered whether a separate classification for non-current assets held for sale would create unnecessary complexity in IFRSs and introduce an element of management intent into the accounting. Some commentators suggested that the categorisation 'assets held for sale' is unnecessary, and that if the focus were changed to 'assets *retired* from active use' much of the complexity could be eliminated, because the latter classification would be based on actuality rather than what they perceive as management intent. They assert that it is the potential abuse of the classification that necessitates many of the detailed requirements in SFAS 144. Others suggested that, if existing IFRSs were amended to specify that assets retired from active use are measured at fair value less costs to sell and to require additional disclosure, some convergence with SFAS 144 could be achieved without creating a new IFRS.

* The Board acknowledges that not all financial assets within the scope of IAS 39 are recognised at fair value with changes in fair value recognised in profit or loss but it did not want to make any further changes to the accounting for financial assets at this time.

BC17 However, the Board concluded that providing information about assets and groups of assets and liabilities to be disposed of is of benefit to users of financial statements. Such information should assist users in assessing the timing, amount and uncertainty of future cash flows. The Board understands that this was also the assessment underpinning SFAS 144. Therefore the Board concluded that introducing the notion of assets and disposal groups held for sale makes IFRSs more complete.

BC18 Furthermore, although the held for sale classification begins from an intention to sell the asset, the other criteria for this classification are tightly drawn and are significantly more objective than simply specifying an intention or commitment to sell. Some might argue that the criteria are too specific. However, the Board believes that the criteria should be specific to achieve comparability of classification between entities. The Board does not believe that a classification 'retired from active use' would necessarily require fewer criteria to support it. For example, it would be necessary to establish a distinction between assets retired from active use and those that are held as back-up spares or are temporarily idle.

BC19 Lastly, if the classification and measurement of assets held for sale in IFRSs are the same as in US GAAP, convergence will have been achieved in an area of importance to users of financial statements.

BC20 Most respondents to ED 4 agreed that a separate classification for non-current assets that are no longer held to be used is desirable. However, the proposals in ED 4 were criticised for the following reasons:

(a) the criteria were too restrictive and rules-based.

(b) a commitment to sell needs to be demonstrated, consistently with the requirements of IAS 37 *Provisions, Contingent Liabilities and Contingent Assets* relating to restructuring provisions.

(c) the classification should be for assets retired from active use.

(d) assets to be abandoned should be treated in the same way as assets to be sold.

BC21 The Board noted that a more flexible definition would be open to abuse. Further, changing the criteria for classification could cause divergence from US GAAP. The Board has, however, reordered the criteria to highlight the principles.

BC22 The Board also noted that the requirements of IAS 37 establish when a liability is incurred, whereas the requirements of the IFRS relate to the measurement and presentation of assets that are already recognised.

BC23 Finally, the Board reconfirmed the principle behind the classification proposals in ED 4, which is that the carrying amount of the assets will be recovered principally through sale. Applying this principle to assets retired from active use, the Board decided that assets retired from active use that do not meet the criteria for classification as assets held for sale should not be presented separately because the carrying amount of the asset may not be recovered principally through sale. Conversely, the Board decided that assets that meet the criteria to be classified as held for sale and are being used should not be precluded from being separately classified. This is because, if a non-current asset is available for immediate sale, the remaining use of the asset is incidental to its recovery through sale and the carrying amount of the asset will be recovered principally through sale.

BC24 Applying the same principle to assets to be abandoned, the Board noted that their carrying value will never be recovered principally through sale.

Assets to be exchanged for other non-current assets

BC25 Under SFAS 144, long-lived assets that are to be exchanged for similar productive assets cannot be classified as held for sale. They are regarded as disposed of only when exchanged. The Basis for Conclusions on SFAS 144 explains that this is because the exchange of such assets is accounted for at amounts based on the carrying amount of the assets, not at fair value, and that using the carrying amount is more consistent with the accounting for a long-lived asset to be held and used than for a long-lived asset to be sold.

BC26 Under IAS 16 *Property, Plant and Equipment*, as revised in 2003, an exchange of assets is normally measured at fair value. The SFAS 144 reasoning for the classification of such assets as held for sale does not, therefore, apply. Consistently with IAS 16, the IFRS treats an exchange of assets as a disposal and acquisition of assets unless the exchange has no commercial substance.

BC27 The FASB has published an exposure draft proposing to converge with the requirements in IAS 16 for an exchange of assets to be measured at fair value. The exposure draft also proposes a consequential amendment to SFAS 144 that would make exchanges of assets that have commercial substance eligible for classification as held for sale.

Measurement of non-current assets held for sale

BC28 SFAS 144 requires a long-lived asset or a disposal group classified as held for sale to be measured at the lower of its carrying amount and fair value less costs to sell. A long-lived asset classified as held for sale (or included within a disposal group) is not depreciated, but interest and other expenses attributable to the liabilities of a disposal group are recognised.

BC29 As explained in the Basis for Conclusions on SFAS 144, the remaining use in operations of an asset that is to be sold is incidental to the recovery of the carrying amount through sale. The accounting for such an asset should therefore be a process of valuation rather than allocation.

BC30 The FASB further observed that once the asset is remeasured, to depreciate the asset would reduce its carrying amount below its fair value less costs to sell. It also noted that should there be a decline in the value of the asset after initial classification as held for sale and before eventual sale, the loss would be recognised in the period of decline because the fair value less costs to sell is evaluated each period.

BC31 The counter-argument is that, although classified as held for sale, the asset is still being used in operations, and hence cessation of depreciation is inconsistent with the basic principle that the cost of an asset should be allocated over the period during which benefits are obtained from its use. Furthermore, although the decline in the value of the asset through its use would be reflected in the recognised change in fair value, it might also be masked by an increase arising from changes in the market prices of the asset.

BC32 However, the Board noted that IAS 16 requires an entity to keep the expected useful life and residual values of property. plant and equipment up to date, and IAS 36 *Impairment of Assets* requires an immediate write-down to the higher of value in use and fair value less costs to sell. An entity should, therefore, often achieve a measurement effect for individual assets that are about to be sold under other IFRSs similar to that required by this IFRS as follows. Under other IFRSs, if the fair value less costs to sell is higher than carrying amount there will be no impairment and no depreciation (because the residual value will have been updated). If fair value less costs to sell is lower than carrying amount, there will be an impairment loss that reduces the carrying amount to fair value less costs to sell and then no depreciation (because the residual value will have been updated), unless value in use is higher than fair value less costs to sell. If value in use is higher than fair value less costs to sell, there would be small differences between the treatment that would arise under other IFRSs and the treatment under IFRS 5. Under other IFRSs there would be an impairment loss to the extent that the carrying amount exceeds value in use rather than to the extent that the carrying amount exceeds fair value less costs to sell. Under other IFRSs, there would also then be depreciation of the excess of value in use (the new carrying amount of the asset) over fair value less costs to sell (its residual value). However, for assets classified as held for sale, value in use will differ from fair value less costs to sell only to the extent of the net cash flows expected to arise before the sale. If the period to sale is short, this amount will usually be relatively small. The difference in impairment loss recognised and subsequent depreciation under other IFRSs compared with the impairment loss and no subsequent depreciation under IFRS 5 would, therefore, also be small.

BC33 The Board concluded that the measurement requirements of IFRS 5 for individual assets would often not involve a significant change from the requirements of other IFRSs. Furthermore, the Board agreed with the FASB that the cash flows arising from the asset's remaining use were incidental to the recovery of the asset through sale and, hence, concluded that individual assets classified as held for sale should be measured at the lower of carrying amount and fair value less costs to sell and should not be depreciated.

BC34 For disposal groups, there could be greater differences between the requirements in other IFRSs and the requirements of IFRS 5. For example, the fair value less costs to sell of a disposal group may reflect internally generated goodwill to the extent that it is higher than the carrying value of the net assets in the disposal group. The residual value of the non-current assets in the disposal group may, nonetheless, be such that, if they were accounted for in accordance with IAS 16, those assets would be depreciated.

BC35 In such a situation, some might view the requirements in IFRS 5 as allowing internally generated goodwill to stop the depreciation of non-current assets. However, the Board does not agree with that view. Rather, the Board believes that the internally generated goodwill provides a buffer against the recognition of an impairment loss on the disposal group. The same effect arises from the impairment requirements in IAS 36. The non-depreciation of the non-current assets in the disposal group is, as with individual assets, a consequence of the basic principle underlying the separate classification, that the carrying amount of the asset will be recovered principally through sale, not continuing use, and that amounts recovered through continuing use will be incidental.

BC36 In addition, it is important to emphasise that IFRS 5 permits only an asset (or disposal group) that is to be *sold* to be classified as held for sale. Assets to be abandoned are classified as held and used until disposed of, and thus are depreciated. The Board agrees with the FASB's observation that a distinction can be drawn between an asset that is to be sold and an asset that is to be abandoned, because the former will be recovered principally through sale and the latter through its continuing use. Therefore, it is logical that depreciation should cease in the former but not the latter case.

BC37 When an asset or a disposal group held for sale is part of a foreign operation with a functional currency that is different from the presentation currency of the group, an exchange difference will have been recognised in equity arising from the translation of the asset or disposal group into the presentation currency of the group. IAS 21 *The Effects of Changes in Foreign Exchange Rates* requires the exchange difference to be 'recycled' from equity to profit or loss on disposal of the operation. The question arises whether classification as held for sale should trigger the recycling of any exchange differences. Under US GAAP (EITF 01-5 *Application of FASB Statement No. 52 to an Investment Being Evaluated for Impairment That Will Be Disposed Of*) the accumulated foreign currency translation adjustments previously recognised in other comprehensive income that are expected to be recycled in income at the time of sale are included in the carrying amount of the asset (or disposal group) being tested for impairment.

BC38 In its project on reporting comprehensive income, the Board may reconsider the issue of recycling. Therefore, it did not wish to make any interim changes to the requirements in IAS 21. Hence, the IFRS does not permit any exchange differences to be recycled on the classification of an asset or a disposal group as held for sale. The recycling will take place when the asset or disposal group is sold.

The allocation of an impairment loss to a disposal group

BC39 Under SFAS 144 and the proposals in ED 4, assets within the disposal group that are not within the scope of the IFRS are adjusted in accordance with other standards before measuring the fair value less costs to sell of the disposal group. Any loss or gain recognised on adjusting the carrying amount of the disposal group is allocated to the carrying amount of the long-lived assets of the group.

BC40 This is different from the requirements of IAS 36 for the allocation of an impairment loss arising on a cash-generating unit. IAS 36 requires an impairment loss on a cash-generating unit to be allocated first to reduce the carrying amount of goodwill and then to reduce pro rata the carrying amounts of the other assets in the unit.

BC41 The Board considered whether the allocation of an impairment loss for a disposal group should be consistent with the requirements of IAS 36 or with the requirements of SFAS 144. The Board concluded that it would be simplest to require the same allocation as is required by IAS 36 for cash-generating units. Although this is different from SFAS 144, the disposal group as a whole will be measured at the same amount.

Newly acquired assets

BC42 SFAS 144 requires, and ED 4 proposed, newly acquired assets that meet the criteria to be classified as held for sale to be measured at fair value less costs to sell on initial recognition. So, in those instances, other than in a business combination, in which an entity acquires a non-current asset that meets the criteria to be classified as held for sale, a loss is recognised in profit or loss if the cost of the asset exceeds its fair value less costs to sell. In the more common cases in which an entity acquires, as part of a business combination, a non-current asset (or disposal group) that meets the criteria to be classified as held for sale, the difference between fair value and fair value less costs to sell is recognised in goodwill.

BC43 Some respondents to ED 4 noted that measuring newly acquired assets not part of a business combination at fair value less costs to sell was inconsistent with the general proposal that assets classified as held for sale should be measured at *the lower of carrying amount* and fair value less costs to sell. The Board agreed and amended the requirement so that it is clear that the newly acquired assets (or disposal groups) are measured on initial recognition at the lower of what their carrying amount would be were they not classified as held for sale (ie cost) and fair value less costs to sell.

BC44 In relation to business combinations, the Board noted that conceptually the assets should be recognised initially at fair value and then immediately classified as held for sale, with the result that the costs to sell are recognised in profit or loss, not goodwill. In theory, if the entity had factored the costs to sell into the purchase price, the reduced price would lead to the creation of negative goodwill, the immediate recognition of which in profit or loss would offset the loss arising from the costs to sell. Of course, in practice, the reduced price will usually result in lower net positive goodwill rather than negative goodwill to be recognised in profit or loss. For that reason, and for the sake of convergence, the Board concluded that in a business combination non-current assets that meet the criteria to be classified as held for sale on acquisition should be measured at fair value less costs to sell on initial recognition.

BC45 The Board and the FASB are considering which items should form part of the business combination transaction more generally in their joint project on the application of the purchase method. This consideration includes whether the assets and liabilities recognised in the transaction should be based on the acquirer's or the acquiree's perspective. The outcome of those deliberations may affect the decision discussed in paragraph BC44.

Recognition of subsequent increases in fair value less costs to sell

BC46 The Board considered whether a subsequent increase in fair value less costs to sell should be recognised to the extent that it reversed previous impairments. SFAS 144 requires the recognition of a subsequent increase in fair value less costs to sell, but not in excess of the cumulative loss previously recognised for a write-down to fair value less costs to sell. The Board decided that, under IFRSs, a gain should be recognised to the extent that it reverses any impairment of the asset, either in accordance with the IFRS or previously in accordance with IAS 36.

Recognising a gain for the reversal of an impairment that occurred before the classification of the asset as held for sale is consistent with the requirement in IAS 36 to recognise reversals of impairment.

Recognition of impairment losses and subsequent gains for assets that, before classification as held for sale, were measured at revalued amounts in accordance with another IFRS

BC47 ED 4 proposed that impairment losses and subsequent gains for assets that, before classification as held for sale, were measured at revalued amounts in accordance with another IFRS should be treated as revaluation decreases and increases according to the standard under which the assets had previously been revalued, consistently with the requirements of IAS 36, except to the extent that the losses and gains are caused by the initial recognition of, or changes in, costs to sell. ED 4 also proposed that costs to sell should always be recognised in profit or loss.

BC48 Many respondents disagreed with these proposals, because of their complexity and because of the resulting inconsistent treatment of assets classified as held for sale. The Board considered the issues raised and decided that assets that were already carried at fair value with changes in fair value recognised in profit or loss should not be subject to the measurement requirements of the IFRS. The Board believes that, for such assets, continued measurement at fair value gives better information than measurement at the lower of carrying amount and fair value less costs to sell. The Board did not, however, believe that such treatment was appropriate for assets that had been revalued in accordance with IAS 16 and IAS 38, because those standards require depreciation to continue and the revaluation change would not necessarily be recognised in profit or loss. The Board concluded that assets that had been revalued in accordance with IAS 16 and IAS 38 should be treated in the same way as any assets that, before classification as held for sale, had not been revalued. Such an approach results in a consistent treatment for assets that are within the scope of the measurement requirements of the IFRS and, hence, a simpler standard.

Measurement of assets reclassified as held for use

BC49 Under SFAS 144, when an entity changes its plan to sell the asset and reclassifies a long-lived asset from held for sale to held and used, the asset is measured at the lower of (a) the carrying amount before the asset (or disposal group) was classified as held for sale, adjusted for any depreciation (or amortisation) that would have been recognised had the asset (or disposal group) been continuously classified as held and used and (b) its fair value at the date of the decision not to sell.

BC50 The underlying principle is to restore the carrying value of the asset to what it would have been had it never been classified as held for sale, taking into account any impairments that may have occurred. In fact, SFAS 144 requires that, for held and used assets, an impairment is recognised only if the carrying amount of the asset exceeds the sum of the undiscounted cash flows expected to result from its use and eventual disposal. Thus, the carrying amount of the asset if it had never been classified as held for sale might exceed its fair value. As a result, SFAS 144 does not necessarily lead to the asset reverting to its original carrying amount. However, the Basis for Conclusions on SFAS 144 notes that the FASB concluded it would be inappropriate to write up the carrying amount of the asset to an amount greater than its fair value solely on the basis of an undiscounted cash flow test. Hence, it arrived at the requirement for measurement at the lower of (a) the asset's carrying amount had it not been classified as held for sale and (b) fair value at the date of the decision not to sell the asset.

BC51 IAS 36 has a different measurement basis for impaired assets, ie recoverable amount. The Board concluded that to be consistent with the principle of SFAS 144 and also to be consistent with the requirements of IAS 36, an asset that ceases to be classified as held for sale should be measured at the lower of (a) the carrying amount that would have been recognised had the asset not been classified as held for sale and (b) its recoverable amount at the date of reclassification. Whilst this is not full convergence, the difference arises from differences in the US GAAP and IFRS impairment models.

Removal of exemption from consolidation for subsidiaries acquired and held exclusively with a view to resale

BC52 SFAS 144 removed the exemption from consolidation in US GAAP for subsidiaries held on a temporary basis on the grounds that all assets held for sale should be treated in the same way, ie as required by SFAS 144 rather than having some assets consolidated and some not.

BC53 The Board agreed that all subsidiaries should be consolidated and that all assets (and disposal groups) that meet the criteria to be classified as held for sale should be treated in the same way. The exemption from consolidation in IAS 27 *Consolidated and Separate Financial Statements* for subsidiaries acquired and held exclusively with a view to resale prevents those assets and disposal groups within such subsidiaries that meet the criteria to be classified as held for sale from being treated consistently with other assets and disposal groups. ED 4 therefore proposed that the exemption in IAS 27 should be removed.

BC54 Some respondents disagreed with this proposal, on the grounds that the information provided by consolidation of such subsidiaries would be less useful than that provided by the current requirement to measure the investment in such subsidiaries at fair value. The Board noted that the impact of the proposals in ED 4 would be limited to the following:

(a) the measurement of a subsidiary that currently is within the scope of the exemptions would change from fair value as required by IAS 39 to the lower of cost and fair value less costs to sell.

(b) any change in fair value of the investment in the subsidiary would, in accordance with the current requirements in IAS 27, be presented as a single amount in profit or loss as a held-for-trading financial asset in accordance with IAS 39. As discussed in paragraph BC72, the subsidiary would be a discontinued operation and, in accordance with the IFRS's requirements (see paragraphs BC73–BC76), any recognised change in the value of the disposal group that comprises the subsidiary would be presented as a single amount in profit or loss.

(c) the presentation in the balance sheet would change from a single amount for the investment in the subsidiary to two amounts–one for the assets and one for the liabilities of the disposal group that is the subsidiary.*

BC55 The Board reaffirmed its conclusion set out in paragraph BC53. However, it noted that the limited impact of the proposals apply only to the amounts required to be presented on the face of the balance sheet and the income statement. Providing the required analyses of those amounts in the notes could potentially involve the entity having to obtain significantly more information. The Board therefore decided not to require the disclosure of the analyses of the amounts presented on the face of the balance sheet and income statement for newly acquired subsidiaries and to clarify in an example the computational short cuts that could be used to arrive at the amounts to be presented on the face of the balance sheet and income statement.

Presentation of non-current assets held for sale

BC56 SFAS 144 requires an entity to present:

(a) a long-lived asset classified as held for sale separately in the balance sheet; and

(b) the assets and liabilities of a disposal group classified as held for sale separately in the asset and liability sections of the balance sheet. The major classes of those assets and liabilities are separately disclosed either on the face of the balance sheet or in the notes.

BC57 In the Basis for Conclusions on SFAS 144 the FASB noted that information about the nature of both assets and liabilities of a disposal group is useful to users. Separately presenting those items in the balance sheet provides information that is relevant. Separate presentation also distinguishes those assets that are not being depreciated from those that are being depreciated. The Board agreed with the FASB's views.

BC58 Respondents to ED 4 noted that the separate presentation within equity of amounts relating to assets and disposal groups classified as held for sale (such as, for example, unrealised gains and losses on available-for-sale assets and foreign currency translation adjustments) would also provide useful information. The Board agreed and has added such a requirement to the IFRS.

Timing of classification as, and definition of, discontinued operations

BC59 With the introduction of SFAS 144, the FASB broadened the scope of a discontinued operation from a 'segment of a business' to a 'component of an entity'. A component is widely drawn, the criterion being that it comprises 'operations and cash flows that can be clearly distinguished, operationally and for financial reporting purposes, from the rest of the entity'. SFAS 144 states that a component may be a segment, a reporting unit, a subsidiary or an asset group.

* Greater disaggregation of the disposal group on the face of the balance sheet is permitted but not required.

BC60 However, at the same time, the FASB specified more restrictive criteria for determining *when* the component is classified as discontinued and hence when its results are presented as discontinued. SFAS 144 requires a component to be classified as discontinued only if it has been disposed of or if it meets the criteria for classification as an asset 'held for sale'.

BC61 The definition of a discontinuing operation in IAS 35 as a 'major line of business' or 'geographical area of operations' is closer to the former, and narrower, US GAAP definition. The trigger in IAS 35 for classifying the operation as discontinuing is the earlier of (a) the entity entering into a binding sale agreement and (b) the board of directors approving and announcing a formal disposal plan. Although IAS 35 refers to IAS 37 *Provisions, Contingent Liabilities and Contingent Assets* for further guidance on what constitutes a plan, the criteria are less restrictive than those in SFAS 144.

BC62 Paragraph 12 of the *Framework* states that the objective of financial statements is to provide information about the financial position, performance and changes in financial position of an entity that is useful to a wide range of users in making economic decisions. Paragraph 15 of the *Framework* goes on to state that the economic decisions that are taken by users of financial statements require an evaluation of the ability of an entity to generate cash and cash equivalents. Separately highlighting the results of discontinued operations provides users with information that is relevant in assessing the ongoing ability of the entity to generate cash flows.

BC63 In terms of the timing of classifying an operation as discontinued, the Board considered whether more useful information is provided by making the classification conditional upon a firm decision to discontinue an operation (the current IAS 35 approach) or conditional upon the classification of an operation as held for sale.

BC64 The Board decided that, to be consistent with the presentation of assets held for disposal and in the interests of convergence, an operation should be classified as discontinued when it is disposed of or classified as held for sale.

BC65 IAS 35 also adopts a different approach from US GAAP when criteria for classification as discontinued are met after the period-end but before the financial statements are issued. SFAS 144 requires some disclosure; however, the component is *not* presented as a discontinued operation. IAS 35 requires the component to be classified as discontinuing.

BC66 The Board believes that, consistently with IAS 10 *Events after the Balance Sheet Date*, a component should not be classified as discontinued in the financial statements unless it meets the criteria to be so classified at the balance sheet date.

BC67 In terms of the definition of a discontinued operation, ED 4 proposed adopting the SFAS 144 definition of a discontinued operation. The Board argued that under existing IAS 35 there may be disposal transactions that, although likely to have an impact on the ongoing operations of the entity, do not meet the criteria for classification as a discontinuing activity. For example, an entity might dispose of a significant portion, but not all, of its cash-generating units operating in a particular geographical area. Under IAS 35, that might not meet the definition of a discontinuing operation. Under SFAS 144, if the relevant criteria were met, it would.

BC68 However, a substantial majority of respondents to ED 4 disagreed with this proposal. They preferred instead to retain the IAS 35 criterion that a discontinued operation should be a major line of business or geographical area of operations.

BC69 The Board reconsidered the issue in the light of the comments received and concluded that the size of unit that could be classified as discontinued in accordance with SFAS 144 was too small, with the result that the information provided by separately presenting discontinued operations may not be as useful as it could be.

BC70 The Board also noted that the FASB Emerging Issues Task Force (EITF) is considering practical problems that have arisen in implementing the criteria for discontinued operations in SFAS 144. Specifically, the EITF is considering (a) the cash flows of the component that should be considered in the determination of whether cash flows have been or will be eliminated from the ongoing operations of the entity and (b) the types of continuing involvement that constitute significant continuing involvement in the operations of the disposal component. As a result of these practical problems, the Board further concluded that it was not appropriate to change the definition of a discontinued operation in a way that was likely to cause the same problems in practice as have arisen under SFAS 144.

BC71 The Board therefore decided that it would retain the requirement in IAS 35 that a discontinued operation should be a major line of business or geographical area of operations, noting that this will include operations that would have been excluded from the US definition before SFAS 144, which was based on a reporting segment. However, the Board regards this as an interim measure and intends to work with the FASB to arrive at a converged definition within a relatively short time.

BC72 Lastly, the Board considered whether newly acquired subsidiaries that meet the criteria to be classified as held for sale should always be classified as discontinued. The Board concluded that they should be so classified because they are being disposed of for one of the following reasons:

(a) the subsidiary is in a different line of business from the entity, so disposing of it is similar to disposing of a major line of business.

(b) the subsidiary is required to be disposed of by regulators because the entity would otherwise have too much of a particular type of operation in a particular geographical area. In such a case the subsidiary must be a significant operation.

Presentation of discontinued operations

BC73 SFAS 144 requires the results of a discontinued operation to be presented as a separate component in the income statement (net of income tax) for all periods presented.

BC74 IAS 35 did not require the results of a discontinuing operation to be presented as a net amount on the face of the income statement. Instead, specified items are disclosed either in the notes or on the face of the income statement.

BC75 In ED 4, the Board noted that it was considering the presentation of discontinued operations in the income statement in its project on reporting comprehensive income and that it did not wish to prejudge the outcome of that project by changing the requirements of IAS 35 in respect of the components to be disclosed. Given that the project on reporting comprehensive income will not be completed as soon as previously expected, the Board decided to proceed with its decisions on the presentation of discontinued operations in this IFRS.

BC76 The Board believes that discontinued operations should be shown in a section of the income statement separately from continuing operations because of the different cash flows expected to arise from the two types of operations. The Board concluded that it is sufficient to show a single net figure for discontinued operations on the face of the income statement because of the limited future cash flows expected to arise from the operations. The IFRS therefore permits an analysis of the single net amount to be presented either in the notes or on the face of the income statement.

BC77 A substantial majority of the respondents to ED 4 supported such a presentation.

Transitional arrangements

BC78 Some respondents to ED 4 noted that there could be difficulties in obtaining the information necessary to apply the IFRS retrospectively. The Board agreed that hindsight might be involved in determining at what date assets or disposal groups met the criteria to be classified as held for sale and their fair value at that date. Problems might also arise in separating the results of operations that would have been classified as discontinued operations in prior periods and that had been derecognised in full before the effective date of the IFRS.

BC79 The Board therefore decided to require application of the IFRS prospectively and allow retrospective application only when the necessary information had been obtained in the prior periods in question.

Terminology

BC80 Two issues of terminology arose in developing the IFRS:

(a) the use of the term 'probable' and

(b) the use of the term 'fair value less costs to sell'.

BC81 In SFAS 144, the term *probable* is described as referring to a future sale that is 'likely to occur'. For the purposes of IFRSs, probable is defined as 'more likely than not'. To converge on the same meaning as SFAS 144 and to avoid using the term 'probable' with different meanings in IFRSs, this IFRS uses the phrase 'highly probable'. The Board regards 'highly probable' as implying a significantly higher probability than 'more likely than not' and as implying the same probability as the FASB's phrase 'likely to occur'. This is consistent with the Board's use of 'highly probable' in IAS 39.

BC82 The measurement basis 'fair value less costs to sell' used in SFAS 144 is the same as the measurement 'net selling price' used in IAS 36 (as issued in 1998). SFAS 144 defines fair value of an asset as 'the amount at which that asset could be bought or sold in a current transaction between willing parties, that is, other than in a forced or liquidation sale', and costs to sell as 'the incremental direct costs to transact a sale, that is, the costs that result directly from and are essential to a sale transaction and that would not have been incurred by the entity had the decision to sell not been made.' IAS 36 defines net selling price as the amount obtainable from the sale of an asset in an arm's length transaction between knowledgeable, willing parties, less the costs of disposal. Costs of disposal are incremental costs directly attributable to the disposal of an asset, excluding finance costs and income tax expenses.

BC83 The Board considered using the phrase 'net selling price' to be consistent with IAS 36. However, it noted that 'fair value' is used in many IFRSs. The Board concluded that it would be preferable to use the same phrase as SFAS 144 so that it is clear that convergence on this point had been achieved and to amend IAS 36 so that the terminology in IAS 36 is consistent with other IFRSs. Therefore, a consequential amendment made by IFRS 5 replaces 'net selling price' with 'fair value less costs to sell' throughout IAS 36.

Summary of changes from ED 4

BC84 The major changes from the proposals in ED 4 are:

(a) clarification that assets classified as non-current are not reclassified as current until they meet the criteria to be classified as held for sale (paragraph BC10).

(b) goodwill and financial assets under leases are included in the scope of the measurement provisions of the IFRS (paragraphs BC8–BC14).

(c) non-current assets carried at fair value with changes recognised in profit or loss are excluded from the measurement provisions of the IFRS (paragraphs BC8–BC14).

(d) assets that are revalued in accordance with IAS 16 or IAS 38 are, when classified as held for sale, treated consistently with assets that had not previously been revalued (paragraphs BC47 and BC48).

(e) the allocation of an impairment loss on a disposal group is consistent with the order of allocation of impairment losses in IAS 36 (paragraphs BC39–BC41).

(f) the criterion in IAS 35 that a discontinued operation should be a major line of business or area of geographical operations has been added (paragraphs BC67–BC71).

(g) discontinued operations can be presented on the face of the income statement as a single amount (paragraphs BC73–BC77).

Comparison with relevant aspects of SFAS 144

BC85 The following table sets out the extent of convergence with SFAS 144:

Requirement	Extent of convergence with SFAS 144
Scope	Some differences in scope arising from other differences between IFRSs and US GAAP.
Criteria for classification as held for sale	Fully converged.
Treatment of assets to be exchanged	Fully converged if FASB proposals on exchanges of non-monetary assets are finalised.
Treatment of assets to be abandoned	Fully converged.
Measurement on initial classification	Converged, other than cumulative exchange differences recognised directly in equity that are included in the carrying amount of the asset (or disposal group) under US GAAP but are not under IFRS 5.
Subsequent measurement	Converged on the principles, but some differences arising from different requirements on reversals of previous impairments.
Changes to a plan to sell	Converged on reclassification and on measurement, except for differences arising from different requirements on reversals of previous impairments.
Presentation of assets classified as held for sale	Fully converged.
Definition of a discontinued operation	Not converged but the Board intends to work with the FASB to arrive at a converged definition within a relatively short time.
Timing of classification of an operation as discontinued	Fully converged.
Presentation of a discontinued operation	Converged except that SFAS 144 requires the presentation of pre-and post-tax profits on the face of the income statement and IFRS 5 requires the presentation of post-tax profit only (although disaggregation is permitted).

Dissenting opinions on IFRS 5

Dissent of Anthony T Cope and Harry K Schmid

DO1 Messrs Cope and Schmid dissent from the issue of IFRS 5.

Dissent of Anthony T Cope

DO2 Mr Cope dissents because, in his view, the IFRS fails to meet fully the needs of users in this important area.

DO3 In deciding to undertake this project, the Board had two objectives–to improve users' ability to assess the amount, timing and uncertainty of future cash flows, and to converge with US GAAP. The ability to identify assets (or asset groups) whose value will be recovered principally through sale rather than through operations has significant implications for future cash flows. Similarly, separate presentation of discontinued operations enables users to distinguish those parts of a business that will not contribute to future cash flows.

DO4 The importance of identifying and disaggregating these components was emphasised in the 1994 report of the Special Committee on Financial Reporting of the American Institute of Certified Public Accountants (the AICPA Jenkins Committee). The Jenkins Committee report, arguably the most extensive and authoritative survey of user needs ever undertaken, recommended that:

> [The definition of discontinued operations] should be broadened to include all significant discontinued operations whose assets and results of operations and activities can be distinguished physically and operationally and for business reporting purposes.

The sections of SFAS 144 dealing with discontinued operations were the direct response of the FASB to this recommendation.

DO5 Indeed, the Board appeared to agree in its initial deliberations. In ED 4, the Board stated:

> [The Board] further concluded that the definition of discontinued operations in SFAS 144 leads to more useful information being presented and disclosed for a wider range of operations than did the existing definition in IAS 35. That information is important to users in their assessment of the amount, timing and uncertainty of future cash flows.

Mr Cope continues to agree with that statement.

DO6 However, the Board ultimately has decided to retain the definition in IAS 35, thus failing to gain convergence on an important point in a project designed to achieve such convergence, and failing to respond to the stated needs of users.

DO7 The reason given for the Board's action is that implementation problems with SFAS 144 have emerged in the US. (Most of these problems seem to be with the guidance concerning the definition in SFAS 144, rather than the definition itself.) In paragraph BC71, the Board describes its action as an interim measure, and plans to work with the FASB to arrive promptly at a converged solution. In Mr Cope's view, it would have been much preferable to have converged first, and then dealt with any implementation problems jointly with the FASB.

Dissent of Harry K Schmid

DO8 The main reasons for Mr Schmid's dissent are:

(a) depreciation/amortisation of non-current assets that are still in active use should not cease only because of a management decision to sell the assets that has not yet been fully carried out; and

(b) measurement of assets should not be based on a management decision that has not yet been fully carried out, requiring a very rule-based Standard.

DO9 Mr Schmid believes that not depreciating/amortising assets classified as held for sale but still in active use is conceptually wrong and is especially problematic for discontinued operations because such operations represent a separate major line of business or geographical area of operations. Mr Schmid does not accept that measurement at the lower of carrying amount and fair value less costs to sell acts as a proxy for depreciation because, in most such cases, the fair value less costs to sell will be higher than the carrying amount as the fair value of such disposal groups will often reflect internally generated goodwill. Therefore, non-current assets in such disposal groups will simply remain at their carrying amounts even though they are still actively used, up to one year or even longer. In addition, the net profit shown separately in the income statement for discontinued operations will not be meaningful because depreciation/amortisation charges are not deducted for the continued use of the assets and this profit cannot be compared with the information restated in comparative periods where depreciation had been charged.

DO10 The proposed classification 'held for sale' and resulting measurement of non-current assets (or disposal groups) so classified is based on a management decision that has not yet been fully carried out and demands detailed (anti-abuse) rules to define the classification and to fix the time boundaries during which these assets can remain within the classification. The final result is, in Mr Schmid's view, an excessively detailed and rule-based Standard.

DO11 Mr Schmid believes that a more simple and straightforward solution would have been possible by creating a special category of non-current assets retired from active use. The concept 'retired from active use' would have been simple to apply and management intentions would be removed from the Standard. The classification would equally apply to any form of disposal (sale, abandonment, exchange, spin-off etc); no detailed (anti-abuse) rules and no illustrations would be necessary and the Standard would be simple and based on a clear and unambiguous principle. Mr Schmid, on this point, does not agree with the conclusions in paragraph BC18 that a classification 'retired from active use' would not require fewer criteria to support it than the category 'assets held for sale'.

DO12 Mr Schmid agrees with paragraph BC17 of the Basis for Conclusions, but in order to provide information of intended sales of non-current assets, especially discontinued operations, disclosure could have been required to take effect as soon as such assets are likely to be sold, even if they are still in active use.

DO13 Mr Schmid is fully in favour of seeking, whenever possible, convergence with US GAAP, but only if the converged solution is of high quality. He is of the opinion that this is not the case for this Standard for the reasons given.

Contents

GUIDANCE ON IMPLEMENTING IFRS 5 NON-CURRENT ASSETS HELD FOR SALE AND DISCONTINUED OPERATIONS

Guidance on Implementing IFRS 5 Non-current Assets Held for Sale and Discontinued Operations

This guidance accompanies, but is not part of, IFRS 5.

Availability for immediate sale (paragraph 7)

To qualify for classification as held for sale, a non-current asset (or disposal group) must be available for immediate sale in its present condition subject only to terms that are usual and customary for sales of such assets (or disposal groups) (paragraph 7). A non-current asset (or disposal group) is available for immediate sale if an entity currently has the intention and ability to transfer the asset (or disposal group) to a buyer in its present condition. Examples 1–3 illustrate situations in which the criterion in paragraph 7 would or would not be met.

Example 1

An entity is committed to a plan to sell its headquarters building and has initiated actions to locate a buyer.

(a) The entity intends to transfer the building to a buyer after it vacates the building. The time necessary to vacate the building is usual and customary for sales of such assets. The criterion in paragraph 7 would be met at the plan commitment date.

(b) The entity will continue to use the building until construction of a new headquarters building is completed. The entity does not intend to transfer the existing building to a buyer until after construction of the new building is completed (and it vacates the existing building). The delay in the timing of the transfer of the existing building imposed by the entity (seller) demonstrates that the building is not available for immediate sale. The criterion in paragraph 7 would not be met until construction of the new building is completed, even if a firm purchase commitment for the future transfer of the existing building is obtained earlier.

Example 2

An entity is committed to a plan to sell a manufacturing facility and has initiated actions to locate a buyer. At the plan commitment date, there is a backlog of uncompleted customer orders.

(a) The entity intends to sell the manufacturing facility with its operations. Any uncompleted customer orders at the sale date will be transferred to the buyer. The transfer of uncompleted customer orders at the sale date will not affect the timing of the transfer of the facility. The criterion in paragraph 7 would be met at the plan commitment date.

(b) The entity intends to sell the manufacturing facility, but without its operations. The entity does not intend to transfer the facility to a buyer until after it ceases all operations of the facility and eliminates the backlog of uncompleted customer orders. The delay in the timing of the transfer of the facility imposed by the entity (seller) demonstrates that the facility is not available for immediate sale. The criterion in paragraph 7 would not be met until the operations of the facility cease, even if a firm purchase commitment for the future transfer of the facility were obtained earlier.

Example 3

An entity acquires through foreclosure a property comprising land and buildings that it intends to sell.

(a) The entity does not intend to transfer the property to a buyer until after it completes renovations to increase the property's sales value. The delay in the timing of the transfer of the property imposed by the entity (seller) demonstrates that the property is not available for immediate sale. The criterion in paragraph 7 would not be met until the renovations are completed.

(b) After the renovations are completed and the property is classified as held for sale but before a firm purchase commitment is obtained, the entity becomes aware of environmental damage requiring remediation. The entity still intends to sell the property. However, the entity does not have the ability to transfer the property to a buyer until after the remediation is completed. The delay in the timing of the transfer of the property imposed by others before a firm purchase commitment is obtained demonstrates that the property is not available for immediate sale. The criterion in paragraph 7 would not continue to be met. The property would be reclassified as held and used in accordance with paragraph 26.

Completion of sale expected within one year (paragraph 8)

Example 4

To qualify for classification as held for sale, the sale of a non-current asset (or disposal group) must be highly probable (paragraph 7), and transfer of the asset (or disposal group) must be expected to qualify for recognition as a completed sale within one year (paragraph 8). That criterion would not be met if, for example:

(a) an entity that is a commercial leasing and finance company is holding for sale or lease equipment that has recently ceased to be leased and the ultimate form of a future transaction (sale or lease) has not yet been determined.

(b) an entity is committed to a plan to 'sell' a property that is in use, and the transfer of the property will be accounted for as a sale and finance leaseback.

Exceptions to the criterion in paragraph 8

An exception to the one-year requirement in paragraph 8 applies in limited situations in which the period required to complete the sale of a non-current asset (or disposal group) will be (or has been) extended by events or circumstances beyond an entity's control and specified conditions are met (paragraphs 9 and B1). Examples 5–7 illustrate those situations.

Example 5

An entity in the power generating industry is committed to a plan to sell a disposal group that represents a significant portion of its regulated operations. The sale requires regulatory approval, which could extend the period required to complete the sale beyond one year. Actions necessary to obtain that approval cannot be initiated until after a buyer is known and a firm purchase commitment is obtained. However, a firm purchase commitment is highly probable within one year. In that situation, the conditions in paragraph B1(a) for an exception to the one-year requirement in paragraph 8 would be met.

Example 6

An entity is committed to a plan to sell a manufacturing facility in its present condition and classifies the facility as held for sale at that date. After a firm purchase commitment is obtained, the buyer's inspection of the property identifies environmental damage not previously known to exist. The entity is required by the buyer to make good the damage, which will extend the period required to complete the sale beyond one year. However, the entity has initiated actions to make good the damage, and satisfactory rectification of the damage is highly probable. In that situation, the conditions in paragraph B1(b) for an exception to the one-year requirement in paragraph 8 would be met.

Example 7

An entity is committed to a plan to sell a non-current asset and classifies the asset as held for sale at that date.

(a) During the initial one-year period, the market conditions that existed at the date the asset was classified initially as held for sale deteriorate and, as a result, the asset is not sold by the end of that period. During that period, the entity actively solicited but did not receive any reasonable offers to purchase the asset and, in response, reduced the price. The asset continues to be actively marketed at a price that is reasonable given the change in market conditions, and the criteria in paragraphs 7 and 8 are therefore met. In that situation, the conditions in paragraph B1(c) for an exception to the one-year requirement in paragraph 8 would be met. At the end of the initial one-year period, the asset would continue to be classified as held for sale.

(b) During the following one-year period, market conditions deteriorate further, and the asset is not sold by the end of that period. The entity believes that the market conditions will improve and has not further reduced the price of the asset. The asset continues to be held for sale, but at a price in excess of its current fair value. In that situation, the absence of a price reduction demonstrates that the asset is not available for immediate sale as required by paragraph 7. In addition, paragraph 8 also requires an asset to be marketed at a price that is reasonable in relation to its current fair value. Therefore, the conditions in paragraph B1(c) for an exception to the one-year requirement in paragraph 8 would not be met. The asset would be reclassified as held and used in accordance with paragraph 26.

Determining whether an asset has been abandoned

Paragraphs 13 and 14 of the IFRS specify requirements for when assets are to be treated as abandoned. Example 8 illustrates when an asset has not been abandoned.

Example 8

An entity ceases to use a manufacturing plant because demand for its product has declined. However, the plant is maintained in workable condition and it is expected that it will be brought back into use if demand picks up. The plant is not regarded as abandoned.

Presenting a discontinued operation that has been abandoned

Paragraph 13 of the IFRS prohibits assets that will be abandoned from being classified as held for sale. However, if the assets to be abandoned are a major line of business or geographical area of operations, they are reported in discontinued operations at the date at which they are abandoned. Example 9 illustrates this.

Example 9

In October 2005 an entity decides to abandon all of its cotton mills, which constitute a major line of business. All work stops at the cotton mills during the year ended 31 December 2006. In the financial statements for the year ended 31 December 2005, results and cash flows of the cotton mills are treated as continuing operations. In the financial statements for the year ended 31 December 2006, the results and cash flows of the cotton mills are treated as discontinued operations and the entity makes the disclosures required by paragraphs 33 and 34 of the IFRS.

Allocation of an impairment loss on a disposal group

Paragraph 23 of the IFRS requires an impairment loss (or any subsequent gain) recognised for a disposal group to reduce (or increase) the carrying amount of the non-current assets in the group that are within the scope of the measurement requirements of the IFRS, in the order of allocation set out in paragraphs 104 and 122 of IAS 36 (as revised in 2004). Example 10 illustrates the allocation of an impairment loss on a disposal group.

Example 10

An entity plans to dispose of a group of its assets (as an asset sale). The assets form a disposal group, and are measured as follows:

	Carrying amount at the reporting date before classification as held for sale	Carrying amount as remeasured immediately before classification as held for sale
	CU [(a)]	CU
Goodwill	1,500	1,500
Property, plant and equipment (carried at revalued amounts	4,600	4,000
Property, plant and equipment (carried at cost)	5,700	5,700
Inventory	2,400	2,200
AFS financial assets	1,800	1,500
Total	**16,000**	**14,900**

(a) In this guidance, monetary amounts are denominated in 'currency units' (CU).

The entity recognises the loss of CU1,100 (CU16,000 – CU14,900) immediately before classifying the disposal group as held for sale.

The entity estimates that fair value less costs to sell of the disposal group amounts to CU13,000. Because an entity measures a disposal group classified as held for sale at the lower of its carrying amount and fair value less costs to sell, the entity recognises an impairment loss of CU1,900 (CU14,900 – CU13,000) when the group is initially classified as held for sale.

The impairment loss is allocated to non-current assets to which the measurement requirements of the IFRS are applicable. Therefore, no impairment loss is allocated to inventory and AFS financial assets. The loss is allocated to the other assets in the order of allocation set out in paragraphs 104 and 122 of IAS 36 (as revised in 2004).

The allocation can be illustrated as follows:

	Carrying amount as remeasured immediately before classification as held for sale	Allocated impairment loss	Carrying amount after allocation of impairment loss
	CU	CU	CU
Goodwill	1,500	(1,500)	0
Property, plant and equipment (carried at revalued amounts)	4,000	(165)	3,835
Property, plant and equipment (carried at cost)	5,700	(235)	5,465
Inventory	2,200	–	2,200
AFS financial assets	1,500	–	1,500
Total	**14,900**	**(1,900)**	**13,000**

First, the impairment loss reduces any amount of goodwill. Then, the residual loss is allocated to other assets pro rata based on the carrying amounts of those assets.

Presenting discontinued operations in the income statement

Paragraph 33 of the IFRS requires an entity to disclose a single amount on the face of the income statement for discontinued operations with an analysis in the notes or in a section of the income statement separate from continuing operations. Example 11 illustrates how these requirements might be met.

Example 11

XYZ GROUP – INCOME STATEMENT FOR THE YEAR ENDED 31 DECEMBER 20X2 (illustrating the classification of expenses by function)

(in thousands of currency units)	20X2	20X1
Continuing operations		
Revenue	X	X
Cost of sales	(X)	(X)
Gross profit	X	X
Other income	X	X
Distribution costs	(X)	(X)
Administrative expenses	(X)	(X)
Other expenses	(X)	(X)
Finance costs	(X)	(X)
Share of profit of associates	X	X
Profit before tax	X	X
Income tax expense	(X)	(X)
Profit for the period from continuing operations	X	X
Discontinued operations		
Profit for the period from discontinued operations[(a)]	X	X
Profit for the period	X	X
Attributable to:		
Equity holders of the parent	X	X
Minority interest	X	X
	X	X

(a) The required analysis would be given in the notes.

Presenting non-current assets or disposal groups classified as held for sale

Paragraph 38 of the IFRS requires an entity to present a non-current asset classified as held for sale and the assets of a disposal group classified as held for sale separately from other assets in the balance sheet. The liabilities of a disposal group classified as held for sale are also presented separately from other liabilities in the balance sheet. Those assets and liabilities are not offset and presented as a single amount. Example 12 illustrates these requirements.

Example 12

At the end of 20X5, an entity decides to dispose of part of its assets (and directly associated liabilities). The disposal, which meets the criteria in paragraphs 7 and 8 to be classified as held for sale, takes the form of two disposal groups, as follows:

	Carrying amount after classification as held for sale	
	Disposal group I:	Disposal group II:
	CU	CU
Property, plant and equipment	4,900	1,700
AFS financial asset	1,400 [(a)]	–
Liabilities	(2,400)	(900)
Net carrying amount of disposal group	**3,900**	**800**

(a) An amount of CU400 relating to these assets has been recognised directly in equity.

The presentation in the entity's balance sheet of the disposal groups classified as held for sale can be shown as follows:

	20X5	**20X4**
ASSETS		
Non-current assets		
AAA	X	X
BBB	X	X
CCC	X	X
	X	X
Current assets		
DDD	X	X
EEE	X	X
	X	X
Non-current assets classified as held for sale	8,000	–
	X	X
Total assets	X	X

Continued from previous page

	20X5	20X4
EQUITY AND LIABILITIES		
Equity attributable to equity holders of the parent		
FFF	X	X
GGG	X	X
Amounts recognised directly in equity relating to non-current assets held for sale	400	–
	X	X
Minority interest	X	X
Total equity	X	X
Non-current liabilities		
HHH	X	X
III	X	X
JJJ	X	X
	X	X
Current liabilities		
KKK	X	X
LLL	X	X
MMM	X	X
Liabilities directly associated with non-current assets classified as held for sale	3,300	–
	X	X
Total liabilities	X	X
Total equity and liabilities	X	X

The presentation requirements for assets (or disposal groups) classified as held for sale at the end of the reporting period do not apply retrospectively. The comparative balance sheets for any previous periods are therefore not re-presented.

Measuring and presenting subsidiaries acquired with a view to resale and classified as held for sale

A subsidiary acquired with a view to sale is not exempt from consolidation in accordance with IAS 27 *Consolidated and Separate Financial Statements*. However, if it meets the criteria in paragraph 11, it is presented as a disposal group classified as held for sale. Example 13 illustrates these requirements.

Example 13

Entity A acquires an entity H, which is a holding company with two subsidiaries, S1 and S2. S2 is acquired exclusively with a view to sale and meets the criteria to be classified as held for sale. In accordance with paragraph 32(c), S2 is also a discontinued operation.

The estimated fair value less costs to sell of S2 is CU135. A accounts for S2 as follows:

- initially, A measures the identifiable liabilities of S2 at fair value, say at CU40
- initially, A measures the acquired assets as the fair value less costs to sell of S2 (CU135) plus the fair value of the identifiable liabilities (CU40), ie at CU175
- at the balance sheet date, A remeasures the disposal group at the lower of its cost and fair value less costs to sell, say at CU130. The liabilities are remeasured in accordance with applicable IFRSs, say at CU35. The total assets are measured at CU130 + CU35, ie at CU165
- at the balance sheet date, A presents the assets and liabilities separately from other assets and liabilities in its consolidated financial statements as illustrated in Example 12 *Presenting non-current assets or disposal groups classified as held for sale*, and
- in the income statement, A presents the total of the post-tax profit or loss of S2 and the post-tax gain or loss recognised on the subsequent remeasurement of S2, which equals the remeasurement of the disposal group from CU135 to CU130.

Further analysis of the assets and liabilities or of the change in value of the disposal group is not required.

Guidance on the effect of IFRS 5 on IAS 36 (as revised in 2004), IAS 38 (as revised in 2004) and IFRS 3

IAS 36 (as revised in 2004), IAS 38 (as revised in 2004) and IFRS 3 include changes that arise from IFRS 5 as follows.

IAS 36 *Impairment of Assets* was amended as described below.

All references to 'net selling price' were replaced by 'fair value less costs to sell'.

Paragraph 2 was amended to read as follows:

2. This Standard shall be applied in accounting for the impairment of all assets, other than:

(a) ...

(i) **non-current assets (or disposal groups) classified as held for sale in accordance with IFRS 5** *Non-current Assets Held for Sale and Discontinued Operations*.

Paragraph 3 was amended to read as follows:

3. This Standard does not apply to inventories, assets arising from construction contracts, deferred tax assets ~~or~~, assets arising from employee benefits, or assets classified as held for sale (or included in a disposal group that is classified as held for sale) because existing Standards applicable to these assets contain requirements for recognising and measuring these assets.

Paragraph 6 was amended to read as follows:

...

A *cash-generating unit* is the smallest identifiable group of assets that generates cash inflows ~~from continuing use~~ that are largely independent of the cash inflows from other assets or groups of assets.

...

A footnote was added to the last sentence of paragraph 12(f), as follows:

* * Once an asset meets the criteria to be classified as held for sale (or is included in a disposal group that is classified as held for sale), it is excluded from the scope of IAS 36 and is accounted for in accordance with IFRS 5 *Non-current Assets Held for Sale and Discontinued Operations*

IAS 38 *Intangible Assets* was amended as described below.

Paragraph 3 was amended to read as follows:

3. ...For example, this Standard does not apply to:

(a) ...

(h) non-current intangible assets classified as held for sale (or included in a disposal group that is classified as held for sale) in accordance with IFRS 5 *Non-current Assets Held for Sale and Discontinued Operations*.

Paragraph 97 was amended to read as follows:

97. ... Amortisation shall cease at the earlier of the date that the asset is classified as held for sale (or included in a disposal group that is classified as held for sale) in accordance with IFRS 5 and the date that the asset is derecognised.

Paragraph 117 was amended to read as follows:

117 ... Amortisation of an intangible asset with a finite useful life does not cease when the intangible asset is no longer used, unless the asset has been fully depreciated or is classified as held for sale (or included in a disposal group that is classified as held for sale) in accordance with IFRS 5.

Paragraph 118(e)(ii) was amended to read as follows:

(ii) assets classified as held for sale or included in a disposal group classified as held for sale in accordance with IFRS 5 and other disposals;

IFRS 3 *Business Combinations* was amended as described below

Paragraph 36 was amended to read as follows:

36 **The acquirer shall, at the acquisition date, allocate the cost of a business combination by recognising the acquiree's identifiable assets, liabilities and contingent liabilities that satisfy the recognition criteria in paragraph 37 at their fair values at that date, except for non-current assets (or disposal groups) that are classified as held for sale in accordance with IFRS 5** *Non-current Assets Held for Sale and Discontinued Operations*, **which shall be recognised at fair value less costs to sell. Any difference...**

Paragraph 75(b) and (d) was amended to read as follows:

(b) additional goodwill recognised during the period except goodwill included in a disposal group that, on acquisition, meets the criteria to be classified as held for sale in accordance with IFRS 5;

(d) goodwill included in a disposal group classified as held for sale in accordance with IFRS 5 and goodwill derecognised during the period without having previously been included in a disposal group classified as held for sale;

International Financial Reporting Standard 6

Exploration for and Evaluation of Mineral Resources

Contents

International Financial Reporting Standard 6 *Exploration for and Evaluation of Mineral Resources* (IFRS 6) is set out in paragraphs 1–27 and Appendices A and B. All the paragraphs have equal authority. Paragraphs in **bold type** state the main principles. Terms defined in Appendix A are in *italics* the first time they appear in the Standard. Definitions of other terms are given in the Glossary for International Financial Reporting Standards. IFRS 6 should be read in the context of its objective and the Basis for Conclusions, the *Preface to International Financial Reporting Standards* and the *Framework for the Preparation and Presentation of Financial Statements.* IAS 8 *Accounting Policies, Changes in Accounting Estimates and Errors* provides a basis for selecting and applying accounting policies in the absence of explicit guidance.

Introduction

Reasons for issuing the IFRS

IN1 The International Accounting Standards Board decided to develop an International Financial Reporting Standard (IFRS) on exploration for and evaluation of mineral resources because:

(a) until now there has been no IFRS that specifically addresses the accounting for those activities and they are excluded from the scope of IAS 38 *Intangible Assets*. In addition, 'mineral rights and mineral resources such as oil, natural gas and similar non-regenerative resources' are excluded from the scope of IAS 16 *Property, Plant and Equipment*. Consequently, an entity was required to determine its accounting policy for the exploration for and evaluation of mineral resources in accordance with paragraphs 10–12 of IAS 8 *Accounting Policies, Changes in Accounting Estimates and Errors*.

(b) there are different views on how exploration and evaluation expenditures should be accounted for in accordance with IFRSs.

(c) accounting practices for exploration and evaluation assets under the requirements of other standard-setting bodies are diverse and often differ from practices in other sectors for expenditures that may be considered analogous (eg accounting practices for research and development costs in accordance with IAS 38).

(d) exploration and evaluation expenditures are significant to entities engaged in extractive activities.

(e) an increasing number of entities incurring exploration and evaluation expenditures present their financial statements in accordance with IFRSs, and many more are expected to do so from 2005.

IN2 The Board's predecessor organisation, the International Accounting Standards Committee, established a Steering Committee in 1998 to carry out initial work on accounting and financial reporting by entities engaged in extractive activities. In November 2000 the Steering Committee published an Issues Paper *Extractive Industries*.

IN3 In July 2001 the Board announced that it would restart the project only when agenda time permitted. Although the Board recognised the importance of accounting for extractive activities generally, it decided in September 2002 that it was not feasible to complete the detailed analysis required for this project, obtain appropriate input from constituents and undertake the Board's normal due process in time to implement changes before many entities adopted IFRSs in 2005.

IN4 The Board's objectives for this phase of its extractive activities project are:

(a) to make limited improvements to accounting practices for exploration and evaluation expenditures, without requiring major changes that might be reversed when the Board undertakes a comprehensive review of accounting practices used by entities engaged in the exploration for and evaluation of mineral resources.

(b) to specify the circumstances in which entities that recognise exploration and evaluation assets should test such assets for impairment in accordance with IAS 36 *Impairment of Assets*.

(c) to require entities engaged in the exploration for and evaluation of mineral resources to disclose information about exploration and evaluation assets, the level at which such assets are assessed for impairment and any impairment losses recognised.

Main features of the IFRS

IN5 The IFRS:

(a) permits an entity to develop an accounting policy for exploration and evaluation assets without specifically considering the requirements of paragraphs 11 and 12 of IAS 8. Thus, an entity adopting IFRS 6 may continue to use the accounting policies applied immediately before adopting the IFRS. This includes continuing to use recognition and measurement practices that are part of those accounting policies.

(b) requires entities recognising exploration and evaluation assets to perform an impairment test on those assets when facts and circumstances suggest that the carrying amount of the assets may exceed their recoverable amount.

(c) varies the recognition of impairment from that in IAS 36 but measures the impairment in accordance with that Standard once the impairment is identified.

International Financial Reporting Standard 6
Exploration for and Evaluation of Mineral Resources

Objective

1 The objective of this IFRS is to specify the financial reporting for the *exploration for and evaluation of mineral resources.*

2 In particular, the IFRS requires:

(a) limited improvements to existing accounting practices for *exploration and evaluation expenditures.*

(b) entities that recognise *exploration and evaluation assets* to assess such assets for impairment in accordance with this IFRS and measure any impairment in accordance with IAS 36 *Impairment of Assets.*

(c) disclosures that identify and explain the amounts in the entity's financial statements arising from the exploration for and evaluation of mineral resources and help users of those financial statements understand the amount, timing and certainty of future cash flows from any exploration and evaluation assets recognised.

Scope

3 An entity shall apply the IFRS to exploration and evaluation expenditures that it incurs.

4 The IFRS does not address other aspects of accounting by entities engaged in the exploration for and evaluation of mineral resources.

5 An entity shall not apply the IFRS to expenditures incurred:

(a) before the exploration for and evaluation of mineral resources, such as expenditures incurred before the entity has obtained the legal rights to explore a specific area.

(b) after the technical feasibility and commercial viability of extracting a mineral resource are demonstrable.

Recognition of exploration and evaluation assets

Temporary exemption from IAS 8 paragraphs 11 and 12

6 When developing its accounting policies, an entity recognising exploration and evaluation assets shall apply paragraph 10 of IAS 8 *Accounting Policies, Changes in Accounting Estimates and Errors.*

7 Paragraphs 11 and 12 of IAS 8 specify sources of authoritative requirements and guidance that management is required to consider in developing an accounting policy for an item if no IFRS applies specifically to that item. Subject to paragraphs 9 and 10 below, this IFRS exempts an entity from applying those paragraphs to its accounting policies for the recognition and measurement of exploration and evaluation assets.

Measurement of exploration and evaluation assets

Measurement at recognition

8 **Exploration and evaluation assets shall be measured at cost.**

Elements of cost of exploration and evaluation assets

9 An entity shall determine a policy specifying which expenditures are recognised as exploration and evaluation assets and apply the policy consistently. In making this determination, an entity considers the degree to which the expenditure can be associated with finding specific mineral resources. The following are examples of expenditures that might be included in the initial measurement of exploration and evaluation assets (the list is not exhaustive):

(a) acquisition of rights to explore;

(b) topographical, geological, geochemical and geophysical studies;

(c) exploratory drilling;

(d) trenching;

(e) sampling; and

(f) activities in relation to evaluating the technical feasibility and commercial viability of extracting a mineral resource.

10 Expenditures related to the development of mineral resources shall not be recognised as exploration and evaluation assets. The *Framework* and IAS 38 *Intangible Assets* provide guidance on the recognition of assets arising from development.

11 In accordance with IAS 37 *Provisions, Contingent Liabilities and Contingent Assets* an entity recognises any obligations for removal and restoration that are incurred during a particular period as a consequence of having undertaken the exploration for and evaluation of mineral resources.

Measurement after recognition

12 After recognition, an entity shall apply either the cost model or the revaluation model to the exploration and evaluation assets. If the revaluation model is applied (either the model in IAS 16 *Property, Plant and Equipment* or the model in IAS 38) it shall be consistent with the classification of the assets (see paragraph 15).

Changes in accounting policies

13 **An entity may change its accounting policies for exploration and evaluation expenditures if the change makes the financial statements more relevant to the economic decision-making needs of users and no less reliable, or more reliable and no less relevant to those needs. An entity shall judge relevance and reliability using the criteria in IAS 8.**

14 To justify changing its accounting policies for exploration and evaluation expenditures, an entity shall demonstrate that the change brings its financial statements closer to meeting the criteria in IAS 8, but the change need not achieve full compliance with those criteria.

Presentation

Classification of exploration and evaluation assets

15 An entity shall classify exploration and evaluation assets as tangible or intangible according to the nature of the assets acquired and apply the classification consistently.

16 Some exploration and evaluation assets are treated as intangible (eg drilling rights), whereas others are tangible (eg vehicles and drilling rigs). To the extent that a tangible asset is consumed in developing an intangible asset, the amount reflecting that consumption is part of the cost of the intangible asset. However, using a tangible asset to develop an intangible asset does not change a tangible asset into an intangible asset.

Reclassification of exploration and evaluation assets

17 An exploration and evaluation asset shall no longer be classified as such when the technical feasibility and commercial viability of extracting a mineral resource are demonstrable. Exploration and evaluation assets shall be assessed for impairment, and any impairment loss recognised, before reclassification.

Impairment

Recognition and measurement

18 **Exploration and evaluation assets shall be assessed for impairment when facts and circumstances suggest that the carrying amount of an exploration and evaluation asset may exceed its recoverable amount. When facts and circumstances suggest that the carrying amount exceeds the recoverable amount, an entity shall measure, present and disclose any resulting impairment loss in accordance with IAS 36, except as provided by paragraph 21 below.**

19 For the purposes of exploration and evaluation assets only, paragraph 20 of this IFRS shall be applied rather than paragraphs 8–17 of IAS 36 when identifying an exploration and evaluation asset that may be impaired. Paragraph 20 uses the term 'assets' but applies equally to separate exploration and evaluation assets or a cash-generating unit.

20 One or more of the following facts and circumstances indicate that an entity should test exploration and evaluation assets for impairment (the list is not exhaustive):

(a) the period for which the entity has the right to explore in the specific area has expired during the period or will expire in the near future, and is not expected to be renewed.

(b) substantive expenditure on further exploration for and evaluation of mineral resources in the specific area is neither budgeted nor planned.

(c) exploration for and evaluation of mineral resources in the specific area have not led to the discovery of commercially viable quantities of mineral resources and the entity has decided to discontinue such activities in the specific area.

(d) sufficient data exist to indicate that, although a development in the specific area is likely to proceed, the carrying amount of the exploration and evaluation asset is unlikely to be recovered in full from successful development or by sale.

In any such case, or similar cases, the entity shall perform an impairment test in accordance with IAS 36. Any impairment loss is recognised as an expense in accordance with IAS 36.

Specifying the level at which exploration and evaluation assets are assessed for impairment

21 **An entity shall determine an accounting policy for allocating exploration and evaluation assets to cash-generating units or groups of cash-generating units for the purpose of assessing such assets for impairment. Each cash-generating unit or group of units to which an exploration and evaluation asset is allocated shall not be larger than a segment based on either the entity's primary or secondary reporting format determined in accordance with IAS 14** *Segment Reporting*.

22 The level identified by the entity for the purposes of testing exploration and evaluation assets for impairment may comprise one or more cash-generating units.

Disclosure

23 **An entity shall disclose information that identifies and explains the amounts recognised in its financial statements arising from the exploration for and evaluation of mineral resources.**

24 To comply with paragraph 23, an entity shall disclose:

(a) its accounting policies for exploration and evaluation expenditures including the recognition of exploration and evaluation assets.

(b) the amounts of assets, liabilities, income and expense and operating and investing cash flows arising from the exploration for and evaluation of mineral resources.

25 An entity shall treat exploration and evaluation assets as a separate class of assets and make the disclosures required by either IAS 16 or IAS 38 consistent with how the assets are classified.

Effective date

26 **An entity shall apply this IFRS for annual periods beginning on or after 1 January 2006. Earlier application is encouraged. If an entity applies the IFRS for a period beginning before 1 January 2006, it shall disclose that fact.**

Transitional provisions

27 If it is impracticable to apply a particular requirement of paragraph 18 to comparative information that relates to annual periods beginning before 1 January 2006, an entity shall disclose that fact. IAS 8 explains the term 'impracticable'.

Appendix A
Defined terms

This appendix is an integral part of the IFRS.

exploration and evaluation assets	**Exploration and evaluation expenditures** recognised as assets in accordance with the entity's accounting policy.
exploration and evaluation expenditures	Expenditures incurred by an entity in connection with the **exploration for and evaluation of mineral resources** before the technical feasibility and commercial viability of extracting a mineral resource are demonstrable.
exploration for and evaluation of mineral resources	The search for mineral resources, including minerals, oil, natural gas and similar non-regenerative resources after the entity has obtained legal rights to explore in a specific area, as well as the determination of the technical feasibility and commercial viability of extracting the mineral resource.

Appendix B
Amendments to other IFRSs

The amendments in this appendix shall be applied for annual periods beginning on or after 1 January 2006. If an entity applies this IFRS for an earlier period, these amendments shall be applied for that earlier period.

* * * * *

The amendments contained in this appendix when this IFRS was issued in 2004 have been incorporated into the text of IFRS 1 and IASs 16 and 38 as issued at 9 December 2004.

Approval of IFRS 6 by the Board

International Financial Reporting Standard 6 *Exploration for and Evaluation of Mineral Resources* was approved for issue by ten of the fourteen members of the International Accounting Standards Board. Messrs Garnett, Leisenring, McGregor and Smith dissented. Their dissenting opinions are set out after the Basis for Conclusions.

Sir David Tweedie	Chairman
Thomas E Jones	Vice-Chairman
Mary E Barth	
Hans-Georg Bruns	
Anthony T Cope	
Jan Engström	
Robert P Garnett	
Gilbert Gélard	
James J Leisenring	
Warren J McGregor	
Patricia L O'Malley	
John T Smith	
Geoffrey Whittington	
Tatsumi Yamada	

CONTENTS

Basis for Conclusions on IFRS 6 Exploration for and Evaluation of Mineral Resources

This Basis for Conclusions accompanies, but is not part of, IFRS 6.

Introduction

BC1 This Basis for Conclusions summarises the International Accounting Standards Board's considerations in reaching the conclusions in IFRS 6 *Exploration for and Evaluation of Mineral Resources*. Individual Board members gave greater weight to some factors than to others.

Reasons for issuing the IFRS

BC2 Paragraphs 10–12 of IAS 8 *Accounting Policies, Changes in Accounting Estimates and Errors* specify a hierarchy of criteria that an entity should use in developing an accounting policy if no IFRS applies specifically to an item. Without the exemption in IFRS 6, an entity adopting IFRSs in 2005 would have needed to assess whether its accounting policies for the exploration for and evaluation of mineral resources complied with those requirements. In the absence of guidance, there might have been uncertainty about what would be acceptable. Establishing what would be acceptable could have been costly and some entities might have made major changes in 2005 followed by further significant changes once the Board completes its comprehensive review of accounting for extractive activities.

BC3 To avoid unnecessary disruption for both users and preparers at this time, the Board proposed to limit the need for entities to change their existing accounting policies for exploration and evaluation assets. The Board did this by:

(a) creating a temporary exemption from parts of the hierarchy in IAS 8 that specify the criteria an entity uses in developing an accounting policy if no IFRS applies specifically.

(b) limiting the impact of that exemption from the hierarchy by identifying expenditures to be included in and excluded from exploration and evaluation assets and requiring all exploration and evaluation assets to be assessed for impairment.

BC4 The Board published its proposals in January 2004. ED 6 *Exploration for and Evaluation of Mineral Resources* had a comment deadline of 16 April 2004. The Board received 55 comment letters.

BC5 In April 2004 the Board approved a research project to be undertaken by staff from the national standard-setters in Australia, Canada, Norway and South Africa that will address accounting for extractive activities generally. The research project team is assisted by an advisory panel, which includes members from industry (oil and gas and mining sectors), accounting firms, users and securities regulators from around the world.

Scope

BC6 In the Board's view, even though no IFRS has addressed extractive activities directly, all IFRSs (including International Accounting Standards and

Interpretations) are applicable to entities engaged in the exploration for and evaluation of mineral resources that make an unreserved statement of compliance with IFRSs in accordance with IAS 1 *Presentation of Financial Statements*. Consequently, each IFRS must be applied by all such entities.

BC7 Some respondents to ED 6 encouraged the Board to develop standards for other stages in the process of exploring for and evaluating mineral resources, including pre-exploration activities (ie activities preceding the exploration for and evaluation of mineral resources) and development activities (ie activities after the technical feasibility and commercial viability of extracting a mineral resource are demonstrable). The Board decided not to do this for two reasons. First, it did not want to prejudge the comprehensive review of the accounting for such activities. Second, the Board concluded that an appropriate accounting policy for pre-exploration activities could be developed from an application of existing IFRSs, from the *Framework*'s definitions of assets and expenses, and by applying the general principles of asset recognition in IAS 16 *Property, Plant and Equipment* and IAS 38 *Intangible Assets*.

BC8 The Board also decided not to expand the scope of IFRS 6 beyond that proposed in ED 6 because to do so would require additional due process, possibly including another exposure draft. In view of the many entities engaged in extractive activities that would be required to apply IFRSs from 1 January 2005, the Board decided that it should not delay issuing guidance by expanding the scope of the IFRS beyond the exploration for and evaluation of mineral resources.

Definition of exploration and evaluation assets

BC9 Most respondents to ED 6 agreed with the Board's proposed definition of exploration and evaluation assets, but asked for changes or clarifications to make the Board's intentions clearer:

(a) some respondents asked the Board to distinguish between exploration and pre-exploration expenditures.

(b) others asked the Board to define exploration and evaluation activities separately, reflecting the different risk profiles of such activities or the requirements of other jurisdictions.

(c) other respondents asked for further guidance on what constitute mineral resources, principally examples of what constitutes a mineral reserve.

Expenditures incurred before the exploration for and evaluation of mineral resources

BC10 Respondents seemed either to be concerned that the Board was extending the scope of the proposals to include expenditures incurred before the acquisition of legal rights to explore in a specific area in the definition of exploration and evaluation expenditure. Some were concerned that such an extension would open the way for the recognition of such expenditures as assets; others preferred this result. In drafting IFRS 6, the Board could not identify any reason why the *Framework* was not applicable to such expenditures.

BC11 The Board decided not to define pre-acquisition or pre-exploration expenditures. However, the IFRS clarifies that expenditures before the entity has obtained legal rights to explore in a specific area are not exploration and evaluation expenditures and are therefore outside the scope of the IFRS.

BC12 The Board noted that an appropriate application of IFRSs might require pre-acquisition expenditures related to the acquisition of an intangible asset (eg expenditures directly attributable to the acquisition of an exploration licence) to be recognised as part of the intangible asset in accordance with IAS 38. Paragraph 27(a) of IAS 38 states that the cost of a separately acquired intangible asset comprises its purchase price, including import duties and non-refundable purchase taxes, and some directly attributable costs.

BC13 Similarly, the Board understands that expenditures incurred before the exploration for and evaluation of mineral resources cannot usually be associated with any specific mineral property and thus are likely to be recognised as an expense as incurred. However, such expenditures need to be distinguished from expenditures on infrastructure—for example access roads—necessary for the exploration work to proceed. Such expenditures should be recognised as property, plant and equipment in accordance with paragraph 3 of IAS 16.

Separate definitions of 'exploration' and 'evaluation'

BC14 Some respondents asked the Board to provide separate definitions of exploration and evaluation. The Board considered using the definitions provided in the Issues Paper *Extractive Industries* published by its predecessor, the Board of the International Accounting Standards Committee, in November 2000, because those definitions would be acceptable to many respondents, particularly because they are based on definitions that have been used for a number of years in both the mining and the oil and gas sectors.

BC15 The Board concluded that distinguishing between evaluation and exploration would not improve the IFRS. Exploration and evaluation are accounted for in the same way.

Mineral resources

BC16 Some respondents asked the Board to define mineral resources more precisely. The Board concluded that, for the purposes of the IFRS, elaboration was unnecessary. The items listed in the definition of exploration for and evaluation of mineral resources were sufficient to convey the Board's intentions.

Recognition of exploration and evaluation assets

Temporary exemption from IAS 8 paragraphs 11 and 12

BC17 A variety of accounting practices are followed by entities engaged in the exploration for and evaluation of mineral resources. These practices range from deferring on the balance sheet nearly all exploration and evaluation expenditure to recognising all such expenditure in profit or loss as incurred. The IFRS permits these various accounting practices to continue. Given this diversity, some respondents to ED 6 opposed any exemption from paragraphs 11 and 12 of IAS 8. These respondents were concerned that entities could give the appearance of compliance with IFRSs while being inconsistent with the stated objectives of the IASB, ie to provide users of financial statements with financial information that was of high quality, transparent and comparable. The Board did not grant the exemption from parts of IAS 8 lightly, but took this step to minimise disruption, especially in 2006 (or 2005, for those entities that adopt the IFRS early), both for users (eg lack of continuity of trend data) and for preparers (eg systems changes).

BC18 IFRS 4 *Insurance Contracts* provides a temporary exemption from paragraphs 10–12 of IAS 8. That exemption is broader than in IFRS 6 because IFRS 4 leaves many significant aspects of accounting for insurance contracts until phase II of the Board's project on that topic. A requirement to apply paragraph 10 of IAS 8 to insurance contracts would have had much more pervasive effects and insurers would have needed to address matters such as completeness, substance over form and neutrality. In contrast, IFRS 6 leaves a relatively narrow range of issues unaddressed and the Board did not think that an exemption from paragraph 10 of IAS 8 was necessary.

BC19 ED 6 made it clear that the Board intended to suspend only paragraphs 11 and 12 of IAS 8, implying that paragraph 10 should be followed when an entity was determining its accounting policies for exploration and evaluation assets. However, it was apparent from some comments received that the Board's intention had not been understood clearly. Consequently, the IFRS contains a specific statement that complying with paragraph 10 of IAS 8 is mandatory.

BC20 Respondents who objected to the Board's proposal in ED 6 to permit some accounting practices to continue found it difficult to draw a meaningful distinction between the exploration for and evaluation of mineral resources and scientific research. Both activities can be costly and have significant risks of failure. These respondents would support bringing the exploration for and evaluation of mineral resources within the scope of IAS 16 and IAS 38. The Board is similarly concerned that existing accounting practices might result in the inappropriate recognition of exploration and evaluation assets. However, it is also concerned that accounting for exploration and evaluation expenditures in accordance with IAS 38 might result in the overstatement of expenses. In the absence of internationally accepted standards for such expenditures, the Board concluded that it could not make an informed judgement in advance of the comprehensive review of accounting for extractive activities.

BC21 Some suggested that the Board should require an entity to follow its national accounting requirements (ie national GAAP) in accounting for the exploration for and evaluation of mineral resources until the Board completes its comprehensive review of accounting for extractive activities, to prevent the selection of accounting policies that do not form a comprehensive basis of accounting. Consistently with its conclusions in IFRS 4, the Board concluded that defining national GAAP would have posed problems. Further definitional problems could have arisen because some entities do not apply the national GAAP of their own country. For example, some non-US entities with extractive activities in the oil and gas sector apply US GAAP. Moreover, it is unusual and, arguably, beyond the Board's mandate to impose requirements set by another body.

BC22 Therefore, the Board decided that an entity could continue to follow the accounting policies that it was using when it first applied the IFRS's requirements, provided they satisfy the requirements of paragraph 10 of IAS 8 and with some exceptions noted below. An entity could also improve those accounting policies if specified criteria are met (see paragraphs 13 and 14 of the IFRS).

BC23 The Board acknowledges that it is difficult to make piecemeal changes to recognition and measurement practices at this time because many aspects of accounting for extractive activities are interrelated with aspects that will not be considered until the Board completes its comprehensive review of accounting for extractive activities. However, not imposing the requirements in the IFRS would detract from the relevance and reliability of an entity's financial statements to an unacceptable degree.

Elements of cost of exploration and evaluation assets

BC24 ED 6 paragraph 7 listed examples of expenditures related to the exploration for and evaluation of mineral resources that might be included in the cost of an exploration and evaluation asset. ED 6 paragraph 8 listed expenditures that could not be recognised as an exploration and evaluation asset. Respondents expressed a desire for greater clarity with respect to these paragraphs and more examples of types of expenditures that would be included or excluded.

BC25 In the light of the responses, the Board decided to redraft the guidance to state that the list is not exhaustive and that the items noted are examples of expenditures that might, but need not always, satisfy the definition of exploration and evaluation expenditure. In addition, the Board noted that IFRSs require that expenditures should be treated consistently for comparable activities and between reporting periods. Any change in what is deemed to be an expenditure qualifying for recognition as an exploration and evaluation asset should be treated as a change in an accounting policy accounted for in accordance with IAS 8. Pending the comprehensive review of accounting for extractive activities, the Board does not think that it is feasible to define what expenditures should be included or excluded.

BC26 ED 6 paragraph 8 proposed to prohibit expenditure related to the development of a mineral resource from being recognised as an exploration and evaluation asset. Respondents expressed difficulty identifying expenditures on 'development'. The Board did not define 'development of a mineral resource' because this is beyond the scope of the IFRS.

BC27 However, the Board noted that development of a mineral resource once the technical feasibility and commercial viability of extracting the mineral resource had been determined was an example of the development phase of an internal project. Paragraph 57 of IAS 38 provides guidance that should be followed in developing an accounting policy for this activity.

BC28 ED 6 proposed that administration and other general overhead costs should be excluded from the initial measurement of exploration and evaluation assets. Several respondents suggested that general and administrative and overhead costs *directly attributable* to the exploration and evaluation activities should qualify for inclusion in the carrying amount of the asset. These respondents saw this treatment as consistent with the treatment of such costs with respect to inventory (paragraph 11 of IAS 2 *Inventories*) and intangible assets (paragraph 67(a) of IAS 38).

However, the Board noted that such a treatment would seem to be inconsistent with paragraph 19(d) of IAS 16. The IFRS was not regarded as the appropriate Standard in which to resolve this inconsistency, and the Board decided to delete the reference in the IFRS to administrative and other general overheads. The treatment of such expenditures would be an accounting policy choice; the chosen policy should be consistent with one of the treatments available under IFRSs.

Measurement after recognition

BC29 The IFRS permits an entity recognising exploration and evaluation assets to measure such assets, after recognition, using either the cost model or the revaluation model in IAS 16 and IAS 38. The model chosen should be consistent with how the entity classifies the exploration and evaluation assets. Those revaluation models permit the revaluation of assets when specified requirements are met (see paragraphs 31–42 of IAS 16 and paragraphs 72–84 of IAS 38). The revaluation model in IAS 38 can be used only if the asset's fair value can be determined by reference to an active market; the revaluation model in IAS 16 refers only to 'market-based evidence'. The Board was troubled by this inconsistency and was concerned that entities might choose accounting policies to achieve a more advantageous measurement of exploration and evaluation assets.

BC30 A few respondents were also concerned with the option proposed in ED 6. Some did not agree that exploration and evaluation assets should be revalued, preferring an arbitrary prohibition of remeasurement. Others were concerned about the reliability of the measure. The Board concluded that no substantive reasons had been presented for reaching a conclusion different from that in ED 6. Although the revaluation of an exploration asset in accordance with IAS 16 or IAS 38 might not be widespread, it was not appropriate to prohibit remeasurement of specific types of IAS 16 or IAS 38 assets on a selective basis.

BC31 Exploration and evaluation assets may arise as a result of a business combination. The Board noted that IFRS 3 *Business Combinations* applies to all entities asserting compliance with IFRSs and that any exploration and evaluation assets acquired in a business combination should be accounted for in accordance with IFRS 3.

Presentation of exploration and evaluation assets

BC32 ED 6 noted that the Board had not yet considered whether exploration and evaluation assets are tangible or intangible. Several respondents suggested that the Board should give some direction on this issue.

BC33 Some exploration and evaluation assets are treated as intangible assets (eg drilling rights), whereas others are clearly tangible (eg vehicles and drilling rigs). A tangible asset may be used in the development of an intangible one. For example, a portable drilling rig may be used to drill test wells or take core samples, clearly part of the exploration activity. To the extent that the tangible asset is consumed in developing an intangible asset, the amount reflecting that consumption is part of the cost of the intangible asset. However, using the drilling rig to develop an intangible asset does not change a tangible asset into an intangible asset.

BC34 Pending completion of the comprehensive review of accounting practices for extractive activities, the Board did not wish to decide whether and which exploration and evaluation assets should be classified as tangible or intangible. However, the Board concluded that an entity should classify the elements of exploration and evaluation assets as tangible or intangible according to their nature and apply this classification consistently. This classification is the foundation for other accounting policy choices as described in paragraphs BC29–BC31 and for the disclosures required by the IFRS.

Impairment of exploration and evaluation assets

BC35 When it developed ED 6, the Board decided that an entity recognising exploration and evaluation assets should test those assets for impairment, and that the impairment test to be applied should be that in IAS 36. Respondents accepted the general proposition that exploration and evaluation assets should be tested for impairment. However, the Board's proposals for a special 'cash-generating unit for exploration and evaluation assets' (the special CGU) were not thought appropriate or useful.

Assessment of impairment

BC36 In some cases, and particularly in exploration-only entities, exploration and evaluation assets do not generate cash flows and there is insufficient information about the mineral resources in a specific area for an entity to make reasonable estimates of exploration and evaluation assets' recoverable amount. This is because the exploration for and evaluation of the mineral resources has not reached a stage at which information sufficient to estimate future cash flows is available to the entity. Without such information, it is not possible to estimate either fair value less costs to sell or value in use, the two measures of recoverable amount in IAS 36. Respondents noted that this would lead to an immediate write-off of exploration assets in many cases.

BC37 The Board was persuaded by respondents' arguments that recognising impairment losses on this basis was potentially inconsistent with permitting existing methods of accounting for exploration and evaluation assets to continue. Therefore, pending completion of the comprehensive review of accounting for extractive activities, the Board decided to change the approach to recognition of impairment; the assessment of impairment should be triggered by changes in facts and circumstances. However, it also confirmed that, once an entity had determined that an exploration and evaluation asset was impaired, IAS 36 should be used to measure, present and disclose that impairment in the financial statements, subject to special requirements with respect to the level at which impairment is assessed.

BC38 Paragraph 12 of ED 6 proposed that an entity that had recognised exploration and evaluation assets should assess those assets for impairment annually and recognise any resulting impairment loss in accordance with IAS 36. Paragraph 13 proposed a set of indicators of impairment that an entity would consider in addition to those in IAS 36. Respondents stated that these indicators would not achieve the Board's intended result, especially in circumstances in which the information necessary for an assessment of mineral reserves was not available.

BC39 The Board replaced the proposals in paragraphs 12 and 13 of ED 6 with an exception to the recognition requirements in IAS 36. The Board decided that, until the entity had sufficient data to determine technical feasibility and commercial viability, exploration and evaluation assets need not be assessed for impairment. However, when such information becomes available, or other facts and circumstances suggest that the asset might be impaired, the exploration and evaluation assets must be assessed for impairment. The IFRS suggests possible indicators of impairment.

The level at which impairment is assessed

BC40 When it developed ED 6, the Board decided that there was a need for consistency between the level at which costs were accumulated and the level at which impairment was assessed. Without this consistency, there was a danger that expenditures that would form part of the cost of an exploration and evaluation asset under one of the common methods of accounting for the exploration for and evaluation of mineral resources would need to be recognised in profit or loss in accordance with IAS 36. Consequently, ED 6 proposed that an entity recognising exploration and evaluation assets should make a one-time election to test those assets either at the level of the IAS 36 cash-generating unit (CGU) or at the level of a special CGU. ED 6 explained that any assets other than exploration and evaluation assets included within the special CGU should continue to be subject to separate impairment testing in accordance with IAS 36, and that impairment test should be performed before the special CGU was tested for impairment.

BC41 Respondents disagreed with the Board's proposal. In particular, and for various reasons, they did not accept that the special CGU would provide the relief it was intended to provide, because:

(a) small, start-up or exploration-only entities might not have adequate cash flows to support exploration and evaluation assets that were not cash-generating.

(b) entities applying the successful efforts method of accounting typically conduct impairment tests property by property. However, because of the way in which the special CGU was defined in ED 6 such entities would be forced to carry out impairment tests at the CGU level.

(c) the special CGU permitted management extensive discretion.

In addition, there was concern that, because the exploration and evaluation assets could be aggregated with other assets in the special CGU, there would be confusion about the appropriate measurement model to apply (fair value less costs to sell or value in use). As a result, many respondents to ED 6 did not think that the Board had achieved its intention in this respect, and said that they preferred to apply IAS 36 without the special CGU.

BC42 Although the Board disagreed with some of the arguments put forward by respondents, it acknowledged that the special CGU seemed to be more confusing than helpful. This suggested that it was not needed. Paragraph BC20 of the Basis for Conclusions on ED 6 noted the Board's reluctance to introduce a special CGU. Removing the special CGU would eliminate much of the complexity in the proposed IFRS and the confusion among constituents. It would also mean that entities with extractive activities would assess their assets for impairment at the same level as other entities—providing a higher level of comparability than might otherwise be the case.

BC43 Board members noted that paragraph 22 of IAS 36 requires impairment to be assessed at the individual asset level 'unless the asset does not generate cash inflows that are largely independent of those from other assets or groups of assets'. In addition, paragraph 70 of IAS 36 requires that 'if an active market exists for the output produced by an asset or group of assets, that asset or group of assets shall be identified as a cash-generating unit'. In some cases in which exploration and evaluation assets are recognised, eg in the petroleum sector, each well is potentially capable of producing cash inflows that are observable and capable of reliable measurement because there is an active market for crude oil. The Board was concerned that removing the special CGU would cause entities recognising exploration and evaluation assets to test for impairment at a very low level.

BC44 The issue was highlighted in the July 2004 issue of *IASB Update*, in the project summary and in the *Effect of Redeliberations* documents available on the IASB's Website. These documents were also sent to the Board's research project team and others with a request to encourage their constituents to respond to the issues raised. The Board received 16 comment letters.

BC45 The majority of respondents continued to support the elimination of the special CGU. They also supported the notion that entities should test impairment at the level of the cost centre and suggested that the Board should consider defining an 'asset' as it applied to exploration and evaluation assets. The respondents argued that such an approach would reflect more accurately the way in which the industry manages its operations. The Board was persuaded by these arguments and decided that it should permit entities some flexibility in allocating exploration and evaluation assets to cash-generating units or groups of units, subject to an upper limit on the size of the units or groups of units.

BC46 The Board decided that its approach to the impairment of goodwill in the 2004 revisions to IAS 36 paragraphs 80–82 offered the best model available within IFRSs to accomplish its objective. It noted that entities might be able to monitor exploration and evaluation assets for internal management purposes at the level of an oilfield or a contiguous ore body. The Board did not intend to require impairment to be assessed at such a low level. Consequently, the IFRS permits CGUs to be aggregated. However, the Board decided to require the level at which impairment was assessed to be no larger than a segment, based on either the entity's primary or the entity's secondary segment reporting format in accordance with IAS 14 *Segment Reporting*. The Board concluded, consistently with the approach to goodwill in IAS 36, that this approach was necessary to ensure that entities managed on a matrix basis could test exploration and evaluation assets for impairment at the level of reporting that reflects the way they manage their operations. This requirement is no less rigorous than ED 6's requirement that the special CGU should 'be no larger than a segment'.

BC47 Consequently, the Board decided to remove the proposed special CGU. In doing so, it noted that eliminating this requirement would have the following benefits:

(a) once an impairment was identified, the measurement, presentation and disclosure of impairment would be more consistent across entities recognising exploration and evaluation assets.

(b) it would remove the confusion about what practices entities recognising exploration and evaluation assets for the first time should follow.

(c) it would remove the risk noted in some comment letters that the special CGU could become the 'industry norm', limiting the Board's options when the comprehensive review of accounting for extractive activities is completed.

Reversal of impairment losses

BC48 The reversal of impairment losses when specified requirements (ie those set out in paragraphs 109–123 of IAS 36) are met is required of all entities for all assets (excluding goodwill and equity investments classified as available for sale). Respondents to ED 6 who commented on this issue and who disagreed with the ability to reverse impairment losses advanced no new arguments why the Board should prohibit reversal of impairment losses in the case of exploration and evaluation assets. Consequently, the Board reaffirmed its conclusion that it would not be appropriate to propose an exemption from the requirement to reverse impairment losses for exploration and evaluation assets.

Changes in accounting policies

BC49 IAS 8 prohibits a change in accounting policies that is not required by an IFRS, unless the change will result in the provision of reliable and more relevant information. Although the Board wished to avoid imposing unnecessary changes in this IFRS, it did not believe it should exempt entities from the requirement to justify changes in accounting policies. Consistently with its conclusions in IFRS 4, the Board decided to permit changes in accounting policies for exploration and evaluation assets if they make the financial statements more relevant and no less reliable, or more reliable and no less relevant judged by the criteria in IAS 8.

Disclosures

BC50 The disclosure requirements in the IFRS are based on a principle that an entity should disclose information that identifies and explains the amounts recognised in its financial statements that arise from the exploration for and evaluation of mineral resources, supplemented by specified disclosures to meet that objective.

BC51 Although respondents agreed that entities should be allowed flexibility in determining the levels of aggregation and amount of disclosure, they suggested that the Board should introduce more specific and standardised disclosure requirements. Some respondents were concerned that the variety of accounting for the exploration for and evaluation of mineral resources could reduce comparability.

BC52 The Board concluded that the ED 6 approach was superior to requiring a long list of detailed and prescriptive disclosures because concentrating on the underlying principle:

(a) makes it easier for entities to understand the rationale for the requirements, which promotes compliance.

(b) avoids requiring specific disclosures that may not be needed to meet the underlying objectives in the circumstances of every entity and could lead to information overload that obscures important information in a mass of detail.

(c) gives entities flexibility to decide on an appropriate level of aggregation that enables users to see the overall picture, but without combining information that has different characteristics.

(d) permits reporting exploration and evaluation expenditure by segment on either an annual basis or an accumulated basis.

BC53 Some respondents suggested that the Board should require disclosures similar to those in paragraphs 73 and 74 of IAS 16 or in paragraphs 118–125 of IAS 38. Both IAS 16 and IAS 38 contain scope exclusions for exploration and evaluation assets. Therefore, entities recognising these assets could claim that the requirements were not applicable. The Board decided that, although the scope of those standards excludes exploration and evaluation assets, their required disclosures would provide information relevant to an understanding of the financial statements and useful to users. Consequently, the Board concluded that the IFRS should confirm that the disclosures of IASs 16 and 38 are required consistently with how the entity classifies its exploration and evaluation assets (ie tangible (IAS 16) or intangible (IAS 38)).

BC54 In addition, some respondents suggested that the Board should require disclosure of non-financial information, including:

(a) commercial reserve quantities;

(b) rights to explore for, develop and produce wasting resources;

(c) disclosures about stages after exploration and evaluation; and

(d) the number of years since exploration started, and an estimation of the time remaining until a decision could be made about the technical feasibility and commercial viability of extracting the mineral resource.

Commercial reserves

BC55 The Board acknowledged that information about commercial reserve quantities is, perhaps, the most important disclosure for an entity with extractive activities. However, it noted that commercial reserves are usually determined after the exploration and evaluation stage has ended and it concluded that such disclosure was beyond the stated scope of the IFRS.

Stages after exploration and evaluation

BC56 As with commercial reserves, the Board concluded that, although information about stages after exploration and evaluation would be useful to users of financial statements, such disclosure is beyond the scope of the IFRS.

Project timing

BC57 The Board also concluded that disclosure of the number of years since exploration started and the estimated time remaining until a decision could be made about development would apply only to large scale exploration activities. It noted that if the project is significant, paragraph 103(c) of IAS 1 already requires its disclosure, ie as additional information that is necessary for an understanding of the financial statements.

Effective date

BC58 ED 6 proposed that the IFRS should be effective for annual periods beginning on or after 1 January 2005. The Board decided to change the effective date to 1 January 2006 to allow entities more time to make the transition to the IFRS. It also decided to permit an entity that wishes or is required to adopt IFRSs before 1 January 2006 to adopt IFRS 6 early.

Transition

BC59 The Board did not propose any special transition in ED 6. Consequently, paragraphs 14–27 of IAS 8 would apply to any changes in accounting that are necessary as a result of the IFRS.

BC60 Some respondents expressed concern about the application of the proposals to prior periods—especially those related to impairment and the inclusion or exclusion of some expenditures from exploration and evaluation assets. In particular, respondents requested that if the Board were to require restatement, it should give transitional guidance on how to identify elements previously recognised as exploration and evaluation assets now outside the definition.

BC61 IAS 8 would require entities recognising exploration and evaluation assets to determine whether there were any facts and circumstances indicating impairment in prior periods. The Board concluded that retrospective application was not likely to involve the use of hindsight because the facts and circumstances identified in the IFRS are generally objective indicators and whether they existed at a particular date should be a question of fact. However, the Board noted that it provided transitional relief in IFRS 4 for applying the liability adequacy test to comparative periods on the basis of impracticability, principally because the liability adequacy test involves the use of current estimates of future cash flows from an entity's insurance contracts. The Board does not expect that IFRS 6's approach to impairment will involve current estimates of future cash flows and other variables to the same extent. However, it is aware that the variety of approaches to assessing recoverability means that current estimates of future cash flows and other variables are likely to be in use by some entities.

BC62 Therefore, consistently with IFRS 4, the Board concluded that if it is impracticable to apply the impairment test to comparative information that relates to annual periods beginning before 1 January 2006, an entity should disclose that fact.

BC63 Some respondents were concerned that entities would have difficulty in compiling the information necessary for 2004 comparative figures, and suggested that entities should be exempted from restating comparatives on transition, given that the IFRS would be introduced close to 1 January 2005, and could result in substantial changes.

BC64 The Board considered a similar issue when it developed ED 7 *Financial Instruments: Disclosures*, in which it concluded that entities that apply the requirements proposed in ED 7 only when they become mandatory should be required to provide comparative disclosures because such entities will have enough time to prepare the information.

BC65 In ED 7, the Board decided to propose that an entity that both (a) adopts IFRSs for the first time before 1 January 2006 and (b) applies the IFRS before that date should be exempt from the requirement to produce comparative information in the first year of application. The Board compared the concerns raised by constituents in response to ED 6 and the issues it considered in developing ED 7 and decided that its conclusions in ED 7 were also appropriate for the IFRS.

Summary of changes from ED 6

BC66 The following is a summary of the main changes from ED 6 to the IFRS. The Board:

(a) deleted the specific prohibition against including administration and other general overhead costs in the initial measurement of an exploration and evaluation asset (paragraph BC28).

(b) introduced a requirement for the entity to classify exploration and evaluation assets as either tangible or intangible according to the nature of the asset acquired and to apply this classification consistently (paragraphs BC32–BC34).

(c) amended the impairment principle so that an impairment is recognised on the basis of an assessment of facts and circumstances and measured, presented and disclosed in accordance with IAS 36, subject to the modification of the level at which the impairment is assessed (paragraphs BC36–BC39).

(d) deleted the indicators of impairment proposed in ED 6 and replaced them with examples of facts and circumstances that would suggest that an exploration and evaluation asset was impaired (paragraphs BC36–BC39).

(e) deleted the special cash-generating unit for exploration and evaluation assets and instead required that the entity determine an accounting policy for allocating exploration and evaluation assets to a cash-generating unit or units for the purpose of the impairment test (paragraphs BC40–BC47).

(f) amended the effective date of the IFRS so that the IFRS is effective for annual periods beginning on or after 1 January 2006 (paragraph BC58).

(g) provided transitional relief for disclosure for entities adopting IFRSs for the first time and adopting the IFRS before 1 January 2006 (paragraphs BC59–BC65).

Dissenting opinions on IFRS 6

Dissent of Robert P Garnett, James J Leisenring, Warren J McGregor and John T Smith

DO1 Messrs Garnett, Leisenring, McGregor and Smith dissent from the issue of IFRS 6.

DO2 These four Board members dissent because they would not permit entities the alternative of continuing their existing accounting treatment for exploration and evaluation assets. In particular, they believe that all entities should be required to apply paragraphs 11 and 12 of IAS 8 *Accounting Policies, Changes in Accounting Estimates and Errors* when developing an accounting policy for exploration and evaluation assets. These Board members believe that the requirements in IAS 8 have particular relevance and applicability when an IFRS lacks specificities, as is the case for entities recognising exploration and evaluation assets. This is especially true because the IFRS allows the continuation of a variety of measurement bases for these items and, because of the failure to consider the *Framework*, may result in the inappropriate recognition of assets. In the view of these Board members, if an entity cannot meet those requirements, it should not be allowed to describe its financial statements as being in accordance with International Financial Reporting Standards.

DO3 Messrs Garnett and McGregor also disagree with the modifications to the requirements of IAS 36 for the purpose of assessing exploration and evaluation assets for impairment contained in paragraphs 18–22 of the IFRS. They think that the requirements of IAS 36 should be applied in their entirety to exploration and evaluation assets. Failure to do so could result in exploration and evaluation assets continuing to be carried forward when such assets are not known to be recoverable. This could result in the exclusion of relevant information from the financial statements because of the failure to recognise impairment losses on a timely basis and the inclusion of unreliable information because of the inclusion of assets that do not faithfully represent the transactions and other events that they purport to represent.

DO4 The four Board members' concerns are heightened by the absence as yet from the Board's main agenda of a project on accounting for exploration for and evaluation of mineral resources generally. Although a research project has begun, it is unlikely that the Board will be able to develop financial reporting standards in the medium term. Accordingly, it is likely that the concession referred to in paragraph DO2 and, in Messrs Garnett and McGregor's cases, in paragraph DO3, will remain in place for some time.

International Accounting Standard 1

Presentation of Financial Statements

This version includes amendments resulting from Amendment to IAS 19 Employee Benefits—Actuarial Gains and Losses, Group Plans and Disclosures *issued on 16 December 2004.*

CONTENTS

BASIS FOR CONCLUSIONS

IMPLEMENTATION GUIDANCE

TABLE OF CONCORDANCE

International Accounting Standard 1 *Presentation of Financial Statements* (IAS 1) is set out in paragraphs 1–128 and the Appendix. All the paragraphs have equal authority but retain the IASC format of the Standard when it was adopted by the IASB. IAS 1 should be read in the context of its objective and the Basis for Conclusions, the *Preface to International Financial Reporting Standards* and the *Framework for the Preparation and Presentation of Financial Statements.* IAS 8 *Accounting Policies, Changes in Accounting Estimates and Errors* provides a basis for selecting and applying accounting policies in the absence of explicit guidance.

Introduction

IN1 International Accounting Standard 1 *Presentation of Financial Statements* (IAS 1) replaces IAS 1 *Presentation of Financial Statements* (revised in 1997), and should be applied for annual periods beginning on or after 1 January 2005. Earlier application is encouraged.

Reasons for revising IAS 1

IN2 The International Accounting Standards Board developed this revised IAS 1 as part of its project on Improvements to International Accounting Standards. The project was undertaken in the light of queries and criticisms raised in relation to the Standards by securities regulators, professional accountants and other interested parties. The objectives of the project were to reduce or eliminate alternatives, redundancies and conflicts within the Standards, to deal with some convergence issues and to make other improvements.

IN3 For IAS 1, the Board's main objectives were:

(a) to provide a framework within which an entity assesses how to present fairly the effects of transactions and other events, and assesses whether the result of complying with a requirement in a Standard or an Interpretation would be so misleading that it would not give a fair presentation;

(b) to base the criteria for classifying liabilities as current or non-current solely on the conditions existing at the balance sheet date;

(c) to prohibit the presentation of items of income and expense as 'extraordinary items';

(d) to specify disclosures about the judgements management has made in the process of applying the entity's accounting policies, apart from those involving estimations, that have the most significant effect on the amounts recognised in the financial statements; and

(e) to specify disclosures about key sources of estimation uncertainty at the balance sheet date that have a significant risk of causing a material adjustment to the carrying amounts of assets and liabilities within the next financial year.

IN4 The Board did not reconsider the fundamental approach to the presentation of financial statements contained in IAS 1.

Changes from previous requirements

IN5 The main changes from the previous version of IAS 1 are described below.

Fair presentation and departures from IFRSs

IN6 The Standard includes guidance on the meaning of 'present fairly' and emphasises that the application of International Financial Reporting Standards (IFRSs) is presumed to result in financial statements that achieve a fair presentation.

IN7 The Standard requires an entity, in the extremely rare circumstances in which management concludes that compliance with a requirement in a Standard or an Interpretation would be so misleading that it would conflict with the objective of financial statements set out in the *Framework for the Preparation and Presentation of Financial Statements*, to depart from the requirement unless departure is prohibited by the relevant regulatory framework. In either case, the entity is required to make specified disclosures.

Classification of assets and liabilities

IN8 The Standard requires an entity to present assets and liabilities in order of liquidity only when a liquidity presentation provides information that is reliable and is more relevant than a current/non-current presentation.

IN9 The Standard requires a liability held primarily for the purpose of being traded to be classified as current.

IN10 The Standard requires a financial liability that is due within twelve months after the balance sheet date, or for which the entity does not have an unconditional right to defer its settlement for at least twelve months after the balance sheet date, to be classified as a current liability. This classification is required even if an agreement to refinance, or to reschedule payments, on a long-term basis is completed after the balance sheet date and before the financial statements are authorised for issue. (Such an agreement would qualify for disclosure as a non-adjusting event after the balance sheet date in accordance with IAS 10 *Events after the Balance Sheet Date*.) However, this requirement does not affect the classification of a liability as non-current when the entity has, under the terms of an existing loan facility, the discretion to refinance or roll over its obligations for at least twelve months after the balance sheet date.

IN11 In some cases, a long-term financial liability is payable on demand because the entity has breached a condition of its loan agreement on or before the balance sheet date. The Standard requires the liability to be classified as current at the balance sheet date even if, after the balance sheet date, and before the financial statements are authorised for issue, the lender has agreed not to demand payment as a consequence of the breach. (Such an agreement would qualify for disclosure as a non-adjusting event after the balance sheet date in accordance with IAS 10.) However, the liability is to be classified as non-current if the lender agreed by the balance sheet date to provide a period of grace ending at least twelve months after the balance sheet date. In this context, a period of grace is a period within which the entity can rectify the breach and during which the lender cannot demand immediate repayment.

Presentation and disclosure

IN12 The Standard requires the following disclosures:

(a) the judgements, apart from those involving estimations (see (b) below), management has made in the process of applying the entity's accounting policies that have the most significant effect on the amounts recognised in the financial statements (eg management's judgement in determining whether financial assets are held-to-maturity investments); and

(b) the key assumptions concerning the future, and other key sources of estimation uncertainty at the balance sheet date, that have a significant risk of causing a material adjustment to the carrying amounts of assets and liabilities within the next financial year.

IN13 The following disclosures required by the previous version of the Standard have been omitted:

(a) the results of operating activities, and extraordinary items, as line items on the face of the income statement. The revised Standard prohibits disclosure of 'extraordinary items' in financial statements.

(b) the number of an entity's employees.

IN14 The Standard includes all requirements previously set out in other Standards for the presentation of particular line items on the face of the balance sheet and income statement (and makes the necessary consequential amendments to those Standards). The line items are:

(a) biological assets;

(b) liabilities and assets for current tax, deferred tax liabilities and deferred tax assets; and

(c) a single amount comprising the total of (i) the post-tax profit or loss of discontinued operations and (ii) the post-tax gain or loss recognised on the measurement to fair value less costs to sell or on the disposal of the assets or disposal group(s) constituting the discontinued operation.

Other changes

IN15 The requirements for the selection and application of accounting policies have been transferred to the revised IAS 8 *Accounting Policies, Changes in Accounting Estimates and Errors*.

IN16 The presentation requirements for profit or loss for the period, formerly contained in IAS 8 *Net Profit or Loss for the Period, Fundamental Errors and Changes in Accounting Policies*, have been transferred to this Standard.

IN17 A definition of 'material' has been added.

IN18 The Standard requires disclosure, on the face of the income statement, of the entity's profit or loss for the period and the allocation of that amount between 'profit or loss attributable to minority interest' and 'profit or loss attributable to equity holders of the parent'. A similar requirement has been added for the statement of changes in equity. The allocated amounts are not to be presented as items of income or expense.

IN19 The Standard also requires disclosure, on the face of the statement of changes in equity, of total income and expenses for the period (including amounts recognised directly in equity), showing separately the amounts attributable to equity holders of the parent and to minority interest.

International Accounting Standard 1
Presentation of Financial Statements

Objective

1 The objective of this Standard is to prescribe the basis for presentation of general purpose financial statements, to ensure comparability both with the entity's financial statements of previous periods and with the financial statements of other entities. To achieve this objective, this Standard sets out overall requirements for the presentation of financial statements, guidelines for their structure and minimum requirements for their content. The recognition, measurement and disclosure of specific transactions and other events are dealt with in other Standards and in Interpretations.

Scope

2 **This Standard shall be applied to all general purpose financial statements prepared and presented in accordance with International Financial Reporting Standards (IFRSs).**

3 General purpose financial statements are those intended to meet the needs of users who are not in a position to demand reports tailored to meet their particular information needs. General purpose financial statements include those that are presented separately or within another public document such as an annual report or a prospectus. This Standard does not apply to the structure and content of condensed interim financial statements prepared in accordance with IAS 34 *Interim Financial Reporting*. However, paragraphs 13–41 apply to such financial statements. This Standard applies equally to all entities and whether or not they need to prepare consolidated financial statements or separate financial statements, as defined in IAS 27 *Consolidated and Separate Financial Statements*.

4 IAS 30 *Disclosures in the Financial Statements of Banks and Similar Financial Institutions* specifies additional requirements for banks and similar financial institutions that are consistent with the requirements of this Standard.

5 This Standard uses terminology that is suitable for profit-oriented entities, including public sector business entities. Entities with not-for-profit activities in the private sector, public sector or government seeking to apply this Standard may need to amend the descriptions used for particular line items in the financial statements and for the financial statements themselves.

6 Similarly, entities that do not have equity as defined in IAS 32 *Financial Instruments: Disclosure and Presentation* (eg some mutual funds) and entities whose share capital is not equity (eg some co-operative entities) may need to adapt the presentation in the financial statements of members' or unitholders' interests.

Purpose of financial statements

7 Financial statements are a structured representation of the financial position and financial performance of an entity. The objective of general purpose financial statements is to provide information about the financial position, financial

performance and cash flows of an entity that is useful to a wide range of users in making economic decisions. Financial statements also show the results of management's stewardship of the resources entrusted to it. To meet this objective, financial statements provide information about an entity's:

(a) assets;

(b) liabilities;

(c) equity;

(d) income and expenses, including gains and losses;

(e) other changes in equity; and

(f) cash flows.

This information, along with other information in the notes, assists users of financial statements in predicting the entity's future cash flows and, in particular, their timing and certainty.

Components of financial statements

8 **A complete set of financial statements comprises:**

(a) a balance sheet;

(b) an income statement;

(c) a statement of changes in equity showing either:

(i) all changes in equity, or

(ii) changes in equity other than those arising from transactions with equity holders acting in their capacity as equity holders;

(d) a cash flow statement; and

(e) notes, comprising a summary of significant accounting policies and other explanatory notes.

9 Many entities present, outside the financial statements, a financial review by management that describes and explains the main features of the entity's financial performance and financial position and the principal uncertainties it faces. Such a report may include a review of:

(a) the main factors and influences determining financial performance, including changes in the environment in which the entity operates, the entity's response to those changes and their effect, and the entity's policy for investment to maintain and enhance financial performance, including its dividend policy;

(b) the entity's sources of funding and its targeted ratio of liabilities to equity; and

(c) the entity's resources not recognised in the balance sheet in accordance with IFRSs.

10 Many entities also present, outside the financial statements, reports and statements such as environmental reports and value added statements, particularly in industries in which environmental factors are significant and

when employees are regarded as an important user group. Reports and statements presented outside financial statements are outside the scope of IFRSs.

Definitions

11 **The following terms are used in this Standard with the meanings specified:**

Impracticable **Applying a requirement is impracticable when the entity cannot apply it after making every reasonable effort to do so.**

International Financial Reporting Standards (IFRSs) **are Standards and Interpretations adopted by the International Accounting Standards Board (IASB). They comprise:**

(a) International Financial Reporting Standards;

(b) International Accounting Standards; and

(c) Interpretations originated by the International Financial Reporting Interpretations Committee (IFRIC) or the former Standing Interpretations Committee (SIC).

Material **Omissions or misstatements of items are material if they could, individually or collectively, influence the economic decisions of users taken on the basis of the financial statements. Materiality depends on the size and nature of the omission or misstatement judged in the surrounding circumstances. The size or nature of the item, or a combination of both, could be the determining factor.**

Notes **contain information in addition to that presented in the balance sheet, income statement, statement of changes in equity and cash flow statement. Notes provide narrative descriptions or disaggregations of items disclosed in those statements and information about items that do not qualify for recognition in those statements.**

12 Assessing whether an omission or misstatement could influence economic decisions of users, and so be material, requires consideration of the characteristics of those users. The *Framework for the Preparation and Presentation of Financial Statements* states in paragraph 25 that 'users are assumed to have a reasonable knowledge of business and economic activities and accounting and a willingness to study the information with reasonable diligence.' Therefore, the assessment needs to take into account how users with such attributes could reasonably be expected to be influenced in making economic decisions.

Overall considerations

Fair presentation and compliance with IFRSs

13 **Financial statements shall present fairly the financial position, financial performance and cash flows of an entity. Fair presentation requires the faithful representation of the effects of transactions, other events and conditions in accordance with the definitions and recognition criteria for assets, liabilities, income and expenses set out in the** ***Framework*****. The application of IFRSs, with additional disclosure when necessary, is presumed to result in financial statements that achieve a fair presentation.**

14 **An entity whose financial statements comply with IFRSs shall make an explicit and unreserved statement of such compliance in the notes. Financial statements shall not be described as complying with IFRSs unless they comply with all the requirements of IFRSs.**

15 In virtually all circumstances, a fair presentation is achieved by compliance with applicable IFRSs. A fair presentation also requires an entity:

(a) to select and apply accounting policies in accordance with IAS 8 *Accounting Policies, Changes in Accounting Estimates and Errors*. IAS 8 sets out a hierarchy of authoritative guidance that management considers in the absence of a Standard or an Interpretation that specifically applies to an item.

(b) to present information, including accounting policies, in a manner that provides relevant, reliable, comparable and understandable information.

(c) to provide additional disclosures when compliance with the specific requirements in IFRSs is insufficient to enable users to understand the impact of particular transactions, other events and conditions on the entity's financial position and financial performance.

16 **Inappropriate accounting policies are not rectified either by disclosure of the accounting policies used or by notes or explanatory material.**

17 **In the extremely rare circumstances in which management concludes that compliance with a requirement in a Standard or an Interpretation would be so misleading that it would conflict with the objective of financial statements set out in the *Framework*, the entity shall depart from that requirement in the manner set out in paragraph 18 if the relevant regulatory framework requires, or otherwise does not prohibit, such a departure.**

18 **When an entity departs from a requirement of a Standard or an Interpretation in accordance with paragraph 17, it shall disclose:**

(a) that management has concluded that the financial statements present fairly the entity's financial position, financial performance and cash flows;

(b) that it has complied with applicable Standards and Interpretations, except that it has departed from a particular requirement to achieve a fair presentation;

(c) the title of the Standard or Interpretation from which the entity has departed, the nature of the departure, including the treatment that the Standard or Interpretation would require, the reason why that treatment would be so misleading in the circumstances that it would conflict with the objective of financial statements set out in the *Framework*, and the treatment adopted; and

(d) for each period presented, the financial impact of the departure on each item in the financial statements that would have been reported in complying with the requirement.

19 **When an entity has departed from a requirement of a Standard or an Interpretation in a prior period, and that departure affects the amounts recognised in the financial statements for the current period, it shall make the disclosures set out in paragraph 18(c) and (d).**

20 Paragraph 19 applies, for example, when an entity departed in a prior period from a requirement in a Standard or an Interpretation for the measurement of assets or liabilities and that departure affects the measurement of changes in assets and liabilities recognised in the current period's financial statements.

21 **In the extremely rare circumstances in which management concludes that compliance with a requirement in a Standard or an Interpretation would be so misleading that it would conflict with the objective of financial statements set out in the *Framework*, but the relevant regulatory framework prohibits departure from the requirement, the entity shall, to the maximum extent possible, reduce the perceived misleading aspects of compliance by disclosing:**

(a) the title of the Standard or Interpretation in question, the nature of the requirement, and the reason why management has concluded that complying with that requirement is so misleading in the circumstances that it conflicts with the objective of financial statements set out in the *Framework*; and

(b) for each period presented, the adjustments to each item in the financial statements that management has concluded would be necessary to achieve a fair presentation.

22 For the purpose of paragraphs 17–21, an item of information would conflict with the objective of financial statements when it does not represent faithfully the transactions, other events and conditions that it either purports to represent or could reasonably be expected to represent and, consequently, it would be likely to influence economic decisions made by users of financial statements. When assessing whether complying with a specific requirement in a Standard or an Interpretation would be so misleading that it would conflict with the objective of financial statements set out in the *Framework*, management considers:

(a) why the objective of financial statements is not achieved in the particular circumstances; and

(b) how the entity's circumstances differ from those of other entities that comply with the requirement. If other entities in similar circumstances comply with the requirement, there is a rebuttable presumption that the entity's compliance with the requirement would not be so misleading that it would conflict with the objective of financial statements set out in the *Framework*.

Going concern

23 **When preparing financial statements, management shall make an assessment of an entity's ability to continue as a going concern. Financial statements shall be prepared on a going concern basis unless management either intends to liquidate the entity or to cease trading, or has no realistic alternative but to do so. When management is aware, in making its**

assessment, of material uncertainties related to events or conditions that may cast significant doubt upon the entity's ability to continue as a going concern, those uncertainties shall be disclosed. When financial statements are not prepared on a going concern basis, that fact shall be disclosed, together with the basis on which the financial statements are prepared and the reason why the entity is not regarded as a going concern.

24 In assessing whether the going concern assumption is appropriate, management takes into account all available information about the future, which is at least, but is not limited to, twelve months from the balance sheet date. The degree of consideration depends on the facts in each case. When an entity has a history of profitable operations and ready access to financial resources, a conclusion that the going concern basis of accounting is appropriate may be reached without detailed analysis. In other cases, management may need to consider a wide range of factors relating to current and expected profitability, debt repayment schedules and potential sources of replacement financing before it can satisfy itself that the going concern basis is appropriate.

Accrual basis of accounting

25 An entity shall prepare its financial statements, except for cash flow information, using the accrual basis of accounting.

26 When the accrual basis of accounting is used, items are recognised as assets, liabilities, equity, income and expenses (the elements of financial statements) when they satisfy the definitions and recognition criteria for those elements in the *Framework*.

Consistency of presentation

27 The presentation and classification of items in the financial statements shall be retained from one period to the next unless:

(a) it is apparent, following a significant change in the nature of the entity's operations or a review of its financial statements, that another presentation or classification would be more appropriate having regard to the criteria for the selection and application of accounting policies in IAS 8; or

(b) a Standard or an Interpretation requires a change in presentation.

28 A significant acquisition or disposal, or a review of the presentation of the financial statements, might suggest that the financial statements need to be presented differently. An entity changes the presentation of its financial statements only if the changed presentation provides information that is reliable and is more relevant to users of the financial statements and the revised structure is likely to continue, so that comparability is not impaired. When making such changes in presentation, an entity reclassifies its comparative information in accordance with paragraphs 38 and 39.

Materiality and aggregation

29 **Each material class of similar items shall be presented separately in the financial statements. Items of a dissimilar nature or function shall be presented separately unless they are immaterial.**

30 Financial statements result from processing large numbers of transactions or other events that are aggregated into classes according to their nature or function. The final stage in the process of aggregation and classification is the presentation of condensed and classified data, which form line items on the face of the balance sheet, income statement, statement of changes in equity and cash flow statement, or in the notes. If a line item is not individually material, it is aggregated with other items either on the face of those statements or in the notes. An item that is not sufficiently material to warrant separate presentation on the face of those statements may nevertheless be sufficiently material for it to be presented separately in the notes.

31 Applying the concept of materiality means that a specific disclosure requirement in a Standard or an Interpretation need not be satisfied if the information is not material.

Offsetting

32 **Assets and liabilities, and income and expenses, shall not be offset unless required or permitted by a Standard or an Interpretation.**

33 It is important that assets and liabilities, and income and expenses, are reported separately. Offsetting in the income statement or the balance sheet, except when offsetting reflects the substance of the transaction or other event, detracts from the ability of users both to understand the transactions, other events and conditions that have occurred and to assess the entity's future cash flows. Measuring assets net of valuation allowances–for example, obsolescence allowances on inventories and doubtful debts allowances on receivables–is not offsetting.

34 IAS 18 *Revenue* defines revenue and requires it to be measured at the fair value of the consideration received or receivable, taking into account the amount of any trade discounts and volume rebates allowed by the entity. An entity undertakes, in the course of its ordinary activities, other transactions that do not generate revenue but are incidental to the main revenue-generating activities. The results of such transactions are presented, when this presentation reflects the substance of the transaction or other event, by netting any income with related expenses arising on the same transaction. For example:

(a) gains and losses on the disposal of non-current assets, including investments and operating assets, are reported by deducting from the proceeds on disposal the carrying amount of the asset and related selling expenses; and

(b) expenditure related to a provision that is recognised in accordance with IAS 37 *Provisions, Contingent Liabilities and Contingent Assets* and reimbursed under a contractual arrangement with a third party (for example, a supplier's warranty agreement) may be netted against the related reimbursement.

35 In addition, gains and losses arising from a group of similar transactions are reported on a net basis, for example, foreign exchange gains and losses or gains and losses arising on financial instruments held for trading. Such gains and losses are, however, reported separately if they are material.

Comparative information

36 **Except when a Standard or an Interpretation permits or requires otherwise, comparative information shall be disclosed in respect of the previous period for all amounts reported in the financial statements. Comparative information shall be included for narrative and descriptive information when it is relevant to an understanding of the current period's financial statements.**

37 In some cases, narrative information provided in the financial statements for the previous period(s) continues to be relevant in the current period. For example, details of a legal dispute, the outcome of which was uncertain at the last balance sheet date and is yet to be resolved, are disclosed in the current period. Users benefit from information that the uncertainty existed at the last balance sheet date, and about the steps that have been taken during the period to resolve the uncertainty.

38 **When the presentation or classification of items in the financial statements is amended, comparative amounts shall be reclassified unless the reclassification is impracticable. When comparative amounts are reclassified, an entity shall disclose:**

(a) the nature of the reclassification;

(b) the amount of each item or class of items that is reclassified; and

(c) the reason for the reclassification.

39 **When it is impracticable to reclassify comparative amounts, an entity shall disclose:**

(a) the reason for not reclassifying the amounts; and

(b) the nature of the adjustments that would have been made if the amounts had been reclassified.

40 Enhancing the inter-period comparability of information assists users in making economic decisions, especially by allowing the assessment of trends in financial information for predictive purposes. In some circumstances, it is impracticable to reclassify comparative information for a particular prior period to achieve comparability with the current period. For example, data may not have been collected in the prior period(s) in a way that allows reclassification, and it may not be practicable to recreate the information.

41 IAS 8 deals with the adjustments to comparative information required when an entity changes an accounting policy or corrects an error.

Structure and content

Introduction

42 This Standard requires particular disclosures on the face of the balance sheet, income statement and statement of changes in equity and requires disclosure of other line items either on the face of those statements or in the notes. IAS 7 sets out requirements for the presentation of a cash flow statement.

43 This Standard sometimes uses the term 'disclosure' in a broad sense, encompassing items presented on the face of the balance sheet, income statement, statement of changes in equity and cash flow statement, as well as in the notes. Disclosures are also required by other Standards and Interpretations. Unless specified to the contrary elsewhere in this Standard, or in another Standard or Interpretation, such disclosures are made either on the face of the balance sheet, income statement, statement of changes in equity or cash flow statement (whichever is relevant), or in the notes.

Identification of the financial statements

44 The financial statements shall be identified clearly and distinguished from other information in the same published document.

45 IFRSs apply only to financial statements, and not to other information presented in an annual report or other document. Therefore, it is important that users can distinguish information that is prepared using IFRSs from other information that may be useful to users but is not the subject of those requirements.

46 Each component of the financial statements shall be identified clearly. In addition, the following information shall be displayed prominently, and repeated when it is necessary for a proper understanding of the information presented:

(a) the name of the reporting entity or other means of identification, and any change in that information from the preceding balance sheet date;

(b) whether the financial statements cover the individual entity or a group of entities;

(c) the balance sheet date or the period covered by the financial statements, whichever is appropriate to that component of the financial statements;

(d) the presentation currency, as defined in IAS 21 *The Effects of Changes in Foreign Exchange Rates*; **and**

(e) the level of rounding used in presenting amounts in the financial statements.

47 The requirements in paragraph 46 are normally met by presenting page headings and abbreviated column headings on each page of the financial statements. Judgement is required in determining the best way of presenting such information. For example, when the financial statements are presented

electronically, separate pages are not always used; the above items are then presented frequently enough to ensure a proper understanding of the information included in the financial statements.

48 Financial statements are often made more understandable by presenting information in thousands or millions of units of the presentation currency. This is acceptable as long as the level of rounding in presentation is disclosed and material information is not omitted.

Reporting period

49 Financial statements shall be presented at least annually. When an entity's balance sheet date changes and the annual financial statements are presented for a period longer or shorter than one year, an entity shall disclose, in addition to the period covered by the financial statements:

(a) the reason for using a longer or shorter period; and

(b) the fact that comparative amounts for the income statement, statement of changes in equity, cash flow statement and related notes are not entirely comparable.

50 Normally, financial statements are consistently prepared covering a one-year period. However, for practical reasons, some entities prefer to report, for example, for a 52-week period. This Standard does not preclude this practice, because the resulting financial statements are unlikely to be materially different from those that would be presented for one year.

Balance sheet

Current/non-current distinction

51 An entity shall present current and non-current assets, and current and non-current liabilities, as separate classifications on the face of its balance sheet in accordance with paragraphs 57–67 except when a presentation based on liquidity provides information that is reliable and is more relevant. When that exception applies, all assets and liabilities shall be presented broadly in order of liquidity.

52 Whichever method of presentation is adopted, for each asset and liability line item that combines amounts expected to be recovered or settled (a) no more than twelve months after the balance sheet date and (b) more than twelve months after the balance sheet date, an entity shall disclose the amount expected to be recovered or settled after more than twelve months.

53 When an entity supplies goods or services within a clearly identifiable operating cycle, separate classification of current and non-current assets and liabilities on the face of the balance sheet provides useful information by distinguishing the net assets that are continuously circulating as working capital from those used in the entity's long-term operations. It also highlights assets that are expected to be realised within the current operating cycle, and liabilities that are due for settlement within the same period.

54 For some entities, such as financial institutions, a presentation of assets and liabilities in increasing or decreasing order of liquidity provides information that

is reliable and is more relevant than a current/non-current presentation because the entity does not supply goods or services within a clearly identifiable operating cycle.

55 In applying paragraph 51, an entity is permitted to present some of its assets and liabilities using a current/non-current classification and others in order of liquidity when this provides information that is reliable and is more relevant. The need for a mixed basis of presentation might arise when an entity has diverse operations.

56 Information about expected dates of realisation of assets and liabilities is useful in assessing the liquidity and solvency of an entity. IAS 32 requires disclosure of the maturity dates of financial assets and financial liabilities. Financial assets include trade and other receivables, and financial liabilities include trade and other payables. Information on the expected date of recovery and settlement of non-monetary assets and liabilities such as inventories and provisions is also useful, whether or not assets and liabilities are classified as current or non-current. For example, an entity discloses the amount of inventories that are expected to be recovered more than twelve months after the balance sheet date.

Current assets

57 **An asset shall be classified as current when it satisfies any of the following criteria:**

(a) it is expected to be realised in, or is intended for sale or consumption in, the entity's normal operating cycle;

(b) it is held primarily for the purpose of being traded;

(c) it is expected to be realised within twelve months after the balance sheet date; or

(d) it is cash or a cash equivalent (as defined in IAS 7 *Cash Flow Statements*) unless it is restricted from being exchanged or used to settle a liability for at least twelve months after the balance sheet date.

All other assets shall be classified as non-current.

58 This Standard uses the term 'non-current' to include tangible, intangible and financial assets of a long-term nature. It does not prohibit the use of alternative descriptions as long as the meaning is clear.

59 The operating cycle of an entity is the time between the acquisition of assets for processing and their realisation in cash or cash equivalents. When the entity's normal operating cycle is not clearly identifiable, its duration is assumed to be twelve months. Current assets include assets (such as inventories and trade receivables) that are sold, consumed or realised as part of the normal operating cycle even when they are not expected to be realised within twelve months after the balance sheet date. Current assets also include assets held primarily for the purpose of being traded (financial assets within this category are classified as held for trading in accordance with IAS 39 *Financial Instruments: Recognition and Measurement*) and the current portion of non-current financial assets.

Current liabilities

60 **A liability shall be classified as current when it satisfies any of the following criteria:**

(a) it is expected to be settled in the entity's normal operating cycle;

(b) it is held primarily for the purpose of being traded;

(c) it is due to be settled within twelve months after the balance sheet date; or

(d) the entity does not have an unconditional right to defer settlement of the liability for at least twelve months after the balance sheet date.

All other liabilities shall be classified as non-current.

61 Some current liabilities, such as trade payables and some accruals for employee and other operating costs, are part of the working capital used in the entity's normal operating cycle. Such operating items are classified as current liabilities even if they are due to be settled more than twelve months after the balance sheet date. The same normal operating cycle applies to the classification of an entity's assets and liabilities. When the entity's normal operating cycle is not clearly identifiable, its duration is assumed to be twelve months.

62 Other current liabilities are not settled as part of the normal operating cycle, but are due for settlement within twelve months after the balance sheet date or held primarily for the purpose of being traded. Examples are financial liabilities classified as held for trading in accordance with IAS 39, bank overdrafts, and the current portion of non-current financial liabilities, dividends payable, income taxes and other non-trade payables. Financial liabilities that provide financing on a long-term basis (ie are not part of the working capital used in the entity's normal operating cycle) and are not due for settlement within twelve months after the balance sheet date are non-current liabilities, subject to paragraphs 65 and 66.

63 An entity classifies its financial liabilities as current when they are due to be settled within twelve months after the balance sheet date, even if:

(a) the original term was for a period longer than twelve months; and

(b) an agreement to refinance, or to reschedule payments, on a long-term basis is completed after the balance sheet date and before the financial statements are authorised for issue.

64 If an entity expects, and has the discretion, to refinance or roll over an obligation for at least twelve months after the balance sheet date under an existing loan facility, it classifies the obligation as non-current, even if it would otherwise be due within a shorter period. However, when refinancing or rolling over the obligation is not at the discretion of the entity (for example, there is no agreement to refinance), the potential to refinance is not considered and the obligation is classified as current.

65 When an entity breaches an undertaking under a long-term loan agreement on or before the balance sheet date with the effect that the liability becomes payable on demand, the liability is classified as current, even if the lender has agreed, after the balance sheet date and before the authorisation of the financial statements for

issue, not to demand payment as a consequence of the breach. The liability is classified as current because, at the balance sheet date, the entity does not have an unconditional right to defer its settlement for at least twelve months after that date.

66 However, the liability is classified as non-current if the lender agreed by the balance sheet date to provide a period of grace ending at least twelve months after the balance sheet date, within which the entity can rectify the breach and during which the lender cannot demand immediate repayment.

67 In respect of loans classified as current liabilities, if the following events occur between the balance sheet date and the date the financial statements are authorised for issue, those events qualify for disclosure as non-adjusting events in accordance with IAS 10 *Events after the Balance Sheet Date*:

(a) refinancing on a long-term basis;

(b) rectification of a breach of a long-term loan agreement; and

(c) the receipt from the lender of a period of grace to rectify a breach of a long-term loan agreement ending at least twelve months after the balance sheet date.

Information to be presented on the face of the balance sheet

68 **As a minimum, the face of the balance sheet shall include line items that present the following amounts to the extent that they are not presented in accordance with paragraph 68A:**

(a) property, plant and equipment;

(b) investment property;

(c) intangible assets;

(d) financial assets (excluding amounts shown under (e), (h) and (i));

(e) investments accounted for using the equity method;

(f) biological assets;

(g) inventories;

(h) trade and other receivables;

(i) cash and cash equivalents;

(j) trade and other payables;

(k) provisions;

(l) financial liabilities (excluding amounts shown under (j) and (k));

(m) liabilities and assets for current tax, as defined in IAS 12 ***Income Taxes*****;**

(n) deferred tax liabilities and deferred tax assets, as defined in IAS 12;

(o) minority interest, presented within equity; and

(p) issued capital and reserves attributable to equity holders of the parent.

68A The face of the balance sheet shall also include line items that present the following amounts:

(a) the total of assets classified as held for sale and assets included in disposal groups classified as held for sale in accordance with IFRS 5 *Non-current Assets Held for Sale and Discontinued Operations*; **and**

(b) liabilities included in disposal groups classified as held for sale in accordance with IFRS 5.

69 Additional line items, headings and subtotals shall be presented on the face of the balance sheet when such presentation is relevant to an understanding of the entity's financial position.

70 When an entity presents current and non-current assets, and current and non-current liabilities, as separate classifications on the face of its balance sheet, it shall not classify deferred tax assets (liabilities) as current assets (liabilities).

71 This Standard does not prescribe the order or format in which items are to be presented. Paragraph 68 simply provides a list of items that are sufficiently different in nature or function to warrant separate presentation on the face of the balance sheet. In addition:

(a) line items are included when the size, nature or function of an item or aggregation of similar items is such that separate presentation is relevant to an understanding of the entity's financial position; and

(b) the descriptions used and the ordering of items or aggregation of similar items may be amended according to the nature of the entity and its transactions, to provide information that is relevant to an understanding of the entity's financial position. For example, a bank amends the above descriptions to apply the more specific requirements in IAS 30.

72 The judgement on whether additional items are presented separately is based on an assessment of:

(a) the nature and liquidity of assets;

(b) the function of assets within the entity; and

(c) the amounts, nature and timing of liabilities.

73 The use of different measurement bases for different classes of assets suggests that their nature or function differs and, therefore, that they should be presented as separate line items. For example, different classes of property, plant and equipment can be carried at cost or revalued amounts in accordance with IAS 16 *Property, Plant and Equipment*.

Information to be presented either on the face of the balance sheet or in the notes

74 **An entity shall disclose, either on the face of the balance sheet or in the notes, further subclassifications of the line items presented, classified in a manner appropriate to the entity's operations.**

75 The detail provided in subclassifications depends on the requirements of IFRSs and on the size, nature and function of the amounts involved. The factors set out in paragraph 72 also are used to decide the basis of subclassification. The disclosures vary for each item, for example:

(a) items of property, plant and equipment are disaggregated into classes in accordance with IAS 16;

(b) receivables are disaggregated into amounts receivable from trade customers, receivables from related parties, prepayments and other amounts;

(c) inventories are subclassified, in accordance with IAS 2 *Inventories*, into classifications such as merchandise, production supplies, materials, work in progress and finished goods;

(d) provisions are disaggregated into provisions for employee benefits and other items; and

(e) equity capital and reserves are disaggregated into various classes, such as paid-in capital, share premium and reserves.

76 **An entity shall disclose the following, either on the face of the balance sheet or in the notes:**

(a) for each class of share capital:

(i) the number of shares authorised;

(ii) the number of shares issued and fully paid, and issued but not fully paid;

(iii) par value per share, or that the shares have no par value;

(iv) a reconciliation of the number of shares outstanding at the beginning and at the end of the period;

(v) the rights, preferences and restrictions attaching to that class including restrictions on the distribution of dividends and the repayment of capital;

(vi) shares in the entity held by the entity or by its subsidiaries or associates; and

(vii) shares reserved for issue under options and contracts for the sale of shares, including the terms and amounts; and

(b) a description of the nature and purpose of each reserve within equity.

77 **An entity without share capital, such as a partnership or trust, shall disclose information equivalent to that required by paragraph 76(a), showing changes during the period in each category of equity interest, and the rights, preferences and restrictions attaching to each category of equity interest.**

Income statement

Profit or loss for the period

78 **All items of income and expense recognised in a period shall be included in profit or loss unless a Standard or an Interpretation requires otherwise.**

79 Normally, all items of income and expense recognised in a period are included in profit or loss. This includes the effects of changes in accounting estimates. However, circumstances may exist when particular items may be excluded from profit or loss for the current period. IAS 8 deals with two such circumstances: the correction of errors and the effect of changes in accounting policies.

80 Other Standards deal with items that may meet the *Framework* definitions of income or expense but are usually excluded from profit or loss. Examples include revaluation surpluses (see IAS 16), particular gains and losses arising on translating the financial statements of a foreign operation (see IAS 21) and gains or losses on remeasuring available-for-sale financial assets (see IAS 39).

Information to be presented on the face of the income statement

81 **As a minimum, the face of the income statement shall include line items that present the following amounts for the period:**

(a) revenue;

(b) finance costs;

(c) share of the profit or loss of associates and joint ventures accounted for using the equity method;

(d) tax expense;

(e) a single amount comprising the total of (i) the post-tax profit or loss of discontinued operations and (ii) the post-tax gain or loss recognised on the measurement to fair value less costs to sell or on the disposal of the assets or disposal group(s) constituting the discontinued operation; and

(f) profit or loss.

82 **The following items shall be disclosed on the face of the income statement as allocations of profit or loss for the period:**

(a) profit or loss attributable to minority interest; and

(b) profit or loss attributable to equity holders of the parent.

83 **Additional line items, headings and subtotals shall be presented on the face of the income statement when such presentation is relevant to an understanding of the entity's financial performance.**

84 Because the effects of an entity's various activities, transactions and other events differ in frequency, potential for gain or loss and predictability, disclosing the components of financial performance assists in an understanding of the financial performance achieved and in making projections of future results. Additional line items are included on the face of the income statement, and the descriptions used and the ordering of items are amended when this is necessary to explain the elements of financial performance. Factors to be considered include materiality and the nature and function of the components of income and expenses. For example, a bank amends the descriptions to apply the more specific requirements in IAS 30. Income and expense items are not offset unless the criteria in paragraph 32 are met.

85 An entity shall not present any items of income and expense as extraordinary items, either on the face of the income statement or in the notes.

Information to be presented either on the face of the income statement or in the notes

86 When items of income and expense are material, their nature and amount shall be disclosed separately.

87 Circumstances that would give rise to the separate disclosure of items of income and expense include:

(a) write-downs of inventories to net realisable value or of property, plant and equipment to recoverable amount, as well as reversals of such write-downs;

(b) restructurings of the activities of an entity and reversals of any provisions for the costs of restructuring;

(c) disposals of items of property, plant and equipment;

(d) disposals of investments;

(e) discontinued operations;

(f) litigation settlements; and

(g) other reversals of provisions.

88 An entity shall present an analysis of expenses using a classification based on either the nature of expenses or their function within the entity, whichever provides information that is reliable and more relevant.

89 Entities are encouraged to present the analysis in paragraph 88 on the face of the income statement.

90 Expenses are subclassified to highlight components of financial performance that may differ in terms of frequency, potential for gain or loss and predictability. This analysis is provided in one of two forms.

91 The first form of analysis is the nature of expense method. Expenses are aggregated in the income statement according to their nature (for example, depreciation, purchases of materials, transport costs, employee benefits and advertising costs), and are not reallocated among various functions within the

entity. This method may be simple to apply because no allocations of expenses to functional classifications are necessary. An example of a classification using the nature of expense method is as follows:

Revenue		X
Other income		X
Changes in inventories of finished goods and work in progress	X	
Raw materials and consumables used	X	
Employee benefits expense	X	
Depreciation and amortisation expense	X	
Other expenses	X	
Total expenses		(X)
Profit		X

92 The second form of analysis is the function of expense or 'cost of sales' method and classifies expenses according to their function as part of cost of sales or, for example, the costs of distribution or administrative activities. At a minimum, an entity discloses its cost of sales under this method separately from other expenses. This method can provide more relevant information to users than the classification of expenses by nature, but allocating costs to functions may require arbitrary allocations and involve considerable judgement. An example of a classification using the function of expense method is as follows:

Revenue	X
Cost of sales	(X)
Gross profit	X
Other income	X
Distribution costs	(X)
Administrative expenses	(X)
Other expenses	(X)
Profit	X

93 **Entities classifying expenses by function shall disclose additional information on the nature of expenses, including depreciation and amortisation expense and employee benefits expense.**

94 The choice between the function of expense method and the nature of expense method depends on historical and industry factors and the nature of the entity. Both methods provide an indication of those costs that might vary, directly or indirectly, with the level of sales or production of the entity. Because each method of presentation has merit for different types of entities, this Standard requires management to select the most relevant and reliable presentation. However, because information on the nature of expenses is useful in predicting

future cash flows, additional disclosure is required when the function of expense classification is used. In paragraph 93, 'employee benefits' has the same meaning as in IAS 19 *Employee Benefits*.

95 **An entity shall disclose, either on the face of the income statement or the statement of changes in equity, or in the notes, the amount of dividends recognised as distributions to equity holders during the period, and the related amount per share.**

Statement of changes in equity

96 **An entity shall present a statement of changes in equity showing on the face of the statement:**

(a) profit or loss for the period;

(b) each item of income and expense for the period that, as required by other Standards or by Interpretations, is recognised directly in equity, and the total of these items;

(c) total income and expense for the period (calculated as the sum of (a) and (b)), showing separately the total amounts attributable to equity holders of the parent and to minority interest; and

(d) for each component of equity, the effects of changes in accounting policies and corrections of errors recognised in accordance with IAS 8.

A statement of changes in equity that comprises only these items shall be titled a statement of recognised income and expense.

97 **An entity shall also present, either on the face of the statement of changes in equity or in the notes:**

(a) the amounts of transactions with equity holders acting in their capacity as equity holders, showing separately distributions to equity holders;

(b) the balance of retained earnings (ie accumulated profit or loss) at the beginning of the period and at the balance sheet date, and the changes during the period; and

(c) a reconciliation between the carrying amount of each class of contributed equity and each reserve at the beginning and the end of the period, separately disclosing each change.

98 Changes in an entity's equity between two balance sheet dates reflect the increase or decrease in its net assets during the period. Except for changes resulting from transactions with equity holders acting in their capacity as equity holders (such as equity contributions, reacquisitions of the entity's own equity instruments and dividends) and transaction costs directly related to such transactions, the overall change in equity during a period represents the total amount of income and expenses, including gains and losses, generated by the entity's activities during that period (whether those items of income and expenses are recognised in profit or loss or directly as changes in equity).

99 This Standard requires all items of income and expense recognised in a period to be included in profit or loss unless another Standard or an Interpretation requires

otherwise. Other Standards require some gains and losses (such as revaluation increases and decreases, particular foreign exchange differences, gains or losses on remeasuring available-for-sale financial assets, and related amounts of current tax and deferred tax) to be recognised directly as changes in equity. Because it is important to consider all items of income and expense in assessing changes in an entity's financial position between two balance sheet dates, this Standard requires the presentation of a statement of changes in equity that highlights an entity's total income and expenses, including those that are recognised directly in equity.

100 IAS 8 requires retrospective adjustments to effect changes in accounting policies, to the extent practicable, except when the transitional provisions in another Standard or an Interpretation require otherwise. IAS 8 also requires that restatements to correct errors are made retrospectively, to the extent practicable. Retrospective adjustments and retrospective restatements are made to the balance of retained earnings, except when a Standard or an Interpretation requires retrospective adjustment of another component of equity. Paragraph 96(d) requires disclosure in the statement of changes in equity of the total adjustment to each component of equity resulting, separately, from changes in accounting policies and from corrections of errors. These adjustments are disclosed for each prior period and the beginning of the period.

101 The requirements in paragraphs 96 and 97 may be met in various ways. One example is a columnar format that reconciles the opening and closing balances of each element within equity. An alternative is to present only the items set out in paragraph 96 in the statement of changes in equity. Under this approach, the items described in paragraph 97 are shown in the notes.

Cash flow statement

102 Cash flow information provides users of financial statements with a basis to assess the ability of the entity to generate cash and cash equivalents and the needs of the entity to utilise those cash flows. IAS 7 *Cash Flow Statements* sets out requirements for the presentation of the cash flow statement and related disclosures.

Notes

Structure

103 The notes shall:

(a) present information about the basis of preparation of the financial statements and the specific accounting policies used in accordance with paragraphs 108–115;

(b) disclose the information required by IFRSs that is not presented on the face of the balance sheet, income statement, statement of changes in equity or cash flow statement; and

(c) provide additional information that is not presented on the face of the balance sheet, income statement, statement of changes in equity or cash flow statement, but is relevant to an understanding of any of them.

104 **Notes shall, as far as practicable, be presented in a systematic manner. Each item on the face of the balance sheet, income statement, statement of changes in equity and cash flow statement shall be cross-referenced to any related information in the notes.**

105 Notes are normally presented in the following order, which assists users in understanding the financial statements and comparing them with financial statements of other entities:

(a) a statement of compliance with IFRSs (see paragraph 14);

(b) a summary of significant accounting policies applied (see paragraph 108);

(c) supporting information for items presented on the face of the balance sheet, income statement, statement of changes in equity and cash flow statement, in the order in which each statement and each line item is presented; and

(d) other disclosures, including:

   (i) contingent liabilities (see IAS 37) and unrecognised contractual commitments; and

   (ii) non-financial disclosures, eg the entity's financial risk management objectives and policies (see IAS 32).

106 In some circumstances, it may be necessary or desirable to vary the ordering of specific items within the notes. For example, information on changes in fair value recognised in profit or loss may be combined with information on maturities of financial instruments, although the former disclosures relate to the income statement and the latter relate to the balance sheet. Nevertheless, a systematic structure for the notes is retained as far as practicable.

107 Notes providing information about the basis of preparation of the financial statements and specific accounting policies may be presented as a separate component of the financial statements.

Disclosure of accounting policies

108 **An entity shall disclose in the summary of significant accounting policies:**

(a) the measurement basis (or bases) used in preparing the financial statements; and

(b) the other accounting policies used that are relevant to an understanding of the financial statements.

109 It is important for users to be informed of the measurement basis or bases used in the financial statements (for example, historical cost, current cost, net realisable value, fair value or recoverable amount) because the basis on which the financial statements are prepared significantly affects their analysis. When more than one measurement basis is used in the financial statements, for example when particular classes of assets are revalued, it is sufficient to provide an indication of the categories of assets and liabilities to which each measurement basis is applied.

110 In deciding whether a particular accounting policy should be disclosed, management considers whether disclosure would assist users in understanding how transactions, other events and conditions are reflected in the reported

financial performance and financial position. Disclosure of particular accounting policies is especially useful to users when those policies are selected from alternatives allowed in Standards and Interpretations. An example is disclosure of whether a venturer recognises its interest in a jointly controlled entity using proportionate consolidation or the equity method (see IAS 31 *Interests in Joint Ventures*). Some Standards specifically require disclosure of particular accounting policies, including choices made by management between different policies they allow. For example, IAS 16 requires disclosure of the measurement bases used for classes of property, plant and equipment. IAS 23 *Borrowing Costs* requires disclosure of whether borrowing costs are recognised immediately as an expense or capitalised as part of the cost of qualifying assets.

111 Each entity considers the nature of its operations and the policies that the users of its financial statements would expect to be disclosed for that type of entity. For example, an entity subject to income taxes would be expected to disclose its accounting policies for income taxes, including those applicable to deferred tax liabilities and assets. When an entity has significant foreign operations or transactions in foreign currencies, disclosure of accounting policies for the recognition of foreign exchange gains and losses would be expected. When business combinations have occurred, the policies used for measuring goodwill and minority interest are disclosed.

112 An accounting policy may be significant because of the nature of the entity's operations even if amounts for current and prior periods are not material. It is also appropriate to disclose each significant accounting policy that is not specifically required by IFRSs, but is selected and applied in accordance with IAS 8.

113 An entity shall disclose, in the summary of significant accounting policies or other notes, the judgements, apart from those involving estimations (see paragraph 116), that management has made in the process of applying the entity's accounting policies and that have the most significant effect on the amounts recognised in the financial statements.

114 In the process of applying the entity's accounting policies, management makes various judgements, apart from those involving estimations, that can significantly affect the amounts recognised in the financial statements. For example, management makes judgements in determining:

(a) whether financial assets are held-to-maturity investments;

(b) when substantially all the significant risks and rewards of ownership of financial assets and lease assets are transferred to other entities;

(c) whether, in substance, particular sales of goods are financing arrangements and therefore do not give rise to revenue; and

(d) whether the substance of the relationship between the entity and a special purpose entity indicates that the special purpose entity is controlled by the entity.

115 Some of the disclosures made in accordance with paragraph 113 are required by other Standards. For example, IAS 27 requires an entity to disclose the reasons why the entity's ownership interest does not constitute control, in respect of an investee that is not a subsidiary even though more than half of its voting or

potential voting power is owned directly or indirectly through subsidiaries. IAS 40 requires disclosure of the criteria developed by the entity to distinguish investment property from owner-occupied property and from property held for sale in the ordinary course of business, when classification of the property is difficult.

Key sources of estimation uncertainty

116 **An entity shall disclose in the notes information about the key assumptions concerning the future, and other key sources of estimation uncertainty at the balance sheet date, that have a significant risk of causing a material adjustment to the carrying amounts of assets and liabilities within the next financial year. In respect of those assets and liabilities, the notes shall include details of:**

(a) their nature; and

(b) their carrying amount as at the balance sheet date.

117 Determining the carrying amounts of some assets and liabilities requires estimation of the effects of uncertain future events on those assets and liabilities at the balance sheet date. For example, in the absence of recently observed market prices used to measure the following assets and liabilities, future-oriented estimates are necessary to measure the recoverable amount of classes of property, plant and equipment, the effect of technological obsolescence on inventories, provisions subject to the future outcome of litigation in progress, and long-term employee benefit liabilities such as pension obligations. These estimates involve assumptions about such items as the risk adjustment to cash flows or discount rates used, future changes in salaries and future changes in prices affecting other costs.

118 The key assumptions and other key sources of estimation uncertainty disclosed in accordance with paragraph 116 relate to the estimates that require management's most difficult, subjective or complex judgements. As the number of variables and assumptions affecting the possible future resolution of the uncertainties increases, those judgements become more subjective and complex, and the potential for a consequential material adjustment to the carrying amounts of assets and liabilities normally increases accordingly.

119 The disclosures in paragraph 116 are not required for assets and liabilities with a significant risk that their carrying amounts might change materially within the next financial year if, at the balance sheet date, they are measured at fair value based on recently observed market prices (their fair values might change materially within the next financial year but these changes would not arise from assumptions or other sources of estimation uncertainty at the balance sheet date).

120 The disclosures in paragraph 116 are presented in a manner that helps users of financial statements to understand the judgements management makes about the future and about other key sources of estimation uncertainty. The nature and extent of the information provided vary according to the nature of the assumption and other circumstances. Examples of the types of disclosures made are:

(a) the nature of the assumption or other estimation uncertainty;

(b) the sensitivity of carrying amounts to the methods, assumptions and estimates underlying their calculation, including the reasons for the sensitivity;

(c) the expected resolution of an uncertainty and the range of reasonably possible outcomes within the next financial year in respect of the carrying amounts of the assets and liabilities affected; and

(d) an explanation of changes made to past assumptions concerning those assets and liabilities, if the uncertainty remains unresolved.

121 It is not necessary to disclose budget information or forecasts in making the disclosures in paragraph 116.

122 When it is impracticable to disclose the extent of the possible effects of a key assumption or another key source of estimation uncertainty at the balance sheet date, the entity discloses that it is reasonably possible, based on existing knowledge, that outcomes within the next financial year that are different from assumptions could require a material adjustment to the carrying amount of the asset or liability affected. In all cases, the entity discloses the nature and carrying amount of the specific asset or liability (or class of assets or liabilities) affected by the assumption.

123 The disclosures in paragraph 113 of particular judgements management made in the process of applying the entity's accounting policies do not relate to the disclosures of key sources of estimation uncertainty in paragraph 116.

124 The disclosure of some of the key assumptions that would otherwise be required in accordance with paragraph 116 is required by other Standards. For example, IAS 37 requires disclosure, in specified circumstances, of major assumptions concerning future events affecting classes of provisions. IAS 32 requires disclosure of significant assumptions applied in estimating fair values of financial assets and financial liabilities that are carried at fair value. IAS 16 requires disclosure of significant assumptions applied in estimating fair values of revalued items of property, plant and equipment.

Other disclosures

125 An entity shall disclose in the notes:

(a) the amount of dividends proposed or declared before the financial statements were authorised for issue but not recognised as a distribution to equity holders during the period, and the related amount per share; and

(b) the amount of any cumulative preference dividends not recognised.

126 An entity shall disclose the following, if not disclosed elsewhere in information published with the financial statements:

(a) the domicile and legal form of the entity, its country of incorporation and the address of its registered office (or principal place of business, if different from the registered office);

(b) a description of the nature of the entity's operations and its principal activities; and

(c) the name of the parent and the ultimate parent of the group.

Effective date

127 **An entity shall apply this Standard for annual periods beginning on or after 1 January 2005. Earlier application is encouraged. If an entity applies this Standard for a period beginning before 1 January 2005, it shall disclose that fact.**

127A **An entity shall apply the amendment in paragraph 96 for annual periods beginning on or after 1 January 2006. If an entity applies the amendments to IAS 19** *Employee Benefits—Actuarial Gains and Losses, Group Plans and Disclosures* **for an earlier period, that amendment shall be applied for that earlier period.**

Withdrawal of IAS 1 (revised 1997)

128 This Standard supersedes IAS 1 *Presentation of Financial Statements* revised in 1997.

Appendix
Amendments to other pronouncements

The amendments in this appendix shall be applied for annual periods beginning on or after 1 January 2005. If an entity applies this Standard for an earlier period, these amendments shall be applied for that earlier period.

* * * * *

The amendments contained in this appendix when this Standard was revised in 2003 have been incorporated into the relevant pronouncements published in this volume.

Approval of IAS 1 by the Board

International Accounting Standard 1 *Presentation of Financial Statements* was approved for issue by the fourteen members of the International Accounting Standards Board.

Sir David Tweedie	Chairman
Thomas E Jones	Vice-Chairman
Mary E Barth	
Hans-Georg Bruns	
Anthony T Cope	
Robert P Garnett	
Gilbert Gélard	
James J Leisenring	
Warren J McGregor	
Patricia L O'Malley	
Harry K Schmid	
John T Smith	
Geoffrey Whittington	
Tatsumi Yamada	

Basis for Conclusions

This Basis for Conclusions accompanies, but is not part of, IAS 1.

Introduction

BC1 This Basis for Conclusions summarises the International Accounting Standards Board's considerations in reaching its conclusions on revising IAS 1 *Presentation of Financial Statements* in 2003. Individual Board members gave greater weight to some factors than to others.

BC2 In July 2001 the Board announced that, as part of its initial agenda of technical projects, it would undertake a project to improve a number of Standards, including IAS 1. The project was undertaken in the light of queries and criticisms raised in relation to the Standards by securities regulators, professional accountants and other interested parties. The objectives of the Improvements project were to reduce or eliminate alternatives, redundancies and conflicts within Standards, to deal with some convergence issues and to make other improvements. In May 2002 the Board published its proposals in an Exposure Draft of *Improvements to International Accounting Standards*, with a comment deadline of 16 September 2002. The Board received over 160 comment letters on the Exposure Draft.

BC3 Because the Board's intention was not to reconsider the fundamental approach to the presentation of financial statements established by IAS 1, this Basis for Conclusions does not discuss requirements in IAS 1 that the Board has not reconsidered. Various issues concerning the presentation of the income statement were not addressed in the Standard and Implementation Guidance because of the Board's project on reporting comprehensive income.

Departures from standards and interpretations

BC4 Paragraph 13 of the previous version of IAS 1 permitted an entity to depart from a requirement in a Standard 'in the extremely rare circumstances when management concludes that compliance with a requirement in a Standard would be misleading, and therefore that departure from a requirement is necessary to achieve a fair presentation'. When such a departure occurred, paragraph 13 required extensive disclosure of the facts and circumstances surrounding the departure and the treatment adopted.

BC5 The Board decided to clarify in paragraph 13 of the Standard that for financial statements to present fairly the financial position, financial performance and cash flows of an entity, they must represent faithfully the effects of transactions and other events in accordance with the definitions and recognition criteria for assets, liabilities, income and expenses set out in the *Framework for the Preparation and Presentation of Financial Statements*

BC6 The Board decided to limit the occasions on which an entity should depart from a requirement in a Standard or an Interpretation to the extremely rare circumstances in which management concludes that compliance with the requirement would be so misleading that it would conflict with the objective of financial statements set out in the *Framework*. Guidance on this criterion states that an item of information would conflict with the objective of financial statements when it does not represent faithfully the transactions, other events or conditions that it either purports to represent or could reasonably be expected to represent and, consequently, it would be likely to influence economic decisions made by users of financial statements.

BC7 These amendments provide a framework within which an entity assesses how to present fairly the effects of transactions, other events and conditions, and whether the result of complying with a requirement in a Standard or an Interpretation would be so misleading that it would not give a fair presentation.

BC8 The Board considered whether the Standard should be silent regarding departures from IFRSs. The Board decided against that change, noting that such a change would remove its capability to specify the criteria under which departures from IFRSs should occur.

BC9 Departing from a requirement in a Standard or an Interpretation when considered necessary to achieve a fair presentation would conflict with the regulatory framework in some jurisdictions. The revised Standard takes into account the different regulatory frameworks concerning departures from accounting standards in the various jurisdictions in which entities prepare financial statements. It requires that when an entity's circumstances satisfy the criterion described in paragraph BC6 for departure from a requirement in a Standard or an Interpretation, the entity should proceed as follows:

(a) when the relevant regulatory framework requires–or otherwise does not prohibit–a departure from the requirement, the entity is required to make that departure and the disclosures set out in paragraph 18 of the Standard; and

(b) when the relevant regulatory framework prohibits departure from the requirement, the entity is required, to the maximum extent possible, to reduce the perceived misleading aspects of compliance by making the disclosures set out in paragraph 21 of the Standard.

This amendment enables entities to comply with the requirements of the Standard when the relevant regulatory framework prohibits departures from accounting standards, while retaining the principle that entities should, to the maximum extent possible, ensure that financial statements provide a fair presentation.

BC10 After considering the comments received on the Exposure Draft, the Board added to the Standard a requirement in paragraph 19 to disclose the effect of a departure from a requirement of a Standard or an Interpretation in a prior period on the current period's financial statements. Without this disclosure, users of the entity's financial statements could be unaware of the continuing effects of prior period departures.

BC11 In view of the strict criteria for departure from a requirement in a Standard or an Interpretation, the Standard includes a rebuttable presumption that if other entities in similar circumstances comply with the requirement, the entity's compliance with the requirement would not be so misleading that it would conflict with the objective of financial statements set out in the *Framework*.

Results of operating activities

BC12 The Standard omits the requirement in the previous version to disclose the results of operating activities as a line item on the face of the income statement. 'Operating activities' are not defined in the Standard, and the Board decided not to require disclosure of an undefined item.

BC13 The Board recognises that an entity may elect to disclose the results of operating activities, or a similar line item, even though this term is not defined. In such cases, the Board notes that the entity should ensure the amount disclosed is representative of activities that would normally be considered to be 'operating'. In the Board's view, it would be misleading and would impair the comparability of financial statements if items of an operating nature were excluded from the results of operating activities, even if that had been industry practice. For example, it would be inappropriate to exclude items clearly related to operations (such as inventory write-downs and restructuring and relocation expenses) because they occur irregularly or infrequently or are unusual in amount. Similarly, it would be inappropriate to exclude items on the grounds that they do not involve cash flows, such as depreciation and amortisation expenses.

Extraordinary items

BC14 IAS 8 *Net Profit or Loss for the Period, Fundamental Errors and Changes in Accounting Policies* required extraordinary items to be disclosed on the face of the income statement separately from the profit or loss from ordinary activities (paragraph 10). Paragraph 6 of that Standard defined 'extraordinary items' as 'income or expenses that arise from events or transactions that are clearly distinct from the ordinary activities of the enterprise and therefore are not expected to recur frequently or regularly'.

BC15 The Board decided to eliminate the concept of extraordinary items from IAS 8 and to prohibit the presentation of items of income and expense as 'extraordinary items' in the income statement and the notes. Therefore, in accordance with the revised Standard, no items of income and expense are to be presented as arising from outside the entity's ordinary activities.

BC16 Some respondents to the Exposure Draft argued that extraordinary items should be presented in a separate component of the income statement because they are clearly distinct from all of the other items of income and expense, and because such presentation highlights to users of financial statements the items of income and expense to which the least attention should be given when predicting an entity's future performance.

BC17 The Board decided that items treated as extraordinary result from the normal business risks faced by an entity and do not warrant presentation in a separate component of the income statement. The nature or function of a transaction or other event, rather than its frequency, should determine its presentation within the income statement. Items currently classified as 'extraordinary' are only a subset of the items of income and expense that may warrant disclosure to assist users in predicting an entity's future performance.

BC18 Eliminating the category of extraordinary items eliminates the need for arbitrary segregation of the effects of related external events–some recurring and others not–on the profit or loss of an entity for a period. For example, arbitrary allocations would have been necessary to estimate the financial effect of an earthquake on an entity's profit or loss if it occurs during a major cyclical downturn in economic activity. In addition, paragraph 86 of the Standard requires disclosure of the nature and amount of material items of income and expense.

Minority interest

BC19 The Standard requires the 'profit or loss attributable to minority interest' and 'profit or loss attributable to equity holders of the parent' each to be presented on the face of the income statement in accordance with paragraph 82. These amounts are to be presented as allocations of profit or loss, not as items of income or expense. A similar requirement has been added for the statement of changes in equity, in paragraph 96(c) of the Standard. These changes are consistent with the revised IAS 27 *Consolidated and Separate Financial Statements*, which requires that in consolidated balance sheets, minority interest is presented within equity because it does not meet the definition of a liability in the *Framework*.

Effect of events after the balance sheet date on the classification of liabilities

BC20 Paragraph 63 of the previous version of IAS 1 included the following:

> An enterprise should continue to classify its long-term interest-bearing liabilities as non-current, even when they are due to be settled within twelve months of the balance sheet date if:
>
> (a) the original term was for a period of more than twelve months;
>
> (b) the enterprise intends to refinance the obligation on a long-term basis; and
>
> (c) that intention is supported by an agreement to refinance, or to reschedule payments, which is completed before the financial statements are authorised for issue.

BC21 Paragraph 65 of the previous version of IAS 1 stated:

> Some borrowing agreements incorporate undertakings by the borrower (covenants) which have the effect that the liability becomes payable on demand if certain conditions related to the borrower's financial position are breached. In these circumstances, the liability is classified as non-current only when:
>
> (a) the lender has agreed, prior to the authorisation of the financial statements for issue, not to demand payment as a consequence of the breach; and
>
> (b) it is not probable that further breaches will occur within twelve months of the balance sheet date.

BC22 The Board considered the requirements in paragraphs 63 and 65 and concluded that refinancing, or the receipt of a waiver of the lender's right to demand payment, that occurs after the balance sheet date should not be taken into account in the classification of a liability.

BC23 The Exposure Draft proposed the following amendments:

(a) to amend paragraph 63 to specify that a long-term financial liability due to be settled within twelve months of the balance sheet date should not be classified as a non-current liability because an agreement to refinance, or to reschedule payments, on a long-term basis is completed after the balance sheet date and before the financial statements are authorised for issue. This amendment does not affect the classification of a liability as non-current when the entity has, under the terms of an existing loan facility, the discretion to refinance or roll over its obligations for at least twelve months after the balance sheet date.

(b) to amend paragraph 65 to specify that a long-term financial liability that is payable on demand because the entity breached a condition of its loan agreement should be classified as current at the balance sheet date even if the lender has agreed after the balance sheet date, and before the financial statements are authorised for issue, not to demand payment as a consequence of the breach. However, if the lender has agreed by the balance sheet date to provide a period of grace within which the entity can rectify the breach and during which the lender cannot demand immediate repayment, the liability is classified as non-current if it is due for settlement, without that breach of the loan agreement, at least twelve months after the balance sheet date and:

(i) the entity rectifies the breach within the period of grace; or

(ii) when the financial statements are authorised for issue, the period of grace is incomplete and it is probable that the breach will be rectified.

BC24 Some respondents disagreed with these proposals. They advocated classifying a liability as current or non-current according to whether it is expected to use current assets of the entity, rather than strictly on the basis of its date of maturity and whether it is callable at the balance sheet date. In their view, this would provide more relevant information about the liability's future effect on the timing of the entity's resource flows.

BC25 However, the Board decided that the following arguments for changing paragraphs 63 and 65 of the previous version of the Standard were more persuasive:

(a) refinancing a liability after the balance sheet date does not affect the entity's liquidity and solvency *at the balance sheet date*, the reporting of which should reflect contractual arrangements in force on that date. Therefore, it is a non-adjusting event in accordance with IAS 10 *Events after the Balance Sheet Date* and should not affect the presentation of the entity's balance sheet.

(b) it is illogical to adopt a criterion that 'non-current' classification of short-term obligations expected to be rolled over for at least twelve months after the balance sheet date depends on whether the roll-over is at the discretion of the entity, and then to provide an exception based on refinancing occurring after the balance sheet date.

(c) in the circumstances set out in paragraph 65, unless the lender has waived its right to demand immediate repayment or granted a period of grace within which the entity may rectify the breach of the loan agreement, the financial condition of the entity at the balance sheet date was that the entity did not hold an absolute right to defer repayment, based on the terms of the loan agreement. The granting of a waiver or a period of grace changes the terms of the loan agreement. Therefore, an entity's receipt from the lender, after the balance sheet date, of a waiver or a period of grace of at least twelve months does not change the nature of the liability to non-current until it occurs.

BC26 The revised Standard includes the amendments proposed in the Exposure Draft, with one change. The change relates to the classification of a long-term loan when, at the balance sheet date, the lender has provided a period of grace within which a breach of the loan agreement can be rectified, and during which period the lender cannot demand immediate repayment of the loan.

BC27 The Exposure Draft proposed that such a loan should be classified as non-current if it is due for settlement, without the breach, at least twelve months after the balance sheet date and:

(a) the entity rectifies the breach within the period of grace; or

(b) when the financial statements are authorised for issue, the period of grace is incomplete and it is probable that the breach will be rectified.

BC28 After considering the comments received on the Exposure Draft, the Board decided that the occurrence or probability of a rectification of a breach after the balance sheet date is irrelevant to the conditions existing at the balance sheet date. The revised Standard requires that, for the loan to be classified as non-current, the period of grace must end at least twelve months after the balance sheet date (see paragraph 66). Therefore, conditions (a) and (b) in paragraph BC27 are redundant.

BC29 The Board considered arguments that if a period of grace to remedy a breach of a long-term loan agreement is provided before the balance sheet date, the loan should be classified as non-current regardless of the length of the period of grace. These arguments are based on the view that, at the balance sheet date, the lender does not have an unconditional legal right to demand repayment before the original maturity date (ie if the entity remedies the breach during the period of grace, it is entitled to repay the loan on the original maturity date). However, the Board concluded that an entity should classify a loan as non-current only if it has an unconditional right to defer settlement of the loan for at least twelve months after the balance sheet date. This criterion focuses on the legal rights of the entity, rather than those of the lender.

Disclosure of the judgements management has made in the process of applying the entity's accounting policies

BC30 The revised Standard requires disclosure of the judgements, apart from those involving estimations, management has made in the process of applying the entity's accounting policies that have the most significant effect on the amounts recognised in the financial statements (see paragraph 113). An example of these judgements is how management determines whether financial assets are held-to-maturity investments. The Board decided that disclosure of the most important of these judgements would enable users of financial statements to understand better how the accounting policies are applied and to make comparisons between entities regarding the basis on which managements make these judgements.

BC31 Comments received on the Exposure Draft indicated that the purpose of the proposed disclosure was unclear. Accordingly, the Board amended the disclosure explicitly to exclude judgements involving estimations (which are the subject of the disclosure in paragraph 116 of the revised Standard) and added another four examples of the types of judgements disclosed (see paragraphs 114 and 115).

Disclosure of key sources of estimation uncertainty

BC32 The revised Standard requires disclosure of the key assumptions concerning the future, and other key sources of estimation uncertainty at the balance sheet date, that have a significant risk of causing a material adjustment to the carrying amounts of assets and liabilities within the next financial year. For those assets and liabilities, the proposed disclosures include details of:

(a) their nature; and

(b) their carrying amount as at the balance sheet date (see paragraph 116).

BC33 Determining the carrying amounts of some assets and liabilities requires estimation of the effects of uncertain future events on those assets and liabilities at the balance sheet date. For example, in the absence of recently observed market prices used to measure the following assets and liabilities, future-oriented estimates are necessary to measure the recoverable amount of classes of property, plant and equipment, the effect of technological obsolescence of inventories, provisions subject to the future outcome of litigation in progress, and long-term employee benefit liabilities such as pension obligations. These estimates involve assumptions about such items as the risk adjustment to cash flows or discount rates used, future changes in salaries and future changes in prices affecting other costs. No matter how diligently an entity estimates the carrying amounts of assets and liabilities subject to significant estimation uncertainty at the balance sheet date, the reporting of point estimates in the balance sheet cannot provide information about the estimation uncertainties involved in measuring those assets and liabilities and the implications of those uncertainties for the period's profit or loss.

BC34 The *Framework* states that 'The economic decisions that are taken by users of financial statements require an evaluation of the ability of an enterprise to generate cash and cash equivalents and of the timing and certainty of their generation.' The Board decided that disclosure of information about key assumptions and other key sources of estimation uncertainty at the balance sheet date enhances the relevance, reliability and understandability of the information reported in financial statements. These key assumptions and other key sources of estimation uncertainty relate to estimates that require management's most difficult, subjective or complex judgements. Therefore, disclosure in accordance with paragraph 116 of the revised Standard would be made in respect of relatively few assets or liabilities (or classes of them).

BC35 The Exposure Draft proposed the disclosure of some 'sources of measurement uncertainty'. In the light of comments received that the purpose of this disclosure was unclear, the Board decided:

(a) to amend the subject of that disclosure to 'sources of estimation uncertainty at the balance sheet date'; and

(b) to clarify in the revised Standard that the disclosure does not apply to assets and liabilities measured at fair value based on recently observed market prices (see paragraph 119 of the Standard).

BC36 When assets and liabilities are measured at fair value on the basis of recently observed market prices, future changes in carrying amounts would not result from using estimates to measure the assets and liabilities at the balance sheet date. Using observed market prices to measure assets or liabilities obviates the need for estimates at the balance sheet date. The market prices properly reflect the fair values at the balance sheet date, even though future market prices could be different. The objective of fair value measurement is to reflect fair value at the measurement date, not to predict a future value.

BC37 The revised Standard does not prescribe the particular form or detail of the disclosures. Circumstances differ from entity to entity, and the nature of estimation uncertainty at the balance sheet date has many facets. The revised Standard limits the scope of the disclosures to items that have a significant risk of causing a material adjustment to the carrying amounts of assets and liabilities *within the next financial year.* The longer the future period to which the disclosures relate, the greater the range of items that would qualify for disclosure, and the less specific the disclosures that could be made about particular assets or liabilities. A period longer than the next financial year might obscure the most relevant information with other disclosures.

Criterion for exemption from requirements

BC38 The previous version of IAS 1 specified that when the presentation or classification of items in the financial statements is amended, comparative amounts should be reclassified unless it is impracticable to do so (paragraph 40). Applying a requirement is impracticable when the entity cannot apply it after making every reasonable effort to do so.

BC39 The Exposure Draft proposed a different criterion for exemption from particular requirements. For the reclassification of comparative amounts, and its proposed new requirement to disclose key assumptions and other sources of estimation uncertainty at the balance sheet date (discussed in paragraphs BC32–BC37), the Exposure Draft proposed that the criterion for exemption should be that applying the requirements would give rise to undue cost or effort.

BC40 In the light of comments received on the Exposure Draft, the Board decided that an exemption based on management's assessment of undue cost or effort is too subjective to be applied consistently by different entities. Moreover, the Board decided that balancing costs and benefits is a task for the Board when it sets accounting requirements rather than for entities when they apply those requirements. Therefore, the Board decided to retain the 'impracticability' criterion for exemption set out in the previous version of IAS 1. This affects the exemptions set out in paragraphs 38–40 and 122 of the revised Standard. Impracticability is the only basis on which specific exemptions are provided in Standards and Interpretations from applying particular requirements when the effect of applying them is material.

Guidance on Implementing IAS 1

This guidance accompanies, but is not part of, IAS 1.

Illustrative financial statement structure

IG1 The Standard sets out the components of financial statements and minimum requirements for disclosure on the face of the balance sheet and the income statement as well as for the presentation of changes in equity. It also describes further items that may be presented either on the face of the relevant financial statement or in the notes. This guidance provides simple examples of ways in which the requirements of the Standard for the presentation of the balance sheet, income statement and changes in equity might be met. The order of presentation and the descriptions used for line items should be changed when necessary in order to achieve a fair presentation in each entity's particular circumstances.

IG2 The illustrative balance sheet shows one way in which a balance sheet distinguishing between current and non-current items may be presented. Other formats may be equally appropriate, provided the distinction is clear.

IG3 Two income statements are provided, to illustrate the alternative classifications of income and expenses, by nature and by function. Two possible approaches to presenting changes in equity are also illustrated.

IG4 The examples are not intended to illustrate all aspects of IFRSs. Nor do they comprise a complete set of financial statements, which would also include a cash flow statement, a summary of significant accounting policies and other explanatory notes.

XYZ Group – Balance sheet as at 31 December 20X2

(in thousands of currency units)

	20X2	**20X1**
ASSETS		
Non–current assets		
Property, plant and equipment	X	X
Goodwill	X	X
Other intangible assets	X	X
Investments in associates	X	X
Available–for–sale investments	X	X
	X	X
Current assets		
Inventories	X	X
Trade receivables	X	X
Other current assets	X	X
Cash and cash equivalents	X	X
	X	X
Total assets	X	X

Continued from previous page

XYZ Group – Balance sheet as at 31 December 20X2

(in thousands of currency units)

	20X2	20X1
EQUITY AND LIABILITIES		
Equity attributable to equity holders of the parent		
Share capital	X	X
Other reserves	X	X
Retained earnings	X	X
	X	X
Minority interest	X	X
Total equity	X	X
Non–current liabilities		
Long–term borrowings	X	X
Deferred tax	X	X
Long–term provisions	X	X
Total non–current liabilities	X	X
Current liabilities		
Trade and other payables	X	X
Short–term borrowings	X	X
Current portion of long–term borrowings	X	X
Current tax payable	X	X
Short–term provisions	X	X
Total current liabilities	X	X
Total liabilities	X	X
Total equity and liabilities	X	X

XYZ Group – Income statement for the year ended 31 December 20X2

(illustrating the classification of expenses by function)

(in thousands of currency units)

	20X2	**20X1**
Revenue	X	X
Cost of sales	(X)	(X)
Gross profit	X	X
Other income	X	X
Distribution costs	(X)	(X)
Administrative expenses	(X)	(X)
Other expenses	(X)	(X)
Finance costs	(X)	(X)
Share of profit of associates[(a)]	X	X
Profit before tax	X	X
Income tax expense	(X)	(X)
Profit for the period	X	X
Attributable to:		
Equity holders of the parent	X	X
Minority interest	X	X
	X	X

(a) This means the share of associates' profit attributable to equity holders of the associates, ie it is after tax and minority interests in the associates.

XYZ Group – Income statement for the year ended 31 December 20X2

(illustrating the classification of expenses by nature)

(in thousands of currency units)

	20X2	**20X1**
Revenue	X	X
Other income	X	X
Changes in inventories of finished goods and work in progress	(X)	X
Work performed by the entity and capitalised	X	X
Raw material and consumables used	(X)	(X)
Employee benefits expense	(X)	(X)
Depreciation and amortisation expense	(X)	(X)
Impairment of property, plant and equipment[(a)]	(X)	(X)
Other expenses	(X)	(X)
Finance costs	(X)	(X)
Share of profit of associates	X	X
Profit before tax	X	X
Income tax expense	(X)	(X)
Profit for the period	X	X
Attributable to:		
Equity holders of the parent	X	X
Minority interest	X	X
	X	X

(a) In an income statement in which expenses are classified by nature, an impairment of property, plant and equipment is shown as a separate line item. By contrast, if expenses are classified by function, the impairment is included in the function(s) to which it relates

XYZ Group – Statement of changes in equity for the year ended 31 December 20X2

(in thousands of currency units)

	Attributable to equity holders of the parent					Minority interest	Total equity
	Share capital	Other reserves[a]	Translation reserve	Retained earnings	Total		
Balance at 31 December 20X0	X	X	(X)	X	X	X	X
Changes in accounting policy	–	–	–	(X)	(X)	(X)	(X)
Restated balance	X	X	(X)	X	X	X	X
Changes in equity for 20X1							
Gain on property revaluation		X			X	X	X
Available–for–sale investments:							
Valuation gains/(losses) taken to equity		(X)			(X)		(X)
Transferred to profit or loss on sale		(X)			(X)		(X)
Cash flow hedges:							
Gains/(losses) taken to equity		X			X	X	X
Transferred to profit or loss for the period		X			X	X	X
Transferred to initial carrying amount of hedged items		(X)			(X)		(X)
Exchange differences on translating foreign operations			(X)		(X)	(X)	(X)
Tax on items taken directly to or transferred from equity	–	(X)	X	–	(X)	(X)	(X)
Net income recognised directly in equity		X	(X)		X	X	X
Profit for the period	–	–	–	X	X	X	X
Total recognised income and expense for the period		X	(X)	X	X	X	X
Dividends				(X)	(X)	(X)	(X)
Issue of share capital	X				X		X
Equity share options issued	–	X	–	–	X	–	X
Balance at 31 December 20X1 carried forward	X	X	(X)	X	X	X	X

Continued from previous page

XYZ Group – Statement of changes in equity for the year ended 31 December 20X2

(in thousands of currency units)

	Attributable to equity holders of the parent					Minority interest	Total equity
	Share capital	Other reserves[a]	Translation reserve	Retained earnings	Total		
Balance at 31 December 20X1 brought forward	X	X	(X)	X	X	X	X
Changes in equity for 20X2							
Loss on property revaluation		(X)			(X)	(X)	(X)
Available–for–sale investments:							
Valuation gains/(losses) taken to equity		(X)			(X)		(X)
Transferred to profit or loss on sale		X			X		X
Cash flow hedges:							
Gains/(losses) taken to equity		X			X	X	X
Transferred to profit or loss for the period		(X)			(X)	(X)	(X)
Transferred to initial carrying amount of hedged items		(X)			(X)		(X)
Exchange differences on translating foreign operations			(X)		(X)	(X)	(X)
Tax on items taken directly to or transferred from equity	–	X	X	–	X	X	X
Net income recognised directly in equity		(X)	(X)		(X)	(X)	(X)
Profit for the period	–	–	–	X	X	X	X
Total recognised income and expense for the period		(X)	(X)	X	X	X	X
Dividends				(X)	(X)	(X)	(X)
Issue of share capital	X	–	–	–	X	–	X
Balance at 31 December 20X2	X	X	(X)	X	X	X	X

(a) Other reserves are analysed into their components, if material

An alternative method of presenting changes in equity is illustrated on the following page.

XYZ Group – Statement of recognised income and expense for the year ended 31 December 20X2

(in thousands of currency units)

	20X2	20X1
Gain/(loss) on revaluation of properties	(X)	X
Available–for–sale investments:		
Valuation gains/(losses) taken to equity	(X)	(X)
Transferred to profit or loss on sale	X	(X)
Cash flow hedges:		
Gains/(losses) taken to equity	X	X
Transferred to profit or loss for the period	(X)	X
Transferred to the initial carrying amount of hedged items	(X)	(X)
Exchange differences on translation of foreign operations	(X)	(X)
Actuarial gains (losses) on defined benefit plans	X	(X)
Tax on items taken directly to or transferred from equity	X	(X)
Net income recognised directly in equity	(X)	X
Profit for the period	X	X
Total recognised income and expense for the period	X	X
Attributable to:		
Equity holders of the parent	X	X
Minority interest	X	X
	X	X
Effect of changes in accounting policy:		
Equity holders of the parent		(X)
Minority interest		(X)
		(X)

The above example illustrates an approach that presents changes in equity representing income and expense in a separate component of the financial statements. Under this approach, a reconciliation of opening and closing balances of share capital, reserves and accumulated profit, as illustrated on the previous page, is given in the notes.

Table of Concordance

This table shows how the contents of the superseded version of IAS 1 and the current version of IAS 1 correspond. Paragraphs are treated as corresponding if they broadly address the same matter even though the guidance may differ.

Superseded IAS 1 paragraph	Current IAS 1 paragraph	Superseded IAS 1 paragraph	Current IAS 1 paragraph	Superseded IAS 1 paragraph	Current IAS 1 paragraph
Objective	1	29	29	58	58
1	2	30	30	59	59
2	3	31	None	60	60
3	4	32	31	61	61
4	5	33	32	62	62
5	7	34	32	63	63
6	None	35	33	64	64
7	8	36	34	65	65, 66
8	9	37	35	66	68
9	10	38	36	67	69
10	13	39	37	68	71
11	14	40	38, 39	69	None
12	16	41	40, 41	70	72
13	17, 18	42	42	71	73
14	None	43	43	72	74
15	15	44	44	73	75
16	None	45	45	74	76, 77, 125
17	22	46	46	75	81–83
18	None	47	47	76	84
19	None	48	48	77	88
20	IAS 8.7–10	49	49	78	89
21	IAS 8.5	50	None	79	90
22	IAS 8.11, 12	51	50	80	91
23	23	52	None	81	None
24	24	53	51	82	92
25	25	54	52	83	93
26	26	55	53	84	94
27	27	56	56	85	95
28	28	57	57	86	96, 97

Superseded IAS 1 paragraph	Current IAS 1 paragraph
87	98
88	99
89	101
90	102
91	103
92	104
93	None
94	105
95	106
96	107
97	108
98	109
99	110

Superseded IAS 1 paragraph	Current IAS 1 paragraph
100	111
101	112
102	126
103	127
104	128
Appendix A	Guidance on Implementing IAS 1
None	6
None	11, 12
None	19–21
None	54, 55
None	67
None	68 A

Superseded IAS 1 paragraph	Current IAS 1 paragraph
None	70[(a)]
None	78–80[(b)]
None	85[(c)]
None	86, 87[(d)]
None	100
None	113–124

(a) Formerly in IAS 12, paragraph 70

(b) Formerly in IAS 8, paragraphs 7–9

(c) Replaces IAS 8, paragraph 10

(d) Formerly in IAS 8, paragraphs 16 and 18

International Accounting Standard 2

Inventories

This version includes amendments resulting from new and amended IFRSs issued up to 31 December 2004.

CONTENTS

International Accounting Standard 2 *Inventories* (IAS 2) is set out in paragraphs 1–42 and the Appendix. All the paragraphs have equal authority but retain the IASC format of the Standard when it was adopted by the IASB. IAS 2 should be read in the context of its objective and the Basis for Conclusions, the *Preface to International Financial Reporting Standards* and the *Framework for the Preparation and Presentation of Financial Statements.* IAS 8 *Accounting Policies, Changes in Accounting Estimates and Errors* provides a basis for selecting and applying accounting policies in the absence of explicit guidance.

Introduction

IN1 International Accounting Standard 2 *Inventories* (IAS 2) replaces IAS 2 *Inventories* (revised in 1993) and should be applied for annual periods beginning on or after 1 January 2005. Earlier application is encouraged. The Standard also supersedes SIC-1 *Consistency–Different Cost Formulas for Inventories.*

Reasons for revising IAS 2

IN2 The International Accounting Standards Board developed this revised IAS 2 as part of its project on Improvements to International Accounting Standards. The project was undertaken in the light of queries and criticisms raised in relation to the Standards by securities regulators, professional accountants and other interested parties. The objectives of the project were to reduce or eliminate alternatives, redundancies and conflicts within the Standards, to deal with some convergence issues and to make other improvements.

IN3 For IAS 2 the Board's main objective was a limited revision to reduce alternatives for the measurement of inventories. The Board did not reconsider the fundamental approach to accounting for inventories contained in IAS 2.

The main changes

IN4 The main changes from the previous version of IAS 2 are described below.

Objective and scope

IN5 The objective and scope paragraphs of IAS 2 were amended by removing the words 'held under the historical cost system', to clarify that the Standard applies to all inventories that are not specifically excluded from its scope.

Scope clarification

IN6 The Standard clarifies that some types of inventories are outside its scope while certain other types of inventories are exempted only from the measurement requirements in the Standard.

IN7 Paragraph 3 establishes a clear distinction between those inventories that are entirely outside the scope of the Standard (described in paragraph 2) and those inventories that are outside the scope of the measurement requirements but within the scope of the other requirements in the Standard.

Scope exemptions

Producers of agricultural and forest products, agricultural produce after harvest and minerals and mineral products

IN8 The Standard does not apply to the measurement of inventories of producers of agricultural and forest products, agricultural produce after harvest, and minerals and mineral products, to the extent that they are measured at net realisable value in accordance with well-established industry practices. The previous version of

IAS 2 was amended to replace the words 'mineral ores' with 'minerals and mineral products' to clarify that the scope exemption is not limited to the early stage of extraction of mineral ores.

Inventories of commodity broker–traders

IN9 The Standard does not apply to the measurement of inventories of commodity broker-traders to the extent that they are measured at fair value less costs to sell.

Cost of inventories

Costs of purchase

IN10 IAS 2 does not permit exchange differences arising directly on the recent acquisition of inventories invoiced in a foreign currency to be included in the costs of purchase of inventories. This change from the previous version of IAS 2 resulted from the elimination of the allowed alternative treatment of capitalising certain exchange differences in IAS 21 *The Effects of Changes in Foreign Exchange Rates*. That alternative had already been largely restricted in its application by SIC-11 *Foreign Exchange—Capitalisation of Losses from Severe Currency Devaluations*. SIC-11 has been superseded as a result of the revision of IAS 21 in 2003.

Other costs

IN11 Paragraph 18 was inserted to clarify that when inventories are purchased with deferred settlement terms, the difference between the purchase price for normal credit terms and the amount paid is recognised as interest expense over the period of financing.

Cost formulas

Consistency

IN12 The Standard incorporates the requirements of SIC-1 *Consistency—Different Cost Formulas for Inventories* that an entity use the same cost formula for all inventories having a similar nature and use to the entity. SIC-1 is superseded.

Prohibition of LIFO as a cost formula

IN13 The Standard does not permit the use of the last-in, first-out (LIFO) formula to measure the cost of inventories.

Recognition as an expense

IN14 The Standard eliminates the reference to the matching principle.

IN15 The Standard describes the circumstances that would trigger a reversal of a write-down of inventories recognised in a prior period.

Disclosure

Inventories carried at fair value less costs to sell

IN16 The Standard requires disclosure of the carrying amount of inventories carried at fair value less costs to sell.

Write–down of inventories

IN17 The Standard requires disclosure of the amount of any write-down of inventories recognised as an expense in the period and eliminates the requirement to disclose the amount of inventories carried at net realisable value.

International Accounting Standard 2 Inventories

Objective

1 The objective of this Standard is to prescribe the accounting treatment for inventories. A primary issue in accounting for inventories is the amount of cost to be recognised as an asset and carried forward until the related revenues are recognised. This Standard provides guidance on the determination of cost and its subsequent recognition as an expense, including any write-down to net realisable value. It also provides guidance on the cost formulas that are used to assign costs to inventories.

Scope

2 **This Standard applies to all inventories, except:**

(a) **work in progress arising under construction contracts, including directly related service contracts (see IAS 11** *Construction Contracts***);**

(b) **financial instruments; and**

(c) **biological assets related to agricultural activity and agricultural produce at the point of harvest (see IAS 41** *Agriculture***).**

3 **This Standard does not apply to the measurement of inventories held by:**

(a) **producers of agricultural and forest products, agricultural produce after harvest, and minerals and mineral products, to the extent that they are measured at net realisable value in accordance with well-established practices in those industries. When such inventories are measured at net realisable value, changes in that value are recognised in profit or loss in the period of the change.**

(b) **commodity broker-traders who measure their inventories at fair value less costs to sell. When such inventories are measured at fair value less costs to sell, changes in fair value less costs to sell are recognised in profit or loss in the period of the change.**

4 The inventories referred to in paragraph 3(a) are measured at net realisable value at certain stages of production. This occurs, for example, when agricultural crops have been harvested or minerals have been extracted and sale is assured under a forward contract or a government guarantee, or when an active market exists and there is a negligible risk of failure to sell. These inventories are excluded from only the measurement requirements of this Standard.

5 Broker-traders are those who buy or sell commodities for others or on their own account. The inventories referred to in paragraph 3(b) are principally acquired with the purpose of selling in the near future and generating a profit from fluctuations in price or broker-traders' margin. When these inventories are measured at fair value less costs to sell, they are excluded from only the measurement requirements of this Standard.

Definitions

6 **The following terms are used in this Standard with the meanings specified:**

Inventories **are assets:**

(a) held for sale in the ordinary course of business;

(b) in the process of production for such sale; or

(c) in the form of materials or supplies to be consumed in the production process or in the rendering of services.

Net realisable value **is the estimated selling price in the ordinary course of business less the estimated costs of completion and the estimated costs necessary to make the sale.**

Fair value **is the amount for which an asset could be exchanged, or a liability settled, between knowledgeable, willing parties in an arm's length transaction.**

7 Net realisable value refers to the net amount that an entity expects to realise from the sale of inventory in the ordinary course of business. Fair value reflects the amount for which the same inventory could be exchanged between knowledgeable and willing buyers and sellers in the marketplace. The former is an entity-specific value; the latter is not. Net realisable value for inventories may not equal fair value less costs to sell.

8 Inventories encompass goods purchased and held for resale including, for example, merchandise purchased by a retailer and held for resale, or land and other property held for resale. Inventories also encompass finished goods produced, or work in progress being produced, by the entity and include materials and supplies awaiting use in the production process. In the case of a service provider, inventories include the costs of the service, as described in paragraph 19, for which the entity has not yet recognised the related revenue (see IAS 18 *Revenue*).

Measurement of inventories

9 **Inventories shall be measured at the lower of cost and net realisable value.**

Cost of inventories

10 **The cost of inventories shall comprise all costs of purchase, costs of conversion and other costs incurred in bringing the inventories to their present location and condition.**

Costs of purchase

11 The costs of purchase of inventories comprise the purchase price, import duties and other taxes (other than those subsequently recoverable by the entity from the taxing authorities), and transport, handling and other costs directly attributable to the acquisition of finished goods, materials and services. Trade discounts, rebates and other similar items are deducted in determining the costs of purchase.

Costs of conversion

12 The costs of conversion of inventories include costs directly related to the units of production, such as direct labour. They also include a systematic allocation of fixed and variable production overheads that are incurred in converting materials into finished goods. Fixed production overheads are those indirect costs of production that remain relatively constant regardless of the volume of production, such as depreciation and maintenance of factory buildings and equipment, and the cost of factory management and administration. Variable production overheads are those indirect costs of production that vary directly, or nearly directly, with the volume of production, such as indirect materials and indirect labour.

13 The allocation of fixed production overheads to the costs of conversion is based on the normal capacity of the production facilities. Normal capacity is the production expected to be achieved on average over a number of periods or seasons under normal circumstances, taking into account the loss of capacity resulting from planned maintenance. The actual level of production may be used if it approximates normal capacity. The amount of fixed overhead allocated to each unit of production is not increased as a consequence of low production or idle plant. Unallocated overheads are recognised as an expense in the period in which they are incurred. In periods of abnormally high production, the amount of fixed overhead allocated to each unit of production is decreased so that inventories are not measured above cost. Variable production overheads are allocated to each unit of production on the basis of the actual use of the production facilities.

14 A production process may result in more than one product being produced simultaneously. This is the case, for example, when joint products are produced or when there is a main product and a by-product. When the costs of conversion of each product are not separately identifiable, they are allocated between the products on a rational and consistent basis. The allocation may be based, for example, on the relative sales value of each product either at the stage in the production process when the products become separately identifiable, or at the completion of production. Most by-products, by their nature, are immaterial. When this is the case, they are often measured at net realisable value and this value is deducted from the cost of the main product. As a result, the carrying amount of the main product is not materially different from its cost.

Other costs

15 Other costs are included in the cost of inventories only to the extent that they are incurred in bringing the inventories to their present location and condition. For example, it may be appropriate to include non-production overheads or the costs of designing products for specific customers in the cost of inventories.

16 Examples of costs excluded from the cost of inventories and recognised as expenses in the period in which they are incurred are:

(a) abnormal amounts of wasted materials, labour or other production costs;

(b) storage costs, unless those costs are necessary in the production process before a further production stage;

(c) administrative overheads that do not contribute to bringing inventories to their present location and condition; and

(d) selling costs.

17 IAS 23 *Borrowing Costs* identifies limited circumstances where borrowing costs are included in the cost of inventories.

18 An entity may purchase inventories on deferred settlement terms. When the arrangement effectively contains a financing element, that element, for example a difference between the purchase price for normal credit terms and the amount paid, is recognised as interest expense over the period of the financing.

Cost of inventories of a service provider

19 To the extent that service providers have inventories, they measure them at the costs of their production. These costs consist primarily of the labour and other costs of personnel directly engaged in providing the service, including supervisory personnel, and attributable overheads. Labour and other costs relating to sales and general administrative personnel are not included but are recognised as expenses in the period in which they are incurred. The cost of inventories of a service provider does not include profit margins or non-attributable overheads that are often factored into prices charged by service providers.

Cost of agricultural produce harvested from biological assets

20 In accordance with IAS 41 *Agriculture* inventories comprising agricultural produce that an entity has harvested from its biological assets are measured on initial recognition at their fair value less estimated point-of-sale costs at the point of harvest. This is the cost of the inventories at that date for application of this Standard.

Techniques for the measurement of cost

21 Techniques for the measurement of the cost of inventories, such as the standard cost method or the retail method, may be used for convenience if the results approximate cost. Standard costs take into account normal levels of materials and supplies, labour, efficiency and capacity utilisation. They are regularly reviewed and, if necessary, revised in the light of current conditions.

22 The retail method is often used in the retail industry for measuring inventories of large numbers of rapidly changing items with similar margins for which it is impracticable to use other costing methods. The cost of the inventory is determined by reducing the sales value of the inventory by the appropriate percentage gross margin. The percentage used takes into consideration inventory that has been marked down to below its original selling price. An average percentage for each retail department is often used.

Cost formulas

23 The cost of inventories of items that are not ordinarily interchangeable and goods or services produced and segregated for specific projects shall be assigned by using specific identification of their individual costs.

24 Specific identification of cost means that specific costs are attributed to identified items of inventory. This is the appropriate treatment for items that are segregated for a specific project, regardless of whether they have been bought or produced. However, specific identification of costs is inappropriate when there are large numbers of items of inventory that are ordinarily interchangeable. In such circumstances, the method of selecting those items that remain in inventories could be used to obtain predetermined effects on profit or loss.

25 The cost of inventories, other than those dealt with in paragraph 23, shall be assigned by using the first-in, first-out (FIFO) or weighted average cost formula. An entity shall use the same cost formula for all inventories having a similar nature and use to the entity. For inventories with a different nature or use, different cost formulas may be justified.

26 For example, inventories used in one business segment may have a use to the entity different from the same type of inventories used in another business segment. However, a difference in geographical location of inventories (or in the respective tax rules), by itself, is not sufficient to justify the use of different cost formulas.

27 The FIFO formula assumes that the items of inventory that were purchased or produced first are sold first, and consequently the items remaining in inventory at the end of the period are those most recently purchased or produced. Under the weighted average cost formula, the cost of each item is determined from the weighted average of the cost of similar items at the beginning of a period and the cost of similar items purchased or produced during the period. The average may be calculated on a periodic basis, or as each additional shipment is received, depending upon the circumstances of the entity.

Net realisable value

28 The cost of inventories may not be recoverable if those inventories are damaged, if they have become wholly or partially obsolete, or if their selling prices have declined. The cost of inventories may also not be recoverable if the estimated costs of completion or the estimated costs to be incurred to make the sale have increased. The practice of writing inventories down below cost to net realisable value is consistent with the view that assets should not be carried in excess of amounts expected to be realised from their sale or use.

29 Inventories are usually written down to net realisable value item by item. In some circumstances, however, it may be appropriate to group similar or related items. This may be the case with items of inventory relating to the same product line that have similar purposes or end uses, are produced and marketed in the same geographical area, and cannot be practicably evaluated separately from other items in that product line. It is not appropriate to write inventories down on the basis of a classification of inventory, for example, finished goods, or all the inventories in a particular industry or geographical segment. Service providers generally accumulate costs in respect of each service for which a separate selling price is charged. Therefore, each such service is treated as a separate item.

30 Estimates of net realisable value are based on the most reliable evidence available at the time the estimates are made, of the amount the inventories are expected to

realise. These estimates take into consideration fluctuations of price or cost directly relating to events occurring after the end of the period to the extent that such events confirm conditions existing at the end of the period.

31 Estimates of net realisable value also take into consideration the purpose for which the inventory is held. For example, the net realisable value of the quantity of inventory held to satisfy firm sales or service contracts is based on the contract price. If the sales contracts are for less than the inventory quantities held, the net realisable value of the excess is based on general selling prices. Provisions may arise from firm sales contracts in excess of inventory quantities held or from firm purchase contracts. Such provisions are dealt with under IAS 37 *Provisions, Contingent Liabilities and Contingent Assets*.

32 Materials and other supplies held for use in the production of inventories are not written down below cost if the finished products in which they will be incorporated are expected to be sold at or above cost. However, when a decline in the price of materials indicates that the cost of the finished products exceeds net realisable value, the materials are written down to net realisable value. In such circumstances, the replacement cost of the materials may be the best available measure of their net realisable value.

33 A new assessment is made of net realisable value in each subsequent period. When the circumstances that previously caused inventories to be written down below cost no longer exist or when there is clear evidence of an increase in net realisable value because of changed economic circumstances, the amount of the write-down is reversed (ie the reversal is limited to the amount of the original write-down) so that the new carrying amount is the lower of the cost and the revised net realisable value. This occurs, for example, when an item of inventory that is carried at net realisable value, because its selling price has declined, is still on hand in a subsequent period and its selling price has increased.

Recognition as an expense

34 When inventories are sold, the carrying amount of those inventories shall be recognised as an expense in the period in which the related revenue is recognised. The amount of any write-down of inventories to net realisable value and all losses of inventories shall be recognised as an expense in the period the write-down or loss occurs. The amount of any reversal of any write-down of inventories, arising from an increase in net realisable value, shall be recognised as a reduction in the amount of inventories recognised as an expense in the period in which the reversal occurs.

35 Some inventories may be allocated to other asset accounts, for example, inventory used as a component of self-constructed property, plant or equipment. Inventories allocated to another asset in this way are recognised as an expense during the useful life of that asset.

Disclosure

36 The financial statements shall disclose:

(a) the accounting policies adopted in measuring inventories, including the cost formula used;

(b) the total carrying amount of inventories and the carrying amount in classifications appropriate to the entity;

(c) the carrying amount of inventories carried at fair value less costs to sell;

(d) the amount of inventories recognised as an expense during the period;

(e) the amount of any write-down of inventories recognised as an expense in the period in accordance with paragraph 34;

(f) the amount of any reversal of any write-down that is recognised as a reduction in the amount of inventories recognised as expense in the period in accordance with paragraph 34;

(g) the circumstances or events that led to the reversal of a write-down of inventories in accordance with paragraph 34; and

(h) the carrying amount of inventories pledged as security for liabilities.

37 Information about the carrying amounts held in different classifications of inventories and the extent of the changes in these assets is useful to financial statement users. Common classifications of inventories are merchandise, production supplies, materials, work in progress and finished goods. The inventories of a service provider may be described as work in progress.

38 The amount of inventories recognised as an expense during the period, which is often referred to as cost of sales, consists of those costs previously included in the measurement of inventory that has now been sold and unallocated production overheads and abnormal amounts of production costs of inventories. The circumstances of the entity may also warrant the inclusion of other amounts, such as distribution costs.

39 Some entities adopt a format for profit or loss that results in amounts being disclosed other than the cost of inventories recognised as an expense during the period. Under this format, an entity presents an analysis of expenses using a classification based on the nature of expenses. In this case, the entity discloses the costs recognised as an expense for raw materials and consumables, labour costs and other costs together with the amount of the net change in inventories for the period.

Effective date

40 An entity shall apply this Standard for annual periods beginning on or after 1 January 2005. Earlier application is encouraged. If an entity applies this Standard for a period beginning before 1 January 2005, it shall disclose that fact.

Withdrawal of other pronouncements

41 This Standard supersedes IAS 2 *Inventories* (revised in 1993).

42 This Standard supersedes SIC-1 *Consistency—Different Cost Formulas for Inventories*.

Appendix
Amendments to other pronouncements

The amendments in this appendix shall be applied for annual periods beginning on or after 1 January 2005. If an entity applies this Standard for an earlier period, these amendments shall be applied for that earlier period

* * * * *

The amendments contained in this appendix when this Standard was revised in 2003 have been incorporated into the relevant pronouncements published in this volume.

Approval of IAS 2 by the Board

International Accounting Standard 2 *Inventories* was approved for issue by the fourteen members of the International Accounting Standards Board.

Sir David Tweedie	Chairman
Thomas E Jones	Vice-Chairman
Mary E Barth	
Hans-Georg Bruns	
Anthony T Cope	
Robert P Garnett	
Gilbert Gélard	
James J Leisenring	
Warren J McGregor	
Patricia L O'Malley	
Harry K Schmid	
John T Smith	
Geoffrey Whittington	
Tatsumi Yamada	

Basis for Conclusions

This Basis for Conclusions accompanies, but is not part of, IAS 2.

Introduction

BC1 This Basis for Conclusions summarises the International Accounting Standards Board's considerations in reaching its conclusions on revising IAS 2 *Inventories* in 2003. Individual Board members gave greater weight to some factors than to others.

BC2 In July 2001 the Board announced that, as part of its initial agenda of technical projects, it would undertake a project to improve a number of Standards, including IAS 2. The project was undertaken in the light of queries and criticisms raised in relation to the Standards by securities regulators, professional accountants and other interested parties. The objectives of the Improvements project were to reduce or eliminate alternatives, redundancies and conflicts within Standards, to deal with some convergence issues and to make other improvements. In May 2002 the Board published its proposals in an Exposure Draft of *Improvements to International Accounting Standards*, with a comment deadline of 16 September 2002. The Board received over 160 comment letters on the Exposure Draft.

BC3 Because the Board's intention was not to reconsider the fundamental approach to the accounting for inventories established by IAS 2, this Basis for Conclusions does not discuss requirements in IAS 2 that the Board has not reconsidered.

Scope

Reference to historical cost system

BC4 Both the objective and the scope of the previous version of IAS 2 referred to 'the accounting treatment for inventories under the historical cost system.' Some had interpreted those words as meaning that the Standard applied only under a historical cost system and permitted entities the choice of applying other measurement bases, for example fair value.

BC5 The Board agreed that those words could be seen as permitting a choice, resulting in inconsistent application of the Standard. Accordingly, it deleted the words 'in the context of the historical cost system in accounting for inventories' to clarify that the Standard applies to all inventories that are not specifically exempted from its scope.

Inventories of broker–traders

BC6 The Exposure Draft proposed excluding from the scope of the Standard inventories of non-producers of agricultural and forest products and mineral ores to the extent that these inventories are measured at net realisable value in accordance with well-established industry practices. However, some respondents disagreed with this scope exemption for the following reasons:

(a) the scope exemption should apply to all types of inventories of broker-traders;

(b) established practice is for broker-traders to follow a mark–to–market approach rather than to value these inventories at net realisable value;

(c) the guidance on net realisable value in IAS 2 is not appropriate for the valuation of inventories of broker-traders.

BC7 The Board found these comments persuasive. Therefore it decided that the Standard should not apply to the measurement of inventories of:

(a) producers of agricultural and forest products, agricultural produce after harvest, and minerals and mineral products, to the extent that they are measured at net realisable value (as in the previous version of IAS 2), or

(b) commodity broker-traders when their inventories are measured at fair value less costs to sell.

BC8 The Board further decided that the measurement of the effect of inventories on profit or loss for the period needed to be consistent with the measurement attribute of inventories for which such exemption is allowed. Accordingly, to qualify under (a) or (b), the Standard requires changes in the recognised amount of inventories to be included in profit or loss for the period. The Board believes this is particularly appropriate in the case of commodity broker-traders because they seek to profit from fluctuations in prices and trade margins.

Cost formulas

BC9 The combination of the previous version of IAS 2 and SIC-1 *Consistency—Different Cost Formulas for Inventories* allowed some choice between first-in, first-out (FIFO) or weighted average cost formulas (benchmark treatment) and the last-in, first-out (LIFO) method (allowed alternative treatment). The Board decided to eliminate the allowed alternative of using the LIFO method.

BC10 The LIFO method treats the newest items of inventory as being sold first, and consequently the items remaining in inventory are recognised as if they were the oldest. This is generally not a reliable representation of actual inventory flows.

BC11 The LIFO method is an attempt to meet a perceived deficiency of the conventional accounting model (the measurement of cost of goods sold expense by reference to outdated prices for the inventories sold, whereas sales revenue is measured at current prices). It does so by imposing an unrealistic cost flow assumption.

BC12 The use of LIFO in financial reporting is often tax-driven, because it results in cost of goods sold expense calculated using the most recent prices being deducted from revenue in the determination of the gross margin. The LIFO method reduces (increases) profits in a manner that tends to reflect the effect that increased (decreased) prices would have on the cost of replacing inventories sold. However, this effect depends on the relationship between the prices of the most recent inventory acquisitions and the replacement cost at the end of the period. Thus, it is not a truly systematic method for determining the effect of changing prices on profits.

BC13 The use of LIFO results in inventories being recognised in the balance sheet at amounts that bear little relationship to recent cost levels of inventories. However, LIFO can distort profit or loss, especially when 'preserved' older 'layers' of inventory are presumed to have been used when inventories are substantially reduced. It is more likely in these circumstances that relatively new inventories will have been used to meet the increased demands on inventory.

BC14 Some respondents argued that the use of LIFO has merit in certain circumstances because it partially adjusts profit or loss for the effects of price changes. The Board concluded that it is not appropriate to allow an approach that results in a measurement of profit or loss for the period that is inconsistent with the measurement of inventories for balance sheet purposes.

BC15 Other respondents argued that in some industries, such as the oil and gas industry, inventory levels are driven by security considerations and often represent a minimum of 90 days of sales. They argue that, in these industries, the use of LIFO better reflects an entity's performance because inventories held as security stocks are closer to long-term assets than to working capital.

BC16 The Board was not convinced by these arguments because these security stocks do not match historical layers under a LIFO computation.

BC17 Other respondents argued that in some cases, for example, when measuring coal dumps, piles of iron or metal scraps (when stock bins are replenished by 'topping up'), the LIFO method reflects the actual physical flow of inventories.

BC18 The Board concluded that valuation of these inventories follows a direct costing approach where actual physical flows are matched with direct costs, which is a method different from LIFO.

BC19 The Board decided to eliminate the LIFO method because of its lack of representational faithfulness of inventory flows. This decision does not rule out specific cost methods that reflect inventory flows that are similar to LIFO.

BC20 The Board recognised that, in some jurisdictions, use of the LIFO method for tax purposes is possible only if that method is also used for accounting purposes. It concluded, however, that tax considerations do not provide an adequate conceptual basis for selecting an appropriate accounting treatment and that it is not acceptable to allow an inferior accounting treatment purely because of tax regulations and advantages in particular jurisdictions. This may be an issue for local taxation authorities.

BC21 IAS 2 continues to allow the use of both the FIFO and the weighted average methods for interchangeable inventories.

Cost of inventories recognised as an expense in the period

BC22 The Exposure Draft proposed deleting paragraphs in the previous version of IAS 2 that required disclosure of the cost of inventories recognised as an expense in the period, because this disclosure is required in IAS 1 *Presentation of Financial Statements*.

BC23 Some respondents observed that IAS 1 does not specifically require disclosure of the cost of inventories recognised as an expense in the period when presenting an analysis of expenses using a classification based on their function. They argued that this information is important to understand the financial statements. Therefore the Board decided to require this disclosure specifically in IAS 2.

Table of Concordance

This table shows how the contents of the superseded version of IAS 2 and the current version of IAS correspond. Paragraphs are treated as corresponding if they broadly address the same matter even though the guidance may differ.

This table also shows how the requirements of SIC Interpretation SIC-1 have been incorporated into the current version of IAS 2.

Superseded IAS 2 paragraph	Current IAS 2 paragraph
Objective	1
1	2,3
2	None
3	4
4	6
5	8
6	9
7	10
8	11
9	None
10	12
11	13
12	14
13	15
14	16
15	17
16	19

Superseded IAS 2 paragraph	Current IAS 2 paragraph
16 A	20
17	21
18	22
19	23
20	24
21	25
22	27
23	None
24	None
25	28
26	29
27	30
28	31
29	32
30	33
31	34
32	None

Superseded IAS 2 paragraph	Current IAS 2 paragraph
33	35
34	36
35	37
36	None
37	36
38	38
39	39
40	None
41	40
None	3
None	5
None	7
None	18
None	41
None	42
SIC-1	25, 26

International Accounting Standard 7

Cash Flow Statements

This version includes amendments resulting from new and amended IFRSs issued up to 31 December 2004.

Contents

International Accounting Standard 7 *Cash Flow Statements* (IAS 7) is set out in paragraphs 1–53. All the paragraphs have equal authority but retain the IASC format of the Standard when it was adopted by the IASB. IAS 7 should be read in the context of its objective, the *Preface to International Financial Reporting Standards* and the *Framework for the Preparation and Presentation of Financial Statements*. IAS 8 *Accounting Policies, Changes in Accounting Estimates and Errors* provides a basis for selecting and applying accounting policies in the absence of explicit guidance.

International Accounting Standard 7
Cash Flow Statements

Objective

Information about the cash flows of an entity is useful in providing users of financial statements with a basis to assess the ability of the entity to generate cash and cash equivalents and the needs of the entity to utilise those cash flows. The economic decisions that are taken by users require an evaluation of the ability of an entity to generate cash and cash equivalents and the timing and certainty of their generation.

The objective of this Standard is to require the provision of information about the historical changes in cash and cash equivalents of an entity by means of a cash flow statement which classifies cash flows during the period from operating, investing and financing activities.

Scope

1 **An entity shall prepare a cash flow statement in accordance with the requirements of this Standard and shall present it as an integral part of its financial statements for each period for which financial statements are presented.**

2 This Standard supersedes IAS 7 *Statement of Changes in Financial Position*, approved in July 1977.

3 Users of an entity's financial statements are interested in how the entity generates and uses cash and cash equivalents. This is the case regardless of the nature of the entity's activities and irrespective of whether cash can be viewed as the product of the entity, as may be the case with a financial institution. Entities need cash for essentially the same reasons however different their principal revenue-producing activities might be. They need cash to conduct their operations, to pay their obligations, and to provide returns to their investors. Accordingly, this Standard requires all entities to present a cash flow statement.

Benefits of cash flow information

4 A cash flow statement, when used in conjunction with the rest of the financial statements, provides information that enables users to evaluate the changes in net assets of an entity, its financial structure (including its liquidity and solvency) and its ability to affect the amounts and timing of cash flows in order to adapt to changing circumstances and opportunities. Cash flow information is useful in assessing the ability of the entity to generate cash and cash equivalents and enables users to develop models to assess and compare the present value of the future cash flows of different entities. It also enhances the comparability of the reporting of operating performance by different entities because it eliminates the effects of using different accounting treatments for the same transactions and events.

5 Historical cash flow information is often used as an indicator of the amount, timing and certainty of future cash flows. It is also useful in checking the accuracy of past assessments of future cash flows and in examining the relationship between profitability and net cash flow and the impact of changing prices.

Definitions

6 The following terms are used in this Standard with the meanings specified:

Cash **comprises cash on hand and demand deposits.**

Cash equivalents **are short-term, highly liquid investments that are readily convertible to known amounts of cash and which are subject to an insignificant risk of changes in value.**

Cash flows **are inflows and outflows of cash and cash equivalents.**

Operating activities **are the principal revenue-producing activities of the entity and other activities that are not investing or financing activities.**

Investing activities **are the acquisition and disposal of long-term assets and other investments not included in cash equivalents.**

Financing activities **are activities that result in changes in the size and composition of the contributed equity and borrowings of the entity.**

Cash and cash equivalents

7 Cash equivalents are held for the purpose of meeting short-term cash commitments rather than for investment or other purposes. For an investment to qualify as a cash equivalent it must be readily convertible to a known amount of cash and be subject to an insignificant risk of changes in value. Therefore, an investment normally qualifies as a cash equivalent only when it has a short maturity of, say, three months or less from the date of acquisition. Equity investments are excluded from cash equivalents unless they are, in substance, cash equivalents, for example in the case of preferred shares acquired within a short period of their maturity and with a specified redemption date.

8 Bank borrowings are generally considered to be financing activities. However, in some countries, bank overdrafts which are repayable on demand form an integral part of an entity's cash management. In these circumstances, bank overdrafts are included as a component of cash and cash equivalents. A characteristic of such banking arrangements is that the bank balance often fluctuates from being positive to overdrawn.

9 Cash flows exclude movements between items that constitute cash or cash equivalents because these components are part of the cash management of an entity rather than part of its operating, investing and financing activities. Cash management includes the investment of excess cash in cash equivalents.

Presentation of a cash flow statement

10 The cash flow statement shall report cash flows during the period classified by operating, investing and financing activities.

11 An entity presents its cash flows from operating, investing and financing activities in a manner which is most appropriate to its business. Classification by activity provides information that allows users to assess the impact of those activities on the financial position of the entity and the amount of its cash and cash equivalents. This information may also be used to evaluate the relationships among those activities.

12 A single transaction may include cash flows that are classified differently. For example, when the cash repayment of a loan includes both interest and capital, the interest element may be classified as an operating activity and the capital element is classified as a financing activity.

Operating activities

13 The amount of cash flows arising from operating activities is a key indicator of the extent to which the operations of the entity have generated sufficient cash flows to repay loans, maintain the operating capability of the entity, pay dividends and make new investments without recourse to external sources of financing. Information about the specific components of historical operating cash flows is useful, in conjunction with other information, in forecasting future operating cash flows.

14 Cash flows from operating activities are primarily derived from the principal revenue-producing activities of the entity. Therefore, they generally result from the transactions and other events that enter into the determination of profit or loss. Examples of cash flows from operating activities are:

(a) cash receipts from the sale of goods and the rendering of services;

(b) cash receipts from royalties, fees, commissions and other revenue;

(c) cash payments to suppliers for goods and services;

(d) cash payments to and on behalf of employees;

(e) cash receipts and cash payments of an insurance entity for premiums and claims, annuities and other policy benefits;

(f) cash payments or refunds of income taxes unless they can be specifically identified with financing and investing activities; and

(g) cash receipts and payments from contracts held for dealing or trading purposes.

Some transactions, such as the sale of an item of plant, may give rise to a gain or loss which is included in the determination of profit or loss. However, the cash flows relating to such transactions are cash flows from investing activities.

15 An entity may hold securities and loans for dealing or trading purposes, in which case they are similar to inventory acquired specifically for resale. Therefore, cash flows arising from the purchase and sale of dealing or trading securities are classified as operating activities. Similarly, cash advances and loans made by financial institutions are usually classified as operating activities since they relate to the main revenue-producing activity of that entity.

Investing activities

16 The separate disclosure of cash flows arising from investing activities is important because the cash flows represent the extent to which expenditures have been made for resources intended to generate future income and cash flows. Examples of cash flows arising from investing activities are:

(a) cash payments to acquire property, plant and equipment, intangibles and other long-term assets. These payments include those relating to capitalised development costs and self-constructed property, plant and equipment;

(b) cash receipts from sales of property, plant and equipment, intangibles and other long-term assets;

(c) cash payments to acquire equity or debt instruments of other entities and interests in joint ventures (other than payments for those instruments considered to be cash equivalents or those held for dealing or trading purposes);

(d) cash receipts from sales of equity or debt instruments of other entities and interests in joint ventures (other than receipts for those instruments considered to be cash equivalents and those held for dealing or trading purposes);

(e) cash advances and loans made to other parties (other than advances and loans made by a financial institution);

(f) cash receipts from the repayment of advances and loans made to other parties (other than advances and loans of a financial institution);

(g) cash payments for futures contracts, forward contracts, option contracts and swap contracts except when the contracts are held for dealing or trading purposes, or the payments are classified as financing activities; and

(h) cash receipts from futures contracts, forward contracts, option contracts and swap contracts except when the contracts are held for dealing or trading purposes, or the receipts are classified as financing activities.

When a contract is accounted for as a hedge of an identifiable position, the cash flows of the contract are classified in the same manner as the cash flows of the position being hedged.

Financing activities

17 The separate disclosure of cash flows arising from financing activities is important because it is useful in predicting claims on future cash flows by providers of capital to the entity. Examples of cash flows arising from financing activities are:

(a) cash proceeds from issuing shares or other equity instruments;

(b) cash payments to owners to acquire or redeem the entity's shares;

(c) cash proceeds from issuing debentures, loans, notes, bonds, mortgages and other short or long-term borrowings;

(d) cash repayments of amounts borrowed; and

(e) cash payments by a lessee for the reduction of the outstanding liability relating to a finance lease.

Reporting cash flows from operating activities

18 **An entity shall report cash flows from operating activities using either:**

(a) the direct method, whereby major classes of gross cash receipts and gross cash payments are disclosed; or

(b) the indirect method, whereby profit or loss is adjusted for the effects of transactions of a non-cash nature, any deferrals or accruals of past or future operating cash receipts or payments, and items of income or expense associated with investing or financing cash flows.

19 Entities are encouraged to report cash flows from operating activities using the direct method. The direct method provides information which may be useful in estimating future cash flows and which is not available under the indirect method. Under the direct method, information about major classes of gross cash receipts and gross cash payments may be obtained either:

(a) from the accounting records of the entity; or

(b) by adjusting sales, cost of sales (interest and similar income and interest expense and similar charges for a financial institution) and other items in the income statement for:

(i) changes during the period in inventories and operating receivables and payables;

(ii) other non-cash items; and

(iii) other items for which the cash effects are investing or financing cash flows.

20 Under the indirect method, the net cash flow from operating activities is determined by adjusting profit or loss for the effects of:

(a) changes during the period in inventories and operating receivables and payables;

(b) non-cash items such as depreciation, provisions, deferred taxes, unrealised foreign currency gains and losses, undistributed profits of associates, and minority interests; and

(c) all other items for which the cash effects are investing or financing cash flows.

Alternatively, the net cash flow from operating activities may be presented under the indirect method by showing the revenues and expenses disclosed in the income statement and the changes during the period in inventories and operating receivables and payables.

Reporting cash flows from investing and financing activities

21 **An entity shall report separately major classes of gross cash receipts and gross cash payments arising from investing and financing activities, except to the extent that cash flows described in paragraphs 22 and 24 are reported on a net basis.**

Reporting cash flows on a net basis

22 **Cash flows arising from the following operating, investing or financing activities may be reported on a net basis:**

(a) cash receipts and payments on behalf of customers when the cash flows reflect the activities of the customer rather than those of the entity; and

(b) cash receipts and payments for items in which the turnover is quick, the amounts are large, and the maturities are short.

23 Examples of cash receipts and payments referred to in paragraph 22(a) are:

(a) the acceptance and repayment of demand deposits of a bank;

(b) funds held for customers by an investment entity; and

(c) rents collected on behalf of, and paid over to, the owners of properties.

Examples of cash receipts and payments referred to in paragraph 22(b) are advances made for, and the repayment of:

(a) principal amounts relating to credit card customers;

(b) the purchase and sale of investments; and

(c) other short-term borrowings, for example, those which have a maturity period of three months or less.

24 **Cash flows arising from each of the following activities of a financial institution may be reported on a net basis:**

(a) cash receipts and payments for the acceptance and repayment of deposits with a fixed maturity date;

(b) the placement of deposits with and withdrawal of deposits from other financial institutions; and

(c) cash advances and loans made to customers and the repayment of those advances and loans.

Foreign currency cash flows

25 **Cash flows arising from transactions in a foreign currency shall be recorded in an entity's functional currency by applying to the foreign currency amount the exchange rate between the functional currency and the foreign currency at the date of the cash flow.**

26 **The cash flows of a foreign subsidiary shall be translated at the exchange rates between the functional currency and the foreign currency at the dates of the cash flows.**

27 Cash flows denominated in a foreign currency are reported in a manner consistent with IAS 21 *Accounting for the Effects of Changes in Foreign Exchange Rates*. This permits the use of an exchange rate that approximates the actual rate. For example, a weighted average exchange rate for a period may be used for recording foreign currency transactions or the translation of the cash flows of a

foreign subsidiary. However, IAS 21 does not permit use of the exchange rate at the balance sheet date when translating the cash flows of a foreign subsidiary.

28 Unrealised gains and losses arising from changes in foreign currency exchange rates are not cash flows. However, the effect of exchange rate changes on cash and cash equivalents held or due in a foreign currency is reported in the cash flow statement in order to reconcile cash and cash equivalents at the beginning and the end of the period. This amount is presented separately from cash flows from operating, investing and financing activities and includes the differences, if any, had those cash flows been reported at end of period exchange rates.

29 [Deleted]

30 [Deleted]

Interest and dividends

31 **Cash flows from interest and dividends received and paid shall each be disclosed separately. Each shall be classified in a consistent manner from period to period as either operating, investing or financing activities.**

32 The total amount of interest paid during a period is disclosed in the cash flow statement whether it has been recognised as an expense in the income statement or capitalised in accordance with the allowed alternative treatment in IAS 23 *Borrowing Costs*.

33 Interest paid and interest and dividends received are usually classified as operating cash flows for a financial institution. However, there is no consensus on the classification of these cash flows for other entities. Interest paid and interest and dividends received may be classified as operating cash flows because they enter into the determination of profit or loss. Alternatively, interest paid and interest and dividends received may be classified as financing cash flows and investing cash flows respectively, because they are costs of obtaining financial resources or returns on investments.

34 Dividends paid may be classified as a financing cash flow because they are a cost of obtaining financial resources. Alternatively, dividends paid may be classified as a component of cash flows from operating activities in order to assist users to determine the ability of an entity to pay dividends out of operating cash flows.

Taxes on income

35 **Cash flows arising from taxes on income shall be separately disclosed and shall be classified as cash flows from operating activities unless they can be specifically identified with financing and investing activities.**

36 Taxes on income arise on transactions that give rise to cash flows that are classified as operating, investing or financing activities in a cash flow statement. While tax expense may be readily identifiable with investing or financing activities, the related tax cash flows are often impracticable to identify and may arise in a different period from the cash flows of the underlying transaction. Therefore, taxes paid are usually classified as cash flows from operating activities. However, when it is practicable to identify the tax cash flow with an individual transaction that gives rise to cash flows that are classified as investing or

financing activities the tax cash flow is classified as an investing or financing activity as appropriate. When tax cash flows are allocated over more than one class of activity, the total amount of taxes paid is disclosed.

Investments in subsidiaries, associates and joint ventures

37 When accounting for an investment in an associate or a subsidiary accounted for by use of the equity or cost method, an investor restricts its reporting in the cash flow statement to the cash flows between itself and the investee, for example, to dividends and advances.

38 An entity which reports its interest in a jointly controlled entity (see IAS 31 *Interests in Joint Ventures*) using proportionate consolidation, includes in its consolidated cash flow statement its proportionate share of the jointly controlled entity's cash flows. An entity which reports such an interest using the equity method includes in its cash flow statement the cash flows in respect of its investments in the jointly controlled entity, and distributions and other payments or receipts between it and the jointly controlled entity.

Acquisitions and disposals of subsidiaries and other business units

39 The aggregate cash flows arising from acquisitions and from disposals of subsidiaries or other business units shall be presented separately and classified as investing activities.

40 An entity shall disclose, in aggregate, in respect of both acquisitions and disposals of subsidiaries or other business units during the period each of the following:

(a) the total purchase or disposal consideration;

(b) the portion of the purchase or disposal consideration discharged by means of cash and cash equivalents;

(c) the amount of cash and cash equivalents in the subsidiary or business unit acquired or disposed of; and

(d) the amount of the assets and liabilities other than cash or cash equivalents in the subsidiary or business unit acquired or disposed of, summarised by each major category.

41 The separate presentation of the cash flow effects of acquisitions and disposals of subsidiaries and other business units as single line items, together with the separate disclosure of the amounts of assets and liabilities acquired or disposed of, helps to distinguish those cash flows from the cash flows arising from the other operating, investing and financing activities. The cash flow effects of disposals are not deducted from those of acquisitions.

42 The aggregate amount of the cash paid or received as purchase or sale consideration is reported in the cash flow statement net of cash and cash equivalents acquired or disposed of.

Non–cash transactions

43 Investing and financing transactions that do not require the use of cash or cash equivalents shall be excluded from a cash flow statement. Such transactions shall be disclosed elsewhere in the financial statements in a way that provides all the relevant information about these investing and financing activities.

44 Many investing and financing activities do not have a direct impact on current cash flows although they do affect the capital and asset structure of an entity. The exclusion of non-cash transactions from the cash flow statement is consistent with the objective of a cash flow statement as these items do not involve cash flows in the current period. Examples of non-cash transactions are:

(a) the acquisition of assets either by assuming directly related liabilities or by means of a finance lease;

(b) the acquisition of an entity by means of an equity issue; and

(c) the conversion of debt to equity.

Components of cash and cash equivalents

45 An entity shall disclose the components of cash and cash equivalents and shall present a reconciliation of the amounts in its cash flow statement with the equivalent items reported in the balance sheet.

46 In view of the variety of cash management practices and banking arrangements around the world and in order to comply with IAS 1 *Presentation of Financial Statements*, an entity discloses the policy which it adopts in determining the composition of cash and cash equivalents.

47 The effect of any change in the policy for determining components of cash and cash equivalents, for example, a change in the classification of financial instruments previously considered to be part of an entity's investment portfolio, is reported in accordance with IAS 8 *Accounting Policies, Changes in Accounting Estimates and Errors*.

Other disclosures

48 An entity shall disclose, together with a commentary by management, the amount of significant cash and cash equivalent balances held by the entity that are not available for use by the group.

49 There are various circumstances in which cash and cash equivalent balances held by an entity are not available for use by the group. Examples include cash and cash equivalent balances held by a subsidiary that operates in a country where exchange controls or other legal restrictions apply when the balances are not available for general use by the parent or other subsidiaries.

50 Additional information may be relevant to users in understanding the financial position and liquidity of an entity. Disclosure of this information, together with a commentary by management, is encouraged and may include:

(a) the amount of undrawn borrowing facilities that may be available for future operating activities and to settle capital commitments, indicating any restrictions on the use of these facilities;

(b) the aggregate amounts of the cash flows from each of operating, investing and financing activities related to interests in joint ventures reported using proportionate consolidation;

(c) the aggregate amount of cash flows that represent increases in operating capacity separately from those cash flows that are required to maintain operating capacity; and

(d) the amount of the cash flows arising from the operating, investing and financing activities of each reported industry and geographical segment (see IAS 14 *Segment Reporting*).

51 The separate disclosure of cash flows that represent increases in operating capacity and cash flows that are required to maintain operating capacity is useful in enabling the user to determine whether the entity is investing adequately in the maintenance of its operating capacity. An entity that does not invest adequately in the maintenance of its operating capacity may be prejudicing future profitability for the sake of current liquidity and distributions to owners.

52 The disclosure of segmental cash flows enables users to obtain a better understanding of the relationship between the cash flows of the business as a whole and those of its component parts and the availability and variability of segmental cash flows.

Effective date

53 **This Standard becomes operative for financial statements covering periods beginning on or after 1 January 1994.**

Appendix A
Cash flow statement for an entity other than a financial institution

This appendix accompanies, but is not part of, IAS 7.

1 The examples show only current period amounts. Corresponding amounts for the preceding period are required to be presented in accordance with IAS 1 *Presentation of Financial Statements.*

2 Information from the income statement and balance sheet is provided to show how the statements of cash flows under the direct method and indirect method have been derived. Neither the income statement nor the balance sheet is presented in conformity with the disclosure and presentation requirements of other Standards.

3 The following additional information is also relevant for the preparation of the statements of cash flows:

- all of the shares of a subsidiary were acquired for 590. The fair values of assets acquired and liabilities assumed were as follows:

Inventories	100
Accounts receivable	100
Cash	40
Property, plant and equipment	650
Trade payables	100
Long–term debt	200

- 250 was raised from the issue of share capital and a further 250 was raised from long-term borrowings.
- interest expense was 400, of which 170 was paid during the period. Also, 100 relating to interest expense of the prior period was paid during the period.
- dividends paid were 1,200.
- the liability for tax at the beginning and end of the period was 1,000 and 400 respectively. During the period, a further 200 tax was provided for. Withholding tax on dividends received amounted to 100.
- during the period, the group acquired property, plant and equipment with an aggregate cost of 1,250 of which 900 was acquired by means of finance leases. Cash payments of 350 were made to purchase property, plant and equipment.
- plant with original cost of 80 and accumulated depreciation of 60 was sold for 20.
- accounts receivable as at the end of 20X2 include 100 of interest receivable.

Consolidated income statement for the period ended 20X2

Sales	30,650
Cost of sales	(26,000)
Gross profit	4,650
Depreciation	(450)
Administrative and selling expenses	(910)
Interest expense	(400)
Investment income	500
Foreign exchange loss	(40)
Profit before taxation	3,350
Taxes on income	(300)
Profit	3,050

Consolidated balance sheet as at end of 20X2

		20X2		20X1
Assets				
Cash and cash equivalents		230		160
Accounts receivable		1,900		1,200
Inventory		1,000		1,950
Portfolio investments		2,500		2,500
Property, plant and equipment at cost	3,730		1,910	
Accumulated depreciation	(1,450)		(1,060)	
Property, plant and equipment net		2,280		850
Total assets		7,910		6,660
Liabilities				
Trade payables		250		1,890
Interest payable		230		100
Income taxes payable		400		1,000
Long–term debt		2,300		1,040
Total liabilities		3,180		4,030
Shareholder's Equity				
Share capital		1,500		1,250
Retained earnings		3,230		1,380
Total shareholders' equity		4,730		2,630
Total liabilities and shareholders' equity		7,910		6,660

Direct method cash flow statement (paragraph 18a)

		20X2
Cash flows from operating activities		
Cash receipts from customers	30,150	
Cash paid to suppliers and employees	(27,600)	
Cash generated from operations	2,550	
Interest paid	(270)	
Income taxes paid	(900)	
Net cash from operating activities		1,380
Cash flows from investing activities		
Acquisition of subsidiary X, net of cash acquired (Note A)	(550)	
Purchase of property, plant and equipment (Note B)	(350)	
Proceeds from sale of equipment	20	
Interest received	200	
Dividends received	200	
Net cash used in investing activities		(480)
Cash flows from financing activities		
Proceeds from issue of share capital	250	
Proceeds from long–term borrowings	250	
Payment of finance lease liabilities	(90)	
Dividends paid[(a)]	(1,200)	
Net cash used in financing activities		(790)
Net increase in cash and cash equivalents		110
Cash and cash equivalents at beginning of period (Note C)		120
Cash and cash equivalents at end of period (Note C)		230

(a) This could also be shown as an operating cash flow.

Indirect method cash flow statement (paragraph 18b)

		20X2
Cash flows from operating activities		
Profit before taxation	3,350	
Adjustments for:		
Depreciation	450	
Foreign exchange loss	40	
Investment income	(500)	
Interest expense	400	
	3,740	
Increase in trade and other receivables	(500)	
Decrease in inventories	1,050	
Decrease in trade payables	(1,740)	
Cash generated from operations	2,550	
Interest paid	(270)	
Income taxes paid	(900)	
Net cash from operating activities		1,380
Cash flows from investing activities		
Acquisition of subsidiary X net of cash acquired (Note A)	(550)	
Purchase of property, plant and equipment (Note B)	(350)	
Proceeds from sale of equipment	20	
Interest received	200	
Dividends received	200	
Net cash used in investing activities		(480)
Cash flows from financing activities		
Proceeds from issue of share capital	250	
Proceeds from long–term borrowings	250	
Payment of finance lease liabilities	(90)	
Dividends paid[(a)]	(1,200)	
Net cash used in financing activities		(790)
Net increase in cash and cash equivalents		110
Cash and cash equivalents at beginning of period (Note C)		120
Cash and cash equivalents at end of period (Note C)		230

(a) This could also be shown as an operating cash flow.

Notes to the cash flow statement (direct method and indirect method)

A. Acquisition of subsidiary

During the period the Group acquired subsidiary X. The fair value of assets acquired and liabilities assumed were as follows:

Cash	40
Inventories	100
Accounts receivable	100
Property, plant and equipment	650
Trade payables	(100)
Long–term debt	(200)
Total purchase price	590
Less: Cash of X	(40)
Cash flow on acquisition net of cash acquired	550

B. Property, plant and equipment

During the period, the Group acquired property, plant and equipment with an aggregate cost of 1,250 of which 900 was acquired by means of finance leases. Cash payments of 350 were made to purchase property, plant and equipment.

C. Cash and cash equivalents

Cash and cash equivalents consist of cash on hand and balances with banks, and investments in money market instruments. Cash and cash equivalents included in the cash flow statement comprise the following balance sheet amounts:

	20X2	20X1
Cash on hand and balances with banks	40	25
Short–term investments	190	135
Cash and cash equivalents as previously reported	230	160
Effect of exchange rate changes	–	(40)
Cash and cash equivalents as restated	230	120

Cash and cash equivalents at the end of the period include deposits with banks of 100 held by a subsidiary which are not freely remissible to the holding company because of currency exchange restrictions.

The Group has undrawn borrowing facilities of 2,000 of which 700 may be used only for future expansion.

D. Segment information

	Segment A	Segment B	Total
Cash flows from:			
Operating activities	1,520	(140)	1,380
Investing activities	(640)	160	(480)
Financing activities	(570)	(220)	(790)
	310	(200)	110

Alternative presentation (indirect method)

As an alternative, in an indirect method cash flow statement, operating profit before working capital changes is sometimes presented as follows:

Revenues excluding investment income	30,650	
Operating expense excluding depreciation	(26,910)	
Operating profit before working capital changes		3,740

Appendix B
Cash flow statement for a financial institution

This appendix accompanies, but is not part of, IAS 7.

1 The example shows only current period amounts. Comparative amounts for the preceding period are required to be presented in accordance with IAS 1 *Presentation of Financial Statements*.

2 The example is presented using the direct method.

		20X2
Cash flows from operating activities		
Interest and commission receipts	28,447	
Interest payments	(23,463)	
Recoveries on loans previously written off	237	
Cash payments to employees and suppliers	(997)	
	4,224	
(Increase) decrease in operating assets:		
Short–term funds	(650)	
Deposits held for regulatory or monetary control purposes	234	
Funds advanced to customers	(288)	
Net increase in credit card receivables	(360)	
Other short–term negotiable securities	(120)	
Increase (decrease) in operating liabilities:		
Deposits from customers	600	
Negotiable certificates of deposit	(200)	
Net cash from operating activities before income tax	3,440	
Income taxes paid	(100)	
Net cash from operating activities		3,340
Cash flows from investing activities		
Disposal of subsidiary Y	50	
Dividends received	200	
Interest received	300	
Proceeds from sales of non–dealing securities	1,200	
Purchase of non–dealing securities	(600)	
Purchase of property, plant and equipment	(500)	
Net cash from investing activities		650

Continued from previous page

Cash flows from financing activities		
Issue of loan capital	1,000	
Issue of preference shares by subsidiary undertaking	800	
Repayment of long–term borrowings	(200)	
Net decrease in other borrowings	(1,000)	
Dividends paid	(400)	
Net cash from financing activities		200
Effects of exchange rate changes on cash and cash equivalents		600
Net increase in cash and cash equivalents		4,790
Cash and cash equivalents at beginning of period		4,050
Cash and cash equivalents at end of period		8,840

International Accounting Standard 8

Accounting Policies, Changes in Accounting Estimates and Errors

This version includes amendments resulting from new and amended IFRSs issued up to 31 December 2004.

CONTENTS

International Accounting Standard 8 *Accounting Policies, Changes in Accounting Estimates and Errors* (IAS 8) is set out in paragraphs 1–56 and the Appendix. All the paragraphs have equal authority but retain the IASC format of the Standard when it was adopted by the IASB. IAS 8 should be read in the context of its objective and the Basis for Conclusions, the *Preface to International Financial Reporting Standards* and the *Framework for the Preparation and Presentation of Financial Statements*.

Introduction

IN1 International Accounting Standard 8 *Accounting Policies, Changes in Accounting Estimates and Errors* (IAS 8) replaces IAS 8 *Net Profit or Loss for the Period, Fundamental Errors and Changes in Accounting Policies* (revised in 1993) and should be applied for annual periods beginning on or after 1 January 2005. Earlier application is encouraged. The Standard also replaces the following Interpretations:

- SIC-2 *Consistency—Capitalisation of Borrowing Costs*
- SIC-18 *Consistency—Alternative Methods.*

Reasons for revising IAS 8

IN2 The International Accounting Standards Board developed this revised IAS 8 as part of its project on Improvements to International Accounting Standards. The project was undertaken in the light of queries and criticisms raised in relation to the Standards by securities regulators, professional accountants and other interested parties. The objectives of the project were to reduce or eliminate alternatives, redundancies and conflicts within the Standards, to deal with some convergence issues and to make other improvements.

IN3 For IAS 8, the Board's main objectives were:

(a) to remove the allowed alternative to retrospective application of voluntary changes in accounting policies and retrospective restatement to correct prior period errors;

(b) to eliminate the concept of a fundamental error;

(c) to articulate the hierarchy of guidance to which management refers, whose applicability it considers when selecting accounting policies in the absence of Standards and Interpretations that specifically apply;

(d) to define material omissions or misstatements, and describe how to apply the concept of materiality when applying accounting policies and correcting errors; and

(e) to incorporate the consensus in SIC-2 *Consistency–Capitalisation of Borrowing Costs* and in SIC-18 *Consistency–Alternative Methods.*

IN4 The Board did not reconsider the other requirements of IAS 8.

Changes from previous requirements

IN5 The main changes from the previous version of IAS 8 are described below.

Selection of accounting policies

IN6 The requirements for the selection and application of accounting policies in the previous version of IAS 1 *Presentation of Financial Statements* have been transferred to the Standard. The Standard updates the previous hierarchy of guidance to which management refers and whose applicability it considers when selecting accounting policies in the absence of Standards and Interpretations that specifically apply.

Materiality

IN7 The Standard defines material omissions or misstatements. It stipulates that:

(a) the accounting policies in International Financial Reporting Standards (IFRSs) need not be applied when the effect of applying them is immaterial. This complements the statement in IAS 1 that disclosures required by IFRSs need not be made if the information is immaterial.

(b) financial statements do not comply with IFRSs if they contain material errors.

(c) material prior period errors are to be corrected retrospectively in the first set of financial statements authorised for issue after their discovery.

Voluntary changes in accounting policies and corrections of prior period errors

IN8 The Standard requires retrospective application of voluntary changes in accounting policies and retrospective restatement to correct prior period errors. It removes the allowed alternative in the previous version of IAS 8:

(a) to include in profit or loss for the current period the adjustment resulting from changing an accounting policy or the amount of a correction of a prior period error; and

(b) to present unchanged comparative information from financial statements of prior periods.

IN9 As a result of the removal of the allowed alternative, comparative information for prior periods is presented as if new accounting policies had always been applied and prior period errors had never occurred.

Impracticability

IN10 The Standard retains the 'impracticability' criterion for exemption from changing comparative information when changes in accounting policies are applied retrospectively and prior period errors are corrected. The Standard now includes a definition of 'impracticable' and guidance on its interpretation.

IN11 The Standard also states that when it is impracticable to determine the cumulative effect, at the beginning of the current period, of:

(a) applying a new accounting policy to all prior periods, or

(b) an error on all prior periods,

the entity changes the comparative information as if the new accounting policy had been applied, or the error had been corrected, prospectively from the earliest date practicable.

Fundamental errors

IN12 The Standard eliminates the concept of a fundamental error and thus the distinction between fundamental errors and other material errors. The Standard defines prior period errors.

Disclosures

IN13 The Standard now requires, rather than encourages, disclosure of an impending change in accounting policy when an entity has yet to implement a new Standard or Interpretation that has been issued but not yet come into effect. In addition, it requires disclosure of known or reasonably estimable information relevant to assessing the possible impact that application of the new Standard or Interpretation will have on the entity's financial statements in the period of initial application.

IN14 The Standard requires more detailed disclosure of the amounts of adjustments resulting from changing accounting policies or correcting prior period errors. It requires those disclosures to be made for each financial statement line item affected and, if IAS 33 *Earnings per Share* applies to the entity, for basic and diluted earnings per share.

Other changes

IN15 The presentation requirements for profit or loss for the period have been transferred to IAS 1.

IN16 The Standard incorporates the consensus in SIC-18 *Consistency—Alternative Methods*, namely that:

(a) an entity selects and applies its accounting policies consistently for similar transactions, other events and conditions, unless a Standard or an Interpretation specifically requires or permits categorisation of items for which different policies may be appropriate; and

(b) if a Standard or an Interpretation requires or permits such categorisation, an appropriate accounting policy is selected and applied consistently to each category.

The consensus in SIC-18 incorporated the consensus in SIC-2 *Consistency—Capitalisation of Borrowing Costs*, and requires that when an entity has chosen a policy of capitalising borrowing costs, it should apply this policy to all qualifying assets.

IN17 The Standard includes a definition of a change in accounting estimate.

IN18 The Standard includes exceptions from including the effects of changes in accounting estimates prospectively in profit or loss. It states that to the extent that a change in an accounting estimate gives rise to changes in assets or liabilities, or relates to an item of equity, it is recognised by adjusting the carrying amount of the related asset, liability or equity item in the period of the change.

International Accounting Standard 8
Accounting Policies, Changes in Accounting Estimates and Errors

Objective

1 The objective of this Standard is to prescribe the criteria for selecting and changing accounting policies, together with the accounting treatment and disclosure of changes in accounting policies, changes in accounting estimates and corrections of errors. The Standard is intended to enhance the relevance and reliability of an entity's financial statements, and the comparability of those financial statements over time and with the financial statements of other entities.

2 Disclosure requirements for accounting policies, except those for changes in accounting policies, are set out in IAS 1 *Presentation of Financial Statements.*

Scope

3 **This Standard shall be applied in selecting and applying accounting policies, and accounting for changes in accounting policies, changes in accounting estimates and corrections of prior period errors.**

4 The tax effects of corrections of prior period errors and of retrospective adjustments made to apply changes in accounting policies are accounted for and disclosed in accordance with IAS 12 *Income Taxes.*

Definitions

5 **The following terms are used in this Standard with the meanings specified:**

Accounting policies **are the specific principles, bases, conventions, rules and practices applied by an entity in preparing and presenting financial statements.**

A *change in accounting estimate* **is an adjustment of the carrying amount of an asset or a liability, or the amount of the periodic consumption of an asset, that results from the assessment of the present status of, and expected future benefits and obligations associated with, assets and liabilities. Changes in accounting estimates result from new information or new developments and, accordingly, are not corrections of errors.**

International Financial Reporting Standards (IFRSs) **are Standards and Interpretations adopted by the International Accounting Standards Board (IASB). They comprise:**

(a) International Financial Reporting Standards;

(b) International Accounting Standards; and

(c) Interpretations originated by the International Financial Reporting Interpretations Committee (IFRIC) or the former Standing Interpretations Committee (SIC).

Material **Omissions or misstatements of items are material if they could, individually or collectively, influence the economic decisions of users taken on the basis of the financial statements. Materiality depends on the size and nature of the omission or misstatement judged in the surrounding circumstances. The size or nature of the item, or a combination of both, could be the determining factor.**

Prior period errors **are omissions from, and misstatements in, the entity's financial statements for one or more prior periods arising from a failure to use, or misuse of, reliable information that:**

(a) was available when financial statements for those periods were authorised for issue; and

(b) could reasonably be expected to have been obtained and taken into account in the preparation and presentation of those financial statements.

Such errors include the effects of mathematical mistakes, mistakes in applying accounting policies, oversights or misinterpretations of facts, and fraud.

Retrospective application **is applying a new accounting policy to transactions, other events and conditions as if that policy had always been applied.**

Retrospective restatement **is correcting the recognition, measurement and disclosure of amounts of elements of financial statements as if a prior period error had never occurred.**

Impracticable **Applying a requirement is impracticable when the entity cannot apply it after making every reasonable effort to do so. For a particular prior period, it is impracticable to apply a change in an accounting policy retrospectively or to make a retrospective restatement to correct an error if:**

(a) the effects of the retrospective application or retrospective restatement are not determinable;

(b) the retrospective application or retrospective restatement requires assumptions about what management's intent would have been in that period; or

(c) the retrospective application or retrospective restatement requires significant estimates of amounts and it is impossible to distinguish objectively information about those estimates that:

(i) provides evidence of circumstances that existed on the date(s) as at which those amounts are to be recognised, measured or disclosed; and

(ii) would have been available when the financial statements for that prior period were authorised for issue

from other information.

Prospective application **of a change in accounting policy and of recognising the effect of a change in an accounting estimate, respectively, are:**

(a) applying the new accounting policy to transactions, other events and conditions occurring after the date as at which the policy is changed; and

(b) recognising the effect of the change in the accounting estimate in the current and future periods affected by the change.

6 Assessing whether an omission or misstatement could influence economic decisions of users, and so be material, requires consideration of the characteristics of those users. The *Framework for the Preparation and Presentation of Financial Statements* states in paragraph 25 that 'users are assumed to have a reasonable knowledge of business and economic activities and accounting and a willingness to study the information with reasonable diligence.' Therefore, the assessment needs to take into account how users with such attributes could reasonably be expected to be influenced in making economic decisions.

Accounting policies

Selection and application of accounting policies

7 When a Standard or an Interpretation specifically applies to a transaction, other event or condition, the accounting policy or policies applied to that item shall be determined by applying the Standard or Interpretation and considering any relevant Implementation Guidance issued by the IASB for the Standard or Interpretation.

8 IFRSs set out accounting policies that the IASB has concluded result in financial statements containing relevant and reliable information about the transactions, other events and conditions to which they apply. Those policies need not be applied when the effect of applying them is immaterial. However, it is inappropriate to make, or leave uncorrected, immaterial departures from IFRSs to achieve a particular presentation of an entity's financial position, financial performance or cash flows.

9 Implementation Guidance for Standards issued by the IASB does not form part of those Standards, and therefore does not contain requirements for financial statements.

10 In the absence of a Standard or an Interpretation that specifically applies to a transaction, other event or condition, management shall use its judgement in developing and applying an accounting policy that results in information that is:

(a) relevant to the economic decision-making needs of users; and

(b) reliable, in that the financial statements:

(i) represent faithfully the financial position, financial performance and cash flows of the entity;

(ii) reflect the economic substance of transactions, other events and conditions, and not merely the legal form;

(iii) **are neutral, ie free from bias;**

(iv) **are prudent; and**

(v) **are complete in all material respects.**

11 **In making the judgement described in paragraph 10, management shall refer to, and consider the applicability of, the following sources in descending order:**

(a) **the requirements and guidance in Standards and Interpretations dealing with similar and related issues; and**

(b) **the definitions, recognition criteria and measurement concepts for assets, liabilities, income and expenses in the *Framework*.**

12 **In making the judgement described in paragraph 10, management may also consider the most recent pronouncements of other standard-setting bodies that use a similar conceptual framework to develop accounting standards, other accounting literature and accepted industry practices, to the extent that these do not conflict with the sources in paragraph 11.**

Consistency of accounting policies

13 **An entity shall select and apply its accounting policies consistently for similar transactions, other events and conditions, unless a Standard or an Interpretation specifically requires or permits categorisation of items for which different policies may be appropriate. If a Standard or an Interpretation requires or permits such categorisation, an appropriate accounting policy shall be selected and applied consistently to each category.**

Changes in accounting policies

14 **An entity shall change an accounting policy only if the change:**

(a) **is required by a Standard or an Interpretation; or**

(b) **results in the financial statements providing reliable and more relevant information about the effects of transactions, other events or conditions on the entity's financial position, financial performance or cash flows.**

15 Users of financial statements need to be able to compare the financial statements of an entity over time to identify trends in its financial position, financial performance and cash flows. Therefore, the same accounting policies are applied within each period and from one period to the next unless a change in accounting policy meets one of the criteria in paragraph 14.

16 **The following are not changes in accounting policies:**

(a) **the application of an accounting policy for transactions, other events or conditions that differ in substance from those previously occurring; and**

(b) **the application of a new accounting policy for transactions, other events or conditions that did not occur previously or were immaterial.**

17 The initial application of a policy to revalue assets in accordance with IAS 16 *Property, Plant and Equipment* **or IAS 38** *Intangible Assets* **is a change in an accounting policy to be dealt with as a revaluation in accordance with IAS 16 or IAS 38, rather than in accordance with this Standard.**

18 Paragraphs 19–31 do not apply to the change in accounting policy described in paragraph 17.

Applying changes in accounting policies

19 Subject to paragraph 23:

(a) an entity shall account for a change in accounting policy resulting from the initial application of a Standard or an Interpretation in accordance with the specific transitional provisions, if any, in that Standard or Interpretation; and

(b) when an entity changes an accounting policy upon initial application of a Standard or an Interpretation that does not include specific transitional provisions applying to that change, or changes an accounting policy voluntarily, it shall apply the change retrospectively.

20 For the purpose of this Standard, early application of a Standard or an Interpretation is not a voluntary change in accounting policy.

21 In the absence of a Standard or an Interpretation that specifically applies to a transaction, other event or condition, management may, in accordance with paragraph 12, apply an accounting policy from the most recent pronouncements of other standard-setting bodies that use a similar conceptual framework to develop accounting standards. If, following an amendment of such a pronouncement, the entity chooses to change an accounting policy, that change is accounted for and disclosed as a voluntary change in accounting policy.

Retrospective application

22 Subject to paragraph 23, when a change in accounting policy is applied retrospectively in accordance with paragraph 19(a) or (b), the entity shall adjust the opening balance of each affected component of equity for the earliest prior period presented and the other comparative amounts disclosed for each prior period presented as if the new accounting policy had always been applied.

Limitations on retrospective application

23 When retrospective application is required by paragraph 19(a) or (b), a change in accounting policy shall be applied retrospectively except to the extent that it is impracticable to determine either the period-specific effects or the cumulative effect of the change.

24 When it is impracticable to determine the period-specific effects of changing an accounting policy on comparative information for one or more prior periods presented, the entity shall apply the new accounting policy to the carrying amounts of assets and liabilities as at the beginning of the earliest period for which retrospective application is practicable,

which may be the current period, and shall make a corresponding adjustment to the opening balance of each affected component of equity for that period.

25 **When it is impracticable to determine the cumulative effect, at the beginning of the current period, of applying a new accounting policy to all prior periods, the entity shall adjust the comparative information to apply the new accounting policy prospectively from the earliest date practicable.**

26 When an entity applies a new accounting policy retrospectively, it applies the new accounting policy to comparative information for prior periods as far back as is practicable. Retrospective application to a prior period is not practicable unless it is practicable to determine the cumulative effect on the amounts in both the opening and closing balance sheets for that period. The amount of the resulting adjustment relating to periods before those presented in the financial statements is made to the opening balance of each affected component of equity of the earliest prior period presented. Usually the adjustment is made to retained earnings. However, the adjustment may be made to another component of equity (for example, to comply with a Standard or an Interpretation). Any other information about prior periods, such as historical summaries of financial data, is also adjusted as far back as is practicable.

27 When it is impracticable for an entity to apply a new accounting policy retrospectively, because it cannot determine the cumulative effect of applying the policy to all prior periods, the entity, in accordance with paragraph 25, applies the new policy prospectively from the start of the earliest period practicable. It therefore disregards the portion of the cumulative adjustment to assets, liabilities and equity arising before that date. Changing an accounting policy is permitted even if it is impracticable to apply the policy prospectively for any prior period. Paragraphs 50–53 provide guidance on when it is impracticable to apply a new accounting policy to one or more prior periods.

Disclosure

28 **When initial application of a Standard or an Interpretation has an effect on the current period or any prior period, would have such an effect except that it is impracticable to determine the amount of the adjustment, or might have an effect on future periods, an entity shall disclose:**

(a) the title of the Standard or Interpretation;

(b) when applicable, that the change in accounting policy is made in accordance with its transitional provisions;

(c) the nature of the change in accounting policy;

(d) when applicable, a description of the transitional provisions;

(e) when applicable, the transitional provisions that might have an effect on future periods;

(f) for the current period and each prior period presented, to the extent practicable, the amount of the adjustment:

(i) for each financial statement line item affected; and

(ii) **if IAS 33 *Earnings per Share* applies to the entity, for basic and diluted earnings per share;**

(g) **the amount of the adjustment relating to periods before those presented, to the extent practicable; and**

(h) **if retrospective application required by paragraph 19(a) or (b) is impracticable for a particular prior period, or for periods before those presented, the circumstances that led to the existence of that condition and a description of how and from when the change in accounting policy has been applied.**

Financial statements of subsequent periods need not repeat these disclosures.

29 **When a voluntary change in accounting policy has an effect on the current period or any prior period, would have an effect on that period except that it is impracticable to determine the amount of the adjustment, or might have an effect on future periods, an entity shall disclose:**

(a) **the nature of the change in accounting policy;**

(b) **the reasons why applying the new accounting policy provides reliable and more relevant information;**

(c) **for the current period and each prior period presented, to the extent practicable, the amount of the adjustment:**

(i) **for each financial statement line item affected; and**

(ii) **if IAS 33 applies to the entity, for basic and diluted earnings per share;**

(d) **the amount of the adjustment relating to periods before those presented, to the extent practicable; and**

(e) **if retrospective application is impracticable for a particular prior period, or for periods before those presented, the circumstances that led to the existence of that condition and a description of how and from when the change in accounting policy has been applied.**

Financial statements of subsequent periods need not repeat these disclosures.

30 **When an entity has not applied a new Standard or Interpretation that has been issued but is not yet effective, the entity shall disclose:**

(a) **this fact; and**

(b) **known or reasonably estimable information relevant to assessing the possible impact that application of the new Standard or Interpretation will have on the entity's financial statements in the period of initial application.**

31 In complying with paragraph 30, an entity considers disclosing:

(a) the title of the new Standard or Interpretation;

(b) the nature of the impending change or changes in accounting policy;

(c) the date by which application of the Standard or Interpretation is required;

(d) the date as at which it plans to apply the Standard or Interpretation initially; and

(e) either:

(i) a discussion of the impact that initial application of the Standard or Interpretation is expected to have on the entity's financial statements; or

(ii) if that impact is not known or reasonably estimable, a statement to that effect.

Changes in accounting estimates

32 As a result of the uncertainties inherent in business activities, many items in financial statements cannot be measured with precision but can only be estimated. Estimation involves judgements based on the latest available, reliable information. For example, estimates may be required of:

(a) bad debts;

(b) inventory obsolescence;

(c) the fair value of financial assets or financial liabilities;

(d) the useful lives of, or expected pattern of consumption of the future economic benefits embodied in, depreciable assets; and

(e) warranty obligations.

33 The use of reasonable estimates is an essential part of the preparation of financial statements and does not undermine their reliability.

34 An estimate may need revision if changes occur in the circumstances on which the estimate was based or as a result of new information or more experience. By its nature, the revision of an estimate does not relate to prior periods and is not the correction of an error.

35 A change in the measurement basis applied is a change in an accounting policy, and is not a change in an accounting estimate. When it is difficult to distinguish a change in an accounting policy from a change in an accounting estimate, the change is treated as a change in an accounting estimate.

36 The effect of a change in an accounting estimate, other than a change to which paragraph 37 applies, shall be recognised prospectively by including it in profit or loss in:

(a) the period of the change, if the change affects that period only; or

(b) the period of the change and future periods, if the change affects both.

37 To the extent that a change in an accounting estimate gives rise to changes in assets and liabilities, or relates to an item of equity, it shall be recognised by adjusting the carrying amount of the related asset, liability or equity item in the period of the change.

38 Prospective recognition of the effect of a change in an accounting estimate means that the change is applied to transactions, other events and conditions from the date of the change in estimate. A change in an accounting estimate may affect only the current period's profit or loss, or the profit or loss of both the current period and future periods. For example, a change in the estimate of the amount of bad debts affects only the current period's profit or loss and therefore is recognised in the current period. However, a change in the estimated useful life of, or the expected pattern of consumption of the future economic benefits embodied in, a depreciable asset affects depreciation expense for the current period and for each future period during the asset's remaining useful life. In both cases, the effect of the change relating to the current period is recognised as income or expense in the current period. The effect, if any, on future periods is recognised as income or expense in those future periods.

Disclosure

39 **An entity shall disclose the nature and amount of a change in an accounting estimate that has an effect in the current period or is expected to have an effect in future periods, except for the disclosure of the effect on future periods when it is impracticable to estimate that effect.**

40 **If the amount of the effect in future periods is not disclosed because estimating it is impracticable, an entity shall disclose that fact.**

Errors

41 Errors can arise in respect of the recognition, measurement, presentation or disclosure of elements of financial statements. Financial statements do not comply with IFRSs if they contain either material errors or immaterial errors made intentionally to achieve a particular presentation of an entity's financial position, financial performance or cash flows. Potential current period errors discovered in that period are corrected before the financial statements are authorised for issue. However, material errors are sometimes not discovered until a subsequent period, and these prior period errors are corrected in the comparative information presented in the financial statements for that subsequent period (see paragraphs 42–47).

42 **Subject to paragraph 43, an entity shall correct material prior period errors retrospectively in the first set of financial statements authorised for issue after their discovery by:**

(a) restating the comparative amounts for the prior period(s) presented in which the error occurred; or

(b) if the error occurred before the earliest prior period presented, restating the opening balances of assets, liabilities and equity for the earliest prior period presented.

Limitations on retrospective restatement

43 **A prior period error shall be corrected by retrospective restatement except to the extent that it is impracticable to determine either the period-specific effects or the cumulative effect of the error.**

44 **When it is impracticable to determine the period-specific effects of an error on comparative information for one or more prior periods presented, the entity shall restate the opening balances of assets, liabilities and equity for the earliest period for which retrospective restatement is practicable (which may be the current period).**

45 **When it is impracticable to determine the cumulative effect, at the beginning of the current period, of an error on all prior periods, the entity shall restate the comparative information to correct the error prospectively from the earliest date practicable.**

46 The correction of a prior period error is excluded from profit or loss for the period in which the error is discovered. Any information presented about prior periods, including any historical summaries of financial data, is restated as far back as is practicable.

47 When it is impracticable to determine the amount of an error (eg a mistake in applying an accounting policy) for all prior periods, the entity, in accordance with paragraph 45, restates the comparative information prospectively from the earliest date practicable. It therefore disregards the portion of the cumulative restatement of assets, liabilities and equity arising before that date. Paragraphs 50–53 provide guidance on when it is impracticable to correct an error for one or more prior periods.

48 Corrections of errors are distinguished from changes in accounting estimates. Accounting estimates by their nature are approximations that may need revision as additional information becomes known. For example, the gain or loss recognised on the outcome of a contingency is not the correction of an error.

Disclosure of prior period errors

49 **In applying paragraph 42, an entity shall disclose the following:**

(a) the nature of the prior period error;

(b) for each prior period presented, to the extent practicable, the amount of the correction:

(i) for each financial statement line item affected; and

(ii) if IAS 33 applies to the entity, for basic and diluted earnings per share;

(c) the amount of the correction at the beginning of the earliest prior period presented; and

(d) if retrospective restatement is impracticable for a particular prior period, the circumstances that led to the existence of that condition and a description of how and from when the error has been corrected.

Financial statements of subsequent periods need not repeat these disclosures.

Impracticability in respect of retrospective application and retrospective restatement

50 In some circumstances, it is impracticable to adjust comparative information for one or more prior periods to achieve comparability with the current period. For example, data may not have been collected in the prior period(s) in a way that allows either retrospective application of a new accounting policy (including, for the purpose of paragraphs 51–53, its prospective application to prior periods) or retrospective restatement to correct a prior period error, and it may be impracticable to recreate the information.

51 It is frequently necessary to make estimates in applying an accounting policy to elements of financial statements recognised or disclosed in respect of transactions, other events or conditions. Estimation is inherently subjective, and estimates may be developed after the balance sheet date. Developing estimates is potentially more difficult when retrospectively applying an accounting policy or making a retrospective restatement to correct a prior period error, because of the longer period of time that might have passed since the affected transaction, other event or condition occurred. However, the objective of estimates related to prior periods remains the same as for estimates made in the current period, namely, for the estimate to reflect the circumstances that existed when the transaction, other event or condition occurred.

52 Therefore, retrospectively applying a new accounting policy or correcting a prior period error requires distinguishing information that

(a) provides evidence of circumstances that existed on the date(s) as at which the transaction, other event or condition occurred, and

(b) would have been available when the financial statements for that prior period were authorised for issue

from other information. For some types of estimates (eg an estimate of fair value not based on an observable price or observable inputs), it is impracticable to distinguish these types of information. When retrospective application or retrospective restatement would require making a significant estimate for which it is impossible to distinguish these two types of information, it is impracticable to apply the new accounting policy or correct the prior period error retrospectively.

53 Hindsight should not be used when applying a new accounting policy to, or correcting amounts for, a prior period, either in making assumptions about what management's intentions would have been in a prior period or estimating the amounts recognised, measured or disclosed in a prior period. For example, when an entity corrects a prior period error in measuring financial assets previously classified as held-to-maturity investments in accordance with IAS 39 *Financial Instruments: Recognition and Measurement*, it does not change their basis of measurement for that period if management decided later not to hold them to maturity. In addition, when an entity corrects a prior period error in calculating its liability for employees' accumulated sick leave in accordance with IAS 19 *Employee Benefits*, it disregards information about an unusually severe influenza season during the next period that became available after the financial statements for the prior period were authorised for issue. The fact that significant estimates

are frequently required when amending comparative information presented for prior periods does not prevent reliable adjustment or correction of the comparative information.

Effective date

54 **An entity shall apply this Standard for annual periods beginning on or after 1 January 2005. Earlier application is encouraged. If an entity applies this Standard for a period beginning before 1 January 2005, it shall disclose that fact.**

Withdrawal of other pronouncements

55 This Standard supersedes IAS 8 *Net Profit or Loss for the Period, Fundamental Errors and Changes in Accounting Policies*, revised in 1993.

56 This Standard supersedes the following Interpretations:

(a) SIC-2 *Consistency—Capitalisation of Borrowing Costs*; and

(b) SIC-18 *Consistency—Alternative Methods.*

Appendix
Amendments to other pronouncements

The amendments in this appendix shall be applied for annual periods beginning on or after 1 January 2005. If an entity applies this Standard for an earlier period, these amendments shall be applied for that earlier period.

* * * * *

The amendments contained in this appendix when this Standard was revised in 2003 have been incorporated into the relevant pronouncements published in this volume.

Approval of IAS 8 by the Board

International Accounting Standard 8 *Accounting Policies, Changes in Accounting Estimates and Errors* was approved for issue by the fourteen members of the International Accounting Standards Board.

Sir David Tweedie	Chairman
Thomas E Jones	Vice-Chairman
Mary E Barth	
Hans-Georg Bruns	
Anthony T Cope	
Robert P Garnett	
Gilbert Gélard	
James J Leisenring	
Warren J McGregor	
Patricia L O'Malley	
Harry K Schmid	
John T Smith	
Geoffrey Whittington	
Tatsumi Yamada	

Basis for Conclusions

This Basis for Conclusions accompanies, but is not part of, IAS 8.

Introduction

BC1 This Basis for Conclusions summarises the International Accounting Standards Board's considerations in reaching its conclusions on revising IAS 8 *Net Profit or Loss for the Period, Fundamental Errors and Changes in Accounting Policies* in 2003. Individual Board members gave greater weight to some factors than to others.

BC2 In July 2001 the Board announced that, as part of its initial agenda of technical projects, it would undertake a project to improve a number of Standards, including IAS 8. The project was undertaken in the light of queries and criticisms raised in relation to the Standards by securities regulators, professional accountants and other interested parties. The objectives of the Improvements project were to reduce or eliminate alternatives, redundancies and conflicts within Standards, to deal with some convergence issues and to make other improvements. In May 2002 the Board published its proposals in an Exposure Draft of *Improvements to International Accounting Standards*, with a comment deadline of 16 September 2002. The Board received over 160 comment letters on the Exposure Draft.

BC3 The Standard includes extensive changes to the previous version of IAS 8. The Board's intention was not to reconsider all of the previous Standard's requirements for selecting and applying accounting policies, and accounting for changes in accounting policies, changes in accounting estimates and corrections of errors. Accordingly, this Basis for Conclusions does not discuss requirements in IAS 8 that the Board did not reconsider.

Removing allowed alternative treatments

BC4 The previous version of IAS 8 included allowed alternative treatments of voluntary changes in accounting policies (paragraphs 54–57) and corrections of fundamental errors (paragraphs 38–40). Under those allowed alternatives:

(a) the adjustment resulting from retrospective application of a change in an accounting policy was included in profit or loss for the current period; and

(b) the amount of the correction of a fundamental error was included in profit or loss for the current period.

BC5 In both circumstances, comparative information was presented as it was presented in the financial statements of prior periods.

BC6 The Board identified the removal of optional treatments for changes in accounting policies and corrections of errors as an important improvement to the previous version of IAS 8. The Standard removes the allowed alternative treatments and requires changes in accounting policies and corrections of prior period errors to be accounted for retrospectively.

BC7 The Board concluded that retrospective application made by amending the comparative information presented for prior periods is preferable to the previously allowed alternative treatments because, under the now required method of retrospective application:

(a) profit or loss for the period of the change does not include the effects of changes in accounting policies or errors relating to prior periods.

(b) information presented about prior periods is prepared on the same basis as information about the current period, and is therefore comparable. This information possesses a qualitative characteristic identified in the *Framework for the Preparation and Presentation of Financial Statements*, and provides the most useful information for trend analysis of income and expenses.

(c) prior period errors are not repeated in comparative information presented for prior periods.

BC8 Some respondents to the Exposure Draft argued that the previously allowed alternative treatments are preferable because:

(a) correcting prior period errors by restating prior period information involves an unjustifiable use of hindsight;

(b) recognising the effects of changes in accounting policies and corrections of errors in current period profit or loss makes them more prominent to users of financial statements; and

(c) each amount credited or debited to retained earnings as a result of an entity's activities has been recognised in profit or loss in some period.

BC9 The Board concluded that restating prior period information to correct a prior period error does not involve an unjustifiable use of hindsight because prior period errors are defined in terms of a failure to use, or misuse of, reliable information that was available when the prior period financial statements were authorised for issue and could reasonably be expected to have been obtained and taken into account in the preparation and presentation of those financial statements.

BC10 The Board also concluded that the disclosures about changes in accounting policies and corrections of prior period errors in paragraphs 28, 29 and 49 of the Standard should ensure that their effects are sufficiently prominent to users of financial statements.

BC11 The Board further concluded that it is less important for each amount credited or debited to retained earnings as a result of an entity's activities to be recognised in profit or loss in some period than for the profit or loss for each period presented to represent faithfully the effects of transactions and other events occurring in that period.

Eliminating the distinction between fundamental errors and other material prior period errors

BC12 The Standard eliminates the distinction between fundamental errors and other material prior period errors. As a result, all material prior period errors are accounted for in the same way as a fundamental error was accounted for under the retrospective treatment in the previous version of IAS 8. The Board concluded that the definition of 'fundamental errors' in the previous version was difficult to interpret consistently because the main feature of the definition–that the error causes the financial statements of one or more prior periods no longer to be considered to have been reliable–was also a feature of all material prior period errors.

Applying a Standard or an Interpretation that specifically applies to an item

BC13 The Exposure Draft proposed that when a Standard or an Interpretation applies to an item in the financial statements, the accounting policy (or policies) applied to that item is (are) determined by considering the following in descending order:

(a) the Standard (including any Appendices that form part of the Standard);

(b) the Interpretation;

(c) Appendices to the Standard that do not form a part of the Standard; and

(d) Implementation Guidance issued in respect of the Standard.

BC14 The Board decided not to set out a hierarchy of requirements for these circumstances. The Standard requires only applicable Standards and Interpretations to be applied. In addition, it does not mention Appendices.

BC15 The Board decided not to rank Standards above Interpretations because the definition of International Financial Reporting Standards (IFRSs) includes Interpretations, which are equal in status to Standards. The rubric to each Standard clarifies what material constitutes the requirements of an IFRS and what is Implementation Guidance. The term 'Appendix' is retained only for material that is part of an IFRS.

Pronouncements of other standard–setting bodies

BC16 The Exposure Draft proposed that in the absence of a Standard or an Interpretation specifically applying to an item, management should develop and apply an accounting policy by considering, among other guidance, pronouncements of other standard-setting bodies that use a similar conceptual framework to develop accounting standards. Respondents to the Exposure Draft commented that this could *require* entities to consider the pronouncements of various other standard-setting bodies when IASB guidance does not exist. Some commentators argued that, for example, it could require consideration of all components of US GAAP on some topics. After considering these comments, the Board decided that the Standard should indicate that considering such pronouncements is voluntary (see paragraph 12 of the Standard).

BC17 As proposed in the Exposure Draft, the Standard states that pronouncements of other standard-setting bodies are used only if they do not conflict with:

(a) the requirements and guidance in Standards and Interpretations dealing with similar and related issues; and

(b) the definitions, recognition criteria and measurement concepts for assets, liabilities, income and expenses in the *Framework*.

BC18 The Standard refers to the most recent pronouncements of other standard-setting bodies because if pronouncements are withdrawn or superseded, the relevant standard-setting body no longer thinks they include the best accounting policies to apply.

BC19 Comments received indicated that it was unclear from the Exposure Draft whether a change in accounting policy following a change in a pronouncement of another standard-setting body should be accounted for under the transitional provisions in that pronouncement. As noted above, the Standard does not mandate using pronouncements of other standard-setting bodies in any circumstances. Accordingly, the Board decided to clarify that such a change in accounting policy is accounted for and disclosed as a voluntary change in accounting policy (see paragraph 21 of the Standard). Thus, an entity is precluded from applying transitional provisions specified by the other standard-setting body if they are inconsistent with the treatment of voluntary changes in accounting policies specified by the Standard.

Materiality

BC20 The Standard states that accounting policies specified by IFRSs need not be applied when the effect of applying them is immaterial. It also states that financial statements do not comply with IFRSs if they contain material errors, and that material prior period errors are to be corrected in the first set of financial statements authorised for issue after their discovery. The Standard includes a definition of material omissions or misstatements, which is based on the description of materiality in the previous version of IAS 1 *Presentation of Financial Statements* and in the *Framework*.

BC21 The former *Preface to Statements of International Accounting Standards* stated that International Accounting Standards were not intended to apply to immaterial items. There is no equivalent statement in the *Preface to International Financial Reporting Standards*. The Board received comments that the absence of such a statement from the *Preface* could be interpreted as requiring an entity to apply accounting policies (including measurement requirements) specified by IFRSs to immaterial items. However, the Board decided that the application of the concept of materiality should be in Standards rather than in the *Preface*.

BC22 The application of the concept of materiality is set out in two Standards. The revised IAS 1 *Presentation of Financial Statements* continues to specify its application to disclosures. IAS 8 specifies the application of materiality in applying accounting policies and correcting errors (including errors in measuring items).

Criterion for exemption from requirements

BC23 The previous version of IAS 8 included an impracticability criterion for exemption from retrospective application of voluntary changes in accounting policies and retrospective restatement for fundamental errors, and from making related disclosures, when the allowed alternative treatment of those items was not applied. The Exposure Draft proposed instead an exemption from retrospective application and retrospective restatement when it gives rise to undue cost or effort.

BC24 In the light of comments received on the Exposure Draft, the Board decided that an exemption based on management's assessment of undue cost or effort is too subjective to be applied consistently by different entities. Moreover, the Board decided that balancing costs and benefits is a task for the Board when it sets accounting requirements rather than for entities when they apply those requirements. Therefore, the Board decided to retain the impracticability criterion for exemption in the previous version of IAS 8. This affects the exemptions in paragraphs 23–25, 39 and 43–45 of the Standard. Impracticability is the only basis on which specific exemptions are provided in Standards and Interpretations from applying particular requirements when the effect of applying them is material.

Definition of 'impracticable'

BC25 The Board decided to clarify the meaning of 'impracticable' in relation to retrospective application of a change in accounting policy and retrospective restatement to correct a prior period error.

BC26 Some commentators suggested that retrospective application of a change in accounting policy and retrospective restatement to correct a prior period error are impracticable for a particular prior period whenever significant estimates are required as of a date in that period. However, the Board decided to specify a narrower definition of impracticable because the fact that significant estimates are frequently required when amending comparative information presented for prior periods does not prevent reliable adjustment or correction of the comparative information. Thus, the Board decided that an inability to distinguish objectively information that both provides evidence of circumstances that existed on the date(s) as at which those amounts are to be recognised, measured or disclosed and would have been available when the financial statements for that prior period were authorised for issue from other information is the factor that prevents reliable adjustment or correction of comparative information for prior periods (see part (c) of the definition of 'impracticable' and paragraphs 51 and 52 of the Standard).

BC27 The Standard specifies that hindsight should not be used when applying a new accounting policy to, or correcting amounts for, a prior period, either in making assumptions about what management's intentions would have been in a prior period or estimating the amounts in a prior period. This is because management's intentions in a prior period cannot be objectively established in a later period, and using information that would have been unavailable when the financial statements for the prior period(s) affected were authorised for issue is inconsistent with the definitions of retrospective application and retrospective restatement.

Applying the impracticability exemption

BC28 The Standard specifies that when it is impracticable to determine the cumulative effect of applying a new accounting policy to all prior periods, or the cumulative effect of an error on all prior periods, the entity changes the comparative information as if the new accounting policy had been applied, or the error had been corrected, prospectively from the earliest date practicable (see paragraphs 25 and 45 of the Standard). This is similar to paragraph 52 of the previous version of IAS 8, but it is no longer restricted to changes in accounting policies. The Board decided to include such provisions in the Standard because it agrees with comments received that it is preferable to require prospective application from the start of the earliest period practicable than to permit a change in accounting policy only when the entity can determine the cumulative effect of the change for all prior periods at the beginning of the current period.

BC29 Consistently with the Exposure Draft's proposals, the Standard provides an impracticability exemption from retrospective application of changes in accounting policies, including retrospective application of changes made in accordance with the transitional provisions in a Standard or an Interpretation. The previous version of IAS 8 specified the impracticability exemption for retrospective application of only *voluntary* changes in accounting policies. Thus, the applicability of the exemption to changes made in accordance with the transitional provisions in a Standard or an Interpretation depended on the text of that Standard or Interpretation. The Board extended the applicability of the exemption because it decided that the need for the exemption applies equally to all changes in accounting policies applied retrospectively.

Disclosures about impending application of newly issued standards and interpretations

BC30 The Standard requires an entity to provide disclosures when it has not yet applied a new Standard or Interpretation that has been issued but is not yet effective. The entity is required to disclose that it has not yet applied the Standard or Interpretation, and known or reasonably estimable information relevant to assessing the possible impact that initial application of the new Standard or Interpretation will have on the entity's financial statements in the period of initial application (paragraph 30). The Standard also includes guidance on specific disclosures the entity should consider when applying this requirement (paragraph 31).

BC31 Paragraphs 30 and 31 of the Standard differ from the proposals in the Exposure Draft in the following respects:

(a) they specify that an entity needs to disclose information only if it is known or reasonably estimable. This clarification responds to comments on the Exposure Draft that the proposed disclosures would sometimes be impracticable.

(b) whereas the Exposure Draft proposed to mandate the disclosures now in paragraph 31, the Standard sets out these disclosures as items an entity should consider disclosing to meet the general requirement in paragraph 30. This amendment focuses the requirement on the objective of the disclosure, and, in response to comments on the Exposure Draft that the proposed disclosures were more onerous than the disclosures in US GAAP, clarifies that the Board's intention was to converge with US requirements, rather than to be more onerous.

Recognising the effects of changes in accounting estimates

BC32 The Exposure Draft proposed to retain without exception the requirement in the previous version of IAS 8 that the effect of a change in accounting estimate is *recognised in profit or loss* in:

(a) the period of the change, if the change affects that period only; or

(b) the period of the change and future periods, if the change affects both.

BC33 Some respondents to the Exposure Draft disagreed with requiring the effects of all changes in accounting estimates to be recognised in profit or loss. They argued that this is inappropriate to the extent that a change in an accounting estimate gives rise to changes in assets and liabilities, because the entity's equity does not change as a result. These commentators also argued that it is inappropriate to preclude recognising the effects of changes in accounting estimates directly in equity when that is required or permitted by a Standard or an Interpretation. The Board concurs, and decided to provide an exception to the requirement described in paragraph BC32 for these circumstances.

Guidance on Implementing IAS 8

This guidance accompanies, but is not part of, IAS 8.

Example 1 – Retrospective restatement of errors

1.1 During 20X2, Beta Co discovered that some products that had been sold during 20X1 were incorrectly included in inventory at 31 December 20X1 at CU6,500.*

1.2 Beta's accounting records for 20X2 show sales of CU104,000, cost of goods sold of CU86,500 (including CU6,500 for the error in opening inventory), and income taxes of CU5,250.

1.3 In 20X1, Beta reported:

	CU
Sales	73,500
Cost of goods sold	(53,500)
Profit before income taxes	20,000
Income taxes	(6,000)
Profit	14,000

1.4 20X1 opening retained earnings was CU20,000 and closing retained earnings was CU34,000.

1.5 Beta's income tax rate was 30 per cent for 20X2 and 20X1. It had no other income or expenses.

1.6 Beta had CU5,000 of share capital throughout, and no other components of equity except for retained earnings. Its shares are not publicly traded and it does not disclose earnings per share.

Beta Co

Extract from the income statement

	20X2	(restated) 20X1
	CU	CU
Sales	104,000	73,500
Cost of goods sold	(80,000)	(60,000)
Profit before income taxes	24,000	13,500
Income taxes	(7,200)	(4,050)
Profit	16,800	9,450

* In these examples, monetary amounts are denominated in 'currency units' (CU).

Continued from previous page

Beta Co

Statement of changes in equity

	Share capital	Retained earnings	Total
	CU	CU	CU
Balance at 31 December 20X0	5,000	20,000	25,000
Profit for the year ended 31 December 20X1 as restated		9,450	9,450
Balance at 31 December 20X1	5,000	29,450	34,450
Profit for the year ended 31 December 20X2		16,800	16,800
Balance at 31 December 20X2	5,000	46,250	51,250

Extracts from the notes

1 Some products that had been sold in 20X1 were incorrectly included in inventory at 31 December 20X1 at CU6,500. The financial statements of 20X1 have been restated to correct this error. The effect of the restatement on those financial statements is summarised below. There is no effect in 20X2.

	Effect on 20X1
	CU
(Increase) in cost of goods sold	(6,500)
Decrease in income tax expense	1,950
(Decrease) in profit	(4,550)
(Decrease) in inventory	(6,500)
Decrease in income tax payable	1,950
(Decrease) in equity	(4,550)

Example 2 – Change in accounting policy with retrospective application

2.1 During 20X2, Gamma Co changed its accounting policy for the treatment of borrowing costs that are directly attributable to the acquisition of a hydroelectric power station under construction for use by Gamma. In previous periods, Gamma had capitalised such costs. Gamma has now decided to treat these costs as an expense, rather than capitalise them. Management judges that the new policy is preferable because it results in a more transparent treatment of finance costs and is consistent with local industry practice, making Gamma's financial statements more comparable.

2.2 Gamma capitalised borrowing costs incurred of CU2,600 during 20X1 and CU5,200 in periods before 20X1. All borrowing costs incurred in previous years in respect of the acquisition of the power station were capitalised.

2.3 Gamma's accounting records for 20X2 show profit before interest and income taxes of CU30,000; interest expense of CU3,000 (which relates only to 20X2); and income taxes of CU8,100.

2.4 Gamma has not yet recognised any depreciation on the power station because it is not yet in use.

2.5 In 20X1, Gamma reported:

	CU
Profit before interest and income taxes	18,000
Interest expense	–
Profit before income taxes	18,000
Income taxes	(5,400)
Profit	12,600

2.6 20X1 opening retained earnings was CU20,000 and closing retained earnings was CU32,600.

2.7 Gamma's tax rate was 30 per cent for 20X2, 20X1 and prior periods.

2.8 Gamma had CU10,000 of share capital throughout, and no other components of equity except for retained earnings. Its shares are not publicly traded and it does not disclose earnings per share.

Continued from previous page

Gamma Co

Extract from the income statement

	20X2	(restated) 20X1
	CU	CU
Profit before interest and income taxes	30,000	18,000
Interest expense	(3,000)	(2,600)
Profit before income taxes	27,000	15,400
Income taxes	(8,100)	(4,620)
Profit	18,900	10,780

Gamma Co

Statement of changes in equity

	Share capital	(restated) Retained earnings	Total
	CU	CU	CU
Balance at 31 December 20X0 as previously reported	10,000	20,000	30,000
Change in accounting policy for the capitalisation of interest (net of income taxes of CU1,560) (Note 1)		(3,640)	(3,640)
Balance at 31 December 20X0 as restated	10,000	16,360	26,360
Profit for the year ended 31 December 20X1 (restated)		10,780	10,780
Balance at 31 December 20X1	10,000	27,140	37,140
Profit for the year ended 31 December 20X2		18,900	18,900
Balance at 31 December 20X2	10,000	46,040	56,040

Continued from previous page

Extracts from the notes

1 During 20X2, Gamma changed its accounting policy for the treatment of borrowing costs related to a hydro–electric power station under construction for use by Gamma. Previously, Gamma capitalised such costs. They are now written off as expenses as incurred. Management judges that this policy provides reliable and more relevant information because it results in a more transparent treatment of finance costs and is consistent with local industry practice, making Gamma's financial statements more comparable. This change in accounting policy has been accounted for retrospectively, and the comparative statements for 20X1 have been restated. The effect of the change on 20X1 is tabulated below. Opening retained earnings for 20X1 have been reduced by CU3,640, which is the amount of the adjustment relating to periods prior to 20X1.

Effect on 20X1	CU
(Increase) in interest expense	(2,600)
Decrease in income tax expense	780
(Decrease) in profit	(1,820)
Effect on periods prior to 20X1	
(Decrease) in profit (CU5,200 interest expense less tax of CU1,560)	(3,640)
(Decrease) in assets in the course of construction and in retained earnings at 31 December 20X1	(5,460)

Example 3 – Prospective application of a change in accounting policy when retrospective application is not practicable

3.1 During 20X2, Delta Co changed its accounting policy for depreciating property, plant and equipment, so as to apply much more fully a components approach, whilst at the same time adopting the revaluation model.

3.2 In years before 20X2, Delta's asset records were not sufficiently detailed to apply a components approach fully. At the end of 20X1, management commissioned an engineering survey, which provided information on the components held and their fair values, useful lives, estimated residual values and depreciable amounts at the beginning of 20X2. However, the survey did not provide a sufficient basis for reliably estimating the cost of those components that had not previously been accounted for separately, and the existing records before the survey did not permit this information to be reconstructed.

Continued from previous page

3.3 Delta's management considered how to account for each of the two aspects of the accounting change. They determined that it was not practicable to account for the change to a fuller components approach retrospectively, or to account for that change prospectively from any earlier date than the start of 20X2. Also, the change from a cost model to a revaluation model is required to be accounted for prospectively. Therefore, management concluded that it should apply Delta's new policy prospectively from the start of 20X2.

3.4 Additional information:

Delta's tax rate is 30 per cent.

	CU
Property, plant and equipment at the end of 20X1:	
Cost	25,000
Depreciation	(14,000)
Net book value	11,000
Prospective depreciation expense for 20X2 (old basis)	1,500
Some results of the engineering survey:	
Valuation	17,000
Estimated residual value	3,000
Average remaining asset life (years)	7
Depreciation expense on existing property, plant and equipment for 20X2 (new basis)	2,000

Extract from the notes

1 From the start of 20X2, Delta changed its accounting policy for depreciating property, plant and equipment, so as to apply much more fully a components approach, whilst at the same time adopting the revaluation model. Management takes the view that this policy provides reliable and more relevant information because it deals more accurately with the components of property, plant and equipment and is based on up-to-date values. The policy has been applied prospectively from the start of 20X2 because it was not practicable to estimate the effects of applying the policy either retrospectively, or prospectively from any earlier date. Accordingly, the adoption of the new policy has no effect on prior years. The effect on the current year is to increase the carrying amount of property, plant and equipment at the start of the year by CU6,000; increase the opening deferred tax provision by CU1,800; create a revaluation reserve at the start of the year of CU4,200; increase depreciation expense by CU500; and reduce tax expense by CU150.

Table of Concordance

This table shows how the contents of the superseded version of IAS 8 and the current version of IAS 8 correspond. Paragraphs are treated as corresponding if they broadly address the same matter even though the guidance may differ.

This table also shows how the requirements of SIC-2 and SIC-18 have been incorporated into the current version of IAS 8.

Superseded IAS 8 paragraph	Current IAS 8 paragraph	Superseded IAS 8 paragraph	Current IAS 8 paragraph	Superseded IAS 8 paragraph	Current IAS 8 paragraph
Objective	1	24	34	48	30, 31
1	3	25	35	49	22, 23
2	55	26	36	50	26
3	2	27	38	51	None
4	None	28	None	52	24, 25
5	4	29	None	53	28, 29
6	5	30	39, 40	54	None
7	(IAS 1.78)	31	41	55	None
8	(IAS 1.79)	32	41	56	None
9	(IAS 1.80)	33	48	57	None
10	(IAS 1.85)	34	42	58	54
11	None	35	46	Appendix A	Guidance on Implementing IAS 8
12	None	36	None		
13	None	37	49	SIC-2	13
14	None	38	None	SIC-18	13
15	None	39	None	None	6
16	(IAS 1.86)	40	None	None	20, 21
17	None	41	15	None	27
18	(IAS 1.87)	42	14	None	37
19	None	43	14	None	43–45
20	None	44	16–18	None	47
21	None	45	None	None	50–53
22	None	46	19	None	56
23	32, 33	47	None		

International Accounting Standard 10

Events after the Balance Sheet Date

This version includes amendments resulting from new and amended IFRSs issued up to 31 December 2004.

CONTENTS

International Accounting Standard 10 *Events after the Balance Sheet Date* (IAS 10) is set out in paragraphs 1–24 and the Appendix. All the paragraphs have equal authority but retain the IASC format of the Standard when it was adopted by the IASB. IAS 10 should be read in the context of its objective and the Basis for Conclusions, the *Preface to International Financial Reporting Standards* and the *Framework for the Preparation and Presentation of Financial Statements*. IAS 8 *Accounting Policies, Changes in Accounting Estimates and Errors* provides a basis for selecting and applying accounting policies in the absence of explicit guidance.

Introduction

IN1 International Accounting Standard 10 *Events after the Balance Sheet Date* (IAS 10) replaces IAS 10 *Events After the Balance Sheet Date* (revised in 1999) and should be applied for annual periods beginning on or after 1 January 2005. Earlier application is encouraged.

Reasons for revising IAS 10

IN2 The International Accounting Standards Board developed this revised IAS 10 as part of its project on Improvements to International Accounting Standards. The project was undertaken in the light of queries and criticisms raised in relation to the Standards by securities regulators, professional accountants and other interested parties. The objectives of the project were to reduce or eliminate alternatives, redundancies and conflicts within the Standards, to deal with some convergence issues and to make other improvements.

IN3 For IAS 10 the Board's main objective was a limited clarification of the accounting for dividends declared after the balance sheet date. The Board did not reconsider the fundamental approach to the accounting for events after the balance sheet date contained in IAS 10.

The main changes

IN4 The main change from the previous version of IAS 10 was a limited clarification of paragraphs 12 and 13 (paragraphs 11 and 12 of the previous version of IAS 10). As revised, those paragraphs state that if an entity declares dividends after the balance sheet date, the entity shall not recognise those dividends as a liability at the balance sheet date.

International Accounting Standard 10
Events after the Balance Sheet Date

Objective

1 The objective of this Standard is to prescribe:

(a) when an entity should adjust its financial statements for events after the balance sheet date; and

(b) the disclosures that an entity should give about the date when the financial statements were authorised for issue and about events after the balance sheet date.

The Standard also requires that an entity should not prepare its financial statements on a going concern basis if events after the balance sheet date indicate that the going concern assumption is not appropriate.

Scope

2 **This Standard shall be applied in the accounting for, and disclosure of, events after the balance sheet date.**

Definitions

3 **The following terms are used in this Standard with the meanings specified:**

Events after the balance sheet **date are those events, favourable and unfavourable, that occur between the balance sheet date and the date when the financial statements are authorised for issue. Two types of events can be identified:**

(a) those that provide evidence of conditions that existed at the balance sheet date (*adjusting events after the balance sheet date***); and**

(b) those that are indicative of conditions that arose after the balance sheet date (*non-adjusting events after the balance sheet date***).**

4 The process involved in authorising the financial statements for issue will vary depending upon the management structure, statutory requirements and procedures followed in preparing and finalising the financial statements.

5 In some cases, an entity is required to submit its financial statements to its shareholders for approval after the financial statements have been issued. In such cases, the financial statements are authorised for issue on the date of issue, not the date when shareholders approve the financial statements.

> **Example**
>
> The management of an entity completes draft financial statements for the year to 31 December 20X1 on 28 February 20X2. On 18 March 20X2, the board of directors reviews the financial statements and authorises them for issue. The entity announces its profit and selected other financial information on 19 March 20X2. The financial statements are made available to shareholders and others on 1 April 20X2. The shareholders approve the financial statements at their annual meeting on 15 May 20X2 and the approved financial statements are then filed with a regulatory body on 17 May 20X2.
>
> *The financial statements are authorised for issue on 18 March 20X2 (date of board authorisation for issue).*

6 In some cases, the management of an entity is required to issue its financial statements to a supervisory board (made up solely of non-executives) for approval. In such cases, the financial statements are authorised for issue when the management authorises them for issue to the supervisory board.

> **Example**
>
> On 18 March 20X2, the management of an entity authorises financial statements for issue to its supervisory board. The supervisory board is made up solely of non-executives and may include representatives of employees and other outside interests. The supervisory board approves the financial statements on 26 March 20X2. The financial statements are made available to shareholders and others on 1 April 20X2. The shareholders approve the financial statements at their annual meeting on 15 May 20X2 and the financial statements are then filed with a regulatory body on 17 May 20X2.
>
> *The financial statements are authorised for issue on 18 March 20X2 (date of management authorisation for issue to the supervisory board).*

7 Events after the balance sheet date include all events up to the date when the financial statements are authorised for issue, even if those events occur after the public announcement of profit or of other selected financial information.

Recognition and measurement

Adjusting events after the balance sheet date

8 **An entity shall adjust the amounts recognised in its financial statements to reflect adjusting events after the balance sheet date.**

9 The following are examples of adjusting events after the balance sheet date that require an entity to adjust the amounts recognised in its financial statements, or to recognise items that were not previously recognised:

(a) the settlement after the balance sheet date of a court case that confirms that the entity had a present obligation at the balance sheet date. The entity adjusts any previously recognised provision related to this court case in accordance with IAS 37 *Provisions, Contingent Liabilities and Contingent Assets* or recognises a new provision. The entity does not merely disclose a contingent liability because the settlement provides additional evidence that would be considered in accordance with paragraph 16 of IAS 37.

(b) the receipt of information after the balance sheet date indicating that an asset was impaired at the balance sheet date, or that the amount of a previously recognised impairment loss for that asset needs to be adjusted. For example:

(i) the bankruptcy of a customer that occurs after the balance sheet date usually confirms that a loss existed at the balance sheet date on a trade receivable and that the entity needs to adjust the carrying amount of the trade receivable; and

(ii) the sale of inventories after the balance sheet date may give evidence about their net realisable value at the balance sheet date.

(c) the determination after the balance sheet date of the cost of assets purchased, or the proceeds from assets sold, before the balance sheet date.

(d) the determination after the balance sheet date of the amount of profit-sharing or bonus payments, if the entity had a present legal or constructive obligation at the balance sheet date to make such payments as a result of events before that date (see IAS 19 *Employee Benefits*).

(e) the discovery of fraud or errors that show that the financial statements are incorrect.

Non–adjusting events after the balance sheet date

10 **An entity shall not adjust the amounts recognised in its financial statements to reflect non-adjusting events after the balance sheet date.**

11 An example of a non-adjusting event after the balance sheet date is a decline in market value of investments between the balance sheet date and the date when the financial statements are authorised for issue. The decline in market value does not normally relate to the condition of the investments at the balance sheet date, but reflects circumstances that have arisen subsequently. Therefore, an entity does not adjust the amounts recognised in its financial statements for the investments. Similarly, the entity does not update the amounts disclosed for the investments as at the balance sheet date, although it may need to give additional disclosure under paragraph 21.

Dividends

12 **If an entity declares dividends to holders of equity instruments (as defined in IAS 32** *Financial Instruments: Disclosure and Presentation***) after the balance sheet date, the entity shall not recognise those dividends as a liability at the balance sheet date.**

13 If dividends are declared (ie the dividends are appropriately authorised and no longer at the discretion of the entity) after the balance sheet date but before the financial statements are authorised for issue, the dividends are not recognised as a liability at the balance sheet date because they do not meet the criteria of a

present obligation in IAS 37. Such dividends are disclosed in the notes in accordance with IAS 1 *Presentation of Financial Statements*.

Going concern

14 **An entity shall not prepare its financial statements on a going concern basis if management determines after the balance sheet date either that it intends to liquidate the entity or to cease trading, or that it has no realistic alternative but to do so.**

15 Deterioration in operating results and financial position after the balance sheet date may indicate a need to consider whether the going concern assumption is still appropriate. If the going concern assumption is no longer appropriate, the effect is so pervasive that this Standard requires a fundamental change in the basis of accounting, rather than an adjustment to the amounts recognised within the original basis of accounting.

16 IAS 1 specifies required disclosures if:

(a) the financial statements are not prepared on a going concern basis; or

(b) management is aware of material uncertainties related to events or conditions that may cast significant doubt upon the entity's ability to continue as a going concern. The events or conditions requiring disclosure may arise after the balance sheet date.

Disclosure

Date of authorisation for issue

17 **An entity shall disclose the date when the financial statements were authorised for issue and who gave that authorisation. If the entity's owners or others have the power to amend the financial statements after issue, the entity shall disclose that fact.**

18 It is important for users to know when the financial statements were authorised for issue, because the financial statements do not reflect events after this date.

Updating disclosure about conditions at the balance sheet date

19 **If an entity receives information after the balance sheet date about conditions that existed at the balance sheet date, it shall update disclosures that relate to those conditions, in the light of the new information.**

20 In some cases, an entity needs to update the disclosures in its financial statements to reflect information received after the balance sheet date, even when the information does not affect the amounts that it recognises in its financial statements. One example of the need to update disclosures is when evidence becomes available after the balance sheet date about a contingent liability that existed at the balance sheet date. In addition to considering whether it should recognise or change a provision under IAS 37 *Provisions, Contingent Liabilities and Contingent Assets*, an entity updates its disclosures about the contingent liability in the light of that evidence.

Non–adjusting events after the balance sheet date

21 **If non-adjusting events after the balance sheet date are material, non-disclosure could influence the economic decisions of users taken on the basis of the financial statements. Accordingly, an entity shall disclose the following for each material category of non-adjusting event after the balance sheet date:**

(a) the nature of the event; and

(b) an estimate of its financial effect, or a statement that such an estimate cannot be made.

22 The following are examples of non-adjusting events after the balance sheet date that would generally result in disclosure:

(a) a major business combination after the balance sheet date (IFRS 3 *Business Combinations* requires specific disclosures in such cases) or disposing of a major subsidiary;

(b) announcing a plan to discontinue an operation;

(c) major purchases of assets, classification of assets as held for sale in accordance with IFRS 5 *Non-current Assets Held for Sale and Discontinued Operations*, other disposals of assets, or expropriation of major assets by government;

(d) the destruction of a major production plant by a fire after the balance sheet date;

(e) announcing, or commencing the implementation of, a major restructuring (see IAS 37);

(f) major ordinary share transactions and potential ordinary share transactions after the balance sheet date (IAS 33 *Earnings per Share* requires an entity to disclose a description of such transactions, other than when such transactions involve capitalisation or bonus issues, share splits or reverse share splits all of which are required to be adjusted under IAS 33);

(g) abnormally large changes after the balance sheet date in asset prices or foreign exchange rates;

(h) changes in tax rates or tax laws enacted or announced after the balance sheet date that have a significant effect on current and deferred tax assets and liabilities (see IAS 12 *Income Taxes*);

(i) entering into significant commitments or contingent liabilities, for example, by issuing significant guarantees; and

(j) commencing major litigation arising solely out of events that occurred after the balance sheet date.

Effective date

23 **An entity shall apply this Standard for annual periods beginning on or after 1 January 2005. Earlier application is encouraged. If an entity applies this Standard for a period beginning before 1 January 2005, it shall disclose that fact.**

Withdrawal of IAS 10 (revised 1999)

24 This Standard supersedes IAS 10 *Events After the Balance Sheet Date* (revised in 1999).

Appendix
Amendments to other pronouncements

The amendments in this appendix shall be applied for annual periods beginning on or after 1 January 2005. If an entity applies this Standard for an earlier period, these amendments shall be applied for that earlier period.

* * * * *

The amendments contained in this appendix when this Standard was revised in 2003 have been incorporated into the relevant pronouncements published in this volume.

Approval of IAS 10 by the Board

International Accounting Standard 10 *Events after the Balance Sheet Date* was approved for issue by the fourteen members of the International Accounting Standards Board.

Sir David Tweedie	Chairman
Thomas E Jones	Vice-Chairman
Mary E Barth	
Hans-Georg Bruns	
Anthony T Cope	
Robert P Garnett	
Gilbert Gélard	
James J Leisenring	
Warren J McGregor	
Patricia L O'Malley	
Harry K Schmid	
John T Smith	
Geoffrey Whittington	
Tatsumi Yamada	

Basis for Conclusions

This Basis for Conclusions accompanies, but is not part of, IAS 10.

Introduction

BC1 This Basis for Conclusions summarises the International Accounting Standards Board's considerations in reaching its conclusions on revising IAS 10 *Events After the Balance Sheet Date* in 2003. Individual Board members gave greater weight to some factors than to others.

BC2 In July 2001 the Board announced that, as part of its initial agenda of technical projects, it would undertake a project to improve a number of Standards, including IAS 10. The project was undertaken in the light of queries and criticisms raised in relation to the Standards by securities regulators, professional accountants and other interested parties. The objectives of the Improvements project were to reduce or eliminate alternatives, redundancies and conflicts within Standards, to deal with some convergence issues and to make other improvements. In May 2002 the Board published its proposals in an Exposure Draft of *Improvements to International Accounting Standards*, with a comment deadline of 16 September 2002. The Board received over 160 comment letters on the Exposure Draft.

BC3 Because the Board's intention was not to reconsider the fundamental approach to the accounting for events after the balance sheet date established by IAS 10, this Basis for Conclusions does not discuss requirements in IAS 10 that the Board has not reconsidered.

Limited clarification

BC4 For this limited clarification of IAS 10 the main change made is in paragraphs 12 and 13 (paragraphs 11 and 12 of the previous version of IAS 10). As revised, those paragraphs state that if dividends are declared after the balance sheet date, an entity shall not recognise those dividends as a liability at the balance sheet date. This is because undeclared dividends do not meet the criteria of a present obligation in IAS 37 *Provisions, Contingent Liabilities and Contingent Assets*. The Board discussed whether or not an entity's past practice of paying dividends could be considered a constructive obligation. The Board concluded that such practices do not give rise to a liability to pay dividends.

Table of Concordance

This table shows how the contents of the superseded version of IAS 10 and the current version of IAS 10 correspond. Paragraphs are treated as corresponding if they broadly address the same matter even though the guidance may differ.

Superseded IAS 10 paragraph	Current IAS 10 paragraph
Objective	1
1	2
2	3
3	4
4	5
5	6
6	7
7	8
8	9
9	10
10	11
11	12
12	13
13	14
14	15
15	16
16	17
17	18
18	19
19	20
20	21
21	22
22	23
23	None
None	24

International Accounting Standard 11

Construction Contracts

This Standard is effective for financial statements covering periods beginning on or after 1 January 1995.

CONTENTS

International Accounting Standard 11 *Construction Contracts* (IAS 11) is set out in paragraphs 1–46. All the paragraphs have equal authority but retain the IASC format of the Standard when it was adopted by the IASB. IAS 11 should be read in the context of its objective, the *Preface to International Financial Reporting Standards* and the *Framework for the Preparation and Presentation of Financial Statements*. IAS 8 *Accounting Policies, Changes in Accounting Estimates and Errors* provides a basis for selecting and applying accounting policies in the absence of explicit guidance.

International Accounting Standard 11 Construction Contracts

Objective

The objective of this Standard is to prescribe the accounting treatment of revenue and costs associated with construction contracts. Because of the nature of the activity undertaken in construction contracts, the date at which the contract activity is entered into and the date when the activity is completed usually fall into different accounting periods. Therefore, the primary issue in accounting for construction contracts is the allocation of contract revenue and contract costs to the accounting periods in which construction work is performed. This Standard uses the recognition criteria established in the *Framework for the Preparation and Presentation of Financial Statements* to determine when contract revenue and contract costs should be recognised as revenue and expenses in the income statement. It also provides practical guidance on the application of these criteria.

Scope

1 **This Standard shall be applied in accounting for construction contracts in the financial statements of contractors.**

2 This Standard supersedes IAS 11 *Accounting for Construction Contracts* approved in 1978.

Definitions

3 **The following terms are used in this Standard with the meanings specified:**

A *construction contract* **is a contract specifically negotiated for the construction of an asset or a combination of assets that are closely interrelated or interdependent in terms of their design, technology and function or their ultimate purpose or use.**

A *fixed price contract* **is a construction contract in which the contractor agrees to a fixed contract price, or a fixed rate per unit of output, which in some cases is subject to cost escalation clauses.**

A *cost plus contract* **is a construction contract in which the contractor is reimbursed for allowable or otherwise defined costs, plus a percentage of these costs or a fixed fee.**

4 A construction contract may be negotiated for the construction of a single asset such as a bridge, building, dam, pipeline, road, ship or tunnel. A construction contract may also deal with the construction of a number of assets which are closely interrelated or interdependent in terms of their design, technology and function or their ultimate purpose or use; examples of such contracts include those for the construction of refineries and other complex pieces of plant or equipment.

5 For the purposes of this Standard, construction contracts include:

(a) contracts for the rendering of services which are directly related to the construction of the asset, for example, those for the services of project managers and architects; and

(b) contracts for the destruction or restoration of assets, and the restoration of the environment following the demolition of assets.

6 Construction contracts are formulated in a number of ways which, for the purposes of this Standard, are classified as fixed price contracts and cost plus contracts. Some construction contracts may contain characteristics of both a fixed price contract and a cost plus contract, for example in the case of a cost plus contract with an agreed maximum price. In such circumstances, a contractor needs to consider all the conditions in paragraphs 23 and 24 in order to determine when to recognise contract revenue and expenses.

Combining and segmenting construction contracts

7 The requirements of this Standard are usually applied separately to each construction contract. However, in certain circumstances, it is necessary to apply the Standard to the separately identifiable components of a single contract or to a group of contracts together in order to reflect the substance of a contract or a group of contracts.

8 When a contract covers a number of assets, the construction of each asset shall be treated as a separate construction contract when:

(a) separate proposals have been submitted for each asset;

(b) each asset has been subject to separate negotiation and the contractor and customer have been able to accept or reject that part of the contract relating to each asset; and

(c) the costs and revenues of each asset can be identified.

9 A group of contracts, whether with a single customer or with several customers, shall be treated as a single construction contract when:

(a) the group of contracts is negotiated as a single package;

(b) the contracts are so closely interrelated that they are, in effect, part of a single project with an overall profit margin; and

(c) the contracts are performed concurrently or in a continuous sequence.

10 A contract may provide for the construction of an additional asset at the option of the customer or may be amended to include the construction of an additional asset. The construction of the additional asset shall be treated as a separate construction contract when:

(a) the asset differs significantly in design, technology or function from the asset or assets covered by the original contract; or

(b) the price of the asset is negotiated without regard to the original contract price.

Contract revenue

11 **Contract revenue shall comprise:**

(a) **the initial amount of revenue agreed in the contract; and**

(b) **variations in contract work, claims and incentive payments:**

(i) **to the extent that it is probable that they will result in revenue; and**

(ii) **they are capable of being reliably measured.**

12 Contract revenue is measured at the fair value of the consideration received or receivable. The measurement of contract revenue is affected by a variety of uncertainties that depend on the outcome of future events. The estimates often need to be revised as events occur and uncertainties are resolved. Therefore, the amount of contract revenue may increase or decrease from one period to the next. For example:

(a) a contractor and a customer may agree variations or claims that increase or decrease contract revenue in a period subsequent to that in which the contract was initially agreed;

(b) the amount of revenue agreed in a fixed price contract may increase as a result of cost escalation clauses;

(c) the amount of contract revenue may decrease as a result of penalties arising from delays caused by the contractor in the completion of the contract; or

(d) when a fixed price contract involves a fixed price per unit of output, contract revenue increases as the number of units is increased.

13 A variation is an instruction by the customer for a change in the scope of the work to be performed under the contract. A variation may lead to an increase or a decrease in contract revenue. Examples of variations are changes in the specifications or design of the asset and changes in the duration of the contract. A variation is included in contract revenue when:

(a) it is probable that the customer will approve the variation and the amount of revenue arising from the variation; and

(b) the amount of revenue can be reliably measured.

14 A claim is an amount that the contractor seeks to collect from the customer or another party as reimbursement for costs not included in the contract price. A claim may arise from, for example, customer caused delays, errors in specifications or design, and disputed variations in contract work. The measurement of the amounts of revenue arising from claims is subject to a high level of uncertainty and often depends on the outcome of negotiations. Therefore, claims are included in contract revenue only when:

(a) negotiations have reached an advanced stage such that it is probable that the customer will accept the claim; and

(b) the amount that it is probable will be accepted by the customer can be measured reliably.

15 Incentive payments are additional amounts paid to the contractor if specified performance standards are met or exceeded. For example, a contract may allow for an incentive payment to the contractor for early completion of the contract. Incentive payments are included in contract revenue when:

(a) the contract is sufficiently advanced that it is probable that the specified performance standards will be met or exceeded; and

(b) the amount of the incentive payment can be measured reliably.

Contract costs

16 Contract costs shall comprise:

(a) costs that relate directly to the specific contract;

(b) costs that are attributable to contract activity in general and can be allocated to the contract; and

(c) such other costs as are specifically chargeable to the customer under the terms of the contract.

17 Costs that relate directly to a specific contract include:

(a) site labour costs, including site supervision;

(b) costs of materials used in construction;

(c) depreciation of plant and equipment used on the contract;

(d) costs of moving plant, equipment and materials to and from the contract site;

(e) costs of hiring plant and equipment;

(f) costs of design and technical assistance that is directly related to the contract;

(g) the estimated costs of rectification and guarantee work, including expected warranty costs; and

(h) claims from third parties.

These costs may be reduced by any incidental income that is not included in contract revenue, for example income from the sale of surplus materials and the disposal of plant and equipment at the end of the contract.

18 Costs that may be attributable to contract activity in general and can be allocated to specific contracts include:

(a) insurance;

(b) costs of design and technical assistance that are not directly related to a specific contract; and

(c) construction overheads.

Such costs are allocated using methods that are systematic and rational and are applied consistently to all costs having similar characteristics. The allocation is based on the normal level of construction activity. Construction overheads include costs such as the preparation and processing of construction personnel payroll. Costs that may be attributable to contract activity in general and can be allocated to specific contracts also include borrowing costs when the contractor adopts the allowed alternative treatment in IAS 23 *Borrowing Costs*.

19 Costs that are specifically chargeable to the customer under the terms of the contract may include some general administration costs and development costs for which reimbursement is specified in the terms of the contract.

20 Costs that cannot be attributed to contract activity or cannot be allocated to a contract are excluded from the costs of a construction contract. Such costs include:

(a) general administration costs for which reimbursement is not specified in the contract;

(b) selling costs;

(c) research and development costs for which reimbursement is not specified in the contract; and

(d) depreciation of idle plant and equipment that is not used on a particular contract.

21 Contract costs include the costs attributable to a contract for the period from the date of securing the contract to the final completion of the contract. However, costs that relate directly to a contract and are incurred in securing the contract are also included as part of the contract costs if they can be separately identified and measured reliably and it is probable that the contract will be obtained. When costs incurred in securing a contract are recognised as an expense in the period in which they are incurred, they are not included in contract costs when the contract is obtained in a subsequent period.

Recognition of contract revenue and expenses

22 When the outcome of a construction contract can be estimated reliably, contract revenue and contract costs associated with the construction contract shall be recognised as revenue and expenses respectively by reference to the stage of completion of the contract activity at the balance sheet date. An expected loss on the construction contract shall be recognised as an expense immediately in accordance with paragraph 36.

23 In the case of a fixed price contract, the outcome of a construction contract can be estimated reliably when all the following conditions are satisfied:

(a) total contract revenue can be measured reliably;

(b) it is probable that the economic benefits associated with the contract will flow to the entity;

(c) both the contract costs to complete the contract and the stage of contract completion at the balance sheet date can be measured reliably; and

(d) the contract costs attributable to the contract can be clearly identified and measured reliably so that actual contract costs incurred can be compared with prior estimates.

24 In the case of a cost plus contract, the outcome of a construction contract can be estimated reliably when all the following conditions are satisfied:

(a) it is probable that the economic benefits associated with the contract will flow to the entity; and

(b) the contract costs attributable to the contract, whether or not specifically reimbursable, can be clearly identified and measured reliably.

25 The recognition of revenue and expenses by reference to the stage of completion of a contract is often referred to as the percentage of completion method. Under this method, contract revenue is matched with the contract costs incurred in reaching the stage of completion, resulting in the reporting of revenue, expenses and profit which can be attributed to the proportion of work completed. This method provides useful information on the extent of contract activity and performance during a period.

26 Under the percentage of completion method, contract revenue is recognised as revenue in the income statement in the accounting periods in which the work is performed. Contract costs are usually recognised as an expense in the income statement in the accounting periods in which the work to which they relate is performed. However, any expected excess of total contract costs over total contract revenue for the contract is recognised as an expense immediately in accordance with paragraph 36.

27 A contractor may have incurred contract costs that relate to future activity on the contract. Such contract costs are recognised as an asset provided it is probable that they will be recovered. Such costs represent an amount due from the customer and are often classified as contract work in progress.

28 The outcome of a construction contract can only be estimated reliably when it is probable that the economic benefits associated with the contract will flow to the entity. However, when an uncertainty arises about the collectibility of an amount already included in contract revenue, and already recognised in the income statement, the uncollectable amount or the amount in respect of which recovery has ceased to be probable is recognised as an expense rather than as an adjustment of the amount of contract revenue.

29 An entity is generally able to make reliable estimates after it has agreed to a contract which establishes:

(a) each party's enforceable rights regarding the asset to be constructed;

(b) the consideration to be exchanged; and

(c) the manner and terms of settlement.

It is also usually necessary for the entity to have an effective internal financial budgeting and reporting system. The entity reviews and, when necessary, revises the estimates of contract revenue and contract costs as the contract progresses. The need for such revisions does not necessarily indicate that the outcome of the contract cannot be estimated reliably.

30 The stage of completion of a contract may be determined in a variety of ways. The entity uses the method that measures reliably the work performed. Depending on the nature of the contract, the methods may include:

(a) the proportion that contract costs incurred for work performed to date bear to the estimated total contract costs;

(b) surveys of work performed; or

(c) completion of a physical proportion of the contract work.

Progress payments and advances received from customers often do not reflect the work performed.

31 When the stage of completion is determined by reference to the contract costs incurred to date, only those contract costs that reflect work performed are included in costs incurred to date. Examples of contract costs which are excluded are:

(a) contract costs that relate to future activity on the contract, such as costs of materials that have been delivered to a contract site or set aside for use in a contract but not yet installed, used or applied during contract performance, unless the materials have been made specially for the contract; and

(b) payments made to subcontractors in advance of work performed under the subcontract.

32 When the outcome of a construction contract cannot be estimated reliably:

(a) revenue shall be recognised only to the extent of contract costs incurred that it is probable will be recoverable; and

(b) contract costs shall be recognised as an expense in the period in which they are incurred.

An expected loss on the construction contract shall be recognised as an expense immediately in accordance with paragraph 36.

33 During the early stages of a contract it is often the case that the outcome of the contract cannot be estimated reliably. Nevertheless, it may be probable that the entity will recover the contract costs incurred. Therefore, contract revenue is recognised only to the extent of costs incurred that are expected to be recoverable. As the outcome of the contract cannot be estimated reliably, no profit is recognised. However, even though the outcome of the contract cannot be estimated reliably, it may be probable that total contract costs will exceed total contract revenues. In such cases, any expected excess of total contract costs over total contract revenue for the contract is recognised as an expense immediately in accordance with paragraph 36.

34 Contract costs that are not probable of being recovered are recognised as an expense immediately. Examples of circumstances in which the recoverability of contract costs incurred may not be probable and in which contract costs may need to be recognised as an expense immediately include contracts:

(a) that are not fully enforceable, ie their validity is seriously in question;

(b) the completion of which is subject to the outcome of pending litigation or legislation;

(c) relating to properties that are likely to be condemned or expropriated;

(d) where the customer is unable to meet its obligations; or

(e) where the contractor is unable to complete the contract or otherwise meet its obligations under the contract.

35 When the uncertainties that prevented the outcome of the contract being estimated reliably no longer exist, revenue and expenses associated with the construction contract shall be recognised in accordance with paragraph 22 rather than in accordance with paragraph 32.

Recognition of expected losses

36 When it is probable that total contract costs will exceed total contract revenue, the expected loss shall be recognised as an expense immediately.

37 The amount of such a loss is determined irrespective of:

(a) whether work has commenced on the contract;

(b) the stage of completion of contract activity; or

(c) the amount of profits expected to arise on other contracts which are not treated as a single construction contract in accordance with paragraph 9.

Changes in estimates

38 The percentage of completion method is applied on a cumulative basis in each accounting period to the current estimates of contract revenue and contract costs. Therefore, the effect of a change in the estimate of contract revenue or contract costs, or the effect of a change in the estimate of the outcome of a contract, is accounted for as a change in accounting estimate (see IAS 8 *Accounting Policies, Changes in Accounting Estimates and Errors*). The changed estimates are used in the determination of the amount of revenue and expenses recognised in the income statement in the period in which the change is made and in subsequent periods.

Disclosure

39 An entity shall disclose:

(a) the amount of contract revenue recognised as revenue in the period;

(b) the methods used to determine the contract revenue recognised in the period; and

(c) the methods used to determine the stage of completion of contracts in progress.

40 An entity shall disclose each of the following for contracts in progress at the balance sheet date:

(a) the aggregate amount of costs incurred and recognised profits (less recognised losses) to date;

(b) the amount of advances received; and

(c) the amount of retentions.

41 Retentions are amounts of progress billings that are not paid until the satisfaction of conditions specified in the contract for the payment of such amounts or until defects have been rectified. Progress billings are amounts billed for work performed on a contract whether or not they have been paid by the customer. Advances are amounts received by the contractor before the related work is performed.

42 An entity shall present:

(a) the gross amount due from customers for contract work as an asset; and

(b) the gross amount due to customers for contract work as a liability.

43 The gross amount due from customers for contract work is the net amount of:

(a) costs incurred plus recognised profits; less

(b) the sum of recognised losses and progress billings

for all contracts in progress for which costs incurred plus recognised profits (less recognised losses) exceeds progress billings.

44 The gross amount due to customers for contract work is the net amount of:

(a) costs incurred plus recognised profits; less

(b) the sum of recognised losses and progress billings

for all contracts in progress for which progress billings exceed costs incurred plus recognised profits (less recognised losses).

45 An entity discloses any contingent liabilities and contingent assets in accordance with IAS 37 *Provisions, Contingent Liabilities and Contingent Assets*. Contingent liabilities and contingent assets may arise from such items as warranty costs, claims, penalties or possible losses.

Effective date

46 This Standard becomes operative for financial statements covering periods beginning on or after 1 January 1995.

Appendix
Illustrative examples

This appendix accompanies, but is not part of, IAS 11.

Disclosure of accounting policies

The following are examples of accounting policy disclosures:

Revenue from fixed price construction contracts is recognised on the percentage of completion method, measured by reference to the percentage of labour hours incurred to date to estimated total labour hours for each contract.

Revenue from cost plus contracts is recognised by reference to the recoverable costs incurred during the period plus the fee earned, measured by the proportion that costs incurred to date bear to the estimated total costs of the contract.

The determination of contract revenue and expenses

The following example illustrates one method of determining the stage of completion of a contract and the timing of the recognition of contract revenue and expenses (see paragraphs 22–35 of the Standard).

A construction contractor has a fixed price contract for 9,000 to build a bridge. The initial amount of revenue agreed in the contract is 9,000. The contractor's initial estimate of contract costs is 8,000. It will take 3 years to build the bridge.

By the end of year 1, the contractor's estimate of contract costs has increased to 8,050.

In year 2, the customer approves a variation resulting in an increase in contract revenue of 200 and estimated additional contract costs of 150. At the end of year 2, costs incurred include 100 for standard materials stored at the site to be used in year 3 to complete the project.

The contractor determines the stage of completion of the contract by calculating the proportion that contract costs incurred for work performed to date bear to the latest estimated total contract costs. A summary of the financial data during the construction period is as follows:

	Year 1	Year 2	Year 3
Initial amount of revenue agreed in contract	9,000	9,000	9,000
Variation	–	200	200
Total contract revenue	9,000	9,200	9,200
Contract costs incurred to date	2,093	6,168	8,200
Contract costs to complete	5,957	2,032	–
Total estimated contract costs	8,050	8,200	8,200
Estimated profit	950	1,000	1,000
Stage of completion	26%	74%	100%

The stage of completion for year 2 (74%) is determined by excluding from contract costs incurred for work performed to date the 100 of standard materials stored at the site for use in year 3.

The amounts of revenue, expenses and profit recognised in the income statement in the three years are as follows:

	To date	Recognised in prior years	Recognised in current year
Year 1			
Revenue (9,000 × .26)	2,340	–	2,340
Expenses (8,050 × .26)	2,093	–	2,093
Profit	247	–	247
Year 2			
Revenue (9,200 × .74)	6,808	2,340	4,468
Expenses (8,200 × .74)	6,068	2,093	3,975
Profit	740	247	493
Year 3			
Revenue (9,200 × 1.00)	9,200	6,808	2,392
Expenses	8,200	6,068	2,132
Profit	1,000	740	260

Contract disclosures

A contractor has reached the end of its first year of operations. All its contract costs incurred have been paid for in cash and all its progress billings and advances have been received in cash. Contract costs incurred for contracts B, C and E include the cost of materials that have been purchased for the contract but which have not been used in contract performance to date. For contracts B, C and E, the customers have made advances to the contractor for work not yet performed.

The status of its five contracts in progress at the end of year 1 is as follows:

	A	B	C	D	E	Total
Contract revenue recognised in accordance with paragraph 22	145	520	380	200	55	1,300
Contract expenses recognised in accordance with paragraph 22	110	450	350	250	55	1,215
Expected losses recognised in accordance with paragraph 36	–	–	–	40	30	70
Recognised profits less recognised losses	35	70	30	(90)	(30)	15
Contract costs incurred in the period	110	510	450	250	100	1,420
Contract costs incurred recognised as contract expenses in the period in accordance with paragraph 22	110	450	350	250	55	1,215
Contract costs that relate to future activity recognised as an asset in accordance with paragraph 27	–	60	100	–	45	205
Contract revenue (see above)	145	520	380	200	55	1,300
Progress billings (paragraph 41)	100	520	380	180	55	1,235
Unbilled contract revenue	45	–	–	20	–	65
Advances (paragraph 41)	–	80	20	–	25	125

The amounts to be disclosed in accordance with the Standard are as follows:

Contract revenue recognised as revenue in the period (paragraph 39(a))	1,300
Contract costs incurred and recognised profits (less recognised losses) to date paragraph 40(a))	1,435
Advances received (paragraph 40(b))	125
Gross amount due from customers for contract work – presented as an asset in accordance with paragraph 42(a)	220
Gross amount due to customers for contract work – presented as a liability in accordance with paragraph 42(b)	(20)

The amounts to be disclosed in accordance with paragraphs 40(a), 42(a) and 42(b) are calculated as follows:

	Contract					
	A	B	C	D	E	Total
Contract costs incurred	110	510	450	250	100	1,420
Recognised profits less recognised losses	35	70	30	(90)	(30)	15
	145	580	480	160	70	1,435
Progress billings	100	520	380	180	55	1,235
Due from customers	45	60	100	–	15	220
Due to customers	–	–	–	(20)	–	(20)

The amount disclosed in accordance with paragraph 40(a) is the same as the amount for the current period because the disclosures relate to the first year of operation.

International Accounting Standard 12

Income Taxes

This version includes amendments resulting from new and amended IFRSs issued up to 31 December 2004.

The following Interpretations relate to IAS 12:

- SIC-21 *Income Taxes – Recovery of Revalued Non-Depreciable Assets*; and
- SIC-25 *Income Taxes – Changes in the Tax Status of an Entity or its Shareholders.*

CONTENTS

International Accounting Standard 12 *Income Taxes* (IAS 12) is set out in paragraphs 1–91. All the paragraphs have equal authority but retain the IASC format of the Standard when it was adopted by the IASB. IAS 12 should be read in the context of its objective, the *Preface to International Financial Reporting Standards* and the *Framework for the Preparation and Presentation of Financial Statements*. IAS 8 *Accounting Policies, Changes in Accounting Estimates and Errors* provides a basis for selecting and applying accounting policies in the absence of explicit guidance.

Introduction

IN1 This Standard ('IAS 12 (revised)') replaces IAS 12 *Accounting for Taxes on Income* ('the original IAS 12'). IAS 12 (revised) is effective for accounting periods beginning on or after 1 January 1998. The major changes from the original IAS 12 are as follows.

IN2 The original IAS 12 required an entity to account for deferred tax using either the deferral method or a liability method which is sometimes known as the income statement liability method. IAS 12 (revised) prohibits the deferral method and requires another liability method which is sometimes known as the balance sheet liability method.

The income statement liability method focuses on timing differences, whereas the balance sheet liability method focuses on temporary differences. Timing differences are differences between taxable profit and accounting profit that originate in one period and reverse in one or more subsequent periods. Temporary differences are differences between the tax base of an asset or liability and its carrying amount in the balance sheet. The tax base of an asset or liability is the amount attributed to that asset or liability for tax purposes.

All timing differences are temporary differences. Temporary differences also arise in the following circumstances, which do not give rise to timing differences, although the original IAS 12 treated them in the same way as transactions that do give rise to timing differences:

(a) subsidiaries, associates or joint ventures have not distributed their entire profits to the parent or investor;

(b) assets are revalued and no equivalent adjustment is made for tax purposes; and

(c) the cost of a business combination is allocated to the identifiable assets acquired and liabilities assumed by reference to their fair values, but no equivalent adjustment is made for tax purposes.

Furthermore, there are some temporary differences which are not timing differences, for example those temporary differences that arise when:

(a) the non-monetary assets and liabilities of an entity are measured in its functional currency but the taxable profit or tax loss (and, hence, the tax base of its non-monetary assets and liabilities) is determined in a different currency;

(b) non-monetary assets and liabilities are restated under IAS 29 *Financial Reporting in Hyperinflationary Economies*; or

(c) the carrying amount of an asset or liability on initial recognition differs from its initial tax base.

IN3 The original IAS 12 permitted an entity not to recognise deferred tax assets and liabilities where there was reasonable evidence that timing differences would not reverse for some considerable period ahead. IAS 12 (revised) requires an entity to recognise a deferred tax liability or (subject to certain conditions) asset for all temporary differences, with certain exceptions noted below.

IN4 The original IAS 12 required that:

(a) deferred tax assets arising from timing differences should be recognised when there was a reasonable expectation of realisation; and

(b) deferred tax assets arising from tax losses should be recognised as an asset only where there was assurance beyond any reasonable doubt that future taxable income would be sufficient to allow the benefit of the loss to be realised. The original IAS 12 permitted (but did not require) an entity to defer recognition of the benefit of tax losses until the period of realisation.

IAS 12 (revised) requires that deferred tax assets should be recognised when it is probable that taxable profits will be available against which the deferred tax asset can be utilised. Where an entity has a history of tax losses, the entity recognises a deferred tax asset only to the extent that the entity has sufficient taxable temporary differences or there is convincing other evidence that sufficient taxable profit will be available.

IN5 As an exception to the general requirement set out in paragraph IN3 above, IAS 12 (revised) prohibits the recognition of deferred tax liabilities and deferred tax assets arising from certain assets or liabilities whose carrying amount differs on initial recognition from their initial tax base. Because such circumstances do not give rise to timing differences, they did not result in deferred tax assets or liabilities under the original IAS 12.

IN6 The original IAS 12 required that taxes payable on undistributed profits of subsidiaries and associates should be recognised unless it was reasonable to assume that those profits will not be distributed or that a distribution would not give rise to a tax liability. However, IAS 12 (revised) prohibits the recognition of such deferred tax liabilities (and those arising from any related cumulative translation adjustment) to the extent that:

(a) the parent, investor or venturer is able to control the timing of the reversal of the temporary difference; and

(b) it is probable that the temporary difference will not reverse in the foreseeable future.

Where this prohibition has the result that no deferred tax liabilities have been recognised, IAS 12 (revised) requires an entity to disclose the aggregate amount of the temporary differences concerned.

IN7 The original IAS 12 did not refer explicitly to fair value adjustments made on a business combination. Such adjustments give rise to temporary differences and IAS 12 (revised) requires an entity to recognise the resulting deferred tax liability or (subject to the probability criterion for recognition) deferred tax asset with a corresponding effect on the determination of the amount of goodwill or any excess of the acquirer's interest in the net fair value of the acquiree's identifiable assets, liabilities and contingent liabilities over the cost of the combination. However, IAS 12 (revised) prohibits the recognition of deferred tax liabilities arising from the initial recognition of goodwill.

IN8 The original IAS 12 permitted, but did not require, an entity to recognise a deferred tax liability in respect of asset revaluations. IAS 12 (revised) requires an entity to recognise a deferred tax liability in respect of asset revaluations.

IN9 The tax consequences of recovering the carrying amount of certain assets or liabilities may depend on the manner of recovery or settlement, for example:

(a) in certain countries, capital gains are not taxed at the same rate as other taxable income; and

(b) in some countries, the amount that is deducted for tax purposes on sale of an asset is greater than the amount that may be deducted as depreciation.

The original IAS 12 gave no guidance on the measurement of deferred tax assets and liabilities in such cases. IAS 12 (revised) requires that the measurement of deferred tax liabilities and deferred tax assets should be based on the tax consequences that would follow from the manner in which the entity expects to recover or settle the carrying amount of its assets and liabilities.

IN10 The original IAS 12 did not state explicitly whether deferred tax assets and liabilities may be discounted. IAS 12 (revised) prohibits discounting of deferred tax assets and liabilities. Paragraph B16(i) of IFRS 3 *Business Combinations* prohibits discounting of deferred tax assets acquired and deferred tax liabilities assumed in a business combination.

IN11 The original IAS 12 did not specify whether an entity should classify deferred tax balances as current assets and liabilities or as non-current assets and liabilities. IAS 12 (revised) requires that an entity which makes the current/non-current distinction should not classify deferred tax assets and liabilities as current assets and liabilities.

IN12 The original IAS 12 stated that debit and credit balances representing deferred taxes may be offset. IAS 12 (revised) establishes more restrictive conditions on offsetting, based largely on those for financial assets and liabilities in IAS 32 *Financial Instruments: Disclosure and Presentation*.

IN13 The original IAS 12 required disclosure of an explanation of the relationship between tax expense and accounting profit if not explained by the tax rates effective in the reporting entity's country. IAS 12 (revised) requires this explanation to take either or both of the following forms:

(a) a numerical reconciliation between tax expense (income) and the product of accounting profit multiplied by the applicable tax rate(s); or

(b) a numerical reconciliation between the average effective tax rate and the applicable tax rate.

IAS 12 (revised) also requires an explanation of changes in the applicable tax rate(s) compared to the previous accounting period.

IN14 New disclosures required by IAS 12 (revised) include:

(a) in respect of each type of temporary difference, unused tax losses and unused tax credits:

(i) the amount of deferred tax assets and liabilities recognised; and

(ii) the amount of the deferred tax income or expense recognised in the income statement, if this is not apparent from the changes in the amounts recognised in the balance sheet;

(b) in respect of discontinued operations, the tax expense relating to:

   (i) the gain or loss on discontinuance; and

   (ii) the profit or loss from the ordinary activities of the discontinued operation; and

(c) the amount of a deferred tax asset and the nature of the evidence supporting its recognition, when:

   (i) the utilisation of the deferred tax asset is dependent on future taxable profits in excess of the profits arising from the reversal of existing taxable temporary differences; and

   (ii) the entity has suffered a loss in either the current or preceding period in the tax jurisdiction to which the deferred tax asset relates.

International Accounting Standard 12
Income Taxes

Objective

The objective of this Standard is to prescribe the accounting treatment for income taxes. The principal issue in accounting for income taxes is how to account for the current and future tax consequences of:

(a) the future recovery (settlement) of the carrying amount of assets (liabilities) that are recognised in an entity's balance sheet; and

(b) transactions and other events of the current period that are recognised in an entity's financial statements.

It is inherent in the recognition of an asset or liability that the reporting entity expects to recover or settle the carrying amount of that asset or liability. If it is probable that recovery or settlement of that carrying amount will make future tax payments larger (smaller) than they would be if such recovery or settlement were to have no tax consequences, this Standard requires an entity to recognise a deferred tax liability (deferred tax asset), with certain limited exceptions.

This Standard requires an entity to account for the tax consequences of transactions and other events in the same way that it accounts for the transactions and other events themselves. Thus, for transactions and other events recognised in profit or loss, any related tax effects are also recognised in profit or loss. For transactions and other events recognised directly in equity, any related tax effects are also recognised directly in equity. Similarly, the recognition of deferred tax assets and liabilities in a business combination affects the amount of goodwill arising in that business combination or the amount of any excess of the acquirer's interest in the net fair value of the acquiree's identifiable assets, liabilities and contingent liabilities over the cost of the combination.

This Standard also deals with the recognition of deferred tax assets arising from unused tax losses or unused tax credits, the presentation of income taxes in the financial statements and the disclosure of information relating to income taxes.

Scope

1 **This Standard shall be applied in accounting for income taxes.**

2 For the purposes of this Standard, income taxes include all domestic and foreign taxes which are based on taxable profits. Income taxes also include taxes, such as withholding taxes, which are payable by a subsidiary, associate or joint venture on distributions to the reporting entity.

3 [Deleted]

4 This Standard does not deal with the methods of accounting for government grants (see IAS 20 *Accounting for Government Grants and Disclosure of Government Assistance*) or investment tax credits. However, this Standard does deal with the accounting for temporary differences that may arise from such grants or investment tax credits.

Definitions

5 **The following terms are used in this Standard with the meanings specified:**

Accounting profit **is profit or loss for a period before deducting tax expense.**

Taxable profit (tax loss) **is the profit (loss) for a period, determined in accordance with the rules established by the taxation authorities, upon which income taxes are payable (recoverable).**

Tax expense (tax income) **is the aggregate amount included in the determination of profit or loss for the period in respect of current tax and deferred tax.**

Current tax **is the amount of income taxes payable (recoverable) in respect of the taxable profit (tax loss) for a period.**

Deferred tax liabilities **are the amounts of income taxes payable in future periods in respect of taxable temporary differences.**

Deferred tax assets **are the amounts of income taxes recoverable in future periods in respect of:**

(a) deductible temporary differences;

(b) the carryforward of unused tax losses; and

(c) the carryforward of unused tax credits.

Temporary differences **are differences between the carrying amount of an asset or liability in the balance sheet and its tax base. Temporary differences may be either:**

(a) *taxable temporary differences*, **which are temporary differences that will result in taxable amounts in determining taxable profit (tax loss) of future periods when the carrying amount of the asset or liability is recovered or settled; or**

(b) *deductible temporary differences*, **which are temporary differences that will result in amounts that are deductible in determining taxable profit (tax loss) of future periods when the carrying amount of the asset or liability is recovered or settled.**

The *tax base* **of an asset or liability is the amount attributed to that asset or liability for tax purposes.**

6 Tax expense (tax income) comprises current tax expense (current tax income) and deferred tax expense (deferred tax income).

Tax base

7 The tax base of an asset is the amount that will be deductible for tax purposes against any taxable economic benefits that will flow to an entity when it recovers the carrying amount of the asset. If those economic benefits will not be taxable, the tax base of the asset is equal to its carrying amount.

Examples

1 A machine cost 100. For tax purposes, depreciation of 30 has already been deducted in the current and prior periods and the remaining cost will be deductible in future periods, either as depreciation or through a deduction on disposal. Revenue generated by using the machine is taxable, any gain on disposal of the machine will be taxable and any loss on disposal will be deductible for tax purposes. *The tax base of the machine is 70.*

2 Interest receivable has a carrying amount of 100. The related interest revenue will be taxed on a cash basis. *The tax base of the interest receivable is nil.*

3 Trade receivables have a carrying amount of 100. The related revenue has already been included in taxable profit (tax loss). *The tax base of the trade receivables is 100.*

4 Dividends receivable from a subsidiary have a carrying amount of 100. The dividends are not taxable. *In substance, the entire carrying amount of the asset is deductible against the economic benefits. Consequently, the tax base of the dividends receivable is 100.**

5 A loan receivable has a carrying amount of 100. The repayment of the loan will have no tax consequences. *The tax base of the loan is 100.*

* Under this analysis, there is no taxable temporary difference. An alternative analysis is that the accrued dividends receivable have a tax base of nil and that a tax rate of nil is applied to the resulting taxable temporary difference of 100. Under both analyses, there is no deferred tax liability.

8 The tax base of a liability is its carrying amount, less any amount that will be deductible for tax purposes in respect of that liability in future periods. In the case of revenue which is received in advance, the tax base of the resulting liability is its carrying amount, less any amount of the revenue that will not be taxable in future periods.

Examples

1 Current liabilities include accrued expenses with a carrying amount of 100. The related expense will be deducted for tax purposes on a cash basis. *The tax base of the accrued expenses is nil.*

2 Current liabilities include interest revenue received in advance, with a carrying amount of 100. The related interest revenue was taxed on a cash basis. *The tax base of the interest received in advance is nil.*

3 Current liabilities include accrued expenses with a carrying amount of 100. The related expense has already been deducted for tax purposes. *The tax base of the accrued expenses is 100.*

Continued from previous page

Examples

4 Current liabilities include accrued fines and penalties with a carrying amount of 100. Fines and penalties are not deductible for tax purposes. *The tax base of the accrued fines and penalties is 100.*[*]

5 A loan payable has a carrying amount of 100. The repayment of the loan will have no tax consequences. *The tax base of the loan is 100.*

* Under this analysis, there is no deductible temporary difference. An alternative analysis is that the accrued fines and penalties payable have a tax base of nil and that a tax rate of nil is applied to the resulting deductible temporary difference of 100. Under both analyses, there is no deferred tax asset.

9 Some items have a tax base but are not recognised as assets and liabilities in the balance sheet. For example, research costs are recognised as an expense in determining accounting profit in the period in which they are incurred but may not be permitted as a deduction in determining taxable profit (tax loss) until a later period. The difference between the tax base of the research costs, being the amount the taxation authorities will permit as a deduction in future periods, and the carrying amount of nil is a deductible temporary difference that results in a deferred tax asset.

10 Where the tax base of an asset or liability is not immediately apparent, it is helpful to consider the fundamental principle upon which this Standard is based: that an entity shall, with certain limited exceptions, recognise a deferred tax liability (asset) whenever recovery or settlement of the carrying amount of an asset or liability would make future tax payments larger (smaller) than they would be if such recovery or settlement were to have no tax consequences. Example C following paragraph 52 illustrates circumstances when it may be helpful to consider this fundamental principle, for example, when the tax base of an asset or liability depends on the expected manner of recovery or settlement.

11 In consolidated financial statements, temporary differences are determined by comparing the carrying amounts of assets and liabilities in the consolidated financial statements with the appropriate tax base. The tax base is determined by reference to a consolidated tax return in those jurisdictions in which such a return is filed. In other jurisdictions, the tax base is determined by reference to the tax returns of each entity in the group.

Recognition of current tax liabilities and current tax assets

12 Current tax for current and prior periods shall, to the extent unpaid, be recognised as a liability. If the amount already paid in respect of current and prior periods exceeds the amount due for those periods, the excess shall be recognised as an asset.

13 The benefit relating to a tax loss that can be carried back to recover current tax of a previous period shall be recognised as an asset.

14 When a tax loss is used to recover current tax of a previous period, an entity recognises the benefit as an asset in the period in which the tax loss occurs because it is probable that the benefit will flow to the entity and the benefit can be reliably measured.

Recognition of deferred tax liabilities and deferred tax assets

Taxable temporary differences

15 **A deferred tax liability shall be recognised for all taxable temporary differences, except to the extent that the deferred tax liability arises from:**

(a) the initial recognition of goodwill; or

(b) the initial recognition of an asset or liability in a transaction which:

(i) is not a business combination; and

(ii) at the time of the transaction, affects neither accounting profit nor taxable profit (tax loss).

However, for taxable temporary differences associated with investments in subsidiaries, branches and associates, and interests in joint ventures, a deferred tax liability shall be recognised in accordance with paragraph 39.

16 It is inherent in the recognition of an asset that its carrying amount will be recovered in the form of economic benefits that flow to the entity in future periods. When the carrying amount of the asset exceeds its tax base, the amount of taxable economic benefits will exceed the amount that will be allowed as a deduction for tax purposes. This difference is a taxable temporary difference and the obligation to pay the resulting income taxes in future periods is a deferred tax liability. As the entity recovers the carrying amount of the asset, the taxable temporary difference will reverse and the entity will have taxable profit. This makes it probable that economic benefits will flow from the entity in the form of tax payments. Therefore, this Standard requires the recognition of all deferred tax liabilities, except in certain circumstances described in paragraphs 15 and 39.

Example

An asset which cost 150 has a carrying amount of 100. Cumulative depreciation for tax purposes is 90 and the tax rate is 25%.

The tax base of the asset is 60 (cost of 150 less cumulative tax depreciation of 90). To recover the carrying amount of 100, the entity must earn taxable income of 100, but will only be able to deduct tax depreciation of 60. Consequently, the entity will pay income taxes of 10 (40 at 25%) when it recovers the carrying amount of the asset. The difference between the carrying amount of 100 and the tax base of 60 is a taxable temporary difference of 40. Therefore, the entity recognises a deferred tax liability of 10 (40 at 25%) representing the income taxes that it will pay when it recovers the carrying amount of the asset.

17 Some temporary differences arise when income or expense is included in accounting profit in one period but is included in taxable profit in a different period. Such temporary differences are often described as timing differences. The following are examples of temporary differences of this kind which are taxable temporary differences and which therefore result in deferred tax liabilities:

(a) interest revenue is included in accounting profit on a time proportion basis but may, in some jurisdictions, be included in taxable profit when cash is collected. The tax base of any receivable recognised in the balance sheet with respect to such revenues is nil because the revenues do not affect taxable profit until cash is collected;

(b) depreciation used in determining taxable profit (tax loss) may differ from that used in determining accounting profit. The temporary difference is the difference between the carrying amount of the asset and its tax base which is the original cost of the asset less all deductions in respect of that asset permitted by the taxation authorities in determining taxable profit of the current and prior periods. A taxable temporary difference arises, and results in a deferred tax liability, when tax depreciation is accelerated (if tax depreciation is less rapid than accounting depreciation, a deductible temporary difference arises, and results in a deferred tax asset); and

(c) development costs may be capitalised and amortised over future periods in determining accounting profit but deducted in determining taxable profit in the period in which they are incurred. Such development costs have a tax base of nil as they have already been deducted from taxable profit. The temporary difference is the difference between the carrying amount of the development costs and their tax base of nil.

18 Temporary differences also arise when:

(a) the cost of a business combination is allocated by recognising the identifiable assets acquired and liabilities assumed at their fair values, but no equivalent adjustment is made for tax purposes (see paragraph 19);

(b) assets are revalued and no equivalent adjustment is made for tax purposes (see paragraph 20);

(c) goodwill arises in a business combination (see paragraphs 21 and 32);

(d) the tax base of an asset or liability on initial recognition differs from its initial carrying amount, for example when an entity benefits from non-taxable government grants related to assets (see paragraphs 22 and 33); or

(e) the carrying amount of investments in subsidiaries, branches and associates or interests in joint ventures becomes different from the tax base of the investment or interest (see paragraphs 38–45).

Business combinations

19 The cost of a business combination is allocated by recognising the identifiable assets acquired and liabilities assumed at their fair values at the acquisition date. Temporary differences arise when the tax bases of the identifiable assets acquired and liabilities assumed are not affected by the business combination or are

affected differently. For example, when the carrying amount of an asset is increased to fair value but the tax base of the asset remains at cost to the previous owner, a taxable temporary difference arises which results in a deferred tax liability. The resulting deferred tax liability affects goodwill (see paragraph 66).

Assets carried at fair value

20 IFRSs permit or require certain assets to be carried at fair value or to be revalued (see, for example, IAS 16 *Property, Plant and Equipment*, IAS 38 *Intangible Assets*, IAS 39 *Financial Instruments: Recognition and Measurement* and IAS 40 *Investment Property*). In some jurisdictions, the revaluation or other restatement of an asset to fair value affects taxable profit (tax loss) for the current period. As a result, the tax base of the asset is adjusted and no temporary difference arises. In other jurisdictions, the revaluation or restatement of an asset does not affect taxable profit in the period of the revaluation or restatement and, consequently, the tax base of the asset is not adjusted. Nevertheless, the future recovery of the carrying amount will result in a taxable flow of economic benefits to the entity and the amount that will be deductible for tax purposes will differ from the amount of those economic benefits. The difference between the carrying amount of a revalued asset and its tax base is a temporary difference and gives rise to a deferred tax liability or asset. This is true even if:

(a) the entity does not intend to dispose of the asset. In such cases, the revalued carrying amount of the asset will be recovered through use and this will generate taxable income which exceeds the depreciation that will be allowable for tax purposes in future periods; or

(b) tax on capital gains is deferred if the proceeds of the disposal of the asset are invested in similar assets. In such cases, the tax will ultimately become payable on sale or use of the similar assets.

Goodwill

21 Goodwill arising in a business combination is measured as the excess of the cost of the combination over the acquirer's interest in the net fair value of the acquiree's identifiable assets, liabilities and contingent liabilities. Many taxation authorities do not allow reductions in the carrying amount of goodwill as a deductible expense in determining taxable profit. Moreover, in such jurisdictions, the cost of goodwill is often not deductible when a subsidiary disposes of its underlying business. In such jurisdictions, goodwill has a tax base of nil. Any difference between the carrying amount of goodwill and its tax base of nil is a taxable temporary difference. However, this Standard does not permit the recognition of the resulting deferred tax liability because goodwill is measured as a residual and the recognition of the deferred tax liability would increase the carrying amount of goodwill.

21A Subsequent reductions in a deferred tax liability that is unrecognised because it arises from the initial recognition of goodwill are also regarded as arising from the initial recognition of goodwill and are therefore not recognised under paragraph 15(a). For example, if goodwill acquired in a business combination has a cost of 100 but a tax base of nil, paragraph 15(a) prohibits the entity from recognising the resulting deferred tax liability. If the entity subsequently recognises an impairment loss of 20 for that goodwill, the amount of the taxable temporary difference relating to the goodwill is reduced from 100 to 80, with a resulting decrease in the value of the unrecognised deferred tax liability. That decrease in the value of the unrecognised deferred tax liability is also regarded as relating to the initial recognition of the goodwill and is therefore prohibited from being recognised under paragraph 15(a).

21B Deferred tax liabilities for taxable temporary differences relating to goodwill are, however, recognised to the extent they do not arise from the initial recognition of goodwill. For example, if goodwill acquired in a business combination has a cost of 100 that is deductible for tax purposes at a rate of 20 per cent per year starting in the year of acquisition, the tax base of the goodwill is 100 on initial recognition and 80 at the end of the year of acquisition. If the carrying amount of goodwill at the end of the year of acquisition remains unchanged at 100, a taxable temporary difference of 20 arises at the end of that year. Because that taxable temporary difference does not relate to the initial recognition of the goodwill, the resulting deferred tax liability is recognised.

Initial recognition of an asset or liability

22 A temporary difference may arise on initial recognition of an asset or liability, for example if part or all of the cost of an asset will not be deductible for tax purposes. The method of accounting for such a temporary difference depends on the nature of the transaction which led to the initial recognition of the asset:

(a) in a business combination, an entity recognises any deferred tax liability or asset and this affects the amount of goodwill or the amount of any excess over the cost of the combination of the acquirer's interest in the net fair value of the acquiree's identifiable assets, liabilities and contingent liabilities (see paragraph 19);

(b) if the transaction affects either accounting profit or taxable profit, an entity recognises any deferred tax liability or asset and recognises the resulting deferred tax expense or income in the income statement (see paragraph 59);

(c) if the transaction is not a business combination, and affects neither accounting profit nor taxable profit, an entity would, in the absence of the exemption provided by paragraphs 15 and 24, recognise the resulting deferred tax liability or asset and adjust the carrying amount of the asset or liability by the same amount. Such adjustments would make the financial statements less transparent. Therefore, this Standard does not permit an entity to recognise the resulting deferred tax liability or asset, either on initial recognition or subsequently (see example below). Furthermore, an entity does not recognise subsequent changes in the unrecognised deferred tax liability or asset as the asset is depreciated.

Example illustrating paragraph 22(c)

An entity intends to use an asset which cost 1,000 throughout its useful life of five years and then dispose of it for a residual value of nil. The tax rate is 40%. Depreciation of the asset is not deductible for tax purposes.
On disposal, any capital gain would not be taxable and any capital loss would not be deductible.

As it recovers the carrying amount of the asset, the entity will earn taxable income of 1,000 and pay tax of 400. The entity does not recognise the resulting deferred tax liability of 400 because it results from the initial recognition of the asset.

In the following year, the carrying amount of the asset is 800. In earning taxable income of 800, the entity will pay tax of 320. The entity does not recognise the deferred tax liability of 320 because it results from the initial recognition of the asset.

23 In accordance with IAS 32 *Financial Instruments: Disclosure and Presentation* the issuer of a compound financial instrument (for example, a convertible bond) classifies the instrument's liability component as a liability and the equity component as equity. In some jurisdictions, the tax base of the liability component on initial recognition is equal to the initial carrying amount of the sum of the liability and equity components. The resulting taxable temporary difference arises from the initial recognition of the equity component separately from the liability component. Therefore, the exception set out in paragraph 15(b) does not apply. Consequently, an entity recognises the resulting deferred tax liability. In accordance with paragraph 61, the deferred tax is charged directly to the carrying amount of the equity component. In accordance with paragraph 58, subsequent changes in the deferred tax liability are recognised in the income statement as deferred tax expense (income).

Deductible temporary differences

24 A deferred tax asset shall be recognised for all deductible temporary differences to the extent that it is probable that taxable profit will be available against which the deductible temporary difference can be utilised, unless the deferred tax asset arises from the initial recognition of an asset or liability in a transaction that:

(a) is not a business combination; and

(b) at the time of the transaction, affects neither accounting profit nor taxable profit (tax loss).

However, for deductible temporary differences associated with investments in subsidiaries, branches and associates, and interests in joint ventures, a deferred tax asset shall be recognised in accordance with paragraph 44.

25 It is inherent in the recognition of a liability that the carrying amount will be settled in future periods through an outflow from the entity of resources embodying economic benefits. When resources flow from the entity, part or all of their amounts may be deductible in determining taxable profit of a period later than the period in which the liability is recognised. In such cases, a temporary difference exists between the carrying amount of the liability and its tax base. Accordingly, a deferred tax asset arises in respect of the income taxes that will be

recoverable in the future periods when that part of the liability is allowed as a deduction in determining taxable profit. Similarly, if the carrying amount of an asset is less than its tax base, the difference gives rise to a deferred tax asset in respect of the income taxes that will be recoverable in future periods.

Example
An entity recognises a liability of 100 for accrued product warranty costs. For tax purposes, the product warranty costs will not be deductible until the entity pays claims. The tax rate is 25%. *The tax base of the liability is nil (carrying amount of 100, less the amount that will be deductible for tax purposes in respect of that liability in future periods). In settling the liability for its carrying amount, the entity will reduce its future taxable profit by an amount of 100 and, consequently, reduce its future tax payments by 25 (100 at 25%). The difference between the carrying amount of 100 and the tax base of nil is a deductible temporary difference of 100. Therefore, the entity recognises a deferred tax asset of 25 (100 at 25%), provided that it is probable that the entity will earn sufficient taxable profit in future periods to benefit from a reduction in tax payments.*

26 The following are examples of deductible temporary differences which result in deferred tax assets:

(a) retirement benefit costs may be deducted in determining accounting profit as service is provided by the employee, but deducted in determining taxable profit either when contributions are paid to a fund by the entity or when retirement benefits are paid by the entity. A temporary difference exists between the carrying amount of the liability and its tax base; the tax base of the liability is usually nil. Such a deductible temporary difference results in a deferred tax asset as economic benefits will flow to the entity in the form of a deduction from taxable profits when contributions or retirement benefits are paid;

(b) research costs are recognised as an expense in determining accounting profit in the period in which they are incurred but may not be permitted as a deduction in determining taxable profit (tax loss) until a later period. The difference between the tax base of the research costs, being the amount the taxation authorities will permit as a deduction in future periods, and the carrying amount of nil is a deductible temporary difference that results in a deferred tax asset;

(c) the cost of a business combination is allocated by recognising the identifiable assets acquired and liabilities assumed at their fair values at the acquisition date. When a liability assumed is recognised at the acquisition date but the related costs are not deducted in determining taxable profits until a later period, a deductible temporary difference arises which results in a deferred tax asset. A deferred tax asset also arises when the fair value of an identifiable asset acquired is less than its tax base. In both cases, the resulting deferred tax asset affects goodwill (see paragraph 66); and

(d) certain assets may be carried at fair value, or may be revalued, without an equivalent adjustment being made for tax purposes (see paragraph 20). A deductible temporary difference arises if the tax base of the asset exceeds its carrying amount.

27 The reversal of deductible temporary differences results in deductions in determining taxable profits of future periods. However, economic benefits in the form of reductions in tax payments will flow to the entity only if it earns sufficient taxable profits against which the deductions can be offset. Therefore, an entity recognises deferred tax assets only when it is probable that taxable profits will be available against which the deductible temporary differences can be utilised.

28 It is probable that taxable profit will be available against which a deductible temporary difference can be utilised when there are sufficient taxable temporary differences relating to the same taxation authority and the same taxable entity which are expected to reverse:

(a) in the same period as the expected reversal of the deductible temporary difference; or

(b) in periods into which a tax loss arising from the deferred tax asset can be carried back or forward.

In such circumstances, the deferred tax asset is recognised in the period in which the deductible temporary differences arise.

29 When there are insufficient taxable temporary differences relating to the same taxation authority and the same taxable entity, the deferred tax asset is recognised to the extent that:

(a) it is probable that the entity will have sufficient taxable profit relating to the same taxation authority and the same taxable entity in the same period as the reversal of the deductible temporary difference (or in the periods into which a tax loss arising from the deferred tax asset can be carried back or forward). In evaluating whether it will have sufficient taxable profit in future periods, an entity ignores taxable amounts arising from deductible temporary differences that are expected to originate in future periods, because the deferred tax asset arising from these deductible temporary differences will itself require future taxable profit in order to be utilised; or

(b) tax planning opportunities are available to the entity that will create taxable profit in appropriate periods.

30 Tax planning opportunities are actions that the entity would take in order to create or increase taxable income in a particular period before the expiry of a tax loss or tax credit carryforward. For example, in some jurisdictions, taxable profit may be created or increased by:

(a) electing to have interest income taxed on either a received or receivable basis;

(b) deferring the claim for certain deductions from taxable profit;

(c) selling, and perhaps leasing back, assets that have appreciated but for which the tax base has not been adjusted to reflect such appreciation; and

(d) selling an asset that generates non-taxable income (such as, in some jurisdictions, a government bond) in order to purchase another investment that generates taxable income.

Where tax planning opportunities advance taxable profit from a later period to an earlier period, the utilisation of a tax loss or tax credit carryforward still depends on the existence of future taxable profit from sources other than future originating temporary differences.

31 When an entity has a history of recent losses, the entity considers the guidance in paragraphs 35 and 36.

32 [Deleted]

Initial recognition of an asset or liability

33 One case when a deferred tax asset arises on initial recognition of an asset is when a non-taxable government grant related to an asset is deducted in arriving at the carrying amount of the asset but, for tax purposes, is not deducted from the asset's depreciable amount (in other words its tax base); the carrying amount of the asset is less than its tax base and this gives rise to a deductible temporary difference. Government grants may also be set up as deferred income in which case the difference between the deferred income and its tax base of nil is a deductible temporary difference. Whichever method of presentation an entity adopts, the entity does not recognise the resulting deferred tax asset, for the reason given in paragraph 22.

Unused tax losses and unused tax credits

34 A deferred tax asset shall be recognised for the carryforward of unused tax losses and unused tax credits to the extent that it is probable that future taxable profit will be available against which the unused tax losses and unused tax credits can be utilised.

35 The criteria for recognising deferred tax assets arising from the carryforward of unused tax losses and tax credits are the same as the criteria for recognising deferred tax assets arising from deductible temporary differences. However, the existence of unused tax losses is strong evidence that future taxable profit may not be available. Therefore, when an entity has a history of recent losses, the entity recognises a deferred tax asset arising from unused tax losses or tax credits only to the extent that the entity has sufficient taxable temporary differences or there is convincing other evidence that sufficient taxable profit will be available against which the unused tax losses or unused tax credits can be utilised by the entity. In such circumstances, paragraph 82 requires disclosure of the amount of the deferred tax asset and the nature of the evidence supporting its recognition.

36 An entity considers the following criteria in assessing the probability that taxable profit will be available against which the unused tax losses or unused tax credits can be utilised:

(a) whether the entity has sufficient taxable temporary differences relating to the same taxation authority and the same taxable entity, which will result in taxable amounts against which the unused tax losses or unused tax credits can be utilised before they expire;

(b) whether it is probable that the entity will have taxable profits before the unused tax losses or unused tax credits expire;

(c) whether the unused tax losses result from identifiable causes which are unlikely to recur; and

(d) whether tax planning opportunities (see paragraph 30) are available to the entity that will create taxable profit in the period in which the unused tax losses or unused tax credits can be utilised.

To the extent that it is not probable that taxable profit will be available against which the unused tax losses or unused tax credits can be utilised, the deferred tax asset is not recognised.

Re–assessment of unrecognised deferred tax assets

37 At each balance sheet date, an entity re-assesses unrecognised deferred tax assets. The entity recognises a previously unrecognised deferred tax asset to the extent that it has become probable that future taxable profit will allow the deferred tax asset to be recovered. For example, an improvement in trading conditions may make it more probable that the entity will be able to generate sufficient taxable profit in the future for the deferred tax asset to meet the recognition criteria set out in paragraph 24 or 34. Another example is when an entity re-assesses deferred tax assets at the date of a business combination or subsequently (see paragraphs 67 and 68).

Investments in subsidiaries, branches and associates and interests in joint ventures

38 Temporary differences arise when the carrying amount of investments in subsidiaries, branches and associates or interests in joint ventures (namely the parent or investor's share of the net assets of the subsidiary, branch, associate or investee, including the carrying amount of goodwill) becomes different from the tax base (which is often cost) of the investment or interest. Such differences may arise in a number of different circumstances, for example:

(a) the existence of undistributed profits of subsidiaries, branches, associates and joint ventures;

(b) changes in foreign exchange rates when a parent and its subsidiary are based in different countries; and

(c) a reduction in the carrying amount of an investment in an associate to its recoverable amount.

In consolidated financial statements, the temporary difference may be different from the temporary difference associated with that investment in the parent's separate financial statements if the parent carries the investment in its separate financial statements at cost or revalued amount.

39 **An entity shall recognise a deferred tax liability for all taxable temporary differences associated with investments in subsidiaries, branches and associates, and interests in joint ventures, except to the extent that both of the following conditions are satisfied:**

(a) the parent, investor or venturer is able to control the timing of the reversal of the temporary difference; and

(b) it is probable that the temporary difference will not reverse in the foreseeable future.

40 As a parent controls the dividend policy of its subsidiary, it is able to control the timing of the reversal of temporary differences associated with that investment (including the temporary differences arising not only from undistributed profits but also from any foreign exchange translation differences). Furthermore, it would often be impracticable to determine the amount of income taxes that would be payable when the temporary difference reverses. Therefore, when the parent has determined that those profits will not be distributed in the foreseeable future the parent does not recognise a deferred tax liability. The same considerations apply to investments in branches.

41 The non-monetary assets and liabilities of an entity are measured in its functional currency (see IAS 21 *The Effects of Changes in Foreign Exchange Rates*). If the entity's taxable profit or tax loss (and, hence, the tax base of its non-monetary assets and liabilities) is determined in a different currency, changes in the exchange rate give rise to temporary differences that result in a recognised deferred tax liability or (subject to paragraph 24) asset. The resulting deferred tax is charged or credited to profit or loss (see paragraph 58).

42 An investor in an associate does not control that entity and is usually not in a position to determine its dividend policy. Therefore, in the absence of an agreement requiring that the profits of the associate will not be distributed in the foreseeable future, an investor recognises a deferred tax liability arising from taxable temporary differences associated with its investment in the associate. In some cases, an investor may not be able to determine the amount of tax that would be payable if it recovers the cost of its investment in an associate, but can determine that it will equal or exceed a minimum amount. In such cases, the deferred tax liability is measured at this amount.

43 The arrangement between the parties to a joint venture usually deals with the sharing of the profits and identifies whether decisions on such matters require the consent of all the venturers or a specified majority of the venturers. When the venturer can control the sharing of profits and it is probable that the profits will not be distributed in the foreseeable future, a deferred tax liability is not recognised.

44 **An entity shall recognise a deferred tax asset for all deductible temporary differences arising from investments in subsidiaries, branches and associates, and interests in joint ventures, to the extent that, and only to the extent that, it is probable that:**

(a) the temporary difference will reverse in the foreseeable future; and

(b) taxable profit will be available against which the temporary difference can be utilised.

45 In deciding whether a deferred tax asset is recognised for deductible temporary differences associated with its investments in subsidiaries, branches and associates, and its interests in joint ventures, an entity considers the guidance set out in paragraphs 28 to 31.

Measurement

46 **Current tax liabilities (assets) for the current and prior periods shall be measured at the amount expected to be paid to (recovered from) the taxation authorities, using the tax rates (and tax laws) that have been enacted or substantively enacted by the balance sheet date.**

47 **Deferred tax assets and liabilities shall be measured at the tax rates that are expected to apply to the period when the asset is realised or the liability is settled, based on tax rates (and tax laws) that have been enacted or substantively enacted by the balance sheet date.**

48 Current and deferred tax assets and liabilities are usually measured using the tax rates (and tax laws) that have been enacted. However, in some jurisdictions, announcements of tax rates (and tax laws) by the government have the substantive effect of actual enactment, which may follow the announcement by a period of several months. In these circumstances, tax assets and liabilities are measured using the announced tax rate (and tax laws).

49 When different tax rates apply to different levels of taxable income, deferred tax assets and liabilities are measured using the average rates that are expected to apply to the taxable profit (tax loss) of the periods in which the temporary differences are expected to reverse.

50 [Deleted]

51 **The measurement of deferred tax liabilities and deferred tax assets shall reflect the tax consequences that would follow from the manner in which the entity expects, at the balance sheet date, to recover or settle the carrying amount of its assets and liabilities.**

52 In some jurisdictions, the manner in which an entity recovers (settles) the carrying amount of an asset (liability) may affect either or both of:

(a) the tax rate applicable when the entity recovers (settles) the carrying amount of the asset (liability); and

(b) the tax base of the asset (liability).

In such cases, an entity measures deferred tax liabilities and deferred tax assets using the tax rate and the tax base that are consistent with the expected manner of recovery or settlement.

Example A

An asset has a carrying amount of 100 and a tax base of 60. A tax rate of 20% would apply if the asset were sold and a tax rate of 30% would apply to other income.

The entity recognises a deferred tax liability of 8 (40 at 20%) if it expects to sell the asset without further use and a deferred tax liability of 12 (40 at 30%) if it expects to retain the asset and recover its carrying amount through use.

Example B

An asset with a cost of 100 and a carrying amount of 80 is revalued to 150. No equivalent adjustment is made for tax purposes. Cumulative depreciation for tax purposes is 30 and the tax rate is 30%. If the asset is sold for more than cost, the cumulative tax depreciation of 30 will be included in taxable income but sale proceeds in excess of cost will not be taxable.

The tax base of the asset is 70 and there is a taxable temporary difference of 80. If the entity expects to recover the carrying amount by using the asset, it must generate taxable income of 150, but will only be able to deduct depreciation of 70. On this basis, there is a deferred tax liability of 24 (80 at 30%). If the entity expects to recover the carrying amount by selling the asset immediately for proceeds of 150, the deferred tax liability is computed as follows:

	Taxable Temporary Difference	*Tax Rate*	*Deferred Tax Liability*
Cumulative tax depreciation	*30*	*30%*	*9*
Proceeds in excess of cost	*50*	*nil*	*–*
Total	*80*		*9*

(note: in accordance with paragraph 61, the additional deferred tax that arises on the revaluation is charged directly to equity)

Example C

The facts are as in example B, except that if the asset is sold for more than cost, the cumulative tax depreciation will be included in taxable income (taxed at 30%) and the sale proceeds will be taxed at 40%, after deducting an inflation-adjusted cost of 110.

If the entity expects to recover the carrying amount by using the asset, it must generate taxable income of 150, but will only be able to deduct depreciation of 70. On this basis, the tax base is 70, there is a taxable temporary difference of 80 and there is a deferred tax liability of 24 (80 at 30%), as in example B.

If the entity expects to recover the carrying amount by selling the asset immediately for proceeds of 150, the entity will be able to deduct the indexed cost of 110. The net proceeds of 40 will be taxed at 40%. In addition, the cumulative tax depreciation of 30 will be included in taxable income and taxed at 30%. On this basis, the tax base is 80 (110 less 30), there is a taxable temporary difference of 70 and there is a deferred tax liability of 25 (40 at 40% plus 30 at 30%). If the tax base is not immediately apparent in this example, it may be helpful to consider the fundamental principle set out in paragraph 10.

(note: in accordance with paragraph 61, the additional deferred tax that arises on the revaluation is charged directly to equity)

52A In some jurisdictions, income taxes are payable at a higher or lower rate if part or all of the net profit or retained earnings is paid out as a dividend to shareholders of the entity. In some other jurisdictions, income taxes may be refundable or payable if part or all of the net profit or retained earnings is paid out as a dividend to shareholders of the entity. In these circumstances, current and deferred tax assets and liabilities are measured at the tax rate applicable to undistributed profits.

52B In the circumstances described in paragraph 52A, the income tax consequences of dividends are recognised when a liability to pay the dividend is recognised. The income tax consequences of dividends are more directly linked to past transactions or events than to distributions to owners. Therefore, the income tax consequences of dividends are recognised in profit or loss for the period as required by paragraph 58 except to the extent that the income tax consequences of dividends arise from the circumstances described in paragraph 58(a) and (b).

Example illustrating paragraphs 52A and 52B

The following example deals with the measurement of current and deferred tax assets and liabilities for an entity in a jurisdiction where income taxes are payable at a higher rate on undistributed profits (50%) with an amount being refundable when profits are distributed. The tax rate on distributed profits is 35%. At the balance sheet date, 31 December 20X1, the entity does not recognise a liability for dividends proposed or declared after the balance sheet date. As a result, no dividends are recognised in the year 20X1. Taxable income for 20X1 is 100,000. The net taxable temporary difference for the year 20X1 is 40,000.

The entity recognises a current tax liability and a current income tax expense of 50,000. No asset is recognised for the amount potentially recoverable as a result of future dividends. The entity also recognises a deferred tax liability and deferred tax expense of 20,000 (40,000 at 50%) representing the income taxes that the entity will pay when it recovers or settles the carrying amounts of its assets and liabilities based on the tax rate applicable to undistributed profits.

Subsequently, on 15 March 20X2 the entity recognises dividends of 10,000 from previous operating profits as a liability.

On 15 March 20X2, the entity recognises the recovery of income taxes of 1,500 (15% of the dividends recognised as a liability) as a current tax asset and as a reduction of current income tax expense for 20X2.

53 Deferred tax assets and liabilities shall not be discounted.

54 The reliable determination of deferred tax assets and liabilities on a discounted basis requires detailed scheduling of the timing of the reversal of each temporary difference. In many cases such scheduling is impracticable or highly complex. Therefore, it is inappropriate to require discounting of deferred tax assets and liabilities. To permit, but not to require, discounting would result in deferred tax assets and liabilities which would not be comparable between entities. Therefore, this Standard does not require or permit the discounting of deferred tax assets and liabilities.

55 Temporary differences are determined by reference to the carrying amount of an asset or liability. This applies even where that carrying amount is itself determined on a discounted basis, for example in the case of retirement benefit obligations (see IAS 19 *Employee Benefits*).

56 The carrying amount of a deferred tax asset shall be reviewed at each balance sheet date. An entity shall reduce the carrying amount of a deferred tax asset to the extent that it is no longer probable that sufficient taxable profit will be available to allow the benefit of part or all of that deferred tax asset to be utilised. Any such reduction shall be reversed to the extent that it becomes probable that sufficient taxable profit will be available.

Recognition of current and deferred tax

57 Accounting for the current and deferred tax effects of a transaction or other event is consistent with the accounting for the transaction or event itself. Paragraphs 58 to 68C implement this principle.

Income statement

58 **Current and deferred tax shall be recognised as income or an expense and included in profit or loss for the period, except to the extent that the tax arises from:**

(a) a transaction or event which is recognised, in the same or a different period, directly in equity (see paragraphs 61 to 65); or

(b) a business combination (see paragraphs 66 to 68).

59 Most deferred tax liabilities and deferred tax assets arise where income or expense is included in accounting profit in one period, but is included in taxable profit (tax loss) in a different period. The resulting deferred tax is recognised in the income statement. Examples are when:

(a) interest, royalty or dividend revenue is received in arrears and is included in accounting profit on a time apportionment basis in accordance with IAS 18 *Revenue*, but is included in taxable profit (tax loss) on a cash basis; and

(b) costs of intangible assets have been capitalised in accordance with IAS 38 *Intangible Assets* and are being amortised in the income statement, but were deducted for tax purposes when they were incurred.

60 The carrying amount of deferred tax assets and liabilities may change even though there is no change in the amount of the related temporary differences. This can result, for example, from:

(a) a change in tax rates or tax laws;

(b) a re-assessment of the recoverability of deferred tax assets; or

(c) a change in the expected manner of recovery of an asset.

The resulting deferred tax is recognised in the income statement, except to the extent that it relates to items previously charged or credited to equity (see paragraph 63).

Items credited or charged directly to equity

61 **Current tax and deferred tax shall be charged or credited directly to equity if the tax relates to items that are credited or charged, in the same or a different period, directly to equity.**

62 International Financial Reporting Standards require or permit certain items to be credited or charged directly to equity. Examples of such items are:

(a) a change in carrying amount arising from the revaluation of property, plant and equipment (see IAS 16 *Property, Plant and Equipment*);

(b) an adjustment to the opening balance of retained earnings resulting from either a change in accounting policy that is applied retrospectively or the correction of an error (see IAS 8 *Accounting Policies, Changes in Accounting Estimates and Errors*);

(c) exchange differences arising on the translation of the financial statements of a foreign operation (see IAS 21 *The Effects of Changes in Foreign Exchange Rates*); and

(d) amounts arising on initial recognition of the equity component of a compound financial instrument (see paragraph 23).

63 In exceptional circumstances it may be difficult to determine the amount of current and deferred tax that relates to items credited or charged to equity. This may be the case, for example, when:

(a) there are graduated rates of income tax and it is impossible to determine the rate at which a specific component of taxable profit (tax loss) has been taxed;

(b) a change in the tax rate or other tax rules affects a deferred tax asset or liability relating (in whole or in part) to an item that was previously charged or credited to equity; or

(c) an entity determines that a deferred tax asset should be recognised, or should no longer be recognised in full, and the deferred tax asset relates (in whole or in part) to an item that was previously charged or credited to equity.

In such cases, the current and deferred tax related to items that are credited or charged to equity is based on a reasonable pro rata allocation of the current and deferred tax of the entity in the tax jurisdiction concerned, or other method that achieves a more appropriate allocation in the circumstances.

64 IAS 16 *Property, Plant and Equipment* does not specify whether an entity should transfer each year from revaluation surplus to retained earnings an amount equal to the difference between the depreciation or amortisation on a revalued asset and the depreciation or amortisation based on the cost of that asset. If an entity makes such a transfer, the amount transferred is net of any related deferred tax. Similar considerations apply to transfers made on disposal of an item of property, plant or equipment.

65 When an asset is revalued for tax purposes and that revaluation is related to an accounting revaluation of an earlier period, or to one that is expected to be carried out in a future period, the tax effects of both the asset revaluation and the adjustment of the tax base are credited or charged to equity in the periods in which they occur. However, if the revaluation for tax purposes is not related to an accounting revaluation of an earlier period, or to one that is expected to be carried out in a future period, the tax effects of the adjustment of the tax base are recognised in the income statement.

65A When an entity pays dividends to its shareholders, it may be required to pay a portion of the dividends to taxation authorities on behalf of shareholders. In many jurisdictions, this amount is referred to as a withholding tax. Such an amount paid or payable to taxation authorities is charged to equity as a part of the dividends.

Deferred tax arising from a business combination

66 As explained in paragraphs 19 and 26(c), temporary differences may arise in a business combination. In accordance with IFRS 3 *Business Combinations*, an entity recognises any resulting deferred tax assets (to the extent that they meet the recognition criteria in paragraph 24) or deferred tax liabilities as identifiable assets and liabilities at the acquisition date. Consequently, those deferred tax assets and liabilities affect goodwill or the amount of any excess of the acquirer's interest in the net fair value of the acquiree's identifiable assets, liabilities and contingent liabilities over the cost of the combination. However, in accordance with paragraph 15(a), an entity does not recognise deferred tax liabilities arising from the initial recognition of goodwill.

67 As a result of a business combination, an acquirer may consider it probable that it will recover its own deferred tax asset that was not recognised before the business combination. For example, the acquirer may be able to utilise the benefit of its unused tax losses against the future taxable profit of the acquiree. In such cases, the acquirer recognises a deferred tax asset, but does not include it as part of the accounting for the business combination, and therefore does not take it into account in determining the goodwill or the amount of any excess of the acquirer's interest in the net fair value of the acquiree's identifiable assets, liabilities and contingent liabilities over the cost of the combination.

68 If the potential benefit of the acquiree's income tax loss carryforwards or other deferred tax assets did not satisfy the criteria in IFRS 3 for separate recognition when a business combination is initially accounted for but is subsequently realised, the acquirer shall recognise the resulting deferred tax income in profit or loss. In addition, the acquirer shall:

(a) reduce the carrying amount of goodwill to the amount that would have been recognised if the deferred tax asset had been recognised as an identifiable asset from the acquisition date; and

(b) recognises the reduction in the carrying amount of goodwill as an expense.

However, this procedure shall not result in the creation of an excess of the acquirer's interest in the net fair value of the acquiree's identifiable assets, liabilities and contingent liabilities over the cost of the combination, nor shall it increase the amount previously recognised for any such excess.

Example

An entity acquired a subsidiary that had deductible temporary differences of 300. The tax rate at the time of the acquisition was 30 per cent. The resulting deferred tax asset of 90 was not recognised as an identifiable asset in determining the goodwill of 500 that resulted from the business combination. Two years after the combination, the entity assessed that future taxable profit should be sufficient to recover the benefit of all the deductible temporary differences.

The entity recognises a deferred tax asset of 90 and, in profit or loss, deferred tax income of 90. The entity also reduces the carrying amount of goodwill by 90 and recognises an expense for this amount in profit or loss. Consequently, the cost of the goodwill is reduced to 410, being the amount that would have been recognised had the deferred tax asset of 90 been recognised as an identifiable asset at the acquisition date.

If the tax rate had increased to 40 per cent, the entity would have recognised a deferred tax asset of 120 (300 at 40 per cent) and, in profit or loss, deferred tax income of 120. If the tax rate had decreased to 20 per cent, the entity would have recognised a deferred tax asset of 60 (300 at 20 per cent) and deferred tax income of 60. In both cases, the entity would also reduce the carrying amount of goodwill by 90 and recognise an expense for that amount in profit or loss.

Current and deferred tax arising from share–based payment transactions

68A In some tax jurisdictions, an entity receives a tax deduction (ie an amount that is deductible in determining taxable profit) that relates to remuneration paid in shares, share options or other equity instruments of the entity. The amount of that tax deduction may differ from the related cumulative remuneration expense, and may arise in a later accounting period. For example, in some jurisdictions, an entity may recognise an expense for the consumption of employee services received as consideration for share options granted, in accordance with IFRS 2 *Share-based Payment*, and not receive a tax deduction until the share options are exercised, with the measurement of the tax deduction based on the entity's share price at the date of exercise.

68B As with the research costs discussed in paragraphs 9 and 26(b) of this Standard, the difference between the tax base of the employee services received to date (being the amount the taxation authorities will permit as a deduction in future periods), and the carrying amount of nil, is a deductible temporary difference that results in a deferred tax asset. If the amount the taxation authorities will permit as a deduction in future periods is not known at the end of the period, it should be estimated, based on information available at the end of the period. For example, if the amount that the taxation authorities will permit as a deduction in future periods is dependent upon the entity's share price at a future date, the measurement of the deductible temporary difference should be based on the entity's share price at the end of the period.

68C As noted in paragraph 68A, the amount of the tax deduction (or estimated future tax deduction, measured in accordance with paragraph 68B) may differ from the related cumulative remuneration expense. Paragraph 58 of the Standard requires that current and deferred tax should be recognised as income or an expense and included in profit or loss for the period, except to the extent that the tax arises from (a) a transaction or event which is recognised, in the same or a different period, directly in equity, or (b) a business combination. If the amount of the tax deduction (or estimated future tax deduction) exceeds the amount of the related cumulative remuneration expense, this indicates that the tax deduction relates not only to remuneration expense but also to an equity item. In this situation, the excess of the associated current or deferred tax should be recognised directly in equity.

Presentation

Tax assets and tax liabilities

69 [Deleted]

70 [Deleted]

Offset

71 An entity shall offset current tax assets and current tax liabilities if, and only if, the entity:

(a) has a legally enforceable right to set off the recognised amounts; and

(b) intends either to settle on a net basis, or to realise the asset and settle the liability simultaneously.

72 Although current tax assets and liabilities are separately recognised and measured they are offset in the balance sheet subject to criteria similar to those established for financial instruments in IAS 32 *Financial Instruments: Disclosure and Presentation*. An entity will normally have a legally enforceable right to set off a current tax asset against a current tax liability when they relate to income taxes levied by the same taxation authority and the taxation authority permits the entity to make or receive a single net payment.

73 In consolidated financial statements, a current tax asset of one entity in a group is offset against a current tax liability of another entity in the group if, and only if, the entities concerned have a legally enforceable right to make or receive a single net payment and the entities intend to make or receive such a net payment or to recover the asset and settle the liability simultaneously.

74 An entity shall offset deferred tax assets and deferred tax liabilities if, and only if:

(a) the entity has a legally enforceable right to set off current tax assets against current tax liabilities; and

(b) the deferred tax assets and the deferred tax liabilities relate to income taxes levied by the same taxation authority on either:

(i) the same taxable entity; or

(ii) different taxable entities which intend either to settle current tax liabilities and assets on a net basis, or to realise the assets and

settle the liabilities simultaneously, in each future period in which significant amounts of deferred tax liabilities or assets are expected to be settled or recovered.

75 To avoid the need for detailed scheduling of the timing of the reversal of each temporary difference, this Standard requires an entity to set off a deferred tax asset against a deferred tax liability of the same taxable entity if, and only if, they relate to income taxes levied by the same taxation authority and the entity has a legally enforceable right to set off current tax assets against current tax liabilities.

76 In rare circumstances, an entity may have a legally enforceable right of set-off, and an intention to settle net, for some periods but not for others. In such rare circumstances, detailed scheduling may be required to establish reliably whether the deferred tax liability of one taxable entity will result in increased tax payments in the same period in which a deferred tax asset of another taxable entity will result in decreased payments by that second taxable entity.

Tax expense

Tax expense (income) related to profit or loss from ordinary activities

77 The tax expense (income) related to profit or loss from ordinary activities shall be presented on the face of the income statement.

Exchange differences on deferred foreign tax liabilities or assets

78 IAS 21 *The Effects of Changes in Foreign Exchange Rates* requires certain exchange differences to be recognised as income or expense but does not specify where such differences should be presented in the income statement. Accordingly, where exchange differences on deferred foreign tax liabilities or assets are recognised in the income statement, such differences may be classified as deferred tax expense (income) if that presentation is considered to be the most useful to financial statement users.

Disclosure

79 The major components of tax expense (income) shall be disclosed separately.

80 Components of tax expense (income) may include:

(a) current tax expense (income);

(b) any adjustments recognised in the period for current tax of prior periods;

(c) the amount of deferred tax expense (income) relating to the origination and reversal of temporary differences;

(d) the amount of deferred tax expense (income) relating to changes in tax rates or the imposition of new taxes;

(e) the amount of the benefit arising from a previously unrecognised tax loss, tax credit or temporary difference of a prior period that is used to reduce current tax expense;

(f) the amount of the benefit from a previously unrecognised tax loss, tax credit or temporary difference of a prior period that is used to reduce deferred tax expense;

(g) deferred tax expense arising from the write-down, or reversal of a previous write-down, of a deferred tax asset in accordance with paragraph 56; and

(h) the amount of tax expense (income) relating to those changes in accounting policies and errors that are included in profit or loss in accordance with IAS 8, because they cannot be accounted for retrospectively.

81 **The following shall also be disclosed separately:**

(a) the aggregate current and deferred tax relating to items that are charged or credited to equity;

(b) [deleted];

(c) an explanation of the relationship between tax expense (income) and accounting profit in either or both of the following forms:

(i) a numerical reconciliation between tax expense (income) and the product of accounting profit multiplied by the applicable tax rate(s), disclosing also the basis on which the applicable tax rate(s) is (are) computed; or

(ii) a numerical reconciliation between the average effective tax rate and the applicable tax rate, disclosing also the basis on which the applicable tax rate is computed;

(d) an explanation of changes in the applicable tax rate(s) compared to the previous accounting period;

(e) the amount (and expiry date, if any) of deductible temporary differences, unused tax losses, and unused tax credits for which no deferred tax asset is recognised in the balance sheet;

(f) the aggregate amount of temporary differences associated with investments in subsidiaries, branches and associates and interests in joint ventures, for which deferred tax liabilities have not been recognised (see paragraph 39);

(g) in respect of each type of temporary difference, and in respect of each type of unused tax losses and unused tax credits:

(i) the amount of the deferred tax assets and liabilities recognised in the balance sheet for each period presented;

(ii) the amount of the deferred tax income or expense recognised in the income statement, if this is not apparent from the changes in the amounts recognised in the balance sheet;

(h) in respect of discontinued operations, the tax expense relating to:

(i) the gain or loss on discontinuance; and

(ii) the profit or loss from the ordinary activities of the discontinued operation for the period, together with the corresponding amounts for each prior period presented; and

(i) **the amount of income tax consequences of dividends to shareholders of the entity that were proposed or declared before the financial statements were authorised for issue, but are not recognised as a liability in the financial statements.**

82 An entity shall disclose the amount of a deferred tax asset and the nature of the evidence supporting its recognition, when:

(a) **the utilisation of the deferred tax asset is dependent on future taxable profits in excess of the profits arising from the reversal of existing taxable temporary differences; and**

(b) **the entity has suffered a loss in either the current or preceding period in the tax jurisdiction to which the deferred tax asset relates.**

82A In the circumstances described in paragraph 52A, an entity shall disclose the nature of the potential income tax consequences that would result from the payment of dividends to its shareholders. In addition, the entity shall disclose the amounts of the potential income tax consequences practicably determinable and whether there are any potential income tax consequences not practicably determinable.

83 [Deleted]

84 The disclosures required by paragraph 81(c) enable users of financial statements to understand whether the relationship between tax expense (income) and accounting profit is unusual and to understand the significant factors that could affect that relationship in the future. The relationship between tax expense (income) and accounting profit may be affected by such factors as revenue that is exempt from taxation, expenses that are not deductible in determining taxable profit (tax loss), the effect of tax losses and the effect of foreign tax rates.

85 In explaining the relationship between tax expense (income) and accounting profit, an entity uses an applicable tax rate that provides the most meaningful information to the users of its financial statements. Often, the most meaningful rate is the domestic rate of tax in the country in which the entity is domiciled, aggregating the tax rate applied for national taxes with the rates applied for any local taxes which are computed on a substantially similar level of taxable profit (tax loss). However, for an entity operating in several jurisdictions, it may be more meaningful to aggregate separate reconciliations prepared using the domestic rate in each individual jurisdiction. The following example illustrates how the selection of the applicable tax rate affects the presentation of the numerical reconciliation.

Example illustrating paragraph 85

In 19X2, an entity has accounting profit in its own jurisdiction (country A) of 1,500 (19X1: 2,000) and in country B of 1,500 (19X1: 500). The tax rate is 30% in country A and 20% in country B. In country A, expenses of 100 (19X1: 200) are not deductible for tax purposes.

The following is an example of a reconciliation to the domestic tax rate.

	19X1	19X2
Accounting profit	2,500	3,000
Tax at the domestic rate of 30%	750	900
Tax effect of expenses that are not deductible for tax purposes	60	30
Effect of lower tax rates in country B	(50)	(150)
Tax expense	760	780

The following is an example of a reconciliation prepared by aggregating separate reconciliations for each national jurisdiction. Under this method, the effect of differences between the reporting entity's own domestic tax rate and the domestic tax rate in other jurisdictions does not appear as a separate item in the reconciliation. An entity may need to discuss the effect of significant changes in either tax rates, or the mix of profits earned in different jurisdictions, in order to explain changes in the applicable tax rate(s), as required by paragraph 81(d).

Accounting profit	2,500	3,000
Tax at the domestic rates applicable to profits in the country concerned	700	750
Tax effect of expenses that are not deductible for tax purposes	60	30
Tax expense	760	780

86 The average effective tax rate is the tax expense (income) divided by the accounting profit.

87 It would often be impracticable to compute the amount of unrecognised deferred tax liabilities arising from investments in subsidiaries, branches and associates and interests in joint ventures (see paragraph 39). Therefore, this Standard requires an entity to disclose the aggregate amount of the underlying temporary differences but does not require disclosure of the deferred tax liabilities. Nevertheless, where practicable, entities are encouraged to disclose the amounts of the unrecognised deferred tax liabilities because financial statement users may find such information useful.

87A Paragraph 82A requires an entity to disclose the nature of the potential income tax consequences that would result from the payment of dividends to its shareholders. An entity discloses the important features of the income tax systems and the factors that will affect the amount of the potential income tax consequences of dividends.

87B It would sometimes not be practicable to compute the total amount of the potential income tax consequences that would result from the payment of dividends to shareholders. This may be the case, for example, where an entity has a large number of foreign subsidiaries. However, even in such circumstances, some portions of the total amount may be easily determinable. For example, in a consolidated group, a parent and some of its subsidiaries may have paid income taxes at a higher rate on undistributed profits and be aware of the amount that would be refunded on the payment of future dividends to shareholders from consolidated retained earnings. In this case, that refundable amount is disclosed. If applicable, the entity also discloses that there are additional potential income tax consequences not practicably determinable. In the parent's separate financial statements, if any, the disclosure of the potential income tax consequences relates to the parent's retained earnings.

87C An entity required to provide the disclosures in paragraph 82A may also be required to provide disclosures related to temporary differences associated with investments in subsidiaries, branches and associates or interests in joint ventures. In such cases, an entity considers this in determining the information to be disclosed under paragraph 82A. For example, an entity may be required to disclose the aggregate amount of temporary differences associated with investments in subsidiaries for which no deferred tax liabilities have been recognised (see paragraph 81(f)). If it is impracticable to compute the amounts of unrecognised deferred tax liabilities (see paragraph 87) there may be amounts of potential income tax consequences of dividends not practicably determinable related to these subsidiaries.

88 An entity discloses any tax-related contingent liabilities and contingent assets in accordance with IAS 37 *Provisions, Contingent Liabilities and Contingent Assets*. Contingent liabilities and contingent assets may arise, for example, from unresolved disputes with the taxation authorities. Similarly, where changes in tax rates or tax laws are enacted or announced after the balance sheet date, an entity discloses any significant effect of those changes on its current and deferred tax assets and liabilities (see IAS 10 *Events after the Balance Sheet Date*).

Effective date

89 This Standard becomes operative for financial statements covering periods beginning on or after 1 January 1998, except as specified in paragraph 91. If an entity applies this Standard for financial statements covering periods beginning before 1 January 1998, the entity shall disclose the fact it has applied this Standard instead of IAS 12 *Accounting for Taxes on Income*, **approved in 1979.**

90 This Standard supersedes IAS 12 *Accounting for Taxes on Income*, approved in 1979.

91 **Paragraphs 52A, 52B, 65A, 81(i), 82A, 87A, 87B, 87C and the deletion of paragraphs 3 and 50 become operative for annual financial statements* covering periods beginning on or after 1 January 2001. Earlier adoption is encouraged. If earlier adoption affects the financial statements, an entity shall disclose that fact.**

* Paragraph 91 refers to 'annual financial statements' in line with more explicit language for writing effective dates adopted in 1998. Paragraph 89 refers to 'financial statements'.

Appendix A
Examples of temporary differences

The appendix accompanies, but is not part of, IAS 12.

A. Examples of circumstances that give rise to taxable temporary differences

All taxable temporary differences give rise to a deferred tax liability.

Transactions that affect the income statement

1 Interest revenue is received in arrears and is included in accounting profit on a time apportionment basis but is included in taxable profit on a cash basis.

2 Revenue from the sale of goods is included in accounting profit when goods are delivered but is included in taxable profit when cash is collected. *(note: as explained in B3 below, there is also a deductible temporary difference associated with any related inventory).*

3 Depreciation of an asset is accelerated for tax purposes.

4 Development costs have been capitalised and will be amortised to the income statement but were deducted in determining taxable profit in the period in which they were incurred.

5 Prepaid expenses have already been deducted on a cash basis in determining the taxable profit of the current or previous periods.

Transactions that affect the balance sheet

6 Depreciation of an asset is not deductible for tax purposes and no deduction will be available for tax purposes when the asset is sold or scrapped. *(note: paragraph 15(b) of the Standard prohibits recognition of the resulting deferred tax liability unless the asset was acquired in a business combination, see also paragraph 22 of the Standard).*

7 A borrower records a loan at the proceeds received (which equal the amount due at maturity), less transaction costs. Subsequently, the carrying amount of the loan is increased by amortisation of the transaction costs to accounting profit. The transaction costs were deducted for tax purposes in the period when the loan was first recognised. *(notes: (1) the taxable temporary difference is the amount of transaction costs already deducted in determining the taxable profit of current or prior periods, less the cumulative amount amortised to accounting profit; and (2) as the initial recognition of the loan affects taxable profit, the exception in paragraph 15(b) of the Standard does not apply. Therefore, the borrower recognises the deferred tax liability).*

8 A loan payable was measured on initial recognition at the amount of the net proceeds, net of transaction costs. The transaction costs are amortised to accounting profit over the life of the loan. Those transaction costs are not deductible in determining the taxable profit of future, current or prior periods. *(notes: (1) the taxable temporary difference is the amount of unamortised transaction costs; and (2) paragraph 15(b) of the Standard prohibits recognition of the resulting deferred tax liability).*

9 The liability component of a compound financial instrument (for example a convertible bond) is measured at a discount to the amount repayable on maturity (see IAS 32 *Financial Instruments: Disclosure and Presentation*). The discount is not deductible in determining taxable profit (tax loss).

Fair value adjustments and revaluations

10 Financial assets or investment property are carried at fair value which exceeds cost but no equivalent adjustment is made for tax purposes.

11 An entity revalues property, plant and equipment (under the revaluation model treatment in IAS 16 *Property, Plant and Equipment*) but no equivalent adjustment is made for tax purposes. (*note: paragraph 61 of the Standard requires the related deferred tax to be charged directly to equity*).

Business combinations and consolidation

12 The carrying amount of an asset is increased to fair value in a business combination and no equivalent adjustment is made for tax purposes. (*Note that on initial recognition, the resulting deferred tax liability increases goodwill or decreases the amount of any excess of the acquirer's interest in the net fair value of the acquiree's identifiable assets, liabilities and contingent liabilities over the cost of the combination. See paragraph 66 of the Standard*).

13 Reductions in the carrying amount of goodwill are not deductible in determining taxable profit and the cost of the goodwill would not be deductible on disposal of the business. (*Note that paragraph 15(a) of the Standard prohibits recognition of the resulting deferred tax liability*).

14 Unrealised losses resulting from intragroup transactions are eliminated by inclusion in the carrying amount of inventory or property, plant and equipment.

15 Retained earnings of subsidiaries, branches, associates and joint ventures are included in consolidated retained earnings, but income taxes will be payable if the profits are distributed to the reporting parent. (*note: paragraph 39 of the Standard prohibits recognition of the resulting deferred tax liability if the parent, investor or venturer is able to control the timing of the reversal of the temporary difference and it is probable that the temporary difference will not reverse in the foreseeable future*).

16 Investments in foreign subsidiaries, branches or associates or interests in foreign joint ventures are affected by changes in foreign exchange rates. (*notes: (1) there may be either a taxable temporary difference or a deductible temporary difference; and (2) paragraph 39 of the Standard prohibits recognition of the resulting deferred tax liability if the parent, investor or venturer is able to control the timing of the reversal of the temporary difference and it is probable that the temporary difference will not reverse in the foreseeable future*).

17 The non-monetary assets and liabilities of an entity are measured in its functional currency but the taxable profit or tax loss is determined in a different currency. (*notes: (1) there may be either a taxable temporary difference or a deductible temporary difference; (2) where there is a taxable temporary difference, the resulting deferred tax liability is recognised (paragraph 41 of the Standard); and (3) the deferred tax is recognised in profit or loss, see paragraph 58 of the Standard*).

Hyperinflation

18 Non-monetary assets are restated in terms of the measuring unit current at the balance sheet date (see IAS 29 *Financial Reporting in Hyperinflationary Economies*) and no equivalent adjustment is made for tax purposes. *(notes: (1) the deferred tax is charged in the income statement; and (2) if, in addition to the restatement, the non-monetary assets are also revalued, the deferred tax relating to the revaluation is charged to equity and the deferred tax relating to the restatement is charged in the income statement).*

B. Examples of circumstances that give rise to deductible temporary differences

All deductible temporary differences give rise to a deferred tax asset. However, some deferred tax assets may not satisfy the recognition criteria in paragraph 24 of the Standard.

Transactions that affect the income statement

1 Retirement benefit costs are deducted in determining accounting profit as service is provided by the employee, but are not deducted in determining taxable profit until the entity pays either retirement benefits or contributions to a fund. *(note: similar deductible temporary differences arise where other expenses, such as product warranty costs or interest, are deductible on a cash basis in determining taxable profit).*

2 Accumulated depreciation of an asset in the financial statements is greater than the cumulative depreciation allowed up to the balance sheet date for tax purposes.

3 The cost of inventories sold before the balance sheet date is deducted in determining accounting profit when goods or services are delivered but is deducted in determining taxable profit when cash is collected. *(note: as explained in A2 above, there is also a* **taxable** *temporary difference associated with the related trade receivable).*

4 The net realisable value of an item of inventory, or the recoverable amount of an item of property, plant or equipment, is less than the previous carrying amount and an entity therefore reduces the carrying amount of the asset, but that reduction is ignored for tax purposes until the asset is sold.

5 Research costs (or organisation or other start up costs) are recognised as an expense in determining accounting profit but are not permitted as a deduction in determining taxable profit until a later period.

6 Income is deferred in the balance sheet but has already been included in taxable profit in current or prior periods.

7 A government grant which is included in the balance sheet as deferred income will not be taxable in future periods. *(note: paragraph 24 of the Standard prohibits the recognition of the resulting deferred tax asset, see also paragraph 33 of the Standard).*

Fair value adjustments and revaluations

8 Financial assets or investment property are carried at fair value which is less than cost, but no equivalent adjustment is made for tax purposes.

Business combinations and consolidation

9 A liability is recognised at its fair value in a business combination, but none of the related expense is deducted in determining taxable profit until a later period. *(Note that the resulting deferred tax asset decreases goodwill or increases the amount of any excess of the acquirer's interest in the net fair value of the acquiree's identifiable assets, liabilities and contingent liabilities over the cost of the combination. See paragraph 66 of the Standard).*

10 [Deleted]

11 Unrealised profits resulting from intragroup transactions are eliminated from the carrying amount of assets, such as inventory or property, plant or equipment, but no equivalent adjustment is made for tax purposes.

12 Investments in foreign subsidiaries, branches or associates or interests in foreign joint ventures are affected by changes in foreign exchange rates. *(notes: (1) there may be a taxable temporary difference or a deductible temporary difference; and (2) paragraph 44 of the Standard requires recognition of the resulting deferred tax asset to the extent, and only to the extent, that it is probable that: (a) the temporary difference will reverse in the foreseeable future; and (b) taxable profit will be available against which the temporary difference can be utilised).*

13 The non-monetary assets and liabilities of an entity are measured in its functional currency but the taxable profit or tax loss is determined in a different currency. *(notes: (1) there may be either a taxable temporary difference or a deductible temporary difference; (2) where there is a deductible temporary difference, the resulting deferred tax asset is recognised to the extent that it is probable that sufficient taxable profit will be available (paragraph 41 of the Standard); and (3) the deferred tax is recognised in profit or loss, see paragraph 58 of the Standard.)*

C. Examples of circumstances where the carrying amount of an asset or liability is equal to its tax base

1 Accrued expenses have already been deducted in determining an entity's current tax liability for the current or earlier periods.

2 A loan payable is measured at the amount originally received and this amount is the same as the amount repayable on final maturity of the loan.

3 Accrued expenses will never be deductible for tax purposes.

4 Accrued income will never be taxable.

Appendix B
Illustrative computations and presentation

The appendix accompanies, but is not part of, IAS 12. Extracts from income statements and balance sheets are provided to show the effects on these financial statements of the transactions described below. These extracts do not necessarily conform with all the disclosure and presentation requirements of other Standards.

All the examples in this appendix assume that the entities concerned have no transaction other than those described.

Example 1 – Depreciable assets

An entity buys equipment for 10,000 and depreciates it on a straight line basis over its expected useful life of five years. For tax purposes, the equipment is depreciated at 25% per annum on a straight line basis. Tax losses may be carried back against taxable profit of the previous five years. In year 0, the entity's taxable profit was 5,000. The tax rate is 40%.

The entity will recover the carrying amount of the equipment by using it to manufacture goods for resale. Therefore, the entity's current tax computation is as follows:

	Year				
	1	*2*	*3*	*4*	*5*
Taxable income	2,000	2,000	2,000	2,000	2,000
Depreciation for tax purposes	2,500	2,500	2,500	2,500	0
Taxable profit (tax loss)	(500)	(500)	(500)	(500)	2,000
Current tax expense (income) at 40%	(200)	(200)	(200)	(200)	800

The entity recognises a current tax asset at the end of years 1 to 4 because it recovers the benefit of the tax loss against the taxable profit of year 0.

The temporary differences associated with the equipment and the resulting deferred tax asset and liability and deferred tax expense and income are as follows:

	Year				
	1	*2*	*3*	*4*	*5*
Carrying Amount	8,000	6,000	4,000	2,000	0
Tax base	7,500	5,000	2,500	0	0
Taxable temporary difference	200	1,000	1,500	2,000	0
Opening deferred tax liability	0	200	400	600	800
Deferred tax expense (income)	200	200	200	200	(800)
Closing deferred tax liability	200	400	600	800	0

The entity recognises the deferred tax liability in years 1 to 4 because the reversal of the taxable temporary difference will create taxable income in subsequent years. The entity's income statement is as follows:

	Year				
	1	*2*	*3*	*4*	*5*
Income	2,000	2,000	2,000	2,000	2,000
Depreciation	2,000	2,000	2,000	2,000	2,000
Profit before tax	0	0	0	0	0
Current tax expense (income)	(200)	(200)	(200)	(200)	800
Deferred tax expense (income)	200	200	200	200	(800)
Total tax expense (income)	0	0	0	0	0
Net profit for the period	0	0	0	0	0

Example 2 – Deferred tax assets and liabilities

The example deals with an entity over the two year period, X5 and X6. In X5 the enacted income tax rate was 40% of taxable profit. In X6 the enacted income tax rate was 35% of taxable profit.

Charitable donations are recognised as an expense when they are paid and are not deductible for tax purposes.

In X5, the entity was notified by the relevant authorities that they intend to pursue an action against the entity with respect to sulphur emissions. Although as at December X6 the action had not yet come to court the entity recognised a liability of 700 in X5 being its best estimate of the fine arising from the action. Fines are not deductible for tax purposes.

In X2, the entity incurred 1,250 of costs in relation to the development of a new product. These costs were deducted for tax purposes in X2. For accounting purposes, the entity capitalised this expenditure and amortised it on the straight-line basis over five years. At 31/12/X4, the unamortised balance of these product development costs was 500.

In X5, the entity entered into an agreement with its existing employees to provide health care benefits to retirees. The entity recognises as an expense the cost of this plan as employees provide service. No payments to retirees were made for such benefits in X5 or X6. Healthcare costs are deductible for tax purposes when payments are made to retirees. The entity has determined that it is probable that taxable profit will be available against which any resulting deferred tax asset can be utilised.

Buildings are depreciated for accounting purposes at 5% a year on a straight line basis and at 10% a year on a straight line basis for tax purposes. Motor vehicles are depreciated for accounting purposes at 20% a year on a straight-line basis and at 25% a year on a straight-line basis for tax purposes. A full year's depreciation is charged for accounting purposes in the year that an asset is acquired.

At 1/1/X6, the building was revalued to 65,000 and the entity estimated that the remaining useful life of the building was 20 years from the date of the revaluation. The revaluation did not affect taxable profit in X6 and the taxation authorities did not adjust the tax base of the building to reflect the revaluation. In X6, the entity transferred 1,033 from revaluation reserve to retained earnings. This represents the difference of 1,590 between the actual depreciation on the building (3,250) and equivalent depreciation based on the cost of the building (1,660, which is the book value at 1/1/X6 of 33,200 divided by the remaining useful life of 20 years), less the related deferred tax of 557 (see paragraph 64 of the Standard).

Current tax expense

	X5	*X6*
Accounting profit	8,775	8,740
Add		
Depreciation for accounting purposes	4,800	8,250
Charitable donations	500	350
Fine for environmental pollution	700	–
Product development costs	250	250
Healthcare benefits	2,000	1,000
	17,025	18,590
Deduct		
Depreciation for tax purposes	(8,100)	(11,850)
Taxable Profit	8,925	6,740
Current tax expense at 40%	3,570	
Current tax expense at 35%		2,359

Carrying amounts of property, plant and equipment

Cost	*Building*	*Motor vehicles*	*Total*
Balance at 31/12/X4	50,000	10,000	60,000
Additions X5	6,000	–	6,000
Balance at 31/12/X5	56,000	10,000	66,000
Elimination of accumulated depreciation on revaluation at 1/1/X6	(22,800)	–	(22,800)
Revaluation at 1/1/X6	31,800	–	31,800
Balance at 1/1/X6	65,000	10,000	75,000
Additions X6	–	15,000	15,000
	65,000	25,000	90,000

Continued from previous page

Carrying amounts of property, plant and equipment

Cost	***Building***	***Motor vehicles***	***Total***
Accumulated depreciation	5%	20%	
Balance at 31/12/X4	20,000	4,000	24,000
Depreciation X5	2,800	2,000	4,800
Balance at 31/12/X5	22,800	6,000	28,800
Revaluation at 1/1/X6	(22,800)	–	(22,800)
Balance at 1/1/X6	–	6,000	6,000
Depreciation X6	3,250	5,000	8,250
Balance at 31/12/X6	3,250	11,000	14,250
Carrying amount			
31/12/X4	30,000	6,000	36,000
31/12/X5	33,200	4,000	37,200
31/12/X6	61,750	14,000	75,750

Tax base of property, plant and equipment

Cost	*Building*	*Motor vehicles*	*Total*
Balance at 31/12/X4	50,000	10,000	60,000
Additions X5	6,000	–	6,000
Balance at 31/12/X5	56,000	10,000	66,000
Additions X6	–	15,000	15,000
Balance at 31/12/X6	56,000	25,000	81,000
Accumulated depreciation	10%	25%	
Balance at 31/12/X4	40,000	5,000	45,000
Depreciation X5	5,600	2,500	8,100
Balance at 31/12/X5	45,600	7,500	53,100
Depreciation X6	5,600	6,250	11,850
Balance 31/12/X6	51,200	13,750	64,950
Tax base			
31/12/X4	10,000	5,000	15,000
31/12/X5	10,400	2,500	12,900
31/12/X6	4,800	11,250	16,050

Deferred tax assets, liabilities and expense at 31/12/X4

	Carrying amount	*Tax base*	*Temporary differences*
Accounts receivable	500	500	–
Inventory	2,000	2,000	–
Product development costs	500	–	500
Investments	33,000	33,000	–
Property, plant & equipment	36,000	15,000	21,000
TOTAL ASSETS	72,000	50,500	21,500
Current income taxes payable	3,000	3,000	–
Accounts payable	500	500	–
Fines payable	–	–	–
Liability for healthcare benefits	–	–	–
Long–term debt	20,000	20,000	–
Deferred income taxes	8,600	8,600	–
TOTAL LIABILITIES	32,100	32,100	
Share capital	5,000	5,000	–
Revaluation surplus	–	–	–
Retained earnings	34,900	13,400	
TOTAL LIABILITIES / EQUITY	72,000	50,500	
TEMPORARY DIFFERENCES			21,500
Deferred tax liability	21,500 at 40%		8,600
Deferred tax asset	–	–	–
Net deferred tax liability			8,600

Deferred tax assets, liabilities and expense at 31/12/X5

	Carrying amount	Tax base	Temporary differences
Accounts receivable	500	500	–
Inventory	2,000	2,000	–
Product development costs	250	–	250
Investments	33,000	33,000	–
Property, plant & equipment	37,200	12,900	24,300
TOTAL ASSETS	72,950	48,400	24,550
Current income taxes payable	3,570	3,570	–
Accounts payable	500	500	–
Fines payable	700	700	–
Liability for healthcare benefits	2,000	–	(2,000)
Long–term debt	12,475	12,475	–
Deferred income taxes	9,020	9,020	–
TOTAL LIABILITIES	28,265	26,265	(2,000)
Share capital	5,000	5,000	–
Revaluation surplus	–	–	–
Retained earnings	39,685	17,135	
TOTAL LIABILITIES / EQUITY	72,950	48,400	
TEMPORARY DIFFERENCES			22,550

Deferred tax liability	24,550 at 40%	9,820
Deferred tax asset	(2,000) at 40%	(800)
Net deferred tax liability		9,020
Less: Opening deferred tax liability		(8,600)
Deferred tax expense (income) related to the origination and reversal of temporary differences		420

Deferred tax assets, liabilities and expense at 31/12/X6

	Carrying amount	*Tax base*	*Temporary differences*
Accounts receivable	500	500	–
Inventory	2,000	2,000	–
Product development costs	–	–	–
Investments	33,000	33,000	–
Property, plant & equipment	75,750	16,050	59,700
TOTAL ASSETS	111,250	51,550	59,700
Current income taxes payable	2,359	2,359	–
Accounts payable	500	500	–
Fines payable	700	700	–
Liability for healthcare benefits	3,000	–	(3,000)
Long–term debt	12,805	12,805	–
Deferred income taxes	19,845	19,845	–
TOTAL LIABILITIES	39,209	36,209	(3,000)
Share capital	5,000	5,000	–
Revaluation surplus	19,637	–	–
Retained earnings	47,404	10,341	
TOTAL LIABILITIES / EQUITY	111,250	51,550	
TEMPORARY DIFFERENCES			56,700

Deferred tax liability	59,700 at 35%	20,895
Deferred tax asset	(3,000) at 35%	(1,050)
Net deferred tax liability		19,845
Less: Opening deferred tax liability		(9,020)
Adjustment to opening deferred tax liability resulting from reduction in tax rate	22,550 at 5%	1,127
Deferred tax attributable to revaluation surplus	31,800 at 35%	(11,130)
Deferred tax expense (income) related to the origination and reversal of temporary differences		822

Illustrative disclosure

The amounts to be disclosed in accordance with the Standard are as follows:

Major components of tax expense (income) (paragraph 79)

	X5	*X6*
Current tax expense	3,570	2,359
Deferred tax expense relating to the origination and reversal of temporary differences:	420	822
Deferred tax expense (income) resulting from reduction in tax rate	–	(1,127)
Tax expense	3,990	2,054

Aggregate current and deferred tax relating to items charged or credited to equity (paragraph 81(a))

Deferred tax relating to revaluation of building	–	(11,130)

In addition, deferred tax of 557 was transferred in X6 from retained earnings to revaluation reserve. This relates to the difference between the actual depreciation on the building and equivalent depreciation based on the cost of the building.

Explanation of the relationship between tax expense and accounting profit (paragraph 81(c))

The Standard permits two alternative methods of explaining the relationship between tax expense (income) and accounting profit. Both of these formats are illustrated on the next page.

(i) a numerical reconciliation between tax expense (income) and the product of accounting profit multiplied by the applicable tax rate(s), disclosing also the basis on which the applicable tax rate(s) is (are) computed

	X5	*X6*
Accounting profit	8,775	8,740
Tax at the applicable tax rate of 35% (X5: 40%)	3,510	3,059
Tax effect of expenses that are not deductible in determining taxable profit:		
Charitable donations	200	122
Fines for environmental pollution	280	–
Reduction in opening deferred taxes resulting from reduction in tax rate	–	(1,127)
Tax expense	3,990	2,054

The applicable tax rate is the aggregate of the national income tax rate of 30% (X5: 35%) and the local income tax rate of 5%.

(ii) a numerical reconciliation between the average effective tax rate and the applicable tax rate, disclosing also the basis on which the applicable tax rate is computed

	X5	*X6*
	%	%
Applicable tax rate	40.0	35.0
Tax effect of expenses that are not deductible for tax purposes:		
Charitable donations	2.3	1.4
Fines for environmental pollution	3.2	–
Effect on opening deferred taxes of reduction in tax rate	–	(12.9)
Average effective tax rate (tax expense divided by profit before tax)	45.5	23.5

The applicable tax rate is the aggregate of the national income tax rate of 30% (X5: 35%) and the local income tax rate of 5%.

An explanation of changes in the applicable tax rate(s) compared to the previous accounting period (paragraph 81(d))

In X6, the government enacted a change in the national income tax rate from 35% to 30%.

In respect of each type of temporary difference, and in respect of each type of unused tax losses and unused tax credits:

(i) the amount of the deferred tax assets and liabilities recognised in the balance sheet for each period presented;

(ii) the amount of the deferred tax income or expense recognised in the income statement for each period presented, if this is not apparent from the changes in the amounts recognised in the balance sheet (paragraph 81(g))

	X5	*X6*
Accelerated depreciation for tax purposes	9,720	10,322
Liabilities for health care benefits that are deducted for tax purposes only when paid	(800)	(1,050)
Product development costs deducted from taxable profit in earlier years	100	–
Revaluation, net of related depreciation	–	10,573
Deferred tax liability	9,020	19,845

(note: the amount of the deferred tax income or expense recognised in the income statement for the current year is apparent from the changes in the amounts recognised in the balance sheet)

Example 3 – Business combinations

On 1 January X5 entity A acquired 100 per cent of the shares of entity B at a cost of 600. At the acquisition date, the tax base in A's tax jurisdiction of A's investment in B is 600. Reductions in the carrying amount of goodwill are not deductible for tax purposes, and the cost of the goodwill would also not be deductible if B were to dispose of its underlying business. The tax rate in A's tax jurisdiction is 30 per cent and the tax rate in B's tax jurisdiction is 40 per cent.

The fair value of the identifiable assets acquired and liabilities assumed (excluding deferred tax assets and liabilities) by A is set out in the following table, together with their tax bases in B's tax jurisdiction and the resulting temporary differences.

	Cost of acquisition	*Tax base*	*Temporary differences*
Property, plant and equipment	270	155	115
Accounts receivable	210	210	–
Inventory	174	124	50
Retirement benefit obligations	(30)	–	(30)
Accounts payable	(120)	(120)	–
Fair value of the identifiable assets acquired and liabilities assumed, excluding deferred tax	504	369	135

The deferred tax asset arising from the retirement benefit obligations is offset against the deferred tax liabilities arising from the property, plant and equipment and inventory (see paragraph 74 of the Standard).

No deduction is available in B's tax jurisdiction for the cost of the goodwill. Therefore, the tax base of the goodwill in B's jurisdiction is nil. However, in accordance with paragraph 15(a) of the Standard, A recognises no deferred tax liability for the taxable temporary difference associated with the goodwill in B's tax jurisdiction.

The carrying amount, in A's consolidated financial statements, of its investment in B is made up as follows:

Fair value of identifiable assets acquired and liabilities assumed, excluding deferred tax	504
Deferred tax liability (135 at 40%)	(54)
Fair value of identifiable assets acquired and liabilities assumed	450
Goodwill	150
Carrying amount	600

Because, at the acquisition date, the tax base in A's tax jurisdiction, of A's investment in B is 600, no temporary difference is associated in A's tax jurisdiction with the investment.

During X5, B's equity (incorporating the fair value adjustments made as a result of the business combination) changed as follows:

At 1 January X5	450
Retained profit for X5 (net profit of 150, less dividend payable of 80)	70
At 31 December X5	520

A recognises a liability for any withholding tax or other taxes that it will incur on the accrued dividend receivable of 80.

At 31 December X5, the carrying amount of A's underlying investment in B, excluding the accrued dividend receivable, is as follows:

Net assets of B	520
Goodwill	150
Carrying amount	670

The temporary difference associated with A's underlying investment is 70. This amount is equal to the cumulative retained profit since the acquisition date.

If A has determined that it will not sell the investment in the foreseeable future and that B will not distribute its retained profits in the foreseeable future, no deferred tax liability is recognised in relation to A's investment in B (see paragraphs 39 and 40 of the Standard). Note that this exception would apply for an investment in an associate only if there is an agreement requiring that the profits of the associate will not be distributed in the foreseeable future (see paragraph 42 of the Standard). A discloses the amount of the temporary difference for which no deferred tax is recognised, ie 70 (see paragraph 81(f) of the Standard).

If A expects to sell the investment in B, or that B will distribute its retained profits in the foreseeable future, A recognises a deferred tax liability to the extent that the temporary difference is expected to reverse. The tax rate reflects the manner in which A expects to recover the carrying amount of its investment (see paragraph 51 of the Standard). A credits or charges the deferred tax to equity to the extent that the deferred tax results from foreign exchange translation differences which have been charged or credited directly to equity (paragraph 61 of the Standard). A discloses separately:

(a) the amount of deferred tax which has been charged or credited directly to equity (paragraph 81(a) of the Standard); and

(b) the amount of any remaining temporary difference which is not expected to reverse in the foreseeable future and for which, therefore, no deferred tax is recognised (see paragraph 81(f) of the Standard).

Example 4 – Compound financial instruments

An entity receives a non-interest-bearing convertible loan of 1,000 on 31 December X4 repayable at par on 1 January X8. In accordance with IAS 32 *Financial Instruments: Disclosure and Presentation* the entity classifies the instrument's liability component as a liability and the equity component as equity. The entity assigns an initial carrying amount of 751 to the liability component of the convertible loan and 249 to the equity component. Subsequently, the entity recognises imputed discount as interest expense at an annual rate of 10% on the carrying amount of the liability component at the beginning of the year. The tax authorities do not allow the entity to claim any deduction for the imputed discount on the liability component of the convertible loan. The tax rate is 40%.

The temporary differences associated with the liability component and the resulting deferred tax liability and deferred tax expense and income are as follows:

	Year			
	X4	*X5*	*X6*	*X7*
Carrying amount of liability component	751	826	909	1,000
Tax base	1,000	1,000	1,000	1,000
Taxable temporary difference	249	174	91	–
Opening deferred tax liability at 40%	0	100	70	37
Deferred tax charged to equity	100	–	–	–
Deferred tax expense (income)	–	(30)	(33)	(37)
Closing deferred tax liability at 40%	100	70	37	–

As explained in paragraph 23 of the Standard, at 31 December X4, the entity recognises the resulting deferred tax liability by adjusting the initial carrying amount of the equity component of the convertible liability. Therefore, the amounts recognised at that date are as follows:

Liability component	751
Deferred tax liability	100
Equity component (249 less 100)	149
	1,000

Subsequent changes in the deferred tax liability are recognised in the income statement as tax income (see paragraph 23 of the Standard). Therefore, the entity's income statement is as follows:

				Year
	X4	*X5*	*X6*	*X7*
Interest expense (imputed discount)	–	75	83	91
Deferred tax (income)	–	(30)	(33)	(37)
	–	45	50	54

Example 5 – Share-based payment transactions

In accordance with IFRS 2 *Share-based Payment*, an entity has recognised an expense for the consumption of employee services received as consideration for share options granted. A tax deduction will not arise until the options are exercised, and the deduction is based on the options' intrinsic value at exercise date.

As explained in paragraph 68B of the Standard, the difference between the tax base of the employee services received to date (being the amount the taxation authorities will permit as a deduction in future periods in respect of those services), and the carrying amount of nil, is a deductible temporary difference that results in a deferred tax asset. Paragraph 68B requires that, if the amount the taxation authorities will permit as a deduction in future periods is not known at the end of the period, it should be estimated, based on information available at the end of the period. If the amount that the taxation authorities will permit as a deduction in future periods is dependent upon the entity's share price at a future date, the measurement of the deductible temporary difference should be based on the entity's share price at the end of the period. Therefore, in this example, the estimated future tax deduction (and hence the measurement of the deferred tax asset) should be based on the options' intrinsic value at the end of the period.

As explained in paragraph 68C of the Standard, if the tax deduction (or estimated future tax deduction) exceeds the amount of the related cumulative remuneration expense, this indicates that the tax deduction relates not only to remuneration expense but also to an equity item. In this situation, paragraph 68C requires that the excess of the associated current or deferred tax should be recognised directly in equity.

The entity's tax rate is 40 per cent. The options were granted at the start of year 1, vested at the end of year 3 and were exercised at the end of year 5. Details of the expense recognised for employee services received and consumed in each accounting period, the number of options outstanding at each year-end, and the intrinsic value of the options at each year-end, are as follows:

	Employee services expense	Number of options at year–end	Intrinsic value per option
Year 1	188,000	50,000	5
Year 2	185,000	45,000	8
Year 3	190,000	40,000	13
Year 4	0	40,000	17
Year 5	0	40,000	20

The entity recognises a deferred tax asset and deferred tax income in years 1–4 and current tax income in year 5 as follows. In years 4 and 5, some of the deferred and current tax income is recognised directly in equity, because the estimated (and actual) tax deduction exceeds the cumulative remuneration expense.

Year 1

Deferred tax asset and deferred tax income:

(50,000 × 5 × ⅓[(a)] × 0.40) = 33,333

(a) The tax base of the employee services received is based on the intrinsic value of the options, and those options were granted for three years' services. Because only one year's services have been received to date, it is necessary to multiply the option's intrinsic value by one–third to arrive at the tax base of the employee services received in year 1.

The deferred tax income is all recognised in profit or loss, because the estimated future tax deduction of 83,333 (50,000 × 5 × ⅓) is less than the cumulative remuneration expense of 188,000.

Year 2

Deferred tax asset at year–end:		
(45,000 × 8 × ⅔ × 0.40) =	96,000	
Less deferred tax asset at start of year	(33,333)	
Deferred tax income for year		62,667*

* This amount consists of the following:

Deferred tax income for the temporary difference between the tax base of the employee services received during the year and their carrying amount of nil:		
(45,000 × 8 × ⅓ × 0.40)	48,000	
Tax income resulting from an adjustment to the tax base of employee services received in previous years:		
(a) increase in intrinsic value: (45,000 × 3 × ⅓ × 0.40)	18,000	
(b) decrease in number of options: (5,000 × 5 × ⅓ × 0.40)	(3,333)	
Deferred tax income for year		62,667

The deferred tax income is all recognised in profit or loss, because the estimated future tax deduction of 240,000 (45,000 × 8 × ⅔) is less than the cumulative remuneration expense of 373,000 (188,000 + 185,000).

Year 3

Deferred tax asset at year–end:	
(40,000 × 13 × 0.40) =	208,000
Less deferred tax asset at start of year	(96,000)
Deferred tax income for year	112,000

The deferred tax income is all recognised in profit or loss, because the estimated future tax deduction of 520,000 (40,000 × 13) is less than the cumulative remuneration expense of 563,000 (188,000 + 185,000 + 190,000).

Year 4

Deferred tax asset at year–end:		
(40,000 × 17 × 0.40) =	272,000	
Less deferred tax asset at start of year	(208,000)	
Deferred tax income for year		64,000

The deferred tax income is recognised partly in profit or loss and partly directly in equity as follows:

Estimated future tax deduction (40,000 × 17) =	680,000	
Cumulative remuneration expense	563,000	
Excess tax deduction		117,000
Deferred tax income for year	64,000	
Excess recognised directly in equity (117,000 × 0.40) =	46,800	
Recognised in profit or loss		17,200

Year 5

Deferred tax expense (reversal of deferred tax asset)	272,000	
Amount recognised directly in equity (reversal of cumulative deferred tax income recognised directly in equity)	46,800	
Amount recognised in profit or loss		225,200
Current tax income based on intrinsic value of options at exercise date (40,000 × 20 × 0.40) =	320,000	
Amount recognised in profit or loss (563,000 × 0.40) =	225,200	
Amount recognised directly in equity		94,800

Summary

	Income statement				Balance sheet	
	Employee services expense	Current tax expense (income)	Deferred tax expense (income)	Total tax expense (income)	Equity	Deferred tax asset
Year 1	188,000	0	(33,333)	(33,333)	0	33,333
Year 2	185,000	0	(62,667)	(62,667)	0	96,000
Year 3	190,000	0	(112,000)	(112,000)	0	208,000
Year 4	0	0	(17,200)	(17,200)	(46,800)	272,000
Year 5	0	(225,200)	225,200	0	46,800	0
					(94,800)	
Totals	563,000	(225,200)	0	(225,200)	(94,800)	0

International Accounting Standard 14

Segment Reporting

This version includes amendments resulting from new and amended IFRSs issued up to 31 December 2004.

CONTENTS

International Accounting Standard 14 *Segment Reporting* (IAS 14) is set out in paragraphs 1–84. All the paragraphs have equal authority but retain the IASC format of the Standard when it was adopted by the IASB. IAS 14 should be read in the context of its objective, the *Preface to International Financial Reporting Standards* and the *Framework for the Preparation and Presentation of Financial Statements.* IAS 8 *Accounting Policies, Changes in Accounting Estimates and Errors* provides a basis for selecting and applying accounting policies in the absence of explicit guidance.

Introduction

IN1 This Standard (IAS 14 (revised)) replaces IAS 14 *Reporting Financial Information by Segment* ('the original IAS 14'). IAS 14 (revised) is effective for accounting periods beginning on or after 1 July 1998. The major changes from the original IAS 14 are as follows.

IN2 The original IAS 14 applied to entities whose securities are publicly traded and other economically significant entities. IAS 14 (revised) applies to entities whose equity or debt securities are publicly traded, including enterprises in the process of issuing equity or debt securities in a public securities market, but not to other economically significant entities.

IN3 The original IAS 14 required that information be reported for industry segments and geographical segments. It provided only general guidance for identifying industry segments and geographical segments. It suggested that internal organisational groupings may provide a basis for determining reportable segments, or segment reporting may require reclassification of data. IAS 14 (revised) requires that information be reported for business segments and geographical segments. It provides more detailed guidance than the original IAS 14 for identifying business segments and geographical segments. It requires that an entity look to its internal organisational structure and internal reporting system for the purpose of identifying those segments. If internal segments are based neither on groups of related products and services nor on geography, IAS 14 (revised) requires that an entity should look to the next lower level of internal segmentation to identify its reportable segments.

IN4 The original IAS 14 required that the same quantity of information be reported for both industry segments and geographical segments. IAS 14 (revised) provides that one basis of segmentation is primary and the other is secondary, with considerably less information required to be disclosed for secondary segments.

IN5 The original IAS 14 was silent on whether segment information must be prepared using the accounting policies adopted for the consolidated or entity financial statements. IAS 14 (revised) requires that the same accounting policies be followed.

IN6 The original IAS 14 had allowed differences in the definition of segment result among entities. IAS 14 (revised) provides more detailed guidance than the original IAS 14 as to specific items of revenue and expense that should be included in or excluded from segment revenue and segment expense. Accordingly, IAS 14 (revised) provides for a standardised measure of segment result, but only to the extent that items of revenue and operating expense can be directly attributed or reasonably allocated to segments.

IN7 IAS 14 (revised) requires 'symmetry' in the inclusion of items in segment result and in segment assets. If, for example, segment result reflects depreciation expense, the depreciable asset must be included in segment assets. The original IAS 14 was silent on this matter.

IN8 The original IAS 14 was silent on whether segments deemed too small for separate reporting could be combined with other segments or excluded from all reportable segments. IAS 14 (revised) provides that small internally reported segments that are not required to be separately reported may be combined with each other if they share a substantial number of the factors that define a business segment or geographical segment, or they may be combined with a similar significant segment for which information is reported internally if certain conditions are met.

IN9 The original IAS 14 was silent on whether geographical segments should be based on where the entity's assets are located (the origin of its sales) or on where its customers are located (the destination of its sales). IAS 14 (revised) requires that, whichever is the basis of an entity's geographical segments, several items of data must be presented on the other basis if significantly different.

IN10 The original IAS 14 required four principal items of information for both industry segments and geographical segments:

(a) sales or other operating revenues, distinguishing between revenue derived from customers outside the entity and revenue derived from other segments;

(b) segment result;

(c) segment assets employed; and

(d) the basis of inter-segment pricing.

For an entity's primary basis of segment reporting (business segments or geographical segments), IAS 14 (revised) requires those same four items of information plus:

(a) segment liabilities;

(b) cost of property, plant, equipment, and intangible assets acquired during the period;

(c) depreciation and amortisation expense;

(d) non-cash expenses other than depreciation and amortisation; and

(e) the entity's share of the profit or loss of an associate, joint venture, or other investment accounted for under the equity method if substantially all of the associate's operations are within only that segment, and the amount of the related investment.

For an entity's secondary basis of segment reporting, IAS 14 (revised) drops the original IAS 14 requirement for segment result and replaces it with the cost of property, plant, equipment, and intangible assets acquired during the period.

IN11 The original IAS 14 was silent on whether prior period segment information presented for comparative purposes should be restated for a material change in segment accounting policies. IAS 14 (revised) requires restatement unless it is impracticable to do so.

IN12 IAS 14 (revised) requires that if total revenue from external customers for all reportable segments combined is less than 75 per cent of total entity revenue, then additional reportable segments should be identified until the 75 per cent level is reached.

IN13 The original IAS 14 allowed a different method of pricing inter-segment transfers to be used in segment data than was actually used to price the transfers. IAS 14 (revised) requires that inter-segment transfers be measured on the basis that the entity actually used to price the transfers.

IN14 IAS 14 (revised) requires disclosure of revenue for any segment not deemed reportable because it earns a majority of its revenue from sales to other segments if that segment's revenue from sales to external customers is 10 per cent or more of total entity revenue. The original IAS 14 had no comparable requirement.

International Accounting Standard 14
Segment Reporting

Objective

The objective of this Standard is to establish principles for reporting financial information by segment–information about the different types of products and services an entity produces and the different geographical areas in which it operates–to help users of financial statements:

(a) better understand the entity's past performance;

(b) better assess the entity's risks and returns; and

(c) make more informed judgements about the entity as a whole.

Many entities provide groups of products and services or operate in geographical areas that are subject to differing rates of profitability, opportunities for growth, future prospects, and risks. Information about an entity's different types of products and services and its operations in different geographical areas–often called segment information–is relevant to assessing the risks and returns of a diversified or multinational entity but may not be determinable from the aggregated data. Therefore, segment information is widely regarded as necessary to meeting the needs of users of financial statements.

Scope

1 **This Standard shall be applied in complete sets of published financial statements that comply with International Financial Reporting Standards.**

2 A complete set of financial statements includes a balance sheet, income statement, cash flow statement, a statement showing changes in equity, and notes, as provided in IAS 1 *Presentation of Financial Statements*.

3 **This Standard shall be applied by entities whose equity or debt securities are publicly traded and by entities that are in the process of issuing equity or debt securities in public securities markets.**

4 If an entity whose securities are not publicly traded prepares financial statements that comply with International Financial Reporting Standards, that entity is encouraged to disclose financial information by segment voluntarily.

5 **If an entity whose securities are not publicly traded chooses to disclose segment information voluntarily in financial statements that comply with International Financial Reporting Standards, that entity shall comply fully with the requirements of this Standard.**

6 **If a single financial report contains both consolidated financial statements of an entity whose securities are publicly traded and the separate financial statements of the parent or one or more subsidiaries, segment information need be presented only on the basis of the consolidated financial**

statements. If a subsidiary is itself an entity whose securities are publicly traded, it will present segment information in its own separate financial report.

7 **Similarly, if a single financial report contains both the financial statements of an entity whose securities are publicly traded and the separate financial statements of an equity method associate or joint venture in which the entity has a financial interest, segment information need be presented only on the basis of the entity's financial statements. If the equity method associate or joint venture is itself an entity whose securities are publicly traded, it will present segment information in its own separate financial report.**

Definitions

Definitions from other Standards

8 **The following terms are used in this Standard with the meanings specified in IAS 7** *Cash Flow Statements*; **IAS 8** *Accounting Policies, Changes in Accounting Estimates and Errors*; **and IAS 18** *Revenue*:

Operating activities **are the principal revenue-producing activities of an entity and other activities that are not investing or financing activities.**

Accounting policies **are the specific principles, bases, conventions, rules and practices applied by an entity in preparing and presenting financial statements.**

Revenue **is the gross inflow of economic benefits during the period arising in the course of the ordinary activities of an entity when those inflows result in increases in equity, other than increases relating to contributions from equity participants.**

Definitions of business segment and geographical segment

9 **The terms business segment and geographical segment are used in this Standard with the following meanings:**

A *business segment* **is a distinguishable component of an entity that is engaged in providing an individual product or service or a group of related products or services and that is subject to risks and returns that are different from those of other business segments. Factors that shall be considered in determining whether products and services are related include:**

(a) the nature of the products or services;

(b) the nature of the production processes;

(c) the type or class of customer for the products or services;

(d) the methods used to distribute the products or provide the services; and

(e) if applicable, the nature of the regulatory environment, for example, banking, insurance, or public utilities.

A *geographical segment* is a distinguishable component of an entity that is engaged in providing products or services within a particular economic environment and that is subject to risks and returns that are different from those of components operating in other economic environments. Factors that shall be considered in identifying geographical segments include:

(a) similarity of economic and political conditions;

(b) relationships between operations in different geographical areas;

(c) proximity of operations;

(d) special risks associated with operations in a particular area;

(e) exchange control regulations; and

(f) the underlying currency risks.

A *reportable segment* is a business segment or a geographical segment identified based on the foregoing definitions for which segment information is required to be disclosed by this Standard.

10 The factors in paragraph 9 for identifying business segments and geographical segments are not listed in any particular order.

11 A single business segment does not include products and services with significantly differing risks and returns. While there may be dissimilarities with respect to one or several of the factors in the definition of a business segment, the products and services included in a single business segment are expected to be similar with respect to a majority of the factors.

12 Similarly, a geographical segment does not include operations in economic environments with significantly differing risks and returns. A geographical segment may be a single country, a group of two or more countries, or a region within a country.

13 The predominant sources of risks affect how most entities are organised and managed. Therefore, paragraph 27 of this Standard provides that an entity's organisational structure and its internal financial reporting system is the basis for identifying its segments. The risks and returns of an entity are influenced both by the geographical *location of its operations* (where its products are produced or where its service delivery activities are based) and also by the *location of its markets* (where its products are sold or services are rendered). The definition allows geographical segments to be based on either:

(a) the location of an entity's production or service facilities and other assets; or

(b) the location of its markets and customers.

14 An entity's organisational and internal reporting structure will normally provide evidence of whether its dominant source of geographical risks results from the location of its assets (the origin of its sales) or the location of its customers (the destination of its sales). Accordingly, an entity looks to this structure to determine whether its geographical segments should be based on the location of its assets or on the location of its customers.

15 Determining the composition of a business or geographical segment involves a certain amount of judgement. In making that judgement, entity management takes into account the objective of reporting financial information by segment as set forth in this Standard and the qualitative characteristics of financial statements as identified in the IASC *Framework for the Preparation and Presentation of Financial Statements*. Those qualitative characteristics include the relevance, reliability, and comparability over time of financial information that is reported about an entity's different groups of products and services and about its operations in particular geographical areas, and the usefulness of that information for assessing the risks and returns of the entity as a whole.

Definitions of segment revenue, expense, result, assets, and liabilities

16 **The following additional terms are used in this Standard with the meanings specified:**

Segment revenue **is revenue reported in the entity's income statement that is directly attributable to a segment and the relevant portion of entity revenue that can be allocated on a reasonable basis to a segment, whether from sales to external customers or from transactions with other segments of the same entity. Segment revenue does not include:**

(a) [deleted]

(b) interest or dividend income, including interest earned on advances or loans to other segments, unless the segment's operations are primarily of a financial nature; or

(c) gains on sales of investments or gains on extinguishment of debt unless the segment's operations are primarily of a financial nature.

Segment revenue includes an entity's share of profits or losses of associates, joint ventures, or other investments accounted for under the equity method only if those items are included in consolidated or total entity revenue.

Segment revenue includes a joint venturer's share of the revenue of a jointly controlled entity that is accounted for by proportionate consolidation in accordance with IAS 31 *Interests in Joint Ventures*.

Segment expense **is expense resulting from the operating activities of a segment that is directly attributable to the segment and the relevant portion of an expense that can be allocated on a reasonable basis to the segment, including expenses relating to sales to external customers and expenses relating to transactions with other segments of the same entity. Segment expense does not include:**

(a) [deleted]

(b) interest, including interest incurred on advances or loans from other segments, unless the segment's operations are primarily of a financial nature;

(c) losses on sales of investments or losses on extinguishment of debt unless the segment's operations are primarily of a financial nature;

(d) **an entity's share of losses of associates, joint ventures, or other investments accounted for under the equity method;**

(e) **income tax expense; or**

(f) **general administrative expenses, head-office expenses, and other expenses that arise at the entity level and relate to the entity as a whole. However, costs are sometimes incurred at the entity level on behalf of a segment. Such costs are segment expenses if they relate to the segment's operating activities and they can be directly attributed or allocated to the segment on a reasonable basis.**

Segment expense includes a joint venturer's share of the expenses of a jointly controlled entity that is accounted for by proportionate consolidation in accordance with IAS 31.

For a segment's operations that are primarily of a financial nature, interest income and interest expense may be reported as a single net amount for segment reporting purposes only if those items are netted in the consolidated or entity financial statements.

Segment result **is segment revenue less segment expense. Segment result is determined before any adjustments for minority interest.**

Segment assets **are those operating assets that are employed by a segment in its operating activities and that either are directly attributable to the segment or can be allocated to the segment on a reasonable basis.**

If a segment's segment result includes interest or dividend income, its segment assets include the related receivables, loans, investments, or other income-producing assets.

Segment assets do not include income tax assets.

Segment assets include investments accounted for under the equity method only if the profit or loss from such investments is included in segment revenue. Segment assets include a joint venturer's share of the operating assets of a jointly controlled entity that is accounted for by proportionate consolidation in accordance with IAS 31.

Segment assets are determined after deducting related allowances that are reported as direct offsets in the entity's balance sheet.

Segment liabilities **are those operating liabilities that result from the operating activities of a segment and that either are directly attributable to the segment or can be allocated to the segment on a reasonable basis.**

If a segment's segment result includes interest expense, its segment liabilities include the related interest-bearing liabilities.

Segment liabilities include a joint venturer's share of the liabilities of a jointly controlled entity that is accounted for by proportionate consolidation in accordance with IAS 31.

Segment liabilities do not include income tax liabilities.

Segment accounting policies **are the accounting policies adopted for preparing and presenting the financial statements of the consolidated group or entity as well as those accounting policies that relate specifically to segment reporting.**

17 The definitions of segment revenue, segment expense, segment assets, and segment liabilities include amounts of such items that are directly attributable to a segment and amounts of such items that can be allocated to a segment on a reasonable basis. An entity looks to its internal financial reporting system as the starting point for identifying those items that can be directly attributed, or reasonably allocated, to segments. That is, there is a presumption that amounts that have been identified with segments for internal financial reporting purposes are directly attributable or reasonably allocable to segments for the purpose of measuring the segment revenue, segment expense, segment assets, and segment liabilities of reportable segments.

18 In some cases, however, a revenue, expense, asset, or liability may have been allocated to segments for internal financial reporting purposes on a basis that is understood by entity management but that could be deemed subjective, arbitrary, or difficult to understand by external users of financial statements. Such an allocation would not constitute a reasonable basis under the definitions of segment revenue, segment expense, segment assets, and segment liabilities in this Standard. Conversely, an entity may choose not to allocate some item of revenue, expense, asset, or liability for internal financial reporting purposes, even though a reasonable basis for doing so exists. Such an item is allocated pursuant to the definitions of segment revenue, segment expense, segment assets, and segment liabilities in this Standard.

19 Examples of segment assets include current assets that are used in the operating activities of the segment, property, plant, and equipment, assets that are the subject of finance leases (IAS 17 *Leases*), and intangible assets. If a particular item of depreciation or amortisation is included in segment expense, the related asset is also included in segment assets. Segment assets do not include assets used for general entity or head-office purposes. Segment assets include operating assets shared by two or more segments if a reasonable basis for allocation exists. Segment assets include goodwill that is directly attributable to a segment or can be allocated to a segment on a reasonable basis, and segment expense includes any impairment losses recognised for goodwill.

20 Examples of segment liabilities include trade and other payables, accrued liabilities, customer advances, product warranty provisions, and other claims relating to the provision of goods and services. Segment liabilities do not include borrowings, liabilities related to assets that are the subject of finance leases (IAS 17), and other liabilities that are incurred for financing rather than operating purposes. If interest expense is included in segment result, the related interest-bearing liability is included in segment liabilities. The liabilities of segments whose operations are not primarily of a financial nature do not include borrowings and similar liabilities because segment result represents an operating, rather than a net-of-financing, profit or loss. Further, because debt is often

issued at the head-office level on an entity-wide basis, it is often not possible to directly attribute, or reasonably allocate, the interest-bearing liability to the segment.

21 Measurements of segment assets and liabilities include adjustments to the prior carrying amounts of the identifiable segment assets and segment liabilities of an entity acquired in a business combination, even if those adjustments are made only for the purpose of preparing consolidated financial statements and are not recognised in either the parent's separate or the subsidiary's individual financial statements. Similarly, if property, plant or equipment has been revalued after acquisition in accordance with the revaluation model in IAS 16, then measurements of segment assets reflect those revaluations.

22 Some guidance for cost allocation can be found in other Standards. For example, paragraphs 11–20 of IAS 2 *Inventories* (as revised in 2003) provide guidance on attributing and allocating costs to inventories, and paragraphs 16–21 of IAS 11 *Construction Contracts* provide guidance on attributing and allocating costs to contracts. That guidance may be useful in attributing or allocating costs to segments.

23 IAS 7 *Cash Flow Statements* provides guidance as to whether bank overdrafts should be included as a component of cash or should be reported as borrowings.

24 Segment revenue, segment expense, segment assets, and segment liabilities are determined before intragroup balances and intragroup transactions are eliminated as part of the consolidation process, except to the extent that such intragroup balances and transactions are between group entities within a single segment.

25 While the accounting policies used in preparing and presenting the financial statements of the entity as a whole are also the fundamental segment accounting policies, segment accounting policies include, in addition, policies that relate specifically to segment reporting, such as identification of segments, method of pricing inter-segment transfers, and basis for allocating revenues and expenses to segments.

Identifying reportable segments

Primary and secondary segment reporting formats

26 The dominant source and nature of an entity's risks and returns shall govern whether its primary segment reporting format will be business segments or geographical segments. If the entity's risks and rates of return are affected predominantly by differences in the products and services it produces, its primary format for reporting segment information shall be business segments, with secondary information reported geographically. Similarly, if the entity's risks and rates of return are affected predominantly by the fact that it operates in different countries or other geographical areas, its primary format for reporting segment information shall be geographical segments, with secondary information reported for groups of related products and services.

27 **An entity's internal organisational and management structure and its system of internal financial reporting to the board of directors and the chief executive officer shall normally be the basis for identifying the predominant source and nature of risks and differing rates of return facing the entity and, therefore, for determining which reporting format is primary and which is secondary, except as provided in subparagraphs (a) and (b) below:**

(a) if an entity's risks and rates of return are strongly affected both by differences in the products and services it produces and by differences in the geographical areas in which it operates, as evidenced by a 'matrix approach' to managing the company and to reporting internally to the board of directors and the chief executive officer, then the entity shall use business segments as its primary segment reporting format and geographical segments as its secondary reporting format; and

(b) if an entity's internal organisational and management structure and its system of internal financial reporting to the board of directors and the chief executive officer are based neither on individual products or services or on groups of related products/services nor on geography, the directors and management of the entity shall determine whether the entity's risks and returns are related more to the products and services it produces or more to the geographical areas in which it operates and, as a consequence, shall choose either business segments or geographical segments as the entity's primary segment reporting format, with the other as its secondary reporting format.

28 For most entities, the predominant source of risks and returns determines how the entity is organised and managed. An entity's organisational and management structure and its internal financial reporting system normally provide the best evidence of the entity's predominant source of risks and returns for purpose of its segment reporting. Therefore, except in rare circumstances, an entity will report segment information in its financial statements on the same basis as it reports internally to top management. Its predominant source of risks and returns becomes its primary segment reporting format. Its secondary source of risks and returns becomes its secondary segment reporting format.

29 A 'matrix presentation'–both business segments and geographical segments as primary segment reporting formats with full segment disclosures on each basis–often will provide useful information if an entity's risks and rates of return are strongly affected both by differences in the products and services it produces and by differences in the geographical areas in which it operates. This Standard does not require, but does not prohibit, a 'matrix presentation'.

30 In some cases, an entity's organisation and internal reporting may have developed along lines unrelated either to differences in the types of products and services they produce or to the geographical areas in which they operate. For instance, internal reporting may be organised solely by legal entity, resulting in internal segments composed of groups of unrelated products and services. In those unusual cases, the internally reported segment data will not meet the objective of this Standard. Accordingly, paragraph 27(b) requires the directors and

management of the entity to determine whether the entity's risks and returns are more product/service driven or geographically driven and to choose either business segments or geographical segments as the entity's primary basis of segment reporting. The objective is to achieve a reasonable degree of comparability with other entities enhance understandability of the resulting information, and meet the expressed needs of investors, creditors, and others for information about product/service-related and geographically-related risks and returns.

Business and geographical segments

31 **An entity's business and geographical segments for external reporting purposes shall be those organisational units for which information is reported to the board of directors and to the chief executive officer for the purpose of evaluating the unit's past performance and for making decisions about future allocations of resources, except as provided in paragraph 32.**

32 **If an entity's internal organisational and management structure and its system of internal financial reporting to the board of directors and the chief executive officer are based neither on individual products or services or on groups of related products/services nor on geography, paragraph 27(b) requires that the directors and management of the entity shall choose either business segments or geographical segments as the entity's primary segment reporting format based on their assessment of which reflects the primary source of the entity's risks and returns, with the other its secondary reporting format. In that case, the directors and management of the entity must determine its business segments and geographical segments for external reporting purposes based on the factors in the definitions in paragraph 9 of this Standard, rather than on the basis of its system of internal financial reporting to the board of directors and chief executive officer, consistent with the following:**

(a) if one or more of the segments reported internally to the directors and management is a business segment or a geographical segment based on the factors in the definitions in paragraph 9 but others are not, subparagraph (b) below shall be applied only to those internal segments that do not meet the definitions in paragraph 9 (that is, an internally reported segment that meets the definition shall not be further segmented);

(b) for those segments reported internally to the directors and management that do not satisfy the definitions in paragraph 9, management of the entity shall look to the next lower level of internal segmentation that reports information along product and service lines or geographical lines, as appropriate under the definitions in paragraph 9; and

(c) if such an internally reported lower-level segment meets the definition of business segment or geographical segment based on the factors in paragraph 9, the criteria in paragraphs 34 and 35 for identifying reportable segments shall be applied to that segment.

33 Under this Standard, most entities will identify their business and geographical segments as the organisational units for which information is reported to the board of directors (particularly the supervisory non-management directors, if any) and to the chief executive officer (the senior operating decision maker, which in some cases may be a group of several people) for the purpose of evaluating each unit's past performance and for making decisions about future allocations of resources. And even if an entity must apply paragraph 32 because its internal segments are not along product/service or geographical lines, it will look to the next lower level of internal segmentation that reports information along product and service lines or geographical lines rather than construct segments solely for external reporting purposes. This approach of looking to an entity's organisational and management structure and its internal financial reporting system to identify the entity's business and geographical segments for external reporting purposes is sometimes called the 'management approach', and the organisational components for which information is reported internally are sometimes called 'operating segments'.

Reportable segments

34 **Two or more internally reported business segments or geographical segments that are substantially similar may be combined as a single business segment or geographical segment. Two or more business segments or geographical segments are substantially similar only if:**

(a) they exhibit similar long-term financial performance; and

(b) they are similar in all of the factors in the appropriate definition in paragraph 9.

35 **A business segment or geographical segment shall be identified as a reportable segment if a majority of its revenue is earned from sales to external customers and:**

(a) its revenue from sales to external customers and from transactions with other segments is 10 per cent or more of the total revenue, external and internal, of all segments; or

(b) its segment result, whether profit or loss, is 10 per cent or more of the combined result of all segments in profit or the combined result of all segments in loss, whichever is the greater in absolute amount; or

(c) its assets are 10 per cent or more of the total assets of all segments.

36 **If an internally reported segment is below all of the thresholds of significance in paragraph 35:**

(a) that segment may be designated as a reportable segment despite its size;

(b) if not designated as a reportable segment despite its size, that segment may be combined into a separately reportable segment with one or more other similar internally reported segment(s) that are also below all of the thresholds of significance in paragraph 35 (two or more

business segments or geographical segments are similar if they share a majority of the factors in the appropriate definition in paragraph 9); and

(c) **if that segment is not separately reported or combined, it shall be included as an unallocated reconciling item.**

37 **If total external revenue attributable to reportable segments constitutes less than 75 per cent of the total consolidated or entity revenue, additional segments shall be identified as reportable segments, even if they do not meet the 10 per cent thresholds in paragraph 35, until at least 75 per cent of total consolidated or entity revenue is included in reportable segments.**

38 The 10 per cent thresholds in this Standard are not intended to be a guide for determining materiality for any aspect of financial reporting other than identifying reportable business and geographical segments.

39 By limiting reportable segments to those that earn a majority of their revenue from sales to external customers, this Standard does not require that the different stages of vertically integrated operations be identified as separate business segments. However, in some industries, current practice is to report certain vertically integrated activities as separate business segments even if they do not generate significant external sales revenue. For instance, many international oil companies report their upstream activities (exploration and production) and their downstream activities (refining and marketing) as separate business segments even if most or all of the upstream product (crude petroleum) is transferred internally to the entity's refining operation.

40 This Standard encourages, but does not require, the voluntary reporting of vertically integrated activities as separate segments, with appropriate description including disclosure of the basis of pricing inter-segment transfers as required by paragraph 75.

41 **If an entity's internal reporting system treats vertically integrated activities as separate segments and the entity does not choose to report them externally as business segments, the selling segment shall be combined into the buying segment(s) in identifying externally reportable business segments unless there is no reasonable basis for doing so, in which case the selling segment would be included as an unallocated reconciling item.**

42 **A segment identified as a reportable segment in the immediately preceding period because it satisfied the relevant 10 per cent thresholds shall continue to be a reportable segment for the current period notwithstanding that its revenue, result, and assets all no longer exceed the 10 per cent thresholds, if the management of the entity judges the segment to be of continuing significance.**

43 **If a segment is identified as a reportable segment in the current period because it satisfies the relevant 10 per cent thresholds, prior period segment data that is presented for comparative purposes shall be restated to reflect the newly reportable segment as a separate segment, even if that segment did not satisfy the 10 per cent thresholds in the prior period, unless it is impracticable to do so.**

Segment accounting policies

44 **Segment information shall be prepared in conformity with the accounting policies adopted for preparing and presenting the financial statements of the consolidated group or entity.**

45 There is a presumption that the accounting policies that the directors and management of an entity have chosen to use, in preparing its consolidated or entity-wide financial statements, are those that the directors and management believe are the most appropriate for external reporting purposes. Since the purpose of segment information is to help users of financial statements better understand and make more informed judgements about the entity as a whole, this Standard requires the use, in preparing segment information, of the accounting policies that the directors and management have chosen. That does not mean, however, that the consolidated or entity accounting policies are to be applied to reportable segments as if the segments were separate stand-alone reporting entities. A detailed calculation done in applying a particular accounting policy at the entity-wide level may be allocated to segments if there is a reasonable basis for doing so. Pension calculations, for example, often are done for an entity as a whole, but the entity-wide figures may be allocated to segments based on salary and demographic data for the segments.

46 This Standard does not prohibit the disclosure of additional segment information that is prepared on a basis other than the accounting policies adopted for the consolidated or entity financial statements provided that (a) the information is reported internally to the board of directors and the chief executive officer for purposes of making decisions about allocating resources to the segment and assessing its performance and (b) the basis of measurement for this additional information is clearly described.

47 **Assets that are jointly used by two or more segments shall be allocated to segments if, and only if, their related revenues and expenses also are allocated to those segments.**

48 The way in which asset, liability, revenue, and expense items are allocated to segments depends on such factors as the nature of those items, the activities conducted by the segment, and the relative autonomy of that segment. It is not possible or appropriate to specify a single basis of allocation that shall be adopted by all entities. Nor is it appropriate to force allocation of entity asset, liability, revenue, and expense items that relate jointly to two or more segments, if the only basis for making those allocations is arbitrary or difficult to understand. At the same time, the definitions of segment revenue, segment expense, segment assets, and segment liabilities are interrelated, and the resulting allocations shall be consistent. Therefore, jointly used assets are allocated to segments if, and only if, their related revenues and expenses also are allocated to those segments. For example, an asset is included in segment assets if, and only if, the related depreciation or amortisation is deducted in measuring segment result.

Disclosure

49 Paragraphs 50–67 specify the disclosures required for reportable segments for an entity's *primary* segment reporting format. Paragraphs 68–72 identify the

disclosures required for an entity's *secondary* reporting format. Entities are encouraged to present all of the primary-segment disclosures identified in paragraphs 50–67 for each reportable secondary segment, although paragraphs 68–72 require considerably less disclosure on the secondary basis. Paragraphs 74–83 address several other segment disclosure matters. Appendix B to this Standard illustrates application of these disclosure standards.

Primary reporting format

50 **The disclosure requirements in paragraphs 51–67 shall be applied to each reportable segment based on an entity's primary reporting format.**

51 **An entity shall disclose segment revenue for each reportable segment. Segment revenue from sales to external customers and segment revenue from transactions with other segments shall be separately reported.**

52 **An entity shall disclose segment result for each reportable segment, presenting the result from continuing operations separately from the result from discontinued operations.**

52A **An entity shall restate segment results in prior periods presented in the financial statements so that the disclosures required by paragraph 52 relating to discontinued operations relate to all operations that had been classified as discontinued at the balance sheet date of the latest period presented.**

53 If an entity can compute segment profit or loss or some other measure of segment profitability other than segment result without arbitrary allocations, reporting of such amount(s) is encouraged in addition to segment result, appropriately described. If that measure is prepared on a basis other than the accounting policies adopted for the consolidated or entity financial statements, the entity will include in its financial statements a clear description of the basis of measurement.

54 An example of a measure of segment performance above segment result on the income statement is gross margin on sales. Examples of measures of segment performance below segment result on the income statement are profit or loss from ordinary activities (either before or after income taxes) and profit or loss.

55 **An entity shall disclose the total carrying amount of segment assets for each reportable segment.**

56 **An entity shall disclose segment liabilities for each reportable segment.**

57 **An entity shall disclose the total cost incurred during the period to acquire segment assets that are expected to be used during more than one period (property, plant, equipment, and intangible assets) for each reportable segment. While this sometimes is referred to as capital additions or capital expenditure, the measurement required by this principle shall be on an accrual basis, not a cash basis.**

58 **An entity shall disclose the total amount of expense included in segment result for depreciation and amortisation of segment assets for the period for each reportable segment.**

59 **An entity is encouraged, but not required to disclose the nature and amount of any items of segment revenue and segment expense that are of such size, nature, or incidence that their disclosure is relevant to explain the performance of each reportable segment for the period.**

60 IAS 1 requires that when items of income and expense are material, their nature and amount shall be disclosed separately. IAS 1 offers a number of examples, including write-downs of inventories and property, plant, and equipment, provisions for restructurings, disposals of property, plant, and equipment and long-term investments, discontinued operations, litigation settlements, and reversals of provisions. Paragraph 59 is not intended to change the classification of any such items or to change the measurement of such items. The disclosure encouraged by that paragraph, however, does change the level at which the significance of such items is evaluated for disclosure purposes from the entity level to the segment level.

61 **An entity shall disclose, for each reportable segment, the total amount of significant non-cash expenses, other than depreciation and amortisation for which separate disclosure is required by paragraph 58, that were included in segment expense and, therefore, deducted in measuring segment result.**

62 IAS 7 requires that an entity present a cash flow statement that separately reports cash flows from operating, investing, and financing activities. IAS 7 notes that disclosing cash flow information for each reportable industry and geographical segment is relevant to understanding the entity's overall financial position, liquidity, and cash flows. IAS 7 encourages the disclosure of such information. This Standard also encourages the segment cash flow disclosures that are encouraged by IAS 7. Additionally, it encourages disclosure of significant non-cash revenues that were included in segment revenue and, therefore, added in measuring segment result.

63 **An entity that provides the segment cash flow disclosures that are encouraged by IAS 7 need not also disclose depreciation and amortisation expense pursuant to paragraph 58 or non-cash expenses pursuant to paragraph 61.**

64 **An entity shall disclose, for each reportable segment, the aggregate of the entity's share of the profit or loss of associates, joint ventures, or other investments accounted for under the equity method if substantially all of those associates' operations are within that single segment.**

65 While a single aggregate amount is disclosed pursuant to the preceding paragraph, each associate, joint venture, or other equity method investment is assessed individually to determine whether its operations are substantially all within a segment.

66 **If an entity's aggregate share of the profit or loss of associates, joint ventures, or other investments accounted for under the equity method is disclosed by reportable segment, the aggregate investments in those associates and joint ventures shall also be disclosed by reportable segment.**

67 **An entity shall present a reconciliation between the information disclosed for reportable segments and the aggregated information in the consolidated or individual financial statements. In presenting the reconciliation, the entity shall reconcile segment revenue to entity revenue from external customers (including disclosures of the amount of entity revenue from external customers not included in any segment); segment result from continuing operations shall be reconciled to a comparable measure of entity operating profit or loss from continuing operations as well as to entity profit or loss from continuing operations; segment result from discontinued operations shall be reconciled to entity profit or loss from discontinued operations; segment assets shall be reconciled to entity assets; and segment liabilities shall be reconciled to entity liabilities.**

Secondary segment information

68 Paragraphs 50–67 identify the disclosure requirements to be applied to each reportable segment based on an entity's primary reporting format. Paragraphs 69–72 identify the disclosure requirements to be applied to each reportable segment based on an entity's secondary reporting format, as follows:

(a) if an entity's primary format is business segments, the required secondary-format disclosures are identified in paragraph 69;

(b) if an entity's primary format is geographical segments based on location of assets (where the entity's products are produced or where its service delivery operations are based), the required secondary-format disclosures are identified in paragraphs 70 and 71;

(c) if an entity's primary format is geographical segments based on the location of its customers (where its products are sold or services are rendered), the required secondary-format disclosures are identified in paragraphs 70 and 72.

69 **If an entity's primary format for reporting segment information is business segments, it shall also report the following information:**

(a) segment revenue from external customers by geographical area based on the geographical location of its customers, for each geographical segment whose revenue from sales to external customers is 10 per cent or more of total entity revenue from sales to all external customers;

(b) the total carrying amount of segment assets by geographical location of assets, for each geographical segment whose segment assets are 10 per cent or more of the total assets of all geographical segments; and

(c) the total cost incurred during the period to acquire segment assets that are expected to be used during more than one period (property, plant, equipment, and intangible assets) by geographical location of assets, for each geographical segment whose segment assets are 10 per cent or more of the total assets of all geographical segments.

70 **If an entity's primary format for reporting segment information is geographical segments (whether based on location of assets or location of**

customers), it shall also report the following segment information for each business segment whose revenue from sales to external customers is 10 per cent or more of total entity revenue from sales to all external customers or whose segment assets are 10 per cent or more of the total assets of all business segments:

(a) segment revenue from external customers;

(b) the total carrying amount of segment assets; and

(c) the total cost incurred during the period to acquire segment assets that are expected to be used during more than one period (property, plant, equipment, and intangible assets).

71 **If an entity's primary format for reporting segment information is geographical segments that are based on location of assets, and if the location of its customers is different from the location of its assets, then the entity shall also report revenue from sales to external customers for each customer-based geographical segment whose revenue from sales to external customers is 10 per cent or more of total entity revenue from sales to all external customers.**

72 **If an entity's primary format for reporting segment information is geographical segments that are based on location of customers, and if the entity's assets are located in different geographical areas from its customers, then the entity shall also report the following segment information for each asset-based geographical segment whose revenue from sales to external customers or segment assets are 10 per cent or more of related consolidated or total entity amounts:**

(a) the total carrying amount of segment assets by geographical location of the assets; and

(b) the total cost incurred during the period to acquire segment assets that are expected to be used during more than one period (property, plant, equipment, and intangible assets) by location of the assets.

Illustrative segment disclosures

73 Appendix B to this Standard presents an illustration of the disclosures for primary and secondary reporting formats that are required by this Standard.

Other disclosure matters

74 **If a business segment or geographical segment for which information is reported to the board of directors and chief executive officer is not a reportable segment because it earns a majority of its revenue from sales to other segments, but nonetheless its revenue from sales to external customers is 10 per cent or more of total entity revenue from sales to all external customers, the entity shall disclose that fact and the amounts of revenue from (a) sales to external customers and (b) internal sales to other segments.**

75 **In measuring and reporting segment revenue from transactions with other segments, inter-segment transfers shall be measured on the basis that the entity actually used to price those transfers. The basis of pricing inter-segment transfers and any change therein shall be disclosed in the financial statements.**

76 **Changes in accounting policies adopted for segment reporting that have a material effect on segment information shall be disclosed, and prior period segment information presented for comparative purposes shall be restated unless it is impracticable to do so. Such disclosure shall include a description of the nature of the change, the reasons for the change, the fact that comparative information has been restated or that it is impracticable to do so, and the financial effect of the change, if it is reasonably determinable. If an entity changes the identification of its segments and it does not restate prior period segment information on the new basis because it is impracticable to do so, then for the purpose of comparison the entity shall report segment data for both the old and the new bases of segmentation in the year in which it changes the identification of its segments.**

77 Changes in accounting policies applied by the entity are dealt with in IAS 8. IAS 8 requires that changes in accounting policy shall be made only if required by a Standard or Interpretation, or if the change will result in reliable and more relevant information about transactions, other events or conditions in the financial statements of the entity.

78 Changes in accounting policies applied at the entity level that affect segment information are dealt with in accordance with IAS 8. Unless a new Standard or Interpretation specifies otherwise, IAS 8 requires that:

(a) a change in accounting policy shall be applied retrospectively and prior period information restated unless it is impracticable to determine either the cumulative effect or the period-specific effects of the change;

(b) if retrospective application is not practicable for all periods presented, the new accounting policy shall be applied retrospectively from the earliest practicable date; and

(c) if it is impracticable to determine the cumulative effect of applying the new accounting policy at the start of the current period, the policy shall be applied prospectively from the earliest date practicable.

79 Some changes in accounting policies relate specifically to segment reporting. Examples include changes in identification of segments and changes in the basis for allocating revenues and expenses to segments. Such changes can have a significant impact on the segment information reported but will not change aggregate financial information reported for the entity. To enable users to understand the changes and to assess trends, prior period segment information that is included in the financial statements for comparative purposes is restated, if practicable, to reflect the new accounting policy.

80 Paragraph 75 requires that, for segment reporting purposes, inter-segment transfers shall be measured on the basis that the entity actually used to price those transfers. If an entity changes the method that it actually uses to price inter-segment transfers, that is not a change in accounting policy for which prior period segment data shall be restated pursuant to paragraph 76. However, paragraph 75 requires disclosure of the change.

81 An entity shall indicate the types of products and services included in each reported business segment and indicate the composition of each reported geographical segment, both primary and secondary, if not otherwise disclosed in the financial statements or elsewhere in the financial report.

82 To assess the impact of such matters as shifts in demand, changes in the price of inputs or other factors of production, and the development of alternative products and processes on a business segment, it is necessary to know the activities encompassed by that segment. Similarly, to assess the impact of changes in the economic and political environment on the risks and rates of returns of a geographical segment, it is important to know the composition of that geographical segment.

83 Previously reported segments that no longer satisfy the quantitative thresholds are not reported separately. They may no longer satisfy those thresholds, for example, because of a decline in demand or a change in management strategy or because a part of the operations of the segment has been sold or combined with other segments. An explanation of the reasons why a previously reported segment is no longer reported may also be useful in confirming expectations regarding declining markets and changes in entity strategies.

Effective date

84 This Standard becomes operative for financial statements covering periods beginning on or after 1 July 1998. Earlier application is encouraged. If an entity applies this Standard for financial statements covering periods beginning before 1 July 1998 instead of the original IAS 14, the entity shall disclose that fact. If financial statements include comparative information for periods prior to the effective date or earlier voluntary adoption of this Standard, restatement of segment data included therein to conform to the provisions of this Standard is required unless it is not practicable to do so, in which case the entity shall disclose that fact.

Appendix A
Segment definition decision tree

This appendix accompanies, but is not part of, IAS 14. Its purpose is to illustrate the application of paragraphs 27–43.

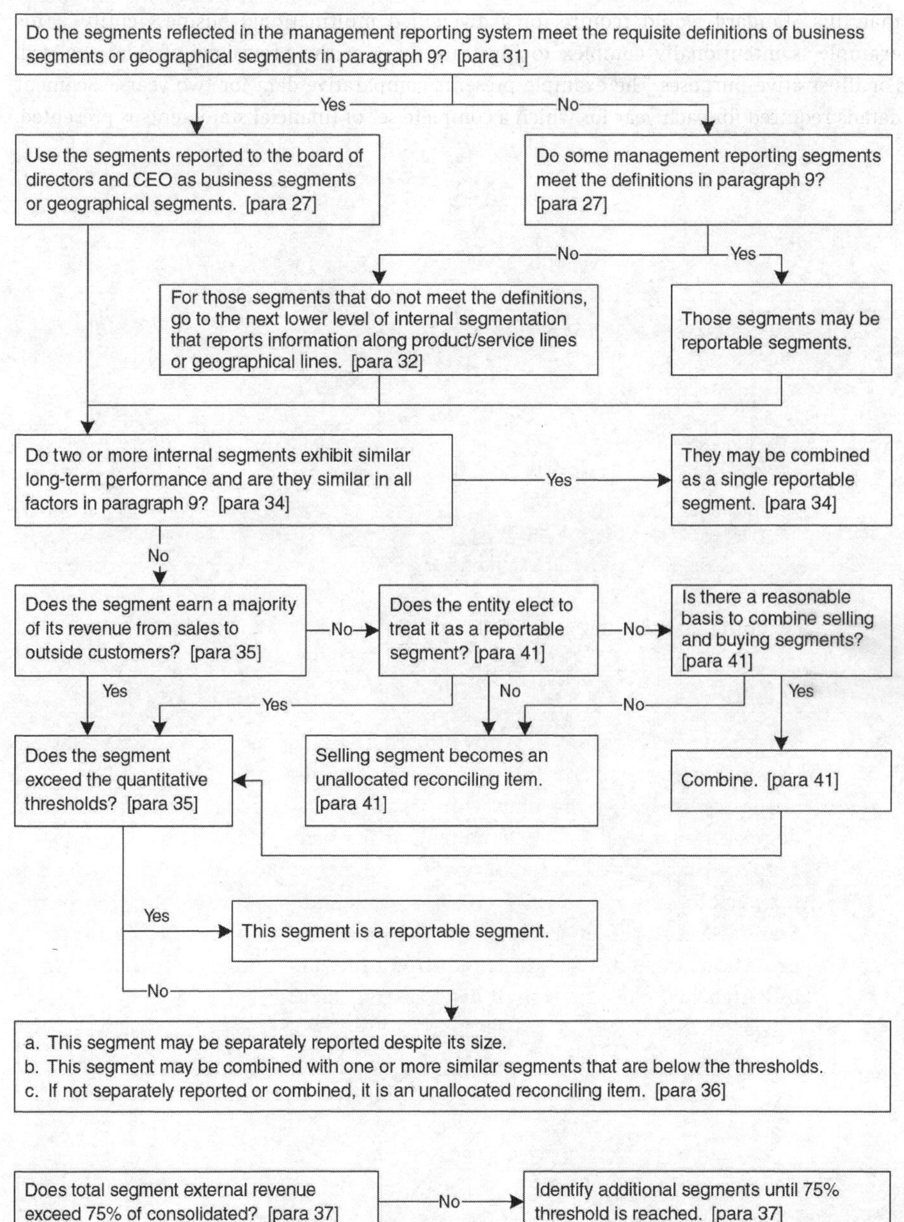

Does total segment external revenue exceed 75% of consolidated? [para 37] —No→ Identify additional segments until 75% threshold is reached. [para 37]

Appendix B
Illustrative segment disclosures

This appendix accompanies, but is not part of, IAS 14.

The schedule and related note presented in this appendix illustrate the segment disclosures that this Standard would require for a diversified multinational business entity. This example is intentionally complex to illustrate most of the provisions of this Standard. For illustrative purposes, the example presents comparative data for two years. Segment data is required for each year for which a complete set of financial statements is presented.

Schedule A Information about business segments (Note 4)
(All amounts million)

	Paper products		Office products		Publishing		Other operations		Elimination		Consolidated	
	20X2	20X1	20X2	20X1	20X2	20X1	20X2	20X1	20X2	20X1	20X2	20X1
Revenue												
External sales	55	50	20	17	19	16	7	7				
Inter–segment sales	15	10	10	14	2	4	2	2	(29)	(30)		
Total revenue	70	60	30	31	21	20	9	9	(29)	(30)	101	90
Result												
Segment result	20	17	9	7	2	1	0	0	(1)	(1)	30	24
Unallocated corporate expenses											(7)	(9)
Operating profit											23	15
Interest expense											(4)	(4)
Interest income											2	3
Share of profits of associates	6	5		2	2						8	7
Income taxes											(7)	(4)
Profit											22	17
Other Information												
Segment assets	54	50	34	30	10	10	10	9			108	99
Investment in equity method associates	20	16					12	10			32	26
Unallocated corporate assets											35	30
Consolidated total assets											175	155
Segment liabilities	25	15	8	11	8	8	1	1			42	35
Unallocated corporate liabilities											40	55
Consolidated total liabilities											82	90
Capital expenditure	12	10	3	5	5		4	3				
Depreciation	9	7	9	7	5	3	3	4				
Non–cash expenses other than depreciation	8	2	7	3	2	2	2	1				

Note 4 Business and geographical segments (all amounts million)

Business segments: for management purposes, the Company is organised on a worldwide basis into three major operating divisions–paper products, office products and publishing–each headed by a senior vice-president. The divisions are the basis on which the Company reports its primary segment information. The paper products segment produces a broad range of writing and publishing papers and newsprint. The office products segment manufactures labels, binders, pens, and markers and also distributes office products made by others. The publishing segment develops and sells loose-leaf services, bound volumes and CD-ROM products in the fields of taxation, law and accounting. Other operations include development of computer software for specialised business applications for unaffiliated customers and development of certain former productive timberlands into vacation home sites. Financial information about business segments is presented in Schedule A.

Geographical segments: although the Company's three divisions are managed on a worldwide basis, they operate in four principal geographical areas of the world. In the United Kingdom, its home country, the Company produces and sells a broad range of papers and office products. Additionally, all of the Company's publishing and computer software development operations are conducted in the United Kingdom, though the published loose-leaf and bound volumes and CD-ROM products are sold throughout the United Kingdom and Western Europe. In the European Union, the Company operates paper and office products manufacturing facilities and sales offices in the following countries: France, Belgium, Germany and the Netherlands. Operations in Canada and the United States are essentially similar and consist of manufacturing papers and newsprint that are sold entirely within those two countries. Most of the paper pulp comes from Company-owned timberlands in the two countries. Operations in Indonesia include the production of paper pulp and the manufacture of writing and publishing papers and office products, almost all of which is sold outside Indonesia, both to other segments of the Company and to external customers.

Sales by market: the following table shows the distribution of the Company's consolidated sales by geographical market, regardless of where the goods were produced:

	Sales revenue by geographical market	
	20X2	**20X1**
United Kingdom	19	22
Other European Union countries	30	31
Canada and the United States	28	21
Mexico and South America	6	2
Southeast Asia (principally Japan and Taiwan)	18	14
	101	90

Assets and additions to property, plant, equipment, and intangible assets by geographical area: the following tables show the carrying amount of segment assets and additions to property, plant, equipment, and intangible assets by geographical area in which the assets are located:

	Carrying amount of segment assets		Additions to property, plant, equipment, and intangible assets	
	20X2	20X1	20X2	20X1
United Kingdom	72	78	8	5
Other European Union countries	47	37	5	4
Canada and the United States	34	20	4	3
Indonesia	22	20	7	6
	175	155	24	18

Segment revenue and expense: in Belgium, paper and office products are manufactured in combined facilities and are sold by a combined sales force. Joint revenues and expenses are allocated to the two business segments. All other segment revenue and expense is directly attributable to the segments.

Segment assets and liabilities: segment assets include all operating assets used by a segment and consist principally of operating cash, receivables, inventories and property, plant and equipment, net of allowances and provisions. While most such assets can be directly attributed to individual segments, the carrying amount of certain assets used jointly by two or more segments is allocated to the segments on a reasonable basis. Segment liabilities include all operating liabilities and consist principally of accounts, wages, and taxes currently payable and accrued liabilities. Segment assets and liabilities do not include deferred income taxes.

Inter-segment transfers: segment revenue, segment expenses and segment result include transfers between business segments and between geographical segments. Such transfers are accounted for at competitive market prices charged to unaffiliated customers for similar goods. Those transfers are eliminated in consolidation.

Unusual item: sales of office products to external customers in 20X2 were adversely affected by a lengthy strike of transportation workers in the United Kingdom, which interrupted product shipments for approximately four months. The Company estimates that sales of office products were approximately half of what they would otherwise have been during the four-month period.

Investment in equity method associates: the Company owns 40 per cent of the capital stock of EuroPaper Ltd, a specialist paper manufacturer with operations principally in Spain and the United Kingdom. The investment is accounted for by the equity method. Although the investment and the Company's share of EuroPaper's net profit are excluded from segment assets and segment revenue, they are shown separately in conjunction with data for the paper products segment. The Company also owns several small equity method investments in Canada and the United States whose operations are dissimilar to any of the three business segments.

Appendix C
Summary of required disclosure

This appendix accompanies, but is not part of, IAS 14. Its purpose is to summarise the disclosures required by paragraphs 49–83 for each of the three possible primary segment reporting formats.

[¶xx] refers to paragraph xx in the Standard.

Primary format is business segments	**Primary format is geographical segments by location of assets**	**Primary format is geographical segments by location of customers**
Required primary disclosures:	***Required primary disclosures:***	***Required primary disclosures:***
Revenue from external customers by business segment [¶51]	Revenue from external customers by location of assets [¶51]	Revenue from external customers by location of customers [¶51]
Revenue from transactions with other segments by business segment [¶51]	Revenue from transactions with other segments by location of assets [¶51]	Revenue from transactions with other segments by location of customers [¶51]
Segment result by business segment [¶52]	Segment result by location of assets [¶52]	Segment result by location of customers [¶52]
Carrying amount of segment assets by business segment [¶55]	Carrying amount of segment assets by location of assets [¶55]	Carrying amount of segment assets by location of customers [¶55]
Segment liabilities by business segment [¶56]	Segment liabilities by location of assets [¶56]	Segment liabilities by location of customers [¶56]
Cost to acquire property, plant, equipment, and intangibles by business segment [¶57]	Cost to acquire property, plant, equipment, and intangibles by location of assets [¶57]	Cost to acquire property, plant, equipment, and intangibles by location of customers [¶57]
Depreciation and amortisation expense by business segment [¶58]	Depreciation and amortisation expense by location of assets [¶58]	Depreciation and amortisation expense by location of customers [¶58]
Non–cash expenses other than depreciation and amortisation by business segment [¶61]	Non–cash expenses other than depreciation and amortisation by location of assets [¶61]	Non–cash expenses other than depreciation and amortisation by location of customers [¶61]

Continued from previous page

Primary format is business segments	**Primary format is geographical segments by location of assets**	**Primary format is geographical segments by location of customers**
Required primary disclosures:	***Required primary disclosures:***	***Required primary disclosures:***
Share of profit or loss of [¶64] and investment in [¶66] equity method associates or joint ventures by business segment (if substantially all within a single business segment)	Share of profit or loss of [¶64] and investment in [¶66] equity method associates or joint ventures by location of assets (if substantially all within a single segment)	Share of profit or loss of [¶64] and investment in [¶66] equity method associates or joint ventures by location of customers (if substantially all within a single segment)
Reconciliation of revenue, result, assets, and liabilities by business segment [¶67]	Reconciliation of revenue, result, assets, and liabilities [¶67]	Reconciliation of revenue, result, assets, and liabilities [¶67]

Primary format is business segments	**Primary format is geographical segments by location of assets**	**Primary format is geographical segments by location of customers**
Required secondary disclosures:	***Required secondary disclosures:***	***Required secondary disclosures:***
Revenue from external customers by location of customers [¶69]	Revenue from external customers by business segment [¶70]	Revenue from external customers by business segment [¶70]
Carrying amount of segment assets by location of assets [¶69]	Carrying amount of segment assets by business segment [¶70]	Carrying amount of segment assets by business segment [¶70]
Cost to acquire property, plant, equipment, and intangibles by location of assets [¶69]	Cost to acquire property, plant, equipment, and intangibles by business segment [¶70]	Cost to acquire property, plant, equipment, and intangibles by business segment [¶70]
–	Revenue from external customers by geographical customers if different from location of assets [¶71]	–
–	–	Carrying amount of segment assets by location of assets if different from location of customers [¶72]
–	–	Cost to acquire property, plant, equipment, and intangibles by location of assets if different from location of customers [¶72]

Primary format is business segments	**Primary format is geographical segments by location of assets**	**Primary format is geographical segments by location of customers**
Other required disclosures:	***Other required disclosures:***	***Other required disclosures:***
Revenue for any business or geographical segment whose external revenue is more than 10 per cent of entity revenue but that is not a reportable segment because a majority of its revenue is from internal transfers [¶74]	Revenue for any business or geographical segment whose external revenue is more than 10 per cent of entity revenue but that is not a reportable segment because a majority of its revenue is from internal transfers [¶74]	Revenue for any business or geographical segment whose external revenue is more than 10 per cent of entity revenue but that is not a reportable segment because a majority of its revenue is from internal transfers [¶74]
Basis of pricing inter–segment transfers and any change therein [¶75]	Basis of pricing inter–segment transfers and any change therein [¶75]	Basis of pricing inter–segment transfers and any change therein [¶75]
Changes in segment accounting policies [¶76]	Changes in segment accounting policies [¶76]	Changes in segment accounting policies [¶76]
Types of products and services in each business segment [¶81]	Types of products and services in each business segment [¶81]	Types of products and services in each business segment [¶81]
Composition of each geographical segment [¶81]	Composition of each geographical segment [¶81]	Composition of each geographical segment [¶81]

International Accounting Standard 16

Property, Plant and Equipment

This version includes amendments from IFRS 6 Exploration for and Evaluation of Mineral Resources *issued on 9 December 2004.*

CONTENTS

International Accounting Standard 16 *Property, Plant and Equipment* (IAS 16) is set out in paragraphs 1–83 and the Appendix. All the paragraphs have equal authority but retain the IASC format of the Standard when it was adopted by the IASB. IAS 16 should be read in the context of its objective and the Basis for Conclusions, the *Preface to International Financial Reporting Standards* and the *Framework for the Preparation and Presentation of Financial Statements*. IAS 8 *Accounting Policies, Changes in Accounting Estimates and Errors* provides a basis for selecting and applying accounting policies in the absence of explicit guidance.

Introduction

IN1 International Accounting Standard 16 *Property, Plant and Equipment* (IAS 16) replaces IAS 16 *Property, Plant and Equipment* (revised in 1998), and should be applied for annual periods beginning on or after 1 January 2005. Earlier application is encouraged. The Standard also replaces the following Interpretations:

- SIC-6 *Costs of Modifying Existing Software*
- SIC-14 *Property, Plant and Equipment—Compensation for the Impairment or Loss of Items*
- SIC-23 *Property, Plant and Equipment—Major Inspection or Overhaul Costs.*

Reasons for revising IAS 16

IN2 The International Accounting Standards Board developed this revised IAS 16 as part of its project on Improvements to International Accounting Standards. The project was undertaken in the light of queries and criticisms raised in relation to the Standards by securities regulators, professional accountants and other interested parties. The objectives of the project were to reduce or eliminate alternatives, redundancies and conflicts within the Standards, to deal with some convergence issues and to make other improvements.

IN3 For IAS 16 the Board's main objective was a limited revision to provide additional guidance and clarification on selected matters. The Board did not reconsider the fundamental approach to the accounting for property, plant and equipment contained in IAS 16.

The main changes

IN4 The main changes from the previous version of IAS 16 are described below.

Scope

IN5 This Standard clarifies that an entity is required to apply the principles of this Standard to items of property, plant and equipment used to develop or maintain (a) biological assets and (b) mineral rights and mineral reserves such as oil, natural gas and similar non-regenerative resources.

Recognition: subsequent costs

IN6 An entity evaluates under the general recognition principle all property, plant and equipment costs at the time they are incurred. Those costs include costs incurred initially to acquire or construct an item of property, plant and equipment and costs incurred subsequently to add to, replace part of, or service an item. The previous version of IAS 16 contained two recognition principles. An entity applied the second recognition principle to subsequent costs.

Measurement at recognition: asset dismantlement, removal and restoration costs

IN7 The cost of an item of property, plant and equipment includes the costs of its dismantlement, removal or restoration, the obligation for which an entity incurs as a consequence of installing the item. Its cost also includes the costs of its dismantlement, removal or restoration, the obligation for which an entity incurs as a consequence of using the item during a particular period for purposes other than to produce inventories during that period. The previous version of IAS 16 included within its scope only the costs incurred as a consequence of installing the item.

Measurement at recognition: asset exchange transactions

IN8 An entity is required to measure an item of property, plant and equipment acquired in exchange for a non-monetary asset or assets, or a combination of monetary and non-monetary assets, at fair value unless the exchange transaction lacks commercial substance. Under the previous version of IAS 16, an entity measured such an acquired asset at fair value unless the exchanged assets were similar.

Measurement after recognition: revaluation model

IN9 If fair value can be measured reliably, an entity may carry all items of property, plant and equipment of a class at a revalued amount, which is the fair value of the items at the date of the revaluation less any subsequent accumulated depreciation and accumulated impairment losses. Under the previous version of IAS 16, use of revalued amounts did not depend on whether fair values were reliably measurable.

Depreciation: unit of measure

IN10 An entity is required to determine the depreciation charge separately for each significant part of an item of property, plant and equipment. The previous version of IAS 16 did not as clearly set out this requirement.

Depreciation: depreciable amount

IN11 An entity is required to measure the residual value of an item of property, plant and equipment as the amount it estimates it would receive currently for the asset if the asset were already of the age and in the condition expected at the end of its useful life. The previous version of IAS 16 did not specify whether the residual value was to be this amount or the amount, inclusive of the effects of inflation, that an entity expected to receive in the future on the asset's actual retirement date.

Depreciation: depreciation period

IN12 An entity is required to begin depreciating an item of property, plant and equipment when it is available for use and to continue depreciating it until it is derecognised, even if during that period the item is idle. The previous version of IAS 16 did not specify when depreciation of an item began and specified that an entity should cease depreciating an item that it had retired from active use and was holding for disposal.

Derecognition: derecognition date

IN13 An entity is required to derecognise the carrying amount of an item of property, plant and equipment that it disposes of on the date the criteria for the sale of goods in IAS 18 *Revenue* would be met. The previous version of IAS 16 did not require an entity to use those criteria to determine the date on which it derecognised the carrying amount of a disposed-of item of property, plant and equipment.

IN14 An entity is required to derecognise the carrying amount of a part of an item of property, plant and equipment if that part has been replaced and the entity has included the cost of the replacement in the carrying amount of the item. The previous version of IAS 16 did not extend its derecognition principle to such parts; rather, its recognition principle for subsequent expenditures effectively precluded the cost of a replacement from being included in the carrying amount of the item.

Derecognition: gain classification

IN15 An entity cannot classify as revenue a gain it realises on the disposal of an item of property, plant and equipment. The previous version of IAS 16 did not contain this provision.

International Accounting Standard 16 Property, Plant and Equipment

Objective

1 The objective of this Standard is to prescribe the accounting treatment for property, plant and equipment so that users of the financial statements can discern information about an entity's investment in its property, plant and equipment and the changes in such investment. The principal issues in accounting for property, plant and equipment are the recognition of the assets, the determination of their carrying amounts and the depreciation charges and impairment losses to be recognised in relation to them.

Scope

2 This Standard shall be applied in accounting for property, plant and equipment except when another Standard requires or permits a different accounting treatment.

3 This Standard does not apply to:

(a) property, plant and equipment classified as held for sale in accordance with IFRS 5 *Non-current Assets Held for Sale and Discontinued Operations*;

(b) biological assets related to agricultural activity (see IAS 41 *Agriculture*);

(c) the recognition and measurement of exploration and evaluation assets (see IFRS 6 *Exploration for and Evaluation of Mineral Resources*); or

(d) mineral rights and mineral reserves such as oil, natural gas and similar non-regenerative resources.

However, this Standard applies to property, plant and equipment used to develop or maintain the assets described in (b)–(d).

4 Other Standards may require recognition of an item of property, plant and equipment based on an approach different from that in this Standard. For example, IAS 17 *Leases* requires an entity to evaluate its recognition of an item of leased property, plant and equipment on the basis of the transfer of risks and rewards. However, in such cases other aspects of the accounting treatment for these assets, including depreciation, are prescribed by this Standard.

5 An entity shall apply this Standard to property that is being constructed or developed for future use as investment property but does not yet satisfy the definition of 'investment property' in IAS 40 *Investment Property*. Once the construction or development is complete, the property becomes investment property and the entity is required to apply IAS 40. IAS 40 also applies to investment property that is being redeveloped for continued future use as investment property. An entity using the cost model for investment property in accordance with IAS 40 shall use the cost model in this Standard.

Definitions

6 **The following terms are used in this Standard with the meanings specified:**

Carrying amount **is the amount at which an asset is recognised after deducting any accumulated depreciation and accumulated impairment losses.**

Cost **is the amount of cash or cash equivalents paid or the fair value of the other consideration given to acquire an asset at the time of its acquisition or construction or, where applicable, the amount attributed to that asset when initially recognised in accordance with the specific requirements of other IFRSs, eg IFRS 2** *Share-based Payment.*

Depreciable amount **is the cost of an asset, or other amount substituted for cost, less its residual value.**

Depreciation **is the systematic allocation of the depreciable amount of an asset over its useful life.**

Entity-specific value **is the present value of the cash flows an entity expects to arise from the continuing use of an asset and from its disposal at the end of its useful life or expects to incur when settling a liability.**

Fair value **is the amount for which an asset could be exchanged between knowledgeable, willing parties in an arm's length transaction.**

An *impairment loss* **is the amount by which the carrying amount of an asset exceeds its recoverable amount.**

Property, plant and equipment **are tangible items that:**

(a) are held for use in the production or supply of goods or services, for rental to others, or for administrative purposes; and

(b) are expected to be used during more than one period.

Recoverable amount **is the higher of an asset's net selling price and its value in use.**

The *residual value* **of an asset is the estimated amount that an entity would currently obtain from disposal of the asset, after deducting the estimated costs of disposal, if the asset were already of the age and in the condition expected at the end of its useful life.**

Useful life **is:**

(a) the period over which an asset is expected to be available for use by an entity; or

(b) the number of production or similar units expected to be obtained from the asset by an entity.

Recognition

7 **The cost of an item of property, plant and equipment shall be recognised as an asset if, and only if:**

(a) it is probable that future economic benefits associated with the item will flow to the entity; and

(b) the cost of the item can be measured reliably.

8 Spare parts and servicing equipment are usually carried as inventory and recognised in profit or loss as consumed. However, major spare parts and stand-by equipment qualify as property, plant and equipment when an entity expects to use them during more than one period. Similarly, if the spare parts and servicing equipment can be used only in connection with an item of property, plant and equipment, they are accounted for as property, plant and equipment.

9 This Standard does not prescribe the unit of measure for recognition, ie what constitutes an item of property, plant and equipment. Thus, judgement is required in applying the recognition criteria to an entity's specific circumstances. It may be appropriate to aggregate individually insignificant items, such as moulds, tools and dies, and to apply the criteria to the aggregate value.

10 An entity evaluates under this recognition principle all its property, plant and equipment costs at the time they are incurred. These costs include costs incurred initially to acquire or construct an item of property, plant and equipment and costs incurred subsequently to add to, replace part of, or service it.

Initial costs

11 Items of property, plant and equipment may be acquired for safety or environmental reasons. The acquisition of such property, plant and equipment, although not directly increasing the future economic benefits of any particular existing item of property, plant and equipment, may be necessary for an entity to obtain the future economic benefits from its other assets. Such items of property, plant and equipment qualify for recognition as assets because they enable an entity to derive future economic benefits from related assets in excess of what could be derived had those items not been acquired. For example, a chemical manufacturer may install new chemical handling processes to comply with environmental requirements for the production and storage of dangerous chemicals; related plant enhancements are recognised as an asset because without them the entity is unable to manufacture and sell chemicals. However, the resulting carrying amount of such an asset and related assets is reviewed for impairment in accordance with IAS 36 *Impairment of Assets*.

Subsequent costs

12 Under the recognition principle in paragraph 7, an entity does not recognise in the carrying amount of an item of property, plant and equipment the costs of the day-to-day servicing of the item. Rather, these costs are recognised in profit or loss as incurred. Costs of day-to-day servicing are primarily the costs of labour and consumables, and may include the cost of small parts. The purpose of these expenditures is often described as for the 'repairs and maintenance' of the item of property, plant and equipment.

13 Parts of some items of property, plant and equipment may require replacement at regular intervals. For example, a furnace may require relining after a specified number of hours of use, or aircraft interiors such as seats and galleys may require replacement several times during the life of the airframe. Items of property, plant and equipment may also be acquired to make a less frequently recurring replacement, such as replacing the interior walls of a building, or to make a nonrecurring replacement. Under the recognition principle in paragraph 7, an entity recognises in the carrying amount of an item of property, plant and equipment the cost of replacing part of such an item when that cost is incurred if the recognition criteria are met. The carrying amount of those parts that are replaced is derecognised in accordance with the derecognition provisions of this Standard (see paragraphs 67–72).

14 A condition of continuing to operate an item of property, plant and equipment (for example, an aircraft) may be performing regular major inspections for faults regardless of whether parts of the item are replaced. When each major inspection is performed, its cost is recognised in the carrying amount of the item of property, plant and equipment as a replacement if the recognition criteria are satisfied. Any remaining carrying amount of the cost of the previous inspection (as distinct from physical parts) is derecognised. This occurs regardless of whether the cost of the previous inspection was identified in the transaction in which the item was acquired or constructed. If necessary, the estimated cost of a future similar inspection may be used as an indication of what the cost of the existing inspection component was when the item was acquired or constructed.

Measurement at recognition

15 **An item of property, plant and equipment that qualifies for recognition as an asset shall be measured at its cost.**

Elements of cost

16 The cost of an item of property, plant and equipment comprises:

(a) its purchase price, including import duties and non-refundable purchase taxes, after deducting trade discounts and rebates.

(b) any costs directly attributable to bringing the asset to the location and condition necessary for it to be capable of operating in the manner intended by management.

(c) the initial estimate of the costs of dismantling and removing the item and restoring the site on which it is located, the obligation for which an entity incurs either when the item is acquired or as a consequence of having used the item during a particular period for purposes other than to produce inventories during that period.

17 Examples of directly attributable costs are:

(a) costs of employee benefits (as defined in IAS 19 *Employee Benefits*) arising directly from the construction or acquisition of the item of property, plant and equipment;

(b) costs of site preparation;

(c) initial delivery and handling costs;

(d) installation and assembly costs;

(e) costs of testing whether the asset is functioning properly, after deducting the net proceeds from selling any items produced while bringing the asset to that location and condition (such as samples produced when testing equipment); and

(f) professional fees.

18 An entity applies IAS 2 *Inventories* to the costs of obligations for dismantling, removing and restoring the site on which an item is located that are incurred during a particular period as a consequence of having used the item to produce inventories during that period. The obligations for costs accounted for in accordance with IAS 2 or IAS 16 are recognised and measured in accordance with IAS 37 *Provisions, Contingent Liabilities and Contingent Assets.*

19 Examples of costs that are not costs of an item of property, plant and equipment are:

(a) costs of opening a new facility;

(b) costs of introducing a new product or service (including costs of advertising and promotional activities);

(c) costs of conducting business in a new location or with a new class of customer (including costs of staff training); and

(d) administration and other general overhead costs.

20 Recognition of costs in the carrying amount of an item of property, plant and equipment ceases when the item is in the location and condition necessary for it to be capable of operating in the manner intended by management. Therefore, costs incurred in using or redeploying an item are not included in the carrying amount of that item. For example, the following costs are not included in the carrying amount of an item of property, plant and equipment:

(a) costs incurred while an item capable of operating in the manner intended by management has yet to be brought into use or is operated at less than full capacity;

(b) initial operating losses, such as those incurred while demand for the item's output builds up; and

(c) costs of relocating or reorganising part or all of an entity's operations.

21 Some operations occur in connection with the construction or development of an item of property, plant and equipment, but are not necessary to bring the item to the location and condition necessary for it to be capable of operating in the manner intended by management. These incidental operations may occur before or during the construction or development activities. For example, income may be earned through using a building site as a car park until construction starts. Because incidental operations are not necessary to bring an item to the location and condition necessary for it to be capable of operating in the manner intended

by management, the income and related expenses of incidental operations are recognised in profit or loss and included in their respective classifications of income and expense.

22 The cost of a self-constructed asset is determined using the same principles as for an acquired asset. If an entity makes similar assets for sale in the normal course of business, the cost of the asset is usually the same as the cost of constructing an asset for sale (see IAS 2). Therefore, any internal profits are eliminated in arriving at such costs. Similarly, the cost of abnormal amounts of wasted material, labour, or other resources incurred in self-constructing an asset is not included in the cost of the asset. IAS 23 *Borrowing Costs* establishes criteria for the recognition of interest as a component of the carrying amount of a self-constructed item of property, plant and equipment.

Measurement of cost

23 The cost of an item of property, plant and equipment is the cash price equivalent at the recognition date. If payment is deferred beyond normal credit terms, the difference between the cash price equivalent and the total payment is recognised as interest over the period of credit unless such interest is recognised in the carrying amount of the item in accordance with the allowed alternative treatment in IAS 23.

24 One or more items of property, plant and equipment may be acquired in exchange for a non-monetary asset or assets, or a combination of monetary and non-monetary assets. The following discussion refers simply to an exchange of one non-monetary asset for another, but it also applies to all exchanges described in the preceding sentence. The cost of such an item of property, plant and equipment is measured at fair value unless (a) the exchange transaction lacks commercial substance or (b) the fair value of neither the asset received nor the asset given up is reliably measurable. The acquired item is measured in this way even if an entity cannot immediately derecognise the asset given up. If the acquired item is not measured at fair value, its cost is measured at the carrying amount of the asset given up.

25 An entity determines whether an exchange transaction has commercial substance by considering the extent to which its future cash flows are expected to change as a result of the transaction. An exchange transaction has commercial substance if:

(a) the configuration (risk, timing and amount) of the cash flows of the asset received differs from the configuration of the cash flows of the asset transferred; or

(b) the entity-specific value of the portion of the entity's operations affected by the transaction changes as a result of the exchange; and

(c) the difference in (a) or (b) is significant relative to the fair value of the assets exchanged.

For the purpose of determining whether an exchange transaction has commercial substance, the entity-specific value of the portion of the entity's operations affected by the transaction shall reflect post-tax cash flows. The result of these analyses may be clear without an entity having to perform detailed calculations.

26 The fair value of an asset for which comparable market transactions do not exist is reliably measurable if (a) the variability in the range of reasonable fair value estimates is not significant for that asset or (b) the probabilities of the various estimates within the range can be reasonably assessed and used in estimating fair value. If an entity is able to determine reliably the fair value of either the asset received or the asset given up, then the fair value of the asset given up is used to measure the cost of the asset received unless the fair value of the asset received is more clearly evident.

27 The cost of an item of property, plant and equipment held by a lessee under a finance lease is determined in accordance with IAS 17 *Leases*.

28 The carrying amount of an item of property, plant and equipment may be reduced by government grants in accordance with IAS 20 *Accounting for Government Grants and Disclosure of Government Assistance*.

Measurement after recognition

29 **An entity shall choose either the cost model in paragraph 30 or the revaluation model in paragraph 31 as its accounting policy and shall apply that policy to an entire class of property, plant and equipment.**

Cost model

30 **After recognition as an asset, an item of property, plant and equipment shall be carried at its cost less any accumulated depreciation and any accumulated impairment losses.**

Revaluation model

31 **After recognition as an asset, an item of property, plant and equipment whose fair value can be measured reliably shall be carried at a revalued amount, being its fair value at the date of the revaluation less any subsequent accumulated depreciation and subsequent accumulated impairment losses. Revaluations shall be made with sufficient regularity to ensure that the carrying amount does not differ materially from that which would be determined using fair value at the balance sheet date.**

32 The fair value of land and buildings is usually determined from market-based evidence by appraisal that is normally undertaken by professionally qualified valuers. The fair value of items of plant and equipment is usually their market value determined by appraisal.

33 If there is no market-based evidence of fair value because of the specialised nature of the item of property, plant and equipment and the item is rarely sold, except as part of a continuing business, an entity may need to estimate fair value using an income or a depreciated replacement cost approach.

34 The frequency of revaluations depends upon the changes in fair values of the items of property, plant and equipment being revalued. When the fair value of a revalued asset differs materially from its carrying amount, a further revaluation is required. Some items of property, plant and equipment experience significant and volatile changes in fair value, thus necessitating annual revaluation. Such frequent revaluations are unnecessary for items of property, plant and equipment

with only insignificant changes in fair value. Instead, it may be necessary to revalue the item only every three or five years.

35 When an item of property, plant and equipment is revalued, any accumulated depreciation at the date of the revaluation is treated in one of the following ways:

(a) restated proportionately with the change in the gross carrying amount of the asset so that the carrying amount of the asset after revaluation equals its revalued amount. This method is often used when an asset is revalued by means of applying an index to its depreciated replacement cost.

(b) eliminated against the gross carrying amount of the asset and the net amount restated to the revalued amount of the asset. This method is often used for buildings.

The amount of the adjustment arising on the restatement or elimination of accumulated depreciation forms part of the increase or decrease in carrying amount that is accounted for in accordance with paragraphs 39 and 40.

36 If an item of property, plant and equipment is revalued, the entire class of property, plant and equipment to which that asset belongs shall be revalued.

37 A class of property, plant and equipment is a grouping of assets of a similar nature and use in an entity's operations. The following are examples of separate classes:

(a) land;

(b) land and buildings;

(c) machinery;

(d) ships;

(e) aircraft;

(f) motor vehicles;

(g) furniture and fixtures; and

(h) office equipment.

38 The items within a class of property, plant and equipment are revalued simultaneously to avoid selective revaluation of assets and the reporting of amounts in the financial statements that are a mixture of costs and values as at different dates. However, a class of assets may be revalued on a rolling basis provided revaluation of the class of assets is completed within a short period and provided the revaluations are kept up to date.

39 If an asset's carrying amount is increased as a result of a revaluation, the increase shall be credited directly to equity under the heading of revaluation surplus. However, the increase shall be recognised in profit or loss to the extent that it reverses a revaluation decrease of the same asset previously recognised in profit or loss.

40 If an asset's carrying amount is decreased as a result of a revaluation, the decrease shall be recognised in profit or loss. However, the decrease shall

be debited directly to equity under the heading of revaluation surplus to the extent of any credit balance existing in the revaluation surplus in respect of that asset.

41 The revaluation surplus included in equity in respect of an item of property, plant and equipment may be transferred directly to retained earnings when the asset is derecognised. This may involve transferring the whole of the surplus when the asset is retired or disposed of. However, some of the surplus may be transferred as the asset is used by an entity. In such a case, the amount of the surplus transferred would be the difference between depreciation based on the revalued carrying amount of the asset and depreciation based on the asset's original cost. Transfers from revaluation surplus to retained earnings are not made through profit or loss.

42 The effects of taxes on income, if any, resulting from the revaluation of property, plant and equipment are recognised and disclosed in accordance with IAS 12 *Income Taxes*.

Depreciation

43 Each part of an item of property, plant and equipment with a cost that is significant in relation to the total cost of the item shall be depreciated separately.

44 An entity allocates the amount initially recognised in respect of an item of property, plant and equipment to its significant parts and depreciates separately each such part. For example, it may be appropriate to depreciate separately the airframe and engines of an aircraft, whether owned or subject to a finance lease.

45 A significant part of an item of property, plant and equipment may have a useful life and a depreciation method that are the same as the useful life and the depreciation method of another significant part of that same item. Such parts may be grouped in determining the depreciation charge.

46 To the extent that an entity depreciates separately some parts of an item of property, plant and equipment, it also depreciates separately the remainder of the item. The remainder consists of the parts of the item that are individually not significant. If an entity has varying expectations for these parts, approximation techniques may be necessary to depreciate the remainder in a manner that faithfully represents the consumption pattern and/or useful life of its parts.

47 An entity may choose to depreciate separately the parts of an item that do not have a cost that is significant in relation to the total cost of the item.

48 The depreciation charge for each period shall be recognised in profit or loss unless it is included in the carrying amount of another asset.

49 The depreciation charge for a period is usually recognised in profit or loss. However, sometimes, the future economic benefits embodied in an asset are absorbed in producing other assets. In this case, the depreciation charge constitutes part of the cost of the other asset and is included in its carrying amount. For example, the depreciation of manufacturing plant and equipment is included in the costs of conversion of inventories (see IAS 2). Similarly,

depreciation of property, plant and equipment used for development activities may be included in the cost of an intangible asset recognised in accordance with IAS 38 *Intangible Assets*.

Depreciable amount and depreciation period

50 **The depreciable amount of an asset shall be allocated on a systematic basis over its useful life.**

51 **The residual value and the useful life of an asset shall be reviewed at least at each financial year-end and, if expectations differ from previous estimates, the change(s) shall be accounted for as a change in an accounting estimate in accordance with IAS 8** *Accounting Policies, Changes in Accounting Estimates and Errors*.

52 Depreciation is recognised even if the fair value of the asset exceeds its carrying amount, as long as the asset's residual value does not exceed its carrying amount. Repair and maintenance of an asset do not negate the need to depreciate it.

53 The depreciable amount of an asset is determined after deducting its residual value. In practice, the residual value of an asset is often insignificant and therefore immaterial in the calculation of the depreciable amount.

54 The residual value of an asset may increase to an amount equal to or greater than the asset's carrying amount. If it does, the asset's depreciation charge is zero unless and until its residual value subsequently decreases to an amount below the asset's carrying amount.

55 Depreciation of an asset begins when it is available for use, ie when it is in the location and condition necessary for it to be capable of operating in the manner intended by management. Depreciation of an asset ceases at the earlier of the date that the asset is classified as held for sale (or included in a disposal group that is classified as held for sale) in accordance with IFRS 5 and the date that the asset is derecognised. Therefore, depreciation does not cease when the asset becomes idle or is retired from active use unless the asset is fully depreciated. However, under usage methods of depreciation the depreciation charge can be zero while there is no production.

56 The future economic benefits embodied in an asset are consumed by an entity principally through its use. However, other factors, such as technical or commercial obsolescence and wear and tear while an asset remains idle, often result in the diminution of the economic benefits that might have been obtained from the asset. Consequently, all the following factors are considered in determining the useful life of an asset:

(a) expected usage of the asset. Usage is assessed by reference to the asset's expected capacity or physical output.

(b) expected physical wear and tear, which depends on operational factors such as the number of shifts for which the asset is to be used and the repair and maintenance programme, and the care and maintenance of the asset while idle.

(c) technical or commercial obsolescence arising from changes or improvements in production, or from a change in the market demand for the product or service output of the asset.

(d) legal or similar limits on the use of the asset, such as the expiry dates of related leases.

57 The useful life of an asset is defined in terms of the asset's expected utility to the entity. The asset management policy of the entity may involve the disposal of assets after a specified time or after consumption of a specified proportion of the future economic benefits embodied in the asset. Therefore, the useful life of an asset may be shorter than its economic life. The estimation of the useful life of the asset is a matter of judgement based on the experience of the entity with similar assets.

58 Land and buildings are separable assets and are accounted for separately, even when they are acquired together. With some exceptions, such as quarries and sites used for landfill, land has an unlimited useful life and therefore is not depreciated. Buildings have a limited useful life and therefore are depreciable assets. An increase in the value of the land on which a building stands does not affect the determination of the depreciable amount of the building.

59 If the cost of land includes the costs of site dismantlement, removal and restoration, that portion of the land asset is depreciated over the period of benefits obtained by incurring those costs. In some cases, the land itself may have a limited useful life, in which case it is depreciated in a manner that reflects the benefits to be derived from it.

Depreciation method

60 The depreciation method used shall reflect the pattern in which the asset's future economic benefits are expected to be consumed by the entity.

61 The depreciation method applied to an asset shall be reviewed at least at each financial year-end and, if there has been a significant change in the expected pattern of consumption of the future economic benefits embodied in the asset, the method shall be changed to reflect the changed pattern. Such a change shall be accounted for as a change in an accounting estimate in accordance with IAS 8.

62 A variety of depreciation methods can be used to allocate the depreciable amount of an asset on a systematic basis over its useful life. These methods include the straight-line method, the diminishing balance method and the units of production method. Straight-line depreciation results in a constant charge over the useful life if the asset's residual value does not change. The diminishing balance method results in a decreasing charge over the useful life. The units of production method results in a charge based on the expected use or output. The entity selects the method that most closely reflects the expected pattern of consumption of the future economic benefits embodied in the asset. That method is applied consistently from period to period unless there is a change in the expected pattern of consumption of those future economic benefits.

Impairment

63 To determine whether an item of property, plant and equipment is impaired, an entity applies IAS 36 *Impairment of Assets*. That Standard explains how an entity reviews the carrying amount of its assets, how it determines the recoverable amount of an asset, and when it recognises, or reverses the recognition of, an impairment loss.

64 [Deleted]

Compensation for impairment

65 Compensation from third parties for items of property, plant and equipment that were impaired, lost or given up shall be included in profit or loss when the compensation becomes receivable.

66 Impairments or losses of items of property, plant and equipment, related claims for or payments of compensation from third parties and any subsequent purchase or construction of replacement assets are separate economic events and are accounted for separately as follows:

(a) impairments of items of property, plant and equipment are recognised in accordance with IAS 36;

(b) derecognition of items of property, plant and equipment retired or disposed of is determined in accordance with this Standard;

(c) compensation from third parties for items of property, plant and equipment that were impaired, lost or given up is included in determining profit or loss when it becomes receivable; and

(d) the cost of items of property, plant and equipment restored, purchased or constructed as replacements is determined in accordance with this Standard.

Derecognition

67 The carrying amount of an item of property, plant and equipment shall be derecognised:

(a) on disposal; or

(b) when no future economic benefits are expected from its use or disposal.

68 The gain or loss arising from the derecognition of an item of property, plant and equipment shall be included in profit or loss when the item is derecognised (unless IAS 17 requires otherwise on a sale and leaseback). Gains shall not be classified as revenue.

69 The disposal of an item of property, plant and equipment may occur in a variety of ways (eg by sale, by entering into a finance lease or by donation). In determining the date of disposal of an item, an entity applies the criteria in IAS 18 *Revenue* for recognising revenue from the sale of goods. IAS 17 applies to disposal by a sale and leaseback.

70 If, under the recognition principle in paragraph 7, an entity recognises in the carrying amount of an item of property, plant and equipment the cost of a

replacement for part of the item, then it derecognises the carrying amount of the replaced part regardless of whether the replaced part had been depreciated separately. If it is not practicable for an entity to determine the carrying amount of the replaced part, it may use the cost of the replacement as an indication of what the cost of the replaced part was at the time it was acquired or constructed.

71 **The gain or loss arising from the derecognition of an item of property, plant and equipment shall be determined as the difference between the net disposal proceeds, if any, and the carrying amount of the item.**

72 The consideration receivable on disposal of an item of property, plant and equipment is recognised initially at its fair value. If payment for the item is deferred, the consideration received is recognised initially at the cash price equivalent. The difference between the nominal amount of the consideration and the cash price equivalent is recognised as interest revenue in accordance with IAS 18 reflecting the effective yield on the receivable.

Disclosure

73 **The financial statements shall disclose, for each class of property, plant and equipment:**

(a) the measurement bases used for determining the gross carrying amount;

(b) the depreciation methods used;

(c) the useful lives or the depreciation rates used;

(d) the gross carrying amount and the accumulated depreciation (aggregated with accumulated impairment losses) at the beginning and end of the period; and

(e) a reconciliation of the carrying amount at the beginning and end of the period showing:

- **(i) additions;**
- **(ii) assets classified as held for sale or included in a disposal group classified as held for sale in accordance with IFRS 5 and other disposals;**
- **(iii) acquisitions through business combinations;**
- **(iv) increases or decreases resulting from revaluations under paragraphs 31, 39 and 40 and from impairment losses recognised or reversed directly in equity in accordance with IAS 36;**
- **(v) impairment losses recognised in profit or loss in accordance with IAS 36;**
- **(vi) impairment losses reversed in profit or loss in accordance with IAS 36;**
- **(vii) depreciation;**
- **(viii) the net exchange differences arising on the translation of the financial statements from the functional currency into a different**

presentation currency, including the translation of a foreign operation into the presentation currency of the reporting entity; and

(ix) other changes.

74 The financial statements shall also disclose:

(a) the existence and amounts of restrictions on title, and property, plant and equipment pledged as security for liabilities;

(b) the amount of expenditures recognised in the carrying amount of an item of property, plant and equipment in the course of its construction;

(c) the amount of contractual commitments for the acquisition of property, plant and equipment; and

(d) if it is not disclosed separately on the face of the income statement, the amount of compensation from third parties for items of property, plant and equipment that were impaired, lost or given up that is included in profit or loss.

75 Selection of the depreciation method and estimation of the useful life of assets are matters of judgement. Therefore, disclosure of the methods adopted and the estimated useful lives or depreciation rates provides users of financial statements with information that allows them to review the policies selected by management and enables comparisons to be made with other entities. For similar reasons, it is necessary to disclose:

(a) depreciation, whether recognised in profit or loss or as a part of the cost of other assets, during a period; and

(b) accumulated depreciation at the end of the period.

76 In accordance with IAS 8 an entity discloses the nature and effect of a change in an accounting estimate that has an effect in the current period or is expected to have an effect in subsequent periods. For property, plant and equipment, such disclosure may arise from changes in estimates with respect to:

(a) residual values;

(b) the estimated costs of dismantling, removing or restoring items of property, plant and equipment;

(c) useful lives; and

(d) depreciation methods.

77 If items of property, plant and equipment are stated at revalued amounts, the following shall be disclosed:

(a) the effective date of the revaluation;

(b) whether an independent valuer was involved;

(c) the methods and significant assumptions applied in estimating the items' fair values;

(d) **the extent to which the items' fair values were determined directly by reference to observable prices in an active market or recent market transactions on arm's length terms or were estimated using other valuation techniques;**

(e) **for each revalued class of property, plant and equipment, the carrying amount that would have been recognised had the assets been carried under the cost model; and**

(f) **the revaluation surplus, indicating the change for the period and any restrictions on the distribution of the balance to shareholders.**

78 In accordance with IAS 36 an entity discloses information on impaired property, plant and equipment in addition to the information required by paragraph 73(e)(iv)–(vi).

79 Users of financial statements may also find the following information relevant to their needs:

(a) the carrying amount of temporarily idle property, plant and equipment;

(b) the gross carrying amount of any fully depreciated property, plant and equipment that is still in use;

(c) the carrying amount of property, plant and equipment retired from active use and not classified as held for sale in accordance with IFRS 5; and

(d) when the cost model is used, the fair value of property, plant and equipment when this is materially different from the carrying amount.

Therefore, entities are encouraged to disclose these amounts.

Transitional provisions

80 **The requirements of paragraphs 24–26 regarding the initial measurement of an item of property, plant and equipment acquired in an exchange of assets transaction shall be applied prospectively only to future transactions.**

Effective date

81 **An entity shall apply this Standard for annual periods beginning on or after 1 January 2005. Earlier application is encouraged. If an entity applies this Standard for a period beginning before 1 January 2005, it shall disclose that fact.**

81A **An entity shall apply the amendments in paragraph 3 for annual periods beginning on or after 1 January 2006. If an entity applies IFRS 6** *Exploration for and Evaluation of Mineral Resources* **for an earlier period, those amendments shall be applied for that earlier period.**

Withdrawal of other pronouncements

82 This Standard supersedes IAS 16 *Property, Plant and Equipment* (revised in 1998).

83 This Standard supersedes the following Interpretations:

(a) SIC-6 *Costs of Modifying Existing Software*;

(b) SIC-14 *Property, Plant and Equipment—Compensation for the Impairment or Loss of Items*; and

(c) SIC-23 *Property, Plant and Equipment—Major Inspection or Overhaul Costs*.

Appendix
Amendments to other pronouncements

The amendments in this appendix shall be applied for annual periods beginning on or after 1 January 2005. If an entity applies this Standard for an earlier period, these amendments shall be applied for that earlier period.

* * * * *

The amendments contained in this appendix when this Standard was issued in 2003 have been incorporated into the relevant pronouncements published in this volume.

Approval of IAS 16 by the Board

International Accounting Standard 16 *Property, Plant and Equipment* was approved for issue by the fourteen members of the International Accounting Standards Board.

Sir David Tweedie	Chairman
Thomas E Jones	Vice-Chairman
Mary E Barth	
Hans-Georg Bruns	
Anthony T Cope	
Robert P Garnett	
Gilbert Gélard	
James J Leisenring	
Warren J McGregor	
Patricia L O'Malley	
Harry K Schmid	
John T Smith	
Geoffrey Whittington	
Tatsumi Yamada	

Basis for Conclusions

This Basis for Conclusions accompanies, but is not part of, IAS 16.

Introduction

BC1 This Basis for Conclusions summarises the International Accounting Standards Board's considerations in reaching its conclusions on revising IAS 16 *Property, Plant and Equipment* in 2003. Individual Board members gave greater weight to some factors than to others.

BC2 In July 2001 the Board announced that, as part of its initial agenda of technical projects, it would undertake a project to improve a number of Standards, including IAS 16. The project was undertaken in the light of queries and criticisms raised in relation to the Standards by securities regulators, professional accountants and other interested parties. The objectives of the Improvements project were to reduce or eliminate alternatives, redundancies and conflicts within Standards, to deal with some convergence issues and to make other improvements. In May 2002 the Board published its proposals in an Exposure Draft of *Improvements to International Accounting Standards*, with a comment deadline of 16 September 2002. The Board received over 160 comment letters on the Exposure Draft.

BC3 Because the Board's intention was not to reconsider the fundamental approach to the accounting for property, plant and equipment that was established by IAS 16, this Basis for Conclusions does not discuss requirements in IAS 16 that the Board has not reconsidered.

Scope

BC4 The Board clarified that the requirements of IAS 16 apply to items of property, plant and equipment that an entity uses to develop or maintain (a) biological assets and (b) mineral rights and mineral reserves such as oil, natural gas and similar non-regenerative resources. The Board noted that items of property, plant and equipment that an entity uses for these purposes possess the same characteristics as other items of property, plant and equipment.

Recognition

BC5 In considering potential improvements to the previous version of IAS 16, the Board reviewed its subsequent expenditure recognition principle for two reasons. First, the existing subsequent expenditure recognition principle did not align with the asset recognition principle in the *Framework*. Second, the Board noted difficulties in practice in making the distinction it required between expenditures that maintain, and those that enhance, an item of property, plant and equipment. Some expenditures seem to do both.

BC6 The Board ultimately decided that the separate recognition principle for subsequent expenditure was not needed. As a result, an entity will evaluate all its property, plant and equipment costs under IAS 16's general recognition principle. Also, if the cost of a replacement for part of an item of property, plant and equipment is recognised in the carrying amount of an asset, then an entity will derecognise the carrying amount of what was replaced to avoid carrying both the replacement and the replaced portion as assets. This derecognition occurs whether or not what is replaced is a part of an item that the entity depreciates separately.

BC7 The Board's decision on how to handle the recognition principles was not reached easily. In the Exposure Draft (ED), the Board proposed to include within IAS 16's general recognition principle only the recognition of subsequent expenditures that are replacements of a part of an item of property, plant and equipment. Also in the ED, the Board proposed to modify the subsequent expenditure recognition principle to distinguish more clearly the expenditures to which it would continue to apply.

BC8 Respondents to the ED agreed that it was appropriate for subsequent expenditures that were replacements of a part of an item of property, plant and equipment that an entity depreciated separately to be covered by the general recognition principle. However, the respondents argued, and the Board agreed, that the modified second principle was not clearer because it would result in an entity recognising in the carrying amount of an asset and then depreciating subsequent expenditures that were for the day-to-day servicing of items of property, plant and equipment, those that might commonly be regarded as for 'repairs and maintenance'. That result was not the Board's intention.

BC9 In its redeliberation of the ED, the Board concluded it could not retain the proposed modified subsequent expenditure recognition principle. It also concluded that it could not revert to the subsequent expenditure principle in the previous version of IAS 16 because, if it did, nothing was improved; the *Framework* conflict was not resolved and the practice issues were not addressed.

BC10 The Board concluded that it was best for all subsequent expenditures to be covered by IAS 16's general recognition principle. This solution had the following advantages:

(a) use of IAS 16's general recognition principle fits the *Framework*.

(b) use of a single recognition principle is a straightforward approach.

(c) retaining IAS 16's general recognition principle and combining it with the derecognition principle will result in financial statements that reflect what is occurring, ie both the flow of property, plant and equipment through an entity and the economics of the acquisition and disposal process.

(d) use of one recognition principle fosters consistency. With two principles, consistency is not achieved unless it is clear when each should apply. Because IAS 16 does not address what constitutes an 'item' of property, plant and equipment, this clarity was not assured because some might characterise a particular cost as the initial cost of a new item of property, plant and equipment and others might regard it as a subsequent cost of an existing item of property, plant and equipment.

BC11 As a consequence of placing all subsequent expenditures under IAS 16's general recognition principle, the Board also included those expenditures under IAS 16's derecognition principle. In the ED, the Board proposed the derecognition of the carrying amount of a part of an item that was depreciated separately and was replaced by a subsequent expenditure that an entity recognised in the carrying amount of the asset under the general recognition principle. With this change, replacements of a part of an item that are not depreciated separately are subject to the same approach.

BC12 The Board noted that some subsequent expenditures on property, plant and equipment, although arguably incurred in the pursuit of future economic benefits, are not sufficiently certain to be recognised in the carrying amount of an asset under the general recognition principle. Thus, the Board decided to state in the Standard that an entity recognises in profit or loss as incurred the costs of the day-to-day servicing of property, plant and equipment.

Measurement at recognition

Asset dismantlement, removal and restoration costs

BC13 The previous version of IAS 16 provided that in initially measuring an item of property, plant and equipment at its cost, an entity would include the cost of dismantling and removing that item and restoring the site on which it is located to the extent it had recognised an obligation for that cost. As part of its deliberations, the Board evaluated whether it could improve this guidance by addressing associated issues that have arisen in practice.

BC14 The Board concluded that the relatively limited scope of the Improvements project warranted addressing only one matter. That matter was whether the cost of an item of property, plant and equipment should include the initial estimate of the cost of dismantlement, removal and restoration that an entity incurs as a consequence of using the item (instead of as a consequence of acquiring it). Therefore, the Board did not address how an entity should account for (a) changes in the amount of the initial estimate of a recognised obligation, (b) the effects of accretion of, or changes in interest rates on, a recognised obligation or (c) the cost of obligations an entity did not face when it acquired the item, such as an obligation triggered by a law change enacted after the asset was acquired.

BC15 The Board observed that whether the obligation is incurred upon acquisition of the item or while it is being used, its underlying nature and its association with the asset are the same. Therefore, the Board decided that the cost of an item should include the costs of dismantlement, removal or restoration, the obligation for which an entity has incurred as a consequence of having used the item during a particular period other than to produce inventories during that period. An entity applies IAS 2 *Inventories* to the costs of these obligations that are incurred as a consequence of having used the item during a particular period to produce inventories during that period. The Board observed that accounting for these costs initially in accordance with IAS 2 acknowledges their nature. Furthermore, doing so achieves the same result as including these costs as an element of the cost of an item of property, plant and equipment, depreciating them over the production period just completed and identifying the depreciation charge as a cost to produce another asset (inventory), in which case the depreciation charge constitutes part of the cost of that other asset.

BC16 The Board noted that because IAS 16's initial measurement provisions are not affected by an entity's subsequent decision to carry an item under the cost model or the revaluation model, the Board's decision applies to assets that an entity carries under either treatment.

Asset exchange transactions

BC17 Paragraph 22 of the previous version of IAS 16 indicated that if (a) an item of property, plant and equipment is acquired in exchange for a similar asset that has a similar use in the same line of business and has a similar fair value or (b) an item of property, plant and equipment is sold in exchange for an equity interest in a similar asset, then no gain or loss is recognised on the transaction. The cost of the new asset is the carrying amount of the asset given up (rather than the fair value of the purchase consideration given for the new asset).

BC18 This requirement in the previous version of IAS 16 was consistent with views that:

(a) gains should not be recognised on exchanges of assets unless the exchanges represent the culmination of an earning process;

(b) exchanges of assets of a similar nature and value are not a substantive event warranting the recognition of gains; and

(c) requiring or permitting the recognition of gains from such exchanges enables entities to 'manufacture' gains by attributing inflated values to the assets exchanged, if the assets do not have observable market prices in active markets.

BC19 The approach described above raised issues about how to identify whether assets exchanged are similar in nature and value. The Board reviewed this topic, and noted views that:

(a) under the *Framework*, the recognition of income from an exchange of assets does not depend on whether the assets exchanged are dissimilar;

(b) income is not necessarily earned only at the culmination of an earning process, and in some cases it is arbitrary to determine when an earning process culminates;

(c) generally, under both measurement bases after recognition that are permitted under IAS 16, gain recognition is not deferred beyond the date at which assets are exchanged; and

(d) removing 'existing carrying amount' measurement of property, plant and equipment acquired in exchange for similar assets would increase the consistency of measurement of acquisitions of assets.

BC20 The Board decided to require in IAS 16 that all items of property, plant and equipment acquired in exchange for non-monetary assets or a combination of monetary and non-monetary assets should be measured at fair value, except that, if the exchange transaction lacks commercial substance or the fair value of neither of the assets exchanged can be determined reliably, then the cost of the asset acquired in the exchange should be measured at the carrying amount of the asset given up.

BC21 The Board added the 'commercial substance' test in response to a concern raised in the comments it received on the ED. This concern was that, under the Board's proposal, an entity would measure at fair value an asset acquired in a transaction that did not have commercial substance, ie the transaction did not have a discernible effect on an entity's economics. The Board agreed that requiring an evaluation of commercial substance would help to give users of the financial statements assurance that the substance of a transaction in which the acquired asset is measured at fair value (and often, consequentially, a gain on the disposal of the transferred asset is recognised in income) is the same as its legal form.

BC22 The Board concluded that in evaluating whether a transaction has commercial substance, an entity should calculate the present value of the post-tax cash flows that it can reasonably expect to derive from the portion of its operations affected by the transaction. The discount rate should reflect the entity's current assessment of the time value of money and the risks specific to those operations rather than those that market place participants would make.

BC23 The Board included the 'reliable measurement' test for using fair value to measure these exchanges to minimise the risk that entities could 'manufacture' gains by attributing inflated values to the assets exchanged. Taking into consideration its project for the convergence of IFRSs and US GAAP, the Board discussed whether to change the manner in which its 'reliable measurement' test is described. The Board observed this was unnecessary because it believes that its guidance and that contained in US GAAP are intended to have the same meaning.

BC24 The Board decided to retain, in IAS 18 *Revenue*, its prohibition on recognising revenue from exchanges or swaps of goods or services of a similar nature and value. The Board has on its agenda a project on revenue recognition and does not propose to make any significant amendments to IAS 18 until that project is completed.

Measurement after recognition

Revaluation model

BC25 The Board is taking part in research activities with national standard-setters on revaluations of property, plant and equipment. This research is intended to promote international convergence of standards. One of the most important issues is identifying the preferred measurement attribute for revaluations. This research could lead to proposals to amend IAS 16.

Depreciation: unit of measure

BC26 The Board's discussions about the potential improvements to the depreciation principle in the previous version of IAS 16 included consideration of the unit of measure an entity uses to depreciate its items of property, plant and equipment. Of particular concern to the Board were situations in which the unit of measure is the 'item as a whole' even though that item may be composed of significant parts with individually varying useful lives or consumption patterns. The Board did not believe that, in these situations, an entity's use of approximation techniques, such as a weighted average useful life for the item as a whole, resulted in depreciation that faithfully represents an entity's varying expectations for the significant parts.

BC27 The Board sought to improve the previous version of IAS 16 by proposing in the ED revisions to existing guidance on separating an item into its parts and then further clarifying in the Standard the need for an entity to depreciate separately any significant parts of an item of property, plant and equipment. By doing so an entity will also separately depreciate the item's remainder.

Depreciation: depreciable amount

BC28 During its discussion of depreciation principles, the Board noted the concern that, under the cost model, the previous version of IAS 16 does not state clearly why an entity deducts an asset's residual value from its cost to determine the asset's depreciable amount. Some argue that the objective is one of precision, ie reducing the amount of depreciation so that it reflects the item's net cost. Others argue that the objective is one of economics, ie stopping depreciation if, because of inflation or otherwise, an entity expects that during its useful life an asset will increase in value by an amount greater than it will diminish.

BC29 The Board decided to improve the previous version of IAS 16 by making clear the objective of deducting a residual value in determining an asset's depreciable amount. In doing so, the Board did not adopt completely either the 'net cost' or the 'economics' objective. Given the concept of depreciation as a cost allocation technique, the Board concluded that an entity's expectation of increases in an asset's value, because of inflation or otherwise, does not override the need to depreciate it. Thus, the Board changed the definition of residual value to the amount an entity could receive for the asset currently (at the financial reporting date) if the asset were already as old and worn as it will be when the entity expects to dispose of it. Thus, an increase in the expected residual value of an asset because of past events will affect the depreciable amount; expectations of future changes in residual value other than the effects of expected wear and tear will not.

Depreciation: depreciation period

BC30 The Board decided that the useful life of an asset should encompass the entire time it is available for use, regardless of whether during that time it is in use or is idle. Idle periods most commonly occur just after an asset is acquired and just before it is disposed of, the latter while the asset is held either for sale or for another form of disposal.

BC31 The Board concluded that, whether idle or not, it is appropriate to depreciate an asset with a limited useful life so that the financial statements reflect the consumption of the asset's service potential that occurs while the asset is held. The Board also discussed but decided not to address the measurement of assets held for sale. The Board concluded that whether to apply a different measurement model to assets held for sale—which may or may not be idle—was a different question and was beyond the scope of the Improvements project.

BC32 In July 2003 the Board published ED 4 *Disposal of Non-current Assets and Presentation of Discontinued Operations*. ED 4 was published as part of the Board's short-term convergence project, the scope of which was broader than that of the Improvements project. In ED 4, the Board proposed that an entity should classify some of its assets as 'assets held for sale' if specified criteria are met. Among other things, the Board proposed that an entity should cease depreciating an asset classified in this manner, irrespective of whether the asset is idle. The basis for this proposal was that the carrying amount of an asset held for sale will be recovered principally through sale rather than future operations, and therefore accounting for the asset should be a process of valuation rather than allocation. The Board will amend IAS 16 accordingly when ED 4 is finalised.

Depreciation: depreciation method

BC33 The Board considered how an entity should account for a change in a depreciation method. The Board concluded that a change in a depreciation method is a change in the technique used to apply the entity's accounting policy to recognise depreciation as an asset's future economic benefits are consumed. Therefore, it is a change in an accounting estimate.

Derecognition

Derecognition date

BC34 The Board decided that an entity should apply the revenue recognition principle in IAS 18 *Revenue* for sales of goods to its gains from the sales of items of property, plant and equipment. The requirements in that principle ensure the representational faithfulness of an entity's recognised revenue. Representational faithfulness is also the appropriate objective for an entity's recognised gains. However, in IAS 16, the revenue recognition principle's criteria drive derecognition of the asset disposed of rather than recognition of the proceeds received. Applying the principle instead to the recognition of the proceeds might lead to the conclusion that an entity will recognise a deferred gain. Deferred gains do not meet the definition of a liability under the *Framework*. Thus, the Board decided that an entity does not derecognise an item of property, plant and equipment until the requirements in IAS 18 to recognise revenue on the sale of goods are met.

Gain classification

BC35 Although the Board concluded that an entity should apply the recognition principle for revenue from sales of goods to its recognition of gains on disposals of items of property, plant and equipment, the Board concluded that the respective approaches to income statement display should differ. The Board concluded that users of financial statements would consider these gains and the proceeds from an entity's sale of goods in the course of its ordinary activities differently in their evaluation of an entity's past results and their projections of future cash flows. This is because revenue from the sale of goods is typically more likely to recur in comparable amounts than are gains from sales of items of property, plant and equipment. Accordingly, the Board concluded that an entity should not classify as revenue gains on disposals of items of property, plant and equipment.

Transitional provisions

BC36 The Board concluded that it would be impracticable for an entity to determine retrospectively whether a previous transaction involving an exchange of non-monetary assets had commercial substance. This is because it would not be possible for management to avoid using hindsight in making the necessary estimates as of earlier dates. Accordingly, the Board decided that in accordance with the provisions of IAS 8 an entity should consider commercial substance only in evaluating the initial measurement of future transactions involving an exchange of non-monetary assets.

Summary of changes from the Exposure Draft

BC37 The main changes from the ED proposals to the revised Standard are as follows:

(a) The ED contained two recognition principles, one applying to subsequent expenditures on existing items of property, plant and equipment. The Standard contains a single recognition principle that applies to costs incurred initially to acquire an item and costs incurred subsequently to add to, replace part of or service an item. An entity applies the recognition principle to the latter costs at the time it incurs them.

(b) Under the approach proposed in the ED, an entity measured an item of property, plant and equipment acquired in exchange for a non-monetary asset at fair value irrespective of whether the exchange transaction in which it was acquired had commercial substance. Under the Standard, a lack of commercial substance is cause for an entity to measure the acquired asset at the carrying amount of the asset given up.

(c) Compared with the Standard, the ED did not as clearly set out the principle that an entity separately depreciates at least the parts of an item of property, plant and equipment that are of significant cost.

(d) Under the approach proposed in the ED, an entity derecognised the carrying amount of a replaced part of an item of property, plant and equipment if it recognised in the carrying amount of the asset the cost of the replacement under the general recognition principle. In the Standard, an entity also applies this approach to a replacement of a part of an item that is not depreciated separately.

(e) In finalising the Standard, the Board identified further necessary consequential amendments to IFRS 1, IAS 14, IAS 34, IAS 36, IAS 37, IAS 38, IAS 40, SIC-13, SIC-21, SIC-22 and SIC-32.

Table of Concordance

This table shows how the contents of the superseded version of IAS 16 and the current version of IAS 16 correspond. Paragraphs are treated as corresponding if they broadly address the same matter even though their guidance may differ.

The table also shows how the requirements of SIC Interpretations SIC-14 and SIC-23 have been incorporated into the current version of IAS 16.

Superseded IAS 16 paragraph	Current IAS 16 paragraph	Superseded IAS 16 paragraph	Current IAS 16 paragraph	Superseded IAS 16 paragraph	Current IAS 16 paragraph
Objective	1	27	13	54	64
1	2	28	30	55	67
2	3	29	31	56	68, 71
3	4	30	32	57	None
4	5	31	32, 33	58	69
5	None	32	34	59	55
6	6	33	35	60	73
7	7	34	36	61	74
8	None	35	37	62	75
9	None	36	38	63	76
10	None	37	39	64	77
11	8, 9	38	40	65	78
12	43–47	39	41	66	79
13	11	40	42	67	81
14	15	41	48, 50, 60	68	82, 83
15	16–18	42	52	SIC-14	65, 66
16	23	43	56	SIC-23	14
17	19, 20	44	57	None	10
18	22	45	58	None	12
19	27	46	51, 53	None	21
20	28	47	62	None	24, 25
21	26	48	49	None	29
22	None	49	51	None	54
23	None	50	None	None	59
24	None	51	None	None	70
25	None	52	61	None	72
26	None	53	63	None	80–82

International Accounting Standard 17

Leases

This version includes amendments resulting from new and amended IFRSs issued up to 31 December 2004.

CONTENTS

International Accounting Standard 17 *Leases* (IAS 17) is set out in paragraphs 1–70 and the Appendix. All the paragraphs have equal authority but retain the IASC format of the Standard when it was adopted by the IASB. IAS 17 should be read in the context of its objective and the Basis for Conclusions, the *Preface to International Financial Reporting Standards* and the *Framework for the Preparation and Presentation of Financial Statements.* IAS 8 *Accounting Policies, Changes in Accounting Estimates and Errors* provides a basis for selecting and applying accounting policies in the absence of explicit guidance.

Introduction

IN1 International Accounting Standard 17 *Leases* (IAS 17) replaces IAS 17 *Leases* (revised in 1997) and should be applied for annual periods beginning on or after 1 January 2005. Earlier application is encouraged.

Reasons for revising IAS 17

IN2 The International Accounting Standards Board developed this revised IAS 17 as part of its project on Improvements to International Accounting Standards. The project was undertaken in the light of queries and criticisms raised in relation to the Standards by securities regulators, professional accountants and other interested parties. The objectives of the project were to reduce or eliminate alternatives, redundancies and conflicts within the Standards, to deal with some convergence issues and to make other improvements.

IN3 For IAS 17 the Board's main objective was a limited revision to clarify the classification of a lease of land and buildings and to eliminate accounting alternatives for initial direct costs in the financial statements of lessors.

IN4 Because the Board's agenda includes a project on leases, the Board did not reconsider the fundamental approach to the accounting for leases contained in IAS 17. For the same reason, the Board decided not to incorporate into IAS 17 relevant SIC Interpretations.

The main changes

Scope

IN5 Although IAS 40 *Investment Property* prescribes the measurement models that can be applied to investment properties held, it requires the finance lease accounting methodology set out in this Standard to be used for investment properties held under leases.

Definitions

Initial direct costs

IN6 Initial direct costs are incremental costs that are directly attributable to negotiating and arranging a lease. The definition of the interest rate implicit in the lease has been amended to clarify that it is the discount rate that results in the present value of the minimum lease payments and any unguaranteed residual value equalling the fair value of the leased asset plus initial direct costs of the lessor.

Inception of the lease/commencement of the lease term

IN7 This Standard distinguishes between the inception of the lease (when leases are classified) and the commencement of the lease term (when recognition takes place).

Unearned finance income/net investment in the lease

IN8 The definitions of these terms have been simplified and articulated more explicitly to complement the changes relating to initial direct costs referred to in paragraphs IN10–IN12 and the change in the definition of the interest rate implicit in the lease referred to in paragraph IN6.

Classification of leases

IN9 When classifying a lease of land and buildings, an entity normally considers the land and buildings elements separately. The minimum lease payments are allocated between the land and buildings elements in proportion to the relative fair values of the leasehold interests in the land and buildings elements of the lease. The land element is normally classified as an operating lease unless title passes to the lessee at the end of the lease term. The buildings element is classified as an operating or finance lease by applying the classification criteria in the Standard.

Initial direct costs

IN10 Lessors include in the initial measurement of finance lease receivables the initial direct costs incurred in negotiating a lease. This treatment does not apply to manufacturer or dealer lessors. Manufacturer or dealer lessors recognise costs of this type as an expense when the selling profit is recognised.

IN11 Initial direct costs incurred by lessors in negotiating an operating lease are added to the carrying amount of the leased asset and recognised over the lease term on the same basis as the lease income.

IN12 The Standard does not permit initial direct costs of lessors to be charged as expenses as incurred.

Transitional provisions

IN13 As discussed in paragraph 68 of the Standard, an entity that has previously applied IAS 17 (revised 1997) is required to apply the amendments made by this Standard retrospectively for all leases, or if IAS 17 (revised 1997) was not applied retrospectively, for all leases entered into since it first applied that Standard.

International Accounting Standard 17
Leases

Objective

1 The objective of this Standard is to prescribe, for lessees and lessors, the appropriate accounting policies and disclosure to apply in relation to leases.

Scope

2 **This Standard shall be applied in accounting for all leases other than:**

(a) leases to explore for or use minerals, oil, natural gas and similar non-regenerative resources; and

(b) licensing agreements for such items as motion picture films, video recordings, plays, manuscripts, patents and copyrights.

However, this Standard shall not be applied as the basis of measurement for:

(a) property held by lessees that is accounted for as investment property (see IAS 40 *Investment Property***);**

(b) investment property provided by lessors under operating leases (see IAS 40);

(c) biological assets held by lessees under finance leases (see IAS 41 *Agriculture***); or**

(d) biological assets provided by lessors under operating leases (see IAS 41).

3 This Standard applies to agreements that transfer the right to use assets even though substantial services by the lessor may be called for in connection with the operation or maintenance of such assets. This Standard does not apply to agreements that are contracts for services that do not transfer the right to use assets from one contracting party to the other.

Definitions

4 **The following terms are used in this Standard with the meanings specified:**

A *lease* **is an agreement whereby the lessor conveys to the lessee in return for a payment or series of payments the right to use an asset for an agreed period of time.**

A *finance lease* **is a lease that transfers substantially all the risks and rewards incidental to ownership of an asset. Title may or may not eventually be transferred.**

An *operating lease* **is a lease other than a finance lease.**

A *non-cancellable lease* **is a lease that is cancellable only:**

(a) upon the occurrence of some remote contingency;

(b) with the permission of the lessor;

(c) if the lessee enters into a new lease for the same or an equivalent asset with the same lessor; or

(d) upon payment by the lessee of such an additional amount that, at inception of the lease, continuation of the lease is reasonably certain.

The *inception* **of the lease is the earlier of the date of the lease agreement and the date of commitment by the parties to the principal provisions of the lease. As at this date:**

(a) a lease is classified as either an operating or a finance lease; and

(b) in the case of a finance lease, the amounts to be recognised at the commencement of the lease term are determined.

The *commencement of the lease term* **is the date from which the lessee is entitled to exercise its right to use the leased asset. It is the date of initial recognition of the lease (ie the recognition of the assets, liabilities, income or expenses resulting from the lease, as appropriate).**

The *lease term* **is the non-cancellable period for which the lessee has contracted to lease the asset together with any further terms for which the lessee has the option to continue to lease the asset, with or without further payment, when at the inception of the lease it is reasonably certain that the lessee will exercise the option.**

Minimum lease payments **are the payments over the lease term that the lessee is or can be required to make, excluding contingent rent, costs for services and taxes to be paid by and reimbursed to the lessor, together with:**

(a) for a lessee, any amounts guaranteed by the lessee or by a party related to the lessee; or

(b) for a lessor, any residual value guaranteed to the lessor by:

(i) the lessee;

(ii) a party related to the lessee; or

(iii) a third party unrelated to the lessor that is financially capable of discharging the obligations under the guarantee.

However, if the lessee has an option to purchase the asset at a price that is expected to be sufficiently lower than fair value at the date the option becomes exercisable for it to be reasonably certain, at the inception of the lease, that the option will be exercised, the minimum lease payments comprise the minimum payments payable over the lease term to the expected date of exercise of this purchase option and the payment required to exercise it.

Fair value **is the amount for which an asset could be exchanged, or a liability settled, between knowledgeable, willing parties in an arm's length transaction.**

Economic life **is either:**

(a) the period over which an asset is expected to be economically usable by one or more users; or

(b) the number of production or similar units expected to be obtained from the asset by one or more users.

Useful life **is the estimated remaining period, from the commencement of the lease term, without limitation by the lease term, over which the economic benefits embodied in the asset are expected to be consumed by the entity.**

Guaranteed residual value **is:**

(a) for a lessee, that part of the residual value that is guaranteed by the lessee or by a party related to the lessee (the amount of the guarantee being the maximum amount that could, in any event, become payable); and

(b) for a lessor, that part of the residual value that is guaranteed by the lessee or by a third party unrelated to the lessor that is financially capable of discharging the obligations under the guarantee.

Unguaranteed residual value **is that portion of the residual value of the leased asset, the realisation of which by the lessor is not assured or is guaranteed solely by a party related to the lessor.**

Initial direct costs **are incremental costs that are directly attributable to negotiating and arranging a lease, except for such costs incurred by manufacturer or dealer lessors.**

Gross investment in the lease **is the aggregate of:**

(a) the minimum lease payments receivable by the lessor under a finance lease, and

(b) any unguaranteed residual value accruing to the lessor.

Net investment in the lease **is the gross investment in the lease discounted at the interest rate implicit in the lease.**

Unearned finance income **is the difference between:**

(a) the gross investment in the lease, and

(b) the net investment in the lease.

The *interest rate implicit in the lease* **is the discount rate that, at the inception of the lease, causes the aggregate present value of (a) the minimum lease payments and (b) the unguaranteed residual value to be equal to the sum of (i) the fair value of the leased asset and (ii) any initial direct costs of the lessor.**

The *lessee's incremental borrowing rate of interest* **is the rate of interest the lessee would have to pay on a similar lease or, if that is not determinable, the rate that, at the inception of the lease, the lessee would incur to borrow over a similar term, and with a similar security, the funds necessary to purchase the asset.**

Contingent rent **is that portion of the lease payments that is not fixed in amount but is based on the future amount of a factor that changes other than with the passage of time (eg percentage of future sales, amount of future use, future price indices, future market rates of interest).**

5 A lease agreement or commitment may include a provision to adjust the lease payments for changes in the construction or acquisition cost of the leased property or for changes in some other measure of cost or value, such as general price levels, or in the lessor's costs of financing the lease, during the period between the inception of the lease and the commencement of the lease term. If so, the effect of any such changes shall be deemed to have taken place at the inception of the lease for the purposes of this Standard.

6 The definition of a lease includes contracts for the hire of an asset that contain a provision giving the hirer an option to acquire title to the asset upon the fulfilment of agreed conditions. These contracts are sometimes known as hire purchase contracts.

Classification of leases

7 The classification of leases adopted in this Standard is based on the extent to which risks and rewards incidental to ownership of a leased asset lie with the lessor or the lessee. Risks include the possibilities of losses from idle capacity or technological obsolescence and of variations in return because of changing economic conditions. Rewards may be represented by the expectation of profitable operation over the asset's economic life and of gain from appreciation in value or realisation of a residual value.

8 A lease is classified as a finance lease if it transfers substantially all the risks and rewards incidental to ownership. A lease is classified as an operating lease if it does not transfer substantially all the risks and rewards incidental to ownership.

9 Because the transaction between a lessor and a lessee is based on a lease agreement between them, it is appropriate to use consistent definitions. The application of these definitions to the differing circumstances of the lessor and lessee may result in the same lease being classified differently by them. For example, this may be the case if the lessor benefits from a residual value guarantee provided by a party unrelated to the lessee.

10 Whether a lease is a finance lease or an operating lease depends on the substance of the transaction rather than the form of the contract.* Examples of situations that individually or in combination would normally lead to a lease being classified as a finance lease are:

(a) the lease transfers ownership of the asset to the lessee by the end of the lease term;

* See also SIC-27 *Evaluating the Substance of Transactions Involving the Legal Form of a Lease.*

(b) the lessee has the option to purchase the asset at a price that is expected to be sufficiently lower than the fair value at the date the option becomes exercisable for it to be reasonably certain, at the inception of the lease, that the option will be exercised;

(c) the lease term is for the major part of the economic life of the asset even if title is not transferred;

(d) at the inception of the lease the present value of the minimum lease payments amounts to at least substantially all of the fair value of the leased asset; and

(e) the leased assets are of such a specialised nature that only the lessee can use them without major modifications.

11 Indicators of situations that individually or in combination could also lead to a lease being classified as a finance lease are:

(a) if the lessee can cancel the lease, the lessor's losses associated with the cancellation are borne by the lessee;

(b) gains or losses from the fluctuation in the fair value of the residual accrue to the lessee (for example, in the form of a rent rebate equalling most of the sales proceeds at the end of the lease); and

(c) the lessee has the ability to continue the lease for a secondary period at a rent that is substantially lower than market rent.

12 The examples and indicators in paragraphs 10 and 11 are not always conclusive. If it is clear from other features that the lease does not transfer substantially all risks and rewards incidental to ownership, the lease is classified as an operating lease. For example, this may be the case if ownership of the asset transfers at the end of the lease for a variable payment equal to its then fair value, or if there are contingent rents, as a result of which the lessee does not have substantially all such risks and rewards.

13 Lease classification is made at the inception of the lease. If at any time the lessee and the lessor agree to change the provisions of the lease, other than by renewing the lease, in a manner that would have resulted in a different classification of the lease under the criteria in paragraphs 7–12 if the changed terms had been in effect at the inception of the lease, the revised agreement is regarded as a new agreement over its term. However, changes in estimates (for example, changes in estimates of the economic life or of the residual value of the leased property), or changes in circumstances (for example, default by the lessee), do not give rise to a new classification of a lease for accounting purposes.

14 Leases of land and of buildings are classified as operating or finance leases in the same way as leases of other assets. However, a characteristic of land is that it normally has an indefinite economic life and, if title is not expected to pass to the lessee by the end of the lease term, the lessee normally does not receive substantially all of the risks and rewards incidental to ownership, in which case the lease of land will be an operating lease. A payment made on entering into or acquiring a leasehold that is accounted for as an operating lease represents prepaid lease payments that are amortised over the lease term in accordance with the pattern of benefits provided.

15 The land and buildings elements of a lease of land and buildings are considered separately for the purposes of lease classification. If title to both elements is expected to pass to the lessee by the end of the lease term, both elements are classified as a finance lease, whether analysed as one lease or as two leases, unless it is clear from other features that the lease does not transfer substantially all risks and rewards incidental to ownership of one or both elements. When the land has an indefinite economic life, the land element is normally classified as an operating lease unless title is expected to pass to the lessee by the end of the lease term, in accordance with paragraph 14. The buildings element is classified as a finance or operating lease in accordance with paragraphs 7–13.

16 Whenever necessary in order to classify and account for a lease of land and buildings, the minimum lease payments (including any lump-sum upfront payments) are allocated between the land and the buildings elements in proportion to the relative fair values of the leasehold interests in the land element and buildings element of the lease at the inception of the lease. If the lease payments cannot be allocated reliably between these two elements, the entire lease is classified as a finance lease, unless it is clear that both elements are operating leases, in which case the entire lease is classified as an operating lease.

17 For a lease of land and buildings in which the amount that would initially be recognised for the land element, in accordance with paragraph 20, is immaterial, the land and buildings may be treated as a single unit for the purpose of lease classification and classified as a finance or operating lease in accordance with paragraphs 7–13. In such a case, the economic life of the buildings is regarded as the economic life of the entire leased asset.

18 Separate measurement of the land and buildings elements is not required when the lessee's interest in both land and buildings is classified as an investment property in accordance with IAS 40 and the fair value model is adopted. Detailed calculations are required for this assessment only if the classification of one or both elements is otherwise uncertain.

19 In accordance with IAS 40, it is possible for a lessee to classify a property interest held under an operating lease as an investment property. If it does, the property interest is accounted for as if it were a finance lease and, in addition, the fair value model is used for the asset recognised. The lessee shall continue to account for the lease as a finance lease, even if a subsequent event changes the nature of the lessee's property interest so that it is no longer classified as investment property. This will be the case if, for example, the lessee:

(a) occupies the property, which is then transferred to owner-occupied property at a deemed cost equal to its fair value at the date of change in use; or

(b) grants a sublease that transfers substantially all of the risks and rewards incidental to ownership of the interest to an unrelated third party. Such a sublease is accounted for by the lessee as a finance lease to the third party, although it may be accounted for as an operating lease by the third party.

Leases in the financial statements of lessees

Finance leases

Initial recognition

20 **At the commencement of the lease term, lessees shall recognise finance leases as assets and liabilities in their balance sheets at amounts equal to the fair value of the leased property or, if lower, the present value of the minimum lease payments, each determined at the inception of the lease. The discount rate to be used in calculating the present value of the minimum lease payments is the interest rate implicit in the lease, if this is practicable to determine; if not, the lessee's incremental borrowing rate shall be used. Any initial direct costs of the lessee are added to the amount recognised as an asset.**

21 Transactions and other events are accounted for and presented in accordance with their substance and financial reality and not merely with legal form. Although the legal form of a lease agreement is that the lessee may acquire no legal title to the leased asset, in the case of finance leases the substance and financial reality are that the lessee acquires the economic benefits of the use of the leased asset for the major part of its economic life in return for entering into an obligation to pay for that right an amount approximating, at the inception of the lease, the fair value of the asset and the related finance charge.

22 If such lease transactions are not reflected in the lessee's balance sheet, the economic resources and the level of obligations of an entity are understated, thereby distorting financial ratios. Therefore, it is appropriate for a finance lease to be recognised in the lessee's balance sheet both as an asset and as an obligation to pay future lease payments. At the commencement of the lease term, the asset and the liability for the future lease payments are recognised in the balance sheet at the same amounts except for any initial direct costs of the lessee that are added to the amount recognised as an asset.

23 It is not appropriate for the liabilities for leased assets to be presented in the financial statements as a deduction from the leased assets. If for the presentation of liabilities on the face of the balance sheet a distinction is made between current and non-current liabilities, the same distinction is made for lease liabilities.

24 Initial direct costs are often incurred in connection with specific leasing activities, such as negotiating and securing leasing arrangements. The costs identified as directly attributable to activities performed by the lessee for a finance lease are added to the amount recognised as an asset.

Subsequent measurement

25 **Minimum lease payments shall be apportioned between the finance charge and the reduction of the outstanding liability. The finance charge shall be allocated to each period during the lease term so as to produce a constant periodic rate of interest on the remaining balance of the liability. Contingent rents shall be charged as expenses in the periods in which they are incurred.**

26 In practice, in allocating the finance charge to periods during the lease term, a lessee may use some form of approximation to simplify the calculation.

27 A finance lease gives rise to depreciation expense for depreciable assets as well as finance expense for each accounting period. The depreciation policy for depreciable leased assets shall be consistent with that for depreciable assets that are owned, and the depreciation recognised shall be calculated in accordance with IAS 16 ***Property, Plant and Equipment*** **and IAS 38** ***Intangible Assets*****. If there is no reasonable certainty that the lessee will obtain ownership by the end of the lease term, the asset shall be fully depreciated over the shorter of the lease term and its useful life.**

28 The depreciable amount of a leased asset is allocated to each accounting period during the period of expected use on a systematic basis consistent with the depreciation policy the lessee adopts for depreciable assets that are owned. If there is reasonable certainty that the lessee will obtain ownership by the end of the lease term, the period of expected use is the useful life of the asset; otherwise the asset is depreciated over the shorter of the lease term and its useful life.

29 The sum of the depreciation expense for the asset and the finance expense for the period is rarely the same as the lease payments payable for the period, and it is, therefore, inappropriate simply to recognise the lease payments payable as an expense. Accordingly, the asset and the related liability are unlikely to be equal in amount after the commencement of the lease term.

30 To determine whether a leased asset has become impaired, an entity applies IAS 36 *Impairment of Assets*.

31 Lessees shall, in addition to meeting the requirements of IAS 32 ***Financial Instruments: Disclosure and Presentation*****, make the following disclosures for finance leases:**

(a) for each class of asset, the net carrying amount at the balance sheet date.

(b) a reconciliation between the total of future minimum lease payments at the balance sheet date, and their present value. In addition, an entity shall disclose the total of future minimum lease payments at the balance sheet date, and their present value, for each of the following periods:

(i) not later than one year;

(ii) later than one year and not later than five years;

(iii) later than five years.

(c) contingent rents recognised as an expense in the period.

(d) the total of future minimum sublease payments expected to be received under non-cancellable subleases at the balance sheet date.

(e) a general description of the lessee's material leasing arrangements including, but not limited to, the following:

(i) the basis on which contingent rent payable is determined;

(ii) the existence and terms of renewal or purchase options and escalation clauses; and

(iii) restrictions imposed by lease arrangements, such as those concerning dividends, additional debt, and further leasing.

32 In addition, the requirements for disclosure in accordance with IAS 16, IAS 36, IAS 38, IAS 40 and IAS 41 apply to lessees for assets leased under finance leases.

Operating leases

33 Lease payments under an operating lease shall be recognised as an expense on a straight-line basis over the lease term unless another systematic basis is more representative of the time pattern of the user's benefit.*

34 For operating leases, lease payments (excluding costs for services such as insurance and maintenance) are recognised as an expense on a straight-line basis unless another systematic basis is representative of the time pattern of the user's benefit, even if the payments are not on that basis.

35 Lessees shall, in addition to meeting the requirements of IAS 32, make the following disclosures for operating leases:

(a) the total of future minimum lease payments under non-cancellable operating leases for each of the following periods:

(i) not later than one year;

(ii) later than one year and not later than five years;

(iii) later than five years.

(b) the total of future minimum sublease payments expected to be received under non-cancellable subleases at the balance sheet date.

(c) lease and sublease payments recognised as an expense in the period, with separate amounts for minimum lease payments, contingent rents, and sublease payments.

(d) a general description of the lessee's significant leasing arrangements including, but not limited to, the following:

(i) the basis on which contingent rent payable is determined;

(ii) the existence and terms of renewal or purchase options and escalation clauses; and

(iii) restrictions imposed by lease arrangements, such as those concerning dividends, additional debt and further leasing.

* See also SIC-15 *Operating Leases—Incentives.*

Leases in the financial statements of lessors

Finance leases

Initial recognition

36 **Lessors shall recognise assets held under a finance lease in their balance sheets and present them as a receivable at an amount equal to the net investment in the lease.**

37 Under a finance lease substantially all the risks and rewards incidental to legal ownership are transferred by the lessor, and thus the lease payment receivable is treated by the lessor as repayment of principal and finance income to reimburse and reward the lessor for its investment and services.

38 Initial direct costs are often incurred by lessors and include amounts such as commissions, legal fees and internal costs that are incremental and directly attributable to negotiating and arranging a lease. They exclude general overheads such as those incurred by a sales and marketing team. For finance leases other than those involving manufacturer or dealer lessors, initial direct costs are included in the initial measurement of the finance lease receivable and reduce the amount of income recognised over the lease term. The interest rate implicit in the lease is defined in such a way that the initial direct costs are included automatically in the finance lease receivable; there is no need to add them separately. Costs incurred by manufacturer or dealer lessors in connection with negotiating and arranging a lease are excluded from the definition of initial direct costs. As a result, they are excluded from the net investment in the lease and are recognised as an expense when the selling profit is recognised, which for a finance lease is normally at the commencement of the lease term.

Subsequent measurement

39 **The recognition of finance income shall be based on a pattern reflecting a constant periodic rate of return on the lessor's net investment in the finance lease.**

40 A lessor aims to allocate finance income over the lease term on a systematic and rational basis. This income allocation is based on a pattern reflecting a constant periodic return on the lessor's net investment in the finance lease. Lease payments relating to the period, excluding costs for services, are applied against the gross investment in the lease to reduce both the principal and the unearned finance income.

41 Estimated unguaranteed residual values used in computing the lessor's gross investment in a lease are reviewed regularly. If there has been a reduction in the estimated unguaranteed residual value, the income allocation over the lease term is revised and any reduction in respect of amounts accrued is recognised immediately.

41A An asset under a finance lease that is classified as held for sale (or included in a disposal group that is classified as held for sale) in accordance with IFRS 5 *Non-current Assets Held for Sale and Discontinued Operations* shall be accounted for in accordance with that IFRS.

42 **Manufacturer or dealer lessors shall recognise selling profit or loss in the period, in accordance with the policy followed by the entity for outright sales. If artificially low rates of interest are quoted, selling profit shall be restricted to that which would apply if a market rate of interest were charged. Costs incurred by manufacturer or dealer lessors in connection with negotiating and arranging a lease shall be recognised as an expense when the selling profit is recognised.**

43 Manufacturers or dealers often offer to customers the choice of either buying or leasing an asset. A finance lease of an asset by a manufacturer or dealer lessor gives rise to two types of income:

(a) profit or loss equivalent to the profit or loss resulting from an outright sale of the asset being leased, at normal selling prices, reflecting any applicable volume or trade discounts; and

(b) finance income over the lease term.

44 The sales revenue recognised at the commencement of the lease term by a manufacturer or dealer lessor is the fair value of the asset, or, if lower, the present value of the minimum lease payments accruing to the lessor, computed at a market rate of interest. The cost of sale recognised at the commencement of the lease term is the cost, or carrying amount if different, of the leased property less the present value of the unguaranteed residual value. The difference between the sales revenue and the cost of sale is the selling profit, which is recognised in accordance with the entity's policy for outright sales.

45 Manufacturer or dealer lessors sometimes quote artificially low rates of interest in order to attract customers. The use of such a rate would result in an excessive portion of the total income from the transaction being recognised at the time of sale. If artificially low rates of interest are quoted, selling profit is restricted to that which would apply if a market rate of interest were charged.

46 Costs incurred by a manufacturer or dealer lessor in connection with negotiating and arranging a finance lease are recognised as an expense at the commencement of the lease term because they are mainly related to earning the manufacturer's or dealer's selling profit.

47 **Lessors shall, in addition to meeting the requirements in IAS 32, disclose the following for finance leases:**

(a) a reconciliation between the gross investment in the lease at the balance sheet date, and the present value of minimum lease payments receivable at the balance sheet date. In addition, an entity shall disclose the gross investment in the lease and the present value of minimum lease payments receivable at the balance sheet date, for each of the following periods:

(i) not later than one year;

(ii) later than one year and not later than five years;

(iii) later than five years.

(b) unearned finance income.

(c) **the unguaranteed residual values accruing to the benefit of the lessor.**

(d) **the accumulated allowance for uncollectible minimum lease payments receivable.**

(e) **contingent rents recognised as income in the period.**

(f) **a general description of the lessor's material leasing arrangements.**

48 As an indicator of growth it is often useful also to disclose the gross investment less unearned income in new business added during the period, after deducting the relevant amounts for cancelled leases.

Operating leases

49 Lessors shall present assets subject to operating leases in their balance sheets according to the nature of the asset.

50 Lease income from operating leases shall be recognised in income on a straight-line basis over the lease term, unless another systematic basis is more representative of the time pattern in which use benefit derived from the leased asset is diminished.*

51 Costs, including depreciation, incurred in earning the lease income are recognised as an expense. Lease income (excluding receipts for services provided such as insurance and maintenance) is recognised on a straight-line basis over the lease term even if the receipts are not on such a basis, unless another systematic basis is more representative of the time pattern in which use benefit derived from the leased asset is diminished.

52 Initial direct costs incurred by lessors in negotiating and arranging an operating lease shall be added to the carrying amount of the leased asset and recognised as an expense over the lease term on the same basis as the lease income.

53 The depreciation policy for depreciable leased assets shall be consistent with the lessor's normal depreciation policy for similar assets, and depreciation shall be calculated in accordance with IAS 16 and IAS 38.

54 To determine whether a leased asset has become impaired, an entity applies IAS 36.

55 A manufacturer or dealer lessor does not recognise any selling profit on entering into an operating lease because it is not the equivalent of a sale.

56 Lessors shall, in addition to meeting the requirements of IAS 32, disclose the following for operating leases:

(a) **the future minimum lease payments under non-cancellable operating leases in the aggregate and for each of the following periods:**

(i) **not later than one year;**

(ii) **later than one year and not later than five years;**

(iii) **later than five years.**

* See also SIC-15 *Operating Leases—Incentives.*

(b) total contingent rents recognised as income in the period.

(c) a general description of the lessor's leasing arrangements.

57 In addition, the disclosure requirements in IAS 16, IAS 36, IAS 38, IAS 40 and IAS 41 apply to lessors for assets provided under operating leases.

Sale and leaseback transactions

58 A sale and leaseback transaction involves the sale of an asset and the leasing back of the same asset. The lease payment and the sale price are usually interdependent because they are negotiated as a package. The accounting treatment of a sale and leaseback transaction depends upon the type of lease involved.

59 If a sale and leaseback transaction results in a finance lease, any excess of sales proceeds over the carrying amount shall not be immediately recognised as income by a seller-lessee. Instead, it shall be deferred and amortised over the lease term.

60 If the leaseback is a finance lease, the transaction is a means whereby the lessor provides finance to the lessee, with the asset as security. For this reason it is not appropriate to regard an excess of sales proceeds over the carrying amount as income. Such excess is deferred and amortised over the lease term.

61 If a sale and leaseback transaction results in an operating lease, and it is clear that the transaction is established at fair value, any profit or loss shall be recognised immediately. If the sale price is below fair value, any profit or loss shall be recognised immediately except that, if the loss is compensated for by future lease payments at below market price, it shall be deferred and amortised in proportion to the lease payments over the period for which the asset is expected to be used. If the sale price is above fair value, the excess over fair value shall be deferred and amortised over the period for which the asset is expected to be used.

62 If the leaseback is an operating lease, and the lease payments and the sale price are at fair value, there has in effect been a normal sale transaction and any profit or loss is recognised immediately.

63 For operating leases, if the fair value at the time of a sale and leaseback transaction is less than the carrying amount of the asset, a loss equal to the amount of the difference between the carrying amount and fair value shall be recognised immediately.

64 For finance leases, no such adjustment is necessary unless there has been an impairment in value, in which case the carrying amount is reduced to recoverable amount in accordance with IAS 36.

65 Disclosure requirements for lessees and lessors apply equally to sale and leaseback transactions. The required description of material leasing arrangements leads to disclosure of unique or unusual provisions of the agreement or terms of the sale and leaseback transactions.

66 Sale and leaseback transactions may trigger the separate disclosure criteria in IAS 1 *Presentation of Financial Statements*.

Transitional provisions

67 **Subject to paragraph 68, retrospective application of this Standard is encouraged but not required. If the Standard is not applied retrospectively, the balance of any pre-existing finance lease is deemed to have been properly determined by the lessor and shall be accounted for thereafter in accordance with the provisions of this Standard.**

68 **An entity that has previously applied IAS 17 (revised 1997) shall apply the amendments made by this Standard retrospectively for all leases or, if IAS 17 (revised 1997) was not applied retrospectively, for all leases entered into since it first applied that Standard.**

Effective date

69 **An entity shall apply this Standard for annual periods beginning on or after 1 January 2005. Earlier application is encouraged. If an entity applies this Standard for a period beginning before 1 January 2005, it shall disclose that fact.**

Withdrawal of IAS 17 (revised 1997)

70 This Standard supersedes IAS 17 *Leases* (revised in 1997).

Appendix
Amendments to other pronouncements

The amendments in this appendix shall be applied for annual periods beginning on or after 1 January 2005. If an entity applies this Standard for an earlier period, these amendments shall be applied for that earlier period.

* * * * *

The amendments contained in this appendix when this Standard was issued in 2003 have been incorporated into the relevant pronouncements published in this volume.

Approval of IAS 17 by the Board

International Accounting Standard 17 *Leases* was approved for issue by the fourteen members of the International Accounting Standards Board.

Sir David Tweedie	Chairman
Thomas E Jones	Vice-Chairman
Mary E Barth	
Hans-Georg Bruns	
Anthony T Cope	
Robert P Garnett	
Gilbert Gélard	
James J Leisenring	
Warren J McGregor	
Patricia L O'Malley	
Harry K Schmid	
John T Smith	
Geoffrey Whittington	
Tatsumi Yamada	

Basis for Conclusions

This Basis for Conclusions accompanies, but is not part of, IAS 17.

Introduction

BC1 This Basis for Conclusions summarises the International Accounting Standards Board's considerations in reaching its conclusions on revising IAS 17 *Leases* in 2003. Individual Board members gave greater weight to some factors than to others.

BC2 In July 2001 the Board announced that, as part of its initial agenda of technical projects, it would undertake a project to improve a number of Standards, including IAS 17. The project was undertaken in the light of queries and criticisms raised in relation to the Standards by securities regulators, professional accountants and other interested parties. The objectives of the Improvements project were to reduce or eliminate alternatives, redundancies and conflicts within existing Standards, to deal with some convergence issues and to make other improvements. In May 2002 the Board published its proposals in an Exposure Draft of *Improvements to International Accounting Standards*, with a comment deadline of 16 September 2002. The Board received over 160 comment letters on the Exposure Draft.

BC3 Because the Board's intention was not to reconsider the fundamental approach to the accounting for leases established by IAS 17, this Basis for Conclusions does not discuss requirements in IAS 17 that the Board has not reconsidered.

Classification of leases—leases of land and buildings

BC4 Paragraph 14 of the Standard requires a lease of land with an indefinite economic life to be normally classified as an operating lease, unless title is expected to pass to the lessee by the end of the lease term. The previous version of IAS 17 was not explicit about how to classify a lease of land and buildings.

BC5 This is a matter of concern in countries where property rights are obtained under long-term leases and the substance of those leases differs little from buying a property. Therefore, the Board decided to deal with this matter in its Improvements project and not to defer its resolution until the more fundamental project on leases was completed.

BC6 The Board noted that two approaches are applied in practice. The first is to treat such a lease as a single unit and to classify it as an operating lease in its entirety. The second is to split the lease into two elements–a lease of land and a lease of buildings. The Board decided that the first approach does not adequately reflect the assets controlled by the entity or their usage and financing. It is also inconsistent with the classification and the measurement of other leases. Therefore, the Board rejected the first approach of classifying a lease of land and buildings as an operating lease in its entirety.

BC7 The Board agreed on the second approach of splitting the lease into two elements–a lease of land and a lease of buildings. The land element would normally be classified as an operating lease in accordance with paragraph 14 of the revised Standard and the buildings element classified as an operating or finance lease by applying the conditions in paragraphs 7–13. The Board noted that generally accepted accounting principles in Australia, Canada and the United States all explicitly require a lease of land and buildings to be split into two elements.

BC8 The Board also discussed a third approach, namely whether to delete the requirement (in paragraph 14 of the Standard) normally to classify a lease of land as an operating lease when title does not pass at the end of the lease and to require such a lease to be classified as a finance lease when all other conditions for finance lease classification in the Standard are met. The Board noted that such an accounting treatment would conflict with the criteria for lease classification in the Standard, which are based on the extent to which the risks and rewards incidental to ownership of a leased asset lie with the lessor or the lessee. Indeed, land normally has an indefinite economic life and hence there are significant risks and rewards associated with the land at the end of the lease term, which do not pass to the lessee. Therefore, the Board rejected this approach.

Allocation of minimum lease payments between land and buildings

BC9 The Exposure Draft proposed that the allocation of the minimum lease payments between land and buildings should be made in proportion to their relative fair values at the inception of the lease. Respondents to the Exposure Draft questioned whether the allocation basis referred to the land and buildings components of the fair value of the property or the fair value of those components to the extent they were the subject of the lease.

BC10 The Board noted that an allocation of the minimum lease payments by reference to the relative fair values of the land and buildings would not reflect the fact that land often has an indefinite economic life, and therefore would be expected to maintain its value beyond the lease term. In contrast, the future economic benefits of a building are likely to be used up, at the least to some extent, over the lease term. Therefore, it would be reasonable to expect that the lease payments relating to the building would be set at a level that enabled the lessor not only to make a return on initial investment, but also to recoup the value of the building used up over the term of the lease. In the case of land, the lessor would not normally need compensation for using up the land.

BC11 Therefore, the Board decided to clarify in the Standard that the allocation of the minimum lease payments is weighted to reflect their role in compensating the lessor, and not by reference to the relative fair values of the land and buildings. In other words, the weighting should reflect the lessee's leasehold interest in the land and the buildings. In the extreme case that a building is fully depreciated over the lease term, the minimum lease payments would need to be weighted to provide a return plus the full depreciation of the building's value at the inception of the lease. The leasehold interest in the land would, assuming a residual value that equals its value at the inception of the lease, have a weighting that reflects only a return on the initial investment.

Impracticability of split between land and buildings

BC12 A question that arises is how to treat leases for which it is not possible to measure the two elements reliably (eg because similar land and buildings are not sold or leased separately). One possibility would be to classify the entire lease as a finance lease. This would prevent a lessee from avoiding finance lease treatment for the buildings by asserting that it cannot separately measure the two elements. However, it may be apparent from the circumstances that classifying the entire lease as a finance lease is not representationally faithful. In view of this, the Board decided that when it is not possible to measure the two elements reliably, the entire lease should be classified as a finance lease unless it is clear that both elements should be classified as an operating lease.

Exception to the requirement to separate the land and buildings elements

BC13 The Board discussed whether to allow or require an exception from the requirement to separate the land and buildings elements in cases in which the present value of the land element at the inception of the lease is small in relation to the value of the entire lease. In such cases the benefits of separating the lease into two elements and accounting for each separately may not outweigh the costs. The Board noted that generally accepted accounting principles in Australia, Canada and the United States allow or require such leases to be classified and accounted for as a single unit, with finance lease treatment being used when the relevant criteria are met. The Board decided to allow land and buildings to be treated as a single unit when the land element is immaterial.

BC14 Some respondents to the Exposure Draft requested guidance on how small the relative value of the land element needs to be in relation to the total value of the lease. The Board decided not to introduce a bright line such as a specific percentage threshold. The Board decided that the normal provisions on materiality should apply.

Transitional provisions

BC15 The Board decided that the requirement to separate the land and buildings elements in a lease of land and buildings should be applied retrospectively. It noted that there will be cases when it will be impracticable to reassess the treatment of these leases retrospectively, because doing so requires estimating what the fair value of the two elements was at the inception of the lease, which may have been many years before. The Board also noted that IAS 8 *Accounting Policies, Changes in Accounting Estimates and Errors* contains guidance on when it is impracticable to apply retrospectively a change in accounting policy and therefore decided not to provide specific transitional provisions for the implementation of this revision to IAS 17.

Inception of the lease and commencement of the lease term

BC16 The previous version of IAS 17 did not define the commencement of the lease term. It implicitly assumed that commencement (when the lease begins) and inception (when the agreement is entered into) are simultaneous. Some respondents questioned what should happen if there is a time lag between the two dates, particularly if the amounts change–for example, because the asset is under construction and the final cost is not known at inception. The Standard now specifies that recognition takes place at commencement, based on values measured at inception. However, if the lease is adjusted for changes in the lessor's costs between the inception of the lease and the commencement of the lease term, the effect of any such changes is deemed to have taken place at inception. These revisions are consistent with generally accepted accounting principles in Australia, Canada and the United States, and are consistent with the present accounting treatment of most ordinary purchases and sales.

BC17 In agreeing on this treatment, the Board noted that measurement at commencement would have been more satisfactory in principle. However, this cannot be done properly within the framework of IAS 17 because the Standard generally requires a finance lease receivable or payable to be recognised at an amount based on the fair value of the asset, which is inappropriate at any date after inception.

Leases in the financial statements of lessors other than manufacturers and dealers

BC18 Lessors may incur direct costs in negotiating a lease, such as commissions, brokers' fees and legal fees. The previous version of IAS 17 contained a choice on how to account for such costs–they might be either charged as an expense as incurred or allocated over the lease term. The choice of treatment applied to operating and finance leases. In the case of a finance lease, paragraph 33 of the previous version of IAS 17 stated that allocation over the lease term might be achieved by recognising the cost as an expense and, in the same period, recognising an equal amount of unearned finance income.

BC19 The Board decided that this treatment was not in accordance with the *Framework for the Preparation and Presentation of Financial Statements*. Its effect was to recognise some future finance income as income and an asset at the commencement of the lease term. However, at that date, the *Framework*'s definitions of income and assets are not met. Therefore, the Board decided that if direct costs incurred by lessors are to be allocated over the lease term, this should be achieved by including them in the carrying amount of the lease asset.

BC20 The Board noted that standard-setters in Australia, Canada, France, Japan, the United Kingdom and the United States either permit or require initial direct costs to be allocated over the lease term. The Board also noted that other Standards permit or require the recognition of a range of similar costs in the carrying amount of assets, generally subject to those costs being directly attributable to the acquisition of the asset in question. Hence, for reasons of convergence and comparability with other Standards, the Board decided to require initial direct costs to be included in the carrying amount of the lease asset.

BC21 For consistency with other Standards, in particular IAS 39 *Financial Instruments: Recognition and Measurement*, the Board decided that recognition in the carrying amount of assets should be restricted to costs that are incremental and directly attributable to negotiating and arranging a lease.

Implementation Guidance

This guidance accompanies, but is not part of, IAS 17.

Illustrative examples of sale and leaseback transactions that result in operating leases

A sale and leaseback transaction that results in an operating lease may give rise to profit or a loss, the determination and treatment of which depends on the leased asset's carrying amount, fair value and selling price. The table below shows the requirements of the Standard in various circumstances.

Sale price at fair value (paragraph 61)	**Carrying amount equal to fair value**	**Carrying amount less than fair value**	**Carrying amount above fair value**
Profit	no profit	recognise profit immediately	not applicable
Loss	no loss	not applicable	recognise loss immediately

Sale price below fair value (paragraph 61)			
Profit	no profit	recognise profit immediately	no profit (note 1)
Loss <u>not</u> compensated for by future lease payments at below market price	recognise loss immediately	recognise loss immediately	(note 1)
Loss compensated for by future lease payments at below market price	defer and amortise loss	defer and amortise loss	(note 1)

Sale price above fair value (paragraph 61)			
Profit	defer and amortise profit	defer and amortise excess profit (note 3)	defer and amortise profit (note 2)
Loss	no loss	no loss	(note 1)

Note 1 These parts of the table represent circumstances dealt with in paragraph 63 of the Standard. Paragraph 63 requires the carrying amount of an asset to be written down to fair value where it is subject to a sale and leaseback.

Note 2 Profit is the difference between fair value and sale price because the carrying amount would have been written down to fair value in accordance with paragraph 63.

Note 3 The excess profit (the excess of sale price over fair value) is deferred and amortised over the period for which the asset is expected to be used.
Any excess of fair value over carrying amount is recognised immediately.

Table of Concordance

This table shows how the contents of the superseded version of IAS 17 and the current version of IAS 17 correspond. Paragraphs are treated as corresponding if they broadly address the same matter even though the guidance may differ.

Superseded IAS 17 paragraph	Current IAS 17 paragraph
Objective	1
1	2
2	3
3	4
4	6
5	7
6	8
7	9
8	10
9	11
10	13
11	14
12	20
13	21
14	22
15	23
16	24
17	25
18	26
19	27
20	28
21	29
22	30
23	31
24	32
25	33
26	34
27	35
28	36
29	37
30	39
31	40
32	41
33	38
34	42
35	43
36	44
37	45
38	46
39	47
40	48
41	49
42	50
43	51
44	52
45	53
46	54
47	55
48	56
48A	57
49	58
50	59
51	60
52	61
53	62
54	63
55	64
56	65
57	66
58	67
59	69
60	70
None	5
None	12
None	15–19
None	68
Appendix A	Implementation Guidance

International Accounting Standard 18

Revenue

This version includes amendments resulting from new and amended IFRSs issued up to 31 December 2004.

The following Interpretations relate to IAS 18:

- SIC-27 *Evaluating the Substance of Transactions in the Legal Form of a Lease*
- SIC-31 *Revenue—Barter Transactions Involving Advertising Services*

CONTENTS

paragraphs

INTERNATIONAL ACCOUNTING STANDARD 18 REVENUE

International Accounting Standard 18 *Revenue* (IAS 18) is set out in paragraphs 1–37. All the paragraphs have equal authority but retain the IASC format of the Standard when it was adopted by the IASB. IAS 18 should be read in the context of its objective, the *Preface to International Financial Reporting Standards* and the *Framework for the Preparation and Presentation of Financial Statements*. IAS 8 *Accounting Policies, Changes in Accounting Estimates and Errors* provides a basis for selecting and applying accounting policies in the absence of explicit guidance.

International Accounting Standard 18 Revenue

Objective

Income is defined in the *Framework for the Preparation and Presentation of Financial Statements* as increases in economic benefits during the accounting period in the form of inflows or enhancements of assets or decreases of liabilities that result in increases in equity, other than those relating to contributions from equity participants. Income encompasses both revenue and gains. Revenue is income that arises in the course of ordinary activities of an entity and is referred to by a variety of different names including sales, fees, interest, dividends and royalties. The objective of this Standard is to prescribe the accounting treatment of revenue arising from certain types of transactions and events.

The primary issue in accounting for revenue is determining when to recognise revenue. Revenue is recognised when it is probable that future economic benefits will flow to the entity and these benefits can be measured reliably. This Standard identifies the circumstances in which these criteria will be met and, therefore, revenue will be recognised. It also provides practical guidance on the application of these criteria.

Scope

1 **This Standard shall be applied in accounting for revenue arising from the following transactions and events:**

(a) the sale of goods;

(b) the rendering of services; and

(c) the use by others of entity assets yielding interest, royalties and dividends.

2 This Standard supersedes IAS 18 *Revenue Recognition* approved in 1982.

3 Goods includes goods produced by the entity for the purpose of sale and goods purchased for resale, such as merchandise purchased by a retailer or land and other property held for resale.

4 The rendering of services typically involves the performance by the entity of a contractually agreed task over an agreed period of time. The services may be rendered within a single period or over more than one period. Some contracts for the rendering of services are directly related to construction contracts, for example, those for the services of project managers and architects. Revenue arising from these contracts is not dealt with in this Standard but is dealt with in accordance with the requirements for construction contracts as specified in IAS 11 *Construction Contracts*.

5 The use by others of entity assets gives rise to revenue in the form of:

(a) interest–charges for the use of cash or cash equivalents or amounts due to the entity;

(b) royalties–charges for the use of long-term assets of the entity, for example, patents, trademarks, copyrights and computer software; and

(c) dividends–distributions of profits to holders of equity investments in proportion to their holdings of a particular class of capital.

6 This Standard does not deal with revenue arising from:

(a) lease agreements (see IAS 17 *Leases*);

(b) dividends arising from investments which are accounted for under the equity method (see IAS 28 *Investments in Associates*);

(c) insurance contracts within the scope of IFRS 4 *Insurance Contracts*;

(d) changes in the fair value of financial assets and financial liabilities or their disposal (see IAS 39 *Financial Instruments: Recognition and Measurement*);

(e) changes in the value of other current assets;

(f) initial recognition and from changes in the fair value of biological assets related to agricultural activity (see IAS 41 *Agriculture*);

(g) initial recognition of agricultural produce (see IAS 41); and

(h) the extraction of mineral ores.

Definitions

7 **The following terms are used in this Standard with the meanings specified:**

Revenue **is the gross inflow of economic benefits during the period arising in the course of the ordinary activities of an entity when those inflows result in increases in equity, other than increases relating to contributions from equity participants.**

Fair value **is the amount for which an asset could be exchanged, or a liability settled, between knowledgeable, willing parties in an arm's length transaction.**

8 Revenue includes only the gross inflows of economic benefits received and receivable by the entity on its own account. Amounts collected on behalf of third parties such as sales taxes, goods and services taxes and value added taxes are not economic benefits which flow to the entity and do not result in increases in equity. Therefore, they are excluded from revenue. Similarly, in an agency relationship, the gross inflows of economic benefits include amounts collected on behalf of the principal and which do not result in increases in equity for the entity. The amounts collected on behalf of the principal are not revenue. Instead, revenue is the amount of commission.

Measurement of revenue

9 **Revenue shall be measured at the fair value of the consideration received or receivable.***

* See also SIC-31 *Revenue–Barter Transactions Involving Advertising Services*

10 The amount of revenue arising on a transaction is usually determined by agreement between the entity and the buyer or user of the asset. It is measured at the fair value of the consideration received or receivable taking into account the amount of any trade discounts and volume rebates allowed by the entity.

11 In most cases, the consideration is in the form of cash or cash equivalents and the amount of revenue is the amount of cash or cash equivalents received or receivable. However, when the inflow of cash or cash equivalents is deferred, the fair value of the consideration may be less than the nominal amount of cash received or receivable. For example, an entity may provide interest free credit to the buyer or accept a note receivable bearing a below-market interest rate from the buyer as consideration for the sale of goods. When the arrangement effectively constitutes a financing transaction, the fair value of the consideration is determined by discounting all future receipts using an imputed rate of interest. The imputed rate of interest is the more clearly determinable of either:

(a) the prevailing rate for a similar instrument of an issuer with a similar credit rating; or

(b) a rate of interest that discounts the nominal amount of the instrument to the current cash sales price of the goods or services.

The difference between the fair value and the nominal amount of the consideration is recognised as interest revenue in accordance with paragraphs 29 and 30 and in accordance with IAS 39 *Financial Instruments: Recognition and Measurement.*

12 When goods or services are exchanged or swapped for goods or services which are of a similar nature and value, the exchange is not regarded as a transaction which generates revenue. This is often the case with commodities like oil or milk where suppliers exchange or swap inventories in various locations to fulfil demand on a timely basis in a particular location. When goods are sold or services are rendered in exchange for dissimilar goods or services, the exchange is regarded as a transaction which generates revenue. The revenue is measured at the fair value of the goods or services received, adjusted by the amount of any cash or cash equivalents transferred. When the fair value of the goods or services received cannot be measured reliably, the revenue is measured at the fair value of the goods or services given up, adjusted by the amount of any cash or cash equivalents transferred.

Identification of the transaction

13 The recognition criteria in this Standard are usually applied separately to each transaction. However, in certain circumstances, it is necessary to apply the recognition criteria to the separately identifiable components of a single transaction in order to reflect the substance of the transaction. For example, when the selling price of a product includes an identifiable amount for subsequent servicing, that amount is deferred and recognised as revenue over the period during which the service is performed. Conversely, the recognition criteria are applied to two or more transactions together when they are linked in such a way that the commercial effect cannot be understood without reference to the series of transactions as a whole. For example, an entity may sell goods and, at the

same time, enter into a separate agreement to repurchase the goods at a later date, thus negating the substantive effect of the transaction; in such a case, the two transactions are dealt with together.

Sale of goods

14 **Revenue from the sale of goods shall be recognised when all the following conditions have been satisfied:**

(a) the entity has transferred to the buyer the significant risks and rewards of ownership of the goods;

(b) the entity retains neither continuing managerial involvement to the degree usually associated with ownership nor effective control over the goods sold;

(c) the amount of revenue can be measured reliably;

(d) it is probable that the economic benefits associated with the transaction will flow to the entity; and

(e) the costs incurred or to be incurred in respect of the transaction can be measured reliably.

15 The assessment of when an entity has transferred the significant risks and rewards of ownership to the buyer requires an examination of the circumstances of the transaction. In most cases, the transfer of the risks and rewards of ownership coincides with the transfer of the legal title or the passing of possession to the buyer. This is the case for most retail sales. In other cases, the transfer of risks and rewards of ownership occurs at a different time from the transfer of legal title or the passing of possession.

16 If the entity retains significant risks of ownership, the transaction is not a sale and revenue is not recognised. An entity may retain a significant risk of ownership in a number of ways. Examples of situations in which the entity may retain the significant risks and rewards of ownership are:

(a) when the entity retains an obligation for unsatisfactory performance not covered by normal warranty provisions;

(b) when the receipt of the revenue from a particular sale is contingent on the derivation of revenue by the buyer from its sale of the goods;

(c) when the goods are shipped subject to installation and the installation is a significant part of the contract which has not yet been completed by the entity; and

(d) when the buyer has the right to rescind the purchase for a reason specified in the sales contract and the entity is uncertain about the probability of return.

17 If an entity retains only an insignificant risk of ownership, the transaction is a sale and revenue is recognised. For example, a seller may retain the legal title to the goods solely to protect the collectibility of the amount due. In such a case, if the entity has transferred the significant risks and rewards of ownership, the transaction is a sale and revenue is recognised. Another example of an entity retaining only an insignificant risk of ownership may be a retail sale when a

refund is offered if the customer is not satisfied. Revenue in such cases is recognised at the time of sale provided the seller can reliably estimate future returns and recognises a liability for returns based on previous experience and other relevant factors.

18 Revenue is recognised only when it is probable that the economic benefits associated with the transaction will flow to the entity. In some cases, this may not be probable until the consideration is received or until an uncertainty is removed. For example, it may be uncertain that a foreign governmental authority will grant permission to remit the consideration from a sale in a foreign country. When the permission is granted, the uncertainty is removed and revenue is recognised. However, when an uncertainty arises about the collectibility of an amount already included in revenue, the uncollectible amount or the amount in respect of which recovery has ceased to be probable is recognised as an expense, rather than as an adjustment of the amount of revenue originally recognised.

19 Revenue and expenses that relate to the same transaction or other event are recognised simultaneously; this process is commonly referred to as the matching of revenues and expenses. Expenses, including warranties and other costs to be incurred after the shipment of the goods can normally be measured reliably when the other conditions for the recognition of revenue have been satisfied. However, revenue cannot be recognised when the expenses cannot be measured reliably; in such circumstances, any consideration already received for the sale of the goods is recognised as a liability.

Rendering of services

20 When the outcome of a transaction involving the rendering of services can be estimated reliably, revenue associated with the transaction shall be recognised by reference to the stage of completion of the transaction at the balance sheet date. The outcome of a transaction can be estimated reliably when all the following conditions are satisfied:

(a) the amount of revenue can be measured reliably;

(b) it is probable that the economic benefits associated with the transaction will flow to the entity;

(c) the stage of completion of the transaction at the balance sheet date can be measured reliably; and

(d) the costs incurred for the transaction and the costs to complete the transaction can be measured reliably.*

21 The recognition of revenue by reference to the stage of completion of a transaction is often referred to as the percentage of completion method. Under this method, revenue is recognised in the accounting periods in which the services are rendered. The recognition of revenue on this basis provides useful information on the extent of service activity and performance during a period. IAS 11 *Construction Contracts* also requires the recognition of revenue on this basis. The requirements

* See also SIC-27 *Evaluating the Substance of Transactions in the Legal Form of a Lease* and SIC-31 *Revenue—Barter Transactions Involving Advertising Services*

of that Standard are generally applicable to the recognition of revenue and the associated expenses for a transaction involving the rendering of services.

22 Revenue is recognised only when it is probable that the economic benefits associated with the transaction will flow to the entity. However, when an uncertainty arises about the collectibility of an amount already included in revenue, the uncollectible amount, or the amount in respect of which recovery has ceased to be probable, is recognised as an expense, rather than as an adjustment of the amount of revenue originally recognised.

23 An entity is generally able to make reliable estimates after it has agreed to the following with the other parties to the transaction:

(a) each party's enforceable rights regarding the service to be provided and received by the parties;

(b) the consideration to be exchanged; and

(c) the manner and terms of settlement.

It is also usually necessary for the entity to have an effective internal financial budgeting and reporting system. The entity reviews and, when necessary, revises the estimates of revenue as the service is performed. The need for such revisions does not necessarily indicate that the outcome of the transaction cannot be estimated reliably.

24 The stage of completion of a transaction may be determined by a variety of methods. An entity uses the method that measures reliably the services performed. Depending on the nature of the transaction, the methods may include:

(a) surveys of work performed;

(b) services performed to date as a percentage of total services to be performed; or

(c) the proportion that costs incurred to date bear to the estimated total costs of the transaction. Only costs that reflect services performed to date are included in costs incurred to date. Only costs that reflect services performed or to be performed are included in the estimated total costs of the transaction.

Progress payments and advances received from customers often do not reflect the services performed.

25 For practical purposes, when services are performed by an indeterminate number of acts over a specified period of time, revenue is recognised on a straight-line basis over the specified period unless there is evidence that some other method better represents the stage of completion. When a specific act is much more significant than any other acts, the recognition of revenue is postponed until the significant act is executed.

26 When the outcome of the transaction involving the rendering of services cannot be estimated reliably, revenue shall be recognised only to the extent of the expenses recognised that are recoverable.

27 During the early stages of a transaction, it is often the case that the outcome of the transaction cannot be estimated reliably. Nevertheless, it may be probable that the entity will recover the transaction costs incurred. Therefore, revenue is recognised only to the extent of costs incurred that are expected to be recoverable. As the outcome of the transaction cannot be estimated reliably, no profit is recognised.

28 When the outcome of a transaction cannot be estimated reliably and it is not probable that the costs incurred will be recovered, revenue is not recognised and the costs incurred are recognised as an expense. When the uncertainties that prevented the outcome of the contract being estimated reliably no longer exist, revenue is recognised in accordance with paragraph 20 rather than in accordance with paragraph 26.

Interest, royalties and dividends

29 Revenue arising from the use by others of entity assets yielding interest, royalties and dividends shall be recognised on the bases set out in paragraph 30 when:

(a) it is probable that the economic benefits associated with the transaction will flow to the entity; and

(b) the amount of the revenue can be measured reliably.

30 Revenue shall be recognised on the following bases:

(a) interest shall be recognised using the effective interest method as set out in IAS 39, paragraphs 9 and AG5–AG8;

(b) royalties shall be recognised on an accrual basis in accordance with the substance of the relevant agreement; and

(c) dividends shall be recognised when the shareholder's right to receive payment is established.

31 [Deleted]

32 When unpaid interest has accrued before the acquisition of an interest-bearing investment, the subsequent receipt of interest is allocated between pre-acquisition and post-acquisition periods; only the post-acquisition portion is recognised as revenue. When dividends on equity securities are declared from pre-acquisition profits, those dividends are deducted from the cost of the securities. If it is difficult to make such an allocation except on an arbitrary basis, dividends are recognised as revenue unless they clearly represent a recovery of part of the cost of the equity securities.

33 Royalties accrue in accordance with the terms of the relevant agreement and are usually recognised on that basis unless, having regard to the substance of the agreement, it is more appropriate to recognise revenue on some other systematic and rational basis.

34 Revenue is recognised only when it is probable that the economic benefits associated with the transaction will flow to the entity. However, when an uncertainty arises about the collectibility of an amount already included in revenue, the uncollectible amount, or the amount in respect of which recovery

has ceased to be probable, is recognised as an expense, rather than as an adjustment of the amount of revenue originally recognised.

Disclosure

35 **An entity shall disclose:**

(a) the accounting policies adopted for the recognition of revenue, including the methods adopted to determine the stage of completion of transactions involving the rendering of services;

(b) the amount of each significant category of revenue recognised during the period, including revenue arising from:

(i) the sale of goods;

(ii) the rendering of services;

(iii) interest;

(iv) royalties;

(v) dividends; and

(c) the amount of revenue arising from exchanges of goods or services included in each significant category of revenue.

36 An entity discloses any contingent liabilities and contingent assets in accordance with IAS 37 *Provisions, Contingent Liabilities and Contingent Assets*. Contingent liabilities and contingent assets may arise from items such as warranty costs, claims, penalties or possible losses.

Effective date

37 **This Standard becomes operative for financial statements covering periods beginning on or after 1 January 1995.**

Appendix

This appendix accompanies, but is not part of, IAS 18. The examples focus on particular aspects of a transaction and are not a comprehensive discussion of all the relevant factors that might influence the recognition of revenue. The examples generally assume that the amount of revenue can be measured reliably, it is probable that the economic benefits will flow to the entity and the costs incurred or to be incurred can be measured reliably.

Sale of goods

The law in different countries may mean the recognition criteria in this Standard are met at different times. In particular, the law may determine the point in time at which the entity transfers the significant risks and rewards of ownership. Therefore, the examples in this section of the appendix need to be read in the context of the laws relating to the sale of goods in the country in which the transaction takes place.

1 *'Bill and hold' sales, in which delivery is delayed at the buyer's request but the buyer takes title and accepts billing.*

Revenue is recognised when the buyer takes title, provided:

(a) it is probable that delivery will be made;

(b) the item is on hand, identified and ready for delivery to the buyer at the time the sale is recognised;

(c) the buyer specifically acknowledges the deferred delivery instructions; and

(d) the usual payment terms apply.

Revenue is not recognised when there is simply an intention to acquire or manufacture the goods in time for delivery.

2 *Goods shipped subject to conditions.*

(a) *installation and inspection.*

Revenue is normally recognised when the buyer accepts delivery, and installation and inspection are complete. However, revenue is recognised immediately upon the buyer's acceptance of delivery when:

(i) the installation process is simple in nature, for example the installation of a factory tested television receiver which only requires unpacking and connection of power and antennae; or

(ii) the inspection is performed only for purposes of final determination of contract prices, for example, shipments of iron ore, sugar or soya beans.

(b) *on approval when the buyer has negotiated a limited right of return.*

If there is uncertainty about the possibility of return, revenue is recognised when the shipment has been formally accepted by the buyer or the goods have been delivered and the time period for rejection has elapsed.

(c) *consignment sales under which the recipient (buyer) undertakes to sell the goods on behalf of the shipper (seller).*

Revenue is recognised by the shipper when the goods are sold by the recipient to a third party.

(d) *cash on delivery sales.*

Revenue is recognised when delivery is made and cash is received by the seller or its agent.

3 *Lay away sales under which the goods are delivered only when the buyer makes the final payment in a series of instalments.*

Revenue from such sales is recognised when the goods are delivered. However, when experience indicates that most such sales are consummated, revenue may be recognised when a significant deposit is received provided the goods are on hand, identified and ready for delivery to the buyer.

4 *Orders when payment (or partial payment) is received in advance of delivery for goods not presently held in inventory, for example, the goods are still to be manufactured or will be delivered directly to the customer from a third party.*

Revenue is recognised when the goods are delivered to the buyer.

5 *Sale and repurchase agreements (other than swap transactions) under which the seller concurrently agrees to repurchase the same goods at a later date, or when the seller has a call option to repurchase, or the buyer has a put option to require the repurchase, by the seller, of the goods.*

For a sale and repurchase agreement on an asset other than a financial asset, the terms of the agreement need to be analysed to ascertain whether, in substance, the seller has transferred the risks and rewards of ownership to the buyer and hence revenue is recognised. When the seller has retained the risks and rewards of ownership, even though legal title has been transferred, the transaction is a financing arrangement and does not give rise to revenue. For a sale and repurchase agreement on a financial asset, IAS 39 *Financial Instruments: Recognition and Measurement* applies.

6 *Sales to intermediate parties, such as distributors, dealers or others for resale.*

Revenue from such sales is generally recognised when the risks and rewards of ownership have passed. However, when the buyer is acting, in substance, as an agent, the sale is treated as a consignment sale.

7 *Subscriptions to publications and similar items.*

When the items involved are of similar value in each time period, revenue is recognised on a straight-line basis over the period in which the items are despatched. When the items vary in value from period to period, revenue is recognised on the basis of the sales value of the item despatched in relation to the total estimated sales value of all items covered by the subscription.

8 *Instalment sales, under which the consideration is receivable in instalments.*

Revenue attributable to the sales price, exclusive of interest, is recognised at the date of sale. The sale price is the present value of the consideration, determined by discounting the instalments receivable at the imputed rate of interest. The interest element is recognised as revenue as it is earned, using the effective interest method.

9 *Real estate sales.*

Revenue is normally recognised when legal title passes to the buyer. However, in some jurisdictions the equitable interest in a property may vest in the buyer before legal title passes and therefore the risks and rewards of ownership have been transferred at that stage. In such cases, provided that the seller has no further substantial acts to complete under the contract, it may be appropriate to recognise revenue. In either case, if the seller is obliged to perform any significant acts after the transfer of the equitable and/or legal title, revenue is recognised as the acts are performed. An example is a building or other facility on which construction has not been completed.

In some cases, real estate may be sold with a degree of continuing involvement by the seller such that the risks and rewards of ownership have not been transferred. Examples are sale and repurchase agreements which include put and call options, and agreements whereby the seller guarantees occupancy of the property for a specified period, or guarantees a return on the buyer's investment for a specified period. In such cases, the nature and extent of the seller's continuing involvement determines how the transaction is accounted for. It may be accounted for as a sale, or as a financing, leasing or some other profit sharing arrangement. If it is accounted for as a sale, the continuing involvement of the seller may delay the recognition of revenue.

A seller also considers the means of payment and evidence of the buyer's commitment to complete payment. For example, when the aggregate of the payments received, including the buyer's initial down payment, or continuing payments by the buyer, provide insufficient evidence of the buyer's commitment to complete payment, revenue is recognised only to the extent cash is received.

Rendering of services

10 *Installation fees.*

Installation fees are recognised as revenue by reference to the stage of completion of the installation, unless they are incidental to the sale of a product, in which case they are recognised when the goods are sold.

11 *Servicing fees included in the price of the product.*

When the selling price of a product includes an identifiable amount for subsequent servicing (for example, after sales support and product enhancement on the sale of software), that amount is deferred and recognised as revenue over the period during which the service is performed. The amount deferred is that which will cover the expected costs of the services under the agreement, together with a reasonable profit on those services.

12 *Advertising commissions.*

Media commissions are recognised when the related advertisement or commercial appears before the public. Production commissions are recognised by reference to the stage of completion of the project.

13 *Insurance agency commissions.*

Insurance agency commissions received or receivable which do not require the agent to render further service are recognised as revenue by the agent on the effective commencement or renewal dates of the related policies. However, when it is probable that the agent will be required to render further services during the life of the policy, the commission, or part thereof, is deferred and recognised as revenue over the period during which the policy is in force.

14 *Financial service fees.*

The recognition of revenue for financial service fees depends on the purposes for which the fees are assessed and the basis of accounting for any associated financial instrument. The description of fees for financial services may not be indicative of the nature and substance of the services provided. Therefore, it is necessary to distinguish between fees that are an integral part of the effective interest rate of a financial instrument, fees that are earned as services are provided, and fees that are earned on the execution of a significant act.

(a) *Fees that are an integral part of the effective interest rate of a financial instrument.*

Such fees are generally treated as an adjustment to the effective interest rate. However, when the financial instrument is measured at fair value with the change in fair value recognised in profit or loss, the fees are recognised as revenue when the instrument is initially recognised.

(i) *Origination fees received by the entity relating to the creation or acquisition of a financial asset other than one that under IAS 39 is classified as a financial asset 'at fair value through profit or loss'.*

Such fees may include compensation for activities such as evaluating the borrower's financial condition, evaluating and recording guarantees, collateral and other security arrangements, negotiating the terms of the instrument, preparing and processing documents and closing the transaction. These fees are an integral part of generating an involvement with the resulting financial instrument and, together with the related direct costs, are deferred and recognised as an adjustment to the effective interest rate.

(ii) *Commitment fees received by the entity to originate a loan when the loan commitment is outside the scope of IAS 39.*

If it is probable that the entity will enter into a specific lending arrangement and the loan commitment is not within the scope of IAS 39, the commitment fee received is regarded as compensation for an ongoing involvement with the acquisition of a financial instrument and, together with the related direct costs, is deferred and recognised as an adjustment to the effective interest rate. If the commitment expires without the entity making the loan, the fee is recognised as revenue on expiry. Loan commitments that are within the scope of IAS 39 are accounted for as derivatives and measured at fair value.

(iii) *Origination fees received on issuing financial liabilities measured at amortised cost.*

These fees are an integral part of generating an involvement with a financial liability. When a financial liability is not classified as 'at fair value through profit or loss', the origination fees received are included, with the related transaction costs incurred, in the initial carrying amount of the financial liability and recognised as an adjustment to the effective interest rate. An entity distinguishes fees and costs that are an integral part of the effective interest rate for the financial liability from origination fees and transaction costs relating to the right to provide services, such as investment management services.

(b) *Fees earned as services are provided.*

(i) *Fees charged for servicing a loan.*

Fees charged by an entity for servicing a loan are recognised as revenue as the services are provided.

(ii) *Commitment fees to originate a loan when the loan commitment is outside the scope of IAS 39.*

If it is unlikely that a specific lending arrangement will be entered into and the loan commitment is outside the scope of IAS 39, the commitment fee is recognised as revenue on a time proportion basis over the commitment period. Loan commitments that are within the scope of IAS 39 are accounted for as derivatives and measured at fair value.

(iii) *Investment management fees.*

Fees charged for managing investments are recognised as revenue as the services are provided.

Incremental costs that are directly attributable to securing an investment management contract are recognised as an asset if they can be identified separately and measured reliably and if it is probable that they will be recovered. As in IAS 39, an incremental cost is one that would not have been incurred if the entity had not secured the investment management contract. The asset represents the entity's contractual right to benefit from providing investment management services, and is amortised as the entity recognises the related revenue. If the entity has a portfolio of investment management contracts, it may assess their recoverability on a portfolio basis.

Some financial services contracts involve both the origination of one or more financial instruments and the provision of investment management services. An example is a long-term monthly saving contract linked to the management of a pool of equity securities. The provider of the contract distinguishes the transaction costs relating to the origination of the financial instrument from the costs of securing the right to provide investment management services.

(c) *Fees that are earned on the execution of a significant act.*

The fees are recognised as revenue when the significant act has been completed, as in the examples below.

(i) *Commission on the allotment of shares to a client.*

The commission is recognised as revenue when the shares have been allotted.

(ii) *Placement fees for arranging a loan between a borrower and an investor.*

The fee is recognised as revenue when the loan has been arranged.

(iii) *Loan syndication fees.*

A syndication fee received by an entity that arranges a loan and retains no part of the loan package for itself (or retains a part at the same effective interest rate for comparable risk as other participants) is compensation for the service of syndication. Such a fee is recognised as revenue when the syndication has been completed.

15 *Admission fees.*

Revenue from artistic performances, banquets and other special events is recognised when the event takes place. When a subscription to a number of events is sold, the fee is allocated to each event on a basis which reflects the extent to which services are performed at each event.

16 *Tuition fees.*

Revenue is recognised over the period of instruction.

17 *Initiation, entrance and membership fees.*

Revenue recognition depends on the nature of the services provided. If the fee permits only membership, and all other services or products are paid for separately, or if there is a separate annual subscription, the fee is recognised as revenue when no significant uncertainty as to its collectibility exists. If the fee entitles the member to services or publications to be provided during the membership period, or to purchase goods or services at prices lower than those charged to non-members, it is recognised on a basis that reflects the timing, nature and value of the benefits provided.

18 *Franchise fees.*

Franchise fees may cover the supply of initial and subsequent services, equipment and other tangible assets, and know-how. Accordingly, franchise fees are recognised as revenue on a basis that reflects the purpose for which the fees were charged. The following methods of franchise fee recognition are appropriate:

(a) *Supplies of equipment and other tangible assets.*

The amount, based on the fair value of the assets sold, is recognised as revenue when the items are delivered or title passes.

(b) *Supplies of initial and subsequent services.*

Fees for the provision of continuing services, whether part of the initial fee or a separate fee, are recognised as revenue as the services are rendered. When the separate fee does not cover the cost of continuing services together with a reasonable profit, part of the initial fee, sufficient to cover the costs of continuing services and to provide a reasonable profit on those services, is deferred and recognised as revenue as the services are rendered.

The franchise agreement may provide for the franchisor to supply equipment, inventories, or other tangible assets, at a price lower than that charged to others or a price that does not provide a reasonable profit on those sales. In these circumstances, part of the initial fee, sufficient to cover estimated costs in excess of that price and to provide a reasonable profit on those sales, is deferred and recognised over the period the goods are likely to be sold to the franchisee. The balance of an initial fee is recognised as revenue when performance of all the initial services and other obligations required of the franchisor (such as assistance with site selection, staff training, financing and advertising) has been substantially accomplished.

The initial services and other obligations under an area franchise agreement may depend on the number of individual outlets established in the area. In this case, the fees attributable to the initial services are recognised as revenue in proportion to the number of outlets for which the initial services have been substantially completed.

If the initial fee is collectible over an extended period and there is a significant uncertainty that it will be collected in full, the fee is recognised as cash instalments are received.

(c) *Continuing franchise fees.*

Fees charged for the use of continuing rights granted by the agreement, or for other services provided during the period of the agreement, are recognised as revenue as the services are provided or the rights used.

(d) *Agency transactions.*

Transactions may take place between the franchisor and the franchisee which, in substance, involve the franchisor acting as agent for the franchisee. For example, the franchisor may order supplies and arrange for their delivery to the franchisee at no profit. Such transactions do not give rise to revenue.

19 *Fees from the development of customised software.*

Fees from the development of customised software are recognised as revenue by reference to the stage of completion of the development, including completion of services provided for post-delivery service support.

Interest, royalties and dividends

20 *Licence fees and royalties.*

Fees and royalties paid for the use of an entity's assets (such as trademarks, patents, software, music copyright, record masters and motion picture films) are normally recognised in accordance with the substance of the agreement. As a practical matter, this may be on a straight-line basis over the life of the agreement, for example, when a licensee has the right to use certain technology for a specified period of time.

An assignment of rights for a fixed fee or non-refundable guarantee under a non-cancellable contract which permits the licensee to exploit those rights freely and the licensor has no remaining obligations to perform is, in substance, a sale. An example is a licensing agreement for the use of software when the licensor has no obligations subsequent to delivery. Another example is the granting of rights to exhibit a motion picture film in markets where the licensor has no control over the distributor and expects to receive no further revenues from the box office receipts. In such cases, revenue is recognised at the time of sale.

In some cases, whether or not a licence fee or royalty will be received is contingent on the occurrence of a future event. In such cases, revenue is recognised only when it is probable that the fee or royalty will be received, which is normally when the event has occurred.

International Accounting Standard 19

Employee Benefits

This version includes amendments resulting from Amendment to IAS 19 Employee Benefits—Actuarial Gains and Losses, Group Plans and Disclosures *issued on 16 December 2004*

CONTENTS

International Accounting Standard 19 *Employee Benefits* (IAS 19) is set out in paragraphs 1–160. All the paragraphs have equal authority but retain the IASC format of the Standard when it was adopted by the IASB. IAS 19 should be read in the context of its objective and the Basis for Conclusions, the *Preface to International Financial Reporting Standards* and the *Framework for the Preparation and Presentation of Financial Statements*. IAS 8 *Accounting Policies, Changes in Accounting Estimates and Errors* provides a basis for selecting and applying accounting policies in the absence of explicit guidance.

Introduction

IN1 The Standard prescribes the accounting and disclosure by employers for employee benefits. It replaces IAS 19 *Retirement Benefit Costs* which was approved in 1993. The major changes from the old IAS 19 are set out in the Basis for Conclusions. The Standard does not deal with reporting by employee benefit plans (see IAS 26 *Accounting and Reporting by Retirement Benefit Plans*).

IN2 The Standard identifies four categories of employee benefits:

(a) short-term employee benefits, such as wages, salaries and social security contributions, paid annual leave and paid sick leave, profit-sharing and bonuses (if payable within twelve months of the end of the period) and non-monetary benefits (such as medical care, housing, cars and free or subsidised goods or services) for current employees;

(b) post-employment benefits such as pensions, other retirement benefits, post-employment life insurance and post-employment medical care;

(c) other long-term employee benefits, including long-service leave or sabbatical leave, jubilee or other long-service benefits, long-term disability benefits and, if they are payable twelve months or more after the end of the period, profit-sharing, bonuses and deferred compensation; and

(d) termination benefits.

IN3 The Standard requires an entity to recognise short-term employee benefits when an employee has rendered service in exchange for those benefits.

IN4 Post-employment benefit plans are classified as either defined contribution plans or defined benefit plans. The Standard gives specific guidance on the classification of multi-employer plans, state plans and plans with insured benefits.

IN5 Under defined contribution plans, an entity pays fixed contributions into a separate entity (a fund) and will have no legal or constructive obligation to pay further contributions if the fund does not hold sufficient assets to pay all employee benefits relating to employee service in the current and prior periods. The Standard requires an entity to recognise contributions to a defined contribution plan when an employee has rendered service in exchange for those contributions.

IN6 All other post-employment benefit plans are defined benefit plans. Defined benefit plans may be unfunded, or they may be wholly or partly funded. The Standard requires an entity to:

(a) account not only for its legal obligation, but also for any constructive obligation that arises from the entity's practices;

(b) determine the present value of defined benefit obligations and the fair value of any plan assets with sufficient regularity that the amounts recognised in the financial statements do not differ materially from the amounts that would be determined at the balance sheet date;

(c) use the Projected Unit Credit Method to measure its obligations and costs;

(d) attribute benefit to periods of service under the plan's benefit formula, unless an employee's service in later years will lead to a materially higher level of benefit than in earlier years;

(e) use unbiased and mutually compatible actuarial assumptions about demographic variables (such as employee turnover and mortality) and financial variables (such as future increases in salaries, changes in medical costs and certain changes in state benefits). Financial assumptions should be based on market expectations, at the balance sheet date, for the period over which the obligations are to be settled;

(f) determine the discount rate by reference to market yields at the balance sheet date on high quality corporate bonds (or, in countries where there is no deep market in such bonds, government bonds) of a currency and term consistent with the currency and term of the post-employment benefit obligations;

(g) deduct the fair value of any plan assets from the carrying amount of the obligation. Certain reimbursement rights that do not qualify as plan assets are treated in the same way as plan assets, except that they are presented as a separate asset, rather than as a deduction from the obligation;

(h) limit the carrying amount of an asset so that it does not exceed the net total of:

  (i) any unrecognised past service cost and actuarial losses; plus

  (ii) the present value of any economic benefits available in the form of refunds from the plan or reductions in future contributions to the plan;

(i) recognise past service cost on a straight-line basis over the average period until the amended benefits become vested;

(j) recognise gains or losses on the curtailment or settlement of a defined benefit plan when the curtailment or settlement occurs. The gain or loss should comprise any resulting change in the present value of the defined benefit obligation and of the fair value of the plan assets and the unrecognised part of any related actuarial gains and losses and past service cost; and

(k) recognise a specified portion of the net cumulative actuarial gains and losses that exceed the greater of:

  (i) 10% of the present value of the defined benefit obligation (before deducting plan assets); and

  (ii) 10% of the fair value of any plan assets.

The portion of actuarial gains and losses to be recognised for each defined benefit plan is the excess that fell outside the 10% 'corridor' at the previous reporting date, divided by the expected average remaining working lives of the employees participating in that plan.

The Standard also permits systematic methods of faster recognition, provided that the same basis is applied to both gains and losses and the basis is applied consistently from period to period. Such permitted methods include immediate recognition of all actuarial gains and losses in profit or loss.

In addition, the Standard permits an entity to recognise all actuarial gains and losses in the period in which they occur outside profit or loss in a statement of recognised income and expense.

IN7 The Standard requires a simpler method of accounting for other long-term employee benefits than for post-employment benefits: actuarial gains and losses and past service cost are recognised immediately.

IN8 Termination benefits are employee benefits payable as a result of either: an entity's decision to terminate an employee's employment before the normal retirement date; or an employee's decision to accept voluntary redundancy in exchange for those benefits. The event which gives rise to an obligation is the termination rather than employee service. Therefore, an entity should recognise termination benefits when, and only when, the entity is demonstrably committed to either:

(a) terminate the employment of an employee or group of employees before the normal retirement date; or

(b) provide termination benefits as a result of an offer made in order to encourage voluntary redundancy.

IN9 An entity is demonstrably committed to a termination when, and only when, the entity has a detailed formal plan (with specified minimum contents) for the termination and is without realistic possibility of withdrawal.

IN10 Where termination benefits fall due more than 12 months after the balance sheet date, they should be discounted. In the case of an offer made to encourage voluntary redundancy, the measurement of termination benefits should be based on the number of employees expected to accept the offer.

IN11 [Deleted]

IN12 The Standard is effective for accounting periods beginning on or after 1 January 1999. Earlier application is encouraged. On first adopting the Standard, an entity is permitted to recognise any resulting increase in its liability for post-employment benefits over not more than five years. If the adoption of the standard decreases the liability, an entity is required to recognise the decrease immediately.

IN13 [Deleted]

International Accounting Standard 19
Employee Benefits

Objective

The objective of this Standard is to prescribe the accounting and disclosure for employee benefits. The Standard requires an entity to recognise:

(a) a liability when an employee has provided service in exchange for employee benefits to be paid in the future; and

(b) an expense when the entity consumes the economic benefit arising from service provided by an employee in exchange for employee benefits.

Scope

1 **This Standard shall be applied by an employer in accounting for all employee benefits, except those to which IFRS 2** *Share-based Payment* **applies.**

2 This Standard does not deal with reporting by employee benefit plans (see IAS 26 *Accounting and Reporting by Retirement Benefit Plans*).

3 The employee benefits to which this Standard applies include those provided:

(a) under formal plans or other formal agreements between an entity and individual employees, groups of employees or their representatives;

(b) under legislative requirements, or through industry arrangements, whereby entities are required to contribute to national, state, industry or other multi-employer plans; or

(c) by those informal practices that give rise to a constructive obligation. Informal practices give rise to a constructive obligation where the entity has no realistic alternative but to pay employee benefits. An example of a constructive obligation is where a change in the entity's informal practices would cause unacceptable damage to its relationship with employees.

4 Employee benefits include:

(a) short-term employee benefits, such as wages, salaries and social security contributions, paid annual leave and paid sick leave, profit-sharing and bonuses (if payable within twelve months of the end of the period) and non-monetary benefits (such as medical care, housing, cars and free or subsidised goods or services) for current employees;

(b) post-employment benefits such as pensions, other retirement benefits, post-employment life insurance and post-employment medical care;

(c) other long-term employee benefits, including long-service leave or sabbatical leave, jubilee or other long-service benefits, long-term disability benefits and, if they are not payable wholly within twelve months after the end of the period, profit-sharing, bonuses and deferred compensation; and

(d) termination benefits.

Because each category identified in (a)-(d) above has different characteristics, this Standard establishes separate requirements for each category.

5 Employee benefits include benefits provided to either employees or their dependants and may be settled by payments (or the provision of goods or services) made either directly to the employees, to their spouses, children or other dependants or to others, such as insurance companies.

6 An employee may provide services to an entity on a full-time, part-time, permanent, casual or temporary basis. For the purpose of this Standard, employees include directors and other management personnel.

Definitions

7 **The following terms are used in this Standard with the meanings specified:**

Employee benefits **are all forms of consideration given by an entity in exchange for service rendered by employees.**

Short-term employee benefits **are employee benefits (other than termination benefits) which fall due wholly within twelve months after the end of the period in which the employees render the related service.**

Post-employment benefits **are employee benefits (other than termination benefits) which are payable after the completion of employment.**

Post-employment benefit plans **are formal or informal arrangements under which an entity provides post-employment benefits for one or more employees.**

Defined contribution plans **are post-employment benefit plans under which an entity pays fixed contributions into a separate entity (a fund) and will have no legal or constructive obligation to pay further contributions if the fund does not hold sufficient assets to pay all employee benefits relating to employee service in the current and prior periods.**

Defined benefit plans **are post-employment benefit plans other than defined contribution plans.**

Multi-employer plans **are defined contribution plans (other than state plans) or defined benefit plans (other than state plans) that:**

(a) pool the assets contributed by various entities that are not under common control; and

(b) use those assets to provide benefits to employees of more than one entity, on the basis that contribution and benefit levels are determined without regard to the identity of the entity that employs the employees concerned.

Other long-term employee benefits **are employee benefits (other than post-employment benefits and termination benefits) which do not fall due wholly within twelve months after the end of the period in which the employees render the related service.**

Termination benefits **are employee benefits payable as a result of either:**

(a) an entity's decision to terminate an employee's employment before the normal retirement date; or

(b) an employee's decision to accept voluntary redundancy in exchange for those benefits.

Vested employee benefits **are employee benefits that are not conditional on future employment.**

The *present value of a defined benefit obligation* **is the present value, without deducting any plan assets, of expected future payments required to settle the obligation resulting from employee service in the current and prior periods.**

Current service cost **is the increase in the present value of the defined benefit obligation resulting from employee service in the current period.**

Interest cost **is the increase during a period in the present value of a defined benefit obligation which arises because the benefits are one period closer to settlement.**

Plan assets **comprise:**

(a) assets held by a long-term employee benefit fund; and

(b) qualifying insurance policies.

Assets held by a long-term employee benefit fund **are assets (other than non-transferable financial instruments issued by the reporting entity) that:**

(a) are held by an entity (a fund) that is legally separate from the reporting entity and exists solely to pay or fund employee benefits; and

(b) are available to be used only to pay or fund employee benefits, are not available to the reporting entity's own creditors (even in bankruptcy), and cannot be returned to the reporting entity, unless either:

- **(i) the remaining assets of the fund are sufficient to meet all the related employee benefit obligations of the plan or the reporting entity; or**
- **(ii) the assets are returned to the reporting entity to reimburse it for employee benefits already paid.**

A qualifying insurance policy **is an insurance policy*** **issued by an insurer that is not a related party (as defined in IAS 24** *Related Party Disclosures*) **of the reporting entity, if the proceeds of the policy:**

(a) can be used only to pay or fund employee benefits under a defined benefit plan; and

(b) are not available to the reporting entity's own creditors (even in bankruptcy) and cannot be paid to the reporting entity, unless either:

- **(i) the proceeds represent surplus assets that are not needed for the policy to meet all the related employee benefit obligations; or**

* A qualifying insurance policy is not necessarily an insurance contract, as defined in IFRS 4 *Insurance Contracts*.

(ii) the proceeds are returned to the reporting entity to reimburse it for employee benefits already paid.

Fair value **is the amount for which an asset could be exchanged or a liability settled between knowledgeable, willing parties in an arm's length transaction.**

The *return on plan assets* **is interest, dividends and other revenue derived from the plan assets, together with realised and unrealised gains or losses on the plan assets, less any costs of administering the plan and less any tax payable by the plan itself.**

Actuarial gains and losses **comprise:**

(a) experience adjustments (the effects of differences between the previous actuarial assumptions and what has actually occurred); and

(b) the effects of changes in actuarial assumptions.

Past service cost **is the increase in the present value of the defined benefit obligation for employee service in prior periods, resulting in the current period from the introduction of, or changes to, post-employment benefits or other long-term employee benefits. Past service cost may be either positive (where benefits are introduced or improved) or negative (where existing benefits are reduced).**

Short-term employee benefits

8 Short-term employee benefits include items such as:

(a) wages, salaries and social security contributions;

(b) short-term compensated absences (such as paid annual leave and paid sick leave) where the absences are expected to occur within twelve months after the end of the period in which the employees render the related employee service;

(c) profit-sharing and bonuses payable within twelve months after the end of the period in which the employees render the related service; and

(d) non-monetary benefits (such as medical care, housing, cars and free or subsidised goods or services) for current employees.

9 Accounting for short-term employee benefits is generally straightforward because no actuarial assumptions are required to measure the obligation or the cost and there is no possibility of any actuarial gain or loss. Moreover, short-term employee benefit obligations are measured on an undiscounted basis.

Recognition and measurement

All short-term employee benefits

10 When an employee has rendered service to an entity during an accounting period, the entity shall recognise the undiscounted amount of short-term employee benefits expected to be paid in exchange for that service:

(a) as a liability (accrued expense), after deducting any amount already paid. If the amount already paid exceeds the undiscounted amount of

the benefits, an entity shall recognise that excess as an asset (prepaid expense) to the extent that the prepayment will lead to, for example, a reduction in future payments or a cash refund; and

(b) as an expense, unless another Standard requires or permits the inclusion of the benefits in the cost of an asset (see, for example, IAS 2 ***Inventories*** **and IAS 16** ***Property, Plant and Equipment*****).**

Paragraphs 11, 14 and 17 explain how an entity shall apply this requirement to short-term employee benefits in the form of compensated absences and profit-sharing and bonus plans.

Short-term compensated absences

11 **An entity shall recognise the expected cost of short-term employee benefits in the form of compensated absences under paragraph 10 as follows:**

(a) in the case of accumulating compensated absences, when the employees render service that increases their entitlement to future compensated absences; and

(b) in the case of non-accumulating compensated absences, when the absences occur.

12 An entity may compensate employees for absence for various reasons including vacation, sickness and short-term disability, maternity or paternity, jury service and military service. Entitlement to compensated absences falls into two categories:

(a) accumulating; and

(b) non-accumulating.

13 Accumulating compensated absences are those that are carried forward and can be used in future periods if the current period's entitlement is not used in full. Accumulating compensated absences may be either vesting (in other words, employees are entitled to a cash payment for unused entitlement on leaving the entity) or non-vesting (when employees are not entitled to a cash payment for unused entitlement on leaving). An obligation arises as employees render service that increases their entitlement to future compensated absences. The obligation exists, and is recognised, even if the compensated absences are non-vesting, although the possibility that employees may leave before they use an accumulated non-vesting entitlement affects the measurement of that obligation.

14 **An entity shall measure the expected cost of accumulating compensated absences as the additional amount that the entity expects to pay as a result of the unused entitlement that has accumulated at the balance sheet date.**

15 The method specified in the previous paragraph measures the obligation at the amount of the additional payments that are expected to arise solely from the fact that the benefit accumulates. In many cases, an entity may not need to make detailed computations to estimate that there is no material obligation for unused compensated absences. For example, a sick leave obligation is likely to be material only if there is a formal or informal understanding that unused paid sick leave may be taken as paid vacation.

Example illustrating paragraphs 14 and 15

An entity has 100 employees, who are each entitled to five working days of paid sick leave for each year. Unused sick leave may be carried forward for one calendar year. Sick leave is taken first out of the current year's entitlement and then out of any balance brought forward from the previous year (a LIFO basis). At 30 December 20X1, the average unused entitlement is two days per employee. The entity expects, based on past experience which is expected to continue, that 92 employees will take no more than five days of paid sick leave in 20X2 and that the remaining eight employees will take an average of six and a half days each.

The entity expects that it will pay an additional 12 days of sick pay as a result of the unused entitlement that has accumulated at 31 December 20X1 (one and a half days each, for eight employees). Therefore, the entity recognises a liability equal to 12 days of sick pay.

16 Non-accumulating compensated absences do not carry forward: they lapse if the current period's entitlement is not used in full and do not entitle employees to a cash payment for unused entitlement on leaving the entity. This is commonly the case for sick pay (to the extent that unused past entitlement does not increase future entitlement), maternity or paternity leave and compensated absences for jury service or military service. An entity recognises no liability or expense until the time of the absence, because employee service does not increase the amount of the benefit.

Profit-sharing and bonus plans

17 An entity shall recognise the expected cost of profit-sharing and bonus payments under paragraph 10 when, and only when:

(a) the entity has a present legal or constructive obligation to make such payments as a result of past events; and

(b) a reliable estimate of the obligation can be made.

A present obligation exists when, and only when, the entity has no realistic alternative but to make the payments.

18 Under some profit-sharing plans, employees receive a share of the profit only if they remain with the entity for a specified period. Such plans create a constructive obligation as employees render service that increases the amount to be paid if they remain in service until the end of the specified period. The measurement of such constructive obligations reflects the possibility that some employees may leave without receiving profit-sharing payments.

Example illustrating paragraph 18

A profit-sharing plan requires an entity to pay a specified proportion of its net profit for the year to employees who serve throughout the year. If no employees leave during the year, the total profit-sharing payments for the year will be 3% of net profit. The entity estimates that staff turnover will reduce the payments to 2.5% of net profit.

The entity recognises a liability and an expense of 2.5% of net profit.

19 An entity may have no legal obligation to pay a bonus. Nevertheless, in some cases, an entity has a practice of paying bonuses. In such cases, the entity has a constructive obligation because the entity has no realistic alternative but to pay the bonus. The measurement of the constructive obligation reflects the possibility that some employees may leave without receiving a bonus.

20 An entity can make a reliable estimate of its legal or constructive obligation under a profit-sharing or bonus plan when, and only when:

(a) the formal terms of the plan contain a formula for determining the amount of the benefit;

(b) the entity determines the amounts to be paid before the financial statements are authorised for issue; or

(c) past practice gives clear evidence of the amount of the entity's constructive obligation.

21 An obligation under profit-sharing and bonus plans results from employee service and not from a transaction with the entity's owners. Therefore, an entity recognises the cost of profit-sharing and bonus plans not as a distribution of net profit but as an expense.

22 If profit-sharing and bonus payments are not due wholly within twelve months after the end of the period in which the employees render the related service, those payments are other long-term employee benefits (see paragraphs 126–131).

Disclosure

23 Although this Standard does not require specific disclosures about short-term employee benefits, other Standards may require disclosures. For example, IAS 24 *Related Party Disclosures* requires disclosures about employee benefits for key management personnel. IAS 1 *Presentation of Financial Statements* requires disclosure of employee benefits expense.

Post-employment benefits: distinction between defined contribution plans and defined benefit plans

24 Post-employment benefits include, for example:

(a) retirement benefits, such as pensions; and

(b) other post-employment benefits, such as post-employment life insurance and post-employment medical care.

Arrangements whereby an entity provides post-employment benefits are post-employment benefit plans. An entity applies this Standard to all such arrangements whether or not they involve the establishment of a separate entity to receive contributions and to pay benefits.

25 Post-employment benefit plans are classified as either defined contribution plans or defined benefit plans, depending on the economic substance of the plan as derived from its principal terms and conditions. Under defined contribution plans:

(a) the entity's legal or constructive obligation is limited to the amount that it agrees to contribute to the fund. Thus, the amount of the post-employment benefits received by the employee is determined by the amount of contributions paid by an entity (and perhaps also the employee) to a post-employment benefit plan or to an insurance company, together with investment returns arising from the contributions; and

(b) in consequence, actuarial risk (that benefits will be less than expected) and investment risk (that assets invested will be insufficient to meet expected benefits) fall on the employee.

26 Examples of cases where an entity's obligation is not limited to the amount that it agrees to contribute to the fund are when the entity has a legal or constructive obligation through:

(a) a plan benefit formula that is not linked solely to the amount of contributions;

(b) a guarantee, either indirectly through a plan or directly, of a specified return on contributions; or

(c) those informal practices that give rise to a constructive obligation. For example, a constructive obligation may arise where an entity has a history of increasing benefits for former employees to keep pace with inflation even where there is no legal obligation to do so.

27 Under defined benefit plans:

(a) the entity's obligation is to provide the agreed benefits to current and former employees; and

(b) actuarial risk (that benefits will cost more than expected) and investment risk fall, in substance, on the entity. If actuarial or investment experience are worse than expected, the entity's obligation may be increased.

28 Paragraphs 29–42 below explain the distinction between defined contribution plans and defined benefit plans in the context of multi–employer plans, state plans and insured benefits.

Multi-employer plans

29 **An entity shall classify a multi-employer plan as a defined contribution plan or a defined benefit plan under the terms of the plan (including any constructive obligation that goes beyond the formal terms). Where a multi-employer plan is a defined benefit plan, an entity shall:**

(a) **account for its proportionate share of the defined benefit obligation, plan assets and cost associated with the plan in the same way as for any other defined benefit plan; and**

(b) **disclose the information required by paragraph 120A.**

30 **When sufficient information is not available to use defined benefit accounting for a multi-employer plan that is a defined benefit plan, an entity shall:**

(a) **account for the plan under paragraphs 44–46 as if it were a defined contribution plan;**

(b) **disclose:**

(i) **the fact that the plan is a defined benefit plan; and**

(ii) **the reason why sufficient information is not available to enable the entity to account for the plan as a defined benefit plan; and**

(c) **to the extent that a surplus or deficit in the plan may affect the amount of future contributions, disclose in addition:**

(i) **any available information about that surplus or deficit;**

(ii) **the basis used to determine that surplus or deficit; and**

(iii) **the implications, if any, for the entity.**

31 One example of a defined benefit multi-employer plan is one where:

(a) the plan is financed on a pay-as-you-go basis such that: contributions are set at a level that is expected to be sufficient to pay the benefits falling due in the same period; and future benefits earned during the current period will be paid out of future contributions; and

(b) employees' benefits are determined by the length of their service and the participating entities have no realistic means of withdrawing from the plan without paying a contribution for the benefits earned by employees up to the date of withdrawal. Such a plan creates actuarial risk for the entity: if the ultimate cost of benefits already earned at the balance sheet date is more than expected, the entity will have to either increase its contributions or persuade employees to accept a reduction in benefits. Therefore, such a plan is a defined benefit plan.

32 Where sufficient information is available about a multi-employer plan which is a defined benefit plan, an entity accounts for its proportionate share of the defined benefit obligation, plan assets and post-employment benefit cost associated with the plan in the same way as for any other defined benefit plan. However, in some cases, an entity may not be able to identify its share of the underlying financial position and performance of the plan with sufficient reliability for accounting purposes. This may occur if:

(a) the entity does not have access to information about the plan that satisfies the requirements of this Standard; or

(b) the plan exposes the participating entities to actuarial risks associated with the current and former employees of other entities, with the result that there is no consistent and reliable basis for allocating the obligation, plan assets and cost to individual entities participating in the plan.

In those cases, an entity accounts for the plan as if it were a defined contribution plan and discloses the additional information required by paragraph 30.

32A There may be a contractual agreement between the multi-employer plan and its participants that determines how the surplus in the plan will be distributed to the participants (or the deficit funded). A participant in a multi-employer plan with such an agreement that accounts for the plan as a defined contribution plan in accordance with paragraph 30 shall recognise the asset or liability that arises from the contractual agreement and the resulting income or expense in profit or loss.

Example illustrating paragraph 32A

An entity participates in a multi-employer defined benefit plan that does not prepare plan valuations on an IAS 19 basis. It therefore accounts for the plan as if it were a defined contribution plan. A non-IAS 19 funding valuation shows a deficit of 100 million in the plan. The plan has agreed under contract a schedule of contributions with the participating employers in the plan that will eliminate the deficit over the next five years. The entity's total contributions under the contract are 8 million.

The entity recognises a liability for the contributions adjusted for the time value of money and an equal expense in profit or loss.

32B IAS 37 *Provisions, Contingent Liabilities and Contingent Assets* requires an entity to recognise, or disclose information about, certain contingent liabilities. In the context of a multi-employer plan, a contingent liability may arise from, for example:

(a) actuarial losses relating to other participating entities because each entity that participates in a multi-employer plan shares in the actuarial risks of every other participating entity; or

(b) any responsibility under the terms of a plan to finance any shortfall in the plan if other entities cease to participate.

33 Multi-employer plans are distinct from group administration plans. A group administration plan is merely an aggregation of single employer plans combined to allow participating employers to pool their assets for investment purposes and reduce investment management and administration costs, but the claims of different employers are segregated for the sole benefit of their own employees. Group administration plans pose no particular accounting problems because information is readily available to treat them in the same way as any other single employer plan and because such plans do not expose the participating entities to actuarial risks associated with the current and former employees of other entities. The definitions in this Standard require an entity to classify a group administration plan as a defined contribution plan or a defined benefit plan in accordance with the terms of the plan (including any constructive obligation that goes beyond the formal terms).

Defined benefit plans that share risks between various entities under common control

34 Defined benefit plans that share risks between various entities under common control, for example, a parent and its subsidiaries, are not multi-employer plans.

34A An entity participating in such a plan shall obtain information about the plan as a whole measured in accordance with IAS 19 on the basis of assumptions that apply to the plan as a whole. If there is a contractual agreement or stated policy for charging the net defined benefit cost for the plan as a whole measured in accordance with IAS 19 to individual group entities, the entity shall, in its separate or individual financial statements, recognise the net defined benefit cost so charged. If there is no such agreement or policy, the net defined benefit cost shall be recognised in the separate or individual financial statements of the group entity that is legally the sponsoring employer for the plan. The other group entities shall, in their separate or individual financial statements, recognise a cost equal to their contribution payable for the period.

34B Participation in such a plan is a related party transaction for each individual group entity. An entity shall therefore, in its separate or individual financial statements, make the following disclosures:

(a) the contractual agreement or stated policy for charging the net defined benefit cost or the fact that there is no such policy.

(b) the policy for determining the contribution to be paid by the entity.

(c) if the entity accounts for an allocation of the net defined benefit cost in accordance with paragraph 34A, all the information about the plan as a whole in accordance with paragraphs 120–121.

(d) if the entity accounts for the contribution payable for the period in accordance with paragraph 34A, the information about the plan as a whole required in accordance with paragraphs 120A(b)–(e), (j), (n), (o), (q) and 121. The other disclosures required by paragraph 120A do not apply.

35 [Deleted]

State plans

36 An entity shall account for a state plan in the same way as for a multi-employer plan (see paragraphs 29 and 30).

37 State plans are established by legislation to cover all entities (or all entities in a particular category, for example, a specific industry) and are operated by national or local government or by another body (for example, an autonomous agency created specifically for this purpose) which is not subject to control or influence by the reporting entity. Some plans established by an entity provide both compulsory benefits which substitute for benefits that would otherwise be covered under a state plan and additional voluntary benefits. Such plans are not state plans.

38 State plans are characterised as defined benefit or defined contribution in nature based on the entity's obligation under the plan. Many state plans are funded on a pay-as-you-go basis: contributions are set at a level that is expected to be sufficient

to pay the required benefits falling due in the same period; future benefits earned during the current period will be paid out of future contributions. Nevertheless, in most state plans, the entity has no legal or constructive obligation to pay those future benefits: its only obligation is to pay the contributions as they fall due and if the entity ceases to employ members of the state plan, it will have no obligation to pay the benefits earned by its own employees in previous years. For this reason, state plans are normally defined contribution plans. However, in the rare cases when a state plan is a defined benefit plan, an entity applies the treatment prescribed in paragraphs 29 and 30.

Insured benefits

39 **An entity may pay insurance premiums to fund a post-employment benefit plan. The entity shall treat such a plan as a defined contribution plan unless the entity will have (either directly, or indirectly through the plan) a legal or constructive obligation to either:**

(a) pay the employee benefits directly when they fall due; or

(b) pay further amounts if the insurer does not pay all future employee benefits relating to employee service in the current and prior periods.

If the entity retains such a legal or constructive obligation, the entity shall treat the plan as a defined benefit plan.

40 The benefits insured by an insurance contract need not have a direct or automatic relationship with the entity's obligation for employee benefits. Post-employment benefit plans involving insurance contracts are subject to the same distinction between accounting and funding as other funded plans.

41 Where an entity funds a post-employment benefit obligation by contributing to an insurance policy under which the entity (either directly, indirectly through the plan, through the mechanism for setting future premiums or through a related party relationship with the insurer) retains a legal or constructive obligation, the payment of the premiums does not amount to a defined contribution arrangement. It follows that the entity:

(a) accounts for a qualifying insurance policy as a plan asset (see paragraph 7); and

(b) recognises other insurance policies as reimbursement rights (if the policies satisfy the criteria in paragraph 104A).

42 Where an insurance policy is in the name of a specified plan participant or a group of plan participants and the entity does not have any legal or constructive obligation to cover any loss on the policy, the entity has no obligation to pay benefits to the employees and the insurer has sole responsibility for paying the benefits. The payment of fixed premiums under such contracts is, in substance, the settlement of the employee benefit obligation, rather than an investment to meet the obligation. Consequently, the entity no longer has an asset or a liability. Therefore, an entity treats such payments as contributions to a defined contribution plan.

Post–employment benefits: defined contribution plans

43 Accounting for defined contribution plans is straightforward because the reporting entity's obligation for each period is determined by the amounts to be contributed for that period. Consequently, no actuarial assumptions are required to measure the obligation or the expense and there is no possibility of any actuarial gain or loss. Moreover, the obligations are measured on an undiscounted basis, except where they do not fall due wholly within twelve months after the end of the period in which the employees render the related service.

Recognition and measurement

44 **When an employee has rendered service to an entity during a period, the entity shall recognise the contribution payable to a defined contribution plan in exchange for that service:**

(a) as a liability (accrued expense), after deducting any contribution already paid. If the contribution already paid exceeds the contribution due for service before the balance sheet date, an entity shall recognise that excess as an asset (prepaid expense) to the extent that the prepayment will lead to, for example, a reduction in future payments or a cash refund; and

(b) as an expense, unless another Standard requires or permits the inclusion of the contribution in the cost of an asset (see, for example, IAS 2 ***Inventories*** **and IAS 16** ***Property, Plant and Equipment*****).**

45 **Where contributions to a defined contribution plan do not fall due wholly within twelve months after the end of the period in which the employees render the related service, they shall be discounted using the discount rate specified in paragraph 78.**

Disclosure

46 **An entity shall disclose the amount recognised as an expense for defined contribution plans.**

47 Where required by IAS 24 *Related Party Disclosures* an entity discloses information about contributions to defined contribution plans for key management personnel.

Post–employment benefits: defined benefit plans

48 Accounting for defined benefit plans is complex because actuarial assumptions are required to measure the obligation and the expense and there is a possibility of actuarial gains and losses. Moreover, the obligations are measured on a discounted basis because they may be settled many years after the employees render the related service.

Recognition and measurement

49 Defined benefit plans may be unfunded, or they may be wholly or partly funded by contributions by an entity, and sometimes its employees, into an entity, or fund, that is legally separate from the reporting entity and from which the

employee benefits are paid. The payment of funded benefits when they fall due depends not only on the financial position and the investment performance of the fund but also on an entity's ability (and willingness) to make good any shortfall in the fund's assets. Therefore, the entity is, in substance, underwriting the actuarial and investment risks associated with the plan. Consequently, the expense recognised for a defined benefit plan is not necessarily the amount of the contribution due for the period.

50 Accounting by an entity for defined benefit plans involves the following steps:

(a) using actuarial techniques to make a reliable estimate of the amount of benefit that employees have earned in return for their service in the current and prior periods. This requires an entity to determine how much benefit is attributable to the current and prior periods (see paragraphs 67–71) and to make estimates (actuarial assumptions) about demographic variables (such as employee turnover and mortality) and financial variables (such as future increases in salaries and medical costs) that will influence the cost of the benefit (see paragraphs 72–91);

(b) discounting that benefit using the Projected Unit Credit Method in order to determine the present value of the defined benefit obligation and the current service cost (see paragraphs 64–66);

(c) determining the fair value of any plan assets (see paragraphs 102–104);

(d) determining the total amount of actuarial gains and losses and the amount of those actuarial gains and losses to be recognised (see paragraphs 92–95);

(e) where a plan has been introduced or changed, determining the resulting past service cost (see paragraphs 96–101); and

(f) where a plan has been curtailed or settled, determining the resulting gain or loss (see paragraphs 109–115).

Where an entity has more than one defined benefit plan, the entity applies these procedures for each material plan separately.

51 In some cases, estimates, averages and computational short cuts may provide a reliable approximation of the detailed computations illustrated in this Standard.

Accounting for the constructive obligation

52 An entity shall account not only for its legal obligation under the formal terms of a defined benefit plan, but also for any constructive obligation that arises from the entity's informal practices. Informal practices give rise to a constructive obligation where the entity has no realistic alternative but to pay employee benefits. An example of a constructive obligation is where a change in the entity's informal practices would cause unacceptable damage to its relationship with employees.

53 The formal terms of a defined benefit plan may permit an entity to terminate its obligation under the plan. Nevertheless, it is usually difficult for an entity to cancel a plan if employees are to be retained. Therefore, in the absence of evidence to the contrary, accounting for post-employment benefits assumes that an entity which is currently promising such benefits will continue to do so over the remaining working lives of employees.

Balance sheet

54 **The amount recognised as a defined benefit liability shall be the net total of the following amounts:**

(a) the present value of the defined benefit obligation at the balance sheet date (see paragraph 64);

(b) plus any actuarial gains (less any actuarial losses) not recognised because of the treatment set out in paragraphs 92 and 93;

(c) minus any past service cost not yet recognised (see paragraph 96);

(d) minus the fair value at the balance sheet date of plan assets (if any) out of which the obligations are to be settled directly (see paragraphs 102–104).

55 The present value of the defined benefit obligation is the gross obligation, before deducting the fair value of any plan assets.

56 **An entity shall determine the present value of defined benefit obligations and the fair value of any plan assets with sufficient regularity that the amounts recognised in the financial statements do not differ materially from the amounts that would be determined at the balance sheet date.**

57 This Standard encourages, but does not require, an entity to involve a qualified actuary in the measurement of all material post-employment benefit obligations. For practical reasons, an entity may request a qualified actuary to carry out a detailed valuation of the obligation before the balance sheet date. Nevertheless, the results of that valuation are updated for any material transactions and other material changes in circumstances (including changes in market prices and interest rates) up to the balance sheet date.

58 **The amount determined under paragraph 54 may be negative (an asset). An entity shall measure the resulting asset at the lower of:**

(a) the amount determined under paragraph 54; and

(b) the total of:

(i) any cumulative unrecognised net actuarial losses and past service cost (see paragraphs 92, 93 and 96); and

(ii) the present value of any economic benefits available in the form of refunds from the plan or reductions in future contributions to the plan. The present value of these economic benefits shall be determined using the discount rate specified in paragraph 78.

58A **The application of paragraph 58 shall not result in a gain being recognised solely as a result of an actuarial loss or past service cost in the current period or in a loss being recognised solely as a result of an actuarial gain in the current period. The entity shall therefore recognise immediately under paragraph 54 the following, to the extent that they arise while the defined benefit asset is determined in accordance with paragraph 58(b):**

(a) net actuarial losses of the current period and past service cost of the current period to the extent that they exceed any reduction in the

present value of the economic benefits specified in paragraph 58(b)(ii). If there is no change or an increase in the present value of the economic benefits, the entire net actuarial losses of the current period and past service cost of the current period shall be recognised immediately under paragraph 54.

(b) net actuarial gains of the current period after the deduction of past service cost of the current period to the extent that they exceed any increase in the present value of the economic benefits specified in paragraph 58(b)(ii). If there is no change or a decrease in the present value of the economic benefits, the entire net actuarial gains of the current period after the deduction of past service cost of the current period shall be recognised immediately under paragraph 54.

58B Paragraph 58A applies to an entity only if it has, at the beginning or end of the accounting period, a surplus* in a defined benefit plan and cannot, based on the current terms of the plan, recover that surplus fully through refunds or reductions in future contributions. In such cases, past service cost and actuarial losses that arise in the period, the recognition of which is deferred under paragraph 54(b)(i), will increase the amount specified in paragraph 58. If that increase is not offset by an equal decrease in the present value of economic benefits that qualify for recognition under paragraph 58(b)(ii), there will be an increase in the net total specified by paragraph 58(b) and, hence, a recognised gain. Paragraph 58A prohibits the recognition of a gain in these circumstances. The opposite effect arises with actuarial gains that arise in the period, the recognition of which is deferred under paragraph 54, to the extent that the actuarial gains reduce cumulative unrecognised actuarial losses. Paragraph 58A prohibits the recognition of a loss in these circumstances. For examples of the application of this paragraph, see Appendix C.

59 An asset may arise where a defined benefit plan has been overfunded or in certain cases where actuarial gains are recognised. An entity recognises an asset in such cases because:

(a) the entity controls a resource, which is the ability to use the surplus to generate future benefits;

(b) that control is a result of past events (contributions paid by the entity and service rendered by the employee); and

(c) future economic benefits are available to the entity in the form of a reduction in future contributions or a cash refund, either directly to the entity or indirectly to another plan in deficit.

60 The limit in paragraph 58(b) does not override the delayed recognition of certain actuarial losses (see paragraphs 92 and 93) and certain past service cost (see paragraph 96), other than as specified in paragraph 58A. However, that limit does override the transitional option in paragraph 155(b). Paragraph 120A(f)(iii) requires an entity to disclose any amount not recognised as an asset because of the limit in paragraph 58(b).

---

* A surplus is an excess of the fair value of the plan assets over the present value of the defined benefit obligation.

Example illustrating paragraph 60

A defined benefit plan has the following characteristics:

Present value of the obligation	1,100
Fair value of plan assets	(1,190)
	(90)
Unrecognised actuarial losses	(110)
Unrecognised past service cost	(70)
Unrecognised increase in the liability on initial adoption of the Standard under paragraph 155(b)	(50)
Negative amount determined under paragraph 54	(320)
Present value of available future refunds and reductions in future contributions	90
The limit under paragraph 58(b) is computed as follows:	
Unrecognised actuarial losses	*110*
Unrecognised past service cost	*70*
Present value of available future refunds and reductions in future contributions	*90*
Limit	*270*

270 is less than 320. Therefore, the entity recognises an asset of 270 and discloses that the limit reduced the carrying amount of the asset by 50 (see paragraph 120A(f)(iii)).

Profit or loss

61 **An entity shall recognise the net total of the following amounts in profit or loss, except to the extent that another Standard requires or permits their inclusion in the cost of an asset:**

(a) current service cost (see paragraphs 63–91);

(b) interest cost (see paragraph 82);

(c) the expected return on any plan assets (see paragraphs 105–107) and on any reimbursement rights (see paragraph 104A);

(d) actuarial gains and losses, as required in accordance with the entity's accounting policy (see paragraphs 92–93D);

(e) past service cost (see paragraph 96);

(f) the effect of any curtailments or settlements (see paragraphs 109 and 110); and

(g) the effect of the limit in paragraph 58(b), unless it is recognised outside profit or loss in accordance with paragraph 93C.

62 Other Standards require the inclusion of certain employee benefit costs within the cost of assets such as inventories or property, plant and equipment (see IAS 2 *Inventories* and IAS 16 *Property, Plant and Equipment*). Any post-employment benefit costs included in the cost of such assets include the appropriate proportion of the components listed in paragraph 61.

Recognition and measurement: present value of defined benefit obligations and current service cost

63 The ultimate cost of a defined benefit plan may be influenced by many variables, such as final salaries, employee turnover and mortality, medical cost trends and, for a funded plan, the investment earnings on the plan assets. The ultimate cost of the plan is uncertain and this uncertainty is likely to persist over a long period of time. In order to measure the present value of the post-employment benefit obligations and the related current service cost, it is necessary to:

(a) apply an actuarial valuation method (see paragraphs 64–66);

(b) attribute benefit to periods of service (see paragraphs 67–71); and

(c) make actuarial assumptions (see paragraphs 72–91).

Actuarial valuation method

64 An entity shall use the Projected Unit Credit Method to determine the present value of its defined benefit obligations and the related current service cost and, where applicable, past service cost.

65 The Projected Unit Credit Method (sometimes known as the accrued benefit method pro-rated on service or as the benefit/years of service method) sees each period of service as giving rise to an additional unit of benefit entitlement (see paragraphs 67–71) and measures each unit separately to build up the final obligation (see paragraphs 72–91).

Example illustrating paragraph 65

A lump sum benefit is payable on termination of service and equal to 1% of final salary for each year of service. The salary in year 1 is 10,000 and is assumed to increase at 7% (compound) each year. The discount rate used is 10% per annum. The following table shows how the obligation builds up for an employee who is expected to leave at the end of year 5, assuming that there are no changes in actuarial assumptions. For simplicity, this example ignores the additional adjustment needed to reflect the probability that the employee may leave the entity at an earlier or later date.

Year	*1*	*2*	*3*	*4*	*5*
Benefit attributed to:					
– prior years	*0*	*131*	*262*	*393*	*524*
– current year (1% of final salary)	*131*	*131*	*131*	*131*	*131*
– current and prior years	*131*	*262*	*393*	*524*	*655*

Continued from previous page

Example illustrating paragraph 65

Year	*1*	*2*	*3*	*4*	*5*
Opening obligation	*–*	*89*	*196*	*324*	*476*
Interest at 10%	*–*	*9*	*20*	*33*	*48*
Current service cost	*89*	*98*	*108*	*119*	*131*
Closing obligation	*89*	*196*	*324*	*476*	*655*

Note:

1. *The opening obligation is the present value of benefit attributed to prior years.*
2. *The current service cost is the present value of benefit attributed to the current year.*
3. *The closing obligation is the present value of benefit attributed to current and prior years.*

66 An entity discounts the whole of a post-employment benefit obligation, even if part of the obligation falls due within twelve months of the balance sheet date.

Attributing benefit to periods of service

67 In determining the present value of its defined benefit obligations and the related current service cost and, where applicable, past service cost, an entity shall attribute benefit to periods of service under the plan's benefit formula. However, if an employee's service in later years will lead to a materially higher level of benefit than in earlier years, an entity shall attribute benefit on a straight-line basis from:

(a) the date when service by the employee first leads to benefits under the plan (whether or not the benefits are conditional on further service); until

(b) the date when further service by the employee will lead to no material amount of further benefits under the plan, other than from further salary increases.

68 The Projected Unit Credit Method requires an entity to attribute benefit to the current period (in order to determine current service cost) and the current and prior periods (in order to determine the present value of defined benefit obligations). An entity attributes benefit to periods in which the obligation to provide post-employment benefits arises. That obligation arises as employees render services in return for post-employment benefits which an entity expects to pay in future reporting periods. Actuarial techniques allow an entity to measure that obligation with sufficient reliability to justify recognition of a liability.

Examples illustrating paragraph 68

1. A defined benefit plan provides a lump-sum benefit of 100 payable on retirement for each year of service.

   A benefit of 100 is attributed to each year. The current service cost is the present value of 100. The present value of the defined benefit obligation is the present value of 100, multiplied by the number of years of service up to the balance sheet date.

   If the benefit is payable immediately when the employee leaves the entity, the current service cost and the present value of the defined benefit obligation reflect the date at which the employee is expected to leave. Thus, because of the effect of discounting, they are less than the amounts that would be determined if the employee left at the balance sheet date.

2. A plan provides a monthly pension of 0.2% of final salary for each year of service. The pension is payable from the age of 65.

   Benefit equal to the present value, at the expected retirement date, of a monthly pension of 0.2% of the estimated final salary payable from the expected retirement date until the expected date of death is attributed to each year of service. The current service cost is the present value of that benefit. The present value of the defined benefit obligation is the present value of monthly pension payments of 0.2% of final salary, multiplied by the number of years of service up to the balance sheet date. The current service cost and the present value of the defined benefit obligation are discounted because pension payments begin at the age of 65.

69 Employee service gives rise to an obligation under a defined benefit plan even if the benefits are conditional on future employment (in other words they are not vested). Employee service before the vesting date gives rise to a constructive obligation because, at each successive balance sheet date, the amount of future service that an employee will have to render before becoming entitled to the benefit is reduced. In measuring its defined benefit obligation, an entity considers the probability that some employees may not satisfy any vesting requirements. Similarly, although certain post-employment benefits, for example, post-employment medical benefits, become payable only if a specified event occurs when an employee is no longer employed, an obligation is created when the employee renders service that will provide entitlement to the benefit if the specified event occurs. The probability that the specified event will occur affects the measurement of the obligation, but does not determine whether the obligation exists.

Examples illustrating paragraph 69

1. A plan pays a benefit of 100 for each year of service. The benefits vest after ten years of service.

   A benefit of 100 is attributed to each year. In each of the first ten years, the current service cost and the present value of the obligation reflect the probability that the employee may not complete ten years of service.

Continued from previous page

Examples illustrating paragraph 69

2. A plan pays a benefit of 100 for each year of service, excluding service before the age of 25. The benefits vest immediately.

   No benefit is attributed to service before the age of 25 because service before that date does not lead to benefits (conditional or unconditional). A benefit of 100 is attributed to each subsequent year.

70 The obligation increases until the date when further service by the employee will lead to no material amount of further benefits. Therefore, all benefit is attributed to periods ending on or before that date. Benefit is attributed to individual accounting periods under the plan's benefit formula. However, if an employee's service in later years will lead to a materially higher level of benefit than in earlier years, an entity attributes benefit on a straight-line basis until the date when further service by the employee will lead to no material amount of further benefits. That is because the employee's service throughout the entire period will ultimately lead to benefit at that higher level.

Examples illustrating paragraph 70

1. A plan pays a lump-sum benefit of 1,000 that vests after ten years of service. The plan provides no further benefit for subsequent service.

   A benefit of 100 (1,000 divided by ten) is attributed to each of the first ten years. The current service cost in each of the first ten years reflects the probability that the employee may not complete ten years of service. No benefit is attributed to subsequent years.

2. A plan pays a lump-sum retirement benefit of 2,000 to all employees who are still employed at the age of 55 after twenty years of service, or who are still employed at the age of 65, regardless of their length of service.

   For employees who join before the age of 35, service first leads to benefits under the plan at the age of 35 (an employee could leave at the age of 30 and return at the age of 33, with no effect on the amount or timing of benefits). Those benefits are conditional on further service. Also, service beyond the age of 55 will lead to no material amount of further benefits. For these employees, the entity attributes benefit of 100 (2,000 divided by 20) to each year from the age of 35 to the age of 55.

   For employees who join between the ages of 35 and 45, service beyond twenty years will lead to no material amount of further benefits. For these employees, the entity attributes benefit of 100 (2,000 divided by 20) to each of the first twenty years.

   For an employee who joins at the age of 55, service beyond ten years will lead to no material amount of further benefits. For this employee, the entity attributes benefit of 200 (2,000 divided by 10) to each of the first ten years.

   For all employees, the current service cost and the present value of the obligation reflect the probability that the employee may not complete the necessary period of service.

Continued from previous page

Examples illustrating paragraph 70

3. A post-employment medical plan reimburses 40% of an employee's post-employment medical costs if the employee leaves after more than ten and less than twenty years of service and 50% of those costs if the employee leaves after twenty or more years of service.

   Under the plan's benefit formula, the entity attributes 4% of the present value of the expected medical costs (40% divided by ten) to each of the first ten years and 1% (10% divided by ten) to each of the second ten years. The current service cost in each year reflects the probability that the employee may not complete the necessary period of service to earn part or all of the benefits. For employees expected to leave within ten years, no benefit is attributed.

4. A post-employment medical plan reimburses 10% of an employee's post-employment medical costs if the employee leaves after more than ten and less than twenty years of service and 50% of those costs if the employee leaves after twenty or more years of service.

   Service in later years will lead to a materially higher level of benefit than in earlier years. Therefore, for employees expected to leave after twenty or more years, the entity attributes benefit on a straight-line basis under paragraph 68. Service beyond twenty years will lead to no material amount of further benefits. Therefore, the benefit attributed to each of the first twenty years is 2.5% of the present value of the expected medical costs (50% divided by twenty).

   For employees expected to leave between ten and twenty years, the benefit attributed to each of the first ten years is 1% of the present value of the expected medical costs. For these employees, no benefit is attributed to service between the end of the tenth year and the estimated date of leaving.

   For employees expected to leave within ten years, no benefit is attributed.

71 Where the amount of a benefit is a constant proportion of final salary for each year of service, future salary increases will affect the amount required to settle the obligation that exists for service before the balance sheet date, but do not create an additional obligation. Therefore:

(a) for the purpose of paragraph 67(b), salary increases do not lead to further benefits, even though the amount of the benefits is dependent on final salary; and

(b) the amount of benefit attributed to each period is a constant proportion of the salary to which the benefit is linked.

Example illustrating paragraph 71

Employees are entitled to a benefit of 3% of final salary for each year of service before the age of 55.

Benefit of 3% of estimated final salary is attributed to each year up to the age of 55. This is the date when further service by the employee will lead to no material amount of further benefits under the plan. No benefit is attributed to service after that age.

Actuarial assumptions

72 **Actuarial assumptions shall be unbiased and mutually compatible.**

73 Actuarial assumptions are an entity's best estimates of the variables that will determine the ultimate cost of providing post-employment benefits. Actuarial assumptions comprise:

(a) demographic assumptions about the future characteristics of current and former employees (and their dependants) who are eligible for benefits. Demographic assumptions deal with matters such as:

  (i) mortality, both during and after employment;

  (ii) rates of employee turnover, disability and early retirement;

  (iii) the proportion of plan members with dependants who will be eligible for benefits; and

  (iv) claim rates under medical plans; and

(b) financial assumptions, dealing with items such as:

  (i) the discount rate (see paragraphs 78–82);

  (ii) future salary and benefit levels (see paragraphs 83–87);

  (iii) in the case of medical benefits, future medical costs, including, where material, the cost of administering claims and benefit payments (see paragraphs 88–91); and

  (iv) the expected rate of return on plan assets (see paragraphs 105–107).

74 Actuarial assumptions are unbiased if they are neither imprudent nor excessively conservative.

75 Actuarial assumptions are mutually compatible if they reflect the economic relationships between factors such as inflation, rates of salary increase, the return on plan assets and discount rates. For example, all assumptions which depend on a particular inflation level (such as assumptions about interest rates and salary and benefit increases) in any given future period assume the same inflation level in that period.

76 An entity determines the discount rate and other financial assumptions in nominal (stated) terms, unless estimates in real (inflation-adjusted) terms are more reliable, for example, in a hyper-inflationary economy (see IAS 29 *Financial Reporting in Hyperinflationary Economies*), or where the benefit is index-linked and there is a deep market in index-linked bonds of the same currency and term.

77 **Financial assumptions shall be based on market expectations, at the balance sheet date, for the period over which the obligations are to be settled.**

Actuarial assumptions: discount rate

78 **The rate used to discount post-employment benefit obligations (both funded and unfunded) shall be determined by reference to market yields at the balance sheet date on high quality corporate bonds. In countries where there is no deep market in such bonds, the market yields (at the balance**

sheet date) on government bonds shall be used. The currency and term of the corporate bonds or government bonds shall be consistent with the currency and estimated term of the post-employment benefit obligations.

79 One actuarial assumption which has a material effect is the discount rate. The discount rate reflects the time value of money but not the actuarial or investment risk. Furthermore, the discount rate does not reflect the entity-specific credit risk borne by the entity's creditors, nor does it reflect the risk that future experience may differ from actuarial assumptions.

80 The discount rate reflects the estimated timing of benefit payments. In practice, an entity often achieves this by applying a single weighted average discount rate that reflects the estimated timing and amount of benefit payments and the currency in which the benefits are to be paid.

81 In some cases, there may be no deep market in bonds with a sufficiently long maturity to match the estimated maturity of all the benefit payments. In such cases, an entity uses current market rates of the appropriate term to discount shorter term payments, and estimates the discount rate for longer maturities by extrapolating current market rates along the yield curve. The total present value of a defined benefit obligation is unlikely to be particularly sensitive to the discount rate applied to the portion of benefits that is payable beyond the final maturity of the available corporate or government bonds.

82 Interest cost is computed by multiplying the discount rate as determined at the start of the period by the present value of the defined benefit obligation throughout that period, taking account of any material changes in the obligation. The present value of the obligation will differ from the liability recognised in the balance sheet because the liability is recognised after deducting the fair value of any plan assets and because some actuarial gains and losses, and some past service cost, are not recognised immediately. [Appendix A illustrates the computation of interest cost, among other things.]

Actuarial assumptions: salaries, benefits and medical costs

83 Post-employment benefit obligations shall be measured on a basis that reflects:

- **(a) estimated future salary increases;**
- **(b) the benefits set out in the terms of the plan (or resulting from any constructive obligation that goes beyond those terms) at the balance sheet date; and**
- **(c) estimated future changes in the level of any state benefits that affect the benefits payable under a defined benefit plan, if, and only if, either:**
  - **(i) those changes were enacted before the balance sheet date; or**
  - **(ii) past history, or other reliable evidence, indicates that those state benefits will change in some predictable manner, for example, in line with future changes in general price levels or general salary levels.**

84 Estimates of future salary increases take account of inflation, seniority, promotion and other relevant factors, such as supply and demand in the employment market.

85 If the formal terms of a plan (or a constructive obligation that goes beyond those terms) require an entity to change benefits in future periods, the measurement of the obligation reflects those changes. This is the case when, for example:

(a) the entity has a past history of increasing benefits, for example, to mitigate the effects of inflation, and there is no indication that this practice will change in the future; or

(b) actuarial gains have already been recognised in the financial statements and the entity is obliged, by either the formal terms of a plan (or a constructive obligation that goes beyond those terms) or legislation, to use any surplus in the plan for the benefit of plan participants (see paragraph 98(c)).

86 Actuarial assumptions do not reflect future benefit changes that are not set out in the formal terms of the plan (or a constructive obligation) at the balance sheet date. Such changes will result in:

(a) past service cost, to the extent that they change benefits for service before the change; and

(b) current service cost for periods after the change, to the extent that they change benefits for service after the change.

87 Some post-employment benefits are linked to variables such as the level of state retirement benefits or state medical care. The measurement of such benefits reflects expected changes in such variables, based on past history and other reliable evidence.

88 Assumptions about medical costs shall take account of estimated future changes in the cost of medical services, resulting from both inflation and specific changes in medical costs.

89 Measurement of post-employment medical benefits requires assumptions about the level and frequency of future claims and the cost of meeting those claims. An entity estimates future medical costs on the basis of historical data about the entity's own experience, supplemented where necessary by historical data from other entities, insurance companies, medical providers or other sources. Estimates of future medical costs consider the effect of technological advances, changes in health care utilisation or delivery patterns and changes in the health status of plan participants.

90 The level and frequency of claims is particularly sensitive to the age, health status and sex of employees (and their dependants) and may be sensitive to other factors such as geographical location. Therefore, historical data is adjusted to the extent that the demographic mix of the population differs from that of the population used as a basis for the historical data. It is also adjusted where there is reliable evidence that historical trends will not continue.

91 Some post-employment health care plans require employees to contribute to the medical costs covered by the plan. Estimates of future medical costs take account of any such contributions, based on the terms of the plan at the balance sheet date

(or based on any constructive obligation that goes beyond those terms). Changes in those employee contributions result in past service cost or, where applicable, curtailments. The cost of meeting claims may be reduced by benefits from state or other medical providers (see paragraphs 83(c) and 87).

Actuarial gains and losses

92 **In measuring its defined benefit liability in accordance with paragraph 54, an entity shall, subject to paragraph 58A, recognise a portion (as specified in paragraph 93) of its actuarial gains and losses as income or expense if the net cumulative unrecognised actuarial gains and losses at the end of the previous reporting period exceeded the greater of:**

(a) 10% of the present value of the defined benefit obligation at that date (before deducting plan assets); and

(b) 10% of the fair value of any plan assets at that date.

These limits shall be calculated and applied separately for each defined benefit plan.

93 **The portion of actuarial gains and losses to be recognised for each defined benefit plan is the excess determined in accordance with paragraph 92, divided by the expected average remaining working lives of the employees participating in that plan. However, an entity may adopt any systematic method that results in faster recognition of actuarial gains and losses, provided that the same basis is applied to both gains and losses and the basis is applied consistently from period to period. An entity may apply such systematic methods to actuarial gains and losses even if they are within the limits specified in paragraph 92.**

93A **If, as permitted by paragraph 93, an entity adopts a policy of recognising actuarial gains and losses in the period in which they occur, it may recognise them outside profit or loss, in accordance with paragraphs 93B–93D, providing it does so for:**

(a) all of its defined benefit plans; and

(b) all of its actuarial gains and losses.

93B Actuarial gains and losses recognised outside profit or loss as permitted by paragraph 93A shall be presented in a statement of changes in equity titled 'statement of recognised income and expense' that comprises only the items specified in paragraph 96 of IAS 1 (as revised in 2003). The entity shall not present the actuarial gains and losses in a statement of changes in equity in the columnar format referred to in paragraph 101 of IAS 1 or any other format that includes the items specified in paragraph 97 of IAS 1.

93C An entity that recognises actuarial gains and losses in accordance with paragraph 93A shall also recognise any adjustments arising from the limit in paragraph 58(b) outside profit or loss in the statement of recognised income and expense.

93D Actuarial gains and losses and adjustments arising from the limit in paragraph 58(b) that have been recognised directly in the statement of recognised income

and expense shall be recognised immediately in retained earnings. They shall not be recognised in profit or loss in a subsequent period.

94 Actuarial gains and losses may result from increases or decreases in either the present value of a defined benefit obligation or the fair value of any related plan assets. Causes of actuarial gains and losses include, for example:

(a) unexpectedly high or low rates of employee turnover, early retirement or mortality or of increases in salaries, benefits (if the formal or constructive terms of a plan provide for inflationary benefit increases) or medical costs;

(b) the effect of changes in estimates of future employee turnover, early retirement or mortality or of increases in salaries, benefits (if the formal or constructive terms of a plan provide for inflationary benefit increases) or medical costs;

(c) the effect of changes in the discount rate; and

(d) differences between the actual return on plan assets and the expected return on plan assets (see paragraphs 105–107).

95 In the long term, actuarial gains and losses may offset one another. Therefore, estimates of post-employment benefit obligations may be viewed as a range (or 'corridor') around the best estimate. An entity is permitted, but not required, to recognise actuarial gains and losses that fall within that range. This Standard requires an entity to recognise, as a minimum, a specified portion of the actuarial gains and losses that fall outside a 'corridor' of plus or minus 10%. [Appendix A illustrates the treatment of actuarial gains and losses, among other things.] The Standard also permits systematic methods of faster recognition, provided that those methods satisfy the conditions set out in paragraph 93. Such permitted methods include, for example, immediate recognition of all actuarial gains and losses, both within and outside the 'corridor'. Paragraph 155(b)(iii) explains the need to consider any unrecognised part of the transitional liability in accounting for subsequent actuarial gains.

Past service cost

96 In measuring its defined benefit liability under paragraph 54, an entity shall, subject to paragraph 58A, recognise past service cost as an expense on a straight-line basis over the average period until the benefits become vested. To the extent that the benefits are already vested immediately following the introduction of, or changes to, a defined benefit plan, an entity shall recognise past service cost immediately.

97 Past service cost arises when an entity introduces a defined benefit plan or changes the benefits payable under an existing defined benefit plan. Such changes are in return for employee service over the period until the benefits concerned are vested. Therefore, past service cost is recognised over that period, regardless of the fact that the cost refers to employee service in previous periods. Past service cost is measured as the change in the liability resulting from the amendment (see paragraph 64).

Example illustrating paragraph 97

An entity operates a pension plan that provides a pension of 2% of final salary for each year of service. The benefits become vested after five years of service. On 1 January 20X5 the entity improves the pension to 2.5% of final salary for each year of service starting from 1 January 20X1. At the date of the improvement, the present value of the additional benefits for service from 1 January 20X1 to 1 January 20X5 is as follows:

Employees with more than five years' service at 1/1/X5	150
Employees with less than five years' service at 1/1/X5 (average period until vesting: three years)	120
	270

The entity recognises 150 immediately because those benefits are already vested. The entity recognises 120 on a straight-line basis over three years from 1 January 20X5.

98 Past service cost excludes:

(a) the effect of differences between actual and previously assumed salary increases on the obligation to pay benefits for service in prior years (there is no past service cost because actuarial assumptions allow for projected salaries);

(b) under and over estimates of discretionary pension increases where an entity has a constructive obligation to grant such increases (there is no past service cost because actuarial assumptions allow for such increases);

(c) estimates of benefit improvements that result from actuarial gains that have already been recognised in the financial statements if the entity is obliged, by either the formal terms of a plan (or a constructive obligation that goes beyond those terms) or legislation, to use any surplus in the plan for the benefit of plan participants, even if the benefit increase has not yet been formally awarded (the resulting increase in the obligation is an actuarial loss and not past service cost, see paragraph 85(b));

(d) the increase in vested benefits when, in the absence of new or improved benefits, employees complete vesting requirements (there is no past service cost because the estimated cost of benefits was recognised as current service cost as the service was rendered); and

(e) the effect of plan amendments that reduce benefits for future service (a curtailment).

99 An entity establishes the amortisation schedule for past service cost when the benefits are introduced or changed. It would be impracticable to maintain the detailed records needed to identify and implement subsequent changes in that amortisation schedule. Moreover, the effect is likely to be material only where there is a curtailment or settlement. Therefore, an entity amends the amortisation schedule for past service cost only if there is a curtailment or settlement.

100 Where an entity reduces benefits payable under an existing defined benefit plan, the resulting reduction in the defined benefit liability is recognised as (negative) past service cost over the average period until the reduced portion of the benefits becomes vested.

101 Where an entity reduces certain benefits payable under an existing defined benefit plan and, at the same time, increases other benefits payable under the plan for the same employees, the entity treats the change as a single net change.

Recognition and measurement: plan assets

Fair value of plan assets

102 The fair value of any plan assets is deducted in determining the amount recognised in the balance sheet under paragraph 54. When no market price is available, the fair value of plan assets is estimated; for example, by discounting expected future cash flows using a discount rate that reflects both the risk associated with the plan assets and the maturity or expected disposal date of those assets (or, if they have no maturity, the expected period until the settlement of the related obligation).

103 Plan assets exclude unpaid contributions due from the reporting entity to the fund, as well as any non-transferable financial instruments issued by the entity and held by the fund. Plan assets are reduced by any liabilities of the fund that do not relate to employee benefits, for example, trade and other payables and liabilities resulting from derivative financial instruments.

104 Where plan assets include qualifying insurance policies that exactly match the amount and timing of some or all of the benefits payable under the plan, the fair value of those insurance policies is deemed to be the present value of the related obligations, as described in paragraph 54 (subject to any reduction required if the amounts receivable under the insurance policies are not recoverable in full).

Reimbursements

104A When, and only when, it is virtually certain that another party will reimburse some or all of the expenditure required to settle a defined benefit obligation, an entity shall recognise its right to reimbursement as a separate asset. The entity shall measure the asset at fair value. In all other respects, an entity shall treat that asset in the same way as plan assets. In the income statement, the expense relating to a defined benefit plan may be presented net of the amount recognised for a reimbursement.

104B Sometimes, an entity is able to look to another party, such as an insurer, to pay part or all of the expenditure required to settle a defined benefit obligation. Qualifying insurance policies, as defined in paragraph 7, are plan assets. An entity accounts for qualifying insurance policies in the same way as for all other plan assets and paragraph 104A does not apply (see paragraphs 39–42 and 104).

104C When an insurance policy is not a qualifying insurance policy, that insurance policy is not a plan asset. Paragraph 104A deals with such cases: the entity recognises its right to reimbursement under the insurance policy as a separate asset, rather than as a deduction in determining the defined benefit liability recognised under paragraph 54; in all other respects, the entity treats that asset in the same way as plan assets. In particular, the defined benefit liability recognised under paragraph 54 is increased (reduced) to the extent that net cumulative actuarial gains (losses) on the defined benefit obligation and on the related reimbursement right remain unrecognised under paragraphs 92 and 93. Paragraph 120A(f)(iv) requires the entity to disclose a brief description of the link between the reimbursement right and the related obligation.

Example illustrating paragraphs 104A–104C

Present value of obligation	1,241
Unrecognised actuarial gains	17
Liability recognised in balance sheet	1,258
Rights under insurance policies that exactly match the amount and timing of some of the benefits payable under the plan. Those benefits have a present value of 1,092.	1,092

The unrecognised actuarial gains of 17 are the net cumulative actuarial gains on the obligation and on the reimbursement rights.

104D If the right to reimbursement arises under an insurance policy that exactly matches the amount and timing of some or all of the benefits payable under a defined benefit plan, the fair value of the reimbursement right is deemed to be the present value of the related obligation, as described in paragraph 54 (subject to any reduction required if the reimbursement is not recoverable in full).

Return on plan assets

105 The expected return on plan assets is one component of the expense recognised in the income statement. The difference between the expected return on plan assets and the actual return on plan assets is an actuarial gain or loss; it is included with the actuarial gains and losses on the defined benefit obligation in determining the net amount that is compared with the limits of the 10% 'corridor' specified in paragraph 92.

106 The expected return on plan assets is based on market expectations, at the beginning of the period, for returns over the entire life of the related obligation. The expected return on plan assets reflects changes in the fair value of plan assets held during the period as a result of actual contributions paid into the fund and actual benefits paid out of the fund.

Example illustrating paragraph 106

At 1 January 20X1, the fair value of plan assets was 10,000 and net cumulative unrecognised actuarial gains were 760. On 30 June 20X1, the plan paid benefits of 1,900 and received contributions of 4,900. At 31 December 20X1, the fair value of plan assets was 15,000 and the present value of the defined benefit obligation was 14,792. Actuarial losses on the obligation for 20X1 were 60.

At 1 January 20X1, the reporting entity made the following estimates, based on market prices at that date:

	%
Interest and dividend income, after tax payable by the fund	9.25
Realised and unrealised gains on plan assets (after tax)	2.00
Administration costs	(1.00)
Expected rate of return	10.25

For 20X1, the expected and actual return on plan assets are as follows:

Return on 10,000 held for 12 months at 10.25%	*1,025*
Return on 3,000 held for six months at 5% (equivalent to 10.25% annually, compounded every six months)	*150*
Expected return on plan assets for 20X1	*1,175*
Fair value of plan assets at 31 December 20X1	*15,000*
Less fair value of plan assets at 1 January 20X1	*(10,000)*
Less contributions received	*(4,900)*
Add benefits paid	*1,900*
Actual return on plan assets	*2,000*

The difference between the expected return on plan assets (1,175) and the actual return on plan assets (2,000) is an actuarial gain of 825. Therefore, the cumulative net unrecognised actuarial gains are 1,525 (760 plus 825 less 60). Under paragraph 92, the limits of the corridor are set at 1,500 (greater of: (i) 10% of 15,000 and (ii) 10% of 14,792). In the following year (20X2), the entity recognises in the income statement an actuarial gain of 25 (1,525 less 1,500) divided by the expected average remaining working life of the employees concerned.

The expected return on plan assets for 20X2 will be based on market expectations at 1/1/X2 for returns over the entire life of the obligation.

107 In determining the expected and actual return on plan assets, an entity deducts expected administration costs, other than those included in the actuarial assumptions used to measure the obligation.

Business combinations

108 In a business combination, an entity recognises assets and liabilities arising from post-employment benefits at the present value of the obligation less the fair value of any plan assets (see IFRS 3 *Business Combinations*). The present value of the obligation includes all of the following, even if the acquiree had not yet recognised them at the acquisition date:

(a) actuarial gains and losses that arose before the acquisition date (whether or not they fell inside the 10% 'corridor');

(b) past service cost that arose from benefit changes, or the introduction of a plan, before the acquisition date; and

(c) amounts that, under the transitional provisions of paragraph 155(b), the acquiree had not recognised.

Curtailments and settlements

109 An entity shall recognise gains or losses on the curtailment or settlement of a defined benefit plan when the curtailment or settlement occurs. The gain or loss on a curtailment or settlement shall comprise:

(a) any resulting change in the present value of the defined benefit obligation;

(b) any resulting change in the fair value of the plan assets;

(c) any related actuarial gains and losses and past service cost that, under paragraphs 92 and 96, had not previously been recognised.

110 Before determining the effect of a curtailment or settlement, an entity shall remeasure the obligation (and the related plan assets, if any) using current actuarial assumptions (including current market interest rates and other current market prices).

111 A curtailment occurs when an entity either:

(a) is demonstrably committed to make a material reduction in the number of employees covered by a plan; or

(b) amends the terms of a defined benefit plan such that a material element of future service by current employees will no longer qualify for benefits, or will qualify only for reduced benefits.

A curtailment may arise from an isolated event, such as the closing of a plant, discontinuance of an operation or termination or suspension of a plan. An event is material enough to qualify as a curtailment if the recognition of a curtailment gain or loss would have a material effect on the financial statements. Curtailments are often linked with a restructuring. Therefore, an entity accounts for a curtailment at the same time as for a related restructuring.

112 A settlement occurs when an entity enters into a transaction that eliminates all further legal or constructive obligation for part or all of the benefits provided under a defined benefit plan, for example, when a lump-sum cash payment is made to, or on behalf of, plan participants in exchange for their rights to receive specified post-employment benefits.

113 In some cases, an entity acquires an insurance policy to fund some or all of the employee benefits relating to employee service in the current and prior periods. The acquisition of such a policy is not a settlement if the entity retains a legal or constructive obligation (see paragraph 39) to pay further amounts if the insurer does not pay the employee benefits specified in the insurance policy. Paragraphs 104A–104D deal with the recognition and measurement of reimbursement rights under insurance policies that are not plan assets.

114 A settlement occurs together with a curtailment if a plan is terminated such that the obligation is settled and the plan ceases to exist. However, the termination of a plan is not a curtailment or settlement if the plan is replaced by a new plan that offers benefits that are, in substance, identical.

115 Where a curtailment relates to only some of the employees covered by a plan, or where only part of an obligation is settled, the gain or loss includes a proportionate share of the previously unrecognised past service cost and actuarial gains and losses (and of transitional amounts remaining unrecognised under paragraph 155(b)). The proportionate share is determined on the basis of the present value of the obligations before and after the curtailment or settlement, unless another basis is more rational in the circumstances. For example, it may be appropriate to apply any gain arising on a curtailment or settlement of the same plan to first eliminate any unrecognised past service cost relating to the same plan.

Example illustrating paragraph 115

An entity discontinues a business segment and employees of the discontinued segment will earn no further benefits. This is a curtailment without a settlement. Using current actuarial assumptions (including current market interest rates and other current market prices) immediately before the curtailment, the entity has a defined benefit obligation with a net present value of 1,000, plan assets with a fair value of 820 and net cumulative unrecognised actuarial gains of 50. The entity had first adopted the Standard one year before. This increased the net liability by 100, which the entity chose to recognise over five years (see paragraph 155(b)). The curtailment reduces the net present value of the obligation by 100 to 900.

Of the previously unrecognised actuarial gains and transitional amounts, 10% (100/1,000) relates to the part of the obligation that was eliminated through the curtailment. Therefore, the effect of the curtailment is as follows:

	Before curtailment	*Curtailment gain*	*After curtailment*
Net present value of obligation	*1,000*	*(100)*	*900*
Fair value of plan assets	*(820)*	*–*	*(820)*
	180	*(100)*	*80*
Unrecognised actuarial gains	*50*	*(5)*	*45*
Unrecognised transitional amount (100 × 4/5)	*(80)*	*8*	*(72)*
Net liability recognised in balance sheet	*150*	*(97)*	*53*

Presentation

Offset

116 **An entity shall offset an asset relating to one plan against a liability relating to another plan when, and only when, the entity:**

(a) has a legally enforceable right to use a surplus in one plan to settle obligations under the other plan; and

(b) intends either to settle the obligations on a net basis, or to realise the surplus in one plan and settle its obligation under the other plan simultaneously.

117 The offsetting criteria are similar to those established for financial instruments in IAS 32 *Financial Instruments: Disclosure and Presentation.*

Current/non-current distinction

118 Some entities distinguish current assets and liabilities from non-current assets and liabilities. This Standard does not specify whether an entity should distinguish current and non-current portions of assets and liabilities arising from post-employment benefits.

Financial components of post–employment benefit costs

119 This Standard does not specify whether an entity should present current service cost, interest cost and the expected return on plan assets as components of a single item of income or expense on the face of the income statement.

Disclosure

120 An entity shall disclose information that enables users of financial statements to evaluate the nature of its defined benefit plans and the financial effects of changes in those plans during the period.

120A An entity shall disclose the following information about defined benefit plans:

(a) the entity's accounting policy for recognising actuarial gains and losses.

(b) a general description of the type of plan.

(c) a reconciliation of opening and closing balances of the present value of the defined benefit obligation showing separately, if applicable, the effects during the period attributable to each of the following:

(i) current service cost,

(ii) interest cost,

(iii) contributions by plan participants,

(iv) actuarial gains and losses,

(v) foreign currency exchange rate changes on plans measured in a currency different from the entity's presentation currency,

(vi) benefits paid,

(vii) past service cost,

(viii) business combinations,

(ix) curtailments and

(x) settlements.

(d) an analysis of the defined benefit obligation into amounts arising from plans that are wholly unfunded and amounts arising from plans that are wholly or partly funded.

(e) a reconciliation of the opening and closing balances of the fair value of plan assets and of the opening and closing balances of any reimbursement right recognised as an asset in accordance with

paragraph 104A showing separately, if applicable, the effects during the period attributable to each of the following:

(i) expected return on plan assets,

(ii) actuarial gains and losses,

(iii) foreign currency exchange rate changes on plans measured in a currency different from the entity's presentation currency,

(iv) contributions by the employer,

(v) contributions by plan participants,

(vi) benefits paid,

(vii) business combinations and

(viii) settlements.

(f) a reconciliation of the present value of the defined benefit obligation in (c) and the fair value of the plan assets in (e) to the assets and liabilities recognised in the balance sheet, showing at least:

(i) the net actuarial gains or losses not recognised in the balance sheet (see paragraph 92);

(ii) the past service cost not recognised in the balance sheet (see paragraph 96);

(iii) any amount not recognised as an asset, because of the limit in paragraph 58(b);

(iv) the fair value at the balance sheet date of any reimbursement right recognised as an asset in accordance with paragraph 104A (with a brief description of the link between the reimbursement right and the related obligation); and

(v) the other amounts recognised in the balance sheet.

(g) the total expense recognised in profit or loss for each of the following, and the line item(s) in which they are included:

(i) current service cost;

(ii) interest cost;

(iii) expected return on plan assets;

(iv) expected return on any reimbursement right recognised as an asset in accordance with paragraph 104A;

(v) actuarial gains and losses;

(vi) past service cost;

(vii) the effect of any curtailment or settlement; and

(viii) the effect of the limit in paragraph 58(b).

(h) the total amount recognised in the statement of recognised income and expense for each of the following:

(i) actuarial gains and losses; and

(ii) the effect of the limit in paragraph 58(b).

(i) for entities that recognise actuarial gains and losses in the statement of recognised income and expense in accordance with paragraph 93A, the cumulative amount of actuarial gains and losses recognised in the statement of recognised income and expense.

(j) for each major category of plan assets, which shall include, but is not limited to, equity instruments, debt instruments, property, and all other assets, the percentage or amount that each major category constitutes of the fair value of the total plan assets.

(k) the amounts included in the fair value of plan assets for:

(i) each category of the entity's own financial instruments; and

(ii) any property occupied by, or other assets used by, the entity.

(l) a narrative description of the basis used to determine the overall expected rate of return on assets, including the effect of the major categories of plan assets.

(m) the actual return on plan assets, as well as the actual return on any reimbursement right recognised as an asset in accordance with paragraph 104A.

(n) the principal actuarial assumptions used as at the balance sheet date, including, when applicable:

(i) the discount rates;

(ii) the expected rates of return on any plan assets for the periods presented in the financial statements;

(iii) the expected rates of return for the periods presented in the financial statements on any reimbursement right recognised as an asset in accordance with paragraph 104A;

(iv) the expected rates of salary increases (and of changes in an index or other variable specified in the formal or constructive terms of a plan as the basis for future benefit increases);

(v) medical cost trend rates; and

(vi) any other material actuarial assumptions used.

An entity shall disclose each actuarial assumption in absolute terms (for example, as an absolute percentage) and not just as a margin between different percentages or other variables.

(o) the effect of an increase of one percentage point and the effect of a decrease of one percentage point in the assumed medical cost trend rates on:

(i) the aggregate of the current service cost and interest cost components of net periodic post-employment medical costs; and

(ii) the accumulated post-employment benefit obligation for medical costs.

For the purposes of this disclosure, all other assumptions shall be held constant. For plans operating in a high inflation environment, the disclosure shall be the effect of a percentage increase or decrease in the assumed medical cost trend rate of a significance similar to one percentage point in a low inflation environment.

(p) the amounts for the current annual period and previous four annual periods of:

(i) the present value of the defined benefit obligation, the fair value of the plan assets and the surplus or deficit in the plan; and

(ii) the experience adjustments arising on:

(A) the plan liabilities expressed either as (1) an amount or (2) a percentage of the plan liabilities at the balance sheet date and

(B) the plan assets expressed either as (1) an amount or (2) a percentage of the plan assets at the balance sheet date.

(q) the employer's best estimate, as soon as it can reasonably be determined, of contributions expected to be paid to the plan during the annual period beginning after the balance sheet date.

121 Paragraph 120A(b) requires a general description of the type of plan. Such a description distinguishes, for example, flat salary pension plans from final salary pension plans and from post-employment medical plans. The description of the plan shall include informal practices that give rise to constructive obligations included in the measurement of the defined benefit obligation in accordance with paragraph 52. Further detail is not required.

122 When an entity has more than one defined benefit plan, disclosures may be made in total, separately for each plan, or in such groupings as are considered to be the most useful. It may be useful to distinguish groupings by criteria such as the following:

(a) the geographical location of the plans, for example, by distinguishing domestic plans from foreign plans; or

(b) whether plans are subject to materially different risks, for example, by distinguishing flat salary pension plans from final salary pension plans and from post-employment medical plans.

When an entity provides disclosures in total for a grouping of plans, such disclosures are provided in the form of weighted averages or of relatively narrow ranges.

123 Paragraph 30 requires additional disclosures about multi-employer defined benefit plans that are treated as if they were defined contribution plans.

124 Where required by IAS 24 *Related Party Disclosures* an entity discloses information about:

(a) related party transactions with post-employment benefit plans; and

(b) post-employment benefits for key management personnel.

125 Where required by IAS 37 *Provisions, Contingent Liabilities and Contingent Assets* an entity discloses information about contingent liabilities arising from post-employment benefit obligations.

Other long–term employee benefits

126 Other long-term employee benefits include, for example:

(a) long-term compensated absences such as long-service or sabbatical leave;

(b) jubilee or other long-service benefits;

(c) long-term disability benefits;

(d) profit-sharing and bonuses payable twelve months or more after the end of the period in which the employees render the related service; and

(e) deferred compensation paid twelve months or more after the end of the period in which it is earned.

127 The measurement of other long-term employee benefits is not usually subject to the same degree of uncertainty as the measurement of post-employment benefits. Furthermore, the introduction of, or changes to, other long-term employee benefits rarely causes a material amount of past service cost. For these reasons, this Standard requires a simplified method of accounting for other long-term employee benefits. This method differs from the accounting required for post-employment benefits as follows:

(a) actuarial gains and losses are recognised immediately and no 'corridor' is applied; and

(b) all past service cost is recognised immediately.

Recognition and measurement

128 The amount recognised as a liability for other long-term employee benefits shall be the net total of the following amounts:

(a) the present value of the defined benefit obligation at the balance sheet date (see paragraph 64);

(b) minus the fair value at the balance sheet date of plan assets (if any) out of which the obligations are to be settled directly (see paragraphs 102–104).

In measuring the liability, an entity shall apply paragraphs 49–91, excluding paragraphs 54 and 61. An entity shall apply paragraph 104A in recognising and measuring any reimbursement right.

129 For other long-term employee benefits, an entity shall recognise the net total of the following amounts as expense or (subject to paragraph 58) income, except to the extent that another Standard requires or permits their inclusion in the cost of an asset:

(a) current service cost (see paragraphs 63–91);

(b) interest cost (see paragraph 82);

(c) **the expected return on any plan assets (see paragraphs 105–107) and on any reimbursement right recognised as an asset (see paragraph 104A);**

(d) **actuarial gains and losses, which shall all be recognised immediately;**

(e) **past service cost, which shall all be recognised immediately; and**

(f) **the effect of any curtailments or settlements (see paragraphs 109 and 110).**

130 One form of other long-term employee benefit is long-term disability benefit. If the level of benefit depends on the length of service, an obligation arises when the service is rendered. Measurement of that obligation reflects the probability that payment will be required and the length of time for which payment is expected to be made. If the level of benefit is the same for any disabled employee regardless of years of service, the expected cost of those benefits is recognised when an event occurs that causes a long-term disability.

Disclosure

131 Although this Standard does not require specific disclosures about other long-term employee benefits, other Standards may require disclosures, for example, where the expense resulting from such benefits is material and so would require disclosure in accordance with IAS 1 *Presentation of Financial Statements*. When required by IAS 24 *Related Party Disclosures*, an entity discloses information about other long-term employee benefits for key management personnel.

Termination benefits

132 This Standard deals with termination benefits separately from other employee benefits because the event which gives rise to an obligation is the termination rather than employee service.

Recognition

133 An entity shall recognise termination benefits as a liability and an expense when, and only when, the entity is demonstrably committed to either:

(a) **terminate the employment of an employee or group of employees before the normal retirement date; or**

(b) **provide termination benefits as a result of an offer made in order to encourage voluntary redundancy.**

134 An entity is demonstrably committed to a termination when, and only when, the entity has a detailed formal plan for the termination and is without realistic possibility of withdrawal. The detailed plan shall include, as a minimum:

(a) **the location, function, and approximate number of employees whose services are to be terminated;**

(b) **the termination benefits for each job classification or function; and**

(c) **the time at which the plan will be implemented. Implementation shall begin as soon as possible and the period of time to complete implementation shall be such that material changes to the plan are not likely.**

135 An entity may be committed, by legislation, by contractual or other agreements with employees or their representatives or by a constructive obligation based on business practice, custom or a desire to act equitably, to make payments (or provide other benefits) to employees when it terminates their employment. Such payments are termination benefits. Termination benefits are typically lump-sum payments, but sometimes also include:

(a) enhancement of retirement benefits or of other post-employment benefits, either indirectly through an employee benefit plan or directly; and

(b) salary until the end of a specified notice period if the employee renders no further service that provides economic benefits to the entity.

136 Some employee benefits are payable regardless of the reason for the employee's departure. The payment of such benefits is certain (subject to any vesting or minimum service requirements) but the timing of their payment is uncertain. Although such benefits are described in some countries as termination indemnities, or termination gratuities, they are post-employment benefits, rather than termination benefits and an entity accounts for them as post-employment benefits. Some entities provide a lower level of benefit for voluntary termination at the request of the employee (in substance, a post-employment benefit) than for involuntary termination at the request of the entity. The additional benefit payable on involuntary termination is a termination benefit.

137 Termination benefits do not provide an entity with future economic benefits and are recognised as an expense immediately.

138 Where an entity recognises termination benefits, the entity may also have to account for a curtailment of retirement benefits or other employee benefits (see paragraph 109).

Measurement

139 Where termination benefits fall due more than 12 months after the balance sheet date, they shall be discounted using the discount rate specified in paragraph 78.

140 In the case of an offer made to encourage voluntary redundancy, the measurement of termination benefits shall be based on the number of employees expected to accept the offer.

Disclosure

141 Where there is uncertainty about the number of employees who will accept an offer of termination benefits, a contingent liability exists. As required by IAS 37 *Provisions, Contingent Liabilities and Contingent Assets* an entity discloses information about the contingent liability unless the possibility of an outflow in settlement is remote.

142 As required by IAS 1, an entity discloses the nature and amount of an expense if it is material. Termination benefits may result in an expense needing disclosure in order to comply with this requirement.

143 Where required by IAS 24 *Related Party Disclosures* an entity discloses information about termination benefits for key management personnel.

144-152 [Deleted]

Transitional provisions

153 This section specifies the transitional treatment for defined benefit plans. Where an entity first adopts this Standard for other employee benefits, the entity applies IAS 8 *Accounting Policies, Changes in Accounting Estimates and Errors*.

154 On first adopting this Standard, an entity shall determine its transitional liability for defined benefit plans at that date as:

(a) the present value of the obligation (see paragraph 64) at the date of adoption;

(b) minus the fair value, at the date of adoption, of plan assets (if any) out of which the obligations are to be settled directly (see paragraphs 102–104);

(c) minus any past service cost that, under paragraph 96, shall be recognised in later periods.

155 If the transitional liability is more than the liability that would have been recognised at the same date under the entity's previous accounting policy, the entity shall make an irrevocable choice to recognise that increase as part of its defined benefit liability under paragraph 54:

(a) immediately, under IAS 8; or

(b) as an expense on a straight-line basis over up to five years from the date of adoption. If an entity chooses (b), the entity shall:

(i) apply the limit described in paragraph 58(b) in measuring any asset recognised in the balance sheet;

(ii) disclose at each balance sheet date: (1) the amount of the increase that remains unrecognised; and (2) the amount recognised in the current period;

(iii) limit the recognition of subsequent actuarial gains (but not negative past service cost) as follows. If an actuarial gain is to be recognised under paragraphs 92 and 93, an entity shall recognise that actuarial gain only to the extent that the net cumulative unrecognised actuarial gains (before recognition of that actuarial gain) exceed the unrecognised part of the transitional liability; and

(iv) include the related part of the unrecognised transitional liability in determining any subsequent gain or loss on settlement or curtailment.

If the transitional liability is less than the liability that would have been recognised at the same date under the entity's previous accounting policy, the entity shall recognise that decrease immediately under IAS 8.

156 On the initial adoption of the Standard, the effect of the change in accounting policy includes all actuarial gains and losses that arose in earlier periods even if they fall inside the 10% 'corridor' specified in paragraph 92.

Example illustrating paragraphs 154 to 156

At 31 December 1998, an entity's balance sheet includes a pension liability of 100. The entity adopts the Standard as of 1 January 1999, when the present value of the obligation under the Standard is 1,300 and the fair value of plan assets is 1,000. On 1 January 1993, the entity had improved pensions (cost for non-vested benefits: 160; and average remaining period at that date until vesting: 10 years).

The transitional effect is as follows:

Present value of the obligation	*1,300*
Fair value of plan assets	*(1,000)*
Less: past service cost to be recognised in later periods (160 × 4/10)	*(64)*
Transitional liability	*236*
Liability already recognised	*100*
Increase in liability	*136*

The entity may choose to recognise the increase of 136 either immediately or over up to 5 years. The choice is irrevocable.

At 31 December 1999, the present value of the obligation under the Standard is 1,400 and the fair value of plan assets is 1,050. Net cumulative unrecognised actuarial gains since the date of adopting the Standard are 120. The expected average remaining working life of the employees participating in the plan was eight years. The entity has adopted a policy of recognising all actuarial gains and losses immediately, as permitted by paragraph 93.

The effect of the limit in paragraph 155(b)(iii) is as follows.

Net cumulative unrecognised actuarial gains	*120*
Unrecognised part of transitional liability (136 × 4/5)	*(109)*
Maximum gain to be recognised (paragraph 155(b)(iii))	*11*

Effective date

157 **This Standard becomes operative for financial statements covering periods beginning on or after 1 January 1999, except as specified in paragraphs 159 and 159A. Earlier adoption is encouraged. If an entity applies this Standard to retirement benefit costs for financial statements covering periods beginning before 1 January 1999, the entity shall disclose the fact that it has applied this Standard instead of IAS 19** *Retirement Benefit Costs* **approved in 1993.**

158 This Standard supersedes IAS 19 *Retirement Benefit Costs* approved in 1993.

159 **The following become operative for annual financial statements[*] covering periods beginning on or after 1 January 2001:**

(a) the revised definition of plan assets in paragraph 7 and the related definitions of assets held by a long-term employee benefit fund and qualifying insurance policy; and

(b) the recognition and measurement requirements for reimbursements in paragraphs 104A, 128 and 129 and related disclosures in paragraphs 120A(iv), 120A(g)(iv), 120A(m) and 120A(n)(iii).

Earlier adoption is encouraged. If earlier adoption affects the financial statements, an entity shall disclose that fact.

159A **The amendment in paragraph 58A becomes operative for annual financial statements covering periods ending on or after 31 May 2002. Earlier adoption is encouraged. If earlier adoption affects the financial statements, an entity shall disclose that fact.**

159B **An entity shall apply the amendments in paragraphs 32A, 34–34B, 61 and 120–121 for annual periods beginning on or after 1 January 2006. Earlier application is encouraged. If an entity applies these amendments for a period beginning before 1 January 2006, it shall disclose that fact.**

159C **The option in paragraphs 93A–93D may be used for annual periods ending on or after 16 December 2004. An entity using the option for annual periods beginning before 1 January 2006 shall also apply the amendments in paragraphs 32A, 34–34B, 61 and 120–121.**

160 IAS 8 applies when an entity changes its accounting policies to reflect the changes specified in paragraphs 159–159C. In applying those changes retrospectively, as required by IAS 8, the entity treats those changes as if they had been applied at the same time as the rest of this Standard, except that an entity may disclose the amounts required by paragraph 120A(p) as the amounts are determined for each annual period prospectively from the first annual period presented in the financial statements in which the entity first applies the amendments in paragraph 120A.

---

* Paragraphs 159 and 159A refer to 'annual financial statements' in line with more explicit language for writing effective dates adopted in 1998. Paragraph 157 refers to 'financial statements'.

Appendix A
Illustrative example

The appendix accompanies, but is not part of, IAS 19.

Extracts from income statements and balance sheets are provided to show the effects of the transactions described below. These extracts do not necessarily conform with all the disclosure and presentation requirements of other Standards.

Background information

The following information is given about a funded defined benefit plan. To keep interest computations simple, all transactions are assumed to occur at the year-end. The present value of the obligation and the fair value of the plan assets were both 1,000 at 1 January 20X1. Net cumulative unrecognised actuarial gains at that date were 140.

	20X1	*20X2*	*20X3*
Discount rate at start of year	10.0%	9.0%	8.0%
Expected rate of return on plan assets at start of year	12.0%	11.1%	10.3%
Current service cost	130	140	150
Benefits paid	150	180	190
Contributions paid	90	100	100
Present value of obligation at 31 December	1,141	1,197	1,295
Fair value of plan assets at 31 December	1,092	1,109	1,093
Expected average remaining working lives of employees (years)	10	10	10

In 20X2, the plan was amended to provide additional benefits with effect from 1 January 20X2. The present value as at 1 January 20X2 of additional benefits for employee service before 1 January 20X2 was 50 for vested benefits and 30 for non-vested benefits. As at 1 January 20X2, the entity estimated that the average period until the non-vested benefits would become vested was three years; the past service cost arising from additional non-vested benefits is therefore recognised on a straight-line basis over three years. The past service cost arising from additional vested benefits is recognised immediately (paragraph 96 of the Standard). The entity has adopted a policy of recognising actuarial gains and losses under the minimum requirements of paragraph 93.

Changes in the present value of the obligation and in the fair value of the plan assets

The first step is to summarise the changes in the present value of the obligation and in the fair value of the plan assets and use this to determine the amount of the actuarial gains or losses for the period. These are as follows:

	20X1	*20X2*	*20X3*
Present value of obligation, 1 January	1,000	1,141	1,197
Interest cost	100	103	96
Current service cost	130	140	150
Past service cost—non-vested benefits	–	30	–
Past service cost—vested benefits	–	50	–
Benefits paid	(150)	(180)	(190)
Actuarial (gain) loss on obligation (balancing figure)	61	(87)	42
Present value of obligation, 31 December	1,141	1,197	1,295
Fair value of plan assets, 1 January	1,000	1,092	1,109
Expected return on plan assets	120	121	114
Contributions	90	100	110
Benefits paid	(150)	(180)	(190)
Actuarial gain (loss) on plan assets (balancing figure)	32	(24)	(50)
Fair value of plan assets, 31 December	1,092	1,109	1,093

Limits of the 'corridor'

The next step is to determine the limits of the corridor and then compare these with the cumulative unrecognised actuarial gains and losses in order to determine the net actuarial gain or loss to be recognised in the following period. Under paragraph 92 of the Standard, the limits of the 'corridor' are set at the greater of:

(a) 10% of the present value of the obligation before deducting plan assets; and

(b) 10% of the fair value of any plan assets.

These limits, and the recognised and unrecognised actuarial gains and losses, are as follows:

	20X1	*20X2*	*20X3*
Net cumulative unrecognised actuarial gains (losses) at 1 January	140	107	170
Limits of 'corridor' at 1 January	100	114	120
Excess [A]	40	–	50
Average expected remaining working lives (years) [B]	10	10	10
Actuarial gain (loss) to be recognised [A/B]	4	–	5
Unrecognised actuarial gains (losses) at 1 January	140	107	170
Actuarial gain (loss) for year—obligation	(61)	87	(42)
Actuarial gain (loss) for year—plan assets	32	(24)	(50)
Subtotal	111	170	78
Actuarial (gain) loss recognised	(4)	–	(5)
Unrecognised actuarial gains (losses) at 31 December	107	170	73

Amounts recognised in the balance sheet and profit or loss, and related analyses

The final step is to determine the amounts to be recognised in the balance sheet and profit or loss, and the related analyses to be disclosed in accordance with paragraph 120A(f), (g) and (l) of the Standard (the analyses required to be disclosed in accordance with paragraph 120A(c) and (e) are given in the section of this Appendix 'Changes in the present value of the obligation and in the fair value of the plan assets'). These are as follows.

	20X1	*20X2*	*20X3*
Present value of the obligation	1,141	1,197	1,295
Fair value of plan assets	(1,092)	(1,109)	(1,093)
	49	88	202
Unrecognised actuarial gains (losses)	107	170	73
Unrecognised past service cost—non-vested benefits	–	(20)	(10)
Liability recognised in balance sheet	**156**	**238**	**265**
Current service cost	130	140	150
Interest cost	100	103	96
Expected return on plan assets	(120)	(121)	(114)
Net actuarial (gain) loss recognised in year	(4)	–	(5)
Past service cost—non-vested benefits	–	10	10
Past service cost—vested benefits	–	50	–
Expense recognised in profit or loss	**106**	**182**	**137**
Actual return on plan assets			
Expected return on plan assets	120	121	114
Actuarial gain (loss) on plan assets	32	(24)	(50)
Actual return on plan assets	152	97	64

Note: see example illustrating paragraphs 104A–104C for presentation of reimbursements.

Appendix B
Illustrative disclosures

This appendix accompanies, but is not part of, IAS 19. Extracts from notes show how the required disclosures may be aggregated in the case of a large multi–national group that provides a variety of employee benefits. These extracts do not necessarily conform with all the disclosure and presentation requirements of IAS 19 and other Standards. In particular, they do not illustrate the disclosure of:

(a) *accounting policies for employee benefits (see IAS 1* Presentation of Financial Statements*). Paragraph 120A(a) of the Standard requires this disclosure to include the entity's accounting policy for recognising actuarial gains and losses.*

(b) *a general description of the type of plan (paragraph 120A(b)).*

(c) *a narrative description of the basis used to determine the overall expected rate of return on assets (paragraph 120A(l)).*

(d) *employee benefits granted to directors and key management personnel (see IAS 24* Related Party Disclosures*).*

(e) *share–based employee benefits (see IFRS 2* Share–based Payment*).*

Employee benefit obligations

The amounts recognised in the balance sheet are as follows:

	Defined benefit pension plans		Post–employment medical benefits	
	20X2	*20X1*	*20X2*	*20X1*
Present value of funded obligations	20,300	17,400	–	–
Fair value of plan assets	18,420	17,280	–	–
	1,880	120	–	–
Present value of unfunded obligations	2,000	1,000	7,337	6,405
Unrecognised actuarial gains (losses)	(1,605)	840	(2,707)	(2,607)
Unrecognised past service cost	(450)	(650)	–	–
Net liability	1,825	1,310	4,630	3,798
Amounts in the balance sheet:				
liabilities	1,825	1,400	4,630	3,798
assets	–	(90)	–	–
Net liability	1,825	1,310	4,630	3,798

The pension plan assets include ordinary shares issued by [name of reporting entity] with a fair value of 317 (20X1: 281). Plan assets also include property occupied by [name of reporting entity] with a fair value of 200 (20X1: 185).

The amounts recognised in profit or loss are as follows:

	Defined benefit pension plans		Post–employment medical benefits	
	20X2	*20X1*	*20X2*	*20X1*
Current service cost	850	750	479	411
Interest on obligation	950	1,000	803	705
Expected return on plan assets	(900)	(650)		
Net actuarial losses (gains) recognised in year	(70)	(20)	150	140
Past service cost	200	200		
Losses (gains) on curtailments and settlements	175	(390)		
Total, included in 'employee benefits expense'	1,205	890	1,432	1,256
Actual return on plan assets	600	2,250	–	–

Changes in the present value of the defined benefit obligation are as follows:

	Defined benefit pension plans		Post–employment medical benefits	
	20X2	*20X1*	*20X2*	*20X1*
Opening defined benefit obligation	18,400	11,600	6,405	5,439
Service cost	850	750	479	411
Interest cost	950	1,000	803	705
Actuarial losses (gains)	2,350	950	250	400
Losses (gains) on curtailments	(500)	–		
Liabilities extinguished on settlements	–	(350)		
Liabilities assumed in a business combination	–	5,000		
Exchange differences on foreign plans	900	(150)		
Benefits paid	(650)	(400)	(600)	(550)
Closing defined benefit obligation	22,300	18,400	7,337	6,405

Changes in the fair value of plan assets are as follows:

	Defined benefit pension plans	
	20X2	*20X1*
Opening fair value of plan assets	17,280	9,200
Expected return	900	650
Actuarial gains and (losses)	(300)	1,600
Assets distributed on settlements	(400)	–
Contributions by employer	700	350
Assets acquired in a business combination	–	6,000
Exchange differences on foreign plans	890	(120)
Benefits paid	(650)	(400)
	18,420	17,280

The group expects to contribute 900 to its defined benefit pension plans in 20X3.

The major categories of plan assets as a percentage of total plan assets are as follows:	*20X2*	*20X1*
European equities	30%	35%
North American equities	16%	15%
European bonds	31%	28%
North American bonds	18%	17%
Property	5%	5%

Principal actuarial assumptions at the balance sheet date (expressed as weighted averages):

	20X2	*20X1*
Discount rate at 31 December	5.0%	6.5%
Expected return on plan assets at 31 December	5.4%	7.0%
Future salary increases	5%	4%
Future pension increases	3%	2%
Proportion of employees opting for early retirement	30%	30%
Annual increase in healthcare costs	8%	8%
Future changes in maximum state healthcare benefits	3%	2%

Assumed healthcare cost trend rates have a significant effect on the amounts recognised in profit or loss. A one percentage point change in assumed healthcare cost trend rates would have the following effects:

	One percentage point increase	One percentage point decrease
Effect on the aggregate of the service cost and interest cost	190	(150)
Effect on defined benefit obligation	1,000	(900)

Amounts for the current and previous four periods are as follows:

Defined benefit pension plans

	20X2	*20X1*	*20X0*	*20W9*	*20W8*
Defined benefit obligation	(22,300)	(18,400)	(11,600)	(10,582)	(9,144)
Plan assets	18,420	17,280	9,200	8,502	10,000
Surplus/(deficit)	(3,880)	(1,120)	(2,400)	(2,080)	856
Experience adjustments on plan liabilities	(1,111)	(768)	(69)	543	(642)
Experience adjustments on plan assets	(300)	1,600	(1,078)	(2,890)	2,777

Post-employment medical benefits

	20X2	*20X1*	*20X0*	*20W9*	*20W8*
Defined benefit obligation	7,337	6,405	5,439	4,923	4,221
Experience adjustments on plan liabilities	(232)	829	490	(174)	(103)

The group also participates in an industry-wide defined benefit plan that provides pensions linked to final salaries and is funded on a pay-as-you-go basis. It is not practicable to determine the present value of the group's obligation or the related current service cost as the plan computes its obligations on a basis that differs materially from the basis used in [name of reporting entity]'s financial statements. [describe basis] On that basis, the plan's financial statements to 30 June 20X0 show an unfunded liability of 27,525. The unfunded liability will result in future payments by participating employers. The plan has approximately 75,000 members, of whom approximately 5,000 are current or former employees of [name of reporting entity] or their dependants. The expense recognised in the income statement, which is equal to contributions due for the year, and is not included in the above amounts, was 230 (20X1: 215). The group's future contributions may be increased substantially if other entities withdraw from the plan.

Appendix C
Illustration of the application of paragraph 58A

The appendix accompanies, but is not part of, IAS 19.

The issue

Paragraph 58 of the Standard imposes a ceiling on the defined benefit asset that can be recognised.

58 The amount determined under paragraph 54 may be negative (an asset). An entity shall measure the resulting asset at the lower of:

(a) the amount determined under paragraph 54 [ie the surplus/deficit in the plan plus (minus) any unrecognised losses (gains)]**; and**

(b) the total of:

(i) any cumulative unrecognised net actuarial losses and past service cost (see paragraphs 92, 93 and 96); and

(ii) the present value of any economic benefits available in the form of refunds from the plan or reductions in future contributions to the plan. The present value of these economic benefits shall be determined using the discount rate specified in paragraph 78.

Without paragraph 58A (see below), paragraph 58(b)(i) has the following consequence: sometimes deferring the recognition of an actuarial loss (gain) in determining the amount specified by paragraph 54 leads to a gain (loss) being recognised in the income statement.

The following example illustrates the effect of applying paragraph 58 without paragraph 58A. The example assumes that the entity's accounting policy is not to recognise actuarial gains and losses within the 'corridor' and to amortise actuarial gains and losses outside the 'corridor'. (Whether the 'corridor' is used is not significant. The issue can arise whenever there is deferred recognition under paragraph 54.)

Example 1

	A	B	C	D=A+C	E=B+C	F= lower of D and E	G
Year	Surplus in plan	Economic benefits available (paragraph 58(b)(ii))	Losses unrecognised under paragraph 54	Paragraph 54	Paragraph 58(b)	Asset ceiling, ie recognised asset	Gain recognised in year 2
1	100	0	0	100	0	0	–
2	70	0	30	100	30	30	30

At the end of year 1, there is a surplus of 100 in the plan (column A in the table above), but no economic benefits are available to the entity either from refunds or reductions in future contributions* (column B). There are no unrecognised gains and losses under paragraph 54 (column C). So, if there were no asset ceiling, an asset of 100 would be recognised, being the amount specified by paragraph 54 (column D). The asset ceiling in paragraph 58 restricts the asset to nil (column F).

In year 2 there is an actuarial loss in the plan of 30 that reduces the surplus from 100 to 70 (column A) the recognition of which is deferred under paragraph 54 (column C). So, if there were no asset ceiling, an asset of 100 (column D) would be recognised. The asset ceiling without paragraph 58A would be 30 (column E). An asset of 30 would be recognised (column F), giving rise to a gain in income (column G) even though all that has happened is that a surplus from which the entity cannot benefit has decreased.

A similarly counter-intuitive effect could arise with actuarial gains (to the extent that they reduce cumulative unrecognised actuarial losses).

Paragraph 58A

Paragraph 58A prohibits the recognition of gains (losses) that arise solely from past service cost and actuarial losses (gains).

58A The application of paragraph 58 shall not result in a gain being recognised solely as a result of an actuarial loss or past service cost in the current period or in a loss being recognised solely as a result of an actuarial gain in the current period. The entity shall therefore recognise immediately under paragraph 54 the following, to the extent that they arise while the defined benefit asset is determined in accordance with paragraph 58(b)

(a) net actuarial losses of the current period and past service cost of the current period to the extent that they exceed any reduction in the present value of the economic benefits specified in paragraph 58(b)(ii). If there is no change or an increase in the present value of the economic benefits, the entire net actuarial losses of the current period and past service cost of the current period shall be recognised immediately under paragraph 54.

(b) net actuarial gains of the current period after the deduction of past service cost of the current period to the extent that they exceed any increase in the present value of the economic benefits specified in paragraph 58(b)(ii). If there is no change or a decrease in the present value of the economic benefits, the entire net actuarial gains of the current period after the deduction of past service cost of the current period shall be recognised immediately under paragraph 54.

* based on the current terms of the plan.

Examples

The following examples illustrate the result of applying paragraph 58A. As above, it is assumed that the entity's accounting policy is not to recognise actuarial gains and losses within the 'corridor' and to amortise actuarial gains and losses outside the 'corridor'. For the sake of simplicity the periodic amortisation of unrecognised gains and losses outside the corridor is ignored in the examples.

Example 1 continued – Adjustment when there are actuarial losses and no change in the economic benefits available

	A	B	C	D=A+C	E=B+C	F= lower of D and E	G
Year	Surplus in plan	Economic benefits available (paragraph 58(b)(ii))	Losses unrecognised under paragraph 54	Paragraph 54	Paragraph 58(b)	Asset ceiling, ie recognised asset	Gain recognised in year 2
1	100	0	0	100	0	0	–
2	70	0	0	70	0	0	0

The facts are as in example 1 above. Applying paragraph 58A, there is no change in the economic benefits available to the entity* so the entire actuarial loss of 30 is recognised immediately under paragraph 54 (column D). The asset ceiling remains at nil (column F) and no gain is recognised.

In effect, the actuarial loss of 30 is recognised immediately, but is offset by the reduction in the effect of the asset ceiling.

	Balance sheet asset under paragraph 54 (column D above)	Effect of the asset ceiling	Asset ceiling (column F above)
Year 1	100	(100)	0
Year 2	70	(70)	0
Gain/(loss)	(30)	30	0

In the above example, there is no change in the present value of the economic benefits available to the entity. The application of paragraph 58A becomes more complex when there are changes in present value of the economic benefits available, as illustrated in the following examples.

* The term 'economic benefits available to the entity' is used to refer to those economic benefits that qualify for recognition under paragraph 58(b)(ii).

Example 2 – Adjustment when there are actuarial losses and a decrease in the economic benefits available

	A	B	C	D=A+C	E=B+C	F= lower of D and E	G
Year	Surplus in plan	Economic benefits available (paragraph 58(b)(ii))	Losses unrecognised under paragraph 54	Paragraph 54	Paragraph 58(b)	Asset ceiling, ie recognised asset	Gain recognised in year 2
1	60	30	40	100	70	70	–
2	25	20	50	75	70	70	0

At the end of year 1, there is a surplus of 60 in the plan (column A) and economic benefits available to the entity of 30 (column B). There are unrecognised losses of 40 under paragraph 54* (column C). So, if there were no asset ceiling, an asset of 100 would be recognised (column D). The asset ceiling restricts the asset to 70 (column F).

In year 2, an actuarial loss of 35 in the plan reduces the surplus from 60 to 25 (column A). The economic benefits available to the entity fall by 10 from 30 to 20 (column B). Applying paragraph 58A, the actuarial loss of 35 is analysed as follows:

Actuarial loss equal to the reduction in economic benefits	10
Actuarial loss that exceeds the reduction in economic benefits	25

In accordance with paragraph 58A, 25 of the actuarial loss is recognised immediately under paragraph 54 (column D). The reduction in economic benefits of 10 is included in the cumulative unrecognised losses that increase to 50 (column C). The asset ceiling, therefore, also remains at 70 (column E) and no gain is recognised.

In effect, an actuarial loss of 25 is recognised immediately, but is offset by the reduction in the effect of the asset ceiling.

	Balance sheet asset under paragraph 54 (column D above)	Effect of the asset ceiling	Asset ceiling (column F above)
Year 1	100	(30)	70
Year 2	75	(5)	70
Gain/(loss)	(25)	25	0

* the application of paragraph 58A allows the recognition of some actuarial gains and losses to be deferred under paragraph 54 and, hence, to be included in the calculation of the asset ceiling. For example, cumulative unrecognised actuarial losses that have built up while the amount specified by paragraph 58(b) is not lower than the amount specified by paragraph 54 will not be recognised immediately at the point that the amount specified by paragraph 58(b) becomes lower. Instead their recognition will continue to be deferred in line with the entity's accounting policy. The cumulative unrecognised losses in this example are losses the recognition of which is deferred even though paragraph 58A applies.

Example 3 – Adjustment when there are actuarial gains and a decrease in the economic benefits available to the entity

	A	B	C	D=A+C	E=B+C	F= lower of D and E	G
Year	Surplus in plan	Economic benefits available (paragraph 58(b)(ii))	Losses unrecognised under paragraph 54	Paragraph 54	Paragraph 58(b)	Asset ceiling, ie recognised asset	Gain recognised in year 2
1	60	30	40	100	70	70	–
2	110	25	40	150	65	65	(5)

At the end of year 1 there is a surplus of 60 in the plan (column A) and economic benefits available to the entity of 30 (column B). There are unrecognised losses of 40 under paragraph 54 that arose before the asset ceiling had any effect (column C). So, if there were no asset ceiling, an asset of 100 would be recognised (column D). The asset ceiling restricts the asset to 70 (column F).

In year 2, an actuarial gain of 50 in the plan increases the surplus from 60 to 110 (column A). The economic benefits available to the entity decrease by 5 (column B). Applying paragraph 58A, there is no increase in economic benefits available to the entity. Therefore, the entire actuarial gain of 50 is recognised immediately under paragraph 54 (column D) and the cumulative unrecognised loss under paragraph 54 remains at 40 (column C). The asset ceiling decreases to 65 because of the reduction in economic benefits. That reduction is not an actuarial loss as defined by IAS 19 and therefore does not qualify for deferred recognition.

In effect, an actuarial gain of 50 is recognised immediately, but is (more than) offset by the increase in the effect of the asset ceiling.

	Balance sheet asset under paragraph 54 (column D above)	**Effect of the asset ceiling**	**Asset ceiling (column F above)**
Year 1	100	(30)	70
Year 2	150	(85)	65
Gain/(loss)	50	(55)	(5)

In both examples 2 and 3 there is a reduction in economic benefits available to the entity. However, in example 2 no loss is recognised whereas in example 3 a loss is recognised. This difference in treatment is consistent with the treatment of changes in the present value of economic benefits before paragraph 58A was introduced. The purpose of paragraph 58A is solely to prevent gains (losses) being recognised because of past service cost or actuarial losses (gains). As far as is possible, all other consequences of deferred recognition and the asset ceiling are left unchanged.

Example 4 – Adjustment in a period in which the asset ceiling ceases to have an effect

	A	B	C	D=A+C	E=B+C	F= lower of D and E	G
Year	Surplus in plan	Economic benefits available (paragraph 58(b)(ii))	Losses unrecognised under paragraph 54	Paragraph 54	Paragraph 58(b)	Asset ceiling, ie recognised asset	Gain recognised in year 2
1	60	25	40	100	65	65	–
2	(50)	0	115	65	115	65	0

At the end of year 1 there is a surplus of 60 in the plan (column A) and economic benefits are available to the entity of 25 (column B). There are unrecognised losses of 40 under paragraph 54 that arose before the asset ceiling had any effect (column C). So, if there were no asset ceiling, an asset of 100 would be recognised (column D). The asset ceiling restricts the asset to 65 (column F).

In year 2, an actuarial loss of 110 in the plan reduces the surplus from 60 to a deficit of 50 (column A). The economic benefits available to the entity decrease from 25 to 0 (column B). To apply paragraph 58A it is necessary to determine how much of the actuarial loss arises while the defined benefit asset is determined in accordance with paragraph 58(b). Once the surplus becomes a deficit, the amount determined by paragraph 54 is lower than the net total under paragraph 58(b). So, the actuarial loss that arises while the defined benefit asset is determined in accordance with paragraph 58(b) is the loss that reduces the surplus to nil, ie 60. The actuarial loss is, therefore, analysed as follows:

Actuarial loss that arises while the defined benefit asset is measured under paragraph 58(b):	
Actuarial loss that equals the reduction in economic benefits	25
Actuarial loss that exceeds the reduction in economic benefits	35
	60
Actuarial loss that arises while the defined benefit asset is measured under paragraph 54	50
Total actuarial loss	110

In accordance with paragraph 58A, 35 of the actuarial loss is recognised immediately under paragraph 54 (column D); 75 (25 + 50) of the actuarial loss is included in the cumulative unrecognised losses which increase to 115 (column C). The amount determined under paragraph 54 becomes 65 (column D) and under paragraph 58(b) becomes 115 (column E). The recognised asset is the lower of the two, ie 65 (column F), and no gain or loss is recognised (column G).

In effect, an actuarial loss of 35 is recognised immediately, but is offset by the reduction in the effect of the asset ceiling.

	Balance sheet asset under paragraph 54 (column D above)	Effect of the asset ceiling	Asset ceiling (column F above)
Year 1	100	(35)	65
Year 2	65	0	65
Gain/(loss)	(35)	35	0

Notes

1 In applying paragraph 58A in situations when there is an increase in the present value of the economic benefits available to the entity, it is important to remember that the present value of the economic benefits available cannot exceed the surplus in the plan.*

2 In practice, benefit improvements often result in a past service cost and an increase in expected future contributions due to increased current service costs of future years. The increase in expected future contributions may increase the economic benefits available to the entity in the form of anticipated reductions in those future contributions. The prohibition against recognising a gain solely as a result of past service cost in the current period does not prevent the recognition of a gain because of an increase in economic benefits. Similarly, a change in actuarial assumptions that causes an actuarial loss may also increase expected future contributions and, hence, the economic benefits available to the entity in the form of anticipated reductions in future contributions. Again, the prohibition against recognising a gain solely as a result of an actuarial loss in the current period does not prevent the recognition of a gain because of an increase in economic benefits.

* The example following paragraph 60 of IAS 19 is corrected so that the present value of available future refunds and reductions in contributions equals the surplus in the plan of 90 (rather than 100), with a further correction to make the limit 270 (rather than 280).

Appendix D
Approval of 2002 amendment by the Board

The 2002 amendment to IAS 19 was approved for issue by an affirmative vote of thirteen members of the International Accounting Standards Board. Ms O'Malley dissented. Her dissenting opinion is set out in the following Appendix.

Sir David Tweedie	Chairman
Thomas E Jones	Vice-Chairman
Mary E Barth	
Hans-Georg Bruns	
Anthony T Cope	
Robert P Garnett	
Gilbert Gélard	
James J Leisenring	
Warren J McGregor	
Patricia L O'Malley	
Harry K Schmid	
John T Smith	
Geoffrey Whittington	
Tatsumi Yamada	

Appendix E
Dissenting opinion (2002 amendment)

Ms O'Malley dissents from this amendment of IAS 19. In her view, the perceived problem being addressed is an inevitable result of the interaction of two fundamentally inconsistent notions in IAS 19. The corridor approach allowed by IAS 19 permits the recognition of amounts on the balance sheet that do not meet the Framework's definition of assets. The asset ceiling then imposes a limitation on the recognition of some of those assets based on a recoverability notion. A far preferable limited amendment would be to delete the asset ceiling in paragraph 58. This would resolve the identified problem and at least remove the internal inconsistency in IAS 19.

It is asserted that the amendment to the standard will result in a more representationally faithful portrayal of economic events. Ms O'Malley believes that it is impossible to improve the representational faithfulness of a standard that permits recording an asset relating to a pension plan that actually has a deficiency, or a liability in respect of a plan that actually has a surplus.

Appendix F
Amendments to other Standards

The amendments in this appendix shall be applied for annual periods beginning on or after 1 January 2006. If an entity applies the amendments to IAS 19 for an earlier period, these amendments shall be applied for that earlier period.

* * * * *

The amendments contained in this appendix when this amended Standard was issued in 2004 have been incorporated into the text of IFRS 1 and IASs 1 and 24 as issued at 16 December 2004.

Appendix G
Approval of 2004 amendment by the Board

The amendment to IAS 19 in December 2004 was approved for issue by twelve of the fourteen members of the International Accounting Standards Board. Messrs Leisenring and Yamada dissented. Their dissenting opinions are set out in Appendix H.

Sir David Tweedie	Chairman
Thomas E Jones	Vice-Chairman
Mary E Barth	
Hans-Georg Bruns	
Anthony T Cope	
Jan Engström	
Robert P Garnett	
Gilbert Gélard	
James J Leisenring	
Warren J McGregor	
Patricia L O'Malley	
John T Smith	
Geoffrey Whittington	
Tatsumi Yamada	

Appendix H
Dissenting opinions (2004 amendment)

Dissenting opinions on December 2004 Amendment to IAS 19 Employee Benefits–*Actuarial Gains and Losses, Group Plans and Disclosures*

Dissent of James J Leisenring

DO1 Mr Leisenring dissents from the issue of the Amendment to IAS 19 Employee Benefits–*Actuarial Gains and Losses, Group Plans and Disclosures.*

DO2 Mr Leisenring dissents because he disagrees with the deletion of the last sentence in paragraph 34 and the addition of paragraphs 34A and 34B. He believes that group entities that give a defined benefit promise to their employees should account for that defined benefit promise in their separate or individual financial statements. He further believes that separate or individual financial statements that purport to be prepared in accordance with IFRSs should comply with the same requirements as other financial statements that are prepared in accordance with IFRSs. He therefore disagrees with the removal of the requirement for group entities to treat defined benefit plans that share risks between entities under common control as defined benefit plans and the introduction instead of the requirements of paragraph 34A.

DO3 Mr Leisenring notes that group entities are required to give disclosures about the plan as a whole but does not believe that disclosures are an adequate substitute for recognition and measurement in accordance with the requirements of IAS 19.

Dissent of Tatsumi Yamada

DO4 Mr Yamada dissents from the issue of the Amendment to IAS 19 Employee Benefits–*Actuarial Gains and Losses, Group Plans and Disclosures.*

DO5 Mr Yamada agrees that an option should be added to IAS 19 that allows entities that recognise actuarial gains and losses in full in the period in which they occur to recognise them outside profit or loss in a statement of recognised income and expense, even though under the existing IAS 19 they can be recognised in profit or loss in full in the period in which they occur. He agrees that the option provides more transparent information than the deferred recognition options commonly chosen under IAS 19. However, he also believes that all items of income and expense should be recognised in profit or loss in some period. Until they have been so recognised, they should be included in a component of equity separate from retained earnings. They should be transferred from that separate component of equity into retained earnings when they are recognised in profit or loss. Mr Yamada does not, therefore, agree with the requirements of paragraph 93D.

DO6 Mr Yamada acknowledges the difficulty in finding a rational basis for recognising actuarial gains and losses in profit or loss in periods after their initial recognition in a statement of recognised income and expense when the plan is ongoing. He also acknowledges that, under IFRSs, some gains and losses are recognised directly in a separate component of equity and are not subsequently recognised in profit or loss. However, Mr Yamada does not believe that this justifies expanding this treatment to actuarial gains and losses.

DO7 The cumulative actuarial gains and losses could be recognised in profit or loss when a plan is wound up or transferred outside the entity. The cumulative amount recognised in a separate component of equity would be transferred to retained earnings at the same time. This would be consistent with the treatment of exchange gains and losses on subsidiaries that have a measurement currency different from the presentation currency of the group.

DO8 Therefore, Mr Yamada believes that the requirements of paragraph 93D mean that the option is not an improvement to financial reporting because it allows gains and losses to be excluded permanently from profit or loss and yet be recognised immediately in retained earnings.

CONTENTS

Basis for Conclusions

[The original text has been marked up to reflect the revision of IAS 39 (as revised in 2003) and subsequently IFRS 2; new text is underlined and deleted text is struck through.]

This appendix gives the Board's reasons for rejecting certain alternative solutions. Individual Board members gave greater weight to some factors than to others. Paragraphs 9A–9D, 10A–10K, 48A–48EE and 85A–85E are added in relation to the amendment to IAS 19 issued in December 2004.

Background

1 The IASC Board (the 'Board') approved IAS 19 *Accounting for Retirement Benefits in the Financial Statements of Employers*, in 1983. Following a limited review, the Board approved a revised Standard IAS 19 *Retirement Benefit Costs* ('the old IAS 19'), in 1993. The Board began a more comprehensive review of IAS 19 in November 1994. In August 1995, the IASC Staff published an Issues Paper on *Retirement Benefit and Other Employee Benefit Costs*. In October 1996, the Board approved E54 *Employee Benefits*, with a comment deadline of 31 January 1997. The Board received more than 130 comment letters on E54 from over 20 countries. The Board approved IAS 19 *Employee Benefits* ('the new IAS 19') in January 1998.

2 The Board believes that the new IAS 19 is a significant improvement over the old IAS 19. Nevertheless, the Board believes that further improvement may be possible in due course. In particular, several Board members believe that it would be preferable to recognise all actuarial gains and losses immediately in a statement of financial performance. However, the Board believes that such a solution is not feasible for actuarial gains and losses until the Board makes further progress on various issues relating to the reporting of financial performance. When the Board makes further progress with those issues, it may decide to revisit the treatment of actuarial gains and losses.

Summary of changes to IAS 19

3 The most significant feature of the new IAS 19 is a market based approach to measurement. The main consequences are that the discount rate is based on market yields at the balance sheet date and any plan assets are measured at fair value. In summary, the main changes from the old IAS 19 are the following:

(a) there is a revised definition of defined contribution plans and related guidance (see paragraphs 5 and 6 below), including more detailed guidance than the old IAS 19 on multi-employer plans and state plans (see paragraphs 7–10 below) and on insured plans;

(b) there is improved guidance on the balance sheet treatment of liabilities and assets arising from defined benefit plans (see paragraphs 11–14 below).

(c) defined benefit obligations should be measured with sufficient regularity that the amounts recognised in the financial statements do not differ materially from the amounts that would be determined at the balance sheet date (see paragraphs 15 and 16 below);

(d) projected benefit methods are eliminated and there is a requirement to use the accrued benefit method known as the Projected Unit Credit Method (see paragraphs 17–22 below). The use of an accrued benefit method makes it essential to give detailed guidance on the attribution of benefit to individual periods of service (see paragraphs 23–25 below);

(e) the rate used to discount post-employment benefit obligations and other long-term employee benefit obligations (both funded and unfunded) should be determined by reference to market yields at the balance sheet date on high quality corporate bonds. In countries where there is no deep market in such bonds, the market yields (at the balance sheet date) on government bonds should be used. The currency and term of the corporate bonds or government bonds should be consistent with the currency and estimated term of the post-employment benefit obligations (see paragraphs 26–34 below);

(f) defined benefit obligations should consider all benefit increases that are set out in the terms of the plan (or result from any constructive obligation that goes beyond those terms) at the balance sheet date (see paragraphs 35–37 below);

(g) an entity should recognise, as a minimum, a specified portion of those actuarial gains and losses (arising from both defined benefit obligations and any related plan assets) that fall outside a 'corridor'. An entity is permitted, but not required, to adopt certain systematic methods of faster recognition. Such methods include, among others, immediate recognition of all actuarial gains and losses (see paragraphs 38–48 below);

(h) an entity should recognise past service cost on a straight-line basis over the average period until the benefits become vested. To the extent that the benefits are already vested immediately, an entity should recognise past service cost immediately (see paragraphs 49–62 below);

(i) plan assets should be measured at fair value. Fair value is estimated by discounting expected future cash flows only if no market price is available (see paragraphs 66–75 below);

(j) amounts recognised by the reporting entity as an asset should not exceed the net total of:

    (i) any unrecognised actuarial losses and past service cost; and

    (ii) the present value of any economic benefits available in the form of refunds from the plan or reductions in contributions to the plan (see paragraphs 76–78 below);

(k) curtailment and settlement losses should be recognised not when it is probable that the settlement or curtailment will occur, but when the settlement or curtailment occurs (see paragraphs 79 and 80 below);

(l) improvements have been made to the disclosure requirements (see paragraphs 81–85 below);

(m) the new IAS 19 deals with all employee benefits, whereas IAS 19 deals only with retirement benefits and certain similar post-employment benefits (see paragraphs 86–94 below); and

(n) the transitional provisions for defined benefit plans are amended (see paragraphs 95 and 96 below).

The Board rejected a proposal to require recognition of an 'additional minimum liability' in certain cases (see paragraphs 63–65 below).

Summary of changes to E54

4 The new IAS 19 makes the following principal changes to the proposals in E54:

(a) an entity should attribute benefit to periods of service following the plan's benefit formula, but the straight-line basis should be used if employee service in later years leads to a materially higher level of benefit than in earlier years (see paragraphs 23–25 below);

(b) actuarial assumptions should include estimates of benefit increases not if there is reliable evidence that they will occur, but only if the increases are set out in the terms of the plan (or result from any constructive obligation that goes beyond those terms) at the balance sheet date (see paragraphs 35–37 below);

(c) actuarial gains and losses that fall outside the 10% 'corridor' need not be recognised immediately as proposed in E54. The minimum amount that an entity should recognise for each defined benefit plan is the part that fell outside the 'corridor' as at the end of the previous reporting period, divided by the expected average remaining working lives of the employees participating in that plan. The new IAS 19 also permits certain systematic methods of faster recognition. Such methods include, among others, immediate recognition of all actuarial gains and losses (see paragraphs 38–48 below);

(d) E54 set out two alternative treatments for past service cost and indicated that the Board would eliminate one of these treatments after considering comments on the Exposure Draft. One treatment was immediate recognition of all past service cost. The other treatment was immediate recognition for former employees, with amortisation for current employees over the remaining working lives of the current employees. The new IAS 19 requires that an entity should recognise past service cost on a straight-line basis over the average period until the benefits become vested. To the extent that the benefits are already vested immediately an entity should recognise past service cost immediately (see paragraphs 49–59 below);

(e) the effect of 'negative plan amendments' should not be recognised immediately (as proposed in E54) but treated in the same way as past service cost (see paragraphs 60–62 below);

(f) non-transferable securities issued by the reporting entity have been excluded from the definition of plan assets (see paragraphs 67 and 68 below);

(g) plan assets should be measured at fair value rather than market value, as defined in E54 (see paragraphs 69 and 70 below);

(h) plan administration costs (not just investment administration costs, as proposed in E54), are to be deducted in determining the return on plan assets (see paragraph 75 below);

(i) the limit on the recognition of plan assets has been changed in two respects from the proposals in E54. The limit does not over-ride the corridor for actuarial losses or the deferred recognition of past service cost. Also, the limit refers to **available** refunds or reductions in future contributions. E54 referred to the **expected** refunds or reductions in future contributions (see paragraphs 76–78 below);

(j) unlike E54, the new IAS 19 does not specify whether an income statement should present interest cost and the expected return on plan assets in the same line item as current service cost. The new IAS 19 requires an entity to disclose the line items in which they are included;

(k) improvements have been made to the disclosure requirements (see paragraphs 81–85 below);

(l) the guidance in certain areas (particularly termination benefits, curtailments and settlements, profit-sharing and bonus plans and various references to constructive obligations) has been conformed to the proposals in E59 *Provisions, Contingent Liabilities and Contingent Assets. Also, the Board has added explicit guidance on the measurement of termination benefits, requiring discounting for termination benefits not payable within one year (see paragraphs 91–93* below); and

(m) on initial adoption of the new IAS 19, there is a transitional option to recognise an increase in defined benefit liabilities over not more than five years. The new IAS 19 is operative for financial statements covering periods beginning on or after 1 January 1999, rather than 2001 as proposed in E54 (see paragraphs 95 and 96 below).

Defined contribution plans (paragraphs 24–47 of the Standard)

5 The old IAS 19 defined:

(a) **defined contribution plans** as retirement benefit plans under which amounts to be paid as retirement benefits are determined by reference to contributions to a fund together with investment earnings thereon; and

(b) **defined benefit plans** as retirement benefit plans under which amounts to be paid as retirement benefits are determined by reference to a formula usually based on employees' remuneration and/or years of service.

The Board considers these definitions unsatisfactory because they focus on the benefit receivable by the employee, rather than on the cost to the entity. The definitions in paragraph 7 of the new IAS 19 focus on the downside risk that the cost to the entity may increase. The definition of defined contribution plans does not exclude the upside potential that the cost to the entity may be less than expected.

6 The new IAS 19 does not change the accounting for defined contribution plans, which is straightforward because there is no need for actuarial assumptions and an entity has no possibility of any actuarial gain or loss. The new IAS 19 gives no guidance equivalent to paragraphs 20 (past service costs in defined contribution plans) and 21 (curtailment of defined contribution plans) of the old IAS 19. The Board believes that these issues are not relevant to defined contribution plans.

Multi–employer plans and state plans (paragraphs 29–38 of the Standard)

7 An entity may not always be able to obtain sufficient information from multi-employer plans to use defined benefit accounting. The Board considered three approaches to this problem:

(a) use defined contribution accounting for some and defined benefit accounting for others;

(b) use defined contribution accounting for all multi-employer plans, with additional disclosure where the multi-employer plan is a defined benefit plan; or

(c) use defined benefit accounting for those multi-employer plans that are defined benefit plans. However, where sufficient information is not available to use defined benefit accounting, an entity should disclose that fact and use defined contribution accounting.

8 The Board believes that there is no conceptually sound, workable and objective way to draw a distinction so that an entity could use defined contribution accounting for some multi-employer defined benefit plans and defined benefit accounting for others. Also, the Board believes that it is misleading to use defined contribution accounting for multi-employer plans that are defined benefit plans. This is illustrated by the case of French banks that used defined contribution accounting for defined benefit pension plans operated under industry-wide collective agreements on a pay–as–you–go basis. Demographic trends made these plans unsustainable and a major reform in 1993 replaced these by defined contribution arrangements for future service. At this point, the banks were compelled to quantify their obligations. Those obligations had previously existed, but had not been recognised as liabilities.

9 The Board concluded that an entity should use defined benefit accounting for those multi-employer plans that are defined benefit plans. However, where sufficient information is not available to use defined benefit accounting, an entity should disclose that fact and use defined contribution accounting. The Board agreed to apply the same principle to state plans. The new IAS 19 notes that most state plans are defined contribution plans.

Multi–employer plans: amendment issued by the IASB in December 2004

9A In April 2004 the International Financial Reporting Interpretations Committee (IFRIC) published a draft Interpretation, D6 *Multi–employer Plans*, which proposed the following guidance on how multi–employer plans should apply defined benefit accounting, if possible:

(a) the plan should be measured in accordance with IAS 19 using assumptions appropriate for the plan as a whole

(b) the plan should be allocated to plan participants so that they recognise an asset or liability that reflects the impact of the surplus or deficit on the future contributions from the participant.

9B The concerns raised by respondents to D6 about the availability of the information about the plan as a whole, the difficulties in making an allocation as proposed and the resulting lack of usefulness of the information provided by defined benefit accounting were such that the IFRIC decided not to proceed with the proposals.

9C The International Accounting Standards Board (IASB), when discussing group plans (see paragraphs 10A–10K) noted that, if there were a contractual agreement between a multi-employer plan and its participants on how a surplus would be distributed or deficit funded, the same principle that applied to group plans should apply to multi-employer plans, ie the participants should recognise an asset or liability. In relation to the funding of a deficit, the IASB regarded this principle as consistent with the recognition of a provision in accordance with IAS 37.

9D The IASB therefore decided to clarify in IAS 19 that, if a participant in a defined benefit multi-employer plan:

(a) accounts for that participation on a defined contribution basis in accordance with paragraph 30 of IAS 19 because it had insufficient information to apply defined benefit accounting but

(b) has a contractual agreement that determined how a surplus would be distributed or a deficit funded,

it recognises the asset or liability arising from that contractual agreement.

10 In response to comments on E54, the Board considered a proposal to exempt wholly owned subsidiaries (and their parents) participating in group defined benefit plans from the recognition and measurement requirements in their individual non-consolidated financial statements, on cost-benefit grounds. The Board concluded that such an exemption would not be appropriate.

Application of IAS 19 in the separate or individual financial statements of entities in a consolidated group: amendment issued by the IASB in December 2004

10A Some constituents asked the IASB to consider whether entities participating in a group defined benefit plan should, in their separate or individual financial statements, either have an unqualified exemption from defined benefit accounting or be able to treat the plan as a multi-employer plan.

10B In developing the exposure draft, the IASB did not agree that an unqualified exemption from defined benefit accounting for group defined benefit plans in the separate or individual financial statements of group entities was appropriate. In principle, the requirements of International Financial Reporting Standards (IFRSs) should apply to separate or individual financial statements in the same way as they apply to any other financial statements. Following that principle would mean amending IAS 19 to allow group entities that participate in a plan that meets the definition of a multi-employer plan, except that the participants are under common control, to be treated as participants in a multi-employer plan in their separate or individual financial statements.

10C However, in the exposure draft, the IASB concluded that entities within a group should always be presumed to be able to obtain the necessary information about the plan as a whole. This implies that, in accordance with the requirements for multi-employer plans, defined benefit accounting should be applied if there is a consistent and reliable basis for allocating the assets and obligations of the plan.

10D In the exposure draft, the IASB acknowledged that entities within a group might not be able to identify a consistent and reliable basis for allocating the plan that results in the entity recognising an asset or liability that reflects the extent to which a surplus or deficit in the plan would affect their future contributions. This is because there may be uncertainty in the terms of the plan about how surpluses will be used or deficits funded across the consolidated group. However, the IASB concluded that entities within a group should always be able to make at least a consistent and *reasonable* allocation, for example on the basis of a percentage of pensionable pay.

10E The IASB then considered whether, for some group entities, the benefits of defined benefit accounting using a consistent and *reasonable* basis of allocation were worth the costs involved in obtaining the information. The IASB decided that this was not the case for entities that meet criteria similar to those in IAS 27 *Consolidated and Separate Financial Statements* for the exemption from preparing consolidated financial statements.

10F The exposure draft therefore proposed that:

(a) entities that participate in a plan that would meet the definition of a multi-employer plan except that the participants are under common control, and that meet the criteria set out in paragraph 34 of IAS 19 as proposed to be amended in the exposure draft, should be treated as if they were participants in a multi-employer plan. This means that if there is no consistent and reliable basis for allocating the assets and liabilities of the plan, the entity should use defined contribution accounting and provide additional disclosures.

(b) all other entities that participate in a plan that would meet the definition of a multi-employer plan except that the participants are under common control should be required to apply defined benefit accounting by making a consistent and reasonable allocation of the assets and liabilities of the plan.

10G Respondents to the exposure draft generally supported the proposal to extend the requirements in IAS 19 on multi-employer plans to group entities. However, many disagreed with the criteria proposed in the exposure draft, for the following reasons:

(a) the proposed amendments and the interaction with D6 were unclear.

(b) the provisions for multi-employer accounting should be extended to a listed parent company.

(c) the provisions for multi-employer accounting should be extended to group entities with listed debt.

(d) the provisions for multi-employer plan accounting should be extended to all group entities, including partly-owned subsidiaries.

(e) there should be a blanket exemption from defined benefit accounting for all group entities.

10H The IASB agreed that the proposed requirements for group plans were unnecessarily complex. The IASB also concluded that it would be better to treat group plans separately from multi-employer plans because of the difference in information available to the participants: in a group plan information about the plan as a whole should generally be available. The IASB further noted that, if the parent wishes to comply with IFRSs in its separate financial statements or wishes its subsidiaries to comply with IFRSs in their individual financial statements, then it must obtain and provide the necessary information for the purposes of disclosure, at least.

10I The IASB noted that, if there were a contractual agreement or stated policy on charging the net defined benefit cost to group entities, that agreement or policy would determine the cost for each entity. If there is no such contractual agreement or stated policy, the entity that is the sponsoring employer by default bears the risk relating to the plan. The IASB therefore concluded that a group plan should be allocated to the individual entities within a group in accordance with any contractual agreement or stated policy. If there is no such agreement or policy, the net defined benefit cost is allocated to the sponsoring employer. The other group entities recognise a cost equal to any contribution collected by the sponsoring employer.

10J This approach has the advantages of (a) all group entities recognising the cost they have to bear for the defined benefit promise and (b) being simple to apply.

10K The IASB also noted that participation in a group plan is a related party transaction. As such, disclosures are required to comply with IAS 24 *Related Party Disclosures*. Paragraph 20 of IAS 24 requires an entity to disclose the nature of the related party relationship as well as information about the transactions and outstanding balances necessary for an understanding of the potential effect of the relationship on the financial statements. The IASB noted that information about each of (a) the policy on charging the defined benefit cost, (b) the policy on charging current contributions and (c) the status of the plan as a whole was required to give an understanding of the potential effect of the participation in the group plan on the entity's separate or individual financial statements.

Defined benefit plans

Recognition and measurement: balance sheet (paragraphs 49–60 of the Standard)

11 Paragraph 54 of the new IAS 19 summarises the recognition and measurement of liabilities arising from defined benefit plans and paragraphs 55–107 of the new IAS 19 describe various aspects of recognition and measurement in greater detail. Although the old IAS 19 did not deal explicitly with the recognition of retirement benefit obligations as a liability, it is likely that most entities would recognise a liability for retirement benefit obligations at the same time under both Standards. However, the two Standards differ in the measurement of the resulting liability.

12 Paragraph 54 of the new IAS 19 is based on the definition of, and recognition criteria for, a liability in IASC's *Framework for the Preparation and Presentation of Financial Statements* (the '*Framework*'). The *Framework* defines a liability as *a present obligation of the entity arising from past events, the settlement of which is expected to result in*

an outflow from the entity of resources embodying economic benefits. The *Framework* states that an item which meets the definition of a liability should be recognised if:

(a) it is probable that any future economic benefit associated with the item will flow from the entity; and

(b) the item has a cost or value that can be measured with reliability.

13 The Board believes that:

(a) an entity has an obligation under a defined benefit plan when an employee has rendered service in return for the benefits promised under the plan. Paragraphs 67–71 of the new IAS 19 deal with the attribution of benefit to individual periods of service in order to determine whether an obligation exists;

(b) an entity should use actuarial assumptions to determine whether the entity will pay those benefits in future reporting periods (see paragraphs 72–91 of the Standard); and

(c) actuarial techniques allow an entity to measure the obligation with sufficient reliability to justify recognition of a liability.

14 The Board believes that an obligation exists even if a benefit is not vested, in other words if the employee's right to receive the benefit is conditional on future employment. For example, consider an entity that provides a benefit of 100 to employees who remain in service for two years. At the end of the first year, the employee and the entity are not in the same position as at the beginning of the first year, because the employee will only need to work for one year, instead of two, before becoming entitled to the benefit. Although there is a possibility that the benefit may not vest, that difference is an obligation and, in the Board's view, should result in the recognition of a liability at the end of the first year. The measurement of that obligation at its present value reflects the entity's best estimate of the probability that the benefit may not vest.

Measurement date (paragraphs 56 and 57 of the Standard)

15 Some national standards permit entities to measure the present value of defined benefit obligations at a date up to three months before the balance sheet date. However, the Board decided that entities should measure the present value of defined benefit obligations, and the fair value of any plan assets, at the balance sheet date. Therefore, if an entity carries out a detailed valuation of the obligation at an earlier date, the results of that valuation should be updated to take account of any significant transactions and other significant changes in circumstances up to the balance sheet date.

16 In response to comments on E54, the Board has clarified that full actuarial valuation is not required at the balance sheet date, provided that an entity determines the present value of defined benefit obligations and the fair value of any plan assets with sufficient regularity that the amounts recognised in the financial statements do not differ materially from the amounts that would be determined at the balance sheet date.

Actuarial valuation method (paragraphs 64–66 of the Standard)

17 The old IAS 19 permitted both accrued benefit valuation methods (benchmark treatment) and projected benefit valuation methods (allowed alternative treatment). The two groups of methods are based on fundamentally different, and incompatible, views of the objectives of accounting for employee benefits:

(a) **accrued benefit methods** (sometimes known as 'benefit', 'unit credit' or 'single premium' methods) determine the present value of employee benefits attributable to service to date; but

(b) **projected benefit methods** (sometimes described as 'cost', 'level contribution' or 'level premium' methods) project the estimated total obligation at retirement and then calculate a level funding cost, taking into account investment earnings, that will provide the total benefit at retirement.

The differences between the two groups of methods were discussed in more detail in the Issues Paper published in August 1995.

18 The two methods may have similar effects on the income statement, but only by chance or if the number and age distribution of participating employees remains relatively stable over time. There can be significant differences in the measurement of liabilities under the two groups of methods. For these reasons, the Board believes that a requirement to use a single group of methods will significantly enhance comparability.

19 The Board considered whether it should continue to permit projected benefit methods as an allowed alternative treatment while introducing a new requirement to disclose information equivalent to the use of an accrued benefit method. However, the Board believes that disclosure cannot rectify inappropriate accounting in the balance sheet and income statement. The Board concluded that projected benefit methods are not appropriate, and should be eliminated, because such methods:

(a) focus on future events (future service) as well as past events, whereas accrued benefit methods focus only on past events;

(b) generate a liability which does not represent a measure of any real amount and can be described only as the result of cost allocations; and

(c) do not attempt to measure fair value and cannot, therefore, be used in a business combination, as required by IAS 22 *Business Combinations*.* If an entity uses an accrued benefit method in a business combination, it would not be feasible for the entity to use a projected benefit method to account for the same obligation in subsequent periods.

20 The old IAS 19 did not specify which forms of accrued benefit valuation method should be permitted under the benchmark treatment. The new IAS 19 requires a single accrued benefit method: the most widely used accrued benefit method,

* IAS 22 was withdrawn in 2004 and replaced by IFRS 3 *Business Combinations*.

which is known as the Projected Unit Credit Method (sometimes known as the 'accrued benefit method pro-rated on service' or as the 'benefit/years of service method').

21 The Board acknowledges that the elimination of projected benefit methods, and of accrued benefit methods other than the Projected Unit Credit Method, has cost implications. However, with modern computing power, it will be only marginally more expensive to run a valuation on two different bases and the advantages of improved comparability will outweigh the additional cost.

22 An actuary may sometimes, for example, in the case of a closed fund, recommend a method other than the Projected Unit Credit Method for funding purposes. Nevertheless, the Board agreed to require the use of the Projected Unit Credit Method in all cases because that method is more consistent with the accounting objectives laid down in the new IAS 19.

Attributing benefit to periods of service (paragraphs 67–71 of the Standard)

23 As explained in paragraph 13 above, the Board believes that an entity has an obligation under a defined benefit plan when an employee has rendered service in return for the benefits promised under the plan. The Board considered three alternative methods of accounting for a defined benefit plan which attributes different amounts of benefit to different periods:

(a) apportion the entire benefit on a straight-line basis over the entire period to the date when further service by the employee will lead to no material amount of further benefits under the plan, other than from further salary increases;

(b) apportion benefit under the plan's benefit formula. However, a straight-line basis should be used if the plan's benefit formula attributes a materially higher benefit to later years; or

(c) apportion the benefit that vests at each interim date on a straight-line basis over the period between that date and the previous interim vesting date.

The three methods are illustrated by the following two examples.

Example 1

A plan provides a benefit of 400 if an employee retires after more than ten and less than twenty years of service and a further benefit of 100 (500 in total) if an employee retires after twenty or more years of service.

The amounts attributed to each year are as follows:

	Years 1–10	*Years 11–20*
Method (a)	25	25
Method (b)	40	10
Method (c)	40	10

Example 2

A plan provides a benefit of 100 if an employee retires after more than ten and less than twenty years of service and a further benefit of 400 (500 in total) if an employee retires after twenty or more years of service.

The amounts attributed to each year are as follows:

	Years 1–10	*Years 11–20*
Method (a)	*25*	*25*
Method (b)	*25*	*25*
Method (c)	*10*	*40*

Note: this plan attributes a higher benefit to later years, whereas the plan in Example 1 attributes a higher benefit to earlier years.

24 In approving E54, the Board adopted method (a) on the grounds that this method was the most straightforward and that there were no compelling reasons to attribute different amounts of benefit to different years, as would occur under either of the other methods.

25 A significant minority of commentators on E54 favoured following the benefit formula (or alternatively, if the final Standard were to retain straight-line attribution, the recognition of a minimum liability based on the benefit formula). The Board agreed with these comments and decided to require method (b).

Actuarial assumptions: discount rate (paragraphs 78–82 of the Standard)

26 One of the most important issues in measuring defined benefit obligations is the selection of the criteria used to determine the discount rate. According to the old IAS 19, the discount rate assumed in determining the actuarial present value of promised retirement benefits reflected the long-term rates, or an approximation thereto, at which such obligations are expected to be settled. The Board rejected the use of such a rate because it is not relevant for an entity that does not contemplate settlement and it is an artificial construct, as there may be no market for settlement of such obligations.

27 Some believe that, for funded benefits, the discount rate should be the expected rate of return on the plan assets actually held by a plan, on the grounds that the return on plan assets represents faithfully the expected ultimate cash outflow (ie future contributions). The Board rejected this approach because the fact that a fund has chosen to invest in certain kinds of asset does not affect the nature or amount of the obligation. In particular, assets with a higher expected return carry more risk and an entity should not recognise a smaller liability merely because the plan has chosen to invest in riskier assets with a higher expected return. Therefore, the measurement of the obligation should be independent of the measurement of any plan assets actually held by a plan.

28 The most significant decision is whether the discount rate should be a risk-adjusted rate (one that attempts to capture the risks associated with the obligation). Some argue that the most appropriate risk-adjusted rate is given by

the expected return on an appropriate portfolio of plan assets that would, over the long term, provide an effective hedge against such an obligation. An appropriate portfolio might include:

(a) fixed-interest securities for obligations to former employees to the extent that the obligations are not linked, in form or in substance, to inflation;

(b) index-linked securities for index-linked obligations to former employees; and

(c) equity securities for benefit obligations towards current employees that are linked to final pay. This is based on the view that the long-term performance of equity securities is correlated with general salary progression in the economy as a whole and hence with the final-pay element of a benefit obligation.

It is important to note that the portfolio actually held need not necessarily be an appropriate portfolio in this sense. Indeed, in some countries, regulatory constraints may prevent plans from holding an appropriate portfolio. For example, in some countries, plans are required to hold a certain proportion of their assets in the form of fixed-interest securities. Furthermore, if an appropriate portfolio is a valid reference point, it is equally valid for both funded and unfunded plans.

29 Those who support using the interest rate on an appropriate portfolio as a risk-adjusted discount rate argue that:

(a) portfolio theory suggests that the expected return on an asset (or the interest rate inherent in a liability) is related to the undiversifiable risk associated with that asset (or liability). Undiversifiable risk reflects not the variability of the returns (payments) in **absolute** terms but the **correlation** of the returns (or payments) with the returns on other assets. If cash inflows from a portfolio of assets react to changing economic conditions over the long term in the same way as the cash outflows of a defined benefit obligation, the undiversifiable risk of the obligation (and hence the appropriate discount rate) must be the same as that of the portfolio of assets;

(b) an important aspect of the economic reality underlying final salary plans is the correlation between final salary and equity returns that arises because they both reflect the same long-term economic forces. Although the correlation is not perfect, it is sufficiently strong that ignoring it will lead to systematic overstatement of the liability. Also, ignoring this correlation will result in misleading volatility due to short-term fluctuations between the rate used to discount the obligation and the discount rate that is implicit in the fair value of the plan assets. These factors will deter entities from operating defined benefit plans and lead to switches from equities to fixed interest investments. Where defined benefit plans are largely funded by equities, this could have a serious impact on share prices. This switch will also increase the cost of pensions. There will be pressure on companies to remove the apparent (but non-existent) shortfall;

(c) if an entity settled its obligation by purchasing an annuity, the insurance company would determine the annuity rates by looking to a portfolio of assets that provides cash inflows that substantially offset all the cash flows from the benefit obligation as those cash flows fall due. Therefore, the expected return on an appropriate portfolio measures the obligation at an amount that is close to its market value. In practice, it is not possible to settle a final pay obligation by buying annuities since no insurance company would insure a final pay decision that remained at the discretion of the person insured. However, evidence can be derived from the purchase/sale of businesses that include a final salary pension scheme. In this situation the vendor and purchaser would negotiate a price for the pension obligation by reference to its present value, discounted at the rate of return on an appropriate portfolio;

(d) although investment risk is present even in a well-diversified portfolio of equity securities, any general decline in securities would, in the long term, be reflected in declining salaries. Since employees accepted that risk by agreeing to a final salary plan, the exclusion of that risk from the measurement of the obligation would introduce a systematic bias into the measurement; and

(e) time-honoured funding practices in some countries use the expected return on an appropriate portfolio as the discount rate. Although funding considerations are distinct from accounting issues, the long history of this approach calls for careful scrutiny of any other proposed approach.

30 Those who oppose a risk-adjusted rate argue that:

(a) it is incorrect to look at returns on assets in determining the discount rate for liabilities;

(b) if a sufficiently strong correlation between asset returns and final pay actually existed, a market for final salary obligations would develop, yet this has not happened. Furthermore, where any such apparent correlation does exist, it is not clear whether the correlation results from shared characteristics of the portfolio and the obligations or from changes in the contractual pension promise;

(c) the return on equity securities does not correlate with other risks associated with defined benefit plans, such as variability in mortality, timing of retirement, disability and adverse selection;

(d) in order to evaluate a liability with uncertain cash flows, an entity would normally use a discount rate lower than the risk-free rate, yet the expected return on an appropriate portfolio is higher than the risk-free rate;

(e) the assertion that final salary is strongly correlated with asset returns implies that final salary will tend to decrease if asset prices fall, yet experience shows that salaries tend not to decline;

(f) the notion that equities are not risky in the long term, and the associated notion of long-term value, are based on the fallacious view that the market always bounces back after a crash. Shareholders do not get credit in the market for any additional long-term value if they sell their shares today. Even if some correlation exists over long periods, benefits must be paid as they become due. An entity that funds its obligations with equity securities runs the risk that equity prices may be down when benefits must be paid.

Also, the hypothesis that the real return on equities is uncorrelated with inflation does not mean that equities offer a risk-free return, even in the long term; and

(g) the expected long-term rate of return on an appropriate portfolio cannot be determined sufficiently objectively in practice to provide an adequate basis for an accounting standard. The practical difficulties include specifying the characteristics of the appropriate portfolio, selecting the time horizon for estimating returns on the portfolio and estimating those returns.

31 The Board has not identified clear evidence that the expected return on an appropriate portfolio of assets provides a relevant and reliable indication of the risks associated with a defined benefit obligation, or that such a rate can be determined with reasonable objectivity. Therefore, the Board decided that the discount rate should reflect the time value of money but should not attempt to capture those risks. Furthermore, the discount rate should not reflect the entity's own credit rating, as otherwise an entity with a lower credit rating would recognise a smaller liability. The rate that best achieves these objectives is the yield on high quality corporate bonds. In countries where there is no deep market in such bonds, the yield on government bonds should be used.

32 Another issue is whether the discount rate should be the long-term average rate, based on past experience over a number of years, or the current market yield at the balance sheet date for an obligation of the appropriate term. Those who support a long-term average rate argue that:

(a) a long-term approach is consistent with the transaction-based historical cost approach that is either required or permitted in other International Accounting Standards;

(b) point in time estimates pursue a level of precision that is not attainable in practice and lead to volatility in reported profit that may not be a faithful representation of changes in the obligation but may simply reflect an unavoidable inability to predict accurately the future events that are anticipated in making period-to-period measures;

(c) for an obligation based on final salary, neither market annuity prices nor simulation by discounting expected future cash flows can determine an unambiguous annuity price; and

(d) over the long term, a suitable portfolio of plan assets may provide a reasonably effective hedge against an employee benefit obligation that increases in line with salary growth. However, there is much less assurance that, at a given measurement date, market interest rates will match the salary growth built into the obligation.

33 The Board decided that the discount rate should be determined by reference to market yields at the balance sheet date as:

(a) there is no rational basis for expecting efficient market prices to drift towards any assumed long-term average, because prices in a market of sufficient liquidity and depth incorporate all publicly available information and are more relevant and reliable than an estimate of long-term trends by any individual market participant;

(b) the cost of benefits attributed to service during the current period should reflect prices of that period;

(c) if expected future benefits are defined in terms of projected future salaries that reflect current estimates of future inflation rates, the discount rate should be based on current market interest rates (in nominal terms), as these also reflect current market expectations of inflation rates; and

(d) if plan assets are measured at a current value (ie fair value), the related obligation should be discounted at a current discount rate in order to avoid introducing irrelevant volatility through a difference in the measurement basis.

34 The reference to market yields at the balance sheet date does not mean that short-term discount rates should be used to discount long-term obligations. The new IAS 19 requires that the discount rate should reflect market yields (at the balance sheet date) on bonds with an expected term consistent with the expected term of the obligations.

Actuarial assumptions: salaries, benefits and medical costs (paragraphs 83–91 of the Standard)

35 Some argue that estimates of future increases in salaries, benefits and medical costs should not affect the measurement of assets and liabilities until they are granted, on the grounds that:

(a) future increases are future events; and

(b) such estimates are too subjective.

36 The Board believes that the assumptions are used not to determine whether an obligation exists, but to measure an existing obligation on a basis which provides the most relevant measure of the estimated outflow of resources. If no increase is assumed, this is an implicit assumption that no change will occur and it would be misleading to assume no change if an entity expects a change. The new IAS 19 maintains the existing requirement that measurement should take account of estimated future salary increases. The Board also believes that increases in future medical costs can be estimated with sufficient reliability to justify incorporation of those estimated increases in the measurement of the obligation.

37 E54 proposed that measurement should also assume future benefit increases if there is reliable evidence that those benefit increases will occur. In response to comments, the Board concluded that future benefit increases do not give rise to a present obligation and that there would be no reliable or objective way of deciding which future benefit increases were reliable enough to be incorporated in actuarial assumptions. Therefore, the new IAS 19 requires that future benefit increases should be assumed only if they are set out in the terms of the plan (or result from any constructive obligation that goes beyond the formal terms) at the balance sheet date.

Actuarial gains and losses (paragraphs 92–95 of the Standard)

38 The Board considered five methods of accounting for actuarial gains and losses:

(a) deferred recognition in both the balance sheet and the income statement over the average expected remaining working life of the employees concerned (see paragraph 39 below);

(b) immediate recognition both in the balance sheet and outside the income statement in equity (IAS 1 *Presentation of Financial Statements* sets out requirements for the presentation or disclosure of such movements in equity) (see paragraphs 40 and 41 below);

(c) a 'corridor' approach, with immediate recognition in both the balance sheet and the income statement for amounts falling outside a 'corridor' (see paragraph 42 below);

(d) a modified 'corridor' approach with deferred recognition of items within the 'corridor' and immediate recognition for amounts falling outside the 'corridor' (see paragraph 43 below); and

(e) deferred recognition for amounts falling outside a 'corridor' (see paragraphs 44–46 below).

39 The old IAS 19 required a deferred recognition approach: actuarial gains and losses were recognised as an expense or as income systematically over the expected remaining working lives of those employees. Arguments for this approach are that:

(a) immediate recognition (even when reduced by a 'corridor') can cause volatile fluctuations in liability and expense and implies a degree of accuracy which can rarely apply in practice. This volatility may not be a faithful representation of changes in the obligation but may simply reflect an unavoidable inability to predict accurately the future events that are anticipated in making period-to-period measures; and

(b) in the long term, actuarial gains and losses may offset one another. Actuarial assumptions are projected over many years, for example, until the expected date of death of the last pensioner, and are, accordingly, long-term in nature. Departures from the assumptions do not normally denote definite changes in the underlying assets or liability, but are indicators which, if not reversed, may accumulate to denote such changes in the future. They are not a gain or loss of the period but a fine tuning of the cost that emerges over the long term; and

(c) the immediate recognition of actuarial gains and losses in the income statement would cause unacceptable volatility.

40 Arguments for an immediate recognition approach are that:

(a) deferred recognition and 'corridor' approaches are complex, artificial and difficult to understand. They add to cost by requiring entities to keep complex records. They also require complex provisions to deal with curtailments, settlements and transitional matters. Also, as such approaches are not used for other uncertain assets and liabilities, it is not clear why they should be used for post-employment benefits;

(b) it requires less disclosure because all actuarial gains and losses are recognised;

(c) it represents faithfully the entity's financial position. An entity will report an asset only when a plan is in surplus and a liability only when a plan has a deficit. Paragraph 95 of the *Framework* notes that the application of the matching concept does not allow the recognition of items in the balance sheet which do not meet the definition of assets or liabilities. Deferred actuarial losses do not represent future benefits and hence do not meet the Framework's definition of an asset, even if offset against a related liability. Similarly, deferred actuarial gains do not meet the *Framework's* definition of a liability;

(d) the balance sheet treatment is consistent with the proposals in the Financial Instruments Steering Committee's March 1997 Discussion Paper *Accounting for Financial Assets and Liabilities;*

(e) it generates income and expense items that are not arbitrary and that have information content;

(f) it is not reasonable to assume that all actuarial gains or losses will be offset in future years; on the contrary, if the original actuarial assumptions are still valid, future fluctuations will, on average, offset each other and thus will not offset past fluctuations;

(g) deferred recognition attempts to avoid volatility. However, a financial measure should be volatile if it purports to represent faithfully transactions and other events that are themselves volatile. Moreover, concerns about volatility could be addressed adequately by using a second performance statement or a statement of changes in equity;

(h) immediate recognition is consistent with IAS 8 *Accounting Policies, Changes in Accounting Estimates and Errors.* Under IAS 8, the effect of changes in accounting estimates should be included in profit or loss for the period if the change affects the current period only but not future periods. Actuarial gains and losses are not an estimate of future events, but result from events before the balance sheet date that resolve a past estimate (experience adjustments) or from changes in the estimated cost of employee service before the balance sheet date (changes in actuarial assumptions);

(i) any amortisation period (or the width of a 'corridor') is arbitrary. In addition, the amount of benefit remaining at a subsequent date is not objectively determinable and this makes it difficult to carry out an impairment test on any expense that is deferred; and

(j) in some cases, even supporters of amortisation or the 'corridor' may prefer immediate recognition. One possible example is where plan assets are stolen. Another possible example is a major change in the basis of taxing pension plans (such as the abolition of dividend tax credits for UK pension plans in 1997). However, although there might be agreement on extreme cases, it would prove very difficult to develop objective and non-arbitrary criteria for identifying such cases.

41 The Board found the immediate recognition approach attractive. However, the Board believes that it is not feasible to use this approach for actuarial gains and losses until the Board resolves substantial issues about performance reporting. These issues include:

(a) whether financial performance includes those items that are recognised directly in equity;

(b) the conceptual basis for determining whether items are recognised in the income statement or directly in equity;

(c) whether net cumulative actuarial losses should be recognised in the income statement, rather than directly in equity; and

(d) whether certain items reported initially in equity should subsequently be reported in the income statement ('recycling').

When the Board makes further progress with those issues, it may decide to revisit the treatment of actuarial gains and losses.

42 E54 proposed a 'corridor approach'. Under this approach, an entity does not recognise actuarial gains and losses to the extent that the cumulative unrecognised amounts do not exceed 10% of the present value of the obligation (or, if greater, 10% of the fair value of plan assets). Arguments for such approaches are that they:

(a) acknowledge that estimates of post-employment benefit obligations are best viewed as a range around the best estimate. As long as any new best estimate of the liability stays within that range, it would be difficult to say that the liability has really changed. However, once the new best estimate moves outside that range, it is not reasonable to assume that actuarial gains or losses will be offset in future years. If the original actuarial assumptions are still valid, future fluctuations will, on average, offset each other and thus will not offset past fluctuations;

(b) are easy to understand, do not require entities to keep complex records and do not require complex provisions to deal with settlements, curtailments and transitional matters;

(c) result in the recognition of an actuarial loss only when the liability (net of plan assets) has increased in the current period and an actuarial gain only when the (net) liability has decreased. By contrast, amortisation methods sometimes result in the recognition of an actuarial loss even if the (net) liability is unchanged or has decreased in the current period, or an actuarial gain even if the (net) liability is unchanged or has increased;

(d) represent faithfully transactions and other events that are themselves volatile. Paragraph 34 of the *Framework* notes that it may be relevant to recognise items and to disclose the risk of error surrounding their recognition and measurement despite inherent difficulties either in identifying the transactions and other events to be measured or in devising and applying measurement and presentation techniques that can convey messages that correspond with those transactions and events; and

(e) are consistent with IAS 8 *Accounting Policies, Changes in Accounting Estimates and Errors*. Under IAS 8, the effect of changes in accounting estimates is included in profit or loss for the period if the change affects the current period only but not future periods. Actuarial gains and losses are not an estimate of future events, but arise from events before the balance sheet date that resolve a past estimate (experience adjustments) or from changes in the estimated cost of employee service before the balance sheet date (changes in actuarial assumptions).

43 Some commentators on E54 argued that an entity should, over a period, recognise actuarial gains and losses within the 'corridor'. Otherwise, certain gains and losses would be deferred permanently, even though it would be more appropriate to recognise them (for example, to recognise gains and losses that persist for a number of years without reversal or to avoid a cumulative effect on the income statement where the net liability returns ultimately to the original level). However, the Board concluded that such a requirement would add complexity for little benefit.

44 The 'corridor' approach was supported by fewer than a quarter of the commentators on E54. In particular, the vast majority of preparers argued that the resulting volatility would not be a realistic portrayal of the long-term nature of post-employment benefit obligations. The Board concluded that there was not sufficient support from its constituents for such a significant change in current practice.

45 Approximately one third of the commentators on E54 supported the deferred recognition approach. Approximately another third of the respondents proposed a version of the corridor approach which applies deferred recognition to amounts falling outside the corridor. It results in less volatility than the corridor alone or deferred recognition alone. In the absence of any compelling conceptual reasons for choosing between these two approaches, the Board concluded that the latter approach would be a pragmatic means of avoiding a level of volatility that many of its constituents consider to be unrealistic.

46 In approving the final Standard, the Board decided to specify the minimum amount of actuarial gains or losses to be recognised, but permit any systematic method of faster recognition, provided that the same basis is applied to both gains and losses and the basis is applied consistently from period to period. The Board was persuaded by the following arguments:

(a) both the extent of volatility reduction and the mechanism adopted to effect it are essentially practical issues. From a conceptual point of view, the Board found the immediate recognition approach attractive. Therefore, the Board saw no reason to preclude entities from adopting faster methods of recognising actuarial gains and losses. In particular, the Board did not wish to discourage entities from adopting a consistent policy of recognising all actuarial gains and losses immediately. Similarly, the Board did not wish to discourage national standard-setters from requiring immediate recognition; and

(b) where mechanisms are in place to reduce volatility, the amount of actuarial gains and losses recognised during the period is largely arbitrary and has little information content. Also, the new IAS 19 requires an entity to disclose both the recognised and unrecognised amounts. Therefore, although there is some loss of comparability in allowing entities to use different mechanisms, the needs of users are not likely to be compromised if faster (and systematic) recognition methods are permitted.

47 The Board noted that changes in the fair value of any plan assets are, in effect, the results of changing estimates by market participants and are, therefore, inextricably linked with changes in the present value of the obligation. Consequently, the Board decided that changes in the fair value of plan assets are actuarial gains and losses and should be treated in the same way as the changes in the related obligation.

48 The width of a 'corridor' (ie the point at which it becomes necessary to recognise gains and losses) is arbitrary. To enhance comparability, the Board decided that the width of the 'corridor' should be consistent with the current requirement in those countries that have already adopted a 'corridor' approach, notably the USA. The Board noted that a significantly narrower 'corridor' would suffer from the disadvantages of the 'corridor', without being large enough to generate the advantages. On the other hand, a significantly wider 'corridor' would lack credibility.

An additional option for the recognition of actuarial gains and losses: amendment adopted by the IASB in December 2004

48A In 2004 the IASB published an exposure draft proposing an additional option for the recognition of actuarial gains and losses. The proposed option allowed an entity that recognised actuarial gains and losses in full in the period in which they occurred to recognise them outside profit or loss in a statement of recognised income and expense.

48B The argument for immediate recognition of actuarial gains and losses is that they are economic events of the period. Recognising them when they occur provides a faithful representation of those events. It also results in a faithful representation of the plan in the balance sheet. In contrast, when recognition is deferred, the information provided is partial and potentially misleading. Furthermore, any net cumulative deferred actuarial losses can give rise to a debit item in the balance sheet that does not meet the definition of an asset. Similarly, any net cumulative deferred actuarial gains can give rise to a credit item in the balance sheet that does not meet the definition of a liability.

48C The arguments put forward for deferred recognition of actuarial gains and losses are, as noted above:

(a) immediate recognition can cause volatile fluctuations in the balance sheet and income statement. It implies a degree of accuracy of measurement that rarely applies in practice. As a result, the volatility may not be a faithful representation of changes in the defined benefit asset or liability, but may simply reflect an unavoidable inability to predict accurately the future events that are anticipated in making period-to-period measurements.

(b) in the long term, actuarial gains and losses may offset one another.

(c) whether or not the volatility resulting from immediate recognition reflects economic events of the period, it is too great to be acceptable in the financial statements. It could overwhelm the profit or loss and financial position of other business operations.

48D The IASB does not accept arguments (a) and (b) as reasons for deferred recognition. It believes that the defined benefit asset or liability can be measured with sufficient reliability to justify its recognition. Recognition in a transparent manner of the current best estimate of the events of the period and the resulting asset and liability provides better information than non-recognition of an arbitrary amount of that current best estimate. Further, it is not reasonable to assume that existing actuarial gains and losses will be offset in future years. This implies an ability to predict future market prices.

48E The IASB also does not accept argument (c) in relation to the balance sheet. If the post-employment benefit amounts are large and volatile, the post-employment plan must be large and risky compared with other business operations. However, the IASB accepts that requiring actuarial gains and losses to be recognised in full in profit or loss in the period in which they occur is not appropriate at this time because the IASB has yet to develop fully the appropriate presentation of profit or loss and other items of recognised income and expense.

48F The IASB noted that the UK standard FRS 17 *Retirement Benefits* requires recognition of actuarial gains and losses in full as they occur outside profit or loss in a statement of total recognised gains and losses.

48G The IASB does not believe that immediate recognition of actuarial gains and losses outside profit or loss is necessarily ideal. However, it provides more transparent information than deferred recognition. The IASB therefore decided to propose such an option pending further developments on the presentation of profit or loss and other items of recognised income and expense.

48H IAS 1 *Presentation of Financial Statements* (as revised in 2003) requires income and expense recognised outside profit or loss to be presented in a statement of changes in equity. The statement of changes in equity must present the total income and expense for the period, being the profit or loss for the period and each item of income and expense for the period that, as required or permitted by other Standards or Interpretations, is recognised directly in equity (IAS 1 paragraph 96(a)–(c)). IAS 1 also permits these items, together with the effect of changes in accounting policies and the correction of errors, to be the only items shown in the statement of changes in equity.

48I To emphasise its view that actuarial gains and losses are items of income or expense, the IASB decided that actuarial gains and losses that are recognised outside profit or loss must be presented in the form of a statement of changes in equity that excludes transactions with equity holders acting in their capacity as equity holders. The IASB decided that this statement should be titled 'the statement of recognised income and expense'.

48J The responses from the UK to the exposure draft strongly supported the proposed option. The responses from outside the UK were divided. The main concerns expressed were:

(a) the option is not a conceptual improvement compared with immediate recognition of actuarial gains and losses in profit or loss.

(b) the option prejudges issues relating to IAS 1 that should be resolved in the project on reporting comprehensive income.

(c) adding options to Standards is not desirable and obstructs comparability.

(d) the IASB should not tinker with IAS 19 before undertaking a comprehensive review of the Standard.

(e) the option could lead to divergence from US GAAP.

(f) deferred recognition is preferable to immediate recognition.

48K The IASB agrees that actuarial gains and losses are items of income and expense. However, it believes that it would be premature to require their immediate recognition in profit or loss before a comprehensive review of both accounting for post-employment benefits and reporting comprehensive income. The requirement that actuarial gains and losses that are recognised outside profit or loss must be recognised in a statement of recognised income and expense does not prejudge any of the discussions the IASB is yet to have on reporting comprehensive income. Rather, the IASB is allowing an accounting treatment currently accepted by a national standard-setter (the UK ASB) to continue, pending the comprehensive review of accounting for post-employment benefits and reporting comprehensive income.

48L The IASB also agrees that adding options to Standards is generally undesirable because of the resulting lack of comparability between entities. However, IAS 19 permits an entity to choose *any* systematic method of recognition for actuarial gains and losses that results in faster recognition than the minimum required by the Standard. Furthermore, the amount to be recognised under any deferral method will depend on when that method was first applied, ie when an entity first adopted IAS 19 or started a defined benefit plan. There is, therefore, little or no comparability because of the existing options in IAS 19.

48M The IASB further agrees that a fundamental review of accounting for post-employment benefits is needed. However, such a review is likely to take some time to complete. In the meantime, the IASB believes that it would be wrong to prohibit a method of recognising actuarial gains and losses that is accepted by a national standard-setter and provides more transparent information about the costs and risks of running a defined benefit plan.

48N The IASB agrees that the new option could lead to divergence from US GAAP. However, although IAS 19 and US GAAP share the same basic approach, they differ in several respects. The IASB has decided not to address these issues now. Furthermore, the option is just that. No entity is obliged to create such divergence.

48O Lastly, as discussed above, the IASB does not agree that deferred recognition is better than immediate recognition of actuarial gains and losses. The amounts recognised under a deferral method are opaque and not representationally faithful, and the inclusion of deferral methods creates a complex difficult standard.

48P The IASB considered whether actuarial gains and losses that have been recognised outside profit or loss should be recognised in profit or loss in a later period (ie recycled). The IASB noted that there is not a consistent policy on recycling in IFRSs and that recycling in general is an issue to be resolved in its project on reporting comprehensive income. Furthermore, it is difficult to see a rational basis on which actuarial gains and losses could be recycled. The exposure draft therefore proposed prohibiting recycling of actuarial gains and losses that have been recognised in the statement of recognised income and expense.

48Q Most respondents supported not recycling actuarial gains and losses. However, many argued in favour of recycling, for the following reasons:

(a) all income and expense should be recognised in profit or loss at some time.

(b) a ban on recycling is a new approach in IFRSs and should not be introduced before a fundamental review of reporting comprehensive income.

(c) to ban recycling could encourage abuse in setting over-optimistic actuarial assumptions.

48R The IASB notes that most items under IFRSs that are recognised outside profit or loss are recycled, but not all. Revaluation gains and losses on property, plant and equipment and intangibles are not recycled. The question of recycling therefore remains open in IFRSs. The IASB does not believe that a general decision on the matter should be made in the context of these amendments. The decision in these amendments not to recycle actuarial gains and losses is made because of the pragmatic inability to identify a suitable basis and does not prejudge the wider debate that will take place in the project on reporting comprehensive income.

48S In the meantime, the IASB acknowledges the concern of some respondents that some items of income or expense will not be recognised in profit or loss in any period. The IASB has therefore required disclosure of the cumulative amounts recognised in the statement of recognised income and expense so that users of the financial statements can assess the effect of this policy.

48T The IASB also notes the argument that to ban recycling could lead to abuse in setting over-optimistic assumptions. A lower cost could be recognised in profit or loss with resulting experience losses being recognised in the statement of recognised income and expense. Some of the new disclosures help to counter such concerns, for example, the narrative description of the basis for the expected rate of return and the five-year history of experience gains and losses. The IASB also notes that under a deferred recognition approach, if over-optimistic assumptions are used, a lower cost is recognised immediately in profit or loss and the resulting experience losses are recognised only gradually over the next 10–15 years. The incentive for such abuse is just as great under deferred recognition as it is under immediate recognition outside profit or loss.

48U The IASB also considered whether actuarial gains and losses recognised outside profit or loss should be recognised immediately in a separate component of equity and transferred to retained earnings at a later period. Again the IASB concluded that there is no rational basis for a transfer to retained earnings in later periods. Hence, the exposure draft proposed that actuarial gains and losses that are recognised outside profit or loss should be recognised in retained earnings immediately.

48V A small majority of the respondents supported this proposal. The arguments put forward against immediate recognition in retained earnings were:

(a) the IASB should not set requirements on the component of equity in which items should be recognised before a fundamental review of the issue.

(b) retained earnings should be the cumulative total of profit or loss less amounts distributed to owners.

(c) the volatility of the amounts means that separate presentation would be helpful.

(d) the impact on distributions needs to be considered.

(e) actuarial gains and losses are temporary in nature and hence should be excluded from retained earnings.

48W In IFRSs, the phrase 'retained earnings' is not defined and the IASB has not discussed what it should mean. In particular, retained earnings is not defined as the cumulative total of profit or loss less amounts distributed to owners. As with recycling, practice varies under IFRSs. Some amounts that are recognised outside profit or loss are required to be presented in a separate component of equity, for example exchange gains and losses on foreign subsidiaries. Other such amounts are not, for example gains and losses on available-for-sale financial assets.

48X The IASB does not believe that it is appropriate to introduce a definition of retained earnings in the context of these amendments to IAS 19. The proposal in the exposure draft was based on practical considerations. As with recycling, there is no rational basis for transferring actuarial gains and losses from a separate component in equity into retained earnings at a later date. As discussed above, the IASB has added a requirement to disclose the cumulative amount recognised in the statement of recognised income and expense to provide users with further information.

48Y Consideration of the implications of IFRSs on the ability of an entity to make distributions to equity holders is not within the IASB's remit. In addition, the IASB does not agree that even if actuarial gains and losses were temporary in nature this would justify excluding them from retained earnings.

48Z Finally, the IASB considered whether, if actuarial gains and losses are recognised when they occur, entities should be required to present separately in retained earnings an amount equal to the defined benefit asset or liability. Such a presentation is required by FRS 17. The IASB noted that such a presentation is not required by IFRSs for any other item, however significant its size or volatility, and that entities can provide the information if they wish. The IASB therefore decided not to require such a presentation.

48AA IAS 19 limits the amount of a surplus that can be recognised as an asset ('the asset ceiling') to the present value of any economic benefits available to an entity in the form of refunds from the plan or reductions in future contributions to the plan.* The IASB considered whether the effect of this limit should be recognised outside profit or loss, if that is the entity's accounting policy for actuarial gains and losses, or treated as an adjustment of the other components of the defined benefit cost and recognised in profit or loss.

48BB The IASB decided that the effect of the limit is similar to an actuarial gain or loss because it arises from a remeasurement of the benefits available to an entity from a surplus in the plan. The IASB therefore concluded that, if the entity's accounting policy is to recognise actuarial gains and losses as they occur outside profit or loss, the effect of the limit should also be recognised outside profit or loss in the statement of recognised income and expense.

48CC Most respondents supported this proposal. The arguments opposing the proposal were:

(a) the adjustment arising from the asset ceiling is not necessarily caused by actuarial gains and losses and should not be treated in the same way.

(b) it is not consistent with FRS 17, which allocates the change in the recoverable surplus to various events and hence to different components of the defined benefit cost.

48DD The IASB agrees that the adjustment from the asset ceiling is not necessarily caused by actuarial gains and losses. The asset ceiling effectively imposes a different measurement basis for the asset to be recognised (present value of refunds and reductions in future contributions) from that used to derive the actuarial gains and losses and other components of the defined benefit cost (fair value of plan assets less projected unit credit value of plan liabilities). Changes in the recognised asset arise from changes in the present value of refunds and reductions in future contributions. Such changes can be caused by events of the same type as those that cause actuarial gains and losses, for example changes in interest rates or assumptions about longevity, or by events that do not cause actuarial gains and losses, for example trustees agreeing to a refund in exchange for benefit enhancements or a management decision to curtail the plan.

48EE Because the asset ceiling imposes a different measurement basis for the asset to be recognised, the IASB does not believe it is possible to allocate the effect of the asset ceiling to the components of the defined benefit cost other than on an arbitrary basis. The IASB reaffirmed its view that the adjustment arising from the asset ceiling should, therefore, be regarded as a remeasurement and similar to an actuarial gain or loss. This treatment also has the advantages of (a) being simple and (b) giving transparent information because the cost of the defined benefit promise (ie the service costs and interest cost) remains unaffected by the funding of the plan.

* The limit also includes unrecognised actuarial gains and losses and past service costs.

Past service cost (paragraphs 96–101 of the Standard)

49 E54 included two alternative treatments for past service cost. The first approach was similar to that used in the old IAS 19 (amortisation for current employees and immediate recognition for former employees). The second approach was immediate recognition of all past service cost.

50 Those who support the first approach argue that:

(a) an entity introduces or improves employee benefits for current employees in order to generate future economic benefits in the form of reduced employee turnover, improved productivity, reduced demands for increases in cash compensation and improved prospects for attracting additional qualified employees;

(b) although it may not be feasible to improve benefits for current employees without also improving benefits for former employees, it would be impracticable to assess the resulting economic benefits for an entity and the period over which those benefits will flow to the entity; and

(c) immediate recognition is too revolutionary. It would also have undesirable social consequences because it would deter companies from improving benefits.

51 Those who support immediate recognition of all past service cost argue that:

(a) amortisation of past service cost is inconsistent with the view of employee benefits as an exchange between an entity and its employees for services rendered: past service cost relates to past events and affects the employer's present obligation arising from employees' past service. Although an entity may improve benefits in the expectation of future benefits, an obligation exists and should be recognised;

(b) deferred recognition of the liability reduces comparability; an entity that retrospectively improves benefits relating to past service will report lower liabilities than an entity that granted identical benefits at an earlier date, yet both have identical benefit obligations. Also, deferred recognition encourages entities to increase pensions instead of salaries;

(c) past service cost does not give an entity control over a resource and thus does not meet the *Framework's* definition of an asset. Therefore, it is not appropriate to defer recognition of the expense; and

(d) there is not likely to be a close relationship between cost–the only available measure of the effect of the amendment–and any related benefits in the form of increased loyalty.

52 Under the old IAS 19, past service cost for current employees was recognised as an expense systematically over the expected remaining working lives of the employees concerned. Similarly, under the first approach set out in E54, past service cost was to be amortised over the average expected remaining working lives of the employees concerned. However, E54 also proposed that the attribution period for current service cost should end when the employee's entitlement to

receive all significant benefits due under the plan is no longer conditional on further service. Some commentators on E54 felt that these two provisions were inconsistent.

53 In the light of comments received, the Board concluded that past service cost should be amortised over the average period until the amended benefits become vested, because:

(a) once the benefits become vested, there is clearly a liability that should be recognised; and

(b) although non-vested benefits give rise to an obligation, any method of attributing non-vested benefits to individual periods is essentially arbitrary. In determining how that obligation builds up, no single method is demonstrably superior to all others.

54 Some argue that a 'corridor' approach should be used for past service cost because the use of a different accounting treatment for past service cost than for actuarial gains and losses may create an opportunity for accounting arbitrage. However, the purpose of the 'corridor' is to deal with the inevitable imprecision in the measurement of defined benefit obligations. Past service cost results from a management decision, rather than inherent measurement uncertainty. Consequently, the Board rejected the 'corridor' approach for past service cost.

55 The Board rejected proposals that:

(a) past service cost should (as under the old IAS 19) be recognised over a shorter period where plan amendments provide an entity with economic benefits over that shorter period: for example, when plan amendments were made regularly, the old IAS 19 stated that the additional cost may be recognised as an expense or income systematically over the period to the next expected plan amendment. The Board believes that the actuarial assumptions should allow for such regular plan amendments and that subsequent differences between the assumed increase and the actual increase are actuarial gains or losses, not a past service cost;

(b) past service cost should be recognised over the remaining life expectancy of the participants if all or most plan participants are inactive. The Board believes that it is not clear that the past service cost will lead to economic benefits to the entity over that period; and

(c) even if past service cost is generally recognised on a delayed basis, past service cost should not be recognised immediately if the past service cost results from legislative changes (such as a new requirement to equalise retirement ages for men and women) or from decisions by trustees who are not controlled, or influenced, by the entity's management. The Board decided that such a distinction would not be practicable.

56 The old IAS 19 did not specify the basis upon which an entity should amortise the unrecognised balance of past service cost. The Board agreed that any amortisation method is arbitrary and decided to require straight-line amortisation, as that is the simplest method to apply and understand. To enhance comparability, the Board decided to require a single method and not to permit alternative methods, such as methods that assign:

(a) an equal amount of past service cost to each expected year of employee service; or

(b) past service cost to each period in proportion to estimated total salaries in that period.

Paragraph 99 confirms that the amortisation schedule is not amended for subsequent changes in the average remaining working life, unless there is a curtailment or settlement.

57 Unlike the old IAS 19, the new IAS 19 treats past service cost for current employees differently from actuarial gains. This means that some benefit improvements may be funded out of actuarial gains that have not yet been recognised in the financial statements. Some argue that the resulting past service cost should not be recognised because:

(a) the cost of the improvements does not meet the *Framework's* definition of an expense, as there is no outflow or depletion of any asset which was previously recognised in the balance sheet; and

(b) in some cases, benefit improvements may have been granted only because of actuarial gains.

The Board decided to require the same accounting treatment for all past service cost (ie recognise over the average period until the amended benefits become vested) whether or not they are funded out of an actuarial gain that is already recognised in the entity's balance sheet.

58 Some commentators on E54 argued that the recognition of actuarial gains should be limited if there is unamortised past service cost. The Board rejected this proposal because it would introduce additional complexity for limited benefit. Other commentators would prohibit the recognition of actuarial gains that are earmarked for future benefit improvements. However, the Board believes that if such earmarking is set out in the formal (or constructive) terms of the plan, the benefit improvements should be included in the actuarial assumptions. In other cases, there is insufficient linkage between the actuarial gains and the benefit improvements to justify an exceptional treatment.

59 The old IAS 19 did not specify the balance sheet treatment for past service cost. Some argue that an entity should recognise past service cost immediately both as an addition to the liability and as an asset (prepaid expense) on the grounds that deferred recognition of the liability offsets a liability against an asset (unamortised past service cost) that cannot be used to settle the liability. However, the Board decided that an entity should recognise past service cost for current employees as an addition to the liability gradually over a period, because:

(a) past service cost does not give an entity control over a resource and thus does not meet the Framework's definition of an asset;

(b) separate presentation of a liability and a prepaid expense may confuse users; and

(c) although non-vested benefits give rise to an obligation, any method of attributing non-vested benefits to individual periods is essentially arbitrary. In determining how that obligation builds up, no single method is demonstrably superior to all others.

60 The old IAS 19 appeared to treat plan amendments that reduce benefits as negative past service cost (ie amortisation for current employees, immediate recognition for former employees). However, some argue that this results in the recognition of deferred income that conflicts with the *Framework*. They also argue that there is only an arbitrary distinction between amendments that should be treated in this way and curtailments or settlements. Therefore, E54 proposed that:

(a) plan amendments are:

(i) a curtailment if the amendment reduces benefits for future service; and

(ii) a settlement if the amendment reduces benefits for past service; and

(b) any gain or loss on the curtailment or settlement should be recognised immediately when the curtailment or settlement occurs.

61 Some commentators on E54 argued that such 'negative plan amendments' should be treated as negative past service cost by being recognised as deferred income and amortised into the income statement over the working lives of the employees concerned. The basis for this view is that 'negative' amendments reduce employee morale in the same way that 'positive' amendments increase morale. Also, a consistent treatment avoids the abuses that might occur if an entity could improve benefits in one period (and recognise the resulting expense over an extended period) and then reduce the benefits (and recognise the resulting income immediately). The Board agreed with this view. Therefore, the new IAS 19 treats both 'positive' and 'negative' plan amendments in the same way.

62 The distinction between negative past service cost and curtailments would be important if:

(a) a material amount of negative past service cost were amortised over a long period (this is unlikely, as the new IAS 19 requires that negative past service cost should be amortised until the time when those (reduced) benefits that relate to prior service are vested); or

(b) unrecognised past service cost or actuarial gains exist. For a curtailment these would be recognised immediately, whereas they would not be affected directly by negative past service cost.

The Board believes that the distinction between negative past service cost and curtailments is unlikely to have any significant effect in practice and that any attempt to deal with exceptional cases would result in excessive complexity.

Recognition and measurement: an additional minimum liability

63 The Board considered whether it should require an entity to recognise an additional minimum liability where:

(a) an entity's immediate obligation if it discontinued a plan at the balance sheet date would be greater than the present value of the liability that would otherwise be recognised in the balance sheet;

(b) vested post-employment benefits are payable at the date when an employee leaves the entity. Consequently, because of the effect of discounting, the present value of the vested benefit would be greater if an employee left immediately after the balance sheet date than if the employee completes the expected period of service; or

(c) the present value of vested benefits exceeds the amount of the liability that would otherwise be recognised in the balance sheet. This could occur where a large proportion of the benefits are fully vested and an entity has not recognised actuarial losses or past service cost.

64 One example of a requirement for an entity to recognise an additional minimum liability is in the US Standard SFAS 87 *Employers' Accounting for Pensions*: the minimum liability is based on current salaries and excludes the effect of deferring certain past service cost and actuarial gains and losses. If the minimum liability exceeds the obligation measured on the normal projected salary basis (with deferred recognition of certain income and expense), the excess is recognised as an intangible asset (not exceeding the amount of any unamortised past service cost, with any further excess deducted directly from equity) and as an additional minimum liability.

65 The Board believes that such additional measures of the liability are potentially confusing and do not provide relevant information. They would also conflict with the *Framework's* going concern assumption and with its definition of a liability. The new IAS 19 does not require the recognition of an additional minimum liability. Certain of the circumstances discussed in the preceding two paragraphs may give rise to contingent liabilities requiring disclosure under IAS 10 *Events after the Balance Sheet Date*.

Plan assets (paragraphs 102–107 of the Standard)

66 The new IAS 19 requires explicitly that defined benefit obligations should be recognised as a liability after deducting plan assets (if any) out of which the obligations are to be settled directly (see paragraph 54 of the Standard). This is already widespread, and probably universal, practice. The Board believes that plan assets reduce (but do not extinguish) an entity's own obligation and result in a single, net liability. Although the presentation of that net liability as a single amount in the balance sheet differs conceptually from the offsetting of separate assets and liabilities, the Board decided in issuing IAS 19 in 1998 that the definition of plan assets should be consistent with the offsetting criteria in IAS 32 *Financial Instruments: Disclosure and Presentation*. IAS 32 states that a financial asset and a financial liability should be offset and the net amount reported in the balance sheet when an entity:

(a) has a legally enforceable right to set off the recognised amounts; and

(b) intends either to settle on a net basis, or to realise the asset and settle the liability simultaneously.

67 IAS 19 (revised 1998) defined plan assets as assets (other than non-transferable financial instruments issued by the reporting entity) held by an entity (a fund) that satisfies all of the following conditions:

(a) the entity is legally separate from the reporting entity;

(b) the assets of the fund are to be used only to settle the employee benefit obligations, are not available to the entity's own creditors and cannot be returned to the entity (or can be returned to the entity only if the remaining assets of the fund are sufficient to meet the plan's obligations); and

(c) to the extent that sufficient assets are in the fund, the entity will have no legal or constructive obligation to pay the related employee benefits directly.

67A In issuing IAS 19 in 1998, the Board considered whether the definition of plan assets should include a fourth condition: that the entity does not control the fund. The Board concluded that control is not relevant in determining whether the assets in a fund reduce an entity's own obligation.

68 In response to comments on E54, the Board decided to modify the definition of plan assets to exclude non-transferable financial instruments issued by the reporting entity. If this were not done, an entity could reduce its liabilities, and increase its equity, by issuing non-transferable equity instruments to a defined benefit plan.

Plan assets: revised definition adopted in 2000

68A In 1999, the Board began a limited scope project to consider the accounting for assets held by a fund that satisfies parts (a) and (b) of the definition set out in paragraph 67 above, but does not satisfy condition (c) because the entity retains a legal or constructive obligation to pay the benefits directly. IAS 19 (revised 1998) did not address assets held by such funds.

68B The Board considered two main approaches to such funds:

(a) a **net** approach – the entity recognises its entire obligation as a liability after deducting the fair value of the assets held by the fund; and

(b) a **gross** approach – the entity recognises its entire obligation as a liability and recognises its rights to a refund from the fund as a separate asset.

68C Supporters of a net approach made one or more of the following arguments:

(a) a gross presentation would be misleading, because:

(i) where conditions (a) and (b) of the definition in paragraph 67 above are met, the entity does not control the assets held by the fund; and

(ii) even if the entity retains a legal obligation to pay the entire amount of the benefits directly, this legal obligation is a matter of form rather than substance;

(b) a gross presentation would be an unnecessary change from current practice, which generally permits a net presentation. It would introduce excessive complexity into the Standard, for limited benefit to users, given that paragraph 120(c) already requires disclosure of the gross amounts;

(c) a gross approach may lead to measurement difficulties because of the interaction with the 10% corridor for the obligation.

(i) One possibility would be to measure the assets at fair value, with all changes in fair value recognised immediately. This might seem inconsistent with the treatment of plan assets, because changes in the fair value of plan assets are one component of the actuarial gains and losses to which the corridor is applied under IAS 19. In other words, this approach would deny entities the opportunity of offsetting gains and losses on the assets against gains and losses on the liability.

(ii) A second possibility would be to defer changes in the fair value of the assets to the extent that there are unrecognised actuarial gains and losses on the obligations. However, the carrying amount of the assets would then have no easily describable meaning. It would probably also require complex and arbitrary rules to match the gains and losses on the assets with gains and losses on the obligation.

(iii) A third possibility would be to measure the assets at fair value, but to aggregate the changes in fair value with actuarial gains and losses on the liability. In other words, the assets would be treated in the same way as plan assets, except the balance sheet presentation would be gross rather than net. However, this would mean that changes in the fair value of the assets could affect the measurement of the obligation; and

(d) a net approach might be viewed as analogous to the treatment of joint and several liabilities under paragraph 29 of IAS 37. An entity recognises a provision for the part of the obligation for which an outflow of resources embodying economic benefits is probable. The part of the obligation that is expected to be met by other parties is treated as a contingent liability.

68D Supporters of a gross approach advocated that approach for one or more of the following reasons:

(a) paragraph 66 above gives an explanation for presenting defined benefit obligations net of plan assets. The explanation focuses on whether offsetting is appropriate. Part (c) of the 1998 definition focuses on offsetting. This suggests that assets that satisfy parts (a) and (b) of the definition, but fail part (c) of the definition, should be treated in the same way as plan assets for recognition and measurement purposes, but should be shown gross on the face of the balance sheet without offsetting;

(b) if offsetting is allowed when condition (c) is not met, this would seem to be equivalent to permitting a net presentation for 'in-substance defeasance' and other analogous cases where IAS 32 indicates explicitly that offsetting is inappropriate. The Board has rejected 'in-substance defeasance' for financial instruments (see IAS 39 Application Guidance, paragraph AG59) and there is no obvious reason to permit it in accounting for defined benefit plans. In these cases the entity retains an obligation that should be recognised as a liability and the entity's right to reimbursement from the plan is a source of economic benefits that should be recognised as an asset. Offsetting would be permitted if the conditions in paragraph ~~33~~42 of IAS 32 are satisfied;

(c) the Board decided in IAS 37 to require a gross presentation for reimbursements related to provisions, even though this was not previously general practice. There is no conceptual reason to require a different treatment for employee benefits;

(d) although some consider that a gross approach requires an entity to recognise assets that it does not control, others believe that this view is incorrect. A gross approach requires the entity to recognise an asset representing its right to receive reimbursement from the fund that holds those assets. It does not require the entity to recognise the underlying assets of the fund;

(e) in a plan with plan assets that meet the definition adopted in 1998, the employees' first claim is against the fund—they have no claim against the entity if sufficient assets are in the fund. In the view of some, the fact that employees must first claim against the fund is more than just a difference in form—it changes the substance of the obligation; and

(f) defined benefit plans might be regarded under SIC-12 *Consolidation—Special Purpose Entities* as special purpose entities that the entity controls—and should consolidate. As the offsetting criterion in IAS 19 is consistent with offsetting criteria in other International Accounting Standards, it is relatively unimportant whether the pension plan is consolidated in cases where the obligation and the plan assets qualify for offset. If the assets are presented as a deduction from the related benefit obligations in cases where condition (c) is not met, it could become important to assess whether the entity should consolidate the plan.

68E Some argued that a net approach should be permitted when an entity retains an obligation to pay the entire amount of the benefits directly, but the obligation is considered unlikely to have any substantive effect in practice. The Board concluded that it would not be practicable to establish guidance of this kind that could be applied in a consistent manner.

68F The Board also considered the possibility of adopting a 'linked presentation' that UK Financial Reporting Standard FRS 5 *Reporting the Substance of Transactions*, requires for non-recourse finance. Under FRS 5, the face of the balance sheet presents both the gross amount of the asset and, as a direct deduction, the related non-recourse debt. Supporters of this approach argued that it portrays the close link between related assets and liabilities without compromising general offsetting requirements. Opponents of the linked presentation argued that it creates a form of balance sheet presentation that IASC has not used previously and may cause confusion. The Board decided not to adopt the linked presentation.

68G The Board concluded that a net presentation is justified where there are restrictions (including restrictions that apply on bankruptcy of the reporting entity) on the use of the assets so that the assets can be used only to pay or fund employee benefits. Accordingly, the Board decided to modify the definition of plan assets set out in paragraph 67 above by:

(a) emphasising that the creditors of the entity should not have access to the assets held by the fund, even on bankruptcy of the reporting entity; and

(b) deleting condition (c), so that the existence of a legal or constructive obligation to pay the employee benefits directly does not preclude a net presentation, and modifying condition (b) to explicitly permit the fund to reimburse the entity for paying the long-term employee benefits.

68H When an entity retains a direct obligation to the employees, the Board acknowledges that the net presentation is inconsistent with the derecognition requirements for financial instruments in IAS 39 and with the offsetting requirements in IAS 32. However, in the Board's view, the restrictions on the use of the assets create a sufficiently strong link with the employee benefit obligations that a net presentation is more relevant than a gross presentation, even if the entity retains a direct obligation to the employees.

68I The Board believes that such restrictions are unique to employee benefit plans and does not intend to permit this net presentation for other liabilities if the conditions in IAS 32 and IAS 39 are not met. Accordingly, condition (a) in the new definition refers to the reason for the existence of the fund. The Board believes that an arbitrary restriction of this kind is the only practical way to permit a pragmatic exception to IASC's general offsetting criteria without permitting an unacceptable extension of this exception to other cases.

68J In some plans that exist in some countries, an entity is entitled to receive a reimbursement of employee benefits from a separate fund but the entity has discretion to delay receipt of the reimbursement or to claim less than the full reimbursement. Some argue that this element of discretion weakens the link between the benefits and the reimbursement so much that a net presentation is not justifiable. They believe that the definition of plan assets should exclude assets held by such funds and that a gross approach should be used in such cases. The Board concluded that the link between the benefits and the reimbursement is strong enough in such cases that a net approach is still appropriate.

68K The Board's proposal for extending the definition of plan assets was set out in Exposure Draft E67 *Pension Plan Assets*, published in July 2000. The vast majority of the 39 respondents to E67 supported the proposal.

68L A number of respondents to E67 proposed a further extension of the definition to include certain insurance policies that have similar economic effects to funds whose assets qualify as plan assets under the revised definition proposed in E67. Accordingly, the Board decided to extend the definition of plan assets to include certain insurance policies (now described in IAS 19 as qualifying insurance policies) that satisfy the same conditions as other plan assets. These decisions were implemented in a revised IAS 19, approved by the Board in October 2000.

Plan assets: measurement

69 The old IAS 19 stated that plan assets are valued at fair value, but did not define fair value. However, other International Accounting Standards define fair value as 'the amount for which an asset could be exchanged or a liability settled between knowledgeable, willing parties in an arm's length transaction'. This may imply that no deduction is made for the estimated costs necessary to sell the asset (in

other words, it is a mid-market value, with no adjustment for transaction costs). However, some argue that a plan will eventually have to dispose of its assets in order to pay benefits. Therefore, the Board concluded in E54 that plan assets should be measured at market value. Market value was defined, as in IAS 25 *Accounting for Investments*,* as the amount obtainable from the sale of an asset in an active market.

70 Some commentators on E54 felt that the proposal to measure plan assets at market value would not be consistent with IAS 22 *Business Combinations*† and with the measurement of financial assets as proposed in the discussion paper *Accounting for Financial Assets and Financial Liabilities* published by IASC's Financial Instruments Steering Committee in March 1997. Therefore, the Board decided that plan assets should be measured at fair value.

71 Some argue that concerns about volatility in reported profit should be countered by permitting or requiring entities to measure plan assets at a market-related value that reflects changes in fair value over an arbitrary period, such as five years. The Board believes that the use of market-related values would add excessive and unnecessary complexity and that the combination of the 'corridor' approach to actuarial gains and losses with deferred recognition outside the 'corridor' is sufficient to deal with concerns about volatility.

72 The old IAS 19 stated that, when fair values were estimated by discounting future cash flows, the long-term rate of return reflected the average rate of total income (interest, dividends and appreciation in value) expected to be earned on the plan assets during the time period until benefits are paid. It was not clear whether the old IAS 19 allowed a free choice between market values and discounted cash flows, or whether discounted cash flows could be used only when no market value was available. The Board decided that plan assets should be measured by techniques such as discounting expected future cash flows only when no market value is available.

73 Some believe that plan assets should be measured on the following basis, which is required by IAS 25 *Accounting for Investments*:*

(a) long-term investments are carried in the balance sheet at either cost, revalued amounts or, in the case of marketable equity securities, the lower of cost and market value determined on a portfolio basis. The carrying amount of a long-term investment is reduced to recognise a decline other than temporary in the value of the investment; and

(b) current investments are carried in the balance sheet at either market value or the lower of cost and market value.

The Board rejected this basis because it is not consistent with the basis used for measuring the related obligations.

74 The Board decided that there should not be a different basis for measuring investments that have a fixed redemption value and that match the obligations of

* superseded by IAS 39 *Financial Instruments: Recognition and Measurement* and IAS 40 *Investment Property*.

† IAS 22 was withdrawn in 2004 and replaced by IFRS 3 *Business Combinations*.

the plan, or specific parts thereof. IAS 26 *Accounting and Reporting by Retirement Benefit Plans* permits such investments to be measured on an amortised cost basis.

75 In response to comments on E54, the Board decided that all plan administration costs (not just investment administration costs, as proposed in E54), should be deducted in determining the return on plan assets.

Reimbursements (paragraphs 104A–104D of the Standard)

75A Paragraph 41 of IAS 19 states that an entity recognises its rights under an insurance policy as an asset if the policy is held by the entity itself. IAS 19 (revised 1998) did not address the measurement of these insurance policies. The entity's rights under the insurance policy might be regarded as a financial asset. However, rights and obligations arising under insurance contracts are excluded from the scope of IAS 39 *Financial Instruments: Recognition and Measurement*. Also, IAS 39 does not apply to 'employers' ~~assets and liabilities~~ rights and obligations under employee benefit plans, to which IAS 19 *Employee Benefits* applies'. Paragraphs 39–42 of IAS 19 discuss insured benefits in distinguishing defined contribution plans and defined benefit plans, but this discussion does not deal with measurement.

75B In reviewing the definition of plan assets (see paragraphs 68A–68L above), the Board decided to review the treatment of insurance policies that an entity holds in order to fund employee benefits. Even under the revised definition adopted in 2000, the entity's rights under an insurance policy that is not a qualifying insurance policy (as defined in the 2000 revision to IAS 19) are not plan assets.

75C In 2000, the Board decided to introduce recognition and measurement requirements for reimbursements under such insurance policies (see paragraphs 104A–104D). The Board based these requirements on the treatment of reimbursements under paragraphs 53–58 of IAS 37 *Provisions, Contingent Liabilities and Contingent Assets*. In particular, the Standard requires an entity to recognise a right to reimbursement of post-employment benefits as a separate asset, rather than as a deduction from the related obligations. In all other respects (for example, the use of the 'corridor') the Standard requires an entity to treat such reimbursement rights in the same way as plan assets. This requirement reflects the close link between the reimbursement right and the related obligation.

75D Paragraph 104 states that where plan assets include insurance policies that exactly match the amount and timing of some or all of the benefits payable under the plan, the plan's rights under those insurance policies are measured at the same amount as the related obligations. Paragraph 104D extends that conclusion to insurance policies that are assets of the entity itself.

75E IAS 37 states that the amount recognised for the reimbursement should not exceed the amount of the provision. Paragraph 104A of the Standard contains no similar restriction, because the asset limit in paragraph 58 already applies to prevent the recognition of an asset that exceeds the available economic benefits.

Limit on the recognition of an asset (paragraphs 58–60 of the Standard)

76 In certain cases, paragraph 54 of the new IAS 19 would require an entity to recognise an asset. E54 proposed that the amount of the asset recognised should not exceed the aggregate of the present values of:

(a) any refunds expected from the plan; and

(b) any expected reduction in future contributions arising from the surplus.

In approving E54, the Board took the view that an entity should not recognise an asset at an amount that exceeds the present value of the future benefits that are expected to flow to the entity from that asset. This view is consistent with the Board's proposal that assets should not be carried at more than their recoverable amount (see E55 *Impairment of Assets*). The old IAS 19 contained no such restriction.

77 On reviewing the responses to E54, the Board concluded that the limit on the recognition of an asset should not over-ride the treatments of actuarial losses or past service cost in order not to defeat the purpose of these treatments. Consequently, the limit is likely to come into play only where:

(a) an entity has chosen the transitional option to recognise the effect of adopting the new IAS 19 over up to five years, but has funded the obligation more quickly; or

(b) the plan is very mature and has a very large surplus that is more than large enough to eliminate all future contributions and cannot be returned to the entity.

78 Some commentators argued that the limit in E54 was not operable because it would require an entity to make extremely subjective forecasts of expected refunds or reductions in contributions. In response to these comments, the Board agreed that the limit should reflect the available refunds or reductions in contributions.

Asset ceiling: amendment adopted in May 2002

78A In April 2002, the Board agreed on an amendment to the limit on the recognition of an asset (the asset ceiling) in paragraph 58 of the Standard. The objective of the amendment was to prevent gains (losses) being recognised solely as a result of the deferred recognition of past service cost and actuarial losses (gains).

78B The asset ceiling is specified in paragraph 58 of IAS 19, which requires a defined benefit asset to be measured at the lower of:

(a) the amount determined under paragraph 54; and

(b) the total of:

(i) any cumulative unrecognised net actuarial losses and past service cost; and

(ii) the present value of any economic benefits available in the form of refunds from the plan or reductions in future contributions to the plan.

78C The problem arises when an entity defers recognition of actuarial losses or past service cost in determining the amount specified in paragraph 54 but is required to measure the defined benefit asset at the net total specified in paragraph 58(b). Paragraph 58(b)(i) could result in the entity recognising an increased asset because of actuarial losses or past service cost in the period. The increase in the asset would be reported as a gain in income. Examples illustrating the issue are given in Appendix C.

78D The Board agreed that recognising gains (losses) arising from past service cost and actuarial losses (gains) is not representationally faithful. Further, the Board holds the view that this issue demonstrates that IAS 19 can give rise to serious problems. The Board intends to undertake a comprehensive review of the aspects of IAS 19 that cause concern, including the interaction of the asset ceiling and the options to defer recognition of certain gains and losses. In the meantime, the Board regards as an improvement a limited amendment to prevent their interaction giving rise to unfaithful representations of events.

78E Paragraph 58A, therefore, prevents gains (losses) from being recognised solely as a result of the deferred recognition of past service cost or actuarial losses (gains).

78F Some Board members and respondents to the exposure draft of this amendment suggested that the issue be dealt with by removing paragraph 58(b)(i). Paragraph 58(b)(i) is the component of the asset ceiling that gives rise to the problem: losses that are unrecognised under paragraph 54 are added to the amount that can be recognised as an asset. However, deleting paragraph 58(b)(i) effectively removes the option of deferred recognition of actuarial losses for all entities that have a defined benefit asset. Removing this option would have wide reaching implications for the deferred recognition approach in IAS 19 that can be considered fully only within the context of the comprehensive review noted above.

Curtailments and settlements (paragraphs 109–115 of the Standard)

79 Under the old IAS 19, curtailment and settlement **gains** were recognised when the curtailment or settlement **occurred**, but **losses** were recognised when it was **probable** that the curtailment or settlement would occur. The Board concluded that management's intent to curtail or settle a defined benefit plan is not a sufficient basis to recognise a loss. The new IAS 19 requires that curtailment and settlement losses, as well as gains, should be recognised when the curtailment or settlement occurs. The guidance on the recognition of curtailments and settlements has been conformed to the proposals in E59 *Provisions, Contingent Liabilities and Contingent Assets*.

80 Under some national standards:

(a) the gain or loss on a curtailment includes any unamortised past service cost (on the grounds that a curtailment eliminates the previously expected motivational effect of the benefit improvement), but excludes unrecognised actuarial gains or losses (on the grounds that the entity is still exposed to actuarial risk); and

(b) the gain or loss on a settlement includes any unrecognised actuarial gains or losses (on the grounds that the entity is no longer exposed to actuarial risk), but excludes unamortised past service cost (on the grounds that the previously expected motivational effect of the benefit improvement is still present).

The Board considers that this approach has some conceptual merit, but it leads to considerable complexity. The new IAS 19 requires that the gain or loss on a curtailment or settlement should include the related unrecognised actuarial gains and losses and past service cost. This is consistent with the old IAS 19.

Presentation and disclosure (paragraphs 116–125 of the Standard)

81 The Board decided not to specify whether an entity should distinguish current and non-current portions of assets and liabilities arising from post-employment benefits, because such a distinction may sometimes be arbitrary.

82 Information about defined benefit plans is particularly important to users of financial statements because other information published by an entity will not allow users to estimate the nature and extent of defined benefit obligations and to assess the risks associated with those obligations. The disclosure requirements are based on the following principles:

(a) the most important information about employee benefits is information about the uncertainty attaching to measures of employee benefit obligations and costs and about the potential consequences of such uncertainty for future cash flows;

(b) employee benefit arrangements are often complex, and this makes it particularly important for disclosures to be clear, concise and relevant;

(c) given the wide range of views on the treatment of actuarial gains and losses and past service cost, the required disclosures should highlight their impact on the income statement and the impact of any unrecognised actuarial gains and losses and unamortised past service cost on the balance sheet; and

(d) the benefits derived from information should exceed the cost of providing it.

83 The Board agreed the following changes to the disclosure requirements proposed in E54:

(a) the description of a defined benefit plan need only be a general description of the type of plan: for example, flat salary pension plans should be distinguished from final salary plans and from post-employment medical plans. Further detail would not be required;

(b) an entity should disclose the amounts, if any, included in the fair value of plan assets not only for each category of the reporting entity's own financial instruments, but also for any property occupied by, or other assets used by, the entity;

(c) an entity should disclose not just the expected return on plan assets, but also the actual return on plan assets;

(d) an entity should disclose a reconciliation of the movements in the net liability (or asset) recognised in its balance sheet; and

(e) an entity should disclose any amount not recognised as an asset because of the new limit in paragraph 58(b) of the Standard.

84 Some commentators on E54, especially preparers, felt that the disclosures were excessive. A particular concern expressed by several respondents was aggregation: how should an entity aggregate information about many different plans in a concise, meaningful and cost-effective way? Two disclosures that seemed to cause special concern were the analysis of the overall charge in the income statement and the actuarial assumptions. In particular, a number of commentators felt that the requirement to disclose expected rates of salary increases would cause difficulties with employees. However, the Board concluded that all the disclosures were essential.

85 The Board considered whether smaller or non-public entities could be exempted from any of the disclosure requirements. However, the Board concluded that any such exemptions would either prevent disclosure of essential information or do little to reduce the cost of the disclosures.

Disclosures: amendment issued by the IASB in December 2004

85A From a review of national standards on accounting for post–employment benefits, the IASB identified the following disclosures that it proposed should be added to IAS 19:

(a) reconciliations showing the changes in plan assets and defined benefit obligations. The IASB believed that these reconciliations give clearer information about the plan. Unlike the reconciliation previously required by IAS 19 that showed the changes in the recognised net liability or asset, the new reconciliations include amounts whose recognition has been deferred. The reconciliation previously required was eliminated.

(b) information about plan assets. The IASB believed that more information is needed about the plan assets because, without such information, users cannot assess the level of risk inherent in the plan. The exposure draft proposed:

   (i) disclosure of the percentage that the major classes of assets held by the plan constitute of the total fair value of the plan assets;

   (ii) disclosure of the expected rate of return for each class of asset; and

   (iii) a narrative description of the basis used to determine the overall expected rate of return on assets.

(c) information about the sensitivity of defined benefit plans to changes in medical cost trend rates. The IASB believed that this is necessary because the effects of changes in a plan's medical cost trend rate are difficult to assess. The way in which healthcare cost assumptions interact with caps, cost–sharing provisions, and other factors in the plan precludes reasonable estimates of the effects of those changes. The IASB also noted that the disclosure of a change of one percentage point would be appropriate for plans operating in low inflation environments but would not provide useful information for plans operating in high inflation environments.

(d) information about trends in the plan. The IASB believed that information about trends is important so that users have a view of the plan over time, not just at the balance sheet date. Without such information, users may misinterpret the future cash flow implications of the plan. The exposure draft proposed disclosure of five-year histories of the plan liabilities, plan assets, the surplus or deficit and experience adjustments.

(e) information about contributions to the plan. The IASB believed that this will provide useful information about the entity's cash flows in the immediate future that cannot be determined from the other disclosures about the plan. It proposed the disclosure of the employer's best estimate, as soon as it can reasonably be determined, of contributions expected to be paid to the plan during the next fiscal year beginning after the balance sheet date.

(f) information about the nature of the plan. The IASB proposed an addition to paragraph 121 of IAS 19 to ensure that the description of the plan is complete and includes all the terms of the plan that are used in the determination of the defined benefit obligation.

85B The proposed disclosures were generally supported by respondents to the exposure draft, except for the expected rate of return for each major category of plan assets, sensitivity information about medical cost trend rates and the information about trends in the plan.

85C In relation to the expected rate of return for each major category of plan assets, respondents argued that the problems of aggregation for entities with many plans in different geographical areas were such that this information would not be useful. The IASB accepted this argument and decided not to proceed with the proposed disclosure. However, the IASB decided to specify that the narrative description of the basis for the overall expected rate of return should include the effect of the major categories of plan assets.

85D Respondents also expressed concerns that the sensitivity information about medical cost trend rates gave undue prominence to that assumption, even though medical costs might not be significant compared with other defined benefit costs. The IASB noted that the sensitivity information need be given only if the medical costs are material and that IAS 1 requires information to be given about all key assumptions and key sources of estimation uncertainty.

85E Finally, some respondents argued that requiring five-year histories would give rise to information overload and was unnecessary because the information was available from previous financial statements. The IASB reconfirmed its view that the trend information was useful and noted that it was considerably easier for an entity to take the information from previous financial statements and present it in the current financial statements than it would be for users to find the figures for previous periods. However, the IASB agreed that as a transitional measure entities should be permitted to build up the trend information over time.

Benefits other than post–employment benefits

Compensated absences (paragraphs 11–16 of the Standard)

86 Some argue that an employee's entitlement to future compensated absences does not create an obligation if that entitlement is conditional on future events other than future service. However, the Board believes that an obligation arises as an employee renders service which increases the employee's entitlement (conditional or unconditional) to future compensated absences; for example, accumulating paid sick leave creates an obligation because any unused entitlement increases the employee's entitlement to sick leave in future periods. The probability that the employee will be sick in those future periods affects the measurement of that obligation, but does not determine whether that obligation exists.

87 The Board considered three alternative approaches to measuring the obligation that results from unused entitlement to accumulating compensated absences:

(a) recognise the entire unused entitlement as a liability, on the basis that any future payments are made first out of unused entitlement and only subsequently out of entitlement that will accumulate in future periods (a FIFO approach);

(b) recognise a liability to the extent that future payments for the employee group as a whole are expected to exceed the future payments that would have been expected in the absence of the accumulation feature (a group LIFO approach); or

(c) recognise a liability to the extent that future payments for individual employees are expected to exceed the future payments that would have been expected in the absence of the accumulation feature (an individual LIFO approach).

These methods are illustrated by the following example.

Example

An entity has 100 employees, who are each entitled to five working days of paid sick leave for each year. Unused sick leave may be carried forward for one year. Such leave is taken first out of the current year's entitlement and then out of any balance brought forward from the previous year (a LIFO basis). At 31 December 20X1, the average unused entitlement is two days per employee. The entity expects, based on past experience which is expected to continue, that 92 employees will take no more than four days of paid sick leave in 20X2 and that the remaining 8 employees will take an average of six and a half days each.

Method (a): *The entity recognises a liability equal to the undiscounted amount of 200 days of sick pay (two days each, for 100 employees). It is assumed that the first 200 days of paid sick leave result from the unused entitlement.*

Continued from previous page **Example**	
Method (b):	*The entity recognises no liability because paid sick leave for the employee group as a whole is not expected to exceed the entitlement of five days each in 20X2.*
Method (c):	*The entity recognises a liability equal to the undiscounted amount of 12 days of sick pay (one and a half days each, for 8 employees).*

88 The Board selected method (c), the individual LIFO approach, because that method measures the obligation at the present value of the additional future payments that are expected to arise solely from the accumulation feature. The new IAS 19 notes that, in many cases, the resulting liability will not be material.

Death–in–service benefits

89 E54 gave guidance on cases where death–in–service benefits are not insured externally and are not provided through a post-employment benefit plan. The Board concluded that such cases will be rare. Accordingly, the Board agreed to delete the guidance on death–in–service benefits.

Other long–term employee benefits (paragraphs 126–131 of the Standard)

90 The Board decided, for simplicity, not to permit or require a 'corridor' approach for other long-term employee benefits, as such benefits do not present measurement difficulties to the same extent as post-employment benefits. For the same reason, the Board decided to require immediate recognition of all past service cost for such benefits and not to permit any transitional option for such benefits.

Termination benefits (paragraphs 132–143 of the Standard)

91 Under some national standards, termination benefits are not recognised until employees have accepted the offer of the termination benefits. However, the Board decided that the communication of an offer to employees (or their representatives) creates an obligation and that obligation should be recognised as a liability if there is a detailed formal plan. The detailed formal plan both makes it probable that there will be an outflow of resources embodying economic benefits and also enables the obligation to be measured reliably.

92 Some argue that a distinction should be made between:

(a) termination benefits resulting from an explicit contractual or legal requirement; and

(b) termination benefits resulting from an offer to encourage voluntary redundancy.

The Board believes that such a distinction is irrelevant; an entity offers termination benefits to encourage voluntary redundancy because the entity already has a constructive obligation. The communication of an offer enables an entity to measure the obligation reliably. E54 proposed some limited flexibility to allow that communication to take place shortly after the balance sheet date. However, in response to comments on E54, and for consistency with E59 *Provisions, Contingent Liabilities and Contingent Assets*, the Board decided to remove that flexibility.

93 Termination benefits are often closely linked with curtailments and settlements and with restructuring provisions. Therefore, the Board decided that there is a need for recognition and measurement principles to be similar. The guidance on the recognition of termination benefits (and of curtailments and settlements) has been conformed to the proposals in E59 *Provisions, Contingent Liabilities and Contingent Assets*. The Board agreed to add explicit guidance (not given in E54) on the measurement of termination benefits, requiring discounting for termination benefits not payable within one year.

Equity compensation benefits (paragraphs 144–152 of the Standard)

94 ~~The Board decided that the new IAS 19 should not:~~

~~(a) include recognition and measurement requirements for equity compensation benefits, in view of the lack of international consensus on the recognition and measurement of the resulting obligations and costs; or~~

~~(b) require disclosure of the fair value of employee share options, in view of the lack of international consensus on the fair value of many employee share options.~~[(a)]

(a) Paragraphs 144–152 of IAS 19 were deleted by IFRS 2 *Share-based Payment*.

Transition and effective date (paragraphs 153–158 of the Standard)

95 The Board recognises that the new IAS 19 will lead to significant changes for some entities. E54 proposed to mitigate this problem by delaying the effective date of the new IAS 19 until 3 years after its approval. In response to comments on E54, the Board introduced a transitional option to amortise an increase in defined benefit liabilities over not more than five years. In consequence, the Board decided that it was not necessary to delay the effective date.

96 E54 proposed no specific transitional provisions. Consequently, an entity applying the new IAS 19 for the first time would have been required to compute the effect of the 'corridor' retrospectively. Some commentators felt that this would be impracticable and would not generate useful information. The Board agreed with these comments. Accordingly, the new IAS 19 confirms that, on initial adoption, an entity does not compute the effect of the 'corridor' retrospectively.

International Accounting Standard 20

Accounting for Government Grants and Disclosure of Government Assistance

This version includes amendments resulting from new and amended IFRSs issued up to 31 December 2004.

One Interpretation relates to IAS 20:

- SIC-10 *Government Assistance—No Specific Relation to Operating Activities.*

CONTENTS

International Accounting Standard 20 *Accounting for Government Grants and Disclosure of Government Assistance* (IAS 20) is set out in paragraphs 1–41. All the paragraphs have equal authority but retain the IASC format of the Standard when it was adopted by the IASB. IAS 20 should be read in the context of the *Preface to International Financial Reporting Standards* and the *Framework for the Preparation and Presentation of Financial Statements*. IAS 8 *Accounting Policies, Changes in Accounting Estimates and Errors* provides a basis for selecting and applying accounting policies in the absence of explicit guidance.

International Accounting Standard 20 Accounting for Government Grants and Disclosure of Government Assistance

Scope

1 **This Standard shall be applied in accounting for, and in the disclosure of, government grants and in the disclosure of other forms of government assistance.**

2 This Standard does not deal with:

(a) the special problems arising in accounting for government grants in financial statements reflecting the effects of changing prices or in supplementary information of a similar nature;

(b) government assistance that is provided for an entity in the form of benefits that are available in determining taxable income or are determined or limited on the basis of income tax liability (such as income tax holidays, investment tax credits, accelerated depreciation allowances and reduced income tax rates);

(c) government participation in the ownership of the entity;

(d) government grants covered by IAS 41 *Agriculture*.

Definitions

3 **The following terms are used in this Standard with the meanings specified:**

Government **refers to government, government agencies and similar bodies whether local, national or international.**

Government assistance **is action by government designed to provide an economic benefit specific to an entity or range of entities qualifying under certain criteria. Government assistance for the purpose of this Standard does not include benefits provided only indirectly through action affecting general trading conditions, such as the provision of infrastructure in development areas or the imposition of trading constraints on competitors.**

Government grants **are assistance by government in the form of transfers of resources to an entity in return for past or future compliance with certain conditions relating to the operating activities of the entity. They exclude those forms of government assistance which cannot reasonably have a value placed upon them and transactions with government which cannot be distinguished from the normal trading transactions of the entity.***

Grants related to assets **are government grants whose primary condition is that an entity qualifying for them should purchase, construct or otherwise**

* See also SIC-10 *Government Assistance—No Specific Relation to Operating Activities*

acquire long-term assets. Subsidiary conditions may also be attached restricting the type or location of the assets or the periods during which they are to be acquired or held.

Grants related to income **are government grants other than those related to assets.**

Forgivable loans **are loans which the lender undertakes to waive repayment of under certain prescribed conditions.**

Fair value **is the amount for which an asset could be exchanged between a knowledgeable, willing buyer and a knowledgeable, willing seller in an arm's length transaction.**

4 Government assistance takes many forms varying both in the nature of the assistance given and in the conditions which are usually attached to it. The purpose of the assistance may be to encourage an entity to embark on a course of action which it would not normally have taken if the assistance was not provided.

5 The receipt of government assistance by an entity may be significant for the preparation of the financial statements for two reasons. Firstly, if resources have been transferred, an appropriate method of accounting for the transfer must be found. Secondly, it is desirable to give an indication of the extent to which the entity has benefited from such assistance during the reporting period. This facilitates comparison of an entity's financial statements with those of prior periods and with those of other entities.

6 Government grants are sometimes called by other names such as subsidies, subventions, or premiums.

Government grants

7 **Government grants, including non-monetary grants at fair value, shall not be recognised until there is reasonable assurance that:**

(a) the entity will comply with the conditions attaching to them; and

(b) the grants will be received.

8 A government grant is not recognised until there is reasonable assurance that the entity will comply with the conditions attaching to it, and that the grant will be received. Receipt of a grant does not of itself provide conclusive evidence that the conditions attaching to the grant have been or will be fulfilled.

9 The manner in which a grant is received does not affect the accounting method to be adopted in regard to the grant. Thus a grant is accounted for in the same manner whether it is received in cash or as a reduction of a liability to the government.

10 A forgivable loan from government is treated as a government grant when there is reasonable assurance that the entity will meet the terms for forgiveness of the loan.

11 Once a government grant is recognised, any related contingent liability or contingent asset is treated in accordance with IAS 37 *Provisions, Contingent Liabilities and Contingent Assets*.

12 Government grants shall be recognised as income over the periods necessary to match them with the related costs which they are intended to compensate, on a systematic basis. They shall not be credited directly to shareholders' interests.

13 Two broad approaches may be found to the accounting treatment of government grants: the capital approach, under which a grant is credited directly to shareholders' interests, and the income approach, under which a grant is taken to income over one or more periods.

14 Those in support of the capital approach argue as follows:

(a) government grants are a financing device and should be dealt with as such in the balance sheet rather than be passed through the income statement to offset the items of expense which they finance. Since no repayment is expected, they should be credited directly to shareholders' interests; and

(b) it is inappropriate to recognise government grants in the income statement, since they are not earned but represent an incentive provided by government without related costs.

15 Arguments in support of the income approach are as follows:

(a) since government grants are receipts from a source other than shareholders, they should not be credited directly to shareholders' interests but should be recognised as income in appropriate periods;

(b) government grants are rarely gratuitous. The entity earns them through compliance with their conditions and meeting the envisaged obligations. They should therefore be recognised as income and matched with the associated costs which the grant is intended to compensate; and

(c) as income and other taxes are charges against income, it is logical to deal also with government grants, which are an extension of fiscal policies, in the income statement.

16 It is fundamental to the income approach that government grants be recognised as income on a systematic and rational basis over the periods necessary to match them with the related costs. Income recognition of government grants on a receipts basis is not in accordance with the accrual accounting assumption (see IAS 1 *Presentation of Financial Statements*) and would only be acceptable if no basis existed for allocating a grant to periods other than the one in which it was received.

17 In most cases the periods over which an entity recognises the costs or expenses related to a government grant are readily ascertainable and thus grants in recognition of specific expenses are recognised as income in the same period as the relevant expense. Similarly, grants related to depreciable assets are usually recognised as income over the periods and in the proportions in which depreciation on those assets is charged.

18 Grants related to non-depreciable assets may also require the fulfilment of certain obligations and would then be recognised as income over the periods which bear the cost of meeting the obligations. As an example, a grant of land may be conditional upon the erection of a building on the site and it may be appropriate to recognise it as income over the life of the building.

19 Grants are sometimes received as part of a package of financial or fiscal aids to which a number of conditions are attached. In such cases, care is needed in identifying the conditions giving rise to costs and expenses which determine the periods over which the grant will be earned. It may be appropriate to allocate part of a grant on one basis and part on another.

20 A government grant that becomes receivable as compensation for expenses or losses already incurred or for the purpose of giving immediate financial support to the entity with no future related costs shall be recognised as income of the period in which it becomes receivable.

21 In some circumstances, a government grant may be awarded for the purpose of giving immediate financial support to an entity rather than as an incentive to undertake specific expenditures. Such grants may be confined to an individual entity and may not be available to a whole class of beneficiaries. These circumstances may warrant recognising a grant as income in the period in which the entity qualifies to receive it, with disclosure to ensure that its effect is clearly understood.

22 A government grant may become receivable by an entity as compensation for expenses or losses incurred in a previous period. Such a grant is recognised as income of the period in which it becomes receivable, with disclosure to ensure that its effect is clearly understood.

Non–monetary government grants

23 A government grant may take the form of a transfer of a non-monetary asset, such as land or other resources, for the use of the entity. In these circumstances it is usual to assess the fair value of the non-monetary asset and to account for both grant and asset at that fair value. An alternative course that is sometimes followed is to record both asset and grant at a nominal amount.

Presentation of grants related to assets

24 Government grants related to assets, including non-monetary grants at fair value, shall be presented in the balance sheet either by setting up the grant as deferred income or by deducting the grant in arriving at the carrying amount of the asset.

25 Two methods of presentation in financial statements of grants (or the appropriate portions of grants) related to assets are regarded as acceptable alternatives.

26 One method sets up the grant as deferred income which is recognised as income on a systematic and rational basis over the useful life of the asset.

27 The other method deducts the grant in arriving at the carrying amount of the asset. The grant is recognised as income over the life of a depreciable asset by way of a reduced depreciation charge.

28 The purchase of assets and the receipt of related grants can cause major movements in the cash flow of an entity. For this reason and in order to show the gross investment in assets, such movements are often disclosed as separate items in the cash flow statement regardless of whether or not the grant is deducted from the related asset for the purpose of balance sheet presentation.

Presentation of grants related to income

29 Grants related to income are sometimes presented as a credit in the income statement, either separately or under a general heading such as 'Other income'; alternatively, they are deducted in reporting the related expense.

30 Supporters of the first method claim that it is inappropriate to net income and expense items and that separation of the grant from the expense facilitates comparison with other expenses not affected by a grant. For the second method it is argued that the expenses might well not have been incurred by the entity if the grant had not been available and presentation of the expense without offsetting the grant may therefore be misleading.

31 Both methods are regarded as acceptable for the presentation of grants related to income. Disclosure of the grant may be necessary for a proper understanding of the financial statements. Disclosure of the effect of the grants on any item of income or expense which is required to be separately disclosed is usually appropriate.

Repayment of government grants

32 A government grant that becomes repayable shall be accounted for as a revision to an accounting estimate (see IAS 8 *Accounting Policies, Changes in Accounting Estimates and Errors***). Repayment of a grant related to income shall be applied first against any unamortised deferred credit set up in respect of the grant. To the extent that the repayment exceeds any such deferred credit, or where no deferred credit exists, the repayment shall be recognised immediately as an expense. Repayment of a grant related to an asset shall be recorded by increasing the carrying amount of the asset or reducing the deferred income balance by the amount repayable. The cumulative additional depreciation that would have been recognised to date as an expense in the absence of the grant shall be recognised immediately as an expense.**

33 Circumstances giving rise to repayment of a grant related to an asset may require consideration to be given to the possible impairment of the new carrying amount of the asset.

Government assistance

34 Excluded from the definition of government grants in paragraph 3 are certain forms of government assistance which cannot reasonably have a value placed upon them and transactions with government which cannot be distinguished from the normal trading transactions of the entity.

35 Examples of assistance that cannot reasonably have a value placed upon them are free technical or marketing advice and the provision of guarantees. An example of

assistance that cannot be distinguished from the normal trading transactions of the entity is a government procurement policy that is responsible for a portion of the entity's sales. The existence of the benefit might be unquestioned but any attempt to segregate the trading activities from government assistance could well be arbitrary.

36 The significance of the benefit in the above examples may be such that disclosure of the nature, extent and duration of the assistance is necessary in order that the financial statements may not be misleading.

37 Loans at nil or low interest rates are a form of government assistance, but the benefit is not quantified by the imputation of interest.

38 In this Standard, government assistance does not include the provision of infrastructure by improvement to the general transport and communication network and the supply of improved facilities such as irrigation or water reticulation which is available on an ongoing indeterminate basis for the benefit of an entire local community.

Disclosure

39 The following matters shall be disclosed:

(a) the accounting policy adopted for government grants, including the methods of presentation adopted in the financial statements;

(b) the nature and extent of government grants recognised in the financial statements and an indication of other forms of government assistance from which the entity has directly benefited; and

(c) unfulfilled conditions and other contingencies attaching to government assistance that has been recognised.

Transitional provisions

40 An entity adopting the Standard for the first time shall:

(a) comply with the disclosure requirements, where appropriate; and

(b) either:

(i) adjust its financial statements for the change in accounting policy in accordance with IAS 8 *Accounting Policies, Changes in Accounting Estimates and Errors;* **or**

(ii) apply the accounting provisions of the Standard only to grants or portions of grants becoming receivable or repayable after the effective date of the Standard.

Effective date

41 This Standard becomes operative for financial statements covering periods beginning on or after 1 January 1984.

International Accounting Standard 21

The Effects of Changes in Foreign Exchange Rates

This version includes amendments resulting from new and amended IFRSs issued up to 31 December 2004.

CONTENTS

International Accounting Standard 21 *The Effects of Changes in Foreign Exchange Rates* (IAS 21) is set out in paragraphs 1–62 and the Appendix. All the paragraphs have equal authority but retain the IASC format of the Standard when it was adopted by the IASB. IAS 21 should be read in the context of its objective and the Basis for Conclusions, the *Preface to International Financial Reporting Standards* and the *Framework for the Preparation and Presentation of Financial Statements*. IAS 8 *Accounting Policies, Changes in Accounting Estimates and Errors* provides a basis for selecting and applying accounting policies in the absence of explicit guidance.

Introduction

IN1 International Accounting Standard 21 *The Effects of Changes in Foreign Exchange Rates* (IAS 21) replaces IAS 21 *The Effects of Changes in Foreign Exchange Rates* (revised in 1993), and should be applied for annual periods beginning on or after 1 January 2005. Earlier application is encouraged. The Standard also replaces the following Interpretations:

- SIC-11 *Foreign Exchange—Capitalisation of Losses Resulting from Severe Currency Devaluations*
- SIC-19 *Reporting Currency—Measurement and Presentation of Financial Statements under IAS 21 and IAS 29*
- SIC-30 *Reporting Currency—Translation from Measurement Currency to Presentation Currency.*

Reasons for revising IAS 21

IN2 The International Accounting Standards Board developed this revised IAS 21 as part of its project on Improvements to International Accounting Standards. The project was undertaken in the light of queries and criticisms raised in relation to the Standards by securities regulators, professional accountants and other interested parties. The objectives of the project were to reduce or eliminate alternatives, redundancies and conflicts within the Standards, to deal with some convergence issues and to make other improvements.

IN3 For IAS 21 the Board's main objective was to provide additional guidance on the translation method and on determining the functional and presentation currencies. The Board did not reconsider the fundamental approach to accounting for the effects of changes in foreign exchange rates contained in IAS 21.

The main changes

IN4 The main changes from the previous version of IAS 21 are described below.

Scope

IN5 The Standard excludes from its scope foreign currency derivatives that are within the scope of IAS 39 *Financial Instruments: Recognition and Measurement.* Similarly, the material on hedge accounting has been moved to IAS 39.

Definitions

IN6 The notion of 'reporting currency' has been replaced with two notions:

- functional currency, ie the currency of the primary economic environment in which the entity operates. The term 'functional currency' is used in place of 'measurement currency' (the term used in SIC-19) because it is the more commonly used term, but with essentially the same meaning.
- presentation currency, ie the currency in which financial statements are presented.

Definitions—functional currency

IN7 When a reporting entity prepares financial statements, the Standard requires each individual entity included in the reporting entity–whether it is a stand-alone entity, an entity with foreign operations (such as a parent) or a foreign operation (such as a subsidiary or branch)–to determine its functional currency and measure its results and financial position in that currency. The new material on functional currency incorporates some of the guidance previously included in SIC-19 on how to determine a measurement currency. However, the Standard gives greater emphasis than SIC-19 gave to the currency of the economy that determines the pricing of transactions, as opposed to the currency in which transactions are denominated.

IN8 As a result of these changes and the incorporation of guidance previously in SIC-19:

- an entity (whether a stand-alone entity or a foreign operation) does not have a free choice of functional currency.
- an entity cannot avoid restatement in accordance with IAS 29 *Financial Reporting in Hyperinflationary Economies* by, for example, adopting a stable currency (such as the functional currency of its parent) as its functional currency.

IN9 The Standard revises the requirements in the previous version of IAS 21 for distinguishing between foreign operations that are integral to the operations of the reporting entity (referred to below as 'integral foreign operations') and foreign entities. The requirements are now among the indicators of an entity's functional currency. As a result:

- there is no distinction between integral foreign operations and foreign entities. Rather, an entity that was previously classified as an integral foreign operation will have the same functional currency as the reporting entity.
- only one translation method is used for foreign operations–namely that described in the previous version of IAS 21 as applying to foreign entities (see paragraph IN13).
- the paragraphs dealing with the distinction between an integral foreign operation and a foreign entity and the paragraph specifying the translation method to be used for the former have been deleted.

Reporting foreign currency transactions in the functional currency—recognition of exchange differences

IN10 The Standard removes the limited option in the previous version of IAS 21 to capitalise exchange differences resulting from a severe devaluation or depreciation of a currency against which there is no means of hedging. Under the Standard, such exchange differences are now recognised in profit or loss. Consequently, SIC-11, which outlined restricted circumstances in which such exchange differences may be capitalised, has been superseded since capitalisation of such exchange differences is no longer permitted in any circumstances.

Reporting foreign currency transactions in the functional currency—change in functional currency

IN11 The Standard replaces the previous requirement for accounting for a change in the classification of a foreign operation (which is now redundant) with a requirement that a change in functional currency is accounted for prospectively.

Use of a presentation currency other than the functional currency—translation to the presentation currency

IN12 The Standard permits an entity to present its financial statements in any currency (or currencies). For this purpose, an entity could be a stand-alone entity, a parent preparing consolidated financial statements or a parent, an investor or a venturer preparing separate financial statements in accordance with IAS 27 *Consolidated and Separate Financial Statements*.

IN13 An entity is required to translate its results and financial position from its functional currency into a presentation currency (or currencies) using the method required for translating a foreign operation for inclusion in the reporting entity's financial statements. Under this method, assets and liabilities are translated at the closing rate, and income and expenses are translated at the exchange rates at the dates of the transactions (or at the average rate for the period when this is a reasonable approximation).

IN14 The Standard requires comparative amounts to be translated as follows:

(a) for an entity whose functional currency is not the currency of a hyperinflationary economy:

(i) assets and liabilities in each balance sheet presented are translated at the closing rate at the date of that balance sheet (ie last year's comparatives are translated at last year's closing rate).

(ii) income and expenses in each income statement presented are translated at exchange rates at the dates of the transactions (ie last year's comparatives are translated at last year's actual or average rate).

(b) for an entity whose functional currency is the currency of a hyperinflationary economy, and for which the comparative amounts are translated into the currency of a different hyperinflationary economy, all amounts (eg balance sheet and income statement amounts) are translated at the closing rate of the most recent balance sheet presented (ie last year's comparatives, as adjusted for subsequent changes in the price level, are translated at this year's closing rate).

(c) for an entity whose functional currency is the currency of a hyperinflationary economy, and for which the comparative amounts are translated into the currency of a non-hyperinflationary economy, all amounts are those presented in the prior year financial statements (ie not adjusted for subsequent changes in the price level or subsequent changes in exchange rates).

This translation method, like that described in paragraph IN13, applies when translating the financial statements of a foreign operation for inclusion in the financial statements of the reporting entity, and when translating the financial statements of an entity into a different presentation currency.

Use of a presentation currency other than the functional currency—translation of a foreign operation

IN15 The Standard requires goodwill and fair value adjustments to assets and liabilities that arise on the acquisition of a foreign entity to be treated as part of the assets and liabilities of the acquired entity and translated at the closing rate.

Disclosure

IN16 The Standard includes most of the disclosure requirements of SIC-30. These apply when a translation method different from that described in paragraphs IN13 and IN14 is used or other supplementary information (such as an extract from the full financial statements) is displayed in a currency other than the functional currency or the presentation currency.

IN17 In addition, entities must disclose when there has been a change in functional currency, and the reasons for the change.

International Accounting Standard 21
The Effects of Changes in Foreign Exchange Rates

Objective

1 An entity may carry on foreign activities in two ways. It may have transactions in foreign currencies or it may have foreign operations. In addition, an entity may present its financial statements in a foreign currency. The objective of this Standard is to prescribe how to include foreign currency transactions and foreign operations in the financial statements of an entity and how to translate financial statements into a presentation currency.

2 The principal issues are which exchange rate(s) to use and how to report the effects of changes in exchange rates in the financial statements.

Scope

3 **This Standard shall be applied:***

(a) **in accounting for transactions and balances in foreign currencies, except for those derivative transactions and balances that are within the scope of IAS 39** *Financial Instruments: Recognition and Measurement*

(b) **in translating the results and financial position of foreign operations that are included in the financial statements of the entity by consolidation, proportionate consolidation or the equity method; and**

(c) **in translating an entity's results and financial position into a presentation currency.**

4 IAS 39 applies to many foreign currency derivatives and, accordingly, these are excluded from the scope of this Standard. However, those foreign currency derivatives that are not within the scope of IAS 39 (eg some foreign currency derivatives that are embedded in other contracts) are within the scope of this Standard. In addition, this Standard applies when an entity translates amounts relating to derivatives from its functional currency to its presentation currency.

5 This Standard does not apply to hedge accounting for foreign currency items, including the hedging of a net investment in a foreign operation. IAS 39 applies to hedge accounting.

6 This Standard applies to the presentation of an entity's financial statements in a foreign currency and sets out requirements for the resulting financial statements to be described as complying with International Financial Reporting Standards. For translations of financial information into a foreign currency that do not meet these requirements, this Standard specifies information to be disclosed.

7 This Standard does not apply to the presentation in a cash flow statement of cash flows arising from transactions in a foreign currency, or to the translation of cash flows of a foreign operation (see IAS 7 *Cash Flow Statements*).

* See also SIC-7 *Introduction of the Euro.*

Definitions

8 **The following terms are used in this Standard with the meanings specified:**

Closing rate **is the spot exchange rate at the balance sheet date.**

Exchange difference **is the difference resulting from translating a given number of units of one currency into another currency at different exchange rates.**

Exchange rate **is the ratio of exchange for two currencies.**

Fair value **is the amount for which an asset could be exchanged, or a liability settled, between knowledgeable, willing parties in an arm's length transaction.**

Foreign currency **is a currency other than the functional currency of the entity.**

Foreign operation **is an entity that is a subsidiary, associate, joint venture or branch of a reporting entity, the activities of which are based or conducted in a country or currency other than those of the reporting entity.**

Functional currency **is the currency of the primary economic environment in which the entity operates.**

A *group* **is a parent and all its subsidiaries.**

Monetary items **are units of currency held and assets and liabilities to be received or paid in a fixed or determinable number of units of currency.**

Net investment in a foreign operation **is the amount of the reporting entity's interest in the net assets of that operation.**

Presentation currency **is the currency in which the financial statements are presented.**

Spot exchange rate **is the exchange rate for immediate delivery.**

Elaboration on the definitions

Functional currency

9 The primary economic environment in which an entity operates is normally the one in which it primarily generates and expends cash. An entity considers the following factors in determining its functional currency:

(a) the currency:

(i) that mainly influences sales prices for goods and services (this will often be the currency in which sales prices for its goods and services are denominated and settled); and

(ii) of the country whose competitive forces and regulations mainly determine the sales prices of its goods and services.

(b) the currency that mainly influences labour, material and other costs of providing goods or services (this will often be the currency in which such costs are denominated and settled).

10 The following factors may also provide evidence of an entity's functional currency:

(a) the currency in which funds from financing activities (ie issuing debt and equity instruments) are generated.

(b) the currency in which receipts from operating activities are usually retained.

11 The following additional factors are considered in determining the functional currency of a foreign operation, and whether its functional currency is the same as that of the reporting entity (the reporting entity, in this context, being the entity that has the foreign operation as its subsidiary, branch, associate or joint venture):

(a) whether the activities of the foreign operation are carried out as an extension of the reporting entity, rather than being carried out with a significant degree of autonomy. An example of the former is when the foreign operation only sells goods imported from the reporting entity and remits the proceeds to it. An example of the latter is when the operation accumulates cash and other monetary items, incurs expenses, generates income and arranges borrowings, all substantially in its local currency.

(b) whether transactions with the reporting entity are a high or a low proportion of the foreign operation's activities.

(c) whether cash flows from the activities of the foreign operation directly affect the cash flows of the reporting entity and are readily available for remittance to it.

(d) whether cash flows from the activities of the foreign operation are sufficient to service existing and normally expected debt obligations without funds being made available by the reporting entity.

12 When the above indicators are mixed and the functional currency is not obvious, management uses its judgement to determine the functional currency that most faithfully represents the economic effects of the underlying transactions, events and conditions. As part of this approach, management gives priority to the primary indicators in paragraph 9 before considering the indicators in paragraphs 10 and 11, which are designed to provide additional supporting evidence to determine an entity's functional currency.

13 An entity's functional currency reflects the underlying transactions, events and conditions that are relevant to it. Accordingly, once determined, the functional currency is not changed unless there is a change in those underlying transactions, events and conditions.

14 If the functional currency is the currency of a hyperinflationary economy, the entity's financial statements are restated in accordance with IAS 29 *Financial Reporting in Hyperinflationary Economies*. An entity cannot avoid restatement in accordance with IAS 29 by, for example, adopting as its functional currency a currency other than the functional currency determined in accordance with this Standard (such as the functional currency of its parent).

Net investment in a foreign operation

15 An entity may have a monetary item that is receivable from or payable to a foreign operation. An item for which settlement is neither planned nor likely to occur in the foreseeable future is, in substance, a part of the entity's net investment in that foreign operation, and is accounted for in accordance with paragraphs 32 and 33. Such monetary items may include long-term receivables or loans. They do not include trade receivables or trade payables.

Monetary items

16 The essential feature of a monetary item is a right to receive (or an obligation to deliver) a fixed or determinable number of units of currency. Examples include: pensions and other employee benefits to be paid in cash; provisions that are to be settled in cash; and cash dividends that are recognised as a liability. Similarly, a contract to receive (or deliver) a variable number of the entity's own equity instruments or a variable amount of assets in which the fair value to be received (or delivered) equals a fixed or determinable number of units of currency is a monetary item. Conversely, the essential feature of a non-monetary item is the absence of a right to receive (or an obligation to deliver) a fixed or determinable number of units of currency. Examples include: amounts prepaid for goods and services (eg prepaid rent); goodwill; intangible assets; inventories; property, plant and equipment; and provisions that are to be settled by the delivery of a non-monetary asset.

Summary of the approach required by this standard

17 In preparing financial statements, each entity—whether a stand-alone entity, an entity with foreign operations (such as a parent) or a foreign operation (such as a subsidiary or branch)—determines its functional currency in accordance with paragraphs 9–14. The entity translates foreign currency items into its functional currency and reports the effects of such translation in accordance with paragraphs 20–37 and 50.

18 Many reporting entities comprise a number of individual entities (eg a group is made up of a parent and one or more subsidiaries). Various types of entities, whether members of a group or otherwise, may have investments in associates or joint ventures. They may also have branches. It is necessary for the results and financial position of each individual entity included in the reporting entity to be translated into the currency in which the reporting entity presents its financial statements. This Standard permits the presentation currency of a reporting entity to be any currency (or currencies). The results and financial position of any individual entity within the reporting entity whose functional currency differs from the presentation currency are translated in accordance with paragraphs 38–50.

19 This Standard also permits a stand-alone entity preparing financial statements or an entity preparing separate financial statements in accordance with IAS 27 *Consolidated and Separate Financial Statements* to present its financial statements in any currency (or currencies). If the entity's presentation currency differs from its functional currency, its results and financial position are also translated into the presentation currency in accordance with paragraphs 38–50.

Reporting foreign currency transactions in the functional currency

Initial recognition

20 A foreign currency transaction is a transaction that is denominated or requires settlement in a foreign currency, including transactions arising when an entity:

(a) buys or sells goods or services whose price is denominated in a foreign currency;

(b) borrows or lends funds when the amounts payable or receivable are denominated in a foreign currency; or

(c) otherwise acquires or disposes of assets, or incurs or settles liabilities, denominated in a foreign currency.

21 A foreign currency transaction shall be recorded, on initial recognition in the functional currency, by applying to the foreign currency amount the spot exchange rate between the functional currency and the foreign currency at the date of the transaction.

22 The date of a transaction is the date on which the transaction first qualifies for recognition in accordance with International Financial Reporting Standards. For practical reasons, a rate that approximates the actual rate at the date of the transaction is often used, for example, an average rate for a week or a month might be used for all transactions in each foreign currency occurring during that period. However, if exchange rates fluctuate significantly, the use of the average rate for a period is inappropriate.

Reporting at subsequent balance sheet dates

23 At each balance sheet date:

(a) foreign currency monetary items shall be translated using the closing rate;

(b) non-monetary items that are measured in terms of historical cost in a foreign currency shall be translated using the exchange rate at the date of the transaction; and

(c) non-monetary items that are measured at fair value in a foreign currency shall be translated using the exchange rates at the date when the fair value was determined.

24 The carrying amount of an item is determined in conjunction with other relevant Standards. For example, property, plant and equipment may be measured in terms of fair value or historical cost in accordance with IAS 16 *Property, Plant and Equipment*. Whether the carrying amount is determined on the basis of historical cost or on the basis of fair value, if the amount is determined in a foreign currency it is then translated into the functional currency in accordance with this Standard.

25 The carrying amount of some items is determined by comparing two or more amounts. For example, the carrying amount of inventories is the lower of cost and net realisable value in accordance with IAS 2 *Inventories*. Similarly, in accordance

with IAS 36 *Impairment of Assets*, the carrying amount of an asset for which there is an indication of impairment is the lower of its carrying amount before considering possible impairment losses and its recoverable amount. When such an asset is non-monetary and is measured in a foreign currency, the carrying amount is determined by comparing:

(a) the cost or carrying amount, as appropriate, translated at the exchange rate at the date when that amount was determined (ie the rate at the date of the transaction for an item measured in terms of historical cost); and

(b) the net realisable value or recoverable amount, as appropriate, translated at the exchange rate at the date when that value was determined (eg the closing rate at the balance sheet date).

The effect of this comparison may be that an impairment loss is recognised in the functional currency but would not be recognised in the foreign currency, or vice versa.

26 When several exchange rates are available, the rate used is that at which the future cash flows represented by the transaction or balance could have been settled if those cash flows had occurred at the measurement date. If exchangeability between two currencies is temporarily lacking, the rate used is the first subsequent rate at which exchanges could be made.

Recognition of exchange differences

27 As noted in paragraph 3, IAS 39 applies to hedge accounting for foreign currency items. The application of hedge accounting requires an entity to account for some exchange differences differently from the treatment of exchange differences required by this Standard. For example, IAS 39 requires that exchange differences on monetary items that qualify as hedging instruments in a cash flow hedge are reported initially in equity to the extent that the hedge is effective.

28 Exchange differences arising on the settlement of monetary items or on translating monetary items at rates different from those at which they were translated on initial recognition during the period or in previous financial statements shall be recognised in profit or loss in the period in which they arise, except as described in paragraph 32.

29 When monetary items arise from a foreign currency transaction and there is a change in the exchange rate between the transaction date and the date of settlement, an exchange difference results. When the transaction is settled within the same accounting period as that in which it occurred, all the exchange difference is recognised in that period. However, when the transaction is settled in a subsequent accounting period, the exchange difference recognised in each period up to the date of settlement is determined by the change in exchange rates during each period.

30 When a gain or loss on a non-monetary item is recognised directly in equity, any exchange component of that gain or loss shall be recognised directly in equity. Conversely, when a gain or loss on a non-monetary item is recognised in profit or loss, any exchange component of that gain or loss shall be recognised in profit or loss.

31 Other Standards require some gains and losses to be recognised directly in equity. For example, IAS 16 requires some gains and losses arising on a revaluation of property, plant and equipment to be recognised directly in equity. When such an asset is measured in a foreign currency, paragraph 23(c) of this Standard requires the revalued amount to be translated using the rate at the date the value is determined, resulting in an exchange difference that is also recognised in equity.

32 Exchange differences arising on a monetary item that forms part of a reporting entity's net investment in a foreign operation (see paragraph 15) shall be recognised in profit or loss in the separate financial statements of the reporting entity or the individual financial statements of the foreign operation, as appropriate. In the financial statements that include the foreign operation and the reporting entity (eg consolidated financial statements when the foreign operation is a subsidiary), such exchange differences shall be recognised initially in a separate component of equity and recognised in profit or loss on disposal of the net investment in accordance with paragraph 48.

33 When a monetary item forms part of a reporting entity's net investment in a foreign operation and is denominated in the functional currency of the reporting entity, an exchange difference arises in the foreign operation's individual financial statements in accordance with paragraph 28. Similarly, if such an item is denominated in the functional currency of the foreign operation, an exchange difference arises in the reporting entity's separate financial statements in accordance with paragraph 28. Such exchange differences are reclassified to the separate component of equity in the financial statements that include the foreign operation and the reporting entity (ie financial statements in which the foreign operation is consolidated, proportionately consolidated or accounted for using the equity method). However, a monetary item that forms part of the reporting entity's net investment in a foreign operation may be denominated in a currency other than the functional currency of either the reporting entity or the foreign operation. The exchange differences that arise on translating the monetary item into the functional currencies of the reporting entity and the foreign operation are not reclassified to the separate component of equity in the financial statements that include the foreign operation and the reporting entity (ie they remain recognised in profit or loss).

34 When an entity keeps its books and records in a currency other than its functional currency, at the time the entity prepares its financial statements all amounts are translated into the functional currency in accordance with paragraphs 20–26. This produces the same amounts in the functional currency as would have occurred had the items been recorded initially in the functional currency. For example, monetary items are translated into the functional currency using the closing rate, and non-monetary items that are measured on a historical cost basis are translated using the exchange rate at the date of the transaction that resulted in their recognition.

Change in functional currency

35 **When there is a change in an entity's functional currency, the entity shall apply the translation procedures applicable to the new functional currency prospectively from the date of the change.**

36 As noted in paragraph 13, the functional currency of an entity reflects the underlying transactions, events and conditions that are relevant to the entity. Accordingly, once the functional currency is determined, it can be changed only if there is a change to those underlying transactions, events and conditions. For example, a change in the currency that mainly influences the sales prices of goods and services may lead to a change in an entity's functional currency.

37 The effect of a change in functional currency is accounted for prospectively. In other words, an entity translates all items into the new functional currency using the exchange rate at the date of the change. The resulting translated amounts for non-monetary items are treated as their historical cost. Exchange differences arising from the translation of a foreign operation previously classified in equity in accordance with paragraphs 32 and 39(c) are not recognised in profit or loss until the disposal of the operation.

Use of a presentation currency other than the functional currency

Translation to the presentation currency

38 An entity may present its financial statements in any currency (or currencies). If the presentation currency differs from the entity's functional currency, it translates its results and financial position into the presentation currency. For example, when a group contains individual entities with different functional currencies, the results and financial position of each entity are expressed in a common currency so that consolidated financial statements may be presented.

39 **The results and financial position of an entity whose functional currency is not the currency of a hyperinflationary economy shall be translated into a different presentation currency using the following procedures:**

(a) assets and liabilities for each balance sheet presented (ie including comparatives) shall be translated at the closing rate at the date of that balance sheet;

(b) income and expenses for each income statement (ie including comparatives) shall be translated at exchange rates at the dates of the transactions; and

(c) all resulting exchange differences shall be recognised as a separate component of equity.

40 For practical reasons, a rate that approximates the exchange rates at the dates of the transactions, for example an average rate for the period, is often used to translate income and expense items. However, if exchange rates fluctuate significantly, the use of the average rate for a period is inappropriate.

41 The exchange differences referred to in paragraph 39(c) result from:

(a) translating income and expenses at the exchange rates at the dates of the transactions and assets and liabilities at the closing rate. Such exchange differences arise both on income and expense items recognised in profit or loss and on those recognised directly in equity.

(b) translating the opening net assets at a closing rate that differs from the previous closing rate.

These exchange differences are not recognised in profit or loss because the changes in exchange rates have little or no direct effect on the present and future cash flows from operations. When the exchange differences relate to a foreign operation that is consolidated but not wholly-owned, accumulated exchange differences arising from translation and attributable to minority interests are allocated to, and recognised as part of, minority interest in the consolidated balance sheet.

42 The results and financial position of an entity whose functional currency is the currency of a hyperinflationary economy shall be translated into a different presentation currency using the following procedures:

(a) all amounts (ie assets, liabilities, equity items, income and expenses, including comparatives) shall be translated at the closing rate at the date of the most recent balance sheet, except that

(b) when amounts are translated into the currency of a non-hyperinflationary economy, comparative amounts shall be those that were presented as current year amounts in the relevant prior year financial statements (ie not adjusted for subsequent changes in the price level or subsequent changes in exchange rates).

43 When an entity's functional currency is the currency of a hyperinflationary economy, the entity shall restate its financial statements in accordance with IAS 29 *Financial Reporting in Hyperinflationary Economies* **before applying the translation method set out in paragraph 42, except for comparative amounts that are translated into a currency of a non-hyperinflationary economy (see paragraph 42(b)). When the economy ceases to be hyperinflationary and the entity no longer restates its financial statements in accordance with IAS 29, it shall use as the historical costs for translation into the presentation currency the amounts restated to the price level at the date the entity ceased restating its financial statements.**

Translation of a foreign operation

44 Paragraphs 45–47, in addition to paragraphs 38–43, apply when the results and financial position of a foreign operation are translated into a presentation currency so that the foreign operation can be included in the financial statements of the reporting entity by consolidation, proportionate consolidation or the equity method.

45 The incorporation of the results and financial position of a foreign operation with those of the reporting entity follows normal consolidation procedures, such as the elimination of intragroup balances and intragroup transactions of a subsidiary

(see IAS 27 *Consolidated and Separate Financial Statements* and IAS 31 *Interests in Joint Ventures*). However, an intragroup monetary asset (or liability), whether short-term or long-term, cannot be eliminated against the corresponding intragroup liability (or asset) without showing the results of currency fluctuations in the consolidated financial statements. This is because the monetary item represents a commitment to convert one currency into another and exposes the reporting entity to a gain or loss through currency fluctuations. Accordingly, in the consolidated financial statements of the reporting entity, such an exchange difference continues to be recognised in profit or loss or, if it arises from the circumstances described in paragraph 32, it is classified as equity until the disposal of the foreign operation.

46 When the financial statements of a foreign operation are as of a date different from that of the reporting entity, the foreign operation often prepares additional statements as of the same date as the reporting entity's financial statements. When this is not done, IAS 27 allows the use of a different reporting date provided that the difference is no greater than three months and adjustments are made for the effects of any significant transactions or other events that occur between the different dates. In such a case, the assets and liabilities of the foreign operation are translated at the exchange rate at the balance sheet date of the foreign operation. Adjustments are made for significant changes in exchange rates up to the balance sheet date of the reporting entity in accordance with IAS 27. The same approach is used in applying the equity method to associates and joint ventures and in applying proportionate consolidation to joint ventures in accordance with IAS 28 *Investments in Associates* and IAS 31.

47 Any goodwill arising on the acquisition of a foreign operation and any fair value adjustments to the carrying amounts of assets and liabilities arising on the acquisition of that foreign operation shall be treated as assets and liabilities of the foreign operation. Thus they shall be expressed in the functional currency of the foreign operation and shall be translated at the closing rate in accordance with paragraphs 39 and 42.

Disposal of a foreign operation

48 On the disposal of a foreign operation, the cumulative amount of the exchange differences deferred in the separate component of equity relating to that foreign operation shall be recognised in profit or loss when the gain or loss on disposal is recognised.

49 An entity may dispose of its interest in a foreign operation through sale, liquidation, repayment of share capital or abandonment of all, or part of, that entity. The payment of a dividend is part of a disposal only when it constitutes a return of the investment, for example when the dividend is paid out of pre-acquisition profits. In the case of a partial disposal, only the proportionate share of the related accumulated exchange difference is included in the gain or loss. A write-down of the carrying amount of a foreign operation does not constitute a partial disposal. Accordingly, no part of the deferred foreign exchange gain or loss is recognised in profit or loss at the time of a write-down.

Tax effects of all exchange differences

50 Gains and losses on foreign currency transactions and exchange differences arising on translating the results and financial position of an entity (including a foreign operation) into a different currency may have tax effects. IAS 12 *Income Taxes* applies to these tax effects.

Disclosure

51 **In paragraphs 53 and 55–57 references to 'functional currency' apply, in the case of a group, to the functional currency of the parent.**

52 **An entity shall disclose:**

(a) the amount of exchange differences recognised in profit or loss except for those arising on financial instruments measured at fair value through profit or loss in accordance with IAS 39; and

(b) net exchange differences classified in a separate component of equity, and a reconciliation of the amount of such exchange differences at the beginning and end of the period.

53 **When the presentation currency is different from the functional currency, that fact shall be stated, together with disclosure of the functional currency and the reason for using a different presentation currency.**

54 **When there is a change in the functional currency of either the reporting entity or a significant foreign operation, that fact and the reason for the change in functional currency shall be disclosed.**

55 **When an entity presents its financial statements in a currency that is different from its functional currency, it shall describe the financial statements as complying with International Financial Reporting Standards only if they comply with all the requirements of each applicable Standard and each applicable Interpretation of those Standards including the translation method set out in paragraphs 39 and 42.**

56 An entity sometimes presents its financial statements or other financial information in a currency that is not its functional currency without meeting the requirements of paragraph 55. For example, an entity may convert into another currency only selected items from its financial statements. Or, an entity whose functional currency is not the currency of a hyperinflationary economy may convert the financial statements into another currency by translating all items at the most recent closing rate. Such conversions are not in accordance with International Financial Reporting Standards and the disclosures set out in paragraph 57 are required.

57 **When an entity displays its financial statements or other financial information in a currency that is different from either its functional currency or its presentation currency and the requirements of paragraph 55 are not met, it shall:**

(a) clearly identify the information as supplementary information to distinguish it from the information that complies with International Financial Reporting Standards;

(b) **disclose the currency in which the supplementary information is displayed; and**

(c) **disclose the entity's functional currency and the method of translation used to determine the supplementary information.**

Effective date and transition

58 **An entity shall apply this Standard for annual periods beginning on or after 1 January 2005. Earlier application is encouraged. If an entity applies this Standard for a period beginning before 1 January 2005, it shall disclose that fact.**

59 **An entity shall apply paragraph 47 prospectively to all acquisitions occurring after the beginning of the financial reporting period in which this Standard is first applied. Retrospective application of paragraph 47 to earlier acquisitions is permitted. For an acquisition of a foreign operation treated prospectively but which occurred before the date on which this Standard is first applied, the entity shall not restate prior years and accordingly may, when appropriate, treat goodwill and fair value adjustments arising on that acquisition as assets and liabilities of the entity rather than as assets and liabilities of the foreign operation. Therefore, those goodwill and fair value adjustments either are already expressed in the entity's functional currency or are non-monetary foreign currency items, which are reported using the exchange rate at the date of the acquisition.**

60 **All other changes resulting from the application of this Standard shall be accounted for in accordance with the requirements of IAS 8** *Accounting Policies, Changes in Accounting Estimates and Errors*.

Withdrawal of other pronouncements

61 This Standard supersedes IAS 21 *The Effects of Changes in Foreign Exchange Rates* (revised in 1993).

62 This Standard supersedes the following Interpretations:

(a) SIC-11 *Foreign Exchange—Capitalisation of Losses Resulting from Severe Currency Devaluations*;

(b) SIC-19 *Reporting Currency—Measurement and Presentation of Financial Statements under IAS 21 and IAS 29*; and

(c) SIC-30 *Reporting Currency—Translation from Measurement Currency to Presentation Currency*.

Appendix
Amendments to other pronouncements

The amendments in this appendix shall be applied for annual periods beginning on or after 1 January 2005. If an entity applies this Standard for an earlier period, these amendments shall be applied for that earlier period.

* * * * *

The amendments contained in this appendix when this Standard was issued in 2003 have been incorporated into the relevant pronouncements published in this volume.

Approval of IAS 21 by the Board

International Accounting Standard 21 *The Effects of Changes in Foreign Exchange Rates* was approved for issue by the fourteen members of the International Accounting Standards Board.

Sir David Tweedie	Chairman
Thomas E Jones	Vice-Chairman
Mary E Barth	
Hans-Georg Bruns	
Anthony T Cope	
Robert P Garnett	
Gilbert Gélard	
James J Leisenring	
Warren J McGregor	
Patricia L O'Malley	
Harry K Schmid	
John T Smith	
Geoffrey Whittington	
Tatsumi Yamada	

Basis for Conclusions

This Basis for Conclusions accompanies, but is not part of, IAS 21.

Introduction

BC1 This Basis for Conclusions summarises the International Accounting Standards Board's considerations in reaching its conclusions on revising IAS 21 *The Effects of Changes in Foreign Exchange Rates* in 2003. Individual Board members gave greater weight to some factors than to others.

BC2 In July 2001 the Board announced that, as part of its initial agenda of technical projects, it would undertake a project to improve a number of Standards, including IAS 21. The project was undertaken in the light of queries and criticisms raised in relation to the Standards by securities regulators, professional accountants and other interested parties. The objectives of the Improvements project were to reduce or eliminate alternatives, redundancies and conflicts within Standards, to deal with some convergence issues and to make other improvements. In May 2,002 the Board published its proposals in an Exposure Draft of *Improvements to International Accounting Standards*, with a comment deadline of 16 September 2002. The Board received over 160 comment letters on the Exposure Draft.

BC3 Because the Board's intention was not to reconsider the fundamental approach to accounting for the effects of changes in foreign exchange rates established by IAS 21, this Basis for Conclusions does not discuss requirements in IAS 21 that the Board has not reconsidered.

Functional currency

BC4 The term 'reporting currency' was previously defined as 'the currency used in presenting the financial statements'. This definition comprises two separate notions (which were identified in SIC-19 *Reporting Currency—Measurement and Presentation of Financial Statements under IAS 21 and IAS 29*):

- the measurement currency (the currency in which the entity measures the items in the financial statements); and
- the presentation currency (the currency in which the entity presents its financial statements).

The Board decided to revise the previous version of IAS 21 to incorporate the SIC-19 approach of separating these two notions. The Board also noted that the term 'functional currency' is more commonly used than 'measurement currency' and decided to adopt the more common term.

BC5 The Board noted a concern that the guidance in SIC-19 on determining a measurement currency could permit entities to choose one of several currencies, or to select an inappropriate currency. In particular, some believed that SIC-19 placed too much emphasis on the currency in which transactions are denominated and too little emphasis on the underlying economy that determines the pricing of those transactions. To meet these concerns, the Board defined functional currency as 'the currency of the primary economic environment in which the entity operates'. The Board also provided guidance on how to determine the functional currency (see paragraphs 9–14 of the Standard). This guidance draws heavily on SIC-19 and equivalent guidance in US and other national standards, but also reflects the Board's decision that some factors merit greater emphasis than others.

BC6 The Board also discussed whether a foreign operation that is integral to the reporting entity (as described in the previous version of IAS 21) could have a functional currency that is different from that of its 'parent'.* The Board decided that the functional currencies will always be the same, because it would be contradictory for an integral foreign operation that 'carries on business as if it were an extension of the reporting enterprise's operations'† to operate in a primary economic environment different from its parent.

BC7 It follows that it is not necessary to translate the results and financial position of an integral foreign operation when incorporating them into the financial statements of the parent—they will already be measured in the parent's functional currency. Furthermore, it is not necessary to distinguish between an integral foreign operation and a foreign entity. When a foreign operation's functional currency is different from that of its parent, it is a foreign entity, and the translation method in paragraphs 38–49 of the Standard applies.

BC8 The Board also decided that the principles in the previous version of IAS 21 for distinguishing an integral foreign operation from a foreign entity are relevant in determining an operation's functional currency. Hence it incorporated these principles into the Standard in that context.

BC9 The Board agreed that the indicators in paragraph 9 are the primary indicators for determining the functional currency and that paragraphs 10 and 11 are secondary. This is because the indicators in paragraphs 10 and 11 are not linked to the primary economic environment in which the entity operates but provide additional supporting evidence to determine an entity's functional currency.

Presentation currency

BC10 A further issue is whether an entity should be permitted to present its financial statements in a currency (or currencies) other than its functional currency. Some believe it should not. They believe that the functional currency, being the currency of the primary economic environment in which the entity operates, most usefully portrays the economic effect of transactions and events on the entity. For a group that comprises operations with a number of functional currencies, they believe that the consolidated financial statements should be presented in the functional currency that management uses when controlling and monitoring the performance and financial position of the group. They also believe that allowing an entity to present its financial statements in more than one currency may confuse, rather than help, users of those financial statements.

* The term 'parent' is used broadly in this context to mean an entity that has a branch, associate or joint venture, as well as one with a subsidiary.

† IAS 21 (revised 1993), paragraph 24

Supporters of this view believe that any presentation in a currency other than that described above should be regarded as a 'convenience translation' that is outside the scope of IFRSs.

BC11 Others believe that the choice of presentation currency should be limited, for example, to the functional currency of one of the substantive entities within a group. However, such a restriction might be easily overcome–an entity that wished to present its financial statements in a different currency might establish a substantive, but relatively small operation with that functional currency.

BC12 Still others believe that, given the rising trend towards globalisation, entities should be permitted to present their financial statements in any currency. They note that most large groups do not have a single functional currency, but rather comprise operations with a number of functional currencies. For such entities, they believe it is not clear which currency should be the presentation currency, or why one currency is preferable to another. They also point out that management may not use a single currency when controlling and monitoring the performance and financial position of such a group. In addition, they note that in some jurisdictions, entities are required to present their financial statements in the local currency, even when this is not the functional currency.* Hence, if IFRSs required the financial statements to be presented in the functional currency, some entities would have to present two sets of financial statements: financial statements that comply with IFRSs presented in the functional currency and financial statements that comply with local regulations presented in a different currency.

BC13 The Board was persuaded by the arguments in the previous paragraph. Accordingly, it decided that entities should be permitted to present their financial statements in any currency (or currencies).

BC14 The Board also clarified that the Standard does not prohibit the entity from providing, as supplementary information, a 'convenience translation'. Such a 'convenience translation' may display financial statements (or selected portions of financial statements) in a currency other than the presentation currency, as a convenience to some users. The 'convenience translation' may be prepared using a translation method other than that required by the Standard. These types of 'convenience translations' should be clearly identified as supplementary information to distinguish them from information required by IFRSs and translated in accordance with the Standard.

Translation method

BC15 The Board debated which method should be used to translate financial statements from an entity's functional currency into a different presentation currency.

BC16 The Board agreed that the translation method should not have the effect of substituting another currency for the functional currency. Put another way, presenting the financial statements in a different currency should not change the

* This includes entities operating in another country and, for example, publishing financial statements to comply with a listing requirement of that country.

way in which the underlying items are measured. Rather, the translation method should merely express the underlying amounts, as measured in the functional currency, in a different currency.

BC17 Given this, the Board considered two possible translation methods. The first is to translate all amounts (including comparatives) at the most recent closing rate. This method has several advantages: it is simple to apply; it does not generate any new gains and losses; and it does not change ratios such as return on assets. This method is supported by those who believe that the process of merely expressing amounts in a different currency should preserve the relationships among amounts as measured in the functional currency and, as such, should not lead to any new gains or losses.

BC18 The second method considered by the Board is the one that the previous version of IAS 21 required for translating the financial statements of a foreign operation.* This method results in the same amounts in the presentation currency regardless of whether the financial statements of a foreign operation are:

(a) first translated into the functional currency of another group entity (eg the parent) and then into the presentation currency, or

(b) translated directly into the presentation currency.

BC19 This method avoids the need to decide the currency in which to express the financial statements of a multinational group before they are translated into the presentation currency. As noted above, many large groups do not have a single functional currency, but comprise operations with a number of functional currencies. For such entities it is not clear which functional currency should be chosen in which to express amounts before they are translated into the presentation currency, or why one currency is preferable to another. In addition, this method produces the same amounts in the presentation currency for a stand-alone entity as for an identical subsidiary of a parent whose functional currency is the presentation currency.

BC20 The Board decided to require the second method, ie that the financial statements of any entity (whether a stand-alone entity, a parent or an operation within a group) whose functional currency differs from the presentation currency used by the reporting entity are translated using the method set out in paragraphs 38–49 of the Standard.

BC21 With respect to translation of comparative amounts, the Board adopted the approach required by SIC-30 for:

(a) an entity whose functional currency is not the currency of the hyperinflationary economy (assets and liabilities in the comparative balance sheet are translated at the closing rate at the date of that balance sheet and income and expenses in the comparative income statement are translated at exchange rates at the dates of the transactions); and

(b) an entity whose functional currency is the currency of a hyperinflationary economy, and for which the comparative amounts are being translated into

* This is to translate balance sheet items at the closing rate and income and expense items at actual (or average) rates, except for an entity whose functional currency is that of a hyperinflationary economy.

the currency of a hyperinflationary economy (both balance sheet and income statement items are translated at the closing rate of the most recent balance sheet presented).

BC22 However, the Board decided not to adopt the SIC-30 approach for the translation of comparatives for an entity whose functional currency is the currency of a hyperinflationary economy, and for which the comparative amounts are being translated into a presentation currency of a non-hyperinflationary economy. The Board noted that in such a case, the SIC-30 approach requires restating the comparative amounts from those shown in last year's financial statements for both the effects of inflation and for changes in exchange rates. If exchange rates fully reflect differing price levels between the two economies to which they relate, the SIC-30 approach will result in the same amounts for the comparatives as were reported as current year amounts in the prior year financial statements. Furthermore, the Board noted that in the prior year, the relevant amounts had been already expressed in the non-hyperinflationary presentation currency, and there was no reason to change them. For these reasons the Board decided to require that all comparative amounts are those presented in the prior year financial statements (ie there is no adjustment for either subsequent changes in the price level or subsequent changes in exchange rates).

BC23 The Board decided to incorporate into the Standard most of the disclosure requirements of SIC-30 *Reporting Currency—Translation from Measurement Currency to Presentation Currency* that apply when a different translation method is used or other supplementary information, such as an extract from the full financial statements, is displayed in a currency other than the functional currency (see paragraph 57 of the Standard). These disclosures enable users to distinguish information prepared in accordance with IFRSs from information that may be useful to users but is not the subject of IFRSs, and also tell users how the latter information has been prepared.

Capitalisation of exchange differences

BC24 The previous version of IAS 21 allowed a limited choice of accounting for exchange differences that arise 'from a severe devaluation or depreciation of a currency against which there is no practical means of hedging and that affects liabilities which cannot be settled and which arise directly on the recent acquisition of an asset'.* The benchmark treatment was to recognise such exchange differences in profit or loss. The allowed alternative was to recognise them as an asset.

BC25 The Board noted that the allowed alternative (of recognition as an asset) was not in accordance with the *Framework for the Preparation and Presentation of Financial Statements* because exchange losses do not meet the definition of an asset. Moreover, recognition of exchange losses as an asset is neither allowed nor required by any liaison standard-setter, so its deletion would improve convergence. Finally, in many cases when the conditions for recognition as an asset are met, the asset would be restated in accordance with IAS 29 *Financial Reporting in Hyperinflationary Economies*. Thus, to the extent that an exchange loss

* IAS 21 (revised 1993), paragraph 21.

reflects hyperinflation, this effect is taken into account by IAS 29. For all of these reasons, the Board removed the allowed alternative treatment and the related SIC Interpretation is superseded.

Goodwill and fair value adjustments

BC26 The previous version of IAS 21 allowed a choice of translating goodwill and fair value adjustments to assets and liabilities that arise on the acquisition of a foreign entity at (a) the closing rate or (b) the historical transaction rate.

BC27 The Board agreed that, conceptually, the correct treatment depends on whether goodwill and fair value adjustments are part of:

(a) the assets and liabilities of the acquired entity (which would imply translating them at the closing rate); or

(b) the assets and liabilities of the parent (which would imply translating them at the historical rate).

BC28 The Board agreed that fair value adjustments clearly relate to the identifiable assets and liabilities of the acquired entity and should therefore be translated at the closing rate.

BC29 Goodwill is more complex, partly because it is measured as a residual. In addition, the Board noted that difficult issues can arise when the acquired entity comprises businesses that have different functional currencies (eg if the acquired entity is a multinational group). The Board discussed how to assess any resulting goodwill for impairment and, in particular, whether the goodwill would need to be 'pushed down' to the level of each different functional currency or could be accounted for and assessed at a higher level.

BC30 One view is that when the parent acquires a multinational operation comprising businesses with many different functional currencies, any goodwill may be treated as an asset of the parent/acquirer and tested for impairment at a consolidated level. Those who support this view believe that, in economic terms, the goodwill is an asset of the parent because it is part of the acquisition price paid by the parent. Thus, they believe, it would be incorrect to allocate the goodwill to the many acquired businesses and translate it into their various functional currencies. Rather, the goodwill, being treated as an asset of the parent, is not exposed to foreign currency risks, and translation differences associated with it should not be recognised. In addition, they believe that such goodwill should be tested for impairment at a consolidated level. Under this view, allocating or 'pushing down' the goodwill to a lower level, such as each different functional currency within the acquired foreign operation, would not serve any purpose.

BC31 Others take a different view. They believe that the goodwill is part of the parent's net investment in the acquired entity. In their view, goodwill should be treated no differently from other assets of the acquired entity, in particular intangible assets, because a significant part of the goodwill is likely to comprise intangible assets that do not qualify for separate recognition. They also note that goodwill arises only because of the investment in the foreign entity and has no existence apart from that entity. Lastly, they point out that when the acquired entity comprises a number of businesses with different functional currencies, the cash flows that support the continued recognition of goodwill are generated in those different functional currencies.

BC32 The Board was persuaded by the reasons set out in the preceding paragraph and decided that goodwill is treated as an asset of the foreign operation and translated at the closing rate. Consequently, goodwill should be allocated to the level of each functional currency of the acquired foreign operation. This means that the level to which goodwill is allocated for foreign currency translation purposes may be different from the level at which the goodwill is tested for impairment. Entities follow the requirements in IAS 36 *Impairment of Assets* to determine the level at which goodwill is tested for impairment.

Table of Concordance

This table shows how the contents of the superseded version of IAS 21 and the current version of IAS 21 correspond. Paragraphs are treated as corresponding if they broadly address the same matter even though the guidance may differ.

This table also shows how the requirements of SIC Interpretations SIC-19 and SIC-30 have been incorporated into the current version of IAS 21.

Superseded IAS 21 paragraph	Current IAS 21 paragraph
Objective	1, 2
1	3
2	4, 5
3	None
4	6
5	None
6	7
7	8
8	20
9	21
10	22
11	23
12	24
13	None
14	27
15	28
16	29
17	32
18	15
19	None
20	None
21	None
22	None
23	None
24	11
25	11
26	11
27	None
28	None
29	None
30	39
31	40
32	41
33	47
34	45
35	46
36	43
37	48
38	49
39	None
40	None
41	50
42	52
43	53, 54
44	None
45	None
46	None
47	None
48	59, 60
49	58
None	9
None	10
None	12–14
None	16–19
None	25, 26
None	30, 31
None	33–38
None	42
None	44
None	51
None	55–57
None	61, 62
SIC-19	8–14, 43, 56, 57
SIC-30	38–43, 51, 56, 57

International Accounting Standard 23

Borrowing Costs

This version includes amendments resulting from new and amended IFRSs issued up to 31 December 2004.

Contents

paragraphs

INTERNATIONAL ACCOUNTING STANDARD 23 BORROWING COSTS

International Accounting Standard 23 *Borrowing Costs* (IAS 23) is set out in paragraphs 1–31. All the paragraphs have equal authority but retain the IASC format of the Standard when it was adopted by the IASB. IAS 23 should be read in the context of its objective, the *Preface to International Financial Reporting Standards* and the *Framework for the Preparation and Presentation of Financial Statements*. IAS 8 *Accounting Policies, Changes in Accounting Estimates and Errors* provides a basis for selecting and applying accounting policies in the absence of explicit guidance.

International Accounting Standard 23
Borrowing Costs

Objective

The objective of this Standard is to prescribe the accounting treatment for borrowing costs. This Standard generally requires the immediate expensing of borrowing costs. However, the Standard permits, as an allowed alternative treatment, the capitalisation of borrowing costs that are directly attributable to the acquisition, construction or production of a qualifying asset.

Scope

1 **This Standard shall be applied in accounting for borrowing costs.**

2 This Standard supersedes IAS 23 *Capitalisation of Borrowing Costs* approved in 1983.

3 This Standard does not deal with the actual or imputed cost of equity, including preferred capital not classified as a liability.

Definitions

4 **The following terms are used in this Standard with the meanings specified:**

Borrowing costs **are interest and other costs incurred by an entity in connection with the borrowing of funds.**

A *qualifying asset* **is an asset that necessarily takes a substantial period of time to get ready for its intended use or sale.**

5 Borrowing costs may include:

(a) interest on bank overdrafts and short-term and long-term borrowings;

(b) amortisation of discounts or premiums relating to borrowings;

(c) amortisation of ancillary costs incurred in connection with the arrangement of borrowings;

(d) finance charges in respect of finance leases recognised in accordance with IAS 17 *Leases;* and

(e) exchange differences arising from foreign currency borrowings to the extent that they are regarded as an adjustment to interest costs.

6 Examples of qualifying assets are inventories that require a substantial period of time to bring them to a saleable condition, manufacturing plants, power generation facilities and investment properties. Other investments, and those inventories that are routinely manufactured or otherwise produced in large quantities on a repetitive basis over a short period of time, are not qualifying assets. Assets that are ready for their intended use or sale when acquired also are not qualifying assets.

Borrowing costs – benchmark treatment

Recognition

7 **Borrowing costs shall be recognised as an expense in the period in which they are incurred.**

8 Under the benchmark treatment borrowing costs are recognised as an expense in the period in which they are incurred regardless of how the borrowings are applied.

Disclosure

9 **The financial statements shall disclose the accounting policy adopted for borrowing costs.**

Borrowing costs – allowed alternative treatment

Recognition

10 **Borrowing costs shall be recognised as an expense in the period in which they are incurred, except to the extent that they are capitalised in accordance with paragraph 11.**

11 **Borrowing costs that are directly attributable to the acquisition, construction or production of a qualifying asset shall be capitalised as part of the cost of that asset. The amount of borrowing costs eligible for capitalisation shall be determined in accordance with this Standard.**

12 Under the allowed alternative treatment, borrowing costs that are directly attributable to the acquisition, construction or production of an asset are included in the cost of that asset. Such borrowing costs are capitalised as part of the cost of the asset when it is probable that they will result in future economic benefits to the entity and the costs can be measured reliably. Other borrowing costs are recognised as an expense in the period in which they are incurred.

Borrowing costs eligible for capitalisation

13 The borrowing costs that are directly attributable to the acquisition, construction or production of a qualifying asset are those borrowing costs that would have been avoided if the expenditure on the qualifying asset had not been made. When an entity borrows funds specifically for the purpose of obtaining a particular qualifying asset, the borrowing costs that directly relate to that qualifying asset can be readily identified.

14 It may be difficult to identify a direct relationship between particular borrowings and a qualifying asset and to determine the borrowings that could otherwise have been avoided. Such a difficulty occurs, for example, when the financing activity of an entity is coordinated centrally. Difficulties also arise when a group uses a range of debt instruments to borrow funds at varying rates of interest, and lends those funds on various bases to other entities in the group. Other complications arise through the use of loans denominated in or linked to foreign currencies, when the group operates in highly inflationary economies, and from fluctuations in exchange rates. As a result, the determination of the amount of borrowing

costs that are directly attributable to the acquisition of a qualifying asset is difficult and the exercise of judgement is required.

15 **To the extent that funds are borrowed specifically for the purpose of obtaining a qualifying asset, the amount of borrowing costs eligible for capitalisation on that asset shall be determined as the actual borrowing costs incurred on that borrowing during the period less any investment income on the temporary investment of those borrowings.**

16 The financing arrangements for a qualifying asset may result in an entity obtaining borrowed funds and incurring associated borrowing costs before some or all of the funds are used for expenditures on the qualifying asset. In such circumstances, the funds are often temporarily invested pending their expenditure on the qualifying asset. In determining the amount of borrowing costs eligible for capitalisation during a period, any investment income earned on such funds is deducted from the borrowing costs incurred.

17 **To the extent that funds are borrowed generally and used for the purpose of obtaining a qualifying asset, the amount of borrowing costs eligible for capitalisation shall be determined by applying a capitalisation rate to the expenditures on that asset. The capitalisation rate shall be the weighted average of the borrowing costs applicable to the borrowings of the entity that are outstanding during the period, other than borrowings made specifically for the purpose of obtaining a qualifying asset. The amount of borrowing costs capitalised during a period shall not exceed the amount of borrowing costs incurred during that period.**

18 In some circumstances, it is appropriate to include all borrowings of the parent and its subsidiaries when computing a weighted average of the borrowing costs; in other circumstances, it is appropriate for each subsidiary to use a weighted average of the borrowing costs applicable to its own borrowings.

Excess of the carrying amount of the qualifying asset over recoverable amount

19 When the carrying amount or the expected ultimate cost of the qualifying asset exceeds its recoverable amount or net realisable value, the carrying amount is written down or written off in accordance with the requirements of other Standards. In certain circumstances, the amount of the write-down or write-off is written back in accordance with those other Standards.

Commencement of capitalisation

20 **The capitalisation of borrowing costs as part of the cost of a qualifying asset shall commence when:**

(a) expenditures for the asset are being incurred;

(b) borrowing costs are being incurred; and

(c) activities that are necessary to prepare the asset for its intended use or sale are in progress.

21 Expenditures on a qualifying asset include only those expenditures that have resulted in payments of cash, transfers of other assets or the assumption of

interest-bearing liabilities. Expenditures are reduced by any progress payments received and grants received in connection with the asset (see IAS 20 *Accounting for Government Grants and Disclosure of Government Assistance*). The average carrying amount of the asset during a period, including borrowing costs previously capitalised, is normally a reasonable approximation of the expenditures to which the capitalisation rate is applied in that period.

22 The activities necessary to prepare the asset for its intended use or sale encompass more than the physical construction of the asset. They include technical and administrative work prior to the commencement of physical construction, such as the activities associated with obtaining permits prior to the commencement of the physical construction. However, such activities exclude the holding of an asset when no production or development that changes the asset's condition is taking place. For example, borrowing costs incurred while land is under development are capitalised during the period in which activities related to the development are being undertaken. However, borrowing costs incurred while land acquired for building purposes is held without any associated development activity do not qualify for capitalisation.

Suspension of capitalisation

23 Capitalisation of borrowing costs shall be suspended during extended periods in which active development is interrupted.

24 Borrowing costs may be incurred during an extended period in which the activities necessary to prepare an asset for its intended use or sale are interrupted. Such costs are costs of holding partially completed assets and do not qualify for capitalisation. However, capitalisation of borrowing costs is not normally suspended during a period when substantial technical and administrative work is being carried out. Capitalisation of borrowing costs is also not suspended when a temporary delay is a necessary part of the process of getting an asset ready for its intended use or sale. For example, capitalisation continues during the extended period needed for inventories to mature or the extended period during which high water levels delay construction of a bridge, if such high water levels are common during the construction period in the geographic region involved.

Cessation of capitalisation

25 Capitalisation of borrowing costs shall cease when substantially all the activities necessary to prepare the qualifying asset for its intended use or sale are complete.

26 An asset is normally ready for its intended use or sale when the physical construction of the asset is complete even though routine administrative work might still continue. If minor modifications, such as the decoration of a property to the purchaser's or user's specification, are all that are outstanding, this indicates that substantially all the activities are complete.

27 When the construction of a qualifying asset is completed in parts and each part is capable of being used while construction continues on other parts, capitalisation of borrowing costs shall cease when substantially all the activities necessary to prepare that part for its intended use or sale are completed.

28 A business park comprising several buildings, each of which can be used individually is an example of a qualifying asset for which each part is capable of being usable while construction continues on other parts. An example of a qualifying asset that needs to be complete before any part can be used is an industrial plant involving several processes which are carried out in sequence at different parts of the plant within the same site, such as a steel mill.

Disclosure

29 **The financial statements shall disclose:**

(a) the accounting policy adopted for borrowing costs;

(b) the amount of borrowing costs capitalised during the period; and

(c) the capitalisation rate used to determine the amount of borrowing costs eligible for capitalisation.

Transitional provisions

30 **When the adoption of this Standard constitutes a change in accounting policy, an entity is encouraged to adjust its financial statements in accordance with IAS 8** *Accounting Policies, Changes in Accounting Estimates and Errors*. **Alternatively, entities shall capitalise only those borrowing costs incurred after the effective date of the Standard that meet the criteria for capitalisation.**

Effective date

31 **This Standard becomes operative for financial statements covering periods beginning on or after 1 January 1995.**

International Accounting Standard 24

Related Party Disclosures

This version includes amendments resulting from Amendment to IAS 19 Employee Benefits–Actuarial Gains and Losses, Group Plans and Disclosures *issued on 16 December 2004.*

CONTENTS

International Accounting Standard 24 *Related Party Disclosures* (IAS 24) is set out in paragraphs 1–24 and the Appendix. All the paragraphs have equal authority but retain the IASC format of the Standard when it was adopted by the IASB. IAS 24 should be read in the context of its objective and the Basis for Conclusions, the *Preface to International Financial Reporting Standards* and the *Framework for the Preparation and Presentation of Financial Statements*. IAS 8 *Accounting Policies, Changes in Accounting Estimates and Errors* provides a basis for selecting and applying accounting policies in the absence of explicit guidance.

Introduction

IN1 International Accounting Standard 24 *Related Party Disclosures* (IAS 24) replaces IAS 24 *Related Party Disclosures* (reformatted in 1994) and should be applied for annual periods beginning on or after 1 January 2005. Earlier application is encouraged.

IN2 The International Accounting Standards Board developed this revised IAS 24 as part of its project on Improvements to International Accounting Standards. The project was undertaken in the light of queries and criticisms raised in relation to the Standards by securities regulators, professional accountants and other interested parties. The objectives of the project were to reduce or eliminate alternatives, redundancies and conflicts within the Standards, to deal with some convergence issues and to make other improvements.

IN3 For IAS 24 the Board's main objective was to provide additional guidance and clarity in the scope of the Standard, the definitions and the disclosures for related parties. The wording of the Standard's objective was amended to clarify that the entity's financial statements should contain the disclosures necessary to draw attention to the possibility that the financial position and profit or loss may have been affected by the existence of related parties and by transactions and outstanding balances with them. The Board did not reconsider the fundamental approach to related party disclosures contained in IAS 24.

The main changes

IN4 The main changes from the previous version of IAS 24 are described below.

Scope

IN5 The Standard requires disclosure of the compensation of key management personnel.

IN6 State-controlled entities are within the scope of International Financial Reporting Standards, ie those that are profit-oriented are no longer exempted from disclosing transactions with other state-controlled entities.

Purpose of related party disclosures

IN7 Discussions on the pricing of transactions and related disclosures between related parties have been removed because the Standard does not apply to the measurement of related party transactions.

Definitions

IN8 The definition of 'related party' has been expanded by adding:

- parties with joint control over the entity;
- joint ventures in which the entity is a venturer; and
- post-employment benefit plans for the benefit of employees of an entity, or of any entity that is a related party to that entity.

IN9 The Standard adds a definition of 'close members of the family of an individual' and clarifies that non-executive directors are key management personnel.

IN10 The Standard clarifies that two venturers are not related parties simply because they share joint control over a joint venture.

Disclosure

IN11 The Standard further clarifies the disclosure requirements about:

- outstanding balances with related parties together with their terms and conditions including whether they are secured, and the nature of the consideration to be provided in settlement.
- details of any guarantees given or received.
- provisions for doubtful debts.
- the settlement of liabilities on behalf of the entity or by the entity on behalf of another party.

IN12 The Standard clarifies that an entity discloses that the terms of related party transactions are equivalent to those that prevail in arm's length transactions only if such terms can be substantiated.

IN13 Other new disclosures required include the following:

- the amounts of transactions and outstanding balances with respect to related parties. Disclosure of proportions of transactions and outstanding balances is no longer sufficient.
- the expense recognised during the period in respect of bad or doubtful debts due from related parties.
- classification of amounts payable to, and receivable from, related parties into different categories of related parties.
- the name of the entity's parent and, if different, the ultimate controlling party. If neither of these two parties produces financial statements available for public use, the name of the next most senior parent that does so is required.

International Accounting Standard 24
Related Party Disclosures

Objective

1 The objective of this Standard is to ensure that an entity's financial statements contain the disclosures necessary to draw attention to the possibility that its financial position and profit or loss may have been affected by the existence of related parties and by transactions and outstanding balances with such parties.

Scope

2 **This Standard shall be applied in:**

(a) identifying related party relationships and transactions;

(b) identifying outstanding balances between an entity and its related parties;

(c) identifying the circumstances in which disclosure of the items in (a) and (b) is required; and

(d) determining the disclosures to be made about those items.

3 **This Standard requires disclosure of related party transactions and outstanding balances in the separate financial statements of a parent, venturer or investor presented in accordance with IAS 27** *Consolidated and Separate Financial Statements*.

4 Related party transactions and outstanding balances with other entities in a group are disclosed in an entity's financial statements. Intragroup related party transactions and outstanding balances are eliminated in the preparation of consolidated financial statements of the group.

Purpose of related party disclosures

5 Related party relationships are a normal feature of commerce and business. For example, entities frequently carry on parts of their activities through subsidiaries, joint ventures and associates. In these circumstances, the entity's ability to affect the financial and operating policies of the investee is through the presence of control, joint control or significant influence.

6 A related party relationship could have an effect on the profit or loss and financial position of an entity. Related parties may enter into transactions that unrelated parties would not. For example, an entity that sells goods to its parent at cost might not sell on those terms to another customer. Also, transactions between related parties may not be made at the same amounts as between unrelated parties.

7 The profit or loss and financial position of an entity may be affected by a related party relationship even if related party transactions do not occur. The mere existence of the relationship may be sufficient to affect the transactions of the entity with other parties. For example, a subsidiary may terminate relations with

a trading partner on acquisition by the parent of a fellow subsidiary engaged in the same activity as the former trading partner. Alternatively, one party may refrain from acting because of the significant influence of another–for example, a subsidiary may be instructed by its parent not to engage in research and development.

8 For these reasons, knowledge of related party transactions, outstanding balances and relationships may affect assessments of an entity's operations by users of financial statements, including assessments of the risks and opportunities facing the entity.

Definitions

9 **The following terms are used in this Standard with the meanings specified:**

Related party **A party is related to an entity if:**

(a) directly, or indirectly through one or more intermediaries, the party:

(i) controls, is controlled by, or is under common control with, the entity (this includes parents, subsidiaries and fellow subsidiaries);

(ii) has an interest in the entity that gives it significant influence over the entity; or

(iii) has joint control over the entity;

(b) the party is an associate (as defined in IAS 28 *Investments in Associates***) of the entity;**

(c) the party is a joint venture in which the entity is a venturer (see IAS 31 *Interests in Joint Ventures***);**

(d) the party is a member of the key management personnel of the entity or its parent;

(e) the party is a close member of the family of any individual referred to in (a) or (d);

(f) the party is an entity that is controlled, jointly controlled or significantly influenced by, or for which significant voting power in such entity resides with, directly or indirectly, any individual referred to in (d) or (e); or

(g) the party is a post-employment benefit plan for the benefit of employees of the entity, or of any entity that is a related party of the entity.

A *related party transaction* **is a transfer of resources, services or obligations between related parties, regardless of whether a price is charged.**

Close members of the family of an individual **are those family members who may be expected to influence, or be influenced by, that individual in their dealings with the entity. They may include:**

(a) the individual's domestic partner and children;

(b) children of the individual's domestic partner; and

(c) dependants of the individual or the individual's domestic partner.

Compensation **includes all employee benefits (as defined in IAS 19** *Employee Benefits***) including employee benefits to which IFRS 2** *Share-based Payment* **applies. Employee benefits are all forms of consideration paid, payable or provided by the entity, or on behalf of the entity, in exchange for services rendered to the entity. It also includes such consideration paid on behalf of a parent of the entity in respect of the entity. Compensation includes:**

(a) short-term employee benefits, such as wages, salaries and social security contributions, paid annual leave and paid sick leave, profit-sharing and bonuses (if payable within twelve months of the end of the period) and non-monetary benefits (such as medical care, housing, cars and free or subsidised goods or services) for current employees;

(b) post-employment benefits such as pensions, other retirement benefits, post-employment life insurance and post-employment medical care;

(c) other long-term employee benefits, including long-service leave or sabbatical leave, jubilee or other long-service benefits, long-term disability benefits and, if they are not payable wholly within twelve months after the end of the period, profit-sharing, bonuses and deferred compensation;

(d) termination benefits; and

(e) share-based payment.

Control **is the power to govern the financial and operating policies of an entity so as to obtain benefits from its activities.**

Joint control **is the contractually agreed sharing of control over an economic activity.**

Key management personnel **are those persons having authority and responsibility for planning, directing and controlling the activities of the entity, directly or indirectly, including any director (whether executive or otherwise) of that entity.**

Significant influence **is the power to participate in the financial and operating policy decisions of an entity, but is not control over those policies. Significant influence may be gained by share ownership, statute or agreement.**

10 In considering each possible related party relationship, attention is directed to the substance of the relationship and not merely the legal form.

11 In the context of this Standard, the following are not necessarily related parties:

(a) two entities simply because they have a director or other member of key management personnel in common, notwithstanding (d) and (f) in the definition of 'related party'.

(b) two venturers simply because they share joint control over a joint venture.

(c) (i) providers of finance,

(ii) trade unions,

(iii) public utilities, and

(iv) government departments and agencies,

simply by virtue of their normal dealings with an entity (even though they may affect the freedom of action of an entity or participate in its decision-making process).

(d) a customer, supplier, franchisor, distributor or general agent with whom an entity transacts a significant volume of business, merely by virtue of the resulting economic dependence.

Disclosure

12 **Relationships between parents and subsidiaries shall be disclosed irrespective of whether there have been transactions between those related parties. An entity shall disclose the name of the entity's parent and, if different, the ultimate controlling party. If neither the entity's parent nor the ultimate controlling party produces financial statements available for public use, the name of the next most senior parent that does so shall also be disclosed.**

13 To enable users of financial statements to form a view about the effects of related party relationships on an entity, it is appropriate to disclose the related party relationship when control exists, irrespective of whether there have been transactions between the related parties.

14 The identification of related party relationships between parents and subsidiaries is in addition to the disclosure requirements in IAS 27, IAS 28 and IAS 31, which require an appropriate listing and description of significant investments in subsidiaries, associates and jointly controlled entities.

15 When neither the entity's parent nor the ultimate controlling party produces financial statements available for public use, the entity discloses the name of the next most senior parent that does so. The next most senior parent is the first parent in the group above the immediate parent that produces consolidated financial statements available for public use.

16 **An entity shall disclose key management personnel compensation in total and for each of the following categories:**

(a) short-term employee benefits;

(b) post-employment benefits;

(c) other long-term benefits;

(d) termination benefits; and

(e) share-based payment.

17 **If there have been transactions between related parties, an entity shall disclose the nature of the related party relationship as well as information about the transactions and outstanding balances necessary for an**

understanding of the potential effect of the relationship on the financial statements. These disclosure requirements are in addition to the requirements in paragraph 16 to disclose key management personnel compensation. At a minimum, disclosures shall include:

(a) the amount of the transactions;

(b) the amount of outstanding balances and:

(i) their terms and conditions, including whether they are secured, and the nature of the consideration to be provided in settlement; and

(ii) details of any guarantees given or received;

(c) provisions for doubtful debts related to the amount of outstanding balances; and

(d) the expense recognised during the period in respect of bad or doubtful debts due from related parties.

18 **The disclosures required by paragraph 17 shall be made separately for each of the following categories:**

(a) the parent;

(b) entities with joint control or significant influence over the entity;

(c) subsidiaries;

(d) associates;

(e) joint ventures in which the entity is a venturer;

(f) key management personnel of the entity or its parent; and

(g) other related parties.

19 The classification of amounts payable to, and receivable from, related parties in the different categories as required in paragraph 18 is an extension of the disclosure requirement in IAS 1 *Presentation of Financial Statements* for information to be presented either on the balance sheet or in the notes. The categories are extended to provide a more comprehensive analysis of related party balances and apply to related party transactions.

20 The following are examples of transactions that are disclosed if they are with a related party:

(a) purchases or sales of goods (finished or unfinished);

(b) purchases or sales of property and other assets;

(c) rendering or receiving of services;

(d) leases;

(e) transfers of research and development;

(f) transfers under licence agreements;

(g) transfers under finance arrangements (including loans and equity contributions in cash or in kind);

(h) provision of guarantees or collateral; and

(i) settlement of liabilities on behalf of the entity or by the entity on behalf of another party.

Participation by a parent or subsidiary in a defined benefit plan that shares risks between group entities is a transaction between related parties (see paragraph 34B of IAS 19).

21 Disclosures that related party transactions were made on terms equivalent to those that prevail in arm's length transactions are made only if such terms can be substantiated.

22 Items of a similar nature may be disclosed in aggregate except when separate disclosure is necessary for an understanding of the effects of related party transactions on the financial statements of the entity.

Effective date

23 An entity shall apply this Standard for annual periods beginning on or after 1 January 2005. Earlier application is encouraged. If an entity applies this Standard for a period beginning before 1 January 2005, it shall disclose that fact.

23A An entity shall apply the amendments in paragraph 20 for annual periods beginning on or after 1 January 2006. If an entity applies the amendments to IAS 19 *Employee Benefits—Actuarial Gains and Losses, Group Plans and Disclosures* **for an earlier period, these amendments shall be applied for that earlier period.**

Withdrawal of IAS 24 (reformatted 1994)

24 This Standard supersedes IAS 24 *Related Party Disclosures* (reformatted in 1994).

Appendix
Amendment to IAS 30

This amendment in this appendix shall be applied for annual periods beginning on or after 1 January 2005. If an entity applies this Standard for an earlier period, this amendment shall be applied for that earlier period.

* * * * *

The amendment contained in this appendix when this Standard was issued in 2003 has been incorporated into the text of IAS 30 published in this volume.

Approval of IAS 24 by the Board

International Accounting Standard 24 *Related Party Disclosures* was approved for issue by the fourteen members of the International Accounting Standards Board.

Sir David Tweedie	Chairman
Thomas E Jones	Vice-Chairman
Mary E Barth	
Hans-Georg Bruns	
Anthony T Cope	
Robert P Garnett	
Gilbert Gélard	
James J Leisenring	
Warren J McGregor	
Patricia L O'Malley	
Harry K Schmid	
John T Smith	
Geoffrey Whittington	
Tatsumi Yamada	

Basis for Conclusions

This Basis for Conclusions accompanies, but is not part of, IAS 24.

Introduction

BC1 This Basis for Conclusions summarises the International Accounting Standards Board's considerations in reaching its conclusions on revising IAS 24 *Related Party Disclosures* in 2003. Individual Board members gave greater weight to some factors than to others.

BC2 In July 2001 the Board announced that, as part of its initial agenda of technical projects, it would undertake a project to improve a number of Standards, including IAS 24. The project was undertaken in the light of queries and criticisms raised in relation to the Standards by securities regulators, professional accountants and other interested parties. The objectives of the Improvements project were to reduce or eliminate alternatives, redundancies and conflicts within existing standards, to deal with some convergence issues and to make other improvements. In May 2002 the Board published its proposals in an Exposure Draft of *Improvements to International Accounting Standards*, with a comment deadline of 16 September 2002. The Board received over 160 comment letters on the Exposure Draft.

BC3 Because the Board's intention was not to reconsider the fundamental approach to related party disclosures established by IAS 24, this Basis for Conclusions does not discuss requirements in IAS 24 that the Board has not reconsidered.

Management compensation

BC4 The previous version of IAS 24 had no exemption for the disclosure of key management personnel compensation. In developing the Exposure Draft, the Board proposed that the disclosure of management compensation, expense allowances and similar items paid in the ordinary course of business should not be required because:

(a) the approval processes for key management personnel compensation in some jurisdictions remove the rationale for related party disclosures;

(b) privacy issues arise in some jurisdictions where accountability mechanisms other than disclosure in financial statements exist; and

(c) requiring these disclosures placed weight on the determination of 'key management personnel' and 'compensation', which was likely to prove contentious. In addition, comparability of these disclosures would be unlikely until measurement requirements are developed for all forms of compensation.

BC5 However, some respondents to the Exposure Draft objected to the proposed exemption because they were concerned that information relating to management compensation is relevant to users' information needs and that an exemption based on 'items paid in the ordinary course of business' could lead to abuse. Establishing a disclosure exemption on such a criterion without a definition of the terms could lead to exempting other transactions with management from being disclosed, because they could all be structured as 'compensation paid in the ordinary course of an entity's operations'. Respondents argued that such an exemption could lead to abuse because it could potentially apply to any transactions with management.

BC6 The Board was persuaded by the respondents' views on the Exposure Draft and decided that the Standard should require disclosure of key management personnel compensation because:

(a) the principle underpinning the requirements in IAS 24 is that transactions with related parties should be disclosed, and key management personnel are related parties of an entity.

(b) key management personnel compensation is relevant to decisions made by users of financial statements when it represents a material amount. The structure and amount of compensation are major drivers in the implementation of the business strategy.

(c) the benefit of this information to users of financial statements largely outweighs the potential lack of comparability arising from the absence of recognition and measurement requirements for all forms of compensation.

BC7 The Board believes that although some jurisdictions have processes for approving compensation for key management personnel in an attempt to ensure an arm's length result, it is clear that some jurisdictions do not. Furthermore, although approval processes for management compensation may involve other parties such as shareholders or investors, key management personnel may still have a significant input. In addition, the Board noted that disclosing key management personnel compensation would improve transparency and comparability, thereby enabling users of financial statements to make a better assessment of the impact of such compensation on the entity's financial position and profit or loss. The Board also noted that the definition of key management personnel and the guidance on compensation in IAS 19 *Employee Benefits* are sufficient to enable entities to disclose the relevant information.

Related party disclosures in separate financial statements

BC8 The previous version of IAS 24 exempted disclosures about related party transactions in:

(a) parent financial statements when they are made available or published with the consolidated statements; and

(b) financial statements of a wholly-owned subsidiary if its parent is incorporated in the same country and provides consolidated financial statements in that country.

BC9 In the Exposure Draft the Board proposed to continue exempting separate financial statements of parents and financial statements of wholly-owned subsidiaries from disclosures about any related parties in specified circumstances. It proposed that disclosure of related party transactions and outstanding balances in the separate financial statements of a parent or the financial statements of a wholly-owned subsidiary would not be required, but only if those statements were made available or published with consolidated financial statements for the group.

BC10 The Board decided to retain this exemption for the Exposure Draft so that entities that are required by law to produce financial statements available for public use in accordance with International Financial Reporting Standards in addition to the group's consolidated financial statements would not be unduly burdened. The Board noted that in some circumstances, users can find sufficient information for their purposes regarding a subsidiary from either its financial statements or the group's consolidated financial statements. In addition, the users of financial statements of a subsidiary often have, or can obtain access to, more information. The Board also noted that users should be aware that amounts recognised in the financial statements of a wholly-owned subsidiary can be affected significantly by the subsidiary's relationship with its parent.

BC11 Respondents to the Exposure Draft objected to this exemption, on the grounds that disclosure of related party transactions and outstanding balances is essential information for external users who need to be aware of the level of support provided by related parties. The respondents also argued that financial statements prepared in accordance with International Financial Reporting Standards could be presented on a stand-alone basis. Therefore, financial statements prepared on the basis of this proposed exemption would not achieve a fair presentation without related party disclosures.

BC12 The Board was persuaded by those arguments and decided to require the disclosure of related party transactions and outstanding balances in separate financial statements of a parent, investor or venturer in addition to the disclosure requirements in IAS 27 *Consolidated and Separate Financial Statements*, IAS 28 *Investments in Associates* and IAS 31 *Interests in Joint Ventures.*

BC13 The Board noted that the financial statements of an entity that is part of a consolidated group may include the effects of extensive intra-group transactions. Indeed, potentially all of the revenues and expenses for such an entity may derive from related party transactions. The Board concluded that the disclosures required by IAS 24 are essential to understanding the financial position and financial performance of such an entity and therefore should be required for separate financial statements presented in accordance with IAS 27.

BC14 The Board also believed that disclosure of such transactions is essential because the external users need to be aware of the interrelationships between related parties, including the level of support provided by related parties, to assist external users in their economic decisions.

Table of Concordance

This table shows how the contents of the superseded version of IAS 24 and the current version of IAS 24 correspond. Paragraphs are treated as corresponding if they broadly address the same matter even though the guidance may differ.

Superseded IAS 24 paragraph	Current IAS 24 paragraph
1	2
2	9, 11
3	9
4	4
5	9
6	11
7	5
8	6
9	7
10	None
11	None
12	None
13	None
14	None
15	None
16	None
17	None
18	None
19	20
20	12
21	13
22	17
23	None
24	22
25	None
26	23
None	1
None	3
None	8
None	10
None	14–16
None	18, 19
None	21
None	24

International Accounting Standard 26

Accounting and Reporting by Retirement Benefit Plans

This Standard is effective for financial statements covering periods beginning on or after 1 January 1988.

Contents

International Accounting Standard 26 *Accounting and Reporting by Retirement Benefit Plans* (IAS 26) is set out in paragraphs 1–37. All the paragraphs have equal authority but retain the IASC format of the Standard when it was adopted by the IASB. IAS 26 should be read in the context of the *Preface to International Financial Reporting Standards* and the *Framework for the Preparation and Presentation of Financial Statements*. IAS 8 *Accounting Policies, Changes in Accounting Estimates and Errors* provides a basis for selecting and applying accounting policies in the absence of explicit guidance.

International Accounting Standard 26
Accounting and Reporting by Retirement Benefit Plans

Scope

1 This Standard shall be applied in the financial statements of retirement benefit plans where such financial statements are prepared.

2 Retirement benefit plans are sometimes referred to by various other names, such as 'pension schemes', 'superannuation schemes' or 'retirement benefit schemes'. This Standard regards a retirement benefit plan as a reporting entity separate from the employers of the participants in the plan. All other Standards apply to the financial statements of retirement benefit plans to the extent that they are not superseded by this Standard.

3 This Standard deals with accounting and reporting by the plan to all participants as a group. It does not deal with reports to individual participants about their retirement benefit rights.

4 IAS 19 *Employee Benefits* is concerned with the determination of the cost of retirement benefits in the financial statements of employers having plans. Hence this Standard complements IAS 19.

5 Retirement benefit plans may be defined contribution plans or defined benefit plans. Many require the creation of separate funds, which may or may not have separate legal identity and may or may not have trustees, to which contributions are made and from which retirement benefits are paid. This Standard applies regardless of whether such a fund is created and regardless of whether there are trustees.

6 Retirement benefit plans with assets invested with insurance companies are subject to the same accounting and funding requirements as privately invested arrangements. Accordingly, they are within the scope of this Standard unless the contract with the insurance company is in the name of a specified participant or a group of participants and the retirement benefit obligation is solely the responsibility of the insurance company.

7 This Standard does not deal with other forms of employment benefits such as employment termination indemnities, deferred compensation arrangements, long-service leave benefits, special early retirement or redundancy plans, health and welfare plans or bonus plans. Government social security type arrangements are also excluded from the scope of this Standard.

Definitions

8 The following terms are used in this Standard with the meanings specified:

Retirement benefit plans **are arrangements whereby an entity provides benefits for employees on or after termination of service (either in the form of an annual income or as a lump sum) when such benefits, or the contributions towards them, can be determined or estimated in advance of retirement from the provisions of a document or from the entity's practices.**

Defined contribution plans **are retirement benefit plans under which amounts to be paid as retirement benefits are determined by contributions to a fund together with investment earnings thereon.**

Defined benefit plans **are retirement benefit plans under which amounts to be paid as retirement benefits are determined by reference to a formula usually based on employees' earnings and/or years of service.**

Funding **is the transfer of assets to an entity (the *fund*) separate from the employer's entity to meet future obligations for the payment of retirement benefits.**

For the purposes of this Standard the following terms are also used:

Participants **are the members of a retirement benefit plan and others who are entitled to benefits under the plan.**

Net assets available for benefits **are the assets of a plan less liabilities other than the actuarial present value of promised retirement benefits.**

Actuarial present value of promised retirement benefits **is the present value of the expected payments by a retirement benefit plan to existing and past employees, attributable to the service already rendered.**

Vested benefits **are benefits, the rights to which, under the conditions of a retirement benefit plan, are not conditional on continued employment.**

9 Some retirement benefit plans have sponsors other than employers; this Standard also applies to the financial statements of such plans.

10 Most retirement benefit plans are based on formal agreements. Some plans are informal but have acquired a degree of obligation as a result of employers' established practices. While some plans permit employers to limit their obligations under the plans, it is usually difficult for an employer to cancel a plan if employees are to be retained. The same basis of accounting and reporting applies to an informal plan as to a formal plan.

11 Many retirement benefit plans provide for the establishment of separate funds into which contributions are made and out of which benefits are paid. Such funds may be administered by parties who act independently in managing fund assets. Those parties are called trustees in some countries. The term trustee is used in this Standard to describe such parties regardless of whether a trust has been formed.

12 Retirement benefit plans are normally described as either defined contribution plans or defined benefit plans, each having their own distinctive characteristics. Occasionally plans exist that contain characteristics of both. Such hybrid plans are considered to be defined benefit plans for the purposes of this Standard.

Defined contribution plans

13 The financial statements of a defined contribution plan shall contain a statement of net assets available for benefits and a description of the funding policy.

14 Under a defined contribution plan, the amount of a participant's future benefits is determined by the contributions paid by the employer, the participant, or both, and the operating efficiency and investment earnings of the fund. An employer's obligation is usually discharged by contributions to the fund. An actuary's advice is not normally required although such advice is sometimes used to estimate future benefits that may be achievable based on present contributions and varying levels of future contributions and investment earnings.

15 The participants are interested in the activities of the plan because they directly affect the level of their future benefits. Participants are interested in knowing whether contributions have been received and proper control has been exercised to protect the rights of beneficiaries. An employer is interested in the efficient and fair operation of the plan.

16 The objective of reporting by a defined contribution plan is periodically to provide information about the plan and the performance of its investments. That objective is usually achieved by providing financial statements including the following:

(a) a description of significant activities for the period and the effect of any changes relating to the plan, and its membership and terms and conditions;

(b) statements reporting on the transactions and investment performance for the period and the financial position of the plan at the end of the period; and

(c) a description of the investment policies.

Defined benefit plans

17 The financial statements of a defined benefit plan shall contain either:

(a) a statement that shows:

(i) the net assets available for benefits;

(ii) the actuarial present value of promised retirement benefits, distinguishing between vested benefits and non-vested benefits; and

(iii) the resulting excess or deficit; or

(b) a statement of net assets available for benefits including either:

(i) a note disclosing the actuarial present value of promised retirement benefits, distinguishing between vested benefits and non-vested benefits; or

(ii) a reference to this information in an accompanying actuarial report.

If an actuarial valuation has not been prepared at the date of the financial statements, the most recent valuation shall be used as a base and the date of the valuation disclosed.

18 For the purposes of paragraph 17, the actuarial present value of promised retirement benefits shall be based on the benefits promised under the terms of the plan on service rendered to date using either current salary levels or projected salary levels with disclosure of the basis used. The effect

of any changes in actuarial assumptions that have had a significant effect on the actuarial present value of promised retirement benefits shall also be disclosed.

19 **The financial statements shall explain the relationship between the actuarial present value of promised retirement benefits and the net assets available for benefits, and the policy for the funding of promised benefits.**

20 Under a defined benefit plan, the payment of promised retirement benefits depends on the financial position of the plan and the ability of contributors to make future contributions to the plan as well as the investment performance and operating efficiency of the plan.

21 A defined benefit plan needs the periodic advice of an actuary to assess the financial condition of the plan, review the assumptions and recommend future contribution levels.

22 The objective of reporting by a defined benefit plan is periodically to provide information about the financial resources and activities of the plan that is useful in assessing the relationships between the accumulation of resources and plan benefits over time. This objective is usually achieved by providing financial statements including the following:

(a) a description of significant activities for the period and the effect of any changes relating to the plan, and its membership and terms and conditions;

(b) statements reporting on the transactions and investment performance for the period and the financial position of the plan at the end of the period;

(c) actuarial information either as part of the statements or by way of a separate report; and

(d) a description of the investment policies.

Actuarial present value of promised retirement benefits

23 The present value of the expected payments by a retirement benefit plan may be calculated and reported using current salary levels or projected salary levels up to the time of retirement of participants.

24 The reasons given for adopting a current salary approach include:

(a) the actuarial present value of promised retirement benefits, being the sum of the amounts presently attributable to each participant in the plan, can be calculated more objectively than with projected salary levels because it involves fewer assumptions;

(b) increases in benefits attributable to a salary increase become an obligation of the plan at the time of the salary increase; and

(c) the amount of the actuarial present value of promised retirement benefits using current salary levels is generally more closely related to the amount payable in the event of termination or discontinuance of the plan.

25 Reasons given for adopting a projected salary approach include:

(a) financial information should be prepared on a going concern basis, irrespective of the assumptions and estimates that must be made;

(b) under final pay plans, benefits are determined by reference to salaries at or near retirement date; hence salaries, contribution levels and rates of return must be projected; and

(c) failure to incorporate salary projections, when most funding is based on salary projections, may result in the reporting of an apparent overfunding when the plan is not overfunded, or in reporting adequate funding when the plan is underfunded.

26 The actuarial present value of promised retirement benefits based on current salaries is disclosed in the financial statements of a plan to indicate the obligation for benefits earned to the date of the financial statements. The actuarial present value of promised retirement benefits based on projected salaries is disclosed to indicate the magnitude of the potential obligation on a going concern basis which is generally the basis for funding. In addition to disclosure of the actuarial present value of promised retirement benefits, sufficient explanation may need to be given so as to indicate clearly the context in which the actuarial present value of promised retirement benefits should be read. Such explanation may be in the form of information about the adequacy of the planned future funding and of the funding policy based on salary projections. This may be included in the financial statements or in the actuary's report.

Frequency of actuarial valuations

27 In many countries, actuarial valuations are not obtained more frequently than every three years. If an actuarial valuation has not been prepared at the date of the financial statements, the most recent valuation is used as a base and the date of the valuation disclosed.

Financial statement content

28 For defined benefit plans, information is presented in one of the following formats which reflect different practices in the disclosure and presentation of actuarial information:

(a) a statement is included in the financial statements that shows the net assets available for benefits, the actuarial present value of promised retirement benefits, and the resulting excess or deficit. The financial statements of the plan also contain statements of changes in net assets available for benefits and changes in the actuarial present value of promised retirement benefits. The financial statements may be accompanied by a separate actuary's report supporting the actuarial present value of promised retirement benefits;

(b) financial statements that include a statement of net assets available for benefits and a statement of changes in net assets available for benefits. The actuarial present value of promised retirement benefits is disclosed in a note to the statements. The financial statements may also be accompanied by a report from an actuary supporting the actuarial present value of promised retirement benefits; and

(c) financial statements that include a statement of net assets available for benefits and a statement of changes in net assets available for benefits with the actuarial present value of promised retirement benefits contained in a separate actuarial report.

In each format a trustees' report in the nature of a management or directors' report and an investment report may also accompany the financial statements.

29 Those in favour of the formats described in paragraphs 28(a) and 28(b) believe that the quantification of promised retirement benefits and other information provided under those approaches help users to assess the current status of the plan and the likelihood of the plan's obligations being met. They also believe that financial statements should be complete in themselves and not rely on accompanying statements. However, some believe that the format described in paragraph 28(a) could give the impression that a liability exists, whereas the actuarial present value of promised retirement benefits does not in their opinion have all the characteristics of a liability.

30 Those who favour the format described in paragraph 28(c) believe that the actuarial present value of promised retirement benefits should not be included in a statement of net assets available for benefits as in the format described in paragraph 28(a) or even be disclosed in a note as in 28(b), because it will be compared directly with plan assets and such a comparison may not be valid. They contend that actuaries do not necessarily compare actuarial present value of promised retirement benefits with market values of investments but may instead assess the present value of cash flows expected from the investments. Therefore, those in favour of this format believe that such a comparison is unlikely to reflect the actuary's overall assessment of the plan and that it may be misunderstood. Also, some believe that, regardless of whether quantified, the information about promised retirement benefits should be contained solely in the separate actuarial report where a proper explanation can be provided.

31 This Standard accepts the views in favour of permitting disclosure of the information concerning promised retirement benefits in a separate actuarial report. It rejects arguments against the quantification of the actuarial present value of promised retirement benefits. Accordingly, the formats described in paragraphs 28(a) and 28(b) are considered acceptable under this Standard, as is the format described in paragraph 28 (c) so long as the financial statements contain a reference to, and are accompanied by, an actuarial report that includes the actuarial present value of promised retirement benefits.

All plans

Valuation of plan assets

32 **Retirement benefit plan investments shall be carried at fair value. In the case of marketable securities fair value is market value. Where plan investments are held for which an estimate of fair value is not possible disclosure shall be made of the reason why fair value is not used.**

33 In the case of marketable securities fair value is usually market value because this is considered the most useful measure of the securities at the report date and of the investment performance for the period. Those securities that have a fixed redemption value and that have been acquired to match the obligations of the plan, or specific parts thereof, may be carried at amounts based on their ultimate redemption value assuming a constant rate of return to maturity. Where plan investments are held for which an estimate of fair value is not possible, such as

total ownership of an entity, disclosure is made of the reason why fair value is not used. To the extent that investments are carried at amounts other than market value or fair value, fair value is generally also disclosed. Assets used in the operations of the fund are accounted for in accordance with the applicable Standards.

Disclosure

34 **The financial statements of a retirement benefit plan, whether defined benefit or defined contribution, shall also contain the following information:**

- **(a) a statement of changes in net assets available for benefits;**
- **(b) a summary of significant accounting policies; and**
- **(c) a description of the plan and the effect of any changes in the plan during the period.**

35 Financial statements provided by retirement benefit plans include the following, if applicable:

- (a) a statement of net assets available for benefits disclosing:
  - (i) assets at the end of the period suitably classified;
  - (ii) the basis of valuation of assets;
  - (iii) details of any single investment exceeding either 5% of the net assets available for benefits or 5% of any class or type of security;
  - (iv) details of any investment in the employer; and
  - (v) liabilities other than the actuarial present value of promised retirement benefits;
- (b) a statement of changes in net assets available for benefits showing the following:
  - (i) employer contributions;
  - (ii) employee contributions;
  - (iii) investment income such as interest and dividends;
  - (iv) other income;
  - (v) benefits paid or payable (analysed, for example, as retirement, death and disability benefits, and lump sum payments);
  - (vi) administrative expenses;
  - (vii) other expenses;
  - (viii) taxes on income;
  - (ix) profits and losses on disposal of investments and changes in value of investments; and
  - (x) transfers from and to other plans;
- (c) a description of the funding policy;

(d) for defined benefit plans, the actuarial present value of promised retirement benefits (which may distinguish between vested benefits and non-vested benefits) based on the benefits promised under the terms of the plan, on service rendered to date and using either current salary levels or projected salary levels; this information may be included in an accompanying actuarial report to be read in conjunction with the related financial statements; and

(e) for defined benefit plans, a description of the significant actuarial assumptions made and the method used to calculate the actuarial present value of promised retirement benefits.

36 The report of a retirement benefit plan contains a description of the plan, either as part of the financial statements or in a separate report. It may contain the following:

(a) the names of the employers and the employee groups covered;

(b) the number of participants receiving benefits and the number of other participants, classified as appropriate;

(c) the type of plan—defined contribution or defined benefit;

(d) a note as to whether participants contribute to the plan;

(e) a description of the retirement benefits promised to participants;

(f) a description of any plan termination terms; and

(g) changes in items (a) to (f) during the period covered by the report.

It is not uncommon to refer to other documents that are readily available to users and in which the plan is described, and to include only information on subsequent changes.

Effective date

37 This Standard becomes operative for financial statements of retirement benefit plans covering periods beginning on or after 1 January 1988.

International Accounting Standard 27

Consolidated and Separate Financial Statements

This version includes amendments resulting from new and amended IFRSs issued up to 31 December 2004.

CONTENTS

International Accounting Standard 27 *Consolidated and Separate Financial Statements* (IAS 27) is set out in paragraphs 1–45 and the Appendix. All the paragraphs have equal authority but retain the IASC format of the Standard when it was adopted by the IASB. IAS 27 should be read in the context of the Basis for Conclusions, the *Preface to International Financial Reporting Standards* and the *Framework for the Preparation and Presentation of Financial Statements*. IAS 8 *Accounting Policies, Changes in Accounting Estimates and Errors* provides a basis for selecting and applying accounting policies in the absence of explicit guidance.

Introduction

IN1 International Accounting Standard 27 *Consolidated and Separate Financial Statements* (IAS 27) replaces IAS 27 (revised 2000) *Consolidated Financial Statements and Accounting for Investments in Subsidiaries* and should be applied for annual periods beginning on or after 1 January 2005. Earlier application is encouraged. The Standard also replaces SIC-33 *Consolidation and Equity Method—Potential Voting Rights and Allocation of Ownership Interests*.

Reasons for revising IAS 27

IN2 The International Accounting Standards Board developed this revised IAS 27 as part of its project on Improvements to International Accounting Standards. The project was undertaken in the light of queries and criticisms raised in relation to the Standards by securities regulators, professional accountants and other interested parties. The objectives of the project were to reduce or eliminate alternatives, redundancies and conflicts within the Standards, to deal with some convergence issues and to make other improvements.

IN3 For IAS 27 the Board's main objective was to reduce alternatives in accounting for subsidiaries in consolidated financial statements and in accounting for investments in the separate financial statements of a parent, venturer or investor. The Board did not reconsider the fundamental approach to consolidation of subsidiaries contained in IAS 27.

The main changes

IN4 The main changes from the previous version of IAS 27 are described below.

Scope

IN5 The Standard applies to accounting for investments in subsidiaries, jointly controlled entities and associates in the separate financial statements of a parent, a venturer or investor. Therefore, the title of the Standard was amended as shown in paragraph IN1.

Exemptions from consolidating investments in subsidiaries

IN6 The Standard modifies the exemption from preparing consolidated financial statements. Paragraph 8 in the previous version of IAS 27 (now paragraph 10) was amended so that a parent need not present consolidated financial statements if:

(a) the parent is itself a wholly-owned subsidiary, or the parent is a partially-owned subsidiary of another entity and its other owners, including those not otherwise entitled to vote, have been informed about, and do not object to, the parent not preparing consolidated financial statements;

(b) the parent's debt or equity instruments are not traded in a public market (a domestic or foreign stock exchange or an over-the-counter market, including local and regional markets);

(c) the parent did not file, nor is it in the process of filing, its financial statements with a securities commission or other regulatory organisation for the purpose of issuing any class of instruments in a public market; and

(d) the ultimate or any intermediate parent of the parent produces consolidated financial statements available for public use that comply with International Financial Reporting Standards.

The Standard clarifies the requirements for a parent exempted from preparing consolidated financial statements when the parent elects, or is required by local regulations, to present separate financial statements (see paragraphs IN13 and IN14).

Temporary control

IN7 The Standard does not require consolidation of a subsidiary acquired when there is evidence that control is intended to be temporary. However, there must be evidence that the subsidiary is acquired with the intention to dispose of it within twelve months and that management is actively seeking a buyer. In addition, the words 'in the near future' were replaced with the words 'within twelve months'. When a subsidiary previously excluded from consolidation is not disposed of within twelve months it must be consolidated as from the date of acquisition unless narrowly specified circumstances apply.*

IN8 The Standard stipulates that the requirement to consolidate investments in subsidiaries applies to venture capital organisations, mutual funds, unit trusts and similar entities. This was added for clarification.

IN9 An entity is not permitted to exclude from consolidation an entity it continues to control simply because that entity is operating under severe long-term restrictions that significantly impair its ability to transfer funds to the parent. Control must be lost for exclusion to occur.

Consolidation procedures

Potential voting rights

IN10 The Standard requires an entity to consider the existence and effect of potential voting rights currently exercisable or convertible when assessing whether it has the power to govern the financial and operating policies of another entity. This requirement was previously included in SIC-33, which has been superseded.

Accounting policies

IN11 The Standard requires an entity to use uniform accounting policies for reporting like transactions and other events in similar circumstances. The previous version of IAS 27 provided an exception to this requirement when it was 'not practicable to use uniform accounting policies'.

* In March 2004, the Board issued IFRS 5 *Non-current Assets Held for Sale and Discontinued Operations*. IFRS 5 removes this scope exclusion and now eliminates the exemption from consolidation when control is intended to be temporary. See IFRS 5 Basis for Conclusions for further discussion.

Minority interests

IN12 This Standard requires an entity to present minority interests in the consolidated balance sheet within equity, separately from the parent shareholders' equity. Though the previous version of IAS 27 precluded presentation of minority interests within liabilities, it did not require presentation within equity.

Separate financial statements

IN13 The Standard prescribes the accounting treatment for investments in subsidiaries, jointly controlled entities and associates when an entity elects, or is required by local regulations, to present separate financial statements. It requires these investments to be accounted for at cost or in accordance with IAS 39 *Financial Instruments: Recognition and Measurement.*

IN14 The Standard retains an alternative for accounting for these investments in an investor's separate financial statements.

International Accounting Standard 27
Consolidated and Separate Financial Statements

Scope

1 **This Standard shall be applied in the preparation and presentation of consolidated financial statements for a group of entities under the control of a parent.**

2 This Standard does not deal with methods of accounting for business combinations and their effects on consolidation, including goodwill arising on a business combination (see IFRS 3 *Business Combinations*).

3 **This Standard shall also be applied in accounting for investments in subsidiaries, jointly controlled entities and associates when an entity elects, or is required by local regulations, to present separate financial statements.**

Definitions

4 **The following terms are used in this Standard with the meanings specified:**

Consolidated financial statements **are the financial statements of a group presented as those of a single economic entity.**

Control **is the power to govern the financial and operating policies of an entity so as to obtain benefits from its activities.**

The *cost method* **is a method of accounting for an investment whereby the investment is recognised at cost. The investor recognises income from the investment only to the extent that the investor receives distributions from accumulated profits of the investee arising after the date of acquisition. Distributions received in excess of such profits are regarded as a recovery of investment and are recognised as a reduction of the cost of the investment.**

A *group* **is a parent and all its subsidiaries.**

Minority interest **is that portion of the profit or loss and net assets of a subsidiary attributable to equity interests that are not owned, directly or indirectly through subsidiaries, by the parent.**

A *parent* **is an entity that has one or more subsidiaries.**

Separate financial statements **are those presented by a parent, an investor in an associate or a venturer in a jointly controlled entity, in which the investments are accounted for on the basis of the direct equity interest rather than on the basis of the reported results and net assets of the investees.**

A *subsidiary* **is an entity, including an unincorporated entity such as a partnership, that is controlled by another entity (known as the parent).**

5 A parent or its subsidiary may be an investor in an associate or a venturer in a jointly controlled entity. In such cases, consolidated financial statements

prepared and presented in accordance with this Standard are also prepared so as to comply with IAS 28 *Investments in Associates* and IAS 31 *Interests in Joint Ventures.*

6 For an entity described in paragraph 5, separate financial statements are those prepared and presented in addition to the financial statements referred to in paragraph 5. Separate financial statements need not be appended to, or accompany, those statements.

7 The financial statements of an entity that does not have a subsidiary, associate or venturer's interest in a jointly controlled entity are not separate financial statements.

8 A parent that is exempted in accordance with paragraph 10 from presenting consolidated financial statements may present separate financial statements as its only financial statements.

Presentation of consolidated financial statements

9 A parent, other than a parent described in paragraph 10, shall present consolidated financial statements in which it consolidates its investments in subsidiaries in accordance with this Standard.

10 A parent need not present consolidated financial statements if and only if:

(a) the parent is itself a wholly-owned subsidiary, or is a partially-owned subsidiary of another entity and its other owners, including those not otherwise entitled to vote, have been informed about, and do not object to, the parent not presenting consolidated financial statements;

(b) the parent's debt or equity instruments are not traded in a public market (a domestic or foreign stock exchange or an over-the-counter market, including local and regional markets);

(c) the parent did not file, nor is it in the process of filing, its financial statements with a securities commission or other regulatory organisation for the purpose of issuing any class of instruments in a public market; and

(d) the ultimate or any intermediate parent of the parent produces consolidated financial statements available for public use that comply with International Financial Reporting Standards.

11 A parent that elects in accordance with paragraph 10 not to present consolidated financial statements, and presents only separate financial statements, complies with paragraphs 37–42.

Scope of consolidated financial statements

12 Consolidated financial statements shall include all subsidiaries of the parent.*

* If on acquisition a subsidiary meets the criteria to be classified as held for sale in accordance with IFRS 5 *Non-current Assets Held for Sale and Discontinued Operations*, it shall be accounted for in accordance with that Standard.

13 Control is presumed to exist when the parent owns, directly or indirectly through subsidiaries, more than half of the voting power of an entity unless, in exceptional circumstances, it can be clearly demonstrated that such ownership does not constitute control. Control also exists when the parent owns half or less of the voting power of an entity when there is:*

(a) power over more than half of the voting rights by virtue of an agreement with other investors;

(b) power to govern the financial and operating policies of the entity under a statute or an agreement;

(c) power to appoint or remove the majority of the members of the board of directors or equivalent governing body and control of the entity is by that board or body; or

(d) power to cast the majority of votes at meetings of the board of directors or equivalent governing body and control of the entity is by that board or body.

14 An entity may own share warrants, share call options, debt or equity instruments that are convertible into ordinary shares, or other similar instruments that have the potential, if exercised or converted, to give the entity voting power or reduce another party's voting power over the financial and operating policies of another entity (potential voting rights). The existence and effect of potential voting rights that are currently exercisable or convertible, including potential voting rights held by another entity, are considered when assessing whether an entity has the power to govern the financial and operating policies of another entity. Potential voting rights are not currently exercisable or convertible when, for example, they cannot be exercised or converted until a future date or until the occurrence of a future event.

15 In assessing whether potential voting rights contribute to control, the entity examines all facts and circumstances (including the terms of exercise of the potential voting rights and any other contractual arrangements whether considered individually or in combination) that affect potential voting rights, except the intention of management and the financial ability to exercise or convert.

16 [Deleted]

17 [Deleted]

18 [Deleted]

19 A subsidiary is not excluded from consolidation simply because the investor is a venture capital organisation, mutual fund, unit trust or similar entity.

20 A subsidiary is not excluded from consolidation because its business activities are dissimilar from those of the other entities within the group. Relevant information is provided by consolidating such subsidiaries and disclosing additional information in the consolidated financial statements about the different business

* See also SIC-12 *Consolidation—Special Purpose Entities.*

activities of subsidiaries. For example, the disclosures required by IAS 14 *Segment Reporting* help to explain the significance of different business activities within the group.

21 A parent loses control when it loses the power to govern the financial and operating policies of an investee so as to obtain benefit from its activities. The loss of control can occur with or without a change in absolute or relative ownership levels. It could occur, for example, when a subsidiary becomes subject to the control of a government, court, administrator or regulator. It could also occur as a result of a contractual agreement.

Consolidation procedures

22 In preparing consolidated financial statements, an entity combines the financial statements of the parent and its subsidiaries line by line by adding together like items of assets, liabilities, equity, income and expenses. In order that the consolidated financial statements present financial information about the group as that of a single economic entity, the following steps are then taken:

(a) the carrying amount of the parent's investment in each subsidiary and the parent's portion of equity of each subsidiary are eliminated (see IFRS 3, which describes the treatment of any resultant goodwill);

(b) minority interests in the profit or loss of consolidated subsidiaries for the reporting period are identified; and

(c) minority interests in the net assets of consolidated subsidiaries are identified separately from the parent shareholders' equity in them. Minority interests in the net assets consist of:

(i) the amount of those minority interests at the date of the original combination calculated in accordance with IFRS 3; and

(ii) the minority's share of changes in equity since the date of the combination.

23 When potential voting rights exist, the proportions of profit or loss and changes in equity allocated to the parent and minority interests are determined on the basis of present ownership interests and do not reflect the possible exercise or conversion of potential voting rights.

24 Intragroup balances, transactions, income and expenses shall be eliminated in full.

25 Intragroup balances and transactions, including income, expenses and dividends, are eliminated in full. Profits and losses resulting from intragroup transactions that are recognised in assets, such as inventory and fixed assets, are eliminated in full. Intragroup losses may indicate an impairment that requires recognition in the consolidated financial statements. IAS 12 *Income Taxes* applies to temporary differences that arise from the elimination of profits and losses resulting from intragroup transactions.

26 The financial statements of the parent and its subsidiaries used in the preparation of the consolidated financial statements shall be prepared as of the same reporting date. When the reporting dates of the parent and a

subsidiary are different, the subsidiary prepares, for consolidation purposes, additional financial statements as of the same date as the financial statements of the parent unless it is impracticable to do so.

27 **When, in accordance with paragraph 26, the financial statements of a subsidiary used in the preparation of consolidated financial statements are prepared as of a reporting date different from that of the parent, adjustments shall be made for the effects of significant transactions or events that occur between that date and the date of the parents financial statements. In any case, the difference between the reporting date of the subsidiary and that of the parent shall be no more than three months. The length of the reporting periods and any difference in the reporting dates shall be the same from period to period.**

28 **Consolidated financial statements shall be prepared using uniform accounting policies for like transactions and other events in similar circumstances.**

29 If a member of the group uses accounting policies other than those adopted in the consolidated financial statements for like transactions and events in similar circumstances, appropriate adjustments are made to its financial statements in preparing the consolidated financial statements.

30 The income and expenses of a subsidiary are included in the consolidated financial statements from the acquisition date as defined in IFRS 3. The income and expenses of a subsidiary are included in the consolidated financial statements until the date on which the parent ceases to control the subsidiary. The difference between the proceeds from the disposal of the subsidiary and its carrying amount as of the date of disposal, including the cumulative amount of any exchange differences that relate to the subsidiary recognised in equity in accordance with IAS 21 *The Effects of Changes in Foreign Exchange Rates*, is recognised in the consolidated income statement as the gain or loss on the disposal of the subsidiary.

31 **An investment in an entity shall be accounted for in accordance with IAS 39** *Financial Instruments: Recognition and Measurement* **from the date that it ceases to be a subsidiary, provided that it does not become an associate as defined in IAS 28 or a jointly controlled entity as described in IAS 31.**

32 **The carrying amount of the investment at the date that the entity ceases to be a subsidiary shall be regarded as the cost on initial measurement of a financial asset in accordance with IAS 39.**

33 **Minority interests shall be presented in the consolidated balance sheet within equity, separately from the parent shareholders' equity. Minority interests in the profit or loss of the group shall also be separately disclosed.**

34 The profit or loss is attributed to the parent shareholders and minority interests. Because both are equity, the amount attributed to minority interests is not income or expense.

35 Losses applicable to the minority in a consolidated subsidiary may exceed the minority interest in the subsidiary's equity. The excess, and any further losses applicable to the minority, are allocated against the majority interest except to

the extent that the minority has a binding obligation and is able to make an additional investment to cover the losses. If the subsidiary subsequently reports profits, such profits are allocated to the majority interest until the minority's share of losses previously absorbed by the majority has been recovered.

36 If a subsidiary has outstanding cumulative preference shares that are held by minority interests and classified as equity, the parent computes its share of profits or losses after adjusting for the dividends on such shares, whether or not dividends have been declared.

Accounting for investments in subsidiaries, jointly controlled entities and associates in separate financial statements

37 When separate financial statements are prepared, investments in subsidiaries, jointly controlled entities and associates that are not classified as held for sale (or included in a disposal group that is classified as held for sale) in accordance with IFRS 5 shall be accounted for either:

(a) at cost, or

(b) in accordance with IAS 39.

The same accounting shall be applied for each category of investments. Investments in subsidiaries, jointly controlled entities and associates that are classified as held for sale (or included in a disposal group that is classified as held for sale) in accordance with IFRS 5 shall be accounted for in accordance with that IFRS.

38 This Standard does not mandate which entities produce separate financial statements available for public use. Paragraphs 37 and 39–42 apply when an entity prepares separate financial statements that comply with International Financial Reporting Standards. The entity also produces consolidated financial statements available for public use as required by paragraph 9, unless the exemption provided in paragraph 10 is applicable.

39 Investments in jointly controlled entities and associates that are accounted for in accordance with IAS 39 in the consolidated financial statements shall be accounted for in the same way in the investor's separate financial statements.

Disclosure

40 The following disclosures shall be made in consolidated financial statements:

(a) [Deleted]

(b) [Deleted]

(c) the nature of the relationship between the parent and a subsidiary when the parent does not own, directly or indirectly through subsidiaries, more than half of the voting power;

(d) the reasons why the ownership, directly or indirectly through subsidiaries, of more than half of the voting or potential voting power of an investee does not constitute control;

(e) the reporting date of the financial statements of a subsidiary when such financial statements are used to prepare consolidated financial statements and are as of a reporting date or for a period that is different from that of the parent, and the reason for using a different reporting date or period; and

(f) the nature and extent of any significant restrictions (eg resulting from borrowing arrangements or regulatory requirements) on the ability of subsidiaries to transfer funds to the parent in the form of cash dividends or to repay loans or advances.

41 **When separate financial statements are prepared for a parent that, in accordance with paragraph 10, elects not to prepare consolidated financial statements, those separate financial statements shall disclose:**

(a) the fact that the financial statements are separate financial statements; that the exemption from consolidation has been used; the name and country of incorporation or residence of the entity whose consolidated financial statements that comply with International Financial Reporting Standards have been produced for public use; and the address where those consolidated financial statements are obtainable;

(b) a list of significant investments in subsidiaries, jointly controlled entities and associates, including the name, country of incorporation or residence, proportion of ownership interest and, if different, proportion of voting power held; and

(c) a description of the method used to account for the investments listed under (b).

42 **When a parent (other than a parent covered by paragraph 41), venturer with an interest in a jointly controlled entity or an investor in an associate prepares separate financial statements, those separate financial statements shall disclose:**

(a) the fact that the statements are separate financial statements and the reasons why those statements are prepared if not required by law;

(b) a list of significant investments in subsidiaries, jointly controlled entities and associates, including the name, country of incorporation or residence, proportion of ownership interest and, if different, proportion of voting power held; and

(c) a description of the method used to account for the investments listed under (b);

and shall identify the financial statements prepared in accordance with paragraph 9 of this Standard, IAS 28 and IAS 31 to which they relate.

Effective date

43 **An entity shall apply this Standard for annual periods beginning on or after 1 January 2005. Earlier application is encouraged. If an entity applies this Standard for a period beginning before 1 January 2005, it shall disclose that fact.**

Withdrawal of other pronouncements

44 This Standard supersedes IAS 27 *Consolidated Financial Statements and Accounting for Investments in Subsidiaries* (revised in 2000).

45 This Standard supersedes SIC-33 *Consolidation and Equity Method—Potential Voting Rights and Allocation of Ownership Interests.*

Appendix
Amendments to other pronouncements

The amendments in this appendix shall be applied for annual periods beginning on or after 1 January 2005. If an entity applies this Standard for an earlier period, these amendments shall be applied for that earlier period.

* * * * *

The amendments contained in this appendix when this Standard was issued in 2003 have been incorporated into the relevant pronouncements published in this volume.

Approval of IAS 27 by the Board

International Accounting Standard 27 *Consolidated and Separate Financial Statements* was approved for issue by thirteen of the fourteen members of the International Accounting Standards Board. Mr Yamada dissented. His dissenting opinion is set out after the Basis for Conclusions.

Sir David Tweedie	Chairman
Thomas E Jones	Vice-Chairman
Mary E Barth	
Hans-Georg Bruns	
Anthony T Cope	
Robert P Garnett	
Gilbert Gélard	
James J Leisenring	
Warren J McGregor	
Patricia L O'Malley	
Harry K Schmid	
John T Smith	
Geoffrey Whittington	
Tatsumi Yamada	

Basis for Conclusions

This Basis for Conclusions accompanies, but is not part of, IAS 27.

Introduction

BC1 This Basis for Conclusions summarises the International Accounting Standards Board's considerations in reaching its conclusions on revising IAS 27 *Consolidated Financial Statements and Accounting for Investments in Subsidiaries* in 2003. Individual Board members gave greater weight to some factors than to others.

BC2 In July 2001 the Board announced that, as part of its initial agenda of technical projects, it would undertake a project to improve a number of Standards, including IAS 27. The project was undertaken in the light of queries and criticisms raised in relation to the Standards by securities regulators, professional accountants and other interested parties. The objectives of the Improvements project were to reduce or eliminate alternatives, redundancies and conflicts within Standards, to deal with some convergence issues and to make other improvements. In May 2002 the Board published its proposals in an Exposure Draft of *Improvements to International Accounting Standards*, with a comment deadline of 16 September 2002. The Board received over 160 comment letters on the Exposure Draft.

BC3 Because the Board's intention was not to reconsider the fundamental approach to consolidation established in IAS 27, this Basis for Conclusions does not discuss requirements in IAS 27 that the Board has not reconsidered.

Presentation of consolidated financial statements

Exemption from preparing consolidated financial statements

BC4 Paragraph 7 of the previous version of IAS 27 required consolidated financial statements to be presented. However, paragraph 8 permitted a parent that is a wholly-owned or virtually wholly-owned subsidiary not to prepare consolidated financial statements. The Board considered whether to withdraw or amend this exemption from the general requirement.

BC5 The Board decided to retain an exemption, so that entities in a group that are required by law to produce financial statements available for public use in accordance with International Financial Reporting Standards, in addition to consolidated financial statements, would not be unduly burdened.

BC6 The Board noted that in some circumstances users can find sufficient information for their purposes regarding a subsidiary from either its separate financial statements or consolidated financial statements. In addition, the users of financial statements of a subsidiary often have, or can get access to, more information.

BC7 Having agreed to retain an exemption, the Board decided to modify the circumstances in which an entity would be exempt and considered the following criteria.

Unanimous agreement of the owners of the minority interests

BC8 The Exposure Draft proposed to extend the exemption to a parent that is not wholly-owned if the owners of the minority interest, including those not otherwise entitled to vote, unanimously agree.

BC9 Some respondents disagreed with the proposal for unanimous agreement of minority shareholders to be a condition for exemption, in particular because of the practical difficulties in obtaining responses from all of those shareholders. The Board decided that the exemption should be available to a parent that is not wholly-owned when the owners of the minority interests have been informed about, and do not object to, consolidated financial statements not being presented.

Exemption available only to non-public entities

BC10 The Board believes that the information needs of users of financial statements of entities whose debt or equity instruments are traded in a public market are best served when investments in subsidiaries, jointly controlled entities and associates are accounted for in accordance with IASs 27, 28 *Investments in Associates* and 31 *Interests in Joint Ventures*. The Board therefore decided that the exemption from preparing such consolidated financial statements should not be available to such entities or to entities in the process of issuing instruments in a public market.

BC11 The Board decided that a parent that meets the criteria for exemption from the requirement to prepare consolidated financial statements should, in its separate financial statements, account for those subsidiaries in the same way as other parents, venturers with interests in jointly controlled entities or investors in associates account for investments in their separate financial statements. The Board draws a distinction between accounting for such investments as equity investments and accounting for the economic entity that the parent controls. In relation to the former, the Board decided that each category of investment should be accounted for consistently.

BC12 The Board decided that the same approach to accounting for investments in separate financial statements should apply irrespective of the circumstances for which they are prepared. Thus, parents that present consolidated financial statements, and those that do not because they are exempted, should present the same form of separate financial statements.

Scope of consolidated financial statements

Scope exclusions

BC13 Paragraph 13 of the previous version of IAS 27 required a subsidiary to be excluded from consolidation when control is intended to be temporary or when the subsidiary operates under severe long-term restrictions.

Temporary control

BC14 The Board considered whether to remove this scope exclusion and thereby converge with other standard-setters that had recently eliminated a similar exclusion. The Board decided to consider this issue as part of a comprehensive standard dealing with asset disposals. It decided to retain an exemption from consolidating a subsidiary when there is evidence that the subsidiary is acquired with the intention to dispose of it within twelve months and that management is actively seeking a buyer. The Board's Exposure Draft ED 4 *Disposal of Non-current Assets and Presentation of Discontinued Operations* proposes to measure and present assets held for sale in a consistent manner irrespective of whether they are held by an investor or in a subsidiary. Therefore, ED 4 proposes to eliminate the exemption from consolidation when control is intended to be temporary and contains a draft consequential amendment to IAS 27 to achieve this.*

Severe long–term restrictions impairing ability to transfer funds to the parent

BC15 The Board decided to remove the exclusion of a subsidiary from consolidation when there are severe long-term restrictions that impair a subsidiary's ability to transfer funds to the parent. It did so because such circumstances may not preclude control. The Board decided that a parent, when assessing its ability to control a subsidiary, should consider restrictions on the transfer of funds from the subsidiary to the parent. In themselves, such restrictions do not preclude control.

Venture capital organisations, private equity entities and similar organisations

BC16 The Exposure Draft of IAS 27 proposed to clarify that a subsidiary should not be excluded from consolidation simply because the entity is a venture capital organisation, mutual fund, unit trust or similar entity. Some respondents from the private equity industry disagreed with this proposed clarification. They argued that private equity entities should not be required to consolidate the investments they control in accordance with the requirements in IAS 27. They argued that they should measure those investments at fair value. Those respondents raised varying arguments–some based on whether control is exercised, some on the length of time that should be provided before consolidation is required, and some on whether consolidation was an appropriate basis for private equity entities or the type of investments they make.

* In March 2004, the Board issued IFRS 5 *Non-current Assets Held for Sale and Discontinued Operations*. IFRS 5 removes this scope exclusion and now eliminates the exemption from consolidation when control is intended to be temporary. See IFRS 5 Basis for Conclusions for further discussion.

BC17 Some respondents also noted that the Board decided to exclude venture capital organisations and similar entities from the scope of IASs 28 and 31 when investments in associates or jointly controlled entities are measured at fair value in accordance with IAS 39 *Financial Instruments: Recognition and Measurement*. In the view of these respondents, the Board was proposing that similar assets should be accounted for in dissimilar ways.

BC18 The Board did not accept these arguments. The Board noted that these issues are not specific to the private equity industry. It confirmed that a subsidiary should not be excluded from consolidation on the basis of the nature of the controlling entity. Consolidation is based on the parent's ability to control the investee, which captures both the power to control (ie the ability exists but it is not exercised) and actual control (ie the ability is exercised). Consolidation is triggered by control and should not be affected by whether management intends to hold an investment in an entity that it controls for the short term.

BC19 The Board noted that the exception from the consolidation principle in the previous version of IAS 27, when control of a subsidiary is intended to be temporary, might have been misread or interpreted loosely. Some respondents to the Exposure Draft had interpreted 'near future' as covering a period of up to five years. The Board decided to remove these words and to restrict the exception to subsidiaries acquired and held exclusively for disposal within twelve months, providing that management is actively seeking a buyer.

BC20 The Board did not agree that it should differentiate between types of entity, or types of investment, when applying a control model of consolidation. It also did not agree that management intention should be a determinant of control. Even if it had wished to make such differentiations, the Board did not see how or why it would be meaningful to distinguish private equity investors from other types of entities.

BC21 The Board believes that the diversity of the investment portfolios of entities operating in the private equity sector is not different from the diversification of portfolios held by a conglomerate, which is an industrial group made up of entities that often have diverse and unrelated interests. The Board acknowledged that financial information about an entity's different types of products and services and its operations in different geographical areas—segment information—is relevant to assessing the risks and returns of a diversified or multinational entity and may not be determinable from the aggregated data presented in the consolidated balance sheet. The Board noted that IAS 14 *Segment Reporting* establishes principles for reporting segment information by entities whose equity or debt instruments are publicly traded, or any entity that discloses segment information voluntarily.

BC22 The Board concluded that for investments under the control of private equity entities, users' information needs are best served by financial statements in which those investments are consolidated, thus revealing the extent of the operations of the entities they control. The Board noted that a parent can either present information about the fair value of those investments in the notes to the consolidated financial statements or prepare separate financial statements in addition to its consolidated financial statements, presenting those investments at cost or at fair value. By contrast, the Board decided that information needs of users of financial statements would not be well served if those controlling investments were measured only at fair value. This would leave unreported the assets and liabilities of a controlled entity. It is conceivable that an investment in a large, highly geared subsidiary would have only a small fair value. Reporting that value alone would preclude a user from being able to assess the financial position, results and cash flows of the group.

Minority interests

BC23 Minority interest is defined in IAS 27 and IFRS 3 *Business Combinations* as that part of the profit or loss and net assets of a subsidiary attributable to equity interests that are not owned, directly or indirectly through subsidiaries, by the parent. Paragraph 26 of the previous version of IAS 27 required minority interests to be presented in the consolidated balance sheet separately from liabilities and the parent shareholders' equity.

BC24 The Board decided to amend this requirement and to require minority interests to be presented in the consolidated balance sheet within equity, separately from the parent shareholders' equity. The Board agreed that a minority interest is not a liability of a group because it does not meet the definition of a liability in the *Framework for the Preparation and Presentation of Financial Statements*.

BC25 Paragraph 49(b) of the *Framework* states that a liability is a present obligation of the entity arising from past events, the settlement of which is expected to result in an outflow from the entity of resources embodying economic benefits. Paragraph 60 of the *Framework* further indicates that an essential characteristic of a liability is that the entity has a present obligation and that an obligation is a duty or responsibility to act or perform in a particular way. The Board noted that the existence of a minority interest in the net assets of a subsidiary does not give rise to a present obligation of the group, the settlement of which is expected to result in an outflow of economic benefits from the group.

BC26 Rather, the Board noted that a minority interest represents the residual interest in the net assets of those subsidiaries held by some of the shareholders of the subsidiaries within the group, and therefore meets the *Framework*'s definition of equity. Paragraph 49(c) of the *Framework* states that equity is the residual interest in the assets of the entity after deducting all its liabilities.

BC27 The Board acknowledged that this decision gives rise to questions about the recognition and measurement of minority interests but it concluded that the proposed presentation is consistent with current standards and the *Framework* and would provide better comparability than presentation in the consolidated balance sheet with either liabilities or parent shareholders' equity. It decided that the recognition and measurement questions should be addressed as part of its project on business combinations.

Measurement of investments in subsidiaries, jointly controlled entities and associates in separate financial statements

BC28 Paragraph 29 of the previous version of IAS 27 permitted investments in subsidiaries to be measured in any one of three ways in a parent's separate financial statements. These were cost, the equity method, or as available-for-sale financial assets in accordance with IAS 39. Paragraph 12 of the previous version of IAS 28 permitted the same choices for investments in associates in separate financial statements, and paragraph 38 of the previous version of IAS 31 mentioned that IAS 31 did not indicate a preference for any particular treatment for accounting for interests in jointly controlled entities in a venturer's separate financial statements. The Board decided to require use of cost or IAS 39 for all investments included in separate financial statements.

BC29 Although the equity method would provide users with some profit and loss information similar to that obtained from consolidation, the Board noted that such information is reflected in the investor's economic entity financial statements and does not need to be provided to the users of its separate financial statements. For separate statements, the focus is upon the performance of the assets as investments. The Board concluded that separate financial statements prepared using either the fair value method in accordance with IAS 39 or the cost method would be relevant. Using the fair value method in accordance with IAS 39 would provide a measure of the economic value of the investments. Using the cost method can result in relevant information, depending on the purpose of preparing the separate financial statements. For example, they may be needed only by particular parties to determine the dividend income from subsidiaries.

BC30 [Deleted]

Dissenting Opinion

DO1 Mr Yamada dissents from this Standard because he believes that the change in classification of minority interests in the consolidated balance sheet, that is to say, the requirement that it be shown as equity, should not be made as part of the Improvements project. He agrees that minority interests do not meet the definition of a liability under the *Framework for the Preparation and Presentation of Financial Statements*, as stated in paragraph BC25 of the Basis for Conclusions, and that the current requirement, for minority interests to be presented separately from liabilities and the parent shareholders' equity, is not desirable. However, he does not believe that this requirement should be altered at this stage. He believes that before making the change in classification, which will have a wide variety of impacts on current consolidation practices, various issues related to this change need to be considered comprehensively by the Board. These include consideration of the objectives of consolidated financial statements and the accounting procedures that should flow from those objectives. Even though the Board concluded as noted in paragraph BC27, he believes that the decision related to the classification of minority interests should not be made until such a comprehensive consideration of recognition and measurement is completed.

DO2 Traditionally, there are two views of the objectives of consolidated financial statements; they are implicit in the parent company view and the economic entity view. Mr Yamada believes that the objectives, that is to say, what information should be provided and to whom, should be considered by the Board before it makes its decision on the classification of minority interests in IAS 27. He is of the view that the Board is taking the economic entity view without giving enough consideration to this fundamental issue.

DO3 Step acquisitions are being discussed in the second phase of the Business Combinations project, which is not yet finalised at the time of finalising IAS 27 under the Improvements project. When the ownership interest of the parent increases, the Board has tentatively decided that the difference between the consideration paid by the parent to minority interests and the carrying value of the ownership interests acquired by the parent is recognised as part of equity, which is different from the current practice of recognising a change in the amount of goodwill. If the parent retains control of a subsidiary but its ownership interest decreases, the difference between the consideration received by the parent and the carrying value of the ownership interests transferred is also recognised as part of equity, which is different from the current practice of recognising a gain or a loss. Mr Yamada believes that the results of this discussion are predetermined by the decision related to the classification of minority interests as equity. The changes in accounting treatments are fundamental and he believes that the decision on which of the two views should govern the consolidated financial statements should be taken only after careful consideration of the ramifications. He believes that the amendment of IAS 27 relating to the classification of minority interests should not be made before completion of the second phase of the Business Combinations project.

Implementation Guidance
Guidance on implementing IAS 27 *Consolidated and Separate Financial Statements*, IAS 28 *Investments in Associates* and IAS 31 *Interests in Joint Ventures*

This guidance accompanies IAS 27, IAS 28 and IAS 31, but is not part of them.

Consideration of potential voting rights

Introduction

IG1 Paragraphs 14, 15 and 23 of IAS 27 *Consolidated and Separate Financial Statements* and paragraphs 8 and 9 of IAS 28 *Investments in Associates* require an entity to consider the existence and effect of all potential voting rights that are currently exercisable or convertible. They also require all facts and circumstances that affect potential voting rights to be examined, except the intention of management and the financial ability to exercise or convert potential voting rights. Because the definition of joint control in paragraph 3 of IAS 31 *Interests in Joint Ventures* depends upon the definition of control, and because that Standard is linked to IAS 28 for application of the equity method, this guidance is also relevant to IAS 31.

Guidance

IG2 Paragraph 4 of IAS 27 defines control as the power to govern the financial and operating policies of an entity so as to obtain benefits from its activities. Paragraph 2 of IAS 28 defines significant influence as the power to participate in the financial and operating policy decisions of the investee but not to control those policies. Paragraph 3 of IAS 31 defines joint control as the contractually agreed sharing of control over an economic activity. In these contexts, power refers to the ability to do or effect something. Consequently, an entity has control, joint control or significant influence when it currently has the ability to exercise that power, regardless of whether control, joint control or significant influence is actively demonstrated or is passive in nature. Potential voting rights held by an entity that are currently exercisable or convertible provide this ability. The ability to exercise power does not exist when potential voting rights lack economic substance (eg the exercise price is set in a manner that precludes exercise or conversion in any feasible scenario). Consequently, potential voting rights are considered when, in substance, they provide the ability to exercise power.

IG3 Control and significant influence also arise in the circumstances described in paragraph 13 of IAS 27 and paragraphs 6 and 7 of IAS 28 respectively, which include consideration of the relative ownership of voting rights. IAS 31 depends on IAS 27 and IAS 28 and references to IAS 27 and IAS 28 from this point onwards should be read as being relevant to IAS 31. Nevertheless it should be borne in mind that joint control involves contractual sharing of control and this contractual aspect is likely to be the critical determinant. Potential voting rights such as share call options and convertible debt are capable of changing an entity's voting power over another entity–if the potential voting rights are exercised or converted, then the relative ownership of the ordinary shares carrying voting rights changes. Consequently, the existence of control (the definition of which permits only one entity to have control of another entity) and significant influence are determined only after assessing all the factors described in paragraph 13 of IAS 27 and paragraphs 6 and 7 of IAS 28 respectively, and considering the existence and effect of potential voting rights. In addition, the entity examines all facts and circumstances that affect potential voting rights except the intention of management and the financial ability to exercise or convert. The intention of management does not affect the existence of power and the financial ability of an entity to exercise or convert is difficult to assess.

IG4 An entity may initially conclude that it controls or significantly influences another entity after considering the potential voting rights that it can currently exercise or convert. However, the entity may not control or significantly influence the other entity when potential voting rights held by other parties are also currently exercisable or convertible. Consequently, an entity considers all potential voting rights held by it and by other parties that are currently exercisable or convertible when determining whether it controls or significantly influences another entity. For example, all share call options are considered, whether held by the entity or another party. Furthermore, the definition of control in paragraph 4 of IAS 27 permits only one entity to have control of another entity. Therefore, when two or more entities each hold significant voting rights, both actual and potential, the factors in paragraph 13 of IAS 27 are reassessed to determine which entity has control.

IG5 The proportion allocated to the parent and minority interests in preparing consolidated financial statements in accordance with IAS 27, and the proportion allocated to an investor that accounts for its investment using the equity method in accordance with IAS 28, are determined solely on the basis of present ownership interests. The proportion allocated is determined taking into account the eventual exercise of potential voting rights and other derivatives that, in substance, give access at present to the economic benefits associated with an ownership interest.

IG6 In some circumstances an entity has, in substance, a present ownership as a result of a transaction that gives it access to the economic benefits associated with an ownership interest. In such circumstances, the proportion allocated is determined taking into account the eventual exercise of those potential voting rights and other derivatives that give the entity access to the economic benefits at present.

IG7 IAS 39 *Financial Instruments: Recognition and Measurement* does not apply to interests in subsidiaries, associates and jointly controlled entities that are consolidated, accounted for using the equity method or proportionately consolidated in accordance with IAS 27, IAS 28 and IAS 31 respectively. When instruments containing potential voting rights in substance currently give access to the economic benefits associated with an ownership interest, and the investment is accounted for in one of the above ways, the instruments are not subject to the requirements of IAS 39. In all other cases, instruments containing potential voting rights are accounted for in accordance with IAS 39.

Illustrative examples

IG8 The five examples below each illustrate one aspect of a potential voting right. In applying IAS 27, IAS 28 or IAS 31, an entity considers all aspects. The existence of control, significant influence and joint control can be determined only after assessing the other factors described in IAS 27, IAS 28 and IAS 31. For the purpose of these examples, however, those other factors are presumed not to affect the determination, even though they may affect it when assessed.

Example 1: Options are out of the money

Entities A and B own 80 per cent and 20 per cent respectively of the ordinary shares that carry voting rights at a general meeting of shareholders of Entity C. Entity A sells one-half of its interest to Entity D and buys call options from Entity D that are exercisable at any time at a premium to the market price when issued, and if exercised would give Entity A its original 80 per cent ownership interest and voting rights.

Though the options are out of the money, they are currently exercisable and give Entity A the power to continue to set the operating and financial policies of Entity C, because Entity A could exercise its options now. The existence of the potential voting rights, as well as the other factors described in paragraph 13 of IAS 27, are considered and it is determined that Entity A controls Entity C.

Example 2: Possibility of exercise or conversion

Entities A, B and C own 40 per cent, 30 per cent and 30 per cent respectively of the ordinary shares that carry voting rights at a general meeting of shareholders of Entity D. Entity A also owns call options that are exercisable at any time at the fair value of the underlying shares and if exercised would give it an additional 20 per cent of the voting rights in Entity D and reduce Entity B's and Entity C's interests to 20 per cent each. If the options are exercised, Entity A will have control over more than one-half of the voting power. The existence of the potential voting rights, as well as the other factors described in paragraph 13 of IAS 27 and paragraphs 6 and 7 of IAS 28, are considered and it is determined that Entity A controls Entity D.

Example 3: Other rights that have the potential to increase an entity's voting power or reduce another entity's voting power

Entities A, B and C own 25 per cent, 35 per cent and 40 per cent respectively of the ordinary shares that carry voting rights at a general meeting of shareholders of Entity D. Entities B and C also have share warrants that are exercisable at any time at a fixed price and provide potential voting rights. Entity A has a call option to purchase these share warrants at any time for a nominal amount. If the call option is exercised, Entity A would have the potential to increase its ownership interest, and thereby its voting rights, in Entity D to 51 per cent (and dilute Entity B's interest to 23 per cent and Entity C's interest to 26 per cent).

Although the share warrants are not owned by Entity A, they are considered in assessing control because they are currently exercisable by Entities B and C. Normally, if an action (eg purchase or exercise of another right) is required before an entity has ownership of a potential voting right, the potential voting right is not regarded as held by the entity. However, the share warrants are, in substance, held by Entity A, because the terms of the call option are designed to ensure Entity A's position. The combination of the call option and share warrants gives Entity A the power to set the operating and financial policies of Entity D, because Entity A could currently exercise the option and share warrants.

The other factors described in paragraph 13 of IAS 27 and paragraphs 6 and 7 of IAS 28 are also considered, and it is determined that Entity A, not Entity B or C, controls Entity D.

Example 4: Management intention

Entities A, B and C each own 33⅓ per cent of the ordinary shares that carry voting rights at a general meeting of shareholders of Entity D. Entities A, B and C each have the right to appoint two directors to the board of Entity D. Entity A also owns call options that are exercisable at a fixed price at any time and if exercised would give it all the voting rights in Entity D. The management of Entity A does not intend to exercise the call options, even if Entities B and C do not vote in the same manner as Entity A. The existence of the potential voting rights, as well as the other factors described in paragraph 13 of IAS 27 and paragraphs 6 and 7 of IAS 28, are considered and it is determined that Entity A controls Entity D. The intention of Entity A's management does not influence the assessment.

Example 5: Financial ability

Entities A and B own 55 per cent and 45 per cent respectively of the ordinary shares that carry voting rights at a general meeting of shareholders of Entity C. Entity B also holds debt instruments that are convertible into ordinary shares of Entity C. The debt can be converted at a substantial price, in comparison with Entity B's net assets, at any time and if converted would require Entity B to borrow additional funds to make the payment. If the debt were to be converted, Entity B would hold 70 per cent of the voting rights and Entity A's interest would reduce to 30 per cent.

Although the debt instruments are convertible at a substantial price, they are currently convertible and the conversion feature gives Entity B the power to set the operating and financial policies of Entity C. The existence of the potential voting rights, as well as the other factors described in paragraph 13 of IAS 27, are considered and it is determined that Entity B, not Entity A, controls Entity C. The financial ability of Entity B to pay the conversion price does not influence the assessment.

Table of Concordance

This table shows how the contents of the superseded version of IAS 27 and the current version of IAS 27 correspond. Paragraphs are treated as corresponding if they broadly address the same matter even though the guidance may differ.

The table also shows how the requirements of SIC Interpretation SIC-33 have been incorporated into the current version of IAS 27.

Superseded IAS 27 paragraph	Current IAS 27 paragraph
1	1
2	3
3	None
4	None
5	2
6	4
7	9
8	10, 41
9	None
10	None
11	12
12	13
13	None
14	20
15	22

Superseded IAS 27 paragraph	Current IAS 27 paragraph
16	None
17	24
18	25
19	26
20	27
21	28
22	29
23	30
24	31
25	32
26	33
27	35
28	36
29	37
30	39

Superseded IAS 27 paragraph	Current IAS 27 paragraph
31	3
32	40
33	43
SIC-33	14, 15
None	5–8
None	11
None	19
None	21
None	23
None	34
None	38
None	41, 42
None	44, 45

International Accounting Standard 28

Investments in Associates

This version includes amendments resulting from new and amended IFRSs issued up to 31 December 2004.

CONTENTS

International Accounting Standard 28 *Investments in Associates* (IAS 28) is set out in paragraphs 1–43 and the Appendix. All the paragraphs have equal authority but retain the IASC format of the Standard when it was adopted by the IASB. IAS 28 should be read in the context of the Basis for Conclusions, the *Preface to International Financial Reporting Standards* and the *Framework for the Preparation and Presentation of Financial Statements*. IAS 8 *Accounting Policies, Changes in Accounting Estimates and Errors* provides a basis for selecting and applying accounting policies in the absence of explicit guidance.

Introduction

IN1 International Accounting Standard 28 *Investments in Associates* replaces IAS 28 *Accounting for Investments in Associates* (revised in 2000) and should be applied for annual periods beginning on or after 1 January 2005. Earlier application is encouraged. The Standard also replaces the following Interpretations:

- SIC-3 *Elimination of Unrealised Profits and Losses on Transactions with Associates*
- SIC-20 *Equity Accounting Method—Recognition of Losses*
- SIC-33 *Consolidation and Equity Method—Potential Voting Rights and Allocation of Ownership Interests.*

Reasons for revising IAS 28

IN2 The International Accounting Standards Board developed this revised IAS 28 as part of its project on Improvements to International Accounting Standards. The project was undertaken in the light of queries and criticisms raised in relation to the Standards by securities regulators, professional accountants and other interested parties. The objectives of the project were to reduce or eliminate alternatives, redundancies and conflicts within the Standards, to deal with some convergence issues and to make other improvements.

IN3 For IAS 28 the Board's main objective was to reduce alternatives in the application of the equity method and in accounting for investments in associates in separate financial statements. The Board did not reconsider the fundamental approach when accounting for investments in associates using the equity method contained in IAS 28.

The main changes

IN4 The main changes from the previous version of IAS 28 are described below.

Scope

IN5 The Standard does not apply to investments that would otherwise be associates or interests of venturers in jointly controlled entities held by venture capital organisations, mutual funds, unit trusts and similar entities when those investments are classified as held for trading and accounted for in accordance with IAS 39 *Financial Instruments: Recognition and Measurement.* Those investments are measured at fair value, with changes in fair value recognised in profit or loss in the period in which they occur.

IN6 Furthermore, the Standard provides exemptions from application of the equity method similar to those provided for certain parents not to prepare consolidated financial statements. These exemptions include when the investor is also a parent exempt in accordance with IAS 27 *Consolidated and Separate Financial Statements* from preparing consolidated financial statements (paragraph 13(b)), and when the investor, though not such a parent, can satisfy the same type of conditions that exempt such parents (paragraph 13(c)).

Significant influence

Potential voting rights

IN7 An entity is required to consider the existence and effect of potential voting rights currently exercisable or convertible when assessing whether it has the power to participate in the financial and operating policy decisions of the investee. This requirement was previously included in SIC-33, which has been superseded.

Equity method

IN8 The Standard clarifies that investments in associates over which the investor has significant influence must be accounted for using the equity method whether or not the investor also has investments in subsidiaries and prepares consolidated financial statements. However, the investor does not apply the equity method when presenting separate financial statements prepared in accordance with IAS 27.

Exemption from applying the equity method

IN9 The Standard does not require the equity method to be applied when an associate is acquired and held with a view to its disposal within twelve months of acquisition. There must be evidence that the investment is acquired with the intention to dispose of it and that management is actively seeking a buyer. The words 'in the near future' were replaced with the words 'within twelve months'. When such an associate is not disposed of within twelve months it must be accounted for using the equity method as from the date of acquisition, except in narrowly specified circumstances.*

IN10 The Standard does not permit an investor that continues to have significant influence over an associate not to apply the equity method when the associate is operating under severe long-term restrictions that significantly impair its ability to transfer funds to the investor. Significant influence must be lost before the equity method ceases to be applicable.

Elimination of unrealised profits and losses on transactions with associates

IN11 Profits and losses resulting from 'upstream' and 'downstream' transactions between an investor and an associate must be eliminated to the extent of the investor's interest in the associate. The consensus in SIC-3 has been incorporated into the Standard.

Non–coterminous year–ends

IN12 When financial statements of an associate used in applying the equity method are prepared as of a reporting date that is different from that of the investor, the difference must be no greater than three months.

---

* In March 2004, the Board issued IFRS 5 *Non-current Assets Held for Sale and Discontinued Operations*. IFRS 5 removes this scope exclusion and now eliminates the exemption from applying the equity method when significant influence over an associate is intended to be temporary. See IFRS 5 Basis for Conclusions for further discussion.

Uniform accounting policies

IN13 The Standard requires an investor to make appropriate adjustments to the associate's financial statements to conform them to the investor's accounting policies for reporting like transactions and other events in similar circumstances. The previous version of IAS 28 provided an exception to this requirement when it was 'not practicable to use uniform accounting policies'.

Recognition of losses

IN14 An investor must consider the carrying amount of its investment in the equity of the associate and its other long-term interests in the associate when recognising its share of losses of the associate. SIC-20 limited the recognition of the investor's share of losses to the carrying amount of its investment in the equity of the associate. Therefore, that Interpretation has been superseded.

Separate financial statements

IN15 The requirements for the preparation of an investor's separate financial statements are established by reference to IAS 27.

International Accounting Standard 28 Investments in Associates

Scope

1 **This Standard shall be applied in accounting for investments in associates. However, it does not apply to investments in associates held by:**

(a) venture capital organisations, or

(b) mutual funds, unit trusts and similar entities including investment-linked insurance funds

that upon initial recognition are designated as at fair value through profit or loss or are classified as held for trading and accounted for in accordance with IAS 39 *Financial Instruments: Recognition and Measurement*. **Such investments shall be measured at fair value in accordance with IAS 39, with changes in fair value recognised in profit or loss in the period of the change.**

Definitions

2 **The following terms are used in this Standard with the meanings specified:**

An *associate* **is an entity, including an unincorporated entity such as a partnership, over which the investor has significant influence and that is neither a subsidiary nor an interest in a joint venture.**

Consolidated financial statements **are the financial statements of a group presented as those of a single economic entity.**

Control **is the power to govern the financial and operating policies of an entity so as to obtain benefits from its activities.**

The *equity method* **is a method of accounting whereby the investment is initially recognised at cost and adjusted thereafter for the post-acquisition change in the investor's share of net assets of the investee. The profit or loss of the investor includes the investor's share of the profit or loss of the investee.**

Joint control **is the contractually agreed sharing of control over an economic activity, and exists only when the strategic financial and operating decisions relating to the activity require the unanimous consent of the parties sharing control (the venturers).**

Separate financial statements **are those presented by a parent, an investor in an associate or a venturer in a jointly controlled entity, in which the investments are accounted for on the basis of the direct equity interest rather than on the basis of the reported results and net assets of the investees.**

Significant influence **is the power to participate in the financial and operating policy decisions of the investee but is not control or joint control over those policies.**

A *subsidiary* is an entity, including an unincorporated entity such as a partnership, that is controlled by another entity (known as the parent).

3 Financial statements in which the equity method is applied are not separate financial statements, nor are the financial statements of an entity that does not have a subsidiary, associate or venturer's interest in a joint venture.

4 Separate financial statements are those presented in addition to consolidated financial statements, financial statements in which investments are accounted for using the equity method and financial statements in which venturers' interests in joint ventures are proportionately consolidated. Separate financial statements may or may not be appended to, or accompany, those financial statements.

5 Entities that are exempted in accordance with paragraph 10 of IAS 27 *Consolidated and Separate Financial Statements* from consolidation, paragraph 2 of IAS 31 *Interests in Joint Ventures* from applying proportionate consolidation or paragraph 13(c) of this Standard from applying the equity method may present separate financial statements as their only financial statements.

Significant influence

6 If an investor holds, directly or indirectly (eg through subsidiaries), 20 per cent or more of the voting power of the investee, it is presumed that the investor has significant influence, unless it can be clearly demonstrated that this is not the case. Conversely, if the investor holds, directly or indirectly (eg through subsidiaries), less than 20 per cent of the voting power of the investee, it is presumed that the investor does not have significant influence, unless such influence can be clearly demonstrated. A substantial or majority ownership by another investor does not necessarily preclude an investor from having significant influence.

7 The existence of significant influence by an investor is usually evidenced in one or more of the following ways:

(a) representation on the board of directors or equivalent governing body of the investee;

(b) participation in policy-making processes, including participation in decisions about dividends or other distributions;

(c) material transactions between the investor and the investee;

(d) interchange of managerial personnel; or

(e) provision of essential technical information.

8 An entity may own share warrants, share call options, debt or equity instruments that are convertible into ordinary shares, or other similar instruments that have the potential, if exercised or converted, to give the entity additional voting power or reduce another party's voting power over the financial and operating policies of another entity (ie potential voting rights). The existence and effect of potential voting rights that are currently exercisable or convertible, including potential voting rights held by other entities, are considered when assessing whether an entity has significant influence. Potential voting rights are not currently

exercisable or convertible when, for example, they cannot be exercised or converted until a future date or until the occurrence of a future event.

9 In assessing whether potential voting rights contribute to significant influence, the entity examines all facts and circumstances (including the terms of exercise of the potential voting rights and any other contractual arrangements whether considered individually or in combination) that affect potential rights, except the intention of management and the financial ability to exercise or convert.

10 An entity loses significant influence over an investee when it loses the power to participate in the financial and operating policy decisions of that investee. The loss of significant influence can occur with or without a change in absolute or relative ownership levels. It could occur, for example, when an associate becomes subject to the control of a government, court, administrator or regulator. It could also occur as a result of a contractual agreement.

Equity method

11 Under the equity method, the investment in an associate is initially recognised at cost and the carrying amount is increased or decreased to recognise the investor's share of the profit or loss of the investee after the date of acquisition. The investor's share of the profit or loss of the investee is recognised in the investor's profit or loss. Distributions received from an investee reduce the carrying amount of the investment. Adjustments to the carrying amount may also be necessary for changes in the investor's proportionate interest in the investee arising from changes in the investee's equity that have not been recognised in the investee's profit or loss. Such changes include those arising from the revaluation of property, plant and equipment and from foreign exchange translation differences. The investor's share of those changes is recognised directly in equity of the investor.

12 When potential voting rights exist, the investor's share of profit or loss of the investee and of changes in the investee's equity is determined on the basis of present ownership interests and does not reflect the possible exercise or conversion of potential voting rights.

Application of the equity method

13 An investment in an associate shall be accounted for using the equity method except when:

(a) the investment is classified as held for sale in accordance with IFRS 5 *Non-current Assets Held for Sale and Discontinued Operations*;

(b) the exception in paragraph 10 of IAS 27, allowing a parent that also has an investment in an associate not to present consolidated financial statements, applies; or

(c) all of the following apply:

(i) the investor is a wholly-owned subsidiary, or is a partially-owned subsidiary of another entity and its other owners, including those not otherwise entitled to vote, have been informed about, and do not object to, the investor not applying the equity method;

(ii) **the investor's debt or equity instruments are not traded in a public market (a domestic or foreign stock exchange or an over-the-counter market, including local and regional markets);**

(iii) **the investor did not file, nor is it in the process of filing, its financial statements with a securities commission or other regulatory organisation, for the purpose of issuing any class of instruments in a public market; and**

(iv) **the ultimate or any intermediate parent of the investor produces consolidated financial statements available for public use that comply with International Financial Reporting Standards.**

14 **Investments described in paragraph 13(a) shall be accounted for in accordance with IFRS 5.**

15 When an investment in an associate previously classified as held for sale no longer meets the criteria to be so classified, it shall be accounted for using the equity method as from the date of its classification as held for sale. Financial statements for the periods since classification as held for sale shall be amended accordingly.

16 [Deleted]

17 The recognition of income on the basis of distributions received may not be an adequate measure of the income earned by an investor on an investment in an associate because the distributions received may bear little relation to the performance of the associate. Because the investor has significant influence over the associate, the investor has an interest in the associate's performance and, as a result, the return on its investment. The investor accounts for this interest by extending the scope of its financial statements to include its share of profits or losses of such an associate. As a result, application of the equity method provides more informative reporting of the net assets and profit or loss of the investor.

18 **An investor shall discontinue the use of the equity method from the date that it ceases to have significant influence over an associate and shall account for the investment in accordance with IAS 39 from that date, provided the associate does not become a subsidiary or a joint venture as defined in IAS 31.**

19 **The carrying amount of the investment at the date that it ceases to be an associate shall be regarded as its cost on initial measurement as a financial asset in accordance with IAS 39.**

20 Many of the procedures appropriate for the application of the equity method are similar to the consolidation procedures described in IAS 27. Furthermore, the concepts underlying the procedures used in accounting for the acquisition of a subsidiary are also adopted in accounting for the acquisition of an investment in an associate.

21 A group's share in an associate is the aggregate of the holdings in that associate by the parent and its subsidiaries. The holdings of the group's other associates or joint ventures are ignored for this purpose. When an associate has subsidiaries, associates, or joint ventures, the profits or losses and net assets taken into account in applying the equity method are those recognised in the associate's financial

statements (including the associate's share of the profits or losses and net assets of its associates and joint ventures), after any adjustments necessary to give effect to uniform accounting policies (see paragraphs 26 and 27).

22 Profits and losses resulting from 'upstream' and 'downstream' transactions between an investor (including its consolidated subsidiaries) and an associate are recognised in the investor's financial statements only to the extent of unrelated investors' interests in the associate. 'Upstream' transactions are, for example, sales of assets from an associate to the investor. 'Downstream' transactions are, for example, sales of assets from the investor to an associate. The investor's share in the associate's profits and losses resulting from these transactions is eliminated.

23 An investment in an associate is accounted for using the equity method from the date on which it becomes an associate. On acquisition of the investment any difference between the cost of the investment and the investor's share of the net fair value of the associate 's identifiable assets, liabilities and contingent liabilities is accounted for in accordance with IFRS 3 *Business Combinations*. Therefore:

(a) goodwill relating to an associate is included in the carrying amount of the investment. However, amortisation of that goodwill is not permitted and is therefore not included in the determination of the investor's share of the associate's profits or losses.

(b) any excess of the investor's share of the net fair value of the associate's identifiable assets, liabilities and contingent liabilities over the cost of the investment is excluded from the carrying amount of the investment and is instead included as income in the determination of the investor's share of the associate's profit or loss in the period in which the investment is acquired.

Appropriate adjustments to the investor's share of the associate's profits or losses after acquisition are also made to account, for example, for depreciation of the depreciable assets based on their fair values at the acquisition date. Similarly, appropriate adjustments to the investor's share of the associate's profits or losses after acquisition are made for impairment losses recognised by the associate, such as for goodwill or property, plant and equipment.

24 The most recent available financial statements of the associate are used by the investor in applying the equity method. When the reporting dates of the investor and the associate are different, the associate prepares, for the use of the investor, financial statements as of the same date as the financial statements of the investor unless it is impracticable to do so.

25 When, in accordance with paragraph 24, the financial statements of an associate used in applying the equity method are prepared as of a different reporting date from that of the investor, adjustments shall be made for the effects of significant transactions or events that occur between that date and the date of the investor's financial statements. In any case, the difference between the reporting date of the associate and that of the investor shall be no more than three months. The length of the reporting periods and any difference in the reporting dates shall be the same from period to period.

26 **The investor's financial statements shall be prepared using uniform accounting policies for like transactions and events in similar circumstances.**

27 If an associate uses accounting policies other than those of the investor for like transactions and events in similar circumstances, adjustments shall be made to conform the associate's accounting policies to those of the investor when the associate's financial statements are used by the investor in applying the equity method.

28 If an associate has outstanding cumulative preference shares that are held by parties other than the investor and classified as equity, the investor computes its share of profits or losses after adjusting for the dividends on such shares, whether or not the dividends have been declared.

29 If an investor's share of losses of an associate equals or exceeds its interest in the associate, the investor discontinues recognising its share of further losses. The interest in an associate is the carrying amount of the investment in the associate under the equity method together with any long-term interests that, in substance, form part of the investor's net investment in the associate. For example, an item for which settlement is neither planned nor likely to occur in the foreseeable future is, in substance, an extension of the entity's investment in that associate. Such items may include preference shares and long-term receivables or loans but do not include trade receivables, trade payables or any long-term receivables for which adequate collateral exists, such as secured loans. Losses recognised under the equity method in excess of the investor's investment in ordinary shares are applied to the other components of the investor's interest in an associate in the reverse order of their seniority (ie priority in liquidation).

30 After the investor's interest is reduced to zero, additional losses are provided for, and a liability is recognised, only to the extent that the investor has incurred legal or constructive obligations or made payments on behalf of the associate. If the associate subsequently reports profits, the investor resumes recognising its share of those profits only after its share of the profits equals the share of losses not recognised.

Impairment losses

31 After application of the equity method, including recognising the associate's losses in accordance with paragraph 29, the investor applies the requirements of IAS 39 to determine whether it is necessary to recognise any additional impairment loss with respect to the investor's net investment in the associate.

32 The investor also applies the requirements of IAS 39 to determine whether any additional impairment loss is recognised with respect to the investor's interest in the associate that does not constitute part of the net investment and the amount of that impairment loss.

33 Because goodwill included in the carrying amount of an investment in an associate is not separately recognised, it is not tested for impairment separately by applying the requirements for impairment testing goodwill in IAS 36 *Impairment of Assets*. Instead, the entire carrying amount of the investment is tested under IAS 36 for impairment, by comparing its recoverable amount (higher of value in

use and fair value less costs to sell) with its carrying amount, whenever application of the requirements in IAS 39 indicates that the investment may be impaired. In determining the value in use of the investment, an entity estimates:

(a) its share of the present value of the estimated future cash flows expected to be generated by the associate, including the cash flows from the operations of the associate and the proceeds on the ultimate disposal of the investment; or

(b) the present value of the estimated future cash flows expected to arise from dividends to be received from the investment and from its ultimate disposal.

Under appropriate assumptions, both methods give the same result.

34 The recoverable amount of an investment in an associate is assessed for each associate, unless the associate does not generate cash inflows from continuing use that are largely independent of those from other assets of the entity.

Separate financial statements

35 **An investment in an associate shall be accounted for in the investor's separate financial statements in accordance with paragraphs 37–42 of IAS 27.**

36 This Standard does not mandate which entities produce separate financial statements available for public use.

Disclosure

37 **The following disclosures shall be made:**

(a) the fair value of investments in associates for which there are published price quotations;

(b) summarised financial information of associates, including the aggregated amounts of assets, liabilities, revenues and profit or loss;

(c) the reasons why the presumption that an investor does not have significant influence is overcome if the investor holds, directly or indirectly through subsidiaries, less than 20 per cent of the voting or potential voting power of the investee but concludes that it has significant influence;

(d) the reasons why the presumption that an investor has significant influence is overcome if the investor holds, directly or indirectly through subsidiaries, 20 per cent or more of the voting or potential voting power of the investee but concludes that it does not have significant influence;

(e) the reporting date of the financial statements of an associate, when such financial statements are used in applying the equity method and are as of a reporting date or for a period that is different from that of the investor, and the reason for using a different reporting date or different period;

(f) **the nature and extent of any significant restrictions (eg resulting from borrowing arrangements or regulatory requirements) on the ability of associates to transfer funds to the investor in the form of cash dividends, or repayment of loans or advances;**

(g) **the unrecognised share of losses of an associate, both for the period and cumulatively, if an investor has discontinued recognition of its share of losses of an associate;**

(h) **the fact that an associate is not accounted for using the equity method in accordance with paragraph 13; and**

(i) **summarised financial information of associates, either individually or in groups, that are not accounted for using the equity method, including the amounts of total assets, total liabilities, revenues and profit or loss.**

38 **Investments in associates accounted for using the equity method shall be classified as non-current assets. The investor's share of the profit or loss of such associates, and the carrying amount of those investments, shall be separately disclosed. The investor's share of any discontinued operations of such associates shall also be separately disclosed.**

39 **The investor's share of changes recognised directly in the associate's equity shall be recognised directly in equity by the investor and shall be disclosed in the statement of changes in equity as required by IAS 1** *Presentation of Financial Statements*.

40 **In accordance with IAS 37** *Provisions, Contingent Liabilities and Contingent Assets* **the investor shall disclose:**

(a) **its share of the contingent liabilities of an associate incurred jointly with other investors; and**

(b) **those contingent liabilities that arise because the investor is severally liable for all or part of the liabilities of the associate.**

Effective date

41 **An entity shall apply this Standard for annual periods beginning on or after 1 January 2005. Earlier application is encouraged. If an entity applies this Standard for a period beginning before 1 January 2005, it shall disclose that fact.**

Withdrawal of other pronouncements

42 This Standard supersedes IAS 28 *Accounting for Investments in Associates* (revised in 2000).

43 This Standard supersedes the following Interpretations:

(a) SIC-3 *Elimination of Unrealised Profits and Losses on Transactions with Associates*;

(b) SIC-20 *Equity Accounting Method—Recognition of Losses*; and

(c) SIC-33 *Consolidation and Equity Method—Potential Voting Rights and Allocation of Ownership Interests*.

Appendix
Amendments to other pronouncements

The amendments in this appendix shall be applied for annual periods beginning on or after 1 January 2005. If an entity applies this Standard for an earlier period, these amendments shall be applied for that earlier period.

* * * * *

The amendments contained in this appendix when this Standard was issued in 2003 have been incorporated into the relevant pronouncements published in this volume.

Approval of IAS 28 by the Board

International Accounting Standard 28 *Investments in Associates* was approved for issue by the fourteen members of the International Accounting Standards Board.

Sir David Tweedie	Chairman
Thomas E Jones	Vice-Chairman
Mary E Barth	
Hans-Georg Bruns	
Anthony T Cope	
Robert P Garnett	
Gilbert Gélard	
James J Leisenring	
Warren J McGregor	
Patricia L O'Malley	
Harry K Schmid	
John T Smith	
Geoffrey Whittington	
Tatsumi Yamada	

Basis for Conclusions

This Basis for Conclusions accompanies, but is not part of, IAS 28.

Introduction

BC1 This Basis for Conclusions summarises the International Accounting Standards Board's considerations in reaching its conclusions on revising IAS 28 *Accounting for Investments in Associates* in 2003. Individual Board members gave greater weight to some factors than to others.

BC2 In July 2001 the Board announced that, as part of its initial agenda of technical projects, it would undertake a project to improve a number of Standards, including IAS 28. The project was undertaken in the light of queries and criticisms raised in relation to the Standards by securities regulators, professional accountants and other interested parties. The objectives of the Improvements project were to reduce or eliminate alternatives, redundancies and conflicts within Standards, to deal with some convergence issues and to make other improvements. In May 2002 the Board published its proposals in an Exposure Draft of *Improvements to International Accounting Standards*, with a comment deadline of 16 September 2002. The Board received over 160 comment letters on the Exposure Draft.

BC3 Because the Board's intention was not to reconsider the fundamental approach to the accounting for investments in associates established by IAS 28, this Basis for Conclusions does not discuss requirements in IAS 28 that the Board has not reconsidered.

Scope exclusion: investments in associates held by venture capital organisations, mutual funds, unit trusts and similar entities

BC4 There are no specific requirements that address accounting for investments by venture capital organisations, mutual funds, unit trusts and similar entities. As a result, depending on whether an entity has control, joint control or significant influence over an investee, one of the following Standards is applied:

(a) IAS 27 *Consolidated and Separate Financial Statements*,

(b) IAS 28 *Investments in Associates*, or

(c) IAS 31 *Interests in Joint Ventures*.

BC5 The Board considered whether another approach is appropriate for these investors when they have joint control or significant influence over their investees. The Board noted that use of the equity or proportionate consolidation methods for investments held by venture capital organisations, mutual funds, unit trusts and similar entities often produces information that is not relevant to their management and investors and that fair value measurement produces more relevant information.

BC6 In addition, the Board noted that there may be frequent changes in the level of ownership in these investments and that financial statements are less useful if there are frequent changes in the method of accounting for an investment.

Measurement at fair value in accordance with IAS 39

BC7 Accordingly, the Board decided that investments held by venture capital organisations, mutual funds, unit trusts and similar entities including investment-linked insurance funds should be excluded from the scope of IAS 28 and IAS 31 when they are measured at fair value in accordance with IAS 39 *Financial Instruments: Recognition and Measurement*. The Board understands that fair value information is often readily available because fair value measurement is a well-established practice in these industries including for investments in entities in the early stages of their development or in non-listed entities.

Treatment of changes in fair value

BC8 The Board decided that if venture capital organisations, mutual funds, unit trusts and similar entities are to be excluded from the scope of IAS 28, it should be only when they recognise changes in the fair value of their investments in associates in profit or loss in the period in which those changes occur. This is to achieve the same treatment as for investments in subsidiaries or associates that are not consolidated or accounted for using the equity method because control or significant influence is intended to be temporary. The Board's approach distinguishes between accounting for the investment and accounting for the economic entity. In relation to the former, the Board decided that there should be consistency in the treatment of all investments, including changes in the fair value of these investments.

BC9 The Board noted that if such investments were classified in accordance with IAS 39, they would not always meet the definition of investments classified as held for trading because venture capital organisations may hold an investment for a period of 3–5 years. In accordance with IAS 39 such an investment is classified as available for sale (unless the entity elects to designate the investment on initial recognition at fair value through profit or loss). Classification as available for sale would not result in recognising changes in fair value in profit or loss. To achieve a similar effect on income to that of applying the equity method, the Board decided to exempt investments held by venture capital organisations, mutual funds, unit trusts and similar entities from this Standard only when they are measured at fair value through profit or loss (either by designation or because they meet the definition in IAS 39 of held for trading).

Reference to 'well-established' industry practices

BC10 The Exposure Draft proposed to limit the availability of the scope exclusion to situations in which well-established industry practice existed. Some respondents noted that the development of industry practice to measure such investments at fair value would have been precluded in industries established in countries already applying IFRSs. The Board confirmed that the main purpose of the reference to 'well-established' practice in the Exposure Draft was to emphasise that the exclusion would apply generally to those investments for which fair value is already available.

BC11 Therefore, the Board decided that the availability of the exclusion should be based only on the nature of an entity's activities and to delete the reference to 'well-established' practices. The Board understands that measurement of these investments at fair value is 'well-established' practice in these industries.

Definition of 'venture capital organisations'

BC12 The Board decided not to define further those 'venture capital organisations and similar entities' excluded from the scope of the Standard. Apart from recognising the difficulties of arriving at a universally applicable definition, the Board did not want inadvertently to make it difficult for entities to measure investments at fair value. However, the Board decided to clarify that the reference to 'similar entities' in the scope exclusion includes investment-linked insurance funds.

BC13 The Board decided, however, that if an investee is a subsidiary in accordance with IAS 27, it should be consolidated. The Board concluded that if an investor controls an investee, the investee is part of a group and part of the structure through which the group operates its business and thus consolidation of the investee is appropriate.

Application of the equity method

Temporary significant influence

BC14 The Board considered whether to remove the exemption from applying the equity method when significant influence over an associate is intended to be temporary. The Board decided to consider this issue as part of a comprehensive standard dealing with asset disposals. It decided to retain an exemption from applying the equity method when there is evidence that an associate is acquired with the intention to dispose of it within twelve months and that management is actively seeking a buyer. The Board's Exposure Draft ED 4 *Disposal of Non-current Assets and Presentation of Discontinued Operations* proposes to measure and present assets held for sale in a consistent manner irrespective of whether they are held by an investor in an associate or in a subsidiary.*

Severe long–term restrictions impairing ability to transfer funds to the investor

BC15 The Board decided to remove the exemption from applying the equity method for an associate that previously applied when severe long-term restrictions impaired an associate's ability to transfer funds to the investor. It did so because such circumstances may not preclude the investor's significant influence over the associate. The Board decided that an investor should, when assessing its ability to exercise significant influence over an entity, consider restrictions on the transfer of funds from the associate to the investor. In themselves, such restrictions do not preclude the existence of significant influence.

* In March 2004, the Board issued IFRS 5 *Non-current Assets Held for Sale and Discontinued Operations.* IFRS 5 removes this scope exclusion and now eliminates the exemption from applying the equity method when significant influence over an associate is intended to be temporary. See IFRS 5 Basis for Conclusions for further discussion.

Non–coterminous year–ends

BC16 The Exposure Draft of May 2002 proposed to limit to three months any difference between the reporting dates of the investor and the associate when applying the equity method. Some respondents to that Exposure Draft believed that it could be impracticable for the investor to prepare financial statements as of the same date when the date of the investor's and the associate's financial statements differ by more than three months. The Board noted that a three-month limit operates in several jurisdictions and it was concerned that a longer period, such as six months, would lead to the recognition of stale information. Therefore, it decided to retain the three-month limit.

Recognition of losses

BC17 The previous version of IAS 28 and SIC-20 *Equity Accounting Method—Recognition of Losses* restricted application of the equity method when, in accounting for the investor's share of losses, the carrying amount of the investment is reduced to zero.

BC18 The Board decided that the base to be reduced to zero should be broader than residual equity interests and should also include other non-equity interests that are in substance part of the net investment in the associate, such as long-term receivables. Therefore, the Board decided to withdraw SIC-20.

BC19 The Board also noted that if non-equity investments are not included in the base to be reduced to zero, an investor could restructure its investment to fund the majority in non-equity investments to avoid recognising the losses of the associate under the equity method.

BC20 In widening the base against which losses are to be recognised, the Board also clarified the application of the impairment provisions of IAS 39 to the financial assets that form part of the net investment.

Table of Concordance

This table shows how the contents of the superseded version of IAS 28 and the current version of IAS 28 correspond. Paragraphs are treated as corresponding if they broadly address the same matter even though the guidance may differ.

The table also shows how the requirements of SIC Interpretations SIC-3, SIC-20 and SIC-33 have been incorporated into the current version of IAS 28.

Superseded IAS 28 paragraph	Current IAS 28 paragraph	Superseded IAS 28 paragraph	Current IAS 28 paragraph	Superseded IAS 28 paragraph	Current IAS 28 paragraph
1	1	16	20	30	None
2	None	17	23	31	None
3	2	18	24	SIC-3	21, 22
4	6	19	25	SIC-20	30–32
5	7	20	26, 27	SIC-33	8, 9, 12
6	11	21	28	None	3–5
7	None	22	29	None	10
8	13	23	33	None	14, 15
9	17	24	34	None	19
11	18	25	None	None	35–37
12	None	26	40	None	39
13	None	27	None	None	42, 43
14	None	28	38		
15	None	29	41		

International Accounting Standard 29

Financial Reporting in Hyperinflationary Economies

This version includes amendments resulting from new and amended IFRSs issued up to 31 December 2004.

CONTENTS

paragraphs

INTERNATIONAL ACCOUNTING STANDARD 29 FINANCIAL REPORTING IN HYPERINFLATIONARY ECONOMIES

International Accounting Standard 29 *Financial Reporting in Hyperinflationary Economies* (IAS 29) is set out in paragraphs 1–41. All the paragraphs have equal authority but retain the IASC format of the Standard when it was adopted by the IASB. IAS 29 should be read in the context of the *Preface to International Financial Reporting Standards* and the *Framework for the Preparation and Presentation of Financial Statements*. IAS 8 *Accounting Policies, Changes in Accounting Estimates and Errors* provides a basis for selecting and applying accounting policies in the absence of explicit guidance.

International Accounting Standard 29
Financial Reporting in Hyperinflationary Economies

Scope

1 **This Standard shall be applied to the financial statements, including the consolidated financial statements, of any entity whose functional currency is the currency of a hyperinflationary economy.**

2 In a hyperinflationary economy, reporting of operating results and financial position in the local currency without restatement is not useful. Money loses purchasing power at such a rate that comparison of amounts from transactions and other events that have occurred at different times, even within the same accounting period, is misleading.

3 This Standard does not establish an absolute rate at which hyperinflation is deemed to arise. It is a matter of judgement when restatement of financial statements in accordance with this Standard becomes necessary. Hyperinflation is indicated by characteristics of the economic environment of a country which include, but are not limited to, the following:

(a) the general population prefers to keep its wealth in non-monetary assets or in a relatively stable foreign currency. Amounts of local currency held are immediately invested to maintain purchasing power;

(b) the general population regards monetary amounts not in terms of the local currency but in terms of a relatively stable foreign currency. Prices may be quoted in that currency;

(c) sales and purchases on credit take place at prices that compensate for the expected loss of purchasing power during the credit period, even if the period is short;

(d) interest rates, wages and prices are linked to a price index; and

(e) the cumulative inflation rate over three years is approaching, or exceeds, 100%.

4 It is preferable that all entities that report in the currency of the same hyperinflationary economy apply this Standard from the same date. Nevertheless, this Standard applies to the financial statements of any entity from the beginning of the reporting period in which it identifies the existence of hyperinflation in the country in whose currency it reports.

The restatement of financial statements

5 Prices change over time as the result of various specific or general political, economic and social forces. Specific forces such as changes in supply and demand and technological changes may cause individual prices to increase or decrease significantly and independently of each other. In addition, general forces may result in changes in the general level of prices and therefore in the general purchasing power of money.

6 In most countries, financial statements are prepared on the historical cost basis of accounting without regard either to changes in the general level of prices or to increases in specific prices of assets held, except to the extent that property, plant and equipment and investments may be revalued. Some entities, however, present financial statements that are based on a current cost approach that reflects the effects of changes in the specific prices of assets held.

7 In a hyperinflationary economy, financial statements, whether they are based on a historical cost approach or a current cost approach, are useful only if they are expressed in terms of the measuring unit current at the balance sheet date. As a result, this Standard applies to the financial statements of entities reporting in the currency of a hyperinflationary economy. Presentation of the information required by this Standard as a supplement to unrestated financial statements is not permitted. Furthermore, separate presentation of the financial statements before restatement is discouraged.

8 The financial statements of an entity whose functional currency is the currency of a hyperinflationary economy, whether they are based on a historical cost approach or a current cost approach, shall be stated in terms of the measuring unit current at the balance sheet date. The corresponding figures for the previous period required by IAS 1 *Presentation of Financial Statements* **and any information in respect of earlier periods shall also be stated in terms of the measuring unit current at the balance sheet date. For the purpose of presenting comparative amounts in a different presentation currency, paragraphs 42(b) and 43 of IAS 21** *The Effects of Changes in Foreign Exchange Rates* **(as revised in 2003) apply.**

9 The gain or loss on the net monetary position shall be included in profit or loss and separately disclosed.

10 The restatement of financial statements in accordance with this Standard requires the application of certain procedures as well as judgement. The consistent application of these procedures and judgements from period to period is more important than the precise accuracy of the resulting amounts included in the restated financial statements.

Historical cost financial statements

Balance sheet

11 Balance sheet amounts not already expressed in terms of the measuring unit current at the balance sheet date are restated by applying a general price index.

12 Monetary items are not restated because they are already expressed in terms of the monetary unit current at the balance sheet date. Monetary items are money held and items to be received or paid in money.

13 Assets and liabilities linked by agreement to changes in prices, such as index linked bonds and loans, are adjusted in accordance with the agreement in order to ascertain the amount outstanding at the balance sheet date. These items are carried at this adjusted amount in the restated balance sheet.

14 All other assets and liabilities are non-monetary. Some non-monetary items are carried at amounts current at the balance sheet date, such as net realisable value and market value, so they are not restated. All other non-monetary assets and liabilities are restated.

15 Most non-monetary items are carried at cost or cost less depreciation; hence they are expressed at amounts current at their date of acquisition. The restated cost, or cost less depreciation, of each item is determined by applying to its historical cost and accumulated depreciation the change in a general price index from the date of acquisition to the balance sheet date. Hence, property, plant and equipment, investments, inventories of raw materials and merchandise, goodwill, patents, trademarks and similar assets are restated from the dates of their purchase. Inventories of partly-finished and finished goods are restated from the dates on which the costs of purchase and of conversion were incurred.

16 Detailed records of the acquisition dates of items of property, plant and equipment may not be available or capable of estimation. In these rare circumstances, it may be necessary, in the first period of application of this Standard, to use an independent professional assessment of the value of the items as the basis for their restatement.

17 A general price index may not be available for the periods for which the restatement of property, plant and equipment is required by this Standard. In these circumstances, it may be necessary to use an estimate based, for example, on the movements in the exchange rate between the functional currency and a relatively stable foreign currency.

18 Some non-monetary items are carried at amounts current at dates other than that of acquisition or that of the balance sheet, for example property, plant and equipment that has been revalued at some earlier date. In these cases, the carrying amounts are restated from the date of the revaluation.

19 The restated amount of a non-monetary item is reduced, in accordance with appropriate Standards, when it exceeds the amount recoverable from the item's future use (including sale or other disposal). Hence, in such cases, restated amounts of property, plant and equipment, goodwill, patents and trademarks are reduced to recoverable amount, restated amounts of inventories are reduced to net realisable value and restated amounts of current investments are reduced to market value.

20 An investee that is accounted for under the equity method may report in the currency of a hyperinflationary economy. The balance sheet and income statement of such an investee are restated in accordance with this Standard in order to calculate the investor's share of its net assets and results of operations. Where the restated financial statements of the investee are expressed in a foreign currency they are translated at closing rates.

21 The impact of inflation is usually recognised in borrowing costs. It is not appropriate both to restate the capital expenditure financed by borrowing and to capitalise that part of the borrowing costs that compensates for the inflation during the same period. This part of the borrowing costs is recognised as an expense in the period in which the costs are incurred.

22 An entity may acquire assets under an arrangement that permits it to defer payment without incurring an explicit interest charge. Where it is impracticable to impute the amount of interest, such assets are restated from the payment date and not the date of purchase.

23 [Deleted]

24 At the beginning of the first period of application of this Standard, the components of owners' equity, except retained earnings and any revaluation surplus, are restated by applying a general price index from the dates the components were contributed or otherwise arose. Any revaluation surplus that arose in previous periods is eliminated. Restated retained earnings are derived from all the other amounts in the restated balance sheet.

25 At the end of the first period and in subsequent periods, all components of owners' equity are restated by applying a general price index from the beginning of the period or the date of contribution, if later. The movements for the period in owners' equity are disclosed in accordance with IAS 1 *Presentation of Financial Statements*.

Income statement

26 This Standard requires that all items in the income statement are expressed in terms of the measuring unit current at the balance sheet date. Therefore all amounts need to be restated by applying the change in the general price index from the dates when the items of income and expenses were initially recorded in the financial statements.

Gain or loss on net monetary position

27 In a period of inflation, an entity holding an excess of monetary assets over monetary liabilities loses purchasing power and an entity with an excess of monetary liabilities over monetary assets gains purchasing power to the extent the assets and liabilities are not linked to a price level. This gain or loss on the net monetary position may be derived as the difference resulting from the restatement of non-monetary assets, owners' equity and income statement items and the adjustment of index linked assets and liabilities. The gain or loss may be estimated by applying the change in a general price index to the weighted average for the period of the difference between monetary assets and monetary liabilities.

28 The gain or loss on the net monetary position is included in net income. The adjustment to those assets and liabilities linked by agreement to changes in prices made in accordance with paragraph 13 is offset against the gain or loss on net monetary position. Other income statement items, such as interest income and expense, and foreign exchange differences related to invested or borrowed funds, are also associated with the net monetary position. Although such items are separately disclosed, it may be helpful if they are presented together with the gain or loss on net monetary position in the income statement.

Current cost financial statements

Balance sheet

29 Items stated at current cost are not restated because they are already expressed in terms of the measuring unit current at the balance sheet date. Other items in the balance sheet are restated in accordance with paragraphs 11 to 25.

Income statement

30 The current cost income statement, before restatement, generally reports costs current at the time at which the underlying transactions or events occurred. Cost of sales and depreciation are recorded at current costs at the time of consumption; sales and other expenses are recorded at their money amounts when they occurred. Therefore all amounts need to be restated into the measuring unit current at the balance sheet date by applying a general price index.

Gain or loss on net monetary position

31 The gain or loss on the net monetary position is accounted for in accordance with paragraphs 27 and 28.

Taxes

32 The restatement of financial statements in accordance with this Standard may give rise to differences between the carrying amount of individual assets and liabilities in the balance sheet and their tax bases. These differences are accounted for in accordance with IAS 12 *Income Taxes*.

Cash flow statement

33 This Standard requires that all items in the cash flow statement are expressed in terms of the measuring unit current at the balance sheet date.

Corresponding figures

34 Corresponding figures for the previous reporting period, whether they were based on a historical cost approach or a current cost approach, are restated by applying a general price index so that the comparative financial statements are presented in terms of the measuring unit current at the end of the reporting period. Information that is disclosed in respect of earlier periods is also expressed in terms of the measuring unit current at the end of the reporting period. For the purpose of presenting comparative amounts in a different presentation currency, paragraphs 42(b) and 43 of IAS 21 *The Effects of Changes in Foreign Exchange Rates* (as revised in 2003) apply.

Consolidated financial statements

35 A parent that reports in the currency of a hyperinflationary economy may have subsidiaries that also report in the currencies of hyperinflationary economies. The financial statements of any such subsidiary need to be restated by applying a general price index of the country in whose currency it reports before they are included in the consolidated financial statements issued by its parent. Where

such a subsidiary is a foreign subsidiary, its restated financial statements are translated at closing rates. The financial statements of subsidiaries that do not report in the currencies of hyperinflationary economies are dealt with in accordance with IAS 21 *The Effects of Changes in Foreign Exchange Rates*.

36 If financial statements with different reporting dates are consolidated, all items, whether non-monetary or monetary, need to be restated into the measuring unit current at the date of the consolidated financial statements.

Selection and use of the general price index

37 The restatement of financial statements in accordance with this Standard requires the use of a general price index that reflects changes in general purchasing power. It is preferable that all entities that report in the currency of the same economy use the same index.

Economies ceasing to be hyperinflationary

38 When an economy ceases to be hyperinflationary and an entity discontinues the preparation and presentation of financial statements prepared in accordance with this Standard, it shall treat the amounts expressed in the measuring unit current at the end of the previous reporting period as the basis for the carrying amounts in its subsequent financial statements.

Disclosures

39 The following disclosures shall be made:

(a) the fact that the financial statements and the corresponding figures for previous periods have been restated for the changes in the general purchasing power of the functional currency and, as a result, are stated in terms of the measuring unit current at the balance sheet date;

(b) whether the financial statements are based on a historical cost approach or a current cost approach; and

(c) the identity and level of the price index at the balance sheet date and the movement in the index during the current and the previous reporting period.

40 The disclosures required by this Standard are needed to make clear the basis of dealing with the effects of inflation in the financial statements. They are also intended to provide other information necessary to understand that basis and the resulting amounts.

Effective date

41 This Standard becomes operative for financial statements covering periods beginning on or after 1 January 1990.

International Accounting Standard 30

Disclosures in the Financial Statements of Banks and Similar Financial Institutions

This version includes amendments resulting from new and amended IFRSs issued up to 31 December 2004.

CONTENTS

International Accounting Standard 30 *Disclosures in the Financial Statements of Banks and Similar Financial Institutions* (IAS 30) is set out in paragraphs 1–59. All the paragraphs have equal authority but retain the IASC format of the Standard when it was adopted by the IASB. IAS 30 should be read in the context of the *Preface to International Financial Reporting Standards* and the *Framework for the Preparation and Presentation of Financial Statements.* IAS 8 *Accounting Policies, Changes in Accounting Estimates and Errors* provides a basis for selecting and applying accounting policies in the absence of explicit guidance.

International Accounting Standard 30
Disclosures in the Financial Statements of Banks and Similar Financial Institutions

Scope

1 **This Standard shall be applied in the financial statements of banks and similar financial institutions (subsequently referred to as banks).**

2 For the purposes of this Standard, the term 'bank' includes all financial institutions, one of whose principal activities is to take deposits and borrow with the objective of lending and investing and which are within the scope of banking or similar legislation. The Standard is relevant to such entities whether or not they have the word 'bank' in their name.

3 Banks represent a significant and influential sector of business worldwide. Most individuals and organisations make use of banks, either as depositors or borrowers. Banks play a major role in maintaining confidence in the monetary system through their close relationship with regulatory authorities and governments and the regulations imposed on them by those governments. Hence there is considerable and widespread interest in the well-being of banks, and in particular their solvency and liquidity and the relative degree of risk that attaches to the different types of their business. The operations, and thus the accounting and reporting requirements, of banks are different from those of other commercial entities. This Standard recognises their special needs. It also encourages the presentation of a commentary on the financial statements which deals with such matters as the management and control of liquidity and risk.

4 This Standard supplements other Standards which also apply to banks unless they are specifically exempted in a Standard.

5 This Standard applies to the separate financial statements and the consolidated financial statements of a bank. Where a group undertakes banking operations, this Standard is applicable in respect of those operations on a consolidated basis.

Background

6 The users of the financial statements of a bank need relevant, reliable and comparable information which assists them in evaluating the financial position and performance of the bank and which is useful to them in making economic decisions. They also need information which gives them a better understanding of the special characteristics of the operations of a bank. Users need such information even though a bank is subject to supervision and provides the regulatory authorities with information that is not always available to the public. Therefore disclosures in the financial statements of a bank need to be sufficiently comprehensive to meet the needs of users, within the constraint of what it is reasonable to require of management.

7 The users of the financial statements of a bank are interested in its liquidity and solvency and the risks related to the assets and liabilities recognised on its balance sheet and to its off balance sheet items. Liquidity refers to the availability of

sufficient funds to meet deposit withdrawals and other financial commitments as they fall due. Solvency refers to the excess of assets over liabilities and, hence, to the adequacy of the bank's capital. A bank is exposed to liquidity risk and to risks arising from currency fluctuations, interest rate movements, changes in market prices and from counterparty failure. These risks may be reflected in the financial statements, but users obtain a better understanding if management provides a commentary on the financial statements which describes the way it manages and controls the risks associated with the operations of the bank.

Accounting policies

8 Banks use differing methods for the recognition and measurement of items in their financial statements. While harmonisation of these methods is desirable, it is beyond the scope of this Standard. In order to comply with IAS 1 *Presentation of Financial Statements* and thereby enable users to understand the basis on which the financial statements of a bank are prepared, accounting policies dealing with the following items may need to be disclosed:

(a) the recognition of the principal types of income (see paragraphs 10 and 11);

(b) the valuation of investment and dealing securities (see paragraphs 24 and 25);

(c) the distinction between those transactions and other events that result in the recognition of assets and liabilities on the balance sheet and those transactions and other events that only give rise to contingencies and commitments (see paragraphs 26–29);

(d) the basis for the determination of impairment losses on loans and advances and for writing off uncollectible loans and advances (see paragraphs 43–49); and

(e) the basis for the determination of charges for general banking risks and the accounting treatment of such charges (see paragraphs 50–52).

Some of these topics are the subject of existing Standards while others may be dealt with at a later date.

Income statement

9 **A bank shall present an income statement which groups income and expenses by nature and discloses the amounts of the principal types of income and expenses.**

10 **In addition to the requirements of other Standards, the disclosures in the income statement or the notes shall include, but are not limited to, the following items of income and expenses:**

Interest and similar income;

Interest expense and similar charges;

Dividend income;

Fee and commission income;

Fee and commission expense;

Gains less losses arising from dealing securities;

Gains less losses arising from investment securities;

Gains less losses arising from dealing in foreign currencies;

Other operating income;

Impairment losses on loans and advances;

General administrative expenses; and

Other operating expenses.

11 The principal types of income arising from the operations of a bank include interest, fees for services, commissions and dealing results. Each type of income is separately disclosed in order that users can assess the performance of a bank. Such disclosures are in addition to those of the source of income required by IAS 14 *Segment Reporting*.

12 The principal types of expenses arising from the operations of a bank include interest, commissions, losses on loans and advances, charges relating to the reduction in the carrying amount of investments and general administrative expenses. Each type of expense is separately disclosed in order that users can assess the performance of a bank.

13 Income and expense items shall not be offset except for those relating to hedges and to assets and liabilities that have been offset in accordance with IAS 32.

14 Offsetting in cases other than those relating to hedges and to assets and liabilities that have been offset as described in IAS 32 prevents users from assessing the performance of the separate activities of a bank and the return that it obtains on particular classes of assets.

15 Gains and losses arising from each of the following are normally reported on a net basis:

(a) disposals and changes in the carrying amount of dealing securities;

(b) disposals of investment securities; and

(c) dealings in foreign currencies.

16 Interest income and interest expense are disclosed separately in order to give a better understanding of the composition of, and reasons for changes in, net interest.

17 Net interest is a product of both interest rates and the amounts of borrowing and lending. It is desirable for management to provide a commentary about average interest rates, average interest earning assets and average interest-bearing liabilities for the period. In some countries, governments provide assistance to banks by making deposits and other credit facilities available at interest rates which are substantially below market rates. In these cases, management's commentary often discloses the extent of these deposits and facilities and their effect on net income.

Balance sheet

18 **A bank shall present a balance sheet that groups assets and liabilities by nature and lists them in an order that reflects their relative liquidity.**

19 **In addition to the requirements of other Standards, the disclosures in the balance sheet or the notes shall include, but are not limited to, the following assets and liabilities.**

Assets

Cash and balances with the central bank;

Treasury bills and other bills eligible for rediscounting with the central bank;

Government and other securities held for dealing purposes;

Placements with, and loans and advances to, other banks;

Other money market placements;

Loans and advances to customers; and

Investment securities.

Liabilities

Deposits from other banks;

Other money market deposits;

Amounts owed to other depositors;

Certificates of deposits;

Promissory notes and other liabilities evidenced by paper; and

Other borrowed funds.

20 The most useful approach to the classification of the assets and liabilities of a bank is to group them by their nature and list them in the approximate order of their liquidity; this may equate broadly to their maturities. Current and non-current items are not presented separately because most assets and liabilities of a bank can be realised or settled in the near future.

21 The distinction between balances with other banks and those with other parts of the money market and from other depositors is relevant information because it gives an understanding of a bank's relations with, and dependence on, other banks and the money market. Hence, a bank discloses separately:

(a) balances with the central bank;

(b) placements with other banks;

(c) other money market placements;

(d) deposits from other banks;

(e) other money market deposits; and

(f) other deposits.

22 A bank generally does not know the holders of its certificates of deposit because they are usually traded on an open market. Hence, a bank discloses separately deposits that have been obtained through the issue of its own certificates of deposit or other negotiable paper.

23 [Deleted]

24 **A bank shall disclose the fair values of each class of its financial assets and liabilities as required by IAS 32** ***Financial Instruments: Disclosure and Presentation*****.**

25 IAS 39 provides for four classifications of financial assets: loans and receivables, held-to-maturity investments, financial assets at fair value through profit or loss, and available-for-sale financial assets. A bank shall disclose the fair values of its financial assets for these four classifications, as a minimum.

Contingencies and commitments including off balance sheet items

26 **A bank shall disclose the following contingent liabilities and commitments:**

(a) the nature and amount of commitments to extend credit that are irrevocable because they cannot be withdrawn at the discretion of the bank without the risk of incurring significant penalty or expense; and

(b) the nature and amount of contingent liabilities and commitments arising from off balance sheet items including those relating to:

(i) direct credit substitutes including general guarantees of indebtedness, bank acceptance guarantees and standby letters of credit serving as financial guarantees for loans and securities;

(ii) certain transaction-related contingent liabilities including performance bonds, bid bonds, warranties and standby letters of credit related to particular transactions;

(iii) short-term self-liquidating trade-related contingent liabilities arising from the movement of goods, such as documentary credits where the underlying shipment is used as security; and

(iv) [Deleted]

(v) [Deleted]

(vi) other commitments, note issuance facilities and revolving underwriting facilities.

27 IAS 37 *Provisions, Contingent Liabilities and Contingent Assets* deals generally with accounting for, and disclosure of, contingent liabilities. The Standard is of particular relevance to banks because banks often become engaged in many types of contingent liabilities and commitments, some revocable and others irrevocable, which are frequently significant in amount and substantially larger than those of other commercial entities.

28 Many banks also enter into transactions that are presently not recognised as assets or liabilities in the balance sheet but which give rise to contingencies and commitments. Such off balance sheet items often represent an important part of

the business of a bank and may have a significant bearing on the level of risk to which the bank is exposed. These items may add to, or reduce, other risks, for example by hedging assets or liabilities on the balance sheet.

29 The users of the financial statements need to know about the contingencies and irrevocable commitments of a bank because of the demands they may put on its liquidity and solvency and the inherent possibility of potential losses. Users also require adequate information about the nature and amount of off balance sheet transactions undertaken by a bank.

Maturities of assets and liabilities

30 A bank shall disclose an analysis of assets and liabilities into relevant maturity groupings based on the remaining period at the balance sheet date to the contractual maturity date.

31 The matching and controlled mismatching of the maturities and interest rates of assets and liabilities is fundamental to the management of a bank. It is unusual for banks ever to be completely matched since business transacted is often of uncertain term and of different types. An unmatched position potentially enhances profitability but can also increase the risk of losses.

32 The maturities of assets and liabilities and the ability to replace, at an acceptable cost, interest-bearing liabilities as they mature, are important factors in assessing the liquidity of a bank and its exposure to changes in interest rates and exchange rates. In order to provide information that is relevant for the assessment of its liquidity, a bank discloses, as a minimum, an analysis of assets and liabilities into relevant maturity groupings.

33 The maturity groupings applied to individual assets and liabilities differ between banks and in their appropriateness to particular assets and liabilities. Examples of periods used include the following:

(a) up to 1 month;

(b) from 1 month to 3 months;

(c) from 3 months to 1 year;

(d) from 1 year to 5 years; and

(e) from 5 years and over.

Frequently the periods are combined, for example, in the case of loans and advances, by grouping those under one year and those over one year. When repayment is spread over a period of time, each instalment is allocated to the period in which it is contractually agreed or expected to be paid or received.

34 It is essential that the maturity periods adopted by a bank are the same for assets and liabilities. This makes clear the extent to which the maturities are matched and the consequent dependence of the bank on other sources of liquidity.

35 Maturities could be expressed in terms of:

(a) the remaining period to the repayment date;

(b) the original period to the repayment date; or

(c) the remaining period to the next date at which interest rates may be changed.

The analysis of assets and liabilities by their remaining periods to the repayment dates provides the best basis to evaluate the liquidity of a bank. A bank may also disclose repayment maturities based on the original period to the repayment date in order to provide information about its funding and business strategy. In addition, a bank may disclose maturity groupings based on the remaining period to the next date at which interest rates may be changed in order to demonstrate its exposure to interest rate risks. Management may also provide, in its commentary on the financial statements, information about interest rate exposure and about the way it manages and controls such exposures.

36 In many countries, deposits made with a bank may be withdrawn on demand and advances given by a bank may be repayable on demand. However, in practice, these deposits and advances are often maintained for long periods without withdrawal or repayment; hence, the effective date of repayment is later than the contractual date. Nevertheless, a bank discloses an analysis expressed in terms of contractual maturities even though the contractual repayment period is often not the effective period because contractual dates reflect the liquidity risks attaching to the bank's assets and liabilities.

37 Some assets of a bank do not have a contractual maturity date. The period in which these assets are assumed to mature is usually taken as the expected date on which the assets will be realised.

38 The users' evaluation of the liquidity of a bank from its disclosure of maturity groupings is made in the context of local banking practices, including the availability of funds to banks. In some countries, short-term funds are available, in the normal course of business, from the money market or, in an emergency, from the central bank. In other countries, this is not the case.

39 In order to provide users with a full understanding of the maturity groupings, the disclosures in the financial statements may need to be supplemented by information as to the likelihood of repayment within the remaining period. Hence, management may provide, in its commentary on the financial statements, information about the effective periods and about the way it manages and controls the risks and exposures associated with different maturity and interest rate profiles.

Concentrations of assets, liabilities and off balance sheet items

40 A bank shall disclose any significant concentrations of its assets, liabilities and off balance sheet items. Such disclosures shall be made in terms of geographical areas, customer or industry groups or other concentrations of risk. A bank shall also disclose the amount of significant net foreign currency exposures.

41 A bank discloses significant concentrations in the distribution of its assets and in the source of its liabilities because it is a useful indication of the potential risks inherent in the realisation of the assets and the funds available to the bank. Such disclosures are made in terms of geographical areas, customer or industry groups or other concentrations of risk which are appropriate in the circumstances

of the bank. A similar analysis and explanation of off balance sheet items is also important. Geographical areas may comprise individual countries, groups of countries or regions within a country; customer disclosures may deal with sectors such as governments, public authorities, and commercial and business entities. Such disclosures are made in addition to any segment information required by IAS 14 *Segment Reporting*.

42 The disclosure of significant net foreign currency exposures is also a useful indication of the risk of losses arising from changes in exchange rates.

Losses on loans and advances

43 A bank shall disclose the following:

(a) the accounting policy that describes the basis on which uncollectible loans and advances are recognised as an expense and written off.

(b) details of the movements in any allowance for impairment losses on loans and advances during the period. It shall disclose separately the amount recognised as an expense in the period for impairment losses on uncollectible loans and advances, the amount charged in the period for loans and advances written off and the amount credited in the period for loans and advances previously written off that have been recovered.

(c) the aggregate amount of any allowance account for impairment losses on loans and advances at the balance sheet date.

44 Any amounts set aside in respect of losses on loans and advances in addition to impairment losses recognised under IAS 39 on loans and advances shall be accounted for as appropriations of retained earnings. Any credits resulting from the reduction of such amounts result in an increase in retained earnings and are not included in the determination of profit or loss for the period.

45 [Deleted]

46 Local circumstances or legislation may require or allow a bank to set aside amounts for impairment losses on loans and advances in addition to those losses that have been recognised under IAS 39. Any such amounts set aside represent appropriations of retained earnings and not expenses in determining profit or loss. Similarly, any credits resulting from the reduction of such amounts result in an increase in retained earnings and are not included in the determination of profit or loss.

47 Users of the financial statements of a bank need to know the impact that impairment losses on loans and advances have had on the financial position and performance of the bank; this helps them judge the effectiveness with which the bank has employed its resources. Therefore a bank discloses the aggregate amount of any allowance account for impairment losses on loans and advances at the balance sheet date and the movements in the allowance account during the period. The movements in the allowance account, including the amounts previously written off that have been recovered during the period, are shown separately.

48 [Deleted]

49 When loans and advances cannot be recovered, they are written off and charged against any allowance account for impairment losses. In some cases, they are not written off until all the necessary legal procedures have been completed and the amount of the impairment loss is finally determined. In other cases, they are written off earlier, for example when the borrower has not paid any interest or repaid any principal that was due in a specified period. As the time at which uncollectible loans and advances are written off differs, the gross amount of loans and advances and of the allowance account for impairment losses may vary considerably in similar circumstances. As a result, a bank discloses its policy for writing off uncollectible loans and advances.

General banking risks

50 **Any amounts set aside for general banking risks, including future losses and other unforeseeable risks or contingencies shall be separately disclosed as appropriations of retained earnings. Any credits resulting from the reduction of such amounts result in an increase in retained earnings and shall not be included in the determination of profit or loss for the period.**

51 Local circumstances or legislation may require or allow a bank to set aside amounts for general banking risks, including future losses or other unforeseeable risks, in addition to the charges for losses on loans and advances determined in accordance with paragraph 45. A bank may also be required or allowed to set aside amounts for contingencies. Such amounts for general banking risks and contingencies do not qualify for recognition as provisions under IAS 37 *Provisions, Contingent Liabilities and Contingent Assets*. Therefore, a bank recognises such amounts as appropriations of retained earnings. This is necessary to avoid the overstatement of liabilities, understatement of assets, undisclosed accruals and provisions and the opportunity to distort net income and equity.

52 The income statement cannot present relevant and reliable information about the performance of a bank if profit or loss for the period includes the effects of undisclosed amounts set aside for general banking risks or additional contingencies, or undisclosed credits resulting from the reversal of such amounts. Similarly, the balance sheet cannot provide relevant and reliable information about the financial position of a bank if the balance sheet includes overstated liabilities, understated assets or undisclosed accruals and provisions.

Assets pledged as security

53 **A bank shall disclose the aggregate amount of secured liabilities and the nature and carrying amount of the assets pledged as security.**

54 In some countries, banks are required, either by law or national custom, to pledge assets as security to support certain deposits and other liabilities. The amounts involved are often substantial and so may have a significant impact on the assessment of the financial position of a bank.

Trust activities

55 Banks commonly act as trustees and in other fiduciary capacities that result in the holding or placing of assets on behalf of individuals, trusts, retirement benefit plans and other institutions. Provided the trustee or similar relationship is legally supported, these assets are not assets of the bank and, therefore, are not included in its balance sheet. If the bank is engaged in significant trust activities, disclosure of that fact and an indication of the extent of those activities is made in its financial statements because of the potential liability if it fails in its fiduciary duties. For this purpose, trust activities do not encompass safe custody functions.

Related party transactions

56 IAS 24 *Related Party Disclosures* deals generally with the disclosures of related party relationships and transactions between a reporting entity and its related parties. In some countries, the law or regulatory authorities prevent or restrict banks entering into transactions with related parties whereas in others such transactions are permitted. IAS 24 is of particular relevance in the presentation of the financial statements of a bank in a country that permits such transactions.

57 Certain transactions between related parties may be effected on different terms from those with unrelated parties. For example, a bank may advance a larger sum or charge lower interest rates to a related party than it would in otherwise identical circumstances to an unrelated party; advances or deposits may be moved between related parties more quickly and with less formality than is possible when unrelated parties are involved. Even when related party transactions arise in the ordinary course of a bank's business, information about such transactions is relevant to the needs of users and its disclosure is required by IAS 24.

58 When a bank has entered into transactions with related parties, it is appropriate to disclose the nature of the related party relationship as well as information about the transactions and outstanding balances necessary for an understanding of the potential effects of the relationship on the financial statements of the bank. The disclosures are made in accordance with IAS 24 and include disclosures relating to a bank's policy for lending to related parties and, in respect of related party transactions, the amount included in:

(a) each of loans and advances, deposits and acceptances and promissory notes; disclosures may include the aggregate amounts outstanding at the beginning and end of the period, as well as advances, deposits, repayments and other changes during the period;

(b) each of the principal types of income, interest expense and commissions paid;

(c) the amount of the expense recognised in the period for impairment losses on loans and advances and the amount of any allowance at the balance sheet date; and

(d) irrevocable commitments and contingencies and commitments arising from off balance sheet items.

Effective date

59 **This Standard becomes operative for the financial statements of banks covering periods beginning on or after 1 January 1991.**

International Accounting Standard 31

Interests in Joint Ventures

This version includes amendments resulting from new and amended IFRSs issued up to 31 December 2004.

CONTENTS

International Accounting Standard 31 *Interests in Joint Ventures* (IAS 31) is set out in paragraphs 1–59 and the Appendix. All the paragraphs have equal authority but retain the IASC format of the Standard when it was adopted by the IASB. IAS 31 should be read in the context of its objective and the Basis for Conclusions, the *Preface to International Financial Reporting Standards* and the *Framework for the Preparation and Presentation of Financial Statements*. IAS 8 *Accounting Policies, Changes in Accounting Estimates and Errors* provides a basis for selecting and applying accounting policies in the absence of explicit guidance.

Introduction

IN1 International Accounting Standard 31 *Interests in Joint Ventures* (IAS 31) replaces IAS 31 *Financial Reporting of Interests in Joint Ventures* (revised in 2000), and should be applied for annual periods beginning on or after 1 January 2005. Earlier application is encouraged.

Reasons for revising IAS 31

IN2 The International Accounting Standards Board developed this revised IAS 31 as part of its project on Improvements to International Accounting Standards. The project was undertaken in the light of queries and criticisms raised in relation to the Standards by securities regulators, professional accountants and other interested parties. The objectives of the project were to reduce or eliminate alternatives, redundancies and conflicts within the Standards, to deal with some convergence issues and to make other improvements.

IN3 For IAS 31 the Board's main objective was to make the amendments necessary to take account of the extensive changes being made to IAS 27 *Consolidated Financial Statements and Accounting for Investments in Subsidiaries* and IAS 28 *Accounting for Investments in Associates* as part of the Improvements project. The Board did not reconsider the fundamental approach to the accounting for interests in joint ventures contained in IAS 31.

The main changes

IN4 The main changes from the previous version of IAS 31 are described below.

Scope

IN5 The Standard does not apply to investments that would otherwise be interests of venturers in jointly controlled entities held by venture capital organisations, mutual funds, unit trusts and similar entities when those investments are classified as held for trading and accounted for in accordance with IAS 39 *Financial Instruments: Recognition and Measurement*. Those investments are measured at fair value, with changes in fair value being recognised in profit or loss in the period in which they occur.

IN6 Furthermore, the Standard provides exemptions from application of proportionate consolidation or the equity method similar to those provided for certain parents not to prepare consolidated financial statements. These exemptions include when the investor is also a parent exempt in accordance with IAS 27 *Consolidated and Separate Financial Statements* from preparing consolidated financial statements (paragraph 2(b)), and when the investor, though not such a parent, can satisfy the same type of conditions that exempt such parents (paragraph 2(c)).

Exemptions from applying proportionate consolidation or the equity method

IN7 The Standard does not require proportionate consolidation or the equity method to be applied when an interest in a joint venture is acquired and held with a view to its disposal within twelve months of acquisition. There must be evidence that the investment is acquired with the intention to dispose of it and that management is actively seeking a buyer. The words 'in the near future' from the previous version of IAS 31 were replaced with the words 'within twelve months'. When such an interest in a joint venture is not disposed of within twelve months it must be accounted for using proportionate consolidation or the equity method as from the date of acquisition, except in narrowly specified circumstances.*

IN8 The Standard does not permit a venturer that continues to have joint control of an interest in a joint venture not to apply proportionate consolidation or the equity method when the joint venture is operating under severe long-term restrictions that significantly impair its ability to transfer funds to the venturer. Joint control must be lost before proportionate consolidation or the equity method ceases to apply.

Separate financial statements

IN9 The requirements for the preparation of an investor's separate financial statements are established by reference to IAS 27.

Disclosure

IN10 The Standard requires a venturer to disclose the method it uses to recognise its interests in jointly controlled entities (ie proportionate consolidation or the equity method).

* In March 2004, the Board issued IFRS 5 *Non-current Assets Held for Sale and Discontinued Operations*. IFRS 5 removes this scope exclusion and now eliminates the exemption from applying proportionate consolidation or the equity method when joint control of a joint venture is intended to be temporary. See IFRS 5 Basis for Conclusions for further discussion.

International Accounting Standard 31
Interests in Joint Ventures

Scope

1 **This Standard shall be applied in accounting for interests in joint ventures and the reporting of joint venture assets, liabilities, income and expenses in the financial statements of venturers and investors, regardless of the structures or forms under which the joint venture activities take place. However, it does not apply to venturers' interests in jointly controlled entities held by:**

(a) venture capital organisations, or

(b) mutual funds, unit trusts and similar entities including investment-linked insurance funds

that upon initial recognition are designated as at fair value through profit or loss or are classified as held for trading and accounted for in accordance with IAS 39 *Financial Instruments: Recognition and Measurement*. **Such investments shall be measured at fair value in accordance with IAS 39, with changes in fair value recognised in profit or loss in the period of the change.**

2 **A venturer with an interest in a jointly controlled entity is exempted from paragraphs 30 (proportionate consolidation) and 38 (equity method) when it meets the following conditions:**

(a) the interest is classified as held for sale in accordance with IFRS 5 *Non-current Assets Held for Sale and Discontinued Operations*;

(b) the exception in paragraph 10 of IAS 27 *Consolidated and Separate Financial Statements* **allowing a parent that also has an interest in a jointly controlled entity not to present consolidated financial statements is applicable; or**

(c) all of the following apply:

(i) the venturer is a wholly-owned subsidiary, or is a partially-owned subsidiary of another entity and its owners, including those not otherwise entitled to vote, have been informed about, and do not object to, the venturer not applying proportionate consolidation or the equity method;

(ii) the venturer's debt or equity instruments are not traded in a public market (a domestic or foreign stock exchange or an over-the-counter market, including local and regional markets);

(iii) the venturer did not file, nor is it in the process of filing, its financial statements with a securities commission or other regulatory organisation, for the purpose of issuing any class of instruments in a public market; and

(iv) **the ultimate or any intermediate parent of the venturer produces consolidated financial statements available for public use that comply with International Financial Reporting Standards.**

Definitions

3 **The following terms are used in this Standard with the meanings specified:**

Control **is the power to govern the financial and operating policies of an economic activity so as to obtain benefits from it.**

The *equity method* **is a method of accounting whereby an interest in a jointly controlled entity is initially recorded at cost and adjusted thereafter for the post-acquisition change in the venturer's share of net assets of the jointly controlled entity. The profit or loss of the venturer includes the venturer's share of the profit or loss of the jointly controlled entity.**

An *investor in a joint venture* **is a party to a joint venture and does not have joint control over that joint venture.**

Joint control **is the contractually agreed sharing of control over an economic activity, and exists only when the strategic financial and operating decisions relating to the activity require the unanimous consent of the parties sharing control (the venturers).**

A *joint venture* **is a contractual arrangement whereby two or more parties undertake an economic activity that is subject to joint control.**

Proportionate consolidation **is a method of accounting whereby a venturer's share of each of the assets, liabilities, income and expenses of a jointly controlled entity is combined line by line with similar items in the venturer's financial statements or reported as separate line items in the venturer's financial statements.**

Separate financial statements **are those presented by a parent, an investor in an associate or a venturer in a jointly controlled entity, in which the investments are accounted for on the basis of the direct equity interest rather than on the basis of the reported results and net assets of the investees.**

Significant influence **is the power to participate in the financial and operating policy decisions of an economic activity but is not control or joint control over those policies.**

A *venturer* **is a party to a joint venture and has joint control over that joint venture.**

4 Financial statements in which proportionate consolidation or the equity method is applied are not separate financial statements, nor are the financial statements of an entity that does not have a subsidiary, associate or venturer's interest in a jointly controlled entity.

5 Separate financial statements are those presented in addition to consolidated financial statements, financial statements in which investments are accounted for using the equity method and financial statements in which venturers' interests in

joint ventures are proportionately consolidated. Separate financial statements need not be appended to, or accompany, those statements.

6 Entities that are exempted in accordance with paragraph 10 of IAS 27 from consolidation, paragraph 13(c) of IAS 28 *Investments in Associates* from applying the equity method or paragraph 2 of this Standard from applying proportionate consolidation or the equity method may present separate financial statements as their only financial statements.

Forms of joint venture

7 Joint ventures take many different forms and structures. This Standard identifies three broad types—jointly controlled operations, jointly controlled assets and jointly controlled entities—that are commonly described as, and meet the definition of, joint ventures. The following characteristics are common to all joint ventures:

(a) two or more venturers are bound by a contractual arrangement; and

(b) the contractual arrangement establishes joint control.

Joint control

8 Joint control may be precluded when an investee is in legal reorganisation or in bankruptcy, or operates under severe long-term restrictions on its ability to transfer funds to the venturer. If joint control is continuing, these events are not enough in themselves to justify not accounting for joint ventures in accordance with this Standard.

Contractual arrangement

9 The existence of a contractual arrangement distinguishes interests that involve joint control from investments in associates in which the investor has significant influence (see IAS 28). Activities that have no contractual arrangement to establish joint control are not joint ventures for the purposes of this Standard.

10 The contractual arrangement may be evidenced in a number of ways, for example by a contract between the venturers or minutes of discussions between the venturers. In some cases, the arrangement is incorporated in the articles or other by-laws of the joint venture. Whatever its form, the contractual arrangement is usually in writing and deals with such matters as:

(a) the activity, duration and reporting obligations of the joint venture;

(b) the appointment of the board of directors or equivalent governing body of the joint venture and the voting rights of the venturers;

(c) capital contributions by the venturers; and

(d) the sharing by the venturers of the output, income, expenses or results of the joint venture.

11 The contractual arrangement establishes joint control over the joint venture. Such a requirement ensures that no single venturer is in a position to control the activity unilaterally.

12 The contractual arrangement may identify one venturer as the operator or manager of the joint venture. The operator does not control the joint venture but acts within the financial and operating policies that have been agreed by the venturers in accordance with the contractual arrangement and delegated to the operator. If the operator has the power to govern the financial and operating policies of the economic activity, it controls the venture and the venture is a subsidiary of the operator and not a joint venture.

Jointly controlled operations

13 The operation of some joint ventures involves the use of the assets and other resources of the venturers rather than the establishment of a corporation, partnership or other entity, or a financial structure that is separate from the venturers themselves. Each venturer uses its own property, plant and equipment and carries its own inventories. It also incurs its own expenses and liabilities and raises its own finance, which represent its own obligations. The joint venture activities may be carried out by the venturer's employees alongside the venturer's similar activities. The joint venture agreement usually provides a means by which the revenue from the sale of the joint product and any expenses incurred in common are shared among the venturers.

14 An example of a jointly controlled operation is when two or more venturers combine their operations, resources and expertise to manufacture, market and distribute jointly a particular product, such as an aircraft. Different parts of the manufacturing process are carried out by each of the venturers. Each venturer bears its own costs and takes a share of the revenue from the sale of the aircraft, such share being determined in accordance with the contractual arrangement.

15 In respect of its interests in jointly controlled operations, a venturer shall recognise in its financial statements:

(a) the assets that it controls and the liabilities that it incurs; and

(b) the expenses that it incurs and its share of the income that it earns from the sale of goods or services by the joint venture.

16 Because the assets, liabilities, income and expenses are recognised in the financial statements of the venturer, no adjustments or other consolidation procedures are required in respect of these items when the venturer presents consolidated financial statements.

17 Separate accounting records may not be required for the joint venture itself and financial statements may not be prepared for the joint venture. However, the venturers may prepare management accounts so that they may assess the performance of the joint venture.

Jointly controlled assets

18 Some joint ventures involve the joint control, and often the joint ownership, by the venturers of one or more assets contributed to, or acquired for the purpose of, the joint venture and dedicated to the purposes of the joint venture. The assets

are used to obtain benefits for the venturers. Each venturer may take a share of the output from the assets and each bears an agreed share of the expenses incurred.

19 These joint ventures do not involve the establishment of a corporation, partnership or other entity, or a financial structure that is separate from the venturers themselves. Each venturer has control over its share of future economic benefits through its share of the jointly controlled asset.

20 Many activities in the oil, gas and mineral extraction industries involve jointly controlled assets. For example, a number of oil production companies may jointly control and operate an oil pipeline. Each venturer uses the pipeline to transport its own product in return for which it bears an agreed proportion of the expenses of operating the pipeline. Another example of a jointly controlled asset is when two entities jointly control a property, each taking a share of the rents received and bearing a share of the expenses.

21 In respect of its interest in jointly controlled assets, a venturer shall recognise in its financial statements:

(a) its share of the jointly controlled assets, classified according to the nature of the assets;

(b) any liabilities that it has incurred;

(c) its share of any liabilities incurred jointly with the other venturers in relation to the joint venture;

(d) any income from the sale or use of its share of the output of the joint venture, together with its share of any expenses incurred by the joint venture; and

(e) any expenses that it has incurred in respect of its interest in the joint venture.

22 In respect of its interest in jointly controlled assets, each venturer includes in its accounting records and recognises in its financial statements:

(a) its share of the jointly controlled assets, classified according to the nature of the assets rather than as an investment. For example, a share of a jointly controlled oil pipeline is classified as property, plant and equipment.

(b) any liabilities that it has incurred, for example those incurred in financing its share of the assets.

(c) its share of any liabilities incurred jointly with other venturers in relation to the joint venture.

(d) any income from the sale or use of its share of the output of the joint venture, together with its share of any expenses incurred by the joint venture.

(e) any expenses that it has incurred in respect of its interest in the joint venture, for example those related to financing the venturer's interest in the assets and selling its share of the output.

Because the assets, liabilities, income and expenses are recognised in the financial statements of the venturer, no adjustments or other consolidation procedures are required in respect of these items when the venturer presents consolidated financial statements.

23 The treatment of jointly controlled assets reflects the substance and economic reality and, usually, the legal form of the joint venture. Separate accounting records for the joint venture itself may be limited to those expenses incurred in common by the venturers and ultimately borne by the venturers according to their agreed shares. Financial statements may not be prepared for the joint venture, although the venturers may prepare management accounts so that they may assess the performance of the joint venture.

Jointly controlled entities

24 A jointly controlled entity is a joint venture that involves the establishment of a corporation, partnership or other entity in which each venturer has an interest. The entity operates in the same way as other entities, except that a contractual arrangement between the venturers establishes joint control over the economic activity of the entity.

25 A jointly controlled entity controls the assets of the joint venture, incurs liabilities and expenses and earns income. It may enter into contracts in its own name and raise finance for the purposes of the joint venture activity. Each venturer is entitled to a share of the profits of the jointly controlled entity, although some jointly controlled entities also involve a sharing of the output of the joint venture.

26 A common example of a jointly controlled entity is when two entities combine their activities in a particular line of business by transferring the relevant assets and liabilities into a jointly controlled entity. Another example is when an entity commences a business in a foreign country in conjunction with the government or other agency in that country, by establishing a separate entity that is jointly controlled by the entity and the government or agency.

27 Many jointly controlled entities are similar in substance to those joint ventures referred to as jointly controlled operations or jointly controlled assets. For example, the venturers may transfer a jointly controlled asset, such as an oil pipeline, into a jointly controlled entity, for tax or other reasons. Similarly, the venturers may contribute into a jointly controlled entity assets that will be operated jointly. Some jointly controlled operations also involve the establishment of a jointly controlled entity to deal with particular aspects of the activity, for example, the design, marketing, distribution or after-sales service of the product.

28 A jointly controlled entity maintains its own accounting records and prepares and presents financial statements in the same way as other entities in conformity with International Financial Reporting Standards.

29 Each venturer usually contributes cash or other resources to the jointly controlled entity. These contributions are included in the accounting records of the venturer and recognised in its financial statements as an investment in the jointly controlled entity.

Financial statements of a venturer

Proportionate consolidation

30 **A venturer shall recognise its interest in a jointly controlled entity using proportionate consolidation or the alternative method described in paragraph 38. When proportionate consolidation is used, one of the two reporting formats identified below shall be used.**

31 A venturer recognises its interest in a jointly controlled entity using one of the two reporting formats for proportionate consolidation irrespective of whether it also has investments in subsidiaries or whether it describes its financial statements as consolidated financial statements.

32 When recognising an interest in a jointly controlled entity, it is essential that a venturer reflects the substance and economic reality of the arrangement, rather than the joint venture's particular structure or form. In a jointly controlled entity, a venturer has control over its share of future economic benefits through its share of the assets and liabilities of the venture. This substance and economic reality are reflected in the consolidated financial statements of the venturer when the venturer recognises its interests in the assets, liabilities, income and expenses of the jointly controlled entity by using one of the two reporting formats for proportionate consolidation described in paragraph 34.

33 The application of proportionate consolidation means that the balance sheet of the venturer includes its share of the assets that it controls jointly and its share of the liabilities for which it is jointly responsible. The income statement of the venturer includes its share of the income and expenses of the jointly controlled entity. Many of the procedures appropriate for the application of proportionate consolidation are similar to the procedures for the consolidation of investments in subsidiaries, which are set out in IAS 27.

34 Different reporting formats may be used to give effect to proportionate consolidation. The venturer may combine its share of each of the assets, liabilities, income and expenses of the jointly controlled entity with the similar items, line by line, in its financial statements. For example, it may combine its share of the jointly controlled entity's inventory with its inventory and its share of the jointly controlled entity's property, plant and equipment with its property, plant and equipment. Alternatively, the venturer may include separate line items for its share of the assets, liabilities, income and expenses of the jointly controlled entity in its financial statements. For example, it may show its share of a current asset of the jointly controlled entity separately as part of its current assets; it may show its share of the property, plant and equipment of the jointly controlled entity separately as part of its property, plant and equipment. Both these reporting formats result in the reporting of identical amounts of profit or loss and of each major classification of assets, liabilities, income and expenses; both formats are acceptable for the purposes of this Standard.

35 Whichever format is used to give effect to proportionate consolidation, it is inappropriate to offset any assets or liabilities by the deduction of other liabilities or assets or any income or expenses by the deduction of other expenses or income, unless a legal right of set-off exists and the offsetting represents the expectation as to the realisation of the asset or the settlement of the liability.

36 A venturer shall discontinue the use of proportionate consolidation from the date on which it ceases to have joint control over a jointly controlled entity.

37 A venturer discontinues the use of proportionate consolidation from the date on which it ceases to share in the control of a jointly controlled entity. This may happen, for example, when the venturer disposes of its interest or when such external restrictions are placed on the jointly controlled entity that the venturer no longer has joint control.

Equity method

38 As an alternative to proportionate consolidation described in paragraph 30, a venturer shall recognise its interest in a jointly controlled entity using the equity method.

39 A venturer recognises its interest in a jointly controlled entity using the equity method irrespective of whether it also has investments in subsidiaries or whether it describes its financial statements as consolidated financial statements.

40 Some venturers recognise their interests in jointly controlled entities using the equity method, as described in IAS 28. The use of the equity method is supported by those who argue that it is inappropriate to combine controlled items with jointly controlled items and by those who believe that venturers have significant influence, rather than joint control, in a jointly controlled entity. This Standard does not recommend the use of the equity method because proportionate consolidation better reflects the substance and economic reality of a venturer's interest in a jointly controlled entity, that is to say, control over the venturer's share of the future economic benefits. Nevertheless, this Standard permits the use of the equity method, as an alternative treatment, when recognising interests in jointly controlled entities.

41 A venturer shall discontinue the use of the equity method from the date on which it ceases to have joint control over, or have significant influence in, a jointly controlled entity.

Exceptions to proportionate consolidation and equity method

42 Interests in jointly controlled entities that are classified as held for sale in accordance with IFRS 5 shall be accounted for in accordance with that IFRS.

43 When an interest in a jointly controlled entity previously classified as held for sale no longer meets the criteria to be so classified, it shall be accounted for using proportionate consolidation or the equity method as from the date of its classification as held for sale. Financial statements for the periods since classification as held for sale shall be amended accordingly.

44 [Deleted]

45 **From the date on which a jointly controlled entity becomes a subsidiary of a venturer, the venturer shall account for its interest in accordance with IAS 27. From the date on which a jointly controlled entity becomes an associate of a venturer, the venturer shall account for its interest in accordance with IAS 28.**

Separate financial statements of a venturer

46 **An interest in a jointly controlled entity shall be accounted for in a venturer's separate financial statements in accordance with paragraphs 37–42 of IAS 27.**

47 This Standard does not mandate which entities produce separate financial statements available for public use.

Transactions between a venturer and a joint venture

48 **When a venturer contributes or sells assets to a joint venture, recognition of any portion of a gain or loss from the transaction shall reflect the substance of the transaction. While the assets are retained by the joint venture, and provided the venturer has transferred the significant risks and rewards of ownership, the venturer shall recognise only that portion of the gain or loss that is attributable to the interests of the other venturers.* The venturer shall recognise the full amount of any loss when the contribution or sale provides evidence of a reduction in the net realisable value of current assets or an impairment loss.**

49 **When a venturer purchases assets from a joint venture, the venturer shall not recognise its share of the profits of the joint venture from the transaction until it resells the assets to an independent party. A venturer shall recognise its share of the losses resulting from these transactions in the same way as profits except that losses shall be recognised immediately when they represent a reduction in the net realisable value of current assets or an impairment loss.**

50 To assess whether a transaction between a venturer and a joint venture provides evidence of impairment of an asset, the venturer determines the recoverable amount of the asset in accordance with IAS 36 *Impairment of Assets*. In determining value in use, the venturer estimates future cash flows from the asset on the basis of continuing use of the asset and its ultimate disposal by the joint venture.

Reporting interests in joint ventures in the financial statements of an investor

51 **An investor in a joint venture that does not have joint control shall account for that investment in accordance with IAS 39 or, if it has significant influence in the joint venture, in accordance with IAS 28.**

* See also SIC-13 *Jointly Controlled Entities—Non-Monetary Contributions by Venturers*.

Operators of joint ventures

52 **Operators or managers of a joint venture shall account for any fees in accordance with IAS 18** ***Revenue*****.**

53 One or more venturers may act as the operator or manager of a joint venture. Operators are usually paid a management fee for such duties. The fees are accounted for by the joint venture as an expense.

Disclosure

54 **A venturer shall disclose the aggregate amount of the following contingent liabilities, unless the probability of loss is remote, separately from the amount of other contingent liabilities:**

(a) any contingent liabilities that the venturer has incurred in relation to its interests in joint ventures and its share in each of the contingent liabilities that have been incurred jointly with other venturers;

(b) its share of the contingent liabilities of the joint ventures themselves for which it is contingently liable; and

(c) those contingent liabilities that arise because the venturer is contingently liable for the liabilities of the other venturers of a joint venture.

55 **A venturer shall disclose the aggregate amount of the following commitments in respect of its interests in joint ventures separately from other commitments:**

(a) any capital commitments of the venturer in relation to its interests in joint ventures and its share in the capital commitments that have been incurred jointly with other venturers; and

(b) its share of the capital commitments of the joint ventures themselves.

56 **A venturer shall disclose a listing and description of interests in significant joint ventures and the proportion of ownership interest held in jointly controlled entities. A venturer that recognises its interests in jointly controlled entities using the line-by-line reporting format for proportionate consolidation or the equity method shall disclose the aggregate amounts of each of current assets, long-term assets, current liabilities, long-term liabilities, income and expenses related to its interests in joint ventures.**

57 **A venturer shall disclose the method it uses to recognise its interests in jointly controlled entities.**

Effective date

58 **An entity shall apply this Standard for annual periods beginning on or after 1 January 2005. Earlier application is encouraged. If an entity applies this Standard for a period beginning before 1 January 2005, it shall disclose that fact.**

Withdrawal of IAS 31 (revised 2000)

59 This Standard supersedes IAS 31 *Financial Reporting of Interests in Joint Ventures* (revised in 2000).

Appendix
Amendments to other pronouncements

The amendments in this appendix shall be applied for annual periods beginning on or after 1 January 2005. If an entity applies this Standard for an earlier period, these amendments shall be applied for that earlier period.

* * * * *

The amendments contained in this appendix when this Standard was issued in 2003 have been incorporated into the relevant pronouncements published in this volume.

Approval of IAS 31 by the Board

International Accounting Standard 31 *Interests in Joint Ventures* was approved for issue by the fourteen members of the International Accounting Standards Board.

Sir David Tweedie	Chairman
Thomas E Jones	Vice-Chairman
Mary E Barth	
Hans-Georg Bruns	
Anthony T Cope	
Robert P Garnett	
Gilbert Gélard	
James J Leisenring	
Warren J McGregor	
Patricia L O'Malley	
Harry K Schmid	
John T Smith	
Geoffrey Whittington	
Tatsumi Yamada	

Basis for Conclusions

This Basis for Conclusions accompanies, but is not part of, IAS 31.

Introduction

BC1 This Basis for Conclusions summarises the International Accounting Standards Board's considerations in reaching its conclusions on revising IAS 31 *Financial Reporting of Interests in Joint Ventures* in 2003. Individual Board members gave greater weight to some factors than to others.

BC2 In July 2001 the Board announced that, as part of its initial agenda of technical projects, it would undertake a project to improve a number of Standards, including IAS 27 *Consolidated Financial Statements and Accounting for Investments in Subsidiaries* and IAS 28 *Accounting for Investments in Associates.* The project was undertaken in the light of queries and criticisms raised in relation to the Standards by securities regulators, professional accountants and other interested parties. The objectives of the Improvements project were to reduce or eliminate alternatives, redundancies and conflicts within Standards, to deal with some convergence issues and to make other improvements. Because of the changes that were to be proposed for the revised versions of IAS 27 *Consolidated and Separate Financial Statements* and IAS 28 *Investments in Associates*, the Board also proposed to make some important consequential amendments to IAS 31 *Financial Reporting of Interests in Joint Ventures.*

BC3 Because the Board's intention was not to reconsider the fundamental approach to the accounting for joint ventures established by IAS 31 and to reflect only those changes related to its decisions in the Improvements project, in particular in relation to IAS 27 and IAS 28, this Basis for Conclusions does not discuss requirements in IAS 31 that the Board has not reconsidered. However, because of the scale of the amendments to the Standard, the Board believes it will be helpful to users to issue IAS 31 along with the Standards that were previously identified for revision as part of the Improvements project.

Scope exclusion: investments in joint ventures held by venture capital organisations, mutual funds, unit trusts and similar entities

BC4 There are no specific requirements that address accounting for investments by venture capital organisations, mutual funds, unit trusts and similar entities. As a result, depending on whether an entity has control, joint control or significant influence over an investee, one of the following Standards is applied:

(a) IAS 27 *Consolidated and Separate Financial Statements*,

(b) IAS 28 *Investments in Associates*, or

(c) IAS 31 *Interests in Joint Ventures.*

BC5 The Board considered whether another approach is appropriate for these investors when they do not have control but have joint control or significant influence over their investees. The Board noted that use of proportionate consolidation or the equity method for investments held by venture capital organisations, mutual funds, unit trusts and similar entities often produces information that is not relevant to their management and investors and that fair value measurement produces more relevant information in these circumstances. As noted in the Basis for Conclusions on IAS 27, the Board confirmed that a subsidiary should not be excluded from consolidation on the basis of the nature of the controlling entity. Consolidation is based on the parent's ability to control the investee and should not be affected by whether management intends to hold an investment in an entity that it controls for the short term. The Board concluded that for investments under the control of private equity entities, users' information needs are best served by financial statements in which those investments are consolidated, thus revealing the extent of the operations of the entities they control.

BC6 In addition, the Board noted that there may be frequent changes in the level of ownership in these investments and that financial statements are less useful if there are frequent changes in the method of accounting for an investment.

Measurement at fair value in accordance with IAS 39

BC7 Accordingly, the Board decided that investments held by venture capital organisations, mutual funds, unit trusts and similar entities including investment-linked insurance funds should be excluded from the scope of IAS 31 when they are measured at fair value in accordance with IAS 39 *Financial Instruments: Recognition and Measurement*. The Board understands that fair value information is often readily available because fair value measurement is a well-established practice in these industries including for investments in entities in the early stages of their development or in non-listed entities.

Treatment of changes in fair value

BC8 The Board decided that if venture capital organisations, mutual funds, unit trusts and similar entities are to be excluded from the scope of IAS 31, it should be only when they recognise changes in the fair value of their interests in joint ventures in profit or loss in the period in which those changes occur. This is to achieve the same treatment as for investments in subsidiaries or associates that are not consolidated or accounted for using the equity method because control or significant influence is intended to be temporary. The Board's approach distinguishes between accounting for the investment and accounting for the economic entity. In relation to the former, the Board decided that there should be consistency in the treatment of all investments, including changes in the fair value of these investments.

BC9 The Board noted that if such investments were classified in accordance with IAS 39, they would not always meet the definition of investments classified as held for trading because venture capital organisations may hold an investment for a period of 3–5 years. In accordance with IAS 39 such an investment is classified as available for sale (unless the entity elects to designate the investment on initial recognition at fair value through profit or loss). Classification as available for sale would not result in recognising changes in fair value in profit or loss. To achieve a similar effect on income to that of applying proportionate consolidation or the equity method, the Board decided to exempt investments held by venture capital organisations, mutual funds, unit trusts and similar entities from this Standard only when they are measured at fair value through profit or loss (either by designation or because they meet the definition in IAS 39 of held for trading).

Reference to 'well–established' industry practices

BC10 The Exposure Draft of IAS 28 proposed to limit the availability of the scope exclusion to situations in which well-established industry practice existed. Some respondents noted that the development of industry practice to measure such investments at fair value would have been precluded in industries established in countries already applying IFRSs. The Board confirmed that the main purpose of the reference to 'well-established' practice in the Exposure Draft was to emphasise that the exclusion would apply generally to those investments for which fair value is already available.

BC11 Therefore, the Board decided that the availability of the exclusion from the scope of IAS 31 should be based only on the nature of an entity's activities and to delete the reference to 'well-established' practices. The Board understands that measurement of these investments at fair value is 'well-established' practice in these industries.

Definition of 'venture capital organisations'

BC12 The Board decided not to define further those 'venture capital organisations and similar entities' excluded from the scope of IAS 31. Apart from recognising the difficulties of arriving at a universally applicable definition, the Board did not want inadvertently to make it difficult for entities to measure investments at fair value. However, the Board decided to clarify that the reference to 'similar entities' in the scope exclusion includes investment-linked insurance funds.

Application of proportionate consolidation or the equity method

Temporary joint control

BC13 The Board considered whether to remove the exemption from applying proportionate consolidation or the equity method when joint control in a joint venture is intended to be temporary. The Board decided to consider this issue as part of a comprehensive standard dealing with asset disposals. It decided to retain an exemption from applying proportionate consolidation or the equity method when there is evidence that an interest in a joint venture is acquired with the intention to dispose of it within twelve months and that management is actively seeking a buyer. The Board's Exposure Draft ED 4 *Disposal of Non-current Assets and Presentation of Discontinued Operations* proposes to measure and present assets held for sale in a consistent manner irrespective of whether they are held by an investor in an associate, a joint venture or a subsidiary.*

* In March 2004 the Board issued IFRS 5 *Non-current Assets Held for Sale and Discontinued Operations*. IFRS 5 removes this scope exclusion and now eliminates the exemption from applying proportionate consolidation or the equity method when joint control of a joint venture is intended to be temporary. See IFRS 5 Basis for Conclusions for further discussion.

Severe long–term restrictions impairing ability to transfer funds to the investor

BC14 The Board decided to remove the exemption from applying proportionate consolidation or the equity method for an interest in a joint venture that previously applied when severe long-term restrictions impaired a venture's ability to transfer funds to the venturer. It did so because such circumstances may not preclude the venturer's joint control over the venture. The Board decided that an investor should, when assessing its ability to exercise joint control over an entity, consider restrictions on the transfer of funds from the entity to the investor. In themselves, such restrictions do not preclude the existence of joint control.

Non–coterminous year–ends

BC15 The Exposure Draft of May 2002 proposed to limit to three months any difference between the reporting dates of the venturer and the venture when applying proportionate consolidation or the equity method. Some respondents to that Exposure Draft believed that it could be impracticable for the venturer to prepare financial statements as of the same date when the date of the venturer's and the venture's financial statements differ by more than three months. The Board noted that a three-month limit operates in several jurisdictions and it was concerned that a longer period, such as six months, would lead to the recognition of stale information. Therefore, it decided to retain the three-month limit.

Table of Concordance

This table shows how the contents of the superseded version of IAS 31 and the current version of IAS 31 correspond. Paragraphs are treated as corresponding if they broadly address the same matter even though the guidance may differ.

Superseded IAS 31 paragraph	Current IAS 31 paragraph
1	1
2	3
3	7
4	9
5	10
6	11
7	12
8	13
9	14
10	15
11	16
12	17
13	18
14	19
15	20
16	21
17	22
18	23
19	24
20	25
21	26
22	27
23	28
24	29
25	30
26	32
27	33
28	34
29	35
30	36
31	37
32	38
33	40
34	41
35	42
36	None
37	45
38	46
39	48
40	49
41	50
42	51
43	52
44	53
45	54
46	55
47	56
48	None
49	None
50	58
51	None
52	None
None	2
None	4–6
None	8
None	31
None	39
None	43
None	47
None	57
None	59

International Accounting Standard 32

Financial Instruments: Disclosure and Presentation

This version includes amendments resulting from new and amended IFRSs issued up to 31 December 2004.

CONTENTS

International Accounting Standard 32 *Financial Instruments: Disclosure and Presentation* (IAS 32) is set out in paragraphs 1–100 and the Appendix. All the paragraphs have equal authority but retain the IASC format of the Standard when it was adopted by the IASB. IAS 32 should be read in the context of its objective and the Basis for Conclusions, the *Preface to International Financial Reporting Standards* and the *Framework for the Preparation and Presentation of Financial Statements*. IAS 8 *Accounting Policies, Changes in Accounting Estimates and Errors* provides a basis for selecting and applying accounting policies in the absence of explicit guidance.

Introduction

Reasons for revising IAS 32

IN1 International Accounting Standard 32 *Financial Instruments: Disclosure and Presentation* (IAS 32) replaces IAS 32 *Financial Instruments: Disclosure and Presentation* (revised in 2000), and should be applied for annual periods beginning on or after 1 January 2005. Earlier application is permitted. The Standard also replaces the following Interpretations and draft Interpretation:

- SIC-5 *Classification of Financial Instruments—Contingent Settlement Provisions*;
- SIC-16 *Share Capital—Reacquired Own Equity Instruments (Treasury Shares)*;
- SIC-17 *Equity—Costs of an Equity Transaction*; and
- draft SIC-D34 *Financial Instruments—Instruments or Rights Redeemable by the Holder*.

IN2 The International Accounting Standards Board developed this revised IAS 32 as part of its project to improve IAS 32 and IAS 39 *Financial Instruments: Recognition and Measurement*. The objective of the project was to reduce complexity by clarifying and adding guidance, eliminating internal inconsistencies and incorporating into the Standards elements of Standing Interpretations Committee (SIC) Interpretations and IAS 39 implementation guidance published by the Implementation Guidance Committee (IGC).

IN3 For IAS 32, the Board's main objective was a limited revision to provide additional guidance on selected matters—such as the measurement of the components of a compound financial instrument on initial recognition, and the classification of derivatives based on an entity's own shares—and to locate all disclosures relating to financial instruments in one Standard. The Board did not reconsider the fundamental approach to the presentation and disclosure of financial instruments contained in IAS 32.

The main changes

IN4 The main changes from the previous version of IAS 32 are described below.

Scope

IN5 The scope of IAS 32 has, where appropriate, been conformed to the scope of IAS 39.

Principle

IN6 In summary, when an issuer determines whether a financial instrument is a financial liability or an equity instrument, the instrument is an equity instrument if, and only if, both conditions (a) and (b) are met.

(a) The instrument includes no contractual obligation:

(i) to deliver cash or another financial asset to another entity; or

(ii) to exchange financial assets or financial liabilities with another entity under conditions that are potentially unfavourable to the issuer.

(b) If the instrument will or may be settled in the issuer's own equity instruments, it is:

(i) a non-derivative that includes no contractual obligation for the issuer to deliver a variable number of its own equity instruments; or

(ii) a derivative that will be settled by the issuer exchanging a fixed amount of cash or another financial asset for a fixed number of its own equity instruments. For this purpose, the issuer's own equity instruments do not include instruments that are themselves contracts for the future receipt or delivery of the issuer's own equity instruments.

IN7 In addition, when an issuer has an obligation to purchase its own shares for cash or another financial asset, there is a liability for the amount that the issuer is obliged to pay.

IN8 The definitions of a financial asset and a financial liability, and the description of an equity instrument, are amended consistently with this principle.

Classification of contracts settled in an entity's own equity instruments

IN9 The classification of derivative and non-derivative contracts indexed to, or settled in, an entity's own equity instruments has been clarified consistently with the principle in paragraph IN6 above. In particular, when an entity uses its own equity instruments 'as currency' in a contract to receive or deliver a variable number of shares whose value equals a fixed amount or an amount based on changes in an underlying variable (eg a commodity price), the contract is not an equity instrument, but is a financial asset or a financial liability.

Puttable instruments

IN10 IAS 32 incorporates the guidance previously proposed in draft SIC Interpretation 34 *Financial Instruments—Instruments or Rights Redeemable by the Holder*. Consequently, a financial instrument that gives the holder the right to put the instrument back to the issuer for cash or another financial asset (a 'puttable instrument') is a financial liability of the issuer. In response to comments received on the Exposure Draft, the Standard provides additional guidance and illustrative examples for entities that, because of this requirement, have no equity or whose share capital is not equity as defined in IAS 32.

Contingent settlement provisions

IN11 IAS 32 incorporates the conclusion previously in SIC-5 *Classification of Financial Instruments—Contingent Settlement Provisions* that a financial instrument is a financial liability when the manner of settlement depends on the occurrence or non-occurrence of uncertain future events or on the outcome of uncertain circumstances that are beyond the control of both the issuer and the holder. Contingent settlement provisions are ignored when they apply only in the event of liquidation of the issuer or are not genuine.

Settlement options

IN12 Under IAS 32, a derivative financial instrument is a financial asset or a financial liability when it gives one of the parties to it a choice of how it is settled unless all of the settlement alternatives would result in it being an equity instrument.

Measurement of the components of a compound financial instrument on initial recognition

IN13 The revisions eliminate the option previously in IAS 32 to measure the liability component of a compound financial instrument on initial recognition either as a residual amount after separating the equity component, or by using a relative-fair-value method. Thus, any asset and liability components are separated first and the residual is the amount of any equity component. These requirements for separating the liability and equity components of a compound financial instrument are conformed to both the definition of an equity instrument as a residual and the measurement requirements in IAS 39.

Treasury shares

IN14 IAS 32 incorporates the conclusion previously in SIC-16 *Share Capital—Reacquired Own Equity Instruments (Treasury Shares)* that the acquisition or subsequent resale by an entity of its own equity instruments does not result in a gain or loss for the entity. Rather it represents a transfer between those holders of equity instruments who have given up their equity interest and those who continue to hold an equity instrument.

Interest, dividends, losses and gains

IN15 IAS 32 incorporates the guidance previously in SIC-17 *Equity—Costs of an Equity Transaction*. Transaction costs incurred as a necessary part of completing an equity transaction are accounted for as part of that transaction and are deducted from equity.

Disclosure

IN16 The limited exemption in IAS 32 from the requirement to disclose fair value of financial assets and financial liabilities has been conformed to the exemption in IAS 39 from the requirement to measure at fair value some investments in unquoted equity instruments and derivatives linked to such equity instruments.

IN17 Disclosure requirements have been added for the following:

(a) information about the use of valuation techniques, including the sensitivities of fair value estimates to significant valuation assumptions;

(b) information about assets retained in transactions that do not qualify for derecognition in their entirety;

(c) the carrying amounts of financial assets and financial liabilities that are classified as held for trading and those designated by the entity upon initial recognition as financial assets and financial liabilities at fair value through profit or loss;

(d) the amount of the change in fair value of a financial liability designated as at fair value through profit or loss that is not attributable to changes in a benchmark interest rate;

(e) the existence of, and specified information about, issued compound financial instruments with multiple embedded derivative features that have interdependent values; and

(f) information about any defaults by the entity on loans payable and other breaches of loan agreements.

IN18 The requirement to disclose separate information about financial assets carried at an amount in excess of fair value has been eliminated because it is redundant. This is because IAS 32 requires the disclosure of fair value information to be given in a way that permits comparison with financial assets' carrying amounts.

IN19 Disclosure requirements previously in IAS 39 have been moved to IAS 32.

Withdrawal of other pronouncements

IN20 As a consequence of the revisions to this Standard, the Board withdrew the three Interpretations and one draft Interpretation of the former Standing Interpretations Committee noted in paragraph IN1.

Potential impact of proposals in exposure drafts

IN21 [Deleted]

International Accounting Standard 32
Financial Instruments: Disclosure and Presentation

Objective

1 The objective of this Standard is to enhance financial statement users' understanding of the significance of financial instruments to an entity's financial position, performance and cash flows.

2 This Standard contains requirements for the presentation of financial instruments and identifies the information that should be disclosed about them. The presentation requirements apply to the classification of financial instruments, from the perspective of the issuer, into financial assets, financial liabilities and equity instruments; the classification of related interest, dividends, losses and gains; and the circumstances in which financial assets and financial liabilities should be offset. The Standard requires disclosure of information about factors that affect the amount, timing and certainty of an entity's future cash flows relating to financial instruments and the accounting policies applied to those instruments. This Standard also requires disclosure of information about the nature and extent of an entity's use of financial instruments, the business purposes they serve, the risks associated with them, and management's policies for controlling those risks.

3 The principles in this Standard complement the principles for recognising and measuring financial assets and financial liabilities in IAS 39 *Financial Instruments: Recognition and Measurement.*

Scope

4 This Standard shall be applied by all entities to all types of financial instruments except:

(a) those interests in subsidiaries, associates and joint ventures that are accounted for under IAS 27 *Consolidated and Separate Financial Statements*, **IAS 28** *Investments in Associates* **or IAS 31** *Interests in Joint Ventures*. **However, entities shall apply this Standard to an interest in a subsidiary, associate or joint venture that according to IAS 27, IAS 28 or IAS 31 is accounted for under IAS 39** *Financial Instruments: Recognition and Measurement*. **In these cases, entities shall apply the disclosure requirements in IAS 27, IAS 28 and IAS 31 in addition to those in this Standard. Entities shall also apply this Standard to all derivatives on interests in subsidiaries, associates or joint ventures.**

(b) employers' rights and obligations under employee benefit plans, to which IAS 19 *Employee Benefits* **applies.**

(c) contracts for contingent consideration in a business combination (see IFRS 3 *Business Combinations*). **This exemption applies only to the acquirer.**

(d) **insurance contracts as defined in IFRS 4** *Insurance Contracts*. **However, this Standard applies to derivatives that are embedded in insurance contracts if IAS 39 requires the entity to account for them separately.**

(e) **financial instruments that are within the scope of IFRS 4 because they contain a discretionary participation feature. The issuer of these instruments is exempt from applying to these features paragraphs 15–32 and AG25–AG35 of this Standard regarding the distinction between financial liabilities and equity instruments. However, these instruments are subject to all other requirements of this Standard. Furthermore, this Standard applies to derivatives that are embedded in these instruments (see IAS 39).**

(f) **financial instruments, contracts and obligations under share-based payment transactions to which IFRS 2** *Share-based Payment* **applies, except for**

(i) **contracts within the scope of paragraphs 8–10 of this Standard, to which this Standard applies,**

(ii) **paragraphs 33 and 34 of this Standard, which shall be applied to treasury shares purchased, sold, issued or cancelled in connection with employee share option plans, employee share purchase plans, and all other share-based payment arrangements.**

5 This Standard applies to recognised and unrecognised financial instruments. Recognised financial instruments include equity instruments issued by the entity and financial assets and financial liabilities that are within the scope of IAS 39. Unrecognised financial instruments include some financial instruments that, although outside the scope of IAS 39, are within the scope of this Standard (such as some loan commitments).

6 [Deleted]

7 Other Standards specific to particular types of financial instrument contain additional presentation and disclosure requirements. For example, IAS 17 *Leases* and IAS 26 *Accounting and Reporting by Retirement Benefit Plans* incorporate specific disclosure requirements relating to finance leases and retirement benefit plan investments, respectively. In addition, some requirements of other Standards, particularly IAS 30 *Disclosures in the Financial Statements of Banks and Similar Financial Institutions*, apply to financial instruments.

8 This Standard shall be applied to those contracts to buy or sell a non-financial item that can be settled net in cash or another financial instrument, or by exchanging financial instruments, as if the contracts were financial instruments, with the exception of contracts that were entered into and continue to be held for the purpose of the receipt or delivery of a non-financial item in accordance with the entity's expected purchase, sale or usage requirements.

9 There are various ways in which a contract to buy or sell a non-financial item can be settled net in cash or another financial instrument or by exchanging financial instruments. These include:

(a) when the terms of the contract permit either party to settle it net in cash or another financial instrument or by exchanging financial instruments;

(b) when the ability to settle net in cash or another financial instrument, or by exchanging financial instruments, is not explicit in the terms of the contract, but the entity has a practice of settling similar contracts net in cash or another financial instrument, or by exchanging financial instruments (whether with the counterparty, by entering into offsetting contracts or by selling the contract before its exercise or lapse);

(c) when, for similar contracts, the entity has a practice of taking delivery of the underlying and selling it within a short period after delivery for the purpose of generating a profit from short-term fluctuations in price or dealer's margin; and

(d) when the non-financial item that is the subject of the contract is readily convertible to cash.

A contract to which (b) or (c) applies is not entered into for the purpose of the receipt or delivery of the non-financial item in accordance with the entity's expected purchase, sale or usage requirements, and, accordingly, is within the scope of this Standard. Other contracts to which paragraph 8 applies are evaluated to determine whether they were entered into and continue to be held for the purpose of the receipt or delivery of the non-financial item in accordance with the entity's expected purchase, sale or usage requirement, and accordingly, whether they are within the scope of this Standard.

10 A written option to buy or sell a non-financial item that can be settled net in cash or another financial instrument, or by exchanging financial instruments, in accordance with paragraph 9(a) or (d) is within the scope of this Standard. Such a contract cannot be entered into for the purpose of the receipt or delivery of the non-financial item in accordance with the entity's expected purchase, sale or usage requirements.

Definitions (see also paragraphs AG3–AG24)

11 **The following terms are used in this Standard with the meanings specified:**

A ***financial instrument*** **is any contract that gives rise to a financial asset of one entity and a financial liability or equity instrument of another entity.**

A ***financial asset*** **is any asset that is:**

(a) cash;

(b) an equity instrument of another entity;

(c) a contractual right:

(i) to receive cash or another financial asset from another entity; or

(ii) to exchange financial assets or financial liabilities with another entity under conditions that are potentially favourable to the entity; or

(d) a contract that will or may be settled in the entity's own equity instruments and is:

(i) a non-derivative for which the entity is or may be obliged to receive a variable number of the entity's own equity instruments; or

(ii) a derivative that will or may be settled other than by the exchange of a fixed amount of cash or another financial asset for a fixed number of the entity's own equity instruments. For this purpose the entity's own equity instruments do not include instruments that are themselves contracts for the future receipt or delivery of the entity's own equity instruments.

A *financial liability* **is any liability that is:**

(a) a contractual obligation:

(i) to deliver cash or another financial asset to another entity; or

(ii) to exchange financial assets or financial liabilities with another entity under conditions that are potentially unfavourable to the entity; or

(b) a contract that will or may be settled in the entity's own equity instruments and is:

(i) a non-derivative for which the entity is or may be obliged to deliver a variable number of the entity's own equity instruments; or

(ii) a derivative that will or may be settled other than by the exchange of a fixed amount of cash or another financial asset for a fixed number of the entity's own equity instruments. For this purpose the entity's own equity instruments do not include instruments that are themselves contracts for the future receipt or delivery of the entity's own equity instruments.

An *equity instrument* **is any contract that evidences a residual interest in the assets of an entity after deducting all of its liabilities.**

Fair value **is the amount for which an asset could be exchanged, or a liability settled, between knowledgeable, willing parties in an arm's length transaction.**

12 The following terms are defined in paragraph 9 of IAS 39 and are used in this Standard with the meaning specified in IAS 39.

- amortised cost of a financial asset or financial liability
- available-for-sale financial assets
- derecognition
- derivative
- effective interest method
- financial asset or financial liability at fair value through profit or loss
- firm commitment
- forecast transaction

- hedge effectiveness
- hedged item
- hedging instrument
- held-to-maturity investments
- loans and receivables
- regular way purchase or sale
- transaction costs.

13 In this Standard, 'contract' and 'contractual' refer to an agreement between two or more parties that has clear economic consequences that the parties have little, if any, discretion to avoid, usually because the agreement is enforceable by law. Contracts, and thus financial instruments, may take a variety of forms and need not be in writing.

14 In this Standard, 'entity' includes individuals, partnerships, incorporated bodies, trusts and government agencies.

Presentation

Liabilities and equity (see also paragraphs AG25–AG29)

15 The issuer of a financial instrument shall classify the instrument, or its component parts, on initial recognition as a financial liability, a financial asset or an equity instrument in accordance with the substance of the contractual arrangement and the definitions of a financial liability, a financial asset and an equity instrument.

16 When an issuer applies the definitions in paragraph 11 to determine whether a financial instrument is an equity instrument rather than a financial liability, the instrument is an equity instrument if, and only if, both conditions (a) and (b) below are met.

(a) The instrument includes no contractual obligation:

(i) to deliver cash or another financial asset to another entity; or

(ii) to exchange financial assets or financial liabilities with another entity under conditions that are potentially unfavourable to the issuer.

(b) If the instrument will or may be settled in the issuer's own equity instruments, it is:

(i) a non-derivative that includes no contractual obligation for the issuer to deliver a variable number of its own equity instruments; or

(ii) a derivative that will be settled only by the issuer exchanging a fixed amount of cash or another financial asset for a fixed number of its own equity instruments. For this purpose the issuer's own equity instruments do not include instruments that are themselves contracts for the future receipt or delivery of the issuer's own equity instruments.

A contractual obligation, including one arising from a derivative financial instrument, that will or may result in the future receipt or delivery of the issuer's own equity instruments, but does not meet conditions (a) and (b) above, is not an equity instrument.

No contractual obligation to deliver cash or another financial asset (paragraph 16(a))

17 A critical feature in differentiating a financial liability from an equity instrument is the existence of a contractual obligation of one party to the financial instrument (the issuer) either to deliver cash or another financial asset to the other party (the holder) or to exchange financial assets or financial liabilities with the holder under conditions that are potentially unfavourable to the issuer. Although the holder of an equity instrument may be entitled to receive a pro rata share of any dividends or other distributions of equity, the issuer does not have a contractual obligation to make such distributions because it cannot be required to deliver cash or another financial asset to another party.

18 The substance of a financial instrument, rather than its legal form, governs its classification on the entity's balance sheet. Substance and legal form are commonly consistent, but not always. Some financial instruments take the legal form of equity but are liabilities in substance and others may combine features associated with equity instruments and features associated with financial liabilities. For example:

(a) a preference share that provides for mandatory redemption by the issuer for a fixed or determinable amount at a fixed or determinable future date, or gives the holder the right to require the issuer to redeem the instrument at or after a particular date for a fixed or determinable amount, is a financial liability.

(b) a financial instrument that gives the holder the right to put it back to the issuer for cash or another financial asset (a 'puttable instrument') is a financial liability. This is so even when the amount of cash or other financial assets is determined on the basis of an index or other item that has the potential to increase or decrease, or when the legal form of the puttable instrument gives the holder a right to a residual interest in the assets of an issuer. The existence of an option for the holder to put the instrument back to the issuer for cash or another financial asset means that the puttable instrument meets the definition of a financial liability. For example, open-ended mutual funds, unit trusts, partnerships and some co-operative entities may provide their unitholders or members with a right to redeem their interests in the issuer at any time for cash equal to their proportionate share of the asset value of the issuer. However, classification as a financial liability does not preclude the use of descriptors such as 'net asset value attributable to unitholders' and 'change in net asset value attributable to unitholders' on the face of the financial statements of an entity that has no contributed equity (such as some mutual funds and unit trusts, see Illustrative Example 7) or the use of additional disclosure to show that total members' interests comprise items such as reserves that meet the definition of equity and puttable instruments that do not (see Illustrative Example 8).

19 If an entity does not have an unconditional right to avoid delivering cash or another financial asset to settle a contractual obligation, the obligation meets the definition of a financial liability. For example:

(a) a restriction on the ability of an entity to satisfy a contractual obligation, such as lack of access to foreign currency or the need to obtain approval for payment from a regulatory authority, does not negate the entity's contractual obligation or the holder's contractual right under the instrument.

(b) a contractual obligation that is conditional on a counterparty exercising its right to redeem is a financial liability because the entity does not have the unconditional right to avoid delivering cash or another financial asset.

20 A financial instrument that does not explicitly establish a contractual obligation to deliver cash or another financial asset may establish an obligation indirectly through its terms and conditions. For example:

(a) a financial instrument may contain a non-financial obligation that must be settled if, and only if, the entity fails to make distributions or to redeem the instrument. If the entity can avoid a transfer of cash or another financial asset only by settling the non-financial obligation, the financial instrument is a financial liability.

(b) a financial instrument is a financial liability if it provides that on settlement the entity will deliver either:

(i) cash or another financial asset; or

(ii) its own shares whose value is determined to exceed substantially the value of the cash or other financial asset.

Although the entity does not have an explicit contractual obligation to deliver cash or another financial asset, the value of the share settlement alternative is such that the entity will settle in cash. In any event, the holder has in substance been guaranteed receipt of an amount that is at least equal to the cash settlement option (see paragraph 21).

Settlement in the entity's own equity instruments (paragraph 16(b))

21 A contract is not an equity instrument solely because it may result in the receipt or delivery of the entity's own equity instruments. An entity may have a contractual right or obligation to receive or deliver a number of its own shares or other equity instruments that varies so that the fair value of the entity's own equity instruments to be received or delivered equals the amount of the contractual right or obligation. Such a contractual right or obligation may be for a fixed amount or an amount that fluctuates in part or in full in response to changes in a variable other than the market price of the entity's own equity instruments (eg an interest rate, a commodity price or a financial instrument price). Two examples are (a) a contract to deliver as many of the entity's own equity instruments as are equal in value to CU100,* and (b) a contract to deliver as many of the entity's own equity instruments as are equal in value to the value of 100 ounces of gold. Such a contract is a financial liability of the entity even

* In this Standard, monetary amounts are denominated in 'currency units' (CU).

though the entity must or can settle it by delivering its own equity instruments. It is not an equity instrument because the entity uses a variable number of its own equity instruments as a means to settle the contract. Accordingly, the contract does not evidence a residual interest in the entity's assets after deducting all of its liabilities.

22 A contract that will be settled by the entity (receiving or) delivering a fixed number of its own equity instruments in exchange for a fixed amount of cash or another financial asset is an equity instrument. For example, an issued share option that gives the counterparty a right to buy a fixed number of the entity's shares for a fixed price or for a fixed stated principal amount of a bond is an equity instrument. Changes in the fair value of a contract arising from variations in market interest rates that do not affect the amount of cash or other financial assets to be paid or received, or the number of equity instruments to be received or delivered, on settlement of the contract do not preclude the contract from being an equity instrument. Any consideration received (such as the premium received for a written option or warrant on the entity's own shares) is added directly to equity. Any consideration paid (such as the premium paid for a purchased option) is deducted directly from equity. Changes in the fair value of an equity instrument are not recognised in the financial statements.

23 A contract that contains an obligation for an entity to purchase its own equity instruments for cash or another financial asset gives rise to a financial liability for the present value of the redemption amount (for example, for the present value of the forward repurchase price, option exercise price or other redemption amount). This is the case even if the contract itself is an equity instrument. One example is an entity's obligation under a forward contract to purchase its own equity instruments for cash. When the financial liability is recognised initially under IAS 39, its fair value (the present value of the redemption amount) is reclassified from equity. Subsequently, the financial liability is measured in accordance with IAS 39. If the contract expires without delivery, the carrying amount of the financial liability is reclassified to equity. An entity's contractual obligation to purchase its own equity instruments gives rise to a financial liability for the present value of the redemption amount even if the obligation to purchase is conditional on the counterparty exercising a right to redeem (eg a written put option that gives the counterparty the right to sell an entity's own equity instruments to the entity for a fixed price).

24 A contract that will be settled by the entity delivering or receiving a fixed number of its own equity instruments in exchange for a variable amount of cash or another financial asset is a financial asset or financial liability. An example is a contract for the entity to deliver 100 of its own equity instruments in return for an amount of cash calculated to equal the value of 100 ounces of gold.

Contingent settlement provisions

25 A financial instrument may require the entity to deliver cash or another financial asset, or otherwise to settle it in such a way that it would be a financial liability, in the event of the occurrence or non-occurrence of uncertain future events (or on the outcome of uncertain circumstances) that are beyond the control of both the issuer and the holder of the instrument, such as a change in a stock market index,

consumer price index, interest rate or taxation requirements, or the issuer's future revenues, net income or debt-to-equity ratio. The issuer of such an instrument does not have the unconditional right to avoid delivering cash or another financial asset (or otherwise to settle it in such a way that it would be a financial liability). Therefore, it is a financial liability of the issuer unless:

(a) the part of the contingent settlement provision that could require settlement in cash or another financial asset (or otherwise in such a way that it would be a financial liability) is not genuine; or

(b) the issuer can be required to settle the obligation in cash or another financial asset (or otherwise to settle it in such a way that it would be a financial liability) only in the event of liquidation of the issuer.

Settlement options

26 **When a derivative financial instrument gives one party a choice over how it is settled (eg the issuer or the holder can choose settlement net in cash or by exchanging shares for cash), it is a financial asset or a financial liability unless all of the settlement alternatives would result in it being an equity instrument.**

27 An example of a derivative financial instrument with a settlement option that is a financial liability is a share option that the issuer can decide to settle net in cash or by exchanging its own shares for cash. Similarly, some contracts to buy or sell a non-financial item in exchange for the entity's own equity instruments are within the scope of this Standard because they can be settled either by delivery of the non-financial item or net in cash or another financial instrument (see paragraphs 8–10). Such contracts are financial assets or financial liabilities and not equity instruments.

Compound financial instruments (see also paragraphs AG30–AG35 and Illustrative Examples 9–12)

28 **The issuer of a non-derivative financial instrument shall evaluate the terms of the financial instrument to determine whether it contains both a liability and an equity component. Such components shall be classified separately as financial liabilities, financial assets or equity instruments in accordance with paragraph 15.**

29 An entity recognises separately the components of a financial instrument that (a) creates a financial liability of the entity and (b) grants an option to the holder of the instrument to convert it into an equity instrument of the entity. For example, a bond or similar instrument convertible by the holder into a fixed number of ordinary shares of the entity is a compound financial instrument. From the perspective of the entity, such an instrument comprises two components: a financial liability (a contractual arrangement to deliver cash or another financial asset) and an equity instrument (a call option granting the holder the right, for a specified period of time, to convert it into a fixed number of ordinary shares of the entity). The economic effect of issuing such an instrument is substantially the same as issuing simultaneously a debt instrument with an early settlement provision and warrants to purchase ordinary shares, or issuing a

debt instrument with detachable share purchase warrants. Accordingly, in all cases, the entity presents the liability and equity components separately on its balance sheet.

30 Classification of the liability and equity components of a convertible instrument is not revised as a result of a change in the likelihood that a conversion option will be exercised, even when exercise of the option may appear to have become economically advantageous to some holders. Holders may not always act in the way that might be expected because, for example, the tax consequences resulting from conversion may differ among holders. Furthermore, the likelihood of conversion will change from time to time. The entity's contractual obligation to make future payments remains outstanding until it is extinguished through conversion, maturity of the instrument or some other transaction.

31 IAS 39 deals with the measurement of financial assets and financial liabilities. Equity instruments are instruments that evidence a residual interest in the assets of an entity after deducting all of its liabilities. Therefore, when the initial carrying amount of a compound financial instrument is allocated to its equity and liability components, the equity component is assigned the residual amount after deducting from the fair value of the instrument as a whole the amount separately determined for the liability component. The value of any derivative features (such as a call option) embedded in the compound financial instrument other than the equity component (such as an equity conversion option) is included in the liability component. The sum of the carrying amounts assigned to the liability and equity components on initial recognition is always equal to the fair value that would be ascribed to the instrument as a whole. No gain or loss arises from initially recognising the components of the instrument separately.

32 Under the approach described in paragraph 31, the issuer of a bond convertible into ordinary shares first determines the carrying amount of the liability component by measuring the fair value of a similar liability (including any embedded non-equity derivative features) that does not have an associated equity component. The carrying amount of the equity instrument represented by the option to convert the instrument into ordinary shares is then determined by deducting the fair value of the financial liability from the fair value of the compound financial instrument as a whole.

Treasury shares (see also paragraph AG36)

33 If an entity reacquires its own equity instruments, those instruments ('treasury shares') shall be deducted from equity. No gain or loss shall be recognised in profit or loss on the purchase, sale, issue or cancellation of an entity's own equity instruments. Such treasury shares may be acquired and held by the entity or by other members of the consolidated group. Consideration paid or received shall be recognised directly in equity.

34 The amount of treasury shares held is disclosed separately either on the face of the balance sheet or in the notes, in accordance with IAS 1 *Presentation of Financial Statements*. An entity provides disclosure in accordance with IAS 24 *Related Party Disclosures* if the entity reacquires its own equity instruments from related parties.

Interest, dividends, losses and gains (see also paragraph AG37)

35 **Interest, dividends, losses and gains relating to a financial instrument or a component that is a financial liability shall be recognised as income or expense in profit or loss. Distributions to holders of an equity instrument shall be debited by the entity directly to equity, net of any related income tax benefit. Transaction costs of an equity transaction, other than costs of issuing an equity instrument that are directly attributable to the acquisition of a business (which shall be accounted for under IFRS 3), shall be accounted for as a deduction from equity, net of any related income tax benefit.**

36 The classification of a financial instrument as a financial liability or an equity instrument determines whether interest, dividends, losses and gains relating to that instrument are recognised as income or expense in profit or loss. Thus, dividend payments on shares wholly recognised as liabilities are recognised as expenses in the same way as interest on a bond. Similarly, gains and losses associated with redemptions or refinancings of financial liabilities are recognised in profit or loss, whereas redemptions or refinancings of equity instruments are recognised as changes in equity. Changes in the fair value of an equity instrument are not recognised in the financial statements.

37 An entity typically incurs various costs in issuing or acquiring its own equity instruments. Those costs might include registration and other regulatory fees, amounts paid to legal, accounting and other professional advisers, printing costs and stamp duties. The transaction costs of an equity transaction are accounted for as a deduction from equity (net of any related income tax benefit) to the extent they are incremental costs directly attributable to the equity transaction that otherwise would have been avoided. The costs of an equity transaction that is abandoned are recognised as an expense.

38 Transaction costs that relate to the issue of a compound financial instrument are allocated to the liability and equity components of the instrument in proportion to the allocation of proceeds. Transaction costs that relate jointly to more than one transaction (for example, costs of a concurrent offering of some shares and a stock exchange listing of other shares) are allocated to those transactions using a basis of allocation that is rational and consistent with similar transactions.

39 The amount of transaction costs accounted for as a deduction from equity in the period is disclosed separately under IAS 1 *Presentation of Financial Statements.* The related amount of income taxes recognised directly in equity is included in the aggregate amount of current and deferred income tax credited or charged to equity that is disclosed under IAS 12 *Income Taxes.*

40 Dividends classified as an expense may be presented in the income statement either with interest on other liabilities or as a separate item. In addition to the requirements of this Standard, disclosure of interest and dividends is subject to the requirements of IAS 1 and IAS 30 *Disclosures in the Financial Statements of Banks and Similar Financial Institutions.* In some circumstances, because of the differences between interest and dividends with respect to matters such as tax deductibility, it

is desirable to disclose them separately in the income statement. Disclosures of the tax effects are made in accordance with IAS 12.

41 Gains and losses related to changes in the carrying amount of a financial liability are recognised as income or expense in profit or loss even when they relate to an instrument that includes a right to the residual interest in the assets of the entity in exchange for cash or another financial asset (see paragraph 18(b)). Under IAS 1 the entity presents any gain or loss arising from remeasurement of such an instrument separately on the face of the income statement when it is relevant in explaining the entity's performance.

Offsetting a financial asset and a financial liability (see also paragraphs AG38 and AG39)

42 **A financial asset and a financial liability shall be offset and the net amount presented in the balance sheet when, and only when, an entity:**

(a) currently has a legally enforceable right to set off the recognised amounts; and

(b) intends either to settle on a net basis, or to realise the asset and settle the liability simultaneously.

In accounting for a transfer of a financial asset that does not qualify for derecognition, the entity shall not offset the transferred asset and the associated liability (see IAS 39, paragraph 36).

43 This Standard requires the presentation of financial assets and financial liabilities on a net basis when doing so reflects an entity's expected future cash flows from settling two or more separate financial instruments. When an entity has the right to receive or pay a single net amount and intends to do so, it has, in effect, only a single financial asset or financial liability. In other circumstances, financial assets and financial liabilities are presented separately from each other consistently with their characteristics as resources or obligations of the entity.

44 Offsetting a recognised financial asset and a recognised financial liability and presenting the net amount differs from the derecognition of a financial asset or a financial liability. Although offsetting does not give rise to recognition of a gain or loss, the derecognition of a financial instrument not only results in the removal of the previously recognised item from the balance sheet but also may result in recognition of a gain or loss.

45 A right of set-off is a debtor's legal right, by contract or otherwise, to settle or otherwise eliminate all or a portion of an amount due to a creditor by applying against that amount an amount due from the creditor. In unusual circumstances, a debtor may have a legal right to apply an amount due from a third party against the amount due to a creditor provided that there is an agreement between the three parties that clearly establishes the debtor's right of set-off. Because the right of setoff is a legal right, the conditions supporting the right may vary from one legal jurisdiction to another and the laws applicable to the relationships between the parties need to be considered.

46 The existence of an enforceable right to set off a financial asset and a financial liability affects the rights and obligations associated with a financial asset and a

financial liability and may affect an entity's exposure to credit and liquidity risk. However, the existence of the right, by itself, is not a sufficient basis for offsetting. In the absence of an intention to exercise the right or to settle simultaneously, the amount and timing of an entity's future cash flows are not affected. When an entity intends to exercise the right or to settle simultaneously, presentation of the asset and liability on a net basis reflects more appropriately the amounts and timing of the expected future cash flows, as well as the risks to which those cash flows are exposed. An intention by one or both parties to settle on a net basis without the legal right to do so is not sufficient to justify offsetting because the rights and obligations associated with the individual financial asset and financial liability remain unaltered.

47 An entity's intentions with respect to settlement of particular assets and liabilities may be influenced by its normal business practices, the requirements of the financial markets and other circumstances that may limit the ability to settle net or to settle simultaneously. When an entity has a right of set-off, but does not intend to settle net or to realise the asset and settle the liability simultaneously, the effect of the right on the entity's credit risk exposure is disclosed in accordance with paragraph 76.

48 Simultaneous settlement of two financial instruments may occur through, for example, the operation of a clearing house in an organised financial market or a face-to-face exchange. In these circumstances the cash flows are, in effect, equivalent to a single net amount and there is no exposure to credit or liquidity risk. In other circumstances, an entity may settle two instruments by receiving and paying separate amounts, becoming exposed to credit risk for the full amount of the asset or liquidity risk for the full amount of the liability. Such risk exposures may be significant even though relatively brief. Accordingly, realisation of a financial asset and settlement of a financial liability are treated as simultaneous only when the transactions occur at the same moment.

49 The conditions set out in paragraph 42 are generally not satisfied and offsetting is usually inappropriate when:

(a) several different financial instruments are used to emulate the features of a single financial instrument (a 'synthetic instrument');

(b) financial assets and financial liabilities arise from financial instruments having the same primary risk exposure (for example, assets and liabilities within a portfolio of forward contracts or other derivative instruments) but involve different counterparties;

(c) financial or other assets are pledged as collateral for non-recourse financial liabilities;

(d) financial assets are set aside in trust by a debtor for the purpose of discharging an obligation without those assets having been accepted by the creditor in settlement of the obligation (for example, a sinking fund arrangement); or

(e) obligations incurred as a result of events giving rise to losses are expected to be recovered from a third party by virtue of a claim made under an insurance contract.

50 An entity that undertakes a number of financial instrument transactions with a single counterparty may enter into a 'master netting arrangement' with that counterparty. Such an agreement provides for a single net settlement of all financial instruments covered by the agreement in the event of default on, or termination of, any one contract. These arrangements are commonly used by financial institutions to provide protection against loss in the event of bankruptcy or other circumstances that result in a counterparty being unable to meet its obligations. A master netting arrangement commonly creates a right of set-off that becomes enforceable and affects the realisation or settlement of individual financial assets and financial liabilities only following a specified event of default or in other circumstances not expected to arise in the normal course of business. A master netting arrangement does not provide a basis for offsetting unless both of the criteria in paragraph 42 are satisfied. When financial assets and financial liabilities subject to a master netting arrangement are not offset, the effect of the arrangement on an entity's exposure to credit risk is disclosed in accordance with paragraph 76.

Disclosure

51 The purpose of the disclosures required by this Standard is to provide information to enhance understanding of the significance of financial instruments to an entity's financial position, performance and cash flows, and assist in assessing the amounts, timing and certainty of future cash flows associated with those instruments.

52 Transactions in financial instruments may result in an entity assuming or transferring to another party one or more of the financial risks described below. The required disclosures provide information to assist users of financial statements in assessing the extent of risk related to financial instruments.

(a) *Market risk* includes three types of risk:

  (i) *currency risk*—the risk that the value of a financial instrument will fluctuate because of changes in foreign exchange rates.

  (ii) *fair value interest rate risk*—the risk that the value of a financial instrument will fluctuate because of changes in market interest rates.

  (iii) *price risk*—the risk that the value of a financial instrument will fluctuate as a result of changes in market prices, whether those changes are caused by factors specific to the individual instrument or its issuer or factors affecting all instruments traded in the market.

  Market risk embodies not only the potential for loss but also the potential for gain.

(b) *Credit risk*—the risk that one party to a financial instrument will fail to discharge an obligation and cause the other party to incur a financial loss.

(c) *Liquidity risk* (also referred to as *funding risk*)—the risk that an entity will encounter difficulty in raising funds to meet commitments associated with financial instruments. Liquidity risk may result from an inability to sell a financial asset quickly at close to its fair value.

(d) *Cash flow interest rate risk*—the risk that the future cash flows of a financial instrument will fluctuate because of changes in market interest rates. In the case of a floating rate debt instrument, for example, such fluctuations result in a change in the effective interest rate of the financial instrument, usually without a corresponding change in its fair value.

Format, location and classes of financial instruments

53 This Standard does not prescribe either the format of the information required to be disclosed or its location within the financial statements. To the extent that the required information is presented on the face of the financial statements, it is unnecessary to repeat it in the notes. Disclosures may include a combination of narrative descriptions and quantified data, as appropriate to the nature of the instruments and their relative significance to the entity.

54 Determining the level of detail to be disclosed about particular financial instruments requires the exercise of judgement taking into account the relative significance of those instruments. It is necessary to strike a balance between overburdening financial statements with excessive detail that may not assist users of financial statements and obscuring important information as a result of too much aggregation. For example, when an entity is party to a large number of financial instruments with similar characteristics and no single contract is individually material, a summary by classes of instruments is appropriate. On the other hand, information about an individual instrument may be important when it is, for example, a material component of an entity's capital structure.

55 The management of an entity groups financial instruments into classes that are appropriate to the nature of the information disclosed, taking into account matters such as the characteristics of the instruments and the measurement basis that has been applied. In general, classes distinguish items measured at cost or amortised cost from items measured at fair value. Sufficient information is provided to permit a reconciliation to relevant line items on the balance sheet. When an entity is a party to financial instruments not within the scope of this Standard, those instruments constitute a class or classes of financial assets or financial liabilities separate from those within the scope of this Standard. Disclosures about those financial instruments are dealt with by other IFRSs.

Risk management policies and hedging activities

56 An entity shall describe its financial risk management objectives and policies, including its policy for hedging each main type of forecast transaction for which hedge accounting is used.

57 In addition to providing specific information about particular balances and transactions related to financial instruments, an entity provides a discussion of the extent to which financial instruments are used, the associated risks and the business purposes served. A discussion of management's policies for controlling the risks associated with financial instruments includes policies on matters such as hedging of risk exposures, avoidance of undue concentrations of risk and requirements for collateral to mitigate credit risk. Such discussion provides a valuable additional perspective that is independent of the specific instruments held or outstanding at a particular time.

58 **An entity shall disclose the following separately for designated fair value hedges, cash flow hedges and hedges of a net investment in a foreign operation (as defined in IAS 39):**

(a) a description of the hedge;

(b) a description of the financial instruments designated as hedging instruments and their fair values at the balance sheet date;

(c) the nature of the risks being hedged; and

(d) for cash flow hedges, the periods in which the cash flows are expected to occur, when they are expected to enter into the determination of profit or loss, and a description of any forecast transaction for which hedge accounting had previously been used but which is no longer expected to occur.

59 **When a gain or loss on a hedging instrument in a cash flow hedge has been recognised directly in equity, through the statement of changes in equity, an entity shall disclose:**

(a) the amount that was so recognised in equity during the period;

(b) the amount that was removed from equity and included in profit or loss for the period; and

(c) the amount that was removed from equity during the period and included in the initial measurement of the acquisition cost or other carrying amount of a non-financial asset or non-financial liability in a hedged highly probable forecast transaction.

Terms, conditions and accounting policies

60 **For each class of financial asset, financial liability and equity instrument, an entity shall disclose:**

(a) information about the extent and nature of the financial instruments, including significant terms and conditions that may affect the amount, timing and certainty of future cash flows; and

(b) the accounting policies and methods adopted, including the criteria for recognition and the basis of measurement applied.

61 **As part of the disclosure of an entity's accounting policies, an entity shall disclose, for each category of financial assets, whether regular way purchases and sales of financial assets are accounted for at trade date or at settlement date (see IAS 39, paragraph 38).**

62 The contractual terms and conditions of a financial instrument affect the amount, timing and certainty of future cash receipts and payments by the parties to the instrument. When financial instruments are significant, either individually or as a class, to the financial position of an entity or its future operating results, their terms and conditions are disclosed. If no single instrument is individually significant to the future cash flows of the entity, the essential characteristics of the instruments are described by reference to appropriate groupings of like instruments.

63 When financial instruments held or issued by an entity, either individually or as a class, create a potentially significant exposure to the risks described in paragraph 52, terms and conditions that warrant disclosure include:

(a) the principal, stated, face or other similar amount, which, for some derivative instruments, such as interest rate swaps, might be the amount (referred to as the notional amount) on which future payments are based;

(b) the date of maturity, expiry or execution;

(c) early settlement options held by either party to the instrument, including the period in which, or date at which, the options can be exercised and the exercise price or range of prices;

(d) options held by either party to the instrument to convert the instrument into, or exchange it for, another financial instrument or some other asset or liability, including the period in which, or date at which, the options can be exercised and the conversion or exchange ratio(s);

(e) the amount and timing of scheduled future cash receipts or payments of the principal amount of the instrument, including instalment repayments and any sinking fund or similar requirements;

(f) stated rate or amount of interest, dividend or other periodic return on principal and the timing of payments;

(g) collateral held, in the case of a financial asset, or pledged, in the case of a financial liability;

(h) in the case of an instrument for which cash flows are denominated in a currency other than the entity's functional currency, the currency in which receipts or payments are required;

(i) in the case of an instrument that provides for an exchange, information described in items (a)–(h) for the instrument to be acquired in the exchange; and

(j) any condition of the instrument or an associated covenant that, if contravened, would significantly alter any of the other terms (for example, a maximum debt-to-equity ratio in a bond covenant that, if contravened, would make the full principal amount of the bond due and payable immediately).

64 When the balance sheet presentation of a financial instrument differs from the instrument's legal form, it is desirable for an entity to explain in the notes the nature of the instrument.

65 The usefulness of information about the extent and nature of financial instruments is enhanced when it highlights any relationship between individual instruments that can significantly affect the amount, timing or certainty of the future cash flows of an entity. For example, it may be important to disclose hedging relationships such as one that might exist when an entity holds an investment in shares for which it has purchased a put option. The extent to which a risk exposure is altered by the relationship among the assets and liabilities may be apparent to financial statement users from information of the type described in paragraph 63, but in some circumstances further disclosure is necessary.

66 In accordance with IAS 1, an entity provides disclosure of all significant accounting policies, including the general principles adopted and the method of applying those principles to transactions, other events and conditions arising in the entity's business. In the case of financial instruments, such disclosure includes:

(a) the criteria applied in determining when to recognise a financial asset or financial liability and when to derecognise it;

(b) the basis of measurement applied to financial assets and financial liabilities on initial recognition and subsequently; and

(c) the basis on which income and expenses arising from financial assets and financial liabilities are recognised and measured.

Interest rate risk

67 For each class of financial assets and financial liabilities, an entity shall disclose information about its exposure to interest rate risk, including:

(a) contractual repricing or maturity dates, whichever dates are earlier; and

(b) effective interest rates, when applicable.

68 An entity provides information about its exposure to the effects of future changes in the prevailing level of interest rates. Changes in market interest rates have a direct effect on the contractually determined cash flows associated with some financial assets and financial liabilities (cash flow interest rate risk) and on the fair value of others (fair value interest rate risk).

69 Information about maturity dates (or repricing dates when they are earlier) indicates the length of time for which interest rates are fixed, and information about effective interest rates indicates the levels at which they are fixed. Disclosure of this information provides users of financial statements with a basis for evaluating the fair value interest rate risk to which an entity is exposed and, thus, the potential for gain or loss. For instruments that are repriced to a market rate of interest before maturity, disclosure of the period until the next repricing is more important for this purpose than disclosure of the period to maturity.

70 To supplement the information about contractual repricing and maturity dates, an entity may elect to disclose information about expected repricing or maturity dates when those dates differ significantly from the contractual dates. For example, such information may be particularly relevant when an entity is able to predict, with reasonable reliability, the amount of fixed rate mortgage loans that will be repaid before maturity and it uses this information as the basis for managing its interest rate risk exposure. The additional information includes disclosure that it is based on management's expectations of future events and an explanation of the assumptions made about repricing or maturity dates and how those assumptions differ from the contractual dates.

71 An entity indicates which of its financial assets and financial liabilities are:

(a) exposed to fair value interest rate risk, such as financial assets and financial liabilities with a fixed interest rate;

(b) exposed to cash flow interest rate risk, such as financial assets and financial liabilities with a floating interest rate that is reset as market rates change; and

(c) not directly exposed to interest rate risk, such as some investments in equity instruments.

72 The requirement in paragraph 67(b) applies to bonds, notes, loans and similar financial instruments involving future payments that create a return to the holder and a cost to the issuer reflecting the time value of money. The requirement does not apply to financial instruments such as investments in equity instruments and derivative instruments that do not bear a determinable effective interest rate. For example, even though instruments such as interest rate derivatives (including swaps, forward rate agreements and options) are exposed to fair value or cash flow risk from changes in market interest rates, disclosure of an effective interest rate is not required. However, when providing effective interest rate information, an entity discloses the effect on its interest rate risk exposure of hedging transactions such as interest rate swaps.

73 An entity may become exposed to interest rate risk as a result of a transaction in which no financial asset or financial liability is recognised on its balance sheet. In such circumstances, the entity discloses information that permits users of its financial statements to understand the nature and extent of its exposure. For example, when an entity has a commitment to lend funds at a fixed interest rate, the disclosure normally includes the stated principal, interest rate and term to maturity of the amount to be lent and the significant terms of the transaction giving rise to the exposure to interest rate risk.

74 The nature of an entity's business and the extent of its activity in financial instruments determine whether information about interest rate risk is presented in narrative form, in tables or by using a combination of the two. When an entity has a variety of financial instruments exposed to fair value or cash flow interest rate risk, it may adopt one or more of the following approaches to presenting information:

(a) The carrying amounts of financial instruments exposed to interest rate risk may be presented in tabular form, grouped by those that are contracted to mature or be repriced in the following periods after the balance sheet date:

(i) in one year or less;

(ii) in more than one year but not more than two years;

(iii) in more than two years but not more than three years;

(iv) in more than three years but not more than four years;

(v) in more than four years but not more than five years; and

(vi) in more than five years.

(b) When the performance of an entity is significantly affected by the level of its exposure to interest rate risk or changes in that exposure, more detailed information is desirable. An entity such as a bank may disclose, for example, separate groupings of the carrying amounts of financial instruments contracted to mature or be repriced:

(i) in one month or less after the balance sheet date;

(ii) in more than one month but not more than three months after the balance sheet date; and

(iii) in more than three months but not more than twelve months after the balance sheet date.

(c) Similarly, an entity may indicate its exposure to cash flow interest rate risk through a table indicating the aggregate carrying amount of groups of floating rate financial assets and financial liabilities maturing within various future time periods.

(d) Interest rate information may be disclosed for individual financial instruments. Alternatively, weighted average rates or a range of rates may be presented for each class of financial instrument. An entity may group into separate classes instruments denominated in different currencies or having substantially different credit risks when those factors result in instruments having substantially different effective interest rates.

75 In some circumstances, an entity may be able to provide useful information about its exposure to interest rate risks by indicating the effect of a hypothetical change in market interest rates on the fair value of its financial instruments and future profit or loss and cash flows. Such information may be based on, for example, an assumed one percentage point (100 basis points) change in market interest rates occurring at the balance sheet date. The effects of a change in interest rates include changes in interest income and expense relating to floating rate financial instruments and gains or losses resulting from changes in the fair value of fixed rate instruments. The reported interest rate sensitivity may be restricted to the direct effects of an interest rate change on interest-bearing financial instruments recognised at the balance sheet date because the indirect effects of a rate change on financial markets and individual entities cannot normally be predicted reliably. When disclosing interest rate sensitivity information, an entity indicates the basis on which it has prepared the information, including any significant assumptions.

Credit risk

76 For each class of financial assets and other credit exposures, an entity shall disclose information about its exposure to credit risk, including:

(a) the amount that best represents its maximum credit risk exposure at the balance sheet date, without taking account of the fair value of any collateral, in the event of other parties failing to perform their obligations under financial instruments; and

(b) significant concentrations of credit risk.

77 An entity provides information relating to credit risk to permit users of its financial statements to assess the extent to which failures by counterparties to discharge their obligations could reduce the amount of future cash inflows from financial assets recognised at the balance sheet date or require a cash outflow from other credit exposures (such as a credit derivative or an issued guarantee of the obligations of a third party). Such failures give rise to a loss recognised in an

entity's profit or loss. Paragraph 76 does not require an entity to disclose an assessment of the probability of losses arising in the future.

78 The purposes of disclosing amounts exposed to credit risk without regard to potential recoveries from realisation of collateral ('an entity's maximum credit risk exposure') are:

(a) to provide users of financial statements with a consistent measure of the amount exposed to credit risk for financial assets and other credit exposures; and

(b) to take into account the possibility that the maximum exposure to loss may differ from the carrying amount of financial assets recognised at the balance sheet date.

79 In the case of financial assets exposed to credit risk, the carrying amount of the assets in the balance sheet, net of any applicable provisions for loss, usually represents the amount exposed to credit risk. For example, in the case of an interest rate swap carried at fair value, the maximum exposure to loss at the balance sheet date is normally the carrying amount because it represents the cost, at current market rates, of replacing the swap in the event of default. In these circumstances, no additional disclosure beyond that provided on the balance sheet is necessary. On the other hand, an entity's maximum potential loss from some financial instruments may differ significantly from their carrying amount and from other disclosed amounts such as their fair value or principal amount. In such circumstances, additional disclosure is necessary to meet the requirements of paragraph 76(a).

80 A financial asset subject to a legally enforceable right of set-off against a financial liability is not presented on the balance sheet net of the liability unless settlement is intended to take place on a net basis or simultaneously. Nevertheless, an entity discloses the existence of the legal right of set-off when providing information in accordance with paragraph 76. For example, when an entity is due to receive the proceeds from realisation of a financial asset before settlement of a financial liability of equal or greater amount against which the entity has a legal right of setoff, the entity has the ability to exercise that right of set-off to avoid incurring a loss in the event of a default by the counterparty. However, if the entity responds, or is likely to respond, to the default by extending the term of the financial asset, an exposure to credit risk would exist if the revised terms are such that collection of the proceeds is expected to be deferred beyond the date on which the liability is required to be settled. To inform users of financial statements of the extent to which exposure to credit risk at a particular point in time has been reduced, the entity discloses the existence and effect of the right of set-off when the financial asset is expected to be collected in accordance with its terms. When the financial liability against which a right of set-off exists is due to be settled before the financial asset, the entity is exposed to credit risk on the full carrying amount of the asset if the counterparty defaults after the liability has been settled.

81 An entity may have entered into one or more master netting arrangements that serve to mitigate its exposure to credit loss but do not meet the criteria for offsetting. When a master netting arrangement significantly reduces the credit risk associated with financial assets not offset against financial liabilities with the

same counterparty, an entity provides additional information concerning the effect of the arrangement. Such disclosure indicates that:

(a) the credit risk associated with financial assets subject to a master netting arrangement is eliminated only to the extent that financial liabilities due to the same counterparty will be settled after the assets are realised; and

(b) the extent to which an entity's overall exposure to credit risk is reduced through a master netting arrangement may change substantially within a short period following the balance sheet date because the exposure is affected by each transaction subject to the arrangement.

It is also desirable for an entity to disclose the terms of its master netting arrangements that determine the extent of the reduction in its credit risk.

82 An entity may be exposed to credit risk as a result of a transaction in which no financial asset is recognised on its balance sheet, such as for a financial guarantee or credit derivative contract. Guaranteeing an obligation of another party creates a liability and exposes the guarantor to credit risk that is taken into account in making the disclosures required by paragraph 76.

83 Concentrations of credit risk are disclosed when they are not apparent from other disclosures about the nature of the business and financial position of the entity and result in a significant exposure to loss in the event of default by other parties. Identification of such concentrations requires judgement by management taking into account the circumstances of the entity and its debtors. IAS 14 *Segment Reporting* provides guidance in identifying industry and geographical segments within which credit risk concentrations may arise.

84 Concentrations of credit risk may arise from exposures to a single debtor or to groups of debtors having such a similar characteristic that their ability to meet their obligations is expected to be affected similarly by changes in economic or other conditions. Characteristics that may give rise to a concentration of risk include the nature of the activities undertaken by debtors, such as the industry in which they operate, the geographical area in which activities are undertaken and the level of creditworthiness of groups of borrowers. For example, a manufacturer of equipment for the oil and gas industry will normally have trade accounts receivable from sales of its products for which the risk of non-payment is affected by economic changes in the oil and gas industry. A bank that normally lends on an international scale may have many loans outstanding to less developed nations and the bank's ability to recover them may be adversely affected by local economic conditions.

85 Disclosure of concentrations of credit risk includes a description of the shared characteristic that identifies each concentration and the amount of the maximum credit risk exposure associated with all financial assets sharing that characteristic.

Fair value

86 Except as set out in paragraph 90 and 91A , for each class of financial assets and financial liabilities, an entity shall disclose the fair value of that class of assets and liabilities in a way that permits it to be compared with the corresponding carrying amount in the balance sheet. (IAS 39 provides guidance for determining fair value.)

87 Fair value information is widely used for business purposes in determining an entity's overall financial position and in making decisions about individual financial instruments. It is also relevant to many decisions made by users of financial statements because, in many circumstances, it reflects the judgement of the financial markets about the present value of expected future cash flows relating to an instrument. Fair value information permits comparisons of financial instruments having substantially the same economic characteristics, regardless of why they are held and when and by whom they were issued or acquired. Fair values provide a neutral basis for assessing management's stewardship by indicating the effects of its decisions to buy, sell or hold financial assets and to incur, maintain or discharge financial liabilities. When an entity does not measure a financial asset or financial liability in its balance sheet at fair value, it provides fair value information through supplementary disclosures.

88 For financial instruments such as short-term trade receivables and payables, no disclosure of fair value is required when the carrying amount is a reasonable approximation of fair value.

89 In disclosing fair values, an entity groups financial assets and financial liabilities into classes and offsets them only to the extent that their related carrying amounts are offset in the balance sheet.

90 If investments in unquoted equity instruments or derivatives linked to such equity instruments are measured at cost under IAS 39 because their fair value cannot be measured reliably, that fact shall be disclosed together with a description of the financial instruments, their carrying amount, an explanation of why fair value cannot be measured reliably and, if possible, the range of estimates within which fair value is highly likely to lie. Furthermore, if financial assets whose fair value previously could not be reliably measured are sold, that fact, the carrying amount of such financial assets at the time of sale and the amount of gain or loss recognised shall be disclosed.

91 If investments in unquoted equity instruments or derivatives linked to such equity instruments are measured at cost under IAS 39 because their fair values cannot be measured reliably, the information about fair value set out in paragraphs 86 and 92 is not required to be disclosed. Instead, information is provided to assist users of the financial statements in making their own judgements about the extent of possible differences between the carrying amount of such financial assets and financial liabilities and their fair value. In addition to an explanation of the principal characteristics of the financial instruments that are pertinent to their value and the reason for not disclosing fair values, information is provided about the market for the instruments. In some cases, the terms and conditions of the instruments disclosed in accordance with paragraph 60 may provide sufficient information. When it has a reasonable basis for doing so, management may indicate its opinion on the relationship between fair value and the carrying amount of financial assets and financial liabilities for which it is unable to determine fair value reliably.

91A Some financial assets and financial liabilities contain a discretionary participation feature as described in IFRS 4 ***Insurance Contracts*****. If an entity cannot measure reliably the fair value of that feature, the entity shall**

disclose that fact together with a description of the contract, its carrying amount, an explanation of why fair value cannot be measured reliably and, if possible, the range of estimates within which fair value is highly likely to lie.

92 **An entity shall disclose:**

(a) the methods and significant assumptions applied in determining fair values of financial assets and financial liabilities separately for significant classes of financial assets and financial liabilities. (Paragraph 55 provides guidance for determining classes of financial assets.)

(b) whether fair values of financial assets and financial liabilities are determined directly, in full or in part, by reference to published price quotations in an active market or are estimated using a valuation technique (see IAS 39, paragraphs AG71–AG79).

(c) whether its financial statements include financial instruments measured at fair values that are determined in full or in part using a valuation technique based on assumptions that are not supported by observable market prices or rates. If changing any such assumption to a reasonably possible alternative would result in a significantly different fair value, the entity shall state this fact and disclose the effect on the fair value of a range of reasonably possible alternative assumptions. For this purpose, significance shall be judged with respect to profit or loss and total assets or total liabilities.

(d) the total amount of the change in fair value estimated using a valuation technique that was recognised in profit or loss during the period.

93 Disclosure of fair value information includes disclosure of the method used in determining fair value and the significant assumptions made in its application. For example, an entity discloses information about the assumptions relating to prepayment rates, rates of estimated credit losses and interest or discount rates if they are significant.

Other disclosures

94 **Derecognition**

(a) An entity may have either transferred a financial asset (see paragraph 18 of IAS 39) or entered into the type of arrangement described in paragraph 19 of IAS 39 in such a way that the arrangement does not qualify as a transfer of a financial asset. If the entity either continues to recognise all of the asset or continues to recognise the asset to the extent of the entity's continuing involvement (see IAS 39, paragraphs 29 and 30) it shall disclose for each class of financial asset:

(i) the nature of the assets;

(ii) the nature of the risks and rewards of ownership to which the entity remains exposed;

(iii) **when the entity continues to recognise all of the asset, the carrying amounts of the asset and of the associated liability; and**

(iv) **when the entity continues to recognise the asset to the extent of its continuing involvement, the total amount of the asset, the amount of the asset that the entity continues to recognise and the carrying amount of the associated liability.**

Collateral

(b) **An entity shall disclose the carrying amount of financial assets pledged as collateral for liabilities, the carrying amount of financial assets pledged as collateral for contingent liabilities, and (consistently with paragraphs 60(a) and 63(g)) any material terms and conditions relating to assets pledged as collateral.**

(c) **When an entity has accepted collateral that it is permitted to sell or repledge in the absence of default by the owner of the collateral, it shall disclose:**

(i) **the fair value of the collateral accepted (financial and non-financial assets);**

(ii) **the fair value of any such collateral sold or repledged and whether the entity has an obligation to return it; and**

(iii) **any material terms and conditions associated with its use of this collateral (consistently with paragraphs 60(a) and 63(g)).**

Compound financial instruments with multiple embedded derivatives

(d) **If an entity has issued an instrument that contains both a liability and an equity component (see paragraph 28) and the instrument has multiple embedded derivative features whose values are interdependent (such as a callable convertible debt instrument), it shall disclose the existence of those features and the effective interest rate on the liability component (excluding any embedded derivatives that are accounted for separately).**

Financial assets and financial liabilities at fair value through profit or loss (see also paragraph AG40)

(e) **An entity shall disclose the carrying amounts of financial assets and financial liabilities that:**

(i) **are classified as held for trading; and**

(ii) **were, upon initial recognition, designated by the entity as financial assets and financial liabilities at fair value through profit or loss (ie those that are not financial instruments classified as held for trading).**

(f) **If the entity has designated a financial liability as at fair value through profit or loss, it shall disclose:**

(i) **the amount of change in its fair value that is not attributable to changes in a benchmark interest rate (eg LIBOR); and**

- (ii) **the difference between its carrying amount and the amount the entity would be contractually required to pay at maturity to the holder of the obligation.**

Reclassification

(g) If the entity has reclassified a financial asset as one measured at cost or amortised cost rather than at fair value (see IAS 39, paragraph 54), it shall disclose the reason for that reclassification.

Income statement and equity

(h) An entity shall disclose material items of income, expense and gains and losses resulting from financial assets and financial liabilities, whether included in profit or loss or as a separate component of equity. For this purpose, the disclosure shall include at least the following items:

- **(i) total interest income and total interest expense (calculated using the effective interest method) for financial assets and financial liabilities that are not at fair value through profit or loss;**
- **(ii) for available-for-sale financial assets, the amount of any gain or loss recognised directly in equity during the period and the amount that was removed from equity and recognised in profit or loss for the period; and**
- **(iii) the amount of interest income accrued on impaired financial assets, in accordance with IAS 39, paragraph AG93.**

Impairment

(i) An entity shall disclose the nature and amount of any impairment loss recognised in profit or loss for a financial asset, separately for each significant class of financial asset (paragraph 55 provides guidance for determining classes of financial assets).

Defaults and breaches

(j) With respect to any defaults of principal, interest, sinking fund or redemption provisions during the period on loans payable recognised as at the balance sheet date, and any other breaches during the period of loan agreements when those breaches can permit the lender to demand repayment (except for breaches that are remedied, or in response to which the terms of the loan are renegotiated, on or before the balance sheet date), an entity shall disclose:

- **(i) details of those breaches;**
- **(ii) the amount recognised as at the balance sheet date in respect of the loans payable on which the breaches occurred; and**
- **(iii) with respect to amounts disclosed under (ii), whether the default has been remedied or the terms of the loans payable renegotiated before the date the financial statements were authorised for issue.**

95 For the purpose of disclosing information on breaches of loan agreements in accordance with paragraph 94(j), loans payable include issued debt instruments and financial liabilities other than short-term trade payables on normal credit terms. When such a breach occurred during the period, and the breach has not been remedied or the terms of the loan payable have not been renegotiated by the balance sheet date, the effect of the breach on the classification of the liability as current or non-current is determined under IAS 1.

Effective date

96 An entity shall apply this Standard for annual periods beginning on or after 1 January 2005. Earlier application is permitted. An entity shall not apply this Standard for annual periods beginning before 1 January 2005 unless it also applies IAS 39 (issued December 2003), including the amendments issued in March 2004. If an entity applies this Standard for a period beginning before 1 January 2005, it shall disclose that fact.

97 This Standard shall be applied retrospectively.

Withdrawal of other pronouncements

98 This Standard supersedes IAS 32 *Financial Instruments: Disclosure and Presentation* revised in 2000.

99 This Standard supersedes the following Interpretations:

(a) SIC-5 *Classification of Financial Instruments—Contingent Settlement Provisions*;

(b) SIC-16 *Share Capital—Reacquired Own Equity Instruments (Treasury Shares)*; and

(c) SIC-17 *Equity—Costs of an Equity Transaction*.

100 This Standard withdraws draft SIC Interpretation D34 *Financial Instruments—Instruments or Rights Redeemable by the Holder*.

Appendix
Application Guidance
IAS 32 *Financial Instruments: Disclosure and Presentation*

This appendix is an integral part of the Standard.

AG1 This Application Guidance explains the application of particular aspects of the Standard.

AG2 The Standard does not deal with the recognition or measurement of financial instruments. Requirements about the recognition and measurement of financial assets and financial liabilities are set out in IAS 39 *Financial Instruments: Recognition and Measurement.*

Definitions (paragraphs 11–14)

Financial assets and financial liabilities

AG3 Currency (cash) is a financial asset because it represents the medium of exchange and is therefore the basis on which all transactions are measured and recognised in financial statements. A deposit of cash with a bank or similar financial institution is a financial asset because it represents the contractual right of the depositor to obtain cash from the institution or to draw a cheque or similar instrument against the balance in favour of a creditor in payment of a financial liability.

AG4 Common examples of financial assets representing a contractual right to receive cash in the future and corresponding financial liabilities representing a contractual obligation to deliver cash in the future are:

(a) trade accounts receivable and payable;

(b) notes receivable and payable;

(c) loans receivable and payable; and

(d) bonds receivable and payable.

In each case, one party's contractual right to receive (or obligation to pay) cash is matched by the other party's corresponding obligation to pay (or right to receive).

AG5 Another type of financial instrument is one for which the economic benefit to be received or given up is a financial asset other than cash. For example, a note payable in government bonds gives the holder the contractual right to receive and the issuer the contractual obligation to deliver government bonds, not cash. The bonds are financial assets because they represent obligations of the issuing government to pay cash. The note is, therefore, a financial asset of the note holder and a financial liability of the note issuer.

AG6 'Perpetual' debt instruments (such as 'perpetual' bonds, debentures and capital notes) normally provide the holder with the contractual right to receive payments on account of interest at fixed dates extending into the indefinite future, either with no right to receive a return of principal or a right to a return of principal under terms that make it very unlikely or very far in the future. For example, an entity may issue a financial instrument requiring it to make annual payments in perpetuity equal to a stated interest rate of 8 per cent applied to a stated par or principal amount of CU1,000.* Assuming 8 per cent to be the market rate of interest for the instrument when issued, the issuer assumes a contractual obligation to make a stream of future interest payments having a fair value (present value) of CU1,000 on initial recognition. The holder and issuer of the instrument have a financial asset and a financial liability, respectively.

AG7 A contractual right or contractual obligation to receive, deliver or exchange financial instruments is itself a financial instrument. A chain of contractual rights or contractual obligations meets the definition of a financial instrument if it will ultimately lead to the receipt or payment of cash or to the acquisition or issue of an equity instrument.

AG8 The ability to exercise a contractual right or the requirement to satisfy a contractual obligation may be absolute, or it may be contingent on the occurrence of a future event. For example, a financial guarantee is a contractual right of the lender to receive cash from the guarantor, and a corresponding contractual obligation of the guarantor to pay the lender, if the borrower defaults. The contractual right and obligation exist because of a past transaction or event (assumption of the guarantee), even though the lender's ability to exercise its right and the requirement for the guarantor to perform under its obligation are both contingent on a future act of default by the borrower. A contingent right and obligation meet the definition of a financial asset and a financial liability, even though such assets and liabilities are not always recognised in the financial statements. Some of these contingent rights and obligations may be insurance contracts within the scope of IFRS 4.

AG9 Under IAS 17 *Leases* a finance lease is regarded as primarily an entitlement of the lessor to receive, and an obligation of the lessee to pay, a stream of payments that are substantially the same as blended payments of principal and interest under a loan agreement. The lessor accounts for its investment in the amount receivable under the lease contract rather than the leased asset itself. An operating lease, on the other hand, is regarded as primarily an uncompleted contract committing the lessor to provide the use of an asset in future periods in exchange for consideration similar to a fee for a service. The lessor continues to account for the leased asset itself rather than any amount receivable in the future under the contract. Accordingly, a finance lease is regarded as a financial instrument and an operating lease is not regarded as a financial instrument (except as regards individual payments currently due and payable).

AG10 Physical assets (such as inventories, property, plant and equipment), leased assets and intangible assets (such as patents and trademarks) are not financial assets. Control of such physical and intangible assets creates an opportunity to generate an inflow of cash or another financial asset, but it does not give rise to a present right to receive cash or another financial asset.

AG11 Assets (such as prepaid expenses) for which the future economic benefit is the receipt of goods or services, rather than the right to receive cash or another financial asset, are not financial assets. Similarly, items such as deferred revenue and most warranty obligations are not financial liabilities because the outflow of

* In this guidance, monetary amounts are denominated in 'currency units' (CU).

economic benefits associated with them is the delivery of goods and services rather than a contractual obligation to pay cash or another financial asset.

AG12 Liabilities or assets that are not contractual (such as income taxes that are created as a result of statutory requirements imposed by governments) are not financial liabilities or financial assets. Accounting for income taxes is dealt with in IAS 12 *Income Taxes*. Similarly, constructive obligations, as defined in IAS 37 *Provisions, Contingent Liabilities and Contingent Assets*, do not arise from contracts and are not financial liabilities.

Equity instruments

AG13 Examples of equity instruments include non-puttable ordinary shares, some types of preference shares (see paragraphs AG25 and AG26), and warrants or written call options that allow the holder to subscribe for or purchase a fixed number of non-puttable ordinary shares in the issuing entity in exchange for a fixed amount of cash or another financial asset. An entity's obligation to issue or purchase a fixed number of its own equity instruments in exchange for a fixed amount of cash or another financial asset is an equity instrument of the entity. However, if such a contract contains an obligation for the entity to pay cash or another financial asset, it also gives rise to a liability for the present value of the redemption amount (see paragraph AG27(a)). An issuer of non-puttable ordinary shares assumes a liability when it formally acts to make a distribution and becomes legally obligated to the shareholders to do so. This may be the case following the declaration of a dividend or when the entity is being wound up and any assets remaining after the satisfaction of liabilities become distributable to shareholders.

AG14 A purchased call option or other similar contract acquired by an entity that gives it the right to reacquire a fixed number of its own equity instruments in exchange for delivering a fixed amount of cash or another financial asset is not a financial asset of the entity. Instead, any consideration paid for such a contract is deducted from equity.

Derivative financial instruments

AG15 Financial instruments include primary instruments (such as receivables, payables and equity instruments) and derivative financial instruments (such as financial options, futures and forwards, interest rate swaps and currency swaps). Derivative financial instruments meet the definition of a financial instrument and, accordingly, are within the scope of this Standard.

AG16 Derivative financial instruments create rights and obligations that have the effect of transferring between the parties to the instrument one or more of the financial risks inherent in an underlying primary financial instrument. On inception, derivative financial instruments give one party a contractual right to exchange financial assets or financial liabilities with another party under conditions that are potentially favourable, or a contractual obligation to exchange financial assets or financial liabilities with another party under conditions that are potentially unfavourable. However, they generally[*] do not result in a transfer of the underlying primary financial instrument on inception of the contract, nor does such a transfer necessarily take place on maturity of the contract. Some instruments embody both a right and an obligation to make an exchange. Because the terms of the exchange are determined on inception of the derivative instrument, as prices in financial markets change those terms may become either favourable or unfavourable.

AG17 A put or call option to exchange financial assets or financial liabilities (ie financial instruments other than an entity's own equity instruments) gives the holder a right to obtain potential future economic benefits associated with changes in the fair value of the financial instrument underlying the contract. Conversely, the writer of an option assumes an obligation to forgo potential future economic benefits or bear potential losses of economic benefits associated with changes in the fair value of the underlying financial instrument. The contractual right of the holder and obligation of the writer meet the definition of a financial asset and a financial liability, respectively. The financial instrument underlying an option contract may be any financial asset, including shares in other entities and interest-bearing instruments. An option may require the writer to issue a debt instrument, rather than transfer a financial asset, but the instrument underlying the option would constitute a financial asset of the holder if the option were exercised. The option-holder's right to exchange the financial asset under potentially favourable conditions and the writer's obligation to exchange the financial asset under potentially unfavourable conditions are distinct from the underlying financial asset to be exchanged upon exercise of the option. The nature of the holder's right and of the writer's obligation are not affected by the likelihood that the option will be exercised.

AG18 Another example of a derivative financial instrument is a forward contract to be settled in six months' time in which one party (the purchaser) promises to deliver CU1,000,000 cash in exchange for CU1,000,000 face amount of fixed rate government bonds, and the other party (the seller) promises to deliver CU1,000,000 face amount of fixed rate government bonds in exchange for CU1,000,000 cash. During the six months, both parties have a contractual right and a contractual obligation to exchange financial instruments. If the market price of the government bonds rises above CU1,000,000, the conditions will be favourable to the purchaser and unfavourable to the seller; if the market price falls below CU1,000,000, the effect will be the opposite. The purchaser has a contractual right (a financial asset) similar to the right under a call option held and a contractual obligation (a financial liability) similar to the obligation under a put option written; the seller has a contractual right (a financial asset) similar to the right under a put option held and a contractual obligation (a financial liability) similar to the obligation under a call option written. As with options, these contractual rights and obligations constitute financial assets and financial liabilities separate and distinct from the underlying financial instruments (the bonds and cash to be exchanged). Both parties to a forward contract have an

* This is true of most, but not all derivatives, eg in some cross-currency interest rate swaps principal is exchanged on inception (and re-exchanged on maturity).

obligation to perform at the agreed time, whereas performance under an option contract occurs only if and when the holder of the option chooses to exercise it.

AG19 Many other types of derivative instruments embody a right or obligation to make a future exchange, including interest rate and currency swaps, interest rate caps, collars and floors, loan commitments, note issuance facilities and letters of credit. An interest rate swap contract may be viewed as a variation of a forward contract in which the parties agree to make a series of future exchanges of cash amounts, one amount calculated with reference to a floating interest rate and the other with reference to a fixed interest rate. Futures contracts are another variation of forward contracts, differing primarily in that the contracts are standardised and traded on an exchange.

Contracts to buy or sell non-financial items (paragraphs 8–10)

AG20 Contracts to buy or sell non-financial items do not meet the definition of a financial instrument because the contractual right of one party to receive a non-financial asset or service and the corresponding obligation of the other party do not establish a present right or obligation of either party to receive, deliver or exchange a financial asset. For example, contracts that provide for settlement only by the receipt or delivery of a non-financial item (eg an option, futures or forward contract on silver) are not financial instruments. Many commodity contracts are of this type. Some are standardised in form and traded on organised markets in much the same fashion as some derivative financial instruments. For example, a commodity futures contract may be bought and sold readily for cash because it is listed for trading on an exchange and may change hands many times. However, the parties buying and selling the contract are, in effect, trading the underlying commodity. The ability to buy or sell a commodity contract for cash, the ease with which it may be bought or sold and the possibility of negotiating a cash settlement of the obligation to receive or deliver the commodity do not alter the fundamental character of the contract in a way that creates a financial instrument. Nevertheless, some contracts to buy or sell non-financial items that can be settled net or by exchanging financial instruments, or in which the non-financial item is readily convertible to cash, are within the scope of the Standard as if they were financial instruments (see paragraph 8).

AG21 A contract that involves the receipt or delivery of physical assets does not give rise to a financial asset of one party and a financial liability of the other party unless any corresponding payment is deferred past the date on which the physical assets are transferred. Such is the case with the purchase or sale of goods on trade credit.

AG22 Some contracts are commodity-linked, but do not involve settlement through the physical receipt or delivery of a commodity. They specify settlement through cash payments that are determined according to a formula in the contract, rather than through payment of fixed amounts. For example, the principal amount of a bond may be calculated by applying the market price of oil prevailing at the maturity of the bond to a fixed quantity of oil. The principal is indexed by reference to a commodity price, but is settled only in cash. Such a contract constitutes a financial instrument.

AG23 The definition of a financial instrument also encompasses a contract that gives rise to a non-financial asset or non-financial liability in addition to a financial asset or financial liability. Such financial instruments often give one party an option to exchange a financial asset for a non-financial asset. For example, an oil-linked bond may give the holder the right to receive a stream of fixed periodic interest payments and a fixed amount of cash on maturity, with the option to exchange the principal amount for a fixed quantity of oil. The desirability of exercising this option will vary from time to time depending on the fair value of oil relative to the exchange ratio of cash for oil (the exchange price) inherent in the bond. The intentions of the bondholder concerning the exercise of the option do not affect the substance of the component assets. The financial asset of the holder and the financial liability of the issuer make the bond a financial instrument, regardless of the other types of assets and liabilities also created.

AG24 Although the Standard was not developed to apply to commodity or other contracts that do not satisfy the definition of a financial instrument or fall within paragraph 8, entities may regard it as appropriate to apply the relevant disclosure requirements of this Standard to such contracts.

Presentation

Liabilities and equity (paragraphs 15–27)

No contractual obligation to deliver cash or another financial asset (paragraphs 17–20)

AG25 Preference shares may be issued with various rights. In determining whether a preference share is a financial liability or an equity instrument, an issuer assesses the particular rights attaching to the share to determine whether it exhibits the fundamental characteristic of a financial liability. For example, a preference share that provides for redemption on a specific date or at the option of the holder contains a financial liability because the issuer has an obligation to transfer financial assets to the holder of the share. The potential inability of an issuer to satisfy an obligation to redeem a preference share when contractually required to do so, whether because of a lack of funds, a statutory restriction or insufficient profits or reserves, does not negate the obligation. An option of the issuer to redeem the shares for cash does not satisfy the definition of a financial liability because the issuer does not have a present obligation to transfer financial assets to the shareholders. In this case, redemption of the shares is solely at the discretion of the issuer. An obligation may arise, however, when the issuer of the shares exercises its option, usually by formally notifying the shareholders of an intention to redeem the shares.

AG26 When preference shares are non-redeemable, the appropriate classification is determined by the other rights that attach to them. Classification is based on an assessment of the substance of the contractual arrangements and the definitions of a financial liability and an equity instrument. When distributions to holders of the preference shares, whether cumulative or non-cumulative, are at the discretion of the issuer, the shares are equity instruments. The classification of a preference share as an equity instrument or a financial liability is not affected by, for example:

(a) a history of making distributions;

(b) an intention to make distributions in the future;

(c) a possible negative impact on the price of ordinary shares of the issuer if distributions are not made (because of restrictions on paying dividends on the ordinary shares if dividends are not paid on the preference shares);

(d) the amount of the issuer's reserves;

(e) an issuer's expectation of a profit or loss for a period; or

(f) an ability or inability of the issuer to influence the amount of its profit or loss for the period.

Settlement in the entity's own equity instruments (paragraphs 21–24)

AG27 The following examples illustrate how to classify different types of contracts on an entity's own equity instruments:

(a) A contract that will be settled by the entity receiving or delivering a fixed number of its own shares for no future consideration, or exchanging a fixed number of its own shares for a fixed amount of cash or another financial asset, is an equity instrument. Accordingly, any consideration received or paid for such a contract is added directly to or deducted directly from equity. One example is an issued share option that gives the counterparty a right to buy a fixed number of the entity's shares for a fixed amount of cash. However, if the contract requires the entity to purchase (redeem) its own shares for cash or another financial asset at a fixed or determinable date or on demand, the entity also recognises a financial liability for the present value of the redemption amount. One example is an entity's obligation under a forward contract to repurchase a fixed number of its own shares for a fixed amount of cash.

(b) An entity's obligation to purchase its own shares for cash gives rise to a financial liability for the present value of the redemption amount even if the number of shares that the entity is obliged to repurchase is not fixed or if the obligation is conditional on the counterparty exercising a right to redeem. One example of a conditional obligation is an issued option that requires the entity to repurchase its own shares for cash if the counterparty exercises the option.

(c) A contract that will be settled in cash or another financial asset is a financial asset or financial liability even if the amount of cash or another financial asset that will be received or delivered is based on changes in the market price of the entity's own equity. One example is a net cash-settled share option.

(d) A contract that will be settled in a variable number of the entity's own shares whose value equals a fixed amount or an amount based on changes in an underlying variable (eg a commodity price) is a financial asset or a financial liability. An example is a written option to buy gold that, if exercised, is settled net in the entity's own instruments by the entity delivering as many of those instruments as are equal to the value of the option contract. Such a contract is a financial asset or financial liability even if the underlying variable is the entity's own share price rather than gold. Similarly, a contract that will be settled in a fixed number of the entity's own shares, but the rights attaching to those shares will be varied so that the settlement value equals a fixed amount or an amount based on changes in an underlying variable, is a financial asset or a financial liability.

Contingent settlement provisions (paragraph 25)

AG28 Paragraph 25 requires that if a part of a contingent settlement provision that could require settlement in cash or another financial asset (or in another way that would result in the instrument being a financial liability) is not genuine, the settlement provision does not affect the classification of a financial instrument. Thus, a contract that requires settlement in cash or a variable number of the entity's own shares only on the occurrence of an event that is extremely rare, highly abnormal and very unlikely to occur is an equity instrument. Similarly, settlement in a fixed number of an entity's own shares may be contractually precluded in circumstances that are outside the control of the entity, but if these circumstances have no genuine possibility of occurring, classification as an equity instrument is appropriate.

Treatment in consolidated financial statements

AG29 In consolidated financial statements, an entity presents minority interests—ie the interests of other parties in the equity and income of its subsidiaries—in accordance with IAS 1 *Presentation of Financial Statements* and IAS 27 *Consolidated and Separate Financial Statements*. When classifying a financial instrument (or a component of it) in consolidated financial statements, an entity considers all terms and conditions agreed between members of the group and the holders of the instrument in determining whether the group as a whole has an obligation to deliver cash or another financial asset in respect of the instrument or to settle it in a manner that results in liability classification. When a subsidiary in a group issues a financial instrument and a parent or other group entity agrees additional terms directly with the holders of the instrument (eg a guarantee), the group may not have discretion over distributions or redemption. Although the subsidiary may appropriately classify the instrument without regard to these additional terms in its individual financial statements, the effect of other agreements between members of the group and the holders of the instrument is considered in order to ensure that consolidated financial statements reflect the contracts and transactions entered into by the group as a whole. To the extent that there is such an obligation or settlement provision, the instrument (or the component of it that is subject to the obligation) is classified as a financial liability in consolidated financial statements.

Compound financial instruments (paragraphs 28–32)

AG30 Paragraph 28 applies only to issuers of non-derivative compound financial instruments. Paragraph 28 does not deal with compound financial instruments from the perspective of holders. IAS 39 deals with the separation of embedded derivatives from the perspective of holders of compound financial instruments that contain debt and equity features.

AG31 A common form of compound financial instrument is a debt instrument with an embedded conversion option, such as a bond convertible into ordinary shares of the issuer, and without any other embedded derivative features. Paragraph 28 requires the issuer of such a financial instrument to present the liability component and the equity component separately on the balance sheet, as follows:

(a) The issuer's obligation to make scheduled payments of interest and principal is a financial liability that exists as long as the instrument is not converted. On initial recognition, the fair value of the liability component is the present value of the contractually determined stream of future cash flows discounted at the rate of interest applied at that time by the market to instruments of comparable credit status and providing substantially the same cash flows, on the same terms, but without the conversion option.

(b) The equity instrument is an embedded option to convert the liability into equity of the issuer. The fair value of the option comprises its time value and its intrinsic value, if any. This option has value on initial recognition even when it is out of the money.

AG32 On conversion of a convertible instrument at maturity, the entity derecognises the liability component and recognises it as equity. The original equity component remains as equity (although it may be transferred from one line item within equity to another). There is no gain or loss on conversion at maturity.

AG33 When an entity extinguishes a convertible instrument before maturity through an early redemption or repurchase in which the original conversion privileges are unchanged, the entity allocates the consideration paid and any transaction costs for the repurchase or redemption to the liability and equity components of the instrument at the date of the transaction. The method used in allocating the consideration paid and transaction costs to the separate components is consistent with that used in the original allocation to the separate components of the proceeds received by the entity when the convertible instrument was issued, in accordance with paragraphs 28–32.

AG34 Once the allocation of the consideration is made, any resulting gain or loss is treated in accordance with accounting principles applicable to the related component, as follows:

(a) the amount of gain or loss relating to the liability component is recognised in profit or loss; and

(b) the amount of consideration relating to the equity component is recognised in equity.

AG35 An entity may amend the terms of a convertible instrument to induce early conversion, for example by offering a more favourable conversion ratio or paying other additional consideration in the event of conversion before a specified date. The difference, at the date the terms are amended, between the fair value of the consideration the holder receives on conversion of the instrument under the revised terms and the fair value of the consideration the holder would have received under the original terms is recognised as a loss in profit or loss.

Treasury shares (paragraphs 33 and 34)

AG36 An entity's own equity instruments are not recognised as a financial asset regardless of the reason for which they are reacquired. Paragraph 33 requires an entity that reacquires its own equity instruments to deduct those equity instruments from equity. However, when an entity holds its own equity on behalf of others, eg a financial institution holding its own equity on behalf of a client, there is an agency relationship and as a result those holdings are not included in the entity's balance sheet.

Interest, dividends, losses and gains (paragraphs 35–41)

AG37 The following example illustrates the application of paragraph 35 to a compound financial instrument. Assume that a non-cumulative preference share is mandatorily redeemable for cash in five years, but that dividends are payable at the discretion of the entity before the redemption date. Such an instrument is a compound financial instrument, with the liability component being the present value of the redemption amount. The unwinding of the discount on this component is recognised in profit or loss and classified as interest expense. Any dividends paid relate to the equity component and, accordingly, are recognised as a distribution of profit or loss. A similar treatment would apply if the redemption was not mandatory but at the option of the holder, or if the share was mandatorily convertible into a variable number of ordinary shares calculated to equal a fixed amount or an amount based on changes in an underlying variable (eg commodity). However, if any unpaid dividends are added to the redemption amount, the entire instrument is a liability. In such a case, any dividends are classified as interest expense.

Offsetting a financial asset and a financial liability (paragraphs 42–50)

AG38 To offset a financial asset and a financial liability, an entity must have a currently enforceable legal right to set off the recognised amounts. An entity may have a conditional right to set off recognised amounts, such as in a master netting agreement or in some forms of non-recourse debt, but such rights are enforceable only on the occurrence of some future event, usually a default of the counterparty. Thus, such an arrangement does not meet the conditions for offset.

AG39 The Standard does not provide special treatment for so-called 'synthetic instruments', which are groups of separate financial instruments acquired and held to emulate the characteristics of another instrument. For example, a floating rate long-term debt combined with an interest rate swap that involves receiving floating payments and making fixed payments synthesises a fixed rate long-term debt. Each of the individual financial instruments that together constitute a 'synthetic instrument' represents a contractual right or obligation with its own terms and conditions and each may be transferred or settled separately. Each financial instrument is exposed to risks that may differ from the risks to which other financial instruments are exposed. Accordingly, when one financial instrument in a 'synthetic instrument' is an asset and another is a liability, they are not offset and presented on an entity's balance sheet on a net basis unless they meet the criteria for offsetting in paragraph 42. Disclosures are provided about the significant terms and conditions of each financial instrument, although an entity may indicate in addition the nature of the relationship between the individual instruments (see paragraph 65).

Disclosure

Financial assets and financial liabilities at fair value through profit or loss (paragraph 94(f))

AG40 If an entity designates a financial liability as at fair value through profit or loss, it is required to disclose the amount of change in the fair value of the liability that is not attributable to changes in a benchmark interest rate (eg LIBOR). For a liability whose fair value is determined on the basis of an observed market price, this amount can be estimated as follows:

(a) First, the entity computes the liability's internal rate of return at the start of the period using the observed market price of the liability and the liability's contractual cash flows at the start of the period. It deducts from this rate of return the benchmark interest rate at the start of the period, to arrive at an instrument-specific component of the internal rate of return.

(b) Next, the entity calculates the present value of the liability using the liability's contractual cash flows at the start of the period and a discount rate equal to the sum of the benchmark interest rate at the end of the period and the instrument-specific component of the internal rate of return at the start of the period as determined in (a).

(c) The amount determined in (b) is then decreased for any cash paid on the liability during the period and increased to reflect the increase in fair value that arises because the contractual cash flows are one period closer to their due date.

(d) The difference between the observed market price of the liability at the end of the period and the amount determined in (c) is the change in fair value that is not attributable to changes in the benchmark interest rate. This is the amount to be disclosed.

Approval of IAS 32 by the Board

International Accounting Standard 32 *Financial Instruments: Disclosure and Presentation* was approved for issue by thirteen of the fourteen members of the International Accounting Standards Board. Mr Leisenring dissented. His dissenting opinion is set out after the Basis for Conclusions.

Sir David Tweedie	Chairman
Thomas E Jones	Vice-Chairman
Mary E Barth	
Hans-Georg Bruns	
Anthony T Cope	
Robert P Garnett	
Gilbert Gélard	
James J Leisenring	
Warren J McGregor	
Patricia L O'Malley	
Harry K Schmid	
John T Smith	
Geoffrey Whittington	
Tatsumi Yamada	

Basis for Conclusions

This Basis for Conclusions accompanies, but is not a part of, IAS 32

BC1 This Basis for Conclusions summarises the International Accounting Standards Board's considerations in reaching its conclusions on revising IAS 32 *Financial Instruments: Disclosure and Presentation* in 2003. Individual Board members gave greater weight to some factors than to others.

BC2 In July 2001 the Board announced that, as part of its initial agenda of technical projects, it would undertake a project to improve a number of Standards, including IAS 32 and IAS 39 *Financial Instruments: Recognition and Measurement.* The objectives of the Improvements project were to reduce the complexity in the Standards by clarifying and adding guidance, eliminating internal inconsistencies, and incorporating into the Standards elements of Standing Interpretations Committee (SIC) Interpretations and IAS 39 implementation guidance. In June 2002 the Board published its proposals in an Exposure Draft of proposed amendments to IAS 32 *Financial Instruments: Disclosure and Presentation* and IAS 39 *Financial Instruments: Recognition and Measurement*, with a comment deadline of 14 October 2002. The Board received over 170 comment letters on the Exposure Draft.

BC3 Because the Board did not reconsider the fundamental approach to the accounting for financial instruments established by IAS 32 and IAS 39, this Basis for Conclusions does not discuss requirements in IAS 32 that the Board has not reconsidered.

Definitions (paragraphs 11–14 and AG3–AG24)

Financial asset, financial liability and equity instrument (paragraphs 11 and AG3–AG14)

BC4 The revised IAS 32 addresses the classification as financial assets, financial liabilities or equity instruments of financial instruments that are indexed to, or settled in, an entity's own equity instruments. As discussed further in paragraphs BC6–BC15, the Board decided to preclude equity classification for such contracts when they (a) involve an obligation to deliver cash or another financial asset or to exchange financial assets or financial liabilities under conditions that are potentially unfavourable to the entity, (b) in the case of a non-derivative, are not for the receipt or delivery of a fixed number of shares or (c) in the case of a derivative, are not for the exchange of a fixed number of shares for a fixed amount of cash or another financial asset. The Board also decided to preclude equity classification for contracts that are derivatives on derivatives on an entity's own equity. Consistently with this decision, the Board also decided to amend the definitions of financial asset, financial liability and equity instrument in IAS 32 to make them consistent with the guidance about contracts on an entity's own equity instruments. The Board did not reconsider other aspects of the definitions as part of this project to revise IAS 32, for example the other changes to the definitions proposed by the Joint Working Group in its Draft Standard *Financial Instruments and Similar Items* published by the Board's predecessor body, IASC, in 2000.

Presentation (paragraphs 15–50 and AG25–AG39)

Liabilities and equity (paragraphs 15–27 and AG25–AG29)

BC5 The revised IAS 32 addresses whether derivative and non-derivative contracts indexed to, or settled in, an entity's own equity instruments are financial assets, financial liabilities or equity instruments. The original IAS 32 dealt with aspects of this issue piecemeal and it was not clear how various transactions (eg net share settled contracts and contracts with settlement options) should be treated under the Standard. The Board concluded that it needed to clarify the accounting treatment for such transactions.

BC6 The approach agreed by the Board can be summarised as follows:

A contract on an entity's own equity is an equity instrument if, and only if:

(a) it contains no contractual obligation to transfer cash or another financial asset, or to exchange financial assets or financial liabilities with another entity under conditions that are potentially unfavourable to the entity; and

(b) if the instrument will or may be settled in the entity's own equity instruments, it is either (i) a non-derivative that includes no contractual obligation for the entity to deliver a variable number of its own equity instruments, or (ii) a derivative that will be settled by the entity exchanging a fixed amount of cash or another financial asset for a fixed number of its own equity instruments.

No contractual obligation to deliver cash or another financial asset (paragraphs 17–20 and AG25–AG26)

Puttable instruments (paragraph 18(b))

BC7 The Board decided that a financial instrument that gives the holder the right to put the instrument back to the entity for cash or another financial asset is a financial liability of the entity. Such financial instruments are commonly issued by mutual funds, unit trusts, co-operative and similar entities, often with the redemption amount being equal to a proportionate share in the net assets of the entity. Although the legal form of such financial instruments often includes a right to the residual interest in the assets of an entity available to holders of such instruments, the inclusion of an option for the holder to put the instrument back to the entity for cash or another financial asset means that the instrument meets the definition of a financial liability. The classification as a financial liability is independent of considerations such as when the right is exercisable, how the amount payable or receivable upon exercise of the right is determined, and whether the puttable instrument has a fixed maturity.

BC8 The Board noted that the classification of a puttable instrument as a financial liability does not preclude the use of descriptors such as 'net assets attributable to unitholders' and 'change in net assets attributable to unitholders' on the face of the financial statements of an entity that has no equity (such as some mutual funds and unit trusts) or whose share capital is a financial liability under IAS 32 (such as some co-operatives). The Board also agreed that it should provide examples of how such entities might present their income statement and balance sheet (see Illustrative Examples 7 and 8).

Implicit obligations (paragraph 20)

BC9 The Board did not debate whether an obligation can be established implicitly rather than explicitly because this is not within the scope of an improvements project. This question will be considered by the Board in its project on revenue, liabilities and equity. Consequently, the Board retained the existing notion that an instrument may establish an obligation indirectly through its terms and conditions (see paragraph 20). However, it decided that the example of a preference share with a contractually accelerating dividend which, within the foreseeable future, is scheduled to yield a dividend so high that the entity will be economically compelled to redeem the instrument, was insufficiently clear. The example was therefore removed and replaced with others that are clearer and deal with situations that have proved problematic in practice.

Settlement in the entity's own equity instruments (paragraphs 21–24 and AG27)

BC10 The approach taken in the revised IAS 32 includes two main conclusions:

(a) When an entity has an obligation to purchase its own shares for cash (such as under a forward contract to purchase its own shares), there is a financial liability for the amount of cash that the entity has an obligation to pay.

(b) When an entity uses its own equity instruments 'as currency' in a contract to receive or deliver a variable number of shares whose value equals a fixed amount or an amount based on changes in an underlying variable (eg a commodity price), the contract is not an equity instrument, but is a financial asset or a financial liability. In other words, when a contract is settled in a variable number of the entity's own equity instruments, or by the entity exchanging a fixed number of its own equity instruments for a variable amount of cash or another financial asset, the contract is not an equity instrument but is a financial asset or a financial liability.

When an entity has an obligation to purchase its own shares for cash, there is a financial liability for the amount of cash that the entity has an obligation to pay.

BC11 An entity's obligation to purchase its own shares establishes a maturity date for the shares that are subject to the contract. Therefore, to the extent of the obligation, those shares cease to be equity instruments when the entity assumes the obligation. This treatment under IAS 32 is consistent with the treatment of shares that provide for mandatory redemption by the entity. Without a requirement to recognise a financial liability for the present value of the share redemption amount, entities with identical obligations to deliver cash in exchange for their own equity instruments could report different information in their financial statements depending on whether the redemption clause is embedded in the equity instrument or is a free-standing derivative contract.

BC12 Some respondents to the Exposure Draft suggested that when an entity writes an option that, if exercised, will result in the entity paying cash in return for receiving its own shares, it is incorrect to treat the full amount of the exercise price as a financial liability because the obligation is conditional upon the option being exercised. The Board rejected this argument because the entity has an obligation to pay the full redemption amount and cannot avoid settlement in cash or another financial asset for the full redemption amount unless the counterparty decides not to exercise its redemption right or specified future events or circumstances beyond the control of the entity occur or do not occur. The Board also noted that a change would require a reconsideration of other provisions in IAS 32 that require liability treatment for obligations that are conditional on events or choices that are beyond the entity's control. These include, for example, (a) the treatment of financial instruments with contingent settlement provisions as financial liabilities for the full amount of the conditional obligation, (b) the treatment of preference shares that are redeemable at the option of the holder as financial liabilities for the full amount of the conditional obligation, and (c) the treatment of financial instruments (puttable instruments) that give the holder the right to put the instrument back to the issuer for cash or another financial asset, the amount of which is determined by reference to an index, and which therefore has the potential to increase and decrease, as financial liabilities for the full amount of the conditional obligation.

When an entity uses its own equity instruments as currency in a contract to receive or deliver a variable number of shares, the contract is not an equity instrument, but is a financial asset or a financial liability.

BC13 The Board agreed that it would be inappropriate to account for a contract as an equity instrument when an entity's own equity instruments are used as currency in a contract to receive or deliver a variable number of shares whose value equals a fixed amount or an amount based on changes in an underlying variable (eg a net share-settled derivative contract on gold or an obligation to deliver as many shares as are equal in value to CU10,000). Such a contract represents a right or obligation of a specified amount rather than a specified equity interest. A contract to pay or receive a specified amount (rather than a specified equity interest) is not an equity instrument. For such a contract, the entity does not know, before the transaction is settled, how many of its own shares (or how much cash) it will receive or deliver and the entity may not even know whether it will receive or deliver its own shares.

BC14 In addition, the Board noted that precluding equity treatment for such a contract limits incentives for structuring potentially favourable or unfavourable transactions to obtain equity treatment. For example, the Board believes that an entity should not be able to obtain equity treatment for a transaction simply by including a share settlement clause when the contract is for a specified value, rather than a specified equity interest.

BC15 The Board rejected the argument that a contract that is settled in the entity's own shares must be an equity instrument because no change in assets or liabilities, and thus no gain or loss, arises on settlement of the contract. The Board noted that any gain or loss arises before settlement of the transaction, not when it is settled.

Contingent settlement provisions (paragraphs 25 and AG28)

BC16 The revised Standard incorporates the conclusion previously in SIC-5 *Classification of Financial Instruments—Contingent Settlement Provisions* that a financial instrument for which the manner of settlement depends on the occurrence or non-occurrence of uncertain future events, or on the outcome of uncertain circumstances that are beyond the control of both the issuer and the holder (ie a 'contingent settlement provision'), is a financial liability.

BC17 The amendments do not include the exception previously provided in paragraph 6 of SIC-5 for circumstances in which the possibility of the entity being required to settle in cash or another financial asset is remote at the time the financial instrument is issued. The Board concluded that it is not consistent with the definitions of financial liabilities and equity instruments to classify an obligation to deliver cash or another financial asset as a financial liability only when settlement in cash is probable. There is a contractual obligation to transfer economic benefits as a result of past events because the entity is unable to avoid a settlement in cash or another financial asset unless an event occurs or does not occur in the future.

BC18 However, the Board also concluded that contingent settlement provisions that would apply only in the event of liquidation of an entity should not influence the classification of the instrument because to do so would be inconsistent with a going concern assumption. A contingent settlement provision that provides for payment in cash or another financial asset only on the liquidation of the entity is similar to an equity instrument that has priority in liquidation and therefore should be ignored in classifying the instrument.

BC19 Additionally, the Board decided that if the part of a contingent settlement provision that could require settlement in cash or a variable number of own shares is not genuine, it should be ignored for the purposes of classifying the instrument. The Board also agreed to provide guidance on the meaning of 'genuine' in this context (see paragraph AG28).

Settlement options (paragraphs 26 and 27)

BC20 The revised Standard requires that if one of the parties to a contract has one or more options as to how it is settled (eg net in cash or by exchanging shares for cash), the contract is a financial asset or a financial liability unless all of the settlement alternatives would result in equity classification. The Board concluded that entities should not be able to circumvent the accounting requirements for financial assets and financial liabilities simply by including an option to settle a contract through the exchange of a fixed number of shares for a fixed amount. The Board had proposed in the Exposure Draft that past practice and management intentions should be considered in determining the classification of such instruments. However, respondents to the Exposure Draft noted that such requirements can be difficult to apply because some entities do not have any history of similar transactions and the assessment of whether an established practice exists and of what is management's intention can be subjective. The Board agreed with these comments and accordingly concluded that past practice and management intentions should not be determining factors.

Alternative approaches considered

BC21 In finalising the revisions to IAS 32 the Board considered, but rejected, a number of alternative approaches:

(a) To classify as an equity instrument any contract that will be settled in the entity's own shares. The Board rejected this approach because it does not deal adequately with transactions in which an entity is using its own shares as currency, eg when an entity has an obligation to pay a fixed or determinable amount that is settled in a variable number of its own shares.

(b) To classify a contract as an equity instrument only if (i) the contract will be settled in the entity's own shares, and (ii) the changes in the fair value of the contract move in the same direction as the changes in the fair value of the shares from the perspective of the counterparty. Under this approach, contracts that will be settled in the entity's own shares would be financial assets or financial liabilities if, from the perspective of the counterparty, their value moves inversely with the price of the entity's own shares. An example is an entity's obligation to buy back its own shares. The Board rejected this approach because its adoption would represent a fundamental shift in the concept of equity. The Board also noted that it would result in a change to the classification of some transactions, compared with the existing *Framework* and IAS 32, that had not been exposed for comment.

(c) To classify as an equity instrument a contract that will be settled in the entity's own shares unless its value changes in response to something other than the price of the entity's own shares. The Board rejected this approach to avoid an exception to the principle that non-derivative contracts that are settled in a variable number of an entity's own shares should be treated as financial assets or financial liabilities.

(d) To limit classification as equity instruments to outstanding ordinary shares, and classify as financial assets or financial liabilities all contracts that involve future receipt or delivery of the entity's own shares. The Board rejected this approach because its adoption would represent a fundamental shift in the concept of equity. The Board also noted that it would result in a change to the classification of some transactions compared with the existing IAS 32 that had not been exposed for comment.

Compound financial instruments (paragraphs 28–32 and AG30–AG35)

BC22 The Standard requires the separate presentation on an entity's balance sheet of liability and equity components of a single financial instrument. It is more a matter of form than a matter of substance that both liabilities and equity interests are created by a single financial instrument rather than two or more separate instruments. The Board believes that an entity's financial position is more faithfully represented by separate presentation of liability and equity components contained in a single instrument.

Allocation of the initial carrying amount to the liability and equity components (paragraphs 31 and 32, AG36–AG38 and Illustrative Examples 9–12)

BC23 The previous version of IAS 32 did not prescribe a particular method for assigning the initial carrying amount of a compound financial instrument to its separated liability and equity components. Rather, it suggested approaches that might be considered, such as:

(a) assigning to the less easily measurable component (often the equity component) the residual amount after deducting from the instrument as a whole the amount separately determined for the component that is more easily determinable (a 'with-and-without' method); and

(b) measuring the liability and equity components separately and, to the extent necessary, adjusting these amounts pro rata so that the sum of the components equals the amount of the instrument as a whole (a 'relative fair value' method).

BC24 This choice was originally justified on the grounds that IAS 32 did not deal with the measurement of financial assets, financial liabilities and equity instruments.

BC25 However, since the issue of IAS 39, IFRSs contain requirements for the measurement of financial assets and financial liabilities. Therefore, the view that IAS 32 should not prescribe a particular method for separating compound financial instruments because of the absence of measurement requirements for financial instruments is no longer valid. IAS 39, paragraph 43, requires a financial liability to be measured on initial recognition at its fair value. Therefore, a relative fair value method could result in an initial measurement of the liability component that is not in compliance with IAS 39.

BC26 After initial recognition, a financial liability that is classified as at fair value through profit or loss is measured at fair value under IAS 39, and other financial liabilities are measured at amortised cost. If the liability component of a compound financial instrument is classified as at fair value through profit or loss, an entity could recognise an immediate gain or loss after initial recognition if it applies a relative fair value method. This is contrary to IAS 32, paragraph 31, which states that no gain or loss arises from recognising the components of the instrument separately.

BC27 Under the *Framework*, and IASs 32 and 39, an equity instrument is defined as any contract that evidences a residual interest in the assets of an entity after deducting all of its liabilities. Paragraph 67 of the *Framework* further states that the amount at which equity is recognised in the balance sheet is dependent on the measurement of assets and liabilities.

BC28 The Board concluded that the alternatives in IAS 32 to measure on initial recognition the liability component of a compound financial instrument as a residual amount after separating the equity component or on the basis of a relative fair value method should be eliminated. Instead the liability component should be measured first (including the value of any embedded non-equity derivative features, such as an embedded call feature), and the residual amount assigned to the equity component.

BC29 The objective of this amendment is to make the requirements about the entity's separation of the liability and equity components of a single compound financial instrument consistent with the requirements about the initial measurement of a financial liability in IAS 39 and the definitions in IAS 32 and the *Framework* of an equity instrument as a residual interest.

BC30 This approach removes the need to estimate inputs to, and apply, complex option pricing models to measure the equity component of some compound financial instruments. The Board also noted that the absence of a prescribed approach led to a lack of comparability among entities applying IAS 32 and that it therefore was desirable to specify a single approach.

BC31 The Board noted that a requirement to use the with-and-without method, under which the liability component is determined first, is consistent with the proposals of the Joint Working Group of Standard Setters in its Draft Standard and Basis for Conclusions in *Financial Instruments and Similar Items*, published by IASC in December 2000 (see Draft Standard, paragraphs 74 and 75 and Application Supplement, paragraph 318).

Treasury shares (paragraphs 33, 34 and AG36)

BC32 The revised Standard incorporates the guidance in SIC-16 *Share Capital—Reacquired Own Equity Instruments (Treasury Shares).* The acquisition and subsequent resale by an entity of its own equity instruments represents a transfer between those holders of equity instruments who have given up their equity interest and those who continue to hold an equity instrument, rather than a gain or loss to the entity.

Interest, dividends, losses and gains (paragraphs 35–41 and AG37)

Costs of an equity transaction (paragraphs 35 and 37–39)

BC33 The revised Standard incorporates the guidance in SIC-17 *Equity—Costs of an Equity Transaction.* Transaction costs incurred as a necessary part of completing an equity transaction are accounted for as part of the transaction to which they relate. Linking the equity transaction and costs of the transaction reflects in equity the total cost of the transaction.

Disclosure (paragraphs 51–95)

Interest rate risk and credit risk (paragraphs 67–85)

BC34 The Board did not consider amendments to the disclosures on interest rate risk and credit risk. It will do so as part of its project to review IAS 30 *Disclosures in the Financial Statements of Banks and Similar Financial Institutions.* This project will also consider requirements for the presentation of financial instruments on the face of the balance sheet and income statement.

Fair value (paragraphs 86–93)

BC35 The exemption from the requirement to provide disclosures about fair value in IAS 32, paragraph 90, is consistent with the exemption from the requirement to measure particular financial assets and financial liabilities at fair value under

IAS 39, paragraphs 46 and 47. Accordingly, disclosure of fair value is not required for investments in unquoted equity instruments and derivatives linked to such equity instruments if their fair value cannot be measured reliably. For all other financial assets and financial liabilities, it is reasonable to expect that fair value can be determined with sufficient reliability within constraints of timeliness and cost. Therefore, the Board concluded that there should be no exception from the requirement to disclose fair value information for such financial assets and financial liabilities.

BC36 To provide users of financial statements with a sense of the potential variability of fair value estimates, the Board decided that information about the use of valuation techniques should be disclosed, such as the sensitivities of fair value estimates to the main valuation assumptions. In forming this conclusion the Board considered the view that disclosure of sensitivities could be difficult, in particular when there are many valuation assumptions to which the disclosure would apply and these assumptions are interdependent. However, the Board noted that a detailed quantitative disclosure of sensitivity to all valuation assumptions is not required (only those that could result in a significantly different estimate of fair value are required) and that the disclosure does not require the entity to reflect all interdependencies between assumptions when making the disclosure. Additionally, the Board considered the view that this disclosure might imply that a fair value established by a valuation technique is less valid than one established by other means. However, the Board noted that fair values that are estimated by valuation techniques are more subjective than those established from an observable market price, and concluded that users should be given information to help them in assessing this subjectivity.

Financial assets carried at an amount in excess of fair value

BC37 The Board eliminated the disclosure requirements in IAS 32 regarding financial assets carried at an amount in excess of fair value, including the reasons for not reducing the carrying amount. IAS 39 requires financial assets classified as either held-to-maturity investments or as loans and receivables to be carried at amortised cost, which may exceed fair value. Because IAS 39 contains requirements governing the measurement of financial assets and IAS 32 requires fair value information to be provided in a way that permits comparisons with the financial assets' carrying amounts, the requirement to disclose separate information about financial assets carried at an amount in excess of fair value is redundant.

Other disclosures (paragraphs 94, 95 and AG40)

Derecognition (paragraph 94(a))

BC38 An entity may have either transferred a financial asset (see IAS 39, paragraph 18) or have entered into the type of arrangement described in paragraph 19 of IAS 39, in such a way that the arrangement does not qualify as a transfer of a financial asset. If the entity either continues to recognise all of the asset or continues to recognise the asset to the extent of its continuing involvement, the revised Standard requires disclosure of the nature and extent of the financial asset and any associated liabilities (see paragraph 94(a)). Such disclosure helps users of the financial statements to evaluate the significance of such transactions and may be relevant, for example, if an entity sells a portfolio of receivables and provides a limited guarantee of only one risk. In that example, the amount of the transferred receivables the transferor continues to recognise may be much riskier than the amount it derecognises.

Multiple embedded derivative features (paragraph 94(d))

BC39 The Board noted that the separation of the liability and equity components of a compound financial instrument is more complicated for compound financial instruments with multiple embedded derivative features whose values are interdependent (for example, a convertible debt instrument that gives the issuer a right to call the instrument back from the holder or the holder a right to put the instrument back to the issuer) than for those without such features. If the embedded equity and non-equity derivative features are interdependent, the sum of the separately determined values of the liability and equity components will not equal the value of the compound financial instrument as a whole.

BC40 For example, the values of an embedded call option feature and an equity conversion option feature in a callable convertible debt instrument depend in part on each other in cases where the holder's equity conversion option is extinguished when the entity exercises the call option or vice versa. The following diagram illustrates the joint value arising from the interaction between a call option and an equity conversion option in a callable convertible bond. Circle L represents the value of the liability component, ie the value of the straight debt and the embedded call option on the straight debt, and Circle E represents the value of the equity component, ie the equity conversion option on the straight debt. The total area covered by the two circles represents the value of the callable convertible bond. The difference between the value of the callable convertible bond as a whole and the sum of the separately determined values for the liability and equity components is the joint value attributable to the interdependence between the call option feature and the equity conversion feature. It is represented by the intersection between the two circles.

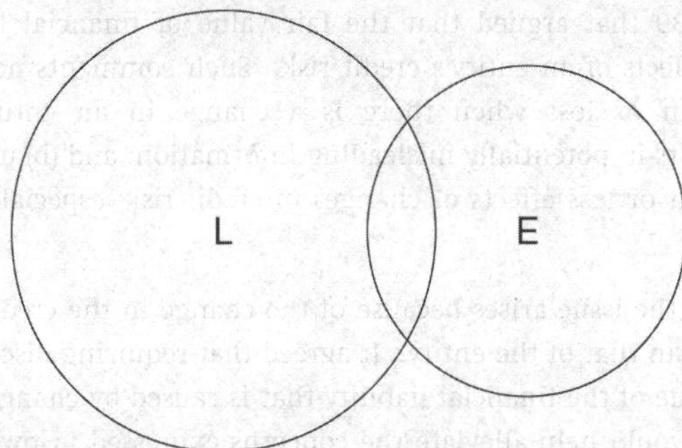

BC41 Under the approach in paragraph BC25, the joint value attributable to the interdependence between multiple embedded derivative features is included in the liability component. A numerical example is set out as Illustrative Example 10.

BC42 Even though this approach is consistent with the definition of equity as a residual interest, the Board recognises that the allocation of the joint value to either the liability component or the equity component is arbitrary because it is, by its nature, joint. Therefore, the Board concluded that disclosure of the existence of issued compound financial instruments with multiple embedded derivative features that have interdependent values and the effective yield on the liability component is important. Such disclosure highlights the impact of multiple embedded derivative features on the amounts reported as liabilities and equity and interest expense for the issuer of a compound financial instrument.

Financial assets and financial liabilities at fair value through profit or loss (paragraphs 94(e), 94(f) and AG40)

BC43 The revised Standard requires disclosure of the carrying amounts of financial assets and financial liabilities that are classified as held for trading and those designated by the entity upon initial recognition as financial assets and financial liabilities at fair value through profit or loss. The Board concluded that an indication of the extent to which an entity designates financial assets and financial liabilities at fair value through profit or loss is useful to users because there are no restrictions on the items that can be so designated and because these items do not meet the definition of held for trading.

BC44 The revisions to IAS 39 include the ability for entities to designate a non-derivative financial liability as held at fair value through profit or loss. Paragraph 94(f)(i) requires disclosure of the change in fair value of such a financial liability that is not attributable to changes in a benchmark interest rate. The Board considered this disclosure in its deliberations on the fair value measurement of financial liabilities and whether changes in the credit risk of a liability should be included in its fair value measurement when the fair value option is used in IAS 39. The Board agreed that such changes should be included (ie the fair value of financial liabilities is not adjusted to exclude the effect of changes in the credit quality of the liability). Its reasons for this decision are set out in the Basis for Conclusions on IAS 39, paragraphs BC87–BC92.

BC45 The Board considered comments received on the Exposure Draft of proposed amendments to IAS 39 that argued that the fair value of financial liabilities should exclude the effects of an entity's credit risk. Such comments noted that (a) recognising a gain or loss when there is a change in an entity's own creditworthiness results in potentially misleading information; and (b) users may misinterpret the profit or loss effects of changes in credit risk, especially in the absence of disclosures.

BC46 The Board noted that the issue arises because of the change in the credit risk of the liability, rather than that of the entity. It agreed that requiring disclosure of the change in fair value of the financial liability that is caused by changes in the liability's credit risk would help alleviate the concerns expressed. However, the Board noted that providing this disclosure would often not be practicable because it may not be possible to separate and measure reliably that part of the change in fair value. Therefore, it decided to require disclosure of the change in fair value of the financial liability that is not attributable to changes in a benchmark interest rate. The Board believes this is a reasonable proxy for the change in fair value that is attributable to changes in the liability's credit risk, in particular when such changes are large, and will provide users with information with which to understand the profit or loss effect of such a change in credit risk.

BC47 The Board concluded that when an entity has designated a financial liability as at fair value through profit or loss, disclosure should be given of the difference between the carrying amount and the amount the entity would contractually be required to pay at maturity to the holders of the liability (see paragraph 94(f)(ii)). The fair value may differ significantly from the settlement amount, in particular for financial liabilities with a long duration when an entity has experienced a significant deterioration in creditworthiness since their issue.

Defaults and breaches (paragraph 94(j))

BC48 The revised Standard requires disclosures of defaults in the payment of principal and interest, breaches of sinking fund or redemption provisions on loans payable, and any other breaches when those breaches can permit the lender to demand repayment of loans payable. Such disclosures provide relevant information about the entity's creditworthiness and its prospects of obtaining future loans.

Summary of changes from the Exposure Draft

BC49 The main changes from the Exposure Draft's proposals are as follows:

(a) The Exposure Draft proposed to define a financial liability as a contractual obligation to deliver cash or another financial asset to another entity or to exchange financial instruments with another entity under conditions that are potentially unfavourable. The definition in the Standard has been expanded to include some contracts that will or may be settled in the entity's own equity instruments. The Standard's definition of a financial asset has been similarly expanded.

(b) The Exposure Draft proposed that a financial instrument that gives the holder the right to put it back to the entity for cash or another financial asset is a financial liability. The Standard retains this conclusion, but provides additional guidance and illustrative examples to assist entities that, as a result of this requirement, either have no equity as defined in IAS 32 or whose share capital is not equity as defined in IAS 32.

(c) The Standard retains and clarifies the proposal in the Exposure Draft that terms and conditions of a financial instrument may indirectly create an obligation.

(d) The Exposure Draft proposed to incorporate in IAS 32 the conclusion previously in SIC-5 *Classification of Financial Instruments—Contingent Settlement Provisions*. This is that a financial instrument for which the manner of settlement depends on the occurrence or non-occurrence of uncertain future events or on the outcome of uncertain circumstances that are beyond the control of both the issuer and the holder is a financial liability. The Standard clarifies this conclusion by requiring contingent settlement provisions that apply only in the event of liquidation of an entity or are not genuine to be ignored.

(e) The Exposure Draft proposed that a derivative contract that contains an option as to how it is settled meets the definition of an equity instrument if the entity had all of the following: (i) an unconditional right and ability to settle the contract gross; (ii) an established practice of such settlement; and (iii) the intention to settle the contract gross. These conditions have not been carried forward into the Standard. Rather, a derivative with settlement options is classified as a financial asset or a financial liability unless all the settlement alternatives would result in equity classification.

(f) The Standard provides explicit guidance on accounting for the repurchase of a convertible instrument.

(g) The Standard provides explicit guidance on accounting for the amendment of the terms of a convertible instrument to induce early conversion.

(h) The Exposure Draft proposed that a financial instrument that is an equity instrument of a subsidiary should be eliminated on consolidation when held by the parent, or presented in the consolidated balance sheet within equity when not held by the parent (as a minority interest separate from the equity of the parent). The Standard requires all terms and conditions agreed between members of the group and the holders of the instrument to be considered when determining if the group as a whole has an obligation that would give rise to a financial liability. To the extent there is such an obligation, the instrument (or component of the instrument that is subject to the obligation) is a financial liability in consolidated financial statements.

(i) The Standard has clarified that the disclosure proposals in the Exposure Draft relating to when fair value is estimated using a valuation technique did not require disclosure of sensitivity to *all* valuation assumptions not supported by observable market prices. Rather, the sensitivity disclosure is required only if:

   (i) the fair value is sensitive to a particular assumption;

   (ii) reasonably possible alternatives for that assumption would result in a significantly different result; and

   (iii) that assumption is not supported by observable market prices or rates.

(j) For financial liabilities designated as at fair value through profit or loss, the Standard requires disclosure of the amount of the change in fair value that is not attributable to changes in a benchmark interest rate. This disclosure gives an indication of how much of the change in fair value is caused by changes in the credit risk of the liability.

Dissenting Opinion

Dissent of James J Leisenring

DO1 Mr Leisenring dissents from IAS 32 because, in his view, the conclusions about the accounting for forward purchase contracts and written put options on an issuer's equity instruments that require physical settlement in exchange for cash are inappropriate. IAS 32 requires a forward purchase contract to be recognised as though the future transaction had already occurred. Similarly it requires a written put option to be accounted for as though the option had already been exercised. Both of these contracts result in combining the separate forward contract and the written put option with outstanding shares to create a synthetic liability.

DO2 Recording a liability for the present value of the fixed forward price as a result of a forward contract is inconsistent with the accounting for other forward contracts. Recording a liability for the present value of the strike price of an option results in recording a liability that is inconsistent with the *Framework* as there is no present obligation for the strike price. In both instances the shares considered to be subject to the contracts are outstanding, have the same rights as any other shares and should be accounted for as outstanding. The forward and option contracts meet the definition of a derivative and should be accounted for as derivatives rather than create an exception to the accounting required by IAS 39. Similarly, if the redemption feature is embedded in the equity instrument (for example, a redeemable preference share) rather than being a free-standing derivative contract, the redemption feature should be accounted for as a derivative.

DO3 Mr Leisenring also objects to the conclusion that a purchased put or call option on a fixed number of an issuer's equity instruments is not an asset. The rights created by these contracts meet the definition of an asset and should be accounted for as assets and not as a reduction in equity. These contracts also meet the definition of derivatives that should be accounted for as such consistently with IAS 39.

Illustrative Examples

These examples accompany, but are not part of, IAS 32.

Accounting for contracts on equity instruments of an entity

IE1 The following examples* illustrate the application of paragraphs 15–27 and IAS 39 to the accounting for contracts on an entity's own equity instruments.

Example 1: Forward to buy shares

IE2 This example illustrates the journal entries for forward purchase contracts on an entity's own shares that will be settled (a) net in cash, (b) net in shares or (c) by delivering cash in exchange for shares. It also discusses the effect of settlement options (see (d) below). To simplify the illustration, it is assumed that no dividends are paid on the underlying shares (ie the 'carry return' is zero) so that the present value of the forward price equals the spot price when the fair value of the forward contract is zero. The fair value of the forward has been computed as the difference between the market share price and the present value of the fixed forward price.

Assumptions:

Contract date	1 February 2002
Maturity date	31 January 2003
Market price per share on 1 February 2002	CU100
Market price per share on 31 December 2002	CU110
Market price per share on 31 January 2003	CU106
Fixed forward price to be paid on 31 January 2003	CU104
Present value of forward price on 1 February 2002	CU100
Number of shares under forward contract	1,000
Fair value of forward on 1 February 2002	CU0
Fair value of forward on 31 December 2002	CU6,300
Fair value of forward on 31 January 2003	CU2,000

* In these examples, monetary amounts are denominated in 'currency units' (CU).

(a) Cash for cash ('net cash settlement')

IE3 In this subsection, the forward purchase contract on the entity's own shares will be settled net in cash, ie there is no receipt or delivery of the entity's own shares upon settlement of the forward contract.

On 1 February 2002, Entity A enters into a contract with Entity B to receive the fair value of 1,000 of Entity A's own outstanding ordinary shares as of 31 January 2003 in exchange for a payment of CU104,000 in cash (ie CU104 per share) on 31 January 2003. The contract will be settled net in cash. Entity A records the following journal entries.

1 February 2002

The price per share when the contract is agreed on 1 February 2002 is CU100. The initial fair value of the forward contract on 1 February 2002 is zero.

No entry is required because the fair value of the derivative is zero and no cash is paid or received.

31 December 2002

On 31 December 2002, the market price per share has increased to CU110 and, as a result, the fair value of the forward contract has increased to CU6,300.

Dr Forward asset	CU6,300	
Cr Gain		CU6,300

To record the increase in the fair value of the forward contract.

31 January 2003

On 31 January 2003, the market price per share has decreased to CU106. The fair value of the forward contract is CU2,000 ([CU106 × 1,000] – CU104,000).

On the same day, the contract is settled net in cash. Entity A has an obligation to deliver CU104,000 to Entity B and Entity B has an obligation to deliver CU106,000 (CU106 ×1,000) to Entity A, so Entity B pays the net amount of CU2,000 to Entity A.

Dr Loss	CU4,300	
Cr Forward asset		CU4,300

To record the decrease in the fair value of the forward contract (ie CU4,300 = CU6,300 – CU2,000).

Dr Cash	CU2,000	
Cr Forward asset		CU2,000

To record the settlement of the forward contract.

(b) Shares for shares ('net share settlement')

IE4 Assume the same facts as in (a) except that settlement will be made net in shares instead of net in cash. Entity A's journal entries are the same as those shown in (a) above, except for recording the settlement of the forward contract, as follows:

31 January 2003

The contract is settled net in shares. Entity A has an obligation to deliver CU104,000 (CU104 × 1,000) worth of its shares to Entity B and Entity B has an obligation to deliver CU106,000 (CU106 × 1,000) worth of shares to Entity A. Thus, Entity B delivers a net amount of CU2,000 (CU106,000 – CU104,000) worth of shares to Entity A, ie 18.9 shares (CU2,000/CU106).

Dr Equity	CU2,000	
Cr Forward asset		CU2,000

To record the settlement of the forward contract.

(c) Cash for shares ('gross physical settlement')

IE5 Assume the same facts as in (a) except that settlement will be made by delivering a fixed amount of cash and receiving a fixed number of Entity A's shares. Similarly to (a) and (b) above, the price per share that Entity A will pay in one year is fixed at CU104. Accordingly, Entity A has an obligation to pay CU104,000 in cash to Entity B (CU104 × 1,000) and Entity B has an obligation to deliver 1,000 of Entity A's outstanding shares to Entity A in one year. Entity A records the following journal entries.

1 February 2002

Dr Equity	CU100,000	
Cr Liability		CU100,000

To record the obligation to deliver CU104,000 in one year at its present value of CU100,000 discounted using an appropriate interest rate (see IAS 39, paragraph AG64).

31 December 2002

Dr Interest expense	CU3,660	
Cr Liability		CU3,660

To accrue interest in accordance with the effective interest method on the liability for the share redemption amount.

31 January 2003

Dr Interest expense	CU340	
Cr Liability		CU340

To accrue interest in accordance with the effective interest method on the liability for the share redemption amount.

Entity A delivers CU104,000 in cash to Entity B and Entity B delivers 1,000 of Entity A's shares to Entity A.

Dr Liability	CU104,000	
Cr Cash		CU104,000

To record the settlement of the obligation to redeem Entity A's own shares for cash.

(d) Settlement options

IE6 The existence of settlement options (such as net in cash, net in shares or by an exchange of cash and shares) has the result that the forward repurchase contract is a financial asset or a financial liability. If one of the settlement alternatives is to exchange cash for shares ((c) above), Entity A recognises a liability for the obligation to deliver cash, as illustrated in (c) above. Otherwise, Entity A accounts for the forward contract as a derivative.

Example 2: Forward to sell shares

IE7 This example illustrates the journal entries for forward sale contracts on an entity's own shares that will be settled (a) net in cash, (b) net in shares or (c) by receiving cash in exchange for shares. It also discusses the effect of settlement options (see (d) below). To simplify the illustration, it is assumed that no dividends are paid on the underlying shares (ie the 'carry return' is zero) so that the present value of the forward price equals the spot price when the fair value of the forward contract is zero. The fair value of the forward has been computed as the difference between the market share price and the present value of the fixed forward price.

Assumptions:

Contract date	1 February 2002
Maturity date	31 January 2003
Market price per share on 1 February 2002	CU100
Market price per share on 31 December 2002	CU110
Market price per share on 31 January 2003	CU106
Fixed forward price to be paid on 31 January 2003	CU104
Present value of forward price on 1 February 2002	CU100
Number of shares under forward contract	1,000
Fair value of forward on 1 February 2002	CU0
Fair value of forward on 31 December 2002	(CU6,300)
Fair value of forward on 31 January 2003	(CU2,000)

(a) Cash for cash ('net cash settlement')

IE8 On 1 February 2002, Entity A enters into a contract with Entity B to pay the fair value of 1,000 of Entity A's own outstanding ordinary shares as of 31 January 2003 in exchange for CU104,000 in cash (ie CU104 per share) on 31 January 2003. The contract will be settled net in cash. Entity A records the following journal entries.

1 February 2002

No entry is required because the fair value of the derivative is zero and no cash is paid or received.

31 December 2002

Dr Loss	CU6,300	
Cr Forward liability		CU6,300

To record the decrease in the fair value of the forward contract.

31 January 2003

Dr Forward gain	CU4,300	
Cr Gain		CU4,300

To record the increase in the fair value of the forward contract (ie CU4,300 = CU6,300 – CU2,000).

The contract is settled net in cash. Entity B has an obligation to deliver CU104,000 to Entity A, and Entity A has an obligation to deliver CU106,000 (CU106 × 1,000) to Entity B. Thus, Entity A pays the net amount of CU2,000 to Entity B.

Dr Forward liability	CU2,000	
Cr Cash		CU2,000

To record the settlement of the forward contract.

(b) Shares for shares ('net share settlement')

IE9 Assume the same facts as in (a) except that settlement will be made net in shares instead of net in cash. Entity A's journal entries are the same as those shown in (a), except:

31 January 2003

The contract is settled net in shares. Entity A has a right to receive CU104,000 (CU104 × 1,000) worth of its shares and an obligation to deliver CU106,000 (CU106 × 1,000) worth of its shares to Entity B. Thus, Entity A delivers a net amount of CU2,000 (CU106,000 – CU104,000) worth of its shares to Entity B, ie 18.9 shares (CU2,000/CU106).

Dr Forward liability	CU2,000	
Cr Equity		CU2,000

To record the settlement of the forward contract. The issue of the entity's own shares is treated as an equity transaction.

(c) Shares for shares ('net share settlement')

IE10 Assume the same facts as in (a), except that settlement will be made by receiving a fixed amount of cash and delivering a fixed number of the entity's own shares. Similarly to (a) and (b) above, the price per share that Entity A will pay in one year is fixed at CU104. Accordingly, Entity A has a right to receive CU104,000 in cash (CU104 × 1,000) and an obligation to deliver 1,000 of its own shares in one year. Entity A records the following journal entries.

1 February 2002

No entry is made on 1 February. No cash is paid or received because the forward has an initial fair value of zero. A forward contract to deliver a fixed number of Entity A's own shares in exchange for a fixed amount of cash or another financial asset meets the definition of an equity instrument because it cannot be settled otherwise than through the delivery of shares in exchange for cash.

31 December 2002

No entry is made on 31 December because no cash is paid or received and a contract to deliver a fixed number of Entity A's own shares in exchange for a fixed amount of cash meets the definition of an equity instrument of the entity.

31 January 2003

On 31 January 2003, Entity A receives CU104,000 in cash and delivers 1,000 shares.

Dr Cash	CU104,000	
Cr Equity		CU104,000

To record the settlement of the forward contract.

(d) Settlement options

IE11 The existence of settlement options (such as net in cash, net in shares or by an exchange of cash and shares) has the result that the forward contract is a financial asset or a financial liability. It does not meet the definition of an equity instrument because it can be settled otherwise than by Entity A repurchasing a fixed number of its own shares in exchange for paying a fixed amount of cash or another financial asset. Entity A recognises a derivative asset or liability, as illustrated in (a) and (b) above. The accounting entry to be made on settlement depends on how the contract is actually settled.

Example 3: Purchased call option on shares

IE12 This example illustrates the journal entries for a purchased call option right on the entity's own shares that will be settled (a) net in cash, (b) net in shares or (c) by delivering cash in exchange for the entity's own shares. It also discusses the effect of settlement options (see (d) below):

Assumptions:

Contract date	1 February 2002
Maturity date	31 January 2003 (European terms, ie it can be exercised only at maturity)
Exercise right holder	Reporting entity (Entity A)
Market price per share on 1 February 2002	CU100
Market price per share on 31 December 2002	CU104
Market price per share on 31 January 2003	CU104
Fixed exercise price to be paid on 31 January 2003	CU102
Number of shares under option contract	1,000
Fair value of option on 1 February 2002	CU5,000
Fair value of option on 31 December 2002	CU3,000
Fair value of option on 31 January 2003	CU2,000

(a) Cash for cash ('net cash settlement')

IE13 On 1 February 2002, Entity A enters into a contract with Entity B that gives Entity B the obligation to deliver, and Entity A the right to receive the fair value of 1,000 of Entity A's own ordinary shares as of 31 January 2003 in exchange for CU102,000 in cash (ie CU102 per share) on 31 January 2003, if Entity A exercises that right. The contract will be settled net in cash. If Entity A does not exercise its right, no payment will be made. Entity A records the following journal entries.

1 February 2002

The price per share when the contract is agreed on 1 February 2002 is CU100. The initial fair value of the option contract on 1 February 2002 is CU5,000, which Entity A pays to Entity B in cash on that date. On that date, the option has no intrinsic value, only time value, because the exercise price of CU102 exceeds the market price per share of CU100 and it would therefore not be economic for Entity A to exercise the option. In other words, the call option is out of the money.

Dr Call option asset	CU5,000	
Cr Cash		CU5,000

To recognise the purchased call option.

31 December 2002

On 31 December 2002, the market price per share has increased to CU104. The fair value of the call option has decreased to CU3,000, of which CU2,000 is intrinsic value ([CU104 – CU102] × 1,000), and CU1,000 is the remaining time value.

Dr Loss	CU2,000	
Cr Call option asset		CU2,000

To record the decrease in the fair value of the call option.

31 January 2003

On 31 January 2003, the market price per share is still CU104. The fair value of the call option has decreased to CU2,000, which is all intrinsic value ([CU104 – CU102] × 1,000) because no time value remains.

Dr Loss	CU1,000	
Cr Call option asset		CU1,000

To record the decrease in the fair value of the call option.

On the same day, Entity A exercises the call option and the contract is settled net in cash. Entity B has an obligation to deliver CU104,000 (CU104 × 1,000) to Entity A in exchange for CU102,000 (CU102 × 1,000) from Entity A, so Entity A receives a net amount of CU2,000.

Dr Cash	CU2,000	
Cr Call option asset		CU2,000

To record the settlement of the option contract.

(b) Shares for shares ('net share settlement')

IE14 Assume the same facts as in (a) except that settlement will be made net in shares instead of net in cash. Entity A's journal entries are the same as those shown in (a) except for recording the settlement of the option contract as follows:

31 January 2003

Entity A exercises the call option and the contract is settled net in shares. Entity B has an obligation to deliver CU104,000 (CU104 × 1,000) worth of Entity A's shares to Entity A in exchange for CU102,000 (CU102 × 1,000) worth of Entity A's shares. Thus, Entity B delivers the net amount of CU2,000 worth of shares to Entity A, ie 19.2 shares (CU2,000/CU104).

Dr Equity	CU2,000	
Cr Call option asset		CU2,000

To record the settlement of the option contract. The settlement is accounted for as a treasury share transaction (ie no gain or loss).

(c) Cash for shares ('gross physical settlement')

IE15 Assume the same facts as in (a) except that settlement will be made by receiving a fixed number of shares and paying a fixed amount of cash, if Entity A exercises the option. Similarly to (a) and (b) above, the exercise price per share is fixed at CU102. Accordingly, Entity A has a right to receive 1,000 of Entity A's own outstanding shares in exchange for CU102,000 (CU102 ×1,000) in cash, if Entity A exercises its option. Entity A records the following journal entries.

1 February 2002

Dr Equity	CU5,000	
Cr Cash		CU5,000

To record the cash paid in exchange for the right to receive Entity A's own shares in one year for a fixed price. The premium paid is recognised in equity.

31 December 2002

No entry is made on 31 December because no cash is paid or received and a contract that gives a right to receive a fixed number of Entity A's own shares in exchange for a fixed amount of cash meets the definition of an equity instrument of the entity.

31 January 2003

Entity A exercises the call option and the contract is settled gross. Entity B has an obligation to deliver 1,000 of Entity A's shares in exchange for CU102,000 in cash.

Dr Equity	CU102,000	
Cr Cash		CU102,000

To record the settlement of the option contract.

(d) Settlement options

IE16 The existence of settlement options (such as net in cash, net in shares or by an exchange of cash and shares) has the result that the call option is a financial asset. It does not meet the definition of an equity instrument because it can be settled otherwise than by Entity A repurchasing a fixed number of its own shares in exchange for paying a fixed amount of cash or another financial asset. Entity A recognises a derivative asset, as illustrated in (a) and (b) above. The accounting entry to be made on settlement depends on how the contract is actually settled.

Example 4: Written call option on shares

IE17 This example illustrates the journal entries for a written call option obligation on the entity's own shares that will be settled (a) net in cash, (b) net in shares or (c) by delivering cash in exchange for shares. It also discusses the effect of settlement options (see (d) below).

Assumptions:

Contract date	1 February 2002
Maturity date	31 January 2003 (European terms, ie it can be exercised only at maturity)
Exercise right holder	Counterparty (Entity B)
Market price per share on 1 February 2002	CU100
Market price per share on 31 December 2002	CU104
Market price per share on 31 January 2003	CU104
Fixed exercise price to be paid on 31 January 2003	CU102
Number of shares under option contract	1,000
Fair value of option on 1 February 2002	CU5,000
Fair value of option on 31 December 2002	CU3,000
Fair value of option on 31 January 2003	CU2,000

(a) Cash for cash ('net cash settlement')

IE18 Assume the same facts as in Example 3(a) above except that Entity A has written a call option on its own shares instead of having purchased a call option on them. Accordingly, on 1 February 2002 Entity A enters into a contract with Entity B that gives Entity B the right to receive and Entity A the obligation to pay the fair value of 1,000 of Entity A's own ordinary shares as of 31 January 2003 in exchange for CU102,000 in cash (ie CU102 per share) on 31 January 2003, if Entity B exercises that right. The contract will be settled net in cash. If Entity B does not exercise its right, no payment will be made. Entity A records the following journal entries.

1 February 2002

Dr Cash	CU5,000	
Cr Call option obligation		CU5,000

To recognise the written call option.

31 December 2002

Dr Call option obligation	CU2,000	
Cr Gain		CU2,000

To record the decrease in the fair value of the call option.

31 January 2003

Dr Call option obligation	CU1,000	
Cr Gain		CU1,000

To record the decrease in the fair value of the option.

On the same day, Entity B exercises the call option and the contract is settled net in cash. Entity A has an obligation to deliver CU104,000 (CU104 × 1,000) to Entity B in exchange for CU102,000 (CU102 × 1,000) from Entity B, so Entity A pays a net amount of CU2,000.

Dr Call option obligation	CU2,000	
Cr Cash		CU2,000

To record the settlement of the option contract.

(b) Shares for shares ('net share settlement')

IE19 Assume the same facts as in (a) except that settlement will be made net in shares instead of net in cash. Entity A's journal entries are the same as those shown in (a), except for recording the settlement of the option contract, as follows:

31 December 2003

Entity B exercises the call option and the contract is settled net in shares. Entity A has an obligation to deliver CU104,000 (CU104 × 1,000) worth of Entity A's shares to Entity B in exchange for CU102,000 (CU102 × 1,000) worth of Entity A's shares. Thus, Entity A delivers the net amount of CU2,000 worth of shares to Entity B, ie 19.2 shares (CU2,000/CU104).

Dr Call option obligation	CU2,000	
Cr Equity		CU2,000

To record the settlement of the option contract. The settlement is accounted for as an equity transaction.

(c) Cash for shares ('gross physical settlement')

IE20 Assume the same facts as in (a) except that settlement will be made by delivering a fixed number of shares and receiving a fixed amount of cash, if Entity B exercises the option. Similarly to (a) and (b) above, the exercise price per share is fixed at CU102. Accordingly, Entity B has a right to receive 1,000 of Entity A's own outstanding shares in exchange for CU102,000 (CU102 × 1,000) in cash, if Entity B exercises its option. Entity A records the following journal entries.

1 February 2002

Dr Cash	CU5,000	
Cr Equity		CU5,000

To record the cash received in exchange for the obligation to deliver a fixed number of Entity A's own shares in one year for a fixed price. The premium received is recognised in equity. Upon exercise, the call would result in the issue of a fixed number of shares in exchange for a fixed amount of cash.

31 December 2002

No entry is made on 31 December because no cash is paid or received and a contract to deliver a fixed number of Entity A's own shares in exchange for a fixed amount of cash meets the definition of an equity instrument of the entity.

31 January 2003

Entity B exercises the call option and the contract is settled gross. Entity A has an obligation to deliver 1,000 shares in exchange for CU102,000 in cash.

Dr Cash	CU102,000	
Cr Equity		CU102,000

To record the settlement of the option contract.

(d) Settlement options

IE21 The existence of settlement options (such as net in cash, net in shares or by an exchange of cash and shares) has the result that the call option is a financial liability. It does not meet the definition of an equity instrument because it can be settled otherwise than by Entity A issuing a fixed number of its own shares in exchange for receiving a fixed amount of cash or another financial asset. Entity A recognises a derivative liability, as illustrated in (a) and (b) above. The accounting entry to be made on settlement depends on how the contract is actually settled.

Example 5: Purchased put option on shares

IE22 This example illustrates the journal entries for a purchased put option on the entity's own shares that will be settled (a) net in cash, (b) net in shares or (c) by delivering cash in exchange for shares. It also discusses the effect of settlement options (see (d) below).

Assumptions:

Contract date	1 February 2002
Maturity date	31 January 2003 (European terms, ie it can be exercised only at maturity)
Exercise right holder	Reporting entity (Entity A)
Market price per share on 1 February 2002	CU100
Market price per share on 31 December 2002	CU95
Market price per share on 31 January 2003	CU95
Fixed exercise price to be paid on 31 January 2003	CU98
Number of shares under option contract	1,000
Fair value of option on 1 February 2002	CU5,000
Fair value of option on 31 December 2002	CU4,000
Fair value of option on 31 January 2003	CU3,000

(a) Cash for cash ('net cash settlement')

IE23 On 1 February 2002, Entity A enters into a contract with Entity B that gives Entity A the right to sell, and Entity B the obligation to buy the fair value of 1,000 of Entity A's own outstanding ordinary shares as of 31 January 2003 at a strike price of CU98,000 (ie CU98 per share) on 31 January 2003, if Entity A exercises that right. The contract will be settled net in cash. If Entity A does not exercise its right, no payment will be made. Entity A records the following journal entries.

1 February 2002

The price per share when the contract is agreed on 1 February 2002 is CU100. The initial fair value of the option contract on 1 February 2002 is CU5,000, which Entity A pays to Entity B in cash on that date. On that date, the option has no intrinsic value, only time value, because the exercise price of CU98 is less than the market price per share of CU100. Therefore it would not be economic for Entity A to exercise the option. In other words, the put option is out of the money.

Dr Put option asset	CU102,000	
Cr Cash		CU102,000

To recognise the purchased put option.

31 December 2002

On 31 December 2002 the market price per share has decreased to CU95. The fair value of the put option has decreased to CU4,000, of which CU3,000 is intrinsic value ([CU98 – CU95] × 1,000) and CU1,000 is the remaining time value.

Dr Loss	CU1,000	
Cr Put option asset		CU1,000

To record the decrease in the fair value of the put option.

31 January 2003

On 31 January 2003 the market price per share is still CU95. The fair value of the put option has decreased to CU3,000, which is all intrinsic value ([CU98 – CU95] × 1,000) because no time value remains.

Dr Loss	CU1,000	
Cr Put option asset		CU1,000

To record the decrease in the fair value of the option.

On the same day, Entity A exercises the put option and the contract is settled net in cash. Entity B has an obligation to deliver CU98,000 to Entity A and Entity A has an obligation to deliver CU95,000 (CU95 × 1,000) to Entity B, so Entity B pays the net amount of CU3,000 to Entity A.

Dr Cash	CU3,000	
Cr Put option asset		CU3,000

To record the settlement of the option contract.

(b) Shares for shares ('net share settlement')

IE24 Assume the same facts as in (a) except that settlement will be made net in shares instead of net in cash. Entity A's journal entries are the same as shown in (a), except:

31 January 2003

Entity A exercises the put option and the contract is settled net in shares. In effect, Entity B has an obligation to deliver CU98,000 worth of Entity A's shares to Entity A, and Entity A has an obligation to deliver CU95,000 worth of Entity A's shares (CU95 × 1,000) to Entity B, so Entity B delivers the net amount of CU3,000 worth of shares to Entity A, ie 31.6 shares (CU3,000/CU95).

Dr Equity	CU3,000	
Cr Put option asset		CU3,000

To record the settlement of the option contract.

(c) Cash for shares ('gross physical settlement')

IE25 Assume the same facts as in (a) except that settlement will be made by receiving a fixed amount of cash and delivering a fixed number of Entity A's shares, if Entity A exercises the option. Similarly to (a) and (b) above, the exercise price per share is fixed at CU98. Accordingly, Entity B has an obligation to pay CU98,000 in cash to Entity A (CU98 × 1,000) in exchange for 1,000 of Entity A's outstanding shares, if Entity A exercises its option. Entity A records the following journal entries.

1 February 2002

Dr Equity	CU5,000	
Cr Cash		CU5,000

To record the cash received in exchange for the right to deliver Entity A's own shares in one year for a fixed price. The premium paid is recognised directly in equity. Upon exercise, it results in the issue of a fixed number of shares in exchange for a fixed price.

31 December 2002

No entry is made on 31 December because no cash is paid or received and a contract to deliver a fixed number of Entity A's own shares in exchange for a fixed amount of cash meets the definition of an equity instrument of Entity A.

31 January 2003

Entity A exercises the put option and the contract is settled gross. Entity B has an obligation to deliver CU98,000 in cash to Entity A in exchange for 1,000 shares.

Dr Cash	CU98,000	
Cr Equity		CU98,000

To record the settlement of the option contract.

(d) Settlement options

IE26 The existence of settlement options (such as net in cash, net in shares or by an exchange of cash and shares) has the result that the put option is a financial asset. It does not meet the definition of an equity instrument because it can be settled otherwise than by Entity A issuing a fixed number of its own shares in exchange for receiving a fixed amount of cash or another financial asset. Entity A recognises a derivative asset, as illustrated in (a) and (b) above. The accounting entry to be made on settlement depends on how the contract is actually settled.

Example 6: Written put option on shares

IE27 This example illustrates the journal entries for a written put option on the entity's own shares that will be settled (a) net in cash, (b) net in shares or (c) by delivering cash in exchange for shares. It also discusses the effect of settlement options (see (d) below).

Assumptions:

Contract date	1 February 2002
Maturity date	31 January 2003 (European terms, ie it can be exercised only at maturity)
Exercise right holder	Counterparty (Entity B)
Market price per share on 1 February 2002	CU100
Market price per share on 31 December 2002	CU95
Market price per share on 31 January 2003	CU95
Fixed exercise price to be paid on 31 January 2003	CU98
Present value of exercise price on 1 February 2002	CU95
Number of shares under option contract	1,000
Fair value of option on 1 February 2002	CU5,000
Fair value of option on 31 December 2002	CU4,000
Fair value of option on 31 January 2003	CU3,000

(a) Cash for cash ('net cash settlement')

IE28 Assume the same facts as in Example 5(a) above, except that Entity A has written a put option on its own shares instead of having purchased a put option on its own shares. Accordingly, on 1 February 2002, Entity A enters into a contract with Entity B that gives Entity B the right to receive and Entity A the obligation to pay the fair value of 1,000 of Entity A's outstanding ordinary shares as of 31 January 2003 in exchange for CU98,000 in cash (ie CU98 per share) on 31 January 2003, if Entity B exercises that right. The contract will be settled net in cash. If Entity B does not exercise its right, no payment will be made. Entity A records the following journal entries.

1 February 2002

Dr Cash	CU5,000	
Cr Put option liability		CU5,000

To recognise the written put option.

31 December 2002

Dr Put option liability	CU1,000	
Cr Gain		CU1,000

To record the decrease in the fair value of the put option.

31 January 2003

Dr Put option liability	CU1,000	
Cr Gain		CU1,000

To record the decrease in the fair value of the put option.

On the same day, Entity B exercises the put option and the contract is settled net in cash. Entity A has an obligation to deliver CU98,000 to Entity B, and Entity B has an obligation to deliver CU95,000 (CU95 × 1,000) to Entity A. Thus, Entity A pays the net amount of CU3,000 to Entity B.

Dr Put option liability	CU3,000	
Cr Cash		CU3,000

To record the settlement of the option contract.

(b) Shares for shares ('net share settlement')

IE29 Assume the same facts as in (a) except that settlement will be made net in shares instead of net in cash. Entity A's journal entries are the same as those in (a), except for the following:

31 January 2003

Entity B exercises the put option and the contract is settled net in shares. In effect, Entity A has an obligation to deliver CU98,000 worth of shares to Entity B, and Entity B has an obligation to deliver CU95,000 worth of Entity A's shares (CU95 × 1,000) to Entity A. Thus, Entity A delivers the net amount of CU3,000 worth of Entity A's shares to Entity B, ie 31.6 shares (3,000/95).

Dr Put option liability	CU3,000	
Cr Equity		CU3,000

To record the settlement of the option contract. The issue of Entity A's own shares is accounted for as an equity transaction.

(c) Cash for shares ('gross physical settlement')

IE30 Assume the same facts as in (a) except that settlement will be made by delivering a fixed amount of cash and receiving a fixed number of shares, if Entity B exercises the option. Similarly to (a) and (b) above, the exercise price per share is fixed at CU98. Accordingly, Entity A has an obligation to pay CU98,000 in cash to Entity B (CU98 × 1,000) in exchange for 1,000 of Entity A's outstanding shares, if Entity B exercises its option. Entity A records the following journal entries.

1 February 2002

Dr Cash	CU5,000	
Cr Equity		CU5,000

To recognise the option premium received of CU5,000 in equity.

Dr Equity	CU95,000	
Cr Liability		CU95,000

To recognise the present value of the obligation to deliver CU98,000 in one year, ie CU95,000, as a liability.

31 December 2002

Dr Interest expense	CU2,750	
Cr Liability		CU2,750

To accrue interest in accordance with the effective interest method on the liability for the share redemption amount.

31 January 2003

Dr Interest expense	CU250	
Cr Liability		CU250

To accrue interest in accordance with the effective interest method on the liability for the share redemption amount.

On the same day, Entity B exercises the put option and the contract is settled gross. Entity A has an obligation to deliver CU98,000 in cash to Entity B in exchange for CU95,000 worth of shares (CU95 × 1,000).

Dr Liability	CU98,000	
Cr Cash		CU98,000

To record the settlement of the option contract.

(d) Settlement options

IE31 The existence of settlement options (such as net in cash, net in shares or by an exchange of cash and shares) has the result that the written put option is a financial liability. If one of the settlement alternatives is to exchange cash for shares ((c) above), Entity A recognises a liability for the obligation to deliver cash, as illustrated in (c) above. Otherwise, Entity A accounts for the put option as a derivative liability.

Entities such as mutual funds and co-operatives whose share capital is not equity as defined in IAS 32

Example 7: Entities with no equity

IE32 The following example illustrates an income statement and balance sheet format that may be used by entities such as mutual funds that do not have equity as defined in IAS 32. Other formats are possible.

Income statement for the year ended 31 December 20X1

	20X1	**20X0**
	CU	CU
Revenue	2,956	1,718
Expenses (classified by nature or function)	(644)	(614)
Profit from operating activities	2,312	1,104
Finance costs		
– other finance costs	(47)	(47)
– distributions to unitholders	(50)	(50)
Change in net assets attributable to unitholders	2,215	1,007

Balance sheet at 31 December 20X1

		20X1		20X0
	CU	CU	CU	CU
ASSETS				
Non–current assets (classified in accordance with IAS 1)	91,374		78,484	
Total non–current assets		91,374		78,484
Current assets (classified in accordance with IAS 1)	1,422		1,769	
Total current assets		1,422		1,769
Total assets		92,796		80,253
LIABILITIES				
Current liabilities (classified in accordance with IAS 1)	647		66	
Total current liabilities		(647)		(66)
Non–current liabilities excluding net assets attributable to unitholders (classified in accordance with IAS 1)	280		136	
		(280)		(136)
Net assets attributable to unitholders		91,869		80,051

Example 8: Entities with some equity

IE33 The following example illustrates an income statement and balance sheet format that may be used by entities whose share capital is not equity as defined in IAS 32 because the entity has an obligation to repay the share capital on demand. Other formats are possible.

Income statement for the year ended 31 December 20X1

	20X1	**20X0**
	CU	CU
Revenue	472	498
Expenses (classified by nature or function)	(367)	(396)
Profit from operating activities	105	102
Finance costs		
– other finance costs	(4)	(4)
– distributions to members	(50)	(50)
Change in net assets attributable to members	51	48

Balance sheet at 31 December 20X1

		20X1		20X0
	CU	CU	CU	CU
ASSETS				
Non–current assets (classified in accordance with IAS 1)	908		830	
Total non–current assets		908		830
Current assets (classified in accordance with IAS 1)	383		350	
Total current assets		383		350
Total assets		1,291		1,180
LIABILITIES				
Current liabilities (classified in accordance with IAS 1)	372		338	
Share capital repayable on demand	202		161	
Total current liabilities		(574)		(499)
Total assets less current liabilities		717		681
Non–current liabilities (classified in accordance with IAS 1)	187		196	
		(187)		(196)
RESERVES[(a)]				
Reserves eg revaluation reserve, retained earnings etc	530		485	
		530		485
		717		681

MEMORANDUM NOTE – Total members' interests

Share capital repayable on demand	202	161
Reserves	530	485
	732	646

(a) In this example, the entity has no obligation to deliver a share of its reserves to its members.

Accounting for compound financial instruments

Example 9: Separation of a compound financial instrument on initial recognition

IE34 Paragraph 28 describes how the components of a compound financial instrument are separated by the entity on initial recognition. The following example illustrates how such a separation is made.

IE35 An entity issues 2,000 convertible bonds at the start of year 1. The bonds have a three-year term, and are issued at par with a face value of CU1,000 per bond, giving total proceeds of CU2,000,000. Interest is payable annually in arrears at a nominal annual interest rate of 6 per cent. Each bond is convertible at any time up to maturity into 250 ordinary shares. When the bonds are issued, the prevailing market interest rate for similar debt without conversion options is 9 per cent.

IE36 The liability component is measured first, and the difference between the proceeds of the bond issue and the fair value of the liability is assigned to the equity component. The present value of the liability component is calculated using a discount rate of 9 per cent, the market interest rate for similar bonds having no conversion rights, as shown below.

	CU
Present value of the principal – CU2,000,000 payable at the end of three years	1,544,367
Present value of the interest – CU120,000 payable annually in arrears for three years	303,755
Total liability component	1,848,122
Equity component (by deduction)	151,878
Proceeds of the bond issue	2,000,000

Example 10: Separation of a compound financial instrument with multiple embedded derivative features

IE37 The following example illustrates the application of paragraph 31 to the separation of the liability and equity components of a compound financial instrument with multiple embedded derivative features.

IE38 Assume that the proceeds received on the issue of a callable convertible bond are CU60. The value of a similar bond without a call or equity conversion option is CU57. Based on an option pricing model, it is determined that the value to the entity of the embedded call feature in a similar bond without an equity conversion option is CU2. In this case, the value allocated to the liability component under paragraph 31 is CU55 (CU57 – CU2) and the value allocated to the equity component is CU5 (CU60 – CU55).

Example 11: Repurchase of a convertible instrument

IE39 The following example illustrates how an entity accounts for a repurchase of a convertible instrument. For simplicity, at inception, the face amount of the instrument is assumed to be equal to the aggregate carrying amount of its liability and equity components in the financial statements, ie no original issue premium or discount exists. Also, for simplicity, tax considerations have been omitted from the example.

IE40 On 1 January 1999, Entity A issued a 10 per cent convertible debenture with a face value of CU1,000 maturing on 31 December 2008. The debenture is convertible into ordinary shares of Entity A at a conversion price of CU25 per share. Interest is payable half-yearly in cash. At the date of issue, Entity A could have issued non-convertible debt with a ten-year term bearing a coupon interest rate of 11 per cent.

IE41 In the financial statements of Entity A the carrying amount of the debenture was allocated on issue as follows:

	CU
Liability component	
Present value of 20 half–yearly interest payments of CU50, discounted at 11%	597
Present value of CU1,000 due in 10 years, discounted at 11%, compounded half–yearly	343
	940
Equity component	
(difference between CU1,000 total proceeds and CU940 allocated above)	60
Total proceeds	1,000

IE42 On 1 January 2004, the convertible debenture has a fair value of CU1,700.

IE43 Entity A makes a tender offer to the holder of the debenture to repurchase the debenture for CU1,700, which the holder accepts. At the date of repurchase, Entity A could have issued non–convertible debt with a five–year term bearing a coupon interest rate of 8 per cent.

IE44 The repurchase price is allocated as follows:

	Carrying value	Fair value	Difference
Liability component:	CU	CU	CU
Present value of 10 remaining half–yearly interest payments of CU50, discounted at 11% and 8%, respectively	377	405	
Present value of CU1,000 due in 5 years, discounted at 11% and 8%, compounded half–yearly, respectively	585	676	
	962	1,081	(119)
Equity component	60	619[(a)]	(559)
Total	1,022	1,700	(678)

(a) This amount represents the difference between the fair value amount allocated to the liability component and the repurchase price of CU1,700.

IE45 Entity A recognises the repurchase of the debenture as follows:

Dr Liability component	CU962	
Dr Debt settlement expense (income statement)	CU119	
Cr Cash		CU1,081

To recognise the repurchase of the liability component.

Dr Equity	CU619	
Cr Cash		CU619

To recognise the cash paid for the equity component.

IE46 The equity component remains as equity, but may be transferred from one line item within equity to another.

Example 12: Amendment of the terms of a convertible instrument to induce early conversion

IE47 The following example illustrates how an entity accounts for the additional consideration paid when the terms of a convertible instrument are amended to induce early conversion.

IE48 On 1 January 1999, Entity A issued a 10 per cent convertible debenture with a face value of CU1,000 with the same terms as described in Example 11. On 1 January 2000, to induce the holder to convert the convertible debenture promptly, Entity A reduces the conversion price to CU20 if the debenture is converted before 1 March 2000 (ie within 60 days).

IE49 Assume the market price of Entity A's ordinary shares on the date the terms are amended is CU40 per share. The fair value of the incremental consideration paid by Entity A is calculated as follows:

Number of ordinary shares to be issued to debenture holders under **amended** *conversion terms:*		
Face amount	CU1,000	
New conversion price	/CU20	per share
Number of ordinary shares to be issued on conversion	50	shares
Number of ordinary shares to be issued to debenture holders under **original** *conversion terms:*		
Face amount	CU1,000	
Original conversion price	/CU25	per share
Number of ordinary shares to be issued on conversion	40	shares
Number of **incremental** *ordinary shares issued upon conversion*	10	shares
Value of incremental ordinary shares issued upon conversion		
CU40 per share x 10 incremental shares	CU400	

IE50 The incremental consideration of CU400 is recognised as a loss in profit or loss.

Table of Concordance

This table shows how the contents of the superseded version of IAS 32 and the current version of IAS 32 correspond. Paragraphs are treated as corresponding if they broadly address the matter even though the guidance may differ.

The table also shows how the consensus and disclosure paragraphs of the superseded SIC Interpretations 5, 16 and 17 and draft SIC Interpretation D34, and the disclosure requirements formerly included in IAS 39, have been incorporated into the current version of IAS 32.

Except where indicated, all references are to IAS 32.

Superseded paragraph	Current paragraph
Objective	1,2,3
1	4,5
2	None
3	None
4	7
5	11
6	13
7	14
8	AG7
9	AG15
10	AG16
11	AG10
12	AG11
13	AG12
14	AG20
15	AG8
16	None
17	AG29
18	15
19	18
20	17, 19(a)
21	16, 17(part)
22	18(a), 20
23	28
24	BC22

Superseded paragraph	Current paragraph
25	29
26	30
27	None
28	31
29	32
30	35
31	36
32	40
33	42
34	43
35	44
36	45
37	46
38	47
39	48
40	49
41	50
42	51, 57
43	52
43A	56
44	53
45	54
46	55
47	60
48	62

Superseded paragraph	Current paragraph
49	63
50	64
51	65
52	66
53	None
54	None
55	None
56	67
57	68
58	69
59	70
60	71
61	None
62	72
63	73
64	74
65	75
66	76
67	77
68	78
69	79
70	80
71	81
72	None
73	82

Superseded paragraph	Current paragraph
74	83
75	84
76	85
77	86, 90
78	87
79	92, 93
80	IAS 39.AG69 (part)
81	IAS 39.AG71, IAS 39.AG72
82	IAS 39.AG64, IAS 39.AG74
83	None
84	None
85	91
86	88
87	86, 89
88	None
89	None
90	None
91	None
92	None
93	None
94	94(e)

Superseded paragraph	Current paragraph
95	96, 97
96	96,97
A1	AG1
A2	AG2
A3	AG3
A4	AG4
A5	AG5
A6	AG9
A7	AG13
A8	AG14(part)
A9	AG16
A10	AG17
A11	AG18
A12	AG19
A13	AG20
A14	AG21
A15	AG22
A16	AG23
A17	AG24
A18	None
A19	AG6
A20	19, AG25
A21	AG26

Superseded paragraph	Current paragraph
A22	AG30
A23	AG31
A24	IE34-IE36
A25	AG39
A26	None
A27	None
SIC-5.5	25
SIC-5.6	25
SIC-16.4	33
SIC-16.5	33
SIC-16.6	34
SIC-16.7	34
SIC-17.5	None
SIC-17.6	31, 35
SIC-17.7	38
SIC-17.8	38
SIC-17.9	39
SIC-D34.6	18
SIC-39.166	None
SIC-39.167	61, 92
SIC-39.168	93
SIC-39.169	56, 58, 59
SIC-39.70	94

International Accounting Standard 33

Earnings per Share

This version includes amendments resulting from new and amended IFRSs issued up to 31 December 2004.

CONTENTS

International Accounting Standard 33 *Earnings per Share* (IAS 33) is set out in paragraphs 1–76 and Appendices A and B. All the paragraphs have equal authority but retain the IASC format of the Standard when it was adopted by the IASB. IAS 33 should be read in the context of its objective and the Basis for Conclusions, the *Preface to International Financial Reporting Standards* and the *Framework for the Preparation and Presentation of Financial Statements*. IAS 8 *Accounting Policies, Changes in Accounting Estimates and Errors* provides a basis for selecting and applying accounting policies in the absence of explicit guidance.

Introduction

IN1 International Accounting Standard 33 *Earnings per Share* (IAS 33) replaces IAS 33 *Earnings Per Share* (issued in 1997), and should be applied for annual periods beginning on or after 1 January 2005. Earlier application is encouraged. The Standard also replaces SIC-24 *Earnings Per Share—Financial Instruments and Other Contracts that May Be Settled in Shares.*

Reasons for revising IAS 33

IN2 The International Accounting Standards Board has developed this revised IAS 33 as part of its project on Improvements to International Accounting Standards. The project was undertaken in the light of queries and criticisms raised in relation to the Standards by securities regulators, professional accountants and other interested parties. The objectives of the project were to reduce or eliminate alternatives, redundancies and conflicts within the Standards, to deal with some convergence issues and to make other improvements.

IN3 For IAS 33 the Board's main objective was a limited revision to provide additional guidance and illustrative examples on selected complex matters, such as the effects of contingently issuable shares; potential ordinary shares of subsidiaries, joint ventures or associates; participating equity instruments; written put options; purchased put and call options; and mandatorily convertible instruments. The Board did not reconsider the fundamental approach to the determination and presentation of earnings per share contained in IAS 33.

International Accounting Standard 33 Earnings per Share

Objective

1 The objective of this Standard is to prescribe principles for the determination and presentation of earnings per share, so as to improve performance comparisons between different entities in the same reporting period and between different reporting periods for the same entity. Even though earnings per share data have limitations because of the different accounting policies that may be used for determining 'earnings', a consistently determined denominator enhances financial reporting. The focus of this Standard is on the denominator of the earnings per share calculation.

Scope

2 **This Standard shall be applied by entities whose ordinary shares or potential ordinary shares are publicly traded and by entities that are in the process of issuing ordinary shares or potential ordinary shares in public markets.**

3 **An entity that discloses earnings per share shall calculate and disclose earnings per share in accordance with this Standard.**

4 **When an entity presents both consolidated financial statements and separate financial statements prepared in accordance with IAS 27** *Consolidated and Separate Financial Statements*, **the disclosures required by this Standard need be presented only on the basis of the consolidated information. An entity that chooses to disclose earnings per share based on its separate financial statements shall present such earnings per share information only on the face of its separate income statement. An entity shall not present such earnings per share information in the consolidated financial statements.**

Definitions

5 **The following terms are used in this Standard with the meanings specified:**

Antidilution **is an increase in earnings per share or a reduction in loss per share resulting from the assumption that convertible instruments are converted, that options or warrants are exercised, or that ordinary shares are issued upon the satisfaction of specified conditions.**

A *contingent share agreement* **is an agreement to issue shares that is dependent on the satisfaction of specified conditions.**

Contingently issuable ordinary shares **are ordinary shares issuable for little or no cash or other consideration upon the satisfaction of specified conditions in a contingent share agreement.**

Dilution **is a reduction in earnings per share or an increase in loss per share resulting from the assumption that convertible instruments are converted,**

that options or warrants are exercised, or that ordinary shares are issued upon the satisfaction of specified conditions.

Options, warrants and their equivalents **are financial instruments that give the holder the right to purchase ordinary shares.**

An *ordinary share* **is an equity instrument that is subordinate to all other classes of equity instruments.**

A *potential ordinary share* **is a financial instrument or other contract that may entitle its holder to ordinary shares.**

Put options **on ordinary shares are contracts that give the holder the right to sell ordinary shares at a specified price for a given period.**

6 Ordinary shares participate in profit for the period only after other types of shares such as preference shares have participated. An entity may have more than one class of ordinary shares. Ordinary shares of the same class have the same rights to receive dividends.

7 Examples of potential ordinary shares are:

(a) financial liabilities or equity instruments, including preference shares, that are convertible into ordinary shares;

(b) options and warrants;

(c) shares that would be issued upon the satisfaction of conditions resulting from contractual arrangements, such as the purchase of a business or other assets.

8 Terms defined in IAS 32 *Financial Instruments: Disclosure and Presentation* are used in this Standard with the meanings specified in paragraph 11 of IAS 32, unless otherwise noted. IAS 32 defines financial instrument, financial asset, financial liability, equity instrument and fair value, and provides guidance on applying those definitions.

Measurement

Basic earnings per share

9 **An entity shall calculate basic earnings per share amounts for profit or loss attributable to ordinary equity holders of the parent entity and, if presented, profit or loss from continuing operations attributable to those equity holders.**

10 **Basic earnings per share shall be calculated by dividing profit or loss attributable to ordinary equity holders of the parent entity (the numerator) by the weighted average number of ordinary shares outstanding (the denominator) during the period.**

11 The objective of basic earnings per share information is to provide a measure of the interests of each ordinary share of a parent entity in the performance of the entity over the reporting period.

Earnings

12 For the purpose of calculating basic earnings per share, the amounts attributable to ordinary equity holders of the parent entity in respect of:

(a) profit or loss from continuing operations attributable to the parent entity; and

(b) profit or loss attributable to the parent entity

shall be the amounts in (a) and (b) adjusted for the after-tax amounts of preference dividends, differences arising on the settlement of preference shares, and other similar effects of preference shares classified as equity.

13 All items of income and expense attributable to ordinary equity holders of the parent entity that are recognised in a period, including tax expense and dividends on preference shares classified as liabilities are included in the determination of profit or loss for the period attributable to ordinary equity holders of the parent entity (see IAS 1 *Presentation of Financial Statements*).

14 The after-tax amount of preference dividends that is deducted from profit or loss is:

(a) the after-tax amount of any preference dividends on non-cumulative preference shares declared in respect of the period; and

(b) the after-tax amount of the preference dividends for cumulative preference shares required for the period, whether or not the dividends have been declared. The amount of preference dividends for the period does not include the amount of any preference dividends for cumulative preference shares paid or declared during the current period in respect of previous periods.

15 Preference shares that provide for a low initial dividend to compensate an entity for selling the preference shares at a discount, or an above-market dividend in later periods to compensate investors for purchasing preference shares at a premium, are sometimes referred to as increasing rate preference shares. Any original issue discount or premium on increasing rate preference shares is amortised to retained earnings using the effective interest method and treated as a preference dividend for the purposes of calculating earnings per share.

16 Preference shares may be repurchased under an entity's tender offer to the holders. The excess of the fair value of the consideration paid to the preference shareholders over the carrying amount of the preference shares represents a return to the holders of the preference shares and a charge to retained earnings for the entity. This amount is deducted in calculating profit or loss attributable to ordinary equity holders of the parent entity.

17 Early conversion of convertible preference shares may be induced by an entity through favourable changes to the original conversion terms or the payment of additional consideration. The excess of the fair value of the ordinary shares or

other consideration paid over the fair value of the ordinary shares issuable under the original conversion terms is a return to the preference shareholders, and is deducted in calculating profit or loss attributable to ordinary equity holders of the parent entity.

18 Any excess of the carrying amount of preference shares over the fair value of the consideration paid to settle them is added in calculating profit or loss attributable to ordinary equity holders of the parent entity.

Shares

19 For the purpose of calculating basic earnings per share, the number of ordinary shares shall be the weighted average number of ordinary shares outstanding during the period.

20 Using the weighted average number of ordinary shares outstanding during the period reflects the possibility that the amount of shareholders' capital varied during the period as a result of a larger or smaller number of shares being outstanding at any time. The weighted average number of ordinary shares outstanding during the period is the number of ordinary shares outstanding at the beginning of the period, adjusted by the number of ordinary shares bought back or issued during the period multiplied by a time-weighting factor. The time-weighting factor is the number of days that the shares are outstanding as a proportion of the total number of days in the period; a reasonable approximation of the weighted average is adequate in many circumstances.

21 Shares are usually included in the weighted average number of shares from the date consideration is receivable (which is generally the date of their issue), for example:

(a) ordinary shares issued in exchange for cash are included when cash is receivable;

(b) ordinary shares issued on the voluntary reinvestment of dividends on ordinary or preference shares are included when dividends are reinvested;

(c) ordinary shares issued as a result of the conversion of a debt instrument to ordinary shares are included from the date that interest ceases to accrue;

(d) ordinary shares issued in place of interest or principal on other financial instruments are included from the date that interest ceases to accrue;

(e) ordinary shares issued in exchange for the settlement of a liability of the entity are included from the settlement date;

(f) ordinary shares issued as consideration for the acquisition of an asset other than cash are included as of the date on which the acquisition is recognised; and

(g) ordinary shares issued for the rendering of services to the entity are included as the services are rendered.

The timing of the inclusion of ordinary shares is determined by the terms and conditions attaching to their issue. Due consideration is given to the substance of any contract associated with the issue.

22 Ordinary shares issued as part of the cost of a business combination are included in the weighted average number of shares from the acquisition date. This is because the acquirer incorporates into its income statement the acquiree's profits and losses from that date.

23 Ordinary shares that will be issued upon the conversion of a mandatorily convertible instrument are included in the calculation of basic earnings per share from the date the contract is entered into.

24 Contingently issuable shares are treated as outstanding and are included in the calculation of basic earnings per share only from the date when all necessary conditions are satisfied (ie the events have occurred). Shares that are issuable solely after the passage of time are not contingently issuable shares, because the passage of time is a certainty. Outstanding ordinary shares that are contingently returnable (ie subject to recall) are not treated as outstanding and are excluded from the calculation of basic earnings per share until the date the shares are no longer subject to recall.

25 [Deleted]

26 The weighted average number of ordinary shares outstanding during the period and for all periods presented shall be adjusted for events, other than the conversion of potential ordinary shares, that have changed the number of ordinary shares outstanding without a corresponding change in resources.

27 Ordinary shares may be issued, or the number of ordinary shares outstanding may be reduced, without a corresponding change in resources. Examples include:

(a) a capitalisation or bonus issue (sometimes referred to as a stock dividend);

(b) a bonus element in any other issue, for example a bonus element in a rights issue to existing shareholders;

(c) a share split; and

(d) a reverse share split (consolidation of shares).

28 In a capitalisation or bonus issue or a share split, ordinary shares are issued to existing shareholders for no additional consideration. Therefore, the number of ordinary shares outstanding is increased without an increase in resources. The number of ordinary shares outstanding before the event is adjusted for the proportionate change in the number of ordinary shares outstanding as if the event had occurred at the beginning of the earliest period presented. For example, on a two-for-one bonus issue, the number of ordinary shares outstanding before the issue is multiplied by three to obtain the new total number of ordinary shares, or by two to obtain the number of additional ordinary shares.

29 A consolidation of ordinary shares generally reduces the number of ordinary shares outstanding without a corresponding reduction in resources. However, when the overall effect is a share repurchase at fair value, the reduction in the number of ordinary shares outstanding is the result of a corresponding reduction in resources. An example is a share consolidation combined with a special dividend. The weighted average number of ordinary shares outstanding for the

period in which the combined transaction takes place is adjusted for the reduction in the number of ordinary shares from the date the special dividend is recognised.

Diluted earnings per share

30 **An entity shall calculate diluted earnings per share amounts for profit or loss attributable to ordinary equity holders of the parent entity and, if presented, profit or loss from continuing operations attributable to those equity holders.**

31 **For the purpose of calculating diluted earnings per share, an entity shall adjust profit or loss attributable to ordinary equity holders of the parent entity, and the weighted average number of shares outstanding, for the effects of all dilutive potential ordinary shares.**

32 The objective of diluted earnings per share is consistent with that of basic earnings per share—to provide a measure of the interest of each ordinary share in the performance of an entity—while giving effect to all dilutive potential ordinary shares outstanding during the period. As a result:

(a) profit or loss attributable to ordinary equity holders of the parent entity is increased by the after-tax amount of dividends and interest recognised in the period in respect of the dilutive potential ordinary shares and is adjusted for any other changes in income or expense that would result from the conversion of the dilutive potential ordinary shares; and

(b) the weighted average number of ordinary shares outstanding is increased by the weighted average number of additional ordinary shares that would have been outstanding assuming the conversion of all dilutive potential ordinary shares.

Earnings

33 **For the purpose of calculating diluted earnings per share, an entity shall adjust profit or loss attributable to ordinary equity holders of the parent entity, as calculated in accordance with paragraph 12, by the after-tax effect of:**

(a) any dividends or other items related to dilutive potential ordinary shares deducted in arriving at profit or loss attributable to ordinary equity holders of the parent entity as calculated in accordance with paragraph 12;

(b) any interest recognised in the period related to dilutive potential ordinary shares; and

(c) any other changes in income or expense that would result from the conversion of the dilutive potential ordinary shares.

34 After the potential ordinary shares are converted into ordinary shares, the items identified in paragraph 33(a)–(c) no longer arise. Instead, the new ordinary shares are entitled to participate in profit or loss attributable to ordinary equity holders of the parent entity. Therefore, profit or loss attributable to ordinary equity holders of the parent entity calculated in accordance with paragraph 12 is

adjusted for the items identified in paragraph 33(a)–(c) and any related taxes. The expenses associated with potential ordinary shares include transaction costs and discounts accounted for in accordance with the effective interest method (see paragraph 9 of IAS 39 *Financial Instruments: Recognition and Measurement*, as revised in 2003).

35 The conversion of potential ordinary shares may lead to consequential changes in income or expenses. For example, the reduction of interest expense related to potential ordinary shares and the resulting increase in profit or reduction in loss may lead to an increase in the expense related to a non-discretionary employee profit-sharing plan. For the purpose of calculating diluted earnings per share, profit or loss attributable to ordinary equity holders of the parent entity is adjusted for any such consequential changes in income or expense.

Shares

36 For the purpose of calculating diluted earnings per share, the number of ordinary shares shall be the weighted average number of ordinary shares calculated in accordance with paragraphs 19 and 26, plus the weighted average number of ordinary shares that would be issued on the conversion of all the dilutive potential ordinary shares into ordinary shares. Dilutive potential ordinary shares shall be deemed to have been converted into ordinary shares at the beginning of the period or, if later, the date of the issue of the potential ordinary shares.

37 Dilutive potential ordinary shares shall be determined independently for each period presented. The number of dilutive potential ordinary shares included in the year-to-date period is not a weighted average of the dilutive potential ordinary shares included in each interim computation.

38 Potential ordinary shares are weighted for the period they are outstanding. Potential ordinary shares that are cancelled or allowed to lapse during the period are included in the calculation of diluted earnings per share only for the portion of the period during which they are outstanding. Potential ordinary shares that are converted into ordinary shares during the period are included in the calculation of diluted earnings per share from the beginning of the period to the date of conversion; from the date of conversion, the resulting ordinary shares are included in both basic and diluted earnings per share.

39 The number of ordinary shares that would be issued on conversion of dilutive potential ordinary shares is determined from the terms of the potential ordinary shares. When more than one basis of conversion exists, the calculation assumes the most advantageous conversion rate or exercise price from the standpoint of the holder of the potential ordinary shares.

40 A subsidiary, joint venture or associate may issue to parties other than the parent, venturer or investor potential ordinary shares that are convertible into either ordinary shares of the subsidiary, joint venture or associate, or ordinary shares of the parent, venturer or investor (the reporting entity). If these potential ordinary shares of the subsidiary, joint venture or associate have a dilutive effect on the basic earnings per share of the reporting entity, they are included in the calculation of diluted earnings per share.

Dilutive potential ordinary shares

41 Potential ordinary shares shall be treated as dilutive when, and only when, their conversion to ordinary shares would decrease earnings per share or increase loss per share from continuing operations.

42 An entity uses profit or loss from continuing operations attributable to the parent entity as the control number to establish whether potential ordinary shares are dilutive or antidilutive. Profit or loss from continuing operations attributable to the parent entity is adjusted in accordance with paragraph 12 and excludes items relating to discontinued operations.

43 Potential ordinary shares are antidilutive when their conversion to ordinary shares would increase earnings per share or decrease loss per share from continuing operations. The calculation of diluted earnings per share does not assume conversion, exercise, or other issue of potential ordinary shares that would have an antidilutive effect on earnings per share.

44 In determining whether potential ordinary shares are dilutive or antidilutive, each issue or series of potential ordinary shares is considered separately rather than in aggregate. The sequence in which potential ordinary shares are considered may affect whether they are dilutive. Therefore, to maximise the dilution of basic earnings per share, each issue or series of potential ordinary shares is considered in sequence from the most dilutive to the least dilutive, ie dilutive potential ordinary shares with the lowest 'earnings per incremental share' are included in the diluted earnings per share calculation before those with a higher earnings per incremental share. Options and warrants are generally included first because they do not affect the numerator of the calculation.

Options, warrants and their equivalents

45 For the purpose of calculating diluted earnings per share, an entity shall assume the exercise of dilutive options and warrants of the entity. The assumed proceeds from these instruments shall be regarded as having been received from the issue of ordinary shares at the average market price of ordinary shares during the period. The difference between the number of ordinary shares issued and the number of ordinary shares that would have been issued at the average market price of ordinary shares during the period shall be treated as an issue of ordinary shares for no consideration.

46 Options and warrants are dilutive when they would result in the issue of ordinary shares for less than the average market price of ordinary shares during the period. The amount of the dilution is the average market price of ordinary shares during the period minus the issue price. Therefore, to calculate diluted earnings per share, potential ordinary shares are treated as consisting of both the following:

(a) a contract to issue a certain number of the ordinary shares at their average market price during the period. Such ordinary shares are assumed to be fairly priced and to be neither dilutive nor antidilutive. They are ignored in the calculation of diluted earnings per share.

(b) a contract to issue the remaining ordinary shares for no consideration. Such ordinary shares generate no proceeds and have no effect on profit or loss attributable to ordinary shares outstanding. Therefore, such shares are dilutive and are added to the number of ordinary shares outstanding in the calculation of diluted earnings per share.

47 Options and warrants have a dilutive effect only when the average market price of ordinary shares during the period exceeds the exercise price of the options or warrants (ie they are 'in the money'). Previously reported earnings per share are not retroactively adjusted to reflect changes in prices of ordinary shares.

47A For share options and other share-based payment arrangements to which IFRS 2 *Share-based Payment* applies, the issue price referred to in paragraph 46 and the exercise price referred to in paragraph 47 shall include the fair value of any goods or services to be supplied to the entity in the future under the share option or other share-based payment arrangement.

48 Employee share options with fixed or determinable terms and non-vested ordinary shares are treated as options in the calculation of diluted earnings per share, even though they may be contingent on vesting. They are treated as outstanding on the grant date. Performance-based employee share options are treated as contingently issuable shares because their issue is contingent upon satisfying specified conditions in addition to the passage of time.

Convertible instruments

49 The dilutive effect of convertible instruments shall be reflected in diluted earnings per share in accordance with paragraphs 33 and 36.

50 Convertible preference shares are antidilutive whenever the amount of the dividend on such shares declared in or accumulated for the current period per ordinary share obtainable on conversion exceeds basic earnings per share. Similarly, convertible debt is antidilutive whenever its interest (net of tax and other changes in income or expense) per ordinary share obtainable on conversion exceeds basic earnings per share.

51 The redemption or induced conversion of convertible preference shares may affect only a portion of the previously outstanding convertible preference shares. In such cases, any excess consideration referred to in paragraph 17 is attributed to those shares that are redeemed or converted for the purpose of determining whether the remaining outstanding preference shares are dilutive. The shares redeemed or converted are considered separately from those shares that are not redeemed or converted.

Contingently issuable shares

52 As in the calculation of basic earnings per share, contingently issuable ordinary shares are treated as outstanding and included in the calculation of diluted earnings per share if the conditions are satisfied (ie the events have occurred). Contingently issuable shares are included from the beginning of the period (or from the date of the contingent share agreement, if later). If the conditions are not satisfied, the number of contingently issuable shares included in the diluted earnings per share calculation is based on the number of shares that would be issuable if the end of the period were the end of the contingency period. Restatement is not permitted if the conditions are not met when the contingency period expires.

53 If attainment or maintenance of a specified amount of earnings for a period is the condition for contingent issue and if that amount has been attained at the end of the reporting period but must be maintained beyond the end of the reporting period for an additional period, then the additional ordinary shares are treated as outstanding, if the effect is dilutive, when calculating diluted earnings per share. In that case, the calculation of diluted earnings per share is based on the number of ordinary shares that would be issued if the amount of earnings at the end of the reporting period were the amount of earnings at the end of the contingency period. Because earnings may change in a future period, the calculation of basic earnings per share does not include such contingently issuable ordinary shares until the end of the contingency period because not all necessary conditions have been satisfied.

54 The number of ordinary shares contingently issuable may depend on the future market price of the ordinary shares. In that case, if the effect is dilutive, the calculation of diluted earnings per share is based on the number of ordinary shares that would be issued if the market price at the end of the reporting period were the market price at the end of the contingency period. If the condition is based on an average of market prices over a period of time that extends beyond the end of the reporting period, the average for the period of time that has lapsed is used. Because the market price may change in a future period, the calculation of basic earnings per share does not include such contingently issuable ordinary shares until the end of the contingency period because not all necessary conditions have been satisfied.

55 The number of ordinary shares contingently issuable may depend on future earnings and future prices of the ordinary shares. In such cases, the number of ordinary shares included in the diluted earnings per share calculation is based on both conditions (ie earnings to date and the current market price at the end of the reporting period). Contingently issuable ordinary shares are not included in the diluted earnings per share calculation unless both conditions are met.

56 In other cases, the number of ordinary shares contingently issuable depends on a condition other than earnings or market price (for example, the opening of a specific number of retail stores). In such cases, assuming that the present status of the condition remains unchanged until the end of the contingency period, the contingently issuable ordinary shares are included in the calculation of diluted earnings per share according to the status at the end of the reporting period.

57 Contingently issuable potential ordinary shares (other than those covered by a contingent share agreement, such as contingently issuable convertible instruments) are included in the diluted earnings per share calculation as follows:

(a) an entity determines whether the potential ordinary shares may be assumed to be issuable on the basis of the conditions specified for their issue in accordance with the contingent ordinary share provisions in paragraphs 52–56; and

(b) if those potential ordinary shares should be reflected in diluted earnings per share, an entity determines their impact on the calculation of diluted earnings per share by following the provisions for options and warrants in paragraphs 45–48, the provisions for convertible instruments in paragraphs

49–51, the provisions for contracts that may be settled in ordinary shares or cash in paragraphs 58–61, or other provisions, as appropriate.

However, exercise or conversion is not assumed for the purpose of calculating diluted earnings per share unless exercise or conversion of similar outstanding potential ordinary shares that are not contingently issuable is assumed.

Contracts that may be settled in ordinary shares or cash

58 When an entity has issued a contract that may be settled in ordinary shares or cash at the entity's option, the entity shall presume that the contract will be settled in ordinary shares, and the resulting potential ordinary shares shall be included in diluted earnings per share if the effect is dilutive.

59 When such a contract is presented for accounting purposes as an asset or a liability, or has an equity component and a liability component, the entity shall adjust the numerator for any changes in profit or loss that would have resulted during the period if the contract had been classified wholly as an equity instrument. That adjustment is similar to the adjustments required in paragraph 33.

60 For contracts that may be settled in ordinary shares or cash at the holder's option, the more dilutive of cash settlement and share settlement shall be used in calculating diluted earnings per share.

61 An example of a contract that may be settled in ordinary shares or cash is a debt instrument that, on maturity, gives the entity the unrestricted right to settle the principal amount in cash or in its own ordinary shares. Another example is a written put option that gives the holder a choice of settling in ordinary shares or cash.

Purchased options

62 Contracts such as purchased put options and purchased call options (ie options held by the entity on its own ordinary shares) are not included in the calculation of diluted earnings per share because including them would be antidilutive. The put option would be exercised only if the exercise price were higher than the market price and the call option would be exercised only if the exercise price were lower than the market price.

Written put options

63 Contracts that require the entity to repurchase its own shares, such as written put options and forward purchase contracts, are reflected in the calculation of diluted earnings per share if the effect is dilutive. If these contracts are 'in the money' during the period (ie the exercise or settlement price is above the average market price for that period), the potential dilutive effect on earnings per share shall be calculated as follows:

(a) it shall be assumed that at the beginning of the period sufficient ordinary shares will be issued (at the average market price during the period) to raise proceeds to satisfy the contract;

(b) it shall be assumed that the proceeds from the issue are used to satisfy the contract (ie to buy back ordinary shares); and

(c) **the incremental ordinary shares (the difference between the number of ordinary shares assumed issued and the number of ordinary shares received from satisfying the contract) shall be included in the calculation of diluted earnings per share.**

Retrospective adjustments

64 **If the number of ordinary or potential ordinary shares outstanding increases as a result of a capitalisation, bonus issue or share split, or decreases as a result of a reverse share split, the calculation of basic and diluted earnings per share for all periods presented shall be adjusted retrospectively. If these changes occur after the balance sheet date but before the financial statements are authorised for issue, the per share calculations for those and any prior period financial statements presented shall be based on the new number of shares. The fact that per share calculations reflect such changes in the number of shares shall be disclosed. In addition, basic and diluted earnings per share of all periods presented shall be adjusted for the effects of errors and adjustments resulting from changes in accounting policies accounted for retrospectively.**

65 An entity does not restate diluted earnings per share of any prior period presented for changes in the assumptions used in earnings per share calculations or for the conversion of potential ordinary shares into ordinary shares.

Presentation

66 **An entity shall present on the face of the income statement basic and diluted earnings per share for profit or loss from continuing operations attributable to the ordinary equity holders of the parent entity and for profit or loss attributable to the ordinary equity holders of the parent entity for the period for each class of ordinary shares that has a different right to share in profit for the period. An entity shall present basic and diluted earnings per share with equal prominence for all periods presented.**

67 Earnings per share is presented for every period for which an income statement is presented. If diluted earnings per share is reported for at least one period, it shall be reported for all periods presented, even if it equals basic earnings per share. If basic and diluted earnings per share are equal, dual presentation can be accomplished in one line on the income statement.

68 **An entity that reports a discontinued operation shall disclose the basic and diluted amounts per share for the discontinued operation either on the face of the income statement or in the notes to the financial statements.**

69 **An entity shall present basic and diluted earnings per share, even if the amounts are negative (ie a loss per share).**

Disclosure

70 **An entity shall disclose the following:**

(a) the amounts used as the numerators in calculating basic and diluted earnings per share, and a reconciliation of those amounts to profit or loss attributable to the parent entity for the period. The reconciliation shall include the individual effect of each class of instruments that affects earnings per share.

(b) the weighted average number of ordinary shares used as the denominator in calculating basic and diluted earnings per share, and a reconciliation of these denominators to each other. The reconciliation shall include the individual effect of each class of instruments that affects earnings per share.

(c) instruments (including contingently issuable shares) that could potentially dilute basic earnings per share in the future, but were not included in the calculation of diluted earnings per share because they are antidilutive for the period(s) presented.

(d) a description of ordinary share transactions or potential ordinary share transactions, other than those accounted for in accordance with paragraph 64, that occur after the balance sheet date and that would have changed significantly the number of ordinary shares or potential ordinary shares outstanding at the end of the period if those transactions had occurred before the end of the reporting period.

71 Examples of transactions in paragraph 70(d) include:

(a) an issue of shares for cash;

(b) an issue of shares when the proceeds are used to repay debt or preference shares outstanding at the balance sheet date;

(c) the redemption of ordinary shares outstanding;

(d) the conversion or exercise of potential ordinary shares outstanding at the balance sheet date into ordinary shares;

(e) an issue of options, warrants, or convertible instruments; and

(f) the achievement of conditions that would result in the issue of contingently issuable shares.

Earnings per share amounts are not adjusted for such transactions occurring after the balance sheet date because such transactions do not affect the amount of capital used to produce profit or loss for the period.

72 Financial instruments and other contracts generating potential ordinary shares may incorporate terms and conditions that affect the measurement of basic and diluted earnings per share. These terms and conditions may determine whether any potential ordinary shares are dilutive and, if so, the effect on the weighted average number of shares outstanding and any consequent adjustments to profit or loss attributable to ordinary equity holders. The disclosure of the terms and conditions of such financial instruments and other contracts is encouraged, if not otherwise required (see IAS 32).

73 **If an entity discloses, in addition to basic and diluted earnings per share, amounts per share using a reported component of the income statement other than one required by this Standard, such amounts shall be calculated using the weighted average number of ordinary shares determined in accordance with this Standard. Basic and diluted amounts per share relating to such a component shall be disclosed with equal prominence and presented in the notes to the financial statements. An entity shall indicate the basis on which the numerator(s) is (are) determined, including whether amounts per share are before tax or after tax. If a component of the income statement is used that is not reported as a line item in the income statement, a reconciliation shall be provided between the component used and a line item that is reported in the income statement.**

Effective date

74 **An entity shall apply this Standard for annual periods beginning on or after 1 January 2005. Earlier application is encouraged. If an entity applies the Standard for a period beginning before 1 January 2005, it shall disclose that fact.**

Withdrawal of other pronouncements

75 This Standard supersedes IAS 33 *Earnings Per Share* (issued in 1997).

76 This Standard supersedes SIC-24 *Earnings Per Share—Financial Instruments and Other Contracts that May Be Settled in Shares.*

Appendix A
Application guidance

This appendix is an integral part of the Standard.

Profit or loss attributable to the parent entity

A1 For the purpose of calculating earnings per share based on the consolidated financial statements, profit or loss attributable to the parent entity refers to profit or loss of the consolidated entity after adjusting for minority interests.

Rights issues

A2 The issue of ordinary shares at the time of exercise or conversion of potential ordinary shares does not usually give rise to a bonus element. This is because the potential ordinary shares are usually issued for full value, resulting in a proportionate change in the resources available to the entity. In a rights issue, however, the exercise price is often less than the fair value of the shares. Therefore, as noted in paragraph 27(b), such a rights issue includes a bonus element. If a rights issue is offered to all existing shareholders, the number of ordinary shares to be used in calculating basic and diluted earnings per share for all periods before the rights issue is the number of ordinary shares outstanding before the issue, multiplied by the following factor:

$$\frac{\text{Fair value per share immediately before the exercise of rights}}{\text{Theoretical ex-rights fair value per share}}$$

The theoretical ex-rights fair value per share is calculated by adding the aggregate market value of the shares immediately before the exercise of the rights to the proceeds from the exercise of the rights, and dividing by the number of shares outstanding after the exercise of the rights. Where the rights are to be publicly traded separately from the shares before the exercise date, fair value for the purposes of this calculation is established at the close of the last day on which the shares are traded together with the rights.

Control number

A3 To illustrate the application of the control number notion described in paragraphs 42 and 43, assume that an entity has profit from continuing operations attributable to the parent entity of CU4,800,* a loss from discontinued operations attributable to the parent entity of (CU7,200), a loss attributable to the parent entity of (CU2,400), and 2,000 ordinary shares and 400 potential ordinary shares outstanding. The entity's basic earnings per share is CU2.40 for continuing operations, (CU3.60) for discontinued operations and (CU1.20) for the loss. The 400 potential ordinary shares are included in the diluted earnings per share calculation because the resulting CU2.00 earnings per share for continuing operations is dilutive, assuming no profit or loss impact of those 400 potential ordinary shares. Because profit from continuing operations attributable to the parent entity is the control number, the entity also includes those 400 potential

* In this guidance, monetary amounts are denominated in 'currency units' (CU).

ordinary shares in the calculation of the other earnings per share amounts, even though the resulting earnings per share amounts are antidilutive to their comparable basic earnings per share amounts, ie the loss per share is less [(CU3.00) per share for the loss from discontinued operations and (CU1.00) per share for the loss].

Average market price of ordinary shares

A4 For the purpose of calculating diluted earnings per share, the average market price of ordinary shares assumed to be issued is calculated on the basis of the average market price of the ordinary shares during the period. Theoretically, every market transaction for an entity's ordinary shares could be included in the determination of the average market price. As a practical matter, however, a simple average of weekly or monthly prices is usually adequate.

A5 Generally, closing market prices are adequate for calculating the average market price. When prices fluctuate widely, however, an average of the high and low prices usually produces a more representative price. The method used to calculate the average market price is used consistently unless it is no longer representative because of changed conditions. For example, an entity that uses closing market prices to calculate the average market price for several years of relatively stable prices might change to an average of high and low prices if prices start fluctuating greatly and the closing market prices no longer produce a representative average price.

Options, warrants and their equivalents

A6 Options or warrants to purchase convertible instruments are assumed to be exercised to purchase the convertible instrument whenever the average prices of both the convertible instrument and the ordinary shares obtainable upon conversion are above the exercise price of the options or warrants. However, exercise is not assumed unless conversion of similar outstanding convertible instruments, if any, is also assumed.

A7 Options or warrants may permit or require the tendering of debt or other instruments of the entity (or its parent or a subsidiary) in payment of all or a portion of the exercise price. In the calculation of diluted earnings per share, those options or warrants have a dilutive effect if (a) the average market price of the related ordinary shares for the period exceeds the exercise price or (b) the selling price of the instrument to be tendered is below that at which the instrument may be tendered under the option or warrant agreement and the resulting discount establishes an effective exercise price below the market price of the ordinary shares obtainable upon exercise. In the calculation of diluted earnings per share, those options or warrants are assumed to be exercised and the debt or other instruments are assumed to be tendered. If tendering cash is more advantageous to the option or warrant holder and the contract permits tendering cash, tendering of cash is assumed. Interest (net of tax) on any debt assumed to be tendered is added back as an adjustment to the numerator.

A8 Similar treatment is given to preference shares that have similar provisions or to other instruments that have conversion options that permit the investor to pay cash for a more favourable conversion rate.

A9 The underlying terms of certain options or warrants may require the proceeds received from the exercise of those instruments to be applied to redeem debt or other instruments of the entity (or its parent or a subsidiary). In the calculation of diluted earnings per share, those options or warrants are assumed to be exercised and the proceeds applied to purchase the debt at its average market price rather than to purchase ordinary shares. However, the excess proceeds received from the assumed exercise over the amount used for the assumed purchase of debt are considered (ie assumed to be used to buy back ordinary shares) in the diluted earnings per share calculation. Interest (net of tax) on any debt assumed to be purchased is added back as an adjustment to the numerator.

Written put options

A10 To illustrate the application of paragraph 63, assume that an entity has outstanding 120 written put options on its ordinary shares with an exercise price of CU35. The average market price of its ordinary shares for the period is CU28. In calculating diluted earnings per share, the entity assumes that it issued 150 shares at CU28 per share at the beginning of the period to satisfy its put obligation of CU4,200. The difference between the 150 ordinary shares issued and the 120 ordinary shares received from satisfying the put option (30 incremental ordinary shares) is added to the denominator in calculating diluted earnings per share.

Instruments of subsidiaries, joint ventures or associates

A11 Potential ordinary shares of a subsidiary, joint venture or associate convertible into either ordinary shares of the subsidiary, joint venture or associate, or ordinary shares of the parent, venturer or investor (the reporting entity) are included in the calculation of diluted earnings per share as follows:

(a) instruments issued by a subsidiary, joint venture or associate that enable their holders to obtain ordinary shares of the subsidiary, joint venture or associate are included in calculating the diluted earnings per share data of the subsidiary, joint venture or associate. Those earnings per share are then included in the reporting entity's earnings per share calculations based on the reporting entity's holding of the instruments of the subsidiary, joint venture or associate.

(b) instruments of a subsidiary, joint venture or associate that are convertible into the reporting entity's ordinary shares are considered among the potential ordinary shares of the reporting entity for the purpose of calculating diluted earnings per share. Likewise, options or warrants issued by a subsidiary, joint venture or associate to purchase ordinary shares of the reporting entity are considered among the potential ordinary shares of the reporting entity in the calculation of consolidated diluted earnings per share.

A12 For the purpose of determining the earnings per share effect of instruments issued by a reporting entity that are convertible into ordinary shares of a subsidiary, joint venture or associate, the instruments are assumed to be converted and the numerator (profit or loss attributable to ordinary equity holders of the parent entity) adjusted as necessary in accordance with paragraph 33. In addition to those adjustments, the numerator is adjusted for any change in the profit or loss recorded by the reporting entity (such as dividend income or equity method income) that is attributable to the increase in the number of ordinary shares of the subsidiary, joint venture or associate outstanding as a result of the assumed conversion. The denominator of the diluted earnings per share calculation is not affected because the number of ordinary shares of the reporting entity outstanding would not change upon assumed conversion.

Participating equity instruments and two–class ordinary shares

A13 The equity of some entities includes:

(a) instruments that participate in dividends with ordinary shares according to a predetermined formula (for example, two for one) with, at times, an upper limit on the extent of participation (for example, up to, but not beyond, a specified amount per share).

(b) a class of ordinary shares with a different dividend rate from that of another class of ordinary shares but without prior or senior rights.

A14 For the purpose of calculating diluted earnings per share, conversion is assumed for those instruments described in paragraph A13 that are convertible into ordinary shares if the effect is dilutive. For those instruments that are not convertible into a class of ordinary shares, profit or loss for the period is allocated to the different classes of shares and participating equity instruments in accordance with their dividend rights or other rights to participate in undistributed earnings. To calculate basic and diluted earnings per share:

(a) profit or loss attributable to ordinary equity holders of the parent entity is adjusted (a profit reduced and a loss increased) by the amount of dividends declared in the period for each class of shares and by the contractual amount of dividends (or interest on participating bonds) that must be paid for the period (for example, unpaid cumulative dividends).

(b) the remaining profit or loss is allocated to ordinary shares and participating equity instruments to the extent that each instrument shares in earnings as if all of the profit or loss for the period had been distributed. The total profit or loss allocated to each class of equity instrument is determined by adding together the amount allocated for dividends and the amount allocated for a participation feature.

(c) the total amount of profit or loss allocated to each class of equity instrument is divided by the number of outstanding instruments to which the earnings are allocated to determine the earnings per share for the instrument.

For the calculation of diluted earnings per share, all potential ordinary shares assumed to have been issued are included in outstanding ordinary shares.

Partly paid shares

A15 Where ordinary shares are issued but not fully paid, they are treated in the calculation of basic earnings per share as a fraction of an ordinary share to the extent that they were entitled to participate in dividends during the period relative to a fully paid ordinary share.

A16 To the extent that partly paid shares are not entitled to participate in dividends during the period they are treated as the equivalent of warrants or options in the calculation of diluted earnings per share. The unpaid balance is assumed to represent proceeds used to purchase ordinary shares. The number of shares included in diluted earnings per share is the difference between the number of shares subscribed and the number of shares assumed to be purchased.

Appendix B
Amendments to other pronouncements

The amendments in this appendix shall be applied for annual periods beginning on or after 1 January 2005. If an entity applies this Standard for an earlier period, these amendments shall be applied for that earlier period.

* * * * *

The amendments contained in this appendix when this Standard was revised in 2003 have been incorporated into the relevant pronouncements published in this volume.

Approval of IAS 33 by the Board

International Accounting Standard 33 *Earnings per Share* was approved for issue by the fourteen members of the International Accounting Standards Board.

Sir David Tweedie	Chairman
Thomas E Jones	Vice-Chairman
Mary E Barth	
Hans-Georg Bruns	
Anthony T Cope	
Robert P Garnett	
Gilbert Gélard	
James J Leisenring	
Warren J McGregor	
Patricia L O'Malley	
Harry K Schmid	
John T Smith	
Geoffrey Whittington	
Tatsumi Yamada	

Basis for Conclusions

This Basis for Conclusions accompanies, but is not part of, IAS 33.

Introduction

BC1 This Basis for Conclusions summarises the International Accounting Standards Board's considerations in reaching its conclusions on revising IAS 33 *Earnings Per Share* in 2003. Individual Board members gave greater weight to some factors than to others.

BC2 In July 2001 the Board announced that, as part of its initial agenda of technical projects, it would undertake a project to improve a number of Standards, including IAS 33. The project was undertaken in the light of queries and criticisms raised in relation to the Standards by securities regulators, professional accountants and other interested parties. The objectives of the Improvements project were to reduce or eliminate alternatives, redundancies and conflicts within Standards, to deal with some convergence issues and to make other improvements. In May 2002 the Board published its proposals in an Exposure Draft of *Improvements to International Accounting Standards*, with a comment deadline of 16 September 2002. The Board received over 160 comment letters on the Exposure Draft.

BC3 Because the Board's intention was not to reconsider the fundamental approach to the determination and presentation of earnings per share established by IAS 33, this Basis for Conclusions does not discuss requirements in IAS 33 that the Board has not reconsidered.

Presentation of parent's separate earnings per share

BC4 The Exposure Draft published in May 2002 proposed deleting paragraphs 2 and 3 of the previous version of IAS 33, which stated that when the parent's separate financial statements and consolidated financial statements are presented, earnings per share need be presented only on the basis of consolidated information.

BC5 Some respondents expressed concern that the presentation of two earnings per share figures (one for the parent's separate financial statements and one for the consolidated financial statements) might be misleading.

BC6 The Board noted that disclosing the parent's separate earnings per share amount is useful in limited situations, and therefore decided to retain the option. However, the Board decided that the Standard should prohibit presentation of the parent's separate earnings per share amounts in the consolidated financial statements (either on the face of the financial statements or in the notes).

Contracts that may be settled in ordinary shares or cash

BC7 The Exposure Draft proposed that an entity should include in the calculation of the number of potential ordinary shares in the diluted earnings per share calculation contracts that may be settled in ordinary shares or cash, at the issuer's option, based on a rebuttable presumption that the contracts will be settled in shares. This proposed presumption could be rebutted if the issuer had acted through an established pattern of past practice, published policies, or by having made a sufficiently specific current statement indicating to other parties the manner in which it expected to settle, and, as a result, the issuer had created a valid expectation on the part of those other parties that it would settle in a manner other than by issuing shares.

BC8 The majority of the respondents on the Exposure Draft agreed with the proposed treatment of contracts that may be settled in ordinary shares or cash at the issuer's option. However, the Board decided to withdraw the notion of a rebuttable presumption and to incorporate into the Standard the requirements of SIC-24 *Earnings Per Share—Financial Instruments and Other Contracts that May Be Settled in Shares*. SIC-24 requires financial instruments or other contracts that may result in the issue of ordinary shares of the entity to be considered potential ordinary shares of the entity.

BC9 Although the proposed treatment would have converged with that required by several liaison standard-setters, for example, in US SFAS 128 *Earnings per Share*, the Board concluded that the notion of a rebuttable presumption is inconsistent with the stated objective of diluted earnings per share. The US Financial Accounting Standards Board has agreed to consider this difference as part of the joint short-term convergence project with the IASB.

Calculation of year-to-date diluted earnings per share

BC10 The Exposure Draft proposed the following approach to the year-to-date calculation of diluted earnings per share:

(a) The number of potential ordinary shares is a year-to-date weighted average of the number of potential ordinary shares included in each interim diluted earnings per share calculation, rather than a year-to-date weighted average of the number of potential ordinary shares weighted for the period they were outstanding (ie without regard for the diluted earnings per share information reported during the interim periods).

(b) The number of potential ordinary shares is computed using the average market price during the interim periods, rather than using the average market price during the year-to-date period.

(c) Contingently issuable shares are weighted for the interim periods in which they were included in the computation of diluted earnings per share, rather than being included in the computation of diluted earnings per share (if the conditions are satisfied) from the beginning of the year-to-date reporting period (or from the date of the contingent share agreement, if later).

BC11 The majority of the respondents on the Exposure Draft disagreed with the proposed approach to the year-to-date calculation of diluted earnings per share. The most significant argument against the proposed approach was that the proposed calculation of diluted earnings per share could result in an amount for year-to-date diluted earnings per share that was different for entities that report more frequently, for example, on a quarterly or half-yearly basis, and for entities that report only annually. It was also noted that this problem would be exacerbated for entities with seasonal businesses.

BC12 The Board considered whether to accept that differences in the frequency of interim reporting would result in different earnings per share amounts being reported. However, IAS 34 *Interim Financial Reporting* states 'the frequency of an entity's reporting (annual, half-yearly, or quarterly) should not affect the measurement of its annual results. To achieve that objective, measurements for interim reporting purposes should be made on a year-to-date basis.'

BC13 The Board also considered whether it could mandate the frequency of interim reporting to ensure consistency between all entities preparing financial statements in accordance with IFRSs, ie those that are brought within the scope of IAS 33 by virtue of issuing publicly traded instruments or because they elect to present earnings per share. However, IAS 34 states that, 'This Standard does not mandate which entities should be required to publish interim financial reports, how frequently, or how soon after the end of an interim period.' The frequency of interim reporting is mandated by securities regulators, stock exchanges, governments, and accountancy bodies, and varies by jurisdiction.

BC14 Although the proposed approach for the calculation of year-to-date diluted earnings per share would have converged with US SFAS 128, the Board concluded that the approach was inconsistent with IAS 34 and that it could not mandate the frequency of interim reporting. The US Financial Accounting Standards Board has agreed to consider this difference as part of the joint short-term convergence project with the IASB as well as the issue noted in paragraph BC9.

Other changes

BC15 Implementation questions have arisen since the previous version of IAS 33 was issued, typically concerning the application of the Standard to complex capital structures and arrangements. In response, the Board decided to provide additional application guidance in the Appendix as well as illustrative examples on more complex matters that were not addressed in the previous version of IAS 33. These matters include the effects of contingently issuable shares, potential ordinary shares of subsidiaries, joint ventures or associates, participating equity instruments, written put options, and purchased put and call options.

CONTENTS

ILLUSTRATIVE EXAMPLES

Illustrative Examples

These examples accompany, but are not part of, IAS 33.

Example 1 Increasing rate preference shares

Reference: IAS 33, paragraphs 12 and 15

Entity D issued non-convertible, non-redeemable class A cumulative preference shares of CU100 par value on 1 January 20X1. The class A preference shares are entitled to a cumulative annual dividend of CU7 per share starting in 20X4.

At the time of issue, the market rate dividend yield on the class A preference shares was 7 per cent a year. Thus, Entity D could have expected to receive proceeds of approximately CU100 per class A preference share if the dividend rate of CU7 per share had been in effect at the date of issue.

In consideration of the dividend payment terms, however, the class A preference shares were issued at CU81.63 per share, ie at a discount of CU18.37 per share. The issue price can be calculated by taking the present value of CU100, discounted at 7 per cent over a three-year period.

Because the shares are classified as equity, the original issue discount is amortised to retained earnings using the effective interest method and treated as a preference dividend for earnings per share purposes. To calculate basic earnings per share, the following imputed dividend per class A preference share is deducted to determine the profit or loss attributable to ordinary equity holders of the parent entity:

Year	*Carrying amount of class A preference shares 1 January*	*Imputed dividend* [(a)]	*Carrying amount of class A preference shares 31 December* [(b)]	*Dividend paid*
	CU	CU	CU	CU
20X1	81.63	5.71	87.34	–
20X2	87.34	6.12	93.46	–
20X3	93.46	6.54	100.00	–
Thereafter:	100.00	7.00	107.00	(7.00)

(a) at 7%

(b) This is before dividend payment.

Example 2 Weighted average number of ordinary shares

Reference: IAS 33, paragraphs 19–21

		Shares issued	*Treasury shares*[a]	*Shares outstanding*
1 January 20X1	Balance at beginning of year	2,000	300	1,700
31 May 20X1	Issue of new shares for cash	800	–	2,500
1 December 20X1	Purchase of treasury shares for cash	–	250	2,250
31 December 20X1	Balance at year–end	2,800	550	2,250

Calculation of weighted average:

(1,700 x $^5/_{12}$) + (2,500 x $^6/_{12}$) + (2,250 x $^1/_{12}$) = 2,146 shares *or*

(1,700 x $^{12}/_{12}$) + (800 x $^7/_{12}$) – (250 x $^1/_{12}$) = 2,146 shares

(a) Treasury shares are equity instruments reacquired and held by the issuing entity itself or by its subsidiaries.

Example 3 Bonus issue

Reference: IAS 33, paragraphs 26, 27(a) and 28

Profit attributable to ordinary equity holders of the parent entity 20X0	CU180
Profit attributable to ordinary equity holders of the parent entity 20X1	CU600
Ordinary shares outstanding until 30 September 20X1	200
Bonus issue 1 October 20X1	2 ordinary shares for each ordinary share outstanding at 30 September 20X1 200 × 2 = 400
Basic earnings per share 20X1	$\frac{\text{CU600}}{(200 + 400)}$ = CU1.00
Basic earnings per share 20X0	$\frac{\text{CU180}}{(200 + 400)}$ = CU0.30

Because the bonus issue was without consideration, it is treated as if it had occurred before the beginning of 20X0, the earliest period presented.

Example 4 Rights issue

Reference: IAS 33, paragraphs 26, 27(b) and A2

	20X0	20X1	20X2
Profit attributable to ordinary equity holders of the parent entity	CU1,100	CU1,500	CU1,800

Shares outstanding before rights issue	500 shares
Rights issue	One new share for each five outstanding shares (100 new shares total) Exercise price: CU5.00 Date of rights issue: 1 January 20X1 Last date to exercise rights: 1 March 20X1
Market price of one ordinary share immediately before exercise on 1 March 20X1:	CU11.00
Reporting date	31 December

Calculation of theoretical ex–rights value per share

$$\frac{\text{Fair value of all outstanding shares before the exercise of rights + total amount received from exercise of rights}}{\text{Number of shares outstanding before exercise + number of shares issued in the exercise}}$$

$$\frac{(\text{CU}11.00 \times 500 \text{ shares}) + (\text{CU}5.00 \times 100 \text{ shares})}{500 \text{ shares} + 100 \text{ shares}}$$

Theoretical ex–rights value per share = CU10.00

Calculation of adjustment factor

$$\frac{\text{Fair value per share before exercise of rights}}{\text{Theoretical ex–rights value per share}} \qquad \frac{\text{CU}11.00}{\text{CU}10.00} = 1.10$$

Calculation of basic earnings per share

		20X0	20X1	20X2
20X0 basic EPS as originally reported:	CU1,100 ÷ 500 shares	CU2.20		
20X0 basic EPS restated for rights issue:	$\frac{\text{CU}1,100}{(500 \text{ shares} \times 1.1)}$	CU2.00		
20X1 basic EPS including effects of rights issue:	$\frac{\text{CU}1,500}{(500 \times 1.1 \times \frac{2}{12}) + (600 \times \frac{10}{12})}$		CU2.54	
20X2 basic EPS:	CU1,800 ÷ 600 shares			CU3.00

Example 5 Effects of share options on diluted earnings per share

Reference: IAS 33, paragraphs 45–47

Profit attributable to ordinary equity holders of the parent entity for year 20X1	CU1,200,000
Weighted average number of ordinary shares outstanding during year 20X1	500,000 shares
Average market price of one ordinary share during year 20X1	CU20.00
Weighted average number of shares under option during year 20X1	100,000 shares
Exercise price for shares under option during year 20X1	CU15.00

Calculation of earnings per share

	Earnings	*Shares*	*Per share*
Profit attributable to ordinary equity holders of the parent entity for year 20X1	CU1,200,000		
Weighted average shares outstanding during year 20X1		500,000	
Basic earnings per share			CU2.40
Weighted average number of shares under option		100,000	
Weighted average number of shares that would have been issued at average market price: (100,000 × CU15.00) ÷ CU20.00	(a)	(75,000)	
Diluted earnings per share	CU1,200,000	525,000	CU2.29

(a) Earnings have not increased because the total number of shares has increased only by the number of shares (25,000) deemed to have been issued for no consideration (see paragraph 46(b) of the Standard).

Example 5A Determining the exercise price of employee share options

Weighted average number of unvested share options per employee	1,000
Weighted average amount per employee to be recognised over the remainder of the vesting period for employee services to be rendered as consideration for the share options, determined in accordance with IFRS 2 *Share–based Payment*	CU1,200
Cash exercise price of unvested share options	CU15
Calculation of adjusted exercise price	
Fair value of services yet to be rendered per employee:	CU1,200
Fair value of services yet to be rendered per option: (CU1,200 ÷ 1,000)	CU1.20
Total exercise price of share options: (CU15.00 + CU1.20)	CU16.20

Example 6 Convertible bonds*

Reference: IAS 33, paragraphs 33, 34, 36 and 49

Profit attributable to ordinary equity holders of the parent entity	CU1,004
Ordinary shares outstanding	1,000
Basic earnings per share	CU1.00
Convertible bonds	100
Each block of 10 bonds is convertible into three ordinary shares	
Interest expense for the current year relating to the liability component of the convertible bonds	CU10
Current and deferred tax relating to that interest expense	CU4
Note: the interest expense includes amortisation of the discount arising on initial recognition of the liability component (see IAS 32 Financial Instruments: Disclosure and Presentation*).*	
Adjusted profit attributable to ordinary equity holders of the parent entity	CU1,004 + CU10 – CU4 = CU1,010
Number of ordinary shares resulting from conversion of bonds	30
Number of ordinary shares used to calculate diluted earnings per share	1,000 + 30 = 1,030
Diluted earnings per share	$\frac{\text{CU1,010}}{\text{1,030}}$ = CU0.98

* This example does not illustrate the classification of the components of convertible financial instruments as liabilities and equity or the classification of related interest and dividends as expenses and equity as required by IAS 32.

Example 7 Contingently issuable shares

Reference: IAS 33, paragraphs 19, 24, 36, 37, 41–43 and 52

Ordinary shares outstanding during 20X1	1,000,000 (there were no options, warrants or convertible instruments outstanding during the period)

An agreement related to a recent business combination provides for the issue of additional ordinary shares based on the following conditions:

	5,000 additional ordinary shares for each new retail site opened during 20X1
	1,000 additional ordinary shares for each CU1,000 of consolidated profit in excess of CU2,000,000 for the year ended 31 December 20X1
Retail sites opened during the year:	one on 1 May 20X1
	one on 1 September 20X1
Consolidated year–to–date profit attributable to ordinary equity holders of the parent entity:	CU1,100,000 as of 31 March 20X1
	CU2,300,000 as of 30 June 20X1
	CU1,900,000 as of 30 September 20X1 (including a CU450,000 loss from a discontinued operation)
	CU2,900,000 as of 31 December 20X1

Basic earnings per share

	First quarter	Second quarter	Third quarter	Fourth quarter	Full year
Numerator (CU)	1,100,000	1,200,000	(400,000)	1,000,000	2,900,000
Denominator:					
Ordinary shares outstanding	1,000,000	1,000,000	1,000,000	1,000,000	1,000,000
Retail site contingency	–	3,333 [(a)]	6,667 [(b)]	10,000	5,000 [(c)]
Earnings contingency[(d)]	–	–	–	–	–
Total shares	1,000,000	1,003,333	1,006,667	1,010,000	1,005,000
Basic earnings per share (CU)	1.10	1.20	(0.40)	0.99	2.89

(a) 5,000 shares × ⅔

(b) 5,000 shares + (5,000 shares × ⅓)

(c) (5,000 shares × 8⁄12) + (5,000 shares × 4⁄12)

(d) The earnings contingency has no effect on basic earnings per share because it is not certain that the condition is satisfied until the end of the contingency period. The effect is negligible for the fourth-quarter and full-year calculations because it is not certain that the condition is met until the last day of the period.

Diluted earnings per share

	First quarter	*Second quarter*	*Third quarter*	*Fourth quarter*	*Full year*
Numerator (CU)	1,100,000	1,200,000	(400,000)	1,000,000	2,900,000
Denominator:					
Ordinary shares outstanding	1,000,000	1,000,000	1,000,000	1,000,000	1,000,000
Retail site contingency	–	5,000	10,000	10,000	10,000
Earnings contingency	– (a)	300,000 (b)	– (c)	900,000 (d)	900,000 (d)
Total shares	1,000,000	1,305,000	1,010,000	1,910,000	1,910,000
Basic earnings per share (CU)	1.10	0.92	(0.40) (e)	0.52	1.52

(a) Company A does not have year-to-date profit exceeding CU2,000,000 at 31 March 20X1. The Standard does not permit projecting future earnings levels and including the related contingent shares.

(b) [(CU2,300,000 – CU2,000,000) ÷ 1,000] × 1,000 shares = 300,000 shares.

(c) Year-to-date profit is less than CU2,000,000.

(d) [(CU2,900,000 – CU2,000,000) ÷ 1,000] × 1,000 shares = 900,000 shares.

(e) Because the loss during the third quarter is attributable to a loss from a discontinued operation, the antidilution rules do not apply. The control number (ie profit or loss from continuing operations attributable to the equity holders of the parent entity) is positive. Accordingly, the effect of potential ordinary shares is included in the calculation of diluted earnings per share.

Example 8 Convertible bonds settled in shares or cash at the issuer's option

Reference: IAS 33, paragraphs 31–33, 36, 58 and 59

An entity issues 2,000 convertible bonds at the beginning of Year 1. The bonds have a three-year term, and are issued at par with a face value of CU1,000 per bond, giving total proceeds of CU2,000,000. Interest is payable annually in arrears at a nominal annual interest rate of 6 per cent. Each bond is convertible at any time up to maturity into 250 common shares. The entity has an option to settle the principal amount of the convertible bonds in ordinary shares or in cash.

When the bonds are issued, the prevailing market interest rate for similar debt without a conversion option is 9 per cent. At the issue date, the market price of one common share is CU3. Income tax is ignored.

Profit attributable to ordinary equity holders of the parent entity Year 1	CU1,000,000
Ordinary shares outstanding	1,200,000
Convertible bonds outstanding	2,000
Allocation of proceeds of the bond issue:	
Liability component	CU1,848,122*
Equity component	CU151,878
	CU2,000,000

The liability and equity components would be determined in accordance with IAS 32 *Financial Instruments: Disclosure and Presentation*. These amounts are recognised as the initial carrying amounts of the liability and equity components. The amount assigned to the issuer conversion option equity element is an addition to equity and is not adjusted.

Basic earnings per share Year 1:

$$\frac{CU1{,}000{,}000}{1{,}200{,}000} = CU0.83 \text{ per ordinary share}$$

Diluted earnings per share Year 1:

It is presumed that the issuer will settle the contract by the issue of ordinary shares. The dilutive effect is therefore calculated in accordance with paragraph 59 of the Standard.

$$\frac{CU1{,}000{,}000 + CU166{,}331^{(a)}}{1{,}200{,}000 + 500{,}000^{(b)}} = CU0.69 \text{ per ordinary share}$$

(a) Profit is adjusted for the accretion of CU166,331 (CU1,848,122 × 9%) of the liability because of the passage of time.

(b) 500,000 ordinary shares = 250 ordinary shares × 2,000 convertible bonds

* This represents the present value of the principal and interest discounted at 9% – CU2,000,000 payable at the end of three years; CU120,000 payable annually in arrears for three years.

Example 9 Calculation of weighted average number of shares: determining the order in which to include dilutive instruments*

Primary reference: IAS 33, paragraph 44

Secondary reference: IAS 33, paragraphs 10, 12, 19, 31–33, 36, 41–47, 49 and 50

Earnings	CU
Profit from continuing operations attributable to the parent entity	16,400,000
Less dividends on preference shares	(6,400,000)
Profit from continuing operations attributable to ordinary equity holders of the parent entity	10,000,000
Loss from discontinued operations attributable to the parent entity	(4,000,000)
Profit attributable to ordinary equity holders of the parent entity	6,000,000
Ordinary shares outstanding	2,000,000
Average market price of one ordinary share during year	CU75.00

Potential ordinary shares

Options	100,000 with exercise price of CU60
Convertible preference shares	800,000 shares with a par value of CU100 entitled to a cumulative dividend of CU8 per share. Each preference share is convertible to two ordinary shares.
5% convertible bonds	Nominal amount CU100,000,000. Each CU1,000 bond is convertible to 20 ordinary shares. There is no amortisation of premium or discount affecting the determination of interest expense.
Tax rate	40%

* This example does not illustrate the classification of the components of convertible financial instruments as liabilities and equity or the classification of related interest and dividends as expenses and equity as required by IAS 32.

Increase in earnings attributable to ordinary equity holders on conversion of potential ordinary shares

		Increase in earnings	*Increase in number of ordinary shares*	*Earnings per incremental share*
		CU		CU
Options				
Increase in earnings		Nil		
Incremental shares issued for no consideration	100,000 × (CU75 – CU60) ÷ CU75		20,000	Nil
Convertible preference shares				
Increase in profit	CU800,000 × 100 × 0.08	6,400,000		
Incremental shares	2 × 800,000		1,600,000	4.00
5% convertible bonds				
Increase in profit	CU100,000,000 × 0.05 × (1 – 0.40)	3,000,000		
Incremental shares	100,000 × 20		2,000,000	1.50

The order in which to include the dilutive instruments is therefore:

(a) Options

(b) 5% convertible bonds

(c) Convertible preference shares

Calculation of diluted earnings per share

	Profit from continuing operations attributable to ordinary equity holders of the parent entity (control number)	*Ordinary shares*	*Per share*	
	CU		CU	
As reported	10,000,000	2,000,000	5.00	
Options	–	20,000		
	10,000,000	2,020,000	4.95	Dilutive
5% convertible bonds	3,000,000	2,000,000		
	13,000,000	4,020,000	3.23	Dilutive
Convertible preference shares	6,400,000	1,600,000		
	19,400,000	5,620,000	3.45	Antidilutive

Because diluted earnings per share is increased when taking the convertible preference shares into account (from CU3.23 to CU3.45), the convertible preference shares are antidilutive and are ignored in the calculation of diluted earnings per share. Therefore, diluted earnings per share for profit from continuing operations is CU3.23:

	Basic EPS	*Diluted EPS*
	CU	CU
Profit from continuing operations attributable to ordinary equity holders of the parent entity	5.00	3.23
Loss from discontinued operations attributable to ordinary equity holders of the parent entity	(2.00)[(a)]	(0.99)[(b)]
Profit attributable to ordinary equity holders of the parent entity	3.00 [(c)]	2.24 [(d)]

(a) (CU4,000,000) ÷ 2,000,000 = (CU2.00)

(b) (CU4,000,000) ÷ 4,020,000 = (CU0.99)

(c) CU6,000,000 ÷ 2,000,000 = CU3.00

(d) (CU6,000,000 + CU3,000,000) ÷ 4,020,000 = CU2.24

Example 10 Instruments of a subsidiary: calculation of basic and diluted earnings per share*

Reference: IAS 33, paragraphs 40, A11 and A12

Parent:

Profit attributable to ordinary equity holders of the parent entity	CU12,000 (excluding any earnings of, or dividends paid by, the subsidiary)
Ordinary shares outstanding	10,000
Instruments of subsidiary owned by the parent	800 ordinary shares 30 warrants exercisable to purchase ordinary shares of subsidiary 300 convertible preference shares

Subsidiary:

Profit	CU5,400
Ordinary shares outstanding	1,000
Warrants	150, exercisable to purchase ordinary shares of the subsidiary
Exercise price	CU10
Average market price of one ordinary share	CU20
Convertible preference shares	400, each convertible into one ordinary share
Dividends on preference shares	CU1 per share

No inter–company eliminations or adjustments were necessary except for dividends.

For the purposes of this illustration, income taxes have been ignored.

* This example does not illustrate the classification of the components of convertible financial instruments as liabilities and equity or the classification of related interest and dividends as expenses and equity as required by IAS 32.

Subsidiary's earnings per share

Basic EPS CU5.00 calculated: $\dfrac{\text{CU5,400}^{(a)} - \text{CU400}^{(b)}}{\text{1,000}^{(c)}}$

Diluted EPS CU3.66 calculated: $\dfrac{\text{CU5,400}^{(d)}}{(\text{1,000} + 75^{(e)} + 400^{(f)})}$

(a) Subsidiary's profit attributable to ordinary equity holders.

(b) Dividends paid by subsidiary on convertible preference shares.

(c) Subsidiary's ordinary shares outstanding.

(d) Subsidiary's profit attributable to ordinary equity holders (CU5,000) increased by CU400 preference dividends for the purpose of calculating diluted earnings per share.

(e) Incremental shares from warrants, calculated: [(CU20 – CU10) ÷ CU20] × 150.

(f) Subsidiary's ordinary shares assumed outstanding from conversion of convertible preference shares, calculated: 400 convertible preference shares × conversion factor of 1.

Consolidated earnings per share

Basic EPS CU1.63 calculated: $\dfrac{\text{CU12,000}^{(a)} + \text{CU4,300}^{(b)}}{\text{10,000}^{(c)}}$

Diluted EPS CU1.61 calculated: $\dfrac{\text{CU12,000} + \text{CU2,928}^{(d)} + \text{CU55}^{(e)} + \text{CU1,098}^{(f)}}{\text{10,000}}$

(a) Parent's profit attributable to ordinary equity holders of the parent entity.

(b) Portion of subsidiary's profit to be included in consolidated basic earnings per share, calculated: (800 × CU5.00) + (300 × CU1.00).

(c) Parent's ordinary shares outstanding.

(d) Parent's proportionate interest in subsidiary's earnings attributable to ordinary shares, calculated: (800 ÷ 1,000) × (1,000 shares × CU3.66 per share).

(e) Parent's proportionate interest in subsidiary's earnings attributable to warrants, calculated: (30 ÷ 150) × (75 incremental shares × CU3.66 per share).

(f) Parent's proportionate interest in subsidiary's earnings attributable to convertible preference shares, calculated: (300 ÷ 400) × (400 shares from conversion × CU3.66 per share).

Example 11 Participating equity instruments and two-class ordinary shares*

Reference: IAS 33, paragraphs A13 and A14

Profit attributable to equity holders of the parent entity	CU100,000
Ordinary shares outstanding	10,000
Non–convertible preference shares	6,000
Non–cumulative annual dividend on preference shares (before any dividend is paid on ordinary shares)	CU5.50 per share

After ordinary shares have been paid a dividend of CU2.10 per share, the preference shares participate in any additional dividends on a 20:80 ratio with ordinary shares (ie after preference and ordinary shares have been paid dividends of CU5.50 and CU2.10 per share, respectively, preference shares participate in any additional dividends at a rate of one–fourth of the amount paid to ordinary shares on a per–share basis).

Dividends on preference shares paid	CU33,000	(CU5.50 per share)
Dividends on ordinary shares paid	CU21,000	(CU2.10 per share)

* This example does not illustrate the classification of the components of convertible financial instruments as liabilities and equity or the classification of related interest and dividends as expenses and equity as required by IAS 32.

Continued from previous page

Basic earnings per share is calculated as follows:

	CU	CU
Profit attributable to equity holders of the parent entity		100,000
Less dividends paid:		
Preference	33,000	
Ordinary	21,000	
		(54,000)
Undistributed earnings		46,000

Allocation of undistributed earnings:

Allocation per ordinary share = A

Allocation per preference share = B; B = ¼ A

$$(A \times 10{,}000) + (\tfrac{1}{4} \times A \times 6{,}000) = CU46{,}000$$

$$A = CU46{,}000 \div (10{,}000 + 1{,}500)$$

$$A = CU4.00$$

$$B = \tfrac{1}{4} A$$

$$B = CU1.00$$

Basic per share amounts:

	Preference shares	*Ordinary shares*
Distributed earnings	CU5.50	CU2.10
Undistributed earnings	CU1.00	CU4.00
Totals	CU6.50	CU6.10

Example 12 Calculation of basic and diluted earnings per share and income statement presentation (comprehensive example)*

This example illustrates the quarterly and annual calculations of basic and diluted earnings per share in the year 20X1 for Company A, which has a complex capital structure. The control number is profit or loss from continuing operations attributable to the parent entity. Other facts assumed are as follows:

Average market price of ordinary shares: The average market prices of ordinary shares for the calendar year 20X1 were as follows:

First quarter	CU49
Second quarter	CU60
Third quarter	CU67
Fourth quarter	CU67

The average market price of ordinary shares from 1 July to 1 September 20X1 was CU65.

Ordinary shares: The number of ordinary shares outstanding at the beginning of 20X1 was 5,000,000. On 1 March 20X1, 200,000 ordinary shares were issued for cash.

Convertible bonds: In the last quarter of 20X0, 5 per cent convertible bonds with a principal amount of CU12,000,000 due in 20 years were sold for cash at CU1,000 (par). Interest is payable twice a year, on 1 November and 1 May. Each CU1,000 bond is convertible into 40 ordinary shares. No bonds were converted in 20X0. The entire issue was converted on 1 April 20X1 because the issue was called by Company A.

Convertible preference shares: In the second quarter of 20X0, 800,000 convertible preference shares were issued for assets in a purchase transaction. The quarterly dividend on each convertible preference share is CU0.05, payable at the end of the quarter for shares outstanding at that date. Each share is convertible into one ordinary share. Holders of 600,000 convertible preference shares converted their preference shares into ordinary shares on 1 June 20X1.

Warrants: Warrants to buy 600,000 ordinary shares at CU55 per share for a period of five years were issued on 1 January 20X1. All outstanding warrants were exercised on 1 September 20X1.

Options: Options to buy 1,500,000 ordinary shares at CU75 per share for a period of 10 years were issued on 1 July 20X1. No options were exercised during 20X1 because the exercise price of the options exceeded the market price of the ordinary shares.

Tax rate: The tax rate was 40 per cent for 20X1.

* This example does not illustrate the classification of the components of convertible financial instruments as liabilities and equity or the classification of related interest and dividends as expenses and equity as required by IAS 32.

20X1	*Profit (loss) from continuing operations attributable to the parent entity* [(a)]	*Profit (loss) attributable to the parent entity*
	CU	CU
First quarter	5,000,000	5,000,000
Second quarter	6,500,000	6,500,000
Third quarter	1,000,000	(1,000,000)[(b)]
Fourth quarter	(700,000)	(700,000)
Full year	11,800,000	9,800,000

(a) This is the control number (before adjusting for preference dividends).

(b) Company A had a CU2,000,000 loss (net of tax) from discontinued operations in the third quarter.

First Quarter 20X1

Basic EPS calculation	CU
Profit from continuing operations attributable to the parent entity	5,000,000
Less: preference shares dividends	(40,000)[(a)]
Profit attributable to ordinary equity holders of the parent entity	4,960,000

Dates	*Shares outstanding*	*Fraction of period*	*Weighted–average shares*
1 January–28 February	5,000,000	⅔	3,333,333
Issue of ordinary shares on 1 March	200,000		
1 March–31 March	5,200,000	⅓	1,733,333
Weighted–average shares			5,066,666
Basic EPS			**CU0.98**

(a) 800,000 shares × CU0.05

Continued from previous page

Diluted EPS calculation

Profit attributable to ordinary equity holders of the parent entity		CU4,960,000
Plus: profit impact of assumed conversions		
Preference share dividends	CU40,000 (b)	
Interest on 5% convertible bonds	CU90,000 (c)	
Effect of assumed conversions		CU130,000
Profit attributable to ordinary equity holders of the parent entity including assumed conversions		CU5,090,000
Weighted–average shares		5,066,666
Plus: incremental shares from assumed conversions		
Warrants	0 (d)	
Convertible preference shares	80,000	
5% convertible bonds	480,000	
Dilutive potential ordinary shares		1,280,000
Adjusted weighted–average shares		6,346,666
Diluted EPS		**CU0.80**

(b) 800,000 shares × CU0.05

(c) (CU12,000,000 × 5%) ÷ 4; less taxes at 40%

(d) The warrants were not assumed to be exercised because they were antidilutive in the period (CU55 [exercise price] > CU49 [average price]).

Second Quarter 20X1

Basic EPS calculation			CU
Profit from continuing operations attributable to the parent entity			6,500,000
Less: preference shares dividends			(10,000)[(a)]
Profit attributable to ordinary equity holders of the parent entity			6,490,000

Dates	*Shares outstanding*	*Fraction of period*	*Weighted–average shares*
1 April	5,200,000		
Conversion of 5% bonds on 1 April	480,000		
1 April–31 May	5,680,000	⅔	3,786,666
Conversion of preference shares 1 June	600,000		
1 June–30 June	6,280,000	⅓	2,093,333
Weighted–average shares			5,880,000
Basic EPS			**CU1.10**

(a) 200,000 shares × CU0.05

Continued from previous page

Diluted EPS calculation

Profit attributable to ordinary equity holders of the parent entity		CU6,490,000
Plus: profit impact of assumed conversions		
Preference share dividends	CU10,000 (b)	
Effect of assumed conversions		CU10,000
Profit attributable to ordinary equity holders of the parent entity including assumed conversions		CU6,500,000
Weighted–average shares		5,880,000
Plus: incremental shares from assumed conversions		
Warrants	50,000 (c)	
Convertible preference shares	600,000 (d)	
Dilutive potential ordinary shares		650,000
Adjusted weighted–average shares		6,530,000
Diluted EPS		**CU1.00**

(b) 200,000 shares × CU0.05

(c) CU55 × 600,000 = CU33,000,000; CU33,000,000 ÷ CU60 = 550,000; 600,000 − 550,000 = 50,000 shares OR [(CU60 − CU55) ÷ CU60] × 600,000 shares = 50,000 shares

(d) (800,000 shares × ⅔) + (200,000 shares × ⅓)

Third Quarter 20X1			
Basic EPS calculation			CU
Profit from continuing operations attributable to the parent entity			1,000,000
Less: preference shares dividends			(10,000)
Profit from continuing operations attributable to ordinary equity holders of the parent entity			990,000
Loss from discontinued operations attributable to the parent entity			(2,000,000)
Loss attributable to ordinary equity holders of the parent entity			(1,010,000)
Dates	*Shares outstanding*	*Fraction of period*	*Weighted–average shares*
1 July–31 August	6,280,000	⅔	4,186,666
Exercise of warrants on 1 September	600,000		
1 September–30 September	6,880,000	⅓	2,293,333
Weighted–average shares			6,480,000
Basic EPS			
Profit from continuing operations			**CU0.15**
Loss from discontinued operations			**(CU0.31)**
Loss			**(CU0.16)**

Continued from previous page

Diluted EPS calculation		
Profit from continuing operations attributable to ordinary equity holders of the parent entity		CU990,000
Plus: profit impact of assumed conversions		
Preference share dividends	CU10,000	
Effect of assumed conversions		CU10,000
Profit from continuing operations attributable to ordinary equity holders of the parent entity including assumed conversions		CU1,000,000
Loss from discontinued operations attributable to the parent entity		(CU2,000,000)
Loss attributable to ordinary equity holders of the parent entity including assumed conversions		(CU1,000,000)
Weighted–average shares		6,480,000
Plus: incremental shares from assumed conversions		
Warrants	50,000 [(a)]	
Convertible preference shares	200,000	
Dilutive potential ordinary shares		261,538
Adjusted weighted–average shares		6,741,538

Diluted EPS	
Profit from continuing operations	**CU0.15**
Loss from discontinued operations	**(CU0.30)**
Loss	**(CU0.15)**

(a) [(CU65 − CU55) ÷ CU65] × 600,000 = 92,308 shares; 92,308 × ⅔ = 61,538 shares

Note: The incremental shares from assumed conversions are included in calculating the diluted per-share amounts for the loss from discontinued operations and loss even though they are antidilutive. This is because the control number (profit from continuing operations attributable to ordinary equity holders of the parent entity, adjusted for preference dividends) was positive (ie profit, rather than loss).

Fourth Quarter 20X1

Basic EPS calculation			CU
Loss from continuing operations attributable to the parent entity			(700,000)
Add: preference shares dividends			(10,000)
Loss attributable to ordinary equity holders of the parent entity			(710,000)
Dates	*Shares outstanding*	*Fraction of period*	*Weighted–average shares*
1 October–31 December	6,880,000	3/3	6,880,000
Weighted–average shares			6,880,000
Basic and diluted EPS			
Loss attributable to ordinary equity holders of the parent entity			**(CU0.10)**

Note: The incremental shares from assumed conversions are not included in calculating the diluted per-share amounts because the control number (loss from continuing operations attributable to ordinary equity holders of the parent entity adjusted for preference dividends) was negative (ie a loss, rather than profit).

Full Year 20X1

Basic EPS calculation	CU
Profit from continuing operations attributable to the parent entity	11,800,000
Less: preference shares dividends	(70,000)
Profit from continuing operations attributable to ordinary equity holders of the parent entity	11,730,000
Loss from discontinued operations attributable to the parent entity	(2,000,000)
Profit attributable to ordinary equity holders of the parent entity	9,730,000

Dates	*Shares outstanding*	*Fraction of period*	*Weighted–average shares*
1 January–28 February	5,000,000	2/12	833,333
Issue of ordinary shares on 1 March	200,000		
1 March–31 March	5,200,000	1/12	433,333
Conversion of 5% bonds on 1 April	480,000		
1 April–31 May	5,680,000	2/12	946,667
Conversion of preference shares on 1 June	600,000		
1 June–31 August	6,280,000	3/12	1,570,000
Exercise of warrants on 1 September	600,000		
1 September–31 December	6,880,000	4/12	2,293,333
Weighted–average shares			6,076,667

Basic EPS	
Profit from continuing operations	**CU1.93**
Loss from discontinued operations	**(CU0.33)**
Profit	**CU1.60**

Continued from previous page

Diluted EPS calculation

Profit from continuing operations attributable to ordinary equity holders of the parent entity		CU11,730,000
Plus: profit impact of assumed conversions		
Preference share dividends	CU70,000	
Interest on 5% convertible bonds	CU90,000 [(a)]	
Effect of assumed conversions		CU160,000
Profit from continuing operations attributable to ordinary equity holders of the parent entity including assumed conversions		CU11,890,000
Loss from discontinued operations attributable to the parent entity		(CU2,000,000)
Profit attributable to ordinary equity holders of the parent entity including assumed conversions		CU9,890,000
Weighted–average shares		6,076,667
Plus: incremental shares from assumed conversions		
Warrants	14,880 [(b)]	
Convertible preference shares	450,000 [(c)]	
5% convertible bonds	120,000 [(d)]	
Dilutive potential ordinary shares		584,880
Adjusted weighted–average shares		6,661,547
Diluted EPS		
Profit from continuing operations		**CU1.78**
Loss from discontinued operations		**(CU0.30)**
Profit		**CU1.48**

(a) (CU12,000,000 × 5%) ÷ 4; less taxes at 40%

(b) [(CU57.125* − CU55) ÷ CU57.125] × 600,000 = 22,320 shares; 22,320 × 8⁄12 = 14,880 shares
*The average market price from 1 January 20X1 to 1 September 20X1

(c) (800,000 shares × 5⁄12) + (200,000 shares × 7⁄12)

(d) 480,000 shares × 3⁄12

The following illustrates how Company A might present its earnings per share data on its income statement. Note that the amounts per share for the loss from discontinued operations are not required to be presented on the face of the income statement.

	For the year ended 20X1
	CU
Earnings per ordinary share	
Profit from continuing operations	1.93
Loss from discontinued operations	(0.33)
Profit	1.60
Diluted earnings per ordinary share	
Profit from continuing operations	1.78
Loss from discontinued operations	(0.30)
Profit	1.48

The following table includes the quarterly and annual earnings per share data for Company A. The purpose of this table is to illustrate that the sum of the four quarters' earnings per share data will not necessarily equal the annual earnings per share data. The Standard does not require disclosure of this information.

	First quarter	*Second quarter*	*Third quarter*	*Fourth quarter*	*Full year*
	CU	CU	CU	CU	CU
Basic EPS					
Profit (loss) from continuing operations	0.98	1.10	0.15	(0.10)	1.93
Loss from discontinued operations	–	–	(0.31)	–	(0.33)
Profit (loss)	0.98	1.10	(0.16)	(0.10)	1.60
Diluted EPS					
Profit (loss) from continuing operations	0.80	1.00	0.15	(0.10)	1.78
Loss from discontinued operations	–	–	(0.30)	–	(0.30)
Profit (loss)	0.80	1.00	(0.15)	(0.10)	1.48

Table of Concordance

This table shows how the contents of the superseded version of IAS 33 and the current version of IAS 33 correspond. Paragraphs are treated as corresponding if they broadly address the same matter even though the guidance may differ.

This table also shows how the requirements of SIC Interpretation SIC-24 have been incorporated into the current version of IAS 33.

Superseded IAS 33 paragraph	Current IAS 33 paragraph
Objective	1
1	2
2	4
3	None
4	3
5	3
6	5
7	6
8	7
9	8
10	10
11	12
12	13
13	14
14	19
15	20
Example following paragraph 15	Illustrative Example 2
16	21
17	22
18	A15
19	24, 25
20	26
21	27
22	28
23	A2
Example following paragraph 23	Illustrative Examples 3 and 4
24	31
25	32
26	33
27	34
Example following paragraph 27	Illustrative Example 6
28	35
29	36
30	39
31	52
32	40
33	45
34	45, A4
35	46
Example following paragraph 35	Illustrative Example 5
36	None
37	A16
38	41
39	42
40	43
41	44
Example following paragraph 41	Illustrative Example 9
42	38
43	64
44	65
45	70(d), 71
46	71
47	69
48	69
49	70(a), (b)
50	72
51	73
52	None
53	74
SIC-24	58–61
None	IN1–IN3
None	9
None	11
None	15–18
None	23
None	29, 30
None	37
None	47–51
None	53–57
None	62, 63
None	67, 68
None	70(c)
None	75, 76
None	A1
None	A3
None	A5–A14
None	Illustrative Examples 1, 7, 8, 10, 11, 12

International Accounting Standard 34

Interim Financial Reporting

This version includes amendments resulting from new and amended IFRSs issued up to 31 December 2004.

CONTENTS

International Accounting Standard 34 *Interim Financial Reporting* (IAS 34) is set out in paragraphs 1–46. All the paragraphs have equal authority but retain the IASC format of the Standard when it was adopted by the IASB. IAS 34 should be read in the context of its objective, the *Preface to International Financial Reporting Standards* and the *Framework for the Preparation and Presentation of Financial Statements*. IAS 8 *Accounting Policies, Changes in Accounting Estimates and Errors* provides a basis for selecting and applying accounting policies in the absence of explicit guidance.

Introduction

IN1 This Standard (IAS 34) addresses interim financial reporting, a matter not covered in a prior Standard. IAS 34 is effective for accounting periods beginning on or after 1 January 1999.

IN2 An interim financial report is a financial report that contains either a complete or condensed set of financial statements for a period shorter than an entity's full financial year.

IN3 This Standard does not mandate which entities should publish interim financial reports, how frequently, or how soon after the end of an interim period. In IASC's judgement, those matters should be decided by national governments, securities regulators, stock exchanges, and accountancy bodies. This Standard applies if a company is required or elects to publish an interim financial report in accordance with Standards.

IN4 This Standard:

(a) defines the minimum content of an interim financial report, including disclosures; and

(b) identifies the accounting recognition and measurement principles that should be applied in an interim financial report.

IN5 Minimum content of an interim financial report is a condensed balance sheet, condensed income statement, condensed cash flow statement, condensed statement showing changes in equity, and selected explanatory notes.

IN6 On the presumption that anyone who reads an entity's interim report will also have access to its most recent annual report, virtually none of the notes to the annual financial statements are repeated or updated in the interim report. Instead, the interim notes include primarily an explanation of the events and changes that are significant to an understanding of the changes in financial position and performance of the entity since the last annual reporting date.

IN7 An entity should apply the same accounting policies in its interim financial report as are applied in its annual financial statements, except for accounting policy changes made after the date of the most recent annual financial statements that are to be reflected in the next annual financial statements. The frequency of an entity's reporting—annual, half-yearly, or quarterly—should not affect the measurement of its annual results. To achieve that objective, measurements for interim reporting purposes are made on a year-to-date basis.

IN8 An appendix to this Standard provides guidance for applying the basic recognition and measurement principles at interim dates to various types of asset, liability, income, and expense. Income tax expense for an interim period is based on an estimated average annual effective income tax rate, consistent with the annual assessment of taxes.

IN9 In deciding how to recognise, classify, or disclose an item for interim financial reporting purposes, materiality is to be assessed in relation to the interim period financial data, not forecasted annual data.

International Accounting Standard 34
Interim Financial Reporting

Objective

The objective of this Standard is to prescribe the minimum content of an interim financial report and to prescribe the principles for recognition and measurement in complete or condensed financial statements for an interim period. Timely and reliable interim financial reporting improves the ability of investors, creditors, and others to understand an entity's capacity to generate earnings and cash flows and its financial condition and liquidity.

Scope

1 This Standard does not mandate which entities should be required to publish interim financial reports, how frequently, or how soon after the end of an interim period. However, governments, securities regulators, stock exchanges, and accountancy bodies often require entities whose debt or equity securities are publicly traded to publish interim financial reports. This Standard applies if an entity is required or elects to publish an interim financial report in accordance with International Financial Reporting Standards. The International Accounting Standards Committee* encourages publicly traded entities to provide interim financial reports that conform to the recognition, measurement, and disclosure principles set out in this Standard. Specifically, publicly traded entities are encouraged:

(a) to provide interim financial reports at least as of the end of the first half of their financial year; and

(b) to make their interim financial reports available not later than 60 days after the end of the interim period.

2 Each financial report, annual or interim, is evaluated on its own for conformity to International Financial Reporting Standards. The fact that an entity may not have provided interim financial reports during a particular financial year or may have provided interim financial reports that do not comply with this Standard does not prevent the entity's annual financial statements from conforming to International Financial Reporting Standards if they otherwise do so.

3 If an entity's interim financial report is described as complying with International Financial Reporting Standards, it must comply with all of the requirements of this Standard. Paragraph 19 requires certain disclosures in that regard.

* The International Accounting Standards Committee was succeeded by the International Accounting Standards Board, which began operations in 2001.

Definitions

4 **The following terms are used in this Standard with the meanings specified:**

Interim period **is a financial reporting period shorter than a full financial year.**

Interim financial report **means a financial report containing either a complete set of financial statements (as described in IAS 1** *Presentation of Financial Statements*) **or a set of condensed financial statements (as described in this Standard) for an interim period.**

Content of an interim financial report

5 IAS 1 defines a complete set of financial statements as including the following components:

(a) a balance sheet;

(b) an income statement;

(c) a statement of changes in equity showing either:

(i) all changes in equity, or

(ii) changes in equity other than those arising from transactions with equity holders acting in their capacity as equity holders;

(d) a cash flow statement; and

(e) notes, comprising a summary of significant accounting policies and other explanatory notes.

6 In the interest of timeliness and cost considerations and to avoid repetition of information previously reported, an entity may be required to or may elect to provide less information at interim dates as compared with its annual financial statements. This Standard defines the minimum content of an interim financial report as including condensed financial statements and selected explanatory notes. The interim financial report is intended to provide an update on the latest complete set of annual financial statements. Accordingly, it focuses on new activities, events, and circumstances and does not duplicate information previously reported.

7 Nothing in this Standard is intended to prohibit or discourage an entity from publishing a complete set of financial statements (as described in IAS 1) in its interim financial report, rather than condensed financial statements and selected explanatory notes. Nor does this Standard prohibit or discourage an entity from including in condensed interim financial statements more than the minimum line items or selected explanatory notes as set out in this Standard. The recognition and measurement guidance in this Standard applies also to complete financial statements for an interim period, and such statements would include all of the disclosures required by this Standard (particularly the selected note disclosures in paragraph 16) as well as those required by other Standards.

Minimum components of an interim financial report

8 **An interim financial report shall include, at a minimum, the following components:**

(a) condensed balance sheet;

(b) condensed income statement;

(c) condensed statement showing either (i) all changes in equity or (ii) changes in equity other than those arising from capital transactions with owners and distributions to owners;

(d) condensed cash flow statement; and

(e) selected explanatory notes.

Form and content of interim financial statements

9 **If an entity publishes a complete set of financial statements in its interim financial report, the form and content of those statements shall conform to the requirements of IAS 1 for a complete set of financial statements.**

10 **If an entity publishes a set of condensed financial statements in its interim financial report, those condensed statements shall include, at a minimum, each of the headings and subtotals that were included in its most recent annual financial statements and the selected explanatory notes as required by this Standard. Additional line items or notes shall be included if their omission would make the condensed interim financial statements misleading.**

11 **Basic and diluted earnings per share shall be presented on the face of an income statement, complete or condensed, for an interim period.**

12 IAS 1 provides guidance on the structure of financial statements. The Implementation Guidance for IAS 1 illustrates ways in which the balance sheet, income statement and statement of changes in equity may be presented.

13 IAS 1 requires a statement of changes in equity be presented as a separate component of an entity's financial statements, and permits information about changes in equity arising from transactions with equity holders acting in their capacity as equity holders (including distributions to equity holders) to be shown either on the face of the statement or in the notes. An entity follows the same format in its interim statement of changes in equity as it did in its most recent annual statement.

14 An interim financial report is prepared on a consolidated basis if the entity's most recent annual financial statements were consolidated statements. The parent's separate financial statements are not consistent or comparable with the consolidated statements in the most recent annual financial report. If an entity's annual financial report included the parent's separate financial statements in addition to consolidated financial statements, this Standard neither requires nor prohibits the inclusion of the parent's separate statements in the entity's interim financial report.

Selected explanatory notes

15 A user of an entity's interim financial report will also have access to the most recent annual financial report of that entity. It is unnecessary, therefore, for the notes to an interim financial report to provide relatively insignificant updates to the information that was already reported in the notes in the most recent annual report. At an interim date, an explanation of events and transactions that are significant to an understanding of the changes in financial position and performance of the entity since the last annual reporting date is more useful.

16 **An entity shall include the following information, as a minimum, in the notes to its interim financial statements, if material and if not disclosed elsewhere in the interim financial report. The information shall normally be reported on a financial year-to-date basis. However, the entity shall also disclose any events or transactions that are material to an understanding of the current interim period:**

(a) a statement that the same accounting policies and methods of computation are followed in the interim financial statements as compared with the most recent annual financial statements or, if those policies or methods have been changed, a description of the nature and effect of the change;

(b) explanatory comments about the seasonality or cyclicality of interim operations;

(c) the nature and amount of items affecting assets, liabilities, equity, net income, or cash flows that are unusual because of their nature, size, or incidence;

(d) the nature and amount of changes in estimates of amounts reported in prior interim periods of the current financial year or changes in estimates of amounts reported in prior financial years, if those changes have a material effect in the current interim period;

(e) issuances, repurchases, and repayments of debt and equity securities;

(f) dividends paid (aggregate or per share) separately for ordinary shares and other shares;

(g) segment revenue and segment result for business segments or geographical segments, whichever is the entity's primary basis of segment reporting (disclosure of segment data is required in an entity's interim financial report only if IAS 14 *Segment Reporting* **requires that entity to disclose segment data in its annual financial statements);**

(h) material events subsequent to the end of the interim period that have not been reflected in the financial statements for the interim period;

(i) the effect of changes in the composition of the entity during the interim period, including business combinations, acquisition or disposal of subsidiaries and long-term investments, restructurings, and discontinued operations. In the case of business combinations,

the entity shall disclose the information required to be disclosed under paragraphs 66–73 of IFRS 3 ***Business Combinations*****; and**

(j) changes in contingent liabilities or contingent assets since the last annual balance sheet date.

17 Examples of the kinds of disclosures that are required by paragraph 16 are set out below. Individual Standards and Interpretations provide guidance regarding disclosures for many of these items:

(a) the write-down of inventories to net realisable value and the reversal of such a write-down;

(b) recognition of a loss from the impairment of property, plant, and equipment, intangible assets, or other assets, and the reversal of such an impairment loss;

(c) the reversal of any provisions for the costs of restructuring;

(d) acquisitions and disposals of items of property, plant, and equipment;

(e) commitments for the purchase of property, plant, and equipment;

(f) litigation settlements;

(g) corrections of prior period errors;

(h) [deleted]

(i) any loan default or breach of a loan agreement that has not been remedied on or before the balance sheet date; and

(j) related party transactions.

18 Other Standards specify disclosures that should be made in financial statements. In that context, financial statements means complete sets of financial statements of the type normally included in an annual financial report and sometimes included in other reports. Except as required by paragraph 16(i), the disclosures required by those other Standards are not required if an entity's interim financial report includes only condensed financial statements and selected explanatory notes rather than a complete set of financial statements.

Disclosure of compliance with IFRSs

19 If an entity's interim financial report is in compliance with this Standard, that fact shall be disclosed. An interim financial report shall not be described as complying with Standards unless it complies with all of the requirements of International Financial Reporting Standards.

Periods for which interim financial statements are required to be presented

20 Interim reports shall include interim financial statements (condensed or complete) for periods as follows:

(a) balance sheet as of the end of the current interim period and a comparative balance sheet as of the end of the immediately preceding financial year;

(b) income statements for the current interim period and cumulatively for the current financial year to date, with comparative income statements for the comparable interim periods (current and year-to-date) of the immediately preceding financial year;

(c) statement showing changes in equity cumulatively for the current financial year to date, with a comparative statement for the comparable year-to-date period of the immediately preceding financial year; and

(d) cash flow statement cumulatively for the current financial year to date, with a comparative statement for the comparable year-to-date period of the immediately preceding financial year.

21 For an entity whose business is highly seasonal, financial information for the twelve months ending on the interim reporting date and comparative information for the prior twelve-month period may be useful. Accordingly, entities whose business is highly seasonal are encouraged to consider reporting such information in addition to the information called for in the preceding paragraph.

22 Appendix A illustrates the periods required to be presented by an entity that reports half-yearly and an entity that reports quarterly.

Materiality

23 In deciding how to recognise, measure, classify, or disclose an item for interim financial reporting purposes, materiality shall be assessed in relation to the interim period financial data. In making assessments of materiality, it shall be recognised that interim measurements may rely on estimates to a greater extent than measurements of annual financial data.

24 IAS 1 *Presentation of Financial Statements* and IAS 8 *Accounting Policies, Changes in Accounting Estimates and Errors* define an item as material if its omission or misstatement could influence the economic decisions of users of the financial statements. IAS 1 requires separate disclosure of material items, including (for example) discontinued operations, and IAS 8 requires disclosure of changes in accounting estimates, errors, and changes in accounting policies. The two Standards do not contain quantified guidance as to materiality.

25 While judgement is always required in assessing materiality, this Standard bases the recognition and disclosure decision on data for the interim period by itself for reasons of understandability of the interim figures. Thus, for example, unusual items, changes in accounting policies or estimates, and errors are recognised and disclosed on the basis of materiality in relation to interim period data to avoid misleading inferences that might result from non-disclosure. The overriding goal is to ensure that an interim financial report includes all information that is relevant to understanding an entity's financial position and performance during the interim period.

Disclosure in annual financial statements

26 **If an estimate of an amount reported in an interim period is changed significantly during the final interim period of the financial year but a separate financial report is not published for that final interim period, the nature and amount of that change in estimate shall be disclosed in a note to the annual financial statements for that financial year.**

27 IAS 8 requires disclosure of the nature and (if practicable) the amount of a change in estimate that either has a material effect in the current period or is expected to have a material effect in subsequent periods. Paragraph 16(d) of this Standard requires similar disclosure in an interim financial report. Examples include changes in estimate in the final interim period relating to inventory write-downs, restructurings, or impairment losses that were reported in an earlier interim period of the financial year. The disclosure required by the preceding paragraph is consistent with the IAS 8 requirement and is intended to be narrow in scope—relating only to the change in estimate. An entity is not required to include additional interim period financial information in its annual financial statements.

Recognition and measurement

Same accounting policies as annual

28 **An entity shall apply the same accounting policies in its interim financial statements as are applied in its annual financial statements, except for accounting policy changes made after the date of the most recent annual financial statements that are to be reflected in the next annual financial statements. However, the frequency of an entity's reporting (annual, half-yearly, or quarterly) shall not affect the measurement of its annual results. To achieve that objective, measurements for interim reporting purposes shall be made on a year-to-date basis.**

29 Requiring that an entity apply the same accounting policies in its interim financial statements as in its annual statements may seem to suggest that interim period measurements are made as if each interim period stands alone as an independent reporting period. However, by providing that the frequency of an entity's reporting shall not affect the measurement of its annual results, paragraph 28 acknowledges that an interim period is a part of a larger financial year. Year-to-date measurements may involve changes in estimates of amounts reported in prior interim periods of the current financial year. But the principles for recognising assets, liabilities, income, and expenses for interim periods are the same as in annual financial statements.

30 To illustrate:

(a) the principles for recognising and measuring losses from inventory write-downs, restructurings, or impairments in an interim period are the same as those that an entity would follow if it prepared only annual financial statements. However, if such items are recognised and measured in one interim period and the estimate changes in a subsequent interim period of that financial year, the original estimate is changed in the subsequent interim period either by accrual of an additional amount of loss or by reversal of the previously recognised amount;

(b) a cost that does not meet the definition of an asset at the end of an interim period is not deferred on the balance sheet either to await future information as to whether it has met the definition of an asset or to smooth earnings over interim periods within a financial year; and

(c) income tax expense is recognised in each interim period based on the best estimate of the weighted average annual income tax rate expected for the full financial year. Amounts accrued for income tax expense in one interim period may have to be adjusted in a subsequent interim period of that financial year if the estimate of the annual income tax rate changes.

31 Under the *Framework for the Preparation and Presentation of Financial Statements* (the *Framework*), recognition is the 'process of incorporating in the balance sheet or income statement an item that meets the definition of an element and satisfies the criteria for recognition'. The definitions of assets, liabilities, income, and expenses are fundamental to recognition, both at annual and interim financial reporting dates.

32 For assets, the same tests of future economic benefits apply at interim dates and at the end of an entity's financial year. Costs that, by their nature, would not qualify as assets at financial yearend would not qualify at interim dates either. Similarly, a liability at an interim reporting date must represent an existing obligation at that date, just as it must at an annual reporting date.

33 An essential characteristic of income (revenue) and expenses is that the related inflows and outflows of assets and liabilities have already taken place. If those inflows or outflows have taken place, the related revenue and expense are recognised; otherwise they are not recognised. The *Framework* says that 'expenses are recognised in the income statement when a decrease in future economic benefits related to a decrease in an asset or an increase of a liability has arisen that can be measured reliably... [The] *Framework* does not allow the recognition of items in the balance sheet which do not meet the definition of assets or liabilities.'

34 In measuring the assets, liabilities, income, expenses, and cash flows reported in its financial statements, an entity that reports only annually is able to take into account information that becomes available throughout the financial year. Its measurements are, in effect, on a year-to-date basis.

35 An entity that reports half-yearly uses information available by mid-year or shortly thereafter in making the measurements in its financial statements for the first six-month period and information available by year-end or shortly thereafter for the twelve-month period. The twelve-month measurements will reflect possible changes in estimates of amounts reported for the first six-month period. The amounts reported in the interim financial report for the first six-month period are not retrospectively adjusted. Paragraphs 16(d) and 26 require, however, that the nature and amount of any significant changes in estimates be disclosed.

36 An entity that reports more frequently than half-yearly measures income and expenses on a year-to-date basis for each interim period using information available when each set of financial statements is being prepared. Amounts of

income and expenses reported in the current interim period will reflect any changes in estimates of amounts reported in prior interim periods of the financial year. The amounts reported in prior interim periods are not retrospectively adjusted. Paragraphs 16(d) and 26 require, however, that the nature and amount of any significant changes in estimates be disclosed.

Revenues received seasonally, cyclically, or occasionally

37 **Revenues that are received seasonally, cyclically, or occasionally within a financial year shall not be anticipated or deferred as of an interim date if anticipation or deferral would not be appropriate at the end of the entity's financial year.**

38 Examples include dividend revenue, royalties, and government grants. Additionally, some entities consistently earn more revenues in certain interim periods of a financial year than in other interim periods, for example, seasonal revenues of retailers. Such revenues are recognised when they occur.

Costs incurred unevenly during the financial year

39 **Costs that are incurred unevenly during an entity's financial year shall be anticipated or deferred for interim reporting purposes if, and only if, it is also appropriate to anticipate or defer that type of cost at the end of the financial year.**

Applying the recognition and measurement principles

40 Appendix B provides examples of applying the general recognition and measurement principles set out in paragraphs 28–39.

Use of estimates

41 **The measurement procedures to be followed in an interim financial report shall be designed to ensure that the resulting information is reliable and that all material financial information that is relevant to an understanding of the financial position or performance of the entity is appropriately disclosed. While measurements in both annual and interim financial reports are often based on reasonable estimates, the preparation of interim financial reports generally will require a greater use of estimation methods than annual financial reports.**

42 Appendix C provides examples of the use of estimates in interim periods.

Restatement of previously reported interim periods

43 **A change in accounting policy, other than one for which the transition is specified by a new Standard or Interpretation, shall be reflected by:**

(a) restating the financial statements of prior interim periods of the current financial year and the comparable interim periods of any prior financial years that will be restated in the annual financial statements in accordance with IAS 8; or

(b) when it is impracticable to determine the cumulative effect at the beginning of the financial year of applying a new accounting policy to

all prior periods, adjusting the financial statements of prior interim periods of the current financial year, and comparable interim periods of prior financial years to apply the new accounting policy prospectively from the earliest date practicable.

44 One objective of the preceding principle is to ensure that a single accounting policy is applied to a particular class of transactions throughout an entire financial year. Under IAS 8, a change in accounting policy is reflected by retrospective application, with restatement of prior period financial data as far back as is practicable. However, if the cumulative amount of the adjustment relating to prior financial years is impracticable to determine, then under IAS 8 the new policy is applied prospectively from the earliest date practicable. The effect of the principle in paragraph 43 is to require that within the current financial year any change in accounting policy is applied either retrospectively or, if that is not practicable, prospectively, from no later than the beginning of the financial year.

45 To allow accounting changes to be reflected as of an interim date within the financial year would allow two differing accounting policies to be applied to a particular class of transactions within a single financial year. The result would be interim allocation difficulties, obscured operating results, and complicated analysis and understandability of interim period information.

Effective date

46 This Standard becomes operative for financial statements covering periods beginning on or after 1 January 1999. Earlier application is encouraged.

Appendix A
Illustration of periods required to be presented

This appendix, which accompanies, but is not part of, IAS 34, provides examples to illustrate application of the principle in paragraph 20.

Entity publishes interim financial reports half–yearly

A1 The entity's financial year ends 31 December (calendar year). The entity will present the following financial statements (condensed or complete) in its half-yearly interim financial report as of 30 June 2001:

Balance sheet:			
	At	30 June 2001	31 December 2000
Income statement:			
	6 months ending	30 June 2001	30 June 2000
Cash flow statement:			
	6 months ending	30 June 2001	30 June 2000
Statement of changes in equity:			
	6 months ending	30 June 2001	30 June 2000

Entity publishes interim financial reports quarterly

A2 The entity's financial year ends 31 December (calendar year). The entity will present the following financial statements (condensed or complete) in its quarterly interim financial report as of 30 June 2001:

Balance sheet:			
	At	30 June 2001	31 December 2000
Income statement:			
	6 months ending	30 June 2001	30 June 2000
	3 months ending	30 June 2001	30 June 2000
Cash flow statement:			
	6 months ending	30 June 2001	30 June 2000
Statement of changes in equity:			
	6 months ending	30 June 2001	30 June 2000

Appendix B
Examples of applying the recognition and measurement principles

This appendix, which accompanies, but is not part of, IAS 34, provides examples of applying the general recognition and measurement principles set out in paragraphs 28–39.

Employer payroll taxes and insurance contributions

B1 If employer payroll taxes or contributions to government-sponsored insurance funds are assessed on an annual basis, the employer's related expense is recognised in interim periods using an estimated average annual effective payroll tax or contribution rate, even though a large portion of the payments may be made early in the financial year. A common example is an employer payroll tax or insurance contribution that is imposed up to a certain maximum level of earnings per employee. For higher income employees, the maximum income is reached before the end of the financial year, and the employer makes no further payments through the end of the year.

Major planned periodic maintenance or overhaul

B2 The cost of a planned major periodic maintenance or overhaul or other seasonal expenditure that is expected to occur late in the year is not anticipated for interim reporting purposes unless an event has caused the entity to have a legal or constructive obligation. The mere intention or necessity to incur expenditure related to the future is not sufficient to give rise to an obligation.

Provisions

B3 A provision is recognised when an entity has no realistic alternative but to make a transfer of economic benefits as a result of an event that has created a legal or constructive obligation. The amount of the obligation is adjusted upward or downward, with a corresponding loss or gain recognised in the income statement, if the entity's best estimate of the amount of the obligation changes.

B4 This Standard requires that an entity apply the same criteria for recognising and measuring a provision at an interim date as it would at the end of its financial year. The existence or non-existence of an obligation to transfer benefits is not a function of the length of the reporting period. It is a question of fact.

Year–end bonuses

B5 The nature of year-end bonuses varies widely. Some are earned simply by continued employment during a time period. Some bonuses are earned based on a monthly, quarterly, or annual measure of operating result. They may be purely discretionary, contractual, or based on years of historical precedent.

B6 A bonus is anticipated for interim reporting purposes if, and only if, (a) the bonus is a legal obligation or past practice would make the bonus a constructive obligation for which the entity has no realistic alternative but to make the payments, and (b) a reliable estimate of the obligation can be made. IAS 19 *Employee Benefits* provides guidance.

Contingent lease payments

B7 Contingent lease payments can be an example of a legal or constructive obligation that are recognised as a liability. If a lease provides for contingent payments based on the lessee achieving a certain level of annual sales, an obligation can arise in the interim periods of the financial year before the required annual level of sales has been achieved, if that required level of sales is expected to be achieved and the entity, therefore, has no realistic alternative but to make the future lease payment.

Intangible assets

B8 An entity will apply the definition and recognition criteria for an intangible asset in the same way in an interim period as in an annual period. Costs incurred before the recognition criteria for an intangible asset are met are recognised as an expense. Costs incurred after the specific point in time at which the criteria are met are recognised as part of the cost of an intangible asset. 'Deferring' costs as assets in an interim balance sheet in the hope that the recognition criteria will be met later in the financial year is not justified.

Pensions

B9 Pension cost for an interim period is calculated on a year-to-date basis by using the actuarially determined pension cost rate at the end of the prior financial year, adjusted for significant market fluctuations since that time and for significant curtailments, settlements, or other significant one-time events.

Vacations, holidays, and other short-term compensated absences

B10 Accumulating compensated absences are those that are carried forward and can be used in future periods if the current period's entitlement is not used in full. IAS 19 *Employee Benefits* requires that an entity measure the expected cost of and obligation for accumulating compensated absences at the amount the entity expects to pay as a result of the unused entitlement that has accumulated at the balance sheet date. That principle is also applied at interim financial reporting dates. Conversely, an entity recognises no expense or liability for non-accumulating compensated absences at an interim reporting date, just as it recognises none at an annual reporting date.

Other planned but irregularly occurring costs

B11 An entity's budget may include certain costs expected to be incurred irregularly during the financial year, such as charitable contributions and employee training costs. Those costs generally are discretionary even though they are planned and tend to recur from year to year. Recognising an obligation at an interim financial reporting date for such costs that have not yet been incurred generally is not consistent with the definition of a liability.

Measuring interim income tax expense

B12 Interim period income tax expense is accrued using the tax rate that would be applicable to expected total annual earnings, that is, the estimated average annual effective income tax rate applied to the pre-tax income of the interim period.

B13 This is consistent with the basic concept set out in paragraph 28 that the same accounting recognition and measurement principles shall be applied in an interim financial report as are applied in annual financial statements. Income taxes are assessed on an annual basis. Interim period income tax expense is calculated by applying to an interim period's pre-tax income the tax rate that would be applicable to expected total annual earnings, that is, the estimated average annual effective income tax rate. That estimated average annual rate would reflect a blend of the progressive tax rate structure expected to be applicable to the full year's earnings including enacted or substantively enacted changes in the income tax rates scheduled to take effect later in the financial year. IAS 12 *Income Taxes* provides guidance on substantively enacted changes in tax rates. The estimated average annual income tax rate would be re-estimated on a year-to-date basis, consistent with paragraph 28 of this Standard. Paragraph 16(d) requires disclosure of a significant change in estimate.

B14 To the extent practicable, a separate estimated average annual effective income tax rate is determined for each taxing jurisdiction and applied individually to the interim period pre-tax income of each jurisdiction. Similarly, if different income tax rates apply to different categories of income (such as capital gains or income earned in particular industries), to the extent practicable a separate rate is applied to each individual category of interim period pre-tax income. While that degree of precision is desirable, it may not be achievable in all cases, and a weighted average of rates across jurisdictions or across categories of income is used if it is a reasonable approximation of the effect of using more specific rates.

B15 To illustrate the application of the foregoing principle, an entity reporting quarterly expects to earn 10,000 pre-tax each quarter and operates in a jurisdiction with a tax rate of 20 per cent on the first 20,000 of annual earnings and 30 per cent on all additional earnings. Actual earnings match expectations. The following table shows the amount of income tax expense that is reported in each quarter:

	1st Quarter	2nd Quarter	3rd Quarter	4th Quarter	Annual
Tax expense	2,500	2,500	2,500	2,500	10,000

10,000 of tax is expected to be payable for the full year on 40,000 of pre-tax income.

B16 As another illustration, an entity reports quarterly, earns 15,000 pre-tax profit in the first quarter but expects to incur losses of 5,000 in each of the three remaining quarters (thus having zero income for the year), and operates in a jurisdiction in which its estimated average annual income tax rate is expected to be 20 per cent.

The following table shows the amount of income tax expense that is reported in each quarter:

	1st Quarter	2nd Quarter	3rd Quarter	4th Quarter	Annual
Tax expense	3,000	(1,000)	(1,000)	(1,000)	0

Difference in financial reporting year and tax year

B17 If the financial reporting year and the income tax year differ, income tax expense for the interim periods of that financial reporting year is measured using separate weighted average estimated effective tax rates for each of the income tax years applied to the portion of pre-tax income earned in each of those income tax years.

B18 To illustrate, an entity's financial reporting year ends 30 June and it reports quarterly. Its taxable year ends 31 December. For the financial year that begins 1 July, Year 1 and ends 30 June, Year 2, the entity earns 10,000 pre-tax each quarter. The estimated average annual income tax rate is 30 per cent in Year 1 and 40 per cent in Year 2.

	Quarter ending 30 Sept	Quarter ending 31 Dec	Quarter ending 31 Mar	Quarter ending 30 June	Year ending 30 June
	Year 1	Year 1	Year 2	Year 2	Year 2
Tax expense	3,000	3,000	4,000	4,000	14,000

Tax credits

B19 Some tax jurisdictions give taxpayers credits against the tax payable based on amounts of capital expenditures, exports, research and development expenditures, or other bases. Anticipated tax benefits of this type for the full year are generally reflected in computing the estimated annual effective income tax rate, because those credits are granted and calculated on an annual basis under most tax laws and regulations. On the other hand, tax benefits that relate to a one-time event are recognised in computing income tax expense in that interim period, in the same way that special tax rates applicable to particular categories of income are not blended into a single effective annual tax rate. Moreover, in some jurisdictions tax benefits or credits, including those related to capital expenditures and levels of exports, while reported on the income tax return, are more similar to a government grant and are recognised in the interim period in which they arise.

Tax loss and tax credit carrybacks and carryforwards

B20 The benefits of a tax loss carryback are reflected in the interim period in which the related tax loss occurs. IAS 12 provides that 'the benefit relating to a tax loss that can be carried back to recover current tax of a previous period shall be recognised as an asset'. A corresponding reduction of tax expense or increase of tax income is also recognised.

B21 IAS 12 provides that 'a deferred tax asset shall be recognised for the carryforward of unused tax losses and unused tax credits to the extent that it is probable that future taxable profit will be available against which the unused tax losses and unused tax credits can be utilised'. IAS 12 provides criteria for assessing the probability of taxable profit against which the unused tax losses and credits can be utilised. Those criteria are applied at the end of each interim period and, if they are met, the effect of the tax loss carryforward is reflected in the computation of the estimated average annual effective income tax rate.

B22 To illustrate, an entity that reports quarterly has an operating loss carryforward of 10,000 for income tax purposes at the start of the current financial year for which a deferred tax asset has not been recognised. The entity earns 10,000 in the first quarter of the current year and expects to earn 10,000 in each of the three remaining quarters. Excluding the carryforward, the estimated average annual income tax rate is expected to be 40 per cent. Tax expense is as follows:

	1st Quarter	2nd Quarter	3rd Quarter	4th Quarter	Annual
Tax expense	3,000	3,000	3,000	3,000	12,000

Contractual or anticipated purchase price changes

B23 Volume rebates or discounts and other contractual changes in the prices of raw materials, labour, or other purchased goods and services are anticipated in interim periods, by both the payer and the recipient, if it is probable that they have been earned or will take effect. Thus, contractual rebates and discounts are anticipated but discretionary rebates and discounts are not anticipated because the resulting asset or liability would not satisfy the conditions in the *Framework* that an asset must be a resource controlled by the entity as a result of a past event and that a liability must be a present obligation whose settlement is expected to result in an outflow of resources.

Depreciation and amortisation

B24 Depreciation and amortisation for an interim period is based only on assets owned during that interim period. It does not take into account asset acquisitions or dispositions planned for later in the financial year.

Inventories

B25 Inventories are measured for interim financial reporting by the same principles as at financial year-end. IAS 2 *Inventories* establishes standards for recognising and measuring inventories. Inventories pose particular problems at any financial reporting date because of the need to determine inventory quantities, costs, and net realisable values. Nonetheless, the same measurement principles are applied for interim inventories. To save cost and time, entities often use estimates to measure inventories at interim dates to a greater extent than at annual reporting dates. Following are examples of how to apply the net realisable value test at an interim date and how to treat manufacturing variances at interim dates.

Net realisable value of inventories

B26 The net realisable value of inventories is determined by reference to selling prices and related costs to complete and dispose at interim dates. An entity will reverse a write-down to net realisable value in a subsequent interim period only if it would be appropriate to do so at the end of the financial year.

B27 [Deleted]

Interim period manufacturing cost variances

B28 Price, efficiency, spending, and volume variances of a manufacturing entity are recognised in income at interim reporting dates to the same extent that those variances are recognised in income at financial year end. Deferral of variances that are expected to be absorbed by year end is not appropriate because it could result in reporting inventory at the interim date at more or less than its portion of the actual cost of manufacture.

Foreign currency translation gains and losses

B29 Foreign currency translation gains and losses are measured for interim financial reporting by the same principles as at financial year end.

B30 IAS 21 *The Effects of Changes in Foreign Exchange Rates* specifies how to translate the financial statements for foreign operations into the presentation currency, including guidelines for using average or closing foreign exchange rates and guidelines for recognising the resulting adjustments in profit of loss or in equity. Consistently with IAS 21, the actual average and closing rates for the interim period are used. Entities do not anticipate some future changes in foreign exchange rates in the remainder of the current financial year in translating foreign operations at an interim date.

B31 If IAS 21 requires translation adjustments to be recognised as income or expense in the period in which they arise, that principle is applied during each interim period. Entities do not defer some foreign currency translation adjustments at an interim date if the adjustment is expected to reverse before the end of the financial year.

Interim financial reporting in hyperinflationary economies

B32 Interim financial reports in hyperinflationary economies are prepared by the same principles as at financial year end.

B33 IAS 29 *Financial Reporting in Hyperinflationary Economies* requires that the financial statements of an entity that reports in the currency of a hyperinflationary economy be stated in terms of the measuring unit current at balance sheet date, and the gain or loss on the net monetary position is included in net income. Also, comparative financial data reported for prior periods is restated to the current measuring unit.

B34 Entities follow those same principles at interim dates, thereby presenting all interim data in the measuring unit as of the end of the interim period, with the resulting gain or loss on the net monetary position included in the interim period's net income. Entities do not annualise the recognition of the gain or loss.

Nor do they use an estimated annual inflation rate in preparing an interim financial report in a hyperinflationary economy.

Impairment of assets

B35 IAS 36 *Impairment of Assets* requires that an impairment loss be recognised if the recoverable amount has declined below carrying amount.

B36 This Standard requires that an entity apply the same impairment testing, recognition, and reversal criteria at an interim date as it would at the end of its financial year. That does not mean, however, that an entity must necessarily make a detailed impairment calculation at the end of each interim period. Rather, an entity will review for indications of significant impairment since the end of the most recent financial year to determine whether such a calculation is needed.

Appendix C
Examples of the use of estimates

This appendix, which accompanies, but is not part of, IAS 34, provides examples to illustrate application of the principle in paragraph 41.

C1 **Inventories:** Full stock-taking and valuation procedures may not be required for inventories at interim dates, although it may be done at financial year-end. It may be sufficient to make estimates at interim dates based on sales margins.

C2 **Classifications of current and non-current assets and liabilities:** Entities may do a more thorough investigation for classifying assets and liabilities as current or non-current at annual reporting dates than at interim dates.

C3 **Provisions:** Determination of the appropriate amount of a provision (such as a provision for warranties, environmental costs, and site restoration costs) may be complex and often costly and time-consuming. Entities sometimes engage outside experts to assist in the annual calculations. Making similar estimates at interim dates often entails updating of the prior annual provision rather than the engaging of outside experts to do a new calculation.

C4 **Pensions:** IAS 19 *Employee Benefits* requires that an entity determine the present value of defined benefit obligations and the market value of plan assets at each balance sheet date and encourages an entity to involve a professionally qualified actuary in measurement of the obligations. For interim reporting purposes, reliable measurement is often obtainable by extrapolation of the latest actuarial valuation.

C5 **Income taxes:** Entities may calculate income tax expense and deferred income tax liability at annual dates by applying the tax rate for each individual jurisdiction to measures of income for each jurisdiction. Paragraph 14 of Appendix B acknowledges that while that degree of precision is desirable at interim reporting dates as well, it may not be achievable in all cases, and a weighted average of rates across jurisdictions or across categories of income is used if it is a reasonable approximation of the effect of using more specific rates.

C6 **Contingencies:** The measurement of contingencies may involve the opinions of legal experts or other advisers. Formal reports from independent experts are sometimes obtained with respect to contingencies. Such opinions about litigation, claims, assessments, and other contingencies and uncertainties may or may not also be needed at interim dates.

C7 **Revaluations and fair value accounting:** IAS 16 *Property, Plant and Equipment* allows an entity to choose as its accounting policy the revaluation model whereby items of property, plant and equipment are revalued to fair value. Similarly, IAS 40 *Investment Property* requires an entity to determine the fair value of investment property. For those measurements, an entity may rely on professionally qualified valuers at annual reporting dates though not at interim reporting dates.

C8 **Intercompany reconciliations:** Some intercompany balances that are reconciled on a detailed level in preparing consolidated financial statements at financial year end might be reconciled at a less detailed level in preparing consolidated financial statements at an interim date.

C9 **Specialised industries:** Because of complexity, costliness, and time, interim period measurements in specialised industries might be less precise than at financial year end. An example would be calculation of insurance reserves by insurance companies.

International Accounting Standard 36

Impairment of Assets

This version includes amendments resulting from new and amended IFRSs issued up to 31 December 2004.

CONTENTS

International Accounting Standard 36 *Impairment of Assets* (IAS 36) is set out in paragraphs 1–141 and Appendices A and B. All the paragraphs have equal authority but retain the IASC format of the Standard when it was adopted by the IASB. IAS 36 should be read in the context of its objective and the Basis for Conclusions, the *Preface to International Financial Reporting Standards* and the *Framework for the Preparation and Presentation of Financial Statements*. IAS 8 *Accounting Policies, Changes in Accounting Estimates and Errors* provides a basis for selecting and applying accounting policies in the absence of explicit guidance.

Introduction

IN1 International Accounting Standard 36 *Impairment of Assets* (IAS 36) replaces IAS 36 *Impairment of Assets* (issued in 1998), and should be applied:

(a) on acquisition to goodwill and intangible assets acquired in business combinations for which the agreement date is on or after 31 March 2004.

(b) to all other assets, for annual periods beginning on or after 31 March 2004.

Earlier application is encouraged.

Reasons for revising IAS 36

IN2 The International Accounting Standards Board developed this revised IAS 36 as part of its project on business combinations. The project's objective is to improve the quality of, and seek international convergence on, the accounting for business combinations and the subsequent accounting for goodwill and intangible assets acquired in business combinations.

IN3 The project has two phases. The first phase resulted in the Board issuing simultaneously IFRS 3 *Business Combinations* and revised versions of IAS 36 and IAS 38 *Intangible Assets*. The Board's deliberations during the first phase of the project focused primarily on the following issues:

(a) the method of accounting for business combinations;

(b) the initial measurement of the identifiable assets acquired and liabilities and contingent liabilities assumed in a business combination;

(c) the recognition of provisions for terminating or reducing the activities of an acquiree;

(d) the treatment of any excess of the acquirer's interest in the fair values of identifiable net assets acquired in a business combination over the cost of the combination; and

(e) the accounting for goodwill and intangible assets acquired in a business combination.

IN4 Therefore, the Board's intention while revising IAS 36 was to reflect only those changes related to its decisions in the Business Combinations project, and *not* to reconsider all of the requirements in IAS 36. The changes that have been made in the Standard are primarily concerned with the impairment test for goodwill.

Summary of main changes

Frequency of impairment testing

IN5 The previous version of IAS 36 required the recoverable amount of an asset to be measured whenever there is an indication that the asset may be impaired. This requirement is included in the Standard. However, the Standard also requires:

(a) the recoverable amount of an intangible asset with an indefinite useful life to be measured annually, irrespective of whether there is any indication that it may be impaired. The most recent detailed calculation of recoverable amount made in a preceding period may be used in the impairment test for that asset in the current period, provided specified criteria are met.

(b) the recoverable amount of an intangible asset not yet available for use to be measured annually, irrespective of whether there is any indication that it may be impaired.

(c) goodwill acquired in a business combination to be tested for impairment annually.

Measuring value in use

IN6 The Standard clarifies that the following elements should be reflected in the calculation of an asset's value in use:

(a) an estimate of the future cash flows the entity expects to derive from the asset;

(b) expectations about possible variations in the amount or timing of those future cash flows;

(c) the time value of money, represented by the current market risk-free rate of interest;

(d) the price for bearing the uncertainty inherent in the asset; and

(e) other factors, such as illiquidity, that market participants would reflect in pricing the future cash flows the entity expects to derive from the asset.

The Standard also clarifies that the second, fourth and fifth of these elements can be reflected either as adjustments to the future cash flows or adjustments to the discount rate.

IN7 The Standard carries forward from the previous version of IAS 36 the requirement for the cash flow projections used to measure value in use to be based on reasonable and supportable assumptions that represent management's best estimate of the economic conditions that will exist over the remaining useful life of the asset. However, the Standard clarifies that management:

(a) should assess the reasonableness of the assumptions on which its current cash flow projections are based by examining the causes of differences between past cash flow projections and actual cash flows.

(b) should ensure that the assumptions on which its current cash flow projections are based are consistent with past actual outcomes, provided the effects of subsequent events or circumstances that did not exist when those actual cash flows were generated make this appropriate.

IN8 The previous version of IAS 36 required the cash flow projections used to measure value in use to be based on the most recent financial budgets/forecasts approved by management. The Standard carries forward this requirement, but clarifies that the cash flow projections exclude any estimated cash inflows or outflows expected to arise from:

(a) future restructurings to which the entity is not yet committed; or

(b) improving or enhancing the asset's performance.

IN9 Additional guidance on using present value techniques in measuring an asset's value in use is included in Appendix A of the Standard. In addition, the guidance in the previous version of IAS 36 on estimating the discount rate when an asset-specific rate is not directly available from the market has been relocated to Appendix A.

Identifying the cash–generating unit to which an asset belongs

IN10 The Standard carries forward from the previous version of IAS 36 the requirement that if an active market exists for the output produced by an asset or a group of assets, that asset or group of assets should be identified as a cash-generating unit, even if some or all of the output is used internally. However, the previous version of IAS 36 required that, in such circumstances, management's best estimate of future market prices for the output should be used in estimating the future cash flows used to determine the unit's value in use. It also required that when an entity was estimating future cash flows to determine the value in use of cash-generating units using the output, management's best estimate of future market prices for the output should be used. The Standard requires that if the cash inflows generated by *any* asset or cash-generating unit are affected by internal transfer pricing, an entity should use management's best estimate of future price(s) that could be achieved in arm's length transactions in estimating:

(a) the future cash inflows used to determine the asset's or cash-generating unit's value in use; and

(b) the future cash outflows used to determine the value in use of other assets or cash-generating units affected by the internal transfer pricing.

Allocating goodwill to cash–generating units

IN11 The previous version of IAS 36 required goodwill acquired in a business combination to be tested for impairment as part of impairment testing the cash-generating unit(s) to which it related. It employed a 'bottom-up/top-down' approach under which the goodwill was, in effect, tested for impairment by allocating its carrying amount to each cash-generating unit or smallest group of cash-generating units to which a portion of that carrying amount could be allocated on a reasonable and consistent basis. The Standard similarly requires goodwill acquired in a business combination to be tested for impairment as part of impairment testing the cash-generating unit(s) to which it relates. However, the Standard clarifies that:

(a) the goodwill should, from the acquisition date, be allocated to each of the acquirer's cash-generating units, or groups of cash-generating units, that are expected to benefit from the synergies of the business combination, irrespective of whether other assets or liabilities of the acquiree are assigned to those units or groups of units.

(b) each unit or group of units to which the goodwill is allocated should:

(i) represent the lowest level within the entity at which the goodwill is monitored for internal management purposes; and

(ii) not be larger than a segment based on either the entity's primary or the entity's secondary reporting format determined in accordance with IAS 14 *Segment Reporting*.

IN12 The Standard also clarifies the following:

(a) if the initial allocation of goodwill acquired in a business combination cannot be completed before the end of the annual period in which the business combination occurs, that initial allocation should be completed before the end of the first annual period beginning after the acquisition date.

(b) when an entity disposes of an operation within a cash-generating unit (group of units) to which goodwill has been allocated, the goodwill associated with that operation should be:

(i) included in the carrying amount of the operation when determining the gain or loss on disposal; and

(ii) measured on the basis of the relative values of the operation disposed of and the portion of the cash-generating unit (group of units) retained, unless the entity can demonstrate that some other method better reflects the goodwill associated with the operation disposed of.

(c) when an entity reorganises its reporting structure in a manner that changes the composition of cash-generating units (groups of units) to which goodwill has been allocated, the goodwill should be reallocated to the units (groups of units) affected. This reallocation should be performed using a relative value approach similar to that used when an entity disposes of an operation within a cash-generating unit (group of units), unless the entity can demonstrate that some other method better reflects the goodwill associated with the reorganised units (groups of units).

Timing of impairment tests for goodwill

IN13 The Standard permits:

(a) the annual impairment test for a cash-generating unit (group of units) to which goodwill has been allocated to be performed at any time during an annual reporting period, provided the test is performed at the same time every year.

(b) different cash-generating units (groups of units) to be tested for impairment at different times.

However, if some of the goodwill allocated to a cash-generating unit (group of units) was acquired in a business combination during the current annual period, the Standard requires that unit (group of units) to be tested for impairment before the end of the current period.

IN14 The Standard permits the most recent detailed calculation made in a preceding period of the recoverable amount of a cash-generating unit (group of units) to which goodwill has been allocated to be used in the impairment test for that unit (group of units) in the current period, provided specified criteria are met.

Reversals of impairment losses for goodwill

IN15 The previous version of IAS 36 required an impairment loss recognised for goodwill in a previous period to be reversed when the impairment loss was caused by a specific external event of an exceptional nature that is not expected to recur and subsequent external events have occurred that reverse the effect of that event. The Standard prohibits the recognition of reversals of impairment losses for goodwill.

Disclosure

IN16 The Standard requires that if any portion of the goodwill acquired in a business combination during the period has not been allocated to a cash-generating unit at the reporting date, an entity should disclose the amount of the unallocated goodwill together with the reasons why that amount remains unallocated.

IN17 The Standard requires disclosure of information for each cash-generating unit (group of units) for which the carrying amount of goodwill or intangible assets with indefinite useful lives allocated to that unit (group of units) is significant in comparison with the entity's total carrying amount of goodwill or intangible assets with indefinite lives. That information is concerned primarily with the key assumptions used to measure the recoverable amounts of such units (groups of units).

IN18 The Standard also requires specified information to be disclosed if some or all of the carrying amount of goodwill or intangible assets with indefinite lives is allocated across multiple cash-generating units (groups of units), and the amount so allocated to each unit (group of units) is not significant in comparison with the total carrying amount of goodwill or intangible assets with indefinite lives. Further disclosures are required if, in such circumstances, the recoverable amounts of any of those units (groups of units) are based on the same key assumption(s) and the aggregate carrying amount of goodwill or intangible assets with indefinite lives allocated to them is significant in comparison with the entity's total carrying amount of goodwill or intangible assets with indefinite lives.

International Accounting Standard 36 Impairment of Assets

Objective

1 The objective of this Standard is to prescribe the procedures that an entity applies to ensure that its assets are carried at no more than their recoverable amount. An asset is carried at more than its recoverable amount if its carrying amount exceeds the amount to be recovered through use or sale of the asset. If this is the case, the asset is described as impaired and the Standard requires the entity to recognise an impairment loss. The Standard also specifies when an entity should reverse an impairment loss and prescribes disclosures.

Scope

2 **This Standard shall be applied in accounting for the impairment of all assets, other than:**

- **(a) inventories (see IAS 2** *Inventories***);**
- **(b) assets arising from construction contracts (see IAS 11** *Construction Contracts***);**
- **(c) deferred tax assets (see IAS 12** *Income Taxes***);**
- **(d) assets arising from employee benefits (see IAS 19** *Employee Benefits***);**
- **(e) financial assets that are within the scope of IAS 39** *Financial Instruments: Recognition and Measurement***;**
- **(f) investment property that is measured at fair value (see IAS 40** *Investment Property***);**
- **(g) biological assets related to agricultural activity that are measured at fair value less estimated point-of-sale costs (see IAS 41** *Agriculture***);**
- **(h) deferred acquisition costs, and intangible assets, arising from an insurer's contractual rights under insurance contracts within the scope of IFRS 4** *Insurance Contracts***; and**
- **(i) non-current assets (or disposal groups) classified as held for sale in accordance with IFRS 5** *Non-current Assets Held for Sale and Discontinued Operations***.**

3 This Standard does not apply to inventories, assets arising from construction contracts, deferred tax assets, assets arising from employee benefits, or assets classified as held for sale (or included in a disposal group that is classified as held for sale) because existing Standards applicable to these assets contain requirements for recognising and measuring these assets.

4 This Standard applies to financial assets classified as:

- (a) subsidiaries, as defined in IAS 27 *Consolidated and Separate Financial Statements*;
- (b) associates, as defined in IAS 28 *Investments in Associates*; and
- (c) joint ventures, as defined in IAS 31 *Interests in Joint Ventures*.

For impairment of other financial assets, refer to IAS 39.

5 This Standard does not apply to financial assets within the scope of IAS 39, investment property measured at fair value in accordance with IAS 40, or biological assets related to agricultural activity measured at fair value less estimated point-of-sale costs in accordance with IAS 41. However, this Standard applies to assets that are carried at revalued amount (ie fair value) in accordance with other Standards, such as the revaluation model in IAS 16 *Property, Plant and Equipment*. Identifying whether a revalued asset may be impaired depends on the basis used to determine fair value:

(a) if the asset's fair value is its market value, the only difference between the asset's fair value and its fair value less costs to sell is the direct incremental costs to dispose of the asset:

(i) if the disposal costs are negligible, the recoverable amount of the revalued asset is necessarily close to, or greater than, its revalued amount (ie fair value). In this case, after the revaluation requirements have been applied, it is unlikely that the revalued asset is impaired and recoverable amount need not be estimated.

(ii) if the disposal costs are not negligible, the fair value less costs to sell of the revalued asset is necessarily less than its fair value. Therefore, the revalued asset will be impaired if its value in use is less than its revalued amount (ie fair value). In this case, after the revaluation requirements have been applied, an entity applies this Standard to determine whether the asset may be impaired.

(b) if the asset's fair value is determined on a basis other than its market value, its revalued amount (ie fair value) may be greater or lower than its recoverable amount. Hence, after the revaluation requirements have been applied, an entity applies this Standard to determine whether the asset may be impaired.

Definitions

6 **The following terms are used in this Standard with the meanings specified:**

An *active market* is a market in which all the following conditions exist:

(a) the items traded within the market are homogeneous;

(b) willing buyers and sellers can normally be found at any time; and

(c) prices are available to the public.

The *agreement date* for a business combination is the date that a substantive agreement between the combining parties is reached and, in the case of publicly listed entities, announced to the public. In the case of a hostile takeover, the earliest date that a substantive agreement between the combining parties is reached is the date that a sufficient number of the acquiree's owners have accepted the acquirer's offer for the acquirer to obtain control of the acquiree.

Carrying amount **is the amount at which an asset is recognised after deducting any accumulated depreciation (amortisation) and accumulated impairment losses thereon.**

A *cash-generating unit* **is the smallest identifiable group of assets that generates cash inflows that are largely independent of the cash inflows from other assets or groups of assets.**

Corporate assets **are assets other than goodwill that contribute to the future cash flows of both the cash-generating unit under review and other cash-generating units.**

Costs of disposal **are incremental costs directly attributable to the disposal of an asset or cash-generating unit, excluding finance costs and income tax expense.**

Depreciable amount **is the cost of an asset, or other amount substituted for cost in the financial statements, less its residual value.**

Depreciation (Amortisation) **is the systematic allocation of the depreciable amount of an asset over its useful life.***

Fair value less costs to sell **is the amount obtainable from the sale of an asset or cash-generating unit in an arm's length transaction between knowledgeable, willing parties, less the costs of disposal.**

An *impairment loss* **is the amount by which the carrying amount of an asset or a cash-generating unit exceeds its recoverable amount.**

The *recoverable amount* **of an asset or a cash-generating unit is the higher of its fair value less costs to sell and its value in use.**

Useful life **is either:**

(a) the period of time over which an asset is expected to be used by the entity; or

(b) the number of production or similar units expected to be obtained from the asset by the entity.

Value in use **is the present value of the future cash flows expected to be derived from an asset or cash-generating unit.**

Identifying an asset that may be impaired

7 Paragraphs 8–17 specify when recoverable amount shall be determined. These requirements use the term 'an asset' but apply equally to an individual asset or a cash-generating unit. The remainder of this Standard is structured as follows:

(a) paragraphs 18–57 set out the requirements for measuring recoverable amount. These requirements also use the term 'an asset' but apply equally to an individual asset and a cash-generating unit.

(b) paragraphs 58–108 set out the requirements for recognising and measuring impairment losses. Recognition and measurement of impairment losses for

* In the case of an intangible asset, the term 'amortisation' is generally used instead of 'depreciation'. The two terms have the same meaning.

individual assets other than goodwill are dealt with in paragraphs 58–64. Paragraphs 65–108 deal with the recognition and measurement of impairment losses for cash-generating units and goodwill.

(c) paragraphs 109–116 set out the requirements for reversing an impairment loss recognised in prior periods for an asset or a cash-generating unit. Again, these requirements use the term 'an asset' but apply equally to an individual asset or a cash-generating unit. Additional requirements for an individual asset are set out in paragraphs 117–121, for a cash-generating unit in paragraphs 122 and 123, and for goodwill in paragraphs 124 and 125.

(d) paragraphs 126–133 specify the information to be disclosed about impairment losses and reversals of impairment losses for assets and cash-generating units. Paragraphs 134–137 specify additional disclosure requirements for cash-generating units to which goodwill or intangible assets with indefinite useful lives have been allocated for impairment testing purposes.

8 An asset is impaired when its carrying amount exceeds its recoverable amount. Paragraphs 12–14 describe some indications that an impairment loss may have occurred. If any of those indications is present, an entity is required to make a formal estimate of recoverable amount. Except as described in paragraph 10, this Standard does not require an entity to make a formal estimate of recoverable amount if no indication of an impairment loss is present.

9 An entity shall assess at each reporting date whether there is any indication that an asset may be impaired. If any such indication exists, the entity shall estimate the recoverable amount of the asset.

10 Irrespective of whether there is any indication of impairment, an entity shall also:

(a) test an intangible asset with an indefinite useful life or an intangible asset not yet available for use for impairment annually by comparing its carrying amount with its recoverable amount. This impairment test may be performed at any time during an annual period, provided it is performed at the same time every year. Different intangible assets may be tested for impairment at different times. However, if such an intangible asset was initially recognised during the current annual period, that intangible asset shall be tested for impairment before the end of the current annual period.

(b) test goodwill acquired in a business combination for impairment annually in accordance with paragraphs 80–99.

11 The ability of an intangible asset to generate sufficient future economic benefits to recover its carrying amount is usually subject to greater uncertainty before the asset is available for use than after it is available for use. Therefore, this Standard requires an entity to test for impairment, at least annually, the carrying amount of an intangible asset that is not yet available for use.

12 **In assessing whether there is any indication that an asset may be impaired, an entity shall consider, as a minimum, the following indications:**

External sources of information

(a) **during the period, an asset's market value has declined significantly more than would be expected as a result of the passage of time or normal use.**

(b) **significant changes with an adverse effect on the entity have taken place during the period, or will take place in the near future, in the technological, market, economic or legal environment in which the entity operates or in the market to which an asset is dedicated.**

(c) **market interest rates or other market rates of return on investments have increased during the period, and those increases are likely to affect the discount rate used in calculating an asset's value in use and decrease the asset's recoverable amount materially.**

(d) **the carrying amount of the net assets of the entity is more than its market capitalisation.**

Internal sources of information

(e) **evidence is available of obsolescence or physical damage of an asset.**

(f) **significant changes with an adverse effect on the entity have taken place during the period, or are expected to take place in the near future, in the extent to which, or manner in which, an asset is used or is expected to be used. These changes include the asset becoming idle, plans to discontinue or restructure the operation to which an asset belongs, plans to dispose of an asset before the previously expected date, and reassessing the useful life of an asset as finite rather than indefinite.***

(g) **evidence is available from internal reporting that indicates that the economic performance of an asset is, or will be, worse than expected.**

13 The list in paragraph 12 is not exhaustive. An entity may identify other indications that an asset may be impaired and these would also require the entity to determine the asset's recoverable amount or, in the case of goodwill, perform an impairment test in accordance with paragraphs 80–99.

14 Evidence from internal reporting that indicates that an asset may be impaired includes the existence of:

(a) cash flows for acquiring the asset, or subsequent cash needs for operating or maintaining it, that are significantly higher than those originally budgeted;

(b) actual net cash flows or operating profit or loss flowing from the asset that are significantly worse than those budgeted;

* Once an asset meets the criteria to be classified as held for sale (or is included in a disposal group that is classified as held for sale), it is excluded from the scope of this Standard and is accounted for in accordance with IFRS 5 *Non-current Assets Held for Sale and Discontinued Operations*.

(c) a significant decline in budgeted net cash flows or operating profit, or a significant increase in budgeted loss, flowing from the asset; or

(d) operating losses or net cash outflows for the asset, when current period amounts are aggregated with budgeted amounts for the future.

15 As indicated in paragraph 10, this Standard requires an intangible asset with an indefinite useful life or not yet available for use and goodwill to be tested for impairment, at least annually. Apart from when the requirements in paragraph 10 apply, the concept of materiality applies in identifying whether the recoverable amount of an asset needs to be estimated. For example, if previous calculations show that an asset's recoverable amount is significantly greater than its carrying amount, the entity need not re-estimate the asset's recoverable amount if no events have occurred that would eliminate that difference. Similarly, previous analysis may show that an asset's recoverable amount is not sensitive to one (or more) of the indications listed in paragraph 12.

16 As an illustration of paragraph 15, if market interest rates or other market rates of return on investments have increased during the period, an entity is not required to make a formal estimate of an asset's recoverable amount in the following cases:

(a) if the discount rate used in calculating the asset's value in use is unlikely to be affected by the increase in these market rates. For example, increases in short-term interest rates may not have a material effect on the discount rate used for an asset that has a long remaining useful life.

(b) if the discount rate used in calculating the asset's value in use is likely to be affected by the increase in these market rates but previous sensitivity analysis of recoverable amount shows that:

(i) it is unlikely that there will be a material decrease in recoverable amount because future cash flows are also likely to increase (eg in some cases, an entity may be able to demonstrate that it adjusts its revenues to compensate for any increase in market rates); or

(ii) the decrease in recoverable amount is unlikely to result in a material impairment loss.

17 If there is an indication that an asset may be impaired, this may indicate that the remaining useful life, the depreciation (amortisation) method or the residual value for the asset needs to be reviewed and adjusted in accordance with the Standard applicable to the asset, even if no impairment loss is recognised for the asset.

Measuring recoverable amount

18 This Standard defines recoverable amount as the higher of an asset's or cash-generating unit's fair value less costs to sell and its value in use. Paragraphs 19–57 set out the requirements for measuring recoverable amount. These requirements use the term 'an asset' but apply equally to an individual asset or a cash-generating unit.

19 It is not always necessary to determine both an asset's fair value less costs to sell and its value in use. If either of these amounts exceeds the asset's carrying amount, the asset is not impaired and it is not necessary to estimate the other amount.

20 It may be possible to determine fair value less costs to sell, even if an asset is not traded in an active market. However, sometimes it will not be possible to determine fair value less costs to sell because there is no basis for making a reliable estimate of the amount obtainable from the sale of the asset in an arm's length transaction between knowledgeable and willing parties. In this case, the entity may use the asset's value in use as its recoverable amount.

21 If there is no reason to believe that an asset's value in use materially exceeds its fair value less costs to sell, the asset's fair value less costs to sell may be used as its recoverable amount. This will often be the case for an asset that is held for disposal. This is because the value in use of an asset held for disposal will consist mainly of the net disposal proceeds, as the future cash flows from continuing use of the asset until its disposal are likely to be negligible.

22 Recoverable amount is determined for an individual asset, unless the asset does not generate cash inflows that are largely independent of those from other assets or groups of assets. If this is the case, recoverable amount is determined for the cash-generating unit to which the asset belongs (see paragraphs 65–103), unless either:

(a) the asset's fair value less costs to sell is higher than its carrying amount; or

(b) the asset's value in use can be estimated to be close to its fair value less costs to sell and fair value less costs to sell can be determined.

23 In some cases, estimates, averages and computational short cuts may provide reasonable approximations of the detailed computations illustrated in this Standard for determining fair value less costs to sell or value in use.

Measuring the recoverable amount of an intangible asset with an indefinite useful life

24 Paragraph 10 requires an intangible asset with an indefinite useful life to be tested for impairment annually by comparing its carrying amount with its recoverable amount, irrespective of whether there is any indication that it may be impaired. However, the most recent detailed calculation of such an asset's recoverable amount made in a preceding period may be used in the impairment test for that asset in the current period, provided all of the following criteria are met:

(a) if the intangible asset does not generate cash inflows from continuing use that are largely independent of those from other assets or groups of assets and is therefore tested for impairment as part of the cash-generating unit to which it belongs, the assets and liabilities making up that unit have not changed significantly since the most recent recoverable amount calculation;

(b) the most recent recoverable amount calculation resulted in an amount that exceeded the asset's carrying amount by a substantial margin; and

(c) based on an analysis of events that have occurred and circumstances that have changed since the most recent recoverable amount calculation, the likelihood that a current recoverable amount determination would be less than the asset's carrying amount is remote.

Fair value less costs to sell

25 The best evidence of an asset's fair value less costs to sell is a price in a binding sale agreement in an arm's length transaction, adjusted for incremental costs that would be directly attributable to the disposal of the asset.

26 If there is no binding sale agreement but an asset is traded in an active market, fair value less costs to sell is the asset's market price less the costs of disposal. The appropriate market price is usually the current bid price. When current bid prices are unavailable, the price of the most recent transaction may provide a basis from which to estimate fair value less costs to sell, provided that there has not been a significant change in economic circumstances between the transaction date and the date as at which the estimate is made.

27 If there is no binding sale agreement or active market for an asset, fair value less costs to sell is based on the best information available to reflect the amount that an entity could obtain, at the balance sheet date, from the disposal of the asset in an arm's length transaction between knowledgeable, willing parties, after deducting the costs of disposal. In determining this amount, an entity considers the outcome of recent transactions for similar assets within the same industry. Fair value less costs to sell does not reflect a forced sale, unless management is compelled to sell immediately.

28 Costs of disposal, other than those that have been recognised as liabilities, are deducted in determining fair value less costs to sell. Examples of such costs are legal costs, stamp duty and similar transaction taxes, costs of removing the asset, and direct incremental costs to bring an asset into condition for its sale. However, termination benefits (as defined in IAS 19 *Employee Benefits*) and costs associated with reducing or reorganising a business following the disposal of an asset are not direct incremental costs to dispose of the asset.

29 Sometimes, the disposal of an asset would require the buyer to assume a liability and only a single fair value less costs to sell is available for both the asset and the liability. Paragraph 78 explains how to deal with such cases.

Value in use

30 The following elements shall be reflected in the calculation of an asset's value in use:

(a) an estimate of the future cash flows the entity expects to derive from the asset;

(b) expectations about possible variations in the amount or timing of those future cash flows;

(c) the time value of money, represented by the current market risk-free rate of interest;

(d) the price for bearing the uncertainty inherent in the asset; and

(e) **other factors, such as illiquidity, that market participants would reflect in pricing the future cash flows the entity expects to derive from the asset.**

31 Estimating the value in use of an asset involves the following steps:

(a) estimating the future cash inflows and outflows to be derived from continuing use of the asset and from its ultimate disposal; and

(b) applying the appropriate discount rate to those future cash flows.

32 The elements identified in paragraph 30(b), (d) and (e) can be reflected either as adjustments to the future cash flows or as adjustments to the discount rate. Whichever approach an entity adopts to reflect expectations about possible variations in the amount or timing of future cash flows, the result shall be to reflect the expected present value of the future cash flows, ie the weighted average of all possible outcomes. Appendix A provides additional guidance on the use of present value techniques in measuring an asset's value in use.

Basis for estimates of future cash flows

33 In measuring value in use an entity shall:

(a) base cash flow projections on reasonable and supportable assumptions that represent management's best estimate of the range of economic conditions that will exist over the remaining useful life of the asset. Greater weight shall be given to external evidence.

(b) base cash flow projections on the most recent financial budgets/forecasts approved by management, but shall exclude any estimated future cash inflows or outflows expected to arise from future restructurings or from improving or enhancing the asset's performance. Projections based on these budgets/forecasts shall cover a maximum period of five years, unless a longer period can be justified.

(c) estimate cash flow projections beyond the period covered by the most recent budgets/forecasts by extrapolating the projections based on the budgets/forecasts using a steady or declining growth rate for subsequent years, unless an increasing rate can be justified. This growth rate shall not exceed the long-term average growth rate for the products, industries, or country or countries in which the entity operates, or for the market in which the asset is used, unless a higher rate can be justified.

34 Management assesses the reasonableness of the assumptions on which its current cash flow projections are based by examining the causes of differences between past cash flow projections and actual cash flows. Management shall ensure that the assumptions on which its current cash flow projections are based are consistent with past actual outcomes, provided the effects of subsequent events or circumstances that did not exist when those actual cash flows were generated make this appropriate.

35 Detailed, explicit and reliable financial budgets/forecasts of future cash flows for periods longer than five years are generally not available. For this reason,

management's estimates of future cash flows are based on the most recent budgets/forecasts for a maximum of five years. Management may use cash flow projections based on financial budgets/forecasts over a period longer than five years if it is confident that these projections are reliable and it can demonstrate its ability, based on past experience, to forecast cash flows accurately over that longer period.

36 Cash flow projections until the end of an asset's useful life are estimated by extrapolating the cash flow projections based on the financial budgets/forecasts using a growth rate for subsequent years. This rate is steady or declining, unless an increase in the rate matches objective information about patterns over a product or industry lifecycle. If appropriate, the growth rate is zero or negative.

37 When conditions are favourable, competitors are likely to enter the market and restrict growth. Therefore, entities will have difficulty in exceeding the average historical growth rate over the long term (say, twenty years) for the products, industries, or country or countries in which the entity operates, or for the market in which the asset is used.

38 In using information from financial budgets/forecasts, an entity considers whether the information reflects reasonable and supportable assumptions and represents management's best estimate of the set of economic conditions that will exist over the remaining useful life of the asset.

Composition of estimates of future cash flows

39 Estimates of future cash flows shall include:

(a) projections of cash inflows from the continuing use of the asset;

(b) projections of cash outflows that are necessarily incurred to generate the cash inflows from continuing use of the asset (including cash outflows to prepare the asset for use) and can be directly attributed, or allocated on a reasonable and consistent basis, to the asset; and

(c) net cash flows, if any, to be received (or paid) for the disposal of the asset at the end of its useful life.

40 Estimates of future cash flows and the discount rate reflect consistent assumptions about price increases attributable to general inflation. Therefore, if the discount rate includes the effect of price increases attributable to general inflation, future cash flows are estimated in nominal terms. If the discount rate excludes the effect of price increases attributable to general inflation, future cash flows are estimated in real terms (but include future specific price increases or decreases).

41 Projections of cash outflows include those for the day-to-day servicing of the asset as well as future overheads that can be attributed directly, or allocated on a reasonable and consistent basis, to the use of the asset.

42 When the carrying amount of an asset does not yet include all the cash outflows to be incurred before it is ready for use or sale, the estimate of future cash outflows includes an estimate of any further cash outflow that is expected to be incurred before the asset is ready for use or sale. For example, this is the case for a building under construction or for a development project that is not yet completed.

43 To avoid double-counting, estimates of future cash flows do not include:

(a) cash inflows from assets that generate cash inflows that are largely independent of the cash inflows from the asset under review (for example, financial assets such as receivables); and

(b) cash outflows that relate to obligations that have been recognised as liabilities (for example, payables, pensions or provisions).

44 Future cash flows shall be estimated for the asset in its current condition. Estimates of future cash flows shall not include estimated future cash inflows or outflows that are expected to arise from:

(a) a future restructuring to which an entity is not yet committed; or

(b) improving or enhancing the asset's performance.

45 Because future cash flows are estimated for the asset in its current condition, value in use does not reflect:

(a) future cash outflows or related cost savings (for example reductions in staff costs) or benefits that are expected to arise from a future restructuring to which an entity is not yet committed; or

(b) future cash outflows that will improve or enhance the asset's performance or the related cash inflows that are expected to arise from such outflows.

46 A restructuring is a programme that is planned and controlled by management and materially changes either the scope of the business undertaken by an entity or the manner in which the business is conducted. IAS 37 *Provisions, Contingent Liabilities and Contingent Assets* contains guidance clarifying when an entity is committed to a restructuring.

47 When an entity becomes committed to a restructuring, some assets are likely to be affected by this restructuring. Once the entity is committed to the restructuring:

(a) its estimates of future cash inflows and cash outflows for the purpose of determining value in use reflect the cost savings and other benefits from the restructuring (based on the most recent financial budgets/forecasts approved by management); and

(b) its estimates of future cash outflows for the restructuring are included in a restructuring provision in accordance with IAS 37.

Illustrative Example 5 illustrates the effect of a future restructuring on a value in use calculation.

48 Until an entity incurs cash outflows that improve or enhance the asset's performance, estimates of future cash flows do not include the estimated future cash inflows that are expected to arise from the increase in economic benefits associated with the cash outflow (see Illustrative Example 6).

49 Estimates of future cash flows include future cash outflows necessary to maintain the level of economic benefits expected to arise from the asset in its current condition. When a cash-generating unit consists of assets with different estimated useful lives, all of which are essential to the ongoing operation of the unit, the replacement of assets with shorter lives is considered to be part of the day-to-day

servicing of the unit when estimating the future cash flows associated with the unit. Similarly, when a single asset consists of components with different estimated useful lives, the replacement of components with shorter lives is considered to be part of the day-to-day servicing of the asset when estimating the future cash flows generated by the asset.

50 Estimates of future cash flows shall not include:

(a) cash inflows or outflows from financing activities; or

(b) income tax receipts or payments.

51 Estimated future cash flows reflect assumptions that are consistent with the way the discount rate is determined. Otherwise, the effect of some assumptions will be counted twice or ignored. Because the time value of money is considered by discounting the estimated future cash flows, these cash flows exclude cash inflows or outflows from financing activities. Similarly, because the discount rate is determined on a pre-tax basis, future cash flows are also estimated on a pre-tax basis.

52 The estimate of net cash flows to be received (or paid) for the disposal of an asset at the end of its useful life shall be the amount that an entity expects to obtain from the disposal of the asset in an arm's length transaction between knowledgeable, willing parties, after deducting the estimated costs of disposal.

53 The estimate of net cash flows to be received (or paid) for the disposal of an asset at the end of its useful life is determined in a similar way to an asset's fair value less costs to sell, except that, in estimating those net cash flows:

(a) an entity uses prices prevailing at the date of the estimate for similar assets that have reached the end of their useful life and have operated under conditions similar to those in which the asset will be used.

(b) the entity adjusts those prices for the effect of both future price increases due to general inflation and specific future price increases or decreases. However, if estimates of future cash flows from the asset's continuing use and the discount rate exclude the effect of general inflation, the entity also excludes this effect from the estimate of net cash flows on disposal.

Foreign currency future cash flows

54 Future cash flows are estimated in the currency in which they will be generated and then discounted using a discount rate appropriate for that currency. An entity translates the present value using the spot exchange rate at the date of the value in use calculation.

Discount rate

55 The discount rate (rates) shall be a pre-tax rate (rates) that reflect(s) current market assessments of:

(a) the time value of money; and

(b) the risks specific to the asset for which the future cash flow estimates have not been adjusted.

56 A rate that reflects current market assessments of the time value of money and the risks specific to the asset is the return that investors would require if they were to choose an investment that would generate cash flows of amounts, timing and risk profile equivalent to those that the entity expects to derive from the asset. This rate is estimated from the rate implicit in current market transactions for similar assets or from the weighted average cost of capital of a listed entity that has a single asset (or a portfolio of assets) similar in terms of service potential and risks to the asset under review. However, the discount rate(s) used to measure an asset's value in use shall not reflect risks for which the future cash flow estimates have been adjusted. Otherwise, the effect of some assumptions will be double-counted.

57 When an asset-specific rate is not directly available from the market, an entity uses surrogates to estimate the discount rate. Appendix A provides additional guidance on estimating the discount rate in such circumstances.

Recognising and measuring an impairment loss

58 Paragraphs 59–64 set out the requirements for recognising and measuring impairment losses for an individual asset other than goodwill. Recognising and measuring impairment losses for cash-generating units and goodwill are dealt with in paragraphs 65–108.

59 If, and only if, the recoverable amount of an asset is less than its carrying amount, the carrying amount of the asset shall be reduced to its recoverable amount. That reduction is an impairment loss.

60 An impairment loss shall be recognised immediately in profit or loss, unless the asset is carried at revalued amount in accordance with another Standard (for example, in accordance with the revaluation model in IAS 16 ***Property, Plant and Equipment*****). Any impairment loss of a revalued asset shall be treated as a revaluation decrease in accordance with that other Standard.**

61 An impairment loss on a non-revalued asset is recognised in profit or loss. However, an impairment loss on a revalued asset is recognised directly against any revaluation surplus for the asset to the extent that the impairment loss does not exceed the amount in the revaluation surplus for that same asset.

62 When the amount estimated for an impairment loss is greater than the carrying amount of the asset to which it relates, an entity shall recognise a liability if, and only if, that is required by another Standard.

63 After the recognition of an impairment loss, the depreciation (amortisation) charge for the asset shall be adjusted in future periods to allocate the asset's revised carrying amount, less its residual value (if any), on a systematic basis over its remaining useful life.

64 If an impairment loss is recognised, any related deferred tax assets or liabilities are determined in accordance with IAS 12 *Income Taxes* by comparing the revised carrying amount of the asset with its tax base (see Illustrative Example 3).

Cash–generating units and goodwill

65 Paragraphs 66–108 set out the requirements for identifying the cash-generating unit to which an asset belongs and determining the carrying amount of, and recognising impairment losses for, cash-generating units and goodwill.

Identifying the cash–generating unit to which an asset belongs

66 **If there is any indication that an asset may be impaired, recoverable amount shall be estimated for the individual asset. If it is not possible to estimate the recoverable amount of the individual asset, an entity shall determine the recoverable amount of the cash-generating unit to which the asset belongs (the asset's cash-generating unit).**

67 The recoverable amount of an individual asset cannot be determined if:

(a) the asset's value in use cannot be estimated to be close to its fair value less costs to sell (for example, when the future cash flows from continuing use of the asset cannot be estimated to be negligible); and

(b) the asset does not generate cash inflows that are largely independent of those from other assets.

In such cases, value in use and, therefore, recoverable amount, can be determined only for the asset's cash-generating unit.

Example
A mining entity owns a private railway to support its mining activities. The private railway could be sold only for scrap value and it does not generate cash inflows that are largely independent of the cash inflows from the other assets of the mine. *It is not possible to estimate the recoverable amount of the private railway because its value in use cannot be determined and is probably different from scrap value. Therefore, the entity estimates the recoverable amount of the cash-generating unit to which the private railway belongs, ie the mine as a whole.*

68 As defined in paragraph 6, an asset's cash-generating unit is the smallest group of assets that includes the asset and generates cash inflows that are largely independent of the cash inflows from other assets or groups of assets. Identification of an asset's cash-generating unit involves judgement. If recoverable amount cannot be determined for an individual asset, an entity identifies the lowest aggregation of assets that generate largely independent cash inflows.

Example

A bus company provides services under contract with a municipality that requires minimum service on each of five separate routes. Assets devoted to each route and the cash flows from each route can be identified separately. One of the routes operates at a significant loss.

Because the entity does not have the option to curtail any one bus route, the lowest level of identifiable cash inflows that are largely independent of the cash inflows from other assets or groups of assets is the cash inflows generated by the five routes together. The cash-generating unit for each route is the bus company as a whole.

69 Cash inflows are inflows of cash and cash equivalents received from parties external to the entity. In identifying whether cash inflows from an asset (or group of assets) are largely independent of the cash inflows from other assets (or groups of assets), an entity considers various factors including how management monitors the entity's operations (such as by product lines, businesses, individual locations, districts or regional areas) or how management makes decisions about continuing or disposing of the entity's assets and operations. Illustrative Example 1 gives examples of identification of a cash-generating unit.

70 If an active market exists for the output produced by an asset or group of assets, that asset or group of assets shall be identified as a cash-generating unit, even if some or all of the output is used internally. If the cash inflows generated by any asset or cash-generating unit are affected by internal transfer pricing, an entity shall use management's best estimate of future price(s) that could be achieved in arm's length transactions in estimating:

(a) the future cash inflows used to determine the asset's or cash-generating unit's value in use; and

(b) the future cash outflows used to determine the value in use of any other assets or cash-generating units that are affected by the internal transfer pricing.

71 Even if part or all of the output produced by an asset or a group of assets is used by other units of the entity (for example, products at an intermediate stage of a production process), this asset or group of assets forms a separate cash-generating unit if the entity could sell the output on an active market. This is because the asset or group of assets could generate cash inflows that would be largely independent of the cash inflows from other assets or groups of assets. In using information based on financial budgets/forecasts that relates to such a cash-generating unit, or to any other asset or cash-generating unit affected by internal transfer pricing, an entity adjusts this information if internal transfer prices do not reflect management's best estimate of future prices that could be achieved in arm's length transactions.

72 Cash-generating units shall be identified consistently from period to period for the same asset or types of assets, unless a change is justified.

73 If an entity determines that an asset belongs to a cash-generating unit different from that in previous periods, or that the types of assets aggregated for the asset's cash-generating unit have changed, paragraph 130 requires disclosures about the cash-generating unit, if an impairment loss is recognised or reversed for the cash-generating unit.

Recoverable amount and carrying amount of a cash–generating unit

74 The recoverable amount of a cash-generating unit is the higher of the cash-generating unit's fair value less costs to sell and its value in use. For the purpose of determining the recoverable amount of a cash-generating unit, any reference in paragraphs 19–57 to 'an asset' is read as a reference to 'a cash-generating unit'.

75 The carrying amount of a cash-generating unit shall be determined on a basis consistent with the way the recoverable amount of the cash-generating unit is determined.

76 The carrying amount of a cash-generating unit:

(a) includes the carrying amount of only those assets that can be attributed directly, or allocated on a reasonable and consistent basis, to the cash-generating unit and will generate the future cash inflows used in determining the cash-generating unit's value in use; and

(b) does not include the carrying amount of any recognised liability, unless the recoverable amount of the cash-generating unit cannot be determined without consideration of this liability.

This is because fair value less costs to sell and value in use of a cash-generating unit are determined excluding cash flows that relate to assets that are not part of the cash-generating unit and liabilities that have been recognised (see paragraphs 28 and 43).

77 When assets are grouped for recoverability assessments, it is important to include in the cash-generating unit all assets that generate or are used to generate the relevant stream of cash inflows. Otherwise, the cash-generating unit may appear to be fully recoverable when in fact an impairment loss has occurred. In some cases, although some assets contribute to the estimated future cash flows of a cash-generating unit, they cannot be allocated to the cash-generating unit on a reasonable and consistent basis. This might be the case for goodwill or corporate assets such as head office assets. Paragraphs 80–103 explain how to deal with these assets in testing a cash-generating unit for impairment.

78 It may be necessary to consider some recognised liabilities to determine the recoverable amount of a cash-generating unit. This may occur if the disposal of a cash-generating unit would require the buyer to assume the liability. In this case, the fair value less costs to sell (or the estimated cash flow from ultimate disposal) of the cash-generating unit is the estimated selling price for the assets of the cash-generating unit and the liability together, less the costs of disposal. To perform a meaningful comparison between the carrying amount of the

cash-generating unit and its recoverable amount, the carrying amount of the liability is deducted in determining both the cash-generating unit's value in use and its carrying amount.

Example

A company operates a mine in a country where legislation requires that the owner must restore the site on completion of its mining operations. The cost of restoration includes the replacement of the overburden, which must be removed before mining operations commence. A provision for the costs to replace the overburden was recognised as soon as the overburden was removed. The amount provided was recognised as part of the cost of the mine and is being depreciated over the mine's useful life. The carrying amount of the provision for restoration costs is CU500,[a] which is equal to the present value of the restoration costs.

The entity is testing the mine for impairment. The cash-generating unit for the mine is the mine as a whole. The entity has received various offers to buy the mine at a price of around CU800. This price reflects the fact that the buyer will assume the obligation to restore the overburden. Disposal costs for the mine are negligible. The value in use of the mine is approximately CU1,200, excluding restoration costs. The carrying amount of the mine is CU1,000.

The cash-generating unit's fair value less costs to sell is CU800. This amount considers restoration costs that have already been provided for. As a consequence, the value in use for the cash-generating unit is determined after consideration of the restoration costs and is estimated to be CU700 (CU1,200 less CU500). The carrying amount of the cash-generating unit is CU500, which is the carrying amount of the mine (CU1,000) less the carrying amount of the provision for restoration costs (CU500.) Therefore, the recoverable amount of the cash-generating unit exceeds its carrying amount.

(a) In this Standard, monetary amounts are denominated in 'currency units' (CU).

79 For practical reasons, the recoverable amount of a cash-generating unit is sometimes determined after consideration of assets that are not part of the cash-generating unit (for example, receivables or other financial assets) or liabilities that have been recognised (for example, payables, pensions and other provisions). In such cases, the carrying amount of the cash-generating unit is increased by the carrying amount of those assets and decreased by the carrying amount of those liabilities.

Goodwill

Allocating goodwill to cash–generating units

80 **For the purpose of impairment testing, goodwill acquired in a business combination shall, from the acquisition date, be allocated to each of the acquirer's cash-generating units, or groups of cash-generating units, that are expected to benefit from the synergies of the combination, irrespective**

of whether other assets or liabilities of the acquiree are assigned to those units or groups of units. Each unit or group of units to which the goodwill is so allocated shall:

(a) represent the lowest level within the entity at which the goodwill is monitored for internal management purposes; and

(b) not be larger than a segment based on either the entity's primary or the entity's secondary reporting format determined in accordance with IAS 14 *Segment Reporting*.

81 Goodwill acquired in a business combination represents a payment made by an acquirer in anticipation of future economic benefits from assets that are not capable of being individually identified and separately recognised. Goodwill does not generate cash flows independently of other assets or groups of assets, and often contributes to the cash flows of multiple cash-generating units. Goodwill sometimes cannot be allocated on a non-arbitrary basis to individual cash-generating units, but only to groups of cash-generating units. As a result, the lowest level within the entity at which the goodwill is monitored for internal management purposes sometimes comprises a number of cash-generating units to which the goodwill relates, but to which it cannot be allocated. References in paragraphs 83–99 to a cash-generating unit to which goodwill is allocated should be read as references also to a group of cash-generating units to which goodwill is allocated.

82 Applying the requirements in paragraph 80 results in goodwill being tested for impairment at a level that reflects the way an entity manages its operations and with which the goodwill would naturally be associated. Therefore, the development of additional reporting systems is typically not necessary.

83 A cash-generating unit to which goodwill is allocated for the purpose of impairment testing may not coincide with the level at which goodwill is allocated in accordance with IAS 21 *The Effects of Changes in Foreign Exchange Rates* for the purpose of measuring foreign currency gains and losses. For example, if an entity is required by IAS 21 to allocate goodwill to relatively low levels for the purpose of measuring foreign currency gains and losses, it is not required to test the goodwill for impairment at that same level unless it also monitors the goodwill at that level for internal management purposes.

84 If the initial allocation of goodwill acquired in a business combination cannot be completed before the end of the annual period in which the business combination is effected, that initial allocation shall be completed before the end of the first annual period beginning after the acquisition date.

85 In accordance with IFRS 3 *Business Combinations*, if the initial accounting for a business combination can be determined only provisionally by the end of the period in which the combination is effected, the acquirer:

(a) accounts for the combination using those provisional values; and

(b) recognises any adjustments to those provisional values as a result of completing the initial accounting within twelve months of the acquisition date.

In such circumstances, it might also not be possible to complete the initial allocation of the goodwill acquired in the combination before the end of the annual period in which the combination is effected. When this is the case, the entity discloses the information required by paragraph 133.

86 **If goodwill has been allocated to a cash-generating unit and the entity disposes of an operation within that unit, the goodwill associated with the operation disposed of shall be:**

(a) included in the carrying amount of the operation when determining the gain or loss on disposal; and

(b) measured on the basis of the relative values of the operation disposed of and the portion of the cash-generating unit retained, unless the entity can demonstrate that some other method better reflects the goodwill associated with the operation disposed of.

Example

An entity sells for CU100 an operation that was part of a cash-generating unit to which goodwill has been allocated. The goodwill allocated to the unit cannot be identified or associated with an asset group at a level lower than that unit, except arbitrarily. The recoverable amount of the portion of the cash-generating unit retained is CU300.

Because the goodwill allocated to the cash-generating unit cannot be non-arbitrarily identified or associated with an asset group at a level lower than that unit, the goodwill associated with the operation disposed of is measured on the basis of the relative values of the operation disposed of and the portion of the unit retained. Therefore, 25 per cent of the goodwill allocated to the cash-generating unit is included in the carrying amount of the operation that is sold.

87 **If an entity reorganises its reporting structure in a way that changes the composition of one or more cash-generating units to which goodwill has been allocated, the goodwill shall be reallocated to the units affected. This reallocation shall be performed using a relative value approach similar to that used when an entity disposes of an operation within a cash-generating unit, unless the entity can demonstrate that some other method better reflects the goodwill associated with the reorganised units.**

Example

Goodwill had previously been allocated to cash-generating unit A. The goodwill allocated to A cannot be identified or associated with an asset group at a level lower than A, except arbitrarily. A is to be divided and integrated into three other cash-generating units, B, C and D.

Because the goodwill allocated to A cannot be non-arbitrarily identified or associated with an asset group at a level lower than A, it is reallocated to units B, C and D on the basis of the relative values of the three portions of A before those portions are integrated with B, C and D.

Testing cash–generating units with goodwill for impairment

88 **When, as described in paragraph 81, goodwill relates to a cash-generating unit but has not been allocated to that unit, the unit shall be tested for impairment, whenever there is an indication that the unit may be impaired, by comparing the unit's carrying amount, excluding any goodwill, with its recoverable amount. Any impairment loss shall be recognised in accordance with paragraph 104.**

89 If a cash-generating unit described in paragraph 88 includes in its carrying amount an intangible asset that has an indefinite useful life or is not yet available for use and that asset can be tested for impairment only as part of the cash-generating unit, paragraph 10 requires the unit also to be tested for impairment annually.

90 **A cash-generating unit to which goodwill has been allocated shall be tested for impairment annually, and whenever there is an indication that the unit may be impaired, by comparing the carrying amount of the unit, including the goodwill, with the recoverable amount of the unit. If the recoverable amount of the unit exceeds the carrying amount of the unit, the unit and the goodwill allocated to that unit shall be regarded as not impaired. If the carrying amount of the unit exceeds the recoverable amount of the unit, the entity shall recognise the impairment loss in accordance with paragraph 104.**

Minority interest

91 In accordance with IFRS 3, goodwill recognised in a business combination represents the goodwill acquired by a parent based on the parent's ownership interest, rather than the amount of goodwill controlled by the parent as a result of the business combination. Therefore, goodwill attributable to a minority interest is not recognised in the parent's consolidated financial statements. Accordingly, if there is a minority interest in a cash-generating unit to which goodwill has been allocated, the carrying amount of that unit comprises:

(a) both the parent's interest and the minority interest in the identifiable net assets of the unit; and

(b) the parent's interest in goodwill.

However, part of the recoverable amount of the cash-generating unit determined in accordance with this Standard is attributable to the minority interest in goodwill.

92 Consequently, for the purpose of impairment testing a non–wholly–owned cash-generating unit with goodwill, the carrying amount of that unit is notionally adjusted, before being compared with its recoverable amount. This is accomplished by grossing up the carrying amount of goodwill allocated to the unit to include the goodwill attributable to the minority interest. This notionally adjusted carrying amount is then compared with the recoverable amount of the unit to determine whether the cash-generating unit is impaired. If it is, the entity allocates the impairment loss in accordance with paragraph 104 first to reduce the carrying amount of goodwill allocated to the unit.

93 However, because goodwill is recognised only to the extent of the parent's ownership interest, any impairment loss relating to the goodwill is apportioned between that attributable to the parent and that attributable to the minority interest, with only the former being recognised as a goodwill impairment loss.

94 If the total impairment loss relating to goodwill is less than the amount by which the notionally adjusted carrying amount of the cash-generating unit exceeds its recoverable amount, paragraph 104 requires the remaining excess to be allocated to the other assets of the unit pro rata on the basis of the carrying amount of each asset in the unit.

95 Illustrative Example 7 illustrates the impairment testing of a non-wholly-owned cash-generating unit with goodwill.

Timing of impairment tests

96 The annual impairment test for a cash-generating unit to which goodwill has been allocated may be performed at any time during an annual period, provided the test is performed at the same time every year. Different cash-generating units may be tested for impairment at different times. However, if some or all of the goodwill allocated to a cash-generating unit was acquired in a business combination during the current annual period, that unit shall be tested for impairment before the end of the current annual period.

97 If the assets constituting the cash-generating unit to which goodwill has been allocated are tested for impairment at the same time as the unit containing the goodwill, they shall be tested for impairment before the unit containing the goodwill. Similarly, if the cash-generating units constituting a group of cash-generating units to which goodwill has been allocated are tested for impairment at the same time as the group of units containing the goodwill, the individual units shall be tested for impairment before the group of units containing the goodwill.

98 At the time of impairment testing a cash-generating unit to which goodwill has been allocated, there may be an indication of an impairment of an asset within the unit containing the goodwill. In such circumstances, the entity tests the asset for impairment first, and recognises any impairment loss for that asset before testing for impairment the cash-generating unit containing the goodwill. Similarly, there may be an indication of an impairment of a cash-generating unit within a group of units containing the goodwill. In such circumstances, the entity tests the cash-generating unit for impairment first, and recognises any impairment loss for that unit, before testing for impairment the group of units to which the goodwill is allocated.

99 The most recent detailed calculation made in a preceding period of the recoverable amount of a cash-generating unit to which goodwill has been allocated may be used in the impairment test of that unit in the current period provided all of the following criteria are met:

(a) the assets and liabilities making up the unit have not changed significantly since the most recent recoverable amount calculation;

(b) **the most recent recoverable amount calculation resulted in an amount that exceeded the carrying amount of the unit by a substantial margin; and**

(c) **based on an analysis of events that have occurred and circumstances that have changed since the most recent recoverable amount calculation, the likelihood that a current recoverable amount determination would be less than the current carrying amount of the unit is remote.**

Corporate assets

100 Corporate assets include group or divisional assets such as the building of a headquarters or a division of the entity, EDP equipment or a research centre. The structure of an entity determines whether an asset meets this Standard's definition of corporate assets for a particular cash-generating unit. The distinctive characteristics of corporate assets are that they do not generate cash inflows independently of other assets or groups of assets and their carrying amount cannot be fully attributed to the cash-generating unit under review.

101 Because corporate assets do not generate separate cash inflows, the recoverable amount of an individual corporate asset cannot be determined unless management has decided to dispose of the asset. As a consequence, if there is an indication that a corporate asset may be impaired, recoverable amount is determined for the cash-generating unit or group of cash-generating units to which the corporate asset belongs, and is compared with the carrying amount of this cash-generating unit or group of cash-generating units. Any impairment loss is recognised in accordance with paragraph 104.

102 In testing a cash-generating unit for impairment, an entity shall identify all the corporate assets that relate to the cash-generating unit under review. If a portion of the carrying amount of a corporate asset:

(a) **can be allocated on a reasonable and consistent basis to that unit, the entity shall compare the carrying amount of the unit, including the portion of the carrying amount of the corporate asset allocated to the unit, with its recoverable amount. Any impairment loss shall be recognised in accordance with paragraph 104.**

(b) **cannot be allocated on a reasonable and consistent basis to that unit, the entity shall:**

  (i) **compare the carrying amount of the unit, excluding the corporate asset, with its recoverable amount and recognise any impairment loss in accordance with paragraph 104;**

  (ii) **identify the smallest group of cash-generating units that includes the cash-generating unit under review and to which a portion of the carrying amount of the corporate asset can be allocated on a reasonable and consistent basis; and**

  (iii) **compare the carrying amount of that group of cash-generating units, including the portion of the carrying amount of the corporate asset allocated to that group of units, with the**

recoverable amount of the group of units. Any impairment loss shall be recognised in accordance with paragraph 104.

103 Illustrative Example 8 illustrates the application of these requirements to corporate assets.

Impairment loss for a cash-generating unit

104 An impairment loss shall be recognised for a cash-generating unit (the smallest group of cash-generating units to which goodwill or a corporate asset has been allocated) if, and only if, the recoverable amount of the unit (group of units) is less than the carrying amount of the unit (group of units). The impairment loss shall be allocated to reduce the carrying amount of the assets of the unit (group of units) in the following order:

(a) first, to reduce the carrying amount of any goodwill allocated to the cash-generating unit (group of units); and

(b) then, to the other assets of the unit (group of units) pro rata on the basis of the carrying amount of each asset in the unit (group of units).

These reductions in carrying amounts shall be treated as impairment losses on individual assets and recognised in accordance with paragraph 60.

105 In allocating an impairment loss in accordance with paragraph 104, an entity shall not reduce the carrying amount of an asset below the highest of:

(a) its fair value less costs to sell (if determinable);

(b) its value in use (if determinable); and

(c) zero.

The amount of the impairment loss that would otherwise have been allocated to the asset shall be allocated pro rata to the other assets of the unit (group of units).

106 If it is not practicable to estimate the recoverable amount of each individual asset of a cash-generating unit, this Standard requires an arbitrary allocation of an impairment loss between the assets of that unit, other than goodwill, because all assets of a cash-generating unit work together.

107 If the recoverable amount of an individual asset cannot be determined (see paragraph 67):

(a) an impairment loss is recognised for the asset if its carrying amount is greater than the higher of its fair value less costs to sell and the results of the allocation procedures described in paragraphs 104 and 105; and

(b) no impairment loss is recognised for the asset if the related cash-generating unit is not impaired. This applies even if the asset's fair value less costs to sell is less than its carrying amount.

Example

A machine has suffered physical damage but is still working, although not as well as before it was damaged. The machine's fair value less costs to sell is less than its carrying amount. The machine does not generate independent cash inflows. The smallest identifiable group of assets that includes the machine and generates cash inflows that are largely independent of the cash inflows from other assets is the production line to which the machine belongs. The recoverable amount of the production line shows that the production line taken as a whole is not impaired.

Assumption 1: budgets/forecasts approved by management reflect no commitment of management to replace the machine.

The recoverable amount of the machine alone cannot be estimated because the machine's value in use:

(a) may differ from its fair value less costs to sell; and

(b) can be determined only for the cash-generating unit to which the machine belongs (the production line).

The production line is not impaired. Therefore, no impairment loss is recognised for the machine. Nevertheless, the entity may need to reassess the depreciation period or the depreciation method for the machine. Perhaps a shorter depreciation period or a faster depreciation method is required to reflect the expected remaining useful life of the machine or the pattern in which economic benefits are expected to be consumed by the entity.

Assumption 2: budgets/forecasts approved by management reflect a commitment of management to replace the machine and sell it in the near future. Cash flows from continuing use of the machine until its disposal are estimated to be negligible.

The machine's value in use can be estimated to be close to its fair value less costs to sell. Therefore, the recoverable amount of the machine can be determined and no consideration is given to the cash-generating unit to which the machine belongs (ie the production line). Because the machine's fair value less costs to sell is less than its carrying amount, an impairment loss is recognised for the machine.

108 **After the requirements in paragraphs 104 and 105 have been applied, a liability shall be recognised for any remaining amount of an impairment loss for a cash-generating unit if, and only if, that is required by another Standard.**

Reversing an impairment loss

109 Paragraphs 110–116 set out the requirements for reversing an impairment loss recognised for an asset or a cash-generating unit in prior periods. These requirements use the term 'an asset' but apply equally to an individual asset or a cash-generating unit. Additional requirements for an individual asset are set out in paragraphs 117–121, for a cash-generating unit in paragraphs 122 and 123 and for goodwill in paragraphs 124 and 125.

110 **An entity shall assess at each reporting date whether there is any indication that an impairment loss recognised in prior periods for an asset other than goodwill may no longer exist or may have decreased. If any such indication exists, the entity shall estimate the recoverable amount of that asset.**

111 **In assessing whether there is any indication that an impairment loss recognised in prior periods for an asset other than goodwill may no longer exist or may have decreased, an entity shall consider, as a minimum, the following indications:**

External sources of information

(a) **the asset's market value has increased significantly during the period.**

(b) **significant changes with a favourable effect on the entity have taken place during the period, or will take place in the near future, in the technological, market, economic or legal environment in which the entity operates or in the market to which the asset is dedicated.**

(c) **market interest rates or other market rates of return on investments have decreased during the period, and those decreases are likely to affect the discount rate used in calculating the asset's value in use and increase the asset's recoverable amount materially.**

Internal sources of information

(d) **significant changes with a favourable effect on the entity have taken place during the period, or are expected to take place in the near future, in the extent to which, or manner in which, the asset is used or is expected to be used. These changes include costs incurred during the period to improve or enhance the asset's performance or restructure the operation to which the asset belongs.**

(e) **evidence is available from internal reporting that indicates that the economic performance of the asset is, or will be, better than expected.**

112 Indications of a potential decrease in an impairment loss in paragraph 111 mainly mirror the indications of a potential impairment loss in paragraph 12.

113 If there is an indication that an impairment loss recognised for an asset other than goodwill may no longer exist or may have decreased, this may indicate that the remaining useful life, the depreciation (amortisation) method or the residual value may need to be reviewed and adjusted in accordance with the Standard applicable to the asset, even if no impairment loss is reversed for the asset.

114 **An impairment loss recognised in prior periods for an asset other than goodwill shall be reversed if, and only if, there has been a change in the estimates used to determine the asset's recoverable amount since the last impairment loss was recognised. If this is the case, the carrying amount of the asset shall, except as described in paragraph 117, be increased to its recoverable amount. That increase is a reversal of an impairment loss.**

115 A reversal of an impairment loss reflects an increase in the estimated service potential of an asset, either from use or from sale, since the date when an entity last recognised an impairment loss for that asset. Paragraph 130 requires an entity to identify the change in estimates that causes the increase in estimated service potential. Examples of changes in estimates include:

(a) a change in the basis for recoverable amount (ie whether recoverable amount is based on fair value less costs to sell or value in use);

(b) if recoverable amount was based on value in use, a change in the amount or timing of estimated future cash flows or in the discount rate; or

(c) if recoverable amount was based on fair value less costs to sell, a change in estimate of the components of fair value less costs to sell.

116 An asset's value in use may become greater than the asset's carrying amount simply because the present value of future cash inflows increases as they become closer. However, the service potential of the asset has not increased. Therefore, an impairment loss is not reversed just because of the passage of time (sometimes called the 'unwinding' of the discount), even if the recoverable amount of the asset becomes higher than its carrying amount.

Reversing an impairment loss for an individual asset

117 The increased carrying amount of an asset other than goodwill attributable to a reversal of an impairment loss shall not exceed the carrying amount that would have been determined (net of amortisation or depreciation) had no impairment loss been recognised for the asset in prior years.

118 Any increase in the carrying amount of an asset other than goodwill above the carrying amount that would have been determined (net of amortisation or depreciation) had no impairment loss been recognised for the asset in prior years is a revaluation. In accounting for such a revaluation, an entity applies the Standard applicable to the asset.

119 A reversal of an impairment loss for an asset other than goodwill shall be recognised immediately in profit or loss, unless the asset is carried at revalued amount in accordance with another Standard (for example, the revaluation model in IAS 16 *Property, Plant and Equipment*). Any reversal of an impairment loss of a revalued asset shall be treated as a revaluation increase in accordance with that other Standard.

120 A reversal of an impairment loss on a revalued asset is credited directly to equity under the heading revaluation surplus. However, to the extent that an impairment loss on the same revalued asset was previously recognised in profit or loss, a reversal of that impairment loss is also recognised in profit or loss.

121 After a reversal of an impairment loss is recognised, the depreciation (amortisation) charge for the asset shall be adjusted in future periods to allocate the asset's revised carrying amount, less its residual value (if any), on a systematic basis over its remaining useful life.

Reversing an impairment loss for a cash-generating unit

122 **A reversal of an impairment loss for a cash-generating unit shall be allocated to the assets of the unit, except for goodwill, pro rata with the carrying amounts of those assets. These increases in carrying amounts shall be treated as reversals of impairment losses for individual assets and recognised in accordance with paragraph 119.**

123 **In allocating a reversal of an impairment loss for a cash-generating unit in accordance with paragraph 122, the carrying amount of an asset shall not be increased above the lower of:**

(a) its recoverable amount (if determinable); and

(b) the carrying amount that would have been determined (net of amortisation or depreciation) had no impairment loss been recognised for the asset in prior periods.

The amount of the reversal of the impairment loss that would otherwise have been allocated to the asset shall be allocated pro rata to the other assets of the unit, except for goodwill.

Reversing an impairment loss for goodwill

124 **An impairment loss recognised for goodwill shall not be reversed in a subsequent period.**

125 IAS 38 *Intangible Assets* prohibits the recognition of internally generated goodwill. Any increase in the recoverable amount of goodwill in the periods following the recognition of an impairment loss for that goodwill is likely to be an increase in internally generated goodwill, rather than a reversal of the impairment loss recognised for the acquired goodwill.

Disclosure

126 **An entity shall disclose the following for each class of assets:**

(a) the amount of impairment losses recognised in profit or loss during the period and the line item(s) of the income statement in which those impairment losses are included.

(b) the amount of reversals of impairment losses recognised in profit or loss during the period and the line item(s) of the income statement in which those impairment losses are reversed.

(c) the amount of impairment losses on revalued assets recognised directly in equity during the period.

(d) the amount of reversals of impairment losses on revalued assets recognised directly in equity during the period.

127 A class of assets is a grouping of assets of similar nature and use in an entity's operations.

128 The information required in paragraph 126 may be presented with other information disclosed for the class of assets. For example, this information may

be included in a reconciliation of the carrying amount of property, plant and equipment, at the beginning and end of the period, as required by IAS 16 *Property, Plant and Equipment*.

129 **An entity that reports segment information in accordance with IAS 14** *Segment Reporting* **shall disclose the following for each reportable segment based on an entity's primary reporting format:**

- **(a) the amount of impairment losses recognised in profit or loss and directly in equity during the period.**
- **(b) the amount of reversals of impairment losses recognised in profit or loss and directly in equity during the period.**

130 **An entity shall disclose the following for each material impairment loss recognised or reversed during the period for an individual asset, including goodwill, or a cash-generating unit:**

- **(a) the events and circumstances that led to the recognition or reversal of the impairment loss.**
- **(b) the amount of the impairment loss recognised or reversed.**
- **(c) for an individual asset:**
  - **(i) the nature of the asset; and**
  - **(ii) if the entity reports segment information in accordance with IAS 14, the reportable segment to which the asset belongs, based on the entity's primary reporting format.**
- **(d) for a cash-generating unit:**
  - **(i) a description of the cash-generating unit (such as whether it is a product line, a plant, a business operation, a geographical area, or a reportable segment as defined in IAS 14);**
  - **(ii) the amount of the impairment loss recognised or reversed by class of assets and, if the entity reports segment information in accordance with IAS 14, by reportable segment based on the entity's primary reporting format; and**
  - **(iii) if the aggregation of assets for identifying the cash-generating unit has changed since the previous estimate of the cash-generating unit's recoverable amount (if any), a description of the current and former way of aggregating assets and the reasons for changing the way the cash-generating unit is identified.**
- **(e) whether the recoverable amount of the asset (cash-generating unit) is its fair value less costs to sell or its value in use.**
- **(f) if recoverable amount is fair value less costs to sell, the basis used to determine fair value less costs to sell (such as whether fair value was determined by reference to an active market).**
- **(g) if recoverable amount is value in use, the discount rate(s) used in the current estimate and previous estimate (if any) of value in use.**

131 **An entity shall disclose the following information for the aggregate impairment losses and the aggregate reversals of impairment losses recognised during the period for which no information is disclosed in accordance with paragraph 130:**

(a) the main classes of assets affected by impairment losses and the main classes of assets affected by reversals of impairment losses.

(b) the main events and circumstances that led to the recognition of these impairment losses and reversals of impairment losses.

132 An entity is encouraged to disclose assumptions used to determine the recoverable amount of assets (cash-generating units) during the period. However, paragraph 134 requires an entity to disclose information about the estimates used to measure the recoverable amount of a cash-generating unit when goodwill or an intangible asset with an indefinite useful life is included in the carrying amount of that unit.

133 **If, in accordance with paragraph 84, any portion of the goodwill acquired in a business combination during the period has not been allocated to a cash-generating unit (group of units) at the reporting date, the amount of the unallocated goodwill shall be disclosed together with the reasons why that amount remains unallocated.**

Estimates used to measure recoverable amounts of cash–generating units containing goodwill or intangible assets with indefinite useful lives

134 **An entity shall disclose the information required by (a)–(f) for each cash-generating unit (group of units) for which the carrying amount of goodwill or intangible assets with indefinite useful lives allocated to that unit (group of units) is significant in comparison with the entity's total carrying amount of goodwill or intangible assets with indefinite useful lives:**

(a) the carrying amount of goodwill allocated to the unit (group of units).

(b) the carrying amount of intangible assets with indefinite useful lives allocated to the unit (group of units).

(c) the basis on which the unit's (group of units') recoverable amount has been determined (ie value in use or fair value less costs to sell).

(d) if the unit's (group of units') recoverable amount is based on value in use:

(i) a description of each key assumption on which management has based its cash flow projections for the period covered by the most recent budgets/forecasts. Key assumptions are those to which the unit's (group of units') recoverable amount is most sensitive.

(ii) a description of management's approach to determining the value(s) assigned to each key assumption, whether those value(s) reflect past experience or, if appropriate, are consistent with external sources of information, and, if not, how and why they differ from past experience or external sources of information.

(iii) the period over which management has projected cash flows based on financial budgets/forecasts approved by management and, when a period greater than five years is used for a cash-generating unit (group of units), an explanation of why that longer period is justified.

(iv) the growth rate used to extrapolate cash flow projections beyond the period covered by the most recent budgets/forecasts, and the justification for using any growth rate that exceeds the long-term average growth rate for the products, industries, or country or countries in which the entity operates, or for the market to which the unit (group of units) is dedicated.

(v) the discount rate(s) applied to the cash flow projections.

(e) if the unit's (group of units') recoverable amount is based on fair value less costs to sell, the methodology used to determine fair value less costs to sell. If fair value less costs to sell is not determined using an observable market price for the unit (group of units), the following information shall also be disclosed:

(i) a description of each key assumption on which management has based its determination of fair value less costs to sell. Key assumptions are those to which the unit's (group of units') recoverable amount is most sensitive.

(ii) a description of management's approach to determining the value(s) assigned to each key assumption, whether those value(s) reflect past experience or, if appropriate, are consistent with external sources of information, and, if not, how and why they differ from past experience or external sources of information.

(f) if a reasonably possible change in a key assumption on which management has based its determination of the unit's (group of units') recoverable amount would cause the unit's (group of units') carrying amount to exceed its recoverable amount:

(i) the amount by which the unit's (group of units') recoverable amount exceeds its carrying amount.

(ii) the value assigned to the key assumption.

(iii) the amount by which the value assigned to the key assumption must change, after incorporating any consequential effects of that change on the other variables used to measure recoverable amount, in order for the unit's (group of units') recoverable amount to be equal to its carrying amount.

135 **If some or all of the carrying amount of goodwill or intangible assets with indefinite useful lives is allocated across multiple cash-generating units (groups of units), and the amount so allocated to each unit (group of units) is not significant in comparison with the entity's total carrying amount of goodwill or intangible assets with indefinite useful lives, that fact shall be disclosed, together with the aggregate carrying amount of goodwill or intangible assets with indefinite useful lives allocated to those units**

(groups of units). In addition, if the recoverable amounts of any of those units (groups of units) are based on the same key assumption(s) and the aggregate carrying amount of goodwill or intangible assets with indefinite useful lives allocated to them is significant in comparison with the entity's total carrying amount of goodwill or intangible assets with indefinite useful lives, an entity shall disclose that fact, together with:

(a) the aggregate carrying amount of goodwill allocated to those units (groups of units).

(b) the aggregate carrying amount of intangible assets with indefinite useful lives allocated to those units (groups of units).

(c) a description of the key assumption(s).

(d) a description of management's approach to determining the value(s) assigned to the key assumption(s), whether those value(s) reflect past experience or, if appropriate, are consistent with external sources of information, and, if not, how and why they differ from past experience or external sources of information.

(e) if a reasonably possible change in the key assumption(s) would cause the aggregate of the units' (groups of units') carrying amounts to exceed the aggregate of their recoverable amounts:

(i) the amount by which the aggregate of the units' (groups of units') recoverable amounts exceeds the aggregate of their carrying amounts.

(ii) the value(s) assigned to the key assumption(s).

(iii) the amount by which the value(s) assigned to the key assumption(s) must change, after incorporating any consequential effects of the change on the other variables used to measure recoverable amount, in order for the aggregate of the units' (groups of units') recoverable amounts to be equal to the aggregate of their carrying amounts.

136 The most recent detailed calculation made in a preceding period of the recoverable amount of a cash-generating unit (group of units) may, in accordance with paragraph 24 or 99, be carried forward and used in the impairment test for that unit (group of units) in the current period provided specified criteria are met. When this is the case, the information for that unit (group of units) that is incorporated into the disclosures required by paragraphs 134 and 135 relate to the carried forward calculation of recoverable amount.

137 Illustrative Example 9 illustrates the disclosures required by paragraphs 134 and 135.

Transitional provisions and effective date

138 If an entity elects in accordance with paragraph 85 of IFRS 3 ***Business Combinations*** **to apply IFRS 3 from any date before the effective dates set out in paragraphs 78–84 of IFRS 3, it also shall apply this Standard prospectively from that same date.**

139 **Otherwise, an entity shall apply this Standard:**

(a) to goodwill and intangible assets acquired in business combinations for which the agreement date is on or after 31 March 2004; and

(b) to all other assets prospectively from the beginning of the first annual period beginning on or after 31 March 2004.

140 **Entities to which paragraph 139 applies are encouraged to apply the requirements of this Standard before the effective dates specified in paragraph 139. However, if an entity applies this Standard before those effective dates, it also shall apply IFRS 3 and IAS 38** *Intangible Assets* **(as revised in 2004) at the same time.**

Withdrawal of IAS 36 (issued 1998)

141 This Standard supersedes IAS 36 *Impairment of Assets* (issued in 1998).

Appendix A
Using present value techniques to measure value in use

This appendix is an integral part of the Standard. It provides guidance on the use of present value techniques in measuring value in use. Although the guidance uses the term 'asset', it equally applies to a group of assets forming a cash-generating unit.

The components of a present value measurement

A1 The following elements together capture the economic differences between assets:

(a) an estimate of the future cash flow, or in more complex cases, series of future cash flows the entity expects to derive from the asset;

(b) expectations about possible variations in the amount or timing of those cash flows;

(c) the time value of money, represented by the current market risk-free rate of interest;

(d) the price for bearing the uncertainty inherent in the asset; and

(e) other, sometimes unidentifiable, factors (such as illiquidity) that market participants would reflect in pricing the future cash flows the entity expects to derive from the asset.

A2 This appendix contrasts two approaches to computing present value, either of which may be used to estimate the value in use of an asset, depending on the circumstances. Under the 'traditional' approach, adjustments for factors (b)–(e) described in paragraph A1 are embedded in the discount rate. Under the 'expected cash flow' approach, factors (b), (d) and (e) cause adjustments in arriving at risk-adjusted expected cash flows. Whichever approach an entity adopts to reflect expectations about possible variations in the amount or timing of future cash flows, the result should be to reflect the expected present value of the future cash flows, ie the weighted average of all possible outcomes.

General principles

A3 The techniques used to estimate future cash flows and interest rates will vary from one situation to another depending on the circumstances surrounding the asset in question. However, the following general principles govern any application of present value techniques in measuring assets:

(a) interest rates used to discount cash flows should reflect assumptions that are consistent with those inherent in the estimated cash flows. Otherwise, the effect of some assumptions will be double-counted or ignored. For example, a discount rate of 12 per cent might be applied to contractual cash flows of a loan receivable. That rate reflects expectations about future defaults from loans with particular characteristics. That same 12 per cent rate should not be used to discount expected cash flows because those cash flows already reflect assumptions about future defaults.

(b) estimated cash flows and discount rates should be free from both bias and factors unrelated to the asset in question. For example, deliberately understating estimated net cash flows to enhance the apparent future profitability of an asset introduces a bias into the measurement.

(c) estimated cash flows or discount rates should reflect the range of possible outcomes rather than a single most likely, minimum or maximum possible amount.

Traditional and expected cash flow approaches to present value

Traditional approach

A4 Accounting applications of present value have traditionally used a single set of estimated cash flows and a single discount rate, often described as 'the rate commensurate with the risk'. In effect, the traditional approach assumes that a single discount rate convention can incorporate all the expectations about the future cash flows and the appropriate risk premium. Therefore, the traditional approach places most of the emphasis on selection of the discount rate.

A5 In some circumstances, such as those in which comparable assets can be observed in the marketplace, a traditional approach is relatively easy to apply. For assets with contractual cash flows, it is consistent with the manner in which marketplace participants describe assets, as in 'a 12 per cent bond'.

A6 However, the traditional approach may not appropriately address some complex measurement problems, such as the measurement of non-financial assets for which no market for the item or a comparable item exists. A proper search for 'the rate commensurate with the risk' requires analysis of at least two items–an asset that exists in the marketplace and has an observed interest rate and the asset being measured. The appropriate discount rate for the cash flows being measured must be inferred from the observable rate of interest in that other asset. To draw that inference, the characteristics of the other asset's cash flows must be similar to those of the asset being measured. Therefore, the measurer must do the following:

(a) identify the set of cash flows that will be discounted;

(b) identify another asset in the marketplace that appears to have similar cash flow characteristics;

(c) compare the cash flow sets from the two items to ensure that they are similar (for example, are both sets contractual cash flows, or is one contractual and the other an estimated cash flow?);

(d) evaluate whether there is an element in one item that is not present in the other (for example, is one less liquid than the other?); and

(e) evaluate whether both sets of cash flows are likely to behave (ie vary) in a similar fashion in changing economic conditions.

Expected cash flow approach

A7 The expected cash flow approach is, in some situations, a more effective measurement tool than the traditional approach. In developing a measurement, the expected cash flow approach uses all expectations about possible cash flows instead of the single most likely cash flow. For example, a cash flow might be

CU100, CU200 or CU300 with probabilities of 10 per cent, 60 per cent and 30 per cent, respectively. The expected cash flow is CU220. The expected cash flow approach thus differs from the traditional approach by focusing on direct analysis of the cash flows in question and on more explicit statements of the assumptions used in the measurement.

A8 The expected cash flow approach also allows use of present value techniques when the timing of cash flows is uncertain. For example, a cash flow of CU1,000 may be received in one year, two years or three years with probabilities of 10 per cent, 60 per cent and 30 per cent, respectively. The example below shows the computation of expected present value in that situation.

Present value of CU1,000 in 1 year at 5%	CU952.38	
Probability	10.00%	CU95.24
Present value of CU1,000 in 2 years at 5.25%	CU902.73	
Probability	60.00%	CU541.64
Present value of CU1,000 in 3 years at 5.50%	CU851.61	
Probability	30.00%	CU255.48
Expected present value		CU892.36

A9 The expected present value of CU892.36 differs from the traditional notion of a best estimate of CU902.73 (the 60 per cent probability). A traditional present value computation applied to this example requires a decision about which of the possible timings of cash flows to use and, accordingly, would not reflect the probabilities of other timings. This is because the discount rate in a traditional present value computation cannot reflect uncertainties in timing.

A10 The use of probabilities is an essential element of the expected cash flow approach. Some question whether assigning probabilities to highly subjective estimates suggests greater precision than, in fact, exists. However, the proper application of the traditional approach (as described in paragraph A6) requires the same estimates and subjectivity without providing the computational transparency of the expected cash flow approach.

A11 Many estimates developed in current practice already incorporate the elements of expected cash flows informally. In addition, accountants often face the need to measure an asset using limited information about the probabilities of possible cash flows. For example, an accountant might be confronted with the following situations:

(a) the estimated amount falls somewhere between CU50 and CU250, but no amount in the range is more likely than any other amount. Based on that limited information, the estimated expected cash flow is CU150 [(50 + 250)/2].

(b) the estimated amount falls somewhere between CU50 and CU250, and the most likely amount is CU100. However, the probabilities attached to each amount are unknown. Based on that limited information, the estimated expected cash flow is CU133.33 [(50 + 100 + 250)/3].

(c) the estimated amount will be CU50 (10 per cent probability), CU250 (30 per cent probability), or CU100 (60 per cent probability). Based on that limited information, the estimated expected cash flow is CU140 [(50 × 0.10) + (250 × 0.30) + (100 × 0.60)].

In each case, the estimated expected cash flow is likely to provide a better estimate of value in use than the minimum, most likely or maximum amount taken alone.

A12 The application of an expected cash flow approach is subject to a cost-benefit constraint. In some cases, an entity may have access to extensive data and may be able to develop many cash flow scenarios. In other cases, an entity may not be able to develop more than general statements about the variability of cash flows without incurring substantial cost. The entity needs to balance the cost of obtaining additional information against the additional reliability that information will bring to the measurement.

A13 Some maintain that expected cash flow techniques are inappropriate for measuring a single item or an item with a limited number of possible outcomes. They offer an example of an asset with two possible outcomes: a 90 per cent probability that the cash flow will be CU10 and a 10 per cent probability that the cash flow will be CU1,000. They observe that the expected cash flow in that example is CU109 and criticise that result as not representing either of the amounts that may ultimately be paid.

A14 Assertions like the one just outlined reflect underlying disagreement with the measurement objective. If the objective is accumulation of costs to be incurred, expected cash flows may not produce a representationally faithful estimate of the expected cost. However, this Standard is concerned with measuring the recoverable amount of an asset. The recoverable amount of the asset in this example is not likely to be CU10, even though that is the most likely cash flow. This is because a measurement of CU10 does not incorporate the uncertainty of the cash flow in the measurement of the asset. Instead, the uncertain cash flow is presented as if it were a certain cash flow. No rational entity would sell an asset with these characteristics for CU10.

Discount rate

A15 Whichever approach an entity adopts for measuring the value in use of an asset, interest rates used to discount cash flows should not reflect risks for which the estimated cash flows have been adjusted. Otherwise, the effect of some assumptions will be double-counted.

A16 When an asset-specific rate is not directly available from the market, an entity uses surrogates to estimate the discount rate. The purpose is to estimate, as far as possible, a market assessment of:

(a) the time value of money for the periods until the end of the asset's useful life; and

(b) factors (b), (d) and (e) described in paragraph A1, to the extent those factors have not caused adjustments in arriving at estimated cash flows.

A17 As a starting point in making such an estimate, the entity might take into account the following rates:

(a) the entity's weighted average cost of capital determined using techniques such as the Capital Asset Pricing Model;

(b) the entity's incremental borrowing rate; and

(c) other market borrowing rates.

A18 However, these rates must be adjusted:

(a) to reflect the way that the market would assess the specific risks associated with the asset's estimated cash flows; and

(b) to exclude risks that are not relevant to the asset's estimated cash flows or for which the estimated cash flows have been adjusted.

Consideration should be given to risks such as country risk, currency risk and price risk.

A19 The discount rate is independent of the entity's capital structure and the way the entity financed the purchase of the asset, because the future cash flows expected to arise from an asset do not depend on the way in which the entity financed the purchase of the asset.

A20 Paragraph 55 requires the discount rate used to be a pre-tax rate. Therefore, when the basis used to estimate the discount rate is post-tax, that basis is adjusted to reflect a pre-tax rate.

A21 An entity normally uses a single discount rate for the estimate of an asset's value in use. However, an entity uses separate discount rates for different future periods where value in use is sensitive to a difference in risks for different periods or to the term structure of interest rates.

Appendix B
Amendment to IAS 16

The amendment in this appendix shall be applied when an entity applies IAS 16 Property, Plant and Equipment *(as revised in 2003). It is superseded when IAS 36* Impairment of Assets *(as revised in 2004) becomes effective. This appendix replaces the consequential amendments made by IAS 16 (as revised in 2003) to IAS 36* Impairment of Assets *(issued in 1998). IAS 36 (as revised in 2004) incorporates the requirements of the paragraphs in this appendix. Consequently, the amendments from IAS 16 (as revised in 2003) are not necessary once an entity is subject to IAS 36 (as revised in 2004). Accordingly, this appendix is applicable only to entities that elect to apply IAS 16 (as revised in 2003) before its effective date.*

* * * * *

The text of this appendix has been omitted from this volume.

Approval of IAS 36 by the Board

International Accounting Standard 36 *Impairment of Assets* was approved for issue by eleven of the fourteen members of the International Accounting Standards Board. Messrs Cope and Leisenring and Professor Whittington dissented. Their dissenting opinions are set out after the Basis for Conclusions on IAS 36.

Sir David Tweedie	Chairman
Thomas E Jones	Vice-Chairman
Mary E Barth	
Hans-Georg Bruns	
Anthony T Cope	
Robert P Garnett	
Gilbert Gélard	
James J Leisenring	
Warren J McGregor	
Patricia L O'Malley	
Harry K Schmid	
John T Smith	
Geoffrey Whittington	
Tatsumi Yamada	

CONTENTS

---

* In IFRS 5 *Non-current Assets Held for Sale and Discontinued Operations*, issued by the IASB in 2004, the term 'net selling price' was replaced in IAS 36 by 'fair value less costs to sell'.

Basis for Conclusions on IAS 36 Impairment of Assets

The International Accounting Standards Board revised IAS 36 as part of its project on business combinations. It was not the Board's intention to reconsider as part of that project all of the requirements in IAS 36.

The previous version of IAS 36 was accompanied by a Basis for Conclusions summarising the former International Accounting Standards Committee's considerations in reaching some of its conclusions in that Standard. For convenience the Board has incorporated into its own Basis for Conclusions material from the previous Basis for Conclusions that discusses (a) matters the Board did not reconsider and (b) the history of the development of a standard on impairment of assets. That material is contained in paragraphs denoted by numbers with the prefix BCZ. Paragraphs describing the Board's considerations in reaching its own conclusions are numbered with the prefix BC.

Introduction

BC1 This Basis for Conclusions summarises the International Accounting Standards Board's considerations in reaching the conclusions in IAS 36 *Impairment of Assets*. Individual Board members gave greater weight to some factors than to others.

BC2 The International Accounting Standards Committee (IASC) issued the previous version of IAS 36 in 1998. It has been revised by the Board as part of its project on business combinations. That project has two phases. The first has resulted in the Board issuing simultaneously IFRS 3 *Business Combinations* and revised versions of IAS 36 and IAS 38 *Intangible Assets*. Therefore, the Board's intention in revising IAS 36 as part of the first phase of the project was not to reconsider all of the requirements in IAS 36. The changes to IAS 36 are primarily concerned with the impairment tests for intangible assets with indefinite useful lives (hereafter referred to as 'indefinite-lived intangibles') and goodwill. The Board has not deliberated the other requirements in IAS 36. Those other requirements will be considered by the Board as part of a future project on impairment of assets.

BC3 The previous version of IAS 36 was accompanied by a Basis for Conclusions summarising IASC's considerations in reaching some of its conclusions in that Standard. For convenience, the Board has incorporated into this Basis for Conclusions material from the previous Basis for Conclusions that discusses matters the Board did not consider. That material is contained in paragraphs denoted by numbers with the prefix BCZ. The views expressed in paragraphs denoted by numbers with the prefix BCZ are those of IASC.

Scope (paragraph 2)

BCZ4 IAS 2 *Inventories* requires an enterprise to measure the recoverable amount of inventory at its net realisable value. IASC believed that there was no need to revise this requirement because it was well accepted as an appropriate test for recoverability of inventories. No major difference exists between IAS 2 and the requirements included in IAS 36 (see paragraphs BCZ37–BCZ39).

BCZ5 IAS 11 *Construction Contracts* and IAS 12 *Income Taxes* already deal with the impairment of assets arising from construction contracts and deferred tax assets respectively. Under both IAS 11 and IAS 12, recoverable amount is, in effect, determined on an undiscounted basis. IASC acknowledged that this was inconsistent with the requirements of IAS 36. However, IASC believed that it was not possible to eliminate that inconsistency without fundamental changes to IAS 11 and IAS 12. IASC had no plans to revise IAS 11 or IAS 12.

BCZ6 IAS 19 *Employee Benefits* contains an upper limit on the amount at which an enterprise should recognise an asset arising from employee benefits. Therefore, IAS 36 does not deal with such assets. The limit in IAS 19 is determined on a discounted basis that is broadly compatible with the requirements of IAS 36. The limit does not override the deferred recognition of certain actuarial losses and certain past service costs.

BCZ7 IAS 39 *Financial Instruments: Recognition and Measurement* sets out the requirements for impairment of financial assets.

BCZ8 IAS 36 is applicable to all assets, unless specifically excluded, regardless of their classification as current or non-current. Before IAS 36 was issued, there was no International Accounting Standard on accounting for the impairment of current assets other than inventories.

Measuring recoverable amount (paragraphs 18–57)

BCZ9 In determining the principles that should govern the measurement of recoverable amount, IASC considered, as a first step, what an enterprise will do if it discovers that an asset is impaired. IASC concluded that, in such cases, an enterprise will either keep the asset or dispose of it. For example, if an enterprise discovers that the service potential of an asset has decreased:

(a) the enterprise may decide to sell the asset if the net proceeds from the sale would provide a higher return on investment than continuing use in operations; or

(b) the enterprise may decide to keep the asset and use it, even if its service potential is lower than originally expected. Some reasons may be that:

   (i) the asset cannot be sold or disposed of immediately;

   (ii) the asset can be sold only at a low price;

   (iii) the asset's service potential can still be recovered but only with additional efforts or expenditure; or

   (iv) the asset could still be profitable although not to the same extent as expected originally.

IASC concluded that the resulting decision from a rational enterprise is, in substance, an investment decision based on estimated net future cash flows expected from the asset.

BCZ10 IASC then considered which of the following four alternatives for determining the recoverable amount of an asset would best reflect this conclusion:

(a) recoverable amount should be the sum of undiscounted future cash flows.

(b) recoverable amount should be the asset's fair value: more specifically, recoverable amount should be derived primarily from the asset's market value. If market value cannot be determined, then recoverable amount should be based on the asset's value in use as a proxy for market value.

(c) recoverable amount should be the asset's value in use.

(d) recoverable amount should be the higher of the asset's net selling price and value in use.*

Each of these alternatives is discussed below.

BCZ11 It should be noted that fair value, net selling price and value in use all reflect a present value calculation (implicit or explicit) of estimated net future cash flows expected from an asset:

(a) fair value reflects the market's expectation of the present value of the future cash flows to be derived from the asset;

(b) net selling price reflects the market's expectation of the present value of the future cash flows to be derived from the asset, less the direct incremental costs to dispose of the asset; and

(c) value in use is the enterprise's estimate of the present value of the future cash flows to be derived from continuing use and disposal of the asset.

These bases all consider the time value of money and the risks that the amount and timing of the actual cash flows to be received from an asset might differ from estimates. Fair value and net selling price may differ from value in use because the market may not use the same assumptions as an individual enterprise.

Recoverable amount based on the sum of undiscounted cash flows

BCZ12 Some argue that recoverable amount should be measured as the sum of undiscounted future cash flows from an asset. They argue that:

(a) historical cost accounting is not concerned with measuring the economic value of assets. Therefore, the time value of money should not be considered in estimating the amount that will be recovered from an asset.

(b) it is premature to use discounting techniques without further research and debates on:

(i) the role of discounting in the financial statements; and

(ii) how assets should be measured generally.

If financial statements include assets that are carried on a variety of different bases (historical cost, discounted amounts or other bases), this will be confusing for users.

(c) identifying an appropriate discount rate will often be difficult and subjective.

(d) discounting will increase the number of impairment losses recognised. This, coupled with the requirement for reversals of impairment losses, introduces a volatile element into the income statement. It will make it harder for users to understand the performance of an enterprise.

* In IFRS 5 *Non-current Assets Held for Sale and Discontinued Operations*, issued by the IASB in 2004, the term 'net selling price' was replaced in IAS 36 by 'fair value less costs to sell'.

A minority of commentators on E55 *Impairment of Assets* supported this view.

BCZ13 IASC rejected measurement of recoverable amount based on the sum of undiscounted cash flows because:

(a) the objective of the measurement of recoverable amount is to reflect an investment decision. Money has a time value, even when prices are stable. If future cash flows were not discounted, two assets giving rise to cash flows of the same amount but with different timings would show the same recoverable amount. However, their current market values would be different because all rational economic transactions take account of the time value of money.

(b) measurements that take into consideration the time value of money are more relevant to investors, other external users of financial statements and management for resource allocation decisions, regardless of the general measurement basis adopted in the financial statements.

(c) many enterprises were already familiar with the use of discounting techniques, particularly for supporting investment decisions.

(d) discounting was already required for other areas of financial statements that are based on expectations of future cash flows, such as long-term provisions and employee benefit obligations.

(e) users are better served if they are aware on a timely basis of assets that will not generate sufficient returns to cover, at least, the time value of money.

Recoverable amount based on fair value

BCZ14 IAS 32 *Financial Instruments: Disclosure and Presentation* and a number of other International Accounting Standards define fair value as:

'... the amount for which an asset could be exchanged, or a liability settled, between knowledgeable, willing parties in an arm's length transaction...'

BCZ15 International Accounting Standards include the following requirements or guidance for measuring fair value:

(a) for the purpose of revaluation of an item of property, plant or equipment to its fair value, IAS 16 *Property, Plant and Equipment* indicates that fair value is usually an asset's market value, normally determined by appraisal undertaken by professionally qualified valuers and, if no market exists, fair value is based on the asset's depreciated replacement cost.

(b) for the purpose of revaluation of an intangible asset to its fair value, IASC proposed in E60 *Intangible Assets* that fair value be determined by reference to market values obtained from an active market. E60 proposed a definition of an active market.*

(c) IASC proposed revisions to IAS 22 (see E61 *Business Combinations*) so that fair value would be determined without consideration of the acquirer's intentions for the future use of an asset.†

* IASC approved an International Accounting Standard on intangible assets in 1998.

† IASC approved revisions to IAS 22 *Business Combinations* in 1998.

(d) IAS 39[*] indicates that if an active market exists, the fair value of a financial instrument is based on a quoted market price. If there is no active market, fair value is determined by using estimation techniques such as market values of similar types of financial instruments, discounted cash flow analysis and option pricing models.

BCZ16 Some argue that the only appropriate measurement for the recoverable amount of an asset is fair value (based on observable market prices or, if no observable market prices exist, estimated considering prices for similar assets and the results of discounted future cash flow calculations). Proponents of fair value argue that:

(a) the purpose of measuring recoverable amount is to estimate a market value, not an enterprise-specific value. An enterprise's estimate of the present value of future cash flows is subjective and in some cases may be abused. Observable market prices that reflect the judgement of the market place are a more reliable measurement of the amounts that will be recovered from an asset. They reduce the use of management's judgement.

(b) if an asset is expected to generate greater net cash inflows for the enterprise than for other participants, the superior returns are almost always generated by internally generated goodwill stemming from the synergy of the business and its management team. For consistency with IASC's proposals in E60 that internally generated goodwill should not be recognised as an asset, these above-market cash flows should be excluded from assessments of an asset's recoverable amount.

(c) determining recoverable amount as the higher of net selling price and value in use is tantamount to determining two diverging measures whilst there should be only one measure to estimate recoverable amount.

A minority of commentators on E55 supported measuring recoverable amount at fair value (based on observable market prices or, if no observable market prices exist, estimated considering prices for similar assets and the results of discounted future cash flow calculations).

BCZ17 IASC rejected the proposal that an asset's recoverable amount should be determined by reference to its fair value (based on observable market prices or, if no observable market prices exist, estimated considering prices for similar assets and the results of discounted future cash flow calculations). The reasons are the following:

(a) IASC believed that no preference should be given to the market's expectation of the recoverable amount of an asset (basis for fair value when market values are available and for net selling price) over a reasonable estimate performed by the individual enterprise that owns the asset (basis for fair value when market values are not available and for value in use). For example, an enterprise may have information about future cash flows that is superior to the information available in the market place. Also, an enterprise may plan to use an asset in a manner different from the market's view of the best use.

* The IASB's project to revise IAS 32 and IAS 39 in 2003 resulted in the relocation of the requirements on fair value measurement from IAS 32 to IAS 39.

(b) market values are a way to estimate fair value but only if they reflect the fact that both parties, the acquirer and the seller, are willing to enter a transaction. If an enterprise can generate greater cash flows by using an asset than by selling it, it would be misleading to base recoverable amount on the market price of the asset because a rational enterprise would not be willing to sell the asset. Therefore, recoverable amount should not refer only to a transaction between two parties (which is unlikely to happen) but should also consider an asset's service potential from its use by the enterprise.

(c) IASC believed that in assessing the recoverable amount of an asset, it is the amount that an enterprise can expect to recover from that asset, including the effect of synergy with other assets, that is relevant.

The following two examples illustrate the proposal (rejected by IASC) that an enterprise should measure an asset's recoverable amount at its fair value (primarily based on observable market values if these values are available).

Example 1

10 years ago, an enterprise bought its headquarters building for 2,000. Since then, the real estate market has collapsed and the building's market value at balance sheet date is estimated to be 1,000. Disposal costs of the building would be negligible. The building's carrying amount at the balance sheet date is 1,500 and its remaining useful life is 30 years. The building meets all the enterprise's expectations and it is likely that these expectations will be met for the foreseeable future. As a consequence, the enterprise has no plans to move from its current headquarters. The value in use of the building cannot be determined because the building does not generate independent cash inflows. Therefore, the enterprise assesses the recoverable amount of the building's cash-generating unit, that is, the enterprise as a whole. That calculation shows that the building's cash-generating unit is not impaired.

Proponents of fair value (primarily based on observable market values if these values are available) would measure the recoverable amount of the building at its market value (1,000) and, hence, would recognise an impairment loss of 500 (1,500 less 1,000), even though calculations show that the building's cash-generating unit is not impaired.

IASC did not support this approach and believed that the building was not impaired. IASC believed that, in the situation described, the enterprise would not be willing to sell the building for 1,000 and that the assumption of a sale was not relevant.

Example 2

At the end of 20X0, an enterprise purchased a computer for 100 for general use in its operations. The computer is depreciated over 4 years on a straight-line basis. Residual value is estimated to be nil. At the end of 20X2, the carrying amount of the computer is 50. There is an active market for second-hand computers of this type. The market value of the computer is 30. The enterprise does not intend to replace the computer before the end of its useful life. The computer's cash-generating unit is not impaired.

Proponents of fair value (primarily based on observable market values if these values are available) would measure the recoverable amount of the computer at its market value (30) and, therefore, would recognise an impairment loss of 20 (50 less 30) even though the computer's cash-generating unit is not impaired.

IASC did not support this approach and believed that the computer was not impaired as long as:

(a) *the enterprise was not committed to dispose of the computer before the end of its expected useful life; and*

(b) *the computer's cash-generating unit was not impaired.*

BCZ18 If no deep and liquid market exists for an asset, IASC considered that value in use would be a reasonable estimate of fair value. This is likely to happen for many assets within the scope of IAS 36: observable market prices are unlikely to exist for goodwill, most intangible assets and many items of property, plant and equipment. Therefore, it is likely that the recoverable amount of these assets, determined in accordance with IAS 36, will be similar to the recoverable amount based on the fair value of these assets.

BCZ19 For some assets within the scope of IAS 36, observable market prices exist or consideration of prices for similar assets is possible. In such cases, the asset's net selling price will differ from the asset's fair value only by the direct incremental costs of disposal. IASC acknowledged that recoverable amount as the higher of net selling price and value in use would sometimes differ from fair value primarily based on market prices (even if the disposal costs are negligible). This is because, as explained in paragraph BCZ17(a), the market may not use the same assumptions about future cash flows as an individual enterprise.

BCZ20 IASC believed that IAS 36 included sufficient requirements to prevent an enterprise from using assumptions different from the market place that are unjustified. For example, an enterprise is required to determine value in use using:

(a) cash flow projections based on reasonable and supportable assumptions and giving greater weight to external evidence; and

(b) a discount rate that reflects current market assessments of the time value of money and the risks specific to the asset.

Recoverable amount based on value in use

BCZ21 Some argue that value in use is the only appropriate measurement for the recoverable amount of an asset because:

(a) financial statements are prepared under a going concern assumption. Therefore, no consideration should be given to an alternative measurement that reflects a disposal, unless this reflects the enterprise's intentions.

(b) assets should not be carried at amounts higher than their service potential from use by the enterprise. Unlike value in use, a market value does not necessarily reflect the service potential of an asset.

Few commentators on E55 supported this view.

BCZ22 IASC rejected this proposal because:

(a) if an asset's net selling price is higher than its value in use, a rational enterprise will dispose of the asset. In this situation, it is logical to base recoverable amount on the asset's net selling price to avoid recognising an impairment loss that is unrelated to economic reality.

(b) if an asset's net selling price is greater than its value in use, but management decides to keep the asset, the extra loss (the difference between net selling price and value in use) properly falls in later periods because it results from management's decision in these later periods to keep the asset.

Recoverable amount based on the higher of net selling price and value in use*

BCZ23 The requirement that recoverable amount should be the higher of net selling price and value in use stems from the decision that measurement of the recoverable amount of an asset should reflect the likely behaviour of a rational management. Furthermore, no preference should be given to the market's expectation of the recoverable amount of an asset (basis for net selling price) over a reasonable estimate performed by the individual enterprise which owns the asset (basis for value in use) or vice versa (see paragraphs BCZ17–BCZ20 and BCZ22). It is uncertain whether the assumptions of the market or the enterprise are more likely to be true. Currently, perfect markets do not exist for many of the assets within the scope of IAS 36 and it is unlikely that predictions of the future will be entirely accurate, regardless of who makes them.

BCZ24 IASC acknowledged that an enterprise would use judgement in determining whether an impairment loss needed to be recognised. For this reason, IAS 36 included some safeguards to limit the risk that an enterprise may make an over-optimistic (pessimistic) estimate of recoverable amount:

(a) IAS 36 requires a formal estimate of recoverable amount whenever there is an indication that:

(i) an asset may be impaired; or

(ii) an impairment loss may no longer exist or may have decreased.

* In IFRS 5 *Non-current Assets Held for Sale and Discontinued Operations*, issued by the IASB in 2004, the term 'net selling price' was replaced in IAS 36 by 'fair value less costs to sell'.

For this purpose, IAS 36 includes a relatively detailed (although not exhaustive) list of indicators that an asset may be impaired (see paragraphs 12 and 111 of IAS 36).

(b) IAS 36 provides guidelines for the basis of management's projections of future cash flows to be used to estimate value in use (see paragraph 33 of IAS 36).

BCZ25 IASC considered the cost of requiring an enterprise to determine both net selling price and value in use, if the amount determined first is below an asset's carrying amount. IASC concluded that the benefits of such a requirement outweigh the costs.

BCZ26 The majority of the commentators on E55 supported IASC's view that recoverable amount should be measured at the higher of net selling price and value in use.

Assets held for disposal

BCZ27 IASC considered whether the recoverable amount of an asset held for disposal should be measured only at the asset's net selling price. When an enterprise expects to dispose of an asset within the near future, the net selling price of the asset is normally close to its value in use. Indeed, the value in use usually consists mostly of the net proceeds to be received for the asset, since future cash flows from continuing use are usually close to nil. Therefore, IASC believed that the definition of recoverable amount as included in IAS 36 is appropriate for assets held for disposal without a need for further requirements or guidance.

Other refinements to the measurement of recoverable amount

Replacement cost as a ceiling

BCZ28 Some argue that the replacement cost of an asset should be adopted as a ceiling for its recoverable amount. They argue that the value of an asset to the business would not exceed the amount that the enterprise would be willing to pay for the asset at the balance sheet date.

BCZ29 IASC believed that replacement cost techniques are not appropriate to measuring the recoverable amount of an asset. This is because replacement cost measures the cost of an asset and not the future economic benefits recoverable from its use and/or disposal.

Appraisal values

BCZ30 In some cases, an enterprise might seek external appraisal of recoverable amount. External appraisal is not a separate technique in its own right. IASC believed that if appraisal values are used, an enterprise should verify that the external appraisal follows the requirements of IAS 36.

Net selling price (paragraphs 25–29)*

BCZ31 IAS 36 defines net selling price as the amount obtainable from the sale of an asset in an arm's length transaction between knowledgeable, willing parties, less the incremental costs directly attributable to the disposal of the asset.

BCZ32 In other words, net selling price reflects the market's expectations of the future cash flows for an asset after the market's consideration of the time value of money and the risks inherent in receiving those cash flows, less the disposal costs.

BCZ33 Some argue that direct incremental costs of disposal should not be deducted from the amount obtainable from the sale of an asset because, unless management has decided to dispose of the asset, the going concern assumption should apply.

BCZ34 IASC believed that it is appropriate to deduct direct incremental costs of disposal in determining net selling price because the purpose of the exercise is to determine the net amount that an enterprise could recover from the sale of an asset at the date of the measurement and to compare it with the alternative of keeping the asset and using it.

BCZ35 IAS 36 indicates that termination benefits (as defined in IAS 19 *Employee Benefits*) and costs associated with reducing or reorganising a business following the disposal of an asset are not direct incremental costs to dispose of the asset. IASC considered these costs as incidental to (rather than a direct consequence of) the disposal of an asset. In addition, this guidance is consistent with the direction of the project on provisions.†

BCZ36 Although the definition of 'net selling price' would be similar to a definition of 'net fair value', IASC decided to use the term 'net selling price' instead of 'net fair value'. IASC believed that the term 'net selling price' better describes the amount that an enterprise should determine and that will be compared with an asset's value in use.

Net realisable value

BCZ37 IAS 2 *Inventories* defines net realisable value as:

'... the estimated selling price in the ordinary course of business ... less the estimated costs necessary to make the sale...'

BCZ38 For the purpose of determining recoverable amount, IASC decided not to use the term 'net realisable value' as defined in IAS 2 because:

(a) IAS 2's definition of net realisable value does not refer explicitly to transactions carried out on an arm's length basis.

(b) net realisable value refers to an estimated selling price in the ordinary course of business. In certain cases, net selling price will reflect a forced sale, if management is compelled to sell immediately.

* In IFRS 5 *Non-current Assets Held for Sale and Discontinued Operations*, issued by the IASB in 2004, the term 'net selling price' was replaced in IAS 36 by 'fair value less costs to sell'.

† IASC approved an International Accounting Standard on provisions, contingent liabilities and contingent assets in 1998.

(c) it is important that net selling price uses, as a starting point, a selling price agreed between knowledgeable, willing buyers and sellers. This is not explicitly mentioned in the definition of net realisable value.

BCZ39 In most cases, net selling price and net realisable value will be similar. However, IASC did not believe that it was necessary to change the definition of net realisable value used in IAS 2 because, for inventories, the definition of net realisable value is well understood and seems to work satisfactorily.

Value in use (paragraphs 30–57 and the Appendix)

BCZ40 IAS 36 defines value in use as the present value of the future cash flows expected to be derived from an asset.

Expected value approach

BCZ41 Some argue that, to better reflect uncertainties in timing and amounts inherent in estimated future cash flows, expected future cash flows should be used in determining value in use. An expected value approach considers all expectations about possible future cash flows instead of the single, most likely, future cash flows.

Example
An enterprise estimates that there are two scenarios for future cash flows: a first possibility of future cash flows amounts to 120 with a 40 per cent probability and a second possibility amounts to 80 with a 60 per cent probability. *The most likely future cash flows would be 80 and the expected future cash flows would be 96 (80 × 60% + 120 × 40%).*

BCZ42 In most cases, it is likely that budgets/forecasts that are the basis for cash flow projections will reflect a single estimate of future cash flows only. For this reason, IASC decided that an expected value approach should be permitted but not required.

Future cash flows from internally generated goodwill and synergy with other assets

BCZ43 IASC rejected a proposal that estimates of future cash inflows should reflect only future cash inflows relating to the asset that was initially recognised (or the remaining portion of that asset if part of it has already been consumed or sold). The purpose of such a requirement would be to avoid including in an asset's value in use future cash inflows from internally generated goodwill or from synergy with other assets. This would be consistent with IASC's proposal in E60 *Intangible Assets* to prohibit the recognition of internally generated goodwill as an asset.*

BCZ44 In many cases, it will not be possible in practice to distinguish future cash inflows from the asset initially recognised from the future cash inflows from internally generated goodwill or a modification of the asset. This is particularly true when

* IASC approved an International Accounting Standard on intangible assets in 1998.

businesses are merged or once an asset has been enhanced by subsequent expenditure. IASC concluded that it is more important to focus on whether the carrying amount of an asset will be recovered rather than on whether the recovery stems partly from internally generated goodwill.

BCZ45 The proposal–that future cash inflows should reflect only future cash inflows relating to the asset that was initially recognised–would also conflict with the requirement under IAS 36 that cash flow projections should reflect reasonable and supportable assumptions that represent management's best estimate of the set of economic conditions that will exist over the remaining useful life of the asset (see paragraph 33 of IAS 36). Therefore, the Standard requires that future cash inflows should be estimated for an asset in its current condition, whether or not these future cash inflows are from the asset that was initially recognised or from its subsequent enhancement or modification.

Example

Several years ago, an enterprise purchased a customer list with 10,000 addresses that it recognised as an intangible asset. The enterprise uses this list for direct marketing of its products. Since initial recognition, about 2,000 customer addresses have been deleted from the list and 3,000 new customer addresses added to it. The enterprise is determining the value in use of the customer list.

Under the proposal (rejected by IASC) that an enterprise should reflect only future cash inflows relating to the asset that was initially recognised, the enterprise would consider only those future cash inflows generated by the remaining 8,000 (10,000 less 2,000) customers from the list acquired.

Under IAS 36, an enterprise considers the future cash inflows generated by the customer list in its current condition, ie by all 11,000 customers (8,000 plus 3,000).

Value in use estimated in a foreign currency (paragraph 54)

BCZ46 In response to comments from field test participants, paragraph 54 of IAS 36 includes guidance on calculating the value in use of an asset that generates future cash flows in a foreign currency. IAS 36 indicates that value in use in a foreign currency is translated into the reporting currency* using the spot exchange rate at the balance sheet date.

BCZ47 If a currency is freely convertible and traded in an active market, the spot rate reflects the market's best estimate of future events that will affect that currency. Therefore, the only available unbiased estimate of a future exchange rate is the current spot rate, adjusted by the difference in expected future rates of general inflation in the two countries to which the currencies belong.

* In IAS 21 *The Effects of Changes in Foreign Exchange Rates*, as revised by the IASB in 2003, the term 'reporting currency' was replaced by 'functional currency'.

BCZ48 A value in use calculation already deals with the effect of general inflation since it is calculated either by:

(a) estimating future cash flows in nominal terms (ie including the effect of general inflation and specific price changes) and discounting them at a rate that includes the effects of general inflation; or

(b) estimating future cash flows in real terms (ie excluding the effect of general inflation but including the effect of specific price changes) and discounting them at a rate that excludes the effect of general inflation.

BCZ49 To use a forward rate to translate value in use expressed in a foreign currency would be inappropriate. This is because a forward rate reflects the market's adjustment for the differential in interest rates. Using such a rate would result in double-counting the time value of money (first in the discount rate and then in the forward rate).

BCZ50 Even if a currency is not freely convertible or is not traded in an active market—with the consequence that it can no longer be assumed that the spot exchange rate reflects the market's best estimate of future events that will affect that currency—IAS 36 indicates that an enterprise uses the spot exchange rate at the balance sheet date to translate value in use estimated in a foreign currency. This is because IASC believed that it is unlikely that an enterprise can make a more reliable estimate of future exchange rates than the current spot exchange rate.

BCZ51 An alternative to estimating the future cash flows in the currency in which they are generated would be to estimate them in another currency as a proxy and discount them at a rate appropriate for this other currency. This solution may be simpler, particularly where cash flows are generated in the currency of a hyperinflationary economy (in such cases, some would prefer using a hard currency as a proxy) or in a currency other than the reporting currency. However, this solution may be misleading if the exchange rate varies for reasons other than changes in the differential between the general inflation rates in the two countries to which the currencies belong. In addition, this solution is inconsistent with the approach under IAS 29 *Financial Reporting in Hyperinflationary Economies*, which does not allow, if the reporting currency* is the currency of a hyperinflationary economy, translation into a hard currency as a proxy for restatement in terms of the measuring unit current at the balance sheet date.

Discount rate (paragraphs 55–57 and A15–A21)

BCZ52 The purpose of discounting future cash flows is to reflect the time value of money and the uncertainties attached to those cash flows:

(a) assets that generate cash flows soon are worth more than those generating the same cash flows later. All rational economic transactions will take account of the time value of money. The cost of not receiving a cash inflow until some date in the future is an opportunity cost that can be measured by considering what income has been lost by not investing that money for the

* In IAS 21 *The Effects of Changes in Foreign Exchange Rates*, as revised by the IASB in 2003, the term 'reporting currency' was replaced by 'functional currency'.

period. The time value of money, before consideration of risk, is given by the rate of return on a risk-free investment, such as government bonds of the same duration.

(b) the value of the future cash flows is affected by the variability (ie the risks) associated with the cash flows. Therefore, all rational economic transactions will take risk into account.

BCZ53 As a consequence IASC decided:

(a) to reject a discount rate based on a historical rate–ie the effective rate implicit when an asset was acquired. A subsequent estimate of recoverable amount has to be based on prevailing interest rates because management's decisions about whether to keep the asset are based on prevailing economic conditions. Historical rates do not reflect prevailing economic conditions.

(b) to reject a discount rate based on a risk-free rate, unless the future cash flows have been adjusted for all the risks specific to the asset.

(c) to require that the discount rate should be a rate that reflects current market assessments of the time value of money and the risks specific to the asset. This rate is the return that investors would require if they were to choose an investment that would generate cash flows of amounts, timing and risk profile equivalent to those that the enterprise expects to derive from the asset.

BCZ54 In principle, value in use should be an enterprise-specific measure determined in accordance with the enterprise's own view of the best use of that asset. Logically, the discount rate should be based on the enterprise's own assessment both of the time value of money and of the risks specific to the future cash flows from the asset. However, IASC believed that such a rate could not be verified objectively. Therefore, IAS 36 requires that the enterprise should make its own estimate of future cash flows but that the discount rate should reflect, as far as possible, the market's assessment of the time value of money. Similarly, the discount rate should reflect the premium that the market would require from uncertain future cash flows based on the distribution estimated by the enterprise.

BCZ55 IASC acknowledged that a current asset-specific market-determined rate would rarely exist for the assets covered by IAS 36. Therefore, an enterprise uses current market-determined rates for other assets (as similar as possible to the asset under review) as a starting point and adjusts these rates to reflect the risks specific to the asset for which the cash flow projections have not been adjusted.

Additional guidance included in the Standard in 2004

Elements reflected in value in use (paragraphs 30–32)

BC56 The Exposure Draft of Proposed Amendments to IAS 36 proposed, and the revised Standard includes, additional guidance to clarify:

(a) the elements that are reflected in an asset's value in use; and

(b) that some of those elements (ie expectations about possible variations in the amount or timing of future cash flows, the price for bearing the uncertainty inherent in the asset, and other factors that market participants would reflect in pricing the future cash flows the entity expects to derive from the asset) can be reflected either as adjustments to the future cash flows or as adjustments to the discount rate.

The Board decided to include this additional guidance in the Exposure Draft in response to a number of requests from its constituents for clarification of the requirements in the previous version of IAS 36 on measuring value in use.

BC57 Respondents to the Exposure Draft generally agreed with the proposals. Those that disagreed varied widely in their views, arguing that:

(a) IAS 36 should be amended to permit entities to measure value in use using methods other than discounting of future cash flows.

(b) when measuring the value in use of an intangible asset, entities should be required to reflect the price for bearing the uncertainty inherent in the asset as adjustments to the future cash flows.

(c) it is inconsistent with the definition of value in use to reflect in that measure the other factors that market participants would reflect in pricing the future cash flows the entity expects to derive from the asset—this element refers to market pricing of an asset rather than to the value to the entity of the asset. Other factors should be reflected in value in use only to the extent that they affect the cash flows the entity can achieve from the asset.

BC58 In considering (a) above, the Board observed that the measure of recoverable amount in IAS 36 (ie higher of value in use and fair value less costs to sell) stems from IASC's decision that an asset's recoverable amount should reflect the likely behaviour of a rational management, with no preference given to the market's expectation of the recoverable amount of an asset (ie fair value less costs to sell) over a reasonable estimate performed by the entity that controls the asset (ie value in use) or vice versa (see paragraph BCZ23). In developing the Exposure Draft and revising IAS 36, the Board concluded that it would be inappropriate to modify the measurement basis adopted in the previous version of IAS 36 for determining recoverable amount until the Board considers and resolves the broader question of the appropriate measurement objective(s) in accounting. Moreover, IAS 36 does not preclude the use of other valuation techniques in estimating fair value less costs to sell. For example, paragraph 27 of the Standard states that 'If there is no binding sale agreement or active market for an asset, fair value less costs to sell is based on the best information available to reflect the amount that an entity could obtain, at the balance sheet date, from the disposal of the asset in an arm's length transaction between knowledgeable, willing parties, after deducting the costs of disposal.'

BC59 In considering (b) above, the Board observed that the previous version of IAS 36 permitted risk adjustments to be reflected either in the cash flows or in the discount rate, without indicating a preference. The Board could see no justification for amending this approach to require risk adjustments for uncertainty to be factored into the cash flows, particularly given the Board's inclination to avoid modifying the requirements in the previous version of IAS 36 for determining recoverable amount until it considers and resolves the broader question of measurement in accounting. Additionally, the Board as part of its consultative process conducted field visits and round-table discussions during the comment period for the Exposure Draft.* Many field visit participants indicated a preference for reflecting such risk adjustments in the discount rate.

BC60 In considering (c) above, the Board observed that the measure of value in use adopted in IAS 36 is not a pure 'entity-specific' measure. Although the cash flows used as the starting point in the calculation represent entity-specific cash flows (ie they are derived from the most recent financial budgets/forecasts approved by management and represent management's best estimate of the set of economic conditions that will exist over the remaining useful life of the asset), their present value is required to be determined using a discount rate that reflects current market assessments of the time value of money and the risks specific to the asset. Paragraph 56 of the Standard (paragraph 49 of the previous version of IAS 36) clarifies that 'A rate that reflects current market assessments of the time value of money and the risks specific to the asset is the return that investors would require if they were to choose an investment that would generate cash flows of amounts, timing and risk profile equivalent to those that the entity expects to derive from the asset.' In other words, an asset's value in use reflects how the market would price the cash flows that management expects to derive from that asset.

BC61 Therefore, the Board concluded that:

(a) it is consistent with the measure of value in use adopted in IAS 36 to include in the list of elements the other factors that market participants would reflect in pricing the future cash flows the entity expects to derive from the asset.

(b) all of the elements proposed in the Exposure Draft (and listed in paragraph 30 of the revised Standard) should be reflected in the calculation of an asset's value in use.

Estimates of future cash flows (paragraphs 33, 34 and 44)

BC62 The Exposure Draft proposed requiring cash flow projections used in measuring value in use to be based on reasonable and supportable assumptions that take into account both past actual cash flows and management's past ability to forecast cash flows accurately.

BC63 Many respondents to the Exposure Draft disagreed with this proposal, arguing that:

(a) the reasons for past cash flow forecasts differing from actual cash flows may be irrelevant to the current projections. For example, if there has been a major change in management, management's past ability to forecast cash flows might not be relevant to the current projections. Additionally, a poor record of forecasting cash flows accurately might be the result of factors

* The field visits were conducted from early December 2002 to early April 2003, and involved IASB members and staff in meetings with 41 companies in Australia, France, Germany, Japan, South Africa, Switzerland and the United Kingdom. IASB members and staff also took part in a series of round-table discussions with auditors, preparers, accounting standard-setters and regulators in Canada and the United States on implementation issues encountered by North American companies during first-time application of US Statements of Financial Accounting Standards 141 *Business Combinations* and 142 *Goodwill and Other Intangible Assets*, and the equivalent Canadian Handbook Sections, which were issued in June 2001.

outside of management's control (such as the events of September 11, 2001), rather than indicative of management bias.

(b) it is unclear how, in practice, the assumptions on which the cash flow projections are based could take into account past differences between management's forecasts and actual cash flows.

(c) the proposal is inconsistent with the requirement to base cash flow projections on the most recent financial budgets/forecasts approved by management.

BC64 The Board observed that, as worded, the proposal would have *required* the assumptions on which the cash flow forecasts are based to be adjusted for past actual cash flows and management's past ability to forecast cash flows accurately. The Board agreed with respondents that it is not clear how, in practice, this might be achieved, and that in some circumstances past actual cash flows and management's past ability to forecast cash flows accurately might not be relevant to the development of current forecasts. However, the Board remained of the view that in developing the assumptions on which the cash flow forecasts are based, management should remain mindful of, and when appropriate make the necessary adjustments for, an entity's actual past performance or previous history of management consistently overstating or understating cash flow forecasts.

BC65 Therefore, the Board decided not to proceed with the proposal, but instead to include in paragraph 34 of the Standard guidance clarifying that management:

(a) should assess the reasonableness of the assumptions on which its current cash flow projections are based by examining the causes of differences between past cash flow projections and actual cash flows; and

(b) should ensure that the assumptions on which its current cash flow projections are based are consistent with past actual outcomes, provided the effects of subsequent events or circumstances that did not exist when those actual cash flows were generated make this appropriate.

BC66 In finalising the Standard the Board also considered two issues identified by respondents to the Exposure Draft and referred to the Board by the International Financial Reporting Interpretations Committee. Both issues related to the application of paragraphs 27(b) and 37 of the previous version of IAS 36 (now paragraphs 33(b) and 44). The Board did not reconsider those paragraphs when developing the Exposure Draft.

BC67 Paragraph 27(b) required the cash flow projections used to measure value in use to be based on the most recent financial budgets/forecasts that have been approved by management. Paragraph 37, however, required the future cash flows to be estimated for the asset [or cash-generating unit] in its current condition and excluded estimated future cash inflows or outflows that are expected to arise from: (a) a future restructuring to which an enterprise is not yet committed; or (b) future capital expenditure that will improve or enhance the asset [or cash-generating unit] in excess of its originally assessed standard of performance.*

BC68 The first issue the Board considered related to the acquisition of a cash-generating unit when:

(a) the price paid for the unit was based on projections that included a major restructuring expected to result in a substantial increase in the net cash inflows derived from the unit; and

(b) there is no observable market from which to estimate the unit's fair value less costs to sell.

Respondents expressed concern that if the net cash inflows arising from the restructuring were not reflected in the unit's value in use, comparison of the unit's recoverable amount and carrying amount immediately after the acquisition would result in the recognition of an impairment loss.

BC69 The Board agreed with respondents that, all else being equal, the value in use of a newly acquired unit would, in accordance with IAS 36, be less than the price paid for the unit to the extent that the price includes the net benefits of a future restructuring to which the entity is not yet committed. However, this does not mean that a comparison of the unit's recoverable amount with its carrying amount immediately after the acquisition will result in the recognition of an impairment loss. The Board observed that:

(a) recoverable amount is measured in accordance with IAS 36 as the higher of value in use and fair value less costs to sell. Fair value less costs to sell is defined in the Standard as 'the amount obtainable from the sale of an asset or cash-generating unit in an arm's length transaction between knowledgeable, willing parties, less the costs of disposal.'

(b) paragraphs 25–27 of the Standard provide guidance on estimating fair value less costs to sell. In accordance with that guidance, the best evidence of a recently acquired unit's fair value less costs to sell is likely to be the arm's length price the entity paid to acquire the unit, adjusted for disposal costs and for any changes in economic circumstances between the transaction date and the date at which the estimate is made.

(c) if the unit's fair value less costs to sell were to be otherwise estimated, it would also reflect the market's assessment of the expected net benefits any acquirer would be able to derive from restructuring the unit or from future capital expenditure on the unit.

* The requirement to exclude future capital expenditure that will improve or enhance the asset in excess of its originally assessed standard of performance was amended in 2003 as a consequential amendment arising from the revision of IAS 16 *Property, Plant and Equipment*. Paragraph 44 of IAS 36 now requires estimates of future cash flows to exclude future cash inflows or outflows that are expected to arise from improving or enhancing the asset's performance.

BC70 Therefore, all else being equal, the unit's recoverable amount would be its fair value less costs to sell, rather than its value in use. As such, the net benefits of the restructuring would be reflected in the unit's recoverable amount, meaning that an impairment loss would arise only to the extent of any material disposal costs.

BC71 The Board acknowledged that treating the newly acquired unit's fair value less costs to sell as its recoverable amount seems inconsistent with the reason underpinning a 'higher of fair value less costs to sell and value in use' recoverable amount measurement objective. Measuring recoverable amount as the higher of fair value less costs to sell and value in use is intended to reflect the economic decisions that are made when an asset becomes impaired: is it better to sell or keep using the asset?

BC72 Nevertheless, the Board concluded that:

(a) amending IAS 36 to include in value in use calculations the costs and benefits of future restructurings to which the entity is not yet committed would be a significant change to the concept of value in use adopted in the previous version of IAS 36. That concept is 'value in use for the asset in its current condition'.

(b) the concept of value in use in IAS 36 should not be modified as part of the Business Combinations project, but should be reconsidered only once the Board considers and resolves the broader question of the appropriate measurement objectives in accounting.

BC73 The second issue the Board considered related to what some respondents suggested was a conflict between the requirements in paragraphs 27(b) and 37 of the previous version of IAS 36 (now paragraphs 33(b) and 44). Paragraph 27(b) required value in use to be based on the most recent forecasts approved by management–which would be likely to reflect management's intentions in relation to future restructurings and future capital expenditure–whereas paragraph 37 required value in use to exclude the effects of a future restructuring to which the enterprise is not yet committed and future capital expenditure that will improve or enhance the asset in excess of its originally assessed standard of performance.

BC74 The Board concluded that it is clear from the Basis for Conclusions on the previous version of IAS 36 that IASC's intention was that value in use should be calculated using estimates of future cash inflows for an asset in its current condition. The Board nevertheless agreed with respondents that the requirement for value in use to be based on the most recent forecasts approved by management could be viewed as inconsistent with paragraph 37 of the previous version of IAS 36 when those forecasts include either future restructurings to which the entity is not yet committed or future cash flows associated with improving or enhancing the asset's performance.

* The requirement to exclude future capital expenditure that will improve or enhance the asset in excess of its originally assessed standard of performance was amended in 2003 as a consequential amendment arising from the revision of IAS 16 *Property, Plant and Equipment*. Paragraph 44 of IAS 36 now requires estimates of future cash flows to exclude future cash inflows or outflows that are expected to arise from improving or enhancing the asset's performance.

BC75 Therefore, the Board decided to clarify, in what is now paragraph 33(b) of the revised Standard, that cash flow projections should be based on the most recent financial budgets/forecasts that have been approved by management, but should exclude any estimated future cash inflows or outflows expected to arise from future restructurings or from improving or enhancing the asset's performance. The Board also decided to clarify that when a cash-generating unit contains assets with different estimated useful lives (or, similarly, when an asset comprises components with different estimated useful lives), the replacement of assets (components) with shorter lives is considered to be part of the day-to-day servicing of the unit (asset) when estimating the future cash flows associated with the unit (asset).

Using present value techniques to measure value in use (paragraphs A1–A14)

BC76 The Exposure Draft proposed additional application guidance on using present value techniques in measuring value in use. The Board decided to include this additional guidance in the Exposure Draft in response to requests for clarification of the requirements in the previous version of IAS 36 on measuring value in use.

BC77 Respondents to the Exposure Draft were generally supportive of the additional guidance. Those that were not varied in their views, suggesting that:

(a) limiting the guidance to a brief appendix to IAS 36 is insufficient.

(b) although the guidance is useful, it detracts from the main purpose of IAS 36, which is to establish accounting principles for impairment testing assets. Therefore, the guidance should be omitted from the Standard.

(c) entities should be required to use an expected cash flow approach to measure value in use.

(d) an expected cash flow approach is not consistent with how transactions are priced by management and should be prohibited.

BC78 In considering (a) and (b) above, the Board noted that the respondents that commented on the additional guidance generally agreed that it is useful and sufficient.

BC79 In considering (c) and (d) above, the Board observed that the previous version of IAS 36 did not require value in use to be calculated using an expected cash flow approach, nor did it prohibit such an approach. The Board could see no justification for requiring or prohibiting the use of an expected cash flow approach, particularly given the Board's inclination to avoid modifying the requirements in the previous version of IAS 36 for determining recoverable amount until it considers and resolves the broader measurement issues in accounting. Additionally, in relation to (d), some field visit participants said that they routinely undertake sensitivity and statistical analysis as the basis for using an expected value approach to budgeting/forecasting and strategic decision-making.

BC80 Therefore, the Board decided to include in the revised Standard the application guidance on using present value techniques that was proposed in the Exposure Draft.

Income taxes

Consideration of future tax cash flows

BCZ81 Future income tax cash flows may affect recoverable amount. It is convenient to analyse future tax cash flows into two components:

(a) the future tax cash flows that would result from any difference between the tax base of an asset (the amount attributed to it for tax purposes) and its carrying amount, after recognition of any impairment loss. Such differences are described in IAS 12 *Income Taxes* as 'temporary differences'.

(b) the future tax cash flows that would result if the tax base of the asset were equal to its recoverable amount.

BCZ82 For most assets, an enterprise recognises the tax consequences of temporary differences as a deferred tax liability or deferred tax asset in accordance with IAS 12. Therefore, to avoid double-counting, the future tax consequences of those temporary differences–the first component referred to in paragraph BCZ81–are not considered in determining recoverable amount (see further discussion in paragraphs BCZ86–BCZ89).

BCZ83 The tax base of an asset on initial recognition is normally equal to its cost. Therefore, net selling price* implicitly reflects market participants' assessment of the future tax cash flows that would result if the tax base of the asset were equal to its recoverable amount. Therefore, no adjustment is required to net selling price to reflect the second component referred to in paragraph BCZ81.

BCZ84 In principle, value in use should include the present value of the future tax cash flows that would result if the tax base of the asset were equal to its value in use–the second component referred to in paragraph BCZ81. Nevertheless it may be burdensome to estimate the effect of that component. This is because:

(a) to avoid double-counting, it is necessary to exclude the effect of temporary differences; and

(b) value in use would need to be determined by an iterative and possibly complex computation so that value in use itself reflects a tax base equal to that value in use.

For these reasons, IASC decided to require an enterprise to determine value in use by using pre-tax future cash flows and, hence, a pre-tax discount rate.

Determining a pre–tax discount rate

BCZ85 In theory, discounting post-tax cash flows at a post-tax discount rate and discounting pre-tax cash flows at a pre-tax discount rate should give the same result, as long as the pre-tax discount rate is the post-tax discount rate adjusted to reflect the specific amount and timing of the future tax cash flows. The pre-tax discount rate is not always the post-tax discount rate grossed up by a standard rate of tax.

* In IFRS 5 *Non-current Assets Held for Sale and Discontinued Operations*, issued by the IASB in 2004, the term 'net selling price' was replaced in IAS 36 by 'fair value less costs to sell'.

Example

This example illustrates that a post-tax discount rate grossed-up by a standard rate of tax is not always an appropriate pre-tax discount rate.

At the end of 20X0, the carrying amount of an asset is 1,757 and its remaining useful life is 5 years. The tax base in 20X0 is the cost of the asset. The cost is fully deductible at the end of 20X1. The tax rate is 20%. The discount rate for the asset can be determined only on a post-tax basis and is estimated to be 10%. At the end of 20X0, cash flow projections determined on a pre-tax basis are as follows:

		20X1	20X2	20X3	20X4	20X5
(1)	Pre–tax cash flows (CF)	800	600	500	200	100

Value in use determined using post-tax cash flows and a post-tax discount rate

End of 20X0		*20X1*	*20X2*	*20X3*	*20X4*	*20X5*
(2)	*Deduction of the cost of the asset*	*(1,757)*	–	–	–	–
(3)	*Tax CF [((1)–(2))×20%]*	*(191)*	*120*	*100*	*40*	*20*
(4)	*Post–tax CF [(1)–(3)]*	*991*	*480*	*400*	*160*	*80*
(5)	*Post–tax CF discounted at 10%*	*901*	*396*	*301*	*109*	*50*
Value in use [Σ(5)] =						*1,757*

Value in use determined using pre-tax cash flows and a pre-tax discount rate (determined by grossing-up the post-tax discount rate)

Pre–tax discount rate (grossed–up) [10%/(100%–20%)] 12.5%

End of 20X0		*20X1*	*20X2*	*20X3*	*20X4*	*20X5*
(6)	*Pre–tax CF discounted at 12.5%*	*711*	*475*	*351*	*125*	*55*
Value in use [Σ(6)] =						*1,717*

Continued from previous page

Example

Determination of the 'real' pre-tax discount rate

A pre-tax discount rate can be determined by an iterative computation so that value in use determined using pre-tax cash flows and a pre-tax discount rate equals value in use determined using post-tax cash flows and a post-tax discount rate. In the example, the pre-tax discount rate would be 11.2%.

End of 20X0	*20X1*	*20X2*	*20X3*	*20X4*	*20X5*
(7) Pre–tax CF discounted at 11.2%	*718*	*485*	*364*	*131*	*59*
Value in use [Σ(7)] =					*1,757*

The 'real' pre-tax discount rate differs from the post-tax discount rate grossed-up by the standard rate of tax depending on the tax rate, the post-tax discount rate, the timing of the future tax cash flows and the useful life of the asset. Note that the tax base of the asset in this example has been set equal to its cost at the end of 20X0. Therefore, there is no deferred tax to consider in the balance sheet.

Interaction with IAS 12

BCZ86 IAS 36 requires that recoverable amount should be based on present value calculations, whereas under IAS 12 an enterprise determines deferred tax assets and liabilities by comparing the carrying amount of an asset (a present value if the carrying amount is based on recoverable amount) with its tax base (an undiscounted amount).

BCZ87 One way to eliminate this inconsistency would be to measure deferred tax assets and liabilities on a discounted basis. In developing the revised version of IAS 12 (approved in 1996), there was not enough support to require that deferred tax assets and liabilities should be measured on a discounted basis. IASC believed there was still not consensus to support such a change in existing practice. Therefore, IAS 36 requires an enterprise to measure the tax effects of temporary differences using the principles set out in IAS 12.

BCZ88 IAS 12 does not permit an enterprise to recognise certain deferred tax liabilities and assets. In such cases, some believe that the value in use of an asset, or a cash-generating unit, should be adjusted to reflect the tax consequences of recovering its pre-tax value in use. For example, if the tax rate is 25 per cent, an enterprise must receive pre-tax cash flows with a present value of 400 in order to recover a carrying amount of 300.

BCZ89 IASC acknowledged the conceptual merit of such adjustments but concluded that they would add unnecessary complexity. Therefore, IAS 36 neither requires nor permits such adjustments.

Comments by field visit participants and respondents to the December 2002 Exposure Draft

BC90 In revising IAS 36, the Board considered the requirement in the previous version of IAS 36 for:

(a) income tax receipts and payments to be excluded from the estimates of future cash flows used to measure value in use; and

(b) the discount rate used to measure value in use to be a pre-tax rate that reflects current market assessments of the time value of money and the risks specific to the asset for which the future cash flow estimates have not been adjusted.

BC91 The Board had not considered these requirements when developing the Exposure Draft. However, some field visit participants and respondents to the Exposure Draft stated that using pre-tax cash flows and pre-tax discount rates would be a significant implementation issue for entities. This is because typically an entity's accounting and strategic decision-making systems are fully integrated and use post-tax cash flows and post-tax discount rates to arrive at present value measures.

BC92 In considering this issue, the Board observed that the definition of value in use in the previous version of IAS 36 and the associated requirements on measuring value in use were not sufficiently precise to give a definitive answer to the question of what tax attribute an entity should reflect in value in use. For example, although IAS 36 specified discounting pre-tax cash flows at a pre-tax discount rate—with the pre-tax discount rate being the post-tax discount rate adjusted to reflect the specific amount and timing of the future tax cash flows—it did not specify *which* tax effects the pre-tax rate should include. Arguments could be mounted for various approaches.

BC93 The Board decided that any decision to amend the requirement in the previous version of IAS 36 for pre-tax cash flows to be discounted at a pre-tax discount rate should be made only after the Board has resolved the issue of what tax attribute should be reflected in value in use. The Board decided that it should not try to resolve this latter issue as part of the Business Combinations project—decisions on the treatment of tax in value in use calculations should be made only as part of its conceptual project on measurement. Therefore, the Board concluded it should not amend as part of the current revision of IAS 36 the requirement to use pre-tax cash flows and pre-tax discount rates when measuring value in use.

BC94 However, the Board observed that, conceptually, discounting post-tax cash flows at a post-tax discount rate and discounting pre-tax cash flows at a pre-tax discount rate should give the same result, as long as the pre-tax discount rate is the post-tax discount rate adjusted to reflect the specific amount and timing of the future tax cash flows. The pre-tax discount rate is generally not the post-tax discount rate grossed up by a standard rate of tax.

Recognition of an impairment loss (paragraphs 58–64)

BCZ95 IAS 36 requires that an impairment loss should be recognised whenever the recoverable amount of an asset is below its carrying amount. IASC considered various criteria for recognising an impairment loss in the financial statements:

(a) recognition if it is considered that the impairment loss is permanent ('permanent criterion');

(b) recognition if it is considered probable that an asset is impaired, ie if it is probable that an enterprise will not recover the carrying amount of the asset ('probability criterion'); and

(c) immediate recognition whenever recoverable amount is below the carrying amount ('economic criterion').

Recognition based on a 'permanent' criterion

BCZ96 Supporters of the 'permanent' criterion argue that:

(a) this criterion avoids the recognition of temporary decreases in the recoverable amount of an asset.

(b) the recognition of an impairment loss refers to future operations; it is contrary to the historical cost system to account for future events. Also, depreciation (amortisation) will reflect these future losses over the expected remaining useful life of the asset.

This view was supported by only a few commentators on E55 *Impairment of Assets*.

BCZ97 IASC decided to reject the 'permanent' criterion because:

(a) it is difficult to identify whether an impairment loss is permanent. There is a risk that, by using this criterion, recognition of an impairment loss may be delayed.

(b) this criterion is at odds with the basic concept that an asset is a resource that will generate future economic benefits. Cost-based accrual accounting cannot reflect events without reference to future expectations. If the events that led to a decrease in recoverable amount have already taken place, the carrying amount should be reduced accordingly.

Recognition based on a 'probability' criterion

BCZ98 Some argue that an impairment loss should be recognised only if it is considered probable that the carrying amount of an asset cannot be fully recovered. Proponents of a 'probability' criterion are divided between:

(a) those who support the use of a recognition trigger based on the sum of the future cash flows (undiscounted and without allocation of interest costs) as a practical approach to implementing the 'probability' criterion; and

(b) those who support reflecting the requirements in IAS 10 (reformatted 1994) *Contingencies and Events Occurring After the Balance Sheet Date*.*

Sum of undiscounted future cash flows (without interest costs)

BCZ99 Some national standard-setters use the 'probability' criterion as a basis for recognition of an impairment loss and require, as a practical approach to implementing that criterion, that an impairment loss should be recognised only if the sum of the future cash flows from an asset (undiscounted and without allocation of interest costs) is less than the carrying amount of the asset. An impairment loss, when recognised, is measured as the difference between the carrying amount of the asset and its recoverable amount measured at fair value (based on quoted market prices or, if no quoted market prices exist, estimated considering prices for similar assets and the results of valuation techniques, such as the sum of cash flows discounted to their present value, option-pricing models, matrix pricing, option-adjusted spread models and fundamental analysis).

BCZ100 One of the characteristics of this approach is that the bases for recognition and measurement of an impairment loss are different. For example, even if the fair value of an asset is lower than its carrying amount, no impairment loss will be recognised if the sum of undiscounted cash flows (without allocation of interest costs) is greater than the asset's carrying amount. This might occur, especially if an asset has a long useful life.

BCZ101 Those who support using the sum of undiscounted future cash flows (without allocation of interest costs) as a recognition trigger argue that:

(a) using a recognition trigger based on undiscounted amounts is consistent with the historical cost framework.

(b) it avoids recognising temporary impairment losses and creating potentially volatile earnings that may mislead users of financial statements.

(c) net selling price† and value in use are difficult to substantiate–a price for the disposal of an asset or an appropriate discount rate is difficult to estimate.

(d) it is a higher threshold for recognising impairment losses. It should be relatively easy to conclude that the sum of undiscounted future cash flows will equal or exceed the carrying amount of an asset without incurring the cost of allocating projected cash flows to specific future periods.

This view was supported by a minority of commentators on E55 *Impairment of Assets*.

BCZ102 IASC considered the arguments listed above but rejected this approach because:

(a) when it identifies that an asset may be impaired, a rational enterprise will make an investment decision. Therefore, it is relevant to consider the time value of money and the risks specific to an asset in determining whether an asset is impaired. This is particularly true if an asset has a long useful life.

* The requirements relating to contingencies in the 1994 version of IAS 10 were replaced in 1998 with the requirements in IAS 37 *Provisions, Contingent Liabilities and Contingent Assets*.

† In IFRS 5 *Non-current Assets Held for Sale and Discontinued Operations*, issued by the IASB in 2004, the term 'net selling price' was replaced in IAS 36 by 'fair value less costs to sell'.

(b) IAS 36 does not require an enterprise to estimate the recoverable amount of each [depreciable] asset every year but only if there is an indication that an asset may be materially impaired. An asset that is depreciated (amortised) in an appropriate manner is unlikely to become materially impaired unless events or changes in circumstances cause a sudden reduction in the estimate of recoverable amount.

(c) probability factors are already encompassed in the determination of value in use, in projecting future cash flows and in requiring that recoverable amount should be the higher of net selling price and value in use.

(d) if there is an unfavourable change in the assumptions used to determine recoverable amount, users are better served if they are informed about this change in assumptions on a timely basis.

Probability criterion based on IAS 10 (reformatted 1994)

BCZ103 IAS 10 required the amount of a contingent loss to be recognised as an expense and a liability if:

(a) it was probable that future events will confirm that, after taking into account any related probable recovery, an asset had been impaired or a liability incurred at the balance sheet date; and

(b) a reasonable estimate of the amount of the resulting loss could be made.

BCZ104 IASC rejected the view that an impairment loss should be recognised based on the requirements in IAS 10 because:

(a) the requirements in IAS 10 were not sufficiently detailed and would have made a 'probability' criterion difficult to apply.

(b) those requirements would have introduced another unnecessary layer of probability. Indeed, as mentioned above, probability factors are already encompassed in estimates of value in use and in requiring that recoverable amount should be the higher of net selling price and value in use.

Recognition based on an 'economic' criterion

BCZ105 IAS 36 relies on an 'economic' criterion for the recognition of an impairment loss—an impairment loss is recognised whenever the recoverable amount of an asset is below its carrying amount. This criterion was already used in many International Accounting Standards before IAS 36, such as IAS 9 *Research and Development Costs*, IAS 22 *Business Combinations*, and IAS 16 *Property, Plant and Equipment*.

BCZ106 IASC considered that an 'economic' criterion is the best criterion to give information which is useful to users in assessing future cash flows to be generated by the enterprise as a whole. In estimating the time value of money and the risks specific to an asset in determining whether the asset is impaired, factors, such as the probability or permanence of the impairment loss, are subsumed in the measurement.

BCZ107 The majority of commentators on E55 supported IASC's view that an impairment loss should be recognised based on an 'economic' criterion.

Revalued assets: recognition in the income statement versus directly in equity

BCZ108 IAS 36 requires that an impairment loss on a revalued asset should be recognised as an expense in the income statement immediately, except that it should be recognised directly in equity to the extent that it reverses a previous revaluation on the same asset.

BCZ109 Some argue that, when there is a clear reduction in the service potential (for example, physical damage) of a revalued asset, the impairment loss should be recognised in the income statement.

BCZ110 Others argue that an impairment loss should always be recognised as an expense in the income statement. The logic of this argument is that an impairment loss arises only where there is a reduction in the estimated future cash flows that form part of the business's operating activities. Indeed, according to IAS 16, whether or not an asset is revalued, the depreciation charge is always recognised in the income statement. Supporters of this view question why the treatment of an impairment loss on a revalued asset should be different to depreciation.

BCZ111 IASC believed that it would be difficult to identify whether an impairment loss is a downward revaluation or a reduction in service potential. Therefore, IASC decided to retain the treatment used in IAS 16 and to treat an impairment loss of a revalued asset as a revaluation decrease (and similarly, a reversal of an impairment loss as a subsequent revaluation increase).

BCZ112 For a revalued asset, the distinction between an 'impairment loss' ('reversal of an impairment loss') and another 'revaluation decrease' ('revaluation increase') is important for disclosure purposes. If an impairment loss that is material to the enterprise as a whole has been recognised or reversed, more information on how this impairment loss is measured is required by IAS 36 than for the recognition of a revaluation in accordance with IAS 16.

Cash-generating units (paragraphs 66–73)

BCZ113 Some support the principle of determining recoverable amount on an individual asset basis only. This view was expressed by a few commentators on E55. They argued that:

(a) it would be difficult to identify cash-generating units at a level other than the business as a whole and, therefore, impairment losses would never be recognised for individual assets; and

(b) it should be possible to recognise an impairment loss, regardless of whether an asset generates cash inflows that are independent from those of other assets or groups of assets. Commentators quoted examples of assets that have become under-utilised or obsolete but that are still in use.

BCZ114 IASC acknowledged that identifying the lowest level of independent cash inflows for a group of assets would involve judgement. However, IASC believed that the concept of cash-generating units is a matter of fact: assets work together to generate cash flows.

BCZ115 In response to requests from commentators on E55, IAS 36 includes additional guidance and examples for identifying cash-generating units and for determining the carrying amount of cash-generating units. IAS 36 emphasises that cash-generating units should be identified for the lowest level of aggregation of assets possible.

Internal transfer pricing (paragraph 70)

BC116 The previous version of IAS 36 required that if an active market exists for the output produced by an asset or a group of assets:

(a) that asset or group of assets should be identified as a cash-generating unit, even if some or all of the output is used internally; and

(b) management's best estimate of the future market prices for the output should be used in estimating:

(i) the future cash inflows that relate to the internal use of the output when determining the value in use of this cash-generating unit; and

(ii) the future cash outflows that relate to the internal use of the output when determining the value in use of the entity's other cash-generating units.

BC117 The requirement in (a) above has been carried forward in the revised Standard. However, some respondents to the Exposure Draft asked for additional guidance to clarify the role of internal transfer pricing versus prices in an arm's length transaction when developing cash flow forecasts. The Board decided to address this issue by amending the requirement in (b) above to deal more broadly with cash-generating units whose cash flows are affected by internal transfer pricing, rather than just cash-generating units whose internally consumed output could be sold on an active market.

BC118 Therefore, the Standard clarifies that if the cash inflows generated by *any* asset or cash-generating unit are affected by internal transfer pricing, an entity should use management's best estimate of future prices that could be achieved in arm's length transactions in estimating:

(a) the future cash inflows used to determine the asset's or cash-generating unit's value in use; and

(b) the future cash outflows used to determine the value in use of other assets or cash-generating units affected by the internal transfer pricing.

Testing indefinite–lived intangibles for impairment

BC119 As part of the first phase of its Business Combinations project, the Board concluded that:

(a) an intangible asset should be regarded as having an indefinite useful life when, based on an analysis of all relevant factors (eg legal, regulatory, contractual, competitive and economic), there is no foreseeable limit on the period over which the asset is expected to generate net cash inflows for the entity; and

(b) an indefinite-lived intangible should not be amortised, but should be tested regularly for impairment.

An outline of the Board's deliberations on each of these issues is provided in the Basis for Conclusions on IAS 38 *Intangible Assets.*

BC120 Having reached these conclusions, the Board then considered the form that the impairment test for indefinite-lived intangibles should take. The Board concluded that:

(a) an indefinite-lived intangible should be tested for impairment annually, or more frequently if there is any indication that it may be impaired; and

(b) the recoverable amounts of such assets should be measured, and impairment losses (and reversals of impairment losses) in respect of those assets should be accounted for, in accordance with the requirements in IAS 36 for assets other than goodwill.

Paragraphs BC121–BC126 outline the Board's deliberations in reaching its conclusion about the frequency and timing of impairment testing indefinite-lived intangibles. Paragraphs BC129 and BC130 outline the Board's deliberations in reaching its conclusions about measuring the recoverable amount of such assets and accounting for impairment losses and reversals of impairment losses.

Frequency and timing of impairment testing (paragraphs 9 and 10(a))

BC121 In developing the Exposure Draft, the Board observed that requiring assets to be remeasured when they are impaired is a valuation concept rather than one of cost allocation. This concept, which some have termed 'the recoverable cost concept', focuses on the benefits to be derived from the asset in the future, rather than on the process by which the cost or other carrying amount of the asset should be allocated to particular accounting periods. Therefore, the purpose of an impairment test is to assess whether the carrying amount of an asset will be recovered through use or sale of the asset. Nevertheless, allocating the depreciable amount of an asset with a limited useful life on a systematic basis over that life provides some assurance against the asset's carrying amount exceeding its recoverable amount. The Board acknowledged that non-amortisation of an intangible asset increases the reliance that must be placed on impairment reviews of that asset to ensure that its carrying amount does not exceed its recoverable amount.

BC122 Accordingly, the Exposure Draft proposed that indefinite-lived intangibles should be tested for impairment at the end of each annual reporting period. The Board concluded, however, that testing such assets annually for impairment is not a substitute for management being aware of events occurring or circumstances changing between annual tests that indicate a possible impairment. Therefore, the Exposure Draft also proposed that an entity should be required to test such assets for impairment whenever there is an indication of possible impairment, and not wait until the next annual test.

BC123 The respondents to the Exposure Draft generally supported the proposal to test indefinite-lived intangibles for impairment annually and whenever there is an indication of possible impairment. Those that disagreed argued that requiring an annual impairment test would be excessively burdensome, and recommended requiring an impairment test only when there is an indication that an indefinite-lived intangible might be impaired. After considering these comments the Board:

(a) reaffirmed its view that non-amortisation of an intangible asset increases the reliance that must be placed on impairment reviews of that asset to ensure that its carrying amount does not exceed its recoverable amount.

(b) concluded that IAS 36 should require indefinite-lived intangibles to be tested for impairment annually and whenever there is an indication of possible impairment.

BC124 However, as noted in paragraph BC122, the Exposure Draft proposed that the annual impairment tests for indefinite-lived intangibles should be performed at the end of each annual period. Many respondents to the Exposure Draft disagreed that IAS 36 should mandate the timing of the annual impairment tests. They argued that:

(a) it would be inconsistent with the proposal (now a requirement) that the annual impairment test for a cash-generating unit to which goodwill has been allocated may be performed at any time during an annual period, provided the test is performed at the same time every year. There is no justification for providing less flexibility in the timing of the annual impairment test for indefinite-lived intangibles.

(b) if the impairment test for an indefinite-lived intangible is linked to the impairment test for goodwill (ie if the indefinite-lived intangible is assessed for impairment at the same cash-generating unit level as goodwill, rather than individually or as part of a smaller cash-generating unit), the requirement to measure its recoverable amount at the end of the annual period could result in the cash-generating unit to which it (and the goodwill) belongs being tested for impairment at least twice each annual period, which is too burdensome. For example, assume a cash-generating unit contains goodwill and an indefinite-lived intangible, and that the indefinite-lived intangible is assessed for impairment at the same cash-generating unit level as goodwill. Assume also that the entity reports quarterly, has a December year-end, and decides to test goodwill for impairment at the end of the third quarter to coincide with the completion of its annual strategic planning/budgeting process. The proposal that the annual impairment test for an indefinite-lived intangible should be performed at the end of each annual period would mean that the entity would be required:

    (i) to calculate at the end of each September the recoverable amount of the cash-generating unit, compare it with its carrying amount, and, if the carrying amount exceeds the recoverable amount, recognise an impairment loss for the unit by reducing the carrying amount of goodwill and allocating any remaining impairment loss to the other assets in the unit, including the indefinite-lived intangible.

    (ii) to perform the same steps again each December to test the indefinite-lived intangible for impairment.

(iii) to perform the same steps again at any other time throughout the annual period if there is an indication that the cash-generating unit, the goodwill or the indefinite-lived intangible may be impaired.

BC125 In considering these comments, the Board indicated a preference for requiring entities to perform the recoverable amount calculations for both goodwill and indefinite-lived intangibles at the end of the annual period. However, the Board acknowledged that, as outlined in paragraph BC124(b), impairment tests for indefinite-lived intangibles will sometimes be linked to impairment tests for goodwill, and that many entities would find it difficult to perform all those tests at the end of the annual period.

BC126 Therefore, consistently with the annual impairment test for goodwill, the Standard permits the annual impairment test for an indefinite-lived intangible to be performed at any time during an annual period, provided it is performed at the same time every year.

Carrying forward a recoverable amount calculation (paragraph 24)

BC127 The Standard permits the most recent detailed calculation of the recoverable amount of an indefinite-lived intangible to be carried forward from a preceding period for use in the current period's impairment test, provided all of the criteria in paragraph 24 of the Standard are met.

BC128 Integral to the Board's decision that indefinite-lived intangibles should be tested for impairment annually was the view that many entities should be able to conclude that the recoverable amount of such an asset is greater than its carrying amount without actually recomputing recoverable amount. However, the Board concluded that this would be the case only if the last recoverable amount determination exceeded the carrying amount by a substantial margin, and nothing had happened since then to make the likelihood of an impairment loss other than remote. The Board concluded that, in such circumstances, permitting a detailed calculation of the recoverable amount of an indefinite-lived intangible to be carried forward from the preceding period for use in the current period's impairment test would significantly reduce the costs of applying the impairment test, without compromising its integrity.

Measuring recoverable amount and accounting for impairment losses and reversals of impairment losses

BC129 The Board could see no compelling reason why the measurement basis adopted for determining recoverable amount and the treatment of impairment losses and reversals of impairment losses for one group of identifiable assets should differ from those applying to other identifiable assets. Adopting different methods would impair the usefulness of the information provided to users about an entity's identifiable assets, because both comparability and reliability, which rest on the notion that similar transactions are accounted for in the same way, would be diminished. Therefore, the Board concluded that the recoverable amounts of indefinite-lived intangibles should be measured, and impairment losses and reversals of impairment losses in respect of those assets should be accounted for, consistently with other identifiable assets covered by the Standard.

BC130 The Board expressed some concern over the measurement basis adopted in the previous version of IAS 36 for determining recoverable amount (ie higher of value in use and net selling price) and its treatment of impairment losses and reversals of impairment losses for assets other than goodwill. However, the Board's intention in revising IAS 36 was *not* to reconsider the general approach to impairment testing. Accordingly, the Board decided that it should address concerns over that general approach as part of its future re-examination of IAS 36 in its entirety, rather than as part of its Business Combinations project.

Testing goodwill for impairment (paragraphs 80–99)

BC131 The Board concluded that if a rigorous and operational impairment test could be devised, more useful information would be provided to users of an entity's financial statements under an approach in which goodwill is not amortised, but is instead tested for impairment annually or more frequently if events or changes in circumstances indicate that the goodwill might be impaired. An outline of the Board's deliberations in reaching this conclusion is provided in the Basis for Conclusions on IFRS 3 *Business Combinations.*

BC132 Paragraphs BC133–BC177 outline the Board's deliberations on the form that the impairment test for goodwill should take:

(a) paragraphs BC137–BC159 discuss the requirements relating to the allocation of goodwill to cash-generating units and the level at which goodwill is tested for impairment.

(b) paragraphs BC160–BC170 discuss the requirements relating to the recognition and measurement of impairment losses for goodwill, including the frequency of impairment testing.

(c) paragraphs BC171–BC177 discuss the requirements relating to the timing of goodwill impairment tests.

BC133 As a first step in its deliberations, the Board considered the objective of the goodwill impairment test and the measure of recoverable amount that should be adopted for such a test. The Board observed that recent North American standards use fair value as the basis for impairment testing goodwill, whereas the previous version of IAS 36 and the United Kingdom standard are based on an approach under which recoverable amount is measured as the higher of value in use and net selling price.

BC134 The Board also observed that goodwill acquired in a business combination represents a payment made by an acquirer in anticipation of future economic benefits from assets that are not capable of being individually identified and separately recognised. Goodwill does not generate cash flows independently of other assets or groups of assets and therefore cannot be measured directly. Instead, it is measured as a residual amount, being the excess of the cost of a business combination over the acquirer's interest in the net fair value of the acquiree's identifiable assets, liabilities and contingent liabilities. Moreover, goodwill acquired in a business combination and goodwill generated after that business combination cannot be separately identified, because they contribute jointly to the same cash flows.

BC135 The Board concluded that because it is not possible to measure separately goodwill generated internally after a business combination and to factor that measure into the impairment test for acquired goodwill, the carrying amount of goodwill will always be shielded from impairment by that internally generated goodwill. Therefore, the Board took the view that the objective of the goodwill impairment test could at best be to ensure that the carrying amount of goodwill is recoverable from future cash flows expected to be generated by both acquired goodwill and goodwill generated internally after the business combination.

BC136 The Board noted that because goodwill is measured as a residual amount, the starting point in any goodwill impairment test would have to be the recoverable amount of the operation or unit to which the goodwill relates, regardless of the measurement basis adopted for determining recoverable amount. The Board decided that until it considers and resolves the broader question of the appropriate measurement objective(s) in accounting, identifying the appropriate measure of recoverable amount for that unit would be problematic. Therefore, although the Board expressed concern over the measurement basis adopted in IAS 36 for determining recoverable amount, it decided that it should not depart from that basis when measuring the recoverable amount of a unit whose carrying amount includes acquired goodwill. The Board noted that this would have the added advantage of allowing the impairment test for goodwill to be integrated with the impairment test in IAS 36 for other assets and cash-generating units that include goodwill.

Allocating goodwill to cash–generating units (paragraphs 80–87)

BC137 The previous version of IAS 36 required goodwill to be tested for impairment as part of impairment testing the cash-generating units to which it relates. It employed a 'bottom–up/top–down' approach under which the goodwill was in effect tested for impairment by allocating its carrying amount to each of the smallest cash-generating units to which a portion of that carrying amount could be allocated on a reasonable and consistent basis.

BC138 Consistently with the previous version of IAS 36, the Exposure Draft proposed that:

(a) goodwill should be tested for impairment as part of impairment testing the cash-generating units to which it relates; and

(b) the carrying amount of goodwill should be allocated to each of the smallest cash-generating units to which a portion of that carrying amount can be allocated on a reasonable and consistent basis.

However, the Exposure Draft proposed additional guidance clarifying that a portion of the carrying amount of goodwill should be regarded as capable of being allocated to a cash-generating unit on a reasonable and consistent basis only when that unit represents the lowest level at which management monitors the return on investment in assets that include the goodwill. That cash-generating unit could not, however, be larger than a segment based on the entity's primary reporting format determined in accordance with IAS 14 *Segment Reporting*.

BC139 In developing this proposal, the Board noted that because acquired goodwill does not generate cash flows independently of other assets or groups of assets, it can be tested for impairment only as part of impairment testing the cash-generating units to which it relates. However, the Board was concerned that in the absence of any guidance on the precise meaning of 'allocated on a reasonable and consistent basis', some might conclude that when a business combination enhances the value of all of the acquirer's pre-existing cash-generating units, any goodwill acquired in that business combination should be tested for impairment only at the level of the entity itself. The Board concluded that this should not be the case. Rather, there should be a link between the level at which goodwill is tested for impairment and the level of internal reporting that reflects the way an entity manages its operations and with which the goodwill naturally would be associated. Therefore, it was important to the Board that goodwill should be tested for impairment at a level at which information about the operations of an entity and the assets that support them is provided for internal reporting purposes.

BC140 In redeliberating this issue, the Board noted that respondents' and field visit participants' comments indicated that the Board's intention relating to the allocation of goodwill had been widely misunderstood, with many concluding that goodwill would need to be allocated to a much lower level than that intended by the Board. For example, some respondents and field visit participants were concerned that the proposal to allocate goodwill to such a low level would force entities to allocate goodwill arbitrarily to cash-generating units, and therefore to develop new or additional reporting systems to perform the test. The Board confirmed that its intention was that there should be a link between the level at which goodwill is tested for impairment and the level of internal reporting that reflects the way an entity manages its operations. Therefore, except for entities that do not monitor goodwill at or below the segment level, the proposals relating to the level of the goodwill impairment test should *not* cause entities to allocate goodwill arbitrarily to cash-generating units. Nor should they create the need for entities to develop new or additional reporting systems.

BC141 The Board observed from its discussions with field visit participants that much of the confusion stemmed from the definition of a 'cash-generating unit', when coupled with the proposal in paragraph 73 of the Exposure Draft for goodwill to be allocated to each 'smallest cash-generating unit to which a portion of the carrying amount of the goodwill can be allocated on a reasonable and consistent basis'. Additionally, field visit participants and respondents were unclear about the reference in paragraph 74 of the Exposure Draft to 'the lowest level at which management monitors the return on investments in assets that include goodwill', the most frequent question being 'what level of management?' (eg board of directors, chief executive officer, or segment management).

BC142 The Board noted that once its intention on this issue was clarified for field visit participants, they all, with the exception of one company that believes goodwill should be tested for impairment at the entity level, supported the level at which the Board believes goodwill should be tested for impairment.

BC143 The Board also noted the comment from a number of respondents and field visit participants that for some organisations, particularly those managed on a matrix basis, the proposal for cash-generating units to which the goodwill is allocated to be no larger than a segment based on the entity's *primary* reporting format could result in an outcome that is inconsistent with the Board's intention, ie that there should be a link between the level at which goodwill is tested for impairment and the level of internal reporting that reflects the way an entity manages its operations. The following example illustrates this point:

> A company managed on a matrix basis is organised primarily on a geographical basis, with product groups providing the secondary basis of segmentation. Goodwill is acquired as part of an acquisition of a product group that is present in several geographical regions, and is then monitored on an ongoing basis for internal reporting purposes as part of the product group/secondary segment. It is feasible that the secondary segment might, depending on the definition of 'larger', be 'larger' than a primary segment.

BC144 Therefore, the Board decided:

(a) that the Standard should require each unit or group of units to which goodwill is allocated to represent the lowest level within the entity at which the goodwill is monitored for internal management purposes.

(b) to clarify in the Standard that acquired goodwill should, from the acquisition date, be allocated to each of the acquirer's cash-generating units, or groups of cash-generating units, that are expected to benefit from the combination, irrespective of whether other assets or liabilities of the acquiree are assigned to those units or groups of units.

(c) to replace the proposal for cash–generating units or groups of units to which goodwill is allocated to be no larger than a segment based on the entity's *primary* reporting format, with the requirement that they be no larger than a segment based on either the entity's primary or the entity's secondary reporting format. The Board concluded that this amendment is necessary to ensure that entities managed on a matrix basis are able to test goodwill for impairment at the level of internal reporting that reflects the way they manage their operations.

BC145 Some respondents to the Exposure Draft raised the following additional concerns on the allocation of goodwill for impairment testing purposes:

(a) mandating that goodwill should be allocated to at least the segment level is inappropriate—it will often result in arbitrary allocations, and entities would need to develop new or additional reporting systems.

(b) for convergence reasons, the level of the goodwill impairment test should be the same as the level in US Financial Accounting Standards Board Statement of Financial Accounting Standards No. 142 *Goodwill and Other Intangible Assets* (SFAS 142) (ie the reporting unit level).

(c) cash-generating units that constitute businesses with similar characteristics should, as is required by SFAS 142, be aggregated and treated as single units, notwithstanding that they may be monitored independently for internal purposes.

BC146 In relation to (a), the Board reaffirmed the conclusion it reached when developing the Exposure Draft that requiring goodwill to be allocated to at least the segment level is necessary to avoid entities erroneously concluding that, when a business combination enhances the value of all of the acquirer's pre-existing cash-generating units, any goodwill acquired in that combination could be tested for impairment only at the level of the entity itself.

BC147 In relation to (b), the Board noted that SFAS 142 requires goodwill to be tested for impairment at a level of reporting referred to as a 'reporting unit'. A reporting unit is an operating segment (as defined in SFAS 131 *Disclosures about Segments of an Enterprise and Related Information**) or one level below an operating segment (referred to as a component). A component of an operating segment is a reporting unit if the component constitutes a business for which discrete financial information is available and segment management regularly reviews the operating results of that component. However, two or more components of an operating segment must be aggregated and deemed a single reporting unit if the components have similar economic characteristics. An operating segment is deemed to be a reporting unit if all of its components are similar, if none of its components is a reporting unit, or if it comprises only a single component.

BC148 Therefore, unlike IAS 36, SFAS 142 places a limit on how far goodwill can be 'pushed down' for impairment testing (ie one level below an operating segment).

BC149 In deciding not to converge with SFAS 142 on the level of the goodwill impairment test, the Board noted the following findings from the field visits and North American round-table discussions:

(a) most of the US registrant field visit participants stated that the Board's proposals on the level of the goodwill impairment test would result, in practice, in goodwill being tested for impairment at the same level at which it is tested in accordance with SFAS 142. However, several stated that under the Board's proposals, goodwill would be tested for impairment at a lower level than under SFAS 142. Nevertheless, they believe that the Board's approach provides users and management with more useful information.

(b) several round-table participants stated that they (or, in the case of audit firm participants, their clients) manage and have available information about their investments in goodwill at a lower level than the level of the SFAS 142 impairment test. They expressed a high level of dissatisfaction at being prevented by SFAS 142 from recognising goodwill impairments that they knew existed at these lower levels, but which 'disappeared' once the lower level units were aggregated with other units containing sufficient 'cushions' to offset the impairment loss.

BC150 In considering suggestion (c) in paragraph BC145, the Board observed that aggregating units that constitute businesses with similar characteristics could result in the disappearance of an impairment loss that management *knows* exists

* The basis for identifying 'operating segments' under SFAS 131 differs from the basis for identifying segments based on the entity's primary reporting format under IAS 14. SFAS 131 defines an operating segment as a component of an enterprise (a) that engages in business activities from which it may earn revenues and incur expenses, including revenues and expenses relating to transactions with other components of the enterprise; (b) whose operating results are regularly reviewed by the enterprise's chief operating decision maker to make decisions about resources to be allocated to the segment and assess its performance; and (c) for which discrete financial information is available.

in a cash-generating unit because the units with which it is aggregated contain sufficient cushions to offset the impairment loss. In the Board's view, if, because of the way an entity is managed, information about goodwill impairment losses is available to management at a particular level, that information should also be available to the users of the entity's financial statements.

Completing the initial allocation of goodwill (paragraphs 84 and 85)

BC151 If the initial allocation of goodwill acquired in a business combination cannot be completed before the end of the annual period in which the business combination is effected, the Exposure Draft proposed, and the revised Standard requires, that the initial allocation should be completed before the end of the first annual period beginning after the acquisition date. In contrast, ED 3 proposed, and IFRS 3 requires, that if the initial accounting for a business combination can be determined only provisionally by the end of the period in which the combination is effected, the acquirer should:

(a) account for the combination using those provisional values; and

(b) recognise any adjustments to those provisional values as a result of completing the initial accounting within twelve months of the acquisition date.

BC152 Some respondents to the Exposure Draft questioned why the period to complete the initial allocation of goodwill should differ from the period to complete the initial accounting for a business combination. The Board's view is that acquirers should be allowed a longer period to complete the goodwill allocation, because that allocation often might not be able to be performed until after the initial accounting for the combination is complete. This is because the cost of the combination or the fair values at the acquisition date of the acquiree's identifiable assets, liabilities or contingent liabilities, and therefore the amount of goodwill acquired in the combination, would not be finalised until the initial accounting for the combination in accordance with IFRS 3 is complete.

Disposal of a portion of a cash–generating unit containing goodwill (paragraph 86)

BC153 The Exposure Draft proposed that when an entity disposes of an operation within a cash-generating unit to which goodwill has been allocated, the goodwill associated with that operation should be:

(a) included in the carrying amount of the operation when determining the gain or loss on disposal; and

(b) measured on the basis of the relative values of the operation disposed of and the portion of the cash-generating unit retained.

BC154 This proposal has been carried forward in the Standard with one modification. The Standard requires the goodwill associated with the operation disposed of to be measured on the basis of the relative values of the operation disposed of and the portion of the cash-generating unit retained, unless the entity can demonstrate that some other method better reflects the goodwill associated with the operation disposed of.

BC155 In developing the Exposure Draft, the Board concluded that the proposed level of the impairment test would mean that goodwill could not be identified or associated with an asset group at a level lower than the cash-generating unit to which the goodwill is allocated, except arbitrarily. However, the Board also concluded that when an operation within that cash-generating unit is being disposed of, it is appropriate to presume that some amount of goodwill is associated with that operation. Thus, an allocation of the goodwill should be required when the part of the cash-generating unit being disposed of constitutes an operation.

BC156 Some respondents to the Exposure Draft suggested that although in most circumstances goodwill could not be identified or associated with an asset group at a level lower than the cash-generating unit or group of cash-generating units to which it is allocated for impairment testing, there may be some instances when this is not so. For example, assume an acquiree is integrated with one of the acquirer's pre-existing cash-generating units that did not include any goodwill in its carrying amount. Assume also that almost immediately after the business combination the acquirer disposes of a loss-making operation within the cash-generating unit. The Board agreed with respondents that in such circumstances, it might reasonably be concluded that no part of the carrying amount of goodwill has been disposed of, and therefore no part of its carrying amount should be derecognised by being included in the determination of the gain or loss on disposal.

Reorganisation of reporting structure (paragraph 87)

BC157 The Exposure Draft proposed that when an entity reorganises its reporting structure in a way that changes the composition of cash-generating units to which goodwill has been allocated, the goodwill should be reallocated to the units affected using a relative value approach similar to that used when an entity disposes of an operation within a cash-generating unit.

BC158 In developing the Exposure Draft, the Board concluded that a reorganisation that changes the composition of a cash-generating unit to which goodwill has been allocated gives rise to the same allocation problem as disposing of an operation within that unit. Therefore, the same allocation methodology should be used in both cases.

BC159 As a result, and consistently with the Board's decision to modify its proposal on allocating goodwill when an entity disposes of an operation, the revised Standard requires an entity that reorganises its reporting structure in a way that changes the composition of one or more cash-generating units to which goodwill has been allocated:

(a) to reallocate the goodwill to the units affected; and

(b) to perform this reallocation using a relative value approach similar to that used when an entity disposes of an operation within a cash-generating unit (group of cash-generating units), unless the entity can demonstrate that some other method better reflects the goodwill associated with the reorganised units (groups of units).

Recognition and measurement of impairment losses (paragraphs 88–99 and 104)

Background to the proposals in the Exposure Draft

BC160 The Exposure Draft proposed a two-step approach for impairment testing goodwill. The first step involved using a screening mechanism for identifying potential goodwill impairments, whereby goodwill allocated to a cash-generating unit would be identified as potentially impaired only when the carrying amount of the unit exceeded its recoverable amount. if an entity identified the goodwill allocated to a cash-generating unit as potentially impaired, an entity would then determine whether the goodwill allocated to the unit was impaired by comparing its recoverable amount, measured as the 'implied value' of the goodwill, with its carrying amount. The implied value of goodwill would be measured as a residual, being the excess of:

(a) the recoverable amount of the cash-generating unit to which the goodwill has been allocated, over

(b) the net fair value of the identifiable assets, liabilities and contingent liabilities the entity would recognise if it acquired the cash-generating unit in a business combination on the date of the impairment test (excluding any identifiable asset that was acquired in a business combination but not recognised separately from goodwill at the acquisition date).

BC161 In developing the Exposure Draft, the Board's discussion focused first on how the recoverable amount of goodwill allocated to a cash-generating unit could be separated from the recoverable amount of the unit as a whole, given that goodwill generated internally after a business combination could not be measured separately. The Board concluded that a method similar to the method an acquirer uses to allocate the cost of a business combination to the net assets acquired could be used to measure the recoverable amount of goodwill after its initial recognition. Thus, the Board decided that some measure of the net assets of a cash-generating unit to which goodwill has been allocated should be subtracted from the recoverable amount of that unit to determine a current implied value for the goodwill. The Board concluded that the measure of the net assets of a cash-generating unit described in paragraph BC160(b) would result in the best estimate of the current implied value of the goodwill, given that goodwill generated internally after a business combination could not be measured separately.

BC162 Having decided on the most appropriate measure of the recoverable amount of goodwill, the Board then considered how often an entity should be required to test goodwill for impairment. Consistently with its conclusions about indefinite-lived intangibles, the Board concluded that non-amortisation of goodwill increases the reliance that must be placed on impairment tests to ensure that the carrying amount of goodwill does not exceed its recoverable amount. Accordingly, the Board decided that goodwill should be tested for impairment annually. However, the Board also concluded that the annual test is not a substitute for management being aware of events occurring or circumstances changing between annual tests indicating a possible impairment of goodwill. Therefore, the Board decided that an entity should also be required to test goodwill for impairment whenever there is an indication of possible impairment.

BC163 After the Board decided on the frequency of impairment testing, it expressed some concern that the proposed test would not be cost-effective. This concern related primarily to the requirement to determine the fair value of each identifiable asset, liability and contingent liability within a cash-generating unit that would be recognised by the entity if it had acquired the cash-generating unit in a business combination on the date of the impairment test (to estimate the implied value of goodwill).

BC164 Therefore, the Board decided to propose as a first step in the impairment test for goodwill a screening mechanism similar to that in SFAS 142. Under SFAS 142, goodwill is tested for impairment by first comparing the fair value of the reporting unit to which the goodwill has been allocated for impairment testing purposes with the carrying amount of that unit. If the fair value of the unit exceeds its carrying amount, the goodwill is regarded as not impaired. An entity need estimate the implied fair value of goodwill (using an approach consistent with that described in paragraph BC160) only if the fair value of the unit is less than its carrying amount.

The Board's redeliberations

BC165 Many respondents disagreed with the proposal to adopt a two-step approach to impairment testing goodwill. In particular, the second step of the proposed impairment test and the method for measuring any impairment loss for the goodwill caused considerable concern. Respondents provided the following conceptual arguments against the proposed approach:

(a) by drawing on only some aspects of the SFAS 142 two-step approach, the result is a hybrid between fair values and value in use. More particularly, not measuring goodwill's implied value as the difference between the unit's fair value and the net fair value of the identifiable net assets in the unit, but instead measuring it as the difference between the unit's recoverable amount (ie higher of value in use and fair value less costs to sell) and the net fair value of the identifiable net assets in the unit, results in a measure of goodwill that conceptually is neither fair value nor recoverable amount. This raises questions about the conceptual validity of measuring goodwill impairment losses as the difference between goodwill's implied value and carrying amount.

(b) it seems inconsistent to consider goodwill separately for impairment testing when other assets within a unit are not considered separately but are instead considered as part of the unit as a whole, particularly given that goodwill, unlike many other assets, cannot generate cash inflows independently of other assets. The previous version of IAS 36 is premised on the notion that if a series of independent cash flows can be generated only by a group of assets operating together, impairment losses should be considered only for that group of assets as a whole—individual assets within the group should not be considered separately.

(c) concluding that the recoverable amount of goodwill—which cannot generate cash inflows independently of other assets—should be measured separately for measuring impairment losses makes it difficult to understand how the Board could in the future reasonably conclude that such an approach to measuring impairment losses is also not appropriate for other assets. In other words, if it adopts the proposed two-step approach for goodwill, the Board could in effect be committing itself to an 'individual asset/fair value' approach for measuring impairments of all other assets. A decision on this issue should be made only as part of a broad reconsideration of the appropriate measurement objective for impairment testing generally.

(d) if goodwill is considered separately for impairment testing using an implied value calculation when other assets within a unit are considered only as part of the unit as a whole, there will be asymmetry: unrecognised goodwill will shield the carrying value of other assets from impairment, but the unrecognised value of other assets will not shield the carrying amount of goodwill from impairment. This seems unreasonable given that the unrecognised value of those other assets cannot then be recognised. Additionally, the carrying amount of a unit will be less than its recoverable amount whenever an impairment loss for goodwill exceeds the unrecognised value of the other assets in the unit.

BC166 Additionally, respondents, field visit participants and North American round-table participants raised the following concerns about the practicability and costs of applying the proposed two-step approach:

(a) many companies would be required regularly to perform the second step of the impairment test, and therefore would need to determine the fair values of each identifiable asset, liability and contingent liability within the impaired unit(s) that the entity would recognise if it acquired the unit(s) in a business combination on the date of the impairment test. Although determining these fair values would not, for some companies, pose significant practical challenges (because, for example, fair value information for their significant assets is readily available), most would need to engage, on a fairly wide scale and at significant cost, independent valuers for some or all of the unit's assets. This is particularly the case for identifying and measuring the fair values of unrecognised internally generated intangible assets.

(b) determining the fair values of each identifiable asset, liability and contingent liability within an impaired unit is likely to be impracticable for multi-segmented manufacturers that operate multi-product facilities servicing more than one cash-generating unit. For example, assume an entity's primary basis of segmentation is geographical (eg Europe, North America, South America, Asia, Oceania and Africa) and that its secondary basis of segmentation is based on product groups (vaccinations, over–the–counter medicines, prescription medicines and vitamins/dietary supplements). Assume also that:

(i) the lowest level within the entity at which the goodwill is monitored for internal management purposes is one level below primary segment (eg the vitamins business in North America), and that goodwill is therefore tested for impairment at this level;

(ii) the plants and distribution facilities in each geographical region manufacture and distribute for all product groups; and

(iii) to determine the carrying amount of each cash-generating unit containing goodwill, the carrying amount of each plant and distribution facility has been allocated between each product group it services.

If, for example, the recoverable amount of the North American vitamins unit were less than its carrying amount, measuring the implied value of goodwill in that unit would require a valuation exercise to be undertaken for *all* North American assets so that a portion of each asset's fair value can then be allocated to the North American vitamins unit. These valuations are likely to be extremely costly and virtually impossible to complete within a reasonable time period (field visit participants' estimates ranged from six to twelve months). The degree of impracticability will be even greater for those entities that monitor, and therefore test, goodwill at the segment level.

BC167 In considering the above comments, the Board noted that:

(a) all of the US registrant field visit participants and North American round-table participants that have had to perform the second step of the SFAS 142 impairment test were compelled to engage, at significant cost, independent valuers.

(b) the impairment model proposed in the Exposure Draft, although based on the two-step approach in SFAS 142, differed from the SFAS 142 test and would be unlikely to result in convergence for the following reasons:

(i) the recoverable amount of a unit to which goodwill is allocated in accordance with IAS 36 would be the higher of the unit's value in use and fair value less costs to sell, rather than fair value. Many of the US registrant field visit participants stated that the measure of recoverable amount they would use under IAS 36 would differ from the fair value measure they would be required to use under SFAS 142.

(ii) the level at which goodwill is tested for impairment in accordance with SFAS 142 will often be higher than the level at which it would be tested under IAS 36. Many of the US registrant field visit participants stated that goodwill would be tested for impairment in accordance with IAS 36 at a lower level than under SFAS 142 because of either: (1) the limit SFAS 142 places on how far goodwill can be 'pushed down' for impairment testing (ie one level below an operating segment); or (2) the requirement in SFAS 142 to aggregate components with similar economic characteristics. Nevertheless, these participants unanimously agreed that the IAS 36 approach provides users and management with more useful information. The Board also noted that many of the North American round-table participants stated that they (or, in the case of audit firm participants, their clients) manage and have available information about their investments in goodwill at a level lower than a reporting unit as defined in SFAS 142. Many of these participants expressed a high level of dissatisfaction at being prevented by SFAS 142 from recognising goodwill impairments that they knew existed at these lower levels, but 'disappeared' once the lower level units were aggregated with other units containing sufficient 'cushions' to offset the impairment loss.

BC168 The Board also noted that, unlike SFAS 142, it had as its starting point an impairment model in IAS 36 that integrates the impairment testing of *all* assets within a cash-generating unit, including goodwill. Unlike US generally accepted accounting principles (GAAP), which use an undiscounted cash flow screening mechanism for impairment testing long-lived assets other than goodwill, IAS 36 requires the recoverable amount of an asset or cash-generating unit to be measured whenever there is an indication of possible impairment. Therefore, if at the time of impairment testing a 'larger' unit to which goodwill has been allocated there is an indication of a possible impairment in an asset or 'smaller' cash-generating unit included in that larger unit, an entity is required to test that asset or smaller unit for impairment first. Consequently, the Board concluded that it would be reasonable in an IAS 36 context to presume that an impairment loss for the larger unit would, after all other assets and smaller units are assessed for impairment, be likely to relate to the goodwill in the unit. Such a presumption would not be reasonable if an entity were following US GAAP.

BC169 The Board considered converging fully with the SFAS 142 approach. However, although supporting convergence, the Board was concerned that the SFAS 142 approach would not provide better information than an approach under which goodwill is tested for impairment at a lower level (thereby removing many of the 'cushions' protecting the goodwill from impairment) but with the amount of any impairment loss for goodwill measured in accordance with the one-step approach in the previous version of IAS 36.

BC170 The Board concluded that the complexity and costs of applying the two-step approach proposed in the Exposure Draft would outweigh the benefits of that approach. Therefore, the Board decided to retain the approach to measuring impairments of goodwill included in the previous version of IAS 36. Thus, the Standard requires any excess of the carrying amount of a cash-generating unit (group of units) to which goodwill has been allocated over its recoverable amount to be recognised first as an impairment loss for goodwill. Any excess remaining after the carrying amount of goodwill has been reduced to zero is then recognised by being allocated to the other assets of the unit pro rata with their carrying amounts.

Timing of impairment tests (paragraphs 96–99)

BC171 To reduce the costs of applying the test, and consistently with the proposals in the Exposure Draft, the Standard permits the annual impairment test for a cash-generating unit (group of units) to which goodwill has been allocated to be performed at any time during an annual period, provided the test is performed at the same time every year. Different cash-generating units (groups of units) may be tested for impairment at different times. However, if some or all of the goodwill allocated to a unit (group of units) was acquired in a business combination during the current annual period, that unit (group of units) must be tested for impairment before the end of the current annual period.

BC172 The Board observed that acquirers can sometimes 'overpay' for an acquiree, resulting in the amount initially recognised for the business combination and the resulting goodwill exceeding the recoverable amount of the investment. The Board concluded that the users of an entity's financial statements are provided with representationally faithful, and therefore useful, information about a business combination if such an impairment loss is recognised by the acquirer in the annual period in which the business combination occurs.

BC173 The Board was concerned that it might be possible for entities to delay recognising such an impairment loss until the annual period after the business combination if the Standard included only a requirement to impairment test cash-generating units (groups of units) to which goodwill has been allocated on an annual basis at any time during a period. Therefore, the Board decided to include in the Standard the added requirement that if some or all of the goodwill allocated to a unit (group of units) was acquired in a business combination during the current annual period, the unit (group of units) should be tested for impairment before the end of that period.

Sequence of impairment tests (paragraph 97)

BC174 The Standard requires that if the assets (cash-generating units) constituting the cash-generating unit (group of units) to which goodwill has been allocated are tested for impairment at the same time as the unit (group of units) containing the goodwill, those other assets (units) should be tested for impairment before the unit (group of units) containing the goodwill.

BC175 The Board observed that assets or cash-generating units making up a unit or group of units to which goodwill has been allocated might need to be tested for impairment at the same time as the unit or group of units containing the goodwill when there is an indication of a possible impairment of the asset or smaller unit. The Board concluded that to assess whether the unit or group of units containing the goodwill, and therefore whether the goodwill, is impaired, the carrying amount of the unit or group of units containing the goodwill would need first to be adjusted by recognising any impairment losses relating to the assets or smaller units within that unit or group of units.

Carrying forward a recoverable amount calculation (paragraph 99)

BC176 Consistently with the impairment test for indefinite-lived intangibles, the Standard permits the most recent detailed calculation of the recoverable amount of a cash-generating unit (group of units) to which goodwill has been allocated to be carried forward from a preceding period for use in the current period's impairment test, provided all of the criteria in paragraph 99 are met.

BC177 Integral to the Board's decision that goodwill should be tested for impairment annually was the view that many entities should be able to conclude that the recoverable amount of a cash-generating unit (group of units) to which goodwill has been allocated is greater than its carrying amount without actually recomputing recoverable amount. However, again consistently with its conclusions about indefinite-lived intangibles, the Board concluded that this would be the case only if the last recoverable amount determination exceeded the carrying amount of the unit (group of units) by a substantial margin, and nothing had happened since that last determination to make the likelihood of an impairment loss other than remote. The Board concluded that in such circumstances, permitting a detailed calculation of the recoverable amount of a cash-generating unit (group of units) to which goodwill has been allocated to be carried forward from the preceding period for use in the current period's impairment test would significantly reduce the costs of applying the impairment test, without compromising its integrity.

Allocating an impairment loss between the assets of a cash-generating unit (paragraphs 104–107)

BCZ178 IAS 36 includes requirements for the allocation of an impairment loss for a cash-generating unit that differ from the proposals in E55. In particular, E55 proposed that an impairment loss should be allocated:

(a) first, to goodwill;

(b) secondly, to intangible assets for which no active market exists;

(c) thirdly, to assets whose net selling price* is less than their carrying amount; and

(d) then, to the other assets of the unit on a pro-rata basis based on the carrying amount of each asset in the unit.

BCZ179 The underlying reasons for making this proposal were that:

(a) an impairment loss for a cash-generating unit should be allocated, in priority, to assets with the most subjective values. Goodwill and intangible assets for which there is no active market were considered to be in that category. Intangible assets for which there is no active market were considered to be similar to goodwill (IASC was thinking of brand names, publishing titles etc).

(b) if the net selling price of an asset is less than its carrying amount, this was considered a reasonable basis for allocating part of the impairment loss to that asset rather than to other assets.

BCZ180 Many commentators on E55 objected to the proposal on the grounds that:

(a) not all intangible assets for which no active market exists are similar to goodwill (for example, licences and franchise rights). They disagreed that the value of intangible assets is always more subjective than the value of tangible assets (for example, specialised plant and equipment).

(b) the concept of cash-generating units implies a global approach for the assets of the units and not an asset-by-asset approach.

In response to these comments, IASC decided to withdraw E55's proposal for the allocation of an impairment loss to intangible assets and assets whose net selling price is less than their carrying amount.

* In IFRS 5 *Non-current Assets Held for Sale and Discontinued Operations*, issued by the IASB in 2004, the term 'net selling price' was replaced in IAS 36 by 'fair value less costs to sell'.

BCZ181 IASC rejected a proposal that an impairment loss for a cash-generating unit should be allocated first to any obviously impaired asset. IASC believed that if the recoverable amount of an obviously impaired asset can be determined for the individual asset, there is no need to estimate the recoverable amount of the asset's cash-generating unit. If the recoverable amount of an individual asset cannot be determined, it cannot be said that the asset is obviously impaired because an impairment loss for a cash-generating unit relates to all of the assets of that unit.

Reversing impairment losses for assets other than goodwill (paragraphs 110–123)

BCZ182 IAS 36 requires that an impairment loss for an asset other than goodwill should be reversed if, and only if, there has been a change in the estimates used to determine an asset's recoverable amount since the last impairment loss was recognised.

BCZ183 Opponents of reversals of impairment losses argue that:

(a) reversals of impairment losses are contrary to the historical cost accounting system. When the carrying amount is reduced, recoverable amount becomes the new cost basis for an asset. Consequently, reversing an impairment loss is no different from revaluing an asset upward. Indeed, in many cases, recoverable amount is similar to the measurement basis used for the revaluation of an asset. Hence, reversals of impairment losses should be either prohibited or recognised directly in equity as a revaluation.

(b) reversals of impairment losses introduce volatility in reported earnings. Periodic, short-term income measurements should not be affected by unrealised changes in the measurement of a long-lived asset.

(c) the result of reversals of impairment losses would not be useful to users of financial statements since the amount of a reversal under IAS 36 is limited to an amount that does not increase the carrying amount of an asset above its depreciated historical cost. Neither the amount reversed nor the revised carrying amount have any information content.

(d) in many cases, reversals of impairment losses will result in the implicit recognition of internally generated goodwill.

(e) reversals of impairment losses open the door to abuse and income 'smoothing' in practice.

(f) follow-up to verify whether an impairment loss needs to be reversed is costly.

BCZ184 IASC's reasons for requiring reversals of impairment losses were the following:

(a) it is consistent with the *Framework* and the view that future economic benefits that were not previously expected to flow from an asset have been reassessed as probable.

(b) a reversal of an impairment loss is not a revaluation and is consistent with the historical cost accounting system as long as the reversal does not result in the carrying amount of an asset exceeding its original cost less amortisation/depreciation, had the impairment loss not been recognised. Accordingly, the reversal of an impairment loss should be recognised in the income statement and any amount in excess of the depreciated historical cost should be accounted for as a revaluation.

(c) impairment losses are recognised and measured based on estimates. Any change in the measurement of an impairment loss is similar to a change in estimate. IAS 8 *Net Profit or Loss for the Period, Fundamental Errors and Changes in Accounting Policies** requires that a change in accounting estimate should be included in the determination of the net profit or loss in (a) the period of the change, if the change affects the period only, or (b) the period of the change and future periods, if the change affects both.

(d) reversals of impairment losses provide users with a more useful indication of the potential for future benefits of an asset or group of assets.

(e) results of operations will be more fairly stated in the current period and in future periods because depreciation or amortisation will not reflect a previous impairment loss that is no longer relevant. Prohibition of reversals of impairment losses may lead to abuses such as recording a significant loss one year with the resulting lower amortisation/depreciation charge and higher profits in subsequent years.

BCZ185 The majority of commentators on E55 supported IASC's proposals for reversals of impairment losses.

BCZ186 IAS 36 does not permit an enterprise to recognise a reversal of an impairment loss just because of the unwinding of the discount. IASC supported this requirement for practical reasons only. Otherwise, if an impairment loss is recognised and recoverable amount is based on value in use, a reversal of the impairment loss would be recognised in each subsequent year for the unwinding of the discount. This is because, in most cases, the pattern of depreciation of an asset is different from the pattern of value in use. IASC believed that, when there is no change in the assumptions used to estimate recoverable amount, the benefits from recognising the unwinding of the discount each year after an impairment loss has been recognised do not justify the costs involved. However, if a reversal is recognised because assumptions have changed, the discount unwinding effect is included in the amount of the reversal recognised.

Reversing goodwill impairment losses (paragraph 124)

BC187 Consistently with the proposal in the Exposure Draft, the Standard prohibits the recognition of reversals of impairment losses for goodwill. The previous version of IAS 36 required an impairment loss for goodwill recognised in a previous period to be reversed when the impairment loss was caused by a specific external event of an exceptional nature that was not expected to recur, and subsequent external events had occurred that reversed the effect of that event.

BC188 Most respondents to the Exposure Draft agreed that reversals of impairment losses for goodwill should be prohibited. Those that disagreed argued that reversals of impairment losses for goodwill should be treated in the same way as reversals of

* IAS 8 *Net Profit or Loss for the Period, Fundamental Errors and Changes in Accounting Policies* was superseded in 2003 by IAS 8 *Accounting Policies, Changes in Accounting Estimates and Errors*.

impairment losses for other assets, but limited to circumstances in which the impairment loss was caused by specific events beyond the entity's control.

BC189 In revising IAS 36, the Board noted that IAS 38 *Intangible Assets* prohibits the recognition of internally generated goodwill. Therefore, if reversals of impairment losses for goodwill were permitted, an entity would need to establish the extent to which a subsequent increase in the recoverable amount of goodwill is attributable to the recovery of the acquired goodwill within a cash-generating unit, rather than an increase in the internally generated goodwill within the unit. The Board concluded that this will seldom, if ever, be possible. Because the acquired goodwill and internally generated goodwill contribute jointly to the same cash flows, any subsequent increase in the recoverable amount of the acquired goodwill is indistinguishable from an increase in the internally generated goodwill. Even if the specific external event that caused the recognition of the impairment loss is reversed, it will seldom, if ever, be possible to determine that the effect of that reversal is a corresponding increase in the recoverable amount of the acquired goodwill. Therefore, the Board concluded that reversals of impairment losses for goodwill should be prohibited.

BC190 The Board expressed some concern that prohibiting the recognition of reversals of impairment losses for goodwill so as to avoid recognising internally generated goodwill might be viewed by some as inconsistent with the impairment test for goodwill. This is because the impairment test results in the carrying amount of goodwill being shielded from impairment by internally generated goodwill. This has been described by some as 'backdoor' capitalisation of internally generated goodwill.

BC191 However, the Board was not as concerned about goodwill being shielded from the recognition of impairment losses by internally generated goodwill as it was about the direct recognition of internally generated goodwill that might occur if reversals of impairment losses for goodwill were permitted. As discussed in paragraph BC135, the Board is of the view that it is not possible to devise an impairment test for acquired goodwill that removes the cushion against the recognition of impairment losses provided by goodwill generated internally after a business combination.

Disclosures for cash–generating units containing goodwill or indefinite–lived intangibles (paragraphs 134 and 135)

Background to the proposals in the Exposure Draft

BC192 The Exposure Draft proposed requiring an entity to disclose a range of information about cash-generating units whose carrying amounts included goodwill or indefinite-lived intangibles. That information included:

(a) the carrying amount of goodwill and the carrying amount of indefinite-lived intangibles.

(b) the basis on which the unit's recoverable amount had been determined (ie value in use or net selling price).

(c) the amount by which the unit's recoverable amount exceeded its carrying amount.

(d) the key assumptions and estimates used to measure the unit's recoverable amount and information about the sensitivity of that recoverable amount to changes in the key assumptions and estimates.

BC193 If an entity reports segment information in accordance with IAS 14 *Segment Reporting*, the Exposure Draft proposed that this information should be disclosed in aggregate for each segment based on the entity's primary reporting format. However, the Exposure Draft also proposed that the information would be disclosed separately for a cash-generating unit when:

(a) the carrying amount of the goodwill or indefinite-lived intangibles allocated to the unit was significant in relation to the total carrying amount of goodwill or indefinite-lived intangibles; or

(b) the basis for determining the unit's recoverable amount differed from the basis used for the other units within the segment whose carrying amounts include goodwill or indefinite-lived intangibles; or

(c) the nature of, or value assigned to the key assumptions or growth rate on which management based its determination of the unit's recoverable amount differed significantly from that used for the other units within the segment whose carrying amounts include goodwill or indefinite-lived intangibles.

BC194 In deciding to propose these disclosure requirements in the Exposure Draft, the Board observed that non-amortisation of goodwill and indefinite-lived intangibles increases the reliance that must be placed on impairment tests of those assets to ensure that their carrying amounts do not exceed their recoverable amounts. However, the nature of impairment tests means that the carrying amounts of such assets and the related assertion that those carrying amounts are recoverable will normally be supported only by management's projections. Therefore, the Board decided to examine ways in which the reliability of the impairment tests for goodwill and indefinite-lived intangibles could be improved. As a first step, the Board considered including a subsequent cash flow test in the revised Standard, similar to that included in UK Financial Reporting Standard 11 *Impairment of Fixed Assets and Goodwill* (FRS 11).

Subsequent cash flow test

BC195 FRS 11 requires an entity to perform a subsequent cash flow test to confirm, ex post, the cash flow projections used to measure a unit's value in use when testing goodwill for impairment. Under FRS 11, for five years following each impairment test for goodwill in which recoverable amount has been based on value in use, the actual cash flows achieved must be compared with those forecast. If the actual cash flows are so much less than those forecast that use of the actual cash flows in the value in use calculation could have required recognition of an impairment in previous periods, the original impairment calculations must be re-performed using the actual cash flows, but without revising any other cash flows or assumptions (except those that change as a direct consequence of the occurrence of the actual cash flows, for example where a major cash inflow has been delayed for a year). Any impairment identified must then be recognised in the current period, unless the impairment has reversed and the reversal of the loss satisfies the criteria in FRS 11 regarding reversals of impairment losses for goodwill.

BC196 The Board noted the following arguments in support of including a similar test in the revised Standard:

(a) it would enhance the reliability of the goodwill impairment test by preventing the possibility of entities avoiding the recognition of impairment losses by using over-optimistic cash flow projections in the value in use calculations.

(b) it would provide useful information to users of an entity's financial statements because a record of actual cash flows continually less than forecast cash flows tends to cast doubt on the reliability of current estimates.

BC197 However, the subsequent cash flow test is designed only to prevent entities from avoiding goodwill write-downs. The Board observed that, given current trends in 'big bath' restructuring charges, the greater risk to the quality of financial reporting might be from entities trying to write off goodwill without adequate justification in an attempt to 'manage' the balance sheet. The Board also observed that:

(a) the focus of the test on cash flows ignores other elements in the measurement of value in use. As a result, it does not produce representationally faithful results in a present value measurement system. The Board considered incorporating into the recalculation performed under the test corrections of estimates of other elements in the measurement of value in use. However, the Board concluded that specifying which elements to include would be problematic. Moreover, adding corrections of estimates of those other elements to the test would, in effect, transform the test into a requirement to perform a comprehensive recalculation of value in use for each of the five annual reporting periods following an impairment test.

(b) the amount recognised as an impairment loss under the test is the amount of the impairment that would have been recognised, provided changes in estimates of remaining cash flows and changes in discount and growth rates are ignored. Therefore, it is a hypothetical amount that does not provide decision-useful information—it is neither an estimate of a current amount nor a prediction of ultimate cash flows.

(c) the requirement to perform the test for each of the five annual reporting periods following an impairment test could result in an entity having to maintain as many as five sets of 5-year computations for each cash-generating unit to which goodwill has been allocated. Therefore, the test is likely to be extremely burdensome, particularly if an entity has a large number of such units, without producing understandable or decision-useful information.

BC198 Therefore, the Board decided not to propose a subsequent cash flow test in the Exposure Draft. However, the Board remained committed to finding some way of improving the reliability of the impairment tests for goodwill and indefinite-lived intangibles, and decided to explore improving that reliability through disclosure requirements.

Including disclosure requirements in the revised Standard

BC199 In developing the Exposure Draft, the Board observed that the *Framework* identifies reliability as one of the key qualitative characteristics that information must possess to be useful to users in making economic decisions. To be reliable, information must be free from material error and bias and be able to be depended upon to represent faithfully that which it purports to represent. The *Framework* identifies relevance as another key qualitative characteristic that information must possess to be useful to users in making economic decisions. To be relevant, information must help users to evaluate past, present or future events, or confirm or correct their past evaluations.

BC200 The Board observed that information that assists users in evaluating the reliability of other information included in the financial statements is itself relevant, increasing in relevance as the reliability of that other information decreases. For example, information that assists users in evaluating the reliability of the amount recognised for a provision is relevant because it helps users to evaluate the effect of both a past event (ie the economic consequences of the past event giving rise to the present obligation) and a future event (ie the amount of the expected future outflow of economic benefits required to settle the obligation). Accordingly, IAS 37 *Provisions, Contingent Liabilities and Contingent Assets* requires an entity to disclose, for each class of provision, information about the uncertainties surrounding the amount and timing of expected outflows of economic benefits, and the major assumptions concerning future events that may affect the amount required to settle the obligation and have been reflected in the amount of the provision.

BC201 The Board concluded that because information that assists users in evaluating the reliability of other information is itself relevant, an entity should disclose information that assists users in evaluating the reliability of the estimates used by management to support the carrying amounts of goodwill and indefinite-lived intangibles.

BC202 The Board also concluded that such disclosures would provide users with more useful information for evaluating the reliability of the impairment tests for goodwill and indefinite-lived intangibles than the information that would be provided by a subsequent cash flow test.

BC203 The Board then considered how some balance might be achieved between the objective of providing users with useful information for evaluating the reliability of the estimates used by management to support the carrying amounts of goodwill and indefinite-lived intangibles, and the potential magnitude of those disclosures.

BC204 The Board decided that a reasonable balance might be achieved between the objective of the disclosures and their potential magnitude by requiring:

(a) information to be disclosed on an aggregate basis for each segment based on the entity's primary reporting format that includes in its carrying amount goodwill or indefinite-lived intangibles; but

(b) information for a particular cash-generating unit within that segment to be excluded from the aggregate information and disclosed separately when either:

(i) the basis (ie net selling price or value in use), methodology or key assumptions used to measure its recoverable amount differ from those used to measure the recoverable amounts of the other units in the segment; or

(ii) the carrying amount of the goodwill or indefinite-lived intangibles in the unit is significant in relation to the total carrying amount of goodwill or indefinite-lived intangibles.

The Board's redeliberations

BC205 After considering respondents' and field visit participants' comments, the Board confirmed its previous conclusion that information that assists users in evaluating the reliability of other information is itself relevant, increasing in relevance as the reliability of that other information decreases. Therefore, entities should be required to disclose information that assists users in evaluating the reliability of the estimates used by management to support the carrying amounts of goodwill and indefinite-lived intangibles. The Board noted that almost all field visit participants and many respondents expressed explicit support of its conclusion that, because non-amortisation of goodwill and indefinite-lived intangibles increases the reliance that must be placed on impairment tests of those assets, some additional disclosure is necessary to provide users with information for evaluating the reliability of those impairment tests.

BC206 However, it was clear from field visit participants' responses that the proposed disclosures could not be meaningfully aggregated at the segment level to the extent the Board had hoped might be the case. As a result, the proposal to require the information to be disclosed on an aggregate basis for each segment, but with disaggregated disclosures for cash-generating units in the circumstances set out in paragraph BC193 would not result in a reasonable balance between the objective of the disclosures and their potential magnitude.

BC207 The Board was also sympathetic to field visit participants' and respondents' concerns that the proposed disclosures went beyond their intended objective of providing users with relevant information for evaluating the reliability of the impairment tests for goodwill and indefinite-lived intangibles. For example, field visit participants and respondents argued that:

(a) it would be extremely difficult to distil the recoverable amount calculations into concise but meaningful disclosures because those calculations typically are complex and do not normally result in a single point estimate of recoverable amount—a single value for recoverable amount would normally be determined only when the bottom-end of the recoverable amount range is less than a cash-generating unit's carrying amount. These difficulties make it doubtful that the information, particularly the sensitivity analyses, could be produced on a timely basis.

(b) disclosing the proposed information, particularly the values assigned to, and the sensitivity of, each key assumption on which recoverable amount calculations are based, could cause significant commercial harm to an entity. Users of financial statements might, for example, use the quantitative disclosures as the basis for initiating litigation against the entity, its board of directors or management in the highly likely event that those assumptions prove less than accurate. The increased litigation risk would either encourage management to use super-conservative assumptions, thereby resulting in improper asset write-downs, or compel management to engage independent experts to develop all key assumptions and perform the recoverable amount calculations. Additionally, many of the field visit participants expressed concern over the possible impact that disclosing such information might have on their ability to defend themselves in various legal proceedings.

BC208 Therefore, the Board considered the following two interrelated issues:

(a) if the proposed disclosures went beyond their intended objective, what information *should* be disclosed so that users have sufficient information for evaluating the reliability of impairment tests for goodwill and indefinite-lived intangibles?

(b) how should this information be presented so that there is an appropriate balance between providing users with information for evaluating the reliability of the impairment tests, and the potential magnitude of those disclosures?

BC209 As a result of its redeliberations, the Board decided:

(a) not to proceed with the proposal to require information for evaluating the reliability of the impairment tests for goodwill and indefinite-lived intangibles to be disclosed in aggregate for each segment and separately for cash-generating units within a segment in specified circumstances. Instead, the Standard requires this information to be disclosed only for each cash-generating unit (group of units) for which the carrying amount of goodwill or indefinite-lived intangibles allocated to that unit (group of units) is significant in comparison with the entity's total carrying amount of goodwill or indefinite-lived intangibles.

(b) not to proceed with the proposal to require an entity to disclose the amount by which the recoverable amount of a cash-generating unit exceeds its carrying amount. Instead, the Standard requires an entity to disclose this information only if a reasonably possible change in a key assumption on which management has based its determination of the unit's (group of units') recoverable amount would cause the unit's (group of units') carrying amount to exceed its recoverable amount.

(c) not to proceed with the proposal to require an entity to disclose the value assigned to each key assumption on which management based its recoverable amount determination, and the amount by which that value must change, after incorporating any consequential effects of that change on the other variables used to measure recoverable amount, in order for the unit's recoverable amount to be equal to its carrying amount. Instead, the Standard requires an entity to disclose a description of each key assumption on which management has based its recoverable amount determination, management's approach to determining the value(s) assigned to each key assumption, whether those value(s) reflect past experience or, if appropriate, are consistent with external sources of information, and, if not, how and why they differ from past experience or external sources of information. However, if a reasonably possible change in a key assumption would cause the unit's (group of units') carrying amount to exceed its recoverable amount, the entity is also required to disclose the value assigned to the key assumption, and the amount by which that value must change, after incorporating any consequential effects of that change on the other variables used to measure recoverable amount, in order for the unit's (group of units') recoverable amount to be equal to its carrying amount.

(d) to require information about key assumptions to be disclosed also for any key assumption that is relevant to the recoverable amount determination of multiple cash-generating units (groups of units) that individually contain insignificant amounts of goodwill or indefinite-lived intangibles, but contain, in aggregate, significant amounts of goodwill or indefinite-lived intangibles.

Transitional provisions (paragraphs 138–140)

BC210 If an entity elects to apply IFRS 3 from any date before the effective dates outlined in IFRS 3, it is also required to apply IAS 36 from that same date. Paragraphs BC181–BC184 of the Basis for Conclusions on IFRS 3 outline the Board's deliberations on this issue.

BC211 Otherwise, IAS 36 is applied:

(a) to goodwill and intangible assets acquired in business combinations for which the agreement date is on or after 31 March 2004; and

(b) to all other assets prospectively from the beginning of the first annual period beginning on or after 31 March 2004.

BC212 In developing the requirements set out in paragraph BC211, the Board considered whether entities should be required:

(a) to apply retrospectively the revised impairment test for goodwill; and

(b) to apply retrospectively the requirement prohibiting reversals of impairment losses for goodwill and therefore eliminate any reversals recognised before the date the revised Standard was issued.

BC213 The Board concluded that retrospective application of the revised impairment test for goodwill would be problematic for the following reasons:

(a) it was likely to be impossible in many cases because the information needed may not exist or may no longer be obtainable.

(b) it would require the determination of estimates that would have been made at a prior date, and therefore would raise the problem of how the effect of hindsight could be separated from the factors existing at the date of the impairment test.

BC214 The Board also noted that the requirement for goodwill to be tested for impairment annually, irrespective of whether there is any indication that it may be impaired, will ensure that by the end of the first period in which the Standard is effective, all recognised goodwill acquired before its effective date would be tested for impairment.

BC215 In the case of reversals of impairment losses for goodwill, the Board acknowledged that requiring the elimination of reversals recognised before the revised Standard's effective date might seem appropriate, particularly given the Board's reasons for prohibiting reversals of impairment losses for goodwill (see paragraphs BC187–BC191). The Board concluded, however, that the previous amortisation of that goodwill, combined with the requirement for goodwill to be tested for impairment at least annually, ensures that the carrying amount of the goodwill does not exceed its recoverable amount at the end of the reporting period in which the Standard is effective. Therefore, the Board concluded that the Standard should apply on a prospective basis.

Transitional impairment test for goodwill

BC216 Given that one of the objectives of the first phase of the Business Combinations project was to seek international convergence on the accounting for goodwill, the Board considered whether IAS 36 should include a transitional goodwill impairment test similar to that included in SFAS 142. SFAS 142 requires goodwill to be tested for impairment annually, and between annual tests if an event occurs or circumstances change and would be more likely than not to reduce the fair value of a reporting unit below its carrying amount. The transitional provisions in SFAS 142 require the impairment test for goodwill to be applied prospectively. However, a transitional goodwill impairment test must be performed as of the *beginning* of the fiscal year in which SFAS 142 is applied in its entirety. An impairment loss recognised as a result of a transitional test is recognised as the effect of a change in accounting principle, rather than as an impairment loss. In addition to the transitional test, SFAS 142 requires an entity to perform the required annual goodwill impairment test in the year that SFAS 142 is initially applied in its entirety. In other words, the transitional goodwill impairment test may not be regarded as the initial year's annual test unless an entity designates the beginning of its fiscal year as the date for its annual goodwill impairment test.

BC217 The FASB concluded that goodwill that was not regarded as impaired under US GAAP before SFAS 142 was issued could be determined to be impaired if the SFAS 142 impairment test was applied to that goodwill at the date an entity initially applied SFAS 142. This is because, under previous US GAAP, entities typically tested goodwill for impairment using undiscounted estimates of future cash flows. The FASB further concluded that:

(a) the preponderance of any transitional impairment losses was likely to result from the change in methods and treating those losses as stemming from changes in accounting principles would therefore be more representationally faithful.

(b) given that a transitional impairment loss should be reported as a change in accounting principle, the transitional goodwill impairment test should ideally apply as of the date SFAS 142 is initially applied.

BC218 The Board observed that under the previous version of IAS 36, goodwill that was amortised over a period exceeding 20 years was required to be tested for impairment at least at each financial year-end. Goodwill that was amortised over a period not exceeding 20 years was required to be tested for impairment at the balance sheet date if there was an indication that it might be impaired. The revised Standard requires goodwill to be tested for impairment annually or more frequently if there is an indication the goodwill might be impaired. It also carries forward from the previous version of IAS 36 (a) the indicators of impairment, (b) the measure of recoverable amount (ie higher of value in use and fair value less costs to sell), and (c) the requirement for an impairment loss for a cash-generating unit to be allocated first to reduce the carrying amount of any goodwill allocated to the unit.

BC219 Therefore, goodwill tested for impairment in accordance with the previous version of the revised Standard immediately before the beginning of the reporting period in which the revised Standard becomes effective (because it was being amortised over a period exceeding 20 years or because there was an indicator of impairment) could not be identified as impaired under IAS 36 at the beginning of the period in which it becomes effective. This is because application of the Standard results in a goodwill impairment loss being identified only if the carrying amount of the cash-generating unit (group of units) to which the goodwill has been allocated exceeds its recoverable amount, and the impairment test in the previous version of IAS 36 ensures that this will not be the case.

BC220 The Board concluded that there would be only one possible situation in which a transitional impairment test might give rise to the recognition of an impairment loss for goodwill. This would be when goodwill being amortised over a period not exceeding 20 years was, immediately before the beginning of the period in which the revised Standard becomes effective, impaired in the absence of any indicator of impairment that ought reasonably to have been considered by the entity. The Board concluded that this is likely to be a rare occurrence.

BC221 The Board observed that any such impairment loss would nonetheless be recognised as a consequence of applying the requirement in IAS 36 to test goodwill for impairment at least annually. Therefore, the only benefit of applying a transitional impairment test would be, in those rare cases, to separate the impairment loss arising before the period in which the revised Standard is effective from any impairment loss arising after the beginning of that period.

BC222 The Board concluded that given the rare circumstances in which this issue would arise, the benefit of applying a transitional goodwill impairment test would be outweighed by the added costs of the test. Therefore, the Board decided that the revised Standard should not require a transitional goodwill impairment test.

Transitional impairment test for indefinite–lived intangibles

BC223 SFAS 142 also requires a transitional impairment test to be applied, as of the beginning of the fiscal year in which that Standard is initially applied, to intangible assets recognised before the effective date of SFAS 142 that are reassessed as having indefinite useful lives. An impairment loss arising from that transitional impairment test is recognised as the effect of a change in accounting principle rather than as an impairment loss. As with goodwill:

(a) intangible assets that cease being amortised upon initial application of SFAS 142 are tested for impairment in accordance with SFAS 142 using a different method from what had previously applied to those assets. Therefore, it is possible that such an intangible asset not previously regarded as impaired might be determined to be impaired under SFAS 142.

(b) the FASB concluded that the preponderance of any transitional impairment losses would be likely to result from the change in impairment testing methods. Treating those losses as stemming from changes in accounting principles is therefore more representationally faithful.

BC224 The Board considered whether IAS 36 should include a transitional impairment test for indefinite-lived intangibles similar to that in SFAS 142.

BC225 The Board observed that the previous version of IAS 38 *Intangible Assets* required an intangible asset being amortised over a period exceeding 20 years to be tested for impairment at least at each financial year-end in accordance with the previous version of IAS 36. An intangible asset being amortised over a period not exceeding 20 years was required, under the previous version of IAS 36, to be tested for impairment at the balance sheet date only if there was an indication the asset might be impaired. The revised Standard requires an indefinite-lived intangible to be tested for impairment at least annually. However, it also requires that the recoverable amount of such an asset should continue to be measured as the higher of the asset's value in use and fair value less costs to sell.

BC226 As with goodwill, the Board concluded that the revised Standard should not require a transitional impairment test for indefinite-lived intangibles because:

(a) the only circumstance in which a transitional impairment test might give rise to the recognition of an impairment loss would be when an indefinite-lived intangible previously being amortised over a period not exceeding 20 years was, immediately before the beginning of the period in which the revised Standard is effective, impaired in the absence of any indicator of impairment that ought reasonably to have been considered by the entity.

(b) any such impairment loss would nonetheless be recognised as a consequence of applying the requirement in the Standard to test such assets for impairment at least annually. Therefore, the only benefit of such a test would be to separate the impairment loss arising before the period in which the revised Standard is effective from any impairment loss arising after the beginning of that period.

(c) given the extremely rare circumstances in which this issue is likely to arise, the benefit of applying a transitional impairment test is outweighed by the added costs of the test.

Early application (paragraph 140)

BC227 The Board noted that the issue of any Standard demonstrates its opinion that application of the Standard will result in more useful information being provided to users about an entity's financial position, performance or cash flows. On that basis, a case exists for permitting, and indeed encouraging, entities to apply IAS 36 before its effective date. However, the Board also considered that permitting a revised Standard to be applied before its effective date potentially diminishes comparability between entities in the period(s) leading up to that effective date, and has the effect of providing entities with an option.

BC228 The Board concluded that the benefit of providing users with more useful information about an entity's financial position, performance and cash flows by permitting early application of IAS 36 outweighs the disadvantages of potentially diminished comparability. Therefore, entities are encouraged to apply the requirements of IAS 36 before its effective date. However, given that the revision of IAS 36 is part of an integrated package, IAS 36 requires IFRS 3 and IAS 38 (as revised in 2004) to be applied at the same time.

Summary of main changes from the Exposure Draft

BC229 The following are the main changes from the Exposure Draft:

(a) the Exposure Draft proposed that an intangible asset with an indefinite useful life should be tested for impairment at the end of each annual period by comparing its carrying amount with its recoverable amount. The Standard requires such an intangible asset to be tested for impairment annually by comparing its carrying amount with its recoverable amount. The impairment test may be performed at any time during an annual period, provided it is performed at the same time every year, and different intangible assets may be tested for impairment at different times. However, if such an intangible asset was initially recognised during the current annual period, the Standard requires that intangible asset to be tested for impairment before the end of the current annual period.

(b) the Exposure Draft proposed that the cash flow projections used to measure value in use should be based on reasonable and supportable assumptions that take into account both past actual cash flows and management's past ability to forecast cash flows accurately. This proposal has not been included in the Standard. Instead, the Standard includes guidance clarifying that management:

(i) should assess the reasonableness of the assumptions on which its current cash flow projections are based by examining the causes of differences between past cash flow projections and actual cash flows; and

(ii) should ensure that the assumptions on which its current cash flow projections are based are consistent with past actual outcomes, provided the effects of subsequent events or circumstances that did not exist when those actual cash flows were generated make this appropriate.

(c) the Exposure Draft proposed that if an active market exists for the output produced by an asset or a group of assets, that asset or group of assets should be identified as a cash-generating unit, even if some or all of the output is used internally. In such circumstances, management's best estimate of future market prices for the output should be used in estimating the future cash flows used to determine the unit's value in use. The Exposure Draft also proposed that when estimating future cash flows to determine the value in use of cash-generating units using the output, management's best estimate of future market prices for the output should be used.

The Standard similarly requires that if an active market exists for the output produced by an asset or a group of assets, that asset or group of assets should be identified as a cash-generating unit, even if some or all of the output is used internally. However, the Standard clarifies that if the cash inflows generated by *any* asset or cash-generating unit are affected by internal transfer pricing, an entity should use management's best estimate of future price(s) that could be achieved in arm's length transactions in estimating:

(i) the future cash inflows used to determine the asset's or cash-generating unit's value in use; and

(ii) the future cash outflows used to determine the value in use of other assets or cash-generating units affected by the internal transfer pricing.

(d) the Exposure Draft proposed that goodwill acquired in a business combination should be allocated to one or more cash-generating units, with each of those units representing the smallest cash-generating unit to which a portion of the carrying amount of the goodwill could be allocated on a reasonable and consistent basis. The Exposure Draft also proposed that:

(i) a portion of the carrying amount of goodwill should be regarded as capable of being allocated to a cash-generating unit on a reasonable and consistent basis only when that unit represents the lowest level at which management monitors the return on investment in assets that include the goodwill.

(ii) each cash-generating unit should not be larger than a segment based on the entity's primary reporting format determined in accordance with IAS 14 *Segment Reporting*.

The Standard requires goodwill acquired in a business combination to be allocated to each of the acquirer's cash-generating units, or groups of cash-generating units, that are expected to benefit from the synergies of the combination, irrespective of whether other assets or liabilities of the acquiree are assigned to those units or groups of units. The Standard also requires each unit or group of units to which the goodwill is so allocated: (1) to represent the lowest level within the entity at which the goodwill is monitored for internal management purposes; and (2) to be not larger than a segment based on either the entity's primary or the entity's secondary reporting format determined in accordance with IAS 14.

(e) the Exposure Draft proposed that when an entity disposes of an operation within a cash-generating unit to which goodwill has been allocated, the goodwill associated with that operation should be:

(i) included in the carrying amount of the operation when determining the gain or loss on disposal; and

(ii) measured on the basis of the relative values of the operation disposed of and the portion of the cash-generating unit retained.

This proposal has been included in the Standard with one modification. The Standard requires the goodwill associated with the operation disposed of to be measured on the basis of the relative values of the operation disposed of and the portion of the cash-generating unit retained, unless the entity can demonstrate that some other method better reflects the goodwill associated with the operation disposed of.

(f) the Exposure Draft proposed that when an entity reorganises its reporting structure in a way that changes the composition of cash-generating units to which goodwill has been allocated, the goodwill should be reallocated to the units affected using a relative value approach similar to that used when an entity disposes of an operation within a cash-generating unit. The Standard similarly requires an entity that reorganises its reporting structure in a way that changes the composition of one or more cash-generating units to which goodwill has been allocated to reallocate the goodwill to the units (groups of units) affected. However, the Standard requires this reallocation to be performed using a relative value approach similar to that used when an entity disposes of an operation within a cash-generating unit, unless the entity can demonstrate that some other method better reflects the goodwill associated with the reorganised units (groups of units).

(g) the Exposure Draft proposed a two-step approach for impairment testing goodwill. The first step involved using a screening mechanism for identifying potential goodwill impairments, whereby goodwill allocated to a cash-generating unit would be identified as potentially impaired only when the carrying amount of the unit exceeded its recoverable amount. If an entity identified the goodwill allocated to a cash-generating unit as potentially impaired, an entity would then determine whether the goodwill allocated to the unit was impaired by comparing its recoverable amount, measured as the implied value of the goodwill, with its carrying amount. The implied value of goodwill would be measured as a residual, being the excess of the recoverable amount of the cash-generating unit to which the goodwill has been allocated, over the net fair value of the identifiable assets, liabilities and contingent liabilities the entity would recognise if it acquired the cash-generating unit in a business combination on the date of the impairment test. The Standard requires any excess of the carrying amount of a cash-generating unit (group of units) to which goodwill has been allocated over its recoverable amount to be recognised first as an impairment loss for goodwill. Any excess remaining after the carrying amount of goodwill has been reduced to zero is then recognised by being allocated to the other assets of the unit pro rata with their carrying amounts.

(h) the Exposure Draft proposed requiring an entity to disclose information about cash-generating units whose carrying amounts included goodwill or indefinite-lived intangibles. That information included the carrying amount of goodwill and the carrying amount of indefinite-lived intangibles, the basis on which the unit's recoverable amount had been determined (ie value in use or net selling price), the amount by which the unit's recoverable amount exceeded its carrying amount, the key assumptions and estimates used to measure the unit's recoverable amount and information about the sensitivity of that recoverable amount to changes in the key assumptions and estimates. If an entity reports segment information in accordance with IAS 14, the Exposure Draft proposed that this information should be disclosed in aggregate for each segment based on the entity's primary reporting format. However, the Exposure Draft also proposed that the information would be disclosed separately for a cash-generating unit if specified criteria were met. The Standard:

(i) does not require information for evaluating the reliability of the impairment tests for goodwill and indefinite-lived intangibles to be disclosed in aggregate for each segment and separately for cash-generating units within a segment when specified criteria are met. Instead, the Standard requires this information to be disclosed for each cash-generating unit (group of units) for which the carrying amount of goodwill or indefinite-lived intangibles allocated to that unit (group of units) is significant in comparison with the entity's total carrying amount of goodwill or indefinite-lived intangibles.

(ii) does not require an entity to disclose the amount by which the recoverable amount of a cash-generating unit exceeds its carrying amount. Instead, the Standard requires an entity to disclose this information only if a reasonably possible change in a key assumption on which management has based its determination of the unit's (group of units') recoverable amount would cause the unit's (group of units') carrying amount to exceed its recoverable amount.

(iii) does not require an entity to disclose the value assigned to each key assumption on which management has based its recoverable amount determination, and the amount by which that value must change, after incorporating any consequential effects of that change on the other variables used to measure recoverable amount, in order for the unit's recoverable amount to be equal to its carrying amount. Instead, the Standard requires an entity to disclose a description of each key assumption on which management has based its recoverable amount determination, management's approach to determining the value(s) assigned to each key assumption, whether those value(s) reflect past experience or, if appropriate, are consistent with external sources of information, and, if not, how and why they differ from past experience or external sources of information. However, if a reasonably possible change in a key assumption would cause the unit's (group of units') carrying amount to exceed its recoverable amount, the entity is also required to disclose the value assigned to the key assumption, and the amount by which that value must change, after incorporating any consequential effects of that change on the other variables used to measure recoverable amount, in order for the unit's (group of units') recoverable amount to be equal to its carrying amount.

(iv) requires information about key assumptions to be disclosed for any key assumption that is relevant to the recoverable amount determination of multiple cash-generating units (groups of units) that individually contain insignificant amounts of goodwill or indefinite-lived intangibles, but which contain, in aggregate, significant amounts of goodwill or indefinite-lived intangibles.

History of the development of a standard on impairment of assets

BCZ230 In June 1996, IASC decided to prepare an International Accounting Standard on Impairment of Assets. The reasons for developing a Standard on impairment of assets were:

(a) to combine the requirements for identifying, measuring, recognising and reversing an impairment loss in one Standard to ensure that those requirements are consistent;

(b) the previous requirements and guidance in International Accounting Standards were not detailed enough to ensure that enterprises identified, recognised and measured impairment losses in a similar way, eg there was a need to eliminate certain alternatives for measuring an impairment loss, such as the former option not to use discounting; and

(c) IASC decided in March 1996 to explore whether the amortisation period of intangible assets and goodwill could, in certain rare circumstances, exceed 20 years if those assets were subject to detailed and reliable annual impairment tests.

BCZ231 In April 1997, IASC approved Exposure Draft E55 *Impairment of Assets*. IASC received more than 90 comment letters from over 20 countries. IASC also performed a field test of E55's proposals. More than 20 companies from various business sectors and from 10 different countries participated in the field test. About half of the field test participants prepared their financial statements using International Accounting Standards and the other half reported using other Standards. Field test participants completed a detailed questionnaire and most of them were visited by IASC staff to discuss the results of the application of E55's proposals to some of their assets. A brief summary of the comment letters received on E55 and the results of the field test was published in IASC *Insight* in December 1997.

BCZ232 In October 1997, IASC, together with the Accounting Standards Boards in Australia, Canada, New Zealand, the United Kingdom and the United States, published a discussion paper entitled *International Review of Accounting Standards Specifying the Recoverable Amount Test* for Long-Lived Assets (Jim Paul, from the staff of the Australian Accounting Research Foundation, was the principal author). This discussion paper resulted from the discussions of a 'working group' consisting of some Board members and senior staff members from the standard-setting bodies listed above and IASC. The paper:

(a) noted the key features of the working group members' existing or proposed accounting standards that require an impairment test, and compared those standards; and

(b) proposed the views of the working group on the major issues.

BCZ233 In April 1998, after considering the comments received on E55 and the results of the field test, IASC approved IAS 36 *Impairment of Assets*.

Dissenting Opinions

Dissent of Anthony T Cope, James J Leisenring and Geoffrey Whittington

DO1 Messrs Cope and Leisenring and Professor Whittington dissent from the issue of IAS 36.

DO2 Messrs Cope and Leisenring and Professor Whittington dissent because they object to the impairment test that the Standard requires for goodwill.

DO3 Messrs Cope and Leisenring agree with the prohibition, in paragraph 54 of IFRS 3 *Business Combinations*, of amortisation of goodwill. Research and experience have demonstrated that the amortisation of goodwill produces data that is meaningless, and perhaps even misleading. However, if goodwill is not amortised, its special nature mandates that it should be accounted for with caution. The Basis for Conclusions on IAS 36 (paragraph BC131) states that 'if a rigorous and operational impairment test [for goodwill] could be devised, more useful information would be provided to users of an entity's financial statements under an approach in which goodwill is not amortised, but instead tested for impairment annually or more frequently if events or changes in circumstances indicate that the goodwill might be impaired.' Messrs Cope and Leisenring agree with that statement. However, they believe that the impairment test to which a majority of the Board has agreed lacks the rigour to satisfy that condition.

DO4 Messrs Cope and Leisenring share the reservations of some Board members, as noted in paragraph BC130 of the Basis for Conclusions on IAS 36, about an impairment test based on measuring the recoverable amount of an asset, and particularly an asset with an indefinite life, as the higher of fair value less costs to sell or value in use. Messrs Cope and Leisenring are content, however, for the time being to defer consideration of that general measurement issue, pending more research and debate on measurement principles. (They note that the use of fair value would achieve significant convergence with US GAAP.) But a much more rigorous effort must be made to determine the recoverable amount of goodwill, however measured, than the Board's revised impairment test. The 'two-step' method originally proposed by the Board in the Exposure Draft of Proposed Amendments to IAS 36 and IAS 38 was a more useful approach to determining the 'implied value' of goodwill. That test should have been retained.

DO5 Messrs Cope and Leisenring recognise that some constituents raised objections to the complexity and potential cost of the requirements proposed in the Exposure Draft. However, they believe that many commentators misunderstood the level at which the Board intended impairment testing to be undertaken. This was demonstrated during the field-testing of the Exposure Draft. Furthermore, the provisions of paragraph 99 of IAS 36, specifying when impairment testing need not be undertaken, provide generous relief from the necessity of making frequent calculations. They would have preferred to meet those objections by specifying that the goodwill impairment test should be at the level set out in US Financial Accounting Standards Board's Statement of Financial Accounting Standards No. 142 *Goodwill and Other Intangible Assets*.

DO6 Professor Whittington believes that there are two aspects of the proposed impairment test that are particularly unsatisfactory. First, the failure to eliminate the shield from impairment provided by the internally generated goodwill of the acquiring entity at acquisition. This is discussed in paragraph DO7. Second, the lack of a subsequent cash flow test. This is discussed in paragraphs DO8–DO10. The inability to eliminate the shield from impairment provided by internally generated goodwill accruing after the acquisition date is also a problem. However, there is no obvious practical way of dealing with this problem within the framework of conventional impairment tests.

DO7 When an acquired business is merged with an acquirer's existing operations, the impairment test in IAS 36 does not take account of the acquirer's pre-existing internally generated goodwill. Thus, the pre-existing internally generated goodwill of the acquirer provides a shield against impairment additional to that provided by subsequent internally generated goodwill. Professor Whittington believes that the impairment test would be more rigorous if it included a requirement similar to that in UK Financial Reporting Standard 11 *Impairment of Fixed Assets and Goodwill*, which recognises, for purposes of impairment testing, the implied value of the acquirer's goodwill existing at the time of acquisition.

DO8 The subsequent cash flow test is discussed in paragraphs BC195–BC198 of the Basis for Conclusions on IAS 36. A subsequent cash flow test substitutes in past impairment tests the cash flows that actually occurred for those that were estimated at the time of the impairment tests, and requires a write-down if the revised estimates would have created an impairment loss for goodwill. It is thus a correction of an estimate. Such a test is incorporated in FRS 11.

DO9 The Board's reasons for rejecting the subsequent cash flow test are given in paragraph BC197(a)–(c). The preamble to paragraph BC197 claims that the subsequent cash flow test is misdirected because excessive write-downs of goodwill may be a problem that should be prevented. However, the subsequent cash flow test requires only realistic write-downs (based on actual outcomes), not excessive ones. If the statement in paragraph BC197 is correct, this may point to another deficiency in the impairment testing process that requires a different remedy.

DO10 Paragraph BC197(a) asserts that 'it does not produce representationally faithful results' because it ignores other elements in the measurement of value in use. As explained above, it merely substitutes the outcome cash flow for the estimate, which should have a clear meaning and provides a safeguard against over-optimism in the estimation of cash flows. If corrections of estimates of other elements, such as variations that have occurred in interest rates, were considered important in this context, they could be incorporated in the calculation. Paragraph BC197(b) seems to raise the same point as paragraph BC197(a), as to the meaning of the impairment loss under the test. Paragraph BC197(c) complains about the excessive burden that a subsequent cash flow test might impose. Professor Whittington notes that the extent of the burden depends, of course, upon the frequency with which the test is applied. He also notes that the extensive disclosure requirements currently associated with the impairment test might be reduced if the subsequent cash flow test were in place.

CONTENTS

Illustrative Examples

These examples accompany, but are not part of, IAS 36. All the examples assume that the entities concerned have no transactions other than those described. In the examples monetary amounts are denominated in 'currency units' (CU).

Example 1 Identification of cash–generating units

The purpose of this example is:

(a) to indicate how cash-generating units are identified in various situations; and

(b) to highlight certain factors that an entity may consider in identifying the cash-generating unit to which an asset belongs.

A – Retail store chain

Background

IE1 Store X belongs to a retail store chain M. X makes all its retail purchases through M's purchasing centre. Pricing, marketing, advertising and human resources policies (except for hiring X's cashiers and sales staff) are decided by M. M also owns five other stores in the same city as X (although in different neighbourhoods) and 20 other stores in other cities. All stores are managed in the same way as X. X and four other stores were purchased five years ago and goodwill was recognised.

What is the cash-generating unit for X (X's cash-generating unit)?

Analysis

IE2 In identifying X's cash-generating unit, an entity considers whether, for example:

(a) internal management reporting is organised to measure performance on a store–by–store basis; and

(b) the business is run on a store–by–store profit basis or on a region/city basis.

IE3 All M's stores are in different neighbourhoods and probably have different customer bases. So, although X is managed at a corporate level, X generates cash inflows that are largely independent of those of M's other stores. Therefore, it is likely that X is a cash-generating unit.

IE4 If X's cash-generating unit represents the lowest level within M at which the goodwill is monitored for internal management purposes, M applies to that cash-generating unit the impairment test described in paragraph 90 of IAS 36. If information about the carrying amount of goodwill is not available and monitored for internal management purposes at the level of X's cash-generating unit, M applies to that cash-generating unit the impairment test described in paragraph 88 of IAS 36.

B – Plant for an intermediate step in a production process

Background

IE5 A significant raw material used for plant Y's final production is an intermediate product bought from plant X of the same entity. X's products are sold to Y at a transfer price that passes all margins to X. Eighty per cent of Y's final production is sold to customers outside of the entity. Sixty per cent of X's final production is sold to Y and the remaining 40 per cent is sold to customers outside of the entity.

For each of the following cases, what are the cash-generating units for X and Y?

Case 1: X could sell the products it sells to Y in an active market. Internal transfer prices are higher than market prices.

Case 2: There is no active market for the products X sells to Y.

Analysis

Case 1

IE6 X could sell its products in an active market and, so, generate cash inflows that would be largely independent of the cash inflows from Y. Therefore, it is likely that X is a separate cash-generating unit, although part of its production is used by Y (see paragraph 70 of IAS 36).

IE7 It is likely that Y is also a separate cash-generating unit. Y sells 80 per cent of its products to customers outside of the entity. Therefore, its cash inflows can be regarded as largely independent.

IE8 Internal transfer prices do not reflect market prices for X's output. Therefore, in determining value in use of both X and Y, the entity adjusts financial budgets/forecasts to reflect management's best estimate of future prices that could be achieved in arm's length transactions for those of X's products that are used internally (see paragraph 70 of IAS 36).

Case 2

IE9 It is likely that the recoverable amount of each plant cannot be assessed independently of the recoverable amount of the other plant because:

(a) the majority of X's production is used internally and could not be sold in an active market. So, cash inflows of X depend on demand for Y's products. Therefore, X cannot be considered to generate cash inflows that are largely independent of those of Y.

(b) the two plants are managed together.

IE10 As a consequence, it is likely that X and Y together are the smallest group of assets that generates cash inflows that are largely independent.

C – Single product entity

Background

IE11 Entity M produces a single product and owns plants A, B and C. Each plant is located in a different continent. A produces a component that is assembled in either B or C. The combined capacity of B and C is not fully utilised. M's products are sold worldwide from either B or C. For example, B's production can be sold in C's continent if the products can be delivered faster from B than from C. Utilisation levels of B and C depend on the allocation of sales between the two sites.

For each of the following cases, what are the cash-generating units for A, B and C?

Case 1: There is an active market for A's products.

Case 2: There is no active market for A's products.

Analysis

Case 1

IE12 It is likely that A is a separate cash-generating unit because there is an active market for its products (see Example B – Plant for an intermediate step in a production process, Case 1).

IE13 Although there is an active market for the products assembled by B and C, cash inflows for B and C depend on the allocation of production across the two sites. It is unlikely that the future cash inflows for B and C can be determined individually. Therefore, it is likely that B and C together are the smallest identifiable group of assets that generates cash inflows that are largely independent.

IE14 In determining the value in use of A and B plus C, M adjusts financial budgets/forecasts to reflect its best estimate of future prices that could be achieved in arm's length transactions for A's products (see paragraph 70 of IAS 36).

Case 2

IE15 It is likely that the recoverable amount of each plant cannot be assessed independently because:

(a) there is no active market for A's products. Therefore, A's cash inflows depend on sales of the final product by B and C.

(b) although there is an active market for the products assembled by B and C, cash inflows for B and C depend on the allocation of production across the two sites. It is unlikely that the future cash inflows for B and C can be determined individually.

IE16 As a consequence, it is likely that A, B and C together (ie M as a whole) are the smallest identifiable group of assets that generates cash inflows that are largely independent.

D – Magazine titles

Background

IE17 A publisher owns 150 magazine titles of which 70 were purchased and 80 were self-created. The price paid for a purchased magazine title is recognised as an intangible asset. The costs of creating magazine titles and maintaining the existing titles are recognised as an expense when incurred. Cash inflows from direct sales and advertising are identifiable for each magazine title. Titles are managed by customer segments. The level of advertising income for a magazine title depends on the range of titles in the customer segment to which the magazine title relates. Management has a policy to abandon old titles before the end of their economic lives and replace them immediately with new titles for the same customer segment.

What is the cash-generating unit for an individual magazine title?

Analysis

IE18 It is likely that the recoverable amount of an individual magazine title can be assessed. Even though the level of advertising income for a title is influenced, to a certain extent, by the other titles in the customer segment, cash inflows from direct sales and advertising are identifiable for each title. In addition, although titles are managed by customer segments, decisions to abandon titles are made on an individual title basis.

IE19 Therefore, it is likely that individual magazine titles generate cash inflows that are largely independent of each other and that each magazine title is a separate cash-generating unit.

E – Building half–rented to others and half–occupied for own use

Background

IE20 M is a manufacturing company. It owns a headquarters building that used to be fully occupied for internal use. After down-sizing, half of the building is now used internally and half rented to third parties. The lease agreement with the tenant is for five years.

What is the cash-generating unit of the building?

Analysis

IE21 The primary purpose of the building is to serve as a corporate asset, supporting M's manufacturing activities. Therefore, the building as a whole cannot be considered to generate cash inflows that are largely independent of the cash inflows from the entity as a whole. So, it is likely that the cash-generating unit for the building is M as a whole.

IE22 The building is not held as an investment. Therefore, it would not be appropriate to determine the value in use of the building based on projections of future market related rents.

Example 2 Calculation of value in use and recognition of an impairment loss

In this example, tax effects are ignored.

Background and calculation of value in use

IE23 At the end of 20X0, entity T acquires entity M for CU10,000. M has manufacturing plants in three countries.

Schedule 1. Data at the end of 20X0

End of 20X0	*Allocation of purchase price*	*Fair value of identifiable assets*	*Goodwill*
	CU	CU	CU[(a)]
Activities in Country A	3,000	2,000	1,000
Activities in Country B	2,000	1,500	500
Activities in Country C	5,000	3,500	1,500
Total	10,000	7,000	3,000

(a) Activities in each country represent the lowest level at which the goodwill is monitored for internal management purposes (determined as the difference between the purchase price of the activities in each country, as specified in the purchase agreement, and the fair value of the identifiable assets).

IE23A Because goodwill has been allocated to the activities in each country, each of those activities must be tested for impairment annually or more frequently if there is any indication that it may be impaired (see paragraph 90 of IAS 36).

IE24 The recoverable amounts (ie higher of value in use and fair value less costs to sell) of the cash-generating units are determined on the basis of value in use calculations. At the end of 20X0 and 20X1, the value in use of each cash-generating unit exceeds its carrying amount. Therefore the activities in each country and the goodwill allocated to those activities are regarded as not impaired.

IE25 At the beginning of 20X2, a new government is elected in Country A. It passes legislation significantly restricting exports of T's main product. As a result, and for the foreseeable future, T's production in Country A will be cut by 40 per cent.

IE26 The significant export restriction and the resulting production decrease require T also to estimate the recoverable amount of the Country A operations at the beginning of 20X2.

IE27 T uses straight-line depreciation over a 12-year life for the Country A identifiable assets and anticipates no residual value.

IE28 To determine the value in use for the Country A cash-generating unit (see Schedule 2), T:

(a) prepares cash flow forecasts derived from the most recent financial budgets/forecasts for the next five years (years 20X2–20X6) approved by management.

(b) estimates subsequent cash flows (years 20X7–20Y2) based on declining growth rates. The growth rate for 20X7 is estimated to be 3 per cent. This rate is lower than the average long-term growth rate for the market in Country A.

(c) selects a 15 per cent discount rate, which represents a pre-tax rate that reflects current market assessments of the time value of money and the risks specific to the Country A cash-generating unit.

Recognition and measurement of impairment loss

IE29 The recoverable amount of the Country A cash-generating unit is CU1,360.

IE30 T compares the recoverable amount of the Country A cash-generating unit with its carrying amount (see Schedule 3).

IE31 Because the carrying amount exceeds the recoverable amount by CU1,473, T recognises an impairment loss of CU1,473 immediately in profit or loss. The carrying amount of the goodwill that relates to the Country A operations is reduced to zero before reducing the carrying amount of other identifiable assets within the Country A cash-generating unit (see paragraph 104 of IAS 36).

IE32 Tax effects are accounted for separately in accordance with IAS 12 *Income Taxes* (see Illustrative Example 3A).

Schedule 2. Calculation of the value in use of the Country A cash-generating unit at the beginning of 20X2

Year	*Long–term growth rates*	*Future cash flows* CU	*Present value factor at 15% discount rate*[3]	*Discounted future cash flows* CU
20X2 (n=1)		230[1]	0.86957	200
20X3		253[1]	0.75614	191
20X4		273[1]	0.65752	180
20X5		290[1]	0.57175	166
20X6		304[1]	0.49718	151
20X7	3%	313[2]	0.43233	135
20X8	(2)%	307[2]	0.37594	115
20X9	(6)%	289[2]	0.32690	94
20Y0	(15)%	245[2]	0.28426	70
20Y1	(25)%	184[2]	0.24719	45
20Y2	(67)%	61[2]	0.21494	13
Value in use				1,360

1 Based on management's best estimate of net cash flow projections (after the 40% cut).

2 Based on an extrapolation from preceding year cash flow using declining growth rates.

3 The present value factor is calculated as $k = 1/(1+a)^n$, where a = discount rate and n = period of discount.

Schedule 3. Calculation and allocation of the impairment loss for the Country A cash–generating unit at the beginning of 20X2

Beginning of 20X2	*Goodwill*	*Identifiable assets*	*Total*
	CU	CU	CU
Historical cost	1,000	2,000	3,000
Accumulated depreciation (20X1)	–	(167)	(167)
Carrying amount	1,000	1,833	2,833
Impairment loss	(1,000)	(473)	(1,473)
Carrying amount after impairment loss	–	1,360	1,360

Example 3 Deferred tax effects

A – Deferred tax effects of the recognition of an impairment loss

Use the data for entity T as presented in Example 2, with supplementary information as provided in this example.

IE33 At the beginning of 20X2, the tax base of the identifiable assets of the Country A cash-generating unit is CU900. Impairment losses are not deductible for tax purposes. The tax rate is 40 per cent.

IE34 The recognition of an impairment loss on the assets of the Country A cash-generating unit reduces the taxable temporary difference related to those assets. The deferred tax liability is reduced accordingly.

Beginning of 20X2	*Identifiable assets before impairment loss*	*Impairment loss*	*Identifiable assets after impairment loss*
	CU	CU	CU
Carrying amount (Example 2)	1,833	(473)	1,360
Tax base	900	–	900
Taxable temporary difference	933	(473)	460
Deferred tax liability at 40%	373	(189)	184

IE35 In accordance with IAS 12 *Income Taxes*, no deferred tax relating to the goodwill was recognised initially. Therefore, the impairment loss relating to the goodwill does not give rise to a deferred tax adjustment.

B – Recognition of an impairment loss creates a deferred tax asset

IE36 An entity has an identifiable asset with a carrying amount of CU1,000. Its recoverable amount is CU650. The tax rate is 30 per cent and the tax base of the asset is CU800. Impairment losses are not deductible for tax purposes. The effect of the impairment loss is as follows:

	Before impairment	*Effect of impairment*	*After impairment*
	CU	CU	CU
Carrying amount	1,000	(350)	650
Tax base	800	–	800
Taxable (deductible) temporary difference	200	(350)	(150)
Deferred tax liability (asset) at 30%	60	(105)	45

IE37 In accordance with IAS 12, the entity recognises the deferred tax asset to the extent that it is probable that taxable profit will be available against which the deductible temporary difference can be utilised.

Example 4 Reversal of an impairment loss

Use the data for entity T as presented in Example 2, with supplementary information as provided in this example. In this example, tax effects are ignored.

Background

IE38 In 20X3, the government is still in office in Country A, but the business situation is improving. The effects of the export laws on T's production are proving to be less drastic than initially expected by management. As a result, management estimates that production will increase by 30 per cent. This favourable change requires T to re-estimate the recoverable amount of the net assets of the Country A operations (see paragraphs 110 and 111 of IAS 36). The cash-generating unit for the net assets of the Country A operations is still the Country A operations.

IE39 Calculations similar to those in Example 2 show that the recoverable amount of the Country A cash-generating unit is now CU1,910.

Reversal of impairment loss

IE40 T compares the recoverable amount and the net carrying amount of the Country A cash-generating unit.

Schedule 1. Calculation of the carrying amount of the Country A cash-generating unit at the end of 20X3

	Goodwill	*Identifiable assets*	*Total*
	CU	CU	CU
Beginning of 20X2 (Example 2)			
Historical cost	1,000	2,000	3,000
Accumulated depreciation	–	(167)	(167)
Impairment loss	(1,000)	(473)	(1,473)
Carrying amount after impairment loss	–	1,360	1,360
End of 20X3			
Additional depreciation (2 years)[(a)]	–	(247)	(247)
Carrying amount	–	1,113	1,113
Recoverable amount			1,910
Excess of recoverable amount over carrying amount			797

(a) After recognition of the impairment loss at the beginning of 20X2, T revised the depreciation charge for the Country A identifiable assets (from CU166.7 per year to CU123.6 per year), based on the revised carrying amount and remaining useful life (11 years).

IE41 There has been a favourable change in the estimates used to determine the recoverable amount of the Country A net assets since the last impairment loss was recognised. Therefore, in accordance with paragraph 114 of IAS 36, T recognises a reversal of the impairment loss recognised in 20X2.

IE42 In accordance with paragraphs 122 and 123 of IAS 36, T increases the carrying amount of the Country A identifiable assets by CU387 (see Schedule 3), ie up to the lower of recoverable amount (CU1,910) and the identifiable assets' depreciated historical cost (CU1,500) (see Schedule 2). This increase is recognised immediately in profit or loss.

IE43 In accordance with paragraph 124 of IAS 36, the impairment loss on goodwill is not reversed.

Schedule 2. Determination of the depreciated historical cost of the Country A identifiable assets at the end of 20X3

End of 20X3	*Identifiable assets*
	CU
Historical cost	2,000
Accumulated depreciation *(166.7 × 3 years)*	(500)
Depreciated historical cost	1,500
Carrying amount (Schedule 1)	1,113
Difference	387

Schedule 3. Carrying amount of the Country A assets at the end of 20X3

End of 20X3	*Goodwill*	*Identifiable assets*	*Total*
	CU	CU	CU
Gross carrying amount	1,000	2,000	3,000
Accumulated amortisation	–	(414)	(414)
Accumulated impairment loss	(1,000)	(473)	(1,473)
Carrying amount	–	1,113	1,113
Reversal of impairment loss	0	387	387
Carrying amount after reversal of impairment loss	–	1,500	1,500

Example 5 Treatment of a future restructuring

In this example, tax effects are ignored.

Background

IE44 At the end of 20X0, entity K tests a plant for impairment. The plant is a cash-generating unit. The plant's assets are carried at depreciated historical cost. The plant has a carrying amount of CU3,000 and a remaining useful life of 10 years.

IE45 The plant's recoverable amount (ie higher of value in use and fair value less costs to sell) is determined on the basis of a value in use calculation. Value in use is calculated using a pre-tax discount rate of 14 per cent.

IE46 Management approved budgets reflect that:

(a) at the end of 20X3, the plant will be restructured at an estimated cost of CU100. Since K is not yet committed to the restructuring, a provision has not been recognised for the future restructuring costs.

(b) there will be future benefits from this restructuring in the form of reduced future cash outflows.

IE47 At the end of 20X2, K becomes committed to the restructuring. The costs are still estimated to be CU100 and a provision is recognised accordingly. The plant's estimated future cash flows reflected in the most recent management approved budgets are given in paragraph IE51 and a current discount rate is the same as at the end of 20X0.

IE48 At the end of 20X3, actual restructuring costs of CU100 are incurred and paid. Again, the plant's estimated future cash flows reflected in the most recent management approved budgets and a current discount rate are the same as those estimated at the end of 20X2.

At the end of 20X0

Schedule 1. Calculation of the plant's value in use at the end of 20X0

Year	*Future cash flows*	*Discounted at 14%*
	CU	CU
20X1	300	263
20X2	280	215
20X3	420 [1]	283
20X4	520 [2]	308
20X5	350 [2]	182
20X6	420 [2]	191
20X7	480 [2]	192
20X8	480 [2]	168
20X9	460 [2]	141
20X10	400 [2]	108
Value in use		2,051

[1] Excludes estimated restructuring costs reflected in management budgets.

[2] Excludes estimated benefits expected from the restructuring reflected in management budgets.

IE49 The plant's recoverable amount (ie value in use) is less than its carrying amount. Therefore, K recognises an impairment loss for the plant.

Schedule 2. Calculation of the impairment loss at the end of 20X0

	Plant
	CU
Carrying amount before impairment loss	3,000
Recoverable amount (Schedule 1)	2,051
Impairment loss	(949)
Carrying amount after impairment loss	2,051

At the end of 20X1

IE50 No event occurs that requires the plant's recoverable amount to be re-estimated. Therefore, no calculation of the recoverable amount is required to be performed.

At the end of 20X2

IE51 The entity is now committed to the restructuring. Therefore, in determining the plant's value in use, the benefits expected from the restructuring are considered in forecasting cash flows. This results in an increase in the estimated future cash flows used to determine value in use at the end of 20X0. In accordance with paragraphs 110 and 111 of IAS 36, the recoverable amount of the plant is re-determined at the end of 20X2.

Schedule 3. Calculation of the plant's value in use at the end of 20X2

Year	*Future cash flows*	*Discounted at 14%*
	CU	CU
20X3	420 [1]	368
20X4	570 [2]	439
20X5	380 [2]	256
20X6	450 [2]	266
20X7	510 [2]	265
20X8	510 [2]	232
20X9	480 [2]	192
20X10	410 [2]	144
Value in use		2,162

1 Excludes estimated restructuring costs because a liability has already been recognised.

2 Includes estimated benefits expected from the restructuring reflected in management budgets.

IE52 The plant's recoverable amount (value in use) is higher than its carrying amount (see Schedule 4). Therefore, K reverses the impairment loss recognised for the plant at the end of 20X0.

Schedule 4. Calculation of the reversal of the impairment loss at the end of 20X2

	Plant
	CU
Carrying amount at the end of 20X0 (Schedule 2)	2,051
End of 20X2	
Depreciation charge (for 20X1 and 20X2–Schedule 5)	(410)
Carrying amount before reversal	1,641
Recoverable amount (Schedule 3)	2,162
Reversal of the impairment loss	521
Carrying amount after reversal	2,162
Carrying amount: depreciated historical cost (Schedule 5)	2,400 [(a)]

(a) The reversal does not result in the carrying amount of the plant exceeding what its carrying amount would have been at depreciated historical cost. Therefore, the full reversal of the impairment loss is recognised.

At the end of 20X3

IE53 There is a cash outflow of CU100 when the restructuring costs are paid. Even though a cash outflow has taken place, there is no change in the estimated future cash flows used to determine value in use at the end of 20X2. Therefore, the plant's recoverable amount is not calculated at the end of 20X3.

Schedule 5. Summary of the carrying amount of the plant

End of year	*Depreciated historical cost*	*Recoverable amount*	*Adjusted depreciation charge*	*Impairment loss*	*Carrying amount after impairment*
	CU	CU	CU	CU	CU
20X0	3,000	2,051	0	(949)	2,051
20X1	2,700	nc	(205)	0	1,846
20X2	2,400	2,162	(205)	521	2,162
20X3	2,100	nc	(270)	0	1,892

nc = not calculated as there is no indication that the impairment loss may have increased/decreased.

Example 6 Treatment of future costs

In this example, tax effects are ignored.

Background

IE54 At the end of 20X0, entity F tests a machine for impairment. The machine is a cash-generating unit. It is carried at depreciated historical cost and its carrying amount is CU150,000. It has an estimated remaining useful life of 10 years.

IE55 The machine's recoverable amount (ie higher of value in use and fair value less costs to sell) is determined on the basis of a value in use calculation. Value in use is calculated using a pre-tax discount rate of 14 per cent.

IE56 Management approved budgets reflect:

(a) estimated costs necessary to maintain the level of economic benefit expected to arise from the machine in its current condition; and

(b) that in 20X4, costs of CU25,000 will be incurred to enhance the machine's performance by increasing its productive capacity.

IE57 At the end of 20X4, costs to enhance the machine's performance are incurred. The machine's estimated future cash flows reflected in the most recent management approved budgets are given in paragraph IE60 and a current discount rate is the same as at the end of 20X0.

At the end of 20X0

Schedule 1. Calculation of the machine's value in use at the end of 20X0

Year	*Future cash flows*	*Discounted at 14%*
	CU	CU
20X1	22,165 [1]	19,443
20X2	21,450 [1]	16,505
20X3	20,550 [1]	13,871
20X4	24,725 [1, 2]	14,639
20X5	25,325 [1, 3]	13,153
20X6	24,825 [1, 3]	11,310
20X7	24,123 [1, 3]	9,640
20X8	25,533 [1, 3]	8,951
20X9	24,234 [1, 3]	7,452
20X10	22,850 [1, 3]	6,164
Value in use		121,128

1 Includes estimated costs necessary to maintain the level of economic benefit expected to arise from the machine in its current condition.

2 Excludes estimated costs to enhance the machine's performance reflected in management budgets.

3 Excludes estimated benefits expected from enhancing the machine's performance reflected in management budgets.

IE58 The machine's recoverable amount (value in use) is less than its carrying amount. Therefore, F recognises an impairment loss for the machine.

Schedule 2. Calculation of the impairment loss at the end of 20X0

	Machine
	CU
Carrying amount before impairment loss	150,000
Recoverable amount (Schedule 1)	121,128
Impairment loss	(28,872)
Carrying amount after impairment loss	121,128

Years 20X1–20X3

IE59 No event occurs that requires the machine's recoverable amount to be re-estimated. Therefore, no calculation of recoverable amount is required to be performed.

At the end of 20X4

IE60 The costs to enhance the machine's performance are incurred. Therefore, in determining the machine's value in use, the future benefits expected from enhancing the machine's performance are considered in forecasting cash flows. This results in an increase in the estimated future cash flows used to determine value in use at the end of 20X0. As a consequence, in accordance with paragraphs 110 and 111 of IAS 36, the recoverable amount of the machine is recalculated at the end of 20X4.

Schedule 3. Calculation of the machine's value in use at the end of 20X4

Year	*Future cash flows*[a]	*Discounted at 14%*
	CU	CU
20X5	30,321	26,597
20X6	32,750	25,200
20X7	31,721	21,411
20X8	31,950	18,917
20X9	33,100	17,191
20X10	27,999	12,756
Value in use		122,072

(a) Includes estimated benefits expected from enhancing the machine's performance reflected in management budgets.

IE61 The machine's recoverable amount (ie value in use) is higher than the machine's carrying amount and depreciated historical cost (see Schedule 4). Therefore, K reverses the impairment loss recognised for the machine at the end of 20X0 so that the machine is carried at depreciated historical cost.

Schedule 4. Calculation of the reversal of the impairment loss at the end of 20X4

	Machine
	CU
Carrying amount at the end of 20X0 (Schedule 2)	121,128
End of 20X4	
Depreciation charge (20X1 to 20X4 – Schedule 5)	(48,452)
Costs to enhance the asset's performance	25,000
Carrying amount before reversal	97,676
Recoverable amount (Schedule 3)	122,072
Reversal of the impairment loss	17,324
Carrying amount after reversal	115,000
Carrying amount: depreciated historical cost (Schedule 5)	115,000 [(a)]

(a) The value in use of the machine exceeds what its carrying amount would have been at depreciated historical cost. Therefore, the reversal is limited to an amount that does not result in the carrying amount of the machine exceeding depreciated historical cost.

Schedule 5. Summary of the carrying amount of the machine

Year	*Depreciated historical cost*	*Recoverable amount*	*Adjusted depreciated charge*	*Impairment loss*	*Carrying amount after impairment*
	CU	CU	CU	CU	CU
20X0	150,000	121,128	0	(28,872)	121,128
20X1	135,000	nc	(12,113)	0	109,015
20X2	120,000	nc	(12,113)	0	96,902
20X3	105,000	nc	(12,113)	0	84,789
20X4	90,000		(12,113)		
enhancement	25,000		–		
	115,000	122,072	(12,113)	17,324	115,000
20X5	95,833	nc	(19,167)	0	95,833

nc = not calculated as there is no indication that the impairment loss may have increased/decreased.

Example 7 Impairment testing cash-generating units with goodwill and minority interests

In this example, tax effects are ignored.

Background

IE62 Entity X acquires an 80 per cent ownership interest in Entity Y for CU1,600 on 1 January 20X3. At that date, Y's identifiable net assets have a fair value of CU1,500. Y has no contingent liabilities. Therefore, X recognises in its consolidated financial statements:

(a) goodwill of CU400, being the difference between the cost of the business combination of CU1,600 and X's 80 per cent interest in Y's identifiable net assets;

(b) Y's identifiable net assets at their fair value of CU1,500; and

(c) a minority interest of CU300, being the 20 per cent interest in Y's identifiable net assets held by parties outside X.

IE63 The assets of Y together are the smallest group of assets that generate cash inflows that are largely independent of the cash inflows from other assets or groups of assets. Therefore Y is a cash-generating unit. Because this cash-generating unit includes goodwill within its carrying amount, it must be tested for impairment annually, or more frequently if there is an indication that it may be impaired (see paragraph 90 of IAS 36).

IE64 At the end of 20X3, X determines that the recoverable amount of cash-generating unit Y is CU1,000. X uses straight-line depreciation over a 10-year life for Y's identifiable assets and anticipates no residual value.

Testing Y for impairment

IE65 A portion of Y's recoverable amount of CU1,000 is attributable to the unrecognised minority interest in goodwill. Therefore, in accordance with paragraph 92 of IAS 36, the carrying amount of Y must be notionally adjusted to include goodwill attributable to the minority interest, before being compared with the recoverable amount of CU1,000.

Schedule 1. Testing Y for impairment at the end of 20X3

End of 20X3	*Goodwill*	*Identifiable net assets*	*Total*
	CU	CU	CU
Gross carrying amount	400	1,500	1,900
Accumulated depreciation	–	(150)	(150)
Carrying amount	400	1,350	1,750
Unrecognised minority interest	100[(a)]	–	100
Notionally adjusted carrying amount	500	1,350	1,850
Recoverable amount			1,000
Impairment loss			850

(a) Goodwill attributable to X's 80% interest in Y at the acquisition date is CU400. Therefore, goodwill notionally attributable to the 20% minority interest in Y at the acquisition date is CU100.

IE66 In accordance with paragraph 104 of IAS 36, the impairment loss of CU850 is allocated to the assets in the unit by first reducing the carrying amount of goodwill to zero.

IE67 Therefore, CU500 of the CU850 impairment loss for the unit is allocated to the goodwill. However, because the goodwill is recognised only to the extent of X's 80 per cent ownership interest in Y, X recognises only 80 per cent of that goodwill impairment loss (ie CU400).

IE68 The remaining impairment loss of CU350 is recognised by reducing the carrying amounts of Y's identifiable assets (see Schedule 2).

Schedule 2. Allocation of the impairment loss for Y at the end of 20X3

End of 20X3	*Goodwill*	*Identifiable net assets*	*Total*
	CU	CU	CU
Gross carrying amount	400	1,500	1,900
Accumulated depreciation	–	(150)	(150)
Carrying amount	400	1,350	1,750
Impairment loss	(400)	(350)	(750)
Carrying amount after impairment loss	–	1,000	1,000

Example 8 Allocation of corporate assets

In this example, tax effects are ignored.

Background

IE69 Entity M has three cash-generating units: A, B and C. The carrying amounts of those units do not include goodwill. There are adverse changes in the technological environment in which M operates. Therefore, M conducts impairment tests of each of its cash-generating units. At the end of 20X0, the carrying amounts of A, B and C are CU100, CU150 and CU200 respectively.

IE70 The operations are conducted from a headquarters. The carrying amount of the headquarters is CU200: a headquarters building of CU150 and a research centre of CU50. The relative carrying amounts of the cash-generating units are a reasonable indication of the proportion of the headquarters building devoted to each cash-generating unit. The carrying amount of the research centre cannot be allocated on a reasonable basis to the individual cash-generating units.

IE71 The remaining estimated useful life of cash-generating unit A is 10 years. The remaining useful lives of B, C and the headquarters are 20 years. The headquarters is depreciated on a straight-line basis.

IE72 The recoverable amount (ie higher of value in use and fair value less costs to sell) of each cash-generating unit is based on its value in use. Value in use is calculated using a pre-tax discount rate of 15 per cent.

Identification of corporate assets

IE73 In accordance with paragraph 102 of IAS 36, M first identifies all the corporate assets that relate to the individual cash-generating units under review. The corporate assets are the headquarters building and the research centre.

IE74 M then decides how to deal with each of the corporate assets:

(a) the carrying amount of the headquarters building can be allocated on a reasonable and consistent basis to the cash-generating units under review; and

(b) the carrying amount of the research centre cannot be allocated on a reasonable and consistent basis to the individual cash-generating units under review.

Allocation of corporate assets

IE75 The carrying amount of the headquarters building is allocated to the carrying amount of each individual cash-generating unit. A weighted allocation basis is used because the estimated remaining useful life of A's cash-generating unit is 10 years, whereas the estimated remaining useful lives of B and C's cash-generating units are 20 years.

Schedule 1. Calculation of a weighted allocation of the carrying amount of the headquarters building

End of 20X0	*A*	*B*	*C*	*Total*
	CU	CU	CU	CU
Carrying amount	100	150	200	450
Useful life	10 years	20 years	20 years	
Weighting based on useful life	1	2	2	
Carrying amount after weighting	100	300	400	800
Pro–rata allocation of the building	12% *(100/800)*	38% *(300/800)*	50% *(400/800)*	100%
Allocation of the carrying amount of the building (based on pro–rata above)	19	56	75	150
Carrying amount (after allocation of the building)	119	206	275	600

Determination of recoverable amount and calculation of impairment losses

IE76 Paragraph 102 of IAS 36 requires first that the recoverable amount of each individual cash–generating unit be compared with its carrying amount, including the portion of the carrying amount of the headquarters building allocated to the unit, and any resulting impairment loss recognised. Paragraph 102 of IAS 36 then requires the recoverable amount of M as a whole (ie the smallest group of cash–generating units that includes the research centre) to be compared with its carrying amount, including both the headquarters building and the research centre.

Schedule 2. Calculation of A, B, C and M's value in use at the end of 20X0

	A		*B*		*C*		*M*	
Year	*Future cash flows*	*Discount at 15%*	*Future cash flows*	*Discount at 15%*	*Future cash flows*	*Discount at 15%*	*Future cash flows*	*Discount at 15%*
	CU	CU	CU	CU	CU	CU	CU	CU
1	18	16	9	8	10	9	39	34
2	31	23	16	12	20	15	72	54
3	37	24	24	16	34	22	105	69
4	42	24	29	17	44	25	128	73
5	47	24	32	16	51	25	143	71
6	52	22	33	14	56	24	155	67
7	55	21	34	13	60	22	162	61
8	55	18	35	11	63	21	166	54
9	53	15	35	10	65	18	167	48
10	48	12	35	9	66	16	169	42
11			36	8	66	14	132	28
12			35	7	66	12	131	25
13			35	6	66	11	131	21
14			33	5	65	9	128	18
15			30	4	62	8	122	15
16			26	3	60	6	115	12
17			22	2	57	5	108	10
18			18	1	51	4	97	8
19			14	1	43	3	85	6
20			10	1	35	2	71	4
Value in use		199		164		271		720 [(a)]

(a) It is assumed that the research centre generates additional future cash flows for the entity as a whole. Therefore, the sum of the value in use of each individual cash-generating unit is less than the value in use of the business as a whole. The additional cash flows are not attributable to the headquarters building.

Schedule 3. Impairment testing A, B and C

End of 20X0	*A*	*B*	*C*
	CU	CU	CU
Carrying amount (after allocation of the building) (Schedule 1)	119	206	275
Recoverable amount (Schedule 2)	199	164	271
Impairment loss	0	(42)	(4)

IE77 The next step is to allocate the impairment losses between the assets of the cash-generating units and the headquarters building.

Schedule 4. Allocation of the impairment losses for cash-generating units B and C

Cash-generating unit	*B*		*C*	
	CU		CU	
To headquarters building	(12)	*(42 x 56/206)*	(1)	*(4 x 75/275)*
To assets in cash-generating unit	(30)	*(42 x 150/206)*	(3)	*(4 x 200/275)*
	(42)		(4)	

IE78 Because the research centre could not be allocated on a reasonable and consistent basis to A, B and C's cash-generating units, M compares the carrying amount of the smallest group of cash-generating units to which the carrying amount of the research centre can be allocated (ie M as a whole) to its recoverable amount.

Schedule 5. Impairment testing the smallest group of cash-generating units to which the carrying amount of the research centre can be allocated (ie M as a whole)

End of 20X0	*A*	*B*	*C*	*Building*	*Research centre*	*M*
	CU	CU	CU	CU	CU	CU
Carrying amount	100	150	200	150	50	650
Impairment loss arising from the first step of the test	–	(30)	(3)	(13)	–	(46)
Carrying amount after the first step of the test	100	120	197	137	50	604
Recoverable amount (Schedule 2)						720
Impairment loss for the 'larger' cash-generating unit						0

IE79 Therefore, no additional impairment loss results from the application of the impairment test to M as a whole. Only an impairment loss of CU46 is recognised as a result of the application of the first step of the test to A, B and C.

Example 9 Disclosures about cash-generating units with goodwill or intangible assets with indefinite useful lives

The purpose of this example is to illustrate the disclosures required by paragraphs 134 and 135 of IAS 36.

Background

IE80 Entity M is a multinational manufacturing firm that uses geographical segments as its primary format for reporting segment information. M's three reportable segments based on that format are Europe, North America and Asia. Goodwill has been allocated for impairment testing purposes to three individual cash-generating units–two in Europe (units A and B) and one in North America (unit C)–and to one group of cash-generating units (comprising operation XYZ) in Asia. Units A, B and C and operation XYZ each represent the lowest level within M at which the goodwill is monitored for internal management purposes.

IE81 M acquired unit C, a manufacturing operation in North America, in December 20X2. Unlike M's other North American operations, C operates in an industry with high margins and high growth rates, and with the benefit of a 10-year patent on its primary product. The patent was granted to C just before M's acquisition of C. As part of accounting for the acquisition of C, M recognised, in addition to the patent, goodwill of CU3,000 and a brand name of CU1,000. M's management has determined that the brand name has an indefinite useful life. M has no other intangible assets with indefinite useful lives.

IE82 The carrying amounts of goodwill and intangible assets with indefinite useful lives allocated to units A, B and C and to operation XYZ are as follows:

	Goodwill	*Intangible assets with indefinite useful lives*
	CU	CU
A	350	
B	450	
C	3,000	1,000
XYZ	1,200	
Total	5,000	1,000

IE83 During the year ending 31 December 20X3, M determines that there is no impairment of any of its cash-generating units or group of cash-generating units containing goodwill or intangible assets with indefinite useful lives. The recoverable amounts (ie higher of value in use and fair value less costs to sell) of those units and group of units are determined on the basis of value in use calculations. M has determined that the recoverable amount calculations are most sensitive to changes in the following assumptions:

Units A and B	*Unit C*	*Operation XYZ*
Gross margin during the budget period (budget period is 4 years)	5–year US government bond rate during the budget period (budget period is 5 years)	Gross margin during the budget period (budget period is 5 years)
Raw materials price inflation during the budget period	Raw materials price inflation during the budget period	Japanese yen/US dollar exchange rate during the budget period
Market share during the budget period	Market share during the budget period	Market share during the budget period
Growth rate used to extrapolate cash flows beyond the budget period	Growth rate used to extrapolate cash flows beyond the budget period	Growth rate used to extrapolate cash flows beyond the budget period

IE84 Gross margins during the budget period for A, B and XYZ are estimated by M based on average gross margins achieved in the period immediately before the start of the budget period, increased by 5 per cent per year for anticipated efficiency improvements. A and B produce complementary products and are operated by M to achieve the same gross margins.

IE85 Market shares during the budget period are estimated by M based on average market shares achieved in the period immediately before the start of the budget period, adjusted each year for any anticipated growth or decline in market shares. M anticipates that:

(a) market shares for A and B will differ, but will each grow during the budget period by 3 per cent per year as a result of ongoing improvements in product quality.

(b) C's market share will grow during the budget period by 6 per cent per year as a result of increased advertising expenditure and the benefits from the protection of the 10–year patent on its primary product.

(c) XYZ's market share will remain unchanged during the budget period as a result of the combination of ongoing improvements in product quality and an anticipated increase in competition.

IE86 A and B purchase raw materials from the same European suppliers, whereas C's raw materials are purchased from various North American suppliers. Raw materials price inflation during the budget period is estimated by M to be consistent with forecast consumer price indices published by government agencies in the relevant European and North American countries.

IE87 The 5–year US government bond rate during the budget period is estimated by M to be consistent with the yield on such bonds at the beginning of the budget period. The Japanese yen/US dollar exchange rate is estimated by M to be consistent with the average market forward exchange rate over the budget period.

IE88 M uses steady growth rates to extrapolate beyond the budget period cash flows for A, B, C and XYX. The growth rates for A, B and XYZ are estimated by M to be consistent with publicly available information about the long-term average growth rates for the markets in which A, B and XYZ operate. However, the growth rate for C exceeds the long-term average growth rate for the market in which C operates. M's management is of the opinion that this is reasonable in the light of the protection of the 10-year patent on C's primary product.

IE89 M includes the following disclosure in the notes to its financial statements for the year ending 31 December 20X3.

Impairment Tests for Goodwill and Intangible Assets with Indefinite Lives

Goodwill has been allocated for impairment testing purposes to three individual cash-generating units—two in Europe (units A and B) and one in North America (unit C)—and to one group of cash-generating units (comprising operation XYZ) in Asia. The carrying amount of goodwill allocated to unit C and operation XYZ is significant in comparison with the total carrying amount of goodwill, but the carrying amount of goodwill allocated to each of units A and B is not. Nevertheless, the recoverable amounts of units A and B are based on some of the same key assumptions, and the aggregate carrying amount of goodwill allocated to those units is significant.

Operation XYZ

The recoverable amount of operation XYZ has been determined based on a value in use calculation. That calculation uses cash flow projections based on financial budgets approved by management covering a five-year period, and a discount rate of 8.4 per cent. Cash flows beyond that five-year period have been extrapolated using a steady 6.3 per cent growth rate. This growth rate does not exceed the long-term average growth rate for the market in which XYZ operates. Management believes that any reasonably possible change in the key assumptions on which XYZ's recoverable amount is based would *not* cause XYZ's carrying amount to exceed its recoverable amount.

Unit C

The recoverable amount of unit C has also been determined based on a value in use calculation. That calculation uses cash flow projections based on financial budgets approved by management covering a five-year period, and a discount rate of 9.2 per cent. C's cash flows beyond the five-year period are extrapolated using a steady 12 per cent growth rate. This growth rate exceeds by 4 percentage points the long-term average growth rate for the market in which C operates. However, C benefits from the protection of a 10-year patent on its primary product, granted in December 20X2. Management believes that a 12 per cent growth rate is reasonable in the light of that patent. Management also believes that any reasonably possible change in the key assumptions on which C's recoverable amount is based would *not* cause C's carrying amount to exceed its recoverable amount.

Units A and B

The recoverable amounts of units A and B have been determined on the basis of value in use calculations. Those units produce complementary products, and their recoverable amounts are based on some of the same key assumptions. Both value in use calculations use cash flow projections based on financial budgets approved by management covering a four-year period, and a discount rate of 7.9 per cent. Both sets of cash flows beyond the four-year period are extrapolated using a steady 5 per cent growth rate. This growth rate does not exceed the long-term average growth rate for the market in which A and B operate. Cash flow projections during the budget period for both A and B are also based on the same expected gross margins during the budget period and the same raw materials price inflation during the budget period. Management believes that any reasonably possible change in any of these key assumptions would *not* cause the aggregate carrying amount of A and B to exceed the aggregate recoverable amount of those units.

	Operation XYZ	*Unit C*	*Units A and B (in aggregate)*
Carrying amount of goodwill	CU1,200	CU3,000	CU800
Carrying amount of brand name with indefinite useful life	–	CU1,000	–
Key assumptions used in value in use calculations[(a)]			
• Key assumption	• Budgeted gross margins	• 5-year US government bond rate	• Budgeted gross margins
• Basis for determining value(s) assigned to key assumption	• Average gross margins achieved in period immediately before the budget period, increased for expected efficiency improvements.	• Yield on 5-year US government bonds at the beginning of the budget period.	• Average gross margins achieved in period immediately before the budget period, increased for expected efficiency improvements.
	• Values assigned to key assumption reflect past experience, except for efficiency improvements. Management believes improvements of 5% per year are reasonably achievable.	• Value assigned to key assumption is consistent with external sources of information	• Values assigned to key assumption reflect past experience, except for efficiency improvements. Management believes improvements of 5% per year are reasonably achievable.

• Key assumption	• Japanese yen/US dollar exchange rate during the budget period	• Raw materials price inflation	• Raw materials price inflation
• Basis for determining value(s) assigned to key assumption	• Average market forward exchange rate over the budget period.	• Forecast consumer price indices during the budget period for North American countries from which raw materials are purchased.	• Forecast consumer price indices during the budget period for European countries from which raw materials are purchased.
	• Value assigned to key assumption is consistent with external sources of information.	• Value assigned to key assumption is consistent with external sources of information.	• Value assigned to key assumption is consistent with external sources of information.
• Key assumption	• Budgeted market share	• Budgeted market share	
• Basis for determining value(s) assigned to key assumption	• Average market share in period immediately before the budget period.	• Average market share in period immediately before the budget period, increased each year for anticipated growth in market share.	
	• Value assigned to key assumption reflects past experience. No change in market share expected as a result of ongoing product quality improvements coupled with anticipated increase in competition.	• Management believes market share growth of 6% per year is reasonably achievable due to increased advertising expenditure, the benefits from the protection of the 10-year patent on C's primary product, and the expected synergies to be achieved from operating C as part of M's North American segment.	

(a) The key assumptions shown in this table for units A and B are only those that are used in the recoverable amount calculations for both units.

Table of Concordance

This table shows the contents of the superseded version of IAS 36 and the current version of IAS 36 correspond. Paragraphs are treated as corresponding if they broadly address the same matter even though their guidance may differ.

Superseded IAS 36 paragraph	Current IAS 36 paragraph	Superseded IAS 36 paragraph	Current IAS 36 paragraph	Superseded IAS 36 paragraph	Current IAS 36 paragraph
Objective	1	29	36	58	59
1	2	30	37	59	60
2	3	31	38	60	61
3	4	32	39	61	62
4	5	33	40	62	63
5	6	34	41	63	64
6	7	35	42	64	65
7	8	36	43	65	66
8	9	37	44	66	67
9	12	38	45	67	68
10	13	39	46	68	69
11	14	40	47	69	70
12	15	41	48	70	71
13	16	42	49	71	72
14	17	43	50	72	73
15	18	44	51	73	74
16	19	45	52	74	75
17	20	46	53	75	76
18	21	47	54	76	77
19	22	48	55	77	78
20	23	49	56	78	79
21	25	50	57, A16	79	81
22	26	51	A17	80–82	80, 82, 88, 90
23	27	52	A18	83	None
24	28	53	A15	84	100
25	29	54	A19	85	101
26	31	55	A20	86	102
27	33	56	A21	87	103
28	35	57	58	88	104

Superseded IAS 36 paragraph	Current IAS 36 paragraph
89	105
90	None
91	106
92	107
93	108
94	109
95	110
96	111
97	112
98	113
99	114
100	115
101	116
102	117
103	118
104	119
105	120
106	121
107	122
108	123
109	124
110	125
111	124
112	None
113	126
114	127
115	128
116	129
117	130
118	131
119	132
120	138, 139
121	None
122	139
A1	IE1
A2	IE2
A3	IE3
A4	IE4
A5	IE5
A6	IE6
A7	IE7
A8	IE8
A9	IE9
A10	IE10
A11	IE11
A12	IE12
A13	IE13
A14	IE14
A15	IE15
A16	IE16
A17	IE17
A18	IE18
A19	IE19
A20	IE20
A21	IE21
A22	IE22
A23	IE23
A24	IE27
A25	IE25
A26	IE23A, IE24, IE26
A27	None
A28	IE28
A29	IE29
A30	IE30
A31	IE31
A32	IE32
A33	IE33
A34	IE34
A35	IE35
A36	IE36
A37	IE37
A38	IE38
A39	IE39
A40	IE40
A41	IE41
A42	IE42
A43	IE43
A44	IE44
A45	IE45
A46	IE46
A47	IE47
A48	IE48
A49	IE49
A50	IE50
A51	IE51
A52	IE52
A53	IE53
A54	IE54
A55	IE55
A56	IE56
A57	IE57
A58	IE58
A59	IE59
A60	IE60
A61	IE61
A62	None
A63	None
A64	None
A65	None

Superseded IAS 36 paragraph	Current IAS 36 paragraph
A66	None
A67	None
A68	None
A69	None
A70	None
A71	None
A72	IE69
A73	IE70
A74	IE71
A75	IE72
A76	IE73
A77	IE74
A78	IE75
A79	IE76
A80	IE76
A81	IE77
A82	IE78
A83	IE79
None	10, 11
None	24
None	30
None	32
None	34
None	83–87
None	89
None	91–99
None	133–137
None	140, 141
None	A1–A14
None	IE62–IE68
None	IE80–IE89

International Accounting Standard 37

Provisions, Contingent Liabilities and Contingent Assets

This version includes amendments resulting from new and amended IFRSs issued up to 31 December 2004.

CONTENTS

International Accounting Standard 37 *Provisions, Contingent Liabilities and Contingent Assets* (IAS 37) is set out in paragraphs 1–95. All the paragraphs have equal authority but retain the IASC format of the Standard when it was adopted by the IASB. IAS 37 should be read in the context of its objective, the *Preface to International Financial Reporting Standards* and the *Framework for the Preparation and Presentation of Financial Statements*. IAS 8 *Accounting Policies, Changes in Accounting Estimates and Errors* provides a basis for selecting and applying accounting policies in the absence of explicit guidance.

Introduction

IN1 IAS 37 prescribes the accounting and disclosure for all provisions, contingent liabilities and contingent assets, except:

(a) those resulting from financial instruments that are carried at fair value;

(b) those resulting from executory contracts, except where the contract is onerous. Executory contracts are contracts under which neither party has performed any of its obligations or both parties have partially performed their obligations to an equal extent;

(c) those arising in insurance entities from contracts with policyholders; or

(d) those covered by another Standard.

Provisions

IN2 The Standard defines provisions as liabilities of uncertain timing or amount. A provision should be recognised when, and only when:

(a) an entity has a present obligation (legal or constructive) as a result of a past event;

(b) it is probable (ie more likely than not) that an outflow of resources embodying economic benefits will be required to settle the obligation; and

(c) a reliable estimate can be made of the amount of the obligation. The Standard notes that it is only in extremely rare cases that a reliable estimate will not be possible.

IN3 The Standard defines a constructive obligation as an obligation that derives from an entity's actions where:

(a) by an established pattern of past practice, published policies or a sufficiently specific current statement, the entity has indicated to other parties that it will accept certain responsibilities; and

(b) as a result, the entity has created a valid expectation on the part of those other parties that it will discharge those responsibilities.

IN4 In rare cases, for example in a law suit, it may not be clear whether an entity has a present obligation. In these cases, a past event is deemed to give rise to a present obligation if, taking account of all available evidence, it is more likely than not that a present obligation exists at the balance sheet date. An entity recognises a provision for that present obligation if the other recognition criteria described above are met. If it is more likely than not that no present obligation exists, the entity discloses a contingent liability, unless the possibility of an outflow of resources embodying economic benefits is remote.

IN5 The amount recognised as a provision should be the best estimate of the expenditure required to settle the present obligation at the balance sheet date, in other words, the amount that an entity would rationally pay to settle the obligation at the balance sheet date or to transfer it to a third party at that time.

IN6 The Standard requires that an entity should, in measuring a provision:

(a) take risks and uncertainties into account. However, uncertainty does not justify the creation of excessive provisions or a deliberate overstatement of liabilities;

(b) discount the provisions, where the effect of the time value of money is material, using a pre-tax discount rate (or rates) that reflect(s) current market assessments of the time value of money and those risks specific to the liability that have not been reflected in the best estimate of the expenditure. Where discounting is used, the increase in the provision due to the passage of time is recognised as an interest expense;

(c) take future events, such as changes in the law and technological changes, into account where there is sufficient objective evidence that they will occur; and

(d) not take gains from the expected disposal of assets into account, even if the expected disposal is closely linked to the event giving rise to the provision.

IN7 An entity may expect reimbursement of some or all of the expenditure required to settle a provision (for example, through insurance contracts, indemnity clauses or suppliers' warranties). An entity should:

(a) recognise a reimbursement when, and only when, it is virtually certain that reimbursement will be received if the entity settles the obligation. The amount recognised for the reimbursement should not exceed the amount of the provision; and

(b) recognise the reimbursement as a separate asset. In the income statement, the expense relating to a provision may be presented net of the amount recognised for a reimbursement.

IN8 Provisions should be reviewed at each balance sheet date and adjusted to reflect the current best estimate. If it is no longer probable that an outflow of resources embodying economic benefits will be required to settle the obligation, the provision should be reversed.

IN9 A provision should be used only for expenditures for which the provision was originally recognised.

Provisions – specific applications

IN10 The Standard explains how the general recognition and measurement requirements for provisions should be applied in three specific cases: future operating losses; onerous contracts; and restructurings.

IN11 Provisions should not be recognised for future operating losses. An expectation of future operating losses is an indication that certain assets of the operation may be impaired. In this case, an entity tests these assets for impairment under IAS 36 *Impairment of Assets*.

IN12 If an entity has a contract that is onerous, the present obligation under the contract should be recognised and measured as a provision. An onerous contract is one in which the unavoidable costs of meeting the obligations under the contract exceed the economic benefits expected to be received under it.

IN13 The Standard defines a restructuring as a programme that is planned and controlled by management, and materially changes either:

(a) the scope of a business undertaken by an entity; or

(b) the manner in which that business is conducted.

IN14 A provision for restructuring costs is recognised only when the general recognition criteria for provisions are met. In this context, a constructive obligation to restructure arises only when an entity:

(a) has a detailed formal plan for the restructuring identifying at least:

(i) the business or part of a business concerned;

(ii) the principal locations affected;

(iii) the location, function, and approximate number of employees who will be compensated for terminating their services;

(iv) the expenditures that will be undertaken; and

(v) when the plan will be implemented; and

(b) has raised a valid expectation in those affected that it will carry out the restructuring by starting to implement that plan or announcing its main features to those affected by it.

IN15 A management or board decision to restructure does not give rise to a constructive obligation at the balance sheet date unless the entity has, before the balance sheet date:

(a) started to implement the restructuring plan; or

(b) communicated the restructuring plan to those affected by it in a sufficiently specific manner to raise a valid expectation in them that the entity will carry out the restructuring.

IN16 Where a restructuring involves the sale of an operation, no obligation arises for the sale until the entity is committed to the sale, ie there is a binding sale agreement.

IN17 A restructuring provision should include only the direct expenditures arising from the restructuring, which are those that are both:

(a) necessarily entailed by the restructuring; and

(b) not associated with the ongoing activities of the entity. Thus, a restructuring provision does not include such costs as: retraining or relocating continuing staff; marketing; or investment in new systems and distribution networks.

Contingent liabilities

IN18 The Standard defines a contingent liability as:

(a) a possible obligation that arises from past events and whose existence will be confirmed only by the occurrence or non-occurrence of one or more uncertain future events not wholly within the control of the entity; or

(b) a present obligation that arises from past events but is not recognised because:

(i) it is not probable that an outflow of resources embodying economic benefits will be required to settle the obligation; or

(ii) the amount of the obligation cannot be measured with sufficient reliability.

IN19 An entity should not recognise a contingent liability. An entity should disclose a contingent liability, unless the possibility of an outflow of resources embodying economic benefits is remote.

Contingent assets

IN20 The Standard defines a contingent asset as a possible asset that arises from past events and whose existence will be confirmed only by the occurrence or non-occurrence of one or more uncertain future events not wholly within the control of the entity. An example is a claim that an entity is pursuing through legal processes, where the outcome is uncertain.

IN21 An entity should not recognise a contingent asset. A contingent asset should be disclosed where an inflow of economic benefits is probable.

IN22 When the realisation of income is virtually certain, then the related asset is not a contingent asset and its recognition is appropriate.

Effective date

IN23 The Standard becomes operative for annual financial statements covering periods beginning on or after 1 July 1999. Earlier application is encouraged.

International Accounting Standard 37
Provisions, Contingent Liabilities and Contingent Assets

Objective

The objective of this Standard is to ensure that appropriate recognition criteria and measurement bases are applied to provisions, contingent liabilities and contingent assets and that sufficient information is disclosed in the notes to the financial statements to enable users to understand their nature, timing and amount.

Scope

1 **This Standard shall be applied by all entities in accounting for provisions, contingent liabilities and contingent assets, except:**

(a) **those resulting from executory contracts, except where the contract is onerous; and**

(b) [deleted]

(c) **those covered by another Standard.**

2 This Standard does not apply to financial instruments (including guarantees) that are within the scope of IAS 39 *Financial Instruments: Recognition and Measurement*.

3 Executory contracts are contracts under which neither party has performed any of its obligations or both parties have partially performed their obligations to an equal extent. This Standard does not apply to executory contracts unless they are onerous.

4 [Deleted]

5 Where another Standard deals with a specific type of provision, contingent liability or contingent asset, an entity applies that Standard instead of this Standard. For example, IFRS 3 *Business Combinations* addresses the treatment by an acquirer of contingent liabilities assumed in a business combination. Similarly, certain types of provisions are also addressed in Standards on:

(a) construction contracts (see IAS 11 *Construction Contracts*);

(b) income taxes (see IAS 12 *Income Taxes*);

(c) leases (see IAS 17 *Leases*). However, as IAS 17 contains no specific requirements to deal with operating leases that have become onerous, this Standard applies to such cases;

(d) employee benefits (see IAS 19 *Employee Benefits*); and

(e) insurance contracts (see IFRS 4 *Insurance Contracts*). However, this Standard applies to provisions, contingent liabilities and contingent assets of an insurer, other than those arising from its contractual obligations and rights under insurance contracts within the scope of IFRS 4.

6 Some amounts treated as provisions may relate to the recognition of revenue, for example where an entity gives guarantees in exchange for a fee. This Standard

does not address the recognition of revenue. IAS 18 *Revenue* identifies the circumstances in which revenue is recognised and provides practical guidance on the application of the recognition criteria. This Standard does not change the requirements of IAS 18.

7 This Standard defines provisions as liabilities of uncertain timing or amount. In some countries the term 'provision' is also used in the context of items such as depreciation, impairment of assets and doubtful debts: these are adjustments to the carrying amounts of assets and are not addressed in this Standard.

8 Other Standards specify whether expenditures are treated as assets or as expenses. These issues are not addressed in this Standard. Accordingly, this Standard neither prohibits nor requires capitalisation of the costs recognised when a provision is made.

9 This Standard applies to provisions for restructurings (including discontinued operations). When a restructuring meets the definition of a discontinued operation, additional disclosures may be required by IFRS 5 *Non-current Assets Held for Sale and Discontinued Operations*.

Definitions

10 **The following terms are used in this Standard with the meanings specified:**

A *provision* **is a liability of uncertain timing or amount.**

A *liability* **is a present obligation of the entity arising from past events, the settlement of which is expected to result in an outflow from the entity of resources embodying economic benefits.**

An *obligating event* **is an event that creates a legal or constructive obligation that results in an entity having no realistic alternative to settling that obligation.**

A *legal obligation* **is an obligation that derives from:**

(a) a contract (through its explicit or implicit terms);

(b) legislation; or

(c) other operation of law.

A *constructive obligation* **is an obligation that derives from an entity's actions where:**

(a) by an established pattern of past practice, published policies or a sufficiently specific current statement, the entity has indicated to other parties that it will accept certain responsibilities; and

(b) as a result, the entity has created a valid expectation on the part of those other parties that it will discharge those responsibilities.

A *contingent liability* **is:**

(a) a possible obligation that arises from past events and whose existence will be confirmed only by the occurrence or non-occurrence of one or more uncertain future events not wholly within the control of the entity; or

(b) a present obligation that arises from past events but is not recognised because:

(i) it is not probable that an outflow of resources embodying economic benefits will be required to settle the obligation; or

(ii) the amount of the obligation cannot be measured with sufficient reliability.

A *contingent asset* is a possible asset that arises from past events and whose existence will be confirmed only by the occurrence or non-occurrence of one or more uncertain future events not wholly within the control of the entity.

An *onerous contract* is a contract in which the unavoidable costs of meeting the obligations under the contract exceed the economic benefits expected to be received under it.

A *restructuring* is a programme that is planned and controlled by management, and materially changes either:

(a) the scope of a business undertaken by an entity; or

(b) the manner in which that business is conducted.

Provisions and other liabilities

11 Provisions can be distinguished from other liabilities such as trade payables and accruals because there is uncertainty about the timing or amount of the future expenditure required in settlement. By contrast:

(a) trade payables are liabilities to pay for goods or services that have been received or supplied and have been invoiced or formally agreed with the supplier; and

(b) accruals are liabilities to pay for goods or services that have been received or supplied but have not been paid, invoiced or formally agreed with the supplier, including amounts due to employees (for example, amounts relating to accrued vacation pay). Although it is sometimes necessary to estimate the amount or timing of accruals, the uncertainty is generally much less than for provisions.

Accruals are often reported as part of trade and other payables, whereas provisions are reported separately.

Relationship between provisions and contingent liabilities

12 In a general sense, all provisions are contingent because they are uncertain in timing or amount. However, within this Standard the term 'contingent' is used for liabilities and assets that are not recognised because their existence will be confirmed only by the occurrence or non-occurrence of one or more uncertain future events not wholly within the control of the entity. In addition, the term 'contingent liability' is used for liabilities that do not meet the recognition criteria.

13 This Standard distinguishes between:

(a) provisions – which are recognised as liabilities (assuming that a reliable estimate can be made) because they are present obligations and it is probable that an outflow of resources embodying economic benefits will be required to settle the obligations; and

(b) contingent liabilities – which are not recognised as liabilities because they are either:

(i) possible obligations, as it has yet to be confirmed whether the entity has a present obligation that could lead to an outflow of resources embodying economic benefits; or

(ii) present obligations that do not meet the recognition criteria in this Standard (because either it is not probable that an outflow of resources embodying economic benefits will be required to settle the obligation, or a sufficiently reliable estimate of the amount of the obligation cannot be made).

Recognition

Provisions

14 **A provision shall be recognised when:**

(a) an entity has a present obligation (legal or constructive) as a result of a past event;

(b) it is probable that an outflow of resources embodying economic benefits will be required to settle the obligation; and

(c) a reliable estimate can be made of the amount of the obligation.

If these conditions are not met, no provision shall be recognised.

Present obligation

15 **In rare cases it is not clear whether there is a present obligation. In these cases, a past event is deemed to give rise to a present obligation if, taking account of all available evidence, it is more likely than not that a present obligation exists at the balance sheet date.**

16 In almost all cases it will be clear whether a past event has given rise to a present obligation. In rare cases, for example in a law suit, it may be disputed either whether certain events have occurred or whether those events result in a present obligation. In such a case, an entity determines whether a present obligation exists at the balance sheet date by taking account of all available evidence, including, for example, the opinion of experts. The evidence considered includes any additional evidence provided by events after the balance sheet date. On the basis of such evidence:

(a) where it is more likely than not that a present obligation exists at the balance sheet date, the entity recognises a provision (if the recognition criteria are met); and

(b) where it is more likely that no present obligation exists at the balance sheet date, the entity discloses a contingent liability, unless the possibility of an outflow of resources embodying economic benefits is remote (see paragraph 86).

Past event

17 A past event that leads to a present obligation is called an obligating event. For an event to be an obligating event, it is necessary that the entity has no realistic alternative to settling the obligation created by the event. This is the case only:

(a) where the settlement of the obligation can be enforced by law; or

(b) in the case of a constructive obligation, where the event (which may be an action of the entity) creates valid expectations in other parties that the entity will discharge the obligation.

18 Financial statements deal with the financial position of an entity at the end of its reporting period and not its possible position in the future. Therefore, no provision is recognised for costs that need to be incurred to operate in the future. The only liabilities recognised in an entity's balance sheet are those that exist at the balance sheet date.

19 It is only those obligations arising from past events existing independently of an entity's future actions (ie the future conduct of its business) that are recognised as provisions. Examples of such obligations are penalties or clean-up costs for unlawful environmental damage, both of which would lead to an outflow of resources embodying economic benefits in settlement regardless of the future actions of the entity. Similarly, an entity recognises a provision for the decommissioning costs of an oil installation or a nuclear power station to the extent that the entity is obliged to rectify damage already caused. In contrast, because of commercial pressures or legal requirements, an entity may intend or need to carry out expenditure to operate in a particular way in the future (for example, by fitting smoke filters in a certain type of factory). Because the entity can avoid the future expenditure by its future actions, for example by changing its method of operation, it has no present obligation for that future expenditure and no provision is recognised.

20 An obligation always involves another party to whom the obligation is owed. It is not necessary, however, to know the identity of the party to whom the obligation is owed–indeed the obligation may be to the public at large. Because an obligation always involves a commitment to another party, it follows that a management or board decision does not give rise to a constructive obligation at the balance sheet date unless the decision has been communicated before the balance sheet date to those affected by it in a sufficiently specific manner to raise a valid expectation in them that the entity will discharge its responsibilities.

21 An event that does not give rise to an obligation immediately may do so at a later date, because of changes in the law or because an act (for example, a sufficiently specific public statement) by the entity gives rise to a constructive obligation. For example, when environmental damage is caused there may be no obligation to remedy the consequences. However, the causing of the damage will become an

obligating event when a new law requires the existing damage to be rectified or when the entity publicly accepts responsibility for rectification in a way that creates a constructive obligation.

22 Where details of a proposed new law have yet to be finalised, an obligation arises only when the legislation is virtually certain to be enacted as drafted. For the purpose of this Standard, such an obligation is treated as a legal obligation. Differences in circumstances surrounding enactment make it impossible to specify a single event that would make the enactment of a law virtually certain. In many cases it will be impossible to be virtually certain of the enactment of a law until it is enacted.

Probable outflow of resources embodying economic benefits

23 For a liability to qualify for recognition there must be not only a present obligation but also the probability of an outflow of resources embodying economic benefits to settle that obligation. For the purpose of this Standard*, an outflow of resources or other event is regarded as probable if the event is more likely than not to occur, ie the probability that the event will occur is greater than the probability that it will not. Where it is not probable that a present obligation exists, an entity discloses a contingent liability, unless the possibility of an outflow of resources embodying economic benefits is remote (see paragraph 86).

24 Where there are a number of similar obligations (eg product warranties or similar contracts) the probability that an outflow will be required in settlement is determined by considering the class of obligations as a whole. Although the likelihood of outflow for any one item may be small, it may well be probable that some outflow of resources will be needed to settle the class of obligations as a whole. If that is the case, a provision is recognised (if the other recognition criteria are met).

Reliable estimate of the obligation

25 The use of estimates is an essential part of the preparation of financial statements and does not undermine their reliability. This is especially true in the case of provisions, which by their nature are more uncertain than most other balance sheet items. Except in extremely rare cases, an entity will be able to determine a range of possible outcomes and can therefore make an estimate of the obligation that is sufficiently reliable to use in recognising a provision.

26 In the extremely rare case where no reliable estimate can be made, a liability exists that cannot be recognised. That liability is disclosed as a contingent liability (see paragraph 86).

Contingent liabilities

27 An entity shall not recognise a contingent liability.

28 A contingent liability is disclosed, as required by paragraph 86, unless the possibility of an outflow of resources embodying economic benefits is remote.

* The interpretation of 'probable' in this Standard as 'more likely than not' does not necessarily apply in other Standards.

29 Where an entity is jointly and severally liable for an obligation, the part of the obligation that is expected to be met by other parties is treated as a contingent liability. The entity recognises a provision for the part of the obligation for which an outflow of resources embodying economic benefits is probable, except in the extremely rare circumstances where no reliable estimate can be made.

30 Contingent liabilities may develop in a way not initially expected. Therefore, they are assessed continually to determine whether an outflow of resources embodying economic benefits has become probable. If it becomes probable that an outflow of future economic benefits will be required for an item previously dealt with as a contingent liability, a provision is recognised in the financial statements of the period in which the change in probability occurs (except in the extremely rare circumstances where no reliable estimate can be made).

Contingent assets

31 An entity shall not recognise a contingent asset.

32 Contingent assets usually arise from unplanned or other unexpected events that give rise to the possibility of an inflow of economic benefits to the entity. An example is a claim that an entity is pursuing through legal processes, where the outcome is uncertain.

33 Contingent assets are not recognised in financial statements since this may result in the recognition of income that may never be realised. However, when the realisation of income is virtually certain, then the related asset is not a contingent asset and its recognition is appropriate.

34 A contingent asset is disclosed, as required by paragraph 89, where an inflow of economic benefits is probable.

35 Contingent assets are assessed continually to ensure that developments are appropriately reflected in the financial statements. If it has become virtually certain that an inflow of economic benefits will arise, the asset and the related income are recognised in the financial statements of the period in which the change occurs. If an inflow of economic benefits has become probable, an entity discloses the contingent asset (see paragraph 89).

Measurement

Best estimate

36 The amount recognised as a provision shall be the best estimate of the expenditure required to settle the present obligation at the balance sheet date.

37 The best estimate of the expenditure required to settle the present obligation is the amount that an entity would rationally pay to settle the obligation at the balance sheet date or to transfer it to a third party at that time. It will often be impossible or prohibitively expensive to settle or transfer an obligation at the balance sheet date. However, the estimate of the amount that an entity would rationally pay to settle or transfer the obligation gives the best estimate of the expenditure required to settle the present obligation at the balance sheet date.

38 The estimates of outcome and financial effect are determined by the judgement of the management of the entity, supplemented by experience of similar transactions and, in some cases, reports from independent experts. The evidence considered includes any additional evidence provided by events after the balance sheet date.

39 Uncertainties surrounding the amount to be recognised as a provision are dealt with by various means according to the circumstances. Where the provision being measured involves a large population of items, the obligation is estimated by weighting all possible outcomes by their associated probabilities. The name for this statistical method of estimation is 'expected value'. The provision will therefore be different depending on whether the probability of a loss of a given amount is, for example, 60 per cent or 90 per cent. Where there is a continuous range of possible outcomes, and each point in that range is as likely as any other, the mid-point of the range is used.

Example

An entity sells goods with a warranty under which customers are covered for the cost of repairs of any manufacturing defects that become apparent within the first six months after purchase. If minor defects were detected in all products sold, repair costs of 1 million would result. If major defects were detected in all products sold, repair costs of 4 million would result. The entity's past experience and future expectations indicate that, for the coming year, 75 per cent of the goods sold will have no defects, 20 per cent of the goods sold will have minor defects and 5 per cent of the goods sold will have major defects. In accordance with paragraph 24, an entity assesses the probability of an outflow for the warranty obligations as a whole.

The expected value of the cost of repairs is:

(75% of nil) + (20% of 1m) + (5% of 4m) = 400,000

40 Where a single obligation is being measured, the individual most likely outcome may be the best estimate of the liability. However, even in such a case, the entity considers other possible outcomes. Where other possible outcomes are either mostly higher or mostly lower than the most likely outcome, the best estimate will be a higher or lower amount. For example, if an entity has to rectify a serious fault in a major plant that it has constructed for a customer, the individual most likely outcome may be for the repair to succeed at the first attempt at a cost of 1,000, but a provision for a larger amount is made if there is a significant chance that further attempts will be necessary.

41 The provision is measured before tax, as the tax consequences of the provision, and changes in it, are dealt with under IAS 12 *Income Taxes*.

Risks and uncertainties

42 The risks and uncertainties that inevitably surround many events and circumstances shall be taken into account in reaching the best estimate of a provision.

43 Risk describes variability of outcome. A risk adjustment may increase the amount at which a liability is measured. Caution is needed in making judgements under conditions of uncertainty, so that income or assets are not overstated and expenses or liabilities are not understated. However, uncertainty does not justify the creation of excessive provisions or a deliberate overstatement of liabilities. For example, if the projected costs of a particularly adverse outcome are estimated on a prudent basis, that outcome is not then deliberately treated as more probable than is realistically the case. Care is needed to avoid duplicating adjustments for risk and uncertainty with consequent overstatement of a provision.

44 Disclosure of the uncertainties surrounding the amount of the expenditure is made under paragraph 85(b).

Present value

45 Where the effect of the time value of money is material, the amount of a provision shall be the present value of the expenditures expected to be required to settle the obligation.

46 Because of the time value of money, provisions relating to cash outflows that arise soon after the balance sheet date are more onerous than those where cash outflows of the same amount arise later. Provisions are therefore discounted, where the effect is material.

47 The discount rate (or rates) shall be a pre-tax rate (or rates) that reflect(s) current market assessments of the time value of money and the risks specific to the liability. The discount rate(s) shall not reflect risks for which future cash flow estimates have been adjusted.

Future events

48 Future events that may affect the amount required to settle an obligation shall be reflected in the amount of a provision where there is sufficient objective evidence that they will occur.

49 Expected future events may be particularly important in measuring provisions. For example, an entity may believe that the cost of cleaning up a site at the end of its life will be reduced by future changes in technology. The amount recognised reflects a reasonable expectation of technically qualified, objective observers, taking account of all available evidence as to the technology that will be available at the time of the clean-up. Thus it is appropriate to include, for example, expected cost reductions associated with increased experience in applying existing technology or the expected cost of applying existing technology to a larger or more complex clean-up operation than has previously been carried out. However, an entity does not anticipate the development of a completely new technology for cleaning up unless it is supported by sufficient objective evidence.

50 The effect of possible new legislation is taken into consideration in measuring an existing obligation when sufficient objective evidence exists that the legislation is virtually certain to be enacted. The variety of circumstances that arise in practice makes it impossible to specify a single event that will provide sufficient, objective evidence in every case. Evidence is required both of what legislation will demand

and of whether it is virtually certain to be enacted and implemented in due course. In many cases sufficient objective evidence will not exist until the new legislation is enacted.

Expected disposal of assets

51 **Gains from the expected disposal of assets shall not be taken into account in measuring a provision.**

52 Gains on the expected disposal of assets are not taken into account in measuring a provision, even if the expected disposal is closely linked to the event giving rise to the provision. Instead, an entity recognises gains on expected disposals of assets at the time specified by the Standard dealing with the assets concerned.

Reimbursements

53 **Where some or all of the expenditure required to settle a provision is expected to be reimbursed by another party, the reimbursement shall be recognised when, and only when, it is virtually certain that reimbursement will be received if the entity settles the obligation. The reimbursement shall be treated as a separate asset. The amount recognised for the reimbursement shall not exceed the amount of the provision.**

54 **In the income statement, the expense relating to a provision may be presented net of the amount recognised for a reimbursement.**

55 Sometimes, an entity is able to look to another party to pay part or all of the expenditure required to settle a provision (for example, through insurance contracts, indemnity clauses or suppliers' warranties). The other party may either reimburse amounts paid by the entity or pay the amounts directly.

56 In most cases the entity will remain liable for the whole of the amount in question so that the entity would have to settle the full amount if the third party failed to pay for any reason. In this situation, a provision is recognised for the full amount of the liability, and a separate asset for the expected reimbursement is recognised when it is virtually certain that reimbursement will be received if the entity settles the liability.

57 In some cases, the entity will not be liable for the costs in question if the third party fails to pay. In such a case the entity has no liability for those costs and they are not included in the provision.

58 As noted in paragraph 29, an obligation for which an entity is jointly and severally liable is a contingent liability to the extent that it is expected that the obligation will be settled by the other parties.

Changes in provisions

59 **Provisions shall be reviewed at each balance sheet date and adjusted to reflect the current best estimate. If it is no longer probable that an outflow of resources embodying economic benefits will be required to settle the obligation, the provision shall be reversed.**

60 Where discounting is used, the carrying amount of a provision increases in each period to reflect the passage of time. This increase is recognised as borrowing cost.

Use of provisions

61 A provision shall be used only for expenditures for which the provision was originally recognised.

62 Only expenditures that relate to the original provision are set against it. Setting expenditures against a provision that was originally recognised for another purpose would conceal the impact of two different events.

Application of the recognition and measurement rules

Future operating losses

63 Provisions shall not be recognised for future operating losses.

64 Future operating losses do not meet the definition of a liability in paragraph 10 and the general recognition criteria set out for provisions in paragraph 14.

65 An expectation of future operating losses is an indication that certain assets of the operation may be impaired. An entity tests these assets for impairment under IAS 36 *Impairment of Assets*.

Onerous contracts

66 If an entity has a contract that is onerous, the present obligation under the contract shall be recognised and measured as a provision.

67 Many contracts (for example, some routine purchase orders) can be cancelled without paying compensation to the other party, and therefore there is no obligation. Other contracts establish both rights and obligations for each of the contracting parties. Where events make such a contract onerous, the contract falls within the scope of this Standard and a liability exists which is recognised. Executory contracts that are not onerous fall outside the scope of this Standard.

68 This Standard defines an onerous contract as a contract in which the unavoidable costs of meeting the obligations under the contract exceed the economic benefits expected to be received under it. The unavoidable costs under a contract reflect the least net cost of exiting from the contract, which is the lower of the cost of fulfilling it and any compensation or penalties arising from failure to fulfil it.

69 Before a separate provision for an onerous contract is established, an entity recognises any impairment loss that has occurred on assets dedicated to that contract (see IAS 36 *Impairment of Assets*).

Restructuring

70 The following are examples of events that may fall under the definition of restructuring:

(a) sale or termination of a line of business;

(b) the closure of business locations in a country or region or the relocation of business activities from one country or region to another;

(c) changes in management structure, for example, eliminating a layer of management; and

(d) fundamental reorganisations that have a material effect on the nature and focus of the entity's operations.

71 A provision for restructuring costs is recognised only when the general recognition criteria for provisions set out in paragraph 14 are met. Paragraphs 72–83 set out how the general recognition criteria apply to restructurings.

72 A constructive obligation to restructure arises only when an entity:

(a) has a detailed formal plan for the restructuring identifying at least:

(i) the business or part of a business concerned;

(ii) the principal locations affected;

(iii) the location, function, and approximate number of employees who will be compensated for terminating their services;

(iv) the expenditures that will be undertaken; and

(v) when the plan will be implemented; and

(b) has raised a valid expectation in those affected that it will carry out the restructuring by starting to implement that plan or announcing its main features to those affected by it.

73 Evidence that an entity has started to implement a restructuring plan would be provided, for example, by dismantling plant or selling assets or by the public announcement of the main features of the plan. A public announcement of a detailed plan to restructure constitutes a constructive obligation to restructure only if it is made in such a way and in sufficient detail (ie setting out the main features of the plan) that it gives rise to valid expectations in other parties such as customers, suppliers and employees (or their representatives) that the entity will carry out the restructuring.

74 For a plan to be sufficient to give rise to a constructive obligation when communicated to those affected by it, its implementation needs to be planned to begin as soon as possible and to be completed in a timeframe that makes significant changes to the plan unlikely. If it is expected that there will be a long delay before the restructuring begins or that the restructuring will take an unreasonably long time, it is unlikely that the plan will raise a valid expectation on the part of others that the entity is at present committed to restructuring, because the timeframe allows opportunities for the entity to change its plans.

75 A management or board decision to restructure taken before the balance sheet date does not give rise to a constructive obligation at the balance sheet date unless the entity has, before the balance sheet date:

(a) started to implement the restructuring plan; or

(b) announced the main features of the restructuring plan to those affected by it in a sufficiently specific manner to raise a valid expectation in them that the entity will carry out the restructuring.

If an entity starts to implement a restructuring plan, or announces its main features to those affected, only after the balance sheet date, disclosure is required under IAS 10 *Events after the Balance Sheet Date*, if the restructuring is material and nondisclosure could influence the economic decisions of users taken on the basis of the financial statements.

76 Although a constructive obligation is not created solely by a management decision, an obligation may result from other earlier events together with such a decision. For example, negotiations with employee representatives for termination payments, or with purchasers for the sale of an operation, may have been concluded subject only to board approval. Once that approval has been obtained and communicated to the other parties, the entity has a constructive obligation to restructure, if the conditions of paragraph 72 are met.

77 In some countries, the ultimate authority is vested in a board whose membership includes representatives of interests other than those of management (eg employees) or notification to such representatives may be necessary before the board decision is taken. Because a decision by such a board involves communication to these representatives, it may result in a constructive obligation to restructure.

78 No obligation arises for the sale of an operation until the entity is committed to the sale, ie there is a binding sale agreement.

79 Even when an entity has taken a decision to sell an operation and announced that decision publicly, it cannot be committed to the sale until a purchaser has been identified and there is a binding sale agreement. Until there is a binding sale agreement, the entity will be able to change its mind and indeed will have to take another course of action if a purchaser cannot be found on acceptable terms. When the sale of an operation is envisaged as part of a restructuring, the assets of the operation are reviewed for impairment, under IAS 36 *Impairment of Assets*. When a sale is only part of a restructuring, a constructive obligation can arise for the other parts of the restructuring before a binding sale agreement exists.

80 A restructuring provision shall include only the direct expenditures arising from the restructuring, which are those that are both:

(a) necessarily entailed by the restructuring; and

(b) not associated with the ongoing activities of the entity.

81 A restructuring provision does not include such costs as:

(a) retraining or relocating continuing staff;

(b) marketing; or

(c) investment in new systems and distribution networks.

These expenditures relate to the future conduct of the business and are not liabilities for restructuring at the balance sheet date. Such expenditures are recognised on the same basis as if they arose independently of a restructuring.

82 Identifiable future operating losses up to the date of a restructuring are not included in a provision, unless they relate to an onerous contract as defined in paragraph 10.

83 As required by paragraph 51, gains on the expected disposal of assets are not taken into account in measuring a restructuring provision, even if the sale of assets is envisaged as part of the restructuring.

Disclosure

84 **For each class of provision, an entity shall disclose:**

(a) the carrying amount at the beginning and end of the period;

(b) additional provisions made in the period, including increases to existing provisions;

(c) amounts used (ie incurred and charged against the provision) during the period;

(d) unused amounts reversed during the period; and

(e) the increase during the period in the discounted amount arising from the passage of time and the effect of any change in the discount rate.

Comparative information is not required.

85 **An entity shall disclose the following for each class of provision:**

(a) a brief description of the nature of the obligation and the expected timing of any resulting outflows of economic benefits;

(b) an indication of the uncertainties about the amount or timing of those outflows. Where necessary to provide adequate information, an entity shall disclose the major assumptions made concerning future events, as addressed in paragraph 48; and

(c) the amount of any expected reimbursement, stating the amount of any asset that has been recognised for that expected reimbursement.

86 **Unless the possibility of any outflow in settlement is remote, an entity shall disclose for each class of contingent liability at the balance sheet date a brief description of the nature of the contingent liability and, where practicable:**

(a) an estimate of its financial effect, measured under paragraphs 36–52;

(b) an indication of the uncertainties relating to the amount or timing of any outflow; and

(c) the possibility of any reimbursement.

87 In determining which provisions or contingent liabilities may be aggregated to form a class, it is necessary to consider whether the nature of the items is sufficiently similar for a single statement about them to fulfil the requirements of paragraphs 85(a) and (b) and 86(a) and (b). Thus, it may be appropriate to treat as a single class of provision amounts relating to warranties of different products, but it would not be appropriate to treat as a single class amounts relating to normal warranties and amounts that are subject to legal proceedings.

88 Where a provision and a contingent liability arise from the same set of circumstances, an entity makes the disclosures required by paragraphs 84–86 in a way that shows the link between the provision and the contingent liability.

89 **Where an inflow of economic benefits is probable, an entity shall disclose a brief description of the nature of the contingent assets at the balance sheet date, and, where practicable, an estimate of their financial effect, measured using the principles set out for provisions in paragraphs 36–52.**

90 It is important that disclosures for contingent assets avoid giving misleading indications of the likelihood of income arising.

91 **Where any of the information required by paragraphs 86 and 89 is not disclosed because it is not practicable to do so, that fact shall be stated.**

92 **In extremely rare cases, disclosure of some or all of the information required by paragraphs 84–89 can be expected to prejudice seriously the position of the entity in a dispute with other parties on the subject matter of the provision, contingent liability or contingent asset. In such cases, an entity need not disclose the information, but shall disclose the general nature of the dispute, together with the fact that, and reason why, the information has not been disclosed.**

Transitional provisions

93 **The effect of adopting this Standard on its effective date (or earlier) shall be reported as an adjustment to the opening balance of retained earnings for the period in which the Standard is first adopted. Entities are encouraged, but not required, to adjust the opening balance of retained earnings for the earliest period presented and to restate comparative information. If comparative information is not restated, this fact shall be disclosed.**

94 [Deleted]

Effective date

95 **This Standard becomes operative for annual financial statements covering periods beginning on or after 1 July 1999. Earlier application is encouraged. If an entity applies this Standard for periods beginning before 1 July 1999, it shall disclose that fact.**

96 [Deleted]

Appendix A
Tables – Provisions, contingent liabilities, contingent assets and reimbursements

This appendix accompanies, but is not part of, IAS 37. Its purpose is to summarise the main requirements of the Standard.

Provisions and contingent liabilities

Where, as a result of past events, there may be an outflow of resources embodying future economic benefits in settlement of: (a) a present obligation; or (b) a possible obligation whose existence will be confirmed only by the occurrence or non-occurrence of one or more uncertain future events not wholly within the control of the entity.		
There is a present obligation that probably requires an outflow of resources.	**There is a possible obligation or a present obligation that may, but probably will not, require an outflow of resources.**	**There is a possible obligation or a present obligation where the likelihood of an outflow of resources is remote.**
A provision is recognised (paragraph 14).	No provision is recognised (paragraph 27).	No provision is recognised (paragraph 27).
Disclosures are required for the provision (paragraphs 84 and 85).	Disclosures are required for the contingent liability (paragraph 86).	No disclosure is required (paragraph 86).

A contingent liability also arises in the extremely rare case where there is a liability that cannot be recognised because it cannot be measured reliably. Disclosures are required for the contingent liability.

Contingent assets

Where, as a result of past events, there is a possible asset whose existence will be confirmed only by the occurrence or non-occurrence of one or more uncertain future events not wholly within the control of the entity.		
The inflow of economic benefits is virtually certain.	**The inflow of economic benefits is probable, but not virtually certain.**	**The inflow is not probable.**
The asset is not contingent (paragraph 33).	No asset is recognised (paragraph 31).	No asset is recognised (paragraph 31).
	Disclosures are required (paragraph 89).	No disclosure is required (paragraph 89).

Reimbursements

Some or all of the expenditure required to settle a provision is expected to be reimbursed by another party.		
The entity has no obligation for the part of the expenditure to be reimbursed by the other party.	**The obligation for the amount expected to be reimbursed remains with the entity and it is virtually certain that reimbursement will be received if the entity settles the provision.**	**The obligation for the amount expected to be reimbursed remains with the entity and the reimbursement is not virtually certain if the entity settles the provision.**
The entity has no liability for the amount to be reimbursed (paragraph 57).	The reimbursement is recognised as a separate asset in the balance sheet and may be offset against the expense in the income statement. The amount recognised for the expected reimbursement does not exceed the liability (paragraphs 53 and 54).	The expected reimbursement is not recognised as an asset (paragraph 53).
No disclosure is required.	The reimbursement is disclosed together with the amount recognised for the reimbursement (paragraph 85(c)).	The expected reimbursement is disclosed (paragraph 85(c)).

Appendix B

Decision tree

This appendix accompanies, but is not part of, IAS 37. Its purpose is to summarise the main recognition requirements of the Standard for provisions and contingent liabilities.

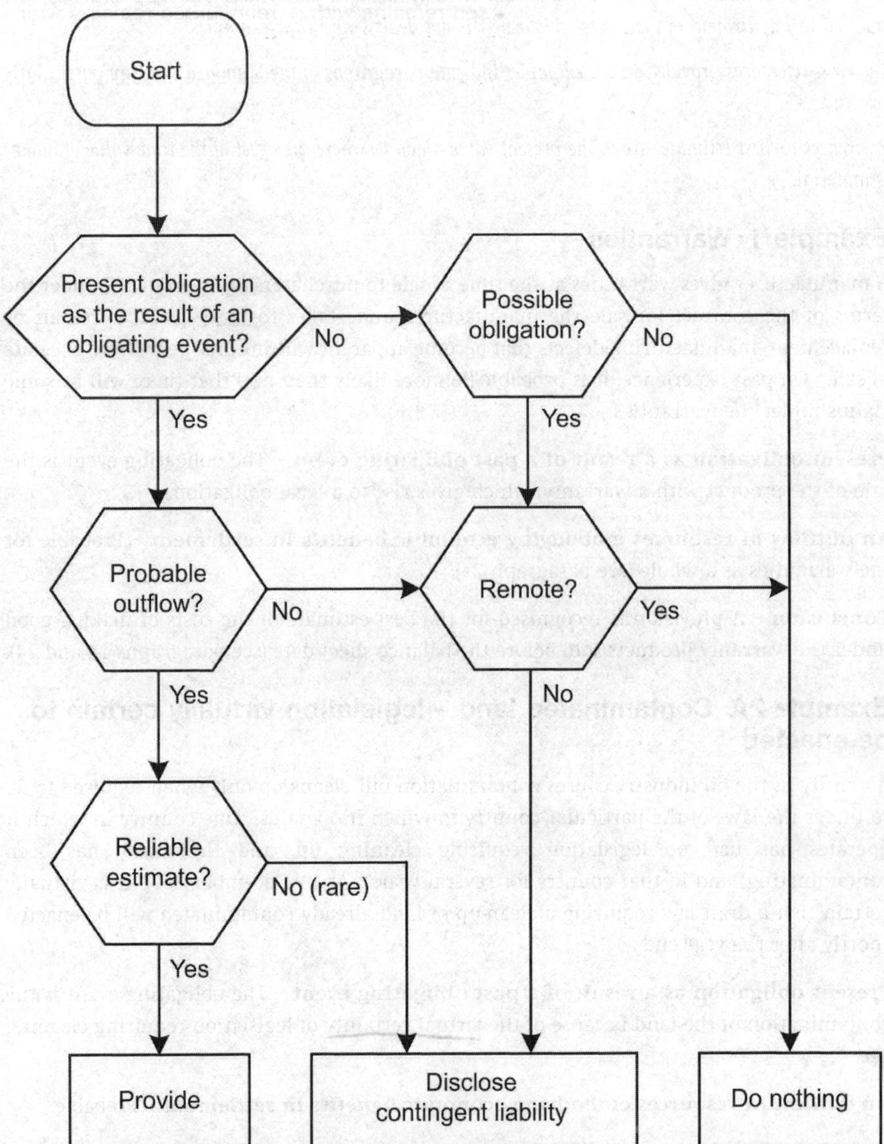

Note: in rare cases, it is not clear whether there is a present obligation. In these cases, a past event is deemed to give rise to a present obligation if, taking account of all available evidence, it is more likely than not that a present obligation exists at the balance sheet date (paragraph 15 of the Standard).

Appendix C
Examples: recognition

This appendix accompanies, but is not part of, IAS 37.

All the entities in the examples have 31 December year-ends. In all cases, it is assumed that a reliable estimate can be made of any outflows expected. In some examples the circumstances described may have resulted in impairment of the assets—this aspect is not dealt with in the examples.

The cross-references provided in the examples indicate paragraphs of the Standard that are particularly relevant.

References to 'best estimate' are to the present value amount, where the effect of the time value of money is material.

Example 1 Warranties

A manufacturer gives warranties at the time of sale to purchasers of its product. Under the terms of the contract for sale the manufacturer undertakes to make good, by repair or replacement, manufacturing defects that become apparent within three years from the date of sale. On past experience, it is probable (ie more likely than not) that there will be some claims under the warranties.

Present obligation as a result of a past obligating event – The obligating event is the sale of the product with a warranty, which gives rise to a legal obligation.

An outflow of resources embodying economic benefits in settlement – Probable for the warranties as a whole (see paragraph 24).

Conclusion – A provision is recognised for the best estimate of the costs of making good under the warranty products sold before the balance sheet date (see paragraphs 14 and 24).

Example 2A Contaminated land – legislation virtually certain to be enacted

An entity in the oil industry causes contamination but cleans up only when required to do so under the laws of the particular country in which it operates. One country in which it operates has had no legislation requiring cleaning up, and the entity has been contaminating land in that country for several years. At 31 December 2000 it is virtually certain that a draft law requiring a clean-up of land already contaminated will be enacted shortly after the year end.

Present obligation as a result of a past obligating event – The obligating event is the contamination of the land because of the virtual certainty of legislation requiring cleaning up.

An outflow of resources embodying economic benefits in settlement – Probable.

Conclusion– A provision is recognised for the best estimate of the costs of the clean-up (see paragraphs 14 and 22).

Example 2B Contaminated land and constructive obligation

An entity in the oil industry causes contamination and operates in a country where there is no environmental legislation. However, the entity has a widely published environmental policy in which it undertakes to clean up all contamination that it causes. The entity has a record of honouring this published policy.

Present obligation as a result of a past obligating event– The obligating event is the contamination of the land, which gives rise to a constructive obligation because the conduct of the entity has created a valid expectation on the part of those affected by it that the entity will clean up contamination.

An outflow of resources embodying economic benefits in settlement – Probable.

Conclusion – A provision is recognised for the best estimate of the costs of clean-up (see paragraphs 10 (the definition of a constructive obligation), 14 and 17).

Example 3 Offshore oilfield

An entity operates an offshore oilfield where its licensing agreement requires it to remove the oil rig at the end of production and restore the seabed. Ninety per cent of the eventual costs relate to the removal of the oil rig and restoration of damage caused by building it, and 10 per cent arise through the extraction of oil. At the balance sheet date, the rig has been constructed but no oil has been extracted.

Present obligation as a result of a past obligating event – The construction of the oil rig creates a legal obligation under the terms of the licence to remove the rig and restore the seabed and is thus an obligating event. At the balance sheet date, however, there is no obligation to rectify the damage that will be caused by extraction of the oil.

An outflow of resources embodying economic benefits in settlement – Probable.

Conclusion– A provision is recognised for the best estimate of ninety per cent of the eventual costs that relate to the removal of the oil rig and restoration of damage caused by building it (see paragraph 14). These costs are included as part of the cost of the oil rig. The 10 per cent of costs that arise through the extraction of oil are recognised as a liability when the oil is extracted.

Example 4 Refunds policy

A retail store has a policy of refunding purchases by dissatisfied customers, even though it is under no legal obligation to do so. Its policy of making refunds is generally known.

Present obligation as a result of a past obligating event – The obligating event is the sale of the product, which gives rise to a constructive obligation because the conduct of the store has created a valid expectation on the part of its customers that the store will refund purchases.

An outflow of resources embodying economic benefits in settlement – Probable, a proportion of goods are returned for refund (see paragraph 24).

Conclusion – A provision is recognised for the best estimate of the costs of refunds (see paragraphs 10 (the definition of a constructive obligation), 14, 17 and 24).

Example 5A Closure of a division – no implementation before balance sheet date

On 12 December 2000 the board of an entity decided to close down a division. Before the balance sheet date (31 December 2000) the decision was not communicated to any of those affected and no other steps were taken to implement the decision.

Present obligation as a result of a past obligating event– There has been no obligating event and so there is no obligation.

Conclusion – No provision is recognised (see paragraphs 14 and 72).

Example 5B Closure of a division – communication/implementation before balance sheet date

On 12 December 2000, the board of an entity decided to close down a division making a particular product. On 20 December 2000 a detailed plan for closing down the division was agreed by the board; letters were sent to customers warning them to seek an alternative source of supply and redundancy notices were sent to the staff of the division.

Present obligation as a result of a past obligating event – The obligating event is the communication of the decision to the customers and employees, which gives rise to a constructive obligation from that date, because it creates a valid expectation that the division will be closed.

An outflow of resources embodying economic benefits in settlement – Probable.

Conclusion – A provision is recognised at 31 December 2000 for the best estimate of the costs of closing the division (see paragraphs 14 and 72).

Example 6 Legal requirement to fit smoke filters

Under new legislation, an entity is required to fit smoke filters to its factories by 30 June 2000. The entity has not fitted the smoke filters.

(a) At the balance sheet date of 31 December 1999

Present obligation as a result of a past obligating event – There is no obligation because there is no obligating event either for the costs of fitting smoke filters or for fines under the legislation.

Conclusion – No provision is recognised for the cost of fitting the smoke filters (see paragraphs 14 and 17–19).

(b) At the balance sheet date of 31 December 2000

Present obligation as a result of a past obligating event – There is still no obligation for the costs of fitting smoke filters because no obligating event has occurred (the fitting of the filters). However, an obligation might arise to pay fines or penalties under the legislation because the obligating event has occurred (the non-compliant operation of the factory).

An outflow of resources embodying economic benefits in settlement– Assessment of probability of incurring fines and penalties by non-compliant operation depends on the details of the legislation and the stringency of the enforcement regime.

Conclusion – No provision is recognised for the costs of fitting smoke filters. However, a provision is recognised for the best estimate of any fines and penalties that are more likely than not to be imposed (see paragraphs 14 and 17–19).

Example 7 Staff retraining as a result of changes in the income tax system

The government introduces a number of changes to the income tax system. As a result of these changes, an entity in the financial services sector will need to retrain a large proportion of its administrative and sales workforce in order to ensure continued compliance with financial services regulation. At the balance sheet date, no retraining of staff has taken place.

Present obligation as a result of a past obligating event – There is no obligation because no obligating event (retraining) has taken place.

Conclusion – No provision is recognised (see paragraphs 14 and 17–19).

Example 8 An onerous contract

An entity operates profitably from a factory that it has leased under an operating lease. During December 2000 the entity relocates its operations to a new factory. The lease on the old factory continues for the next four years, it cannot be cancelled and the factory cannot be re-let to another user.

Present obligation as a result of a past obligating event – The obligating event is the signing of the lease contract, which gives rise to a legal obligation.

An outflow of resources embodying economic benefits in settlement – When the lease becomes onerous, an outflow of resources embodying economic benefits is probable. (Until the lease becomes onerous, the entity accounts for the lease under IAS 17 *Leases*).

Conclusion – A provision is recognised for the best estimate of the unavoidable lease payments (see paragraphs 5(c), 14 and 66).

Example 9 A single guarantee

On 31 December 1999, Entity A gives a guarantee of certain borrowings of Entity B, whose financial condition at that time is sound. During 2000, the financial condition of Entity B deteriorates and at 30 June 2000 Entity B files for protection from its creditors.

This contract meets the definition of an insurance contract in IFRS 4 *Insurance Contracts*. IFRS 4 permits the issuer to continue its existing accounting policies for insurance contracts if specified minimum requirements are satisfied. IFRS 4 also permits changes in accounting policies that meet specified criteria. The following is an example of an accounting policy that IFRS 4 permits.

(a) At 31 December 1999

Present obligation as a result of a past obligating event – The obligating event is the giving of the guarantee, which gives rise to a legal obligation.

An outflow of resources embodying economic benefits in settlement – No outflow of benefits is probable at 31 December 1999.

Conclusion – The guarantee is recognised at fair value.

(b) At 31 December 2000

Present obligation as a result of a past obligating event – The obligating event is the giving of the guarantee, which gives rise to a legal obligation.

An outflow of resources embodying economic benefits in settlement – At 31 December 2000, it is probable that an outflow of resources embodying economic benefits will be required to settle the obligation.

Conclusion – The guarantee is subsequently measured at the higher of (a) the best estimate of the obligation (see paragraphs 14 and 23), and (b) the amount initially recognised less, when appropriate, cumulative amortisation in accordance with IAS 18 *Revenue*.

Note: Where an entity gives guarantees in exchange for a fee, revenue is recognised under IAS 18 *Revenue*.

Example 10 A court case

After a wedding in 2000, ten people died, possibly as a result of food poisoning from products sold by the entity. Legal proceedings are started seeking damages from the entity but it disputes liability. Up to the date of authorisation of the financial statements for the year to 31 December 2000 for issue, the entity's lawyers advise that it is probable that the entity will not be found liable. However, when the entity prepares the financial statements for the year to 31 December 2001, its lawyers advise that, owing to developments in the case, it is probable that the entity will be found liable.

(a) At 31 December 2000

Present obligation as a result of a past obligating event – On the basis of the evidence available when the financial statements were approved, there is no obligation as a result of past events.

Conclusion – No provision is recognised (see paragraphs 15–16). The matter is disclosed as a contingent liability unless the probability of any outflow is regarded as remote (paragraph 86).

(b) At 31 December 2001

Present obligation as a result of a past obligating event – On the basis of the evidence available, there is a present obligation.

An outflow of resources embodying economic benefits in settlement – Probable.

Conclusion – A provision is recognised for the best estimate of the amount to settle the obligation (paragraphs 14–16).

Example 11 Repairs and maintenance

Some assets require, in addition to routine maintenance, substantial expenditure every few years for major refits or refurbishment and the replacement of major components. IAS 16 *Property, Plant and Equipment* gives guidance on allocating expenditure on an asset to its component parts where these components have different useful lives or provide benefits in a different pattern.

Example 11A Refurbishment costs – no legislative requirement

A furnace has a lining that needs to be replaced every five years for technical reasons. At the balance sheet date, the lining has been in use for three years.

Present obligation as a result of a past obligating event – There is no present obligation.

Conclusion – No provision is recognised (see paragraphs 14 and 17–19).

The cost of replacing the lining is not recognised because, at the balance sheet date, no obligation to replace the lining exists independently of the company's future actions—even the intention to incur the expenditure depends on the company deciding to continue operating the furnace or to replace the lining. Instead of a provision being recognised, the depreciation of the lining takes account of its consumption, ie it is depreciated over five years. The re-lining costs then incurred are capitalised with the consumption of each new lining shown by depreciation over the subsequent five years.

Example 11B Refurbishment costs – legislative requirement

An airline is required by law to overhaul its aircraft once every three years.

Present obligation as a result of a past obligating event – There is no present obligation.

Conclusion – No provision is recognised (see paragraphs 14 and 17–19).

The costs of overhauling aircraft are not recognised as a provision for the same reasons as the cost of replacing the lining is not recognised as a provision in example 11A. Even a legal requirement to overhaul does not make the costs of overhaul a liability, because no obligation exists to overhaul the aircraft independently of the entity's future actions–the entity could avoid the future expenditure by its future actions, for example by selling the aircraft. Instead of a provision being recognised, the depreciation of the aircraft takes account of the future incidence of maintenance costs, ie an amount equivalent to the expected maintenance costs is depreciated over three years.

Appendix D
Examples: disclosures

The appendix accompanies, but is not part of, IAS 37.

Two examples of the disclosures required by paragraph 85 are provided below.

Example 1 Warranties

A manufacturer gives warranties at the time of sale to purchasers of its three product lines. Under the terms of the warranty, the manufacturer undertakes to repair or replace items that fail to perform satisfactorily for two years from the date of sale. At the balance sheet date, a provision of 60,000 has been recognised. The provision has not been discounted as the effect of discounting is not material. The following information is disclosed:

A provision of 60,000 has been recognised for expected warranty claims on products sold during the last three financial years. It is expected that the majority of this expenditure will be incurred in the next financial year, and all will be incurred within two years of the balance sheet date.

Example 2 Decommissioning costs

In 2000, an entity involved in nuclear activities recognises a provision for decommissioning costs of 300 million. The provision is estimated using the assumption that decommissioning will take place in 60–70 years' time. However, there is a possibility that it will not take place until 100–110 years' time, in which case the present value of the costs will be significantly reduced. The following information is disclosed:

A provision of 300 million has been recognised for decommissioning costs. These costs are expected to be incurred between 2060 and 2070; however, there is a possibility that decommissioning will not take place until 2100–2110. If the costs were measured based upon the expectation that they would not be incurred until 2100–2110 the provision would be reduced to 136 million. The provision has been estimated using existing technology, at current prices, and discounted using a real discount rate of 2 per cent.

An example is given below of the disclosures required by paragraph 92 where some of the information required is not given because it can be expected to prejudice seriously the position of the entity.

Example 3 Disclosure exemption

An entity is involved in a dispute with a competitor, who is alleging that the entity has infringed patents and is seeking damages of 100 million. The entity recognises a provision for its best estimate of the obligation, but discloses none of the information required by paragraphs 84 and 85 of the Standard. The following information is disclosed:

Litigation is in process against the company relating to a dispute with a competitor who alleges that the company has infringed patents and is seeking damages of 100 million. The information usually required by IAS 37 Provisions, Contingent Liabilities and Contingent Assets *is not disclosed on the grounds that it can be expected to prejudice seriously the outcome of the litigation. The directors are of the opinion that the claim can be successfully resisted by the company.*

International Accounting Standard 38

Intangible Assets

This version includes amendments from IFRS 6 Exploration for and Evaluation of Mineral Resources *issued on 9 December 2004.*

CONTENTS

International Accounting Standard 38 *Intangible Assets* (IAS 38) is set out in paragraphs 1–133. All the paragraphs have equal authority but retain the IASC format of the Standard when it was adopted by the IASB. IAS 38 should be read in the context of its objective and the Basis for Conclusions, the Preface to *International Financial Reporting Standards* and the *Framework for the Preparation and Presentation of Financial Statements*. IAS 8 *Accounting Policies, Changes in Accounting Estimates and Errors* provides a basis for selecting and applying accounting policies in the absence of explicit guidance.

Introduction

IN1 International Accounting Standard 38 *Intangible Assets* (IAS 38) replaces IAS 38 *Intangible Assets* (issued in 1998), and should be applied:

(a) on acquisition to the accounting for intangible assets acquired in business combinations for which the agreement date is on or after 31 March 2004.

(b) to all other intangible assets, for annual periods beginning on or after 31 March 2004.

Earlier application is encouraged.

Reasons for revising IAS 38

IN2 The International Accounting Standards Board developed this revised IAS 38 as part of its project on business combinations. The project's objective is to improve the quality of, and seek international convergence on, the accounting for business combinations and the subsequent accounting for goodwill and intangible assets acquired in business combinations.

IN3 The project has two phases. The first phase resulted in the Board issuing simultaneously IFRS 3 *Business Combinations* and revised versions of IAS 38 and IAS 36 *Impairment of Assets*. The Board's deliberations during the first phase of the project focused primarily on:

(a) the method of accounting for business combinations;

(b) the initial measurement of the identifiable assets acquired and liabilities and contingent liabilities assumed in a business combination;

(c) the recognition of provisions for terminating or reducing the activities of an acquiree;

(d) the treatment of any excess of the acquirer's interest in the fair values of identifiable net assets acquired in a business combination over the cost of the combination; and

(e) the accounting for goodwill and intangible assets acquired in a business combination.

IN4 Therefore, the Board's intention while revising IAS 38 was to reflect only those changes related to its decisions in the Business Combinations project, and *not* to reconsider all of the requirements in IAS 38. The changes that have been made in the Standard are primarily concerned with clarifying the notion of 'identifiability' as it relates to intangible assets, the useful life and amortisation of intangible assets, and the accounting for in-process research and development projects acquired in business combinations.

Summary of main changes

Definition of an intangible asset

IN5 The previous version of IAS 38 defined an intangible asset as an identifiable non-monetary asset without physical substance held for use in the production or supply of goods or services, for rental to others, or for administrative purposes. The requirement for the asset to be held for use in the production or supply of goods or services, for rental to others, or for administrative purposes has been removed from the definition of an intangible asset.

IN6 The previous version of IAS 38 did not define 'identifiability', but stated that an intangible asset could be distinguished clearly from goodwill if the asset was separable, but that separability was not a necessary condition for identifiability. The Standard states that an asset meets the identifiability criterion in the definition of an intangible asset when it:

(a) is separable, ie capable of being separated or divided from the entity and sold, transferred, licensed, rented or exchanged, either individually or together with a related contract, asset or liability; or

(b) arises from contractual or other legal rights, regardless of whether those rights are transferable or separable from the entity or from other rights and obligations.

Criteria for initial recognition

IN7 The previous version of IAS 38 required an intangible asset to be recognised if, and only if, it was probable that the expected future economic benefits attributable to the asset would flow to the entity, and its cost could be measured reliably. These recognition criteria have been included in the Standard. However, additional guidance has been included to clarify that:

(a) the probability recognition criterion is always considered to be satisfied for intangible assets that are acquired separately or in a business combination.

(b) the fair value of an intangible asset acquired in a business combination can normally be measured with sufficient reliability to be recognised separately from goodwill. If an intangible asset acquired in a business combination has a finite useful life, there is a rebuttable presumption that its fair value can be measured reliably.

Subsequent expenditure

IN8 Under the previous version of IAS 38, the treatment of subsequent expenditure on an in-process research and development project acquired in a business combination and recognised as an asset separately from goodwill was unclear. The Standard requires such expenditure to be:

(a) recognised as an expense when incurred if it is research expenditure;

(b) recognised as an expense when incurred if it is development expenditure that does not satisfy the criteria in IAS 38 for recognising such expenditure as an intangible asset; and

(c) recognised as an intangible asset if it is development expenditure that satisfies the criteria in IAS 38 for recognising such expenditure as an intangible asset.

Useful life

IN9 The previous version of IAS 38 was based on the assumption that the useful life of an intangible asset is always finite, and included a rebuttable presumption that the useful life cannot exceed twenty years from the date the asset is available for use. That rebuttable presumption has been removed. The Standard requires an intangible asset to be regarded as having an indefinite useful life when, based on an analysis of all of the relevant factors, there is no foreseeable limit to the period over which the asset is expected to generate net cash inflows for the entity.

IN10 The previous version of IAS 38 required that if control over the future economic benefits from an intangible asset was achieved through legal rights granted for a finite period, the useful life of the intangible asset could not exceed the period of those rights, unless the rights were renewable and renewal was virtually certain. The Standard requires that:

(a) the useful life of an intangible asset arising from contractual or other legal rights should not exceed the period of those rights, but may be shorter depending on the period over which the asset is expected to be used by the entity; and

(b) if the rights are conveyed for a limited term that can be renewed, the useful life should include the renewal period(s) only if there is evidence to support renewal by the entity without significant cost.

Intangible assets with indefinite useful lives

IN11 The Standard requires that:

(a) an intangible asset with an indefinite useful life should not be amortised.

(b) the useful life of such an asset should be reviewed each reporting period to determine whether events and circumstances continue to support an indefinite useful life assessment for that asset. If they do not, the change in the useful life assessment from indefinite to finite should be accounted for as a change in an accounting estimate.

Impairment testing intangible assets with finite useful lives

IN12 The previous version of IAS 38 required the recoverable amount of an intangible asset that was amortised over a period exceeding twenty years from the date it was available for use to be estimated at least at each financial year-end, even if there was no indication that the asset was impaired. This requirement has been removed. Therefore, an entity needs to determine the recoverable amount of an intangible asset with a finite useful life that is amortised over a period exceeding twenty years from the date it is available for use only when, in accordance with IAS 36, there is an indication that the asset may be impaired.

Disclosure

IN13 If an intangible asset is assessed as having an indefinite useful life, the Standard requires an entity to disclose the carrying amount of that asset and the reasons supporting the indefinite useful life assessment.

International Accounting Standard 38 Intangible Assets

Objective

1 The objective of this Standard is to prescribe the accounting treatment for intangible assets that are not dealt with specifically in another Standard. This Standard requires an entity to recognise an intangible asset if, and only if, specified criteria are met. The Standard also specifies how to measure the carrying amount of intangible assets and requires specified disclosures about intangible assets.

Scope

2 This Standard shall be applied in accounting for intangible assets, except:

- **(a) intangible assets that are within the scope of another Standard;**
- **(b) financial assets, as defined in IAS 39** *Financial Instruments: Recognition and Measurement*;
- **(c) the recognition and measurement of exploration and evaluation assets (see IFRS 6** *Exploration for and Evaluation of Mineral Resources*); **and**
- **(d) expenditure on the development and extraction of, minerals, oil, natural gas and similar non-regenerative resources.**

3 If another Standard prescribes the accounting for a specific type of intangible asset, an entity applies that Standard instead of this Standard. For example, this Standard does not apply to:

- (a) intangible assets held by an entity for sale in the ordinary course of business (see IAS 2 *Inventories* and IAS 11 *Construction Contracts*).
- (b) deferred tax assets (see IAS 12 *Income Taxes*).
- (c) leases that are within the scope of IAS 17 *Leases*.
- (d) assets arising from employee benefits (see IAS 19 *Employee Benefits*).
- (e) financial assets as defined in IAS 39. The recognition and measurement of some financial assets are covered by IAS 27 *Consolidated and Separate Financial Statements*, IAS 28 *Investments in Associates* and IAS 31 *Interests in Joint Ventures*.
- (f) goodwill acquired in a business combination (see IFRS 3 *Business Combinations*).
- (g) deferred acquisition costs, and intangible assets, arising from an insurer's contractual rights under insurance contracts within the scope of IFRS 4 *Insurance Contracts*. IFRS 4 sets out specific disclosure requirements for those deferred acquisition costs but not for those intangible assets. Therefore, the disclosure requirements in this Standard apply to those intangible assets.
- (h) non-current intangible assets classified as held for sale (or included in a disposal group that is classified as held for sale) in accordance with IFRS 5 *Non-current Assets Held for Sale and Discontinued Operations*.

4 Some intangible assets may be contained in or on a physical substance such as a compact disc (in the case of computer software), legal documentation (in the case of a licence or patent) or film. In determining whether an asset that incorporates both intangible and tangible elements should be treated under IAS 16 *Property, Plant and Equipment* or as an intangible asset under this Standard, an entity uses judgement to assess which element is more significant. For example, computer software for a computer-controlled machine tool that cannot operate without that specific software is an integral part of the related hardware and it is treated as property, plant and equipment. The same applies to the operating system of a computer. When the software is not an integral part of the related hardware, computer software is treated as an intangible asset.

5 This Standard applies to, among other things, expenditure on advertising, training, start-up, research and development activities. Research and development activities are directed to the development of knowledge. Therefore, although these activities may result in an asset with physical substance (eg a prototype), the physical element of the asset is secondary to its intangible component, ie the knowledge embodied in it.

6 In the case of a finance lease, the underlying asset may be either tangible or intangible. After initial recognition, a lessee accounts for an intangible asset held under a finance lease in accordance with this Standard. Rights under licensing agreements for items such as motion picture films, video recordings, plays, manuscripts, patents and copyrights are excluded from the scope of IAS 17 and are within the scope of this Standard.

7 Exclusions from the scope of a Standard may occur if activities or transactions are so specialised that they give rise to accounting issues that may need to be dealt with in a different way. Such issues arise in the accounting for expenditure on the exploration for, or development and extraction of, oil, gas and mineral deposits in extractive industries and in the case of insurance contracts. Therefore, this Standard does not apply to expenditure on such activities and contracts. However, this Standard applies to other intangible assets used (such as computer software), and other expenditure incurred (such as start-up costs), in extractive industries or by insurers.

Definitions

8 **The following terms are used in this Standard with the meanings specified:**

An *active market* **is a market in which all the following conditions exist:**

(a) the items traded in the market are homogeneous;

(b) willing buyers and sellers can normally be found at any time; and

(c) prices are available to the public.

The *agreement date* **for a business combination is the date that a substantive agreement between the combining parties is reached and, in the case of publicly listed entities, announced to the public. In the case of a hostile takeover, the earliest date that a substantive agreement between the**

combining parties is reached is the date that a sufficient number of the acquiree's owners have accepted the acquirer's offer for the acquirer to obtain control of the acquiree.

Amortisation **is the systematic allocation of the depreciable amount of an intangible asset over its useful life.**

An *asset* **is a resource:**

(a) controlled by an entity as a result of past events; and

(b) from which future economic benefits are expected to flow to the entity.

Carrying amount **is the amount at which an asset is recognised in the balance sheet after deducting any accumulated amortisation and accumulated impairment losses thereon.**

Cost **is the amount of cash or cash equivalents paid or the fair value of other consideration given to acquire an asset at the time of its acquisition or construction, or, when applicable, the amount attributed to that asset when initially recognised in accordance with the specific requirements of other IFRSs, eg IFRS 2** *Share-based Payment*.

Depreciable amount **is the cost of an asset, or other amount substituted for cost, less its residual value.**

Development **is the application of research findings or other knowledge to a plan or design for the production of new or substantially improved materials, devices, products, processes, systems or services before the start of commercial production or use.**

Entity-specific value **is the present value of the cash flows an entity expects to arise from the continuing use of an asset and from its disposal at the end of its useful life or expects to incur when settling a liability.**

Fair value of an asset **is the amount for which that asset could be exchanged between knowledgeable, willing parties in an arm's length transaction.**

An *impairment loss* **is the amount by which the carrying amount of an asset exceeds its recoverable amount.**

An *intangible asset* **is an identifiable non-monetary asset without physical substance.**

Monetary assets **are money held and assets to be received in fixed or determinable amounts of money.**

Research **is original and planned investigation undertaken with the prospect of gaining new scientific or technical knowledge and understanding.**

The *residual value* **of an intangible asset is the estimated amount that an entity would currently obtain from disposal of the asset, after deducting the estimated costs of disposal, if the asset were already of the age and in the condition expected at the end of its useful life.**

Useful life **is:**

(a) the period over which an asset is expected to be available for use by an entity; or

(b) the number of production or similar units expected to be obtained from the asset by an entity.

Intangible assets

9 Entities frequently expend resources, or incur liabilities, on the acquisition, development, maintenance or enhancement of intangible resources such as scientific or technical knowledge, design and implementation of new processes or systems, licences, intellectual property, market knowledge and trademarks (including brand names and publishing titles). Common examples of items encompassed by these broad headings are computer software, patents, copyrights, motion picture films, customer lists, mortgage servicing rights, fishing licences, import quotas, franchises, customer or supplier relationships, customer loyalty, market share and marketing rights.

10 Not all the items described in paragraph 9 meet the definition of an intangible asset, ie identifiability, control over a resource and existence of future economic benefits. If an item within the scope of this Standard does not meet the definition of an intangible asset, expenditure to acquire it or generate it internally is recognised as an expense when it is incurred. However, if the item is acquired in a business combination, it forms part of the goodwill recognised at the acquisition date (see paragraph 68).

Identifiability

11 The definition of an intangible asset requires an asset to be identifiable to distinguish it from goodwill. Goodwill acquired in a business combination represents a payment made by the acquirer in anticipation of future economic benefits from assets that are not capable of being individually identified and separately recognised. The future economic benefits may result from synergy between the identifiable assets acquired or from assets that, individually, do not qualify for recognition in the financial statements but for which the acquirer is prepared to make a payment in the business combination.

12 An asset meets the identifiability criterion in the definition of an intangible asset when it:

(a) is separable, ie is capable of being separated or divided from the entity and sold, transferred, licensed, rented or exchanged, either individually or together with a related contract, asset or liability; or

(b) arises from contractual or other legal rights, regardless of whether those rights are transferable or separable from the entity or from other rights and obligations.

Control

13 An entity controls an asset if the entity has the power to obtain the future economic benefits flowing from the underlying resource and to restrict the access of others to those benefits. The capacity of an entity to control the future

economic benefits from an intangible asset would normally stem from legal rights that are enforceable in a court of law. In the absence of legal rights, it is more difficult to demonstrate control. However, legal enforceability of a right is not a necessary condition for control because an entity may be able to control the future economic benefits in some other way.

14 Market and technical knowledge may give rise to future economic benefits. An entity controls those benefits if, for example, the knowledge is protected by legal rights such as copyrights, a restraint of trade agreement (where permitted) or by a legal duty on employees to maintain confidentiality.

15 An entity may have a team of skilled staff and may be able to identify incremental staff skills leading to future economic benefits from training. The entity may also expect that the staff will continue to make their skills available to the entity. However, an entity usually has insufficient control over the expected future economic benefits arising from a team of skilled staff and from training for these items to meet the definition of an intangible asset. For a similar reason, specific management or technical talent is unlikely to meet the definition of an intangible asset, unless it is protected by legal rights to use it and to obtain the future economic benefits expected from it, and it also meets the other parts of the definition.

16 An entity may have a portfolio of customers or a market share and expect that, because of its efforts in building customer relationships and loyalty, the customers will continue to trade with the entity. However, in the absence of legal rights to protect, or other ways to control, the relationships with customers or the loyalty of the customers to the entity, the entity usually has insufficient control over the expected economic benefits from customer relationships and loyalty for such items (eg portfolio of customers, market shares, customer relationships and customer loyalty) to meet the definition of intangible assets. In the absence of legal rights to protect customer relationships, exchange transactions for the same or similar non-contractual customer relationships (other than as part of a business combination) provide evidence that the entity is nonetheless able to control the expected future economic benefits flowing from the customer relationships. Because such exchange transactions also provide evidence that the customer relationships are separable, those customer relationships meet the definition of an intangible asset.

Future economic benefits

17 The future economic benefits flowing from an intangible asset may include revenue from the sale of products or services, cost savings, or other benefits resulting from the use of the asset by the entity. For example, the use of intellectual property in a production process may reduce future production costs rather than increase future revenues.

Recognition and measurement

18 The recognition of an item as an intangible asset requires an entity to demonstrate that the item meets:

(a) the definition of an intangible asset (see paragraphs 8–17); and

(b) the recognition criteria (see paragraphs 21–23).

This requirement applies to costs incurred initially to acquire or internally generate an intangible asset and those incurred subsequently to add to, replace part of, or service it.

19 Paragraphs 25–32 deal with the application of the recognition criteria to separately acquired intangible assets, and paragraphs 33–43 deal with their application to intangible assets acquired in a business combination. Paragraph 44 deals with the initial measurement of intangible assets acquired by way of a government grant, paragraphs 45–47 with exchanges of intangible assets, and paragraphs 48–50 with the treatment of internally generated goodwill. Paragraphs 51–67 deal with the initial recognition and measurement of internally generated intangible assets.

20 The nature of intangible assets is such that, in many cases, there are no additions to such an asset or replacements of part of it. Accordingly, most subsequent expenditures are likely to maintain the expected future economic benefits embodied in an existing intangible asset rather than meet the definition of an intangible asset and the recognition criteria in this Standard. In addition, it is often difficult to attribute subsequent expenditure directly to a particular intangible asset rather than to the business as a whole. Therefore, only rarely will subsequent expenditure—expenditure incurred after the initial recognition of an acquired intangible asset or after completion of an internally generated intangible asset—be recognised in the carrying amount of an asset. Consistently with paragraph 63, subsequent expenditure on brands, mastheads, publishing titles, customer lists and items similar in substance (whether externally acquired or internally generated) is always recognised in profit or loss as incurred. This is because such expenditure cannot be distinguished from expenditure to develop the business as a whole.

21 An intangible asset shall be recognised if, and only if:

(a) it is probable that the expected future economic benefits that are attributable to the asset will flow to the entity; and

(b) the cost of the asset can be measured reliably.

22 An entity shall assess the probability of expected future economic benefits using reasonable and supportable assumptions that represent management's best estimate of the set of economic conditions that will exist over the useful life of the asset.

23 An entity uses judgement to assess the degree of certainty attached to the flow of future economic benefits that are attributable to the use of the asset on the basis of the evidence available at the time of initial recognition, giving greater weight to external evidence.

24 An intangible asset shall be measured initially at cost.

Separate acquisition

25 Normally, the price an entity pays to acquire separately an intangible asset reflects expectations about the probability that the expected future economic benefits embodied in the asset will flow to the entity. In other words, the effect of

probability is reflected in the cost of the asset. Therefore, the probability recognition criterion in paragraph 21(a) is always considered to be satisfied for separately acquired intangible assets.

26 In addition, the cost of a separately acquired intangible asset can usually be measured reliably. This is particularly so when the purchase consideration is in the form of cash or other monetary assets.

27 The cost of a separately acquired intangible asset comprises:

(a) its purchase price, including import duties and non-refundable purchase taxes, after deducting trade discounts and rebates; and

(b) any directly attributable cost of preparing the asset for its intended use.

28 Examples of directly attributable costs are:

(a) costs of employee benefits (as defined in IAS 19 *Employee Benefits*) arising directly from bringing the asset to its working condition;

(b) professional fees arising directly from bringing the asset to its working condition; and

(c) costs of testing whether the asset is functioning properly.

29 Examples of expenditures that are not part of the cost of an intangible asset are:

(a) costs of introducing a new product or service (including costs of advertising and promotional activities);

(b) costs of conducting business in a new location or with a new class of customer (including costs of staff training); and

(c) administration and other general overhead costs.

30 Recognition of costs in the carrying amount of an intangible asset ceases when the asset is in the condition necessary for it to be capable of operating in the manner intended by management. Therefore, costs incurred in using or redeploying an intangible asset are not included in the carrying amount of that asset. For example, the following costs are not included in the carrying amount of an intangible asset:

(a) costs incurred while an asset capable of operating in the manner intended by management has yet to be brought into use; and

(b) initial operating losses, such as those incurred while demand for the asset's output builds up.

31 Some operations occur in connection with the development of an intangible asset, but are not necessary to bring the asset to the condition necessary for it to be capable of operating in the manner intended by management. These incidental operations may occur before or during the development activities. Because incidental operations are not necessary to bring an asset to the condition necessary for it to be capable of operating in the manner intended by management, the income and related expenses of incidental operations are recognised immediately in profit or loss, and included in their respective classifications of income and expense.

32 If payment for an intangible asset is deferred beyond normal credit terms, its cost is the cash price equivalent. The difference between this amount and the total payments is recognised as interest expense over the period of credit unless it is capitalised in accordance with the capitalisation treatment permitted in IAS 23 *Borrowing Costs*.

Acquisition as part of a business combination

33 In accordance with IFRS 3 *Business Combinations*, if an intangible asset is acquired in a business combination, the cost of that intangible asset is its fair value at the acquisition date. The fair value of an intangible asset reflects market expectations about the probability that the future economic benefits embodied in the asset will flow to the entity. In other words, the effect of probability is reflected in the fair value measurement of the intangible asset. Therefore, the probability recognition criterion in paragraph 21(a) is always considered to be satisfied for intangible assets acquired in business combinations.

34 Therefore, in accordance with this Standard and IFRS 3, an acquirer recognises at the acquisition date separately from goodwill an intangible asset of the acquiree if the asset's fair value can be measured reliably, irrespective of whether the asset had been recognised by the acquiree before the business combination. This means that the acquirer recognises as an asset separately from goodwill an in-process research and development project of the acquiree if the project meets the definition of an intangible asset and its fair value can be measured reliably. An acquiree's in-process research and development project meets the definition of an intangible asset when it:

(a) meets the definition of an asset; and

(b) is identifiable, ie is separable or arises from contractual or other legal rights.

Measuring the fair value of an intangible asset acquired in a business combination

35 The fair value of intangible assets acquired in business combinations can normally be measured with sufficient reliability to be recognised separately from goodwill. When, for the estimates used to measure an intangible asset's fair value, there is a range of possible outcomes with different probabilities, that uncertainty enters into the measurement of the asset's fair value, rather than demonstrates an inability to measure fair value reliably. If an intangible asset acquired in a business combination has a finite useful life, there is a rebuttable presumption that its fair value can be measured reliably.

36 An intangible asset acquired in a business combination might be separable, but only together with a related tangible or intangible asset. For example, a magazine's publishing title might not be able to be sold separately from a related subscriber database, or a trademark for natural spring water might relate to a particular spring and could not be sold separately from the spring. In such cases, the acquirer recognises the group of assets as a single asset separately from goodwill if the individual fair values of the assets in the group are not reliably measurable.

37 Similarly, the terms 'brand' and 'brand name' are often used as synonyms for trademarks and other marks. However, the former are general marketing terms that are typically used to refer to a group of complementary assets such as a trademark (or service mark) and its related trade name, formulas, recipes and technological expertise. The acquirer recognises as a single asset a group of complementary intangible assets comprising a brand if the individual fair values of the complementary assets are not reliably measurable. If the individual fair values of the complementary assets are reliably measurable, an acquirer may recognise them as a single asset provided the individual assets have similar useful lives.

38 The only circumstances in which it might not be possible to measure reliably the fair value of an intangible asset acquired in a business combination are when the intangible asset arises from legal or other contractual rights and either:

(a) is not separable; or

(b) is separable, but there is no history or evidence of exchange transactions for the same or similar assets, and otherwise estimating fair value would be dependent on immeasurable variables.

39 Quoted market prices in an active market provide the most reliable estimate of the fair value of an intangible asset (see also paragraph 78). The appropriate market price is usually the current bid price. If current bid prices are unavailable, the price of the most recent similar transaction may provide a basis from which to estimate fair value, provided that there has not been a significant change in economic circumstances between the transaction date and the date at which the asset's fair value is estimated.

40 If no active market exists for an intangible asset, its fair value is the amount that the entity would have paid for the asset, at the acquisition date, in an arm's length transaction between knowledgeable and willing parties, on the basis of the best information available. In determining this amount, an entity considers the outcome of recent transactions for similar assets.

41 Entities that are regularly involved in the purchase and sale of unique intangible assets may have developed techniques for estimating their fair values indirectly. These techniques may be used for initial measurement of an intangible asset acquired in a business combination if their objective is to estimate fair value and if they reflect current transactions and practices in the industry to which the asset belongs. These techniques include, when appropriate:

(a) applying multiples reflecting current market transactions to indicators that drive the profitability of the asset (such as revenue, market shares and operating profit) or to the royalty stream that could be obtained from licensing the intangible asset to another party in an arm's length transaction (as in the 'relief from royalty' approach); or

(b) discounting estimated future net cash flows from the asset.

Subsequent expenditure on an acquired in-process research and development project

42 **Research or development expenditure that:**

(a) relates to an in-process research or development project acquired separately or in a business combination and recognised as an intangible asset; and

(b) is incurred after the acquisition of that project

shall be accounted for in accordance with paragraphs 54–62.

43 Applying the requirements in paragraphs 54–62 means that subsequent expenditure on an in-process research or development project acquired separately or in a business combination and recognised as an intangible asset is:

(a) recognised as an expense when incurred if it is research expenditure;

(b) recognised as an expense when incurred if it is development expenditure that does not satisfy the criteria for recognition as an intangible asset in paragraph 57; and

(c) added to the carrying amount of the acquired in-process research or development project if it is development expenditure that satisfies the recognition criteria in paragraph 57.

Acquisition by way of a government grant

44 In some cases, an intangible asset may be acquired free of charge, or for nominal consideration, by way of a government grant. This may happen when a government transfers or allocates to an entity intangible assets such as airport landing rights, licences to operate radio or television stations, import licences or quotas or rights to access other restricted resources. In accordance with IAS 20 *Accounting for Government Grants and Disclosure of Government Assistance*, an entity may choose to recognise both the intangible asset and the grant initially at fair value. If an entity chooses not to recognise the asset initially at fair value, the entity recognises the asset initially at a nominal amount (the other treatment permitted by IAS 20) plus any expenditure that is directly attributable to preparing the asset for its intended use.

Exchanges of assets

45 One or more intangible assets may be acquired in exchange for a non-monetary asset or assets, or a combination of monetary and non-monetary assets. The following discussion refers simply to an exchange of one non-monetary asset for another, but it also applies to all exchanges described in the preceding sentence. The cost of such an intangible asset is measured at fair value unless (a) the exchange transaction lacks commercial substance or (b) the fair value of neither the asset received nor the asset given up is reliably measurable. The acquired asset is measured in this way even if an entity cannot immediately derecognise the asset given up. If the acquired asset is not measured at fair value, its cost is measured at the carrying amount of the asset given up.

46 An entity determines whether an exchange transaction has commercial substance by considering the extent to which its future cash flows are expected to change as a result of the transaction. An exchange transaction has commercial substance if:

(a) the configuration (ie risk, timing and amount) of the cash flows of the asset received differs from the configuration of the cash flows of the asset transferred; or

(b) the entity-specific value of the portion of the entity's operations affected by the transaction changes as a result of the exchange; and

(c) the difference in (a) or (b) is significant relative to the fair value of the assets exchanged.

For the purpose of determining whether an exchange transaction has commercial substance, the entity-specific value of the portion of the entity's operations affected by the transaction shall reflect post-tax cash flows. The result of these analyses may be clear without an entity having to perform detailed calculations.

47 Paragraph 21(b) specifies that a condition for the recognition of an intangible asset is that the cost of the asset can be measured reliably. The fair value of an intangible asset for which comparable market transactions do not exist is reliably measurable if (a) the variability in the range of reasonable fair value estimates is not significant for that asset or (b) the probabilities of the various estimates within the range can be reasonably assessed and used in estimating fair value. If an entity is able to determine reliably the fair value of either the asset received or the asset given up, then the fair value of the asset given up is used to measure cost unless the fair value of the asset received is more clearly evident.

Internally generated goodwill

48 Internally generated goodwill shall not be recognised as an asset.

49 In some cases, expenditure is incurred to generate future economic benefits, but it does not result in the creation of an intangible asset that meets the recognition criteria in this Standard. Such expenditure is often described as contributing to internally generated goodwill. Internally generated goodwill is not recognised as an asset because it is not an identifiable resource (ie it is not separable nor does it arise from contractual or other legal rights) controlled by the entity that can be measured reliably at cost.

50 Differences between the market value of an entity and the carrying amount of its identifiable net assets at any time may capture a range of factors that affect the value of the entity. However, such differences do not represent the cost of intangible assets controlled by the entity.

Internally generated intangible assets

51 It is sometimes difficult to assess whether an internally generated intangible asset qualifies for recognition because of problems in:

(a) identifying whether and when there is an identifiable asset that will generate expected future economic benefits; and

(b) determining the cost of the asset reliably. In some cases, the cost of generating an intangible asset internally cannot be distinguished from the cost of maintaining or enhancing the entity's internally generated goodwill or of running day-to-day operations.

Therefore, in addition to complying with the general requirements for the recognition and initial measurement of an intangible asset, an entity applies the requirements and guidance in paragraphs 52–67 to all internally generated intangible assets.

52 To assess whether an internally generated intangible asset meets the criteria for recognition, an entity classifies the generation of the asset into:

(a) a research phase; and

(b) a development phase.

Although the terms 'research' and 'development' are defined, the terms 'research phase' and 'development phase' have a broader meaning for the purpose of this Standard.

53 If an entity cannot distinguish the research phase from the development phase of an internal project to create an intangible asset, the entity treats the expenditure on that project as if it were incurred in the research phase only.

Research phase

54 No intangible asset arising from research (or from the research phase of an internal project) shall be recognised. Expenditure on research (or on the research phase of an internal project) shall be recognised as an expense when it is incurred.

55 In the research phase of an internal project, an entity cannot demonstrate that an intangible asset exists that will generate probable future economic benefits. Therefore, this expenditure is recognised as an expense when it is incurred.

56 Examples of research activities are:

(a) activities aimed at obtaining new knowledge;

(b) the search for, evaluation and final selection of, applications of research findings or other knowledge;

(c) the search for alternatives for materials, devices, products, processes, systems or services; and

(d) the formulation, design, evaluation and final selection of possible alternatives for new or improved materials, devices, products, processes, systems or services.

Development phase

57 An intangible asset arising from development (or from the development phase of an internal project) shall be recognised if, and only if, an entity can demonstrate all of the following:

(a) the technical feasibility of completing the intangible asset so that it will be available for use or sale.

(b) **its intention to complete the intangible asset and use or sell it.**

(c) **its ability to use or sell the intangible asset.**

(d) **how the intangible asset will generate probable future economic benefits. Among other things, the entity can demonstrate the existence of a market for the output of the intangible asset or the intangible asset itself or, if it is to be used internally, the usefulness of the intangible asset.**

(e) **the availability of adequate technical, financial and other resources to complete the development and to use or sell the intangible asset.**

(f) **its ability to measure reliably the expenditure attributable to the intangible asset during its development.**

58 In the development phase of an internal project, an entity can, in some instances, identify an intangible asset and demonstrate that the asset will generate probable future economic benefits. This is because the development phase of a project is further advanced than the research phase.

59 Examples of development activities are:

(a) the design, construction and testing of pre-production or pre-use prototypes and models;

(b) the design of tools, jigs, moulds and dies involving new technology;

(c) the design, construction and operation of a pilot plant that is not of a scale economically feasible for commercial production; and

(d) the design, construction and testing of a chosen alternative for new or improved materials, devices, products, processes, systems or services.

60 To demonstrate how an intangible asset will generate probable future economic benefits, an entity assesses the future economic benefits to be received from the asset using the principles in IAS 36 *Impairment of Assets*. If the asset will generate economic benefits only in combination with other assets, the entity applies the concept of cash-generating units in IAS 36.

61 Availability of resources to complete, use and obtain the benefits from an intangible asset can be demonstrated by, for example, a business plan showing the technical, financial and other resources needed and the entity's ability to secure those resources. In some cases, an entity demonstrates the availability of external finance by obtaining a lender's indication of its willingness to fund the plan.

62 An entity's costing systems can often measure reliably the cost of generating an intangible asset internally, such as salary and other expenditure incurred in securing copyrights or licences or developing computer software.

63 Internally generated brands, mastheads, publishing titles, customer lists and items similar in substance shall not be recognised as intangible assets.

64 Expenditure on internally generated brands, mastheads, publishing titles, customer lists and items similar in substance cannot be distinguished from the cost of developing the business as a whole. Therefore, such items are not recognised as intangible assets.

Cost of an internally generated intangible asset

65 The cost of an internally generated intangible asset for the purpose of paragraph 24 is the sum of expenditure incurred from the date when the intangible asset first meets the recognition criteria in paragraphs 21, 22 and 57. Paragraph 71 prohibits reinstatement of expenditure previously recognised as an expense.

66 The cost of an internally generated intangible asset comprises all directly attributable costs necessary to create, produce, and prepare the asset to be capable of operating in the manner intended by management. Examples of directly attributable costs are:

(a) costs of materials and services used or consumed in generating the intangible asset;

(b) costs of employee benefits (as defined in IAS 19 *Employee Benefits*) arising from the generation of the intangible asset;

(c) fees to register a legal right; and

(d) amortisation of patents and licences that are used to generate the intangible asset.

IAS 23 *Borrowing Costs* specifies criteria for the recognition of interest as an element of the cost of an internally generated intangible asset.

67 The following are not components of the cost of an internally generated intangible asset:

(a) selling, administrative and other general overhead expenditure unless this expenditure can be directly attributed to preparing the asset for use;

(b) identified inefficiencies and initial operating losses incurred before the asset achieves planned performance; and

(c) expenditure on training staff to operate the asset.

Example illustrating paragraph 65

An entity is developing a new production process. During 20X5, expenditure incurred was CU1,000[a], of which CU900 was incurred before 1 December 20X5 and CU100 was incurred between 1 December 20X5 and 31 December 20X5. The entity is able to demonstrate that, at 1 December 20X5, the production process met the criteria for recognition as an intangible asset. The recoverable amount of the know-how embodied in the process (including future cash outflows to complete the process before it is available for use) is estimated to be CU500.

At the end of 20X5, the production process is recognised as an intangible asset at a cost of CU100 (expenditure incurred since the date when the recognition criteria were met, ie 1 December 20X5). The CU900 expenditure incurred before 1 December 20X5 is recognised as an expense because the recognition criteria were not met until 1 December 20X5. This expenditure does not form part of the cost of the production process recognised in the balance sheet.

During 20X6, expenditure incurred is CU2,000. At the end of 20X6, the recoverable amount of the know-how embodied in the process (including future cash outflows to complete the process before it is available for use) is estimated to be CU1,900.

At the end of 20X6, the cost of the production process is CU2,100 (CU100 expenditure recognised at the end of 20X5 plus CU2,000 expenditure recognised in 20X6). The entity recognises an impairment loss of CU200 to adjust the carrying amount of the process before impairment loss (CU2,100) to its recoverable amount (CU1,900). This impairment loss will be reversed in a subsequent period if the requirements for the reversal of an impairment loss in IAS 36 are met.

(a) In this Standard, monetary amounts are denominated in 'currency units'

Recognition of an expense

68 **Expenditure on an intangible item shall be recognised as an expense when it is incurred unless:**

(a) it forms part of the cost of an intangible asset that meets the recognition criteria (see paragraphs 18–67); or

(b) the item is acquired in a business combination and cannot be recognised as an intangible asset. If this is the case, this expenditure (included in the cost of the business combination) shall form part of the amount attributed to goodwill at the acquisition date (see IFRS 3 ***Business Combinations*****).**

69 In some cases, expenditure is incurred to provide future economic benefits to an entity, but no intangible asset or other asset is acquired or created that can be recognised. In these cases, the expenditure is recognised as an expense when it is incurred. For example, except when it forms part of the cost of a business

combination, expenditure on research is recognised as an expense when it is incurred (see paragraph 54). Other examples of expenditure that is recognised as an expense when it is incurred include:

(a) expenditure on start-up activities (ie start-up costs), unless this expenditure is included in the cost of an item of property, plant and equipment in accordance with IAS 16 *Property, Plant and Equipment*. Start-up costs may consist of establishment costs such as legal and secretarial costs incurred in establishing a legal entity, expenditure to open a new facility or business (ie pre-opening costs) or expenditures for starting new operations or launching new products or processes (ie pre-operating costs).

(b) expenditure on training activities.

(c) expenditure on advertising and promotional activities.

(d) expenditure on relocating or reorganising part or all of an entity.

70 Paragraph 68 does not preclude recognising a prepayment as an asset when payment for the delivery of goods or services has been made in advance of the delivery of goods or the rendering of services.

Past expenses not to be recognised as an asset

71 Expenditure on an intangible item that was initially recognised as an expense shall not be recognised as part of the cost of an intangible asset at a later date.

Measurement after recognition

72 An entity shall choose either the cost model in paragraph 74 or the revaluation model in paragraph 75 as its accounting policy. If an intangible asset is accounted for using the revaluation model, all the other assets in its class shall also be accounted for using the same model, unless there is no active market for those assets.

73 A class of intangible assets is a grouping of assets of a similar nature and use in an entity's operations. The items within a class of intangible assets are revalued simultaneously to avoid selective revaluation of assets and the reporting of amounts in the financial statements representing a mixture of costs and values as at different dates.

Cost model

74 After initial recognition, an intangible asset shall be carried at its cost less any accumulated amortisation and any accumulated impairment losses.

Revaluation model

75 After initial recognition, an intangible asset shall be carried at a revalued amount, being its fair value at the date of the revaluation less any subsequent accumulated amortisation and any subsequent accumulated impairment losses. For the purpose of revaluations under this Standard, fair value shall be determined by reference to an active market.

Revaluations shall be made with such regularity that at the balance sheet date the carrying amount of the asset does not differ materially from its fair value.

76 The revaluation model does not allow:

(a) the revaluation of intangible assets that have not previously been recognised as assets; or

(b) the initial recognition of intangible assets at amounts other than cost.

77 The revaluation model is applied after an asset has been initially recognised at cost. However, if only part of the cost of an intangible asset is recognised as an asset because the asset did not meet the criteria for recognition until part of the way through the process (see paragraph 65), the revaluation model may be applied to the whole of that asset. Also, the revaluation model may be applied to an intangible asset that was received by way of a government grant and recognised at a nominal amount (see paragraph 44).

78 It is uncommon for an active market with the characteristics described in paragraph 8 to exist for an intangible asset, although this may happen. For example, in some jurisdictions, an active market may exist for freely transferable taxi licences, fishing licences or production quotas. However, an active market cannot exist for brands, newspaper mastheads, music and film publishing rights, patents or trademarks, because each such asset is unique. Also, although intangible assets are bought and sold, contracts are negotiated between individual buyers and sellers, and transactions are relatively infrequent. For these reasons, the price paid for one asset may not provide sufficient evidence of the fair value of another. Moreover, prices are often not available to the public.

79 The frequency of revaluations depends on the volatility of the fair values of the intangible assets being revalued. If the fair value of a revalued asset differs materially from its carrying amount, a further revaluation is necessary. Some intangible assets may experience significant and volatile movements in fair value, thus necessitating annual revaluation. Such frequent revaluations are unnecessary for intangible assets with only insignificant movements in fair value.

80 If an intangible asset is revalued, any accumulated amortisation at the date of the revaluation is either:

(a) restated proportionately with the change in the gross carrying amount of the asset so that the carrying amount of the asset after revaluation equals its revalued amount; or

(b) eliminated against the gross carrying amount of the asset and the net amount restated to the revalued amount of the asset.

81 If an intangible asset in a class of revalued intangible assets cannot be revalued because there is no active market for this asset, the asset shall be carried at its cost less any accumulated amortisation and impairment losses.

82 If the fair value of a revalued intangible asset can no longer be determined by reference to an active market, the carrying amount of the asset shall be its revalued amount at the date of the last revaluation by reference to the

active market less any subsequent accumulated amortisation and any subsequent accumulated impairment losses.

83 The fact that an active market no longer exists for a revalued intangible asset may indicate that the asset may be impaired and that it needs to be tested in accordance with IAS 36 *Impairment of Assets*.

84 If the fair value of the asset can be determined by reference to an active market at a subsequent measurement date, the revaluation model is applied from that date.

85 If an intangible asset's carrying amount is increased as a result of a revaluation, the increase shall be credited directly to equity under the heading of revaluation surplus. However, the increase shall be recognised in profit or loss to the extent that it reverses a revaluation decrease of the same asset previously recognised in profit or loss.

86 If an intangible asset's carrying amount is decreased as a result of a revaluation, the decrease shall be recognised in profit or loss. However, the decrease shall be debited directly to equity under the heading of revaluation surplus to the extent of any credit balance in the revaluation surplus in respect of that asset.

87 The cumulative revaluation surplus included in equity may be transferred directly to retained earnings when the surplus is realised. The whole surplus may be realised on the retirement or disposal of the asset. However, some of the surplus may be realised as the asset is used by the entity; in such a case, the amount of the surplus realised is the difference between amortisation based on the revalued carrying amount of the asset and amortisation that would have been recognised based on the asset's historical cost. The transfer from revaluation surplus to retained earnings is not made through the income statement.

Useful life

88 An entity shall assess whether the useful life of an intangible asset is finite or indefinite and, if finite, the length of, or number of production or similar units constituting, that useful life. An intangible asset shall be regarded by the entity as having an indefinite useful life when, based on an analysis of all of the relevant factors, there is no foreseeable limit to the period over which the asset is expected to generate net cash inflows for the entity.

89 The accounting for an intangible asset is based on its useful life. An intangible asset with a finite useful life is amortised (see paragraphs 97–106), and an intangible asset with an indefinite useful life is not (see paragraphs 107–110). The Illustrative Examples accompanying this Standard illustrate the determination of useful life for different intangible assets, and the subsequent accounting for those assets based on the useful life determinations.

90 Many factors are considered in determining the useful life of an intangible asset, including:

(a) the expected usage of the asset by the entity and whether the asset could be managed efficiently by another management team;

(b) typical product life cycles for the asset and public information on estimates of useful lives of similar assets that are used in a similar way;

(c) technical, technological, commercial or other types of obsolescence;

(d) the stability of the industry in which the asset operates and changes in the market demand for the products or services output from the asset;

(e) expected actions by competitors or potential competitors;

(f) the level of maintenance expenditure required to obtain the expected future economic benefits from the asset and the entity's ability and intention to reach such a level;

(g) the period of control over the asset and legal or similar limits on the use of the asset, such as the expiry dates of related leases; and

(h) whether the useful life of the asset is dependent on the useful life of other assets of the entity.

91 The term 'indefinite' does not mean 'infinite'. The useful life of an intangible asset reflects only that level of future maintenance expenditure required to maintain the asset at its standard of performance assessed at the time of estimating the asset's useful life, and the entity's ability and intention to reach such a level. A conclusion that the useful life of an intangible asset is indefinite should not depend on planned future expenditure in excess of that required to maintain the asset at that standard of performance.

92 Given the history of rapid changes in technology, computer software and many other intangible assets are susceptible to technological obsolescence. Therefore, it is likely that their useful life is short.

93 The useful life of an intangible asset may be very long or even indefinite. Uncertainty justifies estimating the useful life of an intangible asset on a prudent basis, but it does not justify choosing a life that is unrealistically short.

94 The useful life of an intangible asset that arises from contractual or other legal rights shall not exceed the period of the contractual or other legal rights, but may be shorter depending on the period over which the entity expects to use the asset. If the contractual or other legal rights are conveyed for a limited term that can be renewed, the useful life of the intangible asset shall include the renewal period(s) only if there is evidence to support renewal by the entity without significant cost.

95 There may be both economic and legal factors influencing the useful life of an intangible asset. Economic factors determine the period over which future economic benefits will be received by the entity. Legal factors may restrict the period over which the entity controls access to these benefits. The useful life is the shorter of the periods determined by these factors.

96 Existence of the following factors, among others, indicates that an entity would be able to renew the contractual or other legal rights without significant cost:

(a) there is evidence, possibly based on experience, that the contractual or other legal rights will be renewed. If renewal is contingent upon the consent of a third party, this includes evidence that the third party will give its consent;

(b) there is evidence that any conditions necessary to obtain renewal will be satisfied; and

(c) the cost to the entity of renewal is not significant when compared with the future economic benefits expected to flow to the entity from renewal.

If the cost of renewal is significant when compared with the future economic benefits expected to flow to the entity from renewal, the 'renewal' cost represents, in substance, the cost to acquire a new intangible asset at the renewal date.

Intangible assets with finite useful lives

Amortisation period and amortisation method

97 **The depreciable amount of an intangible asset with a finite useful life shall be allocated on a systematic basis over its useful life. Amortisation shall begin when the asset is available for use, ie when it is in the location and condition necessary for it to be capable of operating in the manner intended by management. Amortisation shall cease at the earlier of the date that the asset is classified as held for sale (or included in a disposal group that is classified as held for sale) in accordance with IFRS 5** *Non-current Assets Held for Sale and Discontinued Operations* **and the date that the asset is derecognised. The amortisation method used shall reflect the pattern in which the asset's future economic benefits are expected to be consumed by the entity. If that pattern cannot be determined reliably, the straight-line method shall be used. The amortisation charge for each period shall be recognised in profit or loss unless this or another Standard permits or requires it to be included in the carrying amount of another asset.**

98 A variety of amortisation methods can be used to allocate the depreciable amount of an asset on a systematic basis over its useful life. These methods include the straight-line method, the diminishing balance method and the unit of production method. The method used is selected on the basis of the expected pattern of consumption of the expected future economic benefits embodied in the asset and is applied consistently from period to period, unless there is a change in the expected pattern of consumption of those future economic benefits. There is rarely, if ever, persuasive evidence to support an amortisation method for intangible assets with finite useful lives that results in a lower amount of accumulated amortisation than under the straight-line method.

99 Amortisation is usually recognised in profit or loss. However, sometimes the future economic benefits embodied in an asset are absorbed in producing other assets. In this case, the amortisation charge constitutes part of the cost of the other asset and is included in its carrying amount. For example, the amortisation of intangible assets used in a production process is included in the carrying amount of inventories (see IAS 2 *Inventories*).

Residual value

100 **The residual value of an intangible asset with a finite useful life shall be assumed to be zero unless:**

(a) **there is a commitment by a third party to purchase the asset at the end of its useful life; or**

(b) **there is an active market for the asset and:**

(i) **residual value can be determined by reference to that market; and**

(ii) **it is probable that such a market will exist at the end of the asset's useful life.**

101 The depreciable amount of an asset with a finite useful life is determined after deducting its residual value. A residual value other than zero implies that an entity expects to dispose of the intangible asset before the end of its economic life.

102 An estimate of an asset's residual value is based on the amount recoverable from disposal using prices prevailing at the date of the estimate for the sale of a similar asset that has reached the end of its useful life and has operated under conditions similar to those in which the asset will be used. The residual value is reviewed at least at each financial year-end. A change in the asset's residual value is accounted for as a change in an accounting estimate in accordance with IAS 8 *Accounting Policies, Changes in Accounting Estimates and Errors*.

103 The residual value of an intangible asset may increase to an amount equal to or greater than the asset's carrying amount. If it does, the asset's amortisation charge is zero unless and until its residual value subsequently decreases to an amount below the asset's carrying amount.

Review of amortisation period and amortisation method

104 The amortisation period and the amortisation method for an intangible asset with a finite useful life shall be reviewed at least at each financial year-end. If the expected useful life of the asset is different from previous estimates, the amortisation period shall be changed accordingly. If there has been a change in the expected pattern of consumption of the future economic benefits embodied in the asset, the amortisation method shall be changed to reflect the changed pattern. Such changes shall be accounted for as changes in accounting estimates in accordance with IAS 8.

105 During the life of an intangible asset, it may become apparent that the estimate of its useful life is inappropriate. For example, the recognition of an impairment loss may indicate that the amortisation period needs to be changed.

106 Over time, the pattern of future economic benefits expected to flow to an entity from an intangible asset may change. For example, it may become apparent that a diminishing balance method of amortisation is appropriate rather than a straight-line method. Another example is if use of the rights represented by a licence is deferred pending action on other components of the business plan. In this case, economic benefits that flow from the asset may not be received until later periods.

Intangible assets with indefinite useful lives

107 **An intangible asset with an indefinite useful life shall not be amortised.**

108 In accordance with IAS 36 *Impairment of Assets*, an entity is required to test an intangible asset with an indefinite useful life for impairment by comparing its recoverable amount with its carrying amount

(a) annually, and

(b) whenever there is an indication that the intangible asset may be impaired.

Review of useful life assessment

109 **The useful life of an intangible asset that is not being amortised shall be reviewed each period to determine whether events and circumstances continue to support an indefinite useful life assessment for that asset. If they do not, the change in the useful life assessment from indefinite to finite shall be accounted for as a change in an accounting estimate in accordance with IAS 8** *Accounting Policies, Changes in Accounting Estimates and Errors*.

110 In accordance with IAS 36, reassessing the useful life of an intangible asset as finite rather than indefinite is an indicator that the asset may be impaired. As a result, the entity tests the asset for impairment by comparing its recoverable amount, determined in accordance with IAS 36, with its carrying amount, and recognising any excess of the carrying amount over the recoverable amount as an impairment loss.

Recoverability of the carrying amount – impairment losses

111 To determine whether an intangible asset is impaired, an entity applies IAS 36 *Impairment of Assets*. That Standard explains when and how an entity reviews the carrying amount of its assets, how it determines the recoverable amount of an asset and when it recognises or reverses an impairment loss.

Retirements and disposals

112 **An intangible asset shall be derecognised:**

(a) on disposal; or

(b) when no future economic benefits are expected from its use or disposal.

113 **The gain or loss arising from the derecognition of an intangible asset shall be determined as the difference between the net disposal proceeds, if any, and the carrying amount of the asset. It shall be recognised in profit or loss when the asset is derecognised (unless IAS 17** *Leases* **requires otherwise on a sale and leaseback). Gains shall not be classified as revenue.**

114 The disposal of an intangible asset may occur in a variety of ways (eg by sale, by entering into a finance lease, or by donation). In determining the date of disposal of such an asset, an entity applies the criteria in IAS 18 *Revenue* for recognising revenue from the sale of goods. IAS 17 applies to disposal by a sale and leaseback.

115 If in accordance with the recognition principle in paragraph 21 an entity recognises in the carrying amount of an asset the cost of a replacement for part of an intangible asset, then it derecognises the carrying amount of the replaced part. If it is not practicable for an entity to determine the carrying amount of the replaced part, it may use the cost of the replacement as an indication of what the cost of the replaced part was at the time it was acquired or internally generated.

116 The consideration receivable on disposal of an intangible asset is recognised initially at its fair value. If payment for the intangible asset is deferred, the consideration received is recognised initially at the cash price equivalent. The difference between the nominal amount of the consideration and the cash price equivalent is recognised as interest revenue in accordance with IAS 18 reflecting the effective yield on the receivable.

117 Amortisation of an intangible asset with a finite useful life does not cease when the intangible asset is no longer used, unless the asset has been fully depreciated or is classified as held for sale (or included in a disposal group that is classified as held for sale) in accordance with IFRS 5.

Disclosure

General

118 An entity shall disclose the following for each class of intangible assets, distinguishing between internally generated intangible assets and other intangible assets:

(a) whether the useful lives are indefinite or finite and, if finite, the useful lives or the amortisation rates used;

(b) the amortisation methods used for intangible assets with finite useful lives;

(c) the gross carrying amount and any accumulated amortisation (aggregated with accumulated impairment losses) at the beginning and end of the period;

(d) the line item(s) of the income statement in which any amortisation of intangible assets is included;

(e) a reconciliation of the carrying amount at the beginning and end of the period showing:

(i) additions, indicating separately those from internal development, those acquired separately, and those acquired through business combinations;

(ii) assets classified as held for sale or included in a disposal group classified as held for sale in accordance with IFRS 5 and other disposals;

(iii) increases or decreases during the period resulting from revaluations under paragraphs 75, 85 and 86 and from impairment losses recognised or reversed directly in equity in accordance with IAS 36 ***Impairment of Assets*** **(if any);**

(iv) impairment losses recognised in profit or loss during the period in accordance with IAS 36 (if any);

(v) impairment losses reversed in profit or loss during the period in accordance with IAS 36 (if any);

(vi) any amortisation recognised during the period;

(vii) net exchange differences arising on the translation of the financial statements into the presentation currency, and on the translation of a foreign operation into the presentation currency of the entity; and

(viii) other changes in the carrying amount during the period.

119 A class of intangible assets is a grouping of assets of a similar nature and use in an entity's operations. Examples of separate classes may include:

(a) brand names;

(b) mastheads and publishing titles;

(c) computer software;

(d) licences and franchises;

(e) copyrights, patents and other industrial property rights, service and operating rights;

(f) recipes, formulae, models, designs and prototypes; and

(g) intangible assets under development.

The classes mentioned above are disaggregated (aggregated) into smaller (larger) classes if this results in more relevant information for the users of the financial statements.

120 An entity discloses information on impaired intangible assets in accordance with IAS 36 in addition to the information required by paragraph 118(e)(iii)–(v).

121 IAS 8 requires an entity to disclose the nature and amount of a change in an accounting estimate that has a material effect in the current period or is expected to have a material effect in subsequent periods. Such disclosure may arise from changes in:

(a) the assessment of an intangible asset's useful life;

(b) the amortisation method; or

(c) residual values.

122 An entity shall also disclose:

(a) for an intangible asset assessed as having an indefinite useful life, the carrying amount of that asset and the reasons supporting the assessment of an indefinite useful life. In giving these reasons, the entity shall describe the factor(s) that played a significant role in determining that the asset has an indefinite useful life.

(b) a description, the carrying amount and remaining amortisation period of any individual intangible asset that is material to the entity's financial statements.

(c) for intangible assets acquired by way of a government grant and initially recognised at fair value (see paragraph 44):

(i) the fair value initially recognised for these assets;

(ii) their carrying amount; and

(iii) whether they are measured after recognition under the cost model or the revaluation model.

(d) the existence and carrying amounts of intangible assets whose title is restricted and the carrying amounts of intangible assets pledged as security for liabilities.

(e) the amount of contractual commitments for the acquisition of intangible assets.

123 When an entity describes the factor(s) that played a significant role in determining that the useful life of an intangible asset is indefinite, the entity considers the list of factors in paragraph 90.

Intangible assets measured after recognition using the revaluation model

124 **If intangible assets are accounted for at revalued amounts, an entity shall disclose the following:**

(a) by class of intangible assets:

(i) the effective date of the revaluation;

(ii) the carrying amount of revalued intangible assets; and

(iii) the carrying amount that would have been recognised had the revalued class of intangible assets been measured after recognition using the cost model in paragraph 74;

(b) the amount of the revaluation surplus that relates to intangible assets at the beginning and end of the period, indicating the changes during the period and any restrictions on the distribution of the balance to shareholders; and

(c) the methods and significant assumptions applied in estimating the assets' fair values.

125 It may be necessary to aggregate the classes of revalued assets into larger classes for disclosure purposes. However, classes are not aggregated if this would result in the combination of a class of intangible assets that includes amounts measured under both the cost and revaluation models.

Research and development expenditure

126 **An entity shall disclose the aggregate amount of research and development expenditure recognised as an expense during the period.**

127 Research and development expenditure comprises all expenditure that is directly attributable to research or development activities (see paragraphs 66 and 67 for guidance on the type of expenditure to be included for the purpose of the disclosure requirement in paragraph 126).

Other information

128 An entity is encouraged, but not required, to disclose the following information:

(a) a description of any fully amortised intangible asset that is still in use; and

(b) a brief description of significant intangible assets controlled by the entity but not recognised as assets because they did not meet the recognition criteria in this Standard or because they were acquired or generated before the version of IAS 38 *Intangible Assets* issued in 1998 was effective.

Transitional provisions and effective date

129 **If an entity elects in accordance with paragraph 85 of IFRS 3** *Business Combinations* **to apply IFRS 3 from any date before the effective dates set out in paragraphs 78–84 of IFRS 3, it also shall apply this Standard prospectively from that same date. Thus, the entity shall not adjust the carrying amount of intangible assets recognised at that date. However, the entity shall, at that date, apply this Standard to reassess the useful lives of its recognised intangible assets. If, as a result of that reassessment, the entity changes its assessment of the useful life of an asset, that change shall be accounted for as a change in an accounting estimate in accordance with IAS 8** *Accounting Policies, Changes in Accounting Estimates and Errors***.**

130 **Otherwise, an entity shall apply this Standard:**

(a) to the accounting for intangible assets acquired in business combinations for which the agreement date is on or after 31 March 2004; and

(b) to the accounting for all other intangible assets prospectively from the beginning of the first annual period beginning on or after 31 March 2004. Thus, the entity shall not adjust the carrying amount of intangible assets recognised at that date. However, the entity shall, at that date, apply this Standard to reassess the useful lives of such intangible assets. If, as a result of that reassessment, the entity changes its assessment of the useful life of an asset, that change shall be accounted for as a change in an accounting estimate in accordance with IAS 8.

130A An entity shall apply the amendments in paragraph 2 for annual periods beginning on or after 1 January 2006. If an entity applies IFRS 6 *Exploration for and Evaluation of Mineral Resources* for an earlier period, those amendments shall be applied for that earlier period.

Exchanges of similar assets

131 The requirement in paragraphs 129 and 130(b) to apply this Standard prospectively means that if an exchange of assets was measured before the effective date of this Standard on the basis of the carrying amount of the asset given up, the entity does not restate the carrying amount of the asset acquired to reflect its fair value at the acquisition date.

Early application

132 Entities to which paragraph 130 applies are encouraged to apply the requirements of this Standard before the effective dates specified in paragraph 130. However, if an entity applies this Standard before those effective dates, it also shall apply IFRS 3 and IAS 36 ***Impairment of Assets*** **(as revised in 2004) at the same time.**

Withdrawal of IAS 38 (issued 1998)

133 This Standard supersedes IAS 38 *Intangible Assets* (issued in 1998).

Approval of IAS 38 by the Board

International Accounting Standard 38 *Intangible Assets* was approved for issue by thirteen of the fourteen members of the International Accounting Standards Board. Professor Whittington dissented. His dissenting opinion is set out after the Basis for Conclusions on IAS 38.

Sir David Tweedie	Chairman
Thomas E Jones	Vice-Chairman
Mary E Barth	
Hans-Georg Bruns	
Anthony T Cope	
Robert P Garnett	
Gilbert Gélard	
James J Leisenring	
Warren J McGregor	
Patricia L O'Malley	
Harry K Schmid	
John T Smith	
Geoffrey Whittington	
Tatsumi Yamada	

CONTENTS

Basis for Conclusions on IAS 38 Intangible Assets

The International Accounting Standards Board revised IAS 38 as part of its project on business combinations. It was not the Board's intention to reconsider as part of that project all of the requirements in IAS 38.

The previous version of IAS 38 was accompanied by a Basis for Conclusions summarising the former International Accounting Standards Committee's considerations in reaching some of its conclusions in that Standard. For convenience the Board has incorporated into its own Basis for Conclusions material from the previous Basis for Conclusions that discusses (a) matters the Board did not reconsider and (b) the history of the development of a standard on intangible assets. That material is contained in paragraphs denoted by numbers with the prefix BCZ. Paragraphs describing the Board's considerations in reaching its own conclusions are numbered with the prefix BC.

Introduction

BC1 This Basis for Conclusions summarises the International Accounting Standards Board's considerations in reaching the conclusions in IAS 38 *Intangible Assets*. Individual Board members gave greater weight to some factors than to others.

BC2 The International Accounting Standards Committee (IASC) issued the previous version of IAS 38 in 1998. It has been revised by the Board as part of its project on business combinations. That project has two phases. The first has resulted in the Board issuing simultaneously IFRS 3 *Business Combinations* and revised versions of IAS 38 and IAS 36 *Impairment of Assets*. Therefore, the Board's intention in revising IAS 38 as part of the first phase of the project was not to reconsider all of the requirements in IAS 38. The changes to IAS 38 are primarily concerned with:

(a) the notion of 'identifiability' as it relates to intangible assets;

(b) the useful life and amortisation of intangible assets; and

(c) the accounting for in-process research and development projects acquired in business combinations.

BC3 With the exception of research and development projects acquired in business combinations, the Board did not reconsider the requirements in the previous version of IAS 38 on the recognition of internally generated intangible assets. The previous version of IAS 38 was accompanied by a Basis for Conclusions summarising IASC's considerations in reaching some of its conclusions in that Standard. For convenience, the Board has incorporated into this Basis for Conclusions material from the previous Basis for Conclusions that discusses the recognition of internally generated intangible assets (see paragraphs BCZ29–BCZ46) and the history of the development of a standard on intangible assets (see paragraphs BCZ104–BCZ110). The views expressed in paragraphs BCZ29–BCZ46 and BCZ104–BCZ110 are those of IASC.

Definition of an intangible asset (paragraph 8)

BC4 An intangible asset was defined in the previous version of IAS 38 as 'an identifiable non-monetary asset without physical substance held for use in the production or supply of goods or services, for rental to others, or for administrative services'.

The definition in the revised Standard eliminates the requirement for the asset to be held for use in the production or supply of goods or services, for rental to others, or for administrative services.

BC5 The Board observed that the essential characteristics of intangible assets are that they:

(a) are resources controlled by the entity from which future economic benefits are expected to flow to the entity;

(b) lack physical substance; and

(c) are identifiable.

The Board concluded that the purpose for which an entity holds an item with these characteristics is not relevant to its classification as an intangible asset, and that all such items should be within the scope of the Standard.

Identifiability (paragraph 12)

BC6 Under the Standard, as under the previous version of IAS 38, a non-monetary asset without physical substance must be identifiable to meet the definition of an intangible asset. The previous version of IAS 38 did not define 'identifiability', but stated that an intangible asset could be distinguished from goodwill if the asset was separable, but that separability was not a necessary condition for identifiability. The revised Standard requires an asset to be treated as meeting the identifiability criterion in the definition of an intangible asset when it is separable, or when it arises from contractual or other legal rights, regardless of whether those rights are transferable or separable from the entity or from other rights and obligations.

Background to the Board's deliberations

BC7 The Board was prompted to consider the issue of 'identifiability' as part of the first phase of its Business Combinations project as a result of changes during 2001 to the requirements in Canadian and United States standards on the separate recognition of intangible assets acquired in business combinations. The Board observed that intangible assets comprise an increasing proportion of the assets of many entities, and that intangible assets acquired in a business combination are often included in the amount recognised as goodwill, despite the requirements in IAS 22 *Business Combinations* and IAS 38 for them to be recognised separately from goodwill. The Board agreed with the conclusion reached by the Canadian and US standard-setters that the usefulness of financial statements would be enhanced if intangible assets acquired in a business combination were distinguished from goodwill. Therefore, the Board concluded that the IFRS arising from the first phase of the Business Combinations project should provide a definitive basis for identifying and recognising intangible assets acquired in a business combination separately from goodwill.

BC8 In revising IAS 38 and developing IFRS 3, the Board affirmed the view in the previous version of IAS 38 that identifiability is the characteristic that conceptually distinguishes other intangible assets from goodwill. The Board concluded that to provide a definitive basis for identifying and recognising intangible assets separately from goodwill, the concept of identifiability needed to be articulated more clearly.

Clarifying identifiability (paragraph 12)

BC9 Consistently with the guidance in the previous version of IAS 38, the Board concluded that an intangible asset can be distinguished from goodwill if it is separable, ie capable of being separated or divided from the entity and sold, transferred, licensed, rented or exchanged. Therefore, in the context of intangible assets, separability signifies identifiability, and intangible assets with that characteristic that are acquired in a business combination should be recognised as assets separately from goodwill.

BC10 However, again consistently with the guidance in the previous version of IAS 38, the Board concluded that separability is not the only indication of identifiability. The Board observed that, in contrast to goodwill, the values of many intangible assets arise from rights conveyed legally by contract or statute. In the case of acquired goodwill, its value arises from the collection of assembled assets that make up an acquired entity or the value created by assembling a collection of assets through a business combination, such as the synergies that are expected to result from combining entities or businesses. The Board also observed that, although many intangible assets are both separable and arise from contractual-legal rights, some contractual-legal rights establish property interests that are not readily separable from the entity as a whole. For example, under the laws of some jurisdictions some licences granted to an entity are not transferable except by sale of the entity as a whole. The Board concluded that the fact that an intangible asset arises from contractual or other legal rights is a characteristic that distinguishes it from goodwill. Therefore, intangible assets with that characteristic that are acquired in a business combination should be recognised as assets separately from goodwill.

Non–contractual customer relationships (paragraph 16)

BC11 The previous version of IAS 38 and the Exposure Draft of Proposed Amendments to IAS 38 stated that 'An entity controls an asset if the entity has the power to obtain the future economic benefits flowing from the underlying resource and also can restrict the access of others to those benefits.' The documents then expanded on this by stating that 'in the absence of legal rights to protect, or other ways to control, the relationships with customers or the loyalty of the customers to the entity, the entity usually has insufficient control over the economic benefits from customer relationships and loyalty to consider that such items meet the definition of intangible assets.'

BC12 However, the Draft Illustrative Examples accompanying ED 3 *Business Combinations* stated that 'If a customer relationship acquired in a business combination does not arise from a contract, the relationship is recognised as an intangible asset separately from goodwill if it meets the separability criterion. Exchange transactions for the same asset or a similar asset provide evidence of separability of a non-contractual customer relationship and might also provide information about exchange prices that should be considered when estimating fair value.' Whilst respondents to the Exposure Draft generally agreed with the Board's conclusions on the definition of identifiability, some were uncertain about the relationship between the separability criterion for establishing whether a non-contractual customer relationship is identifiable, and the control concept for establishing whether the relationship meets the definition of an asset. Additionally, some respondents suggested that non-contractual customer relationships would, under the proposal in the Exposure Draft, be separately recognised if acquired in a business combination, but not if acquired in a separate transaction.

BC13 The Board observed that exchange transactions for the same or similar non-contractual customer relationships provide evidence not only that the item is separable, but also that the entity is able to control the expected future economic benefits flowing from that relationship. Similarly, if an entity separately acquires a non-contractual customer relationship, the existence of an exchange transaction for that relationship provides evidence both that the item is separable, and that the entity is able to control the expected future economic benefits flowing from the relationship. Therefore, the relationship would meet the intangible asset definition and be recognised as such. However, in the absence of exchange transactions for the same or similar non-contractual customer relationships, such relationships acquired in a business combination would not normally meet the definition of an 'intangible asset'—they would not be separable, nor would the entity be able to demonstrate that it controls the expected future economic benefits flowing from that relationship.

BC14 Therefore, the Board decided to clarify in paragraph 16 of IAS 38 that in the absence of legal rights to protect customer relationships, exchange transactions for the same or similar non-contractual customer relationships (other than as part of a business combination) provide evidence that the entity is nonetheless able to control the future economic benefits flowing from the customer relationships. Because such exchange transactions also provide evidence that the customer relationships are separable, those customer relationships meet the definition of an intangible asset.

Criteria for initial recognition

BC15 In accordance with the Standard, as with the previous version of IAS 38, an intangible asset is recognised if, and only if:

(a) it is probable that the expected future economic benefits that are attributable to the asset will flow to the entity; and

(b) the cost of the asset can be measured reliably.

In revising IAS 38 the Board considered the application of these recognition criteria to intangible assets acquired in business combinations. The Board's deliberations on this issue are set out in paragraphs BC16–BC25.

Acquisition as part of a business combination (paragraphs 33–38)

BC16 The Exposure Draft of Proposed Amendments to IAS 38 proposed that the recognition criteria in paragraph BC15 would, with the exception of an assembled workforce, always be satisfied for an intangible asset acquired in a business combination. Therefore, those criteria were not included in ED 3 *Business Combinations*. ED 3 proposed requiring an acquirer to recognise separately at the acquisition date all of the acquiree's intangible assets as defined in IAS 38, other than an assembled workforce. After considering respondents' comments, the Board decided:

(a) to proceed with the proposal that the probability recognition criterion is always considered to be satisfied for intangible assets acquired in a business combination; and

(b) not to proceed with the proposal that, with the exception of an assembled workforce, sufficient information should always exist to measure reliably the fair value of an intangible asset acquired in a business combination.

Probability recognition criterion

BC17 In revising IAS 38, the Board observed that the fair value of an intangible asset reflects market expectations about the probability that the future economic benefits associated with the intangible asset will flow to the acquirer. In other words, the effect of probability is reflected in the fair value measurement of an intangible asset. Therefore, the probability recognition criterion is always considered to be satisfied for intangible assets acquired in business combinations.

BC18 The Board observed that this highlights a general inconsistency between the recognition criteria for assets and liabilities in the *Framework* (which states that an item meeting the definition of an element should be recognised only if it is probable that any future economic benefits associated with the item will flow to or from the entity, and the item can be measured reliably) and the fair value measurements required in, for example, a business combination. However, the Board concluded that the role of probability as a criterion for recognition in the *Framework* should be considered more generally as part of a forthcoming Concepts project.

Reliability of measurement recognition criterion

BC19 In developing the Exposure Draft, the Board concluded that, except for an assembled workforce, sufficient information should exist to measure reliably the fair value of an asset that has an underlying contractual or legal basis or is capable of being separated from the entity. Respondents generally disagreed with this conclusion, arguing that:

(a) it might not always be possible to measure reliably the fair value of an asset that has an underlying contractual or legal basis or is capable of being separated from the entity.

(b) a similar presumption does not exist in IFRSs for identifiable tangible assets acquired in a business combination. Indeed, the Board decided when developing IFRS 3 *Business Combinations* to carry forward from IAS 22 *Business Combinations* the general principle that an acquirer should recognise separately from goodwill the acquiree's identifiable tangible assets, but only provided they can be measured reliably.

BC20 Additionally, as part of its consultative process, the Board conducted field visits and round-table discussions during the comment period for the Exposure Draft.* Field visit and round-table participants were asked a series of questions aimed at improving the Board's understanding of whether there might exist non-monetary assets without physical substance that are separable or arise from legal or other contractual rights, but for which there may *not* be sufficient information to measure fair value reliably.

BC21 The field visit and round-table participants provided numerous examples of intangible assets they had acquired in recent business combinations whose fair values might not be reliably measurable. For example, one participant acquired water acquisition rights as part of a business combination. The rights are extremely valuable to many manufacturers operating in the same jurisdiction as the participant–the manufacturers cannot acquire water and, in many cases, cannot operate their plants without them. Local authorities grant the rights at little or no cost, but in limited numbers, for fixed periods (normally ten years), and renewal is certain at little or no cost. The rights cannot be sold other than as part of the sale of a business as a whole, therefore there exists no secondary market in the rights. If a manufacturer hands the rights back to the local authority, it is prohibited from reapplying. The participant argued that it could not value these rights separately from its business (and therefore from goodwill), because the business would cease to exist without the rights.

BC22 After considering respondents' comments and the experiences of field visit and round-table participants, the Board concluded that, in some instances, there might not be sufficient information to measure reliably the fair value of an intangible asset separately from goodwill, notwithstanding that the asset is identifiable. The Board observed that, except as outlined in paragraph BC25, the intangible assets whose fair values respondents and field visit and round-table participants could not measure reliably arose either:

(a) from legal or other contractual rights and are not separable (ie could be transferred only as part of the sale of a business as a whole); or

(b) from legal or other contractual rights and are separable (ie capable of being separated or divided from the entity and sold, transferred, licensed, rented or exchanged, either individually or together with a related contract, asset or liability), but there is no history or evidence of exchange transactions for the same or similar assets, and otherwise estimating fair value would be dependent on immeasurable variables.

BC23 Nevertheless, the Board remained of the view that the usefulness of financial statements would be enhanced if intangible assets acquired in a business combination were distinguished from goodwill, particularly given the Board's decision to regard goodwill as an indefinite-lived asset that is not amortised.

* The field visits were conducted from early December 2002 to early April 2003, and involved IASB members and staff in meetings with 41 companies in Australia, France, Germany, Japan, South Africa, Switzerland and the United Kingdom. IASB members and staff also took part in a series of round-table discussions with auditors, preparers, accounting standard-setters and regulators in Canada and the United States on implementation issues encountered by North American companies during first-time application of US Statements of Financial Accounting Standards 141 *Business Combinations* and 142 *Goodwill and Other Intangible Assets*, and the equivalent Canadian Handbook Sections, which were issued in June 2001.

The Board also remained concerned that failing the recognition criterion of reliability of measurement might be inappropriately used by entities as a basis for not recognising intangible assets separately from goodwill. For example, IAS 22 and the previous version of IAS 38 required an acquirer to recognise an intangible asset of the acquiree separately from goodwill at the acquisition date if it was probable that any associated future economic benefits would flow to the acquirer and the asset's fair value could be measured reliably. The Board observed when developing the Exposure Draft that although intangible assets constitute an increasing proportion of the assets of many entities, those acquired in business combinations were often included in the amount recognised as goodwill, despite the requirements in IAS 22 and the previous version of IAS 38 that they be recognised separately from goodwill.

BC24 Therefore, although the Board decided not to proceed with the proposal that, with the exception of an assembled workforce, sufficient information should always exist to measure reliably the fair value of an intangible asset acquired in a business combination, the Board also decided:

(a) to clarify in paragraph 35 of the Standard that the fair value of an intangible asset acquired in a business combination can normally be measured with sufficient reliability for it to be recognised separately from goodwill. When, for the estimates used to measure an intangible asset's fair value, there is a range of possible outcomes with different probabilities, that uncertainty enters into the measurement of the asset's fair value, rather than demonstrates an inability to measure fair value reliably.

(b) to include in paragraph 35 of the Standard a rebuttable presumption that the fair value of a finite-lived intangible asset acquired in a business combination can be measured reliably.

(c) to clarify in paragraph 38 of the Standard that the only circumstances in which it might not be possible to measure reliably the fair value of an intangible asset acquired in a business combination are when the intangible asset arises from legal or other contractual rights and it either (i) is not separable or (ii) is separable but there is no history or evidence of exchange transactions for the same or similar assets and otherwise estimating fair value would be dependent on immeasurable variables.

(d) to include in paragraph 67(h) of IFRS 3 a requirement for entities to disclose a description of each asset that meets the definition of an intangible asset and was acquired in a business combination during the period but was not recognised separately from goodwill, and an explanation of why its fair value could not be measured reliably.

BC25 Some respondents and field visit participants suggested that it might also not be possible to measure reliably the fair value of an intangible asset when it is separable, but only together with a related contract, asset or liability (ie it is not individually separable), there is no history of exchange transactions for the same or similar assets on a stand-alone basis, and, because the related items produce jointly the same cash flows, the fair value of each could be estimated only by arbitrarily allocating those cash flows between the two items. The Board disagreed that such circumstances provide a basis for subsuming the value of the intangible asset within the carrying amount of goodwill. Although some intangible assets are so closely related to other identifiable assets or liabilities that they are usually sold as a package, it would still be possible to measure reliably the fair value of that package. Therefore, the Board decided to include the following clarifications in paragraphs 36 and 37 of the Standard:

(a) when an intangible asset acquired in a business combination is separable but only together with a related tangible or intangible asset, the acquirer recognises the group of assets as a single asset separately from goodwill if the individual fair values of the assets in the group are not reliably measurable.

(b) similarly, an acquirer recognises as a single asset a group of complementary intangible assets constituting a brand if the individual fair values of the complementary assets are not reliably measurable. If the individual fair values of the complementary assets are reliably measurable, the acquirer may recognise them as a single asset separately from goodwill, provided the individual assets have similar useful lives.

Separate acquisition (paragraphs 25 and 26)

BC26 Having decided to include paragraphs 33–38 in IAS 38, the Board also decided that it needed to consider the role of the probability and reliability of measurement recognition criteria for separately acquired intangible assets.

BC27 Consistently with its conclusion about the role of probability in the recognition of intangible assets acquired in business combinations, the Board concluded that the probability recognition criterion is always considered to be satisfied for separately acquired intangible assets. This is because the price an entity pays to acquire separately an intangible asset normally reflects expectations about the probability that the expected future economic benefits associated with the intangible asset will flow to the entity. In other words, the effect of probability is reflected in the cost of the intangible asset.

BC28 The Board also concluded that when an intangible asset is separately acquired in exchange for cash or other monetary assets, sufficient information should exist to measure the cost of that asset reliably. However, this might not be the case when the purchase consideration comprises non-monetary assets. Therefore, the Board decided to carry forward from the previous version of IAS 38 guidance clarifying that the cost of a separately acquired intangible asset can usually be measured reliably, particularly when the purchase consideration is cash or other monetary assets.

Internally generated intangible assets (paragraphs 51–67)

BCZ29 The controversy relating to internally generated intangible assets surrounds whether there should be:

(a) a requirement to recognise internally generated intangible assets in the balance sheet whenever certain criteria are met;

(b) a requirement to recognise expenditure on all internally generated intangible assets as an expense;

(c) a requirement to recognise expenditure on all internally generated intangible assets as an expense, with certain specified exceptions; or

(d) an option to choose between the treatments described in (a) and (b) above.

Background on the requirements for internally generated intangible assets

BCZ30 Before IAS 38 was issued in 1998, some internally generated intangible assets (those that arose from development expenditure) were dealt with under IAS 9 *Research and Development Costs*. The development of, and revisions to, IAS 9 had always been controversial.

BCZ31 Proposed and approved requirements for the recognition of an asset arising from development expenditure and other internally generated intangible assets had been the following:

(a) in 1978, IASC approved IAS 9 *Accounting for Research and Development Activities*. It required expenditure on research and development to be recognised as an expense when incurred, except that an enterprise had the option to recognise an asset arising from development expenditure whenever certain criteria were met.

(b) in 1989, Exposure Draft E32 *Comparability of Financial Statements* proposed retaining IAS 9's option to recognise an asset arising from development expenditure if certain criteria were met and identifying:

(i) as a preferred treatment, recognising all expenditure on research and development as an expense when incurred; and

(ii) as an allowed alternative treatment, recognising an asset arising from development expenditure whenever certain criteria were met.

The majority of commentators on E32 did not support maintaining an option or the proposed preferred treatment.

(c) in 1991, Exposure Draft E37 *Research and Development Costs* proposed requiring the recognition of an asset arising from development expenditure whenever certain criteria were met. In 1993, IASC approved IAS 9 *Research and Development Costs* based on E37.

(d) in 1995, consistently with IAS 9, Exposure Draft E50 *Intangible Assets* proposed requiring internally generated intangible assets—other than those arising from development expenditure, which would still have been covered by IAS 9—to be recognised as assets whenever certain criteria were met.

(e) in 1997, Exposure Draft E60 *Intangible Assets* proposed:

(i) retaining E50's proposals for the recognition of internally generated intangible assets; but

(ii) extending the scope of the Standard on intangible assets to deal with all internally generated intangible assets—including those arising from development expenditure.

(f) in 1998, IASC approved:

(i) IAS 38 *Intangible Assets* based on E60, with a few minor changes; and

(ii) the withdrawal of IAS 9.

BCZ32 From 1989, the majority view at IASC and from commentators was that there should be only one treatment that would require an internally generated intangible asset–whether arising from development expenditure or other expenditure–to be recognised as an asset whenever certain recognition criteria are met. Several minority views were strongly opposed to this treatment but there was no clear consensus on any other single treatment.

Combination of IAS 9 with the Standard on intangible assets

BCZ33 The reasons for not retaining IAS 9 as a separate Standard were that:

(a) IASC believed that an identifiable asset that results from research and development activities is an intangible asset because knowledge is the primary outcome of these activities. Therefore, IASC supported treating expenditure on research and development activities similarly to expenditure on activities intended to create any other internally generated intangible assets.

(b) some commentators on E50, which proposed to exclude research and development expenditures from its scope,

   (i) argued that it was sometimes difficult to identify whether IAS 9 or the proposed Standard on intangible assets should apply, and

   (ii) perceived differences in accounting treatments between IAS 9 and E50's proposals, whereas this was not IASC's intent.

BCZ34 A large majority of commentators on E60 supported including certain aspects of IAS 9 with the proposed Standard on intangible assets and the withdrawal of IAS 9. A minority of commentators on E60 supported maintaining two separate Standards. This minority supported the view that internally generated intangible assets should be dealt with on a case-by-case basis with separate requirements for different types of internally generated intangible assets. These commentators argued that E60's proposed recognition criteria were too general to be effective in practice for all internally generated intangible assets.

BCZ35 IASC rejected a proposal to develop separate standards (or detailed requirements within one standard) for specific types of internally generated intangible assets because, as explained above, IASC believed that the same recognition criteria should apply to all types of internally generated intangible assets.

Consequences of combining IAS 9 with IAS 38

BCZ36 The requirements in IAS 38 and IAS 9 differ in the following main respects:

(a) IAS 9 limited the amount of expenditure that could initially be recognised for an asset arising from development expenditure (ie the amount that formed the cost of such an asset) to the amount that was probable of being recovered from the asset. Instead, IAS 38 requires that:

   (i) all expenditure incurred from when the recognition criteria are met until the asset is available for use should be accumulated to form the cost of the asset; and

   (ii) an enterprise should test for impairment, at least annually, an intangible asset that is not yet available for use. If the cost recognised for the asset exceeds its recoverable amount, an enterprise recognises an impairment loss accordingly. This impairment loss should be reversed if the conditions for reversals of impairment losses under IAS 36 *Impairment of Assets* are met.

(b) IAS 38 permits an intangible asset to be measured after recognition at a revalued amount less subsequent amortisation and subsequent impairment losses. IAS 9 did not permit this treatment. However, it is highly unlikely that an active market (the condition required to revalue intangible assets) will exist for an asset that arises from development expenditure.

(c) IAS 38 requires consideration of residual values in determining the depreciable amount of an intangible asset. IAS 9 prohibited the consideration of residual values. However, IAS 38 sets criteria that make it highly unlikely that an asset that arises from development expenditure would have a residual value above zero.

BCZ37 IASC believed that, in practice, it would be unlikely that the application of IAS 38 would result in differences from the application of IAS 9.

Recognition of expenditure on all internally generated intangible assets as an expense

BCZ38 Those who favour the recognition of expenditure on all internally generated intangible assets (including development expenditure) as an expense argue that:

(a) internally generated intangible assets do not meet the *Framework's* requirements for recognition as an asset because:

(i) the future economic benefits that arise from internally generated intangible assets cannot be distinguished from future economic benefits that arise from internally generated goodwill; and/or

(ii) it is impossible to distinguish reliably the expenditure associated with internally generated intangible assets from the expenditure associated with enhancing internally generated goodwill.

(b) comparability of financial statements will not be achieved. This is because the judgement involved in determining whether it is probable that future economic benefits will flow from internally generated intangible assets is too subjective to result in similar accounting under similar circumstances.

(c) it is not possible to assess reliably the amount that can be recovered from an internally generated intangible asset, unless its fair value can be determined by reference to an active market. Therefore, recognising an internally generated intangible asset for which no active market exists at an amount other than zero may mislead investors.

(d) a requirement to recognise internally generated intangible assets at cost if certain criteria are met results in little, if any, decision-useful or predictive information because:

(i) demonstration of technological feasibility or commercial success in order to meet the recognition criteria will generally not be achieved until substantial expenditure has been recognised as an expense.

Therefore, the cost recognised for an internally generated intangible asset will not reflect the total expenditure on that asset.

(ii) the cost of an internally generated intangible asset may not have any relationship to the value of the asset.

(e) in some countries, users are suspicious about an enterprise that recognises internally generated intangible assets.

(f) the added costs of maintaining the records necessary to justify and support the recognition of internally generated intangible assets do not justify the benefits.

Recognition of internally generated intangible assets

BCZ39 Those who support the mandatory recognition of internally generated intangible assets (including those resulting from development expenditure) whenever certain criteria are met argue that:

(a) recognition of an internally generated intangible asset if it meets the definition of an asset and the recognition criteria is consistent with the *Framework*. An enterprise can, in some instances:

(i) determine the probability of receiving future economic benefits from an internally generated intangible asset; and

(ii) distinguish the expenditure on this asset from expenditure on internally generated goodwill.

(b) there has been massive investment in intangible assets in the last two decades. There have been complaints that:

(i) the non-recognition of investments in intangible assets in the financial statements distorts the measurement of an enterprise's performance and does not allow an accurate assessment of returns on investment in intangible assets; and

(ii) if enterprises do not track the returns on investment in intangible assets better, there is a risk of over- or under-investing in important assets. An accounting system that encourages such behaviour will become an increasingly inadequate signal, both for internal control purposes and for external purposes.

(c) certain research studies, particularly in the United States, have established a cost-value association for research and development expenditures. The studies establish that capitalisation of research and development expenditure yields value-relevant information to investors.

(d) the fact that some uncertainties exist about the value of an asset does not justify a requirement that no cost should be recognised for the asset.

(e) it should not matter for recognition purposes whether an asset is purchased externally or developed internally. Particularly, there should be no opportunity for accounting arbitrage depending on whether an enterprise decides to outsource the development of an intangible asset or develop it internally.

IASC's view in approving IAS 38

BCZ40 IASC's view–consistently reflected in previous proposals for intangible assets–was that there should be no difference between the requirements for:

(a) intangible assets that are acquired externally; and

(b) internally generated intangible assets, whether they arise from development activities or other types of activities.

Therefore, an internally generated intangible asset should be recognised whenever the definition of, and recognition criteria for, an intangible asset are met. This view was also supported by a majority of commentators on E60.

BCZ41 IASC rejected a proposal for an allowed alternative to recognise expenditure on internally generated intangible assets (including development expenditure) as an expense immediately, even if the expenditure results in an asset that meets the recognition criteria. IASC believed that a free choice would undermine the comparability of financial statements and the efforts of IASC to reduce the number of alternative treatments in International Accounting Standards.

Differences in recognition criteria for internally generated intangible assets and purchased intangible assets

BCZ42 IAS 38 includes specific recognition criteria for internally generated intangible assets that expand on the general recognition criteria for intangible assets. It is assumed that these criteria are met implicitly whenever an enterprise acquires an intangible asset. Therefore, IAS 38 requires an enterprise to demonstrate that these criteria are met for internally generated intangible assets only.

Initial recognition at cost

BCZ43 Some commentators on E50 and E60 argued that the proposed recognition criteria in E50 and E60 were too restrictive and that they would prevent the recognition of many intangible assets, particularly internally generated intangible assets. Specifically, they disagreed with the proposals (retained in IAS 38) that:

(a) an intangible asset should not be recognised at an amount other than its cost, even if its fair value can be determined reliably; and

(b) expenditure on an intangible asset that has been recognised as an expense in prior periods should not be reinstated.

They argued that these principles contradict the *Framework* and quoted paragraph 83 of the *Framework*, which specifies that an item that meets the definition of an asset should be recognised if, among other things, its '*cost or value* can be measured with reliability'. These commentators supported recognising an intangible asset–an internally generated intangible asset–at its fair value, if, among other things, its fair value can be measured reliably.

BCZ44 IASC rejected a proposal to allow the initial recognition of an intangible asset at fair value (except if the asset is acquired in a business combination, in exchange for a dissimilar asset* or by way of a government grant) because:

(a) this is consistent with IAS 16 *Property, Plant and Equipment.* IAS 16 prohibits the initial recognition of an item of property, plant or equipment at fair value (except in the specific limited cases as those in IAS 38).

(b) it is difficult to determine the fair value of an intangible asset reliably if no active market exists for the asset. Since active markets with the characteristics set out in IAS 38 are highly unlikely to exist for internally generated intangible assets, IASC did not believe that it was necessary to make an exception to the principles generally applied for the initial recognition and measurement of non-financial assets.

(c) the large majority of commentators on E50 supported the initial recognition of intangible assets at cost and the prohibition of the reinstatement of expenditure on an intangible item that was initially recognised as an expense.

Application of the recognition criteria for internally generated intangible assets

BCZ45 IAS 38 specifically prohibits the recognition as intangible assets of brands, mastheads, publishing titles, customer lists and items similar in substance that are internally generated. IASC believed that internally generated intangible items of this kind would rarely, and perhaps never, meet the recognition criteria in IAS 38. However, to avoid any misunderstanding, IASC decided to set out this conclusion in the form of an explicit prohibition.

BCZ46 IAS 38 also clarifies that expenditure on research, training, advertising and start-up activities will not result in the creation of an intangible asset that can be recognised in the financial statements. Whilst some view these requirements and guidance as being too restrictive and arbitrary, they are based on IASC's interpretation of the application of the recognition criteria in IAS 38. They also reflect the fact that it is sometimes difficult to determine whether there is an internally generated intangible asset distinguishable from internally generated goodwill.

Subsequent accounting for intangible assets

BC47 The Board initially decided that the scope of the first phase of its Business Combinations project should include a consideration of the subsequent accounting for intangible assets acquired in business combinations. To that end, the Board initially focused its attention on the following three issues:

* IAS 16 *Property, Plant and Equipment* (as revised in 2003) requires an entity to measure an item of property, plant and equipment acquired in exchange for a non-monetary asset or assets, or a combination of monetary and non-monetary assets, at fair value unless the exchange transaction lacks commercial substance. Previously, an entity measured such an acquired asset at fair value unless the exchanged assets were similar. The IASB concluded that the same measurement criteria should apply to intangible assets acquired in exchange for a non-monetary asset or assets, or a combination of monetary and non-monetary assets.

(a) whether an intangible asset with a finite useful life and acquired in a business combination should continue to be accounted for after initial recognition in accordance with IAS 38.

(b) whether, and under what circumstances, an intangible asset acquired in a business combination could be regarded as having an indefinite useful life.

(c) how an intangible asset with an indefinite useful life (assuming such an asset exists) acquired in a business combination should be accounted for after initial recognition.

BC48 However, during its deliberations of the issues in (b) and (c) of paragraph BC47, the Board decided that any conclusions it reached on those issues would equally apply to recognised intangible assets obtained other than in a business combination. The Board observed that amending the requirements in the previous version of IAS 38 only for intangible assets acquired in business combinations would create inconsistencies in the accounting for intangible assets depending on how they are obtained. Thus, similar items would be accounted for in dissimilar ways. The Board concluded that creating such inconsistencies would impair the usefulness of the information provided to users about an entity's intangible assets, because both comparability and reliability (which rests on the notion of representational faithfulness, ie that similar transactions are accounted for in the same way) would be diminished. Therefore, the Board decided that any amendments to the requirements in the previous version of IAS 38 to address the issues in (b) and (c) of paragraph BC47 should apply to all recognised intangible assets, whether generated internally or acquired separately or as part of a business combination.

BC49 Before beginning its deliberations of the issues identified in paragraph BC47, the Board noted the concern expressed by some that, because of the subjectivity involved in distinguishing goodwill from other intangible assets as at the acquisition date, differences between the subsequent treatment of goodwill and other intangible assets increases the potential for intangible assets to be misclassified at the acquisition date. The Board concluded, however, that adopting the separability and contractual or other legal rights criteria provides a reasonably definitive basis for separately identifying and recognising intangible assets acquired in a business combination. Therefore, the Board decided that its analysis of the accounting for intangible assets after initial recognition should have regard only to the nature of those assets and not to the subsequent treatment of goodwill.

Accounting for intangible assets with finite useful lives acquired in business combinations

BC50 The Board observed that the previous version of IAS 38 required an intangible asset to be measured after initial recognition:

(a) at cost less any accumulated amortisation and any accumulated impairment losses; or

(b) at a revalued amount, being the asset's fair value, determined by reference to an active market, at the date of revaluation less any subsequent accumulated amortisation and any subsequent accumulated impairment losses. Under this approach, revaluations must be made with such regularity that at the balance sheet date the carrying amount of the asset does not differ materially from its fair value.

Whichever of the above methods was used, the previous version of IAS 38 required the depreciable amount of the asset to be amortised on a systematic basis over the best estimate of its useful life.

BC51 The Board observed that underpinning the requirement for all intangible assets to be amortised is the notion that they all have determinable and finite useful lives. Setting aside the question of whether, and under what circumstances, an intangible asset could be regarded as having an indefinite useful life, an important issue for the Board to consider was whether a departure from the above requirements would be warranted for intangible assets acquired in a business combination that have finite useful lives.

BC52 The Board observed that any departure from the above requirements for intangible assets with finite lives acquired in business combinations would create inconsistencies between the accounting for recognised intangible assets based wholly on the means by which they are obtained. In other words, similar items would be accounted for in dissimilar ways. The Board concluded that creating such inconsistencies would impair the usefulness of the information provided to users about an entity's intangible assets, because both comparability and reliability would be diminished.

BC53 Therefore, the Board decided that intangible assets with finite useful lives acquired in business combinations should continue to be accounted for in accordance with the above requirements after initial recognition.

Impairment testing intangible assets with finite useful lives (paragraph 111)

BC54 The previous version of IAS 38 required the recoverable amount of an intangible asset with a finite useful life that is being amortised over a period of more than 20 years, whether or not acquired in a business combination, to be measured at least at each financial year-end.

BC55 The Board observed that the recoverable amount of a long-lived tangible asset needs to be measured only when, in accordance with IAS 36 *Impairment of Assets*, there is an indication that the asset may be impaired. The Board could see no conceptual reason for requiring the recoverable amounts of some identifiable assets being amortised over very long periods to be determined more regularly than for other identifiable assets being amortised or depreciated over similar periods. Therefore, the Board concluded that the recoverable amount of an intangible asset with a finite useful life that is amortised over a period of more than 20 years should be determined only when, in accordance with IAS 36, there is an indication that the asset may be impaired. Consequently, the Board decided to remove the requirement in the previous version of IAS 38 for the recoverable amount of such an intangible asset to be measured at least at each financial year-end.

BC56 The Board also decided that all of the requirements relating to impairment testing intangible assets should be included in IAS 36 rather than in IAS 38. Therefore, the Board relocated to IAS 36 the requirement in the previous version of IAS 38 that an entity should estimate at the end of each annual reporting period the recoverable amount of an intangible asset not yet available for use, irrespective of whether there is any indication that it may be impaired.

Residual value of an intangible asset with a finite useful life (paragraph 100)

BC57 In revising IAS 38, the Board considered whether to retain for intangible assets with finite useful lives the requirement in the previous version of IAS 38 for the residual value of an intangible asset to be assumed to be zero unless:

(a) there is a commitment by a third party to purchase the asset at the end of its useful life; or

(b) there is an active market for the asset and:

(i) the asset's residual value can be determined by reference to that market; and

(ii) it is probable that such a market will exist at the end of the asset's useful life.

BC58 The Board observed that the definition in the previous version of IAS 38 (as amended by IAS 16 when revised in 2003) of residual value required it to be estimated as if the asset were already of the age and in the condition expected at the end of the asset's useful life. Therefore, if the useful life of an intangible asset was shorter than its economic life because the entity expected to sell the asset before the end of that economic life, the asset's residual value would not be zero, irrespective of whether the conditions in paragraph BC57(a) or (b) are met.

BC59 Nevertheless, the Board observed that the requirement for the residual value of an intangible asset to be assumed to be zero unless the specified criteria are met was included in the previous version of IAS 38 as a means of preventing entities from circumventing the requirement in that Standard to amortise all intangible assets. Excluding this requirement from the revised Standard for finite-lived intangible assets would similarly provide a means of circumventing the requirement to amortise such intangible assets—by claiming that the residual value of such an asset was equal to or greater than its carrying amount, an entity could avoid amortising the asset, even though its useful life is finite. The Board concluded that it should not, as part of the Business Combinations project, modify the criteria for permitting a finite-lived intangible asset's residual value to be other than zero. However, the Board decided that this issue should be addressed as part of a forthcoming project on intangible assets.

Useful lives of intangible assets (paragraphs 88–96)

BC60 Consistently with the proposals in the Exposure Draft of Proposed Amendments to IAS 38, the Standard requires an intangible asset to be regarded by an entity as having an indefinite useful life when, based on an analysis of all of the relevant factors, there is no foreseeable limit to the period over which the asset is expected to generate net cash inflows for the entity.

BC61 In developing the Exposure Draft and the revised Standard, the Board observed that the useful life of an intangible asset is related to the expected cash inflows that are associated with that asset. The Board observed that, to be representationally faithful, the amortisation period for an intangible asset generally should reflect that useful life and, by extension, the cash flow streams associated with the asset. The Board concluded that it is possible for management to have the intention and the ability to maintain an intangible asset in such a way that there is no foreseeable limit on the period over which that particular asset is expected to generate net cash inflows for the entity. In other words, it is conceivable that an analysis of all the relevant factors (ie legal, regulatory, contractual, competitive, economic and other) could lead to a conclusion that there is no foreseeable limit to the period over which a particular intangible asset is expected to generate net cash inflows for the entity.

BC62 For example, the Board observed that some intangible assets are based on legal rights that are conveyed in perpetuity rather than for finite terms. As such, those assets may have cash flows associated with them that may be expected to continue for many years or even indefinitely. The Board concluded that if the cash flows are expected to continue for a finite period, the useful life of the asset is limited to that finite period. However, if the cash flows are expected to continue indefinitely, the useful life is indefinite.

BC63 The previous version of IAS 38 prescribed a presumptive maximum useful life for intangible assets of 20 years. In developing the Exposure Draft and the revised Standard, the Board concluded that such a presumption is inconsistent with the view that the amortisation period for an intangible asset should, to be representationally faithful, reflect its useful life and, by extension, the cash flow streams associated with the asset. Therefore, the Board decided not to include in the revised Standard a presumptive maximum useful life for intangible assets, even if they have finite useful lives.

BC64 Respondents to the Exposure Draft generally supported the Board's proposal to remove from IAS 38 the presumptive maximum useful life and instead to require useful life to be regarded as indefinite when, based on an analysis of all of the relevant factors, there is no foreseeable limit to the period of time over which the intangible asset is expected to generate net cash inflows for the entity. However, some respondents suggested that an inability to determine clearly the useful life of an asset applies equally to many items of property, plant and equipment. Nonetheless, entities are required to determine the useful lives of those items of property, plant and equipment, and allocate their depreciable amounts on a systematic basis over those useful lives. Those respondents suggested that there is no conceptual reason for treating intangible assets differently.

BC65 In considering these comments, the Board noted the following:

(a) an intangible asset's useful life would be regarded as indefinite in accordance with IAS 38 only when, based on an analysis of all of the relevant factors, there is no foreseeable limit to the period of time over which the asset is expected to generate net cash inflows for the entity. Difficulties in accurately determining an intangible asset's useful life do not provide a basis for regarding that useful life as indefinite.

(b) although the useful lives of both intangible and tangible assets are directly related to the period during which they are expected to generate net cash inflows for the entity, the expected physical utility to the entity of a tangible asset places an upper limit on the asset's useful life. In other words, the useful life of a tangible asset could never extend beyond the asset's expected physical utility to the entity.

The Board concluded that tangible assets (other than land) could not be regarded as having indefinite useful lives because there is always a foreseeable limit to the expected physical utility of the asset to the entity.

Useful life constrained by contractual or other legal rights (paragraphs 94–96)

BC66 The Board noted that the useful life of an intangible asset that arises from contractual or other legal rights is constrained by the duration of those rights. The useful life of such an asset cannot extend beyond the duration of those rights, and may be shorter. Accordingly, the Board concluded that in determining the useful life of an intangible asset, consideration should be given to the period that the entity expects to use the intangible asset, which is subject to the expiration of the contractual or other legal rights.

BC67 However, the Board also observed that such rights are often conveyed for limited terms that may be renewed. It therefore considered whether renewals should be assumed in determining the useful life of such an intangible asset. The Board noted that some types of licences are initially issued for finite periods but renewals are routinely granted at little cost, provided that licensees have complied with the applicable rules and regulations. Such licences are traded at prices that reflect more than the remaining term, thereby indicating that renewal at minimal cost is the general expectation. However, renewals are not assured for other types of licences and, even if they are renewed, substantial costs may be incurred to secure their renewal.

BC68 The Board concluded that because the useful lives of some intangible assets depend, in economic terms, on renewal and on the associated costs of renewal, the useful lives assigned to those assets should reflect renewal when there is evidence to support renewal without significant cost.

BC69 Respondents to the Exposure Draft generally supported this conclusion. Those that disagreed suggested that:

(a) when the renewal period depends on the decision of a third party and not merely on the fulfilment of specified conditions by the entity, it gives rise to a contingent asset because the third-party decision affects not only the cost of renewal but also the probability of obtaining it. Therefore, useful life should reflect renewal only when renewal is not subject to third-party approval.

(b) such a requirement would be inconsistent with the basis used to measure intangible assets at the date of a business combination, particularly contractual customer relationships. For example, it is not clear whether the fair value of a contractual customer relationship includes an amount that reflects the probability that the contract will be renewed. The possibility of renewal would have a fair value regardless of the costs required to renew.

This means the useful life of a contractual customer relationship could be inconsistent with the basis used to determine the fair value of the relationship.

BC70 In relation to (a) above, the Board observed that if renewal by the entity is subject to third-party (eg government) approval, the requirement that there be evidence to support the entity's ability to renew would compel the entity to make an assessment of the likely effect of the third-party approval process on the entity's ability to renew. The Board could see no conceptual basis for narrowing the requirement to situations in which the contractual or legal rights are not subject to the approval of third parties.

BC71 In relation to (b) above, the Board observed the following:

(a) the requirements relating to renewal periods address circumstances in which *the entity* is able to renew the contractual or other legal rights, notwithstanding that such renewal may, for example, be conditional on the entity satisfying specified conditions, or subject to third-party approval. Paragraph 94 of the Standard states that '... the useful life of the intangible asset shall include the renewal period(s) only if there is evidence to support renewal *by the entity* [emphasis added] without significant cost.' The ability to renew a customer contract normally rests with the customer and not with the entity.

(b) the respondents seem to regard as a single intangible asset what is, in substance, two intangible assets–one being the customer contract and the other being the related customer relationship. Expected renewals by the customer would affect the fair value of the customer relationship intangible asset, rather than the fair value of the customer contract. Therefore, the useful life of the customer contract would not, under the Standard, extend beyond the term of the contract, nor would the fair value of that customer contract reflect expectations of renewal by the customer. In other words, the useful life of the customer contract would not be inconsistent with the basis used to determine its fair value.

BC72 However, in response to respondents' suggestions, the Board included paragraph 96 in the Standard to provide additional guidance on the circumstances in which an entity should be regarded as being able to renew the contractual or other legal rights without significant cost.

Accounting for intangible assets with indefinite useful lives (paragraphs 107–110)

BC73 Consistently with the proposals in the Exposure Draft, the Standard prohibits the amortisation of intangible assets with indefinite useful lives. Therefore, such assets are measured after initial recognition at:

(a) cost less any accumulated impairment losses; or

(b) a revalued amount, being fair value determined by reference to an active market less any accumulated impairment losses.

Non–amortisation

BC74 In developing the Exposure Draft and the revised Standard, the Board observed that many assets yield benefits to an entity over several periods. Amortisation is the systematic allocation of the cost (or revalued amount) of an asset, less any residual value, to reflect the consumption over time of the future economic benefits embodied in that asset. Thus, if there is no foreseeable limit on the period during which an entity expects to consume the future economic benefits embodied in an asset, amortisation of that asset over, for example, an arbitrarily determined maximum period would not be representationally faithful. Respondents to the Exposure Draft generally supported this conclusion.

BC75 Consequently, the Board decided that intangible assets with indefinite useful lives should not be amortised, but should be subject to regular impairment testing. The Board's deliberations on the form of the impairment test, including the frequency of impairment testing, are included in the Basis for Conclusions on IAS 36. The Board further decided that regular re-examinations should be required of the useful life of an intangible asset that is not being amortised to determine whether circumstances continue to support the assessment that the useful life is indefinite.

Revaluations

BC76 Having decided that intangible assets with indefinite useful lives should not be amortised, the Board considered whether an entity should be permitted to carry such assets at revalued amounts. The Board could see no conceptual justification for precluding some intangible assets from being carried at revalued amounts solely on the basis that there is no foreseeable limit to the period over which an entity expects to consume the future economic benefits embodied in those assets.

BC77 As a result, the Board decided that the Standard should permit intangible assets with indefinite useful lives to be carried at revalued amounts.

Research and development projects acquired in business combinations

BC78 The Board considered the following issues in relation to in-process research and development (IPR&D) projects acquired in a business combination:

(a) whether the proposed criteria for recognising intangible assets acquired in a business combination separately from goodwill should also be applied to IPR&D projects;

(b) the subsequent accounting for IPR&D projects recognised as assets separately from goodwill; and

(c) the treatment of subsequent expenditure on IPR&D projects recognised as assets separately from goodwill.

The Board's deliberations on issue (a), although included in the Basis for Conclusions on IFRS 3, are also, for the sake of completeness, outlined below.

BC79 The Board did not reconsider as part of the first phase of its Business Combinations project the requirements in the previous version of IAS 38 for internally generated intangibles and expenditure on the research or development phase of an internal project. The Board decided that a reconsideration of those requirements is outside the scope of this project.

Initial recognition separately from goodwill

BC80 The Board observed that the criteria in IAS 22 *Business Combinations* and the previous version of IAS 38 for recognising an intangible asset acquired in a business combination separately from goodwill applied to all intangible assets, including IPR&D projects. Therefore, in accordance with those Standards, any intangible item acquired in a business combination was recognised as an asset separately from goodwill when it was identifiable and could be measured reliably, and it was probable that any associated future economic benefits would flow to the acquirer. If these criteria were not satisfied, the expenditure on the cost or value of that item, which was included in the cost of the combination, was part of the amount attributed to goodwill.

BC81 The Board could see no conceptual justification for changing the approach in IAS 22 and the previous version of IAS 38 of using the same criteria for all intangible assets acquired in a business combination when assessing whether those assets should be recognised separately from goodwill. The Board concluded that adopting different criteria would impair the usefulness of the information provided to users about the assets acquired in a combination because both comparability and reliability would be diminished. Therefore, IAS 38 and IFRS 3 require an acquirer to recognise as an asset separately from goodwill any of the acquiree's IPR&D projects that meet the definition of an intangible asset. This will be the case when the IPR&D project meets the definition of an asset and is identifiable, ie is separable or arises from contractual or other legal rights.

BC82 Some respondents to the Exposure Draft of Proposed Amendments to IAS 38 expressed concern that applying the same criteria to all intangible assets acquired in a business combination to assess whether they should be recognised separately from goodwill results in treating some IPR&D projects acquired in business combinations differently from similar projects started internally. The Board acknowledged this point, but concluded that this does not provide a basis for subsuming those acquired intangible assets within goodwill. Rather, it highlights a need to reconsider the conclusion in the Standard that an intangible asset can never exist in respect of an in-process research project and can exist in respect of an in-process development project only once all of the Standard's criteria for deferral have been satisfied. The Board decided that such a reconsideration is outside the scope of its Business Combinations project.

Subsequent accounting for IPR&D projects acquired in a business combination and recognised as intangible assets

BC83 The Board observed that the previous version of IAS 38 required all recognised intangible assets to be accounted for after initial recognition at:

(a) cost less any accumulated amortisation and any accumulated impairment losses; or

(b) revalued amount, being the asset's fair value, determined by reference to an active market, at the date of revaluation less any subsequent accumulated amortisation and any subsequent accumulated impairment losses.

Such assets included: IPR&D projects acquired in a business combination that satisfied the criteria for recognition separately from goodwill; separately acquired IPR&D projects that satisfied the criteria for recognition as an intangible asset; and recognised internally developed intangible assets arising from development or the development phase of an internal project.

BC84 The Board could see no conceptual justification for changing the approach in the previous version of IAS 38 of applying the same requirements to the subsequent accounting for all recognised intangible assets. Therefore, the Board decided that IPR&D projects acquired in a business combination that satisfy the criteria for recognition as an asset separately from goodwill should be accounted for after initial recognition in accordance with the requirements applying to the subsequent accounting for other recognised intangible assets.

Subsequent expenditure on IPR&D projects acquired in a business combination and recognised as intangible assets (paragraphs 42 and 43)

BC85 The Standard requires subsequent expenditure on an IPR&D project acquired separately or in a business combination and recognised as an intangible asset to be:

(a) recognised as an expense when incurred if it is research expenditure;

(b) recognised as an expense when incurred if it is development expenditure that does not satisfy the criteria for recognition as an intangible asset in paragraph 57; and

(c) added to the carrying amount of the acquired IPR&D project if it is development expenditure that satisfies the recognition criteria in paragraph 57.

BC86 In developing this requirement the Board observed that the treatment required under the previous version of IAS 38 of subsequent expenditure on an IPR&D project acquired in a business combination and recognised as an asset separately from goodwill was unclear. Some suggested that the requirements in the previous version of IAS 38 relating to expenditure on research, development, or the research or development phase of an internal project should be applied. However, others argued that those requirements were ostensibly concerned with the initial recognition and measurement of internally generated intangible assets. Instead, the requirements in the previous version of IAS 38 dealing with subsequent expenditure should be applied. Under those requirements, subsequent expenditure on an intangible asset after its purchase or completion would have been recognised as an expense when incurred unless:

(a) it was probable that the expenditure would enable the asset to generate future economic benefits in excess of its originally assessed standard of performance; and

(b) the expenditure could be measured and attributed to the asset reliably.

If these conditions were satisfied, the subsequent expenditure would be added to the carrying amount of the intangible asset.

BC87 The Board observed that this uncertainty also existed for separately acquired IPR&D projects that satisfied the criteria in the previous version of IAS 38 for recognition as intangible assets.

BC88 The Board noted that applying the requirements in the Standard for expenditure on research, development, or the research or development phase of an internal project to subsequent expenditure on IPR&D projects acquired in a business combination and recognised as assets separately from goodwill would result in such subsequent expenditure being treated inconsistently with subsequent expenditure on other recognised intangible assets. However, applying the subsequent expenditure requirements in the previous version of IAS 38 to subsequent expenditure on IPR&D projects acquired in a business combination and recognised as assets separately from goodwill would result in research and development expenditure being accounted for differently depending on whether a project is acquired or started internally.

BC89 The Board concluded that until it has had the opportunity to review the requirements in IAS 38 for expenditure on research, development, or the research or development phase of an internal project, more useful information will be provided to users of an entity's financial statements if all such expenditure is accounted for consistently. This includes subsequent expenditure on a separately acquired IPR&D project that satisfies the Standard's criteria for recognition as an intangible asset.

Transitional provisions (paragraphs 129–132)

BC90 If an entity elects to apply IFRS 3 from any date before the effective dates outlined in IFRS 3, it is also required to apply IAS 38 prospectively from that same date. Otherwise, IAS 38 applies to the accounting for intangible assets acquired in business combinations for which the agreement date is on or after 31 March 2004, and to the accounting for all other intangible assets prospectively from the beginning of the first annual reporting period beginning on or after 31 March 2004. IAS 38 also requires an entity, on initial application, to reassess the useful lives of intangible assets. If, as a result of that reassessment, the entity changes its useful life assessment for an asset, that change is accounted for as a change in an accounting estimate in accordance with IAS 8 *Accounting Policies, Changes in Accounting Estimates and Errors*.

BC91 The Board's deliberations on the transitional issues relating to the initial recognition of intangible assets acquired in business combinations and the impairment testing of intangible assets are addressed in the Basis for Conclusions on IFRS 3 and the Basis for Conclusions on IAS 36, respectively.

BC92 In developing the requirements outlined in paragraph BC90, the Board considered the following three questions:

(a) should the useful lives of, and the accounting for, intangible assets already recognised at the effective date of the Standard continue to be determined in accordance with the requirements in the previous version of IAS 38 (ie by amortising over a presumptive maximum period of twenty years), or in accordance with the requirements in the revised Standard?

(b) if the revised Standard is applied to intangible assets already recognised at its effective date, should the effect of a reassessment of an intangible asset's useful life as a result of the initial application of the Standard be recognised retrospectively or prospectively?

(c) should entities be required to apply the requirements in the Standard for subsequent expenditure on an acquired IPR&D project recognised as an intangible asset retrospectively to expenditure incurred before the effective date of the revised Standard?

BC93 In relation to the first question above, the Board noted its previous conclusion that the most representationally faithful method of accounting for intangible assets is to amortise those with finite useful lives over their useful lives with no limit on the amortisation period, and not to amortise those with indefinite useful lives. Thus, the Board concluded that the reliability and comparability of financial statements would be diminished if the Standard was not applied to intangible assets recognised before its effective date.

BC94 On the second question, the Board observed that a reassessment of an asset's useful life is regarded throughout IFRSs as a change in an accounting estimate, rather than a change in an accounting policy. For example, in accordance with the Standard, as with the previous version of IAS 38, if a new estimate of the expected useful life of an intangible asset is significantly different from previous estimates, the change must be accounted for as a change in accounting estimate in accordance with IAS 8. IAS 8 requires a change in an accounting estimate to be accounted for prospectively by including the effect of the change in profit or loss in:

(a) the period of the change, if the change in estimate affects that period only; or

(b) the period of the change and future periods, if the change in estimate affects both.

BC95 Similarly, in accordance with IAS 16 *Property, Plant and Equipment*, if a new estimate of the expected useful life of an item of property, plant and equipment is significantly different from previous estimates, the change must be accounted for prospectively by adjusting the depreciation expense for the current and future periods.

BC96 Therefore, the Board decided that a reassessment of useful life resulting from the initial application of IAS 38, including a reassessment from a finite to an indefinite useful life, should be accounted for as a change in an accounting estimate. Consequently, the effect of such a change should be recognised prospectively.

BC97 The Board considered the view that because the previous version of IAS 38 required intangible assets to be treated as having a finite useful life, a change to an assessment of indefinite useful life for an intangible asset represents a change in an accounting policy, rather than a change in an accounting estimate. The Board concluded that, even if this were the case, the useful life reassessment should nonetheless be accounted for prospectively. This is because retrospective application would require an entity to determine whether, at the end of each reporting period before the effective date of the Standard, the useful life of an intangible asset was indefinite. Such an assessment requires an entity to make estimates that would have been made at a prior date, and therefore raises problems in relation to the role of hindsight, in particular, whether the benefit of hindsight should be included or excluded from those estimates and, if excluded, how the effect of hindsight can be separated from the other factors existing at the date for which the estimates are required.

BC98 On the third question, and as noted in paragraph BC86, it was not clear whether the previous version of IAS 38 required subsequent expenditure on acquired IPR&D projects recognised as intangible assets to be accounted for:

(a) in accordance with its requirements for expenditure on research, development, or the research or development phase of an internal project; or

(b) in accordance with its requirements for subsequent expenditure on an intangible asset after its purchase or completion.

The Board concluded that subsequent expenditure on an acquired IPR&D project that was capitalised under (b) above before the effective date of the Standard might not have been capitalised had the Standard applied when the subsequent expenditure was incurred. This is because the Standard requires such expenditure to be capitalised as an intangible asset only when it is development expenditure and all of the criteria for deferral are satisfied. In the Board's view, those criteria represent a higher recognition threshold than (b) above.

BC99 Thus, retrospective application of the revised Standard to subsequent expenditure on acquired IPR&D projects incurred before its effective date could result in previously capitalised expenditure being reversed. Such reversal would be required if the expenditure was research expenditure, or it was development expenditure and one or more of the criteria for deferral were not satisfied at the time the expenditure was incurred. The Board concluded that determining whether, at the time the subsequent expenditure was incurred, the criteria for deferral were satisfied raises the same hindsight issues discussed in paragraph BC97: it would require assessments to be made as of a prior date, and therefore raises problems in relation to how the effect of hindsight can be separated from factors existing at the date of the assessment. In addition, such assessments could, in many cases, be impossible: the information needed may not exist or no longer be obtainable.

BC100 Therefore, the Board decided that the Standard's requirements for subsequent expenditure on acquired IPR&D projects recognised as intangible assets should not be applied retrospectively to expenditure incurred before the revised Standard's effective date. The Board noted that any amounts previously included in the carrying amount of such an asset would, in any event, be subject to the requirements for impairment testing in IAS 36.

Early application (paragraph 132)

BC101 The Board noted that the issue of any Standard reflects its opinion that application of the Standard will result in more useful information being provided to users about an entity's financial position, performance or cash flows. On that basis, a case exists for permitting, and indeed encouraging, entities to apply the revised Standard before its effective date. However, the Board also considered the assertion that permitting a revised Standard to be applied before its effective date potentially diminishes comparability between entities in the period(s) leading up to that effective date, and has the effect of providing entities with an option.

BC102 The Board concluded that the benefit of providing users with more useful information about an entity's financial position and performance by permitting early application of the Standard outweighs the disadvantages of potentially diminished comparability. Therefore, entities are encouraged to apply the requirements of the revised Standard before its effective date, provided they also apply IFRS 3 and IAS 36 (as revised in 2004) at the same time.

Summary of main changes from the Exposure Draft

BC103 The following are the main changes from the Exposure Draft of Proposed Amendments to IAS 38:

(a) The Standard includes additional guidance clarifying the relationship between the separability criterion for establishing whether a non-contractual customer relationship is identifiable, and the control concept for establishing whether the relationship meets the definition of an asset. In particular, the Standard clarifies that in the absence of legal rights to protect customer relationships, exchange transactions for the same or similar non-contractual customer relationships (other than as part of a business combination) provide evidence that the entity is nonetheless able to control the future economic benefits flowing from the customer relationships. Because such exchange transactions also provide evidence that the customer relationships are separable, those customer relationships meet the definition of an intangible asset (see paragraphs BC11–BC14).

(b) The Exposure Draft proposed that, except for an assembled workforce, an intangible asset acquired in a business combination should always be recognised separately from goodwill; there was a presumption that sufficient information would always exist to measure reliably its fair value. The Standard states that the fair value of an intangible asset acquired in a business combination can *normally* be measured with sufficient reliability to qualify for recognition separately from goodwill. If an intangible asset acquired in a business combination has a finite useful life, there is a rebuttable presumption that its fair value can be measured reliably (see paragraphs BC16–BC25).

(c) The Exposure Draft proposed, and the Standard requires, that the useful life of an intangible asset arising from contractual or other legal rights should not exceed the period of those rights. However, if the rights are conveyed for a limited term that can be renewed, the useful life should include the renewal period(s) only if there is evidence to support renewal by the entity without significant cost. Additional guidance has been included in the Standard to clarify the circumstances in which an entity should be regarded as being able to renew the contractual or other legal rights without significant cost (see paragraphs BC66–BC72).

History of the development of a standard on intangible assets

BCZ104 IASC published a Draft Statement of Principles on Intangible Assets in January 1,994 and an Exposure Draft E50 *Intangible Assets* in June 1995. Principles in both documents were consistent as far as possible with those in IAS 16 *Property, Plant and Equipment*. The principles were also greatly influenced by the decisions reached in 1993 during the revisions to the treatment of research and development costs and goodwill.

BCZ105 IASC received about 100 comment letters on E50 from over 20 countries. Comment letters on E50 showed that the proposal for the amortisation period for intangible assets—a 20-year ceiling for almost all intangible assets, as required for goodwill in IAS 22 (revised 1993)—raised significant controversy and created serious concerns about the overall acceptability of the proposed standard on intangible assets. IASC considered alternative solutions and concluded in March 1996 that, if an impairment test that is sufficiently robust and reliable could be developed, IASC would propose deleting the 20-year ceiling on the amortisation period for both intangible assets and goodwill.

BCZ106 In August 1997, IASC published proposals for revised treatments for intangible assets and goodwill in Exposure Drafts E60 *Intangible Assets* and E61 *Business Combinations*. This followed the publication of Exposure Draft E55 *Impairment of Assets* in May 1997, which set out detailed proposals for impairment testing.

BCZ107 E60 proposed two major changes to the proposals in E50:

(a) as explained above, revised proposals for the amortisation of intangible assets; and

(b) combining the requirements relating to all internally generated intangible assets in one standard. This meant including certain aspects of IAS 9 *Research and Development Costs* in the proposed standard on intangible assets and withdrawing IAS 9.

BCZ108 Among other proposed changes, E61 proposed revisions to IAS 22 to make the requirements for the amortisation of goodwill consistent with those proposed for intangible assets.

BCZ109 IASC received about 100 comment letters on E60 and E61 from over 20 countries. The majority of the commentators supported most of the proposals in E60 and E61, although some proposals still raised significant controversy. The proposals for impairment tests were also supported by most commentators on E55.

BCZ110 After considering the comments received on E55, E60 and E61, IASC approved:

(a) IAS 36 *Impairment of Assets* (April 1998);

(b) IAS 38 *Intangible Assets* (July 1998);

(c) a revised IAS 22 *Business Combinations* (July 1998); and

(d) withdrawal of IAS 9 *Research and Development Costs* (July 1998).

Dissenting Opinion

Dissent of Geoffrey Whittington

DO1 Professor Whittington dissents from the issue of this Standard because it does not explicitly require the probability recognition criterion in paragraph 21(a) to be applied to intangible assets acquired in a business combination, notwithstanding that it applies to all other intangible assets.

DO2 The reason given for this (paragraphs 33 and BC17) is that fair value is the required measurement on acquisition of an intangible asset as part of a business combination, and fair value incorporates probability assessments. Professor Whittington does not believe that the *Framework* precludes having a prior recognition test based on probability, even when subsequent recognition is at fair value. Moreover, the application of probability may be different for recognition purposes: for example, it may be the 'more likely than not' criterion used in IAS 37 *Provisions, Contingent Liabilities and Contingent Assets*, rather than the 'expected value' approach used in the measurement of fair value.

DO3 This inconsistency between the recognition criteria in the *Framework* and fair values is acknowledged in paragraph BC18. In Professor Whittington's view, the inconsistency should be resolved before changing the recognition criteria for intangible assets acquired in a business combination.

IAS 38 Intangible Assets Illustrative Examples

These examples accompany, but are not part of, IAS 38.

Assessing the useful lives of intangible assets

The following guidance provides examples on determining the useful life of an intangible asset in accordance with IAS 38.

Each of the following examples describes an acquired intangible asset, the facts and circumstances surrounding the determination of its useful life, and the subsequent accounting based on that determination.

Example 1 An acquired customer list

A direct-mail marketing company acquires a customer list and expects that it will be able to derive benefit from the information on the list for at least one year, but no more than three years.

The customer list would be amortised over management's best estimate of its useful life, say 18 months. Although the direct-mail marketing company may intend to add customer names and other information to the list in the future, the expected benefits of the acquired customer list relate only to the customers on that list at the date it was acquired. The customer list also would be reviewed for impairment in accordance with IAS 36 *Impairment of Assets* by assessing at each reporting date whether there is any indication that the customer list may be impaired.

Example 2 An acquired patent that expires in 15 years

The product protected by the patented technology is expected to be a source of net cash inflows for at least 15 years. The entity has a commitment from a third party to purchase that patent in five years for 60 per cent of the fair value of the patent at the date it was acquired, and the entity intends to sell the patent in five years.

The patent would be amortised over its five-year useful life to the entity, with a residual value equal to the present value of 60 per cent of the patent's fair value at the date it was acquired. The patent would also be reviewed for impairment in accordance with IAS 36 by assessing at each reporting date whether there is any indication that it may be impaired.

Example 3 An acquired copyright that has a remaining legal life of 50 years

An analysis of consumer habits and market trends provides evidence that the copyrighted material will generate net cash inflows for only 30 more years.

The copyright would be amortised over its 30-year estimated useful life. The copyright also would be reviewed for impairment in accordance with IAS 36 by assessing at each reporting date whether there is any indication that it may be impaired.

Example 4 An acquired broadcasting licence that expires in five years

The broadcasting licence is renewable every 10 years if the entity provides at least an average level of service to its customers and complies with the relevant legislative requirements. The licence may be renewed indefinitely at little cost and has been renewed twice before the most recent acquisition. The acquiring entity intends to renew the licence indefinitely and evidence supports its ability to do so. Historically, there has been no compelling challenge to the licence renewal. The technology used in broadcasting is not expected to be replaced by another technology at any time in the foreseeable future. Therefore, the licence is expected to contribute to the entity's net cash inflows indefinitely.

The broadcasting licence would be treated as having an indefinite useful life because it is expected to contribute to the entity's net cash inflows indefinitely. Therefore, the licence would not be amortised until its useful life is determined to be finite. The licence would be tested for impairment in accordance with IAS 36 annually and whenever there is an indication that it may be impaired.

Example 5 The broadcasting licence in Example 4

The licensing authority subsequently decides that it will no longer renew broadcasting licences, but rather will auction the licences. At the time the licensing authority's decision is made, the entity's broadcasting licence has three years until it expires. The entity expects that the licence will continue to contribute to net cash inflows until the licence expires.

Because the broadcasting licence can no longer be renewed, its useful life is no longer indefinite. Thus, the acquired licence would be amortised over its remaining three-year useful life and immediately tested for impairment in accordance with IAS 36.

Example 6 An acquired airline route authority between two European cities that expires in three years

The route authority may be renewed every five years, and the acquiring entity intends to comply with the applicable rules and regulations surrounding renewal. Route authority renewals are routinely granted at a minimal cost and historically have been renewed when the airline has complied with the applicable rules and regulations. The acquiring entity expects to provide service indefinitely between the two cities from its hub airports and expects that the related supporting infrastructure (airport gates, slots, and terminal facility leases) will remain in place at those airports for as long as it has the route authority. An analysis of demand and cash flows supports those assumptions.

Because the facts and circumstances support the acquiring entity's ability to continue providing air service indefinitely between the two cities, the intangible asset related to the route authority is treated as having an indefinite useful life. Therefore, the route authority would not be amortised until its useful life is determined to be finite. It would be tested for impairment in accordance with IAS 36 annually and whenever there is an indication that it may be impaired.

Example 7 An acquired trademark used to identify and distinguish a leading consumer product that has been a market-share leader for the past eight years

The trademark has a remaining legal life of five years but is renewable every 10 years at little cost. The acquiring entity intends to renew the trademark continuously and evidence supports its ability to do so. An analysis of (1) product life cycle studies, (2) market, competitive and environmental trends, and (3) brand extension opportunities provides evidence that the trademarked product will generate net cash inflows for the acquiring entity for an indefinite period.

The trademark would be treated as having an indefinite useful life because it is expected to contribute to net cash inflows indefinitely. Therefore, the trademark would not be amortised until its useful life is determined to be finite. It would be tested for impairment in accordance with IAS 36 annually and whenever there is an indication that it may be impaired.

Example 8 A trademark acquired 10 years ago that distinguishes a leading consumer product

The trademark was regarded as having an indefinite useful life when it was acquired because the trademarked product was expected to generate net cash inflows indefinitely. However, unexpected competition has recently entered the market and will reduce future sales of the product. Management estimates that net cash inflows generated by the product will be 20 per cent less for the foreseeable future. However, management expects that the product will continue to generate net cash inflows indefinitely at those reduced amounts.

As a result of the projected decrease in future net cash inflows, the entity determines that the estimated recoverable amount of the trademark is less than its carrying amount, and an impairment loss is recognised. Because it is still regarded as having an indefinite useful life, the trademark would continue not to be amortised but would be tested for impairment in accordance with IAS 36 annually and whenever there is an indication that it may be impaired.

Example 9 A trademark for a line of products that was acquired several years ago in a business combination

At the time of the business combination the acquiree had been producing the line of products for 35 years with many new models developed under the trademark. At the acquisition date the acquirer expected to continue producing the line, and an analysis of various economic factors indicated there was no limit to the period the trademark would contribute to net cash inflows. Consequently, the trademark was not amortised by the acquirer. However, management has recently decided that production of the product line will be discontinued over the next four years.

Because the useful life of the acquired trademark is no longer regarded as indefinite, the carrying amount of the trademark would be tested for impairment in accordance with IAS 36 and amortised over its remaining four-year useful life.

Table of Concordance

This table shows how the contents of the superseded version of IAS 38 and the current version of IAS 38 correspond. Paragraphs are treated as corresponding if they broadly address the same matter.

Superseded IAS 38 paragraph	Current IAS 38 paragraph	Superseded IAS 38 paragraph	Current IAS 38 paragraph	Superseded IAS 38 paragraph	Current IAS 38 paragraph
Objective	1	29	40	58	70
1	2	30	41	59	71
2	3	31	34	60	18, 21
3	4	32	None	61	20
4	5	33	44	62	20
5	6	34	45–47	63	72, 74
6	7	35	45–47	64	72, 75
7	8	36	48	65	76
8	9	37	40	66	77
9	10	38	50	67	78
10	11	39	51	68	79
11	12	40	52	69	80
12	12	41	53	70	72
13	13	42	54	71	73
14	14	43	55	72	81
15	15	44	56	73	82
16	16	45	57	74	83
17	17	46	58	75	84
18	18	47	59	76	85
19	21	48	60	77	86
20	22	49	61	78	87
21	23, 25, 33	50	62	79	97
22	24	51	63	80	90
23	26	52	64	81	92
24	27, 28	53	65	82	None
25	32	54	66	83	None
26	None[(a)]	55	67	84	93
27	33	56	68	85	94
28	35, 38, 39	57	69	86	95

Superseded IAS 38 paragraph	Current IAS 38 paragraph
87	96
88	97
89	98
90	99
91	100
92	101
93	102
94	104
95	105
96	106
97	111
98	None
99	None[(b)]
100	None[(c)]
101	None
102	None

Superseded IAS 38 paragraph	Current IAS 38 paragraph
103	112
104	113
105	None
106	None
107	118
108	119
109	120
110	121
111	122
112	123
113	124
114	125
115	126
116	127
117	128
118–122	129–131

Superseded IAS 38 paragraph	Current IAS 38 paragraph
123	133
None	19
None	29–31
None	36, 37
None	42, 43
None	88, 89
None	91
None	103
None	107–110
None	114–117
None	132
None	Illustrative Examples

(a) Now addressed in IFRS 2 *Share-based Payment*

(b) Modified and relocated to IAS 36 *Impairment of Assets*

(c) Relocated to IAS 36

International Accounting Standard 39

Financial Instruments: Recognition and Measurement

This version includes amendments resulting from IFRIC 5 Rights to Interests arising from Decommissioning, Restoration and Environmental Rehabilitation Funds *and the amendment to IAS 39* Financial Instruments: Recognition and Measurement—Transition and Initial Recognition of Financial Assets and Financial Liabilities *issued in December 2004.*

CONTENTS

ILLUSTRATIVE EXAMPLE

TABLE OF CONCORDANCE OF IAS 39

IMPLEMENTATION GUIDANCE

TABLE OF CONCORDANCE OF IMPLEMENTATION GUIDANCE

International Accounting Standard 39 *Financial Instruments: Recognition and Measurement* (IAS 39) is set out in paragraphs 1–110 and Appendices A and B. All the paragraphs have equal authority but retain the IASC format of the Standard when it was adopted by the IASB. IAS 39 should be read in the context of its objective and the Basis for Conclusions, the *Preface to International Financial Reporting Standards* and the *Framework for the Preparation and Presentation of Financial Statements*. IAS 8 *Accounting Policies, Changes in Accounting Estimates and Errors* provides a basis for selecting and applying accounting policies in the absence of explicit guidance.

Introduction

Reasons for revising IAS 39

IN1 International Accounting Standard 39 *Financial Instruments: Recognition and Measurement* (IAS 39) replaces IAS 39 *Financial Instruments: Recognition and Measurement* (revised in 2000) and should be applied for annual periods beginning on or after 1 January 2005. Earlier application is permitted. Implementation Guidance accompanying this revised IAS 39 replaces the Questions and Answers published by the former Implementation Guidance Committee (IGC).

IN2 The International Accounting Standards Board has developed this revised IAS 39 as part of its project to improve IAS 32 *Financial Instruments: Disclosure and Presentation* and IAS 39. The objective of this project was to reduce complexity by clarifying and adding guidance, eliminating internal inconsistencies and incorporating into the Standard elements of Standing Interpretations Committee (SIC) Interpretations and Questions and Answers published by the IGC.

IN3 For IAS 39, the Board's main objective was a limited revision to provide additional guidance on selected matters such as derecognition, when financial assets and financial liabilities may be measured at fair value, how to assess impairment, how to determine fair value and some aspects of hedge accounting. The Board did not reconsider the fundamental approach to the accounting for financial instruments contained in IAS 39.

The main changes

IN4 The main changes from the previous version of IAS 39 are described below.

Scope

IN5 The treatment of financial guarantee contracts has been reviewed. Such a contract is within the scope of this Standard if it is not an insurance contract, as defined in IFRS 4 *Insurance Contracts.* Furthermore, if an entity entered into, or retained, a financial guarantee on transferring to another party financial assets or financial liabilities within the scope of the Standard, the entity applies the Standard to that contract, even if the contract meets the definition of an insurance contract. The Board expects to issue in the near future an Exposure Draft proposing amendments to the treatment of financial guarantees within the scope of IFRS 4.

IN6 A second scope exclusion has been added for loan commitments that are not classified as at fair value through profit or loss and cannot be settled net. A commitment to provide a loan at a below-market interest rate is measured at the higher of (a) the amount that would be recognised under IAS 37 and (b) the amount initially recognised less, where appropriate, cumulative amortisation recognised in accordance with IAS 18 *Revenue*.

IN7 The Standard continues to require that a contract to buy or sell a non-financial item is within the scope of IAS 39 if it can be settled net in cash or another financial instrument, unless it is entered into and continues to be held for the purpose of receipt or delivery of a non-financial item in accordance with the entity's expected purchase, sale or usage requirements. However, the Standard clarifies that there are various ways in which a contract to buy or sell a non-financial asset can be settled net. These include: when the entity has a practice of settling similar contracts net in cash or another financial instrument, or by exchanging financial instruments; when the entity has a practice of taking delivery of the underlying and selling it within a short period after delivery for the purpose of generating a profit from short-term fluctuations in price or dealer's margin; and when the non-financial item that is the subject of the contract is readily convertible to cash. The Standard also clarifies that a written option that can be settled net in cash or another financial instrument, or by exchanging financial instruments, is within the scope of the Standard.

Definitions

IN8 The Standard amends the definition of 'originated loans and receivables' to become 'loans and receivables'. Under the revised definition, an entity is permitted to classify as loans and receivables purchased loans that are not quoted in an active market.

Derecognition of a financial asset

IN9 Under the original IAS 39, several concepts governed when a financial asset should be derecognised. Although the revised Standard retains the two main concepts of *risks and rewards* and *control*, it clarifies that the evaluation of the transfer of risks and rewards of ownership precedes the evaluation of the transfer of control for all derecognition transactions.

IN10 Under the Standard, an entity determines what asset is to be considered for derecognition. The Standard requires a part of a larger financial asset to be considered for derecognition if, and only if, the part is one of:

(a) specifically identified cash flows from a financial asset; or

(b) a fully proportionate (pro rata) share of the cash flows from a financial asset; or

(c) a fully proportionate (pro rata) share of specifically identified cash flows from a financial asset.

In all other cases, the Standard requires the financial asset to be considered for derecognition in its entirety.

IN11 The Standard introduces the notion of a 'transfer' of a financial asset. A financial asset is derecognised when (a) an entity has transferred a financial asset and (b) the transfer qualifies for derecognition.

IN12 The Standard states that an entity has transferred a financial asset if, and only if, it either:

(a) retains the contractual rights to receive the cash flows of the financial asset, but assumes a contractual obligation to pay those cash flows to one or more recipients in an arrangement that meets three specified conditions; or

(b) transfers the contractual rights to receive the cash flows of a financial asset.

IN13 Under the Standard, if an entity has transferred a financial asset, it assesses whether it has transferred substantially all the risks and rewards of ownership of the transferred asset. If an entity has retained substantially all such risks and rewards, it continues to recognise the transferred asset. If it has transferred substantially all such risks and rewards, it derecognises the transferred asset.

IN14 The Standard specifies that if an entity has neither transferred nor retained substantially all the risks and rewards of ownership of the transferred asset, it assesses whether it has retained control over the transferred asset. If it has retained control, the entity continues to recognise the transferred asset to the extent of its continuing involvement in the transferred asset. If it has not retained control, the entity derecognises the transferred asset.

IN15 The Standard provides guidance on how to apply the concepts of risks and rewards and of control.

Measurement: fair value option

IN16 The Standard permits an entity to designate any financial asset or financial liability on initial recognition as one to be measured at fair value, with changes in fair value recognised in profit or loss. To impose discipline on this categorisation, an entity is precluded from reclassifying financial instruments into or out of this category.

IN17 The option previously contained in IAS 39 to recognise in profit or loss gains and losses on available-for-sale financial assets has been eliminated. Such an option is no longer necessary because under the amendments to IAS 39 an entity is now permitted by designation to measure any financial asset or financial liability at fair value with gains and losses recognised in profit or loss.

How to determine fair value

IN18 The Standard provides the following additional guidance about how to determine fair values using valuation techniques.

- The objective is to establish what the transaction price would have been on the measurement date in an arm's length exchange motivated by normal business considerations.
- A valuation technique (a) incorporates all factors that market participants would consider in setting a price and (b) is consistent with accepted economic methodologies for pricing financial instruments.
- In applying valuation techniques, an entity uses estimates and assumptions that are consistent with available information about the estimates and assumptions that market participants would use in setting a price for the financial instrument.
- The best estimate of fair value at initial recognition of a financial instrument that is not quoted in an active market is the transaction price unless the fair value of the instrument is evidenced by other observable market transactions or is based on a valuation technique whose variables include only data from observable markets.

IN19 The Standard also clarifies that the fair value of a liability with a demand feature, eg a demand deposit, is not less than the amount payable on demand, discounted from the first date that the amount could be required to be paid.

Impairment of financial assets

IN20 The Standard clarifies that an impairment loss is recognised only when it has been incurred. It also provides additional guidance on what events provide objective evidence of impairment for investments in equity instruments.

IN21 The Standard provides additional guidance about how to evaluate impairment that is inherent in a group of loans, receivables or held-to-maturity investments, but cannot yet be identified with any individual financial asset in the group, as follows:

- An asset that is individually assessed for impairment and found to be impaired should not be included in a group of assets that are collectively assessed for impairment.
- An asset that has been individually assessed for impairment and found *not* to be individually impaired should be included in a collective assessment of impairment. The occurrence of an event or a combination of events should not be a precondition for including an asset in a group of assets that are collectively evaluated for impairment.
- When performing a collective assessment of impairment, an entity groups assets by similar credit risk characteristics that are indicative of the debtors' ability to pay all amounts due according to the contractual terms.
- Contractual cash flows and historical loss experience provide the basis for estimating expected cash flows. Historical loss rates are adjusted on the basis of relevant observable data that reflect current economic conditions.
- The methodology for measuring impairment should ensure that an impairment loss is not recognised on the initial recognition of an asset.

IN22 The Standard requires that impairment losses on available-for-sale equity instruments cannot be reversed through profit or loss, ie any subsequent increase in fair value is recognised in equity.

Hedge accounting

IN23 Hedges of firm commitments are now treated as fair value hedges rather than cash flow hedges. However, the Standard clarifies that a hedge of the foreign currency risk of a firm commitment can be treated as either a cash flow hedge or a fair value hedge.

IN24 The Standard requires that when a hedged forecast transaction occurs and results in the recognition of a *financial* asset or a *financial* liability, the gain or loss deferred in equity does not adjust the initial carrying amount of the asset or liability (ie basis adjustment is prohibited), but remains in equity and is recognised in profit or loss consistently with the recognition of gains and losses on the asset or liability. For hedges of forecast transactions that result in the recognition of a *non-financial* asset or a *non-financial* liability, the entity has a choice of whether to apply basis adjustment or retain the hedging gain or loss in equity and report it in profit or loss when the asset or liability affects profit or loss.

IN24A This Standard permits fair value hedge accounting to be used more readily for a portfolio hedge of interest rate risk than previous versions of IAS 39. In particular, for such a hedge, it allows:

(a) the hedged item to be designated as an amount of a currency (eg an amount of dollars, euro, pounds or rand) rather than as individual assets (or liabilities).

(b) the gain or loss attributable to the hedged item to be presented either:

(i) in a single separate line item within assets, for those repricing time periods for which the hedged item is an asset; or

(ii) in a single separate line item within liabilities, for those repricing time periods for which the hedged item is a liability.

(c) prepayment risk to be incorporated by scheduling prepayable items into repricing time periods based on expected, rather than contractual, repricing dates. However, when the portion hedged is based on expected repricing dates, the effect that changes in the hedged interest rate have on those expected repricing dates are included when determining the change in the fair value of the hedged item. Consequently, if a portfolio that contains prepayable items is hedged with a non-prepayable derivative, ineffectiveness arises if the dates on which items in the hedged portfolio are expected to prepay are revised, or actual prepayment dates differ from those expected.

Disclosure

IN25 The disclosure requirements previously in IAS 39 have been moved to IAS 32.

Amendments to and withdrawal of other pronouncements

IN26 As a consequence of the revisions to this Standard, the Implementation Guidance developed by IASC's IAS 39 Implementation Guidance Committee is superseded by this Standard and its accompanying Implementation Guidance.

Potential impact of proposals in exposure drafts

IN27 [Deleted]

International Accounting Standard 39
Financial Instruments: Recognition and Measurement

Objective

1 The objective of this Standard is to establish principles for recognising and measuring financial assets, financial liabilities and some contracts to buy or sell non-financial items. Requirements for presenting and disclosing information about financial instruments are set out in IAS 32 *Financial Instruments: Disclosure and Presentation.*

Scope

2 **This Standard shall be applied by all entities to all types of financial instruments except:**

(a) those interests in subsidiaries, associates and joint ventures that are accounted for under IAS 27 *Consolidated and Separate Financial Statements,* **IAS 28** *Investments in Associates* **or IAS 31** *Interests in Joint Ventures.* **However, entities shall apply this Standard to an interest in a subsidiary, associate or joint venture that according to IAS 27, IAS 28 or IAS 31 is accounted for under this Standard. Entities shall also apply this Standard to derivatives on an interest in a subsidiary, associate or joint venture unless the derivative meets the definition of an equity instrument of the entity in IAS 32.**

(b) rights and obligations under leases to which IAS 17 *Leases* **applies. However:**

(i) lease receivables recognised by a lessor are subject to the derecognition and impairment provisions of this Standard (see paragraphs 15–37, 58, 59, 63–65 and Appendix A paragraphs AG36–AG52 and AG84–AG93);

(ii) finance lease payables recognised by a lessee are subject to the derecognition provisions of this Standard (see paragraphs 39–42 and Appendix A paragraphs AG57–AG63); and

(iii) derivatives that are embedded in leases are subject to the embedded derivatives provisions of this Standard (see paragraphs 10–13 and Appendix A paragraphs AG27–AG33).

(c) employers' rights and obligations under employee benefit plans, to which IAS 19 *Employee Benefits* **applies.**

(d) financial instruments issued by the entity that meet the definition of an equity instrument in IAS 32 (including options and warrants). However, the holder of such equity instruments shall apply this Standard to those instruments, unless they meet the exception in (a) above.

(e) rights and obligations under an insurance contract as defined in IFRS 4 *Insurance Contracts* **or under a contract that is within the scope of**

IFRS 4 because it contains a discretionary participation feature. However, this Standard applies to a derivative that is embedded in such a contract if the derivative is not itself a contract within the scope of IFRS 4 (see paragraphs 10–13 and Appendix A paragraphs AG23–AG33). Furthermore, if an insurance contract is a financial guarantee contract entered into, or retained, on transferring to another party financial assets or financial liabilities within the scope of this Standard, the issuer shall apply this Standard to the contract (see paragraph 3 and Appendix A paragraph AG4A).

(f) **contracts for contingent consideration in a business combination (see IFRS 3 *Business Combinations*). This exemption applies only to the acquirer.**

(g) **contracts between an acquirer and a vendor in a business combination to buy or sell an acquiree at a future date.**

(h) **except as described in paragraph 4, loan commitments that cannot be settled net in cash or another financial instrument. A loan commitment is not regarded as settled net merely because the loan is paid out in instalments (for example, a mortgage construction loan that is paid out in instalments in line with the progress of construction). An issuer of a commitment to provide a loan at a below-market interest rate shall initially recognise it at fair value, and subsequently measure it at the higher of (i) the amount recognised under IAS 37 and (ii) the amount initially recognised less, where appropriate, cumulative amortisation recognised in accordance with IAS 18. An issuer of loan commitments shall apply IAS 37 to other loan commitments that are not within the scope of this Standard. Loan commitments are subject to the derecognition provisions of this Standard (see paragraphs 15–42 and Appendix A paragraphs AG36–AG63).**

(i) **financial instruments, contracts and obligations under share-based payment transactions to which IFRS 2 *Share-based Payment* applies, except for contracts within the scope of paragraphs 5–7 of this Standard, to which this Standard applies.**

(j) **rights to payments to reimburse the entity for expenditure it is required to make to settle a liability that it recognises as a provision in accordance with IAS 37 *Provisions, Contingent Liabilities and Contingent Assets*, or for which, in an earlier period, it recognised a provision in accordance with IAS 37.**

3 Some financial guarantee contracts require the issuer to make specified payments to reimburse the holder for a loss it incurs because a specified debtor fails to make payment when due under the original or modified terms of a debt instrument. If that requirement transfers significant risk to the issuer, the contract is an insurance contract as defined in IFRS 4 (see paragraphs 2(e) and AG4A). Other financial guarantee contracts require payments to be made in response to changes in a specified interest rate, financial instrument price, commodity price, foreign exchange rate, index of prices or rates, credit rating or credit index, or other

variable, provided in the case of a non-financial variable that the variable is not specific to a party to the contract. Such contracts are within the scope of this Standard.

4 **Loan commitments that the entity designates as financial liabilities at fair value through profit or loss are within the scope of this Standard. An entity that has a past practice of selling the assets resulting from its loan commitments shortly after origination shall apply this Standard to all its loan commitments in the same class.**

5 **This Standard shall be applied to those contracts to buy or sell a non-financial item that can be settled net in cash or another financial instrument, or by exchanging financial instruments, as if the contracts were financial instruments, with the exception of contracts that were entered into and continue to be held for the purpose of the receipt or delivery of a non-financial item in accordance with the entity's expected purchase, sale or usage requirements.**

6 There are various ways in which a contract to buy or sell a non-financial item can be settled net in cash or another financial instrument or by exchanging financial instruments. These include:

(a) when the terms of the contract permit either party to settle it net in cash or another financial instrument or by exchanging financial instruments;

(b) when the ability to settle net in cash or another financial instrument, or by exchanging financial instruments, is not explicit in the terms of the contract, but the entity has a practice of settling similar contracts net in cash or another financial instrument or by exchanging financial instruments (whether with the counterparty, by entering into offsetting contracts or by selling the contract before its exercise or lapse);

(c) when, for similar contracts, the entity has a practice of taking delivery of the underlying and selling it within a short period after delivery for the purpose of generating a profit from short-term fluctuations in price or dealer's margin; and

(d) when the non-financial item that is the subject of the contract is readily convertible to cash.

A contract to which (b) or (c) applies is not entered into for the purpose of the receipt or delivery of the non-financial item in accordance with the entity's expected purchase, sale or usage requirements and, accordingly, is within the scope of this Standard. Other contracts to which paragraph 5 applies are evaluated to determine whether they were entered into and continue to be held for the purpose of the receipt or delivery of the non-financial item in accordance with the entity's expected purchase, sale or usage requirements and, accordingly, whether they are within the scope of this Standard.

7 A written option to buy or sell a non-financial item that can be settled net in cash or another financial instrument, or by exchanging financial instruments, in accordance with paragraph 6(a) or (d) is within the scope of this Standard. Such a

contract cannot be entered into for the purpose of the receipt or delivery of the non-financial item in accordance with the entity's expected purchase, sale or usage requirements.

Definitions

8 The terms defined in IAS 32 are used in this Standard with the meanings specified in paragraph 11 of IAS 32. IAS 32 defines the following terms:

- financial instrument
- financial asset
- financial liability
- equity instrument

and provides guidance on applying those definitions.

9 **The following terms are used in this Standard with the meanings specified:**

Definition of a derivative

A *derivative* **is a financial instrument or other contract within the scope of this Standard (see paragraphs 2–7) with all three of the following characteristics:**

(a) its value changes in response to the change in a specified interest rate, financial instrument price, commodity price, foreign exchange rate, index of prices or rates, credit rating or credit index, or other variable, provided in the case of a non-financial variable that the variable is not specific to a party to the contract (sometimes called the 'underlying');

(b) it requires no initial net investment or an initial net investment that is smaller than would be required for other types of contracts that would be expected to have a similar response to changes in market factors; and

(c) it is settled at a future date.

Definitions of four categories of financial instruments

A *financial asset or financial liability at fair value through profit or loss* **is a financial asset or financial liability that meets either of the following conditions.**

(a) It is classified as held for trading. A financial asset or financial liability is classified as held for trading if it is:

(i) acquired or incurred principally for the purpose of selling or repurchasing it in the near term;

(ii) part of a portfolio of identified financial instruments that are managed together and for which there is evidence of a recent actual pattern of short-term profit-taking; or

(iii) a derivative (except for a derivative that is a designated and effective hedging instrument).

(b) Upon initial recognition it is designated by the entity as at fair value through profit or loss. Any financial asset or financial liability within the scope of this Standard may be designated when initially recognised as a financial asset or financial liability at fair value through profit or loss except for investments in equity instruments that do not have a quoted market price in an active market, and whose fair value cannot be reliably measured (see paragraph 46(c) and Appendix A paragraphs AG80 and AG81).

Held-to-maturity investments **are non-derivative financial assets with fixed or determinable payments and fixed maturity that an entity has the positive intention and ability to hold to maturity (see Appendix A paragraphs AG16–AG25) other than:**

(a) those that the entity upon initial recognition designates as at fair value through profit or loss;

(b) those that the entity designates as available for sale; and

(c) those that meet the definition of loans and receivables.

An entity shall not classify any financial assets as held to maturity if the entity has, during the current financial year or during the two preceding financial years, sold or reclassified more than an insignificant amount of held-to-maturity investments before maturity (more than insignificant in relation to the total amount of held-to-maturity investments) other than sales or reclassifications that:

(i) are so close to maturity or the financial asset's call date (for example, less than three months before maturity) that changes in the market rate of interest would not have a significant effect on the financial asset's fair value;

(ii) occur after the entity has collected substantially all of the financial asset's original principal through scheduled payments or prepayments; or

(iii) are attributable to an isolated event that is beyond the entity's control, is non-recurring and could not have been reasonably anticipated by the entity.

Loans and receivables **are non-derivative financial assets with fixed or determinable payments that are not quoted in an active market, other than:**

(a) those that the entity intends to sell immediately or in the near term, which shall be classified as held for trading, and those that the entity upon initial recognition designates as at fair value through profit or loss;

(b) those that the entity upon initial recognition designates as available for sale; or

(c) those for which the holder may not recover substantially all of its initial investment, other than because of credit deterioration, which shall be classified as available for sale.

An interest acquired in a pool of assets that are not loans or receivables (for example, an interest in a mutual fund or a similar fund) is not a loan or receivable.

Available-for-sale financial assets **are those non-derivative financial assets that are designated as available for sale or are not classified as (a) loans and receivables, (b) held-to-maturity investments or (c) financial assets at fair value through profit or loss.**

Definitions relating to recognition and measurement

The *amortised cost of a financial asset or financial liability* **is the amount at which the financial asset or financial liability is measured at initial recognition minus principal repayments, plus or minus the cumulative amortisation using the effective interest method of any difference between that initial amount and the maturity amount, and minus any reduction (directly or through the use of an allowance account) for impairment or uncollectibility.**

The *effective interest method* **is a method of calculating the amortised cost of a financial asset or a financial liability (or group of financial assets or financial liabilities) and of allocating the interest income or interest expense over the relevant period. The** *effective interest rate* **is the rate that exactly discounts estimated future cash payments or receipts through the expected life of the financial instrument or, when appropriate, a shorter period to the net carrying amount of the financial asset or financial liability. When calculating the effective interest rate, an entity shall estimate cash flows considering all contractual terms of the financial instrument (for example, prepayment, call and similar options) but shall not consider future credit losses. The calculation includes all fees and points paid or received between parties to the contract that are an integral part of the effective interest rate (see IAS 18), transaction costs, and all other premiums or discounts. There is a presumption that the cash flows and the expected life of a group of similar financial instruments can be estimated reliably. However, in those rare cases when it is not possible to estimate reliably the cash flows or the expected life of a financial instrument (or group of financial instruments), the entity shall use the contractual cash flows over the full contractual term of the financial instrument (or group of financial instruments).**

Derecognition **is the removal of a previously recognised financial asset or financial liability from an entity's balance sheet.**

Fair value **is the amount for which an asset could be exchanged, or a liability settled, between knowledgeable, willing parties in an arm's length transaction.***

* Paragraphs 48, 49 and AG69–AG82 of Appendix A contain requirements for determining the fair value of a financial asset or financial liability.

A *regular way purchase or sale* is a purchase or sale of a financial asset under a contract whose terms require delivery of the asset within the time frame established generally by regulation or convention in the marketplace concerned.

***Transaction costs* are incremental costs that are directly attributable to the acquisition, issue or disposal of a financial asset or financial liability (see Appendix A paragraph AG13). An incremental cost is one that would not have been incurred if the entity had not acquired, issued or disposed of the financial instrument.**

Definitions relating to hedge accounting

A *firm commitment* is a binding agreement for the exchange of a specified quantity of resources at a specified price on a specified future date or dates.

A *forecast transaction* is an uncommitted but anticipated future transaction.

A *hedging instrument* is a designated derivative or (for a hedge of the risk of changes in foreign currency exchange rates only) a designated non-derivative financial asset or non-derivative financial liability whose fair value or cash flows are expected to offset changes in the fair value or cash flows of a designated hedged item (paragraphs 72–77 and Appendix A paragraphs AG94–AG97 elaborate on the definition of a hedging instrument).

A *hedged item* is an asset, liability, firm commitment, highly probable forecast transaction or net investment in a foreign operation that (a) exposes the entity to risk of changes in fair value or future cash flows and (b) is designated as being hedged (paragraphs 78–84 and Appendix A paragraphs AG98–AG101 elaborate on the definition of hedged items).

***Hedge effectiveness* is the degree to which changes in the fair value or cash flows of the hedged item that are attributable to a hedged risk are offset by changes in the fair value or cash flows of the hedging instrument (see Appendix A paragraphs AG105–AG113).**

Embedded derivatives

10 An embedded derivative is a component of a hybrid (combined) instrument that also includes a non-derivative host contract—with the effect that some of the cash flows of the combined instrument vary in a way similar to a stand-alone derivative. An embedded derivative causes some or all of the cash flows that otherwise would be required by the contract to be modified according to a specified interest rate, financial instrument price, commodity price, foreign exchange rate, index of prices or rates, credit rating or credit index, or other variable, provided in the case of a non-financial variable that the variable is not specific to a party to the contract. A derivative that is attached to a financial instrument but is contractually transferable independently of that instrument, or has a different counterparty from that instrument, is not an embedded derivative, but a separate financial instrument.

11 **An embedded derivative shall be separated from the host contract and accounted for as a derivative under this Standard if, and only if:**

(a) the economic characteristics and risks of the embedded derivative are not closely related to the economic characteristics and risks of the host contract (see Appendix A paragraphs AG30 and AG33);

(b) a separate instrument with the same terms as the embedded derivative would meet the definition of a derivative; and

(c) the hybrid (combined) instrument is not measured at fair value with changes in fair value recognised in profit or loss (ie a derivative that is embedded in a financial asset or financial liability at fair value through profit or loss is not separated).

If an embedded derivative is separated, the host contract shall be accounted for under this Standard if it is a financial instrument, and in accordance with other appropriate Standards if it is not a financial instrument. This Standard does not address whether an embedded derivative shall be presented separately on the face of the financial statements.

12 **If an entity is required by this Standard to separate an embedded derivative from its host contract, but is unable to measure the embedded derivative separately either at acquisition or at a subsequent financial reporting date, it shall treat the entire combined contract as a financial asset or financial liability that is held for trading.**

13 If an entity is unable to determine reliably the fair value of an embedded derivative on the basis of its terms and conditions (for example, because the embedded derivative is based on an unquoted equity instrument), the fair value of the embedded derivative is the difference between the fair value of the hybrid instrument and the fair value of the host contract, if those can be determined under this Standard. If the entity is unable to determine the fair value of the embedded derivative using this method, paragraph 12 applies and the combined instrument is treated as held for trading.

Recognition and derecognition

Initial recognition

14 **An entity shall recognise a financial asset or a financial liability on its balance sheet when, and only when, the entity becomes a party to the contractual provisions of the instrument. (See paragraph 38 with respect to regular way purchases of financial assets.)**

Derecognition of a financial asset

15 In consolidated financial statements, paragraphs 16–23 and Appendix A paragraphs AG34–AG52 are applied at a consolidated level. Hence, an entity first consolidates all subsidiaries in accordance with IAS 27 and SIC-12 *Consolidation—Special Purpose Entities* and then applies paragraphs 16–23 and Appendix A paragraphs AG34–AG52 to the resulting group.

16 **Before evaluating whether, and to what extent, derecognition is appropriate under paragraphs 17–23, an entity determines whether those paragraphs should be applied to a part of a financial asset (or a part of a group of similar financial assets) or a financial asset (or a group of similar financial assets) in its entirety, as follows.**

(a) Paragraphs 17–23 are applied to a part of a financial asset (or a part of a group of similar financial assets) if, and only if, the part being considered for derecognition meets one of the following three conditions.

(i) The part comprises only specifically identified cash flows from a financial asset (or a group of similar financial assets). For example, when an entity enters into an interest rate strip whereby the counterparty obtains the right to the interest cash flows, but not the principal cash flows from a debt instrument, paragraphs 17–23 are applied to the interest cash flows.

(ii) The part comprises only a fully proportionate (pro rata) share of the cash flows from a financial asset (or a group of similar financial assets). For example, when an entity enters into an arrangement whereby the counterparty obtains the rights to a 90 per cent share of all cash flows of a debt instrument, paragraphs 17–23 are applied to 90 per cent of those cash flows. If there is more than one counterparty, each counterparty is not required to have a proportionate share of the cash flows provided that the transferring entity has a fully proportionate share.

(iii) The part comprises only a fully proportionate (pro rata) share of specifically identified cash flows from a financial asset (or a group of similar financial assets). For example, when an entity enters into an arrangement whereby the counterparty obtains the rights to a 90 per cent share of interest cash flows from a financial asset, paragraphs 17–23 are applied to 90 per cent of those interest cash flows. If there is more than one counterparty, each counterparty is not required to have a proportionate share of the specifically identified cash flows provided that the transferring entity has a fully proportionate share.

(b) In all other cases, paragraphs 17–23 are applied to the financial asset in its entirety (or to the group of similar financial assets in their entirety). For example, when an entity transfers (i) the rights to the first or the last 90 per cent of cash collections from a financial asset (or a group of financial assets), or (ii) the rights to 90 per cent of the cash flows from a group of receivables, but provides a guarantee to compensate the buyer for any credit losses up to 8 per cent of the principal amount of the receivables, paragraphs 17–23 are applied to the financial asset (or a group of similar financial assets) in its entirety.

In paragraphs 17–26, the term 'financial asset' refers to either a part of a financial asset (or a part of a group of similar financial assets) as identified in (a) above or, otherwise, a financial asset (or a group of similar financial assets) in its entirety.

17 **An entity shall derecognise a financial asset when, and only when:**

- **(a) the contractual rights to the cash flows from the financial asset expire; or**
- **(b) it transfers the financial asset as set out in paragraphs 18 and 19 and the transfer qualifies for derecognition in accordance with paragraph 20.**

(See paragraph 38 for regular way sales of financial assets.)

18 **An entity transfers a financial asset if, and only if, it either:**

- **(a) transfers the contractual rights to receive the cash flows of the financial asset; or**
- **(b) retains the contractual rights to receive the cash flows of the financial asset, but assumes a contractual obligation to pay the cash flows to one or more recipients in an arrangement that meets the conditions in paragraph 19.**

19 **When an entity retains the contractual rights to receive the cash flows of a financial asset (the 'original asset'), but assumes a contractual obligation to pay those cash flows to one or more entities (the 'eventual recipients'), the entity treats the transaction as a transfer of a financial asset if, and only if, all of the following three conditions are met.**

- **(a) The entity has no obligation to pay amounts to the eventual recipients unless it collects equivalent amounts from the original asset. Short-term advances by the entity with the right of full recovery of the amount lent plus accrued interest at market rates do not violate this condition.**
- **(b) The entity is prohibited by the terms of the transfer contract from selling or pledging the original asset other than as security to the eventual recipients for the obligation to pay them cash flows.**
- **(c) The entity has an obligation to remit any cash flows it collects on behalf of the eventual recipients without material delay. In addition, the entity is not entitled to reinvest such cash flows, except for investments in cash or cash equivalents (as defined in IAS 7 *Cash Flow Statements*) during the short settlement period from the collection date to the date of required remittance to the eventual recipients, and interest earned on such investments is passed to the eventual recipients.**

20 **When an entity transfers a financial asset (see paragraph 18), it shall evaluate the extent to which it retains the risks and rewards of ownership of the financial asset. In this case:**

(a) **if the entity transfers substantially all the risks and rewards of ownership of the financial asset, the entity shall derecognise the financial asset and recognise separately as assets or liabilities any rights and obligations created or retained in the transfer.**

(b) **if the entity retains substantially all the risks and rewards of ownership of the financial asset, the entity shall continue to recognise the financial asset.**

(c) **if the entity neither transfers nor retains substantially all the risks and rewards of ownership of the financial asset, the entity shall determine whether it has retained control of the financial asset. In this case:**

(i) **if the entity has not retained control, it shall derecognise the financial asset and recognise separately as assets or liabilities any rights and obligations created or retained in the transfer.**

(ii) **if the entity has retained control, it shall continue to recognise the financial asset to the extent of its continuing involvement in the financial asset (see paragraph 30).**

21 The transfer of risks and rewards (see paragraph 20) is evaluated by comparing the entity's exposure, before and after the transfer, with the variability in the amounts and timing of the net cash flows of the transferred asset. An entity has retained substantially all the risks and rewards of ownership of a financial asset if its exposure to the variability in the present value of the future net cash flows from the financial asset does not change significantly as a result of the transfer (eg because the entity has sold a financial asset subject to an agreement to buy it back at a fixed price or the sale price plus a lender's return). An entity has transferred substantially all the risks and rewards of ownership of a financial asset if its exposure to such variability is no longer significant in relation to the total variability in the present value of the future net cash flows associated with the financial asset (eg because the entity has sold a financial asset subject only to an option to buy it back at its fair value at the time of repurchase or has transferred a fully proportionate share of the cash flows from a larger financial asset in an arrangement, such as a loan sub-participation, that meets the conditions in paragraph 19).

22 Often it will be obvious whether the entity has transferred or retained substantially all risks and rewards of ownership and there will be no need to perform any computations. In other cases, it will be necessary to compute and compare the entity's exposure to the variability in the present value of the future net cash flows before and after the transfer. The computation and comparison is made using as the discount rate an appropriate current market interest rate. All reasonably possible variability in net cash flows is considered, with greater weight being given to those outcomes that are more likely to occur.

23 Whether the entity has retained control (see paragraph 20(c)) of the transferred asset depends on the transferee's ability to sell the asset. If the transferee has the practical ability to sell the asset in its entirety to an unrelated third party and is

able to exercise that ability unilaterally and without needing to impose additional restrictions on the transfer, the entity has not retained control. In all other cases, the entity has retained control.

Transfers that qualify for derecognition (see paragraph 20(a) and (c)(i))

24 **If an entity transfers a financial asset in a transfer that qualifies for derecognition in its entirety and retains the right to service the financial asset for a fee, it shall recognise either a servicing asset or a servicing liability for that servicing contract. If the fee to be received is not expected to compensate the entity adequately for performing the servicing, a servicing liability for the servicing obligation shall be recognised at its fair value. If the fee to be received is expected to be more than adequate compensation for the servicing, a servicing asset shall be recognised for the servicing right at an amount determined on the basis of an allocation of the carrying amount of the larger financial asset in accordance with paragraph 27.**

25 **If, as a result of a transfer, a financial asset is derecognised in its entirety but the transfer results in the entity obtaining a new financial asset or assuming a new financial liability, or a servicing liability, the entity shall recognise the new financial asset, financial liability or servicing liability at fair value.**

26 **On derecognition of a financial asset in its entirety, the difference between:**

(a) the carrying amount and

(b) the sum of (i) the consideration received (including any new asset obtained less any new liability assumed) and (ii) any cumulative gain or loss that had been recognised directly in equity (see paragraph 55(b))

shall be recognised in profit or loss.

27 **If the transferred asset is part of a larger financial asset (eg when an entity transfers interest cash flows that are part of a debt instrument, see paragraph 16(a)) and the part transferred qualifies for derecognition in its entirety, the previous carrying amount of the larger financial asset shall be allocated between the part that continues to be recognised and the part that is derecognised, based on the relative fair values of those parts on the date of the transfer. For this purpose, a retained servicing asset shall be treated as a part that continues to be recognised. The difference between:**

(a) the carrying amount allocated to the part derecognised and

(b) the sum of (i) the consideration received for the part derecognised (including any new asset obtained less any new liability assumed) and (ii) any cumulative gain or loss allocated to it that had been recognised directly in equity (see paragraph 55(b))

shall be recognised in profit or loss. A cumulative gain or loss that had been recognised in equity is allocated between the part that continues to be recognised and the part that is derecognised, based on the relative fair values of those parts.

28 When an entity allocates the previous carrying amount of a larger financial asset between the part that continues to be recognised and the part that is derecognised, the fair value of the part that continues to be recognised needs to be determined. When the entity has a history of selling parts similar to the part that continues to be recognised or other market transactions exist for such parts, recent prices of actual transactions provide the best estimate of its fair value. When there are no price quotes or recent market transactions to support the fair value of the part that continues to be recognised, the best estimate of the fair value is the difference between the fair value of the larger financial asset as a whole and the consideration received from the transferee for the part that is derecognised.

Transfers that do not qualify for derecognition (see paragraph 20(b))

29 **If a transfer does not result in derecognition because the entity has retained substantially all the risks and rewards of ownership of the transferred asset, the entity shall continue to recognise the transferred asset in its entirety and shall recognise a financial liability for the consideration received. In subsequent periods, the entity shall recognise any income on the transferred asset and any expense incurred on the financial liability.**

Continuing involvement in transferred assets (see paragraph 20(c)(ii))

30 **If an entity neither transfers nor retains substantially all the risks and rewards of ownership of a transferred asset, and retains control of the transferred asset, the entity continues to recognise the transferred asset to the extent of its continuing involvement. The extent of the entity's continuing involvement in the transferred asset is the extent to which it is exposed to changes in the value of the transferred asset. For example:**

(a) when the entity's continuing involvement takes the form of guaranteeing the transferred asset, the extent of the entity's continuing involvement is the lower of (i) the amount of the asset and (ii) the maximum amount of the consideration received that the entity could be required to repay ('the guarantee amount').

(b) when the entity's continuing involvement takes the form of a written or purchased option (or both) on the transferred asset, the extent of the entity's continuing involvement is the amount of the transferred asset that the entity may repurchase. However, in case of a written put option on an asset that is measured at fair value, the extent of the entity's continuing involvement is limited to the lower of the fair value of the transferred asset and the option exercise price (see paragraph AG48).

(c) when the entity's continuing involvement takes the form of a cash-settled option or similar provision on the transferred asset, the

extent of the entity's continuing involvement is measured in the same way as that which results from non-cash settled options as set out in (b) above.

31 **When an entity continues to recognise an asset to the extent of its continuing involvement, the entity also recognises an associated liability. Despite the other measurement requirements in this Standard, the transferred asset and the associated liability are measured on a basis that reflects the rights and obligations that the entity has retained. The associated liability is measured in such a way that the net carrying amount of the transferred asset and the associated liability is:**

(a) the amortised cost of the rights and obligations retained by the entity, if the transferred asset is measured at amortised cost; or

(b) equal to the fair value of the rights and obligations retained by the entity when measured on a stand-alone basis, if the transferred asset is measured at fair value.

32 **The entity shall continue to recognise any income arising on the transferred asset to the extent of its continuing involvement and shall recognise any expense incurred on the associated liability.**

33 **For the purpose of subsequent measurement, recognised changes in the fair value of the transferred asset and the associated liability are accounted for consistently with each other in accordance with paragraph 55, and shall not be offset.**

34 **If an entity's continuing involvement is in only a part of a financial asset (eg when an entity retains an option to repurchase part of a transferred asset, or retains a residual interest that does not result in the retention of substantially all the risks and rewards of ownership and the entity retains control), the entity allocates the previous carrying amount of the financial asset between the part it continues to recognise under continuing involvement, and the part it no longer recognises on the basis of the relative fair values of those parts on the date of the transfer. For this purpose, the requirements of paragraph 28 apply. The difference between:**

(a) the carrying amount allocated to the part that is no longer recognised; and

(b) the sum of (i) the consideration received for the part no longer recognised and (ii) any cumulative gain or loss allocated to it that had been recognised directly in equity (see paragraph 55(b))

shall be recognised in profit or loss. A cumulative gain or loss that had been recognised in equity is allocated between the part that continues to be recognised and the part that is no longer recognised on the basis of the relative fair values of those parts.

35 If the transferred asset is measured at amortised cost, the option in this Standard to designate a financial liability as at fair value through profit or loss is not applicable to the associated liability.

All transfers

36 **If a transferred asset continues to be recognised, the asset and the associated liability shall not be offset. Similarly, the entity shall not offset any income arising from the transferred asset with any expense incurred on the associated liability (see IAS 32 paragraph 42).**

37 **If a transferor provides non-cash collateral (such as debt or equity instruments) to the transferee, the accounting for the collateral by the transferor and the transferee depends on whether the transferee has the right to sell or repledge the collateral and on whether the transferor has defaulted. The transferor and transferee shall account for the collateral as follows:**

(a) If the transferee has the right by contract or custom to sell or repledge the collateral, then the transferor shall reclassify that asset in its balance sheet (eg as a loaned asset, pledged equity instruments or repurchase receivable) separately from other assets.

(b) If the transferee sells collateral pledged to it, it shall recognise the proceeds from the sale and a liability measured at fair value for its obligation to return the collateral.

(c) If the transferor defaults under the terms of the contract and is no longer entitled to redeem the collateral, it shall derecognise the collateral, and the transferee shall recognise the collateral as its asset initially measured at fair value or, if it has already sold the collateral, derecognise its obligation to return the collateral.

(d) Except as provided in (c), the transferor shall continue to carry the collateral as its asset, and the transferee shall not recognise the collateral as an asset.

Regular way purchase or sale of a financial asset

38 **A regular way purchase or sale of financial assets shall be recognised and derecognised, as applicable, using trade date accounting or settlement date accounting (see Appendix A paragraphs AG53–AG56).**

Derecognition of a financial liability

39 **An entity shall remove a financial liability (or a part of a financial liability) from its balance sheet when, and only when, it is extinguished—ie when the obligation specified in the contract is discharged or cancelled or expires.**

40 **An exchange between an existing borrower and lender of debt instruments with substantially different terms shall be accounted for as an extinguishment of the original financial liability and the recognition of a new financial liability. Similarly, a substantial modification of the terms of an existing financial liability or a part of it (whether or not attributable to the financial difficulty of the debtor) shall be accounted for as an extinguishment of the original financial liability and the recognition of a new financial liability.**

41 **The difference between the carrying amount of a financial liability (or part of a financial liability) extinguished or transferred to another party and the consideration paid, including any non-cash assets transferred or liabilities assumed, shall be recognised in profit or loss.**

42 If an entity repurchases a part of a financial liability, the entity shall allocate the previous carrying amount of the financial liability between the part that continues to be recognised and the part that is derecognised based on the relative fair values of those parts on the date of the repurchase. The difference between (a) the carrying amount allocated to the part derecognised and (b) the consideration paid, including any non-cash assets transferred or liabilities assumed, for the part derecognised shall be recognised in profit or loss.

Measurement

Initial measurement of financial assets and financial liabilities

43 **When a financial asset or financial liability is recognised initially, an entity shall measure it at its fair value plus, in the case of a financial asset or financial liability not at fair value through profit or loss, transaction costs that are directly attributable to the acquisition or issue of the financial asset or financial liability.**

44 When an entity uses settlement date accounting for an asset that is subsequently measured at cost or amortised cost, the asset is recognised initially at its fair value on the trade date (see Appendix A paragraphs AG53–AG56).

Subsequent measurement of financial assets

45 For the purpose of measuring a financial asset after initial recognition, this Standard classifies financial assets into the following four categories defined in paragraph 9:

(a) financial assets at fair value through profit or loss;

(b) held-to-maturity investments;

(c) loans and receivables; and

(d) available-for-sale financial assets.

These categories apply to measurement and profit or loss recognition under this Standard. The entity may use other descriptors for these categories or other categorisations when presenting information on the face of the financial statements. The entity shall disclose in the notes the information required by IAS 32.

46 **After initial recognition, an entity shall measure financial assets, including derivatives that are assets, at their fair values, without any deduction for transaction costs it may incur on sale or other disposal, except for the following financial assets:**

(a) loans and receivables as defined in paragraph 9, which shall be measured at amortised cost using the effective interest method;

(b) **held-to-maturity investments as defined in paragraph 9, which shall be measured at amortised cost using the effective interest method; and**

(c) **investments in equity instruments that do not have a quoted market price in an active market and whose fair value cannot be reliably measured and derivatives that are linked to and must be settled by delivery of such unquoted equity instruments, which shall be measured at cost (see Appendix A paragraphs AG80 and AG81).**

Financial assets that are designated as hedged items are subject to measurement under the hedge accounting requirements in paragraphs 89–102. All financial assets except those measured at fair value through profit or loss are subject to review for impairment in accordance with paragraphs 58–70 and Appendix A paragraphs AG84–AG93.

Subsequent measurement of financial liabilities

47 **After initial recognition, an entity shall measure all financial liabilities at amortised cost using the effective interest method, except for:**

(a) **financial liabilities at fair value through profit or loss. Such liabilities, including derivatives that are liabilities, shall be measured at fair value except for a derivative liability that is linked to and must be settled by delivery of an unquoted equity instrument whose fair value cannot be reliably measured, which shall be measured at cost.**

(b) **financial liabilities that arise when a transfer of a financial asset does not qualify for derecognition or is accounted for using the continuing involvement approach. Paragraphs 29 and 31 apply to the measurement of such financial liabilities.**

Financial liabilities that are designated as hedged items are subject to measurement under the hedge accounting requirements in paragraphs 89–102.

Fair value measurement considerations

48 **In determining the fair value of a financial asset or a financial liability for the purpose of applying this Standard or IAS 32, an entity shall apply paragraphs AG69–AG82 of Appendix A.**

49 The fair value of a financial liability with a demand feature (eg a demand deposit) is not less than the amount payable on demand, discounted from the first date that the amount could be required to be paid.

Reclassifications

50 **An entity shall not reclassify a financial instrument into or out of the fair value through profit or loss category while it is held or issued.**

51 **If, as a result of a change in intention or ability, it is no longer appropriate to classify an investment as held to maturity, it shall be reclassified as available for sale and remeasured at fair value, and the difference between its carrying amount and fair value shall be accounted for in accordance with paragraph 55(b).**

52 **Whenever sales or reclassification of more than an insignificant amount of held-to-maturity investments do not meet any of the conditions in paragraph 9, any remaining held-to-maturity investments shall be reclassified as available for sale. On such reclassification, the difference between their carrying amount and fair value shall be accounted for in accordance with paragraph 55(b).**

53 **If a reliable measure becomes available for a financial asset or financial liability for which such a measure was previously not available, and the asset or liability is required to be measured at fair value if a reliable measure is available (see paragraphs 46(c) and 47), the asset or liability shall be remeasured at fair value, and the difference between its carrying amount and fair value shall be accounted for in accordance with paragraph 55.**

54 **If, as a result of a change in intention or ability or in the rare circumstance that a reliable measure of fair value is no longer available (see paragraphs 46(c) and 47) or because the 'two preceding financial years' referred to in paragraph 9 have passed, it becomes appropriate to carry a financial asset or financial liability at cost or amortised cost rather than at fair value, the fair value carrying amount of the financial asset or the financial liability on that date becomes its new cost or amortised cost, as applicable. Any previous gain or loss on that asset that has been recognised directly in equity in accordance with paragraph 55(b) shall be accounted for as follows:**

(a) In the case of a financial asset with a fixed maturity, the gain or loss shall be amortised to profit or loss over the remaining life of the held-to-maturity investment using the effective interest method. Any difference between the new amortised cost and maturity amount shall also be amortised over the remaining life of the financial asset using the effective interest method, similar to the amortisation of a premium and a discount. If the financial asset is subsequently impaired, any gain or loss that has been recognised directly in equity is recognised in profit or loss in accordance with paragraph 67.

(b) In the case of a financial asset that does not have a fixed maturity, the gain or loss shall remain in equity until the financial asset is sold or otherwise disposed of, when it shall be recognised in profit or loss. If the financial asset is subsequently impaired any previous gain or loss that has been recognised directly in equity is recognised in profit or loss in accordance with paragraph 67.

Gains and losses

55 **A gain or loss arising from a change in the fair value of a financial asset or financial liability that is not part of a hedging relationship (see paragraphs 89–102), shall be recognised, as follows.**

(a) A gain or loss on a financial asset or financial liability classified as at fair value through profit or loss shall be recognised in profit or loss.

(b) A gain or loss on an available-for-sale financial asset shall be recognised directly in equity, through the statement of changes in

equity (see IAS 1 *Presentation of Financial Statements*), except for impairment losses (see paragraphs 67–70) and foreign exchange gains and losses (see Appendix A paragraph AG83), until the financial asset is derecognised, at which time the cumulative gain or loss previously recognised in equity shall be recognised in profit or loss. However, interest calculated using the effective interest method (see paragraph 9) is recognised in profit or loss (see IAS 18 *Revenue*). Dividends on an available-for-sale equity instrument are recognised in profit or loss when the entity's right to receive payment is established (see IAS 18).

56 **For financial assets and financial liabilities carried at amortised cost (see paragraphs 46 and 47), a gain or loss is recognised in profit or loss when the financial asset or financial liability is derecognised or impaired, and through the amortisation process. However, for financial assets or financial liabilities that are hedged items (see paragraphs 78–84 and Appendix A paragraphs AG98–AG101) the accounting for the gain or loss shall follow paragraphs 89–102.**

57 **If an entity recognises financial assets using settlement date accounting (see paragraph 38 and Appendix A paragraphs AG53 and AG56), any change in the fair value of the asset to be received during the period between the trade date and the settlement date is not recognised for assets carried at cost or amortised cost (other than impairment losses). For assets carried at fair value, however, the change in fair value shall be recognised in profit or loss or in equity, as appropriate under paragraph 55.**

Impairment and uncollectibility of financial assets

58 **An entity shall assess at each balance sheet date whether there is any objective evidence that a financial asset or group of financial assets is impaired. If any such evidence exists, the entity shall apply paragraph 63 (for financial assets carried at amortised cost), paragraph 66 (for financial assets carried at cost) or paragraph 67 (for available-for-sale financial assets) to determine the amount of any impairment loss.**

59 A financial asset or a group of financial assets is impaired and impairment losses are incurred if, and only if, there is objective evidence of impairment as a result of one or more events that occurred after the initial recognition of the asset (a 'loss event') and that loss event (or events) has an impact on the estimated future cash flows of the financial asset or group of financial assets that can be reliably estimated. It may not be possible to identify a single, discrete event that caused the impairment. Rather the combined effect of several events may have caused the impairment. Losses expected as a result of future events, no matter how likely, are not recognised. Objective evidence that a financial asset or group of assets is impaired includes observable data that comes to the attention of the holder of the asset about the following loss events:

(a) significant financial difficulty of the issuer or obligor;

(b) a breach of contract, such as a default or delinquency in interest or principal payments;

(c) the lender, for economic or legal reasons relating to the borrower's financial difficulty, granting to the borrower a concession that the lender would not otherwise consider;

(d) it becoming probable that the borrower will enter bankruptcy or other financial reorganisation;

(e) the disappearance of an active market for that financial asset because of financial difficulties; or

(f) observable data indicating that there is a measurable decrease in the estimated future cash flows from a group of financial assets since the initial recognition of those assets, although the decrease cannot yet be identified with the individual financial assets in the group, including:

   (i) adverse changes in the payment status of borrowers in the group (eg an increased number of delayed payments or an increased number of credit card borrowers who have reached their credit limit and are paying the minimum monthly amount); or

   (ii) national or local economic conditions that correlate with defaults on the assets in the group (eg an increase in the unemployment rate in the geographical area of the borrowers, a decrease in property prices for mortgages in the relevant area, a decrease in oil prices for loan assets to oil producers, or adverse changes in industry conditions that affect the borrowers in the group).

60 The disappearance of an active market because an entity's financial instruments are no longer publicly traded is not evidence of impairment. A downgrade of an entity's credit rating is not, of itself, evidence of impairment, although it may be evidence of impairment when considered with other available information. A decline in the fair value of a financial asset below its cost or amortised cost is not necessarily evidence of impairment (for example, a decline in the fair value of an investment in a debt instrument that results from an increase in the risk-free interest rate).

61 In addition to the types of events in paragraph 59, objective evidence of impairment for an investment in an equity instrument includes information about significant changes with an adverse effect that have taken place in the technological, market, economic or legal environment in which the issuer operates, and indicates that the cost of the investment in the equity instrument may not be recovered. A significant or prolonged decline in the fair value of an investment in an equity instrument below its cost is also objective evidence of impairment.

62 In some cases the observable data required to estimate the amount of an impairment loss on a financial asset may be limited or no longer fully relevant to current circumstances. For example, this may be the case when a borrower is in financial difficulties and there are few available historical data relating to similar borrowers. In such cases, an entity uses its experienced judgement to estimate the amount of any impairment loss. Similarly an entity uses its experienced judgement to adjust observable data for a group of financial assets to reflect

current circumstances (see paragraph AG89). The use of reasonable estimates is an essential part of the preparation of financial statements and does not undermine their reliability.

Financial assets carried at amortised cost

63 **If there is objective evidence that an impairment loss on loans and receivables or held-to-maturity investments carried at amortised cost has been incurred, the amount of the loss is measured as the difference between the asset's carrying amount and the present value of estimated future cash flows (excluding future credit losses that have not been incurred) discounted at the financial asset's original effective interest rate (ie the effective interest rate computed at initial recognition). The carrying amount of the asset shall be reduced either directly or through use of an allowance account. The amount of the loss shall be recognised in profit or loss.**

64 An entity first assesses whether objective evidence of impairment exists individually for financial assets that are individually significant, and individually or collectively for financial assets that are not individually significant (see paragraph 59). If an entity determines that no objective evidence of impairment exists for an individually assessed financial asset, whether significant or not, it includes the asset in a group of financial assets with similar credit risk characteristics and collectively assesses them for impairment. Assets that are individually assessed for impairment and for which an impairment loss is or continues to be recognised are not included in a collective assessment of impairment.

65 **If, in a subsequent period, the amount of the impairment loss decreases and the decrease can be related objectively to an event occurring after the impairment was recognised (such as an improvement in the debtor's credit rating), the previously recognised impairment loss shall be reversed either directly or by adjusting an allowance account. The reversal shall not result in a carrying amount of the financial asset that exceeds what the amortised cost would have been had the impairment not been recognised at the date the impairment is reversed. The amount of the reversal shall be recognised in profit or loss.**

Financial assets carried at cost

66 **If there is objective evidence that an impairment loss has been incurred on an unquoted equity instrument that is not carried at fair value because its fair value cannot be reliably measured, or on a derivative asset that is linked to and must be settled by delivery of such an unquoted equity instrument, the amount of the impairment loss is measured as the difference between the carrying amount of the financial asset and the present value of estimated future cash flows discounted at the current market rate of return for a similar financial asset (see paragraph 46(c) and Appendix A paragraphs AG80 and AG81). Such impairment losses shall not be reversed.**

Available-for-sale financial assets

67 **When a decline in the fair value of an available-for-sale financial asset has been recognised directly in equity and there is objective evidence that the asset is impaired (see paragraph 59), the cumulative loss that had been recognised directly in equity shall be removed from equity and recognised in profit or loss even though the financial asset has not been derecognised.**

68 **The amount of the cumulative loss that is removed from equity and recognised in profit or loss under paragraph 67 shall be the difference between the acquisition cost (net of any principal repayment and amortisation) and current fair value, less any impairment loss on that financial asset previously recognised in profit or loss.**

69 **Impairment losses recognised in profit or loss for an investment in an equity instrument classified as available for sale shall not be reversed through profit or loss.**

70 **If, in a subsequent period, the fair value of a debt instrument classified as available for sale increases and the increase can be objectively related to an event occurring after the impairment loss was recognised in profit or loss, the impairment loss shall be reversed, with the amount of the reversal recognised in profit or loss.**

Hedging

71 **If there is a designated hedging relationship between a hedging instrument and a hedged item as described in paragraphs 85–88 and Appendix A paragraphs AG102–AG104, accounting for the gain or loss on the hedging instrument and the hedged item shall follow paragraphs 89–102.**

Hedging instruments

Qualifying instruments

72 This Standard does not restrict the circumstances in which a derivative may be designated as a hedging instrument provided the conditions in paragraph 88 are met, except for some written options (see Appendix A paragraph AG94). However, a non-derivative financial asset or non-derivative financial liability may be designated as a hedging instrument only for a hedge of a foreign currency risk.

73 For hedge accounting purposes, only instruments that involve a party external to the reporting entity (ie external to the group, segment or individual entity that is being reported on) can be designated as hedging instruments. Although individual entities within a consolidated group or divisions within an entity may enter into hedging transactions with other entities within the group or divisions within the entity, any such intragroup transactions are eliminated on consolidation. Therefore, such hedging transactions do not qualify for hedge accounting in the consolidated financial statements of the group. However, they may qualify for hedge accounting in the individual or separate financial

statements of individual entities within the group or in segment reporting provided that they are external to the individual entity or segment that is being reported on.

Designation of hedging instruments

74 There is normally a single fair value measure for a hedging instrument in its entirety, and the factors that cause changes in fair value are co-dependent. Thus, a hedging relationship is designated by an entity for a hedging instrument in its entirety. The only exceptions permitted are:

(a) separating the intrinsic value and time value of an option contract and designating as the hedging instrument only the change in intrinsic value of an option and excluding change in its time value; and

(b) separating the interest element and the spot price of a forward contract.

These exceptions are permitted because the intrinsic value of the option and the premium on the forward can generally be measured separately. A dynamic hedging strategy that assesses both the intrinsic value and time value of an option contract can qualify for hedge accounting.

75 A proportion of the entire hedging instrument, such as 50 per cent of the notional amount, may be designated as the hedging instrument in a hedging relationship. However, a hedging relationship may not be designated for only a portion of the time period during which a hedging instrument remains outstanding.

76 A single hedging instrument may be designated as a hedge of more than one type of risk provided that (a) the risks hedged can be identified clearly; (b) the effectiveness of the hedge can be demonstrated; and (c) it is possible to ensure that there is specific designation of the hedging instrument and different risk positions.

77 Two or more derivatives, or proportions of them (or, in the case of a hedge of currency risk, two or more non-derivatives or proportions of them, or a combination of derivatives and non-derivatives or proportions of them), may be viewed in combination and jointly designated as the hedging instrument, including when the risk(s) arising from some derivatives offset(s) those arising from others. However, an interest rate collar or other derivative instrument that combines a written option and a purchased option does not qualify as a hedging instrument if it is, in effect, a net written option (for which a net premium is received). Similarly, two or more instruments (or proportions of them) may be designated as the hedging instrument only if none of them is a written option or a net written option.

Hedged items

Qualifying items

78 A hedged item can be a recognised asset or liability, an unrecognised firm commitment, a highly probable forecast transaction or a net investment in a foreign operation. The hedged item can be (a) a single asset, liability, firm commitment, highly probable forecast transaction or net investment in a foreign operation, (b) a group of assets, liabilities, firm commitments, highly probable

forecast transactions or net investments in foreign operations with similar risk characteristics or (c) in a portfolio hedge of interest rate risk only, a portion of the portfolio of financial assets or financial liabilities that share the risk being hedged.

79 Unlike loans and receivables, a held-to-maturity investment cannot be a hedged item with respect to interest-rate risk or prepayment risk because designation of an investment as held to maturity requires an intention to hold the investment until maturity without regard to changes in the fair value or cash flows of such an investment attributable to changes in interest rates. However, a held-to-maturity investment can be a hedged item with respect to risks from changes in foreign currency exchange rates and credit risk.

80 For hedge accounting purposes, only assets, liabilities, firm commitments or highly probable forecast transactions that involve a party external to the entity can be designated as hedged items. It follows that hedge accounting can be applied to transactions between entities or segments in the same group only in the individual or separate financial statements of those entities or segments and not in the consolidated financial statements of the group. As an exception, the foreign currency risk of an intragroup monetary item (eg a payable/receivable between two subsidiaries) may qualify as a hedged item in the consolidated financial statements if it results in an exposure to foreign exchange rate gains or losses that are not fully eliminated on consolidation under IAS 21 *The Effects of Changes in Foreign Exchange Rates*. Under IAS 21, foreign exchange gains and losses on intragroup monetary items are not fully eliminated on consolidation when the intragroup monetary item is transacted between two group entities that have different functional currencies.

Designation of financial items as hedged items

81 If the hedged item is a financial asset or financial liability, it may be a hedged item with respect to the risks associated with only a portion of its cash flows or fair value (such as one or more selected contractual cash flows or portions of them or a percentage of the fair value) provided that effectiveness can be measured. For example, an identifiable and separately measurable portion of the interest rate exposure of an interest-bearing asset or interest-bearing liability may be designated as the hedged risk (such as a risk-free interest rate or benchmark interest rate component of the total interest rate exposure of a hedged financial instrument).

81A In a fair value hedge of the interest rate exposure of a portfolio of financial assets or financial liabilities (and only in such a hedge), the portion hedged may be designated in terms of an amount of a currency (eg an amount of dollars, euro, pounds or rand) rather than as individual assets (or liabilities). Although the portfolio may, for risk management purposes, include assets and liabilities, the amount designated is an amount of assets or an amount of liabilities. Designation of a net amount including assets and liabilities is not permitted. The entity may hedge a portion of the interest rate risk associated with this designated amount. For example, in the case of a hedge of a portfolio containing prepayable assets, the entity may hedge the change in fair value that is attributable to a change in the hedged interest rate on the basis of expected, rather than contractual, repricing dates. When the portion hedged is based on expected repricing dates, the effect that changes in the hedged interest rate have on those expected repricing dates shall be included when determining the change in the fair value of the hedged item. Consequently, if a portfolio that contains prepayable items is hedged with a non-prepayable derivative, ineffectiveness arises if the dates on which items in the hedged portfolio are expected to prepay are revised, or actual prepayment dates differ from those expected.

Designation of non-financial items as hedged items

82 **If the hedged item is a non-financial asset or non-financial liability, it shall be designated as a hedged item (a) for foreign currency risks, or (b) in its entirety for all risks, because of the difficulty of isolating and measuring the appropriate portion of the cash flows or fair value changes attributable to specific risks other than foreign currency risks.**

Designation of groups of items as hedged items

83 Similar assets or similar liabilities shall be aggregated and hedged as a group only if the individual assets or individual liabilities in the group share the risk exposure that is designated as being hedged. Furthermore, the change in fair value attributable to the hedged risk for each individual item in the group shall be expected to be approximately proportional to the overall change in fair value attributable to the hedged risk of the group of items.

84 Because an entity assesses hedge effectiveness by comparing the change in the fair value or cash flow of a hedging instrument (or group of similar hedging instruments) and a hedged item (or group of similar hedged items), comparing a hedging instrument with an overall net position (eg the net of all fixed rate assets and fixed rate liabilities with similar maturities), rather than with a specific hedged item, does not qualify for hedge accounting.

Hedge accounting

85 Hedge accounting recognises the offsetting effects on profit or loss of changes in the fair values of the hedging instrument and the hedged item.

86 **Hedging relationships are of three types:**

(a) *fair value hedge*: **a hedge of the exposure to changes in fair value of a recognised asset or liability or an unrecognised firm commitment, or an identified portion of such an asset, liability or firm commitment, that is attributable to a particular risk and could affect profit or loss.**

(b) *cash flow hedge*: **a hedge of the exposure to variability in cash flows that (i) is attributable to a particular risk associated with a recognised asset or liability (such as all or some future interest payments on variable rate debt) or a highly probable forecast transaction and (ii) could affect profit or loss.**

(c) *hedge of a net investment in a foreign operation* **as defined in IAS 21.**

87 A hedge of the foreign currency risk of a firm commitment may be accounted for as a fair value hedge or as a cash flow hedge.

88 **A hedging relationship qualifies for hedge accounting under paragraphs 89–102 if, and only if, all of the following conditions are met.**

(a) At the inception of the hedge there is formal designation and documentation of the hedging relationship and the entity's risk management objective and strategy for undertaking the hedge. That documentation shall include identification of the hedging instrument, the hedged item or transaction, the nature of the risk being hedged and how the entity will assess the hedging instrument's effectiveness in offsetting the exposure to changes in the hedged item's fair value or cash flows attributable to the hedged risk.

(b) The hedge is expected to be highly effective (see Appendix A paragraphs AG105–AG113) in achieving offsetting changes in fair value or cash flows attributable to the hedged risk, consistently with the originally documented risk management strategy for that particular hedging relationship.

(c) For cash flow hedges, a forecast transaction that is the subject of the hedge must be highly probable and must present an exposure to variations in cash flows that could ultimately affect profit or loss.

(d) The effectiveness of the hedge can be reliably measured, ie the fair value or cash flows of the hedged item that are attributable to the hedged risk and the fair value of the hedging instrument can be reliably measured (see paragraphs 46 and 47 and Appendix A paragraphs AG80 and AG81 for guidance on determining fair value).

(e) The hedge is assessed on an ongoing basis and determined actually to have been highly effective throughout the financial reporting periods for which the hedge was designated.

Fair value hedges

89 **If a fair value hedge meets the conditions in paragraph 88 during the period, it shall be accounted for as follows:**

(a) the gain or loss from remeasuring the hedging instrument at fair value (for a derivative hedging instrument) or the foreign currency component of its carrying amount measured in accordance with IAS 21 (for a non-derivative hedging instrument) shall be recognised in profit or loss; and

(b) the gain or loss on the hedged item attributable to the hedged risk shall adjust the carrying amount of the hedged item and be recognised in profit or loss. This applies if the hedged item is otherwise measured at cost. Recognition of the gain or loss attributable to the hedged risk in profit or loss applies if the hedged item is an available-for-sale financial asset.

89A For a fair value hedge of the interest rate exposure of a portion of a portfolio of financial assets or financial liabilities (and only in such a hedge), the requirement in paragraph 89(b) may be met by presenting the gain or loss attributable to the hedged item either:

(a) in a single separate line item within assets, for those repricing time periods for which the hedged item is an asset; or

(b) in a single separate line item within liabilities, for those repricing time periods for which the hedged item is a liability.

The separate line items referred to in (a) and (b) above shall be presented next to financial assets or financial liabilities. Amounts included in these line items shall be removed from the balance sheet when the assets or liabilities to which they relate are derecognised.

90 If only particular risks attributable to a hedged item are hedged, recognised changes in the fair value of the hedged item unrelated to the hedged risk are recognised as set out in paragraph 55.

91 An entity shall discontinue prospectively the hedge accounting specified in paragraph 89 if:

(a) the hedging instrument expires or is sold, terminated or exercised (for this purpose, the replacement or rollover of a hedging instrument into another hedging instrument is not an expiration or termination if such replacement or rollover is part of the entity's documented hedging strategy);

(b) the hedge no longer meets the criteria for hedge accounting in paragraph 88; or

(c) the entity revokes the designation.

92 Any adjustment arising from paragraph 89(b) to the carrying amount of a hedged financial instrument for which the effective interest method is used (or, in the case of a portfolio hedge of interest rate risk, to the separate balance sheet line item described in paragraph 89A) shall be amortised to profit or loss. Amortisation may begin as soon as an adjustment exists and shall begin no later than when the hedged item ceases to be adjusted for changes in its fair value attributable to the risk being hedged. The adjustment is based on a recalculated effective interest rate at the date amortisation begins. However, if, in the case of a fair value hedge of the interest rate exposure of a portfolio of financial assets or financial liabilities (and only in such a hedge), amortising using a recalculated effective interest rate is not practicable, the adjustment shall be amortised using a straight-line method. The adjustment shall be amortised fully by maturity of the financial instrument or, in the case of a portfolio hedge of interest rate risk, by expiry of the relevant repricing time period.

93 When an unrecognised firm commitment is designated as a hedged item, the subsequent cumulative change in the fair value of the firm commitment attributable to the hedged risk is recognised as an asset or liability with a corresponding gain or loss recognised in profit or loss (see paragraph 89(b)). The changes in the fair value of the hedging instrument are also recognised in profit or loss.

94 When an entity enters into a firm commitment to acquire an asset or assume a liability that is a hedged item in a fair value hedge, the initial carrying amount of the asset or liability that results from the entity meeting the firm commitment is

adjusted to include the cumulative change in the fair value of the firm commitment attributable to the hedged risk that was recognised in the balance sheet.

Cash flow hedges

95 **If a cash flow hedge meets the conditions in paragraph 88 during the period, it shall be accounted for as follows:**

(a) the portion of the gain or loss on the hedging instrument that is determined to be an effective hedge (see paragraph 88) shall be recognised directly in equity through the statement of changes in equity (see IAS 1); and

(b) the ineffective portion of the gain or loss on the hedging instrument shall be recognised in profit or loss.

96 More specifically, a cash flow hedge is accounted for as follows:

(a) the separate component of equity associated with the hedged item is adjusted to the lesser of the following (in absolute amounts):

(i) the cumulative gain or loss on the hedging instrument from inception of the hedge; and

(ii) the cumulative change in fair value (present value) of the expected future cash flows on the hedged item from inception of the hedge;

(b) any remaining gain or loss on the hedging instrument or designated component of it (that is not an effective hedge) is recognised in profit or loss; and

(c) if an entity's documented risk management strategy for a particular hedging relationship excludes from the assessment of hedge effectiveness a specific component of the gain or loss or related cash flows on the hedging instrument (see paragraphs 74, 75 and 88(a)), that excluded component of gain or loss is recognised in accordance with paragraph 55.

97 **If a hedge of a forecast transaction subsequently results in the recognition of a financial asset or a financial liability, the associated gains or losses that were recognised directly in equity in accordance with paragraph 95 shall be reclassified into profit or loss in the same period or periods during which the asset acquired or liability assumed affects profit or loss (such as in the periods that interest income or interest expense is recognised). However, if an entity expects that all or a portion of a loss recognised directly in equity will not be recovered in one or more future periods, it shall reclassify into profit or loss the amount that is not expected to be recovered.**

98 **If a hedge of a forecast transaction subsequently results in the recognition of a non-financial asset or a non-financial liability, or a forecast transaction for a non-financial asset or non-financial liability becomes a firm commitment for which fair value hedge accounting is applied, then the entity shall adopt (a) or (b) below:**

(a) **It reclassifies the associated gains and losses that were recognised directly in equity in accordance with paragraph 95 into profit or loss in the same period or periods during which the asset acquired or liability assumed affects profit or loss (such as in the periods that depreciation expense or cost of sales is recognised). However, if an entity expects that all or a portion of a loss recognised directly in equity will not be recovered in one or more future periods, it shall reclassify into profit or loss the amount that is not expected to be recovered.**

(b) **It removes the associated gains and losses that were recognised directly in equity in accordance with paragraph 95, and includes them in the initial cost or other carrying amount of the asset or liability.**

99 **An entity shall adopt either (a) or (b) in paragraph 98 as its accounting policy and shall apply it consistently to all hedges to which paragraph 98 relates.**

100 **For cash flow hedges other than those covered by paragraphs 97 and 98, amounts that had been recognised directly in equity shall be recognised in profit or loss in the same period or periods during which the hedged forecast transaction affects profit or loss (for example, when a forecast sale occurs).**

101 **In any of the following circumstances an entity shall discontinue prospectively the hedge accounting specified in paragraphs 95–100:**

(a) **The hedging instrument expires or is sold, terminated or exercised (for this purpose, the replacement or rollover of a hedging instrument into another hedging instrument is not an expiration or termination if such replacement or rollover is part of the entity's documented hedging strategy). In this case, the cumulative gain or loss on the hedging instrument that remains recognised directly in equity from the period when the hedge was effective (see paragraph 95(a)) shall remain separately recognised in equity until the forecast transaction occurs. When the transaction occurs, paragraph 97, 98 or 100 applies.**

(b) **The hedge no longer meets the criteria for hedge accounting in paragraph 88. In this case, the cumulative gain or loss on the hedging instrument that remains recognised directly in equity from the period when the hedge was effective (see paragraph 95(a)) shall remain separately recognised in equity until the forecast transaction occurs. When the transaction occurs, paragraph 97, 98 or 100 applies.**

(c) **The forecast transaction is no longer expected to occur, in which case any related cumulative gain or loss on the hedging instrument that remains recognised directly in equity from the period when the hedge was effective (see paragraph 95(a)) shall be recognised in profit or loss. A forecast transaction that is no longer highly probable (see paragraph 88(c)) may still be expected to occur.**

(d) **The entity revokes the designation. For hedges of a forecast transaction, the cumulative gain or loss on the hedging instrument that remains recognised directly in equity from the period when the**

hedge was effective (see paragraph 95(a)) shall remain separately recognised in equity until the forecast transaction occurs or is no longer expected to occur. When the transaction occurs, paragraph 97, 98 or 100 applies. If the transaction is no longer expected to occur, the cumulative gain or loss that had been recognised directly in equity shall be recognised in profit or loss.

Hedges of a net investment

102 **Hedges of a net investment in a foreign operation, including a hedge of a monetary item that is accounted for as part of the net investment (see IAS 21), shall be accounted for similarly to cash flow hedges:**

(a) the portion of the gain or loss on the hedging instrument that is determined to be an effective hedge (see paragraph 88) shall be recognised directly in equity through the statement of changes in equity (see IAS 1); and

(b) the ineffective portion shall be recognised in profit or loss.

The gain or loss on the hedging instrument relating to the effective portion of the hedge that has been recognised directly in equity shall be recognised in profit or loss on disposal of the foreign operation.

Effective date and transition

103 **An entity shall apply this Standard (including the amendments issued in March 2004) for annual periods beginning on or after 1 January 2005. Earlier application is permitted. An entity shall not apply this Standard (including the amendments issued in March 2004) for annual periods beginning before 1 January 2005 unless it also applies IAS 32 (issued December 2003). If an entity applies this Standard for a period beginning before 1 January 2005, it shall disclose that fact.**

103A **An entity shall apply the amendment in paragraph 2(j) for annual periods beginning on or after 1 January 2006. If an entity applies IFRIC 5** *Rights to Interests arising from Decommissioning, Restoration and Environmental Rehabilitation Funds* **for an earlier period, this amendment shall be applied for that earlier period.**

104 **This Standard shall be applied retrospectively except as specified in paragraphs 105–108. The opening balance of retained earnings for the earliest prior period presented and all other comparative amounts shall be adjusted as if this Standard had always been in use unless restating the information would be impracticable. If restatement is impracticable, the entity shall disclose that fact and indicate the extent to which the information was restated.**

105 **When this Standard is first applied, an entity is permitted to designate a previously recognised financial asset or financial liability as a financial asset or financial liability at fair value through profit or loss or available for sale despite the requirement in paragraph 9 to make such designation upon initial recognition. For any such financial asset designated as available for sale, the entity shall recognise all cumulative changes in fair**

value in a separate component of equity until subsequent derecognition or impairment, when the entity shall transfer that cumulative gain or loss to profit or loss. For any financial instrument designated as at fair value through profit or loss or available for sale, the entity shall:

(a) restate the financial asset or financial liability using the new designation in the comparative financial statements; and

(b) disclose the fair value of the financial assets or financial liabilities designated into each category and the classification and carrying amount in the previous financial statements.

106 Except as permitted by paragraph 107, an entity shall apply the derecognition requirements in paragraphs 15–37 and Appendix A paragraphs AG36–AG52 prospectively. Accordingly, if an entity derecognised financial assets under IAS 39 (revised 2000) as a result of a transaction that occurred before 1 January 2,004 and those assets would not have been derecognised under this Standard, it shall not recognise those assets.

107 Notwithstanding paragraph 106, an entity may apply the derecognition requirements in paragraphs 15–37 and Appendix A paragraphs AG36–AG52 retrospectively from a date of the entity's choosing, provided that the information needed to apply IAS 39 to assets and liabilities derecognised as a result of past transactions was obtained at the time of initially accounting for those transactions.

107A Notwithstanding paragraph 104, an entity may apply the requirements in the last sentence of paragraph AG76, and paragraph AG76A, in either of the following ways:

(a) prospectively to transactions entered into after 25 October 2002; or

(b) prospectively to transactions entered into after 1 January 2004.

108 An entity shall not adjust the carrying amount of non-financial assets and non-financial liabilities to exclude gains and losses related to cash flow hedges that were included in the carrying amount before the beginning of the financial year in which this Standard is first applied. At the beginning of the financial period in which this Standard is first applied, any amount recognised directly in equity for a hedge of a firm commitment that under this Standard is accounted for as a fair value hedge shall be reclassified as an asset or liability, except for a hedge of foreign currency risk that continues to be treated as a cash flow hedge.

Withdrawal of other pronouncements

109 This Standard supersedes IAS 39 *Financial Instruments: Recognition and Measurement* revised in October 2000.

110 This Standard and the accompanying Implementation Guidance supersede the Implementation Guidance issued by the IAS 39 Implementation Guidance Committee, established by the former IASC.

Appendix A
Application guidance

This appendix is an integral part of the Standard.

Scope (paragraphs 2–7)

AG1 Some contracts require a payment based on climatic, geological or other physical variables. (Those based on climatic variables are sometimes referred to as 'weather derivatives'.) If those contracts are not within the scope of IFRS 4 *Insurance Contracts*, they are within the scope of this Standard.

AG2 This Standard does not change the requirements relating to employee benefit plans that comply with IAS 26 *Accounting and Reporting by Retirement Benefit Plans* and royalty agreements based on the volume of sales or service revenues that are accounted for under IAS 18 *Revenue*.

AG3 Sometimes, an entity makes what it views as a 'strategic investment' in equity instruments issued by another entity, with the intention of establishing or maintaining a long-term operating relationship with the entity in which the investment is made. The investor entity uses IAS 28 *Investments in Associates* to determine whether the equity method of accounting is appropriate for such an investment. Similarly, the investor entity uses IAS 31 *Interests in Joint Ventures* to determine whether proportionate consolidation or the equity method is appropriate for such an investment. If neither the equity method nor proportionate consolidation is appropriate, the entity applies this Standard to that strategic investment.

AG4 This Standard applies to the financial assets and financial liabilities of insurers, other than rights and obligations that paragraph 2(e) excludes because they arise under contracts within the scope of IFRS 4.

AG4A Financial guarantee contracts may have various legal forms, such as a financial guarantee, letter of credit, credit default contract or insurance contract. Their accounting treatment does not depend on their legal form. The following are examples of the appropriate treatment (see paragraphs 2(e) and 3):

(a) If the contract is not an insurance contract, as defined in IFRS 4, the issuer applies this Standard. Thus, a financial guarantee contract that requires payments if the credit rating of a debtor falls below a particular level is within the scope of this Standard.

(b) If the issuer incurred or retained the financial guarantee on transferring to another party financial assets or financial liabilities within the scope of this Standard, the issuer applies this Standard.

(c) If the contract is an insurance contract, as defined in IFRS 4, the issuer applies IFRS 4 unless (b) applies.

(d) If the issuer gave a financial guarantee in connection with the sale of goods, the issuer applies IAS 18 in determining when it recognises the resulting revenue.

Definitions (paragraphs 8 and 9)

Effective interest rate

AG5 In some cases, financial assets are acquired at a deep discount that reflects incurred credit losses. Entities include such incurred credit losses in the estimated cash flows when computing the effective interest rate.

AG6 When applying the effective interest method, an entity generally amortises any fees, points paid or received, transaction costs and other premiums or discounts included in the calculation of the effective interest rate over the expected life of the instrument. However, a shorter period is used if this is the period to which the fees, points paid or received, transaction costs, premiums or discounts relate. This will be the case when the variable to which the fees, points paid or received, transaction costs, premiums or discounts relate is repriced to market rates before the expected maturity of the instrument. In such a case, the appropriate amortisation period is the period to the next such repricing date. For example, if a premium or discount on a floating rate instrument reflects interest that has accrued on the instrument since interest was last paid, or changes in market rates since the floating interest rate was reset to market rates, it will be amortised to the next date when the floating interest is reset to market rates. This is because the premium or discount relates to the period to the next interest reset date because, at that date, the variable to which the premium or discount relates (ie interest rates) is reset to market rates. If, however, the premium or discount results from a change in the credit spread over the floating rate specified in the instrument, or other variables that are not reset to market rates, it is amortised over the expected life of the instrument.

AG7 For floating rate financial assets and floating rate financial liabilities, periodic re-estimation of cash flows to reflect movements in market rates of interest alters the effective interest rate. If a floating rate financial asset or floating rate financial liability is recognised initially at an amount equal to the principal receivable or payable on maturity, re-estimating the future interest payments normally has no significant effect on the carrying amount of the asset or liability.

AG8 If an entity revises its estimates of payments or receipts, the entity shall adjust the carrying amount of the financial asset or financial liability (or group of financial instruments) to reflect actual and revised estimated cash flows. The entity recalculates the carrying amount by computing the present value of estimated future cash flows at the financial instrument's original effective interest rate. The adjustment is recognised as income or expense in profit or loss.

Derivatives

AG9 Typical examples of derivatives are futures and forward, swap and option contracts. A derivative usually has a notional amount, which is an amount of currency, a number of shares, a number of units of weight or volume or other units specified in the contract. However, a derivative instrument does not require the holder or writer to invest or receive the notional amount at the inception of the contract. Alternatively, a derivative could require a fixed payment or payment of an amount that can change (but not proportionally with a change in the underlying) as a result of some future event that is unrelated to a notional amount. For example, a contract may require a fixed payment of CU1,000[*] if six-month LIBOR increases by 100 basis points. Such a contract is a derivative even though a notional amount is not specified.

AG10 The definition of a derivative in this Standard includes contracts that are settled gross by delivery of the underlying item (eg a forward contract to purchase a fixed rate debt instrument). An entity may have a contract to buy or sell a non-financial item that can be settled net in cash or another financial instrument or by exchanging financial instruments (eg a contract to buy or sell a commodity at a fixed price at a future date). Such a contract is within the scope of this Standard unless it was entered into and continues to be held for the purpose of delivery of a non-financial item in accordance with the entity's expected purchase, sale or usage requirements (see paragraphs 5–7).

AG11 One of the defining characteristics of a derivative is that it has an initial net investment that is smaller than would be required for other types of contracts that would be expected to have a similar response to changes in market factors. An option contract meets that definition because the premium is less than the investment that would be required to obtain the underlying financial instrument to which the option is linked. A currency swap that requires an initial exchange of different currencies of equal fair values meets the definition because it has a zero initial net investment.

AG12 A regular way purchase or sale gives rise to a fixed price commitment between trade date and settlement date that meets the definition of a derivative. However, because of the short duration of the commitment it is not recognised as a derivative financial instrument. Rather, this Standard provides for special accounting for such regular way contracts (see paragraphs 38 and AG53–AG56).

AG12A The definition of a derivative refers to non-financial variables that are not specific to a party to the contract. These include an index of earthquake losses in a particular region and an index of temperatures in a particular city. Non-financial variables specific to a party to the contract include the occurrence or non-occurrence of a fire that damages or destroys an asset of a party to the contract. A change in the fair value of a non-financial asset is specific to the owner if the fair value reflects not only changes in market prices for such assets (a financial variable) but also the condition of the specific non-financial asset held (a non-financial variable). For example, if a guarantee of the residual value of a specific car exposes the guarantor to the risk of changes in the car's physical condition, the change in that residual value is specific to the owner of the car.

Transaction costs

AG13 Transaction costs include fees and commissions paid to agents (including employees acting as selling agents), advisers, brokers and dealers, levies by regulatory agencies and securities exchanges, and transfer taxes and duties. Transaction costs do not include debt premiums or discounts, financing costs or internal administrative or holding costs.

---

* In this Standard, monetary amounts are denominated in 'currency units' (CU).

Financial assets and financial liabilities held for trading

AG14 Trading generally reflects active and frequent buying and selling, and financial instruments held for trading generally are used with the objective of generating a profit from short-term fluctuations in price or dealer's margin.

AG15 Financial liabilities held for trading include:

(a) derivative liabilities that are not accounted for as hedging instruments;

(b) obligations to deliver financial assets borrowed by a short seller (ie an entity that sells financial assets it has borrowed and does not yet own);

(c) financial liabilities that are incurred with an intention to repurchase them in the near term (eg a quoted debt instrument that the issuer may buy back in the near term depending on changes in its fair value); and

(d) financial liabilities that are part of a portfolio of identified financial instruments that are managed together and for which there is evidence of a recent pattern of short-term profit-taking.

The fact that a liability is used to fund trading activities does not in itself make that liability one that is held for trading.

Held–to–maturity investments

AG16 An entity does not have a positive intention to hold to maturity an investment in a financial asset with a fixed maturity if:

(a) the entity intends to hold the financial asset for an undefined period;

(b) the entity stands ready to sell the financial asset (other than if a situation arises that is non-recurring and could not have been reasonably anticipated by the entity) in response to changes in market interest rates or risks, liquidity needs, changes in the availability of and the yield on alternative investments, changes in financing sources and terms or changes in foreign currency risk; or

(c) the issuer has a right to settle the financial asset at an amount significantly below its amortised cost.

AG17 A debt instrument with a variable interest rate can satisfy the criteria for a held–to–maturity investment. Equity instruments cannot be held–to–maturity investments either because they have an indefinite life (such as ordinary shares) or because the amounts the holder may receive can vary in a manner that is not predetermined (such as for share options, warrants and similar rights). With respect to the definition of held–to–maturity investments, fixed or determinable payments and fixed maturity mean that a contractual arrangement defines the amounts and dates of payments to the holder, such as interest and principal payments. A significant risk of non-payment does not preclude classification of a financial asset as held to maturity as long as its contractual payments are fixed or determinable and the other criteria for that classification are met. If the terms of a perpetual debt instrument provide for interest payments for an indefinite period, the instrument cannot be classified as held to maturity because there is no maturity date.

AG18 The criteria for classification as a held-to-maturity investment are met for a financial asset that is callable by the issuer if the holder intends and is able to hold it until it is called or until maturity and the holder would recover substantially all of its carrying amount. The call option of the issuer, if exercised, simply accelerates the asset's maturity. However, if the financial asset is callable on a basis that would result in the holder not recovering substantially all of its carrying amount, the financial asset cannot be classified as a held-to-maturity investment. The entity considers any premium paid and capitalised transaction costs in determining whether the carrying amount would be substantially recovered.

AG19 A financial asset that is puttable (ie the holder has the right to require that the issuer repay or redeem the financial asset before maturity) cannot be classified as a held-to-maturity investment because paying for a put feature in a financial asset is inconsistent with expressing an intention to hold the financial asset until maturity.

AG20 For most financial assets, fair value is a more appropriate measure than amortised cost. The held-to-maturity classification is an exception, but only if the entity has a positive intention and the ability to hold the investment to maturity. When an entity's actions cast doubt on its intention and ability to hold such investments to maturity, paragraph 9 precludes the use of the exception for a reasonable period of time.

AG21 A disaster scenario that is only remotely possible, such as a run on a bank or a similar situation affecting an insurer, is not something that is assessed by an entity in deciding whether it has the positive intention and ability to hold an investment to maturity.

AG22 Sales before maturity could satisfy the condition in paragraph 9—and therefore not raise a question about the entity's intention to hold other investments to maturity—if they are attributable to any of the following:

(a) a significant deterioration in the issuer's creditworthiness. For example, a sale following a downgrade in a credit rating by an external rating agency would not necessarily raise a question about the entity's intention to hold other investments to maturity if the downgrade provides evidence of a significant deterioration in the issuer's creditworthiness judged by reference to the credit rating at initial recognition. Similarly, if an entity uses internal ratings for assessing exposures, changes in those internal ratings may help to identify issuers for which there has been a significant deterioration in creditworthiness, provided the entity's approach to assigning internal ratings and changes in those ratings give a consistent, reliable and objective measure of the credit quality of the issuers. If there is evidence that a financial asset is impaired (see paragraphs 58 and 59), the deterioration in creditworthiness is often regarded as significant.

(b) a change in tax law that eliminates or significantly reduces the tax-exempt status of interest on the held-to-maturity investment (but not a change in tax law that revises the marginal tax rates applicable to interest income).

(c) a major business combination or major disposition (such as a sale of a segment) that necessitates the sale or transfer of held-to-maturity investments to maintain the entity's existing interest rate risk position or credit risk policy (although the business combination is an event within the entity's control, the changes to its investment portfolio to maintain an interest rate risk position or credit risk policy may be consequential rather than anticipated).

(d) a change in statutory or regulatory requirements significantly modifying either what constitutes a permissible investment or the maximum level of particular types of investments, thereby causing an entity to dispose of a held-to-maturity investment.

(e) a significant increase in the industry's regulatory capital requirements that causes the entity to downsize by selling held-to-maturity investments.

(f) a significant increase in the risk weights of held-to-maturity investments used for regulatory risk-based capital purposes.

AG23 An entity does not have a demonstrated ability to hold to maturity an investment in a financial asset with a fixed maturity if:

(a) it does not have the financial resources available to continue to finance the investment until maturity; or

(b) it is subject to an existing legal or other constraint that could frustrate its intention to hold the financial asset to maturity. (However, an issuer's call option does not necessarily frustrate an entity's intention to hold a financial asset to maturity—see paragraph AG18.)

AG24 Circumstances other than those described in paragraphs AG16–AG23 can indicate that an entity does not have a positive intention or the ability to hold an investment to maturity.

AG25 An entity assesses its intention and ability to hold its held-to-maturity investments to maturity not only when those financial assets are initially recognised, but also at each subsequent balance sheet date.

Loans and receivables

AG26 Any non-derivative financial asset with fixed or determinable payments (including loan assets, trade receivables, investments in debt instruments and deposits held in banks) could potentially meet the definition of loans and receivables. However, a financial asset that is quoted in an active market (such as a quoted debt instrument, see paragraph AG71) does not qualify for classification as a loan or receivable. Financial assets that do not meet the definition of loans and receivables may be classified as held-to-maturity investments if they meet the conditions for that classification (see paragraphs 9 and AG16–AG25). On initial recognition of a financial asset that would otherwise be classified as a loan or receivable, an entity may designate it as a financial asset at fair value through profit or loss, or available for sale.

Embedded derivatives (paragraphs 10–13)

AG27 If a host contract has no stated or predetermined maturity and represents a residual interest in the net assets of an entity, then its economic characteristics and risks are those of an equity instrument, and an embedded derivative would need to possess equity characteristics related to the same entity to be regarded as closely related. If the host contract is not an equity instrument and meets the definition of a financial instrument, then its economic characteristics and risks are those of a debt instrument.

AG28 An embedded non-option derivative (such as an embedded forward or swap) is separated from its host contract on the basis of its stated or implied substantive terms, so as to result in it having a fair value of zero at initial recognition. An embedded option-based derivative (such as an embedded put, call, cap, floor or swaption) is separated from its host contract on the basis of the stated terms of the option feature. The initial carrying amount of the host instrument is the residual amount after separating the embedded derivative.

AG29 Generally, multiple embedded derivatives in a single instrument are treated as a single compound embedded derivative. However, embedded derivatives that are classified as equity (see IAS 32 *Financial Instruments: Disclosure and Presentation*) are accounted for separately from those classified as assets or liabilities. In addition, if an instrument has more than one embedded derivative and those derivatives relate to different risk exposures and are readily separable and independent of each other, they are accounted for separately from each other.

AG30 The economic characteristics and risks of an embedded derivative are not closely related to the host contract (paragraph 11(a)) in the following examples. In these examples, assuming the conditions in paragraph 11(b) and (c) are met, an entity accounts for the embedded derivative separately from the host contract.

(a) A put option embedded in an instrument that enables the holder to require the issuer to reacquire the instrument for an amount of cash or other assets that varies on the basis of the change in an equity or commodity price or index is not closely related to a host debt instrument.

(b) A call option embedded in an equity instrument that enables the issuer to reacquire that equity instrument at a specified price is not closely related to the host equity instrument from the perspective of the holder (from the issuer's perspective, the call option is an equity instrument provided it meets the conditions for that classification under IAS 32, in which case it is excluded from the scope of this Standard).

(c) An option or automatic provision to extend the remaining term to maturity of a debt instrument is not closely related to the host debt instrument unless there is a concurrent adjustment to the approximate current market rate of interest at the time of the extension. If an entity issues a debt instrument and the holder of that debt instrument writes a call option on the debt instrument to a third party, the issuer regards the call option as extending the term to maturity of the debt instrument provided the issuer can be required to participate in or facilitate the remarketing of the debt instrument as a result of the call option being exercised.

(d) Equity-indexed interest or principal payments embedded in a host debt instrument or insurance contract—by which the amount of interest or principal is indexed to the value of equity instruments—are not closely related to the host instrument because the risks inherent in the host and the embedded derivative are dissimilar.

(e) Commodity-indexed interest or principal payments embedded in a host debt instrument or insurance contract–by which the amount of interest or principal is indexed to the price of a commodity (such as gold)–are not closely related to the host instrument because the risks inherent in the host and the embedded derivative are dissimilar.

(f) An equity conversion feature embedded in a convertible debt instrument is not closely related to the host debt instrument from the perspective of the holder of the instrument (from the issuer's perspective, the equity conversion option is an equity instrument and excluded from the scope of this Standard provided it meets the conditions for that classification under IAS 32).

(g) A call, put, or prepayment option embedded in a host debt contract or host insurance contract is not closely related to the host contract unless the option's exercise price is approximately equal on each exercise date to the amortised cost of the host debt instrument or the carrying amount of the host insurance contract. From the perspective of the issuer of a convertible debt instrument with an embedded call or put option feature, the assessment of whether the call or put option is closely related to the host debt contract is made before separating the equity element under IAS 32.

(h) Credit derivatives that are embedded in a host debt instrument and allow one party (the 'beneficiary') to transfer the credit risk of a particular reference asset, which it may not own, to another party (the 'guarantor') are not closely related to the host debt instrument. Such credit derivatives allow the guarantor to assume the credit risk associated with the reference asset without directly owning it.

AG31 An example of a hybrid instrument is a financial instrument that gives the holder a right to put the financial instrument back to the issuer in exchange for an amount of cash or other financial assets that varies on the basis of the change in an equity or commodity index that may increase or decrease (a 'puttable instrument'). Unless the issuer on initial recognition designates the puttable instrument as a financial liability at fair value through profit or loss, it is required to separate an embedded derivative (ie the indexed principal payment) under paragraph 11 because the host contract is a debt instrument under paragraph AG27 and the indexed principal payment is not closely related to a host debt instrument under paragraph AG30(a). Because the principal payment can increase and decrease, the embedded derivative is a non-option derivative whose value is indexed to the underlying variable.

AG32 In the case of a puttable instrument that can be put back at any time for cash equal to a proportionate share of the net asset value of an entity (such as units of an open-ended mutual fund or some unit-linked investment products), the effect of separating an embedded derivative and accounting for each component is to measure the combined instrument at the redemption amount that is payable at the balance sheet date if the holder exercised its right to put the instrument back to the issuer.

AG33 The economic characteristics and risks of an embedded derivative are closely related to the economic characteristics and risks of the host contract in the following examples. In these examples, an entity does not account for the embedded derivative separately from the host contract.

(a) An embedded derivative in which the underlying is an interest rate or interest rate index that can change the amount of interest that would otherwise be paid or received on an interest-bearing host debt contract or insurance contract is closely related to the host contract unless the combined instrument can be settled in such a way that the holder would not recover substantially all of its recognised investment or the embedded derivative could at least double the holder's initial rate of return on the host contract and could result in a rate of return that is at least twice what the market return would be for a contract with the same terms as the host contract.

(b) An embedded floor or cap on the interest rate on a debt contract or insurance contract is closely related to the host contract, provided the cap is at or above the market rate of interest and the floor is at or below the market rate of interest when the contract is issued, and the cap or floor is not leveraged in relation to the host contract. Similarly, provisions included in a contract to purchase or sell an asset (eg a commodity) that establish a cap and a floor on the price to be paid or received for the asset are closely related to the host contract if both the cap and floor were out of the money at inception and are not leveraged.

(c) An embedded foreign currency derivative that provides a stream of principal or interest payments that are denominated in a foreign currency and is embedded in a host debt instrument (eg a dual currency bond) is closely related to the host debt instrument. Such a derivative is not separated from the host instrument because IAS 21 *The Effects of Changes in Foreign Exchange Rates* requires foreign currency gains and losses on monetary items to be recognised in profit or loss.

(d) An embedded foreign currency derivative in a host contract that is an insurance contract or not a financial instrument (such as a contract for the purchase or sale of a non-financial item where the price is denominated in a foreign currency) is closely related to the host contract provided it is not leveraged, does not contain an option feature, and requires payments denominated in one of the following currencies:

  (i) the functional currency of any substantial party to that contract;

  (ii) the currency in which the price of the related good or service that is acquired or delivered is routinely denominated in commercial transactions around the world (such as the US dollar for crude oil transactions); or

  (iii) a currency that is commonly used in contracts to purchase or sell non-financial items in the economic environment in which the transaction takes place (eg a relatively stable and liquid currency that is commonly used in local business transactions or external trade).

(e) An embedded prepayment option in an interest-only or principal-only strip is closely related to the host contract provided the host contract (i) initially resulted from separating the right to receive contractual cash flows of a financial instrument that, in and of itself, did not contain an embedded derivative, and (ii) does not contain any terms not present in the original host debt contract.

(f) An embedded derivative in a host lease contract is closely related to the host contract if the embedded derivative is (i) an inflation-related index such as an index of lease payments to a consumer price index (provided that the lease is not leveraged and the index relates to inflation in the entity's own economic environment), (ii) contingent rentals based on related sales or (iii) contingent rentals based on variable interest rates.

(g) A unit-linking feature embedded in a host financial instrument or host insurance contract is closely related to the host instrument or host contract if the unit-denominated payments are measured at current unit values that reflect the fair values of the assets of the fund. A unit-linking feature is a contractual term that requires payments denominated in units of an internal or external investment fund.

(h) A derivative embedded in an insurance contract is closely related to the host insurance contract if the embedded derivative and host insurance contract are so interdependent that an entity cannot measure the embedded derivative separately (ie without considering the host contract).

Recognition and derecognition (paragraphs 14–42)

Initial recognition (paragraph 14)

AG34 As a consequence of the principle in paragraph 14, an entity recognises all of its contractual rights and obligations under derivatives in its balance sheet as assets and liabilities, respectively, except for derivatives that prevent a transfer of financial assets from being accounted for as a sale (see paragraph AG49). If a transfer of a financial asset does not qualify for derecognition, the transferee does not recognise the transferred asset as its asset (see paragraph AG50).

AG35 The following are examples of applying the principle in paragraph 14:

(a) unconditional receivables and payables are recognised as assets or liabilities when the entity becomes a party to the contract and, as a consequence, has a legal right to receive or a legal obligation to pay cash.

(b) assets to be acquired and liabilities to be incurred as a result of a firm commitment to purchase or sell goods or services are generally not recognised until at least one of the parties has performed under the agreement. For example, an entity that receives a firm order does not generally recognise an asset (and the entity that places the order does not recognise a liability) at the time of the commitment but, rather, delays recognition until the ordered goods or services have been shipped, delivered or rendered. If a firm commitment to buy or sell non-financial items is within the scope of this Standard under paragraphs 5–7, its net fair value is recognised as an asset or liability on the commitment date (see (c) below). In addition, if a previously unrecognised firm commitment is designated as a hedged item in a fair value hedge, any change in the net fair value attributable to the hedged risk is recognised as an asset or liability after the inception of the hedge (see paragraphs 93 and 94).

(c) a forward contract that is within the scope of this Standard (see paragraphs 2–7) is recognised as an asset or a liability on the commitment date, rather than on the date on which settlement takes place. When an entity becomes a party to a forward contract, the fair values of the right and obligation are often equal, so that the net fair value of the forward is zero. If the net fair value of the right and obligation is not zero, the contract is recognised as an asset or liability.

(d) option contracts that are within the scope of this Standard (see paragraphs 2–7) are recognised as assets or liabilities when the holder or writer becomes a party to the contract.

(e) planned future transactions, no matter how likely, are not assets and liabilities because the entity has not become a party to a contract.

Derecognition of a financial asset (paragraphs 15–37)

AG36 The following flow chart illustrates the evaluation of whether and to what extent a financial asset is derecognised.

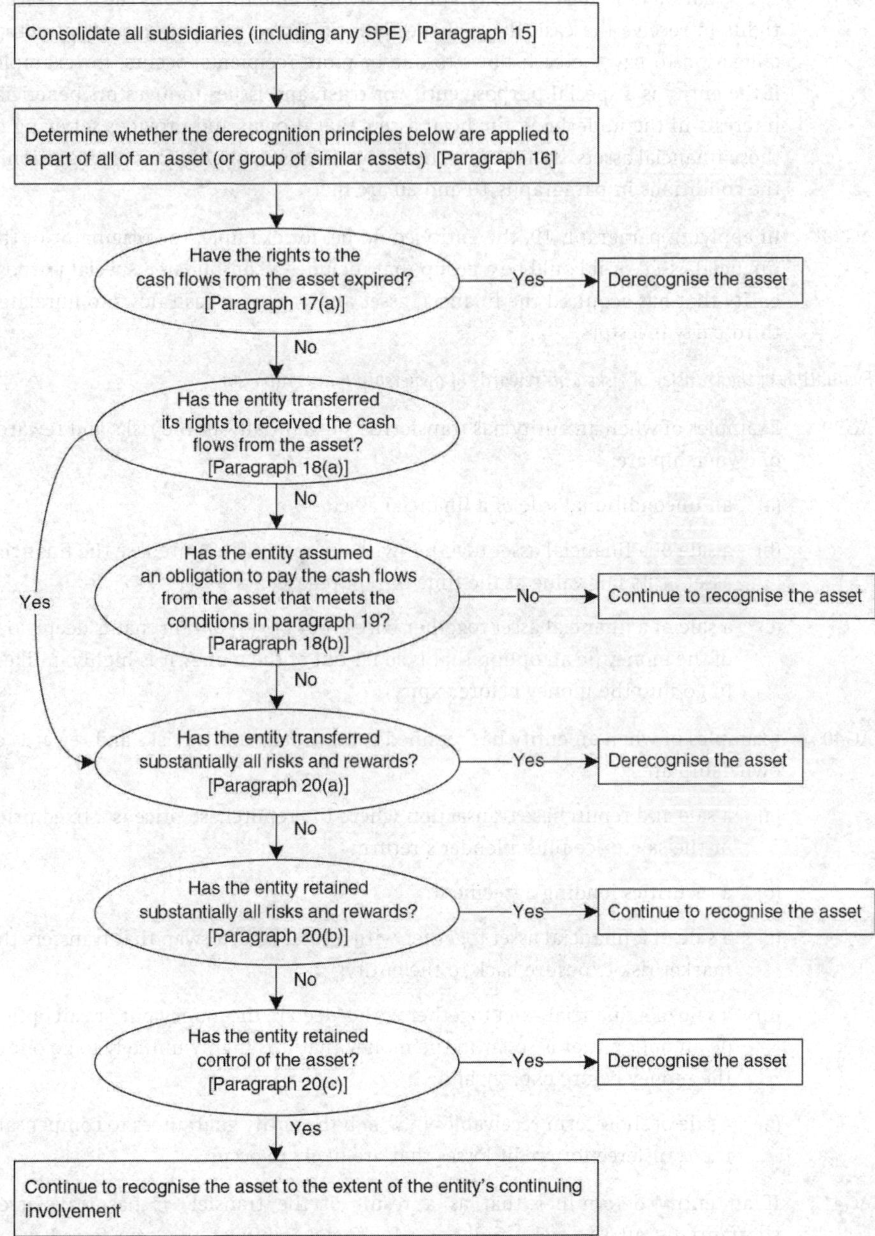

Arrangements under which an entity retains the contractual rights to receive the cash flows of a financial asset, but assumes a contractual obligation to pay the cash flows to one or more recipients (paragraph 18(b))

AG37 The situation described in paragraph 18(b) (when an entity retains the contractual rights to receive the cash flows of the financial asset, but assumes a contractual obligation to pay the cash flows to one or more recipients) occurs, for example, if the entity is a special purpose entity or trust, and issues to investors beneficial interests in the underlying financial assets that it owns and provides servicing of those financial assets. In that case, the financial assets qualify for derecognition if the conditions in paragraphs 19 and 20 are met.

AG38 In applying paragraph 19, the entity could be, for example, the originator of the financial asset, or it could be a group that includes a consolidated special purpose entity that has acquired the financial asset and passes on cash flows to unrelated third party investors.

Evaluation of the transfer of risks and rewards of ownership (paragraph 20)

AG39 Examples of when an entity has transferred substantially all the risks and rewards of ownership are:

(a) an unconditional sale of a financial asset;

(b) a sale of a financial asset together with an option to repurchase the financial asset at its fair value at the time of repurchase; and

(c) a sale of a financial asset together with a put or call option that is deeply out of the money (ie an option that is so far out of the money it is highly unlikely to go into the money before expiry).

AG40 Examples of when an entity has retained substantially all the risks and rewards of ownership are:

(a) a sale and repurchase transaction where the repurchase price is a fixed price or the sale price plus a lender's return;

(b) a securities lending agreement;

(c) a sale of a financial asset together with a total return swap that transfers the market risk exposure back to the entity;

(d) a sale of a financial asset together with a deep in-the-money put or call option (ie an option that is so far in the money that it is highly unlikely to go out of the money before expiry); and

(e) a sale of short-term receivables in which the entity guarantees to compensate the transferee for credit losses that are likely to occur.

AG41 If an entity determines that as a result of the transfer, it has transferred substantially all the risks and rewards of ownership of the transferred asset, it does not recognise the transferred asset again in a future period, unless it reacquires the transferred asset in a new transaction.

Evaluation of the transfer of control

AG42 An entity has not retained control of a transferred asset if the transferee has the practical ability to sell the transferred asset. An entity has retained control of a transferred asset if the transferee does not have the practical ability to sell the transferred asset. A transferee has the practical ability to sell the transferred asset if it is traded in an active market because the transferee could repurchase the transferred asset in the market if it needs to return the asset to the entity. For example, a transferee may have the practical ability to sell a transferred asset if the transferred asset is subject to an option that allows the entity to repurchase it, but the transferee can readily obtain the transferred asset in the market if the option is exercised. A transferee does not have the practical ability to sell the transferred asset if the entity retains such an option and the transferee cannot readily obtain the transferred asset in the market if the entity exercises its option.

AG43 The transferee has the practical ability to sell the transferred asset only if the transferee can sell the transferred asset in its entirety to an unrelated third party and is able to exercise that ability unilaterally and without imposing additional restrictions on the transfer. The critical question is what the transferee is able to do in practice, not what contractual rights the transferee has concerning what it can do with the transferred asset or what contractual prohibitions exist. In particular:

(a) a contractual right to dispose of the transferred asset has little practical effect if there is no market for the transferred asset; and

(b) an ability to dispose of the transferred asset has little practical effect if it cannot be exercised freely. For that reason:

(i) the transferee's ability to dispose of the transferred asset must be independent of the actions of others (ie it must be a unilateral ability); and

(ii) the transferee must be able to dispose of the transferred asset without needing to attach restrictive conditions or 'strings' to the transfer (eg conditions about how a loan asset is serviced or an option giving the transferee the right to repurchase the asset).

AG44 That the transferee is unlikely to sell the transferred asset does not, of itself, mean that the transferor has retained control of the transferred asset. However, if a put option or guarantee constrains the transferee from selling the transferred asset, then the transferor has retained control of the transferred asset. For example, if a put option or guarantee is sufficiently valuable it constrains the transferee from selling the transferred asset because the transferee would, in practice, not sell the transferred asset to a third party without attaching a similar option or other restrictive conditions. Instead, the transferee would hold the transferred asset so as to obtain payments under the guarantee or put option. Under these circumstances the transferor has retained control of the transferred asset.

Transfers that qualify for derecognition

AG45 An entity may retain the right to a part of the interest payments on transferred assets as compensation for servicing those assets. The part of the interest payments that the entity would give up upon termination or transfer of the servicing contract is allocated to the servicing asset or servicing liability. The part of the interest payments that the entity would not give up is an interest-only strip receivable. For example, if the entity would not give up any interest upon termination or transfer of the servicing contract, the entire interest spread is an interest-only strip receivable. For the purposes of applying paragraph 27, the fair values of the servicing asset and interest-only strip receivable are used to allocate the carrying amount of the receivable between the part of the asset that is derecognised and the part that continues to be recognised. If there is no servicing fee specified or the fee to be received is not expected to compensate the entity adequately for performing the servicing, a liability for the servicing obligation is recognised at fair value.

AG46 In estimating the fair values of the part that continues to be recognised and the part that is derecognised for the purposes of applying paragraph 27, an entity applies the fair value measurement requirements in paragraphs 48, 49 and AG69–AG82 in addition to paragraph 28.

Transfers that do not qualify for derecognition

AG47 The following is an application of the principle outlined in paragraph 29. If a guarantee provided by the entity for default losses on the transferred asset prevents a transferred asset from being derecognised because the entity has retained substantially all the risks and rewards of ownership of the transferred asset, the transferred asset continues to be recognised in its entirety and the consideration received is recognised as a liability.

Continuing involvement in transferred assets

AG48 The following are examples of how an entity measures a transferred asset and the associated liability under paragraph 30.

All assets

(a) If a guarantee provided by an entity to pay for default losses on a transferred asset prevents the transferred asset from being derecognised to the extent of the continuing involvement, the transferred asset at the date of the transfer is measured at the lower of (i) the carrying amount of the asset and (ii) the maximum amount of the consideration received in the transfer that the entity could be required to repay ('the guarantee amount'). The associated liability is initially measured at the guarantee amount plus the fair value of the guarantee (which is normally the consideration received for the guarantee). Subsequently, the initial fair value of the guarantee is recognised in profit or loss on a time proportion basis (see IAS 18) and the carrying value of the asset is reduced by any impairment losses.

Assets measured at amortised cost

(b) If a put option obligation written by an entity or call option right held by an entity prevents a transferred asset from being derecognised and the entity measures the transferred asset at amortised cost, the associated liability is measured at its cost (ie the consideration received) adjusted for the amortisation of any difference between that cost and the amortised cost of the transferred asset at the expiration date of the option. For example, assume that the amortised cost and carrying amount of the asset on the date of the transfer is CU98 and that the consideration received is CU95. The amortised cost of the asset on the option exercise date will be CU100. The initial carrying amount of the associated liability is CU95 and the difference between CU95 and CU100 is recognised in profit or loss using the effective interest method. If the option is exercised, any difference between the carrying amount of the associated liability and the exercise price is recognised in profit or loss.

Assets measured at fair value

(c) If a call option right retained by an entity prevents a transferred asset from being derecognised and the entity measures the transferred asset at fair value, the asset continues to be measured at its fair value. The associated liability is measured at (i) the option exercise price less the time value of the option if the option is in or at the money, or (ii) the fair value of the transferred asset less the time value of the option if the option is out of the money. The adjustment to the measurement of the associated liability ensures that the net carrying amount of the asset and the associated liability is the fair value of the call option right. For example, if the fair value of the underlying asset is CU80, the option exercise price is CU95 and the time value of the option is CU5, the carrying amount of the associated liability is CU75 (CU80 – CU5) and the carrying amount of the transferred asset is CU80 (ie its fair value).

(d) If a put option written by an entity prevents a transferred asset from being derecognised and the entity measures the transferred asset at fair value, the associated liability is measured at the option exercise price plus the time value of the option. The measurement of the asset at fair value is limited to the lower of the fair value and the option exercise price because the entity has no right to increases in the fair value of the transferred asset above the exercise price of the option. This ensures that the net carrying amount of the asset and the associated liability is the fair value of the put option obligation. For example, if the fair value of the underlying asset is CU120, the option exercise price is CU100 and the time value of the option is CU5, the carrying amount of the associated liability is CU105 (CU100 + CU5) and the carrying amount of the asset is CU100 (in this case the option exercise price).

(e) If a collar, in the form of a purchased call and written put, prevents a transferred asset from being derecognised and the entity measures the asset at fair value, it continues to measure the asset at fair value. The associated liability is measured at (i) the sum of the call exercise price and fair value of the put option less the time value of the call option, if the call option is in or at the money, or (ii) the sum of the fair value of the asset and the fair value of the put option less the time value of the call option if the call option is out of the money. The adjustment to the associated liability ensures that the net carrying amount of the asset and the associated liability is the fair value of the options held and written by the entity. For example, assume an entity transfers a financial asset that is measured at fair value while simultaneously purchasing a call with an exercise price of CU120 and writing a put with an exercise price of CU80. Assume also that the fair value of the asset is CU100 at the date of the transfer. The time value of the put and call are CU1 and CU5 respectively. In this case, the entity recognises an asset of CU100 (the fair value of the asset) and a liability of CU96 [(CU100 + CU1) – CU5]. This gives a net asset value of CU4, which is the fair value of the options held and written by the entity.

All transfers

AG49 To the extent that a transfer of a financial asset does not qualify for derecognition, the transferor's contractual rights or obligations related to the transfer are not accounted for separately as derivatives if recognising both the derivative and either the transferred asset or the liability arising from the transfer would result in recognising the same rights or obligations twice. For example, a call option retained by the transferor may prevent a transfer of financial assets from being accounted for as a sale. In that case, the call option is not separately recognised as a derivative asset.

AG50 To the extent that a transfer of a financial asset does not qualify for derecognition, the transferee does not recognise the transferred asset as its asset. The transferee derecognises the cash or other consideration paid and recognises a receivable from the transferor. If the transferor has both a right and an obligation to reacquire control of the entire transferred asset for a fixed amount (such as under a repurchase agreement), the transferee may account for its receivable as a loan or receivable.

Examples

AG51 The following examples illustrate the application of the derecognition principles of this Standard.

(a) *Repurchase agreements and securities lending.* If a financial asset is sold under an agreement to repurchase it at a fixed price or at the sale price plus a lender's return or if it is loaned under an agreement to return it to the transferor, it is not derecognised because the transferor retains substantially all the risks and rewards of ownership. If the transferee obtains the right to sell or pledge the asset, the transferor reclassifies the asset on its balance sheet, for example, as a loaned asset or repurchase receivable.

(b) *Repurchase agreements and securities lending—assets that are substantially the same.* If a financial asset is sold under an agreement to repurchase the same or substantially the same asset at a fixed price or at the sale price plus a lender's return or if a financial asset is borrowed or loaned under an agreement to return the same or substantially the same asset to the transferor, it is not derecognised because the transferor retains substantially all the risks and rewards of ownership.

(c) *Repurchase agreements and securities lending—right of substitution.* If a repurchase agreement at a fixed repurchase price or a price equal to the sale price plus a lender's return, or a similar securities lending transaction, provides the transferee with a right to substitute assets that are similar and of equal fair value to the transferred asset at the repurchase date, the asset sold or lent under a repurchase or securities lending transaction is not derecognised because the transferor retains substantially all the risks and rewards of ownership.

(d) *Repurchase right of first refusal at fair value.* If an entity sells a financial asset and retains only a right of first refusal to repurchase the transferred asset at fair value if the transferee subsequently sells it, the entity derecognises the asset because it has transferred substantially all the risks and rewards of ownership.

(e) *Wash sale transaction.* The repurchase of a financial asset shortly after it has been sold is sometimes referred to as a wash sale. Such a repurchase does not preclude derecognition provided that the original transaction met the derecognition requirements. However, if an agreement to sell a financial asset is entered into concurrently with an agreement to repurchase the same asset at a fixed price or the sale price plus a lender's return, then the asset is not derecognised.

(f) *Put options and call options that are deeply in the money.* If a transferred financial asset can be called back by the transferor and the call option is deeply in the money, the transfer does not qualify for derecognition because the transferor has retained substantially all the risks and rewards of ownership. Similarly, if the financial asset can be put back by the transferee and the put option is deeply in the money, the transfer does not qualify for derecognition because the transferor has retained substantially all the risks and rewards of ownership.

(g) *Put options and call options that are deeply out of the money.* A financial asset that is transferred subject only to a deep out-of-the-money put option held by the transferee or a deep out-of-the-money call option held by the transferor is derecognised. This is because the transferor has transferred substantially all the risks and rewards of ownership.

(h) *Readily obtainable assets subject to a call option that is neither deeply in the money nor deeply out of the money.* If an entity holds a call option on an asset that is readily obtainable in the market and the option is neither deeply in the money nor deeply out of the money, the asset is derecognised. This is because the entity (i) has neither retained nor transferred substantially all the risks and rewards of ownership, and (ii) has not retained control. However, if the asset is not readily obtainable in the market, derecognition is precluded to the extent of the amount of the asset that is subject to the call option because the entity has retained control of the asset.

(i) *A not readily obtainable asset subject to a put option written by an entity that is neither deeply in the money nor deeply out of the money.* If an entity transfers a financial asset that is not readily obtainable in the market, and writes a put option that is not deeply out of the money, the entity neither retains nor transfers substantially all the risks and rewards of ownership because of the written put option. The entity retains control of the asset if the put option is sufficiently valuable to prevent the transferee from selling the asset, in which case the asset continues to be recognised to the extent of the transferor's continuing involvement (see paragraph AG44). The entity transfers control of the asset if the put option is not sufficiently valuable to prevent the transferee from selling the asset, in which case the asset is derecognised.

(j) *Assets subject to a fair value put or call option or a forward repurchase agreement.* A transfer of a financial asset that is subject only to a put or call option or a forward repurchase agreement that has an exercise or repurchase price equal to the fair value of the financial asset at the time of repurchase results in derecognition because of the transfer of substantially all the risks and rewards of ownership.

(k) *Cash settled call or put options.* An entity evaluates the transfer of a financial asset that is subject to a put or call option or a forward repurchase agreement that will be settled net in cash to determine whether it has retained or transferred substantially all the risks and rewards of ownership. If the entity has not retained substantially all the risks and rewards of ownership of the transferred asset, it determines whether it has retained control of the transferred asset. That the put or the call or the forward repurchase agreement is settled net in cash does not automatically mean that the entity has transferred control (see paragraphs AG44 and (g), (h) and (i) above).

(l) *Removal of accounts provision.* A removal of accounts provision is an unconditional repurchase (call) option that gives an entity the right to reclaim assets transferred subject to some restrictions. Provided that such an option results in the entity neither retaining nor transferring substantially all the risks and rewards of ownership, it precludes derecognition only to the extent of the amount subject to repurchase (assuming that the transferee cannot sell the assets). For example, if the carrying amount and proceeds from the transfer of loan assets are CU100,000 and any individual loan could be called back but the aggregate amount of loans that could be repurchased could not exceed CU10,000, CU90,000 of the loans would qualify for derecognition.

(m) *Clean–up calls.* An entity, which may be a transferor, that services transferred assets may hold a clean-up call to purchase remaining transferred assets when the amount of outstanding assets falls to a specified level at which the cost of servicing those assets becomes burdensome in relation to the benefits of servicing. Provided that such a clean-up call results in the entity neither retaining nor transferring substantially all the risks and rewards of ownership and the transferee cannot sell the assets, it precludes derecognition only to the extent of the amount of the assets that is subject to the call option.

(n) *Subordinated retained interests and credit guarantees.* An entity may provide the transferee with credit enhancement by subordinating some or all of its interest retained in the transferred asset. Alternatively, an entity may provide the transferee with credit enhancement in the form of a credit guarantee that could be unlimited or limited to a specified amount. If the entity retains substantially all the risks and rewards of ownership of the transferred asset, the asset continues to be recognised in its entirety. If the entity retains some, but not substantially all, of the risks and rewards of ownership and has retained control, derecognition is precluded to the extent of the amount of cash or other assets that the entity could be required to pay.

(o) *Total return swaps.* An entity may sell a financial asset to a transferee and enter into a total return swap with the transferee, whereby all of the interest payment cash flows from the underlying asset are remitted to the entity in exchange for a fixed payment or variable rate payment and any increases or declines in the fair value of the underlying asset are absorbed by the entity. In such a case, derecognition of all of the asset is prohibited.

(p) *Interest rate swaps.* An entity may transfer to a transferee a fixed rate financial asset and enter into an interest rate swap with the transferee to receive a fixed interest rate and pay a variable interest rate based on a notional amount that is equal to the principal amount of the transferred financial asset. The interest rate swap does not preclude derecognition of the transferred asset provided the payments on the swap are not conditional on payments being made on the transferred asset.

(q) *Amortising interest rate swaps.* An entity may transfer to a transferee a fixed rate financial asset that is paid off over time, and enter into an amortising interest rate swap with the transferee to receive a fixed interest rate and pay a variable interest rate based on a notional amount. If the notional amount of the swap amortises so that it equals the principal amount of the transferred financial asset outstanding at any point in time, the swap would generally result in the entity retaining substantial prepayment risk, in which case the entity either continues to recognise all of the transferred asset or continues to recognise the transferred asset to the extent of its continuing involvement. Conversely, if the amortisation of the notional amount of the swap is not linked to the principal amount outstanding of the transferred asset, such a swap would not result in the entity retaining prepayment risk on the asset. Hence, it would not preclude derecognition of the transferred asset provided the payments on the swap are not conditional on interest payments being made on the transferred asset and the swap does not result in the entity retaining any other significant risks and rewards of ownership on the transferred asset.

AG52 This paragraph illustrates the application of the continuing involvement approach when the entity's continuing involvement is in a part of a financial asset.

> Assume an entity has a portfolio of prepayable loans whose coupon and effective interest rate is 10 per cent and whose principal amount and amortised cost is CU10,000. It enters into a transaction in which, in return for a payment of CU9,115, the transferee obtains the right to CU9,000 of any collections of principal plus interest thereon at 9.5 per cent. The entity retains rights to CU1,000 of any collections of principal plus interest thereon at 10 per cent, plus the excess spread of 0.5 per cent on the remaining CU9,000 of principal. Collections from prepayments are allocated between the entity and the transferee proportionately in the ratio of 1:9, but any defaults are deducted from the entity's interest of CU1,000 until that interest is exhausted. The fair value of the loans at the date of the transaction is CU10,100 and the estimated fair value of the excess spread of 0.5 per cent is CU40.

Continued from previous page

The entity determines that it has transferred some significant risks and rewards of ownership (for example, significant prepayment risk) but has also retained some significant risks and rewards of ownership (because of its subordinated retained interest) and has retained control. It therefore applies the continuing involvement approach.

To apply this Standard, the entity analyses the transaction as (a) a retention of a fully proportionate retained interest of CU1,000, plus (b) the subordination of that retained interest to provide credit enhancement to the transferee for credit losses.

The entity calculates that CU9,090 (90 per cent × CU10,100) of the consideration received of CU9,115 represents the consideration for a fully proportionate 90 per cent share. The remainder of the consideration received (CU25) represents consideration received for subordinating its retained interest to provide credit enhancement to the transferee for credit losses. In addition, the excess spread of 0.5 per cent represents consideration received for the credit enhancement. Accordingly, the total consideration received for the credit enhancement is CU65 (CU25 + CU40).

The entity calculates the gain or loss on the sale of the 90 per cent share of cash flows. Assuming that separate fair values of the 90 per cent part transferred and the 10 per cent part retained are not available at the date of the transfer, the entity allocates the carrying amount of the asset in accordance with paragraph 28 as follows:

	Estimated fair value	*Percentage*	*Allocated carrying amount*
Portion transferred	9,090	90%	9,000
Portion retained	1,010	10%	1,000
Total	**10,100**		**10,000**

The entity computes its gain or loss on the sale of the 90 per cent share of the cash flows by deducting the allocated carrying amount of the portion transferred from the consideration received, ie CU90 (CU9,090 – CU9,000). The carrying amount of the portion retained by the entity is CU1,000.

In addition, the entity recognises the continuing involvement that results from the subordination of its retained interest for credit losses. Accordingly, it recognises an asset of CU1,000 (the maximum amount of the cash flows it would not receive under the subordination), and an associated liability of CU1,065 (which is the maximum amount of the cash flows it would not receive under the subordination, ie CU1,000 plus the fair value of the subordination of CU65).

The entity uses all of the above information to account for the transaction as follows:

Continued from previous page

	Debit	Credit
Original asset	–	9,000
Asset recognised for subordination or the residual interest	1,000	–
Asset for the consideration received in the form of excess spread	40	–
Profit or loss (gain on transfer)	–	90
Liability	–	90
Cash received	9,115	–
Total	**10,155**	**10,155**

Immediately following the transaction, the carrying amount of the asset is CU2,040 comprising CU1,000, representing the allocated cost of the portion retained, and CU1,040, representing the entity's additional continuing involvement from the subordination of its retained interest for credit losses (which includes the excess spread of CU40).

In subsequent periods, the entity recognises the consideration received for the credit enhancement (CU65) on a time proportion basis, accrues interest on the recognised asset using the effective interest method and recognises any credit impairment on the recognised assets. As an example of the latter, assume that in the following year there is a credit impairment loss on the underlying loans of CU300. The entity reduces its recognised asset by CU600 (CU300 relating to its retained interest and CU300 relating to the additional continuing involvement that arises from the subordination of its retained interest for credit losses), and reduces its recognised liability by CU300. The net result is a charge to profit or loss for credit impairment of CU300.

Regular way purchase or sale of a financial asset (paragraph 38)

AG53 A regular way purchase or sale of financial assets is recognised using either trade date accounting or settlement date accounting as described in paragraphs AG55 and AG56. The method used is applied consistently for all purchases and sales of financial assets that belong to the same category of financial assets defined in paragraph 9. For this purpose assets that are held for trading form a separate category from assets designated at fair value through profit and loss.

AG54 A contract that requires or permits net settlement of the change in the value of the contract is not a regular way contract. Instead, such a contract is accounted for as a derivative in the period between the trade date and the settlement date.

AG55 The trade date is the date that an entity commits itself to purchase or sell an asset. Trade date accounting refers to (a) the recognition of an asset to be received and the liability to pay for it on the trade date, and (b) derecognition of an asset that is sold, recognition of any gain or loss on disposal and the recognition of a receivable from the buyer for payment on the trade date. Generally, interest does not start to accrue on the asset and corresponding liability until the settlement date when title passes.

AG56 The settlement date is the date that an asset is delivered to or by an entity. Settlement date accounting refers to (a) the recognition of an asset on the day it is received by the entity, and (b) the derecognition of an asset and recognition of any gain or loss on disposal on the day that it is delivered by the entity. When settlement date accounting is applied an entity accounts for any change in the fair value of the asset to be received during the period between the trade date and the settlement date in the same way as it accounts for the acquired asset. In other words, the change in value is not recognised for assets carried at cost or amortised cost; it is recognised in profit or loss for assets classified as financial assets at fair value through profit or loss; and it is recognised in equity for assets classified as available for sale.

Derecognition of a financial liability (paragraphs 39–42)

AG57 A financial liability (or part of it) is extinguished when the debtor either:

(a) discharges the liability (or part of it) by paying the creditor, normally with cash, other financial assets, goods or services; or

(b) is legally released from primary responsibility for the liability (or part of it) either by process of law or by the creditor. (If the debtor has given a guarantee this condition may still be met.)

AG58 If an issuer of a debt instrument repurchases that instrument, the debt is extinguished even if the issuer is a market maker in that instrument or intends to resell it in the near term.

AG59 Payment to a third party, including a trust (sometimes called 'in-substance defeasance'), does not, by itself, relieve the debtor of its primary obligation to the creditor, in the absence of legal release.

AG60 If a debtor pays a third party to assume an obligation and notifies its creditor that the third party has assumed its debt obligation, the debtor does not derecognise the debt obligation unless the condition in paragraph AG57(b) is met. If the debtor pays a third party to assume an obligation and obtains a legal release from its creditor, the debtor has extinguished the debt. However, if the debtor agrees to make payments on the debt to the third party or direct to its original creditor, the debtor recognises a new debt obligation to the third party.

AG61 Although legal release, whether judicially or by the creditor, results in derecognition of a liability, the entity may recognise a new liability if the derecognition criteria in paragraphs 15–37 are not met for the financial assets transferred. If those criteria are not met, the transferred assets are not derecognised, and the entity recognises a new liability relating to the transferred assets.

AG62 For the purpose of paragraph 40, the terms are substantially different if the discounted present value of the cash flows under the new terms, including any fees paid net of any fees received and discounted using the original effective interest rate, is at least 10 per cent different from the discounted present value of the remaining cash flows of the original financial liability. If an exchange of debt instruments or modification of terms is accounted for as an extinguishment, any costs or fees incurred are recognised as part of the gain or loss on the extinguishment. If the exchange or modification is not accounted for as an extinguishment, any costs or fees incurred adjust the carrying amount of the liability and are amortised over the remaining term of the modified liability.

AG63 In some cases, a creditor releases a debtor from its present obligation to make payments, but the debtor assumes a guarantee obligation to pay if the party assuming primary responsibility defaults. In this circumstance the debtor:

(a) recognises a new financial liability based on the fair value of its obligation for the guarantee; and

(b) recognises a gain or loss based on the difference between (i) any proceeds paid and (ii) the carrying amount of the original financial liability less the fair value of the new financial liability.

Measurement (paragraphs 43–70)

Initial measurement of financial assets and financial liabilities (paragraph 43)

AG64 The fair value of a financial instrument on initial recognition is normally the transaction price (ie the fair value of the consideration given or received, see also paragraph AG76). However, if part of the consideration given or received is for something other than the financial instrument, the fair value of the financial instrument is estimated, using a valuation technique (see paragraphs AG74–AG79). For example, the fair value of a long-term loan or receivable that carries no interest can be estimated as the present value of all future cash receipts discounted using the prevailing market rate(s) of interest for a similar instrument (similar as to currency, term, type of interest rate and other factors) with a similar credit rating. Any additional amount lent is an expense or a reduction of income unless it qualifies for recognition as some other type of asset.

AG65 If an entity originates a loan that bears an off-market interest rate (eg 5 per cent when the market rate for similar loans is 8 per cent), and receives an up-front fee as compensation, the entity recognises the loan at its fair value, ie net of the fee it receives. The entity accretes the discount to profit or loss using the effective interest rate method.

Subsequent measurement of financial assets (paragraphs 45 and 46)

AG66 If a financial instrument that was previously recognised as a financial asset is measured at fair value and its fair value falls below zero, it is a financial liability measured in accordance with paragraph 47.

AG67 The following example illustrates the accounting for transaction costs on the initial and subsequent measurement of an available-for-sale financial asset. An asset is acquired for CU100 plus a purchase commission of CU2. Initially, the asset is recognised at CU102. The next financial reporting date occurs one day later, when the quoted market price of the asset is CU100. If the asset were sold, a commission of CU3 would be paid. On that date, the asset is measured at CU100 (without regard to the possible commission on sale) and a loss of CU2 is recognised in equity. If the available-for-sale financial asset has fixed or determinable payments, the transaction costs are amortised to profit or loss using the effective interest method. If the available-for-sale financial asset does not have fixed or determinable payments, the transaction costs are recognised in profit or loss when the asset is derecognised or becomes impaired.

AG68 Instruments that are classified as loans and receivables are measured at amortised cost without regard to the entity's intention to hold them to maturity.

Fair value measurement considerations (paragraphs 48 and 49)

AG69 Underlying the definition of fair value is a presumption that an entity is a going concern without any intention or need to liquidate, to curtail materially the scale of its operations or to undertake a transaction on adverse terms. Fair value is not, therefore, the amount that an entity would receive or pay in a forced transaction, involuntary liquidation or distress sale. However, fair value reflects the credit quality of the instrument.

AG70 This Standard uses the terms 'bid price' and 'asking price' (sometimes referred to as 'current offer price') in the context of quoted market prices, and the term 'the bid-ask spread' to include only transaction costs. Other adjustments to arrive at fair value (eg for counterparty credit risk) are not included in the term 'bid-ask spread'.

Active market: quoted price

AG71 A financial instrument is regarded as quoted in an active market if quoted prices are readily and regularly available from an exchange, dealer, broker, industry group, pricing service or regulatory agency, and those prices represent actual and regularly occurring market transactions on an arm's length basis. Fair value is defined in terms of a price agreed by a willing buyer and a willing seller in an arm's length transaction. The objective of determining fair value for a financial instrument that is traded in an active market is to arrive at the price at which a transaction would occur at the balance sheet date in that instrument (ie without modifying or repackaging the instrument) in the most advantageous active market to which the entity has immediate access. However, the entity adjusts the price in the more advantageous market to reflect any differences in counterparty credit risk between instruments traded in that market and the one being valued. The existence of published price quotations in an active market is the best evidence of fair value and when they exist they are used to measure the financial asset or financial liability.

AG72 The appropriate quoted market price for an asset held or liability to be issued is usually the current bid price and, for an asset to be acquired or liability held, the asking price. When an entity has assets and liabilities with offsetting market risks, it may use mid-market prices as a basis for establishing fair values for the offsetting risk positions and apply the bid or asking price to the net open position as appropriate. When current bid and asking prices are unavailable, the price of the most recent transaction provides evidence of the current fair value as long as there has not been a significant change in economic circumstances since the time of the transaction. If conditions have changed since the time of the transaction (eg a change in the risk-free interest rate following the most recent price quote for a corporate bond), the fair value reflects the change in conditions by reference to current prices or rates for similar financial instruments, as appropriate. Similarly, if the entity can demonstrate that the last transaction price is not fair value (eg because it reflected the amount that an entity would receive or pay in a forced transaction, involuntary liquidation or distress sale), that price is adjusted. The fair value of a portfolio of financial instruments is the product of the number of units of the instrument and its quoted market price. If a published price quotation in an active market does not exist for a financial instrument in its entirety, but active markets exist for its component parts, fair value is determined on the basis of the relevant market prices for the component parts.

AG73 If a rate (rather than a price) is quoted in an active market, the entity uses that market-quoted rate as an input into a valuation technique to determine fair value. If the market-quoted rate does not include credit risk or other factors that market participants would include in valuing the instrument, the entity adjusts for those factors.

No active market: valuation technique

AG74 If the market for a financial instrument is not active, an entity establishes fair value by using a valuation technique. Valuation techniques include using recent arm's length market transactions between knowledgeable, willing parties, if available, reference to the current fair value of another instrument that is substantially the same, discounted cash flow analysis and option pricing models. If there is a valuation technique commonly used by market participants to price the instrument and that technique has been demonstrated to provide reliable estimates of prices obtained in actual market transactions, the entity uses that technique.

AG75 The objective of using a valuation technique is to establish what the transaction price would have been on the measurement date in an arm's length exchange motivated by normal business considerations. Fair value is estimated on the basis of the results of a valuation technique that makes maximum use of market inputs, and relies as little as possible on entity-specific inputs. A valuation technique would be expected to arrive at a realistic estimate of the fair value if (a) it reasonably reflects how the market could be expected to price the instrument and (b) the inputs to the valuation technique reasonably represent market expectations and measures of the risk-return factors inherent in the financial instrument.

AG76 Therefore, a valuation technique (a) incorporates all factors that market participants would consider in setting a price and (b) is consistent with accepted economic methodologies for pricing financial instruments. Periodically, an entity calibrates the valuation technique and tests it for validity using prices from any observable current market transactions in the same instrument (ie without modification or repackaging) or based on any available observable market data. An entity obtains market data consistently in the same market where the instrument was originated or purchased. The best evidence of the fair value of a financial instrument at initial recognition is the transaction price (ie the fair value of the consideration given or received) unless the fair value of that instrument is evidenced by comparison with other observable current market transactions in the same instrument (ie without modification or repackaging) or based on a valuation technique whose variables include only data from observable markets.

AG76A The subsequent measurement of the financial asset or financial liability and the subsequent recognition of gains and losses shall be consistent with the requirements of this Standard. The application of paragraph AG76 may result in no gain or loss being recognised on the initial recognition of a financial asset or financial liability. In such a case, IAS 39 requires that a gain or loss shall be recognised after initial recognition only to the extent that it arises from a change in a factor (including time) that market participants would consider in setting a price.

AG77 The initial acquisition or origination of a financial asset or incurrence of a financial liability is a market transaction that provides a foundation for estimating the fair value of the financial instrument. In particular, if the financial instrument is a debt instrument (such as a loan), its fair value can be determined by reference to the market conditions that existed at its acquisition or origination date and current market conditions or interest rates currently charged by the entity or by others for similar debt instruments (ie similar remaining maturity, cash flow pattern, currency, credit risk, collateral and interest basis). Alternatively, provided there is no change in the credit risk of the debtor and applicable credit spreads after the origination of the debt instrument, an estimate of the current market interest rate may be derived by using a benchmark interest rate reflecting a better credit quality than the underlying debt instrument, holding the credit spread constant, and adjusting for the change in the benchmark interest rate from the origination date. If conditions have changed since the most recent market transaction, the corresponding change in the fair value of the financial instrument being valued is determined by reference to current prices or rates for similar financial instruments, adjusted as appropriate, for any differences from the instrument being valued.

AG78 The same information may not be available at each measurement date. For example, at the date that an entity makes a loan or acquires a debt instrument that is not actively traded, the entity has a transaction price that is also a market price. However, no new transaction information may be available at the next measurement date and, although the entity can determine the general level of market interest rates, it may not know what level of credit or other risk market participants would consider in pricing the instrument on that date. An entity may not have information from recent transactions to determine the appropriate credit spread over the basic interest rate to use in determining a discount rate for a present value computation. It would be reasonable to assume, in the absence of evidence to the contrary, that no changes have taken place in the spread that existed at the date the loan was made. However, the entity would be expected to make reasonable efforts to determine whether there is evidence that there has been a change in such factors. When evidence of a change exists, the entity would consider the effects of the change in determining the fair value of the financial instrument.

AG79 In applying discounted cash flow analysis, an entity uses one or more discount rates equal to the prevailing rates of return for financial instruments having substantially the same terms and characteristics, including the credit quality of the instrument, the remaining term over which the contractual interest rate is fixed, the remaining term to repayment of the principal and the currency in which payments are to be made. Short-term receivables and payables with no stated interest rate may be measured at the original invoice amount if the effect of discounting is immaterial.

No active market: equity instruments

AG80 The fair value of investments in equity instruments that do not have a quoted market price in an active market and derivatives that are linked to and must be settled by delivery of such an unquoted equity instrument (see paragraphs 46(c) and 47) is reliably measurable if (a) the variability in the range of reasonable fair value estimates is not significant for that instrument or (b) the probabilities of the various estimates within the range can be reasonably assessed and used in estimating fair value.

AG81 There are many situations in which the variability in the range of reasonable fair value estimates of investments in equity instruments that do not have a quoted market price and derivatives that are linked to and must be settled by delivery of such an unquoted equity instrument (see paragraphs 46(c) and 47) is likely not to be significant. Normally it is possible to estimate the fair value of a financial asset that an entity has acquired from an outside party. However, if the range of reasonable fair value estimates is significant and the probabilities of the various estimates cannot be reasonably assessed, an entity is precluded from measuring the instrument at fair value.

Inputs to valuation techniques

AG82 An appropriate technique for estimating the fair value of a particular financial instrument would incorporate observable market data about the market conditions and other factors that are likely to affect the instrument's fair value. The fair value of a financial instrument will be based on one or more of the following factors (and perhaps others).

(a) *The time value of money (ie interest at the basic or risk-free rate).* Basic interest rates can usually be derived from observable government bond prices and are often quoted in financial publications. These rates typically vary with the expected dates of the projected cash flows along a yield curve of interest rates for different time horizons. For practical reasons, an entity may use a well-accepted and readily observable general rate, such as LIBOR or a swap rate, as the benchmark rate. (Because a rate such as LIBOR is not the risk-free interest rate, the credit risk adjustment appropriate to the particular financial instrument is determined on the basis of its credit risk in relation to the credit risk in this benchmark rate.) In some countries, the central government's bonds may carry a significant credit risk and may not provide a stable benchmark basic interest rate for instruments denominated in that currency. Some entities in these countries may have a better credit standing and a lower borrowing rate than the central government. In such a case, basic interest rates may be more appropriately determined by reference to interest rates for the highest rated corporate bonds issued in the currency of that jurisdiction.

(b) *Credit risk.* The effect on fair value of credit risk (ie the premium over the basic interest rate for credit risk) may be derived from observable market prices for traded instruments of different credit quality or from observable interest rates charged by lenders for loans of various credit ratings.

(c) *Foreign currency exchange prices.* Active currency exchange markets exist for most major currencies, and prices are quoted daily in financial publications.

(d) *Commodity prices.* There are observable market prices for many commodities.

(e) *Equity prices.* Prices (and indexes of prices) of traded equity instruments are readily observable in some markets. Present value based techniques may be used to estimate the current market price of equity instruments for which there are no observable prices.

(f) *Volatility (ie magnitude of future changes in price of the financial instrument or other item).* Measures of the volatility of actively traded items can normally be reasonably estimated on the basis of historical market data or by using volatilities implied in current market prices.

(g) *Prepayment risk and surrender risk.* Expected prepayment patterns for financial assets and expected surrender patterns for financial liabilities can be estimated on the basis of historical data. (The fair value of a financial liability that can be surrendered by the counterparty cannot be less than the present value of the surrender amount–see paragraph 49.)

(h) *Servicing costs for a financial asset or a financial liability.* Costs of servicing can be estimated using comparisons with current fees charged by other market participants. If the costs of servicing a financial asset or financial liability are significant and other market participants would face comparable costs, the issuer would consider them in determining the fair value of that financial asset or financial liability. It is likely that the fair value at inception of a contractual right to future fees equals the origination costs paid for them, unless future fees and related costs are out of line with market comparables.

Gains and losses (paragraphs 55–57)

AG83 An entity applies IAS 21 to financial assets and financial liabilities that are monetary items in accordance with IAS 21 and denominated in a foreign currency. Under IAS 21, any foreign exchange gains and losses on monetary assets and monetary liabilities are recognised in profit or loss. An exception is a monetary item that is designated as a hedging instrument in either a cash flow hedge (see paragraphs 95–101) or a hedge of a net investment (see paragraph 102). For the purpose of recognising foreign exchange gains and losses under IAS 21, a monetary available-for-sale financial asset is treated as if it were carried at amortised cost in the foreign currency. Accordingly, for such a financial asset, exchange differences resulting from changes in amortised cost are recognised in profit or loss and other changes in carrying amount are recognised in accordance with paragraph 55(b). For available-for-sale financial assets that are not monetary items under IAS 21 (for example, equity instruments), the gain or loss that is recognised directly in equity under paragraph 55(b) includes any related foreign exchange component. If there is a hedging relationship between a non-derivative monetary asset and a non-derivative monetary liability, changes in the foreign currency component of those financial instruments are recognised in profit or loss.

Impairment and uncollectibility of financial assets (paragraphs 58–70)

Financial assets carried at amortised cost (paragraphs 63–65)

AG84 Impairment of a financial asset carried at amortised cost is measured using the financial instrument's original effective interest rate because discounting at the current market rate of interest would, in effect, impose fair value measurement on financial assets that are otherwise measured at amortised cost. If the terms of a loan, receivable or held-to-maturity investment are renegotiated or otherwise modified because of financial difficulties of the borrower or issuer, impairment is measured using the original effective interest rate before the modification of terms. Cash flows relating to short-term receivables are not discounted if the effect of discounting is immaterial. If a loan, receivable or held-to-maturity investment has a variable interest rate, the discount rate for measuring any impairment loss under paragraph 63 is the current effective interest rate(s) determined under the contract. As a practical expedient, a creditor may measure impairment of a financial asset carried at amortised cost on the basis of an instrument's fair value using an observable market price. The calculation of the present value of the estimated future cash flows of a collateralised financial asset reflects the cash flows that may result from foreclosure less costs for obtaining and selling the collateral, whether or not foreclosure is probable.

AG85 The process for estimating impairment considers all credit exposures, not only those of low credit quality. For example, if an entity uses an internal credit grading system it considers all credit grades, not only those reflecting a severe credit deterioration.

AG86 The process for estimating the amount of an impairment loss may result either in a single amount or in a range of possible amounts. In the latter case, the entity recognises an impairment loss equal to the best estimate within the range* taking into account all relevant information available before the financial statements are issued about conditions existing at the balance sheet date.

AG87 For the purpose of a collective evaluation of impairment, financial assets are grouped on the basis of similar credit risk characteristics that are indicative of the debtors' ability to pay all amounts due according to the contractual terms (for example, on the basis of a credit risk evaluation or grading process that considers asset type, industry, geographical location, collateral type, past-due status and other relevant factors). The characteristics chosen are relevant to the estimation of future cash flows for groups of such assets by being indicative of the debtors' ability to pay all amounts due according to the contractual terms of the assets being evaluated. However, loss probabilities and other loss statistics differ

* IAS 37, paragraph 39 contains guidance on how to determine the best estimate in a range of possible outcomes.

at a group level between (a) assets that have been individually evaluated for impairment and found not to be impaired and (b) assets that have not been individually evaluated for impairment, with the result that a different amount of impairment may be required. If an entity does not have a group of assets with similar risk characteristics, it does not make the additional assessment.

AG88 Impairment losses recognised on a group basis represent an interim step pending the identification of impairment losses on individual assets in the group of financial assets that are collectively assessed for impairment. As soon as information is available that specifically identifies losses on individually impaired assets in a group, those assets are removed from the group.

AG89 Future cash flows in a group of financial assets that are collectively evaluated for impairment are estimated on the basis of historical loss experience for assets with credit risk characteristics similar to those in the group. Entities that have no entity-specific loss experience or insufficient experience, use peer group experience for comparable groups of financial assets. Historical loss experience is adjusted on the basis of current observable data to reflect the effects of current conditions that did not affect the period on which the historical loss experience is based and to remove the effects of conditions in the historical period that do not exist currently. Estimates of changes in future cash flows reflect and are directionally consistent with changes in related observable data from period to period (such as changes in unemployment rates, property prices, commodity prices, payment status or other factors that are indicative of incurred losses in the group and their magnitude). The methodology and assumptions used for estimating future cash flows are reviewed regularly to reduce any differences between loss estimates and actual loss experience.

AG90 As an example of applying paragraph AG89, an entity may determine, on the basis of historical experience, that one of the main causes of default on credit card loans is the death of the borrower. The entity may observe that the death rate is unchanged from one year to the next. Nevertheless, some of the borrowers in the entity's group of credit card loans may have died in that year, indicating that an impairment loss has occurred on those loans, even if, at the year-end, the entity is not yet aware which specific borrowers have died. It would be appropriate for an impairment loss to be recognised for these 'incurred but not reported' losses. However, it would not be appropriate to recognise an impairment loss for deaths that are expected to occur in a future period, because the necessary loss event (the death of the borrower) has not yet occurred.

AG91 When using historical loss rates in estimating future cash flows, it is important that information about historical loss rates is applied to groups that are defined in a manner consistent with the groups for which the historical loss rates were observed. Therefore, the method used should enable each group to be associated with information about past loss experience in groups of assets with similar credit risk characteristics and relevant observable data that reflect current conditions.

AG92 Formula-based approaches or statistical methods may be used to determine impairment losses in a group of financial assets (eg for smaller balance loans) as long as they are consistent with the requirements in paragraphs 63–65 and AG87–AG91. Any model used would incorporate the effect of the time value of money, consider the cash flows for all of the remaining life of an asset (not only the next year), consider the age of the loans within the portfolio and not give rise to an impairment loss on initial recognition of a financial asset.

Interest income after impairment recognition

AG93 Once a financial asset or a group of similar financial assets has been written down as a result of an impairment loss, interest income is thereafter recognised using the rate of interest used to discount the future cash flows for the purpose of measuring the impairment loss.

Hedging (paragraphs 71–102)

Hedging instruments (paragraphs 72–77)

Qualifying instruments (paragraphs 72 and 73)

AG94 The potential loss on an option that an entity writes could be significantly greater than the potential gain in value of a related hedged item. In other words, a written option is not effective in reducing the profit or loss exposure of a hedged item. Therefore, a written option does not qualify as a hedging instrument unless it is designated as an offset to a purchased option, including one that is embedded in another financial instrument (for example, a written call option used to hedge a callable liability). In contrast, a purchased option has potential gains equal to or greater than losses and therefore has the potential to reduce profit or loss exposure from changes in fair values or cash flows. Accordingly, it can qualify as a hedging instrument.

AG95 A held-to-maturity investment carried at amortised cost may be designated as a hedging instrument in a hedge of foreign currency risk.

AG96 An investment in an unquoted equity instrument that is not carried at fair value because its fair value cannot be reliably measured or a derivative that is linked to and must be settled by delivery of such an unquoted equity instrument (see paragraphs 46(c) and 47) cannot be designated as a hedging instrument.

AG97 An entity's own equity instruments are not financial assets or financial liabilities of the entity and therefore cannot be designated as hedging instruments.

Hedged items (paragraphs 78–84)

Qualifying items (paragraphs 78–80)

AG98 A firm commitment to acquire a business in a business combination cannot be a hedged item, except for foreign exchange risk, because the other risks being hedged cannot be specifically identified and measured. These other risks are general business risks.

AG99 An equity method investment cannot be a hedged item in a fair value hedge because the equity method recognises in profit or loss the investor's share of the associate's profit or loss, rather than changes in the investment's fair value. For a similar reason, an investment in a consolidated subsidiary cannot be a hedged item in a fair value hedge because consolidation recognises in profit or loss the subsidiary's profit or loss, rather than changes in the investment's fair value.

A hedge of a net investment in a foreign operation is different because it is a hedge of the foreign currency exposure, not a fair value hedge of the change in the value of the investment.

Designation of financial items as hedged items (paragraphs 81 and 81A)

AG99A If a portion of the cash flows of a financial asset or financial liability is designated as the hedged item, that designated portion must be less than the total cash flows of the asset or liability. For example, in the case of a liability whose effective interest rate is below LIBOR, an entity cannot designate (a) a portion of the liability equal to the principal amount plus interest at LIBOR and (b) a negative residual portion. However, the entity may designate all of the cash flows of the entire financial asset or financial liability as the hedged item and hedge them for only one particular risk (eg only for changes that are attributable to changes in LIBOR). For example, in the case of a financial liability whose effective interest rate is 100 basis points below LIBOR, an entity can designate as the hedged item the entire liability (ie principal plus interest at LIBOR minus 100 basis points) and hedge the change in the fair value or cash flows of that entire liability that is attributable to changes in LIBOR. The entity may also choose a hedge ratio of other than one to one in order to improve the effectiveness of the hedge as described in paragraph AG100.

AG99B In addition, if a fixed rate financial instrument is hedged some time after its origination and interest rates have changed in the meantime, the entity can designate a portion equal to a benchmark rate that is higher than the contractual rate paid on the item. The entity can do so provided that the benchmark rate is less than the effective interest rate calculated on the assumption that the entity had purchased the instrument on the day it first designates the hedged item. For example, assume an entity originates a fixed rate financial asset of CU100 that has an effective interest rate of 6 per cent at a time when LIBOR is 4 per cent. It begins to hedge that asset some time later when LIBOR has increased to 8 per cent and the fair value of the asset has decreased to CU90. The entity calculates that if it had purchased the asset on the date it first designates it as the hedged item for its then fair value of CU90, the effective yield would have been 9.5 per cent. Because LIBOR is less than this effective yield, the entity can designate a LIBOR portion of 8 per cent that consists partly of the contractual interest cash flows and partly of the difference between the current fair value (ie CU90) and the amount repayable on maturity (ie CU100).

Designation of non-financial items as hedged items (paragraph 82)

AG100 Changes in the price of an ingredient or component of a non-financial asset or non-financial liability generally do not have a predictable, separately measurable effect on the price of the item that is comparable to the effect of, say, a change in market interest rates on the price of a bond. Thus, a non-financial asset or non-financial liability is a hedged item only in its entirety or for foreign exchange risk. If there is a difference between the terms of the hedging instrument and the hedged item (such as for a hedge of the forecast purchase of Brazilian coffee using a forward contract to purchase Colombian coffee on otherwise similar terms), the hedging relationship nonetheless can qualify as a hedge relationship provided all the conditions in paragraph 88 are met, including that the hedge is expected to be highly effective. For this purpose, the amount of the hedging instrument may be greater or less than that of the hedged item if this improves the effectiveness of the hedging relationship. For example, a regression analysis could be performed to establish a statistical relationship between the hedged item (eg a transaction in Brazilian coffee) and the hedging instrument (eg a transaction in Colombian coffee). If there is a valid statistical relationship between the two variables (ie between the unit prices of Brazilian coffee and Colombian coffee), the slope of the regression line can be used to establish the hedge ratio that will maximise expected effectiveness. For example, if the slope of the regression line is 1.02, a hedge ratio based on 0.98 quantities of hedged items to 1.00 quantities of the hedging instrument maximises expected effectiveness. However, the hedging relationship may result in ineffectiveness that is recognised in profit or loss during the term of the hedging relationship.

Designation of groups of items as hedged items (paragraphs 83 and 84)

AG101 A hedge of an overall net position (eg the net of all fixed rate assets and fixed rate liabilities with similar maturities), rather than of a specific hedged item, does not qualify for hedge accounting. However, almost the same effect on profit or loss of hedge accounting for this type of hedging relationship can be achieved by designating as the hedged item part of the underlying items. For example, if a bank has CU100 of assets and CU90 of liabilities with risks and terms of a similar nature and hedges the net CU10 exposure, it can designate as the hedged item CU10 of those assets. This designation can be used if such assets and liabilities are fixed rate instruments, in which case it is a fair value hedge, or if they are variable rate instruments, in which case it is a cash flow hedge. Similarly, if an entity has a firm commitment to make a purchase in a foreign currency of CU100 and a firm commitment to make a sale in the foreign currency of CU90, it can hedge the net amount of CU10 by acquiring a derivative and designating it as a hedging instrument associated with CU10 of the firm purchase commitment of CU100.

Hedge accounting (paragraphs 85–102)

AG102 An example of a fair value hedge is a hedge of exposure to changes in the fair value of a fixed rate debt instrument as a result of changes in interest rates. Such a hedge could be entered into by the issuer or by the holder.

AG103 An example of a cash flow hedge is the use of a swap to change floating rate debt to fixed rate debt (ie a hedge of a future transaction where the future cash flows being hedged are the future interest payments).

AG104 A hedge of a firm commitment (eg a hedge of the change in fuel price relating to an unrecognised contractual commitment by an electric utility to purchase fuel at a fixed price) is a hedge of an exposure to a change in fair value. Accordingly, such a hedge is a fair value hedge. However, under paragraph 87 a hedge of the foreign currency risk of a firm commitment could alternatively be accounted for as a cash flow hedge.

Assessing hedge effectiveness

AG105 A hedge is regarded as highly effective only if both of the following conditions are met:

(a) At the inception of the hedge and in subsequent periods, the hedge is expected to be highly effective in achieving offsetting changes in fair value or cash flows attributable to the hedged risk during the period for which the hedge is designated. Such an expectation can be demonstrated in various ways, including a comparison of past changes in the fair value or cash flows of the hedged item that are attributable to the hedged risk with past changes in the fair value or cash flows of the hedging instrument, or by demonstrating a high statistical correlation between the fair value or cash flows of the hedged item and those of the hedging instrument. The entity may choose a hedge ratio of other than one to one in order to improve the effectiveness of the hedge as described in paragraph AG100.

(b) The actual results of the hedge are within a range of 80–125 per cent. For example, if actual results are such that the loss on the hedging instrument is CU120 and the gain on the cash instrument is CU100, offset can be measured by 120/100, which is 120 per cent, or by 100/120, which is 83 per cent. In this example, assuming the hedge meets the condition in (a), the entity would conclude that the hedge has been highly effective.

AG106 Effectiveness is assessed, at a minimum, at the time an entity prepares its annual or interim financial statements.

AG107 This Standard does not specify a single method for assessing hedge effectiveness. The method an entity adopts for assessing hedge effectiveness depends on its risk management strategy. For example, if the entity's risk management strategy is to adjust the amount of the hedging instrument periodically to reflect changes in the hedged position, the entity needs to demonstrate that the hedge is expected to be highly effective only for the period until the amount of the hedging instrument is next adjusted. In some cases, an entity adopts different methods for different types of hedges. An entity's documentation of its hedging strategy includes its procedures for assessing effectiveness. Those procedures state whether the assessment includes all of the gain or loss on a hedging instrument or whether the instrument's time value is excluded.

AG107A If an entity hedges less than 100 per cent of the exposure on an item, such as 85 per cent, it shall designate the hedged item as being 85 per cent of the exposure and shall measure ineffectiveness based on the change in that designated 85 per cent exposure. However, when hedging the designated 85 per cent exposure, the entity may use a hedge ratio of other than one to one if that improves the expected effectiveness of the hedge, as explained in paragraph AG100.

AG108 If the principal terms of the hedging instrument and of the hedged asset, liability, firm commitment or highly probable forecast transaction are the same, the changes in fair value and cash flows attributable to the risk being hedged may be likely to offset each other fully, both when the hedge is entered into and afterwards. For example, an interest rate swap is likely to be an effective hedge if the notional and principal amounts, term, repricing dates, dates of interest and principal receipts and payments, and basis for measuring interest rates are the same for the hedging instrument and the hedged item. In addition, a hedge of a highly probable forecast purchase of a commodity with a forward contract is likely to be highly effective if:

(a) the forward contract is for the purchase of the same quantity of the same commodity at the same time and location as the hedged forecast purchase;

(b) the fair value of the forward contract at inception is zero; and

(c) either the change in the discount or premium on the forward contract is excluded from the assessment of effectiveness and recognised in profit or loss or the change in expected cash flows on the highly probable forecast transaction is based on the forward price for the commodity.

AG109 Sometimes the hedging instrument offsets only part of the hedged risk. For example, a hedge would not be fully effective if the hedging instrument and hedged item are denominated in different currencies that do not move in tandem. Also, a hedge of interest rate risk using a derivative would not be fully effective if part of the change in the fair value of the derivative is attributable to the counterparty's credit risk.

AG110 To qualify for hedge accounting, the hedge must relate to a specific identified and designated risk, and not merely to the entity's general business risks, and must ultimately affect the entity's profit or loss. A hedge of the risk of obsolescence of a physical asset or the risk of expropriation of property by a government is not eligible for hedge accounting; effectiveness cannot be measured because those risks are not measurable reliably.

AG111 In the case of interest rate risk, hedge effectiveness may be assessed by preparing a maturity schedule for financial assets and financial liabilities that shows the net interest rate exposure for each time period, provided that the net exposure is associated with a specific asset or liability (or a specific group of assets or liabilities or a specific portion of them) giving rise to the net exposure, and hedge effectiveness is assessed against that asset or liability.

AG112 In assessing the effectiveness of a hedge, an entity generally considers the time value of money. The fixed interest rate on a hedged item need not exactly match the fixed interest rate on a swap designated as a fair value hedge. Nor does the variable interest rate on an interest-bearing asset or liability need to be the same as the variable interest rate on a swap designated as a cash flow hedge. A swap's fair value derives from its net settlements. The fixed and variable rates on a swap can be changed without affecting the net settlement if both are changed by the same amount.

AG113 If an entity does not meet hedge effectiveness criteria, the entity discontinues hedge accounting from the last date on which compliance with hedge effectiveness was demonstrated. However, if the entity identifies the event or change in circumstances that caused the hedging relationship to fail the effectiveness criteria, and demonstrates that the hedge was effective before the event or change in circumstances occurred, the entity discontinues hedge accounting from the date of the event or change in circumstances.

Fair value hedge accounting for a portfolio hedge of interest rate risk

AG114 For a fair value hedge of interest rate risk associated with a portfolio of financial assets or financial liabilities, an entity would meet the requirements of this Standard if it complies with the procedures set out in (a)–(i) and paragraphs AG115–AG132 below.

(a) As part of its risk management process the entity identifies a portfolio of items whose interest rate risk it wishes to hedge. The portfolio may comprise only assets, only liabilities or both assets and liabilities. The entity may identify two or more portfolios (eg the entity may group its available-for-sale assets into a separate portfolio), in which case it applies the guidance below to each portfolio separately.

(b) The entity analyses the portfolio into repricing time periods based on expected, rather than contractual, repricing dates. The analysis into repricing time periods may be performed in various ways including scheduling cash flows into the periods in which they are expected to occur, or scheduling notional principal amounts into all periods until repricing is expected to occur.

(c) On the basis of this analysis, the entity decides the amount it wishes to hedge. The entity designates as the hedged item an amount of assets or liabilities (but not a net amount) from the identified portfolio equal to the amount it wishes to designate as being hedged. This amount also determines the percentage measure that is used for testing effectiveness in accordance with paragraph AG126(b).

(d) The entity designates the interest rate risk it is hedging. This risk could be a portion of the interest rate risk in each of the items in the hedged position, such as a benchmark interest rate (eg LIBOR).

(e) The entity designates one or more hedging instruments for each repricing time period.

(f) Using the designations made in (c)–(e) above, the entity assesses at inception and in subsequent periods, whether the hedge is expected to be highly effective during the period for which the hedge is designated.

(g) Periodically, the entity measures the change in the fair value of the hedged item (as designated in (c)) that is attributable to the hedged risk (as designated in (d)), on the basis of the expected repricing dates determined in (b). Provided that the hedge is determined actually to have been highly effective when assessed using the entity's documented method of assessing effectiveness, the entity recognises the change in fair value of the hedged item as a gain or loss in profit or loss and in one of two line items in the balance sheet as described in paragraph 89A. The change in fair value need not be allocated to individual assets or liabilities.

(h) The entity measures the change in fair value of the hedging instrument(s) (as designated in (e)) and recognises it as a gain or loss in profit or loss. The fair value of the hedging instrument(s) is recognised as an asset or liability in the balance sheet.

(i) Any ineffectiveness* will be recognised in profit or loss as the difference between the change in fair value referred to in (g) and that referred to in (h).

AG115 This approach is described in more detail below. The approach shall be applied only to a fair value hedge of the interest rate risk associated with a portfolio of financial assets or financial liabilities.

AG116 The portfolio identified in paragraph AG114(a) could contain assets and liabilities. Alternatively, it could be a portfolio containing only assets, or only liabilities. The portfolio is used to determine the amount of the assets or liabilities the entity wishes to hedge. However, the portfolio is not itself designated as the hedged item.

AG117 In applying paragraph AG114(b), the entity determines the expected repricing date of an item as the earlier of the dates when that item is expected to mature or to reprice to market rates. The expected repricing dates are estimated at the inception of the hedge and throughout the term of the hedge, based on historical experience and other available information, including information and expectations regarding prepayment rates, interest rates and the interaction between them. Entities that have no entity-specific experience or insufficient experience use peer group experience for comparable financial instruments. These estimates are reviewed periodically and updated in the light of experience. In the case of a fixed rate item that is prepayable, the expected repricing date is the date on which the item is expected to prepay unless it reprices to market rates on an earlier date. For a group of similar items, the analysis into time periods based on expected repricing dates may take the form of allocating a percentage of the group, rather than individual items, to each time period. An entity may apply other methodologies for such allocation purposes. For example, it may use a prepayment rate multiplier for allocating amortising loans to time periods based on expected repricing dates. However, the methodology for such an allocation shall be in accordance with the entity's risk management procedures and objectives.

AG118 As an example of the designation set out in paragraph AG114(c), if in a particular repricing time period an entity estimates that it has fixed rate assets of CU100 and fixed rate liabilities of CU80 and decides to hedge all of the net position of CU20, it designates as the hedged item assets in the amount of CU20 (a portion of the assets).† The designation is expressed as an 'amount of a currency' (eg an amount of dollars, euro, pounds or rand) rather than as individual assets. It follows that all of the assets (or liabilities) from which the hedged amount is drawn–ie all of the CU100 of assets in the above example–must be:

(a) items whose fair value changes in response to changes in the interest rate being hedged; and

* The same materiality considerations apply in this context as apply throughout IFRSs.

† The Standard permits an entity to designate any amount of the available qualifying assets or liabilities, ie in this example any amount of assets between CU0 and CU100.

(b) items that could have qualified for fair value hedge accounting if they had been designated as hedged individually. In particular, because the Standard* specifies that the fair value of a financial liability with a demand feature (such as demand deposits and some types of time deposits) is not less than the amount payable on demand, discounted from the first date that the amount could be required to be paid, such an item cannot qualify for fair value hedge accounting for any time period beyond the shortest period in which the holder can demand payment. In the above example, the hedged position is an amount of assets. Hence, such liabilities are not a part of the designated hedged item, but are used by the entity to determine the amount of the asset that is designated as being hedged. If the position the entity wished to hedge was an amount of liabilities, the amount representing the designated hedged item must be drawn from fixed rate liabilities other than liabilities that the entity can be required to repay in an earlier time period, and the percentage measure used for assessing hedge effectiveness in accordance with paragraph AG126(b) would be calculated as a percentage of these other liabilities. For example, assume that an entity estimates that in a particular repricing time period it has fixed rate liabilities of CU100, comprising CU40 of demand deposits and CU60 of liabilities with no demand feature, and CU70 of fixed rate assets. If the entity decides to hedge all of the net position of CU30, it designates as the hedged item liabilities of CU30 or 50 per cent† of the liabilities with no demand feature.

AG119 The entity also complies with the other designation and documentation requirements set out in paragraph 88(a). For a portfolio hedge of interest rate risk, this designation and documentation specifies the entity's policy for all of the variables that are used to identify the amount that is hedged and how effectiveness is measured, including the following:

(a) which assets and liabilities are to be included in the portfolio hedge and the basis to be used for removing them from the portfolio.

(b) how the entity estimates repricing dates, including what interest rate assumptions underlie estimates of prepayment rates and the basis for changing those estimates. The same method is used for both the initial estimates made at the time an asset or liability is included in the hedged portfolio and for any later revisions to those estimates.

(c) the number and duration of repricing time periods.

(d) how often the entity will test effectiveness and which of the two methods in paragraph AG126 it will use.

(e) the methodology used by the entity to determine the amount of assets or liabilities that are designated as the hedged item and, accordingly, the percentage measure used when the entity tests effectiveness using the method described in paragraph AG126(b).

---

* see paragraph 49

† CU30 ÷ (CU100 – CU40) = 50 per cent

(f) when the entity tests effectiveness using the method described in paragraph AG126(b), whether the entity will test effectiveness for each repricing time period individually, for all time periods in aggregate, or by using some combination of the two.

The policies specified in designating and documenting the hedging relationship shall be in accordance with the entity's risk management procedures and objectives. Changes in policies shall not be made arbitrarily. They shall be justified on the basis of changes in market conditions and other factors and be founded on and consistent with the entity's risk management procedures and objectives.

AG120 The hedging instrument referred to in paragraph AG114(e) may be a single derivative or a portfolio of derivatives all of which contain exposure to the hedged interest rate risk designated in paragraph AG114(d) (eg a portfolio of interest rate swaps all of which contain exposure to LIBOR). Such a portfolio of derivatives may contain offsetting risk positions. However, it may not include written options or net written options, because the Standard[*] does not permit such options to be designated as hedging instruments (except when a written option is designated as an offset to a purchased option). If the hedging instrument hedges the amount designated in paragraph AG114(c) for more than one repricing time period, it is allocated to all of the time periods that it hedges. However, the whole of the hedging instrument must be allocated to those repricing time periods because the Standard[†] does not permit a hedging relationship to be designated for only a portion of the time period during which a hedging instrument remains outstanding.

AG121 When the entity measures the change in the fair value of a prepayable item in accordance with paragraph AG114(g), a change in interest rates affects the fair value of the prepayable item in two ways: it affects the fair value of the contractual cash flows and the fair value of the prepayment option that is contained in a prepayable item. Paragraph 81 of the Standard permits an entity to designate a portion of a financial asset or financial liability, sharing a common risk exposure, as the hedged item, provided effectiveness can be measured. For prepayable items, paragraph 81A permits this to be achieved by designating the hedged item in terms of the change in the fair value that is attributable to changes in the designated interest rate on the basis of *expected*, rather than *contractual*, repricing dates. However, the effect that changes in the hedged interest rate have on those expected repricing dates shall be included when determining the change in the fair value of the hedged item. Consequently, if the expected repricing dates are revised (eg to reflect a change in expected prepayments), or if actual repricing dates differ from those expected, ineffectiveness will arise as described in paragraph AG126. Conversely, changes in expected repricing dates that (a) clearly arise from factors other than changes in the hedged interest rate, (b) are uncorrelated with changes in the hedged interest rate and (c) can be reliably separated from changes that are attributable to the hedged interest rate (eg changes in prepayment rates clearly arising from a change in demographic factors or tax regulations rather than changes in interest rate) are

* see paragraphs 77 and AG94

† see paragraph 75

excluded when determining the change in the fair value of the hedged item, because they are not attributable to the hedged risk. If there is uncertainty about the factor that gave rise to the change in expected repricing dates or the entity is not able to separate reliably the changes that arise from the hedged interest rate from those that arise from other factors, the change is assumed to arise from changes in the hedged interest rate.

AG122 The Standard does not specify the techniques used to determine the amount referred to in paragraph AG114(g), namely the change in the fair value of the hedged item that is attributable to the hedged risk. If statistical or other estimation techniques are used for such measurement, management must expect the result to approximate closely that which would have been obtained from measurement of all the individual assets or liabilities that constitute the hedged item. It is not appropriate to assume that changes in the fair value of the hedged item equal changes in the value of the hedging instrument.

AG123 Paragraph 89A requires that if the hedged item for a particular repricing time period is an asset, the change in its value is presented in a separate line item within assets. Conversely, if the hedged item for a particular repricing time period is a liability, the change in its value is presented in a separate line item within liabilities. These are the separate line items referred to in paragraph AG114(g). Specific allocation to individual assets (or liabilities) is not required.

AG124 Paragraph AG114(i) notes that ineffectiveness arises to the extent that the change in the fair value of the hedged item that is attributable to the hedged risk differs from the change in the fair value of the hedging derivative. Such a difference may arise for a number of reasons, including:

(a) actual repricing dates being different from those expected, or expected repricing dates being revised;

(b) items in the hedged portfolio becoming impaired or being derecognised;

(c) the payment dates of the hedging instrument and the hedged item being different; and

(d) other causes (eg when a few of the hedged items bear interest at a rate below the benchmark rate for which they are designated as being hedged, and the resulting ineffectiveness is not so great that the portfolio as a whole fails to qualify for hedge accounting).

Such ineffectiveness* shall be identified and recognised in profit or loss.

AG125 Generally, the effectiveness of the hedge will be improved:

(a) if the entity schedules items with different prepayment characteristics in a way that takes account of the differences in prepayment behaviour.

(b) when the number of items in the portfolio is larger. When only a few items are contained in the portfolio, relatively high ineffectiveness is likely if one of the items prepays earlier or later than expected. Conversely, when the portfolio contains many items, the prepayment behaviour can be predicted more accurately.

* The same materiality considerations apply in this context as apply throughout IFRSs.

(c) when the repricing time periods used are narrower (eg 1-month as opposed to 3-month repricing time periods). Narrower repricing time periods reduces the effect of any mismatch between the repricing and payment dates (within the repricing time period) of the hedged item and those of the hedging instrument.

(d) the greater the frequency with which the amount of the hedging instrument is adjusted to reflect changes in the hedged item (eg because of changes in prepayment expectations).

AG126 An entity tests effectiveness periodically. If estimates of repricing dates change between one date on which an entity assesses effectiveness and the next, it shall calculate the amount of effectiveness either:

(a) as the difference between the change in the fair value of the hedging instrument (see paragraph AG114(h)) and the change in the value of the entire hedged item that is attributable to changes in the hedged interest rate (including the effect that changes in the hedged interest rate have on the fair value of any embedded prepayment option); or

(b) using the following approximation. The entity:

(i) calculates the percentage of the assets (or liabilities) in each repricing time period that was hedged, on the basis of the estimated repricing dates at the last date it tested effectiveness.

(ii) applies this percentage to its revised estimate of the amount in that repricing time period to calculate the amount of the hedged item based on its revised estimate.

(iii) calculates the change in the fair value of its revised estimate of the hedged item that is attributable to the hedged risk and presents it as set out in paragraph AG114(g).

(iv) recognises ineffectiveness equal to the difference between the amount determined in (iii) and the change in the fair value of the hedging instrument (see paragraph AG114(h)).

AG127 When measuring effectiveness, the entity distinguishes revisions to the estimated repricing dates of existing assets (or liabilities) from the origination of new assets (or liabilities), with only the former giving rise to ineffectiveness. All revisions to estimated repricing dates (other than those excluded in accordance with paragraph AG121), including any reallocation of existing items between time periods, are included when revising the estimated amount in a time period in accordance with paragraph AG126(b)(ii) and hence when measuring effectiveness. Once ineffectiveness has been recognised as set out above, the entity establishes a new estimate of the total assets (or liabilities) in each repricing time period, including new assets (or liabilities) that have been originated since it last tested effectiveness, and designates a new amount as the hedged item and a new percentage as the hedged percentage. The procedures set out in paragraph AG126(b) are then repeated at the next date it tests effectiveness.

AG128 Items that were originally scheduled into a repricing time period may be derecognised because of earlier than expected prepayment or writeoffs caused by impairment or sale. When this occurs, the amount of change in fair value included in the separate line item referred to in paragraph AG114(g) that relates to the derecognised item shall be removed from the balance sheet, and included in the gain or loss that arises on derecognition of the item. For this purpose, it is necessary to know the repricing time period(s) into which the derecognised item was scheduled, because this determines the repricing time period(s) from which to remove it and hence the amount to remove from the separate line item referred to in paragraph AG114(g). When an item is derecognised, if it can be determined in which time period it was included, it is removed from that time period. If not, it is removed from the earliest time period if the derecognition resulted from higher than expected prepayments, or allocated to all time periods containing the derecognised item on a systematic and rational basis if the item was sold or became impaired.

AG129 In addition, any amount relating to a particular time period that has not been derecognised when the time period expires is recognised in profit or loss at that time (see paragraph 89A). For example, assume an entity schedules items into three repricing time periods. At the previous redesignation, the change in fair value reported in the single line item on the balance sheet was an asset of CU25. That amount represents amounts attributable to periods 1, 2 and 3 of CU7, CU8 and CU10, respectively. At the next redesignation, the assets attributable to period 1 have been either realised or rescheduled into other periods. Therefore, CU7 is derecognised from the balance sheet and recognised in profit or loss. CU8 and CU10 are now attributable to periods 1 and 2, respectively. These remaining periods are then adjusted, as necessary, for changes in fair value as described in paragraph AG114(g).

AG130 As an illustration of the requirements of the previous two paragraphs, assume that an entity scheduled assets by allocating a percentage of the portfolio into each repricing time period. Assume also that it scheduled CU100 into each of the first two time periods. When the first repricing time period expires, CU110 of assets are derecognised because of expected and unexpected repayments. In this case, all of the amount contained in the separate line item referred to in paragraph AG114(g) that relates to the first time period is removed from the balance sheet, plus 10 per cent of the amount that relates to the second time period.

AG131 If the hedged amount for a repricing time period is reduced without the related assets (or liabilities) being derecognised, the amount included in the separate line item referred to in paragraph AG114(g) that relates to the reduction shall be amortised in accordance with paragraph 92.

AG132 An entity may wish to apply the approach set out in paragraphs AG114–AG131 to a portfolio hedge that had previously been accounted for as a cash flow hedge in accordance with IAS 39. Such an entity would revoke the previous designation of a cash flow hedge in accordance with paragraph 101(d), and apply the requirements set out in that paragraph. It would also redesignate the hedge as a fair value hedge and apply the approach set out in paragraphs AG114–AG131 prospectively to subsequent accounting periods.

Appendix B
Amendments to other pronouncements

The amendments in this appendix shall be applied for annual periods beginning on or after 1 January 2005. If an entity applies this Standard for an earlier period, these amendments shall be applied for that earlier period.

* * * * *

The amendments contained in this appendix when this Standard was revised in 2003 have been incorporated into the relevant pronouncements published in this volume.

Approval of IAS 39 by the Board

International Accounting Standard 39 *Financial Instruments: Recognition and Measurement* was approved for issue by eleven of the fourteen members of the International Accounting Standards Board. Messrs Cope, Leisenring and McGregor dissented. Their dissenting opinions are set out after the Basis for Conclusions.

Sir David Tweedie	Chairman
Thomas E Jones	Vice-Chairman
Mary E Barth	
Hans-Georg Bruns	
Anthony T Cope	
Robert P Garnett	
Gilbert Gélard	
James J Leisenring	
Warren J McGregor	
Patricia L O'Malley	
Harry K Schmid	
John T Smith	
Geoffrey Whittington	
Tatsumi Yamada	

Approval of Amendments to IAS 39 by the Board

These Amendments to International Accounting Standard 39 *Financial Instruments: Recognition and Measurement—Fair Value Hedge Accounting for a Portfolio Hedge of Interest Rate Risk* were approved for issue by thirteen of the fourteen members of the International Accounting Standards Board. Mr Smith dissented. His dissenting opinion is set out after the Basis for Conclusions.

Sir David Tweedie	Chairman
Thomas E Jones	Vice-Chairman
Mary E Barth	
Hans-Georg Bruns	
Anthony T Cope	
Robert P Garnett	
Gilbert Gélard	
James J Leisenring	
Warren J McGregor	
Patricia L O'Malley	
Harry K Schmid	
John T Smith	
Geoffrey Whittington	
Tatsumi Yamada	

Approval of Amendments to IAS 39 by the Board

These Amendments to International Accounting Standard 39 *Financial Instruments: Recognition and Measurement—Transition and Initial Recognition of Financial Assets and Financial Liabilities* were approved for issue by the fourteen members of the International Accounting Standards Board.

Sir David Tweedie	Chairman
Thomas E Jones	Vice-Chairman
Mary E Barth	
Hans-Georg Bruns	
Anthony T Cope	
Jan Engström	
Robert P Garnett	
Gilbert Gélard	
James J Leisenring	
Warren J McGregor	
Patricia L O'Malley	
John T Smith	
Geoffrey Whittington	
Tatsumi Yamada	

CONTENTS

Basis for Conclusions

This Basis for Conclusions accompanies, but is not part of, IAS 39.

BC1 This Basis for Conclusions summarises the International Accounting Standards Board's considerations in reaching the conclusions on revising IAS 39 *Financial Instruments: Recognition and Measurement* in 2003. Individual Board members gave greater weight to some factors than to others.

BC2 In July 2001 the Board announced that, as part of its initial agenda of technical projects, it would undertake a project to improve a number of Standards, including IAS 32 *Financial Instruments: Disclosure and Presentation* and IAS 39 *Financial Instruments: Recognition and Measurement*. The objectives of the Improvements project were to reduce the complexity in the Standards by clarifying and adding guidance, eliminating internal inconsistencies and incorporating into the Standards elements of Standing Interpretations Committee (SIC) Interpretations and IAS 39 implementation guidance. In June 2002 the Board published its proposals in an Exposure Draft of Proposed Amendments to IAS 32 *Financial Instruments: Disclosure and Presentation* and IAS 39 *Financial Instruments: Recognition and Measurement*, with a comment deadline of 14 October 2002. In August 2003 the Board published a further Exposure Draft of Proposed Amendments to IAS 39 on *Fair Value Hedge Accounting for a Portfolio Hedge of Interest Rate Risk*, with a comment deadline of 14 November 2003.

BC3 Because the Board's intention was not to reconsider the fundamental approach to the accounting for financial instruments established by IAS 32 and IAS 39, this Basis for Conclusions does not discuss requirements in IAS 39 that the Board has not reconsidered.

Background

BC4 The original version of IAS 39 became effective for financial statements covering financial years beginning on or after 1 January 2001. It reflected a mixed measurement model in which some financial assets and financial liabilities are measured at fair value and others at cost or amortised cost, depending in part on an entity's intention in holding an instrument.

BC5 The Board recognises that accounting for financial instruments is a difficult and controversial subject. The Board's predecessor body, the International Accounting Standards Committee (IASC) began its work on the issue some 15 years ago, in 1988. During the next eight years it published two Exposure Drafts, culminating in the issue of IAS 32 on disclosure and presentation in 1995. IASC decided that its initial proposals on recognition and measurement should not be progressed to a Standard, in view of:

- the critical response they had attracted;
- evolving practices in financial instruments; and
- the developing thinking by national standard-setters.

BC6 Accordingly, in 1997 IASC published, jointly with the Canadian Accounting Standards Board, a discussion paper that proposed a different approach, namely that all financial assets and financial liabilities should be measured at fair value.

The responses to that paper indicated both widespread unease with some of its proposals and that more work needed to be done before a standard requiring a full fair value approach could be contemplated.

BC7 In the meantime, IASC concluded that a standard on the recognition and measurement of financial instruments was needed urgently. It noted that although financial instruments were widely held and used throughout the world, few countries apart from the United States had any recognition and measurement standards for them. In addition, IASC had agreed with the International Organization of Securities Commissions (IOSCO) that it would develop a set of 'core' International Accounting Standards that could be endorsed by IOSCO for the purpose of cross-border capital raising and listing in all global markets. Those core standards included one on the recognition and measurement of financial instruments. Accordingly, IASC developed the version of IAS 39 that was issued in 2000.

BC8 In December 2000 a Financial Instruments Joint Working Group of Standard Setters (JWG), comprising representatives or members of accounting standardsetters and professional organisations from a range of countries, published a Draft Standard and Basis for Conclusions entitled *Financial Instruments and Similar Items*. That Draft Standard proposed far-reaching changes to accounting for financial instruments and similar items, including the measurement of virtually all financial instruments at fair value. In the light of feedback on the JWG's proposals, it is evident that much more work is needed before a comprehensive fair value accounting model could be introduced.

BC9 In July 2001 the Board announced that it would undertake a project to improve the existing requirements on the accounting for financial instruments in IAS 32 and IAS 39. The improvements deal with practice issues identified by audit firms, national standard-setters, regulators and others, and issues identified in the IAS 39 implementation guidance process or by IASB staff.

BC10 In June 2002 the Board published an Exposure Draft of proposed amendments to IAS 32 and IAS 39 for a 116-day comment period. More than 170 comment letters were received.

BC11 Subsequently, the Board took steps to enable constituents to inform it better about the main issues arising out of the comment process, and to enable the Board to explain its views of the issues and its tentative conclusions. These consultations included:

(a) discussions with the Standards Advisory Council on the main issues raised in the comment process.

(b) nine roundtable discussions with constituents during March 2003 conducted in Brussels and London. Over 100 organisations and individuals took part in those discussions.

(c) discussions with the Board's liaison standard-setters of the issues raised in the roundtable discussions.

(d) meetings between members of the Board and its staff and various groups of constituents to explore further issues raised in comment letters and at the roundtable discussions.

BC11A Some of the comment letters on the June 2002 Exposure Draft and participants in the roundtables raised a significant issue for which the June 2003 Exposure Draft had not proposed any changes. This was hedge accounting for a portfolio hedge of interest rate risk (sometimes referred to as 'macro hedging') and the related question of the treatment in hedge accounting of deposits with a demand feature (sometimes referred to as 'demand deposits' or 'demandable liabilities'). In particular, some were concerned that it was very difficult to achieve fair value hedge accounting for a macro hedge in accordance with previous versions of IAS 39.

BC11B In the light of these concerns, the Board decided to explore whether and how IAS 39 might be amended to enable fair value hedge accounting to be used more readily for a portfolio hedge of interest rate risk. This resulted in a further Exposure Draft of Proposed Amendments to IAS 39 that was published in August 2003 and on which more than 120 comment letters were received. The amendments proposed in the Exposure Draft were finalised in March 2004.

BC12 The Board did not reconsider the fundamental approach to accounting for financial instruments contained in IAS 39. Some of the complexity in existing requirements is inevitable in a mixed measurement model based in part on management's intentions for holding financial instruments and given the complexity of finance concepts and fair value estimation issues. The amendments reduce some of the complexity by clarifying the Standard, eliminating internal inconsistencies and incorporating additional guidance into the Standard.

BC13 The amendments also eliminate or mitigate some differences between IAS 39 and US GAAP related to the measurement of financial instruments. Already, the measurement requirements in IAS 39 are, to a large extent, similar to equivalent requirements in US GAAP, in particular, those in FASB SFAS 114 *Accounting by Creditors for Impairment of a Loan*, SFAS 115 *Accounting for Certain Investments in Debt and Equity Securities* and SFAS 133 *Accounting for Derivative Instruments and Hedging Activities.*

BC14 The Board will continue its consideration of issues related to the accounting for financial instruments. However, it expects that the basic principles in the improved IAS 39 will be in place for a considerable period.

Scope

Loan commitments (paragraphs 2(i) and 4)

BC15 Loan commitments are firm commitments to provide credit under pre-specified terms and conditions. In the IAS 39 implementation guidance process, the question was raised whether a bank's loan commitments are derivatives accounted for at fair value under IAS 39. This question arises because a commitment to make a loan at a specified rate of interest during a fixed period of time meets the definition of a derivative. In effect, it is a written option for the potential borrower to obtain a loan at a specified rate.

BC16 To simplify the accounting for holders and issuers of loan commitments, the Board decided to exclude particular loan commitments from the scope of IAS 39. The effect of the exclusion is that an entity will not recognise and measure changes in fair value of these loan commitments that result from changes in market interest rates or credit spreads. This is consistent with the measurement of the loan that results if the holder of the loan commitment exercises its right to obtain financing, because changes in market interest rates do not affect the measurement of an asset measured at amortised cost (assuming it is not designated in a category other than loans and receivables).

BC17 However, the Board decided that an entity should be permitted to measure a loan commitment at fair value with changes in fair value recognised in profit or loss on the basis of designation at inception of the loan commitment as a financial liability through profit or loss. This may be appropriate, for example, if the entity manages risk exposures related to loan commitments on a fair value basis.

BC18 The Board further decided that a loan commitment should be excluded from the scope of IAS 39 only if it cannot be settled net. If the value of a loan commitment can be settled net in cash or another financial instrument, including when the entity has a past practice of selling the resulting loan assets shortly after origination, it is difficult to justify its exclusion from the requirement in IAS 39 to measure at fair value similar instruments that meet the definition of a derivative.

BC19 Some comments received on the Exposure Draft disagreed with the Board's proposal that an entity that has a past practice of selling the assets resulting from its loan commitments shortly after origination should apply IAS 39 to all of its loan commitments. The Board considered this concern and agreed that the words in the Exposure Draft did not reflect the Board's intention. Thus, the Board clarified that if an entity has a past practice of selling the assets resulting from its loan commitments shortly after origination, it applies IAS 39 only to its loan commitments in the same class.

BC20 Finally, the Board decided that commitments to provide a loan at a below-market interest rate should be initially measured at fair value, and subsequently measured at the higher of (a) the amount that would be recognised under IAS 37 and (b) the amount initially recognised less, where appropriate, cumulative amortisation recognised in accordance with IAS 18 *Revenue*. It noted that without such a requirement, liabilities that result from such commitments might not be recognised in the balance sheet, because in many cases no cash consideration is received.

Financial guarantee contracts (paragraphs 2(e), 3 and AG4A)

BC21 The Exposure Draft proposed that financial guarantee contracts that provide for specified payments to be made to reimburse the holder for a loss it has incurred because a specified debtor fails to make payment when due should be initially recognised and measured by the issuer in accordance with IAS 39. Subsequently, they should be measured in accordance with IAS 37 *Provisions, Contingent Liabilities and Contingent Assets* at the amount an entity would rationally be expected to pay to settle the obligation or to transfer it to a third party. This amendment would have clarified that an issued financial guarantee contract meets the definition of a liability and should be recognised as such.

BC22 Some of the comments received on the Exposure Draft expressed concern that applying IAS 37 after initial recognition would result in individual financial guarantees being measured at nil immediately after initial recognition if the probability threshold in IAS 37 was not met, and thus the entity would recognise an immediate gain.

BC23 In finalising IFRS 4 *Insurance Contracts*, the Board decided that a financial guarantee should, regardless of its legal form (eg financial guarantee, letter of credit, credit default contract, insurance contract) be within the scope of:

(a) this Standard if it is not an insurance contract, as defined in IFRS 4.

(b) this Standard, for accounting by the issuer, if the issuer incurred or retained the financial guarantee when it transferred to another party financial assets or financial liabilities within the scope of this Standard.

(c) IFRS 4 if it is an insurance contract, as defined in IFRS 4, unless (b) applies. However, the Board also decided to develop an Exposure Draft proposing that financial guarantees within the scope of IFRS 4 should be measured initially at fair value and subsequently in the same way as commitments to provide a loan at a below-market interest rate (see paragraph BC20).

Contracts to buy or sell a non–financial item (paragraphs 5–7 and AG10)

BC24 Before the amendments, IAS 39 and IAS 32 were not consistent with respect to the circumstances in which a commodity-based contract meets the definition of a financial instrument and is accounted for as a derivative. The Board concluded that the amendments should make them consistent on the basis of the notion that a contract to buy or sell a non-financial item should be accounted for as a derivative when it (i) can be settled net or by exchanging financial instruments and (ii) is not held for the purpose of receipt or delivery of the non-financial item in accordance with the entity's expected purchase, sale or usage requirements (a 'normal' purchase or sale). In addition, the Board concluded that the notion of when a contract can be settled net should include contracts:

(a) where the entity has a practice of settling similar contracts net in cash or another financial instrument or by exchanging financial instruments;

(b) for which the entity has a practice of taking delivery of the underlying and selling it within a short period after delivery for the purpose of generating a profit from short-term fluctuations in price or dealer's margin; and

(c) in which the non-financial item that is the subject of the contract is readily convertible to cash.

Because practices of settling net or taking delivery of the underlying and selling it within a short period after delivery also indicate that the contracts are not 'normal' purchases or sales, such contracts are within the scope of IAS 39 and are accounted for as derivatives. The Board also decided to clarify that a written option that can be settled net in cash or another financial instrument, or by exchanging financial instruments, is within the scope of the Standard and cannot qualify as a 'normal' purchase or sale.

Definitions

Loans and receivables (paragraphs 9, 46(a) and AG26)

BC25 The principal difference between loans and receivables and other financial assets is that loans and receivables are not subject to the tainting provisions that apply to held-to-maturity investments. Loans and receivables that are not held for trading may be measured at amortised cost even if an entity does not have the positive intention and ability to hold the loan asset until maturity.

BC26 The Board decided that the ability to measure a financial asset at amortised cost without consideration of the entity's intention and ability to hold the asset until maturity is most appropriate when there is no liquid market for the asset. It is less appropriate to extend the category to debt instruments traded in liquid markets. The distinction for measurement purposes between liquid debt instruments that are acquired upon issue and liquid debt instruments that are acquired shortly afterwards is difficult to justify on conceptual grounds. Why should a liquid debt instrument that is purchased on the day of issue be treated differently from a liquid debt instrument that is purchased one week after issue? Why should it not be possible to classify a liquid debt instrument that is acquired directly from the issuer as available for sale, with fair value gains and losses recognised in equity? Why should a liquid debt instrument that is bought shortly after it is issued be subject to tainting provisions, if a liquid debt instrument that is bought at the time of issue is not subject to tainting provisions?

BC27 The Board therefore decided to add a condition to the definition of a loan or receivable. More specifically, an entity should not be permitted to classify as a loan or receivable an investment in a debt instrument that is quoted in an active market. For such an investment, an entity should be required to demonstrate its positive intention and ability to hold the investment until maturity to be permitted to measure the investment at amortised cost by classifying it as held to maturity.

BC28 The Board considered comments received on the proposal in the Exposure Draft (which was unchanged from the requirement in the original IAS 39) that 'loans and receivables' must be originated (rather than purchased) to meet that classification. Such comments suggested that purchased loans should be eligible for classification as loans and receivables, for example, if an entity buys a loan portfolio, and the purchased loans meet the definition other than the fact that they were purchased. Such comments also noted that (a) some entities typically manage purchased and originated loans together, and (b) there are systems problems of segregating purchased loans from originated loans given that a distinction between them is likely to be made only for accounting purposes. In the light of these concerns, the Board decided to remove the requirement that loans or receivables must be originated by the entity to meet the definition of 'loans and receivables'.

BC29 However, the Board was concerned that removing this requirement might result in some instruments that should be measured at fair value meeting the definition of loans and receivables and thus being measured at amortised cost. In particular, the Board was concerned that this would be the case for a debt instrument in which the purchaser may not recover its investment, for example a fixed rate interest-only strip created in a securitisation and subject to prepayment risk. The Board therefore decided to exclude from the definition of loans and receivables instruments for which the holder may not recover substantially all of its initial investment, other than because of credit deterioration. Such assets are accounted for as available for sale or at fair value through profit or loss.

Effective interest rate (paragraphs 9 and AG5–AG8)

BC30 The Board considered whether the effective interest rate for all financial instruments should be calculated on the basis of estimated cash flows (consistently with the original IAS 39) or whether the use of estimated cash flows should be restricted to groups of financial instruments with contractual cash flows being used for individual financial instruments. The Board agreed to reconfirm the position in the original IAS 39 because it achieves consistent application of the effective interest method throughout the Standard.

BC31 The Board noted that future cash flows and the expected life can be reliably estimated for most financial assets and financial liabilities, in particular for a group of similar financial assets or similar financial liabilities. However, the Board acknowledged that in some rare cases it might not be possible to estimate the timing or amount of future cash flows reliably. It therefore decided to require that if it is not possible to estimate reliably the future cash flows or the expected life of a financial instrument, the entity should use contractual cash flows over the full contractual term of the financial instrument.

BC32 The Board also decided to clarify that expected future defaults should not be included in estimates of cash flows because this would be a departure from the incurred loss model for impairment recognition. At the same time, the Board noted that in some cases, for example, when a financial asset is acquired at a deep discount, credit losses have occurred and are reflected in the price. If an entity does not take into account such credit losses in the calculation of the effective interest rate, the entity would recognise a higher interest income than that inherent in the price paid. The Board therefore decided to clarify that such credit losses are included in the estimated cash flows when computing the effective interest rate.

BC33 The revised IAS 39 refers to all fees 'that are an integral part of the effective interest rate'. The Board included this reference to clarify that IAS 39 relates only to those fees that are determined to be an integral part of the effective interest rate in accordance with IAS 18.

BC34 Some commentators noted that it was not always clear how to interpret the requirement in the original IAS 39 that the effective interest rate must be based on discounting cash flows through maturity or the next market-based repricing date. In particular, it was not always clear whether fees, transaction costs and other premiums or discounts included in the calculation of the effective interest rate should be amortised over the period until maturity or the period to the next market-based repricing date.

BC35 For consistency with the estimated cash flows approach, the Board decided to clarify that the effective interest rate is calculated over the expected life of the instrument or, when applicable, a shorter period. A shorter period is used when the variable (eg interest rates) to which the fee, transaction costs, discount or premium relates is repriced to market rates before the expected maturity of the instrument. In such a case, the appropriate amortisation period is the period to the next such repricing date.

Accounting for a change in estimates

BC36 The Board considered the accounting for a change in the estimates used in calculating the effective interest rate. The Board agreed that if an entity revises its estimates of payments or receipts, it should adjust the carrying amount of the financial instrument to reflect actual and revised estimated cash flows. The adjustment is recognised as income or expense in profit or loss. The entity recalculates the carrying amount by computing the present value of remaining cash flows at the original effective interest rate of the financial instrument. The Board noted that this approach has the practical advantage that it does not require recalculation of the effective interest rate, ie the entity simply recognises the remaining cash flows at the original rate. As a result, this approach avoids a possible conflict with the requirement when assessing impairment to discount estimated cash flows using the original effective interest rate.

Embedded derivatives

Embedded foreign currency derivatives (paragraphs 10 and AG33(d))

BC37 A rationale for the embedded derivatives requirements is that an entity should not be able to circumvent the recognition and measurement requirements for derivatives merely by embedding a derivative in a non-derivative financial instrument or other contract, for example, a commodity forward in a debt instrument. To achieve consistency in accounting for such embedded derivatives, all derivatives embedded in financial instruments that are not measured at fair value with gains and losses recognised in profit or loss ought to be accounted for separately as derivatives. However, as a practical expedient IAS 39 provides that an embedded derivative need not be separated if it is regarded as closely related to its host contract. When the embedded derivative bears a close economic relationship to the host contract, such as a cap or a floor on the interest rate on a loan, it is less likely that the derivative was embedded to achieve a desired accounting result.

BC38 The original IAS 39 specified that a foreign currency derivative embedded in a non-financial host contract (such as a supply contract denominated in a foreign currency) was not separated if it required payments denominated in the currency of the primary economic environment in which any substantial party to the contract operates (their functional currencies) or the currency in which the price of the related good or service that is acquired or delivered is routinely denominated in international commerce (such as the US dollar for crude oil transactions). Such foreign currency derivatives are regarded as bearing such a close economic relationship to their host contracts that they do not have to be separated.

BC39 The requirement to separate embedded foreign currency derivatives may be burdensome for entities that operate in economies in which business contracts denominated in a foreign currency are common. For example, entities domiciled in small countries may find it convenient to denominate business contracts with entities from other small countries in an internationally liquid currency (such as the US dollar, euro or yen) rather than the local currency of any of the parties to the transaction. In addition, an entity operating in a hyperinflationary economy may use a price list in a hard currency to protect against inflation, for example, an entity that has a foreign operation in a hyperinflationary economy that denominates local contracts in the functional currency of the parent.

BC40 In revising IAS 39, the Board concluded that an embedded foreign currency derivative may be integral to the contractual arrangements in the cases mentioned in the previous paragraph. It decided that a foreign currency derivative in a contract should not be required to be separated if it is denominated in a currency that is commonly used in business transactions (that are not financial instruments) in the environment in which the transaction takes place. A foreign currency derivative would be viewed as closely related to the host contract if the currency is commonly used in local business transactions, for example, when monetary amounts are viewed by the general population not in terms of the local currency but in terms of a relatively stable foreign currency, and prices may be quoted in that foreign currency (see IAS 29 *Financial Reporting in Hyperinflationary Economies*).

Recognition and derecognition

Derecognition of a financial asset (paragraphs 15–37)

The original IAS 39

BC41 Under the original IAS 39, several concepts governed when a financial asset should be derecognised. It was not always clear when and in what order to apply these concepts. As a result, the derecognition requirements in the original IAS 39 were not applied consistently in practice.

BC42 As an example, the original IAS 39 was unclear about the extent to which risks and rewards of a transferred asset should be considered for the purpose of determining whether derecognition is appropriate and how risks and rewards should be assessed. In some cases (eg transfers with total returns swaps or unconditional written put options), the Standard specifically indicated whether derecognition was appropriate, whereas in others (eg credit guarantees) it was unclear. Also, some questioned whether the assessment should focus on risks and rewards or only risks and how different risks and rewards should be aggregated and weighed.

BC43 To illustrate, assume an entity sells a portfolio of short-term receivables of CU100* and provides a guarantee to the buyer for credit losses up to a specified amount (say CU20) that is less than the total amount of the receivables, but higher than the amount of expected losses (say CU5). In this case, should (a) the entire portfolio continue to be recognised, (b) the portion that is guaranteed continue to be recognised or (c) the portfolio be derecognised in full and a guarantee be recognised as a financial liability? The original IAS 39 did not give a clear answer

* In this Basis for Conclusions, monetary amounts are denominated in 'currency units' (CU).

and the IAS 39 Implementation Guidance Committee–a group set up by the Board's predecessor body to resolve interpretive issues raised in practice–was unable to reach an agreement on how IAS 39 should be applied in this case. In developing proposals for improvements to IAS 39, the Board concluded that it was important that IAS 39 should provide clear and consistent guidance on how to account for such a transaction.

Exposure draft

BC44 To resolve the problems, the Exposure Draft proposed an approach to derecognition under which a transferor of a financial asset continues to recognise that asset to the extent the transferor has a continuing involvement in it. Continuing involvement could be established in two ways: (a) a reacquisition provision (such as a call option, put option or repurchase agreement) and (b) a provision to pay or receive compensation based on changes in value of the transferred asset (such as a credit guarantee or net cash settled option).

BC45 The purpose of the approach proposed in the Exposure Draft was to facilitate consistent implementation and application of IAS 39 by eliminating conflicting concepts and establishing an unambiguous, more internally consistent and workable approach to derecognition. The main benefits of the proposed approach were that it would greatly clarify IAS 39 and provide transparency on the face of the balance sheet about any continuing involvement in a transferred asset.

Comments received

BC46 Many respondents agreed that there were inconsistencies in the existing derecognition requirements in IAS 39. However, there was limited support for the continuing involvement approach proposed in the Exposure Draft. Respondents expressed conceptual and practical concerns, including:

(a) any benefits of the proposed changes did not outweigh the burden of adopting a different approach that had its own set of (as yet unidentified and unsolved) problems;

(b) the proposed approach was a fundamental change from that in the original IAS 39;

(c) the proposal did not achieve convergence with US GAAP;

(d) the proposal was untested; and

(e) the proposal was not consistent with the *Framework*.

BC47 Many respondents expressed the view that the basic approach in the original IAS 39 should be retained in the revised Standard and the inconsistencies removed. The reasons included: (a) the existing IAS 39 was proven to be reasonable in concept and operational in practice and (b) the approach should not be changed until the Board developed an alternative comprehensive approach.

Revisions to IAS 39

BC48 In response to the comments received, the Board decided to revert to the derecognition concepts in the original IAS 39 and to clarify how and in what order the concepts should be applied. In particular, the Board decided that an evaluation of the transfer of risks and rewards should precede an evaluation of the transfer of control for all types of transactions.

BC49 Although the structure and wording of the derecognition requirements have been substantially amended, the Board concluded that the requirements in the revised IAS 39 are not substantially different from those in the original IAS 39. In support of this conclusion, it noted that the application of the requirements in the revised IAS 39 generally results in answers that could have been obtained under the original IAS 39. In addition, although there will be a need to apply judgement to evaluate whether substantially all risks and rewards have been retained, this type of judgement is not new compared with the original IAS 39. However, the revised requirements clarify the application of the concepts in circumstances in which it was previously unclear how IAS 39 should be applied. The Board concluded that it would be inappropriate to revert to the original IAS 39 without such clarifications.

BC50 The Board also decided to include guidance in the Standard that clarifies how to evaluate the concepts of risks and rewards and of control. The Board regards such guidance as important to provide a framework for applying the concepts in IAS 39. Although judgement is still necessary to apply the concepts in practice, the guidance should increase consistency in how the concepts are applied.

BC51 More specifically, the Board decided that the transfer of risks and rewards should be evaluated by comparing the entity's exposure before and after the transfer to the variability in the amounts and timing of the net cash flows of the transferred asset. If the entity's exposure, on a present value basis, has not changed significantly, the entity would conclude that it has retained substantially all risks and rewards. In this case, the Board concluded that the asset should continue to be recognised. This accounting treatment is consistent with the treatment of repurchase transactions and some assets subject to deep in-the-money options under the original IAS 39. It is also consistent with how some interpreted the original IAS 39 when an entity sells a portfolio of short-term receivables but retains all substantive risks through the issue of a guarantee to compensate for all expected credit losses (see the example in paragraph BC43).

BC52 The Board decided that control should be evaluated by looking to whether the transferee has the practical ability to sell the asset. If the transferee can sell the asset (eg because the asset is readily obtainable in the market and the transferee can obtain a replacement asset should it need to return the asset to the transferor), the transferor has not retained control because the transferor does not control the transferee's use of the asset. If the transferee cannot sell the asset (eg because the transferor has a call option and the asset is not readily obtainable in the market, so that the transferee cannot obtain a replacement asset), the transferor has retained control because the transferee is not free to use the asset as its own.

BC53 The original IAS 39 also did not contain guidance on when a part of a financial asset could be considered for derecognition. The Board decided to include such guidance in the Standard to clarify the issue. It decided that an entity should apply the derecognition principles to a part of a financial asset only if that part contains no risks and rewards relating to the part not being considered for derecognition. Accordingly, a part of a financial asset is considered for derecognition only if it comprises:

(a) only specifically identified cash flows from a financial asset (or a group of similar financial assets);

(b) only a fully proportionate (pro rata) share of the cash flows from a financial asset (or a group of similar financial assets); or

(c) only a fully proportionate (pro rata) share of specifically identified cash flows from a financial asset (or a group of similar financial assets).

In all other cases the derecognition principles are applied to the financial asset in its entirety.

Arrangements under which an entity retains the contractual rights to receive the cash flows of a financial asset but assumes a contractual obligation to pay the cash flows to one or more recipients (paragraph 19)

BC54 The original IAS 39 did not provide explicit guidance about the extent to which derecognition is appropriate for contractual arrangements in which an entity retains its contractual right to receive the cash flows from an asset, but assumes a contractual obligation to pay those cash flows to another entity (a 'pass-through arrangement'). Questions were raised in practice about the appropriate accounting treatment and divergent interpretations evolved for more complex structures.

BC55 To illustrate the issue using a simple example, assume the following. Entity A makes a five-year interest-bearing loan (the 'original asset') of CU100 to Entity B. Entity A then enters into an agreement with Entity C in which, in exchange for a cash payment of CU90, Entity A agrees to pass to Entity C 90 per cent of all principal and interest payments collected from Entity B (as, when and if collected). Entity A accepts no obligation to make any payments to Entity C other than 90 per cent of exactly what has been received from Entity B. Entity A provides no guarantee to Entity C about the performance of the loan and has no rights to retain 90 per cent of the cash collected from Entity B nor any obligation to pay cash to Entity C if cash has not been received from Entity B. In the example above, does Entity A have a loan asset of CU100 and a liability of CU90 or does it have an asset of CU10? To make the example more complex, what if Entity A first transfers the loan to a consolidated special purpose entity (SPE), which in turn passes through to investors the cash flows from the asset? Does the accounting treatment change because Entity A first sold the asset to an SPE?

BC56 To address these issues, the Exposure Draft of proposed amendments to IAS 39 included guidance to clarify under which conditions pass-through arrangements can be treated as a transfer of the underlying financial asset. The Board concluded that an entity does not have an asset and a liability, as defined in the *Framework*, when it enters into an arrangement to pass through cash flows from an asset and that arrangement meets specified conditions. In these cases, the entity acts more as an agent of the eventual recipients of the cash flows than as an owner of the asset. Accordingly, to the extent that those conditions are met the arrangement is treated as a transfer and considered for derecognition even though the entity may continue to collect cash flows from the asset. Conversely, to the extent the conditions are not met, the entity acts more as an owner of the asset with the result that the asset should continue to be recognised.

BC57 Respondents to the Exposure Draft were generally supportive of the proposed changes. Some respondents asked for further clarification of the requirements and the interaction with the requirements for consolidation of special purpose entities (in SIC-12). Respondents in the securitisation industry noted that under the proposed guidance many securitisation structures would not qualify for derecognition.

BC58 Considering these and other comments, the Board decided to proceed with its proposals to issue guidance on pass-through arrangements and to clarify that guidance in finalising the revised IAS 39.

BC59 The Board concluded that the following three conditions must be met for treating a contractual arrangement to pass through cash flows from a financial asset as a transfer of that asset:

(a) The entity has no obligation to pay amounts to the eventual recipients unless it collects equivalent amounts from the original asset. However, the entity is allowed to make short-term advances to the eventual recipient so long as it has the right of full recovery of the amount lent plus accrued interest.

(b) The entity is prohibited by the terms of the transfer contract from selling or pledging the original asset other than as security to the eventual recipients for the obligation to pay them cash flows.

(c) The entity has an obligation to remit any cash flows it collects on behalf of the eventual recipients without material delay. In addition, during the short settlement period, the entity is not entitled to reinvest such cash flows except for investments in cash or cash equivalents and where any interest earned from such investments is remitted to the eventual recipients.

BC60 These conditions follow from the definitions of assets and liabilities in the *Framework*. Condition (a) indicates that the transferor has no liability (because there is no present obligation to pay cash), and conditions (b) and (c) indicate that the transferor has no asset (because the transferor does not control the future economic benefits associated with the transferred asset).

BC61 The Board decided that the derecognition tests that apply to other transfers of financial assets (ie the tests of transferring substantially all the risks and rewards and control) should also apply to arrangements to pass through cash flows that meet the three conditions but do not involve a fully proportional share of all or specifically identified cash flows. Thus, if the three conditions are met and the entity passes on a fully proportional share, either of all cash flows (as in the example in paragraph BC55) or of specifically identified cash flows (eg 10 per cent of all interest cash flows), the proportion sold is derecognised, provided the entity has transferred substantially all the risks and rewards of ownership. Thus, in the example in paragraph BC55, Entity A would report a loan asset of CU10 and derecognise CU90. Similarly, if an entity enters into an arrangement that meets the three conditions above, but the arrangement is not on a fully proportionate basis, the contractual arrangement would have to meet the general derecognition conditions to qualify for derecognition. This ensures consistency in the application of the derecognition model, whether a transaction is structured as a transfer of the contractual right to receive the cash flows of a financial asset or as an arrangement to pass through cash flows.

BC62 To illustrate a disproportionate arrangement using a simple example, assume the following. Entity A originates a portfolio of five-year interest-bearing loans of CU10,000. Entity A then enters into an agreement with Entity C in which, in exchange for a cash payment of CU9,000, Entity A agrees to pay to Entity C the first CU9,000 (plus interest) of cash collected from the loan portfolio. Entity A retains rights to the last CU1,000 (plus interest), ie it retains a subordinated residual interest. If Entity A collects, say, only CU8,000 of its loans of CU10,000 because some debtors default, Entity A would pass on to Entity C all of the CU8,000 collected and Entity A keeps nothing of the CU8,000 collected. If Entity A collects CU9,500, it passes CU9,000 to Entity C and retains CU500. In this case, if Entity A retains substantially all the risks and rewards of ownership because the subordinated retained interest absorbs all of the likely variability in net cash flows, the loans continue to be recognised in their entirety even if the three pass-through conditions are met.

BC63 The Board recognises that many securitisations may fail to qualify for derecognition either because one or more of the three conditions in paragraph 19 are not met or because the entity has retained substantially all the risks and rewards of ownership.

BC64 Whether a transfer of a financial asset qualifies for derecognition does not differ depending on whether the transfer is direct to investors or through a consolidated SPE or trust that obtains the financial assets and, in turn, transfers a portion of those financial assets to third party investors.

Transfers that do not qualify for derecognition (paragraph 29)

BC65 The original IAS 39 did not provide guidance about how to account for a transfer of a financial asset that does not qualify for derecognition. The amendments include such guidance. To ensure that the accounting reflects the rights and obligations that the transferor has in relation to the transferred asset, there is a need to consider the accounting for the asset as well as the accounting for the associated liability.

BC66 When an entity retains substantially all the risks and rewards of the asset (eg in a repurchase transaction), there are generally no special accounting considerations because the entity retains upside and downside exposure to gains and losses resulting from the transferred asset. Therefore, the asset continues to be recognised in its entirety and the proceeds received are recognised as a liability. Similarly, the entity continues to recognise any income from the asset along with any expense incurred on the associated liability.

Continuing involvement in a transferred asset (paragraphs 30–35)

BC67 The Board decided that if the entity determines that it has neither retained nor transferred substantially all of the risks and rewards of an asset and that it has retained control, the entity should continue to recognise the asset to the extent of its continuing involvement. This is to reflect the transferor's continuing exposure to the risks and rewards of the asset and that this exposure is not related to the entire asset, but is limited in amount. The Board noted that precluding derecognition to the extent of the continuing involvement is useful to users of financial statements in such cases, because it reflects the entity's retained exposure to the risks and rewards of the financial asset better than full derecognition.

BC68 When the entity transfers some significant risks and rewards and retains others and derecognition is precluded because the entity retains control of the transferred asset, the entity no longer retains all the upside and downside exposure to gains and losses resulting from the transferred asset. Therefore, the revised IAS 39 requires the asset and the associated liability to be measured in a way that ensures that any changes in value of the transferred asset that are not attributed to the entity are not recognised by the entity.

BC69 For example, special measurement and income recognition issues arise if derecognition is precluded because the transferor has retained a call option or written a put option and the asset is measured at fair value. In those situations, in the absence of additional guidance, application of the general measurement and income recognition requirements for financial assets and financial liabilities in IAS 39 may result in accounting that does not represent the transferor's rights and obligations related to the transfer.

BC70 As another example, if the transferor retains a call option on a transferred available-for-sale financial asset and the fair value of the asset decreases below the exercise price, the transferor does not suffer a loss because it has no obligation to exercise the call option. In that case, the Board decided that it is appropriate to adjust the measurement of the liability to reflect that the transferor has no exposure to decreases in the fair value of the asset below the option exercise price. Similarly, if a transferor writes a put option and the fair value of the asset exceeds the exercise price, the transferee need not exercise the put. Because the transferor has no right to increases in the fair value of the asset above the option exercise price, it is appropriate to measure the asset at the lower of (a) the option exercise price and (b) the fair value of the asset.

Measurement

Fair value measurement option (paragraph 9)

BC71 The Board concluded that it could simplify the application of IAS 39 for some entities by permitting the use of fair value measurement for any financial instrument. With one exception (see paragraph BC82), this greater use of fair value is optional. The fair value measurement option does not require entities to measure more financial instruments at fair value.

BC72 The previous version of IAS 39 did not permit an entity to measure particular categories of financial instruments at fair value with changes in fair value recognised in profit or loss. Examples included:

(a) originated loans and receivables, including a debt instrument acquired directly from the issuer, unless they met the conditions for classification as held for trading in paragraph 9.

(b) financial assets classified as available for sale, unless they met the conditions for classification as held for trading in paragraph 9.

(c) non-derivative financial liabilities even if the entity had a policy and practice of actively repurchasing such liabilities or they formed part of an arbitrage/customer facilitation strategy or fund trading activities.

BC73 The Board decided to permit entities to designate irrevocably on initial recognition any financial instrument as one to be measured at fair value with gains and losses recognised in profit or loss ('fair value through profit or loss'). To impose discipline on this approach, the Board decided that financial instruments should not be reclassified into or out of the category of fair value through profit or loss. In particular, some comments received on the Exposure Draft suggested that entities could use the fair value option to recognise selectively changes in fair value in profit or loss. The Board noted that the requirement to designate irrevocably on initial recognition the financial instruments for which the fair value option is to be applied results in an entity being unable to 'cherry pick' in this way. This is because it will not be known at initial recognition whether the fair value of the instrument will increase or decrease.

BC74 The change simplifies the application of IAS 39 by mitigating some anomalies that result from the different measurement attributes in the Standard. In particular, for financial instruments designated in this way:

(a) it eliminates the need for hedge accounting for hedges of fair value exposures when there are natural offsets, and thereby eliminates the related burden of designating, tracking and analysing hedge effectiveness.

(b) it eliminates the burden of separating embedded derivatives.

(c) it eliminates problems arising from a mixed measurement model where financial assets are measured at fair value and related financial liabilities are measured at amortised cost. In particular, it eliminates volatility in profit or loss and equity that results when matched positions of financial assets and financial liabilities are not measured consistently.

(d) the option to recognise unrealised gains and losses on available-for-sale financial assets in profit or loss is no longer necessary.

(e) it de-emphasises interpretative issues around what constitutes trading.

BC75 Permitting entities to designate at inception any financial instrument at fair value through profit or loss reduces the need for hedge accounting for hedges of fair value exposures and the resulting complexity in accounting for such hedges. Rather than being designated as a hedged item, the item could be designated at fair value through profit or loss to achieve recognition of offsetting fair value gains and losses in the same periods.

BC76 Permitting classification by designation also reduces the burden of separating embedded derivatives from hybrid instruments into host instruments and embedded derivative contracts. For example, under the previous version of IAS 39, an entity did not separate embedded derivatives in financial instruments that were held for trading. The Board noted that many preparers, auditors and others find the requirements to separate embedded derivatives difficult to apply in practice. For example, when applying these requirements an entity will need to carry out a detailed analysis of its financial instruments to identify embedded derivatives. Often it may be easier for the entity to determine the fair value of the combined instrument as a whole rather than to identify the terms of the embedded derivative and separately measure the embedded derivative at fair value, if, for example, the combined instrument is traded in an active market.

BC77 An additional benefit of permitting classification by designation is that the choice in the original IAS 39 of recognising fair value gains and losses on available-for-sale financial assets either in equity or in profit or loss is no longer necessary. An entity can achieve recognition of gains and losses on such assets in profit or loss by designating the asset at fair value through profit or loss. It also increases comparability across entities in how gains and losses on available-for-sale financial assets are recognised. Accordingly, the Board decided that the choice that was in the original IAS 39 should be removed and that gains and losses on available-for-sale financial assets should be recognised in equity.

BC78 Permitting designation at fair value through profit or loss mitigates problems arising from a mixed measurement model when assets are measured at fair value and related liabilities are measured at amortised cost. For example, the inability to classify non-derivative liabilities as held for trading under IAS 39 creates problems for entities with matched asset and liability positions. Under IAS 39, an entity is not permitted to designate non-derivative financial assets or non-derivative financial liabilities as hedging instruments, except for foreign currency exposures, and thus cannot use hedge accounting to eliminate such a mismatch. Because financial liabilities may now be designated at fair value through profit or loss, an entity can consistently recognise fair value changes on matched financial asset and financial liability positions.

BC79 The fair value measurement option enables (but does not require) entities to measure financial instruments at fair value with changes in fair value recognised in profit or loss. Accordingly, it does not restrict an entity's ability to use other accounting methods (such as amortised cost). Some respondents to the Exposure Draft would have preferred more pervasive changes to expand the use of fair values and limit the choices available to entities, such as the elimination of the held-to-maturity category or the cash flow hedge accounting approach. Although such changes have the potential to make the principles in IAS 39 more coherent and less complex, the Board did not consider such changes as part of this project to improve IAS 39.

BC80 Some comments received on the Exposure Draft suggested limiting the scope of the fair value option (eg to instruments that are traded in an active market or to exclude financial liabilities—see paragraphs BC87–BC92). The Board concluded it should not restrict the fair value option because to do so would limit its main benefits, discussed above.

BC81 Comments received on the Exposure Draft also questioned the proposal that all items measured at fair value through profit or loss should have the descriptor 'held for trading'. Some comments noted that 'held for trading' is commonly used with a narrower meaning, and it may be confusing for users if instruments designated at fair value through profit or loss are also called 'held for trading'. Therefore the Board considered using a fifth category of financial instruments—'fair value through profit or loss'—to distinguish those instruments to which the fair value option was applied from those classified as held for trading. The Board rejected this possibility because it believed adding a fifth category of financial instruments would unnecessarily complicate the Standard. Rather, the Board concluded that 'fair value through profit or loss' should be used to describe a category that encompasses financial instruments classified as held for trading and those to which the fair value option is applied.

BC82 In addition, the Board decided to include a requirement for an entity to classify a financial liability as held for trading if it is incurred principally for the purpose of repurchasing it in the near term or it is part of a portfolio of identified financial instruments that are managed together and for which there is evidence of a recent pattern of short-term profit-taking. In these circumstances, the absence of a requirement to measure such financial liabilities at fair value permits cherry-picking of unrealised gains or losses. For example, if an entity wishes to recognise a gain, it can repurchase a fixed rate debt instrument that was issued in an environment where interest rates were lower than in the reporting period and if it wishes to recognise a loss, it can repurchase an issued debt instrument that was issued in an environment in which interest rates were higher than in the reporting period. However, a financial liability is not classified as held for trading merely because it funds assets that are held for trading.

BC83 The Board decided to include in revised IAS 32 a requirement to disclose the settlement amount repayable at maturity of a liability that is designated as at fair value through profit or loss. This gives users of financial statements information about the amount owed by the entity to its creditors in the event of its liquidation.

BC84 The Board also decided to include in IAS 39 the ability for entities to designate a loan or receivable as available for sale (see paragraph 9). The Board decided that, in the context of the existing mixed measurement model, there are no reasons to limit to any particular type of asset the ability to designate an asset as available for sale.

Application of the fair value measurement option to a portion (rather than the entirety) of a financial asset or a financial liability

BC85 Some comments received on the Exposure Draft argued that the fair value measurement option should be extended so that it could also be applied to a portion of a financial asset or a financial liability (eg one risk). The arguments included (a) concerns regarding inclusion of own credit risk in the measurement of financial liabilities and (b) the prohibition on using non-derivatives as hedging instruments (cash instrument hedging).

BC86 The Board concluded that IAS 39 should not extend the fair value measurement option to portions of financial assets or financial liabilities. It was concerned (a) about difficulties in measuring the change in value of the portion because of ordering issues and joint effects (ie if the portion is affected by more than one risk, it may be difficult to isolate accurately and measure the portion); (b) that the amounts recognised in the balance sheet would be neither fair value nor cost; and (c) that a fair value adjustment for a portion may move the carrying amount of an instrument away from its fair value. The Board agreed to address separately the issue of cash instrument hedging.

Own credit risk

BC87 The Board discussed the issue of including changes in own credit risk in the fair value measurement of financial liabilities. It considered responses to the Exposure Draft that expressed concern about the effect of including this component in the fair value measurement and that suggested the fair value option should be restricted to exclude all or some financial liabilities. However, the Board concluded that the fair value option could be applied to any financial liability, and decided not to restrict the option in the Standard because doing so would negate some of the benefits of the fair value option set out in paragraph BC74.

BC88 The Board considered comments on the Exposure Draft that disagreed with the view that, in applying the fair value option to financial liabilities, an entity should recognise income as a result of deteriorating credit quality (and a loan expense as a result of improving credit quality). Commentators noted that it is not useful to report lower liabilities when an entity is in financial difficulty precisely because its debt levels are too high, and that it would be difficult to explain to users of financial statements the reasons why income would be recognised when an entity's creditworthiness deteriorates. These comments suggested that fair value should exclude the effects of changes in own credit risk.

BC89 However, the Board noted that because financial statements are prepared on a going concern basis, credit risk affects the value at which liabilities could be repurchased or settled. Accordingly, the fair value of a financial liability reflects the credit risk relating to that liability. Therefore, it decided to include credit risk relating to a financial liability in the fair value measurement of that liability for the following reasons:

(a) entities realise changes in fair value, including fair value attributable to own credit risk, for example, by renegotiating or repurchasing liabilities or by using derivatives;

(b) changes in credit risk affect the observed market price of a financial liability and hence its fair value;

(c) it is difficult from a practical standpoint to exclude changes in credit risk from an observed market price; and

(d) the fair value of a financial liability (ie the price of that liability in an exchange between a knowledgeable, willing buyer and a knowledgeable, willing seller) on initial recognition reflects the credit risk relating to that liability. The Board believes that it is inappropriate to include credit risk in the initial fair value measurement of financial liabilities, but not subsequently.

BC90 The Board also considered whether the portion of the fair value of a financial liability attributable to changes in credit quality should be specifically disclosed, separately presented in the income statement, or separately presented in equity. The Board decided that separately presenting or disclosing such changes would often not be practicable because it might not be possible to separate and measure reliably that part of the change in fair value. However, it noted that disclosure of such information would be useful to users of financial statements and would help alleviate the concerns expressed. Therefore, it decided in IAS 32 to require disclosure of the changes in fair value of a financial liability that is not attributable to changes in a benchmark rate. The Board believes this is a reasonable proxy for the change in fair value that is attributable to changes in the liability's credit risk, in particular when such changes are large, and will provide users with information with which to understand the profit or loss effect of such a change in credit risk.

BC91 The Board decided to clarify that this issue relates to the credit risk of the financial liability, rather than the creditworthiness of the entity. The Board noted that this more appropriately describes the objective of what is included in the fair value measurement of financial liabilities.

BC92 The Board also noted that the fair value of liabilities secured by valuable collateral, guaranteed by third parties or ranking ahead of virtually all other liabilities is generally unaffected by changes in the entity's creditworthiness.

Measurement of financial liabilities with a demand feature

BC93 Some comments received on the Exposure Draft requested clarification of how to determine fair value for financial liabilities with a demand feature (eg demand deposits), when the fair value measurement option is applied or the liability is otherwise measured at fair value. In other words, could the fair value be less than the amount payable on demand, discounted from the first date that an amount could be required to be paid (the 'demand amount'), such as the amount of the deposit discounted for the period that the entity expects the deposit to be outstanding? Some commentators believe that the fair value of financial liabilities with a demand feature is less than the demand amount, for reasons that include the consistency of such measurement with how those financial liabilities are treated for risk management purposes.

BC94 The Board agreed that this issue should be clarified in IAS 39. It confirmed that the fair value of a financial liability with a demand feature is not less than the amount payable on demand discounted from the first date that the amount could be required to be paid. This conclusion is the same as in the original IAS 32. The Board noted that in many cases, the market price observed for such financial liabilities is the price at which they are originated between the customer and the deposit-taker–ie the demand amount. It also noted that recognising a financial liability with a demand feature at less than the demand amount would give rise to an immediate gain on the origination of such a deposit, which the Board believes is inappropriate.

Fair value measurement guidance (paragraphs AG69–AG82)

BC95 The Board decided to include in the revised IAS 39 expanded guidance about how to determine fair values, in particular for financial instruments for which no quoted market price is available (Appendix A paragraphs AG74–AG82). The Board decided that it is desirable to provide clear and reasonably detailed guidance about the objective and use of valuation techniques to achieve reliable and comparable fair value estimates when financial instruments are measured at fair value.

Use of quoted prices in active markets (paragraphs AG71–AG73)

BC96 The Board considered comments received that disagreed with the proposal in the Exposure Draft that a quoted price is the appropriate measure of fair value for an instrument quoted in an active market. Some respondents argued that (a) valuation techniques are more appropriate for measuring fair value than a quoted price in an active market (eg for derivatives) and (b) valuation models are consistent with industry best practice, and are justified because of their acceptance for regulatory capital purposes.

BC97 However, the Board confirmed that a quoted price is the appropriate measure of fair value for an instrument quoted in an active market, notably because (a) in an active market, the quoted price is the best evidence of fair value, given that fair value is defined in terms of a price agreed by a knowledgeable, willing buyer and a knowledgeable, willing seller; (b) it results in consistent measurement across entities; and (c) fair value as defined in the Standard does not depend on entity-specific factors. The Board further clarified that a quoted price includes market-quoted rates as well as prices.

Entities that have access to more than one active market (paragraph AG71)

BC98 The Board considered situations in which entities operate in different markets. An example is a trader that originates a derivative with a corporate in an active corporate retail market and offsets the derivative by taking out a derivative with a dealer in an active dealers' wholesale market. The Board decided to clarify that the objective of fair value measurement is to arrive at the price at which a transaction would occur at the balance sheet date in the same instrument (ie without modification or repackaging) in the most advantageous active market to which an entity has immediate access. Thus, if a dealer enters into a derivative instrument with the corporate, but has immediate access to a more advantageously priced dealers' market, the entity recognises a profit on initial recognition of the derivative instrument. However, the entity adjusts the price observed in the dealer market for any differences in counterparty credit risk between the derivative instrument with the corporate and that with the dealers' market.

Bid–ask spreads in active markets (paragraph AG72)

BC99 The Board confirmed the proposal in the Exposure Draft that the appropriate quoted market price for an asset held or liability to be issued is usually the current bid price and, for an asset to be acquired or liability held, the asking price. It concluded that applying mid-market prices to an individual instrument is not appropriate because it would result in entities recognising up-front gains or losses for the difference between the bid-ask price and the mid-market price.

BC100 The Board discussed whether the bid-ask spread should be applied to the net open position of a portfolio containing offsetting market risk positions, or to each instrument in the portfolio. It noted the concerns raised by constituents that applying the bid-ask spread to the net open position better reflects the fair value of the risk retained in the portfolio. The Board concluded that for offsetting risk positions, entities could use mid-market prices to determine fair value, and hence may apply the bid or asking price to the net open position as appropriate. The Board believes that when an entity has offsetting risk positions, using the mid-market price is appropriate because the entity (a) has locked in its cash flows from the asset and liability and (b) potentially could sell the matched position without incurring the bid-ask spread.

BC101 Comments received on the Exposure Draft revealed that some interpret the term 'bid-ask spread' differently from others and from the Board. Thus, IAS 39 clarifies that the spread represents only transaction costs.

No active market (paragraphs AG74–AG82)

BC102 The Exposure Draft proposed a three-tier fair value measurement hierarchy as follows:

(a) For instruments traded in active markets, use a quoted price.

(b) For instruments for which there is not an active market, use a recent market transaction.

(c) For instruments for which there is neither an active market nor a recent market transaction, use a valuation technique.

BC103 The Board decided to simplify the proposed fair value measurement hierarchy by requiring the fair value of financial instruments for which there is not an active market to be determined on the basis of valuation techniques, including the use of recent market transactions between knowledgeable, willing parties in an arm's length transaction.

BC104 The Board also considered constituents' comments regarding whether an instrument should always be recognised on initial recognition at the transaction price or whether gains or losses may be recognised on initial recognition when an entity uses a valuation technique to estimate fair value. The Board concluded that an entity may recognise a gain or loss at inception only if fair value is evidenced by comparison with other observable current market transactions in the same instrument (ie without modification or repackaging) or is based on a valuation technique incorporating only observable market data. The Board concluded that those conditions were necessary and sufficient to provide reasonable assurance that fair value was other than the transaction price for the purpose of recognising up-front gains or losses. The Board decided that in other cases, the transaction price gave the best evidence of fair value. The Board also noted that its decision achieved convergence with US GAAP.

Impairment and uncollectibility of financial assets

Impairment of investments in equity instruments (paragraph 61)

BC105 Under IAS 39, investments in equity instruments that are classified as available for sale and investments in unquoted equity instruments whose fair value cannot be reliably measured are subject to an impairment assessment. The original IAS 39 did not include guidance about impairment indicators that are specific to investments in equity instruments. Questions were raised about when in practice such investments become impaired.

BC106 The Board agreed that for marketable investments in equity instruments any impairment trigger other than a decline in fair value below cost is likely to be arbitrary to some extent. If markets are reasonably efficient, today's market price is the best estimate of the discounted value of the future market price. However, the Board also concluded that it is important to provide guidance to address the questions raised in practice.

BC107 The revised IAS 39 includes impairment triggers that the Board concluded were reasonable in the case of investments in equity instruments (paragraph 61). They apply in addition to those specified in paragraph 59, which focus on the assessment of impairment in debt instruments.

Incurred versus expected losses

BC108 Some respondents to the Exposure Draft were confused about whether the Exposure Draft reflected an 'incurred loss' model or an 'expected loss' model. Others expressed concern about the extent to which 'future losses' could be recognised as impairment losses. They suggested that losses should be recognised only when they are incurred (ie a deterioration in the credit quality of an asset or a group of assets after their initial recognition). Other respondents favoured the use of an expected loss approach. They suggested that expected future losses should be considered in the determination of the impairment loss for a group of assets even if the credit quality of a group of assets has not deteriorated from original expectations.

BC109 In considering these comments, the Board decided that impairment losses should be recognised only if they have been incurred. The Board reasoned that it was inconsistent with an amortised cost model to recognise impairment on the basis of expected future transactions and events. The Board also decided that guidance should be provided about what 'incurred' means when assessing whether impairment exists in a group of financial assets. The Board was concerned that, in the absence of such guidance, there could be a range of interpretations about when a loss is incurred or what events cause a loss to be incurred in a group of assets.

BC110 Therefore, the Board included guidance in IAS 39 that specifies that for a loss to be incurred, an event that provides objective evidence of impairment must have occurred after the initial recognition of the financial asset, and IAS 39 now identifies types of such events. Possible or expected future trends that may lead to a loss in the future (eg an expectation that unemployment will rise or a recession will occur) do not provide objective evidence of impairment. In addition, the loss event must have a reliably measurable effect on the present value of estimated future cash flows and be supported by current observable data.

Assets assessed individually and found not to be impaired (paragraphs 59(f) and 64)

BC111 It was not clear in the original IAS 39 whether loans and receivables and some other financial assets, when reviewed for impairment and determined not to be impaired, could or should subsequently be included in the assessment of impairment for a group of financial assets with similar characteristics.

BC112 The Exposure Draft proposed that a loan asset or other financial asset that is measured at amortised cost and has been individually assessed for impairment and found not to be impaired should be included in a collective assessment of impairment. The Exposure Draft also included proposed guidance about how to evaluate impairment inherent in a group of financial assets.

BC113 The comment letters received on the Exposure Draft indicated considerable support for the proposal to include in a collective evaluation of impairment an individually assessed financial asset that is found not to be impaired.

BC114 The Board noted the following arguments in favour of an additional portfolio assessment for individually assessed assets that are found not to be impaired.

(a) Impairment that cannot be identified with an individual loan may be identifiable on a portfolio basis. The *Framework* states that for a large population of receivables, some degree of non-payment is normally regarded as probable. In that case, an expense representing the expected reduction in economic benefits is recognised (*Framework*, paragraph 85). For example, a lender may have some concerns about identified loans with similar characteristics, but not have sufficient evidence to conclude that an impairment loss has occurred on any of those loans on the basis of an individual assessment. Experience may indicate that some of those loans are impaired even though an individual assessment may not reveal this. The amount of loss in a large population of items can be estimated on the basis of experience and other factors by weighing all possible outcomes by their associated probabilities.

(b) Some time may elapse between an event that affects the ability of a borrower to repay a loan and actual default of the borrower. For example, if the market forward price for wheat decreases by 10 per cent, experience may indicate that the estimated payments from borrowers that are wheat farmers will decrease by 1 per cent over a one-year period. When the forward price decreases, there may be no objective evidence that any individual wheat farmer will default on an individually significant loan. On a portfolio basis, however, the decrease in the forward price may provide objective evidence that the estimated future cash flows on loans to wheat farmers have decreased by 1 per cent over a one-year period.

(c) Under IAS 39, impairment of loans is measured on the basis of the present value of estimated future cash flows. Estimations of future cash flows may change because of economic factors affecting a group of loans, such as country and industry factors, even if there is no objective evidence of impairment of an individual loan. For example, if unemployment increases by 10 per cent in a quarter in a particular region, the estimated future cash flows from loans to borrowers in that region for the next quarters may have decreased even though no objective evidence of impairment exists that is based on an individual assessment of loans to borrowers in that region. In that case, objective evidence of impairment exists for the group of financial assets, even though it does not exist for an individual asset.

A requirement for objective evidence to exist to recognise and measure impairment in individually significant loans might result in delayed recognition of loan impairment that has already occurred.

(d) Accepted accounting practice in some countries is to establish a provision to cover impairment losses that, although not specifically identified to individual assets, are known from experience to exist in a loan portfolio as of the balance sheet date.

(e) If assets that are individually not significant are collectively assessed for impairment and assets that are individually significant are not, assets will not be measured on a consistent basis because impairment losses are more difficult to identify asset by asset.

(f) What is an individually significant loan that is assessed on its own will differ from one entity to another. Thus, identical exposures will be evaluated on different bases (individually or collectively), depending on their significance to the entity holding them. If a collective evaluation were not to be required, an entity that wishes to minimise its recognised impairment losses could elect to assess all loans individually. Requiring a collective assessment of impairment for all exposures judged not to be impaired individually enhances consistency between entities rather than reduces it.

BC115 Arguments against an additional portfolio assessment for individually assessed loans that are found not to be impaired are as follows.

(a) It appears illogical to make an impairment provision on a group of loans that have been assessed for impairment on an individual basis and have been found not to be impaired.

(b) The measurement of impairment should not depend on whether a lender has only one loan or a group of similar loans. If the measurement of impairment is affected by whether the lender has groups of similar loans, identical loans may be measured differently by different lenders. To ensure consistent measurement of identical loans, impairment in individually significant financial assets should be recognised and measured asset by asset.

(c) The *Framework* specifies that financial statements are prepared on the accrual basis of accounting, according to which the effects of transactions and events are recognised when they occur and are recognised in the financial statements in the periods to which they relate. Financial statements should reflect the outcome of events that took place before the balance sheet date and should not reflect events that have not yet occurred. If an impairment loss cannot be attributed to a specifically identified financial asset or a group of financial assets that are not individually significant, it is questionable whether an event has occurred that justifies the recognition of impairment. Even though the risk of loss may have increased, a loss has not yet materialised.

(d) The *Framework*, paragraph 94, requires an expense to be recognised only if it can be measured reliably. The process of estimating impairment in a group of loans that have been individually assessed for impairment but found not to be impaired may involve a significant degree of subjectivity. There may be a wide range of reasonable estimates of impairment. In practice, the establishment of general loan loss provisions is sometimes viewed as more of an art than a science. This portfolio approach should be applied only if it is necessary on practical grounds and not to override an assessment made on an individual loan, which must provide a better determination of whether an allowance is necessary.

(e) IAS 39 requires impairment to be measured on a present value basis using the original effective interest rate. Mechanically, it may not be obvious how to do this for a group of loans with similar characteristics that have different effective interest rates. In addition, measurement of impairment in a group of loans based on the present value of estimated cash flows discounted using the original effective interest rate may result in double-counting of losses that were expected on a portfolio basis when the loans were originated because the lender included compensation for those losses in the contractual interest rate charged. As a result, a portfolio assessment of impairment may result in the recognition of a loss almost as soon as a loan is issued. (This question arises also in measuring impairment on a portfolio basis for loans that are not individually assessed for impairment under IAS 39.)

BC116 The Board was persuaded by the arguments in favour of a portfolio assessment for individually assessed assets that are found not to be impaired and decided to confirm that a loan or other financial asset measured at amortised cost that is individually assessed for impairment and found not to be impaired should be included in a group of similar financial assets that are assessed for impairment on a portfolio basis. This is to reflect that, in the light of the law of large numbers, impairment may be evident in a group of assets, but not yet meet the threshold for recognition when any individual asset in that group is assessed. The Board also confirmed that it is important to provide guidance about how to assess impairment on a portfolio basis to introduce discipline into a portfolio assessment. Such guidance promotes consistency in practice and comparability of information across entities. It should also mitigate concerns that collective assessments of impairment should not be used to conceal changes in asset values or as a cushion for potential future losses.

BC117 Some respondents expressed concerns about some of the detailed guidance proposed in the Exposure Draft, such as the guidance about adjusting the discount rate for expected losses. Many entities indicated that they do not have the data and systems necessary to implement the proposed approach. The Board decided to eliminate some of the detailed application guidance (eg whether to make an adjustment of the discount rate for originally expected losses and an illustration of the application of the guidance).

Assets that are assessed individually and found to be impaired (paragraph 64)

BC118 In making a portfolio assessment of impairment, one issue that arises is whether the collective assessment should include assets that have been individually evaluated and identified as impaired.

BC119 One view is that methods used to estimate impairment losses on a portfolio basis are equally valid whether or not an asset has been specifically identified as impaired. Those who support this view note that the law of large numbers applies equally whether or not an asset has been individually identified as impaired and that a portfolio assessment may enable a more accurate prediction to be made of estimated future cash flows.

BC120 Another view is that there should be no need to complement an individual assessment of impairment for an asset that is specifically identified as impaired by an additional portfolio assessment, because objective evidence of impairment exists on an individual basis and expectations of losses can be incorporated in the measurement of impairment for the individual assets. Double-counting of losses in terms of estimated future cash flows should not be permitted. Moreover, recognition of impairment losses for groups of assets should not be a substitute for the recognition of impairment losses on individual assets.

BC121 The Board decided that assets that are individually assessed for impairment and identified as impaired should be excluded from a portfolio assessment of impairment. Excluding assets that are individually identified as impaired from a portfolio assessment of impairment is consistent with the view that collective evaluation of impairment is an interim step pending the identification of impairment losses on individual assets. A collective evaluation identifies losses that have been incurred on a group basis as of the balance sheet date, but cannot yet be identified with individual assets. As soon as information is available to identify losses on individually impaired assets, those assets are removed from the group that is collectively assessed for impairment.

Grouping of assets that are collectively evaluated for impairment (paragraphs 64 and AG87)

BC122 The Board considered how assets that are collectively assessed for impairment should be grouped for the purpose of assessing impairment on a portfolio basis. In practice, different methods are conceivable for grouping assets for the purposes of assessing impairment and computing historical and expected loss rates. For example, assets may be grouped on the basis of one or more of the following characteristics: (a) estimated default probabilities or credit risk grades; (b) type (for example, mortgage loans or credit card loans); (c) geographical location; (d) collateral type; (e) counterparty type (for example, consumer, commercial or sovereign); (f) past-due status; and (g) maturity. More sophisticated credit risk models or methodologies for estimating expected future cash flows may combine several factors, for example, a credit risk evaluation or grading process that considers asset type, industry, geographical location, collateral type, past-due status, and other relevant characteristics of the assets being evaluated and associated loss data.

BC123 The Board decided that for the purpose of assessing impairment on a portfolio basis, the method employed for grouping assets should, as a minimum, ensure that individual assets are allocated to groups of assets that share similar credit risk characteristics. It also decided to clarify that when assets that are assessed individually and found not to be impaired are grouped with assets with similar credit risk characteristics that are assessed only on a collective basis, the loss probabilities and other loss statistics differ between the two types of asset with the result that a different amount of impairment may be required.

Estimates of future cash flows in groups (paragraphs AG89–AG92)

BC124 The Board decided that to promote consistency in the estimation of impairment on groups of financial assets that are collectively evaluated for impairment, guidance should be provided about the process for estimating future cash flows in such groups. It identified the following elements as critical to an adequate process:

(a) Historical loss experience should provide the basis for estimating future cash flows in a group of financial assets that are collectively assessed for impairment.

(b) Entities that have no loss experience of their own or insufficient experience should use peer group experience for comparable groups of financial assets.

(c) Historical loss experience should be adjusted, on the basis of observable data, to reflect the effects of current conditions that did not affect the period on which the historical loss experience is based and to remove the effects of conditions in the historical period that do not exist currently.

(d) Changes in estimates of future cash flows should be directionally consistent with changes in underlying observable data.

(e) Estimation methods should be adjusted to reduce differences between estimates of future cash flows and actual cash flows.

Impairment of investments in available-for-sale financial assets (paragraphs 67–70)

BC125 In the Exposure Draft, the Board proposed that impairment losses on debt and equity instruments classified as available for sale should not be reversed through profit or loss if conditions changed after the recognition of the impairment loss. The Board arrived at this decision because of the difficulties in determining objectively when impairment losses on debt and equity instruments classified as available-for-sale have been recovered and hence of distinguishing a reversal of an impairment (recognised in profit or loss) from other increases in value (recognised in equity). Accordingly, the Board proposed that any increase in the fair value of an available-for-sale financial asset would be recognised directly in equity even though the entity had previously recognised an impairment loss on that asset. The Board noted that this was consistent with the recognition of changes in the fair value of available-for-sale financial assets directly in equity (see paragraph 55(b)).

BC126 The Board considered the comments received on its proposal to preclude reversals of impairment on available-for-sale financial assets. It concluded that available-for-sale debt instruments and available-for-sale equity instruments should be treated differently.

Reversals of impairment on available-for-sale debt instruments (paragraph 70)

BC127 For available-for-sale debt instruments, the Board decided that impairment should be reversed through profit or loss when fair value increases and the increase can be objectively related to an event occurring after the loss was recognised.

BC128 The Board noted that (a) other Standards require the reversal of impairment losses if circumstances change (eg IAS 2 *Inventories*, IAS 16 *Property, Plant and Equipment* and IAS 38 *Intangible Assets*); (b) the decision provides consistency with the requirement to reverse impairment losses on loans and receivables, and on assets classified as held to maturity; and (c) reversals of impairment in debt instruments (ie determining an increase in fair value attributable to an improvement in credit standing) are more objectively determinable than those in equity instruments.

Reversals of impairment on available-for-sale equity instruments (paragraph 69)

BC129 For available-for-sale equity instruments, the Board concluded that if impairment is recognised, and the fair value subsequently increases, the increase in value should be recognised in equity (and not as a reversal of the impairment loss through profit or loss).

BC130 The Board could not find an acceptable way to distinguish reversals of impairment losses from other increases in fair value. Therefore, it decided that precluding reversals of impairment on available-for-sale equity instruments was the only appropriate solution. In its deliberations, the Board considered:

(a) limiting reversals to those cases in which specific facts that caused the original impairment reverse. However, the Board questioned the operationality of applying this approach (ie how to decide whether the same event that caused the impairment caused the reversal).

(b) recognising all changes in fair value below cost as impairments and reversals of impairment through profit or loss, ie all changes in fair value below cost would be recognised in profit or loss, and all changes above cost would be recognised in equity. Although this approach achieves consistency with IAS 16 and IAS 38, and eliminates any subjectivity involved in determining what constitutes impairment or reversal of impairment, the Board noted that it would significantly change the notion of 'available for sale' in practice. The Board believed that introducing such a change to the available-for-sale category was not appropriate at this time.

Hedging

BC131 The Exposure Draft proposed few changes to the hedge accounting guidance in the original IAS 39. The comments on the Exposure Draft raised several issues in the area of hedge accounting suggesting that the Board should consider these issues in the revised IAS 39. The Board's decisions with regard to these issues are presented in the following paragraphs.

Consideration of the shortcut method in SFAS 133

BC132 SFAS 133 *Accounting for Derivative Instruments and Hedging Activities* issued by the FASB allows an entity to assume no ineffectiveness in a hedge of interest rate risk using an interest rate swap as the hedging instrument, provided specified criteria are met (the 'shortcut method').

BC133 The original IAS 39 and the Exposure Draft precluded the use of the shortcut method. Many comments received on the Exposure Draft argued that IAS 39 should permit use of the shortcut method. The Board considered the issue in developing the Exposure Draft, and discussed it in the roundtable discussions that were held in the process of finalising IAS 39.

BC134 The Board noted that, if the shortcut method were permitted, an exception would have to be made to the principle in IAS 39 that ineffectiveness in a hedging relationship is measured and recognised in profit or loss. The Board agreed that no exception to this principle should be made, and therefore concluded that IAS 39 should not permit the shortcut method.

BC135 Additionally, IAS 39 permits the hedging of portions of financial assets and financial liabilities in cases when US GAAP does not. The Board noted that under IAS 39 an entity may hedge a portion of a financial instrument (eg interest rate risk or credit risk), and that if the critical terms of the hedging instrument and the hedged item are the same, the entity would, in many cases, recognise no ineffectiveness.

Hedges of portions of financial assets and financial liabilities (paragraphs 81, 81A, AG99A and AG99B)

BC135 IAS 39 permits a hedged item to be designated as a portion of the cash flows or fair value of a financial asset or financial liability. In finalising the Exposure Draft *Fair Value Hedge Accounting for a Portfolio Hedge of Interest Rate Risk*, the Board received comments that demonstrated that the meaning of a 'portion' was unclear in this context. Accordingly, the Board decided to amend IAS 39 to provide further guidance on what may be designated as a hedged portion, including confirmation that it is not possible to designate a portion that is greater than the total cash flows of the asset or liability.

Expected effectiveness (paragraphs AG105–AG113)

BC136 Qualification for hedge accounting is based on expectations of future effectiveness (prospective) and evaluation of actual effectiveness (retrospective). In the original IAS 39, the prospective test was expressed as 'almost fully offset', whereas the retrospective test was 'within a range of 80–125 per cent'. The Board considered whether to amend IAS 39 to permit the prospective effectiveness to be within the range of 80–125 per cent rather than 'almost fully offset'. The Board noted that an undesirable consequence of such an amendment could be that entities would deliberately underhedge a hedged item in a cash flow hedge so as to reduce recognised ineffectiveness. Therefore, the Board initially decided to retain the guidance in the original IAS 39.

BC136A However, when subsequently finalising the requirements for portfolio hedges of interest rate risk, the Board received representations from constituents that some hedges would fail the 'almost fully offset' test in IAS 39, including some hedges that would qualify for the short-cut method in US GAAP and thus be assumed to be 100 per cent effective. The Board was persuaded that the concern described in the previous paragraph that an entity might deliberately underhedge would be met by an explicit statement that an entity could not deliberately hedge less than 100 per cent of the exposure on an item and designate the hedge as a hedge of 100 per cent of the exposure. Therefore, the Board decided to amend IAS 39:

(a) to remove the words 'almost fully offset' from the prospective effectiveness test, and replace them by a requirement that the hedge is expected to be 'highly effective'. (This amendment is consistent with the wording in US GAAP.)

(b) to include a statement in the Application Guidance in IAS 39 that if an entity hedges less than 100 per cent of the exposure on an item, such as 85 per cent, it shall designate the hedged item as being 85 per cent of the exposure and shall measure ineffectiveness on the basis of the change in the whole of that designated 85 per cent exposure.

BC136B Additionally, comments made in response to the Exposure Draft *Fair Value Hedge Accounting for a Portfolio Hedge of Interest Rate Risk* demonstrated that it was unclear how the prospective effectiveness test was to be applied. The Board noted that the objective of the test was to ensure there was firm evidence to support an expectation of high effectiveness. Therefore, the Board decided to amend the Standard to clarify that an expectation of high effectiveness may be demonstrated in various ways, including a comparison of past changes in the fair value or cash flows of the hedged item that are attributable to the hedged risk with past changes in the fair value or cash flows of the hedging instrument, or by demonstrating a high statistical correlation between the fair value of cash flows of the hedged item and those of the hedging instrument. The Board noted that the entity may choose a hedge ratio of other than one to one in order to improve the effectiveness of the hedge as described in paragraph AG100.

Hedges of portions of non–financial assets and non–financial liabilities for risk other than foreign currency risk (paragraph 82)

BC137 The Board considered comments on the Exposure Draft that suggested that IAS 39 should permit designating as the hedged risk a risk portion of a non-financial item other than foreign currency risk.

BC138 The Board concluded that IAS 39 should not be amended to permit such designation. It noted that in many cases, changes in the cash flows or fair value of a portion of a non-financial hedged item are difficult to isolate and measure. Moreover, the Board noted that permitting portions of non-financial assets and non-financial liabilities to be designated as the hedged item for risk other than foreign currency risk would compromise the principles of identification of the hedged item and effectiveness testing that the Board has confirmed because the portion could be designated so that no ineffectiveness would ever arise.

BC139 The Board confirmed that non-financial items may be hedged in their entirety when the item the entity is hedging is not the standard item underlying contracts traded in the market. In this context, the Board decided to clarify that a hedge ratio of other than one–to–one may maximise expected effectiveness, and to include guidance on how the hedge ratio that maximises expected effectiveness can be determined.

Loan servicing rights

BC140 The Board also considered whether IAS 39 should permit the interest rate risk portion of loan servicing rights to be designated as the hedged item.

BC141 The Board considered the argument that interest rate risk can be separately identified and measured in loan servicing rights, and that changes in market interest rates have a predictable and separately measurable effect on the value of loan servicing rights. The Board also considered the possibility of treating loan servicing rights as financial assets (rather than non-financial assets).

BC142 However, the Board concluded that no exceptions should be permitted for this matter. The Board noted that (a) the interest rate risk and prepayment risk in loan servicing rights are interdependent, and thus inseparable, (b) the fair values of loan servicing rights do not change in a linear fashion as interest rates increase or decrease, and (c) concerns exist about how to isolate and measure the interest rate risk portion of a loan servicing right. Moreover, the Board expressed concern that in jurisdictions in which loan servicing right markets are not developed, the interest rate risk portion may not be measurable.

BC143 The Board also considered whether IAS 39 should be amended to allow, on an elective basis, the inclusion of loan servicing rights in its scope provided that they are measured at fair value with changes in fair value recognised immediately in profit or loss. The Board noted that this would create two exceptions to the general principles in IAS 39. First, it would create a scope exception because IAS 39 applies only to financial assets and financial liabilities; loan servicing rights are non-financial assets. Second, *requiring* an entity to measure loan servicing rights at fair value through profit or loss would create a further exception, because this treatment is optional (except for items that are held for trading). The Board therefore decided not to amend the scope of IAS 39 for loan servicing rights.

Whether to permit hedge accounting using cash instruments

BC144 In finalising the amendments to IAS 39, the Board discussed whether an entity should be permitted to designate a financial asset or financial liability other than a derivative (ie a 'cash instrument') as a hedging instrument in hedges of risks other than foreign currency risk. The original IAS 39 precluded such designation because of the different bases for measuring derivatives and cash instruments. The Exposure Draft did not propose a change to this limitation. However, some commentators suggested a change, noting that entities do not distinguish between derivative and non-derivative financial instruments in their hedging and other risk management activities and that entities may have to use a non-derivative financial instrument to hedge risk if no suitable derivative financial instrument exists.

BC145 The Board acknowledged that some entities use non-derivatives to manage risk. However, it decided to retain the restriction against designating non-derivatives as hedging instruments in hedges of risks other than foreign currency risk. It noted the following arguments in support of this conclusion:

(a) The need for hedge accounting arises in part because derivatives are measured at fair value, whereas the items they hedge may be measured at cost or not recognised at all. Without hedge accounting, an entity might recognise volatility in profit or loss for matched positions. For non-derivative items that are not measured at fair value or for which changes in fair value are not recognised in profit or loss, there is generally no need to adjust the accounting of the hedging instrument or the hedged item to achieve matched recognition of gains and losses in profit or loss.

(b) To allow designation of cash instruments as hedging instruments would diverge from US GAAP: SFAS 133 precludes the designation of non-derivative instruments as hedging instruments except for some foreign currency hedges.

(c) To allow designation of cash instruments as hedging instruments would add complexity to the Standard. More financial instruments would be measured at an amount that represents neither amortised cost nor fair value. Hedge accounting is, and should be, an exception to the normal measurement requirements.

(d) If cash instruments were permitted to be designated as hedging instruments, there would be much less discipline in the accounting model because, in the absence of hedge accounting, a non-derivative may not be selectively measured at fair value. If the entity subsequently decides that it would rather not apply fair value measurement to a cash instrument that had been designated as a hedging instrument, it can breach one of the hedge accounting requirements, conclude that the non-derivative no longer qualifies as a hedging instrument and selectively avoid recognising the changes in fair value of the non-derivative instrument in equity (for a cash flow hedge) or profit or loss (for a fair value hedge).

(e) The most significant use of cash instruments as hedging instruments is to hedge foreign currency exposures, which is permitted under IAS 39.

Whether to treat hedges of forecast transactions as fair value hedges

BC146 The Board considered a suggestion made in some of the comment letters received on the Exposure Draft that a hedge of a forecast transaction should be treated as a fair value hedge, rather than as a cash flow hedge. Some argued that the hedge accounting provisions should be simplified by having only one type of hedge accounting. Some also raised concern about an entity's ability, in some cases, to choose between two hedge accounting methods for the same hedging strategy (ie the choice between designating a forward contract to sell an existing asset as a fair value hedge of the asset or a cash flow hedge of a forecast sale of the asset).

BC147 The Board acknowledged that the hedge accounting provisions would be simplified, and their application more consistent in some situations, if the Standard permitted only one type of hedge accounting. However, the Board concluded that IAS 39 should continue to distinguish between fair value hedge accounting and cash flow hedge accounting. It noted that removing either type of hedge accounting would narrow the range of hedging strategies that could qualify for hedge accounting.

BC148 The Board also noted that treating a hedge of a forecast transaction as a fair value hedge is not appropriate for the following reasons: (a) it would result in the recognition of an asset or liability before the entity has become a party to the contract; (b) amounts would be recognised in the balance sheet that do not meet the definitions of assets and liabilities in the *Framework*; and (c) transactions in which there is no fair value exposure would be treated as if there were a fair value exposure.

Hedges of firm commitments (paragraphs 93 and 94)

BC149 The previous version of IAS 39 required a hedge of a firm commitment to be accounted for as a cash flow hedge. In other words, hedging gains and losses, to the extent that the hedge is effective, were initially recognised in equity and were subsequently 'recycled' to profit or loss in the same period(s) that the hedged firm commitment affected profit or loss (although, when basis adjustment was used, they adjusted the initial carrying amount of an asset or liability recognised in the meantime). Some believe this is appropriate because cash flow hedge accounting for hedges of firm commitments avoids partial recognition of the firm commitment that would otherwise not be recognised. Moreover, some believe it is conceptually incorrect to recognise the hedged fair value exposure of a firm commitment as an asset or liability merely because it has been hedged.

BC150 The Board considered whether hedges of firm commitments should be treated as cash flow hedges or fair value hedges. The Board concluded that hedges of firm commitments should be accounted for as fair value hedges.

BC151 The Board noted that, in concept, a hedge of a firm commitment is a fair value hedge. This is because the fair value of the item being hedged (the firm commitment) changes with changes in the hedged risk.

BC152 The Board was not persuaded by the argument that it is conceptually incorrect to recognise an asset or liability for a firm commitment merely because it has been hedged. It noted that for all fair value hedges, applying hedge accounting has the effect that amounts are recognised as assets or liabilities that would otherwise not be recognised. For example, assume an entity hedges a fixed rate loan asset with a pay-fixed, receive-variable interest rate swap. If there is a loss on the swap, applying fair value hedge accounting requires the offsetting gain on the loan to be recognised, ie the carrying amount of the loan is increased. Thus, applying hedge accounting has the effect of recognising a part of an asset (the increase in the loan's value attributable to interest rate movements) that would otherwise not have been recognised. The only difference in the case of a firm commitment is that, without hedge accounting, none of the commitment is recognised, ie the carrying amount is zero. However, this difference merely reflects that the historical cost of a firm commitment is usually zero. It is not a fundamental difference in concept.

BC153 Furthermore, the Board's decision converges with SFAS 133, and thus eliminates practical problems and eases implementation for entities that report under both standards.

BC154 However, the Board clarified that a hedge of the foreign currency risk of a firm commitment may be treated as either a fair value hedge or a cash flow hedge because foreign currency risk affects both the cash flows and the fair value of the hedged item. Accordingly a foreign currency cash flow hedge of a forecast transaction need not be re-designated as a fair value hedge when the forecast transaction becomes a firm commitment.

Basis adjustments (paragraphs 97–99)

BC155 The question of basis adjustment arises when an entity hedges the future purchase of an asset or the future issue of a liability. One example is that of a US entity that expects to make a future purchase of a German machine that it will pay for in euro. The entity enters into a derivative to hedge against possible future changes in the US dollar/euro exchange rate. Such a hedge is classified as a cash flow hedge under IAS 39, with the effect that gains and losses on the hedging instrument (to the extent that the hedge is effective) are initially recognised in equity. The question the Board considered is what the accounting should be once the future transaction takes place. In its deliberations on this issue, the Board discussed the following approaches:

(a) to remove the hedging gain or loss from equity and recognise it as part of the initial carrying amount of the asset or liability (in the example above, the machine). In future periods, the hedging gain or loss is automatically recognised in profit or loss by being included in amounts such as depreciation expense (for a fixed asset), interest income or expense (for a financial asset or financial liability), or cost of sales (for inventories). This treatment is commonly referred to as 'basis adjustment'.

(b) to leave the hedging gain or loss in equity. In future periods, the gain or loss on the hedging instrument is 'recycled' to profit or loss in the same period(s) as the acquired asset or liability affects profit or loss. This recycling requires a separate adjustment and is not automatic.

BC156 It should be noted that both approaches have the same effect on profit or loss and net assets for all periods affected, so long as the hedge is accounted for as a cash flow hedge. The difference relates to balance sheet presentation and, possibly, the line item in the income statement.

BC157 In the Exposure Draft, the Board proposed that the 'basis adjustment' approach for forecast transactions (approach (a)) should be eliminated and replaced by approach (b) above. It further noted that eliminating the basis adjustment approach would enable IAS 39 to converge with SFAS 133.

BC158 Many of the comments received from constituents disagreed with the proposal in the Exposure Draft. Those responses argued that it would unnecessarily complicate the accounting to leave the hedging gain or loss in equity when the hedged forecast transaction occurs. They particularly noted that tracking the effects of cash flow hedges after the asset or liability is acquired would be complicated and would require systems changes. They also pointed out that treating hedges of firm commitments as fair value hedges has the same effect as a basis adjustment when the firm commitment results in the recognition of an asset or liability. For example, for a perfectly effective hedge of the foreign currency risk of a firm commitment to buy a machine, the effect is to recognise the machine initially at its foreign currency price translated at the forward rate in effect at the inception of the hedge rather than the spot rate. Therefore, they questioned whether it is consistent to treat a hedge of a firm commitment as a fair value hedge while precluding basis adjustments for hedges of forecast transactions.

BC159 Others believe that a basis adjustment is difficult to justify in principle for forecast transactions, and also argue that such basis adjustments impair comparability of financial information. In other words, two identical assets that are purchased at the same time and in the same way, except for the fact that one was hedged, should not be recognised at different amounts.

BC160 The Board concluded that IAS 39 should distinguish between hedges of forecast transactions that will result in the recognition of a *financial* asset or a *financial* liability and those that will result in the recognition of a *non-financial* asset or a *non-financial* liability.

Basis adjustments for hedges of forecast transactions that will result in the recognition of a financial asset or a financial liability

BC161 For hedges of forecast transactions that will result in the recognition of a financial asset or a financial liability, the Board concluded that basis adjustments are not appropriate. Its reason was that basis adjustments cause the initial carrying amount of acquired assets (or assumed liabilities) arising from forecast transactions to move away from fair value and hence would override the requirement in IAS 39 to measure a financial instrument initially at its fair value.

Basis adjustments for hedges of forecast transactions that will result in the recognition of a non-financial asset or a non-financial liability

BC162 For hedges of forecast transactions that will result in the recognition of a non-financial asset or a non-financial liability, the Board decided to permit entities a choice of whether to apply basis adjustment.

BC163 The Board considered the argument that changes in the fair value of the hedging instrument are appropriately included in the initial carrying amount of the recognised asset or liability because such changes represent a part of the 'cost' of that asset or liability. Although the Board has not yet considered the broader issue of what costs may be capitalised at initial recognition, the Board believes that its decision to provide an option for basis adjustments in the case of non-financial items will not pre-empt that future discussion. The Board also recognised that financial items and non-financial items are not necessarily measured at the same amount on initial recognition, because financial items are measured at fair value and non-financial items are measured at cost.

BC164 The Board concluded that, on balance, providing entities with a choice in this case was appropriate. The Board took the view that allowing basis adjustments addresses the concern that precluding basis adjustments complicates the accounting for hedges of forecast transactions. In addition, the number of balance sheet line items that could be affected is quite small, generally being only property, plant and equipment, inventory and the cash flow hedge line item in equity. The Board also noted that US GAAP precludes basis adjustments and that applying a basis adjustment is inconsistent with the accounting for hedges of forecast transactions that will result in the recognition of a financial asset or a financial liability. The Board acknowledged the merits of these arguments, and recognised that by permitting a choice in IAS 39, entities could apply the accounting treatment required by US GAAP.

Hedging using internal contracts

BC165 IAS 39 does not preclude entities from using internal contracts as a risk management tool, or as a tracking device in applying hedge accounting for external contracts that hedge external positions. Furthermore, IAS 39 permits hedge accounting to be applied to transactions between entities in the same group or between segments in the *separate reporting* of those entities or segments. However, IAS 39 does not permit hedge accounting for transactions between entities in the same group in consolidated financial statements. The reason is the fundamental requirement of consolidation that the accounting effects of internal contracts should be eliminated in consolidated financial statements, including any internally generated gains or losses. Designating internal contracts as hedging instruments could result in non-elimination of internal gains and losses and have other accounting effects. The Exposure Draft did not propose any change in this area.

BC166 To illustrate, assume the banking book division of Bank A enters into an internal interest rate swap with the trading book division of the same bank. The purpose is to hedge the net interest rate risk exposure in the banking book of a group of similar fixed rate loan assets funded by floating rate liabilities. Under the swap, the banking book pays fixed interest payments to the trading book and receives variable interest rate payments in return. The bank wants to designate the internal interest rate swap in the banking book as a hedging instrument in its consolidated financial statements.

BC167 If the internal swap in the banking book is designated as a hedging instrument in a cash flow hedge of the liabilities, and the internal swap in the trading book is classified as held for trading, internal gains and losses on that internal swap would not be eliminated. This is because the gains and losses on the internal swap in the banking book would be recognised in equity to the extent the hedge is effective and the gains and losses on the internal swap in the trading book would be recognised in profit or loss.

BC168 If the internal swap in the banking book is designated as a hedging instrument in a fair value hedge of the loan assets and the internal swap in the trading book is classified as held for trading, the changes in the fair value of the internal swap would offset both in total net assets in the balance sheet and profit or loss. However, without elimination of the internal swap, there would be an adjustment to the carrying amount of the hedged loan asset in the banking book to reflect the change in the fair value attributable to the risk hedged by the internal contract. Moreover, to reflect the effect of the internal swap the bank would in effect recognise the fixed rate loan at a floating interest rate and recognise an offsetting trading gain or loss in the income statement. Hence the internal swap would have accounting effects.

BC169 Some respondents to the Exposure Draft and some participants in the roundtables objected to not being able to obtain hedge accounting in the consolidated financial statements for internal contracts between subsidiaries or between a subsidiary and the parent (as illustrated above). Among other things, they emphasised that the use of internal contracts is a key risk management tool and that the accounting should reflect the way in which risk is managed. Some suggested that IAS 39 should be changed to make it consistent with US GAAP, which allows the designation of internal derivative contracts as hedging instruments in cash flow hedges of forecast foreign currency transactions in specified, limited circumstances.

BC170 In considering these comments, the Board noted that the following principles apply to consolidated financial statements:

(a) financial statements provide financial information about an entity or group as a whole (as that of a single entity). Financial statements do not provide financial information about an entity as if it were two separate entities.

(b) a fundamental principle of consolidation is that intragroup balances and intragroup transactions are eliminated in full. Permitting the designation of internal contracts as hedging instruments would require a change to the consolidation principles.

(c) it is conceptually wrong to permit an entity to recognise internally generated gains and losses or make other accounting adjustments because of internal transactions. No external event has occurred.

(d) an ability to recognise internally generated gains and losses could result in abuse in the absence of requirements about how entities should manage and control the associated risks. It is not the purpose of accounting standards to prescribe how entities should manage and control risks.

(e) permitting the designation of internal contracts as hedging instruments violates the following requirements in IAS 39:

   (i) the prohibition against designating as a hedging instrument a non-derivative financial asset or non-derivative financial liability for other than foreign currency risk. To illustrate, if an entity has two offsetting internal contracts and one is the designated hedging instrument in a fair value hedge of a non-derivative asset and the other is the designated hedging instrument in a fair value hedge of a non-derivative liability, from the entity's perspective the effect is to designate a hedging relationship between the asset and the liability (ie a non-derivative asset or non-derivative liability is used as the hedging instrument).

   (ii) the prohibition on designating a net position of assets and liabilities as the hedged item. To illustrate, an entity has two internal contracts. One is designated in a fair value hedge of an asset and the other in a fair value hedge of a liability. The two internal contracts do not fully offset, so the entity lays off the net risk exposure by entering into a net external derivative. In that case, the effect from the entity's perspective is to designate a hedging relationship between the net external derivative and a net position of an asset and a liability.

   (iii) the option to fair value assets and liabilities does not extend to portions of assets and liabilities.

(f) the Board is considering separately whether to make an amendment to IAS 39 to facilitate fair value hedge accounting for portfolio hedges of interest rate risk. The Board believes that that is a better way to address the concerns raised about symmetry with risk management systems than permitting the designation of internal contracts as hedging instruments.

(g) the Board decided to permit an option to measure any financial asset or financial liability at fair value with changes in fair value recognised in profit or loss. This enables an entity to measure matching asset/liability positions at fair value without a need for hedge accounting.

BC171 The Board reaffirmed that it is a fundamental principle of consolidation that any accounting effect of internal contracts is eliminated on consolidation. The Board decided that no exception to this principle should be made in IAS 39. Consistently with this decision, the Board also decided not to explore an amendment to permit internal derivative contracts to be designated as hedging instruments in hedges of some forecast foreign currency transactions, as is permitted by SFAS 138 *Accounting for Certain Derivative Instruments and Certain Hedging Activities.*

BC172 The Board also decided to clarify that IAS 39 does not preclude hedge accounting for transactions between entities in the same group or transactions between segments in individual or separate financial statements of those entities or reporting segments because they are not internal to the entity (ie the individual entity or segment).

Fair value hedge accounting for a portfolio hedge of interest rate risk

Background

BC173 The Exposure Draft of proposed improvements to IAS 39 published in June 2002 did not propose any substantial changes to the requirements for hedge accounting as they applied to a portfolio hedge of interest rate risk. However, some of the comment letters on the Exposure Draft and participants in the roundtable discussions raised this issue. In particular, some were concerned that portfolio hedging strategies they regarded as effective hedges would not have qualified for fair value hedge accounting in accordance with previous versions of IAS 39. Rather, they would have either:

(a) not qualified for hedge accounting at all, with the result that reported profit or loss would be volatile; or

(b) qualified only for cash flow hedge accounting, with the result that reported equity would be volatile.

BC174 In the light of these concerns, the Board decided to explore whether and how IAS 39 could be amended to enable fair value hedge accounting to be used more readily for portfolio hedges of interest rate risk. As a result, in August 2003 the Board published a second Exposure Draft, *Fair Value Hedge Accounting for a Portfolio Hedge of Interest Rate Risk*, with a comment deadline of 14 November 2003. More than 120 comment letters were received. The amendments proposed in this second Exposure Draft were finalised in March 2004. Paragraphs BC135A–BC136B and BC175–BC220 summarise the Board's considerations in reaching conclusions on the issues raised.

Scope

BC175 The Board decided to limit any amendments to IAS 39 to applying fair value hedge accounting to a hedge of interest rate risk on a portfolio of items. In making this decision it noted that:

(a) implementation guidance on IAS 39* explains how to apply cash flow hedge accounting to a hedge of the interest rate risk on a portfolio of items.

(b) the issues that arise for a portfolio hedge of interest rate risk are different from those that arise for hedges of individual items and for hedges of other risks. In particular, the three issues discussed in paragraph BC176 do not arise in combination for such other hedging arrangements.

The issue: why fair value hedge accounting was difficult to achieve in accordance with previous versions of IAS 39

BC176 The Board identified the following three main reasons why a portfolio hedge of interest rate risk might not have qualified for fair value hedge accounting in accordance with previous versions of IAS 39.

(a) Typically, many of the assets that are included in a portfolio hedge are prepayable, ie the counterparty has a right to repay the item before its contractual repricing date. Such assets contain a prepayment option whose fair value changes as interest rates change. However, the derivative that is used as the hedging instrument typically is not prepayable, ie it does not contain a prepayment option. When interest rates change, the resulting change in the fair value of the hedged item (which is prepayable) differs from the change in fair value of the hedging derivative (which is not prepayable), with the result that the hedge may not meet IAS 39's effectiveness tests.† Furthermore, prepayment risk may have the effect that the items included in a portfolio hedge fail the requirement§ that a group of hedged assets or liabilities must be 'similar' and the related requirement$^{\phi}$ that 'the change in fair value attributable to the hedged risk for each individual item in the group shall be expected to be approximately proportional to the overall change in fair value attributable to the hedged risk of the group of items'.

(b) IAS 39‡ prohibits the designation of an overall net position (eg the net of fixed rate assets and fixed rate liabilities) as the hedged item. Rather, it requires individual assets (or liabilities), or groups of similar assets (or similar liabilities), that share the risk exposure equal in amount to the net position to be designated as the hedged item. For example, if an entity has a portfolio of CU100 of assets and CU80 of liabilities, IAS 39 requires that individual assets or a group of similar assets of CU20 are designated as the hedged item. However, for risk management purposes, entities often seek to hedge the net position. This net position changes each period as items are repriced or

* see Q&A F.6.1 and F.6.2

† see IAS 39, paragraph AG105

§ see IAS 39, paragraph 78

ϕ see IAS 39, paragraph 83

‡ see IAS 39, paragraph AG101

derecognised and as new items are originated. Hence, the individual items designated as the hedged item also need to be changed each period. This requires de- and redesignation of the individual items that constitute the hedged item, which gives rise to significant systems needs.

(c) Fair value hedge accounting requires the carrying amount of the hedged item to be adjusted for the effect of changes in the hedged risk.* Applied to a portfolio hedge, this could involve changing the carrying amounts of many thousands of individual items. Also, for any items subsequently de-designated from being hedged, the revised carrying amount must be amortised over the item's remaining life.† This, too, gives rise to significant systems needs.

BC177 The Board decided that any change to IAS 39 must be consistent with the principles that underlie IAS 39's requirements on derivatives and hedge accounting. The three principles that are most relevant to a portfolio hedge of interest rate risk are:

(a) derivatives should be measured at fair value;

(b) hedge ineffectiveness should be identified and recognised in profit or loss;§ and

(c) only items that are assets and liabilities should be recognised as such in the balance sheet. Deferred losses are not assets and deferred gains are not liabilities. However, if an asset or liability is hedged, any change in its fair value that is attributable to the hedged risk should be recognised in the balance sheet.

Prepayment risk

BC178 In considering the issue described in paragraph BC176(a), the Board noted that a prepayable item can be viewed as a combination of a non-prepayable item and a prepayment option. It follows that the fair value of a fixed rate prepayable item changes for two reasons when interest rates move:

(a) the fair value of the contracted cash flows to the contractual repricing date changes (because the rate used to discount them changes); and

(b) the fair value of the prepayment option changes (reflecting, among other things, that the likelihood of prepayment is affected by interest rates).

BC179 The Board also noted that, for risk management purposes, many entities do not consider these two effects separately. Instead they incorporate the effect of prepayments by grouping the hedged portfolio into repricing time periods based on *expected* repayment dates (rather than contractual repayment dates). For example, an entity with a portfolio of 25-year mortgages of CU100 may expect 5 per cent of that portfolio to repay in one year's time, in which case it schedules an amount of CU5 into a 12-month time period. The entity schedules all other

* see IAS 39, paragraph 89(b)

† see IAS 39, paragraph 92

§ Subject to the same materiality considerations that apply in this context as throughout IFRSs.

items contained in its portfolio in a similar way (ie on the basis of expected repayment dates) and hedges all or part of the resulting overall net position in each repricing time period.

BC180 The Board decided to permit the scheduling that is used for risk management purposes, ie on the basis of expected repayment dates, to be used as a basis for the designation necessary for hedge accounting. As a result, an entity would not be required to compute the effect that a change in interest rates has on the fair value of the prepayment option embedded in a prepayable item. Instead, it could incorporate the effect of a change in interest rates on prepayments by grouping the hedged portfolio into repricing time periods based on expected repayment dates. The Board noted that this approach has significant practical advantages for preparers of financial statements, because it allows them to use the data they use for risk management. The Board also noted that the approach is consistent with paragraph 81 of IAS 34, which permits hedge accounting for a portion of a financial asset or financial liability. However, as discussed further in paragraphs BC193–BC206, the Board also concluded that if the entity changes its estimates of the time periods in which items are expected to repay (eg in the light of recent prepayment experience), ineffectiveness will arise, regardless of whether the revision in estimates results in more or less being scheduled in a particular time period.

BC181 The Board also noted that if the items in the hedged portfolio are subject to different amounts of prepayment risk, they may fail the test in paragraph 78 of being similar and the related requirement in paragraph 83 that the change in fair value attributable to the hedged risk for each individual item in the group is expected to be approximately proportional to the overall change in fair value attributable to the hedged risk of the group of items. The Board decided that, in the context of a portfolio hedge of interest rate risk, these requirements could be inconsistent with the Board's decision, set out in the previous paragraph, on how to incorporate the effects of prepayment risk. Accordingly, the Board decided that they should not apply. Instead, the financial assets or financial liabilities included in a portfolio hedge of interest rate risk need only share the risk being hedged.

Designation of the hedged item and liabilities with a demand feature

BC182 The Board considered two main ways to overcome the issue noted in paragraph BC176(b). These were:

(a) to designate the hedged item as the overall net position that results from a portfolio containing assets and liabilities. For example, if a repricing time period contains CU100 of fixed rate assets and CU90 of fixed rate liabilities, the net position of CU10 would be designated as the hedged item.

(b) to designate the hedged item as a portion of the assets (ie assets of CU10 in the above example), but not to require individual assets to be designated.

BC183 Some of those who commented on the Exposure Draft favoured designation of the overall net position in a portfolio that contains assets and liabilities. In their view, existing asset-liability management (ALM) systems treat the identified assets and liabilities as a natural hedge. Management's decisions about additional hedging focus on the entity's remaining net exposure. They observe that designation based on a portion of either the assets or the liabilities is not consistent with existing ALM systems and would entail additional systems costs.

BC184 In considering questions of designation, the Board was also concerned about questions of measurement. In particular, the Board observed that fair value hedge accounting requires measurement of the change in fair value of the hedged item attributable to the risk being hedged. Designation based on the net position would require the assets and the liabilities in a portfolio each to be measured at fair value (for the risk being hedged) in order to compute the fair value of the net position. Although statistical and other techniques can be used to estimate these fair values, the Board concluded that it is not appropriate to assume that the change in fair value of the hedging instrument is equal to the change in fair value of the net position.

BC185 The Board noted that under the first approach in paragraph BC182 (designating an overall net position), an issue arises if the entity has liabilities that are repayable on demand or after a notice period (referred to below as 'demandable liabilities'). This includes items such as demand deposits and some types of time deposits. The Board was informed that, when managing interest rate risk, many entities that have demandable liabilities include them in a portfolio hedge by scheduling them to the date when they *expect* the total amount of demandable liabilities in the portfolio to be due because of net withdrawals from the accounts in the portfolio. This expected repayment date is typically a period covering several years into the future (eg 0–10 years hence). The Board was also informed that some entities wish to apply fair value hedge accounting based on this scheduling, ie they wish to include demandable liabilities in a fair value portfolio hedge by scheduling them on the basis of their expected repayment dates. The arguments for this view are:

(a) it is consistent with how demandable liabilities are scheduled for risk management purposes. Interest rate risk management involves hedging the interest rate margin resulting from assets and liabilities and not the fair value of all or part of the assets and liabilities included in the hedged portfolio. The interest rate margin of a specific period is subject to variability as soon as the amount of fixed rate assets in that period differs from the amount of fixed rate liabilities in that period.

(b) it is consistent with the treatment of prepayable assets to include demandable liabilities in a portfolio hedge based on expected repayment dates.

(c) as with prepayable assets, expected maturities for demandable liabilities are based on the historical behaviour of customers.

(d) applying the fair value hedge accounting framework to a portfolio that includes demandable liabilities would not entail an immediate gain on origination of such liabilities because all assets and liabilities enter the hedged portfolio at their carrying amounts. Furthermore, IAS 39* requires the carrying amount of a financial liability on its initial recognition to be its fair value, which normally equates to the transaction price (ie the amount deposited).

* see IAS 39, paragraph AG76

(e) historical analysis shows that a base level of a portfolio of demandable liabilities, such as chequing accounts, is very stable. Whilst a portion of the demandable liabilities varies with interest rates, the remaining portion—the base level—does not. Hence, entities regard this base level as a long-term fixed rate item and include it as such in the scheduling that is used for risk management purposes.

(f) the distinction between 'old' and 'new' money makes little sense at a portfolio level. The portfolio behaves like a long-term item even if individual liabilities do not.

BC186 The Board noted that this issue is related to that of how to measure the fair value of a demandable liability. In particular, it interrelates with the requirement in IAS 39* that the fair value of a liability with a demand feature is not less than the amount payable on demand, discounted from the first date that the amount could be required to be paid. This requirement applies to all liabilities with a demand feature, not only to those included in a portfolio hedge.

BC187 The Board also noted that:

(a) although entities, when managing risk, may schedule demandable liabilities based on the expected repayment date of the total balance of a portfolio of accounts, the deposit liabilities included in that balance are unlikely to be outstanding for an extended period (eg several years). Rather, these deposits are usually expected to be withdrawn within a short time (eg a few months or less), although they may be replaced by new deposits. Put another way, the balance of the portfolio is relatively stable only because withdrawals on some accounts (which usually occur relatively quickly) are offset by new deposits into others. Thus, the liability being hedged is actually the forecast replacement of existing deposits by the receipt of new deposits. IAS 39 does not permit a hedge of such a forecast transaction to qualify for fair value hedge accounting. Rather, fair value hedge accounting can be applied only to the liability (or asset) or firm commitment that exists today.

(b) a portfolio of demandable liabilities is similar to a portfolio of trade payables. Both comprise individual balances that usually are expected to be paid within a short time (eg a few months or less) and replaced by new balances. Also, for both, there is an amount—the base level—that is expected to be stable and present indefinitely. Hence, if the Board were to permit demandable liabilities to be included in a fair value hedge on the basis of a stable base level created by expected replacements, it should similarly allow a hedge of a portfolio of trade payables to qualify for fair value hedge accounting on this basis.

(c) a portfolio of similar core deposits is not different from an individual deposit, other than that, in the light of the 'law of large numbers', the behaviour of the portfolio is more predictable. There are no diversification effects from aggregating many similar items.

(d) it would be inconsistent with the requirement in IAS 39 that the fair value of a liability with a demand feature is not less than the amount payable on

* see IAS 39, paragraph 49

demand, discounted from the first date that the amount could be required to be paid, to schedule such liabilities for hedging purposes using a different date. For example, consider a deposit of CU100 that can be withdrawn on demand without penalty. IAS 39 states that the fair value of such a deposit is CU100. That fair value is unaffected by interest rates and does not change when interest rates move. Accordingly, the demand deposit cannot be included in a fair value hedge of interest rate risk–there is no fair value exposure to hedge.

BC188 For these reasons, the Board concluded that demandable liabilities should not be included in a portfolio hedge on the basis of the expected repayment date of the *total balance of a portfolio* of demandable liabilities, ie including expected rollovers or replacements of existing deposits by new ones. However, as part of its consideration of comments received on the Exposure Draft, the Board also considered whether a demandable liability, such as a demand deposit, could be included in a portfolio hedge based on the expected repayment date of the *existing balance of individual deposits*, ie ignoring any rollovers or replacements of existing deposits by new deposits. The Board noted the following.

(a) For many demandable liabilities, this approach would imply a much earlier expected repayment date than is generally assumed for risk management purposes. In particular, for chequing accounts it would probably imply an expected maturity of a few months or less. However, for other demandable liabilities, such as fixed term deposits that can be withdrawn only by the depositor incurring a significant penalty, it might imply an expected repayment date that is closer to that assumed for risk management.

(b) This approach implies that the *fair value* of the demandable liability should also reflect the expected repayment date of the existing balance, ie that the fair value of a demandable deposit liability is the present value of the amount of the deposit discounted from the expected repayment date. The Board noted that it would be inconsistent to permit fair value hedge accounting to be based on the expected repayment date, but to measure the fair value of the liability on initial recognition on a different basis. The Board also noted that this approach would give rise to a difference on initial recognition between the amount deposited and the fair value recognised in the balance sheet. This, in turn, gives rise to the issue of what the difference represents. Possibilities the Board considered include (i) the value of the depositor's option to withdraw its money before the expected maturity, (ii) prepaid servicing costs or (iii) a gain. The Board did not reach a conclusion on what the difference represents, but agreed that if it were to require such differences to be recognised, this would apply to all demandable liabilities, not only to those included in a portfolio hedge. Such a requirement would represent a significant change from present practice.

(c) If the fair value of a demandable deposit liability at the date of initial recognition is deemed to equal the amount deposited, a fair value portfolio hedge based on an expected repayment date is unlikely to be effective. This is because such deposits typically pay interest at a rate that is significantly lower than that being hedged (eg the deposits may pay interest at zero or at very low rates, whereas the interest rate being hedged may be LIBOR or a similar benchmark rate). Hence, the fair value of the deposit will be significantly less sensitive to interest rate changes than that of the hedging instrument.

(d) The question of how to fair value a demandable liability is closely related to issues being debated by the Board in other projects, including Insurance (phase II), Revenue Recognition, Leases and Measurement. The Board's discussions in these other projects are continuing and it would be premature to reach a conclusion in the context of portfolio hedging without considering the implications for these other projects.

BC189 As a result, the Board decided:

(a) to confirm the requirement in IAS 39[*] that 'the fair value of a financial liability with a demand feature (eg a demand deposit) is not less than the amount payable on demand, discounted from the first date that the amount could be required to be paid', and

(b) consequently, that a demandable liability cannot qualify for fair value hedge accounting for any time period beyond the shortest period in which the counterparty can demand payment.

The Board noted that, depending on the outcome of its discussions in other projects (principally Insurance (phase II), Revenue Recognition, Leases and Measurement), it might reconsider these decisions at some time in the future.

BC190 The Board also noted that what is designated as the hedged item in a portfolio hedge affects the relevance of this issue, at least to some extent. In particular, if the hedged item is designated as a portion *of the assets* in a portfolio, this issue is irrelevant. To illustrate, assume that in a particular repricing time period an entity has CU100 of fixed rate assets and CU80 of what it regards as fixed rate liabilities and the entity wishes to hedge its net exposure of CU20. Also assume that all of the liabilities are demandable liabilities and the time period is later than that containing the earliest date on which the items can be repaid. If the hedged item is designated as CU20 of *assets*, then the demandable *liabilities* are not included in the hedged item, but rather are used only to determine how much of the assets the entity wishes to designate as being hedged. In such a case, whether the demandable liabilities can be designated as a hedged item in a fair value hedge is irrelevant. However, if the overall net position were to be designated as the hedged item, because the net position comprises CU100 of assets and CU80 of demandable liabilities, whether the demandable liabilities can be designated as a hedged item in a fair value hedge becomes critical.

BC191 Given the above points, the Board decided that a portion of assets or liabilities (rather than an overall net position) may be designated as the hedged item, to overcome part of the demandable liabilities issue. It also noted that this approach is consistent with IAS 39[†], whereas designating an overall net position is not. IAS 39[§] prohibits an overall net position from being designated as the hedged

* see paragraph 49

† see IAS 39, paragraph 84

§ see IAS 39, paragraph AG101

item, but permits a similar effect to be achieved by designating an amount of assets (or liabilities) equal to the net position.

BC192 However, the Board also recognised that this method of designation would not fully resolve the demandable liabilities issue. In particular, the issue is still relevant if, in a particular repricing time period, the entity has so many demandable liabilities whose earliest repayment date is before that time period that (a) they comprise nearly all of what the entity regards as its fixed rate liabilities and (b) its fixed rate liabilities (including the demandable liabilities) exceed its fixed rate assets in this repricing time period. In this case, the entity is in a net liability position. Thus, it needs to designate an amount of the *liabilities* as the hedged item. But unless it has sufficient fixed rate liabilities other than those that can be demanded before that time period, this implies designating the demandable liabilities as the hedged item. Consistently with the Board's decision discussed above, such a hedge does not qualify for fair value hedge accounting. (If the liabilities are non-interest bearing, they cannot be designated as the hedged item in a cash flow hedge because their cash flows do not vary with changes in interest rates, ie there is no cash flow exposure to interest rates.* However, the hedging relationship may qualify for cash flow hedge accounting if designated as a hedge of associated assets.)

What portion of assets should be designated and the impact on ineffectiveness

BC193 Having decided that a portion of assets (or liabilities) could be designated as the hedged item, the Board considered how to overcome the systems problems noted in paragraph BC176(b) and (c). The Board noted that these problems arise from designating individual assets (or liabilities) as the hedged item. Accordingly, the Board decided that the hedged item could be expressed as an *amount* (of assets or liabilities) rather than as individual assets or liabilities.

BC194 The Board noted that this decision–that the hedged item may be designated as an amount of assets or liabilities rather than as specified items–gives rise to the issue of how the amount designated should be specified. The Board considered comments received on the Exposure Draft that it should not specify any method for designating the hedged item and hence measuring effectiveness. However, the Board concluded that if it provided no guidance, entities might designate in different ways, resulting in little comparability between them. The Board also noted that its objective, when permitting an amount to be designated, was to overcome the systems problems associated with designating individual items whilst achieving a very similar accounting result. Accordingly, it concluded that it should require a method of designation that closely approximates the accounting result that would be achieved by designating individual items.

BC195 Additionally, the Board noted that designation determines how much, if any, ineffectiveness arises if actual repricing dates in a particular repricing time period vary from those estimated or if the estimated repricing dates are revised. Taking the above example of a repricing time period in which there are CU100 of fixed

* see Guidance on Implementing IAS 39, Question and Answer F.6.3.

rate assets and the entity designates as the hedged item an amount of CU20 of assets, the Board considered two approaches (a layer approach and a percentage approach) that are summarised below.

Layer approach

BC196 The first of these approaches, illustrated in figure 1, designates the hedged item as a 'layer' (eg (a) the bottom layer, (b) the top layer or (c) a portion of the top layer) of the assets (or liabilities) in a repricing time period. In this approach, the portfolio of CU100 in the above example is considered to comprise a hedged layer of CU20 and an unhedged layer of CU80.

Figure 1: Illustrating the designation of an amount of assets as a layer

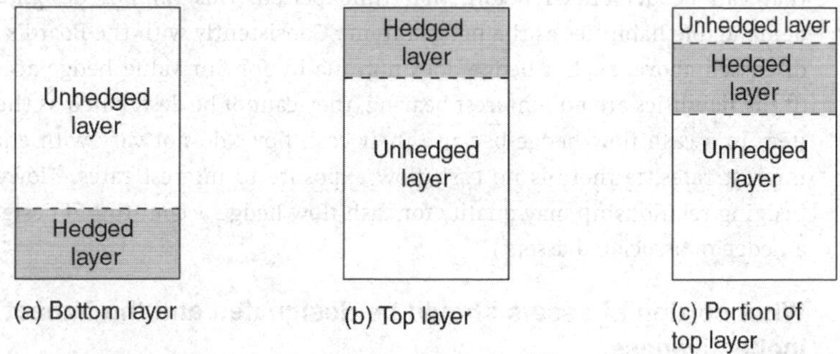

(a) Bottom layer (b) Top layer (c) Portion of top layer

BC197 The Board noted that the layer approach does not result in the recognition of ineffectiveness in all cases when the estimated amount of assets (or liabilities) changes. For example, in a bottom layer approach (see figure 2), if some assets prepay earlier than expected so that the entity revises downward its estimate of the amount of assets in the repricing time period (eg from CU100 to CU90), these reductions are assumed to come first from the unhedged top layer (figure 2(b)). Whether any ineffectiveness arises depends on whether the downward revision reaches the hedged layer of CU20. Thus, if the bottom layer is designated as the hedged item, it is unlikely that the hedged (bottom) layer will be reached and that any ineffectiveness will arise. Conversely, if the top layer is designated (see figure 3), any downward revision to the estimated amount in a repricing time period will reduce the hedged (top) layer and ineffectiveness will arise (figure 3(b)).

Figure 2: Illustrating the effect on changes in prepayments in a bottom layer approach

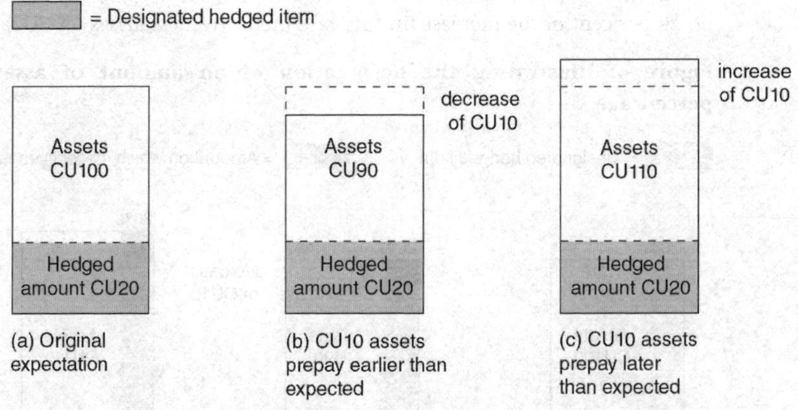

Figure 3: Illustrating the effect on changes in prepayments in a top layer approach

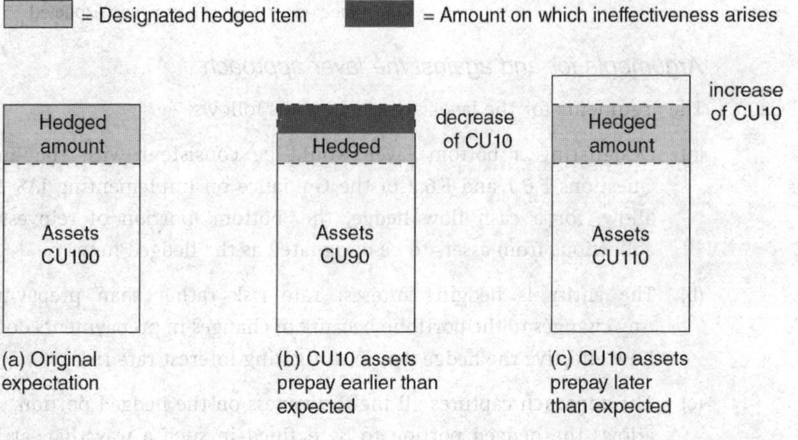

BC198 Finally, if some assets prepay *later* than expected so that the entity revises *upward* its estimate of the amount of assets in this repricing time period (eg from CU100 to CU110, see figures 2(c) and 3(c)), no ineffectiveness arises no matter how the layer is designated, on the grounds that the hedged layer of CU20 is still there and that was all that was being hedged.

Percentage approach

BC199 The percentage approach, illustrated in figure 4, designates the hedged item as a percentage of the assets (or liabilities) in a repricing time period. In this approach, in the portfolio in the above example, 20 per cent of the assets of CU100 in this repricing time period is designated as the hedged item (figure 4(a)). As a result, if some assets prepay *earlier* than expected so that the entity revises *downwards* its estimate of the amount of assets in this repricing time period (eg from CU100 to CU90, figure 4(b)), ineffectiveness arises on 20 per cent of the decrease (in this case ineffectiveness arises on CU2). Similarly, if some assets prepay *later* than expected so that the entity revises *upwards* its estimate of the amount of assets in this repricing time period (eg from CU100 to CU110, figure 4(c)), ineffectiveness arises on 20 per cent of the increase (in this case ineffectiveness arises on CU2).

Figure 4: Illustrating the designation of an amount of assets as a percentage

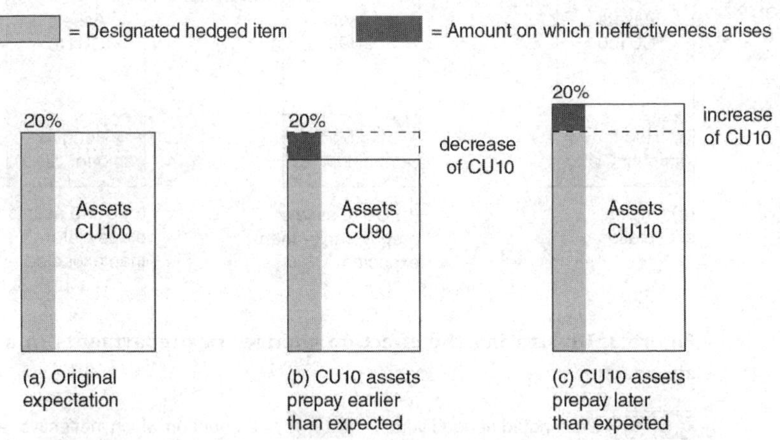

Arguments for and against the layer approach

BC200 The arguments for the layer approach are as follows:

(a) Designating a bottom layer would be consistent with the answers to Questions F.6.1 and F.6.2 of the Guidance on Implementing IAS 39, which allow, for a cash flow hedge, the 'bottom' portion of reinvestments of collections from assets to be designated as the hedged item.

(b) The entity is hedging interest rate risk rather than prepayment risk. Any changes to the portfolio because of changes in prepayments do not affect how effective the hedge was in mitigating interest rate risk.

(c) The approach captures all ineffectiveness on the hedged portion. It merely allows the hedged portion to be defined in such a way that, at least in a bottom layer approach, the first of any potential ineffectiveness relates to the unhedged portion.

(d) It is correct that no ineffectiveness arises if changes in prepayment estimates cause more assets to be scheduled into that repricing time period. So long as assets equal to the hedged layer remain, there is no ineffectiveness and upward revisions of the amount in a repricing time period do not affect the hedged layer.

(e) A prepayable item can be viewed as a combination of a non-prepayable item and a prepayment option. The designation of a bottom layer can be viewed as hedging a part of the life of the non-prepayable item, but none of the prepayment option. For example, a 25-year prepayable mortgage can be viewed as a combination of (i) a non-prepayable, fixed term, 25-year mortgage and (ii) a written prepayment option that allows the borrower to repay the mortgage early. If the entity hedges this asset with a 5-year derivative, this is equivalent to hedging the first five years of component (i). If the position is viewed in this way, no ineffectiveness arises when interest rate changes cause the value of the prepayment option to change (unless the option is exercised and the asset prepaid) because the prepayment option was not hedged.

BC201 The arguments against the layer approach are as follows:

(a) The considerations that apply to a fair value hedge are different from those that apply to a cash flow hedge. In a cash flow hedge, it is the cash flows associated with the reinvestment of probable future collections that are hedged. In a fair value hedge it is the fair value of the assets that currently exist.

(b) The fact that no ineffectiveness is recognised if the amount in a repricing time period is re-estimated upwards (with the effect that the entity becomes underhedged) is not in accordance with IAS 39. For a fair value hedge, IAS 39 requires that ineffectiveness is recognised both when the entity becomes overhedged (ie the derivative exceeds the hedged item) and when it becomes underhedged (ie the derivative is smaller than the hedged item).

(c) As noted in paragraph BC200(e), a prepayable item can be viewed as a combination of a non-prepayable item and a prepayment option. When interest rates change, the fair value of both of these components changes.

(d) The objective of applying fair value hedge accounting to a hedged item designated in terms of an amount (rather than as individual assets or liabilities) is to obtain results that closely approximate those that would have been obtained if individual assets or liabilities had been designated as the hedged item. If individual prepayable assets had been designated as the hedged item, the change in both the components noted in (c) above (to the extent they are attributable to the hedged risk) would be recognised in profit or loss, both when interest rates increase and when they decrease. Accordingly, the change in the fair value of the hedged asset would differ from the change in the fair value of the hedging derivative (unless that derivative includes an equivalent prepayment option) and ineffectiveness would be recognised for the difference. It follows that in the simplified approach of designating the hedged item as an amount, ineffectiveness should similarly arise.

(e) *All* prepayable assets in a repricing time period, and not just a layer of them, contain a prepayment option whose fair value changes with changes in interest rates. Accordingly, when interest rates change, the fair value of the hedged assets (which include a prepayment option whose fair value has changed) will change by an amount different from that of the hedging derivative (which typically does not contain a prepayment option), and ineffectiveness will arise. This effect occurs regardless of whether interest rates increase or decrease—ie regardless of whether re-estimates of prepayments result in the amount in a time period being more or less.

(f) Interest rate risk and prepayment risk are so closely interrelated that it is not appropriate to separate the two components referred to in paragraph BC200(e) and designate only one of them (or a part of one of them) as the hedged item. Often the biggest single cause of changes in prepayment rates is changes in interest rates. This close relationship is the reason why IAS 39[*] prohibits a held-to-maturity asset from being a hedged item with respect to either interest rate risk or prepayment risk. Furthermore, most entities do not separate the two components for risk management purposes. Rather, they incorporate the prepayment option by scheduling amounts based on expected maturities. When entities choose to use risk management practices—based on not separating prepayment and interest rate risk—as the basis for designation for hedge accounting purposes, it is not appropriate to separate the two components referred to in paragraph BC200(e) and designate only one of them (or a part of one of them) as the hedged item.

(g) If interest rates change, the effect on the fair value of a portfolio of prepayable items will be different from the effect on the fair value of a portfolio of otherwise identical but non-prepayable items. However, using a layer approach, this difference would not be recognised—if both portfolios were hedged to the same extent, both would be recognised in the balance sheet at the same amount.

BC202 The Board was persuaded by the arguments in paragraph BC201 and rejected layer approaches. In particular, the Board concluded that the hedged item should be designated in such a way that if the entity changes its estimates of the repricing time periods in which items are expected to repay or mature (eg in the light of recent prepayment experience), ineffectiveness arises. It also concluded that ineffectiveness should arise both when estimated prepayments decrease, resulting in more assets in a particular repricing time period, and when they increase, resulting in fewer.

Arguments for a third approach—measuring directly the change in fair value of the entire hedged item

BC203 The Board also considered comments on the Exposure Draft that:

(a) some entities hedge prepayment risk and interest rate risk separately, by hedging to the expected prepayment date using interest rate swaps, and hedging possible variations in these expected prepayment dates using swaptions.

(b) the embedded derivatives provisions of IAS 39 require some prepayable assets to be separated into a prepayment option and a non-prepayable host contract[†] (unless the entity is unable to measure separately the prepayment option, in which case it treats the entire asset as held for trading[§]). This seems to conflict with the view in the Exposure Draft that the two risks are too difficult to separate for the purposes of a portfolio hedge.

BC204 In considering these arguments, the Board noted that the percentage approach described in paragraph AG126(b) is a proxy for measuring the change in the fair value of the *entire* asset (or liability)—including any embedded prepayment option—that is attributable to changes in interest rates. The Board had developed this proxy in the Exposure Draft because it had been informed that most entities

[*] see IAS 39, paragraph 79

[†] see IAS 39, paragraphs 11 and AG30(g)

[§] see IAS 39, paragraph 12

(a) do not separate interest rate risk and prepayment risk for risk management purposes and hence (b) were unable to value the change in the value of the entire asset (including any embedded prepayment option) that is attributable to changes in the hedged interest rates. However, the comments described in paragraph BC203 indicated that in some cases, entities may be able to measure this change in value directly. The Board noted that such a direct method of measurement is conceptually preferable to the proxy described in paragraph AG126(b) and, accordingly, decided to recognise it explicitly. Thus, for example, if an entity that hedges prepayable assets using a combination of interest rate swaps and swaptions is able to measure directly the change in fair value of the entire asset, it could measure effectiveness by comparing the change in the value of the swaps and swaptions with the change in the fair value of the entire asset (including the change in the value of the prepayment option embedded in them) that is attributable to changes in the hedged interest rate. However, the Board also decided to permit the proxy proposed in the Exposure Draft for those entities that are unable to measure directly the change in the fair value of the entire asset.

Consideration of systems requirements

BC205 Finally, the Board was informed that, to be practicable in terms of systems needs, any approach should not require tracking of the amount in a repricing time period for multiple periods. Therefore it decided that ineffectiveness should be calculated by determining the change in the estimated amount in a repricing time period between one date on which effectiveness is measured and the next, as described more fully in paragraphs AG126 and AG127. This requires the entity to track how much of the change in each repricing time period between these two dates is attributable to revisions in estimates and how much is attributable to the origination of new assets (or liabilities). However, once ineffectiveness has been determined as set out above, the entity in essence starts again, ie it establishes the new amount in each repricing time period (including new items that have been originated since it last tested effectiveness), designates a new hedged item, and repeats the procedures to determine ineffectiveness at the next date it tests effectiveness. Thus the tracking is limited to movements between one date when effectiveness is measured and the next. It is not necessary to track for multiple periods. However, the entity will need to keep records relating to each repricing time period (a) to reconcile the amounts for each repricing time period with the total amounts in the two separate line items in the balance sheet (see paragraph AG114(f)), and (b) to ensure that amounts in the two separate line items are derecognised no later than when the repricing time period to which they relate expires.

BC206 The Board also noted that the amount of tracking required by the percentage approach is no more than what would be required by any of the layer approaches. Thus, the Board concluded that none of the approaches was clearly preferable from the standpoint of systems needs.

The carrying amount of the hedged item

BC207 The last issue noted in paragraph BC176 is how to present in the balance sheet the change in fair value of the hedged item. The Board noted the concern of respondents that the hedged item may contain many—even thousands of–individual assets (or liabilities) and that to change the carrying amounts of each of these individual items would be impracticable. The Board considered dealing with this concern by permitting the change in value to be presented in a single line item in the balance sheet. However, the Board noted that this could result in a decrease in the fair value of a financial asset (financial liability) being recognised as a financial liability (financial asset). Furthermore, for some repricing time periods the hedged item may be an asset, whereas for others it may be a liability. The Board concluded that it would be incorrect to present together the changes in fair value for such repricing time periods, because to do so would combine changes in the fair value of assets with changes in the fair value of liabilities.

BC208 Accordingly, the Board decided that two line items should be presented, as follows:

(a) for those repricing time periods for which the hedged item is an asset, the change in its fair value is presented in a single separate line item within assets; and

(b) for those repricing time periods for which the hedged item is a liability, the change in its fair value is presented in a single separate line item within liabilities.

BC209 The Board noted that these line items represent changes in the fair value of the hedged item. For this reason, the Board decided that they should be presented next to financial assets or financial liabilities.

Derecognition of amounts included in the separate line items

Derecognition of an asset (or liability) in the hedged portfolio

BC210 The Board discussed how and when amounts recognised in the separate balance sheet line items should be removed from the balance sheet. The Board noted that the objective is to remove such amounts from the balance sheet in the same periods as they would have been removed had individual assets or liabilities (rather than an amount) been designated as the hedged item.

BC211 The Board noted that this objective could be fully met only if the entity schedules individual assets or liabilities into repricing time periods and tracks both for how long the scheduled individual items have been hedged and how much of each item was hedged in each time period. In the absence of such scheduling and tracking, some assumptions would need to be made about these matters and, hence, about how much should be removed from the separate balance sheet line items when an asset (or liability) in the hedged portfolio is derecognised. In addition, some safeguards would be needed to ensure that amounts included in the separate balance sheet line items are removed from the balance sheet over a reasonable period and do not remain in the balance sheet indefinitely. With these points in mind, the Board decided to require that:

(a) whenever an asset (or liability) in the hedged portfolio is derecognised–whether through earlier than expected prepayment, sale or write-off from impairment–any amount included in the separate balance sheet line item relating to that derecognised asset (or liability) should be removed from the balance sheet and included in the gain or loss on derecognition.

(b) if an entity cannot determine into which time period(s) a derecognised asset (or liability) was scheduled:

(i) it should assume that higher than expected prepayments occur on assets scheduled into the first available time period; and

(ii) it should allocate sales and impairments to assets scheduled into all time periods containing the derecognised item on a systematic and rational basis.

(c) the entity should track how much of the total amount included in the separate line items relates to each repricing time period, and should remove the amount that relates to a particular time period from the balance sheet no later than when that time period expires.

Amortisation

BC212 The Board also noted that if the designated hedged amount for a repricing time period is reduced, IAS 39* requires that the separate balance sheet line item described in paragraph 89A relating to that reduction is amortised on the basis of a recalculated effective interest rate. The Board noted that for a portfolio hedge of interest rate risk, amortisation based on a recalculated effective interest rate could be complex to determine and could demand significant additional systems requirements. Consequently, the Board decided that in the case of a portfolio hedge of interest rate risk (and only in such a hedge), the line item balance may be amortised using a straight-line method when a method based on a recalculated effective interest rate is not practicable.

The hedging instrument

BC213 The Board was asked by commentators to clarify whether the hedging instrument may be a portfolio of derivatives containing offsetting risk positions. Commentators noted that previous versions of IAS 39 were unclear on this point.

BC214 The issue arises because the assets and liabilities in each repricing time period change over time as prepayment expectations change, as items are derecognised and as new items are originated. Thus the net position, and the amount the entity wishes to designate as the hedged item, also changes over time. If the hedged item decreases, the hedging instrument needs to be reduced. However, entities do not normally reduce the hedging instrument by disposing of some of the derivatives contained in it. Instead, entities adjust the hedging instrument by entering into new derivatives with an offsetting risk profile.

BC215 The Board decided to permit the hedging instrument to be a portfolio of derivatives containing offsetting risk positions for both individual and portfolio hedges. It noted that all of the derivatives concerned are measured at fair value. It also noted that the two ways of adjusting the hedging instrument described in

* see paragraph 92

the previous paragraph can achieve substantially the same effect. Therefore the Board clarified paragraph 77 to this effect.

Hedge effectiveness for a portfolio hedge of interest rate risk

BC216 Some respondents to the Exposure Draft questioned whether IAS 39's effectiveness tests* should apply to a portfolio hedge of interest rate risk. The Board noted that its objective in amending IAS 39 for a portfolio hedge of interest rate risk is to permit fair value hedge accounting to be used more easily, whilst continuing to meet the principles of hedge accounting. One of these principles is that the hedge is highly effective. Thus, the Board concluded that the effectiveness requirements in IAS 39 apply equally to a portfolio hedge of interest rate risk.

BC217 Some respondents to the Exposure Draft sought guidance on how the effectiveness tests are to be applied to a portfolio hedge. In particular, they asked how the prospective effectiveness test is to be applied when an entity periodically 'rebalances' a hedge (ie adjusts the amount of the hedging instrument to reflect changes in the hedged item). The Board decided that if the entity's risk management strategy is to change the amount of the hedging instrument periodically to reflect changes in the hedged position, that strategy affects the determination of the term of the hedge. Thus, the entity needs to demonstrate that the hedge is expected to be highly effective only for the period until the amount of the hedging instrument is next adjusted. The Board noted that this decision does not conflict with the requirement in paragraph 75 that 'a hedging relationship may not be designated for only a portion of the time period during which a hedging instrument remains outstanding'. This is because the entire hedging instrument is designated (and not only some of its cash flows, for example, those to the time when the hedge is next adjusted). However, expected effectiveness is assessed by considering the change in the fair value of the entire hedging instrument only for the period until it is next adjusted.

BC218 A third issue raised in the comment letters was whether, for a portfolio hedge, the retrospective effectiveness test should be assessed for all time buckets in aggregate or individually for each time bucket. The Board decided that entities could use any method to assess retrospective effectiveness, but noted that the chosen method would form part of the documentation of the hedging relationship made at the inception of the hedge in accordance with paragraph 88(a) and hence could not be decided at the time the retrospective effectiveness test is performed.

Transition to fair value hedge accounting for portfolios of interest rate risk

BC219 In finalising the amendments to IAS 39, the Board considered whether to provide additional guidance for entities wishing to apply fair value hedge accounting to a portfolio hedge that had previously been accounted for using cash flow hedge accounting. The Board noted that such entities could apply paragraph 101(d) to revoke the designation of a cash flow hedge and re-designate a new fair value hedge using the same hedged item and hedging instrument, and decided to clarify

* see paragraph AG105

this in the Application Guidance. Additionally, the Board concluded that clarification was not required for first-time adopters because IFRS 1 already contained sufficient guidance.

BC220 The Board also considered whether to permit retrospective designation of a portfolio hedge. The Board noted that this would conflict with the principle in paragraph 88(a) that 'at the inception of the hedge there is formal designation and documentation of the hedging relationship' and accordingly, decided not to permit retrospective designation.

Elimination of selected differences from US GAAP

BC221 The Board considered opportunities to eliminate differences between IAS 39 and US GAAP. The guidance on measurement and hedge accounting under revised IAS 39 is generally similar to that under US GAAP. The amendments will further reduce or eliminate differences between IAS 39 and US GAAP in the areas listed below. In some other areas, a difference will remain. For example, US GAAP in many, but not all, areas is more detailed, which may result in a difference in accounting when an entity applies an accounting approach under IAS 39 that would not be permitted under US GAAP.

Contracts to buy or sell a non-financial item

(a) The Board decided that a contract to buy or sell a non-financial item is a derivative within the scope of IAS 39 if the non-financial item that is the subject of the contract is readily convertible to cash and the contract is not a 'normal' purchase or sale. This requirement is comparable to the definition of a derivative in SFAS 133, which also includes contracts for which the underlying is readily convertible to cash, and to the scope exclusion in SFAS 133 for 'normal' purchases and sales.

Scope: loan commitments

(b) The Board decided to add a paragraph to IAS 39 to exclude particular loan commitments that are not settled net. Such loan commitments were within the scope of the original IAS 39. The amendment moves IAS 39 closer to US GAAP.

Unrealised gains and losses on available-for-sale financial assets

(c) The Board decided to eliminate the option to recognise in profit or loss gains and losses on available-for-sale financial assets (IAS 39, paragraph 55(b)), and thus require such gains and losses to be recognised in equity. The change is consistent with SFAS 115, which does not provide the option in the original IAS 39 to recognise gains and losses on available-for-sale financial assets in profit or loss. SFAS 115 requires those unrealised gains and losses to be recognised in other comprehensive income (not profit or loss).

Fair value in active markets

(d) The Board decided to amend the wording in IAS 39, paragraph AG71, to state that, instead of a quoted market price *normally* being the best evidence of fair value, a quoted market price *is* the best evidence of fair value. This is similar to SFAS 107 *Disclosures about Fair Value of Financial Instruments*.

Fair value in inactive markets

(e) The Board decided to include in IAS 39 a requirement that the best evidence of the fair value of an instrument that is not traded in an active market is the transaction price, unless the fair value is evidenced by comparison with other observable current market transactions in the same instrument (ie without modification or repackaging) or based on a valuation technique incorporating only observable market data. This is similar to the requirements of EITF 023 *Issues Involved in Accounting for Derivative Contracts Held for Trading Purposes and Contracts Involved in Energy Trading and Risk Management Activities.*

Impaired fixed rate loans: observable market price.

(f) The Board decided to permit an impaired fixed interest rate loan to be measured using an observable market price. SFAS 114 allows impairment to be measured on the basis of a loan's observable market price.

Reversal of impairment losses on investments in equity instruments

(g) The Board decided that if an entity recognises an impairment loss on an available–for–sale equity investment and the fair value of the investment subsequently increases, the increase in fair value should be recognised in equity. This is comparable to US GAAP under which reversals of impairment losses are not permitted.

Hedges of firm commitments

(h) The Board decided to require hedges of firm commitments to be treated as fair value hedges instead of cash flow hedges as was required under the original IAS 39 (except foreign currency risk when the hedge may be designated as either a cash flow hedge or a fair value hedge). This change brings IAS 39 closer to SFAS 133.

Basis adjustments to financial assets or financial liabilities resulting from hedges of forecast transactions

(i) Basis adjustments to financial assets or financial liabilities resulting from hedges of forecast transactions are not permitted under SFAS 133. The revised IAS 39 also precludes such basis adjustments.

Basis adjustments to non–financial assets or non–financial liabilities resulting from hedges of forecast transactions

(j) The Board decided to permit entities to apply basis adjustments to non-financial assets or non-financial liabilities that result from hedges of forecast transactions. Although US GAAP precludes basis adjustments, permitting a choice in IAS 39 allows entities to meet the US GAAP requirements.

Summary of changes from the Exposure Draft

BC222 The main changes from the Exposure Draft's proposals are as follows:

Scope

(a) The Standard adopts the proposal in the Exposure Draft that loan commitments that cannot be settled net and are not classified at fair value through profit or loss are excluded from the scope of the Standard. The Standard requires, however, that a commitment to extend a loan at a below-market interest rate is initially recognised at fair value, and subsequently measured at the higher of (i) the amount determined under IAS 37 and (ii) the amount initially recognised, less where appropriate, cumulative amortisation recognised in accordance with IAS 18.

(b) The Standard adopts the proposal in the Exposure Draft that financial guarantees are initially recognised at fair value, but clarifies that subsequently they are measured at the higher of (a) the amount determined under IAS 37 and (b) the amount initially recognised, less, where appropriate, cumulative amortisation recognised in accordance with IAS 18.

Definitions

(c) The Standard amends the definition of 'originated loans and receivables' to 'loans and receivables'. Under the revised definition, an entity is permitted to classify as loans and receivables purchased loans that are not quoted in an active market.

(d) The Standard amends the definition of transaction costs in the Exposure Draft to include internal costs, provided they are incremental and directly attributable to the acquisition, issue or disposal of a financial asset or financial liability.

(e) The Standard amends the definition of the effective interest rate proposed in the Exposure Draft so that the effective interest rate is calculated using estimated cash flows for all instruments. An exception is made for those rare cases in which it is not possible to estimate cash flows reliably, when the Standard requires the use of contractual cash flows over the contractual life of the instrument. The Standard further stipulates that when accounting for a change in estimates, entities adjust the carrying amount of the instrument in the period of change with a corresponding gain or loss recognised in profit or loss. To calculate the new carrying amount, entities discount revised estimated cash flows at the original effective rate.

Derecognition of a financial asset

(f) The Exposure Draft proposed that an entity would continue to recognise a financial asset to the extent of its continuing involvement in that asset. Hence, an entity would derecognise a financial asset only if it did not have any continuing involvement in that asset. The Standard uses the concepts of control and of risks and rewards of ownership to determine whether, and to what extent, a financial asset is derecognised. The continuing involvement approach applies only if an entity retains some, but not substantially all, the risks and rewards of ownership and also retains control (see also (i) below).

(g) Unlike the Exposure Draft, the Standard clarifies when a part of a larger financial asset should be considered for derecognition. The Standard requires a part of a larger financial asset to be considered for derecognition if, and only if, the part is one of:

- only specifically identified cash flows from a financial asset;
- only a fully proportionate (pro rata) share of the cash flows from a financial asset; or
- only a fully proportionate (pro rata) share of specifically identified cash flows from a financial asset.

In all other cases, the Standard requires the financial asset to be considered for derecognition in its entirety.

(h) The Standard retains the conditions proposed in the Exposure Draft for 'pass-through arrangements' in which an entity retains the contractual rights to receive cash flows of a financial asset, but assumes a contractual obligation to pay those cash flows to one or more entities. However, because of confusion over the meaning of the term 'pass-through arrangements', the Standard does not use this term.

(i) The Standard requires that an entity first assesses whether it has transferred substantially all the risks and rewards of ownership. If an entity has retained substantially all such risks and rewards, it continues to recognise the transferred asset. If it has transferred substantially all such risks and rewards, it derecognises the transferred asset. If an entity has neither transferred nor retained substantially all the risks and rewards of ownership of the transferred asset, it assesses whether it has retained control over the transferred asset. If it has retained control, the Standard requires the entity to continue recognising the transferred asset to the extent of its continuing involvement in the transferred asset. If it has not retained control, the entity derecognises the transferred asset.

(j) The Standard provides guidance on how to evaluate the concepts of risks and rewards and of control for derecognition purposes.

Measurement

(k) The Standard adopts the option proposed in the Exposure Draft to permit designation of any financial asset or financial liability on initial recognition as one to be measured at fair value, with changes in fair value recognised in profit or loss. However, the Standard clarifies that the fair value of liabilities with a demand feature, for example, demand deposits, is not less than the amount payable on demand discounted from the first date that the amount could be required to be paid.

(l) The Standard adopts the proposal in the Exposure Draft that quoted prices in active markets should be used to determine fair value in preference to other valuation techniques. The Standard adds guidance that if a rate (rather than a price) is quoted, these quoted rates are used as inputs into valuation techniques to determine the fair value. The Standard further clarifies that if an entity operates in more than one active market, the entity uses the price at which a transaction would occur at the balance sheet date in the same instrument (ie without modification or repackaging) in the most advantageous active market to which the entity has immediate access.

(m) The Standard simplifies the fair value measurement hierarchy in an inactive market so that recent market transactions do not take precedence over a valuation technique. Rather, when there is not a price in an active market, a valuation technique is used. Such valuation techniques include using recent arm's length market transactions.

(n) The Standard also clarifies that the best estimate of fair value at initial recognition of a financial instrument that is not quoted in an active market is the transaction price, unless the fair value of the instrument is evidenced by other observable market transactions or is based on a valuation technique whose variables include only data from observable markets.

Impairment of financial assets

(o) The Standard clarifies that an impairment loss is recognised only when it has been incurred. The Standard eliminates some of the detailed guidance in the Exposure Draft, in particular, the example of how to calculate the discount rate for the purpose of measuring impairment in a group of financial assets.

(p) The Exposure Draft proposed that impairment losses recognised on investments in debt or equity instruments that are classified as available for sale cannot be reversed through profit or loss. The Standard requires that for available-for-sale debt instruments, an impairment loss is reversed through profit or loss when fair value increases and the increase can be objectively related to an event occurring after the loss was recognised. Impairment losses recognised on available-for-sale equity instruments cannot be reversed through profit or loss, ie any subsequent increase in fair value is recognised in equity.

Hedge accounting

(q) The Standard requires that when a hedged forecast transaction actually occurs and results in the recognition of a financial asset or a financial liability, the gain or loss deferred in equity does not adjust the initial carrying amount of the asset or liability (ie 'basis adjustment' is prohibited), but remains in equity and is recognised in profit or loss consistently with the recognition of gains and losses on the asset or liability. For hedges of forecast transactions that will result in the recognition of a non-financial asset or a non-financial liability, the entity has a choice of whether to apply basis adjustment or retain the hedging gain or loss in equity and recognise it in profit or loss when the asset or liability affects profit or loss.

(r) The Exposure Draft proposed to treat hedges of firm commitments as fair value hedges (rather than as cash flow hedges). The Standard adopts this requirement but clarifies that a hedge of the foreign currency risk of a firm commitment may be accounted for as either a fair value hedge or a cash flow hedge.

Transition

(s) The revised Standard adopts the proposal in the Exposure Draft that, on transition, an entity is permitted to designate a previously recognised financial asset or financial liability as a financial asset or a financial liability at fair value through profit or loss or available for sale. However, a disclosure requirement has been added to IAS 32 to provide information about the fair value of the financial assets or financial liabilities designated into each category and the classification and carrying amount in the previous financial statements.

(t) The Exposure Draft proposed retrospective application of the derecognition provisions of the revised IAS 39 to financial assets derecognised under the original IAS 39. The Standard requires prospective application, namely that entities do not recognise those assets that were derecognised under the original Standard, but permits retrospective application from a date of the entity's choosing, provided that the information needed to apply IAS 39 to assets and liabilities derecognised as a result of past transactions was obtained at the time of initially accounting for those transactions.

(u) The Exposure Draft proposed, and the revised Standard originally required, retrospective application of the 'day 1' gain or loss recognition requirements in paragraph AG76. After the revised Standard was issued, constituents raised concerns that retrospective application would diverge from the requirements of US GAAP, would be difficult and expensive to implement, and might require subjective assumptions about what was observable and what was not. In response to these concerns, the Board decided:

(i) to permit entities to apply the requirements in the last sentence of paragraph AG76 in any one of the following ways:

- retrospectively, as previously required by IAS 39
- prospectively to transactions entered into after 25 October 2002, the effective date of equivalent US GAAP requirements
- prospectively to transactions entered into after 1 January 2004, the date of transition to IFRSs for many entities.

(ii) to clarify that a gain or loss should be recognised after initial recognition only to the extent that it arises from a change in a factor (including time) that market participants would consider in setting a price. Some constituents asked the Board to clarify that straight-line amortisation is an appropriate method of recognising the difference between a transaction price (used as fair value in accordance with paragraph AG76) and a valuation made at the time of the transaction that was not based solely on data from observable markets. The Board decided not to do this. It concluded that although straight-line amortisation may be an appropriate method in some cases, it will not be appropriate in others.

Dissenting opinions

Dissent of Anthony T Cope, James J Leisenring and Warren J McGregor from the issue of IAS 39 in December 2003

DO1 Messrs Cope, Leisenring and McGregor dissent from the issue of this Standard.

DO2 Mr Leisenring dissents because he disagrees with the conclusions concerning derecognition, impairment of certain assets and the adoption of basis adjustment hedge accounting in certain circumstances.

DO3 The Standard requires in paragraphs 30 and 31 that to the extent of an entity's continuing involvement in an asset, a liability should be recognised for the consideration received. Mr Leisenring believes that the result of that accounting is to recognise assets that fail to meet the definition of assets and to record liabilities that fail to meet the definition of liabilities. Furthermore, the Standard fails to recognise forward contracts, puts or call options and guarantees that are created, but instead records a fictitious 'borrowing' as a result of rights and obligations created by those contracts. There are other consequences of the continuing involvement approach that has been adopted. For transferors, it results in very different accounting by two entities when they have identical contractual rights and obligations only because one entity once owned the transferred financial asset. Furthermore, the 'borrowing' that is recognised is not accounted for like other loans, so no interest expense may be recorded. Indeed, implementing the proposed approach requires the specific override of measurement and presentation standards applicable to other similar financial instruments that do not arise from derecognition transactions. For example, derivatives created by derecognition transactions are not accounted for at fair value. For transferees, the approach also requires the override of the recognition and measurement requirements applicable to other similar financial instruments. If an instrument is acquired in a transfer transaction that fails the derecognition criteria, the transferee recognises and measures it differently from an instrument that is acquired from the same counterparty separately.

DO4 Mr Leisenring also disagrees with the requirement in paragraph 64 to include an asset that has been individually judged not to be impaired in a portfolio of similar assets for an additional portfolio assessment of impairment. Once an asset is judged not to be impaired, it is irrelevant whether the entity owns one or more similar assets as those assets have no implications for whether the asset that was individually considered for impairment is or is not impaired. The result of this accounting is that two entities could each own 50 per cent of a single loan. Both entities could conclude the loan is not impaired. However, if one of the two entities happens to have other loans that are similar, it would be allowed to recognise an impairment with respect to the loan where the other entity is not. Accounting for identical exposures differently is unacceptable. Mr Leisenring believes that the arguments in paragraph BC115 are compelling.

DO5 Mr Leisenring also dissents from paragraph 98 which allows but does not require basis adjustment for hedges of forecast transactions that result in the recognition of non-financial assets or liabilities. This accounting results in always adjusting the recorded asset or liability at the date of initial recognition away from its fair value. It also records an asset, if the basis adjustment alternative is selected, at an amount other than its cost as defined in IAS 16 *Property, Plant and Equipment* and further described in paragraph 16 of that Standard. If a derivative were to be considered a part of the cost of acquiring an asset, hedge accounting in these circumstances should not be elective to be consistent with IAS 16. Mr Leisenring also objects to creating this alternative as a result of an improvement project that ostensibly had as an objective the reduction of alternatives. The non-comparability that results from this alternative is both undesirable and unnecessary.

DO6 Mr Leisenring also dissents from the application guidance in paragraph AG71 and in particular the conclusion contained in paragraph BC98. He does not believe that an entity that originates a contract in one market should measure the fair value of the contract by reference to a different market in which the transaction did not take place. If prices change in the transacting market, that price change should be recognised when subsequently measuring the fair value of the contract. However, there are many implications of switching between markets when measuring fair value that the Board has not yet addressed. Mr Leisenring believes a gain or loss should not be recognised based on the fact a transaction could occur in a different market.

DO7 Mr Cope dissents from paragraph 64 and agrees with Mr Leisenring's analysis and conclusions on loan impairment as set out above in paragraph DO4. He finds it counter-intuitive that a loan that has been determined not to be impaired following careful analysis should be subsequently accounted for as if it were impaired when included in a portfolio.

DO8 Mr Cope also dissents from paragraph 98, and, in particular, the Board's decision to allow a free choice over whether basis adjustment is used when accounting for hedges of forecast transactions that result in the recognition of non-financial assets or non-financial liabilities. In his view, of the three courses of action open to the Board— retaining IAS 39's requirement to use basis adjustment, prohibiting basis adjustment as proposed in the June 2002 Exposure Draft, or providing a choice—the Board has selected the worst course. Mr Cope believes that the best approach would have been to prohibit basis adjustment, as proposed in the Exposure Draft, because, in his opinion, basis adjustments result in the recognition of assets and liabilities at inappropriate amounts.

DO9 Mr Cope believes that increasing the number of choices in international standards is bad policy. The Board's decision potentially creates major differences between entities choosing one option and those choosing the other. This lack of comparability will adversely affect users' ability to make sound economic decisions.

D10 In addition, Mr Cope notes that entities that are US registrants may choose not to adopt basis adjustment in order to avoid a large reconciling difference to US GAAP. Mr Cope believes that increasing differences between IFRS-compliant entities that are US registrants and those that are not is undesirable.

DO11 Mr McGregor dissents from paragraph 98 and agrees with Mr Cope's and Mr Leisenring's analyses and conclusions as set out above in paragraphs DO5 and DO8–DO10.

DO12 Mr McGregor also dissents from this Standard because he disagrees with the conclusions about impairment of certain assets.

DO13 Mr McGregor disagrees with paragraphs 67 and 69, which deal with the impairment of equity investments classified as available for sale. These paragraphs require impairment losses on such assets to be recognised in profit or loss when there is objective evidence that the asset is impaired. Previously recognised impairment losses are not to be reversed through profit and loss when the assets' fair value increases. Mr McGregor notes that the Board's reasoning for prohibiting reversals through profit or loss of previously impaired available-for-sale equity investments, set out in paragraph BC130 of the Basis for Conclusions, is that it '..could not find an acceptable way to distinguish reversals of impairment losses from other increases in fair value'. He agrees with this reasoning but believes that it applies equally to the recognition of impairment losses in the first place. Mr McGregor believes that the significant subjectivity involved in assessing whether a reduction in fair value represents an impairment (and thus should be recognised in profit or loss) or another decrease in value (and should be recognised directly in equity) will at best lead to a lack of comparability within an entity over time and between entities, and at worst provide an opportunity for entities to manage reported profit or loss.

DO14 Mr McGregor believes that all changes in the fair value of assets classified as available for sale should be recognised in profit or loss. However, such a major change to the Standard would need to be subject to the Board's full due process. At this time, to overcome the concerns expressed in paragraph DO13, he believes that for equity investments classified as available for sale, the Standard should require all changes in fair value below cost to be recognised in profit or loss as impairments and reversals of impairments and all changes in value above cost to be recognised in equity. This approach treats all changes in value the same way, no matter what their cause. The problem of how to distinguish an impairment loss from another decline in value (and of deciding whether there is an impairment in the first place) is eliminated because there is no longer any subjectivity involved. In addition, the approach is consistent with IAS 16 *Property, Plant and Equipment* and IAS 38 *Intangible Assets*.

DO15 Mr McGregor disagrees with paragraph 106 of the Standard and with the consequential amendments to paragraph 27 of IFRS 1 *First-time Adoption of International Financial Reporting Standards*. Paragraph 106 requires entities to apply the derecognition provisions prospectively to financial assets. Paragraph 27 of IFRS 1 requires first-time adopters to apply the derecognition provisions of IAS 39 (as revised in 2003) prospectively to non-derivative financial assets and financial liabilities. Mr McGregor believes that existing IAS 39 appliers should apply the derecognition provisions retrospectively to financial assets, and that first-time adopters should apply the derecognition provisions of IAS 39 retrospectively to all financial assets and financial liabilities. He is concerned that financial assets may have been derecognised under the original IAS 39 by entities that were subject to it, which might not have been derecognised under the revised IAS 39. He is also concerned that non-derivative financial assets and financial liabilities may have been derecognised by first-time adopters under previous GAAP that would not have been derecognised under the revised IAS 39. These amounts may be significant in many cases. Not requiring recognition of such amounts will result in the loss of relevant information and will impair the ability of users of financial statements to make sound economic decisions.

Dissent of John T Smith from the issue in March 2004 of amendments to IAS 39 on fair value hedge accounting for a portfolio hedge of interest rate risk

DO1 Mr Smith dissents from these Amendments to IAS 39 Financial Instruments: Recognition and Measurement *Fair Value Hedge Accounting for a Portfolio Hedge of Interest Rate Risk*. He agrees with the objective of finding a macro hedging solution that would reduce systems demands without undermining the fundamental accounting principles related to derivative instruments and hedging activities. However, Mr Smith believes that some respondents' support for these Amendments and their willingness to accept IAS 39 is based more on the extent to which the Amendments reduce recognition of ineffectiveness, volatility of profit or loss, and volatility of equity than on whether the Amendments reduce systems demands without undermining the fundamental accounting principles.

DO2 Mr Smith believes some decisions made during the Board's deliberations result in an approach to hedge accounting for a portfolio hedge that does not capture what was originally intended, namely a result that is substantially equivalent to designating an individual asset or liability as the hedged item. He understands some respondents will not accept IAS 39 unless the Board provides still another alternative that will further reduce reported volatility. Mr Smith believes that the Amendments already go beyond their intended objective. In particular, he believes that features of these Amendments can be applied to smooth out ineffectiveness and achieve results substantially equivalent to the other methods of measuring ineffectiveness that the Board considered when developing the Exposure Draft. The Board rejected those methods because they did not require the immediate recognition of all ineffectiveness. He also believes those features could be used to manage earnings.

Illustrative Example

This example accompanies, but is not part of, IAS 39.

Facts

IE1 On 1 January 20X1, Entity A identifies a portfolio comprising assets and liabilities whose interest rate risk it wishes to hedge. The liabilities include demandable deposit liabilities that the depositor may withdraw at any time without notice. For risk management purposes, the entity views all of the items in the portfolio as fixed rate items.

IE2 For risk management purposes, Entity A analyses the assets and liabilities in the portfolio into repricing time periods based on expected repricing dates. The entity uses monthly time periods and schedules items for the next five years (ie it has 60 separate monthly time periods).* The assets in the portfolio are prepayable assets that Entity A allocates into time periods based on the expected prepayment dates, by allocating a percentage of all of the assets, rather than individual items, into each time period. The portfolio also includes demandable liabilities that the entity expects, on a portfolio basis, to repay between one month and five years and, for risk management purposes, are scheduled into time periods on this basis. On the basis of this analysis, Entity A decides what amount it wishes to hedge in each time period.

IE3 This example deals only with the repricing time period expiring in three months' time, ie the time period maturing on 31 March 20X1 (a similar procedure would be applied for each of the other 59 time periods). Entity A has scheduled assets of CU100 million and liabilities of CU80 million into this time period. All of the liabilities are repayable on demand.

IE4 Entity A decides, for risk management purposes, to hedge the net position of CU20 million and accordingly enters into an interest rate swap† on 1 January 20X1 to pay a fixed rate and receive LIBOR, with a notional principal amount of CU20 million and a fixed life of three months.

IE5 This Example makes the following simplifying assumptions:

(a) the coupon on the fixed leg of the swap is equal to the fixed coupon on the asset;

(b) the coupon on the fixed leg of the swap becomes payable on the same dates as the interest payments on the asset; and

(c) the interest on the variable leg of the swap is the overnight LIBOR rate. As a result, the entire fair value change of the swap arises from the fixed leg only, because the variable leg is not exposed to changes in fair value due to changes in interest rates.

* In this Example principal cash flows have been scheduled into time periods but the related interest cash flows have been included when calculating the change in the fair value of the hedged item. Other methods of scheduling assets and liabilities are also possible. Also, in this Example, monthly repricing time periods have been used. An entity may choose narrower or wider time periods.

† The Example uses a swap as the hedging instrument. An entity may use forward rate agreements or other derivatives as hedging instruments.

In cases when these simplifying assumptions do not hold, greater ineffectiveness will arise. (The ineffectiveness arising from (a) could be eliminated by designating as the hedged item a portion of the cash flows on the asset that are equivalent to the fixed leg of the swap.)

IE6 It is also assumed that Entity A tests effectiveness on a monthly basis.

IE7 The fair value of an equivalent non-prepayable asset of CU20 million, ignoring changes in value that are not attributable to interest rate movements, at various times during the period of the hedge is as follows:

	1 Jan 20X1	31 Jan 20X1	1 Feb 20X1	28 Feb 20X1	31 Mar 20X1
Fair value (asset) (CU)	20,000,000	20,047,408	20,047,408	20,023,795	Nil

IE8 The fair value of the swap at various times during the period of the hedge is as follows:

	1 Jan 20X1	31 Jan 20X1	1 Feb 20X1	28 Feb 20X1	31 Mar 20X1
Fair value (liability) (CU)	Nil	(47,408)	(47,408)	(23,795)	Nil

Accounting treatment

IE9 On 1 January 20X1, Entity A designates as the hedged item an amount of CU20 million of assets in the three-month time period. It designates as the hedged risk the change in the value of the hedged item (ie the CU20 million of assets) that is attributable to changes in LIBOR. It also complies with the other designation requirements set out in paragraphs 88(d) and AG119 of the Standard.

IE10 Entity A designates as the hedging instrument the interest rate swap described in paragraph IE4.

End of month 1 (31 January 20X1)

IE11 On 31 January 20X1 (at the end of month 1) when Entity A tests effectiveness, LIBOR has decreased. Based on historical prepayment experience, Entity A estimates that, as a consequence, prepayments will occur faster than previously estimated. As a result it re-estimates the amount of assets scheduled into this time period (excluding new assets originated during the month) as CU96 million.

IE12 The fair value of the designated interest rate swap with a notional principal of CU20 million is (CU47,408)* (the swap is a liability).

IE13 Entity A computes the change in the fair value of the hedged item, taking into account the change in estimated prepayments, as follows.

(a) First, it calculates the percentage of the initial estimate of the assets in the time period that was hedged. This is 20 per cent (CU20 million ÷ CU100 million).

* see paragraph IE8.

(b) Second, it applies this percentage (20 per cent) to its revised estimate of the amount in that time period (CU96 million) to calculate the amount that is the hedged item based on its revised estimate. This is CU19.2 million.

(c) Third, it calculates the change in the fair value of this revised estimate of the hedged item (CU19.2 million) that is attributable to changes in LIBOR. This is CU45,511 (CU47,408* × (CU19.2 million ÷ CU20 million)).

IE14 Entity A makes the following accounting entries relating to this time period:

Dr Cash	CU172,097	
Cr Income statement (interest income)[(a)]		CU172,097

To recognise the interest received on the hedged amount (CU19.2 million).

Dr Income statement (interest expense)	CU179,268	
Cr Income statement (interest income)		CU179,268
Cr Cash		Nil

To recognise the interest received and paid on the swap designated as the hedging instrument.

Dr Income statement (loss)	CU47,408	
Cr Derivative liability		CU47,408

To recognise the change in the fair value of the swap.

Dr Separate balance sheet line item	CU45,511	
Cr Income statement (gain)		CU45,511

To recognise the change in the fair value of the hedged amount.

(a) This Example does not show how amounts of interest income and interest expense are calculated.

IE15 The net result on profit or loss (excluding interest income and interest expense) is to recognise a loss of (CU1,897.) This represents ineffectiveness in the hedging relationship that arises from the change in estimated prepayment dates.

Bginning of month 2

IE16 On 1 February 20X1 Entity A sells a proportion of the assets in the various time periods. Entity A calculates that it has sold 8⅓ per cent of the entire portfolio of assets. Because the assets were allocated into time periods by allocating a percentage of the assets (rather than individual assets) into each time period, Entity A determines that it cannot ascertain into which specific time periods the sold assets were scheduled. Hence it uses a systematic and rational basis of allocation. Based on the fact that it sold a representative selection of the assets in the portfolio, Entity A allocates the sale proportionately over all time periods.

IE17 On this basis, Entity A computes that it has sold 8⅓ per cent of the assets allocated to the three-month time period, ie CU8 million (8⅓ per cent of CU96 million).

* ie CU20,047,408 – CU20,000,000. See paragraph IE7.

The proceeds received are CU8,018,400, equal to the fair value of the assets.* On derecognition of the assets, Entity A also removes from the separate balance sheet line item an amount that represents the change in the fair value of the hedged assets that it has now sold. This is 8⅓ per cent of the total line item balance of CU45,511, ie CU3,793.

IE18 Entity A makes the following accounting entries to recognise the sale of the asset and the removal of part of the balance in the separate balance sheet line item:

Dr Cash	CU8,018,400	
Cr Asset		CU8,000,000
Cr Separate balance sheet line item		CU3,793
Cr Income statement (gain)		CU14,607

To recognise the sale of the asset at fair value and to recognise a gain on sale.

Because the change in the amount of the assets is not attributable to a change in the hedged interest rate no ineffectiveness arises.

IE19 Entity A now has CU88 million of assets and CU80 million of liabilities in this time period. Hence the net amount Entity A wants to hedge is now CU8 million and, accordingly, it designates CU8 million as the hedged amount.

IE20 Entity A decides to adjust the hedging instrument by designating only a proportion of the original swap as the hedging instrument. Accordingly, it designates as the hedging instrument CU8 million or 40 per cent of the notional amount of the original swap with a remaining life of two months and a fair value of CU18,963.† It also complies with the other designation requirements in paragraphs 88(a) and AG119 of the Standard. The CU12 million of the notional amount of the swap that is no longer designated as the hedging instrument is either classified as held for trading with changes in fair value recognised in profit or loss, or is designated as the hedging instrument in a different hedge.§

IE21 As at 1 February 20X1 and after accounting for the sale of assets, the separate balance sheet line item is CU41,718 (CU45,511 – CU3,793), which represents the cumulative change in fair value of CU17.6ɸ million of assets. However, as at 1 February 20X1, Entity A is hedging only CU8 million of assets that have a cumulative change in fair value of CU18,963.‡ The remaining separate balance sheet line item of CU22,755# relates to an amount of assets that Entity A still holds but is no longer hedging. Accordingly Entity A amortises this amount over the remaining life of the time period, ie it amortises CU22,755 over two months.

* The amount realised on sale of the asset is the fair value of a prepayable asset, which is less than the fair value of the equivalent non-prepayable asset shown in paragraph IE7.

† CU47,408 × 40 per cent

§ The entity could instead enter into an offsetting swap with a notional principal of CU12 million to adjust its position and designate as the hedging instrument all CU20 million of the existing swap and all CU12 million of the new offsetting swap.

ɸ CU19.2 million–(8⅓% × CU19.2 million)

‡ CU41,718 × (CU8 million ÷ CU17.6 million)

CU41,718 – CU18,963

IE22 Entity A determines that it is not practicable to use a method of amortisation based on a recalculated effective yield and hence uses a straight-line method.

End of month 2 (28 February 20X1)

IE23 On 28 February 20X1 when Entity A next tests effectiveness, LIBOR is unchanged. Entity A does not revise its prepayment expectations. The fair value of the designated interest rate swap with a notional principal of CU8 million is (CU9,518)* (the swap is a liability). Also, Entity A calculates the fair value of the CU8 million of the hedged assets as at 28 February 20X1 as CU8,009,518†.

IE24 Entity A makes the following accounting entries relating to the hedge in this time period:

Dr Cash	CU71,707	
Cr Income statement (interest income)		CU71,707

To recognise the interest received on the hedged amount (CU8 million).

Dr Income statement (interest expense)	CU71,707	
Cr Income statement (interest income)		CU62,115
Cr Cash		CU9,592

To recognise the interest received and paid on the portion of the swap designated as the hedging instrument (CU8 million).

Dr Derivative liability	CU9,445	
Cr Income statement (gain)		CU9,445

To recognise the change in the fair value of the portion of the swap designated as the hedging instrument (CU8 million) (CU9,518 – CU18,963).

Dr Income statement (loss)	CU9,445	
Cr Separate balance sheet line item		CU9,445

To recognise the change in the fair value of the hedged amount (CU8,009,518 – CU8,018,963).

IE25 The net effect on profit or loss (excluding interest income and interest expense) is nil reflecting that the hedge is fully effective.

IE26 Entity A makes the following accounting entry to amortise the line item balance for this time period:

Dr Income statement (loss)	CU11,378	
Cr Separate balance sheet line item		CU11,378[(a)]

To recognise the amortisation charge for the period.

(a) CU22,755 ÷ 2

* CU23,795 [see paragraph IE8] × (CU8 million ÷ CU20 million)

† CU20,023,795 [see paragraph IE7] × (CU8 million ÷ CU20 million)

End of month 3

IE27 During the third month there is no further change in the amount of assets or liabilities in the three-month time period. On 31 March 20X1 the assets and the swap mature and all balances are recognised in profit or loss.

IE28 Entity A makes the following accounting entries relating to this time period:

Dr Cash	CU8,071,707	
Cr Asset (balance sheet)		CU8,000,000
Cr Income statement (interest income)		CU71,707

To recognise the interest and cash received on maturity of the hedged amount (CU8 million).

Dr Income statement (interest expense)	CU71,707	
Cr Income statement (interest income)		CU62,115
Cr Cash		CU9,592

To recognise the interest received and paid on the portion of the swap designated as the hedging instrument (CU8 million).

Dr Derivative liability	CU9,518	
Cr Income statement (gain)		CU9,518

To recognise the expiry of the portion of the swap designated as the hedging instrument (CU8 million).

Dr Income statement (loss)	CU9,518	
Cr Separate balance sheet line item		CU9,518

To remove the remaining line item balance on expiry of the time period.

IE29 The net effect on profit or loss (excluding interest income and interest expense) is nil reflecting that the hedge is fully effective.

IE30 Entity A makes the following accounting entry to amortise the line item balance for this time period:

Dr Income statement (loss)	CU11,377	
Cr Separate balance sheet line item		CU11,377[(a)]

To recognise the amortisation charge for the period.

(a) CU22,755 ÷ 2

Summary

IE31 The tables below summarise:

(a) changes in the separate balance sheet line item;

(b) the fair value of the derivative;

(c) the profit or loss effect of the hedge for the entire three-month period of the hedge; and

(d) interest income and interest expense relating to the amount designated as hedged.

Description	1 Jan 20X1 CU	31 Jan 20X1 CU	1 Feb 20X1 CU	28 Feb 20X1 CU	31 Mar 20X1 CU
Amount of asset hedged	**20,000,000**	**19,200,000**	**8,000,000**	**8,000,000**	**8,000,000**
(a) Changes in the separate balance sheet line item					
Brought forward:					
Balance to be amortised	Nil	Nil	Nil	22,755	11,377
Remaining balance	Nil	Nil	45,511	18,963	9,518
Less: Adjustment on sale of asset	Nil	Nil	(3,793)	Nil	Nil
Adjustment for change in fair value of the hedged asset	Nil	45,511	Nil	(9,445)	(9,518)
Amortisation	Nil	Nil	Nil	(11,378)	(11,377)
Carried forward:					
Balance to be amortised	**Nil**	**Nil**	**22,755**	**11,377**	**Nil**
Remaining balance	**Nil**	**45,511**	**18,963**	**9,518**	**Nil**

(b) The fair value of the derivative

	1 Jan 20X1	31 Jan 20X1	1 Feb 20X1	28 Feb 20X1	31 Mar 20X1
CU20,000,000	Nil	47,408	–	–	–
CU12,000,000	Nil	–	28,445	No longer designated as the hedging instrument.	
CU8,000,000	Nil	–	18,963	9,518	Nil
Total	**Nil**	**47,408**	**47,408**	**9,518**	**Nil**

Continued from previous page

(c) Profit or loss effect of the hedge

	1 Jan 20X1	31 Jan 20X1	1 Feb 20X1	28 Feb 20X1	31 Mar 20X1
Change in line item: asset	Nil	45,511	N/A	(9,445)	(9,518)
Change in derivative fair value	Nil	(47,408)	N/A	9,445	9,518
Net effect	**Nil**	**(1,897)**	**N/A**	**Nil**	**Nil**
Amortisation	**Nil**	**Nil**	**N/A**	**(11,378)**	**(11,377)**

In addition, there is a gain on sale of assets of CU14,607 at 1 February 20X1.

(d) Interest income and interest expense relating to the amount designated as hedged

Profit or loss recognised for the amount hedged	**1 Jan 20X1**	**31 Jan 20X1**	**1 Feb 20X1**	**28 Feb 20X1**	**31 Mar 20X1**
Interest income					
– on the asset	Nil	172,097	N/A	71,707	71,707
– on the swap	Nil	179,268	N/A	62,115	62,115
Interest expense					
– on the swap	Nil	(179,268)	N/A	(71,707)	(71,707)

Table of Concordance

The table shows how the contents of the superseded version of IAS 39 and the current version of IAS 39 correspond. Paragraphs are treated as corresponding if they broadly address the same matter even though the guidance may differ.

The table also shows how the disclosure requirements formerly included in IAS 39 have been incorporated into the current version of IAS 32.

Except where indicated, all references are to IAS 39.

Superseded paragraph	Current paragraph
Objective	1
1	2
2	AG1
3	AG2
4	AG3
5	AG4
6	5
7	6
8	9, IAS 32.11
9	IAS 32.14
10	9
11	IAS 32.11(d), IAS 32.21
12	IAS 32.11, IAS 32.21
13	AG9
14	6, 7
15	AG11
16	AG12
17	AG13
18	AG15
19	None
20	None
21	9
22	10
23	11
24	AG30

Superseded paragraph	Current paragraph
25	AG33
26	12
27	14
28	AG34
29	AG35
30	38, AG53
31	AG54
32	AG55
33	AG56
34	D.2.1[(a)]
35–56	15–37, AG36–AG52
57	39
58	AG57
59	AG59
60	AG61
61	40
62	AG62
63	41
64	AG63
65	None
66	43
67	AG64
68	45
69	46
70	None

Superseded paragraph	Current paragraph
71	None
72	AG66
73	46
74	AG79, AG84
75	AG68
76	AG6–AG8
77	AG67
78	AG83
79	AG16
80	AG17
81	AG18
82	AG19
83	9
84	AG20
85	AG21
86	AG22
87	AG23
88	AG24
89	AG25
90	51
91	53
92	54
93	47
94	AG83
95	AG80, AG81
96	None

Superseded paragraph	Current paragraph
97	AG74–AG76
98	AG69
99	AG71, AG72
100	AG74, AG79
101	AG72, AG74
102	AG81
103	55
104	None
105	None
106	57
107	50
108	56
109	58
110	59, 61
111	63, AG84 (part)
112	64
113	AG84
114	65
115	66
116	AG93
117	67
118	68
119	69, 70
120	None
121	71
122	72
123	AG97
124	AG94
125	AG95
126	AG96
127	78, 79
128	81

Superseded paragraph	Current paragraph
129	82
130	AG100
131	76
132	83
133	84, AG101
134	73
135	AG98
136	85
137	86
138	AG102
139	AG103
140	AG104
141	None
142	88
143	AG111
144	74
145	75
146	AG105
147	AG107, AG108
148	AG109
149	AG110
150	AG99
151	AG106–AG108
152	AG111
153	89
154	None
155	90
156	91
157	92
158	95
159	96
160	97, 98

Superseded paragraph	Current paragraph
161	97
162	100
163	101
164	102
165	None
166	None
167	IAS 32.61, IAS 32.92
168	IAS 32.93
169	IAS 32.56, IAS 32.58, IAS 32.59
170(a)	IAS 32.94(h)(ii)
170(b)	IAS 32.90
170(c)	IAS 32.94(h)
170(d)	IAS 32.94(a)
170(e)	IAS 32.94(g)
170(f)	IAS 32.94(i)
170(g)	IAS 32.94(b)
170(h)	IAS 32.94(c)
171	104
172	105

(a) This paragraph of the standard has been moved to the Implementation Guidence

CONTENTS

GUIDANCE ON IMPLEMENTING IAS 39 FINANCIAL INSTRUMENTS: RECOGNITION AND MEASUREMENT

SECTION F HEDGING

Guidance on Implementing IAS 39 Financial Instruments: Recognition and Measurement

This guidance accompanies, but is not part of, IAS 39.

Section A Scope

A.1 Practice of settling net: forward contract to purchase a commodity

Entity XYZ enters into a fixed price forward contract to purchase one million kilograms of copper in accordance with its expected usage requirements. The contract permits XYZ to take physical delivery of the copper at the end of twelve months or to pay or receive a net settlement in cash, based on the change in fair value of copper. Is the contract accounted for as a derivative?

While such a contract meets the definition of a derivative, it is not necessarily accounted for as a derivative. The contract is a derivative instrument because there is no initial net investment, the contract is based on the price of copper, and it is to be settled at a future date. However, if XYZ intends to settle the contract by taking delivery and has no history for similar contracts of settling net in cash or of taking delivery of the copper and selling it within a short period after delivery for the purpose of generating a profit from short-term fluctuations in price or dealer's margin, the contract is not accounted for as a derivative under IAS 39. Instead, it is accounted for as an executory contract.

A.2 Option to put a non–financial asset

Entity XYZ owns an office building. XYZ enters into a put option with an investor that permits XYZ to put the building to the investor for CU150 million. The current value of the building is CU175* million. The option expires in five years. The option, if exercised, may be settled through physical delivery or net cash, at XYZ's option. How do both XYZ and the investor account for the option?

XYZ's accounting depends on XYZ's intention and past practice for settlement. Although the contract meets the definition of a derivative, XYZ does not account for it as a derivative if XYZ intends to settle the contract by delivering the building if XYZ exercises its option and there is no past practice of settling net (IAS 39.5 and IAS 39.AG10).

The investor, however, cannot conclude that the option was entered into to meet the investor's expected purchase, sale or usage requirements because the investor does not have the ability to require delivery (IAS 39.7). In addition, the option may be settled net in cash. Therefore, the investor has to account for the contract as a derivative. Regardless of past practices, the investor's intention does not affect whether settlement is by delivery or in cash. The investor has written an option, and a written option in which the holder has a choice of physical settlement or net cash settlement can never satisfy the normal delivery requirement for the exemption from IAS 39 because the option writer does not have the ability to require delivery.

However, if the contract were a forward contract rather than an option, and if the contract required physical delivery and the reporting entity had no past practice of settling net in cash or of taking delivery of the building and selling it within a short period after delivery for the purpose of generating a profit from short-term fluctuations in price or dealer's margin, the contract would not be accounted for as a derivative.

* In this Guidance, monetary amounts are denominated in 'currency units' (CU).

Section B Definitions

B.1 Definition of a financial instrument: gold bullion

Is gold bullion a financial instrument (like cash) or is it a commodity?

It is a commodity. Although bullion is highly liquid, there is no contractual right to receive cash or another financial asset inherent in bullion.

B.2 Definition of a derivative: examples of derivatives and underlyings

What are examples of common derivative contracts and the identified underlying?

IAS 39 defines a derivative as follows:

A *derivative* is a financial instrument or other contract within the scope of this Standard with all three of the following characteristics:

(a) its value changes in response to the change in a specified interest rate, financial instrument price, commodity price, foreign exchange rate, index of prices or rates, credit rating or credit index, or other variable, provided in the case of a non-financial variable that the variable is not specific to a party to the contract (sometimes called the 'underlying');

(b) it requires no initial net investment or an initial net investment that is smaller than would be required for other types of contracts that would be expected to have a similar response to changes in market factors; and

(c) it is settled at a future date.

Type of contract	Main pricing–settlement variable (underlying variable)
Interest rate swap	Interest rates
Currency swap (foreign exchange swap)	Currency rates
Commodity swap	Commodity prices
Equity swap	Equity prices (equity of another entity)
Credit swap	Credit rating, credit index or credit price
Total return swap	Total fair value of the reference asset and interest rates
Purchased or written treasury bond option (call or put)	Interest rates
Purchased or written currency option (call or put)	Currency rates
Purchased or written commodity option (call or put)	Commodity prices
Purchased or written stock option (call or put)	Equity prices (equity of another entity)
Interest rate futures linked to government debt (treasury futures)	Interest rates

Continued from previous page

Type of contract	Main pricing–settlement variable (underlying variable)
Currency futures	Currency rates
Commodity futures	Commodity prices
Interest rate forward linked to government debt (treasury forward)	Interest rates
Currency forward	Currency rates
Commodity forward	Commodity prices
Equity forward	Equity prices (equity of another entity)

The above list provides examples of contracts that normally qualify as derivatives under IAS 39. The list is not exhaustive. Any contract that has an underlying may be a derivative. Moreover, even if an instrument meets the definition of a derivative contract, special provisions of IAS 39 may apply, for example, if it is a weather derivative (see IAS 39.AG1), a contract to buy or sell a non-financial item such as commodity (see IAS 39.5 and IAS 39.AG10) or a contract settled in an entity's own shares (see IAS 32.21–IAS 32.24). Therefore, an entity must evaluate the contract to determine whether the other characteristics of a derivative are present and whether special provisions apply.

B.3 Definition of a derivative: settlement at a future date, interest rate swap with net or gross settlement

For the purpose of determining whether an interest rate swap is a derivative financial instrument under IAS 39, does it make a difference whether the parties pay the interest payments to each other (gross settlement) or settle on a net basis?

No. The definition of a derivative does not depend on gross or net settlement.

To illustrate: Entity ABC enters into an interest rate swap with a counterparty (XYZ) that requires ABC to pay a fixed rate of 8 per cent and receive a variable amount based on three-month LIBOR, reset on a quarterly basis. The fixed and variable amounts are determined based on a CU100 million notional amount. ABC and XYZ do not exchange the notional amount. ABC pays or receives a net cash amount each quarter based on the difference between 8 per cent and three-month LIBOR. Alternatively, settlement may be on a gross basis.

The contract meets the definition of a derivative regardless of whether there is net or gross settlement because its value changes in response to changes in an underlying variable (LIBOR), there is no initial net investment, and settlements occur at future dates.

B.4 Definition of a derivative: prepaid interest rate swap (fixed rate payment obligation prepaid at inception or subsequently)

If a party prepays its obligation under a pay-fixed, receive-variable interest rate swap at inception, is the swap a derivative financial instrument?

Yes.

To illustrate: Entity S enters into a CU100 million notional amount five-year pay-fixed, receive-variable interest rate swap with Counterparty C. The interest rate of the variable part of the swap is reset on a quarterly basis to three-month LIBOR. The interest rate of the fixed part of the swap is 10 per cent per year. Entity S prepays its fixed obligation under the swap of CU50 million (CU100 million × 10 per cent × 5 years) at inception, discounted using market interest rates, while retaining the right to receive interest payments on the CU100 million reset quarterly based on three-month LIBOR over the life of the swap.

The initial net investment in the interest rate swap is significantly less than the notional amount on which the variable payments under the variable leg will be calculated. The contract requires an initial net investment that is smaller than would be required for other types of contracts that would be expected to have a similar response to changes in market factors, such as a variable rate bond. Therefore, the contract fulfils the 'no initial net investment or an initial net investment that is smaller than would be required for other types of contracts that would be expected to have a similar response to changes in market factors' provision of IAS 39. Even though Entity S has no future performance obligation, the ultimate settlement of the contract is at a future date and the value of the contract changes in response to changes in the LIBOR index. Accordingly, the contract is regarded as a derivative contract.

Would the answer change if the fixed rate payment obligation is prepaid subsequent to initial recognition?

If the fixed leg is prepaid during the term, that would be regarded as a termination of the old swap and an origination of a new instrument that is evaluated under IAS 39.

B.5 Definition of a derivative: prepaid pay–variable, receive–fixed interest rate swap

If a party prepays its obligation under a pay-variable, receive-fixed interest rate swap at inception of the contract or subsequently, is the swap a derivative financial instrument?

No. A prepaid pay-variable, receive-fixed interest rate swap is not a derivative if it is prepaid at inception and it is no longer a derivative if it is prepaid after inception because it provides a return on the prepaid (invested) amount comparable to the return on a debt instrument with fixed cash flows. The prepaid amount fails the 'no initial net investment or an initial net investment that is smaller than would be required for other types of contracts that would be expected to have a similar response to changes in market factors' criterion of a derivative.

To illustrate: Entity S enters into a CU100 million notional amount five-year pay-variable, receive-fixed interest rate swap with Counterparty C. The variable leg of the swap is reset on a quarterly basis to three-month LIBOR. The fixed interest payments under the swap are calculated as 10 per cent times the swap's notional amount, ie CU10 million per year.

Entity S prepays its obligation under the variable leg of the swap at inception at current market rates, while retaining the right to receive fixed interest payments of 10 per cent on CU100 million per year.

The cash inflows under the contract are equivalent to those of a financial instrument with a fixed annuity stream since Entity S knows it will receive CU10 million per year over the life of the swap. Therefore, all else being equal, the initial investment in the contract should equal that of other financial instruments that consist of fixed annuities. Thus, the initial net investment in the pay-variable, receive-fixed interest rate swap is equal to the investment required in a non-derivative contract that has a similar response to changes in market conditions. For this reason, the instrument fails the 'no initial net investment or an initial net investment that is smaller than would be required for other types of contracts that would be expected to have a similar response to changes in market factors' criterion of IAS 39. Therefore, the contract is not accounted for as a derivative under IAS 39. By discharging the obligation to pay variable interest rate payments, Entity S in effect provides a loan to Counterparty C.

B.6 Definition of a derivative: offsetting loans

Entity A makes a five-year fixed rate loan to Entity B, while B at the same time makes a five-year variable rate loan for the same amount to A. There are no transfers of principal at inception of the two loans, since A and B have a netting agreement. Is this a derivative under IAS 39?

Yes. This meets the definition of a derivative (that is to say, there is an underlying variable, no initial net investment or an initial net investment that is smaller than would be required for other types of contracts that would be expected to have a similar response to changes in market factors, and future settlement). The contractual effect of the loans is the equivalent of an interest rate swap arrangement with no initial net investment. Non-derivative transactions are aggregated and treated as a derivative when the transactions result, in substance, in a derivative. Indicators of this would include:

- they are entered into at the same time and in contemplation of one another
- they have the same counterparty
- they relate to the same risk
- there is no apparent economic need or substantive business purpose for structuring the transactions separately that could not also have been accomplished in a single transaction.

The same answer would apply if Entity A and Entity B did not have a netting agreement, because the definition of a derivative instrument in IAS 39.9 does not require net settlement.

B.7 Definition of a derivative: option not expected to be exercised

The definition of a derivative in IAS 39.9 requires that the instrument 'is settled at a future date'. Is this criterion met even if an option is expected not to be exercised, for example, because it is out of the money?

Yes. An option is settled upon exercise or at its maturity. Expiry at maturity is a form of settlement even though there is no additional exchange of consideration.

B.8 Definition of a derivative: foreign currency contract based on sales volume

Entity XYZ, whose functional currency is the US dollar, sells products in France denominated in euro. XYZ enters into a contract with an investment bank to convert euro to US dollars at a fixed exchange rate. The contract requires XYZ to remit euro based on its sales volume in France in exchange for US dollars at a fixed exchange rate of 6.00. Is that contract a derivative?

Yes. The contract has two underlying variables (the foreign exchange rate and the volume of sales), no initial net investment or an initial net investment that is smaller than would be required for other types of contracts that would be expected to have a similar response to changes in market factors, and a payment provision. IAS 39 does not exclude from its scope derivatives that are based on sales volume.

B.9 Definition of a derivative: prepaid forward

An entity enters into a forward contract to purchase shares of stock in one year at the forward price. It prepays at inception based on the current price of the shares. Is the forward contract a derivative?

No. The forward contract fails the 'no initial net investment or an initial net investment that is smaller than would be required for other types of contracts that would be expected to have a similar response to changes in market factors' test for a derivative.

To illustrate: Entity XYZ enters into a forward contract to purchase one million T ordinary shares in one year. The current market price of T is CU50 per share; the one-year forward price of T is CU55 per share. XYZ is required to prepay the forward contract at inception with a CU50 million payment. The initial investment in the forward contract of CU50 million is less than the notional amount applied to the underlying, one million shares at the forward price of CU55 per share, ie CU55 million. However, the initial net investment approximates the investment that would be required for other types of contracts that would be expected to have a similar response to changes in market factors because T's shares could be purchased at inception for the same price of CU50. Accordingly, the prepaid forward contract does not meet the initial net investment criterion of a derivative instrument.

B.10 Definition of a derivative: initial net investment

Many derivative instruments, such as futures contracts and exchange traded written options, require margin accounts. Is the margin account part of the initial net investment?

No. The margin account is not part of the initial net investment in a derivative instrument. Margin accounts are a form of collateral for the counterparty or clearing house and may take the form of cash, securities or other specified assets, typically liquid assets. Margin accounts are separate assets that are accounted for separately.

B.11 Definition of held for trading: portfolio with a recent actual pattern of short-term profit taking

The definition of a financial asset or financial liability held for trading states that 'a financial asset or financial liability is classified as held for trading if it is ... part of a portfolio of identified financial instruments that are managed together and for which there is evidence of a recent actual pattern of short-term profit taking'. What is a 'portfolio' for the purposes of applying this definition?

Although the term 'portfolio' is not explicitly defined in IAS 39, the context in which it is used suggests that a portfolio is a group of financial assets or financial liabilities that are managed as part of that group (IAS 39.9). If there is evidence of a recent actual pattern of short-term profit taking on financial instruments included in such a portfolio, those financial instruments qualify as held for trading even though an individual financial instrument may in fact be held for a longer period of time.

B.12 Definition of held for trading: balancing a portfolio

Entity A has an investment portfolio of debt and equity instruments. The documented portfolio management guidelines specify that the equity exposure of the portfolio should be limited to between 30 and 50 per cent of total portfolio value. The investment manager of the portfolio is authorised to balance the portfolio within the designated guidelines by buying and selling equity and debt instruments. Is Entity A permitted to classify the instruments as available for sale?

It depends on Entity A's intentions and past practice. If the portfolio manager is authorised to buy and sell instruments to balance the risks in a portfolio, but there is no intention to trade and there is no past practice of trading for short-term profit, the instruments can be classified as available for sale. If the portfolio manager actively buys and sells instruments to generate short-term profits, the financial instruments in the portfolio are classified as held for trading.

B.13 Definition of held–to–maturity financial assets: index–linked principal

Entity A purchases a five-year equity-index-linked note with an original issue price of CU10 at a market price of CU12 at the time of purchase. The note requires no interest payments before maturity. At maturity, the note requires payment of the original issue price of CU10 plus a supplemental redemption amount that depends on whether a specified share price index exceeds a predetermined level at the maturity date. If the share index does not exceed or is equal to the predetermined level, no supplemental redemption amount is paid. If the share index exceeds the predetermined level, the supplemental redemption amount equals the product of 1.15 and the difference between the level of the share index at maturity and the level of the share index when the note was issued divided by the level of the share index at the time of issue. Entity A has the positive intention and ability to hold the note to maturity. Can Entity A classify the note as a held-to-maturity investment?

Yes. The note can be classified as a held-to-maturity investment because it has a fixed payment of CU10 and fixed maturity and Entity A has the positive intention and ability to hold it to maturity (IAS 39.9). However, the equity index feature is a call option not closely related to the debt host, which must be separated as an embedded derivative under IAS 39.11. The purchase price of CU12 is allocated between the host debt instrument and the embedded derivative. For example, if the fair value of the embedded option at acquisition is CU4, the host debt instrument is measured at CU8 on initial recognition. In this case, the discount of CU2 that is implicit in the host bond (principal of CU10 minus the original carrying amount of CU8) is amortised to profit or loss over the term to maturity of the note using the effective interest method.

B.14 Definition of held–to–maturity financial assets: index-linked interest

Can a bond with a fixed payment at maturity and a fixed maturity date be classified as a held–to–maturity investment if the bond's interest payments are indexed to the price of a commodity or equity, and the entity has the positive intention and ability to hold the bond to maturity?

Yes. However, the commodity-indexed or equity-indexed interest payments result in an embedded derivative that is separated and accounted for as a derivative at fair value (IAS 39.11). IAS 39.12 is not applicable since it should be straightforward to separate the host debt investment (the fixed payment at maturity) from the embedded derivative (the index-linked interest payments).

B.15 Definition of held–to–maturity financial assets: sale following rating downgrade

Would a sale of a held–to–maturity investment following a downgrade of the issuer's credit rating by a rating agency raise a question about the entity's intention to hold other investments to maturity?

Not necessarily. A downgrade is likely to indicate a decline in the issuer's creditworthiness. IAS 39 specifies that a sale due to a significant deterioration in the issuer's creditworthiness could satisfy the condition in IAS 39 and therefore not raise a question about the entity's intention to hold other investments to maturity. However, the deterioration in creditworthiness must be significant judged by reference to the credit rating at initial recognition. Also, the rating downgrade must not have been reasonably anticipated when the entity classified the investment as held to maturity in order to meet the condition in IAS 39. A credit downgrade of a notch within a class or from one rating class to the immediately lower rating class could often be regarded as reasonably anticipated. If the rating downgrade in combination with other information provides evidence of impairment, the deterioration in creditworthiness often would be regarded as significant.

B.16 Definition of held–to–maturity financial assets: permitted sales

Would sales of held–to–maturity financial assets due to a change in management compromise the classification of other financial assets as held to maturity?

Yes. A change in management is not identified under IAS 39.AG22 as an instance where sales or transfers from held–to–maturity do not compromise the classification as held to maturity. Sales in response to such a change in management would, therefore, call into question the entity's intention to hold investments to maturity.

To illustrate: Entity X has a portfolio of financial assets that is classified as held to maturity. In the current period, at the direction of the board of directors, the senior management team has been replaced. The new management wishes to sell a portion of the held-to-maturity financial assets in order to carry out an expansion strategy designated and approved by the board. Although the previous management team had been in place since the entity's inception and Entity X had never before undergone a major restructuring, the sale nevertheless calls into question Entity X's intention to hold remaining held-to-maturity financial assets to maturity.

B.17 Definition of held-to-maturity investments: sales in response to entity-specific capital requirements

In some countries, regulators of banks or other industries may set *entity-specific* capital requirements that are based on an assessment of the risk in that particular entity. IAS 39.AG22(e) indicates that an entity that sells held-to-maturity investments in response to an unanticipated significant increase by the regulator in the industry's capital requirements may do so under IAS 39 without necessarily raising a question about its intention to hold other investments to maturity. Would sales of held-to-maturity investments that are due to a significant increase in *entity-specific* capital requirements imposed by regulators (ie capital requirements applicable to a particular entity, but not to the industry) raise such doubt?

Yes, such sales 'taint' the entity's intention to hold other financial assets as held to maturity unless it can be demonstrated that the sales fulfil the condition in IAS 39.9 in that they result from an increase in capital requirements, which is an isolated event that is beyond the entity's control, is non-recurring and could not have been reasonably anticipated by the entity.

B.18 Definition of held–to–maturity financial assets: pledged collateral, repurchase agreements (repos) and securities lending agreements

An entity cannot have a demonstrated ability to hold to maturity an investment if it is subject to a constraint that could frustrate its intention to hold the financial asset to maturity. Does this mean that a debt instrument that has been pledged as collateral, or transferred to another party under a repo or securities lending transaction, and continues to be recognised cannot be classified as a held-to-maturity investment?

No. An entity's intention and ability to hold debt instruments to maturity is not necessarily constrained if those instruments have been pledged as collateral or are subject to a repurchase agreement or securities lending agreement. However, an entity does not have the positive intention and ability to hold the debt instruments until maturity if it does not expect to be able to maintain or recover access to the instruments.

B.19 Definition of held–to–maturity financial assets: 'tainting'

In response to unsolicited tender offers, Entity A sells a significant amount of financial assets classified as held to maturity on economically favourable terms. Entity A does not classify any financial assets acquired after the date of the sale as held to maturity. However, it does not reclassify the remaining held–to–maturity investments since it maintains that it still intends to hold them to maturity. Is Entity A in compliance with IAS 39?

No. Whenever a sale or transfer of more than an insignificant amount of financial assets classified as held to maturity (HTM) results in the conditions in IAS 39.9 and IAS 39.AG22 not being satisfied, no instruments should be classified in that category. Accordingly, any remaining HTM assets are reclassified as available–for–sale financial assets. The reclassification is recorded in the reporting period in which the sales or transfers occurred and is accounted for as a change in classification under IAS 39.51. IAS 39.9 makes it clear that at least two full financial years must pass before an entity can again classify financial assets as HTM.

B.20 Definition of held–to–maturity investments: sub–categorisation for the purpose of applying the 'tainting' rule

Can an entity apply the conditions for held–to–maturity classification in IAS 39.9 separately to different categories of held–to–maturity financial assets, such as debt instruments denominated in US dollars and debt instruments denominated in euro?

No. The 'tainting rule' in IAS 39.9 is clear. If an entity has sold or reclassified more than an insignificant amount of held–to–maturity investments, it cannot classify any financial assets as held–to–maturity financial assets.

B.21 Definition of held–to–maturity investments: application of the 'tainting' rule on consolidation

Can an entity apply the conditions in IAS 39.9 separately to held–to–maturity financial assets held by different entities in a consolidated group, for example, if those group entities are in different countries with different legal or economic environments?

No. If an entity has sold or reclassified more than an insignificant amount of investments classified as held–to–maturity in the consolidated financial statements, it cannot classify any financial assets as held–to–maturity financial assets in the consolidated financial statements unless the conditions in IAS 39.9 are met.

B.22 Definition of loans and receivables: equity instrument

Can an equity instrument, such as a preference share, with fixed or determinable payments be classified within loans and receivables by the holder?

Yes. If a non–derivative equity instrument would be recorded as a liability by the issuer, and it has fixed or determinable payments and is not quoted in an active market, it can be classified within loans and receivables by the holder, provided the definition is otherwise met. IAS 32.15–IAS 32.22 provide guidance about the classification of a financial instrument as a liability or as equity from the perspective of the issuer of a financial instrument. If an instrument meets the definition of an equity instrument under IAS 32, it cannot be classified within loans and receivables by the holder.

B.23 Definition of loans and receivables: banks' deposits in other banks

Banks make term deposits with a central bank or other banks. Sometimes, the proof of deposit is negotiable, sometimes not. Even if negotiable, the depositor bank may or may not intend to sell it. Would such a deposit fall within loans and receivables under IAS 39.9?

Such a deposit meets the definition of loans and receivables, whether or not the proof of deposit is negotiable, unless the depositor bank intends to sell the instrument immediately or in the near term, in which case the deposit is classified as a financial asset held for trading.

B.24 Definition of amortised cost: perpetual debt instruments with fixed or market-based variable rate

Sometimes entities purchase or issue debt instruments that are required to be measured at amortised cost and in respect of which the issuer has no obligation to repay the principal amount. Interest may be paid either at a fixed rate or at a variable rate. Would the difference between the initial amount paid or received and zero ('the maturity amount') be amortised immediately on initial recognition for the purpose of determining amortised cost if the rate of interest is fixed or specified as a market-based variable rate?

No. Since there are no repayments of principal, there is no amortisation of the difference between the initial amount and the maturity amount if the rate of interest is fixed or specified as a market-based variable rate. Because interest payments are fixed or market-based and will be paid in perpetuity, the amortised cost (the present value of the stream of future cash payments discounted at the effective interest rate) equals the principal amount in each period (IAS 39.9).

B.25 Definition of amortised cost: perpetual debt instruments with decreasing interest rate

If the stated rate of interest on a perpetual debt instrument decreases over time, would amortised cost equal the principal amount in each period?

No. From an economic perspective, some or all of the interest payments are repayments of the principal amount. For example, the interest rate may be stated as 16 per cent for the first ten years and as zero per cent in subsequent periods. In that case, the initial amount is amortised to zero over the first ten years using the effective interest method, since a portion of the interest payments represents repayments of the principal amount. The amortised cost is zero after year 10 because the present value of the stream of future cash payments in subsequent periods is zero (there are no further cash payments of either principal or interest in subsequent periods).

B.26 Example of calculating amortised cost: financial asset

Financial assets that are excluded from fair valuation and have a fixed maturity should be measured at amortised cost. How is amortised cost calculated?

Under IAS 39, amortised cost is calculated using the effective interest method. The effective interest rate inherent in a financial instrument is the rate that exactly discounts the estimated cash flows associated with the financial instrument through the expected life of the instrument or, where appropriate, a shorter period to the net carrying amount at initial recognition. The computation includes all fees and points paid or received that are an integral part of the effective interest rate, directly attributable transaction costs and all other premiums or discounts.

The following example illustrates how amortised cost is calculated using the effective interest method. Entity A purchases a debt instrument with five years remaining to maturity for its fair value of CU1,000 (including transaction costs). The instrument has a principal amount of CU1,250 and carries fixed interest of 4.7 per cent that is paid annually (CU1,250 × 4.7 per cent = CU59 per year). The contract also specifies that the borrower has an option to prepay the instrument and that no penalty will be charged for prepayment. At inception, the entity expects the borrower not to prepay.

It can be shown that in order to allocate interest receipts and the initial discount over the term of the debt instrument at a constant rate on the carrying amount, they must be accrued at the rate of 10 per cent annually. The table below provides information about the amortised cost, interest income and cash flows of the debt instrument in each reporting period.

Year	(a) Amortised cost at the beginning of the year	(b = a × 10%) Interest income	(c) Cash flows	(d = a + b – c) Amortised cost at the end of the year
20X0	1,000	100	59	1,041
20X1	1,041	104	59	1,086
20X2	1,086	109	59	1,136
20X3	1,136	113	59	1,190
20X4	1,190	119	1,250+59	–

On the first day of 20X2 the entity revises its estimate of cash flows. It now expects that 50 per cent of the principal will be prepaid at the end of 20X2 and the remaining 50 per cent at the end of 20X4. In accordance with IAS 39.AG8, the opening balance of the debt instrument in 20X2 is adjusted. The adjusted amount is calculated by discounting the amount the entity expects to receive in 20X2 and subsequent years using the original effective interest rate (10 per cent). This results in the new opening balance in 20X2 of CU1,138. The adjustment of CU52 (CU1,138 – CU1,086) is recorded in profit or loss in 20X2. The table below provides information about the amortised cost, interest income and cash flows as they would be adjusted taking into account the change in estimate.

Year	(a) Amortised cost at the beginning of the year	(b = a × 10%) Interest income	(c) Cash flows	(d = a + b – c) Amortised cost at the end of the year
20X0	1,000	100	59	1,041
20X1	1,041	104	59	1,086
20X2	1,086+52	114	625+59	568
20X3	568	57	30	595
20X4	595	60	625+30	–

If the debt instrument becomes impaired, say, at the end of 20X3, the impairment loss is calculated as the difference between the carrying amount (CU595) and the present value of estimated future cash flows discounted at the original effective interest rate (10 per cent).

B.27 Example of calculating amortised cost: debt instruments with stepped interest payments

Sometimes entities purchase or issue debt instruments with a predetermined rate of interest that increases or decreases progressively ('stepped interest') over the term of the debt instrument. If a debt instrument with stepped interest and no embedded derivative is issued at CU1,250 and has a maturity amount of CU1,250, would the amortised cost equal CU1,250 in each reporting period over the term of the debt instrument?

No. Although there is no difference between the initial amount and maturity amount, an entity uses the effective interest method to allocate interest payments over the term of the debt instrument to achieve a constant rate on the carrying amount (IAS 39.9).

The following example illustrates how amortised cost is calculated using the effective interest method for an instrument with a predetermined rate of interest that increases or decreases over the term of the debt instrument ('stepped interest').

On 1 January 2000, Entity A issues a debt instrument for a price of CU1,250. The principal amount is CU1,250 and the debt instrument is repayable on 31 December 2004. The rate of interest is specified in the debt agreement as a percentage of the principal amount as follows: 6.0 per cent in 2000 (CU75), 8.0 per cent in 2001 (CU100), 10.0 per cent in 2002 (CU125), 12.0 per cent in 2003 (CU150), and 16.4 per cent in 2004 (CU205). In this case, the interest rate that exactly discounts the stream of future cash payments through maturity is 10 per cent. Therefore, cash interest payments are reallocated over the term of the debt instrument for the purposes of determining amortised cost in each period. In each period, the amortised cost at the beginning of the period is multiplied by the effective interest rate of 10 per cent and added to the amortised cost. Any cash payments in the period are deducted from the resulting number. Accordingly, the amortised cost in each period is as follows:

Year	(a) Amortised cost at the beginning of the year	(b = a × 10%) Interest income	(c) Cash flows	(d = a + b – c) Amortised cost at the end of the year
2000	1,250	125	75	1,300
2001	1,300	130	100	1,330
2002	1,330	133	125	1,338
2003	1,338	134	150	1,322
2004	1,322	133	1,250+205	–

B.28 Regular way contracts: no established market

Can a contract to purchase a financial asset be a regular way contract if there is no established market for trading such a contract?

Yes. IAS 39.9 refers to terms that require delivery of the asset within the time frame established generally by regulation or convention in the marketplace concerned. Marketplace, as that term is used in IAS 39.9, is not limited to a formal stock exchange or organised over–the–counter market. Rather, it means the environment in which the financial asset is customarily exchanged. An acceptable time frame would be the period reasonably and customarily required for the parties to complete the transaction and prepare and execute closing documents.

For example, a market for private issue financial instruments can be a marketplace.

B.29 Regular way contracts: forward contract

Entity ABC enters into a forward contract to purchase one million of M's ordinary shares in two months for CU10 per share. The contract is with an individual and is not an exchange-traded contract. The contract requires ABC to take physical delivery of the shares and pay the counterparty CU10 million in cash. M's shares trade in an active public market at an average of 100,000 shares a day. Regular way delivery is three days. Is the forward contract regarded as a regular way contract?

No. The contract must be accounted for as a derivative because it is not settled in the way established by regulation or convention in the marketplace concerned.

B.30 Regular way contracts: which customary settlement provisions apply?

If an entity's financial instruments trade in more than one active market, and the settlement provisions differ in the various active markets, which provisions apply in assessing whether a contract to purchase those financial instruments is a regular way contract?

The provisions that apply are those in the market in which the purchase actually takes place.

To illustrate: Entity XYZ purchases one million shares of Entity ABC on a US stock exchange, for example, through a broker. The settlement date of the contract is six business days later. Trades for equity shares on US exchanges customarily settle in three business days. Because the trade settles in six business days, it does not meet the exemption as a regular way trade.

However, if XYZ did the same transaction on a foreign exchange that has a customary settlement period of six business days, the contract would meet the exemption for a regular way trade.

B.31 Regular way contracts: share purchase by call option

Entity A purchases a call option in a public market permitting it to purchase 100 shares of Entity XYZ at any time over the next three months at a price of CU100 per share. If Entity A exercises its option, it has 14 days to settle the transaction according to regulation or convention in the options market. XYZ shares are traded in an active public market that requires three-day settlement. Is the purchase of shares by exercising the option a regular way purchase of shares?

Yes. The settlement of an option is governed by regulation or convention in the marketplace for options and, therefore, upon exercise of the option it is no longer accounted for as a derivative because settlement by delivery of the shares within 14 days is a regular way transaction.

B.32 Recognition and derecognition of financial liabilities using trade date or settlement date accounting

IAS 39 has special rules about recognition and derecognition of financial assets using trade date or settlement date accounting. Do these rules apply to transactions in financial instruments that are classified as financial liabilities, such as transactions in deposit liabilities and trading liabilities?

No. IAS 39 does not contain any specific requirements about trade date accounting and settlement date accounting in the case of transactions in financial instruments that are classified as financial liabilities. Therefore, the general recognition and derecognition requirements in IAS 39.14 and IAS 39.39 apply. IAS 39.14 states that financial liabilities are recognised on the date the entity 'becomes a party to the contractual provisions of the instrument'. Such contracts generally are not recognised unless one of the parties has performed or the contract is a derivative contract not exempted from the scope of IAS 39. IAS 39.39 specifies that financial liabilities are derecognised only when they are extinguished, ie when the obligation specified in the contract is discharged or cancelled or expires.

Section C Embedded derivatives

C.1 Embedded derivatives: separation of host debt instrument

If an embedded non-option derivative is required to be separated from a host debt instrument, how are the terms of the host debt instrument and the embedded derivative identified? For example, would the host debt instrument be a fixed rate instrument, a variable rate instrument or a zero coupon instrument?

The terms of the host debt instrument reflect the stated or implied substantive terms of the hybrid instrument. In the absence of implied or stated terms, the entity makes its own judgement of the terms. However, an entity may not identify a component that is not specified or may not establish terms of the host debt instrument in a manner that would result in the separation of an embedded derivative that is not already clearly present in the hybrid instrument, that is to say, it cannot create a cash flow that does not exist. For example, if a five-year debt instrument has fixed interest payments of CU40,000 annually and a principal payment at maturity of CU1,000,000 multiplied by the change in an equity price index, it would be inappropriate to identify a floating rate host contract and an embedded equity swap that has an offsetting floating rate leg in lieu of identifying a fixed rate host. In that example, the host contract is a fixed rate debt instrument that pays CU40,000 annually because there are no floating interest rate cash flows in the hybrid instrument.

In addition, the terms of an embedded non-option derivative, such as a forward or swap, must be determined so as to result in the embedded derivative having a fair value of zero at the inception of the hybrid instrument. If it were permitted to separate embedded non-option derivatives on other terms, a single hybrid instrument could be decomposed into an infinite variety of combinations of host debt instruments and embedded derivatives, for example, by separating embedded derivatives with terms that create leverage, asymmetry or some other risk exposure not already present in the hybrid instrument. Therefore, it is inappropriate to separate an embedded non-option derivative on terms that result in a fair value other than zero at the inception of the hybrid instrument. The determination of the terms of the embedded derivative is based on the conditions existing when the financial instrument was issued.

C.2 Embedded derivatives: separation of embedded option

The response to Question C.1 states that the terms of an embedded non-option derivative should be determined so as to result in the embedded derivative having a fair value of zero at the initial recognition of the hybrid instrument. When an embedded option-based derivative is separated, must the terms of the embedded option be determined so as to result in the embedded derivative having either a fair value of zero or an intrinsic value of zero (that is to say, be at the money) at the inception of the hybrid instrument?

No. The economic behaviour of a hybrid instrument with an option-based embedded derivative depends critically on the strike price (or strike rate) specified for the option feature in the hybrid instrument, as discussed below. Therefore, the separation of an option-based embedded derivative (including any embedded put, call, cap, floor, caption, floortion or swaption feature in a hybrid instrument) should be based on the stated terms of the option feature documented in the hybrid instrument. As a result, the embedded derivative would not necessarily have a fair value or intrinsic value equal to zero at the initial recognition of the hybrid instrument.

If an entity were required to identify the terms of an embedded option-based derivative so as to achieve a fair value of the embedded derivative of zero, the strike price (or strike rate) generally would have to be determined so as to result in the option being infinitely out of the money. This would imply a zero probability of the option feature being exercised. However, since the probability of the option feature in a hybrid instrument being exercised generally is not zero, it would be inconsistent with the likely economic behaviour of the hybrid instrument to assume an initial fair value of zero. Similarly, if an entity were required to identify the terms of an embedded option-based derivative so as to achieve an intrinsic value of zero for the embedded derivative, the strike price (or strike rate) would have to be assumed to equal the price (or rate) of the underlying variable at the initial recognition of the hybrid instrument. In this case, the fair value of the option would consist only of time value. However, such an assumption would not be consistent with the likely economic behaviour of the hybrid instrument, including the probability of the option feature being exercised, unless the agreed strike price was indeed equal to the price (or rate) of the underlying variable at the initial recognition of the hybrid instrument.

The economic nature of an option-based embedded derivative is fundamentally different from a forward-based embedded derivative (including forwards and swaps), because the terms of a forward are such that a payment based on the difference between the price of the underlying and the forward price will occur at a specified date, while the terms of an option are such that a payment based on the difference between the price of the underlying and the strike price of the option may or may not occur depending on the relationship between the agreed strike price and the price of the underlying at a specified date or dates in the future. Adjusting the strike price of an option-based embedded derivative, therefore, alters the nature of the hybrid instrument. On the other hand, if the terms of a non-option embedded derivative in a host debt instrument were determined so as to result in a fair value of any amount other than zero at the inception of the hybrid instrument, that amount would essentially represent a borrowing or lending. Accordingly, as discussed in the answer to Question C.1, it is not appropriate to separate a non-option embedded derivative in a host debt instrument on terms that result in a fair value other than zero at the initial recognition of the hybrid instrument.

C.3 Embedded derivatives: accounting for a convertible bond

What is the accounting treatment of an investment in a bond (financial asset) that is convertible into shares of the issuing entity or another entity before maturity?

An investment in a convertible bond that is convertible before maturity generally cannot be classified as a held-to-maturity investment because that would be inconsistent with paying for the conversion feature—the right to convert into equity shares before maturity.

An investment in a convertible bond can be classified as an available-for-sale financial asset provided it is not purchased for trading purposes. The equity conversion option is an embedded derivative.

If the bond is classified as available for sale (ie fair value changes recognised directly in equity until the bond is sold), the equity conversion option (the embedded derivative) is separated. The amount paid for the bond is split between the debt instrument without the conversion option and the equity conversion option. Changes in the fair value of the equity conversion option are recognised in profit or loss unless the option is part of a cash flow hedging relationship.

If the convertible bond is measured at fair value with changes in fair value recognised in profit or loss, separating the embedded derivative from the host bond is not permitted.

C.4 Embedded derivatives: equity kicker

In some instances, venture capital entities providing subordinated loans agree that if and when the borrower lists its shares on a stock exchange, the venture capital entity is entitled to receive shares of the borrowing entity free of charge or at a very low price (an 'equity kicker') in addition to interest and repayment of principal. As a result of the equity kicker feature, the interest on the subordinated loan is lower than it would otherwise be. Assuming that the subordinated loan is not measured at fair value with changes in fair value recognised in profit or loss (IAS 39.11(c)), does the equity kicker feature meet the definition of an embedded derivative even though it is contingent upon the future listing of the borrower?

Yes. The economic characteristics and risks of an equity return are not closely related to the economic characteristics and risks of a host debt instrument (IAS 39.11(a)). The equity kicker meets the definition of a derivative because it has a value that changes in response to the change in the price of the shares of the borrower, it requires no initial net investment or an initial net investment that is smaller than would be required for other types of contracts that would be expected to have a similar response to changes in market factors, and it is settled at a future date (IAS 39.11(b) and IAS 39.9(a)). The equity kicker feature meets the definition of a derivative even though the right to receive shares is contingent upon the future listing of the borrower. IAS 39.AG9 states that a derivative could require a payment as a result of some future event that is unrelated to a notional amount. An equity kicker feature is similar to such a derivative except that it does not give a right to a fixed payment, but an option right, if the future event occurs.

C.5 Embedded derivatives: debt or equity host contract

Entity A purchases a five-year 'debt' instrument issued by Entity B with a principal amount of CU1 million that is indexed to the share price of Entity C. At maturity, Entity A will receive from Entity B the principal amount plus or minus the change in the fair value of 10,000 shares of Entity C. The current share price is CU110. No separate interest payments are made by Entity B. The purchase price is CU1 million. Entity A classifies the debt instrument as available for sale. Entity A concludes that the instrument is a hybrid instrument with an embedded derivative because of the equity-indexed principal. For the purposes of separating an embedded derivative, is the host contract an equity instrument or a debt instrument?

The host contract is a debt instrument because the hybrid instrument has a stated maturity, ie it does not meet the definition of an equity instrument (IAS 32.11 and IAS 32.16). It is accounted for as a zero coupon debt instrument. Thus, in accounting for the host instrument, Entity A imputes interest on CU1 million over five years using the applicable market interest rate at initial recognition. The embedded non-option derivative is separated so as to have an initial fair value of zero (see Question C.1).

C.6 Embedded derivatives: synthetic instruments

Entity A acquires a five-year floating rate debt instrument issued by Entity B. At the same time, it enters into a five-year pay-variable, receive-fixed interest rate swap with Entity C. Entity A regards the combination of the debt instrument and swap as a synthetic fixed rate instrument and classifies the instrument as a held-to-maturity investment, since it has the positive intention and ability to hold it to maturity. Entity A contends that separate accounting for the swap is inappropriate since IAS 39.AG33(a) requires an embedded derivative to be classified together with its host instrument if the derivative is linked to an interest rate that can change the amount of interest that would otherwise be paid or received on the host debt contract. Is the entity's analysis correct?

No. Embedded derivative instruments are terms and conditions that are included in non-derivative host contracts. It is generally inappropriate to treat two or more separate financial instruments as a single combined instrument ('synthetic instrument' accounting) for the purpose of applying IAS 39. Each of the financial instruments has its own terms and conditions and each may be transferred or settled separately. Therefore, the debt instrument and the swap are classified separately. The transactions described here differ from the transactions discussed in Question B.6, which had no substance apart from the resulting interest rate swap.

C.7 Embedded derivatives: purchases and sales contracts in foreign currency instruments

A supply contract provides for payment in a currency other than (a) the functional currency of either party to the contract, (b) the currency in which the product is routinely denominated in commercial transactions around the world and (c) the currency that is commonly used in contracts to purchase or sell non-financial items in the economic environment in which the transaction takes place. Is there an embedded derivative that should be separated under IAS 39?

Yes. To illustrate: a Norwegian entity agrees to sell oil to an entity in France. The oil contract is denominated in Swiss francs, although oil contracts are routinely denominated in US dollars in commercial transactions around the world, and Norwegian krone are commonly used in contracts to purchase or sell non-financial items in Norway. Neither entity carries out any significant activities in Swiss francs. In this case, the Norwegian entity regards the supply contract as a host contract with an embedded foreign currency forward to purchase Swiss francs. The French entity regards the supply contact as a host contract with an embedded foreign currency forward to sell Swiss francs. Each entity includes fair value changes on the currency forward in profit or loss unless the reporting entity designates it as a cash flow hedging instrument, if appropriate.

C.8 Embedded foreign currency derivatives: unrelated foreign currency provision

Entity A, which measures items in its financial statements on the basis of the euro (its functional currency), enters into a contract with Entity B, which has the Norwegian krone as its functional currency, to purchase oil in six months for 1,000 US dollars. The host oil contract is not within the scope of IAS 39 because it was entered into and continues to be for the purpose of delivery of a non-financial item in accordance with the entity's expected purchase, sale or usage requirements (IAS 39.5 and IAS 39.AG10). The oil contract includes a leveraged foreign exchange provision that states that the parties, in addition to the provision of, and payment for, oil will exchange an amount equal to the fluctuation in the exchange rate of the US dollar and Norwegian krone applied to a notional amount of 100,000 US dollars. Under IAS 39.11, is that embedded derivative (the leveraged foreign exchange provision) regarded as closely related to the host oil contract?

No, that leveraged foreign exchange provision is separated from the host oil contract because it is not closely related to the host oil contract (IAS 39.AG33(d)).

The payment provision under the host oil contract of 1,000 US dollars can be viewed as a foreign currency derivative because the US dollar is neither Entity A's nor Entity B's functional currency. This foreign currency derivative would not be separated because it follows from IAS 39.AG33(d) that a crude oil contract that requires payment in US dollars is not regarded as a host contract with a foreign currency derivative.

The leveraged foreign exchange provision that states that the parties will exchange an amount equal to the fluctuation in the exchange rate of the US dollar and Norwegian krone applied to a notional amount of 100,000 US dollars is in addition to the required payment for the oil transaction. It is unrelated to the host oil contract and therefore separated from the host oil contract and accounted for as an embedded derivative under IAS 39.11.

C.9 Embedded foreign currency derivatives: currency of international commerce

IAS 39.AG33(d) refers to the currency in which the price of the related goods or services is routinely denominated in commercial transactions around the world. Could it be a currency that is used for a certain product or service in commercial transactions within the local area of one of the substantial parties to the contract?

No. The currency in which the price of the related goods or services is routinely denominated in commercial transactions around the world is only a currency that is used for similar transactions all around the world, not just in one local area. For example, if cross-border transactions in natural gas in North America are routinely denominated in US dollars and such transactions are routinely denominated in euro in Europe, neither the US dollar nor the euro is a currency in which the goods or services is routinely denominated in commercial transactions around the world.

C.10 Embedded derivatives: holder permitted, but not required, to settle without recovering substantially all of its recognised investment

If the terms of a combined instrument permit, but do not require, the holder to settle the combined instrument in a manner that causes it not to recover substantially all of its recognised investment and the issuer does not have such a right (for example, a puttable debt instrument), does the contract satisfy the condition in IAS 39.AG33(a) that the holder would not recover substantially all of its recognised investment?

No. The condition that 'the holder would not recover substantially all of its recognised investment' is not satisfied if the terms of the combined instrument permit, but do not require, the investor to settle the combined instrument in a manner that causes it not to recover substantially all of its recognised investment and the issuer has no such right. Accordingly, an interest-bearing host contract with an embedded interest rate derivative with such terms is regarded as closely related to the host contract. The condition that 'the holder would not recover substantially all of its recognised investment' applies to situations in which the holder can be forced to accept settlement at an amount that causes the holder not to recover substantially all of its recognised investment.

C.11 Embedded derivatives: reliable determination of fair value

If an embedded derivative that is required to be separated cannot be reliably measured because it will be settled by an unquoted equity instrument whose fair value cannot be reliably measured, is the embedded derivative measured at cost?

No. In this case, the entire combined contract is treated as a financial instrument held for trading (IAS 39.12). If the fair value of the combined instrument can be reliably measured, the combined contract is measured at fair value. The entity might conclude, however, that the equity component of the combined instrument may be sufficiently significant to preclude it from obtaining a reliable estimate of the entire instrument. In that case, the combined instrument is measured at cost less impairment.

Section D Recognition and derecognition

D.1 Initial recognition

D.1.1 Recognition: cash collateral

Entity B transfers cash to Entity A as collateral for another transaction with Entity A (for example, a securities borrowing transaction). The cash is not legally segregated from Entity A's assets. Should Entity A recognise the cash collateral it has received as an asset?

Yes. The ultimate realisation of a financial asset is its conversion into cash and, therefore, no further transformation is required before the economic benefits of the cash transferred by Entity B can be realised by Entity A. Therefore, Entity A recognises the cash as an asset and a payable to Entity B while Entity B derecognises the cash and recognises a receivable from Entity A.

D.2 Regular way purchase or sale of a financial asset

D.2.1 Trade date vs settlement date: amounts to be recorded for a purchase

How are the trade date and settlement date accounting principles in the Standard applied to a purchase of a financial asset?

The following example illustrates the application of the trade date and settlement date accounting principles in the Standard for a purchase of a financial asset. On 29 December 20X1, an entity commits itself to purchase a financial asset for CU1,000, which is its fair value on commitment (trade) date. Transaction costs are immaterial. On 31 December 20X1 (financial year-end) and on 4 January 20X2 (settlement date) the fair value of the asset is CU1,002 and CU1,003, respectively. The amounts to be recorded for the asset will depend on how it is classified and whether trade date or settlement date accounting is used, as shown in the two tables below.

Settlement date accounting			
Balances	**Held–to–maturity investments carried at amortised cost**	**Available–for–sale assets remeasured to fair value with changes in equity**	**Assets at fair value through profit or loss remeasured to fair value with changes in profit or loss**
29 December 20X1			
Financial asset	–	–	–
Financial liability	–	–	–
31 December 20X1			
Receivable	–	2	2
Financial asset	–	–	–
Financial liability	–	–	–
Equity (fair value adjustment)	–	(2)	–
Retained earnings (through profit or loss)	–	–	(2)
4 January 20X2			
Receivable	–	–	–
Financial asset	1,000	1,003	1,003
Financial liability	–	–	–
Equity (fair value adjustment)	–	(3)	–
Retained earnings (through profit or loss)	–	–	(3)

Trade date accounting			
Balances	**Held–to–maturity investments carried at amortised cost**	**Available–for–sale assets remeasured to fair value with changes in equity**	**Assets at fair value through profit or loss remeasured to fair value with changes in profit or loss**
29 December 20X1			
Financial asset	1,000	1,000	1,000
Financial liability	(1,000)	(1,000)	(1,000)
31 December 20X1			
Receivable	–	–	–
Financial asset	1,000	1,002	1,002
Financial liability	(1,000)	(1,000)	(1,000)
Equity (fair value adjustment)	–	(2)	–
Retained earnings (through profit or loss)	–	–	(2)
4 January 20X2			
Receivable	–	–	–
Financial asset	1,000	1,003	1,003
Financial liability	–	–	–
Equity (fair value adjustment)	–	(3)	–
Retained earnings (through profit or loss)	–	–	(3)

D.2.2 Trade date vs settlement date: amounts to be recorded for a sale

How are the trade date and settlement date accounting principles in the Standard applied to a sale of a financial asset?

The following example illustrates the application of the trade date and settlement date accounting principles in the Standard for a sale of a financial asset. On 29 December 20X2 (trade date) an entity enters into a contract to sell a financial asset for its current fair value of CU1,010. The asset was acquired one year earlier for CU1,000 and its amortised cost is CU1,000. On 31 December 20X2 (financial year-end), the fair value of the asset is CU1,012. On 4 January 20X3 (settlement date), the fair value is CU1,013. The amounts to be recorded will depend on how the asset is classified and whether trade date or settlement date accounting is used as shown in the two tables below (any interest that might have accrued on the asset is disregarded).

A change in the fair value of a financial asset that is sold on a regular way basis is not recorded in the financial statements between trade date and settlement date even if the entity applies settlement date accounting because the seller's right to changes in the fair value ceases on the trade date.

Settlement date accounting			
Balances	**Held–to–maturity investments carried at amortised cost**	**Available–for–sale assets remeasured to fair value with changes in equity**	**Assets at fair value through profit or loss remeasured to fair value with changes in profit or loss**
29 December 20X2			
Receivable	–	–	–
Financial asset	1,000	1,010	1,010
Equity (fair value adjustment)	–	10	–
Retained earnings (through profit or loss)	–	–	10
31 December 20X2			
Receivable	–	–	–
Financial asset	1,000	1,010	1,010
Equity (fair value adjustment)	–	10	–
Retained earnings (through profit or loss)	–	–	10
4 January 20X3			
Equity (fair value adjustment)	–	–	–
Retained earnings (through profit or loss)	10	10	10

Trade date accounting			
Balances	**Held–to–maturity investments carried at amortised cost**	**Available–for–sale assets remeasured to fair value with changes in equity**	**Assets at fair value through profit or loss remeasured to fair value with changes in profit or loss**
29 December 20X2			
Receivable	1,010	1,010	1,010
Financial asset	–	–	–
Equity (fair value adjustment)	–	–	–
Retained earnings (through profit or loss)	10	10	10
31 December 20X2			
Receivable	1,010	1,010	1,010
Financial asset	–	–	–
Equity (fair value adjustment)	–	–	–
Retained earnings (through profit or loss)	10	10	10
4 January 20X3			
Equity (fair value adjustment)	–	–	–
Retained earnings (through profit or loss)	10	10	10

D.2.3 Settlement date accounting: exchange of non–cash financial assets

If an entity recognises sales of financial assets using settlement date accounting, would a change in the fair value of a financial asset to be received in exchange for the non-cash financial asset that is sold be recognised in accordance with IAS 39.57?

It depends. Any change in the fair value of the financial asset to be received would be accounted for under IAS 39.57 if the entity applies settlement date accounting for that category of financial assets. However, if the entity classifies the financial asset to be received in a category for which it applies trade date accounting, the asset to be received is recognised on the trade date as described in IAS 39.AG55. In that case, the entity recognises a liability of an amount equal to the carrying amount of the financial asset to be delivered on settlement date.

To illustrate: on 29 December 20X2 (trade date) Entity A enters into a contract to sell Note Receivable A, which is carried at amortised cost, in exchange for Bond B, which will be classified as held for trading and measured at fair value. Both assets have a fair value of CU1,010 on 29 December, while the amortised cost of Note Receivable A is CU1,000. Entity A uses settlement date accounting for loans and receivables and trade date accounting for assets held for trading. On 31 December 20X2 (financial year-end), the fair value of Note Receivable A is CU1,012 and the fair value of Bond B is CU1,009. On 4 January 20X3, the fair value of Note Receivable A is CU1,013 and the fair value of Bond B is CU1,007. The following entries are made:

29 December 20X2		
Dr Bond B	CU1,010	
Cr Payable		CU1,010
31 December 20X2		
Dr Trading loss	CU1	
Cr Bond B		CU1
4 January 20X3		
Dr Payable	CU1,010	
Dr Trading loss	CU2	
Cr Note Receivable A		CU1,000
Cr Bond B		CU2
Cr Realisation gain		CU10

Section E Measurement

E.1 Initial measurement of financial assets and financial liabilities

E.1.1 Initial measurement: transaction costs

Transaction costs should be included in the initial measurement of financial assets and financial liabilities other than those at fair value through profit or loss. How should this requirement be applied in practice?

For financial assets, incremental costs that are directly attributable to the acquisition of the asset, for example fees and commissions, are added to the amount originally recognised. For financial liabilities, directly related costs of issuing debt are deducted from the amount of debt originally recognised. For financial instruments that are measured at fair value through profit or loss, transaction costs are not added to the fair value measurement at initial recognition.

For financial instruments that are carried at amortised cost, such as held-to-maturity investments, loans and receivables, and financial liabilities that are not at fair value through profit or loss, transaction costs are included in the calculation of amortised cost using the effective interest method and, in effect, amortised through profit or loss over the life of the instrument.

For available-for-sale financial assets, transaction costs are recognised in equity as part of a change in fair value at the next remeasurement. If an available-for-sale financial asset has fixed or determinable payments and does not have an indefinite life, the transaction costs are amortised to profit or loss using the effective interest method. If an available-for-sale financial asset does not have fixed or determinable payments and has an indefinite life, the transaction costs are recognised in profit or loss when the asset is derecognised or becomes impaired.

Transaction costs expected to be incurred on transfer or disposal of a financial instrument are not included in the measurement of the financial instrument.

E.2 Fair value measurement considerations

E.2.1 Fair value measurement considerations for investment funds

IAS 39.AG72 states that the current bid price is usually the appropriate price to be used in measuring the fair value of an asset held. The rules applicable to some investment funds require net asset values to be reported to investors on the basis of mid-market prices. In these circumstances, would it be appropriate for an investment fund to measure its assets on the basis of mid-market prices?

No. The existence of regulations that require a different measurement for specific purposes does not justify a departure from the general requirement in IAS 39.AG72 to use the current bid price in the absence of a matching liability position. In its financial statements, an investment fund measures its assets at current bid prices. In reporting its net asset value to investors, an investment fund may wish to provide a reconciliation between the fair values recognised on its balance sheet and the prices used for the net asset value calculation.

E.2.2 Fair value measurement: large holding

Entity A holds 15 per cent of the share capital in Entity B. The shares are publicly traded in an active market. The currently quoted price is CU100. Daily trading volume is 0.1 per cent of outstanding shares. Because Entity A believes that the fair value of the Entity B shares it owns, if sold as a block, is greater than the quoted market price, Entity A obtains several independent estimates of the price it would obtain if it sells its holding. These estimates indicate that Entity A would be able to obtain a price of CU105, ie a 5 per cent premium above the quoted price. Which figure should Entity A use for measuring its holding at fair value?

Under IAS 39.AG71, a published price quotation in an active market is the best estimate of fair value. Therefore, Entity A uses the published price quotation (CU100). Entity A cannot depart from the quoted market price solely because independent estimates indicate that Entity A would obtain a higher (or lower) price by selling the holding as a block.

E.3 Gains and losses

E.3.1 Available-for-sale financial assets: exchange of shares

Entity A holds a small number of shares in Entity B. The shares are classified as available for sale. On 20 December 2000, the fair value of the shares is CU120 and the cumulative gain recognised in equity is CU20. On the same day, Entity B is acquired by Entity C, a large public entity. As a result, Entity A receives shares in Entity C in exchange for those it had in Entity B of equal fair value. Under IAS 39.55(b), should Entity A recognise the cumulative gain of CU20 recognised in equity in profit or loss?

Yes. The transaction qualifies for derecognition under IAS 39. IAS 39.55(b) requires that the cumulative gain or loss that has been recognised in equity on an available-for-sale financial asset be recognised in profit or loss when the asset is derecognised. In the exchange of shares, Entity A disposes of the shares it had in Entity B and receives shares in Entity C.

E.3.2 IAS 39 and IAS 21 Available-for-sale financial assets: separation of currency component

For an available-for-sale monetary financial asset, the entity reports changes in the carrying amount relating to changes in foreign exchange rates in profit or loss in accordance with IAS 21.23(a) and IAS 21.28 and other changes in the carrying amount in equity in accordance with IAS 39. How is the cumulative gain or loss that is recognised in equity determined?

It is the difference between the amortised cost (adjusted for impairment, if any) and fair value of the available-for-sale monetary financial asset in the functional currency of the reporting entity. For the purpose of applying IAS 21.28 the asset is treated as an asset measured at amortised cost in the foreign currency.

To illustrate: on 31 December 2001 Entity A acquires a bond denominated in a foreign currency (FC) for its fair value of FC1,000. The bond has five years remaining to maturity and a principal amount of FC1,250, carries fixed interest of 4.7 per cent that is paid annually (FC1,250 × 4.7 per cent = FC59 per year), and has an effective interest rate of 10 per cent. Entity A classifies the bond as available for sale, and thus recognises gains and losses in equity. The entity's functional currency is its local currency (LC). The exchange rate is FC1 to LC1.5 and the carrying amount of the bond is LC1,500 (= FC1,000 × 1.5).

Dr Bond	LC1,500	
Cr Cash		LC1,500

On 31 December 2002, the foreign currency has appreciated and the exchange rate is FC1 to LC2. The fair value of the bond is FC1,060 and thus the carrying amount is LC2,120 (= FC1,060 × 2). The amortised cost is FC1,041 (= LC2,082). In this case, the cumulative gain or loss to be recognised directly in equity is the difference between the fair value and the amortised cost on 31 December 2002, ie LC38 (= LC2,120 – LC2,082).

Interest received on the bond on 31 December 2002 is FC59 (= LC118). Interest income determined in accordance with the effective interest method is FC100 (= 1,000 × 10 per cent). The average exchange rate during the year is FC1 to LC1.75. For the purpose of this question, it is assumed that the use of the average exchange rate provides a reliable approximation of the spot rates applicable to the accrual of interest income during the year (IAS 21.22). Thus, reported interest income is LC175 (= FC100 × 1.75) including accretion of the initial discount of LC72 (= [FC100 – FC59] × 1.75). Accordingly, the exchange difference on the bond that is recognised in profit or loss is LC510 (= LC2,082 – LC1,500 – LC72). Also, there is an exchange gain on the interest receivable for the year of LC15 (= LC59 × [2.00 – 1.75]).

Dr Bond	LC620	
Dr Cash	LC118	
Cr Interest income		LC175
Cr Exchange gain		LC525
Cr Fair value change in equity		LC38

On 31 December 2003, the foreign currency has appreciated further and the exchange rate is FC1 to LC2.50. The fair value of the bond is FC1,070 and thus the carrying amount is LC2,675 (= FC1,070 × 2.50). The amortised cost is FC1,086 (= LC2,715). The cumulative gain or loss to be recognised directly in equity is the difference between the fair value and the amortised cost on 31 December 2003, ie negative LC40 (= LC2,675 – LC2,715). Thus, there is a debit to equity equal to the change in the difference during 2003 of LC78 (= LC40 + LC38).

Interest received on the bond on 31 December 2003 is FC59 (= LC148). Interest income determined in accordance with the effective interest method is FC104 (= FC1,041 × 10 per cent). The average exchange rate during the year is FC1 to LC2.25. For the purpose of this question, it is assumed that the use of the average exchange rate provides a reliable approximation of the spot rates applicable to the accrual of interest income during the year (IAS 21.22). Thus, recognised interest income is LC234 (= FC104 × 2.25) including accretion of the initial discount of LC101 (= [FC104 – FC59] × 2.25). Accordingly, the exchange difference on the bond that is recognised in profit or loss is LC532 (= LC2,715 – LC2,082 – LC101). Also, there is an exchange gain on the interest receivable for the year of LC15 (= FC59 × [2.50 – 2.25]).

Dr Bond	LC555	
Dr Cash	LC148	
Dr Fair value change in equity	LC78	
Cr Interest income		LC234
Cr Exchange gain		LC547

E.3.3 IAS 39 and IAS 21 Exchange differences arising on translation of foreign entities: equity or income?

IAS 21.32 and IAS 21.48 states that all exchange differences resulting from translating the financial statements of a foreign operation should be recognised in equity until disposal of the net investment. This would include exchange differences arising from financial instruments carried at fair value, which would include both financial assets classified as at fair value through profit or loss and financial assets that are available for sale.

IAS 39.55 requires that changes in fair value of financial assets classified as at fair value through profit or loss should be recognised in profit or loss and changes in fair value of available-for-sale investments should be reported in equity.

If the foreign operation is a subsidiary whose financial statements are consolidated with those of its parent, in the consolidated financial statements how are IAS 39.55 and IAS 21.39 applied?

IAS 39 applies in the accounting for financial instruments in the financial statements of a foreign operation and IAS 21 applies in translating the financial statements of a foreign operation for incorporation in the financial statements of the reporting entity.

To illustrate: Entity A is domiciled in Country X and its functional currency and presentation currency are the local currency of Country X (LCX). A has a foreign subsidiary (Entity B) in Country Y whose functional currency is the local currency of Country Y (LCY). B is the owner of a debt instrument, which is held for trading and therefore carried at fair value under IAS 39.

In B's financial statements for year 20X0, the fair value and carrying amount of the debt instrument is LCY100 in the local currency of Country Y. In A's consolidated financial statements, the asset is translated into the local currency of Country X at the spot exchange rate applicable at the balance sheet date (2.00). Thus, the carrying amount is LCX200 (= LCY100 × 2.00) in the consolidated financial statements.

At the end of year 20X1, the fair value of the debt instrument has increased to LCY110 in the local currency of Country Y. B recognises the trading asset at LCY110 in its balance sheet and recognises a fair value gain of LCY10 in its income statement. During the year, the spot exchange rate has increased from 2.00 to 3.00 resulting in an increase in the fair value of the instrument from LCX200 to LCX330 (= LCY110 × 3.00) in the currency of Country X. Therefore, Entity A recognises the trading asset at LCX330 in its consolidated financial statements.

Entity A translates the income statement of B 'at the exchange rates at the dates of the transactions' (IAS 21.39(b)). Since the fair value gain has accrued through the year, A uses the average rate as a practical approximation ([3.00 + 2.00] / 2 = 2.50, in accordance with

IAS 21.22). Therefore, while the fair value of the trading asset has increased by LCX130 (= LCX330 – LCX200), Entity A recognises only LCX25 (= LCY10 × 2.5) of this increase in consolidated profit or loss to comply with IAS 21.39(b). The resulting exchange difference, ie the remaining increase in the fair value of the debt instrument (LCX130 – LCX25 = LCX105), is classified as equity until the disposal of the net investment in the foreign operation in accordance with IAS 21.48.

E.3.4 IAS 39 and IAS 21 Interaction between IAS 39 and IAS 21

IAS 39 includes requirements about the measurement of financial assets and financial liabilities and the recognition of gains and losses on remeasurement in profit or loss. IAS 21 includes rules about the reporting of foreign currency items and the recognition of exchange differences in profit or loss. In what order are IAS 21 and IAS 39 applied?

Balance sheet

Generally, the measurement of a financial asset or financial liability at fair value, cost or amortised cost is first determined in the foreign currency in which the item is denominated in accordance with IAS 39. Then, the foreign currency amount is translated into the functional currency using the closing rate or a historical rate in accordance with IAS 21 (IAS 39.AG83). For example, if a monetary financial asset (such as a debt instrument) is carried at amortised cost under IAS 39, amortised cost is calculated in the currency of denomination of that financial asset. Then, the foreign currency amount is recognised using the closing rate in the entity's financial statements (IAS 21.23). That applies regardless of whether a monetary item is measured at cost, amortised cost or fair value in the foreign currency (IAS 21.24). A non-monetary financial asset (such as an investment in an equity instrument) is translated using the closing rate if it is carried at fair value in the foreign currency (IAS 21.23(c)) and at a historical rate if it is not carried at fair value under IAS 39 because its fair value cannot be reliably measured (IAS 21.23(b) and IAS 39.46(c)).

As an exception, if the financial asset or financial liability is designated as a hedged item in a fair value hedge of the exposure to changes in foreign currency rates under IAS 39, the hedged item is remeasured for changes in foreign currency rates even if it would otherwise have been recognised using a historical rate under IAS 21 (IAS 39.89), ie the foreign currency amount is recognised using the closing rate. This exception applies to non-monetary items that are carried in terms of historical cost in the foreign currency and are hedged against exposure to foreign currency rates (IAS 21.23(b)).

Income statement

The recognition of a change in the carrying amount of a financial asset or financial liability in profit or loss depends on a number of factors, including whether it is an exchange difference or other change in carrying amount, whether it arises on a monetary item (for example, most debt instruments) or non-monetary item (such as most equity investments), whether the associated asset or liability is designated as a cash flow hedge of an exposure to changes in foreign currency rates, and whether it results from translating the financial statements of a foreign operation. The issue of recognising changes in the carrying amount of a financial asset or financial liability held by a foreign operation is addressed in a separate question (see Question E.3.3).

Any exchange difference arising on recognising a *monetary item* at a rate different from that at which it was initially recognised during the period, or recognised in previous financial statements, is recognised in profit or loss or in equity in accordance with IAS 21 (IAS 39.AG83, IAS 21.28 and IAS 21.32), unless the monetary item is designated as a cash flow hedge of a highly probable forecast transaction in foreign currency, in which case the requirements for recognition of gains and losses on cash flow hedges in IAS 39 apply (IAS 39.95). Differences arising from recognising a monetary item at a foreign currency amount different from that at which it was previously recognised are accounted for in a similar manner, since all changes in the carrying amount relating to foreign currency movements should be treated consistently. All other changes in the balance sheet measurement of a monetary item are recognised in profit or loss or in equity in accordance with IAS 39. For example, although an entity recognises gains and losses on available-for-sale monetary financial assets in equity (IAS 39.55(b)), the entity nevertheless recognises the changes in the carrying amount relating to changes in foreign exchange rates in profit or loss (IAS 21.23(a)).

Any changes in the carrying amount of a *non-monetary item* are recognised in profit or loss or in equity in accordance with IAS 39 (IAS 39.AG83). For example, for available-for-sale financial assets the entire change in the carrying amount, including the effect of changes in foreign currency rates, is reported in equity. If the non-monetary item is designated as a cash flow hedge of an unrecognised firm commitment or a highly probable forecast transaction in foreign currency, the requirements for recognition of gains and losses on cash flow hedges in IAS 39 apply (IAS 39.95).

When some portion of the change in carrying amount is recognised in equity and some portion is recognised in profit or loss, for example, if the amortised cost of a foreign currency bond classified as available for sale has increased in foreign currency (resulting in a gain in profit or loss) but its fair value has decreased in the functional currency (resulting in a loss in equity), an entity cannot offset those two components for the purposes of determining gains or losses that should be recognised in profit or loss or in equity.

E.4 Impairment and uncollectibility of financial assets

E.4.1 Objective evidence of impairment

Does IAS 39 require that an entity be able to identify a single, distinct past causative event to conclude that it is probable that an impairment loss on a financial asset has been incurred?

No. IAS 39.59 states 'It may not be possible to identify a single, discrete event that caused the impairment. Rather the combined effect of several events may have caused the impairment.' Also, IAS 39.60 states that 'a downgrade of an entity's credit rating is not, of itself, evidence of impairment, although it may be evidence of impairment when considered with other available information'. Other factors that an entity considers in determining whether it has objective evidence that an impairment loss has been incurred include information about the debtors' or issuers' liquidity, solvency and business and financial risk exposures, levels of and trends in delinquencies for similar financial assets, national and local economic trends and conditions, and the fair value of collateral and guarantees. These and other factors may, either individually or taken together, provide sufficient objective evidence that an impairment loss has been incurred in a financial asset or group of financial assets.

E.4.2 Impairment: future losses

Does IAS 39 permit the recognition of an impairment loss through the establishment of an allowance for future losses when a loan is given? For example, if Entity A lends CU1,000 to Customer B, can it recognise an immediate impairment loss of CU10 if Entity A, based on historical experience, expects that 1 per cent of the principal amount of loans given will not be collected?

No. IAS 39.43 requires a financial asset to be initially measured at fair value. For a loan asset, the fair value is the amount of cash lent adjusted for any fees and costs (unless a portion of the amount lent is compensation for other stated or implied rights or privileges). In addition, IAS 39.58 requires that an impairment loss is recognised only if there is objective evidence of impairment as a result of a past event that occurred after initial recognition. Accordingly, it is inconsistent with IAS 39.43 and IAS 39.58 to reduce the carrying amount of a loan asset on initial recognition through the recognition of an immediate impairment loss.

E.4.3 Assessment of impairment: principal and interest

Because of Customer B's financial difficulties, Entity A is concerned that Customer B will not be able to make all principal and interest payments due on a loan in a timely manner. It negotiates a restructuring of the loan. Entity A expects that Customer B will be able to meet its obligations under the restructured terms. Would Entity A recognise an impairment loss if the restructured terms are as reflected in any of the following cases?

(a) Customer B will pay the full principal amount of the original loan five years after the original due date, but none of the interest due under the original terms.

(b) Customer B will pay the full principal amount of the original loan on the original due date, but none of the interest due under the original terms.

(c) Customer B will pay the full principal amount of the original loan on the original due date with interest only at a lower interest rate than the interest rate inherent in the original loan.

(d) Customer B will pay the full principal amount of the original loan five years after the original due date and all interest accrued during the original loan term, but no interest for the extended term.

(e) Customer B will pay the full principal amount of the original loan five years after the original due date and all interest, including interest for both the original term of the loan and the extended term.

IAS 39.58 indicates that an impairment loss has been incurred if there is objective evidence of impairment. The amount of the impairment loss for a loan measured at amortised cost is the difference between the carrying amount of the loan and the present value of future principal and interest payments discounted at the loan's original effective interest rate. In cases (a)–(d) above, the present value of the future principal and interest payments discounted at the loan's original effective interest rate will be lower than the carrying amount of the loan. Therefore, an impairment loss is recognised in those cases.

In case (e), even though the timing of payments has changed, the lender will receive interest on interest, and the present value of the future principal and interest payments discounted at the loan's original effective interest rate will equal the carrying amount of the loan. Therefore, there is no impairment loss. However, this fact pattern is unlikely given Customer B's financial difficulties.

E.4.4 Assessment of impairment: fair value hedge

A loan with fixed interest rate payments is hedged against the exposure to interest rate risk by a receive-variable, pay-fixed interest rate swap. The hedge relationship qualifies for fair value hedge accounting and is reported as a fair value hedge. Thus, the carrying amount of the loan includes an adjustment for fair value changes attributable to movements in interest rates. Should an assessment of impairment in the loan take into account the fair value adjustment for interest rate risk?

Yes. The loan's original effective interest rate before the hedge becomes irrelevant once the carrying amount of the loan is adjusted for any changes in its fair value attributable to interest rate movements. Therefore, the original effective interest rate and amortised cost of the loan are adjusted to take into account recognised fair value changes. The adjusted effective interest rate is calculated using the adjusted carrying amount of the loan.

An impairment loss on the hedged loan is calculated as the difference between its carrying amount after adjustment for fair value changes attributable to the risk being hedged and the estimated future cash flows of the loan discounted at the adjusted effective interest rate. When a loan is included in a portfolio hedge of interest rate risk, the entity should allocate the change in the fair value of the hedged portfolio to the loans (or groups of similar loans) being assessed for impairment on a systematic and rational basis.

E.4.5 Impairment: provision matrix

A financial institution calculates impairment in the unsecured portion of loans and receivables on the basis of a provision matrix that specifies fixed provision rates for the number of days a loan has been classified as non-performing (zero per cent if less than 90 days, 20 per cent if 90–180 days, 50 per cent if 181–365 days and 100 per cent if more than 365 days). Can the results be considered to be appropriate for the purpose of calculating the impairment loss on loans and receivables under IAS 39.63?

Not necessarily. IAS 39.63 requires impairment or bad debt losses to be calculated as the difference between the asset's carrying amount and the present value of estimated future cash flows discounted at the financial instrument's original effective interest rate.

E.4.6 Impairment: excess losses

Does IAS 39 permit an entity to recognise impairment or bad debt losses in excess of impairment losses that are determined on the basis of objective evidence about impairment in identified individual financial assets or identified groups of similar financial assets?

No. IAS 39 does not permit an entity to recognise impairment or bad debt losses in addition to those that can be attributed to individually identified financial assets or identified groups of financial assets with similar credit risk characteristics (IAS 39.64) on the basis of objective evidence about the existence of impairment in those assets (IAS 39.58). Amounts that an entity might want to set aside for additional possible impairment in financial assets, such as reserves that cannot be supported by objective evidence about impairment, are not recognised as impairment or bad debt losses under IAS 39. However, if an entity determines that no objective evidence of impairment exists for an individually assessed financial asset, whether significant or not, it includes the asset in a group of financial assets with similar credit risk characteristics (IAS 39.64).

E.4.7 Recognition of impairment on a portfolio basis

IAS 39.63 requires that impairment be recognised for financial assets carried at amortised cost. IAS 39.64 states that impairment may be measured and recognised individually or on a portfolio basis for a group of similar financial assets. If one asset in the group is impaired but the fair value of another asset in the group is above its amortised cost, does IAS 39 allow non-recognition of the impairment of the first asset?

No. If an entity knows that an individual financial asset carried at amortised cost is impaired, IAS 39.63 requires that the impairment of that asset should be recognised. It states: 'the amount of the loss is measured as the difference between *the asset's* carrying amount and the present value of estimated future cash flows (excluding future credit losses that have not been incurred) discounted at the financial asset's original effective interest rate' (emphasis added). Measurement of impairment on a portfolio basis under IAS 39.64 may be applied to groups of small balance items and to financial assets that are individually assessed and found not to be impaired when there is indication of impairment in a group of similar assets and impairment cannot be identified with an individual asset in that group.

E.4.8 Impairment: recognition of collateral

If an impaired financial asset is secured by collateral and foreclosure is probable, is the collateral recognised as an asset separate from the impaired financial asset?

No. The measurement of the impaired financial asset reflects the fair value of the collateral. The collateral would generally not meet the recognition criteria until it is transferred to the lender. Accordingly, the collateral is not recognised as an asset separate from the impaired financial asset before foreclosure.

E.4.9 Impairment of non–monetary available–for–sale financial asset

If a non-monetary financial asset, such as an equity instrument, measured at fair value with gains and losses recognised in equity becomes impaired, should the cumulative net loss recognised in equity, including any portion attributable to foreign currency changes, be recognised in profit or loss?

Yes. IAS 39.67 states that when a decline in the fair value of an available–for–sale financial asset has been recognised directly in equity and there is objective evidence that the asset is impaired, the cumulative net loss that had been recognised directly in equity should be removed from equity and recognised in profit or loss even though the asset has not been derecognised. Any portion of the cumulative net loss that is attributable to foreign currency changes on that asset that had been recognised in equity is also recognised in profit or loss. Any subsequent losses, including any portion attributable to foreign currency changes, are also recognised in profit or loss until the asset is derecognised.

E.4.10 Impairment: whether the available–for–sale reserve in equity can be negative

IAS 39.67 requires that gains and losses arising from changes in fair value on available–for–sale financial assets are recognised directly in equity. If the aggregate fair value of such assets is less than their carrying amount, should the aggregate net loss that has been recognised directly in equity be removed from equity and recognised in profit or loss?

Not necessarily. The relevant criterion is not whether the aggregate fair value is less than the carrying amount, but whether there is objective evidence that a financial asset or group of assets is impaired. An entity assesses at each balance sheet date whether there is any objective evidence that a financial asset or group of assets may be impaired, in accordance with IAS 39.59–61. IAS 39.60 states that a downgrade of an entity's credit rating is not, of itself, evidence of impairment, although it may be evidence of impairment when considered with other available information. Additionally, a decline in the fair value of a financial asset below its cost or amortised cost is not necessarily evidence of impairment (for example, a decline in the fair value of an investment in a debt instrument that results from an increase in the basic, risk-free interest rate).

Section F Hedging

F.1 Hedging instruments

F.1.1 Hedging the fair value exposure of a bond denominated in a foreign currency

Entity J, whose functional currency is the Japanese yen, has issued 5 million five-year US dollar fixed rate debt. Also, it owns a 5 million five-year fixed rate US dollar bond which it has classified as available for sale. Can Entity J designate its US dollar liability as a hedging instrument in a fair value hedge of the entire fair value exposure of its US dollar bond?

No. IAS 39.72 permits a non-derivative to be used as a hedging instrument only for a hedge of a foreign currency risk. Entity J's bond has a fair value exposure to foreign currency and interest rate changes and credit risk.

Alternatively, can the US dollar liability be designated as a fair value hedge or cash flow hedge of the foreign currency component of the bond?

Yes. However, hedge accounting is unnecessary because the amortised cost of the hedging instrument and the hedged item are both remeasured using closing rates. Regardless of whether Entity J designates the relationship as a cash flow hedge or a fair value hedge, the effect on profit or loss is the same. Any gain or loss on the non-derivative hedging instrument designated as a cash flow hedge is immediately recognised in profit or loss to correspond with the recognition of the change in spot rate on the hedged item in profit or loss as required by IAS 21.

F.1.2 Hedging with a non-derivative financial asset or liability

Entity J's functional currency is the Japanese yen. It has issued a fixed rate debt instrument with semi-annual interest payments that matures in two years with principal due at maturity of 5 million US dollars. It has also entered into a fixed price sales commitment for 5 million US dollars that matures in two years and is not accounted for as a derivative because it meets the exemption for normal sales in paragraph 5. Can Entity J designate its US dollar liability as a fair value hedge of the entire fair value exposure of its fixed price sales commitment and qualify for hedge accounting?

No. IAS 39.72 permits a non-derivative asset or liability to be used as a hedging instrument only for a hedge of a foreign currency risk.

Alternatively, can Entity J designate its US dollar liability as a cash flow hedge of the foreign currency exposure associated with the future receipt of US dollars on the fixed price sales commitment?

Yes. IAS 39 permits the designation of a non-derivative asset or liability as a hedging instrument in either a cash flow hedge or a fair value hedge of the exposure to changes in foreign exchange rates of a firm commitment (IAS 39.87). Any gain or loss on the non-derivative hedging instrument that is recognised in equity during the period preceding the future sale is recognised in profit or loss when the sale takes place (IAS 39.95).

Alternatively, can Entity J designate the sales commitment as the hedging instrument instead of the hedged item?

No. Only a derivative instrument or a non-derivative financial asset or liability can be designated as a hedging instrument in a hedge of a foreign currency risk. A firm commitment cannot be designated as a hedging instrument. However, if the foreign currency component of the sales commitment is required to be separated as an embedded derivative under IAS 39.11 and IAS 39.AG33(d), it could be designated as a hedging instrument in a hedge of the exposure to changes in the fair value of the maturity amount of the debt attributable to foreign currency risk.

F.1.3 Hedge accounting: use of written options in combined hedging instruments

Issue (a) – Does IAS 39.AG94 preclude the use of an interest rate collar or other derivative instrument that combines a written option component and a purchased option component as a hedging instrument?

It depends. An interest rate collar or other derivative instrument that includes a written option cannot be designated as a hedging instrument if it is a net written option, because IAS 39.AG94 precludes the use of a written option as a hedging instrument unless it is designated as an offset to a purchased option. An interest rate collar or other derivative instrument that includes a written option may be designated as a hedging instrument, however, if the combination is a net purchased option or zero cost collar.

Issue (b) – What factors indicate that an interest rate collar or other derivative instrument that combines a written option component and a purchased option component is not a net written option?

The following factors taken together suggest that an interest rate collar or other derivative instrument that includes a written option is not a net written option.

(a) No net premium is received either at inception or over the life of the combination of options. The distinguishing feature of a written option is the receipt of a premium to compensate the writer for the risk incurred.

(b) Except for the strike prices, the critical terms and conditions of the written option component and the purchased option component are the same (including underlying variable or variables, currency denomination and maturity date). Also, the notional amount of the written option component is not greater than the notional amount of the purchased option component.

F.1.4 Internal hedges

Some entities use internal derivative contracts (internal hedges) to transfer risk exposures between different companies within a group or divisions within a single legal entity. Does IAS 39.73 prohibit hedge accounting in such cases?

Yes, if the derivative contracts are internal to the entity being reported on. IAS 39 does not specify how an entity should manage its risk. However, it states that internal hedging transactions do not qualify for hedge accounting. This applies both (a) in consolidated financial statements for intragroup hedging transactions, and (b) in the individual or separate financial statements of a legal entity for hedging transactions between divisions in the entity. The principles of preparing consolidated financial statements in IAS 27.24 require that 'intragroup balances, transactions, income and expenses shall be eliminated in full'.

On the other hand, an intragroup hedging transaction may be designated as a hedge in the individual or separate financial statements of a group entity, if the intragroup transaction is an external transaction from the perspective of the group entity. In addition, if the internal contract is offset with an external party the external contract may be regarded as the hedging instrument and the hedging relationship may qualify for hedge accounting.

The following summarises the application of IAS 39 to internal hedging transactions.

- IAS 39 does not preclude an entity from using internal derivative contracts for risk management purposes and it does not preclude internal derivatives from being accumulated at the treasury level or some other central location so that risk can be managed on an entity-wide basis or at some higher level than the separate legal entity or division.
- Internal derivative contracts between two separate entities within a consolidated group can qualify for hedge accounting by those entities in their individual or separate financial statements, even though the internal contracts are not offset by derivative contracts with a party external to the consolidated group.
- Internal derivative contracts between two separate divisions within the same legal entity can qualify for hedge accounting in the individual or separate financial statements of that legal entity only if those contracts are offset by derivative contracts with a party external to the legal entity.
- Internal derivative contracts between separate divisions within the same legal entity and between separate entities within the consolidated group can qualify for hedge accounting in the consolidated financial statements only if the internal contracts are offset by derivative contracts with a party external to the consolidated group.
- If the internal derivative contracts are not offset by derivative contracts with external parties, the use of hedge accounting by group entities and divisions using internal contracts must be reversed on consolidation.

To illustrate: the banking division of Entity A enters into an internal interest rate swap with the trading division of the same entity. The purpose is to hedge the interest rate risk exposure of a loan (or group of similar loans) in the loan portfolio. Under the swap, the banking division pays fixed interest payments to the trading division and receives variable interest rate payments in return.

If a hedging instrument is not acquired from an external party, IAS 39 does not allow hedge accounting treatment for the hedging transaction undertaken by the banking and trading divisions. IAS 39.73 indicates that only derivatives that involve a party external to the entity can be designated as hedging instruments and, further, that any gains or losses on intragroup or intra-entity transactions should be eliminated on consolidation. Therefore, transactions between different divisions within Entity A do not qualify for hedge accounting treatment in the financial statements of Entity A. Similarly, transactions between different entities within a group do not qualify for hedge accounting treatment in consolidated financial statements.

However, if in addition to the internal swap in the above example the trading division enters into an interest rate swap or other contract with an external party that offsets the exposure hedged in the internal swap, hedge accounting is permitted under IAS 39. For the purposes of IAS 39, the hedged item is the loan (or group of similar loans) in the banking division and the hedging instrument is the external interest rate swap or other contract.

The trading division may aggregate several internal swaps or portions of them that are not offsetting each other and enter into a single third party derivative contract that offsets the aggregate exposure. Under IAS 39, such external hedging transactions may qualify for hedge accounting treatment provided that the hedged items in the banking division are identified and the other conditions for hedge accounting are met. It should be noted, however, that IAS 39.79 does not permit hedge accounting treatment for held-to-maturity investments if the hedged risk is the exposure to interest rate changes.

F.1.5 Offsetting internal derivative contracts used to manage interest rate risk

If a central treasury function enters into internal derivative contracts with subsidiaries and various divisions within the consolidated group to manage interest rate risk on a centralised basis, can those contracts qualify for hedge accounting in the consolidated financial statements if, before laying off the risk, the internal contracts are first netted against each other and only the net exposure is offset in the marketplace with external derivative contracts?

No. An internal contract designated at the subsidiary level or by a division as a hedge results in the recognition of changes in the fair value of the item being hedged in profit or loss (a fair value hedge) or in the recognition of the changes in the fair value of the internal derivative in equity (a cash flow hedge). There is no basis for changing the measurement attribute of the item being hedged in a fair value hedge unless the exposure is offset with an external derivative. There is also no basis for including the gain or loss on the internal derivative in equity for one entity and recognising it in profit or loss by the other entity unless it is offset with an external derivative. In cases where two or more internal derivatives are used to manage interest rate risk on assets or liabilities at the subsidiary or division level and those internal derivatives are offset at the treasury level, the effect of designating the internal derivatives as hedging instruments is that the hedged non-derivative exposures at the subsidiary or division levels would be used to offset each other on consolidation. Accordingly, since IAS 39.72 does not permit designating non-derivatives as hedging instruments, except for foreign currency exposures, the results of hedge accounting from the use of internal derivatives at the subsidiary or division level that are not laid off with external parties must be reversed on consolidation.

It should be noted, however, that there will be no effect on profit or loss and equity of reversing the effect of hedge accounting in consolidation for internal derivatives that offset each other at the consolidation level if they are used in the same type of hedging relationship at the subsidiary or division level and, in the case of cash flow hedges, where the hedged items affect profit or loss in the same period. Just as the internal derivatives offset at the treasury level, their use as fair value hedges by two separate entities or divisions within the consolidated group will also result in the offset of the fair value amounts recognised in profit or loss, and their use as cash flow hedges by two separate entities or divisions within the consolidated group will also result in the fair value amounts being offset against each other in equity. However, there may be an effect on individual line items in both the consolidated income statement and the consolidated balance sheet, for example when internal derivatives that hedge assets (or liabilities) in a fair value hedge are offset by internal derivatives that are used as a fair value hedge of other assets (or liabilities) that are recognised in a different balance sheet or income statement line item. In addition, to the extent that one of the internal contracts is used as a cash flow hedge and the other is used in a fair value hedge, the effect on profit or loss and equity would not offset since the gain (or loss) on the internal derivative used as a fair value hedge would be recognised in profit or loss and the corresponding loss (or gain) on the internal derivative used as a cash flow hedge would be recognised in equity.

Question F.1.4 describes the application of IAS 39 to internal hedging transactions.

F.1.6 Offsetting internal derivative contracts used to manage foreign currency risk

If a central treasury function enters into internal derivative contracts with subsidiaries and various divisions within the consolidated group to manage foreign currency risk on a centralised basis, can those contracts be used as a basis for identifying external transactions that qualify for hedge accounting in the consolidated financial statements if, before laying off the risk, the internal contracts are first netted against each other and only the net exposure is offset by entering into a derivative contract with an external party?

It depends. IAS 27 *Consolidated and Separate Financial Statements* requires all internal transactions to be eliminated in consolidated financial statements. As stated in IAS 39.73, internal hedging transactions do not qualify for hedge accounting in the consolidated financial statements of the group. Therefore, if an entity wishes to achieve hedge accounting in the consolidated financial statements, it must designate a hedging relationship between a qualifying external hedging instrument and a qualifying hedged item.

As discussed in Question F.1.5, the accounting effect of two or more internal derivatives that are used to manage interest rate risk at the subsidiary or division level and are offset at the treasury level is that the hedged non-derivative exposures at those levels would be used to offset each other on consolidation. There is no effect on profit or loss or equity if (a) the internal derivatives are used in the same type of hedge relationship (ie fair value or cash flow hedges) and (b), in the case of cash flow hedges, any derivative gains and losses that are initially recognised in equity are recognised in profit or loss in the same period(s). When these two conditions are met, the gains and losses on the internal derivatives that are recognised in profit or loss or in equity will offset on consolidation resulting in the same profit or loss and equity as if the derivatives had been eliminated. However, there may be an effect on individual line items, in both the consolidated income statement and the consolidated balance sheet, that would need to be eliminated. In addition, there is an effect on profit or loss and equity if some of the offsetting internal derivatives are used in cash flow hedges, while others are used in fair value hedges. There is also an effect on profit or loss and equity for offsetting internal derivatives that are used in cash flow hedges if the derivative gains and losses that are initially recognised in equity are recognised in profit or loss in different periods (because the hedged items affect profit or loss in different periods).

As regards foreign currency risk, provided that the internal derivatives represent the transfer of foreign currency risk on underlying non-derivative financial assets or liabilities, hedge accounting can be applied because IAS 39.72 permits a non-derivative financial asset or liability to be designated as a hedging instrument for hedge accounting purposes for a hedge of a foreign currency risk. Accordingly, in this case the internal derivative contracts can be used as a basis for identifying external transactions that qualify for hedge accounting in the consolidated financial statements even if they are offset against each other. However, for consolidated financial statements, it is necessary to designate the hedging relationship so that it involves only external transactions.

Furthermore, the entity cannot apply hedge accounting to the extent that two or more offsetting internal derivatives represent the transfer of foreign currency risk on underlying forecast transactions or unrecognised firm commitments. This is because an unrecognised firm commitment or forecast transaction does not qualify as a hedging instrument under IAS 39. Accordingly, in this case the internal derivatives cannot be used as a basis for identifying external transactions that qualify for hedge accounting in the consolidated financial statements. As a result, any cumulative net gain or loss on an internal derivative that has been included in the initial carrying amount of an asset or liability (basis adjustment) or deferred in equity would have to be reversed on consolidation if it cannot be demonstrated that the offsetting internal derivative represented the transfer of a foreign currency risk on a financial asset or liability to an external hedging instrument.

F.1.7 Internal derivatives: examples of applying Question F.1.6

In each case, FC = foreign currency, LC = local currency (which is the entity's functional currency), and TC = treasury centre.

Case 1 Offset of fair value hedges

Subsidiary A has trade receivables of FC100, due in 60 days, which it hedges using a forward contract with TC. Subsidiary B has payables of FC50, also due in 60 days, which it hedges using a forward contact with TC.

TC nets the two internal derivatives and enters into a net external forward contract to pay FC50 and receive LC in 60 days.

At the end of month 1, FC weakens against LC. A incurs a foreign exchange loss of LC10 on its receivables, offset by a gain of LC10 on its forward contract with TC. B makes a foreign exchange gain of LC5 on its payables offset by a loss of LC5 on its forward contract with TC. TC makes a loss of LC10 on its internal forward contract with A, a gain of LC5 on its internal forward contract with B, and a gain of LC5 on its external forward contract.

At the end of month 1, the following entries are made in the individual or separate financial statements of A, B and TC. Entries reflecting intragroup transactions or events are shown in italics.

A's entries

Dr Foreign exchange loss	LC10	
Cr Receivables		LC10
Dr Internal contract TC	*LC10*	
Cr Internal gain TC		*LC10*

B's entries

Dr Payables	LC5	
Cr Foreign exchange gain		LC5
Dr Internal loss TC	*LC5*	
Cr Internal contract TC		*LC5*

TC's entries

Dr Internal loss A	*LC10*	
Cr Internal contract A		*LC10*
Dr Internal contract B	*LC5*	
Cr Internal gain B		*LC5*
Dr External forward contract	LC5	
Cr Foreign exchange gain		LC5

Both A and B could apply hedge accounting in their individual financial statements provided all conditions in IAS 39 are met. However, in this case, no hedge accounting is required because gains and losses on the internal derivatives and the offsetting losses and gains on the hedged receivables and payables are recognised immediately in the income statements of A and B without hedge accounting.

In the consolidated financial statements, the internal derivative transactions are eliminated. In economic terms, the payable in B hedges FC50 of the receivables in A. The external forward contract in TC hedges the remaining FC50 of the receivable in A. Hedge accounting is not necessary in the consolidated financial statements because monetary items are measured at spot foreign exchange rates under IAS 21 irrespective of whether hedge accounting is applied.

The net balances before and after elimination of the accounting entries relating to the internal derivatives are the same, as set out below. Accordingly, there is no need to make any further accounting entries to meet the requirements of IAS 39.

	Debit	*Credit*
Receivables	–	LC10
Payables	LC5	–
External forward contract	LC5	–
Gains and losses	–	–
Internal contracts	–	–

Case 2 Offset of cash flow hedges

To extend the example, A also has highly probable future revenues of FC200 on which it expects to receive cash in 90 days. B has highly probable future expenses of FC500 (advertising cost), also to be paid for in 90 days. A and B enter into separate forward contracts with TC to hedge these exposures and TC enters into an external forward contract to receive FC300 in 90 days.

As before, FC weakens at the end of month 1. A incurs a 'loss' of LC20 on its anticipated revenues because the LC value of these revenues decreases. This is offset by a 'gain' of LC20 on its forward contract with TC.

B incurs a 'gain' of LC50 on its anticipated advertising cost because the LC value of the expense decreases. This is offset by a 'loss' of LC50 on its transaction with TC.

TC incurs a 'gain' of LC50 on its internal transaction with B, a 'loss' of LC20 on its internal transaction with A and a loss of LC30 on its external forward contract.

A and B complete the necessary documentation, the hedges are effective, and both A and B qualify for hedge accounting in their individual financial statements. A defers the gain of LC20 on its internal derivative transaction in a hedging reserve in equity and B defers the loss of LC50 in its hedging reserve in equity. TC does not claim hedge accounting, but measures both its internal and external derivative positions at fair value, which net to zero.

At the end of month 1, the following entries are made in the individual or separate financial statements of A, B and TC. Entries reflecting intragroup transactions or events are shown in italics.

A's entries

Dr Internal contract TC	*LC20*	
Cr Equity		*LC20*

B's entries

Dr Equity	*LC50*	
Cr Internal contract TC		*LC50*

TC's entries

Dr Internal loss A	*LC20*	
Cr Internal contract A		*LC20*
Dr Internal contract B	*LC50*	
Cr Internal gain B		*LC50*
Dr Foreign exchange loss	LC30	
Cr External forward contract		LC30

For the consolidated financial statements, TC's external forward contract on FC300 is designated, at the beginning of month 1, as a hedging instrument of the first FC300 of B's highly probable future expenses. IAS 39 requires that in the consolidated financial statements at the end of month 1, the accounting effects of the internal derivative transactions must be eliminated.

However, the net balances before and after elimination of the accounting entries relating to the internal derivatives are the same, as set out below. Accordingly, there is no need to make any further accounting entries in order for the requirements of IAS 39 to be met.

	Debit	*Credit*
External forward contract	–	LC30
Equity	LC30	–
Gains and losses	–	–
Internal contracts	–	–

Case 3 Offset of fair value and cash flow hedges

Assume that the exposures and the internal derivative transactions are the same as in cases 1 and 2. However, instead of entering into two external derivatives to hedge separately the fair value and cash flow exposures, TC enters into a single net external derivative to receive FC250 in exchange for LC in 90 days.

TC has four internal derivatives, two maturing in 60 days and two maturing in 90 days. These are offset by a net external derivative maturing in 90 days. The interest rate differential between FC and LC is minimal, and therefore the ineffectiveness resulting from the mismatch in maturities is expected to have a minimal effect on profit or loss in TC.

As in cases 1 and 2, A and B apply hedge accounting for their cash flow hedges and TC measures its derivatives at fair value. A defers a gain of LC20 on its internal derivative transaction in equity and B defers a loss of LC50 on its internal derivative transaction in equity.

At the end of month 1, the following entries are made in the individual or separate financial statements of A, B and TC. Entries reflecting intragroup transactions or events are shown in italics.

A's entries

Dr Foreign exchange loss	LC10	
Cr Receivables		LC10
Dr Internal contract TC	*LC10*	
Cr Internal contract TC		*LC10*
Dr Internal contract TC	*LC20*	
Cr Equity		*LC20*

B's entries

Dr Payables	LC5	
Cr Foreign exchange gain		LC5
Dr Internal loss TC	*LC5*	
Cr Internal contract TC		*LC5*
Dr Equity	*LC50*	
Cr Internal contract TC		*LC50*

Continued from previous page

TC's entries

Dr	*Internal loss A*	*LC10*	
	Cr Internal contract A		*LC10*
Dr	*Internal loss A*	*LC20*	
	Cr Internal contract A		*LC20*
Dr	*Internal contract B*	*LC5*	
	Cr Internal gain B		*LC5*
Dr	*Internal contract B*	*LC50*	
	Cr Internal gain B		*LC50*
Dr	Foreign exchange loss	LC25	
	Cr External forward contract		LC25

TOTAL (for the internal derivatives)	*A*	*B*	*Total*
	LC	*LC*	*TC*
Income (fair value hedges)	10	(5)	5
Equity (cash flow hedges)	20	(50)	(30)
Total	30	(55)	(25)

Combining these amounts with the external transactions (ie those not marked in italics above) produces the total net balances before elimination of the internal derivatives as follows:

	Debit	*Credit*
Receivables	–	LC10
Payables	LC5	–
Forward contract	–	LC25
Equity	LC30	–
Gains and losses	–	–
Internal contracts	–	–

For the consolidated financial statements, the following designations are made at the beginning of month 1:

- the payable of FC50 in B is designated as a hedge of the first FC50 of the highly probable future revenues in A. Therefore, at the end of month 1, the following entries are made in the consolidated financial statements: Dr Payable LC5; Cr Equity LC5;
- the receivable of FC100 in A is designated as a hedge of the first FC100 of the highly probable future expenses in B. Therefore, at the end of month 1, the following entries are made in the consolidated financial statements: Dr Equity LC10, Cr Receivable LC10; and

- the external forward contract on FC250 in TC is designated as a hedge of the next FC250 of highly probable future expenses in B. Therefore, at the end of month 1, the following entries are made in the consolidated financial statements: Dr Equity LC25; Cr External forward contract LC25.

In the consolidated financial statements at the end of month 1, IAS 39 requires the accounting effects of the internal derivative transactions to be eliminated.

However, the total net balances before and after elimination of the accounting entries relating to the internal derivatives are the same, as set out below. Accordingly, there is no need to make any further accounting entries to meet the requirements of IAS 39.

	Debit	*Credit*
Receivables	–	LC10
Payables	LC5	–
Forward contract	–	LC25
Equity	LC30	–
Gains and losses	–	–
Internal contracts	–	–

Case 4 Offset of fair value and cash flow hedges with adjustment to carrying amount of inventory

Assume similar transactions as in case 3, except that the anticipated cash outflow of FC500 in B relates to the purchase of inventory that is delivered after 60 days. Assume also that the entity has a policy of basis-adjusting hedged forecast non-financial items. At the end of month 2, there are no further changes in exchange rates or fair values. At that date, the inventory is delivered and the loss of LC50 on B's internal derivative, deferred in equity in month 1, is adjusted against the carrying amount of inventory in B. The gain of LC20 on A's internal derivative is deferred in equity as before.

In the consolidated financial statements, there is now a mismatch compared with the result that would have been achieved by unwinding and redesignating the hedges. The external derivative (FC250) and a proportion of the receivable (FC50) offset FC300 of the anticipated inventory purchase. There is a natural hedge between the remaining FC200 of anticipated cash outflow in B and the anticipated cash inflow of FC200 in A. This relationship does not qualify for hedge accounting under IAS 39 and this time there is only a partial offset between gains and losses on the internal derivatives that hedge these amounts.

At the end of months 1 and 2, the following entries are made in the individual or separate financial statements of A, B and TC. Entries reflecting intragroup transactions or events are shown in italics.

A's entries (all at the end of month 1)

Dr Foreign exchange loss	LC10	
Cr Receivables		LC10
Dr Internal contract TC	*LC10*	
Cr Internal gain TC		*LC10*
Dr Internal contract TC	*LC20*	
Cr Equity		*LC20*

B's entries

At the end of month 1:

Dr Payables	LC5	
Cr Foreign exchange gain		LC5
Dr Internal loss TC	*LC5*	
Cr Internal contract TC		*LC5*
Dr Equity	*LC50*	
Cr Internal contract TC		*LC50*

At the end of month 2:

Dr Inventory	LC50	
Cr Equity		LC50

TC's entries (all at the end of month 1)

Dr Internal loss A	*LC10*	
Cr Internal contract A		*LC10*
Dr Internal loss A	*LC20*	
Cr Internal contract A		*LC20*
Dr Internal contract B	*LC5*	
Cr Internal gain B		*LC5*
Dr Internal contract B	*LC50*	
Cr Internal gain B		*LC50*
Dr Foreign exchange loss	LC25	
Cr Forward		LC25

TOTAL (for the internal derivatives)	*A*	*B*	*Total*
	LC	*LC*	*TC*
Income (fair value hedges)	10	(5)	5
Equity (cash flow hedges)	20	–	20
Basis adjustment (inventory)	–	(50)	(50)
Total	30	(55)	(25)

Combining these amounts with the external transactions (ie those not marked in italics above) produces the total net balances before elimination of the internal derivatives as follows:

	Debit	*Credit*
Receivables	–	LC10
Payables	LC5	–
Forward contract	–	LC25
Equity	–	LC20
Basis adjustment (inventory)	LC50	–
Gains and losses	–	–
Internal contracts	–	–

For the consolidated financial statements, the following designations are made at the beginning of month 1:

- the payable of FC50 in B is designated as a hedge of the first FC50 of the highly probable future revenues in A. Therefore, at the end of month 1, the following entry is made in the consolidated financial statements: Dr Payables LC5; Cr Equity LC5.
- the receivable of FC100 in A is designated as a hedge of the first FC100 of the highly probable future expenses in B. Therefore, at the end of month 1, the following entries are made in the consolidated financial statements: Dr Equity LC10; Cr Receivable LC10; and at the end of month 2, Dr Inventory LC10; Cr Equity LC10.
- the external forward contract on FC250 in TC is designated as a hedge of the next FC250 of highly probable future expenses in B. Therefore, at the end of month 1, the following entry is made in the consolidated financial statements: Dr Equity LC25; Cr External forward contract LC25; and at the end of month 2, Dr Inventory LC25; Cr Equity LC25.

The total net balances after elimination of the accounting entries relating to the internal derivatives are as follows:

	Debit	*Credit*
Receivables	–	LC10
Payables	LC5	–
Forward contract	–	LC25
Equity	–	LC5
Basis adjustment (inventory)	LC35	–
Gains and losses	–	–
Internal contracts	–	–

These total net balances are different from those that would be recognised if the internal derivatives were not eliminated, and it is these net balances that IAS 39 requires to be included in the consolidated financial statements. The accounting entries required to adjust the total net balances before elimination of the internal derivatives are as follows:

(a) to reclassify LC15 of the loss on B's internal derivative that is included in inventory to reflect that FC150 of the forecast purchase of inventory is not hedged by an external instrument (neither the external forward contract of FC250 in TC nor the external payable of FC100 in A); and

(b) to reclassify the gain of LC15 on A's internal derivative to reflect that the forecast revenues of FC150 to which it relates is not hedged by an external instrument.

The net effect of these two adjustments is as follows:

Dr Equity	LC15	
Cr Inventory		LC15

F.1.8 Combination of written and purchased options

In most cases, IAS 39.AG94 prohibits the use of written options as hedging instruments. If a combination of a written option and purchased option (such as an interest rate collar) is transacted as a single instrument with one counterparty, can an entity split the derivative instrument into its written option component and purchased option component and designate the purchased option component as a hedging instrument?

No. IAS 39.74 specifies that a hedging relationship is designated by an entity for a hedging instrument in its entirety. The only exceptions permitted are splitting the time value and intrinsic value of an option and splitting the interest element and spot price on a forward. Question F.1.3 addresses the issue of whether and when a combination of options is considered as a written option.

F.1.9 Delta–neutral hedging strategy

Does IAS 39 permit an entity to apply hedge accounting for a 'delta-neutral' hedging strategy and other dynamic hedging strategies under which the quantity of the hedging instrument is constantly adjusted in order to maintain a desired hedge ratio, for example, to achieve a delta-neutral position insensitive to changes in the fair value of the hedged item?

Yes. IAS 39.74 states that 'a dynamic hedging strategy that assesses both the intrinsic value and time value of an option contract can qualify for hedge accounting'. For example, a portfolio insurance strategy that seeks to ensure that the fair value of the hedged item does not drop below a certain level, while allowing the fair value to increase, may qualify for hedge accounting.

To qualify for hedge accounting, the entity must document how it will monitor and update the hedge and measure hedge effectiveness, be able to track properly all terminations and redesignations of the hedging instrument, and demonstrate that all other criteria for hedge accounting in IAS 39.88 are met. Also, it must be able to demonstrate an expectation that the hedge will be highly effective for a specified short period of time during which the hedge is not expected to be adjusted.

F.1.10 Hedging instrument: out of the money put option

Entity A has an investment in one share of Entity B, which it has classified as available for sale. To give itself partial protection against decreases in the share price of Entity B, Entity A acquires a put option on one share of Entity B and designates the change in the intrinsic value of the put as a hedging instrument in a fair value hedge of changes in the fair value of its share in Entity B. The put gives Entity A the right to sell one share of Entity B at a strike price of CU90. At the inception of the hedging relationship, the share has a quoted price of CU100. Since the put option gives Entity A the right to dispose of the share at a price of CU90, the put should normally be fully effective in offsetting price declines below CU90 on an intrinsic value basis. Price changes above CU90 are not hedged. In this case, are changes in the fair value of the share of Entity B for prices above CU90 regarded as hedge ineffectiveness under IAS 39.88 and recognised in profit or loss under IAS 39.89?

No. IAS 39.74 permits Entity A to designate changes in the intrinsic value of the option as the hedging instrument. The changes in the intrinsic value of the option provide protection against the risk of variability in the fair value of one share of Entity B below or equal to the strike price of the put of CU90. For prices above CU90, the option is out of the money and has no intrinsic value. Accordingly, gains and losses on one share of Entity B for prices above CU90 are not attributable to the hedged risk for the purposes of assessing hedge effectiveness and recognising gains and losses on the hedged item.

Therefore, Entity A reports changes in the fair value of the share in equity if it is associated with variation in its price above CU90 (IAS 39.55 and IAS 39.90). Changes in the fair value of the share associated with price declines below CU90 form part of the designated fair value hedge and are recognised in profit or loss under IAS 39.89(b). Assuming the hedge is effective, those changes are offset by changes in the intrinsic value of the put, which are also recognised in profit or loss (IAS 39.89(a)). Changes in the time value of the put are excluded from the designated hedging relationship and recognised in profit or loss under IAS 39.55(a).

F.1.11 Hedging instrument: proportion of the cash flows of a cash instrument

In the case of foreign exchange risk, a non-derivative financial asset or non-derivative financial liability can potentially qualify as a hedging instrument. Can an entity treat the cash flows for specified periods during which a financial asset or financial liability that is designated as a hedging instrument remains outstanding as a proportion of the hedging instrument under IAS 39.75, and exclude the other cash flows from the designated hedging relationship?

No. IAS 39.75 indicates that a hedging relationship may not be designated for only a portion of the time period in which the hedging instrument is outstanding. For example, the cash flows during the first three years of a ten-year borrowing denominated in a foreign currency cannot qualify as a hedging instrument in a cash flow hedge of the first three years of revenue in the same foreign currency. On the other hand, a non-derivative financial asset or financial liability denominated in a foreign currency may potentially qualify as a hedging instrument in a hedge of the foreign currency risk associated with a hedged item that has a remaining time period until maturity that is equal to or longer than the remaining maturity of the hedging instrument (see Question F.2.17).

F.1.12 Hedges of more than one type of risk

Issue (a) – Normally a hedging relationship is designated between an entire hedging instrument and a hedged item so that there is a single measure of fair value for the hedging instrument. Does this preclude designating a single financial instrument simultaneously as a hedging instrument in both a cash flow hedge and a fair value hedge?

No. For example, entities commonly use a combined interest rate and currency swap to convert a variable rate position in a foreign currency to a fixed rate position in the functional currency. IAS 39.76 allows the swap to be designated separately as a fair value hedge of the currency risk and a cash flow hedge of the interest rate risk provided the conditions in IAS 39.76 are met.

Issue (b) – If a single financial instrument is a hedging instrument in two different hedges, is special disclosure required?

IAS 32.58 requires disclosures separately for designated fair value hedges, cash flow hedges and hedges of a net investment in a foreign operation. The instrument in question would be reported in the IAS 32.58 disclosures separately for each type of hedge.

F.1.13 Hedging instrument: dual foreign currency forward exchange contract

Entity A's functional currency is the Japanese yen. Entity A has a five-year floating rate US dollar liability and a ten-year fixed rate pound sterling-denominated note receivable. The principal amounts of the asset and liability when converted into the Japanese yen are the same. Entity A enters into a single foreign currency forward contract to hedge its foreign currency exposure on both instruments under which it receives US dollars and pays pounds sterling at the end of five years. If Entity A designates the forward exchange contract as a hedging instrument in a cash flow hedge against the foreign currency exposure on the principal repayments of both instruments, can it qualify for hedge accounting?

Yes. IAS 39.76 permits designating a single hedging instrument as a hedge of multiple types of risk if three conditions are met. In this example, the derivative hedging instrument satisfies all of these conditions, as follows.

(a) The risks hedged can be identified clearly. The risks are the exposures to changes in the exchange rates between US dollars and yen, and yen and pounds, respectively.

(b) The effectiveness of the hedge can be demonstrated. For the pound sterling loan, the effectiveness is measured as the degree of offset between the fair value of the principal repayment in pounds sterling and the fair value of the pound sterling payment on the forward exchange contract. For the US dollar liability, the effectiveness is measured as the degree of offset between the fair value of the principal repayment in US dollars and the US dollar receipt on the forward exchange contract. Even though the receivable has a ten-year life and the forward protects it for only the first five years, hedge accounting is permitted for only a portion of the exposure as described in Question F.2.17.

(c) It is possible to ensure that there is specific designation of the hedging instrument and different risk positions. The hedged exposures are identified as the principal amounts of the liability and the note receivable in their respective currency of denomination.

F.1.14 Concurrent offsetting swaps and use of one as a hedging instrument

Entity A enters into an interest rate swap and designates it as a hedge of the fair value exposure associated with fixed rate debt. The fair value hedge meets the hedge accounting criteria of IAS 39. Entity A simultaneously enters into a second interest rate swap with the same swap counterparty that has terms that fully offset the first interest rate swap. Is Entity A required to view the two swaps as one unit and therefore precluded from applying fair value hedge accounting to the first swap?

It depends. IAS 39 is transaction-based. If the second swap was not entered into in contemplation of the first swap or there is a substantive business purpose for structuring the transactions separately, then the swaps are not viewed as one unit.

For example, some entities have a policy that requires a centralised dealer or treasury subsidiary to enter into third-party derivative contracts on behalf of other subsidiaries within the organisation to hedge the subsidiaries' interest rate risk exposures. The dealer or treasury subsidiary also enters into internal derivative transactions with those subsidiaries in order to track those hedges operationally within the organisation. Because the dealer or treasury subsidiary also enters into derivative contracts as part of its trading operations, or because it may wish to rebalance the risk of its overall portfolio, it may enter into a derivative contract with the same third party during the same business day that has substantially the same terms as a contract entered into as a hedging instrument on behalf of another subsidiary. In this case, there is a valid business purpose for entering into each contract.

Judgement is applied to determine whether there is a substantive business purpose for structuring the transactions separately. For example, if the sole purpose is to obtain fair value accounting treatment for the debt, there is no substantive business purpose.

F.2 Hedged items

F.2.1 Whether a derivative can be designated as a hedged item

Does IAS 39 permit designating a derivative instrument (whether a standalone or separately recognised embedded derivative) as a hedged item either individually or as part of a hedged group in a fair value or cash flow hedge, for example, by designating a pay-variable, receive-fixed Forward Rate Agreement (FRA) as a cash flow hedge of a pay-fixed, receive-variable FRA?

No. Derivative instruments are always deemed held for trading and measured at fair value with gains and losses recognised in profit or loss unless they are designated and effective hedging instruments (IAS 39.9). As an exception, IAS 39.AG94 permits the designation of a purchased option as the hedged item in a fair value hedge.

F.2.2 Cash flow hedge: anticipated issue of fixed rate debt

Is hedge accounting allowed for a hedge of an anticipated issue of fixed rate debt?

Yes. This would be a cash flow hedge of a highly probable forecast transaction that will affect profit or loss (IAS 39.86) provided that the conditions in IAS 39.88 are met.

To illustrate: Entity R periodically issues new bonds to refinance maturing bonds, provide working capital and for various other purposes. When Entity R decides it will be issuing bonds, it may hedge the risk of changes in the long-term interest rate from the date it decides to issue the bonds to the date the bonds are issued. If long-term interest rates go up, the bond will be issued either at a higher rate or with a higher discount or smaller premium than was originally expected. The higher rate being paid or decrease in proceeds is normally offset by the gain on the hedge. If long-term interest rates go down, the bond will be issued either at a lower rate or with a higher premium or a smaller discount than was originally expected. The lower rate being paid or increase in proceeds is normally offset by the loss on the hedge.

For example, in August 2000 Entity R decided it would issue CU200 million seven-year bonds in January 2001. Entity R performed historical correlation studies and determined that a seven-year treasury bond adequately correlates to the bonds Entity R expected to issue, assuming a hedge ratio of 0.93 futures contracts to one debt unit. Therefore, Entity R hedged the anticipated issue of the bonds by selling (shorting) CU186 million worth of futures on seven-year treasury bonds. From August 2000 to January 2001 interest rates increased. The short futures positions were closed in January 2001, the date the bonds were issued, and resulted in a CU1.2 million gain that will offset the increased interest payments on the bonds and, therefore, will affect profit or loss over the life of the bonds. The hedge qualifies as a cash flow hedge of the interest rate risk on the forecast issue of debt.

F.2.3 Hedge accounting: core deposit intangibles

Is hedge accounting treatment permitted for a hedge of the fair value exposure of core deposit intangibles?

It depends on whether the core deposit intangible is generated internally or acquired (eg as part of a business combination).

Internally generated core deposit intangibles are not recognised as intangible assets under IAS 38. Because they are not recognised, they cannot be designated as a hedged item.

If a core deposit intangible is acquired together with a related portfolio of deposits, the core deposit intangible is required to be recognised separately as an intangible asset (or as part of the related acquired portfolio of deposits) if it meets the recognition criteria in paragraph 21 of IAS 38 *Intangible Assets*. A recognised core deposit intangible asset could be designated as a hedged item, but only if it meets the conditions in paragraph 88, including the requirement in paragraph 88(d) that the effectiveness of the hedge can be measured reliably. Because it is often difficult to measure reliably the fair value of a core deposit intangible asset other than on initial recognition, it is unlikely that the requirement in paragraph 88(d) will be met.

F.2.4 Hedge accounting: hedging of future foreign currency revenue streams

Is hedge accounting permitted for a currency borrowing that hedges an expected but not contractual revenue stream in foreign currency?

Yes, if the revenues are highly probable. Under IAS 39.86(b) a hedge of an anticipated sale may qualify as a cash flow hedge. For example, an airline entity may use sophisticated models based on experience and economic data to project its revenues in various currencies. If it can demonstrate that forecast revenues for a period of time into the future in a particular currency are 'highly probable', as required by IAS 39.88, it may designate a currency borrowing as a cash flow hedge of the future revenue stream. The portion of the gain or loss on the borrowing that is determined to be an effective hedge is recognised directly in equity through the statement of changes in equity until the revenues occur.

It is unlikely that an entity can reliably predict 100 per cent of revenues for a future year. On the other hand, it is possible that a portion of predicted revenues, normally those expected in the short term, will meet the 'highly probable' criterion.

F.2.5 Cash flow hedges: 'all in one' hedge

If a derivative instrument is expected to be settled gross by delivery of the underlying asset in exchange for the payment of a fixed price, can the derivative instrument be designated as the hedging instrument in a cash flow hedge of that gross settlement assuming the other cash flow hedge accounting criteria are met?

Yes. A derivative instrument that will be settled gross can be designated as the hedging instrument in a cash flow hedge of the variability of the consideration to be paid or received in the future transaction that will occur on gross settlement of the derivative contract itself because there would be an exposure to variability in the purchase or sale price without the derivative. This applies to all fixed price contracts that are accounted for as derivatives under IAS 39.

For example, if an entity enters into a fixed price contract to sell a commodity and that contract is accounted for as a derivative under IAS 39 (for example, because the entity has a practice of settling such contracts net in cash or of taking delivery of the underlying and selling it within a short period after delivery for the purpose of generating a profit from short-term fluctuations in price or dealer's margin), the entity may designate the fixed price contract as a cash flow hedge of the variability of the consideration to be received on the sale of the asset (a future transaction) even though the fixed price contract is the contract under which the asset will be sold. Also, if an entity enters into a forward contract to purchase a debt instrument that will be settled by delivery, but the forward contract is a derivative because its term exceeds the regular way delivery period in the marketplace, the entity may designate the forward as a cash flow hedge of the variability of the consideration to be paid to acquire the debt instrument (a future transaction), even though the derivative is the contract under which the debt instrument will be acquired.

F.2.6 Hedge relationships: entity–wide risk

An entity has a fixed rate asset and a fixed rate liability, each having the same principal amount. Under the terms of the instruments, interest payments on the asset and liability occur in the same period and the net cash flow is always positive because the interest rate on the asset exceeds the interest rate on the liability. The entity enters into an interest rate swap to receive a floating interest rate and pay a fixed interest rate on a notional amount equal to the principal of the asset and designates the interest rate swap as a fair value hedge of the fixed rate asset. Does the hedging relationship qualify for hedge accounting even though the effect of the interest rate swap on an entity-wide basis is to create an exposure to interest rate changes that did not previously exist?

Yes. IAS 39 does not require risk reduction on an entity-wide basis as a condition for hedge accounting. Exposure is assessed on a transaction basis and, in this instance, the asset being hedged has a fair value exposure to interest rate increases that is offset by the interest rate swap.

F.2.7 Cash flow hedge: forecast transaction related to an entity's equity

Can a forecast transaction in the entity's own equity instruments or forecast dividend payments to shareholders be designated as a hedged item in a cash flow hedge?

No. To qualify as a hedged item, the forecast transaction must expose the entity to a particular risk that can affect profit or loss (IAS 39.86). The classification of financial instruments as liabilities or equity generally provides the basis for determining whether transactions or other payments relating to such instruments are recognised in profit or loss (IAS 32). For example, distributions to holders of an equity instrument are debited by the issuer directly to equity (IAS 32.35). Therefore, such distributions cannot be designated as a hedged item. However, a declared dividend that has not yet been paid and is recognised as a financial liability may qualify as a hedged item, for example, for foreign currency risk if it is denominated in a foreign currency.

F.2.8 Hedge accounting: risk of a transaction not occurring

Does IAS 39 permit an entity to apply hedge accounting to a hedge of the risk that a transaction will not occur, for example, if that would result in less revenue to the entity than expected?

No. The risk that a transaction will not occur is an overall business risk that is not eligible as a hedged item. Hedge accounting is permitted only for risks associated with recognised assets and liabilities, firm commitments, highly probable forecast transactions and net investments in foreign operations (IAS 39.86).

F.2.9 Held–to–maturity investments: hedging variable interest rate payments

Can an entity designate a pay–variable, receive–fixed interest rate swap as a cash flow hedge of a variable rate, held–to–maturity investment?

No. It is inconsistent with the designation of a debt investment as being held to maturity to designate a swap as a cash flow hedge of the debt investment's variable interest rate payments. IAS 39.79 states that a held–to–maturity investment cannot be a hedged item with respect to interest rate risk or prepayment risk 'because designation of an investment as held to maturity requires an intention to hold the investment until maturity without regard to changes in the fair value or cash flows of such an investment attributable to changes in interest rates'.

F.2.10 Hedged items: purchase of held–to–maturity investment

An entity forecasts the purchase of a financial asset that it intends to classify as held to maturity when the forecast transaction occurs. It enters into a derivative contract with the intent to lock in the current interest rate and designates the derivative as a hedge of the forecast purchase of the financial asset. Can the hedging relationship qualify for cash flow hedge accounting even though the asset will be classified as a held–to–maturity investment?

Yes. With respect to interest rate risk, IAS 39 prohibits hedge accounting for financial assets that are classified as held–to–maturity (IAS 39.79). However, even though the entity intends to classify the asset as held to maturity, the instrument is not classified as such until the transaction occurs.

F.2.11 Cash flow hedges: reinvestment of funds obtained from held–to–maturity investments

An entity owns a variable rate asset that it has classified as held to maturity. It enters into a derivative contract with the intention to lock in the current interest rate on the reinvestment of variable rate cash flows, and designates the derivative as a cash flow hedge of the forecast future interest receipts on debt instruments resulting from the reinvestment of interest receipts on the held–to–maturity asset. Assuming that the other hedge accounting criteria are met, can the hedging relationship qualify for cash flow hedge accounting even though the interest payments that are being reinvested come from an asset that is classified as held to maturity?

Yes. IAS 39.79 states that a held–to–maturity investment cannot be a hedged item with respect to interest rate risk. Question F.2.9 specifies that this applies not only to fair value hedges, ie hedges of the exposure to fair value interest rate risk associated with held–to–maturity investments that pay fixed interest, but also to cash flow hedges, ie hedges of the exposure to cash flow interest rate risk associated with held–to–maturity investments that pay variable interest at current market rates. However, in this instance, the derivative is designated as an offset of the exposure to cash flow risk associated with forecast future interest receipts on debt instruments resulting from the forecast reinvestment of variable rate cash flows on the held–to–maturity investment. The source of the funds forecast to be reinvested is not relevant in determining whether the reinvestment risk can be hedged. Accordingly, designation of the derivative as a cash flow hedge is permitted. This answer applies also to a hedge of the exposure to cash flow risk associated with the forecast future interest receipts on debt instruments resulting from the reinvestment of interest receipts on a fixed rate asset classified as held to maturity.

F.2.12 Hedge accounting: prepayable financial asset

If the issuer has the right to prepay a financial asset, can the investor designate the cash flows after the prepayment date as part of the hedged item?

Cash flows after the prepayment date may be designated as the hedged item to the extent it can be demonstrated that they are 'highly probable' (IAS 39.88). For example, cash flows after the prepayment date may qualify as highly probable if they result from a group or pool of similar assets (for example, mortgage loans) for which prepayments can be estimated with a high degree of accuracy or if the prepayment option is significantly out of the money. In addition, the cash flows after the prepayment date may be designated as the hedged item if a comparable option exists in the hedging instrument.

F.2.13 Fair value hedge: risk that could affect profit or loss

Is fair value hedge accounting permitted for exposure to interest rate risk in fixed rate loans that are classified as loans and receivables?

Yes. Under IAS 39, loans and receivables are carried at amortised cost. Banking institutions in many countries hold the bulk of their loans and receivables until maturity. Thus, changes in the fair value of such loans and receivables that are due to changes in market interest rates will not affect profit or loss. IAS 39.86 specifies that a fair value hedge is a hedge of the exposure to changes in fair value that is attributable to a particular risk and that can affect profit or loss. Therefore, IAS 39.86 may appear to preclude fair value hedge accounting for loans and receivables. However, it follows from IAS 39.79 that loans and receivables can be hedged items with respect to interest rate risk since they are not designated as held-to-maturity investments. The entity could sell them and the change in fair values would affect profit or loss. Thus, fair value hedge accounting is permitted for loans and receivables.

F.2.14 Intragroup and intra–entity hedging transactions

An Australian entity, whose functional currency is the Australian dollar, has forecast purchases in Japanese yen that are highly probable. The Australian entity is wholly owned by a Swiss entity, which prepares consolidated financial statements (which include the Australian subsidiary) in Swiss francs. The Swiss parent entity enters into a forward contract to hedge the change in yen relative to the Australian dollar. Can that hedge qualify for hedge accounting in the consolidated financial statements, or must the Australian subsidiary that has the foreign currency exposure be a party to the hedging transaction?

Yes. The hedge can qualify for hedge accounting provided the other hedge accounting criteria in IAS 39 are met. Since the Australian entity did not hedge the foreign currency exchange risk associated with the forecast purchases in yen, the effects of exchange rate changes between the Australian dollar and the yen will affect the Australian entity's profit or loss and, therefore, would also affect consolidated profit or loss. IAS 39 does not require that the operating unit that is exposed to the risk being hedged be a party to the hedging instrument.

F.2.15 Internal contracts: single offsetting external derivative

An entity uses what it describes as internal derivative contracts to document the transfer of responsibility for interest rate risk exposures from individual divisions to a central treasury function. The central treasury function aggregates the internal derivative contracts and enters into a single external derivative contract that offsets the internal derivative contracts on a net basis. For example, if the central treasury function has entered into three internal receive-fixed, pay-variable interest rate swaps that lay off the exposure to variable interest cash flows on variable rate liabilities in other divisions and one internal receive-variable, pay-fixed interest rate swap that lays off the exposure to variable interest cash flows on variable rate assets in another division, it would enter into an interest rate swap with an external counterparty that exactly offsets the four internal swaps. Assuming that the hedge accounting criteria are met, in the entity's financial statements would the single offsetting external derivative qualify as a hedging instrument in a hedge of a part of the underlying items on a gross basis?

Yes, but only to the extent the external derivative is designated as an offset of cash inflows or cash outflows on a gross basis. IAS 39.84 indicates that a hedge of an overall net position does not qualify for hedge accounting. However, it does permit designating a part of the underlying items as the hedged position on a gross basis. Therefore, even though the purpose of entering into the external derivative was to offset internal derivative contracts on a net basis, hedge accounting is permitted if the hedging relationship is defined and documented as a hedge of a part of the underlying cash inflows or cash outflows on a gross basis. An entity follows the approach outlined in IAS 39.84 and IAS 39.AG101 to designate part of the underlying cash flows as the hedged position.

F.2.16 Internal contracts: external derivative contracts that are settled net

Issue (a) – An entity uses internal derivative contracts to transfer interest rate risk exposures from individual divisions to a central treasury function. For each internal derivative contract, the central treasury function enters into a derivative contract with a single external counterparty that offsets the internal derivative contract. For example, if the central treasury function has entered into a receive-5 per cent-fixed, pay-LIBOR interest rate swap with another division that has entered into the internal contract with central treasury to hedge the exposure to variability in interest cash flows on a pay-LIBOR borrowing, central treasury would enter into a pay-5 per cent-fixed, receive-LIBOR interest rate swap on the same principal terms with the external counterparty. Although each of the external derivative contracts is formally documented as a separate contract, only the net of the payments on all of the external derivative contracts is settled since there is a netting agreement with the external counterparty. Assuming that the other hedge accounting criteria are met, can the individual external derivative contracts, such as the pay-5 per cent-fixed, receive-LIBOR interest rate swap above, be designated as hedging instruments of underlying gross exposures, such as the exposure to changes in variable interest payments on the pay-LIBOR borrowing above, even though the external derivatives are settled on a net basis?

Generally, yes. External derivative contracts that are legally separate contracts and serve a valid business purpose, such as laying off risk exposures on a gross basis, qualify as hedging instruments even if those external contracts are settled on a net basis with the same external counterparty, provided the hedge accounting criteria in IAS 39 are met. See also Question F.1.14.

Issue (b) – Treasury observes that by entering into the external offsetting contracts and including them in the centralised portfolio, it is no longer able to evaluate the exposures on a net basis. Treasury wishes to manage the portfolio of offsetting external derivatives separately from other exposures of the entity. Therefore, it enters into an additional, single derivative to offset the risk of the portfolio. Can the individual external derivative contracts in the portfolio still be designated as hedging instruments of underlying gross exposures even though a single external derivative is used to offset fully the market exposure created by entering into the external contracts?

Generally, yes. The purpose of structuring the external derivative contracts in this manner is consistent with the entity's risk management objectives and strategies. As indicated above, external derivative contracts that are legally separate contracts and serve a valid business purpose qualify as hedging instruments. Moreover, the answer to Question F.1.14 specifies that hedge accounting is not precluded simply because the entity has entered into a swap that mirrors exactly the terms of another swap with the same counterparty if there is a substantive business purpose for structuring the transactions separately.

F.2.17 Partial term hedging

IAS 39.75 indicates that a hedging relationship may not be designated for only a portion of the time period during which a hedging instrument remains outstanding. Is it permitted to designate a derivative as hedging only a portion of the time period to maturity of a hedged item?

Yes. A financial instrument may be a hedged item for only a portion of its cash flows or fair value, if effectiveness can be measured and the other hedge accounting criteria are met.

To illustrate: Entity A acquires a 10 per cent fixed rate government bond with a remaining term to maturity of ten years. Entity A classifies the bond as available for sale. To hedge itself against fair value exposure on the bond associated with the present value of the interest rate payments until year 5, Entity A acquires a five-year pay-fixed, receive-floating swap. The swap may be designated as hedging the fair value exposure of the interest rate payments on the government bond until year 5 and the change in value of the principal payment due at maturity to the extent affected by changes in the yield curve relating to the five years of the swap.

F.2.18 Hedging instrument: cross–currency interest rate swap

Entity A's functional currency is the Japanese yen. Entity A has a five-year floating rate US dollar liability and a 10-year fixed rate pound sterling-denominated note receivable. Entity A wishes to hedge the foreign currency exposure on its asset and liability and the fair value interest rate exposure on the receivable and enters into a matching cross-currency interest rate swap to receive floating rate US dollars and pay fixed rate pounds sterling and to exchange the dollars for the pounds at the end of five years. Can Entity A designate the swap as a hedging instrument in a fair value hedge against both foreign currency risk and interest rate risk, although both the pound sterling and US dollar are foreign currencies to Entity A?

Yes. IAS 39.81 permits hedge accounting for components of risk, if effectiveness can be measured. Also, IAS 39.76 permits designating a single hedging instrument as a hedge of more than one type of risk if the risks can be identified clearly, effectiveness can be demonstrated, and specific designation of the hedging instrument and different risk positions can be ensured. Therefore, the swap may be designated as a hedging instrument in a fair value hedge of the pound sterling receivable against exposure to changes in its fair value associated with changes in UK interest rates for the initial partial term of five years and the exchange rate between pounds and US dollars. The swap is measured at fair value with changes in fair value recognised in profit or loss. The carrying amount of the receivable is adjusted for changes in its fair value caused by changes in UK interest rates for the first five-year portion of the yield curve. The receivable and payable are remeasured using spot exchange rates under IAS 21 and the changes to their carrying amounts recognised in profit or loss.

F.2.19 Hedged items: hedge of foreign currency risk of publicly traded shares

Entity A acquires shares in Entity B on a foreign stock exchange for their fair value of 1,000 in foreign currency (FC). It classifies the shares as available for sale. To protect itself from the exposure to changes in the foreign exchange rate associated with the shares, it enters into a forward contract to sell FC750. Entity A intends to roll over the forward exchange contract for as long as it retains the shares. Assuming that the other hedge accounting criteria are met, could the forward exchange contract qualify as a hedge of the foreign exchange risk associated with the shares?

Yes, but only if there is a clear and identifiable exposure to changes in foreign exchange rates. Therefore, hedge accounting is permitted if (a) the equity instrument is not traded on an exchange (or in another established marketplace) where trades are denominated in the same currency as the functional currency of Entity A and (b) dividends to Entity A are not denominated in that currency. Thus, if a share is traded in multiple currencies and one of those currencies is the functional currency of the reporting entity, hedge accounting for the foreign currency component of the share price is not permitted.

If so, could the forward exchange contract be designated as a hedging instrument in a hedge of the foreign exchange risk associated with the portion of the fair value of the shares up to FC750 in foreign currency?

Yes. IAS 39 permits designating a portion of the cash flow or fair value of a financial asset as the hedged item if effectiveness can be measured (IAS 39.81). Therefore, Entity A may designate the forward exchange contract as a hedge of the foreign exchange risk associated with only a portion of the fair value of the shares in foreign currency. It could either be designated as a fair value hedge of the foreign exchange exposure of FC750 associated with the shares or as a cash flow hedge of a forecast sale of the shares, provided the timing of the sale is identified. Any variability in the fair value of the shares in foreign currency would not affect the assessment of hedge effectiveness unless the fair value of the shares in foreign currency was to fall below FC750.

F.2.20 Hedge accounting: stock index

An entity may acquire a portfolio of shares to replicate a stock index and a put option on the index to protect itself from fair value losses. Does IAS 39 permit designating the put on the stock index as a hedging instrument in a hedge of the portfolio of shares?

No. If similar financial instruments are aggregated and hedged as a group, IAS 39.83 states that the change in fair value attributable to the hedged risk for each individual item in the group is expected to be approximately proportional to the overall change in fair value attributable to the hedged risk of the group. In the scenario above, the change in the fair value attributable to the hedged risk for each individual item in the group (individual share prices) is not expected to be approximately proportional to the overall change in fair value attributable to the hedged risk of the group.

F.2.21 Hedge accounting: netting of assets and liabilities

May an entity group financial assets together with financial liabilities for the purpose of determining the net cash flow exposure to be hedged for hedge accounting purposes?

An entity's hedging strategy and risk management practices may assess cash flow risk on a net basis but IAS 39.84 does not permit designating a net cash flow exposure as a hedged item for hedge accounting purposes. IAS 39.AG101 provides an example of how a bank might assess its risk on a net basis (with similar assets and liabilities grouped together) and then qualify for hedge accounting by hedging on a gross basis.

F.3 Hedge accounting

F.3.1 Cash flow hedge: fixed interest rate cash flows

An entity issues a fixed rate debt instrument and enters into a receive-fixed, pay-variable interest rate swap to offset the exposure to interest rate risk associated with the debt instrument. Can the entity designate the swap as a cash flow hedge of the future interest cash outflows associated with the debt instrument?

No. IAS 39.86(b) states that a cash flow hedge is 'a hedge of the exposure to variability in cash flows'. In this case, the issued debt instrument does not give rise to any exposure to variability in cash flows since the interest payments are fixed. The entity may designate the swap as a fair value hedge of the debt instrument, but it cannot designate the swap as a cash flow hedge of the future cash outflows of the debt instrument.

F.3.2 Cash flow hedge: reinvestment of fixed interest rate cash flows

An entity manages interest rate risk on a net basis. On 1 January 2001, it forecasts aggregate cash inflows of CU100 on fixed rate assets and aggregate cash outflows of CU90 on fixed rate liabilities in the first quarter of 2002. For risk management purposes it uses a receive-variable, pay-fixed Forward Rate Agreement (FRA) to hedge the forecast net cash inflow of CU10. The entity designates as the hedged item the first CU10 of cash inflows on fixed rate assets in the first quarter of 2002. Can it designate the receive-variable, pay-fixed FRA as a cash flow hedge of the exposure to variability to cash flows in the first quarter of 2002 associated with the fixed rate assets?

No. The FRA does not qualify as a cash flow hedge of the cash flow relating to the fixed rate assets because they do not have a cash flow exposure. The entity could, however, designate the FRA as a hedge of the fair value exposure that exists before the cash flows are remitted.

In some cases, the entity could also hedge the interest rate exposure associated with the forecast reinvestment of the interest and principal it receives on fixed rate assets (see Question F.6.2). However, in this example, the FRA does not qualify for cash flow hedge accounting because it increases rather than reduces the variability of interest cash flows resulting from the reinvestment of interest cash flows (for example, if market rates increase, there will be a cash inflow on the FRA and an increase in the expected interest cash inflows resulting from the reinvestment of interest cash inflows on fixed rate assets). However, potentially it could qualify as a cash flow hedge of a portion of the refinancing of cash outflows on a gross basis.

F.3.3 Foreign currency hedge

Entity A has a foreign currency liability payable in six months' time and it wishes to hedge the amount payable on settlement against foreign currency fluctuations. To that end, it takes out a forward contract to buy the foreign currency in six months' time. Should the hedge be treated as:

(a) a fair value hedge of the foreign currency liability with gains and losses on revaluing the liability and the forward contract at the year-end both recognised in the income statement; or

(b) a cash flow hedge of the amount to be settled in the future with gains and losses on revaluing the forward contract recognised in equity?

IAS 39 does not preclude either of these two methods. If the hedge is treated as a fair value hedge, the gain or loss on the fair value remeasurement of the hedging instrument and the gain or loss on the fair value remeasurement of the hedged item for the hedged risk are recognised immediately in profit or loss. If the hedge is treated as a cash flow hedge with the gain or loss on remeasuring the forward contract recognised in equity, that amount is recognised in profit or loss in the same period or periods during which the hedged item (the liability) affects profit or loss, ie when the liability is remeasured for changes in foreign exchange rates. Therefore, if the hedge is effective, the gain or loss on the derivative is released to profit or loss in the same periods during which the liability is remeasured, not when the payment occurs. See Question F.3.4.

F.3.4 Foreign currency cash flow hedge

An entity exports a product at a price denominated in a foreign currency. At the date of the sale, the entity obtains a receivable for the sale price payable in 90 days and takes out a 90-day forward exchange contract in the same currency as the receivable to hedge its foreign currency exposure.

Under IAS 21, the sale is recorded at the spot rate at the date of sale, and the receivable is restated during the 90-day period for changes in exchange rates with the difference being taken to profit or loss (IAS 21.23 and IAS 21.28).

If the foreign exchange contract is designated as a hedging instrument, does the entity have a choice whether to designate the foreign exchange contract as a fair value hedge of the foreign currency exposure of the receivable or as a cash flow hedge of the collection of the receivable?

Yes. If the entity designates the foreign exchange contract as a fair value hedge, the gain or loss from remeasuring the forward exchange contract at fair value is recognised immediately in profit or loss and the gain or loss on remeasuring the receivable is also recognised in profit or loss.

If the entity designates the foreign exchange contract as a cash flow hedge of the foreign currency risk associated with the collection of the receivable, the portion of the gain or loss that is determined to be an effective hedge is recognised directly in equity, and the ineffective portion in profit or loss (IAS 39.95). The amount recognised directly in equity is transferred to profit or loss in the same period or periods during which changes in the measurement of the receivable affect profit or loss (IAS 39.100).

F.3.5 Fair value hedge: variable rate debt instrument

Does IAS 39 permit an entity to designate a portion of the risk exposure of a variable rate debt instrument as a hedged item in a fair value hedge?

Yes. A variable rate debt instrument may have an exposure to changes in its fair value due to credit risk. It may also have an exposure to changes in its fair value relating to movements in the market interest rate in the periods between which the variable interest rate on the debt instrument is reset. For example, if the debt instrument provides for annual interest payments reset to the market rate each year, a portion of the debt instrument has an exposure to changes in fair value during the year.

F.3.6 Fair value hedge: inventory

IAS 39.86(a) states that a fair value hedge is 'a hedge of the exposure to changes in fair value of a recognised asset or liability ... that is attributable to a particular risk and could affect profit or loss'. Can an entity designate inventories, such as copper inventory, as the hedged item in a fair value hedge of the exposure to changes in the price of the inventories, such as the copper price, although inventories are measured at the lower of cost and net realisable value under IAS 2 ***Inventories*****?**

Yes. The inventories may be hedged for changes in fair value due to changes in the copper price because the change in fair value of inventories will affect profit or loss when the inventories are sold or their carrying amount is written down. The adjusted carrying amount becomes the cost basis for the purpose of applying the lower of cost and net realisable value test under IAS 2. The hedging instrument used in a fair value hedge of inventories may alternatively qualify as a cash flow hedge of the future sale of the inventory.

F.3.7 Hedge accounting: forecast transaction

For cash flow hedges, a forecast transaction that is subject to a hedge must be 'highly probable'. How should the term 'highly probable' be interpreted?

The term 'highly probable' indicates a much greater likelihood of happening than the term 'more likely than not'. An assessment of the likelihood that a forecast transaction will take place is not based solely on management's intentions because intentions are not verifiable. A transaction's probability should be supported by observable facts and the attendant circumstances.

In assessing the likelihood that a transaction will occur, an entity should consider the following circumstances:

(a) the frequency of similar past transactions;

(b) the financial and operational ability of the entity to carry out the transaction;

(c) substantial commitments of resources to a particular activity (for example, a manufacturing facility that can be used in the short run only to process a particular type of commodity);

(d) the extent of loss or disruption of operations that could result if the transaction does not occur;

(e) the likelihood that transactions with substantially different characteristics might be used to achieve the same business purpose (for example, an entity that intends to raise cash may have several ways of doing so, ranging from a short-term bank loan to an offering of ordinary shares); and

(f) the entity's business plan.

The length of time until a forecast transaction is projected to occur is also a factor in determining probability. Other factors being equal, the more distant a forecast transaction is, the less likely it is that the transaction would be regarded as highly probable and the stronger the evidence that would be needed to support an assertion that it is highly probable.

For example, a transaction forecast to occur in five years may be less likely to occur than a transaction forecast to occur in one year. However, forecast interest payments for the next 20 years on variable rate debt would typically be highly probable if supported by an existing contractual obligation.

In addition, other factors being equal, the greater the physical quantity or future value of a forecast transaction in proportion to the entity's transactions of the same nature, the less likely it is that the transaction would be regarded as highly probable and the stronger the evidence that would be required to support an assertion that it is highly probable. For example, less evidence generally would be needed to support forecast sales of 100,000 units in the next month than 950,000 units in that month when recent sales have averaged 950,000 units per month for the past three months.

A history of having designated hedges of forecast transactions and then determining that the forecast transactions are no longer expected to occur would call into question both an entity's ability to predict forecast transactions accurately and the propriety of using hedge accounting in the future for similar forecast transactions.

F.3.8 Retrospective designation of hedges

Does IAS 39 permit an entity to designate hedge relationships retrospectively?

No. Designation of hedge relationships takes effect prospectively from the date all hedge accounting criteria in IAS 39.88 are met. In particular, hedge accounting can be applied only from the date the entity has completed the necessary documentation of the hedge relationship, including identification of the hedging instrument, the related hedged item or transaction, the nature of the risk being hedged, and how the entity will assess hedge effectiveness.

F.3.9 Hedge accounting: designation at the inception of the hedge

Does IAS 39 permit an entity to designate and formally document a derivative contract as a hedging instrument after entering into the derivative contract?

Yes, prospectively. For hedge accounting purposes, IAS 39 requires a hedging instrument to be designated and formally documented as such from the inception of the hedge relationship (IAS 39.88); in other words, a hedge relationship cannot be designated retrospectively. Also, it precludes designating a hedging relationship for only a portion of the time period during which the hedging instrument remains outstanding (IAS 39.75). However, it does not require the hedging instrument to be acquired at the inception of the hedge relationship.

F.3.10 Hedge accounting: identification of hedged forecast transaction

Can a forecast transaction be identified as the purchase or sale of the last 15,000 units of a product in a specified period or as a percentage of purchases or sales during a specified period?

No. The hedged forecast transaction must be identified and documented with sufficient specificity so that when the transaction occurs, it is clear whether the transaction is or is not the hedged transaction. Therefore, a forecast transaction may be identified as the sale of the first 15,000 units of a specific product during a specified three-month period, but it could not be identified as the last 15,000 units of that product sold during a three-month period because the last 15,000 units cannot be identified when they are sold. For the same reason, a forecast transaction cannot be specified solely as a percentage of sales or purchases during a period.

F.3.11 Cash flow hedge: documentation of timing of forecast transaction

For a hedge of a forecast transaction, should the documentation of the hedge relationship that is established at inception of the hedge identify the date on, or time period in which, the forecast transaction is expected to occur?

Yes. To qualify for hedge accounting, the hedge must relate to a specific identified and designated risk (IAS 39.AG110) and it must be possible to measure its effectiveness reliably (IAS 39.88(d)). Also, the hedged forecast transaction must be highly probable (IAS 39.88(c)). To meet these criteria, an entity is not required to predict and document the exact date a forecast transaction is expected to occur. However, it is required to identify and document the time period during which the forecast transaction is expected to occur within a reasonably specific and generally narrow range of time from a most probable date, as a basis for assessing hedge effectiveness. To determine that the hedge will be highly effective in accordance with IAS 39.88(d), it is necessary to ensure that changes in the fair value of the expected cash flows are offset by changes in the fair value of the hedging instrument and this test may be met only if the timing of the cash flows occur within close proximity to each other. If the forecast transaction is no longer expected to occur, hedge accounting is discontinued in accordance with IAS 39.101(c).

F.4 Hedge effectiveness

F.4.1 Hedging on an after–tax basis

Hedging is often done on an after-tax basis. Is hedge effectiveness assessed after taxes?

IAS 39 permits, but does not require, assessment of hedge effectiveness on an after-tax basis. If the hedge is undertaken on an after-tax basis, it is so designated at inception as part of the formal documentation of the hedging relationship and strategy.

F.4.2 Hedge effectiveness: assessment on cumulative basis

IAS 39.88(b) requires that the hedge is expected to be highly effective. Should expected hedge effectiveness be assessed separately for each period or cumulatively over the life of the hedging relationship?

Expected hedge effectiveness may be assessed on a cumulative basis if the hedge is so designated, and that condition is incorporated into the appropriate hedging documentation. Therefore, even if a hedge is not expected to be highly effective in a particular period, hedge accounting is not precluded if effectiveness is expected to remain sufficiently high over the life of the hedging relationship. However, any ineffectiveness is required to be recognised in profit or loss as it occurs.

To illustrate: an entity designates a LIBOR-based interest rate swap as a hedge of a borrowing whose interest rate is a UK base rate plus a margin. The UK base rate changes, perhaps, once each quarter or less, in increments of 25–50 basis points, while LIBOR changes daily. Over a period of 1–2 years, the hedge is expected to be almost perfect. However, there will be quarters when the UK base rate does not change at all, while LIBOR has changed significantly. This would not necessarily preclude hedge accounting.

F.4.3 Hedge effectiveness: counterparty credit risk

Must an entity consider the likelihood of default by the counterparty to the hedging instrument in assessing hedge effectiveness?

Yes. An entity cannot ignore whether it will be able to collect all amounts due under the contractual provisions of the hedging instrument. When assessing hedge effectiveness, both at the inception of the hedge and on an ongoing basis, the entity considers the risk that the counterparty to the hedging instrument will default by failing to make any contractual payments to the entity. For a cash flow hedge, if it becomes probable that a counterparty will default, an entity would be unable to conclude that the hedging relationship is expected to be highly effective in achieving offsetting cash flows. As a result, hedge accounting would be discontinued. For a fair value hedge, if there is a change in the counterparty's creditworthiness, the fair value of the hedging instrument will change, which affects the assessment of whether the hedge relationship is effective and whether it qualifies for continued hedge accounting.

F.4.4 Hedge effectiveness: effectiveness tests

How should hedge effectiveness be measured for the purposes of initially qualifying for hedge accounting and for continued qualification?

IAS 39 does not provide specific guidance about how effectiveness tests are performed. IAS 39.AG105 specifies that a hedge is normally regarded as highly effective only if (a) at inception and in subsequent periods, the hedge is expected to be highly effective in achieving offsetting changes in fair value or cash flows attributable to the hedged risk during the period for which the hedge is designated, and (b) the actual results are within a range of 80–125 per cent. IAS 39.AG105 also states that the expectation in (a) can be demonstrated in various ways.

The appropriateness of a given method of assessing hedge effectiveness will depend on the nature of the risk being hedged and the type of hedging instrument used. The method of assessing effectiveness must be reasonable and consistent with other similar hedges unless different methods are explicitly justified. An entity is required to document at the inception of the hedge how effectiveness will be assessed and then to apply that effectiveness test on a consistent basis for the duration of the hedge.

Several mathematical techniques can be used to measure hedge effectiveness, including ratio analysis, ie a comparison of hedging gains and losses with the corresponding gains and losses on the hedged item at a point in time, and statistical measurement techniques such as regression analysis. If regression analysis is used, the entity's documented policies for assessing effectiveness must specify how the results of the regression will be assessed.

F.4.5 Hedge effectiveness: less than 100 per cent offset

If a cash flow hedge is regarded as highly effective because the actual risk offset is within the allowed 80–125 per cent range of deviation from full offset, is the gain or loss on the ineffective portion of the hedge recognised in equity?

No. IAS 39.95(a) indicates that only the effective portion is recognised directly in equity. IAS 39.95(b) requires the ineffective portion to be recognised in profit or loss.

F.4.7 Assuming perfect hedge effectiveness

If the principal terms of the hedging instrument and of the entire hedged asset or liability or hedged forecast transaction are the same, can an entity assume perfect hedge effectiveness without further effectiveness testing?

No. IAS 39.88(e) requires an entity to assess hedges on an ongoing basis for hedge effectiveness. It cannot assume hedge effectiveness even if the principal terms of the hedging instrument and the hedged item are the same, since hedge ineffectiveness may arise because of other attributes such as the liquidity of the instruments or their credit risk (IAS 39.AG109). It may, however, designate only certain risks in an overall exposure as being hedged and thereby improve the effectiveness of the hedging relationship. For example, for a fair value hedge of a debt instrument, if the derivative hedging instrument has a credit risk that is equivalent to the AA-rate, it may designate only the risk related to AA-rated interest rate movements as being hedged, in which case changes in credit spreads generally will not affect the effectiveness of the hedge.

F.5 Cash flow hedges

F.5.1 Hedge accounting: non–derivative monetary asset or non-derivative monetary liability used as a hedging instrument

If an entity designates a non-derivative monetary asset as a foreign currency cash flow hedge of the repayment of the principal of a non-derivative monetary liability, would the exchange differences on the hedged item be recognised in profit or loss (IAS 21.28) and the exchange differences on the hedging instrument be recognised in equity until the repayment of the liability (IAS 39.95)?

No. Exchange differences on the monetary asset and the monetary liability are both recognised in profit or loss in the period in which they arise (IAS 21.28). IAS 39.AG83 specifies that if there is a hedge relationship between a non-derivative monetary asset and a non-derivative monetary liability, changes in fair values of those financial instruments are recognised in profit or loss.

F.5.2 Cash flow hedges: performance of hedging instrument (1)

Entity A has a floating rate liability of CU1,000 with five years remaining to maturity. It enters into a five-year pay-fixed, receive-floating interest rate swap in the same currency and with the same principal terms as the liability to hedge the exposure to variable cash flow payments on the floating rate liability attributable to interest rate risk. At inception, the fair value of the swap is zero. Subsequently, there is an increase of CU49 in the fair value of the swap. This increase consists of a change of CU50 resulting from an increase in market interest rates and a change of minus CU1 resulting from an increase in the credit risk of the swap counterparty. There is no change in the fair value of the floating rate liability, but the fair value (present value) of the future cash flows needed to offset the exposure to variable interest cash flows on the liability increases by CU50. Assuming that Entity A determines that the hedge is still highly effective, is there ineffectiveness that should be recognised in profit or loss?

No. A hedge of interest rate risk is not fully effective if part of the change in the fair value of the derivative is attributable to the counterparty's credit risk (IAS 39.AG109). However, because Entity A determines that the hedge relationship is still highly effective, it credits the effective portion of the change in fair value of the swap, ie the net change in fair value of CU49, to equity. There is no debit to profit or loss for the change in fair value of the swap attributable to the deterioration in the credit quality of the swap counterparty, because the cumulative change in the present value of the future cash flows needed to offset the exposure to variable interest cash flows on the hedged item, ie CU50, exceeds the cumulative change in value of the hedging instrument, ie CU49.

Dr Swap	CU49	
Cr Equity		CU49

If Entity A concludes that the hedge is no longer highly effective, it discontinues hedge accounting prospectively as from the date the hedge ceased to be highly effective in accordance with IAS 39.101.

Would the answer change if the fair value of the swap instead increases to CU51 of which CU50 results from the increase in market interest rates and CU1 from a decrease in the credit risk of the swap counterparty?

Yes. In this case, there is a credit to profit or loss of CU1 for the change in fair value of the swap attributable to the improvement in the credit quality of the swap counterparty. This is because the cumulative change in the value of the hedging instrument, ie CU51, exceeds the cumulative change in the present value of the future cash flows needed to offset the exposure to variable interest cash flows on the hedged item, ie CU50. The difference of CU1 represents the excess ineffectiveness attributable to the derivative hedging instrument, the swap, and is recognised in profit or loss.

Dr Swap	CU51	
Cr Equity		CU50
Cr Proft or loss		CU1

F.5.3 Cash flow hedges: performance of hedging instrument (2)

On 30 September 2001, Entity A hedges the anticipated sale of 24 tonnes of pulp on 1 March 2002 by entering into a short forward contract on 24 tonnes of pulp. The contract requires net settlement in cash determined as the difference between the future spot price of pulp on a specified commodity exchange and CU1,000. Entity A expects to sell the pulp in a different, local market. Entity A determines that the forward contract is an effective hedge of the anticipated sale and that the other conditions for hedge accounting are met. It assesses hedge effectiveness by comparing the entire change in the fair value of the forward contract with the change in the fair value of the expected cash inflows. On 31 December, the spot price of pulp has increased both in the local market and on the exchange. The increase in the local market exceeds the increase on the exchange. As a result, the present value of the expected cash inflow from the sale on the local market is CU1,100. The fair value of Entity A's forward contract is negative CU80. Assuming that Entity A determines that the hedge is still highly effective, is there ineffectiveness that should be recognised in profit or loss?

No. In a cash flow hedge, ineffectiveness is not recognised in the financial statements when the cumulative change in the fair value of the hedged cash flows exceeds the cumulative change in the value of the hedging instrument. In this case, the cumulative change in the fair value of the forward contract is CU80, while the fair value of the cumulative change in expected future cash flows on the hedged item is CU100. Since the fair value of the cumulative change in expected future cash flows on the hedged item from the inception of the hedge exceeds the cumulative change in fair value of the hedging instrument (in absolute amounts), no portion of the gain or loss on the hedging instrument is recognised in profit or loss (IAS 39.95(b)). Because Entity A determines that the hedge relationship is still highly effective, it debits the entire change in fair value of the forward contract (CU80) to equity.

Dr Equity	CU80	
Cr Forward		CU80

If Entity A concludes that the hedge is no longer highly effective, it discontinues hedge accounting prospectively as from the date the hedge ceases to be highly effective in accordance with IAS 39.101.

F.5.4 Cash flow hedges: forecast transaction occurs before the specified period

An entity designates a derivative as a hedging instrument in a cash flow hedge of a forecast transaction, such as a forecast sale of a commodity. The hedging relationship meets all the hedge accounting conditions, including the requirement to identify and document the period in which the transaction is expected to occur within a reasonably specific and narrow range of time (see Question F.1.17). If, in a subsequent period, the forecast transaction is expected to occur in an earlier period than originally anticipated, can the entity conclude that this transaction is the same as the one that was designated as being hedged?

Yes. The change in timing of the forecast transaction does not affect the validity of the designation. However, it may affect the assessment of the effectiveness of the hedging relationship. Also, the hedging instrument would need to be designated as a hedging instrument for the whole remaining period of its existence in order for it to continue to qualify as a hedging instrument (see IAS 39.75 and Question F.2.17).

F.5.5 Cash flow hedges: measuring effectiveness for a hedge of a forecast transaction in a debt instrument

A forecast investment in an interest-earning asset or forecast issue of an interest-bearing liability creates a cash flow exposure to interest rate changes because the related interest payments will be based on the market rate that exists when the forecast transaction occurs. The objective of a cash flow hedge of the exposure to interest rate changes is to offset the effects of future changes in interest rates so as to obtain a single fixed rate, usually the rate that existed at the inception of the hedge that corresponds with the term and timing of the forecast transaction. During the period of the hedge, it is not possible to determine what the market interest rate for the forecast transaction will be at the time the hedge is terminated or when the forecast transaction occurs. In this case, how is the effectiveness of the hedge assessed and measured?

During this period, effectiveness can be measured on the basis of changes in interest rates between the designation date and the interim effectiveness measurement date. The interest rates used to make this measurement are the interest rates that correspond with the term and occurrence of the forecast transaction that existed at the inception of the hedge and that exist at the measurement date as evidenced by the term structure of interest rates.

Generally it will not be sufficient simply to compare cash flows of the hedged item with cash flows generated by the derivative hedging instrument as they are paid or received, since such an approach ignores the entity's expectations of whether the cash flows will offset in subsequent periods and whether there will be any resulting ineffectiveness.

The discussion that follows illustrates the mechanics of establishing a cash flow hedge and measuring its effectiveness. For the purpose of the illustrations, assume that an entity expects to issue a CU100,000 one-year debt instrument in three months. The instrument will pay interest quarterly with principal due at maturity. The entity is exposed to interest rate increases and establishes a hedge of the interest cash flows of the debt by entering into a forward starting interest rate swap. The swap has a term of one year and will start in three months to correspond with the terms of the forecast debt issue. The entity will pay a fixed rate and receive a variable rate, and the entity designates the risk being hedged as the LIBOR-based interest component in the forecast issue of the debt.

Yield curve

The yield curve provides the foundation for computing future cash flows and the fair value of such cash flows both at the inception of, and during, the hedging relationship. It is based on current market yields on applicable reference bonds that are traded in the marketplace. Market yields are converted to spot interest rates ('spot rates' or 'zero coupon rates') by eliminating the effect of coupon payments on the market yield. Spot rates are used to discount future cash flows, such as principal and interest rate payments, to arrive at their fair value. Spot rates also are used to compute forward interest rates that are used to compute variable and estimated future cash flows. The relationship between spot rates and one-period forward rates is shown by the following formula:

Spot–forward relationship

$$F = \frac{(1 + SR_t)^t}{(1 + SR_{t-1})^{t-1}} - 1$$

where F = forward rate (%)

SR = spot rate (%)

t = period in time (eg 1, 2, 3, 4, 5)

Also, for the purpose of this illustration, assume that the following quarterly-period term structure of interest rates using quarterly compounding exists at the inception of the hedge.

Yield curve at inception – (beginning of period 1)					
Forward periods	*1*	*2*	*3*	*4*	*5*
Spot rates	3.75%	4.50%	5.50%	6.00%	6.25%
Forward rates	3.75%	5.25%	7.51%	7.50%	7.25%

The one-period forward rates are computed on the basis of spot rates for the applicable maturities. For example, the current forward rate for Period 2 calculated using the formula above is equal to $[1.0450^2/1.0375] - 1 = 5.25$ per cent. The current one-period forward rate for Period 2 is different from the current spot rate for Period 2, since the spot rate is an interest rate from the beginning of Period 1 (spot) to the end of Period 2, while the forward rate is an interest rate from the beginning of Period 2 to the end of Period 2.

Hedged item

In this example, the entity expects to issue a CU100,000 one-year debt instrument in three months with quarterly interest payments. The entity is exposed to interest rate increases and would like to eliminate the effect on cash flows of interest rate changes that may happen before the forecast transaction takes place. If that risk is eliminated, the entity would obtain an interest rate on its debt issue that is equal to the one-year forward coupon rate currently available in the marketplace in three months. That forward coupon rate, which is different from the forward (spot) rate, is 6.86 per cent, computed from the term structure of interest rates shown above. It is the market rate of interest that exists at the inception of the hedge, given the terms of the forecast debt instrument. It results in the fair value of the debt being equal to par at its issue.

At the inception of the hedging relationship, the expected cash flows of the debt instrument can be calculated on the basis of the existing term structure of interest rates. For this purpose, it is assumed that interest rates do not change and that the debt would be issued at 6.86 per cent at the beginning of Period 2. In this case, the cash flows and fair value of the debt instrument would be as follows at the beginning of Period 2.

Issue of fixed rate debt Beginning of period 2 – No rate changes (spot based on forward rates)						
	Total					
Original forward periods		*1*	*2*	*3*	*4*	*5*
Remaining periods			*1*	*2*	*3*	*4*
Spot rates			5.25%	6.38%	6.75%	6.88%
Forward rates			5.25%	7.51%	7.50%	7.25%
	CU		*CU*	*CU*	*CU*	*CU*
Cash flows:						
Fixed interest @6.86%			1,716	1,716	1,716	1,716
Principal						100,000
Fair value:						
Interest	6,592		1,694	1,663	1,632	1,603
Principal	93,408					93,408[(a)]
Total	100,000					

(a) $\text{CU}100{,}000/(1 + [0.0688/4])^{4}$

Since it is assumed that interest rates do not change, the fair value of the interest and principal amounts equals the par amount of the forecast transaction. The fair value amounts are computed on the basis of the spot rates that exist at the inception of the hedge for the applicable periods in which the cash flows would occur had the debt been issued at the date of the forecast transaction. They reflect the effect of discounting those cash flows on the basis of the periods that will remain after the debt instrument is issued.

For example, the spot rate of 6.38 per cent is used to discount the interest cash flow that is expected to be paid in Period 3, but it is discounted for only two periods because it will occur two periods after the forecast transaction.

The forward interest rates are the same as shown previously, since it is assumed that interest rates do not change. The spot rates are different but they have not actually changed. They represent the spot rates one period forward and are based on the applicable forward rates.

Hedging instrument

The objective of the hedge is to obtain an overall interest rate on the forecast transaction and the hedging instrument that is equal to 6.86 per cent, which is the market rate at the inception of the hedge for the period from Period 2 to Period 5. This objective is accomplished by entering into a forward starting interest rate swap that has a fixed rate of 6.86 per cent. Based on the term structure of interest rates that exist at the inception of the hedge, the interest rate swap will have such a rate. At the inception of the hedge, the fair value of the fixed rate payments on the interest rate swap will equal the fair value of the variable rate payments, resulting in the interest rate swap having a fair value of zero. The expected cash flows of the interest rate swap and the related fair value amounts are shown as follows.

Interest rate swap						
	Total					
Original forward periods		*1*	*2*	*3*	*4*	*5*
Remaining periods			*1*	*2*	*3*	*4*
	CU		*CU*	*CU*	*CU*	*CU*
Cash flows:						
Fixed interest @6.86%			1,716	1,716	1,716	1,716
Forecast variable interest			1,313	1,877	1,876	1,813
Forecast based on forward rate			*5.25%*	*7.51%*	*7.50%*	*7.25%*
Net interest			(403)	161	160	97
Fair value:						
Discount rate (spot)			*5.25%*	*6.38%*	*6.75%*	*6.88%*
Fixed interest	6,592		1,694	1,663	1,632	1,603
Forecast variable interest	6,592		1,296	1,819	1,784	1,693
Fair value of interest rate swap	0		(398)	156	152	90

At the inception of the hedge, the fixed rate on the forward swap is equal to the fixed rate the entity would receive if it could issue the debt in three months under terms that exist today.

Measuring hedge effectiveness

If interest rates change during the period the hedge is outstanding, the effectiveness of the hedge can be measured in various ways.

Assume that interest rates change as follows immediately before the debt is issued at the beginning of Period 2.

Yield curve – Rates increase 200 basis points					
Forward periods	*1*	*2*	*3*	*4*	*5*
Remaining periods		*1*	*2*	*3*	*4*
Spot rates		5.75%	6.50%	7.50%	8.00%
Forward rates		5.75%	7.25%	9.51%	9.50%

Under the new interest rate environment, the fair value of the pay-fixed at 6.86 per cent, receive-variable interest rate swap that was designated as the hedging instrument would be as follows.

Fair value of interest rate swap						
	Total					
Original forward periods		*1*	*2*	*3*	*4*	*5*
Remaining periods			*1*	*2*	*3*	*4*
	CU	*CU*	*CU*	*CU*	*CU*	*CU*
Cash flows:						
Fixed interest @6.86%			1,716	1,716	1,716	1,716
Forecast variable interest			1,438	1,813	2,377	2,376
Forecast based on new forward rate			*5.25%*	*7.25%*	*9.51%*	*9.50%*
Net interest			(279)	97	661	660
Fair value:						
New discount rate (spot)			*5.75%*	*6.50%*	*7.50%*	*8.00%*
Fixed interest	6,562		1,692	1,662	1,623	1,585
Forecast variable interest	7,615		1,417	1,755	2,248	2,195
Fair value of net interest	1,053		(275)	93	625	610

In order to compute the effectiveness of the hedge, it is necessary to measure the change in the present value of the cash flows or the value of the hedged forecast transaction. There are at least two methods of accomplishing this measurement.

Method A	**Compute change in fair value of debt**					
	Total					
Original forward periods		*1*	*2*	*3*	*4*	*5*
Remaining periods			*1*	*2*	*3*	*4*
	CU		*CU*	*CU*	*CU*	*CU*
Cash flows:						
Fixed interest @6.86%			1,716	1,716	1,716	1,716
Principal				100,000		
Fair value:						
New discount rate (spot)			*5.75%*	*6.50%*	*7.50%*	*8.00%*
Interest	6,562		1,692	1,662	1,623	1,585
Principal	92,385					92,385[(a)]
Total	98,947					
Fair value at inception	100,000					
Fair value difference	(1,053)					

(a) $CU100,000/(1 + [0.08/4])^4$

Under Method A, a computation is made of the fair value in the new interest rate environment of debt that carries interest that is equal to the coupon interest rate that existed at the inception of the hedging relationship (6.86 per cent). This fair value is compared with the expected fair value as of the beginning of Period 2 that was calculated on the basis of the term structure of interest rates that existed at the inception of the hedging relationship, as illustrated above, to determine the change in the fair value. Note that the difference between the change in the fair value of the swap and the change in the expected fair value of the debt exactly offset in this example, since the terms of the swap and the forecast transaction match each other.

Method B Compute change in fair value of cash flows						
	Total					
Original forward periods		*1*	*2*	*3*	*4*	*5*
Remaining periods			*1*	*2*	*3*	*4*
Market rate at inception			6.86%	6.86%	6.86%	6.86%
Current forward rate			5.75%	7.25%	9.51%	9.50%
Rate difference			1.11%	(0.39%)	(2.64%)	(2.64%)
Cash flow difference (principal rate)			CU279	(CU97)	(CU661)	(CU660)
Discount rate (spot)			5.75%	6.50%	7.50%	8.00%
Fair value of difference	(CU1,053)		CU275	(CU93)	(CU625)	(CU610)

Under Method B, the present value of the change in cash flows is computed on the basis of the difference between the forward interest rates for the applicable periods at the effectiveness measurement date and the interest rate that would have been obtained if the debt had been issued at the market rate that existed at the inception of the hedge. The market rate that existed at the inception of the hedge is the one-year forward coupon rate in three months. The present value of the change in cash flows is computed on the basis of the current spot rates that exist at the effectiveness measurement date for the applicable periods in which the cash flows are expected to occur. This method also could be referred to as the 'theoretical swap' method (or 'hypothetical derivative' method) because the comparison is between the hedged fixed rate on the debt and the current variable rate, which is the same as comparing cash flows on the fixed and variable rate legs of an interest rate swap.

As before, the difference between the change in the fair value of the swap and the change in the present value of the cash flows exactly offset in this example, since the terms match.

Other considerations

There is an additional computation that should be performed to compute ineffectiveness before the expected date of the forecast transaction that has not been considered for the purpose of this illustration. The fair value difference has been determined in each of the illustrations as of the expected date of the forecast transaction immediately before the forecast transaction, ie at the beginning of Period 2. If the assessment of hedge effectiveness is done before the forecast transaction occurs, the difference should be discounted to the current date to arrive at the actual amount of ineffectiveness. For example, if the measurement date were one month after the hedging relationship was established and the forecast transaction is now expected to occur in two months, the amount would have to be discounted for the remaining two months before the forecast transaction is expected to occur to arrive at the actual fair value. This step would not be necessary in the examples provided above because there was no ineffectiveness. Therefore, additional discounting of the amounts, which net to zero, would not have changed the result.

Under Method B, ineffectiveness is computed on the basis of the difference between the forward coupon interest rates for the applicable periods at the effectiveness measurement date and the interest rate that would have been obtained if the debt had been issued at the market rate that existed at the inception of the hedge. Computing the change in cash flows based on the difference between the forward interest rates that existed at the inception of the hedge and the forward rates that exist at the effectiveness measurement date is inappropriate if the objective of the hedge is to establish a single fixed rate for a series of forecast interest payments. This objective is met by hedging the exposures with an interest rate swap as illustrated in the above example. The fixed interest rate on the swap is a blended interest rate composed of the forward rates over the life of the swap. Unless the yield curve is flat, the comparison between the forward interest rate exposures over the life of the swap and the fixed rate on the swap will produce different cash flows whose fair values are equal only at the inception of the hedging relationship. This difference is shown in the table below.

	Total					
Original forward periods		*1*	*2*	*3*	*4*	*5*
Remaining periods			*1*	*2*	*3*	*4*
Forward rate at inception			5.25%	7.51%	7.50%	7.25%
Current forward rate			5.75%	7.25%	9.51%	9.50%
Rate difference			(0.50%)	0.26%	(2.00%)	(2.25%)
Cash flow difference (principal rate)			(CU125)	CU64	(CU501)	(CU563)
Discount rate (spot)			5.75%	6.50%	7.50%	8.00%
Fair value of difference	(CU1,055)		(CU123)	CU62	(CU474)	(CU520)
Fair value of interest rate swap	CU1,053					
Ineffectiveness	(CU2)					

If the objective of the hedge is to obtain the forward rates that existed at the inception of the hedge, the interest rate swap is ineffective because the swap has a single blended fixed coupon rate that does not offset a series of different forward interest rates. However, if the objective of the hedge is to obtain the forward coupon rate that existed at the inception of the hedge, the swap is effective, and the comparison based on differences in forward interest rates suggests ineffectiveness when none may exist. Computing ineffectiveness based on the difference between the forward interest rates that existed at the inception of the hedge and the forward rates that exist at the effectiveness measurement date would be an appropriate measurement of ineffectiveness if the hedging objective is to lock in those forward interest rates. In that case, the appropriate hedging instrument would be a series of forward contracts each of which matures on a repricing date that corresponds with the date of the forecast transactions.

It also should be noted that it would be inappropriate to compare only the variable cash flows on the interest rate swap with the interest cash flows in the debt that would be generated by the forward interest rates. That methodology has the effect of measuring ineffectiveness only on a portion of the derivative, and IAS 39 does not permit the bifurcation of a derivative for the purposes of assessing effectiveness in this situation (IAS 39.74). It is recognised, however, that if the fixed interest rate on the interest rate swap is equal to the fixed rate that would have been obtained on the debt at inception, there will be no ineffectiveness assuming that there are no differences in terms and no change in credit risk or it is not designated in the hedging relationship.

F.5.6 Cash flow hedges: firm commitment to purchase inventory in a foreign currency

Entity A has the Local Currency (LC) as its functional currency and presentation currency. On 30 June 2001, it enters into a forward exchange contract to receive Foreign Currency (FC) 100,000 and deliver LC109,600 on 30 June 2002 at an initial cost and fair value of zero. It designates the forward exchange contract as a hedging instrument in a cash flow hedge of a firm commitment to purchase a certain quantity of paper on 31 March 2002 and the resulting payable of FC100,000, which is to be paid on 30 June 2002. All hedge accounting conditions in IAS 39 are met.

As indicated in the table below, on 30 June 2001, the spot exchange rate is LC1.072 to FC1, while the twelve-month forward exchange rate is LC1.096 to FC1. On 31 December 2001, the spot exchange rate is LC1.080 to FC1, while the six-month forward exchange rate is LC1.092 to FC1. On 31 March 2002, the spot exchange rate is LC1.074 to FC1, while the three-month forward rate is LC1.076 to FC1. On 30 June 2002, the spot exchange rate is LC1.072 to FC1. The applicable yield curve in the local currency is flat at 6 per cent per year throughout the period. The fair value of the forward exchange contract is negative LC388 on 31 December 2001 {([1.092 × 100,000] – 109,600)/$1.06^{(6/12)}$}, negative LC1.971 on 31 March 2002 {([1.076 × 100,000] – 109,600)/1.06($^{(3/12)}$)}, and negative LC2,400 on 30 June 2002 {1.072 × 100,000 – 109,600}.

Date	Spot rate	Forward rate to 30 June 2002	Fair value of forward contract
30 June 2001	1.072	1.096	–
31 December 2001	1.080	1.092	(388)
31 March 2002	1.074	1.076	(1,971)
30 June 2002	1.072	–	(2,400)

Issue (a) – What is the accounting for these transactions if the hedging relationship is designated as being for changes in the fair value of the forward exchange contract and the entity's accounting policy is to apply basis adjustment to non-financial assets that result from hedged forecast transactions?

The accounting entries are as follows.

30 June 2001

Dr Forward	LC0	
Cr Cash		LC0

To record the forward exchange contract at its initial amount of zero (IAS 39.43). The hedge is expected to be fully effective because the critical terms of the forward exchange contract and the purchase contract and the assessment of hedge effectiveness are based on the forward price (IAS 39.AG108).

31 December 2001

Dr Equity	LC388	
Cr Forward liability		LC388

To record the change in the fair value of the forward exchange contract between 30 June 2001 and 31 December 2001, ie LC388 – 0 = LC388, directly in equity (IAS 39.95). The hedge is fully effective because the loss on the forward exchange contract (LC388) exactly offsets the change in cash flows associated with the purchase contract based on the forward price [(LC388) = {([1.092 × 100,000] – 109,600)/$1.06^{(6/12)}$} – {([1.096 × 100,000] – 109,600)/1.06}].

31 March 2002

Dr Equity	LC1,583	
Cr Forward liability		LC1,583

To record the change in the fair value of the forward exchange contract between 1 January 2002 and 31 March 2002 (ie LC1,971 – LC388 = LC1,583), directly in equity (IAS 39.94). The hedge is fully effective because the loss on the forward exchange contract (LC1,583) exactly offsets the change in cash flows associated with the purchase contract based on the forward price [(LC1,583) = {([1.076 × 100,000] – 109,600)/$1.06^{(3/12)}$} – {([1.092 × 100,000] – 109,600)/$1.06^{(6/12)}$}].

Dr Paper (purchase price)	LC107,400	
Dr Paper (hedging loss)	LC1,971	
Cr Equity		LC1,971
Cr Payable		LC107,400

To recognise the purchase of the paper at the spot rate (1.074 × FC100,000) and remove the cumulative loss on the forward exchange contract that has been recognised directly in equity (LC1,971) and include it in the initial measurement of the purchased paper. Accordingly, the initial measurement of the purchased paper is LC109,371 consisting of a purchase consideration of LC107,400 and a hedging loss of LC1,971.

30 June 2002

Dr Payable	LC107,400	
Cr Cash		LC107,200
Cr Profit or loss		LC200

To record the settlement of the payable at the spot rate (FC100,000 × 1.072 = 107,200) and the associated exchange gain of LC200 (LC107,400 – LC107,200).

Dr Profit or loss	LC429	
Cr Forward liability		LC429

To record the loss on the forward exchange contract between 1 April 2002 and 30 June 2002 (ie LC2,400 – LC1,971 = LC429) in profit or loss. The hedge is regarded as fully effective because the loss on the forward exchange contract (LC429) exactly offsets the change in the fair value of the payable based on the forward price (LC429 = ([1.072 × 100,000] – 109,600 – {([1.076 × 100,000] – 109,600)/1.06$^{(3/12)}$}).

Dr Forward liability	LC2,400	
Cr Cash		LC2,400

To record the net settlement of the forward exchange contract.

Issue (b) – What is the accounting for these transactions if the hedging relationship instead is designated as being for changes in the spot element of the forward exchange contract and the interest element is excluded from the designated hedging relationship (IAS 39.74)?

The accounting entries are as follows.

30 June 2001

Dr Forward	LC0	
Cr Cash		LC0

To record the forward exchange contract at its initial amount of zero (IAS 39.43). The hedge is expected to be fully effective because the critical terms of the forward exchange contract and the purchase contract are the same and the change in the premium or discount on the forward contract is excluded from the assessment of effectiveness (IAS 39.AG108).

31 December 2001

Dr Profit or loss (interest element)	LC1,165	
Cr Equity (spot element)		LC777
Cr Forward liability		LC388

To record the change in the fair value of the forward exchange contract between 30 June 2001 and 31 December 2001, ie LC388 – 0 = LC388. The change in the present value of spot settlement of the forward exchange contract is a gain of LC777 ({([1.080 × 100,000] – 107,200)/1.06$^{(6/12)}$} – {([1.072 × 100,000] – 107,200)/1.06}), which is recognised directly in equity (IAS 39.95(a)). The change in the interest element of the forward exchange contract (the residual change in fair value) is a loss of LC1,165 (388 + 777), which is recognised in profit or loss (IAS 39.74 and IAS 39.55(a)). The hedge is fully effective because the gain in the spot element of the forward contract (LC777) exactly offsets the change in the purchase price at spot rates (LC777 = {([1.080 × 100,000] – 107,200)/1.06$^{(6/12)}$} – {([1.072 × 100,000] – 107,200)/1.06}).

31 March 2002

Dr Equity (spot element)	LC580	
Dr Profit or loss (interest element)	LC1,003	
Cr Forward liability		LC1,583

To record the change in the fair value of the forward exchange contract between 1 January 2002 and 31 March 2002, ie LC1,971 – LC388 = LC1,583. The change in the present value of the spot settlement of the forward exchange contract is a loss of LC580 ({([1.074 × 100,000] – 107,200)/1.06$^{(3/12)}$} – {([1.080 × 100,000] – 107,200)/1.06$^{(6/12)}$}), which is recognised directly in equity (IAS 39.95(a)). The change in the interest element of the forward exchange contract (the residual change in fair value) is a loss of LC1,003 (LC1,583 – LC580), which is recognised in profit or loss (IAS 39.74 and IAS 39.55(a)). The hedge is fully effective because the loss in the spot element of the forward contract (LC580) exactly offsets the change in the purchase price at spot rates [(580) = {([1.074 × 100,000] – 107,200)/1.06$^{(3/12)}$} – {([1.080 × 100,000] – 107,200) /1.06$^{(6/12)}$}].

Dr Paper (purchase price)	LC107,400	
Dr Equity	LC197	
Cr Paper (hedging gain)		LC197
Cr Payable		LC107,400

To recognise the purchase of the paper at the spot rate (= 1.074 × FC100,000) and remove the cumulative gain on the spot element of the forward exchange contract that has been recognised directly in equity (LC777 – LC580 = LC197) and include it in the initial measurement of the purchased paper. Accordingly, the initial measurement of the purchased paper is LC107,203, consisting of a purchase consideration of LC107,400 and a hedging gain of LC197.

30 June 2002

Dr Payable	LC107,400	
Cr Cash		LC107,200
Cr Profit or loss		LC200

To record the settlement of the payable at the spot rate (FC100,000 × 1.072 = LC107,200) and the associated exchange gain of LC200 (– [1.072 – 1.074] × FC100,000).

Dr Profit or loss (spot element)	LC197	
Dr Profit or loss (interest element)	LC232	
Cr Forward liability		LC429

To record the change in the fair value of the forward exchange contract between 1 April 2002 and 30 June 2002 (ie LC2,400 – LC1,971 = LC429). The change in the present value of the spot settlement of the forward exchange contract is a loss of LC197 ([1.072 × 100,000] – 107,200 – {([1.074 × 100,000] – 107,200)/$1.06^{(3/12)}$}), which is recognised in profit or loss. The change in the interest element of the forward exchange contract (the residual change in fair value) is a loss of LC232 (LC429 – LC197), which is recognised in profit or loss. The hedge is fully effective because the loss in the spot element of the forward contract (LC197) exactly offsets the change in the present value of the spot settlement of the payable [(LC197) = {[1.072 × 100,000] – 107,200 – {([1.074 × 100,000] – 107,200)/$1.06^{(3/12)}$}].

Dr Forward liability	LC2,400	
Cr Cash		LC2,400

To record the net settlement of the forward exchange contract.

The following table provides an overview of the components of the change in fair value of the hedging instrument over the term of the hedging relationship. It illustrates that the way in which a hedging relationship is designated affects the subsequent accounting for that hedging relationship, including the assessment of hedge effectiveness and the recognition of gains and losses.

Period ending	*Change in spot settlement*	*Fair value of change in spot settlement*	*Change in forward settlement*	*Fair value of change in forward settlement*	*Fair value of change in interest element*
	LC	*LC*	*LC*	*LC*	*LC*
June 2001	–	–	–	–	–
December 2001	800	777	(400)	(388)	(1,165)
March 2002	(600)	(580)	(1,600)	(1,583)	(1,003)
June 2002	(200)	(197)	(400)	(429)	(232)
Total	–	–	(2,400)	(2,400)	(2,400)

F.6 Hedges: other issues

F.6.1 Hedge accounting: management of interest rate risk in financial institutions

Banks and other financial institutions often manage their exposure to interest rate risk on a net basis for all or parts of their activities. They have systems to accumulate critical information throughout the entity about their financial assets, financial liabilities and forward commitments, including loan commitments. This information is used to estimate and aggregate cash flows and to schedule such estimated cash flows into the applicable future periods in which they are expected to be paid or received. The systems generate estimates of cash flows based on the contractual terms of the instruments and other factors, including estimates of prepayments and defaults. For risk management purposes, many financial institutions use derivative contracts to offset some or all exposure to interest rate risk on a net basis.

If a financial institution manages interest rate risk on a net basis, can its activities potentially qualify for hedge accounting under IAS 39?

Yes. However, to qualify for hedge accounting the derivative hedging instrument that hedges the net position for risk management purposes must be designated for accounting purposes as a hedge of a gross position related to assets, liabilities, forecast cash inflows or forecast cash outflows giving rise to the net exposure (IAS 39.84, IAS 39.AG101 and IAS 39.AG111). It is not possible to designate a net position as a hedged item under IAS 39 because of the inability to associate hedging gains and losses with a specific item being hedged and, correspondingly, to determine objectively the period in which such gains and losses should be recognised in profit or loss.

Hedging a net exposure to interest rate risk can often be defined and documented to meet the qualifying criteria for hedge accounting in IAS 39.88 if the objective of the activity is to offset a specific, identified and designated risk exposure that ultimately affects the entity's profit or loss (IAS 39.AG110) and the entity designates and documents its interest rate risk exposure on a gross basis. Also, to qualify for hedge accounting the information systems must capture sufficient information about the amount and timing of cash flows and the effectiveness of the risk management activities in accomplishing their objective.

The factors an entity must consider for hedge accounting purposes if it manages interest rate risk on a net basis are discussed in Question F.6.2.

F.6.2 Hedge accounting considerations when interest rate risk is managed on a net basis

If an entity manages its exposure to interest rate risk on a net basis, what are the issues the entity should consider in defining and documenting its interest rate risk management activities to qualify for hedge accounting and in establishing and accounting for the hedge relationship?

Issues (a)–(l) below deal with the main issues. First, Issues (a) and (b) discuss the designation of derivatives used in interest rate risk management activities as fair value hedges or cash flow hedges. As noted there, hedge accounting criteria and accounting consequences differ between fair value hedges and cash flow hedges. Since it may be easier to achieve hedge accounting treatment if derivatives used in interest rate risk management activities are designated as cash flow hedging instruments, Issues (c)–(l) expand on various aspects of the accounting for cash flow hedges. Issues (c)–(f) consider the application of the hedge accounting criteria for cash flow hedges in IAS 39, and Issues (g) and (h) discuss the required accounting treatment. Finally, Issues (i)–(l) elaborate on other specific issues relating to the accounting for cash flow hedges.

Issue (a) – Can a derivative that is used to manage interest rate risk on a net basis be designated under IAS 39 as a hedging instrument in a fair value hedge or a cash flow hedge of a gross exposure?

Both types of designation are possible under IAS 39. An entity may designate the derivative used in interest rate risk management activities either as a fair value hedge of assets, liabilities and firm commitments or as a cash flow hedge of forecast transactions, such as the anticipated reinvestment of cash inflows, the anticipated refinancing or rollover of a financial liability, and the cash flow consequences of the resetting of interest rates for an asset or a liability.

In economic terms, it does not matter whether the derivative instrument is regarded as a fair value hedge or as a cash flow hedge. Under either perspective of the exposure, the derivative has the same economic effect of reducing the net exposure. For example, a receive-fixed, pay-variable interest rate swap can be considered to be a cash flow hedge of a variable rate asset or a fair value hedge of a fixed rate liability. Under either perspective, the fair value or cash flows of the interest rate swap offset the exposure to interest rate changes. However, accounting consequences differ depending on whether the derivative is designated as a fair value hedge or a cash flow hedge, as discussed in Issue (b).

To illustrate: a bank has the following assets and liabilities with a maturity of two years.

	Variable interest	Fixed interest
	CU	CU
Assets	60	100
Liabilities	(100)	(60)
Net	(40)	40

The bank takes out a two-year swap with a notional principal of CU40 to receive a variable interest rate and pay a fixed interest rate to hedge the net exposure. As discussed above, this may be regarded and designated either as a fair value hedge of CU40 of the fixed rate assets or as a cash flow hedge of CU40 of the variable rate liabilities.

Issue (b) – What are the critical considerations in deciding whether a derivative that is used to manage interest rate risk on a net basis should be designated as a hedging instrument in a fair value hedge or a cash flow hedge of a gross exposure?

Critical considerations include the assessment of hedge effectiveness in the presence of prepayment risk and the ability of the information systems to attribute fair value or cash flow changes of hedging instruments to fair value or cash flow changes, respectively, of hedged items, as discussed below.

For accounting purposes, the designation of a derivative as hedging a fair value exposure or a cash flow exposure is important because both the qualification requirements for hedge accounting and the recognition of hedging gains and losses for these categories are different. It is often easier to demonstrate high effectiveness for a cash flow hedge than for a fair value hedge.

Effects of prepayments

Prepayment risk inherent in many financial instruments affects the fair value of an instrument and the timing of its cash flows and impacts on the effectiveness test for fair value hedges and the highly probable test for cash flow hedges, respectively.

Effectiveness is often more difficult to achieve for fair value hedges than for cash flow hedges when the instrument being hedged is subject to prepayment risk. For a fair value hedge to qualify for hedge accounting, the changes in the fair value of the derivative hedging instrument must be expected to be highly effective in offsetting the changes in the fair value of the hedged item (IAS 39.88(b)). This test may be difficult to meet if, for example, the derivative hedging instrument is a forward contract having a fixed term and the financial assets being hedged are subject to prepayment by the borrower. Also, it may be difficult to conclude that, for a portfolio of fixed rate assets that are subject to prepayment, the changes in the fair value for each individual item in the group will be expected to be approximately proportional to the overall changes in fair value attributable to the hedged risk of the group. Even if the risk being hedged is a benchmark interest rate, to be able to conclude that fair value changes will be proportional for each item in the portfolio, it may be necessary to disaggregate the asset portfolio into categories based on term, coupon, credit, type of loan and other characteristics.

In economic terms, a forward derivative instrument could be used to hedge assets that are subject to prepayment but it would be effective only for small movements in interest rates. A reasonable estimate of prepayments can be made for a given interest rate environment and the derivative position can be adjusted as the interest rate environment changes. If an entity's risk management strategy is to adjust the amount of the hedging instrument periodically to reflect changes in the hedged position, the entity needs to demonstrate that the hedge is expected to be highly effective only for the period until the amount of the hedging instrument is next adjusted. However, for that period, the expectation of effectiveness has to be based on existing fair value exposures and the potential for interest rate movements without consideration of future adjustments to those positions. Furthermore, the fair value exposure attributable to prepayment risk can generally be hedged with options.

For a cash flow hedge to qualify for hedge accounting, the forecast cash flows, including the reinvestment of cash inflows or the refinancing of cash outflows, must be highly probable (IAS 39.88(c)) and the hedge expected to be highly effective in achieving offsetting changes in the cash flows of the hedged item and hedging instrument (IAS 39.88(b)). Prepayments affect the timing of cash flows and, therefore, the probability of occurrence of the forecast transaction. If the hedge is established for risk management purposes on a net basis, an entity may have sufficient levels of highly probable cash flows on a gross basis to support the designation for accounting purposes of forecast transactions associated with a portion of the gross cash flows as the hedged item. In this case, the portion of the gross cash flows designated as being hedged may be chosen to be equal to the amount of net cash flows being hedged for risk management purposes.

Systems considerations

The accounting for fair value hedges differs from that for cash flow hedges. It is usually easier to use existing information systems to manage and track cash flow hedges than it is for fair value hedges.

Under fair value hedge accounting, the assets or liabilities that are designated as being hedged are remeasured for those changes in fair values during the hedge period that are attributable to the risk being hedged. Such changes adjust the carrying amount of the hedged items and, for interest sensitive assets and liabilities, may result in an adjustment of the effective interest rate of the hedged item (IAS 39.89). As a consequence of fair value hedging activities, the changes in fair value have to be allocated to the assets or liabilities being hedged in order for the entity to be able to recompute their effective interest rate, determine the subsequent amortisation of the fair value adjustment to profit or loss, and determine the amount that should be recognised in profit or loss when assets are sold or liabilities extinguished (IAS 39.89 and IAS 39.92). To comply with the requirements for fair value hedge accounting, it will generally be necessary to establish a system to track the changes in the fair value attributable to the hedged risk, associate those changes with individual hedged items, recompute the effective interest rate of the hedged items, and amortise the changes to profit or loss over the life of the respective hedged item.

Under cash flow hedge accounting, the cash flows relating to the forecast transactions that are designated as being hedged reflect changes in interest rates. The adjustment for changes in the fair value of a hedging derivative instrument is initially recognised in equity (IAS 39.95). To comply with the requirements for cash flow hedge accounting, it is necessary to determine when the adjustments to equity from changes in the fair value of a hedging instrument should be recognised in profit or loss (IAS 39.100 and IAS 39.101). For cash flow hedges, it is not necessary to create a separate system to make this determination. The system used to determine the extent of the net exposure provides the basis for scheduling the changes in the cash flows of the derivative and the recognition of such changes in profit or loss.

The timing of the recognition in profit or loss can be predetermined when the hedge is associated with the exposure to changes in cash flows. The forecast transactions that are being hedged can be associated with a specific principal amount in specific future periods composed of variable rate assets and cash inflows being reinvested or variable rate liabilities and cash outflows being refinanced, each of which creates a cash flow exposure to changes in interest rates. The specific principal amounts in specific future periods are equal to the notional amount of the derivative hedging instruments and are hedged only for the period that corresponds to the repricing or maturity of the derivative hedging instruments so that the cash flow changes resulting from changes in interest rates are matched with the derivative hedging instrument. IAS 39.100 specifies that the amounts recognised in equity should be recognised in profit or loss in the same period or periods during which the hedged item affects profit or loss.

Issue (c) – If a hedging relationship is designated as a cash flow hedge relating to changes in cash flows resulting from interest rate changes, what would be included in the documentation required by IAS 39.88(a)?

The following would be included in the documentation.

The hedging relationship – The maturity schedule of cash flows used for risk management purposes to determine exposures to cash flow mismatches on a net basis would provide part of the documentation of the hedging relationship.

The entity's risk management objective and strategy for undertaking the hedge – The entity's overall risk management objective and strategy for hedging exposures to interest rate risk would provide part of the documentation of the hedging objective and strategy.

The type of hedge – The hedge is documented as a cash flow hedge.

The hedged item – The hedged item is documented as a group of forecast transactions (interest cash flows) that are expected to occur with a high degree of probability in specified future periods, for example, scheduled on a monthly basis. The hedged item may include interest cash flows resulting from the reinvestment of cash inflows, including the resetting of interest rates on assets, or from the refinancing of cash outflows, including the resetting of interest rates on liabilities and rollovers of financial liabilities. As discussed in Issue (e), the forecast transactions meet the probability test if there are sufficient levels of highly probable cash flows in the specified future periods to encompass the amounts designated as being hedged on a gross basis.

The hedged risk – The risk designated as being hedged is documented as a portion of the overall exposure to changes in a specified market interest rate, often the risk-free interest rate or an interbank offered rate, common to all items in the group. To help ensure that the hedge effectiveness test is met at inception of the hedge and subsequently, the designated hedged portion of the interest rate risk could be documented as being based on the same yield curve as the derivative hedging instrument.

The hedging instrument – Each derivative hedging instrument is documented as a hedge of specified amounts in specified future time periods corresponding with the forecast transactions occurring in the specified future time periods designated as being hedged.

The method of assessing effectiveness – The effectiveness test is documented as being measured by comparing the changes in the cash flows of the derivatives allocated to the applicable periods in which they are designated as a hedge to the changes in the cash flows of the forecast transactions being hedged. Measurement of the cash flow changes is based on the applicable yield curves of the derivatives and hedged items.

Issue (d) – If the hedging relationship is designated as a cash flow hedge, how does an entity satisfy the requirement for an expectation of high effectiveness in achieving offsetting changes in IAS 39.88(b)?

An entity may demonstrate an expectation of high effectiveness by preparing an analysis demonstrating high historical and expected future correlation between the interest rate risk designated as being hedged and the interest rate risk of the hedging instrument. Existing documentation of the hedge ratio used in establishing the derivative contracts may also serve to demonstrate an expectation of effectiveness.

Issue (e) – If the hedging relationship is designated as a cash flow hedge, how does an entity demonstrate a high probability of the forecast transactions occurring as required by IAS 39.88(c)?

An entity may do this by preparing a cash flow maturity schedule showing that there exist sufficient aggregate gross levels of expected cash flows, including the effects of the resetting of interest rates for assets or liabilities, to establish that the forecast transactions that are designated as being hedged are highly probable to occur. Such a schedule should be supported by management's stated intentions and past practice of reinvesting cash inflows and refinancing cash outflows.

For example, an entity may forecast aggregate gross cash inflows of CU100 and aggregate gross cash outflows of CU90 in a particular time period in the near future. In this case, it may wish to designate the forecast reinvestment of gross cash inflows of CU10 as the hedged item in the future time period. If more than CU10 of the forecast cash inflows are contractually specified and have low credit risk, the entity has strong evidence to support an assertion that gross cash inflows of CU10 are highly probable to occur and to support the designation of the forecast reinvestment of those cash flows as being hedged for a particular portion of the reinvestment period. A high probability of the forecast transactions occurring may also be demonstrated under other circumstances.

Issue (f) – If the hedging relationship is designated as a cash flow hedge, how does an entity assess and measure effectiveness under IAS 39.88(d) and IAS 39.88(e)?

Effectiveness is required to be measured at a minimum at the time an entity prepares its annual or interim financial reports. However, an entity may wish to measure it more frequently on a specified periodic basis, at the end of each month or other applicable reporting period. It is also measured whenever derivative positions designated as hedging instruments are changed or hedges are terminated to ensure that the recognition in profit or loss of the changes in the fair value amounts on assets and liabilities and the recognition of changes in the fair value of derivative instruments designated as cash flow hedges are appropriate.

Changes in the cash flows of the derivative are computed and allocated to the applicable periods in which the derivative is designated as a hedge and are compared with computations of changes in the cash flows of the forecast transactions. Computations are based on yield curves applicable to the hedged items and the derivative hedging instruments and applicable interest rates for the specified periods being hedged.

The schedule used to determine effectiveness could be maintained and used as the basis for determining the period in which the hedging gains and losses recognised initially in equity are reclassified out of equity and recognised in profit or loss.

Issue (g) – If the hedging relationship is designated as a cash flow hedge, how does an entity account for the hedge?

The hedge is accounted for as a cash flow hedge in accordance with the provisions in IAS 39.95–IAS 39.100, as follows:

(i) the portion of gains and losses on hedging derivatives determined to result from effective hedges is recognised in equity whenever effectiveness is measured; and

(ii) the ineffective portion of gains and losses resulting from hedging derivatives is recognised in profit or loss.

IAS 39.100 specifies that the amounts recognised in equity should be recognised in profit or loss in the same period or periods during which the hedged item affects profit or loss. Accordingly, when the forecast transactions occur, the amounts previously recognised in equity are recognised in profit or loss. For example, if an interest rate swap is designated as a hedging instrument of a series of forecast cash flows, the changes in the cash flows of the swap are recognised in profit or loss in the periods when the forecast cash flows and the cash flows of the swap offset each other.

Issue (h) – If the hedging relationship is designated as a cash flow hedge, what is the treatment of any net cumulative gains and losses recognised in equity if the hedging instrument is terminated prematurely, the hedge accounting criteria are no longer met, or the hedged forecast transactions are no longer expected to take place?

If the hedging instrument is terminated prematurely or the hedge no longer meets the criteria for qualification for hedge accounting, for example, the forecast transactions are no longer highly probable, the net cumulative gain or loss recognised in equity remains in equity until the forecast transaction occurs (IAS 39.101(a) and IAS 39.101(b)). If the hedged forecast transactions are no longer expected to occur, the net cumulative gain or loss is recognised in profit or loss (IAS 39.101(c)).

Issue (i) – IAS 39.75 states that a hedging relationship may not be designated for only a portion of the time period in which a hedging instrument is outstanding. If the hedging relationship is designated as a cash flow hedge, and the hedge subsequently fails the test for being highly effective, does IAS 39.75 preclude redesignating the hedging instrument?

No. IAS 39.75 indicates that a derivative instrument may not be designated as a hedging instrument for only a portion of its remaining period to maturity. IAS 39.75 does not refer to the derivative instrument's original period to maturity. If there is a hedge effectiveness failure, the ineffective portion of the gain or loss on the derivative instrument is recognised immediately in profit or loss (IAS 39.95(b)) and hedge accounting based on the previous designation of the hedge relationship cannot be continued (IAS 39.101). In this case, the derivative instrument may be redesignated prospectively as a hedging instrument in a new hedging relationship provided this hedging relationship satisfies the necessary conditions. The derivative instrument must be redesignated as a hedge for the entire time period it remains outstanding.

Issue (j) – For cash flow hedges, if a derivative is used to manage a net exposure to interest rate risk and the derivative is designated as a cash flow hedge of forecast interest cash flows or portions of them on a gross basis, does the occurrence of the hedged forecast transaction give rise to an asset or liability that will result in a portion of the hedging gains and losses that were recognised in equity remaining in equity?

No. In the hedging relationship described in Issue (c) above, the hedged item is a group of forecast transactions consisting of interest cash flows in specified future periods. The hedged forecast transactions do not result in the recognition of assets or liabilities and the effect of interest rate changes that are designated as being hedged is recognised in profit or loss in the period in which the forecast transactions occur. Although this is not relevant for the types of hedges described here, if instead the derivative is designated as a hedge of a forecast purchase of a financial asset or issue of a financial liability, the associated gains or losses that were recognised directly in equity are reclassified into profit or loss in the same period or periods during which the asset acquired or liability incurred affects profit or loss (such as in the periods that interest expenses are recognised). However, if an entity expects at any time that all or a portion of a net loss recognised directly in equity will not be recovered in one or more future periods, it shall reclassify immediately into profit or loss the amount that is not expected to be recovered.

Issue (k) – In the answer to Issue (c) above it was indicated that the designated hedged item is a portion of a cash flow exposure. Does IAS 39 permit a portion of a cash flow exposure to be designated as a hedged item?

Yes. IAS 39 does not specifically address a hedge of a portion of a cash flow exposure for a forecast transaction. However, IAS 39.81 specifies that a financial asset or liability may be a hedged item with respect to the risks associated with only a portion of its cash flows or fair value, if effectiveness can be measured. The ability to hedge a portion of a cash flow exposure resulting from the resetting of interest rates for assets and liabilities suggests that a portion of a cash flow exposure resulting from the forecast reinvestment of cash inflows or the refinancing or rollover of financial liabilities can also be hedged. The basis for qualification as a hedged item of a portion of an exposure is the ability to measure effectiveness. This is further supported by IAS 39.82, which specifies that a non-financial asset or liability can be hedged only in its entirety or for foreign currency risk but not for a portion of other risks because of the difficulty of isolating and measuring the appropriate portion of the cash flows or fair value changes attributable to a specific risk. Accordingly, assuming effectiveness can be measured, a portion of a cash flow exposure of forecast transactions associated with, for example, the resetting of interest rates for a variable rate asset or liability can be designated as a hedged item.

Issue (l) – In the answer to Issue (c) above it was indicated that the hedged item is documented as a group of forecast transactions. Since these transactions will have different terms when they occur, including credit exposures, maturities and option features, how can an entity satisfy the tests in IAS 39.78 and IAS 39.83 requiring the hedged group to have similar risk characteristics?

IAS 39.78 provides for hedging a group of assets, liabilities, firm commitments or forecast transactions with similar risk characteristics. IAS 39.83 provides additional guidance and specifies that portfolio hedging is permitted if two conditions are met, namely: the individual items in the portfolio share the same risk for which they are designated, and the change in the fair value attributable to the hedged risk for each individual item in the group will be expected to be approximately proportional to the overall change in fair value.

When an entity associates a derivative hedging instrument with a gross exposure, the hedged item typically is a group of forecast transactions. For hedges of cash flow exposures relating to a group of forecast transactions, the overall exposure of the forecast transactions and the assets or liabilities that are repriced may have very different risks. The exposure from forecast transactions may differ depending on the terms that are expected as they relate to credit exposures, maturities, options and other features. Although the overall risk exposures may be different for the individual items in the group, a specific risk inherent in each of the items in the group can be designated as being hedged.

The items in the portfolio do not necessarily have to have the same overall exposure to risk, provided they share the same risk for which they are designated as being hedged. A common risk typically shared by a portfolio of financial instruments is exposure to changes in the risk-free or benchmark interest rate or to changes in a specified rate that has a credit exposure equal to the highest credit-rated instrument in the portfolio (ie the instrument with the lowest credit risk). If the instruments that are grouped into a portfolio have different credit exposures, they may be hedged as a group for a portion of the exposure. The risk they have in common that is designated as being hedged is the exposure to interest rate changes from the highest credit rated instrument in the portfolio. This ensures that the change in fair value attributable to the hedged risk for each individual item in the group is expected to be approximately proportional to the overall change in fair value attributable to the hedged risk of the group. It is likely there will be some ineffectiveness if the hedging instrument has a credit quality that is inferior to the credit quality of the highest credit-rated instrument being hedged, since a hedging relationship is designated for a hedging instrument in its entirety (IAS 39.74). For example, if a portfolio of assets consists of assets rated A, BB and B, and the current market interest rates for these assets are LIBOR+20 basis points, LIBOR+40 basis points and LIBOR+60 basis points, respectively, an entity may use a swap that pays fixed interest rate and for which variable interest payments based on LIBOR are made to hedge the exposure to variable interest rates. If LIBOR is designated as the risk being hedged, credit spreads above LIBOR on the hedged items are excluded from the designated hedge relationship and the assessment of hedge effectiveness.

F.6.3 Illustrative example of applying the approach in Question F.6.2

The purpose of this example is to illustrate the process of establishing, monitoring and adjusting hedge positions and of qualifying for cash flow hedge accounting in applying the approach to hedge accounting described in Question F.6.2 when a financial institution manages its interest rate risk on an entity-wide basis. To this end, this example identifies a methodology that allows for the use of hedge accounting and takes advantage of existing risk management systems so as to avoid unnecessary changes to it and to avoid unnecessary bookkeeping and tracking.

The approach illustrated here reflects only one of a number of risk management processes that could be employed and could qualify for hedge accounting. Its use is not intended to suggest that other alternatives could not or should not be used. The approach being illustrated could also be applied in other circumstances (such as for cash flow hedges of commercial entities), for example, hedging the rollover of commercial paper financing.

Identifying, assessing and reducing cash flow exposures

The discussion and illustrations that follow focus on the risk management activities of a financial institution that manages its interest rate risk by analysing expected cash flows in a particular currency on an entity-wide basis. The cash flow analysis forms the basis for identifying the interest rate risk of the entity, entering into hedging transactions to manage the risk, assessing the effectiveness of risk management activities, and qualifying for and applying cash flow hedge accounting.

The illustrations that follow assume that an entity, a financial institution, had the following expected future net cash flows and hedging positions outstanding in a specific currency, consisting of interest rate swaps, at the beginning of Period X0. The cash flows shown are expected to occur at the end of the period and, therefore, create a cash flow interest exposure in the following period as a result of the reinvestment or repricing of the cash inflows or the refinancing or repricing of the cash outflows.

The illustrations assume that the entity has an ongoing interest rate risk management programme. Schedule I shows the expected cash flows and hedging positions that existed at the beginning of Period X0. It is included here to provide a starting point in the analysis. It provides a basis for considering existing hedges in connection with the evaluation that occurs at the beginning of Period X1.

Schedule I End of period: expected cash flows and hedging positions							
Quarterly period	*X0*	*X1*	*X2*	*X3*	*X4*	*X5*	*…n*
(units)	*CU*	*CU*	*CU*	*CU*	*CU*	*CU*	*CU*
Expected net cash flows		1,100	1,500	1,200	1,400	1,500	x,xxx
Outstanding interest rate swaps:							
Receive–fixed, pay–variable (notional amounts)	2,000	2,000	2,000	1,200	1,200	1,200	x,xxx
Pay–fixed, receive–variable (notional amounts)	(1,000)	(1,000)	(1,000)	(500)	(500)	(500)	x,xxx
Net exposure after outstanding swaps		100	500	500	700	800	x.xxx

The schedule depicts five quarterly periods. The actual analysis would extend over a period of many years, represented by the notation '...n'. A financial institution that manages its interest rate risk on an entity-wide basis re-evaluates its cash flow exposures periodically. The frequency of the evaluation depends on the entity's risk management policy.

For the purposes of this illustration, the entity is re-evaluating its cash flow exposures at the end of Period X0. The first step in the process is the generation of forecast net cash flow exposures from existing interest-earning assets and interest-bearing liabilities, including the rollover of short-term assets and short-term liabilities. Schedule II below illustrates the forecast of net cash flow exposures. A common technique for assessing exposure to interest rates for risk management purposes is an interest rate sensitivity gap analysis showing the gap between interest rate-sensitive assets and interest rate-sensitive liabilities over different time intervals. Such an analysis could be used as a starting point for identifying cash flow exposures to interest rate risk for hedge accounting purposes.

Schedule II Forecast net cash flow and repricing exposures							
Quarterly period	*Notes*	*X1*	*X2*	*X3*	*X4*	*X5*	*…n*
(units)		*CU*	*CU*	*CU*	*CU*	*CU*	*CU*
CASH INFLOW AND REPRICING EXPOSURES – from assets							
Principal and interest payments:							
Long–term fixed rate	(1)	2,400	3,000	3,000	1,000	1,200	x,xxx
Short–term (roll over)	(1)(2)	1,575	1,579	1,582	1,586	1,591	x,xxx
Variable rate – principal payments	(1)	2,000	1,000	–	500	500	x,xxx
Variable rate – estimated interest	(2)	125	110	105	114	118	x,xxx
Total expected cash inflows		*6,100*	*5,689*	*4,687*	*3,200*	*3,409*	*x,xxx*
Variable rate asset balances	(3)	8,000	7,000	7,000	6,500	6,000	x,xxx
Cash inflows and repricings	**(4)**	**14,100**	**12,689**	**11,687**	**9,700**	**9,409**	**x,xxx**
CASH OUTFLOW AND REPRICING EXPOSURES – from liabilities							
Principal and interest payments:							
Long–term fixed rate	(1)	2,100	400	500	500	301	x,xxx
Short–term (roll over)	(1)(2)	735	737	738	740	742	x,xxx
Variable rate – principal payments	(1)	–	–	2,000	–	1,000	x,xxx
Variable rate – estimated interest	(2)	100	110	120	98	109	x,xxx
Total expected cash outflows		*2,935*	*1,247*	*3,358*	*1,338*	*2,152*	*x,xxx*
Variable rate liability balances	(3)	8,000	8,000	6,000	6,000	5,000	x,xxx
Cash outflows and repricings	**(4)**	**10,935**	**9,247**	**9,358**	**7,338**	**7,152**	**x,xxx**
NET EXPOSURES	*(5)*	*3,165*	*3,442*	*2,329*	*2,362*	*2,257*	*x,xxx*

(1) The cash flows are estimated using contractual terms and assumptions based on management's intentions and market factors. It is assumed that short-term assets and liabilities will continue to be rolled over in succeeding periods. Assumptions about prepayments and defaults and the withdrawal of deposits are based on market and historical data. It is assumed that principal and interest inflows and outflows will be

reinvested and refinanced, respectively, at the end of each period at the then current market interest rates and share the benchmark interest rate risk to which they are exposed.

(2) Forward interest rates obtained from Schedule VI are used to forecast interest payments on variable rate financial instruments and expected rollovers of short-term assets and liabilities. All forecast cash flows are associated with the specific time periods (3 months, 6 months, 9 months and 12 months) in which they are expected to occur. For completeness, the interest cash flows resulting from reinvestments, refinancings and repricings are included in the schedule and shown gross even though only the net margin may actually be reinvested. Some entities may choose to disregard the forecast interest cash flows for risk management purposes because they may be used to absorb operating costs and any remaining amounts would not be significant enough to affect risk management decisions.

(3) The cash flow forecast is adjusted to include the variable rate asset and liability balances in each period in which such variable rate asset and liability balances are repriced. The principal amounts of these assets and liabilities are not actually being paid and, therefore, do not generate a cash flow. However, since interest is computed on the principal amounts for each period based on the then current market interest rate, such principal amounts expose the entity to the same interest rate risk as if they were cash flows being reinvested or refinanced.

(4) The forecast cash flow and repricing exposures that are identified in each period represent the principal amounts of cash inflows that will be reinvested or repriced and cash outflows that will be refinanced or repriced at the market interest rates that are in effect when those forecast transactions occur.

(5) The net cash flow and repricing exposure is the difference between the cash inflow and repricing exposures from assets and the cash outflow and repricing exposures from liabilities. In the illustration, the entity is exposed to interest rate declines because the exposure from assets exceeds the exposure from liabilities and the excess (ie the net amount) will be reinvested or repriced at the current market rate and there is no offsetting refinancing or repricing of outflows.

Note that some banks regard some portion of their non-interest bearing demand deposits as economically equivalent to long-term debt. However, these deposits do not create a cash flow exposure to interest rates and would therefore be excluded from this analysis for accounting purposes.

Schedule II *Forecast net cash flow and repricing exposures* provides no more than a starting point for assessing cash flow exposure to interest rates and for adjusting hedging positions. The complete analysis includes outstanding hedging positions and is shown in Schedule III *Analysis of expected net exposures and hedging positions*. It compares the forecast net cash flow exposures for each period (developed in Schedule II) with existing hedging positions (obtained from Schedule I), and provides a basis for considering whether adjustment of the hedging relationship should be made.

Schedule III Analysis of expected net exposures and hedging positions						
Quarterly period	*X1*	*X2*	*X3*	*X4*	*X5*	*…n*
(units)	*CU*	*CU*	*CU*	*CU*	*CU*	*CU*
Net cash flow and repricing exposures (Schedule II)	3,165	3,442	2,329	2,362	2,257	x,xxx
Pre–existing swaps outstanding:						
Receive–fixed, pay–variable (notional amounts)	2,000	2,000	1,200	1,200	1,200	x,xxx
Pay–fixed, receive–variable (notional amounts)	(1,000)	(1,000)	(500)	(500)	(500)	x,xxx
Net exposure after pre–existing swaps	*2,165*	*2,442*	*1,629*	*1,662*	*1,557*	*x,xxx*
Transactions to adjust outstanding hedging positions:						
Receive–fixed, pay variable swap 1 (notional amount, 10-years)	2,000	2,000	2,000	2,000	2,000	x,xxx
Pay–fixed, receive–variable swap 2 (notional amount, 3-years)			(1,000)	(1,000)	(1,000)	x,xxx
Swaps …X						x,xxx
Unhedged cash flow and repricing exposure	*165*	*442*	*629*	*662*	*557*	*x,xxx*

The notional amounts of the interest rate swaps that are outstanding at the analysis date are included in each of the periods in which the interest rate swaps are outstanding to illustrate the impact of the outstanding interest rate swaps on the identified cash flow exposures. The notional amounts of the outstanding interest rate swaps are included in each period because interest is computed on the notional amounts each period, and the variable rate components of the outstanding swaps are repriced to the current market rate quarterly. The notional amounts create an exposure to interest rates that in part is similar to the principal balances of variable rate assets and variable rate liabilities.

The exposure that remains after considering the existing positions is then evaluated to determine the extent to which adjustments of existing hedging positions are necessary. The bottom portion of Schedule III shows the beginning of Period X1 using interest rate swap transactions to reduce the net exposures further to within the tolerance levels established under the entity's risk management policy.

Note that in the illustration, the cash flow exposure is not entirely eliminated. Many financial institutions do not fully eliminate risk but rather reduce it to within some tolerable limit.

Various types of derivative instruments could be used to manage the cash flow exposure to interest rate risk identified in the schedule of forecast net cash flows (Schedule II). However, for the purpose of the illustration, it is assumed that interest rate swaps are used for all hedging activities. It is also assumed that in periods in which interest rate swaps should be reduced, rather than terminating some of the outstanding interest rate swap positions, a new swap with the opposite return characteristics is added to the portfolio.

In the illustration in Schedule III above, swap 1, a receive-fixed, pay-variable swap, is used to reduce the net exposure in Periods X1 and X2. Since it is a 10-year swap, it also reduces exposures identified in other future periods not shown. However, it has the effect of creating an over-hedged position in Periods X3–X5. Swap 2, a forward starting pay-fixed, receive-variable interest rate swap, is used to reduce the notional amount of the outstanding receive-fixed, pay-variable interest rate swaps in Periods X3–X5 and thereby reduce the over-hedged positions.

It also is noted that in many situations, no adjustment or only a single adjustment of the outstanding hedging position is necessary to bring the exposure to within an acceptable limit. However, when the entity's risk management policy specifies a very low tolerance of risk a greater number of adjustments to the hedging positions over the forecast period would be needed to further reduce any remaining risk.

To the extent that some of the interest rate swaps fully offset other interest rate swaps that have been entered into for hedging purposes, it is not necessary to include them in a designated hedging relationship for hedge accounting purposes. These offsetting positions can be combined, de-designated as hedging instruments, if necessary, and reclassified for accounting purposes from the hedging portfolio to the trading portfolio. This procedure limits the extent to which the gross swaps must continue to be designated and tracked in a hedging relationship for accounting purposes. For the purposes of this illustration it is assumed that CU500 of the pay-fixed, receive-variable interest rate swaps fully offset CU500 of the receive-fixed, pay-variable interest rate swaps at the beginning of Period X1 and for Periods X1–X5, and are de-designated as hedging instruments and reclassified to the trading account.

After reflecting these offsetting positions, the remaining gross interest rate swap positions from Schedule III are shown in Schedule IV as follows.

Schedule IV Interest rate swaps designated as hedges

Quarterly period	*X1*	*X2*	*X3*	*X4*	*X5*	*…n*
(units)	*CU*	*CU*	*CU*	*CU*	*CU*	*CU*
Receive–fixed, pay–variable (notional amounts)	3,500	3,500	2,700	2,700	2,700	x,xxx
Pay–fixed, receive–variable (notional amounts)	(500)	(500)	(1,000)	(1,000)	(1,000)	x,xxx
Net outstanding swaps positions	*3,000*	*3,000*	*1,700*	*1,700*	*1,700*	*x,xxx*

For the purposes of the illustrations, it is assumed that Swap 2, entered into at the beginning of Period X1, only partially offsets another swap being accounted for as a hedge and therefore continues to be designated as a hedging instrument.

Hedge accounting considerations

Illustrating the designation of the hedging relationship

The discussion and illustrations thus far have focused primarily on economic and risk management considerations relating to the identification of risk in future periods and the adjustment of that risk using interest rate swaps. These activities form the basis for designating a hedging relationship for accounting purposes.

The examples in IAS 39 focus primarily on hedging relationships involving a single hedged item and a single hedging instrument, but there is little discussion and guidance on portfolio hedging relationships for cash flow hedges when risk is being managed centrally. In this illustration, the general principles are applied to hedging relationships involving a component of risk in a portfolio having multiple risks from multiple transactions or positions.

Although designation is necessary to achieve hedge accounting, the way in which the designation is described also affects the extent to which the hedging relationship is judged to be effective for accounting purposes and the extent to which the entity's existing system for managing risk will be required to be modified to track hedging activities for accounting purposes. Accordingly, an entity may wish to designate the hedging relationship in a manner that avoids unnecessary systems changes by taking advantage of the information already generated by the risk management system and avoids unnecessary bookkeeping and tracking. In designating hedging relationships, the entity may also consider the extent to which ineffectiveness is expected to be recognised for accounting purposes under alternative designations.

The designation of the hedging relationship needs to specify various matters. These are illustrated and discussed here from the perspective of the hedge of the interest rate risk associated with the cash inflows, but the guidance can also be applied to the hedge of the risk associated with the cash outflows. It is fairly obvious that only a portion of the gross exposures relating to the cash inflows is being hedged by the interest rate swaps. Schedule V *The general hedging relationship* illustrates the designation of the portion of the gross reinvestment risk exposures identified in Schedule II as being hedged by the interest rate swaps.

Schedule V The general hedging relationship

Quarterly period	*X1*	*X2*	*X3*	*X4*	*X5*	*...n*
(units)	*CU*	*CU*	*CU*	*CU*	*CU*	*CU*
Cash inflow repricing exposure (Schedule II)	14,100	12,689	11,687	9,700	9,409	x,xxx
Receive–fixed, pay–variable swaps (Schedule IV)	3,500	3,500	2,700	2,700	2,700	x,xxx
Hedged exposure percentage	*24.8%*	*27.6%*	*23.1%*	*27.8%*	*28.7%*	*xx.x%*

The hedged exposure percentage is computed as the ratio of the notional amount of the receive-fixed, pay-variable swaps that are outstanding divided by the gross exposure. Note that in Schedule V there are sufficient levels of forecast reinvestments in each period to offset more than the notional amount of the receive-fixed, pay-variable swaps and satisfy the accounting requirement that the forecast transaction is highly probable.

It is not as obvious, however, how the interest rate swaps are specifically related to the cash flow interest risks designated as being hedged and how the interest rate swaps are effective in reducing that risk. The more specific designation is illustrated in Schedule VI *The specific hedging relationship* below. It provides a meaningful way of depicting the more complicated narrative designation of the hedge by focusing on the hedging objective to eliminate the cash flow variability associated with future changes in interest rates and to obtain an interest rate equal to the fixed rate inherent in the term structure of interest rates that exists at the commencement of the hedge.

The expected interest from the reinvestment of the cash inflows and repricings of the assets is computed by multiplying the gross amounts exposed by the forward rate for the period. For example, the gross exposure for Period X2 of CU14,100 is multiplied by the forward rate for Periods X2–X5 of 5.50 per cent, 6.00 per cent, 6.50 per cent and 7.25 per cent, respectively, to compute the expected interest for those quarterly periods based on the current term structure of interest rates. The hedged expected interest is computed by multiplying the expected interest for the applicable three-month period by the hedged exposure percentage.

Schedule VI The specific hedging relationship								
			Term structure of interest rates					
Quarterly period			*X1*	*X2*	*X3*	*X4*	*X5*	*...n*
Spot rates			5.00%	5.25%	5.50%	5.75%	6.05%	x.xx%
Forward rates[(a)]			5.00%	5.50%	6.00%	6.50%	7.25%	x.xx%
Cash flow exposures and expected interest amounts								
Repricing period	Time to forecast transaction	Gross amounts exposed	Expected interest					
			CU	CU	CU	CU	CU	CU
2	3 months	14,100	→	**194**	212	229	256	
3	6 months	12,689			**190**	206	230	xxx
4	9 months	11,687				**190**	212	xxx
5	12 months	9,700					**176**	xxx
6	15 months	9,409						**xxx**
Hedged percentage (Schedule V) in the previous period				24.8%	27.6%	23.1%	27.8%	xx.x%
Hedged expected interest				48	52	44	49	xx

(a) The forward interest rates are computed from the spot interest rates and rounded for the purposes of the presentation. Computations that are based on the forward interest rates are made based on the actual computed forward rate and then rounded for the purposes of the presentation.

It does not matter whether the gross amount exposed is reinvested in long-term fixed rate debt or variable rate debt, or in short-term debt that is rolled over in each subsequent period. The exposure to changes in the forward interest rate is the same. For example, if the CU14,100 is reinvested at a fixed rate at the beginning of Period X2 for six months, it will be reinvested at 5.75 per cent. The expected interest is based on the forward interest rates for Period X2 of 5.50 per cent and for Period X3 of 6.00 per cent, equal to a blended rate of 5.75 per cent $(1.055 \times 1.060)^{0.5}$, which is the Period X2 spot rate for the next six months.

However, only the expected interest from the reinvestment of the cash inflows or repricing of the gross amount for the first three-month period after the forecast transaction occurs is designated as being hedged. The expected interest being hedged is represented by the shaded cells. The exposure for the subsequent periods is not hedged. In the example, the portion of the interest rate exposure being hedged is the forward rate of 5.50 per cent for Period X2. In order to assess hedge effectiveness and compute actual hedge ineffectiveness on an ongoing basis, the entity may use the information on hedged interest cash inflows in Schedule VI and compare it with updated estimates of expected interest cash inflows (for example, in a table that looks like Schedule II). As long as expected interest cash inflows exceed hedged interest cash inflows, the entity may compare the cumulative change in the fair value of the hedged cash inflows with the cumulative change in the fair value of the hedging instrument to compute actual hedge effectiveness. If there are insufficient expected interest cash inflows, there will be ineffectiveness. It is measured by comparing the cumulative change in the fair value of the expected interest cash flows to the extent they are less than the hedged cash flows with the cumulative change in the fair value of the hedging instrument.

Describing the designation of the hedging relationship

As mentioned previously, there are various matters that should be specified in the designation of the hedging relationship that complicate the description of the designation but are necessary to limit ineffectiveness to be recognised for accounting purposes and to avoid unnecessary systems changes and bookkeeping. The example that follows describes the designation more fully and identifies additional aspects of the designation not apparent from the previous illustrations.

Example designation

Hedging objective

The hedging objective is to eliminate the risk of interest rate fluctuations over the hedging period, which is the life of the interest rate swap, and in effect obtain a fixed interest rate during this period that is equal to the fixed interest rate on the interest rate swap.

Type of hedge

Cash flow hedge.

Hedging instrument

The receive-fixed, pay-variable swaps are designated as the hedging instrument. They hedge the cash flow exposure to interest rate risk.

Each repricing of the swap hedges a three-month portion of the interest cash inflows that results from:

- the forecast reinvestment or repricing of the principal amounts shown in Schedule V.
- unrelated investments or repricings that occur after the repricing dates on the swap over its life and involve different borrowers or lenders.

The hedged item General

The hedged item is a portion of the gross interest cash inflows that will result from the reinvestment or repricing of the cash flows identified in Schedule V and are expected to occur within the periods shown on such schedule. The portion of the interest cash inflow that is being hedged has three components:

- the principal component giving rise to the interest cash inflow and the period in which it occurs,
- the interest rate component, and
- the time component or period covered by the hedge.

Continued from previous page

Example designation

The hedged item The principal component

The portion of the interest cash inflows being hedged is the amount that results from the first portion of the principal amounts being invested or repriced in each period:

- that is equal to the sum of the notional amounts of the received-fixed, pay-variable interest rate swaps that are designated as hedging instruments and outstanding in the period of the reinvestment or repricing, and
- that corresponds to the first principal amounts of cash flow exposures that are invested or repriced at or after the repricing dates of the interest rate swaps.

The hedged item The interest rate component

The portion of the interest rate change that is being hedged is the change in both of the following:

- the credit component of the interest rate being paid on the principal amount invested or repriced that is equal to the credit risk inherent in the interest rate swap. It is that portion of the interest rate on the investment that is equal to the interest index of the interest rate swap, such as LIBOR, and
- the yield curve component of the interest rate that is equal to the repricing period on the interest rate swap designated as the hedging instrument.

The hedged item The hedged period

The period of the exposure to interest rate changes on the portion of the cash flow exposures being hedged is:

- the period from the designation date to the repricing date of the interest rate swap that occurs within the quarterly period in which, but not before, the forecast transactions occur, and
- its effects for the period after the forecast transactions occur equal to the repricing interval of the interest rate swap.

It is important to recognise that the swaps are not hedging the cash flow risk for a single investment over its entire life. The swaps are designated as hedging the cash flow risk from different principal investments and repricings that are made in each repricing period of the swaps over their entire term. The swaps hedge only the interest accruals that occur in the first period following the reinvestment. They are hedging the cash flow impact resulting from a change in interest rates that occurs up to the repricing of the swap. The exposure to changes in rates for the period from the repricing of the swap to the date of the hedged reinvestment of cash inflows or repricing of variable rate assets is not hedged. When the swap is repriced, the interest rate on the swap is fixed until the next repricing date and the accrual of the net swap settlements is determined. Any changes in interest rates after that date that affect the amount of the interest cash inflow are no longer hedged for accounting purposes.

Designation objectives

Systems considerations

Many of the tracking and bookkeeping requirements are eliminated by designating each repricing of an interest rate swap as hedging the cash flow risk from forecast reinvestments of cash inflows and repricings of variable rate assets for only a portion of the lives of the related assets. Much tracking and bookkeeping would be necessary if the swaps were instead designated as hedging the cash flow risk from forecast principal investments and repricings of variable rate assets over the entire lives of these assets.

This type of designation avoids keeping track of deferred derivative gains and losses in equity after the forecast transactions occur (IAS 39.97 and IAS 39.98) because the portion of the cash flow risk being hedged is that portion that will be recognised in profit or loss in the period immediately following the forecast transactions that corresponds with the periodic net cash settlements on the swap. If the hedge were to cover the entire life of the assets being acquired, it would be necessary to associate a specific interest rate swap with the asset being acquired. If a forecast transaction is the acquisition of a fixed rate instrument, the fair value of the swap that hedged that transaction would be reclassified out of equity to adjust the interest income on the asset when the interest income is recognised. The swap would then have to be terminated or redesignated in another hedging relationship. If a forecast transaction is the acquisition of a variable rate asset, the swap would continue in the hedging relationship but it would have to be tracked back to the asset acquired so that any fair value amounts on the swap recognised in equity could be recognised in profit or loss upon the subsequent sale of the asset.

It also avoids the necessity of associating with variable rate assets any portion of the fair value of the swaps that is recognised in equity. Accordingly, there is no portion of the fair value of the swap that is recognised in equity that should be reclassified out of equity when a forecast transaction occurs or upon the sale of a variable rate asset.

This type of designation also permits flexibility in deciding how to reinvest cash flows when they occur. Since the hedged risk relates only to a single period that corresponds with the repricing period of the interest rate swap designated as the hedging instrument, it is not necessary to determine at the designation date whether the cash flows will be reinvested in fixed rate or variable rate assets or to specify at the date of designation the life of the asset to be acquired.

Effectiveness considerations

Ineffectiveness is greatly reduced by designating a specific portion of the cash flow exposure as being hedged.

- Ineffectiveness due to credit differences between the interest rate swap and hedged forecast cash flow is eliminated by designating the cash flow risk being hedged as the risk attributable to changes in the interest rates that correspond with the rates inherent in the swap, such as the AA rate curve. This type of designation prevents changes resulting from changes in credit spreads from being considered as ineffectiveness.
- Ineffectiveness due to duration differences between the interest rate swap and hedged forecast cash flow is eliminated by designating the interest rate risk being hedged as the risk relating to changes in the portion of the yield curve that corresponds with the period in which the variable rate leg of the interest rate swap is repriced.

- Ineffectiveness due to interest rate changes that occur between the repricing date of the interest rate swap and the date of the forecast transactions is eliminated by simply not hedging that period of time. The period from the repricing of the swap and the occurrence of the forecast transactions in the period immediately following the repricing of the swap is left unhedged. Therefore, the difference in dates does not result in ineffectiveness.

Accounting considerations

The ability to qualify for hedge accounting using the methodology described here is founded on provisions in IAS 39 and on interpretations of its requirements. Some of those are described in the answer to Question F.6.2 *Hedge accounting considerations when interest rate risk is managed on a net basis.* Some additional and supporting provisions and interpretations are identified below.

Hedging a portion of the risk exposure

The ability to identify and hedge only a portion of the cash flow risk exposure resulting from the reinvestment of cash flows or repricing of variable rate instruments is found in IAS 39.81 as interpreted in the answers to Questions F.6.2 Issue (k) and F.2.17 *Partial term hedging*.

Hedging multiple risks with a single instrument

The ability to designate a single interest rate swap as a hedge of the cash flow exposure to interest rates resulting from various reinvestments of cash inflows or repricings of variable rate assets that occur over the life of the swap is founded on IAS 39.76 as interpreted in the answer to Question F.1.12 *Hedges of more than one type of risk*.

Hedging similar risks in a portfolio

The ability to specify the forecast transaction being hedged as a portion of the cash flow exposure to interest rates for a portion of the duration of the investment that gives rise to the interest payment without specifying at the designation date the expected life of the instrument and whether it pays a fixed or variable rate is founded on the answer to Question F.6.2 Issue (l), which specifies that the items in the portfolio do not necessarily have to have the same overall exposure to risk, providing they share the same risk for which they are designated as being hedged.

Hedge terminations

The ability to de-designate the forecast transaction (the cash flow exposure on an investment or repricing that will occur after the repricing date of the swap) as being hedged is provided for in IAS 39.101 dealing with hedge terminations. While a portion of the forecast transaction is no longer being hedged, the interest rate swap is not de-designated, and it continues to be a hedging instrument for the remaining transactions in the series that have not occurred. For example, assume that an interest rate swap having a remaining life of one year has been designated as hedging a series of three quarterly reinvestments of cash flows. The next forecast cash flow reinvestment occurs in three months. When the interest rate swap is repriced in three months at the then current variable rate, the fixed rate and the variable rate on the interest rate swap become known and no longer provide hedge protection for the next three months. If the next forecast transaction does not occur until three months and ten days, the ten-day period that remains after the repricing of the interest rate swap is not hedged.

F.6.4 Hedge accounting: premium or discount on forward exchange contract

A forward exchange contract is designated as a hedging instrument, for example, in a hedge of a net investment in a foreign operation. Is it permitted to amortise the discount or premium on the forward exchange contract to profit or loss over the term of the contract?

No. The premium or discount on a forward exchange contract may not be amortised to profit or loss under IAS 39. Derivatives are always measured at fair value in the balance sheet. The gain or loss resulting from a change in the fair value of the forward exchange contract is always recognised in profit or loss unless the forward exchange contract is designated and effective as a hedging instrument in a cash flow hedge or in a hedge of a net investment in a foreign operation, in which case the effective portion of the gain or loss is recognised in equity. In that case, the amounts recognised in equity are released to profit or loss when the hedged future cash flows occur or on the disposal of the net investment, as appropriate. Under IAS 39.74(b), the interest element (time value) of the fair value of a forward may be excluded from the designated hedge relationship. In that case, changes in the interest element portion of the fair value of the forward exchange contract are recognised in profit or loss.

F.6.5 IAS 39 and IAS 21 Fair value hedge of asset measured at cost

If the future sale of a ship carried at historical cost is hedged against the exposure to currency risk by foreign currency borrowing, does IAS 39 require the ship to be remeasured for changes in the exchange rate even though the basis of measurement for the asset is historical cost?

No. In a fair value hedge, the hedged item is remeasured. However, a foreign currency borrowing cannot be classified as a fair value hedge of a ship since a ship does not contain any separately measurable foreign currency risk. If the hedge accounting conditions in IAS 39.88 are met, the foreign currency borrowing may be classified as a cash flow hedge of an anticipated sale in that foreign currency. In a cash flow hedge, the hedged item is not remeasured.

To illustrate: a shipping entity in Denmark has a US subsidiary that has the same functional currency (the Danish krone). The shipping entity measures its ships at historical cost less depreciation in the consolidated financial statements. In accordance with IAS 21.23(b), the ships are recognised in Danish krone using the historical exchange rate. To hedge, fully or partly, the potential currency risk on the ships at disposal in US dollars, the shipping entity normally finances its purchases of ships with loans denominated in US dollars.

In this case, a US dollar borrowing (or a portion of it) may be designated as a cash flow hedge of the anticipated sale of the ship financed by the borrowing provided the sale is highly probable, for example, because it is expected to occur in the immediate future, and the amount of the sales proceeds designated as being hedged is equal to the amount of the foreign currency borrowing designated as the hedging instrument. The gains and losses on the currency borrowing that are determined to constitute an effective hedge of the anticipated sale are recognised directly in equity through the statement of changes in equity in accordance with IAS 39.95(a).

Section G Other

G.1 Disclosure of changes in fair value

IAS 39 requires financial assets classified as available for sale (AFS) and financial assets and financial liabilities at fair value through profit or loss to be remeasured to fair value. Unless a financial asset or a financial liability is designated as a cash flow hedging instrument, fair value changes for financial assets and financial liabilities at fair value through profit or loss are recognised in profit or loss, and fair value changes for AFS assets are recognised in equity. What disclosures are required regarding the amounts of the fair value changes during a reporting period?

IAS 32.94(h) requires material items of income, expense and gains and losses to be disclosed whether included in profit or loss or in equity. This disclosure requirement encompasses material items of income, expense and gains and losses that arise on remeasurement to fair value. Therefore, an entity provides disclosures of material fair value changes, distinguishing between changes that are recognised in profit or loss and changes that are recognised in equity. Further breakdown is provided of changes that relate to:

(a) AFS assets;

(b) financial assets and financial liabilities at fair value through profit or loss; and

(c) hedging instruments.

IAS 32 neither requires nor prohibits disclosure of components of the change in fair value by the way items are classified for internal purposes. For example, an entity may choose to disclose separately the change in fair value of those derivatives that IAS 39 classifies as held for trading but the entity classifies as part of risk management activities outside the trading portfolio.

In addition, IAS 32.94(e) requires disclosure of the carrying amounts of financial assets and financial liabilities that: (i) are classified as held for trading and (ii) were, upon initial recognition, designated by the entity as financial assets and financial liabilities at fair value through profit or loss (ie those not financial instruments classified as held for trading).

G.2 IAS 39 and IAS 7 Hedge accounting: cash flow statements

How should cash flows arising from hedging instruments be classified in cash flow statements?

Cash flows arising from hedging instruments are classified as operating, investing or financing activities, on the basis of the classification of the cash flows arising from the hedged item. While the terminology in IAS 7 has not been updated to reflect IAS 39, the classification of cash flows arising from hedging instruments in the cash flow statement should be consistent with the classification of these instruments as hedging instruments under IAS 39.

Table of Concordance of Implementation Guidance

This table shows how the contents of the superseded Implementation Guidance issued by the IAS 39 Implementation Guidance Committee correspond to IAS 39 and the accompanying Guidance on Implementing IAS 39. Questions and Answers that have been incorporated into IAS 39 and the accompanying Guidance on Implementing IAS 39 may have been amended to reflect the revisions made to IAS 39 by the IASB.

Except where indicated, all references are to the Guidance on Implementing IAS 39.

Superseded Q&A	Current Reference
1–1	IAS 39.2(f)
1–2	IAS 39.2(f)
1–3–a	IAS 39.2(d)
1–3–b	IAS 39.2(d)
1–4	None
1–5–a	IAS 39.2(f)
1–5–b	IAS 39.2(f)
1–6	IAS 39.2(h)
8–1	B.1
10–1	B.2
10–2	B.3
10–3	IAS 39.AG11
10–4–a	B.4
10–4–b	B.5
10–5	IAS 39.AG10
10–6	IAS 39.AG9
10–7	B.23
10–8	B.6
10–9	B.12
10–10	IAS 39.AG11
10–11–a	None
10–11–b	B.22
10–12	B.27
10–13	B.24
10–14	B.25

Superseded Q&A	Current Reference
10–15	None
10–16	IAS 39.AG17
10–17	IAS 39.AG17
10–18	B.7
10–19	IAS 39.9
10–20	None
10–21	B.11
11–1	None
13–1	IAS 39.AG2
13–2	B.8
14–1	A.1
14–2	IAS 39.6
14–3	A.2
15–1	B.9
15–2	B.10
16–1	B.28
16–2	B.29
16–3	B.30
16–4	B.31
18–1	IAS 39.AG15
18–2	IAS 39.AG15
22–1	C.1
22–2	C.2
23–1	IAS 39.11
23–2	C.3

Superseded Q&A	Current Reference
23–3	IAS 39.AG28, IAS 32.31
23–4	IAS 39.AG33
23–5	IAS 39.AG30(e)
23–6	IAS 39.10
23–7	IAS 39.10
23–8	IAS 39.AG29
23–9	C.4
23–10	IAS 39.12, 13
23–11	IAS 39.AG30(g)
23–12	C.5
25–1	C.6
25–2	C.7
25–3	IAS 39.AG33(c)
25–4	C.8
25–5	C.9
25–6	None
25–7	C.10
25–8	IAS 39.AG3, 3(b)
27–1	B.32
27–2	D.1.1
30–1	None
30–2	IAS 39.AG54
34–1	D.2.2

Superseded Q&A	Current Reference
35–1	IAS 39.16, 20
35–2	None
35–3	IAS 39.18, IAS 39.AG37
35–4	IAS 39.AG50
35–5	IAS 39.AG51(e)
36–1	IAS 39.AG49
37–1	IAS 39.AG51(n)
38–1	IAS 39.AG51(d)
38–2	IAS 39.AG51(i)
38–3	IAS 39.AG51(a)-(c)
38–4	IAS 39.AG51(f)
38–5	IAS 39.AG51 (m)
41–1	IAS 39.AG51 (f)–(h)
47–1	IAS 39.27, 28
47–2	IAS 39.27, 28, IAS 39. AG52
50–1	IAS 39.16(a)(i), IAS 39.AG24, IAS 39.AG45
57–1	IAS 39.AG60
57–2	IAS 39.AG58
57–3	IAS 39.AG60, AG61
62–1	IAS 39.AG62
66–1	E.1.1
66–2	IAS 39.43
66–3	IAS 39.AG64
70–1	IAS 39.46, 47
70–2	IAS 39.AG81
70–3	C.11

Superseded Q&A	Current Reference
73–1	B.26
76–1	IAS 39.AG6
78–1	F.5.1
80–1	B.13
80–2	B.14
83–1	IAS 39.9
83–2	IAS 39.9
83–3	IAS 39.9
83–4	B.19
83–5	B.20
83–6	B.21
83–7	B.15
83–8	IAS 39.AG22(a)
86–1	B.16
86–2	B.17
87–1	B.18
93–1	IAS 39.47
99–1	E.2.1
100–1	E.2.2
103–1	IAS 39.55(b)
103–2	E.3.1
106–1	IAS 39.57
106–2	D.2.3
107–1	None
107–2	IAS 39.50
109–1	E.4.1
110–1	E.4.2
111–1	E.4.3
111–2	E.4.4
111–3	E.4.5
111–4	E.4.6

Superseded Q&A	Current Reference
112–1	E.4.7
112–2	IAS 39.64
113–1	IAS 39.AG84
113–2	E.4.8
113–3	None
115–1	None
117–1	IAS 39.61
117–2	E.4.9
117–3	E4.10
118–1	None
121–1	F.6.1
121–2	F.6.2
122–1	IAS 39.77
122–2	F.1.1
122–3	F.1.2
124–1	F.1.3
127–1	F.2.21
127–2	F.2.9
127–3	F.2.10
127–4	F.2.11
127–5	F.2.1
127–6	IAS 39.79
128–1	F.2.12
128–2	F2.17
128–3	IAS 39.81
128–4	F.2.19
131–1	F.1.12
131–2	F.2.18
131–3	F.1.13
132–1	F.2.20
134–1	F.1.4

Superseded Q&A	Current Reference
134–1–a	F.1.5
134–1–b	F.1.6
134–2	F.2.14
134–3	F.2.15
134–4	F.2.16
137–1	F.2.13
137–2	F.2.2
137–3	F.2.3
137–4	F.2.4
137–5	F.2.5
137–6	F.2.6
137–7	F.3.1
137–8	F.3.2
137–9	F.3.3
137–10	F.3.4
137–11	F.3.5
137–12	F.3.6
137–13	IAS 39.80
137–14	None
137–15	F.1.14
137–16	F.2.7
142–1	F.3.7
142–2	F.4.1

Superseded Q&A	Current Reference
142–3	F.4.2
142–4	F.3.8
142–5	F.3.10
142–6	F.4.3
142–7	F.3.9
142–8	F.3.11
144–1	F.1.8
144–2	F.1.9
144–3	F.1.10
145–1	F.1.11
146–1	F.4.4
146–2	F.4.5
146–3	F.4.6
147–1	F.4.7
149–1	F.2.8
153–1	IAS 39.89(a)
157–1	IAS 39.92
158–1	F.5.2
158–2	F.5.3
158–3	F.5.4
158–4	F.5.5
158–5	F.5.6
160–1	None

Superseded Q&A	Current Reference
163–1	IAS 39.101(c)
164–1	F.6.4
170–1	G.1
170–2	None
172–1	IFRS 1.IG59
172–2	IFRS 1.IG60B
172–3	IFRS 1.IG59
172–4	IFRS 1.27, 27A
172–5	IFRS 1.29
172–6	IFRS 1.30
172–7	IFRS 1.IG56(a)
172–8	IFRS 1.60
172–9	IFRS 1.30 (implied)
172–10	IFRS 1.IG58A (implied)
Other–1	G.2
Other–2	None
Other–3	E.3.3
Other–4	F.6.5
Other–5	E.3.4
Other–6	E.3.2
Appendices to the IAS 39 Implementation Guidance	F.1.7, F.6.3

International Accounting Standard 40

Investment Property

This version includes amendments resulting from new and amended IFRSs issued up to 31 March 2004.

CONTENTS

International Accounting Standard 40 *Investment Property* (IAS 40) is set out in paragraphs 1–86. All the paragraphs have equal authority but retain the IASC format of the Standard when it was adopted by the IASB. IAS 40 should be read in the context of its objective and the IASB's Basis for Conclusions, the *Preface to International Financial Reporting Standards* and the *Framework for the Preparation and Presentation of Financial Statements*. IAS 8 *Accounting Policies, Changes in Accounting Estimates and Errors* provides a basis for selecting and applying accounting policies in the absence of explicit guidance.

Introduction

IN1 International Accounting Standard 40 *Investment Property* (IAS 40) replaces IAS 40 *Investment Property* (issued in 2000), and should be applied for annual periods beginning on or after 1 January 2005. Earlier application is encouraged.

Reasons for revising IAS 40

IN2 The International Accounting Standards Board developed this revised IAS 40 as part of its project on Improvements to International Accounting Standards. The project was undertaken in the light of queries and criticisms raised in relation to the Standards by securities regulators, professional accountants and other interested parties. The objectives of the project were to reduce or eliminate alternatives, redundancies and conflicts within the Standards, to deal with some convergence issues and to make other improvements.

IN3 For IAS 40 the Board's main objective was a limited revision to permit a property interest held by a lessee under an operating lease to qualify as investment property under specified conditions. Those conditions include requirements that the property must otherwise meet the definition of an investment property, and that the lessee must account for the lease as if it were a finance lease and measure the resulting lease asset using the fair value model. The Board did not reconsider the fundamental approach to the accounting for investment property contained in IAS 40.

The main changes

IN4 The main changes from the previous version of IAS 40 are described below.

IN5 A property interest that is held by a lessee under an operating lease may be classified and accounted for as investment property provided that:

(a) the rest of the definition of investment property is met;

(b) the operating lease is accounted for as if it were a finance lease in accordance with IAS 17 *Leases*; and

(c) the lessee uses the fair value model set out in this Standard for the asset recognised.

IN6 The classification alternative described in paragraph IN5 is available on a property-by-property basis. However, because it is a general requirement of the Standard that all investment property should be consistently accounted for using the fair value or cost model, once this alternative is selected for one such property, all property classified as investment property is to be accounted for consistently on a fair value basis.

IN7 The Standard requires an entity to disclose:

(a) whether it applies the fair value model or the cost model; and

(b) if it applies the fair value model, whether, and in what circumstances, property interests held under operating leases are classified and accounted for as investment property.

IN8 When a valuation obtained for investment property is adjusted significantly for the purpose of the financial statements, a reconciliation is required between the valuation obtained and the valuation included in the financial statements.

IN9 The Standard clarifies that if a property interest held under a lease is classified as investment property, the item accounted for at fair value is that interest and not the underlying property.

IN10 Comparative information is required for all disclosures.

IN11 Some significant changes have been incorporated into the Standard as a result of amendments that the Board made to IAS 16 *Property, Plant and Equipment* as part of the Improvements project:

(a) to specify what costs are included in the cost of investment property and when replaced items should be derecognised;

(b) to specify when exchange transactions (ie transactions in which investment property is acquired in exchange for non-monetary assets, in whole or in part) have commercial substance and how such transactions, with or without commercial substance, are accounted for; and

(c) to specify the accounting for compensation from third parties for investment property that was impaired, lost or given up.

Summary of the approach required by the Standard

IN12 The Standard permits entities to choose either:

(a) a fair value model, under which an investment property is measured, after initial measurement, at fair value with changes in fair value recognised in profit or loss; or

(b) a cost model. The cost model is specified in IAS 16 and requires an investment property to be measured after initial measurement at depreciated cost (less any accumulated impairment losses). An entity that chooses the cost model discloses the fair value of its investment property.

IN13 The choice between the cost and fair value models is not available to a lessee accounting for a property interest held under an operating lease that it has elected to classify and account for as investment property. The Standard requires such investment property to be measured using the fair value model.

IN14 The fair value model differs from the revaluation model that is permitted for some non-financial assets. Under the revaluation model, increases in carrying amount above a cost-based measure are recognised as revaluation surplus. However, under the fair value model, all changes in fair value are recognised in profit or loss.

IN15 The Standard requires an entity to apply its chosen model to all of its investment property. However, this does not mean that all eligible operating leases must be classified as investment properties.

IN16 In exceptional cases, when an entity has adopted the fair value model, there may be clear evidence when an entity first acquires an investment property (or when an existing property first becomes investment property following the completion of construction or development, or after a change in use) that its fair value will not be reliably determinable on a continuing basis. In such cases, the Standard requires the entity to measure that investment property using the cost model in IAS 16 until disposal of the investment property. The residual value of the investment property is assumed to be zero.

IN17 A change from one model to the other is made only if the change results in a more appropriate presentation. The Standard states that this is highly unlikely to be the case for a change from the fair value model to the cost model.

IN18 IAS 40 depends upon IAS 17 for requirements for the classification of leases, the accounting for finance and operating leases and for some of the disclosures relevant to leased investment properties. When a property interest held under an operating lease is classified and accounted for as an investment property, IAS 40 overrides IAS 17 by requiring that the lease is accounted for as if it were a finance lease. Paragraphs 14–18 of IAS 17 apply to the classification of leases of land and buildings. In particular, paragraph 18 specifies when it is not necessary to measure separately the land and building elements of such a lease.

International Accounting Standard 40 Investment Property

Objective

1 The objective of this Standard is to prescribe the accounting treatment for investment property and related disclosure requirements.

Scope

2 **This Standard shall be applied in the recognition, measurement and disclosure of investment property.**

3 Among other things, this Standard applies to the measurement in a lessee's financial statements of investment property interests held under a lease accounted for as a finance lease and to the measurement in a lessor's financial statements of investment property provided to a lessee under an operating lease. This Standard does not deal with matters covered in IAS 17 *Leases*, including:

(a) classification of leases as finance leases or operating leases;

(b) recognition of lease income from investment property (see also IAS 18 *Revenue*);

(c) measurement in a lessee's financial statements of property interests held under a lease accounted for as an operating lease;

(d) measurement in a lessor's financial statements of its net investment in a finance lease;

(e) accounting for sale and leaseback transactions; and

(f) disclosure about finance leases and operating leases.

4 This Standard does not apply to:

(a) biological assets related to agricultural activity (see IAS 41 *Agriculture*); and

(b) mineral rights and mineral reserves such as oil, natural gas and similar non-regenerative resources.

Definitions

5 **The following terms are used in this Standard with the meanings specified:**

Carrying amount **is the amount at which an asset is recognised in the balance sheet.**

Cost **is the amount of cash or cash equivalents paid or the fair value of other consideration given to acquire an asset at the time of its acquisition or construction or, where applicable, the amount attributed to that asset when initially recognised in accordance with the specific requirements of other IFRSs, eg IFRS 2** *Share-based Payment*.

Fair value **is the amount for which an asset could be exchanged between knowledgeable, willing parties in an arm's length transaction.**

Investment property **is property (land or a building—or part of a building—or both) held (by the owner or by the lessee under a finance lease) to earn rentals or for capital appreciation or both, rather than for:**

(a) use in the production or supply of goods or services or for administrative purposes; or

(b) sale in the ordinary course of business.

Owner-occupied property **is property held (by the owner or by the lessee under a finance lease) for use in the production or supply of goods or services or for administrative purposes.**

6 **A property interest that is held by a lessee under an operating lease may be classified and accounted for as investment property if, and only if, the property would otherwise meet the definition of an investment property and the lessee uses the fair value model set out in paragraphs 33–55 for the asset recognised. This classification alternative is available on a property-by-property basis. However, once this classification alternative is selected for one such property interest held under an operating lease, all property classified as investment property shall be accounted for using the fair value model. When this classification alternative is selected, any interest so classified is included in the disclosures required by paragraphs 74–78.**

7 Investment property is held to earn rentals or for capital appreciation or both. Therefore, an investment property generates cash flows largely independently of the other assets held by an entity. This distinguishes investment property from owner-occupied property. The production or supply of goods or services (or the use of property for administrative purposes) generates cash flows that are attributable not only to property, but also to other assets used in the production or supply process. IAS 16 *Property, Plant and Equipment* applies to owner-occupied property.

8 The following are examples of investment property:

(a) land held for long-term capital appreciation rather than for short-term sale in the ordinary course of business.

(b) land held for a currently undetermined future use. (If an entity has not determined that it will use the land as owner-occupied property or for short-term sale in the ordinary course of business, the land is regarded as held for capital appreciation.)

(c) a building owned by the entity (or held by the entity under a finance lease) and leased out under one or more operating leases.

(d) a building that is vacant but is held to be leased out under one or more operating leases.

9 The following are examples of items that are not investment property and are therefore outside the scope of this Standard:

(a) property intended for sale in the ordinary course of business or in the process of construction or development for such sale (see IAS 2 *Inventories*), for example, property acquired exclusively with a view to subsequent disposal in the near future or for development and resale.

(b) property being constructed or developed on behalf of third parties (see IAS 11 *Construction Contracts*).

(c) owner-occupied property (see IAS 16), including (among other things) property held for future use as owner-occupied property, property held for future development and subsequent use as owner-occupied property, property occupied by employees (whether or not the employees pay rent at market rates) and owner-occupied property awaiting disposal.

(d) property that is being constructed or developed for future use as investment property. IAS 16 applies to such property until construction or development is complete, at which time the property becomes investment property and this Standard applies. However, this Standard applies to existing investment property that is being redeveloped for continued future use as investment property (see paragraph 58).

(e) property that is leased to another entity under a finance lease.

10 Some properties comprise a portion that is held to earn rentals or for capital appreciation and another portion that is held for use in the production or supply of goods or services or for administrative purposes. If these portions could be sold separately (or leased out separately under a finance lease), an entity accounts for the portions separately. If the portions could not be sold separately, the property is investment property only if an insignificant portion is held for use in the production or supply of goods or services or for administrative purposes.

11 In some cases, an entity provides ancillary services to the occupants of a property it holds. An entity treats such a property as investment property if the services are insignificant to the arrangement as a whole. An example is when the owner of an office building provides security and maintenance services to the lessees who occupy the building.

12 In other cases, the services provided are significant. For example, if an entity owns and manages a hotel, services provided to guests are significant to the arrangement as a whole. Therefore, an owner-managed hotel is owner-occupied property, rather than investment property.

13 It may be difficult to determine whether ancillary services are so significant that a property does not qualify as investment property. For example, the owner of a hotel sometimes transfers some responsibilities to third parties under a management contract. The terms of such contracts vary widely. At one end of the spectrum, the owner's position may, in substance, be that of a passive investor. At the other end of the spectrum, the owner may simply have outsourced day-to-day functions while retaining significant exposure to variation in the cash flows generated by the operations of the hotel.

14 Judgement is needed to determine whether a property qualifies as investment property. An entity develops criteria so that it can exercise that judgement consistently in accordance with the definition of investment property and with the related guidance in paragraphs 7–13. Paragraph 75(c) requires an entity to disclose these criteria when classification is difficult.

15 In some cases, an entity owns property that is leased to, and occupied by, its parent or another subsidiary. The property does not qualify as investment property in the consolidated financial statements, because the property is owner-occupied from the perspective of the group. However, from the perspective of the entity that owns it, the property is investment property if it meets the definition in paragraph 5. Therefore, the lessor treats the property as investment property in its individual financial statements.

Recognition

16 Investment property shall be recognised as an asset when, and only when:

(a) it is probable that the future economic benefits that are associated with the investment property will flow to the entity; and

(b) the cost of the investment property can be measured reliably.

17 An entity evaluates under this recognition principle all its investment property costs at the time they are incurred. These costs include costs incurred initially to acquire an investment property and costs incurred subsequently to add to, replace part of, or service a property.

18 Under the recognition principle in paragraph 16, an entity does not recognise in the carrying amount of an investment property the costs of the day-to-day servicing of such a property. Rather, these costs are recognised in profit or loss as incurred. Costs of day-to-day servicing are primarily the cost of labour and consumables, and may include the cost of minor parts. The purpose of these expenditures is often described as for the 'repairs and maintenance' of the property.

19 Parts of investment properties may have been acquired through replacement. For example, the interior walls may be replacements of original walls. Under the recognition principle, an entity recognises in the carrying amount of an investment property the cost of replacing part of an existing investment property at the time that cost is incurred if the recognition criteria are met. The carrying amount of those parts that are replaced is derecognised in accordance with the derecognition provisions of this Standard.

Measurement at recognition

20 An investment property shall be measured initially at its cost. Transaction costs shall be included in the initial measurement.

21 The cost of a purchased investment property comprises its purchase price and any directly attributable expenditure. Directly attributable expenditure includes, for example, professional fees for legal services, property transfer taxes and other transaction costs.

22 The cost of a self-constructed investment property is its cost at the date when the construction or development is complete. Until that date, an entity applies IAS 16. At that date, the property becomes investment property and this Standard applies (see paragraphs 57(e) and 65).

23 The cost of an investment property is not increased by:

(a) start-up costs (unless they are necessary to bring the property to the condition necessary for it to be capable of operating in the manner intended by management),

(b) operating losses incurred before the investment property achieves the planned level of occupancy, or

(c) abnormal amounts of wasted material, labour or other resources incurred in constructing or developing the property.

24 If payment for an investment property is deferred, its cost is the cash price equivalent. The difference between this amount and the total payments is recognised as interest expense over the period of credit.

25 The initial cost of a property interest held under a lease and classified as an investment property shall be as prescribed for a finance lease by paragraph 20 of IAS 17, ie the asset shall be recognised at the lower of the fair value of the property and the present value of the minimum lease payments. An equivalent amount shall be recognised as a liability in accordance with that same paragraph.

26 Any premium paid for a lease is treated as part of the minimum lease payments for this purpose, and is therefore included in the cost of the asset, but is excluded from the liability. If a property interest held under a lease is classified as investment property, the item accounted for at fair value is that interest and not the underlying property. Guidance on determining the fair value of a property interest is set out for the fair value model in paragraphs 33–52. That guidance is also relevant to the determination of fair value when that value is used as cost for initial recognition purposes.

27 One or more investment properties may be acquired in exchange for a non-monetary asset or assets, or a combination of monetary and non-monetary assets. The following discussion refers to an exchange of one non-monetary asset for another, but it also applies to all exchanges described in the preceding sentence. The cost of such an investment property is measured at fair value unless (a) the exchange transaction lacks commercial substance or (b) the fair value of neither the asset received nor the asset given up is reliably measurable. The acquired asset is measured in this way even if an entity cannot immediately derecognise the asset given up. If the acquired asset is not measured at fair value, its cost is measured at the carrying amount of the asset given up.

28 An entity determines whether an exchange transaction has commercial substance by considering the extent to which its future cash flows are expected to change as a result of the transaction. An exchange transaction has commercial substance if:

(a) the configuration (risk, timing and amount) of the cash flows of the asset received differs from the configuration of the cash flows of the asset transferred, or

(b) the entity-specific value of the portion of the entity's operations affected by the transaction changes as a result of the exchange, and

(c) the difference in (a) or (b) is significant relative to the fair value of the assets exchanged.

For the purpose of determining whether an exchange transaction has commercial substance, the entity-specific value of the portion of the entity's operations affected by the transaction shall reflect post-tax cash flows. The result of these analyses may be clear without an entity having to perform detailed calculations.

29 The fair value of an asset for which comparable market transactions do not exist is reliably measurable if (a) the variability in the range of reasonable fair value estimates is not significant for that asset or (b) the probabilities of the various estimates within the range can be reasonably assessed and used in estimating fair value. If the entity is able to determine reliably the fair value of either the asset received or the asset given up, then the fair value of the asset given up is used to measure cost unless the fair value of the asset received is more clearly evident.

Measurement after recognition

Accounting policy

30 With the exceptions noted in paragraphs 32A and 34, an entity shall choose as its accounting policy either the fair value model in paragraphs 33–55 or the cost model in paragraph 56 and shall apply that policy to all of its investment property.

31 IAS 8 *Accounting Policies, Changes in Accounting Estimates and Errors* states that a voluntary change in accounting policy shall be made only if the change will result in a more appropriate presentation of transactions, other events or conditions in the entity's financial statements. It is highly unlikely that a change from the fair value model to the cost model will result in a more appropriate presentation.

32 This Standard requires all entities to determine the fair value of investment property, for the purpose of either measurement (if the entity uses the fair value model) or disclosure (if it uses the cost model). An entity is encouraged, but not required, to determine the fair value of investment property on the basis of a valuation by an independent valuer who holds a recognised and relevant professional qualification and has recent experience in the location and category of the investment property being valued.

32A An entity may:

(a) choose either the fair value model or the cost model for all investment property backing liabilities that pay a return linked directly to the fair value of, or returns from, specified assets including that investment property; and

(b) choose either the fair value model or the cost model for all other investment property, regardless of the choice made in (a).

32B Some insurers and other entities operate an internal property fund that issues notional units, with some units held by investors in linked contracts and others held by the entity. Paragraph 32A does not permit an entity to measure the property held by the fund partly at cost and partly at fair value.

32C If an entity chooses different models for the two categories described in paragraph 32A, sales of investment property between pools of assets measured using different models shall be recognised at fair value and the cumulative change in fair value shall be recognised in profit or loss. Accordingly, if an investment property is sold from a pool in which the fair value model is used into a pool in which the cost model is used, the property's fair value at the date of the sale becomes its deemed cost.

Fair value model

33 **After initial recognition, an entity that chooses the fair value model shall measure all of its investment property at fair value, except in the cases described in paragraph 53.**

34 **When a property interest held by a lessee under an operating lease is classified as an investment property under paragraph 6, paragraph 30 is not elective; the fair value model shall be applied.**

35 **A gain or loss arising from a change in the fair value of investment property shall be recognised in profit or loss for the period in which it arises.**

36 The fair value of investment property is the price at which the property could be exchanged between knowledgeable, willing parties in an arm's length transaction (see paragraph 5). Fair value specifically excludes an estimated price inflated or deflated by special terms or circumstances such as atypical financing, sale and leaseback arrangements, special considerations or concessions granted by anyone associated with the sale.

37 An entity determines fair value without any deduction for transaction costs it may incur on sale or other disposal.

38 **The fair value of investment property shall reflect market conditions at the balance sheet date.**

39 Fair value is time-specific as of a given date. Because market conditions may change, the amount reported as fair value may be incorrect or inappropriate if estimated as of another time. The definition of fair value also assumes simultaneous exchange and completion of the contract for sale without any variation in price that might be made in an arm's length transaction between knowledgeable, willing parties if exchange and completion are not simultaneous.

40 The fair value of investment property reflects, among other things, rental income from current leases and reasonable and supportable assumptions that represent what knowledgeable, willing parties would assume about rental income from future leases in the light of current conditions. It also reflects, on a similar basis, any cash outflows (including rental payments and other outflows) that could be expected in respect of the property. Some of those outflows are reflected in the liability whereas others relate to outflows that are not recognised in the financial statements until a later date (eg periodic payments such as contingent rents).

41 Paragraph 25 specifies the basis for initial recognition of the cost of an interest in a leased property. Paragraph 33 requires the interest in the leased property to be remeasured, if necessary, to fair value. In a lease negotiated at market rates, the

fair value of an interest in a leased property at acquisition, net of all expected lease payments (including those relating to recognised liabilities), should be zero. This fair value does not change regardless of whether, for accounting purposes, a leased asset and liability are recognised at fair value or at the present value of minimum lease payments, in accordance with paragraph 20 of IAS 17. Thus, remeasuring a leased asset from cost in accordance with paragraph 25 to fair value in accordance with paragraph 33 should not give rise to any initial gain or loss, unless fair value is measured at different times. This could occur when an election to apply the fair value model is made after initial recognition.

42 The definition of fair value refers to 'knowledgeable, willing parties'. In this context, 'knowledgeable' means that both the willing buyer and the willing seller are reasonably informed about the nature and characteristics of the investment property, its actual and potential uses, and market conditions at the balance sheet date. A willing buyer is motivated, but not compelled, to buy. This buyer is neither over-eager nor determined to buy at any price. The assumed buyer would not pay a higher price than a market comprising knowledgeable, willing buyers and sellers would require.

43 A willing seller is neither an over-eager nor a forced seller, prepared to sell at any price, nor one prepared to hold out for a price not considered reasonable in current market conditions. The willing seller is motivated to sell the investment property at market terms for the best price obtainable. The factual circumstances of the actual investment property owner are not a part of this consideration because the willing seller is a hypothetical owner (eg a willing seller would not take into account the particular tax circumstances of the actual investment property owner).

44 The definition of fair value refers to an arm's length transaction. An arm's length transaction is one between parties that do not have a particular or special relationship that makes prices of transactions uncharacteristic of market conditions. The transaction is presumed to be between unrelated parties, each acting independently.

45 The best evidence of fair value is given by current prices in an active market for similar property in the same location and condition and subject to similar lease and other contracts. An entity takes care to identify any differences in the nature, location or condition of the property, or in the contractual terms of the leases and other contracts relating to the property.

46 In the absence of current prices in an active market of the kind described in paragraph 45, an entity considers information from a variety of sources, including:

(a) current prices in an active market for properties of different nature, condition or location (or subject to different lease or other contracts), adjusted to reflect those differences;

(b) recent prices of similar properties on less active markets, with adjustments to reflect any changes in economic conditions since the date of the transactions that occurred at those prices; and

(c) discounted cash flow projections based on reliable estimates of future cash flows, supported by the terms of any existing lease and other contracts and (when possible) by external evidence such as current market rents for similar properties in the same location and condition, and using discount rates that reflect current market assessments of the uncertainty in the amount and timing of the cash flows.

47 In some cases, the various sources listed in the previous paragraph may suggest different conclusions about the fair value of an investment property. An entity considers the reasons for those differences, in order to arrive at the most reliable estimate of fair value within a range of reasonable fair value estimates.

48 In exceptional cases, there is clear evidence when an entity first acquires an investment property (or when an existing property first becomes investment property following the completion of construction or development, or after a change in use) that the variability in the range of reasonable fair value estimates will be so great, and the probabilities of the various outcomes so difficult to assess, that the usefulness of a single estimate of fair value is negated. This may indicate that the fair value of the property will not be reliably determinable on a continuing basis (see paragraph 53).

49 Fair value differs from value in use, as defined in IAS 36 *Impairment of Assets*. Fair value reflects the knowledge and estimates of knowledgeable, willing buyers and sellers. In contrast, value in use reflects the entity's estimates, including the effects of factors that may be specific to the entity and not applicable to entities in general. For example, fair value does not reflect any of the following factors to the extent that they would not be generally available to knowledgeable, willing buyers and sellers:

(a) additional value derived from the creation of a portfolio of properties in different locations;

(b) synergies between investment property and other assets;

(c) legal rights or legal restrictions that are specific only to the current owner; and

(d) tax benefits or tax burdens that are specific to the current owner.

50 In determining the fair value of investment property, an entity does not double-count assets or liabilities that are recognised as separate assets or liabilities. For example:

(a) equipment such as lifts or air-conditioning is often an integral part of a building and is generally included in the fair value of the investment property, rather than recognised separately as property, plant and equipment.

(b) if an office is leased on a furnished basis, the fair value of the office generally includes the fair value of the furniture, because the rental income relates to the furnished office. When furniture is included in the fair value of investment property, an entity does not recognise that furniture as a separate asset.

(c) the fair value of investment property excludes prepaid or accrued operating lease income, because the entity recognises it as a separate liability or asset.

(d) the fair value of investment property held under a lease reflects expected cash flows (including contingent rent that is expected to become payable). Accordingly, if a valuation obtained for a property is net of all payments expected to be made, it will be necessary to add back any recognised lease liability, to arrive at the fair value of the investment property for accounting purposes.

51 The fair value of investment property does not reflect future capital expenditure that will improve or enhance the property and does not reflect the related future benefits from this future expenditure.

52 In some cases, an entity expects that the present value of its payments relating to an investment property (other than payments relating to recognised liabilities) will exceed the present value of the related cash receipts. An entity applies IAS 37 *Provisions, Contingent Liabilities and Contingent Assets* to determine whether to recognise a liability and, if so, how to measure it.

Inability to determine fair value reliably

53 **There is a rebuttable presumption that an entity can reliably determine the fair value of an investment property on a continuing basis. However, in exceptional cases, there is clear evidence when an entity first acquires an investment property (or when an existing property first becomes investment property following the completion of construction or development, or after a change in use) that the fair value of the investment property is not reliably determinable on a continuing basis. This arises when, and only when, comparable market transactions are infrequent and alternative reliable estimates of fair value (for example, based on discounted cash flow projections) are not available. In such cases, an entity shall measure that investment property using the cost model in IAS 16. The residual value of the investment property shall be assumed to be zero. The entity shall apply IAS 16 until disposal of the investment property.**

54 In the exceptional cases when an entity is compelled, for the reason given in the previous paragraph, to measure an investment property using the cost model in accordance with IAS 16, it measures all its other investment property at fair value. In these cases, although an entity may use the cost model for one investment property, the entity shall continue to account for each of the remaining properties using the fair value model.

55 **If an entity has previously measured an investment property at fair value, it shall continue to measure the property at fair value until disposal (or until the property becomes owner-occupied property or the entity begins to develop the property for subsequent sale in the ordinary course of business) even if comparable market transactions become less frequent or market prices become less readily available.**

Cost model

56 **After initial recognition, an entity that chooses the cost model shall measure all of its investment property in accordance with IAS 16's requirements for that model, other than those that meet the criteria to be classified as held for sale (or are included in a disposal group that is classified as held for sale) in accordance with IFRS 5** *Non-current Assets Held for Sale and Discontinued Operations*. **Investment properties that meet the criteria to be classified as held for sale (or are included in a disposal group that is classified as held for sale) shall be measured in accordance with IFRS 5.**

Transfers

57 **Transfers to, or from, investment property shall be made when, and only when, there is a change in use, evidenced by:**

(a) commencement of owner-occupation, for a transfer from investment property to owner-occupied property;

(b) commencement of development with a view to sale, for a transfer from investment property to inventories;

(c) end of owner-occupation, for a transfer from owner-occupied property to investment property;

(d) commencement of an operating lease to another party, for a transfer from inventories to investment property; or

(e) end of construction or development, for a transfer from property in the course of construction or development (covered by IAS 16) to investment property.

58 Paragraph 57(b) requires an entity to transfer a property from investment property to inventories when, and only when, there is a change in use, evidenced by commencement of development with a view to sale. When an entity decides to dispose of an investment property without development, it continues to treat the property as an investment property until it is derecognised (eliminated from the balance sheet) and does not treat it as inventory. Similarly, if an entity begins to redevelop an existing investment property for continued future use as investment property, the property remains an investment property and is not reclassified as owner-occupied property during the redevelopment.

59 Paragraphs 60–65 apply to recognition and measurement issues that arise when an entity uses the fair value model for investment property. When an entity uses the cost model, transfers between investment property, owner-occupied property and inventories do not change the carrying amount of the property transferred and they do not change the cost of that property for measurement or disclosure purposes.

60 **For a transfer from investment property carried at fair value to owner-occupied property or inventories, the property's deemed cost for subsequent accounting in accordance with IAS 16 or IAS 2 shall be its fair value at the date of change in use.**

61 **If an owner-occupied property becomes an investment property that will be carried at fair value, an entity shall apply IAS 16 up to the date of change in use. The entity shall treat any difference at that date between the carrying amount of the property in accordance with IAS 16 and its fair value in the same way as a revaluation in accordance with IAS 16.**

62 Up to the date when an owner-occupied property becomes an investment property carried at fair value, an entity depreciates the property and recognises any impairment losses that have occurred. The entity treats any difference at that date between the carrying amount of the property in accordance with IAS 16 and its fair value in the same way as a revaluation in accordance with IAS 16. In other words:

(a) any resulting decrease in the carrying amount of the property is recognised in profit or loss. However, to the extent that an amount is included in revaluation surplus for that property, the decrease is charged against that revaluation surplus.

(b) any resulting increase in the carrying amount is treated as follows:

(i) to the extent that the increase reverses a previous impairment loss for that property, the increase is recognised in profit or loss. The amount recognised in profit or loss does not exceed the amount needed to restore the carrying amount to the carrying amount that would have been determined (net of depreciation) had no impairment loss been recognised.

(ii) any remaining part of the increase is credited directly to equity in revaluation surplus. On subsequent disposal of the investment property, the revaluation surplus included in equity may be transferred to retained earnings. The transfer from revaluation surplus to retained earnings is not made through profit or loss.

63 **For a transfer from inventories to investment property that will be carried at fair value, any difference between the fair value of the property at that date and its previous carrying amount shall be recognised in profit or loss.**

64 The treatment of transfers from inventories to investment property that will be carried at fair value is consistent with the treatment of sales of inventories.

65 **When an entity completes the construction or development of a self-constructed investment property that will be carried at fair value, any difference between the fair value of the property at that date and its previous carrying amount shall be recognised in profit or loss.**

Disposals

66 **An investment property shall be derecognised (eliminated from the balance sheet) on disposal or when the investment property is permanently withdrawn from use and no future economic benefits are expected from its disposal.**

67 The disposal of an investment property may be achieved by sale or by entering into a finance lease. In determining the date of disposal for investment property,

an entity applies the criteria in IAS 18 for recognising revenue from the sale of goods and considers the related guidance in the Appendix to IAS 18. IAS 17 applies to a disposal effected by entering into a finance lease and to a sale and leaseback.

68 If, in accordance with the recognition principle in paragraph 16, an entity recognises in the carrying amount of an asset the cost of a replacement for part of an investment property, it derecognises the carrying amount of the replaced part. For investment property accounted for using the cost model, a replaced part may not be a part that was depreciated separately. If it is not practicable for an entity to determine the carrying amount of the replaced part, it may use the cost of the replacement as an indication of what the cost of the replaced part was at the time it was acquired or constructed. Under the fair value model, the fair value of the investment property may already reflect that the part to be replaced has lost its value. In other cases it may be difficult to discern how much fair value should be reduced for the part being replaced. An alternative to reducing fair value for the replaced part, when it is not practical to do so, is to include the cost of the replacement in the carrying amount of the asset and then to reassess the fair value, as would be required for additions not involving replacement.

69 Gains or losses arising from the retirement or disposal of investment property shall be determined as the difference between the net disposal proceeds and the carrying amount of the asset and shall be recognised in profit or loss (unless IAS 17 requires otherwise on a sale and leaseback) in the period of the retirement or disposal.

70 The consideration receivable on disposal of an investment property is recognised initially at fair value. In particular, if payment for an investment property is deferred, the consideration received is recognised initially at the cash price equivalent. The difference between the nominal amount of the consideration and the cash price equivalent is recognised as interest revenue in accordance with IAS 18 using the effective interest method.

71 An entity applies IAS 37 or other Standards, as appropriate, to any liabilities that it retains after disposal of an investment property.

72 Compensation from third parties for investment property that was impaired, lost or given up shall be recognised in profit or loss when the compensation becomes receivable.

73 Impairments or losses of investment property, related claims for or payments of compensation from third parties and any subsequent purchase or construction of replacement assets are separate economic events and are accounted for separately as follows:

(a) impairments of investment property are recognised in accordance with IAS 36;

(b) retirements or disposals of investment property are recognised in accordance with paragraphs 66–71 of this Standard;

(c) compensation from third parties for investment property that was impaired, lost or given up is recognised in profit or loss when it becomes receivable; and

(d) the cost of assets restored, purchased or constructed as replacements is determined in accordance with paragraphs 20–29 of this Standard.

Disclosure

Fair value model and cost model

74 The disclosures below apply in addition to those in IAS 17. In accordance with IAS 17, the owner of an investment property provides lessors' disclosures about leases into which it has entered. An entity that holds an investment property under a finance or operating lease provides lessees' disclosures for finance leases and lessors' disclosures for any operating leases into which it has entered.

75 **An entity shall disclose:**

(a) whether it applies the fair value model or the cost model.

(b) if it applies the fair value model, whether, and in what circumstances, property interests held under operating leases are classified and accounted for as investment property.

(c) when classification is difficult (see paragraph 14), the criteria it uses to distinguish investment property from owner-occupied property and from property held for sale in the ordinary course of business.

(d) the methods and significant assumptions applied in determining the fair value of investment property, including a statement whether the determination of fair value was supported by market evidence or was more heavily based on other factors (which the entity shall disclose) because of the nature of the property and lack of comparable market data.

(e) the extent to which the fair value of investment property (as measured or disclosed in the financial statements) is based on a valuation by an independent valuer who holds a recognised and relevant professional qualification and has recent experience in the location and category of the investment property being valued. If there has been no such valuation, that fact shall be disclosed.

(f) the amounts recognised in profit or loss for:

(i) rental income from investment property;

(ii) direct operating expenses (including repairs and maintenance) arising from investment property that generated rental income during the period; and

(iii) direct operating expenses (including repairs and maintenance) arising from investment property that did not generate rental income during the period.

(iv) the cumulative change in fair value recognised in profit or loss on a sale of investment property from a pool of assets in which the cost model is used into a pool in which the fair value model is used (see paragraph 32C).

(g) **the existence and amounts of restrictions on the realisability of investment property or the remittance of income and proceeds of disposal.**

(h) **contractual obligations to purchase, construct or develop investment property or for repairs, maintenance or enhancements.**

Fair value model

76 **In addition to the disclosures required by paragraph 75, an entity that applies the fair value model in paragraphs 33–55 shall disclose a reconciliation between the carrying amounts of investment property at the beginning and end of the period, showing the following:**

(a) **additions, disclosing separately those additions resulting from acquisitions and those resulting from subsequent expenditure recognised in the carrying amount of an asset;**

(b) **additions resulting from acquisitions through business combinations;**

(c) **assets classified as held for sale or included in a disposal group classified as held for sale in accordance with IFRS 5 and other disposals;**

(d) **net gains or losses from fair value adjustments;**

(e) **the net exchange differences arising on the translation of the financial statements into a different presentation currency, and on translation of a foreign operation into the presentation currency of the reporting entity;**

(f) **transfers to and from inventories and owner-occupied property; and**

(g) **other changes.**

77 **When a valuation obtained for investment property is adjusted significantly for the purpose of the financial statements, for example to avoid double-counting of assets or liabilities that are recognised as separate assets and liabilities as described in paragraph 50, the entity shall disclose a reconciliation between the valuation obtained and the adjusted valuation included in the financial statements, showing separately the aggregate amount of any recognised lease obligations that have been added back, and any other significant adjustments.**

78 **In the exceptional cases referred to in paragraph 53, when an entity measures investment property using the cost model in IAS 16, the reconciliation required by paragraph 76 shall disclose amounts relating to that investment property separately from amounts relating to other investment property. In addition, an entity shall disclose:**

(a) **a description of the investment property;**

(b) **an explanation of why fair value cannot be determined reliably;**

(c) **if possible, the range of estimates within which fair value is highly likely to lie; and**

(d) on disposal of investment property not carried at fair value:

(i) the fact that the entity has disposed of investment property not carried at fair value;

(ii) the carrying amount of that investment property at the time of sale; and

(iii) the amount of gain or loss recognised.

Cost model

79 **In addition to the disclosures required by paragraph 75, an entity that applies the cost model in paragraph 56 shall disclose:**

(a) the depreciation methods used;

(b) the useful lives or the depreciation rates used;

(c) the gross carrying amount and the accumulated depreciation (aggregated with accumulated impairment losses) at the beginning and end of the period;

(d) a reconciliation of the carrying amount of investment property at the beginning and end of the period, showing the following:

(i) additions, disclosing separately those additions resulting from acquisitions and those resulting from subsequent expenditure recognised as an asset;

(ii) additions resulting from acquisitions through business combinations;

(iii) assets classified as held for sale or included in a disposal group classified as held for sale in accordance with IFRS 5 and other disposals;

(iv) depreciation;

(v) the amount of impairment losses recognised, and the amount of impairment losses reversed, during the period in accordance with IAS 36;

(vi) the net exchange differences arising on the translation of the financial statements into a different presentation currency, and on translation of a foreign operation into the presentation currency of the reporting entity;

(vii) transfers to and from inventories and owner-occupied property; and

(viii) other changes; and

(e) the fair value of investment property. In the exceptional cases described in paragraph 53, when an entity cannot determine the fair value of the investment property reliably, it shall disclose:

(i) a description of the investment property;

(ii) an explanation of why fair value cannot be determined reliably; and

(iii) if possible, the range of estimates within which fair value is highly likely to lie.

Transitional provisions

Fair value model

80 **An entity that has previously applied IAS 40 (2000) and elects for the first time to classify and account for some or all eligible property interests held under operating leases as investment property shall recognise the effect of that election as an adjustment to the opening balance of retained earnings for the period in which the election is first made. In addition:**

(a) if the entity has previously disclosed publicly (in financial statements or otherwise) the fair value of those property interests in earlier periods (determined on a basis that satisfies the definition of fair value in paragraph 5 and the guidance in paragraphs 36–52), the entity is encouraged, but not required:

(i) to adjust the opening balance of retained earnings for the earliest period presented for which such fair value was disclosed publicly; and

(ii) to restate comparative information for those periods; and

(b) if the entity has not previously disclosed publicly the information described in (a), it shall not restate comparative information and shall disclose that fact.

81 This Standard requires a treatment different from that required by IAS 8. IAS 8 requires comparative information to be restated unless such restatement is impracticable.

82 When an entity first applies this Standard, the adjustment to the opening balance of retained earnings includes the reclassification of any amount held in revaluation surplus for investment property.

Cost model

83 IAS 8 applies to any change in accounting policies that is made when an entity first applies this Standard and chooses to use the cost model. The effect of the change in accounting policies includes the reclassification of any amount held in revaluation surplus for investment property.

84 **The requirements of paragraphs 27–29 regarding the initial measurement of an investment property acquired in an exchange of assets transaction shall be applied prospectively only to future transactions.**

Effective date

85 **An entity shall apply this Standard for annual periods beginning on or after 1 January 2005. Earlier application is encouraged. If an entity applies this Standard for a period beginning before 1 January 2005, it shall disclose that fact.**

Withdrawal of IAS 40 (2000)

86 This Standard supersedes IAS 40 *Investment Property* (issued in 2000).

Approval of IAS 40 by the Board

International Accounting Standard 40 *Investment Property* was approved for issue by the fourteen members of the International Accounting Standards Board.

Sir David Tweedie	Chairman
Thomas E Jones	Vice-Chairman
Mary E Barth	
Hans-Georg Bruns	
Anthony T Cope	
Robert P Garnett	
Gilbert Gélard	
James J Leisenring	
Warren J McGregor	
Patricia L O'Malley	
Harry K Schmid	
John T Smith	
Geoffrey Whittington	
Tatsumi Yamada	

Basis for Conclusions on IAS 40 (as revised in 2003)

This Basis for Conclusions accompanies, but is not part of, IAS 40.

Introduction

BC1 This Basis for Conclusions summarises the International Accounting Standards Board's considerations in reaching its conclusions on revising IAS 40 *Investment Property* in 2003. Individual Board members gave greater weight to some factors than to others.

BC2 In July 2001 the Board announced that, as part of its initial agenda of technical projects, it would undertake a project to improve a number of Standards, including IAS 40. The project was undertaken in the light of queries and criticisms raised in relation to the Standards by securities regulators, professional accountants and other interested parties. The objectives of the Improvements project were to reduce or eliminate alternatives, redundancies and conflicts within Standards, to deal with some convergence issues and to make other improvements. In May 2002 the Board published its proposals in an Exposure Draft of *Improvements to International Accounting Standards*, with a comment deadline of 16 September 2002. The Board received over 160 comment letters on the Exposure Draft.

BC3 Because the Board's intention was not to reconsider the fundamental approach to the accounting for investment property established by IAS 40, this Basis for Conclusions does not discuss requirements in IAS 40 that the Board has not reconsidered. The IASC Basis for Conclusions on IAS 40 (2000) follows this Basis.

Scope

Property interests held under an operating lease

BC4 Paragraph 14 of IAS 17 *Leases* requires a lease of land with an indefinite economic life to be classified as an operating lease, unless title is expected to pass to the lessee by the end of the lease term. Without the provisions of IAS 40 as amended, this operating lease classification would prevent a lessee from classifying its interest in the leased asset as an investment property in accordance with IAS 40. As a result, the lessee could not remeasure its interest in the leased asset to fair value and recognise any change in fair value in profit or loss. However, in some countries, interests in property (including land) are commonly—or exclusively—held under long-term operating leases. The effect of some of these leases differs little from buying a property outright. As a result, some contended that such leases should be accounted for as finance leases or investment property, or as both.

BC5 The Board discussed possible solutions to this issue. In particular, it considered deleting paragraph 14 of IAS 17, so that a long-term lease of land would be classified as a finance lease (and hence could qualify as an investment property) when the conditions for finance lease classification in paragraphs 4–13 of IAS 17 are met. However, the Board noted that this would not resolve all cases encountered in practice. Some leasehold interests held for investment would remain classified as operating leases (eg leases with significant contingent rents), and hence could not be investment property in accordance with IAS 40.

BC6 In the light of this, the Board decided to state separately in paragraph 6 (rather than amend IAS 40's definition of investment property) that a lessee's interest in property that arises under an operating lease could qualify as investment property. The Board decided to limit this amendment to entities that use the fair value model in IAS 40, because the objective of the amendment is to permit use of the fair value model for similar property interests held under finance and operating leases. Put another way, a lessee that uses the cost model for a property would not be permitted to recognise operating leases as assets. The Board also decided to make the change optional, ie a lessee that has an interest in property under an operating lease is allowed, but not required, to classify that property interest as investment property (provided the rest of the definition of investment property is met). The Board confirmed that this classification alternative is available on a property-by-property basis.

BC7 When a lessee's interest in property held under an operating lease is accounted for as an investment property, the Board decided that the initial carrying amounts of that interest and the related liability are to be accounted for as if the lease were a finance lease. This decision places such leases in the same position as investment properties held under finance leases in accordance with the previous version of IAS 40.

BC8 In doing so, the Board acknowledged that this results in different measurement bases for the lease asset and the lease liability. This is also true for owned investment properties and debt that finances them. However, in accordance with IAS 39 *Financial Instruments: Recognition and Measurement*, as revised in 2003, an entity can elect to measure such debt at fair value, but lease liabilities cannot be remeasured in accordance with IAS 17.

BC9 The Board considered changing the scope of IAS 39, but concluded that this would lead to a fundamental review of lease accounting, especially in relation to contingent rentals. The Board decided that this was beyond the limited revisions to IAS 40 to facilitate application of the fair value model to some operating leases classified as investment properties. The Board did, however, indicate that it wished to revisit this issue in a later project on lease accounting. The Board also noted that this was the view of the Board of the former IASC as expressed in its Basis for Conclusions, in paragraphs 25 and 26.*

BC10 Finally, the Board noted that the methodology described in paragraphs 40 and 50(d) of IAS 40, whereby a fair valuation of the property that takes all lease obligations into account is adjusted by adding back any liability that is recognised for these obligations, would, in practice, enable entities to ensure that net assets in respect of the leased interest are not affected by the use of different measurement bases.

* These paragraphs in the IASC Basis are shown as struck through because they may be misleading when read in isolation from IAS 39 (as revised in 2003), which permits liabilities within its scope to be marked to market, with changes in fair value recognised in profit or loss in the period in which the changes occur.

The choice between the cost model and the fair value model

BC11 The Board also discussed whether to remove the choice in IAS 40 of accounting for investment property using a fair value model or a cost model.

BC12 The Board noted that IASC had included a choice for two main reasons. The first was to give preparers and users time to gain experience with using a fair value model. The second was to allow time for countries with less-developed property markets and valuation professions to mature. The Board decided that more time is needed for these events to take place (IAS 40 became mandatory only for periods beginning on or after 1 January 2001). The Board also noted that requiring the fair value model would not converge with the treatment required by most of its liaison standard-setters. For these reasons, the Board decided not to eliminate the choice as part of the Improvements project, but rather to keep the matter under review with a view to reconsidering the option to use the cost model at a later date.

BC13 The Board did not reconsider IAS 40 in relation to the accounting by lessors. The definition of investment property requires that such a property is held by the owner or a lessee under a finance lease. As indicated above, the Board agreed to allow a lessee under an operating lease, in specified circumstances, also to be a 'holder'. However, a lessor that has provided a property to a lessee under a finance lease cannot be a 'holder'. Such a lessor has a lease receivable, not an investment property.

BC14 The Board did not change the requirements for a lessor that leases property under an operating lease that is classified and accounted for by the lessee as investment property. The Board acknowledged that this would mean that two parties could both account as if they 'hold' interests in the property. This could occur at various levels of lessees who become lessors in a manner consistent with the definition of an investment property and the election provided for operating leases. Lessees who use the property in the production or supply of goods or services or for administrative purposes would not be able to classify that property as an investment property.

Basis for Conclusions on IAS 40 (2000)

Contents

Basis for Conclusions on IAS 40 (2000) Investment Property

This Basis for Conclusions accompanies, but is not part of, IAS 40. It was issued by the Board of the former International Accounting Standards Committee (IASC) in 2000. Apart from the deletion of paragraphs B10–B15, B25 and B26, this Basis has not been revised by the IASB. Those paragraphs are no longer relevant and have been deleted to avoid the risk that they might be read out of context. In addition, the text has been annotated where references to material in other standards are no longer valid, following the revision of those standards. Reference should be made to the IASB's Basis for Conclusions on the amendments made in 2003.

Background

B1 The IASC Board (the "Board") approved IAS 25, Accounting for Investments, in 1986. In 1994, the Board approved a reformatted version of IAS 25 presented in the revised format adopted for International Accounting Standards from 1991. Certain terminology was also changed at that time to bring it into line with then current IASC practice. No substantive changes were made to the original approved text.

B2 IAS 25 was one of the standards that the Board identified for possible revision in E32 *Comparability of Financial Statements*. Following comments on the proposals in E32, the Board decided to defer consideration of IAS 25, pending further work on Financial Instruments. In 1998, the Board approved IAS 38 *Intangible Assets* and IAS 39 *Financial Instruments: Recognition and Measurement*, leaving IAS 25 to cover investments in real estate, commodities and tangible assets such as vintage cars and other collectors' items.

B3 In July 1999, the Board approved E64 *Investment Property*, with a comment deadline of 31 October 1999. The Board received 121 comment letters on E64. Comment letters came from various international organisations, as well as from 28 individual countries. The Board approved IAS 40 *Investment Property* in March 2000. Paragraph B67 below summarises the changes that the Board made to E64 in finalising IAS 40.

B4 IAS 40 permits entities to choose between a fair value model and a cost model. As explained in paragraphs B47–B48 below, the Board believes that it is impracticable, at this stage, to require a fair value model for all investment property. At the same time, the Board believes that it is desirable to permit a fair value model. This evolutionary step forward will allow preparers and users to gain greater experience working with a fair value model and will allow time for certain property markets to achieve greater maturity.

Need for a Separate Standard

B5 Some commentators argued that investment property should fall within the scope of IAS 16 *Property, Plant and Equipment*, and that there is no reason to have a separate standard on investment property. They believe that:

(a) it is not possible to distinguish investment property rigorously from owner-occupied property covered by IAS 16 and without reference to management intent. Thus, a distinction between investment property and owner-occupied property will lead to a free choice of different accounting treatments in some cases; and

(b) the fair value accounting model proposed in E64 is not appropriate, on the grounds that fair value is not relevant and, in some cases, not reliable in the case of investment property. The accounting treatments in IAS 16 are appropriate not only for owner-occupied property, but also for investment property.

B6 Having reviewed the comment letters, the Board still believes that the characteristics of investment property differ sufficiently from the characteristics of owner-occupied property that there is a need for a separate Standard on investment property. In particular, the Board believes that information about the fair value of investment property, and about changes in its fair value, is highly relevant to users of financial statements. The Board believes that it is important to permit a fair value model for investment property, so that entities can report fair value information prominently. The Board tried to maintain consistency with IAS 16, except for differences dictated by the choice of a different accounting model.

Scope

Investment Property Entities

B7 Some commentators argued that the Standard should cover only investment property held by entities that specialise in owning such property (and, perhaps, also other investments) and not cover investment property held by other entities. The Board rejected this view because the Board could find no conceptual and practical way to distinguish rigorously any class of entities for which the fair value model would be less or more appropriate.

Investment Property Reportable Segments

B8 Some commentators suggested that the Board should limit the scope of the Standard to entities that have a reportable segment whose main activity is investment property. These commentators argued that an approach linked to reportable segments would require an entity to adopt the fair value model when the entity considers investment property activities to be an important element of its financial performance and would allow an entity to adopt IAS 16 in other cases.

B9 An approach linked to reportable segments would lead to lack of comparability between investment property held in investment property segments and investment property held in other segments. For this reason, the Board rejected such an approach.

~~Long Operating Leases~~

B10 ~~As proposed in E64, the Standard does not permit a lessee to treat its interest in property held under an operating lease as investment property, even if the lessee acquired its interest in exchange for a large up-front payment or the lease has a very long term. Instead, IAS 17, Leases, requires the lessee to recognise the lease payments as an expense on a straight line basis over the lease term unless another systematic basis is more representative of the time pattern of the user's benefit.~~

B11 ~~In some countries, such as Hong Kong and the United Kingdom, enterprises commonly make a large up-front payment to acquire a long-term interest in property (sometimes known as a leasehold interest). Some lessees consider that a leasehold interest is, in economic substance, virtually indistinguishable from rights acquired on buying a property. Indeed, some commentators noted that outright ownership of land or buildings is impossible in some markets, such as Hong Kong, and that property "ownership" in these markets is invariably transferred by selling rights under operating leases. Some commentators, particularly from these countries, felt that lessees should be permitted to use the fair value model to account for such interests.~~

B12 ~~Some commentators suggested amending paragraph 11 of IAS 17, Leases, so that such leases could be classified as finance leases. This paragraph states that a lessee of land does not receive substantially all of the risks and rewards incident to ownership if title is not expected to pass to the lessee by the end of the lease term.~~

B13 ~~The Board found no conceptual basis for distinguishing one class of operating leases for which a fair value model might be appropriate from another class of operating leases where it might be more appropriate to continue the existing cost-based accounting model under IAS 17. In particular, the Board concluded that an up-front payment does not change the economic substance of a lease sufficiently to justify an accounting treatment that differs from the treatment used for otherwise similar leases with no up-front payment. A distinction based on the presence or absence of an up-front payment is difficult to reconcile with the accrual basis of accounting.~~

B14 ~~The Board concluded that the Standard on investment property should not deal with property held under an operating lease and that IAS 17, Leases, should continue to deal with all operating leases. The Board also concluded that no other solution is practicable without a fundamental review of lease accounting.~~

B15 ~~Some commentators urged IASC to begin a fundamental review of lease accounting as soon as possible. The G4+1 group of standard setters is currently undertaking such a review and published a paper on this subject in December 1999. The Board is monitoring progress on this project with interest. However, the Board does not currently have such a review on its own work plan.~~

Investment Property under Construction

B16 E64 proposed that investment property under construction should be measured at fair value. E64 argued that fair value is the most relevant measure and that fair value of investment property under construction is not necessarily more difficult to measure than completed investment property. For example, where an investment property under construction is largely pre-leased, there may be less uncertainty about future cash inflows than for a completed investment property that is largely vacant.

B17 Some commentators argued that it is difficult to estimate fair value reliably for investment property under construction, because a market may not exist for property under construction. They argued that there may be considerable uncertainty about the cost to complete investment property under construction and about the income that such property will generate. Therefore, they suggested that an entity should not measure investment property at more than cost if the investment property is still under construction.

B18 The Board was persuaded by this argument and concluded that investment property under construction should be excluded from the scope of this Standard and should be covered by IAS 16.

B19 Paragraph 52 of the Standard addresses cases where an entity begins to redevelop an existing investment property for continued future use as investment property. One approach would be to require a temporary transfer out of investment property into property under development (subject to IAS 16) for the duration of the redevelopment. However, the Board felt that such temporary transfers would be confusing and would be of little or no benefit to users of financial statements. This approach would also need arbitrary rules to distinguish major redevelopments that would result in such a temporary transfer from less significant works that would not lead to such a transfer. Accordingly, paragraph 52 states that the property remains an investment property and is not reclassified as owner-occupied property during the redevelopment.

B20 When an entity completes the construction or development of a self-constructed investment property that will be carried at fair value, there is likely to be a difference between the fair value of the property at that date and its previous carrying amount. The Board considered two approaches to accounting for such differences under the fair value model.

(a) Under the first approach, the difference would be transferred to revaluation surplus. This approach would be consistent with the Standard's approach to transfers from owner-occupied property to investment property.

(b) Under the second approach, the difference would be recognised in profit or loss for the period. The Board concluded that this second approach gives a more meaningful picture of performance (see paragraph 59).

Property Occupied by Another Entity in the Same Group

B21 In some cases, an entity owns property that is leased to, and occupied by, another entity in the same group. The property does not qualify as investment property in consolidated financial statements that include both entities, because the property is owner-occupied from the perspective of the group as a whole. However, from the perspective of the individual entity that owns it, the property is investment property if it meets the definition set out in the Standard.

B22 Some commentators believe that the definition of investment property should exclude properties that are occupied by another entity in the same group. Alternatively, they suggest that the Standard should not require investment property accounting in individual financial statements for properties that do not qualify as investment property in consolidated financial statements. They believe that:

(a) it could be argued (at least in some such cases) that the property does not meet the definition of investment property from the perspective of a subsidiary whose property is occupied by another entity in the same group—the subsidiary's motive for holding the property is to comply with a directive from its parent and not necessarily to earn rentals or to benefit from capital appreciation. Indeed, the intragroup lease may not be priced on an arm's length basis;

(b) this requirement would lead to additional valuation costs that would not be justified by the limited benefits to users. For groups with subsidiaries that are required to prepare individual financial statements, the cost could be extensive as entities may create a separate subsidiary to hold each property;

(c) some users may be confused if the same property is classified as investment property in the individual financial statements of a subsidiary and as owner-occupied property in the consolidated financial statements of the parent; and

(d) there is a precedent for a similar exemption (relating to disclosure, rather than measurement) in paragraph 4(c) of IAS 24 *Related Party Disclosures*, which does not require disclosures in a wholly-owned subsidiary's financial statements if its parent is incorporated in the same country and provides consolidated financial statements in that country.[*]

B23 Some commentators believe that the definition of investment property should exclude property occupied by any related party. They argue that related parties often do not pay rent on an arm's length basis, that it is often difficult to establish whether the rent is consistent with pricing on an arm's length basis and that rental rates may be subject to arbitrary change. They suggest that fair values are less relevant where property is subject to leases that are not priced on an arm's length basis.

B24 The Board could find no justification for treating property leased to another entity in the same group (or to another related party) differently from property leased to other parties. Therefore, the Board decided that an entity should use the same accounting treatment, regardless of the identity of the lessee.

~~Liabilities Related to Investment Property~~

B25 ~~Some commentators suggested that the Standard should address the measurement of liabilities incurred to acquire investment property. Under IAS 39, Financial Instruments: Recognition and Measurement, such liabilities are, in many cases, measured on an amortised cost basis. These commentators believe that there will be a mismatch if the property is measured at fair value.~~

B26 ~~The Board concluded that it should not, at this stage, permit or require a fair value model for liabilities incurred to acquire investment properties. The Board also decided not to modify the fair value model for investment property to adjust for mismatches caused by using an amortised-cost basis for related financial liabilities. Under IAS 39, the possibility already exists of a similar mismatch between those financial assets measured at fair value and financial liabilities. The Board is participating in an international Joint Working Group on financial instruments, which is pursuing the possibility of measuring all financial assets and financial liabilities at fair value.~~

* IAS 24 *Related Party Disclosures* as revised by the IASB in 2003 no longer provides the exemption mentioned in paragraph B22(d).

Government Grants

B27 IAS 20 *Accounting for Government Grants and Disclosure of Government Assistance* permits two methods of presenting grants relating to assets—either setting up a grant as deferred income and amortising the income over the useful life of the asset or deducting the grant in arriving at the carrying amount of the asset. Some believe that both of those methods reflect a historical cost model and are inconsistent with the fair value model set out in this Standard. Indeed, Exposure Draft E65 *Agriculture*, which proposes a fair value model for biological assets, addresses certain aspects of government grants, as these are a significant factor in accounting for agriculture in some countries.

B28 Some commentators urged IASC to change the accounting treatment of government grants related to investment property. However, most commentators agreed that IASC should not deal with this aspect of government grants now. The Board decided not to revise this aspect of IAS 20 in the project on Investment Property.

B29 Some commentators suggested that IASC should begin a wider review of IAS 20 as a matter of urgency. In early 2000, the G4+1 group of standard setters published a Discussion Paper *Accounting by Recipients for Non-Reciprocal Transfers, Excluding Contributions by Owners: Their Definition, Recognition and Measurement*. The Board's work plan does not currently include a project on the accounting for government grants or other forms of non-reciprocal transfer.

Definition of Investment Property

B30 The definition of investment property excludes:

(a) owner-occupied property—covered by IAS 16 *Property, Plant and Equipment*. Under IAS 16, such property is carried at either depreciated cost or revalued amount less subsequent depreciation. In addition, such property is subject to an impairment test; and

(b) property held for sale in the ordinary course of business—covered by IAS 2 *Inventories*. IAS 2 requires an entity to carry such property at the lower of cost and net realisable value.

B31 These exclusions are consistent with the existing definitions of property, plant and equipment in IAS 16 and inventories in IAS 2. This ensures that all property is covered by one, and only one, of the three Standards.

B32 Some commentators suggested that property held for sale in the ordinary course of business should be treated as investment property rather than as inventories (covered by IAS 2). They argued that:

(a) it is difficult to distinguish property held for sale in the ordinary course of business from property held for capital appreciation; and

(b) it is illogical to require a fair value model for land and buildings held for long-term capital appreciation (investment property) when a cost model is still used for land and buildings held for short-term sale in the ordinary course of business (inventories).

B33 The Board rejected this suggestion because:

(a) if fair value accounting is used for property held for sale in the ordinary course of business, this would raise wider questions about inventory accounting that go beyond the scope of this project; and

(b) it is arguably more important to use fair value accounting for property that may have been acquired over a long period and held for several years (investment property) than for property that was acquired over a shorter period and held for a relatively short time (inventories). With the passage of time, cost-based measurements become increasingly irrelevant. Also, an aggregation of costs incurred over a long period is of questionable relevance.

B34 Some commentators suggested requiring (or at least permitting) entities, particularly financial institutions such as insurance companies, to use the fair value model for their owner-occupied property. They argued that some financial institutions regard their owner-occupied property as an integral part of their investment portfolio and treat it for management purposes in the same way as property leased to others. In the case of insurance companies, the property may be held to back policyholder liabilities. The Board believes that property used for similar purposes should be subject to the same accounting treatment. Accordingly, the Board concluded that no class of entities should use the fair value model for their owner-occupied property.

B35 Some commentators suggested that the definition of investment property should exclude property held for rentals, but not for capital appreciation. In their view, a fair value model may be appropriate for dealing activities, but is inappropriate where an entity has historically held rental property for many years and has no intention of selling it in the foreseeable future. They consider that holding property for long-term rental is a service activity and the assets used in that activity should be treated in the same way as assets used to support other service activities. In their view, holding an investment in property in such cases is similar to holding "held-to-maturity investments", which are measured at amortised cost under IAS 39.

B36 In the Board's view, the fair value model provides useful information about property held for rental, even if there is no immediate intention to sell the property. The economic performance of a property can be regarded as being made up of both rental income earned during the period (net of expenses) and changes in the value of future net rental income. The fair value of an investment property can be regarded as a market-based representation of the value of the future net rental income, regardless of whether the entity is likely to sell the property in the near future. Also, the Standard notes that fair value is determined without deducting costs of disposal—in other words, the use of the fair value model is not intended as a representation that a sale could, or should, be made in the near future.

B37 The classification of hotels and similar property was controversial throughout the project and commentators on E64 had mixed views on this subject. Some see hotels essentially as investments, while others see them essentially as operating properties. Some requested a detailed rule to specify whether hotels (and, perhaps, other categories of property, such as restaurants, bars and nursing homes) should be classified as investment property or as owner-occupied property.

B38 The Board concluded that it is preferable to distinguish investment property from owner-occupied property on the basis of general principles, rather than have arbitrary rules for specific classes of property. Also, it would inevitably be difficult to establish rigorous definitions of specific classes of property to be covered by such rules. Paragraphs 9–11 of the Standard discuss cases such as hotels in the context of the general principles that apply when an entity provides ancillary services.

B39 Some commentators requested quantitative guidance (such as a percentage) to clarify whether an "insignificant portion" is owner-occupied (paragraph 8) and whether ancillary services are "significant" (paragraphs 9–11 of the Standard). As for similar cases in other Standards, the Board concluded that quantitative guidance would create arbitrary distinctions.

Subsequent Expenditure

B40 Some believe that there is no need to capitalise subsequent expenditure in a fair value model and that all subsequent expenditure should be recognised as an expense. However, others believe—and the Board agreed—that the failure to capitalise subsequent expenditure would lead to a distortion of the reported components of financial performance. Therefore, the Standard requires that an entity should determine whether subsequent expenditure should be capitalised using a test similar to the test used for owner-occupied property in IAS 16.

B41 Some commentators suggested that the test for capitalising subsequent expenditure should not refer to the originally assessed standard of performance. They felt that it is impractical and irrelevant to judge against the originally assessed standard of performance, which may relate to many years in the past. Instead, they suggested that subsequent expenditure should be capitalised if it enhances the previously assessed standard of performance—for example, if it increases the current market value of the property or is intended to maintain its competitiveness in the market. The Board saw some merit in this suggestion.

B42 Nevertheless, the Board believes that a reference to the previously assessed standard of performance would require substantial additional guidance, might not change the way the Standard is applied in practice and might cause confusion. The Board also concluded that it was important to retain the existing reference to the originally assessed standard of performance* to be consistent with IAS 16 and IAS 38.

Subsequent Measurement

Accounting Model

B43 Under IAS 25, an entity was permitted to choose from among a variety of accounting treatments for investment property (depreciated cost under the

* IAS 16 *Property, Plant and Equipment* as revised by the IASB in 2003 requires all subsequent costs to be covered by its general recognition principle and eliminated the requirement to reference the originally assessed standard of performance. IAS 40 was amended as a consequence of the change to IAS 16.

benchmark treatment in IAS 16 *Property, Plant and Equipment*, revaluation with depreciation under the allowed alternative treatment in IAS 16, cost less impairment under IAS 25 or revaluation under IAS 25).*

B44 E64 proposed that all investment property should be measured at fair value. Supporters of the fair value model believe that fair values give users of financial statements more useful information than other measures, such as depreciated cost. In their view, rental income and changes in fair value are inextricably linked as integral components of the financial performance of an investment property and measurement at fair value is necessary if that financial performance is to be reported in a meaningful way.

B45 Supporters of the fair value model also note that an investment property generates cash flows largely independently of the other assets held by an entity. In their view, the generation of independent cash flows through rental or capital appreciation distinguishes investment property from owner-occupied property. The production or supply of goods or services (or the use of property for administrative purposes) generates cash flows that are attributable not merely to property, but also to other assets used in the production or supply process. Proponents of the fair value model for investment property argue that this distinction makes a fair value model more appropriate for investment property than for owner-occupied property.

B46 Those who oppose measurement of investment property at fair value argue that:

(a) there is often no active market for investment property (unlike for many financial instruments). Real estate transactions are not frequent and not homogeneous. Each investment property is unique and each sale is subject to significant negotiations. As a result, fair value measurement will not enhance comparability because fair values are not determinable on a reliable basis, especially in countries where the valuation profession is less well established. A depreciated cost measurement provides a more consistent, less volatile, and less subjective measurement;

(b) IAS 39 does not require fair value measurement for all financial assets, even some that are realised more easily than investment property. It would be premature to consider extending the fair value model until the Joint Working Group on financial instruments has completed its work;

(c) a cost basis is used for "shorter term" assets (such as inventories) for which fair value is, arguably, more relevant than for "held for investment" assets; and

(d) measurement at fair value is too costly in relation to the benefits to users.

B47 This is the first time that the Board has proposed requiring a fair value accounting model for non-financial assets. The comment letters on E64 showed that although many support this step, many others still have significant conceptual and practical reservations about extending a fair value model to non-financial assets, particularly (but not exclusively) for entities whose main activity is not to hold

* IAS 16 *Property, Plant and Equipment* as revised by the IASB in 2003 eliminated all references to 'benchmark' treatment and 'allowed alternative' treatments. They are replaced with cost model and revaluation model.

property for capital appreciation. Also, some entities feel that certain property markets are not yet sufficiently mature for a fair value model to work satisfactorily. Furthermore, some believe that it is impossible to create a rigorous definition of investment property and that this makes it impracticable to require a fair value model at present.

B48 For those reasons, the Board believes that it is impracticable, at this stage, to require a fair value model for investment property. At the same time, the Board believes that it is desirable to permit a fair value model. This evolutionary step forward will allow preparers and users to gain greater experience working with a fair value model and will allow time for certain property markets to achieve greater maturity.

B49 IAS 40 permits entities to choose between a fair value model and a cost model. An entity should apply the model chosen to all its investment property. [This choice is not available to a lessee accounting for an investment property under an operating lease as if it were a finance lease–refer to the IASB's Basis for Conclusions on the amendments made in 2003.] The fair value model is the model proposed in E64: investment property should be measured at fair value and changes in fair value should be recognised in the income statement. The cost model is the benchmark treatment* in IAS 16 *Property, Plant and Equipment*: investment property should be measured at depreciated cost (less any accumulated impairment losses). An entity that chooses the cost model should disclose the fair value of its investment property.

B50 Under IAS 8 *Net Profit or Loss for the Period, Fundamental Errors and Changes in Accounting Policies*, a change in accounting policies from one model to the other model should be made only if the change will result in a more appropriate presentation of events or transactions. The Board concluded that this is highly unlikely to be the case for a change from the fair value model to the cost model and paragraph 25 of the Standard reflects this conclusion.

B51 The Board believes that it is undesirable to permit three different accounting treatments for investment property. Accordingly, if an entity does not adopt the fair value model, the Standard requires the entity to use the benchmark treatment in IAS 16 and does not permit the use of the allowed alternative treatment. However, an entity may still use the allowed alternative for other properties covered by IAS 16.*

Guidance on Fair Value

B52 The valuation profession will have an important role in implementing the Standard. Accordingly, in developing its guidance on the fair value of investment property, the Board considered not only similar guidance in other IASC literature, but also International Valuation Standards (IVS) issued by the International Valuation Standards Committee (IVSC). The Board understands that IVSC intends to review, and perhaps revise, its Standards in the near future.

* IAS 16 *Property, Plant and Equipment* as revised by the IASB in 2003 eliminated all references to 'benchmark' treatment and 'allowed alternative' treatments.

B53 The Board believes that IASC's concept of fair value is similar to the IVSC concept of market value. IVSC defines market value as "the estimated amount for which an asset should exchange on the date of valuation between a willing buyer and a willing seller in an arm's length transaction after proper marketing wherein the parties had each acted knowledgeably, prudently and without compulsion." The Board believes that the guidance in paragraphs 29–30 and 32–38 of the Standard is, in substance (and largely in wording as well), identical with guidance in IVS 1.

B54 Paragraphs 31 and 39–46 of IAS 40 have no direct counterpart in the IVSC literature. The Board developed much of this material in response to commentators on E64, who asked for more detailed guidance on determining the fair value of investment property. In developing this material, the Board considered guidance on fair value in other IASC Standards and Exposure Drafts, particularly those on financial instruments (IAS 32 and IAS 39), intangible assets (IAS 38) and agriculture (E65).

Independent Valuation

B55 Some commentators believe that fair values should be determined on the basis of an independent valuation, to enhance the reliability of the fair values reported. Others believe, on cost-benefit grounds, that IASC should not require (and perhaps not even encourage) an independent valuation. They believe that it is for preparers to decide, in consultation with auditors, whether an entity has sufficient internal resources to determine reliable fair values. Some also believe that independent valuers with appropriate expertise are not available in some markets.

B56 The Board concluded that an independent valuation is not always necessary. Therefore, as proposed in E64, the Standard encourages, but does not require, an entity to determine the fair value of all investment property on the basis of a valuation by an independent valuer who holds a recognised and relevant professional qualification and who has recent experience in the location and category of the investment property being valued. This approach is consistent with the approach to actuarial valuations in IAS 19 *Employee Benefits* (see IAS 19, paragraph 57).

Inability to Measure Fair Value Reliably

B57 E64 included a rebuttable presumption that an entity will be able to determine reliably the fair value of property held to earn rentals or for capital appreciation. E64 also proposed a reliability exception: IAS 16 should be applied if evidence indicates clearly, when an entity acquires or constructs a property, that fair value will not be determinable reliably on a continuing basis.

B58 Some commentators opposed various aspects of this proposal, on one or more of the following grounds:

(a) the rebuttable presumption underestimates the difficulties of determining fair value reliably. This will often be impossible, particularly where markets are thin or where there is not a well-established valuation profession;

(b) the accounting model under IAS 16 includes an impairment test under IAS 36. However, it is illogical to rely on an impairment test when fair value cannot be determined using cash flow projections, because an impairment test under IAS 36 is also difficult in such cases;

(c) where fair value cannot be determined reliably, this fact does not justify charging depreciation. Instead, the property in question should be measured at cost less impairment losses; and

(d) to avoid the danger of manipulation, all efforts should be made to determine fair values, even in a relatively inactive market. Even without an active market, a range of projected cash flows is available. If there are problems in determining fair value, an entity should measure the property at the best estimate of fair value and disclose limitations on the reliability of the estimate. If it is completely impossible to determine fair value, fair value should be deemed to be zero.

B59 The Board concluded that the rebuttable presumption and the reliability exception should be retained, but decided to implement them in a different way. In E64, they were implemented by excluding a property from the definition of investment property if the rebuttable presumption was overcome. Some commentators felt that it was confusing to include such a reliability exception in a definition. Accordingly, the Board moved the reliability exception from the definition to the section on subsequent measurement (paragraphs 47–49).

B60 Under E64, an entity should not stop using the fair value model if comparable market transactions become less frequent or market prices become less readily available. Some commentators disagreed with this proposal. They argued that there may be cases when reliable estimates are no longer available and that it would be misleading to continue fair value accounting in such cases. The Board decided that it is important to keep the E64 approach, because otherwise entities might use a reliability exception as an excuse to discontinue fair value accounting in a falling market.

B61 In cases where the reliability exception applies, E64 proposed that an entity should continue to apply IAS 16 until disposal of the property. Some commentators proposed that an entity should start applying the fair value model once the fair value becomes measurable reliably. The Board rejected this proposal because it would inevitably be a subjective decision to determine when fair value has become measurable reliably and this subjectivity could lead to inconsistent application.

B62 E64 proposed no specific disclosure where the reliability exception applies. Some commentators felt that disclosure would be important in such cases. The Board agreed and decided to include disclosures consistent with paragraph 170(b) of IAS 39 (see paragraphs 68 and 69(e) of IAS 40). Paragraph 170(b) of IAS 39 requires disclosures for financial assets whose fair value cannot be reliably measured.

Gains and Losses on Remeasurement to Fair Value

B63 Some commentators argued that there should be either a requirement or an option to recognise changes in the fair value of investment property in equity,* on the grounds that:

(a) the market for property is not liquid enough and market values are uncertain and variable. Investment property is not as liquid as financial instruments and IAS 39 allows an option for available-for-sale investments;

(b) until performance reporting issues are resolved more generally, it is premature to require recognition of fair value changes in the income statement;

(c) recognition of unrealised gains and losses in the income statement increases volatility and does not enhance transparency, because revaluation changes will blur the assessment of an entity's operating performance. It may also cause a presumption that the unrealised gains are available for distribution as dividends;

(d) recognition in equity is more consistent with the historical cost and modified historical cost conventions that are a basis for much of today's accounting. For example, it is consistent with IASC's treatment of revaluations of property, plant and equipment under IAS 16 and with the option available for certain financial instruments under IAS 39;

(e) for properties financed by debt, changes in the fair value of the properties resulting from interest rate changes should not be recognised in the income statement, since the corresponding changes in the fair value of the debt are not recognised under IAS 39;

(f) under paragraphs 92 and 93 of the *Framework*, income should be recognised only when it can be measured with sufficient certainty. For example, IAS 11 *Construction Contracts* requires certain conditions before an entity can use the percentage-of-completion method. These conditions are not normally met for investment property; and

(g) results from operations should be distinguished from changes in values. For example, under IAS 21, unrealised exchange differences on a foreign entity† are recognised in equity.

B64 Some commentators suggested that increases should be recognised in equity and decreases should be recognised in profit or loss. This is similar to the revaluation model that forms the allowed alternative treatment§ in IAS 16 (except for the lack of depreciation).

---

* Under IAS 1 *Presentation of Financial Statements*, all such changes reported in equity are presented in a statement showing changes in equity.

† In IAS 21 *The Effects of Changes in Foreign Exchange Rates*, as revised by the IASB in 2003, the term 'foreign entity' was replaced by 'foreign operation'.

§ IAS 16 *Property, Plant and Equipment* as revised by the IASB in 2003 eliminated all references to 'benchmark' treatment and 'allowed alternative' treatments.

B65 As proposed in E64, the Board concluded that, in a fair value model, changes in the fair value of investment property should be recognised in the income statement as part of profit or loss for the period. The arguments for this approach include the following:

(a) the conceptual case for the fair value model is built largely on the view that this provides the most relevant and transparent view of the financial performance of investment property. Given this, it would be inconsistent to permit or require recognition in equity;

(b) recognition of fair value changes in equity would create a mismatch because net rental income would be recognised in the income statement, whereas the related consumption of the service potential (recognised as depreciation under IAS 16) would be recognised in equity. Similarly, maintenance expenditure would be recognised as an expense while related increases in fair value would be recognised in equity;

(c) using this approach, there is no need to resolve some difficult and controversial issues that would arise if changes in the fair value of investment property were recognised in equity. These issues include the following:

(i) should fair value changes previously recognised in equity be transferred ("recycled") to profit or loss on disposal of investment property; and

(ii) should fair value changes previously recognised in equity be transferred ("recycled") to profit or loss when investment property is impaired? If so, how should such impairment be identified and measured; and

(d) given the difficulty in defining investment property rigorously, entities will sometimes have the option of applying the investment property standard or either of the two treatments in IAS 16. It would be undesirable to include two choices in the investment property standard, as this would give entities a choice (at least occasionally) between four different treatments.

Transfers

B66 When an owner-occupied property carried under the benchmark treatment under IAS 16 becomes an investment property, the measurement basis for the property changes from depreciated cost to fair value. The Board concluded that the effect of this change in measurement basis should be treated as a revaluation under IAS 16 at the date of change in use. The result is that:

(a) the income statement excludes cumulative net increases in fair value that arose before the property became investment property. The portion of this change that arose before the beginning of the current period does not represent financial performance of the current period; and

(b) this treatment creates comparability between entities that had previously revalued the property under the allowed alternative treatment in IAS 16 and those entities that had previously used the IAS 16 benchmark treatment.*

* IAS 16 *Property, Plant and Equipment* as revised by the IASB in 2003 eliminated all references to 'benchmark' treatment and 'allowed alternative' treatments.

Summary of Changes to E64

B67 The most important change between E64 and the final Standard was the introduction of the cost model as an alternative to the fair value model. The other main changes are listed below.

(a) The guidance on determining fair value was expanded, to clarify the following:

(i) the fair value of investment property is not reduced by transaction costs that may be incurred on sale or other disposal (paragraph 30 of the Standard). This is consistent with the measurement of financial assets under paragraph 69 of IAS 39. E64 was silent on the treatment of such costs;

(ii) measurement is based on valuation at the balance sheet date (paragraph 31);

(iii) the best evidence of fair value is normally given by current prices on an active market for similar property in the same location and condition and subject to similar lease and other contracts (paragraph 39). In the absence of such evidence, fair value reflects information from a variety of sources and an entity needs to investigate reasons for any differences between the information from different sources (paragraphs 40–41);

(iv) market value differs from value in use as defined in IAS 36 *Impairment of Assets* (paragraph 43);

(v) there is a need to avoid double counting of investment property and separately recognised assets and liabilities. Integral equipment (such as elevators or air-conditioning) is generally included in the investment property, rather than recognised separately (paragraph 44);

(vi) the fair value of investment property does not reflect future capital expenditure that will improve or enhance the asset and does not reflect the related future benefits from this future expenditure (paragraph 45);

(vii) an entity uses IAS 37 to account for any provisions associated with investment property (paragraph 46); and

(viii) in the exceptional cases when fair value cannot be determined reliably, measurement is under the IAS 16 benchmark treatment* only (in such cases, revaluation under IAS 16 would also not be reliable) and residual value is assumed to be zero (given that fair value cannot be determined reliably) (paragraphs 47–48).

(b) In relation to the scope of the Standard and the definition of investment property:

(i) paragraph 3 now clarifies that the Standard does not apply to forests and similar regenerative natural resources and to mineral rights, the exploration for and extraction of minerals, oil, natural gas and similar non-regenerative resources. This wording is consistent with a similar

* IAS 16 *Property, Plant and Equipment* as revised by the IASB in 2003 eliminated all references to 'benchmark' treatment and 'allowed alternative' treatments.

scope exclusion in IAS 16 *Property, Plant and Equipment*. The Board did not wish to prejudge its decision on the treatment of such items in the current projects on Agriculture and the Extractive Industries;

(ii) land held for a currently undetermined future use is a further example of investment property (paragraph 6(b)), on the grounds that a subsequent decision to use such land as inventory or for development as owner-occupied property would be an investment decision;

(iii) new examples of items that are not investment property are: property held for future use as owner-occupied property, property held for future development and subsequent use as owner-occupied property, property occupied by employees (whether or not the employees pay rent at market rates) and owner-occupied property awaiting disposal (paragraph 7(c));

(iv) property that is being constructed or developed for future use as investment property is now covered by IAS 16 and measured at cost, less impairment losses, if any (paragraph 7(d)). E64 proposed that investment property under construction should be measured at fair value; and

(v) the reference to reliable measurement of fair value (and the related requirements in paragraphs 14–15 of E64) was moved from the definition of investment property into the section on subsequent measurement (paragraphs 47–49).

(c) New paragraph 20 deals with start up costs, initial operating losses and abnormal wastage (based on paragraphs 17 and 18 of IAS 16). The Board considered adding guidance on the treatment of incidental revenue earned during the construction of investment property. However, the Board concluded that this raised an issue in the context of IAS 16 and decided that it was beyond the scope of this project to deal with this.

(d) There is an explicit requirement on determining gains or losses on disposal (paragraph 62). This is consistent with IAS 16, paragraph 56. There are also new cross-references to:

(i) IAS 17 *Leases* and IAS 18 *Revenue*, as guidance for determining the date of disposal (paragraph 61); and

(ii) IAS 37 *Provisions, Contingent Liabilities and Contingent Assets*, for liabilities retained after disposal (paragraph 64).

(e) The Standard states explicitly that an entity should transfer an investment property to inventories when the entity begins to develop the property for subsequent sale in the ordinary course of business (paragraphs 51(b) and 52). E64 proposed that all transfers from investment properties to inventories should be prohibited. The Standard also deals more explicitly than E64 with certain other aspects of transfers.

(f) New disclosure requirements include:

(i) extension of the required disclosure on methods and significant assumptions, which are now to include disclosure of whether fair value was supported by market evidence, or whether the estimate is based on other data (which the entity should disclose) because of the nature of the property and the lack of comparable market data (paragraph 66(b));

(ii) disclosures of rental income and direct operating expenses (paragraph 66(d)); and

(iii) disclosures in the exceptional cases when fair value is not reliably determinable (paragraphs 68 and 69(e)).

(g) E64 proposed a requirement to disclose the carrying amount of unlet or vacant investment property. Some commentators argued that this disclosure was impracticable, particularly for property that is partly vacant. Some also felt that this is a matter for disclosure in a financial review by management, rather than in the financial statements. The Board deleted this disclosure requirement. It should be noted that some indication of vacancy levels may be available from the required disclosure of rental income and from the IAS 17 requirement to disclose cash flows from non-cancellable operating leases (split into less than one year, one to five years and more than five years).

(h) E64 included no specific transitional provisions, which means that IAS 8 would apply. There is a risk that restatement of prior periods might allow entities to manipulate their reported profit or loss for the period by selective use of hindsight in determining fair values in prior periods. Accordingly, the Board decided to prohibit restatement in the fair value model, except where an entity has already publicly disclosed fair values for prior periods (paragraph 70).

Table of Concordance

This table shows how the contents of the superseded version of IAS 40 and the current version of IAS 40 correspond. Paragraphs are treated as corresponding if they broadly address the same matter even though the guidance may differ.

Superseded IAS 40 paragraph	Current IAS 40 paragraph
Objective	1
1	2
2	3
3	4
4	5
5	7
6	8
7	9
8	10
9	11
10	12
11	13
12	14
13	None
14	15
15	16
16	None
17	20
18	21
19	22
20	23
21	24
22	17–19, 69
23	None
24	30
25	31
26	32
None	68
None	72, 73

Superseded IAS 40 paragraph	Current IAS 40 paragraph
27	33
28	35
29	36
30	37
31	38
32	39
33	40
34	42
35	42
36	43
37	None
38	44
39	45
40	46
41	47
42	48
43	49
44	50
45	51
46	52
47	53
48	54
49	55
50	56
51	57
52	58
53	59
None	77
None	84

Superseded IAS 40 paragraph	Current IAS 40 paragraph
54	60
55	61
56	62
57	63
58	64
59	65
60	66
61	67
62	69
63	70
64	71
65	74
66	75
67	76
68	78
69	79
70	80
71	81
72	82
73	83
74	85
75	None
Appendix A	None
None	6
None	25–29
None	32A–32C
None	34
None	41
None	86

International Accounting Standard 41

Agriculture

This version includes amendments resulting from new and amended IFRSs issued up to 31 December 2004.

Contents

International Accounting Standard 41 *Agriculture* (IAS 41) is set out in paragraphs 1–59. All the paragraphs have equal authority but retain the IASC format of the Standard when it was adopted by the IASB. IAS 41 should be read in the context of its objective and the Basis for Conclusions, the *Preface to International Financial Reporting Standards* and the *Framework for the Preparation and Presentation of Financial Statements*. IAS 8 *Accounting Policies, Changes in Accounting Estimates and Errors* provides a basis for selecting and applying accounting policies in the absence of explicit guidance.

Introduction

IN1 IAS 41 prescribes the accounting treatment, financial statement presentation, and disclosures related to agricultural activity, a matter not covered in other Standards. Agricultural activity is the management by an entity of the biological transformation of living animals or plants (biological assets) for sale, into agricultural produce, or into additional biological assets.

IN2 IAS 41 prescribes, among other things, the accounting treatment for biological assets during the period of growth, degeneration, production, and procreation, and for the initial measurement of agricultural produce at the point of harvest. It requires measurement at fair value less estimated point-of-sale costs from initial recognition of biological assets up to the point of harvest, other than when fair value cannot be measured reliably on initial recognition. However, IAS 41 does not deal with processing of agricultural produce after harvest; for example, processing grapes into wine and wool into yarn.

IN3 There is a presumption that fair value can be measured reliably for a biological asset. However, that presumption can be rebutted only on initial recognition for a biological asset for which market-determined prices or values are not available and for which alternative estimates of fair value are determined to be clearly unreliable. In such a case, IAS 41 requires an entity to measure that biological asset at its cost less any accumulated depreciation and any accumulated impairment losses. Once the fair value of such a biological asset becomes reliably measurable, an entity should measure it at its fair value less estimated point-of-sale costs. In all cases, an entity should measure agricultural produce at the point of harvest at its fair value less estimated point-of-sale costs.

IN4 IAS 41 requires that a change in fair value less estimated point-of-sale costs of a biological asset be included in profit or loss for the period in which it arises. In agricultural activity, a change in physical attributes of a living animal or plant directly enhances or diminishes economic benefits to the entity. Under a transaction-based, historical cost accounting model, a plantation forestry entity might report no income until first harvest and sale, perhaps 30 years after planting. On the other hand, an accounting model that recognises and measures biological growth using current fair values reports changes in fair value throughout the period between planting and harvest.

IN5 IAS 41 does not establish any new principles for land related to agricultural activity. Instead, an entity follows IAS 16 *Property, Plant and Equipment* or IAS 40 *Investment Property*, depending on which standard is appropriate in the circumstances. IAS 16 requires land to be measured either at its cost less any accumulated impairment losses, or at a revalued amount. IAS 40 requires land that is investment property to be measured at its fair value, or cost less any accumulated impairment losses. Biological assets that are physically attached to land (for example, trees in a plantation forest) are measured at their fair value less estimated point-of-sale costs separately from the land.

IN6 IAS 41 requires that an unconditional government grant related to a biological asset measured at its fair value less estimated point-of-sale costs be recognised as income when, and only when, the government grant becomes receivable. If a government grant is conditional, including where a government grant requires an entity not to engage in specified agricultural activity, an entity should recognise the government grant as income when, and only when, the conditions attaching to the government grant are met. If a government grant relates to a biological asset measured at its cost less any accumulated depreciation and any accumulated impairment losses, IAS 20 *Accounting for Government Grants and Disclosure of Government Assistance* is applied.

IN7 IAS 41 is effective for annual financial statements covering periods beginning on or after 1 January 2003. Earlier application is encouraged.

IN8 IAS 41 does not establish any specific transitional provisions. The adoption of IAS 41 is accounted for in accordance with IAS 8 *Accounting Policies, Changes in Accounting Estimates and Errors.*

IN9 The Appendix provides illustrative examples of the application of IAS 41. The Basis for Conclusions summarises the Board's reasons for adopting the requirements set out in IAS 41.

International Accounting Standard 41 Agriculture

Objective

The objective of this Standard is to prescribe the accounting treatment and disclosures related to agricultural activity.

Scope

1 **This Standard shall be applied to account for the following when they relate to agricultural activity:**

(a) biological assets;

(b) agricultural produce at the point of harvest; and

(c) government grants covered by paragraphs 34–35.

2 This Standard does not apply to:

(a) land related to agricultural activity (see IAS 16 *Property, Plant and Equipment* and IAS 40 *Investment Property*); and

(b) intangible assets related to agricultural activity (see IAS 38 *Intangible Assets*).

3 This Standard is applied to agricultural produce, which is the harvested product of the entity's biological assets, only at the point of harvest. Thereafter, IAS 2 *Inventories* or another applicable Standard is applied. Accordingly, this Standard does not deal with the processing of agricultural produce after harvest; for example, the processing of grapes into wine by a vintner who has grown the grapes. While such processing may be a logical and natural extension of agricultural activity, and the events taking place may bear some similarity to biological transformation, such processing is not included within the definition of agricultural activity in this Standard.

4 The table below provides examples of biological assets, agricultural produce, and products that are the result of processing after harvest:

Biological assets	Agricultural produce	Products that are the result of processing after harvest
Sheep	Wool	Yarn, carpet
Trees in a plantation forest	Logs	Lumber
Plants	Cotton	Thread, clothing
	Harvested cane	Sugar
Dairy cattle	Milk	Cheese
Pigs	Carcass	Sausages, cured hams

Continued from previous page

Biological assets	Agricultural produce	Products that are the result of processing after harvest
Bushes	Leaf	Tea, cured tobacco
Vines	Grapes	Wine
Fruit trees	Picked fruit	Processed fruit

Definitions

Agriculture–related definitions

5 **The following terms are used in this Standard with the meanings specified:**

Agricultural activity **is the management by an entity of the biological transformation of biological assets for sale, into agricultural produce, or into additional biological assets.**

Agricultural produce **is the harvested product of the entity's biological assets.**

A *biological asset* **is a living animal or plant.**

Biological transformation **comprises the processes of growth, degeneration, production, and procreation that cause qualitative or quantitative changes in a biological asset.**

A *group of biological assets* **is an aggregation of similar living animals or plants.**

Harvest **is the detachment of produce from a biological asset or the cessation of a biological asset's life processes.**

6 Agricultural activity covers a diverse range of activities; for example, raising livestock, forestry, annual or perennial cropping, cultivating orchards and plantations, floriculture, and aquaculture (including fish farming). Certain common features exist within this diversity:

(a) *Capability to change.* Living animals and plants are capable of biological transformation;

(b) *Management of change.* Management facilitates biological transformation by enhancing, or at least stabilising, conditions necessary for the process to take place (for example, nutrient levels, moisture, temperature, fertility, and light). Such management distinguishes agricultural activity from other activities. For example, harvesting from unmanaged sources (such as ocean fishing and deforestation) is not agricultural activity; and

(c) *Measurement of change.* The change in quality (for example, genetic merit, density, ripeness, fat cover, protein content, and fibre strength) or quantity (for example, progeny, weight, cubic metres, fibre length or diameter, and number of buds) brought about by biological transformation is measured and monitored as a routine management function.

7 Biological transformation results in the following types of outcomes:

(a) asset changes through (i) growth (an increase in quantity or improvement in quality of an animal or plant), (ii) degeneration (a decrease in the quantity or deterioration in quality of an animal or plant), or (iii) procreation (creation of additional living animals or plants); or

(b) production of agricultural produce such as latex, tea leaf, wool, and milk.

General definitions

8 **The following terms are used in this Standard with the meanings specified:**

An *active market* **is a market where all the following conditions exist:**

(a) the items traded within the market are homogeneous;

(b) willing buyers and sellers can normally be found at any time; and

(c) prices are available to the public.

Carrying amount **is the amount at which an asset is recognised in the balance sheet.**

Fair value **is the amount for which an asset could be exchanged, or a liability settled, between knowledgeable, willing parties in an arm's length transaction.**

Government grants **are as defined in IAS 20** *Accounting for Government Grants and Disclosure of Government Assistance.*

9 The fair value of an asset is based on its present location and condition. As a result, for example, the fair value of cattle at a farm is the price for the cattle in the relevant market less the transport and other costs of getting the cattle to that market.

Recognition and measurement

10 **An entity shall recognise a biological asset or agricultural produce when, and only when:**

(a) the entity controls the asset as a result of past events;

(b) it is probable that future economic benefits associated with the asset will flow to the entity; and

(c) the fair value or cost of the asset can be measured reliably.

11 In agricultural activity, control may be evidenced by, for example, legal ownership of cattle and the branding or otherwise marking of the cattle on acquisition, birth, or weaning. The future benefits are normally assessed by measuring the significant physical attributes.

12 **A biological asset shall be measured on initial recognition and at each balance sheet date at its fair value less estimated point-of-sale costs, except for the case described in paragraph 30 where the fair value cannot be measured reliably.**

13 **Agricultural produce harvested from an entity's biological assets shall be measured at its fair value less estimated point-of-sale costs at the point of harvest. Such measurement is the cost at that date when applying IAS 2** *Inventories* **or another applicable Standard.**

14 Point-of-sale costs include commissions to brokers and dealers, levies by regulatory agencies and commodity exchanges, and transfer taxes and duties. Point-of-sale costs exclude transport and other costs necessary to get assets to a market.

15 The determination of fair value for a biological asset or agricultural produce may be facilitated by grouping biological assets or agricultural produce according to significant attributes; for example, by age or quality. An entity selects the attributes corresponding to the attributes used in the market as a basis for pricing.

16 Entities often enter into contracts to sell their biological assets or agricultural produce at a future date. Contract prices are not necessarily relevant in determining fair value, because fair value reflects the current market in which a willing buyer and seller would enter into a transaction. As a result, the fair value of a biological asset or agricultural produce is not adjusted because of the existence of a contract. In some cases, a contract for the sale of a biological asset or agricultural produce may be an onerous contract, as defined in IAS 37 *Provisions, Contingent Liabilities and Contingent Assets*. IAS 37 applies to onerous contracts.

17 If an active market exists for a biological asset or agricultural produce, the quoted price in that market is the appropriate basis for determining the fair value of that asset. If an entity has access to different active markets, the entity uses the most relevant one. For example, if an entity has access to two active markets, it would use the price existing in the market expected to be used.

18 If an active market does not exist, an entity uses one or more of the following, when available, in determining fair value:

(a) the most recent market transaction price, provided that there has not been a significant change in economic circumstances between the date of that transaction and the balance sheet date;

(b) market prices for similar assets with adjustment to reflect differences; and

(c) sector benchmarks such as the value of an orchard expressed per export tray, bushel, or hectare, and the value of cattle expressed per kilogram of meat.

19 In some cases, the information sources listed in paragraph 18 may suggest different conclusions as to the fair value of a biological asset or agricultural produce. An entity considers the reasons for those differences, in order to arrive at the most reliable estimate of fair value within a relatively narrow range of reasonable estimates.

20 In some circumstances, market-determined prices or values may not be available for a biological asset in its present condition. In these circumstances, an entity uses the present value of expected net cash flows from the asset discounted at a current market-determined pre-tax rate in determining fair value.

21 The objective of a calculation of the present value of expected net cash flows is to determine the fair value of a biological asset in its present location and condition.

An entity considers this in determining an appropriate discount rate to be used and in estimating expected net cash flows. The present condition of a biological asset excludes any increases in value from additional biological transformation and future activities of the entity, such as those related to enhancing the future biological transformation, harvesting, and selling.

22 An entity does not include any cash flows for financing the assets, taxation, or re-establishing biological assets after harvest (for example, the cost of replanting trees in a plantation forest after harvest).

23 In agreeing an arm's length transaction price, knowledgeable, willing buyers and sellers consider the possibility of variations in cash flows. It follows that fair value reflects the possibility of such variations. Accordingly, an entity incorporates expectations about possible variations in cash flows into either the expected cash flows, or the discount rate, or some combination of the two. In determining a discount rate, an entity uses assumptions consistent with those used in estimating the expected cash flows, to avoid the effect of some assumptions being double-counted or ignored.

24 Cost may sometimes approximate fair value, particularly when:

(a) little biological transformation has taken place since initial cost incurrence (for example, for fruit tree seedlings planted immediately prior to a balance sheet date); or

(b) the impact of the biological transformation on price is not expected to be material (for example, for the initial growth in a 30-year pine plantation production cycle).

25 Biological assets are often physically attached to land (for example, trees in a plantation forest). There may be no separate market for biological assets that are attached to the land but an active market may exist for the combined assets, that is, for the biological assets, raw land, and land improvements, as a package. An entity may use information regarding the combined assets to determine fair value for the biological assets. For example, the fair value of raw land and land improvements may be deducted from the fair value of the combined assets to arrive at the fair value of biological assets.

Gains and losses

26 A gain or loss arising on initial recognition of a biological asset at fair value less estimated point-of-sale costs and from a change in fair value less estimated point-of-sale costs of a biological asset shall be included in profit or loss for the period in which it arises.

27 A loss may arise on initial recognition of a biological asset, because estimated point-of-sale costs are deducted in determining fair value less estimated point-of-sale costs of a biological asset. A gain may arise on initial recognition of a biological asset, such as when a calf is born.

28 A gain or loss arising on initial recognition of agricultural produce at fair value less estimated point-of-sale costs shall be included in profit or loss for the period in which it arises.

29 A gain or loss may arise on initial recognition of agricultural produce as a result of harvesting.

Inability to measure fair value reliably

30 **There is a presumption that fair value can be measured reliably for a biological asset. However, that presumption can be rebutted only on initial recognition for a biological asset for which market-determined prices or values are not available and for which alternative estimates of fair value are determined to be clearly unreliable. In such a case, that biological asset shall be measured at its cost less any accumulated depreciation and any accumulated impairment losses. Once the fair value of such a biological asset becomes reliably measurable, an entity shall measure it at its fair value less estimated point-of-sale costs. Once a non-current biological asset meets the criteria to be classified as held for sale (or is included in a disposal group that is classified as held for sale) in accordance with IFRS 5** *Non-current Assets Held for Sale and Discontinued Operations*, **it is presumed that fair value can be measured reliably.**

31 The presumption in paragraph 30 can be rebutted only on initial recognition. An entity that has previously measured a biological asset at its fair value less estimated point-of-sale costs continues to measure the biological asset at its fair value less estimated point-of-sale costs until disposal.

32 In all cases, an entity measures agricultural produce at the point of harvest at its fair value less estimated point-of-sale costs. This Standard reflects the view that the fair value of agricultural produce at the point of harvest can always be measured reliably.

33 In determining cost, accumulated depreciation and accumulated impairment losses, an entity considers IAS 2 *Inventories*, IAS 16 *Property, Plant and Equipment* and IAS 36 *Impairment of Assets*.

Government grants

34 **An unconditional government grant related to a biological asset measured at its fair value less estimated point-of-sale costs shall be recognised as income when, and only when, the government grant becomes receivable.**

35 **If a government grant related to a biological asset measured at its fair value less estimated point-of-sale costs is conditional, including where a government grant requires an entity not to engage in specified agricultural activity, an entity shall recognise the government grant as income when, and only when, the conditions attaching to the government grant are met.**

36 Terms and conditions of government grants vary. For example, a government grant may require an entity to farm in a particular location for five years and require the entity to return all of the government grant if it farms for less than five years. In this case, the government grant is not recognised as income until the five years have passed. However, if the government grant allows part of the government grant to be retained based on the passage of time, the entity recognises the government grant as income on a time proportion basis.

37 If a government grant relates to a biological asset measured at its cost less any accumulated depreciation and any accumulated impairment losses (see paragraph 30), IAS 20 *Accounting for Government Grants and Disclosure of Government Assistance* is applied.

38 This Standard requires a different treatment from IAS 20, if a government grant relates to a biological asset measured at its fair value less estimated point-of-sale costs or a government grant requires an entity not to engage in specified agricultural activity. IAS 20 is applied only to a government grant related to a biological asset measured at its cost less any accumulated depreciation and any accumulated impairment losses.

Disclosure

39 [Deleted]

General

40 **An entity shall disclose the aggregate gain or loss arising during the current period on initial recognition of biological assets and agricultural produce and from the change in fair value less estimated point-of-sale costs of biological assets.**

41 **An entity shall provide a description of each group of biological assets.**

42 The disclosure required by paragraph 41 may take the form of a narrative or quantified description.

43 An entity is encouraged to provide a quantified description of each group of biological assets, distinguishing between consumable and bearer biological assets or between mature and immature biological assets, as appropriate. For example, an entity may disclose the carrying amounts of consumable biological assets and bearer biological assets by group. An entity may further divide those carrying amounts between mature and immature assets. These distinctions provide information that may be helpful in assessing the timing of future cash flows. An entity discloses the basis for making any such distinctions.

44 Consumable biological assets are those that are to be harvested as agricultural produce or sold as biological assets. Examples of consumable biological assets are livestock intended for the production of meat, livestock held for sale, fish in farms, crops such as maize and wheat, and trees being grown for lumber. Bearer biological assets are those other than consumable biological assets; for example, livestock from which milk is produced, grape vines, fruit trees, and trees from which firewood is harvested while the tree remains. Bearer biological assets are not agricultural produce but, rather, are self-regenerating.

45 Biological assets may be classified either as mature biological assets or immature biological assets. Mature biological assets are those that have attained harvestable specifications (for consumable biological assets) or are able to sustain regular harvests (for bearer biological assets).

46 **If not disclosed elsewhere in information published with the financial statements, an entity shall describe:**

(a) the nature of its activities involving each group of biological assets; and

(b) non-financial measures or estimates of the physical quantities of:

(i) each group of the entity's biological assets at the end of the period; and

(ii) output of agricultural produce during the period.

47 **An entity shall disclose the methods and significant assumptions applied in determining the fair value of each group of agricultural produce at the point of harvest and each group of biological assets.**

48 **An entity shall disclose the fair value less estimated point-of-sale costs of agricultural produce harvested during the period, determined at the point of harvest.**

49 **An entity shall disclose:**

(a) the existence and carrying amounts of biological assets whose title is restricted, and the carrying amounts of biological assets pledged as security for liabilities;

(b) the amount of commitments for the development or acquisition of biological assets; and

(c) financial risk management strategies related to agricultural activity.

50 **An entity shall present a reconciliation of changes in the carrying amount of biological assets between the beginning and the end of the current period. The reconciliation shall include:**

(a) the gain or loss arising from changes in fair value less estimated point-of-sale costs;

(b) increases due to purchases;

(c) decreases attributable to sales and biological assets classified as held for sale (or included in a disposal group that is classified as held for sale) in accordance with IFRS 5;

(d) decreases due to harvest;

(e) increases resulting from business combinations;

(f) net exchange differences arising on the translation of financial statements into a different presentation currency, and on the translation of a foreign operation into the presentation currency of the reporting entity; and

(g) other changes.

51 The fair value less estimated point-of-sale costs of a biological asset can change due to both physical changes and price changes in the market. Separate disclosure of physical and price changes is useful in appraising current period performance and future prospects, particularly when there is a production cycle

of more than one year. In such cases, an entity is encouraged to disclose, by group or otherwise, the amount of change in fair value less estimated point-of-sale costs included in profit or loss due to physical changes and due to price changes. This information is generally less useful when the production cycle is less than one year (for example, when raising chickens or growing cereal crops).

52 Biological transformation results in a number of types of physical change–growth, degeneration, production, and procreation, each of which is observable and measurable. Each of those physical changes has a direct relationship to future economic benefits. A change in fair value of a biological asset due to harvesting is also a physical change.

53 Agricultural activity is often exposed to climatic, disease and other natural risks. If an event occurs that gives rise to a material item of income or expense, the nature and amount of that item are disclosed in accordance with IAS 1 *Presentation of Financial Statements*. Examples of such an event include an outbreak of a virulent disease, a flood, a severe drought or frost, and a plague of insects.

Additional disclosures for biological assets where fair value cannot be measured reliably

54 If an entity measures biological assets at their cost less any accumulated depreciation and any accumulated impairment losses (see paragraph 30) at the end of the period, the entity shall disclose for such biological assets:

(a) a description of the biological assets;

(b) an explanation of why fair value cannot be measured reliably;

(c) if possible, the range of estimates within which fair value is highly likely to lie;

(d) the depreciation method used;

(e) the useful lives or the depreciation rates used; and

(f) the gross carrying amount and the accumulated depreciation (aggregated with accumulated impairment losses) at the beginning and end of the period.

55 If, during the current period, an entity measures biological assets at their cost less any accumulated depreciation and any accumulated impairment losses (see paragraph 30), an entity shall disclose any gain or loss recognised on disposal of such biological assets and the reconciliation required by paragraph 50 shall disclose amounts related to such biological assets separately. In addition, the reconciliation shall include the following amounts included in profit or loss related to those biological assets:

(a) impairment losses;

(b) reversals of impairment losses; and

(c) depreciation.

56 **If the fair value of biological assets previously measured at their cost less any accumulated depreciation and any accumulated impairment losses becomes reliably measurable during the current period, an entity shall disclose for those biological assets:**

(a) a description of the biological assets;

(b) an explanation of why fair value has become reliably measurable; and

(c) the effect of the change.

Government grants

57 **An entity shall disclose the following related to agricultural activity covered by this Standard:**

(a) the nature and extent of government grants recognised in the financial statements;

(b) unfulfilled conditions and other contingencies attaching to government grants; and

(c) significant decreases expected in the level of government grants.

Effective date and transition

58 **This Standard becomes operative for annual financial statements covering periods beginning on or after 1 January 2003. Earlier application is encouraged. If an entity applies this Standard for periods beginning before 1 January 2003, it shall disclose that fact.**

59 This Standard does not establish any specific transitional provisions. The adoption of this Standard is accounted for in accordance with IAS 8 *Accounting Policies, Changes in Accounting Estimates and Errors.*

Appendix
Illustrative examples

This appendix, which was prepared by the IASC staff but was not approved by the IASC Board, accompanies, but is not part of, IAS 41.

A1 Example 1 illustrates how the disclosure requirements of this Standard might be put into practice for a dairy farming entity. This Standard encourages the separation of the change in fair value less estimated point-of-sale costs of an entity's biological assets into physical change and price change. That separation is reflected in Example 1. Example 2 illustrates how to separate physical change and price change.

A2 The financial statements in Example 1 do not conform to all of the disclosure and presentation requirements of other Standards. Other approaches to presentation and disclosure may also be appropriate.

Example 1 XYZ Dairy Ltd

Balance sheet

XYZ Dairy Ltd **Balance sheet**	**Notes**	**31 December 20X1**	**31 December 20X0**
ASSETS			
Non–current assets			
Dairy livestock – immature[(a)]		52,060	47,730
Dairy livestock – mature[(a)]		372,990	411,840
Subtotal – biological assets	3	425,050	459,570
Property, plant and equipment		1,462,650	1,409,800
Total non–current assets		**1,887,700**	**1,869,370**
Current assets			
Inventories		82,950	70,650
Trade and other receivables		88,000	65,000
Cash		10,000	10,000
Total current assets		**180,950**	**145,650**
Total assets		**2,068,650**	**2,015,020**
EQUITY AND LIABILITIES			
Equity			
Issued capital		1,000,000	1,000,000
Accumulated profits		902,828	865,000
Total equity		**1,902,828**	**1,865,000**
Current liabilities			
Trade and other payables		165,822	150,020
Total current liabilities		**165,822**	**150,020**
Total equity and liabilities		**2,068,650**	**2,015,020**

(a) An entity is encouraged, but not required, to provide a quantified description of each group of biological assets, distinguishing between consumable and bearer biological assets or between mature and immature biological assets, as appropriate. An entity discloses the basis for making any such distinctions.

Income statement*

XYZ Dairy Ltd **Income statement**	**Notes**	**Year ended 31 December 20X1**
Fair value of milk produced		518,240
Gains arising from changes in fair value less estimated point–of–sale costs of dairy livestock	3	39,930
		558,170
Inventories used		(137,523)
Staff costs		(127,283)
Depreciation expense		(15,250)
Other operating expenses		(197,092)
		(477,148)
Profit from operations		**81,022**
Income tax expense		(43,194)
Profit for the period		**37,828**

* This income statement presents an analysis of expenses using a classification based on the nature of expenses. IAS 1 *Presentation of Financial Statements* requires that an entity present, either on the face of the income statement or in the notes, an analysis of expenses using a classification based on either the nature of expenses or their function within the entity. IAS 1 encourages presentation of an analysis of expenses on the face of the income statement.

Statement of changes in equity*

XYZ Dairy Ltd			
Statement of changes in equity		**Year ended 31 December 20X1**	
	Share capital	**Accumulated profits**	**Total**
Balance at 1 January 20X1	1,000,000	865,000	**1,865,000**
Profit for the period		37,828	**37,828**
Balance at 31 December 20X1	**1,000,000**	**902,828**	**1,902,828**

Cash flow statement†

XYZ Dairy Ltd **Cash flow statement**	**Notes**	**Year ended 31 December 20X1**
Cash flows from operating activities		
Cash receipts from sales of milk		498,027
Cash receipts from sales of livestock		97,913
Cash paid for supplies and to employees		(460,831)
Cash paid for purchases of livestock		(23,815)
		111,294
Income taxes paid		(43,194)
Net cash from operating activities		**68,100**
Cash flows from investing activities		
Purchase of property, plant and equipment		(68,100)
Net cash used in investing activities		**(68,100)**
Net increase in cash		**0**
Cash at beginning of period		**10,000**
Cash at end of period		**10,000**

* This is one of several formats for the statement of changes in equity permitted by IAS 1.

† This cash flow statement reports cash flows from operating activities using the direct method. IAS 7 *Cash Flow Statements* requires that an equity report cash flows from operating activities using either the direct method or the indirect method. IAS 7 encourages use of the direct method.

Notes

1 **Operations and principal activities**

XYZ Dairy Ltd ('the Company') is engaged in milk production for supply to various customers. At 31 December 20X1, the Company held 419 cows able to produce milk (mature assets) and 137 heifers being raised to produce milk in the future (immature assets). The Company produced 157,584kg of milk with a fair value less estimated point-of-sale costs of 518,240 (that is determined at the time of milking) in the year ended 31 December 20X1.

2 **Accounting policies**

Livestock and milk

Livestock are measured at their fair value less estimated point-of-sale costs. The fair value of livestock is determined based on market prices of livestock of similar age, breed, and genetic merit. Milk is initially measured at its fair value less estimated point-of-sale costs at the time of milking. The fair value of milk is determined based on market prices in the local area.

3 **Biological assets**

Reconciliation of carrying amounts of dairy livestock	**20X1**
Carrying amount at 1 January 20X1	**459,570**
Increases due to purchases	26,250
Gain arising from changes in fair value less estimated point-of-sale costs attributable to physical changes*	15,350
Gain arising from changes in fair value less estimated point-of-sale costs attributable to price changes*	24,580
Decreases due to sales	(100,700)
Carrying amount at 31 December 20X1	**425,050**

4 **Financial risk management strategies**

The Company is exposed to financial risks arising from changes in milk prices. The Company does not anticipate that milk prices will decline significantly in the foreseeable future and, therefore, has not entered into derivative or other contracts to manage the risk of a decline in milk prices. The Company reviews its outlook for milk prices regularly in considering the need for active financial risk management.

* Separating the increase in fair value less estimated point-of-sale costs between the portion attributable to physical changes and the portion attributable to price changes is encouraged but not required by this Standard.

Example 2 Physical change and price change

The following example illustrates how to separate physical change and price change. Separating the change in fair value less estimated point-of-sale costs between the portion attributable to physical changes and the portion attributable to price changes is encouraged but not required by this Standard.

A herd of 10 2 year old animals was held at 1 January 20X1. One animal aged 2.5 years was purchased on 1 July 20X1 for 108, and one animal was born on 1 July 20X1. No animals were sold or disposed of during the period. Per-unit fair values less estimated point-of-sale costs were as follows:

2 year old animal at 1 January 20X1	100	
Newborn animal at 1 July 20X1	70	
2.5 year old animal at 1 July 20X1	108	
Newborn animal at 31 December 20X1	72	
0.5 year old animal at 31 December 20X1	80	
2 year old animal at 31 December 20X1	105	
2.5 year old animal at 31 December 20X1	111	
3 year old animal at 31 December 20X1	120	
Fair value less estimated point-of-sale costs of herd at 1 January 20X1 (10 x 100)		1,000
Purchase on 1 July 20X1 (1 x 108)		108
Increase in fair value less estimated point-of-sale costs due to price change:		
10 × (105 – 100)	50	
1 × (111 – 108)	3	
1 × (72 – 70)	2	55
Increase in fair value less estimated point-of-sale costs due to physical change:		
10 × (120 – 105)	150	
1 × (120 – 111)	9	
1 × (80 – 72)	8	
1 × 70	70	237
Fair value less estimated point-of-sale costs of herd at 31 December 20X1		
11 × 120	1,320	
1 × 80	80	1,400

CONTENTS

paragraphs

BASIS FOR CONCLUSIONS

Basis for Conclusions

This appendix, which was prepared by the IASC Staff but was not approved by the IASC Board, summarises the Board's reasons for:

(a) initiating and proposing an International Accounting Standard on agriculture; and

(b) accepting or rejecting certain alternative views.

Individual Board members gave greater weight to some factors than to others.

Background

B1 In 1994, the IASC Board (the 'Board') decided to develop an International Accounting Standard on agriculture and appointed a Steering Committee to help define the issues and develop possible solutions. In 1996, the Steering Committee published a Draft Statement of Principles ('DSOP') setting out the issues, alternatives, and the Steering Committee's proposals for resolving the issues and inviting public comment. In response, 42 comment letters were received. The Steering Committee reviewed the comments, revised certain of its recommendations, and submitted them to the Board.

B2 In July 1999, the Board approved Exposure Draft E65 *Agriculture* with a comment deadline of 31 January 2000. The Board received 62 comment letters on E65. They came from various international organisations, as well as from 28 individual countries. In April 2000, the IASC Staff sent a questionnaire to entities that undertake agricultural activity in an attempt to determine the reliability of the fair value measurement proposed in E65 and received 20 responses from 11 countries. In December 2000, after considering the comments on E65 and responses to the questionnaire, the Board approved IAS 41 *Agriculture* (the Standard). Paragraph B82 below summarises the changes that the Board made to E65 in finalising the Standard.

The need for an International Accounting Standard on agriculture

B3 A main objective of the IASC is to develop International Accounting Standards that are relevant in the general purpose financial statements of all businesses. While most International Accounting Standards apply to entities in all activities, some International Accounting Standards, for example IAS 30 *Disclosures in the Financial Statements of Banks and Similar Financial Institutions* and IAS 40 *Investment Property*, deal with issues that arise in particular activities. IASC has also undertaken industry-specific projects on insurance and extractive industries.

B4 Diversity in accounting for agricultural activity has occurred because:

(a) prior to the development of the Standard, assets related to agricultural activity and changes in those assets were excluded from the scope of International Accounting Standards:

(i) IAS 2 *Inventories* excluded 'producers' inventories of livestock, agricultural and forest products... to the extent that they are measured at net realisable value in accordance with well established practices in certain industries';

(ii) IAS 16 *Property, Plant and Equipment* did not apply to 'forests and similar regenerative natural resources';

(iii) IAS 18 *Revenue* did not deal with revenue arising from 'natural increases in herds, and agricultural and forest products'; and

(iv) IAS 40 *Investment Property* did not apply to 'forests and similar regenerative natural resources';

(b) accounting guidelines for agricultural activity developed by national standard setters have, in general, been piecemeal, developed to resolve a specific issue related to a form of agricultural activity of significance to that country; and

(c) the nature of agricultural activity creates uncertainty or conflicts when applying traditional accounting models, particularly because the critical events associated with biological transformation (growth, degeneration, production, and procreation) that alter the substance of biological assets are difficult to deal with in an accounting model based on historical cost and realisation.

B5 Most business organisations involved in agricultural activity are small, independent, cash and tax focused, family-operated business units, often perceived as not being required to produce general purpose financial statements. Some believe that because of this an International Accounting Standard on agriculture would not have widespread application. However, even small agricultural entities seek outside capital and subsidies, particularly from banks or government agencies, and these capital providers increasingly request financial statements. Moreover, an international trend towards deregulation, an increasing number of cross-border listings and more investment have resulted in increasing scale, scope, and commercialism of agricultural activity. This has created a greater need for financial statements based on sound and generally accepted accounting principles. For the above reasons, in 1994 the Board added to its agenda a project on agriculture.

B6 The DSOP specifically asked for views on the feasibility of developing a comprehensive International Accounting Standard on agriculture. Some commentators felt that the diversity of agricultural activity prevents the development of a single International Accounting Standard on accounting for all agricultural activities. Others said that different principles should attach to agricultural activity with short and long production cycles. Some cited the need to develop International Accounting Standards that are simple to apply and broad in application. Commentators on the DSOP also noted that agriculture is a significant industry in many countries, particularly in developing and newly industrialised countries. In many such countries it is the most important industry.

B7 After considering the comments on the DSOP, the Board reaffirmed its conclusion that an International Accounting Standard is needed. The Board believes that the principles set forth in the Standard have wide application and provide a clear set of principles.

Scope

B8 The Standard prescribes, among other things, the accounting treatment for biological assets and for the initial measurement of agricultural produce harvested from an entity's biological assets at the point of harvest. However, the Standard does not deal with the processing of agricultural produce after harvest, since the Board did not consider it appropriate to undertake a partial revision of IAS 2 *Inventories* which deals with the accounting treatment for inventories under the historical cost system.* The processing after harvest is accounted for under IAS 2 or another applicable International Accounting Standard (for example, if an entity harvests logs and decides to use them for constructing its own building, IAS 16 *Property, Plant and Equipment* is applied in accounting for the logs).

B9 Some may think of such processing as agricultural activity, particularly if it is done by the same entity that developed the agricultural produce (for example, the processing of grapes into wine by a vintner who has grown the grapes). While such processing may be a logical and natural extension of agricultural activity, and the events taking place may bear some similarity to biological transformation, such processing is not included within the definition of agricultural activity in the Standard.

B10 In particular, the Board considered whether to include circumstances where there is a long ageing or maturation process after harvest (for example, for wine production from grapes and cheese production from milk) in the scope of the Standard. Those who believe that the Standard should cover such processing argue that:

(a) such a long ageing or maturation process is similar to biological transformation and fundamental to assessing the performance of an entity; and

(b) many agricultural entities are vertically integrated and involved in, for example, producing both grapes and wine.

B11 The Board decided not to include such circumstances in the scope of the Standard because of concerns about difficulties in differentiating them from other manufacturing processes (such as conversion of raw materials into marketable inventories as defined in IAS 2). The Board concluded that the requirements in IAS 2 or another applicable International Accounting Standard would be suited to accounting for such processes.

B12 The Board also considered whether to deal with contracts for the sale of a biological asset or agricultural produce and government grants related to agricultural activity in the Standard. These issues are discussed below (see paragraphs B47–54 and B63–73).

* The term 'historical cost system' is no longer applicable owing to revisions made to IAS 2 in December 2003.

Measurement

Biological assets

Fair value versus cost

B13 The Standard requires an entity to use a fair value approach in measuring its biological assets related to agricultural activity as proposed in the DSOP and E65, except for cases where the fair value cannot be measured reliably on initial recognition.

B14 Those who support fair value measurement argue that the effects of changes brought about by biological transformation are best reflected by reference to the fair value changes in biological assets. They believe that fair value changes in biological assets have a direct relationship to changes in expectations of future economic benefits to the entity.

B15 Those who support fair value measurement also note that the transactions entered into to effect biological transformation often have only a weak relationship with the biological transformation itself and, thus, a more distant relationship to expected future economic benefits. For example, patterns of growth in a plantation forest directly affect expectations of future economic benefits but differ markedly, in timing, from patterns of cost incurrence. No income might be reported until first harvest and sale (perhaps 30 years) in a plantation forestry entity using a transaction-based, historical cost accounting model. On the other hand, income is measured and reported throughout the period until initial harvest if an accounting model is used that recognises and measures biological growth using current fair values.

B16 Further, those who support fair value measurement cite reasons for concluding that fair value has greater relevance, reliability, comparability, and understandability as a measurement of future economic benefits expected from biological assets than historical cost, including:

(a) many biological assets are traded in active markets with observable market prices. Active markets for these assets provide a reliable measure of market expectations of future economic benefits. The presence of such markets significantly increases the reliability of market value as an indicator of fair value;

(b) measures of the cost of biological assets are sometimes less reliable than measures of fair value because joint products and joint costs can create situations in which the relationship between inputs and outputs is ill-defined, leading to complex and arbitrary allocations of cost between the different outcomes of biological transformation. Such allocations become even more arbitrary if biological assets generate additional biological assets (offspring) and the additional biological assets are also used in the entity's own agricultural activity;

(c) relatively long and continuous production cycles, with volatility in both the production and market environment, mean that the accounting period often does not depict a full cycle. Therefore, period-end measurement (as opposed to time of transaction) assumes greater significance in deriving a measure of current period financial performance or position. The less significant current year harvest is in relation to total biological transformation, the greater the significance of period-end measures of asset change (growth and degeneration). In relatively high turnover, short production cycle, highly controlled agricultural systems (for example, broiler chicken or mushroom production) in which the majority of biological transformation and harvesting occurs within a year, the relationship between cost and future economic benefits appears more stable. This apparent stability does not alter the relationship between current market value and future economic benefits, but it makes the difference in measurement method less significant; and

(d) different sources of replacement animals and plants (home-grown or purchased) give rise to different costs in a historical cost approach. Similar assets should give rise to similar expectations with regard to future benefits. Considerably enhanced comparability and understandability result when similar assets are measured and reported using the same basis.

B17 Those who oppose measuring biological assets at fair value believe there is superior reliability in cost measurement because historical cost is the result of arm's length transactions, and therefore provides evidence of an open-market value at that point in time, and is independently verifiable. More importantly, they believe fair value is sometimes not reliably measurable and that users of financial statements may be misled by presentation of numbers that are indicated as being fair value but are based on subjective and unverifiable assumptions. Information regarding fair value can be provided other than in a single number in the financial statements. They believe the scope of the Standard is too broad. They also argue that:

(a) market prices are often volatile and cyclical and not appropriate as a basis of measurement;

(b) it may be onerous to require fair valuation at each balance sheet date, especially if interim reports are required;

(c) the historical cost convention is well established and commonly used. The use of any other basis should be accompanied by a change in the IASC *Framework for the Preparation and Presentation of Financial Statements* (the '*Framework*'). For consistency with other International Accounting Standards and other activities, biological assets should be measured at their cost;

(d) cost measurement provides more objective and consistent measurement;

(e) active markets may not exist for some biological assets in some countries. In such cases, fair value cannot be measured reliably, especially during the period of growth in the case of a biological asset that has a long growth period (for example, trees in a plantation forest);

(f) fair value measurement results in recognition of unrealised gains and losses and contradicts principles in International Accounting Standards on recognition of revenue; and

(g) market prices at a balance sheet date may not bear a close relationship to the prices at which assets will be sold, and many biological assets are not held for sale.

B18 The *Framework* is neutral with respect to the choice of measurement basis, identifying that a number of different bases are employed to different degrees and in varying combinations, though noting that historical cost is most commonly adopted. The alternatives specifically identified are historical cost, current cost, realisable value, and present value. Precedents for fair value measurement exist in other International Accounting Standards.

B19 The Board concluded that the Standard should require a fair value model for biological assets related to agricultural activity because of the unique nature and characteristics of agricultural activity. However, the Board also concluded that, in some cases, fair value cannot be measured reliably. Some respondents to the questionnaire, as well as some commentators on E65, expressed significant concern about the reliability of fair value measurement for some biological assets, arguing that:

(a) active markets do not exist for some biological assets, in particular for those with a long growth period;

(b) present value of expected net cash flows is often an unreliable measure of fair value due to the need for, and use of, subjective assumptions (for example, about weather); and

(c) fair value cannot be measured reliably prior to harvest.

Some commentators on E65 suggested that the Standard should include a reliability exception for cases where no active market exists.

B20 The Board decided there was a need to include a reliability exception for cases where market-determined prices or values are not available and alternative estimates of fair value are determined to be clearly unreliable. In those cases, biological assets should be measured at their cost less any accumulated depreciation and any accumulated impairment losses. In determining cost, accumulated depreciation and accumulated impairment losses, an entity considers IAS 2 *Inventories*, IAS 16 *Property, Plant and Equipment* and IAS 36 *Impairment of Assets*.

B21 The Board rejected a benchmark treatment of fair value and an allowed alternative treatment of historical cost because of the greater comparability and understandability achieved by a mandatory fair value approach in the presence of active markets. The Board is also uncomfortable with options in International Accounting Standards.

Treatment of point–of–sale costs

B22 The Standard requires that a biological asset should be measured at its fair value less estimated point–of–sale costs. Point–of–sale costs include commissions to brokers and dealers, levies by regulatory agencies and commodity exchanges, and transfer taxes and duties. Point–of–sale costs exclude transport and other costs necessary to get assets to a market. Such transport and other costs are deducted in determining fair value (that is, fair value is a market price less transport and other costs necessary to get an asset to a market).

B23 E65 proposed that pre-sale disposal costs that will be incurred to place an asset on the market (such as transport costs) should be deducted in determining fair value, if a biological asset will be sold in an active market in another location. However, E65 did not specify the treatment of point-of-sale costs. Some commentators suggested that the Standard should clarify the treatment of point-of-sale costs, as well as pre-sale disposal costs.

B24 Some argue that point-of-sale costs should not be deducted in a fair value model. They argue that fair value less estimated point-of-sale costs would be a biased estimate of markets' estimate of future cash flows, because point-of-sale costs would in effect be recognised as an expense twice if the acquirer pays point-of-sale costs on acquisition; once related to the initial acquisition of biological assets and once related to the immediate measurement at fair value less estimated point-of-sale costs. This would occur even when point-of-sale costs would not be incurred until a future period or would not be paid at all for a bearer biological asset that will not be sold.

B25 On the other hand, some believe that point-of-sale costs should be deducted in a fair value model. They .believe that the carrying amount of an asset should represent the economic benefits that are expected to flow from the asset. They argue that fair value less estimated point-of-sale costs would represent the markets' estimate of the economic benefits that are expected to flow to the entity from that asset at the balance sheet date. They also argue that failure to deduct estimated point-of-sale costs could result in a loss being deferred until a sale occurs.

B26 The Board concluded that fair value less estimated point-of-sale costs is a more relevant measurement of biological assets, acknowledging that, in particular, failure to deduct estimated point-of-sale costs could result in a loss being deferred.

Hierarchy in fair value measurement

B27 The Standard requires that, if an active market exists for a biological asset, the quoted price in that market is the appropriate basis for determining the fair value of that asset. If an active market does not exist, an entity uses market-determined prices or values (such as the most recent market transaction price) when available. However, in some circumstances, market-determined prices or values may not be available for a biological asset in its present condition. In these circumstances, the Standard indicates that an entity uses the present value of expected net cash flows from the asset.

B28 E65 proposed that, if an active market exists for a biological asset, an entity should use the market price in the active market. If an active market does not exist, E65 proposed that an entity should consider other measurement bases such as the price of the most recent transaction for the same type of asset, sector benchmarks, and present value of expected net cash flows. E65 did not set a hierarchy in cases where no active market exists; that is, E65 did not indicate which basis is preferable to the other bases.

B29 The Board considered setting an explicit hierarchy in cases where no active market exists. Some believe that using market-determined prices or values; for example, the most recent market transaction price, would always be preferable to present value of expected net cash flows. On the other hand, some believe that market-determined prices or values would not necessarily be preferable to present value of expected net cash flows, especially when an entity uses market prices for similar assets with adjustment to reflect differences.

B30 The Board concluded that a detailed hierarchy would not provide sufficient flexibility to appropriately deal with all the circumstances that may arise and decided not to set a detailed hierarchy in cases where no active market exists. However, the Board decided to indicate that an entity uses all available market-determined prices or values since otherwise there is a possibility that entities may opt to use present value of expected net cash flows from the asset even when useful market-determined prices or values are available. Of the 20 companies that responded to the questionnaire, six companies used present value of expected net cash flows as a basis of fair value measurement and, in addition, two companies indicated that it was impossible to measure their biological assets reliably since the present value of expected net cash flows would not be reliable (as they would need to use present value as a basis).

B31 When an entity has access to different markets, the Standard indicates that the entity uses the most relevant one. For example, if an entity has access to two active markets, it uses the price existing in the market expected to be used. Some believe that the most advantageous price in the accessible markets should be used. The Standard reflects the view that the most relevant measurement results from using the market expected to be used.

Frequency of fair value measurement

B32 Some argue that less frequent measurement of fair value should be permitted because of concerns about burdens on entities. The Board rejected this approach because of the:

(a) continuous nature of biological transformation;

(b) lack of direct relationships between financial transactions and the outcomes of biological transformation; and

(c) general availability of reliable measures of fair value at reasonable cost.

Independent valuation

B33 A significant number of commentators on the DSOP indicated that, if present value of expected net cash flows is used to determine fair value, an external independent valuation should be required. The Board rejected this proposal since it believes that external independent valuations are not commonly used for certain agricultural activity and it would be burdensome to require an external independent valuation. The Board believes that it is for entities to decide how to determine fair value reliably, including the extent to which independent valuers need to be involved.

Inability to measure fair value reliably

B34 As noted previously, the Board decided to include a reliability exception in the Standard for cases where fair value cannot be measured reliably on initial recognition. The Standard indicates a presumption that fair value can be measured reliably for a biological asset. However, that presumption can be rebutted only on initial recognition for a biological asset for which market-determined prices or values are not available and for which alternative estimates of fair value are determined to be clearly unreliable. In such a case, that biological asset should be measured at its cost less any accumulated depreciation and any accumulated impairment losses. Once the fair value of such a biological asset becomes reliably measurable, the Standard requires that an entity should start measuring the biological asset at its fair value less estimated point-of-sale costs.

B35 Some believe that, if an entity was previously using the reliability exception, the entity should not be allowed to start fair value measurement (that is, an entity should continue to use a cost basis). They argue that it could be a subjective decision to determine when fair value has become reliably measurable and that this subjectivity could lead to inconsistent application and, potentially, abuse. The Board noted, however, that in agricultural activity, it is likely that fair value becomes measurable more reliably as biological transformation occurs and that fair value measurement is preferable to cost in those cases. Thus, the Board decided to require fair value measurement once fair value becomes reliably measurable.

B36 If an entity has previously measured a biological asset at its fair value less estimated point-of-sale costs, the Standard requires that the entity should continue to measure the biological asset at its fair value less estimated point-of-sale costs until disposal. Some argue that reliable estimates may cease to be available. The Board believed that this would rarely, if ever, occur. Accordingly, the Board decided to prohibit entities from changing their measurement basis from fair value to cost, because otherwise an entity might use a reliability exception as an excuse to discontinue fair value accounting in a falling market.

B37 If an entity uses the reliability exception, the Standard requires additional disclosures. The additional disclosures include information on biological assets held at the end of the period such as a description of the assets and an explanation of why fair value cannot be measured reliably. The additional disclosures also include the gain or loss recognised for the period on disposal of biological assets measured at cost less any accumulated depreciation and any accumulated impairment losses, even though those biological assets are not held at the end of the period.

Gains and losses

B38 The Standard requires that a gain or loss arising on initial recognition of a biological asset and from a change in fair value less estimated point-of-sale costs of a biological asset should be included in net profit or loss[*] for the period in which it arises. Those who support this treatment argue that biological transformation is a significant event that should be included in net profit or loss because:

(a) the event is fundamental to understanding an entity's performance; and

* IAS 1 *Presentation of Financial Statements* (revised in 2003) replaced the term 'net profit or loss' with 'profit or loss'.

(b) this is consistent with the accrual basis of accounting.

B39 Some commentators on the DSOP and E65 argued that fair value changes should be included directly in equity, through the statement of changes in equity, until realised, arguing that:

(a) the effects of biological transformation cannot be measured reliably and, therefore, should not be reported as income;

(b) fair value changes should only be included in net profit or loss when the earnings process is complete;

(c) recognition of unrealised gains and losses in net profit or loss increases volatility of earnings;

(d) the results of biological transformation may never be realised, particularly given the risks to which biological assets are exposed; and

(e) it is premature to require recognition of fair value changes in net profit or loss, until performance reporting issues are resolved.

B40 The Board rejected requiring changes in fair value to be included directly in equity since it is difficult to find any conceptual basis for reporting any portion of the changes in fair value of biological assets related to agricultural activity directly in equity. No distinction is made in the *Framework* between recognition in the balance sheet and recognition in the income statement.

Agricultural produce

B41 The Standard requires that agricultural produce harvested from an entity's biological assets should be measured at its fair value less estimated point-of-sale costs at the point of harvest. Such measurement is the cost at that date when applying IAS 2 *Inventories* or another applicable International Accounting Standard.

B42 The Board noted that the same basis of measurement should generally be applied to agricultural produce on initial recognition and to the biological asset from which it is harvested. Because the fair value of a biological asset takes into account the condition of the agricultural produce that will be harvested from the biological asset, it would be illogical to measure the agricultural produce at cost when the biological asset is measured at fair value. For example, the fair value of a sheep with half fleece will differ from the fair value of a similar sheep with full fleece. It would be inconsistent and distort reporting of current period performance if, upon shearing, the shorn fleece is measured at its cost when the fair value of the sheep is reduced by the fair value of the fleece.

B43 As noted previously, certain biological assets are measured at their cost less any accumulated depreciation and any accumulated impairment losses, if the reliability exception is applied. Some argue that a reliability exception should exist for measurement of agricultural produce. The Board rejected this view because many of the arguments for a reliability exception do not apply to agricultural produce. For example, markets more often exist for agricultural produce than for biological assets. The Board also noted that it is generally not practicable to reliably determine the cost of agricultural produce harvested from biological assets.

B44 With regard to measurement after harvest, some argue that agricultural produce should be measured at its fair value both at the point of harvest and at each balance sheet date until sold, consumed, or otherwise disposed of. They argue that this approach would ensure that all agricultural produce of a similar type is measured similarly irrespective of date of harvest, thus enhancing comparability and consistency.

B45 The Board concluded that fair value less estimated point-of-sale costs at the point of harvest should be the cost when applying IAS 2 or another applicable International Accounting Standard, since this is consistent with the historical cost accounting model applied to manufacturing processes in general and other types of inventory.

B46 In reaching the above conclusion, the Board noted that entities undertaking agricultural activity sometimes purchase agricultural produce for resale, and other entities often engage in processing purchased agricultural produce into consumable products. If agricultural produce would be measured at its fair value after harvest, a desire for consistency would suggest revaluing purchased inventories as well, and such a treatment would be inconsistent with IAS 2. The Board did not consider it appropriate to undertake a partial revision of IAS 2.

Sales contracts

B47 Entities often enter into contracts to sell at a future date their biological assets or agricultural produce. The Standard indicates that contract prices are not necessarily relevant in determining fair value and that the fair value of a biological asset or agricultural produce is not adjusted because of the existence of a contract.

B48 E65 did not propose how to account for a contract for the sale of a biological asset or agricultural produce. Some commentators suggested prescribing the treatment of sales contracts since such sales contracts are common in certain agricultural activity. Some commentators also pointed out that certain sales contracts are not within the scope of IAS 39 *Financial Instruments: Recognition and Measurement* and that no other International Accounting Standards deal with those contracts.

B49 Some argue that contract prices should be used in measuring the related biological assets when an entity expects to settle the contract by delivery and believe this would result in the most relevant carrying amount for the biological asset. Others argue that contract prices are not necessarily relevant in measuring the biological assets at fair value since fair value reflects the current market in which a willing buyer and seller would enter into a transaction.

B50 The Board concluded that contract prices should not be used in measuring related biological assets, because contract prices do not necessarily reflect the current market in which a willing buyer and seller would enter into a transaction and therefore do not necessarily represent the fair value of assets. The Board wished to maintain a consistent approach to the measurement of assets. The Board instead considered whether it might require that sales contracts be measured at fair value. It is logical to measure a sales contract at fair value to the extent that a related biological asset is also measured at fair value.

B51 However, the Board noted that to achieve symmetry between the measurement of a biological asset and a related sales contract the Standard would have to carefully restrict the sales contracts to be measured at fair value. An entity may enter into a contract to sell agricultural produce to be harvested from the entity's biological assets. The Board concluded that it would not be appropriate to require fair value measurement for a contract to sell agricultural produce that does not yet exist (for example, milk to be harvested from a cow), since no related asset has yet been recognised or measured at fair value and to do so would be beyond the scope of the project on agriculture.

B52 Thus, the Board considered restricting the sales contracts to be measured at fair value to those for the sale of an entity's existing biological assets and agricultural produce. However, the Board noted that it is difficult to differentiate existing agricultural produce from agricultural produce that does not exist. For example:

(a) if an entity enters into a contract to sell fully-grown wheat at a future date and has half-grown wheat at a balance sheet date, it seems clear that the wheat to be delivered under the contract does not yet exist at the balance sheet date; but

(b) on the other hand, if an entity enters into a contract to sell mature cattle at a future date and has mature cattle at a balance sheet date, it could be argued that the cattle exist in the form in which they will be sold at the balance sheet date. However, it could also be argued that the cattle do not yet exist in the form in which they will be sold at the balance sheet date since further biological transformation will occur between the balance sheet date and the date of delivery.

B53 The Board also noted that the Standard would have to require an entity to stop fair value measurement for sales contracts once agricultural produce to be sold under the contract is harvested from an entity's biological assets, since accounting for agricultural produce is not dealt with in the Standard except for initial measurement and IAS 2 *Inventories* or another applicable International Accounting Standard applies after harvest. It would be illogical to continue fair value measurement when the agricultural produce is measured at historical cost. The Board noted that it would be anomalous to require an entity to start measuring a contract at fair value once the related asset exists and to stop doing that at a later date.

B54 The Board concluded that no solution is practicable without a complete review of the accounting for commodity contracts that are not within the scope of IAS 39. Because of the above difficulties, the Board concluded that the Standard should not deal with the measurement of sales contracts that are not within the scope of IAS 39. Instead, the Board decided to include an observation that those sales contracts may be onerous contracts under IAS 37 *Provisions, Contingent Liabilities and Contingent Assets*.

Land related to agricultural activity

B55 The Standard does not establish any new principles for land related to agricultural activity. Rather, an entity follows IAS 16 *Property, Plant and Equipment* or IAS 40 *Investment Property* depending on which standard is appropriate in the circumstances. IAS 16 requires land to be measured either at its cost less any accumulated impairment losses, or at a revalued amount. IAS 40 requires land that is investment property to be measured at its fair value, or cost less any accumulated impairment losses.

B56 Some argue that land attached to biological assets related to agricultural activity should also be measured at its fair value. They argue that fair value measurement of land results in consistency of measurement with the fair value measurement of biological assets. They also argue that it is sometimes difficult to measure the fair value of such biological assets separately from the land since an active market often exists for the combined assets (that is, land and biological assets; for example, trees in a plantation forest).

B57 The Board rejected this approach, primarily because requiring the fair value measurement of land related to agricultural activity would be inconsistent with IAS 16.

Intangible assets

B58 The Standard does not establish any new principles for intangible assets related to agricultural activity. Rather, an entity follows IAS 38 *Intangible Assets*. IAS 38 requires an intangible asset, after initial recognition, to be measured at its cost less any accumulated amortisation and impairment losses, or at a revalued amount.

B59 E65 proposed that an entity should be encouraged to follow the revaluation alternative in IAS 38 for intangible assets related to agricultural activity, to enhance consistency of measurement with the fair value measurement of biological assets. Some commentators on E65 disagreed with having the encouragement. They argued that a unique treatment for intangible assets related to agricultural activity is not warranted.

B60 The Board did not include the encouragement in E65 in the Standard. The Board concluded that IAS 38 should be applied to intangible assets related to agricultural activity, as it is to intangible assets related to other activities.

Subsequent expenditure

B61 The Standard does not explicitly prescribe how to account for subsequent expenditure related to biological assets. E65 proposed that costs of producing and harvesting biological assets should be charged to expense when incurred and that costs that increase the number of units of biological assets owned or controlled by the entity should be added to the carrying amount of the asset.

B62 Some believe that there is no need to capitalise subsequent expenditure in a fair value model and that all subsequent expenditure should be recognised as an expense. Some also argue that it would sometimes be difficult to prescribe which costs should be recognised as expenses and which costs should be capitalised; for example, in the case of vet fees paid for delivering a calf. The Board decided not to explicitly prescribe the accounting for subsequent expenditure related to biological assets in the Standard, because it believes to do so is unnecessary with a fair value measurement approach.

Government grants

B63 The Standard requires that an unconditional government grant related to a biological asset measured at its fair value less estimated point-of-sale costs should be recognised as income when, and only when, the government grant becomes receivable. If a government grant is conditional, including where a government grant requires an entity not to engage in specified agricultural activity, an entity should recognise the government grant as income when, and only when, the conditions attaching to the government grant are met.

B64 The Standard requires a different treatment from IAS 20 *Accounting for Government Grants and Disclosure of Government Assistance* in the circumstances described above. IAS 20 is to be applied only to government grants related to biological assets measured at cost less any accumulated depreciation and any accumulated impairment losses.

B65 IAS 20 requires that government grants should not be recognised until there is reasonable assurance that:

(a) the entity will comply with the conditions attaching to them; and

(b) the grants will be received.

IAS 20 also requires that government grants should be recognised as income over the periods necessary to match them with the related costs that they are intended to compensate, on a systematic basis. In relation to the presentation of government grants related to assets, IAS 20 permits two methods—setting up a government grant as deferred income or deducting the government grant from the carrying amount of the asset.

B66 The latter method of presentation—deducting a government grant from the carrying amount of the related asset—is inconsistent with a fair value model in which an asset is measured and presented at its fair value. Using the deduction from carrying value approach, an entity would first deduct the government grant from the carrying amount of the related asset and then measure that asset at its fair value. In effect, an entity would recognise a government grant as income immediately, even for a conditional government grant. This conflicts with the requirement in IAS 20 that government grants should not be recognised until there is reasonable assurance that the entity will comply with the conditions attaching to them.

B67 Because of the above, the Board concluded that there was a need to deal with government grants related to biological assets measured at their fair value. Some argued that IASC should begin a wider review of IAS 20 rather than provide special rules in individual International Accounting Standards. The Board acknowledged that this might be a more appropriate approach, but concluded that such a review would be beyond the scope of the project on agriculture. Instead, the Board decided to deal with government grants in the Standard, since the Board noted that government grants related to agricultural activity are common in some countries.

B68 E65 proposed that, if an entity receives a government grant in respect of a biological asset that is measured at its fair value and the grant is unconditional, the entity should recognise the grant as income when the government grant becomes receivable. E65 also proposed that, if a government grant is conditional, the entity should recognise it as income when there is reasonable assurance that the conditions are met.

B69 The Board noted that, if a government grant is conditional, an entity is likely to have costs and ongoing obligations associated with satisfying the conditions attaching to the government grant. It may be possible that the inflow of economic benefits is much less than the amount of the government grant. Given that possibility, the Board acknowledged that the criterion for recognising income from a conditional government grant in E65, when there is reasonable assurance that the conditions are met, may give rise to income recognition that is inconsistent with the *Framework*. The *Framework* indicates that income is recognised in the income statement when an increase in future economic benefits related to an increase in an asset or a decrease in a liability has arisen that can be measured reliably. The Board also noted that it would inevitably be a subjective decision as to when there is reasonable assurance that the conditions are met and that this subjectivity could lead to inconsistent income recognition.

B70 The Board considered two alternative approaches:

(a) an entity should recognise a conditional government grant as income when it is probable that the entity will meet the conditions attaching to the government grant; and

(b) an entity should recognise a conditional government grant as income when the entity meets the conditions attaching to the government grant.

B71 Proponents of approach (a) argue that this approach is generally consistent with the revenue recognition requirements in IAS 18 *Revenue*. IAS 18 requires that revenue should be recognised, among other things, when it is probable that the economic benefits associated with the transaction will flow to the entity.

B72 Proponents of approach (b) believe that, until the conditions attaching to the government grant are met, a liability should be recognised under the *Framework* rather than income since an entity has a present obligation to satisfy the conditions arising from past events. They also argue that income recognition under approach (a) would still be subjective and inconsistent with the recognition criteria indicated in the *Framework*.

B73 The Board concluded that approach (b) is more appropriate. The Board also decided that a government grant that requires an entity not to engage in specified agricultural activity should also be accounted for in the same way as a conditional government grant related to a biological asset measured at its fair value less estimated point-of-sale costs.

Disclosure

Separate disclosure of physical and price changes

B74 The Standard encourages, but does not require, separate disclosure of the effects of the factors resulting in changes to the carrying amount of biological assets, physical change and price change, when there is a production cycle of more than one year. Physical change is attributable to changes in the assets themselves while price change is attributable to changes in unit fair values.

B75 Some argue that the separate disclosure should be required since it is useful in appraising current period performance and future prospects in relation to production from, and maintenance and renewal of, biological assets. Others argue that it may be impracticable to separate these elements and the two components cannot be separated reliably.

B76 The Board concluded that the separate disclosure should not be required because of practicability concerns. However, the Board decided to encourage the separate disclosure, given that such disclosure may be useful and practically determinable in some circumstances. The separate disclosure is not encouraged when the production cycle is less than one year (for example, when raising broiler chickens or growing cereal crops) since that information is less useful in that circumstance.

B77 Some argue that physical changes should be included in net profit or loss and that price changes should be included directly in equity, through the statement of changes in equity. The Board rejected this approach because both components are indicative of management's performance.

Disaggregation of the gain or loss

B78 The Standard requires that an entity should disclose the aggregate gain or loss arising during the current period on initial recognition of biological assets and agricultural produce and from the change in fair value less estimated point-of-sale costs of biological assets. The Standard does not require or encourage disaggregating the gain or loss, except that the Standard encourages separate disclosure of physical changes and price changes as discussed above.

B79 The Board considered requiring, or encouraging, disclosure of the gain or loss on a disaggregated basis; for example, requiring separate disclosure of the gain or loss related to biological assets and the gain or loss related to agricultural produce. Those who supported disaggregating the gain or loss believe that such information is useful in appraising current period performance in relation to biological transformation. Others argued that disaggregation would be impracticable and require a subjective procedure.

Other disclosures

B80 E65 proposed disclosing the:

(a) extent to which the carrying amount of biological assets reflects a valuation by an external independent valuer, or if there has been no valuation by an external independent valuer, that fact;

(b) activities that are unsustainable with an estimated date of cessation of the activities;

(c) aggregate carrying amount of an entity's agricultural land and the basis (cost or revalued amount) on which the carrying amount was determined under IAS 16 *Property, Plant and Equipment*; and

(d) carrying amount of agricultural produce either on the face of the balance sheet or in the notes.

B81 The Board did not include the above disclosures in the Standard. The Board noted that requiring item (a) above would not be appropriate since external independent valuations are not commonly used for assets related to agricultural activity, unlike for certain other assets such as investment property. The Board also noted that item (b) is not required in other International Accounting Standards and a unique disclosure requirement is not warranted for agricultural activity. Items (c) and (d) would be outside the scope of the Standard and covered by other International Accounting Standards (IAS 16 or IAS 2 *Inventories*).

Summary of changes to E65

B82 The Standard made the following principal changes to the proposals in E65:

(a) The Standard includes a reliability exception for biological assets on initial recognition. If the exception is applied, the biological asset should be measured at its cost less any accumulated depreciation and any accumulated impairment losses (paragraph 30 of the Standard). As a consequence, the Standard includes disclosure requirements consistent with paragraph 170(b) of IAS 39 *Financial Instruments: Recognition and Measurement* and paragraph 68 of IAS 40 *Investment Property* (paragraphs 54(a)–(c) and 55 of the Standard), and consistent with paragraphs 60(b)–(d) and 60(e)(v)–(vii) of IAS 16 *Property, Plant and Equipment* (paragraphs 54(d)–(f) and 55).

(b) If the reliability exception is applied but fair value subsequently becomes reliably measurable and, therefore, an entity has started measuring the biological assets at their fair value less estimated point-of-sale costs, the Standard requires the entity to disclose a description of the biological assets, an explanation of why fair value has become reliably measurable, and the effect of the change (paragraph 56).

(c) E65 did not specify how to account for point-of-sale costs (such as commissions to brokers). The Standard requires that biological assets and agricultural produce should be measured at their fair value less estimated point-of-sale costs (paragraphs 12–13).

(d) E65 included net realisable value as one of the measurement bases in cases where no active market exists. Net realisable value was deleted from the bases since it is not a market-determined value.

(e) The Standard indicates that market-determined prices or values are used when available. The Standard also indicates that, in some circumstances, market-determined prices or values may not be available for an asset in its present condition. In these circumstances, an entity uses the present value of expected net cash flows (paragraphs 18–20).

(f) Guidance on the performance of present value calculations was added (paragraphs 21–23).

(g) E65 did not specify how to account for contracts for the sale of a biological asset or agricultural produce. The Standard indicates that the fair value of a biological asset or agricultural produce is not adjusted because of the existence of a sales contract (paragraph 16).

(h) E65 did not explicitly indicate that a gain or loss may arise on initial recognition of agricultural produce. The Standard clarifies that a gain or loss may arise on initial recognition of agricultural produce; for example, as a result of harvesting and that such a gain or loss should be included in net profit or loss for the period in which it arises (paragraphs 28–29).

(i) E65 proposed that costs of producing and harvesting biological assets should be charged to expense when incurred, and that costs that increase the number of units of biological assets owned or controlled by the entity should be added to the carrying amount of the asset. The Standard does not explicitly prescribe how to account for subsequent expenditure related to biological assets.

(j) E65 proposed that an entity should recognise a conditional government grant as income when there is reasonable assurance that the conditions are met. The Standard requires that a conditional government grant related to a biological asset measured at its fair value less estimated point-of-sale costs, including where a government grant requires an entity not to engage in specified agricultural activity, should be recognised as income when, and only when, the conditions attaching to the government grant are met. The Standard also indicates that IAS 20 *Accounting for Government Grants and Disclosure of Government Assistance* is applied to a government grant related to a biological asset measured at its cost less any accumulated depreciation and any accumulated impairment losses (paragraphs 34–35 and 37).

(k) E65 provided the following encouragements specific to agricultural activity with regard to alternative treatments allowed in other International Accounting Standards, to achieve consistency with the accounting treatment of activities covered by E65:

   (i) analysing expenses by nature, as set out in IAS 1 *Presentation of Financial Statements*; and

   (ii) revaluing certain intangible assets used in agricultural activity if an active market exists, as set out in IAS 38 *Intangible Assets.*

   The Board did not include these encouragements in the Standard. The Board noted that IAS 1 and IAS 38 apply to entities that undertake agricultural activity, as well as to those in other activities.

(l) New disclosure requirements include disclosing the:

   (i) basis for making distinctions between consumable and bearer biological assets or between mature and immature biological assets, when an entity provides a quantified description of each group of biological assets (paragraph 43);

   (ii) methods and significant assumptions applied in determining the fair value of each group of agricultural produce at the point of harvest (paragraph 47);

   (iii) fair value less estimated point-of-sale costs of agricultural produce harvested during the period, determined at the point of harvest (paragraph 48);

   (iv) increases resulting from business combinations in the reconciliation of the carrying amount of biological assets (paragraph 50(e)); and

(v) significant decreases expected in the level of government grants related to agricultural activity covered by the Standard (paragraph 57(c)).

(m) E65 proposed disclosing the:

(i) extent to which the carrying amount of biological assets reflects a valuation by an external independent valuer or, if there has been no valuation by an external independent valuer, that fact;

(ii) activities that are unsustainable with an estimated date of cessation of the activities;

(iii) aggregate carrying amount of an entity's agricultural land and the basis (cost or revalued amount) on which the carrying amount was determined under IAS 16; and

(iv) carrying amount of agricultural produce either on the face of the balance sheet or in the notes.

The Standard does not include the above disclosures.

(n) The amendment to IAS 17 *Leases* now clarifies that IAS 17 should not be applied to the measurement by:

(i) lessees of biological assets held under finance leases; and

(ii) lessors of biological assets leased out under operating leases.

Biological assets held under finance leases and those leased out under operating leases are measured under the Standard rather than IAS 17. A lease of a biological asset is classified as a finance lease or operating lease under IAS 17. If a lease is classified as a finance lease, the lessee recognises the leased biological asset under IAS 17 and thereafter measures and presents it under the Standard. In that case, the lessee makes disclosures both under the Standard and IAS 17. A lessor of a biological asset under an operating lease measures and presents the biological asset under the Standard, and makes disclosures both under the Standard and IAS 17.

Preface to International Financial Reporting Interpretations Committee

1 The International Financial Reporting Interpretations Committee (IFRIC) is a committee of the IASB that assists the IASB in establishing and improving standards of financial accounting and reporting for the benefit of users, preparers and auditors of financial statements. The IFRIC was established in March 2002 by the Trustees of the International Accounting Standards Committee Foundation, when it replaced the previous interpretations committee, the Standing Interpretations Committee. The role of the IFRIC is to provide timely guidance on newly identified financial reporting issues not specifically addressed in International Financial Reporting Standards (IFRSs) or issues where unsatisfactory or conflicting interpretations have developed, or seem likely to develop. It thus promotes the rigorous and uniform application of IFRSs.

2 The IFRIC assists the IASB in achieving international convergence of accounting standards by working with similar groups sponsored by national standard-setters to reach similar conclusions on issues where underlying standards are substantially similar.

Responsibilities

3 The IFRIC reviews, on a timely basis, newly identified financial reporting issues not specifically addressed in IFRSs or issues where unsatisfactory or conflicting interpretations have developed, or seem likely to develop in the absence of authoritative guidance, with a view to reaching a consensus on the appropriate treatment.

4 In keeping with the IASB's own approach to setting standards, the IFRIC applies a principles-based approach in providing interpretive guidance. To this end, the IFRIC looks first to the *Framework for the Preparation and Presentation of Financial Statements* as the foundation for formulating a consensus. It then looks to the principles articulated in the applicable standard, if any, to develop its interpretive guidance and to determine that the proposed guidance does not conflict with provisions in the IFRS. In reaching its consensus views, the IFRIC also has due regard for the need for international convergence.

5 In discharging its responsibilities, the IFRIC does not reach a consensus that changes or conflicts with IFRSs or the *Framework*. If the IFRIC concludes that the requirements of an IFRS differ from the *Framework*, it obtains direction from the IASB before providing guidance.

6 The IFRIC informs the IASB of any existing or emerging issues that it perceives as indicative of inadequacies in existing IFRSs or the *Framework*. If the IFRIC believes that an existing IFRS or the *Framework* should be modified or an additional IFRS should be developed, it refers such conclusions to the IASB for its consideration.

7 When the IFRIC reaches a consensus on an issue, that consensus view is made publicly available to interested parties on a timely basis in a document entitled an IFRIC Interpretation. The Interpretations issued by the IFRIC are developed in

accordance with a due process of consultation and debate including making Draft Interpretations available for public comment.

Authority of IFRIC Interpretations

8 IFRIC Interpretations set out consensus views that entities shall apply if their financial statements are described as being prepared in accordance with IFRSs (see paragraph 11 of IAS 1 (revised 1997)).

9 IFRIC Interpretations apply to current and future reporting periods from the date of issue or other specified effective date. Transitional provisions that apply on initial application of an IFRIC consensus view are specified in the Interpretation.

10 An IFRIC consensus view becomes inoperative and is withdrawn when an IFRS or other authoritative document issued by the IASB that overrides or confirms a previously issued IFRIC consensus view becomes effective. Those IFRIC consensus views that would be affected by an authoritative IASB document are identified in the Exposure Draft of that document. The IASB informs the IFRIC when such an IFRS or other authoritative document is issued.

Membership

11 The IFRIC has twelve voting members appointed by the Trustees. The members are selected for their ability to maintain an awareness of current issues as they arise and the technical ability to resolve them. They would normally include accountants in industry and public practice and users of financial statements, with a reasonably broad geographic representation. The lack of a full complement of members, due to resignations or otherwise, does not restrict the IFRIC's ability to meet or alter quorum or voting requirements.

12 Members of the IFRIC are appointed for fixed renewable terms of up to three years. It is recognised that continuity of membership is important to its work. Accordingly, it is expected that a number of members will be appointed for more than one term.

13 The IFRIC is chaired by a member of the IASB, the Director of Technical Activities or another senior member of the IASB staff, or another appropriately qualified individual. The Chair of the IFRIC is appointed by the Trustees on the recommendation of the IASB. The Chair has the right to speak to the technical issues being considered but not to vote.

14 The IFRIC also includes Observers (currently from IOSCO and the European Commission) and two liaison members of the IASB. Observers and liaison IASB members have the right to speak but not to vote. Similarly, members of the IASB other than the two specifically designated to liaise with the IFRIC may attend IFRIC meetings, with the right to speak but not to vote.

15 IFRIC members and Observers are expected to attend all meetings. Membership is personal; members vote in accordance with their own independent views, not as representatives voting according to the views of the firm, organisation or constituency with which they are associated. If an IFRIC member or Observer is unable to attend a meeting, he or she may designate an alternate who will attend in his or her stead. The alternate is nominated in advance in consultation with,

and with the agreement of, the Chair and should be fully briefed by the member in advance of the meeting. Alternates have the right to speak but are not included in determining whether quorum requirements are satisfied and do not have the right to vote.

16 A member's continued membership will be reconsidered by the Trustees if the member is absent from two successive meetings of the IFRIC or is absent from three meetings of the IFRIC held during a period of one year. The member's appointment will be terminated unless reasonable grounds for the absence and an assurance of future attendance are provided.

Meetings and voting

17 Nine voting members of the IFRIC represent a quorum.

18 The IFRIC meets in public following procedures similar to the IASB's general policy for its Board meetings. Meetings may be held utilising a teleconference telephone or any other communication facilities that permit simultaneous communication among all members and Observers, and public observation. Members participating through any communications facility are included in determining whether quorum requirements are satisfied.

19 Each IFRIC member has one vote. Members vote in accordance with their own independent views, not as representatives voting according to the views of any firm, organisation or constituency with which they may be associated.

20 A consensus is achieved when no more than three members present at the meeting have voted against the proposal.

21 The Chair may invite others to attend meetings of the IFRIC as advisers when specialised input is required. A member or Observer may also, with the prior consent of the Chair, bring to a meeting an adviser who has specialised knowledge of a topic to be discussed. Such invited advisers will have the right to speak.

22 The IFRIC may conduct business electronically or by mail between meetings, for example to confirm redrafting of a proposed Draft or final Interpretation, or for the IASB staff to poll initial views on a proposed topic so that it can be developed appropriately for public discussion. All technical decisions, however, are made in meetings that are open for public observation.

Identification of agenda items

23 The primary responsibility for identifying issues to be considered by the IFRIC is that of its members and Observers. Preparers, auditors and others with an interest in financial reporting are encouraged to refer issues to the IFRIC when they believe that divergent practices have emerged regarding the accounting for particular transactions or circumstances or when there is doubt about the appropriate accounting treatment and it is important that a standard treatment be established.

24 Suggested agenda topics may be put forward to the Chair by any individual or organisation for consideration by the IFRIC. A suggestion should contain both a detailed description of the issue (including a description of alternative solutions

referring to the pertinent IASB literature) and an evaluation of the issue using the criteria for agenda items set out in paragraph 27 below.

25 Consensus views of the IFRIC have general applicability. The IFRIC does not resolve issues that are specific to the circumstances of a particular entity.

Agenda Committee and new agenda items

26 The IFRIC Agenda Committee consists of the Chair, one of the IASB liaison members and three IFRIC members. IFRIC members have renewable two-year terms on the Agenda Committee. The Agenda Committee assesses issues suggested to the Chair for addition to the IFRIC agenda and recommends whether the IFRIC should include the issue on its agenda. The Chair does not indicate the source of a suggested agenda item to the Agenda Committee or others.

27 In determining whether to recommend that an issue be included on the IFRIC agenda, the Agenda Committee considers the following criteria, although each issue does not have to satisfy all criteria. To be added to the agenda, an issue should:

(a) have practical and widespread relevance.

(b) involve significantly divergent interpretations (either emerging or already existing in practice).

(c) be likely to result in a consensus view of the IFRIC on a timely basis.

(d) be unrelated to a Board project that is expected to be completed in the near future (ie if a Board project exists that is expected to resolve the issue in a short period, the IFRIC is unlikely to add the issue to its agenda).

28 The Agenda Committee will generally conduct its business electronically or by mail, and will not meet in public.

29 The Agenda Committee reports to the IFRIC at its regular meetings on all the issues the Agenda Committee considered for addition to the IFRIC's agenda and the Agenda Committee's recommendation on each suggested issue. The IFRIC assesses proposed agenda items against the same criteria used by the Agenda Committee. A simple majority of IFRIC members present can agree to add any issue included in the Agenda Committee's report to the IFRIC's agenda, regardless of the Agenda Committee's recommendation.

30 The Agenda Committee or the IFRIC may direct IASB staff to reply to those whose suggestions were not added to the agenda, giving the reasons why the IFRIC decided not to deal with the issue.

Due process

31 The IFRIC reaches its conclusions on the basis of information contained in Issues Summaries that are prepared under the supervision of IASB staff. An Issues Summary describes the issue to be discussed and provides the information necessary for IFRIC members to gain an understanding of the issue and make decisions about it. Issues Summaries are developed for IFRIC consideration after a thorough review of the authoritative accounting literature and possible

alternatives, including consultation with similar groups at liaison national standard-setters. An Issues Summary includes:

(a) a brief description of the transaction or event to be discussed.

(b) the specific issues or questions to be considered by the IFRIC.

(c) the key concepts from the *Framework* that apply.

(d) a description of potential appropriate alternative treatments based on those concepts, with the arguments in favour and against each alternative.

(e) a list of the authoritative IASB accounting literature on the issue as well as pronouncements and views of liaison national standard-setters, identifying any inconsistency between the alternative treatments, the key concepts, or the standards.

(f) recommendations on the appropriate accounting treatment.

32 IASB members have access to all IFRIC agenda papers. They are expected to comment on technical matters as the issues are being considered, particularly if they have concerns about alternatives the IFRIC is seriously considering. IASB members will be informed when the IFRIC reaches a consensus. The Draft Interpretation will be released for public comment unless five or more IASB members object to its release within a week of being informed of its completion. If a Draft Interpretation is not released because of IASB members' objections, the issue will be considered at the next IASB meeting. Based on the discussion at the meeting, the IASB will decide whether the matter should be referred back to the IFRIC, added to its own agenda or not be the subject of any further action.

33 Draft Interpretations are made available for public comments for a suitable period, given the nature of the topic in question. In the case of emergencies this period may be as short as 30 days. Any comments received during the comment period will be considered by the IFRIC before an Interpretation is finalised. Unless confidentiality is requested by the commentator, the comment letters will be made publicly available. A staff summary and analysis of the comment letters will be provided to both the IFRIC and the Board.

34 If Draft Interpretations are changed in the light of new aspects identified by the public comments, re-exposure will be considered. The IFRIC votes to confirm the consensus set out in the final Interpretation. It also approves transmission of the final Interpretation to the IASB. If the IFRIC is aware that the proposed final Interpretation is not consistent with pronouncements of national standard-setters, the transmission to the IASB will include a notification to that effect and the reasons for the inconsistency.

35 When the IFRIC has concluded a final Interpretation, the Interpretation will be put to the IASB for approval before being issued. Approval by the IASB requires at least eight IASB members to be in favour. The IASB votes on the text of the Interpretation put forward by the IFRIC. If an Interpretation is not approved by the IASB, the IASB will subsequently provide the IFRIC with an analysis of the objections and concerns of those voting against approving the Interpretation. Based on this analysis, the IASB will decide whether the matter should be referred back to the IFRIC, added to its own agenda or not be the subject of any further action.

36 Approved Interpretations are issued by the IASB. An Interpretation includes a summary of the accounting issues identified; the consensus view reached on the appropriate accounting and the reasons for that view together with any notes on related points to be considered; and references to relevant IFRSs, parts of the *Framework* and other pronouncements that have been drawn upon to support the consensus view; it also specifies the application date and transitional provisions.

37 To ensure that the IFRIC considers only issues on which timely guidance can be provided, the IFRIC reviews issues at the time agenda decisions are made and subsequently keeps them under review, to assess whether they can be appropriately addressed within the mandate. If an issue has been considered at three meetings and there is still no consensus, the IFRIC reassesses the issue to determine whether it should be deleted from the agenda. The IFRIC may extend consideration of the issue for an additional period, normally not more than one or two meetings. If the IFRIC has concluded that it will not be able to reach a consensus, it will discontinue work on the issue, inform the IASB and publish the fact that work has been discontinued. The IFRIC may recommend that the matter be taken up by the IASB.

Confidentiality

38 IFRIC members and Observers are encouraged to discuss, in general terms, technical issues being considered by the IFRIC with associates who have an interest and expertise in such matters. Informal consultation of this kind offers members the opportunity to bring a variety of views to bear on the decisions to be made. During such consultation, members protect the confidentiality of the specific contents of IFRIC documents.

Communications

39 Information about the deliberations of the IFRIC is made available to users, preparers and auditors of financial information in a variety of ways. The IASB staff publishes summarised information on recent developments regarding the IFRIC on the IASB Website. In addition, IASB staff issue a newsletter after each IFRIC meeting.

Governance

40 The IFRIC provides minutes of its meetings to the IASB and regularly reports to the IASB on matters relating to its procedures, progress with its agenda and other administrative matters.

41 The IFRIC reviews its mandate and operating procedures at least every five years. The results of this review are communicated to the IASB for consideration and, after consultation with the Standards Advisory Council, the IASB may make recommendations for change to the Trustees.

IFRIC Interpretation 1

Changes in Existing Decommissioning, Restoration and Similar Liabilities

CONTENTS

IFRIC Interpretation 1 *Changes in Existing Decommissioning, Restoration and Similar Liabilities* (IFRIC 1) is set out in paragraphs 1–10 and the Appendix. IFRIC 1 is accompanied by Illustrative Examples and a Basis for Conclusions. The scope and authority of Interpretations are set out in paragraphs 1 and 8(10) of the *IFRIC Preface*.

IFRIC Interpretation 1
Changes in Existing Decommissioning, Restoration and Similar Liabilities

References

- IAS 1 *Presentation of Financial Statements* (as revised in 2003)
- IAS 8 *Accounting Policies, Changes in Accounting Estimates and Errors*
- IAS 16 *Property, Plant and Equipment* (as revised in 2003)
- IAS 23 *Borrowing Costs*
- IAS 36 *Impairment of Assets* (as revised in 2004)
- IAS 37 *Provisions, Contingent Liabilities and Contingent Assets*

Background

1 Many entities have obligations to dismantle, remove and restore items of property, plant and equipment. In this Interpretation such obligations are referred to as 'decommissioning, restoration and similar liabilities'. Under IAS 16, the cost of an item of property, plant and equipment includes the initial estimate of the costs of dismantling and removing the item and restoring the site on which it is located, the obligation for which an entity incurs either when the item is acquired or as a consequence of having used the item during a particular period for purposes other than to produce inventories during that period. IAS 37 contains requirements on how to measure decommissioning, restoration and similar liabilities. This Interpretation provides guidance on how to account for the effect of changes in the measurement of existing decommissioning, restoration and similar liabilities.

Scope

2 This Interpretation applies to changes in the measurement of any existing decommissioning, restoration or similar liability that is both:

(a) recognised as part of the cost of an item of property, plant and equipment in accordance with IAS 16; and

(b) recognised as a liability in accordance with IAS 37.

For example, a decommissioning, restoration or similar liability may exist for decommissioning a plant, rehabilitating environmental damage in extractive industries, or removing equipment.

Issue

3 This Interpretation addresses how the effect of the following events that change the measurement of an existing decommissioning, restoration or similar liability should be accounted for:

(a) a change in the estimated outflow of resources embodying economic benefits (eg cash flows) required to settle the obligation;

(b) a change in the current market-based discount rate as defined in paragraph 47 of IAS 37 (this includes changes in the time value of money and the risks specific to the liability); and

(c) an increase that reflects the passage of time (also referred to as the unwinding of the discount).

Consensus

4 Changes in the measurement of an existing decommissioning, restoration and similar liability that result from changes in the estimated timing or amount of the outflow of resources embodying economic benefits required to settle the obligation, or a change in the discount rate, shall be accounted for in accordance with paragraphs 5–7 below.

5 If the related asset is measured using the cost model:

(a) subject to (b), changes in the liability shall be added to, or deducted from, the cost of the related asset in the current period.

(b) the amount deducted from the cost of the asset shall not exceed its carrying amount. If a decrease in the liability exceeds the carrying amount of the asset, the excess shall be recognised immediately in profit or loss.

(c) if the adjustment results in an addition to the cost of an asset, the entity shall consider whether this is an indication that the new carrying amount of the asset may not be fully recoverable. If it is such an indication, the entity shall test the asset for impairment by estimating its recoverable amount, and shall account for any impairment loss, in accordance with IAS 36.

6 If the related asset is measured using the revaluation model:

(a) changes in the liability alter the revaluation surplus or deficit previously recognised on that asset, so that:

(i) a decrease in the liability shall (subject to (b)) be credited directly to revaluation surplus in equity, except that it shall be recognised in profit or loss to the extent that it reverses a revaluation deficit on the asset that was previously recognised in profit or loss;

(ii) an increase in the liability shall be recognised in profit or loss, except that it shall be debited directly to revaluation surplus in equity to the extent of any credit balance existing in the revaluation surplus in respect of that asset.

(b) in the event that a decrease in the liability exceeds the carrying amount that would have been recognised had the asset been carried under the cost model, the excess shall be recognised immediately in profit or loss.

(c) a change in the liability is an indication that the asset may have to be revalued in order to ensure that the carrying amount does not differ materially from that which would be determined using fair value at the balance sheet date. Any such revaluation shall be taken into account in determining the amounts to be taken to profit or loss and equity under (a). If a revaluation is necessary, all assets of that class shall be revalued.

(d) IAS 1 requires disclosure on the face of the statement of changes in equity of each item of income or expense that is recognised directly in equity. In complying with this requirement, the change in the revaluation surplus arising from a change in the liability shall be separately identified and disclosed as such.

7 The adjusted depreciable amount of the asset is depreciated over its useful life. Therefore, once the related asset has reached the end of its useful life, all subsequent changes in the liability shall be recognised in profit or loss as they occur. This applies under both the cost model and the revaluation model.

8 The periodic unwinding of the discount shall be recognised in profit or loss as a finance cost as it occurs. The allowed alternative treatment of capitalisation under IAS 23 is not permitted.

Effective date

9 An entity shall apply this Interpretation for annual periods beginning on or after 1 September 2004. Earlier application is encouraged. If an entity applies the Interpretation for a period beginning before 1 September 2004, it shall disclose that fact.

Transition

10 Changes in accounting policies shall be accounted for according to the requirements of IAS 8 *Accounting Policies, Changes in Accounting Estimates and Errors*.*

* If an entity applies this Interpretation for a period beginning before 1 January 2005, the entity shall follow the requirements of the previous version of IAS 8, which was entitled *Net Profit or Loss for the Period, Fundamental Errors and Changes in Accounting Policies*, unless the entity is applying the revised version of that Standard for that earlier period.

Appendix
Amendments to IFRS 1 *First–time Adoption of International Financial Reporting Standards*

The amendments in this appendix shall be applied for annual periods beginning on or after 1 September 2004. If an entity applies this Interpretation for an earlier period, these amendments shall be applied for that earlier period.

* * * * *

The amendments contained in this appendix when this Interpretation was issued in 2004 have been incorporated into IFRS 1 as issued on and after 27 May 2004.

Illustrative examples

These examples accompany, but are not part of, IFRIC 1.

Common facts

IE1 An entity has a nuclear power plant and a related decommissioning liability. The nuclear power plant started operating on 1 January 2000. The plant has a useful life of 40 years. Its initial cost was CU120,000*; this included an amount for decommissioning costs of CU10,000, which represented CU70,400 in estimated cash flows payable in 40 years discounted at a risk-adjusted rate of 5 per cent. The entity's financial year ends on 31 December.

Example 1: Cost model

IE2 On 31 December 2009, the plant is 10 years old. Accumulated depreciation is CU30,000 (CU120,000 × 10/40 years). Because of the unwinding of discount (5 per cent) over the 10 years, the decommissioning liability has grown from CU10,000 to CU16,300.

IE3 On 31 December 2009, the discount rate has not changed. However, the entity estimates that, as a result of technological advances, the net present value of the decommissioning liability has decreased by CU8,000. Accordingly, the entity adjusts the decommissioning liability from CU16,300 to CU8,300. On this date, the entity makes the following journal entry to reflect the change:

	CU	CU
Dr decommissioning liability	8,000	
Cr cost of asset		8,000

IE4 Following this adjustment, the carrying amount of the asset is CU82,000 (CU120,000 – CU8,000 – CU30,000), which will be depreciated over the remaining 30 years of the asset's life giving a depreciation expense for the next year of CU2,733 (CU82,000 ÷ 30). The next year's finance cost for the unwinding of the discount will be CU415 (CU8,300 × 5 per cent).

IE5 If the change in the liability had resulted from a change in the discount rate, instead of a change in the estimated cash flows, the accounting for the change would have been the same but the next year's finance cost would have reflected the new discount rate.

Example 2: Revaluation model

IE6 The entity adopts the revaluation model in IAS 16 whereby the plant is revalued with sufficient regularity that the carrying amount does not differ materially from fair value. The entity's policy is to eliminate accumulated depreciation at the revaluation date against the gross carrying amount of the asset.

* In these examples, monetary amounts are denominated in currency units (CU).

IE7 When accounting for revalued assets to which decommissioning liabilities attach, it is important to understand the basis of the valuation obtained. For example:

(a) if an asset is valued on a discounted cash flow basis, some valuers may value the asset without deducting any allowance for decommissioning costs (a 'gross' valuation), whereas others may value the asset after deducting an allowance for decommissioning costs (a 'net' valuation), because an entity acquiring the asset will generally also assume the decommissioning obligation. For financial reporting purposes, the decommissioning obligation is recognised as a separate liability, and is not deducted from the asset. Accordingly, if the asset is valued on a net basis, it is necessary to adjust the valuation obtained by adding back the allowance for the liability, so that the liability is not counted twice.*

(b) if an asset is valued on a depreciated replacement cost basis, the valuation obtained may not include an amount for the decommissioning component of the asset. If it does not, an appropriate amount will need to be added to the valuation to reflect the depreciated replacement cost of that component.

IE8 Assume that a market-based discounted cash flow valuation of CU115,000 is obtained at 31 December 2002. It includes an allowance of CU11,600 for decommissioning costs, which represents no change to the original estimate, after the unwinding of three years' discount. The amounts included in the balance sheet at 31 December 2002 are therefore:

	CU
Asset at valuation (1)	126,600
Accumulated depreciation	nil
Decommissioning liability	(11,600)
Net assets	115,000
Retained earnings (2)	(10,600)
Revaluation surplus (3)	15,600

Notes:

(1) Valuation obtained of CU115,000 plus decommissioning costs of CU11,600, allowed for in the valuation but recognised as a separate liability = CU126,600.

(2) Three years' depreciation on original cost CU120,000 × $\frac{3}{40}$ = CU9,000 plus cumulative discount on CU10,000 at 5 per cent compound = CU1,600; total CU10,600.

(3) Revalued amount CU126,600 less previous net book value of CU111,000 (cost CU120,000 less accumulated depreciation CU9,000).

IE9 The depreciation expense for 2003 is therefore CU3,420 (CU126,600 × $\frac{1}{37}$) and the discount expense for 2003 is CU600 (5 per cent of CU11,600). On 31 December 2003, the decommissioning liability (before any adjustment) is CU12,200 and the

* For examples of this principle, see IAS 36 *Impairment of Assets* and IAS 40 *Investment Property*.

discount rate has not changed. However, on that date, the entity estimates that, as a result of technological advances, the present value of the decommissioning liability has decreased by CU5,000. Accordingly, the entity adjusts the decommissioning liability from CU12,200 to CU7,200.

IE10 The whole of this adjustment is taken to revaluation surplus, because it does not exceed the carrying amount that would have been recognised had the asset been carried under the cost model. If it had done, the excess would have been taken to profit or loss in accordance with paragraph 6(b). The entity makes the following journal entry to reflect the change:

	CU	CU
Dr decommissioning liability	5,000	
Cr revaluation surplus		5,000

IE11 The entity decides that a full valuation of the asset is needed at 31 December 2003, in order to ensure that the carrying amount does not differ materially from fair value. Suppose that the asset is now valued at CU107,000, which is net of an allowance of CU7,200 for the reduced decommissioning obligation that should be recognised as a separate liability. The valuation of the asset for financial reporting purposes, before deducting this allowance, is therefore CU114,200. The following additional journal entry is needed:

	CU	CU
Dr accumulated depreciation (1)	3,420	
Cr asset at valuation		3,420
Dr revaluation surplus (2)	8,980	
Cr asset at valuation (3)		8,980

Notes:

(1) Eliminating accumulated depreciation of CU3,420 in accordance with the entity's accounting policy.

(2) The debit is to revaluation surplus because the deficit arising on the revaluation does not exceed the credit balance existing in the revaluation surplus in respect of the asset.

(3) Previous valuation (before allowance for decommissioning costs) CU126,600, less cumulative depreciation CU3,420, less new valuation (before allowance for decommissioning costs) CU114,200.

IE12 Following this valuation, the amounts included in the balance sheet are:

	CU
Asset at valuation	114,200
Accumulated depreciation	nil
Decommissioning liability	(7,200)
Net assets	107,000
Retained earnings (1)	(14,620)
Revaluation surplus (2)	11,620

Notes:

(1) CU10,600 at 31 December 2002 plus 2003's depreciation expense of CU3,420 and discount expense of CU600 = CU14,620.

(2) CU15,600 at 31 December 2002, plus CU5,000 arising on the decrease in the liability, less CU8,980 deficit on revaluation = CU11,620.

Example 3: Transition

IE13 The following example illustrates retrospective application of the Interpretation for preparers that already apply IFRSs. Retrospective application is required by IAS 8 *Accounting Policies, Changes in Accounting Estimates and Errors*, where practicable, and is the benchmark treatment in the previous version of IAS 8. The example assumes that the entity:

(a) adopted IAS 37 on 1 July 1999;

(b) adopts the Interpretation on 1 January 2005; and

(c) before the adoption of the Interpretation, recognised changes in estimated cash flows to settle decommissioning liabilities as income or expense.

IE14 On 31 December 2000, because of the unwinding of the discount (5 per cent) for one year, the decommissioning liability has grown from CU10,000 to CU10,500. In addition, based on recent facts, the entity estimates that the present value of the decommissioning liability has increased by CU1,500 and accordingly adjusts it from CU10,500 to CU12,000. In accordance with its then policy, the increase in the liability is recognised in profit or loss.

IE15 On 1 January 2005, the entity makes the following journal entry to reflect the adoption of the Interpretation:

	CU	CU
Dr cost of asset	1,500	
Cr accumulated depreciation		154
Cr opening retained earnings		1,346

IE16 The cost of the asset is adjusted to what it would have been if the increase in the estimated amount of decommissioning costs at 31 December 2000 had been capitalised on that date. This additional cost would have been depreciated over 39 years. Hence, accumulated depreciation on that amount at 31 December 2004 would be CU154 (CU1,500 × 4⁄39 years).

IE17 Because, before adopting the Interpretation on 1 January 2005, the entity recognised changes in the decommissioning liability in profit or loss, the net adjustment of CU1,346 is recognised as a credit to opening retained earnings. This credit is not required to be disclosed in the financial statements, because of the restatement described below.

IE18 IAS 8 requires the comparative financial statements to be restated and the adjustment to opening retained earnings at the start of the comparative period to be disclosed. The equivalent journal entries at 1 January 2004 are shown below. In addition, depreciation expense for the year ended 31 December 2004 is increased by CU39 from the amount previously reported:

	CU	CU
Dr cost of asset	1,500	
Cr accumulated depreciation		115
Cr opening retained earnings		1,385

Basis for Conclusions

This Basis for Conclusions accompanies, but is not part of, IFRIC 1.

Introduction

BC1 This Basis for Conclusions summarises the IFRIC's considerations in reaching its consensus. Individual IFRIC members gave greater weight to some factors than to others.

Background

BC2 IAS 16 *Property, Plant and Equipment* requires the cost of an item of property, plant and equipment to include the initial estimate of the costs of dismantling and removing an asset and restoring the site on which it is located, the obligation for which an entity incurs either when the item is acquired or as a consequence of having used the item during a particular period for purposes other than to produce inventories during that period.

BC3 IAS 37 *Provisions, Contingent Liabilities and Contingent Assets* requires that the measurement of the liability, both initially and subsequently, should be the estimated expenditure required to settle the present obligation at the balance sheet date and should reflect a current market-based discount rate. It requires provisions to be reviewed at each balance sheet date and adjusted to reflect the current best estimate. Hence, when the effect of a change in estimated outflows of resources embodying economic benefits and/or the discount rate is material, that change should be recognised.

BC4 The IFRIC was asked to address how to account for changes in decommissioning, restoration and similar liabilities. The issue is whether changes in the liability should be recognised in current period profit or loss, or added to (or deducted from) the cost of the related asset. IAS 16 contains requirements for the initial capitalisation of decommissioning costs and IAS 37 contains requirements for measuring the resulting liability; neither specifically addresses accounting for the effect of changes in the liability. The IFRIC was informed that differing views exist, resulting in a risk of divergent practices developing.

BC5 Accordingly, the IFRIC decided to develop guidance on accounting for the changes. In so doing, the IFRIC recognised that the estimation of the liability is inherently subjective, since its settlement may be very far in the future and estimating (a) the timing and amount of the outflow of resources embodying economic benefits (eg cash flows) required to settle the obligation and (b) the discount rate often involves the exercise of considerable judgement. Hence, it is likely that revisions to the initial estimate will be made.

Scope

BC6 The scope of the Interpretation addresses the accounting for changes in estimates of existing liabilities to dismantle, remove and restore items of property, plant and equipment that fall within the scope of IAS 16 and are recognised as a provision under IAS 37. The Interpretation does not apply to changes in estimated liabilities in respect of costs that fall within the scope of other IFRSs, for example, inventory or production costs that fall within the scope of IAS 2 *Inventories*. The IFRIC noted that decommissioning obligations associated with the extraction of minerals are a cost either of the property, plant and equipment used to extract them, in which case they are within the scope of IAS 16 and the Interpretation, or of the inventory produced, which should be accounted for under IAS 2.

Basis for Consensus

BC7 The IFRIC reached a consensus that changes in an existing decommissioning, restoration or similar liability that result from changes in the estimated timing or amount of the outflow of resources embodying economic benefits required to settle the obligation, or a change in the discount rate, should be added to or deducted from the cost of the related asset and depreciated prospectively over its useful life.

BC8 In developing its consensus, the IFRIC also considered the following three alternative approaches for accounting for changes in the outflow of resources embodying economic benefits and changes in the discount rate:

(a) capitalising only the effect of a change in the outflow of resources embodying economic benefits that relate to future periods, and recognising in current period profit or loss all of the effect of a change in the discount rate.

(b) recognising in current period profit or loss the effect of all changes in both the outflow of resources embodying economic benefits and the discount rate.

(c) treating changes in an estimated decommissioning, restoration and similar liability as revisions to the initial liability and the cost of the asset. Under this approach, amounts relating to the depreciation of the asset that would have been recognised to date would be reflected in current period profit or loss and amounts relating to future depreciation would be capitalised.

BC9 The IFRIC rejected alternative (a), because this approach does not treat changes in the outflow of resources embodying economic benefits and in the discount rate in the same way, which the IFRIC agreed is important, given that matters such as inflation can affect both the outflow of economic benefits and the discount rate.

BC10 In considering alternative (b), the IFRIC observed that recognising all of the change in the discount rate in current period profit or loss correctly treats a change in the discount rate as an event of the present period. However, the IFRIC decided against alternative (b) because recognising changes in the estimated outflow of resources embodying economic benefits in current period profit or loss would be inconsistent with the initial capitalisation of decommissioning costs under IAS 16.

BC11 Alternative (c) was the approach proposed in draft Interpretation D2 *Changes in Decommissioning, Restoration and Similar Liabilities*, published on 4 September 2003. In making that proposal, the IFRIC regarded the asset, from the time the liability for decommissioning is first incurred until the end of the asset's useful life, as the unit of account to which decommissioning costs relate. It therefore took the view that revisions to the estimates of those costs, whether through revisions to estimated outflows of resources embodying economic benefits or revisions to the discount rate, ought to be accounted for in the same manner as the initial estimated cost. The IFRIC still sees merit in this proposal, but concluded on balance that, under current standards, full prospective capitalisation should be required for the reasons set out in paragraphs BC12–BC18.

IAS 8 and a change in accounting estimate

BC12 IAS 8 *Accounting Policies, Changes in Accounting Estimates and Errors* requires an entity to recognise a change in an accounting estimate prospectively by including it in profit or loss in the period of the change, if the change affects that period only, or the period of the change and future periods, if the change affects both. To the extent that a change in an accounting estimate gives rise to changes in assets or liabilities, or relates to an item of equity, it is required to be recognised by adjusting the asset, liability or equity item in the period of change.

BC13 Although the IFRIC took the view that the partly retrospective treatment proposed in D2 is consistent with these requirements of IAS 8, most responses to the draft Interpretation suggested that IAS 8 would usually be interpreted as requiring a fully prospective treatment. The IFRIC agreed that IAS 8 would support a fully prospective treatment also, and this is what the Interpretation requires.

IAS 16 and changes in accounting estimates for property, plant and equipment

BC14 Many responses to the draft Interpretation argued that the proposal in D2 was inconsistent with IAS 16, which requires other kinds of change in estimate for property, plant and equipment to be dealt with prospectively. For example, as IAS 8 also acknowledges, a change in the estimated useful life of, or the expected pattern of consumption of the future economic benefits embodied in, a depreciable asset affects depreciation expense for the current period and for each future period during the asset's remaining useful life. In both cases, the effect of the change relating to the current period is recognised in profit or loss in the current period. The effect, if any, on future periods is recognised in profit or loss in those future periods.

BC15 Some responses to the draft Interpretation noted that a change in the estimate of a residual value is accounted for prospectively and does not require a catch-up adjustment. They observed that liabilities relating to decommissioning costs can be regarded as negative residual values, and suggested that the Interpretation should not introduce inconsistent treatment for similar events. Anomalies could result if two aspects of the same change are dealt with differently—for example, if the useful life of an asset was extended and the present value of the decommissioning liability reduced as a result.

BC16 The IFRIC agreed that it had not made a sufficient case for treating changes in estimates of decommissioning and similar liabilities differently from other changes in estimates for property, plant and equipment. The IFRIC understood that there was no likelihood of the treatment of other changes in estimate for such assets being revisited in the near future.

BC17 The IFRIC also noted that the anomalies that could result from its original proposal, if other changes in estimate were dealt with prospectively, were more serious than it had understood previously, and that a fully prospective treatment would be easier to apply consistently.

BC18 The IFRIC had been concerned that a fully prospective treatment could result in either unrealistically large assets or negative assets, particularly if there are large changes in estimates toward the end of an asset's life. The IFRIC noted that the first concern could be dealt with if the assets were reviewed for impairment in accordance with IAS 36 *Impairment of Assets*, and that a zero asset floor could be applied to ensure that an asset did not become negative if cost estimates reduced significantly towards the end of its life. The credit would first be applied to write the carrying amount of the asset down to nil and then any residual credit adjustment would be recognised in profit or loss. These safeguards are included in the final consensus.

Comparison with US GAAP

BC19 In reaching its consensus, the IFRIC considered the US GAAP approach in Statement of Financial Accounting Standards No. 143, *Accounting for Asset Retirement Obligations* (SFAS 143). Under that standard, changes in estimated cash flows are capitalised as part of the cost of the asset and depreciated prospectively, but the decommissioning obligation is not required to be revised to reflect the effect of a change in the current market-assessed discount rate.

BC20 The treatment of changes in estimated cash flows required by this Interpretation is consistent with US GAAP, which the proposal in D2 was not. However, the IFRIC agreed that because IAS 37 requires a decommissioning obligation to reflect the effect of a change in the current market-based discount rate (see paragraph BC3), it was not possible to disregard changes in the discount rate. Furthermore, SFAS 143 did not treat changes in cash flows and discount rates in the same way, which the IFRIC had agreed was important.

The interaction of the Interpretation and initial recognition under IAS 16

BC21 In developing the Interpretation, the IFRIC considered the improvements that have been made to IAS 16 by the Board and agreed that it would explain the interaction of the two.

BC22 IAS 16 (as revised in 2003) clarifies that the initial measurement of the cost of an item of property, plant and equipment should include the cost of dismantling and removing the item and restoring the site on which it is located, if this obligation is incurred either when the item is acquired or as a consequence of having used the item during a particular period for purposes other than to produce inventories during that period. This is because the Board concluded that whether the obligation is incurred upon acquisition of the item or as a consequence of using it, the underlying nature of the cost and its association with the asset are the same.

BC23 However, in considering the improvements to IAS 16, the Board did not address how an entity would account for (a) changes in the amount of the initial estimate of a recognised obligation, (b) the effects of accretion of, or changes in interest rates on, a recognised obligation or (c) the cost of obligations that did not exist when the entity acquired the item, such as an obligation triggered by a change in a law enacted after the asset is acquired. The Interpretation addresses issues (a) and (b).

The interaction of the Interpretation and the choice of measurement model under IAS 16

BC24 IAS 16 allows an entity to choose either the cost model or the revaluation model for measuring its property, plant and equipment, on a class-by-class basis. The IFRIC's view is that the measurement model that an entity chooses under IAS 16 would not be affected by the Interpretation.

BC25 Several responses to the draft Interpretation sought clarification of how it should be applied to revalued assets. The IFRIC noted that:

(a) if the entity chooses the revaluation model, IAS 16 requires the valuation to be kept sufficiently up to date that the carrying amount does not differ materially from that which would be determined using fair value at the balance sheet date. This Interpretation requires a change in a recognised decommissioning, restoration or similar liability generally to be added to or deducted from the cost of the asset. However, a change in the liability does not, of itself, affect the *valuation* of the asset for financial reporting purposes, because (to ensure that it is not counted twice) the separately recognised liability is excluded from its valuation.

(b) rather than changing the valuation of the asset, a change in the liability affects the difference between what would have been reported for the asset under the cost model, under this Interpretation, and its valuation. In other words, it changes the revaluation surplus or deficit that has previously been recognised for the asset. For example, if the liability increases by CU20, which under the cost model would have been added to the cost of the asset, the revaluation surplus reduces (or the revaluation deficit increases) by CU20. Under the revaluation model set out in IAS 16, cumulative revaluation surpluses for an asset are accounted for in equity, and cumulative revaluation deficits are accounted for in profit or loss. The IFRIC decided that changes in the liability relating to a revalued asset should be accounted for in the same way as other changes in revaluation surpluses and deficits under IAS 16.

(c) although a change in the liability does not directly affect the value of the asset for financial reporting purposes, many events that change the value of the liability may also affect the value of the asset, by either a greater or lesser amount. The IFRIC therefore decided that, for revalued assets, a change in a decommissioning liability indicates that a revaluation may be required. Any such revaluation should be taken into account in determining the amount taken to profit or loss under (b) above. If a revaluation is done, IAS 16 requires all assets of the same class to be revalued.

(d) the depreciated cost of an asset (less any impairment) should not be negative, regardless of the valuation model, and the revaluation surplus on an asset should not exceed its value. The IFRIC therefore decided that, if the reduction in a liability exceeds the carrying amount that would have been recognised had the asset been carried under the cost model, the excess reduction should always be taken to profit or loss. For example, if the depreciated cost of an unimpaired asset is CU25, and its revalued amount is CU100, there is a revaluation surplus of CU75. If the decommissioning liability associated with the asset is reduced by CU30, the depreciated cost of the asset should be reduced to nil, the revaluation surplus should be increased to CU100 (which equals the value of the asset), and the remaining CU5 of the reduction in the liability should be taken to profit or loss.

The unwinding of the discount

BC26 The IFRIC considered whether the unwinding of the discount is a borrowing cost for the purposes of IAS 23 *Borrowing Costs*. This question arises because if the unwinding of the discount rate were deemed a borrowing cost for the purposes of IAS 23, in certain circumstances this amount might be capitalised under the allowed alternative treatment of capitalisation. The IFRIC noted that IAS 23 addresses funds borrowed specifically for the purpose of obtaining a particular asset. It agreed that a decommissioning liability does not fall within this description since it does not reflect funds (ie cash) borrowed. Hence, the IFRIC concluded that the unwinding of the discount is not a borrowing cost as defined in IAS 23.

BC27 The IFRIC agreed that the unwinding of the discount as referred to in paragraph 60 of IAS 37 should be reported in profit or loss in the period it occurs.

Disclosures

BC28 The IFRIC considered whether the Interpretation should include disclosure guidance and agreed that it was largely unnecessary because IAS 16 and IAS 37 contain relevant guidance, for example:

(a) IAS 16 explains that IAS 8 requires the disclosure of the nature and effect of changes in accounting estimates that have an effect in the current period or are expected to have a material effect in subsequent periods, and that such disclosure may arise from changes in the estimated costs of dismantling, removing or restoring items of property, plant and equipment.

(b) IAS 37 requires the disclosure of:

(i) a reconciliation of the movements in the carrying amount of the provision for the period.

(ii) the increase during the period in the discounted amount arising from the passage of time and the effect of any change in the discount rate.

(iii) a brief description of the nature of the obligation and the expected timing of any resulting outflows of economic benefits.

(iv) an indication of the uncertainties about the amount or timing of those outflows, and where necessary the disclosure of the major assumptions made concerning future events (eg future interest rates, future changes in salaries, and future changes in prices).

BC29 However, in respect of assets measured using the revaluation model, the IFRIC noted that changes in the liability would often be taken to the revaluation reserve. These changes reflect an event of significance to users, and the IFRIC agreed that they should be given prominence by being separately disclosed and described as such in the statement of changes in equity.

Transition

BC30 The IFRIC agreed that preparers that already apply IFRSs should apply the Interpretation in the manner required by IAS 8, which is usually retrospectively. The IFRIC could not justify another application method, especially when IAS 37 requires retrospective application.

BC31 The IFRIC noted that, in order to apply the Interpretation retrospectively, it is necessary to determine both the timing and amount of any changes that would have been required by the Interpretation. However, IAS 8 specifies that:

(a) if retrospective application is not practicable for all periods presented, the new accounting policy shall be applied retrospectively from the earliest practicable date; and

(b) if it is impracticable to determine the cumulative effect of applying the new accounting policy at the start of the current period, the policy shall be applied prospectively from the earliest date practicable.

BC32 The IFRIC noted that IAS 8 defines a requirement as impracticable when an entity cannot apply it after making every reasonable effort to do so, and gives guidance on when this is so.

BC33 However, the provisions of IAS 8 on practicability do not apply to IFRS 1 *First-time Adoption of International Financial Reporting Standards*. Retrospective application of this Interpretation at the date of transition to IFRSs, which is the treatment required by IFRS 1 in the absence of any exemptions, would require first-time adopters to construct a historical record of all such adjustments that would have been made in the past. In many cases this will not be practicable. The IFRIC agreed that, as an alternative to retrospective application, an entity should be permitted to include in the depreciated cost of the asset at the date of transition an amount calculated by discounting the liability at that date back to, and depreciating it from, when it was first incurred. This Interpretation amends IFRS 1 accordingly.

IFRIC Interpretation 2

Members' Shares in Co-operative Entities and Similar Instruments

CONTENTS

IFRIC Interpretation 2 *Members' Shares in Co-operative Entities and Similar Instruments* (IFRIC 2) is set out in paragraphs 1–14 and the Appendix. IFRIC 2 is accompanied by a Basis for Conclusions. The scope and authority of Interpretations are set out in paragraphs 1 and 8–10 of the *IFRIC Preface*.

IFRIC Interpretation 2
Members' Shares in Co-operative Entities and Similar Instruments

References

- IAS 32 *Financial Instruments: Disclosure and Presentation* (as revised in 2003)
- IAS 39 *Financial Instruments: Recognition and Measurement* (as revised in 2003)

Background

1 Co-operatives and other similar entities are formed by groups of persons to meet common economic or social needs. National laws typically define a co-operative as a society endeavouring to promote its members' economic advancement by way of a joint business operation (the principle of self-help). Members' interests in a co-operative are often characterised as members' shares, units or the like, and are referred to below as 'members' shares'.

2 IAS 32 establishes principles for the classification of financial instruments as financial liabilities or equity. In particular, those principles apply to the classification of puttable instruments that allow the holder to put those instruments to the issuer for cash or another financial instrument. The application of those principles to members' shares in co-operative entities and similar instruments is difficult. Some of the International Accounting Standards Board's constituents have asked for help in understanding how the principles in IAS 32 apply to members' shares and similar instruments that have certain features, and the circumstances in which those features affect the classification as liabilities or equity.

Scope

3 This Interpretation applies to financial instruments within the scope of IAS 32, including financial instruments issued to members of co-operative entities that evidence the members' ownership interest in the entity. This Interpretation does not apply to financial instruments that will or may be settled in the entity's own equity instruments.

Issue

4 Many financial instruments, including members' shares, have characteristics of equity, including voting rights and rights to participate in dividend distributions. Some financial instruments give the holder the right to request redemption for cash or another financial asset, but may include or be subject to limits on whether the financial instruments will be redeemed. How should those redemption terms be evaluated in determining whether the financial instruments should be classified as liabilities or equity?

Consensus

5 The contractual right of the holder of a financial instrument (including members' shares in co-operative entities) to request redemption does not, in itself, require that financial instrument to be classified as a financial liability. Rather, the entity must consider all of the terms and conditions of the financial instrument in determining its classification as a financial liability or equity. Those terms and conditions include relevant local laws, regulations and the entity's governing charter in effect at the date of classification, but not expected future amendments to those laws, regulations or charter.

6 Members' shares that would be classified as equity if the members did not have a right to request redemption are equity if either of the conditions described in paragraphs 7 and 8 is present. Demand deposits, including current accounts, deposit accounts and similar contracts that arise when members act as customers are financial liabilities of the entity.

7 Members' shares are equity if the entity has an unconditional right to refuse redemption of the members' shares.

8 Local law, regulation or the entity's governing charter can impose various types of prohibitions on the redemption of members' shares, eg unconditional prohibitions or prohibitions based on liquidity criteria. If redemption is unconditionally prohibited by local law, regulation or the entity's governing charter, members' shares are equity. However, provisions in local law, regulation or the entity's governing charter that prohibit redemption only if conditions—such as liquidity constraints—are met (or are not met) do not result in members' shares being equity.

9 An unconditional prohibition may be absolute, in that all redemptions are prohibited. An unconditional prohibition may be partial, in that it prohibits redemption of members' shares if redemption would cause the number of members' shares or amount of paid-in capital from members' shares to fall below a specified level. Members' shares in excess of the prohibition against redemption are liabilities, unless the entity has the unconditional right to refuse redemption as described in paragraph 7. In some cases, the number of shares or the amount of paid-in capital subject to a redemption prohibition may change from time to time. Such a change in the redemption prohibition leads to a transfer between financial liabilities and equity.

10 At initial recognition, the entity shall measure its financial liability for redemption at fair value. In the case of members' shares with a redemption feature, the entity measures the fair value of the financial liability for redemption at no less than the maximum amount payable under the redemption provisions of its governing charter or applicable law discounted from the first date that the amount could be required to be paid (see example 3).

11 As required by paragraph 35 of IAS 32, distributions to holders of equity instruments are recognised directly in equity, net of any income tax benefits. Interest, dividends and other returns relating to financial instruments classified as financial liabilities are expenses, regardless of whether those amounts paid are legally characterised as dividends, interest or otherwise.

12 The Appendix, which is an integral part of the consensus, provides examples of the application of this consensus.

Disclosure

13 When a change in the redemption prohibition leads to a transfer between financial liabilities and equity, the entity shall disclose separately the amount, timing and reason for the transfer.

Effective date

14 The effective date and transition requirements of this Interpretation are the same as those for IAS 32 (as revised in 2003). An entity shall apply this Interpretation for annual periods beginning on or after 1 January 2005. If an entity applies this Interpretation for a period beginning before 1 January 2005, it shall disclose that fact. This Interpretation shall be applied retrospectively.

Appendix
Examples of application of the consensus

This appendix is an integral part of the Interpretation.

A1 This appendix sets out seven examples of the application of the IFRIC consensus. The examples do not constitute an exhaustive list; other fact patterns are possible. Each example assumes that there are no conditions other than those set out in the facts of the example that would require the financial instrument to be classified as a financial liability.

Unconditional right to refuse redemption (paragraph 7)

Example 1

Facts

A2 The entity's charter states that redemptions are made at the sole discretion of the entity. The charter does not provide further elaboration or limitation on that discretion. In its history, the entity has never refused to redeem members' shares, although the governing board has the right to do so.

Classification

A3 The entity has the unconditional right to refuse redemption and the members' shares are equity. IAS 32 establishes principles for classification that are based on the terms of the financial instrument and notes that a history of, or intention to make, discretionary payments does not trigger liability classification. Paragraph AG26 of IAS 32 states:

> When preference shares are non-redeemable, the appropriate classification is determined by the other rights that attach to them. Classification is based on an assessment of the substance of the contractual arrangements and the definitions of a financial liability and an equity instrument. When distributions to holders of the preference shares, whether cumulative or non-cumulative, are at the discretion of the issuer, the shares are equity instruments. The classification of a preference share as an equity instrument or a financial liability is not affected by, for example:
>
> (a) a history of making distributions;
>
> (b) an intention to make distributions in the future;
>
> (c) a possible negative impact on the price of ordinary shares of the issuer if distributions are not made (because of restrictions on paying dividends on the ordinary shares if dividends are not paid on the preference shares);
>
> (d) the amount of the issuer's reserves;
>
> (e) an issuer's expectation of a profit or loss for a period; or
>
> (f) an ability or inability of the issuer to influence the amount of its profit or loss for the period.

Example 2

Facts

A4 The entity's charter states that redemptions are made at the sole discretion of the entity. However, the charter further states that approval of a redemption request is automatic unless the entity is unable to make payments without violating local regulations regarding liquidity or reserves.

Classification

A5 The entity does not have the unconditional right to refuse redemption and the members' shares are a financial liability. The restrictions described above are based on the entity's ability to settle its liability. They restrict redemptions only if the liquidity or reserve requirements are not met and then only until such time as they are met. Hence, they do not, under the principles established in IAS 32, result in the classification of the financial instrument as equity. Paragraph AG25 of IAS 32 states:

> Preference shares may be issued with various rights. In determining whether a preference share is a financial liability or an equity instrument, an issuer assesses the particular rights attaching to the share to determine whether it exhibits the fundamental characteristic of a financial liability. For example, a preference share that provides for redemption on a specific date or at the option of the holder contains a financial liability because the issuer has an obligation to transfer financial assets to the holder of the share. *The potential inability of an issuer to satisfy an obligation to redeem a preference share when contractually required to do so, whether because of a lack of funds, a statutory restriction or insufficient profits or reserves, does not negate the obligation.* [Emphasis added]

Prohibitions against redemption (paragraphs 8 and 9)

Example 3

Facts

A6 A co-operative entity has issued shares to its members at different dates and for different amounts in the past as follows:

(a) 1 January 20X1 100,000 shares at CU10 each (CU1,000,000);

(b) 1 January 20X2 100,000 shares at CU20 each (a further CU2,000,000, so that the total for shares issued is CU3,000,000).

Shares are redeemable on demand at the amount for which they were issued.

A7 The entity's charter states that cumulative redemptions cannot exceed 20 per cent of the highest number of its members' shares ever outstanding. At 31 December 20X2 the entity has 200,000 of outstanding shares, which is the highest number of members' shares ever outstanding and no shares have been redeemed in the past. On 1 January 20X3 the entity amends its governing charter and increases the permitted level of cumulative redemptions to 25 per cent of the highest number of its members' shares ever outstanding.

Classification

Before the governing charter is amended

A8 Members' shares in excess of the prohibition against redemption are financial liabilities. The co-operative entity measures this financial liability at fair value at initial recognition. Because these shares are redeemable on demand, the co-operative entity determines the fair value of such financial liabilities as required by paragraph 49 of IAS 39, which states: 'The fair value of a financial liability with a demand feature (eg a demand deposit) is not less than the amount payable on demand ...' Accordingly, the co-operative entity classifies as financial liabilities the maximum amount payable on demand under the redemption provisions.

A9 On 1 January 20X1 the maximum amount payable under the redemption provisions is 20,000 shares at CU10 each and accordingly the entity classifies CU200,000 as financial liability and CU800,000 as equity. However, on 1 January 20X2 because of the new issue of shares at CU20, the maximum amount payable under the redemption provisions increases to 40,000 shares at CU20 each. The issue of additional shares at CU20 creates a new liability that is measured on initial recognition at fair value. The liability after these shares have been issued is 20 per cent of the total shares in issue (200,000), measured at CU20, or CU800,000. This requires recognition of an additional liability of CU600,000. In this example no gain or loss is recognised. Accordingly the entity now classifies CU800,000 as financial liabilities and CU2,200,000 as equity. This example assumes these amounts are not changed between 1 January 20X1 and 31 December 20X2.

After the governing charter is amended

A10 Following the change in its governing charter the co-operative entity can now be required to redeem a maximum of 25 per cent of its outstanding shares or a maximum of 50,000 shares at CU20 each. Accordingly, on 1 January 20X3 the co-operative entity classifies as financial liabilities an amount of CU1,000,000 being the maximum amount payable on demand under the redemption provisions, as determined in accordance with paragraph 49 of IAS 39. It therefore transfers on 1 January 20X3 from equity to financial liabilities an amount of CU200,000, leaving CU2,000,000 classified as equity. In this example the entity does not recognise a gain or loss on the transfer.

Example 4

Facts

A11 Local law governing the operations of co-operatives, or the terms of the entity's governing charter, prohibit an entity from redeeming members' shares if, by redeeming them, it would reduce paid-in capital from members' shares below 75 per cent of the highest amount of paid-in capital from members' shares. The highest amount for a particular co-operative is CU1,000,000. At the balance sheet date the balance of paid-in capital is CU900,000.

Classification

A12 In this case, CU750,000 would be classified as equity and CU150,000 would be classified as financial liabilities. In addition to the paragraphs already cited, paragraph 18(b) of IAS 32 states in part:

> ...a financial instrument that gives the holder the right to put it back to the issuer for cash or another financial asset (a 'puttable instrument') is a financial liability. This is so even when the amount of cash or other financial assets is determined on the basis of an index or other item that has the potential to increase or decrease, or when the legal form of the puttable instrument gives the holder a right to a residual interest in the assets of an issuer. The existence of an option for the holder to put the instrument back to the issuer for cash or another financial asset means that the puttable instrument meets the definition of a financial liability.

A13 The redemption prohibition described in this example is different from the restrictions described in paragraphs 19 and AG25 of IAS 32. Those restrictions are limitations on the ability of the entity to pay the amount due on a financial liability, ie they prevent payment of the liability only if specified conditions are met. In contrast, this example describes an unconditional prohibition on redemptions beyond a specified amount, regardless of the entity's ability to redeem members' shares (eg given its cash resources, profits or distributable reserves). In effect, the prohibition against redemption prevents the entity from incurring any financial liability to redeem more than a specified amount of paid-in capital. Therefore, the portion of shares subject to the redemption prohibition is not a financial liability. While each member's shares may be redeemable individually, a portion of the total shares outstanding is not redeemable in any circumstances other than liquidation of the entity.

Example 5

Facts

A14 The facts of this example are as stated in example 4. In addition, at the balance sheet date, liquidity requirements imposed in the local jurisdiction prevent the entity from redeeming any members' shares unless its holdings of cash and short-term investments are greater than a specified amount. The effect of these liquidity requirements at the balance sheet date is that the entity cannot pay more than CU50,000 to redeem the members' shares.

Classification

A15 As in example 4, the entity classifies CU750,000 as equity and CU150,000 as a financial liability. This is because the amount classified as a liability is based on the entity's unconditional right to refuse redemption and not on conditional restrictions that prevent redemption only if liquidity or other conditions are not met and then only until such time as they are met. The provisions of paragraphs 19 and AG25 of IAS 32 apply in this case.

Example 6

Facts

A16 The entity's governing charter prohibits it from redeeming members' shares, except to the extent of proceeds received from the issue of additional members' shares to new or existing members during the preceding three years. Proceeds from issuing members' shares must be applied to redeem shares for which members have requested redemption. During the three preceding years, the proceeds from issuing members' shares have been CU12,000 and no member's shares have been redeemed.

Classification

A17 The entity classifies CU12,000 of the members' shares as financial liabilities. Consistently with the conclusions described in example 4, members' shares subject to an unconditional prohibition against redemption are not financial liabilities. Such an unconditional prohibition applies to an amount equal to the proceeds of shares issued before the preceding three years, and accordingly, this amount is classified as equity. However, an amount equal to the proceeds from any shares issued in the preceding three years is not subject to an unconditional prohibition on redemption. Accordingly, proceeds from the issue of members' shares in the preceding three years give rise to financial liabilities until they are no longer available for redemption of members' shares. As a result the entity has a financial liability equal to the proceeds of shares issued during the three preceding years, net of any redemptions during that period.

Example 7

Facts

A18 The entity is a co-operative bank. Local law governing the operations of co-operative banks state that at least 50 per cent of the entity's total 'outstanding liabilities' (a term defined in the regulations to include members' share accounts) has to be in the form of members' paid-in capital. The effect of the regulation is that if all of a co-operative's outstanding liabilities are in the form of members' shares, it is able to redeem them all. On 31 December 20X1 the entity has total outstanding liabilities of CU200,000, of which CU125,000 represent members' share accounts. The terms of the members' share accounts permit the holder to redeem them on demand and there are no limitations on redemption in the entity's charter.

Classification

A19 In this example members' shares are classified as financial liabilities. The redemption prohibition is similar to the restrictions described in paragraphs 19 and AG25 of IAS 32. The restriction is a conditional limitation on the ability of the entity to pay the amount due on a financial liability, ie they prevent payment of the liability only if specified conditions are met. More specifically, the entity could be required to redeem the entire amount of members' shares (CU125,000) if it repaid all of its other liabilities (CU75,000). Consequently, the prohibition against redemption does not prevent the entity from incurring a financial liability to redeem more than a specified number of members' shares or amount of paid-in capital. It allows the entity only to defer redemption until a condition is met, ie the repayment of other liabilities. Members' shares in this example are not subject to an unconditional prohibition against redemption and are therefore classified as financial liabilities.

Basis for Conclusions

This Basis for Conclusions accompanies, but is not part of, the Interpretation.

Introduction

BC1 This Basis for Conclusions summarises the IFRIC's considerations in reaching its consensus. Individual IFRIC members gave greater weight to some factors than to others.

Background

BC2 In September 2001, the Standing Interpretations Committee instituted by the former International Accounting Standards Committee (IASC) published Draft Interpretation SIC D-34 *Financial Instruments – Instruments or Rights Redeemable by the Holder*. The Draft Interpretation stated: 'The issuer of a Puttable Instrument should classify the entire instrument as a liability.'

BC3 In 2001 the International Accounting Standards Board (IASB) began operations in succession to IASC. The IASB's initial agenda included a project to make limited amendments to the financial instruments standards issued by IASC. The IASB decided to incorporate the consensus from Draft Interpretation D-34 as part of those amendments. In June 2002 the IASB published an exposure draft of amendments to IAS 32 *Financial Instruments: Disclosure and Presentation* that incorporated the proposed consensus from Draft Interpretation D-34.

BC4 In their responses to the Exposure Draft and in their participation in public round-table discussions held in March 2003, representatives of co-operative banks raised questions about the application of the principles in IAS 32 to members' shares. This was followed by a series of meetings between IASB members and staff and representatives of the European Association of Co-operative Banks. After considering questions raised by the bank group, the IASB concluded that the principles articulated in IAS 32 should not be modified, but that there were questions about the application of those principles to co-operative entities that should be considered by the IFRIC.

BC5 In considering the application of IAS 32 to co-operative entities, the IFRIC recognised that a variety of entities operate as co-operatives and these entities have a variety of capital structures. The IFRIC decided that its proposed Interpretation should address some features that exist in a number of co-operatives. However, the IFRIC noted that its conclusions and the examples in the Interpretation are not limited to the specific characteristics of members' shares in European co-operative banks.

Basis for consensus

BC6 Paragraph 15 of IAS 32 states:

> The issuer of a financial instrument shall classify the instrument, or its component parts, on initial recognition as a financial liability, a financial asset or an equity instrument in accordance with the *substance of the contractual arrangement* and the definitions of a financial liability, a financial asset and an equity instrument. [Emphasis added]

BC7 In many jurisdictions, local law or regulations state that members' shares are equity of the entity. However, paragraph 17 of IAS 32 states:

> A critical feature in differentiating a financial liability from an equity instrument is *the existence of a contractual obligation of one party to the financial instrument (the issuer) either to deliver cash or another financial asset to the other party (the holder)* or to exchange financial assets or financial liabilities with the holder under conditions that are potentially unfavourable to the issuer. Although the holder of an equity instrument may be entitled to receive a pro rata share of any dividends or other distributions of equity, the issuer does not have a contractual obligation to make such distributions because it cannot be required to deliver cash or another financial asset to another party. [Emphasis added]

BC8 Paragraphs cited in the examples in the Appendix and in the paragraphs above show that, under IAS 32, the terms of the contractual agreement govern the classification of a financial instrument as a financial liability or equity. If the terms of an instrument create an unconditional obligation to transfer cash or another financial asset, circumstances that might restrict an entity's ability to make the transfer when due do not alter the classification as a financial liability. If the terms of the instrument give the entity an unconditional right to avoid delivering cash or another financial asset, the instrument is classified as equity. This is true even if other factors make it likely that the entity will continue to distribute dividends or make or other payments. In view of those principles, the IFRIC decided to focus on circumstances that would indicate that the entity has the unconditional right to avoid making payments to a member who has requested that his or her shares be redeemed.

BC9 The IFRIC identified two situations in which a co-operative entity has an unconditional right to avoid the transfer of cash or another financial asset. The IFRIC acknowledges that there may be other situations that may raise questions about the application of IAS 32 to members' shares. However, it understands that the two situations are often present in the contractual and other conditions surrounding members' shares and that interpretation of those two situations would eliminate many of the questions that may arise in practice.

BC10 The IFRIC also noted that an entity assesses whether it has an unconditional right to avoid the transfer of cash or another financial asset on the basis of local laws, regulations and its governing charter in effect at the date of classification. This is because it is local laws, regulations and the governing charter in effect at the classification date, together with the terms contained in the instrument's documentation that constitute the terms and conditions of the instrument at that date. Accordingly, an entity does not take into account expected future amendments to local law, regulation or its governing charter.

The right to refuse redemption (paragraph 7)

BC11 An entity may have the unconditional right to refuse redemption of a member's shares. If such a right exists, the entity does not have the obligation to transfer cash or another financial asset that IAS 32 identifies as a critical characteristic of a financial liability.

BC12 The IFRIC considered whether the entity's history of making redemptions should be considered in deciding whether the entity's right to refuse requests is, in fact, unconditional. The IFRIC observed that a history of making redemptions may create a reasonable expectation that all future requests will be honoured. However, holders of many equity instruments have a reasonable expectation that an entity will continue a past practice of making payments. For example, an entity may have made dividend payments on preference shares for decades. Failure to make those payments would expose the entity to significant economic costs, including damage to the value of its ordinary shares. Nevertheless, as outlined in IAS 32 paragraph AG26 (cited in paragraph A3), a holder's expectations about dividends do not cause a preferred share to be classified as a financial liability.

Prohibitions against redemption (paragraphs 8 and 9)

BC13 An entity may be prohibited by law or its governing charter from redeeming members' shares if doing so would cause the number of members' shares, or the amount of paid-in capital from members' shares, to fall below a specified level. While each individual share might be puttable, a portion of the total shares outstanding is not.

BC14 The IFRIC concluded that conditions limiting an entity's ability to redeem members' shares must be evaluated sequentially. Unconditional prohibitions like those noted in paragraph 8 of the consensus prevent the entity from *incurring a liability* for redemption of all or some of the members' shares, regardless of whether it would otherwise be able to satisfy that financial liability. This contrasts with conditional prohibitions that prevent payments being made only if specified conditions—such as liquidity constraints—are met. Unconditional prohibitions prevent a liability from coming into existence, whereas the conditional prohibitions may only defer the payment of a liability already incurred. Following this analysis, an unconditional prohibition affects classification when an instrument subject to the prohibition is issued or when the prohibition is enacted or added to the entity's governing charter. In contrast, conditional restrictions such as those described in paragraphs 19 and AG25 of IAS 32 do not result in equity classification.

BC15 The IFRIC discussed whether the requirements in IAS 32 can be applied to the classification of members' shares as a whole subject to a partial redemption prohibition. IAS 32 refers to 'a financial instrument', 'a financial liability' and 'an equity instrument'. It does not refer to groups or portfolios of instruments. In view of this the IFRIC considered whether it could apply the requirements in IAS 32 to the classification of members' shares subject to partial redemption prohibitions. The application of IAS 32 to a prohibition against redeeming some portion of members' shares (eg 500,000 shares of an entity with 1,000,000 shares outstanding) is unclear.

BC16 The IFRIC noted that classifying a group of members' shares using the individual instrument approach could lead to misapplication of the principle of 'substance of the contract' in IAS 32. The IFRIC also noted that paragraph 23 of IAS 32 requires an entity that has entered into an agreement to purchase its own equity instruments to recognise a financial liability for the present value of the redemption amount (eg for the present value of the forward repurchase price, option exercise price or other redemption amount) even though the shares subject to the repurchase agreement are not individually identified. Accordingly, the IFRIC decided that for purposes of classification there are instances when IAS 32 does not require the individual instrument approach.

BC17 In many situations, looking at either individual instruments or all of the instruments governed by a particular contract would result in the same classification as financial liability or equity under IAS 32. Thus, if an entity is prohibited from redeeming any of its members' shares, the shares are not puttable and are equity. On the other hand, if there is no prohibition on redemption and no other conditions apply, members' shares are puttable and the shares are financial liabilities. However, in the case of partial prohibitions against redemption, the classification of members' shares governed by the same charter will differ, depending on whether such a classification is based on individual members' shares or the group of members' shares as a whole. For example, consider an entity with a partial prohibition that prevents it from redeeming 99 per cent of the highest number of members' shares ever outstanding. The classification based on individual shares considers each share to be potentially puttable and therefore a financial liability. This is different from the classification based on all of the members' shares. While each member's share may be redeemable individually, 99 per cent of the highest number of shares ever outstanding is not redeemable in any circumstances other than liquidation of the entity and therefore is equity.

Measurement on initial recognition (paragraph 10)

BC18 The IFRIC noted that when the financial liability for the redemption of members' shares that are redeemable on demand is initially recognised, the financial liability is measured at fair value in accordance with paragraph 49 of IAS 39 *Financial Instruments: Recognition and Measurement*. Paragraph 49 states: 'The fair value of a financial liability with a demand feature (eg a demand deposit) is not less than the amount payable on demand, discounted from the first date that the amount could be required to be paid'. Accordingly, the IFRIC decided that the fair value of the financial liability for redemption of members' shares redeemable on demand is the maximum amount payable under the redemption provisions of its governing charter or applicable law. The IFRIC also considered situations in which the number of members' shares or the amount of paid-in capital subject to prohibition against redemption may change. The IFRIC concluded that a change in the level of a prohibition against redemption should lead to a transfer between financial liabilities and equity.

Subsequent measurement

BC19 Some respondents requested additional guidance on subsequent measurement of the liability for redemption of members' shares. The IFRIC noted that the focus of this Interpretation was on clarifying the classification of financial instruments rather than their subsequent measurement. Also, the IASB has on its agenda a project to address the accounting for financial instruments (including members' shares) that are redeemable at a pro rata share of the fair value of the residual interest in the entity issuing the financial instrument. The IASB will consider certain measurement issues in this project. The IFRIC was also informed that the majority of members' shares in co-operative entities are not redeemable at a pro rata share of the fair value of the residual interest in the co-operative entity thereby obviating the more complex measurement issues. In view of the above, the IFRIC decided not to provide additional guidance on measurement in the Interpretation.

Presentation

BC20 The IFRIC noted that entities whose members' shares are not equity could use the presentation formats included in paragraphs IE32 and IE33 of the Illustrative Examples with IAS 32.

Alternatives considered

BC21 The IFRIC considered suggestions that:

(a) members' shares should be classified as equity until a member has requested redemption. That member's share would then be classified as a financial liability and this treatment would be consistent with local laws. Some commentators believe this is a more straightforward approach to classification.

(b) the classification of members' shares should incorporate the probability that members will request redemption. Those who suggest this view observe that experience shows this probability to be small, usually within 1-5 per cent, for some types of co-operative. They see no basis for classifying 100 per cent of the members' shares as liabilities on the basis of the behaviour of 1 per cent.

BC22 The IFRIC did not accept those views. Under IAS 32, the classification of an instrument as financial liability or equity is based on the 'substance of the contractual arrangement and the definitions of a financial liability, a financial asset and an equity instrument.' In paragraph BC7 of the Basis for Conclusions on IAS 32, the IASB observed:

> Although the legal form of such financial instruments often includes a right to the residual interest in the assets of an entity available to holders of such instruments, the inclusion of an option for the holder to put the instrument back to the entity for cash or another financial asset means that the instrument meets the definition of a financial liability. The classification as a financial liability is independent of considerations such as when the right is exercisable, how the amount payable or receivable upon exercise of the right is determined, and whether the puttable instrument has a fixed maturity.

BC23 The IFRIC also observed that an approach similar to that in paragraph BC21(a) is advocated in the Dissenting Opinion of one Board member on IAS 32. As the IASB did not adopt that approach its adoption here would require an amendment to IAS 32.

Transition and effective date (paragraph 14)

BC24 The IFRIC considered whether its Interpretation should have the same transition and effective date as IAS 32, or whether a later effective date should apply with an exemption from IAS 32 for members' shares in the interim. Some co-operatives may wish to amend their governing charter in order to continue their existing practice under national accounting requirements of classifying members' shares as equity. Such amendments usually require a general meeting of members and holding a meeting may not be possible before the effective date of IAS 32.

BC25 After considering a number of alternatives, the IFRIC decided against any exemption from the transition requirements and effective date in IAS 32. In reaching this conclusion, the IFRIC noted that it was requested to provide guidance on the application of IAS 32 when it is first adopted by co-operative entities, ie from 1 January 2005. Also, the vast majority of those who commented on the draft Interpretation did not object to the proposed effective date of 1 January 2005. Finally, the IFRIC observed that classifying members' shares as financial liabilities before the date that the terms of these shares are amended will affect only 2005 financial statements, as first-time adopters are not required to apply IAS 32 to earlier periods. As a result, any effect of the Interpretation on first-time adopters is expected to be limited. Furthermore, the IFRIC noted that regulators are familiar with the accounting issues involved. A co-operative entity may be required to present members' shares as a liability until the governing charter is amended. The IFRIC understands that such amendments, if adopted, could be in place by mid-2005. Accordingly, the IFRIC decided that the effective date for the Interpretation would be annual periods beginning on or after 1 January 2005.

IFRIC Interpretation 3

Emission Rights

CONTENTS

IFRIC Interpretation 3 *Emission Rights* (IFRIC 3) is set out in paragraphs 1–11. IFRIC 3 is accompanied by an Illustrative Example and a Basis for Conclusions. The scope and authority of Interpretations are set out in paragraphs 1 and 8–10 of the *IFRIC Preface*.

IFRIC Interpretation 3
Emission Rights

References

- IAS 8 *Accounting Policies, Changes in Accounting Estimates and Errors*
- IAS 20 *Accounting for Government Grants and Disclosure of Government Assistance*
- IAS 36 *Impairment of Assets* (as revised in 2004)
- IAS 37 *Provisions, Contingent Liabilities and Contingent Assets*
- IAS 38 *Intangible Assets* (as revised in 2004)

Background

1 This Interpretation deals with how to account for a 'cap and trade' emission rights scheme. Such a scheme typically has the following features:

(a) An entity participating in the scheme (participant) is set a target to reduce its emissions to a specified level (the cap). The participant is issued allowances* equal in number to its cap by a government or government agency. Allowances may be issued free of charge, or participants may pay the government for them.

(b) The scheme operates for defined–often annual–compliance periods. Usually, allowances for a compliance period are issued to each participant at the beginning of a period. Actual emissions are normally verified after the end of the period in question.

(c) Participants are free to buy and sell allowances. Thus a participant has three options:

- it can limit its emissions to its cap
- it can reduce its emissions to below its cap and sell (or carry forward–see (e) below) the allowances that it does not require
- it can produce emissions in excess of its cap, in which case it must buy additional allowances for the excess emissions and/or incur a penalty (see (d) below).

A participant can also sell some or even all of its allowances in the expectation of later buying allowances equal to its actual emissions.

(d) At the end of a compliance period (and any additional 'reconciliation period', during which actual emissions are verified and participants may undertake any further trading necessary to ensure they hold enough allowances to meet actual emissions), a participant is required to deliver allowances equal to its actual emissions. If a participant does not deliver sufficient allowances, it will incur a penalty (and will typically be required to deliver the shortfall of allowances in the future). The penalty may take a variety of forms, including

* The term 'allowance' is used throughout this Interpretation. However, some schemes may describe the emission reduction instrument as a right, a certificate or a credit.

a cash payment, reductions in the allowances issued to the participant in subsequent periods, and restrictions on the participant's operations.

(e) In some schemes, unused allowances may be carried forward to be used against future emissions either within the current scheme or, in some cases, in subsequent schemes.

(f) The scheme provides for brokers or other position-taking institutions, ie entities that buy allowances from and sell allowances to participants in the scheme. The presence of such brokers may encourage an active market in allowances as defined in IAS 38.

Scope

2 This Interpretation deals with the accounting by a participant for a cap and trade scheme that is operational. It does not address the purchase of allowances by entities that are not yet subject to such a scheme but expect to be subject to such a scheme in the future. Nor does it address the accounting treatment to be adopted by those brokers or other position-taking institutions to whom allowances are not issued.

3 This Interpretation deals with the accounting for a cap and trade scheme as described above, but some of its requirements may be relevant to other schemes that are also designed to encourage reduced levels of emissions and share some of the features outlined in paragraph 1.

Issues

4 The issues dealt with in this Interpretation are:

(a) does a cap and trade scheme give rise to (i) a net asset or liability or (ii) an asset (for allowances held) and a liability, deferred income and/or income?

(b) if a separate asset is recognised, what is the nature of that asset?

(c) if a separate liability, deferred income and/or income is recognised, what is the nature of that item and how is it measured?

Consensus

5 A cap and trade scheme gives rise to:

(a) an asset for allowances held, as set out in paragraph 6;

(b) a government grant, as set out in paragraph 7; and

(c) a liability for the obligation to deliver allowances equal to emissions that have been made, as set out in paragraph 8.

It does not give rise to a net asset or liability.

6 Allowances, whether issued by government or purchased, are intangible assets that shall be accounted for in accordance with IAS 38. Allowances that are issued for less than fair value shall be measured initially at their fair value.

7 When allowances are issued for less than fair value, the difference between the amount paid and fair value is a government grant that is within the scope of

IAS 20. Initially the grant shall be recognised as deferred income in the balance sheet and subsequently recognised as income on a systematic basis over the compliance period for which the allowances were issued, regardless of whether the allowances are held or sold.

8 As emissions are made, a liability is recognised for the obligation to deliver allowances equal to emissions that have been made. This liability is a provision that is within the scope of IAS 37. It shall be measured at the best estimate of the expenditure required to settle the present obligation at the balance sheet date. This will usually be the present market price of the number of allowances required to cover emissions made up to the balance sheet date.

9 The existence or requirements of an emission rights scheme may cause a reduction in the cash flows expected to be generated by certain assets. Such a reduction is an indication that those assets may be impaired and hence requires those assets to be tested for impairment in accordance with IAS 36.

Effective date

10 An entity shall apply this Interpretation for annual periods beginning on or after 1 March 2005. Earlier adoption is encouraged. If an entity applies this Interpretation for a period beginning before 1 March 2005, it shall disclose that fact.

Transition

11 Changes in accounting policies shall be accounted for according to the transition requirements of IAS 8.

Illustrative example

This example accompanies, but is not part of, IFRIC 3.

Facts

IE1 Company A is a participant in a cap and trade scheme in which allowances are traded in an active market, as defined in IAS 38 *Intangible Assets*. The scheme operates for annual compliance periods that coincide with Company A's reporting periods. On the first day of the first period, Company A is issued, free of charge, allowances for the year to emit 12,000 tonnes of carbon dioxide. The market price of the allowances on that day is CU10* per tonne, giving a fair value of CU120,000.

IE2 Six months later (at its interim reporting date) Company A has emitted 5,500 tonnes of carbon dioxide. It expects its emissions for the whole year to be 12,000 tonnes (ie equal to the allowances issued to it). The market price for allowances has risen to CU12 per tonne.

IE3 At the year-end, Company A measures its emissions for the year at 12,500 tonnes. On the last day of the year, it buys 500 allowances to cover the emissions in excess of the allowances it holds. The market price of allowances at the year-end (and which Company A pays for the extra 500 allowances) is CU11 per tonne.

IE4 Company A does not produce emissions in the course of making inventories (or other assets). Therefore the cost of producing emissions is recognised as an expense in profit or loss.

Accounting under the cost model in IAS 38

Accounting entries

On the first day of the year

IE5 Company A makes the following accounting entry to record receiving the allowances free of charge:

Dr Allowances (an intangible asset)	CU120,000	
Cr Government grant (deferred income)		CU120,000

To recognise the allowances at their fair value (12,000 tonnes at CU10 per tonne).

* In this example, monetary amounts are denominated in currency units (CU).

At the end of the first six months

IE6 Company A makes the following accounting entries in respect of the first six months of the year:

Dr Government grant (deferred income)	CU55,000	
Cr Income		CU55,000

*To recognise as income the portion of the government grant that offsets the cost of emissions in the period.**

Dr Emissions expense	CU66,000	
Cr Liability to deliver allowances		CU66,000

To recognise the increase in the liability for emissions to date (5,500 tonnes measured at CU12 per tonne).

At the end of the year

IE7 Company A makes the following accounting entries in respect of the last six months of the year:

Dr Government grant (deferred income)	CU65,000	
Cr Income		CU65,000

To recognise as income the remaining portion of the government grant.

Dr Emissions expense	CU71,500	
Cr Liability to deliver allowances		CU71,500

To recognise the increase in the liability for emissions to date (12,500 tonnes measured at CU11 per tonne, less the CU66,000 recognised at the interim reporting date).

Dr Allowances (an intangible asset)	CU5,500	
Cr Cash		CU5,500

To recognise the purchase of an additional 500 tonnes of allowances at CU11 per tonne.

* In this example, Company A has chosen to amortise the deferred income using the proportion of actual emissions to estimated total emissions.

IE8 Company A will therefore report as follows:

Income/expense recognised in profit or loss	**First half**	**Second half**	**Full year**
	CU	CU	CU
Government grant	55,000	65,000	120,000
Emissions expense	(66,000)	(71,500)	(137,500)
	(11,000)	(6,500)	(17,500)

Balance sheet	**Date of allocation**	**Interim date**	**Year–end**
	CU	CU	CU
Assets			
Allowances	120,000	120,000	125,500
Cash	–	–	(5,500)
	120,000	120,000	120,000
Liabilities			
Liability to deliver allowances	–	66,000	137,500
Government grant	120,000	65,000	–
	120,000	131,000	137,500
Equity	–	(11,000)	(17,500)

Accounting entries on settling the obligation

IE9 Company A continues to account for the allowances at cost less impairment and to remeasure its liability to deliver allowances until it makes the following accounting entries, when it settles the liability for emissions made in the year:

Dr Liability to deliver allowances	CU137,500	
Cr Allowances		CU125,500
Cr Profit or loss		CU12,000

To recognise the settlement of the obligation.

Accounting under the revaluation model in IAS 38

IE10 In this example, the allowances are traded in an active market, as defined in IAS 38. Therefore, Company A can choose to use the revaluation model in IAS 38 to account for the allowances.

Accounting entries

On the first day of the year

IE11 Company A makes the following accounting entry to record receiving the allowances free of charge:

Dr Allowances (an intangible asset)	CU120,000	
Cr Government grant (deferred income)		CU120,000

To recognise the allowances at their fair value (12,000 tonnes at CU10 per tonne).

At the end of the first six months

IE12 Company A makes the following accounting entries in respect of the first six months of the year:

Dr Allowances (an intangible asset)	CU24,000	
Cr Equity (revaluation surplus)		CU24,000

To recognise the increase in the fair value of the allowances held (12,000 tonnes whose price has increased from CU10 to CU12 per tonne).

Dr Government grant (deferred income)	CU55,000	
Cr Income		CU55,000

To recognise as income the portion of the government grant that offsets the cost of emissions in the period.

Dr Emissions expense	CU66,000	
Cr Liability to deliver allowances		CU66,000

To recognise the increase in the liability for emissions to date (5,500 tonnes measured at CU12 per tonne).

At the end of the year

IE13 Company A makes the following accounting entries in respect of the last six months of the year:

Dr Equity (revaluation surplus)	CU12,000	
Cr Allowances (an intangible asset)		CU12,000

To recognise the decrease in the fair value of the allowances held (12,000 tonnes whose price has decreased from CU12 to CU11 per tonne).

Dr Government grant (deferred income)	CU65,000	
Cr Income		CU65,000

To recognise as income the remaining portion of the government grant.

Dr Emissions expense	CU71,500	
Cr Liability to deliver allowances		CU71,500

To recognise the increase in the liability for emissions to date (12,500 tonnes measured at CU11 per tonne, less the CU66,000 recognised at the interim reporting date).

Dr Allowances (an intangible asset)	CU5,500	
Cr Cash		CU5,500

To recognise the purchase of an additional 500 tonnes of allowances at CU11 per tonne.

IE14 Company A will therefore report as follows:

Income/expense recognised in profit or loss	First half	Second half	Full year
	CU	CU	CU
Government grant	55,000	65,000	120,000
Emissions expense	(66,000)	(71,500)	(137,500)
	(11,000)	(6,500)	(17,500)
Income/expense recognised directly in equity			
Revaluation of allowances	24,000	(12,000)	12,000

Balance sheet	Date of allocation	Interim date	Year–end
	CU	CU	CU
Assets			
Allowances	120,000	144,000	137,500
Cash	–	–	(5,500)
	120,000	144,000	132,000
Liabilities			
Liability to deliver allowances	–	66,000	137,500
Government grant	120,000	65,000	–
	120,000	131,000	137,500
Equity	–	13,000	(5,500)

Accounting entries on settling the obligation

IE15 Company A continues to remeasure the allowances and its liability to deliver allowances until it makes the following accounting entries, when it settles the liability for emissions made in the year:

Dr Liability to deliver allowances	CU137,500	
Cr Allowances		CU137,500

To recognise the settlement of the obligation.

IE16 Company A may transfer its revaluation surplus of CU12,000 directly to retained earnings in accordance with paragraph 87 of IAS 38.

Basis for Conclusions

This Basis for Conclusions accompanies, but is not part of, IFRIC 3.

Introduction

BC1 This Basis for Conclusions summarises the IFRIC's considerations in reaching its consensus. Individual IFRIC members gave greater weight to some factors than to others.

Background

BC2 The IFRIC noted that several governments have, or are developing, schemes to encourage reduced levels of emissions. In particular, schemes are being developed to encourage reductions of greenhouse gas emissions in the light of the Kyoto agreement, which comes into effect in 2008. Some such schemes are based on a cap and trade model as described in paragraph 1 of the Interpretation.

BC3 The IFRIC observed that many companies are, or will be, subject to such schemes. In particular, the IFRIC noted that a European Union scheme for greenhouse gas emissions trading will start in 2005. It also noted that there is at present no guidance on the accounting for such schemes. The IFRIC was informed that no consensus had emerged among market participants on what the accounting treatment should be. Because there is a risk of divergent practices developing, the IFRIC concluded that it should develop an Interpretation. As part of that process, the IFRIC published Draft Interpretation D1 *Emission Rights* for public comment in May 2003 and received 40 comment letters in response to its proposals.

BC4 Most respondents to D1 supported the IFRIC's proposal to develop an Interpretation. However, although agreeing that the IFRIC should add the topic to its agenda, some respondents suggested that the IFRIC should not finalise its proposals at present. Two main reasons were given:

(a) emission rights schemes are in their infancy. Therefore, the IFRIC should wait until the design of the various schemes becomes clearer so that, if necessary, the Interpretation could deal with a broader range of accounting issues.

(b) the International Accounting Standards Board has on its active agenda a project to amend IAS 20 *Accounting for Government Grants and Disclosure of Government Assistance*. Given that IAS 20 is an important reference for the Interpretation, the IFRIC should wait until it is able to interpret the revised IAS 20.

BC5 In considering these comments, the IFRIC initially decided to defer finalising its Interpretation pending (a) the Board's project to revise IAS 20 and (b) a possible amendment of IAS 38 *Intangible Assets* to require allowances to be measured at fair value with changes recognised in profit or loss (this possible amendment is discussed in paragraph BC18 below). However, it became clear that these changes could not be made before a number of schemes started. The IFRIC concluded that the need for timely guidance to prevent divergent practices developing outweighs the disadvantage that the Interpretation might be amended in the medium term. It therefore decided to finalise its Interpretation. It acknowledged that the

Interpretation might need to be amended if the Board amends IAS 20 or IAS 38, but noted that any such amendments would be made as consequential amendments by those revised Standards.

Scope and issues

BC6 The IFRIC noted that there is no universal form of scheme being developed. Rather, individual countries (or, in some cases, groups of countries) are developing schemes tailored to local circumstances. As a result, features that are present in some schemes are not present in others. The IFRIC therefore decided to address the three main accounting issues raised by a generic cap and trade scheme (as set out in paragraph 4 of the Interpretation). The IFRIC understands that such schemes have features that are common to most schemes and that, at present, those features give rise to the biggest issues in practice.

BC7 Whilst focusing on a cap and trade scheme, the IFRIC has highlighted that the requirements of the Interpretation might be relevant to other schemes designed to reduce emissions. The IFRIC noted that although other schemes may not have all of the features outlined in paragraph 1, or may have additional features, they are likely to raise some of the accounting issues addressed in the Interpretation, particularly the question of whether there is a net asset (or liability) or a separate asset and liability. The IFRIC believes that, in accordance with paragraph 11 of IAS 8 *Accounting Policies, Changes in Accounting Estimates and Errors*, an entity should take account of the Interpretation in developing and applying an appropriate accounting policy for other emission reduction schemes.

BC8 Some respondents to D1 asked the IFRIC:

(a) to explain how its requirements apply to other schemes (eg renewable energy certificates and baseline schemes); and

(b) to consider some additional questions raised by cap and trade schemes (including, for example, the accounting treatment of non-cash penalties, measurement of allowances and obligations to deliver allowances when there is no active market for allowances, and the recognition and measurement of impairment losses).

BC9 However, the IFRIC observed that the additional questions that it was being asked to consider were not the most significant issues in practice or were not specifically relevant to emission rights schemes. The IFRIC therefore confirmed its view that the Interpretation should address the three issues set out in paragraph 4. Nonetheless, the IFRIC agreed that, if necessary, it would supplement the Interpretation to deal with any further matters requiring authoritative guidance once more experience has been gained with emission rights schemes.

BC10 The IFRIC noted that some companies that are not yet subject to such a scheme but expect to be subject to such a scheme in the future are buying emission rights in the hope of being able to use them in a future scheme. Also, some companies are entering into contracts for emission 'credits', ie emission rights that are not yet verified. For example, a company may pay a cash sum to a second company to enable that second company to undertake a project to reduce emissions, which it is hoped will result in verified emission rights that would then be delivered back to the first company. The IFRIC noted that these cases raise the question whether allowances should be recognised as assets. Because the IFRIC also did not regard this question as one of the most important issues in practice at present, it decided to limit the scope of the Interpretation to participants in a scheme that is operational.

Consensus

Does a cap and trade scheme give rise to (i) a net asset or liability or (ii) an asset (for allowances held) and a liability, deferred income and/or income?

BC11 In D1 the IFRIC proposed that a cap and trade scheme gives rise to an asset (for allowances held) and a liability, deferred income and/or income. Although most respondents agreed with this proposal, some argued that a cap and trade scheme gives rise to a net position. They suggested that a participant that produces emissions to the extent of its allowances should not recognise either an asset for allowances issued free of charge, or a liability for its emissions. Instead, they proposed that the participant should recognise a liability only when it has produced emissions and holds insufficient allowances to cover them (or, recognise an asset when it holds allowances in excess of its requirements). Those respondents argued that accounting for an emission rights scheme in this way would reflect that a participant that produces emissions to the extent of its allowances is acting in accordance with the rights granted to it, whereas a participant that produces emissions in excess of its allowances is obliged to acquire additional allowances.

BC12 The IFRIC rejected these arguments and decided that its original arguments for concluding that an emission rights scheme gives rise to an asset (for allowances held) and a liability, deferred income and/or income were valid. In support of its conclusion, the IFRIC noted:

- An allowance meets the definition of an asset in the *Framework*, namely it is 'a resource controlled by the entity as a result of past events and from which future economic benefits are expected to flow to the entity.' This is evidenced by the nature of an allowance as a transferable certificate, which the participant can either sell or use to settle an obligation.

- Once emissions have occurred the participant has a liability within the definition in the *Framework*, namely it has 'a present obligation ... arising from past events, the settlement of which is expected to result in an outflow from the entity of resources embodying economic benefits.' The obligation is to deliver allowances.

- The allowance and the obligation exist independently. Although a participant may *intend* to use the allowances it holds to settle its obligation, it cannot be compelled to do so. Instead it may choose to sell allowances and either reduce emissions or buy allowances at a future date. Thus, there is no contractual link between the asset and the liability, even though many participants will hold the allowances solely for the purpose of settling their obligations.

- Under some schemes, participants need to hold an emissions permit in order to produce emissions. This confirms that an allowance itself does not confer a right to emit. Rather it is the instrument that must be delivered in order to settle the obligation that arises from emissions.

- In some cases, a participant may be able to choose which of a number of different allowances (issued under different schemes) it uses to settle its obligation. This feature is likely to become more common as schemes are developed in various countries, with the ability to use allowances issued under one scheme to settle obligations arising in another.
- A cap and trade scheme does not merely represent a 'tax' on emissions in excess of the cap. An important feature of a cap and trade scheme is the ability it gives participants to trade allowances. Accordingly, some participants will purchase allowances from other participants for cash and recognise these purchased allowances as assets. However, purchased allowances are indistinguishable from those issued by government, which confirms that allowances issued by government are assets in their own right.
- There is no right of offset between the allowances and the obligation to deliver allowances, nor is there a debtor/creditor relationship. It is therefore inappropriate to offset the asset and liability.

What is the nature of the asset for allowances held by participants?

Is the asset within the scope of IAS 38 or IAS 39?

BC13 The IFRIC concluded that allowances held by participants are intangible assets within the scope of IAS 38, because they meet the definition of an intangible asset in paragraph 8 of IAS 38: 'an identifiable non-monetary asset without physical substance.'

BC14 Some respondents disagreed with this conclusion and suggested that allowances should be accounted for as financial assets under IAS 39 *Financial Instruments: Recognition and Measurement*. Some also proposed that the allowance should then be treated as the hedging instrument of a forecast transaction (ie future emissions). However, the IFRIC noted that:

- Allowances do not meet the definition of a financial asset in IAS 32 *Financial Instruments: Disclosure and Presentation*, since they are neither equity instruments nor contractual rights to receive cash or other financial assets.
- Allowances do not fall within the scope extension in IAS 39 for contracts to buy or sell a non-financial item, since they are not a contract to buy or sell a non-financial item.
- Allowances are not a derivative because they do not have 'no initial net investment or an initial net investment that is smaller than would be required for other types of contracts that would be expected to have a similar response to changes in market factors' and are not 'settled at a future date'. Therefore, they cannot be designated as a hedging instrument. (The fact that the allowances may be instruments obtained by the entity free of charge does not mean that they have 'no initial net investment'.)
- Being readily tradeable does not make allowances financial assets any more than, say, a readily tradeable commodity.

BC15 The IFRIC therefore concluded that it could not *interpret* allowances as falling within the scope of IAS 39. It also concluded that it would be inappropriate to ask the Board to amend the scope of IAS 38 and IAS 39 to bring allowances within the scope of IAS 39.

BC16 Nonetheless, the IFRIC acknowledged that allowances have some features that are more commonly found in financial assets than in intangible assets. In particular, many are traded in a ready market and are a mechanism for 'pricing' a particular product (eg a tonne of carbon dioxide). Some respondents to D1 therefore suggested that allowances would be best measured at fair value with changes in value recognised in profit or loss. Those respondents were particularly troubled about the mismatch that would arise in profit or loss if allowances were accounted using the cost model in IAS 38, because IAS 37 requires the liability for the obligation to deliver allowances to be measured at a current value. Furthermore, they noted that even if allowances were measured at fair value using the revaluation model in IAS 38, there would be a mismatch in the recognition of changes in the assets and liabilities. This is because changes in the value of the allowances above cost would be recognised in equity, whereas changes in the liability are recognised in profit or loss.

BC17 When the IFRIC developed D1, it noted that the Board was considering removing the present distinction between changes in value recognised in equity and those recognised in profit or loss as part of its project on reporting financial performance. For a participant using the revaluation model in IAS 38, this would have alleviated some of the mismatch referred to above. However, during its redeliberations the IFRIC noted that the Board had revised the timetable for the project on reporting financial performance, and thus that the distinction of recognising some changes in value in profit or loss and others in equity is likely to remain for some time.

BC18 In the light of this, the IFRIC considered whether it should ask the Board to amend IAS 38 so that *all* changes in the value of an allowance measured at fair value would be recognised in profit or loss. The IFRIC noted that the Board would be unlikely for two reasons to reconsider the recognition of changes in value of all intangible assets under the revaluation model in IAS 38: this treatment is the same as IAS 16 *Property, Plant and Equipment* and the Board has a research project on intangible assets. Therefore, to justify an amendment to IAS 38 the IFRIC reasoned that it would need to distinguish allowances from other intangible assets that qualify to be measured subsequently at fair value. The IFRIC noted that it might be possible to identify a subclass of currency-like intangible assets (to include allowances), ie intangible assets that have value only because they are used to settle obligations. However, the IFRIC concluded that it would not be possible to formulate, expose and finalise an amendment to IAS 38 in time for 2005.

Should allowances be amortised?

BC19 Having concluded that allowances fall into the scope of IAS 38, the IFRIC proposed in D1 that allowances should not be amortised but should be tested for impairment in accordance with IAS 36 *Impairment of Assets.*

BC20 Many respondents to D1 disagreed with the conclusion that allowances should not be amortised. Some respondents suggested that the allowance represents a right to produce emissions and therefore that a participant should amortise its allowances as it produces emissions to reflect the consumption of that right. Other respondents broadly agreed with the IFRIC's proposal but noted that the IFRIC's basis for non-amortisation, which was that the residual value of an allowance would be the same as its cost (or revalued amount), would apply only if the allowances were traded in an active market. This is because paragraph 100 of IAS 38 states that the residual value should be assumed to be zero unless there is a commitment by a third party to purchase the asset at the end of its useful life or an active market for the asset.

BC21 As noted in paragraph BC12, the IFRIC concluded that an allowance is not a right to produce emissions and it has confirmed this view with scheme administrators. The allowance is the instrument that a participant surrenders to settle its obligation that arises from its emissions. It therefore follows that a participant in a cap and trade scheme does not consume the economic benefits of an allowance as a result of its emissions. Rather, a participant realises the benefits of that allowance by surrendering it to settle the obligation that arises from producing emissions (or by selling it to another entity). Therefore, the IFRIC observed that amortisation, which is the systematic allocation of the cost of an asset to reflect the consumption of the economic benefits of that asset over its useful life, is incompatible with the way the benefits of the allowances are realised. Although the IFRIC agreed that this observation pointed to precluding amortisation, it agreed with those respondents who highlighted that in some cases such a requirement could be inconsistent with the requirements of IAS 38. The IFRIC therefore decided not to proceed with its proposal in D1 that allowances should not be amortised. Nonetheless, for most allowances traded in an active market, no amortisation will be required, because the residual value will be the same as cost and hence the depreciable amount will be zero.

What is the nature of the separate liability, government grant and/or income that is recognised and how is it measured?

When is a liability recognised?

BC22 The IFRIC discussed when a liability arises for the obligation to deliver allowances equal to actual emissions. The IFRIC concluded that a liability for this obligation arises only as emissions are made. This follows from IAS 37 *Provisions, Contingent Liabilities and Contingent Assets*, which states that there is no liability until an 'obligating event' occurs. In an emission rights scheme, the obligating event—ie the event that obliges the entity to deliver allowances—is the production of emissions (not the receipt of allowances). At the start of the compliance period when allowances are issued this has not yet happened, and hence there is no liability for the obligation to deliver allowances. This view is supported by paragraph 19 of IAS 37, which states: 'It is only those obligations arising from past events existing independently of an entity's future actions (ie the future conduct of its business) that are recognised as provisions.' The IFRIC noted that the obligation to deliver allowances depends entirely on the participant's future actions, ie whether it produces emissions.

BC23 The IFRIC therefore concluded that once emissions are made, a liability will arise that should be accounted for in accordance with IAS 37. Those respondents to D1 who argued that allowances represent a right to produce emissions (ie those who proposed a net model–see paragraph BC11–or those who proposed that allowances should be amortised as the entity produces emissions–see paragraph BC20) disagreed with this conclusion. They argued that a liability arises only when a participant holds insufficient allowances to cover its emissions (ie it has produced emissions outside its allowed right) and is therefore obliged to acquire additional allowances. However, as noted in paragraph BC21, the IFRIC observed that an allowance is not a right to produce emissions. Rather, it is the instrument that is surrendered to government in order to settle the obligation that arises from emissions. This obligation is incurred regardless of whether the participant holds allowances. The fact that a participant may hold assets to meet its obligation for emissions does not relieve the participant of that obligation.

How should the liability be measured?

BC24 The Interpretation specifies that the obligation to deliver allowances for past emissions will normally be measured at the present market price of the number of allowances required to cover emissions made at the balance sheet date. The IFRIC's view is that this follows from paragraph 36 of IAS 37, which requires a provision to be measured at 'the best estimate of the expenditure required to settle the present obligation at the balance sheet date.' This is described as the amount that an entity would rationally pay to settle the obligation or to transfer it to a third party.

BC25 Some respondents to D1 disagreed with this interpretation of IAS 37. They argued that the 'best estimate' could be interpreted to refer to the cost of the allowances held by the participant rather than their current market price. However, the IFRIC noted that the cost of allowances (or their initial fair value, if issued for less than fair value) is not the amount that the participant would rationally pay to settle its obligation. Rather, the amount required to settle an obligation at the balance sheet date would reflect current values. The IFRIC also noted that liabilities are measured independently of how those liabilities will be funded.

Government grant

BC26 Having concluded that there is no liability to deliver allowances at the start of the compliance period when allowances are issued, the IFRIC then considered if there is an element of government grant. The IFRIC concluded that the issue of allowances for less than their fair value (eg free of charge) gives rise to a government grant. Such an award comes within the definition of a government grant in IAS 20: 'assistance by government in the form of transfers of resources to an entity in return for past or future compliance with certain conditions relating to the operating activities of the entity.' In particular, the IFRIC noted that the obligation imposed by an emission rights scheme to reduce emissions or deliver allowances is a condition 'relating to the operating activities of the entity.' It also noted that an award of allowances for less than their fair value comes within paragraph 23 of IAS 20: 'A government grant may take the form of a transfer of a non-monetary asset, such as land or other resources, for the use of the entity.'

BC27 The IFRIC decided that when allowances are issued for less than fair value, they should be recognised initially at their fair value. The IFRIC acknowledged that IAS 20 would permit allowances issued for less than fair value to be recognised at the amount paid for them. However, the IFRIC observed that if this treatment were adopted, participants would not recognise allowances issued free of charge on their balance sheet but they would recognise purchased allowances. The IFRIC concluded that this treatment would not be a faithful representation of the resources controlled by the participant, because purchased allowances are indistinguishable from those issued free of charge.

BC28 Whilst not necessarily disagreeing with the IFRIC's conclusion, some respondents to D1 argued that, in precluding participants from recognising allowances issued for less than fair value at the amount paid for them, the IFRIC was eliminating a choice of accounting treatment from IAS 20. Consequently, in their view, IFRIC was amending a Standard. In its redeliberations, the IFRIC noted that the treatment it was requiring did not conflict with IAS 20. Given this, and because the IFRIC believes that initially recognising allowances at an amount other than their fair value would be inappropriate, the IFRIC reaffirmed its decision to measure the grant and allowances initially at fair value.

BC29 The IFRIC also discussed what method should be used to recognise the grant as income and where in the balance sheet (ie as a deferred credit or as a reduction in the carrying amount of an asset) the grant should be presented if not recognised as income on initial recognition. It noted that paragraph 12 of IAS 20 requires grants to be recognised in income 'over the periods necessary to match them with the related costs which they are intended to compensate, on a systematic basis.' The question therefore is: what are the costs that an award of allowances for less than fair value is intended to compensate for?

BC30 The IFRIC noted that the grant is intended to compensate for higher operating costs in the compliance period. Accordingly, the IFRIC agreed that the grant should initially be recognised as deferred income in the balance sheet. Subsequently the requirement in paragraph 12 of IAS 20 is met by amortising the deferred income on a systematic basis over the compliance period for which the allowances were allocated. The IFRIC observed that any relationship between the allowances and a compliance period other than the one for which they were allocated would be tenuous. The IFRIC also observed that the appropriate amortisation method will depend on how the participant chooses to respond to the emission rights scheme, and accordingly decided that it should not specify a particular method.

BC31 A few respondents to D1 asked the IFRIC to clarify the accounting treatment for the outstanding deferred credit if a participant sold its allowances. These respondents suggested that the outstanding deferred credit should be recognised in income to reflect the realisation of the grant. However, the IFRIC's view is that the grant has been awarded to compensate for the higher operating costs incurred as a result of being subject to a cap and trade scheme. The IFRIC therefore concluded that the deferred credit should not be derecognised when the allowances are sold and should continue to be amortised.

BC32 As discussed in paragraph BC16, many respondents were concerned about the mixed measurement model of the Interpretation. Whilst some noted that this could be dealt with by measuring allowances at fair value, with changes in value recognised in profit or loss, others noted that the effects of the mixed measurement model in profit or loss could be fully addressed only by subsequently remeasuring the deferred credit to take account of changes in the market value of the allowances. However, the IFRIC concluded that since a deferred credit is not a liability under the *Framework*, it would be inappropriate for it to be remeasured.

Penalties

BC33 In D1, the IFRIC proposed that a (cash) penalty, which would be incurred if a participant fails to deliver sufficient allowances to cover its actual emissions, should be taken into account in measuring the provision for the obligation to deliver allowances. In other words, the IFRIC suggested that the obligation to deliver allowances could, in some circumstances, be settled by paying a cash penalty. Some respondents to D1 noted that it would be unusual for a cap and trade scheme to allow a participant to satisfy its environmental obligation with a cash payment. For example, in the EU emissions trading scheme, the penalty does not relieve the participant from its obligation to deliver allowances: the participant pays a penalty *and* delivers allowances the following year. The IFRIC therefore concluded that the penalty should be treated separately from the obligation to deliver allowances. It noted that the penalty would be within the scope of IAS 37 but decided there was no need to provide specific guidance on this point.

Impairment

BC34 The IFRIC noted that the existence of an emission rights scheme might cause certain assets to become impaired, since it might have the effect of reducing the future cash flows expected to arise from an asset (eg a power station) and hence reduce that asset's value in use. As noted in paragraph BC9 the IFRIC concluded that it should not provide guidance on recognition and measurement of impairment losses. Apart from noting that this issue was not specific to emission rights schemes, the IFRIC doubted whether it could add much to the present requirements in IAS 36. However, the IFRIC agreed it would be useful to include a reminder in the Interpretation that an emission rights scheme falls within the indication in paragraph 12(b) of IAS 36 that an asset may be impaired.

Disclosure

BC35 Some respondents to D1 noted that the IFRIC did not propose any disclosure requirements. In its redeliberations, the IFRIC noted that in accordance with IAS 1 *Presentation of Financial Statements*, a participant would be required to disclose the accounting policy followed for a significant cap and trade scheme. In addition, IASs 20, 37 and 38 specify disclosure of details of, respectively, the government grant, liability and asset. The IFRIC has not specified these disclosures in the Interpretation because it believes that, in general, an Interpretation should not reiterate requirements of Standards.

BC36 The IFRIC considered whether any disclosures beyond those required by existing Standards were required by users of the financial statements to allow them to evaluate the effects on a participant of a cap and trade scheme. The IFRIC noted that schemes are evolving and that it might be premature to mandate specific disclosure requirements. The IFRIC also noted that a participant was unlikely to be able to explain its accounting policy without providing some details of the scheme. Therefore, the IFRIC concluded that it would not require additional disclosure.

Effective date and transition

BC37 The IFRIC noted that emission rights schemes are still developing–most have been implemented only in recent years or are still being developed. Accordingly, it is likely that few participants will have been subject to material emission rights schemes for many years. For this reason the IFRIC decided that no special transitional provisions are required and that the effective date of the Interpretation should be 1 March 2005. The IFRIC decided for similar reasons that no special transitional provisions are required for those adopting IFRSs for the first time.

IFRIC Interpretation 4

Determining whether an Arrangement contains a Lease

CONTENTS

IFRIC Interpretation 4 *Determining whether an Arrangement contains a Lease* (IFRIC 4) is set out in paragraphs 1–17 and the Appendix. IFRIC 4 is accompanied by Illustrative Examples and a Basis for Conclusions. The scope and authority of Interpretations are set out in paragraphs 1 and 8–10 of the *IFRIC Preface*.

IFRIC Interpretation 4
Determining whether an Arrangement contains a Lease

References

- IAS 8 *Accounting Policies, Changes in Accounting Estimates and Errors*
- IAS 16 *Property, Plant and Equipment* (as revised in 2003)
- IAS 17 *Leases* (as revised in 2003)
- IAS 38 *Intangible Assets* (as revised in 2004)

Background

1 An entity may enter into an arrangement, comprising a transaction or a series of related transactions, that does not take the legal form of a lease but conveys a right to use an asset (eg an item of property, plant or equipment) in return for a payment or series of payments. Examples of arrangements in which one entity (the supplier) may convey such a right to use an asset to another entity (the purchaser), often together with related services, include:

- outsourcing arrangements (eg the outsourcing of the data processing functions of an entity).
- arrangements in the telecommunications industry, in which suppliers of network capacity enter into contracts to provide purchasers with rights to capacity.
- take-or-pay and similar contracts, in which purchasers must make specified payments regardless of whether they take delivery of the contracted products or services (eg a take-or-pay contract to acquire substantially all of the output of a supplier's power generator).

2 This Interpretation provides guidance for determining whether such arrangements are, or contain, leases that should be accounted for in accordance with IAS 17. It does not provide guidance for determining how such a lease should be classified under that Standard.

3 In some arrangements, the underlying asset that is the subject of the lease is a portion of a larger asset. This Interpretation does not address how to determine when a portion of a larger asset is itself the underlying asset for the purposes of applying IAS 17. Nevertheless, arrangements in which the underlying asset would represent a unit of account in either IAS 16 or IAS 38 are within the scope of this Interpretation.

Scope

4 This Interpretation does not apply to arrangements that are, or contain, leases excluded from the scope of IAS 17.

Issues

5 The issues addressed in this Interpretation are:

(a) how to determine whether an arrangement is, or contains, a lease as defined in IAS 17;

(b) when the assessment or a reassessment of whether an arrangement is, or contains, a lease should be made; and

(c) if an arrangement is, or contains, a lease, how the payments for the lease should be separated from payments for any other elements in the arrangement.

Consensus

Determining whether an arrangement is, or contains, a lease

6 Determining whether an arrangement is, or contains, a lease shall be based on the substance of the arrangement and requires an assessment of whether:

(a) fulfilment of the arrangement is dependent on the use of a specific asset or assets (the asset); and

(b) the arrangement conveys a right to use the asset.

Fulfilment of the arrangement is dependent on the use of a specific asset

7 Although a specific asset may be explicitly identified in an arrangement, it is not the subject of a lease if fulfilment of the arrangement is not dependent on the use of the specified asset. For example, if the supplier is obliged to deliver a specified quantity of goods or services and has the right and ability to provide those goods or services using other assets not specified in the arrangement, then fulfilment of the arrangement is not dependent on the specified asset and the arrangement does not contain a lease. A warranty obligation that permits or requires the substitution of the same or similar assets when the specified asset is not operating properly does not preclude lease treatment. In addition, a contractual provision (contingent or otherwise) permitting or requiring the supplier to substitute other assets for any reason on or after a specified date does not preclude lease treatment before the date of substitution.

8 An asset has been implicitly specified if, for example, the supplier owns or leases only one asset with which to fulfil the obligation and it is not economically feasible or practicable for the supplier to perform its obligation through the use of alternative assets.

Arrangement conveys a right to use the asset

9 An arrangement conveys the right to use the asset if the arrangement conveys to the purchaser (lessee) the right to control the use of the underlying asset. The right to control the use of the underlying asset is conveyed if any one of the following conditions is met:

(a) The purchaser has the ability or right to operate the asset or direct others to operate the asset in a manner it determines while obtaining or controlling more than an insignificant amount of the output or other utility of the asset.

(b) The purchaser has the ability or right to control physical access to the underlying asset while obtaining or controlling more than an insignificant amount of the output or other utility of the asset.

(c) Facts and circumstances indicate that it is remote that one or more parties other than the purchaser will take more than an insignificant amount of the output or other utility that will be produced or generated by the asset during the term of the arrangement, and the price that the purchaser will pay for the output is neither contractually fixed per unit of output nor equal to the current market price per unit of output as of the time of delivery of the output.

Assessing or reassessing whether an arrangement is, or contains, a lease

10 The assessment of whether an arrangement contains a lease shall be made at the inception of the arrangement, being the earlier of the date of the arrangement and the date of commitment by the parties to the principal terms of the arrangement, on the basis of all of the facts and circumstances. A reassessment of whether the arrangement contains a lease after the inception of the arrangement shall be made only if any one of the following conditions is met:

(a) There is a change in the contractual terms, unless the change only renews or extends the arrangement.

(b) A renewal option is exercised or an extension is agreed to by the parties to the arrangement, unless the term of the renewal or extension had initially been included in the lease term in accordance with paragraph 4 of IAS 17. A renewal or extension of the arrangement that does not include modification of any of the terms in the original arrangement before the end of the term of the original arrangement shall be evaluated under paragraphs 6–9 only with respect to the renewal or extension period.

(c) There is a change in the determination of whether fulfilment is dependent on a specified asset.

(d) There is a substantial change to the asset, for example a substantial physical change to property, plant or equipment.

11 A reassessment of an arrangement shall be based on the facts and circumstances as of the date of reassessment, including the remaining term of the arrangement. Changes in estimate (for example, the estimated amount of output to be delivered to the purchaser or other potential purchasers) would not trigger a reassessment. If an arrangement is reassessed and is determined to contain a lease (or not to contain a lease), lease accounting shall be applied (or cease to apply) from:

(a) in the case of (a), (c) or (d) in paragraph 10, when the change in circumstances giving rise to the reassessment occurs;

(b) in the case of (b) in paragraph 10, the inception of the renewal or extension period.

Separating payments for the lease from other payments

12 If an arrangement contains a lease, the parties to the arrangement shall apply the requirements of IAS 17 to the lease element of the arrangement, unless exempted from those requirements in accordance with paragraph 2 of IAS 17. Accordingly, if an arrangement contains a lease, that lease shall be classified as a finance lease or an operating lease in accordance with paragraphs 7–19 of IAS 17. Other elements of the arrangement not within the scope of IAS 17 shall be accounted for in accordance with other Standards.

13 For the purpose of applying the requirements of IAS 17, payments and other consideration required by the arrangement shall be separated at the inception of the arrangement or upon a reassessment of the arrangement into those for the lease and those for other elements on the basis of their relative fair values. The minimum lease payments as defined in paragraph 4 of IAS 17 include only payments for the lease (ie the right to use the asset) and exclude payments for other elements in the arrangement (eg for services and the cost of inputs).

14 In some cases, separating the payments for the lease from payments for other elements in the arrangement will require the purchaser to use an estimation technique. For example, a purchaser may estimate the lease payments by reference to a lease agreement for a comparable asset that contains no other elements, or by estimating the payments for the other elements in the arrangement by reference to comparable agreements and then deducting these payments from the total payments under the arrangement.

15 If a purchaser concludes that it is impracticable to separate the payments reliably, it shall:

(a) in the case of a finance lease, recognise an asset and a liability at an amount equal to the fair value of the underlying asset that was identified in paragraphs 7 and 8 as the subject of the lease. Subsequently the liability shall be reduced as payments are made and an imputed finance charge on the liability recognised using the purchaser's incremental borrowing rate of interest.[*]

(b) in the case of an operating lease, treat all payments under the arrangement as lease payments for the purposes of complying with the disclosure requirements of IAS 17, but

(i) disclose those payments separately from minimum lease payments of other arrangements that do not include payments for non-lease elements, and

(ii) state that the disclosed payments also include payments for non-lease elements in the arrangement.

* ie the lessee's incremental borrowing rate of interest as defined in paragraph 4 of IAS 17.

Effective date

16 An entity shall apply this Interpretation for annual periods beginning on or after 1 January 2006. Earlier application is encouraged. If an entity applies this Interpretation for a period beginning before 1 January 2006, it shall disclose that fact.

Transition

17 IAS 8 specifies how an entity applies a change in accounting policy resulting from the initial application of an Interpretation. An entity is not required to comply with those requirements when first applying this Interpretation. If an entity uses this exemption, it shall apply paragraphs 6–9 of the Interpretation to arrangements existing at the start of the earliest period for which comparative information under IFRSs is presented on the basis of facts and circumstances existing at the start of that period.

Appendix
Amendments to IFRS 1 *First–time Adoption of International Financial Reporting Standards*

The amendments in this appendix shall be applied for annual periods beginning on or after 1 September 2004. If an entity applies this Interpretation for an earlier period, these amendments shall be applied for that earlier period.

* * * * *

The amendments contained in this appendix when this Interpretation was issued in 2004 have been incorporated into IFRS 1 as issued on and after 2 December 2004.

Illustrative Examples

These examples accompany, but are not part of, IFRIC 4.

Example of an arrangement that contains a lease

Facts

IE1 A production company (the purchaser) enters into an arrangement with a third party (the supplier) to supply a minimum quantity of gas needed in its production process for a specified period of time. The supplier designs and builds a facility adjacent to the purchaser's plant to produce the needed gas and maintains ownership and control over all significant aspects of operating the facility. The agreement provides for the following:

- The facility is explicitly identified in the arrangement, and the supplier has the contractual right to supply gas from other sources. However, supplying gas from other sources is not economically feasible or practicable.
- The supplier has the right to provide gas to other customers and to remove and replace the facility's equipment and modify or expand the facility to enable the supplier to do so. However, at inception of the arrangement, the supplier has no plans to modify or expand the facility. The facility is designed to meet only the purchaser's needs.
- The supplier is responsible for repairs, maintenance, and capital expenditures.
- The supplier must stand ready to deliver a minimum quantity of gas each month.
- Each month, the purchaser will pay a fixed capacity charge and a variable charge based on actual production taken. The purchaser must pay the fixed capacity charge irrespective of whether it takes any of the facility's production. The variable charge includes the facility's actual energy costs, which amount to about 90 per cent of the facility's total variable costs. The supplier is subject to increased costs resulting from the facility's inefficient operations.
- If the facility does not produce the stated minimum quantity, the supplier must return all or a portion of the fixed capacity charge.

Assessment

IE2 The arrangement contains a lease within the scope of IAS 17 *Leases*. An asset (the facility) is explicitly identified in the arrangement and fulfilment of the arrangement is dependent on the facility. Although the supplier has the right to supply gas from other sources, its ability to do so is not substantive. The purchaser has obtained the right to use the facility because, on the facts presented–in particular, that the facility is designed to meet only the purchaser's needs and the supplier has no plans to expand or modify the facility–it is remote that one or more parties other than the purchaser will take more than an insignificant amount of the facility's output and the price the purchaser will pay is neither contractually fixed per unit of output nor equal to the current market price per unit of output as of the time of delivery of the output.

Example of an arrangement that does not contain a lease

Facts

IE3 A manufacturing company (the purchaser) enters into an arrangement with a third party (the supplier) to supply a specific component part of its manufactured product for a specified period of time. The supplier designs and constructs a plant adjacent to the purchaser's factory to produce the component part. The designed capacity of the plant exceeds the purchaser's current needs, and the supplier maintains ownership and control over all significant aspects of operating the plant. The arrangement provides for the following:

- The supplier's plant is explicitly identified in the arrangement, but the supplier has the right to fulfil the arrangement by shipping the component parts from another plant owned by the supplier. However, to do so for any extended period of time would be uneconomic.
- The supplier is responsible for repairs, maintenance, and capital expenditures of the plant.
- The supplier must stand ready to deliver a minimum quantity. The purchaser is required to pay a fixed price per unit for the actual quantity taken. Even if the purchaser's needs are such that they do not need the stated minimum quantity, they still pay only for the actual quantity taken.
- The supplier has the right to sell the component parts to other customers and has a history of doing so (by selling in the replacement parts market), so it is expected that parties other than the purchaser will take more than an insignificant amount of the component parts produced at the supplier's plant.

Assessment

IE4 The arrangement does not contain a lease within the scope of IAS 17. An asset (the plant) is explicitly identified in the arrangement and fulfilment of the arrangement is dependent on the facility. Although the supplier has the right to supply component parts from other sources, the supplier would not have the ability to do so because it would be uneconomic. However, the purchaser has not obtained the right to use the plant because the purchaser does not have the ability or right to operate or direct others to operate the plant or control physical access to the plant, and the likelihood that parties other than the purchaser will take more than an insignificant amount of the component parts produced at the plant is more than remote, on the basis of the facts presented. In addition, the price that the purchaser pays is fixed per unit of output taken.

Basis for Conclusions

This Basis for Conclusions accompanies, but is not part of, IFRIC 4.

Introduction

BC1 This Basis for Conclusions summarises the IFRIC's considerations in reaching its consensus. Individual IFRIC members gave greater weight to some factors than to others.

Background (paragraphs 1–3)

BC2 The IFRIC noted that arrangements have developed in recent years that do not take the legal form of a lease but convey rights to use items for agreed periods of time in return for a payment or series of payments. Examples of such arrangements are set out in paragraph 1 of the Interpretation. The IFRIC observed that these arrangements share many features of a lease because a lease is defined in paragraph 4 of IAS 17 *Leases* as 'an agreement whereby the lessor conveys to the lessee in return for a payment or series of payments *the right to use an asset* for an agreed period of time' (emphasis added). The IFRIC noted that all arrangements meeting the definition of a lease should be accounted for in accordance with IAS 17 (subject to the scope of that Standard) regardless of whether they take the legal form of a lease. In other words, just as the Standing Interpretations Committee concluded in SIC-27 *Evaluating the Substance of Transactions Involving the Legal Form of a Lease* that an arrangement that is described as a lease is not necessarily accounted for as a lease, the IFRIC concluded that an arrangement can be within the scope of IAS 17 even if it is not described as a lease. The IFRIC therefore decided that it should issue guidance to assist in determining whether an arrangement is, or contains, a lease.

BC3 The IFRIC published Draft Interpretation D3 *Determining whether an Arrangement contains a Lease* for public comment in January 2004 and received 51 comment letters in response to its proposals. In addition, in order to understand better the practical issues that would have arisen on implementing the proposed Interpretation, IASB staff met a number of preparer constituents.

BC4 There was broad support for the IFRIC issuing an Interpretation on this topic (even among those respondents who disagreed with the criteria in D3 for determining whether a lease exists). However, some respondents to D3 questioned whether the proposals were a legitimate *interpretation* of IAS 17. In particular, some suggested that the proposals anticipated the Board's current research project on leasing.

BC5 In considering these comments, the IFRIC concluded that they primarily arose from its observation in the Basis for Conclusions on D3 that 'the lease asset under IAS 17 is the right to use [and] that this asset should not be confused with the underlying item [in the arrangement]' (eg an item of property, plant or equipment). As a result, the IFRIC understood that some respondents were concerned that D3 was requiring (or permitting) purchasers (lessees) to recognise an intangible asset for the right of use, even for leases classified as operating leases.

BC6 During redeliberation, the IFRIC affirmed its view that conceptually IAS 17 regards the asset as the right of use (although it acknowledged that in a finance lease, a lessee recognises an asset and accounts for that asset as if it were within the scope of IAS 16 *Property, Plant and Equipment* or IAS 38 *Intangible Assets*). However, the IFRIC decided to emphasise that the objective of the Interpretation is only to identify whether an arrangement contains a lease, not to change the requirements of IAS 17. Accordingly, having identified a lease, an entity accounts for that lease in accordance with IAS 17. This includes following the requirements of paragraphs 7–19 of IAS 17 to determine whether the lease should be classified as an operating lease or as a finance lease. This means, for example, that if a purchaser satisfies the criteria in the Interpretation, it (a) recognises an asset only if substantially all the risks and rewards incidental to ownership are transferred and (b) treats the recognised asset as a leased item, rather than an intangible asset for the right to use that item.

BC7 The IFRIC reconsidered its use of the term 'item' in D3 (as in right to use an item). The IFRIC noted that it had used 'item' rather than 'asset' to refer to the underlying asset in the arrangement (eg an item of property, plant or equipment) in order to emphasise that the asset that is the subject of the Interpretation is the right of use and not the underlying item or asset. However, given that many found the use of the term confusing, the IFRIC decided in finalising the Interpretation to revert to the phrase in IAS 17 'right to use an asset'.

Multiple-element arrangements

BC8 The IFRIC observed that many of the arrangements that fall within the scope of the Interpretation are likely to involve services as well as a right to use an asset. In other words, the arrangement is what is sometimes referred to as a multiple-element arrangement. The IFRIC concluded that IAS 17 allows for separate recognition of a lease that is embedded or contained within a multiple-element arrangement because IAS 17 states (paragraph 3) that it applies to 'agreements that transfer the right to use assets even though substantial services by the lessor may be called for in connection with the operation or maintenance of such assets.' In addition, the definition of minimum lease payments in paragraph 4 of IAS 17 clarifies that such payments exclude costs for services. The Interpretation therefore addresses whether a multiple-element arrangement contains a lease and not just whether an *entire* arrangement is a lease.

Portions of an asset (paragraph 3)

BC9 The Interpretation (like D3) does not address what constitutes the underlying asset in the arrangement. In other words, it does not address when a portion of a larger asset can be the subject of a lease.

BC10 Some respondents to D3 suggested that this omission pointed to a flaw in the proposals. They were troubled by the potential inconsistency between the accounting for a take-or-pay arrangement for substantially all of the output from a specific asset (which could have contained a lease) and one for a smaller portion of the output (which would not have been required to be treated as containing a lease). Other respondents argued that D3 would have allowed undue flexibility and that the IFRIC should either explicitly rule out portions or provide additional guidance to clarify which portions should be recognised (for example, those that are physically distinguishable).

BC11 From an early stage in this project, the IFRIC decided that it should not address the issue of portions and should focus on the main question, ie what constitutes a lease. The IFRIC noted that the subject of portions was important in itself and had much wider applicability than the Interpretation. The IFRIC affirmed this view during its redeliberations and therefore rejected the suggestion that it also should address portions in the Interpretation. The IFRIC also concluded that it would be inappropriate to specify that the Interpretation should not be applied to an arrangement that contains a right to use a portion of an asset (whether that portion be a physically distinguishable portion of an asset, or defined by reference to the output of the asset or the time the asset is made available) because this would conflict with IAS 17. The IFRIC agreed that the phrase 'right to use an asset' does not preclude the asset being a portion of a larger asset.

BC12 However, in the light of comments from respondents, the IFRIC decided to clarify that the Interpretation should be applied to arrangements in which the underlying asset would represent the unit of account in either IAS 16 or IAS 38.

Scope (paragraph 4)

BC13 The objective of the Interpretation is to determine whether an arrangement contains a lease that falls within the scope of IAS 17. The lease is then accounted for in accordance with that Standard. Because the Interpretation should not be read as overriding any of the requirements of IAS 17, the IFRIC decided that it should clarify that if an arrangement is found to be, or contains, a lease or licensing agreement that is excluded from the scope of IAS 17, an entity need not apply IAS 17 to that lease or licensing agreement.

BC14 The IFRIC considered whether the scope of the Interpretation might overlap with IAS 39 *Financial Instruments: Recognition and Measurement*. In particular it noted the view that an arrangement for output might meet the definition of a derivative under IAS 39 but also be determined to contain a lease under this Interpretation. The IFRIC concluded that there should not be an overlap because an arrangement for output that is a derivative would not meet the criteria in paragraphs 6–9 of the Interpretation. In particular, the IFRIC noted that such an arrangement would be for a product with a quoted market price available in an active market and would therefore be unlikely to depend upon the use of a specifically identified asset.

Consensus (paragraphs 6–15)

Criteria for determining whether an arrangement contains a lease (paragraphs 6–9)

BC15 In D3 the IFRIC proposed that three criteria would all need to be satisfied for an arrangement to be, or contain, a lease:

(a) The arrangement depends upon a specific item or items (the item). The item need not be explicitly identified by the contractual provisions of the arrangement. Rather it may be implicitly identified because it is not economically feasible or practical for the supplier to fulfil the arrangement by providing use of alternative items.

(b) The arrangement conveys a right to use the item for a specific period of time such that the purchaser is able to exclude others from using the item.

(c) Payments under the arrangement are made for the time that the item is made available for use rather than for actual use of the item.

BC16 D3 also proposed that arrangements in which there is only a remote possibility that parties other than the purchaser will take more than an insignificant amount of the output produced by an item would meet the second of the criteria above.

BC17 In its Basis for Conclusions on D3, the IFRIC drew attention to the similarities between its Interpretation and Issue No. 01–8 *Determining Whether an Arrangement Contains a Lease* published by the US Emerging Issues Task Force (EITF) in May 2003. The IFRIC concluded that '[a]lthough the wording of Issue 01–8 and the draft Interpretation differ, ...a similar assessment of whether an arrangement contains a lease is likely under both interpretations.'

BC18 Some respondents disagreed with the IFRIC's conclusion and suggested that the differences between the two interpretations were, in fact, significant. The IFRIC, however, maintained its original conclusion. In particular, it noted that both it and the EITF had concluded that a right of use can be conveyed in arrangements in which purchasers have rights to acquire the output that will be produced by an asset, regardless of any right or ability physically to operate or control access to that asset. Accordingly, many take-or-pay (and similar contracts) would have been similarly assessed under the two interpretations.

BC19 Nonetheless, the IFRIC agreed that some arrangements would be regarded as leases under Issue 01–8 but not under D3. The IFRIC concluded that there were two main reasons for this. First, the effect of the third criterion in D3 ('payments under the arrangement are made for the time that the item is made available for use rather than for actual use of the item') was that a purchaser would always be required to assume some pricing risk in an arrangement for there to be a lease. This is not the case under Issue 01–8. Secondly, the second criterion in D3 ('the arrangement conveys a right to use the item ...such that the purchaser is able to exclude others from using the item') suggested that a right of use is conveyed in an arrangement for the output from an asset only when the purchaser is taking *substantially all* of the output from a specific asset. Under Issue 01–8, a right of use is also conveyed if the purchaser controls or operates the underlying specific asset while taking more than a *minor amount* of the output from an asset.

BC20 The IFRIC noted that the definition of a lease in IAS 17 is similar to its definition in the US standard SFAS 13 *Accounting for Leases*. Given this, the IFRIC concluded that there was no compelling reason for different assessments of whether an arrangement contains a lease under IFRSs and US GAAP. Furthermore, the IFRIC was sympathetic to the practical difficulties highlighted by some respondents that would arise in cases when an agreement would need to be assessed against two similar, but different, sets of criteria. Therefore, the IFRIC decided that it should seek to eliminate the differences between the approach in D3 and Issue 01–8 for determining whether an arrangement contains a lease. The IFRIC concluded that the most effective way of achieving this objective would be to modify its criteria to conform them more fully to the approach in Issue 01–8.

BC21 The IFRIC decided that as far as possible it should adopt the actual words from Issue 01–8, subject to differences between IAS 17 and SFAS 13. It concluded that differences in wording would not promote convergence and would be likely to cause confusion. Therefore, paragraphs 7–9 are virtually identical to Issue 01–8, except that:

(a) the Interpretation uses the term 'asset' rather than 'property, plant or equipment' as in Issue 01–8. The IFRIC noted that IAS 17 covers a broader range of leases than SFAS 13 and that there was no reason for restricting this Interpretation only to items of property, plant or equipment.

(b) the phrase 'more than a minor amount of the output' in Issue 01–8 has been expressed as 'more than an insignificant amount of the output'. This is because the latter is the more customary form of words under IFRSs and is therefore consistent with other Standards. In this context, however, the IFRIC intends 'minor' and 'insignificant' to have the same meaning.

BC22 Apart from small modifications to the wording of the first criterion in D3, the effect of converging fully with the criteria in Issue 01–8 for determining whether an arrangement contains a lease is that the second and third criteria in D3 are replaced by one criterion, requiring the arrangement to convey to the purchaser the right to control the use of the underlying asset.

BC23 Although the requirements for determining whether an arrangement contains a lease are the same under IFRSs and US GAAP, the IFRIC emphasises that any lease identified by the Interpretation may be accounted for differently under IFRSs and US GAAP because of differences between their respective leasing standards.

Fulfilment of the arrangement is dependent on the use of a specific asset (paragraphs 7 and 8)

BC24 The IFRIC agreed that a specific asset needs to be identified in the arrangement for there to be a lease. The IFRIC concluded that this follows from the definition of a lease, which refers to a 'right to use *an* asset' (emphasis added). The IFRIC also observed that dependence on a specifically identified asset is a feature that distinguishes a lease from other arrangements that also convey rights to use assets but are not leases (eg some service arrangements).

BC25 However, the IFRIC concluded that the identification of the asset in the arrangement need not be explicit. Rather, the facts and circumstances could implicitly identify an asset because it would not be economically feasible or practical for the supplier to perform its obligation by providing the use of alternative assets. Examples of when an asset may be implicitly identified are when the supplier owns only one suitable asset; the asset used to fulfil the contract needs to be at a particular location or specialised to the purchaser's needs; and the supplier is a special purpose entity formed for a limited purpose.

BC26 Some respondents to D3 noted that the effect of this first criterion is that the *purchaser's* accounting could depend on how the *supplier* chooses to fulfil the arrangement. They noted that the purchaser might have no control over this because (in form) the purchaser has contracted for output. Some respondents were also troubled by the lack of comparability, because similar arrangements for the output of an asset could be accounted for differently according to whether they depend on the use of a specific asset.

BC27 In response to the first of these comments, the IFRIC noted that how an entity chooses to obtain a product normally determines the accounting treatment; for example, an entity requiring power may choose to lease a power plant or connect to the grid and the two options would result in different accounting. Although in the respondents' example the choice is the supplier's (rather than the purchaser's), the IFRIC concluded that the critical matter is the end position of the entity (ie is there a lease?) not how it got to that position (ie whether it chose that outcome or it was imposed).

BC28 In response to the second comment, the IFRIC observed that it is important to consider the combined effect of the criteria in the Interpretation rather than considering the criteria individually. On reconsidering the proposals in D3 and the requirements of Issue 01-8, the IFRIC concluded that in the context of current IFRSs, in which executory contracts are generally not accounted for, the Interpretation identifies contracts (or an element therein) that for a purchaser warrant recognition (if the definition of a finance lease is satisfied). The IFRIC concluded that identifying and accounting for the lease element would represent an improvement to existing accounting practice.

Arrangement conveys a right to use the asset (paragraph 9)

BC29 Following Issue 01-8, the Interpretation specifies that a right of use can be conveyed if any of three criteria is satisfied.

BC30 The first two criteria consider the purchaser's ability to control physically the use of the underlying asset, either through operations or access, while obtaining or controlling more than an insignificant amount of the output of the asset. For example, a purchaser's ability to operate the asset may be evidenced by its ability to hire, fire or replace the operator of the asset or its ability to specify significant operating policies and procedures in the arrangement (as opposed to a right to monitor the supplier's activities) with the supplier having no ability to change such policies and procedures.

BC31 In D3 the IFRIC explained that it did not regard the ability of a purchaser to operate physically the underlying asset as determinative of whether a right of use has been conveyed. The IFRIC noted that asset managers 'operate' assets, but this does not necessarily convey a right of use. However, the IFRIC noted that under Issue 01-8, in addition to the ability to operate the asset, the purchaser has to be taking more than a minor amount of the output. The IFRIC agreed that in such cases the arrangement would convey a right of use.

BC32 The IFRIC agreed with the EITF that a right of use has been conveyed in arrangements in which the purchaser has the ability to control physically the use of the underlying asset through access (while obtaining or controlling more than a minor amount of the output of the asset). The IFRIC noted that in such arrangements the purchaser would have the ability to restrict the access of others to economic benefits of the underlying asset.

BC33 The third criterion for determining whether a right of use has been conveyed considers whether the purchaser is taking all or substantially all of the output or other utility of the underlying asset.

BC34 As noted above, D3 similarly specified that a right of use could be conveyed in arrangements in which there is only a remote possibility that other parties could take more than an insignificant amount of the output of an asset. Among the respondents who disagreed with the proposals in D3, it was this criterion that was considered most troublesome. They disagreed that, in certain specified circumstances, a purchaser's right to acquire the output from an asset could be equated with a right of use that asset. Among the arguments put to the IFRIC were:

(a) A right of use requires the purchaser to have the ability to control the way in which the underlying asset is used during the term of the arrangement: for example, the right for the purchaser's employees to assist or supervise the operation of the asset.

(b) In addition to the right to the output, the purchaser needs to have control over the delivery profile of the output; in other words it also needs the ability to determine when the output flows, otherwise it is simply consuming the output of the underlying asset rather than using the asset in its business.

(c) In most supply arrangements, the purchaser would not have access to the plant in the event of default by the supplier but would receive damages. The absence of this right points to there not being a lease. If the arrangement did contain a lease, the purchaser would have the ability to receive the output from the plant in the arrangement by replacing the original supplier with another service provider.

(d) D3 dismisses 'risks and rewards incidental to ownership' of the asset in determining whether an arrangement contains a lease. Therefore, arrangements in which the supplier retains significantly all of the risks and rewards of operation and ownership of the asset could be deemed to contain leases. However, in such arrangements the supplier's cash flows may have significantly more potential for variability than a 'true' lessor and the supplier may demand a return significantly above the market rate for a lessor.

BC35 In its redeliberations, the IFRIC reaffirmed its view that a purchaser that is taking substantially all of the output from an asset has the ability to restrict the access of others to the output from that asset. The purchaser therefore has a right of use because it controls access to the economic benefits to be derived from the asset. The IFRIC therefore did not agree that the absence of the ability to control physically the way in which the underlying asset is used precludes the existence of a right of use (although, as noted above, such an ability may indicate that a right of use has been conveyed).

BC36 With respect to the other points, the IFRIC noted the following:

(a) A purchaser that is taking substantially all of the output from an asset in cases when it is remote that others will be taking more than an insignificant amount of the output does in effect determine when the output flows.

(b) In most straightforward leases, any lessee that terminates the lease because of default by the lessor would no longer have access to the asset. Furthermore, in many leases that contain both a right of use and a service element, the related service contract does not operate independently (eg the lessee cannot terminate the service element alone). Indeed, the IFRIC noted that the purchaser's entitlement to damages in the event of default by the supplier indicates that a right of use was originally conveyed, and that the supplier is compensating the purchaser for withdrawing that right.

(c) Risks and rewards are in general relevant for determining lease classification rather than whether an arrangement is a lease. The IFRIC noted that in many straightforward short-term operating leases, substantially all the risks and rewards are retained by the lessor. Even if it were desirable to specify that a certain level of risks and rewards needed to be transferred for there to be a lease, the IFRIC was doubtful that such a criterion could be made operable. Nonetheless, an arrangement that conveys the right to use an asset will also convey certain risks and rewards incidental to ownership. Therefore, the transfer of risks and rewards of ownership may indicate that the arrangement conveys the right to use an asset. For example, if an arrangement's pricing provides for a fixed capacity charge designed to recover the supplier's capital investment in the underlying asset, the pricing may be persuasive evidence that it is remote that parties other than the purchaser will take more than an insignificant amount of the output or other utility that will be produced or generated by the asset, and the criterion in paragraph 9(c) is satisfied.

BC37 In adopting the approach from Issue 01-8, the IFRIC has specified that an arrangement for all or substantially all of the output from a specific asset does not convey the right to use the asset if the price that the purchaser will pay is contractually fixed per unit of output or equal to the current market price per unit of output as of the time of delivery of the output. This is because in such cases the purchaser is paying for a product or service rather than paying for the right to use the asset. In D3, the IFRIC proposed making a similar distinction by the combination of the second and third criteria (see paragraph BC15(b) and (c) above).

BC38 The IFRIC noted that its Interpretation could result in take-or-pay arrangements, in which purchasers are committed to purchase substantially all of the output from specific assets, being determined to contain leases. This is because in such arrangements the purchaser makes payments for the time that the underlying asset is made available for use rather than on the basis of actual use or output (resulting in the arrangement's pricing being neither fixed per unit of output nor equal to the current market price per unit of output). In many take-or-pay arrangements, the purchaser is contractually committed to pay the supplier regardless of whether the purchaser uses the underlying asset or obtains the output from that asset. Payments are therefore made for the right to use that asset. The IFRIC agreed that the overall effect of such a take-or-pay arrangement is similar to that of a lease plus contracts for related services and supplies (such as contracts for the operation of the asset and the purchase of inputs).

BC39 The IFRIC observed that if an arrangement contains a lease, and the lease is an operating lease, applying the Interpretation is likely to result in the same assets, liabilities and expenses being recognised as if no lease had been identified. However, the IFRIC noted that IAS 17 requires lessors and lessees to recognise operating lease payments on a straight-line basis over the lease term (unless another systematic basis is more representative of the time pattern of the benefit derived from the leased asset), and thus adjustments to the recognition profile of the payments for the lease element might be required in some instances. Also, the IFRIC noted that the Interpretation would often result in additional disclosure, because IAS 17 requires the lessor and lessee to disclose the future minimum lease payments. The IFRIC observed that, for a purchaser, the arrangements discussed in the Interpretation typically represent significant future commitments, and yet these commitments are not specifically required to be disclosed in the financial statements by Standards other than IAS 17. The IFRIC concluded that bringing such arrangements within the scope of IAS 17 would provide users of financial statements with relevant information that is useful for assessing the purchaser's solvency, liquidity and adaptability. The IFRIC acknowledged that the disclosed information might relate only to the lease element of the arrangement; however, it agreed that it would be beyond the scope of this Interpretation to address disclosure of executory contracts more generally.

Assessing or reassessing whether an arrangement contains a lease (paragraphs 10 and 11)

BC40 In D3 the IFRIC proposed that the assessment of whether an arrangement contains a lease should be made at the inception of the arrangement on the basis of the facts and circumstances existing at that time and that, consistently with IAS 17, an arrangement should be reassessed only if there was a change in the terms of the arrangement. Hence, under D3, a supplier that subsequently obtained additional assets with which it could fulfil the arrangement, would not have reassessed the arrangement.

BC41 Some respondents disagreed with this conclusion and argued that the analogy with the requirements for reclassifying a lease in IAS 17 was not relevant because the objective of the Interpretation is to determine whether an arrangement is within the scope of IAS 17. They noted that since this depends on factors such as whether the arrangement depends on a specific asset, it was logical that reassessment should be required if those factors change.

BC42 The IFRIC was persuaded by this argument and concluded that it outweighed the concerns that it had expressed in D3 about it being unduly burdensome to require purchasers to reassess arrangements. The IFRIC also noted that its proposal in D3 was different from Issue 01-8. Given that it had modified its approach to determining whether a lease exists to converge with Issue 01-8, the IFRIC decided that it should also specify the same treatment as Issue 01-8 for reassessments.

BC43 The IFRIC noted that the requirements in paragraphs 10 and 11 relate only to determining when the arrangement should be reassessed and that they do not alter the requirements of IAS 17. Hence if an arrangement that contains a lease is required to be reassessed and found still to contain a lease, the lease is reclassified as a finance lease or operating lease only if so required by paragraph 13 of IAS 17.

Separating payments for the lease from other payments (paragraphs 12–15)

BC44 D3 proposed, and the Interpretation requires, payments in an arrangement containing both a lease and other elements (eg services) to be separated into those for the lease and those for other elements on the basis of their relative fair values. The IFRIC concluded that fair value is the most relevant and faithful representation of the underlying economics of the transaction.

BC45 The IFRIC noted that this requirement could be more onerous for purchasers than for suppliers, particularly when a purchaser has no access to the supplier's pricing information. The IFRIC therefore agreed that it should provide some guidance to assist purchasers in separating the lease from other elements in the arrangement. Nonetheless, the IFRIC acknowledged that in rare cases it might be impracticable for the purchaser to separate the payments reliably. The IFRIC noted that if this was the case and the lease was a finance lease, then the requirements of IAS 17 would ensure that the purchaser would not capitalise an amount greater than the fair value of the asset (since paragraph 20 of IAS 17 requires a lessee to recognise a finance lease asset at the fair value of the leased property or, if lower, the present value of the minimum lease payments). Accordingly, the IFRIC decided to specify that in such cases the purchaser should recognise the fair value of the underlying asset as the leased asset. If the lease is an operating lease and it is impracticable to separate the payments reliably, the IFRIC agreed, as a practical accommodation, that the purchaser should disclose all the payments under the arrangement when disclosing the minimum lease payments, and state that these also include payment for other elements in the arrangement.

BC46 Some respondents to D3 noted that if a purchaser with an operating lease does not separate the payments, the usefulness of the disclosures required by IAS 17 would be reduced. The IFRIC agreed that the minimum lease payments are often used by users of financial statements to estimate the value of assets held under operating leases and therefore concluded that lease payments that also include payments for other elements should be disclosed separately.

Transition (paragraph 17)

BC47 D3 proposed, and the Interpretation requires, retrospective application. Some respondents proposed that the Interpretation should be applied only to new arrangements starting after its effective date. Two main arguments were put forward in support of this view:

(a) convergence with Issue 01-8 (which applies to arrangements starting or modified after the beginning of an entity's next reporting period beginning after 28 May 2003); and

(b) to ease transition, particularly in the case of longer arrangements that started some years ago and where it might be difficult to make the assessments required by D3 retrospectively.

BC48 The IFRIC noted that EITF Abstracts are usually applied prospectively. In contrast, IFRSs (including Interpretations) are applied retrospectively following the principle articulated in IAS 8 *Accounting Policies, Changes in Accounting Estimates and Errors*. The IFRIC could see no compelling argument from departing from this principle. The IFRIC also noted that unless it were to specify exactly the same effective date as Issue 01–8 (which was before D3 was published), reconciling items with US GAAP would still arise.

BC49 In addition, the IFRIC decided that the continuation of some arrangements for many years emphasised the need for retrospective application. Without retrospective application, an entity could be accounting for similar arrangements differently for many years with a consequent loss of comparability.

BC50 However, the IFRIC was sympathetic to the practical difficulties raised by full retrospective application, in particular the difficulty of going back potentially many years and determining whether the criteria would have been satisfied at that time. Although IAS 8 provides relief from fully retrospective application in cases where such treatment would be impracticable, the IFRIC decided that it should provide transitional relief for existing preparers of IFRSs in the Interpretation itself. The IFRIC emphasises that this relief does not alter the transition requirements of IAS 17 and therefore if an arrangement is determined to contain a lease an entity applies IAS 17 from the inception of the arrangement.

IFRIC Interpretation 5

Rights to Interests arising from Decommissioning, Restoration and Environmental Rehabilitation Funds

CONTENTS

IFRIC Interpretation 5 *Rights to Interests arising from Decommissioning, Restoration and Environmental Rehabilitation Funds* (IFRIC 5) is set out in paragraphs 1–15 and the Appendix. IFRIC 5 is accompanied by a Basis for Conclusions. The scope and authority of Interpretations are set out in paragraphs 1 and 8–10 of the *IFRIC Preface*.

References

- IAS 8 *Accounting Policies, Changes in Accounting Estimates and Errors*
- IAS 27 *Consolidated and Separate Financial Statements*
- IAS 28 *Investments in Associates*
- IAS 31 *Interests in Joint Ventures*
- IAS 37 *Provisions, Contingent Liabilities and Contingent Assets*
- IAS 39 *Financial Instruments: Recognition and Measurement* (as revised in 2003)
- SIC-12 *Consolidation—Special Purpose Entities* (as revised in 2004)

Background

1 The purpose of decommissioning, restoration and environmental rehabilitation funds, hereafter referred to as 'decommissioning funds' or 'funds', is to segregate assets to fund some or all of the costs of decommissioning plant (such as a nuclear plant) or certain equipment (such as cars), or in undertaking environmental rehabilitation (such as rectifying pollution of water or restoring mined land), together referred to as 'decommissioning'.

2 Contributions to these funds may be voluntary or required by regulation or law. The funds may have one of the following structures:

(a) funds that are established by a single contributor to fund its own decommissioning obligations, whether for a particular site, or for a number of geographically dispersed sites.

(b) funds that are established with multiple contributors to fund their individual or joint decommissioning obligations, when contributors are entitled to reimbursement for decommissioning expenses to the extent of their contributions plus any actual earnings on those contributions less their share of the costs of administering the fund. Contributors may have an obligation to make additional contributions, for example, in the event of the bankruptcy of another contributor.

(c) funds that are established with multiple contributors to fund their individual or joint decommissioning obligations when the required level of contributions is based on the current activity of a contributor and the benefit obtained by that contributor is based on its past activity. In such cases there is a potential mismatch in the amount of contributions made by a contributor (based on current activity) and the value realisable from the fund (based on past activity).

3 Such funds generally have the following features:

(a) the fund is separately administered by independent trustees.

(b) entities (contributors) make contributions to the fund, which are invested in a range of assets that may include both debt and equity investments, and are available to help pay the contributors' decommissioning costs. The trustees determine how contributions are invested, within the constraints set by the fund's governing documents and any applicable legislation or other regulations.

(c) the contributors retain the obligation to pay decommissioning costs. However, contributors are able to obtain reimbursement of decommissioning costs from the fund up to the lower of the decommissioning costs incurred and the contributor's share of assets of the fund.

(d) the contributors may have restricted access or no access to any surplus of assets of the fund over those used to meet eligible decommissioning costs.

Scope

4 This Interpretation applies to accounting in the financial statements of a contributor for interests arising from decommissioning funds that have both of the following features:

(a) the assets are administered separately (either by being held in a separate legal entity or as segregated assets within another entity); and

(b) a contributor's right to access the assets is restricted.

5 A residual interest in a fund that extends beyond a right to reimbursement, such as a contractual right to distributions once all the decommissioning has been completed or on winding up the fund, may be an equity instrument within the scope of IAS 39 and is not within the scope of this Interpretation.

Issues

6 The issues addressed in this Interpretation are:

(a) how should a contributor account for its interest in a fund?

(b) when a contributor has an obligation to make additional contributions, for example, in the event of the bankruptcy of another contributor, how should that obligation be accounted for?

Consensus

Accounting for an interest in a fund

7 The contributor shall recognise its obligation to pay decommissioning costs as a liability and recognise its interest in the fund separately unless the contributor is not liable to pay decommissioning costs even if the fund fails to pay.

8 The contributor shall determine whether it has control, joint control or significant influence over the fund by reference to IAS 27, IAS 28, IAS 31 and SIC-12. If it does, the contributor shall account for its interest in the fund in accordance with those Standards.

9 If a contributor does not have control, joint control or significant influence over the fund, the contributor shall recognise the right to receive reimbursement from the fund as a reimbursement in accordance with IAS 37. This reimbursement shall be measured at the lower of:

(a) the amount of the decommissioning obligation recognised; and

(b) the contributor's share of the fair value of the net assets of the fund attributable to contributors.

Changes in the carrying value of the right to receive reimbursement other than contributions to and payments from the fund shall be recognised in profit or loss in the period in which these changes occur.

Accounting for obligations to make additional contributions

10 When a contributor has an obligation to make potential additional contributions, for example, in the event of the bankruptcy of another contributor or if the value of the investment assets held by the fund decreases to an extent that they are insufficient to fulfil the fund's reimbursement obligations, this obligation is a contingent liability that is within the scope of IAS 37. The contributor shall recognise a liability only if it is probable that additional contributions will be made.

Disclosure

11 A contributor shall disclose the nature of its interest in a fund and any restrictions on access to the assets in the fund.

12 When a contributor has an obligation to make potential additional contributions that is not recognised as a liability (see paragraph 10), it shall make the disclosures required by paragraph 86 of IAS 37.

13 When a contributor accounts for its interest in the fund in accordance with paragraph 9, it shall make the disclosures required by paragraph 85(c) of IAS 37.

Effective date

14 An entity shall apply this Interpretation for annual periods beginning on or after 1 January 2006. Earlier application is encouraged. If an entity applies this Interpretation to a period beginning before 1 January 2006, it shall disclose that fact.

Transition

15 Changes in accounting policies shall be accounted for in accordance with the requirements of IAS 8.

Appendix
Amendment to IAS 39 *Financial Instruments: Recognition and Measurement*

The amendment in this appendix shall be applied for annual periods beginning on or after 1 January 2006. If an entity applies this Interpretation for an earlier period, the amendment shall be applied for that earlier period.

* * * * *

The amendment contained in this appendix when this Interpretation was issued in 2004 has been incorporated into IAS 39 as issued on and after 16 December 2004.

Basis for Conclusions

This Basis for Conclusions accompanies, but is not part of, IFRIC 5.

Introduction

BC1 This Basis for Conclusions summarises the IFRIC's considerations in reaching its consensus. Individual IFRIC members gave greater weight to some factors than to others.

Background (paragraphs 1–3)

BC2 The IFRIC was informed that an increasing number of entities with decommissioning obligations are contributing to a separate fund established to help fund those obligations. The IFRIC was also informed that questions have arisen in practice over the accounting treatment of interests in such funds and that there is a risk that divergent practices may develop. The IFRIC therefore concluded that it should provide guidance to assist in answering the questions in paragraph 6, in particular on the accounting for the asset of the right to receive reimbursement from a fund. On the issue of whether the fund should be consolidated or equity accounted, the IFRIC concluded that the normal requirements of IAS 27 *Consolidated and Separate Financial Statements*, SIC-12 *Consolidation—Special Purpose Entities*, IAS 28 *Investments in Associates* or IAS 31 *Interests in Joint Ventures* apply and that there is no need for interpretative guidance. The IFRIC published its proposed Interpretation on 15 January 2004 as D4 *Decommissioning, Restoration and Environmental Rehabilitation Funds.*

BC3 Paragraphs 1–3 describe ways in which entities might arrange to fund their decommissioning obligations. Those that are within the scope of the Interpretation are specified in paragraphs 4–6.

Scope (paragraphs 4 and 5)

BC4 D4 did not precisely define the scope because the IFRIC believed that the large variety of schemes in operation would make any definition inappropriate. However, some respondents to D4 disagreed and commented that the absence of any definition made it unclear when the Interpretation should be applied. As a result, the IFRIC has specified the scope by identifying the features that make an arrangement a decommissioning fund. It has also described the different types of fund and the features that may (or may not) be present.

BC5 The IFRIC considered whether it should issue a wider Interpretation that addresses similar forms of reimbursement, or whether it should prohibit the application of the Interpretation to other situations by analogy. The IFRIC rejected any widening of the scope, deciding instead to concentrate on the matter referred to it. The IFRIC also decided that there was no reason to prohibit the application of the Interpretation to other situations by analogy and thus the hierarchy of criteria in paragraphs 7–12 of IAS 8 *Accounting Policies, Changes in Accounting Estimates and Errors* would apply, resulting in similar accounting for reimbursements under arrangements that are not decommissioning funds, but have similar features.

BC6 The IFRIC considered comments from respondents that a contributor may have an interest in the fund that extends beyond its right to reimbursement. In response, the IFRIC added clarification that a residual interest in a fund, such as a contractual right to distributions once all the decommissioning has been completed or on winding up the fund, may be an equity instrument within the scope of IAS 39 *Financial Instruments: Recognition and Measurement*.

Basis for Consensus

Accounting for an interest in a fund (paragraphs 7–9)

BC7 The IFRIC concluded that the contributor should recognise a liability unless the contributor is not liable to pay decommissioning costs even if the fund fails to pay. This is because the contributor remains liable for the decommissioning costs. Additionally, IAS 37 *Provisions, Contingent Liabilities and Contingent Assets* provides that:

(a) when an entity remains liable for expenditure, a provision should be recognised even where reimbursement is available; and

(b) if the reimbursement is virtually certain to be received when the obligation is settled, then it should be treated as a separate asset.

BC8 In concluding that the contributor should recognise separately its liability to pay decommissioning costs and its interest in the fund, the IFRIC also noted the following:

(a) There is no legally enforceable right to set off the rights under the decommissioning fund against the decommissioning liabilities. Also, given that the main objective is reimbursement, it is likely that settlement will not be net or simultaneous. Accordingly, treating these rights and liabilities as analogous to financial assets and financial liabilities would not result in offset because the offset criteria in IAS 32 *Financial Instruments: Disclosure and Presentation* are not met.

(b) Treating the decommissioning obligation as analogous to a financial liability would not result in derecognition through extinguishment. If the fund does not assume the obligation for decommissioning, the criteria in IAS 39 for derecognition of financial liabilities through extinguishment are not met. At best, the fund acts like an in-substance defeasance that does not qualify for derecognition of the liability.

(c) It would not be appropriate to treat decommissioning funds as analogous to pension funds, which are presented net of the related liability. This is because, in allowing a net presentation for pension plans in IAS 19 *Employee Benefits*, the International Accounting Standards Board's predecessor organisation, IASC, stated that it believed the situation is 'unique to employee benefit plans and [it did] not intend to permit this net presentation for other liabilities if the conditions in IAS 32 and IAS 39 are not met' (IAS 19, Basis for Conclusions paragraph 68I).

BC9 As to the accounting for the contributor's interest in the fund, the IFRIC noted that some interests in funds would be within the scope of IAS 27, IAS 28, IAS 31 or

SIC-12. As noted in paragraph BC2, the IFRIC concluded that, in such cases, the normal requirements of those Standards would apply and there is no need for interpretative guidance.

BC10 Otherwise, the IFRIC concluded that the contributor has an asset for its right to receive amounts from the fund.

The right to receive reimbursement from a fund and amendment to the scope of IAS 39

BC11 The IFRIC noted that under existing IFRSs, there are two forms of rights to reimbursement that would be accounted for differently:

(a) A contractual right to receive reimbursement in the form of cash. This meets the definition of a financial asset and is within the scope of IAS 39. Such a financial asset would be classified as an available-for-sale financial asset (unless accounted for using the fair value option) because it does not meet the definitions of a financial asset held for trading, a held-to-maturity investment or a loan or receivable.*

(b) A right to reimbursement other than a contractual right to receive cash. This does not meet the definition of a financial asset and is within the scope of IAS 37.

BC12 The IFRIC concluded that both these forms of reimbursement have economically identical effects. Therefore accounting for both forms in the same way would provide relevant and reliable information to a user of the financial statements. However, the IFRIC noted that this did not appear possible under existing IFRSs because some such rights are within the scope of IAS 39, and others are not. Therefore, it asked the Board to amend the scope of IAS 39 to exclude rights to reimbursement for expenditure required to settle:

(a) a provision that has been recognised in accordance with IAS 37; and

(b) obligations that had been originally recognised as provisions in accordance with IAS 37, but are no longer provisions because their timing or amount is no longer uncertain. An example of such a liability is one that was originally recognised as a provision because of uncertainty about the timing of the cash outflow, but subsequently becomes another type of liability because the timing is now certain.

BC13 This amendment was approved by the Board and is set out in the Appendix of IFRIC 5.† As a result, all such rights to reimbursement are within the scope of IAS 37.

BC14 The IFRIC noted that paragraph 53 of IAS 37 specifies the accounting for rights to receive reimbursement. It requires this right to reimbursement to be separately recognised when it is virtually certain that reimbursement will be received if the

* An interest in a decommissioning fund would not meet the definition of held for trading because it is not acquired or incurred principally for the purpose of selling or repurchasing it in the near term, nor of a held-to-maturity investment because it does not have fixed or determinable maturity. In addition, an interest in a fund is excluded from the definition of loans and receivables in IAS 39 since it is 'an interest acquired in a pool of assets that are not loans and receivables'.

† The amendment has been incorporated into the text of IAS 39 as published in this volume.

contributor settles the obligation. The IFRIC also noted that this paragraph prohibits the recognition of an asset in excess of the recognised liability. For example, rights to receive reimbursement to meet decommissioning liabilities that have yet to be recognised as a provision are not recognised. Accordingly, the IFRIC concluded that when the right to reimbursement is virtually certain to be received if the contributor settles its decommissioning obligation, it should be measured at the lower of the amount of the decommissioning obligation recognised and the reimbursement right.

BC15 The IFRIC discussed whether the reimbursement right should be measured at:

(a) the contributor's share of the fair value of the net assets of the fund attributable to contributors, taking into account any inability to access any surplus of the assets of the fund over eligible decommissioning costs (with any obligation to make good potential defaults of other contributors being treated separately as a contingent liability); or

(b) the fair value of the reimbursement right (which would normally be lower than (a) because of the risks involved, such as the possibility that the contributor may be required to make good defaults of other contributors).

BC16 The IFRIC noted that the right to reimbursement relates to a decommissioning obligation for which a provision would be recognised and measured in accordance with IAS 37. Paragraph 36 of IAS 37 requires such provisions to be measured at 'the best estimate of the expenditure required to settle the present obligation at the balance sheet date'. The IFRIC noted that the amount in paragraph BC15(a)—ie the contributor's share of the fair value of the net assets of the fund attributable to contributors, taking into account any inability to access any surplus of the assets of the fund over eligible decommissioning costs—is the best estimate of the amount available to the contributor to reimburse it for expenditure it had incurred to pay for decommissioning. Thus, the amount of the asset recognised would be consistent with the amount of the liability recognised.

BC17 In contrast, the IFRIC noted that the amount in paragraph BC15(b)—ie the fair value of the reimbursement right—would take into account the factors such as liquidity that the IFRIC believed to be difficult to measure reliably. Furthermore, this amount would be lower than that in paragraph BC15(a) because it reflects the possibility that the contributor may be required to make potential additional contributions in the event of default by other contributors. The IFRIC noted that its decision that the obligation to make potential additional contributions should be treated as a contingent liability in accordance with IAS 37 (see paragraphs BC22–BC25) would result in double-counting of the risk of the additional contribution being required if the measure in paragraph BC15(b) were to be used.

BC18 Consequently, the IFRIC concluded that the approach in paragraph BC15(a) would provide the most useful information to users.

The asset cap

BC19 Many respondents to D4 expressed concern about the 'asset cap' that is imposed by the requirement in paragraph 9. This asset cap limits the amount recognised as a reimbursement asset to the amount of the decommissioning obligation recognised. These respondents argued that rights to benefit in excess of this amount give rise to an additional asset, separate from the reimbursement asset. Such an additional asset may arise in a number of ways, for example:

(a) the contributor has the right to benefit from a repayment of any surplus in the fund that exists once all the decommissioning has been completed or on winding up the fund.

(b) the contributor has the right to benefit from reduced contributions to the fund or increased benefits from the fund (eg by adding new sites to the fund for no additional contributions) in the future.

(c) the contributor expects to obtain benefit from past contributions in the future, based on the current and planned level of activity. However, because contributions are made before the decommissioning obligation is incurred, IAS 37 prevents recognition of an asset in excess of the obligation.

BC20 The IFRIC concluded that a right to benefit from a repayment of any surplus in the fund that exists once all the decommissioning has been completed or on winding up the fund may be an equity instrument within the scope of IAS 39, in which case IAS 39 would apply. However, the IFRIC agreed that an asset should not be recognised for other rights to receive reimbursement from the fund. Although the IFRIC had sympathy with the concerns expressed by constituents that there may be circumstances in which it would seem appropriate to recognise an asset in excess of the reimbursement right, it concluded that it would be inconsistent with paragraph 53 of IAS 37 (which requires that 'the amount recognised for the reimbursement should not exceed the amount of the provision') to recognise this asset. The IFRIC also noted that the circumstances in which this additional asset exists are likely to be limited, and apply only when a contributor has restricted access to a surplus of fund assets that does not give it control, joint control or significant influence over a fund. The IFRIC expects that most such assets would not meet the recognition criteria in the *Framework* because they are highly uncertain and cannot be measured reliably.

BC21 The IFRIC also considered arguments that there should not be a difference between the treatment of a surplus when a fund is accounted for as a subsidiary, joint venture or associate, and when it is not. However, the IFRIC noted that, under IFRSs, restrictions on assets in subsidiaries, joint ventures or associates do not affect recognition of those assets. Hence it concluded that the difference in treatment between funds accounted for as subsidiaries, joint ventures or associates and those accounted for as a reimbursement right is inherent in IFRSs. The IFRIC also concluded that this is appropriate because, in the former case, the contributor exercises a degree of control not present in the latter case.

Obligations to make additional contributions (paragraph 10)

BC22 In some cases, a contributor has an obligation to make potential additional contributions, for example, in the event of the bankruptcy of another contributor.

BC23 The IFRIC noted that by 'joining' the fund, a contributor may assume the position of guarantor of the contributions of the other contributors, and hence become jointly and severally liable for the obligations of other contributors. Such an obligation is a present obligation of the contributor, but the outflow of resources associated with it may not be probable. The IFRIC noted a parallel with the example in paragraph 29 of IAS 37, which states that 'where an entity is jointly and severally liable for an obligation, the part of the obligation that is expected to be met by other parties is treated as a contingent liability.' Accordingly, the IFRIC concluded that a liability would be recognised by the contributor only if it is probable that it will make additional contributions. The IFRIC noted that such a contingent liability may arise both when the contributor's interest in the fund is accounted for as a reimbursement right and when it is accounted for in accordance with IAS 27, IAS 28, IAS 31 or SIC-12.

BC24 The IFRIC considered the argument that an obligation to make good potential shortfalls of other contributors is a financial instrument (ie a financial guarantee) as defined in IAS 32 and hence should be accounted for in accordance with IAS 39. The grounds for this point of view are that the contributor has an obligation to deliver cash to the fund, and the fund has a right to receive cash from the contributor if a shortfall in contributions arises. However, the IFRIC noted that:

(a) a contractual obligation to make good shortfalls of other contributors is a financial guarantee. Financial guarantee contracts that provide for payments to be made if the debtor fails to make payment when due are excluded from the scope of IAS 39.

(b) when the obligation is not contractual, but rather arises as a result of regulation, it is not a financial liability as defined in IAS 32 nor is it within the scope of IAS 39.

BC25 Therefore, the IFRIC concluded that an obligation to make additional contributions in the event of specified circumstances should be treated as a contingent liability in accordance with IAS 37.

Disclosure (paragraphs 11–13)

BC26 The IFRIC noted that the contributor may not be able to access the assets of the fund (including cash or cash equivalents) for many years (eg until it undertakes the decommissioning), if ever. Therefore, the IFRIC concluded that the nature of the contributor's interest and the restriction on access should be disclosed. The IFRIC also concluded that this disclosure is equally relevant when a contributor's interest in a fund is accounted for by consolidation, proportional consolidation or using the equity method because the contributor's ability to access the underlying assets may be similarly restricted.

Effective date and transition (paragraphs 14 and 15)

BC27 D4 proposed that the Interpretation should be effective for annual periods beginning on a date set at three months after the Interpretation was finalised. The IFRIC considered the view of some respondents that the Interpretation should apply from 1 January 2005 (an earlier date) on the grounds that this is the date from which many entities will adopt IFRSs, and hence adopting the Interpretation at that time would promote comparability between periods. However, the IFRIC noted its general practice is to allow at least three months between finalising an Interpretation and its application, to enable entities to obtain the Interpretation and implement any necessary systems changes. In addition, the IFRIC considered the Board's concern that the amendment to IAS 39 issued as part of the Interpretation would change the 'stable platform' of Standards that are in force for entities that will apply IFRSs for the first time in 2005. Therefore, the IFRIC decided to require that the Interpretation should be applied for annual periods beginning on or after 1 January 2006, with earlier application encouraged.

BC28 The IFRIC observed that the implementation of the Interpretation is not expected to be problematic. Therefore, the IFRIC concluded that IAS 8 should apply. Respondents to D4 did not disagree with this conclusion.

SIC Interpretation 7

Introduction of the Euro

This version includes amendments resulting from new and amended IFRSs issued up to 31 December 2004.

SIC Interpretation 7 *Introduction of the Euro* (SIC-7) is set out in paragraphs 3 and 4. SIC-7 is accompanied by a Basis for Conclusions. The scope and authority of Interpretations are set out in paragraphs 1 and 8–10 of the IFRIC *Preface*.

References

- IAS 10 *Events after the Balance Sheet Date* (as revised in 2003)
- IAS 21 *The Effects of Changes in Foreign Exchange Rates* (as revised in 2003)

Issue

1 From 1 January 1999, the effective start of Economic and Monetary Union (EMU), the euro will become a currency in its own right and the conversion rates between the euro and the participating national currencies will be irrevocably fixed, ie the risk of subsequent exchange differences related to these currencies is eliminated from this date on.

2 The issue is the application of IAS 21 to the changeover from the national currencies of participating Member States of the European Union to the euro ('the changeover').

Consensus

3 The requirements of IAS 21 regarding the translation of foreign currency transactions and financial statements of foreign operations should be strictly applied to the changeover. The same rationale applies to the fixing of exchange rates when countries join EMU at later stages.

4 This means that, in particular:

(a) foreign currency monetary assets and liabilities resulting from transactions shall continue to be translated into the functional currency at the closing rate. Any resultant exchange differences shall be recognised as income or expense immediately, except that an entity shall continue to apply its existing accounting policy for exchange gains and losses related to hedges of the currency risk of a forecast transaction;

(b) cumulative exchange differences relating to the translation of financial statements of foreign operations shall continue to be classified as equity and shall be recognised as income or expense only on the disposal of the net investment in the foreign operation; and

(c) exchange differences resulting from the translation of liabilities denominated in participating currencies shall not be included in the carrying amount of related assets.

Basis for Conclusions

[The original text has been marked up to reflect the revision of IAS 21 in 2003: new text is underlined and deleted text is struck through.]

5 IAS 21.23~~11~~ (a) requires that foreign currency monetary items (as defined by IAS 21.8~~07~~) be reported using the closing rate at each balance sheet date. According to IAS 21.28~~15~~, exchange differences arising from the translation of monetary items generally should be recognised as income or as expenses in the period in which they arise. The effective start of the EMU after the balance sheet date does not change the application of these requirements at the balance sheet date; in accordance with IAS 10.10 ~~28~~* it is not relevant whether or not the closing rate can fluctuate after the balance sheet date.

* ~~IAS 10 (revised in 1999), paragraph 20, contains similar requirements.~~

6 IAS 21.5~~14~~ states that the Standard does not apply to ~~deal with~~ hedge accounting, ~~except in restricted circumstances~~. Therefore, this Interpretation does not address how foreign currency hedges should be accounted for. IAS 8.~~42~~ would allow such a change in accounting policy only if the change would result in a more appropriate presentation of events or transactions. The effective start of EMU, of itself, does not justify a change to an entity's established accounting policy related to ~~anticipatory~~ hedges of forecast transactions because the changeover does not affect the economic rationale of such hedges.[*] Therefore, the changeover should not alter the accounting policy where gains and losses on financial instruments used as ~~anticipatory~~ hedges of forecast transactions are ~~currently deferred~~ initially recognised in equity and matched with the related income or expense in a future period.

7 IAS 21.48~~37~~ requires the cumulative amount of exchange differences relating to the translation of the financial statements of a foreign operation ~~entity~~ which have been deferred in equity in accordance with IAS 21.~~17, 19 or 30~~32 or 39(c) to be recognised as income or expenses in the same period in which the gain or loss on disposal of the foreign operation ~~entity~~ is recognised. The fact that the cumulative amount of exchange differences will be fixed under EMU does not justify immediate recognition as income or expenses since the wording and the rationale of IAS 21.48~~37~~ clearly preclude such a treatment.

8 ~~Under the Allowed Alternative Treatment of IAS 21.21, exchange differences resulting from severe devaluations of currencies are included in the carrying amount of the related assets in certain limited circumstances. Those circumstances do not apply to the currencies participating in the changeover since the event of severe devaluation is incompatible with the required stability of participating currencies.~~

Date of consensus

October 1997

Effective date

This Interpretation becomes effective on 1 June 1998. Changes in accounting policies shall be accounted for according to the requirements of IAS 8.

[*] The accounting for hedges is now covered under IAS 39 *Financial Instruments: Recognition and Measurement*. As SIC-7 was issued before IAS 39, the previous version of this Interpretation could refer only to the entity's own accounting policies on the matter.

SIC Interpretation 10

Government Assistance—No Specific Relation to Operating Activities

SIC Interpretation 10 *Government Assistance—No Specific Relation to Operating Activities* (SIC-10) is set out in paragraph 3. SIC-10 is accompanied by a Basis for Conclusions. The scope and authority of Interpretations are set out in paragraphs 1 and 8–10 of the *IFRIC Preface*.

Reference

- IAS 20 *Accounting for Government Grants and Disclosure of Government Assistance*

Issue

1 In some countries government assistance to entities may be aimed at encouragement or long-term support of business activities either in certain regions or industry sectors. Conditions to receive such assistance may not be specifically related to the operating activities of the entity. Examples of such assistance are transfers of resources by governments to entities which:

(a) operate in a particular industry;

(b) continue operating in recently privatised industries; or

(c) start or continue to run their business in underdeveloped areas.

2 The issue is whether such government assistance is a 'government grant' within the scope of IAS 20 and, therefore, should be accounted for in accordance with this Standard.

Consensus

3 Government assistance to entities meets the definition of government grants in IAS 20, even if there are no conditions specifically relating to the operating activities of the entity other than the requirement to operate in certain regions or industry sectors. Such grants shall therefore not be credited directly to equity.

Basis for Conclusions

4 IAS 20.03 defines government grants as assistance by the government in the form of transfers of resources to an entity in return for past or future compliance with certain conditions relating to the operating activities of the entity. The general requirement to operate in certain regions or industry sectors in order to qualify for the government assistance constitutes such a condition in accordance with IAS 20.03. Therefore, such assistance falls within the definition of government grants and the requirements of IAS 20 apply, in particular paragraphs 12 and 20, which deal with the timing of recognition as income.

Date of consensus

January 1998

Effective date

This Interpretation becomes effective on 1 August 1998. Changes in accounting policies shall be accounted for in accordance with IAS 8.

SIC Interpretation 12

Consolidation—Special Purpose Entities

Note: This version includes the amendment resulting from IFRIC Amendment to SIC-12 issued on 11 November 2004. In paragraph 6 new text is underlined and deleted text is struck through. In the Basis for Conclusions, paragraphs 15A–15E have been added.

SIC Interpretation 12 *Consolidation—Special Purpose Entities* (SIC-12) is set out in paragraphs 8–10. SIC-12 is accompanied by a Basis for Conclusions and an appendix illustrating the application of the Interpretation. The scope and authority of Interpretations are set out in paragraphs 1 and 8–10 of the *IFRIC Preface*.

References

- IAS 8 *Accounting Policies, Changes in Accounting Estimates and Errors*
- IAS 19 *Employee Benefits*
- IAS 27 *Consolidated and Separate Financial Statements*
- IAS 32 *Financial Instruments: Disclosure and Presentation*
- IFRS 2 *Share-based Payment*

Issue

1 An entity may be created to accomplish a narrow and well-defined objective (eg to effect a lease, research and development activities or a securitisation of financial assets). Such a special purpose entity ('SPE') may take the form of a corporation, trust, partnership or unincorporated entity. SPEs often are created with legal arrangements that impose strict and sometimes permanent limits on the decision-making powers of their governing board, trustee or management over the operations of the SPE. Frequently, these provisions specify that the policy guiding the ongoing activities of the SPE cannot be modified, other than perhaps by its creator or sponsor (ie they operate on so-called 'autopilot').

2 The sponsor (or entity on whose behalf the SPE was created) frequently transfers assets to the SPE, obtains the right to use assets held by the SPE or performs services for the SPE, while other parties ('capital providers') may provide the funding to the SPE. An entity that engages in transactions with an SPE (frequently the creator or sponsor) may in substance control the SPE.

3 A beneficial interest in an SPE may, for example, take the form of a debt instrument, an equity instrument, a participation right, a residual interest or a lease. Some beneficial interests may simply provide the holder with a fixed or stated rate of return, while others give the holder rights or access to other future economic benefits of the SPE's activities. In most cases, the creator or sponsor (or the entity on whose behalf the SPE was created) retains a significant beneficial interest in the SPE's activities, even though it may own little or none of the SPE's equity.

4 IAS 27 requires the consolidation of entities that are controlled by the reporting entity. However, the Standard does not provide explicit guidance on the consolidation of SPEs.

5 The issue is under what circumstances an entity should consolidate an SPE.

6 This Interpretation does not apply to post-employment benefit plans or ~~equity compensation plans~~ other long-term employee benefit plans to which IAS 19 applies.

7 A transfer of assets from an entity to an SPE may qualify as a sale by that entity. Even if the transfer does qualify as a sale, the provisions of IAS 27 and this Interpretation may mean that the entity should consolidate the SPE. This Interpretation does not address the circumstances in which sale treatment should apply for the entity or the elimination of the consequences of such a sale upon consolidation.

Consensus

8 An SPE shall be consolidated when the substance of the relationship between an entity and the SPE indicates that the SPE is controlled by that entity.

9 In the context of an SPE, control may arise through the predetermination of the activities of the SPE (operating on 'autopilot') or otherwise. IAS 27.13 indicates several circumstances which result in control even in cases where an entity owns one half or less of the voting power of another entity. Similarly, control may exist even in cases where an entity owns little or none of the SPE's equity. The application of the control concept requires, in each case, judgement in the context of all relevant factors.

10 In addition to the situations described in IAS 27.13, the following circumstances, for example, may indicate a relationship in which an entity controls an SPE and consequently should consolidate the SPE (additional guidance is provided in the Appendix to this Interpretation):

(a) in substance, the activities of the SPE are being conducted on behalf of the entity according to its specific business needs so that the entity obtains benefits from the SPE's operation;

(b) in substance, the entity has the decision-making powers to obtain the majority of the benefits of the activities of the SPE or, by setting up an 'autopilot' mechanism, the entity has delegated these decision-making powers;

(c) in substance, the entity has rights to obtain the majority of the benefits of the SPE and therefore may be exposed to risks incident to the activities of the SPE; or

(d) in substance, the entity retains the majority of the residual or ownership risks related to the SPE or its assets in order to obtain benefits from its activities.

11 [Deleted]

Basis for Conclusions

[The original text has been marked up to reflect the revision of IAS 27 in 2003: new text is underlined and deleted text is struck through. Paragraphs 15A–15E were added by IFRIC Amendment to SIC-12 issued on 11 November 2004.]

12 IAS 27.12 ~~11~~ states that '~~a parent which issues~~ Consolidated financial statements shall include ~~should consolidate~~ all subsidiaries of the parent'. IAS 27.04~~06~~ defines a parent as 'an entity that has one or more subsidiaries', a subsidiary as 'an entity, including an unincorporated entity such as a partnership, that is controlled by another entity (known as the parent)', and control as 'the power to govern the financial and operating policies of an entity so as to obtain benefits from its activities.' Paragraph 35 of the *Framework* and IAS 8.10(b)(ii) ~~1.20(b)(ii) (revised 1997)~~ require that transactions and other events are accounted for in accordance with their substance and economic reality, and not merely their legal form.

13 Control over another entity requires having the ability to direct or dominate its decision-making, regardless of whether this power is actually exercised. Under the definitions of IAS 27.04~~06~~, the ability to govern decision-making alone, however, is not sufficient to establish control. The ability to govern decision-making must be accompanied by the objective of obtaining benefits from the entity's activities.

14 SPEs frequently operate in a predetermined way so that no entity has explicit decision-making authority over the SPE's ongoing activities after its formation (ie they operate on 'autopilot'). Virtually all rights, obligations, and aspects of activities that could be controlled are predefined and limited by contractual provisions specified or scheduled at inception. In these circumstances, control may exist for the sponsoring party or others with a beneficial interest, even though it may be particularly difficult to assess, because virtually all activities are predetermined. However, the predetermination of the activities of the SPE through an 'autopilot' mechanism often provides evidence that the ability to control has been exercised by the party making the predetermination for its own benefit at the formation of the SPE and is being perpetuated.

~~15~~ ~~IAS 27.13(b) indicates that a subsidiary should be excluded from consolidation when it 'operates under severe long-term restrictions which significantly impair its ability to transfer funds to the parent.' Predetermination of the activities of an SPE by an enterprise (the sponsor or other party with a beneficial interest) is often a demonstration of control over ongoing activities as determined by that enterprise and would not represent the type of restrictions referred to in IAS 27.13(b).~~

15A In 2004, the IFRIC amended the scope of SIC-12. That Amendment is effective for annual periods beginning on or after 1 January 2005, unless an entity applied IFRS 2 for an earlier period, in which case the Amendment is effective for that earlier period. Before that Amendment, SIC-12 excluded from its scope equity compensation plans and post-employment benefit plans. Paragraphs 15B–15E summarise the IFRIC's considerations in reaching its consensus to amend the scope of SIC-12. Individual IFRIC members gave greater weight to some factors than to others.

15B The IFRIC was asked by the IASB to consider whether the scope exclusion in SIC-12 for equity compensation plans should be removed when IFRS 2 becomes effective. Equity compensation plans were excluded from the scope of SIC-12 because they were within the scope of IAS 19 and that Standard did not specify recognition and measurement requirements for equity compensation benefits. However, once IFRS 2 became effective, IAS 19 would no longer apply to equity compensation plans. IFRS 2 specifies recognition and measurement requirements for equity compensation benefits.

15C Also, IFRS 2 amended IAS 32, to state that paragraphs 33 and 34, which relate to the treatment of treasury shares, should be applied to treasury shares purchased, sold, issued or cancelled in connection with employee share option plans, employee share purchase plans, and all other share-based payment arrangements. However, in some cases, those shares might be held by an employee benefit trust (or similar entity) set up by the entity for the purposes of its share-based payment arrangements. Removing the scope exclusion in SIC-12 would require an entity that controls such a trust to consolidate the trust and, in so doing, to apply the requirements of IAS 32 to treasury shares held by the trust.

15D The IFRIC therefore concluded that, to ensure consistency with IFRS 2 and IAS 32, the scope of SIC-12 should be amended by removing the exclusion of equity compensation plans.

15E At the same time, the IFRIC discussed the scope exclusion in SIC-12 for post-employment benefit plans. The IFRIC noted that, although SIC-12 did not exclude other long-term employee benefit plans from its scope, IAS 19 nevertheless requires those plans to be accounted for in a manner similar to the accounting for post-employment benefit plans. The IFRIC therefore concluded that, to ensure consistency with IAS 19, the scope exclusion in SIC-12 should also apply to other long-term employee benefit plans.

Date of consensus

June 1998

Effective date

This Interpretation becomes effective for annual financial periods beginning on or after 1 July 1999; earlier application is encouraged. Changes in accounting policies shall be accounted in accordance with IAS 8.

An entity shall apply the amendment in paragraph 6 for annual periods beginning on or after 1 January 2005. If an entity applies IFRS 2 for an earlier period, this amendment shall be applied for that earlier period.

Appendix to SIC-12

This appendix accompanies, but is not part of, SIC-12.

Indicators of control over an SPE

The examples in paragraph 10 of this Interpretation are intended to indicate types of circumstances that should be considered in evaluating a particular arrangement in light of the substance–over–form principle. The guidance provided in the Interpretation and in this Appendix is not intended to be used as 'a comprehensive checklist' of conditions that must be met cumulatively in order to require consolidation of an SPE.

(a) *Activities*

The activities of the SPE, in substance, are being conducted on behalf of the reporting entity, which directly or indirectly created the SPE according to its specific business needs.

Examples are:

- the SPE is principally engaged in providing a source of long-term capital to an entity or funding to support an entity's ongoing major or central operations; or
- the SPE provides a supply of goods or services that is consistent with an entity's ongoing major or central operations which, without the existence of the SPE, would have to be provided by the entity itself.

Economic dependence of an entity on the reporting entity (such as relations of suppliers to a significant customer) does not, by itself, lead to control.

(b) *Decision–making*

The reporting entity, in substance, has the decision-making powers to control or to obtain control of the SPE or its assets, including certain decision-making powers coming into existence after the formation of the SPE. Such decision-making powers may have been delegated by establishing an 'autopilot' mechanism.

Examples are:

- power to unilaterally dissolve an SPE;
- power to change the SPE's charter or bylaws; or
- power to veto proposed changes of the SPE's charter or bylaws.

(c) *Benefits*

The reporting entity, in substance, has rights to obtain a majority of the benefits of the SPE's activities through a statute, contract, agreement, or trust deed, or any other scheme, arrangement or device. Such rights to benefits in the SPE may be indicators of control when they are specified in favour of an entity that is engaged in transactions with an SPE and that entity stands to gain those benefits from the financial performance of the SPE.

Examples are:

- rights to a majority of any economic benefits distributed by an entity in the form of future net cash flows, earnings, net assets, or other economic benefits; or
- rights to majority residual interests in scheduled residual distributions or in a liquidation of the SPE.

(d) *Risks*

An indication of control may be obtained by evaluating the risks of each party engaging in transactions with an SPE. Frequently, the reporting entity guarantees a return or credit protection directly or indirectly through the SPE to outside investors who provide substantially all of the capital to the SPE. As a result of the guarantee, the entity retains residual or ownership risks and the investors are, in substance, only lenders because their exposure to gains and losses is limited.

Examples are:

- the capital providers do not have a significant interest in the underlying net assets of the SPE;
- the capital providers do not have rights to the future economic benefits of the SPE;
- the capital providers are not substantively exposed to the inherent risks of the underlying net assets or operations of the SPE; or
- in substance, the capital providers receive mainly consideration equivalent to a lender's return through a debt or equity interest.

SIC Interpretation 13

Jointly Controlled Entities— Non-Monetary Contributions by Venturers

This version includes amendments resulting from new and amended IFRSs issued up to 31 December 2004.

SIC Interpretation 13 *Jointly Controlled Entities—Non-Monetary Contributions by Venturers* (SIC-13) is set out in paragraphs 5–7. SIC-13 is accompanied by a Basis for Conclusions. The scope and authority of Interpretations are set out in paragraphs 1 and 8–10 of the *IFRIC Preface*.

References

- IAS 18 *Revenue*
- IAS 31 *Interests in Joint Ventures*

Issue

1 IAS 31.48 refers to both contributions and sales between a venturer and a joint venture as follows: 'When a venturer contributes or sells assets to a joint venture, recognition of any portion of a gain or loss from the transaction shall reflect the substance of the transaction'. In addition, IAS 31.24 says that 'a jointly controlled entity is a joint venture that involves the establishment of a corporation, partnership or other entity in which each venturer has an interest'. There is no explicit guidance on the recognition of gains and losses resulting from contributions of non-monetary assets to jointly controlled entities ('JCEs').

2 Contributions to a JCE are transfers of assets by venturers in exchange for an equity interest in the JCE. Such contributions may take various forms. Contributions may be made simultaneously by the venturers either upon establishing the JCE or subsequently. The consideration received by the venturer(s) in exchange for assets contributed to the JCE may also include cash or other consideration that does not depend on future cash flows of the JCE ('additional consideration').

3 The issues are:

(a) when the appropriate portion of gains or losses resulting from a contribution of a non-monetary asset to a JCE in exchange for an equity interest in the JCE should be recognised by the venturer in the income statement;

(b) how additional consideration should be accounted for by the venturer; and

(c) how any unrealised gain or loss should be presented in the consolidated financial statements of the venturer.

4 This Interpretation deals with the venturer's accounting for non-monetary contributions to a JCE in exchange for an equity interest in the JCE that is accounted for using either the equity method or proportionate consolidation.

Consensus

5 In applying IAS 31.48 to non-monetary contributions to a JCE in exchange for an equity interest in the JCE, a venturer shall recognise in profit or loss for the period the portion of a gain or loss attributable to the equity interests of the other venturers except when:

(a) the significant risks and rewards of ownership of the contributed non-monetary asset(s) have not been transferred to the JCE; or

(b) the gain or loss on the non-monetary contribution cannot be measured reliably; or

(c) the contribution transaction lacks commercial substance, as that term is described in IAS 16 *Property, Plant and Equipment*.

If exception (a), (b) or (c) applies, the gain or loss is regarded as unrealised and therefore is not recognised in profit or loss unless paragraph 6 also applies.

6 If, in addition to receiving an equity interest in the JCE, a venturer receives monetary or non-monetary assets, an appropriate portion of gain or loss on the transaction shall be recognised by the venturer in profit or loss.

7 Unrealised gains or losses on non-monetary assets contributed to JCEs shall be eliminated against the underlying assets under the proportionate consolidation method or against the investment under the equity method. Such unrealised gains or losses shall not be presented as deferred gains or losses in the venturer's consolidated balance sheet.

Basis for Conclusions

[The original text has been marked up to reflect the revision of IAS 16 and IAS 31 in 2003; new text is underlined and deleted text is struck through.]

8 IAS 31.48~~39~~ requires that, while the assets are retained in the joint venture, the venturer should recognise only that portion of the gain or loss which is attributable to the interests of the other venturers. Additional losses are recognised if required by IAS 31.48~~39~~.

9 IAS 31.48~~39~~ refers to the transfer of the 'significant risks and rewards of ownership' as a condition for recognition of gains or losses resulting from transactions between venturers and joint ventures. IAS 18.16(a) to (d) contain examples of situations where the risks and rewards of ownership are typically not transferred. This guidance also applies by analogy to the recognition of gains or losses resulting from contributions of non-monetary assets to JCEs. Since the venturer participates in joint control of the JCE, it retains some 'continuing managerial involvement' in the asset transferred. However, this does not generally preclude the recognition of gains or losses since joint control does not constitute control to the degree usually associated with ownership (IAS 18.14(b)).

10 Paragraph 92 of the *Framework* states: 'income is recognised in the income statement when an increase in future economic benefits related to an increase in an asset or a decrease of a liability has arisen that can be measured reliably'. IAS 18.14(c) requires, among other conditions, that revenue from the sale of goods should be recognised when 'the amount of revenue can be measured reliably'. The requirement for reliable measurement also applies to the recognition of gains or losses resulting from a contribution of non-monetary assets to a JCE.

11 IAS 18.12 explains that 'when goods and services are exchanged or swapped for goods or services which are of similar nature and value, the exchange is not regarded as a transaction which generates revenue'. ~~IAS 16.22 says that 'an item of property, plant and equipment may be acquired in exchange for a similar asset that has a similar use in the same line of business and which has a similar fair value. An item of property, plant and equipment may also be sold in exchange for an equity interest in a similar asset. In both cases, since the earnings process is~~

~~incomplete, no gain or loss is recognised on the transaction'.~~* The same rationale applies to a contribution of non-monetary assets since a contribution to a JCE is, in substance, an exchange of assets with the other venturers at the level of the JCE.

12 To the extent that the venturer also receives cash or non-monetary assets dissimilar to the assets contributed in addition to equity interests in the JCE, the realisation of which is not dependent on the future cash flows of the JCE, the earnings process is complete. Accordingly, the appropriate portion of the gain on the non-monetary contribution is recognised in profit or loss for the period.

13 It is not appropriate to present unrealised gains or losses on non-monetary assets contributed to JCEs as deferred items since such items do not meet the recognition criteria for assets or liabilities as defined in the *Framework* (paragraphs 53 to 64 and paragraphs 89 to 91).

Date of consensus

June 1998

Effective date

This Interpretation becomes effective for annual financial periods beginning on or after 1 January 1999; earlier application is encouraged. Changes in accounting policies shall be accounted for in accordance with IAS 8.

14 The amendments to the accounting for the non-monetary contribution transactions specified in paragraph 5 shall be applied prospectively to future transactions.

15 An entity shall apply the amendments to this Interpretation made by IAS 16 *Property, Plant and Equipment* for annual periods beginning on or after 1 January 2005. If an entity applies that Standard for an earlier period, it shall also apply these amendments for that earlier period.

* IAS 16 *Property, Plant and Equipment* as revised by the IASB in 2003 requires an entity to measure an item of property, plant and equipment acquired in exchange for a non-monetary asset or assets, or a combination of monetary and non-monetary assets, at fair value unless the exchange transaction lacks commercial substance. Previously, an entity measured such an acquired asset at fair value unless the exchanged assets were similar.

SIC Interpretation 15

Operating Leases—Incentives

This version includes amendments resulting from new and amended IFRSs issued up to 31 December 2004.

SIC Interpretation 15 *Operating Leases—Incentives* (SIC-15) is set out in paragraphs 3–6. SIC-15 is accompanied by a Basis for Conclusions and appendix illustrating the application of the Interpretation. The scope and authority of Interpretations are set out in paragraphs 1 and 8–10 of the *IFRIC Preface*.

Reference

- IAS 17 *Leases* (as revised in 2003)

Issue

1 In negotiating a new or renewed operating lease, the lessor may provide incentives for the lessee to enter into the agreement. Examples of such incentives are an up-front cash payment to the lessee or the reimbursement or assumption by the lessor of costs of the lessee (such as relocation costs, leasehold improvements and costs associated with a pre-existing lease commitment of the lessee). Alternatively, initial periods of the lease term may be agreed to be rent-free or at a reduced rent.

2 The issue is how incentives in an operating lease should be recognised in the financial statements of both the lessee and the lessor.

Consensus

3 All incentives for the agreement of a new or renewed operating lease shall be recognised as an integral part of the net consideration agreed for the use of the leased asset, irrespective of the incentive's nature or form or the timing of payments.

4 The lessor shall recognise the aggregate cost of incentives as a reduction of rental income over the lease term, on a straight-line basis unless another systematic basis is representative of the time pattern over which the benefit of the leased asset is diminished.

5 The lessee shall recognise the aggregate benefit of incentives as a reduction of rental expense over the lease term, on a straight-line basis unless another systematic basis is representative of the time pattern of the lessee's benefit from the use of the leased asset.

6 Costs incurred by the lessee, including costs in connection with a pre-existing lease (for example costs for termination, relocation or leasehold improvements), shall be accounted for by the lessee in accordance with the Standards applicable to those costs, including costs which are effectively reimbursed through an incentive arrangement.

Basis for Conclusions

[The original text has been marked up to reflect the revision of IAS 17 in 2003: new text is underlined and deleted text is struck through]

7 Paragraph 35 of the *Framework* explains that if information is to represent faithfully the transactions and events that it purports to represent, it is necessary that transactions and events are accounted for and presented in accordance with their substance and economic reality and not merely their legal form. IAS ~~1.20(b)(ii)~~ 8.10(b)(ii) also requires the application of accounting policies which reflect economic substance.

8 Paragraph 22 of the *Framework* and IAS 1.25 require the preparation of financial statements under the accrual basis of accounting. IAS 17.33~~25~~ and IAS 17.50~~42~~

specify the basis on which lessees and lessors respectively should recognise amounts payable or receivable under operating leases.

9 The underlying substance of operating lease arrangements is that the lessor and lessee exchange the use of an asset for a specified period for the consideration of a net amount of money. The accounting periods in which this net amount is recognised by either the lessor or the lessee is not affected by the form of the agreement or the timing of payments. Payments made by a lessor to or on behalf of a lessee, or allowances in rental cost made by a lessor, as incentives for the agreement of a new or renewed lease are an inseparable part of the net amount receivable or payable under the operating lease.

10 Costs incurred by the lessor as incentives for the agreement of new or renewed operating leases are not considered to be part of those initial costs which ~~may be recognised as an expense in the income statements in the period in which they are incurred~~ are added to the carrying amount of the leased asset and recognised as an expense over the lease term on the same basis as the lease income in accordance with ~~under~~ IAS 17.52~~44~~. Initial costs, such as direct costs for administration, advertising and consulting or legal fees, are incurred by a lessor to arrange a contract, whereas incentives in an operating lease are, in substance, related to the consideration for the use of the leased asset.

11 Costs incurred by the lessee on its own behalf are accounted for using the applicable recognition requirements. For example, relocation costs are recognised as an expense in the income statement in the period in which they are incurred. The accounting for such costs does not depend on whether or not they are effectively reimbursed through an incentive arrangement as they are not related to the consideration for the use of the leased asset.

Date of consensus

June 1998

Effective date

This Interpretation becomes effective for lease terms beginning on or after 1 January 1999.

Appendix to SIC-15

This appendix accompanies, but is not part of, SIC-15.

Example application of SIC-15

Example 1

An entity agrees to enter into a new lease arrangement with a new lessor. The lessor agrees to pay the lessee's relocation costs as an incentive to the lessee for entering into the new lease. The lessee's moving costs are 1,000. The new lease has a term of 10 years, at a fixed rate of 2,000 per year.

The accounting is:

The lessee recognises relocation costs of 1,000 as an expense in Year 1. Net consideration of 19,000 consists of 2,000 for each of the 10 years in the lease term, less a 1,000 incentive for relocation costs. Both the lessor and lessee would recognise the net rental consideration of 19,000 over the 10 year lease term using a single amortisation method in accordance with paragraphs 4 and 5 of this Interpretation.

Example 2

An entity agrees to enter into a new lease arrangement with a new lessor. The lessor agrees to a rent-free period for the first three years as incentive to the lessee for entering into the new lease. The new lease has a term of 20 years, at a fixed rate of 5,000 per annum for years 4 through 20.

The accounting is:

Net consideration of 85,000 consists of 5,000 for each of 17 years in the lease term. Both the lessor and lessee would recognise the net consideration of 85,000 over the 20 year lease term using a single amortisation method in accordance with paragraphs 4 and 5 of this Interpretation.

SIC Interpretation 21

Income Taxes—Recovery of Revalued Non-Depreciable Assets

This version includes amendments resulting from new and amended IFRSs issued up to 31 December 2004.

SIC Interpretation 21 *Income Taxes—Recovery of Revalued Non-Depreciable Assets* (SIC-21) is set out in paragraph 5. SIC-21 is accompanied by a Basis for Conclusions. The scope and authority of Interpretations are set out in paragraphs 1 and 8–10 of the *IFRIC Preface.*

References

- IAS 12 *Income Taxes*
- IAS 16 *Property, Plant and Equipment* (as revised in 2003)

Issue

1 Under IAS 12.51, the measurement of deferred tax liabilities and assets should reflect the tax consequences that would follow from the manner in which the entity expects, at the balance sheet date, to recover or settle the carrying amount of those assets and liabilities that give rise to temporary differences.

2 IAS 12.20 notes that the revaluation of an asset does not always affect taxable profit (tax loss) in the period of the revaluation and that the tax base of the asset may not be adjusted as a result of the revaluation. If the future recovery of the carrying amount will be taxable, any difference between the carrying amount of the revalued asset and its tax base is a temporary difference and gives rise to a deferred tax liability or asset.

3 The issue is how to interpret the term 'recovery' in relation to an asset that is not depreciated (non-depreciable asset) and is revalued in accordance with paragraph 31 of IAS 16.

4 This Interpretation also applies to investment properties that are carried at revalued amounts under IAS 40.33 but would be considered non-depreciable if IAS 16 were to be applied.

Consensus

5 The deferred tax liability or asset that arises from the revaluation of a non-depreciable asset in accordance with IAS 16.31 shall be measured on the basis of the tax consequences that would follow from recovery of the carrying amount of that asset through sale, regardless of the basis of measuring the carrying amount of that asset. Accordingly, if the tax law specifies a tax rate applicable to the taxable amount derived from the sale of an asset that differs from the tax rate applicable to the taxable amount derived from using an asset, the former rate is applied in measuring the deferred tax liability or asset related to a non-depreciable asset.

Basis for Conclusions

6 The *Framework* indicates that an entity recognises an asset if it is probable that the future economic benefits associated with the asset will flow to the entity. Generally, those future economic benefits will be derived (and therefore the carrying amount of an asset will be recovered) through sale, through use, or through use and subsequent sale. Recognition of depreciation implies that the carrying amount of a depreciable asset is expected to be recovered through use to the extent of its depreciable amount, and through sale at its residual value. Consistent with this, the carrying amount of a non-depreciable asset, such as land having an unlimited life, will be recovered only through sale. That is, because the asset is not depreciated, no part of its carrying amount is expected to be recovered

(that is, consumed) through use. Deferred taxes associated with the non-depreciable asset reflect the tax consequences of selling the asset.

7 The expected manner of recovery is not predicated on the basis of measuring the carrying amount of the asset. For example, if the carrying amount of a non-depreciable asset is measured at its value in use, the basis of measurement does not imply that the carrying amount of the asset is expected to be recovered through use, but through its residual value upon ultimate disposal.

Date of consensus

August 1999

Effective date

This consensus becomes effective on 15 July 2000. Changes in accounting policies shall be accounted for in accordance with IAS 8.

SIC Interpretation 25

Income Taxes—Changes in the Tax Status of an Entity or its Shareholders

This version includes amendments resulting from new and amended IFRSs issued up to 31 December 2004.

SIC Interpretation 25 *Income Taxes—Changes in the Tax Status of an Entity or its Shareholders* (SIC-25) is set out in paragraph 4. SIC-25 is accompanied by a Basis for Conclusions. The scope and authority of Interpretations are set out in paragraphs 1 and 8–10 of the *IFRIC Preface*.

Reference

- IAS 12 *Income Taxes*

Issue

1 A change in the tax status of an entity or of its shareholders may have consequences for an entity by increasing or decreasing its tax liabilities or assets. This may, for example, occur upon the public listing of an entity's equity instruments or upon the restructuring of an entity's equity. It may also occur upon a controlling shareholder's move to a foreign country. As a result of such an event, an entity may be taxed differently; it may for example gain or lose tax incentives or become subject to a different rate of tax in the future.

2 A change in the tax status of an entity or its shareholders may have an immediate effect on the entity's current tax liabilities or assets. The change may also increase or decrease the deferred tax liabilities and assets recognised by the entity, depending on the effect the change in tax status has on the tax consequences that will arise from recovering or settling the carrying amount of the entity's assets and liabilities.

3 The issue is how an entity should account for the tax consequences of a change in its tax status or that of its shareholders.

Consensus

4 A change in the tax status of an entity or its shareholders does not give rise to increases or decreases in amounts recognised directly in equity. The current and deferred tax consequences of a change in tax status shall be included in profit or loss for the period, unless those consequences relate to transactions and events that result, in the same or a different period, in a direct credit or charge to the recognised amount of equity. Those tax consequences that relate to changes in the recognised amount of equity, in the same or a different period (not included in profit or loss), shall be charged or credited directly to equity.

Basis for Conclusions

[The original text has been marked up to reflect the revision of IAS 38 in 2004: deleted text is struck through]

5 IAS 12.58 requires current and deferred tax to be included in the net profit or loss for the period, except to the extent the tax arises from a transaction or event that is recognised directly in equity, in the same or a different period, (or arises from a business combination ~~that is an acquisition~~). IAS 12.61 requires that current and deferred tax be charged or credited directly to equity if the tax relates to items that are credited or charged, in the same or a different period, directly to equity.

6 IAS 12.62 identifies examples of circumstances in which a transaction or event is recognised directly in equity as is permitted or required by another International Accounting Standard. All of these circumstances result in changes in the recognised amount of equity through recognition of a credit or charge directly to equity.

7 IAS 12.65 explains that where the tax base of a revalued asset changes, any tax consequence is recognised directly in equity only to the extent a related accounting revaluation was or is expected to be recognised directly in equity (revaluation surplus).

8 Because tax consequences recognised directly in equity must relate to a transaction or event recognised directly in equity in the same or a different period, the cumulative amount of tax charged or credited directly to equity can be expected to be the same amount that would have been charged or credited directly to equity if the new tax status had applied previously. IAS 12.63(b) acknowledges that determining the tax consequences of a change in the tax rate or other tax rules that affects a deferred tax asset or liability and relates to an item previously charged or credited to equity may prove to be difficult. Because of this, IAS 12.63 suggests that an allocation may be necessary.

Date of consensus

August 1999

Effective date

This consensus becomes effective on 15 July 2000. Changes in accounting policies shall be accounted for in accordance with IAS 8.

SIC Interpretation 27

Evaluating the Substance of Transactions Involving the Legal Form of a Lease

This version includes amendments resulting from new and amended IFRSs issued up to 31 December 2004.

SIC Interpretation 27 *Evaluating the Substance of Transactions Involving the Legal Form of a Lease* (SIC-27) is set out in paragraphs 3–11. SIC-27 is accompanied by a Basis for Conclusions and appendices illustrating the application of the Interpretation. The scope and authority of Interpretations are set out in paragraphs 1 and 8–10 of the *IFRIC Preface*.

References

- IAS 1 *Presentation of Financial Statements* (as revised in 2003)
- IAS 17 *Leases* (as revised in 2003)
- IAS 18 *Revenue*
- IFRS 4 *Insurance Contracts*

Issue

1 An Entity may enter into a transaction or a series of structured transactions (an arrangement) with an unrelated party or parties (an Investor) that involves the legal form of a lease. For example, an Entity may lease assets to an Investor and lease the same assets back, or alternatively, legally sell assets and lease the same assets back. The form of each arrangement and its terms and conditions can vary significantly. In the lease and leaseback example, it may be that the arrangement is designed to achieve a tax advantage for the Investor that is shared with the Entity in the form of a fee, and not to convey the right to use an asset.

2 When an arrangement with an Investor involves the legal form of a lease, the issues are:

(a) how to determine whether a series of transactions is linked and should be accounted for as one transaction;

(b) whether the arrangement meets the definition of a lease under IAS 17; and, if not,

(i) whether a separate investment account and lease payment obligations that might exist represent assets and liabilities of the Entity (eg consider the example described in paragraph A2(a) of Appendix A);

(ii) how the Entity should account for other obligations resulting from the arrangement; and

(iii) how the Entity should account for a fee it might receive from an Investor.

Consensus

3 A series of transactions that involve the legal form of a lease is linked and shall be accounted for as one transaction when the overall economic effect cannot be understood without reference to the series of transactions as a whole. This is the case, for example, when the series of transactions are closely interrelated, negotiated as a single transaction, and takes place concurrently or in a continuous sequence. (Appendix A provides illustrations of application of this Interpretation.)

4 The accounting shall reflect the substance of the arrangement. All aspects and implications of an arrangement shall be evaluated to determine its substance, with weight given to those aspects and implications that have an economic effect.

5 IAS 17 applies when the substance of an arrangement includes the conveyance of the right to use an asset for an agreed period of time. Indicators that individually

demonstrate that an arrangement may not, in substance, involve a lease under IAS 17 include (Appendix B provides illustrations of application of this Interpretation):

(a) an Entity retains all the risks and rewards incident to ownership of an underlying asset and enjoys substantially the same rights to its use as before the arrangement;

(b) the primary reason for the arrangement is to achieve a particular tax result, and not to convey the right to use an asset; and

(c) an option is included on terms that make its exercise almost certain (eg a put option that is exercisable at a price sufficiently higher than the expected fair value when it becomes exercisable).

6 The definitions and guidance in paragraphs 49–64 of the *Framework* shall be applied in determining whether, in substance, a separate investment account and lease payment obligations represent assets and liabilities of the Entity. Indicators that collectively demonstrate that, in substance, a separate investment account and lease payment obligations do not meet the definitions of an asset and a liability and shall not be recognised by the Entity include:

(a) the Entity is not able to control the investment account in pursuit of its own objectives and is not obligated to pay the lease payments. This occurs when, for example, a prepaid amount is placed in a separate investment account to protect the Investor and may only be used to pay the Investor, the Investor agrees that the lease payment obligations are to be paid from funds in the investment account, and the Entity has no ability to withhold payments to the Investor from the investment account;

(b) the Entity has only a remote risk of reimbursing the entire amount of any fee received from an Investor and possibly paying some additional amount, or, when a fee has not been received, only a remote risk of paying an amount under other obligations (eg a guarantee). Only a remote risk of payment exists when, for example, the terms of the arrangement require that a prepaid amount is invested in risk-free assets that are expected to generate sufficient cash flows to satisfy the lease payment obligations; and

(c) other than the initial cash flows at inception of the arrangement, the only cash flows expected under the arrangement are the lease payments that are satisfied solely from funds withdrawn from the separate investment account established with the initial cash flows.

7 Other obligations of an arrangement, including any guarantees provided and obligations incurred upon early termination, shall be accounted for under IAS 37, IAS 39 or IFRS 4, depending on the terms.

8 The criteria in paragraph 20 of IAS 18 shall be applied to the facts and circumstances of each arrangement in determining when to recognise a fee as income that an Entity might receive. Factors such as whether there is continuing involvement in the form of significant future performance obligations necessary to earn the fee, whether there are retained risks, the terms of any guarantee arrangements, and the risk of repayment of the fee, shall be considered.

Indicators that individually demonstrate that recognition of the entire fee as income when received, if received at the beginning of the arrangement, is inappropriate include:

(a) obligations either to perform or to refrain from certain significant activities are conditions of earning the fee received, and therefore execution of a legally binding arrangement is not the most significant act required by the arrangement;

(b) limitations are put on the use of the underlying asset that have the practical effect of restricting and significantly changing the Entity's ability to use (eg deplete, sell or pledge as collateral) the asset;

(c) the possibility of reimbursing any amount of the fee and possibly paying some additional amount is not remote. This occurs when, for example,

   (i) the underlying asset is not a specialised asset that is required by the Entity to conduct its business, and therefore there is a possibility that the Entity may pay an amount to terminate the arrangement early; or

   (ii) the Entity is required by the terms of the arrangement, or has some or total discretion, to invest a prepaid amount in assets carrying more than an insignificant amount of risk (eg currency, interest rate or credit risk). In this circumstance, the risk of the investment's value being insufficient to satisfy the lease payment obligations is not remote, and therefore there is a possibility that the Entity may be required to pay some amount.

9 The fee shall be presented in the income statement based on its economic substance and nature.

Disclosure

10 All aspects of an arrangement that does not, in substance, involve a lease under IAS 17 shall be considered in determining the appropriate disclosures that are necessary to understand the arrangement and the accounting treatment adopted. An Entity shall disclose the following in each period that an arrangement exists:

(a) a description of the arrangement including:

   (i) the underlying asset and any restrictions on its use;

   (ii) the life and other significant terms of the arrangement;

   (iii) the transactions that are linked together, including any options; and

(b) the accounting treatment applied to any fee received, the amount recognised as income in the period, and the line item of the income statement in which it is included.

11 The disclosures required in accordance with paragraph 10 of this Interpretation shall be provided individually for each arrangement or in aggregate for each class of arrangement. A class is a grouping of arrangements with underlying assets of a similar nature (eg power plants).

Basis for Conclusions

[The original text has been marked up to reflect the revision of IAS 39 in 2003 and subsequently the issue of IFRS 4: new text is underlined and deleted text is struck through]

12 Paragraph 9 of IAS 11 *Construction Contracts* requires a group of contracts to be treated as a single contract when the group of contracts is negotiated as a single package, the contracts are so closely interrelated that they are, in effect, part of a single project with an overall profit margin, and the contracts are performed concurrently or in a continuous sequence. In such a situation, a series of transactions that involve the legal form of a lease are linked and accounted for as one transaction, because the overall economic effect cannot be understood without reference to the series of transactions as a whole.

13 An agreement is accounted for as a lease in accordance with IAS 17 when it conveys to the lessee in return for a payment or series of payments the right to use an asset for an agreed period of time. For information to represent faithfully the transactions it purports to represent, paragraph 35 of the *Framework* indicates that it is necessary that transactions are accounted for and presented in accordance with their substance and economic reality, not merely their legal form.

14 When an Entity does not control the assets that will be used to satisfy the lease payment obligations, and is not obligated to pay the lease payments, it does not recognise the assets and lease payment obligations, because the definitions of an asset and a liability have not been met. This is different from the circumstance when an Entity controls the assets, is obligated to pay the lease payments, and then later transfers assets to a third party (including a trust). In that circumstance, the transfer of assets (sometimes called an 'in-substance' defeasance) does not by itself relieve the Entity of its primary obligation, in the absence of legal release. A financial asset and a financial liability, or a portion of either, are derecognised only when the requirements of ~~IAS 39.35–65~~ paragraphs 15–37 and 39–42 of IAS 39 are met.

15 ~~In addition to addressing the general requirements for recognition of a provision, IAS 37 IAS 39~~ IFRS 4 provides guidance for recognising and measuring financial guarantees and similar instruments that provide for payments to be made if the debtor fails to make payments when due, if that contract transfers significant insurance risk to the issuer. ~~IAS 37 also provides guidance when disclosure of a contingent liability is required.~~ Financial guarantee contracts that provide for payments to be made in response to changes in relation to a variable (sometimes referred to as an 'underlying') are subject to IAS 39.

16 IAS 18 addresses the accounting treatment of revenue. Paragraph 75 of the *Framework* indicates that gains are no different in nature from revenue. Therefore, the requirements of IAS 18 apply by analogy or otherwise. Example 14(c) in the Appendix of IAS 18 states that a fee earned on the execution of a significant act, which is much more significant than any other act, is recognised as income when the significant act has been completed. The example also indicates that it is necessary to distinguish between fees earned on completion of a significant act and fees related to future performance or risks retained.

Date of consensus

February 2000

Effective date

This Interpretation becomes effective on 31 December 2001. Changes in accounting policies shall be accounted for in accordance with IAS 8.

Appendix A
Linked transactions

This appendix accompanies, but is not part of, SIC-27.

A1 The Interpretation requires consideration of whether a series of transactions that involve the legal form of a lease are linked to determine whether the transactions are accounted for as one transaction.

A2 Extreme examples of transactions that are viewed as a whole and accounted for as single transactions, include:

(a) An Entity leases an asset to an Investor (the headlease) and leases the same asset back for a shorter period of time (the sublease). At the end of the sublease period, the Entity has the right to buy back the rights of the Investor under a purchase option. If the Entity does not exercise its purchase option, the Investor has options available to it under each of which the Investor receives a minimum return on its investment in the headlease—the Investor may put the underlying asset back to the Entity, or require the Entity to provide a return on the Investor's investment in the headlease.

The predominant purpose of the arrangement is to achieve a tax advantage for the Investor, which is shared with the Entity in the form of a fee, and not to convey the right to use an asset. The Investor pays the fee and prepays the lease payment obligations under the headlease. The agreement requires the amount prepaid to be invested in risk-free assets and, as a requirement of finalising the execution of the legally binding arrangement, placed into a separate investment account held by a Trustee outside of the control of the Entity. The fee is retained by the Entity.

Over the term of the sublease, the sublease payment obligations are satisfied with funds of an equal amount withdrawn from the separate investment account. The Entity guarantees the sublease payment obligations, and will be required to satisfy the guarantee should the separate investment account have insufficient funds. The Entity, but not the Investor, has the right to terminate the sublease early under certain circumstances (eg a change in local or international tax law causes the Investor to lose part or all of the tax benefits, or the Entity decides to dispose of (eg replace, sell or deplete) the underlying asset) and upon payment of a termination value to the Investor. If the Entity chooses early termination, then it would pay the termination value from funds withdrawn from the separate investment account, and if the amount remaining in the separate investment account is insufficient, the difference would be paid by the Entity. The underlying asset is a specialised asset that the Entity requires to conduct its business.

(b) An entity leases an asset to another entity for its entire economic life and leases the same asset back under the same terms and conditions as the original lease. The two entities have a legally enforceable right to set off the amounts owing to one another, and an intention to settle these amounts on a net basis.

(c) An entity (Entity A) leases an asset to another entity (Entity B), and obtains a non-recourse loan from a financier (by using the lease rentals and the asset as collateral). Entity A sells the asset subject to the lease and the loan to a trustee, and leases the same asset back. Entity A also concurrently agrees to repurchase the asset at the end of the lease for an amount equal to the sale price. The financier legally releases Entity A from the primary responsibility for the loan, and Entity A guarantees repayment of the non-recourse loan if Entity B defaults on the payments under the original lease. Entity B's credit rating is assessed as AAA and the amounts of the payments under each of the leases are equal. Entity A has a legally enforceable right to set-off the amounts owing under each of the leases, and an intention to settle the rights and obligations under the leases on a net basis.

(d) An entity (Entity A) legally sells an asset to another entity (Entity B) and leases the same asset back. Entity B is obligated to put the asset back to Entity A at the end of the lease period at an amount that has the overall practical effect, when also considering the lease payments to be received, of providing Entity B with a yield of LIBOR plus 2 per cent per year on the purchase price.

Appendix B
The substance of an arrangement

This appendix accompanies, but is not part of, SIC-27.

B1 The Interpretation requires consideration of the substance of an arrangement to determine whether it includes the conveyance of the right to use an asset for an agreed period of time.

B2 In each of the examples described in Appendix A, the arrangement does not, in substance, involve a lease under IAS 17 for the following reasons:

(a) in the example described in paragraph A2(a), the arrangement is designed predominantly to generate tax benefits that are shared between the two entities. Even though the periods of the headlease and sublease are different, the options available to each of the entities at the end of the sublease period are structured such that the Investor assumes only an insignificant amount of asset risk during the headlease period. The substance of the arrangement is that the Entity receives a fee for executing the agreements, and retains the risks and rewards incident to ownership of the underlying asset.

(b) in the example described in paragraph A2(b), the terms and conditions and period of each of the leases are the same. Therefore, the risks and rewards incident to ownership of the underlying asset are the same as before the arrangement. Further, the amounts owing are offset against one another, and so there is no retained credit risk. The substance of the arrangement is that no transaction has occurred.

(c) in the example described in paragraph A2(c), Entity A retains the risks and rewards incident to ownership of the underlying asset, and the risk of payment under the guarantee is only remote (due to the AAA credit rating). The substance of the arrangement is that Entity A borrows cash, secured by the underlying asset.

(d) in the example described in paragraph A2(d), Entity A's risks and rewards incident to owning the underlying asset do not substantively change. The substance of the arrangement is that Entity A borrows cash, secured by the underlying asset and repayable in instalments over the lease period and in a final lump sum at the end of the lease period. The terms of the option preclude recognition of a sale. Normally, in a sale and leaseback transaction, the risks and rewards incident to owning the underlying asset sold are retained by the seller only during the period of the lease.

SIC Interpretation 29

Disclosure—
Service Concession Arrangements

This version includes amendments resulting from new and amended IFRSs issued up to 31 December 2004.

SIC Interpretation 29 *Disclosure—Service Concession Arrangements* (SIC-29) is set out in paragraphs 6 and 7. SIC-29 is accompanied by a Basis for Conclusions. The scope and authority of Interpretations are set out in paragraphs 1 and 8–10 of the *IFRIC Preface*.

Reference

- IAS 1 *Presentation of Financial Statements* (as revised in 2003)

Issue

1 An entity (the Concession Operator) may enter into an arrangement with another entity (the Concession Provider) to provide services that give the public access to major economic and social facilities. The Concession Provider may be a public or private sector entity, including a governmental body. Examples of service concession arrangements involve water treatment and supply facilities, motorways, car parks, tunnels, bridges, airports and telecommunication networks. Examples of arrangements that are not service concession arrangements include an entity outsourcing the operation of its internal services (eg employee cafeteria, building maintenance, and accounting or information technology functions).

2 A service concession arrangement generally involves the Concession Provider conveying for the period of the concession to the Concession Operator:

(a) the right to provide services that give the public access to major economic and social facilities, and

(b) in some cases, the right to use specified tangible assets, intangible assets, or financial assets,

in exchange for the Concession Operator:

(c) committing to provide the services according to certain terms and conditions during the concession period, and

(d) when applicable, committing to return at the end of the concession period the rights received at the beginning of the concession period and/or acquired during the concession period.

3 The common characteristic of all service concession arrangements is that the Concession Operator both receives a right and incurs an obligation to provide public services.

4 The issue is what information should be disclosed in the notes in the financial statements of a Concession Operator and a Concession Provider.

5 Certain aspects and disclosures relating to some service concession arrangements are already addressed by existing International Accounting Standards (eg IAS 16 applies to acquisitions of items of property, plant and equipment, IAS 17 applies to leases of assets, and IAS 38 applies to acquisitions of intangible assets). However, a service concession arrangement may involve executory contracts that are not addressed in International Accounting Standards, unless the contracts are onerous, in which case IAS 37 applies. Therefore, this Interpretation addresses additional disclosures of service concession arrangements.

Consensus

6 All aspects of a service concession arrangement shall be considered in determining the appropriate disclosures in the notes. A Concession Operator and a Concession Provider shall disclose the following in each period:

(a) a description of the arrangement;

(b) significant terms of the arrangement that may affect the amount, timing and certainty of future cash flows (eg the period of the concession, re-pricing dates and the basis upon which re-pricing or re-negotiation is determined);

(c) the nature and extent (eg quantity, time period or amount as appropriate) of:

(i) rights to use specified assets;

(ii) obligations to provide or rights to expect provision of services;

(iii) obligations to acquire or build items of property, plant and equipment;

(iv) obligations to deliver or rights to receive specified assets at the end of the concession period;

(v) renewal and termination options; and

(vi) other rights and obligations (eg major overhauls); and

(d) changes in the arrangement occurring during the period.

7 The disclosures required in accordance with paragraph 6 of this Interpretation shall be provided individually for each service concession arrangement or in aggregate for each class of service concession arrangements. A class is a grouping of service concession arrangements involving services of a similar nature (eg toll collections, telecommunications and water treatment services).

Basis for Conclusions

[The original text has been marked up to reflect the revision of IAS 1 in 2003: new text is underlined and deleted text is struck through]

8 Paragraph 15 of the *Framework* states that the economic decisions taken by users of financial statements require an evaluation of the ability of the entity to generate cash and cash equivalents and of the timing and certainty of their generation. Paragraph 21 of the *Framework* states that financial statements also contain notes and supplementary schedules and other information. For example, they may contain additional information that is relevant to the needs of users about the items in the balance sheet and income statement. They may also include disclosures about the risks and uncertainties affecting the entity and any resources and obligations not recognised in the balance sheet.

9 A service concession arrangement often has provisions or significant features that warrant disclosure of information necessary to assist in assessing the amount, timing and certainty of future cash flows, and the nature and extent of the various rights and obligations involved. The rights and obligations associated with the services to be provided usually involve a high level of public involvement (eg to provide electricity to a city). Other obligations could include significant acts such

as building an infrastructure asset (eg power plant) and delivering that asset to the Concession Provider at the end of the concession period.

10 IAS 1.~~91~~103(c) requires ~~the~~ an entity's notes ~~to the financial statements of an enterprise~~ to provide additional information ~~which~~ that is not presented on the face of the ~~financial statements~~ balance sheet, income statement, statement of changes in equity or cash flow statement, but ~~that~~ is ~~necessary for a fair presentation~~ relevant to an understanding of any of them. ~~IAS 1.93~~ The definition of notes in IAS 1.11 indicates that ~~the~~ notes ~~to the financial statements include~~ provide narrative descriptions or ~~more detailed analyses~~ disaggregations of ~~amounts shown on the face of~~ items disclosed in the balance sheet, income statement, statement of changes in equity and cash flow statement ~~and statement of changes in equity~~, as well as ~~additional~~ information ~~such as contingent liabilities and commitments~~ about items that do not qualify for recognition in those statements.

Date of consensus

May 2001

Effective date

This Interpretation becomes effective on 31 December 2001.

SIC Interpretation 31

Revenue—Barter Transactions Involving Advertising Services

This version includes amendments resulting from new and amended IFRSs issued up to 31 December 2004.

SIC Interpretation 31 *Revenue—Barter Transactions Involving Advertising Services* (SIC-31) is set out in paragraph 5. SIC-31 is accompanied by a Basis for Conclusions. The scope and authority of Interpretations are set out in paragraphs 1 and 8–10 of the *IFRIC Preface*.

Reference

- IAS 18 *Revenue*

Issue

1 An entity (Seller) may enter into a barter transaction to provide advertising services in exchange for receiving advertising services from its customer (Customer). Advertisements may be displayed on the Internet or poster sites, broadcast on the television or radio, published in magazines or journals, or presented in another medium.

2 In some cases, no cash or other consideration is exchanged between the entities. In some other cases, equal or approximately equal amounts of cash or other consideration are also exchanged.

3 A Seller that provides advertising services in the course of its ordinary activities recognises revenue under IAS 18 from a barter transaction involving advertising when, amongst other criteria, the services exchanged are dissimilar (IAS 18.12) and the amount of revenue can be measured reliably (IAS 18.20(a)). This Interpretation only applies to an exchange of dissimilar advertising services. An exchange of similar advertising services is not a transaction that generates revenue under IAS 18.

4 The issue is under what circumstances can a Seller reliably measure revenue at the fair value of advertising services received or provided in a barter transaction.

Consensus

5 Revenue from a barter transaction involving advertising cannot be measured reliably at the fair value of advertising services received. However, a Seller can reliably measure revenue at the fair value of the advertising services it provides in a barter transaction, by reference only to non-barter transactions that:

(a) involve advertising similar to the advertising in the barter transaction;

(b) occur frequently;

(c) represent a predominant number of transactions and amount when compared to all transactions to provide advertising that is similar to the advertising in the barter transaction;

(d) involve cash and/or another form of consideration (eg marketable securities, non-monetary assets, and other services) that has a reliably measurable fair value; and

(e) do not involve the same counterparty as in the barter transaction.

Basis for Conclusions

6 IAS 18.9 requires revenue to be measured at the fair value of the consideration received or receivable. When the fair value of the services received cannot be measured reliably, the revenue is measured at the fair value of the services provided, adjusted by the amount of any cash or cash equivalents transferred. IAS 18.26 states that when the outcome of a transaction involving the rendering of services cannot be estimated reliably (eg the amount of revenue cannot be measured reliably), revenue should be recognised only to the extent of the expenses recognised that are recoverable. As explained in IAS 18.27, this means that revenue is recognised only to the extent of costs incurred that are expected to be recoverable and, as the outcome of the transactions cannot be estimated reliably, no profit is recognised.

7 Paragraph 31 of the *Framework* states that information has the quality of reliability when it is free from material error and bias and is representationally faithful. Measuring revenue at the fair value of advertising services received from the Customer in a barter transaction is impracticable, because reliable information not available to the Seller is required to support the measurement. Consequently, revenue from a barter transaction involving advertising services is measured at the fair value of the advertising services provided by the Seller to the Customer.

8 IAS 18.7 defines fair value as the amount for which an asset could be exchanged, or a liability settled, between knowledgeable, willing parties in an arm's length transaction. A published price of a service does not constitute reliable evidence of its fair value, unless the price is supported by transactions with knowledgeable and willing parties in an arm's length transaction. For transactions to provide a relevant and reliable basis for support, the services involved are similar, there are many transactions, valuable consideration that can be reliably measured is exchanged, and independent third parties are involved. Consequently, the fair value of advertising services provided in a barter transaction is reliably measurable only when it is supportable by reference to non-barter transactions that have these characteristics.

9 However, a swap of cheques, for example, for equal or substantially equal amounts between the same entities that provide and receive advertising services does not provide reliable evidence of fair value. An exchange of advertising services that also includes only partial cash payment provides reliable evidence of the fair value of the transaction to the extent of the cash component (except when partial cash payments of equal or substantially equal amounts are swapped), but does not provide reliable evidence of the fair value of the entire transaction.

10 Reliable measurement of the fair value of a service also depends on a number of other factors, including the industry, the number of market participants, the nature of the services, and the number of market transactions. In the case of barter transactions involving advertising, the fair value of advertising services is reliably measurable when independent non-barter transactions involving similar advertising provide reliable evidence to substantiate the fair value of the barter exchange.

Date of consensus

May 2001

Effective date

This Interpretation becomes effective on 31 December 2001. Changes in accounting policies shall be accounted for in accordance with IAS 8.

SIC Interpretation 32

Intangible Assets—Web Site Costs

This version includes amendments resulting from new and amended IFRSs issued up to 31 December 2004.

SIC Interpretation 32 *Intangible Assets—Web Site Costs* (SIC-32) is set out in paragraphs 7–10. SIC-32 is accompanied by a Basis for Conclusions and an appendix illustrating the application of the Interpretation. The scope and authority of Interpretations are set out in paragraphs 1 and 8–10 of the *IFRIC Preface*.

References

- IAS 1 *Presentation of Financial Statements* (as revised in 2003)
- IAS 2 *Inventories* (as revised in 2003)
- IAS 11 *Construction Contracts*
- IAS 16 *Property, Plant and Equipment* (as revised in 2003)
- IAS 17 *Leases* (as revised in 2003)
- IAS 36 *Impairment of Assets* (as revised in 2004)
- IAS 38 *Intangible Assets* (as revised in 2004)
- IFRS 3 *Business Combinations*

Issue

1 An entity may incur internal expenditure on the development and operation of its own web site for internal or external access. A web site designed for external access may be used for various purposes such as to promote and advertise an entity's own products and services, provide electronic services, and sell products and services. A web site designed for internal access may be used to store company policies and customer details, and search relevant information.

2 The stages of a web site's development can be described as follows:

(a) Planning – includes undertaking feasibility studies, defining objectives and specifications, evaluating alternatives and selecting preferences.

(b) Application and Infrastructure Development – includes obtaining a domain name, purchasing and developing hardware and operating software, installing developed applications and stress testing.

(c) Graphical Design Development – includes designing the appearance of web pages.

(d) Content Development – includes creating, purchasing, preparing and uploading information, either textual or graphical in nature, on the web site before the completion of the web site's development. This information may either be stored in separate databases that are integrated into (or accessed from) the web site or coded directly into the web pages.

3 Once development of a web site has been completed, the Operating stage begins. During this stage, an entity maintains and enhances the applications, infrastructure, graphical design and content of the web site.

4 When accounting for internal expenditure on the development and operation of an entity's own web site for internal or external access, the issues are:

(a) whether the web site is an internally generated intangible asset that is subject to the requirements of IAS 38; and

(b) the appropriate accounting treatment of such expenditure.

5 This Interpretation does not apply to expenditure on purchasing, developing, and operating hardware (eg web servers, staging servers, production servers and

Internet connections) of a web site. Such expenditure is accounted for under IAS 16. Additionally, when an entity incurs expenditure on an Internet service provider hosting the entity's web site, the expenditure is recognised as an expense under IAS 1.78 and the *Framework* when the services are received.

6 IAS 38 does not apply to intangible assets held by an entity for sale in the ordinary course of business (see IAS 2 and IAS 11) or leases that fall within the scope of IAS 17. Accordingly, this Interpretation does not apply to expenditure on the development or operation of a web site (or web site software) for sale to another entity. When a web site is leased under an operating lease, the lessor applies this Interpretation. When a web site is leased under a finance lease, the lessee applies this Interpretation after initial recognition of the leased asset.

Consensus

7 An entity's own web site that arises from development and is for internal or external access is an internally generated intangible asset that is subject to the requirements of IAS 38.

8 A web site arising from development shall be recognised as an intangible asset if, and only if, in addition to complying with the general requirements described in IAS 38.21 for recognition and initial measurement, an entity can satisfy the requirements in IAS 38.57. In particular, an entity may be able to satisfy the requirement to demonstrate how its web site will generate probable future economic benefits in accordance with IAS 38.57(d) when, for example, the web site is capable of generating revenues, including direct revenues from enabling orders to be placed. An entity is not able to demonstrate how a web site developed solely or primarily for promoting and advertising its own products and services will generate probable future economic benefits, and consequently all expenditure on developing such a web site shall be recognised as an expense when incurred.

9 Any internal expenditure on the development and operation of an entity's own web site shall be accounted for in accordance with IAS 38. The nature of each activity for which expenditure is incurred (eg training employees and maintaining the web site) and the web site's stage of development or post-development shall be evaluated to determine the appropriate accounting treatment (additional guidance is provided in the Appendix to this Interpretation). For example:

(a) the Planning stage is similar in nature to the research phase in IAS 38.54–.56. Expenditure incurred in this stage shall be recognised as an expense when it is incurred.

(b) the Application and Infrastructure Development stage, the Graphical Design stage and the Content Development stage, to the extent that content is developed for purposes other than to advertise and promote an entity's own products and services, are similar in nature to the development phase in IAS 38.57–.64. Expenditure incurred in these stages shall be included in the cost of a web site recognised as an intangible asset in accordance with paragraph 8 of this Interpretation when the expenditure can be directly attributed and is necessary to creating, producing or preparing the web site for it to be capable of operating in the manner intended by management. For example, expenditure on purchasing or creating content (other than content that advertises and promotes an entity's own products and services) specifically for a web site, or expenditure to enable use of the content (eg a fee for acquiring a licence to reproduce) on the web site, shall be included in the cost of development when this condition is met. However, in accordance with IAS 38.71, expenditure on an intangible item that was initially recognised as an expense in previous financial statements shall not be recognised as part of the cost of an intangible asset at a later date (eg if the costs of a copyright have been fully amortised, and the content is subsequently provided on a web site).

(c) expenditure incurred in the Content Development stage, to the extent that content is developed to advertise and promote an entity's own products and services (eg digital photographs of products), shall be recognised as an expense when incurred in accordance with IAS 38.69(c). For example, when accounting for expenditure on professional services for taking digital photographs of an entity's own products and for enhancing their display, expenditure shall be recognised as an expense as the professional services are received during the process, not when the digital photographs are displayed on the web site.

(d) the Operating stage begins once development of a web site is complete. Expenditure incurred in this stage shall be recognised as an expense when it is incurred unless it meets the recognition criteria in IAS 38.18.

10 A web site that is recognised as an intangible asset under paragraph 8 of this Interpretation shall be measured after initial recognition by applying the requirements of IAS 38.72–.87. The best estimate of a web site's useful life should be short.

Basis for Conclusions

[The original text has been marked up to reflect the revision of IAS 16 in 2003 and the subsequent issue of IFRS 3: new text is underlined and deleted text is struck through]

11 An intangible asset is defined in IAS 38.8~~7~~ as an identifiable non-monetary asset without physical substance ~~held for use in the production or supply of goods or services, for rental to others, or for administrative purposes.~~ IAS 38.9~~8~~ provides computer software as a common example of an intangible asset. By analogy, a web site is another example of an intangible asset.

12 IAS 38.68~~56~~ requires expenditure on an intangible item to be recognised as an expense when incurred unless it forms part of the cost of an intangible asset that meets the recognition criteria in IAS 38.18–.67~~55.~~ IAS 38.69~~57~~ requires expenditure on start-up activities to be recognised as an expense when incurred. An entity developing its own web site for internal or external access is not undertaking a start-up activity to the extent that an internally generated intangible asset is created. The requirements and guidance in IAS 38.52–.67~~40–.55~~, in addition to the general requirements described in IAS 38.21~~19~~ for recognition and initial measurement of an intangible asset, apply to expenditure incurred on the development of an entity's own web site. As described in IAS 38.65–.67~~53–.55~~, the cost of a web site recognised as an internally generated intangible asset comprises all expenditure that can be directly

attributed~~, or allocated on a reasonable and consistent basis,~~ and is necessary to creating, producing and preparing the asset for it to be capable of operating in the manner intended by management ~~its intended use~~.

13 IAS 38.54~~42~~ requires expenditure on research (or on the research phase of an internal project) to be recognised as an expense when incurred. The examples provided in IAS 38.56~~44~~ are similar to the activities undertaken in the Planning stage of a web site's development. Consequently, expenditure incurred in the Planning stage of a web site's development is recognised as an expense when incurred.

14 IAS 38.57~~45~~ requires an intangible asset arising from the development phase of an internal project to be recognised only if an entity can demonstrate fulfilment of the six criteria specified. One of the criteria is to demonstrate how a web site will generate probable future economic benefits (IAS 38.57~~45~~(d)). IAS 38.60~~48~~ indicates that this criterion is met by assessing the economic benefits to be received from the web site and using the principles in IAS 36 *Impairment of Assets*, which considers the present value of estimated future cash flows from continuing use of the web site. Future economic benefits flowing from an intangible asset, as stated in IAS 38.17, may include revenue from the sale of products or services, cost savings, or other benefits resulting from the use of the asset by the entity. Therefore, future economic benefits from a web site may be assessed when the web site is capable of generating revenues. A web site developed solely or primarily for advertising and promoting an entity's own products and services is not recognised as an intangible asset, because the entity cannot demonstrate the future economic benefits that will flow. Consequently, all expenditure on developing a web site solely or primarily for promoting and advertising an entity's own products and services is recognised as an expense when incurred.

15 Under IAS 38.21~~19~~, an intangible asset is recognised if, and only if, it meets specified criteria. IAS 38.65~~53~~ indicates that the cost of an internally generated intangible asset is the sum of expenditure incurred from the date when the intangible asset first meets the specified recognition criteria. When an entity acquires or creates content for purposes other than to advertise and promote an entity's own products and services, it may be possible to identify an intangible asset (eg a licence or a copyright) separate from a web site. However, a separate asset is not recognised when expenditure is directly attributed, ~~or allocated on a reasonable and consistent basis,~~ to creating, producing, and preparing the web site for it to be capable of operating in the manner intended by management ~~its intended use~~ –the expenditure is included in the cost of developing the web site.

16 IAS 38.69~~57~~(c) requires expenditure on advertising and promotional activities to be recognised as an expense when incurred. Expenditure incurred on developing content that advertises and promotes an entity's own products and services (eg digital photographs of products) is an advertising and promotional activity, and consequently recognised as an expense when incurred ~~in accordance with IAS 38.57(c)~~.

17 ~~Once development of a web site is complete, an enterprise begins the activities described in the Operating stage. Subsequent expenditure to enhance or maintain an enterprise's own web site is recognised as an expense when incurred unless it meets the recognition criteria in IAS 38.60. IAS 38.61 explains that if the~~

~~expenditure is required to maintain the asset at its originally assessed standard of performance, then the expenditure is recognised as an expense when incurred.~~[*] Once development of a web site is complete, an entity begins the activities described in the Operating stage. Subsequent expenditure to enhance or maintain an entity's own web site is recognised as an expense when incurred unless it meets the recognition criteria in IAS 38.18. IAS 38.20 explains that most subsequent expenditures are likely to maintain the future economic benefits embodied in an existing intangible asset rather than meet the definition of an intangible asset and the recognition criteria set out in IAS 38. In addition, it is often difficult to attribute subsequent expenditure directly to a particular intangible asset rather than to the business as a whole. Therefore, only rarely will subsequent expenditure–expenditure incurred after the initial recognition of a purchased intangible asset or after completion of an internally generated intangible asset–be recognised in the carrying amount of an asset.[†]

18 An intangible asset is measured after initial recognition by applying the requirements of IAS 38.72–.87~~63–.78~~. The revaluation model ~~Allowed Alternative Treatment~~ in IAS 38.75~~64~~ is applied only when the fair value of an intangible asset can be determined by reference to an active market. However, as an active market is unlikely to exist for web sites, the cost model ~~Benchmark Treatment~~ applies. Additionally, ~~since IAS 38.84 states that an intangible asset always has a finite useful life, a web site that is recognised as an asset is amortised over the best estimate of its useful life under IAS 38.79. As~~ as indicated in IAS 38.92~~81~~, many intangible assets are susceptible to technological obsolescence, and given the history of rapid changes in technology, the useful life of web sites will be short.

Date of consensus

May 2001

Effective date

This Interpretation becomes effective on 25 March 2002. The effects of adopting this Interpretation shall be accounted for using the transition requirements in the version of IAS 38 that was issued in 1998. Therefore, when a web site does not meet the criteria for recognition as an intangible asset, but was previously recognised as an asset, the item shall be derecognised at the date when this Interpretation becomes effective. When a web site exists and the expenditure to develop it meets the criteria for recognition as an intangible asset, but was not previously recognised as an asset, the intangible asset shall not be recognised at the date when this Interpretation becomes effective. When a web site exists and the expenditure to develop it meets the criteria for recognition as an intangible asset, was previously recognised as an asset and initially measured at cost, the amount initially recognised is deemed to have been properly determined.

* ~~IAS 16 *Property, Plant and Equipment* as revised by the IASB in 2003 requires all subsequent costs to be covered by its general recognition principle and eliminated the requirement to reference the originally assessed standard of performance. IAS 38 was amended as a consequence of the change to IAS 16 and the paragraphs specifically referred to were eliminated. This paragraph has been struck through to avoid any confusion.~~

† The new text was added by IFRS 3 *Business Combinations* in 2004.

Appendix to SIC-32

This appendix is illustrative only and does not form part of the Interpretation. The purpose of the appendix is to illustrate examples of expenditure that occur during each of the stages described in paragraphs 2 and 3 of the Interpretation and illustrate application of the Interpretation to assist in clarifying its meaning. It is not intended to be a comprehensive checklist of expenditure that might be incurred.

Example application of SIC-32

Stage/nature of expenditure	Accounting treatment
Planning • undertaking feasibility studies • defining hardware and software specifications • evaluating alternative products and suppliers • selecting preferences	Recognise as an expense when incurred in accordance with IAS 38.54
Application and infrastructure development • purchasing or developing hardware	Apply the requirements of IAS 16
• obtaining a domain name • developing operating software (eg operating system and server software) • developing code for the application • installing developed applications on the web server • stress testing	Recognise as an expense when incurred, unless the expenditure can be directly attributed to preparing the web site to operate in the manner intended by management, and the web site meets the recognition criteria in IAS 38.21 and IAS 38.57[(a)]
Graphical design development • designing the appearance (eg layout and colour) of web pages	Recognise as an expense when incurred, unless the expenditure can be directly attributed to preparing the web site to operate in the manner intended by management, and the web site meets the recognition criteria in IAS 38.21 and IAS 38.57[(a)]

Continued from previous page

Stage/nature of expenditure	Accounting treatment
Content development	
• creating, purchasing, preparing (eg creating links and identifying tags), and uploading information, either textual or graphical in nature, on the web site before the completion of the web site's development. Examples of content include information about an entity, products or services offered for sale, and topics that subscribers access	Recognise as an expense when incurred in accordance with IAS 38.69(c) to the extent that content is developed to advertise and promote an entity's own products and services (eg digital photographs of products). Otherwise, recognise as an expense when incurred, unless the expenditure can be directly attributed to preparing the web site to operate in the manner intended by management, and the web site meets the recognition criteria in IAS 38.21 and IAS 38.57[(a)]
Operating	
• updating graphics and revising content • adding new functions, features and content • registering the web site with search engines • backing up data • reviewing security access • analysing usage of the web site	Assess whether it meets the definition of an intangible asset and the recognition criteria set out in IAS 38.18, in which case the expenditure is recognised in the carrying amount of the web site asset
Other	
• selling, administrative and other general overhead expenditure unless it can be directly attributed to preparing the web site for use to operate in the manner intended by management • clearly identified inefficiencies and initial operating losses incurred before the web site achieves planned performance [eg false start testing] • training employees to operate the web site	Recognise as an expense when incurred in accordance with IAS 38.65–.70

(a) All expenditure on developing a web site solely or primarily for promoting and advertising an entity's own products and services is recognised as an expense when incurred in accordance with IAS 38.68.

Glossary of Terms

This glossary is extracted from the International Financial Reporting Standards (IFRSs), International Accounting Standards (IASs) and Interpretations (SICs) as included in this Bound Volume. References are by Standard and paragraph number.

This glossary also includes extracts from the *Framework for the Preparation and Presentation of Financial Statements*. References to the *Framework* are preceded by F.

References set out below in (brackets) indicate minor variations in wording.

Term	Definition	Reference
accounting policies	The specific principles, bases, conventions, rules and practices applied by an entity in preparing and presenting financial statements.	IAS 8.5
accounting profit	The profit or loss for a period before deducting tax expense.	IAS 12.5
accrual basis of accounting	The effects of transactions and other events are recognised when they occur (and not as cash or its equivalent is received or paid) and they are recorded in the accounting records and reported in the financial statements of the periods to which they relate.	F.22
Accumulating compensated absences	Compensated absences that are carried forward and can be used in future periods if the current period's entitlement is not used in full.	IAS 19.13
acquisition date	The date on which the acquirer effectively obtains control of the acquiree.	IFRS 3.A
active market	A market in which all the following conditions exist: (a) the items traded within the market are homogeneous; (b) willing buyers and sellers can normally be found at any time; and (c) prices are available to the public.	IAS 36.6, IAS 38.8
actuarial assumptions	An entity's unbiased and mutually compatible best estimates of the demographic and financial variables that will determine the ultimate cost of providing post-employment benefits.	IAS 19.72–73
actuarial gains and losses	Actuarial gains and losses comprise: (a) experience adjustments (the effects of differences between the previous actuarial assumptions and what has actually occurred); and (b) the effects of changes in actuarial assumptions.	IAS 19.7
actuarial present value of promised retirement benefits	The present value of the expected payments by a retirement benefit plan to existing and past employees, attributable to the service already rendered.	IAS 26.8
adjusting events after the balance sheet date	See events after the balance sheet date	

agreement date (for a business combination)	The date that a substantive agreement between the combining parties is reached and, in the case of publicly listed entities, announced to the public. In the case of a hostile takeover, the earliest date that a substantive agreement between the combining parties is reached is the date that a sufficient number of the acquiree's owners have accepted the acquirer's offer for the acquirer to obtain control of the acquiree.	IAS 36.6, (IAS 38.8), IFRS 3.A
agricultural activity	The management by an entity of the biological transformation of biological assets for sale, into agricultural produce, or into additional biological assets.	IAS 41.5
agricultural produce	The harvested product of the entity's biological assets.	IAS 41.5
Amortisation[*] (Depreciation)	The systematic allocation of the depreciable amount of an asset over its useful life.	IAS 36.6, IAS 38.8
amortised cost of a financial asset or financial liability	The amount at which the financial asset or liability is measured at initial recognition minus principal repayments, plus or minus the cumulative amortisation using the effective interest method of any difference between that initial amount and the maturity amount, and minus any reduction (directly or through the use of an allowance account) for impairment or uncollectability.	IAS 39.9
antidilution	An increase in earnings per share or a reduction in loss per share resulting from the assumption that convertible instruments are converted, that options or warrants are exercised, or that ordinary shares are issued upon the satisfaction of specified conditions.	IAS 33.5
asset	A resource: (a) controlled by an entity as a result of past events; and (b) from which future economic benefits are expected to flow to the entity.	IAS 38.8, (F.49(a))

[*] In the case of an intangible asset or goodwill, the term 'amortisation' is generally used instead of 'depreciation'. Both terms have the same meaning.

assets held by a long-term employee benefit fund	Assets (other than non-transferable financial instruments issued by the reporting entity) that: (a) are held by an entity (a fund) that is legally separate from the reporting entity and exists solely to pay or fund employee benefits; and (b) are available to be used only to pay or fund employee benefits, are not available to the reporting entity's own creditors (even in bankruptcy), and cannot be returned to the reporting entity, unless either: (i) the remaining assets of the fund are sufficient to meet all the related employee benefit obligations of the plan or the reporting entity; or (ii) the assets are returned to the reporting entity to reimburse it for employee benefits already paid.	IAS 19.7
associate	An entity, including an unincorporated entity such as a partnership, over which the investor has significant influence and that is neither a subsidiary nor an interest in a joint venture.	IAS 28.2
available-for-sale financial assets	Those non-derivative financial assets that are designated as available for sale or are not classified as (a) loans and receivables, (b) held-to-maturity investments, or (c) financial assets at fair value through profit or loss.	IAS 39.9
bank	A financial institution one of whose principal activities is to take deposits and borrow with the objective of lending and investing and which is within the scope of banking or similar legislation.	IAS 30.2
basic earnings per share	Profit for the period that is attributable to ordinary shareholders (the numerator) divided by the weighted average number of ordinary shares outstanding during the period (the denominator).	IAS 33.10
biological asset	A living animal or plant.	IAS 41.5
biological transformation	The processes of growth, degeneration, production, and procreation that cause qualitative or quantitative changes in a biological asset.	IAS 41.5
borrowing costs	Interest and other costs incurred by an entity in connection with the borrowing of funds.	IAS 23.4

Term	Definition	Source
business	An integrated set of activities and assets conducted and managed for the purpose of providing: (a) a return to investors; or (b) lower costs or other economic benefits directly and proportionately to policyholders or participants. A business generally consists of inputs, processes applied to those inputs, and resulting outputs that are, or will be, used to generate revenues. If goodwill is present in a transferred set of activities and assets, the transferred set shall be presumed to be a business.	IFRS 3.A
business combination	The bringing together of separate entities or businesses into one reporting entity.	IFRS 3.A
business combination involving entities or businesses under common control	A business combination in which all of the combining entities or businesses ultimately are controlled by the same party or parties both before and after the combination, and that control is not transitory.	IFRS 3.A
business segment	A distinguishable component of an entity that is engaged in providing an individual product or service or a group of related products or services and that is subject to risks and returns that are different from those of other business segments.	IAS 14.9
capital	Under a financial concept of capital, such as invested money or invested purchasing power, the net assets or equity of the entity. The financial concept of capital is adopted by most entities. Under a physical concept of capital, such as operating capability, the productive capacity of the entity based on, for example, units of output per day.	F.102
capitalisation	Recognising a cost as part of the cost of an asset.	IAS 23.11
carrying amount	The amount at which an asset is recognised after deducting any accumulated depreciation (amortisation) and accumulated impairment losses thereon.	IAS 36.6, IAS 16.6, IAS 38.8
cash	Cash on hand and demand deposits.	IAS 7.6
cash equivalents	Short-term, highly liquid investments that are readily convertible to known amounts of cash and which are subject to an insignificant risk of changes in value.	IAS 7.6
cash flow interest rate risk	The risk that future cash flows of a monetary financial instrument will fluctuate because of changes in market interest rates. In the case of a floating rate debt instrument, for example, such fluctuations result in a change in the effective interest rate of the financial instrument, usually without a corresponding change in its fair value.	IAS 32.52(d)

cash flows	Inflows and outflows of cash and cash equivalents.	IAS 7.6
cash generating unit	The smallest identifiable group of assets that generates cash inflows that are largely independent of the cash inflows from other assets or groups of assets.	IAS 36.6
cash-settled share-based payment transaction	A share-based payment transaction in which the entity acquires goods or services by incurring a liability to transfer cash or other assets to the supplier of those goods or services for amounts that are based on the price (or value) of the entity's shares or other equity instruments of the entity.	IFRS 2.A
cedant	The policyholder under a reinsurance contract.	IFRS 4.A
change in accounting estimate	An adjustment of the carrying amount of an asset or a liability, or the amount of the periodic consumption of an asset, that results from the assessment of the present status of, and expected future benefits and obligations associated with, assets and liabilities. Changes in accounting estimates result from new information or new developments and, accordingly, are not corrections of errors.	IAS 8.5
class of assets	Grouping of assets of a similar nature and use in an entity's operations.	IAS 16.37, (IAS 32.55)
close members of the family of an individual	Those family members who may be expected to influence, or be influenced by, that individual in their dealings with the entity. They may include: (a) the individual's domestic partner and children; (b) children of the individual's domestic partner; and (c) dependants of the individual or the individual's domestic partner.	IAS 24.9
closing rate	The spot exchange rate at the balance sheet date.	IAS 21.8
commencement of the lease term	The date from which the lessee is entitled to exercise its right to use the leased asset. It is the date of initial recognition of the lease (ie the recognition of the assets, liabilities, income or expenses resulting from the lease, as appropriate).	IAS 17.4

compensation	Includes all employee benefits to which IFRS 2 Share-based Payment applies. Employee benefits are all forms of consideration paid, payable or provided by the entity, or on behalf of the entity, in exchange for services rendered to the entity. It also includes such consideration paid on behalf of a parent of the entity in respect of the entity. Compensation includes: (a) short-term employee benefits, such as wages, salaries and social security contributions, paid annual leave and paid sick leave, profit-sharing and bonuses (if payable within twelve months of the end of the period) and non-monetary benefits (such as medical care, housing, cars and free or subsidised goods or services) for current employees; (b) post-employment benefits such as pensions, other retirement benefits, post-employment life insurance and post-employment medical care; (c) other long-term employee benefits, including long-service leave or sabbatical leave, jubilee or other long-service benefits, long-term disability benefits and, if they are not payable wholly within twelve months after the end of the period, profit-sharing, bonuses and deferred compensation; (d) termination benefits; and (e) share-based payment.	IAS 24.9
compound instrument	A financial instrument that, from the issuer's perspective, contains both a liability and an equity element.	IAS 32.28
consolidated financial statements	The financial statements of a group presented as those of a single economic entity.	IAS 27.4, IAS 28.2
construction contract	A contract specifically negotiated for the construction of an asset or a combination of assets that are closely interrelated or interdependent in terms of their design, technology and function or their ultimate purpose or use.	IAS 11.3
constructive obligation	An obligation that derives from an entity's actions where: (a) by an established pattern of past practice, published policies or a sufficiently specific current statement, the entity has indicated to other parties that it will accept certain responsibilities; and (b) as a result, the entity has created a valid expectation on the part of those other parties that it will discharge those responsibilities.	IAS 37.10

contingent asset	A possible asset that arises from past events and whose existence will be confirmed only by the occurrence or non-occurrence of one or more uncertain future events not wholly within the control of the entity.	IAS 37.10
contingent liability	(a) A possible obligation that arises from past events and whose existence will be confirmed only by the occurrence or non-occurrence of one or more uncertain future events not wholly within the control of the entity; or (b) a present obligation that arises from past events but is not recognised because: (i) it is not probable that an outflow of resources embodying economic benefits will be required to settle the obligation; or (ii) the amount of the obligation cannot be measured with sufficient reliability.	IAS 37.10
contingent rent	That portion of the lease payments that is not fixed in amount but is based on the future amount of a factor that changes other than with the passage of time (eg percentage of future sales, amount of future use, future price indices, future market rates of interest).	IAS 17.4
contingent share agreement	An agreement to issue shares that is dependent on the satisfaction of specified conditions.	IAS 33.5
contingently issuable ordinary shares	Ordinary shares issuable for little or no cash or other consideration upon the satisfaction of specified conditions in a contingent share agreement.	IAS 33.5
contract	An agreement between two or more parties that has clear economic consequences that the parties have little, if any, discretion to avoid, usually because the agreement is enforceable at law. Contracts may take a variety of forms and need not be in writing.	IAS 32.13
control (of an entity)	The power to govern the financial and operating policies of an entity so as to obtain benefits from its activities.	IAS 24.9, IAS 27.4, IAS 28.2, (IAS 31.3), (IFRS 3.A)
corporate assets	Assets other than goodwill that contribute to the future cash flows of both the cash-generating unit under review and other cash-generating units.	IAS 36.6
'corridor'	A range around an entity's best estimate of post-employment benefit obligations. Outside that range, it is not reasonable to assume that actuarial gains or losses will be offset in future years.	IAS 19.95

cost	The amount of cash or cash equivalents paid or the fair value of the other consideration given to acquire an asset at the time of its acquisition or construction, or, when applicable, the amount attributed to that asset when initially recognised in accordance with the specific requirements of other IFRSs, eg IFRS 2 Share-based Payment.	IAS 16.6, IAS 38.8
cost method	A method of accounting for an investment whereby the investment is recognised at cost. The investor recognises income from the investment only to the extent that the investor receives distributions from accumulated profits of the investee arising after the date of acquisition. Distributions received in excess of such profits are regarded as a recovery of investment and are recognised as a reduction of the cost of the investment.	IAS 27.4
cost of conversion	Costs directly related to the units of production, such as direct labour together with a systematic allocation of fixed and variable production overheads that are incurred in converting materials into finished goods.	IAS 2.12
cost of inventories	All costs of purchase, costs of conversion and other costs incurred in bringing the inventories to their present location and condition.	IAS 2.10
cost of purchase	All of the purchase price, import duties and other taxes (other than those subsequently recoverable by the entity from the taxing authorities), and transport, handling and other costs directly attributable to the acquisition of the item. Trade discounts, rebates and other similar items are deducted in determining the costs of purchase.	IAS 2.11
cost plus contract	A construction contract in which the contractor is reimbursed for allowable or otherwise defined costs, plus a percentage of these costs or a fixed fee.	IAS 11.3
costs of disposal	Incremental costs directly attributable to the disposal of an asset, excluding finance costs and income tax expense.	IAS 36.6
costs to sell	The incremental costs directly attributable to the disposal of an asset (or disposal group), excluding finance costs and income tax expense.	IFRS 5.A
credit risk	The risk that one party to a financial instrument will fail to discharge an obligation and cause the other party to incur a financial loss.	IAS 32.52(b)
currency risk	A market risk – The risk that the value of a financial instrument will fluctuate due to changes in foreign exchange rates.	IAS 32.52(a)(i)

current asset	An asset which satisfies any of the following criteria: (a) it is expected to be realised in, or is intended for sale or consumption in, the entity's normal operating cycle; (b) it is held primarily for the purpose of being traded; (c) it is expected to be realised within twelve months after the balance sheet date; or (d) it is cash or a cash equivalent (as defined in IAS 7 Cash Flow Statements) unless it is restricted from being exchanged or used to settle a liability for at least twelve months after the balance sheet date.	IAS 1.57
current cost	The amount of cash or cash equivalents that would have to be paid if the same or an equivalent asset was acquired currently. The undiscounted amount of cash or cash equivalents that would be required to settle an obligation currently.	F.100(b)
current liabilities	A liability shall be classified as current when it satisfies any of the following criteria: (a) it is expected to be settled in the entity's normal operating cycle; (b) it is held primarily for the purpose of being traded; (c) it is due to be settled within twelve months after the balance sheet date; or (d) the entity does not have an unconditional right to defer settlement of the liability for at least twelve months after the balance sheet date. All other liabilities shall be classified as non-current.	IAS 1.60
current service cost	The increase in the present value of the defined benefit obligation resulting from employee service in the current period.	IAS 19.7
current tax	The amount of income taxes payable (recoverable) in respect of the taxable profit (tax loss) for a period.	IAS 12.5
curtailment	A curtailment occurs when an entity either: (a) is demonstrably committed to make a material reduction in the number of employees covered by a plan; or (b) amends the terms of a defined benefit plan such that a material element of future service by current employees will no longer qualify for benefits, or will qualify only for reduced benefits.	IAS 19.111

date of exchange	When a business combination is achieved in a single exchange transaction, the date of exchange is the acquisition date. When a business combination involves more than one exchange transaction, for example when it is achieved in stages by successive share purchases, the date of exchange is the date that each individual investment is recognised in the financial statements of the acquirer.	IFRS 3.A
date of transition to IFRSs	The beginning of the earliest period for which an entity presents full comparative information under IFRSs in its first IFRS financial statements.	IFRS 1.A
deductible temporary difference	A temporary difference that will result in amounts that are deductible in determining taxable profit (tax loss) of future periods when the carrying amount of the asset or liability is recovered or settled.	IAS 12.5
deemed cost	An amount used as a surrogate for cost or depreciated cost at a given date. Subsequent depreciation or amortisation assumes that the entity had initially recognised the asset or liability at the given date and that its cost was equal to the deemed cost.	IFRS 1.A
deferred tax assets	The amounts of income taxes recoverable in future periods in respect of: (a) deductible temporary differences; (b) the carryforward of unused tax losses; and (c) the carryforward of unused tax credits.	IAS 12.5
deferred tax liabilities	The amounts of income taxes payable in future periods in respect of taxable temporary differences.	IAS 12.5
defined benefit liability	The net total of the following amounts: (a) the present value of the defined benefit obligation at the balance sheet date; (b) plus any actuarial gains (less any actuarial losses) not recognised; (c) minus any past service cost not yet recognised; (d) minus the fair value at the balance sheet date of plan assets (if any) out of which the obligations are to be settled directly.	IAS 19.54
defined benefit obligation (present value of)	The present value, without deducting any plan assets, of expected future payments required to settle the obligation resulting from employee service in the current and prior periods.	IAS 19.7
defined benefit plans	Post-employment benefit plans other than defined contribution plans.	IAS 19.7

defined contribution plans	Post-employment benefit plans under which an entity pays fixed contributions into a separate entity (a fund) and will have no legal or constructive obligation to pay further contributions if the fund does not hold sufficient assets to pay all employee benefits relating to employee service in the current and prior periods.	IAS 19.7, (IAS 26.8)
demonstrably committed	An entity is demonstrably committed to pay termination benefits when, and only when, an entity has a detailed formal plan for the termination and is without realistic possibility of withdrawal. The detailed plan shall include, as a minimum: (a) the location, function, and approximate number of employees whose services are to be terminated; (b) the termination benefits for each job classification or function; and (c) the time at which the plan will be implemented. Implementation shall begin as soon as possible and the period of time to complete implementation shall be such that material changes to the plan are not likely.	IAS 19.134
deposit component	A contractual component that is not accounted for as a derivative under IAS 39 and would be within the scope of IAS 39 if it were a separate instrument.	IFRS 4.A
depreciable amount	The cost of an asset, or other amount substituted for cost (in the financial statements), less its residual value.	IAS 16.6, (IAS 36.6, IAS 38.8)
depreciation (amortisation)*	The systematic allocation of the depreciable amount of an asset over its useful life.	IAS 16.6, IAS 36.6
derecognition (of a financial instrument)	Derecognition is the removal of a previously recognised financial asset or financial liability from an entity's balance sheet.	IAS 39.9

* In the case of an intangible asset, the term 'amortisation' is generally used instead of 'depreciation'. The two terms have the same meaning.

derivative — A financial instrument or other contract within the scope of this Standard (see paragraphs 2–7) with all three of the following characteristics: — IAS 39.9

(a) its value changes in response to the change in a specified interest rate, financial instrument price, commodity price, foreign exchange rate, index of prices or rates, credit rating or credit index, or other variable, provided in the case of a non-financial variable that the variable is not specific to a party to the contract (sometimes called the 'underlying');

(b) it requires no initial net investment or an initial net investment that is smaller than would be required for other types of contracts that would be expected to have a similar response to changes in market factors; and

(c) it is settled at a future date.

derivative financial instruments — Financial instruments such as financial options, futures and forwards, interest rate swaps and currency swaps, which create rights and obligations that have the effect of transferring between the parties to the instrument one or more of the financial risks inherent in an underlying primary financial instrument. On inception, derivative financial instruments give one party a contractual right to exchange financial assets or financial liabilities with another party under conditions that are potentially favourable, or a contractual obligation to exchange financial assets or financial liabilities with another party under conditions that are potentially unfavourable. However, they generally do not result in a transfer of the underlying primary financial instrument on inception of the contract, nor does such a transfer necessarily take place on maturity of the contract. Some instruments embody both a right and an obligation to make an exchange. Because the terms of the exchange are determined on inception of the derivative instrument, as prices in financial markets change those terms may become either favourable or unfavourable. — IAS 32AG15–16

development — The application of research findings or other knowledge to a plan or design for the production of new or substantially improved materials, devices, products, processes, systems or services prior to the commencement of commercial production or use. — IAS 38.8

diluted earnings per share	The amount of profit for the period that is attributable to ordinary shareholders divided by the weighted average number of ordinary shares outstanding during the period, both adjusted for the effects of all dilutive potential ordinary shares.	IAS 33.31
dilution	A reduction in earnings per share or an increase in loss per share resulting from the assumption that convertible instruments are converted, that options or warrants are exercised, or that ordinary shares are issued upon the satisfaction of specified conditions.	IAS 33.5
dilutive potential ordinary shares	Potential ordinary shares whose conversion to ordinary shares would decrease earnings per share or increase loss per share from continuing operations.	IAS 33.41
direct insurance contract	An insurance contract that is not a reinsurance contract.	IFRS 4.A
direct method of reporting cash flows from operating activities	A method which discloses major classes of gross cash receipts and gross cash payments.	IAS 7.18(a)
discontinued operation	A component of an entity that either has been disposed of or is classified as held for sale and: (a) represents a separate major line of business or geographical area of operations, (b) is part of a single co-ordinated plan to dispose of a separate major line of business or geographical area of operations or (c) is a subsidiary acquired exclusively with a view to resale.	IFRS 5.A
discretionary participation feature	A contractual right to receive, as a supplement to guaranteed benefits, additional benefits: (a) that are likely to be a significant portion of the total contractual benefits; (b) whose amount or timing is contractually at the discretion of the issuer; and (c) that are contractually based on: (i) the performance of a specified pool of contracts or a specified type of contract; (ii) realised and/or unrealised investment returns on a specified pool of assets held by the issuer; or (iii) the profit or loss of the company, fund or other entity that issues the contract.	IFRS 4.A

disposal group	A group of assets to be disposed of, by sale or otherwise, together as a group in a single transaction, and liabilities directly associated with those assets that will be transferred in the transaction. The group includes goodwill acquired in a business combination if the group is a cash-generating unit to which goodwill has been allocated in accordance with the requirements of paragraphs 80–87 of IAS 36 Impairment of Assets (as revised in 2004) or if it is an operation within such a cash-generating unit.	IFRS 5.A
dividends	Distributions of profits to holders of equity investments in proportion to their holdings of a particular class of capital.	IAS 18.5
economic life	Either: (a) the period over which an asset is expected to be economically usable by one or more users; or (b) the number of production or similar units expected to be obtained from the asset by one or more users.	IAS 17.4
effective interest method	The effective interest method is a method of calculating the amortised cost of a financial asset or a financial liability (or group of financial assets or financial liabilities) and of allocating the interest income or interest expense over the relevant period. The effective interest rate is the rate that exactly discounts estimated future cash payments or receipts through the expected life of the financial instrument or, when appropriate, a shorter period to the net carrying amount of the financial asset or financial liability. When calculating the effective interest rate, an entity shall estimate cash flows considering all contractual terms of the financial instrument (for example, prepayment, call and similar options) but shall not consider future credit losses. The calculation includes all fees and points paid or received between parties to the contract that are an integral part of the effective interest rate (see IAS 18), transaction costs, and all other premiums or discounts. There is a presumption that the cash flows and the expected life of a group of similar financial instruments can be estimated reliably. However, in those rare cases when it is not possible to estimate reliably the cash flows or the expected life of a financial instrument (or group of financial instruments), the entity shall use the contractual cash flows over the full contractual term of the financial instrument (or group of financial instruments).	IAS 39.9

embedded derivative	A component of a hybrid (combined) instrument that also includes a non-derivative host contract–with the effect that some of the cash flows of the combined instrument vary in a way similar to a stand-alone derivative. An embedded derivative causes some or all of the cash flows that otherwise would be required by the contract to be modified according to a specified interest rate, financial instrument price, commodity price, foreign exchange rate, index of prices or rates, credit rating or credit index, or other variable. A derivative that is attached to a financial instrument but is contractually transferable independently of that instrument, or has a different counterparty from that instrument, is not an embedded derivative, but a separate financial instrument.	IAS 39.10
employee benefits	All forms of consideration given by an entity in exchange for service rendered by employees.	IAS 19.7
employees and others providing similar services	Individuals who render personal services to the entity and either (a) the individuals are regarded as employees for legal or tax purposes, (b) the individuals work for the entity under its direction in the same way as individuals who are regarded as employees for legal or tax purposes, or (c) the services rendered are similar to those rendered by employees. For example, the term encompasses all management personnel, ie those persons having authority and responsibility for planning, directing and controlling the activities of the entity, including non-executive directors.	IFRS 2.A
entity-specific value	The present value of the cash flows an entity expects to arise from the continuing use of an asset and from its disposal at the end of its useful life or expects to incur when settling a liability.	IAS 16.6, IAS 38.8
equity	The residual interest in the assets of the entity after deducting all its liabilities.	F.49(c)
equity instrument	A contract that evidences a residual interest in the assets of an entity after deducting all of its liabilities.	IAS 32.11, IFRS 2.A
equity instrument granted	The right (conditional or unconditional) to an equity instrument of the entity conferred by the entity on another party, under a share-based payment arrangement.	IFRS 2.A
equity method	A method of accounting whereby the investment is initially recognised at cost and adjusted thereafter for the post-acquisition change in the investor's share of net assets of the investee. The profit or loss of the investor includes the investor's share of the profit or loss of the investee.	IAS 28.2
equity-settled share-based payment transaction	A share-based payment transaction in which the entity receives goods or services as consideration for equity instruments of the entity (including shares or share options).	IFRS 2.A

events after the balance sheet date	Events after the balance sheet date are those events, favourable and unfavourable, that occur between the balance sheet date and the date when the financial statements are authorised for issue. Two types of events can be identified: (a) those that provide evidence of conditions that existed at the balance sheet date (adjusting events after the balance sheet date); and (b) those that are indicative of conditions that arose after the balance sheet date (non-adjusting events after the balance sheet date).	IAS 10.3
exchange difference	The difference resulting from translating a given number of units of one currency into another currency at different exchange rates.	IAS 21.8
exchange rate	The ratio of exchange for two currencies.	IAS 21.8
expenses	Decreases in economic benefits during the accounting period in the form of outflows or depletions of assets or incurrences of liabilities that result in decreases in equity, other than those relating to distributions to equity participants.	F.70(b)
experience adjustments	The effect of differences between previous actuarial assumptions and what has actually occurred.	IAS 19.7
exploration and evaluation assets	Exploration and evaluation expenditures recognised as assets in accordance with the entity's accounting policy.	IFRS 6.A
exploration and evaluation expenditures	Expenditures incurred by an entity in connection with the exploration for and evaluation of mineral resources before the technical feasibility and commercial viability of extracting a mineral resource are demonstrable.	IFRS 6.A
exploration for and evaluation of mineral resources	The search for mineral resources, including minerals, oil, natural gas and similar non-regenerative resources after the entity has obtained legal rights to explore in a specific area, as well as the determination of the technical feasibility and commercial viability of extracting the mineral resource.	IFRS 6.A

fair value	The amount for which an asset could be exchanged, or a liability settled, between knowledgeable, willing parties in an arm's length transaction.	IAS 2.6, (IAS 16.6), IAS 17.4, IAS 18.7, (IAS 19.7), (IAS 20.3), IAS 21.8, IAS 32.11, (IAS 38.8), IAS 39.9, IFRS 1.A, (IFRS 2.A), IFRS 3.A, IFRS 4.A, IFRS 5.A
fair value interest rate risk	A market risk – The risk that the value of a financial instrument will fluctuate because of changes in market interest rates.	IAS 32.52(a)(ii)
fair value less costs to sell	The amount obtainable from the sale of an asset or cash-generating unit in an arm's length transaction between knowledgeable, willing parties, less the costs of disposal.	IAS 36.6
FIFO (first-in, first-out)	The assumption that the items of inventory that were purchased or produced first are sold first, and consequently the items remaining in inventory at the end of the period are those most recently purchased or produced.	IAS 2.27
finance lease	A lease that transfers substantially all the risks and rewards incident to ownership of an asset. Title may or may not eventually be transferred.	IAS 17.4

financial asset Any asset that is: IAS 32.11

(a) cash;

(b) an equity instrument of another entity;

(c) a contractual right:

(i) to receive cash or another financial asset from another entity; or

(ii) to exchange financial instruments with another entity under conditions that are potentially favourable; or

(d) a contract that will or may be settled in the entity's own equity instruments and is:

(i) a non-derivative for which the entity is or may be obliged to receive a variable number of the entity's own equity instruments; or

(ii) a derivative that will or may be settled other than by the exchange of a fixed amount of cash or another financial asset for a fixed number of the entity's own equity instruments. For this purpose the entity's own equity instruments do not include instruments that are themselves contracts for the future receipt or delivery of the entity's own equity instruments.

financial asset or financial liability at fair value through profit or loss	A financial asset or financial liability that meets either of the following conditions. (a) It is classified as held for trading. A financial asset or financial liability is classified as held for trading if it is: (i) acquired or incurred principally for the purpose of selling or repurchasing it in the near term; (ii) part of a portfolio of identified financial instruments that are managed together and for which there is evidence of a recent actual pattern of short-term profit-taking; or (iii) a derivative (except for a derivative that is a designated and effective hedging instrument). (b) Upon initial recognition it is designated by the entity as at fair value through profit or loss. Any financial asset or financial liability within the scope of this Standard may be designated when initially recognised as a financial asset or financial liability at fair value through profit or loss except for investments in equity instruments that do not have a quoted market price in an active market, and whose fair value cannot be reliably measured (see paragraph 46(c) and Appendix A paragraphs AG80 and AG81).	IAS 39.9
financial instrument	Any contract that gives rise to both a financial asset of one entity and a financial liability or equity instrument of another entity.	IAS 32.11

financial liability	Any liability that is: (a) a contractual obligation: (i) to deliver cash or another financial asset to another entity; or (ii) to exchange financial assets or financial liabilities with another entity under conditions that are potentially unfavourable to the entity; or (b) a contract that will or may be settled in the entity's own equity instruments and is: (i) a non-derivative for which the entity is or may be obliged to deliver a variable number of the entity's own equity instruments; or (ii) a derivative that will or may be settled other than by the exchange of a fixed amount of cash or another financial asset for a fixed number of the entity's own equity instruments. For this purpose the entity's own equity instruments do not include instruments that are themselves contracts for the future receipt or delivery of the entity's own equity instruments.	IAS 32.11
financial position	The relationship of the assets, liabilities, and equities of an entity, as reported in the balance sheet.	F.47
financial risk	The risk of a possible future change in one or more of a specified interest rate, financial instrument price, commodity price, foreign exchange rate, index of prices or rates, credit rating or credit index or other variable, provided in the case of a non-financial variable that the variable is not specific to a party to the contract.	IFRS 4.A
financial statements	A complete set of financial statements comprises: (a) balance sheet; (b) income statement; (c) a statement showing either: (i) all changes in equity; or (ii) changes in equity other than those arising from transactions with equity holders acting in their capacity as equity holders; (d) a cash flow statement; and (e) notes, comprising a summary of significant accounting policies and other explanatory notes.	IAS 1.8, (F.7)

financing activities	Activities that result in changes in the size and composition of the contributed equity and borrowings of the entity.	IAS 7.6
firm commitment	A binding agreement for the exchange of a specified quantity of resources at a specified price on a specified future date or dates.	IAS 39.9
firm purchase commitment	An agreement with an unrelated party, binding on both parties and usually legally enforceable, that (a) specifies all significant terms, including the price and timing of the transactions, and (b) includes a disincentive for non-performance that is sufficiently large to make performance highly probable.	IFRS 5.A
first IFRS financial statements	The first annual financial statements in which an entity adopts International Financial Reporting Standards (IFRSs), by an explicit and unreserved statement of compliance with IFRSs.	IFRS 1.A
first IFRS reporting period	The reporting period ending on the reporting date of an entity's first IFRS financial statements.	IFRS 1.A
first-time adopter	An entity that presents its first IFRS financial statements.	IFRS 1.A
fixed price contract	A contract in which the contractor agrees to a fixed contract price, or a fixed rate per unit of output, which in some cases is subject to cost escalation clauses.	IAS 11.3
fixed production overheads	Those indirect costs of production that remain relatively constant regardless of the volume of production, such as depreciation and maintenance of factory buildings and equipment, and the cost of factory management and administration.	IAS 2.12
forecast transaction	An uncommitted but anticipated future transaction.	IAS 39.9
foreign currency	A currency other than the functional currency of the entity.	IAS 21.8
foreign currency transaction	A transaction that is denominated in or requires settlement in a foreign currency.	IAS 21.20
foreign operation	An entity that is a subsidiary, associate, joint venture or branch of the reporting entity, the activities of which are based or conducted in a country other than the country of the reporting entity.	IAS 21.8
forgivable loans	Loans which the lender undertakes to waive repayment of under certain prescribed conditions.	IAS 20.3
functional currency	The currency of the primary economic environment in which the entity operates.	IAS 21.8
funding	Contributions by an entity, and sometimes its employees, into an entity, or fund, that is legally separate from the reporting entity and from which the employee benefits are paid.	IAS 19.49, (IAS 26.8)

future economic benefit	The potential to contribute, directly or indirectly, to the flow of cash and cash equivalents to the entity. The potential may be a productive one that is part of the operating activities of the entity. It may also take the form of convertibility into cash or cash equivalents or a capability to reduce cash outflows, such as when an alternative manufacturing process lowers the costs of production.	F.53
gains	Increases in economic benefits and as such are no different in nature from revenue.	F.75
geographical segments	A distinguishable component of an entity that is engaged in providing products or services within a particular economic environment and that is subject to risks and returns that are different from those of components operating in other economic environments.	IAS 14.9
going concern	The entity is normally viewed as a going concern, that is, as continuing in operation for the foreseeable future. It is assumed that the entity has neither the intention nor the necessity of liquidation or of curtailing materially the scale of its operations.	IAS 1.23–24, F.23
goodwill	Future economic benefits arising from assets that are not capable of being individually identified and separately recognised.	IFRS 3.A
government	Government, government agencies and similar bodies whether local, national or international.	IAS 20.3
government assistance	Action by government designed to provide an economic benefit specific to an entity or range of entities qualifying under certain criteria.	IAS 20.3
government grants	Assistance by government in the form of transfers of resources to an entity in return for past or future compliance with certain conditions relating to the operating activities of the entity. They exclude those forms of government assistance which cannot reasonably have a value placed upon them and transactions with government which cannot be distinguished from the normal trading transactions of the entity.	IAS 20.3
grant date	The date at which the entity and another party (including an employee) agree to a share-based payment arrangement, being when the entity and the counterparty have a shared understanding of the terms and conditions of the arrangement. At grant date the entity confers on the counterparty the right to cash, other assets, or equity instruments of the entity, provided the specified vesting conditions, if any, are met. If that agreement is subject to an approval process (for example, by shareholders), grant date is the date when that approval is obtained.	IFRS 2.A

grants related to assets	Government grants whose primary condition is that an entity qualifying for them shall purchase, construct or otherwise acquire long-term assets. Subsidiary conditions may also be attached restricting the type or location of the assets or the periods during which they are to be acquired or held.	IAS 20.3
grants related to income	Government grants other than those related to assets.	IAS 20.3
gross investment in the lease	The aggregate of: (a) the minimum lease payments receivable by the lessor under a finance lease, and (b) any unguaranteed residual value accruing to the lessor.	IAS 17.4
group	A parent and all its subsidiaries.	IAS 21.8, IAS 27.4
group administration (employee benefit) plans	An aggregation of single employer plans combined to allow participating employers to pool their assets for investment purposes and reduce investment management and administration costs, but the claims of different employers are segregated for the sole benefit of their own employees.	IAS 19.33
group of biological assets	An aggregation of similar living animals or plants.	IAS 41.5
guaranteed benefits	Payments or other benefits to which a particular policyholder or investor has an unconditional right that is not subject to the contractual discretion of the issuer.	IFRS 4.A
guaranteed element	An obligation to pay guaranteed benefits, included in a contract that contains a discretionary participation feature.	IFRS 4.A
guaranteed residual value	(a) for a lessee, that part of the residual value that is guaranteed by the lessee or by a party related to the lessee (the amount of the guarantee being the maximum amount that could, in any event, become payable); and (b) for a lessor, that part of the residual value that is guaranteed by the lessee or by a third party unrelated to the lessor that is financially capable of discharging the obligations under the guarantee.	IAS 17.4
harvest	The detachment of produce from a biological asset or the cessation of a biological asset's life processes.	IAS 41.5
hedge effectiveness	The degree to which changes in the fair value or cash flows of the hedged item that are attributable to a hedged risk are offset by changes in the fair value or cash flows of the hedging instrument (see IAS 39 Appendix A paragraphs AG105–AG113).	IAS 39.9

hedged item — A hedged item is an asset, liability, firm commitment, highly probable forecast transaction or net investment in a foreign operation that (a) exposes the entity to risk of changes in fair value or future cash flows and (b) is designated as being hedged (IAS 39 paragraphs 78–84 and Appendix A paragraphs AG98–AG101 elaborate on the definition of hedged items). IAS 39.9

hedging instrument — A designated derivative or (for a hedge of the risk of changes in foreign currency exchange rates only) a designated non-derivative financial asset or non-derivative financial liability whose fair value or cash flows are expected to offset changes in the fair value or cash flows of a designated hedged item (IAS 39 paragraphs 72–77 and Appendix A paragraphs AG94–AG97 elaborate on the definition of a hedging instrument). IAS 39.9

held-to-maturity investment — Non-derivative financial assets with fixed or determinable payments and fixed maturity that an entity has the positive intention and ability to hold to maturity (see Appendix A paragraphs AG16–AG25) other than: IAS 39.9

(a) those that the entity upon initial recognition designates as at fair value through profit or loss;

(b) those that the entity designates as available for sale; and

(c) those that meet the definition of loans and receivables.

An entity shall not classify any financial assets as held to maturity if the entity has, during the current financial year or during the two preceding financial years, sold or reclassified more than an insignificant amount of held-to-maturity investments before maturity (more than insignificant in relation to the total amount of held-to-maturity investments) other than sales or reclassifications that:

(a) are so close to maturity or the financial asset's call date (for example, less than three months before maturity) that changes in the market rate of interest would not have a significant effect on the financial asset's fair value;

(b) occur after the entity has collected substantially all of the financial asset's original principal through scheduled payments or prepayments; or

(c) are attributable to an isolated event that is beyond the entity's control, is non-recurring and could not have been reasonably anticipated by the entity.

Term	Definition	Reference
highly probable	Significantly more likely than probable.	IFRS 5.A
hire-purchase contract	The definition of a lease includes contracts for the hire of an asset which contain a provision giving the hirer an option to acquire title to the asset upon the fulfilment of agreed conditions. These contracts are sometimes known as hire purchase contracts.	IAS 17.6
historical cost	Assets are recorded at the amount of cash or cash equivalents paid or the fair value of the consideration given to acquire them at the time of their acquisition. Liabilities are recorded at the amount of proceeds received in exchange for the obligation, or in some circumstances (for example, income taxes), at the amounts of cash or cash equivalents expected to be paid to satisfy the liability in the normal course of business.	F.100(a)
hyperinflation	Loss of purchasing power of money at such a rate that comparison of amounts from transactions and other events that have occurred at different times, even within the same accounting period, is misleading. Hyperinflation is indicated by characteristics of the economic environment of a country which include, but are not limited to, the following: (a) the general population prefers to keep its wealth in non-monetary assets or in a relatively stable foreign currency. Amounts of local currency held are immediately invested to maintain purchasing power; (b) the general population regards monetary amounts not in terms of the local currency but in terms of a relatively stable foreign currency. Prices may be quoted in that currency; (c) sales and purchases on credit take place at prices that compensate for the expected loss of purchasing power during the credit period, even if the period is short; (d) interest rates, wages and prices are linked to a price index; and (e) the cumulative inflation rate over three years is approaching, or exceeds, 100%.	IAS 29.2–3
impairment loss	The amount by which the carrying amount of an asset exceeds its recoverable amount.	IAS 16.6, IAS 36.6, IAS 38.8
impracticable	Applying a requirement is impracticable when the entity cannot apply it after making every reasonable effort to do so.	IAS 1.11

impracticable	Applying a requirement is impracticable when the entity cannot apply it after making every reasonable effort to do so. For a particular prior period, it is impracticable to apply a change in an accounting policy retrospectively or to make a retrospective restatement to correct an error if: (a) the effects of the retrospective application or retrospective restatement are not determinable; (b) the retrospective application or retrospective restatement requires assumptions about what management's intent would have been in that period; or (c) the retrospective application or retrospective restatement requires significant estimates of amounts and it is impossible to distinguish objectively information about those estimates that: (i) provides evidence of circumstances that existed on the date(s) as at which those amounts are to be recognised, measured or disclosed; and (ii) would have been available when the financial statements for that prior period were authorised for issue (d) from other information.	IAS 8.5
imputed rate of interest	The more clearly determinable of either: (a) the prevailing rate for a similar instrument of an issuer with a similar credit rating; or (b) a rate of interest that discounts the nominal amount of the instrument to the current cash sales price of the goods or services.	IAS 18.11
inception of a lease	The earlier of the date of the lease agreement and the date of commitment by the parties to the principal provisions of the lease.	IAS 17.4
income	Increases in economic benefits during the accounting period in the form of inflows or enhancements of assets or decreases of liabilities that result in increases in equity, other than those relating to contributions from equity participants.	F.70(a)
incremental borrowing rate of interest (lessee's)	The rate of interest the lessee would have to pay on a similar lease or, if that is not determinable, the rate that, at the inception of the lease, the lessee would incur to borrow over a similar term, and with a similar security, the funds necessary to purchase the asset.	IAS 17.4

indirect method of reporting cash flows from operating activities	Under this method, profit or loss is adjusted for the effects of transactions of a non-cash nature, any deferrals or accruals of past or future operating cash receipts or payments, and items of income or expense associated with investing or financing cash flows.	IAS 7.18(b)
initial direct costs	Incremental costs that are directly attributable to negotiating and arranging a lease, except for such costs incurred by manufacturer or dealer lessors.	IAS 17.4
insurance asset	An insurer's net contractual rights under an insurance contract.	IFRS 4.A
insurance contract	A contract under which one party (the insurer) accepts significant insurance risk from another party (the policyholder) by agreeing to compensate the policyholder if a specified uncertain future event (the insured event) adversely affects the policyholder. (See Appendix B for guidance on this definition.)	IFRS 4.A
insurance liability	An insurer's net contractual obligations under an insurance contract.	IFRS 4.A
insurance risk	Risk, other than financial risk, transferred from the holder of a contract to the issuer.	IFRS 4.A
insured event	An uncertain future event that is covered by an insurance contract and creates insurance risk.	IFRS 4.A
insurer	The party that has an obligation under an insurance contract to compensate a policyholder if an insured event occurs.	IFRS 4.A
intangible asset	An identifiable non-monetary asset without physical substance.	IAS 38.8
interest cost (for an employee benefit plan)	The increase during a period in the present value of a defined benefit obligation which arises because the benefits are one period closer to settlement.	IAS 19.7
interest rate implicit in the lease	The discount rate that, at the inception of the lease, causes the aggregate present value of (a) the minimum lease payments and (b) the unguaranteed residual value to be equal to the sum of (i) the fair value of the leased asset and (ii) any initial direct costs of the lessor.	IAS 17.4
interim financial report	A financial report containing either a complete set of financial statements (as described in IAS 1) or a set of condensed financial statements (as described in IAS 34) for an interim period.	IAS 34.4
interim period	A financial reporting period shorter than a full financial year.	IAS 34.4

International Financial Reporting Standards (IFRSs)	Standards and Interpretations adopted by the International Accounting Standards Board (IASB). They comprise: (a) International Financial Reporting Standards; (b) International Accounting Standards; and (c) Interpretations originated by the International Financial Reporting Interpretations Committee (IFRIC) or the former Standing Interpretations Committee (SIC).	IFRS 1.A, IAS 1.11, IAS 8.5
intrinsic value	The difference between the fair value of the shares to which the counterparty has the (conditional or unconditional) right to subscribe or which it has the right to receive, and the price (if any) the counterparty is (or will be) required to pay for those shares. For example, a share option with an exercise price of CU15,* on a share with a fair value of CU20, has an intrinsic value of CU5.	IFRS 2.A
inventories	Assets: (a) held for sale in the ordinary course of business; (b) in the process of production for such sale; or (c) in the form of materials or supplies to be consumed in the production process or in the rendering of services. Inventories encompass goods purchased and held for resale including, for example, merchandise purchased by a retailer and held for resale, or land and other property held for resale. Inventories also encompass finished goods produced, or work in progress being produced, by the entity and include materials and supplies awaiting use in the production process. In the case of a service provider, inventories include the costs of the service, as described in paragraph 19, for which the entity has not yet recognised the related revenue (see IAS 18 Revenue).	IAS 2.6, IAS 2.8
investing activities	The acquisition and disposal of long-term assets and other investments not included in cash equivalents.	IAS 7.6
investment property	Property (land or a building – or part of a building – or both) held (by the owner or by the lessee under a finance lease) to earn rentals or for capital appreciation or both, rather than for: (a) use in the production or supply of goods or services or for administrative purposes; or (b) sale in the ordinary course of business.	IAS 40.4
investor in a joint venture	A party to a joint venture and does not have joint control over that joint venture.	IAS 31.3

* Monetary items are denominated in 'currency units' (CU)

joint control	The contractually agreed sharing of control over an economic activity.	IAS 24.9
joint control	Joint control is the contractually agreed sharing of control over an economic activity, and exists only when the strategic and operating decisions relating to the activity require the unanimous consent of the parties sharing control (the venturers).	IAS 28.2, IAS 31.3
joint venture	A contractual arrangement whereby two or more parties undertake an economic activity which is subject to joint control.	IAS 31.3
jointly controlled entity	A joint venture that involves the establishment of a corporation, partnership or other entity in which each venturer has an interest. The entity operates in the same way as other entities, except that a contractual arrangement between the venturers establishes joint control over the economic activity of the entity.	IAS 31.24
key management personnel	Those persons having authority and responsibility for planning, directing and controlling the activities of the entity, directly or indirectly, including any director (whether executive or otherwise) of that entity.	IAS 24.9
lease	An agreement whereby the lessor conveys to the lessee in return for a payment or series of payments the right to use an asset for an agreed period of time.	IAS 17.4
lease term	The non-cancellable period for which the lessee has contracted to lease the asset together with any further terms for which the lessee has the option to continue to lease the asset, with or without further payment, when at the inception of the lease it is reasonably certain that the lessee will exercise.	IAS 17.4
legal obligation	An obligation that derives from: (a) a contract (through its explicit or implicit terms); (b) legislation; or (c) other operation of law.	IAS 37.10
lessee's incremental borrowing rate of interest	The rate of interest the lessee would have to pay on a similar lease or, if that is not determinable, the rate that, at the inception of the lease, the lessee would incur to borrow over a similar term, and with a similar security, the funds necessary to purchase the asset.	IAS 17.4
liability	A present obligation of the entity arising from past events, the settlement of which is expected to result in an outflow from the entity of resources embodying economic benefits.	IAS 37.10, F.49(b)

liability adequacy test	An assessment of whether the carrying amount of an insurance liability needs to be increased (or the carrying amount of related deferred acquisition costs or related intangible assets decreased), based on a review of future cash flows.	IFRS 4.A
liquidity	The availability of sufficient funds to meet deposit withdrawals and other financial commitments as they fall due.	IAS 30.7, (F.16)
liquidity risk	The risk that an entity will encounter difficulty in raising funds to meet commitments associated with financial instruments. Liquidity risk may result from an inability to sell a financial asset quickly at close to its fair value.	IAS 32.52(c)
loans and receivables	Non-derivative financial assets with fixed or determinable payments that are not quoted in an active market, other than: (a) those that the entity intends to sell immediately or in the near term, which shall be classified as held for trading, and those that the entity upon initial recognition designates as at fair value through profit or loss; (b) those that the entity upon initial recognition designates as available for sale; or (c) those for which the holder may not recover substantially all of its initial investment, other than because of credit deterioration, which shall be classified as available for sale. An interest acquired in a pool of assets that are not loans or receivables (for example, an interest in a mutual fund or a similar fund) is not a loan or receivable.	IAS 39.9
losses	Decreases in economic benefits and as such they are no different in nature from other expenses.	F.79
market condition	A condition upon which the exercise price, vesting or exercisability of an equity instrument depends that is related to the market price of the entity's equity instruments, such as attaining a specified share price or a specified amount of intrinsic value of a share option, or achieving a specified target that is based on the market price of the entity's equity instruments relative to an index of market prices of equity instruments of other entities.	IFRS 2.A
market risk	Market risk includes three types of risk[*]. Market risk embodies not only the potential for loss but also the potential for gain.	IAS 32.52(a)

[*] Currency risk, fair value interest rate risk, price risk. See respective definitions.

master netting arrangement	An arrangement providing for an entity that undertakes a number of financial instrument transactions with a single counterparty to make a single net settlement of all financial instruments covered by the agreement in the event of default on, or termination of, any one contract.	IAS 32.50
matching of costs with revenues	Expenses are recognised in the income statement on the basis of a direct association between the costs incurred and the earning of specific items of income. This process involves the simultaneous or combined recognition of revenues and expenses that result directly and jointly from the same transactions or other events. However, the application of the matching concept does not allow the recognition of items in the balance sheet which do not meet the definition of assets or liabilities.	F.95
material	Omissions or misstatements of items are material if they could, individually or collectively, influence the economic decisions of users taken on the basis of the financial statements. Materiality depends on the size and nature of the omission or misstatement judged in the surrounding circumstances. The size or nature of the item, or a combination of both, could be the determining factor.	IAS 1.11, IAS 8.5
materiality	Information is material if its non-disclosure could influence the economic decisions of users taken on the basis of the financial statements.	F.30
measurement	The process of determining the monetary amounts at which the elements of the financial statements are to be recognised and carried in the balance sheet and income statement.	F.99
measurement date	The date at which the fair value of the equity instruments granted is measured for the purposes of this IFRS. For transactions with employees and others providing similar services, the measurement date is grant date. For transactions with parties other than employees (and those providing similar services), the measurement date is the date the entity obtains the goods or the counterparty renders service.	IFRS 2.A

minimum lease payments	The payments over the lease term that the lessee is or can be required to make, excluding contingent rent, costs for services and taxes to be paid by and reimbursed to the lessor, together with: (a) for a lessee, any amounts guaranteed by the lessee or by a party related to the lessee; or (b) for a lessor, any residual value guaranteed to the lessor by: (i) the lessee; (ii) a party related to the lessee; or (iii) a third party unrelated to the lessor that is financially capable of discharging the obligations under the guarantee. However, if the lessee has an option to purchase the asset at a price that is expected to be sufficiently lower than fair value at the date the option becomes exercisable for it to be reasonably certain, at the inception of the lease, that the option will be exercised, the minimum lease payments comprise the minimum payments payable over the lease term to the expected date of exercise of this purchase option and the payment required to exercise it.	IAS 17.4
minority interest	That portion of the profit or loss and net assets of a subsidiary attributable to equity interests that are not owned, directly or indirectly through subsidiaries, by the parent.	IAS 27.4, IFRS 3.A
monetary items	Units of currency held and assets and liabilities to be received or paid in a fixed or determinable number of units of currency.	IAS 21.8, (IAS 29.12), (IAS 38.8)
multi-employer (benefit) plans	Defined contribution plans (other than state plans) or defined benefit plans (other than state plans) that: (a) pool the assets contributed by various entities that are not under common control; and (b) use those assets to provide benefits to employees of more than one entity, on the basis that contribution and benefit levels are determined without regard to the identity of the entity that employs the employees concerned.	IAS 19.7

Term	Definition	Reference
mutual entity	An entity other than an investor-owned entity, such as a mutual insurance company or a mutual cooperative entity, that provides lower costs or other economic benefits directly and proportionately to its policyholders or participants.	IFRS 3.A
net assets available for benefits	The assets of a plan less liabilities other than the actuarial present value of promised retirement benefits.	IAS 26.8
net investment in a foreign operation	The amount of the reporting entity's interest in the net assets of that operation.	IAS 21.8
net investment in the lease	The gross investment in the lease discounted at the interest rate implicit in the lease.	IAS 17.4
net realisable value	The estimated selling price in the ordinary course of business less the estimated costs of completion and the estimated costs necessary to make the sale. Net realisable value refers to the net amount that an entity expects to realise from the sale of inventory in the ordinary course of business. Fair value reflects the amount for which the same inventory could be exchanged between knowledgeable and willing buyers and sellers in the marketplace. The former is an entity-specific value; the latter is not. Net realisable value for inventories may not equal fair value less costs to sell.	IAS 2.6, IAS 2.7
neutrality	Freedom from bias of the information contained in financial statements.	F.36
non-adjusting events after the balance sheet date	See events after the balance sheet date	
non-cancellable lease	A lease that is cancellable only: (a) upon the occurrence of some remote contingency; (b) with the permission of the lessor; (c) if the lessee enters into a new lease for the same or an equivalent asset with the same lessor; or (d) upon payment by the lessee of an additional amount such that, at inception, continuation of the lease is reasonably certain.	IAS 17.4
non-current asset	An asset that does not meet the definition of a current asset.	IFRS 5.A
normal capacity of production facilities	The production expected to be achieved on average over a number of periods or seasons under normal circumstances, taking into account the loss of capacity resulting from planned maintenance.	IAS 2.13

notes	Notes contain information in addition to that presented in the balance sheet, income statement, statement of changes in equity and cash flow statement. Notes provide narrative descriptions or disaggregations of items disclosed in those statements and information about items that do not qualify for recognition in those statements.	IAS 1.11
obligating event	An event that creates a legal or constructive obligation that results in an entity having no realistic alternative to settling that obligation.	IAS 37.10
obligation	A duty or responsibility to act or perform in a certain way. Obligations may be legally enforceable as a consequence of a binding contract or statutory requirement. Obligations also arise, however, from normal business practice, custom and a desire to maintain good business relations or act in an equitable manner.	F.60
offsetting	See set-off, legal right of	
onerous contract	A contract in which the unavoidable costs of meeting the obligations under the contract exceed the economic benefits expected to be received under it.	IAS 37.10
opening IFRS balance sheet	An entity's balance sheet (published or unpublished) at the date of transition to IFRSs.	IFRS 1.A
operating activities	The principal revenue-producing activities of an entity and other activities that are not investing or financing activities.	IAS 7.6
operating cycle	The time between the acquisition of assets for processing and their realisation in cash or cash equivalents.	IAS 1.59
operating lease	A lease other than a finance lease.	IAS 17.4
Options, warrants and their equivalents	Financial instruments that give the holder the right to purchase ordinary shares.	IAS 33.5
ordinary share	An equity instrument that is subordinate to all other classes of equity instruments.	IAS 33.5
originated loans and receivables	See loans and receivables	
other long-term employee benefits	Employee benefits (other than post-employment benefits and termination benefits) which do not fall due wholly within twelve months after the end of the period in which the employees render the related service.	IAS 19.7
owner-occupied property	Property held (by the owner or by the lessee under a finance lease) for use in the production or supply of goods or services or for administrative purposes.	IAS 40.5
parent	An entity that has one or more subsidiaries.	IAS 27.4, IFRS 3.A

Term	Definition	Reference
participants	The members of a retirement benefit plan and others who are entitled to benefits under the plan.	IAS 26.8
past service cost	The increase in the present value of the defined benefit obligation for employee service in prior periods, resulting in the current period from the introduction of, or changes to, post-employment benefits or other long-term employee benefits. Past service cost may be either positive (where benefits are introduced or improved) or negative (where existing benefits are reduced).	IAS 19.7
percentage of completion method	A method by which contract revenue is matched with the contract costs incurred in reaching the stage of completion, resulting in the reporting of revenue, expenses and profit which can be attributed to the proportion of work completed.	IAS 11.25
performance	The relationship of the income and expenses of an entity, as reported in the income statement.	F.47
plan assets (of an employee benefit plan)	(a) assets held by a long-term employee benefit fund; and (b) qualifying insurance policies.	IAS 19.7
policyholder	A party that has a right to compensation under an insurance contract if an insured event occurs.	IFRS 4.A
post-employment benefits	Employee benefits (other than termination benefits) which are payable after the completion of employment.	IAS 19.7
post-employment benefit plans	Formal or informal arrangements under which an entity provides post-employment benefits for one or more employees.	IAS 19.7
potential ordinary share	A financial instrument or other contract that may entitle its holder to ordinary shares.	IAS 33.5
presentation currency	The currency in which the financial statements are presented.	IAS 21.8
present value	A current estimate of the present discounted value of the future net cash flows in the normal course of business.	F.100(d)
present value of a defined benefit obligation	See defined benefit obligation (present value of)	IAS 19.7
previous GAAP	The basis of accounting that a first-time adopter used immediately before adopting IFRSs.	IFRS 1.A
price risk	A market risk – The risk that the value of a financial instrument will fluctuate as a result of changes in market prices whether those changes are caused by factors specific to the individual instrument or its issuer or factors affecting all securities traded in the market.	IAS 32.52 (a)(iii)
primary financial instruments	Financial instruments such as receivables, payables and equity securities, that are not derivative financial instruments.	IAS 32.AG15

Term	Definition	Reference
prior period errors	Omissions from, and misstatements in, the entity's financial statements for one or more prior periods arising from a failure to use, or misuse of, reliable information that: (a) was available when financial statements for those periods were authorised for issue; and (b) could reasonably be expected to have been obtained and taken into account in the preparation and presentation of those financial statements. Such errors include the effects of mathematical mistakes, mistakes in applying accounting policies, oversights or misinterpretations of facts, and fraud.	IAS 8.5
probable	More likely than not.	IFRS 3.A, IFRS 5.A
profit	The residual amount that remains after expenses (including capital maintenance adjustments, where appropriate) have been deducted from income. Any amount over and above that required to maintain the capital at the beginning of the period is profit.	F.105, F.107
projected unit credit method	An actuarial valuation method that sees each period of service as giving rise to an additional unit of benefit entitlement and measures each unit separately to build up the final obligation (sometimes known as the accrued benefit method pro-rated on service or as the benefit/years of service method).	IAS 19.64–66
property, plant and equipment	Are tangible items that: (a) are held for use in the production or supply of goods or services, for rental to others, or for administrative purposes; and (b) are expected to be used during more than one period.	IAS 16.6
proportionate consolidation	A method of accounting and reporting whereby a venturer's share of each of the assets, liabilities, income and expenses of a jointly controlled entity is combined line by line with similar items in the venturer's financial statements or reported as separate line items in the venturer's financial statements.	IAS 31.3
prospective application	Prospective application of a change in accounting policy and of recognising the effect of a change in an accounting estimate, respectively, are: (a) applying the new accounting policy to transactions, other events and conditions occurring after the date as at which the policy is changed; and (b) recognising the effect of the change in the accounting estimate in the current and future periods affected by the change.	IAS 8.5

provision	A liability of uncertain timing or amount.	IAS 37.10
prudence	The inclusion of a degree of caution in the exercise of the judgements needed in making the estimates required under conditions of uncertainty, such that assets or income are not overstated and liabilities or expenses are not understated.	F.37
put options (on ordinary shares)	Contracts that give the holder the right to sell ordinary shares at a specified price for a given period.	IAS 33.5
qualifying insurance policy	An insurance policy issued by an insurer that is not a related party (as defined in IAS 24, Related Party Disclosures) of the reporting entity, if the proceeds of the policy: (a) can be used only to pay or fund employee benefits under a defined benefit plan; (b) are not available to the reporting entity's own creditors (even in bankruptcy) and cannot be paid to the reporting entity, unless either: (i) the proceeds represent surplus assets that are not needed for the policy to meet all the related employee benefit obligations; or (ii) the proceeds are returned to the reporting entity to reimburse it for employee benefits already paid.	IAS 19.7
realisable value	The amount of cash or cash equivalents that could currently be obtained by selling an asset in an orderly disposal.	F.100(c)
recognition	The process of incorporating in the balance sheet or income statement an item that meets the definition of an element and satisfies the following criteria for recognition: (a) it is probable that any future economic benefit associated with the item will flow to or from the entity; and (b) the item has a cost or value that can be measured with reliability.	F.82, F.83
recoverable amount	The higher of an asset's (or cash-generating unit's) fair value less costs to sell and its value in use.	IAS 36.6, IFRS 5.A
recoverable amount	Recoverable amount is the higher of an asset's net selling price and its value in use.	IAS 16.6
regular way purchase or sale	A purchase or sale of a financial asset under a contract whose terms require delivery of the asset within the time frame established generally by regulation or convention in the marketplace concerned.	IAS 39.9

reinsurance assets	A cedant's net contractual rights under a reinsurance contract.	IFRS 4.A
reinsurance contract	An insurance contract issued by one insurer (the reinsurer) to compensate another insurer (the cedant) for losses on one or more contracts issued by the cedant.	IFRS 4.A
reinsurance	The party that has an obligation under a reinsurance contract to compensate a cedant if an insured event occurs.	IFRS 4.A
related party	A party is related to an entity if: (a) directly, or indirectly through one or more intermediaries, the party: (i) controls, is controlled by, or is under common control with, the entity (this includes parents, subsidiaries and fellow subsidiaries); (ii) has an interest in the entity that gives it significant influence over the entity; or (iii) has joint control over the entity; (b) the party is an associate (as defined in IAS 28 Investments in Associates) of the entity; (c) the party is a joint venture in which the entity is a venturer (see IAS 31 Interests in Joint Ventures); (d) the party is a member of the key management personnel of the entity or its parent; (e) the party is a close member of the family of any individual referred to in (a) or (d); (f) the party is an entity that is controlled, jointly controlled or significantly influenced by, or for which significant voting power in such entity resides with, directly or indirectly, any individual referred to in (d) or (e); or (g) the party is a post-employment benefit plan for the benefit of employees of the entity, or of any entity that is a related party of the entity.	IAS 24.9
related party transaction	A transfer of resources, services or obligations between related parties, regardless of whether a price is charged.	IAS 24.9
relevance	Information has the quality of relevance when it influences the economic decisions of users by helping them evaluate past, present or future events or confirming, or correcting, their past evaluations.	F.26

reliability	Information has the quality of reliability when it is free from material error and bias and can be depended upon by users to represent faithfully that which it either purports to represent or could reasonably be expected to represent.	F.31
reload feature	A feature that provides for an automatic grant of additional share options whenever the option holder exercises previously granted options using the entity's shares, rather than cash, to satisfy the exercise price.	IFRS 2.A
reload option	A new share option granted when a share is used to satisfy the exercise price of a previous share option.	IFRS 2.A
reportable segment	A business segment or a geographical segment for which segment information is required to be disclosed.	IAS 14.9
reporting date	The end of the latest period covered by financial statements or by an interim financial report.	IFRS 1.A
reporting entity	An entity for which there are users who rely on the financial statements as their major source of financial information about the entity.	F.8
reporting entity	An entity for which there are users who rely on the entity's general purpose financial statements for information that will be useful to them for making decisions about the allocation of resources. A reporting entity can be a single entity or a group comprising a parent and all of its subsidiaries.	IFRS 3.A
research	Original and planned investigation undertaken with the prospect of gaining new scientific or technical knowledge and understanding.	IAS 38.8
residual value	The net amount which an entity expects to obtain for an asset at the end of its useful life after deducting the expected costs of disposal.	IAS 16.6
residual value (of an intangible asset)	The estimated amount that an entity would currently obtain from disposal of the asset, after deducting the estimated costs of disposal, if the asset were already of the age and in the condition expected at the end of its useful life.	IAS 16.6, IAS 38.8
restructuring	A programme that is planned and controlled by management, and materially changes either: (a) the scope of a business undertaken by an entity; or (b) the manner in which that business is conducted.	IAS 37.10

Term	Definition	Reference
retirement benefit plans	Arrangements whereby an entity provides benefits for its employees on or after termination of service (either in the form of an annual income or as a lump sum) when such benefits, or the employer's contributions towards them, can be determined or estimated in advance of retirement from the provisions of a document or from the entity's practices. (See also post-employment benefit plans)	IAS 26.8
retrospective application	Applying a new accounting policy to transactions, other events and conditions as if that policy had always been applied.	IAS 8.5
retrospective restatement	Correcting the recognition, measurement and disclosure of amounts of elements of financial statements as if a prior period error had never occurred.	IAS 8.5
return on plan assets (of an employee benefit plan)	Interest, dividends and other revenue derived from the plan assets, together with realised and unrealised gains or losses on the plan assets, less any costs of administering the plan and less any tax payable by the plan itself.	IAS 19.7
revaluation	Restatement of assets and liabilities.	F.81
revalued amount of an asset	The fair value of an asset at the date of a revaluation less any subsequent accumulated depreciation and accumulated impairment losses.	IAS 16.31
revenue	The gross inflow of economic benefits during the period arising in the course of the ordinary activities of an entity when those inflows result in increases in equity, other than increases relating to contributions from equity participants.	IAS 18.7
reverse acquisition	An acquisition where the acquirer is the entity whose equity interests have been acquired and the issuing entity is the acquiree. This might be the case when, for example, a private entity arranges to have itself 'acquired' by a smaller public entity as a means of obtaining a stock exchange listing.	IFRS 3.21
rewards associated with a leased asset	Rewards may be represented by the expectation of profitable operation over the asset's economic life and of gain from appreciation in value or realisation of a residual value.	IAS 17.7
risks associated with a leased asset	Risks include possibilities of losses from idle capacity or technological obsolescence and of variations in return due to changing economic conditions.	IAS 17.7
sale and leaseback transaction	The sale of an asset and the leasing back of the same asset. The lease payment and the sale price are usually interdependent because they are negotiated as a package.	IAS 17.58

segment assets	Those operating assets that are employed by a segment in its operating activities and that either are directly attributable to the segment or can be allocated to the segment on a reasonable basis.	IAS 14.16
segment expense	Expense resulting from the operating activities of a segment that is directly attributable to the segment and the relevant portion of an expense that can be allocated on a reasonable basis to the segment, including expenses relating to sales to external customers and expenses relating to transactions with other segments of the same entity.	IAS 14.16
segment result	Segment revenue less segment expense. Segment result is determined before any adjustments for minority interest.	IAS 14.16
segment revenue	Revenue reported in the entity's income statement that is directly attributable to a segment and the relevant portion of entity revenue that can be allocated on a reasonable basis to a segment, whether from sales to external customers or from transactions with other segments of the same entity.	IAS 14.16
separate financial statements	Those presented by a parent, an investor in an associate or a venturer in a jointly controlled entity, in which the investments are accounted for on the basis of the direct equity interest rather than on the basis of the reported results and net assets of the investees.	IAS 27.4, IAS 31.3
set-off, legal right of	A debtor's legal right, by contract or otherwise, to settle or otherwise eliminate all or a portion of an amount due to a creditor by applying against that amount an amount due from the creditor.	IAS 32.40
settlement (of employee benefit obligations)	A transaction that eliminates all further legal or constructive obligation for part or all of the benefits provided under a defined benefit plan, for example, when a lump-sum cash payment is made to, or on behalf of, plan participants in exchange for their rights to receive specified post-employment benefits.	IAS 19.112
settlement date	The date that a financial asset is delivered to the entity that purchased it.	IAS 39.AG56
settlement value	The undiscounted amounts of cash or cash equivalents expected to be paid to satisfy the liabilities in the normal course of business.	F.100(c)
share-based payment arrangement	An agreement between the entity and another party (including an employee) to enter into a share-based payment transaction, which thereby entitles the other party to receive cash or other assets of the entity for amounts that are based on the price of the entity's shares or other equity instruments of the entity, or to receive equity instruments of the entity, provided the specified vesting conditions, if any, are met.	IFRS 2.A

share-based payment transaction	A transaction in which the entity receives goods or services as consideration for equity instruments of the entity (including shares or share options), or acquires goods or services by incurring liabilities to the supplier of those goods or services for amounts that are based on the price of the entity's shares or other equity instruments of the entity.	IFRS 2.A
share option	A contract that gives the holder the right, but not the obligation, to subscribe to the entity's shares at a fixed or determinable price for a specific period of time.	IFRS 2.A
short seller	An entity that sells securities that it has borrowed and does not yet own.	IAS 39.AG15
short-term employee benefits	Employee benefits (other than termination benefits) which fall due wholly within twelve months after the end of the period in which the employees render the related service.	IAS 19.7
significant influence	Significant influence is the power to participate in the financial and operating policy decisions of an entity, but is not control over those policies. (Significant influence may be gained by share ownership, statute or agreement.)	(IAS 24.9), IAS 28.2, IAS 31.3
solvency	The availability of cash over the longer term to meet financial commitments as they fall due.	F.16
spot exchange rate	The exchange rate for immediate delivery.	IAS 21.8
state (employee benefit) plan	Employee benefit plans established by legislation to cover all entities (or all entities in a particular category, for example a specific industry) and operated by national or local government or by another body (for example an autonomous agency created specifically for this purpose) which is not subject to control or influence by the reporting entity.	IAS 19.37
subsidiary	An entity, including an unincorporated entity such as a partnership, that is controlled by another entity (known as the parent).	IFRS 3.A, IAS 27.4, IAS 28.2
substance over form	The principle that transactions and other events are accounted for and presented in accordance with their substance and economic reality and not merely their legal form.	F.35 (IAS 8.7–10)
tax base of an asset or liability	The amount attributed to that asset or liability for tax purposes.	IAS 12.5
tax expense (tax income)	The aggregate amount included in the determination of profit or loss for the period in respect of current tax and deferred tax. Tax expense (tax income) comprises current tax expense (current tax income) and deferred tax expense (deferred tax income).	IAS 12.5, IAS 12.6
taxable profit (tax loss)	The profit (loss) for a period, determined in accordance with the rules established by the taxation authorities, upon which income taxes are payable (recoverable).	IAS 12.5

taxable temporary difference	A temporary difference that will result in taxable amounts in determining taxable profit (tax loss) of future periods when the carrying amount of the asset or liability is recovered or settled.	IAS 12.5
temporary difference	A difference between the carrying amount of an asset or liability in the balance sheet and its tax base. A temporary difference may be either: (a) a taxable temporary difference; or (b) a deductible temporary difference.	IAS 12.5
termination benefits	Employee benefits payable as a result of either: (a) an entity's decision to terminate an employee's employment before the normal retirement date; or (b) an employee's decision to accept voluntary redundancy in exchange for those benefits.	IAS 19.7
trade date	The date that an entity commits itself to purchase or sell an asset.	IAS 39.AG55
transaction costs (financial instruments)	Incremental costs that are directly attributable to the acquisition, issue or disposal of a financial asset or liability (see IAS 39 Appendix A paragraph AG13). An incremental cost is one that would not have been incurred if the entity had not acquired, issued or disposed of the financial instrument.	IAS 39.9
transitional liability (defined benefit plans)	The following total: (a) the present value of the obligation at the date of adopting IAS 19 (revised); (b) minus the fair value, at the date of adoption, of plan assets (if any) out of which the obligations are to be settled directly; (c) minus any past service cost that shall be recognised in later periods.	IAS 19.154
unbundle	Account for the components of a contract as if they were separate contracts.	IFRS 4.A
understandability	Information provided in financial statements has the quality of understandability when is comprehensible to users who have a reasonable knowledge of business and economic activities and accounting and a willingness to study the information with reasonable diligence.	F.25
unearned finance income	The difference between: (a) the gross investment in the lease, and (b) the net investment in the lease.	IAS 17.4
unguaranteed residual value	That portion of the residual value of the leased asset, the realisation of which by the lessor is not assured or is guaranteed solely by a party related to the lessor.	IAS 17.4

useful life	The estimated remaining period, from the commencement of the lease term, without limitation by the lease term, over which the economic benefits embodied in the asset are expected to be consumed by the entity.	IAS 17.4
useful life	Either: (a) the period over which an asset is expected to be available for use by an entity; or (b) the number of production or similar units expected to be obtained from the asset by the entity.	IAS 16.6, IAS 36.6, IAS 38.8
value in use	The present value of estimated future cash flows expected to arise from the continuing use of an asset and from its disposal at the end of its useful life.	IFRS 5.A
value in use	The present value of the future cash flows expected to be derived from an asset or cash-generating unit.	IAS 36.6
variable production overheads	Those indirect costs of production that vary directly, or nearly directly, with the volume of production, such as indirect materials and indirect labour.	IAS 2.12
venturer	A party to a joint venture that has joint control over that joint venture.	IAS 31.3
vest	To become an entitlement. Under share-based payment arrangement, a counterparty's right to receive cash, other assets, or equity instruments of the entity vests upon satisfaction of any specified vesting conditions.	IFRS 2.A
vested employee benefits	Employee benefits that are not conditional on future employment.	IAS 19.7, (IAS 26.8)
vesting conditions	The conditions that must be satisfied for the counterparty to become entitled to receive cash, other assets or equity instruments of the entity, under a share-based payment arrangement. Vesting conditions include service conditions, which require the other party to complete a specified period of service, and performance conditions, which require specified performance targets to be met (such as a specified increase in the entity's profit over a specified period of time).	IFRS 2.A
vesting period	The period during which all the specified vesting conditions of a share-based payment arrangement are to be satisfied.	IFRS 2.A
warrant	A financial instrument that gives the holder the right to purchase ordinary shares.	IAS 33.5

weighted average cost method	Under this method, the cost of each item is determined from the weighted average of the cost of similar items at the beginning of a period and the cost of similar items purchased or produced during the period. The average may be calculated on a periodic basis, or as each additional shipment is received, depending upon the circumstances of the entity.	IAS 2.27
weighted average number of ordinary shares outstanding during the period	Number of ordinary shares outstanding at the beginning of the period, adjusted by the number of ordinary shares bought back or issued during the period multiplied by a time-weighting factor.	IAS 33.20

Index

The index to this volume is a comprehensive index. It references not only all International Financial Reporting Standards—IFRSs, IASs and Interpretations—but also all related documentation including Bases for Conclusions, Implementation Guidance, Application Guidance, Appendices and Illustrative Examples. In addition, it includes references to the IASC Foundation Constitution, the IASB *Framework* and the IFRS and IFRIC Prefaces.

References to IFRSs, IASs, Interpretations and supporting documentation are by Standard number and paragraph number. This method provides an absolute reference rather than a relative one. The index uses prefix notations to identify the document to which paragraphs and subparagraphs belong. These prefix notations are as follows:

Section	Prefix	Examples	Reference
International Financial Reporting Standards (IFRSs) 1–5	IF	**IF1**.1–47A **IF3**.3A(c)	IFRS 1, paragraphs 1 to 47A IFRS 3, paragraph 3A subparagraph c
International Accounting Standards (IASs) 1–41	*no prefix*	**12**.26(a) **37**.10	IAS 12, paragraph 26 subparagraph a IAS 37, paragraph 10
Basis for Conclusions on IFRSs	BC	**IF2**.BC19–22 **IF4**.BC61(d)	Basis for Conclusions on IFRS 2, paragraphs 19 to 22 Basis for Conclusions on IFRS 4, paragraph 61 subparagraph d
Basis for Conclusions on IASs	B, BC or BCZ	**24**.BC8–14 **36**.BCZ108–112	Basis for Conclusions on IAS 24, paragraphs 8 to 14 Basis for Conclusions on IAS 36, paragraphs 108 to 112
Implementation Guidance on IFRSs and IASs	IG	**39**.IG Section E.4.2 **IF4**.IG6–10	Implementation Guidance on IAS 39 Section E, paragraph 4.2 Implementation Guidance on IFRS 4, paragraphs 6 to 10
Illustrative Examples on IFRSs and IASs	IE	**33**.IE1	IAS 33, Illustrative Example 1
Application Guidance	AG	**32**.AG25–26 **39** Appendix A AG84–93	IAS 32: Application Guidance on IAS 32, paragraphs 25 to 26 IAS 39 Appendix A: Application Guidance on IAS 39, paragraphs 84 to 93
Appendices to IFRSs and IASs	Appendix	**IF1** Appendices A-C **41** Appendix A	IFRS 1, Appendices A to C IAS 41, Appendix A

Other prefixes are: IASC Foundation Constitution–**CN**; Preface to International Financial Reporting Standards–**IFRS Preface**; International Financial Reporting Interpretations Committee Preface–**IFRIC Preface**; IFRIC Interpretations–**IFRIC**; SIC Interpretations–**SIC**; IASB Framework–**F**.

NOTES

NOTES

NOTES

NOTES

NOTES

NOTES